All Music Guide to

Jazz

The best CDs, albums & tapes

**Edited by Ron Wynn
with Michael Erlewine,
Vladimir Bogdanov,
and Chris Woodstra**

mf *Miller Freeman Books*
San Francisco

The *All Music Guide* Series
Jazz Editor: Ron Wynn
Editor: Michael Erlewine
Associate Editor: Chris Woodstra
Database Design: Vladimir Bogdanov

Contributors:

Bob Blumenthal
Myles Boisen
Rick Clark
Bill Dahl
Hank Davis
Bruce Eder
Mark C. Gridley
Scot Hacker
Terri Hinte
Michael Katz
Cub Koda
Richard Lieberson
Dan Morgenstern

David Nelson McCarthy
Michael G. Nastos
Buz Overbeck
Harvey Pekar
J. Poet
Bob Porter
Bruce Boyd Raeburn
Bob Rusch
William Ruhlman
Max Salazar
Richard Skelly
Scott Yanow

Thanks to the staffs and contributors of the following
magazines, for reviews reprinted by permission:
Cadence
DOWN BEAT
Jazz Times
Coda
Jazziz
Rock & Roll Disc
Request
Pulse

Published in 1994 by Miller Freeman Books, 600 Harrison Street, San Francisco, CA 94107
Publishers of GPI Books, *Guitar Player, Bass Player,* and *Keyboard* magazines
A member of the United Newspapers Group

Distributed to the book trade in the U.S. and Canada by
    Publishers Group West, P.O. Box 8843, Emeryville, CA 94662
Distributed to the music trade in the U.S. and Canada by
    Hal Leonard Publishing, P.O. Box 13819, Milwaukee, WI 53213

Library of Congress Cataloging-in-Publication Data:
    The All music guide to jazz : the best CDs, albums & tapes / edited by Ron Wynn
        with Michael Erlewine and Vladimir Bogdanov.
            p.   cm.
        Includes bibliographical references and index.
        ISBN 0-87930-308-5
        1. Jazz—Discopgraphy. 2. Sound recordings—Reviews. I. Wynn, Ron.
    II. Erlewine, Michael. III. Bogdanov, Vladimir, 1965-
    ML156.4.J3A45 1994
    781.65'0266—dc20   94-11273
                                                            MN

Cover Design: Tom Erlewine
Copyeditors: Ellyn Hament and Fran Taylor
Proofreaders: Michael Welch, Lauren Hirshson, and Adrienne Armstrong

Printed in the United States of America
    95 96 97 98   9 8 7 6 5 4 3 2

CONTENTS

HOW TO USE THIS BOOK

ARTIST NAME   (Alternate name in parentheses).

VITAL STATISTICS   Date and place of birth and death, if known.

INSTRUMENT(S) / STYLE OF JAZZ   Major instruments for each performer, and other performace-related credits (bandleader, composer, arranger) are listed here, followed by one or more styles of jazz associated with each performer. A description of these styles is provided in a section at the beginning of the book.

BIOGRAPHY   A quick view of the artist's life and musical career. For major performers, proportionately longer biographies are provided.

MAJOR ALBUMS   These are the 9,000+ albums selected by our editors and contributors. An album listed here (even one without a bullet or comment) is considered an important recording. It's worth a listen. Undistinguished albums are not included here.

KEY TO SYMBOLS   ○ ☆ ★

○ LANDMARK RECORDINGS   Albums marked with an open circle are singled out as landmark or career turning points for the particular artist. These are classic albums—prime stuff. A land-mark recording is either a pivotal recording that marked a change in their career or a high point in their recording output.

☆ ESSENTIAL COLLECTIONS   Albums marked with a star should be part of any good collection of the genre. Often, these are also a good first purchase (filled star). By hearing these albums, you can get a good overview of the entire genre. These are must-hear and must-have recordings. You can't go wrong with them.

★ FIRST PURCHASE   Albums marked with a filled star should be your first purchase. This is where to begin to find out if you like this particular artist. These albums are representative of the best this artist has to offer. If you don't like these picks, chances are this artist is not for you. In the case of an artist (like Miles Davis) who has a number of distinct periods, you will find an essential pick marked for each period. It might be best to start with an earlier album (the albums are listed chronologically when possible) and work up to the later ones.

BOOKER ERVIN (Booker (Telleferro, II) Ervin)

b. 1930, Denison, TX, **d.** Jul. 31, 1970
Tenor saxophone / Hard bop, blues & jazz

Flamboyance, excitement, and bluesy fervor were the trademarks of tenor saxophonist Booker Ervin. He was an aggressive, animated soloist whose repertoire of honks, swaggers, smears, and slurs were matched by his thorough harmonic knowledge and his complete command of the sax. He had one of the hardest tones and biggest sounds among '50s and '60s stylists, something that was even more impressive when he played the blues. Ervin's father was a trombonist who had worked with Buddy Tate. Ervin first played the trombone, then taught himself sax while in the air force. He studied music in Boston for two years, then made his earliest recordings with Ernie Fields's R&B band. This association was Ervin's professional debut as well. During the late '50s and early '60s, he was in Charles Mingus's Jazz Workshop, providing energized, powerful solos. Ervin also played in a group with Horace Parlan, George Tucker, and Al Harewood, and with Randy Weston. He recorded with Weston, and began cutting acclaimed albums as a leader in the '60s. Ervin recorded for Bethlehem, Savoy, and Candid. His crowning achievement was nine albums he did for Prestige in the mid and late '60s. These included such memorable dates as his "books." There were also sessions for Blue Note, Fontana, Pacific Jazz, and a partial album for Enja. Ervin spent most of 1964, 1965, and part of 1966 in Europe, and returned in 1968. Ervin died in 1970. Only a handful of Ervin sessions are currently in print, though others, like *Settin' the Pace*, are being reissued steadily. *—Ron Wynn*

○ **Soulful Saxes / i.** Jun. 1960 / Affinity 758

★ **Book Cooks, The** / Jun. 1960 / Affinity
Robust, earthy Ervin throughout. This tremendous combo date was originally on Bethlehem. *—Ron Wynn*

Down in the Dumps / Nov. 26, 1960-Jan. 5, 1961 / Savoy 1119
An explosive set from Ervin's prime period, reissued on disc with additional material from the following year (1961), with trombonist Dr. Billy Howell. *—Ron Wynn*

○ **Cookin'** / Nov. 26, 1960 / Savoy Jazz 150

That's It / Jan. 6, 1961 / Candid 79014

☆ **Back From the Gig** / Feb. 15, 1963+May 24, 1968 / Blue Note 488
Tenor saxophonist Booker Ervin's *Back From the Gig* is a perplexing volume. It is perplexing because it took Blue Note nearly seven years after Ervin's untimely death to release these valuable and infectious recordings. Apparently, both sessions, one recorded under the tutelage of pianist Horace Parlan (whom Michael Cuscuna thoughtfully documents in his liner notes), were scheduled for release years ago but never materialized. The Parlan sextet (1963) was a tough, no-nonsense blues unit. Ervin, trumpeter Johnny Coles, and guitarist Grant Green are the lead voices and are sly, raw, and often dirty. Ervin, in particular, plays with an inciting bounce and masterful range, lean and to the core. His own 1968 recordings, in cahoots with saxophonist Wayne Shorter and pianist Kenny Barron, are more expansive, envincing a knack for melding his blues romanticism to modal foundations and professing some plain big-band-inspired truths. *—Mikal Gilmore*, Down Beat

HOW TO USE THIS BOOK

ALBUM TITLE   The name of the album is listed in bold as it appears on the original when possible. Very long titles have been abbreviated, or repeated in full as part of the comment, where needed.

DATE   The recording date is given as completely as possible. In some cases only the date of issue or release is known; these are marked with an **i.** preceding the date. We have made every attempt to verify album dates. However, if you have more accurate information, please write us; we are continually updating and refining our listings.

RECORD LABEL & NUMBER   Record labels and numbers indicate the current (or most recent) release of this recording.

REVIEWERS   The name of each review's author (and the magazine where the review originally appeared, if applicable) are given at the end of the review.

○ **Soulful Saxes /** i. Jun. 1960 **/** Affinity 758

★ **Book Cooks, The /** Jun. 1960 / Affinity
Robust, earthy Ervin throughout. This tremendous combo date was originally on Bethlehem. —*Ron Wynn*

Down in the Dumps / Nov. 26, 1960-Jan. 5, 1961 **/** Savoy 1119
An explosive set from Ervin's prime period, reissued on disc with additional material from the following year (1961), with trombonist Dr. Billy Howell. —*Ron Wynn*

○ **Cookin' /** Nov. 26, 1960 / Savoy Jazz 150

That's It / Jan. 6, 1961 / Candid 79014

☆ **Back From the Gig /** Feb. 15, 1963+May 24, 1968 / Blue Note 488
Tenor saxophonist Booker Ervin's *Back From the Gig* is a perplexing volume. It is perplexing because it took Blue Note nearly seven years after Ervin's untimely death to release these valuable and infectious recordings. Apparently, both sessions, one recorded under the tutelage of pianist Horace Parlan (whom Michael Cuscuna thoughtfully documents in his liner notes), were scheduled for release years ago but never materialized. The Parlan sextet (1963) was a tough, no-nonsense blues unit. Ervin, trumpeter Johnny Coles, and guitarist Grant Green are the lead voices and are sly, raw, and often dirty. Ervin, in particular, plays with an inciting bounce and masterful range, lean and to the core. His own 1968 recordings, in cahoots with saxophonist Wayne Shorter and pianist Kenny Barron, are more expansive, envincing a knack for melding his blues romanticism to modal foundations and professing some plain big-band-inspired truths. —*Mikal Gilmore*, Down Beat

ABBREVIATIONS

The following abbreviations are used in some reviews following the musicians' names to indicate instruments played on a particular recording or session.

as	alto saxophone	org	organ
b	bass	p	piano
bcl	bass clarinet	per	percussion
bj	banjo	pkt-t	pocket-trumpet
bs	baritone saxophone	sno	sopranino saxophone
cnt	cornet	ss	soprano saxophone
cl	clarinet	syn	synthesizer
clo	cello	tpt	trumpet
d	drums	tb	trombone
euph	euphonium	tba	tuba
f	flute	ts	tenor saxophone
flhn	flugelhorn	vib	vibraphone
frhn	french horn	vn	violin
g	guitar	vtb	valve trombone
k	keyboards		

FOREWORD

The *All Music Guide to Jazz* is the most complete consumer guide to jazz recordings ever made available. It includes biographies of almost 1200 jazz artists and groups, plus more than 9000 of their finest recordings rated and reviewed. Our jazz editor, Ron Wynn, is well known in the Memphis jazz community, and has been a freelance jazz writer for more than 18 years. Ron has served as the editor of the *New Memphis Star*, as chief music critic for the *Memphis Commercial Appeal*, and has contributed to dozens of periodicals including *Rock & Roll Confidential, The Boston Phoenix, Living Blues, Rejoice*, and *Rock & Roll Disc*.

This is the second voume in the **All Music Guide** series, the first being the original *All Music Guide*. The third in our series, the *All Music Guide to World Music*, will be published in 1995.

The *All Music Guide* is also available on CD-ROM (from Selectware Technology, 29200 Vassar, Ste. 200, Livonia, MI 48152; phone 313-477-7340), for hard disk (from Great Bear Technologies, 100 Moraga Way, Moraga, CA 94556; phone 800-795-4325), on Compu-Serve (GO ALLMUSIC), and on Internet (ALLMUSIC. MSEN.COM and ALLMUSIC.FERRIS.EDU).

Finally, the *All Music Guide* is an ongoing database project, the largest collection of substantive album reviews ever assembled, and we welcome your feedback. Perhaps we have left out some of your favorite albums, and/or included ones that you don't consider essential. Let us know about it. We welcome criticism, suggestions, additions, and/or deletions. Perhaps you are expert on the complete output of a particular artist or group and would like to participate in future editions of this book and/or our larger computer database. We would be glad to hear from you. Call or write:

> *All Music Guide*
> 315 Marion Avenue
> Big Rapids, MI 49307
> 616/796-3437
> FAX 616/796-3060
> (A Division of Matrix Software)

> —*Michael Erlewine*

INTRODUCTION

Jazz may be the only musical form that is easier to define by what it *isn't* than explain what it is. It *isn't* pop, though it certainly has been a vital part of America's popular tradition. It *isn't* background, elevator, gospel, R&B, soundtrack, theatrical, or New Age (nor most so-called fusion), though any or all those styles can at times include elements that appear in jazz compositions. It *isn't* exclusively African American or ethnic music, although everyone (except James Lincoln Collier) acknowledges its Black roots and creative, innovative base, and several dictionaries even label jazz as Black-derived music. Making things more interesting is the fact many of jazz's finest practitioners aren't comfortable with the word; *American Negro, Great Black, American classical* and *creative improvised music* are terms often used as substitutes. But contradictions, ironies, and paradoxes aside, one thing is clear: There's a spirit, an essence, that the jazz fan might not be able to precisely define but can certainly hear. Some cite swing, others emphasize improvisation. Whatever the jazz muse, it is among the most compelling in any idiom and its greatest champions and heroes have unquestionably been American, though the day has long passed when country of birth determined the merit of one's jazz credentials (the same holds true for color and gender).

What the *All Music Guide to Jazz* hopes to do is present the mélange of wonderful, wacky, and unpredictable styles that make up this great sound through various reviews, bios, analyses, and histories. We are presenting a capsule look at the many genres and personalities contained within this universe. These include traditional, bebop, free, swing, and many other styles better and more vigorously defined elsewhere. We hope to appeal first and foremost to music lovers. Collectors, music scholars, historians, students, and musicians are certainly welcome, but, in my opinion, this book is geared toward music lovers, the people who hear and are attracted above all else to music and its beauty. They may or may not know the terminology (and we've included a glossary of some recurring terms in jazz lexicon for the total novice) but they can *feel* and *hear* the message.

As an African American who grew up in the South during the final years of institutionalized segregation, then came of age during the Civil Rights era and ongoing struggle for liberation, I consider this book a labor of love, the fruit of years of plowing through jazz criticism and volumes of histories, discographies, dictionaries, essays, books, and articles. To paraphrase what Stanley Dance once said about Amiri Bakara, I'm another of those whose greatest jazz handicap was being born too late. As a member of the rock & roll baby-boomer generation, I can't have a perspective as well-rounded or jazz-centered as someone who grew up when jazz was a dominant part of the nation's musical consciousness. Despite all the lip service paid jazz by the African-American cultural cognoscenti, the harsh truth is that in my lifetime jazz has been at best a second-class citizen to R&B, blues, funk, disco/dance, hip-hop, rap, you name it.

Much of my jazz education was, and continues to be, second hand: records, books, magazines, and concerts. I bow to no one in my admiration for Duke Ellington, Count Basie, Louis Armstrong, Billie Holiday, Charlie Parker, and Coleman Hawkins, but my heroes have been Miles Davis, John Coltrane, Dinah Washington, and Ornette Coleman. Traditional New Orleans, big band/swing, and bebop are styles I treasure; soul-jazz, funk, hard bop, free, and the blues are things I lived. For me, jazz is part of a great musical whole, rather than an insular world. Whereas once the biggest divider in jazz criticism was between pre- and postbebop, I now feel it's between pre- and post-rock & roll. Those whose backgrounds are predominantly or exclusively in jazz often resent those of us from a "nonpure" background.

I can only say I've done my best to demonstrate my love and affection for the idiom. I was never informed that it was necessary to hate everything else in order to enjoy, understand, or appreciate jazz; thus I still maintain a potent love for many types of music, while having a special place for jazz and an admiration for anyone who'd seek a living trying to play a music many profess to respect, but few seem to support. This book also addresses, at least by implication, the biggest canard repeatedly raised regarding jazz in the '90s: the "purist" syndrome. Jazz has never been "pure"; it was a mixture of styles right from the start and has continually absorbed influences and elements from other genres. But it has also been an inherently honest music, one where fakers and frauds were quickly exposed. This, then, is the basic problem with certain styles that lay claim to jazz status (I deliberately avoid use of the loaded term "authenticity"); it's not that they aren't "pure," but that they are dishonest when they insist they're something they're not. Very few jazz fans are elitists, but most of them know musical integrity and honesty when they hear it.

What's even more interesting is that many of the biggest sources of this confusion are the first to loudly proclaim they aren't jazz musicians when others would label them as such. Even they recognize the integrity that separates real jazz musicians from pretenders. It's predominantly marketers, publicity flacks, and bottom-line bean counters who have insisted on labeling pop instrumentalists jazz players, not the musicians themselves. It's no slight on musicians or an argument for cultural bigotry to insist that melodic noodling not be equated with improvisation or interest in jazz piqued by including in the category people whose modus operandi is light-years removed from even a fourth-rate jazz player.

I wouldn't try to offer a pat or concise definition of jazz; I'll leave that to the practicing musicians and scholars. But I know it's not trendy, slick, prepack- aged, disposable fare created in a multitrack studio to be discarded when something else from some other studio becomes in vogue. Its true beacons prided themselves on crafting their own sounds and looking forward, while absorbing the lessons of the past, rather than looking backward and reflecting someone else's vision. I hope that, when you've finished with the *All Music Guide to Jazz*, you'll have a much better idea of what playing the music means and a healthy appreciation for those who've made it, as well as a real understanding of the difference between a jazz musician and a jazz-based, jazz-tinged, or jazz-influenced pop artist. Though this may seem hopelessly naive, someday perhaps the divergent constituencies within the jazz world, be they critics, listeners, musicians, educators, historians, scholars, or just the Joe around the corner, will combine forces on behalf of the music. If jazz has a proud tradition of innovation and artistry, then it also has an equally shameful one of ridiculous conflicts within the ranks; sometimes these have been stylistic, sometimes critical or regional, other times (regrettably) they've been racial or cultural. These problems must be addressed and overcome if the music is ever to really progress and gain the exposure it merits.

Our thanks to all those who've contributed, and especially Harvey Pekar, Scott Yanow, Dr. Mark Gridley, Bob Blumenthal and the publications *Cadence, Down Beat, Jazz Times,* and *Coda.*

—Ron Wynn

STYLES

Bebop

Bebop is the most widely used name for the music of Charlie Parker and Dizzy Gillespie. The term "bop" is used somewhat less often, and "rebop" was used during the early years but faded thereafter. Historians apply "modern" to most post-swing era jazz styles, with bebop as just the first in the category. During the late 1940s, the most prominent musicians in this category were Bud Powell, Thelonious Monk, Max Roach, Dexter Gordon, Miles Davis, Tadd Dameron, Fats Navarro, Sonny Stitt, Lucky Thompson, and J.J. Johnson. During the 1950s other outstanding players also became prominent: Oscar Peterson, Sonny Rollins, Jackie McLean, Clifford Brown, Kenny Dorham, Phil Woods, Barry Harris, and Tommy Flanagan. By contrast with swing, bebop was primarily a combo style, though Dizzy Gillespie led a string of big bands that performed in this style, and occasionally Woody Herman, Stan Kenton, and Claude Thornhill featured bebop-style arrangements with their big bands. By comparison with earlier jazz styles, bebop was somewhat faster, and its melodies had more erratic contours. Its lines scurried over, under, and around the notes in the accompaniment chords more than swing style lines, which had more frequently used the chord notes themselves. Bebop tunes were the most syncopated of any jazz style, and the improvisations had more ideas per solo. The effect was more agitated than swing style. Bebop's emphasis on instrumental virtuosity exceeded the level of most swing style improvisers, and many bebop players approached the virtuosity of swing standouts Roy Eldridge, Art Tatum, and Benny Goodman. Bebop accompaniments were lighter, more varied, and more fleet than in most swing styles. The earlier jazz practice of using guitar as timekeeping accompanist disappeared with this new style. Bebop drummers played their timekeeping rhythms on the cymbals more than on the drums. They also made more sounds that were unrelated to their timekeeping roles, thereby increasing the amount of "chattering" and the dropping of "bombs." Bebop influenced subsequent styles, such as "hard bop" and several streams within "cool jazz." Mastery of the bebop improvisatory style became the benchmark for young musicians, and remained so even in the 1990s, despite the emergence of jazz styles that were unrelated to bebop such as "jazz-rock fusion" and "new age." During the 1970s and 1980s, bebop revivals were initiated by young musicians such as Richie Cole (1970s), Chris Hollyday (1980s), and others.

Bebop Era

The *bebop era* represents for many *the* most significant period in jazz history; several consider it the time when musicians began stressing artistic rather than commercial concerns, put innovation ahead of convention, and looked toward the future instead of paying homage to the past. Others view bebop as jazz's ultimate dead end, the style that instituted solemnity and elitism among the fraternity, stripped jazz of its connection with dance, and made it impossible for anyone except hard-core collectors, academics, and other musicians to enjoy and appreciate the music. Each assessment contains enough grains of truth to merit closer, more extensive examination, and there have been many studies, dissertations, essays, etc., devoted to addressing and evaluating these contentions. But it's undeniable jazz changed forever during the bebop years. This chapter looks at the musicians who made these sweeping changes and what they were.

Big Band

Big band refers to a jazz group of 10 or more musicians, usually featuring at least three trumpets, two or more trombones, four or more saxophones, and a "rhythm section" of accompanists playing some combination of piano, guitar, bass, and drums. "Big-band music" as a concept for music fans is identified most with the swing era, though there were large, jazz-oriented dance bands before the swing era of the 1930s and 1940s, and large jazz-oriented concert bands after the swing era. Classification difficulties occur when music stores shelve recordings by all large jazz ensembles as though it were a single style, despite the shifting harmonic and rhythmic approaches employed by new ensembles of similar instrumentation that have formed since the swing era. By lumping the music of all large jazz bands together, marketers overlook the different kinds of jazz that large groups have performed: swing (Duke Ellington and Count Basie), bebop (Dizzy Gillespie), cool (Gerry Mulligan, Shorty Rogers, Gil Evans), hard bop (Gerald Wilson), free jazz (some of Sun Ra's work after the 1950s) and jazz-rock fusion (Don Ellis's and Maynard Ferguson's groups of the 1970s). Not all of them are "swing" bands. Many listeners consider "big band" to denote an idiom, not just an instrumentation. For them, the strategies of arranging and soloing that were established during the 1930s link all large jazz ensembles more than the different rhythmic and harmonic concepts distinguish those of one era, for example, bebop, from those of another, for example, jazz-rock. Another important consideration that journalists and jazz fans of the 1930s and 1940s drew was the distinction between bands that conveyed the most hard-driving rhythmic qualities and frequent solo improvisations and those that conveyed less pronounced swing feeling and improvisation. The former were called "swing bands" or "hot bands" (for example, Count Basie's and Duke Ellington's bands). The latter were called "sweet bands" (for example, the bands of Glenn Miller, Wayne King, Freddy Martin, and Guy Lombardo).

Bill Evans Style

Bill Evans style represents a particular refinement of the melodic methods of Nat Cole, Bud Powell, Lennie Tristano, and Lee Konitz with the harmonies of French impressionist composer Maurice Ravel. In trio context, the approach is lean enough to allow considerable interaction with a melodically inclined bassist such as Scott LaFaro, Eddie Gomez, or Marc

Johnson. This, together with a coloristically-oriented drummer such as Paul Motian, often creates an improvised modern jazz that does not sound like bebop, swings in more subtle ways than previous jazz styles, and creates a wider variety of moods and rhythmic feelings.

This style became the basis for (a) numerous albums by Bill Evans; (b) the accompaniment style used in Miles Davis bands of the 1960s; (c) the trio style of Herbie Hancock and his many disciples (Marc Copland, for example); (d) the trio style of Keith Jarrett and his disciples (Lyle Mays, for example); (e) aspects of the acoustic style of Chick Corea, beginning in the late 1960s, still evident during the 1980s; and (f) the primary approach used during the 1980s and 1990s by Joey Calderazzo, Kevin Hays, Kenny Kirkland, Jim McNeely, Fred Hersch, Warren Bernhardt, Billy Childs, and many others.

The Bill Evans trio style overlaps with styles devised by Paul Bley, Clare Fischer, and Denny Zeitlin because it draws upon many of the same sources and esthetics. Cross-pollination of these piano styles also occurred, for instance, when Herbie Hancock was additionally influenced by Fischer, and Keith Jarrett was additionally influenced by Bley.

During the 1960s and 1970s, many pianists had assimilated these approaches and combined them with other favorites. For example, Andrew Hill combined this approach with aspects of Thelonious Monk's style. Others combined the Bill Evans-Herbie Hancock approaches with those of McCoy Tyner (for example, Mulgrew Miller, who also assimilated Chick Corea's style). The results and the work of their disciples persisted in the 1990s.

Boogie-Woogie

Boogie-woogie is a jazz piano style using two pulses stated by the left hand for every beat and the 12-bar blues chord progression as its repertory. The brief, continuously repeating patterns from the left hand give the style its identity. Its jazz flavor comes from rhythmically and melodically playful phrases improvised by the pianist's right hand. It was first popularized during the late 1920s by Clarence "Pinetop" Smith. Boogie-woogie experienced a strong revival during the late 1930s and early 1940s through the recordings of Meade "Lux" Lewis, Albert Ammons, Pete Johnson, Jimmy Yancey, "Cripple" Clarence Lofton, and Cow Cow Davenport. This genre had considerable influence on accompaniment styles in the popular music called rhythm & blues, as well as the beginnings of rock & roll.

Charles Mingus Style

Charles Mingus style refers to the output of the composer/bassist/bandleader from 1945 until his death in 1979. His work was sufficiently unique throughout his career to transcend the jazz styles that were in vogue at the time his recordings were made. The recordings he made with his own groups and his own compositions were nearly always avant-garde, regardless of their time period. Almost the only conventional music he recorded was as a sideman on a few swing-style recordings with Lionel Hampton in the 1940s and 1950s. Though some historians apply the "hard bop" classification to a few of his late 1950s pieces that show sanctified church influences, their earthy and gospelish qualities are about all that those recordings have in common with the funky subcategory of hard bop. So they should also be classified "Charles Mingus Style," not "hard bop." Several musicians made some of the best records of their careers while with Mingus, such as Eric Dolphy, Booker Ervin, and Dannie Richmond. For others, their solos on Mingus records were at least among their best: Jimmy Knepper, Roland Hanna, John Handy, Ted Curson, Teo Macero, Thad Jones and others. Mingus's music was sustained long after his death not only because his compositions continue to be performed by many jazz musicians but also because the Mingus Dynasty band traveled and recorded in his style and played his repertory. His concepts were openly imitated by the compositions and recordings of James Newton, John Rapson, and Vinnie Golia during the 1980s and 1990s, and by the Chicago avant-garde musicians affiliated with the Association for the Advancement of Creative Musicians, who first became widely known during the 1960s and then continued productively in the 1990s.

Chicago Avant-Garde

Chicago avant-garde encompasses acoustic improvisational music that began in the 1950s with organizations led by Sun Ra, continued in the 1960s with the colleagues of Richard Abrams and the Association for the Advancement of Creative Musicians, and received widespread critical attention during the 1970s in groups, and in projects by their members. Influenced in part by Ornette Coleman and Albert Ayler, these musicians occasionally included freely improvised passages in their performances, though their music should not be classified with "free jazz," because so much of it emphasizes composition, and its improvisations often contain carefully developed themes and moods. A rough-hewn, "work-in-progress" quality distinguishes this music from concurrent "cool jazz" and "hard bop." Additionally, it usually conveys little or none of their bebop rhythmic feeling or melodic vocabulary. Unlike the bebop practice of generating numerous melodic ideas in each improvisation, many AACM musicians develop a handful of ideas instead. Also distinctive is a striking degree of unpredictability. Though almost as fresh and unconventional as music by Ornette Coleman and Albert Ayler, this style is more like the music of Charles Mingus because it amalgamates raw, colorful sounds into a mix that has more continuity and less explosiveness than Coleman and Ayler's music.

Major names include: Richard Abrams, Henry Threadgill, Steve McCall, Leo Smith, Thurman Barker, Leroy Jenkins, Ray Anderson, George Lewis, Fred Hopkins, Jerome Cooper, Air, The Creative Construction Company, The Revolutionary Ensemble, Roscoe Mitchell, Lester Bowie, Joseph Jarman, Don Moye, Anthony Braxton, and Malachi Favors.

Chicago Traditional

Chicago traditional is historically the second style of jazz. Usually designating White, small-band musicians who came to prominence in Chicago during the 1920s, the term includes the players known as the "Austin High Gang" (Jimmy McPartland, Bud Freeman, Frank Teschemacher, and others) as well as Muggsy Spanier, Eddie Condon, and others who soon became part of the New York combo scene during the late 1920s and early 1930s. Bix Beiderbecke and Frankie Trumbauer are also considered part of the scene, though they contributed music of distinction and originality for which the "Chicago style" or the "Chicago school" labels are not entirely satisfactory.

The "Dixieland" designation is often applied to the Chicago players as well as to a number of musicians featured by Bob Crosby in his orchestrated versions of combo jazz in the 1930s (Yank Lawson, Bob Haggart, Irving Fazola, Eddie Miller, and others). The term "Dixieland" has also been applied to a collection of New York musicians of the late 1920s and early 1930s (Red Nichols, Miff Mole, and others) who not only emulated New Orleans styles but also developed their own. Many of them became defined to the public by their association with each other in frequent performances during the 1940s and 1950s at such New York City night clubs as Nick's and Condon's. A group of California musicians (Lu Watters, Turk Murphy, Bob Scobey, and others) who became known during this later period have also been classified in this way.

Contemporary Funk

Contemporary funk refers to a kind of jazz from the 1970s and 1980s in which accompanists perform in the Black pop style of soul and funk music while extensive solo improvisations ride atop. Instead of using standard vocabularies of any modern jazz saxophonists (Charlie Parker, Lee Konitz, John Coltrane, Ornette Coleman), most saxophone improvisations in this style use their own repertory of simple phrases that are loaded with bluesy wails and moans. They draw upon traditions illustrated by sax solos on "rhythm and blues" vocal recordings, such as those of King Curtis with the Coasters, Junior Walker with the Motown vocal groups, and Dave Sanborn with the Paul Butterfield Blues Band.

A prominent figure in this genre is Grover Washington, Jr., who often solos in a Hank Crawford-like style over funk accompaniments. These instances make up his best known recordings, though he is also capable of playing other styles of jazz. The Jazz Crusaders (Wilton Felder, Joe Sample) achieved wide popularity when they changed their repertory to this approach during the 1970s and dropped "Jazz" from their band name. A considerable portion of music by Michael Brecker, Tom Scott, and their disciples uses this approach, though they can also play in the jazz styles of John Coltrane and Joe Henderson. Najee, Richard Elliot, and their contemporaries also perform in this style. From approximately 1971 to 1992, Miles Davis led bands in a sophisticated variation of this style, though his saxophone soloists also drew upon the methods of John Coltrane, and his guitarists also showed modern jazz thinking and Jimi Hendrix influence.

See also "jazzy pop" and "jazz-rock fusion."

Cool Jazz

Cool jazz is a designation emerging during the early 1950s to catalog modern jazz styles that sounded less brassy and more subdued than other modern approaches. Though considerable overlap exists, the following subcategories encompass much of what journalists and record companies called "cool jazz" from the 1950s to the middle 1960s:

(1) Soft variants of bebop, including (a) the music on Miles Davis recordings of 1948 to 1955, particularly, but not exclusively, those made for Capitol Records in 1949 and 1950 with Gerry Mulligan and Lee Konitz; (b) the entire output of the Modern Jazz Quartet (into the 1990s); (c) music of Gerry Mulligan, particularly with Chet Baker and Bob Brookmeyer (into the 1970s); (d) the music of Stan Kenton's musicians of the late 1940s through the 1950s, particularly Conte Candoli, Art Pepper, Shorty Rogers, Bill Holman, Bud Shank, Bill Perkins, Jack Sheldon, Lennie Niehaus; (e) George Shearing; (f) Stan Getz.

(2) Music made by an assortment of modern players who skipped bebop as their primary inspiration and began instead with foundations in the most advanced figures of the swing era: (a) Lennie Tristano and his disciples, particularly Lee Konitz and Warne Marsh; (b) Dave Brubeck and Paul Desmond; (c) musicians who revived and further developed the Lester Young-Count Basie small group music of the late 1930s, for instance, some of the 1950s recordings by Jimmy Giuffre, Dave Pell and others.

(3) Musicians from the above categories who were active in California from the late 1940s to the early 1960s, collectively termed "West Coast Jazz": Gerry Mulligan, Bud Shank, Jimmy Giuffre, Jack Sheldon, Shelly Manne, Art Pepper, Conte Candoli, Dave Brubeck, Paul Desmond, Lennie Niehaus, Dave Pell, Chico Hamilton, Jim Hall, Shorty Rogers, John Graas, Chet Baker, Zoot Sims, Bill Holman and others.

(4) Exploratory music with a subdued effect by Teddy Charles, Chico Hamilton, John LaPorta, and their colleagues during the 1950s.

Dixieland

Dixieland is an umbrella used by laymen to indicate musical styles of the earliest New Orleans and Chicago jazz musicians, recorded from 1917 to 1923, as well as its developments and revivals, beginning during the late 1930s. It refers to collectively improvised small-band music. Its materials are rags, blues, one-steps, two-steps, marches, and pop tunes. Simultaneous counterlines are supplied by trumpet, clarinet, and trombone, accompanied by combinations of piano, guitar, banjo, tuba, bass violin, and drums. Major proponents include Joe "King" Oliver, Jelly Roll Morton, Louis Armstrong, Sidney Bechet, Kid Ory, Johnny Dodds, Paul Mares, Nick LaRocca, Bix Beiderbecke, Bud Freeman, and Jimmy McPartland. Major developers and revivalists include Bob Crosby's Bobcats, Lu Watters (Yerba Buena Jazz Band), Bob Scobey, Bob Wilber, Yank Lawson and Bob Haggart (World's Greatest Jazz Band), The Dukes of Dixieland, Turk Murphy, Climax Jazz Band, Black Eagle Jazz Band, Original Salty Dogs, Jim Cullum, and James Dapogny's Chicago Jazz Band. Aficionados make distinctions between various streams of traditional New Orleans jazz, the earliest Chicago jazz, and the assorted variations that are performed by revivalist bands. Some historians reserve "Dixieland" for White groups playing traditional jazz. Some restrict it mostly to disciples of the earliest white Chicagoans.

Free Jazz

Free jazz is one name for the music of Ornette Coleman, Cecil Taylor, Albert Ayler, and their colleagues and disciples. Though Coleman and Taylor had recorded before the '60s, the "free jazz" term was not common until then. The "free" designation derives from Coleman's decision to offer performances that were not always organized according to preset melody, tempo, or progression of accompaniment chords. Freedom from these guidelines allows improvisers a greater degree of spontaneity than was available in previous jazz styles. Though nonmusicians find much of Coleman's music indistinguishable from bebop, musicians make distinctions according to the methods used (lack of preset chords) and the melodic vocabulary (original, not bebop-derived).

Much of Cecil Taylor's music is extremely active. It is densely packed with rapidly shifting layers of complex harmonies and rhythms. And some recordings of Albert Ayler, Pharoah Sanders, and Ornette Coleman include loud screeches and shrieks from trumpets and saxophones, combined with nonrepetitive, highly complex sounds from basses and drums. For these reasons, some listeners equate the term "free jazz" with high-energy, seemingly chaotic group improvisations, even though freedom from adhering to preset chord progressions does not necessitate high "energy" playing or any particular tone qualities or ways of organizing tones for melodic lines. For example, some of John Coltrane's music of the middle 1960s is often classified with "free" jazz, probably because of its collectively improvised turbulence, despite its using preset arrangements of the harmonies guiding the improvisers.

Hard Bop

Hard bop is a label that became common among journalists and record companies during the middle 1950s to describe a number of styles deriving from bebop. Though musicians themselves continued to call the music "bebop," the sounds in these styles frequently seemed weightier and more solemn than the bebop of Charlie Parker and Dizzy Gillespie. There was an unrelenting hardness and drive in the music.

Accompaniment sounds were more frequently in the fore-front. By comparison with bebop, it also used more intricate chord changes and less often borrowed song forms from popular tunes. Bands to whom the term is most frequently applied are the Horace Silver Quintet, the Art Blakey Jazz Messengers, the Cannonball and Nat Adderley quintets and sextets, the Art Farmer-Benny Golson Jazztet, and the Jazz Crusaders. The music can be loosely classified by five subcategories.

(1) "1950s bebop": Some parts of the music, such as the solo improvisations of Clifford Brown, Lou Donaldson, Kenny Dorham, and Donald Byrd are almost indistinguishable from the bebop of Fats Navarro and Charlie Parker. Prominence of highly active drum parts in their accompaniment, however, sometimes identifies the ensemble music as hard bop, particularly with highly interactive drummers Art Blakey, Philly Joe Jones, and Louis Hayes.

(2) "Funky hard bop" or "funky jazz" stems partly from music devised by Horace Silver in the middle 1950s, continuing throughout his career (into the 1990s). Though most of Silver's compositions and solo improvisations are not funky, his funky ones have had the greatest popularity ("The Preacher," "Doodlin'," "Señor Blues," "Song for My Father"). They ultimately defined his music for the majority of jazz listeners. The same can be said for the music of Cannonball Adderley, Nat Adderley ("Work Song," "Jive Samba") and Bobby Timmons ("Moanin'"), beginning in the late 1950s and running into the 1970s. The Adderley recording of Joe Zawinul's gospelish "Mercy, Mercy, Mercy" was a huge hit during the late 1960s.

(3) "Soul-jazz" came partly from the funky subcategory of hard bop. Its earthy, bluesy melodic concept and the repetitive, dance-like rhythmic aspects stood as higher priorities than the invention of complex harmonies and intricate solo improvisations. Jazz swing feeling was foremost. Considerably simplified—often only a hint of bebop harmony or rhythmic complexity remained—soul-jazz became the form of hard bop known to the largest audience, particularly in the music of Jimmy Smith, Shirley Scott, Jack McDuff, Richard "Groove" Holmes, Jimmy McGriff, Ramsey Lewis, Les McCann, Hank Crawford, Stanley Turrentine and Houston Person.

Note that some listeners make no distinction between "soul-jazz" and "funky hard bop," and many musicians don't consider "soul-jazz" to be continuous with "hard bop." They consider it more an extension of the jazz-influenced popular music called "rhythm and blues" (as exemplified by Earl Bostic, King Curtis, Clifford Scott, Junior Walker, Bill Doggett). Also remember that many bebop musicians chose to play simply and with bluesy vocabularies for selected contexts: for instance, Kenny Burrell, Stanley Turrentine, J.J. Johnson, Grant Green, David "Fathead" Newman, Gene Ammons, and Ray Bryant. Their overall output is not funky, though a few pieces on isolated recordings meet all the above criteria for "soul-jazz."

(4) "Coltrane-influenced hard bop" is a post-bop school that never acquired a category of its own in the press or among musicians. It was occupied by several innovators whom the public first recognized during the 1960s, not the 1950s: Wayne Shorter, Freddie Hubbard, McCoy Tyner, Herbie Hancock, Joe Henderson, and Joe Zawinul. These musicians devised new harmonic and melodic vocabularies that were distinguishable from the favorite phrases of Charlie Parker and Dizzy Gillespie, though their accompaniments often resembled bebop practices.

Many journalists and musicians do not consider the music of this fourth subcategory to constitute a separate category. They merely include it within "hard bop," and some classify this music as "bebop." And, though it shows the influence of

John Coltrane's work, this school cannot be categorized solely within the large school of Coltrane disciples who were active after the 1950s because players in this fourth subcategory were not disciples of Coltrane so much as borrowers of selected Coltrane movements.

(5) "Mainstream hard bop": The work of jazz musicians during the 1950s and 1960s which, though still clearly tied to bebop, represented unique approaches: Sonny Rollins (before 1962), John Coltrane (before 1957), Pepper Adams, Curtis Fuller, Jimmy Heath, Hank Mobley, Tommy Flanagan, Art Farmer, Barry Harris, Wes Montgomery, Kenny Burrell, Grant Green, Thad Jones, Jackie McLean, Duke Pearson, Red Garland, Wynton Kelly, Clifford Jordan, Booker Ervin, George Coleman, Charlie Rouse, Harold Land, Blue Mitchell, Kenny Dorham, Benny Bailey, Oliver Nelson, and others.

During the 1980s and 1990s, a number of young musicians engaged in a revival of the 1950s-1960s hard bop style: Out of the Blue (a band named in honor of the great hard bop recordings by the Blue Note company), the Harper Brothers, Terence Blanchard, Donald Harrison, Roy Hargrove (a Freddie Hubbard disciple), Marion Jordan, Mark Whitfield (a Wes Montgomery disciple), Branford Marsalis (who sometimes played remarkably like the 1950s approach of Sonny Rollins, the mid-1960s approach of Wayne Shorter, or whomever else he was studying at the moment), Wynton Marsalis (who emulated the mid-1960s Miles Davis style), Benny Green (who performed in various styles of the 1950s and 60s), Joey DeFrancesco (who imitated the Hammond B-3 organ style of Jimmy Smith), and others.

Harlem Stride

Harlem stride is a style of jazz piano playing in which the pianist's left hand maintains a continuous pulse in groups of four beats by percussively playing a bass note on the first and third beats and a chord on the second and fourth beats. The right hand improvises melodies and harmonies, and the result resembles a very energetic one-man band. It was performed by immensely talented pianists who were able to control the piano with a power and virtuosic force previously unknown in popular music. The style originated in New York before the 1920s, as pianists took ragtime and began developing new, more swinging styles. Major proponents were James P. Johnson, Willie "The Lion" Smith, and Luckey Roberts. They influenced Fats Waller, Duke Ellington, Count Basie, and Joe Sullivan who, in turn, went on to be influential themselves. Art Tatum and Ralph Sutton, for instance, were both influenced by Waller.

Jazz-Rock Fusion

Jazz-rock fusion is a variety of hybrid styles that appeared in the late 1960s and early 1970s, fusing the traditions of soul music, rock, and jazz. Subclassifications are:

(1) "Jazz-rock": Singer-based bands that employed (a) horns, (b) a little jazz improvisation, and (c) accompaniment styles similiar to those of James Brown, Sly Stone, the Parliaments, and Jimi Hendrix bands (Tower of Power; Chase; Chicago; Blood, Sweat & Tears, etc.).

(2) "Original Fusion": Instrumental groups of the late 1960s and early 1970s that improvised extensively and created distinctive new music by fusing Indian, Brazilian, funk, Coltrane-styled jazz, and "rhythm & blues" traditions (The Free Spirits, The Fourth Way, Miles Davis bands of 1969-1991, Weather Report, Tony Williams Lifetime, Dreams, Eleventh House, Headhunters, and other bands from the late 1960s through the 1990s led by John McLaughlin, Larry Coryell, Gary Burton, Eddie Harris, Michael White, Herbie Hancock, Billy Cobham, Jean-Luc Ponty, Michael Brecker, Randy Brecker and others).

(3) "Second-generation fusion": A second wave of instrumental groups originating during the 1970s, which, though drawing on similiar sources as the first wave (see #2), were also responsible for their own blends of modern jazz with soul music, funk, and Latin jazz (Spyro Gyra, the Yellowjackets, The Crusaders, Steps Ahead, Word of Mouth, Oracle, Soft Machine, Hiroshima, Jeff Lorber Fusion, Steely Dan, Prime Time, The Decoding Society, and numerous groups led by Bob James, Lee Ritenour, Earl Klugh, Dave Grusin, Pat Metheny, Stanley Clarke, and others). See also "contemporary funk" and "jazzy pop."

(4) "Light fusion": A lighter variant on styles of the second wave (see #3), often heard in "background music" radio airplay (Kenny G, Richard Elliot, Najee, Lee Ritenour, Kim Pensyl, Art Porter, Rob Mullins, and others). Sometimes this music is made by the same musicians as listed for the second wave (Metheny, Ritenour, Spyro Gyra, Grusin, James, etc.). See also "jazzy pop."

Jazzy Pop

Jazzy pop is the collection of styles that convey jazz flavor and contain some improvisation but are not devoted to jazz as their primary approach. These styles have been present throughout jazz history and consist essentially of popular instrumental music. For example: Ted Lewis in the 1920s, Glen Gray in the 1930s, Glen Miller in the 1940s, Ray Anthony in the 1950s, Al Hirt and Herb Alpert in the 1960s, Chuck Mangione in the 1970s and Kenny G in the 1980s and 1990s. See also "jazz-rock fusion" and "contemporary funk."

John Coltrane School

The *John Coltrane school* is a term that can classify the numerous recordings by saxophonist-composer-bandleader John Coltrane and the musicians who assimilated his music and used it as a significant portion of their own styles. Aside from Coltrane's bebop work of 1946-1956, his output is sufficiently unique in style to warrant a category of its own and not be classified with cool jazz, hard bop, free jazz, or other general categories. Therefore only his pre-1957 work can accurately be cross-listed with bebop or hard bop. The saxophonists who showed Coltrane's influence upon their own styles the earliest were David Young and Joe Farrell in the late 1950s. Then, by the early 1960s, Pharoah Sanders and Charles Lloyd; by the middle 1960s, Gato Barbieri and Andrew White. By the late 1960s, Michael Brecker, David Liebman, and Steve Grossman were all making their marks as bandleaders and recording artists, using styles partly inspired by Coltrane's improvisational and compositional concepts. During the 1970s and 1980s, saxophonists were using Coltrane's melodic and harmonic vocabulary more than those of other models. Pianists, guitarists, and trumpeters were also inspired by Coltrane. For instance, trumpeter Freddie Hubbard has cited Coltrane's influence, and pianist-composer Chick Corea acknowledged Coltrane's inspiration for his own compositions and improvisations.

Part of the "Coltrane school" reflects the accompaniment methods that were refined by pianist McCoy Tyner while employed by Coltrane from 1960 to 1965. Many pianists of the 1960s and 1970s assimilated Tyner's favorite chords and his particular ways of rhythmically feeding those chords to soloists: Alice Coltrane, Bill Henderson, Joanne Brackeen, Mulgrew Miller, Allan Gumbs, John Hicks, Hilton Ruiz, Ronnie Matthews, Kenny Gill, Bobo Stinson, Michael Cochran, Hal Galper, Joe Bonner, and others. Much of this is evident in the ensemble styles of the bands led by the saxophonists mentioned above. These pianists also mastered Tyner's approaches to developing solo improvisations. Since these approaches were new and not really "hard bop," the

Tyner disciples might best be categorized with Tyner or with "the Coltrane school."

Latin Jazz

Latin jazz is the popular music of Cuba, Puerto Rico, and South America with jazz improvisations added. Though not all their music contains solo improvisations, these musicians are most often identified with "Latin jazz": Tito Puente, Mongo Santamaria, Eddie Palmieri, Machito, Willie Bobo, Mario Bauza, Ray Barretto, João Gilberto, Poncho Sanchez, Gato Barbieri, Paquito D'Rivera, Arturo Sandoval, and Hilton Ruiz. The most prominent American-born jazz musicians who have incorporated Latin American accompaniments into some of their pieces are Dizzy Gillespie, Stan Kenton, Cal Tjader, Stan Getz, George Shearing, Herbie Mann, and Chick Corea.

Throughout jazz history, various Latin dance rhythms have been common in jazz, from the tango passage in W.C. Handy's "St. Louis Blues" composition of 1914, to Dizzy Gillespie's "Manteca" recording of 1947, to the accompaniments underneath numerous modern jazz renditions for "I'll Remember April" and "On Green Dolphin Street" of the 1950s. During the 1960s and early 1970s, most modern jazz musicians allocated a portion of their repertory to the samba-like "bossa nova" style. All of these selections qualify for the designation of "Latin jazz."

See also "World Fusion."

Miles Davis Avant-Garde Style

Miles Davis avant-garde style is defined by the Davis band output from 1964 to 1969 with Wayne Shorter, Herbie Hancock, Chick Corea, Ron Carter, Dave Holland, Tony Williams, and Jack DeJohnette and the music made by Davis's musicians when they led their own record dates in the same period. Their approach derived initially from (a) the mode-based thinking that Bill Evans brought to previous Davis bands during 1958 and 1959, (b) a new solo style that Davis devised for his trumpet improvisations, (c) the rhythmic and melodic concepts of the Bill Evans-Scott LaFaro-Paul Motian trio of 1959 to 1961, and (d) some of the melodic and harmonic freedoms that were demonstrated by Ornette Coleman and Don Cherry from 1958 to 1964 and elaborated by Wayne Shorter.

Most of the music made by the mid-1960s Davis band does not use bebop harmonies or melodic vocabulary, and it approximates free jazz in its freshness. It uses considerably more varied approaches to improvised accompaniment than in bebop. However, it is not free jazz. Its improvisations nearly always follow a set tempo and a preset scale or series of tone centers. The music revolves around a number of distinctive compositions by Wayne Shorter ("Masqualero," for instance) that are almost entirely unrelated to the forms or sounds of pop tunes or bebop standards. The lengths of sections within them are unusual. The ways their chords move are also unusual, and the melodies and harmonies are unlike any other style.

This approach inspired the 1970s music of Eddie Henderson, Charles Moore, Kenny Cox, Mark Isham, and Art Lande, and the 1980s and 1990s music of Wynton and Branford Marsalis, Bob Belden, Kenny Kirkland, Joey Calderazzo, Kevin Hays, Donald Harrison, Bill Kirchner, Tim Ries, Billy Childs, Fred Hersch, Wallace Roney, Terence Blanchard, Tim Hagans, John McNeil, Jim Powell, Marc Cohen, and others.

New Age

New age jazz refers to instrumental styles originating during the 1980s, which intentionally avoid the type and extent of rhythmic feeling and melodic surprises common to jazz, though it does use improvisation. Harmonies change only very gradually. It was designed to function equally well as listening music and background music. Much of it is light instrumental music that is not related to jazz. However, when it was first heard, many listeners considered it jazz, rather than classical music. So it remained identified with jazz among those who have not given it a category of its own.

The sounds in new age music are soft and smooth, produced with the intention to calm and soothe, not to energize or provoke. They are heavily processed and often depend upon electronic synthesizers. Asian music and South American instrument sounds are often incorporated. Some kinds of new age feature highly stylized jazz-rock fusion. And several jazz musicians have recorded subdued electronic music that is so pleasant and homogeneous it became classified as new age even when the musicians did not have that function in mind. For instance, some recordings from the ECM firm were perceived that way, and selected works by jazz musicians Pat Metheny and Lyle Mays have been pegged "new age." ECM is primarily a jazz label, however, and the firms most closely associated with new age are Narada and Windham Hill.

George Winston was the most popular artist in this genre during the mid-1980s, and he was playing the style before it acquired the name "new age." He devised his approach by imitating the simplest aspects of Keith Jarrett's solo piano improvisations. Harpist Andres Vollenweider, the Paul Winter Consort, and Oregon have also cornered a segment of the new age audience with music that contains improvisation. They made soothing instrumental music that achieved the 1980s market equivalent of Ray Conniff and Roger Williams in the 1960s.

New Orleans Traditional

New Orleans traditional was the first jazz style, and it took the form of a small-band music that was first prominent at the beginning of the 1900s in New Orleans. Though called "Dixieland" by many listeners, this music is distinguished from its descendants because it is somewhat less solo-oriented. Though traditional New Orleans jazz was performed by Blacks, Whites, and African-American Creoles, some historians reserve the term "Dixieland" for White derivatives and revivals of this style, organized mostly by musicians in Chicago, New York, and San Francisco. This music originated with brass bands and "string bands" that performed for parties and dances in the late 1800s and early 1900s. The groups used combinations of cornet, clarinet, saxophone, trombone, tuba, guitar, banjo, bass violin, drums, and piano. The music usually featured several moving parts at the same time. The arrangements contained a memorable amount of flexibility from performance to performance. Many of the solos and embellishments were improvised, and much of the melody was paraphrased for personalization. The musicians refined the syncopations of ragtime and adapted pop tunes, marches, hymns, blues, and rags for their repertory. The music was quite lively and featured a wide assortment of unusual tone qualities and soulful inflections of a melody tone's pitch. The most extensively recorded groups of this time and style were led by Joe "King" Oliver (Creole Jazz Band), Jelly Roll Morton (Red Hot Peppers), Johnny Dodds, Kid Ory, Sidney Bechet, Louis Armstrong, and Nick LaRocca (The Original Dixieland Jazz Band).

New York Avant-Garde

New York avant-garde of the 1980s and '90s refers to a wide assortment of innovative musicians creating new music from odd amalgams of free jazz, Charles Mingus and John Coltrane styles, fusion, 20th-century classical music, ethnic music, and musical theater. Major proponents include John Zorn, Roy Nathanson, Bill Frisell, Tim Berne, Don Byron,

Steve Coleman, Geri Allen, Greg Osby, Anthony Coleman, Marc Ribot, Butch Morris, and their colleagues. Frequently performing at the Manhattan night club The Knitting Factory, the movement has also been termed "the Brooklyn School" because so many of its musicians live and practice in Brooklyn.

A number of important avant-garde jazz musicians who first came to prominence during the 1970s were also making fresh kinds of jazz-derived styles in New York during the 1980s and 90s: Julius Hemphill, David Murray, Oliver Lake (the World Saxophone Quartet), Ray Anderson, George Lewis, Leo Smith, Thurman Barker, and others. They are sometimes called "avant-garde acoustic" to distinguish them from avant-garde instrumental styles that incorporate electronics and/or the accompaniment styles of funk and soul music. Sometimes they are misclassified with "free jazz," though much of their music is extensively composed and only a fraction of their improvisations are entirely free of pre-planning and set chord progressions.

Soul Jazz

Soul-jazz is a subcategory of hard bop that emerged in the 1950s and had its peak during the 1960s. Some of it derives from a foundation of bebop approaches, but mostly it emphasizes the traditions of earthy, gospelish feeling and simple, highly repetitive accompaniment patterns from the pop music styles known as "rhythm and blues" (exemplified by Earl Bostic's work of the late 1940s and early 1950s, Bill Doggett's "Honky Tonk" of 1956, and the saxophone solos King Curtis recorded with the Coasters in the 1950s). It differs from most hard bop by stressing marked consistency of swing feeling and brief, exceedingly bluesy melodic lines instead of complex chord progressions, intricate improvisations, and rhythmic surprises.

Major proponents are Jimmy Smith, Shirley Scott, Jack McDuff, Richard "Groove" Holmes, Jimmy McGriff, Houston Person, Charles Earland, Ramsey Lewis, Gene Harris, and Les McCann. Several musicians known primarily for their "soul-jazz" are also capable of performing bebop: Ray Charles, Hank Crawford, Stanley Turrentine, Willis "Gator" Jackson, and David "Fathead" Newman.

At one time or another, many bebop musicians have chosen to make selected pieces simple and funky in their melody, chord progressions, and solo improvisations while using highly repetitive accompaniment patterns to establish and maintain a dance-like groove. Most of their output is not funky and would rarely be termed "soul jazz." A few such players are Gene Ammons ("Canadian Sunset," "The Jungle Boss"), Ray Bryant, Lee Morgan ("Sidewinder"), Bobby Timmons ("Dis Here," "Dat Dere," "Moanin'"), Kenny Burrell, Grant Green, Eddie Harris ("Listen Here"), Horace Silver ("Señor Blues," "The Preacher," "Song for My Father"), Cannonball Adderley, and Nat Adderley (for example, "Sack o' Woe," "Jive Samba," "Work Song," "Mercy, Mercy, Mercy," "Walk Tall").

Swing

Swing is the jazz style that emerged during the early 1930s and emphasized big bands. It spilled into the late 1940s and then remained popular in recordings, film, and television music long after its main proponents had disbanded. Most swing-style groups had at least 10 musicians and featured at least three or four saxophones, two or three trumpets, two or three trombones, piano, guitar, bass violin, and drums. Guitarists, bassists, and drummers offered repeating rhythms that were sufficiently simple, buoyant, and lilting to inspire social dancers, the style's largest audience. Musicians strove for large, rich tone qualities on their instruments. Solo improvisers did not seek intricacy in their lines so much as lyricism and a hot, confident feeling that was rhythmically compelling. For these reasons, the musical period of the 1930s and 1940s has been called the "swing era" and "big-band era." Not all dance music played by big bands of the 1930s and 1940s was jazz. A large segment of the public, however, considered almost any lively, syncopated popular music to be "jazz."

Journalists and jazz fans drew distinctions between bands that conveyed the most hard-driving rhythmic qualities and extensive solo improvisations and those that conveyed less swing feeling and improvisation. The former were called "swing bands" or "hot bands" (for example, the bands of Count Basie, Jimmie Lunceford, Andy Kirk, and Duke Ellington). The latter were called "sweet" bands (for example, the bands of Glenn Miller, Wayne King, Freddy Martin, and Guy Lombardo). Many listeners, however, did not make such distinctions. They considered all the big dance bands to be "swing bands." This is not surprising because all the bands (even Guy Lombardo's) did play some jazz. And even the hottest of "swing bands" (like Duke Ellington's) featured some "sweet" numbers. Conversely, some of the biggest hits by Glenn Miller's "sweet" band contained brief jazz improvisations and conveyed quite danceable "swing" feeling. An instructive illustration for this confusion regards Tommy Dorsey's immensely popular bands of the 1940s. The groups had first-rate jazz-oriented accompanists, swinging arrangements, and a number of top-notch jazz improvisers. Yet large portions of their repertory were composed of ballads and vocal features. Therefore, though jazz historians don't usually give Dorsey's bands much attention, jazz musicians generally confer high respect upon them.

Though there were large dance bands before the swing era, "big-band music" as a concept for music fans developed most firmly during this era and persisted for decades thereafter. This has caused ambiguity in labeling because, for example, record store clerks often catalog big-band music as though it were a single style, despite the many different harmonic and rhythmic approaches that new ensembles of similiar instrumentation have used since the swing era. Large ensembles have performed almost every kind of jazz: swing, bebop, cool, hard bop, free jazz, and jazz-rock fusion. Not all big bands are "swing bands," and so "big-band style" should not be used routinely to designate the jazz of all large ensembles. But many consider "big band" to denote an idiom, not just an instrumentation. Also note that there were important jazz improvisers in the swing era, such as Art Tatum and Django Reinhardt, who did not earn their reputations in the context of big bands. And there were others, including Lester Young, Charlie Christian, and Coleman Hawkins, who often made their best recordings in small-band formats, though most of their livelihood and exposure came initially as soloists in big bands.

Third-Stream Jazz

Third-stream jazz is a term coined in 1957 by composer-musicologist Gunther Schuller to designate a kind of jazz

that resulted from the converging of the classical stream with the jazz stream. This often involved classical compositional forms and harmonies blending with jazz improvisation and jazz rhythmic feeling. The term was not intended to substitute for "symphonic jazz" or other examples of jazzy music played by huge ensembles without improvisation, as popularized by Paul Whiteman, for instance. The purest examples of third stream include some of the works of Schuller, John Lewis, Ran Blake, Robert Graettinger, and Don Ellis. For a list of examples, see Schuller's article on page 531 of the *New Grove Dictionary of Jazz, Volume 2.*

World Fusion

World fusion refers to a fusion of Third World music, or just "world music," with jazz, specifically:

(1) Ethnic music that has incorporated jazz improvisations (for example, "Latin jazz"). Frequently, only the solos are improvised jazz. The accompaniments and compositions are essentially the same as in the ethnic music.

(2) Jazz that has incorporated limited aspects of a particular non-Western music. Examples include performances of Dizzy Gillespie's "A Night in Tunisia"; music on some of the 1970s quartet recordings by Keith Jarrett's quartet and quintet on Impulse, in which Middle Eastern instruments and harmonic methods are modified and used; and some of Sun Ra's music from the 1950s into the 1990s, in which African rhythms are incorporated; some of Yusef Lateef's recordings that feature traditional Islamic instruments and methods.

(3) New musical styles that result from distinctly original ways of combining jazz improvisation with original ideas and the instruments, harmonies, compositional practices, and rhythms of an existing ethnic tradition. The product is original, but its flavor still reflects some aspects of a nonjazz, ethnic tradition. Examples include Don Cherry's bands Codona and Nu; some of John McLaughlin's music from the 1970s and the 1990s that drew heavily on the traditions of India; some of Don Ellis's music of the 1970s that drew upon the music of India and Bulgaria; and work by Andy Narell in the 1990s that melds the music and instruments of Trinidad with jazz improvisations and funk styles.

World fusion jazz did not first occur with modern jazz, and its trends are not exclusive to American jazz. For instance, Polynesian music was fusing with Western pop styles at the beginning of the twentieth century, and its feeling attracted some of the earliest jazz musicians. Caribbean dance rhythms have been a significant part of American pop culture throughout the twentieth century, and, since jazz musicians frequently improvised when performing in pop music contexts, blends have been occurring almost continuously. Django Reinhardt was melding the traditions of Gypsy music with French impressionist concert music and jazz improvisation during the 1930s in France.

See also "Latin jazz" and "jazz-rock fusion."

—Mark C. Gridley

TERMS

Arco

The bow of a violin. While anyone who uses the bow playing the bass or cello is said to be playing arco, the actual term is *coll' arco* or "with the bow."

Arpeggio

A term for the sounding of the notes of a chord in succession, rather than simultaneously. It also refers to a chord sounded in the same manner.

Arrangement

An adaptation of a work for an instrumentation or scoring for which it was not originally intended that preserves as much as possible of the piece's original character. The term does not quite have a fixed meaning in jazz terminology. Sometimes a new arrangement may change instrument orders or it may use a melody in one song taken from another. Sometimes rhythmic patterns are changed within songs, and there's a question whether this constitutes a new arrangement or fresh composition. Many well-known jazz pieces are frequently rearranged to the point that they're not necessarily new songs but are quite different from their original version.

Articulation

This refers either to the shaping of a musical phrase or the formation of vowels and consonants in singing. It is another important element in the analysis and evaluation of talent and performance in jazz.

Beat

A beat is the basic pulse of measured music.

Blue notes

The flattened third and flattened seventh note of the scale in any particular key. (The flattened fifth is also heard as a blue note when used as a melodic replacement or variation of the normal fifth, but not when it is a harmonic coloring in dense chordal textures.) These notes are often bent or slurred and underlined or embellished through techniques ranging from growls to slurs. They occur in other musical styles as well as jazz, and their sound and expression are far more important than simply their existence in a strict scalar sense.

Cadence

The concluding part of a phrase, movement, or work that affirms the tonality, modality, or musical language of that phrase, movement, or work through resolving dissonance or in some other fashion.

Cadenza

A virtuoso passage, normally designed for a solo instrument or lead vocal (voice). It is intended to be improvised or

have an improvisatory character, can be short or extended, and may have structural importance.

Charts

In jazz and sometimes pop parlance, another word for musical scores, particularly arrangements for a band or ensemble. Now the word more often refers to the weekly surveys tabulated by music magazines, usually *Billboard*, but other publications like *Radio and Records, Cash Box, Gavin Report*, and even *Rolling Stone* have their own "charts" as well.

Chord

The sounding of two or more notes simultaneously defines a chord. The term "changes" refers to harmonic chord progressions, or chord "changes."

Chorus

This has multiple meanings in the jazz lexicon. Normally, a chorus means going through the entire number one time, whether that means as few as 12 bars, as many as 32, or any other number. It dates back to the days when popular songs contained a verse that could be tossed or omitted, followed by "the chorus." It's often used in critical parlance to refer to an extended solo chorus; for example, on Paul Gonsalves's celebrated performance at the 1956 Newport Jazz Festival.

Circular breathing

A technique used principally by players of wind instruments, but also by some brass players. The player breathes in through the nose while the cheeks push air out through the instrument. This enables the musician to produce an unbroken column of air, and hold a note indefinitely, since there's no need to pause and breathe. The creative value is directly proportional to the musician utilizing the technique.

Composition

One of jazz's more misunderstood and widely used terms. It does not have the strict meaning employed in classical or even other popular styles. Its pure meaning is simply any piece that has been written, but jazz "compositions" can range from extensively noted and prepared works to rearranged melodies or revised riffs and licks. There's also extensive debate over whether improvisation constitutes composition. The use of classical standards of composition in evaluating jazz authors, a tricky (at best) proposition, has added difficulty. Basically, when composition is used in jazz circles, it refers strictly to the piece in question. The more intricate matter of what exactly defines or determines jazz composition remains unresolved.

Counterpoint

The interweaving of different melodic lines. It is present in many styles, notably free jazz and New Orleans traditional, but it is rhythmic counterpoint, rather than melodic counterpoint, that is most critical in jazz.

Dissonance

A sound which, in the primary harmonic system, is unstable and must be resolved to a consonant, or stable, sound. When used skillfully, this can be a most creative element in jazz circles; when misused it can be frightening.

Double time

A technique in which the apparent tempo of a performance is increased by doubling the number of notes played.

Downbeat

The first beat of a performance, or the first beat of each bar (often referred to as "one").

Embouchure

This has a dual meaning in jazz. It's both the position of the mouth and lips in playing reed and brass instruments, and also the mouthpiece of a reed instrument.

Ensemble

A general term referring to the entire jazz group, big band, combo, or orchestra. When critics talk about "ensemble" interaction, they're usually talking about the interplay among group members during the performance of a piece. Often unison sections are called "ensemble" portions of a piece.

Harmony

The combination of two or more tones, which produces a chord. These tones may be actual notes sounded simultaneously or they may be implied (chords derived from the context of a melodic line). The term generally connotes the presence of a tonality, and chords are said to contain harmonic and nonharmonic tones, depending on whether the tones are part of the current tonality.

Improvisation

This is the lifeblood of jazz, and it is also sometimes called "spontaneous creation." This is playing without premeditation. It's also among the more misunderstood premises within jazz. Jazz is not the only music to use improvisation, nor should composition be considered the enemy of improvisation. The act may involve departing from the established melody, distorting it, or coloring it. It can also involve inserting quotes from other compositions into the improvisation being crafted. Some composers, notably Duke Ellington, wrote with improvisations in mind for particular players.

Jam session

A group improvisation session and an outgrowth of the term "jam." This has long been a musician's term for an occasion when informal extended playing occurred apart from regular jobs. Jams were often held late nights or in the early morning hours following gigs. During the '30s and '40s, jam sessions were regular occurrences, but in the late '40s the Musicians' Union started to discourage members from participating in jam sessions, even in situations with invited audiences. But the term stuck and now is used to identify almost any setting where musicians gather. Norman Granz's Jazz at the Philharmonic concerts and recordings are perhaps the prime example of "jam sessions," despite the fact they soon became quite predictable and were hardly spontaneous affairs.

Key

The tonal center of a composition as defined by the relationship between the other notes of a scale to a certain note known as the tonic or key note.

Lick

A phrase of a player that's been copied, learned, and/or repeatedly used by another player. It's become an established jazz practice for musicians to copy the phrases of artists they admire. One thing that separates innovators from journeymen is the ability to develop one's own licks. Another is the ability to create new phrases rather than simply recycle favorite licks.

Measure

The space between two bar lines.

Medley

A performance linking a number of songs or other musical works. The songs are usually, but not always, related.

Melisma

A group of notes sung to the same syllable. This is a marvelous technique when done by masters, and is interesting even in the hands of journeymen, though it can be excruciating when performed by hacks.

Melody

A succession of musical tones, usually with a definite rhythm and having a characteristic musical shape.

Meter

The arrangement of the rhythmic units of a composition in a manner that produces a regular pattern of beats that are then grouped into measures. The number of beats in a measure is indicated by the time signature.

Modal

A style of jazz improvisation on a series of scales instead of a sequence of chords. This style, which became popular in the late '50s and early '60s, wasn't that much removed from bop, but tried to avoid the amount of harmonic movement and direction of bop sequences. The emphasis on the part of the soloist was toward melodic creativity rather than simply relying on chord-derived material.

Mode

In its simplest definition, mode is a designation for types of scales or melodies, indicating the range, the pitch center, and the whole- and half-step relationships between the notes. Many non-Western cultures, particularly Asian ones, apply the concept quite differently. George Russell developed an entire system (The Lydian Concept of Tonal Organization) from the seven seven-note scales used in ancient Greece, which, along with certain five- and six-note scales, constitute the basis of all European music.

Multiphonics

A term describing multiple simultaneous tones produced on a wind instrument from a single fingering. Although the technique is most commonly used in contemporary classical music, such jazz artists as John Coltrane and Albert Mangelsdorff are among its most skillful proponents.

Note

A single sound of a specific pitch and duration.

Original

Another all-purpose term with a somewhat confusing meaning. An original refers to a song performed and written by the same person, as opposed to an "original" playing style, of which there have been precious few. Actually, there aren't that many "original" compositions either, at least in the strictest sense of the term.

Ostinato

A musical figure repeated, usually at the same pitch, throughout a composition.

Overblowing

The practice of blowing into a wind instrument with more than usual force and changing the pitch, producing an overtone rather than the customary tone.

Overdubbing

At one time this was considered something radical, but it is now a commonplace studio practice in every category of popular music. Overdubbing came about through the introduction of sound into films, where it became necessary to find ways of blending dialog, sound effects, and music and replacing one actor's voice with another. Sidney Bechet's 1941 recording of five instruments (which to this day is widely celebrated in some circles and just as widely debunked in others) was an overdubbing milestone. Les Paul invented the multitrack tape machine, and gradually the practice gained popularity and, finally, total acceptance. Now almost no pop albums are done without overdubbing, and more and more jazz works use it as well. Many reissues are even including pieces with new parts overdubbed. Overdubbing has led to additional practices. These include "tracking," where the ensemble arrangement gets recorded first and then the improvised solos are taped and inserted. There is also "layering," whereby each instrument gets recorded in turn, or the rhythm section arrangement first and then other parts, and then everything gets spliced together later. Numerous country "duets" are actually each participant singing a part with the performances linked later in studio.

Phrasing

The grouping and articulation of a sequence of notes to form a logical unit or phrase. A musician's phrasing is an integral factor in evaluating his or her skills.

Pizzicato

An indication for string players to pluck rather than bow the strings, though in jazz most bassists play with the fingers far more often than with the bow.

Rhythm

The distinctive grouping of sounds and silence in time based on, among other things, the duration of tone, strong and weak stresses, and other factors like harmony and melodic contour.

Rhythm section

A term for players in a band whose primary function is to maintain the rhythm. Initially, rhythm was kept mainly by guitar and bass, or piano and drums. Later, during the '20s, both large bands and small combos used four rhythm players with banjo and brass rather than guitar or string bass. During the '30s, the rhythm role reverted again to predominantly piano and drums. Today, in the basic jazz combo, rhythm section instruments are usually bass and drums, with piano (and in some bands guitar) alternating as part of the rhythm section and also as a lead/solo instrument. Many

bands now employ additional percussionists on African and/or Latin instruments for extra rhythmic support.

Riff

A repeated phrase of pronounced rhythmic character, often not strikingly melodic. Riffs occur often in solo work, particularly from players who customarily think along such lines.

Scales

Sequences of notes in ascending or descending order of pitch, customarily beginning and ending on the fundamental note of a tonality or mode and considered to have a scope of one or more octaves.

Sideman

Due to nonsexist language requirements, this term has fallen out of favor in some parts of the jazz universe. It refers to anyone not the group leader on a particular session or date.

Solo

This has at least two meanings in jazz terminology. One refers to any performance that is unaccompanied. Coleman Hawkins's "Picasso" was the first solo saxophone example. It is most frequently the case with pianists, though a number of saxophonists have also recorded some celebrated albums, and some string and brass musicians as well. It also refers to any passage in a performance where one person is engaged in prominent melodic improvisation or on a specific chord sequence. Usually, some or all of the other group members are backing or supporting the "soloist."

Staccato

A type of articulation in which each note so marked is separated from the following note and may receive a greater or lesser accent, depending on the notation and the context.

Standard

A designation usually applied to popular songs from the prerock era whose appeal has outlived the original publication and, in many instances, the lifetimes of the composers. These are often songs from musicals, plays, or films, but are also Tin Pan Alley works and even some numbers that were novelty tunes. Some songs, such as "My Favorite Things" or "Green Dolphin Street," are so identified with jazz that their origins have been forgotten. There are also now jazz "standards," that is, works by jazz composers that have become part of the language, like "Perdido," "Tune Up," or "Ornithology."

Syncopation

In European music, syncopation is a simple and steady pulse that is disturbed by an anticipated or delayed accent. In jazz terms, syncopation has a slightly different meaning, as most jazz is naturally polyrhythmic and thus not syncopated in that sense.

Tempo

The rate of speed of a musical passage, indicated by a suggestive word or phrase or by a precise indication. In jazz and popular music a fast tempo is called uptempo, a slow one down tempo, though few contemporary critics use down tempo in their copy, preferring to talk about ballads or slow songs. Out of tempo usually refers to a group or a soloist with a poor sense of rhythm.

Timbre

The color or tonal quality of a sound, determined by its overtones.

Time signature

An indication of the meter of a piece that's placed at the beginning of a composition and at the beginning of any measure where a change in the prevailing meter occurs. The signature is usually a fraction whose numerator is the number of beats per measure and whose denominator is the unit of beat.

Tone

One of the terms with multiple meanings that can greatly confuse the nonjazz listener and someone trying to understand the jazz lexicon. In jazz parlance, tone refers to the qualities that make up a performer's sound. The term also means a musical sound or pitch, but when critics refer to someone's tone, they're describing or evaluating that individual's sound.

Upbeat

The second beat of a piece. In jazz, the upbeat is usually deemed the stronger in the piece. The term also has widespread nonmusical usage as denoting a positive development or personality.

Virtuoso

An often overused word in jazz circles (criminally misused in pop ones), as it is sometimes applied to merely talented people rather than genuine virtuosos. The strictest meaning is a performer with highly developed technical skill. The difference (or similarity) between a virtuoso and a genius makes for interesting discussion.

—Ron Wynn

A

AHMED ABDUL-MALIK (Sam Gill)

b. Jan. 30, 1927, New York, NY
Bass, oud, oriental instruments / Hard bop, world fusion
An early pioneer in fusing African, African-American, and Middle Eastern musical concepts, Ahmed Abdul-Malik divided his time between playing strong, supportive bass and soloing on oud. He was among the earliest to use the oud in a jazz context, playing it on some '50s sessions. Abdul-Malik studied African and Middle Eastern music, plus violin and bass. He played with Art Blakey in the late '40s, Randy Weston and Thelonious Monk in the '50s, Herbie Mann and Earl Hines in the '60s, and Ken McIntyre in the '70s. Abdul-Malik became a Muslim in the '50s, and played oud on a South American tour sponsored by the State Department in the early '60s and at the first jazz festival held at Tangiers, Morocco, in 1972. He also recorded on oud with Johnny Griffin in the '50s, John Coltrane in the '60s, and Hamiet Bluiett in the '70s. Abdul-Malik began teaching at New York University in 1970, and later became an instructor in the department of African Studies at Brooklyn College. He was given BMI's Pioneer in Jazz award in 1984. Abdul-Malik's *Jazz Sahara* session was reissued on CD in 1993. It's currently his only date available, though he recorded others for New Jazz in the '60s. —*Ron Wynn and Michael G. Nastos*

☆ **Jazz Samba** / Oct. 1958 / Riverside 287
○ **East Meets West** / Mar. 16, 1959+Mar. 31, 1959 / RCA 2015
Jazz Sahara / Jul. 9, 1959 / Riverside 1121
Good date fusing hard bop sensibility with North African instruments and influences. Ahmed Abdul-Malik's oud doesn't seem out of place in a group with Johnny Griffin's powerhouse solos. Drummer Al Harewood fits in with the rhythm section while other percussionists play the kanoon, darabeka, and tambourine. There's not a pianist, but there is a violinist. —*Ron Wynn*
★ **Music of Ahmed Abdul-Malik, The** / May 23, 1961 / New Jazz 8266
Sounds of Africa / Aug. 22, 1962 / New Jazz 8282

AHMED ABDULLAH

b. 1947, New York, NY
Trumpet / Modern creative
A sometimes striking, animated trumpeter, Ahmed Abdullah did several sessions during the '70s in New York "loft" jazz circles, and led the Solomonic Quintet in the '80s. He's also played with Chico Freeman, Charles Brackeen, and Malachi Favors. Abdullah's recorded for Silkheart and Cadence Jazz, and has a couple of sessions available on CD. —*Ron Wynn*

○ **Live at Ali's Alley** / Apr. 24, 1978 / Cadence
Trumpeter Ahmed Abdullah features French horn and cello in his instrumental configuration, while also working alongside tenor saxophonist Chico Freeman on this 1978 date. It's symbolic of the decade's "loft" jazz, a freewheeling date with uneven, but often compelling solos, as well as periods of rambling, unproductive, and ragged ensemble work. Freeman's blistering tenor sax is uniformly inspired, while Abdullah's solos are also aggressive and energetic. Vincent

Chancey's French horn and Muneer Abdul Fataah's cello contributions provide interesting contrast, while bassist Jerome Hunter and drummer Rashied Sinan are competent and effective, though not memorable. —*AMG*

★ **Life's Force** / 1978-1979 / About Time 1001
Progressive trumpeter with sextet in an all-original program. Includes Jay Hoggard on vibes and Vincent Chancey on French horn. —*Michael G. Nastos*

Liquid Magic / i. 1987 / Silkheart 104
On trumpeter Abdullah's debut session for Silkheart, he is sometimes eclipsed. This isn't due so much to Abdullah lacking verve or skill, but to the brilliance exhibited by tenor saxophonist Charles Brackeen and bassist Malachi Favors, whose acrobatics threaten to stretch and pull some songs beyond their harmonic fabric. —*Ron Wynn*

And the Solomonic Quintet / Silkheart 109
Trumpeter Ahmed Abdullah sprays around dissonant solos and spearheads an often frenzied set on his second release for Silkheart. The lineup is exceptional, notably the powerful tenor saxophonist David S. Ware, dynamic bassist Fred Hopkins, and underrated drummer Charles Moffett. —*Ron Wynn*

JOHN ABERCROMBIE (John L. Abercrombie)

b. Dec. 16, 1944, Port Chester, NY
Guitar / Early jazz-rock, modern creative
Perhaps the most skilled of the contemporary jazz guitarists who've embraced and utilized rock techniques and electronic devices in an improvisational framework, John Abercrombie has made many superb recordings since the early '70s. He's used phase shifters, volume pedals, guitar synthesizers, and the electric mandolin on a regular basis. Abercrombie is cited (or blamed) in many circles for helping create the "ECM sound," a patchwork of acoustic and electric sounds made by eclectic musicians who combine jazz, European, and Asian/Indian sources, elements, and influences. But Abercrombie can also swing, can play in the distorted, jagged rock style, can execute bebop changes, can improvise in 12-bar blues patterns, or can engage in free dialogues. He began playing guitar at age 14, taking lessons from a local teacher. He attended Berklee in the mid '60s, while playing in rock bands. Abercrombie studied guitar with Jack Petersen, and in 1967 and 1968 toured with Johnny "Hammond" Smith. He moved to New York in 1969 and worked briefly with the group Dreams, then played with Chico Hamilton, in whose band he made his first visit to Europe. Abercrombie later played with Jeremy Steig, Gil Evans, and Gato Barbieri, while recording with Dave Liebman and playing in Billy Cobham's Spectrum. While recording with these musicians, he attracted extensive critical attention. Abercrombie began recording with Jack DeJohnette and also as a leader in the mid-'70s, working mainly for ECM. Since that time, he's done duo albums with Ralph Towner, played in various DeJohnette bands, and headed various groups. Abercrombie's recorded with Jan Hammer, Dave Holland, Mike Brecker, Richie Beirach, George Mraz, Peter Donald, Marc Johnson, Adam Nussbaum, Peter Erskine, Vince Mendoza, and Jon

Christensen, among others. At present, he has many titles available on CD. —*Ron Wynn and David Nelson McCarthy*

★ **Timeless** / Jun. 21, 1974-Jun. 22, 1974 / ECM 829114
Guitarist John Abercrombie debuted on ECM in 1974 working in a trio setting, a format that would become familiar. Jan Hammer is on synthesizer, organ, and piano, and drummer Jack DeJohnette accompanies him on a date that includes crisp, taut riffs and solos from Abercrombie, sparse and tasty fills and licks by DeJohnette, and a bonus in long stretches of first-rate organ work by Hammer, minus the rock gimmicks that eventually plagued his keyboard work. —AMG

☆ **Gateway—Vol. 1** / Mar. 1975 / ECM 829192
The first of two fine trio albums that match guitarist John Abercrombie, bassist Dave Holland, and drummer Jack DeJohnette manages the trick of being both reflective and dynamic, thanks to Abercrombie's intelligent, finely crafted solos and DeJohnette's first-rate, sympathetic rhythms. Though Holland doesn't play with his usual vigor, he remains enough of a force to successfully interact with Abercrombie and DeJohnette. —AMG

Gateway—Vol. 2 / Mar. 1975+Jul. 1977 / ECM 1105
The second meeting between Abercrombie, bassist Dave Holland, and drummer Jack DeJohnette in 1977 features more electric guitar fireworks and less exacting, thoughtful jazz solos. Holland's bass playing is more intense, while DeJohnette is once more rhythmically diverse, supportive, and in control. Those who prefer hearing the rock-tinged side of Abercrombie's musical personality get their wish on the majority of *Gateway 2.* —AMG

☆ **Sargasso Sea** / May 1976 / ECM 835015
A nice session, though not as spectacular as anticipated. It matches guitarists John Abercrombie and Ralph Towner, who also plays piano. Towner's 12-string solos are stronger than his classical ones, which are frequently beautiful, but don't make much of an impression contrasted to Abercrombie's more energetic improvisations. The title track's the best cut on the sessions; the others are more decorative than intriguing. —AMG

○ **Straight Flight** / Mar. 19-20, 1979 / Jam 5001

Five Years Later / 1981 / ECM 1207
With Ralph Towner (g). Abercrombie is more electric in this duet setting. Three pieces cowritten by the duo. Two vastly different sounds mesh nicely. —*Michael G. Nastos*

★ **Night** / Apr. 1984 / ECM 823212
Spirited original featuring Jan Hammer (k). Favorable group setting for guitarist Abercrombie and timeless trio. Michael Brecker (ts). Definitive. —*Michael G. Nastos*

Current Events / Sep. 1985 / ECM 827770
Excellent trio date featuring Abercrombie playing with bassist Marc Johnson and drummer Peter Erskine. The three take chances, converge, collide, alternate time in the spotlight, and make emphatic, unpredictable music while never staying locked into one groove or style. —*Ron Wynn*

Works / i. Jan. 25, 1991 / ECM 837275
A good 1989 compilation of past Abercrombie selections on various ECM releases, spotlighting his versatility and proficiency. Songs feature his fluid guitar in introspective, mainstream, and free contexts, playing everything from new age–tinged originals to covers of standards. —*Ron Wynn*

RABIH ABOU-KHALIL

Oud and flute / World fusion

Rabih Abou-Khalil is a Lebanese oud and flute player who fled into exile to escape the turmoil in his homeland in the late '70s. He has mixed the improvisational flair and harmonic edges of jazz with the sounds and rhythms of Arabic music, playing an 11-string oud. Abou-Khalil has recorded for MMP, Mesa, and Enja, working with Charlie Mariano, Glen Moore, and Glen Velez, as well as various Lebanese musicians. He has a few sessions available on CD. —*Ron Wynn*

★ **Al-Jadida** / Oct. 1990 / Mesa Bluemoon 79674

MUHAL RICHARD ABRAMS

b. Sep. 19, 1930, Chicago, IL
Piano, composer, cello, clarinet / Early free, progressive big band, modern creative

Muhal Richard Abrams's importance as a pianist, bandleader, arranger, composer, and administrator surpasses the importance of almost anyone else in the Chicago avant-garde school. His efforts in founding both the Experimental Band in 1961 and the Association for the Advancement of Creative Musicians (AACM) in 1965 are legendary. Abrams was the AACM's first president and worked tirelessly encouraging musician/community interaction, urging contemporary players to familiarize themselves with the entire Black musical tradition, and helping to craft the organization's tenets. He was one of the individuals most vital to making the AACM a major institution on both the Chicago and the national music scene. Abrams, in interviews and discussions about the AACM and his own career, stresses original composition, knowing the ropes of the music business (including copyright law and distribution economics), and the importance of diversity. His piano, composition, and arranging styles are similarly broad. His piano approach reflects stride, boogie-woogie, blues, bebop, hard bop, and free influences and elements. His compositions have included traditional New Orleans jazz and 20th-century classical references alongside those of James P. Johnson. Abrams has played clarinet, has led octets and big bands, and has made duo and solo albums.

He began studying piano at age 17, and attended Chicago Musical College for four years. He began playing professionally in 1948, and wrote arrangements for King Flemming in 1950. Abrams played in Walter Perkins's MJT + 3 group in the late '50s, and wrote arrangements and compositions for them as well. Abrams did freelance sessions with many top musicians during their visits to Chicago in the late '50s and early '60s, including Miles Davis, Max Roach, Sonny Rollins, and Johnny Griffin. He began the Experimental Band in 1961 with musicians such as Eddie Harris, Roscoe Mitchell, and Donald Garrett. From this band, Abrams and some other Chicago musicians like Henry Threadgill, Joseph Jarman, Fred Anderson, and Steve McCall established the AACM in 1965, complete with an extensive list of principles, goals, and objectives. The AACM became active in the Chicago Black music community, sponsoring festivals and concerts and starting a school for young musicians.

Abrams was featured on several pioneering releases by AACM members on Delmark, and also recorded his own albums. His involvement in AACM affairs continued until he moved to New York in 1977. There he recorded solo piano sessions as well as duo dates with George Lewis, Anthony Braxton, Leroy Jenkins, and Amina Claudine Myers. During the '80s, he worked with the Kronos String Quartet and has led quintets, octets, and large bands. Abrams recorded albums in the '70s and '80s for India Navigation, Arista, Black Saint, and Enja, plus sessions with the Art Ensemble on Atlantic. His earlier albums on Delmark, as well as many Black Saint sessions, are available on CD. —*Ron Wynn*

★ **Levels and Degrees of Light** / Jun. 7, 1967 / Delmark 413
This is one of Muhal Richard Abrams's early gems, a 1967 session that includes him playing both piano and synthesizer and heading a quartet with Anthony Braxton on clarinet, Thurman Barker on drums, and Gordon Emmanuel on vibes. Abrams's superbly interspersed free, hard bop, and blues elements, Braxton's solos, and the intriguing frontline and contrasts provided by vibes and drums rather than bass results in some unusual and striking compositions. This has been reissued on CD. —AMG

☆ **Young at Heart, Wise in Time** / Jul. 2, 1969+Aug. 20, 1969 / Delmark 423
In his work for solo piano, "Young at Heart," Muhal Richard Abrams weaves a gossamer expression, opening the utter

fullness of his heart to the receptive listener in a manner defiant of analysis or description. No, it isn't "jazz"—but then nothing is, now. No other man could build this in such delicate beauty. "Wise in Time" is also appropriate. —*Barry Tepperman,* Coda

Things to Come from Those Now Gone / Oct. 10, 1972 / Delmark 430

A masterpiece and one of the finest works in the contemporary (post '50s) free jazz vernacular. Muhal Richard Abrams's compositions and piano solos illuminate multiple traditions, from stride and ragtime to the percussive style of the '50s and '60s. —*Ron Wynn*

Afrisong / Sep. 9, 1975 / India Navigation 1058

Muhal Richard Abrams seamlessly blends elements of stride, bebop, blues, and free music on this collection of solo piano pieces recorded in 1975 for the Japanese label Trio/Whynot. It was also available briefly on India Navigation. Top numbers include "Hymn to the East," "Blues for M," and the title track. It was also a chance for Abrams to display his instrumental facility and underrated keyboard skills, which often take a back seat to his arranging, compositions, and bandleading. —AMG

Sightsong / Oct. 13-14, 1975 / Black Saint 0003

When someone gets down to writing a history of jazz in the '60s and '70s, there can be little doubt that Muhal Richard Abrams will be cited as one of the most important contributors. Founder of Chicago's Association for the Advancement of Creative Musicians (the most important musical collective in the history of jazz), a composer of immense talent and diversity, leader of a highly charged big band, and a pianist of unquestionable skill, Abrams has never received the kind of publicity (or accolades) from the musical press that one would have expected of such a talented artist. All his Delmark albums contain moments of true inspiration, but it is *Sightsong* that I would recommend as the best introduction to Abrams and his music. Accompanied by the Art Ensemble of Chicago's bassist, Malachi Favors (and just when will he start receiving the praises he so richly deserves?), Abrams presents a music stripped to its barest essentials. These two play with a telepathic understanding of where each is going to take the music. . . . This album was recorded in New York in October of 1975. —*Carl Brauer,* Cadence

○ **Duet 1976** / i. 1976 / Black Saint

This was not Muhal Richard Abrams' session, but Anthony Braxton's, and was issued on Arista under Braxton's name. The duo teamed for intriguing, sometimes intense and other times more introspective performances on material ranging from Braxton's numerical compositions to their unusual version of "Maple Leaf Rag." Braxton played alto and soprano saxophones, plus contrabass clarinet and sax and standard clarinet, while Abrams concentrated on piano and added everything from bop riffs to stride accents, ragtime, and blues lines. —AMG

1-Oqa+19 / Nov. 1977-Dec. 1977 / Black Saint 0017

Muhal Richard Abrams hasn't presided over many small combos with a more imposing lineup than on this 1977 session. Anthony Braxton and Henry Threadgill play numerous instruments—from alto, tenor, and soprano saxes to flutes and clarinets, even adding background vocals. Fiery percussionist Steve McCall and bassist Leonard Jones, who also adds some vocals, complete the lineup. The unit made demanding, harmonically dense, and rhythmically unpredictable material. Braxton's scurrying solos are matched ably by Threadgill's bluesier lines and Abrams's leadership and inventive blend of jazz, blues, and other sources that hold things together. —AMG

Lifelong Ambitions / i. 1977 / Black Saint 33

☆ **Lifea Blinec** / Feb. 1978 / Novus 3000

Muhal Richard Abrams heads one of his finest small combos on this intense quintet session from 1978. Joseph Jarman provides riveting bass saxophone and bassoon contributions in addition to playing alto clarinet, flute, soprano sax, percussion, and creating vocals. His multiple contributions are matched by Douglas Ewart on an equal array of reed instruments, including bass and soprano clarinet, bassoon, alto and tenor sax, and percussion. Abrams divides his time between keyboards, conducting, and percussion, while Amina Claudine Myers is also on hand adding vibrant, bluesy riffs and statements. Thurman Barker takes care of drum duties and doubles on percussion. —AMG

Spiral Live at Montreux 1978 / Jul. 22, 1978 / Arista 3007

Ruthless clarity and a quality of raw unrestrained energy make this solo piano record a masterpiece. Muhal Richard Abrams elicits one of the beauties of solo piano: the open, timeless feeling of being in the hands of one individual. He solves one difficulty of solo piano: the need of the musician to move through many levels that may cause the listener to fall away and wander in response. "D Song" is a high-energy study in crisp hand technique, moving in a ultra-fast, boppish manner. . . . Abrams's arch-like system of improvisation, both left and right hands dealing complicated chromatic bursts, exposes the mid-range of the piano to a wealth of crossing line patterns and block clusters. The result: a tidal wave of ideas progressing along the percussive systems of Bela Bartok and Cecil Taylor. . . . Abrams was definitely a two-handed piano player; note the concluding minutes of "Voice Song" and the range of dynamics covered. There is an intense, drum-like throbbing in the left hand, intermixed with broken chords and the razor-sharp lines of the right. —*Bradley Parker-Sparrow,* Down Beat

Spihumonesty / Jul. 1979 / Black Saint 0032

Mama and Daddy / Jun. 16+19, 1980 / Black Saint 0041

This is a first-rate big band/large group session from 1980. Muhal Richard Abrams's compositions are played by a masterful ensemble, which includes French horn and tuba in its instrumental mix. There are wonderful solos, dashing arrangements, and fiery rhythm support from Thurman Barker on drums, marimba, and percussion, with Andrew Cyrille adding additional percussive assistance. The group also features Baikida Carroll on trumpet and flugelhorn, Wallace McMillan on various reeds, violinist Leroy Jenkins, bassist Brian Smith, Abrams on keyboards, trombonist George Lewis, Bob Stewart on tuba, and Vincent Chancey on French horn. They present adventurous, disciplined, frequently exciting music. —AMG

Duet 1981 / May 11-12, 1981 / Black Saint 0051

○ **Blues for Ever** / Jul. 20, 1981-Jul. 27, 1981 / Black Saint 0061

Tremendous large orchestra session with Abrams heading a crew that includes the cream of '70s and '80s improvisers, plus some '60s survivors. Though every arrangement doesn't click, the band successfully romps and stomps through enough cuts to show the big band sound doesn't just mean "ghost" groups recreating dusty numbers from the '30s and '40s. —*Ron Wynn*

★ **Rejoicing with the Light** / Jan. 8-25, 1983 / Black Saint 0071

Rejoicing with the Light recalls the episodic "watch what happens" serialism of Muhal Richard Abrams's and Anthony Braxton's initial waxings on Delmark circa the late 1960s, a period of sentimental value for me because it marked my introduction to new music. On side one, duet and a cappella "events" for soprano voice, percussion, strings, brass, and clarinets are alternated with controlled, somberly weighted textures from a 15-piece band. During "Bloodline," dedicated to Fletcher Henderson, Don Redman, and Benny Carter, the proceedings show signs of life, albeit nothing special compared to the elan that former Abrams collaborator Henry Threadgill takes on "the tradition." —*Peter Kostakis,* Down Beat

View from Within / Sep. 22+27, 1984 / Black Saint 0091

Abrams's work for mid-sized groups varies markedly from his solo, trio, or large orchestra material. Compositions are even more unpredictable, there's more emphasis on mood and less on rhythm, and solos are crisper and shorter. At times, this '84 date includes some intriguing instrumental

Jazz Accordian

Early Accordian Players
Charles Melrose (Cellar Boys 1930)
1929 Buster Moten (in Bennie Moten orchestra) (1929)
Jack Cornell (recorded with Irving Mills 1929, 1930)

Accordian Popular in Europe
Kamil Behounek (soloist 1936)
Toivo Karki
Nisse Lind
Buddy Bertinat (with Original Teddies) (1936-1948)

First Jazz Use
Joe Mooney Quartet (well known 1946-1947)

Other swing accordionists included:
Mat Mathews (1924)
The Millers (Dutch group) (1947-1950)
Art Van Damme (Norway) (1920)

George Shearing (1949 plays on Cherokee)

1950s and early '60s include:
Mat Mathews (1924)
Art Van Damme (1920)
Leon Sash (1922)
Pete Jolly (1932)
Tommy Gumina (1931)

Not used in jazz-rock or free jazz

Willem Breuker Kollektief (used it for humorous effects)

---

configurations (vibes/flute/percussion, piano/clarinet/bass clarinet) and ranks among his best '80s dates. —*Ron Wynn*

☆ **Roots of Blue** / Jan. 7, 1986 / RPR 1001

Roots of Blue is equivalent to hard-won success that needn't have been so difficult. It pales by comparison to Abrams's '70s masterstroke *Sight Song* (which features bassist Malachi Favors), though this is not because the participants were not up to the previous standards. "Time into Space into Time" points out a problem that characterizes much of this album: Cecil McBee (bass) is simply not heard between the spaces in this music. Abrams' compositional density allows for very little point/counterpoint between himself and the great bassist, thus his contribution is largely implied throughout. "C.C.'s World" finds McBee merely mirroring Abrams' cluttered tones and muted runs. "Metamor" had Abrams abandoning enough of the opaque air of this film-noir-sounding "composed theme" to let McBee contribute a fine solo. The title selection "Roots of Blue" was the latest in Abrams's continuing exploration with this blues form which, coming from this Chicago pianist, was as much a birthright as it was a rite of passage. He confronts the form by transcending pain and masking it with dignity, temporarily abandoning the obsessiveness and self-involvement that make this music rewarding for being so personal. Yet it is frustrating at times, too. ... Lest I be overly critical, Abrams solos imaginatively during the course of the whole album. The upshot isn't so much the way he approaches the compositions (after all, they are his own), but the way they don't seem to allow bassist McBee room to get off. —*Ludwig Van Trikt*, Cadence

○ **Colours in Thirty-Third** / Dec. 19, 1986 / Black Saint 0091

Muhal Richard Abrams constantly varies the lineups on the seven numbers that comprise this 1986 session, alternating between trio, quartet, quintet, and sextet pieces. The title track and "Introspection" feature the entire group, and are the most striking works, though the trio tunes offer the most musically challenging material. John Purcell on soprano and tenor sax and bass clarinet provides several stirring solos, while violinist John Blake is a solid contributor on several selections. The rhythm tandem of bassist Fred Hopkins and drummer Andrew Cyrille are also consistent and engaging, particularly Cyrille. Abrams, as usual, is an inspiring force as an instrumentalist and conceptualist. —AMG

Hearinga Suite, The / Jan. 17-18, 1989 / Black Saint 120103

Cut to the chase. Stated simply, a masterwork—the latest chapter in a career marked by leadership and fierce determination. —*Willard Jenkins*, Jazz Times

Blu Blu Blu / Nov. 9-10, 1990 / Black Saint 120117

His finest pure big band date. Abrams leads a surging, eclectic aggregation through numbers that are mostly uptempo and aggressive. Whistler Joel Brandon gets honors as most distinctive stylist, but the entire crew is showcased favorably in this '90 session. Things are further enhanced by some of Abrams's most intense pieces, especially "One for the Whistler" and "Stretch Time." —*Ron Wynn*

Family Talk / **i.** 1993 / Black Saint 120132

Muhal Richard Abrams never has and never will make simple, unassuming albums. Whether he is heading big bands or playing solo, duo, trio, or in a combo setting, his compositions are never structured in the usual manner. That is the case on his latest session, a quintet outing but one that matches trumpeter Jack Walrath and multireed player Patience Higgins in the front line with Abrams on piano and synthesizer, Warren Smith on vibes, marimba, gongs, and timpani, and bassist Brad Jones. While such songs as "DizBirdMonkMax (A Tribute)" feature the standard hard bop arrangement, the solos and arrangement are not done in a casual manner. Other times, Abrams varies the moods, instrumentation, voicings, and solo order, with lengthy numbers that have both carefully crafted sections and places that allow the musicians to soar. His music does not have catchy hooks; it is rewarding and captivating but requires some effort and attention. It is joyous but challenging, the kind of thing that separates great fare from merely good material. —*Ron Wynn*

ALEX ACUNA & UNKNOWNS

b. Dec. 12, 1944, Pativika, Peru

Drums, percussion / Latin jazz, world fusion

Alex Acuna isn't as well known as some other Latin percussionists, but he was a steady contributor to many fine sessions in the '70s and '80s. He's probably one of the few percussionists with a better reputation as a conventional drummer. Acuna combines a knowledge of vintage rhythms and music from his native Peru with Afro-Latin beats, jazz, funk, R&B, and rock influences. He learned trumpet and piano from his father, and taught himself drums. Acuna was a studio musician in Lima during his teens, and joined Perez Prado in the mid-'60s for some dates in Las Vegas. He commuted between Las Vegas, Puerto Rico, and Los Angeles from the mid-'60s to the mid-'70s. Acuna spent a couple of years with Weather Report in the mid-'70s, first as their percussionist, then as their drummer. He was featured on the *Heavy Weather* album. Acuna worked in the '70s and '80s with Lee Ritenour, Clare Fischer, Ella Fitzgerald, Tania Maria, Chick Corea, Paco De Lucia, and Joni Mitchell. He started his own band, Koinonia, in 1980, and, in the '90s, has led another group, the Unknowns. Currently, Acuna has one album as a leader available on CD, and there are several other releases that feature his percussion contributions. —*Ron Wynn*

GEORGE ADAMS (George Rufus Adams)

b. Apr. 29, 1940, Covington, GA, **d.** 1992
Tenor saxophone, flute, bass clarinet / Blues & jazz, modern creative

George Adams was a compelling tenor saxophonist and flutist who played in several of the finest combos of the '70s and '80s. Adams's style was reminiscent of David Murray's in its spirited blend of swing, bebop, and free influences. His twisting, honking, and screaming solos were fortified by a bluesy, emphatic tone and his relentless energy. Adams was also a solid flutist and his exuberant, throaty vocals added another ingredient to his approach. Adams was tutored by Wayman Carver during his days at Clark College in Atlanta. He later played in organ trios and R&B, blues, and jazz combos. Adams worked with Howlin' Wolf, Lightnin' Hopkins, and Bill Doggett, and with Hank Ballard and Sam Cooke. He settled in New York during the late '60s, joined Roy Haynes in 1969, and recorded and performed with his Hip Ensemble that also included Hannibal Marvin Peterson. Adams played with Art Blakey, Charles Mingus, Gil Evans, and McCoy Tyner during the '70s, and recorded with all these bands. The Mingus group included Don Pullen and Dannie Richmond, who later teamed with Adams and Cameron Brown in the outstanding Don Pullen-George Adams quartet. They made several fine releases from the late '70s until the mid-'80s. Adams recorded as a leader in the '70s and '80s for Timeless, ECM, Palcoscenico, Soul Note, Blue Note, and DIW. Besides co-leading the quartet with Pullen, he worked with Dave Holland, Kenny Wheeler, Jack DeJohnette, Jimmy Knepper, Hugh Lawson, Mike Richmond, John Scofield, and Peterson, among others. Adams's final group was the quartet Phalanx that featured James "Blood" Ulmer. Several of his sessions as a leader, including *America* and *Old Feeling* on Blue Note, and with the Pullen quartet, are available on CD. Some of the albums Adams made with the Mingus combo, *Mingus Moves*, *Changes One*, and *Changes Two*, were reissued by Rhino on CD in 1993 as part of its distribution/reissue deal with Atlantic. *—Ron Wynn*

○ **Suite for Swingers** / Jul. 28, 1976 / Horo 3
Extended compositions, with Don Pullen. One of the great jazz quartets of the last two decades. All albums worthwhile. *—Michael G. Nastos*

Sound Suggestions / May 1979 / ECM 11141

★ **Don't Lose Control** / Nov. 2-3, 1979 / Soul Note 1004
George Adams (tenor sax, flute, vocals) contributed three pieces and Don Pullen (piano) two to this session for Black Saint's mainstream affiliate (Soul Note). Of the Adams lines, the lilting, pristine "Autumn Song" was the most winning. Introduced at medium tempo, it gradually rippled to a fast shuffle as tenor and piano unraveled long, glistening solos. The title track was a jump blues with an exhortative vocal by Adams—an intrinsic novelty, but lots of fun, and his hoarse singing voice really was a natural extension of his tenor. An incendiary player, he sometimes rushed his climaxes; his best solos fired the senses. "Place and Faces" was a feature for his arpeggiated flute, cooler in timbre than his tenor, but equally invigorating. Pullen's compositions were the more ambitious. The pianist began "Remember?" simply and reflectively, becoming more percussive and more complex as bass and drums entered quietly and rose to the surface. Adams's solo here was uncharacteristically tentative, and the piece never realized its brooding promise. "Double Arc Jake" succeeded in drawing two dissimiliar moods and rhythms from Pullen's dense multi-directional solo. As the pianist bunched his left hand into a fist to punch out a chord, and reached with his right to plunk wire inside the housing, the bassist (Cameron Brown) tapped string to wood. As Adams launched an assault in the tenor's false register, the drummer (Dannie Richmond) splashed cymbals below. *— Milo Fine*, Cadence

Paradise Space Shuttle / Dec. 21, 1979 / Timeless 322
Titles seem to imply more than they normally do here; *Paradise Space Shuttle* is the vehicle for George Adams.

Although the band did not work together as a unit regularly, a feeling of musical communication among the members is readily conveyed. . . . "Intentions," the aptly titled opening tune, is a rollicking, uptempo number (with a terrific solo by pianist Ron Burton) that sets the album's entire tone. Adams really plays on this record—he screeches and wails and blows beautifully on tenor and flute. "Send In the Clowns" is hauntingly simple, rendered with Adams's thumbprint. "Metamorphosis for Mingus" is a loving "Changes" tribute. Adams's singular vocal style is featured on one cut. . . . Adams plays flute and sings on "Invisible Funk-A-Roonie Peacock" on *Paradise*, and James Brown is spliced with the *Agharta* Miles Davis. *—Leslie Ladd*, Down Beat

○ **Hand to Hand** / Feb. 13-14, 1980 / Soul Note 1007
This happy quintet was drawn from a Mingus Dynasty that toured Europe earlier this year (1980). What we have here, in essence, is an abbreviated Mingus Dynasty playing its members' own compositions rather than Charles Mingus's. Mingus is present in spirit, however, in the structure of Adams's ballad "Passion," a swaying theme repeated twice with a linking interlude at a faster tempo, reminiscent of many such pieces on *Changes One* and *Changes Two*, and almost as rich. The tenorist's yearning solo here perfectly maintains the mood of the line. On Hugh Lawson's "Cloocker," Adams displays his vertical leap—he liked to begin a phrase down low and twist his way up note by note, breaking off at the very top the way a basketball player will fire a shot only once he has muscled to the peak of his jump. This and other Adams tendencies betray his R&B apprenticeship, of course, but it is exactly this reliance on "common" elements that made his style so exhilarating. He solos on flute only on Dannie Richmond's rather lightweight bossa "Dee J." Knepper is his jibing front-line partner, contributing greatly to the ensemble's sound, especially on the bubbling "Cloocker." In Knepper, Mingus found one trombonist who combined the breadth of the entire Ellington section, from Sam Nanton's spit to Lawrence Brown's polish, and Knepper demonstrates that kind of flexibility here. Oddly enough, his best solo comes on the piece on which one would expect him to be the least comfortable: Lawson's "Joobubie," whose recurring modal vamp he exploits for drama, not tonal reference (Adams, though more used to such material, does not fare nearly as well). Operating from a stylistic area between Powell and Tyner, Lawson delivers fluid solos and decisive accompaniment. Both Richmonds are superb: the bassist (Mike) cutting his notes to fit the drummer's patterns, the drummer (Dannie) questioning and answering each soloist in his irrepressible way. *—Francis Davis*, Cadence

Melodic Excursions / Jun. 6+9, 1982 / Timeless 166

Gentleman's Agreement / Jan. 11-12, 1983 / Soul Note 1057

Live at the Village Vanguard—Vol. 1 / Aug. 19, 1983 / Soul Note 1094
The first of two powerhouse live sessions from 1983 that catch the George Adams/Don Pullen quartet in smashing form at the famed Village Vanguard. Adams, always a dynamo, seems even more explosive and ambitious on his loping tenor solos, while Pullen rivals him in energy and scope, and the Cameron Brown/Dannie Richmond bass and drum tandem stretched out the rhythms without ever losing control. *—Ron Wynn*

Live at the Village Vanguard—Vol. 2 / Aug. 19, 1983 / Soul Note 1141
This second '83 Village Vanguard set is just as frenzied and experimental as its predecessor. While Adams and Pullen move ever further to the outside, Cameron Brown and Dannie Richmond hold the inside, challenging the soloists, then bringing things back to a mutually satisfying conclusion. *—Ron Wynn*

Nightingale / Aug. 1988 / Blue Note 91984
This was a controversial effort when initially issued in 1988. After carving out a niche as a bombastic, furious improviser, George Adams turns almost timid doing pre-rock pop bal-

lads and standards on *Nightingale*. In retrospect, the illness that finally claimed his life in 1993 may have affected his skills; the tenor solos aren't anywhere as riveting or as searing, while his once raspy, catchy vocals are now more diffuse and uneven. Still, it has its charms, and Hugh Lawson's tidy piano solos underneath clean up a lot of problems caused by Adams's leads. —*Ron Wynn*

★ **America** / May 24, 1989-Jul. 1989 / Blue Note 93896
Saxophonist George Adams was nearing the end of his creative road on 1989's *America*, so it was appropriate for him to go back to his roots and play some blues. He alternates between terse, rippling solos and impassioned, almost serene ones, something that puzzled many critics when this was released. Pianist Hugh Lawson, bassist Cecil McBee, and drummer Marc Johnson take their cues from Adams; they mostly play it straight in their roles, and keep things simple and restrained when in the spotlight, except when Adams himself turns up the intensity. —*Ron Wynn*

○ **Old Feeling** / Mar. 11-12, 1991 / Blue Note 96689
Old Feeling ranks as one of George Adams's most exciting and happily eccentric sessions. Unlike some other avant-gardists who seem to lose their personality and purpose when they play standard material, George Adams turns even overplayed songs into his own inventive devices; three standards get the "Adams treatment" on this CD. This "As Time Goes By" is a bit crazier than usual, and a fairly straightforward "Just the Way You Are" sometimes sounds a little sarcastic. Best is a somewhat nutty reworking of "That Old Feeling" which has a happy, funky rhythm, the leader's menacing vocal, and some outside/inside soloing. This version of "Better Git Hit in Yo' Soul" is the most exciting since the original, with the logical anarchy and dangerous chance-taking of a Charles Mingus performance. Adams even shouts throughout the performance in a tribute to his former boss. Hannibal Marvin Peterson's mellow but explosive trumpet is a good match for Adams's extroverted tenor, and Jean-Paul Bourelly's rockish guitar, which overstays its welcome on "The Wanderer," is also a strong asset. *Old Feeling* demonstrates that advanced jazz does not have to lack humor or color. This fun date is highly recommended. —*Scott Yanow*, Cadence

PEPPER ADAMS (Pepper Park Adams III)

b. Oct. 8, 1930, Highland Park, MI, **d.** Sep. 10, 1986, New York, NY
Baritone saxophone / Bop, hard bop
Pepper Adams sparkled on baritone sax from the '50s until the '80s. His style included a gritty, huge sound that was very robust. Adams had complete command of the cumbersome baritone, and played it with the fluidity and speed of an alto or soprano saxophone. His solos were always carefully controlled, yet delivered with conviction and passion. Adams's family moved to Rochester, New York, from Michigan during his childhood, and he played tenor and clarinet in local bands during the mid-'40s, while also working with Ben Smith. Adams's prime influences were Coleman Hawkins and Harry Carney. When he moved to Detroit, Adams worked in the late '40s with Barry Harris and Frank Foster, among others. He served in the army during the early '50s, then became a member of the house band at the Bluebird club in Detroit. There he played with Sonny Stitt, Wardell Gray, and Miles Davis, while serving in Kenny Burrell's group. He recorded with John Coltrane, Paul Chambers, and Curtis Fuller in 1955, then moved to New York in 1956. Adams played in many big bands. These bands included Stan Kenton's, Maynard Ferguson's, Benny Goodman's, Lionel Hampton's, and Thelonious Monk's, as well as Charles Mingus's. Adams co-led quintets with Donald Byrd in the late '50s and early '60s, and recorded again with Coltrane and Mal Waldron in 1957, writing the songs "Mary's Blues" and "Witches Pit" for the *Dakar* album. The groups he led with Byrd did sessions for Prestige, and he cut an album of Mingus compositions in 1963. Adams recorded in the '60s with Elvin Jones, John Lewis, Ron

Carter, Zoot Sims, and Tommy Flanagan, in the '70s with Roland Hanna, then recorded again with Flanagan in the '80s. He did sessions for Spotlite, Workshop, Palo Alto, Prestige, and Muse, among others. He was in the Thad Jones-Mel Lewis orchestra from 1965 to 1976. Adams also recorded with David Amram, and toured England and Europe in the '70s. He was featured on one of Mingus's final albums, *Me, Myself An Eye*, recorded with Kenny Wheeler in the '80s, and participated in a Count Basie tribute in Nice. Adams even dabbled on bassoon on a couple of '70s albums. There's a fair amount of his material available on CD. —*Ron Wynn and Bob Porter*

Pure Pepper / i. 1957 / Savoy 1142
A recently reissued Savoy set from '57 with Pepper Adams establishing the robust hard bop sound that made him one of the era's greatest baritone sax stylists. He's backed by a group that includes Bernard McKinney (who subsequently took the name Kiane Zawadi) on euphonium, Hank Jones on piano, George Duvivier on bass, and Elvin Jones laying down the patented bursts and rhythms that became immortalized in the '60s when he provided them for John Coltrane. —*Ron Wynn*

Pepper Adams Quintet / Jul. 10, 1957 / VSOP 5

Cool Sounds of Pepper Adams, The / Nov. 19, 1957 / Regent 6066

Pepper-Knepper Quintet / Mar. 25, 1958 / Metrojazz 1004

★ **10 to 4 at the Five-Spot** / Apr. 5, 1958 / Riverside 031
The best example of the bebop baritone saxophonist from Detroit. Includes a young Donald Byrd (tpt) and pianist Bobby Timmons. —*David Szatmary*

Motor City Scene / i. 1960 / Bethlehem 6056

○ **Plays Compositions of Charles Mingus** / Sep. 9, 1963 / Jazz Workshop 219

Encounter! / Dec. 11-12, 1968 / Prestige 7677

Ephemera / Sep. 10, 1973 / Spotlite 6

Julian / Aug. 13, 1975 / Inner City 3014

★ **Reflectory** / Jun. 14, 1978 / Muse 5182
Pepper Adams—with the gritty tone and redoubtable spirit—was among the foremost exponents of the baritone sax, after Harry Carney and Gerry Mulligan, and his mettle as a section man soloist was tested and found true during a 13-year charter tenure with the Thad Jones/Mel Lewis Orchestra.... The humors Adams expresses here are more phlegmatic and even melancholic than his often fiery, brittle work with the big band; not a surprising shift for this freed spirit and interior individual. Each side opens with intriguing minor musings from Adams's own pen that involve ringing, long-toned solos by bassist George Mraz, a perfect companion for deep-note philosophizing. Other Mraz and Adams duos crop up in a eulogy for Harry Carney ("Lady") and a brisk Mutt-and-Jeff scamper ("Etude"). Mraz's soloing on five of the six tunes speaks of Adams's modesty, his ability to set mood, and his attention to procedural niceties. Drummer Billy Hart neatly inserts choruses on either side of pianist Roland Hanna's fleet three on "Etude" and rattles along alone under Adams's first on "That's All." —*Fred Bouchard*, Down Beat

Urban Dreams / Sep. 30, 1981 / Quicksilver 4006

Conjuration—Fat Tuesday's Session / Aug. 19-20, 1983 / Reservoir 113
Contains three previously unissued selections from the week-long engagement.... Adams symbolized everything positive about jazz and his presence is already much missed. —*Larry Hollis*, Cadence

CANNONBALL ADDERLEY (Julian Edwin Adderley)

b. Sep. 15, 1928, Tampa, FL, **d.** Aug. 8, 1975, Gary, IN
Alto saxophone, bandleader / Hard bop, soul jazz
Cannonball Adderley was a scintillating, striking alto saxophonist whose style evolved from early Charlie Parker adulation into gospel and blues-tinged fare in the late '60s. Adderley never had a problem reconciling artistry and en-

tertainment, and while some of his hit material walked the fine line between jazz and pop, his solos were always fluid, biting, and expertly played. His tone ranked among the warmest and his phrasing was close to the most lyrical in jazz history. Adderley's ability to expand his horizons and include Latin, African, and blues elements into his repertoire was also impressive.

Adderley played alto sax in bands around Florida in the early '40s. He directed a high school band in Fort Lauderdale in the late '40s to the early '50s, then played in army bands from 1950 to 1953. After his discharge, he resumed teaching until 1955, then moved to New York. His initial plan had been to take graduate studies at New York University and to form a group with his brother, Nat. Instead, he joined Oscar Pettiford's band and signed a record deal with Savoy. Adderley's debut recordings included Paul Chambers and Kenny Clarke. The brothers finally began their group in 1956, but had to disband due to financial difficulties. Adderley replaced Sonny Rollins in the Miles Davis quintet in 1957, and stayed with the quintet until 1959, appearing on classic Davis dates *Kind of Blue* and *Milestones*.

He cut his first quintet session on Blue Note in 1958, using Miles Davis and Art Blakey as sidemen. He then formed a permanent quintet with his brother, which remained intact until 1975, occasionally in an expanded configuration. They scored a fair amount of hits, particularly on their later Capitol recordings, yet maintained their musical integrity. Among the sidemen were pianists Bobby Timmons, Victor Feldman, Joe Zawinul, George Duke, and Michael Wolff; bassist Walter Booker; drummers Louis Hayes and Roy McCurdy; and, during two separate periods as a sextet, tenors Yusef Lateef and Charles Lloyd.

They began to enjoy pop attention when vocalist Nancy Wilson recorded with them on a 1962 Capitol session. After the demise of Riverside, Adderley switched to Capitol where his sessions generally became more commercial. Cannonball Adderley led many workshops at colleges in the '60s and '70s, speaking on jazz history and sociopolitical developments. The Zawinul composition, "Mercy, Mercy, Mercy," reached number 11 on the charts, and the album of the same name hit number 13 in 1966. They continued recording for Capitol and others into the early '70s. They had five singles and 12 albums that made the charts in the '60s and early '70s, including a phenomenal eight live albums. Cannonball Adderley doubled on the soprano in the '70s.

Through the years, he occasionally made recordings outside of the quintet, including memorable collaborations with John Coltrane (in 1958), Bill Evans, Ray Brown, and Eddie "Cleanhead" Vinson. Adderley was also a successful producer; he produced albums by Bud Powell, Wes Montgomery, and Clifford Jordan, and appeared, with the quintet, in Clint Eastwood's 1971 film *Play Misty for Me*. His career was still going strong when Cannonball Adderley suffered a stroke in 1975; he died a few days later. A project he'd wanted issued for several years, an album that featured his composition "Big Man" based on the John Henry legend, was released posthumously. Currently, many of his sessions are available; they span his entire career. —*Ron Wynn*

Discoveries / Jun. 28, 1955 / Savoy 1195
A 1990 reissue of songs that were newly discovered at that time. They're alternate takes or fresh works that were previously unissued. As such, it's interesting to note most of Cannonball Adderley's solos are as explosive and enticing as those that appear on cuts that did make it onto album. There aren't any lost masterpieces, but there's also very little that's tedious or tepid. —*Ron Wynn*

○ **Spontaneous Combustion** / Jul. 14, 1955 / Savoy 70816
These are Cannonball's first recordings. With Donald Byrd (tpt), Horace Silver (p), Paul Chambers (b), Kenny Clarke (d), Nat Adderley (cnt), and Jerome Richardson (ts, f). —*Michael Erlewine*

In the Land of Hi-Fi / Jun. 8+18, 1956 / EmArcy 36077

Sophisticated Swing / Feb. 6+8, 1957 / EmArcy 36110

★ **Somethin' Else** / Mar. 9, 1958 / Blue Note 46338
Since *Somethin' Else* was first released, it's been common knowledge that it was really Miles Davis's session, done under Adderley's name for contractual reasons. A casual listen to the album will tell you that: it is the Davis trumpet that states the melody on "Autumn Leaves" and "Love for Sale," and at the end of the sultry minor blues "Daddy-O," it is the raspy voice of Davis, rather than the deep voice of Adderley, that is heard asking,"Is that what you wanted, Alfred?" (Producer Alfred Lion would have been a fool if he said no.) But if Davis was up front (and, incidentally, in excellent form), that doesn't mean Adderley's contribution was perfunctory. In fact, he comes on like a young tiger, which is what he was at the time, having just joined Davis's group after making a gigantic splash on the New York scene.... His solo on "Leaves," in which smooth, lyrical lines alternate with haunting, banshee-like cries, takes the top off my head every time I hear it, and he does wonderfully low-down things to the sentimental ballad "Dancing in the Dark." For a look at two giants at an early stage of their careers— Adderley as he was just reaching his first bloom, Davis in full middle-period flower—and a sample of the laidback sounds of a just barely bygone day, *Somethin' Else* is something worth hearing. —*Peter Keepnews*, Down Beat

☆ **Portrait of Cannonball** / Jul. 1, 1958 / Riverside 361
This is Cannonball Adderley's debut (July 1, 1958) on Riverside and it's a good one if you like hard open blowing dates. The quintet (Bill Evans, piano; Sam Jones, bass; Philly Joe Jones, drums) includes Blue Mitchell, whose Brownie-like attack was derivative, but quite a nice contribution. It gives a nice balance to the front line, although they do not always appear together on the opening themes (on "Straight Life" things open as if it was the Blue Mitchell quartet, while on "People Will Say We're in Love" it suggests the Adderley quartet). The rhythm section grinds away nicely as a unit, with particularly nice prodding from Jones, though the entire group seems to have ideas and energy in reserve. —*Bob Rusch*, Cadence

☆ **Things Are Getting Better** / 1958 / Riverside 032
Vibist Milt Jackson turns up in the company as a guest with alto saxophonist Cannonball Adderley on this October 28, 1958 date, which was also issued previously as part of a twofer set. The funk blues is the common point here, and *this* would have been the setting for Horace Silver, though pianist Wynton Kelly is an excellent part of the rhythm backup (bassist Percy Heath, drummer Art Blakey). One does not always get what one expects based on packaging; here, the ingredients are pure, natural, and preserving. —*Bob Rusch*, Cadence

○ **Cannonball Adderley Quintet in Chicago** / Feb. 3, 1959 / Mercury 20449

Cannonball and Coltrane / Feb. 3, 1959 / PolyGram 834588

☆ **Cannonball Adderley Quintet in San Francisco** / Oct. 18+20, 1959 / Original Jazz Classics 35
Live date with Bobby Timmons (p), Nat Adderley (cnt), Sam Jones (b), and Louis Hayes (d). Contains the classic and soulful "This Here." —*Hank Davis*

○ **Coast to Coast** / Oct. 18, 1959+Jan. 12, 1962 / Milestone 47039
Tracks taken from two popular Adderley albums: *Cannonball Adderley Quintet in San Francisco* and *The Cannonball Adderley Sextet in New York.* —AMG

Cannonball Adderley Collection—Vol. 1: Them Dirty Blues / Feb. 1, 1960 / Landmark 1301
With Bobby Timmons (p), Nat Adderley (cnt), Barry Harris (p), Sam Jones (b), and Louis Hayes (d). The first studio recording by Cannonball's new quintet. Features two takes of Nat's new tune "Work Song"—a jazz classic. —*Michael Erlewine*

★ **Cannonball Adderley Collection—Vol. 4: The Poll Winners** / May 21, 1960-Jun. 5, 1960 / Landmark 1304

The *Poll Winners* sessions brought Cannonball Adderley (alto sax), at his insistence, together with the astounding Wes Montgomery, who had been on the national scene only a year and was blowing the minds of virtually everyone in jazz, particularly those of guitarists. Montgomery's revolutionary octave technique is in evidence here, but in its natural context as one element of a remarkably full and rounded style. It would be three years and a switch to another label before he was encouraged to let the octaves dominate his recordings and mask his broad and powerful musical identity. But Montgomery's single-note-line solo on the previously unissued, faster take of "Au Privave" is an example of his ability to swing hard while building a logical succession of ideas independent of the octave feature. On the same track, Adderley opens his solo with a bow to Benny Carter, a reminder of his deep schooling in all the jazz styles of the era, not just Charlie Parker and bebop. Ray Brown, perennial poll-winner and role model for bassists, is the remaining acknowledged star of the album and performs powerfully and impeccably, as usual. Twenty-six-year-old Victor Feldman, a good vibist but a powerhouse pianist, more than holds his own with the big three. Louis Hayes, Adderley's regular drummer, keeps time with ball-bearing perfection. —*Doug Ramsey,* Jazz Times

What Is This Thing Called Soul? / Nov. 22, 1960 / Pablo 238
A classic Adderley work, and among the first to illuminate his ability to play with soul, yet also take chances in his solos. The songs are centered enough in funk and blues backbeats to make them entertaining, yet the improvising is hard-edged and extensive. —*Ron Wynn*

Know What I Mean? / Jan. 27, 1961-Feb. 21, 1961 / Riverside 105
Great album. With Bill Evans (p), Percy Heath (b), and Connie Kay (d). Recorded at Bell Sound Studios in New York City. —*Michael Erlewine*

Quintet Plus / May 11, 1961 / Riverside 306
Recorded just after Adderley's group returned from a very successful European tour. The band is tight. The "Plus" is Wynton Kelly (p). Also Victor Feldman (p, vib), Nat Adderley (cnt), Sam Jones (b), Ron Carter (b), and Louis Hayes (d). —*Michael Erlewine*

In New York / Jan. 12+14, 1962 / Riverside 142
Live date at the Village Vanguard in New York City. With Nat Adderley (cnt), Yusef Lateef (ts, f), Joe Zawinul (p), Sam Jones (b), and Louis Hayes (d). —*Michael Erlewine*

○ **Lush Side of Cannonball, The** / i. Mar. 1962 / Mercury 60652

Cannonball Adderley Collection—Vol. 7: Cannonball in Europe / Aug. 4+5, 1962 / Landmark 1307
Live concert at the International Jazz Festival, Comblain-La-Tour, Belgium—over 30,000 people. With Nat Adderley (cnt), Yusef Lateef (ts, f), Joe Zawinul (p), Sam Jones (b), and Louis Hayes (d). —*Michael Erlewine*

Cannonball Adderley Collection—Vol. 3: Jazz Workshop Revisited / Sep. 21, 1962 / Landmark 1303
Return to San Francisco for the second live "Lighthouse" recording with Cannonball's (by this time seasoned) sextet. This album reached No. 11 on the charts! With Nat Adderley (cnt), Yusef Lateef (ts, f), Joe Zawinul (p), Sam Jones (b), and Louis Hayes (d). —*Michael Erlewine*

○ **Sextet, The** / Sep. 21, 1962-Jul. 19, 1963 / Milestone 9106
Some argue that the early '60s Cannonball Adderley sextet was his finest group. That point can be argued; what can't be disputed is that Yusef Lateef, on tenor, oboe, and flute, gave the band an instrumental push and urgency that its more popular soul-jazz material never matched. Both Cannonball and Nat Adderley were often pushed to the limit, and that competitive spirit extended to the rhythm section as well. —*Ron Wynn*

○ **Best of the Capitol Years** / 1962-1969 / Curb 77399
Contains "Mercy, Mercy, Mercy" and Adderley's most successful jazz/gospel/pop fusion work with Joe Zawinul (k). —*Hank Davis*

Nippon Soul / Jul. 9-15, 1963 / Riverside 435
Recorded in Tokyo by Cannonball Adderley, with Yusef Lateef (ts). —*Michael G. Nastos*

★ **Mercy, Mercy, Mercy! Live at 'The Club'** / Jul. 1966 / EMI 5007
Quintet. This is a great live performance with Nat Adderley (cnt), Victor Gaskin (b), Roy McCurdy (d), and Joe Zawinul (p) at The Club in Chicago. "Mercy, Mercy, Mercy" was a pop hit. —*Michael Erlewine*

Cannonball Live in Japan / Aug. 26, 1966 / Capitol 93560

Country Preacher / Oct. 1969 / Capitol 0404

☆ **Black Messiah** / 1970 / Capitol 846
This is an outstanding two-record set from 1970 that finds Cannonball Adderley playing explosive, bluesy alto and soprano sax, heading a band that includes his brother Nat on cornet, pianist George Duke doing some of his most intense and energetic jazz-based soloing, plus bassist Walter Booker and drummer Roy McCurdy. Special guests include guitarist Mike Deasey and, on one number, New Orleans clarinetist Harold Batiste. Airto Moreira adds sympathetic percussion, and the group's extended numbers include "Dr. Honoris Causa," "The Chocolate Nuisance," and the title cut. There is also plenty of Cannonball Adderley's witty asides, excellent support from the rhythm section, and Nat Adderley's blistering cornet solos. Cannonball Adderley has some of his hottest recorded soprano sax improvisations, and his customary biting and bluesy alto solos. —*Ron Wynn*

Price You Got to Pay To Be Free, The / 1970 / Capitol 636

Inside Straight / Jun. 4, 1973 / Fantasy 750
Recorded "live in the studio" before a large (and animated) group of Adderley fans, this album introduces pianist Hal Galper to the Adderley quintet. Galper is featured on three of his own compositions. —AMG

Dizzy's Business / i. 1993 / Milestone 470692
Though the nine songs on this new Cannonball Adderley reissue were originally done live at concerts in Japan and San Francisco in 1963, they nevertheless make a nice tribute to recently departed jazz giant Dizzy Gillespie. The assembled group was among the finest Adderley ever led, with Yusef Lateef proving a dynamic, unpredictable third solo voice on flute, tenor sax, and oboe, contrasting with Cannonball's pungent alto sax and Nat Adderley's pithy cornet solos. Bassist Sam Jones and drummer Louis Hayes were a topflight tandem, while Joe Zawinul was then playing bluesy, funky piano in his pre-synthesizer, Miles Davis/Weather Report phase. Prime cuts include "New Delhi," "Primitivo," and the title track, but everything's illustrative of a prime band enjoying some great nights. —*Ron Wynn*

NAT ADDERLEY (Nathaniel Adderley)

b. Nov. 25, 1931, Tampa, FL
Cornet / Hard bop, soul jazz

Nat Adderley is a fine hard bop soloist and prominent composer known for his bristling lines, creative use of half-valve effects, bent notes, and wavery phrases. Adderley began playing trumpet as a teenager, and later worked with local bands in Florida. He switched to cornet in 1950, and has also played mellophone and French horn. He worked with Lionel Hampton in the '50s, with Cannonball's combo, and with J.J. Johnson and Woody Herman. The Adderleys regrouped in 1959, and, during the '60s and '70s, were among jazz's most popular small units. Adderley had been recording as a leader since 1955, but after Cannonball died in 1975, he intensified the process. He's recorded for Savoy, Jazzland, Riverside, New Jazz, Prestige, Milestone, A&M, Capitol, Galaxy, Teresa, and Landmark, among others. He's also the writer of classics such as "Jive Samba" and "Work Song." Adderley has several sessions available on CD. —*Ron Wynn*

Introducing Nat Adderley / Sep. 6, 1955 / EmArcy 36091

Branching Out / Sep. 1958 / Riverside 255

This 1958 date has some of his hottest playing as a leader. Adderley concentrates on cornet and there haven't been many on that instrument to take it into more abrupt and challenging harmonic contexts. Johnny Griffin's bluesy, taut tenor keeps things moving, while using pianist Gene Harris, bassist Andy Simpkins, and drummer Bill Dowdy (better known as the Three Sounds) for a rhythm section was inspired. —*Ron Wynn*

★ **Work Song** / Jan. 25+27, 1960 / Riverside 363

Guitarist Wes Montgomery was also aboard for *Work Song,* a Nat Adderley date (January 25 and January 27, 1960) with Bobby Timmons (piano), Louis Hayes (drums), Sam Jones, and Keter Betts or Percy Heath (cello, bass). This is, of course, Nat Adderley's date, and Montgomery's role is not so much that of guitarist extraordinaire, but as one of the plucked strings that give this date its particular ambience. Sam Jones and Keter Betts are together, playing cello and bass, and that, along with guitar and an often genteel, subdued approach, gives much of the music here a chamber mainstream profile. This is partially effective on "I've Got a Crush on You" and "Mean to Me." These are the moments that are best. At other times, the flavor is harder and closer to what one might expect from the album's title, one of the anthems of the New York-based hard bop school. A thoughtful and varied date with a multi-dimensional personality, this has been previously issued as part of a twofer. . . . It's good listening and has particularly nice stereo separation among the strings (on CD). —*Bob Rusch,* Cadence

That's Right / Aug. 9, 1960+Sep. 15, 1960 / Riverside 330

In the Bag / Jun. 1962 / Jazzland 648

Interesting album with New Orleans musicians Nat Perilliat (reeds) and Ellis Marsalis (p). —*Michael G. Nastos*

Natural Soul / Sep. 23, 1963 / Milestone 9009

Sayin' Something / Feb. 16, 1966 / Atlantic 1460

Hummin' / Oct. 1976 / Little David 1012

★ **Little New York Midtown Music, A** / Sep. 18-19, 1978 / Galaxy

Cornetist Nat Adderley is a fine jazzman who has gotten better as the years roll on, but on this date he is pretty well upstaged by the solo work of tenor saxophonist Johnny Griffin, pianist Victor Feldman, and bassist Ron Carter. Two of his originals, "Fortune's Child" and "Sunshine Sammy," are blowing lines of the monotonous, minimal chord structure sort, and here Griffin bites in and leaves Adderley in the dust; part of the reason is Adderley's gentle muted cornet sound. Adderley solos twice on the title piece; the second time around, after a Carter solo, is more nearly what we've come to expect from him. Again, though, Griffin's following solo, and an excellent Feldman solo, upstage him. Adderley is at his best on "Yeehaw Junction" and "Come Rain or Come Shine." Feldman sticks to acoustic piano with the exception of "Fortune's Child" and "Sunshine Sammy," and the sound quality of the electric piano, even in the skillful hands of Feldman, contributes to the monotony of these pieces. Carter has a fine solo on "Come Rain or Come Shine," and starts off magnificently on "A Little New York Midtown Music," but gets tangled in his own thoughts towards the end. Just listening to the recording without a view of the leader's name on the album cover would lead one to think this was Griffin's date. —*Shirley Klett,* Cadence

Blue Autumn / i. 1983 / Evidence 22035

This '83 live set at the Keystone Korner is certainly an uneven, sometimes curious event. The opening number is a solo alto workout for Sonny Fortune and seems to amble through midway before he becomes recharged by the end. The last track, "The Tallahassee Kid," fades out early and Adderley provides a run-down of band personnel until the disc ends. There are some fine cuts; "The Fifth Labor of Hercules" and pianist Larry Willis's title tracks have punchy, snappy melodies, some taut solos, and nice rhythm section interaction between Willis, drummer Jimmy Cobb, and

bassist Walter Booker. But overall, this proves a good, but not essential, Nat Adderley date. —*Ron Wynn*

LARRY ADLER (Lawrence Adler)

b. Feb. 10, 1914, Baltimore, MD
Harmonica / Swing, big band

Though not really a jazz musician, Larry Adler has done more than anyone, through his virtuosity and diversity, to make the harmonica accepted as a legitimate instrument. His recording debut came during a 1934 London session. He recorded with Stephane Grappelli and Django Reinhardt in Paris in 1938, and with John Kirby's orchestra in New York in 1944. Adler's also appeared in several films, among them *Many Happy Returns* with Duke Ellington's orchestra, and *Blues in the Night* with John Kirby's orchestra. Adler lived and recorded in London from 1934 to 1959, after which he moved to America. He has worked extensively with Ellis Larkins; they worked together into the '80s, and received widespread critical acclaim for their New York performances in 1986. Adler has also recorded as a pianist and vocalist, and has been active as a teacher, composer, and arranger. Currently, Adler does not have any listed sessions available on CD. —*Ron Wynn*

Live at the Ballroom / Newport Classics 60019

AIR

b. 1975, **d.** 1986
Modern creative

This trio ranks alongside the Art Ensemble of Chicago, the Revolutionary Ensemble, the World Saxophone Quartet, and Ornette Coleman's "harmolodic" ensembles as one of the premier free jazz units of the '70s and '80s. The original lineup was composer/saxophonist Henry Threadgill, bassist Fred Hopkins, and drummer Steve McCall. All were former members of the Association for the Advancement of Creative Musicians (AACM), and Air took some of the same tenets. They functioned as a cooperative venture; members didn't emphasize rigid soloist/accompanist roles. While Threadgill was the primary composer, his writings and others highlighted a group sound, with solos interchanged within the framework of collective improvisation. They were even more closely knit than the Revolutionary Ensemble. Air, and later New Air, incorporated elements of many Black musical styles, among them blues, funk, traditional New Orleans jazz, ragtime, and boogie-woogie.

Their origin dates back to an assignment Threadgill received in the early '70s. In 1971, he was asked to do some arrangements of ragtime composer Scott Joplin's songs for a theatrical production at Columbia College in Chicago. He teamed with Hopkins and McCall, forming a trio called Reflection. They performed the arrangements, and remained together until 1972. McCall went to Europe and Threadgill and Hopkins went their own ways. When McCall returned from Europe in 1975, the three reunited in New York. They took the name Air, and recorded their first album there for Nessa. They became part of the community of musicians who did a lot of performances and conducted rehearsals in New York City lofts. Air contributed a composition to a series of recordings made in the late '70s titled *Wildflowers* that featured many of these "loft" jazz bands. The trio then toured Europe, Japan, and America.

The lineup remained intact until 1982, when McCall returned to Chicago and was replaced by Pheeroan AkLaff. They were renamed New Air. AkLaff was replaced in 1985 by Andrew Cyrille. The group did several albums in the '70s and '80s, among them releases for Nessa, India Navigation, Black Saint, Arista/Novus, and Antilles. New Air finally disbanded in the late '80s, but Threadgill's sextets and large bands continue performing compositions in a similar vein to Air and New Air. Threadgill and Hopkins have sometimes worked together again. McCall went on to play with Cecil Taylor and to lead his own sextet. AkLaff and Cyrille have continued working with other groups. A few Air and some New Air releases are available on CD. —*Ron Wynn*

☆ **Teilweise Kacke.. Aber Stereo** / **i.** 1973 / Eigenbau 12

○ **Air Song** / Sep. 10, 1975 / India Navigation 1057

Originally released on Why Not Records (Japan), this Air excursion is one of their strongest vinyl documents (if not *the* strongest). Drummer Steve McCall is the most unique creative element as he constantly breaks up the regular pulse with colorful textures and dynamic rhythmic variations. This occurs whether he is traveling uptempo during the double time on "Untitled Tango" and the hot cooking section of "Dance of the Beast," or is breaking it up with tender sparse applications on the title cut. He also has some tasteful solo interludes on "Great Body of the Riddle" that, due to the clever arrangement, are often unexpected (especially the last one, which climbs right out of a return to the head). But this is not to diminish the contributions of Henry Threadgill (alto, tenor, and baritone saxes, flute) and Fred Hopkins (bass). While they were known more for their solid musicianship rather than for having heavily distinct voices in the music, they play with an edge here that grabs the listener's attention. Even Threadgill's flute work (on the title cut), which usually suffered from being just doubling work and not much else, really shines. Neither have a weak solo on the whole disk. And their interaction as a unit is the figurative cherry on the confection. With the exception of "Tango," which is more "solo with support" oriented, the pieces feature group dialogue and interaction with the spotlight shifting very quickly among the three men. —*Milo Fine,* Cadence

○ **Live Air** / Jul. 1, 1976 / Black Saint 0034

This is vintage Air, recorded in 1977 less than a month before Air Time, their initial U.S. release. Side one is mainly Henry Threadgill's flute, beginning with a dramatic, elegiac piece dedicated to the late AACM bassist Charles Clark. Threadgill spins out angular oriental lines, and the overall image is of a wind-blown bluff. The wind itself is bassist Fred Hopkins hovering just behind with tense, delicate vibrato blowing, while drummer Steve McCall touches down here and there like the occasional shaft of sunlight glancing off of rocks. Most of the ten-plus minutes is a counterbalancing of these elements, with Hopkins's bow carrying the melody—no bawling here, just gentle tears. A triadic approach is the glue of this trip; perhaps the years playing Joplin rags, or working the pork chop circuit, account for this. *Live Air* is yet another discourse on frame analysis; these three knew that intuition could define a musical context without lapsing either into repetitive form or excess baggage. —*Brent Staples,* Down Beat

★ **Air Time** / Nov. 17-18, 1977 / Nessa 12

Influenced by Asian and African motifs as well as post-Coleman colleagues like the Art Ensemble of Chicago, the Revolutionary Ensemble and Muhal Richard Abrams's bands (big and small), each member of Air always remained attuned to his own music as well as imaginatively responsive to the other musicians. Group collaboration through interplay was the trio's intent, and at this Air was remarkably successful. Air's roots were in the controlled instrumental extremes, with their earnest intellectual tastes showing through in their esoteric explorations of the Great Black Music avant-garde. Tension in the three extended Henry Threadgill-penned pieces arises from detailed textural and dynamic juxtapositions, and is sometimes resolved as mysteriously as clouds disperse. Drummer Steve McCall's opening ballad and bassist Fred Hopkins's folkish, warm, sonorous vamp ("G.v.E."), the shorter tracks, are flawlessly structured. —*Howie Mandel,* Down Beat

○ **Open Air Suite** / Feb. 21-22, 1978 / Novus 3002

Air was all about musical freedom. The horn/bass/drums format was flexible enough to allow any instrument to dominate or to recede. This was not your typical soloist with accompaniment trio—the rhythm section was equal to the horn in the creation of cooperative sound sculptures. Reedman/composer Henry Threadgill's writing was full of elliptical twists and turns, eerie empty spaces, surprising stop and go interplay, and wide vocalized intervallic leaps. His flute playing was glassy and, well, airy, while his saxo-

phones were glassy and guttural. On "Open Air Suit," his soloing is more concerned with developing a sweeping rhythmic impetus than in refining the profound bluesiness he demonstrates on "Untitled Tango," from *Air Song.* Bassist Fred Hopkins had a resilient time feel and a big woody tone. Drummer Steve McCall was a master of dynamics and tuning. He was able to maintain group continuity even as he kept turning the beat around with surging authority; he was playing pulse, not time. —*Chip Stern,* Down Beat

○ **Live at Montreux 1978** / Jul. 22, 1978 / Novus 3008

★ **Air Lore** / May 11-12, 1979 / Bluebird 6578

This is jazz of the absurd. It is a kind of avant-garde vaudeville, infused with a wackiness whereby contradictions are commonplace. Old and new run together; the lines between melancholy, rage, and cornball comedy disappear. Air cultivated naivete to make this music; it courted ambiguity. *Air Lore* is an oddball masterpiece.... Three of the compositions here date from the first decade: Scott Joplin's "Weeping Willow Rag" (1903) and "Ragtime Dance" (1906) and Jelly Roll Morton's "King Porter Stomp" (1905). Air did not recreate these works, but reacted to them in light of 80 years of jazz "lore." What results is a carefully conceived and flawlessly executed set of chamber pieces. Air didn't mess with the original tunes. Consequently, much of this music is outrageously tonal, its rhythms hopelessly regular, its harmonies shockingly simple. Yet it comes as no surprise that the music never sounds dated. —*Douglas Clark,* Down Beat

○ **Air Mail** / Dec. 28, 1980 / Black Saint 0049

The Chicago trio Air was at a high point on this 1980 date, thanks in part to remarkable percussive foundations provided by the late Steve McCall and his interaction with bassist Fred Hopkins, plus the amazing solos and versatility of nominal leader Henry Threadgill. Besides alto and tenor sax and flute and bass flute, Threadgill plays his own unique instrument called the hubkaphone and makes it just as memorable a weapon as the other horns. —*Ron Wynn*

○ **80 Degrees Below 82** / Jan. 23-24, 1982 / Island 1007

Air (Henry Threadgill, alto sax; Fred Hopkins, bass; and Steve McCall, drums) moved to Antilles for the release of their ninth LP; it is one of the group's more straightahead records. The four selections are variations on blues themes; they're highly structured and rarely venture off into freer spaces. There is more emphasis on individual solos than group improvisation. Hopkins sounds very good—his tone is thick and booming. McCall is a joy to hear whether he is just keeping time (impeccably) or soloing. He had the wonderful ability of making the drums dance in a marvelously simple manner. Threadgill sticks to alto sax on this album. His tone is clean, not too heavy on the vibrato, and he creates much tension by holding back during his solos. *80 Degrees Below 82* may seem a bit conservative to some listeners, but they will undoubtedly appreciate the good musicianship. —*Richard Kamins,* Cadence

New Air—Live at the Montreux Int'l Jazz Festival / Jul. 1983 / Black Saint 0084

New drummer Pheeroan AkLaff brought a fresh approach and crackling edge to the trio Air on this 1983 live date, done at the Montreux Festival. Hopkins doesn't mesh as smoothly with AkLaff on this date, though they find a comfortable meeting place by mid-album. As always, Henry Threadgill is a compelling soloist, especially on alto sax. —*Ron Wynn*

○ **Air Show No. 1** / **i.** Jul. 1987 / Black Saint 0099

Air Show No. 1 is the second album by New Air; drummer Steve McCall had been replaced by Pheeroan AkLaff. Fred Hopkins's bass is the dominant force on this album, reverberating majestically throughout every minute of the music. Hopkins is particularly impressive in his arco duet with Henry Threadgill's tenor on "Salute to the Enema Bandit." On three cuts, the trio is joined by the wonderful Cassandra Wilson. Recalling the best of Sarah Vaughan before her baroque phase, Wilson had (then) made one album under her own name and two with Steve Coleman. Wilson's most engaging moments include an interpretation of her own lyrics to Threadgill's composition, "Don't Drink That Corner," a haunting evocation of the tragic, hallucinatory world of the street drinker that extends the thanatoptic themes of Threadgill's early sextet albums.... New Air's broken-field march, "Side Step," is a more schematic version of what Threadgill did with another march, "Gateway"—the skipping, leaping, close-order drill on the sextet album *Just the Facts and Pass the Bucket* (About Time). The least successful performance on this album is "Air Show" which, according to Nat Hentoff's liner notes, is mostly unstructured and spontaneous. Threadgill's an exciting improviser, but the trio was at its best when it relied on his writing. And at its best, Air was intoxicating and exhilarating. —*Krin Gabbard, Cadence*

TOSHIKO AKIYOSHI

b. Dec. 12, 1929, Dairen, China
Piano, composer, bandleader / Big band, bop, progressive big band
Pianist and bandleader Toshiko Akiyoshi has incorporated elements of traditional Japanese music and bebop and has blended them into her arrangements for large bands and small combos. Her playing has evolved and her harmonic skills have sharpened, with Akiyoshi's solos and phrasing reflecting the influence of Bud Powell. But it's her compositions that have earned widespread admiration among the jazz community. These include "Kogun," "American Ballad," and "Long Yellow Road." Gil Evans, Thad Jones, and Mel Lewis were among the musicians who've influenced her arrangements and compositions.

Initially, Akiyoshi studied classical music, and became interested in jazz in 1947 when she moved to Japan from China. Visiting American musicians, among them Oscar Peterson, urged her to pursue a jazz career in America. She studied at Berklee from 1956 to 1959, and worked in groups with her husband at the time, alto saxophonist Charlie Mariano. They co-formed the Toshiko-Mariano quartet, and worked together in Japan in 1961. She also worked with Charles Mingus for several months in 1962, appearing at a Town Hall concert, before returning to Japan for three years. When she returned to New York, Akiyoshi did a radio series and wrote compositions for a newly assembled big band in 1967.

She and her second husband, tenor saxophonist and flutist Lew Tabackin, formed a quartet in 1970. They moved to Los Angeles in 1972, where they began working with a big band of major studio musicians. The Akiyoshi-Tabackin big band made its debut in 1973 with the album *Kogun*. It attracted widespread interest, and they continued heading the band through the '70s and into the early '80s. Gary Foster, Dick Spencer, and Bobby Shew were among major players featured in the orchestra. The Akiyoshi-Tabackin big band made several critically praised releases before the couple returned to New York in 1981. There, they assembled another big band with Tabackin co-leading and Akiyoshi writing the material. Akiyoshi was featured in a 1984 documentary film, *Toshiko Akiyoshi: Jazz Is My Native Language*. She and Tabackin disbanded their collective orchestra in 1985, and Akiyoshi formed a new big band, Toshiko Akiyoshi's New York Jazz Orchestra. Akiyoshi has a number of releases on CD as a solo artist, and there are sessions that feature the Akiyoshi-Tabackin big band available on CD as well. —*Ron Wynn and Michael G. Nastos*

Toshiko's Piano / Nov. 13-14, 1953 / Norgran 22

Amazing Toshiko Akiyoshi / Jul. 5, 1957 / Verve 8236

Many Sides of Toshiko, The / Sep. 28, 1957 / Verve 8273

Toshiko-Mariano Quartet / Mar. 30, 1963 / Takt Jazz 12

At Top of the Gate / Jul. 30, 1968 / Denon 387874

Kogun / Apr. 3+4, 1974 / RCA 6246

★ **Long Yellow Road** / Apr. 4, 1974-Mar. 4, 1975 / RCA 1350

Toshiko Akiyoshi's approach, like Duke Ellington's, was to write solo and ensemble parts tailored to each band member's individual strengths. Her woodwind voicings were especially effective. On "Quadrille, Anyone?," for example, the rich baritone sax intro of Bill Perkins ends with a dramatic upward line, which is taken to its lofty summit by Lew Tabackin's piccolo. After the full band roars, excellent solo voyages are taken by Gary Foster on soprano and Tabackin on tenor. . . . The most outstanding of the band's many strengths include: Lew Tabackin's eclectic, electric soloing on tenor and flute (Tabackin is simply incredible!); Akiyoshi's exotic, kaleidoscopic colors and textures; the band's spirited ensemble work; and the fine improvisations of such gifted players as Gary Foster, Bobby Shew, and Bill Perkins. —*Chuck Berg, Down Beat*

○ **Tales of a Courtesan** / Dec. 1-3, 1975 / RCA 10723
Tales of a Courtesan is the second Toshiko Akiyoshi-Lew Tabackin big band album under the RCA banner and it is every bit as good as its predecessor, *Long Yellow Road*. At the time (1975), this group was probably the best big band in the world, featuring the compositions and arrangements of the miracle Ms. of jazz, Toshiko Akiyoshi. —*Bill Gallagher, Cadence*

○ **Road Time** / Jan. 30, 1976-Feb. 8, 1976 / RCA 2242
Toshiko Akiyoshi juggles her big band forms and capable soloists brilliantly on this two-LP set, which was recorded during the band's early '76 Japanese tour following the surprise success of their first album, *Kogun*. Her co-leader and then husband Lew Tabackin shares the blowing space with a brace of contrasting altoists, a competitive brass section, and thoughtful slide specialists. But it is the particular achievement of Akiyoshi, who cracked the all-male echelon of composing bandleaders, that makes this assemblage sound like no other. How to typify Akiyoshi's sound? First of all, these are not experimental sides—all the players are studio pros, and the compositions are firmly mainstream matter. Only "Kogun" extends itself past the usual instrumentation to include indigenous Eastern devices. The execution of all passages was rehearsed and assured. However, this band stretches out. Each number includes lengthy solo spots balanced against ensembles swollen with distinctive voicings— flutes, broadly harmonized saxes, blendings within the brass, and a lightly supportive rhythm section—and breaks down into a fast succession of effects that fit tight as a collage and move along like a montage. —*Howie Mandel, Down Beat*

Dedications / Jul. 19-21, 1976 / Inner City 6046

★ **Finesse** / May 8, 1978 / Concord Jazz 4069
The material on *Finesse* is mostly ballads interspersed with a few things done at medium tempo; although this had been pianist/bandleader/composer Toshiko Akiyoshi's domain in the past, this time she brings a dirge-like sound to it that breeds impatience in the listener. In her writing for big band, alongside the drama created by her unusual horn voicings, at turns humorous or reflective, introduced by her sense of rhythmic juxtaposition. It was this later feature that is lacking in all but three of the selections on *Finesse*. Akiyoshi is not the only culprit, as bassist Monty Budwig, who shares much of the solo space, plods through most of his solos as if his bass strings were coated with molasses. The three tunes that break out of this somber pattern are "Mr. Jelly Lord," an original from the Akiyoshi-Tabackin band book, "Warning," and an arrangement of a Grieg piece, "Solvejg's Song." The Jelly Roll Morton tune is played as a ballad, but this time instead of a facile explication of the melody, Akiyoshi explores the emotional beauty of the notes, pausing in reflection before continuing. "Warning" and "Solvejg's Song" are both taken at a medium tempo. —*Bob Rusch, Cadence*

Notorious Tourist from the East / Dec. 5-6, 1978 / Inner City 6066
Fine set showcasing the tasty Akiyoshi piano in non-big band setting. Akiyoshi is a good ballad interpreter, excellent

composer and accomplished soloist, qualities that have been obscured by her conducting and arranging skills. This album put those talents in the forefront. —Ron Wynn

Tribute to Billy Strayhorn, The / i. Aug. 1982 / Jazz America 5003

Remembering Bud: Cleopatra's Dream / i. Aug. 1, 1990-Jul. 3, 1990 / Evidence 22034

Bandleader and pianist Toshiko Akiyoshi is a far better player than she claims, and she demonstrates her abilities on these ten tracks recorded in 1990. From the lush, sensitively articulated solos on "Celia," "I'll Keep Loving You," and the title track, to her more forceful phrasing and intervals on "Parisian Thoroughfare" and "Dance of the Intervals," Akiyoshi displays an accomplished rhythmic style, a nice harmonic sense, and a good command of the keyboard. While her touch and volume are not as emphatic as some other pianists', Akiyoshi's melodic sense and her floating lines are strong enough to express what is necessary within each song. She has alternating accompanists; Ray Drummond and George Mraz are both dynamic, aggressive players, though Mraz gets more solo space. Lewis Nash again shows why he is held in such high regard as a drummer; his playing ranks a bit higher and is more explosive than that of Al Harewood, though he is also less capable on the title track and on "Oblivion." For those unaccustomed to hearing Akiyoshi outside the big-band arena, this will be a pleasant departure. Piano fans already knew what she could do in small combo or in solo situations. —Ron Wynn

○ **Carnegie Hall Concert / i.** Sep. 17, 1992 / Columbia 48805

PHEEROAN AKLAFF

b. 1955
Modern creative
Pheeroan AkLaff is a fine contemporary free player who's worked with several outstanding leaders and musicians in the '70s, '80s, and '90s. AkLaff's crisp, rhythmically arresting style proved ideal when he joined Henry Threadgill and Fred Hopkins in the trio New Air, following Steve McCall's departure. AkLaff played with Jay Hoggard in the mid-'70s, then was in Leo Smith's New Dalta Ahkri, where he earned critical praise and increased recognition. AkLaff worked extensively with Oliver Lake and Anthony Davis in the '70s, and was in Lake's trio in 1978 and 1979. He was in the quartet co-led by Davis and James Newton during those same years, and was a member of Davis's Episteme and Lake's reggae/funk/free band, Jump Up, in the '80s. AkLaff recorded with Amina Claudine Myers and Bakida Carroll in the late '70s and '80s, joined New Air in 1982 and also began recording his own dates for Gramavision. Currently, AkLaff does not have any sessions available on CD, though he can be heard on various reissues and releases by Lake, Davis, Myers, and others. —Ron Wynn

JOE ALBANY (Joseph Albani)

b. Jan. 24, 1924, Atlantic City, NJ, **d.** Jan. 11, 1988, New York, NY
Piano / Bop
A good bebop pianist with solid blues sensitivity and accomplished technique, Joe Albany was one of the early players who successfully adapted bebop's harmonic innovations to the keyboard. He was particularly known for long lines, impressive phrases, and extensive ballad statements. Albany studied piano in high school after playing accordion as a child. He relocated to the West Coast at age 17, joining Leo Watson's group. Albany worked with Benny Carter, Stan Getz, and Georgie Auld in the mid-'40s, then met Charlie Parker in New York. They formed a musical and personal friendship. Albany played with Auld again in 1945, then with Boyd Raeburn. He briefly reteamed with Parker the next year in Los Angeles. He also recorded with Lester Young, and a recording of a rehearsal Albany had with Warne Marsh was also released in 1957. Albany's music with Parker and Young stands as his finest. He later wrote com-

positions for Anita O'Day and worked with Charles Mingus in the mid-'60s. Albany divided his time between living in Europe and living in America in the latter part of his career, and recorded in the '70s for Revelation, Steeplechase, Spotlite, and others, and for Elektra in 1981. He was featured in Carole Langer's documentary film, *Joe Albany. . . . A Jazz Life,* in the '80s. Some of the musicians Albany recorded with include Joe Venuti, Niels-Henning Orsted Pedersen, George Duvivier, Charlie Persip, and Al Gafa. He has a few sessions available on CD. —Ron Wynn

★ **Right Combination / Sep.** 1957 / Riverside 1749
The only early documentation of the swinging bebop pianist. Features Warne Marsh (ts). —David Szatmary

Albany Touch / Jul. 5, 1977 / Sea Breeze 1004
One of the early boppers, Albany issued several solo piano records in the '70s. This one is among his finest, with glittering versions of standards and bop anthems like "Night in Tunisia." —Ron Wynn

Bird Lives / Jan. 4, 1979 / Storyville 4164

Portrait of an Artist / 1982 / Elektra 60161
A good recent example of Albany's hard-driving and infectious style. —David Szatmary

GERALD ALBRIGHT

Vocals, saxophone / Instrumental pop
A fusion and pop/jazz saxophonist, Albright is among the most popular on the current Atlantic roster. His recent live album, recorded at Birdland West, demonstrates he can improvise and can do standard jazz in an above-average fashion. His other releases have been more toward the instrumental pop side, though he's a gifted soloist even in a restrictive format. All his dates are available on CD. —Ron Wynn

○ **Dream Come True / Nov.** 6, 1990 / Atlantic 82087
Albright, who is among the most popular instrumental pop/fusion saxophonists around, plays both high-octane uptempo tunes and slick covers of urban contemporary hits. It's well produced, with a minimum of improvisational content, but should attract those who like lite jazz. —Ron Wynn

★ **Live at Birdland West / 1991 / Atlantic 82334**
Saxophonist Gerald Albright seems and sounds fearless on this issue of half standards and half originals, with bonus points for assembling a fine coterie of sidemen. The album opens with John Coltrane's "Impressions," Hoagy Carmichael's "Georgia on My Mind," and three originals. All were recorded live at Birdland West. Albright plays both alto and tenor, with Onaje Allen Gumbs on acoustic piano and synthesizer, Patrick Moten on organ and synths, Tony Dumas on electric and acoustic basses, Land Richards on drums, and Derek Nakamoto on strings. The second half has Albright playing alto in tandem with tenor terror Kirk Whalum on two cleverly titled originals, "Melodius Thunk" (a tribute to Thelonious Monk) and "Boss of Nova" (with Joe Sample at the keys), plus an oldie, "Limehouse Blues." Then he brings in another legend, Eddie Harris, for another original, "Bubblehead McDaddy," adding Patrice Rushen on piano, Oscar Brashear on trumpet, and Ndugu Chancler on drums. The album lives up to its lineup. —Patricia Myers, Jazz Times

HOWARD ALDEN

b. 1958, Newport Beach, CA
Guitar / Swing
One of the young musicians of the '80s for whom swing, rather than bebop, cool, or free has been the muse, Howard Alden has proven himself to be a topflight guitarist. He's a capable accompanist, an excellent soloist, and a steady bandleader. His playing has flair, wit, and subtlety, and is expressive without being flamboyant or flashy. While Alden is effective on electric, his best work comes on acoustic, where his tone, sound, and touch are illuminated more fully. Alden began playing guitar at age ten, and learned by listening to jazz records. He played professionally in Los Angeles in his

early teens, and took lessons from Jimmy Wyble, an ex-member of Red Norvo's trio. Subsequently, Alden formed a friendship with trombonist Dan Barrett, while continuing to do sessions around Los Angeles. He played with Norvo for a season in Los Angeles during the late '70s, then relocated to New York in the early '80s. He stayed busy working with Joe Bushkin, Ruby Braff, Joe Williams, Woody Herman, Warren Vaché, Jr., Kenny Davern, Benny Carter, Monty Alexander, and Flip Phillips. He and Barrett maintained their relationship and began recording and playing together in a quintet during the mid-'80s. Alden continues to record into the '90s, doing mainly Concord sessions, but also records dates for Stomp Off (a fascinating set on banjo playing classic Harry Reser solos) and Chiaroscuro. He's played with Jack Lesberg, Ken Peplowski, Lynn Seaton, Dennis Mackrel, Frank Tate, Keith Copeland, and George Van Eps, as well as Barrett and Phillips. Currently, he has many albums available on CD. —*Ron Wynn*

Swing Street / Sep. 1986 / Concord Jazz 4349

○ **Howard Alden Trio Plus Special Guests Ken Peplowski & Warren Vaché** / Jan. 1989 / Concord Jazz 4378
Guitarist Howard Alden showed not only taste but wide knowledge of the traditions in his selection, which includes: "Gazelle" and "Your Love," two seldom-heard Duke Ellington tunes; a pair of Django Reinhardt gems, "Douce" and "Tears"; Charlie Parker pieces such as "Back Home"; Thelonious Monk's "Reflections"; and Fats Waller's "Keep a Song," all tunes that are not from the obvious top of the jazz stockpile. In its sources of inspiration, Alden's playing is as eclectic as his choice of material. It is nicely unified in its style, which, for lack of a better term, can be described as modern mainstream with swing era tributaries and bop outlets. That full range can be heard when he and Ken Peplowski (tenor sax, clarinet) collaborate on "Douce Ambiance" and "Back Home Blues." Their unison sound is reminiscent of Stan Getz and Jimmy Raney in the early '50s, and the phrasing and rhythmic emphasis in their solos draws from both the ethos of '30s swing and the inflections of bop. Like Alden's work, Peplowski's tenor solos are solid and enjoyable. Vache's cornet solos are rather more than that; they are compelling and riveting. The ferocity of his growl/plunger work on "Purple Gazelle" is as electrifying as Rex Stewart's in the Ellington small groups. His joyous open solo on the Fats Waller piece is thrilling, and his ballad playing on "Where Are You" keeps Bobby Hackett's legacy of smoothness, burnished tone, and harmonic perfection alive. If anyone has doubts about Mel Lewis as a great drummer/accompanist who can also swing you out of the room, listen to him behind Vaché on "Keep a Song in Your Soul." —*Doug Ramsey, Jazz Times*

Salutes Buck Clayton / Jun. 1989 / Concord Jazz 4395

Snowy Morning Blues / Apr. 1990 / Concord Jazz 4424

No Amps Allowed / 1990 / Chiaroscuro 303

★ **Thirteen Strings** / Feb. 1991 / Concord Jazz 4464
With George Van Eps. Alden's six-string and Van Eps's seven-string make the 13. Long overdue for George Van Eps. Excellent. —*Michael G. Nastos*

Misterioso / Apr. 1991 / Concord Jazz 4487

Hand-Crafted Swing / i. Jun. 30, 1992 / Concord Jazz 4513

MONTY ALEXANDER (Montgomery Bernard)

b. Jun. 6, 1944, Kingston, Jamaica
Piano / Bop, world fusion
A glib, exciting pianist, Monty Alexander has been a first-rate player and bandleader since the early '60s. He's infused his work with a Caribbean flavor, and has successfully adapted and gleaned from the styles of prime influences Art Tatum, Erroll Garner, Nat "King" Cole, and Oscar Peterson. Alexander's speed, facility, precision, and soulfulness are especially evident in a trio setting, but he's just as effective with larger combos. Alexander moved to Miami from Kingston in the early '60s, and played in local clubs before

going to New York. He played at Minton's and other clubs while working summers with Milt Jackson and Ray Brown, and recording with them. Alexander formed his own trio in the '70s, toured Europe in 1974 and 1980, and played at the Montreux Jazz Festival in 1976. He's recorded for MPS, Black & Blue, Pausa, Pablo, and Concord Jazz in the '70s, '80s, and '90s. Alexander's played with Herb Ellis, John Clayton, Jeff Hamilton, Brown, and Jackson. He has several sessions available on CD. —*Ron Wynn*

Zing! / Dec. 11+14, 1967 / RCA 3930

This Is Monty Alexander / Jul. 1, 1969 / Verve 68790

Here Comes the Sun / Jun. 6, 1971 / BASF 20913

Live! Montreux Alexander / Jun. 10, 1976 / Verve 817487
Tremendous piano work makes this live set a standout for Alexander, featured performing at the Montreux Festival. The trio includes bassist John Clayton and drummer Jeff Hamilton, and the set is concluded with a vivid rendition of "Battle Hymn of the Republic." —*Ron Wynn*

Soul Fusion / Jun. 1-2, 1977 / Pablo 2310804

Monty Alexander in Tokyo / Jan. 22, 1979 / Pablo 836

Facets / Aug. 1979 / Concord Jazz 4108

Ivory & Steel / Mar. 1980 / Concord Jazz 4124

Trio / Aug. 1980 / Concord Jazz 4136

Overseas Special / Mar. 1982 / Concord Jazz 253

☆ **Triple Treat I** / Mar. 1982 / Concord Jazz 4193
This recording was done in Osaka, Japan, in March 1982. This particular trio worked together before and were well integrated (guitarist Herb Ellis and bassist Ray Brown, of course, had long experience with pianist Oscar Peterson). This is one of those LPs that I've enjoyed several times already, although I wouldn't claim that it is an inspired session. Just straightahead, middle-of-the-road jazz played very professionally. It includes a nice "Body and Soul" and a good "Triple Treat Blues" (Ray Brown stands out on this cut). Alexander's playing was not up the remainder of the session on "But Not for Me," but Herb Ellis is especially good. —*Shirley Klett, Cadence*

Reunion in Europe / Mar. 27, 1983 / Concord Jazz 231

Duke Ellington Songbook / Mar. 29, 1983 / Verve 821151

★ **River, The** / Oct. 1985 / Concord Jazz 4422
Monty Alexander added three appropriate compositions of his own to this wide-ranging and sympathetic program of music from the church. "Ain't Gonna Study War No More" is a traditional theme, which has served to inspire more than one composition; the Lennon-McCartney "Let It Be" is probably the most familiar. This gets an appropriately rousing treatment. Schubert's "Ave Maria," on the other hand, is approached with quiet respect and features the bowed bass of John Clayton. Some of these performances (cf. "Stand Up") have great rhythmic swing while others (including the "Ave Maria") seem like pretty straight renditions until you notice your foot tapping. Omega Studios (Bob Yesbek is listed as chief engineer) did a superior job in recording. One mike on the piano treble is slightly forward in the mix, but the piano sound is otherwise unusually well caught, as are Clayton (including the bow work) and Thigpen. Monty Alexander produced this one himself and, contrary to most Concord releases, the usual extensive liner notes are lacking. . . . No more need be said: the music speaks for itself. —*Shirley Klett, Cadence*

☆ **Triple Treat II** / Jun. 1987 / Concord Jazz 4338
The trio side of this LP is worth the price of the recording. I was of two minds about the quartet side, but in either case the intensity of the jazz music falls off sharply with the addition of violin. John Frigo was a member of the Soft Winds group, as was Herb Ellis. He's no stranger to jazz, but has never been more than a gentle swinger. One technique used to fit him in was a straight violin introduction followed by some choruses, which swings mildly with Frigo (he builds up a pretty good head of steam on "Lester Leaps in"), and swings harder without him. So, while side B has some fine

to outstanding choruses, there is an uneven quality considered strictly from a jazz standpoint. Since the trio alone on side A swings its socks off, the momentum it generates will carry most listeners through the quartet sides in an approving frame of mind. Ray Brown is featured on "It Might as Well Be Spring," and Ellis makes the most of "Seven Come Eleven." I don't want to imply a putdown of Brown, but Alexander and Ellis are both in top form. The recording quality is well above average, although I don't think Brown's bass was done full justice; his remarkable singing tone was not caught, perhaps due to choice of microphones. On the other hand, I've seldom heard Herb Ellis as well recorded. — *Shirley Klett*, Cadence

☆ **Triple Treat III** / Jun. 1987 / Concord Jazz 4394
Alexander is a master at embellishing the standard jazz piano vocabulary with Caribbean rhythms. While the menu of well-worn show tunes, standards, and an occasional Alexander original isn't overwhelming, the participants' taste and artistry elevate things beyond the realm of another good date among old friends. —*Ron Wynn*, Rock & Roll Disc

Jamboree: Monty Alexander's Ivory and Steel / Feb. 1988-Mar. 1988 / Concord Jazz 4359
Alexander featured his group "Ivory and Steel" for session that blended driving jazz feel, breezy Caribbean flavor in effective, catchy fashion. As usual, Alexander's piano solos were upbeat, brisk, and captivating. —*Ron Wynn*

Saturday Night / **i.** 1993 / Limetree 024
Pianist Monty Alexander and company exude the high spirit and spirituality Alexander is known for on this just-released 1985 live recording. Alexander's Caribbean roots frequently rise to the surface, carried along by the hand drums of Robert Thomas, Jr. The other forces are drummer Ed Thigpen and bassist Reggie Johnson. —*Sunsh Stein*, Jazz Times

LOREZ ALEXANDRIA (Nelson [Née Turner], Dolorez Alexandria)

b. Aug. 14, 1929, Chicago, IL
Vocals / Ballads
Veteran vocalist who specializes in ballads and blues. Alexandria's hallmark is her ability to master the subtle and understated. —*Michael G. Nastos*

Lorez Sings Pres: A Tribute to Lester Young / Nov. 6+13, 1957 / King 565
Tribute to Lester Young. Formerly rare, now reissued in original form. —*Hank Davis*

Band Swings, Lorez Sings, The / **i.** 1959 / King 656
Decent set featuring the highly stylized, often erratic vocalist Lorez Alexandria doing conventional jazz and jazz-centered pop tunes and standards. She's backed by a capable band and sometimes has brilliant moments, but overall Alexandria is an average vocalist. —*Ron Wynn*

Sings Standards with a Touch of Jazz / **i.** 1960 / Deluxe 676
Stylish vocals and prerock interpretative standards done by a singer whose delivery, tone, and approach skirt the boundary between jazz-tinged pop and pop-oriented show biz material. —*Ron Wynn*

Early in the Morning / Mar. 15+17, 1960 / Argo 663

For Swingers Only / Jan. 2-3, 1963 / Argo 720

★ **Alexandria the Great** / 1964 / Impulse 62

☆ **Alexandria the Great / More of The Great** / 1964 / MCA 33116
1964-1965. Twofer. Fine jazz vocal stylings. Combines two Impulse albums. —*Hank Davis*

More of the Great Lorez Alexandria / 1964 / Impulse 76

Sings the Songs of Johnny Mercer—Vol. 3: Tangerine / Dec. 5, 1984 / Trend 538
With the Mike Wofford Quartet. Excellent recent work. Jazz vocals. Classy material with solid four-piece backing. — *Hank Davis*

RASHIED ALI (Robert Patterson)

b. Jul. 1, 1935, Philadelphia, PA
Drums / Early free, modern creative
Rashied Ali made history in the mid-'60s when he was recruited by John Coltrane to serve as second drummer in Coltrane's expanded band. Ali didn't remain in that role very long because Elvin Jones quickly departed, leaving Ali as the lone percussionist. Ali was praised for his ability to play what Trane labeled "multidirectional" rhythms, giving the soloist maximum freedom. This could be heard at its fullest on the duet album *Interstellar Space* (issued after Coltrane's death) where Ali's rhythms spiral around Coltrane's furious wails and screams, and don't conflict with or necessarily guide Coltrane's playing, but mesh and complement it while establishing a counterdirection. Ali studied at the Granoff School in Philadelphia, and played drums with both R&B bands and jazz groups before joining Sonny Rollins in 1963 for a tour of Japan. He then moved to New York, where he played with Pharoah Sanders, Bill Dixon, Paul Bley, Sun Ra, Albert Ayler, and Sunny Murray before starting his tenure with Coltrane in 1965. He continued working with Alice Coltrane after John's death in 1967, then began heading his own groups. In the '70s, Ali began efforts to improve the lot of jazz musicians, especially their ability to control their music and its proceeds, and to find venues for work. He helped organize the New York Musicians Festival in 1972, and formed Survival Records in 1973, issuing his own recordings. He also opened a club, Ali's Alley, which he operated as a place for noncommercial and "loft" jazz acts until 1979. Ali participated in a Dialogue of the Drums concert with Milford Graves and Andrew Cyrille in the mid-'70s, but he's had a low profile in the '80s and '90s. —*Ron Wynn*

★ **Rashied Ali Quintet** / 1973 / Survival 102

DON ALIAS

Percussion / Early jazz-rock, world fusion
A veteran percussionist who first came to fame in the early '70s playing with Miles Davis, Don Alias has done many jazz, jazz-rock, and pop sessions. He does not have any sessions available as a leader, but can be heard on CDs by Carla Bley, Michael Brecker, Joey Calderazzo, Terri Lyne Carrington, and Peter Erskine, among many others. —*Ron Wynn*

GERI ALLEN

b. Jun. 12, 1957, Pontiac, MI (raised in Detroit)
Piano, composer / M-base, modern creative
A shining light among '80s pianists, Geri Allen has achieved a synthesis of bebop, free, hard bop, and funk/R&B influences, and has melded them into an individual, exciting style. Her touch, phrasing, and melodic and rhythmic abilities are superb, and she's been both a busy session player with numerous credits and recording dates and a featured artist on the Soul Note, DIW, JMT/Polygram, and Blue Note labels. Allen cites the musical unpredictability of Thelonious Monk and Herbie Nichols, and the virtuosity of Eric Dolphy, as strong influences on her style. She's noted for her ability to solo in a quiet, yet intense fashion. This skill has been illuminated on some remarkable trio dates with Charlie Haden and Paul Motian. Allen once backed the Supremes during her early days in Detroit. After studying music at Howard University and the University of Pittsburgh with Nathan Davis, she studied privately with Roscoe Mitchell. Allen moved to New York in the early '80s, working with James Newton and Lester Bowie before recording her debut for Minor. She's also played with Marcus Belgrave, Kenny Garrett, Robert Hurst, Jeff Watts, Oliver Lake, Andrew Cyrille, and Robin Eubanks. Allen has worked closely with both Coleman's M-Base and the Black Rock Coalition, an organization of musicians, artists, and cultural activists working to improve conditions and opportunities for African-Americans in every area of American music. She's also

played with Betty Carter. Allen has several albums currently available on CD. —*Ron Wynn*

☆ **Printmakers, The** / Feb. 8-9, 1984 / Minor Music 001

For her debut disc, which was released on a new (1985) label from Germany (Minor Music), pianist Geri Allen chose two excellent sidemen in bassist Anthony Cox and percussionist Andrew Cyrille. Chances are the listener will be grabbed first by Cox's melodic phrasing and rock-solid attention to the rhythm, or by Cyrille's brilliant flair. The first selection opens with the drummer presenting an exhibition of "mouth percussion" before setting up the bouncy "Caribbean" rhythm. Allen was not a stunning soloist; she often tended to play in the middle range of the keyboard, which gives a "blockish" feel to some of her solos. Her ballad style is akin to that of Bill Evans, especially on "Eric," a slow tribute to Eric Dolphy. She displays a leaning towards Keith Jarrett on her other solo piece, "When Kabuya Dances." In the way her left hand dances, punctuating the rhythm while the melody line is simple, you can hear that the pianist continuously varies as she wends her way through the song. In the final analysis, the listener does not get a feeling for Geri Allen, the composer, as much as they get for Geri Allen, the performer. Cox and Cyrille provide most of the sparks, but Allen does a decent job. This is an interesting debut. —*Richard B. Kamins*, Cadence

★ **Open on All Sides in the Middle** / Dec. 1986 / PolyGram 850013

Pianist Geri Allen focuses on her rock/funk/pop heritage on her third LP. It isn't bad for what it is, but little of it is jazz. Fronting the band half the time is Shahita Nurallah, whose voice is high and clear and light—so light that it seems almost disembodied in the high-soprano range where Allen placed her. Hypnotic Latin-derived (but not textbook) rhythms drive several of these pieces; Allen pounds out attractive, if static, syncopated patterns. The horns may fill in the background with written riffs; where vamps and rhythms are hot, the topical mix is refreshing. Swaying beats and cool wordless vocals give "I Sang" Flora Purim-and-Airto Moreira overtones. The pretty 6/8 wobble "Open on All Sides" opens out with periodic breaks for Robin Eubanks's garrulous trombone or the tenor of David Murray (ex-Griot Galaxy, home of Shihad and drummer Tanni Tabbal). Steve Coleman's slippery alto solos and Marcus Belgrave's raggedy-ass flugelhorn offer the jazz highlights—save for Lloyd Storey's tap dancing on the engagingly lopey, marimba-flavored "Dancer." This *urbo contempo* set has radio appeal that won't quit. ("Open" even appropriates a National Public Radio jingle for use as a backing riff.) The synthesizer funk of "In the Middle" is busy/cluttered enough to be fun, for a little while at least. "Drummer's Song" has an ersatz "Birdland" bit that is no worse than real Weather Report, but I'd rather listen to Geri Allen's uncouth comping behind Oliver Lake. (Better yet, she could incorporate that complex humor into her own band.) She has more to offer jazz than progressive pop. —*Kevin Whitehead*, Cadence

○ **In the Year of The Dragon** / Mar. 1989 / PolyGram 834428

On *In the Year of the Dragon*, this trio is creative, colorful, and right on the mark, whether the music is classic bop or very free. The musical communication between these three musicians seems telepathic; each of them obviously possessed large ears. The uptempo "Oblivion" gives Geri Allen an opportunity to display her mastery of Bud Powell's style. The slow, mournful ballad "For John Malachi" is more Thelonious Monkish, while the folk melody "Rollano" has its composer Juan Lazaro Mendolas on the quena (a bamboo flute) with Charlie Haden's rumbling bass adding to its atmosphere. The bassist's original blues, "See You at Per Tutti's," features a melody that starts off like Monk and ends up sounding like Ornette Coleman. Paul Motian's "Last Call" has the piano and bass playing independently of each other, and with Motian (drums) setting the pulse, it becomes a three-way musical conversation. Geri Allen's driving "No More Mr. Nice Guy" and Ornette Coleman's "Invisible" allow the trio to indulge in some fiery freebop, while Haden's

"First Song" is a memorable composition full of quiet authority. The concluding "In the Year of the Tiger" finds Geri Allen (with constant musical commentary from Haden) playing with gentle freeness. Scores of trio albums are released each year, but *In the Year of the Dragon* is something special. Although Paul Motian is quite subtle, each of the three musicians are equally responsible for the music's success. —*Scott Yanow*, Cadence

☆ **Twylight** / 1989 / Verve 841152

Geri Allen, one of the most talented of the young pianists on the scene today, occupies a niche in the evolution of jazz somewhere between the modern mainstream of McCoy Tyner/Chick Corea/Herbie Hancock and the atonal power of Cecil Taylor. Her *Twylight* disc, which, from its cover, looks as if it could be a reggae session, is actually a strong example of her originality. The opener, "When Kabuya Dances," is the longest (8:42) and most memorable selection of this date. Starting off as a new-age type ballad, this performance (which could easily serve as background music for a creative dancer) gradually becomes freer and its repetitions more intense, until it approaches the fury of a Cecil Taylor before working its way back to its new-age beginnings. Most of the other selections are brief (ranging from the six-minute "Shadow Series" to the introspective 1:11 title cut), with virtually the entire focus (save Jaribu Shihad's bowed bass solo on "Little Wind" and two forgettable wordless vocals by Clarice Taylor Bell) on the pianist, who wrote all ten sketches. —*Scott Yanow*, Cadence

○ **Nurturer, The** / Jan. 5-6, 1990 / Capitol 95139

☆ **Segments** / i. 1990 / DIW 833

○ **Maroons** / i. 1992 / Capitol 99493

Don't even bother keeping track of the beat on "Mad Money," one of pianist Geri Allen's 13 original compositions on *Maroons*. Just lie back and listen to her sail by with trumpeter Wallace Roney. . . . She revels in off-kilter meters and the harmonic intricacies of "Dolphy's Dance." On "Laila's House," abrupt time changes just click into place. . . . Allen's compositional chops are in order, too. . . . Repeated patterns anchor her compositions even when they veer into abstraction. . . . Trumpeter Marcus Belgrave, her mentor from Detroit days, sounds especially attuned to her work. He weaves and she bobs in perfect choreography on Lawrence Williams's "Number Four." —*Elaine Guregian*, Down Beat

☆ **Live at the Village Vanguard** / DIW 847

☆ **Etudes—Geri Allen-Haden-Motian** / Soul Note

HENRY ALLEN (Allen Jr,. Henry James)

b. Jan. 7, 1908, New Orleans, LA, **d.** Apr. 17, 1967, New York, NY

Trumpet / New Orleans traditional

One of early jazz's most evocative players, Henry "Red" Allen created a singular trumpet vocabulary that proved highly influential. He was the son of the famed New Orleans Brass Band leader Henry Allen, and his uncles, George and Sam Allen, were parade musicians. Allen utilized an array of effects, among them lip trills, smears, glissandos, growls, and splattered notes. He perfected a rhythmic freedom that made his solos sound extremely loose, yet explosive. During the '30s, Allen performed several celebrated upper- and middle-register solos.

After learning trumpet in his father's band and playing in various New Orleans groups, Allen went to St. Louis to join King Oliver in 1927. He went with Oliver to New York, where he recorded with Clarence Williams. Allen played in Fate Marable's Mississippi riverboat band in 1928 and 1929, and was discovered by Victor representatives looking for a trumpeter to help them offset Armstrong at Okeh. Allen immediately returned to New York, and made four sides in 1929 with members of Luis Russell's band. These performances led to a three-year engagement with Russell's orchestra. Allen then played with Fletcher Henderson in 1933 and 1934, and in the Mills Blue Rhythm Band from 1934 to 1937. These engagements, plus some outstanding small-group recording dates, established Allen as a top trumpet soloist in the early swing period. He worked for Lucky Millinder and even briefly subbed with Duke Ellington. Allen rejoined Russell's band in 1937, which was, at the time, accompanying Louis Armstrong. The band's new status bumped Allen from his accustomed rung as principal soloist. He stayed until 1940.

Allen gradually moved away from swing, and led his own combos in the '40s and '50s. He participated in the emerging traditional jazz revival, cutting New Orleans-styled dates with Sidney Bechet and Jelly Roll Morton, as well as his own groups. By the late '40s, Allen was regaining lost momentum, and by the mid-'50s had recaptured his star position. He recorded with Hawkins, Buster Bailey, Kid Ory, Pee Wee Russell, and J. C. Higginbotham; held a residency at New York's Metropole from 1952 until 1965; and toured Europe throughout the '60s. His 1957 recording of "I Cover the Waterfront" was one of the finest renditions of that anthem. Allen's creative exploitation of timbral effects won him admiration and attention in the '60s from free trumpeters. The LP *Feelin' Good* and another session for Prestige were both critically acclaimed Allen releases during the '60s. He appeared frequently at Newport Jazz Festivals beginning in 1957, and that same year was a guest on the acclaimed television program "The Sound of Jazz." Allen kept playing and touring until the end of his life, and concluded a visit to England only weeks before dying of cancer in 1967. —*Ron Wynn and Bruce Boyd Raeburn*

Ridin' with Red / Jul. 16, 1929-Sep. 24, 1929 / 3033

★ **Henry Allen Collection—Vol. 1 (1929-1930), The** / 1929-1930 / JSP 332

○ **Henry Allen Collection—Vol. 2 (1929-1930), The** / 1929-1930 / JSP 333

Henry Allen & Coleman Hawkins / Jul. 21, 1933 / Hep 1028
With Coleman Hawkins (ts). Driving, swing-era favorites mixed with popular songs of the day, delivered by two masters. —*Bruce Raeburn*

Original 1933-1941 Recordings / 1933-1941 / Tax 3
"Red" in various contexts, providing a good sampler of his early recordings. A memorable solo by Allen on "Body and Soul." —*Bruce Raeburn*

★ **World on a String** / Mar. 21, 1957-Apr. 10, 1957 / Bluebird 2497
Red Allen with J. C. Higginbotham (t), Coleman Hawkins (sax), Buster Bailey (cl), and others—a collaboration that shines on "I Cover the Waterfront," tickles on "Ride, Red, Ride." —*Bruce Raeburn*

Ride, Red, Ride in Hi-Fi / Mar. 21, 1957-Mar. 28, 1957 / RCA 1508

○ **Henry Red Allen Meets Kid Ory** / i. 1960 / Verve 6076

○ **Red Allen Plays King Oliver** / Nov. 1960 / Verve 1025

○ **Mr. Allen** / Jun. 5, 1962 / Swingville 2034

MARSHALL ALLEN

b. 1924
Alto saxophone / Modern creative
A longtime member of Sun Ra's Arkestra and one of the most animated, intense, and explosive alto saxophonists in any genre, Marshall Allen can be heard on numerous Ra releases. He's also a gifted flutist, and plays oboe, piccolo, and other wind instruments. Allen played with Art Simmons in France during 1949 and 1950, then toured Europe with James Moody. He moved to Chicago in the early '50s, where he met Sun Ra. Allen recorded, performed, and toured with various Ra ensembles from the late '50s through the '60s, '70s, and '80s. In the mid-'60s, Allen also recorded with Paul Bley. He can be heard on numerous Ra reissues on CD. —*Ron Wynn*

MOSE ALLISON (Mose John (Jr.) Allison)

b. Nov. 11, 1927, Tippo, MS
Piano, vocals, composer, trumpet / Cool, blues & jazz

A charismatic pianist and vocalist, Mose Allison blends Southern wit and wisdom with urbane sophistication. The results are a keyboard approach that doesn't desert the blues, and is delivered in a consistently entertaining, vibrant fashion. Allison grew up in the Mississippi Delta region, and began piano lessons in the first grade. He learned trumpet in high school, was a pianist in the army, and later attended Louisiana State University. He played in a regional trio, before playing with Al Cohn, Zoot Sims, Gerry Mulligan, and Stan Getz in the late '50s. He also began recording on Prestige, and with Cohn and Sims. He did several Prestige albums in the late '50s. Allison visited Europe in 1959 and London in 1966. During the '60s and early '70s, he made arguably his finest recordings for Atlantic, among them the brilliant *Western Man* and *Your Mind Is on Vacation*. He moved to Elektra in the early '80s, cutting another masterpiece, *Middle Class White Boy*. He was later signed by Blue Note. The trio has been his preferred format, and Allison has led bands and has worked with local musicians in the towns he's played. Allison sessions from the '50s and '60s have been reissued, and his current work remains in print. His '70s Atlantic and '80s Elektra recordings are not readily available on CD. —*Ron Wynn*

Back Country Suite / Mar. 7, 1957 / Prestige 075
A wonderful date mixing his country blue warblings, dynamic piano playing, and cabaret-from-the-backwoods styles. —*Ron Wynn*

Mose Allison Plays for Lovers / Mar. 7, 1957-Feb. 13, 1959 / Prestige 7446

○ **Seventh Son, The** / Mar. 7, 1957-Feb. 13, 1959 / Prestige 3003
This is compilation of cuts from Allison's albums from 1957 to 1959: *Back Country Suite, Local Color, Young Man Mose, Ramblin' with Mose, Creek Bank*, and *Autumn Song*. —AMG

Down Home Piano / Nov. 8, 1957-Feb. 13, 1959 / Prestige 7423
Selections from four of Allison's albums: *Local Color, Ramblin' with Mose, Creek Bank*, and *Autumn Song*. —AMG

Local Color / Nov. 8, 1957 / Prestige 457

○ **Greatest Hits** / Nov. 8, 1957-Feb. 13, 1959 / Prestige 6004

Ol' Devil Mose / i. 1958 / Prestige 24089
This is actually a two-album set combining songs from Allison releases *Rambling with Mose* and *Autumn Song*. They are trio dates, and feature prime Allison vocals, excellent solos, and great interaction between the pianist, bassist Addison Farmer, and drummer Ronnie Free. —*Ron Wynn*

Ramblin' with Mose / Apr. 18, 1958 / Prestige 7215

Autumn Song / Feb. 13, 1959 / Prestige 7189
Fine trio outing with the witty, always engaging Mose Allison in good vocal form and also adding sparkling piano accompaniment and solos. He's backed by Addison Farmer (Art's brother) on bass and Ronnie Free on drums. The set includes an early version of the signature song "Eyesight to the Blind." —*Ron Wynn*

Creek Bank / Aug. 15, 1959 / Prestige 24055
Similar themes, performance levels and musical lineup for this session as *Autumn Song*. The tunes were recorded a few months before, and include more definitive Allison including his brilliant "Seventh Son" and dazzling version of "Yardbird Suite." This has been reissued on CD. —*Ron Wynn*

★ **I Love the Life I Live** / Jun. 28, 1960-Sep. 9, 1960 / Columbia 8367

○ **I Don't Worry About a Thing** / Mar. 15, 1962 / Atlantic 1389

○ **Best of Mose Allison** / i. 1962-1982 / Atlantic 1542

Mose Alive! / Oct. 22-31, 1965 / Edsel 153

★ **Western Man** / Feb. 2, 1971-Mar. 4, 1971 / Atlantic 1584

Mose in Your Ear / Apr. 25-26, 1972 / Atlantic 40460

○ **Your Mind Is on Vacation** / Apr. 5-9, 1976 / Atlantic 1691

○ **Middle Class White Boy** / Feb. 2-3, 1982 / Elektra 52391

While the tunes and arrangements on this record are typical of the Mose Allison style, it departs from the Mose Allison instrumentation. On a majority of the tracks, Allison plays the electric piano, which brings a more "contemporary" sound to the music as well as an increased jump and snap; a contemporization that began in the '70s with *Western Man* on Atlantic. However, the contemporary updating doesn't bring with it the warmth and depth of the rhythmic percussion Allison applied with the acoustic piano. The tunes supported by the acoustic piano remain typical of Allison's earlier work. Aside from this, his singing still portrays casualness; the lyrics still reflect his satiric philosophies of life. Featuring tenor sax and flutist Joe Farrell and guitarist Phil Upchurch doesn't take away from the overall effect of the music, but their roles seem unnecessary, and perhaps were included to add glamour to the record. —*Karrah*, Cadence

Lesson in Living / Jul. 21, 1982 / Elektra 9602371
Lou Donaldson (as) brings a welcome blues and soul-jazz flavor to an already impressive cast and musical menu. —*Ron Wynn*

Ever Since the World Ended / May 11, 1987-Jun. 2, 1987 / Blue Note 48015
A wonderful update of his sound, with dauntless work by Mose. With Arthur Blythe (as) and Kenny Burrell (g). —*Ron Wynn*

Parchman Farm / Original Jazz Classics 18003

LAURINDO ALMEIDA

b. Sep. 2, 1917, Sao Paulo, Brazil
Acoustic guitar, composer / Latin jazz, world fusion
An excellent Brazilian guitarist equally adept at Latin, jazz, and classical playing, Laurindo Almeida has been a first-rate stylist since the late '40s. His style is fluid and especially compelling on ballads. Almeida is a strong soloist, and was one of the earliest musicians to mix samba with jazz. He was a staff guitarist on radio in Rio de Janeiro, and a bandleader. Almeida came to Los Angeles in the late '40s, where he played a couple of years with Stan Kenton. He led a trio in Los Angeles that recorded with Bud Shank (cutting *Brazilliance Vols. 1 and 2*), Herbie Mann, and the Four Freshmen. Almeida was an early bossa nova/jazz star; his album *Viva Bossa Nova* reached the number 13 spot on the pop charts in 1962. He recorded and toured Europe with the Modern Jazz Quartet in the early '60s. His album *Guitar from Ipanema* with vocalist Irene Kral won a Grammy in 1964. He began working with Hollywood orchestras in the '50s, and in 1958 won a *Down Beat* poll for film music for *The Old Man and the Sea*. Almeida spent nearly 25 years playing on film and television soundtracks. He continued recording for Capitol in the '60s, and led bands that included Shank and Gary Foster. Almeida also accompanied his wife, vocalist Deltra Eamon, and played with symphony orchestras. He co-founded the LA Four with Shank, Chuck Flores, and Ray Brown in the mid-'70s. The group later featured Shelly Manne and then Jeff Hamilton, and recorded nine albums in the '70s and '80s. Almeida also performed in a duo with Shank and a trio with Larry Coryell and classical guitarist Sharon Isbin. He wrote guitar textbooks in the late '50s and in the '70s. Almeida made a concert album for Concord in 1979, then teamed with Shank for an album of classical works in the early '80s. He recorded another duo date, this time with Charlie Byrd, for Concord in 1982, and recorded other Concord LPs through the '80s and '90s. Almeida's recently done trio sessions with Bob Magnusson and either Jeff Hamilton or Jim Plank, as well as Charlie Byrd and Carlos Barbosa-Lima. He has several current and reissued albums available on CD. —*Ron Wynn*

★ **Brazilliance—Vols. 1 & 2** / Apr. 15-22, 1953 / World Pacific 96339
With Bud Shank (as, f) on both albums. With Gary Peacock (b) and Chuck Flores (d) on the second album. It is almost possible to hear the birth of the bossa nova in these albums. —*Michael Erlewine*

○ **Delightfully Modern** / i. 1957 / Jazztone 1264

Guitar World of Laurindo Almeida / i. Aug. 1961 / Capitol 8546

Reverie for Spanish Guitar / i. Mar. 1962 / Capitol 8571

○ **Broadway Solo Guitar** / i. Jun. 1964 / Capitol 2063

Guitar from Ipanema / Sep. 1, 1964 / Capitol 2197

Jazz Origin—Brazilliance / i. 1973 / PA/USA 9009

Guitar Player / Oct. 4, 1976 / MCA 6002
A workout for guitarist Laurindo Almeida, who usually offers soft, sentimental, or light riffs and Afro-Latin material. He shows his more adventurous, animated side, and also displays his full range of guitar skills. —*Ron Wynn*

Concierto de Aranjuez / Mar. 27-28, 1978 / Inner City 6031
This solo album includes songs from *Black Orpheus* and a Gershwin medley. —*Michael Erlewine*

First Concerto for Guitar Orchestra / Nov. 1979 / Concord Jazz 42001
Guitarist Laurindo Almeida spins delicate melodies, frequently beautiful riffs, and solos backed by the Los Angeles Orchestra da Camera under the direction of Elmer Ramsey. The program on this 1979 set includes both classical and Afro-Latin compositions. —*Ron Wynn*

Latin Odyssey / Dec. 1982 / Concord Jazz 4211

Artistry in Rhythm / Apr. 1983 / Concord Jazz 238
With Bob Magnusson (b) and Milt Holland (per). This is lovely easy-listening music, in the best sense of that term. —*Michael Erlewine*

○ **Tango: Laurindo Almeida and Charlie Byrd** / Aug. 1985 / Concord Jazz 4290
This isn't a jazz LP, but a well-planned and played program of tangos for background and/or dancing. If this appeals at all to you, I can heartily recommend it. If not, both guitarists can be found on earlier recording sessions in music more to your taste. It sounds as though they enjoyed themselves doing this one. —*Shirley Klett*, Cadence

Music of the Brazilian Masters / 1989 / Concord Jazz 4389

BARRY ALTSCHUL

b. Jan. 6, 1943, New York, NY
Drums / World fusion, modern creative
A superb drummer in free and hard bop circles and an instructor, Barry Altschul provides any rhythmic style needed for a session. He's an excellent timekeeper who can drive a date, solo with verve, or participate in collective improvisations. A self-taught drummer, he later studied with Charlie Persip in the '60s. He worked with Paul Bley from the mid-'60s until 1970, and then periodically until 1980. Altschul was also in the Jazz Composers Guild and Jazz Composers Orchestra in the '60s. After spending a few months in Europe, he studied with Sam Ulano. Altschul was part of the great free band, Circle, with Chick Corea, Anthony Braxton, and Dave Holland in the late '60s and early '70s. When they disbanded, Altschul, Holland, Braxton, and Sam Rivers recorded the seminal *Conference of the Birds*, and he and Holland played in Braxton's quartet. Altschul was also part of the innovative Sam Rivers band of the late '70s. He recorded as a leader for Muse in the late '70s and Sackville and Soul Note in the '80s and '90s, and has taught drums since the late '70s. He doesn't have any sessions as a leader available on CD, but he is featured with Bley and Gary Peacock on an Improvising Artists Incorporated CD reissue. —*Ron Wynn*

Virtuosi / IAI 123844
The interplay among the three featured musicians (drummer Barry Altschul, pianist Paul Bley, bassist Gary Peacock) makes for some fascinating listening. Bassist Peacock serves as Bley's foil and alterego, and drummer Altschul fills in the spaces with feather-light stick work as if in a counterpoint.

On this level the record is quite successful, proving the title was not an extravagant claim. —*Carl Brauer*, Cadence

★ **You Can't Name Your Own Tune** / Feb. 8-9, 1977 / Muse 5124

Barry Altschul's *You Can't Name Your Own Tune* jumps right out and grabs you with its authoritative swing and probing free horn lyricism. Altschul has a totally unique sound. His setup is a throwback to 1930s big band drummers (via Harry Partch), combining the best aspects of an incidental percussionist and a small group drummer. On his first outing as a leader, Altschul's musical collaborators are all leaders and virtuosic innovators of the first rank. Bassist Dave Holland had been Altschul's rhythm section partner in excellent group settings such as Circle (with Chick Corea and Anthony Braxton); Sam Rivers and Muhal Richard Abrams also appear on the recording. Abrams is an emotionally flexible pianist and improviser, alternating freely between percussive and lyrical realms as on his thrashing trio composition "Cmbeh." The then youthful trombonist George Lewis had already established himself as the leading voice on his instrument. "King Korn" finds him anarchistic and romantic: a boldly human cry. Sam Rivers is just slightly less possessed than usual. He and Lewis create lots of powerful statements. . . . The improvising on this session is emotional and cohesive, and Altschul's compositions reflect a most cheerful disposition. —*Chip Stern*, Down Beat

Another Time, Another Place / Mar. 13-14, 1978 / Muse 5176

For Stu / Feb. 18, 1979 / SN 1015

Brahma / Jan. 23, 1980 / Sackville 3023

DANNY ALVIN (Viniello Alvin)

b. Nov. 29, 1902, New York, NY, **d.** Dec. 6, 1958, Chicago, IL
Drums, bandleader / New Orleans traditional
Danny Alvin had a lengthy career playing drums in many traditional jazz groups. The father of guitarist Teddy Walters, Alvin's first major job came playing with Sophie Tucker at Reisenweber's in New York in 1919. He moved to Chicago in the early '20s, then divided his time between New York and Chicago. Alvin played and recorded with greats such as Sidney Bechet, George Brunis, Buck Clayton, Wild Bill Davison, Wingy Manone, Joe Marsala, Art Hodes, Mezz Mezzrow, and George Zack. His legacy as a leader is slim; his best release is a 1958 session for Stepheny. —*Ron Wynn*

★ **Play Basin Street** / Jun. 18, 1958 / Stepheny 4002

FRANCO AMBROSETTI

b. Dec. 10, 1941, Lugano, Switzerland, **d.** 1990
Trumpet, flugelhorn, composer / World fusion
The son of musician Flavio Ambrosetti, Swiss trumpeter and flugelhorn player Franco Ambrosetti was both a successful bandleader and a member of various orchestras led by George Gruntz. A former classical pianist, Ambrosetti taught himself trumpet in the early '60s. He's a well-regarded soloist who won first prize in a 1966 competition sponsored by Friedrich Gulda. Ambrosetti, along with his father and Daniel Humair, helped found Gruntz's Concert Jazz Band in 1972, and worked with Gruntz into the '80s while continuing his other career as an important executive in Italy. Ambrosetti recorded several albums for Enja, playing with Benny Wallace, Phil Woods, Mike Brecker, Kenny Kirkland, and Dave Holland, among others, while he continued to work part time in his family's firm. Ambrosetti has several sessions available on CD. —*Ron Wynn*

Movies / Nov. 24-25, 1986 / Enja 5035
A superb album, even though the subject matter could restrict less dynamic players. But this time, trumpeter Ambrosetti rises to the occasion, and his spirited playing sets the tone for a fine band that includes keyboardist Geri Allen and guitarist John Scofield. Though songs like "Yellow Submarine" are shopworn, they inject some life into them. —*Ron Wynn*

★ **Movies Too** / Mar. 22-23, 1988 / Enja 79616

Brilliant playing from Swiss-born trumpet/flugelhorn player. With Geri Allen (p) and an all-star cast. Includes "Superman," "Angel Eyes," and "Peter Gunn." —*Michael G. Nastos*

○ **Music for Symphony & Jazz Band** / 1990 / Enja 79670
Involved, often sprawling work that seeks to link symphonic, improvisational traditions, and also to work in guest stars and a national Radio Orchestra. Things do hold together, and alto saxophonist Greg Osby adds some torrid licks when he gets space. —*Ron Wynn*

Sunday Walk / I Grandi Del Jazz 98
Italian import made with his son, saxophonist Flavio. Great hard bop. —*Michael G. Nastos*

ALBERT AMMONS (Albert C. Ammons)

b. Sep. 23, 1907, Chicago, IL, **d.** Dec. 2, 1949, Chicago, IL
Piano / Boogie-woogie
He wasn't its earliest practitioner or its founder, but Chicago native Albert Ammons ranked among boogie-woogie's greatest stylists, and played a major role in its late '30s and early '40s revival. Ammons began playing piano at age ten, and was a taxi driver in Chicago during the mid-'20s. He started appearing at clubs in the mid-'30s, cutting his first records on Decca in 1936 under the title Albert Ammons Rhythm Kings. Ammons's legendary 1938 Carnegie Hall date with fellow pianists Pete Johnson and Meade Lux Lewis helped fuel the boogie-woogie craze, especially with their recording "Boogie Woogie Prayer" made later that year. Ammons became a star in New York, and, in 1939, did an extensive, impressive series of recordings. These included nine solo numbers, two duets with Lewis, and five songs with the Port of Harlem Jazzmen for Blue Note. Ammons continued riding the boogie-woogie crest in the early '40s. He recorded more duets in 1941, this time with Johnson. Ammons survived a self-imposed potential disaster: he cut off a fingertip while making a sandwich in '41 and eventually suffered paralysis in both hands, but recovered. Besides frequent appearances at the Cafe Society, Ammons made vital recordings for Commodore in 1944 with Don Byas, Vic Dickenson, and Hot Lips Page. He did other sessions on Mercury with classic blues vocalist Sippie Wallace, and cut additional tracks with his son, Gene. Ammons capped his career by playing at President Truman's inauguration in 1949; he died before that year ended at age 42. His early recordings were vibrant, but reflected the influence of predecessors like Pine Top Smith, notably his solos on "Boogie Woogie Stomp" and "Suitcase Blues." By the 1939 concert, Ammons began to find his own voice, and through much of the '40s his work had its own distinctive rhythm patterns and an electrifying intensity. —*Ron Wynn*

★ **Complete Blue Note Albert Ammons** / Jan. 6, 1939 / Mosaic
This is everything you thought you knew about the Albert Ammons-Meade Lux Lewis (both piano) Blue Note recordings, plus eight previously unissued sides. This is a three-record set, which producers Mike Cuscuna and Charlie Lourie made with a limited run of 5,000 copies (a decision that was probably more realistic than limited). . . . It is hard for me to be even relatively objective about this music as it was some of the first jazz I remember hearing and I've been improvising along its structures ever since. . . . And what vivid tales are here! They never made them any better. Ammons plays his music, poised with excitement, but paced by a rich blues as swampy as it is concrete, while Lux Lewis, with frumpy deliberateness, pounds out poetry on the piano. —*Bob Rusch*, Cadence

○ **First Day** / 1939 / Blue Note 98450

○ **King of Boogie Woogie (1939-1949)** / **i.** 1939-1949 / Blues Classics 27
Classic early '30s, '40s boogie-woogie from a giant in the genre. Albert Ammons began emulating the style of Pinetop Smith, then gradually developed his own voice to the point he was a master player. These cuts include both solos and

duets between Ammons and Meade Lux Lewis, and are seminal. —*Ron Wynn*

- ○ **Boogie Piano Stylings** / **i.** 1950 / Mercury 25012
- ○ **Boogie Woogie Classics** / **i.** 1951 / Blue Note 7017
- ○ **8 to the Bar** / **i.** 195? / RCA 9
- ○ **Master of Boogie** / Milan 35628
- ○ **Giants of Boogie Woogie** / Wolf 10
- ○ **Boogie Woogie Trio—Vol. 3** / Storyville 4006

Albert Ammons, Meade Lux Lewis (p), and Pete Johnson (p). Not a trio, but separate cuts (one duo) from 1939 to 1949. —*Michael Erlewine*

GENE AMMONS (Eugene Ammons)

b. Apr. 14, 1925, Chicago, IL, **d.** Aug. 6, 1974, Chicago, IL
Tenor saxophone, bandleader / Bop, soul jazz

Tenor saxophonist Gene Ammons, son of the great boogie-woogie pianist Albert Ammons, blended hard-driving bebop patterns and R&B devices and delivered them with a tone as big as a house. He was one of the greatest ballad players in any era and a superb interpreter. Ammons studied music at Du Sable High School under Walt Dyett, and left Chicago at age 18 to work with King Kolax's band. He later joined Billy Eckstine's orchestra as its primary bebop soloist in the mid-'40s, then began leading small groups and recording as a leader in 1947. Ammons worked during this period with Junior Mance and Gene Wright, among others. He played briefly with Woody Herman in 1949, then returned to heading small combos. He worked in regular partnership with Sonny Stitt from 1950 to 1952 and periodically afterward, engaging in spirited two-tenor collaborations. Ammons's drug problems disrupted his career in the '50s and '60s, though he was allowed to continue playing while in jail from 1958 to 1960 and from 1962 to 1969. An extremely popular player throughout his career, Ammons made numerous recordings. These include sessions for Mercury, Prestige, Chess, and Enja, among the dozens of Ammons dates that have been in print at various times. He worked in organ combos, soul jazz groups, two- and three-horn ensembles, and big bands; recorded with trios; and played blues, honking R&B, standards, and originals. Though Ammons's career contained many memorable periods, among them the tenor battles with Stitt and combo singles in the mid '50s, and jam sessions and small-band works in the late '50s, his most creative period was the early '60s, when he made many magnificent LPs. Ammons died of pneumonia in 1974. Reissue mania has served him well. His complete Mercury output has been reissued along with his Chess recordings and many Prestige dates. Currently, Ammons's dates from 1950 to his final sessions are available on CD. —*Ron Wynn and Bob Porter*

- ○ **Gene Ammons Story: The 78 Era** / Mar. 5, 1950-Nov. 4, 1955 / Prestige 24058

A two-record anthology that gathers Ammons 78 recordings made in early and mid-'50s. Despite the often short length, the power and energy Ammons displays is impressive, as are the twin-tenor battles with Sonny Stitt. Ammons also occasionally plays baritone or does vocals on some selections. —*Ron Wynn*

- ○ **Woofin' and Tweetin': Gene Ammons All Star Session** / Mar. 5, 1950 / Prestige 7050
- ○ **Blues Up and Down—Vol. 1** / Mar. 5, 1950-Jul. 27, 1950 / Prestige 7823
- ★ **All Star Sessions** / 1950-1955 / Original Jazz Classics 014

One side of this session was a 6/16/55 date with the Farmer Bros., Freddie Redd (piano), Lou Donaldson (alto), and Kenny Clarke (drums) and came off part Horace Silver funk and part Miles Davis white heat. Again, nothing that would make the history books, but very sound and with good substance, flaws and all. The second side offered up parts of three sessions, 3/5/50, 10/28/50, and 1/31/51 featuring Gene Ammons in battles with Sonny Stitt (both tenor). —*Bob Rusch*, Cadence

- ○ **Golden Saxophone** / Nov. 18, 1952-Apr. 15, 1953 / Savoy 14033

Red Top / 1953 / Savoy 1103

These early '50s sessions that Ammons recorded for Savoy have since been reissued in two different series. They're now on CD through Denon/Savoy program, and were available as single album vinyl during an earlier Savoy reissue program. The group includes Johnny Coles on trumpet and Benny Stuberville on bass. —*Ron Wynn*

Juganthology / Jun. 16, 1955-Apr. 1, 1957 / Prestige 24036
Compilation of sessions from Jun. 16, 1955, Nov. 4, 1955, Jul. 13, 1956, Jan. 11, 1957, and Apr. 12, 1957. —AMG

- ☆ **Happy Blues, The** / Apr. 23, 1956 / Prestige 013

This April 23, 1956 session with Gene Ammons, Art and Addison Farmer, Jackie McLean, Duke Jordan, Art Taylor, and Candido, was an impromptu jam released as *The Happy Blues*. Ammons plays nicely and there are moments (in particular, Art Farmer on trumpet), but this is about as one might expect from the grouped professionals: sound, but average. —*Bob Rusch*, Cadence

Jammin' with Gene / Jul. 13, 1956 / Prestige 211

- ○ **Funky** / Jan. 11, 1957 / Prestige 244

A blues-oriented bop album that is not "funky" in the soul-jazz sense of that word. An exception is the title cut, a bluesy tune with Kenny Burrell (g). W/ Jackie McLean (as), Art Farmer (tpt), Mal Waldron (p). Recorded in NYC. —*Michael Erlewine*

Jammin' in Hi Fi with Gene Ammons / Apr. 12, 1957 / Prestige 129

Big Sound, The / Jan. 3, 1958 / Original Jazz Classics 651
With Gene Ammons All Stars. John Coltrane (ts) and Pepper Adams (bar sax) are included in the backing group. There are weighty Ammons solos. —*Ron Wynn*

- ○ **Blue Gene** / May 3, 1958 / Prestige 192

This is a wonderful blues date, with great support from Pepper Adams (bar sax), Mal Waldron (p), Art Taylor (d), Doug Watkins (b), Idrees Sulieman (tpt), and Ray Barretto (conga). —*Ron Wynn*

- ○ **Boss Tenor** / Jun. 16, 1960 / Prestige 297

The relaxed, warm, narrative tenor of Gene Ammons takes over on *Boss Tenor*. This is a June 16, 1960 date with Tommy Flanagan (piano), Doug Watkins (bass), Art Taylor (drums), and Ray Barretto (congas). It is inviting and wonderfully typical of Jug's joys. —*Bob Rusch*, Cadence

- ○ **Gene Ammons Story: Organ Combos** / Jun. 17, 1960-Nov. 28, 1961 / Prestige 24071

These Gene Ammons dates are good ones on several counts. Possibly, Jug's (Ammons's) presence on these recordings alone could serve as a holy book for all saxophonists from the rhythm and blues stylists to the "loft" jazz set. His musicianship and saxophone conception were just that basic. For me, Ammons's rendition of "Angel Eyes" is the standout for this collection. It showcases the robustness and headlong changing lyricism of this tenor saxophonist at his best. Other worthwhile tunes included "Moten Swing," "Satin Doll," and "Stormy Monday Blues." Appearances are made by Joe Newman on trumpet and Frank Wess on tenor and flute, but these two records clearly belong to Gene Ammons. —*Spencer R. Weston*, Cadence

Angel Eyes / Jun. 17, 1960 / Prestige 7369

Gene Ammons Story: Gentle Jug / Jan. 26, 1961-Apr. 13, 1962 / Prestige 24079
Two classic albums from 1961/1962: *Nice N' Cool* and *Gene Ammons*. —*Michael Erlewine*

Soul Summit—Vol. 2 / Jun. 13, 1961-Apr. 13, 1962 / Prestige 7275
Four sessions: June 13, 1961, January 23, 1962, December 1, 1961, and April 13, 1962. —AMG

- ★ **Boss Tenors—Straight Ahead from Chicago 1961** / Aug. 27, 1961 / Verve 837440

There are perhaps no better tenors, no better jazz. Definitive. With Sonny Stitt. —*Michael G. Nastos*

Live! in Chicago / Aug. 29, 1961 / Prestige 395

Boss Soul / Oct. 17-18, 1961 / Prestige 7445

○ **Brother Jack Meets the Boss** / Jan. 23, 1962 / Prestige 7228
On *Brother Jack Meets the Boss*, Gene Ammons, one of the fathers of Chicago tenor, teams with Jack McDuff in a quintet setting (Harold Vick, tenor sax; Eddie Diehl, guitar; Joe Dukes, drums) for the usual blues-based romp. Here, McDuff is in particularly good form and Jug maneuvers with as much subtlety and changes as the genre and drummer allow. The pairing of Ammons with Vick (McDuff's regular sax in his quartet at this time—January 23, 1962) does not ignite. Vick leans more to the longer lines of John Coltrane and comes on reasonably strong on "Strollin'," the one title Gene Ammons sat out. With flat and furry sound, this is just short of average, especially considering the participants. —*Bob Rusch*, Cadence

○ **Soulful Moods of Gene Ammons** / Apr. 14, 1962 / Moodsville 28

○ **Blue Groove** / Apr. 27, 1962 / Prestige 2514
Blue Groove is a long-forgotten date full of Gene Ammons's (tenor sax) sour mash, pinched tone. Four of the eight selections employ Clarence Anderson on organ; it varies from late cocktail lounge to early soap opera filler. Ammons's work is strident and startlingly fresh, especially on "It Never Goes Away" as Anderson slows and tempers his often brutal attack. The album's only high point is Ammons's playing, which is charged with big, substantial notation and some splashes of angular soul-fire. "Sleepy," the album's best take, contains the late tenor saxophonist's deceptive, Lester Young-like moods with twisting, melancholic overtones; he is plaintive and robust. —*Christopher Kuhl*, Cadence

Jug and Dodo / May 4, 1962 / Prestige 24021
A very good team. Dodo Marmarosa was a tasty pianist and a highly underrated player. —*Ron Wynn*

Groove Blues / i. 1968 / Original Jazz Classics 723
Nice, often invigorating '68 session that has Ammons playing with a host of great saxophonists. The roster includes John Coltrane, Jerome Richardson, Pepper Adams, and Paul Quinichette, plus the sterling rhythm section of pianist Mal Waldron, bassist Jamil Nasser, and drummer Arthur Taylor. This has been reissued on CD. —*Ron Wynn*

Boss Is Back, The / Nov. 10-11, 1969 / Prestige 10023

Brother Jug / Nov. 10-11, 1969 / Prestige 10021
Stalwart soul-jazz set from 1969, with Ammons blowing fiercely on tenor, backed by a group that includes the swirling organ of Sonny Phillips and funky drumming by Bernard Purdie, plus a nice guest shot by guitarist Billy Butler on "Jungle Strut." —*Ron Wynn*

Chase, The / Jul. 26, 1970 / Prestige 10010

Black Cat / Nov. 11, 1970 / Prestige 10006

You Talk That Talk / Feb. 8, 1971 / Prestige 10019

In Sweden / Jul. 14, 1973 / Enja 3093
Lesser-known, but still interesting, concert dates featuring Ammons heading a group with pianist Horace Parlan, bassist Red Mitchell, and drummer Ed Jones during appearance at 1973 Abus Jazz Festival. It's not that well recorded, but Ammons's playing is furious, funky, and riveting. —*Ron Wynn*

Goodbye / Mar. 18-20, 1974 / Prestige 10093
An album that is more valuable for the date it was recorded and its overall significance in Ammons' catalog than for the music. It was cut in 1974, with Ammons nearing the end, and does have some fine conga support from Ray Barretto and often outstanding piano by Kenny Drew. Ammons doesn't play with the punch or authority of the past, and is eclipsed by Nat Adderley and Gary Bartz. —*Ron Wynn*

DAVID AMRAM (David Werner Amram III)

b. Nov. 17, 1930, Philadelphia, PA

Composer, French horn / World fusion
A knowledgeable, eclectic bandleader and a versatile composer, David Amram is an outstanding French horn player who has written classical and jazz works, as well as film scores. Amram attended Oberlin College Conservatory in the late '40s, then worked as a horn player in Paris while serving the U.S. Army in Europe. He recorded with Lionel Hampton and as a leader in Paris in 1955. Amram moved to New York the next year, and performed with Charles Mingus and Oscar Pettiford's bands. Amram and Julius Watkins dueled on French horns on the piece "Two French Fries" recorded while he was playing with Pettiford. He co-led a band with George Barrow that recorded in 1957, and played regularly at the Five Spot in the mid '60s. Amram wrote music for the New York Shakespeare Festival, composed orchestral pieces, was the New York Philharmonic's composer-in-residence in 1966 and 1967, and conducted concerts and workshops for children on international folk music and jazz. His fluency with world rhythms enabled Amram to record the magnificent *Havana/New York* album in the late '70s, a great union of jazz and Afro-Latin music that features him working with members of Irakere, Candido, and Thad Jones and Pepper Adams. Amram's *Triple Concerto for Woodwind, Brass, and Jazz Quintets and Orchestra* was recorded in the '70s by various orchestras. Currently, his sessions are not available on CD. —*Ron Wynn and Michael G. Nastos*

★ **Havana/New York** / 1977 / Flying Fish 70057
A landmark 1977 recording with Amram, Thad Jones, Pepper Adams, and Irakere. —*Ron Wynn*

No More Walls / 1978 / Flying Fish 27752

At Home / Around the World / i. 1980 / Flying Fish 094
Amram plays an eclectic mix of styles from all over the world. —*AMG*

CURTIS AMY (Curtis (Edward) Amy)

b. Oct. 11, 1929, Houston, TX
Tenor and soprano saxophone / Hard bop, soul jazz
A good hard-jazz and hard bop tenor and soprano saxophonist, Curtis Amy enjoyed a busy period in the '60s, then dropped out of sight. He had a strong tone and a nice, lightly swinging style, though he wasn't a great soloist. Amy began playing clarinet as a child, then started on tenor in an army band. He studied music education at Kentucky State College and earned his bachelor's degree in the early '50s. After teaching school for a while in Tennessee and working in Midwestern clubs, Amy moved to Los Angeles in the mid-'50s. He recorded with Dizzy Gillespie in 1955, then worked in the early '60s with Onzy Matthews and Roy Ayers, and performed and recorded with Gerald Wilson in 1965 and 1966. Amy led bands that featured Bobby Hutcherson, Victor Feldman, Jimmy Owens, Kenny Barron, and Ayers in the '60s, and recorded for Pacific Jazz and Verve. Currently, Amy's sessions are not available on CD. —*Ron Wynn*

This Is the Blues / i. 1960 / Kimberly 11020

Groovin' Blue / 1961 / Pacific Jazz 19

★ **Way Down** / 1962 / Pacific Jazz 46

Katanga / Mar. 1963 / Pacific Jazz 128
Hard bop from Amy, who doubles here on tenor and soprano sax. —*David Szatmary*

ARILD ANDERSEN

b. Nov. 27, 1945, Lillestrom, Norway
Bass / World fusion, new age
Norwegian bassist Arild Andersen has demonstrated fine skills and stylistic versatility. He's performed admirably in free, jazz-rock, and quasi-new age situations since the '60s. Andersen studied bass and the Lydian Chromatic Concept of Tonal Organization with George Russell, and also played with him during the '60s and '70s. He also studied with Karel Netolicka. Andersen began playing at various festivals in Norway during the late '60s. He was tabbed by Don Cherry for his first appearance outside Norway at the Berliner

Jazztage in 1968. Andersen worked with Jan Garbarek from 1969 to 1973, and played with Russell, Sonny Rollins, Karin Krog, Sam Rivers, and Paul Bley at various festivals. He also worked with Bley, Rivers, Joe Farrell, Dave Friedman, Barry Altschul, Steve Kuhn, and Sheila Jordan in New York during the early '70s. Andersen backed vocalist Radka Toneff, and led quartets that featured Knut Riisnaes, Jon Balke, Paal Thowsen, Juhani Aaltonen, and Lars Jansson in the '70s and early '80s. During the '80s, he performed and recorded with Alphonse Mouzon, John Taylor, and Bill Frisell. Andersen led the quintet, Masqualero, with Jon Christensen, Balke, Tore Brunborg, and trumpeter Nils Peter Molvaer. They toured England and Europe, while recording during the '80s. Andersen recorded as a leader for ECM in 1991; currently, that is his only session available on CD. —*Ron Wynn*

★ **Sagn** / Aug. 1990 / ECM 849647
Recent release that puts bassist Andersen in company with percussionist Nana Vasconcelos. The music ranges from lightweight to exciting, and deserves to be heard for the array of colors Vasconcelos can create, plus the usual bright ECM production and sound. —*Ron Wynn*

CAT ANDERSON (William Alonzo Anderson)

b. Sep. 12, 1916, Greenville, SC, **d.** Apr. 29, 1981, Norwalk, CA
Trumpet, flugelhorn / Swing, big band
Duke Ellington never wanted an ordinary trumpeter, and he didn't get one in Cat Anderson. Anderson possessed virtuoso technique and was the trumpet section leader during his tenure in the band. He was also the ear-splitting, high-note champion who played parts a full octave higher than they were written. But those upper-register exploits were part of a complete style that included poignant ballad solos, expressive blues, witty references, melodic inserts, and mastery of the mute. Anderson learned trumpet in the student band at the Jenkins' Orphanage in Charleston. He formed the Carolina Cotton Pickers while a teen. This touring orphanage troupe performed extensively across the country. Anderson left the group in 1935, then played in the big bands of Claude Hopkins, Lionel Hampton, and others before Ellington hired him in 1944. Anderson left to head his own band in 1947, then returned in 1950 and remained until 1959. He was featured in many Ellington suites. Anderson concluded the famous 1956 live Newport Jazz Festival performance of "Diminuendo in Blue/Crescendo in Blue." He returned to Ellington again in 1961 and played periodically until 1971. From that point, Anderson was with the band only on special occasions. He became a session player on the West Coast. Anderson published a teaching manual on trumpet in 1973, and toured with the Ice Capades in the late '70s. He recorded as a leader for Apollo, Gotham, EmArcy, and Classic Jazz, but none of these recordings are available currently. He can be heard on many Ellington dates that are available on CD. —*Ron Wynn*

Cat on a Hot Tin Horn / Aug. 1958 / EmArcy 36142

Cat Anderson & The Ellington All Stars in Paris / Oct. 30, 1958-Mar. 21, 1964 / Disques Swing 8412
This consists of a pair of Ellingtonian sessions with the Duke absent. The earliest date finds trumpeter Cat Anderson in a frontline with two of Ellington's New Orleans-styled representatives: trombonist Quentin Jackson and clarinetist Russell Procope. Anderson, quite possibly the greatest highnote trumpeter in jazz history (he gets my vote), almost always chose to emphasize his other talents on his own records, primarily his plunger work. His only high notes on this sextet date are in the closing choruses of a happy "Ain't Misbehavin'." Procope and Jackson (with his wah-wah mute) are in splendid form on this October 30, 1958 session. (Also included are George Arvantas, piano; Jimmy Woode, bass; Sam Woodyard drums.) The remainder is from March 20, 1964, with Anderson joined by Procope, the tenor of Paul Gonsalves, either Joe Turner or Claude Bolling on piano, bassist Roland Lobligeois, and Woodyard. Anderson is the only horn on "Confessin' the Blues," there are three blues

jams at a variety of tempos with the full group, and they again emphasize his plunger and mutes. He does a close imitation of Cootie Williams on "Don't Get Around Much Anymore." Procope co-stars on this date, taking several excellent clarinet solos and an impressive outing on alto on "For Jammers Only." ... Also refreshing on this album is a chance to hear Joe Turner's boogie-woogie lines behind the soloists on "C Jam Blues." Anderson's "Gatherin' in a Clearing" and a clever Claude Bolling arrangement of "Muskrat Ramble" round out this high-quality LP. (Total time 54:35). —*Scott Yanow, Cadence*

★ **Plays W.C. Handy** / **i.** Jun. 1977+May 1978 / Black & Blue 591632

ERNESTINE ANDERSON (Ernestine Irene Anderson)

b. 1928, Houston, TX
Vocals / Big band, blues & jazz, ballads & blues
A fine vocalist equally gifted at singing upbeat, spirited blues, big band/swing numbers, and jazzy pop standards, Anderson began her career in the early '40s, singing with the bands of Russell Jacquet, Eddie Heywood, Shifty Henry, and Johnny Otis. Her version of "K. C. Loving" in 1947 with Henry was a mild hit. These orchestras modified swing arrangements, added shouting vocalists, and divided their musical menus between their vocals, jump blues, and fast-paced instrumentals. This formula was eventually labeled Rhythm & Blues, or R&B. But Anderson moved away from that style in the '50s, and became a prominent jazz stylist. She worked with Lionel Hampton in 1952 and 1953, and also sang in New York City clubs. While in Hampton's band she met saxophonist Gigi Gryce. Anderson recorded with Quincy Jones in 1953, and Gryce in 1955, then toured Sweden in 1956 with Rolf Ericson's band that included Duke Jordan and Cecil Payne. While in Sweden, she recorded "Hot Cargo" with Harry Arnold's orchestra, which was well received when it was issued on Mercury in America. Her 1958 album, *Ernestine Anderson*, with Pete Rugolo, was also praised, and Anderson won the New Star award from *Down Beat*'s critics in 1959. She did more recording for Mercury, but encountered difficult times in the early '60s, moving to England in 1965. Anderson recorded "He Says He Loves Me" for the soundtrack of Sidney Poitier's film *The Lost Man* in 1969. The song attracted some attention. Ray Brown heard her singing at Turnwater Conservatory in 1975 during a weekend festival in Canada. He became her manager, and helped her get a contract with Concord Records. The 1976 album, *Hello Like Before*, generated great response throughout the jazz community. Anderson was suddenly an in-demand singer. There were recordings with Hank Jones, Ray Brown, and Monty Alexander and, by the mid '80s, Anderson was cutting sessions with her own quartet. Her 1981 album, *Never Make Your Move Too Soon*, received a Grammy nomination. She continued making strong sessions with Benny Carter in 1984 and the Capp-Pierce big band in 1987. She's more visible today than ever, and has become an established star. Her roots weren't fully in bebop, but she's firmly in the jazz camp, though she does include pop and blues material on her albums. —*Ron Wynn*

Hot Cargo! / **i.** Nov. 16, 1956-Nov. 19, 1956 / Mercury 20354

Swingin' Gig, A / **i.** 1957 / Tampa 2

Moanin', Moanin', Moanin' / 1960 / Mercury 20582

Hello Like Before / Oct. 8-10, 1976 / Concord Jazz 4031
A wonderful session marking Anderson's return to the scene in 1976. Classy, brassy, and delightful swing and vocals. —*Ron Wynn*

Live from Concord to London / Oct. 11, 1976 / Concord Jazz 4054

Sunshine / Aug. 1979 / Concord Jazz 4109
More toward the contemporary, flashy side, but a nice basic jazz set. —*Ron Wynn*

Live at the Concord Jazz Festival / **i.** 1979 / Concord Jazz 102

Never Make Your Move Too Soon / Aug. 1980 / Concord Jazz 4147

A great mix of old and new. A little toward blues/pop side, especially the title cut. —*Ron Wynn*

★ **Big City** / Feb. 1983 / Concord Jazz 4214

With sublime Hank Jones (p) and fine vocals. Solid, swinging arrangements. —*Ron Wynn*

When the Sun Goes Down / Aug. 1984 / Concord Jazz 4263

○ **Be Mine Tonight** / Dec. 1986 / Concord Jazz 4319

Whether singing straightforward ballads or swingers, Ernestine Anderson knows how to put a song across. Utilizing pauses for dramatic effect and giving each word of a lyric the proper amount of emotion are two rare skills that only come with experience. With Anderson, these talents seem second nature. Backed by a fine rhythm section (pianist Marshall Otwell deserves a date of his own) and assisted by Benny Carter's alto on several selections, Anderson sounds as if she really enjoyed this session. Best are a rare vocal version of "In a Mellotone" and a Dinah Washington-inspired treatment of "Christopher Columbus," the two most jazz-oriented tracks on this well-rounded album. —*Scott Yanow*, Cadence

Live at the Alley Cat / i. 1987 / Concord Jazz 336

Standard big-band arrangements and solos, but Anderson (v) makes welcome appearances. —*Ron Wynn*

Boogie Down / Sep. 1989 / Concord Jazz 4407

IVIE ANDERSON

b. 1905, **d.** 1949

Vocals / Swing, ballads & blues

If Ivie Anderson wasn't Duke Ellington's finest vocalist, there weren't many Ellington vocalists who were better than she. She had first-rate diction and a great delivery, with a style that mixed sassiness, sultriness, and vulnerability. Anderson was a singer and dancer at the Cotton Club in the mid '20s; she toured in *Shuffle Along*, and worked with Paul Howard and Anson Weeks. Anderson toured Australia in the late '20s, sang with Earl Hines in 1930, then joined Ellington in 1931. Her version of "Stormy Weather" in 1933 rivaled Ethel Waters's as the definitive pre-Lena Horne rendition. Her string of great songs with Ellington included the signature number "It Don't Mean a Thing," plus "Rose of the Rio Grande," "I'm Satisfied," "A Lonely Coed," and "I Don't Mind." She also sang "All God's Chillun Got Rhythm" in the 1937 Marx Brothers film *A Day at the Races*, which was an example of a bravura performance in a stereotyped role. Anderson was forced to retire from full-time performing in the '40s due to asthma; she did her final recording with an all-star band that included Charles Mingus and Willie Smith in the late '40s. Most of her recordings with Ellington have been reissued on CD. —*Ron Wynn*

RAY ANDERSON

b. 1952, Chicago, IL

Trombone, cornet, tuba, slide trumpet / Hard bop, soul-jazz, modern creative

An outstanding trombonist in free, funk, blues, and hard bop contexts, Ray Anderson's facility, style, and skill have placed him squarely among the best musicians of his generation. Anderson studied with Frank Tirro and Dean Hay, and participated in summer jazz workshops sponsored by the University of Illinois. He played in local funk and jazz-rock groups while attending Macalester College for a year. Anderson worked with Keshavan Maslak, and Charles Moffett, and Stanley Crouch in California, during the early '70s, then moved to New York. He co-produced concerts with Maslak, and rehearsed with a band that included George Lewis, Anthony Davis, and others in New Haven. He replaced Lewis in Anthony Braxton's band in the late '70s, and worked with Barry Altschul. Anderson played with the Roscoe Mitchell-Leo Smith orchestra at the Moers Festival in 1979, and toured Europe with his own group in 1980. Anderson led the Slickaphonics band with Mark Helias in

the '80s. He's recorded for Moers, Soul Note, Teldec, Enja, and Gramavision in the '80s and '90s. He has sessions available on CD. —*Ron Wynn*

Harrisburg Half Life / Jun. 1980 / Moers 01074

Right Down Your Alley / Feb. 3, 1984 / Soul Note 1087

A typically fine, frequently electrifying set from trombonist Ray Anderson, among the best of his generation. This is a tricky set, a trio work for trombone/bass/drums. Anderson, Mark Helias, and Gerry Hemingway are more than up to the test of keeping things moving and interesting without any sax or piano for contrast and counterpoint. —*Ron Wynn*

Old Bottles, New Wine / Jun. 14-15, 1987 / Enja 79628

This LP was a long-awaited experiment by trombonist Ray Anderson with standards. His choice of the rhythm section of Kenny Barron (piano), Cecil McBee (bass), and Dannie Richmond (drums) was excellent. As has been written many times in the past, Barron is a wizard when it comes to accompaniment. He never steps on anyone's musical toes and when he solos, what comes out is invariably interesting. McBee and Richmond lock in right from the start, keeping the proceedings jumping. Ah, but 'tis Anderson who is the story here. Whether it is his elephantine blasts on "In a Mellotone" or his sweet musings on "Wine," he is in charge. He explodes with notes on Dizzy Gillespie's "Ow!" He takes to the plunger on "La Rosita," producing a lovely ballad that builds in intensity with the help of rumbling chords from Barron. Anderson's closing lines are stunning as he plumbs the depth of the trombone. His paean to the virtues of wine warm the cockles of my mercantile heart. Appropriately, the vocal and solo are slurred. His solo is a boozy lope, replete with slides and smears—it is all great fun. —*Richard B. Kamins*, Cadence

★ **Blues Bred in the Bone** / Mar. 27-28, 1989 / Gramavision 79445

Trombonist Ray Anderson's *Blues Bred in the Bone* pays homage, stylistically, to such pioneer plumber's helper bonemen as Tricky Sam Nanton and Vic Dickenson. With guitarist John Scofield, no mean blues picker himself, and drummer Johnny Vidacovich, Anderson proves an uncommonly sensitive interpreter of Billy Strayhorn's "A Flower Is a Lovesome Thing," as well as an intrepid voyager into largely uncharted sonic seas. — *W. Royal Stokes*, Jazz Times

Wishbone / Dec. 1990 / Gramavision 79454

Every One of Us / i. 1992 / Gramavision 79471

A '92 session that equals the past high level of Ray Anderson releases. Tingling trombone solos and excellent support from bassist Charlie Haden and the late Ed Blackwell on drums. Anderson's originals are never predictable. —*Ron Wynn*

HAROLD ARLEN

b. Feb. 15, 1905, Buffalo, NY, **d.** Apr. 23, 1986

Vocals, composer

An American songwriting legend and son of a cantor, Harold Arlen was fascinated early in his life with the sound of ragtime. While singing in his father's synagogue, he also played ragtime piano in local Buffalo bands and accompanied silent films. After creating arrangements for the Buffalodians, Arlen moved to New York. His jobs included arranging for Fletcher Henderson, and serving as a rehearsal pianist for radio and theatre. A vamp he devised while practicing was later turned into the song "Get Happy," with lyrics from Ted Koehler. Arlen and Koehler wrote eight revues for the Cotton Club, one of which included the anthem "Stormy Weather," first performed by Ethel Waters. Though he moved to Hollywood in the '30s, Arlen kept penning songs for Broadway, working with other lyricists like Dorothy Fields, Les Robin, Johnny Mercer, Yip Harburg, and Ira Gershwin, as well as Koehler. His list of hits and accomplishments is amazing. It includes songs for the films *Take a Chance, Star-Spangled Rhythm, The Sky's the Limit*, and his most famous, *The Wizard of Oz*. Arlen also composed tunes for the plays *Earl Carroll Vanities, Rhythm Mania*, and *St. Louis Woman*.

The incredible array of unforgettable compositions include "I've Got the World on a String," "I Gotta Right to Sing the Blues," "The Devil and the Deep Blue Sea," "Come Rain or Come Shine," "It's Only a Paper Moon," and "Over the Rainbow." Numerous jazz artists, as well as pop performers across the spectrum, have recorded his songs. Arlen made a few albums as a performer, among them sessions with Duke Ellington and Barbra Streisand. At present, only one Arlen album, *Harold Sings Arlen, with Streisand*, is available, and it's not on CD. —*Ron Wynn*

★ **Harold Sings Arlen (With Friend)** / **i.** 1966 / Vox Cum Laude 2920

LIL ARMSTRONG (Lillian Armstrong)

b. Feb. 3, 1898, Memphis, TN, **d.** Aug. 27, 1971, Chicago, IL
Piano, vocals, composer / New Orleans traditional
A fine rhythmic player and one of the most ambitious, highly organized early jazz musicians, Lil Hardin Armstrong is most famous for encouraging her husband, Louis Armstrong, to leave King Oliver and join Fletcher Henderson. A quote reportedly attributed to her was that she didn't want to be married to any "second" cornetist. Whether that's true or not, her influence led to Armstrong's making the pivotal move. He later joined her group in Chicago in 1925. She wrote songs for his recording groups, the Hot Fives and Hot Sevens, played and sang on many of the sessions, and also led her own groups, one of which was an all-women's band in the '30s. She and Louis Armstrong divorced in the late '30s, following a long separation. Armstrong played and recorded with Freddie Keppard, King Oliver, Johnny Dodds, Red Allen, and Armstrong, and served as Decca's house pianist in the '30s, recording with numerous musicians. She'd studied music at Fisk University, and later resumed her education in the late '20s, earning a teacher's diploma from Chicago Musical College and a postgraduate degree from New York College of Music. Armstrong plugged songs, performed, and wrote tunes. She toured Europe in the early '50s, and died while playing at a concert in her former husband's memory. Fantasy reissued her 1961 album, *Lil Hardin Armstrong and Her Orchestra*, as part of its 1993 Living Legends series spotlighting traditional jazz musicians. There's also a reissued CD of late '30s and early '40s Armstrong material available on Classics. —*Ron Wynn*

★ **Lil Hardin Armstrong** / Sep. 7, 1961 / Riverside 401

LOUIS ARMSTRONG (Louis Daniel Armstrong)

b. Aug. 4, 1901, New Orleans, LA, **d.** Jul. 6, 1971, New York, NY
Trumpet, bandleader, vocals / New Orleans traditional
Arguably the single most talented musician of the 20th century, Louis "Satchmo" Armstrong is considered by many critics to be the most important and influential figure in jazz history. He learned cornet at the Colored Waif's Home in New Orleans where he'd been sent for firing a pistol in the air. Armstrong worked at odd jobs and struggled in various bands before marrying his first wife in 1918. He replaced Joe "King" Oliver in Kid Ory's band in 1919. Armstrong joined Fate Marable's riverboat band a few weeks later, and was away from New Orleans until 1921. A year later, he joined Oliver's band in Chicago, playing second cornet.

In 1923, the Oliver band made jazz's first recorded masterpieces; they cut 41 tracks that wound up on four different labels. Besides Armstrong and Oliver on cornets, others in the band included: Honore Dutrey on trombone, Johnny Dodds on clarinet, Lil Hardin Armstrong on piano, Baby Dodds on drums, either Arthur Scott or Johnny St. Cyr on banjo, and different saxophonists on some cuts; either Charlie Jackson on bass or Paul Anderson Evans on C-melody. There were four cuts made by Columbia that reportedly also had Ed Atkins on trombone and Jimmie Noone on clarinet. Dodds had to play woodblocks on these dates rather than drums due to limitations in the recording process for cumbersome, acoustically made 78s. Armstrong

has been quoted as saying Oliver was both his primary influence and the only one he'd ever need, and he absorbed Oliver's approach. This included constantly changing his style, while ensuring a singular, personalized sound with these variations. He was impressed by the way Oliver's muted tones approximated the human voice, and the honesty and emotional intensity Oliver communicated in his playing. Though he didn't cite them, Armstrong was probably also influenced by others he'd heard in his youth: Bunk Johnson, Buddy Petit, Chris Kelly, Henry "Kid" Rena, and Manuel Perez.

By 1924, Armstrong had married his second wife, the Oliver band's pianist Lil Hardin. She encouraged him to leave, and his next band was the Fletcher Henderson orchestra. In the early '20s, Armstrong was also playing with Sidney Bechet and with small groups directed by Clarence Williams. There were also blues sessions with Bessie Smith, Chippie Hill, and Ma Rainey. Still, the next milestone came in 1925, while working with his wife's band in Chicago. He did a series of sessions with groups assembled solely for studio recording. There were 33 sides cut over a two-year period that became known as the Hot Fives and Hot Sevens. The Hot Five lineup featured Oliver veterans St. Cyr and Johnny Dodds, plus Kid Ory on trombone, with Armstrong and Lil Hardin on piano. The next year, the roster was expanded to seven with the addition of Baby Dodds on drums and Pete Briggs on tuba, plus the substitution of John Thomas for Ory on trombone.

These recordings radically altered jazz's focus; instead of collective playing, Armstrong's spectacular instrumental (and vocal) improvisations redefined the music. Among the innovations Armstrong ushered in were freely improvising in the cornet or trumpet's lower registers, bending notes to place emphasis within them, and playing around the beat. He sang as vividly and emphatically as he played, and though he didn't invent the idea of a stop-time chorus (the band playing one beat in either one or two bars, giving the soloist the option to do as he desired) he exploited it brilliantly. He's credited with inventing the concept of "scat," a vocal in the manner of a jazz horn improvisation, on "Heebie Jeebies." He made the switch to trumpet for brighter sound during the Hot Five dates, then helped make the stop-time chorus part of jazz vocabulary during a brilliant solo on "Potato Head Blues." The Hot Seven dates were highlighted by numerous superb Armstrong moments. Armstrong then led an 11-member contingent called Louis Armstrong and His Stompers, which included pianist Earl Hines. He and Hines also worked together in a band called the Savoy Ballroom Five that did 18 sides worth of recording in 1928. A few more landmark songs were made during that period: "West End Blues," with its superb solos and structure, and "Weather Bird," a duet between Hines and Armstrong.

After 1928, Armstrong shifted gears, and became the featured soloist and front man for larger orchestras. He played in bands led by Luis Russell, Carroll Dickerson, Les Hite, and Zilner Randolph, and began to emphasize a show business component in his stage performances. Armstrong would punctuate lightweight material with high-note bursts, and he developed comedic routines that would forever become part of The Armstrong image. Yet, he regularly turned songs like "The Peanut Vendor" into triumphs through sheer artistry. Armstrong made history in another way during the '30s, cutting songs with country legend Jimmie Rodgers. He'd often work an entire year without a day off in the early '30s, but was forced to take some time off in the mid '30s when he developed what would become a chronic lip problem.

When Armstrong turned to Joe Glaser, who was neither a fan nor a musician but a savvy businessman, Armstrong's material fortunes improved. Glaser took steps to safeguard Armstrong and turn him into a profitable enterprise. He got him into more than 50 films. Armstrong began recording with Bing Crosby, the Mills Brothers, and, later, Gordon

Jenkins; at the same time in the late '30s, he was doing airchecks with Fats Waller, Bud Freeman, Al Casey, and others. His late '30s and '40s dates weren't as devoid of inspiration or excellence as some detractors claim, but they also weren't the trailblazing exploits of the '20s and early '30s. But Armstrong's public appeal had soared, as had his profile. He and Lil Hardin separated in 1931, and by 1938 they were divorced.

Armstrong's continued evolution into pop stardom escalated in the '40s, with the demise of the swing/big band era and his open, outspoken opposition to bop. He hit upon the ideal commercial formula in 1947: he played a Town Hall concert with Jack Teagarden, Bob Haggart, Peanuts Hucko, Sid Catlett, and others, and enjoyed resounding critical and public success. He returned to the small group format, and for the remainder of his career Armstrong led "all-star" units. The early editions merited their name, containing, among others, Earl Hines, Teagarden, and Barney Bigard; subsequent groups would have ringers interspersed throughout and would depend as much on Armstrong's monologues, asides, clowning, and mugging for audience response as they did on his solos and vocals. His early All-Stars didn't make as many records as they should have; later units probably cut a few too many records.

During the late '40s and through the '50s and '60s, things weren't cut and dried for Armstrong. He made some wonderful records in his later years, particularly the brilliant *Satch Plays Fats* in 1956. Both it and *Satchmo at Symphony Hall* were huge sellers, reaching the Top 10. The 1956/57 four-album work, *Satchmo: A Musical Autobiography*, was an ambitious attempt to depict the All-Stars at their best. Political radicals and militant nationalists ranted about the State Department's extensive use of Armstrong as a goodwill ambassador in the '50s, a period when flagrant American racism was being exposed (at least in the South). Both the radicals and the government were caught by surprise when Armstrong, in an image-busting moment in 1957, exploded when he saw the televised spectacle of Black children being spit on in Arkansas during the debacle created when Governor Orville Faubus urged the National Guard to prevent school integration. "Because of the way they are treating my people . . . the government can go to hell," Armstrong was quoted as saying. He also said Eisenhower had "no guts." While it's uncertain how much direct impact those words had, some credited him with helping force direct governmental intervention on the students' behalf.

Armstrong was not only a celebrated elder statesman and institution in America in the '50s and '60s, but scored eight hits in England from 1952 to 1968, three of them reaching the top spot. "Blueberry Hill" was reissued in 1956 and hit the American pop charts, while "Mack the Knife" was also a hit that same year. Armstrong garnered a number-one record eight years later with "Hello, Dolly!" He continued to make periodic television and film appearances, and toured as much as his health would permit until his death in 1971. Scores of reissues have been rereleased, with many others due. Books, articles, and information keep coming. In 1988, critic Gary Giddins discovered that Armstrong was actually born on August 4, rather than the long-accepted July 4. As Miles Davis once said: "There's nothing you can play on that horn that Louis didn't play first." —*Ron Wynn and Bruce Boyd Raeburn*

☆ **Louis Armstrong and King Oliver** / i. Apr. 5, 1923-Dec. 22, 1924 / Milestone
This set has the same 25 selections by Oliver's Creole Jazz Band and the Red Onion Jazz Babies, plus the two King Oliver-Jelly Roll Morton cornet-piano duets of 1924, both of which are now available on Morton Milestone CD. In one form or another, this music is essential. —*Scott Yanow*

★ **Clarence Williams' Blue Five** / i. Jun. 30, 1923-Oct. 8, 1925 / CSB 63092
With Sidney Bechet. This French LP collects together 16 recordings by pianist Clarence Williams's Blue Five from

1923 to 1925. The brilliant soprano saxophonist Sidney Bechet is on nearly every selection, and Louis Armstrong co-stars on a dozen. These hot, small-group sides (some of which feature Eva Taylor's vocals) give Armstrong and Bechet a rare chance to jam together; the results are often magical. Best is Bechet on "Wild Cat Blues" (he takes an odd, but wonderful, solo on sarrusophone during "Mandy Make Up Your Mind") and Armstrong on "Cake Walking Babies From Home." The latter shows just how brilliant a virtuoso Armstrong already was at this early stage. —*Scott Yanow*

○ **Jazz Classics: Great Original Performances 1923-1931** / 1923-1931 / Mobile Fidelity 597

○ **Hot 5's & 7's 1925-1928** / 1925-1928 / Laserlight 15721

★ **Hot Fives—Vol. 1** / i. Jun. 23, 1926-May 13, 1927 / Columbia 44049
Eight apiece from Louis Armstrong's Hot Fives and Sevens with some stunning trumpet on "Willie the Weeper" and "Potato Head Blues." Johnny Dodds very distinctive clarinet can be heard at its best on "Weary Blues." Classic and very influential New Orleans jazz. —*Scott Yanow*

★ **Hot Fives and Sevens—Vol. 2** / May 13, 1927-Jun. 28, 1928 / Columbia 44253
The last (and some of the best) of the Hot Sevens and Fives with Armstrong in brilliant form and followed closely by clarinetist Johnny Dodds' and guest guitarist Lonnie Johnson. Armstrong is wonderful on "Struttin' with Some Barbecue," "Hotter Than That," and (with his new pianist Earl Hines) "A Monday Date." —*Scott Yanow*

★ **Hot Fives and Sevens—Vol. 3** / May 1927-1928 / Columbia 44422
Earl Hines (p) makes his presence felt and Baby Dodds (d) joins the hit parade, yielding "A Monday Date," "Struttin' with Some Barbecue," "S.O.L. Blues," "Savoy Blues," and "Hotter Than That." Brilliant collaboration and soloing. —*Bruce Raeburn*

★ **Louis Armstrong Collection—Vol. 4: Louis Armstrong and Earl Hines** / i. 1928 / Columbia 45142
Louis Armstrong was at his most advanced at the time of these timeless recordings with pianist Earl Hines. Hines constantly challenged Satch to stretch himself. Their duet "Weather Bird" is futuristic for 1928, their version of "Basin Street Blues" is that standard's earliest recording, and the stunning "West End Blues" was Armstrong's personal favorite recording ever. —*Scott Yanow*

○ **Louis Armstrong (1928-1931)** / 1928-1931 / Nimbus 6002

○ **And His Orchestra (1928-1929)** / 1928-1929 / Classics 570

☆ **Louis Armstrong Collection—Vol. 5: Louis in New York** / i. Mar. 5, 1929-Nov. 26, 1929 / CBS 46148
By 1929, Louis Armstrong had switched from New Orleans jazz to fronting a variety of larger orchestras, widening his repertoire to include pop tunes but always leaving room for closing trumpet solos. This set includes all known versions (including a few new alternates) of his recordings of this era, including appearances backing singers Seger Ellis and Victoria Spivey. Highpoints including "Mahogany Hall Stomp" and "Ain't Misbehavin'." —*Scott Yanow*

☆ **Louis Armstrong Collection—Vol. 6: St. Louis Blues** / i. Dec. 10, 1929-Oct. 9, 1930 / CBS 46996
Using different big bands purely as a backdrop by 1930, Louis Armstrong was free to stretch out with flashy virtuosic trumpet solos and often scat-filled vocal choruses. "St. Louis Blues," "Body and Soul," and "Tiger Rag" are classics but his rendition of "I'm A Ding Dong Daddy" (which has a solo that gradually builds to a tremendous finish) is a true gem. —*Scott Yanow*

☆ **V.S.O.P.—Vol. 1** / i. Nov. 3, 1931-Mar. 11, 1932 / Epic 22019
Louis Armstrong fronted Zilner Randolph's orchestra for these 16 selections, alternating some exhibitionistic solo showcases with expressive ballads. Armstrong is the star throughout, really excelling on two versions of "Stardust," "Chinatown," and "Lawd, You Made the Night Too Long." Not

as essential as his recordings of a few years earlier, but enjoyable enough in their own right. —*Scott Yanow*

Stardust / Nov. 4, 1931 / CBS 44093
Beautiful 1930-1932 sessions. The Portrait label didn't last long, but put out some great stuff, both old and new, while it was active. —*Ron Wynn*

1932-1933 / 1932-Apr. 26, 1933 / RCA/Bluebird 25519
The European Classics label may or may not be a "legitimate" record label, but it currently has the best reissue series for those listeners who want the complete output of vintage jazz artists. As with the less complete *Laughin' Louie* set, these 24 selections mostly find Armstrong overcoming an inferior big band to play some pacesetting trumpet. —*Scott Yanow*

○ **1934-1936** / i. Oct. 1934-Feb. 4, 1936 / Classics 509
This valuable CD includes Louis Armstrong's often riotous Paris session from 1934 ("St. Louis Blues" and "Tiger Rag" almost get out of control!). It also includes Satch's first 17 Decca recordings, smooth renditions of pop tunes that he turns into classic jazz. Duplicates and exceeds Decca's *Rhythm Saved the World*. —*Scott Yanow*

Rare Louis Armstrong / i. 1934-1938 / Jazz Anthology 550182
Memorable swing versions of "St. Louis Blues" and "Tiger Rag" recorded during a European tour (1934), plus Louis with the Fats Waller sextet (1938). —*Bruce Raeburn*

☆ **Rhythm Saved the World** / Oct. 3, 1935-Feb. 4, 1936 / GRP 602
The first and so far only domestic volume on CD of Louis Armstrong's swing era recordings for Decca in chronological order. Joined by the musical, but by then somewhat anonymous Luis Russell orchestra, Armstrong's melodic variations turn these pop tunes into fine jazz, even "La Cucaracha"! The 14 selections find Louis Armstrong in consistently smooth form with his warm vocals as notable as his melodic trumpet. —*Scott Yanow*

★ **Rare Items** / i. Dec. 19, 1935-Aug. 9, 1944 / Decca 9225
This particular LP is actually much rarer now than this music. A fine cross-section of Louis Armstrong's big band years with such high points as "Thanks a Million," "Swing That Music," "Jubilee," and "I Double Dare You." Possibly the best single LP of this productive (but much maligned) period in Louis Armstrong's career. —*Scott Yanow*

☆ **1936-1937** / i. Feb. 4, 1936-Apr. 7, 1937 / Classics 512
Continuing the complete chronological reissue of Louis Armstrong's output for Decca during the swing era, this set finds Satch at his most exhibitionistic (hitting dozens of high notes on "Swing That Music"). He fronts Jimmy Dorsey's orchestra, does a "Pennies from Heaven" medley with Bing Crosby, joins in for two collaborations with the Mills Brothers, and, on four selections, even makes charming (if weird) music with a group of Hawaiians. Not essential, but quite enjoyable. —*Scott Yanow*

○ **Pops** / i. Apr. 27, 1946-Aug. 1, 1956 / RCA 5920
This superior double LP contains Louis Armstrong's final big band swing recordings (and two songs from 1956) along with all of his Victor small group sides (which led to the formation of his All-Stars). One can readily understand why he broke up his orchestra; despite Armstrong's fine singing and playing, by the mid '40s the extra horns were operating as a dead weight, anonymously backing Louis. In contrast, the small group inspired Armstrong to some of his finest playing in years (he builds a long, magnificent solo on "Jack Armstrong Blues") and trombonist/singer Jack Teagarden proves to be a perfect musical partner on tunes like "A Song Was Born" and "Rockin' Chair." Fortunately, the combo recordings are now available in CD format on *Pops: 1940s Small-Band Sides.* —*Scott Yanow*

★ **Pops: 1940's Small Band Sides** / Sep. 6, 1946-Oct. 16, 1947 / RCA 6378
Recorded at the time Louis Armstrong was in the film *New Orleans*, and broke up his orchestra and formed his very

popular All-Stars, these 20 tracks feature Satch in prime form whether playing relaxed standards, New Orleans gems, or dueting with trombonist/vocalist Jack Teagarden. High points include: a reunion with his old boss, trombonist Kid Ory; five selections from his classic 1947 Town Hall concert (including definitive versions of "Ain't Misbehavin'," "Rockin' Chair," and "Back O'Town Blues"); sharing the spotlight with Jack T. on "A Song Was Born" and "Please Stop Playing Those Blues, Boy"; and taking one of his greatest solos ever on "Jack Armstrong Blues." An outstanding set. —*Scott Yanow*

☆ **Satchmo at Symphony Hall—Vol. 1** / Nov. 30, 1947 / Decca 195
The first and best version of Louis Armstrong's All-Stars is heard in inspired form throughout this program of standards, played live before an enthusiastic crowd. Trombonist Jack Teagarden and clarinetist Barney Bigard clearly enjoy playing what was then fresh material, and Louis Armstrong (whether leading the ensembles on "Royal Garden Blues," singing a touching "Black and Blue," or jiving with Velma Middleton on a very funny "That's My Desire") is consistently delightful. Last available on this two-LP set. —*Scott Yanow*

○ **Satchmo at Symphony Hall—Vol. 2** / Nov. 30, 1947 / Decca 8038

☆ **California Concerts** / i. Jan. 30, 1951-Jan. 21, 1955 / GRP 613
This four-CD set contains two nearly complete concerts by Louis Armstrong's All-Stars, giving one a very good idea of the type of performance the great trumpeter/vocalist put on every night. Some dated comedy aside, Satch is in exciting form, assisted by trombonists Jack Teagarden and Trummy Young, clarinetist Barney Bigard, and (for the earlier concert) pianist Earl Hines. Actually, it is the later session (which takes up most of the last three CDs) that is quite spirited and lively, with Armstrong enthusiastically leading his All-Stars through timeworn but fresh Dixieland standards. —*Scott Yanow*

○ **Satchmo at Pasadena** / Jan. 30, 1951 / Decca 8041

At Pasadena Civic Auditorium—Vol. 2 / i. Dec. 7, 1951 / GNP 9050
Actually recorded several years before Vol. 1, this somewhat loose concert finds trombonist Jack Teagarden co-starring with Louis Armstrong on several of the selections, and the Les Brown orchestra backing Satch on the final three numbers. Not essential, but Armstrong fans won't be disappointed. —*Scott Yanow*

Louis Armstrong Plays the Blues / i. 1953 / Riverside 1001

☆ **Louis Armstrong Plays W.C. Handy** / Jul. 12, 1954-Jul. 14, 1954 / Columbia 40242
Along with his Fats Waller tribute, this is considered Louis Armstrong's most rewarding recording of the 1950s. But when Columbia reissued it in 1986, the company thought it was doing collectors a favor by substituting alternate takes on six of the songs for the originals. If they had merely augmented the set with the extra material it would have increased its value, but instead the original (and superior) versions of many of these songs are out of print! The result is an interesting, but flawed, tribute with Armstrong's monumental version of "St. Louis Blues" replaced by an imposter! —*Scott Yanow*

○ **Louis Armstrong at the Crescendo—Vol. 1** / Jan. 21, 1955 / Decca 8168

○ **Louis Armstrong at the Crescendo—Vol. 2** / Jan. 21, 1955 / Decca 8169

☆ **Satch Plays Fats: The Music of Fats Waller** / Apr. 26, 1955-May 3, 1955 / CBS 40378
The same criticisms levelled at the CD version of Louis Armstrong's W. C. Handy set apply to this version of his tribute to Fats Waller. Six of the nine songs heard here are actually alternate takes that are inferior to the original releases. The music is still decent, but only a shadow of the real version. —*Scott Yanow*

○ **Classical Autobiography, A** / **i.** 1956 / Decca 155

○ **Chicago Concert** / **i.** Jun. 1, 1956 / Columbia 236426
Originally out on a double LP, this is a definitive set of the Louis Armstrong All-Stars of 1956. The music and many of the solos will be familiar to longtime Armstrong fans, but whether it is "Struttin' with Some Barbecue," "Basin Street," or Louis's hit "Mack the Knife," the spirit and enthusiasm of this music is irresistible. The best live set of Louis Armstrong in the 1950s. — *Scott Yanow*

At Pasadena Civic Auditorium—Vol. 1 / **i.** 1956 / GNP 11001
A well-rounded live concert by Louis Armstrong and the Trummy Young (trombone)/Edmund Hall (clarinet) version of his All-Stars. This double LP has a typical program by this unit, ranging from Dixieland to "How High the Moon." — *Scott Yanow*

○ **Satchmo: A Musical Biography** / **i.** 1956-1957 / Decca 8604
During 1956-1957, Louis Armstrong revisited many of the high points of his career, re-recording his classics from the 1920s and '30s, while backed by augmented members of his All-Stars. Decca made a big production out of it, adding some slightly earlier All-Star performances. The result is a superb four-LP box set that is very much in need of being reissued on CD. — *Scott Yanow*

Porgy and Bess / Aug. 18, 1957 / PolyGram 827475
Louis Armstrong and Ella Fitzgerald, great mutual admirers, team up for 16 songs from the famous George Gershwin opera. Although this not Louis's or Ella's finest moment on record, it may very well be the most satisfying jazz version of *Porgy and Bess*. Russ Garcia's arrangements for the large orchestra work very well with the two singers. — *Scott Yanow*

Louis Armstrong Meets Oscar Peterson / Oct. 14, 1957 / Verve 825713
An unusual set with Louis Armstrong singing a variety of popular standards in a relaxed and easygoing manner while backed by the Oscar Peterson trio and drummer Louis Bellson. Few fireworks occur, but the change of pace for Armstrong (who also contributes some brief trumpet solos) is refreshing. — *Scott Yanow*

Snake Rag / **i.** 1959 / Chiaroscuro 2002
Exuberant, nice traditional jazz date featuring Louis Armstrong and his All-Stars doing the requisite batch of pop songs, spirituals, etc. This has been reissued on CD, and has a lot more straightahead, no-frills trumpet than usual. — *Ron Wynn*

☆ **Definitive Album by Louis Armstrong, The** / **i.** Aug. 3, 1959-Aug. 5, 1959 / Audio Fidelity 6241
Louis Armstrong recorded two sessions with the Dukes of Dixieland, the fine New Orleans band led by trumpeter Frank Assunto. Although undoubtedly in awe of Armstrong, the Dukes fare very well on this LP, and Louis is in often-stunning form, really nailing some high notes, perhaps for the last time in his career. Well worth the search to find it. — *Scott Yanow*

Best of Louis Armstrong, The / **i.** Sep. 30, 1959-Oct. 2, 1959 / Audio Fidelity 6132
In 1959, the All-Stars featured trombonist Trummy Young and clarinetist Peanuts Hucko, but, of course, Louis Armstrong was the main star. Some unusual material like "Old Kentucky Home," "Drop That Sack," and "Chimes Blues" uplift this fine session, and Satch's highly expressive vocal on "St. James Infirmary" makes this LP quite memorable. The best of Louis? Maybe not, but this was a good week. — *Scott Yanow*

Satchmo Plays King Oliver / **i.** Nov. 1960 / Audiophile 1930

☆ **Complete Sessions** / **i.** 1961 / Roulette 93844
An album with Duke Ellington. This is a joyful collaboration by two of the greatest names in jazz. Tunes include "Mood Indigo," "Black and Tan Fantasy," and other Ellington pieces. Sideman Barney Bigard (cl) adds particular charm to "It Don't Mean a Thing." — *Bruce Boyd Raeburn*

○ **Great Reunion, The** / Apr. 3-4, 1961 / Roulette 52103

☆ **Armstrong/Ellington: Together for the First Time/The Great Reunion** / **i.** Apr. 3, 1961-Apr. 1961 / Mobile Fidelity 514
Formerly available as a two-LP set and also put out on CD by Roulette, these 17 selections are the entire results of the only meeting in the studios by Louis Armstrong and Duke Ellington. Although it might have been preferable to have Armstrong perform with Duke's orchestra, Ellington's performance as pianist with Satch's All-Stars is quite satisfying. The all-Ellington program gave Armstrong a rest from his usual repertoire and permitted him an opportunity to work his magic on fresh material. Lots of surprises, and some sensitive vocalizing and fine supporting work from trombonist Trummy Young and clarinetist Barney Bigard. A gem. — *Scott Yanow*

☆ **Hello, Dolly!** / **i.** Dec. 3, 1963-Apr. 18, 1964 / Kapp 3364
Not only does this wonderful album have the original hit version of "Hello, Dolly!" but a great rendition of "A Kiss to Build a Dream On" and Louis Armstrong's last extended trumpet solo during a hot version of "Jeepers Creepers." No matter how many times one hears "Hello, Dolly!" it is still a joy. — *Scott Yanow*

What a Wonderful World (On MCA) / **i.** 1968 / MCA 25204
1988 reissue of 1968 New York/Las Vegas sessions. Some enjoyable material, lots of show biz. — *Ron Wynn*

What a Wonderful World / May 26, 1970-May 29, 1970 / RCA 8310
The title cut and "Cabaret" from this mostly vocal session were big hits, but most of the other selections are only passable due to the charm of Louis Armstrong. There is very little trumpet here with the last version of the All-Stars doing their best to support an ailing, but still cheerful, Armstrong. — *Scott Yanow*

○ **Giants of Jazz: Louis Armstrong** / **i.** Feb. 1979 / Time-Life 1P31
The three records here take us through Louis Armstrong's career from 1923 with King Oliver's Creole Jazz band to 1950 with his own All-Stars. . . . The first three sides of this set (from "Dippermouth Blues" to "Mahogany Hall Stomp" in 1929) offer a well-structured, if quite incomplete, study of Armstrong's sustained growth as a musician and as an influence. However, Time-Life's *Giants of Jazz* is perfect for the informed jazz aficionado who might enjoy the convenience of so many recordings under one roof, as well as the clear sound transfers achieved. — *Linda Prince*, Down Beat

I Like Jazz: The Essence of Louis Armstrong / **i.** Nov. 21, 1991 / Columbia 47916
Another anthology. Good, but one record of any type cannot communicate the essence of such a great musician. — *Ron Wynn*

☆ **Genius of Louis Armstrong, The** /
Despite the title, this two-album set contains recordings made between 1924 and 1932. It is out of print, which is the only reason it is denied the highest possible recommendation. Containing 29 tracks, it traces Armstrong's evolution from sideman to his Hot Fives and Hot Sevens, and is the best one-album look at his early years. — *William Ruhlmann*

○ **Louis Armstrong Story—Vol. 1, The** / Columbia 4383
○ **Louis Armstrong Story—Vol. 2, The** / Columbia 4384
○ **Louis Armstrong Story—Vol. 3, The** / Columbia 4385
○ **Louis Armstrong Story—Vol. 4, The** / Columbia 854
☆ **Disney Songs the Satchmo Way** / Disney 6

HORACEE ARNOLD (Horacee Emmanuel Arnold)

b. Sep. 25, 1937, Wayland, KY
Drums / Modern creative
An effective drummer who's worked with jazz-rock, hard bop, and Latin bands, Horacee Arnold emerged as a steady percussionist, good accompanist, and sometimes engaging

Music Map

Jazz Arrangers

Late 1910s/Early 1920s
Arrangements by Orchestra Leaders

W.C. Handy (1873-1958)
James Reese Europe (1881-1919)
Art Hickman
Isham Jones (1894-1956)
Sammy Stewart

Major Early Composer-Arrangers
Jelly Roll Morton (1890-1941)
Ferde Grofe (1892-1972)

Standardize Orchestration
Isham Jones (1894-1956)
Ferde Grofe (1892-1972)

Pioneer Arrangers: 1920s-1930s
Don Redman (1900-1964) w/Fletcher Henderson
Jelly Roll Morton (1890-1941) w/Red Hot Peppers
Duke Ellington (1899-1974)
John Nesbitt w/McKinney's Cotton Pickers
Bill Challis (1904) w/Paul Whitman's Orchestra

Swing Era
Fletcher Henderson (1897-1952) Benny Goodman's orchestra
Duke Ellington (1899-1974)
Horace Henderson (1904) Benny Goodman's orchestra
Jimmy Mundy (1907-1983)
Count Basie (1904-1984) Kansas City

Early 1940s
Artie Shaw (1910)
Sy Oliver (1910-1988) w/Jimmie Lunceford
Oliver & Axel Stordahl w/Tommy Dorsey
Leroy Holmes & Dave Matthews w/Harry James
Neal Hefti w/Woody Herman
Eddie Sauter (1914-1981) w/Red Norvo, Benny Goodman
Billy Strayhorn 1915-1967) w/Duke Ellington
Buster Harding (1917-1965) w/Count Basie

After 1945
Ralph Burns (1922) w/Woody Herman
Gerald Valentine (1914) & Tadd Dameron (1917-1965) w/Billy Eckstine
John Lewis (1920) & Gil Fuller (1920) w/Dizzy Gillespie
Benny Golson (1929) – Gigi Gryce (1927-1983)
Ernie Wilkins (1922) & Neal Hefti (1922) w/Count Basie
Gerry Mulligan (1927) w/Gene Krupa, Stan Kenton
Pete Rugolo & Bill Russo (1928) w/Stan Kenton
George Williams w/Gene Krupa
Quincy Jones (1933) w/Lionel Hampton, w/Count Basie
George Handy (1920)
Eddie Finckel, Johnny Richards (1911-1968) w/Boyd Raeburn

Also in
Modern Jazz Quartet
Gerry Mulligan (1927) – Shorty Rogers (1924)
Jimmy Giuffre (1921) – Charles Mingus (1922-1979)
Jimmy Knepper (1927) – Eric Dolphy (1928-1964)
Dannie Richmond (1935-1988) – Jackie McLean (1932)
Lennie Tristano (1919-1978) – Sun Ra (1914-1993)

Major Arrangers
Gil Evans (1912-1988) – Oliver Nelson (1932-1975)
Duke Pearson (1932) – Muhal Richard Abrams (1930)
Lawrence Butch Morris (1940) – David Murray (1955)

Major Arrangers – Musicals, Popular Music
David Rose (1910) – Raymond Scott (1910)
Morton Gould (1913)

Andre Kostelanetz (1901-1980) – Henry Mancini (1924)

Lesser:
Michel Legrand (1932) – Jeremy Lubbock
Mantovani (1905-1980) – Billy May (1916)
Nelson Riddle (1921-1985) – Marty Paich (1925)
Alan Broadbent (1947)

Transcriptions:
Hall Overton (1920-1972) – Supersax

---

soloist in the '60s and '70s. He began playing drums during the late '50s when he was in the Coast Guard and was stationed in Los Angeles. Arnold played in Dave Baker's big band in 1959, then worked with Rahsaan Roland Kirk, Charles Mingus, and a trio with Kirk Lightsey and Cecil McBee in 1960. Arnold played with Henry Grimes and Hassan Ibn Ali for two years, then toured Asia with Alvin Ailey's dance company in 1962. He played with Bud Powell, Hugh Masekela, and Miriam Makeba, studied composition with Heiner Stadler, and studied guitar and composition with Ralph Towner during the mid '60s. Arnold formed the Here and Now Company in 1967, continuing it until 1970. Various members included Sam Rivers, Karl Berger, Robin Kenyatta, Joe Farrell, and Mike Lawrence. Arnold began heading sessions in 1970, recording for Columbia. He also played with Return to Forever and with Stan Getz, then toured Japan with Archie Shepp in 1978. He formed Colloquium III with Billy Hart and Freddie Waits in the late '70s, a trio that led workshops at the Drummers' Collective. Arnold worked with Dave Friedman, and did sessions and taught at William Patterson College in the '80s. None of his sessions are available on CD. —*Ron Wynn*

★ **Tribe** / 1973 / Columbia 32150
Tales of the Exonerated Flea / 1974 / Columbia 32869

ART ENSEMBLE OF CHICAGO

Group / Early free, modern creative

The Art Ensemble of Chicago has emerged as the Association for the Advancement of Creative Musicians' (AACM) most dominant, famous group, though for many years it was better known in Europe than in America. Its five members began organizing in 1965 in Chicago. Trumpeter Lester Bowie, multi-reedmen Joseph Jarman and Roscoe Mitchell, bassist Malachi Favors Magostus, and percussionist Famoudou Don Moye (their original drummer was Phillip Wilson), created a band with the motto, "Great Black Music—Ancient to the Future." They stressed musical and thematic diversity, and saw their performances as a logical extension of traditional African precepts, which included integrating music from daily life or from other cultural forms.

They all played a variety of instruments, and in concerts utilized costumes, masks, makeup, pantomime, poetry readings, and even performed elaborate plays.

They stressed original compositions, though in recent years they've also included unique interpretations of jazz classics. The Art Ensemble fused influences from Africa, America, and Europe, and a routine Art Ensemble concert or album might include polyrhythmic West African drumming, waltzes, intense collective improvisation, and a vocalist wailing the blues or doing gospel. Distinctive Art Ensemble of Chicago approaches include taking a melodic fragment and altering it over long stretches during performances, utilizing varied pitch and timbre inflections for their own sake, and avoiding strict tempos. They are also exceptional in their use of silence and variations of performance volume. Mitchell was in Muhal Richard Abrams's Experimental Band in 1961; later, both he and Jarman led their own bands. The five were involved in the early days of the AACM.

The band's official beginning came in Paris in 1969. They started as a quartet with Bowie, Jarman, Mitchell and Favors. Moye joined in 1970. They played in Paris throughout 1970, cutting several albums, making three film scores, doing many government-sponsored European concerts, and appearing on radio and television. When they returned to America in 1971, the group did only large concerts, jazz festivals, and university workshops at first before extending their appearances to clubs in 1975. They also toured the West Coast that year. The Art Ensemble have operated their own record label (AECO) and their own operations and have provided everything from T-shirts to mugs.

They've done albums for many labels, both collectively and as a group. They've made live and studio releases for Atlantic, Delmark, and ECM, and have been recorded by import labels such as BYG and DIW. Bowie's led and recorded with Brass Fantasy and the New York Organ Ensemble, while doing several sessions as a leader for ECM, Black Saint, Muse, and DIW. Mitchell has led and recorded with the Sound and Space Ensemble on Nessa and Black Saint, and has done quartet, quintet, and solo recordings. Jarman has done duo recordings with Moye, and has recorded in a trio known as the Magic Triangle with Don Pullen and Moye. The Art Ensemble was featured in a 1983 film for British television, *Art Ensemble of Chicago*, by the Bright Thoughts Company. They continue to record periodically as a group, and have recently had some of their DIW albums, originally only issued in Japan, released in America through a joint venture between DIW and Sony. There are many albums available on CD by individual members, their groups, and the collective Art Ensemble. —*Ron Wynn and Dan Morgenstern*

Jackson in Your House, A / Jun. 23, 1969-Aug. 1969 / BYG 529302

People in Sorrow / Jul. 7, 1969 / Nessa 3

Message to Our Folks / Aug. 12, 1969 / Affinity 77

Reese and the Smooth Ones / Aug. 12, 1969 / Freedom 22

★ **Jackson in Your House, A** / Aug. 1969 / Affinity 9
Vitality is the key to the success of the Art Ensemble of Chicago's *A Jackson in Your House*, which consists of reissued material from the BYG LP of the same name. This was recorded with just the quartet of Lester Bowie, Roscoe Mitchell, Joseph Jarman, and Malachi Favors (drummer Philip Wilson had left and Don Moye had yet to link up). There is one item of note here: a short piece, "The Waltz," was dropped from that set and a foggy surrealist piece called "Hey Friends" (6:01) exists in its place. In addition, the timing for "Ericka" and "Song for Charles" is broken differently, though the music seems the same. There is better audio on the CD. —*Bob Rusch*, Cadence

Paris Session, The / 1969 / Freedom 1903

Certain Blacks / Feb. 10, 1970 / Inner City 1004
A classic, with spicy, frenetic solos one moment, comic overtones and clever melodies and rhythms the next. At this point, the Art Ensemble were becoming stars overseas, and were finding the going increasingly tougher in America. It's outside or avant-garde jazz with soul and heart and funk. —*Ron Wynn*

Les Stances à Sophie / Jul. 22, 1970 / Nessa 4

Phase One / Feb. 1971 / Prestige 10064

○ **Live at Mandel Hall** / Jan. 15, 1972 / Delmark 432
A sonic barrage recorded live. The Art Ensemble don't give concerts, they present multimedia spectacles, and this one proves no different. There are lengthy, relentless dialogues and solos, then short, snappy interludes and silly comments, all integrated into one seamless, non-stop show. —*Ron Wynn*

★ **Bap-Tizum** / Sep. 9, 1972 / Atlantic 1639
Recorded at Ann Arbor Blues & Jazz Festival. Essential. Improvised music. —*Michael G. Nastos*

☆ **Jazzlore: Fanfare for the Warriors—Vol. 12** / Sep. 6, 1973 / Atlantic 1651
Fanfare for the Warriors, recorded in Chicago in September of 1973, establishes a mood similar to the group's previous Atlantic release *Bap-tizum*, only *Fanfare* has two distinct advantages. First, it was cut in the studio while *Bap-tizum* was recorded at the mercy of the Ann Arbor Blues & Jazz Festival PA system; second, it solicited the aid of the AACM's spiritual leader, pianist Muhal Richard Abrams. The sound quality of *Bap-tizum* is simply embarrassing next to the clear, uninterrupted musical contemplation of *Fanfare*, and after hearing how much Abrams adds to the group's total sound (melodically, harmonically, *and* rhythmically), it will be difficult to ever again listen to the Art Ensemble without feeling that something is missing. Abrams introduces "Barnyard Scuffel Shuffel" with a serious classical fragment, only to have it destroyed by one of those dynamically jolting barrages of total sound employed throughout the album to set off one segment of a composition from the next. . . . As usual, the Art Ensemble gleans the essence from the back-to-the-roots form and, in the process, transforms it into something of a more transcendental nature. —*Ray Townley*, Down Beat

Kabbalaba Live at Montreux / Jul. 4, 1974 / AECO 004

○ **Great Black Music** / **i.** 1978 / Affinity 9

☆ **Nice Guys** / May 1978 / ECM 827876
The Art Ensemble's album *Nice Guys* was their first for Manfred Eicher's ECM label. Though not their best album, *Nice Guys* is possibly their most representative, a variegated showcase illustrating much of what they do best. Each of the six compositions displays a distinct personality and musical profile. . . . The group's sense of humor is in evidence in Joseph Jarman's sprightly reggae romp "Ja" (singing of Lester Bowie's sojourn in Jamaica and reflecting their subsequent incorporation of calypso and folk elements into their aesthetic of "world music"), and the tongue-in-cheek title tune (featuring bicycle horns, Mitchell's parodistically stiff-jointed solo, and Jarman's "They're so nice!" vocal). "Folkus" is Famoudou Don Moye's African rhythmic polyphony and Bartokian "nightmusic" percussion. The finale, Jarman's "Dreaming of the Master," is *more* than an act of homage to one of the AEC's influential ancestors, the Miles Davis Quintet; it is a haunting reminder that great art transcends temporal and spatial boundaries. It is not important that Bowie could recreate, note for note, Davis's cool modal insouciance, or that Jarman could echo John Coltrane's feverishly explosive tenor torments in such a ghostly fashion. It is the spirit that instigates and informs each note and remains universal, direct, and affecting, and the Art Ensemble was a living testimonial to the glories of the past and the promises of the future. —*Art Lange*, Down Beat

Live in Berlin / Mar. 1979 / West Wind 2051

○ **Live Part One** / **i.** 197? / BYG 2401
Live combines confrontational juxtapositions and stretches of seamless fluidity, yet compared to later concert recordings, *Live* is not as dynamically paced and proportioned. Still, there is a lot of engaging material including a relentless opening barrage that segues into one of their patented, pungently humored themes; some fine solos, particularly

from bassist Malachi Favors and trumpeter Lester Bowie; and a funky strut of a closer. Anyone who found this recording to be a particularly fractured listening experience in its previous incarnation as a two-LP set will find the continuity of the CD format to be a blessing. —*Bill Shoemaker,* Down Beat

○ **Full Force** / Jan. 1980 / ECM 829197
The Art Ensemble of Chicago's first go-round with ECM's Manfred Eicher finds them on their best (well, almost) collaborative behavior: they brought a little fire to his ice; they focused their heat into clear blue flame. . . . Specifically (and of course, subjectively), the pop atmospherics opening "Magg" rattle on without the microscopic etching of "Folkus" (or "People in Sorrow"). Among AEC miniatures, "Care Free" is just a punchy Spanish tag for the side-long "Magg," whereas "Nice Guys," also under two minutes, is a total composition. . . . There is little enough of the reedmen on this set. Short, frenzied solos (Roscoe Mitchell's tenor, Joseph Jarman's soprano) spice "Dance," on which drummer Don Moye and bassist Malachi Favors exchange wild twos; flute and small-horn snippets skitter through "Full Force." The one major sax contribution is Roscoe Mitchell's solemnly, stridently ringing, but brief theme statement over Favor's intriguing vamp on "Magg." Jarman maintains his seldom noted stance as colorist (bassoon, vibes), composer, and director of theatrics. Otherwise, they are section men. —*Fred Bouchard,* Down Beat

Urban Bushmen / May 1980 / ECM 829394
This is arguably the greatest avant-garde jazz band of the '60s and '70s. —*Ron Wynn*

Complete Live in Japan, The / i. Apr. 1984 / DIW 8021

Third Decade / Jun. 1984 / ECM 823213

Tutankhamun / i. 1985 / Black Lion 40122

Ancient in the Future—Vol. 1 / Mar. 1987 / DIW 804

America South Africa / Dec. 1989+Jan. 1990 / Columbia 52954
A welcome return to the American recording scene for the premier Chicago outside band. This mixes African rhythms, township melodies, and the Ensemble's usual array of blistering solos, vocal effects, percussive colors, and furious collective improvisations. —*Ron Wynn*

○ **Dreaming of the Masters Suite** / i. Jan. 1990-Mar. 1990 / DIW 854

Thelonious Sphere Monk—Dreaming of the Masters—Vol. 2 / i. May 6, 1992 / Columbia 48962

GEORGES ARVANITAS

b. 1931
Piano / Swing, bop
One of Europe's most consistent and versatile musicians, Georges Arvanitas has been active since the early '50s. He's worked with traditional, swing, and bebop musicians, and has accommodated the demands of the many expatriate Americans who went to Paris. Though far from being an innovator or a daring soloist, Arvanitas is a capable pianist, knowledgeable of bebop fundamentals and able to work effectively in many situations, from recordings to concerts to jam sessions. Arvanitas worked with traditional jazz groups in Marseilles in the '40s, then moved to Paris in the early '50s. He played with Jimmy Archey, Bill Coleman, Dexter Gordon, Sonny Stitt, Donald Byrd, and several others in the '50s and '60s. He was later resident pianist at the Blue Note, and formed his own group. Arvanitas played with Buck Clayton, Don Byas, and Sonny Criss in the early '60s. He visited New York in 1964 and 1965, working with Ted Curson and Yusef Lateef. He paid a return visit in 1966. Arvanitas's trio with Jacky Sampson and Charles Saudrais worked with several major musicians in the late '60s and early '70s, among them Art Farmer and Dexter Gordon, Buddy Tate and Bill Coleman, Slide Hampton, Anita O'Day, and Curson. Arvanitas played with Robin Kenyatta in 1972, toured Japan with Michel Legrand, and worked in Italy with Criss and

Stitt. He later worked with Pepper Adams, Curson, Dizzy Gillespie, and James Moody in the '80s. He's recorded for Columbia and Saravah, among others, as a leader, and for Spotlite, Futura, and Impro as a session musician. Currently, Arvanitas does not have any sessions available as a leader on CD, at least not in America. —*Ron Wynn*

DOROTHY ASHBY (Dorothy Jeanne Ashby)

b. Aug. 6, 1932, Detroit, MI, **d.** 1986
Harp / Bop
Dorothy Ashby was one of the rare jazz harpists and, arguably, the only significant bebop player on that instrument. She was both a good session musician and a bandleader who was recorded heading trios and quartets. Ashby also had some classical training and influence. She studied music education at Wayne State University, and played with Louis Armstrong and Woody Herman in 1957. Ashby hosted a radio program in Detroit during the early '60s, while working and recording in groups with Frank Wess, Art Taylor, Roy Haynes, Jimmy Cobb, and others. She later played on the West Coast on LPs featuring Sonny Criss and Stanley Turrentine. Ashby's album, *In a Minor Groove,* is currently available on CD. —*Ron Wynn and Michael G. Nastos*

○ **Jazz Harpist** / i. Mar. 21, 1957 / Regent 6039
Dorothy Ashby was at the top of a very small and select circle, jazz harpists. Rather than simply provide atmosphere and colors, Ashby improvised on the instrument and exploited it to the fullest, regardless of the song or context. This now-deleted '57 album has some incredible passages, songs that not only anticipate, but, in some ways, exceed things later done by Alice Coltrane and others. —*Ron Wynn*

★ **Hip Harp** / Mar. 21, 1958 / Prestige 7140

Dorothy Plays for Beautiful People / Sep. 19, 1958 / Prestige 24120

Soft Winds / Aug. 15-16, 1961 / Jazzland 61

○ **Fantastic Jazz Harp of Dorothy Ashby, The** / May 3-4, 1965 / Atlantic 1447
Detroiter Ashby is the premier player on her instrument. With horns and percussion from Richard Davis (b), Grady Tate (d), and Willie Bobo (per). —*Michael G. Nastos*

Afro Harping / Apr. 1968 / Chess 91555
The best and most complete album done by a rare performer, jazz harpist Dorothy Ashby. She didn't approach her instrument as if it were a gimmick, and she wasn't content to be a background/mood specialist. She turned the harp into a lead instrument, and offers solos that are as tough and memorable as those done by any reed, brass, or percussive player. —*Ron Wynn*

Concierto de Aranjuez / Philips 814197

HAROLD ASHBY (Harold Kenneth Ashby)

b. Mar. 27, 1925, Kansas City, MO
Tenor saxophone / Swing, big band
A resourceful, swinging, and sometimes surprising tenor saxophonist, Harold Ashby has been a session mainstay and longtime Ellingtonian. His round, full sound, big tone, and general approach reflect the impact of Ben Webster, but he also displays an imaginative use of the tenor's upper register not often heard among swing-oriented players. Ashby played with Tommy Douglas and Walter Brown in Kansas City during the mid '40s, then moved to Chicago in the early '50s. He worked with several blues bands, then moved to New York in 1957. Ashby played with Milt Larkin and Mercer Ellington, and recorded with Ben Webster, Johnny Hodges, Paul Gonsalves, and Lawrence Brown in the late '50s and '60s. He became a regular in the Ellington band in 1968, and remained until 1975. Ashby stayed with the band for a short while after Duke's death. He then made festival appearances and did session work in New York City. In 1984, Ashby presented a concert at St. Peter's Church in New York with assistance from a grant by the National

Endowment of the Arts. He recorded for Progressive in the late '70s, and for Stash in '91, working with Richard Wyands, Modern Jazz Quartet drummer Connie Kay, and Ellington alumnus Aaron Bell on bass. Both those dates are available on CD. —*Ron Wynn*

★ **Born to Swing** / Oct. 9, 1959+Feb. 27, 1960 / Master Jazz 8122

Presenting Harold Ashby / i. 1978 / Progressive 7040
A long-time Ellingtonian steps away from the orchestra and shows his swing roots. Ashby plays with wit, drive, and style, keeping things going even when they threaten to bog down due to average material or arrangements. A pleasant surprise and nice vehicle for someone known more as part of an organization than on his own. —*Ron Wynn*

Viking, The / i. Aug. 1988 / Gemini 60

I'm Old Fashioned / i. Jul. 1991 / Vintage Jazz 545

SVEND ASMUSSEN

b. Feb. 28, 1916, Copenhagen, Denmark
Violin, vocals / Swing
He's been playing the violin since he was seven, and Svend Asmussen shows no signs of ever losing the vitality and flashy skills that have stamped his playing ever since. Asmussen left the Academy of Arts in Copenhagen, Denmark, when his father died and he was forced to find a job. He made his professional debut in 1933 at Copenhagen's version of the Apollo Theater. By 1934, he'd formed his own band along the lines of Joe Venuti's Blue Four. Asmussen joined the Mills Brothers and Fats Waller when they came through Denmark, but then disbanded his group to pursue an acting and comic career in 1943. Asmussen went back to music when World War II concluded, but was unable to pursue lucrative opportunities in America due to strict immigration laws during the '50s when he was most eager to come. He became a huge star in Europe, playing and doing vocals in groups led by Alice Babs on three occasions, as well as working with Ulrik Neumann. His collaborative efforts with violinists Stuff Smith and Stephane Grappelli were acclaimed examples of superb technique, joy, and tasteful, yet exuberant performances. He also appeared on the masterful album *Duke Ellington's Violin Summit.* —*Ron Wynn*

★ **Hot Fiddle** / i. Jul. 29, 1953 / Brunswick 58051

And His Unmelancholy Danes / i. 1955 /

Skol! / 1955 / Epic 3210

Prize Winners / Feb. 12+17, 1978 / Matrix 1001

FRED ASTAIRE (Franz Austerlitz)

b. May 10, 1899, Omaha, NE, **d.** Jun. 22, 1987, Los Angeles, CA
Vocals, dancer, actor / Ballads & blues
Rated as a magnificent all-around talent, many people would deem singing the least of Fred Astaire's skills, and would rank it well behind dancing and acting. Yet Irving Berlin once said he'd rather hear Fred Astaire sing his compositions than any other vocalist. Astaire was an excellent interpreter of classic American tunes, and could interact with great musicians without being overwhelmed or threatened.

He began his professional career at age five, and starred in vaudeville with his sister, Adele, until 1916. Astaire and his sister paralleled that success on the Broadway stage until 1932, when she gave up show business for marriage. George Gershwin penned "Lady Be Good" for them in 1924, and they did his "Funny Face" in 1927, and the Arthur Schwartz/Howard Dietz number "The Band Wagon" in 1931. A role in Cole Porter's *The Gay Divorcee* in 1932 led to a screen test in which the word on Astaire was supposedly: "Can't act, slightly bald, can dance a little." No matter, he teamed with Ginger Rogers and became the epitome, for most Americans (particularly those unaware of or unwilling to consider Bill Robinson), of grace and flair as a dancer.

But throughout his extraordinary film, stage, and television career, Astaire also made superb recordings. He did transcendent versions of "Lady Be Good," "Fascinating Rhythm," "Dancing in the Dark," "Night and Day," and many, many others. Whether doing songs in theatrical productions or interpreting them in the studio, Astaire brought quiet charm, casual elegance, and exquisite timing, as well as distinctive enunciation and understated sense of swing, to every number. He made outstanding records for Brunswick in the '30s, and for Decca in the '40s. The 1953 four-disc set, *The Fred Astaire Story*, is a collection of songs long associated with him, and features Astaire backed by an array of session and jazz greats. He also made *Swings and Sings Irving Berlin* during that same period, and recorded with Oscar Peterson, Ray Brown, and Charlie Shavers. While his vocal triumphs will never get as much ink as his film and dance exploits, Astaire deserves mention as an important singer in the pre-swing era, with links to, if not a complete foothold in, jazz. —*Ron Wynn and Bruce Eder*

Irving Berlin Songbook / i. Dec. 1952 / Verve 829172
An unusual reconsideration of Astaire's best repertoire, with the singer fronting a jazz combo. Uneven but interesting. —*Bruce Eder*

○ **Fred Astaire Story—Vol. 1, The** / Dec. 1952 / Clef 1001
○ **Fred Astaire Story—Vol. 2, The** / Dec. 1952 / Clef 1002
○ **Fred Astaire Story—Vol. 3, The** / Dec. 1952 / Clef 1003
○ **Fred Astaire Story—Vol. 4, The** / Dec. 1952 / Clef 1004
★ **Astaire Story, The** / Dec. 1952 / Verve 829172
○ **Best of Fred Astaire from MGM Classic Films** / MCA 31175
Fred Astaire Sings / MCA 1552
○ **Starring Fred Astaire** / Columbia 44233
The best of Astaire, featuring songs by Berlin, Gershwin, Kern, and others, which were written specifically for him. —*Bruce Eder*

GEORGIE AULD (John Altwerger)

b. May 19, 1919, Toronto, Ontario, Canada, **d.** Jan. 17, 1990
Tenor and alto saxophone / Swing, big band, bop
One of the finest improvisers in the swing era, Georgie Auld was not an innovator, but modified and adjusted his style to accommodate changes in direction from the swing era to the present, while maintaining his own sound and approach. He had a big tone and smooth sound that reflected two primary influences, Coleman Hawkins and Larry Binyon, who played in Ben Pollack's band. His playing has been alternately rugged and sentimental, with a bluesy underpinning. Auld emigrated from his native Canada to New York in the late '20s, and later switched from alto to tenor after hearing Hawkins. He played with Bunny Berigan, Artie Shaw, and Jan Savitt, and with Benny Goodman and Shaw again in the late '30s and early '40s. He recorded with Goodman's sextet in 1940 and 1941, then served in the army. Auld led his own big band after his discharge, with Manny Albam, Al Cohn, and Neal Hefti providing arrangements at various times. His band worked in several clubs, and Sarah Vaughan, Erroll Garner, Sonny Berman, Dizzy Gillespie, Billy Butterfield, and Freddie Webster all played in Auld's orchestra before it disbanded in 1946. He then led small groups and did session and commercial dates in Los Angeles and Las Vegas. Auld was Tony Martin's music director in the late '60s, and toured frequently. He also was an actor on Broadway in the late '40s, and dubbed Robert DeNiro's tenor sax parts in the film *New York, New York* in 1977. Auld recorded for several labels, among them Musicraft, Xanadu, and Hep. He currently has sessions available on Musicraft and Xanadu CDs. —*Ron Wynn*

Manhattan / May 9, 1952 / Coral 56085

★ **In the Land of Hi Fi** / Sep. 29, 1955-Nov. 11, 1955 / EmArcy 36060

George Auld Plays the Winners / i. Oct. 1963 / Phillips 600096

ROY AYERS (Roy E. Ayers Jr.)

b. Sep. 10, 1940, Los Angeles, CA
Vibes, vocals, piano / Soul-jazz, instrumental pop
A very talented vibist, Ayers was among the top jazz players
of the '60s. He had speed, technique, and the good fortune to
appear on some high-profile albums with Herbie Mann.
Ayers turned more and more to R&B and funk in the '70s.
His group, Ubiquity, began playing jazz-based R&B, then
moved more into straight R&B/funk through the '70s. By the
late '70s and early '80s, Ayers was an R&B bandleader, and
had eight albums that made the *Billboard* charts in 1976-
1979. During the '90s, Ayers recorded for the Ichiban label.
He has both recent sessions and some reissued dates available on CD. —*Ron Wynn*

○ **West Coast Vibes** / Jul. 1963 / United Artists 6325

Virgo Vibes / Mar. 6, 1967 / Atlantic 1488

Ubiquity / i. 1971 / Polydor

★ **Mystic Voyage** / 1975 / Polydor 6057
Nice outing, though there's minimal jazz content. Ayers,
once a *Down Beat* New Star winner, decided, at end of the
'60s, to forego the rigors of a straight jazz life and to investigate the world of funk and R&B. He would (and still does)
dabble back into light soul-jazz, but has become far more
known for his funk and R&B releases like this one. —*Ron
Wynn*

Africa, Center of the World / i. 1981 / Polydor 6327

ALBERT AYLER

b. Jul. 13, 1936, Cleveland, OH, **d.** Nov. 1970, New York, NY
Tenor saxophone / Early free
Albert Ayler is remembered by many as the epitome of the
fire-breathing '60s saxophonist. He was a quirky, genre-
crossing tenorist whose raw, bluesy tone combined the archaic vibrato of the early New Orleans jazzmen with the
reed-splitting multiphonics of the R&B screamers. In his day,
he was dismissed as a primitive, a fake, a destroyer of jazz,
and, paradoxically, a sell-out when, on his final albums, he
shifted his attention to blues and rock grooves (anticipating
Miles Davis's more successful fusion efforts).

He got his start touring as a teenager with blues harpist
Little Walter, and later traveled to California and then to
Europe, trying in vain to find musicians and an audience for
his evolving ideas. His first recordings were made in
Scandinavia in 1962-1963, using local musicians. During
those years, he received encouragement from Cecil Taylor,
Don Cherry, Sonny Rollins, and John Coltrane. What little
literature there is about Ayler often assigns a mentor role to
Coltrane, and while Coltrane may have been responsible for
getting Ayler a contract with Impulse Records, the musical
evidence suggests a mutual relationship, with Coltrane ben-
efiting mainly from the liberating influence of their association. During Ayler's most fertile period (1964-1966), he
made several records in the States for Debut, ESP, and
Impulse, and he toured Europe, with many live recordings
as a result of the tour. His mid-sized ensembles followed a
simple, almost formulaic approach: concise sing-along
melodies reminiscent of nursery rhymes, hymns, and brass
band material would segue abruptly into wild collective improvisation, with Albert playing his evocative tenor like a
pied piper gone mad. This was the time for music of eman-
cipation and catharsis, and Ayler's fresh conception, freed of
jazz clichés and delivered with sweat-drenched intensity,
was certainly timely.

In the late '60s his output decreased, although he seemed
more willing than ever to experiment by singing, playing
bagpipes, and adding White rock musicians and soul singers
to his band. One of these vocalists was his companion, Mary
Parks, (a.k.a. Mary Maria), who seemed to dominate the last
few efforts before his death by drowning in 1970. Few figures have generated as much controversy and mystified
speculation as Ayler, but whatever label you choose to apply,
conservative, radical, folk musician, or jazz revolutionary, he
created his own unique sound, and that sound is still relevant today. In the CD era, unissued material is still coming
out, and his best albums are also being reissued, sparking a
long-overdue critical reappraisal of his importance. —*Ron
Wynn and Myles Boisen*

Albert Ayler: The First Recordings—Vol. 1 / Oct. 25, 1962 /
GNP 9022
His initial album, cut in Stockholm with a local bassist and
drummer, is mainly of historical importance, but does show
the influence of Sonny Rollins and John Coltrane. —*Myles
Boisen*

○ **Witches and Devils** / Feb. 24, 1964 / Freedom 741018
This 1964 date was also issued as *Spirits* on the Debut label
and as *Mothers and Children* on Black Lion. Regardless of
its title, it is a fierce, free wheeling, and often poignant session with Ayler, trumpeter Norman Howard, bassist Earle
Henderson, and drummer Sunny Murray. One cut uses two
bassists. —*Ron Wynn*

Spiritual Unity / Jul. 10, 1964 / ESP 1002
Evocative, intense, and searing trio material cut in 1964.
Bassist Gary Peacock and drummer Sunny Murray, neither
shrinking violets, still have to battle to avoid being overwhelmed by the huge, dramatic Ayler tenor. —*Ron Wynn*

★ **New York Eye and Ear Control** / Jul. 17, 1964 / ESP 1016
A summit meeting of the New York City jazz avant-garde.
With Don Cherry (tpt), John Tchicai (as), Roswell Rudd (t),
and Gary Peacock (b). —*Myles Boisen*

Vibrations / Sep. 14, 1964 / Freedom 741000
Another frequently reissued work with trumpeter Don
Cherry has two versions of his memorable "Ghosts." —*Myles
Boisen*

○ **Hilversum Session, The** / Nov. 9, 1964 / Osmosis 6001
Hilversum, Holland in June 1964, the scene of Eric Dolphy's
Last Date concert, five months later became the location for
Albert Ayler's no less great radio performance. This was the
essential year in Albert Ayler's music when he finally found
freedom through ensembles of players willing to join him in
inventing his fantastic idiom. This album is well-recorded,
unlike the ESPs, so the listener can appreciate the group's
responses to the chaos that threatens from Ayler's unearthly
sounds and tornado energy. Bassist Gary Peacock seems the
one player here who appreciates some degree of space, and
while his bass is not really accompaniment, he fills out the
ensemble sound with phrasing that is sometimes quite complex and fast, other times in half- or quarter-tempo. Again,
we hear what a really ingenious drummer Sunny Murray
was with this group. Unpredictability was the key to Murray,
of course. In the two-tempo "Infant" theme statement,
Murray's line crests right away, while his very detailed playing in "Ghosts" approaches an Elvin Jones-like wildness behind Don Cherry, adding (with the bass) tides of density behind the trumpet's flow before joining Peacock's "solo" with
cymbals to make a duet. . . . So in its emotional range, the
Ayler quartet here reaches the limits of its capacity for variety and excellent playing, exceeding even the long Sunny
Murray-led date *Sunny's Time Now*. —*John Litweiler*, Down
Beat

○ **Bells** / May 1, 1965 / ESP 1010
Album-length live piece, with a quintet including Charles
Tyler (as). Dan Morgenstern's insightful notes give a contemporary account of this ensemble's archaic sound and
wild humor. —*Myles Boisen*

★ **Spirits Rejoice** / Sep. 23, 1965 / ESP 1020
Peak Ayler, with the saxophonist churning, wailing, and
soaring over the beat. He's so energetic and combative that
things threaten to implode constantly, yet he keeps right on
going. —*Ron Wynn*

Live at Lorrach: Paris, 1966 / Nov. 7, 1966+Nov. 13, 1966 /
Hat Art 6039
Quintet. Definitive two-record set of Ayler's touring group
featuring his brother Donald (tpt) and Michael Sampson (violin). Clean, live recordings enhance the complexity of this

band at its peak, ranging from town band melodies to pure aural assault. —*Myles Boisen*

○ **Albert Ayler: The Village Concerts—Vol. 7** / 1967 / ABC/Impulse 9336

This release consists of all unreleased material recorded at the Village Theatre (February 26, 1967) and the Village Vanguard (December 18, 1966). Thankfully, the music is better than Ayler's last few rock endeavors that I think did so much harm to his career. . . . The set's problems don't lie with Ayler (tenor sax), who is the one saving grace (his brother Donald also has some fine moments on trumpet), but rather with his compatriots. The use of the string quartet on record one and the trio on record two appear to be intriguing, but the actual results don't measure up. Part of the problem is a less than optimum engineering job, but the main problem is the cluttered sound. No one seems to be listening closely to what Ayler is doing. Nevertheless, I do recommend that you listen to this album. Ayler's use of simple melodies is engaging and his commitment to his music is readily apparent in his playing. An added bonus is "Angles," a tenor sax/piano duet (the pianist is unidentified, but the liners say it was probably Call Cobbs). If you still haven't been swept up by Ayler's spiritual jazz, this is the track to approach first. —*Carl Brauer*, Cadence

○ **Love Cry** / Aug. 31, 1967 / GRP 108

The 1967-1968 *Love Cry* is good introductory Albert Ayler, less loose and forbidding than his earlier, writhing trio classics. Half these pieces are under four minutes, and the singsong/martial themes are crisp ("Universal Indians" is his masterstroke of economical writing: two notes in a repeating phrase). Like the brass band, Ayler seems to spring from everywhere. With his bellyful slow vibrato and an acute, if rarely acknowledged, time sense, dirges float like driftwood, the dances shout with an urgency more civic than spiritual. Ayler has enough in common with now digested late John Coltrane to be accessible at last. (Drummer Milford Graves and bassist Alan Silva and bugling trumpeter Don Ayler are right on him; Call Cobbs's harpsichord swirls don't sustain, so the sound's leaner than Trane's quartets). —*Kevin Whitehead*, Down Beat

Music Is the Healing Force of the Universe / Aug. 26-29, 1969 / Impulse 9191

At a peak of experimentation, Ayler used bagpipes, blues instrumentals, and vocals to expand his challenging sound and to keep his music at the center of controversy. —*Myles Boisen*

○ **Volume 2** / i. Jun. 1970 / Shandar 10004

○ **Nuits de la Fondation Maeght—Vol. 1** / Jul. 25-27, 1970 / Shandar 10000

These recordings were previously available as separate volumes and are now packaged together as a double set. These concerts were recorded after Albert Ayler's attempts at more commercial efforts and shortly before the discovery of his death. After the statement (and in many cases restatement) of Ayler's marvelous themes, it is perhaps the rhythm that is next in awareness. The drumming is a mismatch; Steve Blairman is no Sunny Murray and lays down an often aggressive, regular beat that is really insensitive in shading and development of the only soloist (Ayler). Ayler has a rushed sense to his playing (on soprano), and nearly all of the tempos have a pushing immediacy about them. Ayler is full of reference to his own themes and others (snatches of "The House I Live In" to bits of Sonny Rollins's music), and seems to spend more time with them than in telescoping his development off them. His comparatively short developments, I would assume, are a result of the weak rhythm foundation; it just doesn't build or develop the strength to carry and support. Even so, Ayler's statements, relative to the average statements, are mighty and astoundingly full of energy. A heavy (very heavy) Sonny Rollins influence is in evidence, especially on the July 21 music. Vocalist Mary Maria only appears on "Music Is the Healing Force of the Universe," and it was the only true attempt at interchange with another soloist. Ayler is very attentive to her singing; she is credited as playing soprano sax on the sleeve, but if this is true it wasn't recorded. Without a doubt, this is a historically important recording. If it is not given concentrated attention, it is very satisfying in many ways. —*Bob Rusch*, Cadence

B

ROBERTO BADEN-POWELL
(Roberto Baden Powell de Aquino)

b. Aug. 6, 1936, New York, NY
Guitar / World fusion
A wonderfully lyrical, sentimental guitarist, Baden-Powell is perhaps the finest rhythmic player to emerge from the mixture of Iberian baroque and West African/Latin influences among Brazilian stylists. Baden-Powell makes albums with a transcendent elegance, lasting beauty, and authenticity. He's demonstrated his knowledge and command of jazz, flamenco, classical, and Afro-Latin genres. Both his father and grandfather were prominent musicians, and Baden-Powell was a professional at age 15. He worked with poet Vinicius de Moraes, whose lyrics, coupled with Baden-Powell's playing, won both critical praise and mass popularity. Baden-Powell and Herbie Mann recorded together in the early '60s. Baden-Powell made his debut as a leader in 1966 at the suggestion of critic Joachim Berendt. Baden-Powell later toured Europe, and continued recording through the '70s and '80s, doing bossa nova, samba, and other traditional Brazilian forms. He recorded in the mid '70s with Stephane Grappelli, and played with Stan Getz in America. Baden-Powell has done sessions for Verve, Black Lion, Adda, MPS, and Tropical. He has several sessions available on CD. —*Ron Wynn*

Tristeza on Guitar / Jun. 1-2, 1966 / Verve 817491
A superb Brazilian guitarist and a superb jazz album without the usual pop trappings. —*Myles Boisen*

★ **Solitude on Guitar** / i. Dec. 10-11, 1971 / Columbia 32441

Frankfurt Opera Concert 1975, The / 1975 / Tropical Music 68958

Felicidade / Adda 581011

BENNY BAILEY (Ernest Harold Bailey)

b. Aug. 13, 1925, Cleveland, OH
Trumpet / Bop, hard bop
A tremendous hard bop soloist and an exciting trumpeter, Benny Bailey has resided in Europe since the '60s. His extensive range, dynamic sound and tone, and often striking high-note solos have been heard on many albums with European orchestras, in all-star groups, and in combos. Bailey learned piano and flute, as well as trumpet, at the Cleveland Conservatory of Music, and in private studies with George Russell. He worked in the early '40s with Bull Moose Jackson and Scatman Crothers, then toured with Jay McShann and played with Teddy Edwards. Bailey joined Dizzy Gillespie's big band in the late '40s, and toured Europe with them. He was one of the principal soloists in Lionel Hampton's orchestra from 1948 to the mid '50s, before he settled in Europe. Bailey played with Harry Arnold's band and recorded with Stan Getz in Sweden during the late '50s. He joined Quincy Jones's orchestra in 1959. Bailey returned to America briefly in 1960, then moved to Germany. He recorded with Eric Dolphy in 1961, and contributed many splendid solos to the huge 1969 hit album, *Swiss Movement*, with Eddie Harris and Les McCann. Bailey was a soloist with the Kenny Clarke-Francy Boland big band from the early

'60s until 1973. He played with George Gruntz in the '70s, as well as various radio bands, before joining the Paris Reunion Band in 1986. The band has frequently toured both America and Europe. Bailey has recorded for Candid, Enja, Ego, and Jazzcraft, among others. Some of his session mates have included Mal Waldron, Kenny Clarke, Sal Nistico, Charlie Rouse, Billy Hart, Richard Wyands, Sam Jones, Albert Dailey, Buster Williams, and Keith Copeland. He has a couple of sessions available on CD. —*Ron Wynn and Michael Erlewine*

★ **Big Brass** / Nov. 25, 1960 / Candid 79011
Septet with trumpeter/leader Phil Woods (as, bass cl), Julius Watkins (French horn), Les Spann (f, g), and Tommy Flanagan (p) Trio. Well-known standards and two originals. Extensions from Quincy Jones Big Band; large sound from seven pieces. A fine document. —*Michael G. Nastos*

Islands / May 25-26, 1976 / Enja 2082

Serenade to a Planet / Dec. 1976 / Ego 4004

While My Lady Sleeps / i. Apr. 1990 / Gemini 69

Music of Quincy Jones, The

BUSTER BAILEY (William C. Bailey)

b. Jul. 19, 1902, Memphis, TN, **d.** Apr. 12, 1967, New York, NY
Clarinet, saxophone / Swing, big band
Clarinetist Buster Bailey was a skilled, classically trained player. He was taught by Franz Schoepp, who was an instructor at Chicago Music College, and who later tutored Benny Goodman. Bailey's solos were known for their smooth, straight approach, as well as his speed and accurate playing. Bailey was in W. C. Handy's orchestra in Memphis as a teen. He moved to Chicago in 1919 and played with Erskine Tate and King Oliver, then joined Henderson in New York during the mid '20s. He was featured on several recordings from 1924 until 1937. Bailey also played with Noble Sissle in America and Europe, and with the Mills Rhythm Band. Bailey was part of John Kirby's great small combo from 1937 to 1946, then worked with Wilbur de Paris, Henry "Red" Allen, and Big Chief Moore. He played again with Allen in the mid '50s, then worked with Wild Bill Davison in the early '60s. Following a short stint with the Saints and Sinners, Bailey spent his final two years with Louis Armstrong's All-Stars. He didn't make many sessions as a leader, but recorded for Vocalion, Varsity, Variety, and Felstad. Currently, these recordings are all unavailable. Bailey's featured on some Kirby reissues on Circle CDs, and on reissues by Clarence Williams and Bessie Smith. —*Ron Wynn*

DEREK BAILEY

b. Jan. 29, 1932, Sheffield, England
Guitar / Early free, modern creative
British musician Derek Bailey is one of the world's foremost guitarists, as well as a distinct and unusual player. His arsenal of effects, splintering riffs, flailing lines, and, at times, seemingly atonal music comes close to being the guitar equivalent of Cecil Taylor, without the percussive elements. Rhythmic and harmonic patterns can be identified (occasionally) with some effort, but Bailey's a spontaneous im-

proviser whose solos explode and evolve in a powerful, highly unpredictable fashion. Both his unaccompanied works and collaborations with Anthony Braxton and fellow European improvisers like Evan Parker are not designed for most tastes. Calling them noncommercial doesn't even address their uniqueness; outside of musicians and critics, it's hard to fathom many listeners enjoying, even wanting to sit through much of Bailey's music despite the fact that he's an exceptional talent. But his work is quite different from anything you could hear elsewhere; it's sometimes abstract, other times lyrical, alternately acoustic and electric. Bailey's arsenal includes a 19-string guitar, a ukulele, and a cracklebox. Bailey worked in the '50s and early '60s in theatres, dance halls, and other settings all over Sheffield. He moved to London from Sheffield in 1966, and began playing free music with John Stevens, Parker, Paul Rutherford, and others. He joined the Spontaneous Music Ensemble for a while before working, for five years, in Tony Oxley's sextet where he began to attract international attention. Bailey formed a trio with Rutherford and Barry Guy in 1970, and started the Incus label with Oxley and Parker. He's been featured on over 50 albums since the late '60s, and Incus has also issued numerous recordings that feature Parker and many other European free musicians. Bailey led the group Company during the '70s, which played in Europe, in Africa, in North and South America, and in Japan. He's done more solo dates in the '80s, while continuing to play in duos and small groups. He published a book on improvisation in 1980 in England that's been translated into several languages. Besides Braxton and his fellow English musicians, Bailey's played with Steve Lacy, Dave Holland, George Lewis, and John Zorn, among others. His CDs can be located via mail order. —*Ron Wynn*

Improvisations for Cello and Guitar / Jan. 1971 / ECM 1013

Solo Guitar / Feb. 1971 / Incus 2
Substance abounds in Derek Bailey's *Solo Guitar Volume I.* This reissue consolidates material on two Incus LPs. His linear conception is given weight and counterbalanced by unusual intervallic concerns linking the guitarist to the Viennese 12-tone school (an encounter with Franz Koglmann seems inevitable) and to Thelonious Monk. The regular utilization of harmonic overtones, all manner of overdubbing, chopping and scraping of chordal clusters, and, on electric, feedback and volume pedal phasing are supportively interwoven with grace and finesse. Compared to later a cappella documents, *Volume I* is attractively austere, purposefully ragged, and, on the first four cuts, effectively random in approach. Also of interest here is the hardcore improvising guitarist's meeting with three compositions: Misha Mengelberg's shuffling "Police" augmented by synthesizer enhancement, the fretboard tapping of Gavin Bryars's "Squirrel," and the intricate linearisms of Willem Breuker's "Eddy," where the struggle between score and interpreter *is* the piece, and hilariously so. —*Milo Fine,* Cadence

Views from Six Windows / Jan. 1980-Feb. 1980 / Metalanguage 114

★ **Yankees** / i. 1982 / Celluloid 5006

Notes / i. Apr. 1985-Jul. 1985 / Incus 48

Figuring / i. May 1987+Sep. 1988 / Incus 05

Village Life / i. Sep. 1991 / Incus 09

MILDRED BAILEY (Mildred [Nee Rinker] Bailey)

b. Feb. 27, 1907, Tekoa, WA, **d.** Dec. 12, 1951, Poughkeepsie, NY

Vocals, piano / Swing, ballads & blues
Mildred Bailey was that rare vocalist who used her voice as an instrument. She was one of the earliest White stylists to completely master many nuances of phrasing, enunciation, and emotional intensity that were commonplace among Black vocalists. She was a skilled scatter, had one of jazz's highest-pitched ranges, and could convey the right emotion to embellish any lyric. Bailey began her career on the West Coast as a radio performer and pianist in movie houses. She

made her first recording in 1929 with Eddie Lang, and sang with Paul Whiteman's band from 1929 until 1933. She'd been introduced to him by her brother, Al Rinker, who'd been in Whiteman's Rhythm Boys vocal trio. Bailey was featured on the radio programs of both George Jessel and Willard Robison in the mid-'30s, then recorded with Benny Goodman in 1939. Prior to that, she'd sung tunes arranged by Eddie Sauter for three years in Red Norvo's band (she and Norvo were married in 1933). Bailey made several stunning records, particularly when working with top musicians. At various times during her short career, she sang with Bunny Berigan, Chu Berry, Jimmy and Tommy Dorsey, Coleman Hawkins, Johnny Hodges, Gene Krupa, and Teddy Wilson, besides Goodman and Norvo. Bailey initially got the nickname "The Rockin' Chair Lady" because she'd done renditions of Hoagy Carmichael's "Rockin' Chair," but that soon gave way to the title "Mr. and Mrs. Swing," referring to the Norvos. Bailey had her own radio show in the mid '40s, after going solo in 1940. Her health started failing during the late '40s, and she died in 1951 at age 44. —*Ron Wynn*

★ **Her Greatest Performances (1929-1946)** / 1929-1946 / Columbia 3L22
A superb three-record set that contains the finest performances from the acclaimed female singer many critics consider the finest White woman jazz vocalist ever. Bailey had a distinctive high-pitched range and excellent phrasing; she also had penchant for making comments that would be deemed racist even in an unenlightened area. This anthology has the cream of the crop from 1929-1946, and is out of print. —*Ron Wynn*

☆ **Uncollected Mildred Bailey** / 1944 / Hindsight 133

○ **M.B.** / Mar. 5, 1946-1947 / Savoy 12219

○ **Rockin' Chair Lady, The** / i. 1953 / Decca 5387

Legendary V-Disc Series / Vintage Jazz Classics 1006

CHET BAKER (Chesney Henry Baker)

b. Dec. 23, 1929, Yale, OK, **d.** May 13, 1988, Amsterdam, Holland

Trumpet, vocals / Cool
Chet Baker's trumpet and vocal approach was immediately recognizable and striking, especially in his prime. He was known for his clear tone, reflective and subdued style, soft volume, and careful, restrained approach in his choices of notes for melodic sequences. He played in army bands before working briefly with Charlie Parker in 1952. Then he began a prominent association with baritone saxophonist Gerry Mulligan, working in Mulligan's "pianoless" quartet. Baker's first recordings as a leader came in 1953, and he later started his own quartet with pianist Russ Freeman. Baker also began recording vocals in 1953, and his earliest material demonstrated a stunning innocence. Baker began enjoying enormous popularity as a leader, and dominated jazz critics polls for several years. These results triggered a wave of debate and discussion regarding the merits of cool versus hard bop jazz. Baker recorded for Pacific Jazz and Riverside during the '50s. He lived in Europe at the end of the '50s and into the mid '60s, and began playing flugelhorn in the '60s. Baker made some fine albums for Prestige in the mid '60s, working with George Coleman, where his style became less cool and moved toward hard bop. He reunited with Mulligan in the '70s, and recorded prolifically throughout the '70s and into the '80s, cutting sessions for Pausa, Enja, Soul Note, Choice, Sonet, and many others. He died in 1988; his death triggered a wealth of reissues that hasn't subsided. Bruce Weber's 1989 documentary film, *Let's Get Lost,* and its soundtrack album generated renewed interest in Baker's life and times. Mosaic's deluxe reissued boxed sets of Mulligan/Baker and Baker/Freeman sessions are exceptional. He has an enormous amount of material available on CD. —*Ron Wynn and Bob Porter*

Let's Get Lost (The Best of Chet Baker Sings) / Feb. 1953-Oct. 1956 / Pacific Jazz 92932

★ **Complete Pacific Jazz Live Recordings** / 1953-1957 / Mosaic 113
Also includes a session from October of 1954. Studio recordings, 1953-1957. With Chet Baker Quartet and Russ Freeman. Chet Baker at the height of his powers. —*Michael Katz*

★ **Chet Baker with Strings** / i. Feb. 20, 1954 / Columbia 46174
Chet Baker with Strings is a reissue (with three "new" takes) of the music that Chet Baker recorded *instrumentally* when he was just past his 24th birthday (it was recorded on December 30 and 31, 1953, and on February 20, 1954). The charts for the nine strings and the jazzmen (Zoot Sims, tenor sax; Bud Shank, alto sax, flute; Russ Freeman, piano; Joe Mondragon, bass; Shelly Manne, drums) are by the likes of Marty Paich, Johnny Mandel, Jack Montrose, and Shorty Rogers, and the arrangements generally avoid getting sickly sweet, although I never stop hoping that the strings will disappear. Sims, Shank, and Freeman help out on the more swinging material, but the emphasis is on Baker's soft sound (46:20). —*Scott Yanow, Cadence*

○ **Chet Baker Sextet** / Sep. 9+15, 1954 / Pacific Jazz 15

○ **Chet in Paris—Vol. 1** / Oct. 1955 / Verve 837474

○ **Chet in Paris—Vol. 2: Everything Happens to Me** / Oct. 1955 / Verve 837475
On this session, we encounter a much older Chet Baker with even less control; he misses notes and his tone cracks on numerous occasions. On the one vocal performance, "Oh You Crazy Moon," Baker throws in some especially pedestrian scatting. Again, I recommend the work of the accompanists, especially bassist J. F. Jenny-Clark, who takes a strong solo on Richie Beirach's haunting line, "Broken Wing." Pianist Phil Markowitz regularly builds solos with great finesse. In spite of all these grousings, however, I am perfectly willing to admit that serious listeners can hear introspection and depth in Baker's music. —*Krin Gabbard, Cadence*

○ **Chet in Paris—Vol. 3: Cheryl** / Dec. 1955-Mar. 1956 / Verve 837476

Route, The / Jul. 1956 / Pacific Jazz 92931

Playboys / Oct. 31, 1956 / Pacific Jazz 94474

★ **Chet Baker in New York** / Sep. 1958 / Riverside 207
Paul Chambers (bass) is with Johnny Griffin (tenor sax), Al Haig (piano) and Philly Joe Jones (drums) on this Chet Baker set from September 1958. There is much to listen to here in the parts (not all pleasant), but as a whole LP pulls in different directions and never gives the listener a sense of resolve from either the group or the music. —*Bob Rusch, Cadence*

Chet Baker Introduces Johnny Pace / Sep. 1958 / Riverside 292
Some interesting guests, among them Herbie Mann (f) and Philly Joe Jones (d). —*Ron Wynn*

○ **Chet (The Lyrical Trumpet of Chet Baker)** / Dec. 30, 1958+Jan. 19, 1959 / Riverside 087
This is a lovely record subtitled *The Lyrical Trumpet of Chet Baker*. Recorded in the late '50s, it presents Baker in different settings with Herbie Mann, Pepper Adams, Bill Evans, Kenny Burrell, Paul Chambers, Connie Kay, or Philly Joe Jones over nine tracks. A placid ambience permeates all the music, and while this now appears to be an all-star date, the all-stars were really only in a coloring supportive role, though their sound jazz instincts gives the extra meaning even in understatement. It is Baker's date all the way, though when Pepper Adams (baritone sax) is present, his powerful contributions make themselves obvious. —*Bob Rusch, Cadence*

Chet / Mar. 1959 / Riverside 229

New Blue Horns / Mar. 1959 / Original Jazz Classics 256
This is a compilation of cuts taken from a couple of Baker's late '50s albums, plus tracks from albums by Kenny Dorham, Nat Adderley, Clark Terry, and Blue Mitchell. — AMG

Chet Baker Plays the Best of Lerner and Loewe / Jul. 21-22, 1959 / Riverside 137

○ **Italian Sessions, The** / i. 1962 / RCA 2001

Chet Baker Sings and Plays / Jun. 1964 / Colpix 476

○ **Baker's Holiday—Plays & Sings Billie Holiday** / May 1965 / Emarcy 838204

Polka Dots and Moonbeams / i. Mar. 1967 / Jazzland 990

You Can't Go Home Again / May 1972 / A&M 0805

Live at Nick's / Nov. 1978 / Criss Cross 1027

○ **Chet Baker with Wolfgang Lackerschmid** / i. Nov. 1979 / Inakustik 8571
This is not a record of rhythm (implied) as much as it is a record of tonal coloring, pitch, and reverberation. This is also an avant-garde Chet Baker, without gimmicks, just meeting an interest to expand and to develop further: to invent, to expand, and to create. This is also very beautiful creativity; art for art's sake. Wolfgang Lackerschmid plays vibes in a manner owing itself more to Red Norvo and Gary Burton than Bags (Milt Jackson), and proves himself to be a creator and artist in his ebb and flow with the trumpeter. Bravos for both artists. The set was recorded January 8 and 9, 1979. —*Bob Rusch, Cadence*

My Funny Valentine / 1980-1987 / Philology 30

Mr. B / Mar. 14, 1983-May 25, 1983 / Timeless 192
Good trio date from '83 cut for the Timeless label. Though Baker, at this point, couldn't handle too many fast tempos, he still found ways to generate some moving solos and statements in short spurts. On the songs he's on in the trio, pianist Kirk Lightsey takes honors with aggressive, yet supportive accompaniment and smooth, confident solos. —*Ron Wynn*

○ **Improviser, The** / Aug. 15+30, 1983 / Cadence 1019
These 50 minutes are fairly bustling with drama and tension. As Per Husby's meticulous liner notes point out, trumpeter Chet Baker sounds "beautifully relaxed" on Tadd Dameron's "Gnid" and Hal Galper's "Night," improvising at length and phrasing with the laconic lyricism that was his trademark. And happily, we have here another Baker essay on Sam Rivers's plaintive "Beatrice," wherein the rhythm section (pianist Husby, bassists Terje Vennas, Bjorn Kjellemyr, drummers Old Jacob Hansen, Espen Rud) play with amazing responsiveness. . . . Both rhythm sections, in fact, are attuned and attentive to the trumpeter, and seem totally invested in making the best music possible. Yes, the sound isn't as opulent as we have come to demand, but the balance between the instruments is true. And, yes, there are some fades and splices (nicely handled in the remix) made necessary by taping misadventures, but the honesty and taut beauty of the music overrides any and all such minor warts. —*Alan Bargebuhr, Cadence*

○ **Chet's Choice** / Jun. 25, 1985 / Criss Cross 1016
The brief liner notes to this record speak of Chet Baker's trumpet playing as being "pure poetry," which isn't too inappropriate a description of most of this record. Baker's somewhat low-key and melodic attack provide for some nice listening on this set of ballads and bop tunes. The lack of percussion on this trio recording provides a somewhat spare setting, which perhaps highlights Baker's lyricism. The trio plays with sufficient heat to prevent this date from being too contemplative and chamber-like. . . . Guitarist Philip Catherine is the other expressive voice here, and proves a fine foil for Baker. In his playing, he takes several roles, including comping and soloing. Hein Van de Geijn (bass) provides an anchor for Baker and Catherine on most of this splendid recording, allowing them to make their impressionistic sketches. On ballads such as the closing "Adriano," Baker is particularly enchanting, whereas the trio is playful and gritty on "Doodlin'" and "Conception." —*Ronald B. Weinstock, Cadence*

○ **Silence** / i. Aug. 1990 / Soul Note 121172

○ **My Favourite Songs, Vols. 1 and 2: The Last Great Concert** / **i.** Nov. 1, 1991 / Enja 79600

Chet Baker doesn't try to push his sound on this session. He simply picks his direction on each tune and steadfastly follows it. He transforms the mood of "Django" from its normal melancholic air into one of quiet confidence. Both the small group and large ensemble contain notable players, like expatriates Herb Geller and Walter Norris. They are side by side with some of Europe's best, like Swiss guitarist John Schroeder. The backing arrangements are subdued, but invariably interesting. With tunes like "All Blues," "I Fall in Love Too Easily," and "My Funny Valentine," it is no surprise to hear Baker playing like Miles Davis, whose style he greatly admired. But just where your mind tells your ears that Baker's modal trumpet solo on "All Blues" should be followed by something with a John Coltrane intensity, the band breaks into a swinging, straightahead 12-bar blues line that leaves you saying "Wow!" Baker intrudes on his otherwise poignant rendition of "My Funny Valentine" with an attempt at vocalizing. As on other of his later recordings, his voice is weak, strained, and unable to hold any one key. It is the sound of his horn that will linger with you above all. —*Paul B. Matthews*, Cadence

Live at Ronnie Scott's / PolyGram 81223

SHORTY BAKER (Harold J. Baker)

b. May 26, 1914, St. Louis, MO, **d.** Nov. 8, 1966, New York, NY
Trumpet / Swing, big band
An outstanding section player and trumpet soloist, Harold "Shorty" Baker had a compelling style that was precise and careful, but was also arresting and memorable. Baker's phrasing and playing in the Ellington section was always under control, while his solos were more distinctive, expressive, and alternately bluesy and poignant. He was among the warmest ballad stylists of all trumpeters, gifted with a marvelous tone and superb timing. Baker began on drums, then switched to trumpet in the late '20s while in his brother's, trombonist Winfield Baker's, band. He worked in the early '30s with Fate Marable and Erskine Tate, then played with Don Redman later in the decade. There was a brief stint with Ellington in 1938, then Baker played with Teddy Wilson and Andy Kirk in the early '40s. He was married to Mary Lou Williams and also played with her in 1942, then rejoined Ellington in 1943, remaining until 1951. Baker returned to Wilson's group in 1952, and was in Johnny Hodges's orchestra in 1954 and 1955. After another stint in the Ellington orchestra from 1957 to 1959, Baker did sessions in New York until his death. Baker led a quartet and was a sideman at the Metropole, and also recorded with Bud Freeman and Doc Cheatham. He was featured on Ellington compositions such as "Mood Indigo" and "A Portrait of Florence Mills." His top playing can be heard on the Columbia album *Ellington Indigos*. —*Ron Wynn*

★ **Shorty & Doc** / Jan. 17, 1961 / Prestige 2021

BURT BALES (Burton Frank Bales)

b. Mar. 20, 1916, **d.** Oct. 26, 1989
Piano / New Orleans traditional
Although well established as a pianist, Burt Bales was also quite effective on mellophone and baritone horn. He loved ragtime and early jazz styles, but added his own flavor and distinctiveness with his "rocking" style. Bales started with dance bands in the '30s, but then responded to the '40s "traditional" New Orleans jazz revival in the Bay Area. He played and recorded with Bunk Johnson during Johnson's heralded 1944 appearance in San Francisco, and led his own bands during the mid '40s. Bales also worked with Lu Watters, Turk Murphy, Bob Scobey, and Marty Marsala in the '40s and '50s. He recorded with Murphy, Scobey, and Marsala as a leader from the late '40s until the mid '50s. Bales recorded as a soloist for Good Time Jazz in 1949 and 1955, and played in San Francisco clubs from 1954-1966,

and from 1975 into the '80s. Currently, he has few titles available on CD. —*Ron Wynn and Bruce Boyd Raeburn*

After Hours Piano / Oct. 22, 1949 / Good Time Jazz 19

★ **They Tore My Playhouse Down** / **i.** 1953 / Good Time Jazz 12025

Burt Bale's testament to Jelly Roll Morton, with numbers such as "Wild Man Blues," "New Orleans Joys," and "Midnight Mama," backed with Paul Lingle's mixed bag of W. C. Handy and Jelly Roll blues and stomps, including "Memphis Blues" and "Black Bottom Stomp" (1953). —*Bruce Raeburn*

GABE BALTAZAR (Gabriel Ruiz (Jr) Baltazar)

b. Nov. 1, 1929, Hilo, HI
Alto saxophone / Cool, progressive big band
An infrequent leader and a distinctive big band soloist with a hint of Charlie Mariano, Gabe Baltazar came to America from Hawaii in the late '50s. His alto solos were often aggressive and energetic, but most of Baltazar's work outside of big band circles has not been released or was available only for short periods. He worked in Los Angeles, then made his recording debut with Paul Togawa's quartet in 1957. Baltazar joined Howard Rumsey's Lighthouse All-Stars in 1960, but never recorded. He toured from 1960 to 1965 as lead alto saxophonist for Stan Kenton's orchestra, recording a number of albums with them. Baltazar also played with Onzy Matthews, Ralph Pena, and Terry Gibbs, and recorded with Gil Fuller and Oliver Nelson. He returned to Hawaii and led the Royal Hawaiian Band in 1969. Baltazar made a big band album in 1979, then returned in 1992 with a new session on VSOP/Mode, *Back in Action*. That label has also reissued his debut with Togawa. The Kenton albums, *Stan Kenton's West Side Story* and *Adventures in Jazz*, feature some of Baltazar's finest playing in that organization. So far, *West Side Story* is not available on CD. —*Ron Wynn*

★ **Stan Kenton Presents Gabe Baltazar** / Jan. 9-11, 1979 / Creative World 3005

Alto saxophonist Gabe Baltazar had spent virtually his entire professional life inside an organization. His one solo album hadn't been issued, and he was well known for his contributions to Stan Kenton's orchestra and his work in studios. Kenton repaid the favor in 1979 by issuing this big band LP with Baltazar as front man on his Creative World label. Despite bombast, Baltazar provides some pungent, energetic alto solos, and shows he deserves his own album issued long before this one. —*Ron Wynn*

Back in Action / Oct. 18, 1992+Oct. 19, 1992 / VSOP 85

Gabe Baltazar is best known for his great alto work with Stan Kenton. This recording is his first in many years and his style and technique are better than ever. —*Ron Wynn*

BILLY BANG (Billy [Walker, William Vincent] Bang)

b. Sep. 20, 1947, Mobile, AL
Violin / Modern creative
A master of haunting melodies, sawing effects, and flashy phrases who displays a bluesy tone and a slashing attack, Billy Bang's made his mark since the '70s in free and new music circles. He studied violin briefly in his youth, then quit playing before returning to the violin during the late '60s. Bang became a professional in the early '70s, and studied with Leroy Jenkins. He did his first solo concert in '77, then formed the String Trio of New York with James Emery and John Lindberg. He led this unit until 1986. Bang formed a quintet in the late '70s, and also played with Ronald Shannon Jackson's Decoding Society, and with Material, which featured Sonny Sharrock. He's recorded for Hat Hut, Hat Music, Anima, and Soul Note in the '70s, '80s, and '90s. Currently, Bang has sessions available on CD. —*Ron Wynn*

New York Collage / May 6, 1978 / Anima 40620

Sweet Space / Nov. 15, 1979 / Anima 12741

Billy Bang's Sextet, live at the Loeb Student Center in New York City. —*AMG*

★ **Distinction without a Difference** / **i.** Jan. 1981 / Hat Hut 04

Billy Bang's solo violin recital (recorded in performance at the GAKU Gallery in New York) is a gem. Here, he not only displays an accomplished technique, but a fertile imagination that makes the 40-minute performance seem more like half that length.... Like Leroy Jenkins, Bang shows a classical attitude toward his improvisations. This album's version of "Sweet Space" sets the mood for the entire album as Bang cuts loose with his full arsenal. "Loweski" is an exciting performance that mixes a little blues, folk, bop, and contemporary music. Each succeeding piece matches the preceding one for excitement until the concluding piece, "Skip to My Lou," a perfect way to end the album. Bang gives it an engaging and moving interpretation. — *Carl Brauer*, Cadence

Rainbow Gladiator / Jun. 10-11, 1981 / Soul Note 1016
A tremendous release, possibly Bang's finest session. His solos are not only expertly played, but intensely delivered, while the songs don't simply develop, but seem to burst at the seams. The late Charles Tyler on baritone and alto sax and pianist Michele Rosewoman match Bang in verve, skill, and power. — *Ron Wynn*

Invitation / Apr. 13-14, 1982 / Soul Note 1036

○ **Outline No. 12** / Jul. 1982 / Celluloid 5004
Fine, animated, but tough-to-find album featuring Billy Bang, arguably the most striking violinist to emerge on the jazz scene since Leroy Jenkins. The songs on this set aren't gentle, demure, or bluesy; they are explosive, searching, and combative, and as such are ideal for Bang's sawing effects and sweeping solos. — *Ron Wynn*

Bangception / Aug. 29, 1982 / Hat Music 3512

Fire from Within, The / Sep. 19+29, 1984 / Soul Note 1086
One of Bang's most highly composed and well-executed releases under his own name. The record is a tribute to the writings of Carlos Castaneda, whose individualistic mysticism is reflected in the imaginative and prayerful compositions. Parker and Barker lay tremendous rhythmic foundations, while Abdullah, Sanders, and Bang skirmish lovingly over the top. Deep listening yields rewards, as this is a multi-layered date with levels that build on each other both melodically and harmonically. — *Scot Hacker*

○ **Live at Carlos 1** / Nov. 1986 / Soul Note 121136

Valve No. 10 / i. Feb. 1988 / Soul Note 121186
Valve No. 10 is perhaps Bang's most cohesive recording: firmly rooted in the bebop tradition, but keeping all doors open to imaginative and forward-looking interpretations of improvised music. Two tracks take the form of tributes to John Coltrane. "September 23" (Trane's birthday) is an inspired reading of a poem to the spirit of creativity read over a surly yet meditative improv groove, and "Lonnie's Lament" is a Coltrane cover rendered with conviction and gratitude. The melodies stick in your head, the playing of the whole quartet is nothing short of amazing, and the seven tracks hang together like puzzle pieces in midair. Highly recommended. — *Scot Hacker*

Tribute to Stuff Smith / i. Sep. 1992 /
The connections to the past are worth pointing out here: Sun Ra and violinist Stuff Smith once played together on what is believed to be Ra's first recording, 1953 or 1954. Bang has always considered Smith to be a potent influence on his work. Bang has been playing in Ra's Arkestra for a couple of years off and on, and now that Ra is gone, Bang is staying on with the Arkestra's core, now billing themselves as the "Satellites of the Sun." Bassist John Ore has also been a staple in Ra's bands, and Andrew Cyrille is no stranger to any of this crew. That said, those who like their violin "inside" will want to start their Bang collections with this recording: it is the least avant-garde of his oeuvre. For Sun Ra lovers, this recording will be important for being probably the very last thing he did before passing on to the interplanetary spaceways. The entire date is relaxed and highly structured. Like Smith, Bang plays here well within established boundaries, but still manages to place his notes somewhere just out of reach, in a place that's difficult to put a finger on, and all the more rewarding because of this enigma. — *Scot Hacker*

AMIRI BARAKA (Everett Leroi Jones)

b. Oct. 7, 1934
Poet / Modern creative
A premier poet, playwright, and essayist, the former Leroi Jones has also written a number of distinguished works on jazz and African-American popular music, and, at one time, was a columnist and critic for *Down Beat* magazine. Baraka studied piano, drums, and trumpet, and earned his B.A. degree from Howard University in 1954. He wrote for *Down Beat*, and also contributed to *Jazz* and *Jazz Review*. His '60s books, *Blues People* (1963) and *Black Music* (1967), were among the first critical examinations of jazz and African-American music by a Black writer. Baraka also wrote controversial plays, such as *The Dutchman*, and was a founder of the Black Arts Repertory Theater-School. He's had more than 20 plays and several volumes of poetry published. His 1987 book, *The Music: Reflections on Jazz and Blues*, continued the direction begun by his earlier works, and he also had an album of his poetry readings backed by jazz musicians released by India Navigation in the '80s. Baraka's been an instructor of African studies at SUNY-Stony Brook since 1980. He wrote a foreword for Rhino's 1993 collection of John Coltrane material (primarily on Atlantic) titled *The John Coltrane Anthology*, and has been working on a Coltrane biography and collaboration with drummer Max Roach. — *Ron Wynn and Michael G. Nastos*

★ **New Music New Poetry** / i. Mar. 1982 / India Navigation 1048
Incendiary poet reads in performance with David Murray (ts) and Steve McCall (d). — *Michael G. Nastos*

PAUL BARBARIN (Adolphe Paul Barbarin)

b. May 5, 1899, New Orleans, LA, **d.** Feb. 17, 1969, New Orleans, LA
Drums / New Orleans traditional
A simple, yet influential drummer who seldom took solos, Paul Barbarin was part of an extensive New Orleans musical dynasty. He used only a snare and one large bass drum, plus a cymbal, a tom-tom, and a woodblock. Barbarin only resorted to the cymbal on a composition's last chorus, and adapted his beat from the driving rhythms of parade bands, sometimes using two-beat patterns. He wrote "Bourbon Street Parade" and "The Second Line," both of which became established standards. Barbarin played on New Orleans streets with bands such as Buddy Petit's Young Olympians while in his teens. He left the Crescent City to work in Chicago's stockyards in 1917, but soon found a more amenable occupation playing music with transplanted homeboys King Oliver and Jimmie Noone, and with other Chicago bands. He worked with Oliver's Dixie Syncopators in the mid '20s before joining Luis Russell's Orchestra in 1928. This gave him the chance to work with Jelly Roll Morton and Louis Armstrong in the '30s. Barbarin returned to New Orleans in 1939, then went back to Chicago in 1942 and 1943 to play with Henry "Red" Allen's sextet, then played with Sidney Bechet. He stayed in New Orleans after World War II, working with small combos and brass bands, including the Onward Brass Band. This 1960 group was patterned and named after the original Onward Band led by his father, Isidore, at the turn of the century. Barbarin's final years were spent working with many veterans affiliated with Preservation Hall. They included Sweet Emma Barrett, with whom he recorded. Barbarin recorded several sessions during this period for Atlantic, Nobility, and Southland. He was leading the Onward band in a street parade when he died in 1969, concluding his career in the same manner in which it began. Currently, Barbarin has a few titles available on CD. — *Ron Wynn and Bruce Boyd Raeburn*

★ **And His New Orleans Jazz** / Jan. 7, 1955 / Atlantic 90977
With Danny Barker (g), Willie Humphrey, Lester Santiago, and others, romping through traditional New Orleans favorites such as "Eh La Bas" and Barbarin's own "Bourbon

Street Parade." Milt Hinton fits in nicely. —*Bruce Boyd Raeburn*

New Orleans Jazz Band / Apr. 21, 1956 / Good Time Jazz 12019

CHRIS BARBER

b. Apr. 17, 1930, Welwyn Garden City, England
Trombone, bandleader / New Orleans traditional, blues & jazz

Though he's a good trombonist in the early New Orleans style, Chris Barber's importance stems more from his talent as a bandleader than from his talent as a player. The English conductor/instrumentalist has been an advocate for traditional jazz and blues since the '50s, and has helped keep both forms alive in England with his various groups. Barber studied trombone and bass at London's Guildhall School of Music. He formed his first traditional jazz group in the late '40s, then organized another group led by Ken Colyer in the mid '50s. Barber became its leader in 1954, and the group was soon extremely popular throughout England. During the '60s, Barber's group became a huge attraction during England's "trad" boom; they started playing rags and expanded into more modern jazz material. Barber also stimulated awareness of and interest in blues and R&B, bringing great musicians such as Muddy Waters and the team of Sonny Terry and Brownie McGhee to England for concerts. He began touring in America during the late '50s, and eventually cut two albums with his American Jazz Band that included Sidney De Paris, Edmond Hall, and Hank Duncan. He restructured his band in the '60s, called it Chris Barber's Jazz and Blues Band, and used rock players like John Slaughter and Pete York as guest stars. Barber also recorded an album with Louis Jordan in the '70s, toured Europe extensively, and did an Echoes of Ellington tour with special guests Russell Procope and Wild Bill Davis in 1976. He collaborated with Dr. John in the early '80s for a Take Me Back To New Orleans show that was performed in England, Europe, and America. Barber's made several recordings for both European and American labels, including sessions for Decca, Columbia, and Black Lion, and for Tempo and Marmalade. He has several dates available on CD. —*Ron Wynn and Michael G. Nastos*

Echoes of Harlem / i. Sep. 1955 / Dormouse 8

○ **Louis Jordan Sings** / i. 1962 / Black Lion 30175

★ **Live in East Berlin** / Nov. 26, 1968 / Black Lion 760502
Spirited live "trad" jazz set cut in Berlin in 1968. Barber's music is always enjoyable and catchy, though it's also very derivative and predictable. They tried to change things a bit here by not sticking strictly to trad with the inclusion of "Mercy, Mercy, Mercy." —*Ron Wynn*

In East Berlin 1 / i. 1973 / Polydor 2460175

In East Berlin 2 / i. 1973 / Polydor 2460176

○ **Chris Barber & Lonnie Donegan** / i. 1973 / Boulevard 4110

Tishomingo Blues / i. 1975 / Black Lion 287691

○ **Echoes of Ellington** / i. 1978 / Black Lion 001

Up Jumped the Blues / i. 1979 / Hefty 106

○ **Creole Love Call** / i. 1983 / Timeless 3

GATO BARBIERI (Leandro J. Barbieri)

b. Nov. 28, 1934, Rosario, Argentina
Tenor saxophone, composer / Latin jazz, world fusion, instrumental pop, modern creative

Gato Barbieri has enjoyed success, in several contexts, from the late '60s through the '90s. He's played free, jazz-rock, traditional South American, film, and light pop material, and has scored crossover hits in the '70s and '80s. His early work was influenced heavily by late '60s John Coltrane and Pharoah Sanders sessions. Barbieri's tenor sax solos echoed Coltrane's and Sanders's voice-like effects, with screams, overblowing, false fingering, honks and bleats, and also echoed their accompaniments, which were based on long stretches of simple, repeating two-chord sequences in minor

keys that supported soaring, sustained-tone solo lines. He used a wide vibrato and would sometimes hum and blow at the same time, producing a high-pitched, wailing tone. Later, Barbieri began playing in a more mellow, sentimental fashion on ballads, but retained the energy style on uptempo dates. He still sometimes utilizes the rising, upper-register approach, but has exchanged his once-fiery method for a more restrained approach on pop and fusion dates.

A native of Argentina, Barbieri's family included several musicians, and he studied clarinet as a child. He moved to Buenos Aires in 1947, where he learned alto sax and made an early impact in Lalo Schifrin's band in 1953. Barbieri switched to tenor and formed his own quartet. He moved to Rome in the early '60s, and joined Don Cherry's group in Paris during 1963. He appeared on fierce dates such as *Complete Communion* on Blue Note in 1966, and recorded with Steve Lacy and Abdullah Ibrahim (then known as Dollar Brand). Barbieri combined free jazz and traditional South American rhythms. His late '60s album for Flying Dutchman, *The Third World*, won him his first widespread recognition, though earlier ESP dates introduced the formula. Barbieri's early '70s Flying Dutchman LPs included contributions from Stanley Clarke, John Abercrombie, and Nana Vasconcelos. One live date paired him with Oliver Nelson and Eddie "Cleanhead" Vinson. But the album that made Barbieri a genuine star was his Grammy-winning soundtrack for the film *Last Tango in Paris* in 1972.

He changed direction in 1973, formed a band of South American musicians, and recorded several traditional Latin albums. *Chapter One: Latin America* inaugurated the series, and Barbieri's band was a popular college attraction in the early '70s. Barbieri appeared at various festivals through the '70s, including Newport, Montreux, and Bologna. During the '80s, he had another smash with the LP *Caliente*. Barbieri essentially played pop and fusion while recording for A&M in the '80s, but in 1989 he returned to the traditional South American vein with *Gato . . . Para Los Amigos* for Bob Thiele's Signature label. He's continued working in the '90s, but hasn't enjoyed similar exposure or popularity through '93. Several of Barbieri's recent and vintage sessions are available on CD, but the Flying Dutchman sessions are unavailable. —*Ron Wynn*

○ **Gato Barbieri and Don Cherry** / 1965 / Inner City 1009
Great duo record with Barbieri and Cherry at their most adventurous and outside. This record is miles away from the heavily orchestrated, quasi-pop soundtracks and mood music that Barbieri's had hits with in the '70s and '80s. It is also much different from Cherry's international material. —*Ron Wynn*

In Search of Mystery / Mar. 15, 1967 / Explosive 1049

Confluence / Mar. 1968 / Arista 1003

Third World, The / Nov. 24+25, 1969 / Flying Dutchman 6369403

★ **Fenix** / Apr. 27-28, 1971 / FD 10144
The manic album that won him fame on college campuses in early '70s. It is still his greatest record on all levels. Nana Vasconcelos is tremendous on percussion. —*Ron Wynn*

El Pampero / Jun. 18, 1971 / RCA 42038

Under Fire / 1971 / Flying Dutchman 10156

★ **Last Tango in Paris** / Nov. 20-25, 1972 / United Artists 29440
An incredibly popular soundtrack, dreamy and lush. Still sounds great 20 years later. A Grammy-winning, sensual soundtrack to the controversial film. —*Ron Wynn*

☆ **Chapter 1: Latin America** / i. 1973 / MCA 39124
A major statement of Latin Jazz. Barbieri with a cast of Argentinian musicians. He later toured the U.S. with them to overflow crowds in several places. —*Ron Wynn*

Chapter 2: Hasta Siempre / i. Jun. 1974 / Impulse 9263
Hasta Siempre is, as the title indicates, another chapter of Gato Barbieri's continuing confrontation with his South American roots. As such, it is ethnic music in the same way that Balinese Gamelan music, Louis Armstrong's Hot Five

sessions, and Moroccan pan pipe music are ethnic music. It is close to Barbieri's native folk melodies and rhythms, and the music relation to Afro-American "jazz" is much more subtle than on his Flying Dutchman recordings. This LP is split between Brazilian and Argentinian music, recorded in Rio and Los Angeles ("Juana Azurdy" was done in Buenos Aires at the same time as the *Chapter One* sessions). The new disc begins as the previous one ended, with the engaging "Encontros," a perfectly delightful, happy, Brazilian tune. There are no quarrels with the rest of the music as presented here. I'll just say that the album cooks like a sonuvabitch. — *Chuck Mitchell*, Down Beat

Chapter 3: Viva Emiliano Zapata / Jun. 25, 1974 / GRP 111
After a disappointing sequel, the third volume in the series again has the fire and energy of the first. — *Ron Wynn*

Chapter 4: Alive in New York / Feb. 20-23, 1975 / ABC/Impulse 9303

☆ **Caliente** / 1976 / A&M 3247

Bahia / i. Mar. 1983 / Fania 608

A. SPENCER BAREFIELD

b. 1953
Guitar / Modern creative
A sensitive, understated guitarist despite the fact that he plays with high-voltage bandleader Roscoe Mitchell, A. Spencer Barefield's acoustic riffs, licks, and phrases have found a home in Mitchell's Sound/Space Ensembles. Barefield has also recorded for Sound Aspects and Trans-African as a leader, and has worked with Oliver Lake, Anthony Holland, Hugh Ragin, Richard Davis, Andrew Cyrille, the Ballade String Quartet, and Tani Tabbal, among others. Currently, Barefield's sessions are unavailable on CD, except through mail order. — *Ron Wynn and Michael G. Nastos*

★ **Trans-Dimensional Space Window** / Dec. 1981 / Trans-African 001
Trans-Dimensional Space Window is a progressive, but listenable, venture for the unique guitar sound of innovator Barefield. With Anthony Holland (sax) and Tani Tabbal (per). "In Between Song" is exceptional. — *Michael G. Nastos*

EDDIE BAREFIELD (Eddie Emmanuel Barefield)

b. Dec. 12, 1909, Madrid (Scandia), IA, **d.** Jan. 3, 1991
Alto and tenor saxophone, clarinet / Swing, big band
An always engaging, enjoyable swing era saxophonist, Eddie Barefield contributed many outstanding solos to numerous ensembles from the '30s to the '80s. He was also a gifted arranger and composer. Barefield co-wrote the tune "Toby" with Buster Moten, and penned the arrangement for Bennie Moten's outstanding '30s recording of it. At one time, he was supplying arrangements for Cab Calloway, Glenn Miller, Benny Goodman, Paul Whiteman, and Jimmy Dorsey. Barefield studied piano from the age of ten, and studied alto at age 13. He worked with cornetist Bernie Young in the early '30s, then played with Bennie Moten, Zack Whyte, McKinney's Cotton Pickers, Cab Calloway, Les Hite, Fletcher Henderson, and Don Redman in the '30s. He also appeared in the films *The Swinging Kid* and *Every Day's a Holiday*. Barefield served as an ABC staff musician and worked for WOR radio in the '40s, and also played with Benny Carter, Duke Ellington, and Ella Fitzgerald's band. Barefield wrote arrangements and conducted pit bands on Broadway from the late '40s until 1970. During the '50s, he played with Sammy Price, and in the '60s, he played with Wilbur De Paris and the group Saints and Sinners. Barefield had another film role in the late '60s production *The Night They Raided Minsky's*. Barefield played in the Ringling Brothers and Barnum & Bailey circus orchestra in the '70s and '80s, and worked with Stan Rubin, Dick Vance, Illinois Jacquet, and the Harlem Blues and Jazz Band in the '80s. Barefield's style influenced Frank Wess. Barefield recorded for Sonet and Famous Door, among others, but currently does not have any sessions available on CD. — *Ron Wynn*

★ **Indestructible Eddie Barefield, The** / i. 1977 / Famous Door 113

DANNY BARKER (Daniel Moses Barker)

b. Jan. 13, 1909, New Orleans, LA, **d.** 1994
Guitar, banjo, vocals, composer / New Orleans traditional
A superb guitarist, banjoist, vocalist, composer, and historian, Danny Barker's career ranges from early traditional to contemporary developments. His single-string technique and expertly played chordal style have been a vital part of many sessions. Compositions such as "Save the Bones for Henry Jones," and "Don't You Make Me Feel High" have been recorded by many jazz and blues artists. Barker learned clarinet, ukulele, and banjo as a child growing up in his grandfather, Isidore Barbarin's, home. He played with the Boozan Kings, then toured Mississippi with Little Brother Montgomery and Willie Pajeaud in the early '20s. Barker later toured Florida with Lee Collins and David Jones. He moved to New York in the early '30s, where he worked with Dave Nelson and Harry White, while switching from banjo to guitar. Barker played in the early '30s with Sidney Bechet, Fess Williams, Albert Nicholas, and James P. Johnson, recording with Red Allen and his wife, Blue Lou Barker. In the late '30s, Barker was featured in the big bands of Lucky Millinder, Benny Carter, and Cab Calloway. From that point, he worked mainly in small combos. Barker appeared on the radio series "This Is Jazz" during the late '40s as part of the traditional revival, and recorded with Mutt Carey and Bunk Johnson while adding six-string banjo to his arsenal. After recording sessions in Los Angeles and New Orleans in the late '40s, Barker returned to New York. He became a favorite at Ryan's, working with Conrad Janis and Wilbur De Paris, and with his own band as well. Barker became assistant curator of the New Orleans Jazz Museum on his return to New Orleans in 1965, and remained in that post for ten years while working as a bandleader and guitarist. He was also grand marshal of the Onward Brass Band in the mid '60s and early '70s. Barker has written and lectured extensively on early jazz, and formed the Fairview Baptist Church Brass band. Barker's books include *Bourbon Street Black*, co-written with Jack Buerkle, and an acclaimed autobiography called *A Life in Jazz*, published by Macmillan in 1986. Currently, Barker's albums are listed as unavailable on CD by most publications, but the unaccompanied session, *Save the Bones*, is available on Orleans. — *Ron Wynn and Michael G. Nastos*

★ **Save the Bones** / 1988 / Orleans 1018

EMIL BARNES (Emile [Mile] Barnes)

b. Feb. 18, 1892, New Orleans, LA, **d.** Mar. 2, 1970, New Orleans, LA
Clarinet / New Orleans traditional
A fiery, dashing clarinetist with an intense, bluesy, and rugged approach, Emile Barnes recorded several sessions during the '50s. The brother of Polo Barnes, his early teachers were Lorenzo Tio, Jr., Alphonse Picou, George Bacquet, and Big Eye Nelson. Barnes worked with Buddy Petit before joining Chris Kelly in 1919. They played together through the '20s. For a short time, Barnes worked with Wooden Joe Nicholas's Camellia Band, but left the music world during the Depression to return to his original occupation, making mattresses. Barnes played with Kid Howard during the late '40s, then made several recordings in the '50s. None of them have been reissued in the CD era, or at least none were reissued prior to1993. — *Ron Wynn*

New Orleans Trad Jazz / Aug. 30, 1951 / America Music 641

GEORGE BARNES

b. Jul. 17, 1921, South Chicago Heights, IL, **d.** Sep. 5, 1977, Concord, CA
Guitar / Swing, blues & jazz
A pivotal guitarist, George Barnes actually recorded on electric before Charlie Christian did, when Barnes accompanied blues vocalists. Barnes was a rarity among '30s players in

that he developed his own single-string style and had a joyful, melodic approach that was influenced by saxophonists. Barnes designed his guitar to get the individualistic sound he desired. His great inflections and nuances broke fresh ground for the guitar, and influenced many in the '40s generation who heard him on radio. Barnes made the instrument as important a lead weapon as saxophones or trumpets. His first dates were with blues singers Big Bill Broonzy, Blind John Davis, and Washboard Sam. Barnes toured the Midwest with his quartet in the mid '30s, then was an NBC staff musician in the late '30s and early '40s, and played with Bud Freeman. He joined ABC after an army stint in the mid '40s and early '50s. Barnes later signed an extended contract with Decca as a guitarist, composer, and arranger in New York. He formed a duo with Carl Kress in the early '60s that toured nationally. They recorded with United Artists, but the duo ended when Kress died in 1965. Barnes teamed with Bucky Pizzarelli in the late '60s and early '70s, then worked with Ruby Braff in a quartet until 1975; he also played with Joe Venuti and teamed a final time with Freeman. Despite his importance, at present Barnes doesn't have any sessions available on CD. —*Ron Wynn and Richard Lieberson*

Uncollected: George Barnes and His Octet 1946 / 1946 / Hindsight 106
With an octet. Unusual arrangements by Barnes, featured here with NBC studio musicians. —*Richard Lieberson*

★ **Guitars Anyone** / 1964 / CARNEY 202
Grab this album if you are lucky enough to find a copy. One of the great guitar duos. Carl Kress's rich rhythm guitar playing and chorded solos perfectly complement Barnes's lead work. —*Richard Lieberson*

○ **Swing Guitar** / Aug. 3, 1972 / Famous Door 100

Blues Going Up / Apr. 17, 1977 / Concord Jazz 43

○ **Plays So Good** / Apr. 17, 1977 / Concord Jazz 67

CHARLIE BARNET (Charles Daly Barnet)

b. Oct. 26, 1913, New York, NY, d. Sep. 4, 1991
Bandleader, vocals, saxophone / Swing, big band
Bandleader Charlie Barnet led one of the swing era's most popular bands. He joined Artie Shaw and Benny Goodman in helping to smash racial barriers by hiring Black musicians in the '30s, beginning with Frankie Newton and John Kirby, and continuing with Roy Eldridge, Charlie Shavers, Benny Carter, and Lena Horne. Barnet worshipped the Ellington sound; Johnny Hodges was a major influence and he incorporated many arrangements into the band's book that mirrored Ellington's. He supervised his band's reed section while doubling on soprano. Barnet's family was wealthy, but he alienated them by refusing to become a lawyer. At the age of 16, Barnet was leading a band on an ocean liner.

After working with Eddie Sauter and Tutti Camarata, among others, in the early '30s, Barnet joined Red Norvo's combo in 1934, where he played alongside Shaw and Teddy Wilson. Barnet's band enjoyed it's biggest hit in 1939 with Billy May's arrangement of the Ray Noble song "Cherokee." The orchestra survived the loss of its instruments and charts in the Palomar ballroom fire that year; Barnet subsequently recorded "We're All Burnt Up." They had three big hits in 1940 and 1941: "Where Was I," "Pompton Turnpike," and "I Hear a Rhapsody." They even poked fun at "sweet bands" with the song "The Wrong Idea." The next year, Barnet recorded with Lena Horne, playing songs such as "Good for Nothin' Joe." His 1942 band included Dodo Marmarosa, Buddy DeFranco, and Neal Hefti, and, before the end of the decade, other Barnet band members included Ralph Burns, Trummy Young, Barney Kessel, Oscar Pettiford, Clark Terry, Gil Fuller, and Manny Albam.

Barnet disbanded in 1949. He moved to the West Coast and led small combos. He reassembled the big band in the mid '60s for special assignments; these included a concert recording for television, and the album *Big Band '67*. With Barnet, distinguished critic Stanley Dance co-wrote the en-

tertaining autobiography *Those Swinging Years* in 1984, in which the author unveiled a life story that ranked with Shaw's. Both Barnet and Shaw were married often; Barnet was married at least six times (some accounts claim he was married as many as 11 times). Barnet continued playing into the '70s, did some music publishing, and even ran a restaurant. He died in '92. Several vintage Barnet sessions have been reissued on various CD packages. —*Ron Wynn*

★ **Barnet—Vol. 1 (1935-1939)** / 1935-1939 / EPM
An excellent reissue of late and mid '30s swing cuts. —*Ron Wynn*

○ **Complete Charlie Barnet—Vol. 2** / i. 1939 / RCA 5577
One in series devoted to late '30s swing recordings of Charlie Barnet. The songs, solos, arrangements, and mood are mostly joyous and if you're a big band devotee, these are essential cuts. But you're better served getting the complete multi-disc package rather than in yearly sets. —*Ron Wynn*

○ **Clap Hands, Here Comes Charlie** / i. 1939-1941 / Bluebird 6273
Charlie Barnet had one of the most consistently swinging bands of the era, a fun-loving unit that was into Duke Ellington's style, but, due to its commercial success ("Cherokee," "Redskin Rhumba," "Pompton Turnpike," etc.) and lack of influential soloists, has always been underrated. Barnet was a hard-drivin', stompin' tenor player who was equally effective on alto (where he echoes Johnny Hodges) and occasionally doubled on soprano. Other major soloists are the fine trumpeter Bobby Burnett and the pioneer electric guitarist Bus Etri. This sampler has 21 of Barnet's best recordings (62:46) tracing his band from January 20, 1939, to August 14, 1941, its prime period. Barnetophiles will desire his six twofer sets, but this CD is the definitive single package. —*Scott Yanow, Cadence*

Orchestra—1941 / Jan. 27, 1941 / Circle 65

Orchestra—1945 / 1945 / Circle

○ **Rockin' in Rhythm** / i. 1954 / RCA 3062

Charlie Barnet Big Band—1967 / 1967 / Mobile Fidelity 841
An example of late Barnet. A surprisingly good set. A wonderful recording. —*Ron Wynn*

JOEY BARON

Drums / M-Base, modern creative
Joey Baron is a slashing, excellent drummer who's worked with several of the most eclectic instrumentalists of the '80s and '90s, and has led his own bands. Baron's recorded with Tim Berne, Hank Roberts, Steve Swallow, and Ellery Eskelin, while he's also played with Jim Hall and Toots Thielemans. He's worked, recorded, and toured frequently with alto saxophonist and composer John Zorn. His compositions range from free and collective unison works to funk, fusion, rock, and reggae. Baron's also recorded in trios with Enrico Pieranunzi and Marc Johnson, and with Charlie Haden and Fred Hersch. Baron's done sessions on JMT and Soul Note. He has dates available on CD. —*Ron Wynn*

DAN BARRETT

b. Dec. 14, 1955, Pasadena, CA
Brass, trombone / Swing
Another of the contemporary swing stylists on the Concord roster, Dan Barrett has an impressive command of the trombone and plays in the warm, smooth, and humorous style of the pre-bebop era. His big tone, relaxed phrasing, and fluid approach can be heard on both his dates and on those dates that feature a quintet he co-led with Howard Alden. Barrett began playing trombone as a teen under the supervision of music teacher Ken Owen. He became a professional in high school, and visited Europe in the late '70s to play at the Breda Jazz Festival in Holland. Barrett and Alden met in the early '80s, and discussed their mutual admiration for swing and big band music. Barrett moved to New York and began playing with the Widespread Depression Orchestra in 1983, working at clubs such as Eddie Condon's and Jimmy Ryan's. Alden had also moved to New York and they later formed a

band using several Buck Clayton arrangements, as well as material written for the John Kirby band in the '30s. Barrett kept playing in New York clubs with musicians such as Scott Hamilton, Doc Cheatham, and Benny Goodman. Both he and Alden were later in an orchestra led by Clayton. Barrett made several international tours in the late '80s and the '90s. He visited Europe and Japan for festival dates and club appearances, and worked with Dick Hyman, Flip Phillips, Kenny Davern, and many others. Barrett has several sessions available on Concord CDs, both as a leader and with Alden. — *Ron Wynn*

★ **Strictly Instrumental** / Jun. 1987 / Concord Jazz 4331
To some extent, I would say the writing on this album inhibits the performances, which are neat, but are seldom blessed with abandon. Individually, pianist Dick Wellstood and trombonist Dan Barrett are the stars. To have theme statements made by trombone again is very welcome indeed. On "Old Fashioned Love" there is a kind of Jimmie Lunceford feeling, although here he does not have Trummy Young's impulsive attack. He is at his best using his plunger on "Strictly Instrumental," especially after Wellstood, tiring of too much politeness, breaks out with vigorous play. Significantly, too, this is the longest track; all the others are about three minutes long, as though they are making 78s, a throwback echoed by the Five Pennies' touches in some of the writing. "Sleep" is also energized by Wellstood's abandon. Warren Vaché (cornet) does not get much solo space, but Howard Alden (guitar) gets a lot. He has a tendency to enter a little diffidently and to let the pulse drop. Although he builds from zero to a firmer statement, this is momentarily disconcerting, particularly in this kind of band context. He has excellent, subtle ideas and good tone, but does not bear down and swing as hard as, say, Scott Hamilton's Chris Flory. These reservations aside, this is an enjoyable album and a very promising debut. — *Stanley Dance*, Jazz Times

RAY BARRETTO

b. Apr. 29, 1929, Brooklyn, NY
Composer, conga, percussion, bandleader / Latin jazz, world fusion
A legend among Latin jazz musicians and fans, Ray Barretto helped popularize the conga in jazz, salsa, and other Latin styles, and in R&B and rock. He's arguably the most recorded Latin musician of all time, with numerous recordings, as either a leader or a session player, from the '50s through the '90s. While not quite a polyrhythmic dynamo like Mongo Santamaria or rhythmic innovator like Chano Pozo, Barretto has displayed remarkable flexibility, foresight, and tremendous accompaniment skills, and is a superb soloist and first-class talent scout.

He began on conga while in the army stationed in Germany. When he returned to America, Barretto began working with New York jazz musicians. His first major job was with Eddie Bonnemere's Latin Jazz Combo. After working with Jose Curbelo, Barretto joined Tito Puente, replacing Mongo Santamaria. He stayed in Puente's band for four years, but also did R&B and jazz session work, playing on singles and working with Red Garland, Gene Ammons, and Lou Donaldson in the late '50s. Barretto made his recording debut as a leader in the early '60s on a Riverside session. *Pachanga with Barretto* featured arrangements by Hector Rivera. Barretto later took many of the same musicians and established his own band. He recorded with Kenny Burrell, Freddie Hubbard, and Cal Tjader during the '60s, while cutting albums on Riverside and on Tico for the Latin market. Barretto scored a crossover hit with the single "El Watusi." He helped modernize the charanga style by incorporating brass into his band. Barretto's Tico LPs blended traditional Latin sounds, jazz improvisation, and even pop and rock covers, such as his version of "If I Had a Hammer." He subsequently recorded for United Artists before joining Fania in 1967.

Barretto eventually became music director of the all-star lineup known as the Fania All Stars. They became quite controversial during their heyday, when proponents praised them for introducing pop and rock audiences to Latin jazz and pop, and detractors labelled them Latin muzak. At one point, the group featured Barretto, Willie Colon, band leader Johnny Pacheco, and vocalists Celia Cruz, Cheo Feliciano, Hector Lavoe, and Ismael Rivera. Barretto remained with that group into the '80s. They sold out shows at Madison Square Garden in the '70s, teamed with jazz-fusion stars like Jan Hammer and Billy Cobham and Afropop instrumentalist Manu Dibango, and performed with special guests such as Kris Kristofferson, Rita Coolidge, Stephen Stills, Weather Report, and Steel Pulse. They were even on Columbia as a group, while the members retained separate pacts with other labels.

Barretto's '60s albums included everything from film soundtracks to soul-flavored cuts and two-trumpet conjuntos, as well as straight bebop and Latin jazz. Barretto worked with George Benson, the Average White Band, and the Rolling Stones in the '70s, as well as the Fania All Stars, continuing to update and expand his Latin base. He experimented with a three-trumpet frontline and brought emerging, fresh performers, such as vocalists Ruben Blades and Tito Allen and bassists Andy Gonzalez and Dave Perez, into his band. He was nominated for a Grammy for his '75 album, *Barretto*, and other '70s LPs, *The Other Road* and *Indestructible*, were heavily praised. Barretto headed a large jazz-rock, instrumental pop, and Latin aggregation while recording for Atlantic. He made albums with two trumpets and saxophonists, Blades's vocals, and a trombonist. The Crusaders produced one Barretto album, and Joe Sample and Wilton Felder also played on it. Barretto's albums such as *Rican! Struction* featured adventurous arrangements and blazing, freewheeling solos and rhythms.

Barretto won many honors during the '70s. He was voted top conga player by *Latin New York* magazine in 1975, 1976, and 1980, and Musician of the Year in 1977 and 1980. Barretto remained in the spotlight during the '80s. His CTI LP, *La Cuna*, with Tito Puente, Charlie Palmieri, and Joe Farrell, among others, was hailed as a Latin jazz masterpiece and was also a good seller (despite the fact it had been withheld for nearly two years). He received another Grammy nomination and continued introducing fresh faces, among them vocalists Willie Torres, Cali Aleman, and Ray Babu. Barretto was music director of the "Bravissimo" television show, and got some high-profile rock exposure when he appeared in the antiapartheid video and on the album "Sun City."

He hasn't slowed down in the '90s, with recent albums issued by Messidor and Concord Picante, as well as others on Latin labels. His contributions to Latin jazz, jazz, and popular music are immeasurable. Barretto currently has a few titles available on American jazz labels on CD; many more can be obtained through Latin specialty stores. — *Ron Wynn*

Carnaval / i. 1962 / Fantasy 24713
Whether playing salsa, Latin jazz, or R&B, Ray Barretto has long been perhaps the most versatile conga player ever. *Carnaval* presents his earliest recordings as a leader and contains both extended jams and structured dance cuts. No matter the setting, Barretto lays down spicy beats and accents, sometimes driving his band, other times stretching out cuts into exciting rhythm dialogs. If you've been disappointed by recent Barretto dates that have seemed subdued, these are the cuts that established his reputation and showed a Latin music superstar was emerging. — *Ron Wynn*

Swing La Moderna & Los Cueros / i. 1964 / Tico

Soul Drummer / i. 1967 / Fania

★ **Other Road, The** / 1973 / Fania 00448
With Billy Cobham on drums and Arthur Webb adding lilting flute inflections, this album was a conscious attempt by Ray Barretto to overstep the merely ethnic appeal. With a nod to old times on "Round Midnight" (which features an intriguing arrangement by Dick Mesa), a journey into the more electronic sounds of tomorrow on "Oracion (The Prayer)," and a rock-energized tune like "Lucretia the Cat,"

the album contains an unusual variety of material. The final jam, "Abidjan Revisited," replete with south-of-the-border vocal refrains, is the album's most straightahead Latin tune. The presence of Cobham is most intriguing. His parents are from Panama, and his playing reveals none of the slam-bang rock flourishes for which he's famous. Surprisingly (or really not so surprisingly), it is most relaxed and swinging, blending beautifully with the timbales, congas, and bongos. —*Ray Townley,* Down Beat

Que Viva la Musica / **i.** 1982 / Salsa 00427

La Cuna / **i.** 1982 / CTI 9002

Live in New York / **i.** 1992 / Messidor 115950
Recent release by Messidor of still dynamic Ray Barretto heading a group for live New York concert. He ranks alongside Mongo Santamaria for consistency, staying power, and impact in both Latin and jazz circles, and his conga playing and presence drive a band like almost no other. —*Ron Wynn*

Ancestral Messages / **i.** 1993 / COJ
Veteran Latin jazzman Ray Barretto keeps going, going, going. He has recorded over 40 albums and in 1989 won a Grammy for Best Tropical Latin performance (with Celia Cruz). His latest release, *Ancestral Messages,* swings brightly, propelled by a front line of Young Lions and Barretto's steady conga rhythms. Barretto and New World Spirit work magic with Benny Golson's "Killer Joe," the 1931 tune "Beautiful Love," and the title tune by Barretto. On "Song for Chano," Barretto pays tribute to the famous Cuban conguero. All the cuts display a well-integrated sound, with the focus on team spirit rather than extended solo work. —*Marcela Breton,* Jazz Times

Hard Hands / Charly 127
A '68 album with Barretto in the midst of his most productive period. He'd made inroads into pop and jazz markets and was a dominant figure on the Latin jazz and salsa circuit. The album not only provided the great conga player and percussionist with a nickname, it yielded the hit single "Abidjan" and also brought personnel changes. Joseph Roman replaced Rene Lopez on trumpet (he'd been drafted) and Tony Fuentes joined the group on bongos. —*Ron Wynn*

BILL BARRON (Barron Jr., William)

b. Mar. 27, 1927, Philadelphia, PA, **d.** Sep. 21, 1989
Tenor and soprano saxophone, flute, composer / Hard bop
A sorely underrated and underrecorded tenor and soprano saxophonist and composer, Bill Barron's sturdy tone, resourceful style, and approach have adapted to bandleaders ranging from Jimmy Heath to Cecil Taylor. Barron was a careful player whose solos often seemed to develop slowly, but would suddenly explode and intensify in approach and pace. The brother of pianist Kenny Barron, he worked in Philadelphia with Heath and Red Garland before moving to New York in 1958. Barron recorded and played with Taylor and Philly Joe Jones, and co-formed a band with Ted Curson. He worked with various bebop and hard bop groups in the '60s and '70s, while also directing the Muse Jazz Workshop of the Children's Museum in Brooklyn and teaching at City College of New York. Barron became chairman of the music department at Wesleyan University in 1984. He's recorded for Savoy, Audiophile, and Muse, among others, and currently has some sessions available on CD. —*Ron Wynn*

Tenor Stylings of Bill Barron, The / Feb. 21, 1961 / Savoy 12160

Hot Line / Mar. 31, 1962 / Savoy 1160
Tremendous two-tenor hard bop and blues set from the early '60s, matching Bill Barron and Booker Ervin. The ringer on the date is drummer Andrew Cyrille, light-years away from the music that would make him a rhythm institution years later. This was reissued on CD in 1986. —*Ron Wynn*

Motivation / 1972 / Savoy 12303

Jazz Caper / Aug. 1978 / Muse 5235

★ **Variations in Blue** / Aug. 23-24, 1984 / Muse 5306
A 1983 quintet set and fine release by Bill Barron. He plays in a familiar, warm manner, and is able to shift either into a more animated pace or to move into an interpretive, somber ballad style with ease. Steady, consistent contributions from trumpeter Jimmy Owens, pianist Kenny Barron, bassist Ray Drummond, and drummer Ben Riley. —*Ron Wynn*

Next Plateau, The / Mar. 1987 / Muse 5368

Nebulae / **i.** Aug. 1988 / Savoy 1184
Good, frequently fiery quartet date with trumpeter Ted Curson always threatening to break out of the harmonic framework, and Barron managing to interact with him, then solo in a totally different fashion. Bassist Jimmy Garrison also plays with a lot less abandon than he would later in the Coltrane quartet. —*Ron Wynn*

KENNY BARRON (Kenneth Barron)

b. 1943, Philadelphia, PA
Piano, composer / Hard bop
One of jazz's most flexible, tasteful, and swinging pianists, Kenny Barron has done everything from R&B to Afro-Latin, with plenty of bebop, combo, trio, and large group sessions in between. His solos and accompaniment are disciplined, energetic, and creative. He doesn't play in a flashy or flamboyant manner, but never fails to add something significant to any situation. Barron began playing piano at age 12, and was later in Mel Melvin's R&B orchestra. He worked with Philly Joe Jones, Jimmy Heath, and Yusef Lateef in the late '50s and early '60s, then moved to New York and began regular Five Spot appearances with James Moody in 1961. Dizzy Gillespie added him to his group on Moody's recommendation, and they toured Europe and North America during Barron's early- and mid-'60s stint. Barron played, for a short while, with Stanley Turrentine, and worked in several groups with Freddie Hubbard in the late '60s. He worked with Lateef again from 1971 to 1975, though he spent part of 1974 with Buddy Rich's sextet. Barron was in a group led by Ron Carter from 1976 until 1980, and was a co-founder of the Monk repertory band, Sphere, with Charlie Rouse in the early '80s. Barron made several impressive albums in the '80s and '90s in various contexts. He teamed with Stan Getz on his final sessions in 1992. He's also been an active jazz educator, and was appointed to the faculty of Rutgers in 1973. —*Ron Wynn*

Sunset at Dawn / Apr. 2, 1973 / Muse 6014

Peruvian Blue / Mar. 14, 1974 / Muse 5044
A more experimental, diverse album than Barron's made in quite some time. On this '74 date he plays in varied settings and alternates the size and personnel according to the song. There are solos, duos, tunes with bass and drums, then one with multiple percussion. Barron's playing has grown since then, but his albums, while beautifully played, aren't anywhere as unusual. —*Ron Wynn*

Lucifer / Apr. 28, 1975 / Muse 5070

Golden Lotus / Apr. 4, 1980 / Muse 5220
Solid 1980 session with the always vibrant, challenging pianist Kenny Barron and the underrated saxophonist John Stubblefield in fiery form. Steve Nelson began generating interest in vibes with his playing on this session. It has been reissued on CD. —*Ron Wynn*

At the Piano / Feb. 13, 1981 / Xanadu 188

Spiral / Jun. 21, 1982 / Eastwind 709

Green Chimneys / Jul. 9, 1983 / Criss Cross 1008
Fine trio date, as Barron, bassist Buster Williams, and drummer Ben Riley prove you can inject life into warhorses and constantly played standards. They recorded this for the Criss Cross label in Holland. —*Ron Wynn*

○ **1 + 1 + 1** / Apr. 23-24, 1984 / Blackhawk 506
1+1+1 presents pianist Kenny Barron in the company of either Michael Moore or Ron Carter, two of the world's finest bassists. Both are superb partners who provide such self-

sufficient harmonic and rhythmic support that additional instrumentation would seem superfluous. . . . When Carter starts to walk under Barron's dancing right hand on the former's "United Blues," the resultant groove is temporal perfection. Throughout the remainder of a program of popular and jazz standards that covers the range of tempos, that kind of secure momentum is maintained. The repertoire itself is broad-ranging, within mainstream parameters, and includes two Duke Ellington numbers as well as one each by Dave Brubeck and John Coltrane. Since, melodically, Kenny Barron is the descendant of Charlie Parker and Bud Powell, stylistic juxtapositions provide such interesting moments as a strangely Thelonious Monkish harmonization of Ellington's "C Jam Blues" and swift, Bird-like single-line right-hand phrasing on his piquant "Prelude to a Kiss." *—A. David Franklin,* Cadence

Autumn in New York / Dec. 14, 1984 / Uptown 2726

○ **Scratch** / Mar. 11, 1985 / Enja 4092

Here pianist Kenny Barron takes on a too-infrequent lead date with two of Europe's leading lights (pith-'n-vinegar English bassist Dave Holland and jewelled-movement Swiss drummer Daniel Humair), and the sparks fly! These three override nation, convention, and barline en route to etching an album of rare brilliance. The title tune (Barron penned four specifically for these never-met gentlemen) smacks more of deviltry than mischievousness as Halloween hobgoblins. "Third Eye" also flashes fleet octaves and mercurial pedal points, integrating the drum kit amid the poised phrases (Humair flicks his neural synapses as quickly as his wrists). Both shift madcap flights with Mephisthophelean ostinati, while "And Then Again," a traditional bop blues, finds Barron flying free yet rooted, and Holland lean and potent. What time! Carmen Lundy's profound and pretty "Quiet Times" gives a welcome stretch. Barron's solo to Abdullah Ibrahim is the most apropos and touching of tributes. *—Fred Bouchard,* Jazz Times

Two as One / i. 1986 / Red 123214

Live at Fat Tuesday's / Jan. 15-16, 1988 / Enja 5071

Barron stretches out and plays both flashy and easy, hot and cool, on this '88 set cut at Fat Tuesday's in New York. Bassist Cecil McBee and drummer Victor Lewis drive the rhythms a bit harder than the Riley/Drummond team, while Eddie Henderson and John Stubblefield on trumpet and tenor sax add some welcome intensity and contrasting solo voices. *—Ron Wynn*

Rhythm-a-Ning / Sep. 3, 1989 / Candid 79044

★ **Live at Maybeck Recital Hall—Vol. 10** / Dec. 3, 1990 / Concord Jazz 4466

Invitation / Dec. 20, 1990 / Criss Cross 1044

○ **Quickstep** / Feb. 18, 1991 / Enja 79669

Kenny Barron Quintet. Composer Barron's best group effort. "Big Girls" is a big composition. *—Michael G. Nastos*

Lemuria-Seascape / 1991 / Candid 79508

The Barron/Drummond/Riley trio step forward into the '90s and churn out another impressive collection; this one contains several either Barron or group originals rather than tons of standards. Exacting, carefully constructed, and consistently brilliant playing all around. *—Ron Wynn*

Sambao / i. 1993 / PolyGram 514472

Pianist Kenny Barron has mastered samba rhythm and concept over many years. Here Barron has a fresh go with native sons of Brazil, guitarist Toninho Horta and bassist Nico Assumpcao, and flexible percussionists Victor Lewis and Mino Cinelu (whose surefooted bahiano "Yalele," lightly paced and vocalized, is the only non-Barron piece of the session). One of Barron's catchy originals, "Bacchanal," dates back to Sonny Fortune's *Serengeti Minstrel* (Atlantic, 1977); its tight circles of changes flash by as smooth as glass. Refreshing, delicate, yet with a kick, the champagne cocktails of samba we've come to expect from Barron in small doses are the whole party here. *—Fred Bouchard,* Jazz Times

GARY BARTZ (Gary Lee Bartz)

b. Sep. 26, 1940, Baltimore, MD

Alto and soprano saxophone, composer / Hard bop

An animated, soulful, and surging alto saxophonist when motivated, Gary Bartz has sometimes made fans and critics wonder about him by recording dubious material. But he regrouped in the '80s, and returned to the aggressive hard bop and straight jazz dates that earned him a reputation as one of the better alto players during the '60s and '70s. Bartz learned soprano sax at age 11, and played in his father's jazz club in Baltimore as a teen. He attended Juilliard for two years, and worked with players such as Grachan Moncur III and Lee Morgan. Bartz made his professional debut with Abbey Lincoln and Max Roach in the mid '60s, and was in Art Blakey's Jazz Messengers in 1965 and 1966. He formed the NTU Troop in 1967, and played with Blue Mitchell while recording with McCoy Tyner, Charles Tolliver, and Roach. Bartz would record and play periodically with Tyner from the late '60s until the late '70s. He played with Miles Davis in 1970 and 1971, recorded with Woody Shaw and Pharoah Sanders in the early '70s, and made his own albums. Bartz toured Europe in 1973, and recorded with Lee Konitz and Jackie McLean. He also made a children's album and had an ill-fated flirtation with fusion in the late '70s. Bartz also did some television scores. His '80s dates became more selective and focused. Bartz has recorded for Milestone, Prestige, Steeplechase, Capitol, and Candid, among others. Currently, he has a couple of selections available on CD. *—Ron Wynn and Michael G. Nastos*

○ **Another Earth** / Jun. 19, 1968 / Milestone 9018

The album that brought alto saxophonist Gary Bartz close to stardom in the late '60s. It has lengthy songs, intense, sometimes dramatic solos, and a guest spot from Pharoah Sanders. When he turned in a less challenging direction in the early '70s, many were puzzled and disappointed. *—Ron Wynn*

Home / Mar. 30, 1969 / Milestone 9027

○ **Libra** / May 31, 1969+Jun. 15, 1967 / Milestone 9006

Excellent compositions and playing in a mainstream mode. Features Kenny Barron on piano and Jimmy Owens on trumpet. This is the more lyrical side of Bartz. *—Michael G. Nastos*

Harlem Bush Music: Taifa / Nov. 19+23, 1970 / Milestone 9031

Altissimo / i. Jul. 1974 / Nippon Phillips 5102

○ **I've Known Rivers and Other Bodies** / Jul. 7, 1974 / Prestige 66001

Gary Bartz is a hard-driving, swinging player out of the Jackie McLean tradition who came up with groups led by McCoy Tyner and Miles Davis. His almost spiritual dedication to his music, drawn in part from these associations, is a constant and underlying presence in what he does. *I've Known Rivers* is the NTU Troop's complete performance (with some editing) at the 1973 Montreux Jazz Festival. Side one and two of the double-disc package, in fact, are totally uncut. The first two sides are non-stop music beginning with the blues "Majick Song," Bartz's device for freeing the audience from any evil thoughts they may have brought with them, and evolves naturally through "Zote," "Jujuman," "Baptist," "Feeling," and "Mama's Soul." "Jujuman," for example, is based on John Coltrane's "Love Supreme" theme, while "Feeling" finds drummer Howard King and pianist Hubert Eaves in a rock groove. "Rivers," which opens side three, is based on a Langston Hughes poem, and the melody is beautiful. Bartz's vocal, his best, is warm and infectious. *I've Known Rivers and Other Bodies* is music for everybody; happy, honest, and exciting. It is a celebration. *—Herb Nolan,* Down Beat

Reflections of Monk / i. Nov. 1988 / Steeplechase 1248

★ **West 42nd Street** / Mar. 31, 1990 / Candid 79049

Another fine recent release by Gary Bartz, who seems determined not to let his reputation slip in the '90s. From burning hard bop to convincing blues with a touch of funk, this is someone with something to say, rather than another instrumentalist confused and plugging into the latest trends. —*Ron Wynn*

There Goes the Neighborhood / Nov. 11-12, 1990 / Candid 79506
Though he dismissed notions about a comeback, this '90 album was the triumphant, exuberant vehicle Gary Bartz hadn't made in quite a while. His rippling solos and dominant presence were welcome for fans who wondered if he'd squandered the potential he showed in the '60s. —*Ron Wynn*

Ode to Super / Steeple Chase 1009

PAUL BASCOMB

b. Feb. 12, 1912, Birmingham, AL, **d.** Dec. 2, 1986, Chicago, IL
Tenor saxophone / Swing, big band, soul jazz
The brother of trumpeter Dud Bascomb, Paul Bascomb was one of the swing-influenced tenor saxophonists whose honking, robust sound helped pave the way for the style that eventually became rhythm and blues. Bascomb played tenor sax with the Bama State Collegians who evolved into the Erskine Hawkins band. He remained with Hawkins for several years, occasionally working in the Count Basie orchestra during the early '40s. Bascomb left Hawkins in 1944 and co-led various bands with his brother, Dud. He led his own groups in the '50s and '60s, playing hard-driving, swing-tinged R&B, blues, and soul-jazz. Bascomb was a perennial attraction at festivals in the '70s and '80s. He recorded for Leonard Allen's United label in the early '50s. Delmark reissued these on a compilation, *Bad Bascomb*. He can also be heard on various Erskine Hawkins compilations. —*Ron Wynn and Michael G. Nastos*

★ **Bad Bascomb** / Mar. 3, 1952 / Delmark 431
Vintage honking R&B and blues sax from one of the instrumentalists who ushered in the first generation of R&B. These tracks were cut for the United label, a Black-owned company in Chicago, and are short, hot, and powerful. —*Ron Wynn*

COUNT BASIE (William Basie)

b. Aug. 21, 1904, Red Bank, NJ, **d.** Apr. 26, 1984, Hollywood, CA
Bandleader, piano / Swing, big band
An American music giant, William "Count" Basie ranks among the select handful of artists whose work embodies swing and, by extension, jazz. He may have been the greatest bandleader ever known because of his ability to set tempos for large orchestras or for small combos. He used a system of melodic leads and cues that kept things moving smoothly, enabling them to accelerate or to downshift when necessary. Basie changed the way rhythm sections accompanied soloists. His piano riffs, played in conjunction with bassist Walter Page, drummer Jo Jones, and guitarist Freddie Green, established equal emphasis on every beat as swing's foundation rhythm. Jones put a constant pulse in the high-hat cymbal rather than in the bass drum, which was an innovative, vital move, and Page's "walking" bass lines provided their own liberating component. This section practiced for hours apart from the band, and were extremely disciplined, yet conveyed a relaxed, loose eloquence.
Basie's lean, spare piano style was so concise that it was often mistaken as a subtle masking of his inability to play. He was a savvy technician who created a blues-rooted style, inserting simple, melodic phrases at strategic moments that provided comic relief and acted as transitional links to move to the next soloist. His late-period piano recordings, some done with pianists like Oscar Peterson who boasted far flashier techniques, demonstrated the fallacy of underestimating Basie's keyboard prowess. He influenced several other players, from John Lewis to Mary Lou Williams, and many self-styled "cool" musicians as well.

Basie studied piano with his mother, then got his graduate degree in practical training from James P. Johnson and Fats Waller when Basie moved to New York. By the time he was 20, Basie had toured extensively on the vaudeville circuit as a solo pianist, accompanist, and music director for blues vocalists, dancers, and comics. After getting stranded in Kansas City, he decided to stay there, and began playing organ in silent film theaters. He joined Walter Page's Blue Devils, then moved to Bennie Moten's Orchestra. After Moten's death, the band continued for a short time under Buster Moten, then Basie departed. He formed a new band with Buster Smith and some other Moten alumni, among them Jo Jones and Lester Young. They were known as the Barons of Rhythm, and began a long engagement at Kansas City's Reno Club. By 1936, they had a regular radio program and had deals with a national booking agency and with Decca. The nine-piece band was expanded, and became the Count Basie orchestra. John Hammond, the famed talent scout and producer, heard them on his car radio, quickly went to a live engagement, and eventually got the orchestra a recording deal. Hammond encouraged Basie to do a national tour.
By the end of the '30s, they were established stars, thanks to anthems such as "One O'Clock Jump," "Jumpin' at the Woodside," and "Taxi War Dance." The orchestra had Young and Herschel Evans on tenor saxes, Buck Clayton and, shortly after, Harry Edison on trumpets, plus a superb rhythm section. They were dominant through the '40s, but in 1950 Basie suffered a money crunch and had to disband. He kept going for two years with six-to-nine-piece groups, featuring musicians such as Clark Terry, Buddy DeFranco, Serge Chaloff, and Buddy Rich. He reorganized the big band in 1952, and began the rigorous recording and touring schedule he maintained almost faithfully until the end, to keep the orchestra intact and active.
Among Basie's sidemen during his last three decades were top jazz musicians such as trumpeters Thad Jones and Joe Newman; tenors Frank Foster, Frank Wess (who helped introduce the flute into jazz), Eddie "Lockjaw" Davis, and Jimmy Forrest; trombonist Al Grey; and drummers Sonny Payne, Rufus "Speedy" Jones, and Butch Miles. Vocalist Joe Williams was also a member of the orchestra. The Basie orchestra toured Europe for the first time in 1954, starting what became a tradition. Unlike Art Blakey, Basie was not celebrated for the fact that a fair number of great young players found their voices while in the Basie orchestra. He issued countless recordings on various labels, heading the band and backing singers like Sarah Vaughan, Tony Bennett, and Frank Sinatra. After his death in 1984, first trumpeter Thad Jones took over the reins. Then, longtime saxophone section member, composer, and arranger Frank Foster took over. Basie alumni have also reunited periodically for concerts and tours as the Countsmen. —*Ron Wynn with Dan Morgenstern*

★ **Complete Roulette Live Recordings of Count Basie and His Orchestra (1958-1962), The** / Mosaic 135
Count Basie is one jazz musician who was amply recorded throughout his career and has been the subject of numerous domestic and foreign reissue lines. Yet Mosaic has managed to release Count Basie material in a valuable fashion. This eight-disc set contains Basie recordings for the Roulette label from 1958 to 1962. It is the first of a two-part series covering his full Roulette output. These are live recordings; the studio sessions are coming via their own set. They were recorded in Miami at Birdland and in Sweden. The menu includes the familiar standards "One O'Clock Jump," "Lil' Darlin'," "Moten Swing," and "Jumpin' at the Woodside." There are plenty of blues, relaxed swingers, and superb vocals provided by a roster of singers that includes Joe Williams, Sarah Vaughan, Jon Hendricks, and O.C. Smith. The regular lineup is augmented on the Swedish sessions by guest instrumentalists trumpeter Benny Bailey and trombonist Ake Persson. There is nothing revolutionary about this music, but its consistency and celebratory fiber remain impressive through every disc. Basie's band contained such musical veterans as Frank Wess, Billy Mitchell, Al Grey,

Freddie Green, Marshall Royal, and Sonny Payne. They were pros who played every night with wit, humor, precision, and charm; they could truly play the blues and never wasted energy or emotion. Their songs were short, steady, and always delightful.

While eight discs is a lot of time for one band no matter how great (and they do frequently repeat some songs like "One O'Clock Jump" and 'Lil' Darlin' ") the set provides a chance to replicate the experience of life on the road for a touring band. Basie fanatics probably already have this and are eagerly awaiting the follow-up; those who are not should still get this set. —*Ron Wynn*

☆ **Basie's Basement** / Oct. 23, 1929-Dec. 13, 1932 / Bluebird 61065

With Jimmy Rushing. The genesis of the Count Basie band can be heard in these recordings by Bennie Moten's Kansas City Orchestra. With Count on piano, trumpeter Hot Lips Page, tenor saxophonist Ben Webster, and such future Basieites as trombonist/guitarist Eddie Durham, baritonist Jack Washington, bassist Walter Page, and the great singer Jimmy Rushing, there are times when Moten's orchestra almost sounds like Count's. Eight selections from the 1929-1930 period are followed by eight numbers recorded at Moten's last and greatest session (December 13, 1932). Such tunes as "Moten's Swing," "Lafayette," and "Blue Room" are prime examples of early swing. —*Scott Yanow*

○ **Count Basie in Kansas City** / 1929-1932 / Camden 514

☆ **Essential Count Basie—Vols. 1 and 2** / Oct. 9, 1936-Jun. 24, 1939 / Columbia 40061

Rather than release all of Count Basie's studio recordings (as Decca recently has or as French Columbia did in two large LP sets over a decade ago), CBS has put together three samplers that contain some (but not all) of the essential Basie recordings from the 1936-1939 period. This first volume has Lester Young's great solo on 1936's "Lady Be Good," the classics "Rock-a-Bye Basie" and "Taxi War Dance," and fine examples of the Basie orchestra throughout 1939. —*Scott Yanow*

★ **Super Chief** / i. Oct. 9, 1936-Jul. 24, 1942 / Columbia 31224

This very interesting two-LP set has quite a variety of material from the 1936-1942 period. It includes a few airchecks, small group sessions led by Mildred Bailey, Harry James, Glenn Harriman, and Teddy Wilson (all feature Basie sidemen); and some studio sessions by both the Count's orchestra and small groups from his three big bands. Along with the rarities is the very first post-Bennie Moten Count Basie session, a quintet date (under the pseudonym of Jones-Smith Incorporated) from 1936 that served as the recording debut of Lester Young; "Lady Be Good" is one of his greatest solos. This two-LP set is highly recommended, if you can find it. — *Scott Yanow*

○ **At the Chatterbox: 1937** / Jan. 10, 1937-Feb. 12, 1937 / Jazz Archives 16

This historic LP features broadcasts by Count Basie's orchestra in Pittsburgh during its first visit to the East Coast. The music is primarily head arrangements and charts borrowed from other bands. Two of the soloists (trumpeter Carl "Tatti" Smith and violinist/guitarist Claude Williams) would eventually be replaced. It is fascinating to hear what this orchestra sounded like at this early stage. Tenor saxophonist Lester Young and trumpeter Buck Clayton (along with Basie) quickly emerge as the most impressive soloists. —*Scott Yanow*

☆ **Best of Count Basie, The** / i. 1937-Feb. 2, 1939 / MCA 4050

This two-LP set contains the best of Basie's Decca years, 24 prime selections including the five mentioned in the review for *The Complete Decca Recordings*. A fine general collection, although most collectors will opt for the much more complete three-CD package. —*Scott Yanow*

★ **Complete Decca Recordings (1937-1939), The** / 1937-Feb. 4, 1939 / GRP 36112

This magnificent three-CD set has the first 63 recordings by Count Basie's orchestra, all of his Deccas. The consistency is

remarkable (with not more than two or three turkeys), and the music is the epitome of swing. With soloists such as Lester Young and Herschel Evans on tenors, trumpeters Buck Clayton and Harry "Sweets" Edison, the great blues singer Jimmy Rushing, and that brilliant rhythm section of Basie, guitarist Freddie Green, bassist Walter Page, and drummer Jo Jones, the music is timeless. It's all here: "One O'Clock Jump," "Sent for You Yesterday," "Blue and Sentimental," "Jumpin' at the Woodside," "Jive at Five," and many others. This is the first Count Basie collection to acquire; it should be in every jazz collection. —*Scott Yanow*

☆ **Rock-A-Bye Basie—Vol. 2** / i. Aug. 9, 1938-Mar. 7, 1940

These broadcasts (all but one selection are from 1938 1939) capture Count Basie's orchestra live from the Famous Door. This CD contains 24 performances, a few of which are incomplete or poorly recorded. However, the enthusiastic solos of Lester Young, fellow tenors Herschel Evans and Buddy Tate, trumpeters Buck Clayton and Harry "Sweets" Edison, and Basie himself are fresh and creative, and the ensembles are consistently swinging. These are the best pre-World War II live recordings of the Count Basie orchestra, and are well worth acquiring. —*Scott Yanow*

☆ **Count Basie at the Famous Door (1938-1939)** / 1938-1939 / Jazz Archives 41

These 15 selections are taken from live broadcasts (mostly in 1938) from the Famous Door, capturing Count Basie's men stretching out and really jamming on the material. Since all of the performances on this LP are also included on the CD *Rock-A-Bye Basie*, that set is preferred. —*Scott Yanow*

○ **Golden Years Vol. 1 (1938), The** / 1938 / EPM 5502

○ **Golden Years Vol. 2 (1938), The** / 1938 / EPM 5510

○ **Essential Count Basie—Vol. 2** / Aug. 4, 1939-May 31, 1940 / Columbia 40835

A fine sampler of the 1939-1940 Count Basie orchestra with such classic performances as "Dickie's Dream," "Lester Leaps In," and "Tickle Toe." Lester Young and fellow tenor Buddy Tate, trumpeters Buck Clayton and Harry Edison, and trombonist Dickie Wells all have their chances to star; they can't help swinging with that light, but solid, Basie rhythm section. Count's Columbia recordings deserve to be reissued in full (with all of the alternate takes), but until CBS gets around to it this is a good introduction to that period. — *Scott Yanow*

○ **Lester Young / Charlie Christian (1939-1940)** / 1939-1940 / Jazz Archives 42

Despite the billing, the majority of this LP features the Count Basie orchestra during 1939-1940 with a generous amount of solo space given to the great Lester Young; Harry Edison, Buddy Tate, and Buck Clayton also have their spots during these high-quality performances. Actually, the most interesting selections are taken from a rehearsal during which Basie, Young, Clayton, and the Count's rhythm section collaborated with Benny Goodman and guitarist Charlie Christian. The performances look toward bop and cool jazz and are the epitome of small group swing. —*Scott Yanow*

☆ **Blues by Basie** / i. 1939-1950 / Columbia 901

Because Count Basie streamlined his piano style down to the bare basics, it is often forgotten how strong a pianist he could be when he was inspired. This intriguing LP features live performances taken from a variety of settings and time periods (dating from 1941-1967), all of which put the focus on Basie's piano. Not too surprisingly most of the numbers are blues but Basie is in consistently fine form and there is enough variety to keep one's interest throughout this excellent set. —*Scott Yanow*

☆ **Essential Count Basie—Vol. 3** / Aug. 8, 1940-Apr. 10, 1941 / Columbia 44150

The third and thus far final volume in a sampler series that picks out some of the high points of Count Basie's 1939-1942 period on Columbia. Lester Young's departure in December of 1940 robbed the orchestra of their top soloist, but the band still outswung all of its competitors and the personnel was consistently outstanding. Coleman Hawkins's guest appearances on "9:20 Special" and "Feedin' the Bean" round out this enjoyable set, but when is Columbia going to reissue all of their Count Basie recordings instead of always recycling the same ones? —*Scott Yanow*

○ **Count Basie (1940-1941)** / **i.** Nov. 1940-Apr. 1941 / Classics 623

☆ **Basie's Best** / **i.** Jan. 21, 1942-Feb. 4, 1946 / Charly 1024
Not his best but a nice sampler of Basie during 1942-46 with 10 studio recordings including a remake of "One O'Clock Jump," the classic "It's Sand Man," "Avenue C," two features for tenorman Illinois Jacquet ("The King" and "Rambo"), and the hard-swinging "Taps Miller" among the more memorable selections. Although Lester Young was gone, such distinctive soloists as trumpeter Harry Edison, trombonist Dickie Wells and tenors Buddy Tate, Don Byas, and Jacquet helped fill in the gap. —*Scott Yanow*

☆ **Count Basie V Discs—Vol. 2: 1943-1945** / **i.** Jun. 1943-May 14, 1945 / Jazz Society 506
This second volume of V Discs almost reaches the great heights of the first LP. Covering a slightly wider span of time, the Basie band is heard during one of its peak periods, the otherwise poorly documented war years. The music is consistently exciting and tops much of what Basie would record during the following five years. —*Scott Yanow*

○ **Basie Special, The** / **i.** Apr. 14, 1944-Jul. 28, 1946 / Everybody's 3004
Dating from 1944-1946, this LP set of formerly rare excerpts from radio broadcasts puts the focus on a lesser-known version of Count Basie's orchestra. The soloists, as usual, are top-notch (particularly trumpeters Harry Edison and Joe Newman, trombonist Dickie Wells, and the tenors of Buddy Tate and Lucky Thompson) and the arrangements, although not yet influenced by bebop, are fairly modern for the period. Much of the material is obscure and the swing is irresistible, making this an excellent release of mid '40s Basie. —*Scott Yanow*

☆ **Beaver Junction** / May 27, 1944-Nov. 12, 1947 / Vintage Jazz Classics 1018
A worthy CD full of Basie rarities including unissued and alternate versions of V Discs and two radio broadcasts; the one from 1944 features drummer Buddy Rich filling in for the recently drafted Jo Jones. Rich had so much fun being part of the swing machine that when Basie handed him a blank check for his services, he tore it up! The music throughout this CD is equally fun for the listener. —*Scott Yanow*

☆ **Count Basie V Discs—Vol. 1: 1944-1945** / **i.** May 27, 1944-Jan. 11, 1945 / Jazz Society 505
Among the very best recordings cut by Count Basie's orchestra in the 1940s are the V Discs they recorded exclusively for distribution to people in the service. The first of two volumes, the 11 performances on this LP are quite inspired, with Harry Edison, Dickie Wells, Lester Young (during the half when he is present), Buddy Tate, and Lucky Thompson taking heated solos. This version of "Taps Miller" is a real classic, but there are no weak cuts on this excellent set. —*Scott Yanow*

☆ **And His Orchestra (1944)** / 1944 / Hindsight 224
Taken from radio broadcasts, this LP is comprised of live performances including some fine vocals by Jimmy Rushing and Thelma Carpenter, two numbers that feature guest Artie Shaw on clarinet, and a well-showcased Lester Young (temporarily back with Basie) on "Jumpin' at the Woodside" and "Every Tub." Considering the high quality of the Basie orchestra during the war years, virtually every broadcast of theirs is worth acquiring. —*Scott Yanow*

☆ **Kansas City Style** / **i.** Feb. 1, 1945-Sep. 2, 1954 / Giants of Jazz 1004
The majority of this fine LP captures the Count Basie orchestra live at an outside concert in 1954. It includes several spots for the tenors of Frank Wess and Frank Foster and ballad features for altoist Marshall Royal and trombonist Henry

Coker. Four earlier tracks are from a radio broadcast in 1945 (with one vocal by Jimmy Rushing), while two numbers are from Basie's rare and exciting appearance as a guest with Benny Goodman's 1946 orchestra. —*Scott Yanow*

☆ **Count Basie—The Orchestra and The Octet** / **i.** Jan. 9, 1946-Apr. 10, 1951 / CBS 88675
This French CBS two-LP set has 13 recordings by the 1946 edition of Count Basie's orchestra (including several features for the exciting tenor of Illinois Jacquet), 12 performances by Basie's octet in 1950 (which star trumpeter Clark Terry, clarinetist Buddy DeFranco, and tenor great Wardell Gray, among others), and Basie's first session with his new big band in 1951 (Wardell Gray's showcase "Little Pony" is considered a classic). The music throughout this twofer is consistently memorable, and the octet performances are so swinging that it makes one regret that Basie could not keep it going along with his new orchestra. —*Scott Yanow*

☆ **One Night Stand with Count Basie at the Avalon** / **i.** 1946-Oct. 1951 / Joyce 1075
This obscure Joyce LP has seven songs from a late 1946 radio broadcast by Count Basie's big band and three numbers from Basie's 1951 septet. The former finds Count's orchestra in transition, with standbys such as trumpeter Harry Edison and the classic rhythm section joined by several newcomers, most notably Duke Ellington's future tenor star Paul Gonsalves. The septet, with trumpeter Clark Terry and tenor saxophonist Wardell Gray, is in top form for three jams, making this a rare set worth the search for it. —*Scott Yanow*

○ **Brand New Wagon: Count Basie 1947** / Jan. 3, 1947-Dec. 12, 1947 / Bluebird 2292
While French RCA put out a three-LP set documenting 48 of Count Basie's recordings for that label during 1947-1950, its American counterpart just reissued 21 of those sides (all from 1947) instead on this highly enjoyable CD. Best are the octet and nonet recordings of May 20-21, but none of these tracks are weak. Trumpeter Harry "Sweets" Edison, the tenors of Paul Gonsalves and Buddy Tate, and the long underrated baritonist Jack Washington star, along with vocalist Jimmy Rushing and the rhythm section. Even during what is sometimes written off as a declining period, the Basie orchestra was near the top in quality, if not popularity. —*Scott Yanow*

☆ **Count Basie—Vols. 1-3** / **i.** Jan. 3, 1947-Feb. 2, 1950 / RCA 37053
This three-LP box set from French RCA skips around a bit and fails to give complete personnel information but it is a gem. 95% of Count Basie's studio recordings for RCA during the 1947-1950 period are included and, even during the weaker and more commercial numbers, the band always swings. There are quite a few obscure gems (Basie's orchestra was not getting much publicity during this era) including features for baritonist Jack Washington and the tenor of Paul Gonsalves, a nonet date from 1947 and Basie's octet session of Feb. 2, 1950, cut shortly after economics forced him to disband his classic orchestra. This box is becoming increasingly difficult to locate but it far exceeds anything put out thus far by its American counterpart. —*Scott Yanow*

○ **Paradise Squat** / **i.** Jul. 22, 1952-Dec. 12, 1952 / Verve 2542
In 1952, Count Basie put together his second big band after two years of work with six-to-eight-piece units. This double LP documents his recordings of that year, and it is very interesting to hear the beginnings of his second great orchestra. The soloists are mostly different from the ones he would feature during the remainder of the 1950s. The most impressive voices are the two contrasting tenors of Eddie "Lockjaw" Davis and Paul Quinichette. With new charts by Neal Hefti and Ernie Wilkins, it seems apparent that the band was on its way, even if Al Hibbler was Basie's vocalist at this point (his version of "Goin' to Chicago" sounds a bit odd). This twofer also has a pair of combo performances that are Count Basie's first matchup with pianist Oscar Peterson. —*Scott Yanow*

☆ **Count Basie/Lester Young—Live at Birdland** / i. Dec. 1952 / Jazz Panorama 1803

Lester Young sat in with his former boss Count Basie every once in awhile; this LP documents one such occasion. Young is heard on roughly half of the selections with Basie's new orchestra in late 1952 alongside such fellow tenors as soundalike Paul Quinichette and the rougher and distinctive Eddie "Lockjaw" Davis. These radio airchecks are well worth getting. —*Scott Yanow*

○ **Sixteen Men Swinging** / i. Dec. 12, 1953-Jun. 1954 / Verve 833556

The second Count Basie orchestra stabilized its sound and its personnel on the two solid sessions from 1953-1954 featured on this two-LP set. With Joe Newman and Thad Jones in the trumpet section and the two tenors of Frank Foster and Frank Wess, the band had more than its share of talented soloists, but it was the clean ensemble sound, the lightly but firmly swinging rhythm section, and the inventive and uncluttered arrangements of Ernie Wilkins and Neal Hefti that made this band a surprise success in 1954. This twofer (which includes "Blues Backstage" and "Down for the Count") has 25 examples of 1950s Basie swing. —*Scott Yanow*

○ **Count Basie Sextet** / i. 1954 / Clef 146

○ **Count Basie Big Band** / i. 1954 / Clef 148

☆ **Class of '54** / Sep. 2, 1954-Sep. 7, 1954 / Black Lion 760924

This fine CD consists of two radio airchecks from 1954, and features Count Basie with a nonet and his full orchestra. The smaller group also has trumpeter Joe Newman, trombonist Henry Coker; the tenors of Frank Wess and Frank Foster are well featured. The big-band tracks (which mostly sport Neal Hefti arrangements) find the orchestra on the brink of great success. —*Scott Yanow*

☆ **Count Basie, Lester Young & The Stars of Birdland** / Feb. 1955 / Jass 17

This live CD documents a tour by top performers who appeared regularly at Birdland. Count Basie's orchestra backs Basie alumnus Lester Young on three tracks, welcomes Stan Getz to sit in for four numbers (including an exciting version of "Little Pony"), accompanies Sarah Vaughan during eight songs, and performs seven tunes by itself, four of which feature Joe Williams (who had just recently joined the band). A historic set that will be prized by collectors. —*Scott Yanow*

☆ **Count Basie Swings, Joe Williams Sings** / i. Jul. 17, 1955-Jul. 26, 1955 / Verve 825770

Joe Williams's debut on records with the Basie orchestra was so successful in every way that the band's future was secure for the next few decades. Included on this essential set are the classic versions of "Every Day I Have the Blues," "The Comeback," "Alright Okay, You Win," "In the Evening," and "Teach Me Tonight"—songs that became so popular that audience demand forced Williams and Basie to perform them each night for the remainder of the 1950s. Highly recommended. —*Scott Yanow*

☆ **April in Paris** / Jul. 26, 1955-Jan. 5, 1956 / Verve 825575

A true classic, this studio album includes Count Basie's hit versions of "April in Paris," "Shiny Stockings," and "Corner Pocket," three tunes that have remained in the Basie band's repertoire ever since. Actually, all ten selections are very enjoyable. This exciting and, of course, swinging record is definitive of 1950s Count Basie. —*Scott Yanow*

○ **Lester Leaps In** / i. Aug. 10, 1955 / Epic 3107

★ **Swings with Joe Williams** / i. 1955 / PolyGram 825770

With Joe Williams. Simply glorious after all these years. Williams was the greatest singer in this style in 1955, at least among males. —*Ron Wynn*

○ **Basie Roars Again!** / i. 1956 / Clef 723

○ **King of Swing, The** / i. 1956 / Clef 724

○ **Basie Rides Again!** / i. 1956 / Clef 729

○ **Basie Bash** / i. 1956 / Columbia 2560

☆ **Greatest! Count Basie Plays . . . Joe Williams Sings Standards, The** / i. Apr. 28, 1956 / Verve 833774

With Joe Williams. Joe Williams never wanted to be typecast as just a blues singer, so on his second full album with Count Basie he concentrated on standards. The swinging treatments given to songs such as "Thou Swell," "My Baby Just Cares for Me," and even "Singin' in the Rain" work quite well, even if the band is confined to a mostly supporting role. —*Scott Yanow*

☆ **Count Basie in London** / Sep. 7, 1956 / Verve 833805

The original of this album's title is a bit of a mystery since actually this album was recorded live in Sweden! The Count Basie orchestra plays its usual repertoire (including "Jumpin' at the Woodside," "Shiny Stockings," and "Corner Pocket") with enthusiasm, concise solos, and typical Basie swing. Joe Williams takes a few vocals. This CD is rounded by three previously unreleased performances. —*Scott Yanow*

☆ **Count Basie at Newport** / Sep. 7, 1957 / PolyGram 833776

At the 1957 Newport Jazz Festival the music was consistently inspired and often historic. Count Basie welcomed back tenor great Lester Young and singer Jimmy Rushing for part of a very memorable set highlighted by "Boogie Woogie" and "Evenin'"; Young plays beautifully throughout and Rushing is in prime form. An exciting full-length version of "One O'Clock Jump" features Young, Illinois Jacquet, and trumpeter Roy Eldridge; the Basie band stretches out on "Swingin' at Newport"; and five previously unreleased selections (put out for the first time on this CD) include four Joe Williams vocals. A great set of music. —*Scott Yanow*

○ **Atomic Mr. Basie** / Oct. 21, 1957-Oct. 22, 1957 / Roulette 1309

Known as the Atomic album due to the cover picture of an A-Bomb exploding, this is one of the great Count Basie records, ranking with *April in Paris*. The 1957 edition of the Basie orchestra romps through "The Kid from Red Bank" (a superlative feature for its leader), "Whirly Bird," and "Lil' Darlin'" among others; everything works on this essential album. —*Scott Yanow*

Best of the Roulette Years / 1957-1962 / Roulette 97969

Compilation gathering prime Basie material from his years on Roulette, a period that includes songs cut with Lambert, Hendricks & Ross, Joe Williams, Tony Bennett, and a lineup with Thad Jones, Eddie "Lockjaw" Davis, Frank Foster, and Joe Newman in the band, among others. —*Ron Wynn*

☆ **Basie Plays Hefti** / Apr. 3, 1958-Apr. 14, 1958 / Roulette 52011

The Count Basie orchestra was in top form for this set of Neal Hefti arrangements. Hefti had been one of the main architects of the new Basie sound of the 1950s. On this memorable date, he utilizes the flute of Frank Wess prominently. "Cute" (heard here in its initial recording) became a standard. —*Scott Yanow*

☆ **Basie** / i. May 1958 / Roulette 52003

☆ **Sing Along with Basie** / May 26, 1958-Sep. 3, 1958 / Roulette 95332

The extraordinary jazz vocal group Lambert, Hendricks, and Ross had debuted in 1957 with *Sing a Song of Basie* on which they recreated the Count's orchestra with their overdubbed voices. That album was so successful that the following year they were able to actually team up with the Basie band. Frank Foster put the original head arrangements of the '30s and '40s down on paper for the orchestra, leaving space for the vocalists to recreate the original solos. The result is a colorful and swinging set. Best is a version of "Goin' to Chicago Blues" that has Joe Williams taking his original vocal while L., H. & Ross sing around him. —*Scott Yanow*

☆ **One More Time (Music from the Pen of Quincy Jones)** / Dec. 18, 1958-Jan. 24, 1959 / Roulette 97271

For this studio album from late 1958 and early 1959, the Count Basie orchestra performs ten Quincy Jones compositions; he also contributed all of the arrangements. "I Needs to Be Be'ed With," "For Lena and Lennie," and "The Midnight

Sun Never Sets" all caught on, and Jones's charts helped expand the Basie sound without altering it. An excellent CD. — *Scott Yanow*

○ **Atomic Band in Concert, The** / 1958 / Bandstand 1525

☆ **Basie Swings, Bennett Sings** / Jan. 1959 / Roulette 93899
With Tony Bennett (v). Dynamic meeting of the great singer and great band. —*Ron Wynn*

○ **Chairman of the Board** / Apr. 18-29, 1959 / Roulette 52032

○ **Basie-Eckstine** / May 22-23, 1959 / Roulette 52029

☆ **Everyday I Have the Blues** / Sep. 24, 1959 / Roulette 52033
With Joe Williams. One of Joe Williams's most rewarding recordings with Count Basie. On this set of blues-oriented material, Williams does a fine remake of "Everyday I Have the Blues" and a classic version of "Going to Chicago," but all ten selections are quite enjoyable. —*Scott Yanow*

Hits of the 50's and 60's / i. 1960 / Reprise

○ **Count Basie / Sarah Vaughan** / Apr. 19, 1960+May 15, 1960 / Roulette 52061

○ **String Along with Basie** / May 10, 1960+Sep. 1, 1960 / Roulette 52051

○ **Just the Blues** / Sep. 9, 1960 / Roulette 52054

☆ **Kansas City Suite: The Music of Benny Carter** / Sep. 1960 / Roulette 94575
These two 1960 sessions gave Benny Carter a unique chance to write a full program for Count Basie's orchestra. Arranged as a type of suite, the ten originals pay tribute to the various Kansas City clubs that were active in the 1930s when Basie was a resident. The band swings throughout as usual, with concise solos adding color to this memorable modern session. —*Scott Yanow*

☆ **First Time! The Count Meets The Duke** / Jul. 6, 1961 / Columbia 40586
This session was an impossible dream come true, the teaming up of the entire Count Basie and Duke Ellington orchestras, including the principals on joint pianos. "Take the 'A' Train," "Jumpin' at the Woodside," "Until I Met You," and everything else works on this album, and somehow the ensembles avoid sounding overcrowded. This version of "Segue in C" is the outstanding performance of a unique and highly enjoyable set. —*Scott Yanow*

○ **Basie at Birdland** / Jul. 28, 1961 / Capitol 59039
The Count Basie orchestra was very much at home at New York's Birdland in the 1950s and early '60s, frequently playing there several months a year. This spirited set has swinging versions of such Basie classics as "Segue in C," "Blues Backstage," and "Little Pony" with Jon Hendricks's guest vocal on "Whirly Bird" taking honors. —*Scott Yanow*

○ **Legend, The** / Oct. 30, 1961+Nov. 1, 1961 / Roulette 52086

○ **Count Basie in Sweden** / i. 1962 / Roulette 52099
Twelve of the better performances from an overseas gig are also available on *Basie on Sweden*, which, like Mosaic's *The Complete Roulette Live Recordings of Count Basie and His Orchestra 1959-1962*, was produced by Michael Cuscuna. Most of the charts are Frank Foster's ("Little Pony," "Backwater Blues," "Who Me?," "In a Mellotone," "Blues Backstage," and "Four, Five, Six") but also included are Neal Hefti's "Plymouth Rock" and "Splanky," Ernie Wilkins's "Peace Pipe," Freddie Green's "Corner Pocket," and Wild Bill Davis's famous reworking of "April in Paris." This abbreviated set could provide a worthwhile introduction for those not yet prepared to indulge in the larger investment. —*Jack Sohmer*, Down Beat

☆ **Count Basie and the Kansas City 7** / Mar. 21, 1962 / MCA 5656
One of Count Basie's few small group sessions of the 1960s and his best. With trumpeter Thad Jones and the tenors of Frank Foster and Eric Dixon filling in the septet, Basie is in superlative form on a variety of blues, standards, and two originals apiece from Thad Jones and Frank Wess. Small-group swing at its best. —*Scott Yanow*

☆ **Retrospective Sessions, The** / Mar. 21, 1962-1969 / IA 93512

This excellent two-LP set includes Count Basie's top small-group session of the 1960s and a "live from Las Vegas" big-band performance from 1969. The former features Basie with a septet that includes trumpeter Thad Jones and tenors Frank Foster and Eric Dixon, while the latter finds virtually all of the solo space on the Basie standards being ably taken by trumpeter Harry "Sweets" Edison and tenor saxophonist Eddie "Lockjaw" Davis (in addition to the leader). Together, these two memorable sessions contain plenty of typically swinging music in the Basie tradition. —*Scott Yanow*

Sinatra-Basie / Oct. 2-3, 1962 / Reprise 1008
Just a wonderful collaboration. Sinatra still sounds interested and dynamic. —*Ron Wynn*

Kansas City Seven / i. 1962 / Impulse 15

☆ **Ella and Basie!** / Jul. 15, 1963-Jul. 16, 1963 / Verve
Considering how often they would work together in future years, it is hard to believe that, at the time of this 1963 session, Ella Fitzgerald had never recorded with Count Basie's orchestra. Their first collaboration was a happy one with Quincy Jones providing arrangements to such swingers as "Honeysuckle Rose," "Them There Eyes" (one of two numbers played by a small group from Basie's big band), "Tea for Two," and "On the Sunny Side of the Street." Other than "Shiny Stockings," most of the repertoire isn't strictly from Basie's book, but the results are quite pleasing. —*Scott Yanow*

☆ **Basie's Beat** / Oct. 7, 1965-Feb. 15, 1967 / Verve 8687
During an era when the Count Basie orchestra was often being used as a mere prop behind other singers, this album was quite refreshing. With the exception of trombonist Richard Boone's two eccentric vocals, this is an instrumental date with arrangements provided by bandmembers past and present, and concise solos contributed by quite a few talented players. —*Scott Yanow*

○ **Our Shining Hour** / 1965 / Verve 8605

○ **Basie's Swingin', Voices Singin'** / Jun. 20-22, 1966 / ABC (Import) 570

☆ **Jazz Fest Masters—Count Basie** / Jun. 1969 / Jazz Masters 75245
If one judged them by their studio albums of the 1963-1970 period, it would seem that Count Basie's orchestra was in its decline, but this recently released live CD proves otherwise. Recorded at the 1969 New Orleans Jazz Festival, the Basie band swings such tunes as "Whirly Bird," "Corner Pocket," "Cherokee" (an Eddie "Lockjaw" Davis feature), and "April in Paris" with enthusiasm and power. A fine session. —*Scott Yanow*

○ **Swingin' the Blues** / i. 196z / Arco 111

☆ **Afrique** / Dec. 22, 1970-Dec. 23, 1970 / Doctor Jazz 39520
Possibly the most unusual album by Count Basie and certainly the most modern. For this session, Oliver Nelson arranged eight recent songs including avant-gardist Albert Ayler's "Love Flower" and Pharoah Sanders's "Japan," giving the Basie band a more contemporary setting (utilizing electric bass on half the songs), while not altering its basic sound. Nelson's "Kilimanjaro" and "Hobo Flats" are highlights of this very successful, but never repeated, "experiment." —*Scott Yanow*

☆ **Loose Walk** / Apr. 24, 1972 / Pablo 2310-928
Ironically, the earliest recording by Count Basie for Norman Granz's Pablo label is one of the most recently released. This jam session features trumpeter Roy Eldridge, trombonist Al Grey, and tenor saxophonist Eddie "Lockjaw" Davis on a set of jammable standards. The results are quite fun. —*Scott Yanow*

Basie Jam—Vols. 1-3 / Dec. 10, 1973 / Pablo 2310-718
The official start of Count Basie's decade-long association with Norman Granz's Pablo label is a bit disappointing; an all-star cast (with trumpeter Harry "Sweets" Edison, trombonist J. J. Johnson, and tenors Eddie Davis and Zoot Sims) playing one blues after another. Reasonably pleasing but

uninspired, there would be many better Basie dates. —*Scott Yanow*

○ **Bosses, The** / Dec. 11, 1973 / Pablo 709

Count Basie and an all-star band (including trumpeter Harry Edison, trombonist J. J. Johnson, and the tenors of Eddie Davis and Zoot Sims) back up veteran Kansas City blues singer Big Joe Turner on one of his better later albums. The many fine solos inspire Turner, who is in top form on such tunes as "Night Time Is the Right Time," "Wee Baby Blues," and "Roll 'Em Pete." —*Scott Yanow*

☆ **For the First Time** / May 22, 1974 / Pablo 2310-712

Throughout his career, Count Basie was modest about his own abilities as a pianist, and his success at streamlining his style to the bare essentials often made listeners underrate his playing talents. This 1974 session is a rarity; an opportunity for Basie to be featured in a trio setting (with bassist Ray Brown and drummer Louie Bellson) during which he provides enough variety to hold one's interest and enough technique to lead many to reassessing his pianistic skills. —*Scott Yanow*

Satch and Josh / Dec. 2, 1974 / Pablo 2310-722

Producer Norman Granz occasionally got carried away with the quantity of his recording projects. In 1974, he recorded a full album teaming fellow pianists Count Basie and Oscar Peterson in a rhythm quintet; little did anyone realize that this then-unique matchup would eventually result in five albums! This first one, which finds Basie doubling on organ, is one of the best. Peterson's virtuosic style somehow works very well with Basie's sparse playing, and these ten numbers really swing. —*Scott Yanow*

☆ **Last Decade, The** / i. 1974-1980 / Artistry 2-107

The well-recorded live performances on this two-LP set date from three different periods: Count Basie's pre-Pablo 1974 band with tenor great Eddie "Lockjaw" Davis, the star-studded 1977 orchestra (featuring Jimmy Forrest's tenor, trombonist Al Grey, and drummer Butch Miles) and the very solid 1980 group. Throughout, the various Basie orchestras are consistently exciting and swinging. —*Scott Yanow*

○ **Basie and Zoot** / Apr. 9, 1975 / Pablo/Fantasy

Pianist/bandleader Count Basie and tenor saxophonist Zoot Sims were beautiful and this is a fine pairing. Sims was at an age when he had caught up to the Count and the Count was hip enough to pass the baton and keep right up with him. There are no musical cliches here; the music sustains itself. John Heard's bass is a pleasure, sensitively walking itself throughout the album. Drummer Louis Bellson is near perfect, keeping the music Kansas City light and rolling, only pushing and prodding Sims and Basie with a delicate tension on "I Surrender Dear." The mark of Norman Granz's productions for Pablo was a give-and-response relationship between producer, artist, and listener, and the level remains incredibly high on the album; inventive, timeless, and classic. —*Bob Rusch*, Cadence

☆ **Fun Time: Count Basie Big Band at Montreux '75** / Jul. 19, 1975 / Pablo 2310-945

This big-band performance from the 1975 Montreux Jazz Festival introduces what could be called Count Basie's third great orchestra (although in style, it was a continuation of the second one that he formed in 1952). Trombonist Al Grey, Jimmy Forrest for tenor, and the fiery drummer Butch Miles give this early Pablo version of the band its own personality, and the Basie orchestra is in top form for a strong set. Of special note are two fine vocals by Bill Caffey, who would quickly drift into obscurity. —*Scott Yanow*

○ **Basie Jam at Montreux '75** / Jul. 19, 1975 / Pablo 2310-750

On one of the earliest and best of the Count Basie jams for Pablo, Basie sounds very happy pushing the combative trumpeter Roy Eldridge, tenor saxophonist Johnny Griffin, and vibraphonist Milt Jackson on two blues and a lengthy version of "Lester Leaps In." Plenty of sparks fly. —*Scott Yanow*

For the Second Time / Aug. 28, 1975 / Pablo 600

On Count Basie's second trio album for Pablo, he is reunited with bassist Ray Brown and drummer Louie Bellson. In addition to the expected blues, the main joy of this set is hearing Basie stretch out on such numbers as "If I Could Be with You," "On the Sunny Side of the Street," and "The One I Love," tunes he did not play much with his orchestra in this later period. —*Scott Yanow*

○ **Prime Time** / Jan. 18-20, 1977 / Pablo 2310-797

One of arranger Sammy Nestico's most enjoyable sessions for Count Basie, these eight selections (six composed by Nestico, including the title cut and "Ya Gotta Try") are performed by an inspired Basie orchestra. Tenor saxophonist Jimmy Forrest and trombonist Al Grey star among the soloists. —*Scott Yanow*

Satch and Josh ... Again / Sep. 20, 1977 / Pablo 2310-802

Recorded three years after their first full album together, this second encounter between Count Basie and Oscar Peterson on twin pianos (this time with a quartet) is as strong as the original, alternating standards with blues. Both Peterson and Basie have one number apiece on electric piano, making this album historic as well as quite musical. —*Scott Yanow*

Count Basie Meets Oscar Peterson / i. 1978 / Pablo 843

Milt Jackson + Count Basie + the Big Band—Vol. 1 / Jan. 18, 1978 / Pablo 2310822

Yessir, That's My Baby / Feb. 21, 1978 / Pablo 2310-923

From the same week that resulted in *Night Rider* and *Timekeepers*, this is the fifth album that documents the matchup of Count Basie and Oscar Peterson. The two pianists (backed by bassist John Heard and drummer Louis Bellson) play five standards and three blues with predictable swing, finding much more in common with each other than one might suspect. —*Scott Yanow*

Night Rider / Feb. 21-22, 1978 / Pablo 688

When they first met up for a full album in 1974, the two-piano team of Count Basie and Oscar Peterson must have seemed like an unlikely matchup. After all, Peterson is known for filling up his rapid solos with virtuosic passages, while Basie is the master of the "less is more" approach, making every note count. But because Oscar had such high respect for Count, he showed great self-restraint and left room for Basie's percussive solos. *Night Rider,* like their two previous joint albums, emphasizes the similarities rather than the differences in these two masters' styles. —*Scott Yanow*

Timekeepers, The / Feb. 21-22, 1978 / Pablo 2310-896

From the same sessions that resulted in *Night Rider* and *Yessir,* this quartet date also features the two pianos of Oscar Peterson and Count Basie collaborating and interacting on swing standards and blues. Any of their five albums together are worth acquiring. —*Scott Yanow*

Live in Japan (1978) / May 21, 1978 / Pablo 246

By 1978, trombonist Al Grey and tenor saxophonist Jimmy Forrest were no longer the stars of the Count Basie orchestra, but this superb ensemble band was also no longer dependent on famous names. In fact, one does not miss their presence on this superior live performance, which features such Basie standbys as "Freckle Face," "All of Me," "Shiny Stockings," and "Jumpin' at the Woodside." Although the soloists were no longer household names, they all fare well, particularly Eric Dixon on tenor and flute. —*Scott Yanow*

On the Road / Jul. 12, 1979 / Pablo 112

This release gives one a definitive look at the Count Basie orchestra during its final years. Trumpeter Pete Minger, trombonist Booty Wood, and Eric Dixon on tenor and flute are the main soloists, but it is the classic Basie ensemble sound (which never seems to get dated or lose its charm and power) that carries the day. Whether it is "Wind Machine," "Splanky," or "In a Mellow Tone," this is a highly enjoyable set. —*Scott Yanow*

Get Together / Sep. 4, 1979 / Pablo 2310-924

This typically enjoyable Basie all-star jam is particularly noteworthy because it includes the great (but underrated) tenor of Budd Johnson along with Eddie "Lockjaw" Davis and trumpeters Clark Terry and Harry "Sweets" Edison. The music is quite delightful, topped by a fine ballad medley. — *Scott Yanow*

Basie Reunions / i. 1980 / Prestige 24109
Special jam sessions of Basie alumni organized by Paul Quinichette and recorded for Prestige in 1957 and 1958. These are exuberant, loose affairs with a relaxed, yet combative air that marks all the great Basie bands. They have been reissued on CD. — *Ron Wynn*

Kansas City Shout / Apr. 7, 1980 / Pablo 2310-859
This session from 1980 helps to recreate the atmosphere of 1930s Kansas City. Featured are the great blues singer Joe Turner and the strong singer and altoist Eddie "Cleanhead" Vinson, along with the Count Basie orchestra. "Just A Dream," "Everyday I Have The Blues," "Cherry Red," and "Stormy Monday" receive very spirited renditions as do some newer blues. Since all of the principals are no longer with us, Norman Granz deserves special thanks for organizing this special session. — *Scott Yanow*

○ **Kansas City 7** / Apr. 10, 1980 / Pablo 690
Norman Granz recorded Count Basie in many different settings during Basie's decade with Granz's Pablo label. This jam session set is a little unusual in that trumpeter Freddie Hubbard is in the cast, along with the tenor of Eddie "Lockjaw" Davis, guitarist Joe Pass, trombonist J. J. Johnson, and Basie; pity Hubbard never recorded with the Count Basie orchestra! This happy session is a strong consolation prize, with plenty of fine solos taken over familiar chord changes. — *Scott Yanow*

○ **Warm Breeze** / Sep. 1-2, 1981 / Pablo 2312-131
This big-band album finds Count Basie (at age 77) and his orchestra performing seven charts by longtime friend Sammy Nestico, including six originals and "Satin Doll." Trumpeter Harry "Sweets" Edison sits in on "How Sweet It Is" and trumpeter Willie Cook has a couple of strong spots, but it is the classic Basie ensemble sound that is this enjoyable studio session's strongest asset. — *Scott Yanow*

Kansas City 6 / Nov. 1, 1981 / Pablo 449
This is one of many small-group jam sessions organized by Norman Granz to feature pianist Count Basie. This time around, the proceedings, which utilize a sextet, have plenty of solo space for trumpeter Willie Cook, altoist Eddie "Cleanhead" Vinson (who also takes a vocal), and guitarist Joe Pass. As usual when Basie had his way, the emphasis is on the blues and the music always swings. — *Scott Yanow*

○ **Farmers Market Barbecue** / May 1982 / Pablo 732
An excellent outing by the Count Basie orchestra during its later years. Actually, half of this album (which is not yet out on CD) features a medium-sized group from Basie's big band, but his orchestra usually had the feel of a small group anyway. At this late stage, soloists include Eric Dixon and Kenny Hing on tenors, trombonist Booty Wood, altoist Danny Turner, and four different trumpeters. Of course, the rhythm section is instantly recognizable, and the music is very much in the Basie tradition. — *Scott Yanow*

○ **88 Basie Street** / May 11-12, 1983 / Pablo 2310901
One of Count Basie's final albums, the very appealing title cut seems to sum up Basie's career, a lightly swinging groove with a strong melody. Two small group performances with guest Joe Pass on guitar and the tenor of Kenny Hing add variety to a particularly strong set. — *Scott Yanow*

Mostly Blues . . . And Some Others / Jun. 22, 1983 / Pablo 2310-919
Count Basie's final small-group studio session (one of a countless number for Norman Granz during Basie's last decade), this outing features trumpeter Snooky Young (who was last with Count's orchestra in the early 1960s), tenor great Eddie "Lockjaw" Davis, and the dependable guitarist Joe Pass (along with rhythm guitarist Freddie Green). The

repertoire lives up to the album's title: blues and swing standards all played with joy and spirit. — *Scott Yanow*

Long Live the Chief / Jun. 24, 1986-Jun. 25, 1986 / Denon 1018
After Count Basie's death, his orchestra went through an expected period of turmoil, almost declaring bankruptcy and having a new short-term leader (the late trumpeter Thad Jones). By 1986 its fortunes had improved, and under the leadership of tenor saxophonist Frank Foster it has become the only "ghost" orchestra to still play viable music after the death of its leader. "Long Live the Chief" was recorded only weeks after Foster assumed command, but already his arrangements and leadership were giving fresh life to this great jazz institution. In addition to remakes of "April in Paris," "Lil' Darlin'," "Corner Pocket," and "Shiny Stockings," there was already some new material in the band's books. This enjoyable CD shows just how strong the orchestra was, even during this period of transition. — *Scott Yanow*

☆ **Legend—the Legacy** / May 16, 1989-May 17, 1989 / Denon 73790
Three years after Frank Foster had become leader of the Count Basie orchestra, the group continued to place very well in jazz polls; few big bands were in its class. This fine CD finds Foster extending the tradition of Count Basie with new arrangements and features for both veterans (including trumpeter Sonny Cohn, altoist Danny Turner, and the tenors of Kenny Hing and Eric Dixon) and the newer members (such as trumpeter Byron Stripling and pianist Ace Carter). With Carmen Bradford proving to be the band's best vocalist since Joe Williams, Frank Foster had succeeded at not only reviving the Count Basie orchestra, but at restoring it to its prime. The lengthy "Count Basie Remembrance Suite," "Booze Brothers," and a new version of Neal Hefti's "Whirly Bird" are among this enjoyable CD's highlights. — *Scott Yanow*

Live at El Morocco / Feb. 20, 1992-Feb. 21, 1992 / Telarc 83312
Even without its original leader, the Count Basie orchestra today is one of the finest jazz big bands in existence. Frank Foster has kept the instantly recognizable sound while welcoming younger soloists and infusing the band's repertoire with new charts. This strong, live program is typical of the Basie band in the 1990s, performing older tunes (such as "Corner Pocket" and "Shiny Stockings") that alternate with newer and no less swinging originals, all of which leaves room for the orchestra's many promising soloists. — *Scott Yanow*

○ **Corner Pocket** / . . . Laserlight 15789
The first of two Laserlight CDs documenting Count Basie's orchestra, sometime in the late 1950s, playing before a live audience. Even with the presence of "Corner Pocket," "Cute" and "Lil' Darlin'," the repertoire is mostly pretty fresh. Baritonist Charlie Fowlkes has a rare feature on "Spring Is Here," altoist Marshall Royal gets a few spots, and Snooky Young leads the powerful rhythm section. Add trombonist Al Grey and tenor saxophonist Billy Mitchell to the other strong soloists of the period and one has a very enjoyable and swinging set of Basie music. The playing time is a bit brief, but Laserlight is a very moderately priced label and the music on this CD is superior. — *Scott Yanow*

MICKEY BASS (Lee Odis Bass)

b. 1943
Bass, saxophone / Hard bop
A Pittsburgh bassist who's worked with hard bop bandleaders and combos since the '60s, Lee Odis "Mickey" Bass hasn't recorded often as a leader. He's played with Chico Freeman, John Hicks, and Kiane Zawadi, among others, and has cut sessions for Chiaroscuro and Early Bird. Currently, Bass's dates as a leader aren't available on CD. — *Ron Wynn and Michael G. Nastos*

★ **Another Way Out** / Early Bird 103
Mickey Bass Quartet. Bassist Bass as leader. Might be hard to find, but worth the search. — *Michael G. Nastos*

Music Map

Jazz Bass, Double-Bass, Contrabass

1890s Ragtime Orchestras & String Bands – Tub & stick
Billy Marrero (1874) – Henry Kimball

Early Jazz Bass – Classic Jazz Era
Bill Johnson (1872-1972) – Steve Brown
John Lindsay (1894-1950) – Wellman Braud (1891-1966)

Early Rhythm Section
Pops Foster (1892-1969) – Al Morgan (1908-1974)

Billy Taylor (1906-1986) – Hayes Alvis (1907-1972)
Grachan Moncur II (1915) – George Kelly (1915-1985)

1930s Players
Walter Page (1900-1957)
John Kirby (1908-1952)
Jimmy Blanton (1918-1942)

1940s Players
Ray Brown (1926)
Milt Hinton (1910)
Tommy Potter (1918-1988)
Red Callender (1916-1922)
Charles Mingus (1922-1979)
Oscar Pettiford (1922-1960)
Slam Stewart (1914-1987)

Sing Along with Instrument
Slam Stewart (1914-1987) – Major Holley (1924)

1950s Players
Wilbur Ware (1923-1979)
Ray Brown (1926)
Charles Mingus (1922-1979)
Red Mitchell (1927)
Scott LaFaro (1936-1961)
Gary Peacock (1935)
Eddie Gomez (1944)

Mainstream
Sam Jones (1924) – Doug Watkins (1934-1962)
Bob Cranshaw (1932) – Paul Chambers (1935-1969)
Ron Carter (1937) – Walter Booker Jr. (1933)
Jimmy Garrison (1934-1976)– George Mraz (1944)
Harvey Swartz (1948)

Major Players
Charlie Haden (1937)
Dave Holland (1946)
Barre Phillips (1934)
Arlid Andersen (1945)
Miroslav Vitous (1947)
Niels Henning-Ørsted Pedersen (1946)
Bary Guy (1947)
Henry Grimes (1935)
Alan Silva
Cecil McBee (1935)
Chris White (1936
Clint Houston (1946)
Israel Crosby (1919-1962)
Bill Crow (1927)
Isla Eckinger (1939)
David Izenon (1932-1979)
Gene Ramey (1913-1984)

Electric Bass
Steve Swallow (1940)
Eberhard Weber (1940)
Jamaaladeen Tacuma (1956)
Alex Blake
Alphonso Johnson (1951)
Albert MacDowell
Jymie Merritt (1926)
Chuck Rainey (1940)
Stanley Clarke (1951)
Monk Montgomery (1921-1982)
Jaco Pastorius (1951-1987)

1980s-1990s
Mark Johnson
Eddie Gomez (1944)
Ratso Harris
Christian McBride
Reginald Veal
Charnett Moffitt
Robert Hurst
Rodney Whitaker
Ray Drummond
Rufus Reid (1944)
Charles Fambrough

Sirone (1940) – Ron McClure (1941)

ALVIN BATISTE

b. 1937, New Orleans, LA
Clarinet / New Orleans traditional, bop, hard bop, blues & jazz

Both an influential teacher and an excellent soloist, Alvin Batiste is highly respected by musicians, but unknown by the general public, even many of the jazz faithful. A tremendous clarinetist, Batiste can play effectively in a traditional New Orleans, R&B, blues, bebop, and hard bop situation, and he also excels on classical or free material. He's a good composer who wrote for the New Orleans Philharmonic and contributed to various jazz groups. Batiste played with Edward Blackwell while a high school student, then worked extensively with Ornette Coleman after army service. He participated in jam sessions with Coleman on the West Coast in the late '50s. Batiste toured with Ray Charles's band in 1958. He was a jazz instructor at Southern University from the late '60s until the mid '80s, and worked periodically with Cannonball Adderley. Batiste was featured on a number included in *The Black Messiah* session, and began recording a complete LP with Adderley, but didn't finish it due to his teaching commitments. He did appear on *Lovers*, the final Adderley release, in 1975. Batiste recorded and played at the Montreux Jazz Festival with Billy Cobham, and was in the marvelous group Clarinet Summit in the '80s. He recorded for India Navigation in 1985, and finally got a major label forum when Sony/Columbia issued his session, *Late*, in 1993. It's his only date as a leader available on CD.
—*Ron Wynn*

★ **Musique D'afrique Nouvell Orleans** / 1984 / India
Navigation 1065

Bayou Magic / **i.** 1986 / India Navigation 1069

BILLY BAUER (William Henry Bauer)

b. Nov. 14, 1915, New York, NY
Guitar / Swing, big band, bop
Guitarist Billy Bauer made the transition from merely
chording and playing rhythm to becoming a progressive
soloist in the mid '40s. He performed harmonically and stylistically advanced solos, and was noted for his exacting ensemble and unison playing. Bauer began on banjo as a child,
then moved to guitar in his teens. He played in Jerry Wald's
band before joining Woody Herman's first Herd in the mid
'40s. Bauer then worked with Benny Goodman and Jack
Teagarden. He was a member of Lennie Tristano's groups
from 1946 to 1949, and played on Tristano's 1949 sessions
Intuition and *Digression*. Bauer recorded with Metronome
All Stars from 1947 to 1953, and played with the NBC staff
orchestra. He was an instructor at the New York
Conservatory of Modern Music in the early '50s, and played
with Goodman in Europe. Bauer worked with Lee Konitz in
the late '50s and '60s. He did session work in New York in
the '70s, and taught privately in the '80s. Currently, Bauer
has one session available on CD, and can also be heard on
Tristano reissues. *—Ron Wynn and Michael G. Nastos*

★ **Let's Have a Session** / 1953 / Ad Lib 5501

Plectrist / **i.** 1956 / Norgran 1082

MARIO BAUZA

b. Apr. 28, 1911, Cayo Hueso, Havana, Cuba, **d.** 1993
Oboe, clarinet, trumpet / Latin jazz
A fine trumpeter, Mario Bauza was one of Latin jazz's greatest personalities. His roots were in the swing era, and he was
outspoken about the ties between Latin rhythms and jazz
improvisation. In one of his last interviews, he told *Village
Voice* writer Enrique Fernandez that there was no such thing
as "Latin Jazz." Instead, Bauza insisted it was "Afro-Cuban"
music. He'd been a bass clarinetist in the Havana Symphony
Orchestra before coming to New York in 1930. Bauza
worked with Noble Sissle in 1932, then served as music director and trumpeter for Chick Webb in the mid and late
'30s. He helped Webb discover and recruit Ella Fitzgerald.
Bauza played briefly with Don Redman, then was in Cab
Calloway's orchestra in the late '30s and early '40s. He
helped get Dizzy Gillespie into the band and befriended him
during his tenure. It was Bauza's talks and influence that
triggered Gillespie's lifetime interest in Latin music. Bauza
joined Machito's Afro-Cubans in 1941, and remained until
1976. He became the music director and helped make them
a perennial attraction on the Latin jazz and Latin music circuit, as well as one of the greatest big bands ever in any
style. Machito's sister and Bauza's wife, Graciela, was a vocalist with the band. Bauza combined a Cuban rhythm section with swing-oriented brass writing and arrangements;
he suggested using non-Latin jazz musicians as guest stars
for sessions. Bauza produced albums featuring Graciela,
Gillespie, and Chico O'Farrell. When he finally left, Machito's
son Mario Grillo replaced him. Bauza continued recording,
working with Graciela, Rafael Cortijo, and others. His mid
'80s release, *Mario Bauza and Friends*, included some members of Machito's band. He and Graciela recorded together
for Caiman in the mid '80s. His most recent release was the
fiery album, *Tanga*, on Messidor in 1992. It's currently the
most easily accessible Bauza date. Others, especially with
Machito, can be obtained through Latin music specialty
stores. *—Ron Wynn*

○ **Ahora Mismo, Guateque de Chombo, Simale, Contigo La
D** / **i.** 1976 / Lamp

○ **Mambo Inn, Quedate, El Marelito & Cubanola** / **i.** 1986 /
Caiman

★ **Tanga Suite, The** / **i.** 1992 / Messidor

A swinging orchestra conducted by the redoubtable Mario
Bauza and featuring such exceptional soloists as Paquito
D'Rivera on alto sax, Victor Paz on trumpet, Pablo Calogero
on baritone sax, and Marcus Persiani on piano. Also, the sophisticated arrangements and songwriting genius of Chico
O'Farrill and Ray Santos make "Tanga" a Cuban jazz classic.
The title cut, dubbed the "national anthem of Latin jazz,"
and first composed in the '40s by Bauza, is an Afro-Cuban
jazz suite consisting of five moments: "Cuban Lullaby,"
"Mambo," "Afro-Cuban Ritual," "Bolero," and "Rumba
Abierta." "Tanga" is given its definitive treatment here. This
brilliant composition with its sultry melodies, earthy
rhythms, and biting brass invites comparison with the great
Duke Ellington suites. Other outstanding cuts include "Son
Cubano," which features the scorching trumpet of Victor Paz,
and "Chucho," composed, arranged, and conducted by
Paquito D'Rivera. Everything on this disc is of a high order.
—Marcela Breton, Jazz Times

SIDNEY BECHET (Sidney Joseph Bechet)

b. May 14, 1897, New Orleans, LA, **d.** May 14, 1959, Paris,
France
Clarinet, soprano saxophone / New Orleans traditional
A child prodigy and a remarkable saxophonist and clar-
inetist, Sidney Bechet belongs in the pantheon of New
Orleans' greatest players. He was a professional musician at
age 13, and left home three years later. Bechet played with
Freddie Keppard as a child, and went through the Deep
South touring with Clarence Williams. After playing with
King Oliver in 1916, Bechet went first to Chicago, then to
New York City. While working with Will Marion Cook's
Southern Syncopated Orchestra in 1919, Bechet went to
Europe for the first time. There, he was heralded by Swiss
conductor Ernest Ansermet, who later raved about his ge-
nius in an article. While in London, Bechet bought a straight
model soprano sax. He played in Paris until 1921, when he
returned to New York.
Bechet made his recording debut with Clarence Williams
in the early '20s, then, in 1924, did sessions with the Red
Onion Babies whose roster included Louis Armstrong.
Following brief stints with Duke Ellington and backing
singers, Bechet appeared at the Kentucky Club in 1925 with
James P. Johnson and made an immediate impact on the
New York scene. His most identifiable and striking stylistic
attribute was his heavy vibrato, as well as his verve and enthusiasm. Bechet never abandoned the gripping, hypnotic
lyricism he'd developed in New Orleans, and was the first
jazz figure to concentrate on the soprano sax, though he was
also an excellent clarinet player. He taught and deeply influenced Johnny Hodges, who divided his time between soprano and alto for an early stretch in his career. Bechet
toured with various shows and revues in the mid '20s, and
returned to Europe with Josephine Baker and Claude
Hopkins in 1925. Bechet left Baker's show, then went on a
Russian tour in 1926. From there he went to Berlin, made a
subsequent European tour in 1927, and joined Noble Sissle
in Paris in 1928. He later organized the New Orleans
Feetwarmers with Tommy Ladnier, and recorded for Victor.
He and Ladnier also became partners in a tailor shop.
Sidney Bechet made a string of great records for Victor
from 1938 to 1941 with various groups that included two
vastly different drummers, Baby Dodds and Kenny Clarke.
He made acclaimed sessions for Blue Note in 1939 with the
Port of Harlem Jazzmen. Bechet's 1940 recording of "Wild
Man Blues" was vintage New Orleans music, lifted into another era and turned into an individualized masterpiece.
Besides these recordings, he also played all over the East
Coast and the Midwest in the '30s and '40s. Bechet returned
to Europe in 1949 and made it his home, becoming a
beloved, idolized figure. He cut "Les Oignons" in 1949 with
clarinetist and bandleader Claude Luter, which became a
huge international hit. He revisited his homeland periodically, returning in 1949, 1951, and 1953. He toured England
and Latin America in 1957, and appeared at the Brussels
International Exhibition in 1958. Bechet's autobiography,

Treat It Gentle, was an eye-opener when published in 1960 and still deserves praise for its straightforward account of a jazz legend's life and times. John Chilton's magnificent biography of Bechet, *The Wizard of Jazz,* traces Bechet's fascinating life nearly week-by-week, and is highly recommended. The shivering, wavery Bechet approach hasn't been revered much in recent times, not even among the tradition-conscious young lion set. But his recordings have a timeless brilliance found only in the music of true giants. —*Ron Wynn and Dan Morgenstern*

Unique Sidney / **i.** Jun. 1923-Nov. 16, 1938 / CBS 63093
This out-of-print French LP contains a mixture of Sidney Bechet items including five very early tracks with Clarence Williams's Blue Five, a 1925 session from the Get Happy Band, "Dear Old Southland" with Noble Sissle's big band in 1937, and the four songs (plus three alternates) cut with Sissle's rhythm section. Excellent music that is generally available elsewhere. —*Scott Yanow*

○ **Complete 1923-6 Clarence Williams Sessions: 1, The** / **i.** Jul. 1923-Oct. 1923 / EPM 5197

○ **Chronological Sidney Bechet, 1923-1936, The** / Oct. 1923-Mar. 1936 / Classics 583
The first in a series of Classics CDs focusing on the recordings of Sidney Bechet, this disc features the clarinetist/soprano saxophonist on two early titles with blues singer Rosetta Crawford, his torrid 1932 session with the New Orleans Feetwarmers (which also features trumpeter Tommy Ladnier and is highlighted by "Shag" and "Maple Leaf Rag"), and sides from Noble Sissle's somewhat commercial orchestra. Fortunately, Sissle was wise enough to give Bechet plenty of solo space on some of his selections, most notably "Polka Dot Rag." Even with a few indifferent vocals, this CD is recommended to those who do not already own this music. —*Scott Yanow*

★ **In New York** / **i.** 1923-1925 / Smithsonian

And the Blues Singers—Vol. 1 / **i.** 1923 / Fat Cat 013
Early Bechet with Clarence Williams's Blue Five, Sara Martin, Eva Taylor, and Margaret Johnson. Bechet as accompanist. —*Bruce Raeburn*

○ **Giants of Jazz** / **i.** 1923-1958 / Time-Life 09
A great retrospective package that contains some of everything Sidney Bechet recorded—from the beginning to the middle to the end. It is part of the Time-Life anthology series, is brilliantly mastered, intelligently sequenced, and contains scholarly notes and text. Sadly, this series has been discontinued. —*Ron Wynn*

Wild Cat Blues / **i.** 1923-1937 / Music Memoria
New set covering the years 1923-1937. The first of a series documenting the complete Bechet legacy. Some duplication with other available sets. —*Ron Wynn*

Sidney Bechet (1924-1938) / 1924-1938 / Pearl Flapper 9772
A compendium of Bechet sides with the Blue Five, Red Onion Jazz Babies, Noble Sissle & His International Orchestra, and Noble Sissle's Swingsters, providing good coverage of the clarinetist in differing musical formats (especially on sarrusophone on "Mandy, Make Up Your Mind!"). —*Bruce Raeburn*

○ **Jazz Heritage: Blackstick (1931-1938)** / **i.** 1931-1938 / MCA 1330
This LP from MCA's Jazz Heritage series of the early 1980s mostly features the great Sidney Bechet as a sideman with Noble Sissle's large show band and on a small group date under Sissle's sponsorship. Since these are Sissle's most jazz-oriented tracks and Bechet has plenty of solo space (particularly on "Roll on Mississippi, Roll on," "Polka Dot Rag," and the combo sides), this music is worth acquiring in one form or another. As a bonus, there are four performances from a 1938 blues date by singer Trixie Smith with Bechet and trumpeter Charlie Shavers. —*Scott Yanow*

☆ **Complete Vol. 1 & 2, The** / **i.** Sep. 15, 1932-Jan. 8, 1941 / RCA 42409

Of all the overlapping Sidney Bechet reissue series, this series of two-LP sets released by French RCA is easily the best, with all of the Victor sides by the great soprano saxophonist and clarinetist (including the valuable alternate takes) being issued complete and in chronological order. The first twofer is highlighted by the blazing session by the New Orleans Feetwarmers from 1932, four selections from the "Really The Blues" date with trumpeter Tommy Ladnier and clarinetist Mezz Mezzrow, and such Bechet classics as "Indian Summer," "Old Man Blues," and "Nobody Knows the Way I Feel Dis Mornin'." —*Scott Yanow*

☆ **Legendary, The** / **i.** 1932-1941 / Bluebird 6590
For those not fortunate enough to own *Master Musician, The Legendary* contains some excellent examples of Sidney Bechet's driving soprano, along with good moments from Tommy Ladnier, Earl Hines, and Charlie Shavers, among others. It includes Bechet's historic "one-man band" performance of "Sheik of Araby" (although not "Blues of Bechet") on which Bechet uses overdubbing to play clarinet, soprano, a weird sounding tenor, piano, bass, and drums. —*Scott Yanow, Cadence*

★ **Master Takes: Victor Sessions (1932-1943)** / 1932-1943 / Bluebird 2402
This three-CD set is perfect in all respects except that it leaves out the very interesting alternate takes from Sidney Bechet's Victor sessions. Consisting of 60 selections (mostly from 1939-1941), this release finds soprano saxophonist and clarinetist Sidney Bechet in his prime, making traditional jazz sound modern during the height of the swing era. A true individualist, Bechet is heard romping with the New Orleans Feetwarmers in 1932, dominating a Tommy Ladnier-Mezz Mezzrow session, starring with Jelly Roll Morton in 1939, and creating classic after classic with the all-star groups he headed. Highpoints include "Indian Summer," "Nobody Knows the Way I Feels Dis Mornin'," "Stompy Jones," "Egyptian Fantasy," and his one-man band overdubbed performance of "The Sheik of Araby." A package that is essential for jazz collectors who do not already possess the French RCA twofer series. —*Scott Yanow*

○ **Chronological Sidney Bechet, 1937-1938, The** / Apr. 1937-Nov. 1938 / Classics 593
The second in a series of CDs of reissued recordings featuring Sidney Bechet has quite a bit of variety. The unique soprano saxophonist is heard with Noble Sissle's show band, dominating a small group sponsored by Sissle, backing blues singer Trixie Smith and the team of Grant & Wilson, and leading his own session with a sextet that includes baritonist Ernie Caceres and on "Hold Tight" a vocal by "The Two Fish Mongers!" Enjoyable, if not quite essential, music. —*Scott Yanow*

Jazz from California / **i.** 1937-1953 / Jazz Archives 44
Two unrelated broadcasts are brought together for this LP by the collector's label Jazz Archives. Cornetist Muggsy Spanier is heard playing exuberant New Orleans-styled solos with Ben Pollack's swing band of 1937, and soprano great Sidney Bechet appears with a Dixieland quintet in 1953 that also features trumpeter Marty Marsala. Fans of these musicians should search for this one! —*Scott Yanow*

○ **Superb Sidney** / **i.** Nov. 16, 1938-Jul. 31, 1947 / CBS 62 6 3 6
Although this LP from French Columbia has a Bechet session from 1938 with a group that also finds baritonist Ernie Caceres in the front line, the bulk of this set features the great soprano saxophonist in 1947 either playing fairly modern tunes such as "Just One of Those Things" and "Love for Sale," while fronting a quartet, or interacting with Bob Wilber's Wildcats (a young trad group including pianist Dick Wellstood) on four wonderful performances such as "Polka Dot Stomp" and "If I Had It But It's All Gone Now." A splendid all-round set showcasing the virtuosic Bechet. —*Scott Yanow*

☆ **Complete Vol. 5 & 6, The** / **i.** Nov. 21, 1938-Dec. 8, 1943 / RCA 89751(2)

The third and final twofer in this definitive series concludes the reissuance of every Sidney Bechet recording on Victor (including the alternate takes) with sessions from 1941 (highlighted by a classic rendition of "What Is This Thing Called Love?") and a quintet set from two years later with trombonist Vic Dickenson. Filling out this two-LP set are what was known as "the Panassie sessions," the recordings organized by French critic Hugues Panassie during a visit to New York in 1938-1939. Mezz Mezzrow is heard at length on performances with trumpeters Tommy Ladnier and Sidney DeParis, but it is the six progressive swing tracks from trumpeter Frankie Newton's septet (with pianist James P. Johnson) that are most memorable, particularly a brilliant version of "Rosetta." —*Scott Yanow*

○ **1938-1940** / i. Nov. 28, 1938-Feb. 5, 1940 / Classics 608
This entry in Classics' chronological reissue of the master takes of Sidney Bechet's early recordings finds the soprano great playing with trumpeter Tommy Ladnier and clarinetist Mezz Mezzrow on the famous "Really The Blues" session, performing a hit version of "Summertime," overshadowing the other members of the all-star Port of Harlem Seven, and recording "Indian Summer" and a hot version of "One O'Clock Jump" in a 1940 session for Victor. However, half of this CD is taken up by an odd and surprisingly restrained marathon date with pianist Willie "The Lion" Smith in which they perform Haitian folk songs! An interesting if not essential set. —*Scott Yanow*

★ **Complete Blue Note Recordings** / i. 1939-1953 / Mosaic
Mosaic, a mail-order company, has compiled a series of remarkable box sets that feature the complete recordings of various immortal musicians at the peak of their careers. This limited-edition, six-LP set (get it while you can!) has all of Sidney Bechet's recordings for Blue Note, including three songs with the Port of Harlem Seven (climaxed by his hit version of "Summertime"). It also has two blues with guitarist Josh White, and Bechet's sessions from 1940, 1944, 1945, 1946, 1949, 1950, 1951, and 1953 in which he shares the front line with such trumpeters as Sidney DeParis, Max Kaminsky, Bunk Johnson, Wild Bill Davison, and Jonah Jones. The music ranges from hot swing to exuberant Dixieland, and Bechet somehow always sounds inspired. —*Scott Yanow*

○ **Port at Harlem Jazzmen** / i. 1939 / Blue Note 7022

○ **1940** / i. Mar. 7, 1940-Jun. 4, 1940 / Classics 619
Classics' chronological reissue of Sidney Bechet's recordings (at least the regular takes) continues with a pair of songs made with blues singer Josh White, eight very enjoyable performances cut with a quartet consisting of cornetist Muggsy Spanier, guitarist Carmen Mastren, and bassist Wellman Braud, and a pair of Bechet's Victor sessions. One of the strongest entries in this valuable series. —*Scott Yanow*

○ **1940-1941** / i. Sep. 6, 1940-Oct. 14, 1941 / Classics 638
Classics' Sidney Bechet series continues with this CD, a generous set full of the soprano's prime Victor recordings including appearances by cornetist Rex Stewart and pianist Earl Hines, Bechet's guest shot with the Chamber Music Society of Lower Basin Street, and his innovative "one-man band" recordings of "The Sheik of Araby" and "Blues of Bechet." Timeless music. —*Scott Yanow*

☆ **Complete Vol. 3 & 4, The** / i. Jan. 8, 1941-Oct. 24, 1941 / RCA 43262
The second of three two-LP sets released by French RCA continues the complete chronological repackaging (including alternate takes) of all of Sidney Bechet's Victor recordings. During the 10-month period covered in this valuable set, Bechet recorded such classics as "Egyptian Fantasy," "Swing Parade," "The Mooche," and even the odd "Laughin' in Rhythm." Bechet, a remarkable soprano saxophonist who made traditional jazz sound modern, also is heard on six instruments during his innovative overdubbed "one-man band" performances of a blues and "The Sheik of Araby." This series is highly recommended but is becoming increasingly difficult to find. —*Scott Yanow*

Jazz Nocturne Volume 1 / i. Mar. 10, 1945-Mar. 29, 1945 / Fat Cat's Jazz 001
In 1945, Sidney Bechet achieved his goal of putting together an old-style New Orleans jazz band with trumpeter Bunk Johnson, settling in for a three-month residence in Boston, but Bunk's excessive drinking and erratic personality made his stay in Bechet's group short-lived. Fortunately, many of their nightly radio broadcasts were recorded and this LP is the first of 12 volumes in this fascinating series, three of which feature Johnson's trumpet. This set starts with a brief interview with Bunk in which he talks about his hopes for the group and then one hears three broadcasts featuring the quintet. Bechet largely dominates the music, although he was persuaded by Bunk to play clarinet on some tunes so as to give the veteran trumpeter a chance. Some fireworks would erupt in the near future! —*Scott Yanow*

Jazz Nocturne Volume 2 / i. Apr. 3, 1945 / Fat Cat's Jazz 002
The second of 12 LPs documenting Sidney Bechet's quintet during an extended stay in Boston, this contains a rehearsal by the band and their performance on radio later the same night. Bechet had looked forward to having Bunk Johnson in his band but the veteran trumpeter was frequently drunk, disliked Bechet's dominant soprano playing (getting him to switch to clarinet on some songs), and had become rather erratic. The rehearsal is tense but very interesting, while the nighttime performance shows that the group was doomed. —*Scott Yanow*

Bechet, Bunk and Boston 1945 / i. Apr. 3, 1945-Apr. 5, 1945 / Jazz Archives 48
Duplicating material released in more complete fashion on Volumes 2 and 3 of the Jazz Nocturne series on Fat Cat's Jazz, this LP features the Sidney Bechet-Bunk Johnson New Orleans band during their stay at the Savoy Cafe in Boston. Unfortunately, Bunk's drinking and erratic playing would result in his being dropped from the group soon afterward. This set contains music played at a rehearsal (at the time Johnson and Bechet were not even talking to each other) and parts of two radio broadcasts. Those fans curious about this historic collaboration and not able to find the rarer Fat Cat releases will find this an often fascinating set. —*Scott Yanow*

Jazz Nocturne Volume 3 / i. Apr. 3, 1945-Apr. 7, 1945 / Fat Cat's Jazz 003
The third of 12 LPs documenting the Sidney Bechet quintet's residence in Boston is the last one to include veteran trumpeter Bunk Johnson. The main reason is obvious from these radio broadcasts; Bunk sounds very erratic, making it difficult for Bechet to know whether to play lead or not. True Bechet fans will want all of these volumes anyway for he is in top form despite the music collapsing around him! —*Scott Yanow*

Jazz Nocturne Volume 4 / i. Apr. 10, 1945-Apr. 17, 1945 / Fat Cat's Jazz 004
This is the fourth of a dozen LPs documenting Sidney Bechet's residence in Boston during part of 1945. After Bunk Johnson essentially drank himself out of the band, Bechet sent for the veteran trumpeter Peter Bocage from New Orleans. In the meantime he started using a local 18-year-old trumpeter, Johnny Windhurst, who turned out to be a particularly suitable player for the band. On Volume 4 Windhurst makes two appearances during the April 10 broadcast; by the concluding April 17 aircheck he sounds very much like a member of the band. Since the trumpeter did not record all that much during his relatively short life, his appearances on six volumes of this series are quite valuable. —*Scott Yanow*

○ **Jazz Nocturne Volume 5** / i. Apr. 19, 1945-Apr. 24, 1945 / Fat Cat's Jazz 005
The fifth of 12 LPs in this series features the Sidney Bechet quintet during two radio broadcasts in April 1945. Bechet plays as inspired as usual but this volume (one of the strongest in the program) ranks as one of trumpeter Johnny Windhurst's finest of his career. The 18 year old was unrecorded up to that point, but he fits in surprisingly well

with the volatile Bechet on these trad jazz standards. —Scott Yanow

○ **Jazz Nocturne Volume 6 / i.** Apr. 26, 1945-May 22, 1945 / Fat Cat's Jazz 006
The sixth in this 12-LP series continues the documentation of the Sidney Bechet quintet in Boston. When Bunk Johnson drank himself out of the band, Bechet sent down to New Orleans for veteran trumpeter Peter Bocage, a move he eventually regretted. In the meantime he was persuaded to use Johnny Windhurst who, although just 18, fit in perfectly. This particular LP has Windhurst's last broadcast with Bechet before Bocage's arrival, and his first after Bocage's departure! Windhurst's participation in these broadcasts makes this series quite valuable, as does the consistently exciting playing of the great Sidney Bechet. —Scott Yanow

Jazz Nocturne Volume 7 / i. May 1, 1945-May 3, 1945 / Fat Cat's Jazz 007
The seventh in a 12-LP series documenting Sidney Bechet's 1945 quintet finds New Orleans veteran Peter Bocage joining the band after Bunk Johnson proved to be unreliable and youngster Johnny Windhurst had filled in quite successfully. Bocage, who had probably only been playing part-time and had a quiet melodic style, was an odd choice and was predictably overshadowed by Bechet in this ensemble-oriented music. Recommended to true Bechet fanatics, although these LPs from this collector's label will be difficult to locate. —Scott Yanow

Jazz Nocturne Volume 8 / i. May 8, 1945-May 10, 1945 / Fat Cat's Jazz 008
By the eighth volume in this 12-LP series from Fat Cat's Jazz, the Sidney Bechet quintet (heard on radio airchecks from their lengthy residency at Boston's Savoy Cafe) featured the quiet and subtle trumpeter Peter Bocage, who was predictably overshadowed by Bechet's passionate soprano. Some good New Orleans-oriented jazz is heard but this set is mostly for Bechet collectors. —Scott Yanow

Jazz Nocturne Volume 9 / i. May 15, 1945-May 17, 1945 / Fat Cat's Jazz 009
The ninth of 12 LPs in this very interesting series has the final two broadcasts from the Peter Bocage version of this band. Bocage, a subtle and quiet trumpeter who never really meshed with Bechet, was homesick for New Orleans, where he would soon permanently return. On the May 15 performance, bassist Pops Foster was absent so Brad Gowans filled in, on valve trombone! Bechet's strong playing throughout makes this a worthwhile LP despite the problems. —Scott Yanow

○ **Jazz Nocturne Volume 10 / i.** May 24, 1945-May 31, 1945 / Fat Cat's Jazz 010
With Peter Bocage's decision to return to New Orleans after a short period with Sidney Bechet's quintet, the trumpet chair went immediately back to 18-year-old Johnny Windhurst, who had filled in very well after Bunk Johnson left the band. In fact, a large reason that the final three LPs in this 12-volume series are recommended (if they can be found!) is the interplay between Windhurst (who would not record commercially for two more years) and the great soprano of Bechet. Fine traditional jazz, taken from two radio broadcasts. —Scott Yanow

○ **Jazz Nocturne Volume 11 / i.** Jun. 5, 1945-Jun. 7, 1945 / Fat Cat's Jazz 011
The 11th volume in this 12-LP series features the final Sidney Bechet quintet of the spring of 1945, with the 18-year-old cornetist Johnny Windhurst in very good form along with a typically inspired Bechet and a solid rhythm section during three radio broadcasts dominated by swing and Dixieland standards. Now that the personnel had stabilized, the music was getting hotter during each performance. —Scott Yanow

○ **Jazz Nocturne Volume 12 / i.** Jun. 12, 1945-Jun. 14, 1945 / Fat Cat's Jazz 012
The final volume in Fat Cat's 12-LP series wraps up with two excellent broadcasts featuring Bechet's soprano and young

cornetist Johnny Windhurst playing Dixieland and swing standards with enthusiasm and close interplay. This is a very valuable if now rare series that should be sought after by Bechet collectors. —Scott Yanow

Sidney Bechet Sessions / Sep. 1946-Feb. 1947 / Storyville 4028
This LP features the great New Orleans soprano saxophonist Sidney Bechet in three different settings. He is heard as the star of pianist Joe Sullivan's quartet in 1945, matching power and creativity with pianist James P. Johnson in a 1946 quartet, and on five jams with clarinetist Mezz Mezzrow in 1947. Throughout, Bechet stars and is typically inspired on this familiar material. —Scott Yanow

Sidney Bechet with Mezz Mezzrow / i. 1947 / Classic Jazz 28
This two-LP set contains some of the best recordings made by Mezz Mezzrow for his King Jazz label. With Sidney Bechet starring on the majority of the tracks, trumpeter Hot Lips Page a major asset on four tunes, a few piano solos by Sammy Price, and two vocals from Pleasant Joe, the music is consistently swinging and blues-oriented. Individual tracks are not as memorable as the overall joyful feelings generated by this stomping music. —Scott Yanow

○ **Wingy Manone/Sidney Bechet Together Town Hall / i.** Oct. 11, 1947-Feb. 18, 1950 / Jazz Archives 29
Trumpeter Wingy Manone and soprano saxophonist Sidney Bechet actually only appear together on two selections, but the music is so hot in spots that one does not mind this LP's false advertising! Side one is taken from a 1947 Town Hall concert featuring Manone with two all-star groups that have such players as Bechet, tenorman Bud Freeman, clarinetist Edmond Hall, Peanuts Hucko (normally a clarinetist but here playing some very effective tenor), and pianist Art Hodes. Side two is taken from a 1950 concert featuring Bechet, trumpeter Max Kaminsky, and trombonist Wilbur DeParis. Dixieland fans will certainly enjoy this album. —Scott Yanow

○ **La Legende de Sidney Bechet / i.** Oct. 14, 1949-Jul. 4, 1958 / Vogue 600245
This CD has a cross-section of soprano great Sidney Bechet's '50s European recordings. A national hero in France during this time although relatively unknown to the general public in the United States, Bechet really dominates this set. The music ranges from his 1949 hit "Les Oignons," an early version of "Petite Fleur," and a passionate "Summertime" to romping jams on "Royal Garden Blues" and "When the Saints Go Marchin' In." A fine introduction to late period Bechet, one of the true giants of jazz history. —Scott Yanow

○ **Jazz Classics—Vol. 1 / i.** 1950 / Blue Note 7002

○ **Jazz Classics—Vol. 2 / i.** 1950 / Blue Note 7003

Bechet in Philadelphia—Volume Two / i. Feb. 18, 1950-May 24, 1950 / Jazz Archives 37
This LP features the virtuosic New Orleans soprano saxophonist Sidney Bechet at three different gigs in 1950. For the bulk of this set he leads a sextet with trumpeter Max Kaminsky and trombonist Wilbur DeParis; he's also heard playing "The Mooche" in a quartet with trombonist Vic Dickenson and matching wits with trumpeter Wild Bill Davison on two standards. Spirited Dixieland with few surprises but containing its share of excitement. —Scott Yanow

His Way / i. Oct. 15, 1951-Oct. 19, 1951 / Pumpkin 102
This LP from the collector's label Pumpkin features the great soprano saxophonist Sidney Bechet heading a quintet, which includes trombonist Big Chief Russell Moore and pianist Red Richards, during three nights in October 1951 at a Boston club. The Dixieland standards and blues mostly stomp with "September Song" being the only real ballad. Although hardly Bechet's definitive session, he never sounds less than inspired and is in fine form here. —Scott Yanow

○ **New Orleans Style, Old and New / i.** 1952 / Commodore 20020

○ **Immortal Performances / i.** 1952 / RCA 31

Salle Pleyel: 31 January 52 / i. Jan. 31, 1952 / Vogue 655001

Sidney Bechet is heard on this CD in concert with Claude Luter's orchestra before a semihysterical audience. The crowd shows one just how popular Bechet was in France during the '50s; if only America treated its jazzmen as well! The music is generally rewarding, but does not contain many surprises. It is a variety of standards and Dixieland tunes with Bechet's soprano rightfully dominating the proceedings. — *Scott Yanow*

At Storyville / **i.** 1953 / Black Lion 760902

○ **Olympia Concert, Paris** / **i.** 1954 / Blue Note 7029

King of the Soprano Saxophone / **i.** 1955 / Good Time Jazz 12013
This is an LP that is well deserving of being reissued on CD. Six memorable performances from 1954 find Sidney Bechet sharing the frontline with the great trumpeter Jonah Jones; their ensembles on "Chinatown, My Chinatown" are extremely exciting. The other four tracks feature Bechet with French orchestras. This version of "Roses of Picardy" is quite wonderful. Bechet at his best in his later years; highly recommended. — *Scott Yanow*

Olympia Concert, October 19, 1955 / Oct. 19, 1955 / Vogue 655605
Sidney Bechet is heard on this CD at a 1955 concert held before an adoring crowd in Paris where he was continually honored as a national hero. Backed by a pair of alternating French "trad" bands, Bechet plays some fresher material than usual, bringing back such classics as "Wild Man Blues," "Wild Cat Rag," and "Viper Mad." — *Scott Yanow*

○ **Creole Reeds** / **i.** 1956 / Riverside 12-216

★ **When a Soprano Meets a Piano** / **i.** 1957 / Inner City 7008
This relatively modern quartet session is one of Sidney Bechet's final recordings, and also features pianist Martial Solal. This LP finds Bechet playing melodically and with invention on superior swing (rather than Dixieland) standards, meeting the modern 25-year-old pianist halfway. Bechet's sound was still beautiful, even at this late stage. — *Scott Yanow*

Bechet!/ the Legendary Sidney Bechet / GNP 9012
This LP finds soprano saxophonist Sidney Bechet playing a variety of material in Paris with French "trad" bands during 1950-1952. Even Bechet cannot save some of the tunes (such as "Casey Jones"), but others (most notably "September Song" and his earlier hit "Summertime") come across quite well. Bechet always sounds inspired and enthusiastic, so pick this one up anyway. — *Scott Yanow*

Parisian Encounter / Vogue 600018
One of the most competitive of all jazzmen, Sidney Bechet is well-teamed with the Louis Armstrong-influenced trumpet of Teddy Buckner on this spirited set from late in Bechet's life. Buckner is reasonably respectful to Bechet, but gets in plenty of hot licks during this Dixielandish session; a concert shortly afterward by the two would be very combative. This fine CD shows that Sidney Bechet never did decline or lose any of his formidable power. — *Scott Yanow*

And Friends / PolyGram 840633
Sampler, part of the Walkman jazz series. It features Bechet during the latter stages in France, playing with his comrades. Some songs are delightful, especially "The Onions" with Claude Luter. — *Ron Wynn*

HARRY BECKETT (Harold Winston Beckett)

b. May 30, 1935, Bridgetown, Barbados
Trumpet, flugelhorn / Modern creative
As fierce and fiery as any trumpet and flugelhorn stylist, yet also capable of shimmering lyricism, Barbados's Harry Beckett has been part of Britain's jazz scene since the '50s. He moved to England in 1954, then joined Graham Collier's band in the early '60s, remaining with it until 1977. Beckett was featured in the 1961 film *All Night Long* with Charles Mingus. He also worked with Mike Westbrook's orchestra, and with Chris McGregor's Brotherhood of Breath. Beckett played with the big bands of Neil Ardley, Mike Gibbs, and

John Warren, and was part of the London Jazz Composer's Orchestra. He was also a member of the small combos led by Tony Oxley, John Surman, and Ray Russell. Beckett played with the Stan Tracey Octet in the mid-'70s, and also worked with Elton Dean and Zila, a group led by Dudu Pukwana. He's recorded as a leader for Ogun, Paladin, RCA, and Phillips. Currently, Beckett does not have any sessions on CD available in America. — *Ron Wynn*

★ **Bremen Concert** / **i.** May 1987 / West Wind 0007

BIX BEIDERBECKE (Leon Bix Beiderbecke)

b. May 10, 1903, Davenport, IA, **d.** Aug. 6, 1931, New York, NY
Piano, cornet / New Orleans traditional
Legend and romanticism have often obscured or clouded Bix Beiderbecke's achievements and importance. His backers rate him as Armstrong's equal and claim Beiderbecke might have surpassed him had he enjoyed a normal life span and career. Others insist Beiderbecke has been overrated; they put him in the same class as Beiderbecke's one-time boss, Paul Whiteman, and argue he's merely a good White musician whose color has given him inflated status. But a clearer look at the facts show that Beiderbecke was an outstanding soloist and a highly influential major contributor to the early jazz scene.

He began learning piano at age three; while listening to such records as the Original Dixieland Jazz Band's *Tiger Rag,* Beiderbecke would slow down the turntable speed and pick out the cornet part on the piano. He eventually taught himself cornet, while continuing piano studies. Beiderbecke played in his high school band, but faced stiff opposition from his parents over his jazz playing. They sent him to Lake Forest Academy in 1921, but Beiderbecke's jazz passion caused him to constantly miss classes so that he could attend live concerts in nearby Chicago. He was later expelled. He worked for his father in Iowa for a few months, then began playing in the Chicago area and on excursion boats on Lake Michigan. In 1923, Beiderbecke joined the Wolverines, and made his first records a year later.

Beiderbecke established himself as a superb soloist and a knowledgeable figure. He had a flawless ear, and his tone was one of the most beautiful in brass history. He was one of the first players able to solo effectively over 32 bars without sticking closely to strict melody. His knowledge of advanced harmonic approaches made him an alternative to Armstrong's exuberant radicalism, but the two admired each other, and Armstrong supposedly lent Beiderbecke his horn so he could sit in on a session. Besides his tone, Beiderbecke's unorthodox fingering, expressiveness, and creative pacing in his solos was impressive. He was influenced by classical music, and equally admired by Black and White musicians, notably Rex Stewart, Red Nichols, and Bunny Berigan. Stewart later reproduced exact Beiderbecke solos on some recordings. The Wolverines were hardly a first-rate organization, and their sessions were poorly recorded. Yet they became a sensation on college campuses, and Beiderbecke was soon hired away by Jean Goldkette.

He made several records with Goldkette before joining Paul Whiteman when Goldkette's group disbanded. The Whiteman recordings were stiff with minimal solo content, but they were superior to the Goldkette sessions, which were plagued by inferior material and lightweight vocalists. Beiderbecke stayed with Whiteman until 1929, but his premier records were cut with small bands led by Traumbauer. At times, Beiderbecke played with Eddie Lang, Adrian Rollini, and Jimmy Dorsey while making songs such as "In the Dark," "Flashes," "Candlelight," and his most famous, "In a Mist." His version of Hoagy Carmichael's "Skylark" so captivated the composer that he carried around Beiderbecke's mouthpiece the rest of his life. He did a radio series in New York for a while, playing with the Dorsey Brothers, the Casa Loma Orchestra, and Benny Goodman before dying in 1931 at age 28.

After his death, Beiderbecke's image was immensely distorted. Novelist Dorothy Baker's 1938 *Young Man with a Horn* created a larger-than-life character, and things were embellished even more by the inaccurate 1950 Kirk Douglas film with the same title (though at least Harry James's dubbed trumpet solos reflect the genuine article). A 1974 book *Bix: Man & the Legend* by Beiderbecke authorities Dick Sudhalter and Richard Evans helps to set much of the record straight, as does a 1982 documentary film *Bix*, directed by Brigitte Berman. —*Ron Wynn and Dan Morgenstern*

○ **And the Wolverines** / **i.** 1924 / Riverside 1050

○ **Complete Bix Beiderbecke, The** / **i.** 1924-1930 / Everest 317

○ **Bix Beiderbecke (1924-1930)** / 1924-1930 / BBC 601
By 1927, Bix Beiderbecke had jumped to New York, but his gang's three midwesterners were its more consistent swingers. The whole sextet lifts off by the end of "Since My Best Girl Turned Me Down," once Adrian Rollini gets his bass sax up to speed. (That track shows off Beiderbecke's nice cornet tone and supple bent notes, too.) —*Kevin Whitehead*, Down Beat

★ **And the Chicago Cornets** / Jan. 26, 1925 / Milestone 47019
All the Wolverines recordings are on this release, including two alternate takes and two with Jimmy McPartland replacing Beiderbecke. The faults of the 21-year-old avant-gardist's mates are obvious; the most remarkable is a tuba player who single-handedly drags the whole band's tempo at the slightest excuse. But as historian Max Harrison said, it was a creatively explosive time for Beiderbecke, crackling with excitement in the February 1924 sides, growing in detail by May (the "off" attack and a perfect slur on "Riverboat Shuffle"). In June, he was capable of a truly lovely improvisation on the "Tiger Rag" changes; a total performance, incidentally, that most groups of the period would have been proud of (Beiderbecke's lead was inspired). "Davenport Blues" from the following January is an oddity, a conscious attempt to play Louis Armstrong phrasing, something he supposedly never did. Perhaps no greater contrast can be found than the King Oliver-Armstrong derivations of Muggsy Spanier. His efforts, mutes and all, were perceptive, and point toward a dignity, drama, and passionate expression beyond Beiderbecke's apprehension. Both the exalted lyricism of Beiderbecke and the classic formulations of Armstrong were soon to be realized, in works that affected jazzmen a half century later. —*John Litweiler*, Down Beat

○ **Early Bix** / **i.** Jan. 26, 1925 / Riverside 1023

○ **Bix and Tram** / Feb. 1927-Sep. 1927

★ **Bix Beiderbecke—Vol. I: Singin' the Blues** / Feb. 1927-Sep. 1927 / Columbia 45450

At the Jazz Band Ball—Vol. 2 / Oct. 5, 1927-Apr. 1928 / Columbia 46175

Bix Lives / 1927-1930 / RCA 6845
This album includes Jean Goldkette and Whiteman material. A nice compliment to the Columbia Records compilations (Vols. 1 & 2). —*Richard Lieberson*

Bix N' Bing / 1927-1930 / Living Era 5005

○ **Bix Beiderbecke Story—Vol. 1, The** / **i.** Jul. 7, 1928 / Columbia 844

★ **Giants of Jazz** / **i.** 192? / Time-Life 04
This Time-Life *Giants of Jazz* collation gives the listener a thorough primer on a brief (1927 and 1928) but crucial period in Bix Beiderbecke's career. Beiderbecke was among the first important players in jazz to bring a sense of artistic consciousness to his work. He was schooled in the classics, had a decent foundation in theory, and was articulate enough to talk intelligently about what he played. Whereas Louis Armstrong fulminated with instinctive brilliance and urgent power, Beiderbecke found it possible to create in a bold but circumspect manner. Of the 40 selections included on the three LPs, 34 are from the 1927-1928 period. No significant Beiderbecke landmarks are ignored and some lesser efforts are included, too, like "Crying All Day," which was to

Beiderbecke's "Singin' the Blues" as Coleman Hawkins's "Rainbow Mist" was to his "Body and Soul" or "Humpty Dumpty," with its insinuations of "Charleston Alley" and modest Beiderbecke solo presence. But we get "I'm Coming Virginia," "Jazz Me Blues," the driving and harmonically alert "Lonely Melody" with Paul Whiteman, and many other gems. And of course, there is the eccentric, slightly out-of-register logic of "In a Mist." Unlike other stars in Time-Life's *Giants of Jazz* series, Beiderbecke is the consistent center of interest here. There is little of importance offered by Beiderbecke's co-stars, save for the remarkable, if dated, work of Eddie Lang on guitar, Joe Venuti on violin, and early Bing Crosby, who was the first to demonstrate what a singer of popular songs could learn from jazz musicians. Beiderbecke's most celebrated partner, Frank Trumbauer, has moments of introspective glory ("For No Reason at All in C"), but time has taken its toll on his playing generally, regardless of his historic relationship as an antecedent to Lester Young. —*John McDonough*, Down Beat

○ **Whiteman Days, The** / **i.** 192? /

RICHIE BEIRACH (Richard Beirach)

b. May 23, 1947, New York, NY
Piano / Early jazz-rock, world fusion, modern creative
Though not identified with the Third Stream movement, pianist Richie Beirach has developed a distinctive, dense approach that reflects the influences of Keith Jarrett, Chick Corea, and Bill Evans. He's played hard bop, jazz-rock, and ethnic music. Beirach was trained in jazz and classical music at Berklee and the Manhattan School of Music, where he earned his Bachelors degree in the early '70s. He was in David Liebman's band, Lookout Farm, in the mid-'70s, then formed his own trio after they disbanded. Beirach was in John Abercrombie's quartet, and co-formed Quest with Liebman in the early '80s. They recorded and performed through the '80s. He also recorded in a duo with George Coleman. Beirach has done sessions for Magenta, Owl, Storyville, Concord, CMP, Triloka, and Blue Note. He has several dates available on CD. —*Ron Wynn*

○ **Forgotten Fantasies** / **i.** 1975 / A&M 709
This features brilliant duets with longtime partner David Liebman (f/sax), on the creative side. Beirach wrote three of the six cuts, and shows his original approach to jazz. —*Michael G. Nastos*

○ **Eon** / Nov. 1976 / ECM 1054
Richie Beirach's well-programmed set begins with an intense reworking of Miles Davis's "Nardis." The introductory rhythm vamp, through its numerous reappearances, functions as an *idee fixe*, thereby allowing Beirach to fragment the tune's melodic and harmonic components so that space and the piano's overtonal timbres interact (along with melody and harmony) as coequal musical elements. Dave Liebman's "Places" is a poignant solo essay capturing echoes and images of bittersweet remembrances. Throughout, Beirach is ably assisted by the excellent musicianship of his colleagues from Lookout Farm, bassist Frank Tusa and percussionist Jeff Williams. —*Chuck Berg*, Down Beat

Hubris / Jun. 1977 / ECM 104

Elegy for Bill Evans / May 12, 1981 / Palo Alto 8065
This tribute to Beirach's good friend and influence has trio jazz with Al Foster on drums and George Mraz on bass. It includes three songs cowritten by Evans and Miles Davis, two other standards, and Evans's immortal "Peace Piece." —*Michael G. Nastos*

Rendezvous (w/ George Mraz) / **i.** Apr. 1982 / IPI 1001

○ **Continuum** / Jul. 5, 1983 / Eastwind 704
Another in a solo piano series Bierach cranked out in the '80s. This was done for the Japanese Baybridge label, and like predecessors and successors, it is mostly originals, though this time he does the title track (written by Tadd Dameron) and also covers "Some Other Time" and "Round Midnight." —*Ron Wynn*

○ **Common Heart** / Sep. 28-29, 1987 / Owl 79243

Alternately stunning and uneven solo piano work from 1987, with Bierach covering originals, spinning out melodies, pacing the set, and trying something different besides conventional theme/solo/theme arrangements. This has been reissued on CD. —*Ron Wynn*

★ **Convergence** / Nov. 10-11, 1990 / Triloka 185
Great communications. Pianist Richard Beirach and tenor saxophonist George Coleman. —*Michael G. Nastos*

○ **Chant** / i. 1991 / Creative Music Prod. 40

○ **Self Portraits** / i. 1992 / CMP 51
Recently issued set of solo piano originals by Bierach, done in a manner that gives autobiographical context to the session and also pace and definition to the compositions. —*Ron Wynn*

Live at Maybeck Recital Hall—Vol. 19 / i. Jul. 24, 1992 / Concord Jazz 4518

MARCUS BELGRAVE

b. 1936
Trumpet / Hard bop
Another underrecorded hard bop trumpeter who, in recent years, has gotten more session work, Marcus Belgrave has played funky blues and gutbucket soul with Ray Charles, and adventurous material with Charles Mingus, McCoy Tyner, and George Gruntz. He has the range, imagination, and raw talent to excel in any style, and has played with both giants and with excellent, but unknown, Detroit musicians like Wendell Harrison. Currently, Belgrave doesn't have any sessions available as a leader, but can be heard on everything from Ray Charles anthologies and reissues to Mingus and Tyner sessions. —*Ron Wynn and Michael G. Nastos*

★ **Gemini II** / 1975 / Tribe 4004
Nonet with master trumpeter. Sometimes funky, spacy, or swinging, but always potent. With Roy Brooks, Wendell Harrison, Harold McKinney, and Phil Ranelin. The band sounds twice its size due to the expansive compositional stance of the leader. —*Michael G. Nastos*

AARON BELL (Samuel Aaron Bell)

b. Apr. 24, 1922, Muskogee, OK
Bass, tuba / Swing, big band, progressive big band
Though he studied at Xavier University and played in many New Orleans bands, Aaron Bell was no traditionalist. Instead, he was one of the best bassists ever in the Duke Ellington band. His powerful lines and graceful, yet sturdy support provided a rich presence in the rhythm section alongside drummer Sam Woodyard and the Duke on piano. Bell was in the navy from 1942 to 1946, then worked with Andy Kirk in 1947. He returned to his native Oklahoma and taught music before resuming his own education at New York University. Bell recorded and worked with Lucky Millinder, Teddy Wilson, and Lester Young in the '50s, while leading his own trio. They recorded in 1955 and 1958. Bell backed vocalists, and played with combos and in the Broadway show *Compulsion* before joining Ellington in 1960. He remained with Ellington until 1962, then did sessions and worked in theater. He became resident composer at La Mama, an experimental New Jersey theater, in 1972. Bell also taught music in Newark, and earned his Masters degree at Columbia in 1975. He can be heard on various Ellington and Stan Kenton sessions, but his own albums are unavailable currently on CD. —*Ron Wynn*

★ **Three Swinging Bells** / Sep. 12, 1955 / Herald 0100

LOUIE BELLSON (Luigi Paulino Alfredo Francesco Antonion Balassoni)

b. Jul. 26, 1924, Rock Falls, IL
Drums / Swing, big band
An excellent combo and big-band drummer, Louie Bellson belongs near the top of any list of swing and large-group stylists. He's particularly known for his expert timing and his ability to control a pair of pedal-operated bass drums. He's

one of the more flamboyant soloists, but doesn't substitute flash for rhythmic ideas. Bellson drives any band he plays with, regardless of its size, and has the discipline and restraint to thrive in loose or controlled situations. He's an underrated composer who wrote a jazz ballet (1962's *The Marriage Vows*), and wrote pieces for combos and symphony orchestras. Bellson was the teenage winner of a nationwide drumming contest sponsored by Gene Krupa, and was in Benny Goodman's orchestra at age 17. After completing his military service in 1946, Bellson built his reputation through stints with Goodman, Tommy Dorsey, Harry James, Count Basie, and Duke Ellington in the early '50s. He doubled as a part-time arranger with Duke, and would return periodically to the Ellington band on special occasions, including the recording of *A Drum Is a Woman* and the first sacred concert. Bellson also wrote and arranged "The Hawk Talks" that was featured on the 1951 Columbia album *HiFi Ellington*. For many years, he was Pearl Bailey's music director and her husband, and led his own big bands that featured sidemen such as Cat Anderson, Don Menza, Conte Candoli, Bobby Shew, Joe Romano, John Heard, and George Duvivier, among others. He was active at workshops on college campuses throughout the '70s and '80s. Other Bellson achievements including writing "I Need Your Key" for James Brown's soul/jazz LP *Soul on Top* in 1970. He's recorded for Pablo, Concord Jazz, and Musicmasters, among many others. Bellson currently has several albums available on CD. —*Ron Wynn and Michael G. Nastos*

Exciting Mr. Bellson and His Big Band, The / i. 1954 / Norgran 7

○ **Louis Bellson with Wardell Gray** / i. 1954 / Norgran 14

○ **Concerto for Drums** / i. 1956 / Norgran 1095

Hawk Talks, The / i. 1956 / Norgran 1099

Brilliant Bellson Sound, The / i. 1960 / Verve 2123

Around the World in Percussion / Mar. 9, 1961 / Roulette 65002

Thunderbird / Oct. 1963 / Jasmine

★ **150 M.P.H.** / i. May 25, 1974 / Concord Jazz 36

Louis Bellson Explosion, The / May 21-22, 1975 / Pablo 728
A fine mid-'70s date that is both a showcase for Bellson's bombastic drumming and also a nice straightahead date with great contributions from Blue Mitchell, Snookey Young, Dick Mitchell, and others. It's been reissued on CD. —*Ron Wynn*

Louie Bellson's 7 / Jul. 25, 1976 / Concord Jazz 25

Ecue Ritmos Cubanos / Jan. 21, 1977 / Pablo 632

Prime Time / Nov. 4, 1977 / Concord Jazz 64

Raincheck / May 3, 1978 / Concord Jazz 73

Louis Bellson Jam / Sep. 28-29, 1978 / Pablo 838

Side Track / Jun. 1979 / Concord Jazz 141

Jazz Giants / Apr. 30, 1989 / Music Masters 5035
Excellent 1989 set with some major names; has a good Buddy Rich (d) versus Bellson track. —*Ron Wynn*

★ **Airmail Special: A Salute to the Big Band Masters** / Feb. 15-16, 1990 / Music Masters 5038
A Salute to the Big Band Masters. Powerhouse salute to big-band masters. —*Ron Wynn*

Drum Session / Inner City 6051

SATHIMA BEA BENJAMIN

b. Oct. 17, 1936, Cape Town, South Africa
Vocals / Ballads & blues, world fusion
Sathima Bea Benjamin is an enchanting, evocative vocalist who performs standards, show tunes, and traditional African music, and who improvises on her own originals with equal excellence. She met her husband, pianist Abdullah Ibrahim (then known as Dollar Brand), at the end of the '50s. The couple met Duke Ellington in Switzerland in the early '60s, and he invited them to Paris for a recording date. Though both recorded, only Ibrahim's recording was released.

Benjamin sang with Ellington at the Newport Jazz Festival in 1965. She worked mostly with Ibrahim into the mid-'70s, but has made several recordings as a leader since then, including an Ellington tribute album in 1979. Benjamin has recorded for Blackhawk and Enja. She's played with Ricky Ford, Buster Williams, Billy Higgins, and Kenny Barron, plus Ibrahim. Benjamin has a couple of sessions available on CD. —*Ron Wynn*

Sathima Sings Ellington / Apr. 1979 / Ekapa 001

○ **Windsong** / Jun. 17, 1985 / Black Hawk 50206

★ **Love Light** / Sep. 5, 1987 / Enja 79605

TONY BENNETT (Tony [Anthony Dominick Benedetto] Bennett)

b. Aug. 3, 1926, New York, NY
Vocals / Ballads & blues
Tony Bennett has enjoyed a resurgence of popularity in the late '80s and early '90s that matches his success in the '50s and '60s. He's been the model of consistency, singing with warmth, choosing ideal material, and making excellent albums that have their foundations in jazz regardless of their lyric content. Bennett's admiration for jazz musicians has often been expressed, and he's said to have modeled his phrasing on Art Tatum's piano technique and his delivery on Mildred Bailey's vocal style.

He sang while waiting tables as a teenager, then performed with military bands during World War II, and later had vocal studies at the American Theatre Wing school. Comedian Bob Hope noticed him working with Pearl Bailey, and made some career suggestions; at Hope's suggestion, Bennett changed his name from Joe Bari to Tony Bennett. Bennett's initial success came via several Columbia singles in the '50s. These included "Because of You," a chart topper in 1951, "I Won't Cry Anymore," and a remake of Hank Williams, Sr.'s "Cold, Cold Heart," which also made it to the number-one spot. Bennett had an impressive run of chart entries, with 24 songs making the Top 40 from 1950 to 1964, and had hits for almost 16 consecutive years. "Stranger in Paradise," "Just in Time," "Rags to Riches," and "There'll Be No Teardrops Tonight" were other big '50s hits. In the early '60s, the signature tune, "I Left My Heart in San Francisco," became a hit and won a Grammy. Other hits included "I Wanna Be Around," "The Good Life," and "Who Can I Turn To."

In the '60s and '70s, Bennett made the transition to an album artist, and had 25 LPs on the charts between 1962 and 1972. Robert Farnon provided arrangements for four major LPs. Bennett didn't merely churn out hits; he recorded with Count Basie, Duke Ellington, and Woody Herman. In the '70s, he played with Bill Evans and Jimmy and Marian McPartland. Later came sessions of Rodgers and Hart songs with Ruby Braff that yielded two volumes of material.

Bennett took a sabbatical from the recording studios in the '70s and '80s, and concentrated on touring, performing, and painting. Columbia filled the void with reissues until his '86 release *The Art of Excellence*, which primarily featured Bennett with Ralph Sharon's trio, but also included an intriguing duet with Ray Charles. A two-volume 1987 anthology, *Tony Bennett/Jazz*, featured an unissued track from 1964 with Bennett and Stan Getz. George Benson, Dizzy Gillespie, and Dexter Gordon were guests on the 1987 new album *Bennett and Berlin*.

His profile hasn't decreased in the '90s, thanks to the hit album *Perfectly Frank* devoted to songs popularized by Frank Sinatra, and to another album with numbers sung by Fred Astaire. Bennett continues to perform all over the world, and has made new inroads, appearing on the "Late Show with David Letterman" in 1993. There's plenty of Bennett available on CD from every era. Columbia issued *Forty Years: The Artistry of Tony Bennett* in 1991, a four-disc boxed set. —*Ron Wynn and William Ruhlmann*

Count Basie and His Orchestra Swings/Tony Bennett Sings / **i.** Aug. 6, 1959 / Roulette 25072

○ **Bennett and Basie Strike up the Band** / **i.** 1961 / Roulette 25231

○ **Tony Bennett at Carnegie Hall** / **i.** 1962 / Sony Special Products 823

☆ **Snowfall: The Tony Bennett Christmas Album** / **i.** 1968 / CBS 9739
Tony Bennett at his peak in 1968, adding his uncommon style to the common standards of the day. —*David A. Milberg*

○ **Tony Bennett/Bill Evans Album, The** / Jun. 10, 1975-Jun. 13, 1975 / Fantasy 9489
The *Tony Bennett/Bill Evans Album* is a magnificent musical accomplishment. Bennett was never better and Evans again shows his abilities as a first-class accompanist. The warm, intimate ambiance between these two pros who obviously had such respect for each other's musical personalities provides an unforgettable experience. —*Chuck Berg, Down Beat*

Tony Bennett/Marian & Jimmy McPartland & Friends Make Magnificent Music / May 13, 1977-May 14, 1977 / DRG 910

Jazz / **i.** 1987 / Columbia 40424

Astoria: Portrait of the Artist / **i.** 1990 / CBS 45348

Rodgers & Hart Songbook / **i.** Sep. 11, 1991 / DRG 2102

★ **Forty Years: The Artistry of Tony Bennett** / **i.** Oct. 7, 1991 / Columbia 46843
It's fascinating to hear how Tony Bennett's voice and style have matured over the years represented by the 87 tracks compiled for this four-CD set. Whether his heart's in San Francisco or Astoria, Bennett's a master at getting to the sensual heart of a song without any phony, macho bravado.— *Roy Hemming, Stereo Review*

Perfectly Frank / **i.** 1992 / Columbia 52965
Think no one can touch the Chairman on his own turf? Think again. Bennett's tribute is such an obvious move. It's odd that it's taken this long to materialize. Sinatra has made no secret of his admiration for Bennett, who puts his spin on this collection of Francis Albert classics. In the process, we wind up with Bennett's best in years. —*Steve Aldrich*

★ **Art of Excellence** / **i.** Mar. 4, 1992 / Columbia 40344
First-rate anthology package features the best Tony Bennett jazz and jazz-influenced pop cuts over several years. It shows the evolution of his style, his facility with big bands and string orchestras, his romantic side, and his interpretative and ballad skills. —*Ron Wynn*

Steppin' Out / **i.** 1993 / Columbia
Bennett's tribute to songs that Fred Astaire made famous (including standards by George Gershwin, Cole Porter, Irving Berlin, and Jerome Kern) is as strong a record as anything he has made recently, including the acclaimed *Perfectly Frank*. —*AMG*

Bennett/Berlin / CBS 44029

HAN BENNINK

b. Apr. 17, 1942, Zaandam, Holland
Drums, percussion, multi-instruments / Modern creative
One of Europe's top drummers and percussionists, Han Bennink employs multiple rhythms, colors, and accents in a manner similar to American free-oriented drummers. He's known for playing on anything and everything as part of his arsenal, including the floor or walls, wood blocks, chimes, cowbells, and assorted percussion instruments from around the world. But while Bennink is associated primarily with free players, he's also backed Ben Webster, Dexter Gordon, Don Byas, Johnny Griffin, Sonny Rollins, and Lee Konitz during various tours. Bennink's father was in a radio orchestra and backed singers and dancers in the Netherlands. He began on clarinet, and still plays it occasionally during performances. Sometimes, he also performs on banjo, viola, and various saxophones. Bennink played with Eric Dolphy during Dolphy's final European visit in 1964 and is featured on the *Last Date* album. He's worked with Derek Bailey,

Evan Parker, and Peter Brotzmann, recording with these musicians and others such as Misha Mengelberg, John Tchicai, Dudu Pukwana, and Willem Breuker in the '60s, '70s, and '80s. He's also done solo percussion albums, and recorded as a leader for FMP, Incus, and ICP, among others. Bennink's sessions as a leader are not available on CD via American labels, but can be obtained by mail order. He can be heard on various Soul Note dates with Steve Lacy, Roswell Rudd, Mengelberg, and others. —*Ron Wynn*

★ **Solo** / **i.** Oct. 1978 / FMP 21

DAVID BENOIT

b. 1953, Bakersfield, CA
Piano / Instrumental pop

A competent pianist, David Benoit has found success making well-produced, pleasant, and heavily arranged albums for GRP in the late '80s and early '90s. He issued one comparatively traditional session, *Waiting for Spring*, but otherwise has done light, uptempo, and ballad instrumental pop material. He's worked with Dave Valentin, Stanley Clarke, Brandon Fields, and Eric Marienthal, among others, and has consistently done well on the contemporary jazz charts. He has received extensive airplay on "lite" jazz and new age/adult contemporary radio outlets. All his dates are available on CD. —*Ron Wynn*

Freedom at Midnight / 1985 / GRP 9545

The popular fusion keyboardist added a string section and a large supporting cast on this 1985 session. Part of the assembled group includes fellow label superstars Eric Marienthal and Dave Valentin. This was elaborately produced and mastered, heavily arranged, and extremely successful on the lite jazz and adult contemporary circuit. —*Ron Wynn*

Urban Daydreams / 1988 / GRP 9587

★ **Waiting for Spring** / Feb. 1989-May 1989 / GRP 9595

○ **Letter to Evan** / **i.** 1992 / GRP 9687

GEORGE BENSON

b. Mar. 22, 1943, Pittsburgh, PA

Guitar, vocals / Blues & jazz, soul-jazz, instrumental pop, hard bop

George Benson has emulated the career paths and direction of two of his strongest influences: Wes Montgomery and Nat "King" Cole. Like Montgomery and Cole, Benson is supremely talented and his highly marketable skills have often required him to compromise his musical talents. Benson's guitar playing has a swinging flexibility and bluesy, soulful grit. His solos are deftly played and nicely executed, performed in a manner that makes him the equal of any contemporary stylist. He can accompany a vocalist or a band, can work with, off, or against the beat, can play tasteful ballads or torrid solos, and can do wailing soul jazz or slow, steamy blues. His singing has the sentimental, lush touches of Cole, but recalls the gospel-tinged delivery of Donny Hathaway.

Benson rode to fame in the '70s on the strength of songs just a cut above easy listening. He became an urban contemporary celebrity with a blend of mellow vocals and light instrumental filler, and has sought to keep record labels and urban radio outlets happy with hit fodder while retaining his integrity by doing occasional jazz projects.

Benson sang in clubs as a youngster, and formed a rock band at age 17. He played with Jack McDuff's quartet twice in the '60s, appearing at the Antibes-Juan-les-Pins Jazz Festival in 1964 and playing on a Swedish television broadcast with Jean Luc-Ponty. He briefly had his own trio in Pittsburgh before reteaming with McDuff. Benson later led and recorded with groups that included Ronnie Cuber and Jimmy Smith. He recorded with Billy Cobham, Miles Davis (who sought in vain to get Benson to join his group), Herbie Hancock, Freddie Hubbard, Ron Carter, and Lee Morgan in the '60s. When Creed Taylor, formerly Wes Montgomery's producer, sought a replacement for his departed star he

signed Benson to A&M, and cut the same string-laden, lightweight pop and rock filler that made Montgomery a star. When Taylor began a new label, CTI, Benson was one of his first signees.

Benson continued making pleasant, at times interesting, records through the early and mid '70s until he switched to Warner Bros. His cover of a Leon Russell tune, "This Masquerade," took Benson to the next level: crossover success. The single was a Top 10 pop hit, and the subsequent *Breezin'* album eventually topped the pop charts and won Grammy awards. Both Columbia and A&M promptly reissued his earlier albums, and Benson began a run of hit records that continued into the early '80s. He had seven Top 40 singles between 1976 and 1983, and four more Top 10 albums. But even Benson expressed displeasure at the content of these albums after awhile, and in the '80s began to try to expand without losing his urban contemporary base. He made a command appearance at the White House in 1979, and showed everyone he hadn't lost his jazz chops. Benson recorded with fellow guitarist Earl Klugh in the late '80s, and in '90 did a nice album with the Count Basie orchestra. Almost every album Benson's done over the '60s, '70s, '80s, and '90s has been reissued on CD. Columbia has reissued anthologies of his soul, jazz, and blues cuts, and Prestige has reissued an anthology of his work with McDuff. —*Ron Wynn*

○ **Benson, George/Jack McDuff** / Apr. 23, 1964+Oct. 19, 1965 / Prestige 24072

Here's another in the series of specially priced, two-record sets that Prestige issued in the '70s. This features guitarist George Benson and organist Jack McDuff from the time when Benson was a member of various McDuff groups. It is better than average guitar/tenor sax/organ dates from 1964 and 1965. —*Turner Martin, Cadence*

★ **New Boss Guitar** / May 1, 1964 / Prestige 461

○ **Benson Burner** / **i.** 1965-1966 / CBS 33569

Hot, soulful mid '60s organ combo material when George Benson was playing with bluesy abandon and reflecting the considerable influence of Grant Green. Anyone hearing these songs shouldn't be surprised at his eventual crossover success, but these aren't as overproduced and orchestrated as either his A&M or his Warner Bros. recordings. —*Ron Wynn*

☆ **Cookbook** / Aug. 1, 1966-Oct. 19, 1966 / Columbia 9413

Simmering interplay, fueled by guitarist Benson and baritone saxophonist Ronnie Cuber, make this early '60s effort one to savor. Six Benson originals, four standards. Produced by John Hammond. Lonnie Smith (organ), and Bennie Green (t). —*Michael G. Nastos*

○ **Blue Benson** / **i.** 1967-1968 / Polydor 2486272

Another sampler spotlighting his bluesy, funky material, this time taken from his brief period on Verve when he recorded with the Sweet Inspirations and also played in a quintet with Herbie Hancock and Ron Carter. It's fine material, but not as strong as the Columbia or Prestige fare that preceded it. —*Ron Wynn*

Shape of Things to Come / **i.** 1968 / A&M 3014

Other Side of Abbey Road, The / **i.** 1969 / A&M 3028

The albums that George Benson made for A&M in the late '60s were the trial runs for the huge hits he enjoyed in the '70s. This session follows almost the identical formula as later releases like *Breezin'*; light, yet immaculately played pop instrumentals and orchestrations, with the inclusion of vocals for counterpoint and contrast. —*Ron Wynn*

★ **Beyond the Blue Horizon** / Feb. 1971 / CBS 40810

Essentially a glorified guitar-organ date, this is top-notch in its field. Clarence Palmer's organ is economical and workmanlike and George Benson's guitar is an honest effort and digs in with ideas, though I still think the best George Benson is found in sideman roles. —*Bob Rusch, Cadence*

☆ **White Rabbit** / Nov. 1971 / CBS 40685

○ **Best of George Benson (on CBS)** / i. 1971-1976 / Columbia 45225
This is a 1989 compilation that covers Benson's tenure at CTI Records, and presents his best as a pure jazz guitarist, prior to his move to singing and the pop-jazz approach found in *Breezin'* and later albums. —*William Ruhlmann*

Bad Benson / May 1974 / CBS 40926

In Concert at Carnegie Hall / Jan. 11, 1975 / Columbia 44167

☆ **Good King Bad** / Jul. 1975+Dec. 1975 / Columbia 45226
This is a good place to hear Benson playing at his jazz best, rather than his commercial best. —*Michael Erlewine*

★ **Breezin'** / Jan. 6-9, 1976 / Warner Brothers 3111
Commercially, this is the definitive Benson album; counterpart to Wes Montgomery's pop works of the '60s. A platinum album. —*Ron Wynn*

Benson & Farrell / Mar. 1976-Sep. 1976 / Columbia 44169
Good duo outing matching two brilliant players who struck gold with CTI's pop-jazz. Within the confines of the material, Benson and Farrell found ways to do more than spew out rote solos and execute the arrangements. Though far from their best work, they managed to retain enough integrity to make it worth hearing for the nonfusion audience. —*Ron Wynn*

In Flight / Aug. 1976+Nov. 1976 / Warner Brothers 2983

Weekend in L A / Feb. 1, 1977 / Warner Brothers 3139
A double-album release and extremely popular, particularly the remake of "On Broadway." It's dominated by vocals, but the few times Benson gets to solo he displays enough artistry and flair to make it memorable. This has been reissued on CD. —*Ron Wynn*

20/20 / 1988 / Warner Brothers 25178
Guitarist/vocalist George Benson was at his crossover peak with this two-record set, doing much more singing than playing, and soloing only when necessary. Even operating within these restrictions, however, Benson still demonstrates both a pleasant, occasionally moving voice and a crafty, soulful guitar style. This makes up for the heavy-handed production. —*Ron Wynn*

Big Boss Band / 1990 / Warner Brothers 26295

BOB BERG (Robert Berg)

b. Apr. 7, 1951, New York, NY
Tenor and soprano saxophone / Hard bop, M-Base
An energetic stylist who was heavily influenced, at first, by John Coltrane, Bob Berg's warm, often evocative tenor sax solos are delivered with fury and zest. His later dates have included good use of soul-jazz devices. Berg has worked in groups led by Horace Silver, Tom Harrell, and Sam Jones, among others. Berg studied at the High School of Performing Arts in New York and at Juilliard before touring with Brother Jack McDuff in 1969. He worked with Horace Silver and Cedar Walton in the '70s and '80s, then joined Miles Davis in the mid '80s, where he moved from a hard bop surrounding to a funk/R&B and jazz-rock context. He's since recorded as a leader for Denon and Red; he'd previously done sessions for Xanadu and EPM. Berg has several dates available as a leader on CD. —*Ron Wynn*

★ **New Birth** / May 12, 1978 / Xanadu 159
New Birth displays plenty of enthusiasm, occasionally too much, as on "Pauletta," where Bob Berg's double-timing and gangly phrasing confuse the pleasant changes, add unwanted tension, and never totally mesh with the rhythm section. He works hard to negotiate the fleet changes of the "Giant Steps"-derived "Neptune," but says little of interest. He seems most comfortable on the funky, uncomplicated changes of "Shapes." Luckily, trumpeter Tom Harrell and pianist Cedar Walton satisfy with their less frantic, less cluttered stylings. —*Art Lange*, Down Beat

Short Stories / Mar. 1987 / Denon 1768

Back Roads / 1991 / Denon 9042

A departure from his usual path, Berg explores different musical idioms such as country, jazz, and fusion. —*Paul Kohler*

○ **In the Shadows** / i. Feb. 26, 1992 / Denon 6210
On his third Denon release, Berg ventures into a few jazz standards while maintaining a strong hold on his fusion roots. Jim Beard is featured on keyboards. —*Paul Kohler*

Enter the Spirit / i. 1993 / Stretch/GRP 1105
Bob Berg may be the Picasso of modern tenors. There are, of course, his searing sound, abundant technique, and sheer power. But even more impressive is Berg's ability to create large-scale canvases where sharply etched lines and vibrant colors coalesce. A benchmark is the loping duo version of Sonny Rollins's "No Moe," in which Berg's scooping and rhythmically inflected lines intertwine with the lyrical yet powerful drumming of the great Dennis Chambers. On bass is the equally impressive James Genus. Piano chores are executed with aplomb by Chick Corea, David Kikoski, and Jim Beard. —*Chuck Berg*, Jazz Times

KARL BERGER (Karl Hans Berger)

b. 1935, Heidelberg, Germany
Piano, vibes, composer, percussion / Modern creative
Though he began as a bebop player, German vibist Karl Berger was one of the more challenging soloists on his instrument during the '60s and '70s. He became a top free player, expanding the vibes' role and making it a more percussive instrument through solos that stressed colors and tones more than fast lines or pretty phrases. He was also an early advocate for more jazz/international music interaction, and, during the mid '80s, took a leave from his teaching post to tour and perform at percussion festivals in India, to play with African drummer Olatunji, and to record with shakuhachi player Hozan Yahamoto.
Berger studied classical piano at age ten, then later served as house pianist at the Club 54 in Heidelberg. He learned bebop from visiting American musicians stationed there like Don Ellis, Leo Wright, Cedar Walton, and Lex Humphries. Berger switched to vibes on the advice of French vibist Michel Hausser, with whom he'd played in Germany and Paris. He studied both musicology and philosophy in Heidelberg and Berlin, earning a doctorate in 1963. Berger then joined Don Cherry's free jazz quintet in Paris in 1965. He worked with Cherry for 18 months, then worked for a month with Steve Lacy before rejoining Cherry. When they recorded in America, Berger remained in the States playing in schools for the organization Young Audiences, with Horacee Arnold's group from 1967 to 1971. He also toured periodically with his own bands, playing and recording with Marion Brown and Roswell Rudd.
Berger and Ornette Coleman cofounded the Creative Music Studio in Woodstock, New York, in 1972. He served as its director and helped to craft programs that aided students in determining their own interests rather than establishing a set curriculum. The studio held many workshops and concerts in the '70s and '80s, and Berger attracted musicians such as Anthony Braxton, Lee Konitz, Jack DeJohnette, and Sam Rivers to assist or play at concerts. He led a 28-piece orchestra that appeared at the 1982 Kool Jazz Festival as part of the Jazz and World Music segment. He made an international tour in 1985 and 1986, and served as guest conductor and composer for the Westdeutscher Rundfunk in Cologne, Germany. Berger continued to record periodically for Black Saint/Soul Note and Enja in the '70s and '80s, and is featured on a trio date with Dave Holland and Edward Blackwell issued by Enja in 1993. It's one of only three Berger titles cited as available on CD. —*Ron Wynn*

Tune In / Mar. 1970 / Milestone 9026

All Kinds of Time / Apr. 26, 1976 / Sackville 3010

○ **Live at the Donaueschingen Festival** / Oct. 1979 / MPS 68250
Definitive Berger originals done live in Germany with the Woodstock Workshop Orchestra, a combination of Creative Music Studio students and instructors. —*Michael G. Nastos*

★ **Transit** / Aug. 16-25, 1988 / Black Saint 92

Crystal Fire / **i.** 1993 / Enja 7029

Karl Berger's long association with Don Cherry, Ornette Coleman, and free music is most evident when Berger plays vibes. Berger's "Crystal Fire Suite" improvises from simple folk melodies, reminiscent of Ornette, supported by liberating, urgent accompaniment from Dave Holland and the late Ed Blackwell. Like crystal, Berger's tone is hard, shimmering, and a bit icy. The piano tracks bring out a warmer, more conventional facet of Berger's music.—*Jon Andrews,* Down Beat

○ **Around** / Black Saint 112

BUNNY BERIGAN (Rowland Bernart Berrigan)

b. Nov. 2, 1908, Hilbert, WI, **d.** Jun. 2, 1942, New York, NY

Trumpet, vocals / Swing

If Bix Beiderbecke hadn't been early jazz's quintessential tragic White jazz figure, then Bunny Berigan certainly would have fit the bill. Berigan was a superb trumpeter who absorbed improvisational concepts and favorite phrases from both Louis Armstrong and Bix Beiderbecke, yet was not a clone of either of these men. His command of the trumpet and timbral variety were Armstrong reflections, while the Beiderbecke touches could be heard in his melodic lines. But Berigan's harmonic sense and dramatic pacing, while certainly refinements of Armstrong and Beiderbecke, were part of a style that wasn't eclipsed by anyone. Berigan began playing in local bands around Hilbert, WI, as a teen, then played in college bands before moving to New York in the early '30s. He doubled on violin for a while, but stopped in 1927. He played in Hal Kemp's band in 1930, and even toured Europe with this orchestra. Then came stints with Smith Ballew, Paul Whiteman, Benny Goodman, and the Dorsey Brothers, with whom he enjoyed a huge hit with the song "Marie," before heading his own band from 1937-1940. Berigan turned in a definitive, shattering performance on the song "I Can't Get Started," which he cut twice. The second version was issued on a 12-inch 78 and combined an almost coy vocal with a sizzling intro and solos modeled after Armstrong's "West End Blues." The song was so magnificent that, reportedly, Armstrong didn't want to record it. Berigan recorded several other magnificent solos on material done for Victor between 1937 and 1940. After winning *Metronome* magazine's 1939 poll and getting five times as many votes as the next closest player, Bunny Berigan began a downslide. He had both a combo and big band collapse under him, and a brief reunion with Tommy Dorsey was a disaster. He died in 1942 at age 33. There are some Berigan sessions available on CD. Robert Dupuis's book on Berigan, *Elusive Legend of Jazz,* is quite definitive and is recommended. —*Ron Wynn*

I Can't Get Started / **i.** 1933-1938 / Pro Arte 554

This Bunny Berigan collection is as good a selection of Berigan (trumpet) as can be found short of the original LPV releases—and this sounds better. There are all the usual takes of "I Can't Get Started," "Peg O' My Heart," "Mahogany Hall Stomp," "Davenport Blues," "I Cried For You," "Ain't She Sweet," "Walkin' the Dog," "Can't Help Lovin' Dat Man," and "Night Song." —*Shirley Klett,* Cadence

★ **Complete Bunny Berigan—Vol. 1, The** / Apr. 1, 1934-Oct. 7, 1937 / Bluebird 5584

The Bunny Berigan (trumpet) groups included George Auld (sounding much like Charlie Barnet on tenor sax), Arnold Fishkin, and George Wettling. The tune Berigan seemed to own at the time, "I Can't Get Started," gets its steam after the vocal when Berigan plays around a group of sustained chords, which was very exciting then. "A Study in Brown" and "Mahogany Hall Stomp" are worth hearing. —*Jerry Atkins,* Cadence

Jazz Heritage: The Decca-Champion Sessions / **i.** Jan. 8, 1936-Apr. 3, 1936 / MCA 1362

○ **Bunny Berigan and His Boys** / Apr. 13, 1936-Jun. 9, 1936 / Epic 16006

○ **Sing! Sing! Sing!—Vol. 1: 1936-1938** / Jul. 1936-Jun. 1938 / Vintage Jazz 627

Complete Bunny Berigan—Vol. 2, The / **i.** Oct. 7, 1937-Jun. 8, 1938 / Bluebird 5657

Sing! Sing! Sing!—Vol. 3: 1937-1938 / 1937-Jun. 1938 / Bluebird 9953

○ **Bunny Berigan & His Orchestra (1937-1938)** / 1937-1938 / Hindsight 239

○ **Devil's Holiday—Vol. 2: 1938** / 1938 / Vintage Jazz 638

IRVING BERLIN (Irving Baline)

b. May 11, 1888, Temun, Siberia, Russia, **d.** Sep. 22, 1989

Songwriter

Irving Berlin was America's tunesmith, the architect of many classic songs for shows and films, and the embodiment of Tin Pan Alley. It's fitting that he lived for 100 years, since his songs spanned the development of the American popular music industry. Berlin had a special piano with a mechanism that allowed him to change keys while he played the only key he knew. He never learned to read or to play the piano properly, and later hired a musical secretary. A Russian emigrant whose family arrived in America from Siberia when he was a child, Berlin was a singing waiter and song plugger early in his career. His name changed from Baline to Berlin by accident, when a printer changed the name on his song "Marie from Sunny Italy" to Berlin. Despite the artistry of his music, reportedly Berlin was concerned always and primarily with commerce. If a song sold, he considered it a great song; if it didn't, he didn't consider it great, regardless of its structure. Berlin's hits began in 1911 when vaudeville vocalist Emma Carus sang "Alexander's Ragtime Band." The next year, Eddie Cantor sang "Everybody's Doin' It." The song "When I Lost You" was penned for his wife Dorothy, who died five months after their marriage in 1912. He was once billed as the "King of Ragtime" for a 1913 show in England, one of the early misapplications of musical royalty. Berlin didn't think much of "God Bless America" and left it out of a show he did for the army while a soldier in 1918. Kate Smith sang it on radio from the New York World's Fair 20 years later for Armistice Day. He gave the royalties to the Scouts.

Berlin began buying back his song rights in the '20s and became a hugely successful publisher. He gave his second wife, Ellin MacKay, the rights to "Always" as a wedding present in gratitude for her marrying him against her family's wishes. His run of hits in the '20s and '30s included "Remember," "Blue Skies," "Marie," "Puttin' on the Ritz," "Soft Lights and Sweet Music," "How Deep Is the Ocean," "Cheek to Cheek," "Top Hat, White Tie and Tails," "Let's Face the Music and Dance," and "Say It Isn't So." Berlin's songs were featured in *The Jazz Singer* (the historic first movie with sound), *Follow the Fleet,* and *On the Avenue.* Things continued in the '40s with *Holiday Inn* and the Broadway play *Annie Get Your Gun.* Jerome Kern was to be the show's songwriter, but after he died producers Rogers & Hammerstein hired Berlin. Berlin's score resulted in a record for hit songs in one show; the list included "There's No Business Like Show Business," "The Girl That I Marry," and "They Say It's Wonderful."

Berlin's string of hits continued in the '50s and early '60s, with songs for *Miss Liberty, Call Me Madam,* and a revival of *Annie Get Your Gun* in 1966, but his run was interrupted with 1962's *Mr. President.* Berlin's many honors included the Congressional Medal of Honor in 1954, the Medal of Freedom in 1966, and membership in the French Legion of Honour. He was also a charter member of ASCAP and was on its first board of directors. Both Alexander Woolcoot and David Ewen did comprehensive biographies of Berlin, and there are many others. Berlin never allowed anyone to do a fictional stage or film biography. The number of jazz and popular music artists who've done Berlin songs is staggering; there are many Berlin songbooks available on CD by everyone from Ella Fitzgerald to Billy Eckstine and Sarah

Vaughan. There are also anthologies and special lines that feature renditions of his work. —*Ron Wynn*

★ **Irving Berlin: A Hundred Years** / i. 1988 / Columbia 40035
Issued to commemorate Berlin's 100th birthday, this 21-track compilation of his songs is culled from recordings made primarily in the '30s, though there are also a few from the '40s and '50s. The artists include Connee Boswell, Bing Crosby, Eddie Cantor, Fred Astaire, Benny Goodman, Dinah Shore, Tony Bennett, and Johnny Mathis. —*William Ruhlmann*

TIM BERNE

b. 1954, Syracuse, NY
Alto saxophone / Modern creative

While improvisation and jazz are at the root of Tim Berne's music, he doesn't limit himself. Berne's compositions include snatches and snippets of free jazz and hard bop, rock, pop, fusion, various international styles, and even contemporary classical. His alto sax work is equally eclectic, with odd rhythms, tonal colors, explosive phrases, poignant melodies, vocal effects, screams and squawks along with blues and soulful melodies. Berne's records and concerts emphasize spontaneity and response more than composition and notation, though he's also written some fine pieces. Berne didn't begin playing alto until he was age 19. He studied with Anthony Braxton and Julius Hemphill, then established his own record label. Berne recorded his first two albums on the West Coast, working with Vinny Golia, Alex Cline, and Roberto Miranda. He moved to New York, where he recorded more albums while working with Olu Dara, Ed Schuller, and Paul Motian. Through the rest of the '80s, Berne did sessions for Soul Note and Columbia. He landed his Columbia pact through a chance meeting with longtime friend Gary Lucas, a former Captain Beefheart guitarist and, at that time, a Columbia executive. Lucas recommended Berne to Columbia. He did two fine albums for the label, which responded by cutting him loose. But Berne had options. He formed the group Miniature, with Hank Roberts and Joey Baron, while also playing with John Zorn and Marilyn Crispell. Berne continues recording on the JMT label. He currently has JMT and Soul Note releases available on CD, but his two fine Columbia albums, *Fulton Street Maul* and *Sanctified Dreams,* have been deleted. In addition, Berne's dates for his Empire Productions label and his early West Coast sessions are not available currently on CD. —*Ron Wynn*

○ **7x** / Jan. 8, 1980 / Empire 36
With the exception of "Water People," a tiring AACM-type exotic percussion and reed "atmosphere" piece, the material on alto saxophonist Tim Berne's record is all very good; the pastoral "A Pearl in the Oliver C." and zigzagging "Chang" are examples of particularly well-delineated lines. Berne's tone is like a marriage of Ornette Coleman and Anthony Braxton's, and his best solos—"Flies," for example, or "Showtime"—display a nice balance of passion and logic. Unfortunately, baritone saxophonist Vinnie Golia often relied on passion alone—he didn't always know what to save for last. Neither did guitarist Nels Cline, whose heavy metal call to battle on "7x" is in especially poor taste. Trombonist John Rapson adds a feisty voice to this group on three titles, and bassist Roberto Miranda and drummer Alex Cline listen well to the soloist and to each other. —*Francis Davis,* Down Beat

○ **Songs and Rituals in Real Time** / Jul. 1, 1981 / Empire 60K2
Tim Berne's fourth meticulously produced album on his Empire label is more of a blowing date than any of his earlier LPs. His other LPs emphasize Berne's compositions, although they contain good blowing, and the live *Songs and Rituals* isn't short on compositional sense. But here, Berne's pieces are stretched to accommodate plenty of solo space, the lion's share of which goes to the leader. Berne, the composer of shapely melodies, is most obviously represented by the dirgelike "rituals," "San Antonio," "Shirley's Song," and "The Ancient Ones." But the two-sax heads of the "songs"

make use of the same long notes and appealing plain-interval consonances and subtle dissonances as the rituals did. On the cuts where Mack Goldsbury plays soprano rather than tenor, the saxes' close harmonies have the same glowing airiness as the horns on Dave Holland's much-admired *Conference of the Birds.* Berne's alto has a keening tone, and a nice way of fluttering on one note by using alternate fingerings. His soaring quality, his attention to patterns (in his flying arpeggios) and to the shape of a phrase are reminiscent of Oliver Nelson at his peak, though Berne's alto has much more of a vocal, shouting quality. Second saxophonist Goldsbury is a less inventive soloist, but he is a good foil for the leader, as he shadows Berne through the heads, using the altoist's lines as instant inspiration. On "New Dog/Old Tricks" in particular, he displays a guttural, bluesy sound.... In an unaccompanied section of "Flies," the two saxes buzz together like double-stopped bowed strings. On "Roberto Miguel" and "Mutants," Berne and Goldsbury take churning, simultaneous solos over an agitated, but controlled, rhythm section. Bassist Ed Schuller is often assigned ostinato-based parts under the blowing, and keeps them flexible and alive. He has sure pitch, and a rich, deep tone, which I haven't heard better represented on record.... His finest moments come in "The Ancient One's" extended cadenza. The unit gets extra crackle from drummer Paul Motian, the real standout here, as elsewhere, because his distinctive approach is so far removed from the typical or the expected. His deliberately loud and assertive thrashing-without-egomania over the head of "Unknown Factor" is a case in point. While riding cymbals, Motian uses his snare to mark off heavy accents that have the impact of bass-drum bombs. He takes a short freight-train solo on "New Dog." —*Kevin Whitehead,* Cadence

○ **Ancestors** / Feb. 1983 / Soul Note 1061
Tim Berne's (alto sax) playing on *Ancestors* is fluid, warm, and conveys a relaxed levity. For this live recording (February 19, 1983) Berne enlarged his regular quartet (Mack Goldsburg, tenor sax, soprano sax; Ed Schuller, bass; Paul Motian, percussion) to include Herb Robertson (trumpet) and Ray Anderson (perhaps the finest trombonist of the past five years (1983)). As usual, the tunes are all Berne originals and display the sectional and harmonic structures that so much of his music seems to exhibit. And the music is very much a vehicle to Berne's success. His sax work is strong, though Ray Anderson is perhaps the most brilliant on this date, but it is the large sound foundation of composer and leader that holds this music together so well and propels it through the soloists. The soloists are very solid; in fact, with the exception of some sluggishness about a third of the way into side two, the music is most involving. —*Bob Rusch,* Cadence

○ **Mutant Variations** / Sep. 1984 / Soul Note 1091
Definitely not part of the new traditional scene, alto saxophonist Tim Berne keeps moving forward. This '84 quartet set of all originals is reminiscent, at times, of mid '50s Ornette Coleman, notably due to Herb Robertson's pocket trumpet solos and the dynamics generated by Berne and Robertson's interaction with bassist Ed Schuller and percussionist Paul Motian. —*Ron Wynn*

★ **Fulton Street Maul** / 1986 / Columbia 40530
This album is a radical departure from earlier recordings, though in some ways it seems a return to the past. More clearly than previous outings, it reflects the influence of Tim Berne's teacher, Julius Hemphill. Hank Roberts' rhythmic sawing evokes Hemphill's early classics, even if his cello didn't have Abdul Wadud's heavy blues accent. A strong vocal quality has always been Berne's most conspicuous asset—but here his alto shouts as much as sings, echoing the gnarly anguish of Hemphill's own less polite side. That impassioned heat was a response to his backing trio's energy and dense sound. Berne's early recording groups featured electric guitar, but this band was notably noisier, more flavored with industrial/art tendencies (a by-product, one suspects, of former outsider Berne's entry into the Lower

Manhattan crowd). Calculated density marked his break with tradition; on the surface at least *Fulton Street*—produced by ex-Beefheart guitarist Gary Lucas—is his least jazzy effort; overdubs abound; improvisation, Berne says, is secondary; the churning rhythm section is more relentless than swinging ("Unknown Disaster," "Federico") caught up in an urban tribal dance. Not that the solos are missing. If Berne (and guitarist Bill Frisell) hew to a harder, harsher line than usual, the leader still steps out. And his compositions can still be roughly divided into fast/angular "songs" ("Miniature") and horizontal "rituals"—slowly unfolding, hauntingly rapturous dirges; "Icicles Revisited" (a reprise from *Mutant Variations*, 9/84); the intermittent refrain of the suite "Betsy." But where his "rituals" received straightfoward exposition before, "Icicles" turns into another propulsive spirit-dance; one of "Betsy's" many episodes spotlights Alex Cline's Tibetan harmonic singing, a quiet monastic whine that probably wouldn't carry at Sweet Basil. "Federico" is for Fellini (while an earlier piece honored Kurosawa), so it's not surprising that these shifting panoramas are informed by cinematic sense.... *Fulton Street Maul*'s not Tim Berne's best, but it's certainly no flop—his keening alto sound and appealingly melancholy writing rise above the carefully plotted din. —*Kevin Whitehead*, Cadence

Sanctified Dreams / **i.** Jun. 1988 / Columbia 44073
Alto saxophonist Tim Berne ranks among the more progressive players around, someone who keeps looking ahead rather than behind. This 1988 set is no different; it contains odd passages, moments of indecision, and segments where Berne and associates blaze away. —*Ron Wynn*

Tim Berne's Fractured Fairy Tales / **i.** 1990 / JMT 834431
There are snatches of free music, funk sections, nods to 20th century classical, hints of world-beat connections, and some moments when the whole process falls apart. Don't look that often for the beat, but you will discover (with effort) the melody. — *Ron Wynn*, Rock & Roll Disc

Pace Yourself: Tim Berne's Caos Totale / Nov. 1990 / JMT 834442

Diminutive Mysteries / **i.** 1993 / JMT/Verve
Most fans of David Sanborn's pop-jazz and instrumental R&B albums probably won't recognize his sound here, where he plays a soprano saxophone much of the time, rather than his familiar alto. But Sanborn's connection with Tim Berne, a fellow saxophonist, is not as unlikely as it might seem. *Diminutive Mysteries* is dedicated to the music of Berne's mentor, Julius Hemphill, formerly of the World Saxophone Quartet. One listen confirms that Sanborn understands this music and respects where it's coming from. Berne commissioned Hemphill to write five new pieces, which are grouped into the title suite and radically reinterpreted by Berne's group of drummer Joey Baron, cellist Hank Roberts, and guitarist Marc Ducret. There are also two older Hemphill compositions, "Rites" and "Mystery to Me," and a long piece by Berne called "The Maze (for Julius)." Berne, who lacks Sanborn's facility on alto, compensates by taking a more orchestral approach on baritone sax. Sanborn cuts loose with a few of his patented bluesy funk licks on alto, but his soprano playing is wild and free. —*Rick Mitchell*, Request

WARREN BERNHARDT

b. Nov. 1938, Wausau, WI
Piano, keyboards / Modern creative
A flexible accompanist, fluid soloist, and ardent disciple of Bill Evans, pianist Warren Bernhardt has been a performer, a teacher, and a composer. His playing can be striking and aggressive, but he's known more for his adaptability than for his harmonic or melodic virtuosity. Bernhardt's played hard bop, cool, jazz-rock, fusion, and pop dates. He began studying classical piano as a child, and gave recitals at age nine. Bernhardt played in Chicago as a soloist while attending college, then joined Paul Winter's sextet in the early '60s and toured South America with them. He moved to New York in 1963, and played with Gerry Mulligan, Clark Terry, George

Benson, and Jeremy Steig during the '60s. Bernhardt also did sessions with pop, rock, and folk stars like Richie Havens, Liza Minnelli, and Tim Hardin. He toured and recorded with Jack DeJohnette's group, Directions, in 1976, and was in a duo with Mike Mainieri from 1975 to 1980. During the '80s, Bernhardt led the band Steps Ahead, and was alternately in trios that featured Peter Erskine and Eddie Gomez and Jimmy Cobb and Dave Holland. He's done sessions for Arista/Novus, Digital Music, and DMP in the '70s, '80s, and '90s. He also founded and edits *Letter from Evans*, a scholarly newsletter of information on the contributions and life of Bill Evans. Currently, Bernhardt has sessions available on CD. —*Ron Wynn*

Solo Piano / Apr. 1977 / Novus 3001

★ **Blue Montreux** / **i.** 1979 / Arista 4224

Blue Montreux II / **i.** 1979 / Arista 4245

CHU BERRY (Leon Brown Berry)

b. Sep. 13, 1910, Wheeling, WV, **d.** Oct. 30, 1941, Conneaut, OH
Tenor saxophone / Swing, big band
Chu Berry was a masterful, impressive tenor saxophonist whose swinging skills have often been undervalued because he played during the era dominated by Coleman Hawkins. But Berry's deep, dark tone, rolling phrasing, haunting manner, and spirit were consistently impressive, particularly on uptempo numbers where he could utilize his great breath control and harmonic expertise. He was a smoother player than Hawkins, but didn't sacrifice any swing or intensity. Berry worked in the '30s with Benny Carter, Teddy Hill, and Fletcher Henderson, then was in Cab Calloway's orchestra until Berry died in a car crash. He recorded as a leader with the Stompy Stevedores in 1937, and his "little jazz" group in 1938 included Roy Eldridge. His 1940 jazz ensemble featured Hot Lips Page. Berry also recorded some rare sides with Charlie Ventura in 1941. Among his finest recorded moments were solos on "Krazy Kapers" with the Chocolate Dandies, "Hot Mallets" with Lionel Hampton, and "Blues in C# Minor" with Teddy Wilson. Berry recorded for Commodore, Columbia, and Variety as a leader. He can be heard on various CD compilations with Henderson, Calloway, and Hampton. EPM issued *The Chu Berry Story* on CD in 1991. —*Ron Wynn and Michael G. Nastos*

★ **Indispensable** / **i.** 1936-1939 / RCA 89481
1936-1939. A wide variety of sessions from an immortal stylist. With Gene Krupa (d), Lionel Hampton (vib), Cab Calloway (v), Fletcher Henderson (leader), and Wingy Manone's bands. —*Michael G. Nastos*

Giant of Tenor Sax, A / Nov. 1938-Aug. 1941 / Commodore 7004

○ **Memorial** / **i.** 1954 / Commodore 20024

☆ **Chu** / **i.** 1955 / Epic 3124

☆ **Chu Berry** / **i.** 1959 / Commodore 30017

EDDIE BERT

b. May 16, 1922, Yonkers, NY
Trombone / Swing, big band, bop
A good trombone soloist known for his flexibility and his firm, strong tone, Eddie Bert has recorded successfully in big bands and sextets playing swing or bebop. He studied with Benny Morton as a teen, then joined Sam Donahue's band at age 18. Bert made his recording debut with Red Norvo's orchestra in 1942, and also played with Charlie Barnet, Woody Herman, Herbie Fields, Stan Kenton, and Benny Goodman in the '40s. Though he spent part of that decade in the army, Bert recorded with Fields, Kenton, and Goodman in the late '40s, and with Kenton, Herman, Ray McKinley, and Les Elgart in the early and mid '50s. He joined a three-trombone unit led by Bill Harris in 1952, and also headed groups on Monday nights at Birdland in 1955. Bert played with Charles Mingus's Jazz Workshop in 1955 and 1956, while also recording as a leader. He eventually got his degree in music

education in 1957 from the Manhattan School of Music, and worked again with Goodman in the late '50s and Mingus in 1962, as well as Gil Melle. Bert worked with Thelonious Monk in 1963 and 1964. He'd started playing in Broadway theatres with Elliot Lawrence in 1954, and continued until 1968. In 1968 he joined Dick Cavett's television show orchestra, and remained with them until 1972. He also toured Europe with the Thad Jones-Mel Lewis orchestra. Bert continued recording in the late '70s and early '80s, making albums with Sal Salvador's sextet and with Lionel Hampton in 1978, and with Teo Macero in 1983. He recently had one of his early Savoy albums, *Eddie Bert with the Hank Jones Trio*, and also *Live at Birdland* with J. R. Monterose, reissued on CD. —*Ron Wynn and Michael G. Nastos*

Eddie Bert Quintet / Mar. 19, 1952-Jun. 10, 1953 / Discovery 3020

Musician of the Year / May 31, 1955 / Savoy 12015
This is a solid example of straightahead bebop, with Hank Jones (p). —*David Szatmary*

○ **Let's Dig Bert** / Nov. 1955 / Transworld 208
Brilliant bebop session by neglected trombonist. Includes the equally neglected saxophonist Dave Schildkraut. —*David Szatmary*

Modern Moods / Nov. 1955 / Jazztone 1223

★ **Like Cool** / i. 1958 / Somerset 5200

East Coast Sounds / i. 1959 / Jazztone 1276

GENE BERTONCINI

b. Apr. 6, 1937, New York, NY
Guitar / Swing, bop
One of the more elegant, tasteful, and sensitive guitarists, Gene Bertoncini has perfected the art of playing soft, sentimental music and presenting it in a light, fluid fashion, yet retaining a degree of feeling and spontaneity. He began on guitar at age nine, and was a professional at age 16, playing on a children's television show. Bertoncini took architecture at Notre Dame rather than music, though he later returned to full-time playing. He played with a group led by Buddy Rich that also included Mike Mainieri and Sam Most. Bertoncini worked with Clark Terry, Paul Winter, Nancy Wilson, and in the television orchestras of Merv Griffin and Skitch Henderson in the '60s. He also backed Tony Bennett, and worked with the Metropolitan Opera House orchestra. During the '70s, Bertoncini played with Wayne Shorter and Charles McPherson, then formed a duo with Mike Moore. They've played and recorded together over parts of two decades, with Bertoncini selecting the material and writing arrangements. Their performances blend classical, light (not "lite") jazz, Latin, and popular material. Bertoncini and Moore were joined by Michael Urbaniak in a trio date in 1981. Bertoncini has also led workshops and taught at the Eastman School. He has recorded for Stash, Chiaroscuro, and Omisound. He and Moore have several releases available on CD. —*Ron Wynn*

Art of the Duo / Sep. 1988 / Stash 6

SKEETER BEST

b. 1914, **d.** 1985
Guitar / Swing, bop
A masterful rhythm guitarist, Skeeter Best was also an above-average lead player, though he didn't display these talents often. He was influenced by the duo of Charlie Christian and Freddie Greene, and laid down slick, polished, and enticing riffs and supporting licks. His solo approach was a classic single-string style, with cleanly articulated, bluesy patterns and phrases. He played in Philadelphia during the late '30s, then worked with Earl Hines in 1941 and 1942 until Best joined the navy. Following his discharge from the service, Best spent his time playing with small combos, and participated in the landmark *Soul Brothers* session that featured Ray Charles and Milt Jackson. He recorded with Mercer Ellington in 1958, and later taught in New York City. Best did not make any sessions as a leader,

but can be heard to good advantage on the *Soul Brothers* CD reissue. —*Ron Wynn*

JOHN BETSCH

Drums / Modern creative
A prolific, solid drummer who's played with several major free musicians in the '70s, '80s, and '90s, John Betsch hasn't landed the major label recording pact or high-profile gig that will get him more recognition. Nonetheless, he has produced aggressive, outstanding drumming on many first-rate sessions. Betsch has played with Billy Bang, Thomas Chapin, Marty Cook, Marilyn Crispell, Abdullah Ibrahim, and Steve Lacy, among others. Currently, he doesn't have any sessions as a leader available on CD, but can be heard on the dates of Bang, Lacy, Crispell, and many others. —*Ron Wynn*

Earth Blossom / **i.** May 1975 / Strata East 19748

ANDY BEY (Andrew W. Bey)

b. 1939, Newark, NJ
Vocals / Hard bop, ballads & blues, soul-jazz
Sometimes an emphatic, on-edge singer and other times so soft a singer that he's nearly inaudible, Andy Bey's work hasn't always been universally appreciated. He has a rich, full sound and good command of blues and bebop mechanics, but sometimes tended to sound shrill and tiring during his stints with Horace Silver (some of that may be attributed to the lyrics he was delivering). Bey began playing piano in his childhood, and later sang and played in Newark. He appeared at the Apollo with Louis Jordan in the late '50s, and led a group with his sisters, Salome and Geraldine, in the '50s, '60s, and '70s. They recorded and toured Europe in the '50s, and recorded for Atlantic in the mid-'70s. Bey recorded with Max Roach (his most effective jazz stint), Duke Pearson, Horace Silver, Gary Bartz, and Stanley Clarke in the '60s and '70s. He sang with the Thad Jones-Mel Lewis Orchestra and Bobby Vidal in the '70s, and reunited with Silver in the late '80s. The albums Bey and his sisters made for Atlantic and Fontana are long gone; and the dates he did with Roach, Silver, Bartz, and Clarke are not available on CD. —*Ron Wynn*

★ **Now Hear** / Aug. 17+20, 1964 / Prestige 7346
Expressive vocalists hook up with Jerome Richardson (sax and f) and Kenny Burrell (g) for expansive treatments of jazz. —*Michael G. Nastos*

ED BICKERT (Edward Isaac Bickert)

b. Nov. 29, 1932, Hochfeld, Manitoba, Canada
Guitar / Swing, cool
A first-class session player and soloist, Canadian guitarist Ed Bickert has been a steady presence in the Toronto club and studio scene since the '50s. His specialty is an incendiary, hard-swinging traditional approach that sidesteps bebop angularity, but employs sophisticated, modern harmonies. With his relaxed melodic sense, gentle tone, and expert ability to interact with other band members, he has few equals as a chordal player. Bickert made his debut in Toronto with Ron Collier and Moe Koffman in the mid '50s, then played with Rob McConnell in the '60s and into the '70s. He played and recorded with Paul Desmond in the mid '70s, and worked as a combo leader in the mid-'70s and early '80s, often coheading groups with Don Thompson. Bickert toured Japan with Milt Jackson in 1979, and recorded with Oscar Peterson, Rosemary Clooney, and Benny Carter in the '80s. He's done sessions for Concord and Sackville. Bickert has several dates available on CD. —*Ron Wynn and David Nelson McCarthy*

From Canada with Love / **i.** 1979 / PMR 115

★ **At Toronto's Bourbon Street** / Jan. 1983 / Concord Jazz 216

Bye Bye Baby / Aug. 1983 / Concord Jazz 232
Nice set with a discernible swing influence, though pianist Dave McKenna sometimes seems ready to break into stride or ragtime progression. The quartet never hurries or rushes their playing, and bassist Steve Wallace and drummer Jake

Hanna are sometimes barely audible. This is smooth, so-phisticated, and wonderfully played, though the energy level sometimes seems quite low. —*Ron Wynn*

I Wished on the Moon / Jun. 1985 / Concord Jazz 4284

This Is New / Dec. 1989 / Concord Jazz 4414

BARNEY BIGARD (Albany Leon Bigard)

b. Mar. 3, 1906, New Orleans, LA, **d.** Jun. 27, 1980, Culver City, CA
Clarinet / New Orleans traditional, swing
A member of a New Orleans musical family, clarinetist Barney Bigard established himself as a leading voice in the Ellington reed section during the '20s, '30s, and early '40s. His blend of dramatic runs, vocal effects, and warm, full tone in every clarinet register made Bigard a dynamic player and prime option for Ellington and Strayhorn in their desire to spotlight orchestral colors and textures. His style bridged the traditional New Orleans and swing periods; he made subtle adjustments to his playing throughout his career, but used those two styles as his foundation.

Bigard originally took lessons on *Eb* clarinet, studying with Lorenzo Tio, Jr. He was discouraged initially, and switched to the tenor saxophone, joining Albert Nicholas's band in 1922. Bigard left Nicholas to work with bassist Oke Gaspard and with Amos White, but returned to Nicholas's band in 1923. They traveled to Chicago in 1924, where they played with King Oliver at the Plantation Cafe from 1925 to 1927. Bigard recorded with Oliver for Vocalion, and with Jelly Roll Morton, Johnny Dodds, and Louis Armstrong. He traveled to New York with Oliver's band in 1927, where they played at the Savoy. While on tour, the group disbanded, and Bigard joined Charlie Elgar's group for the summer in Milwaukee. After returning to New York, Bigard played with Luis Russell for two months, then joined Duke Ellington. From late 1927 until 1942, he was a featured Ellingtonian, appearing on hundreds of songs, among them "Clarinet Lament (Barney's Concerto)," "Mood Indigo," "Ducky Wucky," " "Jack the Bear," "Harlem Air Shaft," "Across the Track Blues," and "Saturday Night Function." He also did numerous sessions with combos of Ellington sidemen, while recording again with Oliver in 1928 and Morton in 1929.

Bigard continued a busy career after leaving Ellington. He led and recorded with groups in New York and Los Angeles. He played with Freddie Slack and Kid Ory, appeared with Armstrong in the 1946 film *New Orleans*, and was a first-edition member of Louis Armstrong and His All-Stars. He spent three different periods with the All-Stars: 1947-1952, 1953-1955, and 1960-1961. Bigard toured extensively, in America and around the world, with the All-Stars, did several recording sessions, and often emerged in later editions as one of the few group members in Armstrong's instrumental class. Bigard did freelance dates in Las Vegas, on the West Coast, and even at Disneyland during hiatus periods with the All-Stars. He played with Cozy Cole in 1958 and 1959, and appeared in the 1957 film *St. Louis Blues*. Bigard semiretired from music in 1962, but spent his final years doing occasional concert dates, making recording and television appearances, and playing festivals. Among his record dates were sessions with Art Hodes and Earl Hines, plus albums for RCA and Crescent Jazz Productions. —*Ron Wynn*

Clarinet Gumbo / Jun. 25, 1973-Jul. 18, 1973 / RCA 11744

★ **Bucket's Got a Hole in It** / Delmark 211
In January 1968, a Chicago television station flew Barney Bigard (clarinet) in from Los Angeles to take part in one of pianist Art Hodes's television shows. Bob Koester took the opportunity to record him with a trio consisting of Hodes, Rail Wilson (bass), and Barrett Deems (drums), and then, in another session, added Nap Trottier (trumpet) and Georg Brunis (trombone). As Koester points out in his very informative and personal liner notes, Hodes had been collecting great clarinetists since he started recording. These are his first sessions with Bigard. This album is just so fine in every way that I really am somewhat at a loss for words about it. ... In my opinion, the quartet sides are the most successful ones in

the album, which may seem surprising in view of the fact that Bigard spent a good proportion of his life playing in New Orleans and Dixieland bands. Yet, I think the truth is that Bigard's heart was really in the type of big-band jazz he played with Duke Ellington and Freddy Slack and the kind of combo swing he played with his own groups, rather than in the traditional clarinet role of a New Orleans ensemble. All of the quartet sides are truly wonderful; "Sweet Lorraine" has the kind of breath-taking beauty that marks the very greatest of Bigard's playing. "Hesitation Blues" marks again his mastery of the blues form, and "Three Little Words" epitomizes his swing. —*Ron Anger*, Coda

ACKER BILK (Bernard Stanley Bilk)

b. Jan. 29, 1929, Pensford, Somerset, England
Clarinet / New Orleans traditional
Best known for his left-field hit "Stranger on the Shore" in the early '60s, Acker Bilk was one of the leaders in England's "trad" jazz boom during the '60s. An entertaining, if not particularly original, clarinetist in the early New Orleans style, Bilk worked as a semiprofessional musician in England before joining Ken Colyer's band as a clarinetist in the mid '50s. He scored his first hit in England with the song "Summer Set" in 1958. Bilk and the Paramount Jazz Band were celebrities during the early '60s, performing in their uniform of bowler hats and striped coats. After landing British successes with the songs "Buona Sera" and "That's My Home," Bilk struck gold with "Stranger on the Shore," recorded with the Young String Chorale. It broke a British record by staying on the charts for 55 weeks. Bilk kept recording and performing through the '60s, '70s, and '80s, and returned to the hit parade with the '76 song "Aria." Bilk has several sessions available on American labels GNP Crescendo, Stomp Off, Pickwick, and K-Tel. —*Ron Wynn*

○ **Best of Acker Bilk—Vol. 2** / GNP 2171

★ **Best of Acker Bilk** / GNP 2116
Another European "trad" (traditional jazz) man, Acker Bilk updates (I think) a Pye recording released on GNP Crescendo as *The Best of Acker Bilk*. We'll give the chap credit for an original tone (clarinet), but with the strings and non jazz material there is little else here. ... There are ten tracks, including a medley of his hit "Stranger on the Shore." —*Bob Rusch*, Cadence

Magic Clarinet of Acker Bilk, The / Dominion 6513

WALTER BISHOP, JR.

b. Apr. 10, 1927, New York, NY
Piano / Bop, hard bop
The son of noted songwriter Walter Bishop, Walter Bishop, Jr. has been a top bebop and hard bop pianist whose style reflects his admiration for Art Tatum and Nat "King" Cole. He also utilizes the right-hand chording technique made famous by Erroll Garner. Bishop played with Art Blakey in the late '40s, then worked with Charlie Parker, Miles Davis, Oscar Pettiford, and Kai Winding in the '50s. Bishop played with Curtis Fuller in 1960, then formed a trio with Jimmy Garrison and G. T. Hogan. He toured with Terry Gibbs in the mid '60s, and later studied at Juilliard with Hall Overton. Bishop moved to Los Angeles in 1969, where he mixed studies and recording. His sessions included dates with Supersax and Blue Mitchell. Bishop was an instructor on the West Coast in the '70s before returning to New York. He played with Clark Terry's big band in the late '70s, toured Switzerland, and led his own bands. He began teaching at the University of Hartford in the early '80s, and was featured in a solo concert at Carnegie Hall in 1983. He's recorded for Prestige, Black Jazz, Muse, DIW, Red, Black Lion, and Seabreeze, among others. Bishop wrote a book on jazz theory in 1976. Currently, he has several sessions available on CD. —*Ron Wynn*

Speak Low / Mar. 14, 1961 / Muse 5066

Walter Bishop Trio, The / 1962-1963 / Prestige 7730

○ **Bish Bash** / i. Aug. 1964+May 1968 / Xanadu 114

Music Map

Big Bands

Early New Orleans Style

Marching/Street Bands

Honky Tonk – "Tonk" Bands
Clarence Williams Blue Five
Louis Armstrong (1901-1971)
Sidney Bechet (1897-1959)

Society Bands
A.J. Piron (1888-1943)
John Robichaux (1886-1938)

Dance, Party Bands
Bunk Johnson's Original Superior Orchestra
Imperial Orchestra – Eagle Band
Leaders:
Buddy Bolden (1877-1931) – Buddy Petit (1897-1931)
Kid Ory (1890-1973) – Joe "King" Oliver (1885-1938)

Jazz Bands
Jack "Papa" Laine (1873-1966)
Players:
Nick LaRocca (1889-1961) – Larry Shields (1893-1953)
Leon Roppolo (1902-1943) – Brunies Brothers
Albert Brunies (1900-1978) – George Brunies (1902-1974)

Symphonic Jazz
Original Dixieland Band
Paul Whitman (1890-1967)

Big Bands
Duke Ellington (1899-1974)
Fletcher Henderson (1897-1952)
Jean Goldkette (1899-1962)
Red Nichols (1905-1965)
Erskine Hawkins (1914)
Andy Kirk (1898)
Bennie Moten (1894-1935)
Bill McKinney (1895-1969)
Jay McShann (1916)
Teddy Wilson (1912-1986)

Benny Goodman (1909-1986)

Chick Webb (1909-1939)
Jimmie Lunceford (1902-1947)
Count Basie (1904-1984)
Artie Shaw (1910)
Glenn Miller (1904-1944)
Count Basie (1904-1984)
Charlie Barnet (1913)
Bob Crosby (1913)
Woody Herman (1913-1987)
Boyd Raeburn 1913-1966)

Sweet Novelty Bands
Kay Kyser (1906-1985)

Small Swing Groups (1933)
Benny Goodman Trio – Woody Herman's Woodchoppers
Bob Crosby's Bob Cats
Tommy Dorsey's (1905-1956) Clambake Seven

Dixieland Revival
Eddie Condon (1905-1973) – Lu Watters (1911)
Turk Murphy (1915-1987) – Bob Scobey (1916-1963)
Bill Bissonette – Firehouse Five (Plus Two)
Wilbur DeParis (1900-1973) – Art Hodes (1904)
Bunk Johnson (1889-1949) – Kid Rena (1898-1949)
Muggsy Spanier (1906-1967)

R&B Style
Buddy Johnson (1915-1977) – Roy Milton (1907)
Joe Morris – Lucky Millinder (1900-1966)
Joe & Jimmy Liggins – Johnny Otis (1921)
Lionel Hampton 1940/42 band – Tiny Bradshaw (1905-1958)
Earl Bostic (1913-1965) – Jack McVea (1914)
Louis Jordan (1908-1975)

Bop Bands (early 1940)
Charlie Parker (1920-1955) – Dizzy Gillespie (1917)
Billy Eckstine (1914-1993) 1945 band
Earl Hines (1905-1989) 1940/41 band

Jazz-Rock/Fusion
Miles Davis (1926) - Dreams – Ten Wheel Drive – Compost
Mahavishnu Orchestra I – Return to Forever I, II, III
Fourth Way – If – Soft Machine – Defunkt
Ornette Coleman's Prime – Time – Eleventh House Band
Lounge Lizards – Steely Dan

Free Jazz Groups
Ornette Coleman (1930) – Cecil Taylor (1929)
Lester Bowie (1941) – Albert Ayler (1936-1970)
Anthony Braxton (1945) – Art Ensemble of Chicago – Air
Sun Ra Arkestra – Revolutionary Ensemble
World Saxophone Quartet – Eight Bold Souls
Jazz Passengers – New York Contemporary Five
Globe Unity Orchestra – String Trio of NY – Circle
29th St. Sax Quartet – Rova Saxophone Quartet

Recent Bands
Wynton Marsalis (1961) – Branford Marsalis (1960)
Scott Hamilton (1954) – Warren Vache (1951)
Brecker Brothers – Harper Brothers
Adams/Pullen Quartet – Roy Haynes Hip Ensemble
Phil Woods Quartet/Quintet – Herbie Hancock Sextant
Sphere – Mingus Dynasty – Heath Brothers
Saxophone Choir

Still More
Oregon – Codona – Paul Winter (1939) Consort
David Murray Special Quartet
Jack DeJohnette's Special Edition – Bobby Watson's Horizon

★ **Coral Keys** / 1971 / Black Jazz 2

Soliloquy / Oct. 21, 1976 / Sea Breeze 1002

Soul Village / Jun. 1977 / Muse 5142
Interesting, often intriguing work that plays off the village concept on the title track, but is otherwise a pretty standard, though expertly performed, batch of standards and bop originals. Bishop utilizes the classic Messenger three-horn lineup, except he substitutes a second saxophonist for a trombonist and uses Randy Brecker as trumpeter. —*Ron Wynn*

Hot House / Dec. 14, 1977 / Muse 5183
Excellent bebop session by this pianist, assisted by Junior Cook (ts) and Bill Hardman (tpt). —*David Szatmary*

Cubicle / Jun. 21, 1978 / Muse 5151
On this 1978 session, the fine bop pianist heads a large group of distinguished stars, among them Curtis Fuller, Pepper Adams, Randy Brecker, Billy Hart, and vocalist Carmen Lundy. It's a different atmosphere for Bishop, usually featured in small combos or trios. Songs are nicely played, and there are several sparkling solos. —*Ron Wynn*

What's New / i. Dec. 1991 / DIW 605
Pianist Walter Bishop, Jr. displays his bop proficiency on this 1991 release, one of his finest. His solos are electric, nicely constructed, and often brilliantly executed. He seldom got much recognition except from musicians, but Bishop was certainly among the finest bop and mainstream pianists of his era. —*Ron Wynn*

CINDY BLACKMAN

b. Nov. 18, 1959, Yellow Springs, OH
Drums / Hard bop, modern creative
An accomplished drummer who is not flamboyant or showy, Cindy Blackman has become a well-respected percussionist in a short period of time. Both her mother and grandmother were classical musicians, and her uncle was a vibist. Blackman began playing drums as a child, and studied classical percussion at the University of Hartford and Berklee. Alan Dawson and Lennie Nelson were two of her instructors. Blackman moved to New York in the early '80s, and played with Freddie Hubbard and Sam Rivers. She became Jackie McLean's regular drummer in 1987, and began recording as a leader that year for Muse. Blackman was a big attraction at jam sessions organized at the Blue Note by Ted Curson, and played with Don Pullen's trio in 1990 at several festivals. She has a few sessions available on CD. —*Ron Wynn*

★ **Trio + Two** / i. Aug. 1990 / Free Lance 015

ED BLACKWELL

b. 1927, **d.** 1992
Drums / Early free, modern creative
Ed Blackwell was one of the greatest melodic drummers in modern jazz history. His ringing rhythms frequently sounded like vocals transferred to drums, and his conception linked traditional New Orleans jazz, marching band beats, Afro-Latin and Caribbean elements, R&B, and blues voicings with free, multiple accents and textures. His ability to provide a quick, incisive history of New Orleans styles turned his solos into exciting, freewheeling events. Blackwell patterned his early playing after that of the great traditional drummer Paul Barbarin, and, during his teens, worked in several R&B bands. During the late '40s, he played in Plas Johnson's and Raymond Johnson's groups. Blackwell moved to Los Angeles in 1951, where he first met and played with Ornette Coleman. They worked together again a couple of years later in Texas, before Blackwell returned to New Orleans in 1956. He toured with Ray Charles in 1957, then moved to New York in 1960, and shortly afterward replaced Billy Higgins in Coleman's band. During the '60s, Blackwell emerged as a seminal percussionist, playing on Coleman sessions such as *Science Fiction* and *Free Jazz*. He also recorded with Don Cherry and John Coltrane, with Cherry in duets, with Eric Dolphy and Booker Little at the

Five Spot, and with Randy Weston, Dewey Redman, and Archie Shepp. He toured Africa with Weston in the mid '60s, and lived in Morocco in 1968. Blackwell was an artist-in-residence at Wesleyan in the mid '70s, then toured and recorded with former Coleman band members Cherry, Redman, and Charlie Haden in the group Old and New Dreams. During the '80s, Blackwell played with Cherry again, was in Anthony Braxton's band, and was also in groups led by Redman and David Murray. He toured England and Scotland in the late '80s working in Cherry's group, Nu. He also did recordings as a leader and sideman for the Black Saint/Soul Note label. Blackwell suffered from severe kidney problems through the '80s, and began undergoing dialysis treatment. He finally died of kidney failure. Currently, Blackwell is featured on many albums with others, but doesn't have any listings of his own on CD, at least in the *Spectrum* catalog. Some of his Black Saint albums can be purchased directly from the Sphere distribution outlet. —*Ron Wynn*

EUBIE BLAKE (James Hubert Blake)

b. Feb. 7, 1883, Baltimore, MD, **d.** Feb. 12, 1983, New York, NY
Piano, composer / Ragtime
Blake was one of ragtime's most noted performers, and was an American institution. As a child, he played hymns, but heard the sounds of the then-new form, ragtime, all around him in Baltimore's brass bands, saloons, and dance halls. Blake picked up his technique by playing in medicine shows, by backing vocalists, and by appearing in gaming houses. He wrote his first major number, "The Charleston Rag," in 1899. He teamed with Noble Sissle in 1915 for a vaudeville appearance, and the duo eventually made it to Broadway in 1921 with the musical *Shuffle Along*. Blake subsequently became a prolific composer for shows, among them the famous *Blackbirds Review*, then left the field to study the Schillinger system at New York University after World War II. He became a celebrity on the strength of a 1969 album, *86 Years of Eubie Blake*, and made an acclaimed appearance at the 1970 New Orleans Jazz Festival. He was awarded the James P. Johnson award in 1970 and the Duke Ellington Medal in 1972, and collaborated with Terry Waldo on the comprehensive book, *This Is Ragtime*, in 1976. The 1976 Broadway show *Eubie* was a memorable overview of his career, which was capped off by his receiving the Presidential Medal of Honor in 1981. —*Ron Wynn*

Memories of You—from Rare Piano Rolls / 1915-1973 / Biograph 112

★ **Blues and Ragtime (1917-1921)** / 1917-1921 / Biograph 1011
A collection that features vintage tunes done by ragtime and early jazz great Eubie Blake. The feeling and energy he generates is tremendous, and even when the solos aren't impressive, Blake's attitude and personality keep things moving. —*Ron Wynn*

○ **Blues & Spirituals (1921)** / Mar. 1921-Dec. 1921 / Biograph 1012
More classic songs from pianist Eubie Blake, whose 100-year life span kept him in the public eye through much of the 20th century. He reflected that experience through his playing, which rocks, sways, and rips at times, then is appropriately mournful or reverent. —*Ron Wynn*

Wizard of Ragtime Piano, The / 1958 / 20th Century 3003

○ **Golden Reunion in Ragtime** / 1962 / Stereoddities 1900

86 Years of Eubie Blake, The / Dec. 26, 1968 / Columbia 22223
Solo piano produced by John Hammond. Also includes sessions done on Feb 6, 1969 and Mar 12, 1969. —*AMG*

○ **Live Concert** / May 22, 1973 / Eubie Blake Music 5
Live Concert, recorded at the Yesteryear Museum's "annual salute to show business nostalgia," is regrettably heavy on both show business and remembrances. Some, I suspect, will be bored with Eubie Blake's verbal grandstanding, rem-

iniscing, and half-lame joking. And several tunes here, like "I'm Just Wild About Harry" and "As Long As You Live," are pure schmaltz. Nevertheless, there is also some good music. "Tricky Fingers," one of Blake's best and most difficult compositions, has a really clever right-hand line, brighter and crisper than anything in the Scott Joplin catalog. Blake's playing reminds us that East Coast ragtime was a style much flashier and crisper than the Sedalia school of this genre. Consider the devilishly tricky line on "Dream Rag," for example. A standout is "Rhapsody in Ragtime," an elaborate concert piece in the style of Joplin's *Euphonic Sounds*, which makes impressive use of bravura octaves and like borrowings from the 19th century's keyboard arsenal. *—Jon Balleras*, Down Beat

JOHN BLAKE

b. Jul. 3, 1947, Philadelphia, PA
Violin / Instrumental pop, modern creative
A dashing, eclectic violinist, John Blake has been a crowd favorite in groups as diverse as Isaac Hayes's Movement and McCoy Tyner's combo. Blake played with Hayes and Alice Coltrane in the '70s, then worked with Tyner in the '80s. He's been a more captivating player as a sideman, contributing broken lines, strumming, and dynamic solos to dates by Hayes, Coltrane, and Tyner. Blake's rare solo albums have been less interesting; he recorded a pair of unimpressive sessions for Gramavision in the mid '80s that failed to showcase Blake's violin playing adequately, and were heavily produced instrumental pop vehicles instead. Blake's date for Sunnyside in the early '90s is a more traditional, satisfying effort. He's working with Joey Calderazzo, Charles Fambrough, and Joe Ford, among others. Blake also studied traditional Indian music. Only his Sunnyside session is available on CD. *—Ron Wynn*

Maiden Dance / Dec. 1983 / Gramavision 8309
Decent set alternating experimental, jazz-based songs and more R&B or pop outings. Violinist Blake can provide slashing, dynamic solos or gripping melodies, but also sometimes relies on gimmicks rather than substance. It's better than his '70s albums. *—Ron Wynn*

○ **Rhythm and Blues** / Jun. 1986 / Gramavision 8608
★ **New Beginning, A** / Mar. 1988 / Rhino 79455

RAN BLAKE

b. Apr. 20, 1935, Springfield, MA
Piano, keyboards, composer / Modern creative
A champion of "Third Stream" music, Ran Blake's piano style mixes gospel inflections and rhythms, classical and film score influences, and bebop and free concepts. He's one of the most unpredictable, but invigorating, players around, and can move from a probing, moody work to an upbeat, spirited boogie then back to another somber piece. Blake studied piano with Ray Cassarino in his teens and simultaneously developed an appreciation for gospel and classical music. He attended Bard College from 1956 to 1960 and studied jazz, meeting vocalist Jeanne Lee. He also studied in Lenox with Oscar Peterson, John Lewis, and Gunther Schuller. Blake and Lee toured Europe in the mid '60s. He became music director of the New England Conservatory's community services department in 1967, and gave concerts in prisons and senior citizens' homes in the late '60s and early '70s. Blake was appointed chairman of the Third Stream department in 1973, and has combined teaching, performances, and tours in Europe and Boston. He received a Guggenheim Fellowship and a grant for composition from the National Endowment for the Arts in 1982. Blake began recording for RCA in the early '60s, doing a session with Lee and George Duvivier. He followed that with solo sessions on various labels. Blake has since recorded with Chris Connor, Ricky Ford, Anthony Braxton, Ted Curson, Houston Person, and Jeanne Lee. His albums have been recorded on Owl, Soul Note, Arista/Freedom, and GM. He has several sessions available on CD. *—Ron Wynn*

Ran Blake Plays Solo Piano / May 1, 1965 / ESP 1011
○ **Blue Potato** / Apr. 1970 / Milestone 9021
Pianist Ran Blake's selection of material for this album ranges from an original composition dedicated to three revolutionary heroes to an Italian folk melody to popular American songs. His style was as eclectic as his taste. Sources and influences spanned the history of music. The life in his hands and feet drew the piano to the task of playing events and feelings. The instrument assumed priority over the demands of tunes, which for him existed only as nameable starting points and figural references. Blake could persuade the music without overburdening it with violent emotion. The pale colors of "Vradiazi," "Bella Ciaou," and "Stars Fell on Alabama" create a pensive mood in sharp contrast to the schizophrenic design of "Chicago" (a city that stumbles; in the past, it used to stride). "God Bless the Child" can be heard as a quiet tribute to Billie Holiday, who symbolized the Black woman in the tragedy of America. Rich chords interspersed with lightly pedalled notes combine in a wavelike rhythm that ebbs through this sensitive portrait.... The *Blue Potato* provides a study in variety of solo expression focused on a broad, but pointed, theme. Ran Blake was splendidly recorded and in excellent form on this LP. *—Alan Offstein*, Coda

○ **Breakthru** / Dec. 2+5, 1975 / Improvising Artists 373842
Excellent, haunting melodies and compositions, delivered in a piano style that's completely distinctive and personal. Ran Blake is one of the few "third stream" pianists who never desert or abandon the concept or the style; yet his playing is never rhythmically vapid or harmonically predictable. He's also great at building and varying moods in his pieces. *—Ron Wynn*

Third Stream Recompositions / Jun. 23, 1977 / Owl 017
Third Stream Today / 1977 / Golden Crest 116
Film Noir / Jan. 23+27, 1980 / Novus 3019
Intriguing third-stream arrangements, all-star lineup. Blake's most hypnotic concept statement. Solo piano. *—Ron Wynn*
Improvisations / Jun. 1981 / Soul Note 1022
○ **Duke Dreams** / Sep. 1982 / Soul Note 1027
Pianist Ran Blake's tribute to Billy Strayhorn and Duke Ellington, *Duke Dreams*, was recorded May 27 and June 2, 1981. Now, a tribute to these men might appear to be an "in-the-tradition" gambit, but Blake's realization of his own tribute (the title cut), Dave Brubeck's "The Duke," and the other material is a glance backward actually looking toward the present/future. Some of the very familiar tunes (as well as the more obscure ones and the Brubeck tribute) are given a most creative reworking. None of the original intent/feeling is destroyed (though some would argue this, not wanting to see their museum perceptions of this music tampered with). Instead, the original intent is developed and distilled through this unique artist whose quirky voicings, rhythms, and lines make everything he does unmistakably Blake. The creative listener will find much to joyously chuckle about throughout the set: unexpected twists, turns, and extrapolations (well-chronicled by Gary Giddins in his liners) that draw the listener to the core of the music. It would have been interesting to hear Ellington's and/or Strayhorn's assessment of this interpretation of their music. Most likely, they would have found it challenging (or perhaps even had a bit of a difficult time with it) as it pushes their original ideas to the limit, but this reviewer nonetheless highly recommends it to appreciators of Ellington, Strayhorn, and/or Blake. *—Bob Rusch*, Cadence

○ **Suffield Gothic** / Sep. 28-29, 1983 / Soul Note 1077
His best concept album, with introspective, teeming melodies and alternately limp and joyful rhythms. Ran Blake's piano solos don't bowl anyone over with their speed or intensity, and they are not filled with clever counterpoint, multiple rhythms, or constant reworking of pop tunes. They're dialogs that shift and evolve according to Blake's vision of the moment; this requires listeners to simply respond, rather than to anticipate. *—Ron Wynn*

○ **Painted Rhythms: The Compleat Ran Blake—Vol. 2** / Sep. 1983 / GM 3008

Vol 1. of *Painted Rhythms*, from the same sessions as its partner, is an excellent introduction to pianist Ran Blake's style, for it includes his reharmonizations of a variety of jazz standards and obscurities. Vol. 2 ranges from Blake's often-scary originals ("Shoah!"/"Babbit"/"Storm Warning") to 1,000-year-old melodies written by Spanish Jews and a fourth re-interpretation of "Maple Leaf Rag" (the first three are on Vol. 1). Throughout, Blake is quite concise (only "Shoah!" exceeds four minutes and seven other sketches are under two), very expressive, and as usual, totally individual. My one quibble is that this CD is so brief as to be the equivalent of a 25-minute LP. It's fair to say Ran Blake's records will never make the *Billboard* charts, but a century from now his music will still be undated and highly thought-provoking. *—Scott Yanow,* Cadence

○ **Painted Rhythms: The Compleat Ran Blake—Vol. 1** / Dec. 1985 / GM 3007

First in a projected series dedicated to the work of pianist/composer Ran Blake, a genuine iconoclast. His songs can be moving, muddled, dense, or aggressive, but they're never dull. His playing is the same way; always changing, seldom flashy, and usually rewarding for listeners with open ears. *—Ron Wynn*

☆ **Short Life of Barbara Monk** / Aug. 26, 1986 / Soul Note 1127

Interesting concept work, with Blake's love of "third stream" (jazz and modern classical concepts merging) and film noir uniting in a series of related, yet divergent, compositions. Blake's lines, phrasing, rhythms, and voicings defy easy analysis or fixed patterns. They're as diffuse and diverse as his interests, making every Blake album both a challenge and a delight. *—Ron Wynn*

★ **You Stepped out of a Cloud** / Aug. 11, 1989 / Owl 79238

Pianist Blake and vocalist Jeanne Lee's first record since the mid '60s. *—Michael G. Nastos*

☆ **Epistrophy** / **i.** 1991 / Soul Note 121177

Pianist Ran Blake is a camera: he peels off a roll and a half of halftone snapshots of Thelonious Monk. Artist and subject share stylistic traits: cryptic wit, love of sass and tremolo, fine dynamics. Easy listeners may view Blake's black and whites as bleak and austere; critical ears may reexamine the collection vis-à-vis the originals: Hmm . . . how did Monk play that one? Did he grab a handful of Bartok on "April in Paris"? Blake's lens plumbs layers of feeling, shaves subtle shades of grey. Blake's humor is not bald (swaggering stride), but inside ("holding hands at midnight/'neath Carolina Moon"), even black (downward arpeggios). His gestures are anti-grand: sidelong, backhand. Fleeting passport photos—three views of "Epistrophy"—take not quite complementary angles on the subject and anchor the exhibit. Dark portraits ("Criss Cross") glint eerily like back-lit cobwebs. Foldout triptychs ("Thelonious"), taken round corners, give startling perspectives. Sepia-tint tremolos ("Reflections") conjure old airs. Darkroom techniques (open pedal, "Monk's Mood," "Epistrophy II") effect eerie likenesses (double images?) of Duke Ellington. "Misterioso" is a blur. When he aims full frontal ("Eronel"), Blake disarms with directness. Blake shoots Monk for the grit, not the glossies. *—Fred Bouchard,* Jazz Times

ART BLAKEY (Art [Abdullah Ibn Buhaina] Blakey)

b. Oct. 11, 1919, Pittsburgh, PA, **d.** Oct. 16, 1990
Drums / Hard bop

Art Blakey was hard bop's guru and its ultimate talent scout, and the percussive anchor of countless brilliant bands. Blakey was famous for his technique; his frequent high-volume snare and bass drum accents. Though he sometimes dismissed the idea of an African/jazz rhythm connection, Blakey incorporated some African devices after he visited Africa in the '40s. These devices included rapping on the side of the drum and using his elbow on the tom-tom to alter the pitch. He was also known for the dramatic closing of the hi-hat on every second and fourth beat. Blakey played

with such force and fury that he eventually lost much of his hearing, and at the end of his life, often played strictly by instinct. But he maintained the Jazz Messengers as the idiom's foremost repertory band from its beginnings in the late '40s and mid '50s into the '90s. The roster of greats whose careers Blakey nurtured include Donald Byrd, Bobby Timmons, Horace Silver, Johnny Griffin, Lee Morgan, Wayne Shorter, Freddie Hubbard, Woody Shaw, James Williams, Wynton and Branford Marsalis, Javon Jackson, and JoAnne Brackeen, to name only a few.

Blakey had a few piano lessons in his childhood, and was playing full-time and heading a band by the seventh grade. He switched from piano to drums, essentially teaching himself by listening to players such as Chick Webb and Sid Catlett. He joined Mary Lou Williams in 1942, then played with the Fletcher Henderson Orchestra in 1943 and 1944, touring the South. He briefly led a big band in Boston, then joined Billy Eckstine's new band. During his years with Eckstine, Blakey met many bebop pioneers, including Miles Davis, Fats Navarro, and Dexter Gordon. Blakey organized a rehearsal band he called the 17 Messengers after leaving Eckstine. He later recorded with an octet called the Jazz Messengers.

Blakey traveled to Africa in the late '40s, living there for more than a year and learning about African music and Islam (he eventually converted to Islam and took the name Buhaina). He performed and did radio broadcasts in the '50s with Charlie Parker, Clifford Brown, and Miles Davis, and with Horace Silver. Blakey was in the Buddy DeFranco quartet from 1951 to 1953. He and Silver formed a cooperative group with Hank Mobley and Kenny Dorham in 1955, using the familiar name Jazz Messengers. When Silver left the group in 1956, Blakey became the band's leader, and held that position for the remainder of its existence. They became the prototype hard bop ensemble, playing aggressive, exciting bebop material with a vivid blues foundation. Blakey took pride in holding onto musicians just long enough to develop their talent. Then, he would see them move on, and have new musicians arrive. The coveted position of Messengers' music director belonged to a host of superb players, from Wayne Shorter to Bobby Watson.

At the same time, Blakey never confined his duties to the Messengers. He found time to record with Monk, the Modern Jazz Quartet, John Coltrane, and various African, jazz, and Latin drummers on a summit session. He also found time to do a film sound track with Benny Golson, to tour with the Giants of Jazz (Gillespie, Monk, Sonny Stitt, and Al McKibbon), to appear often as a soloist at the Newport Jazz Festival, and to keep abreast of changes and fresh faces. The Messengers recorded from the '50s until the '90s, primarily on Blue Note, but also on Impulse, Timeless, Concord, and Bethlehem, and on some foreign labels. Though it seemed he would live forever, Blakey finally passed away in 1990. His spirit and presence are celebrated in the music of the '80s and '90s hard bop revivalists. Mosaic issued a tremendous boxed set in 1993 that features the complete 1960 recordings of his group. Blue Note issued a three-disc greatest hits collection, and there are also many single-disc reissues from the different Messengers periods. *—Ron Wynn*

★ **Complete Blue Note Recordings of Art Blakey's 1960 Messengers, The** / March 6, 1960-May 27, 1961 / Mosaic 141

Drummer Art Blakey led many great editions of the Jazz Messengers from the inaugural mid '50s sessions until his death in the '90s. While arguments rage regarding which was his "best," no doubt the 1960-1961 unit figures in the debate. The lineup included several players recruited by former music director Benny Golson in the late '50s: trumpeter Lee Morgan, bassist James "Jymie" Merritt, and pianist Bobby Timmons. Golson left in 1959 when Blakey opted for a less arranged, looser sound than Golson wanted. Wayne Shorter eventually replaced him, and Timmons returned after temporarily leaving to play with Cannonball Adderley. This wonderful six-disc set, notated with care and painstaking detail by Bob Blumenthal, covers studio and live sessions from March 6, 1960, to May 27, 1961, with the same personnel on all but two songs that were recorded on February 18, 1961, when Walter Davis had replaced Timmons. Producer Michael Cuscuna uses only first-issue dates, and, while he includes some alternate takes, he does not litter the discs with second-rate vault material. They smoothly detail the band's evolution, cohesion, and maturation. Blakey's band plays mostly originals supplied by past and present band members. There are several numbers from Shorter, Morgan, and Timmons, plus contributions from Bill Hardman, Hank Mobley, and Kenny Dorham, songs by Clifford Jordan and Thelonious Monk, and an occasional standard like "When Your Lover Is Gone" or "It's Only a Paper Moon." Shorter is at his fiery best on tenor sax, while Morgan is either a furious, note-bending upper-register acrobatic or a mellow, dynamic ballad stylist. Timmons excels at soul/gospel voicings and accompaniment but also demonstrates a flexibility and melodic and harmonic variety sometimes overshadowed by the popularity of such compositions as "Dat Dere" and "Moanin." Merritt brings a rock-solid pulse and consistent edge to the group on bass, having played both R&B and hard bop. Blakey offers his patented "bombs" on drums, driving and pacing the band without dominating it. His solos on such songs as "Afrique" are explosive, creative, and stimulating. This group is effective playing in either a surging or soothing manner, on waltzes, standards, or originals, personifying the mix of emotion and skills that are the essence of great jazz. This set, as with all Mosaic boxes, goes beyond essential. Get it post haste. — *Ron Wynn*

○ **Africaine: Art Blakey and His Jazz Messengers** / i. Nov. 10, 1950 / Blue Note 1088
On this Art Blakey session, trumpeter Lee Morgan is in consistent good form, tenor saxophonist Wayne Shorter is presentable with strong moments, pianist Walter Davis is too laidback, but Blakey is in rhythm glory. He contributes one of his lengthy solo features on "Haina," and generally keeps things swinging. The strongest cuts are "Lester Left Town" and the title track. —*Bob Rusch*, Cadence

★ **Art Blakey and the Jazz Messengers** / Oct. 31, 1953 / Birdland 110

○ **Art Blakey Quintet—Vol. 2** / Feb. 21, 1954 / Blue Note 5038

Night at Birdland—Vols. 1-3, A / Feb. 21, 1954 / Blue Note 46519
Art Blakey Quintet. 1987 CD reissue of early editions of the group. How can you overlook the sets with Horace Silver (p) and others? Many feel they are his best live dates. I agree. — *Michael G. Nastos*

Blakey with the Jazz Messengers / May 20, 1954 / Emarcy 26030

At the Cafe Bohemia—Vols. 2 and 3 / Nov. 23, 1955 / Blue Note 46522
With Jazz Messengers. Art Blakey's group with Horace Silver (p) and Hank Mobley (ts). Super second volume. —*Ron Wynn*

Jazz Messenger, The / i. May 1956-Dec. 1956 / Columbia 467920
At the time of *Jazz Messenger*, Art Blakey's Jazz Messengers were in a state of transition after a year of consistent personnel. Trombonist Curtis Fuller had just joined to make the group a sextet for the first time, while Lee Morgan (trumpet) and Bobby Timmons (piano) would be departing shortly after this recording (and would be replaced by Freddie Hubbard and Cedar Walton). The Messengers' one session for Impulse is typically swinging, but not quite up to the level of their more exciting Blue Note albums. Since there are no individual features for the sidemen, the solos are fairly short on each track, with Wayne Shorter (tenor sax) and Fuller emerging as standouts. Only "I Hear a Rhapsody" catches fire. —*Scott Yanow*, Cadence

Art Blakey and the Jazz Messengers / Dec. 12, 1956 / Columbia 47118

With the Jazz Messengers. Early period (mid '50s) recordings. Excellent. With Jackie McLean (as). —*Michael G. Nastos*

○ **Hard Bop** / Dec. 12, 1956+Dec. 13, 1956 / Columbia 1040
This recording is part of Columbia's "Jazz Odyssey" reissue series; the original's liner notes are included as well as a small picture of the original album jacket. Regarding the music: while not a particularly "classic" recording, the album is a strong example of drummer Art Blakey's driving, swinging style of jazz (the title is certainly applicable). For me, what makes the album a success is the playing of alto saxophonist Jackie McLean. . . . His tone is strong and his ideas are cliché-free. Trumpeter Bill Hardman is heard to better advantage on other Blakey recordings. Here, his playing sounds tentative, for the most part. On another note, I'd just like to thank Columbia for issuing the recording in mono rather than trying to electronically enhance the music for stereo. —*Carl Brauer*, Cadence

Drum Suite / Dec. 13, 1956+Feb. 22, 1957 / Columbia 1002

Hard Drive / i. 1957 / Bethlehem 6037

Cu-Bop / i. 1957 / Jubilee 1049

Orgy in Rhythm—Vol. 1 / Mar. 7, 1957 / Blue Note 1554

Orgy in Rhythm—Vol. 2 / Mar. 7, 1957 / Blue Note 1555

Theory of Art / Apr. 2, 1957 / Bluebird 6286
By way of Bluebird's CD series, RCA has finally reissued Art Blakey & the Jazz Messengers' *A Night in Tunisia* that originally appeared on Vik, its mid '50s jazz subsidiary. . . . The CD release remains wonderful and overpowering, enhanced a bit by digital remastering, and includes two previously unissued nine-piece band tracks. The Jazz Messengers of 1956-1957 had a "Philadelphia rhythm section" in pianist Sam Dockery and bassist Spanky DeBrest (Art Blakey was from the western end of Pennsylvania), with a front line of Johnny Griffin (tenor sax) and Bill Hardman (trumpet) would record on Atlantic with Thelonious Monk. Jackie McLean had just left the band when the first five tracks of this CD, that make up the *Tunisia* album, were recorded on April 8, 1957. After Griffin's permanent stay, McLean returned just for this session, and the six made up of the powerhouse editions of the Jazz Messengers, at least on record. Blakey's lyrical drum opening for "A Night in Tunisia," absolutely vocal in the tradition of African percussion, is followed by the two-saxophone vamp into Bill Hardman's statement of the theme that together catapults the listener into the heights of Messengers' creative mystique. "Tunisia" was this band's signature, especially in the '50s, and this edition is one of sheer power; vintage hard boppers will love its reappearance! Griffin's evocative swinger, "Off the Wall," deserves close attention by today's young players (as do his infectiously personal swing and dynamics), and the cognizant will fondly recall "Couldn't It Be You?," the Blakey-McLean collaboration that the altoist recorded for *Jackie's Bag* (Blue Note) as his own "Fidel." The two other tracks included here are from the previous week and are gems from Gigi Gryce. "A Night at Tony's" and "Social Call" (which has lived on thanks to Jon Hendricks) are cast in muted tones, the writing is both full-bodied and mellow in sound, almost cool in aspect, and quite different from what we'd expect from Blakey. The recording permits an appreciation for trumpeter Hardman, who sporadically refilled the Jazz Messengers' trumpet chair after the '50s, evidence of his maturity and consistency. He was never a powerful soloist with a big sound, but was one of New York's most reliable musicians. The fleet "A Theory of Art," which entitles this CD, is his contribution. —*Ron Weilburn*, Jazz Times

Art Blakey's Jazz Messengers with Thelonious Monk / May 14, 1957+May 15, 1957 / Atlantic 1278

○ **Art Blakey and the Jazz Messengers Live** / Jul. 29, 1957 / Calliope 3008

★ **Moanin': Art Blakey and the Jazz Messengers** / Oct. 30, 1958 / Blue Note 46516

With The Jazz Messengers. Here is a superb session. With Lee Morgan (tpt) and Bobby Timmons (p). —*Hank Davis*

Holiday for Skins—Vols. 1 and 2 / Nov. 9, 1958 / Blue Note 4005

Olympia Concert: Art Blakey's Jazz Messengers / Nov. 22, 1958+Dec. 17, 1958 / PolyGram 32659
With the Jazz Messengers. Prototype Blakey on 1988 reissue. Lee Morgan (tpt), Benny Golson (ts), and Bobby Timmons (p). All superb. —*Michael G. Nastos*

Des Femmes Disparaissent / Dec. 18-19, 1958 / Fontana 660224

Paris 1958 / i. 1958 / Bluebird 61097

Les Liaisons O.S.T. / i. 1959 / PolyGram 812017
Music from a sound track Blakey cocomposed with Benny Golson in 1958 for a Molinaro film *Des Femmes Disparaissent.* The featured group includes Lee Morgan and Bobby Timmons, and was one of Blakey's finest in a hard bop/soul-jazz vein. —*Ron Wynn*

○ **At the Jazz Corner of the World—Vols. 1 and 2** / Apr. 15, 1959 / Blue Note 4016

○ **Paris Concert: Art Blakey and the Jazz Messengers** / Nov. 15, 1959 / Portrait 44120

Live in Copenhagen (1959) / Nov. 1959 / Royal 516

Big Beat / Mar. 6, 1960 / Blue Note 46400

Unforgettable Lee! / i. Apr. 1960-Jun. 1960 / Fresh Sound 1020

☆ **Like Someone in Love** / Aug. 7, 1960 / Blue Note 84245

○ **Meet You at the Jazz Corner of the World—Vol. 1** / Sep. 14, 1960 / Blue Note 84054

○ **Meet You at the Jazz Corner of the World—Vol. 2** / Sep. 14, 1960 / Blue Note 84055

Roots & Herbs / Feb. 18, 1961 / Blue Note 84347

Witch Doctor, The / Mar. 14, 1961 / Blue Note 84258
The significant release of *Witch Doctor* (recorded March 14, 1961), at a time when the jazz community appeared so polarized, made two points very clear: that Art Blakey was a definitive jazz drummer whose playing existed, time out of mind, and that 1961 was not such a bad year or "polarization is an illusion caused by our lost view of present moments." . . . The master of Latin, African, and American rhythms, Blakey, alive in New York, contributed massively to the available influences during the great Eastern dry spell when thirsty visitors went west to see what Kerouac was rapping about, though it wasn't called rapping in those days. . . . So that's why *Witch Doctor* is good and fresh and hot—because it is how people played jazz in those days. It is definitive jazz, strong gut-music made at a time when the music could have perished. The personnel includes Lee Morgan (trumpet), Wayne Shorter (tenor sax), Bobby Timmons (piano), and Jymie Merritt (bass). —*Alan Offstein, Coda*

Freedom Rider, The / May 27, 1961 / Blue Note 4156

☆ **Mosaic** / Oct. 2, 1961 / Blue Note 46523

Live Messengers / Mar. 9-18, 1962 / Blue Note 473J2

Three Blind Mice—Vols. 1 & 2 / Mar. 9-18, 1962 / Blue Note 84451
Super two-record set with arguably his best three-horn front line (Wayne Shorter, Freddie Hubbard, Curtis Fuller), plus consistently fine piano from Cedar Walton. —*Ron Wynn*

☆ **Caravan** / Oct. 23-24, 1962 / Riverside 038
Same band as *Ugetsu.* Shorter wrote "Sweet 'N Sour" and "This Is for Albert," two of his lesser-known but great compositions. His best work. —*Michael G. Nastos*

○ **Ugetsu** / Jun. 16, 1963 / Riverside 090
Blakey's best sextet with Wayne Shorter (sax), Freddie Hubbard (tpt), and Curtis Fuller (t). Cedar Walton is prominent as music director, arranger, and composer. Live at Birdland, New York City. Famous tunes include "One by One," "On the Ginza," and the title track. Among his best work. —*Michael G. Nastos*

☆ **Jazz Message, A** / Jul. 10, 1963 / MCA 5648
Art Blakey Quartet. Not the Jazz Messengers, but featuring McCoy Tyner (p) and Sonny Stitt (ts). Extraordinary version of "Café." —*Michael G. Nastos*

Free for All / Feb. 10, 1964 / Blue Note 84170
With The Jazz Messengers. 1988 reissue of prime '60s set with Wayne Shorter (sax), Freddie Hubbard (tpt), and Curtis Fuller (t). —*Ron Wynn*

☆ **Kyoto** / Feb. 20, 1964 / Riverside 145
Prime examples of blowing dates can usually be found on Art Blakey recordings; *Kyoto* is an example. This is a February 20, 1964, date with the Messengers of that time: Wayne Shorter (tenor sax), Freddie Hubbard (trumpet), Cedar Walton (piano), Reggie Workman (bass). Wellington Blakey, a cousin to Art Blakey (drums/bandleader), does vocals on one of the five tracks ("Wellington's Blues"). "Wellington Blues," credited to Blakey, is notable in that it is one of the infrequent times he strikes out. The singer sounds slightly like a sober Rubberlegs Williams; in addition, the lyrics are terribly superficial and clichéd. The other unusual thing about this set is the rather subdued role of Blakey; no solos and relatively few of his tracks and trademarks are heard throughout. As usual, there is solid Hubbard, Shorter, and Fuller in evidence. —*Bob Rusch, Cadence*

Indestructible / Apr. 24, 1964+May 15, 1964 / Blue Note 46429
With The Jazz Messengers. There's a bonus cut on the 1986 reissue of a very hot date. —*Ron Wynn*

Buttercorn Lady / Jan. 1-9, 1966 / Limelight 86034

Anthenagin / Mar. 1973 / Prestige 10076

Percussion Discussion / i. 1976 / MCA 92511

○ **In My Prime—Vol. 1** / Dec. 29, 1977 / Timeless 114
Drummer Art Blakey was, without a doubt, a massive wielder of percussive pronouncements. Nevertheless, he was thoroughly within the dictates of good taste when he prodded, with merciless insistence, even the most sheltered of his younger charges. For the most part, they respond vigorously to the drummer's initiatory challenges, although tenorman David Schnitter's customarily large sound is ill-served by an unfortunate mixing job. The Clifford Brownian-enamored trumpeter Valery Ponomarev, the eager alto saxophonist Robert (Bobby) Watson, the promising pianist James Williams, and the confident trombonist Curtis Fuller are all equally well within the purview of their leader's stylistic compass, thereby ensuring a healthy future for the brand of hard bop over which Blakey long reigned supreme. —*Jack Sohmer, Cadence*

In This Korner / May 8, 1978 / Concord Jazz 4068
This is one of the Keystone Korner recordings with the Marsalis brothers. —*Michael G. Nastos*

In My Prime—Vol. 2 / Dec. 4, 1978 / Timeless 118

○ **Live at Montreux and NorthSea** / Jul. 13+17, 1980 / Timeless 510
The Jazz Messengers Big Band album on Timeless is culled from tapes recorded in July 1980 at the Montreux and NorthSea jazz festivals, and boasts the additional virtue of more similarly striking soloists. In actuality, the Big Band was more of an extended sextet than it was an orchestra, for the charts (three originals by alto saxophonist Bobby Watson, one by pianist James Williams, and one standard) serve almost exclusively as stepping-stones for the many featured soloists. All are in top-notch shape; trumpeter Valerie Ponomarev and trombonist Robin Eubanks are the most exceptional of those not already mentioned. —*Jack Sohmer, Down Beat*

Live at Bubba's / Oct. 11, 1980 / Who's Who in Jazz 21019

Album of the Year / Apr. 12, 1981 / MCA 33103
With the Jazz Messengers. 1988 reissue, one of the best from Marsalis period. —*Ron Wynn*

Straight Ahead / Jun. 1981 / Concord Jazz 4168

This is one of the Keystone Korner recordings with the Marsalis brothers. It is good early '80s Blakey. Also, there is spry piano playing by James Williams. —*Michael G. Nastos*

★ **Keystone 3** / Jan. 1982 / Concord Jazz 4196

Drummer Art Blakey's Messengers band with trumpeter Wynton Marsalis is destined to be remembered in a league with those incorporating Lee Morgan, Clifford Brown, and Kenny Dorham. All the more reason to savor *Keystone 3*, which comes from a live date at San Francisco's Keystone Korner. Marsalis doesn't dominate *Keystone 3*, a near classic, because Blakey achieves a tremendous balancing act with the headstrong talents of three disparate front liners (including the scholarly Wynton and the freewheeling saxophonist Branford Marsalis). The interest in Wynton Marsalis may have overshadowed the development of saxophonist Bill Pierce, who contributes a wonderfully breathy "In a Sentimental Mood." Much like John Coltrane's way with a ballad, he works subtly with the melody, confident that excess isn't needed to express his own signature, while pianist Donald Brown contributes McCoy Tyneresque chordings. The brothers shine on "Waterfalls." Branford Marsalis plays a broad-ranging solo, both gutty and fluid, on a Wynton Marsalis composition that shows the influence of Herbie Hancock. Wynton Marsalis's drive, crystal-clear tone, and careful phrasing mix best as he steams through Thelonious Monk's "In Walked Bud." And through it all, Blakey is clearly the catalyst, the ubiquitous trapsman who never needs to overpower the listener to show his control, who talks in several tongues simultaneously and distinctly. —*R. Bruce Dold*, Down Beat

☆ **Oh—By the Way** / May 20, 1982 / Timeless 165

Oh—By the Way, recorded four months and three personnel changes after *Keystone 3*, lacks the overwhelming strength of the Marsalis-fed Messengers, yet is an impressive album, showing how Art Blakey could begin, in a short time, to meld musicians with dynamics different from their predecessors into another powerful group. The new band on *Oh—By the Way* lacks the discipline and singularity of purpose of its predecessor, but suggests that the voices are developing, the cohesion is finding a groove. Trumpeter Terence Blanchard, 19 at the time of the recording, avows a love for Miles Davis and unabashedly emulates Davis on "My Funny Valentine." Johnny O'Neal adds quite a different piano color than Donald Brown. O'Neal has an airy, flowing style that gets a workout on "Tropical Breeze," a trio number that is the best chance on either record to hear Blakey's style. —*R. Bruce Dold*, Down Beat

Live at Ronnie Scott's: Art Blakey and the Jazz Messengers / Feb. 25, 1985 / Castle 14

Live at Sweet Basil: Art Blakey and the Jazz Messengers / Mar. 24, 1985 / GNP 2182

Live at Kimball's / Apr. 1985 / Concord Jazz 4307

Dr. Jeckyl: Art Blakey's Jazz Messengers / Dec. 30-31, 1985 / Evidence 22001

A fine '80s Messengers edition, with his New Orleans connection firmly established, plus exciting pianist Mulgrew Miller and steady bassist Lonnie Plaxico. Blakey had reestablished his patented three-horn front line as well, with trumpeter Wynton Marsalis, alto saxophonist Donald Harrison, and tenor saxophonist Jean Toussaint. —*Ron Wynn*

○ **I Get a Kick out of Bu** / Nov. 11, 1988 / Soul Note 121155

One for All / Apr. 10-11, 1990 / A&M 5329

○ **History of Jazz Messengers** / i. 1992 / Blue Note 97190

Three-disc anthology that covers various editions of the Messengers from the beginning to the end. It contains such classics as "Moanin'," and does a good job of showing how much talent passed through the Blakey organization over the decades. It's particularly valuable as an introductory tool, but is not comprehensive enough to substitute for what should come from the label; a true multidisc boxed set featuring his full recordings for the Blue Note label. —*Ron Wynn*

TERENCE BLANCHARD

b. Mar. 13, 1962, New Orleans, LA
Trumpet / Neo bop
Terence Blanchard is one of the best of the '80s and '90s Miles Davis disciples; some think he is more fiery and passionate in his playing than Wynton Marsalis. His lyricism and compelling solos, as well as his range, taste, and overall technique, have won him critical acclaim. There is another Marsalis connection; Blanchard started on trumpet at age 14 while studying at the New Orleans Center for Creative Arts. His instructor was Ellis Marsalis. He began composition studies the next year, and attended Rutgers in 1980. He joined Lionel Hampton the same year, playing for two years in his band before he replaced Wynton Marsalis in Art Blakey's Jazz Messengers. A fellow student and friend, Donald Harrison, replaced Wynton's brother, Branford, in the group at the same time. Blanchard and Harrison were soon compared to the Marsalis brothers, and the two friends departed the Blakey band at the same time and coformed a group. The Blanchard-Harrison band made its debut on Concord in 1983. They remained together throughout the '80s, moving from Concord to Columbia for more acclaimed recordings in the late '80s. They went their separate ways in the '90s, and Blanchard continued to record with Columbia. Both his music for Spike Lee's film, *Malcolm X*, and his recent album, *Simply Stated*, are outstanding releases. His sessions as a soloist, with Donald Harrison, and in Blakey's Messengers are available on CD. —*Ron Wynn*

New York Second Line / Oct. 15-16, 1983 / George Wein Collection 43002
Blanchard-Harrison. The 1984 set that helped cement their status in the emerging crop of '80s young lions. —*Ron Wynn*

Discernment / Dec. 1984 / George Wein Collection 3008

○ **Fire Waltz- Eric Dolphy and Booker Little Remembered** / i. Oct. 3, 1986-Oct. 4, 1986 / Projazz 681
Terence Blanchard and Donald Harrison continued their homage to the Eric Dolphy/Booker Little duo with a second set of performances recorded at Sweet Basil. They feature "Fire Waltz" and "Bee Vamp," two more tunes the duo immortalized during their Five Spot performances. Their versions of these pieces, as well as their version of "Number Eight," are well-intentioned, frequently exciting, and superbly played. But they are not transcendent for the simple reason that Harrison lacks Dolphy's fluency on either alto sax or bass clarinet, and Blanchard's does not possess Little's command of the upper register or his embouchure. That is not a knock; they certainly click with the identical rhythm section of pianist Mal Waldron, bassist Richard Davis, and drummer Ed Blackwell, who did play on the originals. They spur them on, interact well, and chime in with nicely constructed, thoughtful solos when necessary. Both these volumes are highly recommended, but once you finish them, if you have not heard the originals, do whatever it takes to get them. —*Ron Wynn*

★ **Crystal Stair** / i. 1987 / Columbia 40830
Like Michael Cimino's "The Sicilian," Donald Harrison/Terence Blanchard's *Crystal Stair* seemed designed to vindicate their harshest critics. It fit the neo-con stereotype perfectly; technically polished, glossily recorded (the music in New York, the reverb in L.A.) and neo in outlook, and wearing its traditionalism like an ostentatious coat (hear "God Bless the Child"). Having trailed Wynton Marsalis ever upward from Art Blakey's band to impersonating Miles Davis' quintet to signing with CBS, Harrison (alto, soprano, C-melody sax) and Blanchard (trumpet) have had little incentive to think for themselves. (Harrison has played capable freebop before, but his C-melody solo on "Slam" sounded Berklee-mannered). Unless you've been in a cave prior to 1964, little here will surprise. —*Kevin Whitehead*, Cadence

○ **Black Pearl** / **i.** 1988 / Columbia 44216
Blanchard-Harrison. The best by trumpeter Blanchard and
saxophonist Donald Harrison, especially the title track. —
Michael G. Nastos

○ **Simply Stated** / 1991 / Columbia 48903
Nice date from a youthful New Orleans prodigy, one of his
first done after he and onetime alto sax partner Donald
Harrison parted. Blanchard was battling embouchure problems, but still manages some compelling solos. Antonio Hart
makes a fine replacement for Harrison on alto, and a good
second solo voice. —*Ron Wynn*

☆ **Terence Blanchard** / 1991 / Columbia 47354

JIMMY BLANTON

b. 1918, **d.** 1942
Bass / Swing, big band
Jazz's first great bassist outside the traditional New Orleans
idiom, Jimmy Blanton expanded the instrument's possibilities and rewrote its vocabulary. His full, round tone, unparalleled agility, extremely accurate intonation, swinging style,
and harmonic knowledge made Blanton the model for a
generation, especially for players such as Oscar Pettiford,
Charles Mingus, and Ray Brown. Blanton contributed remarkably advanced solos, departing from what had become
the norm, the fixed walking bass, and demonstrating great
command and flexibility. Blanton played in Chattanooga,
Tennessee, in groups led by his mother, who was a pianist.
He attended Tennessee State a short time, then moved to St.
Louis. He played in Fats Marable's riverboat bands and in
the Jeter-Pillars Orchestra, where he was discovered in 1939
by Duke Ellington. Ellington quickly tapped him for his orchestra, and the results were immediate and impressive.
Blanton enriched the band's sound and rhythmic drive, and
helped inspire Ellington into a period of great compositional
productivity. Blanton's bass was a prominent factor in compositions such as "Ko-Ko," "Jack the Bear," and "Concerto for
Cootie." Blanton also participated in small-group sessions
led by Johnny Hodges, and in duets with Ellington. He was
a member of several early sessions at Minton's (the laboratory for the sounds that became bop were nurtured there).
Blanton's health declined in 1941; he suffered from congen-
ital tuberculosis that took his life. He can be heard on a
number of Ellington reissues. —*Ron Wynn*

CARLA BLEY (Carla [nee Borg] Bley)

b. May 11, 1938, Oakland, CA
*Piano, composer, bandleader / Progressive big band, modern
creative*
A wonderful composer whose madcap personality and humor carries over into her songwriting, Carla Bley has been
at the forefront of many music cooperatives and bands since
the '60s. While her piano playing has the unpredictability of
Thelonious Monk's, her compositions reflect multiple music
genres. She includes early jazz references, improvisational
and symphonic elements, and snippets of any and everything from bebop to rock. Bley's father, a church musician,
taught her a few fundamentals, but otherwise she is self-
trained.
    She moved to New York from Oakland at age 17, and di-
vided her time between playing piano and writing songs for
musicians such as George Russell, her husband Paul Bley,
and Jimmy Giuffre. Bley worked with Pharoah Sanders and
Charles Moffett in 1964, then became a full-time musician.
She and Michael Mantler coformed the Jazz Composers
Guild Orchestra in the mid '60s; he became her second husband. The orchestra gave a concert at Town Hall in 1964,
and Bley went to Europe with a quintet in 1965, recording
and appearing on radio and television.
    Bley also cofounded the Jazz Composer's Orchestra
Association (JCOA) in 1966, a nonprofit organization that
commissioned, produced, and distributed a wide range of
material ignored by the major labels. The JCOA distributed
many labels into the '70s before money woes forced them to
close shop. They recorded a two-record (now disc) album on

their own label that year. Bley's 1967 work *A Genuine Tong
Funeral*, recorded by Gary Burton's Quartet, brought her
widespread public and critical attention, as did several compositions and arrangements for Charlie Haden's Liberation
Music Orchestra album on Impulse in 1969. Her most acclaimed composition was 1971's *Escalator over the Hill*. The
album was hailed by both the national and international
jazz press, and Bley received many composing grants.
    She has divided her time between recording, leading vari-
ous large bands, and composing in the '70s, '80s, and '90s.
She and Mantler began their own company, Watt Records,
which is now distributed by ECM. Bley and Mantler have issued many records on Watt, and Bley worked with Roswell
Rudd and others during the '80s. She provided the sound
track for a 1985 film, *Mortelle Randonnee*. Bley contributed
new compositions to another Haden Liberation Music
Orchestra session in 1983, a Monk tribute album in 1984,
and a Kurt Weill tribute in 1986. She played organ on a Steve
Swallow album in 1986, and did her own session in 1988.
She continued recording with a nine- and a ten-piece band
into the '90s, and, in 1993, did another album with Swallow.
There's a good amount of Bley material on CD, though none
of the JCOA sessions are in print currently. —*Ron Wynn*

★ **Genuine Tong Funeral, A** / **i.** 1967 / RCA 42766

○ **Escalator over the Hill** / Nov. 1968-Jun. 1971 / ECM 839310

☆ **European Tour 1977** / Sep. 1977 / ECM 831830
European Tour 1977 is a studio recording made in Munich.
"Rose and Sad Song" is a sort of mambo, highlighted by two
trombone solos (which are separated by one very dull organ
solo). Roswell Rudd is as brash and cocky as Studs Lonigan.
He plays trombone like a loudmouthed braggart, blaring
and daring, but he has a great sense of humor and an honest voice in spite of himself. "Spangled Banner Minor" is the
major work on the album, a 20-minute opus with Carla Bley
as Charles Ives. It begins with a marvelous orchestration of
"The Star Spangled Banner" in a minor key, played with
mock seriousness. Then drummer Andrew Cyrille goes into
a march cadence, and we get a polytonal mixture of "La
Marseillaise," "Yankee Doodle," and other patriotic favorites.
Another grave and ghostly reference to the national anthem
leads into a long section where the band solemnly intones a
dark hymn while Gary Windo goes mad on tenor.... It is a
crazed composition where everything happens at once. —
Douglas Clark, Down Beat

☆ **Musique Mecanique** / Dec. 1978-Aug. 1979 / ECM 839313
Musique Mecanique begins with "440," a composition using
the standard A as a tonal center. After stating the rolling
melodic theme, the band gets into a rock riff reminiscent of
the Rolling Stones circa 1970, complete with a Bobby Keys-
styled tenor solo. At first, it sounds thin without the electric
instruments, but then it finds its own groove with a breathtaking solo by altoist Alan Braufman, a sassy Roswell Rudd
trombone chorus, and a stately one by John Clark on French
horn. "Musique Mecanique" is a 23-minute, three-part composition that takes up all of side two. The title refers to machines like music boxes and calliopes, and so, in Part I, we
got machines imitating musicians. Part II has a lyric, rendered by Rudd with appropriate theatrics, which twists in on
itself like a mobius strip or an Escher print. Part III could
have been the music for some grotesque ballet, where freaks
dance crooked steps. At several points, Bley wrote the score
to sound like a stuck record. You might curse the disc at first,
but it is a trick, like so much of this music: a prank, a sleight
of hand. —*Douglas Clark*, Down Beat

Social Studies / Sep. 1980-Dec. 1980 / ECM 831831
Excellent throughout. Great instrumental compositions. —
Michael G. Nastos

Night-Glo / Jun. 1985-Aug. 1985 / ECM 827640
As usual, Carla Bley's albums offer provocative arrangements, unorthodox playing, and interesting guest musicians.
Randy Brecker and Paul McCandless are among those who
provide interesting solos, while ECM's patented lush, over-

whelming production adds atmosphere and color. —*Ron Wynn*

Sextet / Dec. 1986-Jan. 1987 / ECM 831697

☆ **Duets: Carla Bley and Steve Swallow** / 1988 / ECM 837345
Despite the coy packaging of this set, there is more *music* here than Carla Bley had offered in many a document, including a healthy revisit to "Batteriewoman" from her investigative days of yesteryear. With the exceptions of the static "Utviklingssang" and "Tango," her work throughout shows a mature voice embracing spare lyricism (a bond to her ex, Paul), sly subtle dissonance, and inventive phrasing. Swallow's (bass) work, at times shaded by electronic devices, is less engaging. His support work is fine, but his solos, while fluid, are stilted by an overadherence to simple scale and arpeggio figures. Too bad he didn't take his cue from Bley's more adventurous variations. —*Milo Fine, Cadence*

☆ **Very Big Carla Bley Band** / Oct. 29-30, 1990 / ECM 847942
Her best LP of the last decade. Best cut is the Latin-tinged *Lo Ultimo*. —*Michael G. Nastos*

Go Together / i. 1993 / ECM 517673
Go Together is a beauty from the talented combination of pianist Carla Bley and bassist Steve Swallow, both of whom also contribute as composers on this all-originals session. Bley shies away from the dissonance her playing often gravitates toward in other settings. And Swallow, one of the most versatile electric bassists around, plays his axe more often like a lead guitar than a rhythm instrument. While most of the tunes here are fresh, there is a tasty reprise of Bley's classic big-band work "Fleur Carnivore," performed here with a sense of fresh intimacy, and certainly minus nostalgia. —*Ken Francklin, Jazz Times*

PAUL BLEY

b. Nov. 10, 1932, Montreal, Quebec, Canada
Piano / Early free, modern creative
An intriguing pianist, Canadian Paul Bley has been a fine soloist, accompanist, and bandleader since the early '50s. His playing is famous for subtle harmonic progressions, for a sometimes spacy quality, for unpredictable rhythmic patterns, and for strong phrasing and excellent melodic interpretations.

Bley studied the violin as a child before turning to piano at age eight. He led a quartet in a Montreal hotel in the mid '40s, then played in New York during the early '50s. Bley studied at Julliard before returning to Canada in 1952. He made a jazz film short and did television work, then returned to New York in 1954. He made his first recording as a leader on Charles Mingus's Debut label in 1953. Bley was in Jackie McLean's quintet with Donald Byrd, Doug Watkins, and Art Taylor, and was in a trio with Mingus and Art Blakey. He moved to Los Angeles in the mid '50s, working mainly in clubs and at some colleges. He played with Chet Baker and in a trio with Billy Higgins and Charlie Haden. Bley led a combo in the late '50s that included Ornette Coleman and Don Cherry. They made one recording at the Hillcrest Club which Bley later issued on his own label. He was also married to pianist Carla Bley during the late '50s and early '60s. Bley led a trio with Steve Swallow and Pete La Roca when he returned to the East Coast during the early '60s. He also played with Charles Mingus, recorded some important free jazz albums with Jimmy Giuffre, and worked with Don Ellis. Bley returned briefly to the West Coast to record with Ellis in 1962.

He led trios in New York during most of the '60s, and played with Sonny Rollins in 1963. The next year Bley participated in the famed October Revolution in Jazz dates in New York, and was a founding member of the Jazz Composers Guild. Bley made several trio albums in the '60s for various labels, and worked with Gary Peacock and Barry Altschul, among others. He became interested in electronics and fusion in the late '60s, and, from 1969 to 1971, recorded with electric keyboards exclusively. He sometimes worked with his second wife, singer/electric keyboardist Annette Peacock. Bley abandoned electronics later in the '70s, and co-

founded the label Improvising Artists Incorporated in 1974 with artist Carol Goss. This label recorded some stunning sets by Sam Rivers and Dave Holland, Bley, Sun Ra, and many others that are now being reissued on CD. Bley also recorded solo albums in the '70s, and worked with Dave Holland and Julius Hemphill. He has continued cutting solo and trio dates in the '80s and '90s. In 1986, he did a date with John Surman, Paul Motian, and Bill Frisell. Bley's playing heavily influenced Keith Jarrett's piano style. There's an ample number of Bley sessions, from the '60s to the '90s, available on CD. —*Ron Wynn*

Pyramid / IAI
One of the prizes of the IAI catalog, this collaboration is a lot more playful and upbeat than *Quiet Song*, and alto and soprano saxophonist Lee Konitz is easily up to the challenge of playing both melodically and free (keyboardist is Paul Bley, electric and acoustic guitarist is Bill Connors). —*Scott Yanow, Coda*

Improvisations: Introducing Paul Bley / Nov. 30, 1953 / Original Jazz Classics 201
This is pianist Paul Bley's debut. Recorded November 30, 1953, this has been a most elusive LP over the years. Fantasy added "Santa Claus Is Coming to Town," originally issued only on a sampler, to the original ten-inch program, but it would seem the two unissued tracks from this session with Art Blakey (drums) and Charles Mingus (bass) are lost. What's here is refreshing music. The harmonics and openness (freedom) suggested by the lines remain remarkably in touch with the times over 30 (1985) years later. Paul Bley has a solid recorded history, yet I still think he remains generally overlooked as a strong and continuing original voice in improvising music. One might start right here, at the beginning, with this record. —*Bob Rusch, Cadence*

○ **Live at the Hillcrest Club (1958)** / Oct. 1958 / Inner City 1007
A classic avant-garde (or free or outside if you prefer) recording from 1958. This was considered Ornette Coleman's album for years, but Bley was the actual leader. The sound quality on the original vinyl album is poor at best, but Coleman's searing, jagged solos and Bley's furious answering lines more than compensate. The CD cleans things up a bit, though it's still a sonic nightmare. —*Ron Wynn*

○ **Floater Syndrome, The** / Aug. 17, 1962+Sep. 12, 1963 / Savoy 1148
1962 and 1963. Trio sessions are with Steve Swallow (b) and Pete LaRoca (d). Paul and Carla Bley and Ornette Coleman wrote the music for this dense and wide-ranging trio. —*Michael G. Nastos*

★ **Paul Bley with Gary Peacock** / Apr. 13, 1963 / PolyGram 843162

☆ **Syndrome** / Sep. 12, 1963 / Savoy 1175
The follow-up to *Floater* features more music from Carla Bley. The Savoy albums really introduced her work (through her then husband) to the world. —*Michael G. Nastos*

☆ **Paul Bley Quartet** / Feb. 9, 1964 / ECM 835250
Free jazz proponent Paul Bley's album consists of original compositions by each of his sidemen, as well as two by Bley. Bley's compositions, "Interplay" and the solo piano piece, "Triste," start and end the album. "Triste" is an interesting short piece, which conveys the essence of its name. —*Robert Iannapollo, Cadence*

○ **Closer** / Dec. 18, 1965 / ESP 1021
On *Closer*, the setting for pianist Paul Bley is the more familiar trio format (Barry Altschul, percussion; Steve Swallow, bass). The music here was recorded December 18, 1965, and actually postdates some of the Bley material on ECM that Improvising Artists and Arista released later in the '70s. This LP is much more characteristic of the Paul Bley style: understated, probing, and occasionally passionately percussive, but always with a gently searching ambience. —*Bob Rusch, Cadence*

○ **Mr. Joy** / May 11, 1968 / Limelight 86060

This Paul Bley date has Gary Peacock on bass and Billy Elgart on drums. There are eight tracks: six by Annette Peacock along with Bley's "Only Lovely" and Ornette Coleman's "Ramblin'." These recordings and one made in December 1968 for RCA (#305) are some of Bley's best and last (during that period) acoustic work. Bley utilizes a full range of the piano's tonal qualities, expressing thought and emotions with economy, but plays with an almost Thelonious Monk-like deliberateness. Gary Peacock's bass work is perfectly in tune with Bley's piano. The bass work is often up front and is given equal voicing with the piano; Elgart's drumming is, too, at times. —Cadence

Open for Love / Sep. 11, 1972 / ECM 827751
Paul Bley's approach was more atonal, less rhythmic, more intellectualized, and less spontaneous than Keith Jarrett's. Bley seems to be consciously editing himself (that is, telling his hands what to play), and there seems to be certain things Bley definitely won't allow himself to play (tonal melodies and triads, for example). Additionally, Bley was much more concerned with the implications of musical silence than Jarrett. In a typical piece, one of two high-tension chords are followed by a languid grouping of floating notes in the treble registers. Bley examines and savors the ramifications of each before he makes his next move. Only on "Harlem" does he remotely approach conventional rhythmic and melodic sound. —Jon Balleras, Down Beat

Scorpio: Paul Bley & Scorpio / Oct. 22-24, 1972 / Milestone 9046

Japan Suite / i. Jul. 25, 1975 / Improvising Artists 373849

○ **Copenhagen and Harlem** / i. Oct. 1975 / Arista 1901
Copenhagen and Harlem, recorded and released in Europe in 1965 and 1966, presents Paul Bley's classic trio running through seven short and two long musical pieces.... He and his companions seemed to envision music as pure design. Nothing here is programmatic or didactic. He thought in melodic shapes and rhythmic thrusts, rather than in key signatures, meters, and conventional harmonic cadences. The result is an anthology of intricate, if somewhat dry, musical patterns. (Even telling precisely where one piece ends and the next begins demands attentive listening.) Time is implicit: rhythms and meters float suspended, punctuated only by the occasional splash of a cluster of notes or a cymbal ping. —Jon Balleras, Down Beat

Axis/Solo Piano / Jul. 1+3, 1977 / Improvising Artists 373853
Axis/Solo Piano is a unique recital. Bley had formidable technique, but he was just as concerned with the sonic possibilities of his instrument. He favored a ringing right sound, and made good use of overtones and silences. On George Gershwin's "Porgy," he struts out a four-square pulse under the theme, segues into some rubato colorings, evokes a passionate blues, and finally fades into reflective musings. Prince Lasha's "Music Matador" combines Mexicali tremolos, unusual harmonies, and a Southwestern barrelhouse ambience. Bley's "El Cordobes—Please Don't Ever Leave Me" begins with ominous Cecil Taylorish power, but concludes with rhapsodic longing. —Chip Stern, Down Beat

Quiet Song / i. 1978 / Improvising Artists 373839
IAI debuted in 1975 with this trio date, reuniting pianist Paul Bley with his old boss clarinetist, saxophonist, and flutist Jimmy Giuffre and with former Return To Forever member guitarist Bill Connors, who by then was mostly playing acoustic guitar. The music is largely free (even the abstract version of "Goodbye") and introverted, with some surprising explosions of passion. —Scott Yanow, Coda

Virtuosi / i. 1978 / Improvising Artists 373844
This was released under drummer Barry Altschul's name, but it is actually the Paul Bley trio of the era (bassist Gary Peacock and pianist Bley). This set consists of two very long (around 16-17 minutes apiece) free ballads, and tends to drag in spots despite close interplay. —Scot Yanow, Coda

○ **Ramblin'** / i. 1980 / Affinity 37

Pianist Paul Bley's July 1, 1966 recording, previously released on BYG and Red Records (Italian), was reissued on Affinity as Ramblin'. In many ways, this is typical of Bley's original piano style, but seems even more exaggerated in his use of silence and empty space than some of Bley's better-known and more concise efforts. There are times here when Bley's "hold your breath" approach goes past the stretch of continuity. It is Bley's show and Mark Levison (bass) and Barry Altschul (drums) give perfect support. The only breaks here from the reflective ballad style are "Ramblin'" and "Mazayalon," which Bley infuses with a definite Chicago funk sound almost as if he had been listening to some Ramsey Lewis. —Bob Rusch, Cadence

Sonor / May 22, 1983 / Soul Note 1085

Hot / Mar. 10, 1985 / Soul Note 1140
Excellent playing by Bley keeps things moving on this '84 date. The songs vary in quality, but Bley's moving, teeming solos are consistently impressive, and the production and sound are excellent. —Ron Wynn

Paul Bley Group, The / i. Mar. 1985 / Soul Note 1140

My Standard / Dec. 8, 1985 / Steeple Chase 1214
After a recording hiatus of six years, pianist Paul Bley returned in 1984 as he had left in 1978, with an album of solo piano.... Here, Bley recorded an album of reinterpretations of standards he'd recorded through the years. When one realizes that he hadn't recorded standards since around 1963 (although he did them in concerts), it makes this LP all the more timely. Among the surprises is a version of "Santa Claus Is Coming to Town," a track recorded at his first date in 1953 with Charles Mingus and Art Blakey.... On the version from 1953, Bley was a bebopper much under the influence of Bud Powell. The piece was dominated by Blakey's chang-a-chang rhythm. The version from 32 years later is the work of a mature improviser and group leader. Billy Hart (drums) sets up a pulse rather than a straight rhythm. Jesper Lundgaard (bass) and Bley roam about freely before they lock into the changes. It is a lot of fun and totally unexpected. Bley's interpretations vary. "You'd Be So Nice to Come Home to" and "All the Things You Are" are handled pretty straightforwardly, playfully dotted with occasional dissonances.... Others are handled in the patented Bley ballad style. The beautiful melody line on "If I'm Lucky" is stretched out, forcing the listener to hang onto every note. "I Can't Get Started" (also from the 1953 session) is only implied, never stated. Lundgaard's feature, "Black and Blue," contains a great bass solo and features some marvelous interplay with Bley.... Although drummer Billy Hart has a little problem with the implied time, he adds some new rhythmic dimensions to Bley's music. His work on "I Wish I Knew" meshes nicely with Bley's behind the beat phrasing and he pushes Bley to one of his best solos. All in all, this is another successful date for Bley. —Robert Iannapollo, Cadence

Nearness of You, The / i. Nov. 1988 / Steeple Chase 1246

Blues for Red / i. 1989 / Red 123238

Life of a Trio—Saturday and Sunday / Dec. 16-17, 1989 / Owl 79230

○ **Bebopbebopbebopbebop** / Dec. 22, 1989 / Steeple Chase 31259
A surprising album from Bley, long considered an outside player with little, if any, affinity for straight bop. He shatters that myth on this set, going through a dozen songs including such anthems as "Ornithology" and "The Theme" with vigor, harmonic distinction, and rhythmic edge. He's brilliantly backed by bassist Bob Cranshaw, providing some of his best, less detached playing in quite a while, and drummer Keith Copeland, navigating the tricky changes with grace. —Ron Wynn

Paul Bley/NHOP / Jun. 24, 1990+Jul. 1, 1990 / Steeple Chase 31005

○ **Memoirs** / i. Jul. 1990 / Soul Note 121240

Memoirs serves as a tidy summation of Paul Bley's gifts as an individual and as a musical conversationalist. It helps that he converses with old friends. Paul Motian is, roughly, to the drums what Bley is to the piano, capable of sculpting icy, paradoxical emotions; on moment's notice, they can venture "out" where tonal centers and rhythmic pulses are not invited. And there, always, is the fundamental Charlie Haden, who demonstrates how a few well-placed notes and well-observed silences can lock a group texture into place. *Memoirs* is truly a three-pronged affair, featuring more tunes from Motian's vivid pen than the others, as well as songs by Thelonious Monk, Ornette Coleman ("Latin Genetics," a Bley favorite), and Bley and Haden. Motian's "Enough Is Enough" is as touchingly tender as "This Is the Hour" is wit-lined. —*Josef Woodard,* Down Beat

JANE IRA BLOOM

b. 1955, Newtown, MA
Electric keyboards, soprano saxophone / Modern creative
A progressive and original composer, Jane Ira Bloom plays soprano saxophone and uses electronics live. She's composed music for NASA. Her approach is highly rhythmic, and her songs can be simple or complex. Her music's for the challenged listener. Bloom has current releases available on CDs recorded for Arabesque and Enja. —*Ron Wynn and Michael G. Nastos*

○ **Second Wind** / Jun. 1980 / Outline 138
Here, soprano and alto saxophonist Jane Ira Bloom stretches out a little, varies her formats, portions out additional blowing space, controlled yet joyous, to other thoughtful colleagues as well, either needling vibraphonist Dave Friedman or spare pianist Larry Karush. The firm groundwork of bassist Kent McLagan anchors each track, but drummer Frank Bennett adds kit colors. We hear more of Bloom's spacious, dynamic soprano, but the last track on each side shows her pearly, rounded, yet "straighter" alto. Bloom took as much care with clear production, quality vinyl, and attractive packaging as she did with her music, and the result is a provocative follow-up to an impressive first outing. —*Fred Bouchard,* Down Beat

○ **Modern Drama** / Feb. 1987 / Columbia 40755
A quick glance at the cover of saxophonist/composer Jane Ira Bloom's *Modern Drama* and one might be led to believe it is a funk-fusion collection. Fear not, listener, it is one more step in the evolution of this fine musician. Over the years, critics have compared Bloom's sound and style to various soprano artists such as Steve Lacy and Wayne Shorter. Like both, she is not a frenetic player, using space wisely. But with the addition of electronics, a touch of John Surman's tone can be heard. On the opening cut, "Overstars," you can hear that her tone is extended (with the use of an octave divider). Her phrases leap and stop, much the way Surman's do. She follows the rhythmic drive of drummer Tom Rainey and the percussive chords of longtime collaborator, pianist Fred Hersch. "Cagney" has a sprightly feel and, this time, she is fed by the spongy bass lines of Ratzo Harris. The electronics are used sparingly and to great effect. In the middle of the tune, she plays a marvelous twisted line with vibraharpist Dave Friedman that sets the stage for Hersch to follow with several good choruses. . . . "More than Sinatra" builds quietly, with the soprano leading the piano through the melody. There are moments when her tone sounds like Toots Thielemans's harmonica. Hersch shines, too: his playing is somewhat ornate, but not stilted. "Strange and Completely" was inspired by a television profile of Billie Holiday. Bloom's melody captures the pathos and aura of sadness that surrounded the singer's life. . . . Purists may blanch at the use (or misuse) of the soprano sound, but this is not a sellout album. You can hear that these musicians have played alongside each other many times. . . . A variety of sounds await the listener and, if your ears and mind are open, you cannot help but enjoy Jane Ira Bloom's fine achievement. —*Richard B. Kamins,* Cadence

★ **Slalom** / Jun. 6+9, 1988 / Columbia 44415

Jane Ira Bloom will never supplant Steve Lacy in ideas or ingenuity, but she's on the right track. Her tone suggests Steve Lacy's purity, but is at times a bit raspy. . . . I find Bloom's ballad playing captivating. On "Gershwin's Skyline—I Loves You Porgy," she cleverly punctuates with vibrato at the beginning of the bar lines, and in the middle, not at the end. On the tangoish "Ice Dancing," Bloom's more angular notions escape beautifully. At times, her soprano takes on the sonic characteristics of a chromatic harmonica. At her most playful, Bloom darts in between the rhythmic cracks of percussionist Tom Rainey. As with her previous album, *Modern Drama,* and the tracks "Overstars" and "Vario," Bloom digs down deep on "Drums Like Dancing" and shows a boppish edge, paraphrasing, cutting, and pasting on the title track, her reprised "Mighty Lights," and "Miro." Primarily a tone poetess, Bloom seems to prefer no-time paintings of reflection and spirituality. The remainder of the recording expresses this. Bloom says the idea is to weave in and out of the jazz tradition, and some purists should not read between the lines. This is not a hard-swinging date. It is a well-crafted, artistic statement and perhaps Bloom's most diverse, and definitely most listenable, album so far (1989). —*Michael G. Nastos,* Cadence

HAMIET BLUIETT

b. 1940, Lovejoy, IL
Baritone saxophone, clarinet / Modern creative
The finest baritone saxophonist of the '70s and beyond, Hamiet Bluiett has demonstrated a huge, impressive sound, superb technique, and a mastery of his horn in every register. In his solos, he can provide an array of tonal colors and harmonic options. A first-rate free player who's as proficient on standards as he is on bebop, Bluiett has played in many excellent groups, has led his own bands, and has been featured on numerous magnificent recordings. Bluiett took music lessons from his aunt, who was a choral director. He started on clarinet at age nine. He attended Southern University, where he studied flute and baritone. Following a stint in the navy, Bluiett moved to St. Louis in the mid '60s. He played with Lester and Joseph Bowie, Charles "Bobo" Shaw, Julius Hemphill, and Oliver Lake. He also worked with the Black Artists Group (BAG), the St. Louis equivalent of Chicago's Association for the Advancement of Creative Musicians (AACM). He moved to New York in 1969, and joined Sam Rivers's large ensemble. Bluiett worked with various bands before joining Charles Mingus's quintet in 1972, remaining with Mingus until 1975. A pair of mid '70s Bluiett concerts were later issued as albums on India Navigation. Bluiett, Hemphill, Lake, and David Murray formed a quartet in 1976 for a New Orleans concert. They decided to remain intact as a working unit and named themselves the World Saxophone Quartet. They've continued recording and performing into the '90s, though Arthur Blythe replaced Hemphill. Bluiett has also worked with other bands; he was a coleader of the Clarinet Family group that featured seven clarinetists. It recorded with Black Saint in the '80s. Bluiett recorded on his own for Black Saint, Soul Note, Chiaroscuro, Enja, and Tutu, among others, in the '70s, '80s, and '90s. He played with Lester Bowie, Hemphill, Abdullah Ibrahim, Phillip Wilson, Marcello Melis, Famadou Don Moye, Don Pullen, Fred Hopkins, Billy Hart, Irene Datcher, Buddy Collette, and Ronnie Burrage during the '70s and '80s. A couple of his sessions as a leader are currently available. His dates with the World Saxophone Quartet and Clarinet Family are available, too. —*Ron Wynn*

★ **Endangered Species** / Jun. 19, 1976 / India Navigation 1025
Baritone saxophonist Hamiet Bluiett wrote the four compositions on this session, but trumpeter Olu Dara gets more solo space and uses it to good advantage with some impassioned improvisations. Except for the very short "Ayana," each of the pieces has an open-ended, stark, almost bleak flavor. "The Other" is the best track. Its Far Eastern flavor is evoked through Bluiett's flute and Jumma Santos's balafon. —*Carl Brauer,* Cadence

Resolution / Nov. 1977 / Black Saint 14

Orchestra Duo and Septet / Nov. 1977-Dec. 1977 / Chiaroscuro 182

Array of pieces by Bluiett. Excellent duet with Pullen, good sextet numbers, interesting orchestral piece. —*Ron Wynn*

Birthright / i. Jun. 1978 / India Navigation 1030

Conceptually, *Birthright* is an intensely personal autobiographical sketch (by baritone saxophonist Hamiet Bluiett). "Doll Baby" honors Bluiett's grandmother, "The Mighty Denn" is a father's revelation to his son, and "The Village of Brooklyn, Ill. 62059" pays respect to the baritonist's hometown. In addition, "Ballad for George Hudson" is an appreciation for a music teacher, "My Father's House" devotes three movements to Bluiett's father, mother, and sister, and "In Tribute to Harry Carney" does just that; while "EBU—Helen" is a recognition of Bluiett's wife. —*Chuck Berg*, Down Beat

S.O.S. / Mar. 1980 / India Navigation

An explosive live quartet set that includes slashing piano from Don Pullen. —*Ron Wynn*

○ **Dangerously Suite** / i. Apr. 1981 / Soul Note 1188

This session was recorded on April 9 and April 17, 1981, and tries a bit too hard to cover all the "Black music" bases from ballads to swing to blues to gospel to funk. The group, which consists of drummer Billy Hart, bassist Buster Williams, African percussionist and vocalist Chief Bey, pianist Bob Neloms (again, another of the "new" generation), and vocalist Irene Datcher (only on "Jefferson") plays well, but only a few surface levels of feeling/commitment seem to be explored. —*Milo Fine*, Cadence

○ **Clarinet Family, The** / Nov. 1984 / Black Saint 0097

There's a big problem in the old ploy of presenting a group's most gripping work at the beginning of an album: the listener can only feel let down as the music plays on. That it happens here is almost inevitable. After all, what could possibly follow the heady arrangements and hot solo work of the first two tunes? (Their width and depth almost make for lessons in jazz history, swirling from Africa and South America to the avant-garde.) The next cut, "Nioka," a lush ballad (which, because of its voicings, sounds like a swing standard and thus garners misplaced applause) almost succeeds due to a heartrending reading and the effective change of pace. But from there, the program mainly consisted of inconclusive snippets culled from the remainder of this concert. —*Milo Fine*, Cadence

○ **EBU** / 1984 / Soul Note 1088

Pianist John Hicks is featured on baritonist Hamiet Bluiett's *EBU* with bassist Fred Hopkins and drummer Marvin "Smitty" Smith. Hicks's presence is indicative of the album's neo-traditional leanings. On the riff tunes "New Bones" and "Gumbo (Vegetarian Style)," Bluiett lets more than a touch of R&B honking seep into his playing, exploiting the baritone's power. . . . The sharply punctuated bari-drums duet that begins (and ends) "Things Will Never Be the Same" has more pep and heat, but the trio middle section drops to a less-demanding energy level. Best up is the closer: a rubato "A Night in Tunisia" snapped to a heady pace just in time for a suspenseful, high-wire falsetto solo by the leader, which is tongue-in-cheek without being farcical. —*Kevin Whitehead*, Cadence

○ **Live in Berlin with the Clarinet Family** / Black Saint 0097

ARTHUR BLYTHE (Arthur Murray Blythe)

b. Jul. 5, 1940, Los Angeles, CA

Alto and soprano saxophone / Hard bop, modern creative

Alto saxophonist Arthur Blythe is a gifted soloist with a wide vibrato and a pungent style that reflects the music of artists from Charlie Parker to Cannonball Adderley. He has an interest in unusual configurations and harmonic/melodic possibilities, which has driven him to lead bands with a tuba, a guitar, or a cello. Blythe excels at playing traditional bebop, hard bop, or free music, and has worked effectively in funk, blues, and R&B, too. His solos are tasteful, swinging, and superbly played. From his days as "Black Arthur" on the West Coast (which made some people think that he was a reincarnated Malcolm X on alto) to his ill-fated Columbia era when he was marketed as "the greatest saxophonist in the world," Blythe has suffered exaggerated expectations and false impressions. These misconceptions haven't affected his output as much as they've created an appearance that he is underachieving. Actually, he has accomplished as much, if not more, than virtually any player of his generation.

Blythe played in school bands as a youngster, then, as a teen, studied with Kirtland Bradford, a one-time member of Jimmie Lunceford's orchestra. Blythe worked with Horace Tapscott during the '60s and early '70s in Los Angeles; both men were founding members of the Union of God's Musicians and Artists Ascension. Blythe was part of the West Coast exodus to New York in the '70s that also saw David Murray, James Newton, and Stanley Crouch move east. He played with Chico Hamilton in the mid '70s, and with Gil Evans in the late '70s and early '80s, and was in the "loft jazz" movement of the '70s. Blythe recorded and played with Lester Bowie and Jack DeJohnette's Special Edition in the late '70s and early '80s.

He signed with Columbia in the late '70s, and led two groups in the early '80s. One group, called In the Tradition, was a bebop and swing-oriented ensemble with Steve McCall and either Stanley Cowell or John Hicks. The other group was an unnamed quintet with Abdul Wadud, Bob Stewart, Bobby Battle, and, sometimes, James "Blood" Ulmer and Kelvyn Bell. This group played challenging, nontraditional material, as well as some hard bop and even some pop, R&B, and funk. Blythe joined the Leaders in the mid '80s, replaced Julius Hemphill in the World Saxophone Quartet, and did more sessions with Stewart, Bell, and Battle. He began recording with Crouch in the late '60s and early '70s. His own albums started with sessions in the mid '70s for India Navigation and Adelphi. The Columbia dates began in the late '70s and continued until the mid '80s. Blythe also recorded for Blackhawk, and has recently done sessions for Enja. Many sessions are available on CD. —*Ron Wynn*

Grip, The / Feb. 26, 1977 / India Navigation 1029

Recorded in concert, alto saxophonist Arthur Blythe's sextet was a small orchestra with an historical perspective. As he explained it, the tuba is used to recall the earliest New Orleans jazz, the cello represents the European influence, and Muhammad Abdullah's conga represents the roots of the jazz experience. *The Grip* grasps this orchestra potential firmly, from the texturally dense polyphony of the title cut to the cello/sax duet that emerges from "Sunrise Service," to the throwaway solo piece with which the date ends. Hearing Blythe and cellist Abdul Wadud in tandem provides yet another perspective on the saxist's tone. On "Service," they play in the same registers long enough to show how well Blythe was matched to the cello's dark, sweeping romance. Both Wadud and Steve Reid (a little-known master of shifting energies) instill the necessary tension in "Spirits in the Field" (the only piece Blythe did *not* write), which is a mournful, Ornette-ish dirge. The slightly labored "As of Yet" is notable for all the front line solos, particularly that of trumpeter Ahmed Abdullah, whose considered use of space offsets Blythe's own instrumental juggernaut. —*Neil Tesser*, Down Beat

★ **Metamorphosis** / Feb. 26, 1977 / India Navigation 1038

This album from India Navigation (alto saxophonist Arthur Blythe's second on that bold New York label) uses nearly as traditional foundations as his *In the Tradition* LP, but in "outer" guise. Blythe's writing, as clear and articulate as his playing, was firmly grounded in blues, often limned in gritty riffs. "Duet" for alto and cello builds a blues structure on rising arpeggios; the title track has a bumptious unison theme that never strays far. On his solos, Blythe effectively uses repetition, shouts, Dolphian figures, and—dig this for traditionalism—melodic variation. "Shadows" is appropriately dark-toned and amorphous, but never impenetrable, its vivid alto obligato etched over slow horns. There follows a curiously textured section for the unusual rhythm, Bob Stewart's nimble figures (on tuba) and Abdul Wadud's *col legno* cello skittering to the fore. Even the free sections swing, and Blythe's spirit prevails. —*Fred Bouchard*, Down Beat

Bush Baby / Dec. 1977 / Adelphi 5008

☆ **Lenox Avenue Breakdown** / 1978 / Columbia 84152

First with Chico Hamilton, then with Gil Evans, and more recently with his own groups, alto saxophonist Arthur Blythe garnered New York's critical kudos, culminating in *Lennox Avenue Breakdown*. The less circumspect compare Blythe to Charlie Parker, but the mantle of Cannonball Adderley appears more fitting. Producer Bob Thiele not only rounded off the starker edges in the tone of Blythe, as well as flutist James Newton, he also rounded off the music. The arrangements are glitzy and monolithic; for that matter, Blythe's music is codified, to some degree. Still, everyone gets solo space here: Newton has one grand break on the title tune, guitarist Blood Ulmer recreates the trumpet role on *The Grip* in his fragmented solos, and tuba player Bob Stewart benefits from the superior Columbia recording quality. Drummer Jack DeJohnette is uniformly excellent, enlivening the island vamp of the sprightly "Down San Diego Way" with sudden and inexplicable sunbursts of cymbals. On the title track, Blythe sounds too straightforwardly Trane-like for so true an originator, but he plays hard and wild on the last two cuts. —*Neil Tesser*, Down Beat

In the Tradition / 1979 / Columbia 83350

Two good-humored original blues ("Break Tune," "Hip Dripper") featured on *In The Tradition* are kept short, but offer half the space to pianist Stanley Cowell, who draws on his own rags, paralleled octaves, bop turns, and wellspring of tradition (five years with the Heaths; childhood home sessions from Art Tatum). He also gets into some scorching cross fires with drummer Steve McCall. The standards have less clipped, matter-of-fact solos from alto saxophonist Arthur Blythe (including an astonishing Sidney Bechet homage on "Jitterbug Waltz"), and are taken more romantically and freely, fading into the mists of time via lingering codas. Blythe's ballads shimmer with his sweet vibrato and ecstatic flights to falsetto range, backed exquisitely by the rhythm mates. "Naima," really heady, soars to the stratosphere; Fred Hopkins abandons his role as anchorman to bow all out arpeggios and tremolos on bass. Blythe's history absorbs style and reminiscence, looking over the shoulder as well as straight ahead. —*Fred Bouchard*, Down Beat

Illusions / 1980 / Columbia 36583

There is so much contrast and color, track to track, on *Illusions* that it is one of the most joyously spirited records of 1980. Alto saxophonist Arthur Blythe and his fellow musicians create a unique sense of motion by way of integrating the roles of the accompanist and soloist, and after hearing "Bush Baby" and "Miss Nancy" back to back, you feel as if you've really been somewhere. Blythe expected a more dynamic response from his rhythm section, and he got it. They had to do something in order to keep Blythe's relatively nondescript, dronish vamps interesting. There is an irresistible sense of tension, which guitarist James "Blood" Ulmer, tuba player Bob Stewart, and cellist Abdul Wadud create collectively that is never fully released (on "Bush Baby," "Illusions," and "Carespin"), and their section functions as an artistically valid ensemble distraction from the soloist. Meshed within this unique ensemble is Blythe's searing alto, varying in mood and intensity for each cut. Pianist John Hicks's thunderous entrance on "Miss Nancy" is awesome. Wadud's cello is multipurpose; he can walk convincingly like a bassist, can thrash about percussively, or can combine with Blythe's horn to create haunting sonorities. —*Arthur Moorehead*, Down Beat

Elaboration / 1982 / Columbia 85990

Basic Blythe / 1987 / Columbia 40884

A classic case of questionable judgment turning what could have been a great album into an uneven one. The assembled quartet is a fine one, with pianist John Hicks, bassist Anthony Cox, and drummer Bobby Battle. Blythe plays with conviction, force, and fury, but the string section and orchestrations dilute his impact and greatly muddle the full process. —*Ron Wynn*

Hipmotism / Mar. 15+17, 1991 / Enja 79672

A long time coming for this extremely gifted saxophonist. Originals, too. The ultimate. —*Michael G. Nastos*

JIMMY BLYTHE

b. circa 1901, Louisville, KY, **d.** Jun. 21, 1931

Piano / Boogie-woogie, blues & jazz

Pianist Jimmy Blythe was a wonderful accompanist and leader who often helped elevate sessions by inspiring otherwise routine performers to extend themselves. At various times, Blythe was house pianist for Paramount, Vocalion, and Gennett, and his rolling, steady barrelhouse licks were heard in a number of groups. These included Blythe's Owls and Blue Boys, the State Street Ramblers, Chicago Stompers, Midnight Ramblers, and Jimmy Bertrand's Washboard Wizards. —*Ron Wynn*

Chicago Jazz / i. 1928 / Riverside 1036

★ **Chicago Stomps and the Dixie Four** / i. 192? / Riverside 1031

WILLIE BOBO (William Correa)

b. Feb. 28, 1934, New York, NY, **d.** Sep. 15, 1983, Los Angeles, CA

Percussion, bandleader / Latin jazz

Willie Bobo was a superb percussionist who made major inroads in jazz, Latin jazz, R&B, and pop. Bobo's father was a musician, and he began on bongos at age 14, then played congas, timbales, and trap drums. Bobo was a band boy for Machito's Afro-Cubans, then studied with Mongo Santamaria in the late '40s. Santamaria taught him percussion, and Bobo served as Santamaria's translator. In the early '50s, Bobo recorded with Mary Lou Williams, who gave him his nickname. Bobo replaced Manny Oquendo in Tito Puente's band in 1954, and would double on timbales when Puente took vibes solos. Bobo later played drums and timbales in Shearing's group with Armando Peraza, Cal Tjader, and Santamaria. He appeared on radio in the '50s as Willie Boborosa. Bobo worked in the late '50s with Cal Tjader, and also played with a short-lived Puente splinter group, Orquesta Manhattan. He and Santamaria coformed La Saborsa, a charanga (flute & violin) band in the early '60s; their recording of "Afro-Blue" became both a hit and a standard. Bobo also played on Santamaria's *Our Man in Havana* before starting his own band with Victor Panoja on congas. He recorded for Tico and Roulette in the mid '60s. Bobo participated in Cal Tjader's hit album, *Soul Sauce*, for Verve in the mid '60s. He issued his own albums in the mid '60s, combining soul and funk with Latin beats. The single "Spanish Grease" became an R&B hit. Bobo worked with Miles Davis, Stan Getz, Cannonball Adderley, Sonny Stitt, Herbie Mann, Terry Gibbs, and Herbie Hancock on various '60s sessions. He worked on the West Coast in the late '60s, and made weekly appearances on Bill Cosby's television show. Bobo recorded for Sussex, Blue Note, and Columbia through the '70s. All of his classic albums must be obtained from Latin music stores; currently, there are no listings for Bobo in most record catalogs. —*Ron Wynn*

Bobo's Beat / 1962-1963 / Roulette 52097

Uno, Dos, Tres / Jan. 1966 / Verve 8648

Juicy / Jan. 12, 1967-Feb. 2, 1967 / Verve 8685

★ **New Dimension, A** / Dec. 1968 / Verve 8772

○ **Spanish Grease** / Verve 8631

Bobo, a prolific percussionist, enjoyed some pop attention with this session. The album is a wonderful mix of R&B,

Latin, and jazz elements, has both open-ended, frenetic jams, and catchy, hook-filled songs. —*Ron Wynn*

GEORGE BOHANON (George Roland (Jr.) Bohanon)

b. Aug. 7, 1937, Detroit, MI
Trombone / Hard bop
The ultimate session star, trombonist George Bohannon has played on many dates, and has interacted nicely with bands or has fit into trombone or other sections. He's one of the finest hard bop trombonists around, but since the late '60s has served predominantly as a studio musician in big bands playing any and all types of music. Bohannon played with Chico Hamilton and Roy Brooks in the early '60s, and recorded as a leader. Since 1969, Bohannon's accompanied Sarah Vaughan, Gene Ammons, Sonny Rollins, Lionel Hampton, Benny Carter, and Bobby "Blue" Bland, among many others. He has no sessions available as a leader, but he can be heard on hundreds of dates. —*Ron Wynn*

★ **Bold Bohanon** / **i.** 1963 / Jazz Workshop 214

JOE BONNER (Joseph Leonard Bonner)

b. 1948
Piano / Modern creative
One of the many contemporary hard bop, bebop, or free stylists influenced by McCoy Tyner, pianist Joe Bonner's strong playing has been featured on several sessions since the early '70s. Bonner studied music at Virginia State College, and played in Roy Haynes Hip Ensemble in the early '70s. He also worked with Freddie Hubbard, Pharoah Sanders, and Billy Harper in the '70s, and toured Europe with Harper in 1978 and 1979. Bonner lived in Copenhagen in the late '70s, but returned to America in 1980. He recorded as a soloist, duo, combo, and trio leader in the '70s and '80s, working with Johnny Dyani and Billy Higgins, and with Dyani. Bonner has done sessions for Muse, Steeplechase, and Teresa. He has a couple of dates available on CD. —*Ron Wynn*

○ **Angel Eyes** / Oct. 1974 / Muse 5114
Pianist Joe Bonner's second album for Muse could almost be called schizophrenic because of its diversity of musical settings. "Angel Eyes" and "I Do" are solo piano pieces that show the influence of McCoy Tyner (most evident on the latter selection). "Love Dance" is a trio piece with bassist Juni Booth and drummer Jimmy Hopps that ends somewhat abruptly. "Interlude" is another Bonner solo, but this time he is heard on bamboo flute: he is adequate, but this is hardly necessary to have on the recording. The two remaining pieces, "Variations" and "Celebration," are what make the album successful. Here, Bonner and the rhythm section are joined by tenor saxophonist Billy Harper and violinist Leroy Jenkins. Vocalist Linda Sharrock is aided on the latter selection and melts into the proceedings with accomplished skill. The combination of voices, violin, and tenor is most effective, and I found Bonner's writing for the larger group of greater interest than his solo or trio pieces. —*Carl Brauer,* Cadence

★ **Lifesaver, The** / Nov. 1974 / Muse 5065
Pianist Joe Bonner's primary influence was McCoy Tyner, as he gladly acknowledges. Traces of Bill Evans also appear, particularly on "Native Son," where both the symmetrical, whimsically innocent line and some of the improvisation recall Evans's delicacy, if not his inventiveness. One can also hear Charles Mingus, the pianist, in here, and even some Debussy and Moussorgsky. —*Alan Heineman,* Down Beat

○ **Impressions of Copenhagen** / 1981 / Evidence 22024
Pianist Joe (then known as Joseph) Bonner turns in an intriguing variation on the shopworn concept of jazz artist recording with strings. He conceived a set mixing piano, brass, chimes, woodwinds, and a string quartet, generating an array of enticing backgrounds, frameworks, and delightful sounds around and behind his own lush, sentimental solos. The results are a gentle, enchanting '81 session that Evidence has reissued with an extra track on a '92 CD. "Lush

Life" is a fine bonus. The full date spotlights Bonner's tremendous piano and chimes and great remastering that bring the blend of strings, brass, and keyboards to the center, augmented by the bass/drum interplay of Paul Warburton and J. Thomas Tilton (who also produced) and the trumpet and trombone playing of Eddie Shu and Gary Olson. —*Ron Wynn*

Devotion / Feb. 20, 1983 / Steeple Chase 1182

Suite for Chocolate / **i.** Aug. 1986 / Steeple Chase 31239

New Beginnings / **i.** 1988 / Theresa 125

BERYL BOOKER

b. Jun. 7, 1922, Philadelphia, PA, **d.** Sep. 30, 1978, Berkeley, CA
Piano, bandleader / Postbop, cool
A fine player who deserves wider recognition and exposure, Beryl Booker displayed a steadily swinging, engaging style during her years as a session musician and bandleader. She played in Philadelphia clubs during the early '40s, and joined Slam Stewart after proving her mettle in a jam session. Booker stayed with Stewart for several years, though she also accompanied Dinah Washington and led a trio that was celebrated as an all-women's group. Booker led several trios in the early '50s, and played with various combos in the mid and late '50s, while accompanying Washington on a European tour in 1959. She also recorded with Billie Holiday in the '50s. Opportunities were never plentiful for women musicians, and unfortunately, Booker's musical career was no exception. She recorded for EmArcy, Trip, Discovery, Cadence, and Victor in the '40s and '50s. Much of her material was issued after her 1978 death. Currently, Booker doesn't have any sessions available on CD as a leader, but she is featured on the Stash two-disc anthology called *Forty Years of Women in Jazz.* —*Ron Wynn and Michael G. Nastos*

★ **Girl Met a Piano** / Jan. 1952 / EmArcy 26007

Beryl Booker Trio / Oct. 14, 1953 / Discovery 3021

Beryl Booker / 1954 / Cadence

○ **Beryl Booker with Don Byas** / 1954 / Discovery 3022

WALTER BOOKER

b. 1933
Bass / Hard bop
Not a flashy player, Walter Booker is a reliable bassist and an underrated stylist. His big tone and ability to play well in the bass's highest register reflect his knowledge of vintage and contemporary approaches. He's also an above-average bowed soloist. Booker played clarinet and alto sax in college with a concert band. He began on bass while in the service. After his discharge, Booker worked with Andrew White in Washington, playing in the JFK quintet during the early '60s. He later worked with Donald Byrd, Sonny Rollins and Ray Bryant, Art Farmer, Milt Jackson, and Chick Corea in the '60s before joining Cannonball Adderley. Booker was in Adderley's band, and toured and recorded regularly with the group from the late '60s until Adderley's death in 1975. During the mid '70s and through the '80s, Booker has played and recorded with Betty Carter, Nick Brignola, Billy Higgins, Richie Cole, Phil Woods, John Hicks, Pharoah Sanders, Nat Adderley, Arnett Cobb, and Clifford Jordan. He doesn't have any sessions available as a leader, but can be heard on many CDs by Adderley, Sanders, Jordan, and many others. —*Ron Wynn*

EARL BOSTIC

b. Apr. 25, 1913, Tulsa, OK, **d.** Oct. 28, 1965, Rochester, NY
Alto saxophone / Blues & jazz, soul-jazz
Earl Bostic's roots and foundation were steeped in jazz and swing, but he became a most prolific R&B bandleader. His searing, sometimes bluesy, sometimes soft and moving alto sax style influenced many players, including John Coltrane. His many King releases, which featured limited soloing and basic melodic and rhythmic movements, might have fooled

novices into thinking Bostic possessed minimal skills, but Art Blakey once said: "Nobody knew more about the saxophone than Bostic, I mean technically, and that includes Bird." Bostic worked in several Midwest bands during the early '30s, then studied at Xavier University. He left school to tour with various groups, among them a band co-led by Charlie Creath and Fate Marable. He moved to New York in the late '30s, where he was a soloist in the bands of Don Redman, Edgar Hayes, and Lionel Hampton. Bostic also led his own combos, whose members included Jimmy Cobb, Al Casey, Blue Mitchell, Stanley Turrentine, Benny Golson, and Coltrane. Bostic toured extensively through the '50s, while cutting numerous sessions for King. His recording of "Flamingo" in 1951 was a huge hit, as were the songs "Sleep," "You Go to My Head," "Cherokee," and "Temptation." Bostic recorded for Allegro, Gotham, and King from the late '40s to the mid '60s. He made more than 400 selections for King; the label would use stereo remakes of songs with different personnel, then would use the same album numbers. After a heart attack, Bostic became a part-time player. His mid '60s albums were more soul-jazz than R&B. Several of his King LPs are available on CD. —*Ron Wynn and Michael Erlewine*

Best of Earl Bostic, The / i. 1956 / Deluxe 500
A nice cross-section of this fiery alto saxist's '50s output, including his hits "Sleep" and "Flamingo." —*Bill Dahl*

Alto-Tude / i. 1957 / King 515
Another in the series of releases by alto saxophonist Earl Bostic issued by King in the late '50s. Though some, this one included, have dubious sound quality, Bostic's alto solos are uniformly excellent, regardless of material. —*Ron Wynn*

★ **Dance Time** / i. 1957 / King 525
These are mostly uptempo instrumental R&B, pop, and dance/novelty tunes delivered with style and flair by the great Earl Bostic. He was among the finest honking saxophonists, and King kept pumping out collections of his singles throughout the '50s. —*Ron Wynn*

Let's Dance with Earl Bostic / i. 1957 / Deluxe 529

Bostic for You / i. 1957 / King 503
Bostic's blistering renditions of old dance numbers transcend R&B and jazz barriers. —*Bill Dahl*

Alto Magic in Hi-Fi / i. 1958 / King 597

Bostic Rocks / i. 1958 / King 571
More dance/novelty, honking R&B, and occasional blues numbers from alto saxophonist Earl Bostic, nearing the end of an incredible run with King. Bostic's more than 400 singles were collected, packaged, released, and rereleased by the label. These are among his most pop and upbeat R&B numbers. —*Ron Wynn*

Showcase of Swinging Dance Hits / i. 1958 / King 583
Perhaps his best rocking and uptempo instrumental pop and R&B material. This album was aimed at the jukebox market, and weighted toward the hottest, most furiously played cuts in the Bostic repertoire. Bostic was as technically accomplished as any alto saxophonist in his era, but he wasn't able to show that while on King. This album was one of the few times that he was able to really show his skills on uptempo material. —*Ron Wynn*

Ain't Misbehavin' / i. 1959 / King
Despite the title, this isn't classic blues or that much Fats Waller, but more vintage instrumental pop, novelty material, R&B cuts, and honking items. Bostic sounds as impassioned and gritty as usual, but the selections run dry on side two. —*Ron Wynn*

Sweet Tunes of the Sentimental Forties / i. 1959 / King 640
Recycled material from other albums were funneled onto this anthology/greatest hits date. It showcases the sentimental side of Bostic, with his biting alto refocused onto romantic, light, and enticing fare. He could play that just as effectively, and proves it throughout this date. —*Ron Wynn*

Workshop / i. 1959 / King 613

Earl Bostic has a more varied amount of material on this late '50s King collection. He covers uptempo R&B and blues, dance/novelty instrumentals, and light jazzy pop on this collection. As always, every solo is played with conviction and passion, no matter how trite the arrangement or musical setting. —*Ron Wynn*

Earl Bostic Plays Old Standards / i. 195? / King 95
Some stirring renditions, furious solos, and alternately appealing, soothing alto statements by Earl Bostic. He's among the least recognized, yet important, members of the R&B sax class. His sidemen included Benny Golson, Mickey Baker, and John Coltrane. This collection is one of numerous albums King issued on Bostic during the '50s, and was briefly available on reissue in the Gusto series of the '70s. —*Ron Wynn*

25 Years of Rhythm and Blues Hits / i. 1960 / King 725
One among a handful of really great Earl Bostic albums on King. This isn't merely a bunch of singles slapped together, but Bostic doing the vintage R&B tunes that he loved. He also gets ample space within the commercial restrictions to stretch out and really play rather than just quote the melody and add a few licks around it. —*Ron Wynn*

Earl Bostic Plays Bossa Nova / i. 1963
An intriguing, though flawed, release. Earl Bostic could play almost anything on alto sax, but Afro-Latin music in general, and bossa nova in particular, weren't among his strong points. He does a decent job under the circumstances, but Coleman Hawkins and Stan Getz made far better bossa nova recordings. —*Ron Wynn*

Jazz As I Feel It / Aug. 13, 1963-Aug. 14, 1963 / King 846

New Sound / i. 1964 / King 900
Nice, sometimes exceptional playing by Earl Bostic. Besides the anticipated honking R&B and bluesy ballads, there are a few songs where Bostic tries some tricks with his tone and soars into the upper register. These moments are a reminder that he was a multidimensional player seldom allowed in his career (at least on record) to fully present his talents. —*Ron Wynn*

★ **Harlem Nocturne** / i. 1969 / King 1048
The title track alone makes the rest of the album worth hearing. Bostic plays "Harlem Nocturne" in a dynamic, almost mystical way, retaining the song's blues feeling, but also giving it a spirituality and air that many other musicians never injected. —*Ron Wynn*

Dance Music from the Bostic Workshop / i. 1988 / King
Includes an astonishing display of sax technique over a torrid R&B beat on the breathtaking "Up There in Orbit." —*Bill Dahl*

Plays (16 Sweet Tunes of the Fantastic 50's) / Starday 3022
One of the most underrated and influential honking R&B saxophonists ever, Earl Bostic was a fine blues, ballad, and R&B player. He showed his facility with sentimental songs, love tunes, and light pop on this album which was issued back in the '50s by King. It was reissued by Gusto briefly in the '70s. —*Ron Wynn*

LESTER BOWIE

b. Oct. 11, 1941, Frederick, MD
Trumpet, flugelhorn, composer / Modern creative
While he's well-known as a member of the Art Ensemble of Chicago, Lester Bowie has amassed almost as many credentials for his work as a leader. His remarkable bag of trumpet and flugelhorn tricks includes half-valve effects, growls, slurs, smears, bent notes, and a wide vibrato that punctuates one of the most humorous, yet striking, solo styles among modern brass players. His eclecticism has led Bowie to issue harsh denunciations of contemporary artists that he revere only the bebop and hard bop jazz tradition. He's led groups such as Brass Fantasy and The New York Organ Ensemble through wild versions of Michael Jackson and James Brown compositions. He's also ventured to the furthest reaches during extended free dialogs, blowing frenetic upper-register solos.

Growing up in St. Louis, Bowie played in many blues and R&B bands, including Albert King's and Little Milton's. He moved to Chicago in 1965 to become music director for R&B/soul singer Fontella Bass, who was his wife at the time. Bowie met Joseph Jarman, Roscoe Mitchell, Malachi Favors, and Don Moye through the Association for the Advancement of Creative Musicians (AACM), which, at the time, was just getting organized. Eventually, Bowie became its second president (Muhal Richard Abrams was the first). The album *Numbers 1 & 2* was issued as a Lester Bowie LP on Nessa in 1967, but was actually the first Art Ensemble release (at the time, the group hadn't begun to use that name formally). It was in Paris during 1969 that Bowie, Jarman, Mitchell, and Favors officially formed the Art Ensemble of Chicago. Moye joined the group the next year.

While the Art Ensemble has been a steady proposition since '69, Bowie has never rested on his laurels. He worked in the early '70s with the 50-piece Baden Baden Free Jazz Orchestra along with Jarman and Roscoe Mitchell. He co-led the group From the Root to the Source, which blended jazz, rock, soul, and gospel, and included both Bass and Martha Peaston in the '70s. He later founded, and still heads, both Brass Fantasy and the New York Organ Ensemble. Bowie recorded albums as a leader in the '70s for Muse, Black Saint, and IAI. He played in Jack DeJohnette's New Directions band in the late '70s, and did guest spots on other albums. During the '80s, he recorded for ECM, Muse, and Venture, and for DIW. He's recorded with the New York Organ Ensemble for DIW in the '90s. There's a good supply of Bowie solo albums available on CD. —*Ron Wynn*

Duet / IAI
A most unusual collaboration, for trumpet-drums duets (Bowie and Wilson respectively) are far from commonplace. However, Bowie's wide range of expressiveness (there are times when he sounds like he is imitating the drums) makes this a success, along with Phillip Wilson's large ears. —*Scott Yanow,* Coda

○ **Numbers 1 & 2** / Aug. 11, 1967+Aug. 25, 1967 / Nessa 1

Fast Last / Sep. 10, 1974 / Muse 5055
Tremendous mid '70s album that indicates the array of talent rising to the surface. It's neither outside nor inside, with songs that threaten to explode and others that are more funky than experimental. Besides Bowie, guests include Julius Hemphill in torrid form, Cecil McBee on bass, and Phillip Wilson on drums. It has not yet been issued on CD. —*Ron Wynn*

Rope-A-Dope / Jun. 17, 1975 / Muse 5081
Funny sometimes, chaotic at other times, Bowie worked on this session with Art Ensemble mates bassist Malachi Favors and drummer Don Moye. Compositions are mostly strong, but the playing is uniformly excellent. This has not been reissued on CD. —*Ron Wynn*

Duet / i. Jan. 1978 / IAI 123854
The air is charged with electricity and purpose when drummer Phillip Wilson and trumpeter Lester Bowie go at it. Bowie, one of the most dramatic and dynamic soloists on his instrument since Henry "Red" Allen, makes a strong pair with his old high school pal and AACM associate. Bowie signals most of the turns of direction, Wilson nudging and galloping and pawing like a champion stallion. Bowie not only runs the gamut of sounds to be had from the trumpet, from exquisite clarion calls to Dizzyish kazoo notes so squeezed it sounds like he's coming and going on the Doppler effect, but he also creates little wells of lyrical referents—a bright staccato high-life, "Three Blind Mice" variants, a four-bar descending blues figure built from Wilson's snare brushing pianissimo into a call-and-response argument, two of Bowie's "voices" screaming epithets over Wilson's cymbal and tom bashes—that glue all the pieces together. Wilson's role here is more of collaborator than independent contractor; together they construct a set of sweeping majesty and excitement aplenty. —*Fred Bouchard,* Down Beat

★ **5th Power, The** / Apr. 12+17, 1978 / Black Saint 0020

1978 quintet with Arthur Blythe (as) and Amina Myers (p). Creative jazz and a progressive gospel segment. Bowie at his eclectic best. Essential. —*Michael G. Nastos*

Great Pretender, The / Jun. 1981 / ECM 829369
On *The Great Pretender*, Lester Bowie turns a potential mob of stylistic approaches—including '50s doo-wop, TV themes, free-form electric music, and Latin-infused jazz—into a palatable whole. Though there are elements of satire and nostalgia inherent in both the selection and presentation of much of the program, this is not a novelty item. Pure, rambunctious, torch-carrying Bowie is to be found everywhere, yes, even on its "Howdy Doody Time." The importance of Bowie's amalgamated style does not lie in its expert culling of sources, but in its ability to harness the no-wave mania of "Doom?" as effortlessly as it created the chiaroscuro of "Rose Drops." —*Bill Shoemaker,* Down Beat

All the Magic! / Jun. 1982 / ECM 810625
Bowie's pop/soul band sometimes smokes, other times falters, but generally makes entertaining music. Bowie's trumpet crackles and roars when he gets space, and his array of devices and effects are often impressive. Ari Brown on soprano and tenor sax and Art Matthews on piano are fine, as are bassist Fred Wilson and drummer Phillip Wilson. Vocalist David Peaston and Fontella Bass made more vivid, exciting records on their own, cutting soul tracks. Here, they fit into the concept, but don't illuminate or expand it. —*Ron Wynn*

I Only Have Eyes for You / Feb. 1985 / ECM 825902

Avant Pop / Mar. 1986 / ECM 829563
Pop? Yes. Avant? No. Perhaps this was the logical progression for Lester Bowie, who, in times past, did his stint with various R&B aggregations. . . . And maybe ECM wanted to document his sincere desire to get lightly down in a further attempt to rekindle the affair they had going with a "poppier" audience via ex-ECMer Pat Metheny. . . . The piece of real interest for the discriminating listener is the almost avant opener, which features some lovely syncopated phrasing in the supporting riffs along with some creative textural manipulations of the horns that give the sound an electronic ambience. —*Milo Fine,* Cadence

☆ **Twilight Dreams** / Apr. 1987 / Venture 90650
This Lester Bowie effort is not particularly stimulating listening. . . . "Personality" continues a joke that worked great with "Hello, Dolly!" and the "Great Pretender," but got progressively staler with subsequent Bowie recordings. "Duke's Fantasy" has a good duet between Bowie and Phillip Wilson (drums). —*Tim Smith,* Cadence

○ **Works** / 1989 / PolyGram 837274
1980-1985 anthology with the Art Ensemble of Chicago, Brass Fantasy, Stanton Davis, Rasul Siddik, Vincent Chancey, Steve Turre, Frank Lacy, Phillip Wilson, and Bob Stewart. —AMG

CURTIS BOYD

Drums / Hard bop
A good drummer in either a soul-jazz, light bebop, or hard bop mode, Curtis Boyd hasn't made any sessions as a leader. He's best known for his playing in the Billy Taylor trio of the mid '80s. —*Ron Wynn*

RONNIE BOYKINS

b. 1935, d. 1980
Bass / Modern creative
A veteran bassist who was a major contributor to the Sun Ra Arkestra, Ronnie Boykins's pronounced sound and heady accompaniment were featured on many Ra sessions of the '50s and '60s. His flexibility enabled Boykins to alternate smoothly between free, hard bop, and bebop dates, and to back vocalists such as Sarah Vaughan and Joe Lee Wilson. Boykins studied in Chicago with the famous instructor Walter Dyett and with Ernie Shepard. He began playing regularly with Ra in 1958, and was in the Arkestra full time until 1966, then worked with it periodically for the rest of his

career. Boykins also played with Bill Barron, Elmo Hope, and Archie Shepp, and the New York Contemporary Five in the early and mid '60s. He formed the Free Jazz Society in the late '60s, and recorded with Rahsaan Roland Kirk in 1967 and Charles Tyler, Wilson, and Steve Lacy in the '70s, while he also played with Vaughan and Mary Lou Williams. He can be heard on CD reissues by Ra, Kirk, Tyler, and others. —*Ron Wynn*

CHARLES BRACKEEN

b. 1940, White's Chapel (renamed Eufaula), OK
Tenor saxophone, trumpet / Modern creative
Though an adventurous, powerful tenor saxophonist, Charles Brackeen has recorded for small independents and has not attained much exposure, even within the jazz community. He was married, for a time, to pianist Joanne Brackeen, who's gone on to attain far more recognition and status as a leader and composer than Charles has received. Brackeen's '70s and '80s recordings for Strata-East and Silkheart are unrestrained, alternately exciting and chaotic vehicles. The Silkheart sessions are available on CD. —*Ron Wynn*

★ **Rhythm X** / 1973 / Strata East

Attainment / 1987 / Silkheart 110
Slightly larger and smaller instrumentation, like on *Rhythm X.* Equally well done. —*Michael G. Nastos*

Banner / 1987 / Silkheart 105

Worshippers Come Nigh / i. 1987 / Silkheart 111
Rousing, declarative session from a grossly underrecorded tenor and soprano saxophonist. Charles Brackeen was persuaded to return to the recording scene in 1986 by Silkheart label's managing director, and this is one of three great albums he made in '86 and '87. The pithy, crisp cornet solos supplied by Olu Dara are almost as striking as Brackeen's sax lines, and there aren't better bassists and drummers in this style than Fred Hopkins and Andrew Cyrille. —*Ron Wynn*

JOANNE BRACKEEN (JoAnne [née Grogan] Brackeen)

b. Jul. 26, 1938, Ventura, CA
Piano / Hard bop
An arresting rhythmic stylist who's been influenced by McCoy Tyner and Chick Corea, Joanne Brackeen's solos and original compositions feature stimulating, complex harmonies, expert pacing, and thematic variety. Essentially, Brackeen taught herself jazz piano. She attended the Los Angeles Conservatory, listened to recordings by Frankie Carle, and directly imitated his solos. Brackeen worked with Teddy Edwards, Harold Land, Dexter Gordon, and Charles Lloyd in Los Angeles during the late '50s. She married Charles Brackeen in the early '60s, and they moved to New York in 1965. Brackeen worked with Art Blakey's Jazz Messengers in the late '60s and early '70s, and with Joe Henderson in the mid '70s. Brackeen was Stan Getz's pianist in the late '70s, winning the chance to record as a leader. She's led various groups since then, mostly trios. Brackeen has done sessions for Choice, Antilles, Concord, and Ken Music. She's worked with Eddie Gomez, Jack DeJohnette, Cecil McBee, Al Foster, Terence Blanchard, and Branford Marsalis, and has been part of Concord's Maybeck Recital Hall solo series. Brackeen has several dates available on CD. —*Ron Wynn and Michael G. Nastos*

Snooze / Mar. 1975 / Choice 1009
Joanne Brackeen's attack is similar to many post-Coltrane (John, not Alice) pianists. She is a piano attacker and displays a texture that is close to Chick Corea's work of a few years back, and close to McCoy Tyner's, but there are definite Bud Powell roots and influences in both her playing and compositions. There are 88 keys and she seems determined to get to all of them, using intense hammering to create rich, deep runs of color on a broad horizontal piano plane. Her execution is determined and seemingly with full authority, using her left hand to produce heavy tonal coloring. Always

present are the rich harmonies that give depth and fullness of body to her technique; her compositions are all full and satisfying in depth, especially "C-SRI" and "Snooze." Bassist Cecil McBee takes more than a supporting role, contributing many fine solos, but the choice here is Joanne Brackeen, who was in full command. This is the first album of her own. —*Carol Ober, Cadence*

★ **Tring-A-Ling** / Mar. 20, 1977 / Choice 1016
Brilliant pianist/composer with powerful modern modal music (all originals). With Michael Brecker on sax and two bassists. —*Michael G. Nastos*

Mythical Magic / Sep. 25-26, 1978 / MPS 0068.211

Aft / i. Sep. 1979 / Timeless 302
Describing this grouping as a "piano trio" misses the point, for Joanne Brackeen's ensemble is better understood as a kind of string trio in which one of the instruments happens to be a piano. The result: seemingly leaderless music done as something "in common." What Brackeen meant by "out there" becomes evident on a track like the nimble, modal "Charlotte's Dream." Clint Houston's bass rustles with brittle, hornlike figures, Brackeen comps with terse, ringy chords, and guitarist Ryo Kawasaki adds fluent, plucky guitar lines—exciting three-way cross fire. Throughout, Brackeen alternates lush, full voicings with inspired tingles. Her solos, jammed with asymmetrical ideas, seem to constantly leap ahead of themselves, alternately expanding and compressing time. —*Jon Balleras, Down Beat*

Ancient Dynasty / 1980 / Columbia 36593
Initially, *Ancient Dynasty* sounds overly structured and tedious. Upon closer inspection, however, I found the group's interaction to be at an extraordinarily high level. "Beagle's Boogie" is a marvelous exercise in thrashing, dissonant funk, and tenor saxophonist Joe Henderson executes his ideas with a true veteran's sense of how space and dynamics should work *for* a soloist and not *against* him. Yet, the taunting give-and-take accompaniment of pianist Joanne Brackeen combines with the throbbing, exuberant percussion work of drummer Jack DeJohnette, who is as responsible for the success of this LP as Henderson. Eddie Gomez's bass is a bit too far back in the mix, but it is refreshing to hear Gomez venturing into the deeper, darker, unknown regions of his instrument. —*Arthur Moorehead, Down Beat*

Special Identity / Dec. 8+9, 1981 / Antilles 848813

○ **Havin' Fun** / Jun. 1985 / Concord Jazz 4280
Good trio session by the underrated pianist Joanne Brackeen. She's extended and complemented by bassist Cecil McBee and drummer Al Foster, and shows rhythmic verve and harmonic strength, plus good solo technique throughout the album. This has been reissued on CD. —*Ron Wynn*

Fi-Fi Goes to Heaven / 1986 / Concord Jazz 4316
The CD version features this energized, capable pianist at her best, with some sharp assistance from Branford Marsalis (ts) and Terence Blanchard (tpt). —*Ron Wynn*

Live at Maybeck Recital Hall / i. Jun. 1989 / Concord Jazz 4409

○ **Where Legends Dwell** / Sep. 3+4, 1991 / Ken Music 021
Extraordinary trio with Eddie Gomez on bass and Jack DeJohnette on drums, this is her best work of the past decade. Twelve tracks are all originals. Over 70 minutes of incredibly ingenious jazz is included. This is easy to dig into. —*Michael G. Nastos*

○ **Dr. Chu Chow** / Pathfinder 8851

BOBBY BRADFORD (Bobby Lee Bradford)

b. Jul. 19, 1934, Cleveland, OH
Cornet, trumpet, composer / Early free, modern creative
A fine trumpeter and cornetist best known for his lengthy, musically profitable relationship with composer/clarinetist John Carter, Bobby Bradford has been a stalwart soloist since the '50s. A compelling and lyrical stylist, Bradford has worked in free and bebop/hard bop contexts, has led his

own band, and has played with large groups while teaching at both the elementary school and college levels. Bradford is also the first trumpeter whose style was influenced by Ornette Coleman. He began on cornet in the late '40s, and worked with Leo Wright, Buster Smith, and John Hardee in the early '50s. Bradford moved to Los Angeles from the South in 1953, playing with Eric Dolphy and Coleman before joining the air force, where he worked with military bands. Bradford rejoined Coleman in the early '60s, then later attended Houston-Tillotson College. After his graduation, Bradford returned to Los Angeles in 1964. He co-formed the New Art Jazz Ensemble with Carter. Bradford taught at an elementary school from the mid-'60s until 1971, and briefly rejoined Coleman's group in New York. During the mid '70s, Bradford was an instructor at Pasadena City College and Pomona College. He played with Arthur Blythe, James Newton, Carter, and others in the Little Big Horn Workshop in the late '70s. During the '80s, Bradford played with David Murray, with John Steven's Freebop, and with Charlie Haden's Liberation Music Orchestra, and led his own band, the Mo'tet. His son, Dennis Bradford, cofounded the Jeff Lorber Fusion in 1979. Bradford has recorded for Emanem, Soul Note, and Arista/Freedom, as well as with Carter on Flying Dutchman, Revelation, and Black Saint. Bradford has sessions available on CD both as a leader and with Carter. —*Ron Wynn*

★ **With John Stevens and the Spontaneous Music Ensemble, Vol.** 1 / **i.** Dec. 1971 / Nessa 17

This set was recorded in England in 1971; the jazz avant-garde there was still relatively new at the time, and John Stevens's series of Spontaneous Music Ensembles are among its most notable exponents. It was their good fortune to meet the American Bobby Bradford, who, along with Don Cherry, had invented and defined the trumpet's role in the evolving new music while with Ornette Coleman's early groups. It was Bradford's good fortune to meet five skilled players so enthusiastically moved by the philosophical tenets of Coleman's music, and it is certainly our good fortune to have one of the rare recorded appearances of this master trumpeter. In "Room 408," superb ensemble improvising emerges continually from the bass and horns regrouping around Bradford; "His Majesty Louis" even offers an unconscious space-age polyphony, right down to a trombone smear.... Bradford's greatest originality was certainly his rhythmic sense, combining the poise of Kenny Dorham and the wide-open-spaces feeling of Buddy Tate and other Texas tenors. The spacing of his phrasing and his marvelous gobbling up of the beat were his most immediate qualities; more subtle was his own personal tempo, which ebbed and flowed, somehow maintaining a relationship with the group's tempo. —*John Litweiler*, Down Beat

○ **One Night Stand** / Nov. 1986 / Soul Note 1168

On *One Night Stand*, the underrated but innovative trumpeter Bobby Bradford, playing with a superior rhythm section based in Florida (that he had only met the previous day), performs four free pieces and three others based on standard chord changes. For the former, the Ornette Coleman-like melodies were kept in mind and are often referred to in the improvisations, while the more bop-oriented songs do not ignore the wider variety of choices offered in the free jazz of the '60s. Bradford, best known for his stint with Coleman and a long-term musical partnership with John Carter, actually has a mellow tone that makes his music very accessible, even during the freer moments. A melodic player with a healthy sense of humor who has become more expressive through the years, Bobby Bradford really gets a chance to stretch out on this fine session. Although pianist Frank Sullivan is essentially a bop player, he does a good job of keeping up during the more adventurous performances. Bassist Scott Walton (who has learned from the innovations of Charlie Haden) and drummer Billy Bowker are excellent in support. "Ashes" (a calypso version of "I Got Rhythm") and the mysterious "Woman" are the

high points of this highly recommended disc. —*Scott Yanow*, Cadence

○ **Comin' On** / **i.** Feb. 1990 / Hat Art 6016
An uneven 1988 date that still contains some glorious moments, mostly when Bradford and longtime cohort clarinetist John Carter play together. Bradford's solos aren't as universally sharp or focused as usual, but he doesn't totally falter. Drummer Andrew Cyrille and bassist Richard Davis dominate in the rhythm section. —*Ron Wynn*

WILL BRADLEY (Will [Wilbur Schwichtenberg] Bradley)

b. Jul. 12, 1912, Newton, NJ, **d.** Jul. 1989
Trombone, composer / Swing
An accomplished trombonist who was much better at ballads and slow tunes than at uptempo workouts, Will Bradley was a busy session musician in the '20s, '30s, and '40s. His avid interest in classical music was reflected by his full, clear tone and his reluctance to incorporate such things as "tailgating" into his solos. Bradley met Ray McKinley while working in Milt Shaw's Detroiters in the late '20s. He worked with Red Nichols on the CBS staff from 1931 to 1940, then played with Ray Noble in 1935 and 1936 before returning to more broadcasts. Bradley led a band with Ray McKinley that cashed in on sweetened, reworked versions of boogie-woogie hits. He recorded with Peanuts Hucko and Freddy Slack. Songs such as "Strange Cargo" and "Beat Me Daddy Eight to the Bar" were hits, though others, like "Bounce Me, Brother, With a Solid Four" and "Fry Me, Cookie, With a Can of Lard," annoyed the urbane Bradley. His band made some wartime recordings, then Bradley opted for full-time radio and television work. He played on Benny Goodman's *B. G. in Hi-Fi* in 1955. Reissues of Bradley's sessions, both as a leader and with McKinley, are available on Aircheck and Columbia CDs. —*Ron Wynn*

★ **Best of Big Bands** / Columbia 46151
With Ray McKinley. Part of a recent series on big bands. Lightweight material. —*Ron Wynn*

○ **Celery Stalks at Midnight** / Columbia 33286

RUBY BRAFF (Reuben Braff)

b. Mar. 16, 1927, Boston, MA
Cornet / New Orleans traditional, swing
One of jazz's finer cornet players, Ruby Braff has a raspy vibrato and a glorious, striking sound, which he's also displayed on trumpet and flugelhorn, though he's played mostly cornet since 1967. He's a master at playing in the lower register, where he gets a lush, convincing tone, though his tone remains strong in other registers, too. He uses flurries of notes to embellish and to punctuate melodies, and is a superb ballad stylist and interpreter of standards. Braff worked in the Boston area during the '40s, recorded in 1949 with Edmond Hall, and played at Storyville with Pee Wee Russell in the early '50s. He moved to New York in 1953, and displayed a versatility that allowed him to excel in many styles, notably traditional New Orleans and Dixieland. His two principle influences were Louis Armstrong and Lester Young. But Braff's approach was, and is, rooted firmly in swing. His mid-'50s recordings with Vic Dickenson won attention; his reputation was solidified by sessions with Buck Clayton, Urbie Green, Mel Powell, Bud Freeman, and Benny Goodman, and by his own recordings as well. After acting and playing in Rogers and Hammerstein's *Pipe Dreams* in 1955 and 1956, and playing on Benny Goodman's LP, *B.G. in Hi-Fi*, Braff survived some lean periods. He made good albums for Stereocraft, United Artists, Epic, Warner Bros., and RCA, but found limited opportunities for regular work. Braff resurfaced in the '60s, thanks to his affiliation with George Wein's Newport All Stars, and to Braff's switch to playing the cornet. He began touring across the country and overseas, recording with Red Norvo, Ellis Larkins, Milt Hinton, and others. Things really changed in 1973, when Braff formed a quartet with coleader guitarist George Barnes. The group was critically acclaimed, and Barnes released several excellent repertory albums, cutting Fats Waller, Fred Astaire,

Gershwin, and Rodgers and Hart tributes. He worked with Dick Hyman, Ed Bickert, and Scott Hamilton. The Braff/Barnes venture finally collapsed under the weight of personality differences, but not before they'd made an enormous contribution to swing-influenced combo jazz. Braff remains active currently, recording and playing festivals and tours. He has many sessions available on CD, on various labels. —*Ron Wynn and Dan Morgenstern*

Hustlin' and Bustlin' / Jul. 1951+May 1954 / Black Lion 760908
Nice '54 date putting Braff in the company of a large group filled with traditional and mainstream jazz greats like clarinetist Edmond Hall, trombonist Vic Dickenson, and bassist Milt Hinton. The songs are vintage, the solos are exuberant, and the ensemble's playing and interaction reflects the musicians' love for this classic sound. —*Ron Wynn*

○ **Inventions in Jazz (Volume 2)** / i. 1955 / Vanguard 8020

○ **Adoration of the Melody** / Mar. 17-18, 1955 / Bethlehem 6043
Back in the mid '50s when *Adoration of the Melody* was made, Ruby Braff had a unique sound of great distinction and character. It was thick and fat, and Braff could fine-tune its vibrato with a master's touch. He could taper his notes, hold them on perfect pitch, then drift into a warm, broad vibrato that swung with as much grace and relaxation as his best phrases. The album's best blends are on "Lucky Guy," "Easy Living," "I'll Be Around," "It's Easy," and above all "When You're Smilin'," which contains an exquisite ensemble orchestration of Lester Young's classic "triplet" solo of 1937. Through it all, Braff indulged only the songs, never himself. Four quartet sides, evidently from another session, fill out the LP, but add nothing to the trumpet-reed concept. The sound is muddy as well. —*John McDonough*, Down Beat

★ **Two by Two: Ruby and Ellis Play Rodgers And Hart** / Oct. 14, 1955 / Vanguard 8507

Ruby Braff Special, The / Oct. 17, 1955 / Vanguard 8504

○ **Two Part Inventions in Jazz—Vol. 1** / i. Nov. 2, 1955 / Vanguard 8019

○ **Two Part Inventions in Jazz—Vol. 2** / i. Nov. 2, 1955 / Vanguard 8020

○ **Ball at Bethlehem** / Dec. 31, 1955+Jan. 1, 1956 /

○ **Magic Horn of Ruby Braff, The** / May 28, 1956 / RCA 1332

○ **Ruby Braff Octet with Pee Wee Russell, The** / Jul. 5, 1957 / Verve 8241

○ **This Is My Lucky Day** / i. Aug. 19, 1957-Dec. 26, 1957 / Bluebird 6456
Pee Wee Russell (clarinet) got plenty of exposure on seven tracks of *This Is My Lucky Day* and to these ears he stole the show. Those sides by trumpeter Ruby Braff's octet (w/Benny Morton, trombone; Nat Pierce, piano; Steve Jordan, guitar; Buzzy Drootin, drums and—make no mistake—Walter Page on bass) originally appeared on *Hi Fi Salute to Bunny* or *Bread, Butter and Jam in Hi Fi.* . . . They were recorded March 26, April 5, and April 12, 1957. The Braff sextet sides (with Roy Eldridge, trumpet; Hank Jones, piano; Mundell Lowe, electric guitar; Leonard Gaskin, bass; Don Lamond, drums) were on *Easy Now* and recorded August 19, 1957. On the Berigan tributes, the four-horn front line gave the ensemble a sound almost too fat and generous, giving "It's Been So Long" an almost glib air. (The section works better reduced to a whisper, "Remember?") Braff's own plump sound radiated the joy of living and Beriganesque romanticism, evoking Berigan's balladry on "I Can't Get Started" (natch) and that of Duke Ellington. In another vein, his fleet filigrees behind Morton on "Marie" transcended the tune's banality. Morton's trombone was delightfully full-bodied and heavy, and Russell, as usual, added pungent contrast, with worried squiggles that rendered distinctions between old and new meaningless. . . . Dick Hafer's mooning tenor didn't quite fit in such fast company, but the relative oddity of tenor in this context worked in his favor. Jordan and Page effectively juxtaposed February 4 and April 4, which might

have reminded Page of old Kansas City days; there was some nice, gentle barrelhouse from Pierce. The Braff-Eldridge-Mundell Lowe band may be the most unlikely mainstream crew Norman Granz never assembled. This listener gives the nod to Eldridge's more tart and compact sound and zippier lines; his modernism made Braff sound old-fashioned (just as Braff makes Eldridge sound more current than your average '30s hero, even for the '50s). Anyway, the mix worked, electric guitar and all, "Broadway" in particular rarely sounding so youthful. Hank Jones did an Earl Hines, introducing "Song Is Ended." Trumpeter John Synder's liner notes, while having little direct bearing on these two projects, illuminated Braff's technical accomplishments while maintaining a rabid fan's enthusiasm. —*Kevin Whitehead*, Cadence

○ **Easy Now** / Aug. 11+19, 1958 / RCA 1966

★ **With the Newport All Stars** / Oct. 28, 1967 / Black Lion 760138
With Buddy Tate (ts), George Wein (p), Jack Lesberg (b), and Don Lamond (d). Both Tate and Braff are in top form on this one. —*Michael Erlewine*

○ **Ruby Braff-George Barnes Quartet, The** / 1973 / Chiaroscuro 121
This album by the Ruby Braff-George Barnes quartet is a thing of beauty. If it reminds me of anything, it is the Kansas City Six recording of Lester Young and Buck Clayton because of the floating, even-four-time feel and the diminutively arranged passages. Wayne Wright was a fine rhythm guitarist who knew just how to play behind Braff and Barnes. John Giufridda (later replaced by Mike Moore) provides a solid bass backing. The two soloists are in sterling form. Braff never sounded freer, happier, or more imaginative; he glides through the air with acrobatic ease. Barnes soars also; his sense of humor is a gas. Both were masters of the compact, precise statement. No solo lasts for more than two choruses in a row. The Braff-Barnes record is indispensable. —*Tom Piazza*, Down Beat

Plays Gershwin / Jul. 26, 1974 / Concord Jazz 4005

Salutes Rodgers & Hart / Oct. 1974 / Concord Jazz 6007
Superb small combo repertory fare, with Braff's terse cornet finding excellent company with guitarist Wayne Wright and George Barnes. Bassist Michael Moore more than makes up for the absence of a drummer. —*Ron Wynn*

To Fred Astaire with Love / 1975 / RCA 11008

With the Ed Bickert Trio / Jun. 14, 1979 / Sackville 3022

○ **Mr. Braff to You: The Ruby Braff Quintet** / Dec. 15, 1983 / Phontastic 7568
If you're familiar with the music of Ruby Braff, Scott Hamilton, and John Bunch, the music on this album holds no surprises. The musicians are all at ease with their instruments, with the swing style, and with these swing-era songs. The liner notes refer to this date as "a jam session," although it doesn't come across that way to me. It has the familiar jam session format of lots of solos and little arranging, but the players here don't cut loose. The closest they come is some muted excitement on "China Boy" at the start of the album. But that's not to say they don't play well or that they don't accomplish their obvious goal of playing relaxing, mellow jazz. Braff sets the mood for this record with his cozy cornet tone. Tenor saxist Scott Hamilton gets equal solo time and outplays the leader. He edges a little closer to Lester Young than he once had, with a lighter tone and gracefully flowing linear ideas that hint at "Pres"-ian ancestry. Pianist John Bunch is mainly an accompanist here, tying the solos together with his accomplished backing. —*Doug Long*, Cadence

Sailboat in the Moonlight, A / Feb. 1985 / Concord Jazz 4296

Me, Myself & I / i. Jun. 1988 / Concord Jazz 4381

Bravura Eloquence / Jun. 1988 / Concord Jazz 4423
Ruby Braff Trio. A wonderful set from a great cornetist. With Howard Alden (g) and Jack Lesberg (b). —*Michael Erlewine*

○ **Music from "South Pacific"** / **i.** Jun. 12, 1990-Jun. 13, 1990 / Concord Jazz 4445

○ **Ruby Braff & His New England Songhounds—Vol. 1** / Oct. 25, 1991 / Concord Jazz 4478

Very Sinatra / CBS 53749
The theme of this album is both logical and laudatory, for the idea is to give cornetist Ruby Braff, a highly lyrical improviser, an opportunity to document his interpretations of some favorite Frank Sinatra-associated material plus one original, "Perfectly Frank." The program consists mostly of slow to medium tempos with Braff at his virtuosic best. Pianist Dick Hyman, the other main solo voice, is also extremely effective; but clarinetist Sam Margolis and trombonist Vic Dickenson are heard from on only two tunes, and even there in subordinate roles. Braff, like Louis Armstrong and Bunny Berigan before him, knows how to inject heat into a ballad without compromising the overall mood of the performance, and, at the same time, is able to explore indigenous nooks and crannies few others would even imagine exist. —*Jack Sohmer,* Cadence

WELLMAN BRAUD

b. 1891, **d.** 1966
Bass / Swing
A premier early bass stylist, Wellman Braud helped expand the instrument's popularity and was a huge influence on future generations. He emphasized a big, pure tone, and was one of the first musicians to exploit the bass's harmonic potential. He maintained a vigorous, constantly swinging beat, and, after a few problems getting adjusted, became a vital member of Ellington's orchestra from the late '20s into the mid '30s. Braud began performing on various string instruments in New Orleans in 1910 and 1911. He played guitar with A. J. Piron, and was a drummer in brass bands. He moved to Chicago in 1917, switched to bass, and played with Charlie Elgar from 1920 to 1922. In 1923, Braud went to Europe with Will Vodery's Plantation Revue, then worked in New York until he joined Ellington in 1927. He stayed with Ellington until 1935, and contributed the composition "Double Check Stomp" to the group's repertoire. He then played with and managed the Spirits of Rhythm from 1935 until he formed his own trio in 1937. Braud added pool (billiards) to his career resume in 1940, opening a poolroom in New York. Though this venture forced Braud to end his career as a full-time musician, he continued to play. Braud recorded with Jelly Roll Morton in 1939 and 1940, with Sidney Bechet in 1940 and 1941, and with Bunk Johnson in 1947. There were reunions with Ellington in 1944 and 1961. He toured Europe with Kid Ory in 1956, then moved to California in 1958. Braud played with Joe Darensbourg in 1960. Ellington paid him tribute in 1970, writing "Portrait of Wellman Braud," which appeared on the *New Orleans Suite* album. —*Ron Wynn*

ANTHONY BRAXTON

b. Jun. 4, 1945, Chicago, IL
Saxophone, composer / Cool, modern creative
Anthony Braxton's music challenges assumptions and preconceptions about what constitutes jazz and Black music, and about the role of the creative African-American performer and composer. Braxton's work has clear and significant European influences; as much as, if not more than, African and African-American influences. From his first album in the late '60s, he has been a controversial figure. A brilliant individual who's a chessmaster and has, for years, used symbolic diagrams as the titles of compositions, his critics have labeled him pretentious, stiff, and obsessed with European standards and virtues (polite terminology for calling him an "Uncle Tom"). He's a multi-instrumentalist who's played alto, soprano, sopranino, bass, and contrabass clarinet. But Braxton has always collaborated with Black free performers, including Muhal Richard Abrams, Roscoe Mitchell, Anthony Davis, and Leroy Jenkins. His work blends free improvisation, bebop, contemporary classical,

opera, and dance. He's written compositions for multiple orchestras and solo sax, quartets, quintets, and big bands. His influences range from Charlie Parker and Ornette Coleman to Paul Desmond, Warne Marsh, Eric Dolphy, and Stockhausen.

Braxton began studying music at age 17, and, at one time, taught harmony in the Association for the Advancement of Creative Musicians' (AACM) school after joining the AACM in 1966. Braxton's debut album featured his trio work with Leo Smith and Leroy Jenkins. The threesome played three compositions on about 20 instruments. That was followed by his historic and controversial two-record set of solo alto, which both intrigued and infuriated the jazz community. Braxton formed the Creative Construction Company trio in 1969 and went to Europe, where he played and recorded with that trio and with other musicians and groups, including Steve McCall, Muhal Richard Abrams, and the Art Ensemble of Chicago. Braxton formed the quartet, Circle, in 1970 with Chick Corea, Dave Holland, and Barry Altschul. They made exciting, resolutely noncommercial material; so noncommercial that Corea, in particular, went in a totally different direction once the group disbanded.

Braxton stayed busy throughout the '70s, recording for both European and American labels. He did sessions overseas for BYG and for many Japanese and Italian companies. Braxton gained both notoriety and disdain for a string of albums he cut for Arista in the mid '70s. Some were with a quartet, some were duos, some were with an orchestra. These albums included a three-LP set for four orchestras that featured a piece that lasted for nearly two hours. This, and another album for two pianos, featured only Braxton's compositions. Almost as controversial were two albums of bebop tunes with accompanists titled *In the Tradition–Vols. 1 & 2* in which Braxton did not stick to either bebop rhythmic feeling or to melodic approaches. Alto saxophonist Bob Mover was moved to record an answer to the album, which he named *In the True Tradition.*

Braxton played with a host of musicians during this period, among them Abrams, the Art Ensemble, Derek Bailey, the Robert Schumann String Quartet, and Joseph Jarman. During the late '70s and '80s, he recorded for the Hat Hut, Hat Art, and Nessa labels, and for Leo. He continued playing with everyone from Max Roach to Marilyn Crispell, covering the gamut of improvisational and symphonic material. He's maintained a hectic pace, but in a different direction from the mid '70s. Braxton stopped trying to earn a livelihood strictly as a performer. He had a three-year position as artist-in-residence at Mills College, then became a tenured full-time professor at Wesleyan College. Few musicians evoke such divided sentiment as Anthony Braxton. It will probably be well into the 21st century (if ever) before there is any consensus about the merits of his music. A healthy number of his titles are available on CD. —*Ron Wynn and Myles Boisen*

Three Compositions of New Jazz / Apr. 1968-May 1968 / Delmark 415

★ **For Alto Saxophone** / Oct. 1968 / Delmark 420-421

Live at Wigmor / **i.** 1974 / Inner City 1041

★ **In the Tradition—Vol. 1** / May 29, 1974 / Steeple Chase 1015
The resulting session shows another side of Anthony Braxton: his Arista recordings, where he eschewed his own compositions for a series of jazz classics. The critics who think Braxton isn't a jazz musician (if that's really important) should finally be silenced. His alto playing on "Marshmallow" and "Just Friends" has his unmistakable stylings, but on "Lush Life" he is at his most traditional similar to "Nickie" on his *Duets 1976* album. "Goodbye Pork Pie Hat" is given the full Braxton treatment, beginning with his breathing into his contrabass clarinet followed by squeaks. Only at the end is the familiar melody played by the very low register horn and Niels-Henning Orsted Pedersen's arco bass. —*Carl Brauer,* Cadence

☆ **In the Tradition—Vol. 2** / May 29, 1974 / Inner City 31045

Braxton's set of vintage bop and mainstream songs, done with reverence and, for the most part, extreme competence. These seem to be Braxton's answer to those who claimed he knew little about jazz tradition and even less about how to present it on an album. Reaction to both albums was strong; fellow alto saxophonist Bob Mover even cut an album in answer to them. —*Ron Wynn*

○ **Duo—Vols. 1 and 2** / Jun. 30, 1974 / Emanem 601
These two albums were originally issued as a double album on Emanem and were the results of a concert given June 30, 1974, in London (the rehearsal extract was recorded the preceding day). The music here goes to the furthest borders, where the line between sound and music become most abstract. Following the logical extension beginning, on one hand, with Gregorian chants, Palestrina, Bach, Block, Schoenberg, and Cage, and, on the other hand, with drums, hollers, Scott Joplin, Louis Armstrong, Dizzy Gillespie, Charlie Parker, Ornette Coleman, and Albert Ayler, we not only find two circles, but they converge, forming a musically historical figure eight with the music on these records at the intersecting point. The basis of musical sound is unlimited, but of a common root. The music here is no more than what had preceded it: permutations, combinations and variations on that common root.... Both albums have over 40 minutes of music. —*Bob Rusch*, Cadence

○ **19 (Solo) Compositions (1988)** / Jun. 1974-Apr. 1988 / New Albion 23

New York (Fall 1974) / Sep. 27, 1974 / Arista 4032
This album is a model of thoughtful record production, a superb cross-section of one of our most intriguing avant-gardists, and his first American recording at the time (1974) since 1968.... Alto sax remains Braxton's major medium, and while he had abandoned his earlier virtuoso ambitions, his range had broadened and his expressive capabilities were dramatized by his increasing ease with rhythms and sound-space placement. The most personal statements, I feel, are on the cuts on side one, cut one, and side one, cut three, particularly the latter. Here, the welter of early influences—John Coltrane, Roscoe Mitchell, Eric Dolphy, and Ornette Coleman—are subjugated, resolving into a personal sense of sonoric/expressive techniques (and even structure) that quite transforms "cool" jazz. Unbound by modes or changes, his rhythm is quite at ease, and his often tenuous melodism blossoms. —*John Litweiler*, Down Beat

Five Pieces (1975) / Jul. 1-2, 1975 / Arista 4064

Montreux/Berlin Concerts, The / Jul. 20, 1975 / Arista 5002
This is the first of the records that capture the startling, still-controversial reedman/composer in live performance, and the classic concert factor of audience feedback reveals its unvoiced effect.... Important, too, that these concerts were recorded in Europe, a venue that proved vital in the careers of Eric Dolphy and Lee Konitz (two major Braxton influences), and which traditionally has been more open to new music than America. *Montreux/Berlin* offers a rich cross-section of the music Braxton had performed in concert by placing him in three distinct settings. The Montreux pieces (two pieces on side one, the first piece on side two) date from 1975 and feature the Braxton quartet with trumpeter Kenny Wheeler. The other piece on side two, and both pieces on side three from the 1976 Berlin Jazz Days festival, replace Wheeler with George Lewis, the trombone phenom. The final piece, which fills side four, is a concerto-styled work for Lewis and Braxton, with an orchestral ensemble part of gratifying color and complexity. In general terms, there is Braxton's incisively attractive view of bebop (track two, side one); and a couple of pieces from his legendary Kelvin series of compositions (each employing a snappy rhythmic germ and thematic contour). There are also slow pieces, including the showcase orchestral work, that concentrates on a dreamy, almost dreary "dynamic stasis" that benefits so well from Braxton's rationalism and control. perhaps my favorite of his frequent flashes of humor, . —*Neil Tesser*, Down Beat

○ **Creative Orchestra Music (1976)** / Feb. 1976 / Arista 4080

This was Anthony Braxton's music in an orchestral framework. To perform these six varied compositions Braxton assembled some seminal creative improvisers including multi-instrumentalist Roscoe Mitchell, trumpet and cornet player Leo Smith, and pianist, arranger, composer, and bandleader Muhal Richard Abrams in addition to those musicians who then made up his regular group (trumpeter Kenny Wheeler, bassist Dave Holland, drummer Phillip Wilson). The opening cut got things off to a roaring start with Braxton on alto, Bruce Johnstone on baritone, and Cecil Bridgewater on trumpet rotating solos against the orchestral riffing. The second cut was nearly an antithesis of the first with Braxton more concerned with spacing and sound. Richard Teitelbaum's synthesizer fit in nicely here. Closing out side one was, would you believe, a march, or as Braxton referred to it, "parade music." But this was light-years away from Sousa with some fine solo work by George Lewis on trombone and Braxton on clarinet. A sheer delight. The second side further reinforced the high quality begun on side one with a Duke Ellington-inspired piece and a remarkable feature for Roscoe Mitchell on alto. —*Carl Brauer,* Cadence

Duets 1976 / Aug. 1-2, 1976 / Arista 4101
This Anthony Braxton session features two AACM veterans (Muhal Richard Abrams, piano) who'd worked together often.... The moment of sheer rapture on *Duets 1976* comes during a lighthearted reading of Scott Joplin's memorable "Maple Leaf Rag." Side one, cut three, is one of Braxton's mathematical configurations that comes off as a beautifully wistful ballad. Side two's end is achieved by "Nickie," with Braxton exhorting out that most cumbersome of instruments, the contrabass sax. Suffice to say these two work within a wide range of contexts, from the rag form to complex mathematical compositions. —*Willard Jenkins, Jr.,* Cadence

Anthony Braxton Live / i. 1977 / Bluebird 6626
Multi-instrumentalist Anthony Braxton's albums are always no-holds-barred propositions, and are aimed squarely at his fans. This live set, with its array of squeaks, squawks, squeals, and screaming solos, done without benefit of contrasting backbeats or anything to balance the slate, deserves praise for Braxton's skills. But those who don't love the outside shouldn't even think about it. —*Ron Wynn*

Complete Braxton, The / i. Apr. 1978 / Arista 1902
1971 was a transitional year for Anthony Braxton, who was then a member of the Circle quartet. While this LP does not include any performances with Circle as a band, it does feature each group member individually and also includes the Braxton quartet as it evolved after the breakup of Circle. The two Chick Corea/Braxton duets, both improvisational, reveal an amazing exchange of musical ideas. Side one, cut one, shows a generally more melodic Corea bandying themes and riffs with Braxton on soprano sax. The duet on side four begins as a slow dirgelike ballad with Corea chording behind Braxton's soprano. It builds to a climatic conclusion with Corea first reaching inside the piano to strum the strings, then a furious exchange between the two artists, and finally a return to the slow opening theme. Three tunes feature a quartet comprised of Braxton, drummer Barry Altschul, bassist Dave Holland, and trumpeter Kenny Wheeler. Of the quartet pieces, side three, cut one, is the most conventional (walking bass, theme-solos-theme format). With Holland and Altschul providing a swinging foundation, the horns are free to stretch out on the solos. The most stylistically innovative quartet composition is on side one. Braxton is armed with his usual arsenal (flute, contrabass clarinet, clarinet, alto sax), and Holland helps set up a mood with a slow bowed bass bottom augmented by Altschul's barrage of percussion instruments. The piece is long and employs extended silences and open spaces as a compositional tool. Although it features a quartet, the piece is actually structured as a variety of solos, duets, and trios. Especially effective duets feature Altschul with Braxton on contrabass clarinet and with Holland's bowed bass solo. —*David Less,* Down Beat

For Four Orchestras / May 18-19, 1978 / Arista 3L8900

In its complete realization, *For Four Orchestras* was nearly three hours long. Of course, a recorded performance loses quite a bit of physical immediacy, and the limitations of the recording medium and economic and time factors forced modifications of Anthony Braxton's original conception of the work, so that this set stands as a documentation of what Braxton called "an excellent version of the 'essence' of the piece." The overall contour of the piece is traceable, however, and one absorbs a feeling about it in addition to recognizing occasional specific details. Despite the number of participants, Braxton ordered his material into a transparent, chamber music lucidity, which allows an interior view of the developmental design of the music's fabric. The various episodes of activity and stasis form a consistently evolving variety of coloristic guises, dynamic ranges, spatial maneuvers, timbral juxtapositions, and levels of intensity, which ultimately defined Braxton's individual solutions to "Klangfarbenmelodie" (or melody created through a constantly shifting series of tones and colors), a technique originated by the Second Viennese School composers (Schoenberg, Berg, and Webern). —*Art Lange*, Down Beat

Composition 96 / Jan. 24, 1981 / Hat Art 1984

Six Compositions: Quartet / Oct. 21-22, 1981 / Antilles 848585

More fierce, often shattering compositions from Anthony Braxton on his usual horn arsenal, backed by a wonderful quartet featuring the welcome presence of drummer Ed Blackwell. Even in this setting, Blackwell finds ways to include enticing accents and rhythms, while pianist Anthony Davis ranks alongside Marilyn Crispell as Braxton's best keyboard partners. Bassist Mark Heilas is also a substantial contributor. —*Ron Wynn*

Open Aspects (1982) / Mar. 18, 1982 / Hat Art 1996

Anthony Braxton's (alto sax, sopranino) work as a free improviser can be quite stimulating. Here, he returned for a second vinyl dialog (the first being *Time Zones*) with Richard Teitelbaum (synthesizer, microcomputer). It provided less intense stimulation and more comfortable friendly dialog than their earlier record. Using the free context, they utilized a number of strategies from ballad to sparse to melodic variations to dense passages bordering on blowouts. The most precious was "No. 2," which centered around a major pentatonic scale figure (a nod to "the tradition"?). The only interesting aspect of this cut also used elsewhere was Teitelbaum's seeming recording of Braxton as the reed man played, and then the re-feeding of the material into the ongoing improvisation, having the effect of a "mirage" Braxton playing in the background. Highlights for this listener included the opener (the only cut featuring the sopranino), which shifted dynamics and textures a number of times and had some strong, rough lines and slurred bending tones from the reed man hitting an early stride; "No. 4," a rousing, flurried piece complete with machine-gunlike rhythm box textures, and the haunting textures accompanying the balladlike "No. 5." A word also about Teitelbaum's multilayered sound production: He not only produced obvious textures; but also sounds, lines, and clusters appearing in various distances from the immediate sound, which made for a continuously engaging listening experience. —*Milo Fine*, Cadence

Composition 113 / Dec. 6, 1983 / Sound Aspects 003

★ **Seven Standards (1985)—Vol. 1** / Jan. 30-31, 1985 / Magenta 0203

Saxophonist plays straightahead with the Hank Jones (p) Trio. Very enjoyable. Vol. 2 also excellent. —*Michael G. Nastos*

London (Quartet—1985) / Nov. 13, 1985 / Leo 414415416

In the fall of 1985, Anthony Braxton took a quartet on a tour of England. This three-record set is a complete performance of one of these concerts. Braxton used his encyclopedic collection of compositions in a unique way with this quartet. At various times in the performance, pieces are collaged to-gether. The musicians simultaneously explore various sections of different compositions. The bass and drums may be using the rhythm track of one composition while sax and piano are playing the solo lines from another. This structure might change as any one of the instruments switches to a different composition or switches its role in the ensemble. All of this flows seamlessly into a complex, evolving structure. This may sound daunting, but don't be scared off by the overly theoretical descriptions or Braxton's dry, impenetrable reputation. This music swings, and all of the playing is first-rate. All four players (Marilyn Crispell, piano; Mark Dresser, bass; Gerry Hemingway, percussion; Braxton, clarinet, flute, alto sax, C-melody sax, soprano sax) are masters of their instruments, and on this particular performance, all of the playing clicks. Braxton's clarinet playing and Crispell's charged piano approach are of particular note. What is striking, though, is how carefully these musicians listen to each other and how well this group functions as a unit. . . . This record provides a glimpse of how Braxton's ideas congealed in a concert performance. —*Michael Rosenstein*, Cadence

○ **Five Compositions (1986)** / Jul. 2-3, 1986 / Black Saint 0106

When Anthony Braxton (reeds) installed a piano in his quartet, his music increasingly echoed the classic group Circle in which he worked with Chick Corea circa 1970. Braxton, of course, never turned his back on heady concepts like those Circle limned; his artistic progress has always relied on refining elements first set forth over two decades ago. And while the compositional strategies he employed grew ever more familiar, his sidefolk executed his thorny themes ever more smoothly. (David Rosenbloom's quick-change piano was used variously as a chording, melody, and percussion instrument—sometimes all three in the space of a few seconds.) I was particularly taken with the opening track, where the akilter but propulsive rhythm suggests the sound of a trunk full of loose bricks, kicked down 20 flights of stairs: clunky, but unstoppable. He was also increasingly preoccupied with the organic unity of an LP program; as the numerical titles suggest, distinctive compositions contain echoes of one another. His pictorial song titles continued to get more bizarre. The pictographs contain representations of: a panel truck, its lights left on, atop a gas station lube rack; a paddlewheel riverboat; something that looks like a folded-up futon sitting astride a coffee table; something else that looks like Godzilla in silhouette (Braxton even cracks a joke or two in his liner notes). That he could now allow himself to reveal a zany streak (as on his quartet's last recital, November 1985) suggests he was feeling more relaxed than ever; relaxation was elusive for so long. As his approach grew more holistic—he saw musical thinking as a gateway to sociopolitical thinking—he seemed more comfortable with himself and the world, and the once-arcane structures, which still scare some people off, sounded more and more "normal." —*Kevin Whitehead*, Cadence

○ **Six Monk's Compositions (1987)** / Jun. 30, 1987+Jul. 1, 1987 / Black Saint 1201161

This may be Braxton's finest straight jazz release, and among his best in any style. Bassist Mal Waldron and bassist Buell Neidlinger are fully equipped to handle Monk's tricky passages, chord structures, and movements, while Braxton displays an affinity for Monk's work that his legion of detractors would find astonishing. Drummer Bill Osborne isn't intimidated by Neidlinger or Waldron, and drives the session effectively. —*Ron Wynn*

○ **Vancouver Duets (1989)** / Jun. 30, 1989 / Music & Arts 611

Blistering, compelling duets that are intense, effective, and often frightening in style, volume, and energy. There's little hard bop, mainstream, or even straight bop; just searing, surging alto sax and piano. —*Ron Wynn*

○ **Tristano Compositions (1989)** / Dec. 10-12, 1989 / Hat Art 6052

Braxton tackles works by another keyboard genius, Lennie Tristano, and shows he's just as able to handle Tristano's pieces as those of Monk. Bassist Cecil McBee and drummer Andrew Cyrille threaten but don't overwhelm baritone saxophonist John Raskin and pianist Dred Scott. The album is dedicated to Warne Marsh, a saxophonist whose influence resounds in much of Braxton's work. —*Ron Wynn*

Willisau (Quartet) / **i.** 1991 / Hat Art
The Willisau set consists of four CDs—two live European performances in June of 1991 and two studio dates from the same time period. The quartet had worked together at this point for well over a decade and had developed a fantastic synergy, an ability to take Braxton's elaborate and excruciatingly complex compositions and spin off on wholly independent trajectories that somehow manage to remain recognizably bracketed in the scope of Braxton's architectural majesty. Hemingway, Dresser, and Crispell are all heard at their finest hours, both individually and as a group. Not for the faint of heart, this set will prove a listening challenge that pays off quickly in tangible rewards, namely a foothold on the "hall of mirrors" approach inherent in most of Braxton's writing. Listen for his many classical references and influences, particularly that of Karlheinz Stockhausen. —*Scot Hacker*

Eight Compositions / **i.** May 14, 1992 / Music & Arts 710

JOSHUA BREAKSTONE

b. 1955
Guitar / Postbop
This Canadian guitarist's steady style and pleasant solos have been heard on a series of milestone recordings. Not flashy or exciting, but reliable, Breakstone has a clean sound and reflects the basic full-toned jazz guitar approach that has passed from Charlie Christian on down. —*Ron Wynn*

Wonderful / May 24, 1983 / Sonora 222
This studio date for the guitarist with the Barry Harris Trio features two Breakstone tunes and five standards from Lennie Tristano, Tadd Dameron, George Gershwin, and Django Reinhardt. This was a good portent of things to come. —*Michael G. Nastos*

★ **4/4 = 1** / Jun. 1984 / Sonora 322
With the Kenny Barron (p) Trio, this one features two more from Breakstone, Frank Lacy's great "Theme for Ernie," and four standards. —*Michael G. Nastos*

Echoes / **i.** Feb. 19, 1986 / Contemporary 14025

Self-Portrait in Swing / **i.** Feb. 1990 / Contemporary 14050
Relaxed, smooth guitar date with the accent on easy swinging standards and originals. Breakstone is solidly in the Joe Pass/Barney Kessel school, someone who plays with minimum of intensity but does display total command and confidence. His solos don't so much impress as they tend to comfort, and nothing here will either bore or amaze anyone. —*Ron Wynn*

○ **9 by 3** / **i.** 1990 / Contemporary 14062
Includes seven trio tracks with Dennis Irwin on bass, Kenny Washington on drums. Includes lots of Monk. Breakstone is starting here to break out of a formulaic mold. —*Michael G. Nastos*

Evening Star / **i.** Jan. 14, 1992 / Contemporary 14040

LENNY BREAU (Leonard Breau)

b. Aug. 5, 1941, Auburn, ME, **d.** Aug. 12, 1984, Los Angeles, CA
Guitar / Swing, bop
Breau was an outstanding finger-style jazz guitarist who performed on both acoustic and electric guitars. Breau's right hand drew on classical, flamenco, and country (Merle Travis/Chet Atkins) fingerpicking techniques. He was one of the first guitarists to digest the impressionistic, postbop chord voicings of pianist Bill Evans. Breau developed the ability to comp chords and improvise single-string melodies simultaneously, creating the illusion of two guitarists playing together. His facility with artificial harmonics remains the envy of many guitarists. Late in his career, Breau began using a seven-string guitar that extended the instrument's range in the upper register. Breau's early RCA recordings are

eclectic and technically dazzling. His later work is less flashy, but communicates on a deeper level. —*Richard Lieberson*

Guitar Sounds of Lenny Breau / Apr. 2, 1968 / RCA 4076
The debut album from the amazing guitarist Lenny Breau. Features several pop tunes as well as jazz-flavored melodies. Difficult to find on LP, but well worth the search. —*Paul Kohler*

★ **Five O'Clock Bells** / Oct. 1977-Jan. 1978 / Genes 5006
1977 and 1978. Solo guitar and vocals. This includes five Breau originals, two standards, and McCoy Tyner's "Visions." Guitar students, this is your homework—find this album. —*Michael G. Nastos*

○ **Mo' Breau** / 1977-1978 / Adelphi 5012
1977 and 1978. The companion to *Five O'Clock Bells* features solo versions of four of Breau's originals, one melded to McCoy Tyner's "Ebony Queen," and three nice standards, including "Emily." —*Michael G. Nastos*

Legendary Lenny Breau . . . Now!!, The / **i.** 1979 / Soundhole
Recorded with the help of guitar master Chet Atkins, this record showcases Lenny in the solo guitar spotlight. A few tunes feature Lenny soloing against a separate rhythm guitar track that he also plays. Breau's version of McCoy Tyner's "Visions" is astounding!! —*Paul Kohler*

Quietude / Jun. 14, 1983 / Electric Muse 1001
These are recordings in Toronto with bassist Dave Young. The album includes four standards, one Breau piece, and a reprise (11 minutes plus) on "Visions." Features pristine playing by two virtuosos. —*Michael G. Nastos*

Last Sessions / 1984 / Adelphi 5024

MICHAEL BRECKER

b. Mar. 29, 1949, Philadelphia, PA
Tenor and soprano saxophone, flute, piano / Modern creative
An outstanding soloist in bebop, hard bop, jazz-rock, fusion, and funk, Michael Brecker is one of the most influential tenor sax stylists, after Coltrane and Joe Henderson. His tone, lines, phrasing, and powerful solos incorporate and reflect aspects of the styles of Coltrane, Wayne Shorter, King Curtis, and Junior Walker. Brecker's intensity, drive, and personalized sound have made him one of the most recognizable contemporary tenor sax players around; it's sometimes frustrating to hear that trademark tenor immersed in arrangements that are little more than background music. As a child and a teen, Brecker played clarinet and alto sax, before turning to tenor in high school. He played in rock bands while attending Indiana University, then moved to New York in 1969. Brecker played with R&B groups and formed Dreams that same year, a superb instrumental unit that needed a vocalist (they never found one). Dreams included his brother Randy and Billy Cobham. They recorded two artistically daring, but commercially stiff, Columbia albums. Brecker played with Horace Silver in 1973 and 1974. He reunited briefly with Cobham, then co-led the Brecker Brothers band with his sibling until the end of the '70s. They sometimes played punchy, entertaining R&B-laced funk; other times they degenerated into vapid instrumental pop. When the Brecker Brothers disbanded, Michael Brecker established Steps with Mike Mainieri; they became Steps Ahead in the early '80s. Brecker joined Herbie Hancock's quartet for a late '80s tour of America and Japan. During that tour, Brecker debuted the Electronic Wind Instrument (EWI), a combination of synthesizer and saxophone. Brecker has been featured on many marvelous sessions as a side musician; he's recorded as a leader for MCA/Impulse and GRP. Brecker has several sessions available on CD. —*Ron Wynn*

○ **Cityscape** / **i.** 1983 / Warner Brothers 3698

Michael Brecker / Dec. 1986-1987 / MCA 5980
The highlight of this very good album is "Nothing Personal." With Pat Metheny (g), Charlie Haden (b), and Jack DeJohnette (d). —*Michael G. Nastos*

★ **Don't Try This at Home** / 1988 / MCA 42229
Good follow-up to Brecker's 1987 debut for the revived
Impulse label, though it isn't quite as energized or as passionate as his debut. He has another excellent supporting
cast, but the songs don't seem as interesting, and the session,
at times, merely sounds like a less intense continuation of its
predecessor. —*Ron Wynn*

○ **Now You See It . . . Now You Don't** / 1990 / GRP 9622
Michael Brecker's two Impulse dates definitely fall into the
area of creative jazz. His GRP debut follows in the same
vein. For *Now You See It*, Brecker's third recording as a
leader, the tenor great uses different personnel on most of
the selections, but plays consistently well. Jim Beard's synthesizers are used for atmosphere; to set up a funky groove
or to provide a backdrop for the leader. Some of the music
sounds like updated John Coltrane (Joey Calderazzo's McCoy
Tyner-influenced piano helps), but other pieces can almost
pass for Weather Report, if Wayne Shorter, rather than Joe
Zawinul, had had the lead voice. Most of the originals (either
by Brecker, Jim Beard, or producer Don Grolnick) project
moods rather than featuring strong melodies, but Michael
Brecker's often-raging tenor makes the most of every opportunity; his intensity on the ironically named "Peep" could
easily challenge Courtney Pine. —*Scott Yanow*, Cadence

RANDY BRECKER

b. Nov. 29, 1945, Philadelphia, PA
Trumpet / Modern creative
The older of the two Brecker brothers, trumpeter Randy has
almost as much verve and skill on his instrument as his
brother, Mike, though he doesn't possess the identical soulfulness. He's performed expert bebop, jazz-rock, fusion, and
Afro-Latin, and his phrasing, timbre, and tone are outstanding. Brecker learned classical trumpet in Philadelphia before
attending Indiana University. He studied jazz theory with
Dave Baker, and played in the prize winning big band that
captured first place at the collegiate jazz festival held at
Notre Dame in the mid '60s. Brecker quit school while touring Europe with the band, and remained there for several
months. When he returned, he joined Blood, Sweat, & Tears
in 1967; he left a year later to play with Horace Silver in
1968 and 1969. Brecker also worked with several big bands,
including Clark Terry's, Duke Pearson's, Joe Henderson's,
Frank Foster's, and the Thad Jones-Mel Lewis organization.
He co-formed Dreams in 1969 with Mike and Billy Cobham.
After two commercially dismal albums, Randy Brecker
worked with Larry Coryell's Eleventh House and Cobham in
the mid '70s. The brothers co-led their band from the mid
'70s to 1979. During the '80s, Randy Brecker led a group that
featured his wife, vocalist Eliane Elias, doing Afro-Latin and
light jazz. He's continued doing sessions. Brecker has
recorded as a leader for Columbia, Score, Arista/Novus,
Denon, GNP Crescendo, and MCA. He has several dates
available on CD. —*Ron Wynn and Michael G. Nastos*

Score / i. 1986 / Capitol 81202
Good octet date with Brecker exploring both jazz-rock and
straight mainstream material. This is his debut as a leader
outside the Brecker Brothers, and he displays the wit, fire,
and style that characterize his work as a session player. The
musicians assembled include guitarist Larry Coryell, playing
both nice bop and more interesting rock-tinged solos, and
bassist Eddie Gomez. —*Ron Wynn*

★ **In the Idiom** / Oct. 19-25, 1986 / Denon 1483
Randy Brecker's *In the Idiom* is an October (19, 20, 25) 1986
program in the company of Joe Henderson (tenor sax), Ron
Carter (bass), David Kikoski (piano), and Al Foster (drums).
Surprisingly: a) this is Brecker's first outing as *the* leader, b)
this is a strong hard bop date, c) Brecker's trumpet playing is
strong and inventive. Just how strong a trumpeter Brecker
could be is demonstrated well on "Little Miss P.," a freeish
cooker that winds down into near-orgasmic playing between
trumpet, bass, and drums. The old cliché about this could be
a classic Blue Note '60s date is true here, and there are times
when the trumpet suggests Lee Morgan and then early

Freddie Hubbard. But while suggestive of a bygone era, the
music or—perhaps more accurately—the playing is fresh. Joe
Henderson (tenor sax) is clearly second fiddle, but a strong
one, and he, too, shines brightly on "Little Miss P." Al Foster
plays on top of the drums, and Ron Carter (bass) fills in and
out. They clearly know the territory, but also seem to *listen*
to each other and play off the inspiration. The only weak
point for me is David Kikoski, whose perfunctory left-hand
and bop right-hand runs never seem to lift off the keyboard
into a further or more inspired development. . . . For me, perhaps the most significant message on this date is the overwhelming strength and inventiveness of "Little Miss P.," a
piece that, probably not coincidentally, moves into free bop,
an area that offered the most promise in keeping this style
vital after a run that is now (1987) well over 40 years old.
Even so, as idiomatic expressions of late '60s styled hard
bop, this is quite inventive and excellent, and I suspect it will
last well over the years to come. —*Bob Rusch*, Cadence

Toe to Toe / i. 1990 / MCA 6334

WILLEM BREUKER

b. Nov. 4, 1944, Amsterdam, Netherlands
*Saxophone, clarinet, composer / Progressive big band, mod-
ern creative*
A leader in the European avant-garde and free music community, Dutch saxophonist, clarinetist, composer, and bandleader Willem Breuker has worked to ensure recording and
performance opportunities for many performers. His compositions incorporate several influences: free jazz, contemporary and avant-garde classical and new music, plus film
themes, dance, and European folk sounds. Breuker also includes a large dose of humor and even absurdist lyrics and
sentiments into his works. That same humor carries over
into his playing, which blends screams, shrieks, and various
effects with honking bleats and moments of almost straight,
bebop-inspired soloing. He helped form the Instant
Composers Pool, a nonprofit organization that sponsors performances and recordings of music by European free players. Breuker has played and recorded with the Globe Unity
Orchestra, and with Peter Brotzmann, Misha Mengelberg,
Hans Bennink, Alexander Schlippenbach, Gunther Hampel,
and many others. He formed the Kollektief in the mid '70s,
and toured Europe. The group visited America and Canada
in the '80s. Breuker was awarded the Dutch National Jazz
Prize in 1970 and the Jazz Prize of the West German Music
Critics in 1976. As a leader, he's recorded for MPS, BVHaast
(Holland), Marge (France), and About Time. None of
Breuker's sessions are available on CD in America, but they
can be obtained by mail order. —*Ron Wynn*

★ **Live in Berlin** / i. Nov. 1975 / FMP 06
This is one of reedman Willem Breuker's works for a larger
group, and while there is an obvious set of structures within
these pieces, it is quite open. Breuker seems to have a knack
and impulse to refer to other well-known compositions in
his work; everything from the Funeral March (Brahms—
Beethoven?) to the Carioca. In doing this he runs very close
to becoming cute, but stops just short, moving on to other
ideas. As a result, it is excellent, this sort of free association
jazz. Much here is extremely humorous and a bit maniacal,
but a tremendous joy. All the music here was composed and
arranged by Breuker except, of course, "Our Day Will Come."
—*Bob Rusch*, Cadence

○ **De Klap** / i. 1985 / BVHaast 068

○ **Metropolis** / Jan. 1989-Apr. 1989 / BVHaast 8903

○ **To Remain** / i. Jan. 1989-Apr. 1989 / BVHaast 8904
This album is a retrospective of sorts, exploring Willem
Breuker's compositions and arrangements from the late '70s
through the late '80s. The centerpiece of this document is a
long suite framed by some shorter pieces. This suite, "To
Remain," is a tightly arranged piece composed in 1979,
which, to my knowledge, had gone unrecorded. "To Remain"
showcases Breuker's trademark wit and ear for punchy,
gutsy voicings. He created the opportunity to write for a

fairly stable ensemble and the writing shows a knack for capturing the strong points of his players. The group also develops an acute awareness of how his music works and is able to respond spontaneously. His compositional techniques take themes and twist them through off-kilter harmonic permutations and turbulent rhythmic evolution. The suite features ensemble sections broken by features for soloists. Andre Goudbeek delivers an acid-toned alto solo where his wrenching attack weaved through with big-band punctuations. Henk DeJong (piano) is also featured in a spiky, clustered solo pitted against a densely voiced ensemble part. The themes are played by the ensemble, which was arranged with variations of reeds/brass counterpoint. The writing is from Breuker's usual collection of disparate influences, ranging from martial rhythms, circus carillon, sweet-toned swing bands, and theater music. All of this is filtered through a series of fun-house mirrors and bounced off of the crack ensemble playing. The piece sprawls a bit at times (particularly the end sections), but there are ample rewards. "P.T.T." tightens the reins of the long-form suite and condenses Breuker's approach into a 4-1/2 minute distillation, complete with four wild, yet concise, solos. "Driebergen-Zeist" is the only piece that was released previously (as the title tune on an '83 BVHaast release). This is the most overtly theatrical of the pieces, using a pointillistic approach to the arrangements. . . . For those looking for a good introduction to Breuker as composer and arranger, this is a good place to start. Also of particular note is the packaging of this CD. It is presented in an album-sized cardboard cover with an inner sleeve that has a vinyl envelope for the CD. This is a great graphic and tactile alternative to tiny CD pamphlets packaged in plastic boxes. —*Michael Rosenstein,* Cadence

○ **Bob's Gallery** / BVHaast 8801

CECIL BRIDGEWATER (Cecil Vernon Bridgewater)

b. Oct. 10, 1942, Urbana, IL
Trumpet, arranger, composer / Hard bop
Cecil Bridgewater is the better-known and better-recognized member of the Bridgewater brothers, two of the most competent second-generation hard bop horn soloists around. A slashing trumpeter, he's been featured in many bands, most notably with Max Roach in the '70s, '80s, and '90s. Tenor saxophonist Ron Bridgewater worked with his brother, Cecil, in a late '60s group appropriately called the Bridgewater Brothers Band. But they split in 1970, and Cecil went to work for Horace Silver. Since then, they've sometimes both worked with Roach, but Ron Bridgewater has had a much lower profile than his brother. Cecil Bridgewater recorded as a leader for Bluemoon in 1993. This is the only session that features either brother as a leader that is available on CD. —*Ron Wynn*

★ **I Love Your Smile** / i. Dec. 4, 1992 / Bluemoon 78187
In his 20 years with Max Roach, Cecil Bridgewater has been a model sideman, more craftsman than creator, distinguished by his rich tone and quirky way with a blue note. He's lined up a top-flight crew for this solo outing, which sparkles with ensemble empathy and communal high spirits. Hornmen Antonio Hart, Roger Byam, and Steve Turre toss off sleek, fluid hard bop runs as Hanna comps with masterly ease, leaving Bridgewater, with his slightly off-kilter attack, the odd man out. But it's Roach, playing on only two tracks, who makes the most distinctive mark.—*Larry Birnbaum,* Down Beat

DEE DEE BRIDGEWATER (Dee Dee [Née Garrett] Bridgewater)

b. May 27, 1950, Memphis, TN
Vocals / Ballads & blues
Dee Dee Bridgewater is a supremely talented jazz singer whose records have not always been indicative of her skills. Her best work was with the Thad Jones-Mel Lewis big band. She can sing loud or soft, and can do brassy, upbeat tunes, blues, or sentimental ballads. She became popular overseas in the late '70s for her one-woman show, *Lady Day.*

Bridgewater began performing in Michigan during the '60s, and toured the Soviet Union in 1969 with the University of Illinois big band. After marrying trumpeter Cecil Bridgewater, she moved to New York in 1970. Following their divorce in the mid '70s, Bridgewater was the principal vocalist with the Jones-Lewis band from 1972 to 1974, then appeared in the Broadway musical, *The Wiz,* from 1974 to 1976, winning a Tony award in 1975. After singing at Hopper's in New York in 1976 and studying with Roland Hanna, Bridgewater moved to Los Angeles. Bridgewater lived in Europe for several years during the '80s, appearing in Paris and London in 1986 and 1987 in the featured role of *Lady Day,* Stephen Stahl's play about Billie Holiday's life. Bridgewater returned to New York in 1987 to perform, and later toured the Far East with an all-star jazz band that included James Moody, Clark Terry, and Grady Tate. She's always on the edge of superstardom. Currently, Bridgewater has Verve and Impulse (MCA reissue) dates available on CD. —*Ron Wynn*

★ **Live in Paris** / Nov. 24-25, 1986 / MCA 6331
Here is a Dee Dee Bridgewater album that won't insult your ears and intelligence. Bridgewater shows her roots in both Carmen McRae and Sarah Vaughan, but brings a new sense of maturity and fullness to her singing; she can now be, and is, in command. And the surroundings on this live recording are loose enough to allow the entire group to blow. "Misty" and "On a Clear Day" become vehicles and program beautifully into each, and when she shifts down into the blues of "Dr. Feelgood" she does so with finesse and believability. "Dr. Feelgood" may be Aretha Franklin's, but in this genre Bridgewater makes it a natural jazz blues. "Dr. Feelgood," "Cherokee," "All Blues," "Here's That Rainy Day," and others—quite a range of material—and it's well handled without lapses of taste. —*Bob Rusch,* Cadence

○ **In Montreux** / i. Jan. 7, 1992 / Verve 511895
Dee Dee Bridgewater moved to Paris years ago and is now reappearing on disc. Her flamboyant, energetic, wide-ranging style projects well at Montreux, where she envelopes an adoring audience in a bear hug of brilliant surface emotions, sheer Sassian skill, and deeply thrilling vibrato. A Horace Silver medley is pure xenon, and Billie Holiday's "Strange Fruit" is an untouchable tribute. —*Fred Bouchard,* Down Beat

NICK BRIGNOLA (Nicholas Thomas Brignola)

b. Jul. 17, 1936
Saxophone / Bop, post bop
A hard bop baritone sax master who also plays soprano, alto, and tenor sax, plus clarinet and flute, Nick Brignola has been a reliable soloist and contributor to top big bands and small combos, including Woody Herman's Herd and Ted Curson's fine '70s unit. The first virtuoso baritone saxophonist to equal Pepper Adams in fluency and ferocity, Brignola plays baritone as his primary instrument, and demonstrates extensive range and control in the upper and lower registers. He's very capable on several other instruments, particularly alto and flute, but does his hottest solos on baritone. Brignola studied music theory at Ithaca College and Berklee, but primarily is self-taught. He played and recorded with Reese Markewich in the late '50s, then with Herb Pomeroy in Boston and with Cal Tjader and the Mastersounds on the West Coast in 1958. A native of Troy, New York, Brignola moved to Albany the following year and formed his own band. He worked and recorded with Herman and Sal Salvador in the mid '60s, and toured Europe with Curson in 1967. He returned to the upstate New York area, formed a label, and issued his debut as a leader. Brignola explored jazz-rock and led a group in that style until the mid '70s. He reteamed with Curson, recorded and toured with him in the late '70s, and began cutting his own releases on various labels. Brignola recorded two dates with fellow baritone saxophonists Ronnie Cuber, Cecil Payne, and Pepper Adams in the late '70s, and did sessions through the '80s. He's done dates for Beehive, Priam, Discovery, Night Life, Interplay,

and Trend, among others. Brignola has a few sessions available on CD. —*Ron Wynn and Michael G. Nastos*

This Is It / Apr. 1967 / Priam 101

★ **Baritone Madness** / Dec. 22, 1977 / Bee Hive 7000
While showing considerable imagination in planning and attentive care in production, *Baritone Madness* is fundamentally a blowing date, but it should be emphasized that it produces striking results. Three of its five cuts offer the spark-producing pairing of veteran Pepper Adams and the (then) younger Nick Brignola, their two baritone saxophones joined on "Billie's Bounce" and "Marmeduke" (sic) by Ted Curson, playing trumpet on the former and flugelhorn on the latter. "Body and Soul" is Brignola's feature, while the rhythm section has "Alone Together" to itself. The two baritonists are the most consistently absorbing soloists. Adams performs throughout with relaxed, easy, almost nonchalant mastery, which contrasts nicely with Brignola's much more muscular, aggressive approach. Taken at breakneck tempo, "Donna Lee," Charlie Parker's variation on "Indiana," is easily the set's standout cut, with agile, confident work from Adams, whose solo rarely ventures too far from the "Indiana" boundaries, while showing, at the same time, considerable inventiveness. Brignola's solo is a different matter, however, full of fiery vigor and unrelenting, tumultuous imagination. —*Pete Welding*, Down Beat

Signals . . . In from Somewhere / Jun. 21, 1983 / Discovery 893
Nice release, though not as frenetic or exciting as past Brignola dates. He doubles on soprano and baritone, playing with skill and depth. His supporting unit has good, reliable pros in pianist Bill Dobbins, bassist John Lockwood, and drummer John Calarco, though none of them equal the leader in raw talent. —*Ron Wynn*

○ **Northern Lights** / Jul. 3, 1984 / Discovery 917
Baritone saxophonist Nick Brignola is in command of his materials. He's great at the bob and weave and plays with mercurial ease. He never falters, never flags. And he is not particularly prone to cliché. Whatever he gets into, he gets out of, without getting hung up. Musical labyrinths, if there are such things, must be his meat. . . . I hear energy, enthusiasm, knowledge, skill, confidence, and taste in Brignola's line, but no cry of the barrio or wail of desolation. Nothing seems to rise up from the man through the bowels of his horn. Thus "Lush Life" is lovely, fluent, graceful, but pale. "Shaw Nuff" sparkles and skips like a flat rock on water, but never ignites. Here, Brignola reminds me of Richie Cole's brand of the hand-is-quicker-than-the-eye bop. . . . Pianist Jim McNeely wrote the serviceable "Antares." Bassist John Lockwood and drummer David Calarco are steady and springy and demonstrate that they have benefitted from their reasonably long association with Brignola. Lockwood is credited with "3 A.M.," which speaks, I must believe, to more than a yen for pizza at the quiet and lonely hour. The other originals are Brignola's, and I found the title track to be much catchier. —*Alan Bargebuhr*, Cadence

○ **Raincheck** / Sep. 1988 / Reservoir 108
Nick Brignola's baritone packs a powerful punch, but Brignola prefers the high register to the low, often darting to harmonics well above the horn's written range. . . . "I Wish I Knew" is typical of his approach. Buoyed by Billy Hart's dancing brushwork, Brignola chews up the tune without resorting to merely running the changes. He doesn't improvise thematically, but the playing is organic. His four-chorus solo peaks naturally in the last, thanks to a strong sense of melody and a series of ideas in which each contains the seed for the next. Though he picked up his tenor, soprano, and clarinet on occasion, the baritone is Brignola's most personal voice. So it is not surprising that both ballads, "My Ship" and "Darn That Dream," the latter a duo with the ever-splendid Kenny Barron (piano), are interpreted on the large horn. (The easy swing of Brignola's clarinet essay, "Tenderly," is the best of the three non-bari cuts.) Barron's richly chordal accompaniment is masterful on "Darn That Dream," providing enough strength to keep from collapsing

under the saxophone's weight. (Even soft, the bari needs a firm net.) Hart stretches out on the burners "Hurricane" and "Baubles," both of which include no-prisoners bari-drum duets. Hart is a dangerous sparring partner, but Brignola refuses to be knocked out. This album gives Brignola plenty of elbow room, and he proves he can play the hell out of a standard. —*Mark Stryker*, Cadence

What It Takes / Oct. 9, 1990 / Reservoir 117
Another gem that didn't get widespread exposure because it came out on small label. This time, Brignola is matched with playing equals, and he comes out burning. He also plays alto sax and clarinet in addition to his customary baritone and soprano. Pianist Kenny Barron and bassist Rufus Reid lift any session, while drummer Dick Berk defers to them, but doesn't lose the reins while doing so. Randy Brecker takes a welcome break from fusion and studio work to show his trumpet chops can handle hard bop and mainstream fare. —*Ron Wynn*

It's Time / i. 1992 / Reservoir 123

Live at Sweet Basil—First Set / Reservoir 125
Despite the baritone sax's comparatively widespread use since the '40s and '50s, truly proficient performers are still rare; but we can point to Nick Brignola as one who today looms far above the crowd. Brignola also demonstrates his control of the soprano on "Mahjong" and his alto on "Sister Sadie." But it is his surpassing ease with the baritone that is in light focus on the other tunes: the swinging "Autumn Leaves," the semi-balladic "East of the Sun," the medium bright "I Hear a Rhapsody," and, perhaps best of all, "Everything Happens to Me." Helping to maintain the gig's high energy level are pianist Mike Holober, bassist Rich Syracuse, and drummer Dick Berk. —*Jack Sohmer*, Jazz Times

BOB BROOKMEYER (Robert Brookmeyer)

b. Dec. 19, 1929, Kansas City, MO
Valve trombone, arranger, piano / Cool
The only modern valve trombone soloist in jazz history, Bob Brookmeyer was the first musician since Juan Tizol to make the instrument his specialty. Brookmeyer demonstrated a strong solo voice, swinging, loose energy, and bluesy underpinnings. His style is mostly swing-era derived. Brookmeyer began his career as a pianist, and added rhythmic, aggressive solos on that instrument. He studied at the Kansas City Conservatory, then began playing piano in dance bands. He worked with Claude Thornhill, Woody Herman, and Stan Getz in the early '50s, and replaced Chet Baker in Gerry Mulligan's "pianoless" quartet during the mid '50s. Brookmeyer played with Jimmy Giuffre in 1957 and 1958, then recorded a pivotal album with Bill Evans in 1959, on which he also played piano. He co-led a band with Clark Terry in the early '60s, toured Europe and Japan with Mulligan, and, in 1965, was a founding member of the Thad Jones-Mel Lewis orchestra, to which he contributed several arrangements. Brookmeyer was in the Merv Griffin television show's band. He moved to the West Coast later in the '60s and did numerous studio sessions, including some dates with jazz musicians. During the '70s, there were reunions with Mulligan and the Jones-Lewis orchestra. Brookmeyer teamed with Terry again in the '80s, and became music director of the reorganized Mel Lewis orchestra, performing as a soloist and writing arrangements. Brookmeyer made his recording debut with Al Cohn in the mid '50s, and has done sessions with Giuffre and Jim Hall, Zoot Sims, Terry, and the Jones-Lewis orchestra, among many others. For a musician with his track record and session credits, he has relatively few titles currently available on CD. —*Ron Wynn*

○ **Bob Brookmeyer with Phil Urso** / Apr. 30, 1954 / Savoy 15041

Modernity of Bob Brookmeyer, The / Jan. 17, 1955 / Clef 732

Dual Role of Bob Brookmeyer, The / Jun. 30, 1955 / Prestige 1729

Stan Getz / Bob Brookmeyer / Sep. 12-13, 1961 / Verve 8418

Trombone Jazz Samba / Aug. 21, 1962-Sep. 14, 1962 / Verve 8498

○ **And Friends** / May 25-27, 1964 / Columbia 36804
Cool was not dead in 1964; valve trombonist Bob Brookmeyer and friends here capture that school's careful restraint, and a touch of its wimpiness. As a front line, the mellow tone qualities of the leader's valve trombone and Stan Getz's tenor are well matched. Although the three original tunes are Brookmeyer's, the saxophonist is really the central figure; Gary Burton was working with Getz at the time, and Elvin Jones (drums) and Ron Carter (bass) would record with him on a date with Bill Evans later in the year. Getz is consistently the strongest soloist, putting that sumptuous feathery cry to work, but he distinguishes the music even more when he is not soloing. His ascending figures, under the closing theme of "Misty," are like wisps of smoke in calm air, and on Hoagy Carmichael's "Skylark" he continues to play soothing lines under Brookmeyer and Burton after his own bluesy spot has ended. Getz's kibbutzing tendency is best exemplified by the way he backs the trombonist on a tender "I've Grown Accustomed to Her Face," an out-of-tempo obligato, on poignant quotes from "I Only Have Eyes For You," and on sketched chords and counterlines his harmonic sophistication serves him well. He and Brookmeyer gracefully weave around each other on "Bracket" and Sergei Mihanovic's "Sometime Ago." Gary Burton (vibes) contributes his bell-clear sound to half the tunes. Herbie Hancock (piano) solos well, particularly on the bland, but memorable, "Jive Hoot," but his comping then as now has cocktail tendencies; he is often too self-effacing. Elvin Jones, who was, of course, the regular drummer with a more forceful group in 1964 (the John Coltrane quartet), breaks into a subdued, but effective, stomp on "Jive Hoot," but, like his rhythm mates, is reined in, save for Gershwin's "Who Cares" when everyone gets to cut loose at last. This is pretty, delicately crafted music of the most unassuming kind. —*Kevin Whitehead*, Cadence

★ **Bob Brookmeyer Small Band—Vols. 1 and 2** / Jul. 28-29, 1978 / Gryphon 4042
Live at Sandy's in Beverly, MA, in 1978. With Michael Moore (b), Jack Wilkins (g), and Joe LaBarbera (d). Mostly standards, some music of Andy Laverne. Two Brookmeyer originals. All arrangements by Brookmeyer. Fine group effort. —*Michael G. Nastos*

CECIL BROOKS III

b. 1961
Drums / Neo-bop
A contemporary drummer and an aggressive, polyrhythmic stylist, Cecil Brooks III has worked in the New York area with musicians such as Greg Osby, Geri Allen, and Lonnie Plaxico. He recorded one album as a leader for Muse in 1989, and has also done session work in both a hard bop and bebop setting. His lone session is available on CD. —*Ron Wynn*

★ **Collective, The** / Mar. 27, 1989 / Muse 5377
This is an auspicious debut for a top-rate drummer, with Geri Allen (p). —*Michael G. Nastos*

ROY BROOKS

b. Sep. 3, 1938, Detroit, MI
Drums, percussion / Hard bop
A dynamic, exciting percussionist and drummer who's also worked with dance groups, Roy Brooks fortifies any musical situation or band. Both a powerful accompanist and a sparkling soloist, Brooks got his start with Yusef Lateef. He later joined the Horace Silver Quintet with fellow Detroiters Louis Hayes, Gene Taylor, and Doug Watkins. He stayed in the Silver group from the late '50s to the mid '60s. Brooks worked with Pharoah Sanders, James Moody, Wes Montgomery, Sonny Stitt, Jackie McLean, Dexter Gordon, Abdullah Ibrahim, Randy Weston, Milt Jackson, Charles Mingus, and Lateef through the remainder of the '60s. In 1970 he was a founding member of M'Boom Re with Max Roach

and several other percussionists, and remains a member. In 1976, Brooks founded a center for teaching jazz to young people in Detroit. He also started the Aboriginal Percussion Choir; they performed at the 1980 Detroit/Montreux Jazz Festival. Brooks has recorded as a leader for Muse, Enja, and Bayside; his 1970 album, *The Free Slave*, is a jazz classic. Of course, it's currently unavailable on CD, but he does have a recent recording of duets with Woody Shaw, Geri Allen, Randy Weston, and Don Pullen. —*Ron Wynn and Michael G. Nastos*

★ **Free Slave, The** / Apr. 26, 1970 / Muse 5003
Recorded at Left Bank Jazz Society in Baltimore, MD, this all-star quintet features George Coleman (ts), Woody Shaw (tpt), Hugh Lawson (p), Cecil McBee (b), and Brooks (d/per). There are four originals, all extended, with room to stretch for musicians. A wild club date. —*Michael G. Nastos*

Live at Town Hall / May 26, 1974 / Baystate 6028
New York City. With Marcus Belgrave (tpt), Sonny Fortune (as), Sonny Red (as), and Eddie Jefferson (v). There are three standards and Brooks's famous "Prophet" and "Blues for the Carpenter's Saw." —*Michael G. Nastos*

TINA BROOKS (Harold Floyd Brooks)

b. Jun. 7, 1932, Fayetteville, NC, **d.** Aug. 13, 1974, New York, NY
Tenor saxophone / Hard bop, postbop, soul-jazz
Tina Brooks was another of jazz's overlooked, ignored players who didn't get much chance to display his talents during his lifetime. He had an emphatic, intense, and striking sound, and played with swing and heart. He could play fine blues, funk, and soul-jazz, or hard bop. Brooks made very few sessions as a leader for Blue Note, and even fewer were issued in his lifetime. He studied C-melody sax shortly after his family moved from North Carolina to New York in the early '40s. Brooks received some lessons from his brother, David, who later played with Bill Doggett. Brooks began his professional career with an R&B band led by Sonny Thompson. They recorded for King in 1951. Brooks later toured with Amos Milburn, then played with Lionel Hampton until 1955. He worked as a freelance player in New York, and became friends with Elmo Hope and "Little" Benny Harris. Harris helped him get a recording contract with Blue Note; he cut sessions in 1959, 1960, and 1961. Brooks served as Jackie McLean's understudy in the leading role of Jack Gelber's play *The Connection*. He also played with Freddie Redd and Howard McGhee on an LP that featured the show's music. Brooks did four sessions as a leader for Blue Note, and played on eight others with Art Blakey, Kenny Burrell, Johnny Coles, Kenny Drew, Freddie Hubbard, Jimmy Smith, and others. A prolonged drug habit cut Brooks's life short; he died in 1974 of kidney failure after an illness of several years. In 1985, Mosaic provided the greatest tribute by packing the vast majority of Brooks's sessions into one deluxe package: *The Complete Blue Note Recordings of Tina Brooks*. —*Ron Wynn*

★ **Blue Note Recordings** / 1958-1961 / Mosaic 106
Tenor saxophonist with four different bands, including Lee Morgan, Freddie Hubbard, Blue Mitchell, and Johnny Coles (trumpets), and also Jackie McLean. Trios led by pianists Sonny Clark, Duke Jordan, and Kenny Drew. Fifteen Brooks originals, seven standards. Brooks was an unsung hero. His work deserves your investigation. —*Michael G. Nastos*

○ **True Blue** / Jun. 25, 1960 / Blue Note 4041

○ **Back to the Tracks** / Sep. 1, 1960+Oct. 20, 1960 / Blue Note 84052

PETER BROTZMANN

b. Mar. 6, 1941, Remscheid, Germany
Tenor saxophone / Progressive big band, modern creative
Brotzmann is a longtime champion of Europe's avant-garde, and a self-taught saxophonist famous for animated, swirling solos and lengthy, twisting dialog. Initially, Brotzmann played in local Dixieland bands in Germany, then was an

early member of the Fluxus movement which began playing free jazz by 1964. A year later, Brotzmann, Peter Kowald, and Seven-Ake Johannsson formed a group. Brotzmann toured Europe in 1966 with a quintet that included Mike Mantler and Carla Bley. He also began working with the Globe Unity Orchestra, and continued with them until 1981. Brotzmann was a founder of the cooperative FMP in 1969, an organization that sponsors and issues free jazz releases. He also founded a trio with Han Bennink and Fred Van Hove that became extremely influential through its blend of European theater and folk music and African rhythms. Van Hove left the group in 1976, but continued playing with Bennink until 1979. During the '80s, Brotzmann's associations included Harry Miller, Louis Moholo, Willie Kellers, Andrew Cyrille, the Alarm Orchestra, Cecil Taylor, and Last Exit. —*Ron Wynn*

○ **For Adolphe Sax** / **i.** Jun. 1967 / FMP 0080
○ **Balls** / **i.** Aug. 1970 / FMP 0020
○ **Brotzmann, Van Hove, Bennink** / **i.** Feb. 1973 / FMP 0130
○ **Outspan No. 1** / **i.** Apr. 1974 / FMP 0180
○ **Outspan No. 2** / **i.** May 1974 / FMP 0200
● **The Nearer the Bone, The Sweeter the Meat** / **i.** Aug. 1979 / FMP 0690
○ **Alarm** / **i.** Nov. 1981 / FMP 1030

For most of two (now three) decades, saxman Peter Brotzmann has been a principal catalyst in Europe's free music activity. *Alarm* is by a nine-piece band of, again, Europe's finest. It begins with long unison siren wails; solos follow, both unaccompanied and over a violently charging rhythm section, as horn screaming moves in and out and collective improvisations appear. As the wailing and moaning continues, the amazing East German (at the time) trombonist Johannes Bauer trills, bubbles, and chatters a wayward line that climaxes as the band swells to screams. Saxmen Brotzmann and Willem Breuker duet, unaccompanied, in a peasant fugue. Drummer Louis Moholo and pianist Alexander Schlippenbach are among the other participants in *Alarm*'s madness. It is loud, happy, wild music, packed with event and structured for maximum visceral impact, an ingenious form to enhance energy music materials. —*John Litweiler*, Down Beat

★ **Andrew Cyrille Meets Peter Brotzmann in Berlin** / **i.** Mar. 1982 / FMP 1000

One senses that this encounter (43:27, March 19-21, 1982) could literally just be the tip of the iceberg in terms of what these two could get into. . . . "Wolf Whistle" lasts all of side one. Essentially, Brotzmann begins on tenor with some melodic material and in jumps Cyrille (drums), cooking and driving. Interestingly enough, Brotzmann plays off melodic angles a great deal of the time, though still building to those almost patented multiphonic wails from time to time. There is a break in the dialog about half way through as Cyrille takes a tasteful solo. Upon Brotzmann's reentry, a horn is sounded (most likely by Cyrille). This appears to startle Brotzmann for a moment, as he stops, listens, matches the sound, and then the two are off and running again with occasional drops in intensity and volume. The cut suffers slightly from their constant parallel interaction and the almost monophonic energy level, but it is still fun. Side two features a three-part piece entitled "Quilt." "A" began with Cyrille's ratchet and a brief, *very* quiet drum solo, which ends with a bit more volume on bicycle horn and shakers. Brotzmann enters over this (on alto?) in the overtone register, creating variations around the bicycle horn. This is simple and convincing, perhaps the LP's highlight. "B" also starts with a drum solo, which quickly moves into a dialog with Brotzmann on baritone. It is a succinct hard blower into "A Night in Tunisia." "C" closes the album with another understated and very musical drum solo. —*Milo Fine*, Cadence

Opened, But Hardly Touched / **i.** Apr. 1983 / FMP 084050
Berlin Djungle / **i.** Nov. 1984 / FMP 1120

Low Life / **i.** Jan. 1987 / Celluloid 5016
Wie Das Leben So Spielt / **i.** Sep. 1989 / FMP 22
Last Home / **i.** 1990 / Pathological

CLIFFORD BROWN

b. Oct. 30, 1930, Wilmington, DE, **d.** Jun. 26, 1956, PA
Trumpet / Bop, hard bop

Clifford Brown was an immensely talented trumpeter, and from all accounts, a genuinely kind human being. His death from a car accident in 1956 at age 25 was a shattering tragedy. In his few years, he showed a facility and solo skill that was magnificent. Clifford Brown's trumpet solos were characterized by an animated force and percussive edge. He was exceptional on fast songs, ripping through registers, reaching seemingly impossible notes, and executing amazing passages with ease. Brown's ballad work was equally gripping, with clear, whipping phrases and exploding lines as he played the melody, then embellished or extended it. Brown's solos bubbled over with ideas from opening note to concluding phrase, and were carefully constructed, yet played in a loose, spontaneous manner.

Brown began on trumpet at age 13, and his chops were shaped by his band director, Harry Andrews, in high school. Brown studied mathematics and music at Maryland State College, played with the college jazz band, and occasionally performed in Philadelphia clubs with Fats Navarro, Dizzy Gillespie, and Charlie Parker. A 1950 car accident put Brown in the hospital for a year, but he made his first recordings with Chris Powell's Blue Flames in 1952. He played with Tadd Dameron's band and worked in Atlantic City. He toured Europe in the fall of 1953 with Lionel Hampton's orchestra, working in a trumpet section with Art Farmer and Quincy Jones. When he returned to America, Brown worked with various groups, including one with Art Blakey. He co-formed the Max Roach-Clifford Brown quintet in 1954. Though the group was together for only two years, they made some sensational music. Harold Land was the initial saxophonist, and was later replaced by Sonny Rollins.

Brown's career was cut so short that he didn't have a surplus of recording opportunities. There were Blue Note sessions, dates done in Paris, recordings for EmArcy, and his early and final sessions for Columbia. Brown also recorded for Prestige. Xanadu, Ingo, and Elektra/Musician have unearthed fragments of live sessions over the years, and Columbia issued a poor audio quality two-record set of a great concert at the Bee Hive. Both Mosaic and Polygram have issued comprehensive boxed sets of Brown/Roach material. There are also a few single-volume discs floating around. —*Ron Wynn and Bob Porter*

★ **Beginning and the End, The** / 1952-1956 / Columbia

Clifford Brown Sextet. Side one has his earliest recordings of some Caribbean-influenced R&B material; side two is a live recording of his last performance, the night before he died. Includes the famous "Donna Lee" solo. A touching tribute album. —*David Nelson McCarthy*

○ **Clifford Brown Quartet in Paris** / **i.** 1953 / Prestige 357

This session is one of the poorer Clifford Brown recordings from his prime period. . . . It would be unfair to say that it is a bad session, mind you—the original takes of the various titles are excellent—but the little errors of improvisation that creep in here and there and the totally monotonous effect of the juxtaposed original/alternate takes combine to remove the impact of the music when you try to listen to it all at once. . . . The two single-take selections stand out, in my opinion, above all the others and possibly—just possibly, mind you—above most of Brownie's other recorded output. His performance of "It Might as Well Be Spring" is the most moving and most moved version of this ill-treated standard that I have ever heard. The trumpeter finds and draws out so much more beauty in his exploration of this line than in any other version of this ballad that I'm almost surprised that anyone would attempt to play this again after this version. . . . Clifford Brown was not a natural blues player . . . but "Blue and Brown" is, surprisingly, the most self-consciously funky and genuinely moanful blues performance I have ever heard in Brown's recorded work, and is probably (if and when somebody gets around to writing the definitive critical work on Brown) one of his masterpieces. . . . I guess it isn't really a bad session so much as a session programmed in a bad manner. —*Barry Tepperman*, Coda

Alternate Takes / Jun. 9, 1953-Aug. 28, 1953 / Blue Note 84428

With three groups: Lou Donaldson (tpt), J. J. Johnson (t), and Clifford Brown Sextet. —*Michael Erlewine*

★ **Complete Blue Note and Pacific Jazz** / **Recordings of Clifford Brown, The** / Mosaic

The Complete Blue Note and Pacific Jazz Recordings of Clifford Brown documents six sessions recorded over a period of 14 months. The first nine tracks are from a June 9, 1953, date. The session was co-led by Brown and alto saxophonist Lou Donaldson and included Elmo Hope (piano), Percy Heath (bass), and Philly Joe Jones (drums). This was my first contact with this Donaldson session and I like his sense of swing and the warm feeling that radiates from his playing. No need to discuss Brownie's playing, as it is exemplary throughout the LP. Less than two weeks later (June 22, 1953), Brown participated in a session that was to be J. J. Johnson's first LP in four years. Besides Johnson (trombone), Brown, and Percy Heath, the sextet included Jimmy Heath (tenor sax, baritone sax), John Lewis (piano), and Kenny Clarke (drums). These nine tracks are marked by the fine juxtaposition of Brown's fiery trumpet with the warm sounds of Johnson and the smoothness of Jimmy Heath's tenor sax. Lewis tends to stay in the background, providing chords for the soloists, but his light touch is perfect. The nine tracks that follow are the first to be issued solely under Brown's name. Recorded August 28, 1953, the sextet included Lewis, Percy Heath, Gigi Gryce (alto sax, flute), Charlie Rouse (tenor sax), and Art Blakey (drums). There are several ballads, a setting which is perfect for Brown's gorgeous tone and articulate phrasings. Every note makes sense, and even in the midst of long melody lines, Brown does not swallow his sounds. Listen to how rhythmical his playing is—he seems to pay more attention to the drummer and bassist than to the pianist. The next three tracks are from a July 11 or 12, 1954, session arranged by Jack Montrose and featuring Stu Williamson (valve trombone), Zoot Sims (tenor sax), Bob Gordon (baritone sax), Russ Freeman (piano), Joe Mondragon (bass), and Shelly Manne (drums). "Daahoud" and "Joy Spring" are two of the more famous Brown compositions. Though they are performed nicely, the cuts seem a bit conservative in comparison to the Brown-Max Roach quintet versions. The following five tracks were recorded one month later (August 11 or December 1954) with the same personnel, save for Mondragon, who was replaced by Carson Smith. There is no discernible change in the style of the music, although the group seems to be playing a bit harder. The last four LP sides were culled from a live performance recorded on the evening of February 21, 1954 at Birdland in New York City. The group, led by Art Blakey, featured Brown, Lou Donaldson, Horace Silver (piano), and Curley Russell (bass). These 14 cuts are among the most exciting live tracks ever to be released. The musicians seem to be telepathic—quotes from other songs drop like rain throughout the solos. Blakey is in a jovial mood and the introductions by Pee Wee Marquette are priceless. This is the first time that the complete performance has been issued on one set (this was also issued in Japan on limited editions and three cuts were released on a Blue Note twofer). The notes on the sessions, by Ira Gitler, are informative without being pedantic. —*Bob Rusch*, Cadence

○ **Brownie Eyes** / Aug. 28, 1953 / Blue Note 267

The original Blue Note *Clifford Brown Memorial Album* has five of the six sides done at each of two summer 1953 dates; this collection retains four from Brown's first date as a leader and two from a Lou Donaldson session. An added song from each session appears here, new to 12-inch LP, which means

the label retired four Brown titles from general circulation. Worse, the inclusion of "Get Happy," from Blue Note 1505, implies that their two early J. J. Johnson collections are in imminent danger of disappearing (they're still currently available). At a time when Dizzy Gillespie and Miles Davis dominated the trumpet scene, Brown had the rare perception to use Fats Navarro's stylistic perfection. The acidic and delirious gaiety that flashed through Navarro's sculptures, however, are replaced by a different kind of joy (though parts of Brown's "Get Happy" solo are pure Navarro). Brown's more elaborate approach is all his own; he finds room in his lines for grace notes and delicacies quite inconceivable to his postwar brothers. His art could include the fire of Gillespie, the brilliance of Navarro, and sometimes even a lyricism almost as personal as Davis's. But Brown had a special sweetness of spirit, and now, 21 years (1975) after these tracks were recorded, we understand why they were so influential. —*John Litweiler*, Down Beat

Paris Collection—Vol. 1, The / Sep. 28-29, 1953 / Inner City 7001

Clifford Brown's beautiful, clean, singing trumpet tone is displayed to full advantage on *The Paris Collection*, which is only the first volume of more to follow in the Jazz Legacy series. The first side of the album is Gigi Gryce and his orchestra, a specially formed big band, and the second side is the Gryce-Brown sextet. The first two tracks are the showpieces: two takes of "Brown Skins," a six-minute Gryce composition showcasing the fertile imagination of young Brownie in an introductory slow tempo and a snap doubletime. Brownie's phrases are long, legato creations, which show an overwhelming amount of confidence and authority from the 22-year-old trumpeter. The solos on the two takes are completely different and they come floating over the 16-piece orchestra and out of the poor mix like the song of the sirens. The second side has Brown blowing away a lumpy rhythm section and Gryce's spirited, boppy alto. Brown throws in some teasing triple-tonguing on an "All the Things You Are," minus Dizzy Gillespie's famous introduction. "I Cover the Waterfront" is the best vehicle for Brownie's large, absorbent tone—his solo is simple and joyous. —*Lee Jeske*, Down Beat

Clifford Brown Big Band in Paris / i. Sep. 28, 1953-Oct. 12, 1953 / Prestige 359

This set completes a three-album series devoted to sides made by Clifford Brown in Paris during September and October 1953. . . . This LP has nine performances by units that ranged in size from eight to 17 pieces. Side A comprises two takes each of the remarkable "Brown Skins," based on "Cherokee," and the gorgeous Quincy Jones chart "Keeping Up with Jonesy." "Brown Skins," a Gigi Gryce arrangement, is a fitting showcase for Brown's quicksilver trumpet. Take one is slightly superior, but Brown freaks will be grateful to have both. "Jonesy" sports superb muted exchanges between Brown and Art Farmer. Take one also has an excellent tenor solo by Clifford Solomon. . . . The second take is a trifle faster and not so together, and the solos are generally inferior. This session, incidentally, marks the debut of Alan Dawson, who drums with power and precision, blending well with section mates Henri Renaud (piano) and Pierre Michelot (bass). "Bum's Rush," from an October 9 session, boasts a scintillating Brown solo and an uneasy statement by Gryce. But Gryce was much more at ease the following day, and on "Chez Moi," a very beboppy line by Jones, he is right on. So is Brown in this hard-driving octet. The excerpt called "No Start No End" is just Brown's solo (and a great one) from another take of "Chez Moi." Finally, there are two takes of "All Weird" which, according to Henri Renaud, is the only orchestration by Brownie that was ever recorded. The voicings reflect Tadd Dameron's influence. Dan Morgenstern points this, and a lot more, out in his instructive liner notes. Brown is once again master of the situation, swerving through the complex changes with deceptive ease and getting right to the heart of the matter. —*Mark Gardner*, Coda

Paris Collection—Vol. 2, The / Sep. 29, 1953-Oct. 8, 1953 / Inner City 7011

In the 1970s, a two-volume set was issued featuring material Clifford Brown had cut while in Paris during the '50s; some with a quartet, others with a sextet or big band. This second volume contains some valuable material, but this is best heard intact or on the three single albums that were originally issued. —*Ron Wynn*

○ **Clifford Brown Sextet in Paris, The** / Original Jazz Classics 358

This record, along with its companion *The Clifford Brown Quartet in Paris*, was initially recorded on the French Vogue label. To my knowledge, this is the first time that either is available in North America.... These sessions were recorded in 1952 when Clifford Brown and his friend Gigi Gryce were traveling through Europe as members of the Lionel Hampton band. American expatriate Jimmy Gourley is on guitar; Frenchman Henri Renaud is on piano; Pierre Michelot is on bass; and Jean-Louis Viale is on drums, rounding out the sextet. Altoist Gryce contributed five compositions to the album including such interesting pieces as "Minority," "Blue Concept," and "Salute to the Bandbox." I have always felt his talents are more in evidence through his compositions and arrangements than through his alto or flute playing. On this record, however, he gets in some respectable solo work. I prefer Gourley's Jimmy Raney-style guitar solos and especially Renaud's Al Haig-influenced piano solos to Gryce's often out-of-tune, tentative playing. Michelot and Viale provide intelligent, rhythmic support throughout the LP. It is Brown, though, who clearly steals the show. His clear-toned flowing trumpet solos are a joy to hear.... His fluent solo masterpieces sound as logical, inventive, and beautiful as they must have in 1953, if not more so.... Prestige wisely includes alternate takes of four of the eight tunes on this record. ... Ira Gitler's well-written liner notes analyze each track, and give relevant biographical and historical information. —*Peter Friedman*, Coda

○ **Clifford Brown in Paris** / Oct. 8+15, 1953 / Prestige 24020
Though he's not playing with equals, Clifford Brown's exquisite solos and general trumpet execution make his every note worth hearing on this 1953 date. Pierre Michelot on bass is the best among the European rhythm section. —*Ron Wynn*

Clifford Brown / Gigi Gryce Sextet / Oct. 8, 1953 / Blue Note 5048

○ **Clifford Brown Quartet** / Oct. 15, 1953 / Blue Note 5047
Simply brilliant playing by Brown and his comrades, notably Max Roach. The Brown/Roach unit had everything; they played as a cohesive group, yet everyone could also spin out majestic solos, and in pianist Richie Powell, Clifford's brother, there was a third fantastic soloist. This is essential, as are most Brown recordings. —*Ron Wynn*

○ **Clifford Brown & Max Roach** / i. 1954 / PolyGram 814645
This recording comes from the beginning of the Max Roach-Clifford Brown association. Actually, this is two sessions. The last four titles are from August 30, 1954 with Richie Powell (piano), George Morrow (bass), and Harold Land (tenor sax). The first four titles are from April 1954 and have Carl Perkins instead of Powell. The earlier set is a bit rough, both in audio and ensemble. Even with its raggedness, there are moments when the supreme excitement of Brownie's trumpet work bites through and when that happens, even if it is just for a chorus or two, it makes the recording impossible to ignore. —*Bob Rusch*, Cadence

More Study in Brown / Feb. 23-25, 1954 / EmArcy 814637
More Study in Brown opens with three tracks featuring the 1956 edition of the Clifford Brown/Max Roach Quintet, with Sonny Rollins on tenor, Richie Powell on piano, George Morrow on bass, and, of course, Clifford Brown and Max Roach on trumpet and drums, respectively. "I'll Remember April" is an alternate to the take originally released on *At Basin Street*, while "Junior's Arrival" and "Flossie Lou" were never released anywhere in the 36000 series. They were, however, released later, the former on *Clifford Brown/The Quintet, Vol. 2* and the latter on a Limelight compendium

(*The Immortal*) of Brown's work.... The remaining five tracks date from 1954-1955 and find Harold Land in place of Rollins on tenor. "Mildama" is an alternate to the take on the original *Brown & Roach Incorporated*. "Jordu," edited when it first appeared, was released later in its full length on the Limelight set referred to earlier.... "These Foolish Things" has the horns laying out, while George Morrow grabs the spotlight (as he seldom did.... "Land's End" is an alternate to the take originally issued on *Study in Brown*, and "The Blues Walk" is an alternate to the take on the original *Clifford Brown & Max Roach*, but is it the *same* alternate take as on the Max Roach *Standard Time* set? ... All in all, this LP serves up somewhat less than it seems to promise: there are only three items, all alternate takes, that had never surfaced before. A fourth is available only on an out-of-print album, but has no Clifford Brown on it. —*Alan Bargebuhr*, Cadence

Clifford Brown, The Quintet—Vol. 1 / Aug. 3, 1954 / Mercury 2403
Clifford Brown, The Quintet—Vol. 1 is the beginning of a complete reissue of all the quintet sides on which trumpeter Clifford Brown solos. There is little that needs to be said about the excellence of the music contained here. Brown, tenor saxophonist Harold Land, and drummer Max Roach were a superior bunch in 1954-1955. Pianist Richie Cole sounds better, to my ears, than on previous hearings. —*Jon Goldman*, Cadence

○ **Clifford Brown and Max Roach—Vol. 1** / Aug. 6, 1954 / EmArcy 36036

Jazz Immortal / Aug. 13, 1954 / Pacific Jazz 46850
Sextet. This album includes some takes and Brown material unavailable elsewhere. —*Ron Wynn*

★ **Brownie: The Complete EmArcy Recordings of** / i. 1954-1956 / PolyGram 838306
Comprehensive, multidisc set that contains Clifford Brown's output for the EmArcy label. This is wonderful material, particularly the sessions by the quartet Brown co-led with Max Roach. But he's also heard here with big bands, backing Dinah Washington, and on other occasions outside the quartet. Brown's tone, speed, command, and phrasing are immaculate and amazing; had he lived past his mid-twenties, he'd certainly have become an icon; he influenced hosts of players anyhow. —*Ron Wynn*

Study in Brown, A / Feb. 23-25, 1955 / EmArcy 814646
Study in Brown is almost at the level of *Clifford Brown & Max Roach at Basin Street*, but lacks Sonny Rollins's stimulating work. Harold Land was and is an excellent player who might have made a stronger impression if so much attention had not been focused on Brown. But the association certainly stimulated growth in his playing, particularly in his tone. "Take The 'A' Train" shows Land at his best. But this LP belongs almost entirely to Brown. His "Cherokee" stands as one of the most striking examples of his playing anywhere, but there is sustained excitement running consistently through this record. The group, as a whole, hits its stride by this time, too. "Jacqui and Gerkin for Perkin" contains interesting voicings. —*John McDonough*, Down Beat

○ **Live at the Bee Hive** / Nov. 7, 1955 / Columbia 35969
This long-buried session is a welcome addition to the skimpy legacy left by trumpeter Clifford Brown, and for several reasons. There is the obvious: that *any* new material featuring Brownie, who was unarguably the finest trumpet player of the hard-bopping '50s, has a place waiting for it on the record shelf. But this November 1955 session, recorded at the now-defunct Bee Hive in Chicago, also offered the first documentation of the Brown-Max Roach unit featuring young Sonny Rollins (Rollins was living in Chicago at this time and was just sitting in for the evening, along with the often overlooked Chicago legend Nicky Hill; he didn't permanently join the band until a couple of months later). This is raw, unfettered jazz, played by men interested in pushing their creativity a little further (and a lot longer) than commercial recording limitations would allow. Thus, our picture

of Brownie—the crisp, bold, impeccably controlled horn man who proved so impressive on studio recordings—is augmented by solos that pile chorus upon chorus, building up speed and intensity until they blast off in brilliant stabs of the avant-garde. One need only compare this LP's version of "Cherokee" with the famous studio version done for EmArcy to see the additional scope that *Live at the Bee Hive* offers. —*Neil Tesser*, Down Beat

○ **Jam Sessions—Vol. 1** / EmArcy 814640

Jam Sessions—Vol. 2 / EmArcy 814638

○ **Daahoud** / Mobile Fidelity 00826

Immortal Clifford Brown, The / Limelight 28601
Though he was working here in a less intense, relaxed "West Coast" sphere, Brown still made some striking music on this 1954 date. It shows he could turn to mellow material, but retain his fire and grit. Tenor saxophonist Zoot Sims and pianist Russ Freeman are among the distinguished guests. —*Ron Wynn*

DONALD BROWN

b. 1954, Memphis, TN
Piano / Hard bop
An eclectic pianist and composer whose style incorporates gospel, blues, and R&B elements as well as hard bop, Donald Brown made his initial impact on the jazz scene in the early '80s with Art Blakey's Jazz Messengers. His bright, often soulful solos and compositions have been heard on albums for Sunnyside, Jazz City, and Muse. Brown has battled arthritis, but continues to work and to play. He has produced sessions for Kenny Garrett, and has been an instructor at the University of Tennessee in Knoxville. Brown has several sessions available on CD. —*Ron Wynn*

○ **Early Bird** / Jan. 4-5, 1987 / Sunnyside 1025
Pianist Donald Brown and altoist Donald Harrison are graduates of the Art Blakey band. In a sense, drummer Freddie Waits and bassist Bob Hurst are second-generation Blakeyites, since both played with Wynton Marsalis. The Buhainian influence on these young musicians is unmistakable even if they frequently adopt a studied posture of laid-back modality. The album's strongest elements are the freewheeling, Eric Dolphyesque exuberance of Donald Harrison and the sturdy bass work of Bob Hurst, who takes an amazing, lightning fast solo on "Bassically Simple." I can also recommend Brown as a composer. During his tenure with Blakey, the drummer performed many of Brown's tunes, and it is not difficult to hear what Blakey liked in the pianist's compositions. At the keyboard, Brown has a few privileged moments here, especially on his solo feature, Tadd Dameron's "If You Could See Me Now." "On a Bad Case of the Blues," dedicated to Blakey, the pianist starts out playing high-rent blues à la Oscar Peterson before the band breaks into its most aggressively driving groove. . . . This is a well-produced, often enjoyable example of the facile, often dreamy neo-bop that has captured the imagination of so many young jazz musicians. —*Krin Gabbard*, Cadence

★ **Sources of Inspiration** / Aug. 11, 1989 / Muse 5385
Pianist Donald Brown wrote all the tunes on this session, which includes two ballads ("Do We Have to Say Goodbye?" and "Phineas"), two midtempo numbers ("Overtaken by a Moment" and "New York") and two impassioned tunes with political overtones ("Capetown Ambush" and "The Human Impersonator"). There is a nice swing to Brown's compositions, a bit of a mid '60s Blue Note feel about them. "Capetown Ambush" and "The Human Impersonator" remind me of Wayne Shorter's very productive period at Blue Note. Some of the tunes are not served well by ill-timed fade-outs, though. Eddie Henderson sounds comfortable, though Gary Bartz struggles a bit with his soprano on "Overtaken by a Moment" and seems bored on "Do We Have to Say Goodbye?" He makes a full recovery for the heated "Capetown Ambush" and "The Human Impersonator" with his alto dovetailing nicely with Henderson's angry trumpet. Donald Brown is an engaging and, at times, forceful pianist

in the mainstream, but with a bit of edge to his playing. He avoids the obvious (especially on "Afro Blue" and Steve Nelson's "One") and his *Sources of Inspiration* is well worth a listen. —*Tim Smith*, Cadence

People Music / Mar. 19-21, 1990 / Muse 5406
A fine 1990 date by a Memphis pianist who, unfortunately, has been plagued by arthritis in recent years and whose playing future is in doubt. He plays nice, bluesy chords and gospel-influenced phrases, but is also an effective straightahead and hard bop improviser. He's backed by a large group that features an interesting configuration with a trumpet/alto sax/vibes front line, and also uses vocals at times. Vincent Herring plays with fire on alto, while Steve Nelson adds a different dimension on vibes. —*Ron Wynn*

LAWRENCE BROWN

b. Aug. 3, 1907, Lawrence, KS, **d.** Sep. 5, 1988
Trombone / Swing, big band
A brilliant player and an all-time great as a section member, Lawrence Brown incorporated a full range of effects and gimmicks into his trombone playing without sacrificing tone, artistry, or technique. Brown leaned piano, violin, and tuba before he learned to play the trombone, but settled on the trombone because it could sound like a cello. He recorded with Paul Howard's Quality Serenaders in 1929 and with Les Hite's band (under Louis Armstrong's direction) in 1930 before he was recruited for Duke Ellington's orchestra in 1932 by Irving Mills. He left Ellington in 1951 to work in Johnny Hodges's orchestra, and stayed with Hodges until 1955. For a time, he was a freelance musician in New York and a studio player for CBS. He rejoined Ellington in 1960, and stayed with him for another decade before retiring from music in 1970. After working for the government, Brown retired completely and moved to California in 1974. —*Ron Wynn*

Slide Trombone Featuring Lawrence Brown / Jan. 26, 1955+Sep. 14, 1955 / Clef 682

★ **Inspired Abandon** / Mar. 8, 1965 / Impulse 89

MARION BROWN (Marion Brown (Jr.))

b. Sep. 8, 1935, Atlanta, GA
Alto saxophone, flute / Early free, modern creative
Alto saxophonist Marion Brown has a reputation as a music radical, and has participated in some fiery, no-holds-barred free sessions. But his pungent lines and intense, searing solos are balanced by a tender lyricism on ballads and blues, and an expressive, almost introspective tone. Brown played various horns in high school and army bands. One of his early teachers was Wayman Carver, and he played with Johnny Hodges in the late '50s in Atlanta. Brown attended Clark College in the '60s. He worked with the Jazz Composers Orchestra Association in 1964, and led his own group in 1965. Brown was featured on a USIA film with Bill Dixon. He later moved to New York and recorded with Dixon, Archie Shepp, and John Coltrane, and appeared on the seminal *Ascension* album. He recorded on the ESP label in the mid '60s. Brown worked with Sun Ra, formed his first band in 1967, and recorded with Graechan Moncur III, Kenny Burrell, and others on Impulse in the late '60s. He toured and recorded in Europe from 1968 to 1970, playing with Steve McCall, Ambrose Jackson, and, frequently, with Gunter Hampel. He returned to America in 1970, where he taught African and African-American music at Bowdoin and toured with Leo Smith. He recorded often in the '70s for ECM, Impulse, and Sweet Earth. He made a solo alto album, and did several combo dates with players such as Kenny Barron, Cecil McBee, Philly Jones, Anthony Braxton, Andrew Cyrille, Chick Corea, and even made a duet album with Elliott Schwartz. Brown studied ethnomusicology at Wesleyan in the mid 70s, and worked often with Hampel. He didn't issue as many recordings in the '80s and '90s, but did a quartet date in 1980 on Sweet Earth. Brown had a book of essays and drawings published in Germany in 1984. There

are only a few Brown dates listed as available on CD, at least from conventional sources. —*Ron Wynn*

Juba-Lee / Nov. 1966 / Fontana 881012

○ **Marion Brown Quartet** / Dec. 1, 1966 / ESP 1022

★ **Three for Shepp** / Dec. 1, 1966 / Impulse 9139

 Afternoon of a Georgia Faun / Aug. 10, 1970 / ECM 1004

Duets / Feb. 18, 1973 / Freedom 1904
Sure to be scorned by some as exercises in anarchy and chaos, the works here are anything but those types of exercises. They are structured, ornate pieces of great beauty, and like all classic art, can be appreciated on many levels, from the simple to the complex. Brown, trumpeter Leo Smith, and keyboardist Elliott Schwartz composed much of the sax-trumpet collaborations on these four sides, formulating a complicated web of interrelationships with Brown's horn and with a variety of percussive artifacts that both play. Schwartz, a radical classical pianist trained in the Cage-Webern school, is often heard overlaying space-age ARP bleats over Brown's alto scowl or percussive accompaniment. —*Arnold Shaw*, Down Beat

☆ **Geechee Recollections** / Jun. 4-5, 1973 / Impulse 9252
Geechee Recollections is a somewhat conscious evocation of the spirit of African music. . . . Marion Brown stretches out hauntingly on both alto and soprano sax on parts of the "suite" that comprise the second side ("Introduction—Tokalokaloka—Ending"), and Leo Smith essays an occasional statement on trumpet, but it is those ferocious drummers, and, to almost as great an extent, James Jefferson's firm and sensitive bass work behind them, that captures my attention. Marion Brown has created an album that is evocative and challenging. Taken on its own terms, *Geechee Recollections* is a hell of a record. —*Peter Keepnews*, Down Beat

Sweet Earth Flying / May 6-7, 1974 / Impulse 9275
The solo piano pieces on this album frame a superior alto solo (despite the sound). Note the intrigue of electric piano and organ here, and a recitation, which the alto enters behind then leads. *Sweet Earth* is broken into four tracks, but "Eleven," the superior performance, is a continuous work. Marion Brown's soprano, at least here, is as fully developed as his alto. The unaccompanied opening theme and improvisation are marvelous; his spacing, as the others enter, is nicely done, and the later curved notes are so lovely that you can only wonder what they sounded like in the studio. A brief keyboard duet follows, then more outstanding soprano leads to a break in time and light, free notes over metrically varied percussion, all very, very well played. The others (Paul Bley and Muhal Richard Abrams on piano, electric piano, and organ, respectively; bassist James Jefferson; drummer Steve McCall; and Bill Hasson on percussion and narration) provide imaginative support. —*John Litweiler*, Down Beat

○ **Vista** / Feb. 18-19, 1975 / Impulse 9304
There is nothing at all wrong with this album. It is relaxing, skillfully played, pretty, and features a vocal on Stevie Wonder's "Visions." The whole first side is in a slow, dreamy vein. The vocal on "Visions" is the kind of thing you'd hear on a Quincy Jones album, but harks back to Earl Coleman. The solos don't stand out, but blend into the rhythm section. Most of the songs take a great deal of time to state the melody and a short space to improvise off of it. —*Ira Steingroot*, Down Beat

La Placita / **Live in Willisau** / Mar. 26, 1977 / Timeless 314

Reed 'n Vibes / i. Jan. 1978 / I.A.I. (Improvising Artists, Inc.) 123855
This 1978 session reunited vibist and flutist Gunter Hampel with alto saxophonist, flutist, and percussionist Marion Brown, who previously recorded with him in Europe in the late '60s. The two men produce lines of notes which, because of their sensitivity, cause concepts like "tonality," "polytonality," "atonality" to become meaningless and give way to the overall term of "music." Hampel creates rich full backdrops

for his own ideas (his solo "And Then They Embraced") and for those of Brown. He literally ebbs and flows on the vibes unlike any other practitioner of that instrument. His flute work showcased during the first section of "Flute Song" is also strong. Brown's alto playing, featured on his "Solo" and throughout the duets, is ever growing. "Solo" is a call-to-arms-like piece that Brown uses as a vehicle for his explorations through the various ranges of the horn, always slying, bending, and twisting, constantly stimulating. —*Milo Fine*, Cadence

Recollections: Ballads and Blues for Saxophone / i. 1985 / Creative Works 1001

RAY BROWN (Raymond Matthews Brown)

b. Oct. 13, 1926, Pittsburgh, PA
Bass / Swing, big band, bop
A steady, consistently excellent technician, Ray Brown's precise, fluid sound has backed numerous vocalists, and has contributed to trios, duos, quartets, quintets, and big bands since the '40s. Though he is not an innovative figure, Brown's tone, ability to anticipate and complement soloists, and overall skills have kept him busy as a session player and bandleader. Brown is generally regarded as the most swinging bassist to hire for a rhythm section.

He moved to New York from Pittsburgh in 1945, and was immediately involved in the emerging bebop revolution. He recorded with Charlie Parker, Dizzy Gillespie, and Bud Powell while playing in Gillespie's big band in 1946 and 1947. He became Ella Fitzgerald's music director (as well as her husband) in the late '40s, and worked with her until 1952. Brown played with an early edition of what became the Modern Jazz Quartet, recording with the Milt Jackson Quartet in 1951. He subsequently joined Oscar Peterson's trio, which ranked among jazz's most popular combos of the '50s and '60s. He also toured with the Jazz at the Philharmonic revue, and was voted top bassist consistently in critics' polls during the decade. Brown proved the ideal partner for Peterson's swirling, intricate solos. The Peterson/Brown/Herb Ellis lineup stayed intact until 1957, and Brown remained with Peterson until 1966. There were also albums for Verve, with Kenny Burrell, Hank Jones, Milt Jackson, big bands, and even with gospel singer Marion Williams.

He started playing cello, and became as skilled on it as he was on the bass. In 1960, Brown created a stir when he had a hybrid instrument built for him that combined features of the cello and the bass. The intriguing, unusually pitched sound attracted plenty of interest from bassists and cellists. Eventually, Ron Carter had a piccolo bass designed along the same lines.

Brown relocated to the West Coast after leaving Peterson, and quickly became extremely busy with studio work, recording, and touring. He continued recording with Jackson on Impulse, then became affiliated with Pablo and Concord in the '70s. There were two duet albums with pianist Jimmie Rowles, nine albums as part of the L.A. Four, and a magnificent recording with Duke Ellington. *This One's for Blanton* lovingly recreated the atmosphere and mood of the great bassist's 1939 and 1940 performances with Ellington. Brown was almost house bassist at Concord and Pablo in the '70s, and continued recording at Concord in the '80s. There were also sessions for Jeton, Capri, and Eastwind with guitarist Laurindo Almeida, pianist Monty Alexander, saxophonists Sam Most and Johnny Griffin, and others.

In the late '80s, Brown formed a trio with pianist Gene Harris and drummer Mickey Roker and toured extensively. Brown has been active in concert promotion and artist management. He helped revive Ernestine Anderson's career in the mid '70s, and assisted her in landing a deal with Concord Records. He managed Quincy Jones, and for years produced concerts at the Hollywood Bowl. He has published several bass instruction books. Ray Brown remains an active, vital jazz contributor. —*Ron Wynn and Barry Pearson*

New Sounds in Modern Music / Sep. 25, 1946 / Savoy 9012

Bass Hit! / Nov. 21+23, 1956 / Verve 8022

Jazz Cello / Aug. 31, 1960+Sep. 1, 1960 / Verve 8390

Featuring Cannonball Adderley / Jan. 23, 1962 / Verve

○ **Ray Brown with Milt Jackson** / Jan. 4-5, 1965 / Verve 8615

Brown's Bag / Dec. 1975 / Concord Jazz 4019
Good, occasionally exciting combo set with some pithy trumpet solos by Blue Mitchell, good tenor sax from Kamauca, and generally excellent playing by all involved, even fusion ace Dave Grusin on piano. —*Ron Wynn*

★ **As Good As It Gets** / Dec. 22, 1977 / Concord Jazz 66
In this well-balanced pairing with bassist Ray Brown, pianist Jimmy Rowles predictably comes up with the unexpected: to wit, a James P. Johnson-like interpretation of "Like Someone in Love," in which this seldom-played '40s tune is transformed into a timeless classic. . . . Rowles's artistry may be unfamiliar to many, but followers of both Teddy Wilson and Thelonious Monk will find much to admire in this musician's talents. —*Jack Sohmer*, Cadence

○ **Something for Lester** / Jun. 22-24, 1979 / Contemporary 412
The splendid *Something for Lester* is only bassist Ray Brown's second album as a leader (*Brown's Bag* for Concord Jazz is the first); on all the others he has been a sideman or a coleader. Pianist Cedar Walton and drummer Elvin Jones are apropos partners-in-sound for the superlative bassist, having worked together in J.J. Johnson's hot band of the late '50s alongside Freddie Hubbard. Their intuitive understanding of each other's playing, combined with Brown's obvious talents, let the music flow unencumbered. —*Zan Stewart*, Down Beat

Big Three, The / i. 1982 / Pablo 2310757

Giants, The / i. 1982 / Pablo 2310796

★ **This One's for Blanton** / i. 1982 / Pablo 2310721
Bassist Jimmy Blanton died at the premature age of 21 after serving with the Duke Ellington band in the early '40s. This album is dedicated to him. Ellington (piano) and Ray Brown (bass) excel on the original Blanton showcase tune "Pitter Panther Patter," where both exhibit complete control of their instruments. In addition, the Ma Rainey tune, "See See Rider," is given a thorough airing. The sleeper is side two, "Fragmented Suite for Piano and Bass" in four movements. This is highly recommended; this disc should be in every school music library as a ready reference work for aspiring young jazz pianists and bassists. It was superbly recorded with clear surfaces—an album not to be missed. —*Bill Gallagher*, Cadence

Ray Brown Three / Feb. 1982 / Concord Jazz 213
Brown took a fresh approach for this 1982 date, retaining the trio format but substituting flute for drums and using Monty Alexander instead of regular pianist Gene Harris. The results are intriguing. Most provides colors and sounds that haven't been on a Brown date since, while Alexander adds some Caribbean flavor and a bit more adventurous sound. —*Ron Wynn*

Soular Energy / Aug. 1984 / Concord Jazz 4268

Red Hot Ray Brown Trio / Nov. 1985-Dec. 1985 / Concord Jazz 4315

☆ **Live at the Loa—Summer Wind** / Jul. 1988 / Concord Jazz 426
Brown's trio with Gene Harris (k) and Jeff Hamilton (d). Perhaps Brown's very best. —*Michael G. Nastos*

Moore Makes 4 / May 22, 1990 / Concord Jazz 4477
Prime release in which Brown departs from his usual trio format and adds tenor saxophonist Ralph Moore. Though it seems like a snap decision, Moore put some edge and juice in the session and even relaxed stars Brown, pianist Gene Harris, and drummer Jeff Hamilton seemed to appreciate the lift. —*Ron Wynn*

○ **Super Bass** / i. Dec. 10, 1990 / Capri 74018

Three Dimensional / Aug. 4, 1991 / Concord Jazz 4520
Excellent recent trio date with Brown's formidable bass interaction with drummer Jeff Hamilton and pianist Gene

Harris. Harris plays with his usual bluesy punch and delicate touch, while Hamilton fits like a glove with Brown. This is heady, solidly professional material. —*Ron Wynn*

DAVE BRUBECK (David Warren Brubeck)

b. Dec. 6, 1920, Concord, CA
Piano, bandleader / Cool

Pianist and composer Dave Brubeck introduced and popularized many unusual and unorthodox things in jazz, notably odd time signatures like 5/4 and 9/8. His ability to integrate irregular meters and jazz forms, his adoption of classical devices, and his sometimes decidedly nonswinging style both distinguish Brubeck's music and lead some people to question its jazz pedigree.

Brubeck began studying classical music as a child, and was trained by his mother, a pianist. He performed professionally with local jazz groups as a teen. Brubeck led a 12-piece band while a music major at the College of the Pacific. He also studied classical composition at Mills College with Darius Milhaud. Brubeck was sent to Europe to lead a service band during World War II, then resumed his studies with Milhaud in 1946. A group he formed with other students, the Jazz Workshop Ensemble, eventually recorded in 1948 as the Dave Brubeck octet. Brubeck also organized a trio with Cal Tjader and Norman Bates that recorded in 1949. In 1951, he rounded the group into a quartet by adding Paul Desmond. But the classic Brubeck quartet didn't take shape until much later in the decade; the addition of Joe Morello in 1956 and Gene Wright in 1958 formed the band that stayed together until 1967. Regardless of their personnel, Brubeck's groups were enormously popular in the '50s, and appeared at many colleges and college campuses (they even recorded at Oberlin in 1953). Brubeck made the cover of *Time* in 1954, and was wooed from Fantasy to Columbia. His first Columbia album, *Jazz Goes to College*, made the Top 10. His Columbia albums were huge sellers, and the classic single, "Take Five," reached 25 on the pop charts. *Time Out*, the 1960 album that featured the single, had a different time signature for each tune and proved to be Brubeck's biggest-selling album.

Brubeck recorded with Armstrong, Jimmy Rushing, and Carmen McRae in the early '60s, and, during his career, has made more than 100 albums with Fantasy, Columbia, Atlantic, Horizon, and Concord, among others. Brubeck dominated critics' polls during the '50s and '60s, and he began to write and record large-scale compositions in the '60s. These included two ballets, a musical, an oratorio, four cantatas, a mass, and works for orchestra and jazz groups, plus several solo pieces.

Brubeck disbanded the quartet in the late '60s to concentrate on composition. His sons Darius (David), Chris, and Danny started joining his groups in the '70s. The original quartet reunited in 1976 to celebrate its 25th anniversary. He continued recording heavily through the '80s, and made a historic tour of the Soviet Union. Numerous Brubeck releases are available, from his earliest material to more recent dates. Columbia issued a four-disc boxed set, *Time Signatures—A Career Retrospective*, in 1992. —*Ron Wynn*

○ **Dave Brubeck Trio, The** / Sep. 1949-Nov. 1950 / Fantasy 24726
Early, seminal music by the pianist who made jazz history in the '50s. This trio features Cal Tjader in his pre-Latin impresario days playing either drums or percussion, while Ron Crotty is the bassist. There are glimmers of what Brubeck would later make his signature sound: classical devices interspersed with a modified stride technique, and odd time signatures. —*Ron Wynn*

24 Classic Original Recordings / i. 1949-1950 / Fantasy 24726
Good set of vintage Brubeck recordings arranged and sequenced specifically for newcomers to his music. They're Brubeck's 1949 and 1950 Fantasy cuts, and they're wonderful. Some include Cal Tjader. This is an excellent set for

those who only want a little Brubeck and are seeking a starting point. —*Ron Wynn*

○ **Cal Tjader with the Dave Brubeck Trio—Vol. 1** / i. 1949-1950 / Fantasy 3331

★ **Greatest Hits from the Fantasy Years (1949-1954)** / 1949-1954 / Fantasy 4528

A nice overview of his material in the years before he crossed over and became a celebrity. —*Ron Wynn*

☆ **Dave Brubeck and Paul Desmond** / Sep. 1952-Feb. 1953 / Fantasy 24727

This is a set of various live recordings of the Brubeck quartet on the eve of national prominence when *Time* magazine covered the ridiculous controversy concerning "cool" jazz and East Coast blues. The listener can trace the genesis of Brubeck's music as he molded "new" fragments in search of the trademark: Paul Desmond's inexplicable, ethereal, and cutting reed-thin alto voice and Brubeck's charging, spirited, and shifting jazz pianism. The original producers even included a rehearsal tape of "Trolley Song" for insight. The album is appealing on two levels: the first is the exceptional music and the second is that many of these seminal cuts had been out of print since 1965. This is highly recommended. —*Christopher Kuhl*, Cadence

○ **Jazz at Storyville** / Oct. 1952-Feb. 1953 / Fantasy 8

○ **Brubeck & Desmond at Wilshire-Ebell** / Jun. 20, 1953 / Fantasy 3249

○ **Featuring Paul Desmond in Concert** / i. Jun. 1953 / Fantasy 013

○ **Jazz at the Blackhawk** / Sep. 1953 / Fantasy 210

★ **Jazz at the College of the Pacific** / Dec. 14, 1953 / Fantasy 047

This is one of two live concerts featuring the Dave Brubeck quartet (alto saxophonist Paul Desmond, bassist Ron Crotty, drummers Lloyd Davis or Joe Dodge) on college campuses in 1953. Pianist Brubeck's quartet was unique and was soon to become the rage with White America. The hard baroque swing of Brubeck and the aloof, yet warm, pretty playing of Desmond, combined with a projected intellectualism, caught on with the WASP powers to be. It was equally hip (and has remained so) for critics to say Brubeck didn't swing and to suggest Desmond was wasting his talents. . . . Nonsense. This group did swing, had emotional depth, and had great humor. The cover on this date is slightly changed and poorly reproduced (the red vinyl was not black), but the music remains wonderful. —*Bob Rusch*, Cadence

○ **Stardust** / i. 1954 / Fantasy 24728

○ **Old Sounds from San Francisco** / i. 1954 / Fantasy 16

★ **Jazz Goes to College** / Mar. 1954 / Columbia 45149

One of the great Dave Brubeck recordings (and there are now—in 1989—over 75 to choose from), *Jazz Goes to College* finds the pianist's three-year-old quartet in its early prime. Bassist Bob Bates and drummer Joe Dodge offer quiet and steady support throughout; a perfect backing for the consistently creative and highly original playing of Brubeck and altoist Paul Desmond. On the blues "Balcony Rock," Desmond's nine choruses are filled with nonstop melodic variations as one idea is repeated in different ways until it evolves into a different, but equally rewarding, theme; it all sounds so effortless. Both Desmond and Dodge had developed their own styles by the time of these March 1954 concerts, and would be criticized repeatedly for not sounding like clones of Charlie Parker and Bud Powell. The piano solos have held up very well throughout the years ("Take the 'A' Train" has a gem) and offer more variety in moods than the typical bop solo of the time. *Jazz Goes to College* ranks in the top five among Dave Brubeck's recordings. —*Scott Yanow*, Cadence

Jazz: Red, Hot and Cool / Aug. 8, 1954 / Sony Special Products 8645

These recordings are culled from a 1954 session at the Basin Street Club with Paul Desmond, Bob Bates on bass, and Joe Dodge on drums. They're done in a bit more standard jazz

fashion than usual, though Brubeck does inject some stately passages into his work. This is more West Coast than anything else, and Dodge and Bates don't team as well as Dodge did with longtime rhythm section partner Eugene Wright. —*Ron Wynn*

○ **Brubeck Plays Brubeck** / Mar. 12, 1956-Apr. 19, 1956 / Columbia 878

○ **Dave Brubeck Quartet in Europe, The** / Mar. 5, 1958 / Columbia 1168

★ **Time Out** / Jun. 25, 1959-Aug. 18, 1959 / Columbia 40585

Time Out helped launch a series of Time records, which, for awhile, became a minor fad in jazz, and had a number of musicians, mainly drummers, demonstrating how adroitly they could play in various exotic, or at least nonstandard, time signatures. . . . Not surprisingly, the record that ignited the fad, *Time Out*, was one of the most successful. Its program features six solid Dave Brubeck originals and the classic Paul Desmond original, "Take Five." This 1959 recording has been issued, reissued, and repackaged so often that it has never been out of catalog. Even so, this digital remaster does greatly enhance the sound. . . . If you love this Brubeck-Desmond-Morello and Wright issue, you'll appreciate hearing this cleaner version. —*Bob Rusch*, Cadence

○ **All Night Long** / i. 1960 / Epic 17032

○ **Brubeck and Rushing** / Aug. 4, 1960 / Columbia 8353

Near-Myth with Bill Smith / Mar. 20, 1961 / Fantasy 236

When clarinetist Bill Smith replaced Paul Desmond in the quartet there wasn't a warm response from loyalists. While Smith became a capable player in time and added some intriguing possibilities in terms of his playing, he was quite different in conception and sound from Desmond. These differences are very apparent on this 1961 release. This has been reissued on CD. —*Ron Wynn*

○ **Take Five** / Sep. 6, 1961 / Sony Special Products 9116

○ **Brubeck in Amsterdam** / Dec. 3, 1962 / Columbia 9897

This is an odd little album; "little" because it is almost an antithesis of pianist Dave Brubeck's then hyper-ambitious LPs, and it fills a crevice in Brubeckia whose existence had not occurred to me. Of the eight tracks, six are tunes from *The Real Ambassadors*, Brubeck's "musical" that was committed to wax at various times throughout 1961 (this concert was recorded December 3, 1962). The Ambassadors are Louis Armstrong, Carmen McRae, and the vocal trio of Lambert, Hendricks, and Ross, and it is interesting, if scarcely thrilling, to hear their songs performed as instrumentals. . . . "Since Love Had Its Way," a simple song in conventional 16/16-bar form (it somehow sounds like the "Tonight Show"—it has that "opener" quality) is four choruses of freewheeling Paul Desmond (alto), framed by initial and closing choruses from Brubeck (in "TRA," it was a vehicle for Armstrong and the All-Stars). "King for a Day," originally performed by Armstrong and Trummy Young, becomes a three-minute bass solo here, and Armstrong's "They Say I Look Like God" is a restrained, low-key essay without Desmond. Both "Cultural Exchange" (nearly identical in construction to that delightful barroom refrain, "Ragged But Right") and "The Real Ambassadors" were given to Armstrong and LH&R previously; here, the entire quartet plays them, as it does "Good Reviews," which had been the property of McRae, Armstrong, and the All-Stars. The remaining two tracks are "Dizzy Ditty," a short (edited?) drum feature for Joe Morello, without Desmond; and "Brandenburg Gate," which appeared before on *The Impressions of Eurasia* LP. That the latter album had already received wide circulation and acceptance is revealed by the audience's applause after Brubeck's first few notes. Brubeck collectors will have to have this, naturally. To those interested primarily in the time-signature business, you'll find absolutely none of that here. Morello's little solo tells a good story, and his accompaniment is customarily faultless; Desmond plays like an angel; and Wright, the unsung hero, is heroic. Brubeck is Brubeck. —*Wayne Jones*, Coda

○ **At Carnegie Hall** / Feb. 22, 1963 / Columbia 826

The quartet does its usual mix of standards and originals in a live setting before faithful admirers. There are few surprises. Brubeck goes through his alternately subdued, then lively piano work, while Desmond has his normal swoops and shimmering slow ballads, and the Wright/Morello team works off them impressively. —*Ron Wynn*

☆ **Jazz Impressions of New York** / Jun. 16, 1964-Aug. 21, 1964 / Columbia 46189

Jazz Impressions of New York is not what people would expect from its title—a collection of tunes having something to do with New York. In 1964, Dave Brubeck wrote the music for a now-forgotten TV series called "Mr. Broadway." The 11 themes on this disc (recorded June 16, 18, 24, and 25, and July 15, August 11, 19, and 21, 1964) are not merely cues or incidental music, but full-length performances by Brubeck's quartet (Brubeck, piano; Paul Desmond, alto sax; Eugene Wright, bass; Joe Morello, drums) from which the show's sound track was drawn. Although none of these individual pieces caught on, the quality is generally high with cross rhythms, waltz time, and a variety of options explored. The Jubilant "Something to Sing About," a melancholy "Autumn in Washington Square," and the show's theme song are most memorable. The music stands on its own 25 years later (1991) with Paul Desmond and Brubeck in top form. —*Scott Yanow*, Cadence

○ **Time In** / Jun. 14-15, 1966 / Columbia 2512

○ **Bravo! Brubeck!** / i. Dec. 1967 / Columbia 2695

○ **Compadres** / Apr. 1968 / Columbia 9704

Blues Roots / Oct. 4, 1968 / Columbia 9749
On the several blues in this collection, pianist Dave Brubeck has not a spark of feeling for the form. He can run together a string of superficially bluesy phrases, but there is no emotion in it, no sorrow, no anger, no joy. Only emptiness. The two good ones—"Limehouse Blues" and "Things Ain't What They Used To Be"—are put through the Brubeck mangle and emerge damaged beyond repair with Gerry Mulligan (bar sax) croaking painfully and the pianist attempting to beat the keyboard into submission. The basslines to all these *Blues Roots*, which are shallowness itself, are supplied by Jack Six. Strongly recommended to every Brubeck and Mulligan fan. —*Mark Gardner*, Coda

Last Set at Newport / Jul. 3, 1971 / Atlantic 1607
A fine collaboration with Gerry Mulligan, which seems to put some life into Brubeck. His playing has some force and rhythmic intensity, while Mulligan plays with a grainy bounce and vibrant tone. Jack Six on bass and Alan Dawson on drums weren't usual Brubeck comrades, so they approached his music with no set ways to play it, and made Brubeck take some chances during his performances. This set has been reissued on CD. —*Ron Wynn*

We're All Together Again (for the First Time) / Oct. 28, 1972-Nov. 4, 1972 / Atlantic 1641
Fine collaboration between Brubeck and Gerry Mulligan, their second early '70s get-together. It proves as fruitful as the first, with Mulligan's throaty, booming baritone finding a comfortable middle ground with Brubeck's elegant phrases and often unpredictable solos. —*Ron Wynn*

○ **Brubeck on Campus** / i. Apr. 1973 / Columbia 31298

☆ **All the Things We Are** / Jul. 17, 1973 / Atlantic 1684
Has cuts with Braxton (sax), Lee Konitz (sax), and others. Very different from regular Brubeck. —*Ron Wynn*

Brubeck & Desmond: Duets (1975) / Jun. 1975-Oct. 1975 / A&M 3290
Sometimes, the most logical combinations take a long time to happen. Pianist Dave Brubeck and alto saxophonist Paul Desmond, through all their years of collaboration, had never recorded as a duo until this outing. The results are most pleasing. No new unexplored vistas are discovered by either. Yet there is, and always will be, a place for prettiness, however verbatim. The only fault of the album is that, despite its melodic beauty, it comes off, at times, like a mood piece, with gorgeous sax solos following quiet piano musings on

both sides. "Balcony Rock" and "Summer Song" are the only uptempo breaks. But even the shortcoming of sporadic monotony can be defended with the debatable argument that Brubeck, lacking the self-contained propulsive force of other pianists, was forced to "play quiet" almost by necessity. In addition, the total absence of percussion strikes another prohibitive blow against any thoughts of a swinging jam session. —*Arnold Shaw*, Down Beat

Tritonis / Mar. 1980 / Concord Jazz 129
One of Brubeck's most intriguing contemporary releases, with Jerry Bergonzi (ts). —*Michael G. Nastos*

Paper Moon / Sep. 1981 / Concord Jazz 4178
Interesting early '80s work, with Brubeck updating and changing sound and direction, moving towards accommodation with fusion and light rock. His own playing kept its jazz edge and foundation, but his group now included saxophonist Jerry Bergonzi, Brubeck's son Chris on electric bass and trombone, and drummer Randy Jones. The album also includes a new version of "St. Louis Blues." —*Ron Wynn*

Blue Rondo / Nov. 1986 / Concord Jazz 4317

Live at Montreux / i. 1987 / Tomato 269613
Dave Brubeck played more and more with his offspring during the '70s, and this set was a complete family affair, with Darius on keyboards and synthesizer, Chris on electric bass and trombone, and Danny on percussion. Unfortunately, none of the three sons is as gifted as his father, and Brubeck proves this even more by finding ways of fitting into a sound that's almost by definition not designed for his style. —*Ron Wynn*

Moscow Nights / Mar. 1987 / Concord Jazz 4353

Once When I Was Young / i. 1992 / Music Masters 65083
The early '60s Brubeck sound, when Smith initially replaced Brubeck, is revisited on this recent set. Smith sounds as prickly and unorthodox as ever, while bassist Jack Six and drummer Randy Jones fill their roles efficiently. Brubeck, still a crafty pianist, doesn't try as many usual things with time signatures and rhythms anymore, but manages to make his solos count more often than not. —*Ron Wynn*

★ **Time Signatures: A Career Retrospective** / i. Nov. 17, 1992 / Columbia 52945
Time Signatures samples 46 Dave Brubeck albums and includes work from his years at Fantasy, Atlantic, Concord, and Music Masters; it is not limited to his Columbia catalog. This ambitious package invites consideration of Brubeck's place in jazz cosmology. The art of Brubeck's career started with his Fantasy sessions. These selections emphasize Brubeck's 1949 trio with Cal Tjader on drums, arguably giving short shrift to Brubeck's octet and early quartet work. Brubeck's partnership with Paul Desmond triggered a period of rapid development, including compositions like "The Duke," and "In Your Own Sweet Way." With the arrival of the underrated rhythm section of drummer Joe Morello and bassist Eugene Wright, the quartet reaches a plateau, particularly from 1958 to 1960. Morello and Wright navigate the unconventional, difficult time signatures ("Blue Rondo à La Turk" in 9/8, "World's Fair" in 13/4), while Brubeck adds his trademark block chords and notorious, percussive accompaniment. The "classic" quartet lasted nine years, and its work occupies 2-1/2 discs. This is the prize in the box, a consistent body of work that holds up over time. Post-Desmond selections seem spotty, with little attention given to Brubeck's '70s and '80s work. Desmond and Brubeck were such ideal foils that the pianist's later collaborations with Gerry Mulligan and Jerry Bergonzi could never be as satisfying. Brubeck's controversial inspiration was a conception of jazz that focused on improvisation, but allowed room for nontraditional devices and influences, including classical studies and impressions of world music. Brubeck's conception was brainy, but not highbrow; complex, but not intimidating; and always melodic. It enticed millions who might otherwise have closed their minds to jazz. —*Jon Andrews*, Down Beat

RAY BRYANT (Raphael Bryant)

b. Dec. 24, 1931, Philadelphia, PA

Piano / Bop, hard bop, blues & jazz, soul-jazz

One of the finest pianists to emerge in the post-World War II period, Ray Bryant has mastered many styles and successfully merges them during performances and on recordings. He often blends blues, stride, and boogie-woogie figures in his solos, and displays extensive harmonic knowledge, melodic invention, and rhythmic verve. He was playing jazz at age 14, and began his career working with Tiny Grimes in the late '40s. Bryant was house pianist at the Blue Note in the early '50s, where he played with Charlie Parker, Miles Davis, Lester Young, Sonny Rollins, and others. Bryant was a prolific contributor to many combo dates in the '50s. He also toured with Carmen McRae and Jo Jones and performed and recorded with Coleman Hawkins at the 1957 Newport Jazz Festival. Bryant settled in New York in 1959, played with Rollins again, and also played with Charlie Shavers and Curtis Fuller. He worked with his own trio in the '60s and also did solo dates. Bryant traveled extensively in the '70s, and made many European appearances. He also performed and recorded with Zoot Sims and Benny Carter. Many of his solo and trio dates were recorded for Epic, Prestige, New Jazz, and Signature. Bryant's '60s sessions for Columbia, Sue, and Cadet are varied, and have some commercial outings mixed with straight jazz sessions, though most are fine. "Madison Time," a dance number that features a Baltimore disc jockey's calls over a nice arrangement, was an R&B and pop hit that featured Al Grey, Sweets Edison, and Buddy Tate. His Atlantic '70s releases include a fine solo album, *At Montreux*, but also include some rather dismal attempts at crossover. Bryant's return to Cadet proved disappointing, too, but a mid '70s Black & Blue (France) date, *Hot Turkey,* is recommended, along with his late '80s and '90s EmArcy sessions. Bryant has many dates available on CD. —*Ron Wynn and Bob Porter*

Meet Betty Carter and Ray Bryant / Jul. 13, 1955 / Epic 3202

Me and the Blues / Apr. 5, 1957+Dec. 19, 1958 / Prestige 24038

Alone with the Blues / Dec. 19, 1958 / New Jazz 249

A brilliant, frequently amazing session in which Ray Bryant demonstrates his command of the piano, his facility with the blues, and his superb solo technique. His version of "Lover Man" offers marvelous left-hand chords, while "Blues No. 3" is also a gem. —*Ron Wynn*

Ray Bryant Plays / Oct. 29, 1959-Nov. 6, 1959 / Signature 6008

○ **Con Alma** / Nov. 25, 1960-Jan. 26, 1961 / Columbia 44058

This is a definitive early Ray Bryant album, and includes "Cubano Chant." —*Michael G. Nastos*

Lonesome Traveler / Sep. 1+8, 1966 / Cadet 778

Ray Bryant Touch, The / May 19-20, 1967 / Cadet 793

Sound Ray / Jun. 26+27, 1969 / Cadet 830

○ **Alone at Montreux** / Jul. 1972 / Atlantic 1626

Ray Bryant is a true two-fisted pianist, seemingly ambidextrous, tripping knowledgeably across the keys. Unlike Keith Jarrett's slightly melancholy stance, Bryant is a solo humorist who sounds as though he goes beyond being wrapped up inside himself as are so many solo artists. Among several prior selections, "Jungle Town" was the standout. Bryant's roots showed themselves succinctly on "Heaven": gospel, of course. —*Willard Jenkins Jr.,* Cadence

○ **Solo Flight** / Dec. 21, 1976 / Pablo 798

A tremendous collection of standards, blues, and ballads from Ray Bryant. He shows his knowledge of early tunes like "Blues in de Big Brass Bed," while ripping through "Moanin,'" and nicely reworking "Take The 'A' Train" and "St. Louis Blues." —*Ron Wynn*

Montreux '77 / Jul. 13, 1977 / Pablo 371

○ **All Blues** / Apr. 10, 1978 / Pablo 820

This set is an absolute pleasure from beginning to end, chockful of witty, engaging, buoyant, and always resourcefully imaginative pianism by one of the underappreciated masters of the music. The choice of material is intelligently varied and is undoubtedly a major factor in the program's success, as is the firm, sympathetic, impeccable support furnished by bassist Sam Jones and drummer Grady Tate. The eight-and-a-half-minute reading of Miles Davis's "All Blues" swings with delicate resilience from start to finish. Pianist Ray Bryant finds no end of singing, infectious delights in it; in fact, one is left with the impression that he could spin it out to twice this length without even beginning to exhaust its potential for further, equally absorbing development. The same is true of Duke Ellington's "C Jam Blues," and Lester Young's "Jumpin' with Symphony Sid"; the pianist approaches these much-recorded, overfamiliar staples of the jazz repertoire as if for the first time, discovering all manner of refreshing new possibilities in them. Bryant's own pieces, "Stick with It," a fetching blues ballad, and "Blues Changes," fit perfectly with the balance of the program. —*Pete Welding,* Down Beat

★ **Ray Bryant Trio Today** / Feb. 13-14, 1987 / EmArcy 832589

With the Ray Bryant Trio. Loaded with standards and two Bryant classics: "Tonk" and "Slow Freight." Recommended. —*Michael G. Nastos*

Blue Moods / i. Feb. 15, 1987 / EmArcy 842438

An outstanding trio date with Bryant offering teeming phrases, sweeping statements, and some wonderful ballads, backed by bassist Rufus Reid and drummer Freddie Waits. Not only great playing all around, but an excellent recording as well. —*Ron Wynn*

★ **Plays Basie and Ellington** / Feb. 15-16, 1987 / EmArcy 832 235

Golden Earrings / Jan. 23, 1988-Jun. 26, 1988 / EmArcy 836368

The Bryant/Reid/Waits team crank out another fine session, this one neatly balancing glittering ballads and joyous uptempo numbers. Bryant has gradually earned the respect he's due as a consummate pianist, while Reid's sympathetic bass work and Waits's nicely controlled drumming complete the package with style. —*Ron Wynn*

MILT BUCKNER (Milton Brent Buckner)

b. Jul. 10, 1915, St. Louis, MO, **d.** Jul. 27, 1977

Piano, organ, arranger / Swing, soul-jazz

Milt Buckner was a swing-era pianist and organist who pioneered the use of patterned parallel chords, a technique that became known as the "locked hands" style, and was soon so commonplace that Buckner would complain when he was credited with inventing it. His piano and organ playing was harmonically rich, emphatic, and energetic, and he was a skilled arranger. The brother of saxophonist Ted Buckner, he played in Detroit bands as a teen before joining Don Cox's group in the early '30s. Buckner was staff arranger briefly for McKinney's Cotton Pickers in the mid '30s, then played in Detroit with Cox and Jimmy Raschel. Buckner joined Lionel Hampton as pianist and arranger in the early '40s. He remained with Hampton until 1948, and wrote "Hamp's Boogie Woogie," "The Lamplighter," and "Count's Basement," among other songs. Buckner played and toured with Illinois Jacquet, Roy Eldridge, and Jo Jones in the '50s and '60s, and worked with Hampton again in the '50s and '70s. He reteamed with Jacquet in the '70s. Buckner began recording as a leader on Savoy in the late '40s, then did sessions for Capitol, Argo, Jazztone, Riverboat, and Bethlehem in the '50s and '60s, and for European labels into the late '60s. Buckner later recorded with Prestige, Saba, Black & Blue (France), and Riff (Dutch) in the '70s. Currently, he doesn't have any sessions as a leader available on CD, but is represented on Hampton and Jacquet anthologies and albums. —*Ron Wynn*

Rockin' with Milt / Apr. 17+18, 1955 / Capitol 642

★ **Rockin' Hammond** / Feb. 22, 1956-Mar. 15, 1956 / Capitol 722
A classic organ combo with a master. From blues to ballads. A fine representation of Buckner's brilliance. —*Michael G. Nastos*

New World of Milt Buckner / Nov. 26, 1962-Mar. 5, 1963 / Bethlehem 6072

Milt Buckner in Europe / Nov. 16, 1966 / Prestige 7668

Crazy Rhythm / Dec. 7, 1967-Sep. 1968 / Black & Blue 33018

○ **Play Chords** / i. Jun. 1973 / MPS 20631

Midnight Slows—Vol. 2 / i. Aug. 1, 1973 / Black & Blue 233055

Midnight Slows—Vol. 3 / i. Aug. 1, 1973 / Black & Blue 333055
Straightahead jazz with Gatemouth Brown (g), Arnett Cobb (sax), and Candy Johnson (sax). —*Michael G. Nastos*

○ **Green Onions** / Feb. 21, 1975 / Inner City 141
With French rhythm section, guitarist Roy Gaines, drummer Panama Francis. Funky and groove-laden. —*Michael G. Nastos*

Midnight Slows—Vol. 1 / Black & Blue 233026

TED BUCKNER (John Edward Buckner)

b. Dec. 14, 1913, **d.** Aug. 12, 1976
Alto saxophone / Swing, soul-jazz
A good, if derivative, alto and soprano saxophonist and brother of keyboardist and arranger Milt Buckner, Ted Buckner was a steady session player and soloist. He wasn't the most imaginative or the most daring player, but his lines, tone, and phrasing were proficient, as was his timing and general technique. Buckner played with local bands in St. Louis and briefly played with McKinney's Cotton Pickers. He was in Jimmie Lunceford's orchestra from 1937 to 1943; it was here that he enjoyed his greatest recognition. Buckner worked in combos in the Detroit area, and toured Europe in the mid '70s. He played on many Motown sessions, while leading his own groups and co-heading a big band with Jimmy Wilkins. Buckner periodically worked with McKinney's Cotton Pickers until his death. A couple of his sessions are available on Aircheck CDs, and some dates he played with Kid Ory are available on Vogue. —*Ron Wynn and Michael G. Nastos*

Teddy Buckner in Concert at the Dixieland Jubilee / Oct. 15, 1955 / Dixieland Jubilee 503

Midnight in Moscow / 1961 / GNP 68

★ **Teddy Buckner and the All Stars** / GNP 507
Session modeled along lines of Louis Armstrong small-combo dates, with Buckner operating in Armstrong role as leader and trumpet soloist, and band members including frequent Armstrong collaborators Trummy Young and Billy Kyle. There are some cliched moments and other numbers where Buckner and company mesh, particularly on "Mahogany Hall Romp." —*Ron Wynn*

TEDDY BUNN

b. 1909, **d.** 1978
Guitar, vocal / Swing
Teddy Bunn was a capable guitarist and a good vocalist. He is best known for his engagements at the Onyx Club and at Nicks in New York during the '30s with the Sepia Nephews (later the Spirits of Rhythm), as well as his participation in many great swing and traditional jazz sessions. Bunn began on acoustic guitar, then switched to electric in the early '40s. He played without a pick, using his thumb and forefinger to solo in a heavily melodic rather than chordal fashion. Bunn taught himself the guitar. He was a background singer for a calypso vocalist before joining the Washboard Serenaders in the late '20s. Bunn recorded with Duke Ellington in 1929, serving as a substitute for Freddie Guy. He joined the Sepia Nephews in 1932. They were a featured attraction at both the Onyx and at Nick's, and Bunn became a star due to his

appearances with them. He later led his own combos, recording with Jimmie Noone, Johnny Dodds, Trixie Smith, Mezz Mezzrow and Tommy Ladnier, J. C. Higginbothan, and Sidney Bechet in the late '30s. Bunn rejoined the Spirits of Rhythm in 1940, and moved with them to California. He recorded with that group and as a session player through the '40s. Bunn also recorded in 1940 with Lionel Hampton, where he began using electric rather than acoustic guitar. He later played with Edgar Hayes in the '40s and '50s, and with Louis Jordan in 1959. Bunn toured Hawaii with Jack McVea, and also did some rock & roll dates. He battled health problems in the '60s and '70s, but continued performing occasionally during those decades. He can be heard on CD reissues that feature Johnny Dodds, Trixie Smith, and Mezz Mezzrow. —*Ron Wynn*

RONNIE BURRAGE

b. 1959
Drums / Modern creative
A versatile drummer who also plays vibes and marimba, Ronnie Burrage has forged a style as much at home with the bristling pace of hard bop and bebop as with the heavy backbeats of funk, soul, and R&B. Burrage's mother was a classical pianist. He sang in the St. Louis Cathedral boys' choir, and played drums with various funk bands. He accompanied Arthur Blythe, Jackie McLean, Andrew Hill, and McCoy Tyner during visits to St. Louis while working with the St. Louis Metropolitan Jazz Quintet in the early '80s. Burrage played in the Woody Shaw quintet in the mid '80s, then formed Third Kind of Blue with John Purcell and Anthony Cox in 1986. They recorded that same year, and Burrage later did a session with Barbara Dennerlein. Both dates are available on CD. —*Ron Wynn*

DAVE BURRELL (Herman Davis Burrell)

b. Sep. 10, 1940, Middletown, OH
Piano, composer / Modern creative
A heavily percussive, rhythmic pianist, Dave Burrell has merged African and Caribbean influences adeptly into his compositions and playing style. His solos are often aggressive, sparse, and animated, though he's also effective on ballads and standards, and is a steady accompanist and bandleader. Burrell's mother was a vocalist who helped to generate his early interest in jazz. He attended the University of Hawaii in the late '50s and early '60s, and graduated from Berklee in the mid '60s. Burrell worked in Boston with Tony Williams and Sam Rivers, then moved to New York. He played with Grachan Moncur III and Marion Brown before forming the Untraditional Jazz Improvisational Team with Byard Lancaster. This group included Sirone and Bobby Kapp. In addition, Burrell helped initiate the 360 Degree Music Experience with Moncur and Beaver Harris in 1968. He served as a music instructor for Harlem's Community Thing Organization and appeared at the 1969 Pan African Festival in Algiers. Burrell worked and recorded with Pharoah Sanders, Alan Silva, Sunny Murray, Harris, and with Archie Shepp in particular. Burrell wrote a jazz opera, *Windward Passages*, in the late '70s. He continued recording and playing both solo dates and with musicians such as David Murray, Hamiet Bluiett, and Cecil McBee. Burrell has recorded for Black Saint, Victor, Denon, Hat Hut, Douglas, Gazell, and BYG. He has a few sessions available on CD. —*Ron Wynn*

In: Sanity / i. Mar. 1976 / Black Saint 7

High One High Two / Feb. 1977 / Arista 1906
A creative pianist does it all on this twofer of 1968 recordings. Wonderful ideas. —*Michael G. Nastos*

Windward Passages / Sep. 13, 1979 / Hat Hut 2R05

★ **Jelly Roll Joys** / 1991 / Gazell 4003

Plays Ellington and Monk / Denon 8550

Daybreak / Gazell 4002

KENNY BURRELL (Kenneth Earl Burrell)

b. Jul. 31, 1931, Detroit, MI
Guitar / Bop, hard bop, postbop, soul-jazz

Kenny Burrell reaffirms the proposition that relaxed, smooth playing need not lack expression or energy. He's made restraint an art form. Burrell's simple, straightforward melody lines, elegant phrasing, and mellow tone are delightful and impressive. He disdains distortion, dissonance, feedback, or voicelike effects, but can convey moods and feelings as effectively as musicians who use a barrage of gimmicks. Burrell began playing guitar at age 12, and studied music at Wayne State University in the early '50s. He made his recording debut with Dizzy Gillespie's sextet in 1951. After his graduation in 1955, Burrell toured with Oscar Peterson, then moved to New York. He established his reputation as a supreme accompanist and has since made dozens of records as a leader and has played on more than 200 others as a sideman. He's worked with such diverse musicians as Stan Getz, Billie Holiday, Milt Jackson, John Coltrane, Quincy Jones, Lalo Schifrin, and Jimmy Smith. Burrell has played funky blues and soulful jazz; has accompanied string orchestras; has done Ellington tributes; has worked in three guitar trios, in duos, and in combos; and has played in jam sessions. He's even recorded on banjo with Mercer Ellington. Burrell began leading seminars at colleges in the early '70s, and has taught courses in Duke Ellington's music at various campuses in Los Angeles. Burrell has done sessions for numerous labels, among them Verve, Blue Note, Prestige, Argo, Columbia, Kapp, Cadet, Fantasy, Concord, Muse, and Audio Source. He has many albums available on CD. *—Ron Wynn and Dan Morgenstern*

Kenny Burrell / Mar. 29, 1956-Dec. 28, 1956 / Blue Note 1543
Formative '56 sessions with Burrell playing with his Detroit hard bop comrades such as bassist Paul Chambers, pianist Tommy Flanagan, and drummer Kenny Clarke. His playing is harder, looser, and more explosive than on later dates, when he'd settled into a fluid, lighter groove. *—Ron Wynn*

For Charlie Christian & Benny Goodman / Dec. 15, 1956-Mar. 28, 1967 / Verve 831087

○ **After Hours: Prestige Classic Jam Sessions—Vol. 1 / i.** Dec. 28, 1956-Jan. 4, 1957 / Prestige 24107

All Night Long / Dec. 28, 1956 / JCI 3603
With Donald Byrd (tpt). Outstanding blues, midtempo set with soul-jazz leanings. More Burrell's influence than Byrd's. A pair of fine bonus CD cuts; good help from Hank Mobley (ts), Mal Waldron (p), and Jerome Richardson (reeds). *—Ron Wynn*

All Day Long / Jan. 4, 1957 / Prestige 427

○ **Blue Moods** / Feb. 1, 1957 / Prestige 7308
Smooth, cool, yet musically impressive late '50s date that has both blowing session fervor and soulful undergirding. Burrell's fluid guitar voicings and Cecil Payne's robust baritone make nice partners, while Tommy Flanagan adds his usual sparkling piano riffs and solos. Bassist Doug Watkins teams with Elvin Jones, who shows he can drive a date without dominating things on drums. *—Ron Wynn*

Two Guitars / Mar. 5, 1957 / Prestige 216
Excellent guitar exchanges. Good reissue and remastering. With Jimmy Raney (g), Jackie McLean (as), Mal Waldron (p), and Art Taylor (d). *—Ron Wynn*

Cats, The / i. Apr. 1957 / Original Jazz Classics 079

★ **Kenny Burrell Quintet with John Coltrane, The** / Mar. 7, 1958 / Prestige 7532
Historically, there seems little justification for releasing the Kenny Burrell/John Coltrane set except for the extremely high quality of the music (caught you napping, eh?). This is where aesthetic and historical concerns intersect. It is true that there is plenty of both guitarist Burrell's and tenor saxophonist Coltrane's material available (and from this period, 1957-1958), so it might seem, since this isn't exceptional music from either, that reasons for reissue are weak. Of course, what is exceptional from both Burrell and Coltrane would

be sensational from others. Suffice it to say this is outstanding music, well worth the price. *—Joel Ray,* Cadence

☆ **Blue Lights—Vol. 1** / May 15, 1958 / Blue Note 81596
I would certainly not overlook this pair of small-combo gems. Burrell deftly juggles blues, ballads, and soul-jazz. Tina Brooks (sax), Art Blakey (d), Junior Cook (ts), and others shine on both sets. These are 1989 CD reissues. *—Ron Wynn*

○ **Blue Lights—Vol. 2** / May 15, 1958 / Capitol 81597
Tina Brooks (sax), Art Blakey (d), Junior Cook (ts), and others, shine on both sets. These are 1989 CD reissues. *—Ron Wynn*

☆ **Night at the Vanguard, A** / Sep. 17, 1959 / Chess 9316

Bluesy Burrell / Sep. 14, 1962 / Prestige 24106

Out of This World / Sep. 14, 1962 / Prestige 7578

○ **Midnight Blue** / Jan. 7, 1963 / Blue Note 46399
Best of the Blue Note period, with Stanley Turrentine (ts) and Major Holley (b). A solid album. *—Michael G. Nastos*

Guitar Forms / Dec. 4, 1964+Apr. 1965 / Verve 825576
An experimental "artsy" record arranged by Gil Evans that has become a classic. However, don't look for the usual bluesy format. *—Michael Erlewine*

Tender Gender, The / Apr. 4, 1966-May 1966 / Cadet 772

Blues, the Common Ground / Dec. 15, 1967-Feb. 19, 1968 / Verve 68746

Night Song / Apr. 14, 1968-Feb. 1969 / Verve 8751

Asphalt Canyon Suite / Oct. 8, 1969-Oct. 16, 1969 / verve 8773

God Bless the Child / May 4, 1971 / Columbia 40808
Despite a murky backdrop, Burrell's guitar solos are fluid and hypnotic. *—Ron Wynn*

○ **Both Feet on the Ground** / Feb. 15-19, 1973 / Fantasy 9427

○ **Up the Street, 'round the Corner Down the Block** / Jan. 1974-Feb. 1974 / Fantasy 9458

★ **Ellington Is Forever—Vols. 1 & 2** / Feb. 4-5, 1975 / Fantasy 79005
While Kenny Burrell certainly possessed the credentials to make an album of Ellingtonia that featured his guitar as the principal voice, he also commanded better taste than to weaken such an endeavor by occupying the spotlight too much. Instead, he enlisted a large cast of diverse musicians who shared a common bond of devotion, and who cared deeply about their purpose. As a result, even in the large ensemble numbers, no one's psyche gets in the way of the music. The bounty of impressive moments is too rich to cite wholly, but a few special ones deserve mention. "Chelsea Bridge" is a sleepy, after-hours performance, with Burrell and pianist Jimmy Jones buoying Jerome Richardson and Snooky Young's melodic phrases in classic Ellington style, emphasizing widely spaced chords and doubling the rhythmic drive. "Mood Indigo," a dramatic and tense blues, features Jimmy Smith's best lush organ style and Burrell's fleshiest sound. Ernie Andrews takes the blues uptown for his vocals on "Don't Get Around Much Anymore" and "My Little Brown Book," the latter a duet with Jimmy Jones. *—Mikal Gilmore,* Down Beat

Tin Tin Deo / Mar. 23, 1977 / Concord Jazz 45
Another in a string of trio dates cut in the '70s. Burrell works with bassist Reggie Johnson and drummer Carl Burnett. It's a good menu featuring standards, originals, and soul-jazz tunes alternating with midtempo and sentimental ballads. There's also one good Afro-Latin song, "La Petite Mambo." *—Ron Wynn*

Handcrafted / Feb. 27, 1978-Mar. 1, 1978 / Muse 5144
A steady, consistently swinging trio date with Burrell's fine guitar playing the focus, and bassist Reggie Johnson and drummer Sherman Ferguson effective, but subdued, in a supporting mode. There's nothing exceptional here, but the breezy pace and bluesy feel are nice. *—Ron Wynn*

In New York / Dec. 1978 / Muse 5241

For Duke / **i.** 1981 / Fantasy 4506
Togethering / Apr. 5–23, 1984 / Blue Note 46093
Generation / Oct. 24-25, 1986 / Blue Note 46756
Guiding Spirit / Aug. 4+5, 1989 / Contemporary 14058

GARY BURTON

b. Jan. 23, 1943, Anderson, IN
Vibes / Postbop, early jazz-rock
Vibist Gary Burton made his debut in 1960, but his sensitivity, style, and approach hearken back to '50s cool. He developed a four-mallet playing style quite different from the exuberant, blues-oriented swing of Lionel Hampton or bebop-influenced fare of Milt Jackson. Burton's professed influences are Bill Evans and Thelonious Monk, but he's also drawn from country and contemporary classical sources. He has devised electronic attachments that produce fuzz tones and reverb, has played vibes without a pulsator, and has incorporated Latin American and Afro-Latin elements. Burton is a self-taught player who began recording for RCA at age 17 with country guitarist Hank Garland. Burton spent two years at Berklee, while he continued recording for RCA. He took a group to South America in 1962. Burton joined George Shearing in the early '60s, and toured Japan with Shearing's group in 1963. Shearing cut an album of Burton compositions in 1964. He then joined Stan Getz and earned widespread acclaim. Getz's group even did a White House date, and appeared in two films. Burton formed a quartet in 1967 with Larry Coryell, Steve Swallow, and Bob Moses, who was later replaced by Roy Haynes. This group's material included strains of what would later be called "jazz-rock," plus country, pop, and jazz. Burton recorded with Stephane Grappelli at the end of the '60s, then toured extensively overseas in the '70s, visiting Europe, Japan, and Australia. He made intimate, sparkling duet albums with Chick Corea, Ralph Towner, Keith Jarrett, Astor Piazzolla, and Swallow in the '70s and '80s; led combos with Sam Brown, Mick Goodrick, John Scofield, and Pat Metheny; recorded with Carla Bley; and has been an active educator. During the '80s, Burton helped newcomers Makoto Ozone, Martin Richards, Scottish saxophonist Tommy Smith, and Jim Odgren. He joined the Berklee faculty in 1971, has published several instructional books, and has done nationwide lecture tours and clinics. RCA was Burton's prime label in the '60s, Atlantic was his label in the late '60s and early '70s, then he recorded for ECM through the '70s and '80s. His most recent material has been on JVC, GRP, and GNP Crescendo. Nearly all of Burton's material is available on CD, except the pioneering RCA dates. —*Ron Wynn and Michael G. Nastos*

○ **New Vibe Man in Town** / Jul. 6, 1961 / RCA 2420
○ **Artist's Choice** / 1963-1968 / Bluebird 6280
This session traces vibist Gary Burton's musical evolution during 1963-1968 with selections taken from eight of Burton's 13 RCA LPs. The innovative vibraphonist is heard in a sparse quartet (Jim Hall, guitar; Chuck Israels, bass; Larry Bunker, drums) performing Hall's "Something's Coming" to start this CD. "No More Blues" and the Beatles' "Norwegian Wood" precede a pair of country tunes ("I Want You," "Faded Love"), which he performs with a Nashville rhythm section and a country fiddler (Buddy Spicher). These are all early attempts at carving out an individual sound. Burton was among the very first to incorporate elements of rock, pop, and freer forms of jazz into his own music without trivializing any of the styles. By 1967, when he started teaming with guitarist Larry Coryell (whose electric blues style owed as much to rock as to jazz), Burton had found his sound. His quartet also featured two respected jazz players (Steve Swallow, bass; Roy Haynes, drums) and their performances, with Bob Moses eventually replacing Haynes, form the bulk of this reissue and still sound adventurous with Jerry Hahn taking over from Coryell in 1968. *Artist's Choice* is a fine retrospective of the early Gary Burton, although I wish that these sessions were available in full, rather than piecemeal, form (68:51). —*Scott Yanow*, Cadence

○ **Time Machine, The** / Apr. 5+6, 1966 / RCA 3642
★ **Duster** / Apr. 18-20, 1967 / RCA
A prophetic session with references to everything from country to rock. It suggested new directions for jazz musicians. —*Ron Wynn*

○ **Gary Burton in Concert** / **i.** 1968 / RCA 3985
Throb / Jun. 2+3, 1969 / Atlantic 1531
Good Vibes / Sep. 2-4, 1969 / Atlantic 1560
This album consists of excellent material, sound reproduction, and musicianship. The voicings include: Gary Burton on vibes, piano, and organ; Jerry Hahn, Sam Brown, and Eric Gale on guitar; Steve Swallow and Chuck Rainey on bass; Richard Tee on piano and organ; and Bill Lavorgna and Bernard Purdie on drums and percussion. Thus, the album is a combination of playing by musicians who had long been involved with either jazz or blues.... It is interesting to hear a gutsy R&B feeling interpreted by an instrument like the vibes, which has a somewhat light sound. Nevertheless, Burton manages to obtain the subtle blueness called for by the R&B tunes, and in so doing, maintains continuity with the rest of the album. ... *Good Vibes* is one of the best Burton releases to be recorded and conveys both good spirits and a new direction for Burton. —*Robert Rouda*, Coda

★ **Gary Burton and Keith Jarrett** / Jan. 12, 1971 / Atlantic 1577
It is not surprising that this album by Gary Burton and Keith Jarrett quickly settled in that warm spot listeners reserve for their favorite musical experiences; not because it is an exceptional and rare piece of jazz, but because the beat and the lyric are so well met in the kind emotions these two players shared during their collaboration. With the exception of "The Raven Speaks," each performance hangs on perfection, blending varied rock meters and gentle country baroque embellishments. Visually, it frames grassy meadows, sunny skies, and delicate moods of happiness and reflection in clear projections by Sam Brown on guitar, Steve Swallow on electric bass, and Bill Goodwin on drums. All the tunes, save "Como En Vietnam," bear the individualized signature of Keith Jarrett and follow the soft, bluesy contours of rural harmonies that capture the power of simpler lifestyles. The compositions themselves are not necessarily simple, though. "Fortune Smiles," the first half of Side B, demonstrates the episodic form, opening with unaccompanied, beautifully pedalled piano that smoothly sketches long lines of melody. The second episode is a haunting, parallel melody from the band sans piano set off by a rhythmic "call." It has its own bridge, and a very funky growl, and is set like a tune-within-a-tune. The third episode is a free piano passage whose content creates a needed contrast with the perfectly symmetrical structure of the whole piece, making that symmetry appear quite lovely. —*Alan Offstein*, Coda

Alone at Last / Jun. 19, 1971-Sep. 7, 1971 / Atlantic 1598
○ **Turn of the Century** / Jun. 19, 1971 / Atlantic 2321
Works / 1972-1980 / ECM 823267
New Quartet / Mar. 5+6, 1973 / ECM 835002
Hotel Hello / May 13+14, 1974 / PolyGram 835586
Ring / Jul. 23+24, 1974 / ECM 829191
The idea, as I understand it, was to team the Gary Burton quintet with several European musicians. But ultimately, the sole addition was bassist Eberhard Weber and the results are remarkably dark and brooding.... The six compositions selected for *Ring* attest to Burton's own ongoing infatuation with melody and structure. Three of the pieces ("Sympathy," "Love," and "Intrude") are by English composer Michael Gibbs, with whom Burton had been associated on two previous albums. Gibbs's writing is austere, at times, but nonetheless compelling. The remaining three compositions include one from Mick Goodrick ("Mevlevia"), Weber's "The Colours of Chloe," the title piece from his own ECM album, and "Spring" by Carla Bley. Bley's offering is a lengthy introspective construction based ostensibly on "Stella by Starlight"; it contains a striking bass exchange between Steve Swallow and Weber. An album such as this is difficult

to describe, since it is complex but accessible, bleak yet exhilarating. It demands much from both musician and listener. —*Herb Nolan*, Down Beat

Dreams So Real / Dec. 1975 / ECM 833329

☆ **Passengers** / Nov. 1976 / ECM 835016
Gary Burton Quartet. Includes some stirring originals with Pat Metheny (g), Eberhard Weber (b). —*Michael G. Nastos*

Times Square / Jan. 1978 / ECM 11111

Real Life Hits / Nov. 1984 / ECM 825235

★ **New Tango, The** / **i.** 1988 / Atlantic 81823
An interesting, uneven but often lush and beautiful collaboration between tango master Piazzolla and vibist Gary Burton. Each goes out of his way to accommodate the other, with the results being more complementary than challenging. Still, it yields several enticing selections. —*Ron Wynn*

Reunion (with Pat Metheny) / May 6-10, 1989 / GRP 9598

Times Like These / **i.** Aug. 25, 1992 / GRP 9569

BILLY BUTLER

b. Dec. 15, 1925, Philadelphia, PA, **d.** Mar. 20, 1991
Guitar / Blues & jazz, soul-jazz
A tasty soul-jazz and blues guitarist, Billy Butler adroitly mixed a Charlie Christian approach with '50s R&B grooves and backbeats. He coaxed a warm, fat tone from his hollow-bodied electric guitar, and provided deceptively simple solos and fills that became staples of the R&B guitar vocabulary. Bill Doggett's "Honky Tonk," featuring Butler, is perhaps the prototype R&B guitar instrumental. "Ram-Bunk'-Shush" and "Big Boy" are other highlights of his tenure with Doggett. He began playing with the doo-wop/R&B group, the Harlemaires, in the late '40s, then led combos until 1952 when he joined Doc Bagby's trio. Butler cowrote "Honky Tonk" while playing with Doggett from 1954 to 1961. He also recorded with King Curtis, Dinah Washington, Panama Francis, Johnny Hodges, Jimmy Smith, and David "Fathead" Newman in the '60s. Butler worked in Broadway pit bands beginning in the late '60s, but found time for recording sessions with Houston Person and Norris Turney in the late '60s and '70s. He led his own band and recorded for Prestige in the late '60s and early '70s. Butler also recorded with Al Casey and Jackie Williams. He toured Europe frequently in the '70s and '80s, doing sessions there and in America. Only one Butler date is currently available on CD. —*Ron Wynn and Richard Lieberson*

Right Track / **i.** 1966 / Edsel 147

○ **Guitar Soul!** / Sep. 1969 / Original Jazz Classics 334

★ **This Is Billy Butler** / Dec. 16, 1969 / Prestige 7622

Don't Be That Way / Feb. 1, 1976 / Black & Blue 03104

BILLY BUTTERFIELD (Charles William Butterfield)

b. Jan. 14, 1917, Middletown, OH, **d.** Mar. 18, 1988, North Palm Beach, FL
Trumpet, flugelhorn / Swing, big band
A fine, dynamic traditional jazz and swing trumpeter, Billy Butterfield was arguably the best pure musician in the Bob Crosby band of the late '30s and early '40s. His playing had power, authority, crispness, and energy, and he was a particularly fine ballad player. Butterfield was a versatile stylist and a great sight reader who stayed busy in studios throughout the '40s, and was also head of the house band at Nick's in New York. Butterfield worked in the mid '30s in the bands of Austin Wylie and Andy Anderson, then joined Crosby in 1937. He was featured on recordings such as "What's New (I'm Free)" and "Spain." He later worked with Artie Shaw in the early '40s, and appeared on radio broadcasts in Chicago. Butterfield played on Gramercy Five recordings, was featured on the song "Star Dust" in the film *Second Choruses*, and worked with Benny Goodman and Les Brown in the early '40s. He worked at both NBC and CBS studios prior to joining the service in the mid '40s, then led a big band. Following that venture, Butterfield led the house band at Nick's in 1947, before returning to studio work. He recorded

with Louis Armstrong during the '50s, and made several college tours with combos. Butterfield was also featured on a Jackie Gleason LP series, *For Lovers Only*. Butterfield relocated to Florida in the mid '60s, where he did some occasional sessions. He joined the World's Greatest Jazz Band from 1968 to 1972, then continued recording and performing into the '80s. He has a few sessions available on CD. —*Ron Wynn*

★ **Uncollected Billy Butterfield & His Orchestra (1946)** / 1946 / Hindsight 173

JAKI BYARD (John A. Byard, Jr.)

b. Jun. 15, 1922, Worcester, MA
Piano / Hard bop, progressive big band, bop
Another extremely eclectic player with a vast knowledge of piano styles, Jaki Byard has proven to be a prolific soloist and composer. He can utilize odd rhythms cleverly, can incorporate stride or boogie-woogie elements, can play 12-bar blues, or can dazzle with intricate, teeming bebop statements. Byard's compositions are known for their humor, and he's led one of the great unknown big bands, the Apollo Stompers, in Boston and New York. Byard learned trumpet and piano as a child, then began playing trombone while in the army. He toured and recorded with Earl Bostic in the late '40s and early '50s before moving to Boston. He worked first as a solo pianist, then as a saxophonist in Herb Pomeroy's big band. Byard played piano in Maynard Ferguson's big band in the late '50s and early '60s, and worked with many major figures throughout the '60s. These musicians include Charles Mingus, Eric Dolphy, Don Ellis, Booker Ervin, and Charlie Mariano. He also played on recordings by Eric Kloss. He did his first session as a leader for Columbia in 1960, following it with several small-group dates for Prestige. Byard worked with musicians such as Ron Carter, Rahsaan Roland Kirk, Ray Nance, and Elvin Jones. Some of Byard's sessions were reissued later under Kirk's name. Byard became heavily involved in music education. He taught at several schools, particularly at the New England Conservatory of Music in the late '60s. Byard juggled New York and Boston editions of the Apollo Stompers into the '80s. He did many sessions for Muse, several of them solo, and also did sessions for Soul Note. Byard recorded duet albums with Earl Hines in the '70s, and with Ran Blake in the '80s. A fair amount of his material is available on CD. —*Ron Wynn*

Blues for Smoke / Dec. 16, 1960 / Candid 79018
An early Byard solo set in which he displays an array of influences, ranging from ragtime and stride to bop and free. At this stage, Byard was developing an individualized sound, so sometimes things seem ragged or his tempos are tentative. But the potential and raw power more than compensate for the occasional fluffed note. —*Ron Wynn*

Giant Steps / Jan. 30, 1962 / Prestige 24086
Excellent trio work bolstered by superior drumming from Roy Haynes on several cuts. Ron Carter's throbbing, huge bass sound and interaction with Byard are an added plus. He doesn't play with as much variety as on other occasions, preferring to mesh with the Carter/Haynes or La Roca team in effective dialogs. —*Ron Wynn*

○ **Out Front!** / May 21, 1964 / Prestige 7397

Live! at Lennie's—Vol. 2 / Apr. 5, 1965 / Prestige 7477

○ **Live! at Lennie's—Vol. 1** / Apr. 15, 1965 / Prestige 7419

☆ **With Strings** / Apr. 2, 1968 / Prestige 7573
Top-notch recording for the brilliant pianist with George Benson (g), Ray Nance (tpt), Ron Carter (b), Richard Davis (b), and Alan Dawson (d). —*Michael G. Nastos*

Jaki Byard Experience, The / Sep. 17, 1968 / Prestige 7615
Jaki Byard sits exclusively at the piano on this set and, let's face it, despite his intriguing experience on other instruments, piano is his "boss" horn. Rahsaan Roland Kirk employs tenor, clarinet, manzello, Kirkban, and whistle, but is heard mainly on tenor, which is good news as the Kirk tenor did not generally receive the appreciation it deserved. The opener, a diabolically beautiful version of "Parisian

Thoroughfare," sets the LP's standard. Kirk starts on tenor, switches to manzello and then back to tenor, always in a surging groove. Byard and Davis retained the feeling in this longest cut of the date. "Hazy Eye," a gorgeous slice of Byard impressionism, is a piano/bass duet on which the composer's loving soul is laid bare. Side two closes on a gospelish note with an impromptu head. Kirk utilizes clarinet and tenor and Byard reaches down for some of that basic piano, which he plays so well. "Monk's Evidence" finds Kirk chewing up the bars and jamming in an impossible number of notes (he might even have faxed Johnny Griffin on this sort of form). Byard plays "Mad Bebop" as a counter melody on the theme and takes a stimulating solo. "Memories of You" gets an unexpected tenor/piano duet treatment, very light and relaxed. Kirk is in splendid voice and Byard wrote in stride that "Tatum Lives!" This is a superb track. The sessions swing to a close with "Teach Me Tonight" (containing bells and a taste of "School Days"). After Byard's whimsical introduction, Richard Davis (bass) sets the spry pulse and all four men (Alan Dawson, drums) buckle to a joyful ball. Byard more than hints at his respect for Erroll Garner; Kirk expounds with simplicity, warmth, and humor. —*Mark Gardner,* Coda

○ **Solo Piano** / Jul. 31, 1969 / Prestige 7686

★ **There'll Be Some Changes Made** / Dec. 27, 1972 / Muse 5007

○ **Family Man** / Apr. 28, 1978-May 1, 1978 / Muse 5173
With Major Holley on bass. Includes excerpts from "Family Suite." Challenging listening. —*Michael G. Nastos*

Phantasies—Vol. 1 / Sep. 25-26, 1984 / Soul Note 1075
The Apollo Stompers take in the whole big-band tradition, the same way leader Jaki Byard incorporates the entire jazz piano tradition in his playing. Like Byard, the Stompers don't regurgitate old musics, but combine them with a personal style that reflects modern sensibilities. . . . However, the Stompers and Byard the arranger aren't always as impressive as Byard the pianist. Their theme—"I May Be Wrong (But I Think You're Wonderful)"—is a generic big-band number and Carole King's "It's Too Late" (sung by Denyce Byard) proves to be as uninspiring to a big band as you might imagine. (The other vocal here is more memorable all around. "Do Nothing Till You Hear from Me" is sung by Diane Byard, who has Phoebe Snow's claret-rich timbre, if a somewhat higher range.) But Oscar Pettiford's "Tricotism" melody played by bassist Ralph Hamperian, who did a Charlie Haden impersonation on "Lonely Woman," sounds as good as ever in Byard's ducal reading. Byard's own writing, represented by only four tunes, is most enjoyable. His 5/4 "Boogie Woogie" features his own clunky Thelonious Monkish accents (as does "Tricotism"). "Prelude No. 29" seques from the sound of Charles Mingus's orchestral writing to that of Ellington's jungle style. Byard echoes Mingus by juxtaposing the melodies of two tunes with the same chords, too: "So What" and "Impressions." Byard the pianist is featured elsewhere as well: on a gossamer "Black and Tan Fantasy" and rippling and cascading through "So What." As on any Byard album, ivory tickling's the highlight. It is grand enough to make you overlook the rough spots. —*Kevin Whitehead,* Cadence

Foolin' Myself / Aug. 1988 / Soul Note 1125

○ **Live at Maybeck Recital Hall—Vol. 17** / Sep. 8, 1992 / Concord Jazz 4511
A dynamic, top-flight piano soloist and bandleader gets a chance to present his complete package in another superb Maybeck set. Byard employs stride, shuffle, and hard bop rhythms, playing with a density and controlled force that make each selection a treasure. —*Ron Wynn*

Phantasies—Vol. 2 / Soul Note 121175
I doubt that Jaki Byard and the Apollo Stompers have ventured out of the New York area, which makes them an updated version of a territory band. Like those homegrown groups, the personnel is a mix of seasoned pros and youngbloods learning the ropes; on *Phantasies—Vol. 2* the results show it. It's a sound that won't alienate swing fans, but won't

excite more adventurous listeners—at least until pianist Byard starts soloing. —*Art Lange,* Down Beat

DON BYAS (Carlos Wesley Byas)

b. Oct. 21, 1912, Muskogee, OK, **d.** Aug. 24, 1972
Tenor saxophone / Swing
Don Byas was an innovative, groundbreaking player whose style was a precursor of bop in its use of substitute chords. He was a great soloist, especially on ballads. He was one of the most successful musicians at finding a comfortable way to blend swing and bop influences; the results proved thoroughly personal and distinctive. Byas's style was influenced undoubtedly by Art Tatum, whom he repeatedly cited as a major source of ideas. He began his career under Coleman Hawkins's spell. After hearing Charlie Parker, Byas kept working until he combined swing lyricism with bop harmonic fluency and rhythmic intensity. The results were often stunning. Byas began playing professionally in the '30s, first at college, then with Lionel Hampton, Eddie Barefield, Buck Clayton, Don Redman, Lucky Millinder, and Andy Kirk. He made his first recordings in 1938 with Timme Rosenkrantz. Byas joined Count Basie in 1941, replacing Lester Young. The next year, he recorded with a small band in Hollywood, Count Basie and His All American Rhythm Section. He also recorded with Thelonious Monk that year. After two years, Byas left, and played with small groups from 1943 to 1945, including combos led by Dizzy Gillespie and Coleman Hawkins, plus his own bands. There were sessions with Slam Stewart, Charlie Shavers, Milt Hinton, and Max Roach. He went to Europe in 1946 with Don Redman's band and decided to stay. Byas first settled in France, then in the Netherlands and in Denmark. He visited England in 1965. During his later years, Byas appeared often at European festivals. There was a 1950 date with Duke Ellington, a mid '50s session with various piano trios, and a '59 recording for a Swedish label. During the '60s, there was a Jazz at the Philharmonic tour, a session with Bud Powell, Kenny Clarke, and Idrees Sulieman, a '63 quartet date, and a masterful collaboration with Ben Webster in 1968. After that, Byas remained mostly in Europe, and played with various jazz and pop bands. He made his final American appearance in 1970 at the Newport Jazz Festival, then toured Japan with Art Blakey. Byas recorded with strings in 1971, and, in 1972, cut his final recording, a quartet session with pianist Tete Montoliu, in Holland. He has some sessions available on CD. —*Ron Wynn*

Midnight at Minton's / 1941 / Onyx

★ **Savoy Jam Party** / Aug. 17, 1944 / Savoy 2213

○ **Don Byas in Paris** / Oct. 18, 1946-Jan. 5, 1949 / Prestige 7598
Bluesy, often explosive blues, ballads, and standards cut in Paris by the great swing tenor saxophonist Don Byas. His huge tone, expressive phrasing, and hard blowing were ideal for this collection that's heavy on standards and includes a sterling rendition of "Body and Soul." The backing band proves capable, if unexciting, keyed by pianist Billy Taylor. —*Ron Wynn*

★ **Don Byas on Blue Star** / i. 1950-1952 / PolyGram 833405
Don Byas on Blue Star is a collection of 23 sides cut in Paris between January 13, 1947 and March 1952. Byas shared similar roots with Wardell Gray; both were influenced by Coleman Hawkins and Lester Young, but where it seems evident that Gray would have eventually been one of the leading modern tenors of the '50s and '60s, Byas settled comfortably as a leading mainstreamer. This is quite understandable as Byas began his recording activity in the late '30s (on a session set up by the same Timmie Rosencrantz who recorded the Erroll Garner material. This session included Tyree Glenn, who co-fronted the band: Peanuts Holland, trumpet; Hubert Rostaing, alto sax; Jean Bouchely, bass; Jean Tilche, guitar; Oliver Buford, drums; and Billy Taylor, piano on these '47 sides). Don Byas went to Europe (along with Holland, Glenn, and Taylor) as a member of the Don Redman orchestra, liked what he saw, and stayed. The material on this CD is gracious and generally

mellow, and fans of the mainstream tenor of Byas will have good reason to acquire the material. —*Bob Rusch,* Cadence

Tenor Saxophone Concerto / **i.** 1951 / Dial 216

Tenderly / **i.** Nov. 1951-May 1955 / Vogue 655620

○ **Don Byas** / Feb. 1954 / Inner City 7018

Tribute to Cannonball, A / Dec. 15, 1961 / Columbia 35755
This is primarily Don Byas's album, despite the presence of drummer Kenny Clarke and pianist Bud Powell. The contribution of the other musicians is largely that of providing the stimulating framework for one of the tenor saxophonist's most successful recordings, though Powell's work also repays close attention and Idrees Sulieman's trumpet playing supplies a brassy contrast of Fats Navarroish melodicism to four tunes. Powell limits himself to intuitively perfect accompaniment and brief, stately solos. Indeed, the title is a post facto tribute to "Buckshot's" good taste as a producer (collectors will remember other notable examples), presumably on the part of Columbia's promotion department rather than from the musicians involved. This recording, along with a few others, reveals a Byas with a matured style and vigor fully worthy of his historic contributions to the changing music scene of the '40s. And Byas, perhaps more than any other tenor player, had heralded the changes of that decade of transformation in jazz style. His playing remained true to that transitional state until his death in 1972. —*Terry Martin,* Down Beat

○ **Anthropology** / Jan. 13, 1964 / Black Lion 160
This session was recorded live in Copenhagen with a superior European rhythm section, and, as the tunes indicate, it was a bop-conscious, high-voltage evening. Pianist Brent Axen was a talented Bud Powell disciple who comps beautifully, but gets off fine solos. Bassist Niels-Henning Orsted Pedersen is strong and drummer William Schiopffe is adequate (though how one wishes Kenny Clarke could have been there!). Highlights are the title track and "Don't Blame Me." On the first, tenor saxophonist Don Byas is frantic, jumping into a well-constructed first chorus, working over some of his favorite lines, playing with force and creativity. His sound also speaks of modernity. Axen has his best solo here and Byas must have dug it because he jumps in on it furiously, leading into a bass-tenor then drums-tenor interlude and a wild close. "Don't" is classically played, the exposition melodic and sensitive, the variations determined and beautiful. "Moonlight in Vermont" is almost as good and is colored with brief, but stunning, doubling. For a sampling of late Byas, this is certainly a valuable issue. —*Gary Giddins,* Down Beat

○ **Ballads for Swingers** / **i.** Nov. 1966 / Polydor 623207

CHARLIE BYRD (Charles L. Byrd)

b. Sep. 16, 1925, Chuckatuck, VA
Guitar / Cool, Latin-jazz
Guitarist Charlie Byrd perfected the application of classical guitar techniques to a jazz setting, and helped introduce American audiences to Latin American sounds, particularly samba and bossa nova, in the early '60s. His style is delightful, attractive, and impressive, and reflects the training he received in the '50s from Sophocles Papas and Andres Segovia. Byrd was born into a musical family; his brother, Joe (Gene), studied at the Peabody Conservatory and has worked in Charlie's groups since the mid '60s. Byrd played with Django Reinhardt while in France during World War II. Following his discharge, he worked with Sol Yaged, Joe Marsala, and Freddie Slack. For a while, Byrd changed fields and became a concert guitarist. He spent half the '50s studying with Papas and Segovia. But he began playing regularly around Washington, D.C., and eventually returned to jazz, working and recording with Woody Herman. He began recording as a leader for Savoy in 1957, and did sessions for Riverside, Prestige, Off-Beat, Columbia, and Milestone in the '60s. Visits to South America on State Department-sponsored tours led to an interest in Latin sounds. Byrd and Stan Getz made the chart-topping album, *Jazz Samba,* in 1962. It

was Byrd's suggestion that they do some compositions by Antonio Carlos Jobim. Byrd did other Latin dates, working with Keter Betts, Cal Tjader, and Clark Terry, among others. Along with Barney Kessell and Herb Ellis, Byrd formed the Great Guitars group in the '70s; they made several Concord albums. Byrd also recorded with Nat Adderley and cut his own sessions on Fantasy. He wrote an instruction manual in 1973 that's become widely used. Byrd made other trio dates, as well as quartet and sextet sessions for Concord in the '70s and '80s, working with Laurindo Almeida and Bud Shank. He recorded with the Washington Guitar Quintet in 1990 for the Concord Concerto label. Lots of Byrd sessions from various periods are available on CD. —*Ron Wynn*

Midnight Guitar / Aug. 4, 1957 / Savoy 1121
A late '50s session that shows another side of Byrd's guitar playing. There are low-down blues songs and funky soul-jazz numbers, as well as his now-familiar sentimental pieces. But this lineup, particularly bassist Keeter Betts, was more interested in exuberant than understated material, and Byrd proved he could fill this bill. —*Ron Wynn*

Jazz at the Show Boat—Vol. 2 / 1959 / Off-Beat 3005

Jazz at the Show Boat—Vol. 3 / 1959 / Off-Beat 93006

Mr. Guitar / 1959-1960 / Riverside 9450

○ **Guitar Artistry of Charlie Byrd, The** / 1960 / Riverside 9451

Charlie Byrd at the Village Vanguard / Jan. 15, 1961 / Original Jazz Classics 669

Latin Byrd / 1961-1963 / Milestone 47005

Bossa Nova Pelos Passaros / 1962 / Riverside 107

★ **Byrd at the Gate** / May 9+10, 1963 / Riverside 262
Byrd at the Gate presents the unique jazz guitar approach of Charlie Byrd and his trio (Keter Betts, bass; Bill Reichenbach, drums) live (May 9 and 10, 1963) at the Gate. Clark Terry (trumpet) and/or Sheldon Powell (tenor sax) make guest appearances on five of the tracks. Charlie Byrd has a fragile ambience and it does not compete well, on an open level, with horns. This is an excellent Byrd record (his best work was for Riverside and later Concord) with jazzy ambience (it's *not* a Clark Terry date). In case you were stung by one of those insipid Charlie Byrd commercial discs (mostly on Columbia), reintroduce yourself with this LP. —*Bob Rusch,* Cadence

○ **Brazilian Byrd** / **i.** 1965 / Columbia 9137

Byrd by the Sea / Mar. 1-3, 1974 / Fantasy 9466
A mild, smooth trio date with Byrd playing light jazz, occasional Afro-Latin, and even a mock classical number, backed by bassist Joe Byrd and drummer Bertill Knox. This sometimes comes close to, but never becomes, mood music. —*Ron Wynn*

○ **Great Guitars** / 1974 / Concord Jazz 4004
The presence of guitarists Charlie Byrd, Barney Kessel, and Herb Ellis on one LP (playing as a trio on four cuts plus a medley, as a duo of Kessel and Ellis on "Makin' Whoopee," and alone on the other tunes), holds more promise than it delivers. There is seldom any real close interplay between the guitars, and the soloists do not seem to draw much inspiration from the others. The exceptions are Byrd's solo cuts, Antonio Carlos Jobim's "Amparo," and the rollicking and joyous "Cow Cow Boogie" featuring all three, with two laying down different rhythmic lines while the third solos. There are no improvised solos on "Amparo," but the arrangement is beautiful, with one guitar taking a pizzicato bass role while Joe Byrd bows his bass and Wayne Phillips scrapes various percussion instruments. Byrd is especially beautiful on "Green Dolphin Street," which he plays with a Latin touch in that style of his in which he plays two lines at once, making this almost overworked tune sound fresh. However, his rendition of "Body and Soul," while pleasant, is uninspired. "Outer Drive," with all three, also doesn't jell, though it swings nicely. The last three tunes, played as a medley, are given fresh new workings. Acoustic and electric guitar weave back and forth between lead and accompaniment to beautiful effect on "Nuages," and the various guitars

combine well on the other two tunes. —*Jerry De Muth*, Cadence

Sugarloaf Suite / Aug. 1979 / Concord Jazz 4114

Brazilville / May 1981 / Concord Jazz 4173
A good quartet date with Bud Shank (as). Shank adds spice to Charlie Byrd's cool Afro-Latin setting. —*Ron Wynn*

Isn't It Romantic / Mar. 1984 / Concord Jazz 4252

It's a Wonderful World / 1988 / Concord Jazz 4374

Washington Guitar Quartet / i. 1992 / Concord Jazz 42014
A guitar showcase, as Charlie Byrd and four other premier players team with a qroup that includes more guitarists in Howard Alden and Carlos Barbosa-Lima, plus bassist Joe Byrd and drummer Chuck Redd. Lots of flashy, impressionistic, Afro-Latin and swing licks, plus pretty ballads and light, sentimental tunes. —*Ron Wynn*

Great Guitars (Live) / Concord Jazz 23

DONALD BYRD (Donaldson Toussaint L'Ouverture, Byrd II)

b. Dec. 9, 1932, Detroit, MI
Trumpet / Hard bop, soul-jazz, instrumental pop, contemporary funk

Donald Byrd has been hailed as a visionary and has been condemned as a traitor. He's played vigorous hard bop, has displayed technical skills that put him at the top of his generation, and has presided over inspirational, superb recording sessions. He's also been responsible for hideous, commercially successful, artistically barren releases that, by even the most minimal standards, don't qualify as either good jazz or good pop. He's one of the best-educated musicians around, has worked tirelessly on behalf of music education and African-American culture, yet has been quoted making highly inflammatory, debatable statements. Byrd may be jazz's ultimate loose cannon now that Miles Davis has departed. His '50s solos, with their ringing, assertive lines and wonderfully full tone, can stand with anyone else's solos. But the music he played on many of his '70s dates is immediately forgettable.

Byrd began his music studies at Wayne State University in the early '50s, but they were halted by military service. He played in an air force band, then attended the Manhattan School of Music where he earned his Masters in music education. Byrd served as Prestige's main studio trumpeter in the late '50s, while cutting dates for Transition, Savoy, Columbia, Discovery, Blue Note, and Prestige. He co-led a group with Pepper Adams from the late '50s into the early '60s. Byrd remained an active bandleader in the '60s and recorded for Bethlehem, then cut a string of Blue Note dates, mostly combos in vintage hard bop fashion. At times he'd experiment, as with the mid '60s *Christo Redentor*, a hymn written and arranged by Duke Pearson. The album included the Coleridge Perkinson Choir. Byrd also studied composition in Europe in 1962 and 1963, and later became an active instructor. He taught at Rutgers, Hampton Institute, Howard, and North Carolina Central.

Byrd began changing direction in the '70s. He worked with a 12-member group on *Electric Byrd*, then turned more and more toward fusion, urban contemporary, and instrumental pop. These albums were big sellers; *Black Byrd* was Blue Note's single biggest hit album in 1973. But the barrage of electronics, funk, and urban contemporary arrangements, rigid backbeats, and background vocalists generated enormous controversy. Byrd denounced his critics as "jazz snobs." He earned a law degree from Howard and received his doctorate in 1982 from Columbia. He served as chairman of Black music at Howard and helped turn an unknown student ensemble into a hugely successful pop fusion act called the Blackbyrds. His late '70s and early '80s albums continued in the fusion/urban contemporary/instrumental pop vein. Then, in the late '80s, Byrd returned to the music he'd once championed. He played on a Sonny Rollins session, and did an album with Mulgrew Miller and Kenny Garrett. During the '90s, he's hedged his bets, cutting jazz material

for Landmark and recording with hip-hopper Guru on his rap/jazz project. —*Ron Wynn*

First Flight / Aug. 23, 1955 / Delmark 407
An instructive session; you can hear Byrd's trumpet conception taking form. Backing groups include Yusef Lateef (sax) and Barry Harris (p). Prototype '80s Detroit/Chicago jazz sound. —*Ron Wynn*

Donald Byrd: Long Green / Sep. 29, 1955 / Savoy 1101
Donald Byrd: Long Green from 1955 features straightahead hard bop and is typical of the better blowing sessions from this period. Everyone (saxophonist Frank Foster, pianist Hank Jones, bassist Paul Chambers, drummer Kenny Clarke) is playing very strongly and this spirit infuses the music. —*Jon Goldman*, Cadence

★ **House of Byrd** / Aug. 3, 1956+Nov. 2, 1956 / Prestige 24066
It is slightly inaccurate to have released this Donald Byrd twofer under his leadership, as on the two LPs reissued here he shares the billing with trumpeter Art Farmer on one and with alto saxophonist Phil Woods on the other. The point seems especially moot since Byrd's playing holds one's attention less well than either of his coleaders. Again, there is a list of formidable sidemen: on the first, recorded in August of 1956, alto saxophonist Jackie McLean, pianist Barry Harris, bassist Doug Watkins, and drummer Art Taylor join trumpeters Byrd and Farmer; on the second, three months later, it is pianist Al Haig, bassist Teddy Kotick, and drummer Charlie Persip, in addition to Woods. The first has some good blowing, especially from Farmer, but suffers from the looseness that afflicted postbop blowing sessions, and too much of Byrd's playing relies on repetition and cliché. Art Taylor's drumming seems erratic and intrusive at times. But the second session is a real trip, and Woods is simply tremendous: fluid, imaginative, under the sway of Charlie Parker to be sure, but possessing his own way of thinking about a solo, which always made his playing unmistakable. Also, this was my first extended experience with Al Haig at the piano; I found him a continual pleasure full of little surprises. Byrd himself sounds like a different player in this group, far less brittle and forced, responding well to both Woods and to the crisper, less busy drumming of Persip. But I would buy this reissue mainly for Farmer's playing and, especially, for Woods's. —*Joel Ray*, Cadence

Two Trumpets / Aug. 3, 1956 / Prestige 7062

All Night Long / i. Dec. 28, 1956 / Original Jazz Classics 427

September Afternoon / i. Dec. 28, 1956 / Discovery 869

All Night Long / i. May 2, 1957 / Original Jazz Classics 427

Jazz Eyes / Sep. 10, 1957 / Savoy 1114

Byrd in Paris—Vols. 1 and 2 / Oct. 22, 1958-Oct. 29, 1958 / Polydor 833394
Two-volume set of early hard bop done in Paris. Presence of Bobby Jaspar (f, ts), a well-regarded but little-known international musician, increases importance. These two dates helped Jaspar establish his reputation. Walter Davis (p), Doug Watkins (b), and Art Taylor (d) make a fine rhythm section. —*Ron Wynn*

Byrd in Hand / May 31, 1959 / Blue Note 84019

Fuego / Oct. 4, 1959 / Blue Note 46534
A good one for this Detroit trumpeter, with Jackie McLean (as) and Duke Pearson (p). —*Michael G. Nastos*

Byrd in Flight / Jul. 10, 1960 / Blue Note 4048

Donald Byrd at the Half Note Cafe—Vols. 1 and 2 / Nov. 11, 1960 / Blue Note 46539
It is unlikely that many of baritone saxophonist Pepper Adams's more recent fans are familiar with his earlier association with the then still jazz-pure Donald Byrd. By 1960, the trumpeter, fresh from a productive mid '50s stint with the Jazz Messengers, had not yet forgotten the valuable lessons he had learned while blowing nightly with Art Blakey, Horace Silver, and Hank Mobley, and he had not yet forsaken his personal adaptation of the combined influences of Kenny Dorham and Clifford Brown. Though his playing

lacked the crackling intensity and unflagging imagination of his models and predecessors in the Messengers, it did have an undeniable charm and sincerity about it, which the trumpet player was to abandon soon after becoming intrigued with the possibility of reaching wider markets and earning far greater money than he could have ever done as a jazz musician. Adams, as ever, is right on target throughout, his full, deep, blustering sound presenting an unusually heavy vehicle for the litheness of his rapid delivery, especially when compared with the then still popular vogue among modern saxophonists for the light, airy tonalities of such reigning stylists as Paul Desmond, Stan Getz, and Gerry Mulligan. Without question, Adams's choice to root his sound in Harry Carney, his ideas in Charlie Parker, and his attack in Serge Chaloff was a wise one, for ultimately he was able to swing the pendulum back to where it had been when he first started playing, years before the ascendancy of the cool school. The music on this digitally transferred re-pressing, complete with the original jacket and notes by Leonard Feather, was recorded on location at Greenwich Village's Half Note by the esteemed Rudy Van Gelder on the night of November 11, 1960. With its companion volume, it gives an accurate representation of the Byrd combo's place in the hierarchy of hard bop groups of the time. —*Jack Sohmer,* Jazz Times

○ **Chant** / Apr. 17, 1961 / Blue Note 991
Trumpeter Donald Byrd and baritone saxophonist Pepper Adams recorded and played together for a long time. This unissued material is both a surprise and a winner. It may have been pianist Herbie Hancock's first recording date, and he and bassist Doug Watkins made it a solid quintet with a good, but little-known, drummer (Eddy Robinson) handling the tempos well. "I'm An Old Cowhand" was used before as a jazz vehicle and its structure seems weak, but Pepper roars as always. Byrd struggles a little and the monotonous multi-tag ending is the only real weak material. Byrd contributes two originals with "You're Next," coming off best with a minor mode and a riff full of triplets that is well constructed. Duke Pearson's original "Chant" has Byrd's best playing and shows his maturity. I don't know what else to say about Pepper Adams except he is never short of astounding. His drive on "That's All" was just as strong 18 years ago as it is now (1979). This is first-rate Blue Note material. —*Jerry L. Atkins,* Cadence

Royal Flush / Sep. 21, 1961 / Blue Note 4101

Jazz Message, The / i. 1962 / Savoy 0133

○ **Groovin' for Nat** / Jan. 12, 1962 / Black Lion 760134
Solid early '60s session with Byrd meshing alongside Duke Pearson and Bob Cranshaw. Johnny Coles makes effective appearances. —*Ron Wynn*

Gigi Gryce/Donald Byrd / i. 1963 / Josie 3500

Donald Byrd, Hank Mobley and Kenny Burrell / i. 1963 / New Jazz 8317

New Perspective, A / Jan. 12, 1963 / Blue Note 84124
Includes the remarkable "Christo Redentor," a Duke Pearson hymn. An excellent merger of gospel, choral, and jazz sensibilities and arrangements. —*Ron Wynn*

I'm Tryin' to Get Home / Dec. 17-18, 1964 / Blue Note 84188
Brass with voices. 1986 reissue of an uneven album that takes same tack as "A New Perspective," but with less success. —*Ron Wynn*

★ **Blackjack** / Jan. 9, 1967 / Blue Note 84259
Perhaps his very best of many recordings with Sonny Red (as), Hank Mobley (ts), and Cedar Walton (p). —*Michael G. Nastos*

Fancy Free / Jun. 6, 1969-May 9, 1970 / Blue Note 84319

☆ **Electric Byrd** / May 15, 1970 / Blue Note
Pivotal release with Byrd using a 12-piece group. Duke Pearson on electric piano. The arrangements and mood are harbingers of Byrd's shift into pop, funk, and R&B. —*Ron Wynn*

Ethiopian Knights / Aug. 25-26, 1971 / Blue Note
Interesting jam-session feel. Top jazz players manage to retain credibility in an essentially R&B setting. The album is cited by many as reflective of the label's trend away from its roots in the '70s. The concept was brainchild of George Butler, now Dr. George Butler of Columbia. —*Ron Wynn*

Young Byrd / i. 1984 / Milestone 47044
A reissue of material from two early sessions pairs Byrd with two saxophonists: Art Pepper and Gigi Gryce. The set with Pepper is live at the famous Five Spot Cafe, while the session with Gryce was done in the studio. Here is Donald Byrd at his peak in the late '50s. —*AMG*

Harlem Blues / Sep. 1987 / Landmark 1516

Getting Down to Business / Oct. 10+12, 1989 / Landmark 1523
Donald Byrd Sextet. Byrd back to mainstream with old and new players. Top solos by Joe Henderson (sax), Kenny Garrett (sax), and Donald Brown (piano). Byrd plays with confidence and an edge. —*Ron Wynn*

○ **City Called Heaven, A** / Jan. 1991 / Landmark 1530

DON BYRON

Clarinet / World fusion, modern creative
The 1993 winner of the *Down Beat* Critics Poll on clarinet, Don Byron has blossomed into arguably the finest player on his instrument. He's doing diverse and unusual things, though Eddie Daniels is certainly his technical equal. Byron has played free, classical, and international music, and has even issued a session of klezmer music. His '92 release, *Tuskegee Experiments,* was an artistic success, and helped cement his reputation as an adventurous, superbly gifted soloist. His tone, phrasing, lines, range, and style are immaculate. Byron is similar to Anthony Davis in his willingness to shatter stereotypes and in his refusal to conform to perceptions or preconceived notions about what's appropriate for an African-American musician to play. Both his jazz and klezmer sessions are available on CD. —*Ron Wynn*

★ **Tuskegee Experiments** / i. 1992 / Nonesuch 79280
The album that helped break clarinet sensation Don Byron to a wider audience. Byron's twisting, soaring solos and impressive command of numerous styles had already made him a critical favorite, and he got rave reviews for this release. It contains a mix of social commentary and explosive playing, and was expertly produced and mastered. —*Ron Wynn*

Plays the Music of Mickey Katz / i. 1993 / Elektra Nonesuch 79313
Virtuoso clarinetist Don Byron schvings mit tongue in cheek on this giddy klezmer counterpart to Ivo Paposov & the Bulgarian Wedding band. An homage to Mickey Katz, graduate of Spike Jones's City Slickers and masterful parodist of the early 1950s, it contains faithful renditions of Katz ditties like "Litvak Square Dance" and "Frailach Jamboree." Byron is ably assisted by a stellar group of New Yorkers, including trumpeter Dave Douglas, violinist Mark Feldman, trombonist Josh Roseman, and second clarinetist J.D. Parran. Singers Lorin Sklamberg and Avi Hoffman supply the requisite amount of borscht belt appeal and schmaltz with absurdist Yiddish takes on tango ("Kiss Of Meyer"), Hawaiian ("Mechaye War Chant"), cowboy ("Haim Afen Range"), and French cabaret music ("C'est Si Bon"). —*Bill Milkowski,* Jazz Times

C

GEORGE CABLES (George Andrew Cables)

b. Nov. 14, 1944, New York, NY
Piano / Hard bop

A superb accompanist best known as Art Pepper's favorite pianist in Pepper's last phase, George Cables has preferred being a sideman rather than leading groups or writing compositions. His interpretative skills and ability to respond and to interact with other musicians has kept Cables busy. He displays great dexterity, harmonic knowledge, and sophistication. Cables has cited Thelonious Monk and Herbie Hancock, and by extension Bill Evans, as prime influences. He studied at Mannes College and formed the Jazz Samaritans with Steve Grossman and Billy Cobham at age 18. Cables played with Art Blakey and Sonny Rollins in the late '60s, then gained national recognition for his work with Joe Henderson in the early '70s, and with Freddie Hubbard in the mid '70s. He also played with Gabor Szabo and Bobby Hutcherson, though Cables really achieved notoriety for his numerous dates in the late '70s with Pepper. Cables was a regular member of Dexter Gordon's group in 1977 and 1978. Cables managed to make distinctive, memorable contributions to many recording sessions and to various bands through the '70s. Generally, he played electric piano, but he returned to the acoustic during the late '70s. Cables recorded with Mel Martin's Bebop and Beyond in the mid '80s. He's made a handful of celebrated records over the years, particularly a late '80s album of Gershwin songs on Contemporary. Cables has recently recorded with Frank Morgan and Bruce Forman, and has cut sessions for Fantasy, Contemporary, and DIW. He has a handful of current sessions available on CD, and a couple of '70s dates have been reissued. —*Ron Wynn*

○ **Circles** / Mar. 27-28, 1979 / Contemporary 14015
An aggressive date with robust solos from Joe Farrell (ts) and decisive playing by Cables. —*Ron Wynn*

Cables' Vision / Dec. 17-19, 1979 / Original Jazz Classics 725
Strong late '70s release with Cables leading larger-than-usual group boasting a strong lineup. Freddie Hubbard, Bobby Hutcherson, and Ernie Watts all prove fiery, dynamic soloists, while Cables shows the phrasing and pianistic magic that made him Art Pepper's favorite. The Tony Dumas/Peter Erskine bass and drums duo sparkle behind and underneath the front line. —*Ron Wynn*

★ **Phantom of the City** / May 14-15, 1985 / Contemporary 14014
This LP features strong interplay between the musicians. Bassist John Heard has a big tone and a strong rhythmic feel. Tony Williams plays well on this record—his tasty fills on the title cut are perfect, while his drive is most important to "You Stepped Out of a Dream." . . . George Cables is a two-fisted pianist: his left hand is very active, sometimes locked in step with his right, other times accentuating the bassist's chords ("Waltz for Monday"). Cables plays his melodies with a flourish, almost a swagger, as displayed on the Chick Corea-like "Blue Nights." He also has a bluesy side, which is best heard on the standard "Old Folks." There are no weak moments on either side, and these cuts really swing. —*Richard B. Kamins*, Cadence

☆ **By George** / Feb. 27, 1987 / Contemporary 14030
Pianist George Cables's tribute to George Gershwin is a zebra of a different stripe: various rhythms are used as methods of diversification on the well-known standards, and the leaner instrumentation is varied, to a small extent. It took a certain amount of courage to tackle these overdone songs, but Cables, who also doubled as producer, explains in his brief notes that these are some personal favorites. He meets the self-challenge with inventiveness and versatility. Cables has an encyclopedic command of the keyboard packed into his fingertips, which allowed him to move about wherever his fertile imagination took him, constructing risky, but logical, improvisations on these musty chord patterns that broke some windows and let some fresh air inside. And just listen to how cleanly the man nails those notes! Here is a pianist with both head and heart. Cables, like Tete Montoliu and Martial Solal, to name just two, has gone unrecognized by the general jazz public for too long. —*Larry Hollis*, Cadence

○ **Night and Day** / **i.** May 1991 / DIW 606

RED CALLENDER (George Sylvester Callender)

b. 1916, Haynesville, VA, **d.** Mar. 8, 1992, Los Angeles, CA
Bass, tuba / Swing, big band, bop, cool

Not many jazz musicians made as important a contribution on one instrument as Red Callender did on two; he was a topflight bassist and an equally outstanding tuba soloist. Callender displayed a range and fluidity on tuba that generated new interest in it as a jazz vehicle, while his round, pronounced tone, timing, and swing on bass fortified many combos and recording sessions. Callender was also a solid arranger and composer who wrote such respected numbers as "Pastel" and "Red Light." He worked in New York during the '30s, but resettled in Los Angeles after going there on tour in 1936 with Blanche Thompson and the Brownskin Models. He debuted on record the next year with Louis Armstrong, then worked with various groups in Hollywood. For nearly three years, Callender played with the band coled by Lester and Lee Young, then formed his own trio. Besides touring frequently with the trio, Callender played with both Nat "King" Cole's and Erroll Garner's trios in the '40s, and recorded with Charlie Parker, Wardell Gray, and Dexter Gordon. He appeared with Louis Armstrong in the film *New Orleans* in 1946, and led a trio in Hawaii during the late '40s. During the '50s, he did many television and film projects, and was a pioneer among Black musicians in the studios. Callender also cut some brilliant recordings with Art Tatum, and did some R&B and pop recording dates. One of his compositions, "Primrose Lane," became a Top 10 hit in 1959, performed by Billy Wallace. During the '60s, Callender recorded on tuba with Charles Mingus at Monterey in 1964. He also worked with Stan Kenton. During the '70s, Callender recorded with Earl Hines. He worked in the '80s with James Newton's quintet (on tuba), led duo dates with Gerry Wiggins, and was a member of Jeannie and Jimmy Cheatham's Sweet Baby Blues Band. His list of recording associations includes Billy Many, Art Pepper, Shorty Rogers, Bing Crosby, Carmen McRae, Plas Johnson, Mel Tormé, Pearl Bailey, Garner, Billy

Eckstine, Buddy Collette, and Ry Cooder. Mingus left Callender a bass in his will. He recorded for numerous labels, among them Crown, MGM, Legend, Hemisphere, and Sunset. His mid '80s autobiography, *Unfinished Dream,* offers vivid details of the late '40s and early '50s Los Angeles jazz scene, particularly as it related to Black musicians. He also reissued some of his material on his own label, Red (not the Black Saint/Soul Note subsidiary). Though he can be heard on many other people's sessions, Callender's own albums are not available on CD. —*Ron Wynn and Michael G. Nastos*

Red Callender Speaks Low / 1954 / Crown 5012

★ **Swingin' Suite** / i. 1956 / Modern 1201

Lowest, The / Apr. 30, 1958+May 1, 1958 / Metrojazz 1007

Night Mist Blues / 1984 / Hemisphere 1002

CAB CALLOWAY (Cabell Calloway)

b. Dec. 25, 1907, Rochester, NY
Vocals, bandleader / Swing, big band
Entertainment value has always been, and remains, a prime element in bandleader Cab Calloway's appeal; it's often overshadowed the musicianship that was a regular feature of his best orchestras. Whether clowning or serious, Calloway was a gifted scat singer who composed several popular songs for his groups. More importantly, he promoted and advanced the careers of many great players, including Chu Berry, Ben Webster, Milt Hinton, Cozy Cole, Jonah Jones, and Dizzy Gillespie. Now in his eighties, he is still fairly healthy, and even appeared on a Michael Jackson video a few years ago.

The brother of singer and bandleader Blanche Calloway, Cab grew up in Baltimore, where he sang in the Baltimore Melody Boys. Calloway attended law school briefly, then quit to begin his professional career in Chicago as a singer and dancer. He toured with Blanche's band in the late '20s, then began leading groups, heading the Alabamians in Chicago and New York, then the Missourians. The 1929 revue "Hot Chocolates" made Calloway a star, and, in 1930, the Missourians played and recorded under Calloway's name. They became the Cotton Club's headline act in 1931 and 1932, and supplanted the Ellington orchestra as house band. From the early '30s until the late '40s, the Cab Calloway orchestra proved a bigger attraction than many bands that were considered their musical superiors (a couple of these bands were superior). They appeared in films such as *The Big Broadcast* in 1932, *International House* in 1933, *The Singing Kid* in 1934, *Manhattan Merry-Go-Round* in 1937, and *Stormy Weather* in 1943. During the '30s, Calloway's hit records included "Minnie the Moocher" and "Kicking the Gong Around" in 1931, and "The Scat Song," "Reefer Man," and "Eadie Was a Lady" in 1932. They signed with Victor in 1933 and toured Europe in 1934. That band included Ben Webster, Chu Berry, Shad Collins, Milt Hinton, vocalist June Richmond, and Gillespie.

Calloway's flamboyant stage manner, charisma, costumes, dance steps, flying jet black hair, and personality led George Gershwin to fashion a character in Porgy and Bess, "Sportin' Life," after Calloway. Calloway made "hi-de-ho" both a signature yell and a national catch phrase. The Orchestra scored a Top 10 hit in 1942 with "Blues in the Night," and were annually among the top-grossing bands on the swing circuit, regardless of color, through the '30s and into the mid '40s. Calloway would eventually play "Sportin' Life" in a '50s version of "Porgy and Bess."

He became active in musical theater after his orchestra disbanded in 1948. He appeared with Pearl Bailey in an all-Black version of *Hello, Dolly!* in 1967. But, periodically he'd reassemble the band for special occasions, notably tours of Canada and of South America. Calloway made a solo tour of England in 1955, and was in the film *St. Louis Blues* in 1958. He sometimes was part of the intermission show for Harlem Globetrotters' games in the mid '60s, and his 1976 autobiography, *Of Minnie the Moocher and Me,* hooked new legions of fans. The '80s were a profitable time for Calloway. He

again appeared in a film, *The Blues Brothers,* and starred with his daughter, Chris, in *His Royal Highness of Hi-De-Ho: the Legendary Cab Calloway* in 1987. There was a guest shot on the Muppets television show, and a spot in the theatrical production *Bubbling Brown Sugar.* Actor Larry Marshall portrayed Calloway in the film *The Cotton Club,* and the sound track included three Calloway songs. He made a film for television in England and toured with his daughter in a reworked Cotton Club act. —*Ron Wynn and Cub Koda*

○ **Cab Calloway (1930-1931)** / i. Jul. 1930-Jun. 1931 / Classics 516
This CD reissue was particularly welcome, for the still-active Cab Calloway was long overdue for a reappraisal. Long put down by some writers as mere entertainer, Calloway was a superior jazz-influenced singer whose vocal abilities were often overshadowed by his showmanship. It's true that many of his vocals could be considered silly (such as his scatting on "Basin Street Blues") but even at his most outlandish, Calloway was colorful and swinging. On "It Looks Like Susie," the earliest selection on this generous 23-song collection (which is actually volume two of the complete early Calloway), Calloway shows what he learned from sister Blanche, while on "You Rascal You," "You Dog," and "Kicking the Gong Around," the singer could be no one else but Cab. His early bands always tended to be underrated, especially in comparison to the 1939-1940 edition that featured Chu Berry and Dizzy Gillespie. Calloway originally took over the Missourians, a hot but commercially unsuccessful unit whose personnel was mostly still intact at the time of this session. Although not on Duke Ellington's level, this band had some fine soloists (trumpeters Lammar Wright and Reuben Reeves, clarinetist Arville Harris, and tenorman Walter Thomas) along with usually tight ensembles; check out "Trickeration." The main fault to this otherwise satisfying package is the excess of surface noise, often sounding like a constant light drizzle of rain; "Without Rhythm" even skips once. Didn't Classics have access to the original masters? The material was recorded on 7/9, 9/23, 10/12, 10/21 and 11/18/31, and 2/29, 4/20 and 6/7/32. (68:53). —*Scott Yanow,* Cadence

★ **Jazz Heritage: Mr. Hi-De-Ho (1930-1931)** / 1930-1931 / MCA 1344
A budget compilation of Calloway's early '30s cuts. Despite the uneven sound, a good starter set. —*Ron Wynn*

○ **Cab Calloway (1931-1932)** / i. Jul. 1931-Jun. 1932 / Classics 526
This CD reissue contains Cab Calloway's first 24 recordings done July 24, October 14, November 12, and December 23, 1930, and March 3, March 9, May 7, June 11, and June 17, 1931. From the start, Calloway's style was fully formed and it is particularly interesting to hear his interpretations of tunes associated with others, especially "Happy Feet" (Paul Whiteman), "The Viper's Drag," and "I'm Crazy 'Bout My Baby" (Fats Waller), along with several Duke Ellington hits. A real rarity is "Yaller" on which Calloway bemoans the difficulties of being a light-skinned Black ("Ain't even Black, I ain't even White, I ain't like the day, I ain't like the night . . . "). If only his delivery on this piece wasn't so close to Al Jolson's delivery! Many of these performances are memorable, especially an exciting (if ultimately silly) "St. Louis Blues," "St. James Infirmary," and, of course, the original "Minnie the Moocher." The soloists are uncredited, but I believe Lammar Wright has most of the trumpet solos. Walter Thomas (on tenor and baritone) and Andrew Brown (an early bass clarinet soloist) are also generally quite impressive. Cab Calloway made up for his lapses of taste with excitement and zaniness; from these fun recordings, one can fully understand why he became such a popular celebrity. —*Scott Yanow,* Cadence

○ **Cab Calloway (1932)** / i. Jun. 1932-Dec. 1932 / Classics 537

○ **Cab Calloway (1932-1934)** / i. Dec. 1932-Sep. 1934 / Classics 544

○ **Cab Calloway (1934-1937)** / **i.** Sep. 1934-Mar. 1937 / Classics 554

On Film (1934-1950) / 1934-1950 / Harlequin 2005
A solid collection of performances taken from sound tracks of his many film appearances. High energy makes up for spotty sound on certain tracks. —*Cub Koda*

○ **Cab Calloway (1937-1938)** / **i.** Mar. 1937-Mar. 1938 / Classics 568

Jumpin' Five / **i.** 1938-1946 / Zeta

○ **Cab Calloway (1938-1939)** / **i.** Mar. 1938-Feb. 1939 / Classics 576

Jumpin' Five / **i.** 1938-1946 / Zeta

○ **Cab Calloway (1939-1940)** / **i.** Mar. 1939-Mar. 1940 / Classics 595

Hi-De-Ho Man / **i.** 1958 / RCA

○ **Cab Calloway (1940)** / **i.** Mar. 1940-Jul. 1940 / Classics 614

Hi-De-Ho Man / **i.** 1958 / RCA
Two-album best-of retrospective that's the perfect place to start, featuring the hits and high points. In and out of print for years, it may actually be on CD by the time this is published. —*Cub Koda*

○ **Minnie the Moocher** / MCA Special Products 20366

Best of the Big Bands / Columbia 45336

★ **Kicking the Gong Around** / ASV 5013
Cab's naughtiest side, with the virtues of substance use imbuing the lyrical text of several tunes included here. If you thought drug songs didn't start until the late '60s in rock music, be prepared for a shock. —*Cub Koda*

MICHEL CAMILO

b. Apr. 4, 1952
Piano / Bop, Latin-jazz
A laser-fast, rhythmically invigorating pianist, Dominican-born Michel Camilo exploded onto the jazz scene in the mid '80s. An exuberant personality who seemed to enjoy playing as much as audiences enjoyed listening to him play, Camilo earned a quick reputation in New York clubs for his great technique, often stunning solos, and sometimes dazzling keyboard displays. Some of that initial enthusiasm was tempered by his relatively bland major label albums, but even these releases contain several glorious moments amid the stretches of expertly played, routine hard bop and Afro-Latin material. Camilo made two albums for the independent Electric Bird label in the mid '80s, working with such well-known jazz stars as Dave Weckl and Anthony Jackson. His late '80s date for the short-lived Portrait label included guest stints by Mongo Santamaria and Marc Johnson, while Ralph Bowen, Michael Phillip Mossman, D.K. Dyson, and others appear on his Epic session. Evidence reissued a pair of mid '80s Camilo dates in 1992. Both of these reissues, and recent material for Portrait and Epic, are available on CD. —*Ron Wynn and Michael G. Nastos*

○ **Why Not** / Feb. 25, 1985-Feb. 2, 1985 / Evidence 22002
Pianist Michel Camilo made his recording debut as a leader with this '85 session for the Japanese King label. Camilo was anxious to show everything, and does so on such cuts as "Thinking of You" and the title track. He rips through phrases, adds powerhouse chords and rippling lines, switches tempos and meters, or moves from a hard bop feel to an Afro-Latin groove in the middle of a piece. His intensity and energy are impressive, but at times he tries too much and stumbles getting back to the melody. He is backed by an interesting mix of session players and fusion types. Trumpeter Lew Soloff and alto/tenor saxophonist Chris Hunter are veterans of Gil Evans's band. Hunter's twisting alto sax forays are the closest thing to David Sanborn other than the real article, and while Soloff isn't the most fiery player, he is technically impressive. The bass/drum corps include Anthony Jackson, more of a funk specialist than a mainstream player, and fusion star Dave Weckl, who reins in his excesses and provides good, basic rhythmic foundations. It isn't an unflawed debut, but Camilo showed he'd be a pianist to be reckoned with down the line. —*Ron Wynn*

Michel Camilo / Jan. 30, 1988-Feb. 1, 1988 / Portrait 44482

★ **On Fire** / **i.** 1989 / Epic 45295

○ **On the Other Hand** / **i.** Oct. 16, 1991 / Epic 46236
Suntan with the Michel Camilo Trio (Anthony Jackson, bass; Dave Weckl or Joel Rosenblaff, drums) was recorded June 29 and 30, 1986. The program is little more than technically flashy fusion fingering. . . . Only on "Cha Cha" does some genuine emotional sweet spontaneity suggest itself, but overall, this is playboy jazz: slick, psuedo, artful, superficially impressionistic, or butt-twitchingly soulful. —*Bob Rusch, Cadence*

CANDIDO (Candido [de Guerra] Cameron)

b. 1921
Conga drums / Latin-jazz, world fusion
A great Afro-Cuban percussionist who taught himself conga, bongo, trap drums, bass, and guitar by listening to both Cuban drummers and the recordings of jazz musicians such as Kenny Clarke and Max Roach, Candido (de Guerra) Cameron evolved into a major player during the '50s. He mixed the rhythms of traditional Yourba music with Spanish folk songs, jazz, and Afro-Cuban inflections and rhythms. Candido began playing drums at age 14, and recorded in Cuba with Machito's Latin bands and with other groups. He played with the house band at Cuban radio station CMQ, and with the Tropicana Club's regular group for six years. Dizzy Gillespie encouraged Candido to move to New York, then helped introduce him to various bandleaders in the early '50s. Candido played with Gillespie and recorded with him in 1954. Candido was a prominent part of Billy Taylor's mid '50s trio, and toured and recorded with Stan Kenton in 1954. He began heading his own bands in Miami and New York. Candido worked with players such as Al Cohn and Phil Woods, while recording with Erroll Garner, Gene Ammons, Kenny Burrell, Art Blakey, Sonny Rollins, Wynton Kelly, Illinois Jacquet, Wes Montgomery, Elvin Jones, Lionel Hampton, and Cohn, among others. He became a prolific session player in the '80s. Candido has also been featured in advertisements for companies marketing percussion instruments, notably congas and bongos. He recorded as a leader for ABC-Paramount, Roulette, Solid State, and Blue Note in the '50s, '60s, and '70s. Unfortunately, none of these recordings are available currently on CD. But the album *Billy Taylor Trio with Candido* has been reissued on CD. —*Ron Wynn*

★ **Candido Featuring Al Cohn** / **i.** 1956 / Paramount 125

Candido the Volcano / **i.** Oct. 3, 1957 / ABC 180

Latin Fire / **i.** 1959 / Paramount 286

Beautiful / **i.** 1959 / RCA 2027

Conga Soul / **i.** 1962 / Roulette 52078

Thousand Finger Man / **i.** 1969 / Solid State 18066

CONTE CANDOLI (Conte [Secondo] Candoli)

b. Jul. 12, 1927, Mishawaka, IN
Trumpet / Bop, cool
Conte and Pete Candoli are both solid trumpet players in the cool bop vein. Born in 1927, Pete Candoli is the older of the two brothers. Both men are good ballad soloists, fine interpreters, and technically accomplished trumpeters with reputations for polished playing with a steady, swinging quality. Pete Candoli played with several swing bands in the '40s, among them Sonny Dunham's, Will Bradley's, Ray McKinley's, Tommy Dorsey's, Teddy Powell's, Woody Herman's, and Boyd Raeburn's. He moved to the West Coast in the '50s, and worked with Les Brown and Stan Kenton. He and his brother worked together in the late '50s and early '60s, then Pete Candoli led his own band. He started a nightclub act with his wife, Edie Adams, in the early '70s with Candoli singing, dancing, playing, and directing the band. The Candoli brothers played the 1973 Monterey Jazz Festival, and appeared and recorded at the 1981 Aurex

Festival in Japan with Lionel Hampton. They continued playing together through the '80s.

In addition to the band he played in with his brother, Conte Candoli played with Woody Herman, Chubby Jackson, Stan Kenton, and Charlie Ventura in the '40s. In the '50s, he worked with Charlie Barnet and Kenton again, before moving to Chicago to head his own group. He came back to California later in 1954, and played with both his brother's band and Howard Rumsey's Lighthouse All Stars through the end of the '50s. Conte recorded and played with Terry Gibbs from 1959 to 1962, and recorded with Gerry Mulligan and Sonny Criss during the '60s. He played with Woody Herman at the Monterey Festival and with Kenton's Los Angeles Neophonic Orchestra. Conte also played regularly with Shelly Manne, worked in the studios on film and television projects, and was in the "Tonight Show" band. During the '70s, he recorded with Frank Strazzeri and Teddy Edwards. Conte was a member of Supersax in the '70s.

The brothers have worked together into the '90s, and have recorded as a joint band for Dot, Mercury, Crown, and Somerset, among others. Conte Candoli has recorded solo sessions for Bethlehem, Atlantic, and Andex. Very few of their dates are available on CD. —*Ron Wynn and Michael Erlewine*

Sincerely, Conte Candoli / Nov. 20, 1954 / Bethlehem 1016

West Coast Wailers / Aug. 16-17, 1955 / Atlantic 1268

Rhythm Plus One / Jun. 11, 1956 / Epic 3297

★ **Conte Candoli Quartet** / Jul. 1957 / Mode 109
This features the *Conte Candoli Quartet* (Candoli, trumpet; Vince Guaraldi, piano; Monty Budwig, bass; Stan Levey, drums) in a rather nondescript set of standards and originals by such musicians as Al Cohn ("Something for Liza"), Osie Johnson ("Mediolistic"), fellow trumpeter and brother, Pete Candoli ("Walkie Talkie/Tara Firma"), and the leader himself ("Mambo Blues"). It is all pleasantly polite, efficiently performed, but rather uninspired, displaying, nonetheless, Candoli's modest gifts as a melodist. Nothing lasts long enough to develop, which is not to say it would have, but lasts a little too long to be regarded as a nicely turned little gem . . . as if it could have been. —*Alan Bargebuhr*, Cadence

HOAGY CARMICHAEL (Howard Hoagland Carmichael)

b. 1899, Bloomington, IN, **d.** Dec. 27, 1981, Palm Springs, CA
Vocals, piano, songwriter
A masterful lyricist and composer, Hoagy Carmichael's songs were recorded and performed by jazz and popular musicians from the '20s to the '90s. Carmichael penned works pliable enough for great jazz interpretations, soulful pop presentations, or good-natured film and stage applications. His early works, such as "Boneyard Shuffle," "Manhattan Rag," and "March of the Hoodlums," were made into traditional jazz romps. Later came classics such as "Stardust," "The Nearness of You," and "Skylark," as well as "Georgia on My Mind," "Heart and Soul," "In the Cool, Cool Cool of the Evening," and "Lazy River." He studied piano with his mother, a professional pianist. Indianapolis pianist Reginald DuValle tutored Carmichael on piano. While in high school, he played at dances, then organized a band while at Indiana University. Carmichael became great friends with Bix Beiderbecke in the mid '20s and later maintained that no one could play his songs like Beiderbecke. Reportedly, Carmichael even slept with Beiderbecke's horn under his pillow. The Wolverines recorded one of Carmichael's earliest numbers, "Riverboat Shuffle." He made his recording debut with Hitch's Happy Harmonists in 1925, and later played with Jean Goldkette's orchestra and recorded with Paul Whiteman. Carmichael moved to New York in 1929, and recorded and performed with Louis Armstrong, Mildred Bailey, the Dorsey Brothers, Benny Goodman, Eddie Lang, Bubber Miley, Red Norvo, and Jack Teagarden in the '30s. He moved to Hollywood in 1935 and became a respected character actor. Carmichael had either musical or dramatic roles in 14 films between 1937 and

1954, among them *To Have and Have Not, The Best Years of Our Lives*, and the highly inaccurate *Young Man with a Horn*. He later made the transition to radio and television acting in the '40s and '50s, and wrote autobiographies in 1964 and 1965. Carmichael's singing has been featured on several anthologies available on CD, and countless renditions of his songs are available on many discs. —*Ron Wynn and Bruce Eder*

○ **Stardust (1927-1932)** / 1927-1932 / Historical 37
This session presents a dozen early Hoagy Carmichael sides, which make a nice complement to other recently (1982) reissued Decca sides. These tracks are earlier (1927-1932) and have greater jazz interest in both solos and arrangements. There is also a good helping of Carmichael vocals mixed in with Cliff Williams and Scrappy Lambert. Also notable is a hot accordion solo (Jack Cornell) on "High & Dry," which also sports a nice trumpet solo (Manny Klein?). Other supporting musicians include Art Schutt, Joe Tarto, Jimmy and Tommy Dorsey, Stan King, and Babe Russin. There are two previously unissued tracks, and the overall sound is fair to good. —*Bob Rusch*, Cadence

○ **Hoagy Sings Carmichael** / Sep. 10, 1956-Sep. 13, 1956 / EMI America 46862

○ **Hoagy Charmichael, The Stardust Road** / i. 1958 / MCA 1507
Hoagy Carmichael, The Stardust Road is a set of Decca recordings from the '40s chockfull of the Carmichael vocal charm and ambience, but only of peripheral jazz interest. —*Bob Rusch*, Cadence

★ **Classic Hoagy Carmichael** / i. 1989 / Smithsonian/Folkways 38
Although there are several horrible vocals and some soupy string sections to be avoided here, this collection will prove of considerable interest to the jazz-inclined. In fact, the artistry of the jazz performers, as compared with that of the pop people, cannot help but make one rather proud of them. From that point of view, the juxtapositioning of the hip and the corny is often both instructive and amusing. Louis Armstrong certainly does marvelously well by Carmichael. Of the other singers, Ella Fitzgerald, Mildred Bailey, Billie Holiday, and Ray Charles provide a special lift. The intention here is obviously to demonstrate Carmichael's scope with a wide variety of performers, but it is surprising that you don't find one out of a whole album of Earl Hines solos here or his "Skylark" with Billy Eckstine. And while Carmichael's "One Night in Havana" may not have been published, there are several recordings of it. But it is good to hear unfamiliar numbers like "Charlie Two-Step" and "Serenade to Gabriel" and the crisp little band back of Ethel Waters on "Old Man Harlem." Six versions of "Stardust" (by Armstrong, Artie Shaw, Carmichael, Ella Fitzgerald, Frank Sinatra, and Wynton Marsalis) do different kinds of justice to a masterpiece that tends to contrast sharply with many of the other compositions, where a kind of homespun, folksy, and very American quality prevails, one that is appropriate to the composer's voice. A well-researched, 64-page booklet by John Edward Hasse handsomely supplements the music. —*Stanley Dance*, Jazz Times

Legendary Performer / i. 1991 / RCA 3370

Hoagy Carmichael Collection / Smithsonian
A definitive, triple-volume set, mostly devoted to others' interpretations of his work, including recordings by Louis Armstrong and the Boswell Sisters. —*Bruce Eder*

○ **Stardust & Much More** / Bluebird 8333
A wide-ranging collection of recordings of his work by Carmichael and others, covering 1927 to 1960. A good starter on his work. —*Bruce Eder*

JUDY CARMICHAEL

b. 1952
Piano / Stride, boogie, swing

Early period jazz preserver. Carmichael is an excellent technical pianist capable of great improvisations in this traditional setting. A keeper. —*Michael G. Nastos*

Two Handed Stride / Apr. 4+29, 1980 / Statiras 8072
A contemporary player with a traditional style, Judy Carmichael bangs out the stride rhythms with both passion and authenticity. Though she adheres to the genre's exacting beats, she also does more than just re-create; she adds her own quirks and phrasing, making this a fine combination of the old and the new. —*Ron Wynn*

★ **Jazz Piano** / Jun. 11, 1983 / Statiras 8074
Solo piano from a lady who knows this music well. Interprets music from Earl Hines, Fats Waller, James P. Johnson, and the like. She is one of a kind, and is a very good player. —*Michael G. Nastos*

Old Friends / Nov. 11, 1985 / C&D JC-2
Live session with Warren Vache (cnt) and Howard Alden (g) in 1983 and 1985. More Fats, James P. Johnson, and Jelly Roll Morton. 13 tracks. A very good representation of her capabilities. —*Michael G. Nastos*

Trio / Jan. 6+7, 1989 / C&D JC-1
With Michael Hashim (sax), Chris Flory (g). There are 11 cuts without a bass, but based in early piano swing. Fats Waller, James P. Johnson, Ellington, and Basie repertoire featured. —*Michael G. Nastos*

HARRY CARNEY (Harry Howell Carney)

b. Apr. 1, 1910, Boston, MA, d. Oct. 8, 1974, New York, NY
Baritone saxophone / Swing, big band
Though he was a talented multi-instrumentalist, Harry Carney's greatness came on the cumbersome baritone saxophone. For many years, he was the instrument's greatest, and often only, substantial soloist. His thick, rumbling, and impressive solos and sound were a vital ingredient that helped to anchor Ellington's orchestra; and his mastery of circular breathing to sustain notes and tones was seldom used in a noncreative, gimmicky manner. Carney played piano, then clarinet and alto sax, before finally adding baritone. He began playing professionally in Boston at age 13, and moved to New York in 1927. Shortly after he arrived, he joined Duke Ellington's band as a 17-year-old, after getting his mother's permission. He's credited with co-writing "Rockin' in Rhythm," which was one of the band's themes. Ellington and/or Strayhorn frequently inserted Carney's baritone in the opening bars of a number. He was featured on songs such as "Jive Stomp," "Ko-Ko," "Slap Happy," "I Can't Believe That You're in Love With Me," and "Dancing in the Dark," as well as "Frustration" and "Serious Serenade." In later years, Carney added bass clarinet, and played it with vigor and declarative force equal to the way he played baritone sax. In addition to being a vital member of the sax section, Carney served as Ellington's designated driver, and there are legendary photos of Carney going to a date in his Cadillac, with Ellington riding shotgun. He worked for Ellington for over 46 years, and died in 1974 within months of the Duke's death. —*Ron Wynn*

★ **Harry Carney with Strings** / Dec. 14, 1954 / Clef 640

IAN CARR

b. Apr. 21, 1933, Dumfries, Scotland
Trumpet, flugelhorn, bandleader, composer, teacher / Early jazz-rock, modern creative
Scottish trumpeter and flugelhorn player Ian Carr has achieved fame as a player, composer, and author. A self-taught trumpeter, Carr made effective contributions to many bands in the '60s, '70s, and '80s. He's played with taste and spark in jazz and jazz-rock bands. He's also composed several pieces and written critically acclaimed books. Carr studied English literature in college before serving in the army during the late '50s. He played in his brother Mike Carr's band, the Emcee Five, in the early '60s. Carr co-led a group with Don Rendell from 1962 to 1969; he also played with Joe Harriott, Don Byas, and John McLaughlin during this pe-

riod. He founded Nucleus in 1969, a band that became one of the most popular and influential jazz-rock groups of all time. They played at the Montreux and Newport Jazz Festivals during the '70s, did several international tours, and recorded 13 albums. They also appeared on many radio and television broadcasts. Carr also recorded with Neil Ardley's New Jazz Orchestra, the Spontaneous Music Ensemble, and Keith Tippets's Centipede, and worked with Michael Garrick. He helped form the United Jazz and Rock Ensemble, which performed into the '80s. Carr composed a piece for the 1974 celebration of William Shakespeare's birthday at the Globe Theater in London. His writings on music include *Miles Davis: A Critical Biography*, published in the mid-'70s. He became an associate professor of music at the Guildhall School of Music and Drama in London in 1982. Carr also became a member of the Royal Society of Musicians of Great Britain and won the Calabria Award in 1982. He's recorded for Columbia, Argo, and Capitol, as well as English companies Vertigo and Gull, but doesn't have any sessions currently available on CD in America. —*Ron Wynn*

TERRI LYNE CARRINGTON (Terri Lynne Carrington)

b. 1962
Drums / Instrumental pop, modern creative
A drummer who got an early start playing in Boston area clubs as a child, Terri Lyne Carrington parlayed the fame and exposure she received as a charter member of Arsenio Hall's first "posse" into a recording contract. But long before her stint on Hall's show, she had earned the respect of the jazz community through her contributions to both fusion and to more conventional sessions. Carrington's timing, disciplined playing, and keen rhythmic qualities were about the only interesting thing in Wayne Shorter's late '80s band, and on many nights her playing helped to elevate otherwise routine filler on Hall's program. She made her recording debut as a leader on an all-star session for Verve/Forecast in the late '80s that was a light fusion and instrumental pop workout with a slight jazz tinge. It included guest appearances by everyone from John Scofield to Greg Osby to Carlos Santana, but wasn't the kind of standout date many anticipated. It's still available on CD. —*Ron Wynn*

★ **Real Life Story** / 1989 / Verve/Forecast 837697

BAIKIDA CARROLL (Baikida E. J. Carroll)

b. Jan. 15, 1947, Saint Louis, MO
Trumpet, flugelhorn / Modern creative
One of the better accompanists and section musicians, Baikida Carroll has added textures, colors, and bright solos to various free jazz ensembles and groups, among them the Black Artists Group (BAG) in St. Louis. He's been an active composer, has written film soundtracks and scores, and has displayed a striking, full sound and solo approach. Carroll attended Southern Illinois University and the Armed Forces School of Music before directing the BAG's free jazz band. He went to Europe with other group members in the mid '70s, and recorded in Paris in 1974. Carroll recorded with Oliver Lake, Michael Gregory Jackson, Muhal Richard Abrams, Jack DeJohnette, and David Murray in the '70s and '80s, cut a solo album in the late '70s, and headed a combo in the early '80s. Currently, only his combo date is available on CD. —*Ron Wynn*

★ **Shadows and Reflections** / i. May 1983 / Soul Note 1023
Trumpeter Baikida Carroll is once again in the company of homeboy alto saxophonist Julius Hemphill on a January 13 and 20, 1982 recording with pianist Anthony Davis, bassist Dave Holland, and drummer Pheeroan AkLaff for Soul Note called *Shadows & Reflections*. The material here sounds like it could have been a late Blue Note recording; in fact, there are times when the horns prompt flashbacks of the Jackie McLean-Charles Tolliver front line of the '60s. And for all their avant-garde credentials, this group sounds very comfortable and at home with the squirrelly free bop displayed here. In fact, I think this is Anthony Davis's strongest, most

direct work (1983) to date (on some tracks, the piano itself sounds a bit less than grand). —*Bob Rusch*, Cadence

---

BENNY CARTER (Bennett Lester Carter)

b. Aug. 8, 1907, New York, NY

Alto saxophone, composer, bandleader / Swing, big band

Like Doc Cheatham, Benny Carter's career spans the gamut of American music. He's been a superb soloist on alto sax and trumpet, and a competent pianist and clarinetist; he's written and arranged hundreds of songs for big bands, small combos, and vocalists; he's done film scores; and he's even participated in hit R&B and soul recordings. As an alto saxophonist, he stands beside Johnny Hodges as one of the finest pre-Charlie Parker stylists. He possesses a wonderfully pure tone, great facility, and distinctive, classical phrasing. His trumpet work has a bright sheen and a light, easy vibrato, and his occasional clarinet and piano solos are far from an embarrassment. He's even made some recordings on tenor and soprano sax, and on trombone. Carter contributed the arrangement for "Keep a Song in Your Soul" to Fletcher Henderson's orchestra in 1930, and is known for his block-chord pieces for reed instruments. Later, he expanded his scope to extended pieces, dramatic scores, and suites.

Though he received some instruction from his mother, essentially Carter was self-taught. He began on trumpet, switched to C-melody sax, and then switched to alto. He played in several bands prior to 1928, among them June Clark's and Earl Hines's. Carter led his own orchestra in 1928, then worked with Charlie Johnson and some others, before joining Fletcher Henderson. After leaving Henderson, Carter briefly served as music director for McKinney's Cotton Pickers in Detroit, then returned to New York. By 1933, he'd gotten his own band again, and led it until 1935. Such players as Bill Coleman, Dicky Wells, Ben Webster, Chu Berry, Teddy Wilson, and Sid Catlett were members of the band. Carter then spent three years in Europe, writing for the British Broadcasting Company in London, leading an integrated band in Holland, and becoming a sensation in the Paris studios. He returned to America in 1938 and formed a new orchestra that took a residency at the Savoy ballroom in Harlem through much of 1939 and 1940. He briefly led a sextet, then took a new big band to California and settled in Los Angeles in 1942.

While leading his orchestra (which, at various times, included Miles Davis, J. J. Johnson, and Max Roach) into the mid '40s, Carter turned to film work in 1943. His first venture was *Stormy Weather*, and he composed and wrote arrangements for several feature films and, eventually, for television shows. He also aided in the effort that led to the amalgamation of the Black and White chapters of the Musicians Local, and helped to get other Black players and writers into the Hollywood arena. Carter turned from leading bands to the Jazz at the Philharmonic circuit in 1946. He maintained a steady schedule of recordings, did occasional big band dates, and wrote arrangements for vocalists in the '50s and '60s. He penned charts for Sarah Vaughan, Ella Fitzgerald, Ray Charles, Peggy Lee, Louis Armstrong, and even Jackie Wilson. He expanded his performance schedule in the '70s, and appeared at several major festivals and toured Europe and Japan. He ended a ten-year recording hiatus, and started a new career as an educator, lecturing at prestigious universities and receiving an honorary doctorate from Princeton in 1974. In the '90s, new and old Carter recordings flood the marketplace, and he's the subject of frequent retrospective articles in which he prefers to look ahead rather than reflect back. —*Ron Wynn with Dan Morgenstern*

○ **Chronological Benny Carter (1929-1933), The** / **i.** Sep. 1929-May 1933 / Classics 522

○ **Chronological Benny Carter (1936), The** / **i.** Apr. 1930-Oct. 1936 / Classics 541

Symphony in Riffs / **i.** 1930-1937 / ASV 5075
Early '30s formative sessions, with Carter's charts and alto sax solos spearheading some great combos. The material on

this disc was culled from different recording projects and includes varying personnel, among them some great players like Teddy Wilson, Wilbur de Paris, Chu Berry, and Big Sid Catlett, plus Carter. These cuts are historic and feature great music. —*Ron Wynn*

Benny Carter (1933) / Mar. 14, 1933+Oct. 16, 1933 / Prestige 7643

○ **Chronological Benny Carter (1933-1936), The** / **i.** May 1933-Apr. 1936 / Classics 530

Chocolate Dandies, The / **i.** 1933-1935 / DRG 8448
Classic early swing and combo material written and arranged by the great Benny Carter. Carter's alto playing is joyous, concise, and bluesy, while his arrangements emphasize both ensemble cohesion and individual freedom. They give his soloists just enough space to express themselves, yet never let the pace waver or the ensemble stop swinging. —*Ron Wynn*

○ **Chronological Benny Carter (1937-1939), The** / **i.** Jan. 1937-Jun. 1939 / Classics 552

○ **Chronological Benny Carter (1940-1941), The** / **i.** May 1940-Oct. 1941 / Classics 631

Uncollected Benny Carter / **i.** 1944 / Hindsight 218
Carter, with Eddie "Lockjaw" Davis (ts) and Harry "Sweets" Edison (tpt), shows the youngsters what jazz phrasing, taste, and sophistication are all about. —*Ron Wynn*

3, 4, 5,—the Verve Small Group Sessions / **i.** 1946 / Verve 849395
The Benny Carter disc has 19 titles: eight by a trio, eight by a quartet, and three by a quintet. The 1954 trio sides, with Teddy Wilson and Jo Jones no less, have previously been issued only in Japan . . . (There's more unissued Hodges, too). Carter plays with consistent authority in his suave style. When backed by Don Abney, George Duvivier and Louis Bellson, the depth and color the bass adds, particularly on "Tenderly," is very valuable. "This Can't Be Love," the notes claim, was not on the original LP, and the three final quintet titles with Oscar Peterson on piano were never issued at all! Most of the tempos are slow to medium, so the fast version of Matt Dennis's "Will You Still Be Mine," makes a pleasing change. Given the numerous playing times, the cited "bonuses" are genuine. —*Stanley Dance*, Jazz Times

★ **Complete Benny Carter on Keynote** / Apr. 22, 1946 / PolyGram 830965
Here's a fine representative sampling of prime Carter '40s cuts. With Arnold Ross Quintet, his own L.A. group at the time. —*Ron Wynn*

○ **Swing 1946** / 1946 / Prestige 7604
The first session in this album is by the Chocolate Dandies for which Benny Carter used Al Grey, Sonny White, and John Simmons from his big band, along with Buck Clayton (just out of the army), Ben Webster, and Sid Catlett (both probably leading their own groups on 52nd Street and very active in the recording studios at that time). Their opening number, "Cadillac Slim," is hauntingly familiar. It is an "I Got Rhythm"-variant that I know I've heard under another title in some vaguely Duke Ellingtonian context. The next session is by Gene Sedric's Orchestra, an actual working band which included, besides the leader, two other Fats Wallerites: Al Casey and Slick Jones. These records are the only ones I know of to have solos by Lincoln Mills (a trumpeter formerly with Carter and other big bands) and Freddy Jefferson (piano), and both are fine players. Sedric was, of course, one of *the* great originals on tenor and clarinet. The third session is by Jonah Jones and his Cats, a group made up entirely of Cab Calloway sidemen (except for drummer Kansas Fields). These must be among Jones's finest records, and to hear them is worth the price of the album alone. His playing is soaring, brilliant, daring, and subtle, by turns. Tyree Glenn contributes some beautifully burnished trombone solos and there is a rare opportunity to hear a particular favorite of mine, Rudy Powell, on clarinet. There is an informative liner by Stanley Dance, full discographical details,

and the recording quality is good despite the phony stereo. —Ron Anger, Coda

Cosmopolite / Dec. 1952 / Clef 141

Jazz Giant / Jun. 11, 1957 / Contemporary 167
While very pleasant, this date rarely rises up to really challenge anyone ("Blue Lou" and "Blues My Naughty Sweetie Gives to Me" do that best). One does get a chance to hear Benny Carter's swing-styled trumpet. Carter switched to alto sax after hearing (Frankie Traumbauer) "Tram" (by some accounts) and, like Coleman Hawkins, from that time on incorporated new concepts into his playing (one can hear both Charlie Parker and Art Pepper in his playing, or vice versa). But Carter's trumpet work did not develop in the same manner, so that when he did play trumpet one got a strictly mainstream style. This date is strictly a Carter spotlight (trombonist Frank Rosolino has a few moments; he and tenor saxophonist Ben Webster are out of "Ain't She Sweet" and "Sweetie"), and for that it is recommended, but as a full date its focus is rather singular, especially considering Webster's presence. —Bob Rusch, Cadence

★ **Swingin' the Twenties** / Nov. 2, 1958 / Contemporary 339
Alto saxophonist Benny Carter receives top billing on this album, but Earl Hines didn't exactly assume the role of mere sideman. With Carter, Hines was an equal. These contemporaries obviously enjoyed their first recording session together. The tempos are playful, so are the tones. Their fondness for the material (classics from the '20s) shows, as does a penchant for producing tidy solos that begin, grow, climax, resolve, and end. On *Swingin' the '20s*, Hines gives an exhibition of what jazz piano was, is, and will be. The light, airy right hand on "If I Could Be with You (One Hour Tonight)" is a favorite device of Ramsey Lewis. The thumping chords of "Sweet Lorraine" point to Errol Garner. The spurts of flamboyance decorating "Who's Sorry Now" have been appropriated by Oscar Peterson. The flip stride-ish echoes in "Mary Lou's" opening cadenza recall Fats Waller. —Cliff Radel, Down Beat

○ **Fabulous Benny Carter, The** / i. 1959 / Audio Lab 1505

○ **Jazz Calendar** / i. 1960 / United Artists 5080

★ **Further Definitions** / Nov. 13+15, 1961 / MCA 5651
This is classic, a masterpiece of arranging, playing, and composing. Carter duplicated the instrumental setting and included some cuts from a landmark session he'd done back in Paris during the '30s. It still sounds wonderful 31 years later, though the vinyl album is superior to MCA reissue. —Ron Wynn

○ **B.B.B. & Co.** / i. 1962 / Prestige 758
This is a April 10, 1962 session served up with class and decorum by Benny Carter (alto sax/trumpet), Ben Webster (tenor sax), Barney Bigard (clarinet), Shorty Sherock (trumpet), Jimmy Rowles (piano), Dave Barbour (guitar), Leroy Vinnegar (bass), and Mel Lewis (drums). If you like the slow drag blues, the highlight here will be the anchor track "You Can't Tell," which stretches out over 12 minutes and keeps the pressure, but never breaks its tension or sweat. —Bob Rusch, Cadence

☆ **Additions to Further Definitions** / Mar. 2, 1966 / Impulse 9116
Additions to Further Definitions is a beautiful, timeless date featuring the writing, arranging, and playing of alto saxophonist Benny Carter on ten tracks. Fans of mainstream or modern will find rewards in this music. Joining the Carter triumph are Bud Shank, Buddy Collette, or Teddy Edwards (saxophones); Bill Perkins, Bill Hood, Don Abney (piano); Al Stoller (drums); Ray Brown or Al McKibbon (bass); Mundell Lowe or Barney Kessel (guitar). —Bob Rusch, Cadence

Birdology—Vol. 1 / i. 1971 / Verve 841132

Birdology—Vol. 2 / i. 1971 / Verve 841133

King, The / Feb. 11, 1976 / Pablo 2310-768
A slightly pretentious title, but a wonderful lineup. Sidemen Tommy Flanagan (p), Milt Jackson (vib), and Joe Pass (g) are superb. —Ron Wynn

★ **Carter, Gillespie, Inc.** / Apr. 27, 1977 / Pablo 682
Producer Norman Granz deserves much applause for returning alto sax master Benny Carter to vinyl on a regular basis in the '70s. Here, he is teamed with the bubbly trumpeter Dizzy Gillespie, a pair seemingly made for each other. Carter is primarily a swing-era survivor, while Gillespie was the quintessential bopper. The feelings are meshed together for an album of real pleasure. Add guitarist Joe Pass, pianist Tommy Flanagan, drummer Mickey Roker, and bassist Al McKibbon and you have a real giants-of-jazz session. Five standards and Carter's "The Courtship" are given much more than a cursory run through. A swinging, relaxed time appears to have been had by all, and nowhere is the rapport more evident than during Carter and Gillespie's spirited trade offs on "Broadway." The recording is bell clear and the recording info is well documented. —Willard Jenkins Jr., Cadence

Live and Well in Japan / Apr. 29, 1977 / Pablo 736
Carter has a good workout on this live set. Ray Bryant (p) is impressive. —Ron Wynn

Benny Carter 4: Montreux 1977 / Jul. 13, 1977 / Pablo 2308204

★ **Gentleman and His Music, A** / Aug. 3, 1985 / Concord Jazz 4285
Everyone gets plenty of room on this one. . . . On "Lover Man" and the tribute to George Duvivier, though, Benny Carter (alto sax) gets to stretch out as the front line solos are divided between Carter and Joe Wilder (trumpet)—no Scott Hamilton—with Ed Bickert (guitar) and Gene Harris (piano) getting a spot before and after. Hamilton (tenor sax) takes his turn on each of the remaining titles, and is particularly good on Carter's "A Kiss for You" even though he had just been introduced to it at the session. Joe Wilder, of course, is excellent on both muted and open horn, and Bickert contributes solidly. Of the personnel here, Gene Harris may be unfamiliar. . . . He had a good deal more visibility in the '60s as the lead pianist with the Three Sounds. Here, he is especially good in backing the "Blues For George" and he contributes an ear-catching Earl Hines-drenched solo to "Lover Man," but he is solid throughout the session. Bassist John Clayton was able to add an extra touch with some unusually good bowed work on Carter's "A Kiss for You," and he really makes the Duvivier tribute memorable. —Shirley Klett, Cadence

Meets Oscar Peterson / Nov. 14, 1986 / Pablo 2310-926
The harmonic master gets capable, standout support from the top-flight bassist. —Ron Wynn

Central City Sketches / i. 1987 / Music Masters 5030
With Eddie Bert, Jimmy Knepper, John Purcell, Lew Tabackin, John Lewis, Ron Carter, and Mel Lewis. —AMG

Cookin' at Carlos 1 / Oct. 5-9, 1988 / Music Masters 5033
Fine playing from Carter. Ordinary compositions, but the group romps through them with style. —Ron Wynn

Over the Rainbow / Oct. 18+19, 1988 / Music Masters 5015
Some beautiful solos by Carter. A good release, though not essential. —Ron Wynn

My Man Benny, My Man Phil / Nov. 21-22, 1989 / Music Masters 5036
With Phil Woods (as). A pair of old friends, these alto sax giants make a great team. —Ron Wynn

○ **Harlem Renaissance** / Nov. 7+9, 1992 / Music Masters 65080
Though an elder statesman, alto saxophonist Benny Carter still has a vigorous, emphatic sound and can play with zest on uptempo wailers or slow, churning blues and ballads. He conducts a combined orchestra blending his own big band with the Rutgers University group. Guest stars Frank Wess, Ralph Bowen, Virgil Jones, and others play on several cuts, then join the students. —Ron Wynn

All of Me / Bluebird 3000

Three Great Swing Saxophonists / Bluebird 1989

These are some superb cuts with Carter and fellow jazz statesmen Ben Webster (ts) and Coleman Hawkins (ts). Though the main body of songs can be found elsewhere, the CD has six bonus cuts. —Ron Wynn

BETTY CARTER (Lorraine Carter)

b. May 16, 1930, Flint, MI
Vocals / Bop, ballads & blues
A demanding, uncompromising vocalist, Betty Carter was nicknamed "bebop" once, and has been a longtime champion of the music. Her style includes surging scat, exacting reworkings of lyrics, vigorous interpretations of standards, and a nonstop, driving approach that's modified only slightly for ballads. She's issued her own recordings rather than subscribe to the dictates of record labels. Her disdain for avant-garde and R&B/soul/pop singers who blend jazz into their performances (Chaka Khan is an exception) is legendary. Her temper rivals any instrumentalist's. Stories about her disagreements with musicians are well known; anyone who attends enough Betty Carter concerts will probably observe her expressing displeasure with a musician or a discourteous audience member. That fire and integrity has characterized her music since the inception of her career.

Carter sang with Charlie Parker as a teen when he and other bop musicians visited Detroit. She studied piano at the Detroit Conservatory, and, after winning a local amateur contest, turned pro in 1946. She joined Lionel Hampton's band in 1948, using the stage name Lorraine Carter. Hampton nicknamed her Betty Bebop, and she eventually took Betty for her first name. She traveled to New York in 1951 with Hampton's big band, then settled there. Carter did several shows at the Apollo, and toured with Miles Davis's band in 1958 and 1959. She recorded with Gigi Gryce in 1958 on Peacock. Carter worked for three years in the early '60s with Ray Charles, and recorded a celebrated duet album (she's been quoted as saying she hates the record). She made a single album in 1960 for ABC Paramount, *The Modern Sound of Betty Carter* and the LP with Charles in 1961. Carter also made some fine but poor-selling releases for Roulette. She played in Japan with Sonny Rollins, in London at Annie Ross's club, and in France during the mid and late '60s.

Carter formed her own trio in 1969, and two years later started Bet-Car Productions, her own record label. Her trio proved a popular attraction on college campuses in the early '70s. She issued *Betty Carter I, Betty Carter 2, The Audience With Betty Carter,* and *Whatever Happened to Love* on her label. A 1975 appearance in the musical *Don't Call Me Man* won Carter increased recognition and exposure, and led to several club engagements. She continued performing with her trio in the '80s, made an appearance on the Cosby show, and signed with Verve in 1988. She continues recording for the label, and has a full slate of club, international, festival, and college appearances. Her resolve and performance skills, as well as her wit and opinions, remain sharp. —Ron Wynn

Meet Betty Carter / May 13+16, 1955 / Epic 3202

Social Call / Apr. 25, 1956 / Sony Special Products 36425
Betty Carter may take much pride in *Social Call,* the reissue of material she recorded in 1955 and 1956. It marks, in a tangible manner, the growing audience appreciating her tremendous talent. It also shows that Carter is a natural innovator. This recording reveals some of the early musical choices Carter made, showing both steps and leaps she took from her early, traditionally centered style to her current, profoundly innovative one. Side one consists of material originally released on Epic as *Meet Betty Carter and Ray Bryant.* These tunes were recorded in two sessions, three days apart, in 1955. On side two, a big band led by Gigi Gryce supports Carter in a '56 date. The arrangements on both sides by Quincy Jones and Gryce (respectively) are excellent, as are the sidemen's swinging performances. Carter alternates between traditionally oriented and innovative styles in these early recordings. The traditionally bright tone

quality of "Can't We Be Friends" and "I Could Write a Book" contrasts with the strikingly diffused timbre of "Tell Him I Said Hello" (1956) and "Moonlight in Vermont" (1955). The decision—whether conscious or unconscious—to develop her husky, widely spread timbral quality is one example of the astute musical decisions Carter made. Another was her move to lower keys. On this recording, she sings in a variety of ranges. When she sings in a comfortably low key, she achieves an admirable regularity of timbre throughout her range. While she doesn't exactly have to strain up high on other tunes, her sound is not nearly as personal or affecting. Carter's musical decisions (especially about pitch and timing) were made with an assurance and musicality that, for most musicians, comes only after many years of work. While there is no doubt that Carter is a better singer now than she was then, this recording is an important reminder of the many ways she expanded the jazz singer's role. —*Elaine Guregian,* Down Beat

○ I Can't Help It / i. 1958 / GRP 114
Late '50s session with Carter honing her skills, backed by both a moderate-sized group and the Richard Wess Orchestra. The group includes Kenny Dorham, Melba Liston, Wynton Kelly, and Benny Golson. Carter was still building a reputation, and was then more in standard scat/hard bop mode than in the interpretative style she later patented. —Ron Wynn

Out There / Feb. 1958 / Peacock 90
A dynamic set with Benny Golson, Melba Liston, and Gigi Gryce that's long since been deleted. —Ron Wynn

★ Modern Sound of Betty Carter / Aug. 18, 1960 / ABC (Import) 363

☆ Ray Charles and Betty Carter / 1961 / ABC (Import)
The session with Betty Carter has been an elusive treasure for many; it had only a brief reappearance as a bootleg after its original removal from the ABC catalog. Here, the program (51:41) is augmented by three other Ray Charles items from the back catalog. The collaboration with Betty Carter has become a legendary session because of its limited catalogue stay and the popular following of both artists. It has, for me, always promised more than it delivers; even so, familiarity over the decades (!) has produced a classic session outing. While I'm not quite sure what I expected, both artists emerge with individual artistries intact. Perhaps it is the hoped-for jazz ambience, which is downplayed, that has always disappointed me; Marty Paich's arrangements are memorable. In this setting, Ray Charles is the balladeer and moves back toward his Nat "King" Cole/Charles Brown roots. —*Bob Rusch,* Cadence

Inside Betty Carter / Jun. 1964 / United Artists 3379
Marred only by its ludicrous playing time (25:26), *Inside Betty Carter* is a welcome reissue of a June 1964 session for UA. Save for her stretch on Richard Rodgers's "Look No Further," a brisk "My Favorite Things," and a mostly breakneck "Something Big," this is a showcase for Betty Balladeer, not Betty Bebop. This isn't a scat session, but a study in lyric interpretation and dramatic shading. Her almost uninflected (microshaded) long high notes on "Some Other Time" are alone worth a hear. Like on her bossa-nova tinged shuffle "Open the Door," she features a lighter tonality than one may associate with her power-pipes work. The backing trio—Hal (Harold) Mabern, piano; Bob Cranshaw, bass; Roy McCurdy, drums—is totally at her service, their contributions are to the point. With so little time ("Look No Further" and "Something Big" are two minutes or less) there's no room for digression. Carter's restraint should make this a favorite among those who like to hear venerable tunes treated with suitable respect. Only "Favorite Things" might be considered a familiar choice. Carter avoids mannered gestures and crowd-pleasing stunts; lovely, but too friggin' short. —*Bob Rusch,* Cadence

Finally, Betty Carter / Sep. 1969 / Roulette 5000

☆ 'Round Midnight / Dec. 6, 1969 / Atlantic 80453

Betty Carter's records have never been excessive in number, and have never been easily accessible or well distributed. This record was recorded live in 1969; it is splendid. Carter has a breathy, distorted voice capable of twisting and bending in a manner not unlike Sarah Vaughan's. Unlike Vaughan, at least on this recording, Carter was never affected or presumptuous. She manages to evoke tension and emotion rather than a condescending hipness. She's also capable of great humor in her singing, but she always swings, and an eight-minute outing of "Surrey with the Fringe on Top" is the epitome of this always-present ability. The jazz trio backing her is in perfect complement (pianist Norman Simmons, bassist Lysle Atkinson, drummer Al Harewood) and is an integral part of the absolute success of the album. —*Doug Shaw*, Cadence

Betty Carter—Vols. 1 and 2 / 1971-1972 / Bet-Car 1001
She put these out herself to get the music out in the marketplace. You can get them directly from her. —*Ron Wynn*

Betty Carter Album, The / 1972 / Verve 835682

Now It's My Turn / Mar. 9, 1976-Jun. 22, 1976 / Roulette 5005

☆ **What a Little Moonlight Can Do** / i. 1976 / Impulse
The material on this two-record set is a reissue of material that originally appeared on Progressive Records around 1958, and on a 1960 ABC recording. This recording, in relation to other Betty Carter material, is not her best, although there are moments. However, even with some of the string backing (ABC), the poor choice of material, the occasional intonation problems, and a pretentiousness (abandoned later), I can still enjoy this recording. I must pick out the enjoyment, it is selective, because I am partial to any Betty Carter, and I suspect others so inclined will want to get this recording. Of the two sessions reissued here, my preference is for the Progressive date and for the more straightahead jazz backing, in particular the tenor sax work of Benny Golson. Trumpeters Kenny Dorham and Ray Copeland, trombonist Melba Liston, alto saxophonists Gigi Gryce and Jimmy Powell, baritone saxophonist Sahib Shihab, tenor saxophonist, flutist, and bassoon player Jerome Richardson, bassists Sam Jones and Peck Morrison, pianist Wynton Kelly, and drummer Specs Wright are present on the Progressive date. The personnel for the ABC record is unknown. —*Bob Rusch*, Cadence

★ **Audience with Betty Carter** / Dec. 6-8, 1979 / Verve 835684
This live recording shows Betty Carter at her liveliest and most compelling. Response among all parties was exceptionally alert: Carter's animated, emotionally charged performance receives an enthusiastic reception that encouraged her to bait the delighted audience further—with witticism and, apparently with some visual gesturing—and the sidemen flatten her idiosyncrasies, anticipating and following her infallibly. Standards and new tunes split the bill here. Carter combines two standards ("Can't We Talk" and "Either It's Love") and thoroughly reworks others ("Spring," "Deep Night," "I Could Write"). It would be hard to imagine a better rhythm section than the one on this set. John Hicks on piano, Curtis Lundy on bass, and Kenneth Washington on drums establish absolutely solid time. The rhythmic strength of this performance would be enough to recommend it, but Carter's ironic persona is irresistible. —*Elaine Guregian*, Down Beat

Whatever Happened to Love / Mar. 27, 1982 / Verve 835683

Look What I Got / 1988 / Verve 835661
No one is any better than Betty Carter when it comes to scat singing, and while there's an ample amount of scatting on *Look What I Got*, it's her ballad work that seems to be reaching new heights. Carter truly knows how to caress a song without sounding insincere, and when she reaches for a note, she never misses. The sheer beauty of her voice is enough to carry most ballads, but Carter never coasts. As usual, she employs frequent tempo changes in her material; the most striking example is "The Good Life." Carter joins the band at a nice, loping tempo. After one chorus, the band double-times the tempo while Carter maintains the slower

pace in a most effective manner. Tenor saxophonist Don Braden augments the trio on four cuts and takes a couple of good solos, although his is basically a supporting role. The trio of Benny Green (piano), Michael Bowie (bass), and Winard Harper (drums) is on hand for most of the uptempo tunes: "All I Got" and "Mr. Gentleman," which are fine examples of Carter's abilities with faster tempos. Betty Carter is one of the finest vocalists in jazz. *Look What I Got* is a very good recording and quite representative of her talent. —*Tim Smith*, Cadence

Droppin' Things / May 25-26, 1990 / Verve 843991

○ **It's Not About the Melody** / i. 1992 / Verve 513870
Contemporary Betty Carter session in which her deep, sometimes weary, and often swaying voice sounds defiant as she moves through both uptempo selections and declarative ballads. Carter has become the top jazz vocalist on the scene, and her treatments don't follow any formula or adhere to any set principles other than her own. —*Ron Wynn*

JOHN CARTER (John Wallace Carter)

b. Sep. 24, 1929, Forth Worth, TX, d. Mar. 31, 1991
Clarinet, alto saxophone / Modern creative
John Carter was a virtuoso clarinetist who was as equally superb at playing bebop as he was at stimulating free dialogues with longtime musical companion Bobby Bradford, or at conducting intricate, original symphonic works. He could play anything from traditional jazz stomps to pop and swing. Unfortunately, Carter received only a slight bit of recognition near the end of his life. He ranged over the clarinet, and could play woody, rumbling solos, upper-register squeals, or warm, moving melodies. He studied clarinet and alto sax, and attended Lincoln University in 1949 and the University of Colorado in 1956. Carter played with Ornette Coleman and Charles Moffett in the late '40s. He was a public school teacher in Fort Worth from 1949 to 1961, and taught in Los Angeles from 1961 to 1982. During those years, Carter also played in bands and made recordings. He cofounded the New Art Jazz Ensemble in Los Angeles with Bradford in 1964, and conducted Coleman symphonic works at UCLA in 1965. Carter formed a quartet with Bradford that same year. The group never had enough recording opportunities, but did some fine sessions for tiny labels in the '60s and '70s. Carter doubled on alto sax and clarinet in the '60s, but dropped alto in the '70s. He was in the Little Big Horn workshop with Bradford, James Newton, Arthur Blythe, and others in the late '70s. Carter recorded a quintet date for Moers in 1979 that featured his folk pieces. He formed the Wind College in 1983 with Newton, Red Callender, and Charles Owens, and was a coleader of the great Clarinet Summit in the 1980s. Carter received most of his notoriety in the late '80s for a series of ambitious albums that chronicle the history of African-Americans. They were issued on Gramavision, and include *Castles of Ghana* and *Dance of the Love Ghosts*. Carter had just begun to reap major publicity when he died in 1991. Regrettably, only a few of his titles are available on CD. —*Ron Wynn*

○ **West Coast Hot** / i. 1969 / Novus 3107
The first recordings in 1969 of the quartet co-led by clarinetist John Carter and trumpeter Bobby Bradford undermine the stereotypes of West Coast jazz, and challenge the New York fire-music establishment's exclusive franchise. Material from two Flying Dutchman sessions has been reissued on *West Coast Hot*. Despite the easy comparison, the assets of Carter and Bradford's quartet are markedly different from Ornette Coleman's. Carter, who displays equal facility on alto, tenor, clarinet, and flute on these early recordings was, unlike Coleman, a true multi-instrumentalist. Bradford was by far the most lyrically swinging, post-bop trumpeter of the day. Bassist Tom Williamson stylistically splits the difference between Charlie Haden and Scott LaFaro, and drummer Bruz Freeman adeptly handles the clipped rhythms, straight-up swing, and moody brush work required of him. Additionally, Coleman's patented lexicon was only one of many compositional tools Carter and

Bradford employed. It's a stretch to call them derivative. — *Bill Shoemaker,* Down Beat

○ **Self-Determination Music** / 1969-1970 / Flying Dutchman 128

○ **Dauwhe** / Feb. 25, 1982-Mar. 8, 1982 / Black Saint 0057
This February 25, 28, and March 8, 1982 recording brought together some of the best of the West (cornetist Bobby Bradford, flutist James Newton, soprano saxophonist, clarinetist, and oboe player Charles Owens, bassist Roberto Miranda, drummer Williams Jeffrey, percussionist/waterphone player Luis Peralta) for a set of five John Carter compositions. The title track is brilliant both in its open construction and in solos executed by the leader, Bradford, and Newton. In fact, this is arguably Newton's most inspired work. "Ode," which completes side one, is almost Billy Strayhornish in its impressionism, and is a showcase for the leader's clarinet. Side two offers more wonderful adventures in sound and continues to build a strong case for John Carter as *the* clarinetist of the '80s. . . . "Enter," "Soft," and "Mating" all flow together to make up side two. It is very exciting music. —*Bob Rusch,* Cadence

★ **Castles of Ghana** / Feb. 1985 / Gramavision 79423
John Carter's *Castles of Ghana* was a suite dealing with the crucible of slavery and its devastating consequence on African civilization. It was performed magnificently, attesting to a composer who created a body of work that added graceful formality and personal signature while never losing sight of the art of individual improvisation. This was an ensemble of brillant paired voicings and inspired soloists. It is noteworthy that Carter wrote compositions that didn't rely on the saxophone or traditional rhythm section as its chief voices. Somewhere between the resounding brass of Bobby Bradford, Bakida Carroll, and Benny Powell that announced the opening and the solemn narration of the closing theme ("Postlude"), we were caught up in a musical drama. This music could at once convey the horror of slavery, yet celebrate the dynamic of human courage by an example of an eclecticism via a vamp, a slow blues, or the interplay between clarinetist John Carter and Marty Ehrlich. All seemed so natural and each player added a very assured and unique voice. . . . *Castles of Ghana* stands as one of the seminal works of the '80s, both for the way it enlivened history and because it was in and of itself one more example of the Black Diaspora. —*Ludwig Van Trikt,* Cadence

Dance of the Love Ghosts / Nov. 1986 / Gramavision 79424
Experimental, daring concept work with Andrew Cyrille (d) and Fred Hopkins (b). Excellent clarinet solos and arrangements by Carter. —*Ron Wynn*

Fields / Mar. 1988 / Gramavision 79425
A 1989 reissue of part of his impressive series spotlighting African-American musical achievement. —*Ron Wynn*

Shadows on a Wall / Apr. 1989 / Gramavision 79422
John Carter's ambitious composition *Roots and Folklore: Episodes in the Development of American Folk Music* comes to an end with the release of *Shadows on a Wall.* Since Carter conceived the five albums as one composition, this final installment can be viewed as the last chapter. Taken as a whole, "Roots and Folklore" is certainly one of the most, if not *the* most ambitious work of the '80s by any jazz artist. . . . *Shadows on a Wall* represents both a triumph of perseverance and a victory of sorts for its creator. It is no surprise that it is a musical triumph as well. The previous record, *Fields,* was a tough act to follow and Carter wisely avoided attempting to match or exceed the intensity of the earlier effort. Instead, he chose to present a largely vocal work, which provides a satisfying conclusion to the suite and also has its share of inspired playing. "Sippie Strut" (misspelled "Sippi" on the cover) opens the record with a relentless piano ostinato supported by ensemble textures while Terry Jenoure scats in the background. The initial written theme is stretched across bar lines and Don Preston's keyboards gave an ethereal presence to the music. The piano then changes to an almost boppish figure and the theme is

further developed before the solos take off. On this piece and throughout the record, the octet plays with a cohesion and precision that only an ensemble that had worked together extensively could muster. Jenoure's voice was mixed as another instrument in the octet, rather than as a solo instrument, and the result is effective. Due to the amount of vocals on all pieces, there isn't much of Jenoure's violin to be heard here, but she is used primarily as a wordless improviser, to great advantage. While Jenoure was not the most impressive "singer of songs," she excelled at just the type of creative, scat-and-beyond style that's heard on this record. Particularly impressive is Bradford's cornet solo (not trumpet, as listed on the cover) on "Sippie Strut," but all of the musicians could be singled out for just about any of the pieces. . . . The rhythm section of Fred Hopkins (bass) and Andrew Cyrille (drums) is solid as a rock throughout, and Benny Powell (trombone) adds the low brass timbre and makes the group sound much larger than eight pieces. Don Preston's synthesizer colors are always tasteful and add greatly to the overall ambience of the proceedings. The underrated, but excellent, Marty Ehrlich also contributes significantly to the music and provides the glue that keeps the written themes together. The leader's clarinet is as strong as ever, and his unaccompanied solo on "Spats" is a joy. —*Carl Baugher,* Cadence

Variations on Selected Themes for Jazz Quintet / Moers 01056

RON CARTER (Ronald Levin Carter)

b. May 4, 1937, Ferndale, MI
Bass, cello, bass guitar, composer / Hard bop, post bop, early jazz-rock
The epitome of class and elegance without stuffiness, Ron Carter has been a world-class bassist and cellist since the '60s. He's one of the greatest accompanists of all time, but has also done many albums that exhibit his prodigious technique. He's a brilliant rhythmic and melodic player who uses everything in the bass and cello arsenal: walking lines, thick, full, prominent notes and tones, drones and strumming effects, and melody snippets. His bowed solos are almost as impressive as the solos he plays with his fingers. Carter has been featured in clothing, instrument, and pipe advertisements; his mix of musical and extra-musical interests brings him close to being the bass equivalent of Duke Ellington. Carter is nearly as accomplished in classical music as he is in jazz, and has performed with symphony orchestras all over the world. He's almost exclusively an acoustic player; he did play electric for a short time in the late '60s and early '70s, but hasn't played it in many, many years.

Carter began playing cello at age ten. When his family moved from Ferndale, Michigan, to Detroit, Carter ran into problems with racial stereotypes about cello players, and switched to bass. He played in the Eastman School's Philharmonic Orchestra, and gained his degree in 1959. He moved to New York and played in Chico Hamilton's quintet with Eric Dolphy while he attended the Manhattan School of Music. Carter earned his master's degree in 1961. After Hamilton returned to the West Coast in 1960, Carter stayed in New York and played with Dolphy and Don Ellis, cutting his first records with them. He worked with Randy Weston and Thelonious Monk, while playing and recording with Jaki Byard in the early '60s. Carter also toured and recorded with Bobby Timmons's trio, and played with Cannonball Adderley. He joined Art Farmer's group for a short time in 1963, before being tapped to become a member of Miles Davis's band. Carter remained with Davis until 1968, appearing on every crucial mid-'60s recording and teaming with Herbie Hancock and Tony Williams to craft a new, freer rhythm section sound. The high-profile job led to a reputation that allowed Carter to become possibly the most recorded bassist in jazz history.

Carter's been heard on an unprecedented number of recordings; some sources claim 500, others have estimated it to be as many as 1,000. The list of people he's played with is simply too great to be cited accurately and completely. Carter's been a member of the New York Jazz Sextet and the New York Jazz Quartet, the VSOP tour, the Milestone Jazzstars, and was in one of the groups featured in the film *'Round Midnight* in 1986. He's led his own bands at various intervals since 1972, using a second bassist to keep time and to establish harmony so that he's free to provide solos. Carter even invented his own instrument, a piccolo bass. Carter's also contributed many arrangements and compositions to both his groups and to other bands. He's done duo recordings with either Cedar Walton or Jim Hall. Carter's recorded for Embryo/Atlantic, CTI, Milestone, Timeless, EmArcy, Galaxy, Elektra, and Concord. He's won numerous critics' polls. Currently, there are several Carter titles, both recent and reissued, available on CD. —*Ron Wynn*

Where? / Jun. 20, 1961 / New Jazz 432
Essential session with Carter on both bass and cello. Awesome solos by Eric Dolphy (sax)—stunning pieces. With Mal Waldron. —*Ron Wynn*

○ **Out Front** / i. 1966 / Prestige 7397

★ **Uptown Conversation** / Oct. 6, 1969 / Atlantic 521
Arguably his best release. A 1989 reissue of an Embryo album that features some rangy, vibrant Carter solos. —*Ron Wynn*

Blues Farm / Jan. 10, 1973 / Columbia 40691
One of his best dates as a leader. A good set with Bob James (k), Richard Tee (k), and Hubert Laws (f)—revealing jazz chops they've seldom shown. —*Ron Wynn*

All Blues / Oct. 24, 1973 / CTI 6037
The order of the day here, as the title indicates, is strictly blues feeling from beginning to end. Although several forms of blues, from ballads to post bop, are presented, there is the general presence of cool beauty throughout. Highlights include "Light Blue," an introspective dialogue between bassist Ron Carter and pianist Roland Hanna; the quirky, jumpy "Rufus;" and a version of "All Blues" that could stand with Miles Davis's anytime. Joe Henderson is as relaxed and mellow as I've ever heard him, soloing economically, filling some spaces, leaving others open. Drummer Billy Cobham offers another side of his talent to the listener on this date, skillfully underplaying his role. Hanna and electric pianist Richard Tee, both underrated players, work at their customary high level, straightahead and typical. Through it all, the witty, slippery Ron Carter slides in and out, strangely elusive, yet always in strong support, and more. While there is nothing adventurous to be found here, *All Blues* is all music, no jive. —*Chuck Mitchell*, Down Beat

Spanish Blue / Nov. 1974 / Columbia 40803

Yellow and Green / May 1976 / Columbia 40928

Pastels / Oct. 18+19, 1976 / Milestone 665
Some tremendous playing by Carter, Kenny Barron (p), and Hugh McCracken (g), though the strings get intrusive. —*Ron Wynn*

★ **Piccolo** / Mar. 26+27, 1977 / Milestone 55004
This is a finely crafted recording, abounding in a pleasing variety of cleverly voiced ensemble passages in a wide range of styles and densities. "Saguaro," for example, walks into a light, quasi-string quartet interlude, and features thoughtful rhythmic diversity throughout, from back beat to double-time swing. On tracks like these, Ron Carter comes close to transcending his instrument's idiosyncrasies, and indeed almost capitalizes on them. The other side of Carter the multi-instrumentalist is Carter the composer; and in addition to his minorish, pathetic "Little Waltz," "Tambien Conocideo," one of Carter's many Spanish-tinged pieces, is outstanding, with flamenco-like flourishes throughout, concluding with a poignant, elongated arco cadenza.... Pianist Kenny Barron receives ample solo space, and as always uses it wisely and wittily. The other members of this quartet (bassist Buster Williams and drummer Ben Riley) loan their equally sym-

pathetic support to this provocative, if not entirely successful, experiment. —*Jon Balleras*, Down Beat

☆ **Third Plane** / Jul. 13, 1977 / Milestone 754
Those wishing for these three musicians to get back to consistently playing the energizing and even creative jazz forms they used to explore were probably somewhat disappointed by this session. Drummer Tony Williams was only mediocre, turning in downright stiff solos on the brief "United Blues" and "Dolphin Dance" (though on the latter, his awkwardness was almost saved by Herbie Hancock (piano) and Ron Carter's (bass) entrance in a psuedo-free vein over his solo before returning to the head). He did do some nice syncopating on "Lawra," but this still paled to the inventive and colorful pulsing he used to do with Miles Davis (pre-*In a Silent Way*) and with his own early Lifetime bands. Carter was rich-toned throughout, playing in a relaxed manner and incorporating all sorts of double and triple stops as well as harmonics. His solos were quite solid on "Stella by Starlight," "United Blues," and "Quiet Times," where he energized the ballad with his outing during the double time section. On the title cut and "Stella," Hancock effectively lagged just a shade behind the beat, adding tension to the music. He didn't really exploit that tension on "Third Plane," but during his solo on "Stella," he grew more into the beat directly and also pushed the parameters of the structure and changes with some genuine "out" passages which were well-integrated into his whole statement—by far, his strongest solo on the album. —*Milo Fine*, Cadence

Peg Leg / Nov. 18-22, 1977 / Milestone 621

Song for You, A / Jun. 1978 / Milestone 9086
A change-of-pace session for Carter. He pairs his formidable bass lines and playing against a backdrop of four cellists, outstanding drummer Jack DeJohnette, and, at various times, pianists Kenny Barron or Leon Pendarvis, guitarist Jay Berliner, and percussionist Ralph McDonald. Things generally work, though sometimes the low energy level and lack of tension threaten to turn this into easy-listening material. —*Ron Wynn*

1 + 3 / Jul. 29, 1978 / Fantasy 1032
Exactly the kind of impressive, high-level playing and interaction you'd expect from this trio. Pianist Herbie Hancock, bassist Ron Carter, and drummer Tony Williams comprised the rhythm section on many '60s Miles Davis's classics; nearly three decades later, they're still in sync with each other. While it's Carter's session, there's really no leader or followers, just three wonderful musicians fully attuned to each other. —*Ron Wynn*

Parade / Mar. 1979 / Milestone 9088
Bassist Carter heads a sterling mid-sized band with three trumpeters and saxophonists, two trombones, but no bass or drums. He handles the job of being both the primary and secondary rhythm support, while guests Joe Henderson, Jon Faddis, and Frank Wess, among others, provide some standout solos. The ensemble interaction clicks as well. —*Ron Wynn*

Alone Together / i. 197x / Milestone 904

Etudes / Sep. 1982 / Elektra 0214
Sophisticated, elegant quartet date from '82, with Art Farmer's serene trumpet and flugelhorn playing setting the tone, backed by tenor and soprano saxophonist Bill Evans, who's more restrained than usual. Carter's bass and Tony Williams's drums are both understated and definitive in their support and backing rhythms. —*Ron Wynn*

Live at Village West / Nov. 1982 / Concord Jazz 4245

All Alone / Mar. 29, 1988 / EmArcy 836366

Something in Common / i. Nov. 1990 / Muse 5376

Standard Bearers / Milestone 6010
An overlooked date. Carter and some first-rate players, including Red Garland (p), McCoy Tyner (p), Herbie Hancock (k), and many others, work their way through a program of jazz classics. The CD has a bonus cut. —*Ron Wynn*

MICHAEL CARVIN

b. Dec. 12, 1944, Houston, TX
Drums / Hard bop

One of the most technically talented drummers active on the hard bop and free scene, Michael Carvin has been uniformly impressive in varied recording and performing sessions. He's demonstrated a complete, sharp, and consistently driving style; one that allows him to offer either crisp, just-off-the-beat drumming and constantly reworked tempos, or to play in a completely free manner. Carvin's father was a drummer who taught his son the rudiments. In the mid '60s, Carvin worked in Earl Grant's big band, then made a tour of duty in Vietnam. After his discharge, Carvin played with B.B. King. He worked with Freddie Hubbard, Pharoah Sanders, Lonnie Liston Smith, McCoy Tyner, Jackie McLean, and Clive Stevens's band, Atmospheres, in the '70s. Carvin recorded with Mickey Bass and Charles Davis's band in the early '80s. He's recorded as a leader for Muse and Steeplechase in the '70s, '80s, and '90s. Carvin has a few sessions available on CD. —*Ron Wynn*

Antiquity / **i.** 1974 / Steeple Chase 1028

Camel, The / Jul. 8, 1975 / Inner City 2038
Percussionist Michael Carvin's *The Camel* boasts impressive personnel (Sonny Fortune, Cecil Bridgewater, Ron Burton, Calvin Hill) who also sound better as an ensemble. "Osum," for instance, is an ebullient highlife piece, while John Coltrane's "Naima" features some lovely Sonny Fortune sax and exquisite, waterfalling piano accompaniment by Ron Burton behind Carvin's brush-breaths. There is also a low-down, old-fashioned blues and the title composition, which employs Middle Eastern textures. Carvin, who worked with both Jackie and Rene McLean in the Cosmic Brotherhood, logged an impressive series of jazz credits and also had a stint as a Motown staff drummer in 1968 and 1969, which explains why a funky undercurrent motivates virtually every rhythm he lays down. —*Charles Mitchell*, Down Beat

First Time / Oct. 7, 1986 / Muse 5352
This session's "Dear Trane" presents Ron Bridgewater (tenor sax) in a haunting solo that is an instance of a post-John Coltrane tenor saxophonist reflecting the influence of the master without being swallowed up by it. Claudio Roditi's work on "My Funny Valentine" and "A Night in Tunisia" is further evidence that among the new crop of trumpet soloists he is a model of inventiveness, logic, and clarity. Roditi maintains those qualities without sacrificing emotional heat as he demonstrates here. Cecil Bridgewater (trumpet) and John Stubblefield (tenor sax) solo well, if predictably. Onjae Allen Gumbs (piano) is, as usual, refreshing and very much in command of the music and his instrument, with an approach to comping that has something in common with McCoy Tyner, but a touch that recalls Tommy Flanagan's. David Williams (bass) solos nicely on "Dear Trane" and is strong in support throughout. Frank Lace (trombone) plays only in the ensembles on three pieces. Carvin might not please devotees of bashing exhibitions because he plays with precision, control, and uncannily low volume, even when soloing at fast tempos. He makes use of space and of subtle dynamic variations, so that in his infrequent passages at volume, the contrast creates interest. Both with sticks and brushes, his playing behind the soloists is subtle, with accents fashioned not to fit the drummer's ego but the soloist's needs. In a highlighted quotation on the album jacket, Max Roach says Carvin is one of his favorite drummers. Carvin's work here makes that tribute understandable. —*Doug Ramsey*, Jazz Times

★ **Between Me and You** / Sep. 27, 1988 / Muse 5370

Revelation / Dec. 12, 1989 / Muse 5399
Fine '89 date, with drummer Carvin heading a group loaded with top-flight hard bop players, from trumpeters Claudio Roditi and Cecil Bridgewater to torrid alto saxophonist Sonny Fortune, back on the jazz scene and wailing. Cyrus Chesnutt capably handles piano duties on most tracks, though John Hicks steps in on "Avotcja" and turns in a splendid solo. —*Ron Wynn*

AL CASEY (Albert Aloysius Casey)

b. Sep. 15, 1915, Louisville, KY
Guitar / Swing

An influential guitarist, Al Casey's impact, in the early '30s and '40s, came through his work with Fats Waller. Casey and Waller teamed for over 230 recordings and were their era's equivalent of Count Basie and Freddie Green. Casey was an excellent rhythm player and an able soloist who fused single-string and chordal approaches nicely on acoustic, and who developed a good style on electric as well. His family moved from Kentucky to New York in 1930, and Casey began his association with Waller while still a teen. He recorded with Frankie Newton in 1939 for a session organized by French critic and author Hughes Panassie. He worked often with Billie Holiday in the late '30s and '40s, and played with Teddy Wilson's big band. Casey also worked with Buster Harding and Chu Berry. He began playing with various Waller band members after the leader's death, and led his own trio. Casey recorded for Capitol in 1945, and played with Earl Hines and Big Sid Catlett. He switched to electric in the mid '40s, and joined the R&B revolution in the late '50s, working with King Curtis. Casey teamed with Jay McShann and Helen Humes in the '70s, and worked with the Harlem Blues and Jazz Band in 1980; he maintained his relationship with that organization through the late '80s. Casey also recorded with Moodsville, Fantasy, and JSP. A couple of his sessions are available on CD. —*Ron Wynn and Michael G. Nastos*

★ **Buck Jumpin'** / Mar. 7, 1960 / Prestige 675
Quintet sides with the Herman Foster Trio and reedman Rudy Powell. Nine tracks, mostly old-timey and bluesy, sweet and mellow. Two previously unreleased tracks. —*Michael G. Nastos*

Al Casey Quartet / Nov. 10, 1960 / Moodsville 12

Jumpin' with Al / Jul. 1973-Aug. 1973 / Black & Blue 33056

Guitar Odyssey / **i.** 1976 / Jazz Odyssey 012

Genius of Jazz Guitar / Jul. 1981 / JSP 1062
Side one with pianist Gene Rogers Trio; side two with Jay McShann or Mike Carr's Trio. Swing, blues, and gospel standards. —*Michael G. Nastos*

Al Casey Remembers King Curtis / Jul. 21, 1985 / JSP 1095

PHILIP CATHERINE

b. Oct. 27, 1942, London, England
Guitar / World fusion, modern creative

One of the greatest living exponents of the classic Django Reinhardt guitar style, Phillip Catherine earned the nickname "Young Django" from Charles Mingus. He can play flashy, flamboyant licks, wondrously beautiful lines, expressive melodies, or torrid solos. Catherine's equally accomplished at jazz, classical, and Afro-Latin material. He was born in London, but is a Belgian. Catherine played for Belgian radio stations in the '60s, and also worked with Lou Bennett. He got his jazz induction with Jean-Luc Ponty's Experience at a time when Ponty was heavily into free music. Catherine came to America after leaving Ponty in the early '70s, enrolled at Berklee, and later formed the band Pork Pie with Charlie Mariano and Jasper van't Hof. They recorded in the mid- and late '70s. Catherine teamed with Niels-Henning Ørsted-Pedersen in the mid '70s, and the duo worked on various projects into the mid '80s. Catherine made several dates with Larry Coryell in the '70s, and worked with Stephane Grappelli, Charles Mingus, and Ørsted-Pedersen in the '70s and '80s. He has a few dates available on CD. —*Ron Wynn*

Twin House / **i.** 1977 / Atlantic 50342

★ **I Remember You** / Oct. 1990 / Criss Cross 1048

Spanish Nights / 1992 / Enja 7023

SID CATLETT

b. 1910, **d.** 1951
Drums / Swing, big band

Just as arguments continue today over who's the greatest drummer in jazz, there were similar disputes during the swing era. Buddy Rich and Gene Krupa got more exposure and ink than "Big" Sid Catlett, but both Rich and Krupa loved and admired Catlett, and he loved and admired them. Catlett was one of jazz's premier combo drummers; a sensitive accompanist who knew how to push a beat, but never overpowered or hurried it. He could anticipate a soloist's direction, and usually adjusted his timbres to suit a soloist's style. He functioned just as expertly in a big band setting, and was an extraordinary extended soloist; along with Max Roach, he may have been jazz's greatest builder and developer of lengthy solos that don't become repetitious, that don't rely excessively on flash, and that don't run out of ideas in mid-stream. Catlett made recordings in every conceivable style: traditional New Orleans jazz, swing, '20s Chicago, and bop. Catlett played in several Chicago bands during his youth before moving to New York in 1930. During the '30s, he played with Benny Carter, McKinney's Cotton Pickers, the Jeter-Pillars Orchestra, and with Fletcher Henderson and Don Redman. He joined Louis Armstrong's big band from 1938 to 1942, and worked with Benny Goodman periodically in 1941. Catlett recorded for Commodore with Chu Berry and his "Little Jazz" Ensemble in 1938, and with Coleman Hawkins and the Chocolate Dandies in 1940. He led his own bands for six years. During this period, there was also a 1943 session with Hawkins and Leonard Feather's All-Stars, and sessions with Dizzy Gillespie and Charlie Ventura. Catlett rejoined Armstrong from 1947 to 1949, this time with the smaller edition of the All-Stars. While waiting in the wings at a theater in 1951, Big Sid Catlett died suddenly at age 41. —*Ron Wynn*

EUGENE CHADBOURNE

b. Jan. 4, 1954, Mount Vernon, NY
Guitar / Early jazz-rock, modern creative

Not strictly a jazz musician (some would say not a jazz musician at all), Eugene Chadbourne is certainly an improviser. His sprawling, skittering, bursting guitar forays are among modern music's most anthemic delights. He combines the wildness of the freest jazz with the unpredictability of manic rock, and adds his own convoluted lyrics and vocals/comments. Chadbourne began playing guitar at age 11. He moved from bottleneck blues to bebop and free jazz, then met England's Derek Bailey. Chadbourne's debut included a nod to Anthony Braxton. He began working with Frank Lowe and Billy Bang in the late '70s, then teamed with John Zorn and Tom Cora. Chadbourne's group, Shockabilly, mixed country, rock, free, and just plain noise in an inspired, if at times completely chaotic, frenetic manner. He recorded with Camper Van Beethoven in the '80s. Chadbourne's material is considered too noncommercial for rock and too outrageous for even most free jazz fans. Currently, he has no sessions listed as available, but his dates can be tracked down by those willing to beat the bushes. —*Ron Wynn*

★ **Lsd C&W** / **i.** 1987 / Fundamental 19
The ultimate Chadbourne, featuring medleys of the Beatles, Roger Miller, and Burl Ives, plus much more insanity filtered through post-avant-garde brilliance. —*Jeff Tamarkin*

There'll Be No Tears Tonight / **i.** Jan. 1987 / Fundamental 006
Country fans expecting straight, faithful versions of these covers of Roger Miller, Hank Williams, and Merle Haggard will be in shock. Imagine honky-tonk as free jazz, and that's what you'll get. —*Jeff Tamarkin*

SERGE CHALOFF

b. Nov. 24, 1923, Boston, MA, **d.** Jul. 16, 1957
Baritone saxophone / Bop

Cello

Music Map

| Cello in Erskine Tate's Vendome Orchestra (1925) |

| Harry Babasin (1921) with Dodo Marmarosa in 1947 |

Oscar Pettiford (1922-1960)–1950s

Ray Brown (1926)
Doug Watkins (1934-1962)
Peter Warren (1935)
Charles Mingus (1922-1979)
Ron Carter (1937)
Eldee Young (1936) w/Ramsey Lewis
Eberhard Weber (1940)
Sam Jones (1924-1981)
Percy Heath (1923)

1955-1962 West Coast Jazz
Fred Katz (1919)
& Nat Gershman (1917) w/Chico Hamilton's quintet

Late 1960s
Irene Aebi w/Steve Lacy
Jean-Charles Capon (1936)
David Baker
Dierdre Murray 1955) w/Hannibal Peterson
David Darling (1941) w/Ralph Towner, Terje Rypdal
David Eyges (1950) w/Byard Lancaster, Cecil McBee
Directions in Jazz
Richard Davis (1930)
Dave Holland (1946)
Abdul Wadud (1947)

A virtuoso baritone saxophonist, Serge Chaloff's bridged the swing and bebop eras in his playing. His early work was decidedly swing-oriented, then he absorbed the changes in harmonic and melodic theory and execution instituted during the bebop period. His driving, yet smoothly played, somberly delivered solos fit perfectly into '50s bands. Chaloff studied piano and clarinet, but taught himself the baritone, initially drawing on the styles of Harry Carney and Jack Washington. After playing in various bands during the late '30s and early '40s, Chaloff joined Boyd Raeburn in 1945. He also played with Georgie Auld's orchestra. Chaloff recorded with Sonny Berman for Dial in 1946. When he became part of Woody Herman's band in 1947, Chaloff became part of the famed Four Brothers section. His popularity was immediate, and he soon displaced his idol, Harry Carney, at the top of the jazz polls. He continued recording on Savoy, Mercer, Motif, and Keynote in the late '40s, playing with Al Cohn, Red Rodney, and Oscar Pettiford, among others. He worked with Boston musicians Herb Pomeroy and Boots Mussulli in the '50s, and recorded for Vogue, Storyville, and Capitol, making some masterpieces for Capitol during that decade. He contracted spinal paralysis. Chaloff played at a Metronome All-Star session and a '57 Four Brothers reunion date for RCA/Vik, then died of cancer. Mosaic Records issued a thorough, superb boxed set, *The Complete Capitol Recordings of Serge Chaloff*, in 1993. —*Ron Wynn*

○ **New Stars-New Sounds—Vol. 2** / Mar. 10, 1949 / Mercer 1003

○ **Serge Chaloff and Boots Mussulli** / **i.** 1954 / Storyville 310
Fable of Mable / Sep. 9+10, 1954 / Black Lion 760923

West Coast jazz's finest baritone saxophonist is in prime, keen form on this 1954 session. Chaloff, playing in a group that also includes Charlie Mariano and Herb Pomeroy, dominates the proceedings without ever seeming to strain or sweat. His rolling lines and smooth sound on the generally bulky-sounding baritone remain one of jazz's more impressive sounds. —*Ron Wynn*

○ **Boston Blow-Up** / Apr. 4+5, 1955 / Capitol 6510
Another swinging, boppish session from a musician who was once a mainstay of Woody Herman's band. —*David Szatmary*

★ **Blue Serge** / Mar. 4, 1956 / Capitol 742
An indispensable session from one of the great underrated baritone sax players, featuring Sonny Clark (p) and Philly Joe Jones (d). —*David Szatmary*

DENNIS CHAMBERS

Saxophone / Modern creative
A drummer whose propulsive style and versatility have enabled him to play in combos or large groups and to work with fusion and hard bop bandleaders, Dennis Chambers hasn't issued any dates as a leader. He's recorded and played with Bob Berg, Bill Evans (sax), Victor Bailey, Bob Belden, Kevin Eubanks, and Mike Stern, among others. All of these musicians currently have sessions available on CD that include Chambers. —*Ron Wynn*

JOE CHAMBERS (Joseph Arthur Chambers)

b. Jun. 25, 1942, Stoneacre, VA
Drums, piano / Modern creative
A steady, reliable player who's worked in hard bop, big-band, and free groups, Joe Chambers has never attained stardom, but enjoys healthy respect among musicians and critics in the jazz community. He's not flashy or bombastic, but can provide anything from consistent timekeeping to excellent solos, varied rhythms, multiple accents and colors, and precise interaction within the rhythm section. Chambers worked in the Washington, D.C. area for a few years in the late '50s and early '60s before moving to New York in 1963. He worked with Eric Dolphy, Freddie Hubbard, Jimmy Giuffre, Lou Donaldson, and Andrew Hill. Then, in the mid '60s and early '70s, he performed and recorded with Bobby Hutcherson. Chambers also played with Donald Byrd's quintet, Duke Pearson's big band, and Joe Henderson's group, and recorded with Sam Rivers, Chick Corea, Wayne Shorter, and Miroslav Vitous. He was among the originals in M'Boom Re', the percussion ensemble founded by Max Roach in 1970. He played in the '70s with Sonny Rollins, Tommy Flanagan, and Art Farmer, while recording and performing with Charles Mingus and Joe Zawinul. Chambers was in the Super Jazz Trio with Reggie Workman and Flanagan in the late '70s, recorded with Chet Baker in the early '80s, and played with Ray Mantilla's Space Station. Hubbard, Hutcherson, and M'Boom Re' have performed Chambers's compositions. They've also been featured on his infrequent albums. Chambers co-led a group with Larry Young in the late '70s, and did albums for Muse and a solo date for Denon. He recorded for Candid in 1992 with Philip Harper, Bob Berg, George Cables, and Santi Debriano. That session is one of only two Chambers dates available on CD. His classic album, *The Almoravid*, isn't in print at the present time. —*Ron Wynn*

★ **Almoravid, The** / Oct. 8, 1973-Nov. 1, 1973 / Muse 5035
This set offers glimpses of quite a few facets of Joe Chambers. The tracks with horns (which date from 1971) are reminiscent of Miles Davis's "Filles De Kilimanjaro" set: long, languid lines, generally reflective soloing, and a gradual realization that the drummer, crisp and cryptic, is at the center of things, the smoldering fold to all that sublime coolness. "Catta," by contrast, finds Chambers in the driver's seat of a rather Caribbean juggernaut, directing the rhythmic energy with a calm, casual, half-time cymbal line. Only on the last track does the leader really step out front, erupting from

a rock beat to speak his piece on the fragmentary "Gazelle Suite," then careening ominously around the foreboding landscape of the enigmatic "Jihad." —*Steve Metaliz*, Down Beat

○ **Double Exposure** / Nov. 16, 1977 / Muse 5165
Double Exposure is a suite of related themes and moods that features percussionist Joe Chambers, mostly on acoustic piano, in tandem with the late organist Larry Young. It is not your typical drummer's date, but then Joe Chambers is not your typical drummer. He made his mark during the '60s as much for his tasteful composing as his drum fury. And this is a fully realized, touching work. One cannot say enough good things about Larry Young. His work on the first side of *Double Exposure* is largely supportive, but his embellishments are so driven and subtle that it is like being caught up in a whirlpool of rhythm and harmony—circles of sound. An aura of Chambers' and Young's shared Muslim belief is evident in the compositions. "Hello to the Wind" combines gospel, blues, and Mideastern colors in a way that will remind some of Duke Ellington (and some of Keith Jarrett). Chambers alternates churchy chords and a minor ostinato phrase to create a dreamy canvas of peace; behind him, Young paints swelling watercolors. Chambers redefines idiomatic rock beats with his own jazz sensibility. He uses his ride cymbals and bell tones to drive the beat, rather than the snare-hi hat-bass drum combinations. Chambers's aggressive drum dances are body killers, and Chambers and Young are breathing as one. —*Chip Stern*, Down Beat

Phantom of the City / Mar. 1991 / Candid 79517
Drummer Joe Chambers works with an intriguing lineup on this '91 quintet set. Young Lion trumpeter Phillip Harper teams up with journeyman Bob Berg, who holds his own with the lyrical, energetic Harper. Chambers never hurries or crowds the soloists, and he interacts easily and fully with pianist George Cables and bassist Santi Debriano. —*Ron Wynn*

PAUL CHAMBERS (Paul Laurence Dunbar (Jr.) Chambers)

b. Apr. 22, 1935, Pittsburgh, PA, **d.** Jan. 4, 1969, New York, NY
Bass / Hard bop
A great session bassist and accompanist, Paul Chambers was one of the finest "walking" players and teamed marvelously with Philly Joe Jones and Red Garland in Miles Davis's great '50s bands. Chambers worked for Davis for eight years, the longest stint of any Davis band member. Chambers also found time to record prolifically in the '50s with John Coltrane, Kenny Clarke, Cannonball Adderley, Donald Byrd, Sonny Rollins, Garland, Bud Powell, Kenny Dorham, Freddie Hubbard, and the J.J. Johnson/Kai Winding team. He wasn't a swashbuckling innovator or a rebel like Mingus, but he was a top bassist in terms of improvising pizzicato bebop-style solos (sometimes arco as well) in a swinging, strong manner. Chambers began playing bass in the late '40s, and worked with Kenny Burrell and other Detroit jazz musicians. He toured with Paul Quinichette in the mid-'50s, and went to New York. Chambers later toured the South with Bennie Green, and played with Sonny Stitt, Joe Roland, and the J.J. Johnson/Kai Winding group. He joined Miles Davis's band in October of 1955 and remained until the early '60s, when he left to form a trio with Wynton Kelly and Jimmy Cobb. This ensemble backed Wes Montgomery and recorded with him, and also with Kenny Burrell for Verve. Chambers did several small group sessions as a leader in 1955, 1956, and 1957 on Blue Note, and later recorded for Vee Jay. Chambers didn't work much in the latter '60s, due to his health. His great bass work appears on numerous reissues, but there are only a couple of his own sessions available on CD at present. —*Ron Wynn and Bob Porter*

High Step / Apr. 20, 1955+Nov. 1955 / Blue Note 451

Complete all-star group sessions from the mid '50s that include John Coltrane contributions. Rare two-record set that was part of a mid '70s Blue Note reissue line. —*Ron Wynn*

Delegation from the East: Chambers' Music, A / Mar. 1956 / Jazz: West 7

Whims of Chambers / Sep. 21, 1956 / Blue Note 1534

East/West Controversy, The / i. Jan. 1957 / Xanadu 104

Paul Chambers Quintet / May 9, 1957 / Blue Note 1564

Chambers' Music / May 19, 1957 / Blue Note 84437
Chambers duels and teams with incendiary drummer Philly Joe Jones, as the duo reaffirms the primacy of bass/percussive interplay in hard bop. — *Ron Wynn, Rock & Roll Disc.*

★ **Bass on Top** / Jul. 14, 1957 / Blue Note 46533
Extraordinary bassist. Highly recommended. A definition for modal-jazz expression. —*Michael G. Nastos*

Ease It / Feb. 2, 1959 / Affinity

Go / Feb. 2-3, 1959 / Vee Jay 1014
Super late '50s date from Vee Jay, with Cannonball Adderly on the case playing furious alto sax, Freddie Hubbard equally inspired on trumpet, and Chambers interacting with longtime section mates pianist Wynton Kelly and drummer Philly Joe Jones. There is an '86 CD reissue. —*Ron Wynn*

Just Friends / 1959 / Vee Jay
Rare 1959 and 1960 sessions Chambers led for the Vee Jay label. These were once available as a poorly remastered bootleg; they are tough to locate. —*Ron Wynn*

1st Bassman / May 12, 1960 / Chameleon 2015
Exceptional '59 date with Chambers working in the company of fellow greats Wynton Kelly, Curtis Fuller, and Yuseff Lateff plus solid pros Lex Humphries and Tommy Turrentine. Few have ever equalled Chambers for overall playing quality, either in ensemble sections, accompaniment, or solo work. The '86 CD contains a bonus cut. —*Ron Wynn*

DENNIS CHARLES

b. 1933
Drums / Early free, modern creative
Dennis Charles was a calypso and mambo drummer before he played jazz, and has added a Caribbean tinge to his drumming since the '40s. He's also been a sensitive accompanist and soloist who's participated in many seminal free jazz recording sessions, especially with Cecil Taylor. Charles came to New York from St. Croix in the mid '40s. He worked with Taylor in Jack Gelber's play *The Connection*, and recorded with Taylor frequently from the mid '50s to the early '60s. He also played and recorded with Steve Lacy and Gil Evans in the '50s, with Archie Shepp and Lacy in the '60s, with Lacy again in the '70s, and with Billy Bang and Lacy once more in the '80s. Charles hasn't issued any dates as a leader, but can be heard on reissues by Taylor, Lacy, Shepp, and Evans, and on recent dates by Bang and Lacy. He's featured on the masterful *The Compete Candid Recordings of Cecil Taylor and Buell Neidlinger* Mosaic boxed set. —*Ron Wynn*

TEDDY CHARLES (Theodore Charles Cohen)

b. Apr. 13, 1928, Chicopee Falls, MA
Vibes, composer / Cool, progressive big band
Teddy Charles's conception and approach have changed considerably from his early days when he worked with big bands led by Benny Goodman, Chubby Jackson, Artie Shaw, and Buddy DeFranco. In the '50s, Charles began to play aggressively and to try newer things, both in his own groups and when playing with others, especially as a producer. He created groups for recordings with three trumpets and a rhythm section or a tenor and two baritones. His '50s solos on vibes were far-reaching and a precursor to the things being done currently by Jay Hoggard or Steve Nelson. Charles was both a dedicated and advanced improviser and a superior composer. He was a regular participant in Charles Mingus's Jazz Composers Workshop in 1954 and 1955, and

he wrote such compositions as "Variations on a Theme By Bud" and other pieces that feature unusual arrangements, modality, and polytonality. His 1956 tenet LP has been reissued on CD by Atlantic, and a 1953 duo effort with Shorty Rogers has been reissued on Prestige. Charles has a more recent session on Soul Note, and an earlier date on Bethlehem with Zoot Sims (now on Fresh Sound), available on CD. —*Ron Wynn*

Teddy Charles' West Coasters / Feb. 20, 1953 / Prestige 1307

Teddy Charles and Wardell Gray / Feb. 20, 1953 / Prestige 1307

Evolution / Aug. 31, 1953+Jan. 6, 1955 / Prestige 1731
Composition is the thing on this session, which features vibist Teddy Charles on two dates: August 31, 1953 and January 6, 1955. The earlier date is with Jimmy Giuffre, Shelly Manne, Shorty Rogers, and Curtis Counce, and the music is highly structured along movements of shifting tempos, colors, and instrument features. It is a bit overdrawn and never really flies. The later session includes J.R. Monterose, Charles Mingus, and Gerry Segal (drums). It, too, is somewhat overloaded by its careful and often confining scoring and sameness in its sax-bass-vibes color blend. This music has always had distinguishing characteristics, but after living with it for more than 30 years, I've never felt it lives up to its talents. —*Bob Rusch*, Cadence

New Directions Quartet / Jan. 6, 1955 / New Jazz 1106

★ **Tentet (Jazzlore 48)** / Jan. 6-17, 1956 / Atlantic 90983
This session from 1956 finds vibraphonist Teddy Charles creating new music beyond bop. As with Jimmy Giuffre, Charles's recordings are not particularly influential, but in both cases the individuality of the style makes for a timelessness that keeps the 33-year-old (1989) music from sounding dated. Charles's tentet, which only existed for this record, was a pioneering "third stream" unit that utilized classical dissonances in the many arranged sections, even behind soloists. Giuffre, Mal Waldron, Gil Evans (then emerging from obscurity), and George Russell each contributed an original (and each arranged their own songs), but it is Charles's three charts (especially the multithemed "The Emperor") that are most memorable. This is an album that rewards repeated listenings. —*Scott Yanow*, Cadence

Word from Bird, A / Oct. 12+16, 1956 / Atlantic 1274

Rant Quintet, The / Apr. 1, 1957 / Savoy 12174

Salute to Hamp, A / 1958 / Bethlehem 6032

Teddy Charles on Campus / 1960 / Fresh Sound
A very rare album with the adventurous Charles finding a way to mesh with Zoot Sims (ts). On the Fresh Sounds import label; the Bethlehem original is long gone. —*Ron Wynn*

Teddy Charles Trio Plays Duke Ellington / i. 1963 / Josie 3505

★ **Live at the Verona Jazz Festival (1988)** / Jun. 1988 / Soul Note 1183
Concert date with Harold Danko trio. The highlight is the Mingus composition "Nostalgia in Times Square." —*Michael G. Nastos*

DOC CHEATHAM (Adolphus Anthony Cheatham)

b. Jun. 13, 1905, Nashville, TN
Trumpet / Swing, big band, bop
Doctor George Butler righted a lot of longtime wrongs for many jazz fans when he signed Doc Cheatham to a contract with Columbia and issued an album in 1993. Cheatham's is one jazz story that's not just about survival and perseverance, but is about triumph as well. His career spans jazz's evolution and the evolution of the American music industry. While not in Armstrong's class, Cheatham is a fine soloist, especially known for his articulation and bell-clear tone, plus his ability with the mute. Cheatham's added a rougher edge to his solos in recent years, and plays with a power and vigor missing among players less than half his age.

Cheatham moved to Chicago from Nashville in the '20s, where one of his earliest jobs involved recording with Ma Rainey on soprano sax. He later played with Albert Wynn, then formed his own group in 1926. Cheatham worked in Philadelphia with Wilbur de Paris in 1927 and 1928, and played briefly with Chick Webb before joining Sam Wooding and touring Europe with him. He returned to America in 1930, and played in several big bands. These included McKinney's Cotton Pickers, Cab Calloway's, Teddy Wilson's, Benny Carter's, and Teddy Hill's, plus Eddie Heywood's sextet from 1943-1945. He earned some notoriety as a soloist and composer while with Heywood, but switched gears in 1948. Cheatham joined Afro-Latin bands led by Marcelino Guerra until 1950, then Perez Prado in 1951 and 1952. He continued working with Calloway and de Paris, and toured Africa and Europe with de Paris in 1957 and 1960. Cheatham became a prolific world traveler, returning to Europe in 1958 with Sammy Price and to Africa again with Herbie Mann in 1960.

From the '40s into the '90s, Cheatham has participated in numerous recording sessions. These include dates with Billie Holiday, Heywood, Count Basie, Pee Wee Russell, Machito, de Paris, Buck Clayton, Milt Hinton, Howard Alden, and his own sessions. Cheatham had his own band in New York from 1960 to 1965, and spent 1966 and 1967 playing with Benny Goodman, but since then has been the ultimate freelancer. He cut a few big-band sessions in the '70s, but specializes in intimate, personalized combo dates. Cheatham has been that rare jazz great who's gotten more work as a living elder than he did in his youth. With age, he seems to have become a superior player; his current solos surpass his earlier ones. —*Ron Wynn and Richard Meyer*

Adolphus Doc Cheatham / Apr. 4-9, 1973 / Jezebel 102

Good for What Ails Ya / May 2, 1975 / Classic Jazz 113
Good mid '70s blues, ballads, standards, and traditional jazz numbers originally cut for the Black and Blue label. Cheatham's spry trumpet solos are more enticing and delightful now than they were years ago. Ted Buckner provides some flair, Sammy Price blues and boogie fervor on piano, "Flea" Connors, gutbucket trombone licks, and bassist Carl Pruitt and drummer J.C. Heard handle the rhythm demands. —*Ron Wynn*

★ **Black Beauty** / Oct. 31, 1979 / Sackville 3029
A Salute to Black American Songwriters. Classic music duet with pianist Sammy Price. Mostly pre-'40s music. Trumpet and piano are in perfect harmony—truly a great album with which to start a collection. —*Michael G. Nastos*

It's a Good Life / Dec. 6-7, 1982 / Parkwood 101
With the Chuck Folds Trio. Well recorded and played. A solid effort from all. —*Michael G. Nastos*

Doc and Sammy / i. 1982 / Sackville 3013

○ **At the Bern Jazz Festival** / Apr. 1983-Jan. 1985 / Sackville 3045

Fabulous, The / Nov. 16-17, 1983 / Parkwood 104
With the Dick Wellstood Trio. Old-timey standards that are timeless as the day they were written. Cheatham's personal spark is clearly evident. —*Michael G. Nastos*

JEANNIE AND JIMMY CHEATHAM

Vocals / Blues & jazz, ballads & blues
The husband-and-wife duo of Jimmy and Jeannie Cheatham have been working together since the mid '50s, and have been married since the late '50s. Her energetic, joyful vocals and his good-natured trombone riffs and accompaniment have been featured on a succession of fine Concord albums in the '80s and '90s. Their professional affiliation began after they met on stage in Buffalo during the '50s. Jeannie Cheatham had performed in clubs, while Jimmy Cheatham had played in Broadway bands and on television, as well as with Bill Dixon, Duke Ellington, Lionel Hampton, Thad Jones, and Ornette Coleman. He'd even been Chico Hamilton's music director. Jeannie Cheatham studied piano as a child, and later accompanied Dinah Washington, Al Hibbler, and Jimmy Weatherspoon, among others. They at-

tended the University of Wisconsin in the '70s and taught in the jazz program, then moved to San Diego in the late '70s. While Jimmy Cheatham taught at the University of California, Jeannie was president of the Lower California Jazz Society. The duo worked in clubs and organized weekly jam sessions. Jeannie Cheatham appeared on a public television special with Sippie Wallace and Big Mama Thornton that was shown in 1983. Concord signed the duo in the mid '80s, and they've been recording ever since, working with both their regular band and such special guests as Charles McPherson, Eddie "Lockjaw" Davis, Eddie "Cleanhead" Vinson, and Red Callender. Most of their sessions are available currently on CD. —*Ron Wynn*

Sweet Baby Blues / Sep. 1984 / Concord Jazz 4258

Homeward Bound / Jan. 1987 / Concord Jazz 4321

★ **Back to the Neighborhood** / Nov. 1988 / Concord Jazz 4373

Luv in the Afternoon / May 1990 / Concord Jazz 4429

Basket Full of Blues / Nov. 1991 / Concord Jazz 4501
The fourth album from the husband-and-wife blues and swing/"trad" jazz duo. Jeannie Cheatham has the sassy attitude of classic blues types, but her subject material and style are firmly planted in the urban mode. Jimmy Cheatham keeps things under control, and assists the band playing bass trombone, though it's saxophonists like Frank Wess and Curtis Peagler who get the most extensive solo space. —*Ron Wynn*

DON CHERRY (Donald Eugene Cherry)

b. Nov. 18, 1936, Oklahoma City, OK
Trumpet, piano, organ, wooden flute, vocals / Early free, world fusion, modern creative
Don Cherry has been a pivotal free jazz player, composer, and theorist, and an invigorating, experimental world music improviser. He's learned several non-Western instruments while studying and incorporating aspects of Asian, traditional Indian, and African sounds into his work. Cherry's trumpet approach reflects the influences of traditional beboppers like Miles Davis, hard bop greats Fats Navarro and Clifford Brown, and swing veteran Harry Edison. His technique isn't always the most efficient; frequently, his rapid-fire solos contain numerous missed or muffed notes. But he's a master at exploring the trumpet and cornet's expressive, voice-like properties; he bends notes and adds slurs and smears, and his twisting solos are tightly constructed and executed regardless of their flaws. He can play on the beat, against it, or can totally ignore it, and, in recent years, tends to bypass preset song forms and bebop chord changes in favor of mantras or extended vamps. Currently, Cherry plays bamboo flutes, berimbau, and various percussive devices along with his unusual pocket cornet (he calls it a "pocket trumpet"), trumpet, flugelhorn, and bugle.

He played piano in an R&B band with Billy Higgins as a teen, then attracted attention in the late '50s playing with Ornette Coleman; his "pocket trumpet" and pithy, brittle sound drew almost as much reaction as Coleman's surging solos and concepts. He was featured on Coleman's first seven albums, and accompanied him to New York in 1959. Cherry and Coleman spent the summer of 1959 at the Lenox School of Music, and the Coleman quartet with Charlie Haden and Billy Higgins made a controversial New York debut that autumn. Cherry played with Steve Lacy, Sonny Rollins, and John Coltrane in the early '60s, and recorded with Coltrane. He was in the New York Contemporary Five in 1963 and 1964 with Archie Shepp and John Tchicai, and played in Europe with Albert Ayler. Cherry co-led a quintet with Gato Barbieri in the mid '60s, and did sessions in Europe and America; some of them were released later on Blue Note. He did other dates with Pharoah Sanders and, in 1969, recorded in Berlin with an octet that included European musicians Albert Mangelsdorff and Arild Andersen, plus Sonny Sharrock. Cherry recorded duets with Edward Blackwell for the BYG label. He taught at Dartmouth in 1970, then was based in Sweden for four years.

Cherry traveled through Europe and the Middle East extensively, playing informally while rigorously studying non-Western musical styles. He continued a busy recording schedule for mostly European and Japanese labels in the early '70s. In 1973, Cherry recorded with the Jazz Composers Orchestra of America, then recorded in Sweden before finally doing some dates for a major American company. He cut albums in the mid '70s for A&M, Atlantic, and Chiaroscuoro, playing with Frank Lowe, Charlie Haden, Billy Higgins, Hamiet Bluiett, and Abdullah Ibrahim, among others. Cherry, Haden, Blackwell, and Dewey Redman recorded in the late '70s for ECM as the quartet Old and New Dreams, and Cherry also recorded with Indian musician Latif Khan. He had a highly publicized collaboration with rock guitarist and vocalist Lou Reed. During the '80s, Cherry recorded in the trio Codona with percussionists Colin Walcott and Nana Vasconcelos. He also did another duo session with Blackwell. After Codona disbanded, Cherry formed a new group, Nu, that included Vasconcelos and Carlos Ward. He worked with the more traditional jazz group the Leaders in the mid '80s. Cherry appeared at the Berlin Jazzfest with Jabbo Smith in 1986, and toured England with Nu in 1987. Only a couple of Cherry titles as a leader are available on CD, though he's also represented by his work in groups. In 1993, Mosaic issued a fine boxed set that covers Cherry's Blue Note recordings. —Ron Wynn

★ **Complete Communion** / Dec. 24, 1965 / Blue Note 4226
The tracks "Complete Communion" and "Elephantasy" each occupy one side of the record. In a compositional sense, they both have the same basis: they are both suites divided into four continuous subsections, each part with its own title. It is not necessary to separate the subsections into single tunes, for Cherry's music, as always, is a collective experience that expands from points of departure that enter by chance, or so it appears, rather than stopping and starting by arrangement. The music produced by Cherry (trumpet), Gato Barbieri (tenor sax), Henry Grimes (bass) and Edward Blackwell (drums) is the jazz entity—improvisation. —Bill Smith, Coda

Live at the Montmartre—Vol. 1 / i. 1965 / Magnetic 111

Live at the Montmartre—Vol. 2 / i. 1965 / Magnetic 112

Symphony for Improvisers / Sep. 19, 1966 / Blue Note 4247
The title of this session, Symphony For Improvisers, really gives us the sum total of all the music. There are pulsations within pulsations, with single and collective lines energizing at all levels and all tempos, continuously rhythmically strong. In fact, the music can be described as rhythm notes enclosed in cohesive emotional groupings. All the players understand each others' music well, and contribute to each other, whether together or leading the other into the next moment. . . . Symphony For Improvisers expands the group that was on Complete Communion, adding Pharoah Sanders (tenor sax), Karl Berger (vibes), and Jenny Clark (bass) to the lineup of Cherry (trumpet), Gato Barbieri (tenor sax), Henry Grimes (bass), and Edward Blackwell (drums). . . . After the collective beginning, the record continues with a series of short solos, returning to miniature thematic statements to move into other bursts of solo sound. This record gives us the added opportunity of hearing Pharoah Sanders on piccolo and tenor, and Berger's vibes and piano; two of the great new leaders of their respective instruments. Sanders's and Berger's voices appear strongly throughout, and it is apparent that Berger, as a member of Cherry's European group, had absorbed a great deal of the leader's music. . . . A great number of interesting things happen on this record that do not appear on Complete Communion. One is the underlying sound of much of the ideas created by other important voices, such as Albert Ayler and Miles Davis, making this music an evolution rather than a revolution. Another point that appears is the large number of sequences in "straight" time patterns, which cause an enormous variant of energy and rhythm cycles. Special mention should be made of Edward Blackwell's percussion work. Few "drummers"

seem to really "listen" to the band, but in Blackwell's case, he is this band's generator of all rhythm dynamics. —Bill Smith, Coda

Brooklyn Is Now / Nov. 11, 1966 / Blue Note 84311
Brooklyn Is Now has five separate tracks, and although the music is still very much Don Cherry's form of loose composition, the use of Pharoah Sanders's tenor as the "other horn" causes a complete change of sound content. Sanders's energy directs the proceedings into realms that did not previously exist. A similar direction appears when he joins the John Coltrane group. Unlike most other musicians, Sanders was not as interested only in notes, but rather in the total effect of sound. This transition from mind and spiritual energy into the horn context gives great varieties of communicative sound: sometimes the solos would unfold as patterns of screech/scream/calm/tranquility; other times, as intermingled counterpoint statements to each other and to everyone's music. Also, there appears to be much more of the solo form, giving more opportunity to hear just how beautiful they all are. —Bill Smith, Coda

Eternal Rhythm / Nov. 11-12, 1968 / Saba 15204
Eternal Rhythm, the title of the album, is an apt description of most of Don Cherry's music. . . . Although this is a good record in part, there is a great deal lacking. Possibly it is the fact that, with the exception of Cherry and Sonny Sharrock (guitar), the group was a European band. This is not completely a derogatory statement, for much of the music produced by Europeans is of a very high caliber, but it still has a distinctly formal sound. . . . Side one features Cherry on an assortment of flutes and cornet, with some not very interesting work by Sharrock. In the liner notes, it says that the music was influenced by the age-old sound of the Javanese and Balinese gamelon. . . . Side two is one of those cacophony of sound-type pieces, with solos above assorted chaos, lots of chimes, bells, and other assorted avant-garde. —Bill Smith, Coda

Mu, First Part & Second Part / Aug. 22, 1969 / Actuel 529331
Electrifying duets with Ed Blackwell (d). This music has been released both as one set and as two separate albums. —Ron Wynn

Relativity Suite / Feb. 14, 1973 / JCOA 006
With Jazz Composers Orchestra. Cutting-edge music. Features many of Cherry's familiar themes. —Michael G. Nastos

Brown Rice / 1975 / A&M 0809

Hear and Now / Dec. 1976 / Atlantic 18217

○ **Don Cherry** / i. May 1977 / Horizon 717
This was originally released in Italy on the EMI label and was probably recorded in 1975. There is also a mistake in the instrumental listings on the back cover. Don Cherry does not play trumpet on "Brown Rice," but he does play it on "Degi-Degi," and for the life of me I can't hear Frank Lowe's tenor on that track. These two tracks are also the least interesting. "Brown Rice" is an R&B-style rocker with wah-wah bass, breathy voice, and Memphis blues tenor. "Degi-Degi" has a monotonous ostinato rhythm pattern over which you can hear Cherry's breathy voice recitation. He also plays some rather simple trumpet lines in unison with what sounds like some Asian double-reed instrument, such as the shenai. Both succeed in terms of their limited scope, but would have been better if they were cut somewhat shorter. What makes this record worth your attention are the other two pieces. "Malkauns" opens with a fairly long Charlie Haden bass solo accompanied by Moki's (only name given) tamboura. Then Cherry and drummer Billy Higgins enter, and when you hear that shining trumpet tone reverberating through the air, you can't help but be moved. "Chenrezig" begins with a duet between Cherry's voice and Hakim Jamil's bass. The rhythm section establishes an Eastern flavor for Cherry's first trumpet solo. There is also a short dialogue between trumpet and tenor before things ease down for another voice-bass duet. Instead of ending things here,

Cherry's voice initiates a rhythm change leading to an energetic solo by Lowe. This is Cherry at his finest. —*Carl Brauer*, Cadence

○ **Old and New Dreams** / i. 1978 / PolyGram 29379
This Italian import is full of the swinging, energetic, inventive music that was lacking on trumpeter Don Cherry's American label recording done two months later. Full credit belongs to tenor saxophonist Dewey Redman, bassist Charlie Haden, and drummer Ed Blackwell who, for me, are the real stars of the album (they are given equal billing with Cherry on the album cover). While Cherry's own playing is of a high quality, it is the group interaction that elevates the music above the norm. Also, Cherry's two compositions ("Next to the Quiet Stream" and "Augmented") are the least interesting pieces. Leading off is Ornette Coleman's "Handwoven," which has that giant's characteristic stomp to it. The first of Redman's contributions come out of the bop camp, whereas Haden's "Chairman Mao" captures the feeling of the Far East without being cloying. The title piece is another Redman tune that is highlighted by his musette playing and Haden's arco playing. Blackwell is able to extract an extremely musical sound out of his standard setup. His rhythmic invention is a joy throughout. —*Carl Brauer*, Cadence

★ **El Corazon with Ed Blackwell** / Feb. 1982 / ECM 829199
This digitally recorded opus is the sequel to *Mu, Parts 1 & 2* that trumpeter Don Cherry and drummer/percussionist Ed Blackwell recorded in 1969 for BYG (it was reissued on Affinity). Thanks to the wonderful ECM sound, it is possible to hear how Blackwell utilizes his entire trap set. He was the supreme percussive melodist—in other words, he was more interested in the tone and pitch of what he was playing than in strictly keeping the beat. Listen to the way he shapes the melody on "Near-in," a solo piece for wood drums. His left hand not only keeps the beat, but plays the bass line at the same time. "Street Parade" is another good example, this time using martial beats that hearken back to the street drummers of New Orleans. Cherry spent many years as a wandering ministrel, traveling in Europe, Africa, and points beyond, while immersing himself in the native music. On trumpet, his attack is strong and his tone is hard, but not brittle. When he moves to piano, there is a folk-like quality to the notes he chooses to play. His gospel-like chords on Thelonious Monk's "Bemsha Swing" bring to mind the playing of Abdullah Ibrahim. His solo trumpet piece closes the LP—the echo on his horn broadens his tone and lengthens the notes. Still, there is a great use of the space between the notes. The composition is like a prayer and is a fitting close to the album. —*Richard B. Kamins*, Cadence

☆ **Art Deco** / Aug. 27-30, 1988 / A&M 5258
Don Cherry's *Art Deco* offers more than a reunion of old friends; it offers a thoroughly pleasurable outing by musicians who revolutionized jazz by mastering its traditions. The ever unpredictable Cherry (trumpet) reunited with his pre-Ornette Coleman bandmates for a relaxed set of standards, solo features, and three of Coleman's tunes. James Clay (tenor sax), who was coaxed from retirement for this session, plays with the large tone and direct approach typical of the Texas tradition of tenor saxophone. He brings a fresh interpretation to that test of tenor manhood, "Body and Soul," and undaunted at being the only non-alum in the band, swings hard on Coleman's "The Blessing." Charlie Haden (bass) is as strong as always, and Billy Higgins (drums) moves things right along. Cherry's surprisingly wistful title tune seems to encapsulate the feeling of the session—a proper appreciation of the past without indulging in nostalgia. —*Steven Hahn*, Jazz Times

Multi Kulti / Dec. 1988-Feb. 1990 / A&M 5323
A '90 patchwork quilt combining things from Asian, African, African-American, and European genres, and united by Don Cherry's multi-instrumentalism and presence. Alto saxophonist Carlos Ward adds punch and spark, while special guests include Nana Vasconcelos, Karl Berger, and Ed Blackwell. —*Ron Wynn*

BILLY CHILDS

Piano / Bop, hard bop
One of the rare hard bop pianists and musicians who've recorded for Windham Hill in the '80s and '90s, Billy Childs is a superb soloist and a fine session player who's worked and recorded with Eddie Daniels, Bruce Forman, Bunky Green, and Freddie Hubbard. Childs is an excellent melodic interpreter who was very influenced by Herbie Hancock. Childs's phrases and solos are nicely constructed, alternately lyrical and intense. He has some dates available on CD. —*Ron Wynn*

★ **Take for Example This . . .** / 1988 / Hip Pocket 0113

Twilight Is upon Us / 1989 / Windham Hill 0118

His April Touch / 1991 / Windham Hill 0131
There is intriguing playing and strong melodic songwriting on this, his third solo album. A modern jazz style with great production. —*Paul Kohler*

○ **Portrait of a Player** / i. 1993 / Windham Hill 10144
On his fourth outing for Windham Hill, pianist Billy Childs delivers an excellent collection of interpretations of jazz and pop standards as well as two originals: the reflective "End of Innocence" and a spirited tribute to Tommy Flanagan ("Flanagan"). Childs gets strong rhythmic support from his bass/drum team (Tony Dumas and Billy Kilson), freeing him to fly through John Coltrane's hard-boppin' "Satellite" and the vibrant "It's You or No One." —*Dan Ouellette*, Down Beat

CHOCOLATE DANDIES

b., USA
Group / Swing, big band
The name Chocolate Dandies was used by different bands, and was taken from the title of an extremely successful 1924 show co-written by Eubie Blake and Noble Sissle. The earliest ensemble that used the name was directed by Don Redman and recorded for Okeh in 1928 and 1929. Recordings that Redman supervised for McKinney's Cotton Pickers were issued under that name also. During the early '30s, several groups under Benny Carter's leadership were called Chocolate Dandies. Coleman Hawkins was featured in editions of the group in both the '30s and '40s; others who were featured in subsequent editions include Max Kaminsky, Floyd O'Brien, Buck Clayton, plus members of both Carter's and Fletcher Henderson's bands. —*Ron Wynn*

★ **Chocolate Dandies (1928-1933)** / 1928-1933 / Disques Swing 8448
Pivotal cuts by early jazz greats Benny Carter, Coleman Hawkins, and the like. —*Ron Wynn*

CHARLIE CHRISTIAN (Charles Christian)

b. Jul. 29, 1916, Texas, d. Mar. 2, 1942, New York
Guitar / Bop
He made only a few records during his lifetime, yet Charlie Christian was a seminal guitarist. He was one of the earliest guitarists to amplify his instrument so that it equalled the volume of the other instruments on the bandstand. He was both a blues master and a knowledgeable harmonic improviser who mastered sophisticated chord changes with ease. Christian solos were studied diligently by first-generation bop players, and he was the swing era's dominant guitarist. Christian grew up in an Oklahoma City ghetto; his father had been a blind guitarist and singer, and his brothers, Edward and Clarence, were musicians. Christian built himself "cigar-box" guitars and played them in elementary school. John Hammond heard about Christian from Mary Lou Williams, and notified Benny Goodman. It took only one hearing for Goodman to offer Christian a spot in his new sextet. Though the three-minute limit of 78 rpm recordings restricted his space, Christian consistently produced crisp, inventive solos. He was featured on weekly radio broadcasts and recordings and was a star in the early '40s. (There are several of his sessions available on CD.) He also participated in the Minton's jam sessions, but didn't enjoy

notoriety both a blues master and a knowledgeable harmonic improviser who mastered sophisticated chord changes with ease. Christian solos were studied diligently by first-generation bop players, and he was the swing era's dominant guitarist. Christian grew up in an Oklahoma City ghetto; his father had been a blind guitarist and singer, and his brothers, Edward and Clarence, were musicians. Christian built himself "cigar-box" guitars and played them in elementary school. John Hammond heard about Christian from Mary Lou Williams, and notified Benny Goodman. It took only one hearing for Goodman to offer Christian a spot in his new sextet. Though the three-minute limit of 78 rpm recordings restricted his space, Christian consistently produced crisp, inventive solos. He was featured on weekly radio broadcasts and recordings and was a star in the early '40s. (There are several of his sessions available on CD.) He also participated in the Minton's jam sessions, but didn't enjoy notoriety for long. Christian was hospitalized in 1941 with tuberculosis, and died the following spring. —*Ron Wynn and Dan Morgenstern*

○ **Solo Flight (1939-1941)** / Aug. 19, 1939-Jun. 1941 / Stash 1021
Although not the very first electric guitarist, Charlie Christian was its first major soloist. During the 19 months between his debut with the Benny Goodman sextet and his being stricken with tuberculosis (which killed him less than a year later), Christian displayed an appealing and virtuosic style. He played the guitar with the force and logic of a horn rather than as a barely audible part of the rhythm section, and he became the major influence on virtually all jazz and popular guitarists (whether they realized it or not) until the emergence of rock in the mid-to-late '60s, 25 years after his death. Solo Flight collects together many of Christian's most exciting radio appearances with the Benny Goodman Sextet (which started out with Lionel Hampton and Fletcher Henderson and, by 1941, featured trumpeter Cootie Williams and tenorman Georgie Auld) along with five selections from a very rare (and, at the time, unreleased) session with Goodman, Count Basie, Buck Clayton, and Lester Young. Classic music. —*Scott Yanow*

★ **Genius of the Electric Guitar** / 1939-1941 / Columbia 40846
The great Benny Goodman Sextet sides. Fifty years have passed, but no one has swung harder. —*Richard Lieberson*

○ **Immortal Charlie Christian, The** / i. 1939-1941 / Legacy 373

☆ **With the Benny Goodman Sextet and Orchestra** / Feb. 7, 1940-Nov. 7, 1940 / Columbia 652

○ **Solo Flight with the Benny Goodman Sextet, Septet & Orches** / Nov. 7, 1940 / Columbia 62581

PETE CHRISTLIEB (Peter Christlieb)

b. Feb. 16, 1945, Los Angeles, CA
Tenor saxophone / Bop, cool
Though he is identified with the West Coast where he lives and is therefore assumed to be a cool, detached player, Pete Christlieb has always been one of the more powerful soloists in any style. His blistering lines, especially on uptempo numbers, are often red hot, while he can also play effective blues and stirring ballads. Initially, Christlieb studied violin before starting sax at age 13. He played with Si Zentner, Chet Baker, and Woody Herman in the '60s, then began working with Louis Bellson; they've maintained a musical relationship through the '80s and into the '90s. Christlieb has worked extensively in the studios since the late '60s doing film and television projects, and was a regular member of the "Tonight Show" orchestra. He played in the backing bands of Della Reese and Sarah Vaughan, among other vocalists, and has also done sessions with Count Basie, Quincy Jones, Mel Lewis, Shelly Manne, Gene Ammons, Frank Rosolino, and Carl Fontna. Christlieb headed his own quartet in 1980, and began a record label in 1981. Bosco has issued albums by Bellson, Bob Florence, and Christlieb. He's recorded for RAHMP, Capri, and Warner Bros. A duet album with Warne Marsh in the late '70s was critically praised.

Christlieb has a couple of sessions available on CD. —*Ron Wynn and Michael G. Nastos*

★ **Apogee** / 1978 / Warner Brothers 3236
This music swings hard from note one to the very end. Aside from that, the album is unusual in several ways. For one thing, the featured soloists were both tenor players; for another, both were highly experienced, but not terribly well known. Warne Marsh had been active since he played with Lennie Tristano in the '50s. Pete Christlieb (at that time) was a busy sessionman who also played in the "Tonight Show" band. Also of interest, the album was produced by Walter Becker and Donald Fagen, a.k.a. Steely Dan. There is fire on every cut. Christlieb and Marsh seem to inspire each other, helped along by a good choice of material and Joe Roccisano's charts. The rhythm section (pianist Lou Levy, bassist Jim Hughart, drummer Nick Ceroli) provides plenty of support. Some of the most exciting moments occur when Christlieb and Marsh solo simultaneously, egging each other on. —*Douglas Clark*, Down Beat

Pete Christlieb Quartet Live, The / 1983 / Bosco 5

○ **Mosaic** / Feb. 16, 1990 / Capri 74026
Recorded at the Portland Inn. Christlieb and Bob Cooper swing dual tenors. —*Michael G. Nastos*

JUNE CHRISTY

b. Nov. 20, 1925, Springfield, IL, **d.** Jun. 21, 1990
Vocals / Big band, ballads & blues
June Christy was a dominant vocalist in the '40s and '50s, with a husky, enticing sound and narrow vibrato that fit well into the '50s cool framework. She projected sexiness and sophistication without sacrificing a wholesome, girl-next-door quality, and had a gorgeous voice. Christy began singing in the late '30s in local bands around her Springfield, Illinois, hometown under the name Sharon Leslie. She then worked with Boyd Raeburn and other orchestras in Chicago, before replacing Anita O'Day in Stan Kenton's orchestra in 1945. Christy had an early hit with "Tampico," and subsequent success with "Shoo-Fly Pie" and "How High the Moon." She became quite popular in the late '40s and early '50s. She topped *Down Beat*'s poll four consecutive years as Best Female Vocalist with a Big Band, and also won *Metronome* polls, while making several short films with the Kenton orchestra. After Kenton temporarily disbanded in 1949, Christy began her solo career, but continued to tour with Kenton. She worked with Ted Heath in the '50s, and with Bob Cooper, whom she'd married, in the late '40s. Christy recorded extensively in the '50s, mainly for Capitol, then did sessions for Kenton's label in the '60s. Christy appeared with Kenton at the 1972 Newport Jazz Festival, and recorded for Discovery in 1977. A fair amount of her '50s work has been reissued. Capitol rereleased vintage dates in 1991 and 1992. —*Ron Wynn and Richard Lieberson*

○ **Uncollected June Christy with the Kentones (1946)** / 1946 / Hindsight 219
Previously unissued June Christy material from late '40s and '50s with a knockoff unit from the Stan Kenton orchestra. It's designed for completists, as its alternate takes and unreleased cuts that were adjudged inferior or left over. There's nothing wrong with some of them, but these are not the songs that made Christy famous. —*Ron Wynn*

★ **Something Cool** / Dec. 27, 1954-May 9, 1955 / Capitol 96329
Christy's classic first album, plus 10 other '50s sides. The best introduction to Christy. —*Richard Lieberson*

○ **Misty Miss Christy, The** / 1956 / Capitol 98452
Fine "torch" and jazzy pop late-'50s recording by Christy, backed by a good group with Maynard Ferguson, Laurindo Almeida, Bud Shank, Bob Cooper, and Claude Williamson, among others. It was reissued on compact disc in 1992. —*Ron Wynn*

This Is June Christy! / 1956 / Capitol 1006

Road Show / i. 1959 / Capitol 96328

Music Map

Jazz Clarinet

Sopranino E-Flat Clarinet

First Used in Brass Bands
New Orleans Players – John Casimir – Polo Barnes
George Lewis – Sammy Rimington

Soprano Clarinet

Creole Musicians
Lorenzo Tio Family (1893-1933) – Alphonse Picou (1878-1961)

Vaudeville Use
Wilbur Sweatman (1882-1961) – Ted Lewis (1892-1971)
Jimmy O'Bryant (1896-1928) – Wilton Crawley (1900-1948)

Dixieland
Pete Fountain (1930)

Pupils Lorenzio Tio, Jr.
Sidney Bechet (1897-1959) – Barney Bigard (1906-1927)
Albert Nicholas (1900-1973)

Bechet's Pupil: Jimmie Noone (1895-1944)
Influenced These White Players:

Alcide "Yellow" Nunez (1884-1934)
Larry Shields (1893-1953) – Jimmy Dorsey (1904-1957)
Benny Goodman (1909-1986) – Artie Shaw (1910)
Leon Rappolo (1902-1943)

Major Early Players
Edmond Hall (1901-1967) – Pee Wee Russell (1906-1969)
Frank Teschemacher (1906-1932)
Early Lester Young (1909-1959) – Ernie Caceres (1911-1971)
Bob Wilber (1928) – Kenny Davern (1935)
Albert Nicholas (1900-1970) – Omer Simeon (1902-1959)
Garvin Bushnell (1902)

The rise of the Saxophone limits Clarinet use

Benny Goodman Tradition
Peanuts Hucko (1918) – Alvin Batiste (1937)
Sol Yaged (1922) – Aaron Sachs (1923) – Bob Wilber (1928)
Stan Hasselgard (1922-1948) – Jimmy Hamilton (1917)

Bass Clarinet
Eric Dolphy (1928-1964)
Bennie Maupin (1940)
Roscoe Mitchell (1940)
Hamiet Bluiett (1940)
Howard Johnson (1941)
Gunther Hampel (1937)
Kalaparusha Maurice McIntyre (1936)
David Murray (1955)
Mario Bavza (1911-1993)
Harry Carney (1910-1974)

Contrabass Clarinet
Anthony Braxton (1945)
Rahsaan Roland Kirk (1936-1977)

Flutists
Sam Most (1930)
Paul Horn (1930)
Herbie Mann (1930)

Free Players
John Carter (1929)
Perry Robinson (1938)
Gunter Hampel (1937)
Anthony Braxton (1945)

Sax Players
Art Pepper (1925-1982)
Buddy Tate (1915)
Kim Cusak

Modern Stylists
John La Porta (1920)
Rolf Kuhn (1929)
Jimmy Giuffre (1921)
Tony Scott (1921)
Buddy DeFranco (1923)
Bill Smith (1926)
Rahsaan Roland Kirk (1936-1977)

1980s John Carter's Clarinet Quartet

Clarinet Summit

Classical Soloist Richard Stolzman

1980s-1990s
Eddie Daniels (1941)
Richard Stoltzman
Don Byron
Wendell Harrison

Fine live recording of June Christy with Stan Kenton & the Four Freshmen from 1959. Christy is a bit below par due to a cold on the day of the recording. —*Kenneth M. Cassidy*

Ballads for Night People / 1959 / Capitol 1308

Cool School, The / 1960 / Capitol 1398

That Time of Year / 1961 / Capitol 1605

Intimate June Christy, The / 1962 / Capitol 1953

Something Broadway, Something Latin / 1965 / Capitol 2410

Best Thing for You, The / i. 1986 / Affinity 145
A strong collection of '50s material, with Pete Rugolo arrangements and top West Coast jazzmen. An import and out-of-print. —*Richard Lieberson*

CURTIS CLARK

b. 1945, **d.** 1969
Bass / Early free, modern creative

Curtis Clark was a fine bassist whose budding career was cut short by his premature death at age 24. He studied bass with Wilbur Ware, and turned professional in 1963. He joined Muhal Richard Abrams Experimental Band, and was a founding member of the Association for the Advancement of Creative Musicians (AACM). Clark worked with Abrams from 1966 to 1968, and played cello, koto, and percussion, in addition to bass, on recordings and in concert with Joseph Jarman. His influence led Jarman to join the AACM. His death greatly affected many AACM members, and both Jarman and the Art Ensemble have recorded compositions in his memory. Clark can be heard on Jarman's *As If It Were the Seasons*, which has not been reissued yet on CD. —*Ron Wynn*

SONNY CLARK (Conrad Yeatis Clark)

b. Jul. 21, 1931, Herminie, PA, **d.** Jan. 13, 1963, New York, NY
Piano / Hard bop

One of the most effortless yet crisp and fluid pianists, Sonny Clark's playing was featured in several topflight '50s bands, and on many wonderful albums. He was admired particularly for his right-hand lines and his rhythmic drive. Clark began playing in his childhood, and developed a jazz interest through listening to the radio broadcasts of Duke Ellington and Count Basie, and to recordings by Art Tatum and Fats Waller. He moved to California from the East Coast in the early '50s, and worked briefly in San Francisco with Vido Musso and Oscar Pettiford before settling in Los Angeles. Clark cut his first sessions with Teddy Charles's West Coasters in 1953, then played in Buddy DeFranco's quartet from 1953 to 1956, touring Europe with them in 1954. He played and recorded with Sonny Criss, Frank Rosolino, and in Howard Rumsey's Lighthouse All Stars. Clark was a member of Dinah Washington's trio in 1957 in New York, and made several recordings as a leader until 1962. These included the all-star date *Dial S for Sonny*, and other classics like *Sonny's Crib* and *Cool Struttin'.* Clark later did sessions that were issued on various labels, among them Time, Xanadu, and Bainbridge. He also played and recorded with Sonny Rollins, Hank Mobley, John Jenkins, Curtis Fuller, Clifford Jordan, and Bennie Green. A heart attack claimed Clark's life long before his productivity had diminished. His most famous Blue Note dates, as well as the Bainbridge session, are available on CD. Mosaic issued a deluxe, five-disc box set of the DeFranco quartet dates in 1985. John Zorn did an album of Clark compositions for Black Saint. —*Ron Wynn*

Dial "S" for Sonny / Jul. 21, 1957 / Blue Note 1570

★ **Sonny's Crib** / Oct. 9, 1957 / Blue Note 46819
Striking sextet performances. Memorable efforts from John Coltrane (ts), Curtis Fuller (t), and Donald Byrd (tpt). 1987 CD reissue has three fine bonus cuts. —*Ron Wynn*

Cool Struttin' / Dec. 8, 1957 / Blue Note 46513
Vols. I & II provide an excellent forum for Clark's brilliant composing and bandleading talents. —*Michael G. Nastos*

Sonny Clark Trio / **i.** Mar. 23, 1960 / Bainbridge 1044
Brilliant late '50s material by the great hard bop pianist and equally gifted supporting players bassist Paul Chambers and drummer Philly Joe Jones. Clark was among the most inventive pianists of the period, a masterful ballad interpreter and a dynamic uptempo soloist, while Chambers and Jones had few peers, either as accompanists or in the spotlight. —*Ron Wynn*

★ **Leapin' and Lopin'** / Nov. 13, 1961 / Blue Note 84091
Mainstream, mostly uptempo jazz with a slight taste of funk. One of Clark's best albums as a leader. The CD has two extra tracks. —*Michael Erlewine*

KENNY CLARKE (Kenneth Spearman Clarke)

b. Jan. 9, 1914, Pittsburgh, PA, **d.** Jan. 26, 1985, Paris, France
Drums, vibes, composer / Bop

Along with Max Roach, Kenny Clarke decisively changed the course of jazz drumming in the bebop era. Clarke and Roach followed in the footsteps of Jo Jones and Dave Tough in helping to shift the time-keeping rhythm from the bass drum to the ride cymbal. Clarke was a master at driving a band and at creating an array of rhythms that made the perfect complement to the soloists' phrasing. He also co-wrote "Salt Peanuts" with Gillespie, and "Epistrophy" with Thelonious Monk.

Clarke studied theory and played vibes, piano, and trombone in high school. While in his teens, he started his professional career with Leroy Bradley's band in Pittsburgh. Later, he joined Roy Eldridge's band, and played in the East and Midwest with groups such as the Jeter-Pillars Orchestra in St. Louis, and the bands of Lonnie Simmons, Edgar Hayes, Claude Hopkins, and Teddy Hill. He played with Gillespie in 1939 and 1940, following a 1938 session that featured Kenny Clarke's Kvintett in Stockholm. Clarke became a regular at Minton's Playhouse in the early '40s, working with Gillespie, Monk, Charlie Parker, and Bud Powell, and influencing fellow drummer and frequent participant Roach. Clarke's habit of interjecting off-beat accents on the snare and bass drum against the music's steady pulse earned him the nicknames of "Klook" and "Klook-mop"; Teddy Hill didn't intend for these names to be terms of endearment. Clarke played with Louis Armstrong, Ella Fitzgerald, Benny Carter, and Red Allen in Chicago, then served in Europe during World War II, returning to America in 1946. He played with Gillespie in 1946 and again in 1948, and stayed in France after going there on tour. Clarke also recorded with Gillespie, Tadd Dameron, and Fats Navarro, and Prestige released some sessions he recorded in Paris in 1950. There was a national tour with Billy Eckstine's band, and, in 1951, Clarke became a founding member of the Milt Jackson Quartet. They were renamed the Modern Jazz Quartet the next year, and Clarke remained with them until 1955. He recorded extensively for Savoy from 1954 to 1956, making *Telefunken Blues*, *Bohemia After Dark*, *Kenny Clarke/Ernie Wilkins Septet*, *Klook's Clique*, and *Meets the Detroit Jazzmen*.

Clarke made a permanent move to Paris in 1956. He played in Bud Powell's trio from 1959 to 1962, and, from 1960 to 1973, co-led what became Europe's premier orchestra with Francy Boland. At first, they called themselves the Clarke-Boland Octet and later changed their name to Big Band. Their group regularly included the finest expatriate American and top European musicians, among them Benny Bailey, Johnny Griffin, Sahib Shihab, Zoot Sims, Idrees Sulieman, Derek Humble, Ake Persson, and Ronnie Scott. Clarke recorded with guitarist Elek Bacsik in 1962, and with Dexter Gordon in 1963. The Clarke-Boland big band cut numerous albums over its 13-year tenure, both studio sessions and live concert dates for several companies, but never played in America. A slated 1970 tour was canceled. Clarke and Boland died within weeks of each other. Clarke became a beloved figure in France and a prolific contributor to numerous sessions. He played on the soundtrack for the film *Ascenseur pour l'echafaud* in 1957, appeared in *Les liaisons dangereuses 1960* in 1959, and wrote music for *On n'enterre pas dimanche* in 1959 and *La riviere du hibou* in 1961. He issued *Pieces of Time* in 1983, a session that matched Clarke with fellow drummers Andrew Cyrille, Milford Graves and Don Moye. He remained in Europe until his death in 1985. —*Ron Wynn*

○ **Paris Bebop Sessions, The** / Oct. 9, 1950 / Prestige 7605
Good, though somewhat stiff, sessions done in Paris by Clarke with a French bassist and pianist. Tenor saxophonist James Moody certainly isn't stiff, however, and it's his exuberant, bluesy solos, coupled with Clarke's spinning beats,

that keep the date from bogging down, especially when pianist Ralph Schecroun takes the spotlight. —*Ron Wynn*

Kenny Clarke All-Stars / Nov. 1, 1954+Feb. 7, 1955 / Savoy 12006

An explosive debut as a leader by one of the originators of bebop. With Frank Morgan (sax) and Milt Jackson (vib). —*David Szatmary*

Bohemia After Dark / Jun. 28, 1955 / Savoy 12017

Recorded shortly after Cannonball Adderley's celebrated 1955 explosion onto the New York jazz scene, this album features Adderley (alto sax) and his brother Nat (trumpet) with other newcomers and established players, all led by Kenny Clarke, the dean of bop drummers. Although trumpeter Donald Byrd and Jerome Richardson on tenor get in some good licks, the Adderleys dominate the date with their freshness and enthusiasm. This was a period in Cannonball Adderley's playing career that he later said was characterized by innocence. That is true, but the honesty and unpretentiousness of it is leavened by the tough, downhome blues feeling that remained a major component of his work, no matter how sophisticated it became later. There was no musical reason for Nat Adderley to be in his brother's shadow. His solos here are in the same league, with a particularly stirring one on "With Apologies to Oscar," a variant of "Sweet Georgia Brown." Clarke, bassist Paul Chambers, and pianist Horace Silver were a state-of-the-art rhythm section of the day. As with all the Savoy records reissued by Denon, there is no updating of discographical information or addition of historical perspective. We get the same inadequate liner notes and silly cover art that graced, if that is the word, the 1955 LP. The sound quality is excellent. —*Doug Ramsey, Jazz Times*

★ **Klook's Clique** / Feb. 6, 1956 / Savoy 12083

An indispensable session by the bop pioneer, with John LaPorta (sax) and Donald Byrd (tpt). —*David Szatmary*

○ **Kenny Clarke Meets the Detroit Jazzmen** / Apr. 30, 1956+May 9, 1956 / Savoy 1111

Sensational mid-'50s date that exemplifies the Detroit hard bop sound. Clarke rides herd on a great band that includes baritone saxophonist Pepper Adams, pianist Tommy Flanagan, guitarist Kenny Burrell, and bassist Paul Chambers. This has been reissued on both domestic and import CDs. —*Ron Wynn*

Plays Andre Hodeir / Sep. 23+26, 1957 / Epic 3376

The best example of this drummer's work in France, featuring Martial Solal (p). —*David Szatmary*

Clarke-Boland Big Band / Jan. 25, 1963 / Atlantic 1404

○ **Sax No End** / Jun. 18, 1967 / PA/USA 7097

○ **Let's Face the Music** / May 13-14, 1968 / Prestige 7699

Live at Ronnie Scott's / Feb. 1969 / MPS

★ **Pieces of Time** / i. 1983 / Soul Note 1078

Standout session late in his career, with fellow drummers Andrew Cyrille, Milford Graves, and Don Moye. —*Ron Wynn*

STANLEY CLARKE (Stanley M. Clarke)

b. Jun. 30, 1951, Philadelphia, PA

Bass, composer / Early jazz-rock, instrumental pop, contemporary funk

While many consider Jaco Pastorius the greatest electric bass guitarist of all time, serious consideration should also be given to Stanley Clarke. Clarke brought to the instrument a harmonic and rhythmic excellence normally heard only on acoustic. His blistering, yet precisely articulated lines, huge dense tone, and marvelous syncopation and attack were unprecedented for an instrument that had been regarded previously as either a guitar stepchild or a weak sister to the acoustic. At one time, Clarke's extraordinary skills flourished on acoustic. In recent years, he's returned, on occasion, to playing the hard bop and bebop dates he excelled at before he turned to electric exclusively in the early '70s.

Clark played accordion as a child, then moved to violin and cello before starting on acoustic and electric bass. He played mostly electric in high school, and worked with R&B and rock bands. Prior to graduation, Clarke moved to New York to seek work as a jazz player, and abandoned previous plans to be a classical musician. He worked with Pharoah Sanders on acoustic and electric in the early '70s, and played with Gil Evans, Mel Lewis, and Horace Silver. Clarke also toured and recorded with Stan Getz, Dexter Gordon, and Art Blakey. But his most important collaboration was with Chick Corea. Clarke met Corea during 1971 while working with Joe Henderson. Clarke soon became a founding member of Return to Forever, a pioneering jazz-rock band. He abandoned acoustic bass temporarily and made eight albums with various editions of Return to Forever. Their debut had a pronounced Afro-Latin bent, but subsequent albums turned more and more towards a rock/funk/jazz blend.

Clarke started working as a leader in the mid '70s while still in the band. He cut a number of LPs for Nemperor/Atlantic, notably the 1976 hit *School Days*. Clarke moved to Epic in 1977 after leaving the group. In the late '70s, '80s, and '90s he's divided his time between heading groups, doing sessions with jazz and rock groups, producing, and composing. He's recorded and toured with Larry Coryell, John McLaughlin, Herbie Hancock, Angela Bofill, George Howard, Stewart Copeland, David Sancious, Tony Williams, Jeff Beck, and the New Barbarians. Clarke cofounded a funk and urban contemporary ensemble with George Duke in the late '70s. The Clarke/Duke Project became a popular act on the urban contemporary circuit in the early '80s, and even scored a Top 20 single with "Sweet Baby." Clarke had a reunion tour with Return to Forever in 1983. He also did a funk cover of Bruce Springsteen's "Born in the USA." Clarke began doing film and television scores in the '80s and continued in the '90s, providing the soundtrack for the popular film *Passenger 57* in 1992. He's a prime example of a gifted improviser who's able to retain a modicum of integrity while alternating between the jazz and pop (as opposed to popular) music worlds. At times, Clarke has lashed out at jazz purists in interviews, but has also shown that he understands the difference between making jazz and cutting fusion and pop. A large number of Clarke dates are available on CD. —*Ron Wynn*

Children of Forever / Dec. 26+27, 1972 / Polydor 827559

An early instructive fusion set from super bassist Stanley Clarke, establishing his identity as a leader. Clarke had made many mainstream jazz dates in the '60s, and was also part of Chick Corea's Return to Forever. His bass playing, as always, is remarkable, and while the songs and production are predictable, there are enough electric moments to indicate Clarke had a future in the fusion and pop world. —*Ron Wynn*

★ **Stanley Clarke** / i. 1974 / Epic 36973

The music on this album moves logically with thematic direction and covers an unusually wide range of colors and emotions. At the top, there is Bill Conors articulately soaring electric guitar work, along with Jan Hammer's keyboard and shrewdly applied Moog. At the bottom, bassist Stanley Clarke and drummer Tony Williams are in melodic and rhythmic tandem. These four might have been constant in the mathematics of structure and stress, but this is music of energy, spirit, and imagery that is open and moving—no fixed rules apply. A great deal of this LP's personality comes not only from Clarke, but also from Tony Williams. He is magnificent; his playing is confident and forceful, and his personality is rarely far from the front. The album, however, is not about individuals, but rather unity in pursuit of Clarke's musical concepts. —*Herb Nolan, Down Beat*

Journey to Love / 1975 / Epic 36974

Prolific bassist Stanley Clarke's second jazz-rock album in the early '70s marks the beginning of what proved to be an extremely profitable collaboration with keyboardist George Duke. The album includes guest appearances from Chick

Corea, John McLaughlin, Lenny White, and rocker Jeff Beck. —*Ron Wynn*

School Days / 1976 / Epic 36975

I Wanna Play for You / Nov. 1979 / Epic 88331

A late '70s two-album (now two-disc) set that blends studio and live sessions. Those who only knew Clarke from his heavily produced, sometimes silly urban contemporary dates should check out the frequently amazing bass work. He was a top acoustic jazz player before switching to electric, and those qualities sometimes can be heard even in his plugged-in solos. The live tracks are more ambitious and impressive than the studio cuts. —*Ron Wynn*

Clarke/Duke Project—Vol. 1, The / i. 1981 / Epic 36918

Clarke/Duke Project—Vol. 2, The / 1983 / Columbia 36934

If This Bass Could Only Talk / 1988 / Portrait 40923

One of a few of his contemporary releases with some good music and an indication of his prodigious talent. —*Ron Wynn*

○ **3** / i. 1990 / Epic 46012

Both an accomplished acoustic player and a pioneering electric bassist, Stanley Clarke found new success in two other areas during the '80s and '90s. One was scoring films, the other was cutting urban contemporary hits with George Duke. This is their third venture, and it continues in the path of its predecessors: short songs, little solo space, double-tracked background vocals, and lots of wah-wah and synthesizer effects. —*Ron Wynn*

○ **Funny How Time Flies** / Portrait 08051

JAMES CLAY

b. Sep. 8, 1935

Tenor saxophone / Bop, hard bop, soul-jazz

After being nearly forgotten for many years, James Clay resurfaced in the public consciousness in the early '90s. An underrated, extremely soulful and bluesy tenor saxophonist, Clay was a successful honking stylist in the '50s; he toured and played through the Southwest. He was also an early partner of Ornette Coleman. Clay was a featured member of Ray Charles's orchestra during the '60s, and recorded a marvelous album with David "Fathead" Newman before dropping out of sight. He returned in the late '80s, with a tremendous session of standards and ballads backed by the Cedar Walton trio. Clay continues strong in the '90s, recording for Antilles with Newman and Roy Hargrove. He has several sessions available on CD. —*Ron Wynn*

★ **Sound of the Wide Open Spaces** / Apr. 26, 1960 / Riverside 257

With David Newman. Dueling Texas tenors on an album recorded by Cannonball Adderley. Definitive music. —*Michael G. Nastos*

Double Dose of Soul, A / Oct. 11, 1960 / Riverside 1790

Bluesy, hypnotic, and essential. With Nat Adderley (cnt), Victor Feldman (vib), and the Gene Harris Trio. —*Ron Wynn*

★ **I Let a Song Go out of My Heart** / Jan. 29, 1989 / Antilles 848279

Although he made his early mark on the jazz scene working with Ornette Coleman and Don Cherry, he's far more of a traditional blues-and-ballad stylist than an explosive experimentalist.—*Ron Wynn, Rock & Roll Disc*

Cookin' at the Continental / Jun. 18-19, 1991 / Antilles 510724

With Fathead Newman (sax) and Roy Hargrove (tpt). Three old standards, six more from Horace Silver, Bobby Timmons, Charlie Parker, and Babs Gonzalez. An up mode. —*Michael G. Nastos*

BUCK CLAYTON (Wilbur Dorsey Clayton)

b. Nov. 12, 1911, Parsons, KS, **d.** Dec. 8, 1991

Trumpet, arranger / Swing, big band

An excellent bandleader and accompanist for many vocalists, including Billie Holiday, Buck Clayton was a valued soloist with the Count Basie orchestra during the '30s and '40s. Later, he was a celebrated studio and jam session player, writer, and arranger. His tart, striking tone and melodic dexterity were his trademark, and Clayton provided several charts for Basie's orchestra and for many other groups.

Clayton began his career in California where he organized a big band that had a residency in China in 1934. When he returned, Clayton led a group and played with other local bands. During a 1936 visit to Kansas City, he was invited to join Basie's orchestra as a replacement for Hot Lips Page. Clayton was also featured on sessions with Lester Young, Teddy Wilson, and Holiday in the late '30s. He remained in the Basie band until 1943, when he left to serve in the army. After leaving the army, Clayton did arrangements for Basie, Benny Goodman, and Harry James before forming a sextet in the late '40s. He toured Europe with this group in 1949 and 1950. Clayton continued heading a combo during the '50s, and worked with Joe Bushkin, Tony Parenti, and Jimmy Rushing, among others. He organized a series of outstanding recordings for Columbia in the mid '50s under the title *Jam Session* (compiled and reissued by Mosaic in 1993). There were sessions with Rushing, Ruby Braff, and Nat Pierce. Clayton led a combo with Coleman Hawkins and J.J. Johnson at the 1956 Newport Jazz Festival, then reunited with Goodman in 1957 at the Waldorf Astoria. There was another European tour, this time with Mezz Mezzrow.

He appeared in the 1956 film, *The Benny Goodman Story*, and played the 1958 Brussels World Fair with Sidney Bechet. Clayton later made another European visit with a Newport Jazz Festival tour. He joined Eddie Condon's band in 1959, a year after appearing in the film *Jazz on a Summer's Day*. Clayton toured Japan and Australia with Condon's group in 1964, and continued to revisit Europe throughout the '60s, often with Humphrey Lyttelton's band, while playing festivals across the country. Lip and other health problems virtually ended his playing career in the late '60s. After a period outside of music, Clayton became active in music again, this time as a nonplaying arranger, touring Africa as part of a State Department series in 1977. He provided arrangements and compositions for a 1974 Lyttelton and Buddy Tate album, and did more jam session albums for Chiaroscuro in 1974 and 1975. He also became an educator, teaching at Hunter College in the early '80s. Clayton led a group of Basie sidemen on a European tour in 1983, then headed a big band in 1987 that played his own compositions and arrangements almost exclusively. Clayton's extensive autobiography with Nancy Miller-Elliot, *Buck Clayton's Jazz World*, was published that same year. —*Ron Wynn*

Classic Swing of Buck Clayton / Jul. 24, 1946 / Riverside 1709

A swing era mainstay performs vintage Kansas City early jazz material with a wonderful roster. Tiny Grimes (g), Trummy Young (t), and a host of others make it a worthy romp. Authoritative 1990 reissue of an important 1946 date. —*Ron Wynn*

Meet Buck Clayton / Feb. 4, 1953-May 26, 1953 / Jazztone 1225

○ **Singing Trumpets** / Feb. 4, 1953 / Jazztone 1267

Buck Meets Ruby / Jul. 1, 1954 / Vanguard

With Ruby Braff (cnt) and Mel Powell. A pair of spry, individualistic trumpet masters meet to a good end. —*Ron Wynn*

Jam Sessions from the Vault / Mar. 5, 1956 / Columbia 44291

Limited edition. Hot set with guests ranging from the familiar (Dicky Wells) to the eyebrow-raising (Tommy Newsom). —*Ron Wynn*

All the Cats Join In / Mar. 5, 1956 / Columbia 882

Buck N' the Blues / Mar. 14, 1957 / Vanguard 8514

Big Band at the Savoy Ballroom / Aug. 1957 / RCA 7230

Copenhagen Concert / Sep. 17, 1959 / Steeple Chase 7

★ **Complete CBS Buck Clayton Jam Sessions** / i. 195z / Mosaic 144

In the 1950s, George Avakian and John Hammond produced a series of all-star mainstream jam sessions for Columbia under the leadership of Buck Clayton. A typical session involved 10 to 12 participants, including the likes of Buddy Tate, Woody Herman, Joe Newman, and Al Cohn. On a never-before-released take of "After Hours," even the ensembles are wonderfully rich, and no wonder—on that session you're listening to the full-bodied tones of Coleman Hawkins, Billy Butterfield, Ruby Braff, and of course Clayton.

On "Christopher Columbus," no player shows greater imagination or verve than alto saxist Lem Davis—and half of his solo wound up on the cutting-room floor when this performance was originally released. Give credit to this boxed set's producer Michael Cuscuna for going back to the original sessions whenever possible and issuing unedited performances, including a few never before released. The production of this six-disc boxed set, from sound quality to annotation, is first-rate. —*Chip Deffa,* Jazz Times

Kansas City Nights / Dec. 20, 1960-Sep. 15, 1961 / Prestige 24040

Buck Clayton and Buddy Tate were enjoying something of a revival in 1960-1961 when these quintet sets were done. Tate's style, by this time, had assimilated something of the later Coleman Hawkins's, and while Tate's clarinet work ("Blue Creek") was not his strongest point, his improvisations here rank among the very best of his long career. His Big Boss Man approach made him quite an ideal partner for Clayton, his bold melodics contrasting with the trumpeter's subtlety and variety of effect. Sir Charles Thompson's work is happy throughout—the perfect accompanist, his soloing justifying the immense respect accorded him by lovers of jazz piano. The context is almost ideal for Clayton, who throughout his recording career repeated a level of performance worthy of consideration among the finest jazzmen. These sessions are not Clayton at his most intense, but the blues date works especially. "Rompin' at Red Bank" is almost Clayton-jam-session-quality stuff, and Miles Davis/John Coltrane lovers are especially encouraged to listen to these trumpet-tenor vibrations. —*John Litweiler,* Down Beat

Buck and Buddy / Dec. 20, 1960 / Prestige 757

★ **Olympia Concert (22 April 61)** / Apr. 22, 1961 / Vogue 30

A splendid set with vintage sensibility and a jam session atmosphere. Buddy Tate (ts) and Sir Charles Thompson (p) are on the money. —*Ron Wynn*

○ **Passport to Paradise** / May 15-16, 1961 / Inner City 7009

Trumpeter Buck Clayton's *Passport to Paradise* is a sparkless swing session recorded in 1961. At the time, Clayton was a good trumpet stylist with a fluent command of the horn and a fine, useful range. His solos are mini-melodies and his taste is always correct. The problem with the album is not Clayton's playing, but Clayton's choice of playing the first chorus of each tune with a mute and ending the song with open horn, with a solo by either the pianist (Sir Charles Thompson) or the guitarist (Jean Bonal) in between. It makes for a boring album, frankly. Clayton's isolated solos are pert and attractive, but this similarity between each number and the generally rattly rhythm (caused by the usually resourceful bassist Gene Ramey and drummer Oliver Jackson) produce a simple, unadorned album of background music. —*Lee Jeske,* Down Beat

Buck & Buddy Blow the Blues / Sep. 15, 1961 / Prestige 2030

Meets Joe Turner / Jun. 2, 1965 / Black Lion 760170

Buck Clayton's classy, vibrant trumpet solos and the resolute shouting of Big Joe Turner are the hooks for this mid-'60s session, matching them with a competent European rhythm section. Except for vibist Bosko Petrovic, they're mostly undistinguished, but that doesn't matter because Clayton and Turner don't let them bring down the energy or performance levels. —*Ron Wynn*

Jam Session / Mar. 25-26, 1974 / Chi-Sound 132

Jazz Spectacular / i. Apr. 1977 / Columbia 808

Swingin' Dream, A / Oct. 23, 1988 / Stash 16

Clayton was nearing the end of the line, but still plays with exquisite taste and good arrangements. Mel Lewis drives the date on drums. —*Ron Wynn*

Heart and Soul / Capitol 74028

With Hamilton Jazz Orchestra. Nice repertory/big-band date. Orchestra contains both spotlight soloists and tremendous session players. —*Ron Wynn*

JIMMY CLEVELAND (James Milton Cleveland)

b. May 3, 1926, Wartrace, TN, d. Feb. 9, 1991
Trombone / Bop, hard bop

Jimmy Cleveland possessed one of the greatest trombone tones around; a rich, always even sound that never faltered, even at a furious pace. He surpassed Jack Teagarden and J. J. Johnson in technical mastery, and played, from the '50s through the '80s, in a complete, commanding manner that produced beautiful, imaginative, and astonishing solos with relative ease. Cleveland began playing trombone at age 16 in his family's band and later at Tennessee State University. The TSU band went to Carnegie Hall; Cleveland left the band to join Lionel Hampton in 1950. He remained with Hampton's band until 1953, and toured Europe with the band in 1953. Cleveland played with Oscar Pettiford, Lucky Thompson, James Moody, Eddie Heywood, Johnny Richards, and Gerry Mulligan through the '50s and into the early '60s. Cleveland was a staff trombonist on the Merv Griffin show house band during the '70s. His bond with Quincy Jones, who'd also been in Hampton's band, led to Cleveland's appearances on numerous film and television soundtracks, Broadway musicials, and hundreds of albums. He may be the most recorded trombonist in modern times. Cleveland's played on albums by Dizzy Gillespie, Donald Byrd, Miles Davis, Gil Evans, Michel Legrand, Oliver Nelson, Jimmy Smith, Wes Montgomery, Lalo Schifrin, Kenny Burrell, Stanley Turrentine, Bill Berry, Hampton, and Gerald Wilson. He's perhaps the ultimate session player. Though he recorded for EmArcy, Mercury, Epic, and Phoenix in the mid and late '50s, it's nearly impossible to find a Cleveland session available anywhere in America. —*Ron Wynn*

Trombones / i. Apr. 18, 1957 / Savoy 12086

★ **Cleveland Style** / Dec. 12+15, 1957 / EmArcy 36126

This is a December 12 and 13, 1957, date with trumpeter Art Farmer, saxophonist Benny Golson, pianist Wynton Kelly, drummer Charli Persip, bassist Eddie Jones, and Jay McAllister or Don Butterfield on tuba. Looking at the horn line and the inclusion of a tuba, it is hardly surprising that this is a mellifluous jazz date. But the blend here, while smooth, is never sedentary, and this is a good example of some of the excellent thinking and swinging jazz that was being produced between New York and Chicago at the time. There are some loose ends here as far as some solos fitting tightly into the whole, but the overall quality and Ernie Wilkins's charts are such that there is more than one angle to grab your interest. And, of course, there is Jimmy Cleveland, one of the best bop trombones; he can still blow. —*Bob Rusch,* Cadence

Rhythm Crazy / Feb. 1959 / EmArcy 26003

Sliding Easy / i. Dec. 24, 1959 / United Artists 4041

ROSEMARY CLOONEY

b. May 23, 1928, Maysville, KY
Vocals / Ballads & blues

Vocalist Rosemary Clooney remains in the news during the '90s. She's been in the midst of a career revival since the '80s, and was among the artists who performed in 1993 at the White House jazz concert. She was criticized by Carmen McRae, who cited her as one of the pop artists inaccurately tabbed as a jazz singer by ignorant critics.

Clooney's rise to fame in the '50s came on the strength of songs that, in many instances, were without question novelty tunes; she's not a vocal improviser like McRae, Carter, or Sarah Vaughan. She is an excellent lyric interpreter, has fine timing, phrases skillfully and intelligently, and performs with the dramatic quality evident among all great singers. Her background and her foundation are in jazz, even if her technique doesn't always adhere to rigid jazz scrutiny. Clooney entered amateur events with her sister, Betty, in Cincinnati, and they sang on radio stations. The duo worked in Tony Pastor's band during the late '40s, then Clooney started as a soloist. She joined the Columbia roster in 1950, and made several hits for them, including "You're Just in Love," "Beautiful Brown Eyes," "Half As Much," "Hey There," "This Ole House," the number-one hit "Come on-a My House" (co-written with Ross Bagdasarian of Chipmunks fame) and "If Teardrops Were Pennies." Clooney had 13 Top 40 hits in the early '50s, among them duets with Guy Mitchell and Marlene Dietrich. She also appeared in films such as *The Stars Are Singing, Here Come the Girls, White Christmas,* and *Red Garters* in 1953 and 1954. Clooney recorded with the Benny Goodman sextet, the Hi-Lo's and Duke Ellington in the '50s.

She moved to RCA in the '60s, and recorded with Bing Crosby. There were also dates for Coral, Reprise, and Capitol, among them another session with Crosby. The rock revolution and a decision to spend more time with her family resulted in Clooney going into semiretirement. She returned in the late '70s, singing with renewed power and confidence while making swing-influenced dates and combo sessions for Concord. She's maintained that relationship through the '80s and '90s, doing standards and repertory albums, and demonstrating a resiliency and energy that validates her position among the fine jazz-based vocalists in American music. There's plenty of Clooney available, from the '50s to her most recent release, "Do You Miss New York," a 1993 outing. —*Ron Wynn and Bill Dahl*

Clap Hands, Here Comes Rosie / Feb. 18, 1960-Feb. 27, 1960 / RCA Victor 2212

○ **16 Most Requested Songs** / i. 1964 / Columbia 44403
Vintage hits from the '50s, including a number of the novelty songs done with Mitch Miller. —*Charles S. Wolfe*

Rosie Sings Bing / 1978 / Concord Jazz 60
Rosemary Clooney sings charming, light, and classic material made famous by Bing Crosby. The jazz content varies, but the musical support provided by a nice band with excellent solos by Scott Hamilton in particular, makes this well worth hearing. —*Ron Wynn*

Rosemary Clooney Sings the Lyrics of Ira Gershwin / Oct. 1979 / Concord Jazz 4112
First of a series of '80s albums in which Rosie, backed by a jazz combo, pays tribute to the great pop composers. The whole series is worth having. —*Charles S. Wolfe*

Sings the Music of Cole Porter / 1982 / Concord Jazz 4185
The first in a series of repertory albums that feature Clooney interpretations of songs by America's principal prerock pop composers, these are arguably the best. Clooney brings to Porter songs the sophistication, touches, lyric shadings, and performances that only vocal veterans who truly understood them could provide. —*Ron Wynn*

My Buddy / Aug. 1983 / Concord Jazz 4226
A fine '83 collaboration between Rosemary Clooney and then Woody Herman big band, though Herman was nearing the end of his great career. Excellent arrangements, steadfast vocals, and the usual tidy, though careful, Concord production and engineering. —*Ron Wynn*

★ **Sings the Music of Harold Arlen** / 1983 / Concord Jazz 4210
Here is another of vocalist Rosemary Clooney's fine series for Concord, this time celebrating the music of Harold Arlen. . . . Clooney's support on this one is, as usual, excellent. Warren Vache (cornet) is just right on his fills and Scott Hamilton (tenor sax) is a bit more muscular than usual. Both Dave McKenna (piano) and Ed Bickert (guitar) get some op-

portunities as well, so that the LP has Clooney's fine singing, plus extra, added attractions. Those who enjoy good vocalists will not be disappointed. —*Shirley Klett*, Cadence

Sings Ballads / Apr. 1985 / Concord Jazz 4282

Sings the Music of Jimmy Van Heusen / 1987 / Concord Jazz 4308
Another sparkling repertory work from a top-flight standards and prerock pop vocalist. Clooney does the same delightful job with Jimmy Van Heusen's music that she did with Harold Arlen's, while everything else—production, arrangements, song sequencing, engineering—is equally satisfying. —*Ron Wynn*

○ **Everything's Coming up Rosie** / 1989 / Concord Jazz 4047
This Rosemary Clooney LP is a blowing session with Scott Hamilton the clear instrumental star of the day. Clooney is relaxed and thoroughly at home. The brisk tempos are handled with easy intimacy and without the usual finger-snapping rigidity that pop singers too often pass off as swinging. The ballads ("More Than You Know," "I've Got a Crush on You") are musical and avoid staged melodrama. One of her biggest hits of the '50s, "Hey There," sounds fresher than ever. Pianist Nat Pierce sparkles throughout. —*John McDonough*, Down Beat

Girl Singer / Nov. 1991-Dec. 1991 / Concord Jazz 4496
A contemporary set that reveals Clooney's voice hasn't lost its luster or effectiveness. This set features her singing with a big band comprised of West Coast session pros. The date reflects traditional Concord conservatism in terms of selections and production, but is certainly well done. The CD contains a bonus track. —*Ron Wynn*

○ **Come on-a My House** / Sony 14382
Anthology/greatest hits items from Sony that contains the classic title song plus other tunes Clooney made popular during the '50s. It is a good introductory package, also perfect for those who only want a little Clooney or just the best-known items. —*Ron Wynn*

ARNETT COBB (Arnette Cleophus Cobb)

b. Aug. 10, 1918, Houston, TX, d. Mar. 24, 1989
Tenor saxophone / Swing
Though he suffered from crippling injuries, Arnett Cobb was an animated, energetic fireball saxophonist with a charismatic playing style and a nonstop attitude that made his playing register with audiences and musicians. He was the prototype Texas tenor, with a surging, demonstrative tone and sound, plus a personalized phrasing and style that were always convincing. Though he began his career in the bebop era, he, like others, took an alternative direction, mainly towards honking R&B and blues. But he could play in the bebop mode when he chose, and his later albums often show that side of his playing.

He studied violin, piano, and trumpet before starting saxophone. Cobb worked with Frank Davis, Chester Boone, and Milt Larkin in the mid and late '30s before joining Lionel Hampton's orchestra in 1942, replacing Illinois Jacquet. He had a crowd-pleasing approach identical to Jacquet's, and was a featured attraction until he left Hampton's orchestra in 1947 to begin his own band. Cobb started recording for Apollo, but disaster struck. He had to have an operation on his spine in 1948. After recovering, Cobb went back on tour. He recorded with Dinah Washington and Jimmy Cobb in 1952. Arnett Cobb was in a severe automobile accident in 1956 that crushed his legs; he refused to stop playing and used crutches the remainder of his career. He not only lead a big band but, in 1960, began managing Houston's El Dorado Club.

The '60s and early '70s were tough periods, but Cobb kept working, playing chitlin' circuit outfits, managing the Club Magnavox in Houston in 1970, and making regional records. A 1973 Town Hall concert appearance with Illinois Jacquet (issued by Classic Jazz) was followed by a European tour and put Cobb back in the spotlight. During the '70s, Cobb did more recording. *Wild Man From Texas* was done for Classic

Jazz. There was *Go Power!*, an enjoyable, highly competitive recording with Eddie "Lockjaw" Davis on Prestige, and another Prestige date titled *Very Saxy*. There were superb jam session releases on Muse with Buddy Tate and Eddie "Cleanhead" Vinson, and other albums on Progressive and Bee Hive in the '80s. Cobb frequently toured overseas, going with Hampton in 1978 on a European excursion and traveling to the Netherlands in 1982. He played with friendly rivals Tate and Jacquet in a group called the Texas Tenors. Cobb died in 1989. His marvelous Apollo recordings have been reissued. Some lesser known, but equally fine, regional sessions are available on Home Cooking. —*Ron Wynn with Myles Boisen*

Complete Apollo Sessions, The / 1947 / Jazz Legacy 500116

★ **Go Power!** / Jan. 9, 1959 / Prestige 7835
Madcap exchanges with Eddie "Lockjaw" Davis (ts). If you find it, savor the purchase. —*Ron Wynn*

☆ **Smooth Sailing** / Feb. 27, 1959 / Original Jazz Classics 323
Noteworthy appearance from undervalued Buster Cooper (t). Textbook soul power; exemplary sax technique from Cobb. —*Ron Wynn*

Very Saxy / Apr. 29, 1959 / Prestige

Party Time / May 14, 1959 / Prestige 219
Splendid soul, funk inflections, torrid Cobb at times; reflective and melancholy at other moments. Fine lineup, though Ray Barretto and Art Taylor sometimes seem to dash underneath. —*Ron Wynn*

○ **More Party Time** / Feb. 16, 1960 / Prestige 7175

Again with Milt Buckner / Jul. 23, 1973 / Black & Blue 590522

Jumpin' at the Woodside / May 21, 1974 / Bluebird 33175

Wild Man from Texas / May 6-30, 1976 / Collectables 5228

★ **Arnett Cobb Is Back** / Jun. 27, 1978 / Progressive 7037
Arnett Cobb Is Back was recorded in June 1978. The material is safe and solid standards and blues, and Cobb plays with authority. Cobb was a master of tonal effects and unexpected quotations, and his playing retained the hardswinging power that made him a major star when he came charging out of Lionel Hampton's orchestra in the 1940s. —*Jim Roberts*, Down Beat

Live at Sandy's!—Vols. 1 and 2 / Aug. 25-26, 1978 / Muse 5191
And the Muse All Stars. A stalwart night of ripping tenor exchanges with Cobb, Eddie "Cleanhead" Vinson, and Buddy Tate. —*Ron Wynn*

Funky Butt / Jan. 22, 1980 / Progressive 7054

Keep on Pushin' / Jun. 27, 1984 / Bee Hive 7017
Overlooked soul-jazz, blues, and bop date with sparkling piano by Junior Mance and fine drumming from Panama Francis. —*Ron Wynn*

Showtime / Aug. 10, 1987 / Fantasy 9659
With Dizzy Gillespie and Jewel Brown. Singer Brown isn't everyone's cup of tea. Cobb & Dizzy (tpt) are just what you'd expect. —*Ron Wynn*

Tenor Tribute—Vol. 1 / Apr. 30, 1988 / Soul Note 121184
A single blowing date at the Jazz Action Center in Nuremberg, Germany, back in 1988, has yielded two discs of *Tenor Tribute*, which link Arnett Cobb, Jimmy Heath, and Joe Henderson in an intergenerational tenor-titan triumvirate. A very young Benny Green is on hand at the keys, alongside bassist Walter Schomocker and drummer Doug Hammond. *Volume I* is nudged out by flute-free *Vol 2*, though on both you can clearly hear the contrast and continuity between Cobb's roughhewn Texas sound, Heath's smoother, soulful Philly tone, and Henderson's unique, post-John Coltrane take. The first volume includes Cobb's "Smooth Sailing," with "Steeplechase," "Lester Leaps In," "When Sunny Gets Blue," "I Got Rhythm," and a ballad medley. —*John Corbett*, Down Beat

JIMMY COBB

b. 1929
Drums / Hard bop
A superb, mostly self-taught drummer, Jimmy Cobb has been a dominant accompanist and outstanding soloist. He approaches the drum kit in both a melodic and percussive fashion, and never plays overly long or rambling solos. He's known for working slightly ahead of the beat, has anchored many fine sessions, and spent five years with Miles Davis in the '50s and '60s. Cobb studied briefly with Jack Dennett, a percussionist with extensive symphonic credentials. He played with Charlie Rouse, Leo Parker, Frank Wess, Billie Holiday, and Pearl Bailey in Washington, D.C. Cobb left in 1950 to join Earl Bostic, and cut his first recordings with him. He played with Dinah Washington for over three years, then worked with Cannonball Adderley, Stan Getz, and Dizzy Gillespie. He took over for Philly Joe Jones in the Davis band in 1958, and was on hand for several seminal dates. He finally left, along with Paul Chambers, to team with Wynton Kelly. The trio played and recorded with Wes Montgomery, Kenny Burrell, and J.J. Johnson before it disbanded. Cobb played on the film soundtrack *Seven Days in May*, and later worked with David Amram. He worked with Sarah Vaughan through the '70s, and was featured on a public television film of a Vaughan concert at the Wolf Trap Jazz Festival. Cobb also worked with Richie Cole, Sonny Stitt, Nat Adderley, and Ricky Ford. During the '80s, he worked with the Joe Albany trio. Cobb remains active. Currently, he does not have any albums as a leader listed in Spectrum under his name. —*Ron Wynn*

BILLY COBHAM (William C. Cobham)

b. May 16, 1946, Panama
Drums, composer, bandleader / Early jazz-rock
In jazz-rock's infancy, there was no one, particularly no other drummer, who played better than Billy Cobham. His barrages and array of rhythms had rock's theatricality, R&B's steadiness and passion, and jazz's fluidity. Cobham anchored some of the genre's greatest units, including Dreams, the original Mahavishnu Orchestra, and his own group, Spectrum. Cobham also worked with Miles Davis. Cobham's family came to New York from Panama when he was three. He attended the High School of Music and Art. Cobham played in the New York Jazz Sextet and with Billy Taylor's and Horace Silver's groups in the late '60s, then was involved in creating Dreams with the Brecker Brothers. He also did funk and R&B sessions with James Brown. Cobham became a superstar with the Mahavishnu Orchestra, where he provided rippling beats behind John McLaughlin's blazing guitar and behind the equally energetic contributions of Jerry Goodman, Rick Laird, and Jan Hammer. After the group disbanded, Cobham did session work, playing with Stanley Turrentine and Ron Carter and heading Spectrum. He became involved in music education during the mid '70s, has been an instructor in Europe and Scandinavia during the '80s and '90s, and has played with various European orchestras and combos. Cobham and McLaughlin coformed a revived Mahavishnu Orchestra in the mid '80s, but it was unsuccessful. He recorded as a leader for Atlantic in the '70s and for GRP in the '80s. Cobham has several sessions available as a leader. —*Ron Wynn*

★ **Spectrum** / 1973-1974 / Atlantic 7268

Crosswinds / 1974 / Atlantic 7300

Total Eclipse / 1974 / Atlantic 18121

AL COHN (Alvin Gilbert Cohn)

b. Nov. 24, 1925, New York, NY, **d.** Feb. 15, 1988, Stroudsburg, PA
Tenor saxophone, arranger / Bop
An invigorating, tasteful, and often exciting player, Al Cohn played in a smooth, warm fashion. His tone was broad and heavy, and he never seemed to strain himself. But he was a swinging, joyful soloist, and his two-sax dates with Zoot

Sims show the fallacy of applying strict labels to any musician. Both musicians were influenced directly by Lester Young, and their approaches reflected aspects of cool playing, but neither made detached, unemotional, or overly cerebral music. Cohn studied piano at age 6 and clarinet at age 12, then began playing tenor. He worked with Joe Marsala in the early '40s, then played and wrote arrangements for Georgie Auld before joining Boyd Raeburn in 1946. Cohn played with Alvino Rey and Buddy Rich before replacing Herbie Steward in the Woody Herman band. He eventually became one of the Four Brothers. He worked for a short time with Artie Shaw in 1949, then played through the mid and late '50s with Elliot Lawrence. But Cohn's longest association was with his buddy, Sims; the two worked together, recording and leading groups periodically from the late '50s until the early '80s. They toured Scandinavia and Japan in the '70s. Cohn played on a Manny Albam/Ernie Wilkins album for RCA in the mid '50s, then began recording on his own for RCA. He recorded with Sims and solo for RCA, Epic, Decca, Savoy, and Coral in the '50s; and Zim, Muse, Sonet, Timeless, Xanadu, Gazell, Concord, and Gemini in the '60s, '70s, and '80s. Cohn served as principal arranger for the musicals *Raisin, Music, Music, Music,* and *Sophisticated Ladies* in the '70s and '80s, and did solos on the soundtrack for the film *Lenny* in the '70s. He worked at clubs and festivals through the '80s and, near the end of his career, played with pianist/vocalist Mose Allison. There's a huge amount of Cohn material, both with Sims and as a leader, available on CD. —*Ron Wynn and Michael G. Nastos*

○ **Cohn's Tones** / Jul. 29, 1950 / Savoy 12048

Progressive Al Cohn, The / Jun. 23, 1953 / Savoy 1126
Worthy reissue of some crackling '50s sessions. Horace Silver (p) spurs and spars with Cohn. —*Ron Wynn*

Broadway / i. 1954 / Fantasy/Original 1812
The easy, relaxed, and yet swinging manner with which Al Cohn played tenor was ideal for interpretations of show tunes and standards. He turns in hot, often exceptional solos on every number on the 1954 session *Broadway,* newly reissued on CD with additional takes of the title cut and "Suddenly It's Spring." Hal Stein, the second soloist on alto sax, plays with persistence and force, but doesn't quite approximate Cohn's driving excellence. The rhythm section in turn gets picked up by Cohn's fury, and pianist Harvey Leonard in particular takes things up a notch in his solos. —*Ron Wynn*

Natural Seven, The / Feb. 5, 1955 / Victor 1116

★ **Natural Rhythm** / May 14, 1955 / RCA 45164
Wonderful mid '50s date with Freddie Green (g) stepping outside Basie's orchestra; Joe Newman accents things on trumpet. —*Ron Wynn*

Brothers!, The / Jun. 24, 1955 / Victor 1162

From A to Z / Jan. 24, 1956 / Bluebird 6469

★ **Al and Zoot** / Mar. 27, 1957 / MCA 31372
Red-letter duet date with the Al Cohn Quintet. The Al Cohn/Zoot Sims (ts) dates here are memorable, though you can't say the same thing for MCA's mixes and remastering. With Mose Allison. —*Ron Wynn*

○ **Jazz Legacy** / i. 1968 / Inner City 7022

○ **Body and Soul** / Mar. 23, 1973 / Muse 5356
With Zoot Sims. Immortal tenor pair with Jaki Byard (p), plus George Duvivier (b) and Mel Lewis (d). Can't miss. —*Michael G. Nastos*

★ **True Blue** / Oct. 22, 1976 / Xanadu 136
Excellent reissue of mid '70s duo, quintet, and septet sessions. High-quality pairing of Cohn with Dexter Gordon (ts). —*Ron Wynn*

○ **Silver Blue** / i. Oct. 1976 / Xanadu 137

America / Dec. 6, 1976 / Xanadu 138

Heavy Love / Mar. 15, 1977 / Xanadu 145

Nonpareil / Apr. 1981 / Concord Jazz 4155

Stately, pleasant, and occasionally arresting, though Cohn has been in better combos. —*Ron Wynn*

Tour De Force / Aug. 11, 1981 / Concord Jazz 4172
With Buddy Tate (ts) and Scott Hamilton (ts). A wonderful meeting between Hamilton, Buddy Tate, and Al Cohn. —*Ron Wynn*

Overtones / Apr. 1982 / Concord Jazz 194
Tasty Cohn solos with precise, dignified support from Hank Jones (p) and George Duvivier (b). —*Ron Wynn*

★ **Standards of Excellence** / Nov. 1983 / Concord Jazz 4241
An accurate title. Confident veterans going through their paces with a minimum of flash and a maximum of talent. Herb Ellis (g) shines. —*Ron Wynn*

Rifftide / Jun. 1987 / Timeless 259

East-Coast West-Coast Scene / i. 198? / Fresh Sound
Fruitful meeting of Cohn and Shorty Rogers (tpt). Currently, only available on a high-priced import. —*Ron Wynn*

DOLO COKER (Charles Mitchell Coker)

b. Nov. 16, 1927, Hartford, CT, d. Apr. 13, 1983, Los Angeles, CA
Piano / Bop
A steady, quite accomplished bebop pianist, Dolo Coker has a bigger reputation among musicians than among the general jazz audience, mainly because he has relatively few widely known recordings. Coker demonstrated strong solo ability, versatility, taste, and sensitivity throughout his career, especially during his many sessions with saxophonists. Coker played in the '40s in Philadelphia with Ben Webster and with Kenny Dorham, Sonny Stitt, Gene Ammons, and with Lou Donaldson, and Philly Joe Jones in the '50s, making his recording debut with Stitt. He worked with Dexter Gordon in the early '60s, then moved to Los Angeles, where he formed his own trio. Coker played in the '70s with Herb Ellis, Blue Mitchell, Stitt, Red Rodney, and Lee Konitz, and with Supersax. He and Sonny Criss did several concerts at Los Angeles public schools. Coker recorded as a leader in the late '70s for Xanadu, playing with Art Pepper, Mitchell, Harry Edison, and Frank Butler, as well as playing solo. A number of his Xanadu dates have not been reissued on CD. —*Ron Wynn*

★ **Dolo!** / **i.** Feb. 1978 / Xanadu 139
Amazingly, this is pianist Dolo Coker's debut album as a leader. Like most Don Schlitten/Xanadu projects, the session features straightahead blowing by compatible pros who obviously respected and enjoyed each others' musical company. Stylistically, Coker was a product of the bop era. Within that grind, his zesty improvisations spin out of a fluent technique and an inventive approach to melody, harmony, and rhythm. So, too, do his compositions. Three of his lines included here, originally from the 1959 L.A. production of Jack Gelber's play *The Connection* ("Dolo," "Affair in Havana," and "Field Day"), are puckish, bop-based tunes that neatly set the course for the soloists. Especially attractive is the exotic "Affair in Havana" with its smoky, mysterious south-of-the-border atmosphere. Coker's real showcase is the one trio track, "Never Let Me Go." Opening with shimmering free-time arabesques, Coker displays unusual emotional and intellectual maturity in a series of dramatically interconnected episodes that conclude with a stormy coda of crashing cascades. —*Chuck Berg, Down Beat*

COZY COLE

b. Oct. 17, 1906, East Orange, NJ, d. Jan. 29, 1981, Columbus, OH
Drums / Swing, big band
A versatile and popular drummer, Cozy Cole had a prolific and lengthy career that saw him prosper in many different situations playing traditional jazz, and swing, working with theatrical ensembles, and appearing in films. Both his brothers, Teddy and Donald, were professional pianists, and Cole led his own band by the late '20s, only two years after his family had moved to New York from New Jersey. He

recorded with Jelly Roll Morton in 1930, and worked in the mid '30s for Benny Carter. Cole played with Cab Calloway in the late '30s and early '40s, then joined Benny Goodman. He later did theater work, appeared with his own band at the Onyx club, and studied at Juilliard. Cole led his own bands in the late '40s, then was a member of the Louis Armstrong All-Stars from 1949 to 1953. He began a drum school with Gene Krupa in 1954. Cole's revival of the song "Topsy" earned him a pop hit in 1958; he cut it as a two-sided drum piece and the "A" side topped the charts. Cole toured with his own band in the '60s, then co-led a quartet with Jonah Jones. He was in the films *Make Mine Music* in the '40s and *The Glenn Miller Story* in the '50s, and also played on the soundtrack of *The Strip*. Cole toured Europe in 1976 with Benny Carter's quartet in Barry Martyn's show *A Night in New Orleans*. He recorded for the Keynote, Savoy, MGM, and Love labels. None of Cole's sessions are available currently on CD. —*Ron Wynn*

★ **Concerto for Cozy** / Mar. 13, 1944-May 1, 1944 / Savoy 12197

Drum Beat Dancing Feet / Sep. 12, 1962 / Coral 757423

NAT KING COLE (Nathaniel Adams Cole)

b. Mar. 17, 1919, Montgomery, AL, **d.** Feb. 15, 1965
Piano / Swing, ballads & blues
Nat "King" Cole's career represents perhaps the greatest example of commerce's triumph over artistry. While he made many lovely and enticing pop tunes and romantic ballads, Cole achieved this by sacrificing his piano skills, which were once remarkably potent and tremendously influential. Cole was expanding innovations begun by Earl Hines and Count Basie, blending intricate right-hand patterns and spare left-hand rhythmic swing variations into an approach that was emphatic, harmonically rich, and creative. His trios could play with restraint or energy. Art Tatum, Oscar Peterson, and Ahmad Jamal, as well as Charles Brown and Ray Charles, were among the pianists who adopted either similar lineups (piano/guitar/bass) or styles. But that velvet, striking voice was so appealing that Cole soon made singing his primary occupation. The 1943 hit, "Straighten Up and Fly Right," featured his picture-perfect diction, smooth sound, and hypnotic qualities. Cole cranked out scores of light pop efforts during the '50s and early '60s, all sung magnificently regardless of their content. There were Christmas albums, Spanish and international LPs, standards, sappy sentimental love tunes galore, and an occasional return to jazz-based material.

Before his career transformation, Cole made substantial impact as a pianist. His father was a Baptist minister, and Cole's brothers were musicians. He was playing organ and singing in his father's church at age 12. During his high school years, Cole studied under N. Clark Smith and Walter Dyett. He began leading a band in 1934 and made his recording debut in 1936 with Eddie Cole's Solid Swingers. At that time, Cole was fully under Hines's influence, and early bands, like the Rogues of Rhythm and Twelve Royal Dukes, frequently played Hines's arrangements. Cole left Chicago in 1936 to lead a band in a revival of Eubie Blake's *Shuffle Along* revue. He relocated to Los Angeles when the show disbanded there in 1937, then formed a trio with guitarist Oscar Moore and bassist Wesley Prince in 1939. Originally, they were supposed to be a quartet, but the drummer was a no-show opening night at Hollywood's Swanee Inn, and they decided they didn't need a drummer anyhow. They began as King Cole and his Swingsters, then became the King Cole Trio.

Cole's reputation as a major jazz musician was cemented with some superb early '40s recordings. These included a fabulous session in 1942 with Lester Young and Red Callendar that yielded "Indiana," and seminal versions of "Tea for Two," "I Can't Get Started," and "Body and Soul." Cole toured with Benny Carter in 1944 and 1945, and appeared in the films *Here Comes Elmer* in 1943, *Stars on Parade* in 1944, *Breakfast in Hollywood* in 1946, and *Make*

Believe Ballroom in 1949. When "Straighten Up and Fly Right" generated enormous success, Cole was directed into a vocal career. He began appearing on fewer occasions with his trio from 1944 to 1946, though they continued performing. He also recorded with Jazz at the Philharmonic. Then came another hit in 1946, "The Christmas Song," one of his first vocals with orchestral accompaniment. Cole landed his own weekly radio show in 1948 and 1949, putting him among the first Black jazz artists to land this prestigious honor. There were three more chart-topping hits from 1946 to 1950: "I Love You (For Sentimental Reasons)," "Nature Boy" with the Frank DeVol orchestra, and "Mona Lisa" with Nelson Riddle's arrangements. The trio was history by 1951.

Cole enjoyed 78 chart hits from 1944 to 1964, 49 that reached the Top 40, with the bulk coming in the post-trio era. Some, like "Pretend," were repeat hits ("Pretend" had three chart runs). Other songs, such as "Unforgettable," were remade and reworked by everyone from Dinah Washington to Cole's daughter, Natalie, who transformed herself into a '90s vintage prerock standards and ballads diva by cutting "Unforgettable" as a duet with her late father via studio/electronic gadgetry. The duet became the cornerstone for a career-reviving multiplatinum smash for Natalie Cole. "Too Young," "Send for Me," "Lazy, Hazy Days of Summer," and many other songs remain staples on Adult Contemporary radio. His '57 version of "Stardust" was the first cover since Bix Beiderbecke's that was praised lavishly by its composer, Hoagy Carmichael.

Unfortunately, Cole suffered severe hardships in the midst of this success. These included a beating at a 1956 Birmingham concert from outraged members of the White Citizens Council, who supposedly were out to prevent their sons and daughters (especially their daughters) from being contaminated by exposure to "rock and roll," a sound Cole was miles away from at the time. He became the first Black host of a network television show the next year, only to see it fail because NBC couldn't obtain enough sponsorship and couldn't get full cooperation and clearances from Southern stations. But these problems didn't limit Cole's film exposure. He was in *Blue Gardenia* and *Small Town Girl* in 1953, *Instanbul and China Gate* in 1957, and *St. Louis Blues* in 1958, a film that was quite fast and loose with facts. He also appeared in *Cat Ballou* in 1965.

While Cole was a consistent sales force as a solo artist, his albums also did well. *Love Is the Thing* topped the charts in 1957, while *Ballads of The Day, The Very Thought of You,* and *To Whom It May Concern* were all very successful. Cole had 24 albums make the Top 100 between 1956 and 1966. *After Midnight* in 1956 temporarily recreated the trio with bassist Charlie Harris and guitarist John Collins, added drummer Lee Young, and included special guests alto saxophonist Willie Smith, trumpeter Harry Edison, violinist Stuff Smith, and trombonist Juan Tizol. It was among Cole's last great jazz dates. There was also *Welcome to The Club* in 1958 with Count Basie's band, and Gerald Wiggins on piano. He teamed with pianist George Shearing in 1962 for *Nat Cole Sings/George Shearing Swings*, another nice, though not as explosive, jazz-based date. Cole's vocals influenced singers as diverse as Chuck Berry, Sam Cooke, Otis Redding, Marvin Gaye, and Brook Benton. Countless adults who never knew he was a great pianist idolized his singing in their youth. But jazz fans still wonder what would have happened if Nat King Cole had been born with a horrible singing voice. His records, both vocal and instrumental, were constantly reissued long before the mania began. Mosaic issued the ultimate boxed set a couple of years ago, the complete Nat King Cole Trio Capitol recordings. —*Ron Wynn and William Ruhlman*

★ **Complete Capitol Trio Recordings** / i. 1939-1951 / Mosaic 138
The definitive (18 full CDs!) collection. These are the trio recordings to listen to, with Nat playing and singing throughout. Lovely music for the jazz purist and everyone else as well. —*Michael Erlewine*

○ **Jumpin' at Capitol** / **i.** 1939-1951 / Rhino 71009
A similar vintage to *Straighten Up & Fly Right,* with a
greater emphasis on mellow standards. Excellent West Coast
trio sound. —*Hank Davis*

○ **Hit That Jive Jack: The Earliest Recordings** / **i.** Dec. 1940-
Oct. 1941 / MCA 42350

○ **Nat Cole at J.A.T.P.—Vol. 1** / Jul. 2, 1944 / Verve 14

○ **Nat Cole at J.A.T.P.—Vol. 2** / Jul. 2, 1944+1946 / Verve 25

★ **Anatomy of a Jam Session** / Jun. 1945 / Black Lion 760137
Remarkable album from 1945, when Nat King Cole was
known for piano brilliance rather than singing prowess. He
cut an intimate, swinging session with Charlie Shavers,
Herbie Haymer, John Simmons, and Buddy Rich holding
court on drums. The album was reissued on CD in 1990. It's
arguably his greatest record outside the trio. —*Ron Wynn*

○ **King Cole Trios Live: 1947-1948, The** / **i.** Mar. 1947-Mar.
1948 / Vintage Jazz Classics 1011

○ **Big Band Cole** / 1950-1958 / Blue Note 96259
Outstanding early '50s session with Cole showing his
tremendous piano skills, backed by a big band. His playing
was still loose, bluesy, and exciting at this juncture, and the
arrangements were designed to give him full exposure, yet
also to have the orchestra really punctuating his solos instead of just accompanying them. The original album was
reissued on CD in 1991 with six bonus cuts. —*Ron Wynn*

○ **In the Beginning** / **i.** 1956 / Decca 8260

★ **Complete After Midnight Sessions, The** / **i.** Aug. 15, 1956-
Sep. 24, 1956 / Capitol 7483282
This 1956 session features Cole's trio with a host of distinguished guest stars. The excellent digital remastering, plus a
menu of 17 numbers and some of Cole's less sugary vocals,
make this one of the few Cole items equally valued by pop
and jazz fans alike. — *Ron Wynn,* Rock & Roll Disc

Saint Louis Blues / Jan. 29-31, 1958 / Capitol 993

Nat King Cole Sings, George Shearing Plays / Dec. 1961 /
Capitol 1675

○ **Capitol Collectors Series** / **i.** 1990 / Capitol 93590
Most of Nat King Cole's biggest hits and best-known songs
are here on this terrific 20-track compilation of his solo
Capitol work. Includes "Mona Lisa," "The Christmas Song,"
"Send For Me," "Ramblin' Rose," and "Unforgettable." —
Stephen Thomas Erlewine

○ **Unforgettable Nat King Cole, The** / **i.** 1992 / Capitol 99230
A '92 reissue designed to take advantage of the success
Cole's daughter, Natalie, had, with a reworked version of
"Unforgettable" that features her doing a duet with her fa-
ther via digital technology. The album offers Cole doing the
original and other selected songs in the same vein. —*Ron
Wynn*

○ **Jazz Encounters** / **i.** Apr. 13, 1992 / Blue Note 96693
Nice anthology presenting Cole in instrumental and vocal
outings matched with numerous jazz and some pop artists,
among them Dizzy Gillespie, Stan Kenton, Benny Carter,
Coleman Hawkins, Woody Herman, Charlie Barnet, Max
Roach, Jo Stafford, Kay Starr, Johnny Mercer, and Buddy
DeFranco. —*Ron Wynn*

RICHIE COLE (Richard Cole)

b. Feb. 29, 1948, Trenton, NJ
Alto, tenor, and baritone saxophone / Bop, hard bop
A hard-working, intense alto saxophonist who's deeply indebted to Phil Woods both musically and inspirationally,
Richie Cole makes intriguing, attractive music. At times, it's
derivative and a bit repetitive, but Cole's spirited solos compensate for other shortcomings. While he's grown and matured as a player, his style can be traced directly to Woods,
and from Woods to Charlie Parker, hardly a bad family tree.
Cole's father owned a jazz club in New Jersey, and Richie
heard jazz often as a child. He started on guitar at age five,
and alto at age ten. Cole studied with Woods in high school,
and won a scholarship to Berklee. He attended for two years,

then dropped out to join Buddy Rich's big band in 1969.
Cole played with Doc Severinsen and Lionel Hampton in the
early '70s before forming his own group. He worked closely
with Eddie Jefferson in the mid '70s, and formed a personal
and professional relationship that blossomed until
Jefferson's death in 1979. During the '80s and '90s, Cole has
led various combos. He's recorded for Muse, Palo Alto,
Concord, and Milestone, among others. Cole has several
dates available on CD. —*Ron Wynn*

Battle of Saxes—Vol. 1 / **i.** Mar. 26-27, 1976 / Muse 5082
Entertaining, stimulating match of alto sax styles of Cole
and Eric Kloss. —*Ron Wynn*

★ **New York Afternoon-Alto Madness** / Oct. 13, 1976 / Muse
5119
While this album clearly shows alto saxophonist Richie
Cole's formidable talents as a soloist in the Phil Woods tradition, none of the music is particularly memorable (all but
two selections are by Cole). The tunes merely serve as jump-
ing-off points for the soloists, which in itself isn't necessarily
bad, but except for Cole and a few fleeting moments from
guitarist Vic Juris, the solos are quickly forgettable. On the
two tunes featuring Eddie Jefferson's vocals, "Waltz For a
Rainy Bebop Evening" and "It's the Same Thing
Everywhere," Cole fares better. Jefferson also adds short vocals to "Alto Madness" (an echoey "alto" at the beginning)
and Juris's "You'll Always Be My Friend" (a recitation of the
title at the conclusion). —*Carl Brauer,* Cadence

○ **Keeper of the Flame** / Sep. 6, 1978 / Muse 5192
A straightahead date. He contributes his usual sparkling, energized alto sax, backed by virtually the same personnel as
on the previous release. Pianist Harold Mabern again takes
second soloist honors, while guitarist Vic Juris, drummer
Eddie Gladden, and percussionist Ray Mantilla handle the
rhythm-section responsibilities. —*Ron Wynn*

☆ **Hollywood Madness** / Apr. 15, 1979 / Muse 5207
Unusual instrumental configuration and lineup for this '79
session. Cole heads a band with two bassists, a drummer, a
pianist, a percussionist, and vocalists Eddie Jefferson and the
Manhattan Transfer. This is part concept vehicle, part blowing session, but other than Cole on alto sax, no one else is as
decisive. Jefferson and the Manhattan Transfer provide
bluesy, flashy singing. —*Ron Wynn*

○ **Side by Side** / Jul. 1980 / Muse 6016
What we have here is a standard live blowing date, and quite
a predictable one, too. This sort of predictability has its positive sides, though, as it goes without saying that when players of this caliber play as one would expect them to do, some
quite good music is bound to come out. As with most sessions of this type, the musical output tends to be uneven.
When the session catches fire, as it does on "Scrapple From
the Apple," it is very good. I think that some of the music
was more effective live than on record, though, and on
"Donna Lee" there is no rhythmical unity at all; the track
goes nowhere. Throughout the album, Phil Woods's consistency and maturity of ideas tends to overshadow Richie Cole
(both alto sax) a bit, and Eddie "Lockjaw" Davis's (tenor sax)
guest appearance is pretty undistinguished. This is mostly
for dedicated hard boppers. —*Per Husby,* Cadence

○ **Alto Annie's Theme** / Jul. 31, 1982 / Palo Alto 8036
This was recorded in 1982 while the group was working at
the Keystone Korner in San Francisco. This, however, is a
studio recording; it had to be to get all the effects and overdubbing used to allow Richie Cole to play all the saxophones (alto, tenor, baritone). "Call of the Wild" is indeed
wild with real wolf calls, but what the saxophone group
refers to as "Megauniversal Saxophone Orchestra" is pretty
straightahead. That track and maybe "Easy to Love" are the
uninhibited ones. "Jeanine" is often done with vocalist Eddie
Jefferson and another Alto Madness group. "Key Largo"
comes from the pen of Benny Carter and has added percussion. "Boplicity" is a good vehicle (it was also done on the
February 1982 Kerouac album with vocalist Mark Murphy—
I prefer this version). Dick Hindman's (piano) single lines

and block chords bring back some real excitement and those lines written for alto and piano are superbly done. Credit goes to the two ex-Stan Getz sideman, bassist Brian Bromberg and drummer Victor Jones. I have never heard them play better. The title track is by the leader on the occasion of the birth of his daughter, Annie, in 1982. It is a lovely tune, and this is Cole at his best. —*Jerry Atkins*, Cadence

Pure Imagination / Nov. 1986 / Concord Jazz 4314

Bossa Nova International / Jun. 1987 / Milestone 9180
With the Hank Crawford Quintet. Cole and Hank Crawford (sax) make an effective team. —*Ron Wynn*

Signature / Jul. 1988 / Milestone 9162

EARL COLEMAN •

b. Aug. 12, 1925, Port Huron, MI
Vocals / Ballads & blues
A good blues and ballad stylist, Earl Coleman displays a rich, booming baritone on many blues and ballad selections. He's never been a matinee idol like Billy Eckstine, whose sound he mirrors, but Coleman has worked with several major bandleaders and combos. Coleman started with Jay McShann and Earl Hines in the early '40s. He went to California with McShann in 1945, and his singing was noticed by Charlie Parker, who recorded with him in 1947. Coleman's single, "This Is Always," became a hit. He did solo dates and worked in the '50s and '60s with Gene Ammons, Gerald Wilson, Don Byas, and Frank Foster. Coleman moved to Europe in 1968, but has returned to America often for sessions and concerts. His own recordings include sessions for Dial, Prestige, Atlantic, Xanadu, and Stash. Coleman has some dates available on CD. —*Ron Wynn and Michael G. Nastos*

★ **Earl Coleman Returns** / Mar. 2, 1956-Jun. 8, 1956 / Prestige 187
Earl Coleman was a singer along the lines of Billy Eckstine and Johnny Hartman. And although he's been working professionally for many, many years (since around 1925), he has never been as familiar to the public as Eckstine or Hartman. Part of the reason may be that he has always chosen to record in a solid jazz context with outstanding instrumentalists. While other mellow baritones have had wider commercial exposure, Coleman can get overly saccharin on occasion, but not so on *Earl Coleman Returns*, a Coleman offering worth reissuing for both vocal and instrumental reasons. —*Bob Rusch, Cadence*

GEORGE COLEMAN

b. Mar. 8, 1935, Memphis, TN
Tenor saxophone / Hard bop
One of the most fluid tenor saxophonists around and a masterful blues and ballad stylist, George Coleman has been an impressive player on the modern jazz scene since the late '50s. A Memphian, Coleman's known for his ability to play bebop changes at tremendous speeds and for his marvelous, even tone. Coleman played in blues bands throughout the mid-South in the '50s, and worked twice with B. B. King (in 1952 and in 1955 and 1956). Coleman left Memphis for Chicago in 1957 with fellow Memphian trumpeter Booker Little. They joined the Max Roach quintet in 1958, and Coleman remained with the group until 1959. He then played with Slide Hampton's octet until 1961, and then had stints with Wild Bill Davis in 1962 and with the Miles Davis quintet in 1963 and 1964. Coleman then worked with Lionel Hampton, Lee Morgan, Elvin Jones, Shirley Scott, and Cedar Walton, but, since the late '60s, has been a leader principally. Coleman's headed quintets, quartets, and octets, and has also played alto, soprano, and keyboards. He's recorded for many labels, among them Theresa (now Evidence), Timeless,

Catalyst, and Verve. He has a number of sessions available on CD. —*Ron Wynn and Michael G. Nastos*

Manhattan Panorama / Evidence 22019
Why George Coleman is not immediately mentioned when the discussion turns to great tenor sax veterans baffles me, because there are not many better mainstream/blues stylists. Other than a good-natured but ultimately empty vocal, Coleman is routinely brilliant on every number during this live Village Vanguard set originally issued on Theresa vinyl. It is wonderfully remastered, and all of Coleman's exuberant cries and swirling, driving solos are presented in their full glory. He teams with fellow Memphians pianist Harold Mabern and bassist Jami Nasser. Mabern's bluesy, vibrant phrases and Nasser's supple licks and accompaniment are ably punctuated by Idris Muhammad's capable drumming. There is a no-nonsense (the opener aside), no-frills attitude exemplified by the quartet; they just explode at the beginning of "New York Suite" and never rest until they conclude "Ray of Light." —*Ron Wynn*

★ **Amsterdam After Dark** / Nov. 2-3, 1977 / Timeless
Legendary tenor saxophonist blows up a storm with the Hilton Ruiz Trio. This has been reissued on CD. The best cut is "New Arrival." —*Michael G. Nastos*

○ **At Yoshi's** / Aug. 1987 / Evidence 22021
George Coleman's animated, anguished tenor sax solos are the hook on this seven-track live set done at Yoshi's in Tokyo during 1989. Coleman offers lush, sensitive playing during "Soul Eyes" and "Good Morning Heartache," but rips through chord changes much of the time, expanding through the upper register and burning. Drummer Alvin Queen and bassist Ray Drummond wisely give Coleman extensive space, spreading and splitting the beat while he roars above. Pianist Harold Mabern adds a contrasting element, nice bluesy, passionate solos or sensitive, subtle understatements that follow and reaffirm Coleman's emphatic lines. It is a fine live date, and one that is superbly remastered. —*Ron Wynn*

My Horns of Plenty / Mar. 4-5, 1991 / PolyGram 511922
A recent date by Coleman, stepping into the '90s in style. He displays his versatility by playing alto and soprano along with his usual tenor, and scoring on each one. The rhythm trio this time includes his favorite pianist, Harold Mabern, plus bassist Ray Drummond and drummer Billy Higgins. —*Ron Wynn*

○ **Eastern Rebellion** / Impulse 33102

ORNETTE COLEMAN

b. Mar. 9, 1930, Fort Worth, TX
Alto saxophone, composer / Early free
Other than Anthony Braxton, Albert Ayler, and Cecil Taylor, Ornette Coleman stands as free jazz's most controversial figure. He's regarded in some circles as an innovative genius; in other circles he's viewed as a heretic or a lunatic. Despite his soft-spoken, unassuming manner, reportedly Coleman has been physically threatened on the bandstand, has had his horn either stolen or destroyed by angry mobs, and was left behind in Los Angeles after a disastrous tour with blues musician Pee Wee Crayton. From Coleman's early days on the West Coast and his first Contemporary releases, the critical community and musicians were split widely over his music. Some saw him as jazz's next logical extension, while others viewed him as the ultimate perversion. The Modern Jazz Quartet's John Lewis helped secure Coleman a recording pact with Atlantic, while such Coleman students as Don Cherry, Billy Higgins, Charlie Haden, Scott LaFaro, and Edward Blackwell were early believers.

Coleman's controversial concepts about music began with his elimination of a treasured jazz axiom in place since bebop: a great soloist must be at the music's core. Coleman's work returned to jazz's early days as an ensemble-dominated sound. He sought to remove what he viewed as an over-reliance on chord changes and on melodic variation. Coleman also sought to eliminate other favorite devices, like call-and-response figures and swing in the traditional sense. He advocated spontaneous, collective interaction, nonsymmetrical lines, and what many inaccurately viewed as atonal, chaotic playing. There's no wonder so many had such a feverish response. Yet Coleman was first and foremost a blues player; his swooping, exploding phrases and solos were very rooted in Texas shuffle blues and a gospelized vocal style. He gradually evolved and developed his ideas until the '70s, when he began espousing "harmolodic" patterns. Rock, R&B, and funk lines and beats merged seamlessly into a collective musical brew of wailing sax lines that was similar, but less intricate, to his classic early and mid-'60s free material. It contained elements of 20th-century classical, as well as his beloved blues and R&B.

Coleman began on alto sax at age 14, then started playing tenor in 1946. He worked in many R&B and blues bands throughout the Fort Worth area through the '40s, then settled in Los Angeles where he studied theory and harmony. Coleman began playing a plastic alto because he couldn't afford a more expensive brass sax, though later he became attracted to the plastic instrument's unusual sound. His debut album hit the jazz world like a bomb in 1958. Cherry, Higgins, bassist Don Payne, and pianist Walter Norris were the quintet for that date. The next year Coleman did a quintet session at the Hillcrest Club with bassist Haden and Paul Bley on piano; it was issued briefly on a poorly recorded LP by Bley's Improvising Artists Incorporated label many years later. By then, Coleman's admirers and detractors were quarreling openly in the jazz press. Lewis arranged a summer visit to the Lenox School of Music and a date at the Five Spot in New York, along with the Atlantic recording gig after Coleman's second Contemporary album had been released. Coleman had met Lewis through Red Mitchell, who'd also introduced him to Contemporary Records label head Lester Koenig and bassist Percy Heath, another Modern Jazz Quartet member. The list of Coleman supporters included Gunther Schuller, Nat Hentoff, Martin Williams, and George Russell, while Charles Mingus was first quoted disparaging Coleman, then later supporting him. Coleman played with Mingus, Max Roach, and Kenny Dorham at a 1960 alternative Newport festival, but the performance wasn't recorded. The 1960 LP Free Jazz with Freddie Hubbard, Eric Dolphy, Scott LaFaro, and Ed Blackwell playing with Coleman's regular group further divided the ranks. In retrospect, much of the album didn't work, but the concept and the portion that did click were monumental and influenced a number of subsequent efforts by other bands.

Coleman continued recording for Atlantic in the early '60s, with Cherry, Charlie Haden (later Scott LaFaro) on bass, and with Blackwell. Jimmy Garrison also recorded with Coleman later on bass. Dewey Redman's tenor was a major asset to Coleman's mid-to-late '60s quartet. He added trumpet and violin along with alto, and worked outside the group on selected engagements, including a Blue Note date with Jackie McLean. He also teamed with Dewey Redman on occasion. Coleman continued recording for ESP, Blue Note, RCA, and Atlantic, but had difficulty getting club dates. His son, Denardo, started on drums in the mid-'60s, and was soon featured on his father's albums, a move that now brought cries of nepotism along with everything else. Coleman wrote prolifically, doing pieces for large orchestras and for film soundtracks. His ambitious work, "Skies of America," was performed on July 4, 1972 at the Newport Jazz Festival. It featured the quartet with the London Symphony Orchestra. Though it was hailed as a masterpiece, it was arguably the high point of the decade for Coleman, who often found the going rugged.

Since that era, his group, Prime Time, has utilized Coleman's alto with two guitars, two electric basses, and two drummers. Although influential, it has never been close to a commercial success. Coleman's Dancing in Your Head for A&M in 1973 included contributions from the Master Musicians of Joujouka and was recorded in Joujouka, Morocco. It was praised widely in the rock press, but reaction was less ecstatic and universal among jazz scribes. It was nearly three years later that Coleman followed it with Body Meta; neither album sold well. He recorded some outstanding records on the Artists House label, and another good date on Antilles, but they were also commercial failures. In the '80s, Coleman recorded sporadically until late in the decade. He did some outstanding releases on the Caravan of Dreams label that simply didn't get good, or even adequate, distribution. He got his widest attention from the album Song X, in which guitarist Pat Metheny's widespread clout and name recognition got Coleman his widest notice in years and gave Metheny credibility in circles in which he'd previously been deemed a lightweight. In the '90s, Coleman remains essentially obscure; he's now much more respected among critics, particularly the younger generation who're less enamored of bebop and view him as the last great innovator. Rhino Records repackaged all of Ornette Coleman's ground-breaking Atlantic recordings in a magnificent six-CD set, Beauty Is a Rare Thing, in 1993 (it includes one album previously issued only in Japan). Most of Coleman's other recordings are currently available on CD also. —Ron Wynn and Myles Boisen

★ **Beauty is A Rare Thing: Complete Atlantic Recordings /** Rhino 71410

Ornette Coleman's music has angered, confused, perplexed, and inspired listeners since the '50s. His work is both remarkably simple and extremely complex. Coleman's compositions have never failed to generate reaction and response; his legions of champions and critics are as animated as his performances. Though he was on Atlantic only from the late '50s until the early '60s, the label delayed issuing some of his music until the early '70s, and one album was never released anywhere except in Japan. Now, nearly 34 years after his initial session, Atlantic (in conjunction with Rhino) has finally issued a mammoth six-disc set with exhaustive liner notes by Robert Palmer presenting Ornette Coleman's entire album output for Atlantic, including To Whom Keeps a Record, the Japanese date. There are six previously unissued selections, plus some originally issued on the LP John Lewis Presents Contemporary Music: Jazz Abstractions— Gunther Schuller & Jim Hall. The discs are mostly in chronological order, although on the sixth disc the final Coleman combo dates in 1961 appear in front of the orchestral sets recorded in 1960. This is pure and at times almost frighteningly personal material. Coleman's alto squeaks, screams, soars, and penetrates. He was first and foremost a blues player, and you can hear him inverting and searching in each solo, avoiding repetition and seeking to express something deep and fresh every time. He is backed by the equally invigorating, unorthodox Don Cherry, playing his "pocket trumpet" in pithy, declarative fashion. Their blistering unison lines, buttressed by supportive yet assertive bass work from Charlie Haden or Scott LaFaro and rippling, probing drumming from Billy Higgins or Ed Blackwell make the songs flow despite the proclaimed lack of structure. Sometimes poignant, striking melodies emerge within the Coleman/Cherry dialogs. Other times, especially on later sessions, their interaction and solos merge into a wall of sound: harmonies, melodies, rhythms, beginnings, choruses, and endings. Except for two Schuller compositions and a typically freewheeling cover of "Embraceable You," every song (54 in all) was written by Coleman. This set spotlights every Coleman facet at Atlantic: amazing free sessions with a double quartet, pieces with a large orchestra, and numerous controversial combo sessions. The fierce, anguished, and spiraling solos on such albums as The Art Of The Improvisers and Ornette on Tenor are not for the faint of heart. It is sax playing that rivals John Coltrane's most vivid, energized, and shattering late-'60s work, and it was equally reviled. The booklet compiles numerous quotes from other musicians about Coleman and details his philosophy and insights. His playing and concepts were so progressive that they are still intriguing and scaring many people. The mastering is superb; never has Coleman's alto been so well recorded or his group's interactions documented so effectively. Whether you are a Coleman fan or think he is a fraud, don't bypass this set. Now if only the same thing would be done by Fantasy, MCA, A&M, Capitol, and Columbia. —*Ron Wynn*

Music of Ornette Coleman: Something Else!!!, The / Feb. 10, 1958-Mar. 24, 1953 / Contemporary 163
Coleman's first studio recording is just what the title promises, and the only one with a pianist (Walter Norris). In attendance are longtime bandmates Don Cherry (tpt) and Billy Higgins (d), playing relatively tame straight jazz and Latin numbers. Originally issued on Contemporary. —*Myles Boisen*

○ **Coleman Classics—Vol.1** / Oct. 1958-Nov. 1958 / Improvising Artists 373852
Basically, this is a seminal edition of the Ornette Coleman Quartet that outraged and transmuted the jazz world of the early '60s, but with the addition of pianist Paul Bley, which, of course, made it not quartet at all, but a quintet. Atypical of jazz ensembles—and of jazz notions altogether—up to that time, the harmonic and percussive latitude traditionally afforded by keyboards only serves to bridle Coleman's aims. But still, the Coleman/Bley pairing of 1958 is an invigorating and amiable one, and a particularly productive interval for Coleman. Two of his best early compositions surface here ("When Will The Blues Leave?" and "Ramblin'") cast as heady bop abstractions. Bley, for the most part, is barely audible in this monophonic mix. But when he pokes through, he can be heard playing complex jagged blues patterns and flowering dissonant counterpoint solos, sounding something akin to a double-tracked Thelonious Monk. —*Mikal Gilmore*, Down Beat

○ **Tomorrow Is the Question!** / Jan. 16, 1959-Mar. 10, 1959 / Contemporary 342
More early explorations of his second Contemporary label date. The affinity between Coleman and Don Cherry (tpt) is more obvious here, but the music is still hampered by a less-than-ideal rhythm section. —*Myles Boisen*

☆ **Shape of Jazz to Come** / May 22, 1959 / Atlantic 1317
Another prophetic title, and Coleman's first recording with his own band, including Charlie Haden (b). This New York session marks the beginning of his most innovative period, and contains the jarring "Congeniality." —*Myles Boisen*

Twins / May 22, 1959 / Atlantic 8810
Later release of early Coleman. Features the first take of his classic "Free Jazz." —*Michael Erlewine*

☆ **Change of the Century** / Oct. 8-9, 1959 / Atlantic 81341
Coleman's roots in New Orleans jazz ("Ramblin'") and Charlie Parker ("Bird Food") are still audible here, with the title cut indicating the way of the future. Drummer Ed Blackwell enlivens the whole affair. —*Myles Boisen*

○ **Art of Improvisers, The** / 1959 / Atlantic 90978
1959-1961. From six early Atlantic sessions. Close-to-definitive group interplay. Extraordinary musicianship. —*Michael G. Nastos*

★ **This Is Our Music** / Jul. 19+26, 1960 / Atlantic 1353

★ **Free Jazz (A Collective Improvisation)** / Dec. 21, 1960 / Atlantic 1364
An across-the-board definitive album; a must-buy. Only for open ears. —*Michael G. Nastos*

Ornette! / Jan. 31, 1961 / Atlantic 1378
The follow up to *Free Jazz* enlists Scott LaFaro on bass, and is the rarest of the Atlantic releases. —*Myles Boisen*

☆ **Ornette on Tenor** / Mar. 22+27, 1961 / Atlantic 1394
Coltrane bassist Jimmy Garrison joins Ed Blackwell (d), Don Cherry (tpt), and Coleman. A fascinating date, and his only one on the tenor sax, "Cross Breeding" is an 11-minute tour de force. —*Myles Boisen*

Ornette Coleman Town Hall Concert / Dec. 21, 1962 / ESP 1006

More new ideas were brewing, as Coleman combined his latest trio (David Izenzon and Charles Moffet) with a string quartet, signaling, from the start, an ongoing flirtation with classical music forms. —*Myles Boisen*

○ **At the "Golden Circle" in Stockholm—Vol. 2** / Dec. 3-4, 1965 / Blue Note 84225
Historic trio sessions from Ornette Coleman cut at the Golden Circle. Coleman plays at an inspiring, feverish pace, working off patterns and arrangements he was constructing almost on the spot. His assistants are bassist David Izenzon and drummer Charles Moffett. Both volumes are essential. —*Ron Wynn*

○ **At the "Golden Circle" in Stockholm—Vol. 1** / Dec. 3-4, 1965 / Blue Note 84224
Volumes 1 and 2. At Stockholm. More trio recordings (without the string quartet)—very edgy and uncompromising, with energy to spare. Ornette's violin and trumpet make fine appearances here. —*Myles Boisen*

Empty Foxhole / Sep. 9, 1966 / Blue Note 84246

Who's Crazy / 1966 / Affinity 102
Recorded in the fall of 1965, this two-record set stems from a particularly rich and fertile period in alto saxophonist, violinist, and trumpeter Ornette Coleman's continuing development. It comes between the justly praised Fairfield Hall and Golden Circle concerts of the nine-month European tour, which broke his lengthy early-'60s sabbatical. Therefore, it has not only historical significance, but also enormous musical value, for it is at least the equal of those two recordings, and is, in some ways, superior. This is a trio (with bassist David Izenzon and drummer Charles Moffett) that represents striking renewal in Coleman's music while making important strides in textural exploration. In some cases ("January"), the music is the most radical produced by this group; in others, like "Dans La Niege," "Misused Blues," or "Wedding Day," they play with winning simplicity. Interestingly, they also provide evidence of Coleman's ability to rework material in a variety of ways. Also worth noting is that Coleman's trumpet work—especially on "The Poet"—is perhaps the finest he'd recorded up to that point. His interplay with Izenzon is compelling, as are the shifting lyrical and uptempo passages. Much of this music is impassioned, but there are lighter moments, too—most notably the take-off of "When the Saints Go Marching in" that colors the latter half of "Wedding Day w/Fuzz," re-emerging as the "Fuzz" theme with manic violin development. —*Chris Sheridan*, Down Beat

Forms and Sounds / Mar. 17+31, 1967 / Bluebird 6561
Some of it works, some of it doesn't, but all of it demands your attention. —*Ron Wynn*

○ **Love Call** / Apr. 29, 1968+May 7, 1968 / Blue Note 84356
Ornette's trumpet work goes south sometimes, but his violin and alto sax are always striking. The CD has three bonus cuts. Dewey Redman makes his points as well. —*Ron Wynn*

New York Is Now / Apr. 29, 1968-May 7, 1968 / Blue Note 84287
Another excellent representation of Coleman's creative brilliance. With Dewey Redman (ts), Jimmy Garrison (b), and Elvin Jones (d). —*Michael G. Nastos*

Crisis / Mar. 22, 1969 / Impulse 9187

○ **Ornette at 12** / Jun. 16, 1969 / Impulse 9178
This album is a recapitulation on and a summation of Ornette Coleman's last three recordings (*The Empty Foxhole* and *New York Is Now* are the previous two). Certainly, Ornette Denardo Coleman (drums) had considerably improved technically, and had a much better understanding of and capacity to cope with the demands his father's music made of him and his instrument.... The most striking aspect of this father-son collaboration continues to be Denardo Coleman's obvious desire to play sympathetically; and although still an inconsistent and immature performer, at the time, he possessed most of the tools needed to accomplish this.... Charlie Haden (bass) had a better com-

mand of Coleman's idiom and its peculiar demand than any other bassist (David Izenon excepted) Coleman might have chosen. Despite his overall good contribution to group textures, Dewey Redman was neither powerful nor original enough an improviser to be a fitting partner for Coleman.... Which brings us to the final determining factor here: Coleman himself and his music. If you have any feeling at all for the new music, you cannot possibly go untouched by his alto playing; he leaves you with mouth agape, thinking he's played it all ... and then he comes right back in to show you how wrong you were. His interpretations, on both the impassioned dirge of "New York" and the up "C.O.D.," are masterful, complete. His downfall here, though, lays in his other instruments. The trumpet vehicle, "Rainbows," is perhaps a more pointed solo than some of his other brass excursions; but his chops just aren't in shape for it, and he muffs too much that he attempts. "Bells and Chimes," like the remainder of Coleman's violin work, is flyweight by comparison with the rest of his output.... Redman gets his only really good solo spot here.... In case it's of any concern to you, the playing time is short (just over 31 minutes). Sound quality is excellent for a live recording. —*Barry Tepperman*, Coda

Friends and Neighbors / Feb. 14, 1970 / Flying Dutchman 123

Science Fiction / Sep. 9-13, 1971 / Columbia 31061

Broken Shadows / 1971 / Columbia 38029
These never-before-released recordings come from the less than two years Ornette Coleman (alto sax) was with Columbia. The first five tracks are from the September 1971 sessions that also produced *Science Fiction;* the remaining three were recorded a year later. The personnel on *Broken Shadows* plays in various configurations and includes the most important figures to emerge from the Coleman school. This music sat unreleased for a decade, yet it sounds fresh. More remarkable is that the outstanding tracks like "Happy House," "School Work," and the title cut are on the level of Coleman's finest work. The entire record is not up to this level, but is certainly worth a listen. The strongest tracks on *Broken Shadows* are excellent and, by themselves, make the record worth getting. The remainder contain interesting and pleasant diversions. —*Paul Roger Barnes*, Cadence

Skies of America / May 1972 / Columbia 31562

★ **Dancing in Your Head** / Jan. 1973 / A&M 0807
Seminal album that outlines Ornette Coleman's "harmolodic" concept in its full glory. Besides Coleman's blend of sanctified/blues/honking alto sax, his band includes the slashing drummer Ronald Shannon Jackson, plus formidable bassist Jamaaladeen Tacuma and various guitarists. The music sizzles, shakes, and explodes, never starting or ending the way you'd expect. —*Ron Wynn*

Body Meta / Dec. 19, 1976 / Artists House 1
The music on *Body Meta*, a continuation of a session first released on *Dancing in Your Head*, is as confounding and startling today (1979) as his earlier albums were when first released. Coleman plays alto, backed by two guitars, bass, and drums. Although each piece begins and ends with at least a runthrough of a melodic fragment, the improvising in between seems to begin and end at the players' whim. At the same time, there is a feeling that what is evolving has some unknown logic, if only in the musicians' imagination. With repeated listening, a sense of the complex interplay of the musicians develops, even if their ultimate intentions still remain a mystery. The drummer (Ronald Shannon Jackson) moves in and out of various times and rhythms. Coleman's alto plays against and with those rhythms. The guitarists (Bern Nix and Charlie Ellerbee) sometimes follow the drummer, and at other times follow Coleman's alto, or go off on a third tangent. All this gives the music a lurching quality—forward, backward, and even static. As with earlier Coleman music, *Body Meta* is challenging to the listener. —*Sam Little*, Cadence

Soapsuds, Soapsuds / Jan. 30, 1977 / Artists House 6

Soapsuds, Soapsuds invites close hearing and enjoyment from first spin. Ornette Coleman (on tenor sax and trumpet) and bassist Charlie Haden meet as longtime collaborators and mutual admirers; each brings respect and knowledgeable response to the other. The mock seriousness of the TV theme "Mary Hartman, Mary Hartman" quickly deepens into tenderness for all plagued yet comic human beings; Coleman fleshes out "Mary" by giving her some rhythm, a clear singing voice, gentle turns of phrase with easy swing, surprising complexities, and an oblique tonal angle, ending with a little-kid-looking-for-mom cry. Haden isn't a step behind Coleman, but is thoroughly involved, ending with a fat handful of clustered bass strings. As the album continues with suite-like attention to their particular harmonic relationship, Coleman and Haden swirl about each other like a diaphonous double helix. Coleman grows somewhat looser, using more complex and suggestive strokes, always with a golden-ringing tone, which is quite different from his 1960 *Ornette on Tenor*. Haden tries everything he can think of on his instrument, and his thoughts run not to virtuosic bass stridings, but to deeply felt patterns and subtly intoned touches. —*Howard Mandel*, Down Beat

Of Human Feelings / Apr. 25, 1979 / Antilles 2001

In All Languages / 1985 / Caravan of Dreams 85008
This album features Ornette's late '50s and early '60s quartet with Charlie Haden (b), Don Cherry (tpt), and Billy Higgins (d). Their work is still vital. This recording also features Coleman's electric Prime Time Double Trio. The utterly no-nonsense approach and high intensity make this a recording challenged music listeners must have. —*Michael G. Nastos*

Opening the Caravan of Dreams / 1985 / Caravan Of Dreams 85001
Sometimes chaotic, sometimes uneven, but always hypnotic in its presentation, Ornette Coleman's band went into the Caravan of Dreams for an amazing session that resulted in this superb two-record set. Sadly, it has had very limited distribution. Coleman records have been few and far between, and this one has both vibrant new cuts and excellent reworkings of older material. —*Ron Wynn*

Virgin Beauty / 1988 / Portrait 44301

STEVE COLEMAN

b. Sep. 20, 1956, Chicago, IL
Saxophone, composer / M-base
Though he's been placed repeatedly at the center of a perceived conflict in jazz circles between "neoconservatives" and "progressives," Steve Coleman insists that he has no axe to grind and is not heading any ideological camp. But the many articles and interviews given since he began M-base in the early '80s would lead you to believe otherwise. In reality, M-Base isn't much different from the Association for the Advancement of Creative Musicians in Chicago or from Black Artists Group in St. Louis; it's both a self-help collective for musicians who share common interests and a organization committed to showing, through performance and composition, the relative unity of all African-American based music. The second part of that equation causes the problem; Coleman's mix of soul, R&B, funk, free jazz, hard bop, bebop, reggae, and disco doesn't sit well with everybody, especially since M-Base concerts and recordings are done in a stream-of-consciousness, nonstop fashion. Coleman's been accused of trivializing jazz in a pseudo-political attempt to attack other contemporary players that he views as elitists. Coleman's alto style is as eclectic as he claims; he's played straight bebop, hard bop, and effective free music with Dave Holland's band. He embraced funk, rock, soul, blues, and jazz while growing up on Chicago's south side. Coleman studied violin in school, then turned to alto at age 15, and played in a James Brown cover band. He later studied at Illinois Wesleyan University. When Coleman returned to Chicago, he worked with Von Freeman, getting a crash course in bebop. He moved to New York in 1978, where he

joined the Thad Jones-Mel Lewis Orchestra. Coleman later played in Cecil Taylor's Orchestra and Sam Rivers's Winds of Manhattan group before coforming M-Base with vocalist Cassandra Wilson. Coleman recorded several albums in the mid '80s and early '90s, teaming with Geri Allen, Graham Haynes, Lonnie Plaxico, Kelvyn Bell, Robin Eubanks, Kevin Bruce Harris, Marvin "Smitty" Smith, and Wilson, among others. He surprised some observers by recording an album in '92 with Tommy Flanagan and Freeman, hardly M-Base charter members. Coleman has several releases available on CD. —*Ron Wynn*

Motherland Pulse / Mar. 1985 / JMT 834401
This shows the jazz side of Coleman. With Geri Allen (p), Lonnie Plaxico (b), Graham Haynes (tpt). —*Michael Erlewine*

On the Edge of Tomorrow / Jan. 1986+Feb. 1986 / JMT 834405
Modern soul music. This is real contemporary funk, most of it danceable. With Geri Allen (synth) and Cassandra Wilson (v). —*Michael Erlewine*

★ **World Expansion** / Nov. 1986 / JMT 834410
With Geri Allen (k) and Robin Eubanks (t). Not his jazziest release, but a lot of good clean funk. —*Michael Erlewine*

Strata Institute Cipher Syntax / 1986 / JMT 834425

Rhythm People (The Resurrection of Creative Black) / Nov. 1990 / Novus 3092
And the Five Elements. Funky, creative improvisations along the lines of Ornette Coleman's "harmolodic" music. With Dave Holland (b) and Robin Eubanks (t). —*Michael Erlewine*

Black Science / Dec. 1990 / Jive/Novus 3119

Rhythm in Mind (The Carnegie Project) / Apr. 29, 1991 / Novus 63125
Erratic, but frequently compelling, release from Steve Coleman, whose M-Base theories have been among the late '80s and early '90s more controversial subjects. The album has bits and pieces of everything from free jazz to funk and pop, and Coleman's playing has enough straight jazz content to hold the interest of purists. —*Ron Wynn*

Drop Kick / Jan. 1992 / Novus 63144

JOHNNY COLES (John Coles)

b. Jul. 3, 1926, Trenton, NJ
Trumpet, flugelhorn / Hard bop
A self-taught trumpeter who also plays flugelhorn, Johnny Coles has combined precision with lyricism and has forged an emphatic, distinctive style. A noted Miles Davis disciple who is not enamored of acrobatics or gimmicks, Coles has provided compelling solos on many occasions with diverse bands. He began playing at age 13, and worked in the early '50s with Philly Joe Jones. Coles played in the '60s with James Moody, Gil Evans, and Charles Mingus, and at the Newport Jazz Festival in 1966 with George Coleman. He was in the Herbie Hancock sextet in the late '60s, and was featured on Hancock's *The Prisoner* album. Coles also played with Ray Charles in the '60s and '70s, and with Duke Ellington. He worked with the Count Basie orchestra in the '80s. Coles recorded with Kenny Burrell and Astrud Gilberto, and with Hancock and Mingus. His own recordings include sessions for Epic, Blue Note, Mainstream, and Criss Cross. Currently, his sessions are not available on CD. —*Ron Wynn*

○ **Warm Sound, The** / Apr. 13, 1961 / Epic 16015

★ **Little Johnny** / Aug. 9, 1963 / Blue Note 4144
The best of this hard bop trumpeter, with Leo Wright (as) and Joe Henderson (sax). —*David Szatmary*

New Morning / Dec. 19, 1982 / Criss Cross 1005

BUDDY COLLETTE (William Marcell Collette)

b. Aug. 6, 1921, Los Angeles, CA
Saxophone, clarinet, flute, composer / Bop, cool
One of the pioneers on jazz flute, Buddy Collette helped to increase the instrument's importance and profile with his distinctive solos. An outstanding improviser who's been greatly admired for his taste and sound on both flute and various saxes, Collette took piano lessons in his childhood, and later learned alto sax and other instruments. He eventually began playing tenor and baritone. Collette worked with Les Hite in the early '40s, before joining the Navy and leading a dance band during World War II. He performed and recorded in the late '40s with Lucky Thompson, Edgar Hayes, Louis Jordan, Benny Carter, and Gerald Wilson, and also with Charles Mingus. Collette had many radio and television dates in the '50s, then gained prominence for his playing in Chico Hamilton's mid-'50s quintet. He led various groups, and recorded a number of albums that feature his own compositions. Collette decreased his active playing to concentrate on composing and scoring films in the '60s. He also wrote arrangements and played with Thelonious Monk, and appeared in several films. He was part of the house band at the Monterey festival in the mid '60s and played with Stan Kenton's Neophonic Orchestra in 1965. Collette performed and wrote material in the '70s, and traveled to Japan with Benny Carter in 1978. He cofounded a record label, Legend, in 1973, and became its president in 1975. A collection of his compositions was published in 1985. Collette recorded with James Newton and Geri Allen in 1988. He's made sessions for Contemporary, ABC/Paramount, Dootone, Specialty, Contemporary, Soul Note, and Legend. He has a few albums available on CD. —*Ron Wynn*

★ **Man of Many Parts** / Feb. 13, 1956-Apr. 17, 1956 / Contemporary 239
This is material from three 1956 sessions that made up Buddy Collette's first LP as a leader and seem designed to display his multi-instrumental (flute, alto sax, tenor sax, clarinet) approach. Except for his clarinet work, however, I find little particularly distinctive about the leader's playing. . . . Overall, as an album, it lacks a particularly strong focus, and while individual tracks shine and deserve attention, the average is of a sampler quality. The cumulative personnel over the record include: Gerald Wilson (trumpet); David Wells (trumpet, trombone); Bill Green (alto sax); Jewel Grant (baritone sax); Ernie Freeman (piano); Red Callendar (bass); Max Albright (drums); Gerald Wiggins (piano); Gene Wright (bass); Bill Richmond (drums); Barney Kessel (guitar); Joe Comfort (bass); and Larry Bunker (drums). —*Bob Rusch*, Cadence

Aloha to Jazz / i. 1957 / Bel Canto 1002

Jazz Loves Paris / 1957-1958 / Specialty 1764
A flawed, but intriguing, concept date from the late '50s, and one of the few jazz albums that Specialty ever issued. Collette was part of large group that also included trombonist Frank Rosolino, organist Gerald Wiggins, pianist Pete Jolly, and guitarist Howard Roberts. The songs are either about Paris or have French themes. In many cases, the playing is superior to the material. —*Ron Wynn*

WILLIE COLON

b. Apr. 28, 1950, Bronx, NY
Vocals / Latin jazz
A hero in Latin America and one of the major names in contemporary Latin music, Willie Colon has been a major bandleader, composer, producer, vocalist, and trombonist since the early '60s. He began playing trumpet at age 12, then switched to trombone at age 14. Colon began music studies while he directed a 14-piece group, the Latin Jazz All-Stars. His first professional group used a two-trombone frontline in homage to Eddie Palmieri. Colon signed with Fania at age 17, and his debut album was *El Malo*. He quickly scored hits with the singles "Jazzy" and "I Wish I Had a Watermelon." Vocalist Hector Lavoe, also a Puerto Rican, was Colon's lead vocalist and worked with him until the mid '70s.

Colon helped introduce non-Cuban musical influences and players into the Latin music and Latin jazz mainstream. His albums are famous for their multicultural blends. Colon has drawn from African children's songs, and from Brazilian, Cuban, Caribbean, and Panamanian numbers. He featured Panamanian cuatro (10-string) player Yomo Toro on the hit single "La Murga." Ntozake Shange later used the single "Che Che Cole" in her production of *for colored girls who have considered suicide when the rainbow is enuf.* It was adapted from a Ghanaian children's song. Colon's songs address everything from street crime to politics. He used the Puerto Rican "bomba" rhythm, jazz, and even featured Sha Na Na guitarist Elliott Randall on one cut.

Throughout the '70s and '80s, Colon expanded his musical options and experimented. He gave the reins of his band to Lavoe at one point, then paired him with Rueben Blades. Colon wrote a salsa ballad for a New York television production in the late '70s. He began collaborating with the great vocalist Celia Cruz in the late '70s, and produced a pair of successful Blades albums. Colon won Musician, Producer, Arranger and Trombonist of the Year in 1978 from *Latin New York*'s readers' poll, and repeated as Musician of the Year in 1981, while also winning Album of the Year for *Fantasmas.* Colon maintained his hectic pace during the '80s. He worked with Ismael Miranda, Lavoe, Cruz, and Blades. Colon's '82 album with Blades, *Canciones del Solar de los Aburriodos,* won a Grammy. He visited Europe for the first time in the '80s, and formed a new band. Both Blades and Lavoe went their separate ways, while Colon continued his idiomatic fusions. He recorded songs by Jacques Brel, Carole King, and Mark Knopfler; did a big band date; produced albums with soca and Haitian rhythms; recorded songs by Brazilian composers Caetano Veloso and Wally Salomao; and became more overtly political and satirical with his own lyrics. Colon produced albums for Lavoe and Cruz in the late '80s, and had an international club hit with the single "Set Fire to Me."

Colon was one of several prominent Latin stars involved with David Byrne's controversial, but hugely successful, Latin music album. He viewed the conflict with a bemused attitude, freely admitting Byrne was no Latino or salsero master, but also acknowledging that neither he nor Celia Cruz had the clout to get on Warner Bros. at that point. Despite his involvement at every level of the music business and his international stature, Colon doesn't have an album listed in the *Spectrum* catalog. His numerous Fania releases are available from Latin music stores. —*Ron Wynn and Max Salazar*

Guisando / **i.** 1969 / Fania 370
Colon's third album with, for trivia buffs, his second-favorite cover. Colon was 20 at the time, and this is still the funky, riotous, sometimes mildly ragged, and chaotic sound of his early days. The hallmarks are exuberance, humor, innovation, lots of Colon compositions, and, as a bonus, the fine piano of the band's African-American pianist, Mark Diamond. —*John Storm Roberts*

★ **Good, the Bad, the Ugly, The** / **i.** 1975 / Fania 484
A classic recording by one of the most creative heads in New York salsa. In 1975 *The Good, the Bad, the Ugly,* a New Directions release done after Colon got fed up with the two-trombone sound, was the evidence that he could reach beyond his youthful sound into a wider and deeper idiom. It is also the last album with Hector Lavoe, who had decided to remain a teen idol. *The Big Break, Asalto Navideño,* and this album are pinnacles, in their different ways, of early to mid-'70s salsa. —*John Storm Roberts*

○ **Siembra** / **i.** 1976 / Fania

○ **Solo** / **i.** 1980 / Fania

○ **Metiendo Mano** / Fania 500
Salsa history in the making: the album in which Willie Colon introduces Ruben Blades to the wider world! An obvious classic, given Blades's subsequent history, but also a gorgeous album with Yomo Toro on two tracks (one with guitar), the great pianist Sonny Bravo on two cuts, and ace percussion with Milton Cardona and Nicky Marrero. —*John Storm Roberts*

☆ **Big Break/La Gran Fuga, The** / Fania 394
Colon's third album and the clearest early sign of his individuality, with a Ghanaian children's song, the first of his

Panamanian-influenced numbers, and a prophetic venture into Brazilian rhythms. —*John Storm Roberts*

○ **El Malo** / Fania 337
El Malo is Colon and Hector Lavoe's first-ever recording, made in 1967 when Colon was a mere 17 years old. Every number's a killer: "Jazzy," "Juana Pena," "Borinquen," "El Malo." Plus boogalu! —*Carl Hoyt, Original Music*

○ **Salsa's Bad Boy** / Charly 238

ALICE COLTRANE

b. Aug. 27, 1937, Detroit, MI
Piano, vibes, harp, organ / Early free
Alice Coltrane was a good hard bop pianist with Terry Gibbs who altered her style and became a McCoy Tyner follower when she joined John Coltrane's band in the late '60s. She replaced Tyner in 1966, a move of epic proportions. She added colors and textures to the expansive, constantly shifting wave of sound generated by Coltrane, Pharoah Sanders, and Rashied Ali. Alice Coltrane's harp playing, with its rippling, ethereal impact, and her swirling organ solos heard on later albums, were often more striking than her piano solos. She studied classical music and jazz as a child, and played in church groups. Coltrane worked in the bands of Kenny Burrell, Johnny Griffin, Lucky Thompson, and Yusef Lateef. During the early '60s, while working and recording with Terry Gibbs, she met John Coltrane. They married in 1965, and a year later she was in the group. After his death, Alice Coltrane led various bands, playing with Sanders, Archie Shepp, Joe Henderson, Frank Lowe, and Carlos Ward, and with Cecil McBee, Jimmy Garrison, Ben Riley, and Roy Haynes. Her early '70s albums blended strings; Asian and Eastern melodies, rhythms, instrumentation and influences; plus free jazz elements. Alice Coltrane moved to California in the early '70s. She formed the Vedantic Center in 1975, a retreat for the study of Eastern/Asian religions. Since the 1978 album *Transfiguration,* Coltrane has performed only on rare occasions. She did play in a 1987 tribute to John Coltrane at the Cathedral of St. John the Divine in New York with a quartet that included her sons. Alice Coltrane has only a couple of selections available on CD, but she can be heard on many late-period John Coltrane reissues. —*Ron Wynn*

Monastic Trio / Jan. 29, 1968 / Impulse 9156

Journey in Satchidananda / 1970 / MCA 33119
Before there was new age, there was Alice Coltrane, an amazing composer and instrumentalist . . . who fused her knowledge of world music, jazz, and Eastern spirituality, and created sounds that were to become foundations for a genre. Recorded in 1970, this album combines her virtuosity on harp and piano with Pharoah Sanders's transcendental soprano sax, plus tamboura and oud, yielding original compositions that are evocative, meditative, searching, yearning, and just simply beautiful. Includes "Isis and Osiris," "Something About John Coltrane," and "Shiva-Loka." A personal favorite of this reviewer 20 years ago, and still highly recommended! —*Ladyslipper*

★ **Ptah the El Daoud** / Jan. 26, 1970 / Impulse 9196
Alice Coltrane's album *Ptah the El Daoud* is a portrait of this woman's deep spiritual nature, in addition to her fine talents as a musician. Coltrane, who said that Bud Powell was her biggest influence, created a style of playing that combined the quick, melodic, bop-rooted (in the tradition of Powell) phrasings of her right hand in conjunction with the uniscale, broad spectrum, flowing sound of her left, a style obviously influenced by her close association with John Coltrane. Her album features four of her compositions, three of which include Pharoah Sanders and Joe Henderson (tenor sax, flute). In addition, Ron Carter on bass and Ben Riley on drums are featured throughout the album. . . . Carter, as always, is rich, subtle, and melodic, while Coltrane, when playing piano, is especially fulfilling to hear with her unique combination of neo-Coltrane fullness and bop-blues roots. . . . Both Henderson and Sanders play remarkably well, and I

was especially impressed by Sanders's flexibility. . . . In listening to this album and Sanders's work with Don Cherry, it can only be concluded that Sanders's musicianship could never really be overrated, for it was on the highest of levels. It is evident, too, that both Sanders and Henderson knew exactly where they were going and what they wished to achieve. Their music is, in a word, precise. —*Robert Rouda*, Coda

○ **Universal Consciousness** / Apr. 6, 1971-Jun. 19, 1971 / Impulse 9210

World Galaxy / Nov. 15-16, 1971 / Impulse 9218

JOHN COLTRANE (John William Coltrane)

b. Sep. 23, 1926, Hamlet, NC, **d.** Jul. 17, 1967, New York, NY
Tenor and soprano saxophone, composer / Bop, hard bop, post bop
John Coltrane stands as the supreme jazz icon from the '50s to the present, even though Miles Davis enjoyed a wider profile among the pop and rock crowd. Coltrane's fame and controversial evolution from devoted traditionalist to radical innovator made him the major stylist in an era when saxophonists ruled jazz circles. Coltrane's music moved through many phases; from instrumental R&B and routine though brilliantly played bebop into his "sheets of sound" concept, where he moved from strict chord progressions into a "modal" manner using false fingerings to extend the tenor's upper range and its tone color option. Later came the free era with its human-like cries, amazingly intense delivery, and dense, dissonant sound. Coltrane sometimes played poignant, lovely songs; other times he strained, groaned and screamed, pushing the horn out beyond not just musical, but almost human, boundaries.

Coltrane learned E-flat alto horn, clarinet, and alto sax in his youth. After moving from North Carolina to Philadelphia, he enrolled at the Ornstein School of Music and the Granoff Studios. His studies were disturbed by a stint in the service. He was stationed in Hawaii. Coltrane then played alto sax in Joe Webb's and King Kolax's bands, then switched to tenor when he joined Eddie "Cleanhead" Vinson in 1947 and 1948. He alternated between alto and tenor in the late '40s playing with Jimmy Heath, Howard McGhee, Dizzy Gillespie, and Earl Bostic. He made his first recording with Gillespie in 1949.

Coltrane opted to specialize on tenor by the mid '50s, when he joined Johnny Hodges's band. He didn't perform regularly for a stretch in 1954, then joined Miles Davis in 1955 for Coltrane's first stint with Davis. After that, he played with Monk, but only participated in a few recording sessions due to contractual conflicts. Coltrane rejoined Davis and played in various quintets and sextets, making classic sessions in the late '50s and early '60s. Davis's concept of freeing players from the confines of structure influenced Coltrane. Coltrane worked in the '50s with three invigorating, creative, and distinctive pianists: Monk, Mal Waldron, and Cecil Taylor. He began playing the soprano while with Davis, buying his first instrument in 1960 and recording on it for Atlantic. Coltrane began his own band in 1960, but took a few months to get the personnel he wanted. McCoy Tyner and Elvin Jones joined early in 1960, but Jimmy Garrison wasn't on board until 1961. At times, Coltrane added Eric Dolphy as a second saxophonist, Reggie Workman (Garrison's predecessor) and Art Davis as second bassists, and Roy Haynes as the preferred substitute whenever Elvin Jones wasn't available.

The Coltrane quartet of the early and mid '60s became the sound and voice for a jazz generation. The quartet made records with Duke Ellington guesting on piano and accompanying ballad singer Johnny Hartman, yet also cut furious works with 15- to 20-minute songs. Tyner's solos, with their two-handed, octave-leaping flurries and slow, steadily building pace set the stage for Coltrane's ear-catching entrances and equally awesome solos. Coltrane would repeat lines, phrases, even notes, then suddenly shift direction. His interpretations of "My Favorite Things" and other pop songs cre-

ated, recreated, destroyed, and then rebuilt melodies and statements. Garrison and Jones could interact with Tyner, work off him, duel with Trane, or support him.

By the mid '60s, Coltrane's music had changed one more time, and he made changes in his group. Pharoah Sanders was added as permanent second saxophonist, and Coltrane's wife, Alice, became the pianist. Rashied Ali was briefly the second drummer, then became the only drummer when Elvin Jones left. The music became even more intense, and the Coltrane/Sanders solos were vivid, frenzied dialogues. Right-wing critics were scandalized, while left-wing types were quick to believe Coltrane's late '60s music was an expression of solidarity with the oppressed. Coltrane expressed passionate religious feelings and named compositions and albums after specific phrases. He had studied Asian and Eastern philosophy and music since the early '60s, and embraced it even more in the late '60s. But he managed to win *Down Beat* polls in spite of savage reviews. *A Love Supreme* was widely acclaimed as a masterpiece in 1964; others saw it as the ultimate end to their devotion to his music. Sadly, Coltrane died in 1967 at the age of 40.

As part of their distribution/reissue deal with Atlantic, Rhino issued an interesting anthology in 1993, though they neatly avoided all but a snippet of his late '60s work. MCA/GRP, the holders of the ABC/Impulse masters, have been issuing numerous concept albums, samplers, anthologies, and a few classic dates. Coltrane's complete Prestige recordings (except those available in the Miles Davis boxed set) are available in a multidisc deluxe package. Individual releases on Atlantic, Pablo, and various import labels, plus his sole Blue Note date, *Blue Train*, are available also. Many music publications marked the 25th anniversary of his death in 1992, and there were musical specials on several jazz radio stations as well. —*Ron Wynn with Myles Boisen*

○ **John Coltrane Plays for Lovers** / Oct. 26, 1956-Dec. 26, 1958 / Prestige 7426

○ **On a Misty Night** / Oct. 26, 1956 / Prestige 24084
This John Coltrane twofer was originally released as *Tenor Conclave* and *Mating Call* (the latter under Tadd Dameron's name). *On a Misty Night* is an uneven affair; the first record is relatively unsatisfying. Since the session is a standard "blowing date," the arrangements are minimal and most of the tunes are given over to straightahead blowing. The order of solos is nicely documented so one can compare different tones and improvisational attitudes, which is about the only interest I found in the music. The Dameron date provides an unadorned look at the first-rate mid '50s sound. And, as Andrew White's liner notes attest, one could hear a good example of Trane's "post-bebop lyricism" (on tenor). (White may have ruffled some feathers with his claim that Coltrane wasn't a "genius" or the "Father of the Avant-Garde.") —*Carl Brauer*, Cadence

Dakar / Apr. 20, 1957 / Prestige 393
Releasing *Dakar* under tenor saxophonist John Coltrane's name was more of a marketing decision than a musical one. In point of fact, it could just as easily have been released under pianist Mal Waldron's name, since he appears on all the tracks and also wrote five of the eleven compositions. The album consists of reissues of three Prestige dates: the first six cuts were released as *Dakar*; Jimmy Heath's "C.T.A." was released under Art Taylor's name on *Taylor's Wailers*, and is played by a quartet of Coltrane, Waldron, bassist Paul Chambers, and Taylor (drums); the final four tracks were released as *Interplay For 2 Trumpets and 2 Tenors*. While the album has much to offer, one shouldn't really purchase it only for Coltrane's playing. For as nice as his contributions are, he really doesn't have any more solo space than the other horn players. One can probably find as much enjoyment in the playing of baritone saxophonists Cecil Payne and Pepper Adams, trumpeters Idrees Sulieman and Webster Young, and tenor saxophonist Bobby Jaspar. The music has the atmosphere of a fairly loose blowing date. There is nothing revelatory here, but it's certainly nice jazz. —*Carl Brauer*, Cadence

Wheelin' / Apr. 20, 1957-Sep. 20, 1957 / Prestige 672

☆ **Lush Life** / Aug. 16, 1957 / Prestige 131
Fine session in which Coltrane stripped away his usual surrounding sound and recorded in a trio format. He's backed only by bassist Earl May and drummer Art Taylor, working in pianoless format championed by Sonny Rollins. The extra space seems to benefit him, as his solos on these cuts are emphatic and exuberant. *—Ron Wynn*

★ **Blue Train** / Sep. 15, 1957 / Blue Note 46095
A landmark album—stunning. This is Coltrane's only Blue Note recording as a leader, and he never made a better album in this particular hard bop style. A must-hear for all jazz fans, *Blue Train* includes Coltrane's most impressive early composition, "Moment's Notice." With outstanding performances from sidemen Lee Morgan (tpt), Curtis Fuller (t), and Kenny Drew (p). *—Michael Erlewine*

★ **John Coltrane: The Prestige Recordings** / i. 1957-1958 / Prestige 4405
Coltrane was *the* major sax stylist in a decade when the tenor saxophone reigned supreme, and his 1955-1958 recordings for Prestige live on as marvels of jazz invention. . . . Here is the complete set of 31 albums he made as leader and sideman—that's 125 slices of jazz genius on 16 CDs. The Rudy Van Gelder studio recordings are warm and clear, simply state of the art. *—Myles Boisen, Roots & Rhythm*

Believer, The / Jan. 10, 1958-Dec. 26, 1958 / Prestige 7292

☆ **Soultrane** / Feb. 7, 1958 / Prestige 021
Coltrane works with the Red Garland trio, a busy unit during this period. He tackles these standards with a quiet confidence, sometimes extending his solos, other times merely expanding the original melody. Garland is an excellent soloist on standards and ballads, while Paul Chambers on bass and drummer Art Taylor provide their own sterling counterpoint. *—Ron Wynn*

Settin' the Pace / Mar. 1958 / Prestige 078

Dial Africa / May 13, 1958-Jun. 24, 1958 / Savoy 1110
Dial Africa brings us more transitional Coltrane to complement the previous *Countdown* sessions, also from 1958. These dates, under the leadership of trumpeter/flugelhornist Wilbur Harden, also feature trombonist Curtis Fuller, pianists Howard Williams or Tommy Flanagan, bassist Al Jackson, and drummer Art Taylor. While utilizing the blowing session format, they were distinguished, in the words of annotator Robert Palmer, as "harbingers of a profound musical and social upheaval, one in which the emerging consciousness of an African cultural heritage would play a vital role." The African influence is most predominant in "Oomba," where a mono-chordal ostinato and three-over-four structure allude to Black African musical practices. . . . In his solo, Coltrane's ascetic, sentimentality-drained sound voices assertive short bursts that progressively lengthen into electrically energized sheets of sound. In addition to Coltrane's assured playing, the set is also notable for the flowing lyricism of Harden, whose solid accomplishments as a player and composer deserve greater attention. *—Chuck Berg, Down Beat*

○ **Black Pearls** / May 23, 1958 / Prestige 352
With Donald Byrd (tpt), Red Garland (p), Paul Chambers (b), and Art Taylor (d). *—Michael Erlewine*

Coltrane Time / Oct. 13, 1958 / Blue Note 84461

Bahia / Dec. 26, 1958 / Original Jazz Classics 415
Steady, often excellent hard-blowing and blues date featuring Coltrane in his busiest recording period. He cut numerous sessions for Prestige during the late '50s to satisfy a commitment to the label and to move to Atlantic. Most were done with the same rhythm section: pianist Red Garland, bassist Paul Chambers, and drummer Art Taylor. All are present here, plus trumpeter Wilbur Harden. *—Ron Wynn*

★ **Giant Steps** / May 4, 1959 / Atlantic 1311

Coltrane Jazz / Nov. 24, 1959-Dec. 2, 1959 / Atlantic 1354

○ **Art of John Coltrane: The Atlantic Years, The** / 1959-1961 / Atlantic 313
Good anthology collecting several good tracks from Coltrane's Atlantic period, among them the earliest "My Favorite Things" and other standards and originals. Though these songs aren't as transcendant as the Impulse period, they are an important indicator of future directions. *—Ron Wynn*

☆ **Avant Garde** / Jun. 20, 1960-Jul. 8, 1960 / Atlantic 90041
With Don Cherry (tpt). This meeting of the titans doesn't sound so "out" nowadays. Influenced by Ornette Coleman. *—Michael G. Nastos*

Coltrane Plays the Blues / Oct. 24, 1960 / Atlantic 1382
Single session. Great tunes like "Mr. Day" and "Mr. Knight." A much-neglected, but important, Coltrane album. *—Michael G. Nastos*

Coltrane's Sound / Oct. 24, 1960 / Atlantic 1419
Wonderful early '60s date, with Coltrane playing standards and extending them, straining at times, other times just playing wondrous melodies. The quartet lineup was not yet in place, but McCoy Tyner on piano and Elvin Jones on drums were slowly locking into the Coltrane concept. Bassist Steve Davis does his best to assist things. *—Ron Wynn*

★ **My Favorite Things** / Oct. 24-26, 1960 / Atlantic 1361
Classic early Coltrane. The title cut is most beautiful, and contains unforgettable piano by McCoy Tyner. *—Michael Erlewine*

Coltrane Legacy, The / Oct. 24, 1960-May 25, 1961 / Atlantic 1553

○ **Africa Brass Sessions—Vol. 1 & 2** / May 23, 1961+Jun. 7, 1961 / MCA 42231
This two-volume recording features the orchestral Coltrane. Important recordings, available on one CD. *—Michael G. Nastos*

☆ **Ole Coltrane** / May 25, 1961 / Atlantic 1373
When *Ole Coltrane* first came out in 1961, Eric Dolphy played under the pseudonym George Lane for contractual reasons. The reissue gets the names right in a session that features Coltrane, Dolphy, Freddie Hubbard, McCoy Tyner, Reggie Workman, Art Davis, and Elvin Jones. The original only had three extended tunes: "Ole," "Dahomey Dance," and "Aisha." The reissue has a bonus. It is the lovely Billy Frazier tune "To Her Ladyship," which was called "Original Untitled Ballad" when first released on *The Coltrane Legacy*. *—Ken Franckling, Jazz Times*

○ **Africa Brass Sessions—Vol. 2** / Jun. 7, 1961 / Impulse 42
Alternate takes, previously unissued titles, and some leftovers comprise this anthology featuring material from the early '60s. Coltrane was steadily heading toward the outside, playing with a searing intensity and probing fury that indicated he'd soon be moving beyond established musical frontiers. Eric Dolphy did the arrangements and conducts the orchestra on the main track. *—Ron Wynn*

○ **Other Village Vanguard Tapes** / Nov. 1-5, 1961 / Impulse 9325
Even if you have John Coltrane's *Live at the Village Vanguard* and *Impressions*, and "Spiritual," "India," and "Chasin' the Trane" are on those recordings, don't think that there's no need to have these versions. You'd be making a big mistake, for this is great Coltrane. This version of "Chasin' the Trane" can't match the *Live at the Village Vanguard* one for sheer exuberance and breathtaking intensity, but it does have a very good Eric Dolphy solo on alto between Trane's two sorties. The first version of "Spiritual" finds Trane on soprano and Dolphy on bass clarinet. The second is, for my money, the finest of the three versions available. It is also the longest (20 minutes). Trane starts on tenor, and the invocation is played by Dolphy on bass clarinet and Garvin Bushell on contrabassoon. Trane's tenor solo is a gem as is Dolphy's. McCoy Tyner's piano solo is somewhat anticlimactic, but then Trane brings things back home with an excellent soprano solo leading everyone back to the in-

vocational theme. The "Untitled Original" features Trane on tenor and Dolphy on alto. On this piece, as on parts of the others, Tyner lays out for long stretches, allowing the two horn players the maximum freedom to present their musical visions. "Greensleeves" is a pleasant six-minute soprano and piano feature without Dolphy. Picking a favorite track out of these is truly difficult, but my personal favorite would have to be "India." The two basses and Abdul-Malik's oud establish the bottom, while Dolphy's bass clarinet and Bushell's oboe play the stately theme. Trane and his soprano soar above all this. His first solo is a monster urged on by Jones's maniacal drumming. Dolphy's solo is equal to the challenge, and Trane responds with another other-worldly flight before the piece returns to the beginning theme. These tapes gathered dust for 15 years, but like a fine wine, they improved with age. — *Carl Brauer*, Cadence

★ **Live at the Village Vanguard** / Nov. 2-3, 1961 / MCA 39136
Coltrane's first eye-opening Vanguard release, parts of which feature him in ambitious, relentless songs with partner Eric Dolphy. The others are a superb rendition of "Softly, as in a Morning Sunrise," set up by McCoy Tyner's passionate piano solo, and the other is a furious version of "Impressions." — *Ron Wynn*

○ **Live in Stockholm (1961)** / Nov. 1961 / Charly 117

○ **European Impressions** / i. Nov. 1961 / Bandstand 1514

Ballads / 1961 / MCA 5885
Partly to counter the ridiculous accusation of being an "angry tenor" and partly for variety's sake, John Coltrane decided to stick to standard ballads for this album and, if anything, he is too respectful of the melodies. Trane's tone is frequently gorgeous here, easily the main joy of the album, but I would have preferred that he stretch out more and really explore these tunes as he does on "I Want to Talk About You" (from *Coltrane Live at Birdland*). Most of these performances barely get beyond the melody statements. — *Scott Yanow*, Cadence

☆ **Gentle Side of John Coltrane** / i. 1961-1964 / GRP 107

○ **Coltrane** / i. Jun. 1962 / MCA 5883
Coltrane is a well-rounded set that is a perfect introduction to the classic quartet (John Coltrane, tenor and soprano sax; McCoy Tyner, piano; Jimmy Garrison, bass; Elvin Jones, drums). The 14-minute "Out of This World" (penned by Harold Arlen and Johnny Mercer) gets an intense improvisation that would have shocked its composers (did either one of them ever hear this recording?). "Soul Eyes" is one of Trane's most beautiful ballad performances, "The Inch Worm" is quite playful (especially for Coltrane), "Tunji" sounds dead serious in the same vein as "Alabama," and the boppish "Miles Mode" is such a strong tune that it is surprising how obscure it remains. — *Scott Yanow*, Cadence

○ **Paris Concert** / Nov. 17, 1962 / Pablo 2308-217
The John Coltrane quartet was formed in 1961, and its impact on jazz and popular music was immediate. In pianist McCoy Tyner, bassist Jimmy Garrrison, and drummer Elvin Jones, Coltrane found musicians with the ability not only to play what he wanted, but to inspire and stimulate him nightly in his search for musical nirvana. Although the quartet was in its infancy on these sessions, its emergence can be heard throughout the 26-minute performance of *Mr. P.C.* Coltrane searches through the intervals, choruses, and throughout his solo for alternative ways to express himself, while the Tyner/Garrison/Jones section keeps altering, reshaping, and evolving underneath. Garrison has one of his earliest, flamboyant strumming and bowing bass workouts on the title tune, while Tyner adds rangy, two-hand phrases and Jones explodes in the background. Thankfully, there is not yet another version of *My Favorite Things* consigned to disc. As an all-time Coltrane fanatic, it seems blasphemous to say this, but the world does not need another *My Favorite Things* at this point. Some of Coltrane's Pablo output has been spotty, but here is one that is not at all spotty. — *Ron Wynn*

○ **Best of John Coltrane** / i. 1962 / Pablo 2405-417

Sessions done for the Pablo label, most of them featuring the great Coltrane quartet. McCoy Tyner on piano, Jimmy Garrison on bass, and Elvin Jones on drums were the ultimate rhythm section for Coltrane; they could provide dynamic support, each was a wonderful soloist, and they could interact with brilliance. Not every Coltrane solo during this period was superb, but each one was compelling. — *Ron Wynn*

○ **Retrospective—Impulse** / i. 1962-1967 / GRP 119
A John Coltrane Retrospective is an admirable attempt to encapsulate the seemingly boundless scope of John Coltrane's creativity during his six years with Impulse!. . . . Given that three CDs have barely enough space for a cursory survey of this historic body of work, producer Michael Cuscuna makes a well-constructed case for Coltrane as an artist who reconciled the various facets of his music with a voice of overriding power and clarity. The threads of continuity in Coltrane's development are laid out at the start of the collection. "Greensleeves," the nimble 3/4 modal soprano feature from *Africa Brass*, followed by a posthumously issued "Naima" from the Village Vanguard sessions, succinctly provides linkage to the Atlantic years, while "Impressions," with its compositional similarities to "So What," ties in his stint with Miles Davis. Add "Spiritual," another 3/4 modal vehicle, albeit a more urgent and deeply hued statement, and the marathon blues, "Chasin' the Trane," and that's Disc I. Disc II suggests Coltrane was in something of a holding pattern during '62 and '63. There's "Soul Eyes" and "I Want to Talk About You," updated from the original Prestige readings, and ballads like "What's New," the Ellington session's "In a Sentimental Mood," and "My One and Only Love," featuring vocalist Johnny Hartman. "Afro Blue" is the disc's 3/4 modal soprano feature. "Miles Mode," "After the Rain," and "Alabama" are the disc's only Coltrane compositions; the former again connects his modal investigations to Davis, while the latter two's use of pedal point was first crystallized on "Naima." The final disc is where Cuscuna's choices are particularly interesting. 1964 is represented by a refinement of his modal playing by "Crescent," "Bessie's Blues," and the first movement of "A Love Supreme." Trane's pivotal forays into diminished scales and even more convoluted harmonic resolution on *The John Coltrane Quartet Plays* are represented by "Chim Chim Cheree"—Coltrane's last flirtation with a pop song—and "Nature Boy." The graceful lyricism of "Dear Lord," the simmering contours of "Living Space" (featuring a theme stated by overdubbed sopranos), and Trane's yearning altissimo on "Welcome" bring us to the demise of the classic quartet. 1967's "Offering," where Coltrane lurches from dramatic themes to jagged motives and a boiling duet with Rashied Ali, ends the program with an image of Coltrane trying to break the mold of his own myth. Sure, "Africa," "India," and a section of *Meditations*, among others, should have been included. But Cuscuna has made a detailed survey that retails at about $25, which should attract new and young listeners. And that's a worthy cause. — *Bill Shoemaker*, Jazz Times

○ **Bye Bye Blackbird** / 1962 / Pablo 681
In 1962, probably in Stockholm, the John Coltrane quartet offered these two concert performances. The quartet's complementary qualities had been long established by this time, and if McCoy Tyner was not quite the original he would soon become, his soloing was bright and ever mobile; Jimmy Garrison was big-toned and the two provided the setting for the powerful interplay of Elvin Jones, whose drumming for Coltrane was especially combustible. Coltrane's opening solo in "Blackbird" is one of his very finest middle-period performances, not for its modernity of sound and harmony so much as for a rhythmic variety that seldom entered his playing after 1957. The original 1957 "Traneing In," from Coltrane's second Prestige album, was one of the crucial moments of his career; the first major occasion of his sheets-of-sound style. It is interesting to compare that performance's excitement of discovery with this new, no less en-

thusiastic, but darker and more troubled performance. Indeed, much of the fine spirit of "Blackbird" is here, as is the inevitable Coltrane movement into multiphonics and harmonic extremes, so that for over half of this long solo he is exultant, particularly on that chromatically descending bridge. Though the repetitions and the self-made barriers of harmony and rhythm eventually did return him to a more characteristically tragic stance, Coltrane at least viewed the sunlight beyond the prison of self in this solo. —*John Litweiler*, Down Beat

○ **European Tour, The** / 1962 / Pablo 2308-222
This is not the best available material by the quartet (pianist McCoy Tyner, bassist Jimmy Garrison, drummer Elvin Jones), but it is still inspirational. If you are not yet familiar with John Coltrane's power, this might give you some ideas of just how formidable Coltrane's artistry was/is. This has not *become* inspiring almost 20 years after it was recorded (1981) because the Coltrane mystique has grown and touched so many; this *was* inspiring at the time, as those fortunate enough to hear during its own time can attest. And those just hearing it for the first time now, during the now generation, can share almost the same fortune, for this accurately represents what could have been any one of countless nights of average playing—average playing from a group that was unique in its power, its spirituality, and its inspiration. And when they climbed above their own average they attained levels beyond ordinary definition. There wasn't any big thing to seeing Coltrane—it was always the music, and it is still with us. This is only average, but it puts to shame the combined lot of "Clonetranes" who have passed this way during the past two decades. Not the best, but still strongly recommended. —*Bob Rusch*, Cadence

☆ **John Coltrane and Johnny Hartman** / Mar. 7, 1963 / MCA 5661
This session features six romantic ballads cradled by Johnny Hartman's silky deep baritone vocals, accompanied by the John Coltrane quartet. In case we weren't listening to those earlier Prestige ballads, Trane reveals that he, too, knew how to read a lyric. . . . It was recorded on March 7, 1963. —*Alan Bargebuhr*, Cadence

☆ **Impressions** / Apr. 29, 1963 / MCA 5887
A three-minute blues ("Up Against the Wall") and a pretty, but far from maudlin, ballad ("After the Rain") balance out the two passionate Village Vanguard performances here by John Coltrane's group. While "India" is quite spiritual (and is highlighted by Eric Dolphy's wonderful bass clarinet), the roaring version of "Impressions" displays John Coltrane's ability to break through new musical boundaries. Anti-jazz indeed; this is the true spirit of jazz. —*Scott Yanow*, Cadence

○ **Live at Birdland** / Oct. 8, 1963 / MCA 33109

○ **Afro Blue Impressions** / Oct. 1963 / Pablo 101
Intensity is the keynote of this two-disc set recorded in 1962 by Norman Granz in Stockholm and Berlin. John Coltrane attacks the repertory with the kind of probing vigor characteristic of this period in his career. That vigor, however, is somewhat mellowed by a sense of joy coming from the saxophonist's pleasure at his audiences' warm reaction. Throughout the album, one is impressed by the extraordinary chemistry of the Coltrane/McCoy Tyner/Jimmy Garrison/Elvin Jones unit. In the history of jazz, this is one of the landmark groups. Especially noteworthy here are the energizing dialogues between Trane and Jones. Unquestionably, Jones is the spark plug that constantly fires Coltrane's pistons. —*Chuck Berg*, Down Beat

○ **Crescent** / Apr. 27, 1964+Jun. 1, 1964 / MCA 5889
Crescent finds the classic John Coltrane quartet in prime form in 1964, although none of the five originals they play caught on as standards. There is not enough Coltrane on this album for it to be an essential acquisition. Much of "Lonnie's Lament" is a bass solo (Jimmy Garrison's are always an acquired taste), and "The Drum Thing" is a feature for Elvin Jones. Much more memorable are the intense "Crescent," the spiritual "Wise One" (foreshadowing the upcoming *Love*

Supreme), and the happy, straightforward "Bessie's Blues." —*Scott Yanow*, Cadence

★ **Love Supreme, A** / Dec. 9, 1964 / MCA 5660
A most powerful statement. His most acclaimed and definitive recording. —*Michael G. Nastos*

○ **Selflessness** / i. 1965 / Impulse 9161
I have no hesitations about hailing the 1963 Newport sides from the *Selflessness* album as two further masterpieces of the John Coltrane quartet era. Certainly, "My Favorite Things" ranks with Coltrane's best recordings of the time, and to me, it is the definitive version of this standard. . . . Coltrane was the master of the straight horn (soprano) who no longer desired to overwork the piddlingly closed scalar lines of the original, transmuting the song to a broadly human wail instead, germanely crying in a manner that he had not surpassed before (inadequate command of his mind in the original Atlantic recording, scarcely less so in the alternate) or after (the problem of Pharoah Sanders's overpowering irrelevancies in the final version). Pianist McCoy Tyner bears down on the line to a degree I had not heard from him, or really thought probable, in his quartet recordings before *A Love Supreme*, as he moved away from the filigreed emptiness so tempting for this line into a realm of fascinating harmonic-modal cross-fire, enhanced with a genuine bluesiness so satisfying in the face of the ersatz of the lily waltz. "I Want to Talk About You" is a deeply moved version, played with obvious affection and dedication to the thought of the line, culminating in a spread-winged a cappella cadenza of total personal lyricism (not so much Sonny Rollinsesque as an anticipation of the "Welcome"), transferring the musician's love to a single linear utterance. —*Barry Tepperman*, Coda

Transition / May 26, 1965-Jun. 10, 1965 / GRP 124
Recorded on June 10, 1965, *Transition* can be looked at as a bridge between earthbound John Coltrane projects like *Crescent* (April and June 1964) and more celestially identified works like *Ascension* (June 28, 1965) and *Interstellar Space* (February 22, 1967). After dealing with modal methods on *A Love Supreme* (December 1964), Coltrane sought a freer, uncluttered harmonic base. He achieves that end on the sprawling title track, which begins as a rising blues and reaches a violent climax that tips into Albert Ayler territory. "Welcome," which originally appeared on *Kulu Se Mama* (October 14, 1965) shows Coltrane to be a melodic improviser. You can actually hear snippets of "Happy Birthday" as a theme. And "Virgil," also from *Kulu Se Mama*, is a drums-tenor conversation that inspires a generation of players, notably Michael Brecker. The five-part "Suite" is essentially broken up to feature each member of the quartet. Jimmy Garrison opens with an unaccompanied bass solo on "Prayer and Meditation: Day." McCoy Tyner showers us with cascading notes on "Peace and After." Elvin Jones's mighty drum prowess is showcased on "Affirmation." And Coltrane makes allusions to "Mr. P.C." on the final summing up, "Prayer and Meditation: 4 A.M." —*Bill Milkowski*, Jazz Times

Kulu Se Mama / Jun. 16, 1965-Oct. 14, 1965 / Impulse 9106

★ **Ascension** / Jun. 28, 1965 / Impulse 95

☆ **Major Works of John Coltrane, The** / Jun. 1965-Oct. 1965 / GRP 113
There is no question that these works are major in length. The two versions of "Ascension" run about 40 minutes each, and "Om" runs 29 minutes. Beyond a doubt, they had major impact on the avant-garde of the free jazz movement of the 1960s. Whether they are among John Coltrane's major contributions will be a function of the listener's appreciation of the music made during the final years of the saxophonist's search. In varying degrees, the two "Ascensions," "Om," "Kulu Se Mama," and "Selflessness" find him making his way toward the metaphysical value in which he was to finally obscure himself. His treasured rhythm section of McCoy Tyner (piano), Jimmy Garrison (bass), and Elvin Jones (drums) had yet to face their disillusion and move on, and so in much of this music there is the anchoring reality

of jazz rhythms as understood in the context of the music's traditions. In fact, in the final analysis, the most satisfying moments (apart from the awe induced by the sheer technical virtuosity of Coltrane's tenor playing) come from Jones, a marvel of polytonality who never fully left jazz time behind. By this time, Coltrane had virtually become the instrument, the most complete tenor saxophonist since, and possibly including, Coleman Hawkins. In light of that overpowering saxophonism, it is difficult to take seriously the efforts of reed players Archie Shepp, Pharoah Sanders, and Donald Garrett to emulate Coltrane's gargantuan excursions. The only way the ensemble playing (to be liberal with the term) can be accepted as valid is to buy the theory that the vigorous communal dissipation of energy is an act of creative liberation. So these examples remain as exhibition pieces from the late career of a man driven to perpetually seek. However little they may be heard, they cannot be disregarded, because John Coltrane was one of the most important musicians of the second half of the century. —*Doug Ramsey*, Jazz Times

New Thing at Newport / Jul. 2, 1965 / GRP 105
One of the earliest examples of Coltrane moving in a newer, freer direction. Archie Shepp (sax) makes an immediate impression. —*Michael G. Nastos*

○ **Live in Paris** / Jul. 1965 / Charly 87

Sun Ship / Aug. 26, 1965 / Impulse 9211
Wonderful, compelling quartet sessions that languished for years in the ABC vaults. —*Michael G. Nastos*

First Meditations / Sep. 2, 1965-1970 / GRP 118
Recorded before *Meditations* but released in 1970, then reissued in 1978 and 1992. The CD has the original version of "Joy." "Compassion" is a standout Coltrane anthem. —*Michael G. Nastos*

Live in Seattle / Sep. 30, 1965 / Impulse 9202
This was a blowing session first released in 1972. The group included pianist McCoy Tyner, drummer Elvin Jones, bassist Jimmy Garrison, tenor saxophonist Pharoah Sanders and bass clarinetist Donald Garrett. Recorded 9/30/65, the LP contained four tunes, several of which stretched out for more than one side. Sanders had just begun his association with John Coltrane (tenor sax) and sounds tentative at times. Everyone else blew well, but the overall mix was muddy, making the proceedings sound more like a maelstrom than a concert. . . . The album closed on an odd note—"Tapestry," a six-minute bass solo. —*Richard B. Kamins*, Cadence

Om / Oct. 1, 1965 / MCA 39118
Perhaps Coltrane's only major release of questionable quality, this was reportedly recorded on his first (and only) LSD trip. Featuring screechy playing and moaning vocals, this is for true believers and historical interest only. —*David Nelson McCarthy*

Meditations / Nov. 23, 1965 / MCA 39139
A perfect companion to *A Love Supreme*, and as powerful and pure in spiritual content and intent. There are long, extended, embellished passages in a hymn-like prayer session. With Pharoah Sanders (ts), Elvin Jones (d), Rashied Ali (d), McCoy Tyner (p), and Jimmy Garrison (b). —*Michael G. Nastos*

○ **Live in Antibes (1965)** / **i.** 1965 / France's Concert 119
This session is a remarkable, often stormy, and disquieting transitional one. The classic John Coltrane quartet is clearly in its final days, and you can hear Coltrane searching for new things to say on such songs as "Impressions," "Blue Waltz," and "Afro Blue," where he starts, breaks, and restarts statements and expresses frustration in mid-solo. He also plays many incredible passages on soprano and tenor, but the most instructive cut is the version of "My Favorite Things," one of the least smooth and turbulent renditions available on record. McCoy Tyner's piano forays are equally arresting and uneven, while the bass/drum interplay of Jimmy Garrison and Elvin Jones remains unified and stimulating. Despite occasional engineering problems (noticeable disruptions during "Naima" and "Blue Waltz" that are blamed on problems caused by the sax being too close to the microphone) and even with the tension, this is a pivotal date in the Coltrane legacy. It's one fans should listen to closely; they can hear the shattering of the quartet's musical bonds. —*Ron Wynn*

Cosmic Music / Feb. 2, 1966 / Coast Recorders 4950
Emphatic, surging, and sometimes unfathomable late-period Coltrane. —*Michael G. Nastos*

○ **Live at the Village Vanguard Again!** / May 28, 1966 / Impulse 9124
Live. Shattering, piercing, and unforgettable. Coltrane and Sanders (ts) blast off to places unforeseen. —*Michael G. Nastos*

○ **Concert in Japan** / Jul. 22, 1966 / Impulse 9246
Concert in Japan doesn't unveil any new facets of John Coltrane's last musical phase, except for the fact that on at least one occasion both he and Pharoah Sanders play the Yamaha saxophone, whatever that is (it sounds a little like a C-melody). But it is another example, and a rather beautiful one, of the kind of searing, soaring, fiercely spiritual sounds he was putting out at this point in his life. Late-period Trane is not everybody's trip, but anyone who has taken the time to make the trip knows how rewarding it can be. There isn't much here you can hum along with or tap your foot to, but on the other hand it amazes me how completely accessible it sounds compared to the way 1966 vintage Coltrane first hit my ears. Basically, "Leo" is turbulent in mood and "Peace" is, well, peaceful, but they both have a similar effect: they fire my spirit and cleanse my mind. Sanders has three solos. His bass clarinet spot on "Leo (part two)" seems a bit forced in its Eastern-ness, but the others are both fervid and well thought out. Alice Coltrane's accompaniment is sensitive, and her one solo sounds more eloquent to me than anything on several albums she's made as a leader. Drummer Rashied Ali is a dynamo throughout and in many spots, particularly his long "Leo (part two)," he plays in a fashion that is not always applicable to the Coltrane of this period. Is there any doubt that the man (John Coltrane) was a genius? —*Peter Keepnews*, Down Beat

Expression / Feb. 15, 1967-Mar. 1967 / Impulse 9120
His final recording session. Features more flute than any other of his recordings. —*Michael G. Nastos*

★ **Interstellar Space** / Feb. 22, 1967 / GRP 110
Posthumous, free-wheeling date by Coltrane with drummer Rashied Ali in a series of slashing, complimentary, and explosive duets. At the time, Coltrane was playing more rhythms than anything else, having leaped beyond notions of chord changes, structure, and melody. Ali sometimes supports him, sometimes challenges him, and holds things together as best he can. —*Ron Wynn*

Africa: The Savoy Sessions / Savoy 70818

EDDIE CONDON (Albert Edwin Condon)

b. Nov. 16, 1905, Goodland, IN, **d.** Aug. 4, 1973, New York, NY

Banjo, guitar / Dixieland
A dedicated traditionalist, Eddie Condon had minimal musical talent, but was an exuberant, tireless promoter and advocate. He led jam sessions, organized and played on records, promoted concerts, and had his own New York club for over 20 years. Condon started on the ukulele, then moved to the banjo and four-string guitar. He played in dance bands throughout the Midwest, and worked with members of the Austin High School Gang in the '20s. He began the McKenzie-Condon Chicagoans in 1927, the start of what became a lifetime endeavor; publicizing, pushing, and helping traditional jazz/Dixieland artists. He moved to New York in 1929, and arranged and performed on numerous sessions into the '70s. Many greats played in his bands, among them Joe Sullivan, Gene Krupa, Fats Waller, Jack Teagarden, Sid Catlett, Max Kaminsky, Pee Wee Russell, Bud Freeman, George Wettling, Bobby Hackett, Billy Butterfield, and Wild Bill Davison.

Condon toured with Red Nichols in 1929, then played in New York and Florida with Red McKenzie and the Mound City Blowers in the early '30s. He recorded with the Rhythmakers in 1932, then co-led a band with Joe Marsala in 1936 and 1937. After playing at Nick's from 1937 to 1944, and working with Hackett, Freeman, Marsala, Brad Gowans, and Miff Mole, Condon started his own club in 1945. He also recorded for Commodore in the early '40s. He comanaged Condon's with Pete Pesci in Greenwich Village, and frequently organized racially integrated concerts, something he continued to do when he presented jazz programs on television, at Town Hall, or at Carnegie Hall. He recorded for Columbia in the '50s, cutting his appearances at his club. He toured England in 1957, and Japan, Australia, and New Zealand in the '60s, and played at several jazz festivals. Condon wrote three books on jazz, had articles published, and was famous for his dry, cutting wit and his outspoken manner. Other than Cab Calloway's "Chinese music" putdown of bop, Condon made the most celebrated put-down of the genre: "We don't flatten our fifths, we drink them." He also commented about French critic Hughes Panassie coming to America to produce records: "Do I tell him how to jump on a grape?" His autobiography, *We Called It Music*, came out in 1948 and was rich in detail up to that point, but unfortunately was published far too early to be comprehensive or inclusive. —*Ron Wynn and Bruce Boyd Raeburn*

Jammin' at Commodore / i. 1938 / Commodore 7007
1938-1944. The Windy City Seven date that launched the Commodore label, plus a Bud Freeman-led combo. Musicians include Pee Wee Russell, Bobby Hackett, George Brunies, Dave Tough, Jess Stacy, and others. —*Bruce Raeburn*

Definitive—Vol. 1 / Jun. 1944-Oct. 1944 / Vintage Jazz 530
Prime Condon on this '40s reissue with Pee Wee Russell (cl), Hot Lips Page (tpt), and Bobby Hackett (cnt). —*Ron Wynn*

Jam Sessions (1944) / Dec. 13-14, 1944 / Jazzology 101102

And His Jazz Concert / i. 1944 / Stash 530
A who's who of the Condon clique, including Bobby Hackett (cnt), Pee Wee Russell (cl), Ernie Caceres, Billy Butterfield, as well as Edmond Hall. Tunes include "Ballin' the Jack," "Ja-Da," "That's a Plenty," "Royal Garden Blues," and "Muskrat Ramble," among others. —*Bruce Raeburn*

Dixieland Jam / Aug. 1957-Sep. 1957 / Columbia 45145

Tiger Rag and All That Jazz / 1958 / World Pacific 1292

★ **In Japan /** Mar. 1964-Apr. 1964 / Chiaroscuro 154
Trumpeter Buck Clayton appears in an active role on *Eddie Condon in Japan*, a concert performance recorded in 1964. This is pure Condon. Clarinetist Pee Wee Russell, saxophonist Bud Freeman, Dick Cary, Cliff Leeman, and trombonist Vic Dickenson join Clayton for some delightful sparring. It is particularly good to hear Clayton in top form. The sound is excellent concert-hall quality. —*John McDonough*, Down Beat

Jazz at the New School / i. Jun. 1973 / Chiaroscuro 110

★ **Commodore Years, The / i.** Mar. 1974 / Atlantic 2309
The first two sides of this two-record set offered some of the best recorded evidence available of the mature White Chicago style at a period when it had fully emerged from its New Orleans roots and, as yet, had not been perverted into that middle-aged, middle-brow supreme mediocrity known as Dixieland. But the real musical treasure was unearthed on the second disk of this two-record set. It featured Bud Freeman's lithe but meaty tenor accompanied only by piano and drums—a setting untypically intimate for the period (1938). On these tracks, Freeman proved to be not only one of the premier saxophone stylists of his day, but, interestingly, a precursor of saxophone styles to come. These two albums were important as artifacts and as pure music. They were a throwback to a time when the playing of jazz was first and foremost a fun thing to do. The important thing to keep in mind is that the records were a delight. —*Peter Keepnews*, Down Beat

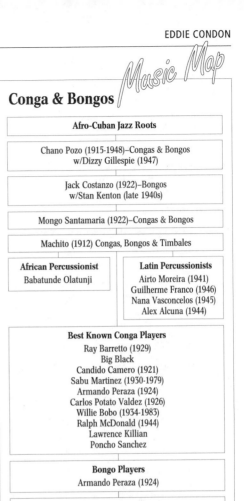

Conga & Bongos

Afro-Cuban Jazz Roots

Chano Pozo (1915-1948)–Congas & Bongos w/Dizzy Gillespie (1947)

Jack Costanzo (1922)–Bongos w/Stan Kenton (late 1940s)

Mongo Santamaria (1922)–Congas & Bongos

Machito (1912) Congas, Bongos & Timbales

African Percussionist	Latin Percussionists
Babatunde Olatunji	Airto Moreira (1941)
	Guilherme Franco (1946)
	Nana Vasconcelos (1945)
	Alex Alcuna (1944)

Best Known Conga Players
Ray Barretto (1929)
Big Black
Candido Camero (1921)
Sabu Martinez (1930-1979)
Armando Peraza (1924)
Carlos Potato Valdez (1926)
Willie Bobo (1934-1983)
Ralph McDonald (1944)
Lawrence Killian
Poncho Sanchez

Bongo Players
Armando Peraza (1924)

Daniel Ponce (1953)
Sammy Figueroa
Willie Bobo (1934-1983)
Cal Tjader (1916-1982)

○ **Real Sound of Jazz, The / i.** Mar. 1990 / Pumpkin 116

○ **Jazzlore: That Toddlin' Town—Chicago Jazz Revisited—Vol. 23** / Atlantic 90461

○ **Town Hall Concerts—Vol. 5** / Jazzology 10

○ **Town Hall Concerts—Vol. 1** / Jazzology 1001
May 27, 1944, marked the first of a year-long series of weekly concerts at Town Hall that were transcribed onto 16-inch discs by the Armed Forces Radio Service and sent over the world for broadcast to people in the service.... The band on that day was an unusual mixture: Max Kaminsky, Bobby Hackett, Miff Mole, Pee Wee Russell, Ernie Caceres, Gene Schroeder, and Eddie Condon from the Regulars, with bassist John Kirby and drummer Sonny Greer, and cameo appearances by Hot Lips Page and Rex Stewart. Kirby, and especially Greer, gave an odd, but not too bothersome, cast to the rhythm section, to one used to a steady diet of George Wettling and Grauso. As collectors of the AFRS series know, the half-hour concerts are a little short on playing time for a 16-inch disc, and usually another title from another concert is tacked on after Fred Robbins's closing announcements and the fadeout. In this case, it is "Ballin' the Jack," with Grauso on drums, which fades out. This title and the preceding blues jam open side two of this release; the remainder of the side is part of the June 24, 1944 concert consisting

of "I've Found a New Baby" (with Condon sitting on top of the only operating mike, thus giving us a clear picture of his method, as well as something to shove up the bleep of his moronic detractors). The transfer is decent, if a little boomy, and near true pitch. — *Wayne Jones*, Coda

○ **Town Hall Concerts—Vol. 2** / Jazzology 1003
○ **Town Hall Concerts—Vol. 3** / Jazzology 6
○ **Town Hall Concerts—Vol. 4** / Jazzology 8
○ **Ballin' the Jack** / Commodore 7015
Eddie Condon and band. Set-piece Condon, as old and conservative as ever. — *Michael G. Nastos*

HARRY CONNICK, JR.

b. Sep. 11, 1967, New Orleans, LA
Vocals, piano / Blues & jazz, ballads & blues
Things seemed to have calmed down a bit for Harry Connick, Jr. At one point in the early '90s, he was simultaneously praised as the next Elvis and Sinatra combined in some quarters, and vilified in others as the ultimate fraud. Connick's actually a good vocalist, a decent pianist, and a product of both excellent training from mentors such as Ellis Marsalis and the late blues great James Booker, and the publicity resources of a multinational conglomerate. His vocal style certainly mirrors Sinatra's and many other prerock, jazz-tinged singers, while his piano work fuses bluesy riffs, bebop progressions, and lush voicings. Connick moved from the realm of curiosity to superstardom when his songs on the soundtrack for the film *When Harry Met Sally* became pop hits. A Grammy award and massive publicity resulted, and Connick was soon doing sold-out concerts and appearing on a syndicated special on public television. A once outspoken advocate for the superiority of vintage jazz and blues to current pop music, Connick has since modified his stance, though he still touts the virtues of Booker, Professor Longhair, and others at every opportunity. All Connick's sessions are available on CD. Negative publicity over a concealed weapon incident may have put a little damper on things, but he remains among the big guns on the Sony label. — *Ron Wynn with Rick Clark and Hank Davis*

20 / **i.** 1989 / Columbia 44369
An attention-grabbing set done when Connick was an unknown 20-year-old. Dr. John (p) and Carmen McRae (v) are in fine form. Connick is a bit more freewheeling, and is not as mannered as he would become later. — *Ron Wynn*

★ **When Harry Met Sally . . .** / **i.** Jun. 1989 / CBS 45319
The soundtrack that made Connick an MOR star. — *Ron Wynn*

○ **We Are in Love** / **i.** 1990 / Columbia 46146

CHRIS CONNOR

b. Nov. 8, 1927, Kansas City, MO
Vocals / Ballads & blues, cool
Chris Connor was one of the most popular '50s vocalists, famous for altering rhythms on ballads, for using little vibrato except on special occasions, and for a husky, lush sound. She was one of the best "torch" artists, and her onstage performance mode, replete with odd facial expressions and postures, drew as many comments as her sound. Connor studied clarinet for eight years as a child, then began singing in her late teens. She was the vocalist with a large band at the University of Missouri led by Bob Brookmeyer, modeled after the Kenton band. After working with a group in Kansas City, Connor moved to New York in 1949. She sang with Claude Thornhill, Herbie Fields, and Thornhill again in the early '50s, performing with Thornhill's vocal group, the Snowflakes. She sang with Jerry Wald, then joined Stan Kenton in 1952 on June Christy's recommendation. She went solo in 1953, and signed with Bethlehem. But the label suspended her two years later because Connor refused to record more than the minimum amount of material required by contract. She moved to Atlantic, and enjoyed success, having two chart singles in the late '50s: "Trust in Me"

and the title cut from the album *I Miss You So*. Connor switched to ABC-Paramount in 1965, and was praised highly for her 1966 appearance at the Austin Jazz Festival. Following a period of semiretirement, Connor made a comeback in the mid '70s, cutting albums with Kenton and with Maynard Ferguson. She continued recording in the '80s for Progressive, Stash, and Contemporary. Her most recent session was a '92 date for Enja. A fair amount of Connor material is available on CD. — *Ron Wynn*

Chris Connor with Ellis Larkin / Aug. 9+11, 1954 / Bethlehem 1001
Lullabies at Birdland / Aug. 21, 1954-Aug. 21, 1954 / Bethlehem 6004
Lullabies for Lovers / Aug. 21, 1954 / Bethlehem 6002
Chris / Apr. 1955 / Bethlehem 56
★ **Cocktails and Dusk** / Apr. 1955 / Bethlehem 6010
A fine album. Unsung vocalist of the '50s. Lots of Cole Porter, with J. J. & Kai (t), Ralph Sharon (p), and Matt Hiaton (b). — *Michael G. Nastos*
Bethlehem Girls / **i.** 1956 / Bethlehem 6006
Jazz Date with Chris Connor, A / Nov. 15, 1956-Dec. 19, 1956 / Atlantic 1286
○ **Sings Gershwin** / Feb. 7, 1957-May 1, 1957 / Atlantic 601
★ **Chris Craft** / Apr. 8, 1958+May 23, 1958 / Atlantic 1290
Ballads of the Sad Cafe / Jan. 29, 1959-Apr. 19, 1959 / Atlantic 1307
Chris in Person / Sep. 13, 1959 / Atlantic 8040
Witchcraft / Oct. 5, 1959 / Atlantic 8032
★ **Portrait of Chris, A** / Dec. 5, 1960-Jan. 23, 1961 / Atlantic 8049
Free Spirits / Dec. 11, 1961-Apr. 30, 1962 / Atlantic 8061
Chris Connor at the Village Gate / 1963 / FM 300
Sings Gentle Bossa Nova / 1965 / Paramount 529
Sweet and Swinging / Feb. 3+28, 1978 / Progressive 7028
Chris Connor with Helen Forrest / **i.** 1983 / Stash
A pair of prime "torch" stylists from the '50s. One classic album from each. — *Ron Wynn*
Classic / Aug. 1986 / Contemporary 14023
A good, though mannered, set from longtime "torch" favorite. A fine lineup, including Paquito D'Rivera (as). — *Ron Wynn*
New Again / Aug. 1987 / Contemporary 14038

BILL CONNORS (William A. Connors)

b. Sep. 24, 1949, Los Angeles, CA
Guitar / Early jazz-rock, modern creative
Equally adept at acoustic and electric guitar, Bill Connors has played jazz-rock, free, and fusion material successfully in the '70s and '80s. His best solos have been in the jazz-rock mode, where his use of distortion and electronics is balanced by fine phrasing and intelligent solos. His free work has tended to be more flash than substance, while the fusion has been routine instrumental pop. Connors played electric guitar with Mike Nock and Steve Swallow in San Francisco in the early '70s, then recorded and toured Europe with Return to Forever in 1973 and 1974. Connors made a solo date for ECM in 1974 on acoustic, and recorded with Stanley Clarke in New York. He made an interesting, if uneven, free release with Lee Konitz in the late '70s, and later recorded with Gary Peacock, Jan Garbarek, and Jack DeJohnette. He worked with Garbarek's band again in 1977 and 1978, and did another solo date in 1979. During the '80s, Connors joined Garbarek's band and played electric. He issued a straight rock album in the mid '80s. Connors has several sessions available on CD. — *Ron Wynn*

★ **Theme to the Guardian** / Nov. 1974 / ECM 829387
An album of terrific solo acoustic guitar from a former member of Return to Forever. — *Paul Kohler*

Of Mist and Melting / Dec. 1977 / ECM 1120
An atmospheric jazz album with Jack DeJohnette (d), Gary Peacock (b), and Jan Garbarek (ts). —*Paul Kohler*

☆ **Swimming with a Hole in My Body** / Aug. 1979 / ECM 1158
Brilliant solo acoustic guitar with some overdubs. Required listening. —*Paul Kohler*

☆ **Step It!** / Jun. 12, 1984-Oct. 15, 1984 / Pathfinder 8503
Superb instrumental fusion album with Connors on electric guitar. Strong compositions. A must! —*Paul Kohler*

Double-Up / 1985 / Pathfinder 8620
Electric trio album, with K. Plainfield replacing Dave Weckl on drums. —*Paul Kohler*

Assembler / Jun. 1987 / Pathfinder 8707
His third electric release, in an Alan Holdsworth style. All his electric albums are highly recommended. —*Paul Kohler*

CHUCK CONNORS

b. 1930
Bass trombone / Swing, big band
A consistent performer on the bass trombone and a long-time member of the Ellington orchestra, Chuck Connors is better known for his section work than for his solo ability. He earned his degree from Boston Conservatory in the mid '50s, then worked with Dizzy Gillespie for nine months in 1957. Connors joined Duke Ellington in 1961. He was with the orchestra until the mid '70s, and remained, for a limited time, after Duke died and Mercer assumed leadership. Connors recorded with Ellington often, and also recorded with many band members on their sessions; among them Ray Nance, Cat Anderson, Johnny Hodges, Paul Gonsalves, and Clark Terry in the '60s and '70s. He and Terry co-led a touring band in 1974, and visited Europe twice in the '70s. Connors can be heard on numerous Ellington recordings on CD, as well as Hodges's sessions. His best known solo was on "Perdido," from the mid '60s RCA album *The Popular Duke Ellington.* —*Ron Wynn*

JUNIOR COOK (Herman Cook)

b. Jul. 22, 1934, Pensacola, FL, **d.** Feb. 4, 1992
Tenor saxophone / Hard bop
Saxophonists like Junior Cook are the lifeblood of jazz; reliable, bluesy, always entertaining players who aren't innovators nor "stars," but frequently outshine others with bigger reputations. Cook plays straightahead, supple, and robust hard bop and blues. His father and older brother were trumpeters, and he played alto in high school before switching to tenor. Cook worked in the late '50s with Dizzy Gillespie, then joined the Horace Silver quintet in 1958. He recorded that same year with Kenny Burrell. Cook stayed with Silver until 1964. When Silver wanted to start a new group, Cook, Blue Mitchell, and the other members also began their own band. Cook and Mitchell worked together until 1969, while Cook also recorded with Barry Harris, John Patton, and Don Patterson. He taught at Berklee in the early '70s, then played with Freddie Hubbard in the mid '70s. Cook worked with Louis Hayes as both coleader and a sideman, then he and Hayes co-led another group in 1975 and 1976. Cook worked with Bill Hardman and Danny Moore in the late '70s, and recorded with Mickey Tucker and Eddie Jefferson. During the '80s, Cook recorded for Muse and worked with Cedar Walton, Buster Williams, and others. Currently, he only has one session available on CD as a leader. —*Ron Wynn*

Junior's Cookin' / Apr. 10, 1961 / Jazzland 58

Ichi-Ban / **i.** 1976 / Timeless 102

○ **Stablemates** / **i.** Nov. 1977 / Affinity 766

Good Cookin' / Jun. 7, 1979 / Muse 5159
All-star hard bop cast, including Bill Hardman (tpt) and Slide Hampton (t). —*David Szatmary*

★ **Somethin's Cookin'** / 1982 / Muse 5470
Something's Cookin' represents tenor saxophonist Junior Cook at his prime, a period that lasted for his entire career. Indeed, consistency marks Cook's work. Right up through

his last session, he was a soulful storyteller. He fills every phrase with meaning and emotion, especially on the ballad "Detour Ahead." He draws on the work of pianists Cedar Walton and Larry Willis for the originals. Walton accompanies on the date. Walton's "Fiesta Espanol" even gets reprised without Walton on the last date. Drummer Billy Higgins and bassist Buster William join Walton in the rhythm section. Given how little Cook recorded as a leader (seven titles under his own name in 30 years, according to discographer Tom Lord), the appearance of this music on CD is welcomed, especially with four alternate takes. (57:25, June 21, 1981). —*David Dupont, Cadence*

○ **Place to Be, The** / Nov. 1988 / Steeple Chase 31240

○ **On a Misty Night** / **i.** Jun. 1989 / Steeple Chase 31266

AL COOPER

b. 1911, **d.** 1981
Alto saxophone, clarinet / Swing, big band
Alto saxophonist, clarinetist, and bandleader Al Cooper was best known as one of the founding members and the leader of the Savoy Sultans from 1937 to 1946. Early in his career, Cooper played at the 101 Club on Lenox Avenue in New York, and at some other clubs in New Jersey and Pleasantville. He was the half brother of Grachan Moncur. —*Ron Wynn*

★ **Jumpin' at the Savoy (1938-1941)** / 1938-1941 / MCA 1345

JEROME COOPER (Jerome D. Cooper)

b. Dec. 14, 1946, Chicago, IL
Percussion / Modern creative
A sparkling drummer and percussionist, Jerome Cooper has played with many fine groups, notably the superb Revolutionary Ensemble. An excellent accompanist, Cooper's solos are noted for their form and pace; he starts slowly, then steadily develops short phrases into powerful, intricate lines and explosive rhythms. He studied drumming with Oliver Coleman and Walter Dyett in the late '50s and early '60s. Cooper attended the American Conservatory and Loop College during the late '60s. He played with Oscar Brown, Jr. and Kalaparusha Maurice McIntyre in 1968, then moved to Europe. Cooper worked there with Steve Lacy, toured Africa with Lou Bennett, and played with the Art Ensemble of Chicago, Alan Silva, Frank Wright, and Noah Howard in the early '70s. He joined the Revolutionary Ensemble with Leroy Jenkins and Sirone when he returned to America in 1971. The trio struggled until 1977, touring extensively, and making far-reaching, critically acclaimed, but low-selling albums. It was truly a cooperative venture, with each member writing compositions and playing multiple instruments. Cooper played piano, bugle, and flute as well as drums and percussion. He also worked with Sam Rivers, George Adams, Karl Berger, Andrew Hill, Anthony Braxton, and McIntyre during this period. During the '80s, Cooper played with Cecil Taylor and with McIntyre again. He recorded as a leader in the '70s for About Time, doing a solo album. It has not been reissued on CD; the Revolutionary Ensemble dates have not been reissued either. Cooper can be heard on reissues by Braxton and Taylor, among others. —*Ron Wynn*

Toot Assumptions / Apr. 14, 1978 / Anima 2J11

For the People / May 12, 1979 / Hat Hut 1R07

★ **Unpredictability of Predictability** / Jul. 6, 1979 / About Time 1002
Jerome Cooper's concert was not the standard virtuoso percussion display (of which he is certainly capable), but rather a series of speculative compositional situations for a one-man band. Some of them work and some don't; that is, while all of them realize their ambitions, some of them are more interesting to contemplate than they are to hear. The title piece (all of side one) opens with a breathy flute repeating a breath-length, untempered, unaccented line, increasing in volume until supplanted by the shriller whistle, agitation implied by the change in timbre. Chiramia, a nasal Mexican

double reed, enters on Movement B, spinning complex, eddying, John Coltrane-like multiphonics, while the bass drum and sock cymbal maintain unshifting patterns independent of each other and of the liners they "accompany." Movement C is a reductive, slow-motion drum solo, the only occasion on the LP in which the entire kit is called into play, mallets probing the skins for resonances as well as rhythms. An anticipatory tom-tom swell announces Movement C1; brushes trace an ascending figure on the cymbal. Cooper switches to sticks and rides the piece out, chanting softly underneath. *Predictability* achieves kinesis through almost aleatory means, but on "Bert the Cat" the beat is more compelling. Consuming all of side two, "Bert" is very possibly a masterpiece, as pivotal and necessary an ode to rhythm as *Dancing in Your Head* (Ornette Coleman). After a few preliminary squibs played in unison with the bass drum, chiramia delineates an infectious six-note theme (da-dada-dadada) over the staggered theme of the bass drums' six (DA-DA-DADA DADA). Conch-like, the balaphone joins the bass drum and the sock cymbal tops off the mix. The bass drum is the tonic, and the supple and strident chirimia and the hollow balaphone each, in turn, explore the interstitial harmonies in its insistent pattern. "Bert" builds in complexity until it ends as simply as it begins. Cooper's coordination is astonishing, and even on chirimia he is fluid and provocative. Side one disintegrates rhythm; side two integrates it. Both strategies are intellectually stimulating, but the latter is more viscerally satisfying. —*Francis Davis,* Cadence

RAY COPELAND

b. 1926, **d.** 1984
Trumpet / Hard bop
An accomplished composer and instructor, Ray Copeland was a solid trumpeter in swing, bebop, hard bop, and even stage bands, from the '40s until the '80s. He taught many workshops and jazz history courses, and his playing demonstrated a confident, engaging tone and crackling energy, as well as effective range and timbre. Copeland studied classical trumpet and played with various rock and pop groups as a teenager in Brooklyn. He toured in the late '40s with Mercer Ellington and with Al Cooper's Savoy Sultans. Copeland played with Andy Kirk and Sy Oliver in the early '50s, and played bebop and swing with Lionel Hampton, Randy Weston, Oscar Pettiford, and others in the late '50s. He was featured in the 1959 film *Kiss Her Goodbye.* Copeland played in the Roxy Theater Orchestra in the late '50s and early '60s, while he also worked with Art Blakey, Cat Anderson, Johnny Richards, Louis Bellson, and Pearl Bailey. Copeland was one of Ella Fitzgerald's accompanists in 1965. He rejoined Weston in 1966, toured Africa on State Department-sponsored events in 1967, and toured Morocco in 1970. He toured Europe with Thelonious Monk in 1968. Copeland played at the 1973 Newport Jazz Festival and continued to perform periodically into the '80s. He also led orchestras in New York during the '70s, and his *Classical Jazz Suite in Six Movements* composition premiered at the Lincoln Center in 1970. Copeland worked in Broadway shows and toured Europe with the revue *The Musical Life of Charlie Parker* in 1974. His book, *The Ray Copeland Method and Approach to the Creative Art of Jazz Improvisation,* was published that same year. Copeland didn't issue any dates as a leader, but can be heard on various reissues by Monk, Weston, Blakey, and Anderson. —*Ron Wynn*

CHICK COREA (Armando Anthony Corea)

b. Jun. 12, 1941, Chelsea, MA
Electric and acoustic piano / Post bop, early free, Latin jazz, early jazz-rock
Chick Corea has refused to sit still or to concentrate on any one style in his career. He's made exquisite free, jazz-rock, fusion, Latin, and classical recordings, and has recorded music that reflects the deep influence of Bill Evans. His playing style expertly mixes aspects from all of these genres as well as rock and funk. Corea has been one of the few keyboardists able to provide a distinctive, personalized sound on electric as well as acoustic, and his barrage of electronic instruments are applied intelligently and musically, not just for their gimmick or commercial appeal. Another contemporary player strongly influenced by Bill Evans, Corea's stint with Miles Davis had great impact on Corea's refusal to stress a particular style. Horace Silver's gospel/Caribbean/bebop synthesis and Bud Powell's bebop vocabulary are other elements that recur in Corea's solo approach, especially in his bebop playing.

Corea began on piano at age four, learning from his father, who was also a professional musician. Listening to classic recordings of such musicians as Charlie Parker and Dizzy Gillespie, Corea became attracted to bebop and began transcribing the solos and compositions of Silver and Powell. He played Latin jazz with Mongo Santamaria and Willie Bobo in the early '60s, then worked and recorded with Blue Mitchell. Corea also recorded his own compositions for the first time while in Mitchell's band. He began making albums as a leader for Solid State (later reissued on Blue Note) in the late '60s, including *Tones for Joan's Bones* in 1966 and the outstanding *Now He Sings, Now He Sobs* in 1968. Corea also played with Stan Getz during 1967, and was featured on the superb albums *Sweet Rain* and *Captain Marvel.* Corea joined Miles Davis in 1968, and was on board during the fertile jazz-rock era, though he left in 1970. Initially, Corea was interested in free music at the start of the '70s, and played in the landmark group Circle with fellow Davis alumnus Dave Holland, Barry Altschul, and Anthony Braxton. But Corea soon found Circle's music confining and isolated. He departed in 1971, and recorded a pair of solo albums in the interim before forming the influential and commercially successful Return To Forever.

The band changed direction during its tenure, beginning as an acoustic jazz-rock unit with an Afro-Latin bent, then becoming a propulsive fusion band with a decided rock tilt in its second incarnation, and concluding as an instrumental pop unit experimenting with orchestrations and featuring a vocalist spouting psuedoreligious, new age rhetoric. But several Corea compositions for Return to Forever became established standards, among them "Spain." Corea's done many things since Return To Forever's demise, including: duos with Gary Burton and Herbie Hancock, trios with Miroslav Vitous and Roy Haynes, a bebop quartet with Mike Brecker, Eddie Gomez, and Steve Gadd, and solo classical dates. Corea's juggled two groups in the '80s and '90s, the Elektric and Akoustic Bands. Each plays the type of music that its name suggests. Corea has done numerous recordings since the late '60s for Solid State, Blue Note, Polydor, ECM, Stretch, Atlantic, Groove Merchant, and his current label, GRP. There are many Corea dates available on CD representing every era and phase of his music. —*Ron Wynn and Michael G. Nastos*

○ **Tones for Joan's Bones** / Nov. 30, 1966-Dec. 1, 1966 / Atlantic 50302

Youthful Corea makes a quick splash. This is an extremely rare album. —*Ron Wynn*

★ **Now He Sings, Now He Sobs** / Feb. 26, 1968 / Blue Note 90055

Now He Sings, Now He Sobs summarized Corea's fresh melodic and harmonic vocabulary for an entire generation of jazz musicians. Young jazz pianists learned these solos note-for-note. The album soon became a staple in the record collections of musicians everywhere. The Miroslav Vitous bass solos were greeted as the most impressive since Scott LaFaro's recordings with Bill Evans in 1961. And this album offers the best Roy Haynes drumming on record. Corea sparkles as he effortlessly darts through his compositional and improvisational innovations at high speed atop the crisp, responsive sounds of Haynes and the facile bass of Vitous. —*Mark C. Gridley*

○ **Chick Corea** / Mar. 14, 1968-Apr. 7, 1970 / Blue Note 39542

This is a two-album set that contains cuts from four sessions, two early sessions in 1968 and 1969, and tracks from two sessions that resulted in the album *Song of Singing*. —AMG

○ **Is** / Jun. 30, 1969 / Solid State 18055
Side one of *Is* is the title track. In the beginning, there is peace (?) with tubular bells, finger cymbals, clacking bits of wood, gongs, bass lines going "boing" with flute overlays, and on into loud, noisy chaos. . . . The quartet without the horns is the highlight of the record. . . . Chick Corea (piano), David Holland (bass), and drummer Jack DeJohnette (the Miles Davis rhythm section at the time), with the addition of Horacee Arnold's percussion, had a beautiful collective sound. It is a great shame that Woody Shaw (trumpet) and Hubert Laws (flute) had to keep intruding on it. —*Bill Smith*, Coda

○ **Sundance** / 1969 / People 09

○ **Early Circle** / Apr. 3, 1970 / Blue Note 84465
Corea in his most experimental, outside period. He was part of the musically advanced group Circle with multi-instrumentalist Anthony Braxton, bassist Dave Holland, and drummer Barry Altschul. These sessions and others won critical acclaim, but attracted little commercial attention. Corea also plays vibes and marimba, Holland occasionally plays guitar, and Altschul plays some marimba along with drums. Braxton's arsenal includes alto and soprano sax, clarinet, and contrabass clarinet. —*Ron Wynn*

Song of Singing / Apr. 7-8, 1970 / Blue Note 84353
Corea in avant-garde free/experimental mode, cutting loose with Dave Holland (b) and Barry Altschul (d). This 1989 reissue contains three bonus cuts. —*Ron Wynn*

Circling In / Oct. 13+19, 1970 / Blue Note 472
This is one of many great trio sessions. Corea would later reunite with rhythm mates Miroslav Vitous (b) and Roy Haynes (d). —*Ron Wynn*

A.R.C. / Jan. 1971 / ECM 833678

★ **Paris Concert** / Feb. 21, 1971 / ECM 843163
This music is constantly changing, and is more concerned, at times, with sound than melody, and strains at its restrictions. A good deal of this cooks. "Nefertitti" starts off at breakneck speed. Anthony Braxton's (reeds, per) solo is exciting, while Chick Corea's accompaniment is filled with quiet chords. The rhythm section (bassist Dave Holland, drummer Barry Altschul) hangs right with the soloist. Braxton and Corea's "Duet" also displays the odd relationship Corea had with the freedom of the music. Braxton's moods range from pensive to roaring, while Corea seems to noodle. I believe the music really comes together on side three, which contains Holland's "Toy Room—Q&A." The music shifts and turns; at times swinging, introspective at other times. The music turns at the suggestions of all the participants—we are hearing this as it was being created with the players relying on their talents and instincts. —*Richard B. Kamins*, Cadence

★ **Return to Forever** / Feb. 2-3, 1972 / ECM 811978
The first and by far the best and most appealing edition. Flora Purim sings wistfully, Stanley Clark dominates on bass, Corea is a sharp, creative pianist. —*Ron Wynn*

☆ **Light As a Feather** / Sep. 1972 / Polydor 827148

☆ **Crystal Silence** / Nov. 6, 1972 / ECM 831331
Gary Burton's debut on ECM with Corea (k). The first of many successful pairings of the two. —*Ron Wynn*

Hymn of the Seventh Galaxy / Aug. 1973 / PolyGram 825336

☆ **Inner Space** / i. 1974 / Atlantic 305
Formative dates from the late '60s reissued as a comprehensive CD anthology. Hubert Laws (f) at his most ambitious. Woody Shaw (tpt), Joe Farrell (ts), and Ron Carter (b) are also on hand. —*Ron Wynn*

Where Have I Known You Before / Jul. 1974-Aug. 1974 / PolyGram 825206

Crackling electric Return To Forever. Includes one killer composition, but marks the beginning of the end if you are looking for a jazz influence. —*Ron Wynn*

Captain Marvel / i. 1975 / Verve 2304225

Leprechaun, The / 1975 / Polydor 2391217

☆ **Romantic Warrior** / Feb. 1976 / Columbia 34076

My Spanish Heart / Oct. 1976 / Polydor 825657
Two-record set that rambles and flounders, but also has some impressive segments. —*Ron Wynn*

○ **Chick Corea and Gary Burton in Concert** / i. Oct. 23+25, 1978 / ECM 821415
One would have thought that recording pianist Chick Corea and vibist Gary Burton in a concert setting would have resulted in some adventurous music, with both parties jabbing the other to produce his best. However, the results on this two-record set are hardly adventurous. Things start off well with "Señor Mouse," as Burton weaves in and out of Corea's comping, creating an infectious mood. But from here on the inspiration is lacking as is the energy. Corea's "Bud Powell" is a pleasant enough swinger, but hardly a memorable tribute to Powell. The last side is somewhat better, but again, neither player seems particularly involved in the music. —*Carl Brauer*, Cadence

Tap Step / Dec. 1978-Jan. 1980 / Warner Brothers 3425
GRP has not confined its reissue program to vintage Impulse and Decca material. They are also rereleasing '70s and '80s fusion and contemporary items by some catalog artists. Chick Corea is among the rare keyboardists able to coax a personalized, arresting sound from synthesizers and electric keyboards. His solos on those instruments are as compelling and interesting as his acoustic piano statements, and his playing provides the disc several moments of glory and beauty. *Tap Step* was a frustrating album when it was originally released, and hearing it digitally reaffirms what initially made it exasperating. Gayle Moran's vocals (why Corea insisted on including them is still a source of wonder) and the rather inane lyrics on *Samba L.A.* and *The Embrace* are sore points. But the good things, which include Corea's solos and those by such guest stars as Joe Farrell, Joe Henderson, and Stanley Clarke, outweigh the forgettable, and Don Alias contributes blistering percussive support. While this is not as consistent or memorable as Corea's early '70s jazz-rock dates, it is far from a failure, and those who overlooked it might be surprised by its quality. —*Ron Wynn*

○ **Three Quartets** / i. 1981 / Warner Brothers 3552
Three Quartets featured dark, pensive lines—more functional than memorable—and exploited nuances of nearly subliminal orchestration and texture: etudes exploring the possibilities of varied instrumental groupings, shadings, and densitites rather than the pure song form. "Quartet No. 1," for example, opened with minorish, disquieting tenor and piano figures, supported by Steve Gadd's well-placed cymbal splashes and Eddie Gomez's unerringly accented tones. An intricate interlude led into a piano/bass parley, which in turn gave way to a gigantic bass solo. "Quartet No. 3" suggested that Chick Corea's writing was interesting as much for what he left out as for what he put in. Free, floating space was punctuated by densely scored sections, all set in relief by subtly shifting moods, textures, and colors. "Quartet No. 2," which comprised the second side of this release, fell into two parts, tributes to Duke Ellington and John Coltrane respectively. An expansive, arpeggiated piano opening, evocative of Ellington's rhapsodic moods, was joined by Mike Brecker's high-register sax lines, leading—again, almost subliminally—into yet another thoughtful solo by Gomez. Here, as throughout, Gadd was pleasingly busy, but not obtrusive. Finally, this album's hottest piece, Corea's tribute to John Coltrane, evoked the spirit of this saxophonist without parodying him. —*Jon Balleras*, Down Beat

Trio Music / Nov. 1981 / PolyGram 827702

Children's Songs / Jul. 1983 / ECM 815680

★ **Trio Music—Live in Europe** / Sep. 1984 / ECM 827769

Jazz Cornet

Originated in France in the 1830s

New Orleans Parade Bands

First Jazz Cornetist
Manuel Perez (1871-1946)
Played with John Robichaux,
Imperial Orchesta and Onward Brass Band (1895)

Buddy Bolden (1877-1931)
First New Orleans Cornet King (1895)

Famous Early Players
Joe "King" Oliver (1885-1938)
Freddie Keppard (1890-1933
Louis Armstrong (1898-1971)
Bunk Johnson (1889-1949)
George Mitchell (1899-1972)
Natty Dominique (1896-1982)
Kid Rena (1898-1949)
Punch Miller (1894-1971)
Lee Collins (1901-1960)
Tommy Ladnier (1900-1939)

Bix Beiderbecke (1903-1931)

Rex Stewart (1907-1967)
Ray Nance (1913-1976)
Bobby Hackett (1915-1976)

Blues Cornet
W.C. Handy (1873-1958)

Traditional Jazz
Jimmy McPartland (1907)
Wild Bill Davison (1906)
Muggsy Spanier (1906-1967)
Ruby Braff (1927)

Revivalists
Warren Vaché Jr. (1951)
John Haim (1929-1949)

Bop Players
Nat Adderley (1931)
Thad Jones (1923-1986)

Free Jazz
Bobby Bradford (1934)
Lawrence Butch Morris
Olu Dara
Don Cherry (1936)
Joe McPhee (1939)

An expert trio date that includes impeccable ensemble interaction and solos from Corea, Miroslav Vitous (b), and Roy Haynes (d). —*Ron Wynn*
○ **Light Years** / 1987 / GRP 9546
○ **Eye of the Beholder** / 1988 / GRP 9564

Corea and his band venture into new territory this time around. Much of this recording sounds as if it could be used with motion pictures. Beautiful soundscapes created by Corea's synthesizers and piano and backed by his very capable band make this album the band's finest work. Recommended. —*Paul Kohler*

Akoustic Band / **i.** 1989 / GRP 9582

Piano Greats / Laserlight 15751

LARRY CORYELL

b. Apr. 2, 1943, Galveston, TX
Guitar / Early jazz-rock, world fusion
Larry Coryell has been a splendid guitar stylist in jazz-rock, bebop, Latin, and classical contexts. His only negative attributes have been inconsistency in choice of supporting musicians and material for his bands and recording projects. Coryell has marvelous skills; he can play entrancing melodies, lightning-fast phrases, spectacular solos, or soothing statements. He's equally masterful on electric or acoustic, and has used wah-wah pedals, attachments, distortion, dissonance, and feedback creatively. He's played 12-string, hollow-bodied, and double neck guitars and guitar synthesizers, as well as conventional acoustic. Coryell has few discernible musical weaknesses besides occasional inconsistency, and his ratio of topflight recorded output to junk has been quite high.

Coryell worked in a band with Mike Mandel as a teenager. He moved to New York from Texas in the mid '60s, where he initially worked with Chico Hamilton and the early jazz-rock band Free Spirits. He played with Gary Burton in 1967 and 1968, doing an intriguing blend of jazz-rock and jazz/country/western swing. Coryell and Mandel formed Foreplay in 1969, and with Steve Marcus continued the group until 1973. Coryell also played in Herbie Mann's band on such crossover hits as *Memphis Underground* and *Memphis Two-Step* during this period. He formed another jazz-rock band with Mandel and Marcus, Eleventh House, in 1973. The group also included Randy Brecker and Alphonse Mouzon, but it degenerated from a promising beginning into an overly loud unit that played second-rate arena rock before its demise. Coryell periodically worked with Miroslav Vitous and John McLaughlin; he and McLaughlin later recorded some superb duets.

Coryell has worked with many duos and small combos, recording and playing with John Scofield, Michael Urbaniak, Steve Khan, Emily Remler, Brian Keane, and Philip Catherine. He's also recorded with Charles Mingus, Stephane Grappelli, and Sonny Rollins. Coryell began cutting his own albums for Vanguard in the late '60s. He continued in the '70s, '80s, and '90s, recording for Vanguard, Flying Dutchman, Arista, Elektra, Atlantic, Mood, Keystone, Flying Fish, Concord, and Shanachie, among others. Coryell's worked with a host of great musicians besides guitarists; these include Jimmy Garrison, Ron Carter, Roy Haynes, Joachim Kuhn, Ray Mantilla, Eddie Gomez, Albert Dailey, Urszula Dudziak, and his wife, Julie. Recent Coryell projects have included a Brazilian session for CTI and some acoustic guitar workouts for Shanachie. He has an ample supply of sessions available on CD. Unfortunately, his best jazz-rock dates (from his time with Gary Burton and his Flying Dutchman recordings) are currently unavailable. —*Ron Wynn*

★ **Essential Larry Coryell** / **i.** 1968-1975 / Vanguard 75-76
○ **Basics (1968-1969)** / 1968-1969 / Vanguard 79375
These are early Larry Coryell takes from 1968-1969, which one might consider either vintage or simply outdated. I suspect Coryell thinks the latter. Vanguard states that the material had not been issued before, but an alternate take of "Sex" was available on an earlier Vanguard release and that might be the case for some of the other material as well. These tracks date back to the period in which Coryell was establishing himself as a premier jazz-rock guitarist, and I suggest this material only if you still find his earlier work in-

teresting. Coryell fans might find cause to purchase this LP, but unless you're familiar with his entire catalog, you'd be better off sampling some of his material that hasn't been stashed away for years. I can't argue with Vanguard's choice of titles here. *Basics* is both brief and accurate, and I couldn't help thinking that if it had been anything more than a basis to build on, these tracks would have been on the racks years ago. *—Mike Joyce*, Cadence

Spaces / Jul. 1970 / Vanguard 79345

At the Village Gate / **i.** 1971 / Vanguard 6573

★ **Barefoot Boy** / 1971 / Philips 6369407
On this recording, Larry Coryell's band might be considered to have two main parts. As one section, we have three drummer/percussionists: Roy Haynes, Lawrence Killian, and Harry Wilkinson. They lock into a rhythm machine of fantastic richness and drive, one that you would do well to make it your business to hear. On the other hand, we have two horns and Coryell (guitar) and Steve Marcus (tenor and soprano sax). Both hornmen are primarily riff players—musicians who mostly function in a strongly delineated rhythmic framework, developing the substance of their solos as embellishments of increasing elegance on and around basically simple ideas. . . . The prime attraction of the album, if it could be said to have one, is Coryell. *—Barry Tepperman*, Coda

Offering / Jan. 17-20, 1972 / Vanguard

Restful Mind / Nov. 1974 / Vanguard 79353

Standing Ovation / Mar. 8+11, 1978 / Mood 33610
A mixed bag with classical, traditional Indian songs, originals, and even modified funk played by Coryell and L. Subramaniam on violin and tampura. Coryell also plays a little piano, and proves an effective partner, though sometimes the stylistic leaping around can be jarring. *—Ron Wynn*

☆ **Just Like Being Born** / 1984 / Flying Fish 337
With Brian Keane (g). Soothing acoustic guitar duets by two excellent players. *—Paul Kohler*

○ **Larry Coryell—Don Lanphere** / **i.** 1990 / Hep 2048

Coryell Plays Ravel & Gershwin / **i.** 1990 / Soundscreen 5152
Eight Gershwin and Ravel tunes (plus one original) appear on this newest disc, overall one of Coryell's more memorable sessions. *— Ron Wynn*, Rock & Roll Disc

Twelve Frets to One Octave / 1991 / Shanachie 97015
A guitar showcase for Coryell, who's always been among the more accomplished players on either electric or acoustic. He goes through old blues, jazz standards, and everything in between. There's absolutely nothing else to support him, enabling Coryell to display his complete technical arsenal. *— Ron Wynn*

Live from Bahia / **i.** 1992 / CTI 79482
Nice Afro-Latin set with Coryell on acoustic guitar, recorded in Bahia. The assembled cast includes drummer Billy Cobham, alto saxophonist Donald Harrison, and several Brazilian musicians, notably vocalist Dori Caymmi. *—Ron Wynn*

EDDIE COSTA (Edwin James Costa)

b. Aug. 14, 1930, Atlas, PA, **d.** Jul. 28, 1962, New York, NY
Vibes, piano / Bop
Eddie Costa was an aggressively rhythmic pianist, known for using the lower half of the keyboard for his rippling lines. He was a highly effective bebop soloist, a fine vibist, and a first-rate reader who was always in demand for studio work. Costa had classical piano training, but taught himself vibes. He worked with Joe Venuti as an 18-year-old, then played in Japan and Korea while in the army. Costa recorded in the mid '50s with Sal Salvador, and later worked with Tal Farlow, Kai Winding, and Don Elliott. A double "New Star" *Down Beat* winner in 1957 on vibes and piano, Costa played in the late '50s with Woody Herman and led a trio with Paul

Motian and Henry Grimes. He was just beginning to explore new harmonic areas when he was killed in a 1962 car crash. Costa recorded for Jubilee, Mode, and Coral. The Mode date, with Art Farmer, Phil Woods, Teddy Kotick and Motian, has been reissued on CD by VSOP. *—Ron Wynn*

Eddie Costa with the Vinnie Burke Trio / Feb. 1956 / Jubilee 1025

★ **Quintet** / Jul. 13, 1958 / Mode 118
A classic bop session with Art Farmer (tpt) and Phil Woods (as). *—David Szatmary*

House of Blue Lights / Jan. 29, 1959+Feb. 2, 1959 / Dot 3206
Adventurous date that borders on the avant-garde. With Paul Motian (d). *—David Szatmary*

CURTIS COUNCE (Curtis Lee Counce)

b. Jan. 23, 1926, Kansas City, MO, **d.** Jul. 31, 1963, Los Angeles, CA
Bass / Hard bop
A first-rate accompanist and session bassist, Curtis Counce played on numerous recording dates in the '50s. He was a solid, swinging player with a great tone; one of the finest "walking" bassists. Counce studied violin, bass, and tuba as a teen, then played in the early '40s with Nat Towles's orchestra. He settled in Los Angeles and worked with Edgar Hayes from 1945 to 1948, followed by stints with Billy Eckstine, Bud Powell, Buddy DeFranco, Wardell Gray, and Hampton Hawes. Counce later played in a group co-led by Benny Carter and Ben Webster, while recording with Lester Young. He studied composition and arranging with Spud Murphy. During the '50s, there were recording sessions with Teddy Charles, Shorty Rogers, Buddy Collette, Claude Williamson, Herb Geller, Bob Cooper, Clifford Brown, and Milt Bernhart. Counce later played with DeFranco again, then toured Europe with Stan Kenton's orchestra. He formed a quintet in the mid '50s that, at various times, included Jack Sheldon, Harold Land, Carl Perkins, and Frank Butler. Some of Counce's recordings were *Landslide, Carl's Blues,* and *Counceltation* (also known as *You Get More Bounce*). He was also a bass teacher and did some film work. Most of Counce's albums have been reissued on CD. *—Ron Wynn*

○ **Sonority** / Jan. 1956 / Contemporary 7655
Curtis Counce Group. A relaxed, yet vibrant, date with Harold Land (ts) and Carl Perkins (p) as standouts. *—Ron Wynn*

★ **Landslide** / Oct. 8+15, 1956 / Contemporary 606
Curtis Counce Group. This is the same lineup as *Sonority,* and the music swings just as hard. *—Ron Wynn*

○ **Counceltation—Vol. 1** / Oct. 15, 1956 / Contemporary 1007539

○ **Counceltation—Vol. 2** / Apr. 15, 1957-Sep. 3, 1957 / Contemporary 7539
This second volume of the three recorded by the Curtis Counce quintet in 1956, '57, and early '58 appeared as a reissue, although the packaging was different from that of the original release, which was known as *You Get more Bounce With Curtis Counce.* It is a welcome reminder of what a tight and joyous group it was. Tenor saxophonist Harold Land, already a veteran in the mid '50s, and the intense, unorthodox young trumpeter Jack Sheldon made a hand-inglove front line. "How Deep" is a prime example of the force and clarity of Harold Land's music. Perkins's development would have been interesting to hear. He was a stomping, blues-based pianist whose style was at the heart of the Counce group and did much to give the band its character. Butler had no solos to equal his famous tour de force on *A Fifth For Frank,* in volume one of the Counce group. But he was in sympathetic attendance throughout, a great drummer, who, like Sheldon, is heard from far too seldom these days. As for Counce, he was a dependable, swinging bassist, a good composer ("Counceltation") and a splendid judge of talent. This album was further evidence that he put together

one of the best small bands of his time. —*Doug Ramsey,* Down Beat

You Get More Bounce with Curtis Counce / Apr. 15, 1957-Sep. 3, 1957 / Contemporary 159

Excellent bassist from the West Coast. Slightly naughty art work. Worth the search to find it. —*Michael G. Nastos*

☆ **Carl's Blues** / Aug. 29, 1957-Jan. 6, 1968 / Contemporary 423

The Curtis Counce (bass) group (Jack Sheldon or Gerald Wilson, trumpet; Harold Wilson, tenor sax; Carl Perkins, piano; Frank Butler, drums) was a working group when they recorded *Carl's Blues.* This album, with its cool-hot late-night ambience, was a sleeper when it was first released and remains so almost 25 years (1983) later. . . . This is music loaded with lots of soul; that's the kind of soul that existed before it was mass-marketed, the kind of soul that screws into your muscle with its muscle. —*Bob Rusch,* Cadence

Exploring the Future / Apr. 1958 / Boplicity 7

STANLEY COWELL (Stanley A. Cowell)

b. May 5, 1941, Toledo, OH
Piano, composer / Bop, hard bop

A top melodic interpreter, pianist Stanley Cowell has played penetrating compositions and inventive solos in trios, combos, and solo situations since he made his debut, in the early '60s, with Rahsaan Roland Kirk while still at Oberlin Conservatory. Cowell's swinging, elegant style and his ability to merge blues, hard bop, and gospel elements have been featured on several memorable recordings. He began playing piano at age four. He earned his Bachelors degree from Oberlin and his Masters degree from the University of Michigan in the '60s. After working with Kirk, Cowell played with Marion Brown and Max Roach through the '60s and into the '70s. He was also in the Harold Land-Bobby Hutcherson quintet from 1968 to 1971. Cowell joined Music, Inc. in 1969 and cofounded Strata-East with Charles Tolliver in 1971. This record label was designed to be owned and operated by and for musicians. The company issued some challenging material until it encountered financial problems in the late '70s; they've resurfaced in the '90s. Cowell recorded with Music, Inc. until 1973, and worked with them again in the late '70s. He also played with the Heath Brothers, Clifford Jordan, and the Piano Choir. Cowell formed Collective Black Artists, Inc. with Reggie Workman and Jimmy Owens, among others, in 1970. He directed the group's ensemble in 1973 and 1974. Cowell worked and recorded principally with the Heath Brothers from 1974 to 1984. He was awarded a grant for composition by the National Endowment for the Arts in 1978, and became a teacher at Lehman College in 1981. Cowell toured internationally as a soloist and in various duos and trios in the '80s and '90s. He's recorded for Galaxy, Trio, PolyGram, Concord, DIW, and Strata-East. Cowell has several sessions available as a leader. —*Ron Wynn and Michael G. Nastos*

○ **Blues for the Viet Cong** / Jun. 5, 1969 / Freedom 41032

This album was recorded in London during 1969 when Stanley Cowell was working with Music, Inc. This was (counting Cowell) a trio perfectly fit to reflect the style of their leader, which was a rolling, gently fierce, modal keyboard attack; a methodical, schooled approach that worked well with artists as varied as Max Roach and Marion Brown. The material here is decidedly *not* avant-garde, postdating a brief period with the likes of Brown and Joseph Jarman of the AACM. As always, the right hand is most active, rocking, and swinging on "Departure," reverting to block-chording near the end as the ferocious bass drums of Jimmy Hopps usher the theme out. The continuous and plentiful examples of dexterous ability on both sides attest to the high standards of quality. All tunes are original, except for an old Art Tatum mantlepiece, Rodgers and Hart's "You Took Advantage of Me." —*Arnold Shaw,* Down Beat

Illusion Suite / Nov. 29, 1972 / ECM 1026

Pianist Stanley Cowell's work with Music, Inc. and elsewhere impressed a lot of people. And even though he has other al-

bums on European labels, this one most directly and accurately pictures his fresh keyboard approach. While Cowell could be thought of as eclectic, it would seem the diversity of his directions was striving toward differences instead of merely taking the easy path. Perhaps the most enchanting element of his style was the gorgeous and telling use he made of dissonance as a tension-builder. "Miss Viki," an acoustic-electric intertwine in oblique funk, is but one example. If you needed more prodding, there is Stanley Clarke's dancing, throbbing, singing bass and his over-dubbed arco work on "Maimoun." Drummer Jimmy Hopps is so right, so tasteful that you (almost) forgot he is there. —*Will Smith,* Down Beat

Regeneration / Apr. 27, 1975 / Strata East 19765

Equipoise / Nov. 28+30, 1978 / Galaxy 5125

★ **Back to the Beautiful** / Jul. 1989 / Concord Jazz 4398

A good session, with Steve Coleman (reeds) in an unusual mainstream role. —*Ron Wynn*

Live at Maybeck Recital Hall—Vol.5 / Jun. 1990 / Concord Jazz 4431

This is part of an outstanding solo piano series. Cowell displays impressive technique and holds his own in the solo setting. —*Ron Wynn*

IDA COX (Ida [Née Prather] Cox)

b. Feb. 25, 1896, Toccoa, GA, d. Nov. 10, 1967, Knoxville, TN
Vocals / Swing, ballads, blues jazz, classic female blues

Blues and jazz vocalist. A stalwart performer whose career began in minstrel shows, Ida Cox was a bawdy, freewheeling performer with a love for "blue" jokes and double-entendre vocals. During the '20s she made memorable cuts with first-rate jazz musicians and was a tent-show star in the '30s. She was one of the earliest, biggest stars on the African-American circuit. She made a final triumphant recording, backed by the Coleman Hawkins group, for Riverside in 1961. —*Ron Wynn*

Ida Cox / i. Jan. 27, 1954 / Riverside 1019

★ **Blues for Rampart Street** / 1961 / Riverside 1758

With Coleman Hawkins. This is latter period Cox, with jazz all-stars. Some of her best tunes. —*Michael G. Nastos*

○ **Wild Women Don't Have the Blues** / i. 1961 / Rosetta 1304

A volume originally recorded in 1961. Many folks have since belted this blues song, but here is the woman who wrote and first sang it in 1924, and it's one of the strongest no-nonsense women's statements ever made. Ida was one of the most important classic blues singers of the golden era ("the only decade when women reigned"). —*Ladyslipper*

○ **Moanin' Groanin' Blues, The** / i. Jul. 1961 / Riverside 147

LOL COXHILL (Lowen Coxhill)

b. Sep. 19, 1932, Portsmouth, England
Soprano saxophone / Modern creative

Famous for his unaccompanied, unorthodox concerts and albums, Lol Coxhill has an immediately identifiable soprano and sopranino style. He's perhaps Steve Lacy's prime rival in getting odd sounds out of the soprano with his wrenching, twisting, quirky solos. While Coxhill's an accomplished saxophonist and can play conventional bebop, it's his winding, flailing soprano and sopranino lines that make him stand out. Early in his career, Coxhill played more conservatively; he backed visiting American soul and blues vocalists in the '60s, playing behind Rufus Thomas, Lowell Fulson, and Champon Jack Dupree. Coxhill worked with Steve Miller's group Delivery in 1969 and 1970, and played with them at the Berlin Music Festival. But his debut album, *Ear of the Beholder,* established a new direction for Coxhill. Since then, he's worked with both bebop and free musicians, among them Chris McGregor, Trevor Watts, Bobby Wellins, and Company. Coxhill's also played with groups such as the Recedents, Standard Conversions, and the Melody Four. Currently, he doesn't have any releases available on CD in America. —*Ron Wynn*

BOB CRANSHAW

b. 1932
Bass / Hard bop
The bass equivalent of a seasoned saxophone veteran who's never been a giant, but is well respected for consistent excellence, Bob Cranshaw has worked steadily with several top jazz musicians. Despite his light tone, Cranshaw's timing, musical knowledge, and versatility have been featured in an impressive array of recording sessions and tours since the late '50s. Cranshaw played piano and drums before switching to bass and tuba in high school. He was a founding member of Walter Perkins's MJT +3 band in 1957. Cranshaw went to New York with the group in 1960, and joined Sonny Rollins when they disbanded in 1962. He also worked with Duke Pearson's small groups and big band. Cranshaw started a parallel career in television, which he has continued, and is known for his years on "Sesame Street." He's also worked in theater orchestras, but his jazz dates have been plentiful. Cranshaw's played with Lee Morgan, Wes Montgomery, Coleman Hawkins, Johnny Hodges, Horace Silver, McCoy Tyner, Thelonious Monk, Jimmy Heath, James Moody, and Buddy Rich, and has toured with George Shearing, Joe Williams, Ella Fitzgerald, and Oscar Peterson. Cranshaw expanded his repertoire and added electric bass in the '70s. He's worked with Rollins frequently in the '80s and '90s. Cranshaw doesn't have any albums as a leader available on CD, but can be heard on numerous current and reissued dates by Rollins, McCoy Tyner, and the MJT + 3, among others. —*Ron Wynn*

HANK CRAWFORD (Bennie Ross (Jr) Crawford)

b. Dec. 21, 1934, Memphis, TN
Alto and baritone saxophone, piano, composer / Blues & jazz, soul-jazz
A brilliant, often hypnotic blues, R&B, and ballad alto saxophonist, Hank Crawford's career was affected negatively by the onslaught of background music and vapid fare issued on the '70s albums that bear his name. While he'd been doing wonderful material with commercial possibilities for years, Crawford was suddenly burdened with glossy, limp, and generic compositions, plus arrangements weighed down by faceless background vocalists. Fortunately, these albums died on the vine and he returned to the gritty blues and sassy R&B, soul-jazz, and occasional bebop that is his specialty. Crawford's tone, one of the most declarative and biting in any jazz era, and his approach were among the finest R&B/blues alto styles since Louis Jordan. At his best, Crawford rivals Eddie "Cleanhead" Vinson in the ability to play in a populist or bebop mode. Crawford also plays baritone and piano, and has been a great arranger and underrated composer. He worked with B. B. King, Bobby "Blue" Bland, and Ike Turner in Memphis before moving to Nashville.

Crawford studied music theory and composition at Tennessee State, leading its dance band and becoming a prominent arranger. He joined Ray Charles in 1958, playing baritone. But a year later, Crawford switched to alto, and became Charles's music director in 1960. The wonderful Charles small combo that included Crawford, David "Fathead" Newman, Leroy "Buster" Cooper, Marcus Belgrave, and Charles (doubling on keyboards and alto), remains one of the finest ever at blending jazz, R&B, and blues. Crawford went solo in 1963, and made a string of wonderful albums for Atlantic in the '60s that were squarely in the same groove as his arrangements for Charles. He even had a couple of hits with the cuts "Misty" and "Skunky Green." During the '70s, Crawford joined Kudu, a division of Creed Taylor's CTI label. His Kudu albums went steadily downhill; fans of the Charles and Atlantic years listened in horror. But Crawford joined Milestone in 1983, and has continued into the '90s cutting the music he does best, working with veterans who share his musical values and can truly play his arrangements. Crawford's recorded a number of albums with Jimmy McGriff. Some of his earlier Atlantic albums are

scheduled to be reissued as part of the company's deal with Rhino. There's one single disc collection of early Atlantic cuts now available. His recent Milestone sessions are available on CD. Thankfully, anyone who didn't endure the Kudu records need not worry; they're currently unavailable. —*Ron Wynn*

Soul Clinic, The / Feb. 24, 1961-May 2, 1961 / Atlantic 1372
Soul of the Ballad / Feb. 16+20, 1963 / Atlantic 1405
True Blues / **i.** 1963-1964 / Atlantic 1423
First album to establish his reputation as a leader outside the Ray Charles orchestra. —*Ron Wynn*
★ **After Hours** / 1965-Jan. 14, 1966 / Atlantic 82364
Soul-jazz and blues with ensembles of varying size from trio up to octet. Detroiters Ali Jackson and Wendell Harrison appear, as well as stalwarts Howard Johnson, Wilbert Hogan, and Joe Dukes (drums), and John Hunt and Fielder Floyd (trumpet). There are four standards including the title track. Originals by Bennie Golson, Ben Tucker, Stanley Turrentine, and the leader. —*Michael G. Nastos*
○ **Double Cross** / Nov. 20, 1967 / Atlantic 1503
Midnight Ramble / Nov. 1982 / Milestone 9112
Indigo Blue / Aug. 1983 / Milestone 9119
With Dr. John (p, organ) and David "Fathead" Newman (ts). Good session with soul-jazz leanings. —*Ron Wynn*
Roadhouse Symphony / Aug. 5-12, 1985 / Milestone 9140
Soul Survivors / Jan. 29+30, 1986 / Milestone 9142
With Jimmy McGriff (organ), George Benson (g), and Mel Lewis (d).
Soul-jazz the way they did it in the '60s (almost). —*Ron Wynn*
Mr. Chips / Nov. 1986 / Milestone 9149
Portrait / 1991 / Milestone 9192
Here is Crawford's latest collection of funky cuts and mellow ballads. —*Ron Wynn*

MARILYN CRISPELL

b. Mar. 30, 1947, Philadelphia, PA
Piano / Modern creative
One of the finest, though one of the least acclaimed modern pianists, Marilyn Crispell has emerged as an exciting, adventurous soloist and composer on the free scene. She's a rarity in that she's not interested in hard bop, jazz/hip-hop, or fusion. Crispell's style, with its slashing phrases, percussive mode, clusters, and speed, pays homage to Cecil Taylor (whom she reveres), but isn't merely an imitation. She's not as dance-oriented as Taylor, and her use of space, African rhythms, and chording also recalls the music of Thelonious Monk and Paul Bley, two other people that she cites as influences, along with Leo Smith. Crispell started piano lessons at age seven at the Peabody Music School in Baltimore. She later studied piano and composition at the New England Conservatory in Boston. Crispell abandoned music for marriage and medical work in 1969. But she returned to the music world six years later, moved to Cape Cod after a divorce, and was introduced to the sound of transitional John Coltrane (*A Love Supreme*) by pianist George Kahn. Crispell attended Karl Berger's Creative Music Studio, and studied jazz harmony with Charlie Banacos in Boston. She met Anthony Braxton at the studio, and toured Europe with his Creative Music Orchestra in 1978, recording on his *Composition 98* album in 1981. Crispell began playing solo and leading groups in the '80s, teaming with Billy Bang and John Betsch in one band. She made several albums on Leo, a British label, working with Reggie Workman, Doug James, Andrew Cyrille, Smith, Anthony Davis, Tim Berne, Marcio Mattos, Eddie Prevost, and several others. Crispell continued recording for Leo in the '90s, playing with Mark Dresser, Gerry Hemingway, Paul Motian, Workman, Braxton, and many others. She's also recorded for Cadence Jazz, and Music & Art Programs of America. The Music & Art Programs of America session is available on CD. Her

other recordings for Leo and Cadence Jazz must be obtained through mail-order services. —*Ron Wynn*

○ **Spirit Music** / May 15, 1981+Jan. 13, 1982 / Cadence 1015
Pianist Marilyn Crispell's music takes some getting used to. It's experimental in the now-familiar manner of players like Cecil Taylor and Anthony Braxton. Crispell plays as if her life depends on it. On *Spirit Music* (also recorded live), the group heads toward a trademark sound, but things don't quite jell; ragged spots break up the flow. One strong point that becomes more apparent after repeated hearings is Crispell's ability to shape a piece with well-defined contours. "ABC," dedicated to Anthony Braxton, is the most impressive example of this control. Clocking in at 23 minutes, it generates, and sustains, the kind of lunatic energy you'd find in a tune by Carla Bley. The performances are never short on excitement. The intensity is ultimately overpowering. Crispell wrote all the tunes on the album, and that fact is more noticeable than it should be. In "Chant," for example, even though the lines are muted, they have the same thunderous temperament as the rest. The tunes are all action, no reflection. Crispell gathered a strong group of musicians together here. They play authoritatively and have moments of inspiration. Violinist Billy Bang brings a very personal brand of virtuosity to the proceedings. German bassist Peter Kowald prods him on with tricks of his own, and drummer John Betsch is strong throughout. —*Elaine Guregian*, Down Beat

Rhythms Hung in Undrawn Sky / May 7, 1983 / Leo 118

★ **Concert in Berlin, A** / Jul. 2, 1983 / Free Music 46
Pianist Marilyn Crispell is close to the Cecil Taylor model on *Live in Berlin*, recorded with violinist Billy Bang, drummer John Betsch, and bassist Peter Kowald. In place of the lean, contrapuntal style she favors elsewhere, her dissonant-and-percussive-as-ever playing here is thicker and more cluttered. Crispell's habit of absentmindedly playing with the sustain pedal down is her undoing here; her sound seems unfocused and fuzzy as a result. Bang's violin playing is one of the highlights of Crispell's *Spirit Music;* regrettably, his distinctive lyricism isn't projected as clearly or consistently here, although he does take a nicely abstract solo and saws off a tailor-made repetitive pattern on "Burundi," his best vehicle. . . . Bang seems to have been swayed from his usual course by the influence of Peter Kowald, whose rubbertones, non-timekeeping bass work is more assured. The rhythm section is the best thing about this date, in fact. Betsch's adaption of Ed Blackwell (or Baby Dodds) mannerisms, on "Burundi" especially, is effective and satisfying. There are moments on this LP when everyone is swept along in an invigorating rush, but in all this busy-ness I miss the originality and clarity that drew me to Crispell's playing in the first place. —*Kevin Whitehead*, Cadence

○ **Live in Zurich** / Apr. 1989 / Leo 122
Crispell keeps cranking out furious, aggressive free dates for the European market. They're devoid of any devices now in vogue on the jazz circuit; no standards, no electronics, no hard bop, adult contemporary, strings, or fusion. If you enjoy hearing spirited dialogues between Crispell, bassist Reggie Workman, and drummer Paul Motian, this one's for you. —*Ron Wynn*

○ **Images** / i. Aug. 1991 / Music & Arts 634
The current piano favorite among the new generation of outside players, Crispell doesn't tone down the intensity until she concludes the session. Her approach, attack, tone, and phrasing have often been compared to her mentor Cecil Taylor, but she's not quite as percussive (no one is). However, this is as close as any living being can get to duplicating his energy and power. —*Ron Wynn*

SONNY CRISS (William Criss)

b. Oct. 23, 1927, Memphis, TN, **d.** Nov. 19, 1977, Los Angeles, CA
Alto and soprano saxophone / Hard bop
Sonny Criss had a searing, energetic alto sax style. Like many other alto players, he was influenced by Charlie

Parker, but Criss forged his own approach. His approach was distinguished by a distinct vibrato and by technical proficiency that allowed him to execute intricate solos and phrases in a smooth, engaging manner. Criss was also a dynamic ballad, blues, and standards player. Criss was one of Eric Dolphy's influences. Though born in Memphis, Criss spent almost all of his professional life on the West Coast. He began playing in Los Angeles in the mid '40s, working in Howard McGhee's band with Charlie Parker and Teddy Edwards. He made his recording debut as a leader in 1947, and cut other sessions for Savoy, Clef, and Imperial with Wardell Gray, Sonny Clark, and Buddy Clark, among others. He also played with Johnny Otis, Billy Eckstine, and Gerald Wilson. Criss toured in a band with Parker under the Jazz at the Philharmonic banner in the late '40s. He played with Eckstine again in '50 and '51, was in Stan Kenton's orchestra in 1955. He worked with Howard Rumsey's Lighthouse All-Stars and Buddy Rich's band, and headed his own groups. He recorded sessions for Impulse, and then for Polydor while living in Europe from 1962 to 1965. He did performances, studio sessions, and radio broadcasts while in Europe. But things got tougher for Criss when he returned to Los Angeles. He made several recordings for Prestige between 1966 and 1969, and cut other dates for Xanadu, Muse, and Impulse in the '70s. But Criss spent more time doing community music projects and working with young people than he did playing dates. He toured Europe in 1973 and 1974, then did more recording in 1975. A couple of years later, Sonny Criss committed suicide. A good amount of his material from the '40s to the '70s has been reissued on CD. —*Ron Wynn*

California Bopping / Apr. 1947-Oct. 1947 / Fresh Sound 156
A session done early in Criss's career that shows formative style and moving solos. —*Ron Wynn*

Memorial Album / 1947-1965 / Xanadu
Good teamup with Hampton Hawes (p). Includes cuts done from 1947-1965. —*Ron Wynn*

Sonny Criss (1949-1957) / 1949-1957 / Fresh Sound 64

Intermission Riff / Oct. 12, 1951 / Pablo 929

★ **Sonny Criss Plays Cole Porter** / 1956 / Imperial 9024

Sonny Criss and Kenny Dorham—Vol. 1: The Bopmasters / i. 1959 / ABC/Impulse 9337
Dating from 1959, the Sonny Criss sides feature Wynton Kelly, perhaps the quintessential combo pianist of the '50s, in a relaxed and swinging set that glows with mellow warmth. Criss's lustrous, penetrating intonation owed much of its pure flavor to the restrained timbres of the cool school, but his effortless liquid phrasing imparts a feelingful cadence that could squeeze juice from the corners of a ballad and render the most tortuous bop harmonics congenially fluid. Criss's debt to the Art Blakey conception is evident on his own "Sylvia," which features the robust, dynamic blues lines of his alto emerging from a Bobby Timmons-like head. His balladic mastery is showcased on "Sweet Lorraine," where his bright tone and mercurial agility more than compensate for his horn's lack of deeper shadings. In contrast to Criss, Kenny Dorham was known as much as a composer as an improviser. . . . Such compositions as "The Prophet" or "Tahitian Suite," however, exude an almost eerie familiarity and possess an uncanny staying power. This was the only waxing of Dorham's Jazz Prophets, a short-lived aggregation he formed between stints with Blakey and Max Roach. The laid-back Lester Youngish delivery of tenorist J.R. Montrose is a perfect foil to Dorham's own relaxed style, and pianist Dick Katz projects a pointed, original chordal matrix out of a post-Powell conception. —*Larry Birnbaum*, Down Beat

○ **Sonny Criss at the Crossroads** / Mar. 1959 / Peacock 91

Portrait of Sonny Criss / Mar. 12, 1967 / Prestige 655
Valuable reissue of a stalwart date. Criss is in piercing form; high-caliber rhythm section work. —*Ron Wynn*

Sonny's Dream / May 8, 1968 / Prestige 707

A fine concept work with Sonny Criss's animated alto sax playing compositions by West Coast writer and bandleader Horace Tapscott. The album, which was originally titled *Birth of the New Cool,* is notable for fine playing from Conte Candoli, Pete Christlieb, and Tommy Flanagan, as well as Criss. It's been reissued on CD. —*Ron Wynn*

○ **I'll Catch the Sun** / Jan. 20, 1969 / Prestige 7628
Torrid uptempo pieces and equally moving ballads from a top-flight saxophonist who never got the credit he deserved while alive. Sonny Criss was as fine a hard bopper and blues-based alto player as anyone in his generation, and this quartet date is ample evidence. Hampton Hawes on piano, Monte Budwig on bass, and Shelly Manne were a capable, supportive rhythm section. —*Ron Wynn*

Crisscraft / Feb. 24, 1975 / Muse 6015
Alto saxophonist Sonny Criss's tone and tasteful ear for improvisation were a joy. Although he stemmed from the Bird school of playing, his delicacy and other qualities gave him a sound that was different. He'd been off the recording scene for six years, re-evaluating himself and re-assuming his own musical gifts. He returned to the studio in 1975 fresh and full of ideas. *Crisscraft* opens with Horace Tapscott's pleasing Latin theme "The Isle of Celia," a fine framework for more than ten minutes of solo features, with Criss leading off and Dolo Coker (on piano) and Larry Gales (on bass) following in tandem. Benny Carter's beautiful "Blues in My Heart," on the other hand, is pure Criss all the way; solid and sure-footed. "All Night Long" is a memorable melodic track, and "Crisscraft" finishes the album with an irresistible straightahead uptempo blues. —*Leonard Maltin,* Down Beat

★ **Saturday Morning** / Mar. 1, 1975 / Xanadu 105
Out of Nowhere / Oct. 20, 1975 / Muse 5089
A tremendous date that reactivated the memory of Criss among long-time jazz fans who had overlooked him. —*Ron Wynn*

BING CROSBY (Harry Lillis Crosby)

b. May 2, 1904, Tacoma, WA, **d.** Oct. 14, 1977, Madrid, Spain
Vocals / Blues & jazz, ballads & blues
Bing Crosby is another icon whose film and television success, and status as a beloved entertainer and celebrity, obscured his musical impact. Crosby wasn't, in the strictest sense, a jazz singer, and through much of his career recorded everything but jazz. Still, this was the style in which he began, and he retained interest in the music, utilizing it when and where he could. He did display excellent vocal jazz skills around 1930, and was also a fine scat singer. Crosby played drums and sang with small jazz groups as a boy. In 1926, Crosby, Al Rinker (Mildred Bailey's brother), and Harry Barris started the Rhythm Boys. They sang with Paul Whiteman's orchestra from 1926 to 1930, then Crosby began his solo career. Crosby's greatest contribution was his ability to understand and exploit the microphone. He was the first vocalist to use it in a manner that personalized songs, and made them intimate experiences for individual listeners. His projection, enunciation, and performances on the microphone changed the course of popular music singing. He was among the earliest crooners, and sometimes seemed to talk or whisper to a melody. Greatly influenced by Louis Armstrong, Crosby exposed the White audience to techniques that were commonplace among Black vocalists; singing on consonants, and using devices like slurs he'd learned from such artists as Harry Mills. He'd ease the weight of breath on the vocal cords by passing into a primary or head voice at a low register.

Crosby was enormously successful in films from the early '30s on, in both musical and dramatic settings. *The Birth of the Blues,* in 1941, was (very) loosely based on the Original Dixieland Jazz Band story, and featured an appearance by Jack Teagarden. Crosby appeared with Louis Armstrong in the 1956 film *High Society,* and recorded with him in 1960. He toured with players such as Milt Hinton and Joe Bushkin,

and employed jazz musicians often on his television specials. His image as the kindly neighborhood singer took a huge hit from a book published by his son, Gary, but his impact on music and on jazz's foundation shouldn't be underestimated. —*Ron Wynn with Cub Koda*

Bing & Basie / **i.** 1972 / EmArcy 824705

★ **Best of Bing Crosby, The** / **i.** 1980 / Decca 184
No single package can hold all of Crosby's hits, but this is a start: original cuts from the '30s and '40s, with many favorites. —*Charles S. Wolfe*

Bing Crosby Story—Vol. 1 (Early Jazz Years) / **i.** 1984 / Sony 201

○ **Bing Crosby (1927-1934)** / **i.** 1987 / BBC
The best-sounding presentation of his formative '20s and '30s cuts. —*Ron Wynn*

★ **And Jazz Friends** / GRP 603
Bing at his best; vintage '40s Decca sides with everyone from Louis Armstrong to Lionel Hampton. —*Charles S. Wolfe*

Crooner, The / Columbia 44229
Classic Columbia sides from 1928 to 1934, with fine remastering and good notes. —*Charles S. Wolfe*

Rare Brunswick Recordings (1930-1931) / MCA 1502
Rare Early Recordings (1929-1933) / Biograph 13

BOB CROSBY (George Robert Crosby)

b. Aug. 25, 1913, Spokane, WA, **d.** Mar. 9, 1993
Vocals, bandleader / Swing, big band
Bob Crosby, Bing's younger brother, often found himself in the odd position of being the least important member of his orchestra. An okay singer, Crosby was much more important as the leader of a memorable swing band that found its own style by looking backwards at the 1920s. To Crosby's credit, he seemed aware of his predicament and comfortable at allocating most of the solo space to his talented sidemen. He featured his sidemen with his big band and with his Bobcats, a hot Dixieland band that came out of his orchestra. After stints with Anson Weeks in 1932 and with the Dorsey Brothers' orchestra during 1934-35, Crosby was voted in as the frontman of a new big band formed out of the remains of Ben Pollack's orchestra. 1935-42 was Crosby's heyday. His band featured classic soloists such as Yank Lawson, Billy Butterfield, Eddie Miller, Matty Matlock, Irving Fazola, Joe Sullivan, Bob Zurke, Jess Stacy, and Muggsy Spanier. During an era when swing was the thing and New Orleans jazz was considered by many to be ancient history, Crosby's crew led the way to the eventual New Orleans revival. Such classic recordings as "South Rampart Street Parade" and "What's New" (both composed by bassist Bob Haggart) along with many Dixieland stomps kept the band quite popular. The orchestra broke up in late 1942. Crosby served in the marines during 1944-45. He spent the rest of his life doing a variety of activities, often bringing back versions of the Bobcats for special concerts and recordings. He took an occasional vocal, but mostly let his sidemen play. Some of Crosby's many Decca recordings are currently available. —*Scott Yanow*

○ **Bob Crosby (1937-1938)** / **i.** 1937-1938 / BBC 688

Bob Crosby & His Orchestra & The Bob Cats / **i.** 193z / EPM 37139
Bob Crosby & Orchestra. A new reissue of prototype late '30s recordings. —*Ron Wynn*

★ **22 Original Big Band Records** / **i.** 1952-1953 / Vanguard 409
Bob Crosby in Hi Fi / Jun. 7-15, 1956 / Coral 57062

ISRAEL CROSBY

b. 1919, **d.** 1962
Bass / Hard bop
A superb bassist, Israel Crosby's supple lines, deep tone, and commanding presence helped the Ahmad Jamal trio of the mid '50s and early '60s become one of the most popular

combos in jazz history. Crosby was a virtuoso who provided dazzling walking lines, soaring solos, and dynamic accompaniment. He played trumpet at age five, then played trombone and tuba before he finally settled on bass. Crosby played with Jess Stacy, Gene Krupa, and Teddy Wilson in the '30s, and with Albert Ammons, Fletcher Henderson, and Horace Henderson. He was a prolific session musician in the '40s, when he worked with Edmond Hall, Georgie Auld, Roy Eldridge, and Coleman Hawkins. Crosby joined Jamal's group in 1954, and when Crosby teamed with drummer Vernell Fournier, Jamal had his strongest lineup. *But Not for Me* was recorded at the Pershing Hotel in 1958, and eventually peaked at number three on the pop charts. Another smash Jamal date with Crosby was *Ahmad Jamal, Volume IV,* which reached number 11 on the charts. Up to the time Crosby died, he was featured on several Jamal sessions; though Jamal would go on to enjoy many other hits, his music was never the same. Crosby also played with Benny Goodman for a short time in 1956 and 1957, and played briefly with George Shearing in 1962. Crosby can be heard on many Jamal reissues. —*Ron Wynn*

CRUSADERS

b., USA
Group / Blues & jazz, soul-jazz, contemporary funk
A once-proud soul-jazz combo, the former Jazz Crusaders of the '60s and '70s are commercial fusion session players today. Wilton Felder, Wayne Henderson, Joe Sample, and Stix Hooper were longtime friends and musical associates who forged a group sound out of the blues, soul, and small-combo jazz they loved. Throughout the '60s, the Jazz Crusaders, featuring an unusual trombone-tenor front line, were the epitome of funky hard bop and became very popular for a jazz group; their many Pacific Jazz albums are still enjoyable. The group dropped "Jazz" from its name in the early '70s, but still created stirring music until Wayne Henderson's departure resulted in a more conventional sound for the group. Switching gradually to commercial funk/R&B, the band had a few major hits in the '80s (most notably "Street Life"), but became somewhat irrelevant to jazz. Stix Hooper's decision to leave in the late '80s virtually ended this group's identity. They have some sessions available on CD. —*Ron Wynn*

Freedom Sounds / May 1961 / Pacific Jazz 96864

Looking Ahead / 1961 / Pacific Jazz 43

★ **Freedom Sounds** / **i.** Apr. 1969 / Atlantic 1512

Old Sox, New Shoes / **i.** 197- / Chisa 804

★ **1** / **i.** 1970 / Chisa
Their finest modern soul-jazz date. Wilton Felder burns on tenor, and the arrangements meld funk beats and jazz licks to maximum success. —*Ron Wynn*

☆ **Second Crusade** / **i.** 1972 / Chisa

Hollywood / **i.** 1973 / MoWest 118

Scratch / 1975 / MCA 37072
Scratch is the result of a concert given at Los Angeles's Roxy Club and it is plainly evident that the Crusaders were among friends. The addition of L.A. session guitarist Larry Carlton and bassist Max Bennett supplied a much-needed embellishment to the formulaic Crusader sound. Trombonist Wayne Henderson, tenor saxophonist Wilton Felder, keyboardist Joe Sample, and drummer Stix Hooper perform in their customary groove; two decades of familiarity bred an astonishing, if sometimes all-too-predictable, precision. The title cut establishes the mood of the set, the clipped but funk-laden urban riff parting to reveal a meaty tenor solo by Felder. The well-worn "Eleanor Rigby" is the most fully realized arrangement; the brooding essence of the tune is assiduously maintained. Carlton sneaks in some fluid guitar runs during the 12-minute piece as the rest of the gang contributes solos (Henderson's comes off most impressively). The bluesy spiritual "Hard Times" is more than a little reminiscent of Cannonball Adderley's "Mercy Mercy Mercy" ren-

dition, with Sample's reflective piano engaging in a delicate interplay with Felder's plaintive sax. —*Marv Hohman,* Down Beat

Chain Reaction / 1975 / MCA 1648

Young Rabbits / **i.** 1976 / Blue Note 4028

Street Life / 1979 / MCA 31024
This album contains their single biggest hit with the title cut. A gold album. —*Ron Wynn*

Those Southern Knights / **i.** 1991 / MCA 1649

○ **Golden Years, The** / **i.** 1992 / GRP 5007
An anthology containing several of the Crusaders's hits and representative songs from their greatest years. It focuses on their '70s records, which were both their most popular and finest. The group's sound began to decline after trombonist Wayne Henderson left, and after they deserted their patented formula, which seamlessly mixed blues, R&B, funk, and soul-jazz. This set features them at their best. —*Ron Wynn*

☆ **Southern Comfort** / MCA 6016

RONNIE CUBER (Ronald Edward Cuber)

b. Dec. 25, 1941, New York, NY
Baritone saxophone / Hard bop, Latin jazz
A well-known baritone saxophonist in both the jazz and Afro-Latin/Latin jazz communities, Ronnie Cuber's trademark thick, robust sound, searing attack, and rumbling phrases have been a familiar ingredient on countless sessions. He played in Marshall Brown's Newport Youth Band at the 1959 Newport Jazz Festival. Cuber recorded and performed with Slide Hampton, Maynard Ferguson, and George Benson in the early and mid '60s, then worked with Lionel Hampton before joining Woody Herman in 1969. Cuber toured Europe with the Herman band, then played with jazz-rock, soul, Afro-Latin, and bebop groups in the '70s. He led various bands in the late '70s and early '80s, and played and recorded with the Lee Konitz nonet, Mickey Tucker, Rein de Graaff, Nick Brignola, and the Xanadu All Stars (Cuber played with the All Stars at the 1978 Montreux Jazz Festival). He led a quartet and composed several pieces in the '80s. Cuber's recorded as a leader for Xanadu and Fresh Sound, and has one session available on CD. —*Ron Wynn*

★ **Cuber Libre** / Aug. 20, 1976 / Xanadu
Baritone sax often sounds awkward in phrasing, lacking flow, with an absence of range, characterized by a squawky sound in the bottom register. Ronnie Cuber's work here has some of those shortcomings, but even when he overcomes them he is often at a loss for ideas during his solos. He seems strongest as an improviser at medium tempos and when he follows good solos by pianist Barry Harris, as on "Tin Tin Deo" and "Sudwest Funk." On the fast "Rifftide," his tone becomes grating. Otherwise, though, Cuber has a big, warm tone with nice vibrato, which is not in the least harsh and is shown to good advantage on this album's only ballad, "Misty," a tune that otherwise is marred by a choppy solo. When stating the melody, his octave range is good, including some nice mellow sections in the upper registers. His playing is best when stating a theme or working over a brief idea in a solo. On the nearly 12-minute long "Star Eyes," he can't build on a solo, relying instead on a close following of the melody or on runs, although he smoothly works in a bit of "There There Eyes" and "I Dream of Jeannie." But when trading fours at the end, he comes up with some nice phrases. "Tin Tin Deo" also has some nice swinging spots when he grabs hold of a phrase and repeats it with some alteration. —*Jerry De Muth,* Cadence

Eleventh Day of Aquarius / Jan. 31, 1978 / Xanadu
A quintet with Tom Harrell (tpt) and the Mickey Tucker Trio playing Latin and jazz. —*Michael G. Nastos*

Passion Fruit / Feb. 29, 1985-Mar. 1985 / King 6347
George Benson (g) makes a guest appearance on this well-engineered recording. —*Ron Wynn*

Two Brothers / Nov. 21, 1985+Dec. 9, 1985 / Pro Arte 623

Some hard bop, some blues, and a few things in between on this '85 set. Cuber's lumbering baritone is backed by a group proficient at either mainstream or more funky material, fueled by drummer Steve Gadd. "Green Dolphin Street" is a high point. —*Ron Wynn*

Live at the Blue Note / Nov. 3, 1986 / Projazz 629
Good, sometimes fiery session, featuring baritone and soprano saxophonist Cuber heading a group with Randy Brecker, organist Lonnie Smith, and drummer Ronnie Burrage. There's plenty of blues, soul-jazz, and hard bop, though no Afro-Latin numbers. —*Ron Wynn*

Best of Ronnie Cuber / Pro Arte 664
A somewhat deceptive title, since Cuber hasn't been a huge name and hasn't scored any "hits" in that sense. But he's been a prolific session and Afro-Latin player, and this collection showcases his thick, bluesy, and hard-hitting baritone style. —*Ron Wynn*

TED CURSON (Theodore Curson)

b. Jun. 3, 1935, Philadelphia, PA
Trumpet, piccolo trumpet, flugelhorn / Hard bop, modern creative
Ted Curson has played some invigorating, highly charged free and hard bop dates, but has never come close to getting widespread exposure or recognition, at least not in America. He hasn't stayed on the scene with the regularity necessary to ensure sustained publicity and coverage. But when he has recorded, Curson's shown extensive range, a strong tone, an aggressive, animated trumpet style, and an approach influenced by Clifford Brown and Lee Morgan. Though not in the same class as Brown and Morgan, Curson's a fine uptempo and ballad player, who more than deserves a regular showcase. Curson studied music in high school and also studied with his Philadelphia friends and neighbors, the Heath brothers. He worked with Charlie Ventura in the early '50s, then met Miles Davis, who encouraged him to move to New York. Curson played with Red Garland, Vera Auer, Mal Waldron, and Cecil Taylor in the late '50s, then with Charles Mingus's Jazz Workshop band of the early '60s that included Eric Dolphy. Curson left Mingus's group to form a band with Bill Barron in 1962. Curson soon grew frustrated with the lack of opportunities and moved to Europe. He cut his most famous album, *Tears for Dolphy*, in Europe. He did some fine sessions for Atlantic and for Supraphon in the '60s. *Tears for Dolphy* was later used in the film *Teorama* in 1969. Curson settled in Denmark for several years, and worked in Europe and on the festival circuit. He returned to America in 1976, and formed a great group with Chris Woods and Nick Brignola. They made a tremendous but low-selling album, *Jubilant Power*, for Inner City. Curson then had to disband the group. He made other good albums for EMI, India Navigation, Interplay, and Chiaroscuro in the '70s, and for Chiaroscuro in the '80s. He also participated in jam sessions at the Blue Note club in the '80s. He's highly respected and well known in Europe, and, in the early '70s, was the first foreign musician awarded a grant by the Finnish government. Presently, he has only a couple of titles available on CD. —*Ron Wynn*

Fire Down Below / Dec. 10, 1962 / Prestige 1744

Flip Top / Aug. 1, 1964 / Freedom 1030
This is a Paris date from one of the music's best trumpeters, with tenor saxophonist Bill Barron. Some of his better originals. —*Michael G. Nastos*

★ **Tears for Dolphy** / Aug. 1, 1964 / Arista
Recorded in Paris, this 1964 session documents Ted Curson's first quartet as a leader. While reflecting his collaborations with Charles Mingus and Cecil Taylor, Curson's approach here is closer to the spirit of the mainstream. Eschewing the more radical techniques of the free approach, Curson and reedman Bill Barron etch tough, but highly melodic, lines above the steady and crisp rhythmic substructure ably provided by bassist Herb Bushler and drummer Dick Berk. —*Chuck Berg*, Down Beat

New Thing and the Blue Thing, The / Mar. 25+29, 1965 / Atlantic 1441

Ode to Booker Ervin / Sep. 3, 1970 / EMI

★ **Jubilant Power** / Oct. 16+17, 1976 / Inner City 1017
Slashing, dynamite exchanges, and an intense approach make this the Curson to grab. —*Ron Wynn*

ANDREW CYRILLE (Andrew Charles Cyrille)

b. Nov. 10, 1939, New York, NY
Drums / Early free, modern creative
Drummer Andrew Cyrille is an outstanding percussionist and is among the more far-sighted players of his generation. His ability to interact with pianist Cecil Taylor seemed almost instinctive on many records; he could provide multiple rhythms and accents, compliment Taylor's direction, change the music's pace, or support the powerful solos of Taylor, saxophonist Jimmy Lyons, and any of the other musicians involved in the dialogue. He was seldom cast in the customary pattern of pushing the beat with Taylor. Cyrille has excelled as a session player and bandleader, too. He began playing drums at age 11, and studied at Juilliard. During the early '50s, he worked with Illinois Jacquet doing swing and bebop and played African and funk/rock/R&B with Olatunji. Cyrille recorded with Coleman Hawkins and Walt Dickerson on Prestige sessions, and Bill Barron on Savoy. He also played with Rahsaan Roland Kirk and Cedar Walton before working, for over a decade, with Taylor. He had one stint at Antioch College as an artist-in-residence. Cyrille was featured on numerous Taylor records for Blue Note, Arista/Freedom, Leo, Shandar, and many other labels. He also recorded with Lyons, the Jazz Composers Orchestra, Grachan Moncur III, and Marion Brown. Cyrille, Milford Graves, and Rashied Ali played and recorded together in the '70s, and Cyrille also did a duo date with Graves. During the '70s and '80s, he began making more dates as a leader; working with a sextet; leading Maono with Ted Daniel; and doing various sessions for Black Saint, FMP, and Ictus. These included a solo percussion set, a trio with Lyons and vocalist Jeannie Lee, and another duet date with German multi-instrumentalist Peter Brotzmann. He was featured on a tremendous session for DIW/Sony with Oliver Lake and Hannibal in 1992. A decent number of Cyrille titles, many of them duets, are available on CD. Some of his output with Taylor is available as well. —*Ron Wynn*

What About / 1971 / Affinity 75
This is a solo drum session from August 11, 1969 that was probably originally recorded for BYG, but I don't believe it was ever issued. The five tracks here are, for the most part, pretty much straightahead, extended drum solos, the type you might hear on a live date in any number of bop or free bop groups. Only "Rims" and "Pioneering," the latter with Cyrille employing various whistle instruments overdubbed, have drum play in a larger, less traditionally structured sense. —*Kevin Whitehead*, Cadence

Dialogue of the Drums / 1974 / Institute Percussive 001
This early 1974 recording of live performances from Columbia University's Wollman Auditorium captures Andrew Cyrille's and Milford Graves's close musical communion in the creation of neo-African settings. As Graves asserts at the end of "Rejuvenation": "The new free, creative Black drumming definitely has a beginning—and that is it!" Other than the battery of percussive devices, the drummers resort only to vocalizations, grunts, and shouts—fragments of chants to provide contrast to their drum work. Such accompaniment seems to grow naturally from the performances, and Graves's drum solo and "Call and Response" provoke undirected answers from the audience, which Cyrille echoes. Forty-five minutes of free percussion music is not everyone's idea of listening pleasure, but these men are masterful, complete musicians. Liner notes mention other performances, including drummer Rashied Ali; that trio of percussion artists would surely provide a further ear-opening experience. —*Howie Mandel*, Down Beat

Loop, The / Jul. 1978 / Ictus 0009

★ Metamusicians' Stomp / Sep. 1978 / Black Saint 0025
Metamusicians Stomp is the group Maono's best-recorded documentation to date (1980), featuring strong solos, interesting compositional structures, and excellent sound quality. If Maono occasionally took on an ensemble sensibility reminiscent of Tony Williams's early Blue Note sessions, it was because of drummer/leader Andrew Cyrille's stylistic flexibility and fastidiousness, forcing his cohorts through a wide range of textural and emotional situations. "5-4-3-2," for example, is a rondo-like structure, which alternates a jaunty, intricate theme with a series of compact, elastic statements from a variety of duo and trio combinations in which each instrumentalist is allowed to speak his piece—all in under five minutes. Kurt Weil's "My Ship" is given a relaxed, partially perfunctory ballad treatment, with Ted Daniel's trumpet succinct and David Ware's tenor playful with a broad, burlesque edge to his burnished tone. "Spiegelgasse 14," which takes up all of the second side, is divided into three parts—"Reflections & Restaurants," "The Park," and "Flight" —though one section flows seamlessly into the next so that the effect is one of a leisurely stroll down a boulevard containing a constantly evolving environment of sights, sounds, and smells. Bassist Nick Di Geronimo is the hero here, maintaining an even, steady, though never monochromatic pulse, over and around which Daniel and Ware alternate bluesy and brassy episodes, while Cyrille flutters in the background like an omnipresent butterfly. —*Art Lange*, Down Beat

○ Nuba / 1979 / Black Saint 0030
The interplay between vocalist Jeanne Lee and alto saxophonist Jimmy Lyons is perfectly offset by the balancing force of drummer Andrew Cyrille. After their long association with pianist Cecil Taylor, Cyrille and Lyons were no strangers to one another and the *Celebration* record provides the common ground for Cyrille and Lee. Lyons's dry tone virtually suggests the desert for "Nuba" (in both its versions), the most fully conceptualized composition on the album. Cyrille's repetitious rhythms visualize the caravan bouncing along through the sands Lyons conjures; Jeanne Lee's vocal becomes the very oasis she sings about. Despite some variances, both versions of "Nuba" are basically similar; Lee's inflections are the major difference. Her amazing ability to "swing" so abstractly, with lyrics, poetry, wordless vocals, or just noises and clucks, is a constant joy. She was no ordinary vocalist, but an instrumentalist of the highest order. Her performance on "In These Last Days" provides a true test for her mettle that she carries out most dynamically. For allowing such space for activity to develop between Lyons (who is as slippery as a snake all throughout

here) and Lee, Cyrille deserves credit. He percolates things without ever being obtrusive, adding just the right color, the most succinct accent. Also worth checking out is Cyrille's thumb piano workout on "Cornbread Picnic (Maize)." This is a very worthwhile recording. —*Mike Cornette*, Cadence

Special People / Oct. 21+22, 1980 / Soul Note 1012

Navigator, The / Sep. 21+22, 1982 / Soul Note 1062
For listeners accustomed to Andrew Cyrille's work with Cecil Taylor and in various percussion-only settings, this album is a surprising change of pace. It features Cyrille's group Maono, a flexible ensemble he led through the '70s, playing a program of six compositions that range from a brief, eccentric bop tune to a freewheeling suite and a long, sensuous ballad. The structured approach is not so surprising in light of Cyrille's total musical background (which included stints with Coleman Hawkins and Mary Lou Williams as well as Cecil Taylor and the JCOA). The album, as a whole, brings to mind Taylor's remark that true musical freedom involves "different ideas and expressions of order." Cyrille's "different ideas" came naturally from his agile mastery of complex rhythmic ideas. He could swing as convincingly in 10/4 as 4/4, and his style was marked by an unmistakable lightness and subtlety. Cyrille's elegant percussive power is balanced by the rough, earthy style of bassist Nick Di Geronimo. Pianist Sonelius Smith works the middle ground, delivering crunching chords when they are needed, but also constructing a stately, lyrical introduction to Cyrille's ballad "So That Life Can Ensure . . . P.S. with Love." Trumpeter Ted Daniel, a charter member of Maono, is critically important to the success of the music, playing with a paradoxically affecting style that combines soft, burnished passages with irregular, probing lines and frenetic outbursts. The tunes frequently develop from individual statements into swirling group "conversations," an approach that is both strikingly contemporary and as old as call-and-response choruses. This is particularly true of "Circumfusion/The Magnificent Bimbo" (Cyrille has a way with song titles), a 10-minute suite that begins with a stark, aleatoric passage. That passage gives way to unison lines that are almost goofy in their looping exuberance. Open-ended, yet tightly constructed, "Circumfusion" is a microcosm of the album as a whole, with its refreshing integration of various elements drawn from the jazz tradition. —*Jim Roberts*, Down Beat

○ My Friend Louis / Nov. 18+19, 1991 / Columbia 52957
Fiery, rampaging session with drummer Andrew Cyrille anchoring a stirring set featuring the dynamic tenor saxophonist David S. Ware. This is uncompromising, exciting material, far from sedate standards or derivative hard bop recitations. —*Ron Wynn*

D

MEREDITH D'AMBROSIO

b. 1941
Vocals / Ballads & blues, modern creative
A soft, polished, yet striking vocalist and pianist, Meredith D'Ambrosio has issued several nice, unimposing albums for Sunnyside. She's sung standards, provided her own lyrics for John Coltrane's "Giant Steps" and Dave Brubeck's "Strange Meadowlark," and has added sparse piano accompaniment. D'Ambrosio's style and sound isn't as quirky as Blossom Dearie's, or as captivating as Mose Allison's, but she's succeeded in making music that's undeniably distinctive and individualistic. She's not a powerful, gripping, or dynamic singer or pianist, yet she retains the listener's attention by an inspired combination of the right material and effective presentation. D'Ambrosio has several sessions available on CD. —*Ron Wynn and Michael G. Nastos*

○ **Little Jazz Bird** / 1982 / Palo Alto 8019
Fine '82 combo session in which D'Ambrosio shows her ability to handle a variety of songs supplied by composers as diverse as harpist Deborah Henson-Conant and vocalist David Frishberg. Phil Woods heads a capable backing band, and supplies his customary heated alto sax solos, while Hank Jones lends some flair on piano. —*Ron Wynn*

It's Your Dance / Mar. 27+28, 1985 / Sunnyside 1011
A first-rate trio date, possibly D'Ambrosio's finest in that format. Her singing has punch, variety, and dimension, and her phrasing is creative and expertly constructed. Kevin Eubanks's guitar contributions are concise, thoughtful, and do not have any gimmicks or wasted riffs. D'Ambrosio and Harold Danko interact smoothly, and his piano backing is delicate and supportive. —*Ron Wynn*

South to a Warmer Place / Feb. 1989 / Sunnyside 1039
Eddie Higgins Trio joined by trumpeter Lou Columbo. Two lyrics by the singer. Sweetness and light. —*Michael G. Nastos*

★ **Love Is Not a Game** / Dec. 19+20, 1990 / Sunnyside 1015
With her husband's Eddie Higgins Trio. Dreamy, soft-voiced D'Ambrosio makes a definitive emotional statement. Fifteen tracks, nine standards (three adapted or modified by D'Ambrosio). Five written by her. Nice twisting on "I Love You/You I Love," "Oh, Look at Me Now/But Now Look at Me," and "Lament/This Lament." —*Michael G. Nastos*

PAQUITO D'RIVERA

b. Jun. 4, 1948, Havana, Cuba
Alto saxophone / Latin jazz, world fusion
An exciting alto saxophonist and clarinetist, Paquito D'Rivera has developed an arresting style that features a hard-edged alto sound, and a rhythmic intensity and fluidity honed from years of working with groups such as Irakere, and working with other Latin bands. He's an excellent soloist in Latin jazz, hard bop, and bebop, and has studied carefully and has absorbed Charlie Parker's style. Not even a few less-than-stellar recordings have prevented D'Rivera from claiming his rightful place among the finest Latin jazz bandleaders and players; his best sessions for Messidor, Chesky, and Candid have shown his skill on blistering uptempo tunes and on poignant ballads, and on his originals and Latin jazz workouts, too. D'Rivera's father, a saxophonist, introduced him to jazz in Havana; he gave his son an introduction to the instrument's pleasures. D'Rivera listened to recordings, then began studies at the Havana Conservatory in 1960. He met Chucho Valdes, who greatly assisted and influenced his career. D'Rivera played in musical theater from the age of 14 and was in an army band during the '60s. He later joined the Orquesta Cubana de Musica Moderna. Several band members later formed Irakere. Irakere attracted international attention during the late '70s and early '80s, particularly on D'Rivera and trumpeter Arturo Sandoval. D'Rivera defected to America in 1980 while the band was in Spain on a European tour. He moved to New York, and worked with David Amram, Dizzy Gillespie, and McCoy Tyner before forming his own band. D'Rivera's recorded for Columbia, Chesky, Messidor, and Candid. His recent Chesky and Messidor dates have been more consistent and Latin-flavored than the Columbias, which were uneven. He reunited with Sandoval on a Messidor date in '92. Most of D'Rivera's releases are available on CD. —*Ron Wynn*

○ **Blowin'** / **i.** 1981 / CBS
Despite the overly-slick production (thankfully with no strings)—including that "magic" touch of reverb, a raw genuine feeling still shines through. It was especially present in alto saxophonist Paquito D'Rivera's fiery bop-oriented (with obvious Latin subtitles) stylings which often climaxed with effective honks and squeals (shades of Gato Barbieri), as well as in bassist Eddie Gomez's solo work on "Waltz For Moe" and "Basstronaut," Ignacio Berroa's rough, slicing drumming style (muted on the rather dull rock/funk/ballad cuts—"Monga" and "Song To My Son"), pianist Hilton Ruiz's solo work on "Chucho" (featuring some wonderful syncopations/time inflections) and "On Green Dolphin Street" (with excellent rough-edged unison lines), and the mostly interesting arrangements. —*Milo Fine*, Cadence

★ **Mariel** / 1982 / Columbia 38177
With pianists Hilton Ruiz and Jorge Dalto. Becoming more funky. Also includes "Moment's Notice." Funk and jazz from Cuban fire-spitter. —*Michael G. Nastos*

Live at Keystone Korner / Jul. 17-18, 1983 / Columbia 38899

○ **Why Not** / Jun. 19-21, 1984 / Columbia 39584
Cuban expatriate Paquito D'Rivera issued a commercially viable, yet fairly musically challenging album with *Why Not*. . . . By combining infectious percussion work, accessible funk-inspired rhythms, and impassioned solo statements, D'Rivera was able to get airplay on adult contemporary radio stations, but without compromising his musical integrity. The June 19-21, 1984, date consists of eight tunes that highlight D'Rivera's alto and clarinet work. Claudio Roditi (trumpet, flugelhorn, valve trombone) also provides some strong solos, but it is the addition of Toots Thielemann (harmonica, guitar, whistle) on some of the tracks that gives more color to the music, making it more interesting. The strong rhythm section is comprised of Michel Camilo (keyboards), Lincoln Goines (electric bass), Portinho, Dave Weckl, Sammy Figueroa, Cucho Martinez, and Manolo

Badrena (drums, percussion). This is accessible, but not insulting. —*Carl Brauer*, Cadence

Manhattan Burn / Sep. 30, 1985-Oct. 1, 1985 / Columbia 40583

Celebration / Sep. 1987-Oct. 1987 / Columbia 44077
1988 release, some high-flying moments. Claudio Roditi (tpt) is great. —*Ron Wynn*

Tico! Tico! / Jul. 1989-Aug. 1989 / Chesky 34

○ **Who's Smoking?!** / May 21-22, 1991 / Candid 79523
Hot, surging Afro-Latin set by alto saxophonist Pacquito D'Rivera, matching him with both celebrated veterans and established session stars. D'Rivera doesn't falter through any of these pieces, and gets strong assistance from special guest James Moody and super trumpet solos by Claudio Roditi. The percussive backgrounds supplied by Danilo Perez and Al Foster are varied and constantly shift and change. —*Ron Wynn*

Reunion / i. 1991 / Messidor 15805
Excellent session done for German label, distributed domestically by Rounder. D'Rivera at top of his game. —*Ron Wynn*

ALBERT DAILEY (Albert Preston Dailey)

b. Jun. 16, 1938, Baltimore, MD, **d.** 1981
Piano, composer / Post bop, hard bop
A sorely neglected and underrated pianist during his lifetime, Albert Dailey's skill and verve as a soloist were appreciated greatly and eulogized following his death. An often hypnotic stylist, his shimmering harmonies and phrases were admired particularly by Stan Getz, with whom he worked in the mid '70s. Daily began piano studies at an early age, then played in the Baltimore Royal Theater's house band in the early and mid '50s. He attended Morgan State and Peabody Conservatory in the late '50s. Dailey toured with vocalist Damita Jo from 1960 to 1963, then led a trio at the Bohemia Caverns in Washington, D.C. before moving to New York in 1964. Dailey played with Dexter Gordon, Roy Haynes, Sarah Vaughan, and Charles Mingus, while recording with Freddie Hubbard. He performed and recorded with Woody Herman at the 1967 Monterey Jazz Festival, and was in Art Blakey's Jazz Messengers during the late '60s and again in the mid '70s. Dailey played periodically with Sonny Rollins, toured and recorded with Stan Getz, and also cut sessions with Elvin Jones and Archie Shepp in the '70s. He performed at Carnegie Hall and in the Mobil Summerpier Concerts series in the '80s, while also playing in the Upper Manhattan Jazz Society with Charlie Rouse, Benny Bailey, and Buster Williams. He recorded for Columbia, Steeplechase, Muse, and Elektra. His '72 debut, *The Day After the Dawn*, received widespread critical praise, but did not make enough sales to keep Columbia from dropping him after that one date. He has only one session currently available on CD. —*Ron Wynn*

Day After the Dawn, The / 1977 / Columbia 31278
Albert Dailey was a unique pianist and composer of the third musical generation after Charlie Parker, who drew his inspiration as an improviser from two sources: the harmonically intricate chord blocks practiced by his predecessors McCoy Tyner and Herbie Hancock, and the spaceless fast-paced horn lines Bud Powell developed. These two streams are clearly identified and segregated in Dailey's solos. . . . Dailey's lines are distinctive, intricate structures that build naturally and easily into harmonic (or, occasionally, contrapuntal) layers, whose logic and form are things of beauty. . . . But the ideas that Dailey, the composer, had on paper don't match those used by Dailey, the pianist, to develop them. The only titles on the album that are really worthy of Dailey's apparent talents are "Free Me," a beautiful overdubbed composition—an improvisation in which he builds interwoven contrapuntal layers on piano, electric piano, bass, drums, and synthesizer, proving himself to be his own best accompanist (as well as one of the very few musicians to whom the Moog is anything but a vacant gimmick); and an unabashedly romantic, unaccompanied "September of My Years". . . . Richard Davis

(bass) is as amazing as ever, and David Lee sounds like a good drummer (even if not quite as attuned to Dailey's conception as Dailey himself is on the overdubbed title track). —*Barry Tepperman*, Coda

★ **Textures** / 1981 / Muse 5256
One of only two in-print releases featuring the engaging, striking piano work of Albert Dailey. This 1981 session has him working with a pianoless trio keyed by saxophonist Arthur Rhames (who reportedly killed himself over bad reviews), plus bassist Rufus Reid and drummer Eddie Gladden. Dailey was a particular favorite of Stan Getz, and was especially strong doing uptempo material. —*Ron Wynn*

TADD DAMERON (Tadley Ewing Peake Dameron)

b. Feb. 21, 1917, Cleveland, OH, **d.** Mar. 8, 1965, New York, NY
Composer, arranger, bandleader, piano / Bop
A prolific composer, arranger, bandleader, and pianist, Tadd Dameron adapted bop compositions for a large band. He wrote many superb compositions that became signature pieces, among them "Good Bait," "Our Delight," "Hot House," "Lyonia," "Sid's Delight," "Lady Bird," and "Casbah." His arrangements for Dizzy Gillespie's orchestra were often compelling, even if the orchestra didn't equal the harmonic and rhythmic intensity and intimacy of a small combo. Dameron's arrangements received their greatest individual treatment by trumpeter Fats Navarro. Navarro's blistering playing illuminated them in a manner that the Gillespie band didn't attain. Dameron worked with several groups before joining Harlan Leonard in Kansas City in 1939. Dameron provided songs and arrangements for Leonard's band, and for Jimmie Lunceford's, Don Redman's, Coleman Hawkins's, Illinois Jacquet's, and Sarah Vaughan's bands. He began writing for Gillespie's big band in the late '40s, and his major orchestral piece, *Soulphony*, debuted at a Carnegie Hall concert in 1948. Dameron began his own group that same year, which included Navarro. He played at the Paris Jazz Fair in 1949 with Miles Davis and James Moody, and recorded for Capitol. Dameron started another group in 1953, this time with Clifford Brown. After that group disbanded, Dameron recorded sessions for Prestige in the mid '50s; one with an octet and the other a quartet date with John Coltrane. He was imprisoned in 1958 on drug charges. After his release in 1961, Dameron wrote pieces that were featured on recordings by Milt Jackson, Sonny Stitt, and Blue Mitchell. He also provided some arrangements for Benny Goodman's '62 Russian tour. Dameron suffered from heart attacks, and died of cancer in 1965. Various musicians and groups emerged to celebrate the beauty of his compositions and arrangements. Pianist Barry Harris did an album of Dameron songs with his trio for Xanadu. Philly Joe Jones led the repertory group, Dameronia, in the early '80s. They recorded Dameron's works and used arrangements transcribed by Don Sickler. Another '80s band, Continuum, with Jimmy Heath and Slide Hampton, made *Mad About Tadd* for the defunct Palo Alto label in 1983. Reissues of Dameron's material on Blue Note (under Navarro's name), Milestone, Capitol, and Affinity (British) are available. —*Ron Wynn and Bob Porter*

○ **Classics of Modern Jazz—Vol. 1: Fats Navarro** / Aug. 28, 1948-Nov. 13, 1948 / Jazzland 950

○ **Classics of Modern Jazz—Vol. 4: The Tadd** / Aug. 28, 1948-Nov. 13, 1948 / Jazzland 968

○ **Tadd Dameron Band 1948** / Oct. 23, 1948 / Jazzland 68

Study in Dameronia, A / Jun. 11, 1953 / Prestige 159

○ **Fontainebleau** / Mar. 9, 1956 / Prestige 055
Fontainebleau puts the emphasis on arrangements; those who might have hoped for a blowing date (March 9, 1956) with Kenny Dorham, Henry Coker, Sahib Shihab, Joe Alexander, Cecil Payne, John Simmons, and Shadow Wilson would be advised to look elsewhere. There are some fine solo moments here; Kenny Dorham seems quite comfortable. It is mostly for the arranging that one would pick this

up, for it does offer some nice examples of the floating, suspended heat that marked this arranger's touch. It is not all fine; the title track falls flat in its impressionistic attempt and hits me with right angles. However, a very hip "Delirium" and "The Scene I Clean" (now almost a standard in arranging) give this record interest beyond the sum of its parts. The remaining tracks are "Flossie Lou" and "Bula-Beige." —*Bob Rusch*, Cadence

★ **Mating Call** / Nov. 30, 1956 / Prestige 212

Magic Touch of Tadd Dameron, The / Feb. 27, 1962 / Riverside 143

○ **Dameronia** / i. 1963 / New Jazz 8300

EDDIE DANIELS (Edward Kenneth Daniels)

b. Oct. 19, 1941, New York, NY
Clarinet, tenor saxophone / Post bop
Depending on whom you choose to believe, Eddie Daniels is currently either the ranking clarinet stylist or is right behind Don Byron. Without question, he is a virtuoso who plays wondrous solos at any tempo, exploits every register, and never seems to hit a clinker or make a mistake. His classical playing is even more faultless; while there are questions about how much blues and soul feeling get into his jazz solos, no one can deny their technical brilliance. Best known, originally, as a tenor saxophonist, Daniels attended the High School of the Performing Arts in New York, and appeared at the 1957 Newport Jazz Festival playing alto in Marshall Brown's Youth band. He earned a Bachelors degree in Brooklyn College in 1963 and a Masters degree from Juilliard in 1966, then played with Tony Scott at the Half Note. As a tenor saxophonist, he was a member of the Thad Jones-Mel Lewis Orchestra for six years, and won first prize in an International Jazz Competition in Vienna. Daniels recorded with Friedrich Gulda and made his debut jazz recording. He played with Freddie Hubbard and Richard Davis in 1969, then recorded with Don Patterson, Bucky Pizzarelli, Airto Moreira, and Morgana King, and did his own dates, in the '70s. Daniels switched exclusively to clarinet in 1984 and premiered Jorge Calandrelli's magnificent "Concerto for Jazz Clarinet and Orchestra" that year. He received a National Endowment for the Arts grant in 1986. Daniels has achieved stardom through a series of records with GRP. He's recorded with Gary Burton and made earlier sessions for Muse and Prestige. Daniels has many releases available on CD. —*Ron Wynn*

First Prize / Sep. 8-12, 1966 / Original Jazz Classics 771
Formative sessions from 1966 featuring Eddie Daniels mainly on tenor sax, and on clarinet on some songs. Daniels was squarely in the cool mode at this point, playing with passion, but not yet confident in his own voice. The menu is predominantly standards, with some light Afro-Latin mixed in. Daniels leads a fine band, with pianist Roland Hanna, bassist Richard Davis, and drummer Mel Lewis—the consummate rhythm section. This has been reissued recently on CD. —*Ron Wynn*

Brief Encounter / Jul. 11, 1977 / Muse 5154
Steady mainstream date by Daniels, who became a clarinet star in the '80s. He plays both clarinet and tenor sax, and does straightahead material backed by pianist Andy Laverne, bassist Rick Laird, and drummer Billy Mintz. It was issued on vinyl in 1977 and reissued on CD in 1986. —*Ron Wynn*

○ **Morning Thunder** / 1978 / Columbia 36290
Morning Thunder is severely blighted by commercial intent, but has passing redemption by featuring Eddie Daniels almost exclusively on clarinet, his alto but a forgettable filigree heard too many other times in the bands of other, even more forgettable players. Unexpectedly, the compositions and background arrangements are no better than commerce deserves. —*Jack Sohmer*, Down Beat

○ **Blackwood** / i. 1979 / GRP 9584

This recording is pleasant and has some fine moments, but for the most part it gives up its delights to too little effort. The backgrounds that Eddie Daniels plays over—mostly Latin, rock, pop, and/or funk with lots of synth—are models of their kind. And Daniels's work is warm and virtuostic. But much of it is also a bit too laidback and, seemingly, unengaged. Consequently, it is not often engaging. Eddie Daniels improvising safe solos over hip pop/fusiony backgrounds is better than a lot of things, but the present master of the jazz clarinet is capable of making better music. If all the other tracks were as interesting as the intriguing title tune of Daniels own "Blue Waltz," where he and Dave Grusin (keyboards) both construct lyrical, inventive solos to a synthesized string accompaniment, it would be another matter altogether. —*David Franklin*, Jazz Times

○ **Memos from Paradise** / Dec. 1987-Jan. 1988 / GRP 9561
Excellent, soaring clarinet solos by Eddie Daniels help overcome occasional compositional defects on this late '80s set. During this decade, Daniels emerged as the clarinet's reigning soloist, and showed why, with plenty of spiraling, exhaustive contributions. Sometimes, the orchestrations get sappy, and Roger Kellaway's piano playing is more nice than exuberant. But the disc is very popular with the light jazz and adult contemporary audience. —*Ron Wynn*

★ **To Bird with Love** / 1987 / GRP 9544
This clarinetist's best solid and swinging studio date, with Fred Hirsch (p) and Al Foster (d). —*Michael G. Nastos*

○ **Nepenthe** / Dec. 1989 / GRP 9607

This Is Now / 1990 / GRP 9635

Under the Influence / i. 1993 / GRP 9716
Eddie Daniels playing sax again? Yes, he who forsook that instrument almost a decade ago in favor of the clarinet exclusively and then proceeded to be responsible as much as anyone for the clarinet's reemergence as a front-line jazz instrument; yes, Eddie Daniels's latest release features his tenor sax playing on 7 of the recording's 11 tracks. This album is a tribute to three of Eddie's major musical influences: Getz, Trane (presumably the balladeer), and Bill Evans. Most of the program of standards and originals clearly reflects this, but an American Southwest/Amerindian dimension is introduced by the intriguing compositions of Santa Fe pianist Allan Pasqua. Despite some wonderful clarinet work on four tracks, Daniels has chosen this occasion to remind us that he also plays tenor sax very well. He plays tenor here with the same lyricism, passion, energy, and tenderness as he plays clarinet on numerous recordings over the last few years. —*Tom Jacobsen*, Jazz Times

---

OLU DARA

b. 1941
Cornet and trumpet / Modern creative
An all-around entertainer whose cornet and trumpet numbers range from blues stomps and rags to screaming free passages, Olu Dara clearly enjoys playing music. His performances and solos encompass the entire Afro-American and American musical vernacular, and draw from marching band numbers, African rhythms, funk and soul tunes, swing, and gospel. Dara also uses mutes in a clever manner that includes wailing choruses, vamps, and exaggerated tones. After navy service, Dara moved from Mississippi to New York in 1963. He's been quite active since the '70s, working with Art Blakey's Jazz Messengers, Oliver Lake, Hamiett Bluiett, David Murray, Henry Threadgill, James Newton, and Don Pullen, among others. Though he doesn't have any sessions as a leader, he can be heard on recent CDs by the musicians listed in this write-up. —*Ron Wynn*

WOLFGANG DAUNER

b. Dec. 30, 1935, Stuttgart, Germany
Piano, composer, bandleader / Early jazz-rock, world fusion, modern creative
An intriguing composer and an ambitious pianist, German musician Wolfgang Dauner has combined jazz, rock, elec-

tronic music, and elements of opera and theater to create broad-based, ranging works. While these compositions sometimes seem too far-reaching, Dauner's best work shows the links between idioms and genres, and offers provocative musical and cultural concepts. He studied trumpet, piano, and composition at the Musikhochschule in Stuttgart, then joined Joki Freund's sextet in the early '60s. Dauner appeared at several German festivals, then made his recording debut heading a trio in 1964. It was one of the first European free jazz recording sessions. Dauner led Radio Jazz Group Stuttgart and wrote compositions for them in 1969. He formed the jazz-rock band Et Cetera in 1970, then co-led the Free Sound & Super Brass Big Band with Hans Koller. He helped organize the United Jazz and Rock Ensemble in 1975, and began featuring theater, opera, and dance segments along with his performances in '70s and '80s concerts. Dauner's composed music for films, radio, and television broadcasts, and has also composed a children's opera. He's recorded for Mood, Columbia, MPS, and ECM, among others. Dauner has a couple of sessions available on CD. —*Ron Wynn*

Solo Piano / **i.** Jun. 1984 / Mood 33600
Though not as rampaging as Don Pullen or Cecil Taylor, Dauner still takes things out on this 1979 solo session issued on a European import label. There's nothing sedate or predictable about these selections; Dauner romps, stomps, breaks off and changes tempos, slashes, and attacks in a nonstop manner. —*Ron Wynn*

KENNY DAVERN (John Kenneth Davern)

b. Jan. 7, 1935, Huntington, NY
Soprano saxophone, clarinet / Dixieland
A first-rate traditional jazz stylist, Kenny Davern has dazzled audiences and critics with his mix of harmonic subtlety and his vintage sound and approach, which is bluesy and woody on the clarinet, and rousing and delightful on the soprano sax. Davern began playing jazz in high school, and turned professional at age 16. He worked with Jack Teagarden in the mid '50s, and made his recording debut with him. Davern worked in New York with Phil Napoleon, Pee Wee Erwin, Red Allen, Buck Clayton, and Jo Jones when Teagarden moved to California. He led a band at Nick's in the early '60s before joining the Dukes of Dixieland in 1962 and 1963 on an extensive domestic tour. Davern played with Eddie Condon, Herman Autrey, and Ruby Braff, then coformed Soprano Summit with Bob Wilber in the '70s. They played together until 1979, then Davern toured alone again and returned to playing more clarinet than soprano. He formed the Blue Three in 1981 with Dick Wellstood and Bobby Rosengarden, and appeared at several European jazz festivals. Davern's recorded in the '80s and '90s on Musicmasters, playing with Howard Alden, Phil Flanigan, Bob Haggert, and Giampaolo Biagi, among others. Davern has mostly recent sessions available on CD. —*Ron Wynn and Michael G. Nastos*

★ **Soprano Summit** / **i.** Mar. 1976 / Concord Jazz 29
Live at the Concord Festival with Bob Wilber and quintet. Two Wilber originals, one by guitarist Marty Grosz. A fine representation of two artists in Dixie-early-swing mode with blues and a touch of Ellington. —*Michael G. Nastos*

Hot Three, The / Jul. 1, 1979 / Monmouth 7091
What a joy it is to hear Kenny Davern in the type of setting he always preferred! This date, then, represents the first time that Davern had ever been permitted to shine completely on his own. Of all the traditionally inspired clarinetists, Davern still ranks as the supreme individualist. This trio recording presents him at his best. In Art Hodes, he had a pianist whose roots went back to the very dawn of swinging jazz. Though never a virtuoso himself, Hodes had lots of experience in compensating for the absence of a bass—indeed, with a player like Hodes, it was almost a preferred condition. Moreover, his solos are exemplary, as always, not only for their Jimmy Yancey-like incisiveness, but for their cakewalking strut as well. Drummer Don DeMicheal, a former

editor of *Down Beat,* may surprise older readers with his revealed competence as a drummer, but musicians have always known that there are mightier tools than the pen. —*Jack Sohmer,* Down Beat

El Rado Schuffle / Jun. 7, 1980 / Kenneth 2050
A tribute to Jimmy Noone with a Swedish sextet. (Two Noone tunes, the rest are played nicely.) —*Michael G. Nastos*

Stretchin' Out / Dec. 1983 / Jazzology 187
A fine swing/traditional date with Dick Wellstood (p) and Chuck Riggs (d). —*Ron Wynn*

Very Thought of You, The / 1983 / Milton Keynes Music 841

○ **Playing for Kicks** / Nov. 1985 / Jazzology 197

Live Hot Jazz / **i.** 1986 / Statiras 8077
Trio with Dick Wellstood (p) and Chuck Riggs (d). Standards played without bass. Davern sticks to clarinet with no clichés. Fine concept and execution. —*Michael G. Nastos*

I'll See You in My Dreams / Jan. 1988 / Music Masters 5020
Outstanding, musically conservative date, with fine playing from Davern and Howard Alden (g). —*Ron Wynn*

One Hour Tonight / **i.** 1988 / Music Masters 5003

ANTHONY DAVIS

b. Feb. 20, 1951, Paterson, NJ
Piano, composer / Modern creative
Pianist/composer Anthony Davis belongs to the class of African-American musicians who reject stereotyping by anyone and insist on following their own course. Davis refuses the designation "jazz musician," and though his father helped found the Black Studies department at Yale (he also knew Art Tatum), Davis has expressed resentment at those who insist he play strictly "Black" music, though he doesn't dispute the existence of that body of work. He freely admits pronounced European as well as African-American influences, and has aimed for a delicate balance of improvised and strictly notated compositions. His playing fuses bebop, Asian, pop, and symphonic influences. His earlier albums and compositions were weighed toward conventional jazz styles, but, since the early '80s, Davis has been composing longer works and operas inspired by either political or ethnic concerns. He's done free music, has participated in big bands, and has played chamber and Third Stream-styled jazz, but lately has been more composer/arranger than improviser. But Davis remains concerned about the plight of musicians. While living in New Haven he cofounded a group called Advent patterned after Chicago's Association for the Advancement of Creative Musicians (AACM).

Davis studied classical music as a child and later attended Yale, receiving his degree in 1975. Besides Advent in 1973, he was also a member of the New Dalta Ahkri led by Leo Smith in the mid and late '70s. He moved to New York in 1977, played with Leroy Jenkins's trio, and co-led a duo and quartet with James Newton. Davis, Newton, and Abdul Wadud have worked together often. Davis formed the octet, Episteme, in 1981; a group conceived to play his mix of improvised and notated material, as well as the works of other composers like Alvin Singleton and Earle Howard. Davis's most controversial project was his opera *X,* based on the life of Malcolm X, with the libretto written by his sister, *Village Voice* editor and writer Thulani Davis. The merits of this work, and the issue of whether it was truly an opera, were discussed in numerous music and general magazines in 1985 and 1986. *X* was performed in Philadelphia in 1985, and was performed by the New York City Opera company in 1986. Davis made his recording debut as a leader on India Navigation in the late '70s, and has recorded combo and solo albums for Red, Sackville, and Gramavision. Besides Wadud, Smith, Jenkins, and Newton, he's worked often with George Lewis and Jay Hoggard. Davis taught composition and history of creative music courses at Yale in the early '80s. Gramavision released *X: The Life and Times Of Malcolm X* in 1992. More cynical types have suggested that Spike Lee's film about Malcolm X generated tons of free publicity, and may have played a part in Gramavision's decision to release the opera recording eight years after it was first performed. Currently, there are only a few Davis titles available on CD. —*Ron Wynn*

Past Lives / Jun. 7, 1978 / Red VPA 134

○ **Of Blues and Dreams** / Jul. 30-31, 1978 / Sackville 3020
Of Blues and Dreams is largely given over to a suite in three movements based on the fantasy writings of pianist/composer Anthony Davis's wife, Deborah Atherton. The title track, a neo-romantic rhapsody in somber hues, sets the stage for a voyage to the planet "Lethe," whose gray mists and phosphorescent waters are conjured up by the swirling, ominous interplay of violin and cello over Davis's brooding piano. An eerie, insistent vamp erupts from amid the fog before unraveling into controlled cacophony, whereupon the ensemble descends to the frightening depths of "Graef," a forbidden drug that foretells the user's death. Violinist Leroy Jenkins and cellist Abdul Wadud supply an appropriately schizoid scenario with pregnant silences that abruptly explodes into chilling tone rows and cluster chords. The suite concludes with the journey of Atherton's protagonist, "Madame Xola," through her interplanetary travels. The lengthy, morose explanation fuses jumpy omnirhythms with a dark Schoenbergian serialism, until at last Jenkins breaks into a nostalgic swing lament that Stuff Smith might have appreciated. —*Larry Birnbaum*, Down Beat

★ **Song for the Old World** / Jul. 1978 / India Navigation 1036
Anthony Davis, then (1978) known in New York as a young pianist/composer from the left side or avant-garde, presents us with his first group record, *Song For the Old World*, and what I think is a distinct return to melody. "Song For the Old World" is a collection of musical folk fragments from Asia, Africa (Ghana), and southern America (New Orleans). The beauty of this composition is in the musical harmonic transitions that float over a very fine percussion line by Ed Blackwell. Generations of string instruments that are from the African hunting bow and also centuries of percussive devices that date from before Christ are but a few of the "interior" musical elements. This is a gentle record, and it takes time for one to hear the beauty, and indeed to *feel* the melody. A great deal of musical history is covered, and it is done in not only a lyrical way, but in an honest way. —*Bradley Parker-Sparrow*, Down Beat

Hidden Voices / Mar. 1979 / India Navigation 1041
This quintet album has great teamwork with George Lewis (t) and James Newton (f). —*Michael G. Nastos*

Under the Double Moon / Sep. 1-2, 1980 / PA/USA 7120

Lady of the Mirrors / 1980 / India Navigation 1047
These solo piano compositions by Anthony Davis are intense, highly symphonic creatures, combining the melodic and rhythmic essence of modern classical music with the textures of jazz. Melodic fragments surge at random, interweaving, crossing, hiding in musical shadows, and exploding. Davis builds modal structures that have the dark, minor essence of Ravel, with the brutal and toying intensity of Bela Bartok. The right-hand configurations in several of these selections sound like a composer's sketch before a symphony or chamber piece. —*Bradley Parker-Sparrow*, Down Beat

Episteme / 1981 / Gramavision 8108
Anthony Davis' role as an active performer on *Episteme* diminished as the composer allowed Mark Helias to conduct this small ensemble in performing Davis's materials. "Wayang No. 11 (Shadowdance)," first performed in 1978, opened the album with an elastic and driving tempo as Davis leavened this seven-minute piece with the symphonic gestations of tension and resolution. "Wayang No. IV (Under The Double Moon)," recorded previously on Davis's solo piano album *Lady of the Mirrors*, was subdivided into two sections: "Opening Dance" and "Sustained Tones." The first section built in a progression of pulsations and percussion with drums, cymbals, chimes, bells, gongs, woodblocks, and agitated strings. The ensemble achieved period of intense sound density and shifting time—a music of changing tempo emerged through the imposition of static rhythms and a light piano resonance; embodying a Phillip Glass-like retentiveness and repetition and evincing a lack of melodic conception and development. "Sustained Tones" exuded more of melodic pulse with the interplay of gongs, the piano and strings—these sounds deliquesced and glimmered, and suggestions evolved. Davis, the pianist, emerged with a serial-line solo full of silence, short phrases building a melodic line (a vision); windows opened allowing the music to stream thorugh as retrograde violin microtones converged in long sustained breaths.... *Episteme* explored indigenous percussiver rhythmic effects, but unfortunately went stale at times. —*Christopher Kuhl*, Cadence

I've Known Rivers / Apr. 1982 / Gramavision 79427
Precious document. Top-notch improvisers team up. Sparks fly! With James Newton on flute and Abdul Wadud on cello. —*Michael G. Nastos*

○ **Mystic Winds, Tropic Breezes** / i. Nov. 1982 / India Navigation 1049

Variations in Dreamtime / i. 1982 / India Navigation 1056
Variations isn't so much an attempt to write classical jazz, but rather to create composed structures for improvisers. Anthony Davis is so successful that the lines between composition and improvisation blur, an appropriate occurrence "in the dreamtime." On the title track, the pianist takes us into the inner world of the dream state with its own logic of order and form. The ominous suspense of Abdul Wadud's droning cello and Davis's tense chords subtly shifts into a Kafkaesque cycle of instruments running from each other, but going nowhere. J.D. Parran's clarinet sings a playful downward scale, while Wadud and trombonist George Lewis enact a call and response. Throughout, the instrumentation is shifting, roles are changing, and like a dream, nothing remains the same for long. Neither "Variations in Dreamtime" nor its flip side, "The Enemy of Light," leaps at you with heroic solos and the swelling crescendos of a linear-time composition. But they have a visceral, compelling presence that makes this Davis's most mature release to date (1982) as a leader. —*John Diliberto*, Down Beat

Hemispheres / Jul. 1983 / Gramavision 79428
Except for the ethereal first and fourth movements, pianist/composer Anthony Davis's suite centers around his evolving concept of rhythmic density. The two varieties of rhythmic density utilized in *Hemispheres* result in a propulsive music ideal for virtuosic, linear improvisation. In the second movement, the juxtaposition of 4/4, 7/4, and 11/4 rhythmic motifs creates a constant polymetric texture, providing a somewhat minimalist groove for a darting George Lewis solo on trombone and a riveting statement from trumpeter Leo Smith. This approach, which also affords Dwight Andrews's soprano ample room in the third movement, promotes an overt soloist/support dynamic within the ensemble. The variety employed in the final movement uses phrases of upwards to 60 beats to establish shifting, intricate relationships between and within the sections of the ensemble while sustaining strong rhythmic momentum. —*Bill Shoemaker*, Down Beat

Middle Passage / 1984 / Gramavision 8401
A 1984 set mixing Davis's studio and tape piano solos and spotlighting originals weaved around the theme of suffering and degradation. The title refers to the many African slaves who died en route from their homeland to America. —*Ron Wynn*

Ghost Factory / i. 1987 / Gramavision 79429
The gifted pianist/composer demonstrates his facility with contemporary classical and jazz pieces, playing sometimes in duos, other times trios, and also interacting with the Kansas City Symphony orchestra. Percussionist Pheeroan AkLaff or Gerry Hemingway and violinist Shem Guibbory are his partners, while all the compositions are Davis's. —*Ron Wynn.*

Trio—Vol. 1 / i. Mar. 1990 / Gramavision 79441
Invigorating follow-up. Has classical as well as improvisational influence and elements. —*Ron Wynn*

Trio—Vol. 2 / i. Nov. 19, 1991 / Gramavision 79441

X: The Life and Times of Malcolm X / i. 1992 / Gramavision 79470

Anthony Davis's harrowingly majestic first opera is as revolutionary as its subject, as it rewrites the rules of what opera can and should be. Davis's most striking overhaul of conventional opera is the inclusion of his working ensemble, Episteme, as an integral performance element. At key points, fully formed solos by reedmen Marty Ehrlich, John Purcell, and others give the score a palpable, spontaneous heat that opera rarely offers. The thunder and lightning provided by Pheeroan AkLaff and Warren Smith's traps in ensemble passages provide intense touches. *X* is Davis's most comprehensive expression of what is essentially a melting-pot compositional sensibility. His music is underpinned by a coalition of seemingly disparate influences, including Thelonious Monk, gamelon, and minimalism (the latter being expressed in a decisively reactionary mode). —*Bill Shoemaker*, Down Beat

○ **Undine** / Mesa Blue Moon 8612

ART DAVIS (Artthur D. Davis)

b. Dec. 5, 1934, Harrisburg, PA
Bass / Hard bop, early free

An accomplished technician who's written books on bass, Art Davis has a distinctive sound, touch, and style that's been heard backing vocalists, in orchestras, and in many combos. He also holds a doctorate in clinical psychology. Davis won a national competition as a tuba player, and studied piano before becoming a bassist in 1951. He worked with Max Roach and Dizzy Gillespie in the late '50s, then with Gigi Gryce and Lena Horne. Davis recorded with Booker Little in 1958 and 1961, and with Quincy Jones, Rahsaan Roland Kirk, Oliver Nelson, Freddie Hubbard, Clark Terry, and Art Blakey in the early '60s. Davis worked with John Coltrane before Jimmy Garrison joined the group, and recorded with Coltrane in 1961 and 1965. Davis belonged to three studio orchestras in the '60s: NBC, CBS, and Westinghouse. He taught at Manhattan Community College in the '70s, and became a psychologist first and musician second after earning his doctorate in the '80s. But Davis did record as a leader for AKM and also performed in a duo with pianist Hilton Ruiz in 1985 and 1986. Currently, he has one session available on CD as a leader, and can also be heard on reissues of the Coltrane albums *Ole Coltrane*, *Africa/Brass*, and *Ascension*. —*Ron Wynn*

○ **Life** / Oct. 1985 / Soul Note 1143

Taped, it appears, on a cassette recorder, the live *Life* is marred by muddy sound, comparable to that on bassist Art Davis's *Live!* from which his feature, "Blues From Concertpiece," was reprised. *Life* is most memorable for the leader's aggressive basswork and not for Davis's functional themes, Pharoah Sanders's training (on the modal "Add" especially), or even John Hicks on piano. . . . Even if you're partial to rhythm sections that "know their place," you have to agree: if any bassist has earned the right *not* to be laid-back, it's Art Davis. Perhaps that's why he hot-dogs all over the LP, most strikingly on the vampy title track. Bearing down on the beat, hyperactively walking, he always seems to lean on the band (instead of letting them lean on him). Some bassists prowl the lower register, some feel at home in the cello range: Davis is one of the few who'll walk from one end of the fingerboard to the other, restlessly exploring the instrument's full range with a consistently plump sound. His mastery was so long denied that it's small wonder he seems driven to display it at every opportunity. . . . His work here is a textbook example of busy playing that works. —*Kevin Whitehead*, Cadence

---

CHARLES DAVIS

b. 1933
Baritone and tenor saxophone / Hard bop

A first-rate baritone saxophonist and a good alto player, Charles Davis has been a fine soloist in swing, big-band, bebop, hard bop, and free situations. His baritone work displays his fluid, easy style, huge tone, and great flexibility and range. Davis attended Du Sable High, and later attended the Chicago School of Music. During the '50s, he worked with Brother Jack McDuff, Ben Webster, Billie Holiday, and Dinah Washington. He gained his greatest notoriety playing with Kenny Dorham from 1959 to 1962. He started playing with Sun Ra in the mid '50s, and worked with the Arkestra regularly until 1956, then worked with the group periodically into the '80s. Davis played in the '60s with Illinois Jacquet, Lionel Hampton, and John Coltrane, and led his own group in 1965 and 1966. Davis played for a decade with the Jazz Composers Orchestra, and with Artistry In Music, the Louis Hayes sextet, Clark Terry's B-A-D band, and the Thad Jones-Mel Lewis orchestra in the '70s. Davis formed the Baritone Saxophone Retinue in 1974, with six baritones and a rhythm section. He worked with Barry Harris, Dameronia and the Philly Joe Jones quartet, and Abdullah Ibrahim in the '80s, and did various sessions in New York as a freelance music director. He's recorded as a leader for Strata-East, West, and Nilva. He has one session available as a leader. —*Ron Wynn*

Dedicated to Tadd / i. Jul. 1980 / West 54 8006

This album features some very adventurous, inventive modern mainstream jazz. Like the music of Tadd Dameron, to whom one assumes this date is dedicated, this music wins through its honesty, its beauty, and its artfulness. Charles Davis first turned heads with his full-range baritone work on a '60s Elvin Jones-Jimmy Garrison date, and he was still a marvel, getting a gurgling, darkly tinged sound while continually coming up with the unexpected musical turn of phrase. His tenor voice can be likened to Johnny Griffin's, buoyant and medium-dark, while his soprano, on which he ekes out a thin, pinched stream, could use some work. Since he plays baritone on three cuts here, all is well. While pianist Kenny Barron is a latter-day Bud Powell, spinning out dazzling ideas with grace and ease, and Clifford Adams is a solid trombonist with a mature, peppy tone who solos with extraordinary fluidity, trumpeter Tex Allen is another potentially major figure who remains virtually unknown to the listening public. He's a fine hornman, pushing out bustling phrases with a crackling, Brownie-like tone. He was also a dashing writer: "Love Gods" and "Sir Charles" are his, the rest are by Davis. Bassist Walter Booker's notes ring on forever, and drummer Billy Hart constantly shifts the cymbal thrust to aid in these processes of tension and release. —*Zan Stewart*, Down Beat

---

EDDIE "LOCKJAW" DAVIS (Edward Davis)

b. 1922, New York, NY, **d.** Nov. 3, 1986, Culver City, CA
Tenor saxophone / Bop, hard bop

Fewer nicknames make more sense than Eddie Davis's "Lockjaw." His twisting, slashing solos, done at what seems like impossible tempos, are funky, bluesy, and tough to beat in jam sessions and cutting contests. His performances in twin tenor situations with longtime friend Johnny Griffin or with other friendly rivals, like Sonny Stitt, were wonders to behold. Though he started at Minton's Playhouse, Davis's style and approach were pure swing and blues. Throughout his career, he proved also that he could master bebop changes in any given situation. A self-taught stylist, Davis began at Minton's in the late '30s. He played with Cootie Williams, Lucky Millinder, Andy Kirk, and Louis Armstrong in the '40s. The songs "You Talk a Little Trash" and "Sweet Lorraine" made some impact as singles for Williams's band. Davis did freelance sessions and began making his own groups. He was a bandleader from 1946 on, though he played with Count Basie in 1952, 1953, 1957, and 1964-1973, serving as road manager during the last period. Davis also played in Shirley Scott's organ trio from 1955 to 1960, making many tremendous gutbucket and soulful releases. The early '60s were the heyday of the two-tenor quintet Davis co-led with Johnny Griffin. The two were ideal matches in speed, volume, dynamics, and fervor, and their records were furious dialogues; *Stolen Moments* and *Live at Minton's* were among their finest. There were equally fine releases for RCA; one was another explosive two-tenor set, this time with Paul Gonsalves. Davis reunited with Griffin for a 1970 Pausa album, and he completed his final stint with Basie in 1973. Davis settled in Las Vegas, and made some European appearances. There were new sessions for Classic Jazz, Pablo, Muse, Enja, MPS, and Vogue in the late '70s and '80s. He died in 1986. Reissues have returned most of Davis's dates with Scott, Griffin, and Basie into general circulation, while many of his own sessions are either currently available or are slated to be reissued. —*Ron Wynn and Bob Porter*

○ **Jaws N' Stitt at Birdland** / i. 1954 / Roulette 97507

Big Beat Jazz / Apr. 19, 1955-Feb. 5, 1957 / King 599

○ **Cookbook—Vols. 1, 2 & 3, The** / Jun. 20, 1958-Dec. 15, 1958 / Original Jazz Classics 652-653-756
A pair of new reissues featuring the late-'50s group, with Davis and Shirley Scott (organ) riding herd on the band. —*Ron Wynn*

Jaws / Sep. 12, 1958 / Prestige 218
With Shirley Scott (organ). This is an excellent reissue of this quartet session. —*Ron Wynn*

Best of Eddie Davis and Shirley Scott, The / Sep. 12, 1958-May 1, 1959 / Prestige 7719
With Shirley Scott. Taken from four sessions of Davis with Shirley Scott. —AMG

Very Saxy / Apr. 29, 1959 / Prestige 458
With Buddy Tate, Coleman Hawkins, and Arnett Cobb. Red-hot jam session. Summit meeting of mainstream veterans. —*Ron Wynn*

Jaws in Orbit / May 1, 1959 / Original Jazz Classics 322
Includes Shirley Scott on the Hammond organ. This is early Scott, who was not all that funky yet. Traditional swinging, uptempo music. —*Michael Erlewine*

Trane Whistle / Sep. 20, 1960 / Prestige 429

Griff and Lock / Nov. 4+10, 1960 / Jazzland 264
Here is the hot, combative team of Eddie Davis and Johnny Griffin (ts). —*Ron Wynn*

○ **Tough Tenors** / Nov. 4+10, 1960 / Philips 821293
A rugged workout with Johnny Griffin (ts); Francy Boland (p) and Kenny Clarke (d) are in the rhythm section. —*Ron Wynn*

★ **Live at Minton's** / Jan. 6, 1961 / Prestige 24099
This duo (tenor saxophonists Eddie "Lockjaw" Davis and Johnny Griffin) made about a dozen LPs together, most for Jazzland and Prestige, and they are all worth investigating. They had a special affinity for pianist Thelonious Monk's music, (I hold on to the unpopular belief that Griffin worked with Monk better than any of Monk's other saxmen worked with Monk). While there are other sets that emphasize that belief better, the Monk pieces ("Straight No Chaser"/"In Walked Bud") included in the program on this live set are among the highlights. Pianist Junior Mance, bassist Larry Gales, and drummer Ben Riley round out this January 6, 1961 set. These are tough tenors of the highest order. —*Bob Rusch*, Cadence

○ **Live! the Midnight Show** / Jan. 6, 1961 / Prestige 7330

○ **Live! the Breakfast Show** / Jan. 6, 1961 / Prestige 7407

○ **Lookin' at Monk** / Feb. 7, 1961 / Jazzland 939

Afro Jaws / May 4+12, 1961 / Riverside 403
1989 reissue of a wild, dashing date with Clark Terry (tpt) and Ernie Royal (tpt). —*Ron Wynn*

Love Calls / Aug. 2, 1967 / RCA 3882

Tough Tenors Again 'n Again / Apr. 24, 1970 / PA/USA
Includes robust duet/duels with longtime comrade Johnny Griffin (ts). —*Ron Wynn*

Sweet and Lovely / i. 1975 / Classic Jazz 116

Jaws Strikes Again / Jan. 1976 / Black & Blue 233101

○ **Singin' 'til the Girls Come Home** / i. Mar. 1976 / Steeple Chase 31058
This is almost as fine an Eddie "Lockjaw" Davis album as you could want. That is not to say it is the best Lockjaw album; the best would be an even more subjective decision, but it is as good as his best. Jaws (Davis) follows a pattern of cool to hot as he advances through a tune, immediately leading to crescendos of gruff, macho, Ben Websterish vibrato on tenor, stopping just short of excessive romanticism. The added spark here is provided by drummer Alex Riel, who really keeps the rhythm on its toes by aggressively mixing up the battery, double timing and challenging with snappy punctuations. —*Bob Rusch*, Cadence

Straight Ahead / May 3, 1976 / Pablo 629

Montreux '77 / Jul. 1977 / Pablo 384

Heavy Hitter, The / Jan. 18, 1979 / Muse 5202

Jaw's Blues / Feb. 11, 1981 / Enja 79644
This hard-to-find session is now generally available on CD. Horace Parlan makes an all-too-infrequent guest spot as pianist. —*Ron Wynn*

○ **Eddie Lockjaw Davis** / i. Feb. 1981 / Enja 3097

○ **Simply Sweets** / i. 1982 / Pablo 2310806

○ **Toughness Tenors** / i. 1986 / Milestone 8212932

★ **Stolen Moments** / Prestige 7834

Best of Eddie "Lockjaw" Davis / Bethlehem 6069

JESSE DAVIS

Tenor and alto saxophone / Neo-bop
Jesse Davis is a twenty-something alto sax star who got his start through a recommendation by a jazz critic. The critic, Ira Gitler, was teaching a class on the history of music and was impressed with Davis. Davis's debut Concord session shows he has much promise as a player and writer. He is a spirited, resourceful player whose compositions reflect tradition as well as a personalized approach. —*Ron Wynn*

○ **Horn of Passion** / i. 1989 / Concord Jazz 4465
A solid debut from a saxophonist who was once in a class taught by Ira Gitler. Decent originals and exuberant performances. The CD version has two bonus cuts. —*Ron Wynn*

★ **Young at Art** / i. Mar. 1993 / Concord Jazz CCD-4565
Concord has a reputation for putting out expertly performed, conservative mainstream material with a swing influence. But the label has also been home to some important dates by such atypical acts as the Terence Blanchard/Donald Harrison duo, drummers Art Blakey and Marvin "Smitty" Smith, and outstanding alto saxophonist Jessie Davis. Davis's third release features his alternately poignant, intense, and introspective treatments of such classics as Cole Porter's "I Love Paris," Thelonious Monk's "Ask Me Now," and his own originals "Brother Roj," "Georgiana," and "One For Cannon." He is backed by some youngsters who play with more drive and less relaxed, steady precision, such as guitarist Peter Bernstein, pianist Brad Mehldau, bassist Dwayne Burno, and drummer Leon Parker. Burno's basslines are big and prominently mixed into the arrangements, while Parker's drumming has plenty of kick and Bernstein's accompaniment is tasty and reserved. Davis's hard-blowing statements add the final ingredient to a date that demonstrates Concord's openness to acts who are not within its usual stylistic sphere but are nonetheless deserving of substantial exposure. —*Ron Wynn*

WALTER DAVIS, JR.

b. Sep. 2, 1932, Richmond, VA, **d.** Jun. 2, 1990
Piano / Bop
An often remarkable and inventive bebop and hard bop pianist, Walter Davis, Jr. once left the music world to be a tailor, but returned. He's a solid soloist, bandleader, and accompanist who's amassed a good body of work, but never became a high-profile name, even within the jazz community. Davis played with Babs Gonzales's Three Bips and a

Bop as a teen, then moved from Richmond to New York in the early '50s. He played with Max Roach and Charlie Parker, recording with Roach in 1953. He joined Dizzy Gillespie's band in 1956, and toured the Middle East and South America. He also played in Paris with Donald Byrd in 1958 and with the Jazz Messengers in 1959. After retiring from music for a while to run his tailor shop, Davis returned in the '60s, producing records and writing arrangements for a local New Jersey group. He studied music in India in 1969, and played with Sonny Rollins in the early '70s. Davis had another stint with the Jazz Messengers in 1975, then led his own group in New York. Davis has recorded for Blue Note, Mapleshade, Debut, Denon, Red, and for French labels. He's done sessions with Roach, Rollins, Sonny Criss, Jackie McLean, Pierre Michelot, Archie Shepp, Kenny Clarke, Byrd, and Blakey, among others. Currently, Davis has some dates available on CD. —Ron Wynn

★ **Davis Cup** / Aug. 2, 1959 / Blue Note 4018
Propulsive hard bop with Donald Byrd (tpt) and Jackie McLean (as).—David Szatmary

Blues Walk / **i.** Nov. 23, 1979 / Red 153

○ **In Walked Thelonious** / **i.** Apr. 1991 / Mapleshade 512631
Some spectacular solo playing by Walter Davis, Jr., a severely underrated pianist. He does 15 Monk classics, among them complex works like "Trinkle, Tinkle" and "Panonica," and makes them his own. All the songs are complete first takes, and there is no overdubbing or multitracking, just Davis displaying his brilliance on each cut. —Ron Wynn

MILES DAVIS (Miles Dewey (III) Davis)

b. May 25, 1926, Alton, IL, **d.** Sep. 25, 1991
Trumpet, keyboards, composer, flugelhorn / Bop, cool, early jazz-rock
Miles Davis forged a definitive alternative jazz style that utilized the middle register, relied on carefully constructed, concise solos, was attuned to colors and textures rather than to volume and speed, and kept reshaping itself, though it seldom strayed far from its basic principles. Periodically, Davis changed everything around him, from lineups to musical surroundings. The shifts through cool, modal improvisation, jazz-rock, and funk weren't as jarring as his detractors claimed they were. While the compositions and arrangements evolved through the decades, Davis never abandoned restrained, demure voicings, understated lines, and wonderfully evocative statements.

Miles Davis achieved a symbolic importance that transcended his genre in a dramatic fashion equaled only by Louis Armstrong, John Coltrane, and Duke Ellington. In the '70s and '80s, Davis was a pop icon who played with Prince, recorded Cyndi Lauper and Michael Jackson songs, appeared at the Fillmore, did fashion shots in Rolling Stone, and made guest appearances on "Miami Vice." He taunted and mocked those he considered stylistic and cultural purists, and tweaked many who admired him with provocative racial comments. Davis delighted in his rebellious image, and often made exaggerated, debatable, outright false statements knowing the response they'd generate. Any nonpartisan look at his career must concede his stature as a bandleader, player, and jazz giant was earned largely via his work in the '50s and '60s. He became a larger-than-life cultural symbol in the '70s; even the worst of his '80s releases usually contained some enjoyable sections. Davis's refusal to recycle or to worship past triumphs, and his willingness to confront the future made him an idol, even among those who shuddered at his sexist comments or who cringed when he made acerbic, harsh put-downs of other musicians.

Davis grew up in East St. Louis where he received a trumpet from his father at age 13. He commented often about his middle-class background, usually as a rejoinder to critics who assumed poverty and suffering were essential ingredients for great jazz musicians. During the early '40s, he played in local bands, once meeting Clark Terry in the process. When the Billy Eckstine band came through town, Davis was introduced to Charlie Parker and Dizzy Gillespie.

He went to New York in 1945 to attend Juilliard, but soon preferred the lessons he could get on 52nd street to those in the academy. Davis wound up playing with Parker, Coleman Hawkins, and others, and, by 1947, had been in both Eckstine's and Benny Carter's bands. He recorded that year with Parker, Hawkins, and Illinois Jacquet for Savoy, Dial, and Aladdin, respectively, and was featured on radio broadcasts with Tadd Dameron. Davis then cut sessions heading the Miles Davis All-Stars with Parker. He led a nine-piece band that did broadcasts at the Royal Roost the next year. In 1949 and 1950, arranger Pete Rugolo suggested to Capitol that the company record a library of the group's music. The nonet, which, at various times, included Gerry Mulligan, John Lewis, Gunther Schuller, Junior Colins, John Barber, Lee Konitz, J.J. Johnson, Max Roach, and Kenny Clarke, used arrangements by Gil Evans, Gerry Mulligan, and John Lewis. Their approach featured a subtle, slower pace, less spirited ensemble interaction, and more relaxed solos. *Birth of the Cool* was not a big, or even moderate, success when it was released, but is now acknowledged as a landmark session, the foundation for a fresh jazz direction.

Yet Davis soon moved beyond this fresh direction. Looking for the next direction became a trend that continued through Davis's musical career. He recorded in the early '50s for Prestige, working with Clarke, Johnson, Lucky Thompson, Horace Silver, Percy Heath, Thelonious Monk, and the Modern Jazz Quartet. He made superb combo sessions for the label in the mid '50s. His original 1955 quartet featured bassist Oscar Pettiford, pianist Red Garland, and drummer Philly Joe Jones. While he made other sessions with Charles Mingus and Jackie McLean, Davis's great '50s band began to emerge. Paul Chambers took over bass duties, and John Coltrane joined the band for his first stint. This quartet cut such marvelous dates as *Working, Steamin',* *Cookin',* and *Relaxin'.* Davis penned "Blues By Five" and contributed impressive interpretations of standards such as "If I Were a Bell" and "I Could Write a Book." The quintet made masterpieces out of compositions by other jazz giants, such as Sonny Rollins and Thelonious Monk. Davis's beautiful muted solos, and teeming, mournful, lyricism made a great contrast to the bustling, aggressive Coltrane, and everything was held together by the communication the rhythm section enjoyed.

During the mid '50s, Davis switched labels to Columbia, and began a nearly three-decade relationship that gave him conglomerate promotional muscle and distribution support. A 1958 Newport Jazz Festival appearance with Monk proved a huge hit. Davis also continued a profitable collaboration with Gil Evans, whose arranging foresight and skill, coupled with a deep personal and professional kinship with Davis, yielded more triumphs. *Round Midnight, Miles Ahead,* an all-star date in Paris, a guest appearance on a great Cannonball Adderly LP, and the music for a French film made 1956 and 1957 fabulous years for Davis. He debuted on flugelhorn for *Miles Ahead.* Davis temporarily replaced Coltrane with Sonny Rollins, but Coltrane returned in 1958, and was joined by Cannonball Adderley. Bill Evans replaced Garland, and Jimmy Cobb was the new drummer, replacing Jones. The revised quintet did sessions with Gil Evans that were later issued on *Porgy and Bess.* Davis recorded with Michel Legrand, and the new lineup cut some tracks in Japan. Davis made history in 1959 with *Kind of Blue.* Wynton Kelly replaced Evans on one track. Evans contributed the composition "Blue in Green," while Gil Evans wrote the introduction to the tune "So What," and Bill Evans brought the vamp for the song "Flamenco Sketches." The album included two songs ("So What" and "Flamenco Sketches") based on modes, plus the 12-bar blues "Freddie Freeloader," which included a Benny Goodman/Charlie Christian riff Davis borrowed. *Sketches of Spain* was another wonderful collaboration between Davis and Gil Evans, and featured Joaquin Rodrigo and Manuel de Falla's music.

More changes came in the '60s. Coltrane left again, this time for good. Adderley also departed, and there were problems with temporary replacements Hank Mobley, George

Coleman, Sonny Stitt (briefly), and Sam Rivers, none of whom gave Davis the second soloist or personality he wanted, though all were fine musicians. Ron Carter came on to replace Chambers, after short stints for pianist Victor Feldman and drummer Frank Butler. Youngbloods Herbie Hancock and Tony Williams took piano and drum duties, joined soon after by Wayne Shorter on tenor. The band cut dates in Europe and New York, some of which were issued, while some weren't. By the mid '60s, they'd hit their stride and Davis had once more remade his identity. Now, he headed a dynamic, animated band that devoured loose, open-ended arrangements. Hancock and Shorter were vigorous, soulful players who could drive a song themselves or in conjunction with Carter and Williams. This quintet from 1966 to 1968 made albums that ranked with any Davis ever recorded in a pure jazz context; *Miles Smiles, Nefertiti, Miles in the Sky* and *Filles de Kilimanjaro* were transitional works, inching Davis toward the eclectic, freewheeling music that came in the late '60s and early '70s.

He began using Dave Holland on some tracks instead of Carter, and encouraged Hancock to try electronic piano. By '69, Davis had either Carter or Holland, Hancock, and newcomers Chick Corea and Joe Zawinul plugged in, along with guitar recruit John McLaughlin. Shorter played mostly soprano sax rather than tenor. Davis used the studio as a laboratory, as Ellington had done. A series of marathon sessions were gradually released; albums *In a Silent Way* and *Bitches Brew* jarred jazz fans, excited rock, pop, and R&B audiences, and left many in all camps bewildered. Davis's alternately jagged, melancholy phrases, his use of echoplex and wah-wah, his extensive pauses and repeated phrases, plus his long absences from the mix were notable. Even more noticeable was the melange of riffs, backbeats, and percussive sounds that swirled around. *Bitches Brew* reached the Top 40, and Davis incorporated contributions from an array of musicians: Bennie Maupin, Jack DeJohnette, Billy Cobham, Airto, Steve Grossman, Sonny Fortune, Mtume, Keith Jarrett, Michael Henderson, and Pete Cosey were among the many players who comprised whoever and whatever his working bands were during the early '70s. Sometimes, albums were sprawling two-record sets, or other times were snippets edited into nonstop suites, or were single extended compositions that covered full album sides.

Miles Davis was at the helm of two significant movements in the '60s and '70s. His mid-'60s unit was extremely influential in jazz and rock/pop circles. This unit included: Wayne Shorter, Herbie Hancock, (later Chick Corea, Keith Jarrett, and Joe Zawinul) Ron Carter (later Dave Holland), and Tony Williams (later Jack DeJohnette), plus John McLaughlin, John Scofield, Pete Cosey, Airto and other drummers, percussionists, and supporting musicians. Many of the sidemen in his groups later led seminal bands themselves and continued developing ideas conceived in his group. The mid- to late '60s band played a superb mix of bebop, blues, originals, pop interpretations, and ostinato numbers. They gradually discarded standards and favored a chordless, tonally flexible approach with songs that allowed Hancock, Carter, and Williams to rework and alter the foundation 4/4 beat. The jazz-rock, funk, and instrumental pop bands Davis led merged acoustic and electric sounds with African-American, African, and Asian percussive instrumentation and rhythms. These bands mixed the surging, personalized, solo approach of jazz with the open-ended jamming of rock and blues. They moved beyond a jazz-rock sandwich to a musical salad that could be unwieldy and chaotic, but also could be imaginative and exciting.

Many '70s Davis albums are montages, with his trumpet or keyboard solos weaving in and out of a continuous wave, and other soloists playing on top of vamps, backbeats, and cross-rhythms. His music became more and more popular among the rock, R&B/soul, urban contemporary, and dance audience, while jazz purists, who'd worshipped his classic bebop and cool material, repeatedly gagged. Illnesses and personal problems took their toll on Davis; his '80s albums,

with a couple of exceptions, were highly forgettable. But his mid-'60s and '70s albums were crucial, and remain as memorable as any he ever made. He's one jazz musician who's had the bulk of his material remain in catalog; Columbia has even reissued such classic albums from these periods as *E.S.P., Miles in the Sky, In a Silent Way, Bitches Brew,* and *Jack Johnson.* Unfortunately, caveats must be in place for any and all Columbia reissues. With Columbia, you're always better off with the vinyl original, if you can find it. — *Ron Wynn*

First Miles / i. 1945-1947 / Savoy Jazz 159

Formative tracks that present an immature, though often compelling, trumpeter struggling to develop a style and a sound. Some cuts are with the Herbie Fields band, and others are with Charlie Parker, John Lewis, Nelson Boyd, and Max Roach. This has been reissued on CD. —*Ron Wynn*

○ **Prebirth of the Cool / i. 1949 / Jazz Live 8003**

Here is an LP of enormous significance, something akin to the Dead Sea Scrolls of modern jazz. We all know, and most accept, the classic stature of the Miles Davis Capitol sessions of 1949 and 1950. Well, here, in airchecks from the Royal Roost, is substantially that same repertoire performed in the group's only public engagement a full four months before the first Capitol date. At this time, Davis was seeking an alternative form of expression to that fashioned by master boppers Charlie Parker, Dizzy Gillespie, Fats Navarro, et al. So Davis found a new direction at the confluence of the harmonic essence of bop and the rich ensemble sense Gil Evans and Gerry Mulligan brought to the bands of Claude Thornhill and Gene Krupa-Elliot Lawrence, respectively. The results heard on this record are a highly restrained, sometimes introspective, bop line disciplined still further within the framework of sensitive and detailed scoring. This is true chamber jazz. —*John McDonough,* Down Beat

★ **Capitol Jazz Classics—Vol. 1 (Complete Birth of the Cool)** / Jan. 21, 1949 / Capitol 16168

This LP contains the great Miles Davis 1949-1950 nonet records. It's called *The Complete Birth of the Cool* because, in addition to the 11 tracks originally issued on Davis's American Capitol LP, it includes "Darn That Dream," a piece featuring Kenny Hagood's singing, which was previously unavailable on an American LP. These performances are extraordinarily important; they mark a turning point in the history of jazz, an evolution from bop into a more restrained, writer-oriented music. Davis and altoist Lee Konitz solo superbly, but the stars here are the guys who provided the charts: Gil Evans, Gerry Mulligan, John Lewis, and John Caris. The ensemble sound that Davis's groups produced was unique. This was due, in part, to the instrumentation; it wasn't common in those days for jazz bands to employ tuba and French horn. Combined with baritone sax and trombone, they gave the group a soft, bottom-heavy ensemble sound. The softness of the ensemble textures tends to mask the harmonically advanced quality of the writing. There is dissonance aplenty here. The compositions are excellent, ranging from the bop pieces "Move" and "Budo" to the standard, "Moon Dreams." John Carisi's blues, "Israel," with its unique melody, full of unusual interval skips, is an exceptional piece. There are all sorts of forecasts of things to come in the charts. The greater emphasis on jazz writing in the '50s was stimulated in part by these records. The ensemble voicings were very influential. And there are all sorts of interesting little things happening here, such as Gerry Mulligan using 3/4 as well as 4/4 meter on "Jeru," and Mulligan and Gil Evans writing a few phrases that depart from the standard four-, eight-, and 16-bar units. "Jeru," for example, contains a nine-bar section. —*Harvey Pekar,* Coda

○ **Complete Birth of the Cool / i. 1949 / Pathe 80798**

A historic album featuring Miles Davis playing in a nonet doing arrangements by Gil Evans and Claude Thornhill. Few realized at the time that the session was launching a musical revolution (some would say a counterrevolution.) The album has been reissued and repackaged so many times, it will always be available somewhere. —*Ron Wynn*

And Horns / Jan. 17+19, 1951 / Original Jazz Classics 53
Instructive early-'50s sessions. Miles emerges out of a "cool" bag, Sonny Rollins (ts) is strong, and Al Cohn (ts) and Zoot Sims (ts) participate. —*Ron Wynn*

Conception / Mar. 3, 1951 / Prestige 1726
With Stan Getz and Lee Konitz. Some thrilling playing. A limited-edition reissue. —*Ron Wynn*

★ **Miles Davis: Chronicle—the Complete Prestige Recordings (1951 1956)** / 1951-1956 / Prestige 012
The complete Prestige recordings. This is an unbelievable eight-disc set of 93 performances containing everything on the Prestige label. —*Ron Wynn*

Volume 1 / May 9, 1952+Apr. 20, 1953 / Blue Note 81501

Collector's Items / Jan. 30, 1953-Mar. 1, 1956 / Original Jazz Classics 71
A good bunch of early Miles sessions. Includes cuts with Charlie Parker (as) and Sonny Rollins (ts). —*Ron Wynn*

Miles Davis—Vol. 2 / Apr. 20, 1953 / Blue Note 81502
Some undervalued dates with Jimmy Heath (sax) and J.J. Johnson (t). —*Ron Wynn*

Tune Up / May 9, 1953-Dec. 24, 1954 / Prestige 24077
From four sessions on May 9, 1953, March 15, 1954, April 3, 1954, and December 24, 1954. —*AMG*

○ **Tallest Trees** / May 19, 1953-Oct. 26, 1956 / Prestige 24012
A two-record grab bag anthology that's lost luster with the issuing of boxed sets and reissues. —*Ron Wynn*

○ **Miles Davis Featuring Sonny Rollins** / May 19, 1953+Mar. 15, 1954 / Prestige 161

Miles Davis Plays for Lovers / May 19, 1953-May 11, 1956 / Prestige 7352

Blue Haze / 1953 / Prestige 093
Fine '50s Davis. The presence of seldom-heard David Schildkraut (as) enhances its value. The supporting cast, which includes Charles Mingus (b), John Lewis (p), Horace Silver (p), et al, isn't too shabby either! —*Ron Wynn*

☆ **Bags Groove** / 1954 / Prestige 245
And Modern Jazz Giants. Sterling sessions with Miles and Monk (p), Milt Jackson (vib), Sonny Rollins (ts), and Horace Silver (p). —*Ron Wynn*

Walkin' / 1954 / Prestige 213
Miles Davis All-Stars. This may well be his best single Prestige date. A wonderful session with Lucky Thompson (sax), Horace Silver (p), and Percy Heath (b). —*Ron Wynn*

○ **Miles Davis & The Modern Jazz Giants** / Dec. 24, 1954 / Prestige 347
Good anthology featuring Miles Davis in sessions with Thelonious Monk, Milt Jackson, John Coltrane, Red Garland, Kenny Clarke, and others. Some are just the Miles Davis mid-'50s quartet that also includes Paul Chambers and Philly Joe Jones; others are specific studio dates. This has been reissued on CD. —*Ron Wynn*

Oleo / i. 1954-1956 / Prestige 7847
More late-'50s tracks, some of which were issued domestically under different titles and on other albums. There's absolutely nothing wrong with this album, but it's been deleted. It was originally only available on European import anyhow. —*Ron Wynn*

Musings of Miles, The / 1955 / Prestige 004
This presents the June 7, 1955 session debut for pianist Red Garland with trumpeter Miles Davis along with bassist Oscar Pettiford and drummer Philly Joe Jones. One can almost see (in hindsight) the conceptualization come together. Red Garland remained still a bit tentative. —*Bob Rusch, Cadence*

Dig / 1955 / Original Jazz Classics 5
Tenor saxophonist Sonny Rollins is present as a member of the Miles Davis sextet (alto saxophonist Jackie McLean, pianist Walter Bishop, bassist Tommy Potter, drummer Art Blakey) on *Dig*, which is part of a October 5, 1951 session, all of which is also on a twofer. I love this music, but I have to admit it sounds dated. This isn't Miles Davis's best, but I've always appreciated it for McLean's cutting sax work. —*Bob Rusch, Cadence*

Miles & Monk at Newport / 1955 / CBS 8978
Outstanding sessions recorded at the Newport Festival. Monk's portion rivals the Miles group. —*Ron Wynn*

Green Haze / i. 1955 / Prestige 24064
A two-record set compiling sessions for two exquisite mid-'50s Miles Davis combo albums: *Musing* and *Miles*. There's little to complain about, between Davis's compelling, concise trumpet solos, and a brilliant supporting cast that includes at various times, Philly Joe Jones, Red Garland, Oscar Pettiford, Charles Mingus, Jackie McLean, Paul Chambers, and John Coltrane. —*Ron Wynn*

Blue Moods / Jul. 9, 1955 / Debut 043
This 1955 date with Britt Woodman (trombone), Charles Mingus (bass), Teddy Charles (vibes), and Elvin Jones (drums) departs from the Miles Davis mode that I was content to be comfortable with at the time . . . It isn't typical Davis (note the heavy Mingus coloring on the arrangements credited to Teddy Charles); it was good Davis, but perhaps the most valuable because it *is* a different setting. —*Bob Rusch, Cadence*

☆ **Round About Midnight** / Oct. 27, 1955-Sep. 10, 1956 / Columbia 40610
Everything about this date, from the black-and-white cover photo, washed in red, of Miles Davis, removed in thought behind dark glasses, to the program, to the performances, is classic. Not surprisingly, careful packaging and exquisite artistry have created a legend and, in this case, one of the essential recordings in the history of recorded music. The group: Philly Joe Jones (drums), Paul Chambers (bass), Red Garland (piano), John Coltrane (tenor sax), and Miles Davis (trumpet). —*Bob Rusch, Cadence*

Circle in the Round / i. Oct. 27, 1955-Dec. 4, 1967 / Columbia 46862

New Miles Davis Quintet, The / Nov. 16, 1955 / Prestige 006
Stirring work from the then-emerging group, with John Coltrane (ts) coming of age. —*Ron Wynn*

Basic Miles / i. 1955-1958 / CBS 32025
Great pieces. These, too, should really be heard in their original sessions. Also aimed at the casual Davis listener. —*Ron Wynn*

Paris Festival International, The / i. 1956 / Columbia 34804
Recorded on May 8, 1949 at the Paris Jazz Festival, this valuable document focuses on the bebop roots of Miles Davis. Though Davis had just waxed some of the classic Capitol sides that helped give birth to the cool, he burned with vigorous abandon a few weeks later in Paris. Davis, of course, had apprenticed with bop giants Charlie Parker and Dizzy Gillespie. Nowhere, however, is his mastery of bop more pronounced than on the Paris tracks. On uptempo romps like "Rifftide," "Allen's Alley," and "Ornithology," Davis unfurls dizzying cascades, arpeggios, and flurries along supercharged dramatic trajectories. The same kind of daring is brought to Davis's ballad feature, "Don't Blame Me." His poignant reworking of the melody and his ability to integrate the unexpected brings the standard to new heights. The Paris session also features the fresh assertiveness of tenorist James Moody. His outing on "Good Bait" includes a nice balance among apish runs, bluesy riffs, and effective quotes like that from "Let's Fall in Love." Aside from his compositions "Good Bait" and "Lady Bird," Tadd Dameron's prime contributions are as accompanist. His rich chordal punctuations and supple swingingness help launch Davis and Moody forays. Additional support is provided by the bedrock bass work of Barney Spieler and the impeccable time-keeping of Kenny Clarke. —*Chuck Berg, Down Beat*

☆ **Workin'** / 1956 / Prestige 296

☆ **Steamin'** / 1956 / Prestige 391
Miles Davis Quintet. This is a landmark '50s work. Both the vinyl and the CD reissue are top-flight. —*Ron Wynn*

☆ **Cookin'** / 1956 / Prestige 128
Classic moments were turned in on *Cookin',* an October 26, 1956 date with Miles Davis (trumpet), John Coltrane (tenor sax), Red Garland (piano), Paul Chambers (bass), and Philly Joe Jones (drums) on five tracks. Everything on the date is right, but perhaps special mention should be made of Red Garland, whose solos and comping have, for some, become an integral part of these compositions. —*Bob Rusch,* Cadence

☆ **Relaxin' with the Miles Davis Quintet** / May 11, 1956-Oct. 26, 1956 / Prestige 190

★ **Miles Davis: The Columbia Years 1955-1985** / i. 1956-1986 / CBS 4K45000
This spans his three decades of activity at the company by splitting the 35 featured tunes into five categories: blues, standards, originals, moods, and electric. Columbia has answered critics of this approach by saying this collection wasn't intended for sophisticated or knowledgeable fans and was designed for novices and casual collectors. Assuming that's true, this set doesn't fully serve that audience either. These criticisms don't mean the set is worthless. There are many memorable and notable selections. Still, these four discs don't give the comprehensive accounting of Davis's Columbia years. —*Ron Wynn,* Rock & Roll Disc

Ascenseur Pour L'echafaud / Dec. 4, 1957 / PolyGram 836305
English translation is "Lift to the Scaffold." An interesting mid-'50s soundtrack album. —*Myles Boisen*

'58 Sessions Featuring "Stella By Starlight" / Mar. 4, 1958-May 26, 1958 / Columbia 47835
Some were recorded May 26, 1958. Rare sessions, never available before. Well worth it. —*Michael G. Nastos*

☆ **Miles & Coltrane** / May 17, 1958-Apr. 2, 1959 / Columbia 44052
It is striking to compare John Coltrane's (tenor sax) playing on "Budo" and "Little Melonae" in October 1955 with his work in the sextet in July 1958. His artistic growth in less than three years is astonishing in terms of conception, technique, execution, intensity, and energy. Indeed, Coltrane's solos on these Newport Festival location recordings of "Two Bass Hit" and "Straight, No Chaser" are more complex and highly charged than those on the studio versions (*Milestones*) made only four months earlier. So rapidly was he changing that hearing his development through his recordings of the late fifties and early sixties is like watching time-lapse film of a flower opening. There are moments, particularly on "Straight, No Chaser," when Coltrane not only chews up the changes, he is so ferocious that he sounds as if he's about to consume the saxophone itself. His "Bye Bye Blackbird" solo has all of the searching inventiveness into which Coltrane plunged when he entered his "sheets of sound" period, but also a kind of logical construction that sometimes goes down under waves of emotion and technique. It is a tribute to Cannonball Adderley (alto sax) that he more than holds his own in the face of Coltrane's creative onslaughts. On "Straight, No Chaser" and the fetching "Fran Dance," he has expansive solos demonstrating such individuality that it's a puzzle why he was sometimes described as a Charlie Parker imitator. As for Davis, "Straight, No Chaser" contains some of his best blues playing, with a hip reharmonized approach to phrases that go back to early jazz history, but sound fresh over 30 (1988) years later. . . . He has some absolutely blistering trumpet work on "Ah-Leu-Cha" and lovely examples of his incomparable muted playing in "Bye Bye Blackbird" and "Fran Dance." Bill Evans's solos are fewer and shorter than those of the horn players, but they are typical of the qualities that attracted Davis: rhythmic tension underlying the lyrical, relaxed, occasionally almost laconic, surface of Evans's improvisation. His and Paul

Chambers (bass) solos are cranked up, but their accompaniments are so faint in the recording balance that they sound phoned in, even after manipulation through a reasonably good graphic equalizer. This session does not represent a milestone in live outdoor recording, but anything by Miles Davis and his "Hot Six" is indispensable. "Little Melonae" and "Ah-Leu-Cha" were made around the time Davis moved from Prestige to Columbia and represent the celebrated quintet at its peak. —*Doug Ramsey,* Jazz Times

Jazz at the Plaza Vol. 1 / Sep. 9, 1958 / Columbia 32470
This is the Miles Davis sextet at very nearly peak form; why this session went unreleased for 15 years is therefore a mystery. Two small gripes: the title cut is clearly and unmistakably Monk's "Straight No Chaser" (I don't understand why it was retitled and credited to Miles); and also, pianist Bill Evans and bassist Paul Chambers are miserably underrecorded. I don't give this five stars (4½) because the recording quality is only fair, and because both alto saxophonist Cannonball Adderley and Evans have been better than they are here. And even tenor saxophonist John Coltrane sometimes overdoes the chord-running number. But that's a relative assessment. When the music is good here—as it is more often than not—the solar system is too low a rating. —*Alan Heineman,* Down Beat

☆ **Porgy & Bess** / 1959 / Columbia 40647
Porgy and Bess is one of the perfect collaborations between Miles Davis and Gil Evans. This was recorded at a time (July/August '58) when America was having a renaissance of interest in *Porgy & Bess,* and when numerous jazz interpretations, most of them quite excellent, were released. This pan-genre effort is amazingly successful in satisfying both the joys of orchestration and improvisation, and it does it in deceptively simple, straightforward terms. For this program, Davis is used first as a colorist with great improvisational skills. —*Bob Rusch,* Cadence

☆ **Milestones** / 1959 / Columbia 40837
A heart-stopping session—wonderful Miles, Coltrane (ts), and Cannonball Adderley (as). Again, get the vinyl if you can find it, though this CD reissue isn't as bad as some others. —*Ron Wynn*

★ **Kind of Blue** / Mar. 2, 1959+Apr. 22, 1959 / CBS 40579
Kind of Blue comes from 1959 (March 2 and April 22) and offers up a program that cements the move to modal playing, which had been developing for the previous few years. Here, the mood is pensive and the playing from the group (Cannonball Adderley, alto sax; John Coltrane, tenor sax; Wynton Kelly, Bill Evans, piano; Paul Chambers, bass; Jimmy Cobb, drums; Miles Davis, trumpet) is superb. Many consider this one of the most essential jazz recordings. . . . It is certainly one of the most influential and it really put the cap on an evolutionary development going back to the *Birth of the Cool* sides of ten years earlier. It also brought to a close the Davis-Coltrane-Evans group (Bill Evans actually left the group in '58). —*Bob Rusch,* Cadence

★ **Sketches of Spain** / i. Nov. 20, 1959 / CBS 40578
Sketches of Spain also roots back to the *Birth of the Cool* period and is one of the concept dates on which Miles Davis and Gil Evans collaborated. With undeniable style, Davis's sighs and Evans's water pastels blossom, spread, and absorb into the fabric of the music. And were it not for their stylistic brilliance, this would have been so much mush. However, this team was so brilliant that even in tedium they were terrific. . . . The music was recorded between autumn of both '59 and '60. Davis is the featured horn with various large ensembles arranged and conducted by Gil Evans. —*Bob Rusch,* Cadence

○ **Legendary Concert, Stockholm, March 22, 1960, The** / Mar. 22, 1960 / Natasha 4011
This is a fascinating document taped by Carl-Erik Lundgren, who also conducted the interview with the saxophonist that is included on the album. The six cuts stretch over four sides, with two long versions of "So What" as the centerpiece of the album. The band is top-notch; it includes Wynton Kelly

(piano), Jimmy Cobb (drums), and Paul Chambers (bass). What a pleasure to listen to this rhythm section! Kelly possessed such a sparse, bluesy style, a distillation of Thelonious Monk and Bud Powell. His right hand dances out riffs and funky phrases while his left hand, oh-so-quietly, dishes out infrequent chords. Cobb is letter-perfect, always singing, his cymbal work never intrusive. Chambers, "Mr. P.C.," is in fine form—he latches onto the beat and "walks" it to death. However, Miles Davis and John Coltrane sound like sparring partners. The trumpeter is sparse and melodic, whether he is creating a tiny squall, as on "All Blues," or a muted masterpiece of balladry as on "Fran Dance." Davis leaves space in his solos, whereas Coltrane never stops blowing. He alternates between short phrases and long streams of notes, yet never abandons the beat. His attack is fierce, especially in relation to the rest of the band. This gig was one of the last that the two leaders played. It is filled with jazz and a touch of blues and plenty of class. —*Richard B. Kamins*, Cadence

○ **Someday My Prince Will Come** / 1961 / Columbia 40947
These are transitional, alternately great and uneven 1961 sessions. Coltrane was on his way out, and Hank Mobley struggles in vain to replace him and satisfy Miles. —*Ron Wynn*

In Person: Friday Night at the Blackhawk / Apr. 21, 1961 / Columbia 44257
By the time *Friday Night at the Blackhawk* (55:00) was recorded in 1961, Hank Mobley had replaced John Coltrane in Miles Davis's quintet and Mobley's tenor solo on "All of You"—excised from the original Columbia LP—is a standout reinclusion in the digital remastering of that fine date. Harmon-muted Davis blows crisp, but complete, on some of the last standards we heard from him (the quietly magnificent Wayne Shorter era followed, but Davis's bands suffered from compositorial poverty from the early '70s on). Wynton Kelly (piano) is lifted into better balance on this new reissue; he prances gaily throughout. —*Fred Bouchard, Jazz Times*

In Person: Saturday Night at the Blackhawk / Apr. 22, 1961 / Columbia 44425
Vol. 2. This concert is available in a complete two-disc set and is best heard that way. Hearing only half or part distorts impact and understanding. —*Ron Wynn*

Directions / Apr. 22, 1961-May 21, 1970 / CBS 88514
Recorded within the same month's time as some of the cuts on *Circle in the Round* (1967), "Water on the Pond" and "Fun" (both on *Directions*) are equally delightful, if less ambitious. By November 1968, with Joe Zawinul's tune ("Directions I" and "Directions II") and the multiple pianos of Zawinul, Herbie Hancock, and Chick Corea replacing the guitar, Miles Davis was charging forth without a glance to the past. On *Direction*'s "Ascent," Davis becomes touchingly tender over four restful pianos. He is feisty on "Duran," a slight riff that his sextet didn't know quite how to engage. But he wouldn't let go of that skeletal format, and on the similar "Willie Nelson," he finds John McLaughlin ready for the challenge. There is a steadily held bass pattern, Steve Grossman is allowed to snake along (on sax), and Jack DeJohnette is frankly rockish. McLaughlin's guitar expansively catches up to Davis, without holding him still. On "Konda," Davis sees how far and freely they can fly, McLaughlin and keyboardist Keith Jarrett twining harmony and rhythm, while Airto Moreira's percussion is mostly for color. —*Howard Mandel*, Down Beat

Live Miles: More Music from the Legendary Carnegie Hall Concert / May 19, 1961 / Columbia 40609
More *Music From the Legendary Carnegie Hall Concert*. These are vault items that didn't make it onto the original 1961 concert recording.

At Carnegie Hall / 1962 / CBS 8612
Transitional early-'60s sessions. Hank Mobley (sax) tries hard, but doesn't really fill Coltrane's shoes. With good Gil Evans orchestra cuts. —*Ron Wynn*

☆ **Miles Ahead** / 1962 / Columbia 40784

The first of CBS's Miles Davis-meets-Gil Evans dates, this recording was acclaimed, and rightly so, on its initial release. Davis plays flugelhorn, an instrument which seemed to suit him better than trumpet: more full-bodied, less shrill, it glosses over his technical deficiencies. Evans's charts were recorded May 6, 10, 23, and 27, 1957 (36:52), and hint at the cathedral resonances of his *Out of the Cool* to come. Evans brought out the best in Davis, and this is an early glimpse at the arranger's mature style. The sound is nice and crisp. —*Kevin Whitehead*, Cadence

Sorcerer / Aug. 21, 1962-May 24, 1967 / Columbia 9532
This vigorous 1967 session has nonmusical significance: Miles put Cicely Tyson's face on the album cover, which scored points for visual impact and the image of Black women. —*Ron Wynn*

☆ **Quiet Nights** / 1962-1963 / CBS 8906

Seven Steps to Heaven / Apr. 16, 1963+May 14, 1963 / CBS 48827
Miles Davis recorded half of this heavily edited 1963 album, *Seven Steps to Heaven*, in Hollywood, and half in New York. Featured are pianist/composer Victor Feldman and drummer Frank Butler (Hollywood), tenor saxist George Coleman, and the rhythm section of pianist Herbie Hancock, bassist Ron Carter, and drummer Tony Williams for the first time (NY). Carter and Coleman were the only holdovers for both sessions. The material is played in a style reminiscent of *Someday My Prince Will Come* (1961): smooth, polished, yet without John Coltrane's heat. The West Coast band's tendency to double-time the slower tunes gives their music a slightly generic quality (Butler's distracting, repetitive snare clicks leading the charge). Despite this, the band's extended treatments of old favorites "Basin Street Blues" and "Baby, Won't You Please Come Home" are memorable. The East Coast band is clearly the more integrated. Definitive, albeit tame, studio versions of "Seven Steps" and Feldman's "Joshua" are slower, elongated progeny for what was to follow in live settings. —*John Ephland*, Down Beat

Miles Davis in Europe / Jul. 26-29, 1963 / Columbia 8983

Miles in Antibes / Jul. 27, 1963 / CBS 6239

○ **Miles in Tokyo** / Jul. 14, 1964 / Columbia 162

★ **My Funny Valentine** / 1965 / CBS 9106
Originally issued as two individual records (one of mostly ballads, the other of cookers), these releases chronicle 1965 sessions at a benefit concert held in New York's Philharmonic Hall at Lincoln Center. Tenor saxophonist George Coleman turns in some inspired playing (according to Miles Davis, his best), particularly on "My Funny Valentine" and Davis's "All Blues" (a late-'50s holdover waltz given an uptempo shot of R&B). Pianist Herbie Hancock, bassist Ron Carter, and drummer Tony Williams all perform with grace, poise, and fire. But it's Davis who plays some of his most impassioned trumpet on record. Gone was the need for formal statements and adherence to melodic shape and contour. Williams's drum solos remain free of the pulse as he chooses to extend the drums' range as a musical instrument. The '60s avant-garde impinges in subtle, delightful ways, providing clues to this transitional band's method of deconstruction. —*John Ephland*, Down Beat

Facets / 1965 / CBS 62637
Various mid- and late-'50s sessions by Miles Davis combos; some performances are great, some are erratic. The album was originally issued in Europe and available only as an import; it has since been deleted. —*Ron Wynn*

Cookin' at the Plugged Nickel / 1965 / Columbia 40645
This session is a CD's worth of more material from the *Live At The Plugged Nickel* sessions recorded at the end of 1965. It has additional songs culled from the club date that feature Miles Davis on trumpet, Herbie Hancock on piano, bassist Ron Carter, saxophonist Wayne Shorter, and drummer Tony Williams. There's also a Japanese import version available, *Complete Live At Plugged Nickel 1965). —John Ephland*, Down Beat

Live at the Plugged Nickel / i. 1965 / CBS 88606
Recorded at the end of 1965, after the innovative January recording of *E.S.P.* and following three canceled engagements at the now-defunct Chicago club due to Davis's serious health problems, the music here has been doled out in parts stateside. It's the clasic quintet blowing standards and blues similiar to the February 1964 concert *My Funny Valentine + Four & More*, with one from the new book, *E.S.P.*, "Agitation." Not surprisingly, there's a fair amount of consistency throughout: the band sounds real loose (Davis's sounds loaded more often than not), playing with a club—as opposed to a more formal concert hall—approach. Of the main soloists, pianist Herbie Hancock gets less time; saxophonist Wayne Shorter is the standout. A blues sensibility pervades whether the music is "Stella By Starlight," "All Of You," or "All Blues"; the recording quality (stereo) is generally very good, with, for example, Tony Williams's deft cymbal and brushwork a marvel, and the occasional off-mic playing of Davis and Shorter adding to the feel of a "you are there" club date. —*John Ephland*, Down Beat

○ **E.S.P.** / Jan. 20-22, 1965 / Columbia 46863
One of numerous mid-'60s standout albums by the great band with Wayne Shorter (sax), Herbie Hancock (p), Ron Carter (b), and Tony Williams (d). Get the vinyl album if at all possible; Columbia's new reissue leaves a lot to be desired. —*Ron Wynn*

In Berlin / 1966 / CBS 62976

☆ **Four & More** / 1966 / CBS 9253
Good material from the mid-'60s period. Herbie Hancock (p) has fine solos. —*Ron Wynn*

Miles Smiles / 1966 / Columbia 48849
This session was issued in 1966. *Miles Smiles* features four originals and one each from composer/saxophonists Eddie Harris and Jimmy Heath. Miles Davis's exquisite waltz, "Circle," showcases his lyrical, muted-trumpet playing laden with sighs, slurs, and the occasional high note. Saxophonist Wayne Shorter and pianist Herbie Hancock follow suit. The rest of the album, however, is more interested in experiments begun with *E.S.P.*'s more aggressive, modal side. Hancock lays out during Davis's and Shorter's solos, with a solo-piano style more hornlike in conception. He forsakes chords for single notes in the treble clef; with scaled-down melodies with few or no harmonic references. (However devised, *Miles Smiles* clearly shows Ornette Coleman's invisible hand.) With a simpler, more austere (and relatively pianoless) sound, the unrehearsed rough *Miles Smiles* holds up so well because it was more of a *jazz* record, spontaneous warts and all. —*John Ephland*, Down Beat

Water Babies / 1966-1968 / CBS 34396
A grab bag sampler of various Miles Davis items that were in the vault from sessions he'd done for Columbia. They issued this during the long time that Davis was off the recording scene recovering from illnesses. There's pre-*Bitches Brew* tracks and other combo pieces. It's nothing extraordinary, but there are some nice cuts, especially the title number. —*Ron Wynn*

Nefertiti / 1967 / Columbia 46113
This tremendous late-'60s cut gives you transcendent Wayne Shorter (sax). I can't say the same about the lackluster Columbia remastering of the new reissue. —*Ron Wynn*

Miles in the Sky / May 15-17, 1968 / Columbia 48954
This suggestive, prophetic date is clearly inching toward *In a Silent Way* and *Bitches Brew* territory. —*Ron Wynn*

Filles de Kilimanjaro / Jun. 20+21, 1968 / Columbia 46116
Filles de Killimanjaro is notable, in part, for its personnel changes (it was the classic quintet's last record) and the total absence of swing rhythms, as well as acoustic keyboards (contrary to the liner note references). Recorded on the heels of *Miles in the Sky*, and at two different points (June and September), the later recordings of "Frelon Burn" and "Mademoiselle Mabry" introduced many fans to keyboardist Chick Corea and English bassist Dave Holland, replace-

ments for Herbie Hancock and Ron Carter. (The new liner notes also maintain incorrect keyboard and bassist personnel for "Frelon Burn" and "Petit Machins," and wrongly note the presence of acoustic basses.) The stylistic precursor to the ever-popular *In a Silent Way* of 1969, *Filles* is performed (and edited) like a suite, with a sense of flow unlike anything Davis had recorded up to that point. As for the classic quintet tracks, "Petit Machins," "Toute de Suite," and "Filles de Kilimanjaro," noted Miles Davis biographer Jack Chambers observes that the band went beyond their usual minimal structures and searched for a common mood, asking listeners to "discover the unity of the pieces instead of just locating it, as viewers must discover the unity in a painting with several simultaneous perspectives." You might say these pieces are a fitting climax to four-plus years of growth from Messrs. Hancock, Carter, Tony Williams, and Wayne Shorter under Miles Davis. In passing, *Filles de Kilimanjaro* is a turning point album unlike any other for Davis: for the first time, his bebop roots were essentially severed, and rockier rhythms, electricity, and ostinato-driven basslines held sway. —*John Ephland*, Down Beat

☆ **In a Silent Way** / 1969 / Columbia 40580
In a Silent Way was recorded on January 18, 1969 and brought Miles Davis together with members of his brilliant group of the '60s (Herbie Hancock/Wayne Shorter/Tony Williams) and emerging musical spirits (Chick Corea/Dave Holland/Joe Zawinul/John McLaughlin), who would launch Davis into the *Bitches Brew* era. On *In a Silent Way*, Davis moves away from "Tunes" while utilizing more electric instrumental coloring and rockish patterns and splicing to manufacture the music, ideas which seemed to take hold a year after his stunning Plugged Nickel recordings. Here, the music continues to show the distinct Davis use of suspension and space, but it is more amorphic and no longer seems rooted in a clear, direct emotion, but is rather indirectly emotional in an illusive sense of reality. —*Bob Rusch*, Cadence

★ **Bitches Brew** / 1970 / Columbia 40577
By the time *Bitches Brew* came along, the new Miles Davis direction was fixed. Recorded just six months after *In a Silent Way*, the music here confused Davis's old fans, but its pop-funky cover art and music quickly sent a message that was picked up by a younger rock audience. I remember my reaction at the time was surprisingly ambivalent. This to me was not *great Black music*, but I cynically saw it as part and parcel of the commercial crap that was beginning to choke and bastardize the catalogs of such dependable companies as Blue Note and Prestige.... I hear it "better" today because there is now so much music that is worse. And relative to his hoary legacy, this shines and is one of the mile markers on a dubious trail. A new musical direction of note, but not, up to this point, a great musical direction. Some may celebrate the talents here of Wayne Shorter, Lenny White, Bennie Maupin, Chick Corea, Jim Riley, Jack DeJohnette, Harvey Brooks, Charles Alia, Dave Holland, John McLaughlin, Joe Zawinul, and Larry Young.... *Bitches Brew*, some of the best of its genre. —*Bob Rusch*, Cadence

Live–Evil / Feb. 6, 1970 / CBS 30954
Here is more transitional early-'70s material. Davis was increasing his R&B and rock content and approach. He plays plenty of organ and wah-wah electric trumpet. Includes fierce solos by Gary Bartz (sax). —*Ron Wynn*

★ **Tribute to Jack Johnson** / Feb. 18, 1970 / Columbia 47036
Superior soundtrack/tribute. Arguably better than any pop/R&B/rock-tinged set, even *Bitches Brew*. Recently reissued on disc. With John McLaughlin (g), Herbie Hancock (k), Steve Grossman (sop sax), Billy Cobham (d), and Michael Henderson (b). —*Ron Wynn*

At the Fillmore / Jun. 17, 1970 / Columbia 30038
Raucous, roughhouse live set; Miles is totally plugged in. Steve Grossman (sop sax) and multiple keyboards—roaring, spewing, and exploding. —*Ron Wynn*

Miles Davis—Vol. 3 / Nov. 26, 1971 / AJ 503
On the Corner / 1973 / CBS 31906

Big Fun / 1974 / One Way 21398

While *Big Fun* is far from prime Davis, it's arresting, sometimes entertaining, and, in its own way, quite representative of his overall work. A two-disc set. — *Ron Wynn, Rock & Roll Disc.*

Get up with It / 1974 / CBS 33236

Agharta / 1975 / Columbia 46799

A CD reissue of a pivotal rock-oriented date. It has rambling, extensive solos with a loose feel. Miles plays keyboards as well as trumpet. There are funk backings with torrid sax by Sonny Fortune and explosive guitar by Pete Cosey. Jazz purists were scandalized. — *Ron Wynn*

Pangaea / i. Feb. 1, 1975 / CBS 46115

There are only two cuts on it, both over 40 minutes in length, and the results are at once intriguing, chaotic, inspired, and maddening. A two-disc set. — *Ron Wynn, Rock & Roll Disc.*

○ **Heard 'round the World** / i. Apr. 1984 / Columbia 238506

Either trying to impress his Japanese audience or simply feeling grand, Miles Davis opens what has long been known as *Miles in Tokyo* fast and happy. The classy young rhythm trio he'd had for a year immediately ignites— Tony Williams a sizzle on his cymbals, bassist Ron Carter so low as to seem subliminal but dependably *there*, pianist Herbie Hancock chording cautiously as though to tend a small blue flame. Then Sam Rivers's tenor bursts forth, scorching the changes and threatening to flare out of control. He doesn't. The trio rises to his pitch and, after three quick choruses in which Rivers singes the edge, regroups behind Hancock, who simmers prettily, like Red Garland. They lay back, under Davis's second, unhurried turn. Davis dares much, trying tempo suspensions, extending his personal technique, sense of harmony, and intonation throughout both the Tokyo and *Miles in Berlin* concerts included on this album. But he insists the second horn, like the rhythm section, underline *his* directions. While Rivers is masterly, emotional, and to the point, there is a hint of friction; at least, the sparks are flying. When Wayne Shorter takes over (on sides three and four) the Quintet still sounds inspired—and, overall, better balanced. The Berlin program is similar to the Tokyo one; Davis again flourishes his singular skills, command, and direct expressiveness. Shorter gets around his tenor as impressively as Rivers, but his attack is not so startlingly ferocious, and his emphasis is less exaggerated. — *Howard Mandel, Down Beat*

Aura / Jan. 1985 / Columbia 45332

This is a very different type of Miles record: A ten-part suite in which he weaves in and out. The moods, feel, and sound keep shifting, thanks to Palle Mikkelborg's compositions and arrangements. — *Ron Wynn*

Tutu / 1986 / Warner Brothers 25490

Music from Siesta / 1987 / Warner Brothers 25655

The ads for the album said "More Than a Soundtrack," but, in fact, this is more of a soundtrack than any composition in recent memory. It is not a collection of compositions as much as a collage of erotic moods. Tracks fade in and out, such as the "Lost in Madrid I through V" themes, and some pieces were so obviously meant to accompany moody visual scenes that one nearly wishes one can watch as well as listen. This is not to say that the album is unlistenable. Indeed, it is interesting and evocative, built on rich classical Spanish motifs and full of lusty woodwinds and castanets and lots of haunting synthesizers. But the avid listener may find himself inexplicably longing for a sip of Sangre de Toro and thinking of things other than the music. The album is often reminiscent of the collaboration between Miles Davis and Gil Evans several decades ago, *Sketches of Spain.* Davis plays those same piercing and muted trumpet solos with pathos and aplomb. This time, thought, the rhythms are augmented by squishy electronic sound and much of the recording technology that the '80s offered. The pieces (somehow that term is very appropriate) are passionate and melancholic. All in all, it is great background music for a seduc-

tion. Maybe that is what they mean by "More Than a Soundtrack". — *Denny Townsend,* Jazz Times

Amandla / 1989 / Warner Brothers 25873

Although nearing the end of his life, Miles plays surprisingly well here. Standard fusion/pop textures provided by Marcus Miller. — *Ron Wynn*

Ballads / i. 1989 / Columbia 44151

These are beautiful, timeless pieces, but should really be heard in their original, intact sessions. This is aimed at casual Davis listeners, novices, or new fans. — *Ron Wynn*

Live at Montreaux / i. 1991 / Warner Brothers 45221

Though Miles Davis did not live to participate in Gerry Mulligan's reunion recordings featuring the nonet that played on the famous late '40s and early '50s "cool" sessions, he did participate in a reunion concert held at Montreux in 1991. This featured both the Gil Evans Orchestra and George Gruntz Concert Jazz Band, plus additional guests Benny Bailey, Grady Tate, Carles Benavent, and various European players. They teamed with Davis to perform Gil Evans's marvelous arrangements. Quincy Jones conducted and conceived the idea of using two orchestras, creating a rich, vital tapestry with reeds and woodwinds offering majestic surroundings for the solos of Davis, fellow trumpeter Wallace Roney, and alto saxophonist Kenny Garrett. Davis was gravely ill, but he manages here to generate memories of the beautiful melodies and entrancing, floating solos of past years. He teams with Roney on "Miles Ahead" in the last chorus and makes clear the difference between teacher and pupil. Roney has been lambasted for a stylistic mimicry of Davis, but he does not imitate here as much as praise his mentor with mellow, striking passages and phrases. Garrett, a fine player in need of one or two great albums to verify his standing, plays with vigor, expressiveness, and depth. Not every moment is golden, but the overall session ranks just a bit below the majestic '50s and '60s dates featuring Miles Davis's trumpet and Gil Evans's arrangements. — *Ron Wynn*

Doo-Bop / 1992 / Warner Brothers 26938

If *On the Corner* suggested hip-hop beats as far back as two decades ago, then consider *Doo-Bop* as offspring. Miles's teaming with producer Easy Mo Bee is a natural—more in league with England's acid jazz scene than anything in the trumpeter's recent canon. Those who've howled over the post-*Bitches Brew* work will find no solace here; instead, chalk this up as one of Miles's most entertaining efforts. — *Steve Aldrich*

NATHAN DAVIS (Nathan Tate Davis)

b. Feb. 15, 1937, Kansas City, KS

Tenor saxophone, educator / Hard bop

An important educator, Nathan Davis has also been a fine player in hard bop and free circles. A strong tenor saxophone soloist, Davis played trombone in high school before turning to clarinet and tenor. He won a scholarship to the University of Kansas, earned his BA in music education, and led a hard bop band that included Carmell Jones. While in the army, Davis was stationed in Berlin and worked in a band. He met and played with Benny Bailey. Davis remained in Europe after his discharge, playing in Paris with Kenny Clarke, Donald Byrd, Art Taylor, and Eric Dolphy, and touring Europe with Art Blakey and the Jazz Messengers in 1965. Davis began cutting albums as a leader in the mid '60s, working with Woody Shaw, Sir Roland Hanna, Richard Davis, Jones, Clarke, and Taylor, among others. He returned to America in 1969, and became director of jazz studies at the University of Pittsburgh. Davis earned a doctorate in ethnomusicology from Wesleyan, and his history of jazz, *Writings in Jazz,* was published in 1985. He's mixed performing and recording with teaching in the '80s and '90s. Davis organized the Paris Reunion Band, an octet that toured Europe, in 1985 as a tribute to Clarke. He's recorded for Saba, Hot House, Segue, and Sonet, among others.

Currently, none of his sessions are available on CD in America. —*Ron Wynn*

★ **Makatuka** / 1971 / Segue 1000

Sixth Sense in the Eleventh House / 1972 / Segue 1002

RICHARD DAVIS

b. Apr. 15, 1930, Chicago, IL
Bass / Bop, hard bop

Richard Davis is a superb bass technician who doesn't have an extensive recorded legacy. Davis has a wonderful tone, is excellent using either the bow or his fingers, and stands out in any situation. He has been a remarkable free, bebop, and hard bop player, has served in world class symphony orchestras, has backed vocalists, and has engaged in stunning duets with fellow bassists. When playing the bass, he does any and everything well: playing accompaniment, playing solos, working with others in the rhythm section, responding to soloists, or playing unison passages. He combines upper-register notes with low sounds coaxed through the use of open strings. Davis studied privately for nearly ten years in the '40s and '50s, while playing with Chicago orchestras. He played with Ahmad Jamal, Charlie Ventura, and Don Shirley in the early and mid '50s, then worked with Sarah Vaughan in the late '50s and early '60s, and with Kenny Burrell. In the '60s, Davis divided his duties between recording and performing sessions with jazz musicians and freelance work with symphony orchestras conducted by Leonard Bernstein and Igor Stravinsky. He recorded often with Eric Dolphy, including the unforgettable dates at the Five Spot. He also worked with Booker Ervin, Andrew Hill, Ben Webster, Stan Getz, Earl Hines, and the Creative Construction Company. Davis teamed with Jaki Byard and Alan Dawson on sessions with Ervin, and teamed with others like Rahsaan Roland Kirk. He also played with Van Morrison. During the '70s, Davis worked with Hank Jones and Billy Cobham, and was a member of the Thad Jones-Mel Lewis Orchestra in the '60s and '70s. Davis left New York in 1977 to teach at the University of Wisconsin in Madison, where he remained into the mid '80s. He appeared at the Aurex Jazz Festival in Tokyo in 1982, playing in a jam session led by trombonists J.J. Johnson and Kai Winding, and at the 1984 Chicago Jazz Festival. Davis was featured in the 1982 film *Jazz in Exile*. He's done relatively few recordings as a leader, though three Muse sessions are now available on CD. The superb *The Philosophy of the Spiritual,* which matched Davis and fellow bassist Bill Lee, is not in print or on CD. —*Ron Wynn*

○ **Philosophy of the Spiritual** / 1971 / Cobblestone 9003

Epistrophy / Now's the Time (Recorded Live at Jazz City) / Sep. 7, 1972 / Muse 6005

Dealin' / Sep. 14, 1972 / Muse 5027

★ **Harvest** / May 3, 1977 / Muse 5115
Premier bassist with groups of varying size. Most interesting listening for the adventurous jazz lover. —*Michael G. Nastos*

With Understanding / i. 1978 / Muse 5083

Way out West / i. 1981 / Muse 5180

Heavy Sounds / Impulse

WILD BILL DAVIS

b. 1918
Organ, piano / Swing, big band

Wild Bill Davis is fine organist, pianist, and arranger who's worked with many big bands and major figures. Davis learned music from his father, a professional singer. He studied music at Tuskegee and Wiley College, then moved to Chicago. Davis played guitar and wrote arrangements for Milt Larkin in the late '30s and early '40s. Then he provided arrangements for Earl Hines and Louis Jordan in the '40s, and also played piano for Jordan. During the '50s, Davis began playing organ and heading his own groups, mostly trios. He also kept writing arrangements, among them one for "April in Paris" by Count Basie in 1955. Davis recorded with

Johnny Hodges and Ella Fitzgerald, among others, in the '60s, then toured and recorded with Duke Ellington from 1969 to 1971. He served as an arranger, organist, and second pianist. Davis toured extensively in the '70s, recording in Paris with Buddy Tate, Al Grey, Slam Stewart, and Illinois Jacquet. He worked with Lionel Hampton in the late '70s and early '80s, led his own group in Europe, and has played at several festivals in the '80s and '90s. —*Ron Wynn*

○ **Wild Bill Davis at Birdland** / Mar. 21, 1955 / Epic 3118

WILD BILL DAVISON (William Stethen Davis)

b. Jan. 5, 1906, Defiance, OH, **d.** Nov. 14, 1989
Cornet / Dixieland

A traditional jazz mainstay who alternated between a flamboyant, combative style on uptempo tunes and a more sentimental, lyrical style on ballads, Wild Bill Davison was active on the jazz scene from the late '20s until the late '80s. Though he was never one of the most elaborate players, Davison parlayed an expressive, dusky tone and distinctive approach that developed greatly from his early days when he patterned his solos after Bix Beiderbecke's. Davison's favorite instrument was cornet, and, during the '30s and early '40s, he also played B-flat valve trombone as well as trumpet. He overcame a lip injury in the '30s. In his teens, Davison played and toured with local Ohio bands, before moving to Chicago. He worked in Chicago from the late '20s to the early '30s, before forming his own band with Frank Teschemacher. He moved to Milwaukee after Teschemacher died, and led various combos. Davison settled in New York in 1941, attracting a great deal of attention with his great Commodore recordings (which featured Pee Wee Russell and George Brunis). After a stint in the army during World War II, he became closely associated with Eddie Condon. Davison was a regular at Condon's clubs during the '40s and '50s, made many recordings, and often headed his own hot groups. With his powerful yet relatively sparse lead, his surprising placement of high notes, and his colorful musical personality (which alternated and sometimes combined sarcasm with sentimentality), Davison was the definitive Dixieland trumpeter. He toured Europe often from the '60s on, played with the Jazz Giants in the late '60s, and kept a very busy schedule until his death. Davison recorded for many labels, among them Savoy, Storyville, Jazzology, Real Time, Sackville, and Audiophile. Davison's reissued sessions are available on CD. They amount to one of the most extensive collections of reissued material of any traditional jazz musician. —*Ron Wynn*

★ **Jazz A-Plenty** / Nov. 27+30, 1943 / Commodore 7011

That's a Plenty / Nov. 27, 1943 / Commodore 14939
Lots of Pee Wee Russell (cl) and George Brunis (t) from old 78s. Nice album to find. —*Michael G. Nastos*

Mild and Wild / Nov. 27+30, 1943 / Commodore 30009

And His Jazz Band, 1943 / Dec. 3, 1943 / Jazzology 103

This Is Jazz—Vol. 1 / Dec. 27, 1947 / Storyville 4067
Sessions with the All-Star Stompers, including George Brunis, Albert Nicholas, Ralph Sutton, Danny Barker, Pops Foster, Baby Dodds, and James P. Johnson. —*Michael G. Nastos*

★ **Individualism Of . . .** / Nov. 7, 1951 / Savoy 2229
1951 sessions at Eddie Condon's in Boston. Features Cutty Cutshall (t), Ed Hall (cl), George Wein (p), and Buzzy Drootin (d). Sextet and septet recordings with two different groups. Dixie to swing standards by the master cornetist. Twenty-three cuts. —*Michael G. Nastos*

Ringside at Condon's / Dec. 10, 1951+Jan. 28, 1952 / Savoy 403
1951 and 1952. Another great swinger with Hall, Cutshall, Drootin, Condon, Cliff Leeman, and others. —*Michael G. Nastos*

Wild Bill Davison with Helen Ward / Apr. 1952 / Paradox 6004

○ **Blowin' Wild** / Feb. 14, 1965 / Jazzology 18

○ **"Wild" Bill Davison/Papa Bue's Viking Jazz Band** / **i.** Feb. 1974 / Storyville 4029

Live at the Rainbow Room / 197z / Chiaroscuro 124

Plays Hoagy Carmichael / Jul. 1981 / Real Time 306
Good record introducing guitarist Howard Alden. Great work from tenor saxophonist Eddie Miller. —*Michael G. Nastos*

○ **Together Again** / Storyville 4027

S' Wonderful / Jazzology 181

ALAN DAWSON

b. 1929
Drums / Bop, hard bop
Both an outstanding drummer and a heralded instructor, Alan Dawson has tutored many first-rate players, and has been showcased on several excellent recordings. His taste, rhythmic sophistication, and drive have been highly praised by musicians and critics alike. Dawson studied with Charles Alden in Boston during the early '50s, and worked with Sabby Lewis. He toured with Lionel Hampton in 1953, played with Lewis again from '53–56, then joined the faculty at Berklee in 1957. He remained there until the mid '70s. Some of Dawson's pupils during that stint included Tony Williams, Clifford Jarvis, Harvey Mason, and Joe LaBarbera. He was also an early mentor to Terry Lyne Carrington, who he spotted working in Boston clubs when she was still a youngster. Dawson did many local gigs as well, and backed visiting greats like Rahsaan Roland Kirk and Sonny Stitt during their dates. His steady, crisply paced drumming with Jakie Byard, Booker Ervin, Tal Farlow, and Dexter Gordon was highlighted on several outstanding Prestige albums in the '60s and '70s, and he was in Dave Brubeck's quartet from 1968 to 1974. Dawson continued to teach privately after leaving Berklee, and has published several instructional manuals. Though he didn't issue any sessions as a leader, Dawson can be heard prominently on many CD reissues by Brubeck, Ervin, Byard, Gordon, and others. —*Ron Wynn*

SIDNEY DE PARIS (De Paris, Sidney)

b. May 30, 1905, Crawfordsville, IN, **d.** Sep. 13, 1967, New York, NY
Trumpet, tuba / New Orleans traditional
Trumpeter and tuba player Sidney De Paris was able to fit his distinctive sound successfully into both traditional jazz and swing bands, showing expertise with mutes and a bright, open sound. He studied music with his father, then worked in the bands of Charlie Johnson and Don Redman in the '20s and '30s, as well as doing some recording with Jelly Roll Morton in 1939. De Paris worked with Zutty Singleton from 1939 to 1941, then played with Benny Carter, Art Hodes, Roy Eldridge, Claude Hopkins, and Sidney Bechet in the '40s. From 1943 until 1967, he was best known for playing with his brother, Wilbur De Paris, in various traditional groups. —*Ron Wynn*

★ **Original Blue Note Jazz—Vol. 2** / Mar. 18, 1944-Oct. 26, 1944 / Blue Note 6506

○ **Sidney Deparis's Blue Note Stompers** / Jun. 14, 1951 / Blue Note 7016

His Rampart Street Ramblers / **i.** 1952 /

WILBUR DE PARIS (De Paris, Wilbur)

b. Jan. 11, 1900, Crawfordsville, IN, **d.** Jan. 3, 1973, New York, NY
Bandleader, trombone / New Orleans traditional
Wilbur De Paris helped keep New Orleans jazz alive from the '20s through the '70s. He started as an alto horn player and played, for a while, with his father's circus band. While visiting New Orleans in 1922, De Paris played C-melody saxophone with Louis Armstrong and worked with A.J. Piron. He led bands in Philadelphia during the mid '20s before coming to New York in 1928. In New York, he recorded and performed with LeRoy Smith, Dave Nelson, Edgar Hayes,

and Noble Sissle, with whom he toured Europe in 1931. De Paris made another European tour in 1936 and '37 with Teddy Hill's band, and recorded with the Mills Blue Rhythm Band in 1937. When Armstrong called in 1937, De Paris answered the summons and remained with the band until 1940. After that, De Paris headed his own groups, and also worked with Ella Fitzgerald. De Paris was a member of Duke Ellington's orchestra from 1945 to 1947. De Paris recorded with Sidney Bechet in 1946, 1949, and 1950. There was an 11-year stint for De Paris at Ryan's in New York; he led a house band that included his brother, Sidney De Paris, and Omer Simeon. De Paris also made a State Department-sponsored trip to Africa in 1957, and worked as both a leader and an arranger until 1972. —*Ron Wynn*

And His Rampart Street Ramblers / Sep. 11, 1952 / Atlantic 141,143

New New Orleans Jazz / Apr. 2, 1955+Apr. 8, 1955 / Atlantic 1219

At Symphony Hall / Oct. 26, 1956 / Atlantic 1253

Plays Cole Porter / Feb. 25, 1957-May 26, 1958 / Atlantic 1288

★ **New Orleans Blues** / Oct. 31, 1957 / Atlantic 1266

Wild Jazz Age, The / May 9+10, 1960 / Atlantic 1336

ELTON DEAN

b. Oct. 28, 1945, Nottingham, England
Alto saxophone, saxello / Modern creative
One of England's better free music soloists, Elton Dean has been both a leader and a busy session musician during the '60s, '70s, and '80s. He played in Bluesology with Long John Baldry in the mid '60s, then began a long musical relationship with Keith Tippett. Dean was in Tippett's sextet in the late '60s and early '70s, then joined Tippett's groups Centipede in the early '70s and Ark in the late '70s. In between, they worked as a duo. Dean was also in the Soft Machine from 1969 to 1971. During the '70s, Dean played in the London Jazz Composers Orchestra, Alan Skidmore's El Skid, Chris McGregor's Brotherhood of Breath, and Carla Bley's band. He also led the bands Just Us and Ninesense, as well as a quintet in the '70s and '80s. Dean's recorded as a leader for Ogun. Currently, he does not have any sessions available on CD in America. —*Ron Wynn*

Edq Live / **i.** Aug. 1989 / ED 03

Duos / **i.** 1989 / ED

Trios / **i.** 1989 / ED 02

★ **Unlimited Saxophone Company** / **i.** 1989 / Ogun 002

BLOSSOM DEARIE

b. Apr. 28, 1926, East Durham, NY
Vocals / Bop, ballads & blues
One of the more unusual acts in jazz or popular music, vocalist/pianist Blossom Dearie has parlayed a light voice and a thin, tight vibrato into a successful recording and cabaret act through distinctive performance techniques. These include a careful use of blues effects, and a controlled, often exaggerated attack and delivery with key words punctuated and emphasized. Her vocals are backed by sparse bop-flavored piano lines. Dearie's professional career began with the Blue Flames, a vocal unit that was part of Woody Herman's orchestra. She also sang with the Blue Reys, another ensemble that was part of Alvino Rey's band. Dearie recorded "Moody's Mood for Love" in 1952, as did King Pleasure. She performed in Paris that same year with Annie Ross. Dearie formed her own group, the Blue Stars, with instrumental backing from such jazz musicians as Fats Sadi and Roger Guerin, and landed a hit with her version of "Lullaby in Birdland," sung in French. The Blue Stars spawned two other vocal groups in the mid '50s: the Double Six Quartet of Paris and the Swingle Singers. Dearie recorded for Barclay Records in Paris in 1954, then returned to America in 1956. She worked in New York and Los Angeles nightclubs, and headed her own trio. Dearie

recorded for Verve in 1956 backed by Herb Ellis, Ray Brown, and Jo Jones, and kept playing and touring through the '60s. She started her own label, Daffodil Records, in the '70s and issued recordings. Dearie was the first recipient of the Mabel Mercer Foundation Award in 1985. She's continued recording, cutting the session *Blossom Dearie Sings Rootin' Songs* in 1987 for DIW. It's available on CD. In addition, some earlier Dearie sessions have been reissued. —*Ron Wynn and Michael G. Nastos*

★ **Blossom Dearie** / i. 1956 / Verve 837934

○ **Blossom Dearie** / i. 1957 / Verve 2037

May I Come In? / Feb. 13-15, 1964 / Daffodil 114

Simply / 1983 / Daffodil 106
Available on vinyl only, this features Bob Dorough on vocals and Jay Berliner on guitar. —*Michael G. Nastos*

Et Tu Bruce? / Apr. 27-28, 1984 / Larrikin 182

Songs of Chelsea / i. 1987 / Daffodil 110

JOEY DEFRANCESCO

b. 1971
Organ, piano, synthesizer, trumpet / Bop, soul-jazz
The current reigning young organ star, twenty-something Joey DeFrancesco has helped to give the Hammond B-3 renewed visibility. DeFrancesco's albums only hint at his abilities, but he shows enough promise to suggest that he's capable of making a genuine soul-jazz classic at some point. His phrasing and style reflect his love and his often expressed admiration for Jimmy Smith. DeFrancesco toured and recorded with Miles Davis, who was another vocal DeFrancesco booster. DeFrancesco plays decent trumpet and piano, and comes from a musical family (his father is also an organist). DeFrancesco turned in a guest trumpet spot on a '93 Jack McDuff album, and displayed a stylistic bond and debt to early '60s Miles Davis. All his releases are available on CD. —*Ron Wynn*

★ **All of Me** / 1989 / Columbia 44463

Part III / 1991 / Columbia 47063
Substantial fluctuation in material quality and performances. DeFrancesco has a good flair for soul-jazz and hard bop, but gets bogged down, at times, in pop-tinged pabulum. —*Ron Wynn*

Where Were You? / 1991 / Columbia 45443
Nice mix-and-match quartet sessions. The lineup is split between esteemed veterans like Illinois Jacquet (sax) and Milt Hinton (b) and the younger Wallace Roney (tpt) and Kirk Whalum (ts). —*Ron Wynn*

○ **Reboppin'** / i. 1992 / Columbia 48624
A recent release by the youthful organ sensation. His powerhouse riffs, solos, and soulful phrasing have made DeFrancesco the top mainstream stylist. This set includes contributions from his father and brother (on one cut), and from a good backing band, despite the absence of major names or stars. —*Ron Wynn*

BUDDY DEFRANCO (Boniface Ferdinand Leonardo DeFranco)

b. Feb. 17, 1923, Camden, NJ
Clarinet, bass clarinet, alto saxophone / Swing, big band, bop
Buddy DeFranco is an extremely talented clarinetist whose technique and tone have often been superior to his material. DeFranco is also a fine bass clarinetist. He's a great bebop artist and his '50s dates mixed bebop, swing, and cool elements. DeFranco won a Philadelphia amateur players' contest sponsored by Tommy Dorsey at age 14. He played in the big bands of Gene Krupa, Charlie Barnet, and Boyd Raeburn in the early '40s, and was Dorsey's principal soloist twice in the mid and late '40s. DeFranco made his recording debut as a leader on Capitol in 1949, then cut sessions for MGM, GNP, Norgran, Verve, and Advance Guard in the '50s, while also recording with Art Tatum and Oscar Peterson. He tried

to lead a big band, but was unsuccessful. DeFranco played in Count Basie's octet and in a quartet with Art Blakey and Kenny Drew. He toured Europe with Billie Holiday in 1954, then settled in California in 1955. DeFranco co-led a quartet in 1954 and 1955 with Sonny Clark that was arguably DeFranco's greatest group. He premiered Nelson Riddle's *Cross-Country Suite* in 1958 at the Hollywood Bowl, while conducting jazz workshops at California schools. Later, he and Riddle recorded the suite for Dot. DeFranco led a unusual clarinet/accordion/bass/drums quartet in the early '60s with Tommy Gumina, and began playing bass clarinet. There were sessions for Mercury, Vee Jay, Delmark, even a Sun Ra date on Saturn. DeFranco led a revived Glenn Miller orchestra in the late '60s and mid '70s, then returned to full-time teaching, making only periodic club appearances. DeFranco did cut some small label sessions in the '70s for Progressive and Pablo, among others. He toured Sweden in 1975. DeFranco co-led a quintet with Terry Gibbs that played in London in 1980 and in New York in 1982. He had a duo in New York with George Duvivier in 1983, and recorded with clarinetist John Denmna and a harpsichord player. DeFranco was in Oscar Peterson's quartet also. He made recordings for Palo Alto and Hep (England). Mosaic has issued the finest DeFranco collection, a five-disc set of his mid-'50s quartet material with Sonny Clark. His most recent session for Concord, *Chip Off the Old Block*, and his quintet material with Gibbs are available, but there's very little other DeFranco material on CD. —*Ron Wynn*

Progressive Mr. Defranco, The / Sep. 28-9, 1953 / Norgran 1006

○ **Buddy Defranco with Strings** / i. 1954 / MGM 253

○ **Buddy Defranco Quartet, The** / i. 1954 / Clef 149

★ **Complete Verve Recordings of Buddy De Franco with Sonny Clark** / Apr. 1954-Aug. 1955 / Mosaic 5117

○ **Cooking the Blues** / 1956-1957 / Verve 8221

○ **Sweet and Lovely** / 1956-1957 / Verve 8224

○ **Closed Session** / Oct. 30, 1957-Nov. 1, 1957 / Verve 8382

Blues Bag / i. 1964 / Affinity

★ **Like Someone in Love** / Mar. 11, 1977 / Mosaic
Simply incredible in every way! Sonny Clark offers moving, heated piano, and this is some of DeFranco's most sumptuous, engaging, and accomplished playing. With majestic Tal Farlow guitar work. —*Ron Wynn*

Mr. Lucky / 1982 / Pablo 2310906

Holiday for Swing / Aug. 22-23, 1988 / Contemporary 14047

JACK DEJOHNETTE

b. Aug. 9, 1942, Chicago, IL
Drums, piano, melodica / Hard bop, modern creative
A premier percussionist and drummer, as well as a fine pianist, composer, electric keyboards and melodica soloist, Jack DeJohnette has been a familiar face on the jazz scene since the '60s. He's often considered the finest modern jazz drummer of the '70s after Elvin Jones and Tony Williams, and has worked and/or led jazz-rock, free, pop, rock, reggae, bebop, and hard bop groups, distinguishing himself regardless of the genre. DeJohnette can provide a steady, sustained pulse indefinitely, or break up the beat and redirect it. He's a marvelous percussionist and can be an equally remarkable timekeeper, he can use brushes expertly, and can provide either booming volume or soft underpinning. DeJohnette was an eclectic drummer and artist long before the term became a defining virtue. He's led numerous bands and done even more recording sessions.

DeJohnette played drums in a high school concert band in Chicago, and took classical piano lessons for ten years. He graduated from the American Conservatory of Music and spent his early days working in all types of bands in Chicago, from R&B and soul to free jazz, while maintaining a busy practice schedule on drums and piano. He moved to

New York in 1966, and worked with Big John Patton. DeJohnette later played with Jackie McLean, Betty Carter, and Abbey Lincoln. His first job that won him major recognition outside jazz circles came in Charles Lloyd's late '60s quartet. They were the first jazz band to visit the Soviet Union and to play several rock halls as well. Lloyd's band toured Europe six times, the Far East once, and enjoyed crossover attention via Lloyd's "Forest Flower" cut. DeJohnette kept busy in New York, working with John Coltrane, Thelonious Monk, Freddie Hubbard, Bill Evans, his Lloyd bandmate Keith Jarrett, Chick Corea, and Stan Getz. DeJohnette also worked with Miles Davis, playing on the *Bitches Brew* album and joining the band full-time in 1970. He remained with them until 1971.

DeJohnette's first band was a jazz-rock group called Compost. He was almost ECM's house drummer in the '70s, appearing on sessions with Kenny Wheeler, Jarrett, John Abercrombie, Jan Garbarek and George Adams. He had a separate deal as a bandleader, and recorded with his groups New Directions in the '70s and Jack DeJohnette's Special Edition in the '80s. New Directions's debut album won the Prix du Jazz Contemporain de l'Academie Charles Cros in 1979. DeJohnette continued recording for ECM in the '80s. He's also recorded for Milestone, Columbia, Landmark, MCA/Impulse, and Prestige. He's played with Bennie Maupin, David Murray, Lester Bowie, Arthur Blythe, Slex Foster, Chico Freeman, Ornette Coleman, Pat Metheny, and Nana Vasconcelos, among others. During the '90s, DeJohnette has been responsible for some original blends of Native American music and jazz. Currently, there are several DeJohnette titles available on CD, including a recent trio session with Metheny and Herbie Hancock. —*Ron Wynn*

DeJohnette Complex, The / Dec. 26, 1968 / Milestone 617
This early session has some appealing cuts. Outstanding personnel; Jack occasionally doubles on melodica. A new reissue. —*Ron Wynn*

★ **Have You Heard?** / Jul. 4, 1970 / Epic 64692

Sorcery / Mar. 1974 / Prestige 10081
Always an imaginative, honest musician, drummer Jack DeJohnette returned to the solo recording scene with a collection of ideas that struck with rough-hewn, experimental directness and bold good humor. "Sorcery #1" and the rest of the first side was recorded at DeJohnette's home in Willow, NY. "The Right Time" and "The Rock Thing" don't fare any better in the recorded sound department than the title tune. The former is a fascinating spoken vocal improvisation of remarkable intensity and imagination; but again, the recording quality eliminates any resonance the voices could have carried in a larger studio. The 14-minute "King Suite" is the album's masterpiece, a disturbing, evocative portrait in sound. DeJohnette's organ work smacks somewhat of both Khalid Yasin and Alice Coltrane, but is far more funkily earthbound. Dave Holland, always a challenging bass player who worked especially well with DeJohnette, is at his most impressive here, guiding the ensemble from serenity to turmoil to eventual peace. It is a very free selection, but each player is strong and versatile enough to meet the responsibilities of that freedom. —*Charles Mitchell,* Down Beat

Ruts and Daitya / i. 1975 / ECM 1021

Cosmic Chicken / Apr. 24+26, 1975 / Prestige 10094
Jack DeJohnette's *Cosmic Chicken* is a wide-open improvement over 1974's *Sorcery.* The difference this time is in an attitude of shared creativity, an approach fostered by the interaction with his excellent quartet. More important, this is music with meaning; it takes chances and consciously avoids contemporary funk stereotypes. The quartet's interaction follows a thoughtfully prescribed format, with Peter Warren's bass lines functioning as the groundwork for the exploratory avenues the others pursue. Tenor and alto saxophonist Alex Foster and guitarist John Abercrombie complement each other's work in their tone colors, range, elections, and unceasing adaptability. DeJohnette's surprise here is his

keyboard playing. On "Memories," he displays competent and intelligent acoustic technique, influenced by the Keith Jarrett school. "Shades of the Phantom" features an intriguing synthesizer solo, reminiscent of the opulent signature of Cesar Franck. —*Mikal Gilmore,* Down Beat

Directions / Feb. 1976 / ECM 1074
The album opens with something that begins nowhere and ends at the same place; that pretty much characterizes a set that never quite knows where it is going. Drummer Jack DeJohnette was trying different combinations, which is refreshing, but never quite found what fit. "Flying Spirits" runs freely into a psuedo-Indian duet of "Pansori Visions" (guitar and drums). "Fantastic" is a guitar and tenor conversation with an R&B beat and miscellaneous noise and percussion. They get into what sounds like total improvisation on "Struttin,'" and here the guitar, tenor, drums trio is really listening to each other: I was reminded of the old Gabor Szabo/Charles Lloyd duets with Chico Hamilton. Warren Bernhardt gets to display his considerable harmonic conceptions on "Morning Star," and then they take it out with a humorous and mercifully brief jump tune. —*Jon Goldman,* Cadence

New Rags / May 1977 / ECM 1103
Directions was distinguished among fusion groups for having seamlessly joined the electronic urge to the improvisational freedoms developed by the most cohesive bands of the last 15 (or so) years. Leader DeJohnette, with his early AACM experience, his success as part of Charles Lloyd's quartet, and his contributions to Miles Davis's rockingest sessions, formed a really cohesive quartet of sympathetic, responsive, and accomplished players. They played what interested them, without pandering to the past or posturing for the pretentious present. DeJohnette's compositional ideas were severe: "Minya's the Mooch" is a dark piece with an elusive melody; "Lydia" is a short, evocative, but exacting effort; and "New Rags" is built on a strident ascending phrase, a series of ensemble stops, and then a calypso take-out chorus. Tenor and soprano saxophonist Alex Foster is the other composer represented. "Flys" and "Steppin Thru" each contain hum-along lines that make good sense as Foster negotiates them. Guitarist John Abercrombie is able to insinuate himself to good results in the latter, as both lead voice and an effective accompanist. —*Howie Mandel,* Down Beat

New Directions / Jun. 1978 / ECM 829374
First for Fantasy and now, releasing their third effort for ECM, Directions always played a freewheeling, anything-goes amalgam of numerous musical styles, accessibly grounded by the impeccable virtuosity of drummer/pianist/composer Jack DeJohnette. *New Directions,* the first release that features bassist Eddie Gomez and trumpeter Lester Bowie, at once contains the band's most exploratory and coherent statement to date—possibly from individual members as well. Here as elsewhere, DeJohnette is all over the kit, dropping tom-tom and bass drum bombs in the midst of compelling cymbal work, double- and triple-timing at will. . . . DeJohnette is absolutely awesome on the extended improvisation "One Handed Woman," accenting his controlled bombast with splashy cymbal flurries and other surprises. Guitarist John Abercrombie alternately sounds like he is filling a small pond with water droplets, or sending poison-tipped darts through the proceedings. Gomez follows Bowie's rises, dips, and shadowboxing before taking off on some arco extensions that provoke thoughts of what violinist Leroy Jenkins might do on a bass. "Woman" eventually evolves into a good-natured, madly swinging shuffle with the quartet singing the title amidst clapping and street-corner jive. —*Michael Zipkin,* Down Beat

★ **Special Edition** / Mar. 1979 / ECM 827694
Arguably his finest small combo. David Murray and Arthur Blythe light up the sky. —*Ron Wynn*

New Directions in Europe / Jun. 1979 / ECM 829158
A 1988 reissue of his other great '70s group, recorded live and on fire. A tremendous group with Lester Bowie (tpt),

John Abercrombie (g), and Eddie Gomez (b) that elevates a menu that, at times, gets ragged. —*Ron Wynn*

○ **Tin Can Alley** / Sep. 1980 / ECM 1189

Tin Can Alley suggests a tonal history of jazz—from the earthy, layered, African rhythmic buildup of Jack DeJohnette's solo feature "The Gri Gri Man" to the ducal sonorities of the drummer's "Pastel Rhapsody." Bassist and cellist Peter Warren's "Riff Raff" completes the circle with a primal collective ad-lib. The leader's title track is boppish and angular. "I Know" dances to a backbeat, while the multitracked horns riff and composer DeJohnette soul-shouts. The horns are particularly forceful, pliant, and varied on the ballad "Pastel Rhapsody." John Purcell solos in an updated Johnny Hodges bag on alto, displaying a lovely timbre, controlled vibrato, and a singing falsetto range. Chico Freeman's tenor solo follows a piano/bass dialogue and is light, rhapsodic, and full of broad scoops and sweeping tonal dips. On this record, DeJohnette scores again with some of the most coherent, thrillingly compelling, multidirectional music around. Rich combinations abound among these exceptional players. —*Owen Cordle*, Down Beat

Album, Album / Jun. 1984 / ECM 823467

Album Album grabs the listener on several levels, gaining depth with each hearing. First, it is the unison horn lines, lush for "Monk's Mood" (baritone saxophonist Howard Johnson's arrangement), spunky for "Festival," recalling a Duke Ellington section here, the World Saxophone Quartet there. Then the listener is grabbed by the way drummer Jack DeJohnette and colleagues continually undercut the chamber aspect of the music (real and potential) with good-time rhythms, hummable melodies, and impassioned solos. Then it is the less obvious things: the way John Purcell (alto, soprano sax) aces the "Ahmad the Terrible" theme; the way David Murray (tenor sax), Purcell, and Johnson take turns on DeJohnette and bassist Rufus Reid in the reprise of "Zoot Suite" (DeJohnette wasn't adverse to consolidating his own past); the way DeJohnette makes the drum synthesizer and electric keyboards work and one-ups the Dirty Dozen Brass Band on "New Orleans Strut" (Murray acts as a ringer here). *Album Album* peaks on "Third World Anthem," a percussive riff giving way to an Abdullah Ibrahim-like folk theme with the horns alternately surging together and setting off on their own (Johnson steps over to tuba here) over the leader's crackling drive. . . . On *Album Album*, DeJohnette's link to Charles Mingus emerges more clearly than ever as an artist who could not only assemble and inspire a superior band, but who could also engage a timeless music with the confidence of putting a personal stamp on it. —*Eric Shepard*, Cadence

Jack DeJohnette Piano Album, The / Jan. 14+15, 1985 / Landmark 1504

Irresistible Force / 1986 / MCA 5992

One of the few substantial albums to emerge from the hyped MCA revival of the Impulse line. —*Ron Wynn*

Audio-Visualscapes / i. Jan. 1989 / MCA 8029

Parallel Realities / i. 1990 / MCA 42313

An overlooked session with Pat Metheny (g) in a definite jazz phase. Herbie Hancock shows his steadfast piano form. —*Ron Wynn*

Music for the Fifth World / i. 1993 / Capitol 99089

Drummer Jack DeJohnette continues on his inspired, twisting path as a leader with this new release. This "world" music involves such seemingly disparate genres as Native American-like chant pieces and a rock-infused jazz ethos featuring the two-guitar attack of John Scofield and Vernon Reid. DeJohnette often engages in a double drum kit rumble with Will Calhoun. Among the tunes are the infectious "Witchi Tai To," by the late Native American saxist Jim Pepper, and a Miles Davis tribute, "Miles," which finds Scofield on familiar stylistic turf. DeJohnette sings over the reggae-lined "Deception Blues." A strange new blend of rock, jazz, native sonorities, and techno-primal energies, De-

Johnette's latest musical experiment opens up new creative possibilities. —*Josef Woodard*, Jazziz

BARBARA DENNERLEIN

b. 1965

Organ / Soul-jazz, modern creative

The really interesting stylist among young organists, Barbara Dennerlein has combined bebop, blues, and soul-jazz in a manner that's alternately intriguing, attractive, and arresting. Unfortunately, she's received more acclaim in Europe than in America, a situation directly attributable to recording on independent labels with limited distribution. Dennerlein's creative use of bass pedals, her incorporation of a MIDI interface and subsequent synthesizer sounds, plus her phrasing, accompaniment, and solos are uniformly impressive. She began playing organ at age 11, and worked in Munich clubs at age 15. Dennerlein accompanied Jimmy Smith and Sonny Fortune during a German tour, and later won two German Record Critics' awards for self-produced albums. She's made several festival appearances and has been featured on German radio and television during the '80s. Dennerlein's recorded in the '80s and '90s with Ronnie Burrage, Ray Anderson, Mark Mondesir, Andy Sheppard, and Bobby Watson, among others. Her sessions for Enja and Bluemoon are available on CD. —*Ron Wynn*

★ **Straight Ahead** / Jul. 1988 / Enja 79608

Organ-fired and guitar-laced modern jazz from this up-and-coming keyboardist. A solid album throughout. —*Michael G. Nastos*

Plays Classics / i. Nov. 1988 / Redken 1188

Hot Stuff / Jun. 1990 / Enja 79654

That's Me / i. 1992 / Blue Moon 79183

Recent release from a compelling organist whose spinning lines, booming bass pedal, and swirling phrases have made her the most intriguing player to emerge since Larry Young. Dennerlein can take things out one moment, then provide soulful, exuberant passages the next. Tenor saxophonist Bob Berg adds some fiery solos in support. —*Ron Wynn*

PAUL DESMOND (Paul Emil Desmond)

b. Nov. 25, 1924, New York, NY, **d.** May 30, 1977, New York, NY

Alto saxophone / Cool

Paul Desmond was an excellent alto saxophonist whose shimmering sound and light airy playing made a sizable impact. The quintessential "cool jazz" saxophonist who was influenced by Pete Brown and Benny Carter, Desmond avoided voice-like effects and seldom played or quoted the blues. He was a fine melodic creator, and the recordings he made apart from the Dave Brubeck quartet emphasized this aspect of his style. Desmond's father played organ in silent movie orchestras, and Paul studied clarinet at San Francisco State University. Desmond worked with several local groups before joining the Dave Brubeck quartet in 1951. He remained with this band until 1967, composing its most popular, and one of jazz's greatest, anthems, "Take Five." When Brubeck ended the group in 1967, Desmond began to gain attention as a solo act, though he'd been making records as a leader since the mid '50s. His first sessions for Fantasy were in 1954, and he cut a quartet set with Gerry Mulligan in 1957. Desmond formed a quartet with Jim Hall in the late '50s, and they played together into the mid '60s. He did sessions for Warner Bros, RCA, A&M, Finesse, and CTI, among others. Desmond worked with both the Modern Jazz Quartet and its bassist and drummer, Percy Heath and Connie Kay. Other recording mates included Ron Carter, Herbie Hancock, Airto, Jack DeJohnette, and, on occasion, Brubeck and Mulligan again. His final quartet included Ed Bickert, Don Thompson and Jerry Fuller. Desmond died of lung cancer in 1977. Another marvelous Mosaic set, a six-disc package of his quartet tracks with Jim Hall, was released in 1987. There are also reissues available of RCA, CTI, Prestige, Mulligan, and MJQ material. Some sessions featuring his final quartet are available also. —*Ron Wynn and Michael Erlewine*

○ **Paul Desmond/Gerry Mulligan Quartet** / **i.** Sep. 2, 1952 / Fantasy 273
Paul Desmond Quintet/Gerry Mulligan Quartet. Lovely. Four dates, from 1952 to 1954. —*Michael Erlewine*

○ **Quintet/Quartet** / **i.** 1954 / Original Jazz Classics 712

Blues in Time / **i.** 1957 / Fantasy

East of the Sun / Sep. 5 07, 1959 / Musicraft 840
Quartet. First-rate quartet session. Jim Hall (g), Percy Heath (b), and Connie Kay (d) are super. —*Ron Wynn*

★ **Paul Desmond—Jim Hall Recordings** / **i.** 1959-1965 / Mosaic
Incredible music! A six-disc boxed set of recordings from 1959 1965 featuring Desmond with Jim Hall. Desmond plays flawless sax, and Jim Hall plays likewise on guitar. In brief, these are classic cuts; the best. Whether you are a beginning listener or a jazz expert, this is satisfying music. Mosaic does it again. —*Michael Erlewine*

Late Lament / Sep. 28, 1961 / Bluebird 5778

Two of a Mind / Jun. 26, 1962-Aug. 13, 1962 / Bluebird 9654

○ **Take Ten** / Jun. 5, 1963-Jun. 25, 1953 / RCA 66146
Early-'60s sessions reissued on a recent Bluebird CD. The title does not refer to a song, but to the number of cuts that Desmond, guitarist Jim Hall, and others recorded. Bassist Percy Heath and drummer Connie Kay also participate. These sessions were partially reissued on CD before; this is the full date. —*Ron Wynn*

○ **Polka Dots & Moonbeams** / 1963-1964 / Bluebird 61066

From the Hot Afternoon / Aug. 13+14, 1969 / A&M 0824

★ **Bridge over Troubled Water** / 1969 / A&M 51204

In Concert at Town Hall / Dec. 25, 1971 / Stet 25101
This delightful collaboration with MJQ has been reissued several times. This is one of the better editions. —*Ron Wynn*

Best of Paul Desmond / **i.** 1972-1975 / Columbia 45484

Skylark / Nov. 1973-Dec. 1973 / Columbia 44170

Pure Desmond / Sep. 1974 / Columbia 40806

★ **Paul Desmond Quartet Live, The** / Oct. 25, 1975-Nov. 1, 1975 / A&M 10
Here are four sides of stylish, rich music performed at Bourbon Street in Toronto by four pros. Everyone had a chance to stretch out (all the pieces are between 7 and 12 minutes) in a setting that was obviously comfortable and yet stimulating. The recording is excellent for a club date. Guitarist Ed Bickert and bassist Don Thompson finally were beginning to be known outside of Canada (although it is unfortunate, in some ways, that this notice depended on their association with American musicians). Alto saxophonist Paul Desmond plays with his usual taste and wit, but I think the album belongs to Bickert and Thompson. Desmond seems to recognize their powerful and sensitive interplay at the end of "Here's That Rainy Day," where he lays out following their solos. And on "Nancy," Desmond's re-entry clearly reveals the effect on him of their solos. Bickert had a fine sense of humor—especially heard on "Things Ain't What They Used to Be"—which must partly account for his compatibility with Desmond, and Thompson plays with that kind of authority that allows him to move us into a predictable phrase and bring it off with aplomb. For the most part, Thompson is a busier soloist than Bickert, who sticks mostly to chording, but Bickert's restraint masks a complicated sense of harmony and rhythm. Listen to his solo on "Nancy," for example. Jerry Fuller's drumming is generally unobtrusive, as it should be on tunes like these. On "Manha de Carnival," though, one suddenly realizes the fineness of his playing; not only does he maintain the crisp looseness of the beat so well that it seems he could play it forever without stopping, but he knows the effect of silence, of not filling in all the empty spaces. —*Joel Ray, Cadence*

VIC DICKENSON (Victor Dickenson)

b. Aug. 6, 1906, Xenia, OH, **d.** Nov. 16, 1984, New York, NY
Trombone / New Orleans traditional
Trombonist Vic Dickenson was the supreme section player, an extremely relaxed-sounding, versatile soloist. His facility enabled him to handle any tempo easily, and his husky, huge sound proved particularly suited for backing singers. He played with local bands in the Midwest before joining Blanche Calloway's band in 1933. Dickenson played with her for three years, then worked with Claude Hopkins and Benny Carter before joining Count Basie in 1940. He played with Frankie Newton from 1941 to 1943, and spent another three years with Eddie Heywood's band. Dickenson remained in California after Heywood's orchestra went there, doing freelance sessions in 1947 and 1948. He recorded for Blue Note with Edmond Hall, James P. Johnson, and Sidney de Paris in 1943 and 1944 (these recordings were reissued by Mosaic in 1985). Dickenson moved to Boston, led a band, and did various dates until the mid '50s, when he relocated to New York. He played with Bill Doggett in 1952, then cut some superb records with Ruby Braff and Edmond Hall for Vanguard in 1953. Dickenson participated in the acclaimed CBS television special, "The Sound of Jazz," with Billie Holiday, Coleman Hawkins, Gerry Mulligan, and others in 1957, then joined Red Allen's band in 1958. During the early '60s, he co-led the Saints and Sinners while he also toured with George Wein's All Stars, worked at Condon's, and played with Wild Bill Davison. He went to Asia and Australia with the Condon band in 1964, then made a solo visit to Europe in 1965. Dickenson co-led a quintet with Bobby Hackett from 1968 to 1970, then played frequently with the '70s' finest traditional jazz group, the World's Greatest Jazz Band. He spent his final years doing freelance dates. —*Ron Wynn*

○ **Vic's Boston Story** / 1956-1957 / Storyville 920

○ **Mainstream** / Oct. 28, 1958 / Atlantic 1303

○ **Vic Dickenson Quintet** / Storyville 4021

★ **Plays Bessie Smith: "Trombone Cholly"** / Gazell 1011
If all the material here is not blues, trombonist Vic Dickenson certainly turns them into the feeling of the blues. Producer Sam Charters wisely picked mid-tempo and slow-tempo material for this classic trombonist (one of the very last). Dickenson worked well in these tempos and, with a controlled vibrato, was able to steer away from some of the Dixie bits he found himself in over the years. Missing here is much of the Dickenson humor, limited mainly to moments when he is playing behind tenor saxophonist Frank Wess. However, the trombonist treats the material here with great respect and gentleness. Frank Wess was not being heard from much during this period (1977) and seems a strange choice for Dickenson and Bessie Smith, but shows a surprising affinity for the material. Even with an occasional Charlie Parkerisms thrown in, Wess proves an asset both behind Dickenson and in his occasional solo spots. Joe Newman's trumpet is primarily full; he neither adds nor detracts as a soloist and serves the best function when carrying the intro melody. —*Geoff Millerman, Cadence*

WALT DICKERSON

b. 1931, Philadelphia, PA
Vibist / Hard bop, modern creative
A solid soloist noted for his complex harmonies, Walt Dickerson provided an alternative voice on the vibes in the '60s before he abruptly stopped playing in 1965. Dickerson uses only two sticks, and dips them in a solution to harden them. His lines, voicings, approach, and technique were quite different from anything else done on vibes at the time, and he was named "new star" by *Down Beat* in 1962. Dickerson teamed with Sun Ra in 1965, recording *Impressions of a Patch of Blue*, a Dickerson arrangement of music for the film of the same name by Jerry Goldsmith, on MGM. A Morgan State graduate, Dickerson served in the army during the early '50s, then played in California, some-

times leading a group that included Andrew Hill and Andrew Cyrille. But he quit playing from 1965 until 1975. After his return, Dickerson worked mainly in Europe. He and Sun Ra recorded together again, this time on Steeplechase in the late '70s. He also made a duo session with Pierre Dorge, and recorded other albums on Steeplechase and Soul Note, including a duet date with Cyrille. Currently, there are a few Dickerson sessions available on CD. —*Ron Wynn and Michael G. Nastos*

This Is Walt Dickerson / Mar. 7, 1961 / Prestige 8254
Early-'60s album by vibist Walt Dickerson, at that time an emerging figure on the avant-garde scene. His long, rambling solos, double-mallet improvisations, and ambitious rhythms set Dickerson apart from the legions who'd patterned themselves after Milt Jackson. Drummer Andrew Cyrille, in his pre-Cecil Taylor period, lays down intricate, effective rhythms, and teams with pianist Austin Crowe and bassist Bob Lewis. This has been reissued on CD. —*Ron Wynn*

Sense of Direction, A / May 5, 1961 / New Jazz 1794
With the Austin Crowe Trio. Three standards, five of Dickerson's boldly tinged originals. A fresh approach to vibes. —*Michael G. Nastos*

○ **Relativity** / Jan. 16, 1962 / New Jazz 8275

★ **Jazz Impressions: "Lawrence Of Arabia"** / 1963 / Dauntless 6313
Jazz Impressions: Lawrence of Arabia. This effort from the vibraphonist stretches the parameters of Maurice Jarre's themes. Rare, but great to have. —*Michael G. Nastos*

○ **Unity** / Mar. 5, 1964 / Audio Fidelity 6131
Vibist Walt Dickerson's intense, circling, John Coltrane-inspired vibes contrasted with pianist Walter Davis's more lighthearted, bop-rooted, locked-hands approach. This contrast is even more evident on *High Moon.* Near the end of his solo, Dickerson beats out a string of high-pitched figures that may be as close to tenor screams as could be reproduced on vibes. Davis follows by comping along without concern in a "My Favorite Things" manner. But the two drummers, Andrew Cyrille and Edgar Bateman, are the most novel aspect of this session: both play in a psuedomelodic polyrhythmic style. The drummers play together in some sections and alternate in others, bringing about a constant shift in density, rhythmic emphasis, and drive, contributing a feeling not necessarily of freedom, but at least of a loosening of metrical structures. Dickerson was clearly heading into new territory at this time (1964), both as vibist and as a leader. It is a shame that his name stopped appearing on record jackets not long after this album was first issued. —*Tom Bingham,* Cadence

Visions / Jul. 11, 1978 / Steeple Chase 1126
Visions features vibist Walt Dickerson with pianist Sun Ra. Because of the addition of the richly harmonic piano, the album's textures are fuller and more orchestral than those found in the unaccompanied *Shades of Love.* The duet session also sounds more forceful, as the two musicians have to play out in order to respond to each other. *Space Dancer,* an especially energetic performance, includes dissonant clusters and flurries delivered at a variety of speeds before tapering off into an exquisite, echolike dialogue. On *Astro,* Dickerson and Ra match ringing sounds, with Dickerson employing the vibraphone's motor and his colleague utilizing the piano's sustaining pedal. *Utopia,* however, features the two musicians in a contrasting counterpoint, pitting the vibraphonist's metallic scraps and fast runs against the pianist's barrage of sounds made mostly inside the instrument. —*Clifford Jay Safane,* Down Beat

AL DI MEOLA

b. Jul. 22, 1954, Jersey City, NJ
Guitar, bandleader, composer / Early jazz-rock, world fusion
Al Di Meola can be a blazing, high-volume electric player or a romantic, lush acoustic soloist. He has been equally successful in both styles, and has done classical guitar dates,

too, since he made his initial splash as a member of Chick Corea's Return to Forever in the mid '70s. Di Meola has as much speed, technique, and harmonic chops as any contemporary player. He's accomplished on electric and a variety of acoustic guitars, including 12-string. He began playing at age 9, and experimented with the steel at age 15. Di Meola attended Berklee, then joined Corea in 1974. Di Meola started recording albums as a leader with Columbia in 1976, and had a string of releases that made the pop charts through the mid '80s. He was a popular fusion and jazz-rock player for several years, then changed direction in 1985 with a solo acoustic date for Manhattan. Di Meola later recorded and toured with John McLaughlin and Paco De Lucia and formed the Al Di Meola Project with Airto Moreira, Phil Markowitz, Danny Gottlieb, and Chip Jackson. Besides his Columbia and Manhattan releases, Di Meola's also recorded for Blue Note and Tomato in the '80s and '90s with his group, World Sinfonia. He has several sessions available on CD. —*Ron Wynn*

Elegant Gypsy / 1976 / Columbia 34461
The frenetic, slashing stylist shows his sentimental, restrained, and romantic side. A gold album. —*Ron Wynn*

Land of the Midnight Sun / 1976 / Columbia 34074
For a solo debut, guitarist Al Di Meola's *Land of the Midnight Sun* is remarkably free of the self-indulgent tinkertoy excesses we have been subjected to on many other coming-out parties. To Di Meola's credit, the mystical, chanting aura of this work is free from a trendy, guru-dictated sense of cosmic dribble. The percussive contributions of Steve Gadd, Lenny White, Mingo Lewis, and Al Mouzon lay a propulsive base for Di Meola's long and exploratory solos. What is special, however, is his well-honed sense of mellow sound. True, when playing with Chick Corea, he has to fit the high-volume demands of the group; but on his own, Di Meola shows his consummate skill as composer and arranger in a more quiet setting, both by transcription and composition. —*Arnold Shaw,* Down Beat

Casino / 1977 / Columbia 47482
Guitarist Al Di Meola was in his electronic fusion phase when this was recorded in the late '70s. He plays frenetic, flashy riffs and solos, and is assisted on a variety of keyboards by Barry Miles, electric bassist Anthony Jackson, and drummer Steve Gadd, who adds a steady array of rock and funk beats. —*Ron Wynn*

★ **Splendido Hotel** / 1979 / Columbia 46117
On *Splendido Hotel,* Al Di Meola combines tight electronic ensemble playing with acoustic forays; some in characteristic territory, and some elsewhere. He maintains a Latin/Mediterranean tone through much of the album, and his emphasis is on composition more than improvisation. Di Meola ended a two-year recording absence with four sides from the studio, stretching out so far as to sing a love song and join Les Paul on the popular standard "Spanish Eyes." "Alien Chase," "Dream Theme," and "Dinner Music" are electric excursions with numerous time changes, stops, and starts. Di Meola's band is not only hot, but inspired. Drummer Robbie Gonzales is a powerhouse, with deep resounding tom-toms and dynamic footwork. Phillip Saisse has many voices on keyboards, adds marimba to three tracks, and is a perfect foil for Di Meola's high-speed guitar pyrotechnics. *Splendido Hotel* is also full of guests. A coy and succinct Jan Hammer Moog solo livens up "Dream Theme." Mingo Lewis sparkles on percussion, when not dropping Syndrum bombs. Anthony Jackson is a fluid bassist, but the lack of a bottom punch in some of his playing is annoying. The redoubtable drummer Steve Gadd was brought in for two tracks and plays surprisingly little. Generally, the playing is not as fresh where the studio players are used as it is when Di Meola is with his own band. Di Meola is reunited with mentor keyboardist Chick Corea on three tracks. The slightly melodramatic acoustic duet "Two to Tango" finds Corea plucking and dampening the piano strings by hand. Corea's composition "Isfaham" features a

boys' choir and is both strikingly beautiful and undeniably overweight. There is an acoustic guitar duet on *Splendido Hotel*, as there is on his *Elegant Gypsy* album. The difference here is that Di Meola plays both parts himself. —*Robin Tolleson*, Down Beat

Friday Night in San Francisco / Dec. 5, 1980 / Columbia 84962
With John McLaughlin (g) and Paco De Lucia (g). The other of two good triple-threat sessions. —*Ron Wynn*

☆ **World Sinfonia** / i. 1991 / Tomato 79750

○ **Kiss My Axe** / i. Feb. 26, 1992 / Tomato 79751

Heart of the Immigrants / i. 1993 / Rhino 79052
After inviting the industry to *Kiss My Axe*, the title of 1992's electric romp, guitarist Di Meola is hoping to charm listeners back into the fold with this year's model, a beautiful tango-flavored acoustic session with strings, dedicated to the memory of the late Astor Piazzolla. Alternating between Piazzolla compositions and originals like the "Carousel Requiem" and the haunting "Under A Dark Moon," Al digs to the depths of his soul on this World Sinfonia project. Bandoneon player Dino Saluzzi adds the tango ambiance while Di Meola caresses each note rather than going for the burn. Their duet on "Someday My Prince Will Come," in tribute to Miles Davis, is particularly moving. —*Bill Milkowski*, Jazz Times

DIRTY DOZEN BRASS BAND

Group / New Orleans traditional
A top-notch ensemble, the Dirty Dozen Brass Band emerged in the mid '70s. They mixed contemporary material from R&B and bebop sources with arrangements that featured more traditional New Orleans brass band numbers; something that angered purists, but drew universal praise from audiences. The group soon became local celebrities, and later became certified stars on the international festival circuit. They've opened the doors for other groups, like the Rebirth Brass band and the Young Olympians. Their music has helped enhance and prolong the brass band tradition. If collaborations with Elvis Costello have given them widespread rock exposure, these collaboration have also brought the musical form to audiences that would otherwise never have heard it. Their brilliance and their jubilant rhythms can be heard on every session they've recorded for Concord, Rounder, and Sony. All of their dates are available on CD. — *Ron Wynn and Bruce Boyd Raeburn*

★ **My Feet Can't Fail Me Now** / i. 1984 / George Wein Collection 43005
The Dirty Dozen's 1984 debut paved the way for a new generation of New Orleans street music—traditional brass band instrumentation meets modern jazz and funk. The Dozen had a number of secret weapons to set them off from the competition, including: veteran baritone player Roger Lewis, a member of Fats Domino's band; Kirk Joseph, the greatest tuba player in jazz; and the ultra-funky Jenell Marshall on snare drum and vocals. While not as gutsy in the recording quality as their later efforts, this CD is highlighted by the Dozen's versions of "Blue Monk" and an early signature tune of theirs, their cover of Dave "Fat Man" Wilson's "I Ate Up the Apple Tree." —*Roundup Newsletter*

Live: Mardi Gras Montreux / Jul. 1985 / Rounder 2052
Dance music in a conceptually revolutionary jazz package— "The Flintstones Meet the President (Meet the Dirty Dozen)" illustrates the band's sense of humor effectively. —*Bruce Raeburn*

Voodoo / Aug. 1987-Sep. 1987 / Columbia 45042
Guest stars Dizzy Gillespie (tpt), Dr. John (p), and Branford Marsalis (ts) fit right in with the band's masterful ensemble work. —*Bruce Raeburn*

New Orleans Album / Dec. 1989 / Columbia 45414
This time, veteran Orleanians Danny Barker, Eddie Bo, and Dave Bartholomew join in, along with Elvis Costello—the

fun quotient runs off the meter with plenty of solos and absolutely infectious rhythms. —*Bruce Raeburn*

○ **Open up—Whatcha Gonna Do for the Rest of Your Life?** / Jan. 1991-Apr. 1991 / Columbia 47383

Jelly / i. 1993 / CBS 53214
The "Jelly" in question is Jelly Roll Morton, the first major composer in jazz as well as an arrogant genius whom the jazz world has never quite known what to do with. Morton's seminal work in the mid to late '20s (check out *The Pearls* on RCA/Bluebird) is essential early jazz. It is also the product of its time, and the DDBB have chosen to be themselves while interpreting his melodies (they ignore Morton's sense of form). What that means is that this is another tasty dollop of second-line rhythms, updated cakewalks, and gumbo backbeat that makes this octet so easy to love. And they're getting better; while the DDBB's early albums didn't have too much variety, there's a lot on *Open Up* and *Jelly*. Each number gets its own particular interpretation (four outside arrangers contributed), and while we might carp here and there (the second theme is missing in this chart of "The Pearls," for instance), on the whole this is joyous, energetic, and celebratory music. —*Bart Grooms*, Option

BILL DIXON (William Robert Dixon)

b. Oct. 5, 1925, Nantucket, MA
Trumpet, composer, flugelhorn, piano / Early free, modern creative
Bill Dixon's recording and performing career has been erratic because he is unwilling to play any music that he doesn't enjoy and respect. He's done free and totally composed/structured material, but has never been featured playing or recording more profitable commercial pop or fusion. Dixon has endured long absences from the musical scene willingly, and has advocated musician involvement in both musical and social causes. His style is seldom comforting; he uses distorted tones purposefully, uses squeezed and bent notes, and often uses exaggerated vibrato and unusual timbres and intonation. His approach is always compelling, but can be disconcerting.
Dixon studied painting at Boston University while working as a trumpeter and arranger. Dixon met Cecil Taylor at the Sportsman's Club in Harlem in 1951, and began a long-term musical and personal friendship. Dixon began heading his own groups in the late '50s, and, during the early '60s, concentrated on compositions, playing only his originals. He formed the United Nations Jazz Society in 1958, and co-led a quartet with Archie Shepp that recorded on Savoy and remained intact into the early '60s. Dixon later formed the New York Contemporary Five with Shepp, Don Cherry, and John Tchicai, writing all their compositions at first. They toured Europe in 1963. Dixon also produced some albums of free music for Savoy in the '60s, and, with filmmaker Peter Sabino, presented a concert series at the Cellar Cafe titled "The October Revolution in Jazz" in 1964. Participants included Sun Ra, Tchicai, Paul Bley, and Milford Graves. These concerts drew large audiences. Dixon organized the Jazz Composers Guild that same year, a collective designed to support jazz artists who wanted to work in venues besides clubs and who wanted to bypass booking agents. Charter members included Cecil Taylor, both Paul and Carla Bley, Mike Mantler, Roswell Rudd, and Shepp. Unfortunately, the Guild didn't last long, and its dreams were unfulfilled.
In the mid '60s, Dixon began working with dancer Judith Dunn, and their decade-long collaboration yielded many concerts that combined free music and dance, including a 1966 Newport Jazz Festival appearance. He recorded infrequently in the '60s, but did a great session for RCA in 1967. Dixon formed the Free Conservatory of the Streets in 1968 in New York, and it eventually received federal funding. That same year, he began teaching at Bennington College, where he started in an advisory/assistant role, and eventually founded a Black music department. Dixon served as visiting professor of music at the University of Wisconsin at Madison in 1971 and 1972, but turned down a permanent appoint-

ment, returning to Vermont to be near his son. He made more sessions in the '70s, particularly for Soul Note, and for Cadence and for Pipe as well. Dixon continued recording for Soul Note in the '80s and '90s, and published a collection of his writings, musical scores, drawings, and photographs in 1986. He also presented new compositions at jazz festivals in Paris, Verona, and Zurich in the late 70s and '80s. Only a handful of his recordings, all recent dates, are available on CD. —*Ron Wynn*

★ **Jazz Artistry of Bill Dixon, The** / Oct. 10, 1966 / RCA 3844

In Italy—Vol. 1 / Jul. 11-13, 1980 / Soul Note 1008
This Soul Note LP, recorded in Milano in the summer of 1980 and distributed in America by Rounder Records (at the time), is trumpeter and composer Bill Dixon's first release since his milestone RCA album *Intents and Purposes* in 1967. While it is less ambitious in scope than *Intents*, it is more intimate, in some ways more immediate, and offers even greater insight into Dixon's total personality. The musical setting is varied, drawing on all of Dixon's capabilities as a group leader and instrumentalist. *Volume One*'s long take of "Evening" begins as an ominous Dixon/Alan Silva trumpet/bass duet and expands to involve the entire sextet for a performance that was thoughtfully conceived and excellently played with moments of agitation and smoky, somber beauty. All six players are present also on three other pieces, with trumpeters Arthur Brooks and Stephen Haynes and saxophonist Stephen Horenstein, all former students of Dixon's at Bennington College (VT), adding splashes of color to the ensembles and taking occasional solo turns. "For Cecil Taylor" conjures its subject with jabbing, anticipatory rhythmic thrusts and features heartfelt Horenstein tenor and, again, good trumpet work. Freddie Waits was a resourceful drummer and Dixon put him to good use. The drum solo here is perfectly placed; it seems to have been brewing to a head all along. This is free music at its very best. —*Francis Davis*, Down Beat

In Italy—Vol. 2 / Jul. 11-13, 1980 / Soul Note 1011
A rare date from a distinctive trumpeter whose approach, clarity of tone, and directness set him apart in the '60s. The set includes a fine three-part song dedicated to Cecil Taylor. The band mixes avant-garde types like bassist Alan Silva with mainstream figures like drummer Freddie Waits. It also has an unusual lineup, with two, sometimes three trumpeters, a saxophonist, a bassist, and a drummer. Dixon occasionally plays piano. —*Ron Wynn*

November 1981 / Nov. 8, 1981 / Soul Note 103738
The music on this two-record set is typical of trumpeter Bill Dixon's hue and perhaps the most *in command* set of his so far released (1983). The first five tracks on sides one and two (November 16 and 17, 1981), struck me as rather unresolved and tedious on first listening. The last four tracks on sides three and four (November 8, 1981), grabbed me with both their immediacy and daring. Both sides impressed me with the dedication to purity, which has always marked all of Dixon's music. Repeated listenings to record number one brought out greater dimensions to the music, displaying an azure mellowness that runs deep with revolving panoramas. Record two opens with "Webern," a bold, biting piece that sets the tone and segues into "Winterset." The record ends with "Velvet," returning to the solace which marks so much of record one, and "Latino Suite," a developing piece of trumpet hues over washes of free rhythm which, by the time it evolves midway into a bowed bass solo, is quite effective. It is interesting how some of this music, "Velvet" in particular, maintains its pacing when it is played at 45 RPM. It plays faster, but the pulse remains the same. —*Bob Rusch*, Cadence

---

BABY DODDS (Baby (Warren) Dodds)

b. Dec. 24, 1898, New Orleans, LA, **d.** Feb. 14, 1959, Chicago, IL
Drums / New Orleans traditional

Along with Bill Johnson and Zutty Singleton, Warren "Baby" Dodds was one of the most important New Orleans drummers. He influenced many of the great stylists in both the traditional and swing genres by playing in a precise, compact, yet dynamic manner. Dodds was one of the first drummers to vary his patterns during performance, creating accents and shadings that were unheard of in an ensemble at that time. His tuning was also a marvel, and was later copied by several drummers, including Dave Tough and Gene Krupa. Late in his career, Dodds documented his technique on a series of Folkways recordings that were complete with commentary. The brother of clarinet wizard Johnny Dodds, he worked in New Orleans with Bunk Johnson, Papa Celestin, and others before joining Fate Marable's riverboat band in 1918. Dodds was invited to join King Oliver in San Francisco in 1922, and recorded with him in Chicago the next year. Dodds stayed in Chicago for over two decades, cutting seminal recordings with Jelly Roll Morton and Louis Armstrong. He also played in bands led by his brother. Dodds was in great demand during the '40s traditional jazz revival, and played with Jimmie Noone, Sidney Bechet, and Johnson, and made radio broadcasts in 1947 and toured Europe with Mezz Mezzrow in 1948. Though he was battling health problems, Dodds kept playing drums until 1957, only two years before his death. His famous series of solos are long gone from print. He can be heard on CD reissues by Armstrong, Johnny Dodds, and Morton. —*Ron Wynn*

○ **Baby Dodds Drum Method: Trio** / Jan. 31, 1944 / American Music 2

Baby Dodds Drum Method: Band / May 14, 1945 / American Music 1

★ **Footnotes to Jazz—Vol. 1** / Jan. 10, 1946 / Smithsonian/ Folkways 2290

Baby Dodds Drum Method: Solo / i. 1951 / American Music

JOHNNY DODDS (John M. Dodds)

b. Apr. 12, 1892, New Orleans, LA, **d.** Aug. 8, 1940, Chicago, IL
Clarinet / New Orleans traditional

Though he wasn't a virtuoso clarinetist, Johnny Dodds was a gifted improviser in the traditional New Orleans style. What set Dodds apart was the flow and energy in his solos. Playing within the restrictive ensemble-dominated early Crescent City style, Dodds injected dramatic lines and unforgettable statements into limited solo space, and did it in a flashy, vibrant manner. His playing had deep blues feeling, and his vibrato proved a marvelous hook for his solos. Dodds grew up in a musical family, and may have been a guitarist before starting clarinet at age 17. After a few lessons from Lorenzo Tio, Jr., Dodds was self-taught. He spent parts of six years with Kid Ory's New Orleans band, first joining the band in 1912. Dodds also toured with Fate Marable's riverboat band in 1917, then returned to Ory's group in 1919 after a brief stint with a road show. He left New Orleans in 1920 to join King Oliver in Chicago. Dodds participated in landmark sessions throughout the '20s, with Oliver's Creole Jazz Band in 1923 and, later, with Louis Armstrong on the Hot Five and Hot Seven studio recordings. While with Oliver, Dodds also played on the West Coast. He directed Freddie Keppard's house band at Kelly's Stables in Chicago from 1924 until 1930. Dodds also worked with Jelly Roll Morton and played frequently with his brother, Baby Dodds, in several small groups, among them the Black Bottom Stompers, Dixieland Thumpers, State Street Ramblers, and Washboard Band. He spent his last decade in Chicago heading a part-time band, sometimes coleading it with Baby Dodds. —*Ron Wynn with Myles Boisen*

○ **Jazz Classics: Great Performances (1923–1929)** / 1923-1929 / Mobile Fidelity 00603

○ **Chronological Johnny Dodds: 1926, The** / i. May 1926-Dec. 1926 / Classics 589

Blue Clarinet Stomp / Dec. 1926-Feb. 1929 / Bluebird 2293
1927 1929. Classic jazz at its best—Dodds with Jelly Roll
Morton's Trio, with his own orchestra, with his Washboard
Band, and with the Dixieland Jug Blowers. Alternate takes
show the improvisational character of Dodd's approach. The
CD has four bonus cuts —*Bruce Raeburn*

Jazz Heritage: Spirit of New Orleans (1926–1927) / 1926-
Apr. 21, 1927 / Jazz Heritage 1328
Traditional jazz's greatest clarinetist is featured on some
late-'20s tracks he cut for Decca. These tracks include
contributions from many immortal figures, among them
Kid Ory, George Mitchell, Jimmy Blythe, and Lil Hardin
Armstrong. —*Ron Wynn*

○ **Johnny Dodds and Kid Ory** / i. 1926-1928 / Epic 16004

○ **King of the New Orleans Clarinet (1926–1938)** / 1926-
1938 / Brunswick 58016

○ **Chronological Johnny Dodds: 1927–1928, The** / i. Jan.
1927-Oct. 1927 / Classics 603

★ **South Side Chicago Jazz** / 1927-1929 / MCA 42326
1927–1929. Dodds in various combinations, from his Trio
through the Black Bottom Stompers to Jimmy Blythe's
Washboard Wizards and the Beale Street Washboard Band.
"Wild Man Blues" shows one of many reasons Dodds was
one of most individual and celebrated clarinetists from New
Orleans. —*Bruce Raeburn*

Sixteen Rare Recordings / Jul. 5, 1928-Jan. 16, 1929 / RCA
558

ERIC DOLPHY (Eric Allan Dolphy)

b. Jun. 20, 1928, Los Angeles, CA, **d.** Jun. 29, 1964, Berlin,
Germany
Alto saxophone, bass clarinet, flute / Hard bop, early free
He was a virtuoso on three instruments and had strong links
to traditional bebop, yet Eric Dolphy endured some of the
worse press given to a major jazz musician during the early
'60s. He was derided as "anti-jazz" and was ridiculed in a
Down Beat blindfold test as a "sad mother" by Miles Davis.
Yet Dolphy was second only to Ornette Coleman as a brilliant '60s avant-garde alto saxophonist and composer. His
soaring, fleeting flute tones were amazingly close to bird
calls, while his loping, register-hopping bass clarinet solos
zoomed from the top to the bottom and back again with incredible ease. His unaccompanied alto sax, bass clarinet, and
flute solos were incredible; he played with the speed and
fury of Charlie Parker, but with a gentility and grace all his
own that mirrored his demure nature. Dolphy was hurt and
bewildered by the attacks, especially since very little of what
he played was uncontrolled or chaotic; it was intense and
vividly personal, but quite smooth. Dolphy loved African
and Indian music as well as jazz, and also played contemporary classical and third-stream music. He alternated between free and traditional bebop fluidly and smoothly.
Influenced by Sonny Criss and Charlie Parker, Dolphy was a
great influence on musicians as diverse as Ken McIntyre and
Anthony Braxton.
　He began playing clarinet at age six, and was doing professional concerts as an alto saxophonist while in junior
high school. He studied music at Los Angeles City College,
then played lead alto in Roy Porter's band from 1948 to
1950. He spent two years in the army, then transferred to the
U.S. Naval School of Music. He returned to Los Angeles in
1953, and played locally in several groups before joining
Chico Hamilton's band in 1958. This was one of Hamilton's
famous "chamber-jazz" groups, and Dolphy's versatility
proved quite handy. He resettled in New York the next year,
and joined Charles Mingus's group. He spent 1960 and 1961
with Mingus, doing several other sessions and cutting his
debut albums as a leader. Dolphy recorded with Ken
McIntyre and Mal Waldron, and with Ron Carter, Jaki Byard,
and Freddie Hubbard. He led a superb quintet with Booker
Little in 1961, but only for a few months. They did stay together long enough to make some magnificent live recordings at the Five Spot. He also did seminal sessions with

Ornette Coleman, Max Roach, and Coltrane, plus another
recording with the Latin Jazz Quintet. Dolphy played in
Europe twice that year and worked, for a short time, with
Coltrane. He formed a group in 1962 that again was short-
lived. Dolphy joined John Lewis's Orchestra U.S.A., and did a
few more dates with Mingus and Coltrane, plus the orchestra. He did some concerts and recording sessions in Europe,
but died in 1964. Fortunately, a great deal of Dolphy material, as well as things he did with other musicians, is available on CD. Several excellent dates have been issued on CD.
—*Ron Wynn and Myles Boisen*

☆ **Outward Bound** / Apr. 1, 1960 / New Jazz 022
Expansive, compelling, and excellent Dolphy with strong
Freddie Hubbard and even better Jaki Byard. —*Ron Wynn*

Status / Apr. 1, 1960-Sep. 8, 1961 / Prestige 24070
Four sessions from 1960–1961. A reissue of two albums: *In
Europe* and *Here and There*. —*AMG*

○ **Here and There** / Apr. 1, 1960-Sep. 8, 1961 / Prestige 673

Other Aspects / Jul. 8, 1960-1962 / Blue Note 48041

☆ **Out There** / Aug. 15, 1960 / New Jazz 023
Dolphy at his evocative best, with wonderful support from
Ron Carter and Roy Haynes.—*Ron Wynn*

Candid Dolphy / Oct. 20, 1960-Apr. 4, 1961 / Candid 79033
From 1960-1961. This is an excellent collection of small
combo sessions with numerous luminaries such as Ted
Curson (tpt), Kenny Dorham (tpt), and Abbey Lincoln (v). —
Ron Wynn

★ **Far Cry** / Dec. 21, 1960 / New Jazz 400
This marks Dolphy's departure from standard jazz repertoire
playing, with originals and exciting Parkerisms. —*Myles
Boisen*

Magic / Dec. 21, 1960+Jun. 27, 1961 / Prestige 24053
With Ron Carter. A reissue of two Prestige albums: *Far Cry*
and the Mal Waldron album, *The Quest*. —*AMG*

★ **Live! at the Five Spot—Vol. 1** / Jul. 16, 1961 / New Jazz 133
The first of the immortal Dolphy live dates, with incredible
interaction between Dolphy and Booker Little (tpt).
Awesome alto sax and bass clarinet, with feverish tempos. —
Ron Wynn

★ **Live! at the Five Spot—Vol. 2** / Jul. 16, 1961 / Prestige 247
Just as vital as its predecessor. Wondrous solos and compositions. 1987 reissues of a landmark concert. —*Ron Wynn*

○ **Eric Dolphy and Booker Little** / Jul. 16, 1961 / Prestige
7334

☆ **Great Concert of Eric Dolphy, The** / Jul. 16, 1961 / Prestige
34002
The complete Five Spot concert recordings in a three-album
package. It may be unavailable now. —*Ron Wynn*

○ **Eric Dolphy Memorial Album** / Jul. 16, 1961 / Prestige
7334
This LP and *Eric Dolphy 1928 1964* are exactly the same,
they're just packaged differently. . . . The music is from Eric
Dolphy's highly regarded 1963 (May June) Douglas sessions,
at which he was surrounded with fellow avant acolytes
(Prince Lasha, flute; Sonny Simmons, alto sax) and players
with more conventional hard bop credentials (Woody Shaw,
trumpet; Clifford Jordan, soprano sax; Bobby Hutcherson,
vibes). The rhythm chores were vouchsafed to Eddie Kahn or
Richard Davis on bass, and Charles Moffitt and J. C. Moses
on drums. "Jitterbug Waltz" is an almost farcical meandering
on that venerable Fats Waller tune. "Music Matador" is a bit
of the calypso-surreal, composed jointly by Lasha and
Simmons. Dolphy is on flute and bass clarinet, respectively,
for these tracks. The flip side, however, contains the disc's
most enduring tracks. "Alone Together" is a duet, which finds
Dolphy's bass clarinet soaring and diving above Richard
Davis's stringent striding. "Love Me" is the full-throated
Dolphy alto along for a three-and-a-half minute investigation of the infrequently heard Victor Young pop tune. *Eric
Dolphy 1928 1964* lists full personnel for each track and has
sensible liner notes (by Leonard Feather). *The Eric Dolphy*

Memorial Album boasts neither of those assets. *—Alan Bargebuhr,* Cadence

Latin Jazz Quintet / Aug. 19, 1961 / New Jazz 8251

Berlin Concerts / Aug. 30, 1961 / Mesa Blue Moon 79636
Tremendous Dolphy with good assistance from Jamil Nasser (b) and Benny Bailey (tpt). *—Ron Wynn*

Eric Dolphy in Europe—Vols. 1–3 / Sep. 6+8, 1961 / Original Jazz Classics 413
Live recordings from two dates, spread over three albums. All feature excellent soloing and capable, if reserved, backing from a Danish trio. *—Myles Boisen*

Copenhagen Concert / Sep. 8, 1961 / Prestige 24027
Remarkable, soaring alto sax, bass clarinet, and flute from the incomparable Eric Dolphy, featured in concert from Copenhagen, Denmark in 1961. Dolphy is so transcendent that he dominates the European rhythm section and renders their contributions, both accompanying him and solo, nearly meaningless. This has been reissued on CD. *—Ron Wynn*

Stockholm Sessions / Sep. 25, 1961-Jan. 1, 19 6 / Enja 79647
Dolphy is typically amazing. Borderline European players and material. The 1990 CD issue has a bonus cut. *—Ron Wynn*

Vintage Dolphy / Mar. 14, 1963-Apr. 18, 1963 / GM 3005
A collection of early-'60s Dolphy recordings that stylistically veer everywhere. Worth having. *—Ron Wynn*

Conversations / May 1963-Jun. 1963 / Restless 72660
For those who want all the Dolphy out there. Often brilliant material, but haphazardly compiled. *—Ron Wynn*

Iron Man / May 1963-Jun. 1963 / Restless 72659
Unheralded, sometimes chaotic set of recordings that includes much of value. Prince Lasha (vib) gets second star. *—Ron Wynn*

★ **Out to Lunch** / Feb. 25, 1964 / Blue Note 46524
His classic. Daring structures and startling solos from a quintet that would all go on to star status. With Freddie Hubbard (tpt) and Bobby Hutcherson (vib). *—Myles Boisen*

☆ **Last Date** / Jun. 2, 1964 / PolyGram 822226
The best of Eric's European sessions, with inspired backing and outstanding solo spots.—Myles Boisen

BARBARA DONALD (Barbara Kay Donald)

b. Feb. 9, 1942, Minneapolis, MN
Trumpet, leader / Modern creative
An often compelling trumpeter, Barbara Donald has worked with several top musicians, among them John Coltrane. Her range, articulation, and hard-edged style are impressive, but she hasn't done many recordings. Donald began playing in R&B groups during the early '60s in New York, and later did a Southern tour with a big band. She worked with Dexter Gordon and Stanley Cowell in Los Angeles, and through the '60s and '70s played with saxophonist Sonny Simmons, who was also her husband. Donald worked with Coltrane, Richard Davis, Prince Lasha, Rahsaan Roland Kirk, and many others during the '60s as well. After a five-year absence, Donald formed her own band in the mid '70s. She recorded for Cadence Jazz in the '80s. Currently, Donald does not have any sessions available on CD. *—Ron Wynn*

★ **Olympia Live** / i. Mar. 1981 / Cadence 1017
The music here is no-frills hard bop with lots of blowing space for the participants. In the case of trumpeter Barbara Donald's recording, she and saxophonist Carter Jefferson take the bulk of the solo space. After a statement of the head, Jefferson takes off on a muscular tenor sax solo with the rhythm section of drums, bass, and piano comping behind him. Donald's trumpet eventually comes in for some impassioned playing. As the interview on the back cover states, Donald shows some of Booker Little's influence, but it is difficult to identify any specific stylist in her playing. Cedar Walton's "Bolivia" has some good solos from Jefferson and Donald with some restrained guitar (Steve Jacobsen)

and piano (Cookie Marenco) in the playground. Thelonious Monk's "Well You Needn't" again has spare comping from the piano and guitar and is a strong performance until Jacobsen comes in for a solo (or at least I think he was supposed to solo). From here, the piece falls into a section where neither the pianist nor guitarist seem willing to take an effective solo. The final two pieces, however, return to the earlier strengths. "Prayer For My Children" is a moving trumpet/piano duet, and "Raisha's Dreams" is a waltz-time performance that is weak only in regards to Jefferson's soprano work, which just is not as strong as his tenor. *—Carl Brauer,* Cadence

○ **Past and Tomorrows, The** / i. Apr. 1982 / Cadence 1017
No doubt that Barbara Donald can play the trumpet with considerable fervor and forcefulness. If that was all there was to it, she would have one terrific LP on her hands. As it is, it is a very good one, marred by a certain unevenness in some aspects. The title track, for example, a Donald composition, is one of those things in which, though the motor is running, the gears never engage, resulting in a sort of musical catalepsy. But the following "Eric," a line by the late Irvin Lovilette (drums), to whom the record is dedicated, is appropriately acidic, with strong soloing from the leader, Carter Jefferson (tenor sax), and Peggy Stern (piano). "Pannonica" is honed into a starkly simple gem, played in less than four minutes, laying bare the beauty of the Thelonious Monk melody. "Ride" contains the date's best bop, in a track that is, perhaps, too brief, but contains more strong soloing from Jefferson. . . . Mike Bisio's (bass) "Charles Too!" (exclamation point added by this writer, taking the cue from the Bisio LP) does not have the power it has on the composer's disk. . . . This is an interesting and varied program, often played with power. *—Alan Bargebuhr,* Cadence

LOU DONALDSON

b. Nov. 1, 1926, Badin, NC
Alto saxophone, vocals / Bop, blues & jazz, soul-jazz
A truly great bebop player, alto saxophonist Lou Donaldson strayed from the path in the early '70s, making some decent soul-jazz and funk records and a couple of mediocre fusion dates. But he returned in the late '70s to his best style: hard-edged, searing bop, played with as much vigor as any living performer. Like Frank Morgan and Phil Woods, Donaldson, at his best, exemplifies the Charlie Parker spirit without being a slavelike imitator. He can insert clever quotes, make dazzling harmonic maneuvers at fast or slow tempos, and play beautiful, compelling blues and ballads.
Donaldson began clarinet studies at age 15, and later joined the navy, continuing his education. Having switched to alto sax, he played in a navy band with Willie Smith, Clark Terry, and Ernie Wilkins. In 1952, Donaldson made his recording debut with Milt Jackson and Thelonious Monk. He began leading various combos, playing with Charlie Parker, Sonny Stitt, Blue Mitchell, Horace Silver, Art Blakey, Clifford Brown, and Philly Joe Jones before joining Blakey's Jazz Messengers with Brown in 1954. Since leaving the Messengers, Donaldson has been a busy leader and session contributor, recording numerous albums and touring frequently nationally and overseas. Initially, he recorded for Blue Note from 1952 to 1962, cutting albums with Silver, Brown, Horace Parlan, Baby Face Willette, and Big John Patton, among others. He started including soul-jazz material on his Blue Note dates, but began to switch more to funk in 1963 when he moved to Argo (later Cadet). Donaldson recorded again with Patton and made a nine-piece session with Oliver Nelson before returning to Blue Note in 1967. There was another nine-piece group date. Donaldson recorded with George Benson, Charles Earland, and Lonnie Smith also. These were mostly soul-jazz and funk, but they were earthy and enjoyable. Donaldson's solos still reflected his bebop heritage.
During the early '70s, Blue Note joined other labels in the jazz-rock/fusion/instrumental pop phase (or craze). Donaldson made albums with overdubbed female vocals,

strings, and heavy electronic backgrounds. He defended albums like *Cosmos* and *Sweet Lou* in magazine and newspaper interviews at the time, but by the late '70s he returned to the music he knew and played best. His '80s sessions for Timeless, Muse, and Blue Note reaffirmed those values; tart, sizzling bop, and animated blues and ballads. He has continued recording in the '90s for Milestone. Donaldson's formative Blue Note dates, both as a leader and with the Jazz Messengers, have been reissued periodically, while the bulk of his other material, except the Argo/Cadet records, is still in print. *—Ron Wynn and Bob Porter*

Lou Donaldson Quartet/Quintet/Sextet, The / Jun. 10, 1952-Aug. 22, 1954 / Blue Note 1537
Both soul-jazz and more mainstream/hard pop sessions. Elmo Hope (p), Horace Silver (p), Blue Mitchell (tpt), Kenny Dorham (tpt), and a cast of all-stars. *—Ron Wynn*

★ **With Clifford Brown** / Jun. 9, 1953 / Blue Note 5030

○ **Wailing with Lou** / Jan. 27, 1955 / Blue Note 1545

○ **Lou Takes Off** / Dec. 15, 1957 / Blue Note 1591

★ **Blues Walk** / Jul. 28, 1958 / Blue Note 46525
Alto saxophonist Lou Donaldson recorded with all manner of groups during his two long stays with Blue Note. Herman Foster, Peck Morrison, Dave Bailey, and Ray Barretto may not have had the hippest reputations vis-à-vis some other Blue Note rhythm players, but on *Blues Walk* they certainly get the job done. Donaldson is in his finest form here. Just how favorably the album is remembered can best be exemplified by the fact that several of the tunes here are among his most requested. Put the pencils and scorecards away, put this album on, and listen to the music; brighten up your day. *—Bob Porter, Jazz Times*

○ **Lou Donaldson with the Three Sounds** / Feb. 12-18, 1959 / Blue Note 4012

Here 'tis / Jan. 23, 1961 / Blue Note 84066
Robust, earthy soul-jazz and blues with overlooked organist Baby Face Willette. *—Ron Wynn*

Natural Soul / May 9, 1962 / Blue Note 84108

Good Gracious / Jan. 24, 1963 / Blue Note 4125

Rough House Blues / Dec. 1964 / Argo
Best and most ambitious of mid-'60s Argo albums. Oliver Nelson supplies the arrangements for this nine-piece band. *—Ron Wynn*

○ **Possum Head** / 1964 / Argo 734

★ **Lush Life** / Jan. 20, 1967 / Blue Note 84254

Alligator Boogaloo / Apr. 7, 1967 / Blue Note 84263
Prototype funk, soul-jazz, blues, boogie, and ballads from a stalwart alto master. *—Ron Wynn*

Sweet Poppa Lou / Jan. 1981 / Muse 5247

Forgotten Man / Jul. 2, 1981 / Timeless
Donaldson breaks into the '80s with verve, contributing an interesting vocal on "Whiskey Drinkin' Woman." *—Ron Wynn*

Back Street / 1982 / Muse 5292

Play the Right Thing / 1990 / Milestone 9190
This is the latest in a long line of sumptuous soul-jazz/funky workouts. *—Ron Wynn*

DOROTHY DONEGAN

Bop
Dorothy Donegan is a captivating, entertaining pianist who's been playing since the '40s. She's a true virtuoso who switches effortlessly between stride, classical music, bebop, and boogie-woogie, sometimes within the same song. Donegan's live appearances often feature unusual medleys in which she plays whatever pops into her head, but few studio recordings really display the power and talents of this unique pianist. Donegan has recorded for Rosetta, Continental, Pontiac, Miltone, Jubilee, Stash, Capitol, Roulette, Regina, Mahogany, Black & Blue, and others. She's recorded mostly in trios or solo situations. *—Ron Wynn*

○ **Dorothy Romps- a Piano Retrospective (1953 1979)** / 1953-1979 / Rosetta 1318

Dorothy Donegan Live! / i. Apr. 30, 1959 / Capitol 1155

Swingin' Jazz in Hi Fi / i. Dec. 1963 / Regina 285

○ **Live at the 1990 Floating Jazz Festival** / 1990 / Chiaroscuro 318

★ **Incredible Dorothy Donegan Trio, The** / i. 1991 / Chiaroscuro 312

○ **Explosive Dorothy Donegan** / i. 1991 / Progressive 7056
An exuberant, frenetic pianist whose albums only partly convey her dynamic personality. Donegan's live act is among jazz's most entertaining, full of sassy, sometimes irreverent commentary that doesn't obscure her command of the instrument. This album has lots of aggressive, raging piano solos, plus some wonderfully played ballads. *—Ron Wynn*

Makin' Whoopie / Black & Blue 59146

Dorothy Romps / Rosetta 1318
This retrospective of the works of one of the most outstanding pianists in jazz history spans 1953-1979, as Volume 9 in Rosetta Records' *Foremothers* series. From boogie-woogie to honky-tonk to blues, pop, and even classical, this album demonstrates the spectacular technique and broad-ranging abilities of the artist. Includes "Greig's Boogie," "Louise," "I Want A Little Girl," "Minuet in G," "Lullaby of Birdland." *—Ladyslipper*

KENNY DORHAM

b. Aug. 30, 1924, Fairfield, TX, **d.** Dec. 5, 1972, New York, NY
Trumpet, composer / Hard bop
Kenny Dorham had a deeply moving, pure tone on trumpet; his sound was clear, sharp, and piercing, especially on ballads. He could rip off phrases and lines, but when he played a melody slowly and sweetly it was an evocative event. Dorham was a gifted, all-around trumpeter, but seldom showcased his complete skills, preferring an understated, subtle approach. Unfortunately, he never received much publicity, and though a highly intelligent, thoughtful individual who wrote insightful commentary on jazz, he's little more than a footnote to many fans.

Dorham studied and played trumpet, tenor sax, and piano. He was a band member in high school and college; Wild Bill Davis was a college band mate. Dorham started during the swing era, but was recruited by Dizzy Gillespie and Billy Eckstine to join their bands in the mid '40s. He even sang blues with Gillespie's band. He recorded with the Be Bop Boys on Savoy in 1946. After short periods with Lionel Hampton and Mercer Ellington, Dorham joined Charlie Parker's group in 1948, and stayed with the group until 1949. He did sessions in New York during the early and mid '50s, and made his recording debut as a leader on Charles Mingus's and Max Roach's Debut label in 1953. He cut *Afro-Cuban* for Blue Note with Cecil Payne, Hank Mobley, and Horace Silver in 1955. Dorham was a founding member of Art Blakey's Jazz Messengers in 1954, and also led a similar short-lived band, the Jazz Prophets. Dorham played on the soundtrack of *A Star Is Born* in 1954, then spent two years with Max Roach from 1956 to 1958.

There were dates for Riverside in the late '50s with Paul Chambers, Tommy Flanagan, and Art Taylor, plus other sessions with ABC Paramount. Dorham did three volumes for Blue Note recorded live at the Cafe Bohemia, and did an intriguing, but uneven, session with John Coltrane and Cecil Taylor, *Coltrane Time*, in 1958. Dorham taught at the Lenox School of Jazz in 1958 and 1959, and wrote scores for the films *Les liaisons dangereuses* and *Un temoin dans la ville* in 1959. During the mid '60s, he co-led a band with tenor saxophonist Joe Henderson that was shamefully neglected. There were classic Blue Note releases such as *Whistle Stop*, *Una Mas*, and *Trumpet Toccata*. Dorham made one album for Cadet in 1970, *Kenny Dorham Sextet* with Muhal Richard Abrams. He died in 1972. Several of his Blue Note albums have been reissued, while his Prestige and Riverside dates have come out in sporadic fashion, some in two-record samplers. Other material for Pacific Jazz, United Artists, Steeplechase, Xanadu, and Time isn't as widely available. — *Ron Wynn*

Kenny Dorham Quintet / Dec. 15, 1953 / Debut 113
A wonderful session originally on Debut. Outstanding Jimmy Heath (sax). — *Ron Wynn*

★ **Afro-Cuban** / Jan. 30, 1955-Mar. 29, 1955 / Blue Note 46815

Round Midnight at the Cafe Bohemia—Vols. 1 & 2 / Jan. 30, 1955-Mar. 29, 1955 / Blue Note 46541
Vol. 1 is tremendous live set at Cafe Bohemia and includes some of Dorham's greatest solos on any record. Vol. 2 is equally strong. — *Ron Wynn*

And the Jazz Prophets / Apr. 4, 1956 / Paramount 122

Jazz Contrasts / May 21, 1957+May 27, 1957 / Riverside 028
A solid session with Sonny Rollins (ts), Max Roach (d), and fellow greats. — *Ron Wynn*

☆ **2 Horns, 2 Rhythms** / Nov. 13, 1957 / Riverside 463
Quartet. Includes the brilliant Ernie Henry (as), who, sadly, has been overlooked, plus more excellent Dorham. — *Ron Wynn*

This Is the Moment / Jul. 7, 1958-Aug. 15, 1958 / Prestige

Blue Spring / Jan. 20, 1959+Feb. 18, 1959 / Riverside 134
Blue Spring, recorded and originally released in 1959, should twist some ears. Trumpeter Kenny Dorham's composing (four scores) and arranging (all six tunes) creates a moving portrait of late-'50s/early-'60s jazz. The melodies are distinct and above average, and the charts resonate with crisp punctuation, flowing internal lines, and warm voicings. The solo payoff between Dorham's dark-toned etchings and Cannonball Adderley's tumbling bop alto adds to the interest here, too. Dorham's low- and middle-register solo on "Spring Is Here" is a gem. — *Owen Cordle, Down Beat*

○ **But Beautiful** / Feb. 18, 1959 / Milestone 47036

Quiet Kenny / Nov. 13, 1959 / Original Jazz Classics 250
An emphatic, remarkable quartet session reissued in 1987. Immaculate Tommy Flanagan (p). — *Ron Wynn*

○ **Showboat** / Dec. 9, 1960 / Bainbridge 1043
A superb quintet date from 1960. Dorham's bright, crackling trumpet contrasts with the smooth, yet vibrant, tenor sax of Jimmy Heath. A dynamic rhythm section features pianist Kenny Drew, bassist Jimmy Garrison, and drummer Art Taylor, and not only compliments and supports the frontline, but frequently spurs and even subtly challenges them during ensemble passages. This has been reissued on CD. — *Ron Wynn*

○ **Whistle Stop** / Jan. 15, 1961 / Blue Note 4063

○ **West 42nd Street** / Mar. 1961 / Black Lion 760119

○ **Osmosis** / Oct. 1961 / Black Lion 760146

○ **Inta Somethin'** / Nov. 1961 / Pacific Jazz 41

Ease It! / i. 1961 / Muse 5053

Matador / Inta Somethin' / Apr. 15, 1962+Nov. 1961 / Capitol 84460

★ **Una Mas** / Apr. 1, 1963 / Blue Note 46515

★ **Trompeta Toccata** / Sep. 4, 1964 / Blue Note 84181
The composer/trumpeter's finest hour. A quintet with Joe Henderson (ts). — *Michael G. Nastos*

Kenny Dorham Sextet / Aug. 20, 1970 / Cadet 60002

DORSEY BROTHERS

Group
Before their different personalities clashed and split the band down the middle, Tommy and Jimmy Dorsey were jointly heading a polished, sophisticated swing band that was extraordinarily popular in the '30s. The brothers' celebrated feud was headline news everywhere. They maintained separate units until their deaths, and even today the ghost bands maintain separate operations and organizations. — *Ron Wynn*

○ **The Dorsey Brothers–Vol. 1** / i. Feb. 14, 1928-Nov. 2, 1928 / 14
This LP (the first of two volumes) has the first 16 recordings led by the Dorsey Brothers. There are no personnel or date listings but this set is well worth acquiring for it includes many fine examples of hot dance music, featuring Tommy Dorsey's trombone, Jimmy's clarinet and alto, and appearances by trumpeters Leo McConville and Phil Napoleon along with a variety of dated singers. Their version of "My Melancholy Baby" is a classic with TD playing some fine trumpet and bass saxophonist Adrian Rollini heard in a prominent role. — *Scott Yanow*

Dorsey Brothers–Vol. 2 / i. Oct. 1928-Nov. 7, 1930 / 15
The second of two LP volumes from the collector's label TOM has 16 more examples of Tommy and Jimmy Dorsey in their early days. The music strikes a balance between hot jazz and commercial dance music with the leaders, tenorman Bud Freeman, and guitarist Eddie Lang having many fine spots even if the varying singers also get plenty of space. Well worth acquiring since most of this material has not been reissued on CD yet. — *Scott Yanow*

○ **Mood Hollywood** / i. Sep. 24, 1932-Oct. 17, 1933 / 1005
This excellent LP features 16 performances (including four alternate takes) by the Dorsey Brothers during 1932-33. Bunny Berigan's trumpet solos are the most memorable aspect of these early swing recordings, many of which feature an octet rather than a big band. Highlights include "Someone Stole Gabriel's Horn," two takes of "I'm Getting Sentimental Over You," and the many fine solos of both Tommy and Jimmy Dorsey. — *Scott Yanow*

Decca Sessions (1934-1935), The / 1934-1935 / MCA 1505
A budget LP from MCA that only includes ten recordings by the Dorsey Brothers Orchestra (less than a half-hour of music) and has a barely readable personnel listing. The only thing that saves this set is the generally strong jazz-oriented music performed by this first-class dance band (heard only a short time before its breakup) including fine versions of "Dippermouth Blues," "Milenberg Joys," and "Honeysuckle Rose." — *Scott Yanow*

The Dorsey Brothers' Orchestra 1935 / i. Jan. 17, 1935 / Circle 20
This LP contains music recorded for radio transcriptions by the Dorsey Brothers Orchestra, one of the most interesting new bands to be heard during this era. The music by this dance band is generally jazz-oriented (although Bob Crosby's three vocals are quite straight) with fine solos from Tommy's trombone and Jimmy's alto and clarinet; the lead trumpet of Charlie Spivak is also heard from. Nice music even if few surprises occur. — *Scott Yanow*

Best of the Big Band / Columbia 48908
The Dorsey Brothers Orchestra was actually just a series of studio groups until Jimmy and Tommy decided to hit the road in 1934. This strong jazz-oriented CD covering the 1932-34 period actually finds the exciting trumpeter Bunny Berigan consistently stealing solo honors. Highlights include Bill Challis's arrangement of "Someone Stole Gabriel's Horn," "The Blue Room," the novelty tune "Annie's Cousin Fanny," and the original version of what would later become Tommy Dorsey's theme song, "I'm Getting Sentimental Over You." — *Scott Yanow*

JIMMY DORSEY (James Dorsey)

b. Feb. 29, 1904, Shenandoah, PA, **d.** Jun. 12, 1957, New York, NY

Clarinet, alto and baritone saxophone / Swing, big band
Jimmy was the older of the Dorsey Brothers. His clarinet playing reflected Jimmie Noone's style, while his sax work was praised by Coleman Hawkins and Lester Young. He had a smooth, polished, and sophisticated approach, and could display a solid rhythmic sense also. Jimmy Dorsey began playing slide trumpet and cornet at age seven, then switched to reed instruments as a teen. After the early years of playing with his brother in various studio bands and with many

of the leading White jazz musicians and bands, Jimmy found himself heading the popular Dorsey orchestra alone in 1935. He began doing extensive radio broadcasts, and recruited top arrangers like Fud Livingston, Don Redman, and Tutti Camarata. Vocalists Bob Eberly and Helen O'Connell also proved quite popular in the late '30s and early '40s. The Jimmy Dorsey orchestra had 23 Top 10 hits between 1940 and 1944, with "Amapoloa," "My Sister and I," "Green Eyes/Maria Elena," "Blue Champagne," and "Tangerine" all topping the charts. The 1947 film *The Fabulous Dorseys* chronicled their lives (to some degree). The brothers re-united in 1953 and continued playing together until Tommy Dorsey's death in 1956. Jimmy Dorsey kept the band going until his battles with cancer forced him to hand the reins over to Lee Castle. Castle's band had the hit "So Rare" four months before Jimmy Dorsey's death in 1957. Thus far, Jimmy Dorsey's part of the Dorsey Brothers equation hasn't been well served by the reissue market, at least domestically. —*Ron Wynn*

○ **The Early Years / i.** Oct. 10, 1935-Dec. 22, 1941 / Bandstand 7104

Jimmy Dorsey was best known during the swing era for leading a rather commercial big band dominated by vocals, so a jazz-oriented retrospective such as this LP is quite welcome. The 16 performances (10 of which are instrumentals) include many rarities such as "Serenade to Nobody in Particular," "Stop! and Reconsider," "Bar Babble," and "Mutiny in the Brass Section." These selections show that, despite its public image, the older Dorsey's orchestra could be a strong jazz band when called upon. —*Scott Yanow*

★ **Contrasts / i.** Jul. 7, 1936-Oct. 7, 1943 / Decca 626

This CD, virtually the only example of Jimmy Dorsey's orchestra currently available on CD, puts the emphasis on JD's jazz sides rather than the vocal best-sellers. Popular singer Helen O'Connell does make three appearances (including the hit "Tangerine"), but most of these selections are instrumentals with Dorsey's alto and clarinet in outstanding form (it was easy to forget his talent as an instrumentalist during these commercial years). Most of the other fine soloists are lesser names although they include future band-leaders Ray McKinley (d) and pianist Freddie Slack. Highlights are "Parade of the Milk Bottle Caps," "I Got Rhythm," "John Silver," "Duks in Upper Sandusky," Dorsey's theme "Contrasts," and "King Porter Stomp," although there isn't a weak track on this release. Recommended, Dorsey's definitive set. —*Scott Yanow*

Uncollected Jimmy Dorsey & His Orchestra—Vol. 1 (1939-1940) / 1939-1940 / Hindsight 101

The first of five Hindsight LPs to document Jimmy Dorsey's radio transcriptions, this set gives a good all-around picture of Dorsey's orchestra shortly before it became a major commercial success. There are four vocals apiece by Helen O'Connell and Bob Eberly, along with eight fine instrumentals. Although Dorsey (on alto and clarinet) is the only distinctive soloist, overall it's first-class swing and dance music. —*Scott Yanow*

☆ **Greatest Hits / i.** 1940-1944 / MCA 252

A sampler containing jazzy pop and big-band songs done by the Jimmy Dorsey band in the immediate period after he left Tommy's orchestra. It's a decent introduction to his music, but far from comprehensive. —*Ron Wynn*

Uncollected Jimmy Dorsey & His Orchestra—Vol. 2 (1942-1944) / 1942-1944 / Hindsight 153

The second of five LPs released by Hindsight that contain performances cut for radio airplay by the Jimmy Dorsey orchestra. This is more jazz-oriented than Dorsey's usual recordings. Helen O'Connell has a pair of vocals, and there are also hot versions of "Just You, Just Me," "I Got Rhythm," "I Would Do Anything For You," and the boppish "Grand Central Getaway," which was composed and arranged by Dizzy Gillespie. Such players as pianist Johnny Guarnieri, trumpeter Ray Linn, and tenorman Babe Russin are heard

from during this fine overview of Dorsey's wartime orchestra. —*Scott Yanow*

○ **Wartime V-Disc Sessions / i.** Oct. 1943-1945 / Sandy Hook 2046

On this excellent LP one gets to hear the overlooked and underrecorded Jimmy Dorsey orchestra of 1943-44 on some strong jazz-oriented performances (with only one vocal) originally recorded for V-discs and not released commercially. A special bonus is the inclusion of three selections from 1945 that find the Jimmy and Tommy Dorsey Orchestras playing together noisily but with coherence. It was the Dorsey Brothers' first musical reunion since their breakup a decade earlier. Overall, this is a fine LP of late-period swing. —*Scott Yanow*

○ **Featuring Maynard Ferguson / i.** Mar. 1949-May 1949 / Big Band Archives 1216

The 1949 Jimmy Dorsey Orchestra was one of the most interesting if overlooked big bands of the era. Although Dorsey had mostly played commercial music earlier in the decade, he had never lost his love for jazz. By 1949 he had hired some bebop musicians and was playing some modern charts, but at the same time was also performing Dixieland with a small group from his orchestra. This LP of radio broadcasts not only features Dorsey's alto and clarinet and the Dixielandish trumpet of Charlie Teagarden but also the outstanding high-note trumpet of Maynard Ferguson, heard a year before he became famous playing with Stan Kenton. Since Ferguson was not with Dorsey long enough to record with him commercially, these radio aircheks are particularly valuable historically in addition to being enjoyable musically. —*Scott Yanow*

Uncollected Jimmy Dorsey & His Orchestra—Vol. 3 (1949-1951) / 1949-1951 / Hindsight 165

The third of five Hindsight LPs featuring Jimmy Dorsey's orchestra is particularly interesting because it features his big bands of 1949 and 1951, a period of time when Dorsey was no longer having hits or prospering financially. In fact, in 1952 he would disband and join brother Tommy's orchestra. Other than one Claire Hogan vocal, these two sessions are comprised of instrumentals that feature both Dorsey and many members of his talented, but no-name, crew. Good late swing music. —*Scott Yanow*

○ **Muscat Ramble / i.** 1950 / Swing House 22

During 1949-50, Jimmy Dorsey enjoyed leading a small group taken out of his big band and playing Dixieland. This English LP finds the hot band, which featured Charlie Teagarden's trumpet and sometimes Cutty Cutshall's trombone, jamming happily on a set of Dixieland standards. Jimmy Dorsey, who mostly sticks to clarinet, clearly enjoyed playing this music; perhaps he should have spent the '50s in similar small combos instead of permanently joining his brother's orchestra in 1952. Recommended music, if you can find this! —*Scott Yanow*

Uncollected Jimmy Dorsey & His Orchestra—Vol. 4 (1950) / 1950 / Hindsight 178

The fourth of five LPs issued by Hindsight that feature rare aircheks of Jimmy Dorsey's orchestra showcases his band in its declining days. Despite the three commercial vocals heard on this set, however, Dorsey's 1950 band was a potentially strong jazz outfit, featuring Charlie Teagarden and Shorty Sherock on trumpets along with the leader's alto and clarinet. JD's workout on "Fingerbustin'" and the renditions of "Lover" and "King Porter Stomp" are high points of this swinging set. —*Scott Yanow*

Uncollected Jimmy Dorsey & His Orchestra—Vol. 5 / 1950 / Hindsight 203

Although he still struggled to keep his orchestra together, during 1949-1950 Jimmy Dorsey often returned to his roots, leading a small contingent out of his big band that he termed "The Original Dorseyland Band." The seven-piece group, featuring Charlie Teagarden's trumpet, trombonist Frank Rehak, Artie Lyons on tenor, and Dorsey mostly on clarinet (but also on alto), is heard playing a variety of

Dixieland tunes in a spirited fashion on these transcriptions. *—Scott Yanow*

★ **Greatest Hits** / Curb 77411

Best of Jimmy Dorsey, The / MCA 4073
This out-of-print, two-LP set has only 20 performances and does not list the personnel or recording dates, but it does contain several fine pictures and offers a good all-around overview of Jimmy Dorsey's commercial recordings. Of the 20 songs, all but four have vocals, mostly by Helen O'Connell and Bob Eberly, and five have vocal duets. Not much is heard from the leader, but it was the singers who made Jimmy Dorsey's orchestra one of the most popular in the early 1940s. Listeners who enjoyed the hits should pick this one up; it includes "Tangerine," "Brazil," "Green Eyes" and "Besame Mucho." *—Scott Yanow*

Fabulous Jimmy Dorsey, The / Fraternity 1008
After Tommy Dorsey's death in 1956, Jimmy Dorsey took over his orchestra, although it turned out that he himself was dying from cancer. Ironically, JD's final recording date resulted in his first hit in over a decade, "So Rare." Dorsey's alto is actually heard on only 4 of the 13 selections on this LP; after he passed away, trumpeter Lee Castle took over the band and altoist Dick Stabile filled in on the remaining selections. Despite its historic value, this mostly forgettable dance and pop music from 1956-57 conclusively proves that by then the big-band era was long dead! *—Scott Yanow*

TOMMY DORSEY (Thomas Dorsey)

b. Nov. 19, 1905, Shenandoah, PA, **d.** Nov. 26, 1956, Greenwich, CT

Trombone, bandleader / Swing, big band
Tommy Dorsey was an excellent ballad player with an elegant, compelling sound and tone, and superior phrasing. Frank Sinatra has often credited Dorsey with teaching him about breathing techniques and phrasing. Dorsey was also a good trumpeter and headed an extremely consistent, popular band. His role in nurturing Sinatra's career alone ensures Dorsey a place in jazz folklore. The Dorsey brothers' father was a coal miner turned music teacher. The brothers co-led bands such as the Novelty Six and Wild Canaries, and were among the earliest jazz groups to be broadcast. They did several studio dates in the '20s, playing with Jean Goldkette, Paul Whiteman, Bix Beiderbecke, Red Nichols, Ted Lewis, and Rudy Vallee, among others. They also organized bands for recording sessions and Broadway shows before starting an eleven-piece group in 1934. They had a three-trombone, one-trumpet band with drummer Ray McKinley. Then, while playing the Glen Island Casino a year later, there was a furious quarrel that caused an irreconcilable dispute between the brothers. Jimmy maintained leadership of the original group, and Tommy formed a band by taking over Joy Haymes's band.

The orchestra scored almost 200 hits between 1935 and 1953. It got things started in 1935 with "Treasure Island" featuring Edythe Wright's vocal. The hit list included "The Music Goes Round and Round," "Alone," "You," "Marie," "Song of India," "Satan Takes a Holiday," "The Big Apple," "Once in a While," and several others. Many brilliant players and singers passed through the ranks, as the Dorsey orchestra was one of the best swing bands with top jazz players. These musicians included Bunny Berigan, Yank Lawson, Charlie Shavers, Max Kaminsky, Buddy DeFranco, Bud Freeman, Dave Tough, Buddy Rich, Louis Bellson, Sy Oliver, Jo Stafford, Jack Leonard, and of course, Frank Sinatra. Dorsey took the advice of a CBS executive and went to hear Sinatra in the early '40s, when Sinatra was with Harry James. James let Sinatra switch to Dorsey's band without extracting a ransom. Sinatra recorded with the vocal quartet the Pied Pipers in 1940. By the middle of the next year, Sinatra was tabbed as outstanding male band vocalist in a *Billboard* survey of colleges, appeared in the film *Las Vegas Nights*, and displaced Bing Crosby in *Down Beat's* poll. The song "Polka Dots and Moonbeams" was Sinatra's first hit with Dorsey, and the songs "I'll Never Smile Again,"

"Delores," "There Are Such Things," and "In the Blue of the Evening" all topped the charts. Sinatra departed in 1942, buying out his contract.

Dorsey's success didn't begin or end with Sinatra. Tactics such as forming a band within a band (the Clambake Seven) or incorporating vocal ensembles as adjuncts scored hits for Dorsey in the pre-Sinatra era. Dorsey was a master at adapting material and at picking fresh talent at exactly the right time. An arrangement of "Pine Top's Boogie Woogie" in 1938 was a huge hit for the band again in 1943 during the ASCAP strike when bands couldn't record. He hired Sy Oliver from Lunceford's band, and Oliver contributed "Easy Does It," "Quiet Please," "Opus One," "Well, Git It!" and "Yes, Indeed" plus popular arrangements of "Chicago" and "On the Sunny Side of the Street." Dorsey took over the strings from Artie Shaw's band in 1942 when Shaw entered the Navy, and at one point had a 34-piece band including vocalists.

But the magic began to fade in the late '40s. A music publication he started, *Bandstand*, folded after six issues. Tommy and Jimmy bought a ballroom in 1944 with partner Harry James that didn't prove the most lucrative investment. Dorsey became popular music director for the Mutual Radio Network in 1945 and 1946, then, at the end of '46, he disbanded the orchestra. He was featured with Jimmy in the film *The Fabulous Dorseys* in 1947. Tommy Dorsey reformed the band two years later. The brothers patched things up and began working together again in 1953. They had a CBS summer series in 1955 and 1956, and guests included Connie Francis and Elvis Presley. Tommy Dorsey died in 1956. The book *Tommy And Jimmy–The Dorsey Years* was published by Herb Sandford in 1972. A ghost band under Warren Covington's leadership had some hits exploiting the cha-cha craze in 1958, and the original band appeared in the opening scene of Martin Scorsese's 1977 film *New York, New York*. RCA has reissued complete Tommy Dorsey and Tommy Dorsey/Frank Sinatra sets. *— Ron Wynn*

○ **Trumpets and Trombones, Vol. 1** / **i.** Aug. 16, 1927-Nov. 18, 1929 / Broadway Intermission 112
This superb LP contains 20 early selections featuring Tommy Dorsey on both trombone and trumpet; he rarely played the latter after 1930. Most of these performances are quite rare (six were issued on this LP for the first time) and they find Dorsey featured with Paul Whiteman, Hoagy Carmichael, Seger Ellis, Arthur Schutt, and, on most selections, the Dorsey Brothers Orchestra. This hot dance music contains many fine jazz solos from some of the top New York studio players of the late '20s and gives one a valuable look at Tommy Dorsey years before he became "the Sentimental Gentleman Of Swing." *—Scott Yanow*

○ **Trumpets and Trombones, Vol. 2** / **i.** Apr. 21, 1930-Feb. 1946 / Broadway Intermission 113
This second LP of Tommy Dorsey rarities features TD both in his early studio days with the Dorsey Brothers' orchestra and with his successful big band. These 14 selections include sound tracks from films, unissued V-discs, radio broadcasts, and early obscure sides from the early '30s. All of the music is quite interesting with "Three Moods" and "Dust" being dance-band classics. Both volumes from this collector's series are highly recommended to all true swing collectors. *— Scott Yanow*

I'm Getting Sentimental Over You / **i.** Sep. 26, 1935-Oct. 1, 1946 / Pickwick 9027
A decent sampling of Tommy Dorsey's recordings including his theme song, four Frank Sinatra vocals (including his final one with TD, "The Song Is You"), "Song of India," a version of "Opus #1" with a string section, and "Well, Git It!" The problem is that this two-LP set only has 18 songs, around 55 minutes of music, making it only worth picking up if at a very inexpensive price! *—Scott Yanow*

○ **Music Goes Round and Round** / Dec. 1935-Feb. 1947 / Bluebird 3140

In 1935, Tommy Dorsey first jammed with musicians from his big band in a Dixieland format, calling the little band the Clambake Seven. He recorded frequently with the unit until 1939, and then on a rare basis until 1950. This particular CD has 21 of the Clambake's better performances, and although it would have been preferable to reissue all of the group's recordings, this serves as a strong introduction to their music. With such soloists as trumpeters Yank Lawson, Max Kaminsky, and Pee Wee Erwin, clarinetists Johnny Mince and Joe Dixon, tenorman Bud Freeman, and TD himself, this music is quite joyous and spirited. Edythe Wright sings ably on many of the songs. Highlights include the title cut, "At the Codfish Ball," two versions of "The Sheik of Araby," and "When the Midnight Choo-Choo Leaves For Alabam." These are Dixieland recordings that predate the New Orleans revival of 1940. —*Scott Yanow*

★ **Seventeen Number Ones** / i. 1935-1942 / RCA 9973

○ **Complete Tommy Dorsey—Vol. 1 (1935)** / 1935 / RCA 5521
The most complete series of Tommy Dorsey reissues is a twofer LP program that succeeded in issuing all of TD's recordings in chronological order from the beginnings of his big band in September 1935 up to March 1939; eight volumes in all before corporate indifference brought the program to a halt at its halfway mark. Since Dorsey led a dance band that performed novelties and commercial vocal features in addition to jazz, not all of the recordings are classics. General collectors might be more satisfied with samplers rather than getting everything. Volume I in this series has, as its high points, "Weary Blues," Dorsey's theme "I'm Getting Sentimental Over You," and the first sides by TD's Clambake Seven including "The Music Goes Round and Round." —*Scott Yanow*

This Is Tommy Dorsey, Vol. 2 / i. Jun. 9, 1936-Jan. 4, 1950 / RCA 6064
A well-conceived sampling of Tommy Dorsey recordings from 1936 to 1950. Unlike the greatest hits that were on the first volume of this early '70s twofer LP series, this set has some of the less obvious but no less enjoyable Dorsey performances including "That's a Plenty," "Milenberg Joys," and "Chicago." Most of this material has since been reissued either on CD or in more complete form on LP. —*Scott Yanow*

Ford V-8 Shows At The Texas Centennial / i. Aug. 1936 / Fanfare 101
This LP features the 1936 Tommy Dorsey orchestra with excellent solos from tenorman Bud Freeman, trumpeter Max Kaminsky, and clarinetist Joe Dixon in addition to the trombonist-leader. There is plenty of fine swinging jazz here from this orchestra including a then-obscure instrumental, "Dancing With You," which a year later with lyrics added would become "Once In A While." —*Scott Yanow*

Radio Days, Vol. 1 / i. Nov. 30, 1936-Jan. 4, 1937 / Starline SG 405
Solid swing music from Tommy Dorsey's orchestra just before he hit it big with "Marie." Although Bunny Berigan is on a few of these songs, the main soloists on this CD are tenorman Bud Freeman, trumpeter Max Kaminsky, and clarinetist Joe Dixon along with Dorsey on trombone. Swinging instrumentals and vocals by Edythe Wright and the Three Esquires are heard in an enjoyable program of Dorsey radio appearances. —*Scott Yanow*

○ **Complete Tommy Dorsey—Vol. 2 (1936)** / 1936 / RCA 5549
The second of eight twofer LPs that trace all of Tommy Dorsey's recordings, completely and in chronological order, from 1935 to March 1939. This set, like the others, includes gems and duds. During 1936, Dorsey's band was popular enough to keep going, but had not broken through to the big time yet. With trumpeter Max Kaminsky, clarinetist Joe Dixon, and the great tenor Bud Freeman contributing solos, and Edythe Wright and the commercial singer Jack Leonard heard on vocals, the music ranges from pop schlock to some big band swing (such as "Royal Garden Blues," "That's a

Plenty," and "After You've Gone"), and two songs by Dorsey's Clambake Seven. —*Scott Yanow*

○ **Complete Tommy Dorsey—Vol. 3 (1936–1937)** / 1936-1937 / RCA 5560
The third LP twofer in this "complete" series (which died after the eighth volume when Bluebird lost interest), this set is the most essential of the bunch because it includes the 18 selections that the great trumpeter Bunny Berigan cut with Dorsey. Not only does this include the major hits "Marie" and "Song of India" (which made Tommy Dorsey into a household name), but it also includes memorable solos on "Mr. Ghost Goes to Town," "Melody in F," "Liebestraum," and "Mendelssohn's Spring Song." Only some of the other songs cut directly before and after Berigan's stint are classics, but there are superior versions of "Keepin' Out of Mischief Now," "Black Eyes," and "Jammin'." —*Scott Yanow*

○ **Complete Tommy Dorsey—Vol. 4 (1937)** / 1937 / RCA 5564
The post-Berigan era found Tommy Dorsey heading one of the most popular of all big bands, rivaling Benny Goodman's. This fourth of eight LP twofers has all of TD's recordings that were cut during a three-month period. These include 15 selections by Dorsey's Clambake Seven (which, at the time, featured trumpeter Pee Wee Erwin, Bud Freeman's tenor, and clarinetist Johnny Mince, in addition to singer Edythe Wright) and a variety of big-band titles, most memorably "Satan Takes a Holiday," "Beale Street Blues," and a truly bizarre version of "Am I Dreaming." Recommended. —*Scott Yanow*

○ **Complete Tommy Dorsey—Vol. 5 (1937)** / 1937 / RCA 5573
The fifth in Bluebird's superb series of LP twofers that trace the "complete" Tommy Dorsey until 1939 is highlighted by 11 performances by his Dixielandish Clambake Seven, along with "Night and Day" and "Once in a While" from his big band. As with the others in this admirable series, there are also plenty of novelties and forgettable vocals included, but Dorsey fanatics should go out of their way to get all of these highly appealing sets. —*Scott Yanow*

○ **Complete Tommy Dorsey—Vol. 6 (1937–1938)** / 1937-1938 / RCA 5578
The sixth out of the eight volumes in the "complete" Tommy Dorsey series of twofer LPs has only two Clambake Seven performances and no major hits, but even with the large amount of so-so Jack Leonard vocals, there are many examples of first-class dance music and swing from the very versatile orchestra. Worth picking up by those Dorsey fans who are wise enough to search for all eight volumes. —*Scott Yanow*

○ **Complete Tommy Dorsey—Vol. 7 (1938)** / 1938 / RCA 5582
The seventh in this series of eight LP twofers contains all of the recordings made by Tommy Dorsey's orchestra during a five-month period in 1938. Seven commercial Jack Leonard vocals are compensated for by seven performances from TD's Clambake Seven, a Dixieland outfit taken out of his big band. With such tunes as "Music, Maestro Please," "Panama," "Chinatown, My Chinatown," "The Sheik of Araby," and the big hit "Boogie Woogie," this set (along with all the others in this valuable series) is recommended to all true Tommy Dorsey fans. —*Scott Yanow*

○ **Complete Tommy Dorsey—Vol. 8 (1938–1939)** / 1938-1939 / RCA 5586
The eighth and, unfortunately, final volume in this superb LP twofer series closed the program of Tommy Dorsey recordings partway through the session of March 8, 1939 thanks to the indifference of RCA Records. This very worthy series reissued all of Tommy Dorsey's studio recordings during the four years since he formed his own band, and although it necessarily included both gems and duds, the former generally outnumber the latter. Vol. 8 is highlighted by "Tin Roof Blues," "Hawaiian War Chant," the two-part "Milenberg Joys," and the Clambake Seven's "You Must Have

Been a Beautiful Baby." All of the volumes in this increasingly hard-to-find series are recommended to serious swing fans. —*Scott Yanow*

○ **Yes, Indeed!** / Jun. 1939-Jun. 1945 / Bluebird 9987
This CD includes many of Tommy Dorsey's very best recordings from 1939 1942 along with four selections dating from 1944 1945. During this period, the sound of Dorsey's orchestra had changed from the earlier days, thanks in large part to Sy Oliver's arrangements and the hard-driving drums of Buddy Rich. With such soloists as trumpeter Ziggy Elman, tenor saxophonist Don Lodice, and clarinetist Johnny Mince (in addition to Dorsey's trombone), this orchestra could play jazz with the best of their contemporaries, although many of their other recordings (not included here) actually showcase vocals and dance music. Highlights of this recommended disc include "Well, All Right," "Stomp It Off," "Quiet Please," "Swing High, "Swanee River," "Deep River" and "Well, Git It!" The later tracks include "Opus #1," the Charlie Shavers feature "At the Fat Man's," and a guest appearance by Duke Ellington on "The Minor Goes Muggin'." —*Scott Yanow*

Tommy Dorsey Featuring Bunny Berigan / i. May 28, 1940-Jun. 2, 1940 / Fanfare 104
Bunny Berigan's second period with Tommy Dorsey's orchestra (which lasted five months) was less successful than his first. In 1937 his solos on "Marie" and "Song of India" had helped TD join the big leagues of swing, but by 1940 Bunny's own band had broken up, he had declared bankruptcy, and the trumpeter was an alcoholic in his declining years. Still Berigan, when he was up to it, remained one of the top jazz trumpeters around (he was only 31). Most of Berigan's later studio recordings with Dorsey have not been reissued in recent times, so this LP, which contains two radio airchecks and one selection from a third, is quite valuable. Although the recording quality is mostly just so-so, Berigan's many solos (Don Lodice's tenor, clarinetist Johnny Mince, and Dorsey's trombone are also heard from) make this a worthwhile release. —*Scott Yanow*

★ **All-Time Greatest Dorsey/Sinatra Hits—Vol. 1 4** / i. 1940-1942 / RCA 8324
With Frank Sinatra. When RCA decided to issue its early-'40s Tommy Dorsey recordings containing Frank Sinatra vocals on compact disc, it abandoned the chronological sequencing found on the Grammy-winning album series *The Dorsey/Sinatra Sessions* and instead jumped back and forth through the catalog. This first volume of four contains some of the biggest hits, notably "I'll Never Smile Again" and "I'll Be Seeing You," and thus is the best selection for beginners. But be sure to move on to Vol. 2 and Vol. 3 and, especially, Vol. 4, which contains Sinatra's first solo session. —*William Ruhlmann*

Dorsey/Sinatra Radio Years—1940-1942 / 1940-1942 / RCA 4741
After reissuing all of Frank Sinatra's studio vocal recordings with Tommy Dorsey on three double LPs, RCA completed the program with this single LP, which consists of Sinatra's radio appearances with TD, his first session as a leader (four titles cut with strings while still with Dorsey), and "I'll Never Smile Again" (from the first volume), which was included as filler because it had recently won an award. Of particular interest is Sinatra's vocal on Jack Leonard's hit "Marie," his participation in a medley with trumpeter Ziggy Elman and fellow singer Jo Stafford, the happy "I'll Take Tallulah," and his farewell to the band on "The Song Is You." —*Scott Yanow*

Well, Get It!—the Td Cd! / 1943-1946 / Jass 14
Tommy Dorsey's wartime orchestra is well featured on these radio airchecks. With such stars as drummer Buddy Rich (and, on three songs, Gene Krupa), clarinetist Buddy DeFranco, and trumpet Charlie Shavers, Dorsey kept up his musical standards despite the change in both the public's taste and the continuing evolution of jazz. With the Sentimentalists, Bonnie Lou Williams, and Stuart Foster contributing vocals, the mixture of jazz and dance music

heard on this CD is typical of Dorsey's mid-'40s music. —*Scott Yanow*

The Great Tommy Dorsey and His Orchestra / i. 1944-1945 / Pickwick 3168
This budget LP contains ten recordings by the mid-'40s Tommy Dorsey orchestra. Despite only having a half-hour of music, there are several strong tracks including the classic version of "Opus #1" with strings, Charlie Shavers's feature "But She's My Buddy's Chick," and Sy Oliver's "Swing High." —*Scott Yanow*

Tommy Dorsey / i. 1950-1952 / First Time Records 1519
In the early 1950s, Tommy Dorsey mostly recorded commercial (and long-out-of-print) music for Decca, so these live performances are quite welcome. Emphasizing the jazz side of TD, this LP features not only Dorsey's trombone but Charlie Shavers's trumpet and Sam Donahue's tenor as well. Bill Finegan contributed some of the arrangements to what would be Tommy Dorsey's last big band before he rejoined forces with his brother Jimmy for a final nostalgia-based orchestra. —*Scott Yanow*

Sentimental Gentleman / i. 1956 / RCA 6003
This two-LP set, which probably was released in the early 1960s and is housed in a very attractive box, has a variety of radio appearances by Tommy Dorsey's orchestra in the early 1940s, some of which are remakes of his hits, although there are a few unusual items. Most interesting are a heated "Hawaiian War Chant" featuring Buddy Rich and Ziggy Elman, Frank Sinatra singing the Jack Leonard hit "Marie," Ziggy Elman reprising "And the Angels Sing," alternate versions of "Well, Git It!" and "Swanee River," and Frank Sinatra's "The Song Is You" from his farewell appearance with the band. This will be a very difficult set to find. —*Scott Yanow*

At the Fat Man's / i. Oct. 1978 / Hep 9
This English LP features three different versions of the Tommy Dorsey orchestra heard in radio performances: his mid-'40s unit, the new big band that he reorganized in 1947, and the unit he led the following year that never did record commercially due to the recording strike. With trumpeter Charlie Shavers, tenorman Don Lodice, and drummer Louis Bellson among the stars, these are good examples of Tommy Dorsey's postwar music, a period of time when the swing he continued to play with enthusiasm was slipping permanently behind the times. —*Scott Yanow*

Dorsey/Sinatra Sessions, Vol. 1 (Feb. 1, 1940–July 17, 1940) / i. 1982 / Bluebird 4334
When RCA ended their "complete Tommy Dorsey" twofer LP series in 1939, they were wise enough to initiate a new (if less ambitious) "complete" series, reissuing all of Frank Sinatra's vocals with TD on three double LPs. The first volume covers the first 51 months and is highlighted by "I'll Be Seeing You," "Polka Dots and Moonbeams," "Fools Rush In," "East of the Sun" (which also includes a brief spot by trumpeter Bunny Berigan), and "I'll Never Smile Again." Obviously, Sinatra fans have to acquire this now out-of-print LP series. —*Scott Yanow*

Dorsey/Sinatra Sessions, Vol. 3 (June 27, 1941–July 2, 1942) / i. 1982 / Bluebird 4336
The third and final LP twofer that reissues all of Frank Sinatra's vocals from his two years with Tommy Dorsey's orchestra has no real hits, but finds Sinatra maturing and sounding particularly strong on "Blue Skies," "A Sinner Kissed an Angel," "Violets For Your Furs," and "Street of Dreams." A fascinating but now out-of-print series. —*Scott Yanow*

Post-War Era, The / i. 1993 / RCA/Bluebird 66156
The funny part about this CD is that there is relatively little Tommy Dorsey on it. His trombone is mostly heard in a cameo role with the exception of "Trombonology." The real stars of this fine CD are arranger Bill Finegan (who wrote the charts for the majority of these 22 performances) and the fiery trumpeter Charlie Shavers, although drummer Louis Bellson also gets featured on "Drumology." After 1946

Tommy Dorsey's music was definitely behind the times (he always had a strong resistance to bebop, and some of these later tracks sound like tired dance music, but this CD does an excellent job of summing up Tommy Dorsey's better recordings of the 1946-50 period, leaving out the real dog tunes and bad vocalists he sometimes utilized. —*Scott Yanow*

Dorsey/Sinatra Sessions, Vol. 2 (July 17, 1940–May 28, 1941) / Bluebird 4335
The second of three twofer LPs that reissue all of Frank Sinatra's vocals with Tommy Dorsey's orchestra contains mostly lesser-known, but enjoyable, ballads. Also included are "Stardust," "Without a Song," and "Let's Get Away From It All." Sinatra collectors should go out of their way to search for this series! —*Scott Yanow*

RAY DRAPER (Raymond Allen Draper)

b. Aug. 3, 1940, New York, NY, **d.** Nov. 1, 1982, New York, NY
Tuba / Hard bop
Another sad case of great potential that was never completely fulfilled, Ray Draper had astonishing skills on tuba. He could play with the speed and energy of a saxophonist, and often presented breakneck solos that were dazzling. But he never got the mental part of his life together, and had problems with discipline and drugs. Draper survived one three-year prison stretch, but was reportedly killed in the midst of a robbery in 1982. He attended the High School of the Performing Arts and Manhattan School of Music. Draper played with Jackie McLean in 1956 and 1957, and recorded with him. Draper then worked with Donald Byrd, and recorded with John Coltrane from 1956 to 1958. He played in Max Roach's group in 1958 and 1959, and played briefly with Don Cherry in the early '60s. Later in the decade, Draper worked with Big Black and Horace Tapscott, then led the jazz-rock group, Red Beans and Rice, in 1968 and 1969. He moved to England in '69, and played with Archie Shepp, Dr. John, and English saxophonist Kenneth Terroade. He recorded with Brother Jack McDuff in 1971, and taught briefly at Wesleyan University. Draper also played with Howard Johnson's group, Gravity. But things worsened, and Draper gradually dropped out of the music scene. Currently, he does not have any sessions available on CD, but can be heard on reissues that feature Roach and McLean. —*Ron Wynn*

★ **Tuba Sounds** / Mar. 15, 1957 / Prestige 7096

Ray Draper Quintet Featuring John Coltrane / Dec. 20, 1957 / New Jazz 8228

Tuba Jazz, A / 1958 / Jubilee 1090

KENNY DREW (Kenneth Sidney Drew)

b. Aug. 28, 1928, New York, NY, **d.** 1993
Piano / Hard bop
The jazz world was rocked again in late '93 when the news broke about Kenny Drew's death. A fine soloist and one of the most in-demand pianists on the jazz scene, Drew was famous for his single-note melodic lines and his versatility. He was equally skilled playing in a denser, chordal method, and was known for his long right hand lines. His albums were delightful; they showed Drew's flexibility with styles and idioms. He began piano studies in his childhood, and was doing recitals at age eight. Drew's approach reflected the equal influences of stride, swing, and bebop. He attended New York's High School of Music and Art, then did his first recording in 1949 with Howard McGhee. Drew became a top player in the '50s, working with Coleman Hawkins, Lester Young, Charlie Parker, Milt Jackson, Art Blakey, and Dinah Washington. He joined Buddy Rich's band in 1958. Drew moved to Europe in 1961, first settling in Paris, then in Copenhagen, where he remained mostly for the rest of his life. Drew formed a duo in the mid '60s with Niels-Ørsted Henning-Pedersen that became the resident rhythm section at the Montmartre. They cut numerous recordings with visiting and expatriate jazz musicians over a 20-year period,

many for Steeple Chase. Drew also formed a publishing company in Copenhagen, Shirew Publishing. He began to increase his compositional output in the '70s, and became more involved in orchestration. Drew did numerous sessions for such labels as Riverside, Fantasy, Blue Note, Timeless, and Soul Note, and has been featured as a sideman on many others. There's a good selection of his material available on CD. —*Ron Wynn*

Introducing the Kenny Drew Trio / i. 1953 /

Modernity of Kenny Drew, The / Jun. 1953 / Norgran 1066

Progressive Piano / i. 1954 / Norgran 1002

Talkin' and Walkin' / Dec. 1955 / Blue Note 84439
Quartet. Prototype hard bop/mainstream Blue Note. Drew is immense on piano. —*Ron Wynn*

Tough Piano Trio / Sep. 20+26, 1956 / Jazzland 9

★ **This Is New** / Mar. 28, 1957+Apr. 3, 1957 / Riverside 483

Hard Bop / Mar. 28, 1957+Apr. 3, 1957 / Jazzland 6

Trio-Quartet-Quintet / i. 1957 / Riverside 6007
A wonderful collection of first-rate pianists in varied contexts, with Donald Byrd (tpt), Paul Chambers (b), and Philly Joe Jones (d) on the job. —*Ron Wynn*

★ **Undercurrent** / Dec. 11, 1960 / Blue Note 84059

Ruby My Dear / Aug. 23, 1977 / Steeple Chase 1129

Home Is Where the Soul Is / Oct. 15, 1978 / Xanadu 166

For Sure / Oct. 16, 1978 / Xanadu 167

It Might As Well Be Spring / Nov. 23, 1981 / Soul Note 1040

And Far Away / Feb. 21, 1983 / Soul Note 1081

Jazz Impressions of Rodgers & Hart / Riverside 1112

RAY DRUMMOND

Bass / Hard bop
A prolific bassist, Ray Drummond has played on dozens of '80s and '90s sessions, often working in tandem with drummer Marvin "Smitty" Smith. His strong tone, outstanding accompaniment, and tasty solos have been featured on his own sessions for Criss Cross, DMP, and Teresa. Drummond's recorded in a duo with John Hicks and in a trio setting with Hank Jones and Billy Higgins. He's also worked with David Newman, Kenny Barron, and Steve Nelson, among others. He has some sessions as a leader available on CD. —*Ron Wynn*

★ **Essence, The** / i. 1991 / Digital Music 480
The third album with premier bassist Ray Drummond stepping out from the rhythm section to serve as leader. This trio outing seems like more of a cooperative venture, as pianist Hank Jones, Drummond, and drummer Billy Higgins zip through the program of standards and originals sounding almost like one player. —*Ron Wynn*

Excursion / i. 1993 / Arabesque 106
Ray Drummond's bass rumbles behind rather than up front on his new release. Although these are mostly his compositions, this is a drum-driven, horn-dominant recording that combines Latin and African rhythms with snatches of free jazz. Danilo Perez's piano lines often provide a soothing current cutting through the crashing waves of Joe Lovano and Craig Handy's horns, though the horns become gently onomatopoeic on "Waterfall," a part of the title track suite "Excursion." The drums and percussion of Marvin "Smitty" Smith and Mor Thiam inspire and enhance much of this recording, sometimes evoking a journey through a jungle or rain forest. The drumming is especially delightful on a fresh arrangement of "Well You Needn't." Drummond's bass is particularly notable on the "Prologue" and "Epilogue" parts of the suite "Excursion" and when he trades off with the drums on "Blues African." —*Sunsh Stein, Jazz Times*

GEORGE DUKE

b. Jan. 12, 1946, San Rafael, CA
Keyboards, producer / Early jazz-rock, instrumental pop, contemporary funk

Music Map

Jazz Drums

African, Caribbean Drummers	Military Marches	Avant-Garde

Avant-Garde
Ed Blackwell (1929)
Paul Motian (1931)
Rashied Ali (1935)
Beaver Harris (1936)
Sunny Murray (1937)
Andrew Cyrille (1939)
Barry Althschul (1943)
Famoudou Don Moye (1946)
Tani Tabbal
M'Boom Ensemble (1970)
Steve McCall (1933-1989)
J.C. Moses (1936-1977)
Clifford Jarvis (1941)

Early Jazz Drummers
Baby Dodds (1898-1959)
Tony Sbarbaro (1897-1969)
Jasper Taylor (1894-1964)

Ragtime Drummers
William Reitz
James Lent
Budd Gilmore

Chicago & New York
Ben Pollack (1903-1971)
Frank Snyder
Vic Berton (1896-1951)
Dave Tough (1907-1948)
Bob Consulman
Paul Kettler
George Stafford–Barrett Deems (1914)
Wayne Jones–Slick Jones (1907-1969)

New Orleans
Baby Dodds (1898-1959)
Zutty Singleton (1898-1975)
Paul Barbarin (1899-1969)

Milton Graves (1941)
Charles "Bobo" Shaw (1947)

Swing Era
Sonny Greer (1895-1982)
Cozy Cole (1906-1981)
Dave Tough (1907-1948)
Gene Krupa (1909-1973)
Chick Webb (1909-1939)
Big Sid Catlett (1910-1951)
Buddy Rich (1917-1987)
Jo Jones (1911-1985)
Kaiser Marshall (1899-1948)

Jazz-Rock
Bobby Colomby (1944)
Billy Cobham (1944)
Tony Williams (1945)
Alphonze Mouzon (1948)
Lenny White (1949)
Bill Bruford (1949)
Peter Erskine (1954)
Simon Phillips (1973)

Solos
Lionel Hampton (1909)
Chick Webb (1901-1939)
George Wettling (1907-1968)
Ray Baudic (1909-1988)

Bop Drumming
Art Blakey (1919-1990)
Philly Joe Jones (1923-1985)
Max Roach (1924)
Roy Haynes (1926)
Kenny Clarke (1929-1985)
Dannie Richmond (1935-1988)

Cool Jazz
Shelly Manne (1920-1984)
Joe Morello (1928)

Roy Brooks (1938)
Dennis Charles (1933)
Jerome Cooper (1946)
Joe Chambers (1942)

Post Bop
Sam Woodyard (1925) – Elvin Jones (1927)
Arthur Taylor (1929) – Louis Hayes (1937)
Roy McCurdy (1936) – Mickey Roker (1932)
Al Foster (1944)
Alan Dawson (1929)
Jimmy Cobb (1929)
Billy Higgins (1936)
Pete LaRoca (1938)

1980s-1990s
Jeff Watts
Jack DeJohnette (1942)
Omar Hakim (1959)
Adam Nussbaum (1955)
Cecil Brooks III
John Vidacovich
Cyndi Blackman
Terri Lyne Carrington
Marvin Smitty Smith (1961)

Duke has had two careers: one artistic, one profitable. His jazz and jazz-rock phase in the '60s and '70s included stints with Cannonball Adderley and Frank Zappa. He co-led a band with Billy Cobham in the mid '70s. Success as a pop producer and the rise of fusion moved him to desert jazz in his second career phase, and he became a big-time pop star, courtesy of the Stan Clarke-George Duke project. —*Ron Wynn*

Faces in Reflection / i. 1975 / MPS 22018

Aura Will Prevail, The / i. 1975 / BASF 25613

Liberated Fantasies / i. 1976 / BASF 22835

★ **Solo Keyboard Album (1976)** / 1976 / Epic 25021

I Love the Blues—She Heard My Cry / i. 1984 / Polydor 8174882

Brazilian Love Affair / i. Dec. 3, 1991 / Epic 36483

TED DUNBAR (Earl Theodore Dunbar)

b. Jan. 17, 1937, Port Arthur, TX

Guitar / Hard bop, modern creative

A self-taught guitarist who later became an instructor, Ted Dunbar's pithy riffs, taut solos, and accompaniment have been featured in hard bop, soul-jazz, jazz-rock, and free situations. Dunbar played trumpet and guitar at Texas Southern in the mid and late '50s. He worked with Arnett Cobb, Don Wilkerson, and Joe Turner. Dunbar studied and played with Dave Baker at Indiana in the early '60s, sometimes subbing for Wes Montgomery. He moved to New York in the mid '60s, and performed and recorded with Gil Evans in the '70s, and with Tony Williams's Lifetime and Frank Foster. Dunbar also worked with Sonny Rollins, Ron Carter, Billy Harper, Roy Haynes, and McCoy Tyner. He was involved with Billy Taylor's Jazzmobile project, the New Jazz Repertory Co., and the National Jazz Ensemble before joining Livingston College's (Rutgers) faculty in 1972. Dunbar has written several books on jazz harmony and guitar. He has recorded as a leader for Xanadu and Muse. Currently, Dunbar does not have any sessions available on CD. —*Ron Wynn*

Jazz Guitarist / **i.** Jul. 1982 / Xanadu 196

CORNELL DUPREE

Guitar / Blues & jazz, soul-jazz
A longtime soul and R&B sessionman, Cornell Dupree plays beautiful fills, tasty licks, and nasty phrases, backing anyone from Aretha to Les McCann. He's a versatile player whose sound was a major component in the group Stuff in the '70s. Dupree sounds at his best on the blues. He can be heard on many soul, R&B, pop, and blues recordings, and on some jazz dates on CD as well. —*Ron Wynn*

○ **Teasin'** / **i.** 1974 / Atlantic
★ **Coast to Coast** / **i.** 1988 / Antilles 842717

BIG JOE DUSKIN

Vocals, piano / Boogie-woogie, blues & jazz
Big Joe Duskin is a fine barrelhouse, blues, and boogie-woogie pianist who's recorded for Arhoolie, King, and other labels over the years. —*Ron Wynn*

★ **Cincinnati Stomp** / **i.** Jan. 1980 / Arhoolie 1080
Fine set presenting vintage barrelhouse piano and stomping blues by Big Joe Duskin, one of the last true stylists in both genres. Duskin's album was done with no fanfare and didn't attract the widespread notice it deserves. —*Ron Wynn*

GEORGE DUVIVIER

b. 1920, **d.** 1985
Bass
A consistently engaging, impressive bassist, George Duvivier's solo specialty was playing fast notes in the upper register while providing steady, deep accompaniment and sharp, strong playing in an ensemble situation. Though he seldom took a leadership role, he was a premier session, studio, and section contributor, and was flexible enough to handle jam sessions, combo, studio, or live dates. During his career, he worked with swing, bop, and cool players, even with the adventurous Eric Dolphy. Duvivier studied violin at the Conservatory of Music and Art in New York, and became assistant concertmaster of the Central Manhattan Symphony Orchestra at age 16. He switched to bass, and later studied composition at New York University. Duvivier played with Coleman Hawkins, Eddie Barefield, and Lucky Millinder in the early '40s, then went into the army. After his discharge, he was Jimmie Lunceford's staff arranger from 1945 to 1947,

then joined Sy Oliver's big band, doubling as bassist and arranger. During the '50s, Duvivier toured Europe extensively with Lena Horne and Nellie Lutcher, and played on many film soundtracks, on commercial jingles, and on television shows. He made a rare date as a leader for the French Coronet label in 1956, playing with Martial Solal. Duvivier stayed busy with jazz dates, playing with Bud Powell from 1953 to 1957, and recording and playing with Chico Hamilton, Benny Goodman, Oliver Nelson, Shelly Manne, Count Basie/Joe Williams, Frank Sinatra, Clark Terry, Ben Webster, Bob Wilber, and Dolphy. He toured with Hank Jones and Benny Carter during the late '70s. Duvivier also recorded with duos Al Cohn and Zoot Sims and Sims with Joe Venuti, and with Warren Vache and Jones. Duvivier died in 1985. —*Ron Wynn*

JOHNNY DYANI (Johnny (Mbizo) Dyani)

b. Nov. 30, 1945, **d.** Jul. 11, 1986
Bass, piano / World fusion, modern creative
A commanding bassist whose booming sound and thick tones were always impressive, Johnny Dyani was a fixture on the English and European free jazz scene beginning in the mid '60s. A South African expatriate, Dyani moved to London in the mid '60s, arriving with Chris McGregor's group, the Blue Notes. He played with the Brotherhood of Breath, McGregor's new band, and with the Spontaneous Music Ensemble, Musicians Co-op, and Steve Lacy. Dyani toured South America and recorded with Lacy, Enrico Rava, and Louis Moholo in the late '60s. He settled in Copenhagen in the early '70s, and made several records across Europe. Dyani recorded with Don Cherry, John Tchicai, Dudu Pukwana, Makaya Ntshoko, Joseph Jarman, and David Murray, and led his own groups as well. He returned briefly to England in 1975 after Mongezi Fesa's death, playing on McGregor's album *Blue Notes for Mongezi*. Dyani can be heard on various CDs featuring Cherry, Murray, and others, but has no sessions available as a leader. —*Ron Wynn*

African Bass / **i.** 1977 / Red 149

Song for Biko / Jul. 18, 1978 / Steeple Chase 1109

Witchdoctor's Son / **i.** Jul. 1980 / Steeple Chase 1098

○ **Mbizo** / Feb. 1981 / Steeple Chase 1163

★ **Afrika** / Oct. 1, 1983 / Steeple Chase 1186
The South African bassist/pianist/composer with a septet. Well respected as a musician worldwide. A unique amalgam of styles. —*Michael G. Nastos*

Angolian Cry / Jul. 23, 1985 / Steeple Chase 1209

E

ALLEN EAGER

b. Jan. 27, 1927, New York, NY
Tenor and alto saxophone / Bop
Tenor saxophonist Eager began as a teenage swing-era player with Tommy Dorsey, but made the switch to bop in the '40s and was one of the finest early players in that genre. Eager's tone and approach merged the influence of Charlie Parker and Lester Young, and was characterized by a swinging, memorable sound and by distinctive phrasing. His playing with Tadd Dameron's combo was praised widely by musicians and critics, and he was featured on several late-'40s Savoy releases. He also worked with Buddy Rich and recorded with Stan Getz in 1949. Eager made infrequent appearances through the mid and late '50s, both abroad and in America. He recorded with Gerry Mulligan in 1951 and with Terry Gibbs in 1952, did some session work at the Open Door in New York, and worked with Howard McGhee, Oscar Pettiford, and Tony Fruscella. While in Paris during the late '50s, Eager began playing alto as well. After recording with Mulligan again in 1957, Eager stopped full-time recording until he returned in 1982, touring Europe and recording with a new combo on the Uptown label. Currently, he can be heard on various CD reissues. *—Ron Wynn*

New Trends in Jazz—Vol. 1 / Mar. 22, 1946 / Savoy 9015
★ **Tenor Sax** / Mar. 22, 1946-Jul. 15, 1947 / Savoy 15044
Renaissance / Mar. 25, 1982 / Uptown 2709

CHARLES EARLAND

b. May 24, 1941, Philadelphia, PA
Organ, soprano saxophone / Hard bop, blues & jazz, soul-jazz
Charles Earland has played organ and other keyboards, as well as soprano sax. His style has been influenced by Jimmy Smith and Jimmy McGriff, and combines elements of soul-jazz with blues, funk, and pop. He doesn't have as heavy a sound as Groove Holmes or Jack McDuff, but has done some solid dates for Prestige, Muse, and other labels. He became one of the most popular organists in the '70s using walking and rolling bass pedal lines in either soul-jazz or jazz-rock and funk contexts. Earland actually began his career as a saxophonist working with McGriff. He began heading his own band in the '60s, and, unable to either attract or to keep organists in his bands, switched to the instrument in 1963. Earland played organ with Lou Donaldson in the late '60s, then issued his own albums on Choice and Prestige. His *Black Talk* album in 1969 featured his own compositions. The LP's success won Earland a long-term deal with Prestige. He started mixing soprano sax, synthesizer, electric piano, and organ in his bands. During the '70s, Earland appeared at the Montreux and Newport jazz festivals, and played on the soundtrack for the film *The Dynamite Brothers*. His '70s Prestige albums alternated between combos, large groups, and some sessions with vocalists. His '73 date, *Leaving This Planet*, included guest appearances from Freddie Hubbard, Eddie Henderson, and Joe Henderson. After a live session recorded in Montreux in 1974, Earland switched labels to Mercury, cutting one studio date, then switched to Muse for four albums. The first three albums reunited Earland with guitarist Jimmy Ponder, who'd played on his first album as a leader. He then recorded with Columbia on sessions ranging from large bands to dates with the Brecker Brothers and female vocalists. During the '80s and '90s, Earland returned to Muse for quartet/combo dates, including one co-led by George Coleman. A few of his '70s Prestige sessions have been reissued on CD, along with more recent Muse releases. *—Ron Wynn and Michael Erlewine*

○ **Black Talk** / Dec. 15, 1969 / Prestige 335
The punchy organ-based music moves along nicely from a group that keeps in the vernacular and also manages to play engagingly on a program of stretchers. *—Bob Rusch, Cadence*

Black Drops / Jun. 1, 1970 / Prestige 10029
Early soul-jazz, occasional R&B, and pop cuts from organist Charles Earland, just cutting his third album as a leader at that time. His organ solos are sometimes churning and impressive, other times they bog down in clichés and repetitive phrases. But the potential Earland shows on most cuts has since materialized. *—Ron Wynn*

Living Black / Sep. 17, 1970 / Prestige 10009
Funky taste of soul done at the Key Club in Newark. With Grover Washington, Jr. *—Ron Wynn*

Charles III / Feb. 16+17, 1972 / Prestige 10061
★ **Leaving This Planet** / Dec. 11-13, 1973 / Fantasy 66002
Great stints by Joe Henderson (sax), Eddie Henderson (tpt), and Freddie Hubbard (tpt). His most ambitious album. *—Ron Wynn*

Odyssey / 1975 / Mercury 1049
Mama Roots / 1977 / Muse 5156
Smokin' / 1977 / Muse 5126
Fine mid-'70s sextet set featuring Earland's customary soul-jazz, blues, and funk uptempo and ballad originals. Tenor saxophonists David Schnitter and George Coleman excel, as does guitarist Jimmy Ponder. *—Ron Wynn*

Pleasant Afternoon / Apr. 19, 1978 / Muse 5201
☆ **Front Burner** / Jun. 27, 1988 / Milestone 9165
Recorded at Englewood Cliffs, NJ. A comeback for a veteran organist. "Mom & Dad" (in 10/4 time) is infectious. *—Michael G. Nastos*

Third Degree Burn / Apr. 15, 1989 / Milestone 9174
Sparkling funky tenor from David "Fathead" Newman and solid organ from Earland. *—Ron Wynn*

Kharma / Prestige 10095

BILL EASLEY

Multi-reeds / Hard bop, modern creative
An extremely versatile and gifted reed player, Bill Easley has displayed a polished, forceful sound on alto, tenor, and baritone saxophones, and on flute and clarinet. He attended Memphis State University during the '60s, and later worked with Isaac Hayes and did sessions at Stax. Easley moved back to New York, and has recorded sessions for Sunnyside and Milestone. He's played with Sir Roland Hanna, James

Williams, Bill Mobley, Mulgrew Miller, Grady Tate, George Caldwell, Victor Gaskin, and Billy Higgins, among others. His sessions are available on CD. —*Ron Wynn*

★ **Wind Inventions** / Sep. 1988 / Sunnyside 1022
Premier clarinetist in a neo-contemporary setting. Very attractive music. —*Michael G. Nastos*

First Call / i. Oct. 20-22, 1990 / Milestone 9186
Blues and bop from a versatile saxophonist. Includes notable appearances by old and new Memphis jazz stars from George Caldwell to Bill Mobley. —*Ron Wynn*

BILLY ECKSTINE (William Clarence Eckstine)

b. Jul. 8, 1914, Pittsburgh, PA, d. Mar. 8, 1993
Vocals, bandleader, trumpet, valve trombone / Swing, big band, bop
The first Black vocalist to be a matinee idol, Billy Eckstine might have been a star as a trombonist, trumpeter, or guitarist if he'd been born with a poor singing voice. Instead, he preceded Nat "King" Cole as a dominant ballads and romantic singer, and was so popular at the end of the '40s and the beginning of the '50s that he signed a huge contract with MGM records. Eckstine was also a gifted talent scout, and helped launch the careers of many bop superstars.

He began his career singing and doubling as an emcee in Pittsburgh clubs. He relocated to Chicago in 1937, and joined the Earl Hines orchestra in 1939, remaining with Hines until 1943. During that time, he learned to play the trumpet, and along with music director/tenor saxophonist Budd Johnson, helped convince Hines to hire several young musicians, including Charlie Parker, Sarah Vaughan, and Dizzy Gillespie. Eckstine went solo in 1943, and began assembling his own big band the next year. Following the advice he'd given Hines, he hired Parker, Gillespie, and Vaughan, plus Gene Ammons, Art Blakey, Miles Davis, Kenny Dorham, Dexter Gordon, Fats Navarro, Lucky Thompson, and Lena Horne during the band's tenure from 1944 to 1947. Johnson and Dameron contributed arrangements, and Eckstine's dynamic baritone leads were the basis for most songs. The group also did a couple of progressive instrumentals, though they couldn't do much recording because of union disputes. The band recorded for the Armed Forces Network and, later, for Savoy. After he disbanded the large group, Eckstine tried to keep things going with an octet, but it soon fell apart due to financial burden.

He then became a solo vocalist, and enjoyed almost immediate success. Between 1949 and 1952, Eckstine had 12 songs reach the Top 30. "My Foolish Heart," "I Apologize," and "I Wanna Be Loved" all made the Top 10. Eckstine was so successful he secured a five-year contract from MGM for what was then a huge amount of money. His hit run didn't last beyond the early '50s, but by then Eckstine was an established star. He began to tour Europe and Australia annually, while playing numerous clubs and festivals also. He was often called to entertain troops overseas. The club act blended lush, sentimental love songs, show business bits and mimicry, some dancing, and a little trumpet or valve trombone. He continued to make occasional recordings, cutting a set of Irving Berlin songs with Vaughan for Mercury and performing in the '60s with the Duke Ellington and Maynard Ferguson bands. There were tours with all-star bands and sessions for Verve, Mercury, and even Motown in the '60s. In 1987, after several years away from the studios, Billy Eckstine surprised everyone with a superb album, *Billy Eckstine Sings With Benny Carter*. Helen Merrill was a special guest, and the session received a Grammy nomination. Eckstine continued working until shortly before his death in 1993. —*Ron Wynn*

○ **I Want to Talk About You** / i. Feb. 1940-Mar. 1945 / Xanadu 207
I Want to Talk About You is a find for fans of the Earl Hines orchestra as well as admirers of singer Billy Eckstine, since most of the titles were taken from Hines's recordings of 1940 and 1941. . . . "If That's the Way You Feel," "I Want to Talk About You," and "Without a Song" are from Air Force

Radio Service transcriptions of the Eckstine band, and are dated March 4, 1945. . . . The sound is satisfactory. —*Shirley Klett, Cadence*

Duke, the Blues and Me, The / Sep. 1945-Apr. 27, 1947 / Regent 6053

★ **Mister B and the Band** / 1945 / Savoy 4401
1945 1946. Landmark recordings from whence bop partly (maybe fully) emerged. The album has incredible personnel and great vocals. —*Ron Wynn*

Mister B Sings / i. 1945-1947 / Savoy

Billy Eckstine Orchestra (1945) / 1945 / Almanac 2415

★ **MGM Years** / i. 1947-1957 / PolyGram 19442

Billy Eckstine Sings / i. 1950 / National 2001(10)

Great Mr. B, The / i. 1954 / King 265

○ **Love Songs of Mr. B** / i. 1954 / EmArcy 26027

○ **Blues for Sale** / 1954 / EmArcy 26025

○ **Mister B with a Beat** / i. 1955 / MGM 3176

Best of Irving Berlin, The / i. 1959 / Mercury 60002

Billy and Sarah / i. 1959 / Lion 70088

Basie and Eckstine, Inc. / i. 1959 / Roulette 52029

Billy Eckstine and His Orchestra / i. 195? / Deluxe 2010

☆ **Mr. B** / i. 1960 / Audio Lab 1549

○ **No Cover, No Minimum** / 1960 / Capitol 98583
An outstanding '60 live set, with Eckstine backed by a good combo doing classics like "Lush Life" and "Moonlight in Vermont." The intimate nightclub setting, coupled with Bobby Tucker's simple, yet effective, arrangements, make this perhaps Eckstine's best album outside his prime '40s and early-'50s dates. It has been reissued on CD with 12 previously unissued cuts. —*Ron Wynn*

☆ **At Basin St. East** / Oct. 1961 / Mercury 832592
A 1990 reissue of a fine live date with Quincy Jones leading the orchestra and writing the tracks. —*Ron Wynn*

★ **Billy Eckstine Sings with Benny Carter** / Nov. 17, 1986-Nov. 18, 1986 / Verve 832011
Billy Eckstine Sings with Benny Carter couples the master balladeer with the great altoist (who plays trumpet on one cut) for a recorded first. There are delicious vocalizations, impeccable accompaniments, and the bonus of Helen Merrill's voice joining Eckstine's on two tracks. —*W. Royal Stokes, Jazz Times*

○ **Stardust** / Polydor 525

Billy Eckstine and Quincy Jones / Mercury 60674

HARRY EDISON (Harry "Sweets" Edison)

b. Oct. 10, 1915, Columbus, OH
Trumpet / Swing
For some unfathomable reason, Harry Edison has lagged behind other swing era trumpet greats in recognition and praise. But he's right near the top among middle-register players, has remarkable timing, and exhibits great humor and strength in his solos. Edison's uncle introduced him to music while he was growing up in Kentucky. He began to play trumpet in local bands after moving to Columbus. Edison joined the Jeter-Pillars orchestra in Cleveland in 1933, then moved with the group to St. Louis the next year, where he remained for two more years. He joined Lucky Millinder's orchestra in New York in 1937, then moved to Count Basie's orchestra six months later. He became a prime soloist with Basie while periodically providing the band with compositions and arrangements. He was featured prominently in the film *Jammin' the Blues* in 1944, and did a comedy vocal on the 1947 hit "Open the Door, Richard." When Basie temporarily disbanded in 1950, Edison split his time between heading bands, doing freelance dates, and traveling with Jazz at the Philharmonic tours. Edison also worked with Buddy Rich. He settled on the West Coast in the early '50s, and was soon busy in various studios, working with Nelson Riddle on Frank Sinatra albums, among other

projects. He co-led a band with tenor saxophonist Jimmy Forrest in 1958 and did some combo recording for Verve. Edison led groups in Los Angeles during the '60s, often re-uniting with Count Basie. He co-led a dynamic combo with saxophonist Eddie "Lockjaw" Davis in the '70s and '80s. They recorded with Storyville, while he, Davis, and Stitt cut another session on Gateway. Edison played with Louis Bellson's band in 1971, and recorded with tenor saxophonist Zoot Sims during some sessions for Norman Granz's Pablo label. He toured Europe with The Countsmen, a Basie alumni/sideman band, in 1983, and cut *Jazz at the Philharmonic 1983* with Davis and trombonist Al Grey. — *Ron Wynn*

○ **Harry Edison Quartet** / **i.** 1953 / Pacific Jazz 4

○ **Sweets at the Haig** / Jul. 1, 1953 / Pacific Jazz 11

★ **Sweets** / Sep. 4, 1956 / Clef 717

☆ **Gee Baby, Ain't I Good to You?** / Mar. 5, 1957+Mar. 30, 1957 / Verve 8211

○ **Swinger, The** / Oct. 1958 / Verve 8295

★ **Jawbreakers** / Apr. 18, 1962 / Riverside 487
Solid, inviting duo work, matching Edison with Eddie "Lockjaw" Davis (ts). — *Ron Wynn*

○ **Ben Webster and Sweets Edison** / Jun. 6, 1962-Jun. 7, 1962 / Columbia 1891

Just Friends / Jul. 26, 1975 / Black & Blue 33106

Opus Funk / Jul. 6, 1976 / Storyville 281

○ **Simply Sweets** / Sep. 22, 1977 / Pablo 2310-806
Another giant of swing trumpet who bridged the gap suc-cessfully, Harry Edison reunites with his old partner, tenor saxophonist Eddie "Lockjaw" Davis, for a tour through what turns out to be primarily blues terrain. Five of the eight tunes are in the 12-bar form, with the title number a bluesy original not wholly unlike "Lil Darlin'" in feeling, if not ex-actly in changes. Sweets (Edison) was known for his under-statement and Jaws (Davis) for his sometimes garrulous pro-lixity, but together they were a well-matched pair. Pianist Dolo Coker, a newcomer to Pablo, earns his keep, as does the lesser-known bassist Harvey Newmark and drummer Jimmie Smith. Coker provides a welcome relief from the trip-hammer perfectionism of Oscar Peterson, Norman Granz's personal favorite. Davis offers little that is unex-pected, but he does it so damned well that few can fault him. Where Edison had seemingly built a style around artfully placed quarter notes and an occasional pronounced flatted fifth, Davis appeared to have decided, a very long time ago, that no phrase could be considered complete without its complement of grace-noted triplets. But, once the listener ac-cepts these habituations with tolerance, he can more easily sweep them away. Personally, I think it is worth the effort. — *Jack Sohmer*, Cadence

Blues for Basie / **i.** 1977 / Pablo

Jazz at the Philharmonic / **i.** 1983 / Pablo
Great exchanges with Al Grey (t) and Eddie "Lockjaw" Davis (ts). Fine solos. — *Ron Wynn*

★ **For My Pals** / Apr. 18, 1988-Apr. 19, 1988 / Pablo 2310-934
Trumpeter Edison never sounded better than on this studio date. Highly recommended. — *Michael G. Nastos*

○ **Swing Summit** / Apr. 1990 / Candid 79050

○ **Harry Sweets Edison and Eddie Lockjaw Davis—Vol. 1** / Storyville 4004

○ **Harry Sweets Edison and Eddie Lockjaw Davis—Vol. 2** / Storyville 4025

TEDDY EDWARDS (Theodore Marcus Edwards)

b. Apr. 26, 1924, Jackson, MS
Tenor saxophone / Bop
Teddy Edwards lacks the reputation his talents have earned him, particularly since he participated in many pivotal be-bop recording sessions at the end of the '40s. The problem is that these recordings were done on the West Coast rather than on the East Coast. Edwards is better known by critics, musicians, historians, and scholars than by the general jazz audience. Edwards's tenor solos reveal certain harmonic distinction, resiliency, and a bluesy underpinning, especially on ballads. He began on alto sax as a child, worked briefly in Michigan and Florida, then joined Ernie Fields's orchestra. Edwards moved to Los Angeles in 1945, playing in Roy Milton's big band. When he was invited to join McGhee's band, Edwards switched to tenor sax. He recorded in the late '40s with Red Callendar, Hampton Hawes, Benny Bailey, Addison Farmer, and Roy Porter. Edwards played with Howard Rumsey in 1949 and 1950, the Max Roach/Clifford Brown quintet in 1954, and with Carter again in 1955. There were tenor bat-tles with Dexter Gordon, and, during the late '50s sessions with Gerald Wilson, there were more tenor battles with Jimmy Witherspoon and Billy Higgins. Edwards continued recording for Contemporary in the early '60s, cutting nice soul-jazz, blues, and bebop dates. There were recordings with Milt Jackson on Impulse, Jimmy Smith on Verve, and as a leader for Prestige in the late '60s. Edwards worked with Benny Goodman in 1964, and played periodically with Wilson's orchestra. He provided compositions for several television and radio programs as well as the films *Any Wednesday* in 1966 and *They Shoot Horses, Don't They* in 1969. Edwards continued touring and recording in the '70s. He played with Sarah Vaughan and recorded for Muse and Xanadu. He made an album for Steeple Chase in the '80s, and played with vocalist Tom Waits. Waits contacted Antilles on his behalf in the '90s. The fine *Mississippi Lad* album with special guest Waits was issued in 1991. Some of Edwards's Contemporary sessions, mostly '60s material including one session with McGhee, have been reissued. — *Ron Wynn*

Foremost, The / 1947-1948 / Onyx 215
Breakout, formative sessions by Delta saxist turned West Coast player. A reissue. — *Ron Wynn*

Central Avenue Breakdown / **i.** 1948 / Onyx
Definitive portrait of emerging Black jazz scene on the West Coast. Not exactly "cool" or "hot." Fine playing by Hampton Hawes (p), Red Callender (b), and Benny Bailey (tpt). — *Ron Wynn*

Teddy's Ready / Aug. 17, 1960 / Contemporary 748
Many feel this album is this West Coast group's finest hour. With Joe Castro (p), Leroy Vinnegar (b), and Billy Higgins (d). — *Michael Erlewine*

○ **Together Again!** / May 15+17, 1961 / Contemporary 424
Dynamite pairing with Howard McGhee (tpt). Incredible pi-ano by Phineas Newborn, Jr. (p) — *Ron Wynn*

Good Gravy! / Aug. 23-25, 1961 / Contemporary 661

Heart and Soul / Apr. 24, 1962 / Contemporary 177

It's Alright / May 24+27, 1967 / Prestige

Nothin' But the Truth / Sep. 1967 / Prestige 7518

★ **Feelin's** / Mar. 25, 1974 / Muse 5045
Teddy Edwards, who had not had a leader's date for more than seven years, far too long for so capable a musician, per-haps tries a little too hard here. Of his four originals, "Tracks" and "April Love" are excellent, "Eleven Twenty Three" and "The Blue Sombrero" are routine, "Ritta Ditta Blues" by Ray Brown is very good indeed, and "Georgia on My Mind" is the famous standard, if we can still identify tunes that most of the young audience no longer knows by that term. Working out of a Gene Ammons bag, Edwards in-vests "Tracks" with plenty of tenor soul; the strategically placed low note is a catchy device. On the pretty bossa "April," his approach is much smoother, but equally convinc-ing, and he displays humor and dexterity on "Ritta." Trumpeter Conte Candoli, more relaxed than with Supersax, is in a very lyrical groove on "April" and bops the blues on "Ritta." Pianist Dolo Coker, long absent from recording stu-dios, is not featured, but when he gets a chance, as on "Tracks," he shows that he had not lost his Bud Powell-in-spired chops. Bassist Ray Brown is beautifully recorded (I

like the balance and mix of the entire date) and is simply masterful. This is solid mainstream fare and, at times, more. —*Dan Morgenstern*, Down Beat

Inimitable / Jun. 25, 1976 / Xanadu

Out of This World / Dec. 5, 1980 / Steeple Chase

Mississippi Lad / Mar. 1991 / Antilles 511411

Blue Saxophone / PolyGram 517527
At age 68 saxophonist Teddy Edwards can boast a formidable resume, having collaborated over the past four decades with Max Roach, Benny Carter, Milt Jackson, Benny Goodman, and Sarah Vaughan. And to judge from *Blue Saxophone*, this versatile tenor remains as vital as ever.

Not that Edwards is a nostalgia buff. Quite the contrary; he's put together a truly idiosyncratic brass-and-strings ensemble for this disc. On "Lennox Lady" or "Them Dirty Old Blues," the strings mimic horn riffs; on one splashy big-band piece, "No Name Number One," Michael White and Dan Weinstein contribute pungent violin and viola (!) solos. —*James Marcus*, Jazz Times

MARTY EHRLICH

Multi-reeds / Modern creative
A tremendous multi-instrumentalist, Marty Ehrlich has displayed just as much versatility in his musical choices. His '80s and '90s releases have covered free, ethnic, collectively improvised, and hard bop material, featuring mostly original compositions. Ehrlich's a pungent soloist on B-flat and bass clarinets, flutes, alto, tenor, and soprano saxophones. He's recorded with Anthony Cox, Pheeroan AkLaff, Stan Strickland, Frank Lacy, Wayne Horovitz, and Andrew Cyrille, among others. Ehrlich has been just as busy as a side musician. He has appeared on sessions by Christy Doran, Julius Hemphill, Muhal Richard Abrams, Leroy Jenkins, John Zorn, Bobby Previte, and George Russell. He's recorded for Muse, Enja, and Sound Aspects. Ehrlich has a couple of sessions available on CD. —*Ron Wynn*

○ **Pliant Plaint** / i. Apr. 1987 / Enja 5065

Traveller's Tale, The / May 1989-Jun. 1989 / Enja 79630
Solid, energized solos by Marty Ehrlich on a variety of saxophones and flute, plus equally animated playing from co-saxophonist Stan Strickland on tenor, soprano, and flute. The two-sax frontline, plus tasteful, probing bass/drum help from Lindsey Horner and Robert Previte, not only fills the spaces open from the absence of a pianist, but periodically shifts the mood, focus, and tempo. —*Ron Wynn*

Emergency Peace / i. Dec. 14-16, 1990 / New World 80409
And Dark Woods Ensemble. A fascinating blend of improvisation and original structures. —*Myles Boisen*

★ **Falling Man** / 1990 / Muse 5398
An intriguing, though sometimes disjointed, duo outing between multi-instrumentalist Marty Erhlich and bassist Anthony Cox. They venture into free, fusion, funk, and rock territory, and while all their duets are exceptionally played, the compositions aren't uniformly interesting. The best cut is their emphatic duet "You Don't Know What Love Is," which was a signature song for Eric Dolphy. —*Ron Wynn*

ROY ELDRIDGE (David Roy Eldridge)

b. Jan. 30, 1911, Pittsburgh, PA, **d.** Feb. 26, 1989
Trumpet / Swing, big band
Roy Eldridge was arguably the swing era's finest trumpet soloist: a combative, rapid-fire player with great rhythmic intensity and extensive range. Eldridge's models were saxophonists, especially Benny Carter and Coleman Hawkins, and he adapted their swift arpeggio style to the trumpet. He was also influenced by trumpeters Louis Armstrong and Jabbo Smith. Eldridge's harmonic knowledge was immense, and his riveting, octave-jumping solos and spectacular high-note climaxes to impressive solos resulted in unforgettable performances and recordings. He stopped playing for health reasons, but his body of work is considerable and is consistently first-rate.

Eldridge began playing professionally as a drummer and trumpeter at age 16, working in carnival shows and territory bands. He moved to New York in 1930, and played in various Harlem dance bands, among them Teddy Hill's. He worked in Pittsburgh and Baltimore in 1933 before returning to New York. He recorded with Hill in 1935, and attracted widespread attention. After joining Fletcher Henderson, his solos and infrequent vocals furthered his growing reputation. He formed a band in 1936 with his brother, Joe. They were broadcast nightly, and Eldridge became famous for marvelous solos on such songs as "Wabash Stomp." He formed a ten-piece group in 1938, and, in 1939, had residencies at New York City's Arcadia Ballroom and, later, at Kelly's Stable. Eldrige smashed racial barriers in 1941, joining Gene Krupa's band and becoming one of the first Blacks with a permanent position in a White orchestra's brass section.

For two years, he enjoyed sustained, across-the-board exposure, and even scored two hits, the duet "Let Me Off Uptown" with Anita O'Day, and "Rockin' Chair." He took a similar position with Artie Shaw in 1944, but, by 1945, disillusioned by ugly racial incidents while on tour with Shaw, Eldridge organized his own big band. He was soon forced to switch to a combo. In 1948, he began a lengthy stint with Norman Granz's Jazz at the Philharmonic tour. Eldridge left America in 1950, opting to remain in Paris while on tour with Benny Goodman. Eldridge remained overseas until 1951, recording and performing before adoring fans. He achieved fresh success upon his return in 1951, finding a niche playing with musicians such as Benny Carter, Johnny Hodges, Ella Fitzgerald, and his idol, Hawkins. From 1970 until 1980, he was a fixture at Ryan's, playing traditional jazz. After a 1980 stroke, Eldridge eventually gave up music, though for many years he made occasional appearances doing vocals and playing drums and piano. Many of his records have resurfaced, thanks to reissue mania. —*Ron Wynn and Dan Morgenstern*

○ **Little Jazz** / i. Feb. 1935-Apr. 1940 / CBS 465684

★ **After You've Gone** / 1936-1946 / GRP 605
Roy Eldridge was a complex trumpet artist, and it is no shame that *After You've Gone* includes several failed attempts to recapture the glory of his 1941 epic/tragic ballad, "Rocking Chair" (for Columbia). The other dominant mood here is the hot, screaming, high-note Eldridge. Most satisfying are the less forced, more modest works, usually at medium tempos, that display the warmth and rasp of his sound. These are mostly big band works from 1943–1946 and contain brief, vivid moments by the likes of tenorist Tom Archia and altoist Porter Kilbert showing bop rearing its lovely head even in this late swing setting. —*John Litweiler*, Down Beat

Early Years, The / i. 1930s / Columbia
This set opens with the rare 1935 ARC "Here Comes Cookie," which boasts a surprisingly startling contribution by trumpeter Roy Eldridge and continues with the entire output of his first issued leader dates, including a previously unissued alternate take of "Wabash Stomp" (except for a recent appearance of "Merritt 8"). The second Eldridge session concludes on side two, which is filled out by four comparatively hard-to-get titles by Teddy Wilson (piano) and Mildred Bailey (vocals), all of which are notable for the trumpeter's unflagging versatility and inventiveness. If all of this was not enough, the entirety of sides three and four constitute the real bonanza for swing fans: ten out of the 12 titles are previously unissued alternate takes of Eldridge features with the Gene Krupa band! Of course, my personal preference lies with Eldridge's work in combo or jam settings, but few can fault the dynamic presence he adds to this large, otherwise undistinguished orchestra. There are some minimally acceptable tunes presented here, to be sure, but the band does its professional best with the material, and Eldridge is, as always, his irrepressible self. —*Jack Sohmer*, Cadence

Uptown / i. 1941-1942 / Columbia 45448

1941–1942. An outstanding compilation of some prime Eldridge cuts with Anita O'Day (v) and Krupa (d). Nice for those who only want a limited amount of his material. — *Ron Wynn*

★ **On Keynote** / i. 1944 / PolyGram 830923
A very good collection of '40s Eldridge done for Keynote. The Coleman Hawkins quintet sides are particularly tasty. — *Ron Wynn*

○ **Rockin' Chair** / Aug. 7, 1951-Dec. 13, 1952 / Clef 704

☆ **Dale's Wail** / Apr. 20, 1953+Dec. 1953 / Clef 705
The expansion of Roy Eldridge's trumpet sonority made all the difference in the world. The bravura passages, as in "Rocking Chair" and "Wrap Your Troubles in Dreams," echo rather than ring. Muted or open, his horn's inflections impress this character on his lines. Eldridge, the third great trumpeter of the generation of Red Allen and Cootie Williams, was and is an emotional player, and the growth of his skill with dynamics finally unified the often disparate elements of his soloing. You could hardly wish for a more complete portrait of an artist than this album. There is a typical almost-bop solo in "The Song Is Ended," a flamboyant tribute to 1930 Armstrong in "Sweethearts on Parade," some rewarding riff-and-ride works in the four structurally isolated choruses of "Feeling a Draft," and just plain superbly skillful playing on "Foggy Day." There is also a courageous attempt at "Echoes of Harlem," that classic Cootie Williams tightrope act, and in the stringing of licks we hear both Eldridge's weakness and the core of his integrity. Eldridge celebrated the spirit of musical adventure, and these '52–'54 works with, incidentally, no other horns and just four Oscar Peterson keyboard solos, constitute an exciting journey. — *John Litweiler*, Down Beat

★ **Little Jazz** / i. 1954 / Columbia 45275
Roy Eldridge was at the top of his form in Paris in June 1950; these sessions show him in magnificent mettle. The rhythm sections are both first rate as Dick Hyman and Ed Shaughnessy take the piano/drum honors on side one, Gerry Wiggins and Kenny Clarke are on side two, and the ubiquitous Pierre Michelot, who appears on six Jazz Legacy LPs, is the bassist on all cuts. The idea of adding Zoot Sims to the first session was useful; Sims's warm, bubbling tenor is a perfect foil for Eldridge's bristling, room-shaking trumpet. Even Eldridge's vocal talents are put to good use here; his singing is as expressive and individualistic as his trumpet playing. On the ballad tempo "Wrap Your Troubles in Dreams," Eldridge takes a second chorus that sizzles, and on the uptempo "Undecided" he buzzes and flies. There is not a single note out of Eldridge's horn that does not absolutely jump off the turntable here. At one point, Wiggins aptly quotes "An American in Paris." Although this album is titled with Eldridge's nickname, "Little Jazz," the trumpeter stands so tall in these sessions that he could have been eating off the top of the Eiffel Tower. — *Lee Jeske*, Down Beat

Roy and Diz—Vol. 2 / Oct. 29, 1954 / Clef 671

Roy and Diz / Oct. 29, 1954 / Clef 641

○ **Trumpet Battle** / Oct. 29, 1954 / Clef 730
Though it's entitled *The Trumpet Battle 1952*, this date devotes only seven minutes of its total (34:17) to any such activity. Side one is entirely taken up with "Jam Session Blues," (16:10) which employs Roy Eldridge and Charlie Shavers on trumpet, Benny Carter on alto, Flip Phillips and Lester Young on tenor, and a rhythm section made up of Oscar Peterson (piano), Ray Brown (bass), Buddy Rich (drums), and Barney Kessel (the latter, of course, on guitar). Side two spends 11:07 on the "Ballad Medley," another Norman Granz JATP convention, Young plays "I Can't Get Started," Shavers essays "Summertime," Phillips does "Sweet Lorraine," Eldridge performs "It's the Talk of the Town," and Benny Carter caps it off with "Cocktails For Two." All of these cuts are marred by some of the worst-recorded sound I've had the misfortune to hear (it is replete with wavering levels and static), and the album bears no cover caveat. The poor sound extends right into the so-called

"Trumpet Battle," distorting what sounds like some fine Benny Carter alto, preceding the Shavers and Eldridge derring-do. The liner notes advise that this material originally appeared as part of a three-LP box set, *JATP Vol. 15*, the last of the JATP series to be issued on the Mercury label. The disc does not look defective, so the explanation for the poor sound must stem from its source. — *Alan Bargebuhr*, Cadence

○ **Roy's Got Rhythm** / i. 1956 / EmArcy 36084

And Benny Carter / i. 1957 /

★ **Mexican Bandit Meets Pittsburg Pirate** / i. Aug. 24, 1973 / Fantasy 9646
Mexican Bandit Meets Pittsburgh Pirate. Interesting title for this wonderful collaboration between Eldridge and Paul Gonsalves (ts); a delightful date. — *Ron Wynn*

Jazz Maturity. . . Where It's Coming From / 1975 / Pablo 2310-816

Happy Time / Jun. 4, 1975 / Pablo 628
This is a 1991 reissue of a pleasant session with Oscar Peterson (p). — *Ron Wynn*

Trumpet Kings at Montreux / i. Jul. 16, 1975 / Pablo 445
With Dizzy Gillespie and Clark Terry. Good workout among these jazz immortals. — *Ron Wynn*

○ **I Remember Harlem** / i. 1976 / Inner City 7012
This is primarily a showcase for the dynamic trumpet style of "Little Jazz." Roy Eldridge plays the blues with so much strength, resiliency, and fun that it is difficult not to get caught up in the excitement. Whether singing the blues in French or playing piano, his music is extremely infectious. His orchestra was basically a Kansas City riff band, which Eldridge used as a perfect foil for his high-powered improvisations. The quintet is notable because of the inclusion of saxophonist Don Byas. Byas and Eldridge play well together and provide the evidence of the transition between swing and bop. — *Spencer R. Weston*, Cadence

○ **Live at the Three Duces** / i. Jun. 1976 / Jazz Archives 24

Montreux 1977 / Jul. 13, 1977 / Pablo 373
A session that is nice and hot. Fine Eldridge and excellent Oscar Peterson (p). — *Ron Wynn*

Roy Eldridge Four / i. 1977 / Pablo

ELIANE ELIAS

b. Mar. 19, 1960, Sao Paulo, Brazil
Piano / Latin, Neo-bop, Jazz
Pianist Elias has found a niche doing updated Afro-Latin music, though she's not as striking or sensual in her delivery as numerous Portuguese and Latin vocalists. Her Blue Note releases have featured better jazz songs than Brazilian cuts. Married to trumpeter Randy Brecker. — *Ron Wynn*

Illusions / Oct. 1986 / Denon 1569

★ **Cross Currents** / i. Jan. 1989 / Denon 2180
This Brazilian pianist's best album to date, though it only scratches the surface of her immense talents. — *Michael G. Nastos*

So Far So Close / i. 1989 / Blue Note 91411

○ **Eliane Elias Plays Jobim** / Dec. 1990 / Blue Note 93089
Good adaptations by Elias of both classic and contemporary Jobim compositions. Her often sultry, soft voice, though not Portuguese, covers the material with conviction and sincerity. She's backed by bassist Eddie Gomez, drummer Jack DeJohnette, and percussionist Nana Vasconcelos. — *Ron Wynn*

Long Story, A / i. 1991 / Blue Note 95476

○ **Fantasia** / i. 1992 / Blue Note 96146
Eliane Elias continues exploring Brazilian music on this latest release, doing both classics such as "The Girl from Ipanema" and a Milton Nascimento medley, plus several Ivan Lins tunes. She uses alternating bassists and drummers, with Eddie Gomez, Marc Johnson, Jack DeJohnette,

and Peter Erskine dividing time, plus Nana Vasconcelos on percussion, with Lins helping out on vocals. —*Ron Wynn*

DUKE ELLINGTON (Edward Kennedy Ellington)

b. Apr. 29, 1899, Washington, DC, **d.** May 24, 1974, New York, NY

Composer, bandleader, piano / Swing, big band

With the 20th century nearing its end, Edward Kennedy "Duke" Ellington looms as its greatest all-around musical figure. Ellington achieved monumental status as a composer, bandleader, arranger, and instrumentalist. No one knows exactly how many songs he wrote, but they're estimated at over 2,000, and the vast majority of songs he recorded were his own. They include an array of short instrumentals and popular songs, extended suites, theatrical pieces, film scores, spirituals, quasi-classical pieces, and one unfinished opera. Ellington understood the difference between composition and improvisational creation. He prepared pieces with specific devices such as call-and-response segments, fragmented motifs, and recurring phrases. There's considerable debate over whether or not his musical abilities declined after the late '30s and early '40s, but it's hard for anyone (other than James Lincoln Collier) to declare, without qualification, that there was marked decline throughout his late period.

A self-taught arranger, Ellington made the orchestra a separate instrument in a manner approached by no one except, perhaps, Charles Mingus, Sun Ra, and Gil Evans. Ellington experimented with tonal effects, unusual voicings, amazing blends, and ensemble pairings. He inverted or switched roles, and had a trumpet change place with a trombone in an arrangement. He exploited the expressive, voicelike styles of players such as Bubber Miley, plunger-muted Cootie Williams, Tricky Sam Nanton, and Cat Anderson, who had a high-register range. Because it seems impossible for any person to do everything well, it was assumed that Ellington was a weak pianist. But he could dazzle when least expected; he rivaled Basie in the strategic insert, and sometimes he wouldn't even play at all. His versatility enabled Ellington to step outside the orchestra in unexpected situations and to succeed at them, from playing in a trio with Max Roach and Charles Mingus to playing with John Coltrane.

His background, particularly his middle-class upbringing, has been the subject of questionable pseudoanalysis over the years. His father was a blueprint maker and an occasional butler, and wanted Ellington to be an artist. Ellington started studying piano at age seven, and was influenced greatly by ragtime stylists. He debuted professionally at age 17 in Washington, D.C., then came to New York in the mid '20s. He had an unprofitable visit in 1923, but, on Fats Waller's suggestion, returned to New York in 1924 with Elmer Snowden's band, the Washingtonians. The roster included Sonny Greer, Otto Hardwicke, and Artie Whetsol. They played the Hollywood and Kentucky clubs on Broadway, and expanded to a ten-piece group by 1927. They became the Cotton Club's house band. Bubber Miley, Sam Nanton, Harry Carney, Rudy Jackson, and Wellman Braud were in the band. Snowden was gone, replaced by Fred Guy, and Ellington was at the helm. They stayed at the Cotton Club from 1927–1931. Barney Bigard replaced Rudy Jackson, and Johnny Hodges, Freddie Jenkins, Cootie Williams were added, and Miley departed. They cut some classic songs in the late '20s, including "East St. Louis Toodle-oo" and "Black and Tan Fantasy." They appeared in the 1930 film *Check and Double Check*, traveling to Hollywood. The orchestra cut some 200 sides in New York, with Ellington's "jungle" style becoming a national sensation.

Ellington began experimenting with extended compositions in 1931 with "Creole Rhapsody," which was followed by "Reminiscing in Tempo," "Diminuendo in Blue," and "Crescendo In Blue." The '30s and '40s proved fertile periods. There were alterations in the instrumental lineup, and the addition of such greats as Ben Webster, Billy Strayhorn, and

Jimmy Blanton. Ray Nance, Shorty Baker, and Jimmy Hamilton joined in the early '40s, and Ellington premiered the celebrated "Black, Brown and Beige" series at Carnegie Hall in 1943. This was an ambitious, three-part piece designed to depict Black history through its various segments. These concerts continued until 1950, while Ellington created increasingly more involved works. The orchestra began a series of foreign tours in the '30s that continued into the '70s. Ellington composed his first film score in 1959, *Anatomy of a Murder.* He recorded with Coltrane and Mingus. Ellington also began writing liturgical music, something that would consume his total interest in his final years. The awards and honors poured in during the '60s and early '70s, though there was also one incredible snub: he failed to receive the Pulitzer Prize despite the unanimous recommendation of the awarding committee. A documentary film, *On the Road with Duke Ellington,* was made in 1974. He worked until the end of his life, then his son, Mercer, took over. The band remains active today, while Ellington reissues and newly discovered sessions from various studio vaults, even Ellington's own collection, keep coming. —*Ron Wynn with Dan Morgenstern*

Vol. 1–the Birth of a Band / Nov. 1924-Dec. 1926 / EPM 5104

This CD contains virtually all of Duke Ellington's recordings before he had developed his own musical identity. Starting off with a piano roll from 1924 and including obscure vocals by Alberta Hunter, Florence Bristol, Alberta Jones, and Jo Trent, this valuable set also has all of Ellington's earliest instrumentals, cut during the years that his Washingtonians successfully struggled and landed an important association with the Kentucky Club. Highly recommended to collectors but certainly too primitive for most of Ellington's fans. —*Scott Yanow*

Complete Vol. 1.–1925-1928 / Sep. 1925-Oct. 1928 / CBS 67264

French Columbia, in the mid to late '70s, put out a perfectly conceived Duke Ellington series that eventually totaled 15 double LPs. As with the French RCA program, Columbia reissued every Ellington recording they owned, including all of the alternate takes, but unfortunately both of these definitive series are very difficult to acquire and current CD programs are less complete. All of the Columbia twofers are worth tracking down if possible. Volume 1 has four early sides from 1925-26 that find Ellington struggling to find his own musical personality. Then suddenly, with "East St. Louis Toodle-oo" from March 22, 1927, Duke emerges as a major force. The contrasting trumpets of Bubber Miley and Arthur Whetsol, along with trombonist Tricky Sam Nanton and a variety of emerging soloists, star throughout this wonderful set which is mostly from 1928. —*Scott Yanow*

Jazz Heritage: Brunswick-Vocalion Rarities / Nov. 29, 1926-Jan. 20, 1931 / MCA 1374

This LP has odds and ends taken from a four-year period during which Duke Ellington emerged as the major bandleader in jazz and popular music. Six of the ten performances on this brief set are rare alternate takes, and although released out of chronological order and a bit haphazardly, veteran collectors will want to find this LP, at least until MCA/Decca gets around to reissuing its contents on CD. —*Scott Yanow*

Brunswick Recordings—Vol. 1 (1926–1929), The / Dec. 29, 1926-Jan. 8, 1929 / MCA 42325

Nice 1990 reissue of his mid- to late-'20s cuts. The sessions have been reissued often. This version is nicely remastered. —*Ron Wynn*

Works of Duke Vols. 1-5, The / Jan. 10, 1927-Nov. 21, 1930 / 731043,7410

In the 1970s, French RCA did a perfect job of reissuing Duke Ellington's priceless recordings for its associated labels, releasing everything cut through 1952 (including all of the alternate takes) on 24 LPs also available in five boxed sets. No other reissue program conducted by RCA (whether on LP or

CD) comes close, although these sets are unfortunately out of print. Vols. 1-5 trace Ellington's legacy from 1927-30 and along with a few period vocals and novelties is overflowing with classics. Get it if you can! —*Scott Yanow*

☆ **Okeh Ellington** / Mar. 22, 1927-Nov. 8, 1930 / Columbia 46177

○ **Flaming Youth** / Oct. 26, 1927-Jan. 6, 1929 / RCA 56
Of all of the single LPs released of early Duke Ellington in the '60s and '70s, *Flaming Youth* is the definitive one, for it seems to include the most exciting versions of each of Ellington's classics of the era. These versions of "Black and Tan Fantasy," "Jubilee Stomp," "The Mooche," and especially "East St. Louis Toodle-oo" have never been topped. This set is a perfect introduction to early Ellington during the LP era, if only to hear the contributions of the unique trumpeter Bubber Miley. —*Scott Yanow*

★ **Sophisticated Ellington** / i. 1927-1966 / RCA 4098
This is a wonderful two-record set of material ranging from the '20s to the '60s. —*Ron Wynn*

○ **Duke Ellington (1927 1934)** / 1927-1934 / Nimbus 6001
This CD, like others in the set, consists of original performances rerecorded in a special "digital stereo" process developed by Robert Parker, an Australian audio engineer. The "enhanced" sound is more likely to appeal to those hearing these old recordings for the first time. To those long familiar with them, the changes Parker has wrought are apt to prove disconcerting at times. But either way, it is good to have the work of these pioneers available on CDs, although it seems likely to be duplicated by the reissue programs of the original owners of the material. Parker's selections and programming verge occasionally on the eccentric, sometimes resulting in the inclusion of rarish items . . . these include "East St. Louis Toodle-oo" by Mills Ten Black Berries, a *nom du disque* for the Ellington band on the Velvetone label. — *Stanley Dance*, Jazz Times

Hot in Harlem Vol. 2 / Oct. 17, 1928-Oct. 29, 1929 / Decca 79241
The second of three LPs covering Duke Ellington's early recordings owned by MCA/Decca contains many high points including "The Mooche," "Rent Party Blues," and a novelty version of "Oklahoma Stomp." Best is a nearly six-minute version of "Tiger Rag" that features six of Ellington's top soloists. Superior to either of the CDs put out by MCA in recent times but hard to find. —*Scott Yanow*

Complete Vol. 2.–1928-1930 / Oct. 1928-Nov. 20, 1929 / CBS 68275
The second volume of this regrettably unavailable series of twofers contains all of CBS's Ellington recordings from October 1928 up to January 29, 1930, a period when trumpeter Cootie Williams replaced Bubber Miley, and altoist Johnny Hodges quickly developed into one of the major soloists in jazz. There are lots of valuable rarities on this highly enjoyable twofer. —*Scott Yanow*

Brunswick Era Vol. 2 / Jan. 8, 1929-Jan. 20, 1931 / Decca 42348
The second of two CDs featuring highlights from MCA's collection of early Duke Ellington (but not as complete as its three LPs from back in the '70s), this enjoyable set is filled with performances from the early Depression years, including the jubilant "Wall Street Wail" (recorded only a short while after the crash of 1929), "Mood Indigo," "Rockin' In Rhythm," and his two-part "Creole Rhapsody." During this period altoist Johnny Hodges emerged as a major soloist and Cootie Williams became more comfortable as the replacement of the great Bubber Miley. —*Scott Yanow*

Complete Vol. 3.–1930-1932, The / Jan. 29, 1930-Feb. 4, 1932 / CBS 88000
The third of 15 volumes that document every Duke Ellington recording for CBS and its related labels up to 1940, this hard-to-find double LP has many alternate takes and even more gems from 1930-32, including rare remakes of "The Mooche" and "Black and Tan Fantasy" and the orig-

inal "It Don't Mean a Thing If It Ain't Got That Swing." —*Scott Yanow*

○ **Duke Ellington (1930)** / i. Jan. 1930-Jun. 1930 / Classics 586

Early Duke Ellington / Jul. 15, 1930-May 20, 1938 / Everest 221
A typical Everest budget production, this LP, despite its title, also has sessions by Jimmy Dorsey (the altoist and clarinetist is backed by an English rhythm section in 1930) and pianist-vocalist Una Mae Carlisle from 1938. In fact, only four of the ten selections are from Ellington, all from a fine date in 1933. Worth picking up if it can be found cheap! —*Scott Yanow*

Works of Duke Vols. 6-10 / Nov. 26, 1930-Jul. 22, 1940 / RCA 741068,7410
The second of five priceless boxed sets put out by French RCA in the 1970s, these five LPs cover Ellington from 1930-34 and also when he returned to Victor in 1940. Loads of brilliant music; even the weaker items have their great moments. —*Scott Yanow*

Duke Ellington Presents Ivie Anderson / Feb. 2, 1932-Feb. 14, 1940 / Columbia 32064
This excellent double LP contains 32 of Ivie Anderson's best vocals with Duke Ellington's orchestra, dating from 1932's "It Don't Mean A Thing" up to 1940's "Stormy Weather." Although Anderson was occasionally saddled with novelty tunes or forgettable items, this set finds her at her very best, and these enjoyable titles also contain many fine solos from Duke's sidemen. —*Scott Yanow*

Reflections in Ellington / Feb. 3, 1932-Sep. 26, 1940 / Everybodys 3005
For this LP, there are previously unissued broadcast performances from 1940 (most of them quite rewarding) that feature one of Duke Ellington's greatest orchestras, along with two medleys from 1932 that are heard for the first time in stereo! Apparently, the latter items were originally recorded using two sets of microphones, and, although the notes are unchanged from the more conventional release, one can hear a bit of separation between the two channels. This LP is well worth searching for. —*Scott Yanow*

Complete Vol. 4.–1932 / Feb. 4, 1932-Dec. 21, 1932 / CBS 88035
From the French CBS series of twofer LPs that reissued all of Duke Ellington's output (including alternate takes) for their associated labels, this set finds Duke's orchestra still flourishing musically at the height of the Depression. Most of these titles generally miss getting reissued by "best of" series, but all are worth hearing. Best known are the two versions of "St. Louis Blues" with guest Bing Crosby and Ellington's famous recording of "The Sheik of Araby" that is highlighted by a famous chorus by trombonist Lawrence Brown. —*Scott Yanow*

Complete Vol. 5.–1932-1933 / Dec. 21, 1932-May 16, 1933 / CBS 88082
The fifth of 15 double LPs from French CBS that document Ellington's long period in the 1930s on Columbia's labels has many fine recordings that often elude reissue. Among the high points are collaborations with guest vocalists like the Mills Brothers, Ethel Waters, and Adelaide Hall, a couple of versions apiece of two medleys from the Blackbirds of 1928, and the original recordings of "Sophisticated Lady" and "Drop Me Off At Harlem." —*Scott Yanow*

Complete Vol. 6.–1933-1936 / Aug. 15, 1933-Jan. 20, 1936 / CBS 88137
It would be difficult to improve upon this French CBS reissue series; if only it were made available on CD! Volume 6 covers a session apiece from 1933 and '34 and then most of 1935. Among the classics are a spirited version of "In The Shade of the Old Apple Tree," "In a Sentimental Mood," "Truckin'," and the four-part "Reminiscing In Tempo." Recommended if it can be found! —*Scott Yanow*

Duke's Men: Small Groups—Vol. 1 / Dec. 12, 1934-Jan. 19, 1938 / Columbia 46995
A fine 1991 reissue of great combos led by the Ellingtonians (a few also with the Duke). —*Ron Wynn*

Complete Vol. 7–1936-1937 / Feb. 27, 1936-Mar. 5, 1937 / CBS 88140
From the definitive French CBS reissue program of two-LP sets, this volume covers 1936 and a bit of '37 with small-group sessions led by Rex Stewart and Barney Bigard (the latter includes the original version of "Caravan") and many lesser-known big-band sides, including a pair of rare solo piano performances by Duke and Rex Stewart's feature "Trumpet In Spades." —*Scott Yanow*

Complete Vol. 8–1937 / Mar. 5, 1937-May 20, 1937 / CBS 88185
Continuing the French CBS definitive reissue series of Duke Ellington's 1930s recordings for its labels, this two-LP set sticks to the first half of 1937. Highlighted by small-group sessions from Cootie Williams and his Rug Cutters, Barney Bigard's Jazzopators, and the first part of Johnny Hodges's initial session as a leader, there are many gems among even the obscurities. —*Scott Yanow*

Volume III / Mar. 18, 1937-Jan. 9, 1940 / Everest 266
A budget LP from Everest, this set features performances by the Duke Ellington orchestra from radio broadcasts dating from 1937 and 1940. Virtually all of Duke's recordings from this era are well worth acquiring. This LP is highlighted by a fine Cootie Williams-Rex Stewart trumpet battle on "Tootin' Through The Roof." —*Scott Yanow*

Complete Vol. 9–1937 / May 20, 1937-Sep. 20, 1937 / CBS 88210
Continuing French CBS's comprehensive mid-'70s reissue of all of Duke Ellington's recordings for its labels during the 1930s, this very enjoyable twofer has small-group sessions led by Johnny Hodges, Barney Bigard, and Rex Stewart and such titles by the big band as "Diminuendo in Blue," "Crescendo in Blue," and the exciting "Harmony in Harlem." Other bands during this era may have been better known to the general public, but in reality Duke Ellington's orchestra had no close competitors. —*Scott Yanow*

Complete Vol. 10–1937-1938 / Oct. 26, 1937-Mar. 28, 1938 / CBS 88220
The majority of this volume from French CBS's complete reissue of Duke Ellington's 1930s recordings focuses on the many rewarding small-group sessions led by his sidemen (and actually directed by Ellington). Cootie Williams, Barney Bigard, and Johnny Hodges all get their chance to act as leader, while the big band is heard on such selections as "The New Black and Tan Fantasy" and "I Let a Song Go Out of My Heart." —*Scott Yanow*

Duke's Men–Volume 2 / Mar. 28, 1938-Mar. 20, 1939 / Columbia/Legacy 2K48835
This second two-CD set, like the first, includes all of the master takes (no alternates) from the small-group sessions led by Duke Ellington's sidemen. During the year covered on this volume, Johnny Hodges, Cootie Williams, and Rex Stewart all had opportunities to head sessions, and the results included early versions of "Jeep's Blues," "Pyramid," "Prelude To A Kiss," "The Jeep Is Jumpin'," and "Hodge Podge," along with many hot obscurities. There are few duds and many memorable performances during these 43 recordings. —*Scott Yanow*

Complete Vol. 11–1938 / Mar. 28, 1938-Aug. 4, 1938 / CBS 88242
This llth of 15 volumes from French CBS continues the complete reissue of all of Duke Ellington's recordings during the 1930s for Columbia's associated labels. With small-group sessions led by Cootie Williams and Johnny Hodges and many fine big-band sessions, this set proves that Duke Ellington had a brilliant orchestra before the 1939-42 edition made history. Included are two versions of Lawrence Brown's famous solo on "Rose of the Rio Grande." —*Scott Yanow*

Complete Vol. 12–1938 / Aug. 4, 1938-Dec. 22, 1938 / CBS 88451
This two-LP set from French CBS's superb reissue series covers a five-month period with small-group sessions by Johnny Hodges (including "Prelude to a Kiss" and "The Jeep Is Jumpin'") and Cootie Williams, along with such big-band selections as "Battle of Swing" and Rex Stewart's famous "Boy Meets Horn." —*Scott Yanow*

Complete Vol. 13–1938-1939 / Dec. 22, 1938-Jun. 2, 1939 / CBS 88518
Taken from the period just prior to bassist Jimmy Blanton joining his orchestra, this two-LP set finds Duke Ellington playing in several formats, including small groups drawn from his orchestra that are led by altoist Johnny Hodges, trumpeter Cootie Williams, and cornetist Rex Stewart, on a pair of rare piano solos (originally unissued) and some big-band classics. High points include "Dooji Wooji," "Pussy Willow," "Finesse," and two versions of "Portrait of the Lion." —*Scott Yanow*

☆ **Braggin' in Brass: The Immortal 1938 Years** / 1938 / Portrait 44395

Complete Vol. 14–1939 / Jun. 2, 1939-Oct. 14, 1939 / CBS 88521
The next-to-last volume in French CBS's definitive (but now out-of-print) LP series, this twofer has combo sides led by altoist Johnny Hodges, clarinetist Barney Bigard, and trumpeter Cootie Williams; a pair of numbers with a vocal group called The Quintones; and bassist Jimmy Blanton's first recordings with Ellington's full orchestra. Whether it be "I'm Checkin' Out Go'om Bye," "The Sergeant Was Shy," "Tootin' Through The Roof," or some of the lesser-known tracks, this music is consistently enjoyable and timeless. —*Scott Yanow*

Complete Vol. 15–1939-1940 / Oct. 14, 1939-Feb. 15, 1940 / CBS 88522
The final two-LP set in French CBS's definitive reissue, this package finds the orchestra poised for greatness just prior to switching to RCA. Bassist Jimmy Blanton was now in the band, tenor saxophonist Ben Webster was aboard by the second half of this set, and such longtime stars as trumpeter Cootie Williams, cornetist Rex Stewart, trombonists Tricky Sam Nanton and Lawrence Brown, clarinetist Barney Bigard, and altoist Johnny Hodges were very much in their prime. Hodges, Bigard, and Cootie get to lead some small-group sessions, Ellington is heard solo on "Blues," there are two Ellington-Blanton piano-bass duets (unpredecented for the time), and the full orchestra backs singer Ivie Anderson on one of her finest sessions. Overall, this series is a brilliant effort that should be duplicated on CD! —*Scott Yanow*

○ **Webster–Blanton Years, The** / i. 1939-1942 / RCA/ Bluebird 5659
A fine three-disc anthology of late-'30s, early-'40s Ellington material covering contributions by pioneer bassist Jimmy Blanton. It includes full orchestra selections, plus bass/piano duets and small combo sessions. While much of this material is also available on more costly packages, this is a good domestic package. —*Ron Wynn*

Jimmy Blanton Years / Jun. 1940-Oct. 9, 1941 / Queen 007
Longtime Ellington collectors should love this LP, for it includes rare radio broadcasts of the Duke Ellington orchestra during 1940-41 and four selections that find Ellington and bassist Jimmy Blanton making guest appearances with John Scott Trotter's studio orchestra. A perfect LP for those Ellington fanatics who think they have everything! —*Scott Yanow*

Works of Duke Vols. 11-15 / Jul. 24, 1940-Jul. 2, 1941 / RCA 17072,FXM17
The third of three brilliant boxed sets put out by French RCA in the 1970s, this five-LP package covers a year in the life of Duke Ellington, one of his very best. Complete with all of the alternate takes, this music has many more than its share of classic performances. Unfortunately, it is long out of print but worth bidding for on auction lists! —*Scott Yanow*

☆ **In a Mellotone** / Sep. 5, 1940 / RCA 1346

Great Ellington Units, The / Nov. 2, 1940-Sep. 29, 1941 / RCA 6751

Beginning in the 1930s, Duke Ellington started recording with small groups taken out of his orchestra under the leadership of his sidemen. These highly enjoyable recordings offered the musicians some variety and the chance to debut some new material. All but two of the small group recordings cut for Victor during 1940–1941 are included on this very enjoyable CD. They include such future Ellington-associated standards as "Day Dream," Things Ain't What They Used to Be," "Passion Flower," and "C Jam Blues." With altoist Johnny Hodges, cornetist Rex Stewart, and clarinetist Barney Bigard acting as leaders (and bassist Jimmy Blanton inspiring the soloists), the music is consistently brilliant. — *Scott Yanow*

☆ **1940 Fargo Concert** / Nov. 7, 1940 / Jazz Society 5201

One winter night in late 1940, Jack Towers (then a young Ellington fan) received permission to record Duke's orchestra on his portable disc cutter at a dance in Fargo, ND. Little did he know that it was a historic night (trumpeter Ray Nance made his debut with the band) and that the band would be in inspired form. Decades later, the music came out on LP and now this double CD includes every scrap of music that has survived. The Duke Ellington orchestra was at one of its peaks during this period, overflowing with distinctive and unique soloists, and propelled by the top bassist in jazz (Jimmy Blanton). With the accelerated writing activity of Ellington and his new musical partner Billy Strayhorn, there was no better orchestra at the time, and there's rarely been a better one since then. Tenor saxophonist Ben Webster is heard in top form on "Star Dust," cornetist Rex Stewart, trombonists Tricky Sam Nanton and Lawrence Brown, clarinetist Barney Bigard and altoist Johnny Hodges also have some very strong moments, and Ray Nance does his best to fit in; many in the band were hearing him for the first time. It is very fortunate indeed that Jack Towers was present for what would have been a forgotten one-night stand. — *Scott Yanow*

☆ **Fargo 1940—Vol. 2 / i.** Nov. 1940 / Tax 3721

○ **Duke Ellington (1940)** / 1940 / Smithsonian 013

○ **Take the 'A' Train: The Legendary Blanton-Webster** / Jan. 15, 1941-Dec. 3, 1941 / Vintage Jazz Classics 1003

During 1941, one of Duke Ellington's peak years, Ellington not only recorded frequently in the studios, but he made this CD's worth of transcriptions for radio. Of the 26 selections on this generous set, eight of the songs were never recorded commercially and six others are heard here in their earliest versions. They include Duke's theme, "Take the 'A' Train," and "Perdido." The all-star orchestra is propelled by the great bassist Jimmy Blanton. Highly recommended. — *Scott Yanow*

☆ **Works of Duke—Vols. 16–20, The** / Jul. 2, 1941-May 15, 1945 / RCA 7201

The fourth of five mammoth boxed sets documenting Duke Ellington's Victor recordings (including all alternate takes), this one has five LPs. Small group sessions by Rex Stewart, Johnny Hodges, and Barney Bigard alternate with full-band classics (including two versions of "Chelsea Bridge" and the original renditions of "Perdido" and "C Jam Blues") during the first half of this set. The remainder traces Ellington's activity in the war years (including his four-part studio version of "Black, Brown and Beige") up to 1945 when he remade many of his hits from the previous decade, most successfully a hot vocal version of "It Don't Mean a Thing." — *Scott Yanow*

Duke Ellington—Vol. 1: 1943 / Nov. 8, 1943 / Circle 101

This is the first in a nine-LP series that contains all of the radio transcriptions that Duke Ellington and his orchestra recorded for the World Broadcasting Series, including alternates and some false starts. Due to the latter, there are generally around five to eight songs per LP, making this nevertheless valuable series of primary interest to collectors. Vol.

1 has previously rare versions of "Rockin' in Rhythm," "Blue Skies," "Boy Meets Horn," "Do Nothing 'Till You Hear From Me," and "Summertime." — *Scott Yanow*

Duke Ellington—Vol. 2: 1943 / Nov. 8, 1943-Nov. 9, 1943 / Circle 102

The second in this nine-LP series of transcriptions documents the 1943 Duke Ellington orchestra shortly after tenor star Ben Webster had departed; the band had so many talented soloists that he was barely missed. Vol. 2 is one of the strongest in this collector's program, containing nine selections (in addition to alternate takes and false starts) that are highlighted by features for Johnny Hodges and Ray Nance. — *Scott Yanow*

○ **Duke Ellington (1943)** / Nov. 9, 1943 / Circle 103

The third of nine volumes in this collector's series features Duke Ellington's transcriptions from 1943 and 1945. Best are strong versions of "Caravan" and "Ain't Misbehavin'" (featuring trumpeter Harold "Shorty" Baker). — *Scott Yanow*

Duke Ellington—Vol. 4: 1943 / Dec. 1, 1943 / Circle 104

Part of a nine-LP series of Duke Ellington's transcriptions for the World Broadcasting system, Vol. 4 has particularly enjoyable versions of "It Don't Mean a Thing," "Johnny Come Lately," and "Creole Love Call." Due to the many alternates, it is recommended mostly to true Ellington collectors. — *Scott Yanow*

Duke Ellington—Vol. 5: 1943–1945 / Dec. 1, 1943-Jan. 2, 1945 / Circle 105

The midway point in this collector's series is reached in Vol. 5, which splits the program between performances by Duke Ellington's orchestras of 1943 and 1945. Although there were some personnel changes, there is a strong consistency to this series. Eight fine numbers (along with some alternate takes and false starts) make this a worthy release. — *Scott Yanow*

At Carnegie Hall / Dec. 11, 1943 / Everest 327

Prestige has, up to this point, released the performances from four of Duke Ellington's Carnegie Hall concerts, but they have not acquired this one, Duke's second recital of 1943. This budget LP has only *some* highlights, but they include exuberant versions of standards and two excerpts from "Black, Brown and Beige." Unless it is released in a more complete form elsewhere, it is worth searching for this LP. — *Scott Yanow*

Duke Ellington—Vol. 6: 1945 / Jan. 2, 1945-Jan. 3, 1945 / Circle 106

The sixth volume in this nine-LP series finds Duke Ellington's orchestra taking its time perfecting six songs to be used for radio transcriptions. Best is Rex Stewart's adventurous "Frantic Fantasy," but because of the many takes, this one is recommended mostly for Ellington collectors. — *Scott Yanow*

○ **Works of Duke—Vols. 21–24, The** / May 16, 1945-Apr. 25, 1953 / RCA 42047

The final boxed set (four LPs this time) put out by French RCA (why doesn't the American counterpart make all of Ellington's recordings available?) finishes off this program with Duke's studio performances from 1945-1946 and a live concert dating from 1952. There is plenty of surprising material (such as "Indiana, "Lover Man," and three W. C. Handy tunes), two trio performances, the original version of "The Perfume Suite," Duke's appearances with several all-star groups, and many other high points. The concert also has a fine version of "Harlem." A strong ending to an exciting but sadly out-of-print series. — *Scott Yanow*

Duke Ellington—Vol. 8: 1945 / Jul. 31, 1945-Aug. 7, 1945 / Circle 108

In contrast to Vol. 7 in this nine-LP series of radio transcriptions by Duke Ellington, this set contains more than its share of interesting selections, including rarely performed arrangements of "Metronome All Out," "Esquire Swank," "Downbeat Shuffle," and "Hollywood Hangover." In addition,

Ray Nance's vocal on "Otto, Make That Riff Staccato" is always a delight. —*Scott Yanow*

Duke Ellington—Vol. 9: 1945 / Aug. 7, 1945 / Circle 109
The final set in this nine-LP series has six fine performances (including a lengthy "In the Shade of the Old Apple Tree"), five false starts, and three complete alternate takes. This is a very valuable collector's series, although more casual listeners are well advised to acquire Ellington's studio recordings of the era first. —*Scott Yanow*

○ **Duke Ellington: October 20, 1945** / Oct. 20, 1945 / Queendisc 006

○ **Happy-Go-Lucky Local** / i. 1946 / Musicraft 52

○ **Uncollected Duke Ellington & His Orchestra—Vol. 5 (1947), The** / Mar. 28, 1946-Jun. 10, 1947 / Hindsight 129
The final volume in this very worthy five-LP series of radio transcriptions, this set features the 1947 Duke Ellington orchestra on plenty of material that is not generally associated with Duke, including "How High the Moon," "Royal Garden Blues," and "Embraceable You." The whole series casts a new light on this often neglected period in Ellington's career and there are more highlights than one can list. For two, try these versions of "Jumpin' Punkins" and "Jump For Joy." —*Scott Yanow*

○ **Uncollected Duke Ellington & His Orchestra—Vol. 1 (1946), The** / Mar. 28, 1946 / Hindsight 125
Hindsight has released five excellent LPs of radio transcriptions by Duke Ellington from 1946-1947, one of his most underrated periods. At the time, the trumpet section starred Taft Jordan and the phenomenal high-note virtuoso Cat Anderson, Tricky Sam Nanton and Lawrence Brown were still in the trombone section, and veterans Harry Carney and Johnny Hodges were joined in the saxophone section by clarinetist Jimmy Hamilton and tenorman Al Sears (not to mention the presence of bassist Oscar Pettiford). Ellington's orchestra was far from in decline! There are lots of colorful moments provided throughout this series by all of the above, and Vol. 1 gets it off to a solid start. —*Scott Yanow*

○ **Uncollected Duke Ellington & His Orchestra—Vol. 2 (1946), The** / Mar. 28, 1946-Nov. 16, 1946 / Hindsight 126
The second of five Hindsight LPs contains Duke Ellington's radio transcriptions from 1946-1947. It has lots of strong moments, including "Perdido," the rousing "Suddenly It Jumped," a 5:12 version of "One O'Clock Jump," and the only performance of a feature for bassist Oscar Pettiford, "Tip Toe Topic." —*Scott Yanow*

○ **Uncollected Duke Ellington & His Orchestra—Vol. 3 (1946), The** / Jul. 16, 1946-Jul. 17, 1946 / Hindsight 127
The third of five volumes in this worthy LP series of Duke Ellington radio transcriptions finds Duke's orchestra in spirited form on a set of standards and obscurities. Al Sears's tenor is powerful on "The Suburbanite," and "Just You, Just Me" and "Indiana" are quite enjoyable, but it is the great Tricky Sam Nanton's solo (recorded four days before his death) on "The Mooche" that takes honors. —*Scott Yanow*

○ **Golden Duke, The** / Oct. 23, 1946-Nov. 1950 / Prestige 24029
This double LP contains some very valuable Duke Ellington studio recordings that have since been reissued as separate sessions. The 13 titles from late-1946 include the hot "Jam-a-Ditty," a classic trumpet battle on "Blue Skies," Ray Nance's colorful vocal on "Tulip or Turnip," and the original version of "Happy-Go-Lucky Local," which Jimmy Forrest would "borrow" a few years later and rename "Night Train." The second half of this twofer features piano duets by Duke Ellington and Billy Strayhorn (the radical-sounding "Tonk" is very memorable), and four showcases for Oscar Pettiford's cello. This music is recommended, in one form or another. —*Scott Yanow*

Duke Ellington's Orchestra / Nov. 25, 1946-Dec. 18, 1946 / Laserlight 15753
This budget CD reissues 11 of the 13 selections recorded by Duke Ellington's orchestra in late 1946. It leaves out the

classic "Tulip or Turnip" and "Overture to a Jam Session" and substitutes later versions of "Satin Doll" and the untraceable "Glory," for some odd reason. The music is strong, even if the packaging and irrelevant liner notes are not. —*Scott Yanow*

○ **Daybreak Express** / i. 1947 / RCA 506

Uncollected Duke Ellington & His Orchestra—Vol. 4 (1947), The / Jan. 7, 1947-Jun. 9, 1947 / Hindsight 128
The fourth in this five-LP series of radio transcriptions from Duke Ellington's underrated orchestra of 1946-1947, all of the sets are enjoyable, often surpassing the level of Ellington's studio recordings of the period. At the time, he had a six-member trumpet section and relatively new soloists in Al Sears, Jimmy Hamilton, and Taft Jordan. Ellington continued his reign as one of the top bandleaders with swinging versions of "Happy Go Lucky Local," three W. C. Handy tunes, and "Jam-a-Ditty." —*Scott Yanow*

☆ **Complete Duke Ellington (1947-1952), The** / Aug. 14, 1947-Dec. 22, 1952 / CBS French 66607
On this six-LP set, French CBS did a perfect job of covering a somewhat forgotten period in the career of Duke Ellington; why doesn't Sony get around to reissuing this valuable material in the same fashion on CD? Big bands were breaking up, rhythm & blues and pop vocalists were taking away the audiences (as was television), yet somehow Ellington kept his orchestra together. This wonderful box set has its share of forgettable vocals and attempts at pop hits, but also contains the "Liberian Suite," "Controversial Suite," and many three-minute classics. The personnel underwent a lot of turnover during these five years, giving one the opportunity to hear such new solo stars as Tyree Glenn (on trombone and vibes), high-note trumpeter Al Killian, and tenor saxophonist Jimmy Forrest (and eventually Paul Gonsalves), along with the usual Ellington greats. This set also finds Ellington surviving the defection of altoist Johnny Hodges in 1951, proving that Ellington never had an off period! —*Scott Yanow*

○ **Complete Duke Ellington—Vol. 1 (1947), The** / Aug. 1947-Oct. 1947 / CBS 462985

○ **Complete Duke Ellington—Vol. 2 (1947-1952), The** / i. Nov. 1947-Dec. 1952 / CBS 462986

Liberian Suite / Dec. 24, 1947 / Sony France 469409

○ **Carnegie Hall Concerts (December 1947)** / Dec. 27, 1947 / Prestige 24075
The final 1947 Carnegie Hall concert featured the premier performance of "Liberian Suite." Although this is called an extended work, the term is misleading. "Liberian" is merely a series of short pieces, no different from any of Ellington's other conventional charts and without any cumulative momentum. The composer's interest seemed much more focused on rhythmic rather than harmonic structures. But then this is a program piece celebrating Liberia's 100th year of independence. "Dance Number Three" is the best of the group of five, a dark absorbing melody played by Ray Nance and Harry Carney. "Cotton Tail" features exciting Al Sears, apparently bitten by the JATP bug. Sonny Greer is boisterous. "Blue Serge" by Mercer Ellington has echoes of 1941. "Triple Play" is a longish piece for Johnny Hodges, Carney, and Lawrence Brown that fails to develop any momentum. Harold Baker is lively on Cootie Williams's piece, "Harlem Airshaft." The rarely played "East St. Louis" was played in tribute to Bubber Miley, who was responsible, perhaps more than any other musician including Duke, for putting the band on the track to its unique sound. "Basso Profoundo" gives off a whiff on "Now's the Time" before being taken over by Raglin and Pettiford. "Echoes of Harlem" and a Hodges medley are beautiful. —*John McDonough*, Down Beat

○ **Carnegie Hall Concerts (November 1948)** / Nov. 13, 1948 / Vintage Jazz Classics 25
The sixth and final of Duke Ellington's acclaimed Carnegie Hall concerts, this two-CD set allows one to hear the largely

undocumented 1948 orchestra, which was kept off record because of a musicians union strike. With Ben Webster temporarily back in the band and solo stylists such as altoist Johnny Hodges, Al Sears on tenor, clarinetist Jimmy Hamilton, and trumpeters Ray Nance and Shorty Baker, the Ellington orchestra performs both newer material (such as "The Tattooed Bride" and several obscurities) and some surprising older compositions. These include a revival of "Reminiscence in Tempo" and a "hits medley." An oddity is one of the very few Ellington performances of Billy Strayhorn's classic "Lush Life." —*Scott Yanow*

○ **1949 Band Salutes Ellington '90, The** / Feb. 1, 1949-Feb. 20, 1949 / Marlor Productions
The 1949 Duke Ellington big band made few worthwhile studio recordings, which makes this LP (consisting of material from radio broadcasts) of great interest to Ellington collectors. Recorded at a time when Al Killian was leading the trumpet section and both Ben Webster and Al Sears were on tenor, this nearly one-hour-long set contains an extended version of "The Tattooed Bride," superior versions of "How High the Moon," and "St. Louis Blues." Even "Singin' in the Rain" is included, as are many fine solos from a somewhat forgotten version of Duke Ellington's orchestra. —*Scott Yanow*

Great Times! Piano Duets with Billy Strayhorn / Oct. 3, 1950-Nov. 1950 / Riverside 108
Co-billing certainly was in order on this 1950 collaboration, which was originally issued on two ten-inch Mercer LPs. The material here brings together, in various combinations, Duke Ellington and Billy Strayhorn (who plays celeste) with Wendell Marshall, Joe Shulman, Lloyd Trotman (bass), Oscar Pettiford (cello), and Jo Jones (drums). There is great vitality here, and the music sounds remarkably current. —*Bob Rusch*, Cadence

Masterpieces by Ellington / Dec. 19, 1950 / Sony France 469407
For this record, and for the first time, Duke Ellington took advantage of the extra time that the LP offered (as opposed to the three-minute 78). Duke and his orchestra perform stretched-out "concert versions" of three of his best-known songs ("Mood Indigo," "Sophisticated Lady," and "Solitude") and the more recently composed "The Tattooed Bride." Superior pacing, careful attention to dynamics and variety, and the strong material itself make this a recommended set. —*Scott Yanow*

West Coast Tour / Jun. 6, 1951-Jun. 30, 1951 / Jazz Bird 2010
This LP contains radio transcriptions that capture the 1951 Duke Ellington orchestra in fine form. Although he did not get as much publicity as many other jazz groups at the time, this edition of Duke's band (which features altoist Willie Smith and drummer Louie Bellson, among others) is excellent. A special highlight is a version of "Diminuendo in Blue" and "Crescendo in Blue" that finds Paul Gonsalves taking a long tenor solo five years before this feature broke up Newport. —*Scott Yanow*

Duke Ellington—Vol. 1 / Jan. 5, 1952-Apr. 29, 1952 / Stardust 201
Although this LP looks like a bootleg, apparently it isn't. The music, taken from live appearances in early 1952, contains some surprising selections including "Margie," "Black Beauty" (25 years after its original recording), "Basin Street Blues," and "One O'Clock Jump." With Ray Nance, Cat Anderson, Willie Cook, and Clark Terry featured among the trumpeters and the famous saxophone section (despite Johnny Hodges's absence) pretty much intact, this all-star orchestra is in good form. —*Scott Yanow*

Two Great Concerts / Mar. 1952-Jan. 30, 1965 / Festival 228
This two-LP set lives up to its title. First, Duke Ellington and his orchestra are heard in 1952 during a period when they were being overlooked by the jazz media, but were still producing a great deal of worthy music. The second half of this release is taken from a European tour in 1965 and features

some prime, late-period playing from trumpeter Cootie Williams. An excellent set, released by a European label and probably very difficult to find. —*Scott Yanow*

First Annual Tour of the Pacific Northwest / 1952 / Smithsonian/Folkways 2968
A long out-of-print two-LP box set from Folkways documents the Duke Ellington orchestra during three concerts in Oregon and Washington during their supposed "off period" in 1952. With four fine trumpet soloists and tenor saxophonist Paul Gonsalves showing increasing individuality, this hard-to-find set is worth a search. —*Scott Yanow*

○ **Showcase** / Apr. 6, 1953-May 18, 1955 / Trio 1551893
This rare three-LP set from a French label contains the majority of Duke Ellington's studio recordings for Capitol during his most neglected period, 1953-1955. Some of the material is lightweight or just remakes of earlier compositions, but there are many strong selections out of these 37 tracks, including the original version of "Satin Doll" and some newer material little heard since (such as "Orson," "The Big Drag," "Ultra Deluxe," and "Frivolous Banta"). Hopefully, this valuable music eventually will be reissued in an even more complete form domestically on CD. —*Scott Yanow*

Rare Broadcast Recordings, The / Apr. 15, 1953 / Jazz Anthology 30JA5220
Since it came out on a now out-of-print English LP, this fine broadcast recording remains rare. The main attraction of this session is that much of the material (including "Liza," "H'Ya Sue," "Primpin' at the Prom," and "Change My Ways") was rarely performed by Ellington. Worthwhile music, if not all that essential. —*Scott Yanow*

Happy Birthday, Duke! the Birthday Sessions—Vols. 1-5 / Apr. 29, 1953-Apr. 29, 1954 / Laserlight 15965
Quite by coincidence, Duke Ellington celebrated his birthday in both 1953 and 1954 by performing with his orchestra at McElroy's Ballroom in Portland, OR. Laserlight has released the results (recorded by engineer Wally Heider) on a five-CD boxed set that is also available as five separate CDs. The 1953-1954 period has never been considered the peak years for Ellington. In fact, his orchestra's popularity was low and he was struggling to keep his group together. However, as these performances show, he still had one of the most exciting big bands in the world, and its commercial difficulties had little to do with the music. There are not many surprises on these dance dates, but it is always fun to hear new solos on Ellington's standards played by his illustrious sidemen. Although they only contain about three hours of music (pretty brief for five CDs), the budget price of Laserlight's releases makes this an excellent buy. —*Scott Yanow*

☆ **Piano Reflections** / Apr. 1953-Dec. 1953 / Capitol 92863
These trio dates from 1953 not only accent the Duke's formidable stride background and rhythmic dexterity, they range from introspective pieces to mournful blues and soulful ballads. —*Ron Wynn, Rock & Roll Disc.*

We Love You Madly / Dec. 15, 1953-Dec. 21, 1953 / Pickwick 3390
This former budget LP only has eight selections (around 27 minutes), but some of the tracks (from Duke's period with Capitol) are very difficult to find elsewhere. Most memorable is a version of "Lady Be Good" that finds Ellington on electric piano, in 1953! —*Scott Yanow*

Ellington (1955) / Dec. 21, 1953-Feb. 2, 1954 / Capitol 521
One of Duke Ellington's better albums for Capitol, this LP features his orchestra stretching out on eight standards, five of them associated with other bandleaders. It is particularly interesting to hear Ellington and his sidemen transform tunes such as "In the Mood," "One O' Clock Jump," and "Stompin' at the Savoy" into a natural part of their repertoire. —*Scott Yanow*

Los Angeles Concert (1954) / Apr. 13, 1954 / GNP 9049

Washington, D. C. Armory Concert, The / Apr. 30, 1955 / Jazz Guild 1002

A particularly enjoyable concert performance by the erratically documented 1955 Duke Ellington orchestra. Both altoist Rick Henderson and bass trombonist John Sanders have rare features, and the orchestra stretches out on "Take the 'A' Train," "Happy Go Lucky Local," and "Harlem." This is one of a countless number of valuable Duke Ellington performances available on record. —*Scott Yanow*

○ **Blue Rose** / Jan. 23, 1956-Jan. 27, 1956 / Sony France 472085
Years before she became a jazz singer through her association with Concord Records, Rosemary Clooney recorded this surprisingly effective album with Duke Ellington's orchestra, revisiting some of his compositions from the 1930s. The Ellington and Strayhorn arrangements leave a liberal amount of space for the many soloists. —*Scott Yanow*

Bethlehem Years—Vol. 1, The / Feb. 7, 1956-Feb. 8, 1956 / Bethlehem 6013
In this two-volume series, Duke Ellington mostly revisits some of his songs from the 1930s, but, as was his custom, the standards were rearranged; they sound nearly brand new. With Johnny Hodges back in the orchestra, the all-star ensemble didn't have any weak points. Other than an overly rapid "Ko-Ko," this set is a gem. —*Scott Yanow*

Duke Ellington Presents . . . / Feb. 1956 / Fantasy 6008
This is actually the second volume of recordings made for Bethlehem in early 1956, a companion to J 4212. In this case, in addition to new versions of "Cotton Tail," "Daydream," and "Everything But You," the emphasis is on Ellingtonian treatments of standards such as "Summertime," "My Funny Valentine," and "Deep Purple." The music is quite enjoyable even if this is not one of Duke's most memorable sets. —*Scott Yanow*

Private Collection—Vol. 1, The / Mar. 17, 1956-Dec. 16, 1956 / Saja 91041
The first of ten CDs of previously unreleased material recorded privately by Ellington between engagements, all of this music was eventually reissued: first on LMR, and then on Saja/Atlantic. Each of the sets has its interesting moments, offering previously unknown compositions and performances. Vol. 1, recorded in Chicago during March and December 1956, has plenty of spots for Clark Terry, Ray Nance, Johnny Hodges, and Paul Gonsalves among the orchestra's many great soloists. —*Scott Yanow*

Ellington at Newport / Jul. 7, 1956 / Columbia 40587
After several years of struggle, Duke Ellington made a spectacular commercial comeback, launched by this memorable appearance at the Newport Jazz Festival. Following an inventive, but somewhat overlooked "Newport Jazz Festival Suite" and a routine version of Johnny Hodges's feature "Jeep's Blues," the orchestra launches into "Diminuendo in Blue" and "Crescendo in Blue" with great intensity. The passion really grows during a marathon 27-chorus blues solo by tenor saxophonist Paul Gonsalves that inspires some wild dancing and a near-riot in the audience; the crowd's reaction can be heard easily on this recording. Following Gonsalves, the full ensemble builds to a tremendous climax with trumpeter Cat Anderson screaming on top. This performance made headlines all around the world and Ellington's "off period" was finally over. It can all be heard on this classic recording. —*Scott Yanow*

○ **Duke (1956–1962)—Vol. 1** / Jul. 7, 1956-Jun. 2, 1959 / CBS 88653
The *Duke (1956–1962)* series (two double LPs and one single album) from French CBS includes a wide variety of unreleased material, alternate takes, and rare recordings by the Duke Ellington orchestra during an era when they recorded 24 albums for Columbia. Vol. 1, a two-LP set, has many valuable performances including a version of "Black and Tan Fantasy" from Duke's famous appearance at Newport in 1956, the four-part "Piano Improvisations," two "new" renditions of "Mood Indigo," and a rare alternate version of Ellington's "Anatomy of a Murder." —*Scott Yanow*

First Annual Connecticut Jazz Festival / Jul. 28, 1956 / IA-JRC 45

From the collector's label IAJRC, this LP, recorded three weeks after Ellington's sensational performance at the 1956 Newport Jazz Festival, features not only Duke's orchestra (best on the three-part "Festival Suite"), but has selections by a sextet led by the great swing trumpeter Buck Clayton. It also has three numbers played by the classic pianist Willie "the Lion" Smith. Lots of fine music. —*Scott Yanow*

○ **Drum Is a Woman, A** / Sep. 1956-Dec. 1956 / Columbia 951

★ **Duke Ellington—Vols. 1-10** / i. 1956 / Atlantic 91041
1956-1970. This essential series comes from his private collection; many brilliant cuts and well worth having. It's hard to separate any of the individual volumes. Studio and dance sessions/suites. —*Ron Wynn*

Duke Ellington—Vol. 7 / Jan. 1957-Jun. 6, 1962 / Atlantic 91231
One of ten CDs of previously unreleased and even unknown studio and concert performances by Duke Ellington's orchestra, these sets allow one to hear Duke experimenting with his ensemble. Some selections are essentially works-in-progress that would develop within the next few years, and others are quickly discarded originals or rearrangements of older tunes. This seventh volume is split between big-band sessions from 1957 and 1962 and a get-together of an octet that includes Duke's former drummer, Sonny Greer, in the latter year. Ellington fans will want all ten in this valuable series. —*Scott Yanow*

Duke Ellington—Vol. 8 / Jan. 1957-Jul. 11, 1967 / Atlantic 91232
The eighth of ten CDs in this valuable series of previously unknown Duke Ellington recordings. The music here is mostly from the 1965–1967 period (with one selection from 1957). It features particularly strong moments from trumpeter Cat Anderson, altoist Johnny Hodges, and tenorman Paul Gonsalves on many little-played Ellington compositions (along with versions of "Cottontail" and "Moon Mist"). Drummer Louie Bellson guests on a few selections. All ten volumes in this series are recommended. —*Scott Yanow*

Happy Reunion / Mar. 1957-Jun. 1958 / CBS 40030

Such Sweet Thunder / Apr. 1957-May 1957 / Sony Special Products 1033
Duke Ellington's tribute to Shakespeare is witty and full of fresh melodies, and gives his famed sidemen many opportunities to solo in unusual settings. Trombonist Britt Woodman stars on "Sonnet to Hank Cinq," trumpeter Cat Anderson gets to go nuts on "Madness in Great Ones," and there are notable features for Johnny Hodges, Paul Gonsalves, and Quentin Jackson. —*Scott Yanow*

○ **Ella Fitzgerald/The Duke Ellington Songbook** / Jun. 25, 1957-Sep. 1957 / Verve 2535
The first lady of song meets the genius of jazz on this delightful two-LP set. Unlike many other albums in which a singer is backed by a big band, there are many spots for Ellington's sidemen to shine; in fact, the four-part "Portrait of Ella Fitzgerald" is purely instrumental until the final movement. It is wonderful to hear Ella sing such songs as "Drop Me Off in Harlem," "Rockin' in Rhythm," and "Perdido" along with the ballads. Recommended. —*Scott Yanow*

○ **All Star Road Band—Vol. 2** / Jun. 1957 / Doctor Jazz 39137

Satin Doll / Jun. 1957-May 31, 1964 / RCA 0337
This French CD duplicates five of the selections from *All Star Road Band* (Doctor Jazz), a dance date by Duke Ellington's orchestra in 1957. The remainder of this set has seven selections from a Chicago concert of 1964, which adds little to the Ellington legacy, but is quite enjoyable on its own terms. —*Scott Yanow*

Live at the 1957 Stratford Festival / Jul. 1957 / Music & Arts 616
Duke Ellington had regained his former commercial success with his performance at the 1956 Newport Jazz Festival, so he was essentially free to play what he pleased for the remainder of his career. This live performance from 1957 ranges from old favorites like "I Got It Bad" and

"Sophisticated Lady" to the spectacular Britt Woodman trombone feature on "Theme Trambene," the whimsical "Pretty and the Wolf," a fresh rendition of "Harlem Air Shaft" featuring trumpeter Clark Terry, and the extended "Harlem Suite." Baritonist Harry Carney, high-note trumpet wizard Cat Anderson, and altoist Johnny Hodges all have their great moments on this enjoyable set. — *Scott Yanow*

☆ **Ellington Indigos** / Sep. 9, 1957-Oct. 10, 1957 / Columbia 44444

○ **Girl's Suite and the Perfume Suite, The** / Dec. 9, 1957-Aug. 20, 1961 / Columbia 38028
This was a rather unusual studio session for Duke Ellington. This is because he chose to allocate all of the solo sections on eight of his standards to tenor saxophonist Paul Gonsalves, including numbers such as "C Jam Blues" and "Jam with Sam," which generally served as features for a variety of players. Obviously, those listeners who most enjoy Gonsalves's harmonically advanced and unpredictable style will have to pick this up. This disc can also serve as a reminder to more general Ellington collectors as to just how power-packed Duke's lineup really was, for Ellington could have given the same treatment to at least six of his other sidemen! — *Scott Yanow*

Dance Dates: California 1958 / i. 1958 / Saja 791230
Ellington always insisted his best music was made for dancers, and this crown jewel of the second set of private recordings recently issued by Atlantic confirms the wisdom of that tenet. These are mainly stomping tunes aimed at making those who hear them react on the floor. There are also dozens of marvelous solos from the likes of Paul Gonsalves, Jimmy Hamilton, Russell Procope, and plenty of lusty stride piano from the Duke as well. — *Ron Wynn*, Rock & Roll Disc

○ **Black, Brown and Beige (1944–1946 Band Recordings)** / Feb. 5, 1958-Feb. 12, 1958 / Bluebird 6641
An outstanding three-disc set that collects his somewhat controversial mid- and late-'40s concert recordings into one nice package. — *Ron Wynn*

Duke Ellington—Vol. 2 / Mar. 4, 1958 / Atlantic 91042
(Also Saja/Atlantic 91042) The second of ten CDs of previously unissued recordings of Duke Ellington, this set differs from the others because it is from a single live session, a dance concert from 1958. At the time, the orchestra boasted such stars as trumpeters Shorty Baker, Clark Terry, and Ray Nance, trombonists Quentin Jackson and Britt Woodman, and a superb saxophone section (although Johnny Hodges was absent temporarily). The music on this CD sticks to standards (some of which are not usually associated with Duke) and can be thought of as a live version of "Ellington Indigos," although the inclusion of some uptempo material (including a totally ad-lib "Lady Be Good") adds more variety. A typically excellent example of 1958 Duke Ellington. — *Scott Yanow*

Duke Ellington—Vol. 6 / Mar. 4, 1958-Mar. 5, 1958 / Atlantic 91230
The sixth of ten CDs in this series of previously unknown "private" recordings is actually related to Vol. 2. Some of these performances are from the same concert at Travis Air Force Base, while the remainder were recorded the next day at Mather Air Force Base. Although altoist Johnny Hodges and high-note trumpeter Cat Anderson are absent, the music does not suffer in the slightest, because Ellington still had 10 other distinctive soloists! Quite informal and sometimes a bit loose, these spirited performances (mostly of standards) give players such as trumpeters Shorty Baker, Clark Terry, and Ray Nance, along with the many other stars, plenty of opportunities to stretch out. Recordings like this one give one a chance to hear how Ellington rearranged tunes to make them sound fresh year after year (sometimes decade after decade). — *Scott Yanow*

Duke Ellington at the Bal Masque / Mar. 1958 / Columbia 8098

One of Duke Ellington's more unusual albums of the 1950s, this live session finds Duke's orchestra performing such songs as "Got a Date with an Angel," "The Peanut Vendor," "Indian Love Call," and even "Who's Afraid of the Big Bad Wolf!" Amazingly enough, the music works quite well for Ellington, and his all-star orchestra manages to transform what could be a set of tired revival swing into superior dance music and swinging jazz. While certainly not the most essential Ellington record, *At the Bal Masque* is a surprise success. — *Scott Yanow*

Cosmic Scene: Duke Ellington's Spacemen / Apr. 12, 1958 / Columbia 1198
This is the original LP version of a fine session featuring a small group from Duke Ellington's orchestra, which due to the time period, he dubbed as his "Spacemen." For this nonet, Duke chose three of his most modern soloists (trumpeter Clark Terry, clarinetist Jimmy Hamilton, and tenor saxophonist Paul Gonsalves) along with his trombone section and the rhythm section. In general, the tunes are standards that give each of the three main horns plenty of space in which to display their distinctive sounds. Part of this has been reissued on *Blues in Orbit* (Columbia). — *Scott Yanow*

○ **Newport Jazz Festival (1958)** / Jul. 3, 1958 / Columbia 1245
Two years after his major success at the Newport Jazz Festival, Duke Ellington returned for another excellent, if somewhat overlooked, performance. Last out on this out-of-print LP, Ellington's set is highlighted by an exciting trumpet feature ("El Gato"), "Jazz Festival Jazzol" (which has a cool and a hot section with impressions of both modern and New Orleans jazz), "Mr. Gentle and Mr. Cool," and a showcase for Clark Terry on flugelhorn ("Juniflip"). A special treat is baritonist Gerry Mulligan's only recording with Ellington, "Prima Bara Dubla," on which he duets with the other great master of the baritone sax, Harry Carney. — *Scott Yanow*

○ **Blues Summit** / Aug. 14, 1958-Feb. 20, 1959 / Verve 8822
Partly reissued on CD, this very enjoyable double-LP includes two related sessions. The main one is both unusual and delightful; it features altoist Johnny Hodges and trumpeter Harry "Sweets" Edison leading a sextet with Duke Ellington on piano. The repertoire is inspired, a variety of jam tunes including several by W. C. Handy, and both Sweets and Hodges are heard at their most expressive. The remainder of this twofer teams Hodges and trombonist Lawrence Brown with tenor great Ben Webster and the exciting trumpeter Roy Eldridge; this time, Billy Strayhorn is on piano and the music is almost as memorable. Highly recommended in one form or another. — *Scott Yanow*

Jazz at the Plaza—Vol. 2 / Sep. 9, 1958 / Columbia 32471
In 1958, Columbia Records hosted a jazz party that resulted in two records: one by the Miles Davis Sextet and the other featuring Duke Ellington's orchestra during a prime period. In addition to features for Johnny Hodges, Clark Terry, and Paul Gonsalves (along with the "Jazz Festival Suite"), Ellington welcomes Count Basie's former vocalist Jimmy Rushing for three numbers. Then, Billie Holiday stops by (in okay form for this late in her life) for two numbers with a small group that includes trumpeter Buck Clayton. Excellent music. — *Scott Yanow*

At the Blue Note in Chicago / Dec. 28, 1958 / Vogue 600062
A typically excellent club appearance by Duke Ellington's orchestra near the end of 1958, which exists on CD because CBS happened to broadcast this set. Nearly all of the selections were composed by Ellington and his associates. Johnny Hodges stars throughout, while trumpeter Clark Terry is tops among the supporting players. Not essential, but well worth owning. — *Scott Yanow*

★ **Anatomy of a Murder** / May 29, 1959-Jun. 2, 1959 / Rykodisc 10039
Duke Ellington's music was used surprisingly little in movies. *Anatomy of a Murder* is a landmark film and Duke's writing fits in perfectly. Like all good soundtracks, the mu-

sic's role was to accompany and to enhance the story, so to hear the soundtrack on CD does leave one with a somewhat incomplete feeling. However, Ellington's writing was colorful enough to stand largely on its own even in this setting, so this set, though not essential, does not disappoint. —*Scott Yanow*

Festival Session / Sep. 8, 1959 / Columbia 36979
This LP includes Ellington's new works for 1959 along with a superior version of "Perdido" (featuring Clark Terry) and a Johnny Hodges workout on "Things Ain't What They Used to Be." None of the newer pieces ("Duael Fuel," "Copout Extension," "Idiom '59," and "Launching Pad") caught on, but all are enjoyable and show that Ellington's creativity, at age 60, had not slowed down in the slightest. —*Scott Yanow*

○ **Duke (1956–1962)—Vol. 2** / Dec. 2, 1959-Jun. 21, 1962 / CBS 88654
The second of three volumes, this two-LP set from French Columbia includes unissued alternate takes and rarities recorded by Duke Ellington for Columbia during 1959-1962. Of primary interest to veteran collectors, there is much to enjoy here, including new renditions of the "Asphalt Jungle Suite," "Tulip or Turnip," "Paris Blues," two versions of "Jingle Bells," and a pair of selections from the one-time meeting on record between the Ellington and Count Basie orchestras that were not included on the original set. —*Scott Yanow*

☆ **Side By Side** / i. 195z / Verve 821578
With Johnny Hodges. Joyous 1986 reissue of magnificent late-'50s small group material. —*Ron Wynn*

Piano in the Background / May 1960-Jun. 1960 / Columbia 1546
One of Ellington's rarer studio sessions and last out on this French CD, the main plot behind this run through of Duke's standards is that the leader's piano is featured at some point in every song. Ellington's sidemen are also heard from, and everyone is in fine form. Duke's solo abilities were always a bit underrated due to his brilliance in other areas, but this set shows just how modern a player he remained through the years. —*Scott Yanow*

Unknown Session / Jul. 14, 1960 / Columbia 35342
Discovered in Columbia's vaults 19 years after it was performed, this recording features a septet from Duke Ellington's orchestra keeping busy in the studios, mostly playing standards and blues. With altoist Johnny Hodges, baritonist Harry Carney, trombonist Lawrence Brown, and cornetist Ray Nance all having ample solo space, these renditions are quite enjoyable; they swing hard and sound fresh. Ellington fans should pick this one up. —*Scott Yanow*

Piano in the Foreground / Mar. 1, 1961 / Columbia 2029
This rare trio session by Duke Ellington (on which he is joined by bassist Aaron Bell and drummer Sam Woodyard) is the first of several sessions in the early 1960s that feature Duke's piano in a variety of settings. It is particularly interesting hearing Ellington performing some of his rarer compositions, such as "Cong-go," "Fontainbleau Forest," "It's Bad to Be Forgotten," and "A Hundred Dreams Ago," along with three standards and a blues. One wishes that today's revivalists would bring back "the Duke Ellington Songbook" along with some of his true obscurities, such as the ones on this somewhat forgotten session. —*Scott Yanow*

○ **Duke Ellington-Louis Armstrong Years, The** / Apr. 3, 1961-Apr. 4, 1961 / Roulette 108
Although Duke Ellington and Louis Armstrong were jazz music's most famous and acclaimed musicians, their only meeting on record (other than a couple of isolated selections in the 1940s) is the music contained on this two-LP set (since reissued on CD). Rather than have Armstrong sit in with Ellington's orchestra, Duke temporarily became a member of Satch's All-Stars. For this all-Ellington program, Louis is inspired by the fresh repertoire and his vocals are often jubilant. With strong assistance from trombonist Trummy Young and clarinetist Barney Bigard (a former Ellington bandmember then travelling with Armstrong), Pops and

Duke created a very memorable and quite unique program of classic music. —*Scott Yanow*

Masters of Jazz—Vol. 6 / Jan. 9, 1962-Feb. 25, 1966 / Storyville 4106
This LP largely duplicates *Duke Ellington & His Orchestra/Johnny Hodges & His Orchestra* (Storyville), featuring six of the seven selections performed by the Duke Ellington orchestra for a half-hour television special. It is the additional material, however, that is of greatest interest, for Duke Ellington is also heard solo in 1966 playing a lengthy medley of his popular numbers and a version of "New World a-Comin'." For that reason, this LP is preferred over the other Storyville set. —*Scott Yanow*

Feeling of Jazz, The / Feb. 13, 1962-Jul. 3, 1962 / Black Lion 760123
A nice all-around set by the 1962 Duke Ellington orchestra. Whether it is the lightweight but fun "Taffy Twist," "I'm Gonna Go Fishin'," (the theme from *Anatomy of a Murder*), or the many songs revived from decades earlier (such as "What Am I Here For," "Black and Tan Fantasy," and "Jump For Joy"), this CD is filled with consistently swinging music. —*Scott Yanow*

New Mood Indigo / Jul. 3, 1962-Mar. 29, 1966 / Doctor Jazz 40359
A very interesting collection of Duke Ellington studio material from 1962–1966 that was first issued in 1985. The title cut finds Ellington giving a rare double-time treatment to his classic "Mood Indigo." Three selections put the focus on the cornet and vocals of Ray Nance. As a special treat, there are four selections from the Mercer Ellington Septet, a combo consisting of six of Duke's sidemen plus a then-unknown 24-year-old pianist named Chick Corea. It gives one a rare chance to hear Corea playing with the likes of Johnny Hodges, Paul Gonsavles, and Harry Carney. Recommended. —*Scott Yanow*

Duke Ellington—Vol. 3 / i. Jul. 25, 1962-Sep. 13, 1962 / Atlantic 91043
This is the third of ten volumes of previously unknown Duke Ellington sessions made available in this valuable CD series. One of the strongest in "the private collection" series these rarities from 1962 include early versions of several selections that were included later in Duke's *Sacred Concerts*, two otherwise unknown but fun Paul Gonsalves originals titled "Major" and "Minor," Thelonious Monk's composition "Monk's Dream" (here mistitled "Blue Monk"), and "September 12th Blues," which welcomes trumpeter Cootie Williams back into the band after a 22-year absence! Recommended. —*Scott Yanow*

○ **Great Tenor Encounters, The** / i. Aug. 18, 1962-Sep. 26, 1962 / Impulse 9350
The Great Tenor Encounters is unique because it contains the only sides Duke Ellington ever recorded with Coleman Hawkins (sides one and two) and John Coltrane (sides three and four). Both sessions took place in 1962. Hawkins should have recorded more with the Duke. His sound and style were perfectly suited to the band. He is surrounded here by the Ellington elite, a septet including Johnny Hodges, Ray Nance, Harry Carney, and Lawrence Brown, and he fits right in. Most of these arrangements are not elaborate and were meant to give everyone room to blow. Some cuts are better than others, but none fail. "Mood Indigo," with Hawkins taking five choruses, and "Solitude," with Nance on violin, have rarely sounded better. Pairing Ellington and Coltrane was an odd idea. Ellington wisely kept the group down to a quartet. Duke's team appears on side three with Aaron Bell on bass and Sam Woodyard on drums, and Trane's team is on side four with Jimmy Garrison on bass and Elvin Jones on drums. The ballads work best because Trane plays them very straight, very beautifully. But even the cuts that do not work are interesting. Rarely did old meet new in such a startling and revealing manner. —*Douglas Clark*, Down Beat

○ **Reevaluations: The Impulse Years** / i. Aug. 18, 1962-Jan. 10, 1966 / ABC/Impulse 9256

This two-LP set is an excellent sampling of Duke Ellington's music as originally released on Impulse. In addition to selections featuring Ellington in small groups with Coleman Hawkins and John Coltrane, there are performances of Duke's music by groups led by Johnny Hodges, McCoy Tyner, Ben Webster, Earl Hines, Clark Terry, Lawrence Brown, and Paul Gonsalves. The most exciting recordings were included through careful selection. A fine introduction to Ellington's legacy, mostly heard through the interpretations of others. —*Scott Yanow*

★ **Money Jungle** / Sep. 17, 1962 / Blue Note 46398
In 1962, Duke Ellington was teamed on record with a trio consisting of bassist Charles Mingus and drummer Max Roach. The setting may have seemed "modern" for a pianist from Duke's generation, but one should realize that he was a major influence on both Thelonious Monk and Cecil Taylor. Ellington, one of the few veterans of the 1920s to make a smooth transition to the relatively modern era, is in superlative form on this date, even when challenged by "Money Jungle" by the potentially combative Mingus. This LP version includes four selections not on the original release; the later CD also adds a couple of "new" alternate takes. Well worth acquiring. —*Scott Yanow*

★ **Duke Ellington and John Coltrane** / Sep. 26, 1962 / MCA 39103
With John Coltrane. Jazz immortals collaborate. Mostly pristine music. —*Michael G. Nastos*

Recollections of the Big Band Era / i. Nov. 29, 1962-Jan. 4, 1963 / Atlantic 90043
Here are some rich, swinging orchestrations combined with resourceful allocations of soloists that display the band in fine form. Standouts include Harry Carney on "Cherokee" against the traditional plunger trombones, Cootie Williams, Ray Nance, and Cat Anderson splitting up "Ciribiribin," and the band in general, in loose, swinging form on "Christopher Columbus" and "Let's Get Together." Other material from these sessions appears on a 1963 Reprise LP. —*John McDonough,* Down Beat

Afro-Bossa / Nov. 29, 1962-Jan. 5, 1963 / Discovery 871
Inspired by their world travels, Duke Ellington and Billy Strayhorn composed eleven new compositions (along with performing the standard "Pyramid") that paid tribute to the rhythms and cultures of many countries. "Purple Gazelle" and "Eighth Veil" became part of the Ellington orchestra's regular repertoire, but each of these dozen selections has its memorable moments. One of Duke's better sessions of the 1960s. —*Scott Yanow*

Symphonic Ellington, The / i. Jan. 31, 1963-Feb. 21, 1963 / Discovery 71003
In 1963, Duke Ellington realized a longtime goal: to record some of his extended works using both a symphony orchestra and his regular big band. Included on this fine CD are the three movements of "Night Creature," the relatively brief "Non-Violent Integration," "La Scala," and an adaptation of Duke's "Harlem Air Shaft." With most of Duke's all-star soloists heard from in this program and his ability to completely avoid making his music so-called "respectable" or self-consciously "third stream," Ellington's arrangements keep the strings from weighing down the proceedings. The music is actually quite successful. —*Scott Yanow*

★ **Great Paris Concert, The** / Feb. 1, 1963-Feb. 23, 1963 / Atlantic 304
A definitive look at the early-1960s edition of the Duke Ellington orchestra, this live two-LP set contains many highlights: fresh versions of "Rockin' in Rhythm," "Concerto For Cootie" (featuring Cootie Williams), "Jam with Sam," extended renditions of "Suite Thursday" and the "Harlem Suite," and a few newer selections. Eleven soloists (not counting the pianist/leader) are heard from in memorable settings, including both Cootie Williams and Ray Nance. Highly recommended music, either as this twofer or on CD. —*Scott Yanow*

Jazz Violin Session / Feb. 22, 1963 / Atlantic 1688
This is a unique entry in Duke Ellington's massive discography. During half of this LP, Ellington and his rhythm section are joined by violinists Stephane Grappelli and Ray Nance, and Svend Asmussen on viola; the remainder of the set adds three horns for background work. On both ancient standards and a few newer pieces put together specifically for this date, the contrasting, but complementary, styles of the three string players and the general infectious enthusiasm makes this a memorable encounter. —*Scott Yanow*

☆ **My People** / i. Aug. 20, 1963-Aug. 28, 1963 / Red Baron 52759
In 1963, Duke Ellington wrote the music for a short-lived show titled *My People*, which was sort of a combination of his early 1940s *Jump For Joy* play along with some of the music from his "Black, Brown and Beige" suite. Using an orchestra comprised of Ellingtonians past, present, and future along with a few compatible outsiders, and featuring a variety of vocalists that include Joya Sherrill, Jimmy Grissom, and Lil Greenwood, Duke created music whose message of racial harmony remains timeless. Due to the high quality of the "Black, Brown and Beige" suite and the shorter originals, this interesting set is more enjoyable than one might expect. —*Scott Yanow*

In the Uncommon Market / i. 1963 / Pablo 2308-247
These tapes from Norman Granz's vaults cover Duke Ellington's tours of Europe in 1963. Seven are primarily rarely performed numbers that feature Duke's orchestra, while three other selections find Ellington romping happily with his trio. A fine all-around set that should delight Ellington collectors. —*Scott Yanow*

Harlem / Mar. 9, 1964 / Pablo 245
Taken from a concert in Stockholm, Sweden, this well-recorded LP mostly features trumpeters Cootie Williams and Cat Anderson, tenor saxophonist Paul Gonsalves, and altoist Johnny Hodges as the main soloists in a set with Duke Ellington's orchestra. "The Opener," "Blow By Blow," and "The Prowling Cat" have rarely been recorded, and even the more familiar pieces are given new life, highlighted by a definitive rendition of "Harlem." —*Scott Yanow*

☆ **All Star Road Band—Vols. 1 and 2** / i. May 31, 1964 / Doctor Jazz 40012
These are albums of mostly familiar things. Johnny Hodges takes us through "Jeep's Blues," "All of Me," "Sunny Side," and "I Got It Bad" (Vol. 1) one more time with no more or less beauty than he gave to hundreds of other performances of those pieces. Clark Terry dances through "Perdido" (Vol. 1) with a precise, brittle trot that outswings his "official" version on the *Festival Session* LP. There really are no surprises here; they were saved for Carnegie Hall, not Carrolltown, PA. Yet the band reaches out across the years and grabs you hard. The resonance and dimension of the recorded quality are nothing short of astounding. —*John McDonough,* Downbeat

Duke Ellington—Vol. 10 / i. Mar. 4, 1965-May 6, 1971 / Atlantic 91234
The tenth and final volume of this valuable series of previously unknown Duke Ellington recordings, this CD contains excerpts from Duke's monumental "Black, Brown and Beige" suite recorded in 1965 (with this version of "The Blues" dating from 1971), a lengthy version of "Ad Lib on Nippon" (which was taken from Ellington's "The Far East Suite"), and a 1966 rendition of "Harlem." Each of these extended works is rich enough to deserve several interpretations, and it is always fascinating to hear how Duke altered his arrangements through the decades. —*Scott Yanow*

Concert in the Virgin Islands / Apr. 14, 1965 / Discovery 841
Although he was in his mid-sixties at the time of this program of mostly new music, Duke Ellington proved that he never declined or lost his creativity. Four of the pieces comprise "The Virgin Islands Suite," there are new versions of "Things Ain't What They Used to Be" and "Chelsea Bridge,"

and there are also a variety of miniature classics. In 1965, the Ellington orchestra had 11 very distinctive soloists; eight are heard from during this memorable set. — *Scott Yanow*

Duke Ellington (1965–1972) / i. 1965-Aug. 2, 1972 / Music Masters 50412
This is the type of CD that Duke Ellington collectors should love, for it contains a variety of unusual and fascinating performances. Highlights include Jimmy Hamilton's stomping tenor on "The Old Circus Train," the colorful "Trombone Buster," early versions of songs later included in "The New Orleans Suite," and three selections featuring organist Wild Bill Davis. — *Scott Yanow*

Great Duke Ellington, The / i. May 1966 / Premier 1009
One of the more obscure Duke Ellington LPs, this session features the orchestra playing ten of Duke's more popular numbers (all at least 20 years old at the time) and "The Twitch." The band's enthusiasm and the wonderfully expressive playing of trumpeter Cootie Williams, however, makes this an album well worth the search you'll have to go through to find it. — *Scott Yanow*

Pianist, The / Jul. 18, 1966-Jan. 7, 1970 / Original Jazz Classics 717
Duke Ellington had so many talents (composer, arranger, bandleader, personality) that his skills as a pianist could be overlooked easily. Fortunately, he did record a fair number of trio albums through the years so there is plenty of evidence as to his unique style, which was both modern and traditional at the same time. *The Pianist* has trio performances from 1966 and 1970, and finds Ellington shifting smoothly between styles and moods yet always remaining himself. — *Scott Yanow*

☆ **Soul Call** / Jul. 28, 1966 / Verve 8701
The centerpiece of this live album is Ellington's "La Plus Belle Africaine," one of his better late-period works. Otherwise, an overly fast "Jam with Sam," two short Paul Gonsalves features, and a lengthy drum solo form the remainder of the program, making this a lesser Ellington item. — *Scott Yanow*

○ **Ella and Duke on the Cote D'azur** / Jul. 28, 1966 / Verve 64072
Ella Fitzgerald and Duke Ellington did not team up in concerts until relatively late in their careers (although Ella did record her *Ellington Songbook* with Duke in the '50s). This live double LP actually finds Ella singing six numbers with the Jimmy Jones Trio and only "Mack the Knife" and a scat-filled "It Don't Mean a Thing" with the orchestra. Ellington has eight numbers for his band, mostly remakes of older tunes, including a guest appearance by former associate Ben Webster on "All Too Soon," a remarkable Buster Cooper trombone feature, and a rowdy version of "The Old Circus Train Turn-Around Blues." This is a spirited set of music that, with better planning, could have been great. — *Scott Yanow*

Far East Suite / Dec. 20, 1966-Dec. 21, 1966 / Bluebird 7640
Duke Ellington could have been forgiven if, by the time he was 67, he had gradually lost his creative desire—not to mention his writing skills. But his genius never dimmed as witnessed by the newer music ("The Far East Suite" and "Ad Lib on Nippon") on this superb set. "The Far East Suite" is really eight separate compositions of which the beautiful "Isfahan" (a memorable Johnny Hodges feature) became the best-known melody. Paul Gonsalves and Jimmy Hamilton are among the main stars; the clarinetist is showcased throughout the 111-minute "Ad Lib on Nippon." But it is the writing of Duke and Strayhorn in their late prime that makes this one of the more memorable Ellington recordings. — *Scott Yanow*

Live in Italy—Vol. 1 / i. Feb. 22, 1967 / Jazz Up 305
The first of two volumes, this CD captures Duke Ellington's orchestra during a European tour late in his career, but when he still retained virtually all of his star sidemen. The inclusion of some lesser-known compositions increases the value of this set as do the excellent solos of tenor saxophon-

ist Paul Gonsalves, trombonist Lawrence Brown, Johnny Hodges, and, on "Salome" and "Wild Onions," the phenomenal high-note trumpeter Cat Anderson. Typically brilliant music from Duke Ellington. — *Scott Yanow*

Intimacy of the Blues / Mar. 15, 1967-Jun. 15, 1970 / Fantasy 624
Lots of rare music was uncovered when these recordings were first released. Duke Ellington did a remarkable number of private recordings with small groups taken from his orchestra; the selections included on this LP are some of the best. A "Combo Suite" from 1967 introduces Billy Strayhorn's "Intimacy of the Blues" along with five forgotten but worthy originals. The music on side two (some of which features organist Wild Bill Davis) dates from 1970; "All Too Soon" showcases Duke's new tenor at the time, Harold Ashby. Excellent music. — *Scott Yanow*

☆ **His Mother Called Him Bill** / Aug. 28, 1967-Sep. 1, 1967 / RCA 6287

Francis A. And Edward K. / Dec. 12, 1967 / Reprise 1024
Frank Sinatra was never a jazz singer, but he always had a strong respect for high musicianship and strong individuals. Since Duke Ellington was recording for Frank's label, Reprise, during this period, it seemed only right that the two would team up eventually. Actually, Ellington's orchestra is primarily stuck in the role of accompanying the singer, who is heard at his best on "I Like the Sunrise" and "Poor Butterfly" (although the inclusion of "Sunny" does not work as well). In reality, this record is more significant in Sinatra's discography than it is in Ellington's. — *Scott Yanow*

☆ **Second Sacred Concert** / 1968 / Prestige 24045

Yale Concert / Jan. 26, 1968 / Fantasy 664
The great Duke Ellington orchestra was still intact and in its late prime at the time of this performance in 1968. With the death of Billy Strayhorn the year before, Ellington (perhaps sensing his own mortality) accelerated his writing activities, proving that even as he neared 70, he was still at his peak. Other than a Johnny Hodges medley and the theme ("Take the 'A' Train"), all of the music on this set was fairly new. Included are showcases for Cootie Williams, Harry Carney, Paul Gonsalves, and Cat Anderson. There is also an 11-minute "The Little Purple Flower," "Swamp Goo" (which gave Russell Procope a chance to play some New Orleans-style clarinet), and a jazz version of Yale's famous "Boola, Boola." — *Scott Yanow*

Latin American Suite / Oct. 1968 / Fantasy 469
Written after his orchestra's successful debut in South America, Duke Ellington's seven-part suite celebrates the atmosphere and rhythms of the many south-of-the-border countries that he visited. The usual horn stars have their moments, but the pianist himself is the main voice throughout this enjoyable set of fresh music. — *Scott Yanow*

○ **Duke Ellington—Vol. 5** / i. Nov. 6, 1968-Jun. 15, 1970 / Atlantic 91045
One of the most interesting of the ten volumes released in "the private collection" series, this CD contains "The Degas Suite" (music for a soundtrack of an art film that was never produced) and a ballet score entitled "The River." Ellington is mostly the lead voice, but his star sidemen are heard from on these formerly very rare and somewhat unusual performances. Clearly, Duke's genius was strong enough to fill three lifetimes full of new music. This CD contains some melodies that might have been more significant if he had lived long enough to find a place for them. — *Scott Yanow*

○ **Duke Ellington—Vol. 9** / i. Nov. 23, 1968-Dec. 3, 1968 / Atlantic 91233
The ninth of ten volumes of music from Duke Ellington's "private collection" of unknown tapes, this CD captures Duke in 1968 shortly after clarinetist Jimmy Hamilton left the band and tenor saxophonist Harold Ashby joined up. Even after 30 years of playing some of these standards, Ellington found new ways to rearrange such songs as "Sophisticated Lady," "Mood Indigo," and "Just Squeeze Me."

In addition, there are a few new obscurities such as "Knuf" (which finds Jeff Castleman switching to electric bass), "Reva," and the somewhat dated Trish Turner vocal on "Cool and Groovy." There are lots of surprises on this fine CD. — *Scott Yanow*

Intimate Ellington, The / Apr. 25, 1969-Jun. 29, 1971 / Pablo 730
This Pablo set has odds and ends taken from nine different recording/rehearsal sessions that find Ellington experimenting a bit with instrumentation and personnel, even taking a vocal on the tongue-in-cheek "Moon Maiden." Performances range from a couple of vigorous trio workouts and spots for Wild Bill Davis's organ to a few big-band performances. Even this late in his life, Duke Ellington had a great deal to say musically and his band continued to rank near the top. —*Scott Yanow*

○ **Seventieth Birthday Concert** / Nov. 25-26, 1969 / Solid State 19000

★ **New Orleans Suite** / Apr. 27, 1970 / Atlantic 1580
The *New Orleans Suite* album is a beautifully conceived, finely executed salute to the Crescent City and some of its most famous sons. Like many of Duke Ellington's longer works, it is a series of sketches that accurately conjure up visions of both the city and its musical heritage. The emphasis is on the blues and gospel traditions that went into the making of jazz, and there is a direct simplicity to much of the orchestration. From a solo point of view, there is much to hear. Most impressive, perhaps, (and not just because it was to be his last recording with the Ellington band) is the passionate blues playing of Johnny Hodges (alto sax) in "Blues For New Orleans" where he improvises extensively over a soft carpet of sound laid down by the velvet-toned organ of Wild Bill Davis. This impassioned segment sets just the right tone. The suite is just about equally divided between the Impressions and the Portraits. Of particular fascination are the contributions of the newer members of the band. Norris Turney's flute floats in and through the orchestral patterns of "Bourbon Street Jingling Jollies," while Harold Ashby's warm tenor saxophone is just right in "Thanks For the Beautiful Land on the Delta." Then there is the skittish, more contemporary, and very rakish flugelhorn of Fred Stone, which blends together perfectly with the always modern sound of Harry Carney's baritone saxophone in "Aristocracy a la Jean LaFitte." One of the most fascinating moments occurs during "Second Line" when trombonists Booty Wood and Julian Priester weave in and out of the ensemble in a solo conversation that evokes the spirit of New Orleans marching music, yet remains far removed stylistically from the original. Special mention should also be made of Russell Procope's warm, wood-toned clarinet in this segment. . . . Unquestionably, Duke Ellington gave us another major contribution from his seemingly inexhaustible pen. —*John Norris, Coda*

Afro-Eurasian Eclipse / Feb. 17, 1971 / Fantasy 645

Toga Brava Suite / Oct. 24, 1971 / United Artists 92

Duke's Big Four, The / Jan. 8, 1973 / Pablo 2310-703
A superb rhythm section with drummer Louis Bellson, guitarist Joe Pass, and bassist Ray Brown complementing Duke Ellington's piano musings over such familiar pieces as "Squeeze Me," "Everything But You," "Hawk Talks," and four others. "Blues" contains some of his more interesting ideas and moves at his best tempo. He simply ignores the rapid pace of "Cotton Tail," preferring to punctuate rather than fill every space with sound. His playing is energetic and swinging in its asymmetrical eccentricity. —*John McDonough, Down Beat*

○ **Date with the Duke—Vols. 1-6, A** / **i**. Jan. 1976 / Fairmount 1001,100
This comprehensive assembly of Duke Ellington's broadcast material from the spring of 1945 is derived from Mel Tormé's personal collection. Some of the selections were previously issued on a French label, but the quality of this authorized edition makes any other version obsolete. Its com-

prehensive nature, of necessity, embraces some lightweight items. But such explosions as "Tootin' Through the Roof" (Vol. 6), an extended "Cotton Tail," "New World-a-Comin'" (Vol. 5), "Diminuendo in Blue" and "Crescendo in Blue" (Vol. 4), and "Perdido and Pitter Patter Panther" with Junior Raglin (Vol. 1) make for some wonderful listening. Rex Stewart, Johnny Hodges, Harry Carney, Sam Nanton, Lawrence Brown, and Al Sears are among the soloists. The ensemble sound is virtually indistinguishable from the 1941 band. —*John McDonough,* Down Beat

○ **Duke Ellington: Eastbourne Performance** / **i**. Jan. 1976 / RCA 1023
This is one of Duke Ellington's last sessions (December 1973), and the orchestra sits this out most of the time as soloists do their numbers with the rhythm section. Cootie Williams and Paul Gonsalves were not around, but Harry Carney's presence is felt. Vocalists Anita Moore and Money Johnson waste valuable time, but "Pitter Patter" and "Woods," a tenor pairing between Harold Ashby and Percy Marion, are lively surprises. —*John McDonough,* Down Beat

○ **Duke Ellington: The Jimmy Blanton Years** / **i**. Jan. 1976 / Queendisc 007
This is a beautifully recorded treasure of Ellingtonia from an "America Dances" broadcast of June 1940. Selections such as "Ko-Ko," "Cotton Tail," "Concerto For Cootie," "Jack the Bear," and "Sergeant Was Shy" are on a par with their definitive studio-made counterparts. A feast! If this is not enough, we also got an Ellington/Blanton duet from a Bing Crosby program. This LP is a real find. —*John McDonough,* Down Beat

○ **Giants of Jazz** / **i**. Oct. 1979 / Time Life 02
There is nothing seriously amiss in this collection. The 40 selections that were agreed upon by the consulting experts John S. Wilson, Stanley Dance, Michael Brooks, and Richard Spottswood are unquestionably among the Ellington band's greatest. Moreover, the consistency of the sound quality achieved in remastering is especially commendable in that the material was drawn from at least eight different original labels. Featured in the first eight selections are those predominantly in the "jungle style" (Bubber Miley, Sam Nanton, Barney Bigard, and Johnny Hodges), but there are also notable solos from Duke Ellington, Wellman Braud, Jabbo Smith, Louis Metcalf, and guest star Lonnie Johnson. The band's next phase is marked by Cootie Williams's replacement of Miley and the subsequent emergence of increasingly more sophisticated compositions. Outstanding solos and orchestrations abound throughout the selections in the '30s, a fruitful period often eclipsed by the even greater years ahead. The universally praised 1940 band, which was defined by the dual presence of Jimmy Blanton and Ben Webster, produced an unprecedented cornucopia of sound and inspired the composer/leader to conceive, to write, and to record some of the most enduring works of his career. That band recorded some 75 titles in two years, not counting alternate takes, and the list of airchecks and documented concerts and dances is still growing. For those who feel, as I do, that the entirety of listenable Ellington should be made generally available in perpetuity, then the reduction of the complete 1940–1942 oeuvre to only 13 titles seems the unkindest cut of all. But the intention of the selection committee must be read as an inducement to further study, for no panel of conscionable jazz savants could ever feel thoroughly confident that it had indeed made an infallible decision where music of this kind is concerned. —*Jack Sohmer,* Down Beat

Jungle Band: Brunswick Era—Vol. 2 (1929-1931), The / 1990 / Decca 42348
Companion volume to the 1990 reissue, second set of late-'20s and early-'30s cuts. —*Ron Wynn*

Cool Rock / **i**. 1992 / Laserlight 15782
Recent release of previously unissued Ellington sessions from the '60s and '70s. Another item best used as an introductory vehicle. —*Ron Wynn*

Greatest Jazz Concert in the World, The / Pablo 2625-704
With Ella Fitzgerald and Coleman Hawkins. A fine three-record set. The title is pretentious, but the album does offer plenty of great music and a cross-section of swing, mainstream, and blues. —*Ron Wynn*

MERCER ELLINGTON (Mercer (Kennedy) Ellington)

b. Mar. 11, 1919, Washington, DC
Trumpet, composer, bandleader / Swing, big band
The son of Duke Ellington and the current leader of the surviving Ellington orchestra. Mercer Ellington has held jobs within the Ellington empire such as arranger and section trumpeter. He also wrote a biography of his famous father in 1978. He studied music in Washington, then in New York at the Institute of Musical Art. Mercer Ellington worked in and around New York in the late '20s and early '30s before forming his own band. The group included musicians such as Clark Terry, Cat Anderson, and Carmen McRae. He contributed some works to the Ellington library, among them "Blue Serge" and "Things Ain't What They Used to Be." While in the army in the mid '40s, Ellington played in a band under Sy Oliver's leadership. From that point on, Ellington led his own groups, and had odd jobs such as disc jockey, sales representative, and record company executive before becoming Cootie Williams's manager and section trumpeter. He joined his father's band in those same two capacities in 1965. Mercer Ellington took the reins of the Ellington orchestra in 1974. He directed the musical *Sophisticated Ladies* from 1981 to 1983. —*Ron Wynn*

★ **Digital Duke** / **i.** 1987 / GRP 9548
This was the new Mercer Ellington record. You wouldn't know that from looking at the front cover, which boasts the *Duke Ellington* orchestra with the flanking words in tiny letters and Duke's name in huge ones. On the back cover, Duke's name appears only in the album's title and Mercer's conductor credit is posted. But it *is* in a paperback-style liner blurb, excerpted from the notes. Leonard Feather appears to opine that Duke's presence "has never been more palpably felt . . . than in this impassioned reminder" of some of his best. . . . To be fair, Feather uncensored doesn't slight Mercer, and this album has some exciting moments. . . . There are a number of Ducalumni aboard: Clark Terry, Britt Woodman, Chuck Connors, Norris Turney, and Louis Bellson. But the standout among the guests, oddly enough, is Branford Marsalis, roaring through the Ducal bop of "Cotton Tail," coming back for a Ben Webster-informed ride on "Take the 'A' Train." On the former, he sounds inspired by Paul Gonsalves's marathons; his solo is as good as or better than any he'd (yet) done on record. The charts were drawn from transcriptions, or were rearranged from Ellington's charts (changing routines and solo orders), or were arranged in his spirit by Barry Lee Hall of Frankie Wechsler. "22 Cent Stomp" retitles an old (how old?) unrecorded up blues, and "Slammer in D Flat" is spirited enough to sound very close to Duke, and as close to new Ellington as the album offers. . . . As indicated, some of it sounds uncannily Dukish. Yet one keeps getting the impression that something is missing—and more often than not, no offense to Charles Owens, that something is the irreplaceable Harry Carney. His booming baritone is the only thing "22 Cent Stomp" lacks. The playing isn't sloppy, but the vets seem to miss the direct encouragement of their flattering, encouraging wicked taskmaster. Even "Take the 'A' Trains'" proudly answering brass lacks their traditional presence, and all the digital sound in town won't change that. . . . So let's remember this is the *Mercer* Ellington orchestra; as no one knows better than me, things weren't what they used to be. —*Kevin Whitehead*, Cadence

DON ELLIS (Donald Johnson Ellis)

b. Jul. 25, 1934, Los Angeles, CA, **d.** Dec. 17, 1978, Hollywood, CA
Trumpet, composer, bandleader / Big band, early jazz-rock, modern creative

An intriguing composer and a virtuoso trumpeter and improviser, Don Ellis was associated with jazz schools ranging from free to third stream and fusion. Sometimes, Ellis blended swing and ethnic/international elements, using Bulgarian and Indian meters in compositions as early as the mid '60s. He also incorporated serialism in his writing, as well as complex meters, amplified trumpet, and electronically distorted timbres. Ellis invented the four-valve trumpet, which was capable of playing quarter-tones. He could play ringing, searing, high notes and breathtaking phrases. Ellis studied composition at Boston University, where he earned a BA in 1956. He played in the bands of Ray McKinley, Charlie Barnet, and Maynard Ferguson in the late '50s, and with George Russell in the early '60s. After moving to New York, he formed his own trio, and was a soloist with the New York Philharmonic in 1963, playing in Larry Austin's "Improvisations" and touring Poland and Scandinavia. Ellis was designated "creative assistant" to Lukas Foss in Buffalo during the mid '60s. He was aided by a Rockefeller grant. Ellis later taught and did graduate study at UCLA. He formed an unusual large jazz orchestra in 1965, which specialized in playing in unusual time signatures (even 15/16!) and featured as many as four bassists and three drummers in the ensembles. In later years, the Don Ellis orchestra utilized electronic devices during some of the horn solos, added a string quartet, and even added a vocal quartet briefly (the latter was unrecorded). Among the sidemen were Glenn Ferris, John Klemmer, Sam Falzone, Frank Strozier, and Milcho Leview. The orchestra's most memorable recordings (none are out yet on CD) were *Autumn, Live at the Fillmore*, and *Tears of Joy* (all for Columbia). They toured the West Coast, recorded at the Monterey Jazz Festival, at Shelly's Manne-Hole, at Stanford University, and at the Fillmore in the mid '60s and early '70s. It was an attraction at the Newport Jazz and Antibes festivals in the '60s and '70s. Ellis won a Grammy for his score of the film *The French Connection* in 1971. After suffering a mid-'70s heart attack, Ellis returned to live performing playing the "superbone." He was a high-profile artist at Columbia during the early '70s, and also recorded for Candid, New Jazz, Pacific Jazz, MPS, and Atlantic. Ellis has a few sessions available as CD reissues. —*Ron Wynn and Michael G. Nastos*

How Time Passes / Oct. 4-5, 1960 / Candid 79004

Out of Nowhere / Apr. 21, 1961 / Candid 79032
Early-'60s Don Ellis, recorded in his pre-big-band days, with bassist Steve Swallow and pianist Paul Bley. It's more conventional material, with Ellis playing in dramatic, high-register fashion. This has been reissued on CD with a bonus track. —*Ron Wynn*

★ **New Ideas** / May 11, 1961 / New Jazz 431
The original thinking-jazz-lover's music. Quintet with unsung vibist Al Francis, and the Jaki Byard Trio. All originals by Ellis, who has a lot to say with combos like this. Variations, nay, mutations of familiar themes crop up, along with staggered and fractured time signatures. A very innovative musician, especially for jazz. —*Michael G. Nastos*

Live in 3 2/3 Time / 1966 / Pacific
Quintet. Unorthodox playing in varying time and musical contexts, done live at Monterey in the mid '60s. —*Ron Wynn*

Electric Bath / **i.** 1968 / Columbia

Don Ellis at Fillmore / 1970 / Columbia
The release that helped break him into a mass audience. It is live, daring, loud, annoying, and distinctive all at once. —*Ron Wynn*

Tears of Joy / May 20-23, 1971 / Columbia 30927

Haiku / 1973 / BASF 21916

Live at Montreux / Jul. 24, 1977 / Atlantic 19178
Six pieces with a big band and strings (21 pieces in all). John McLaughlin-influenced "The Sporting Dance" is a highlight. Lots of interplay, excellent solos from saxophonists Ann Patterson and Ted Nash, and Ellis on quarter-tone trumpet and the superbone. —*Michael G. Nastos*

HERB ELLIS (Mitchel Herbert Ellis)

b. Aug. 4, 1921, Farmersville, TX
Guitar / Swing, bop
As a child, Ellis played banjo then learned the rudiments of guitar on his own before attending North Texas State College with Jimmy Giuffre and Gene Roland. He got his start in the mid '40s with the Casa Loma Orchestra and with the Jimmy Dorsey band. In 1947 he formed the Soft Winds trio, a unit that echoed the influence of the Nat "King" Cole trio right down to Ellis's guitar lines underneath pianist Lou Carter's leads and bassist John Frigo's accompaniment. The trio stayed together until 1952 and had the successful song "Detour Ahead" recorded by Billie Holiday. Ellis replaced Barney Kessel in Oscar Peterson's group in 1953 and attained stature and stardom. He has worked extensively with Ray Brown since the '70s. Exhaustive studio, session, and recording work hasn't dulled his passion. He is a prototype jazz guitarist in the Charlie Christian tradition. —*Ron Wynn*

Nothing But the Blues / Oct. 17, 1957 / Verve

★ **Herb Ellis Meets Jimmy Giuffre** / Mar. 26, 1959 / Verve

Thank You Charlie Christian / 1960 / Verve 68381
Sixties date in tribute to the early jazz guitar great. Ellis does Christian proud. —*Michael G. Nastos*

Three Guitars in Bossa Nova Time / Jan. 16, 1963 / Epic 16036

Herb Ellis and Stuff Smith Together / Jan. 18, 1963 / Columbia

Man with the Guitar / 1965 / Dot 3678

★ **Seven Come Eleven** / Jul. 29, 1973 / Concord Jazz 4002
With Joe Pass. Concord's second record. Titans clash. Great music. Good on CD. First-rate band doing prototype arrangements. —*Ron Wynn*

Two for the Road / Jan. 30, 1974-Feb. 20, 1974 / Pablo 726

Soft Shoe / 1974 / Concord Jazz 4003
"Sweets" Edison (tpt) brings some fire to this Ellis/Ray Brown (b) set. —*Ron Wynn*

Hot Tracks / 1975 / Concord Jazz 4012
With the Ray Brown Sextet. 1989 reissue of this session with Ray Brown (b) sharing the spotlight. —*Ron Wynn*

Pair to Draw / 1976 / Concord Jazz 17

Windflower / Oct. 1977 / Concord Jazz 56

Soft and Mellow / Aug. 1978 / Concord Jazz 4077
On-the-money title. Ellis shows the difference between restraint and detachment. With Ross Tompkins (p). —*Ron Wynn*

Herb Ellis at Montreux / Jul. 1979 / Concord Jazz 116
Tasteful session at the famed Montreux festival. These old pros acquit themselves nicely. —*Ron Wynn*

Herb Mix / Jun. 1981 / Concord Jazz 181

★ **Doggin' Around** / Mar. 1988 / Concord Jazz 4372
With Red Mitchell; certainly a pair of time-tested veterans can't go wrong. The CD has two bonus cuts. —*Ron Wynn*

○ **Roll Call** / **i.** 1992 / Justice 1001
Well-done recent release with Ellis backed by a solid lineup of session and studio pros, among them trumpeter Jay Thomas and violinist Johnny Frigo. They play a mix of blues, traditional jazz stomps, and standards, with organist Mel Rhyne adding soulful support alongside drummer Jake Hanna. —*Ron Wynn*

○ **After You've Gone** / **i.** Mar. 13, 1992 / Concord Jazz 4006

JAMES EMERY

Guitar / Modern creative
An underrated guitarist, James Emery's brisk, nicely articulated solos, complete with strumming, jagged lines and skillful harmonic maneuvers, have been heard with the String Trio of New York and in his solos. Emergy plays both acoustic and electric, and has recorded solo and in a duo with violinist Leroy Jenkins. Emery, Billy Bang, and John

Lindbery were the original String Trio. They began recording for Black Saint in 1979. Charles Burnham replaced Bang in 1987. Emery has recorded as a leader for Lumina and FMP. He has sessions available on CD, both with the String Trio of New York and on his own. —*Ron Wynn*

★ **Exo Eso** / **i.** Oct. 1987 / FMP 59

BOBBY ENRIQUEZ

b. 1943
Piano / Hard bop
Bobby Enriquez carries the nickname "The Madman from Mindinao." The Philippine pianist is an absolutely wired player, on all the time, a virtuoso beyond belief. He plays standards powerfully, and is a great inventor. He mostly plays with a trio, and his live performances are electrifying. Enriquez has a couple of dates available on CD. —*Ron Wynn and Michael G. Nastos*

○ **Wild Man** / 1980 / GNP 2144
Though not as explosive as the title suggests, some strong piano work by Bobby Enriquez in an early-'80s quartet session. The material's divided between originals and standards like "Sweet Georgia Brown" and bop anthems like "Confirmation." Drummer Alex Acuna and Pancho Sanchez on congas provide solid Afro-Latin backgrounds and interact smoothly with star fusion bassist Abe Laboriel. —*Ron Wynn*

Live! in Tokyo—Vol. 2 / **i.** Aug. 6-7, 1982 / GNP 2161

Prodigious Piano / 1982 / GNP 2179

Live at Concerts By the Sea—Vol. 1 and 2 / **i.** 1985 / GNP 2183

★ **Wild Piano** / **i.** Dec. 22, 1987 / Portrait 44160
Filipino "Wild man from Mindanao" plays fiercely probing trio jazz. Look for GNP albums, too. —*Michael G. Nastos*

PETER ERSKINE

b. Jun. 5, 1954, Somers Point, NJ
Drums / Modern creative
A highly skilled, versatile drummer, Peter Erskine has anchored big bands and jazz-rock/ fusion groups. He's known for his sophisticated rhythms, distinctive accompaniment, and powerful, rippling solos. Erskine began drumming at age three, and participated in Stan Kenton's National Stage Band Camps from the age of six. He studied with Alan Dawson and Ed Soph, attending the Interlochen Arts Academy in Michigan and Indiana University. He played with Kenton from 1972 to 1975, then with Maynard Ferguson from 1976 to 1978. Erskine joined Weather Report in 1978, and was their drummer and percussionist until 1982. He also did several West Coast sessions in the late '70s, and was a member of Steps and Steps Ahead. During the '80s, he's worked with John Abercrombie's groups and with the quartet Bass Desires. Erskine has recorded as a leader for Contemporary, Denon, Ah Um, RCA/Novus, and Passport Jazz. He's worked with Joe Farrell, Marc Johnson, Mike Brecker, Randy Brecker, John Scofield, Bob Mintzer, Lew Soloff, Kenny Kirkland, Mike Mandel, and Kenny Werner, among others. He has several sessions available on CD. —*Ron Wynn*

★ **Peter Erskine** / Jun. 22-23, 1982 / Contemporary 610
First release by a first-rate drummer and lots of New York friends. "All's Well that Ends" is a winning track, as is "Leroy St." —*Michael G. Nastos*

Transition / Oct. 16-17, 1986 / Denon 1484

Motion Poet / Apr. 25, 1988-May 1, 1988 / Denon 72582
An excellent percussionist makes an uneven but ambitious statement. —*Ron Wynn*

○ **Sweet Soul** / Mar. 1991 / Novus 63140
A terrific date featuring John Scofield (g), Joe Lovano (s), Bob Mintzer (s) and Kenny Werner (p). Erskine's abilities as a composer are quite evident on this recording. —*Paul Kohler*

You Never Know / **i.** 1993 / PolyGram 517353

On *You Never Know* drummer Peter Erskine is credited with one composition, the quiet, reflective "On The Lake"; a very undrummer-like piece. The remaining tracks are by pianist John Taylor with Cole Porter's "Everything I Love" thrown in for good measure. While Erskine may not seem the dominant force (this seems as much Taylor's album as Erskine's), his subtle drumming provides the pulse and flow to this recording. Both Taylor and bassist Palle Danielsson work from it. Taylor is from the Bill Evans through Herbie Hancock piano tradition and his continually evolving harmonic approach, coupled with a purposeful flow, makes him the ideal pianist for this project. —*Krin Gabbard, Cadence*

BOOKER ERVIN (Booker (Telleferro, II) Ervin)

b. 1930, Denison, TX, **d.** Jul. 31, 1970
Tenor saxophone / Hard bop, blues & jazz
Flamboyance, excitement, and bluesy fervor were the trademarks of tenor saxophonist Booker Ervin. He was an aggressive, animated soloist whose repertoire of honks, swaggers, smears, and slurs were matched by his thorough harmonic knowledge and his complete command of the sax. He had one of the hardest tones and biggest sounds among '50s and '60s stylists, something that was even more impressive when he played the blues. Ervin's father was a trombonist who had worked with Buddy Tate. Ervin first played the trombone, then taught himself sax while in the air force. He studied music in Boston for two years, then made his earliest recordings with Ernie Fields's R&B band. This association was Ervin's professional debut as well. During the late '50s and early '60s, he was in Charles Mingus's Jazz Workshop, providing energized, powerful solos. Ervin also played in a group with Horace Parlan, George Tucker, and Al Harewood, and with Randy Weston. He recorded with Weston, and began cutting acclaimed albums as a leader in the '60s. Ervin recorded for Bethlehem, Savoy, and Candid. His crowning achievement was nine albums he did for Prestige in the mid and late '60s. These included such memorable dates as his "books." There were also sessions for Blue Note, Fontana, Pacific Jazz, and a partial album for Enja. Ervin spent most of 1964, 1965, and part of 1966 in Europe, and returned in 1968. Ervin died in 1970. Only a handful of Ervin sessions are currently in print, though others, like *Settin' the Pace*, are being reissued steadily. —*Ron Wynn*

○ **Soulful Saxes** / **i.** Jun. 1960 / Affinity 758

★ **Book Cooks, The** / Jun. 1960 / Affinity
Robust, earthy Ervin throughout. This tremendous combo date was originally on Bethlehem. —*Ron Wynn*

Down in the Dumps / Nov. 26, 1960-Jan. 5, 1961 / Savoy 1119
An explosive set from Ervin's prime period, reissued on disc with additional material from the following year (1961), with trombonist Dr. Billy Howell. —*Ron Wynn*

○ **Cookin'** / Nov. 26, 1960 / Savoy Jazz 150

That's It / Jan. 6, 1961 / Candid 79014

☆ **Back From the Gig** / Feb. 15, 1963+May 24, 1968 / Blue Note 488
Tenor saxophonist Booker Ervin's *Back From the Gig* is a perplexing volume. It is perplexing because it took Blue Note nearly seven years after Ervin's untimely death to release these valuable and infectious recordings. Apparently, both sessions, one recorded under the tutelage of pianist Horace Parlan (whom Michael Cuscuna thoughtfully documents in his liner notes), were scheduled for release years ago but never materialized. The Parlan sextet (1963) was a tough, no-nonsense blues unit. Ervin, trumpeter Johnny Coles, and guitarist Grant Green are the lead voices and are sly, raw, and often dirty. Ervin, in particular, plays with an inciting bounce and masterful range, lean and to the core. His own 1968 recordings, in cahoots with saxophonist Wayne Shorter and pianist Kenny Barron, are more expansive, envincing a knack for melding his blues romanticism to modal

foundations and professing some plain big-band-inspired truths. —*Mikal Gilmore, Down Beat*

★ **Freedom and Space Sessions** / Dec. 3, 1963+Oct. 2, 1964 / Prestige 7386
With so many new albums being recorded that sound 15 years old, it is refreshing to hear 15-year-old music that doesn't sound its age. The primary reason for this was the exceptional attentiveness of the rhythm section, various permutations of which turn up on almost all of tenor saxophonist Booker Ervin's Prestige LPs. On the uptempo "Lunar Tune," for example, they spontaneously orchestrate, changing textures as if they are all of one mind. Richard Davis takes some astoundingly modern bass solos. On "Grant's Stand," he almost makes the bass talk a la Charles Mingus. Jaki Byard's playing ranges from harplike chords on the slow tunes to forceful, but supportive, dissonances and blocky chords, playing the entire piano from top to bottom. Alan Dawson's shifting coloristic attack is equally engaging; he plays a melodic intro to and a fine melodic solo on "Al's In." On "Mojo," he keeps strict time with his feet while spreading accents around the drum kit with his sticks during Davis's solo. The conversational unity of piano, bass, and drums is particularly evident here, all of which is not to slight the leader. While Byard, Davis, and Dawson push the music into the future, Ervin's tenor reaches beyond the blues (which he intensely digs into on "Grant's Stand") back to the field holler. If his uptempo excursions are shouts, then his ballads are cries. On the slow numbers, he likes long notes with strong terminal vibrato, and he hits some notes a little flat to add to the pathos. Both these qualities are exaggerated on "No Greater Love." On the latter of these sessions, he seems to squeeze more notes into his lines, more in the manner of the times. This reissue contains the complete *Freedom Book* and *Space Book* sessions and one extra cut from each session, "Stella By Starlight" and "The Second #2," both of which originally appeared on Ervin's *Groovin' High. —Kevin Whitehead, Cadence*

The Blues Book / **i.** 1964 / Fantasy/Original 780
Booker Ervin's robust tenor sax was never more authoritative or impressive than when he played the blues. There are only four cuts on this CD reissue of 1964's *The Blues Book*, and two tracks are 14 minutes-plus. Ervin cajoles, moans, screams, and wails through the 12-bar pieces, while trumpeter Carmell Jones and pianist Gildo Mahones take their own blues journeys in answer to Ervin's emphatic laments. Bassist Richard Davis and drummer Alan Dawson nicely keep things simmering without ever letting them slide, as Ervin makes each number a personal testament of skill and resolve. —*Ron Wynn*

Song Book / Feb. 27, 1964 / Original Jazz Classics 779
Another in a series of exceptional quartet dates led by tenor saxophonist Booker Ervin in the mid '60s. This time, Tommy Flanagan replaced Jaki Byard on piano, with absolutely no dip in the quartet's execution. Ervin's solos are once more robust and well played, while the Davis/Dawson bass and drum duo do their customary excellent job. This has been issued on vinyl as part of two-record set, *The Blues Book/The Song Book*, and on both vinyl and CD as a single session. —*Ron Wynn*

Setting the Pace / **i.** 1965 / Fantasy/Original 24123
Booker Ervin's deep, bluesy tone and dramatic, urgent style are extended to their fullest on the lengthy cuts that make up *Setting The Pace*. On the first two numbers, Ervin matches wits with Dexter Gordon, generating furious fire and interesting solos. On the other songs, Ervin handles things alone, often threatening to blow apart the song structure, and constantly reshaping, reworking, and rebuilding his solos before finding the right blend of ideas and energy. Jaki Byard handles the difficult task of switching between supportive and combative roles on piano, with bassist Reggie Workman and drummer Alan Dawson expertly keeping the mood, pace, and tempos steady at times, and then switching gears to take the spotlight or move things in another direction when necessary. —*Ron Wynn*

Lament for Booker Ervin / Oct. 29, 1965 / Enja 2054

○ **Groovin' High** / Jun. 30, 1966-Oct. 30, 1962 / Prestige 7417
Exuberant quartet date from 1964, with Ervin again playing
bluesy, often searing tenor solos. He's supported by an ace
rhythm section that includes pianist Jaki Byard, bassist
Richard Davis, and drummer Alan Dawson. This has been
issued on vinyl as part of two-record set entitled *The
Freedom and Space Sessions* and as a single album under its
original title. It is not available on domestic CD, but on a
Japanese disc. —*Ron Wynn*

The in Between / Jan. 12, 1968 / Blue Note 84283
For the more adventurous. With Bobby Few on piano and
Richard Williams on trumpet. Ervin veers between inside
and outside jazz. —*Ron Wynn*

Booker 'n' Brass / Sep. 1968 / Pacific

PETE ESCOVEDO

Percussion / Latin jazz
A veteran Latin percussionist who's known mostly known to
general audiences as the father of onetime Prince protege,
band member, and confidante Sheila E, Pete Escovedo has
worked with many fine bands on the Latin jazz and dance
circuit. He made two uneven albums for Concord in the late
'80s, though the musicianship of his large group was fine.
The material ranged from arresting Afro-Latin to mild fusion. These sessions are still available on CD. —*Ron Wynn*

★ **Yesterday's Memories—Tomorrow's Dreams** / i. Feb.
16+17, 1985 / Crossover 45002
Yesterday's Memories—Tomorrow's Dreams. Some fusion
mixed in with Latin jazz by Escovedo's 12-piece group. —
Ron Wynn

Mister E / i. Dec. 1987-Jan. 1988 / Crossover 45005
This is a little on the erratic side. Pete Escovedo leads a 16-
piece group. —*Ron Wynn*

KEVIN EUBANKS (Kevin Tyrone Eubanks)

b. Nov. 15, 1957, Philadelphia, PA
Guitar, electric guitar / M-Base, modern creative
Guitarist Kevin Eubanks, currently a member of the
"Tonight Show Starring Jay Leno" band, has played both
acoustic and electric guitar, and has proven to be a capable
soloist and good accompanist in fusion, Afro-Latin, and jazz
settings. He formerly led a jazz-rock band while attending
Berklee, and recorded and toured with Chris Hintze in the
late '70s and Art Blakey in 1980. After moving to New York,
Eubanks worked with Roy Haynes, Ronnie Mathews, and
Slide Hampton, toured with Sam Rivers, and recorded with
Pacquito D'Rivera, Chico Freeman, James Newton, Wynton
Marsalis, and Bobby McFerrin. He's recorded as a leader for
GRP through the '80s, and for Blue Note in the '90s.
Eubanks has worked with Ron Carter, Dave Grusin, Marcus
Miller, Patrice Rushen, Kenny Davis, Dennis Chambers and
Marvin "Smitty" Smith, among others. —*Ron Wynn and
Michael G. Nastos*

Guitarist / May 1982-Aug. 1982 / Elektra 0213
Produced by Michael Gibbs. Acoustic guitar solos and group
works, with Ralph Moore (ts), Roy Haynes (d), Charles David
(p), and Robin Eubanks (t). This is a fine debut album. —
Michael G. Nastos

Opening Night / 1985 / GRP 9520

Promise of Tomorrow / Nov. 1989 / GRP 9604

★ **Turning Point** / i. 1992 / Blue Note 98170
Recent Blue Note session in which Kevin Eubanks disproves
those who've questioned his jazz and improvising credentials. There are only four cuts, and they're designed for intense solos and exacting ensemble interaction. Besides
Eubanks on electric and acoustic guitar, the cast features
alto flutist Kent Jordan, bassist Dave Holland, and drummer
Marvin "Smitty" Smith. —*Ron Wynn*

ROBIN EUBANKS

b. 1959

Trombone, keyboards / M-Base, modern creative
Robin Eubanks is the trombone-playing brother of Kevin
Eubanks. Robin has demonstrated great facility, range, tone,
and style, playing free, hard bop, and even funk and R&B.
He's well versed in progressive techniques, and is skilled in
multiphonics and overdubbing. Eubanks also plays bass
trombone and keyboards. He began recording as a leader in
the early '80s for JMT. Eubanks has worked with Steve
Coleman, Peter Washington, Mulgrew Miller, Branford
Marsalis, Greg Osby, Lonnie Plaxico, Cassandra Wilson, and
his brother, among others. He's also worked frequently with
fellow trombonists such as Steve Turre, Clifton Anderson,
and Slide Hampton. He is a promising young contemporary
jazz player who should do great things. —*Ron Wynn and
Michael G. Nastos*

○ **Different Perspectives** / i. 1988 / JMT 834424
Exceptional first album from this trombonist. A great listening album with many components, mostly in a progressive
vein. —*Michael G. Nastos*

★ **Dedication** / Apr. 1989 / JMT 834433
With Steve Turre. Two trombonists live up to their reputations with much vital music. —*Michael G. Nastos*

Karma / May 1990 / JMT 834446
A noteworthy experimental session with both pop and improvisational elements. —*Ron Wynn*

BILL EVANS (William John Evans)

b. Aug. 16, 1929, Plainfield, NJ, **d.** Sep. 15, 1980
Piano / Cool
An exceptional, intellectual, and greatly influential pianist
whose impact extended far beyond his active career, Bill
Evans looms as a modern keyboard giant. Using a fresh harmonic approach, sensitive touch, and phrasing, Evans created, evolved, extended, and perfected a style based on the
styles of Lennie Tristano, Horace Silver, and Bud Powell. In
its early stages, Evans's playing was more aggressive and bebop-rooted; in time, his music became more lyrical, and employed more subtle voicings, irregular phrase lengths, and a
nonobvious pulse. Evans's solos were constructed painstakingly, with note placements and rhythmic and melodic components cleverly developed. His relationship to his supporting players was equally critical; his work with bassists Scott
LaFaro and Eddie Gomez, or with drummers like Paul
Motian, was a cooperative, reactive process. Evans responded to the light sound and marvelous technique of
LaFaro and Motian's colors and subdued patterns. He had a
similar relationship with guitarist Jim Hall. Evans was an
equally astonishing unaccompanied pianist; these recordings, particularly his overdubbed works, reveal his complete
gifts unencumbered by accompanist duties. Chick Corea,
Keith Jarrett, Herbie Hancock, and Steve Kuhn are just a few
of the names that come to mind when citing the list of
Evans's disciples. He certainly deserves his own
category/school.
Evans attended Southwestern Louisiana University and
worked occasionally with Mundell Lowe and Red Mitchell.
After serving in the army, Evans played with Jerry Wald,
Tony Scott, and George Russell before meeting Paul Motian.
He made his first recording as a leader in 1956. Then Evans
recorded with Charles Mingus, before joining Miles Davis in
1958. His style was cemented the following year on the anthemic *Kind Of Blue* album. Evans began concentrating on
the trio format in 1960, working mainly in either
piano/bass/drums contexts or solo the rest of his career,
though there were many prominent exceptions. He did great
duo dates with vocalist Tony Bennett, valve trombonist Bob
Brookmeyer, and guitarist Jim Hall. Evans contributed to the
soundtrack for the film *Odds Against Tomorrow* in 1959.
During the '60s, Evans topped critics polls and occasionally
won Grammy awards. His first came for the album
Conversations With Myself in 1963, where he accompanied
himself through double and triple tracking. Evans's accompanists included LaFaro, Gomez, Motian, Shelly Manne,
Gary Peacock, and Marc Johnson. His numerous albums in

the '60s and '70s were recorded for Verve, Columbia, CTI, Pausa, Fantasy, Elektra/Musician, and Prestige. The lengthy list of people Evans recorded with includes Oliver Nelson, Jimmy Giuffre, Lee Konitz, Harold Land, Ray Brown, Philly Joe Jones, Kenny Burrell, Toots Thielemans and Warne Marsh, plus regular trio mates. Evans increased his compositional output in the '60s, with such songs as "Waltz for Debby" among his most popular. He chose compositions to perform as carefully as he built his solos.

Evans was among jazz's most entertaining, intriguing personalities when he chose to speak on the record. One of his later interviews included the assessment that jazz wasn't "Black music," at least not in the same manner as blues, R&B, or soul. Evans felt that while jazz had African-American and African roots, its other influences and general stylistic evolution had transformed it into an international sound that was close to being generic rather than ethnic. It was certainly a plausible if debatable view, one that still deserves plenty of discussion. Evans died in 1980. Superb boxed sets of his complete recordings for Fantasy and Riverside have been issued by Prestige. Evans has numerous sessions available on CD. —Ron Wynn

New Jazz Conceptions / Sep. 27, 1956 / Riverside 025
This is pianist Bill Evans's debut as a leader, a September 18 and July 25, 1956 recording. He has backing from bassist Teddy Kotick and drummer Paul Motian. The album swings hard, but really does not develop the grace and cutting execution that would be found on Explorations. —Bob Rusch, Cadence

★ Complete Riverside Recordings (1956–1963) / 1956-1963 / Riverside 018
Twelve CDs. Fantasy/1985. All the marvelous Evans one could ever want is on this incredible 18-disc boxed set. It is a wonderful, comprehensive collection of superb performances, with some of his most majestic trio and solo dates. —Ron Wynn

Everybody Digs Bill Evans / Dec. 15, 1958 / Riverside 068
A worthy session with the great Philly Joe Jones drumming. There's a bonus cut on the CD issue. —Ron Wynn

○ Peace Piece and Other Pieces / Jan. 19, 1959 / Milestone 47024
Half of Peace Pipe and Other Pieces is a reissue of Bill Evans's second Riverside album, Everybody Digs Bill Evans. Recorded in 1958 after Evans left the Miles Davis Sextet, it contains some of the most memorable ballads on record. The remainder of the twofer was cut in 1959, save for one track recorded in 1962. Six of the previously unissued tracks were recorded with two members of that auspicious Davis sextet, Philly Joe Jones and Paul Chambers. "Woodie 'N' You" is typical. The music is straightahead jazz, precise and austere, yet also spirited and brimming with lyric warmth. "Loose Bloose" is one of the few recorded tunes in which Evans leads a quintet. It is the only surviving track from a 1962 session with Zoot Sims, Ron Carter, and Philly Joe Jones. "Bloose" is, as expected, cool, slow, and bluesy. The most celebrated tune is the solo "Peace Pipe." Unified by an entrancing four-note group, the haunting composition achieves its poignancy through Evans's mixture of delicate chords and lush, chromatic arpeggios. The piece is liberated from traditional notions of time and harmony. —Steve Marks, Down Beat

★ Undercurrent / May 15, 1959 / Blue Note 90583
A must-have reissue of a brilliant date with Jim Hall (g). —Ron Wynn

Explorations / Feb. 2, 1961 / Riverside 037
Pianist Bill Evans, like guitarist Wes Montgomery, was a Riverside "discovery." This session was recorded in 1961 by Evans's trio with bassist Scott LaFaro and drummer Paul Motian. The version of "Israel" on this release remains such a continuing, unfolding joy that it alone could justify the album's purchase. Through technique, execution, and imagination, Bill Evans made some very fine "free jazz" that was

also artistically free. This was also issued as part of a twofer. —Bob Rusch, Cadence

○ More from the Vanguard / Jun. 25, 1961 / Milestone 9125
Material recorded live at the Village Vanguard during several sessions with arguably the finest Bill Evans trio: pianist Evans, bassist Scott LaFaro, and drummer Paul Motian. They did enough tracks to fill several albums; these are sessions not included on the original Live at the Village Vanguard dates. —Ron Wynn

○ Sunday at the Village Vanguard / Jun. 25, 1961 / Riverside 140
This represents one of the best-known sessions from the Village Vanguard (most of the material from this June 25, 1961 date was on a previous twofer). Simply put, it sounds like pianist Bill Evans, bassist Scott LaFaro, and drummer Paul Motian, and it sounds like Sunday. —Bob Rusch, Cadence

Village Vanguard Sessions / Jun. 25, 1961 / Milestone 47002
This is a collection of several fine '60s cuts that are all available elsewhere. Aimed at the budget-conscious. —Ron Wynn

Waltz for Debby / Jun. 25, 1961 / Riverside 210
This second issue of the Bill Evans trio (Scott Lafaro, bass; Paul Motian, drums) had a good run on Riverside, as one of the first Milestone twofers and also as part of the 19-LP Bill Evans box. Because of its lasting popularity and the influence of Evans, the material here has become somewhat its own cliché, which, of course, is really an ironic distortion of time and place. For this date, time, place, the artists were right, and for two decades this, for many, continues to be a stimulating comfort. —Bob Rusch, Cadence

How My Heart Sings! / May 17, 1962-Jun. 5, 1962 / Riverside 369
Bill Evans Trio. More from the Evans/Chuck Israels/Paul Motian lineup. —Ron Wynn

Moonbeams / May 17, 1962-Jun. 5, 1962 / Riverside 434
Bill Evans Trio. Top trio again features Evans, Israels (b), and Motian (d). —Ron Wynn

Interplay / Jul. 16, 1962 / Original Jazz Classics 308
Quintet. A dazzling small group date with top-flight Freddie Hubbard (tpt). A 1987 reissue. —Ron Wynn

○ Empathy / a Simple Matter of Conviction / Aug. 14, 1962+Oct. 11, 1966 / PolyGram 837757
Empathy is an August 14, 1962 collaboration between drummer Shelly Manne and pianist Bill Evans that came almost a year after their first pairing. On this date, Monty Budwig is the bassist. This is a bit of an uneven set as there are times when the creative lines taken by Manne and Evans do not really interplay and Budwig tends to straddle between the two. On the other hand, there are individually fine moments, and one particular cut, "Washington Twist" (6:28), matches Manne and Evans equally in creative interplay and involvement. For the most part, however, the grouping on this program falls short of the exciting exchanges one could expect from the combination. —Bob Rusch, Cadence

Conversations with Myself / Jan. 1963-Feb. 1963 / Verve 821984
These stunning multiple-tracked piano solos won a Grammy in a rare acknowledgment of amazing achievement. Great playing and an admirable use of multitrack technology. —Ron Wynn

Bill Evans Trio at Shelly's Manne-Hole / May 30+31, 1963 / Riverside 263
On this 1987 reissue of a super trio date, Chuck Israels is vastly different from Scott LaFaro on bass, yet is equally effective. —Ron Wynn

Time Remembered / May 30+31, 1963 / Milestone 47068
Trio 1964 / Dec. 18, 1963 / Verve 815057

☆ Bill Evans at Town Hall / Feb. 21, 1966 / Verve 831271
★ Intermodulation / Apr. 7, 1966 / Verve 833771

○ **Simple Matter of Conviction, A** / Oct. 11, 1966 / Verve 8675
What separates this from the average good Bill Evans date is the inclusion of Shelly Manne on drums, who inventively pushes and takes unexpected chances. This is, I believe, Eddie Gomez's (bass) debut release with Evans (piano) and it is quite impressive. There are numerous takes at this session, and judging from Chuck Briefer's liners it might be interesting to hear them released. —*Bob Rusch, Cadence*

○ **California Here I Come** / Aug. 17-18, 1967 / Verve 22545
California Here I Come by pianist Bill Evans is not a reissue, but is previously unreleased material from two nights (August 17 and 18, 1967) at the Village Vanguard. This is first-class material, with textbook Evans and drummer Philly Joe Jones pushing the trio (bassist Eddie Gomez) along quite nicely, especially on the uptempos. —*Bob Rusch, Cadence*

☆ **At the Montreux Jazz Festival** / Jun. 15, 1968 / Verve 827844
A superb trio date. Eddie Gomez (b) and Jack DeJohnette (d) are brilliant in accompanying roles. —*Ron Wynn*

Bill Evans Alone / Sep. 1968-Oct. 1968 / Verve 8792

Montreux II / **i.** 1970 / CTI 45219
One of their most stunning, a 1970 trio release featuring alternately beautiful and intense piano improvisations from Bill Evans with bassist Eddie Gomez and drummer Marty Morrell. — *Ron Wynn, Rock & Roll Disc*

From Left to Right / Dec. 1970 / MGM 4723

Bill Evans Album / May 11-20, 1971 / Columbia 30855

Tokyo Concert, The / Jan. 20, 1973 / Fantasy 345

★ **Complete Fantasy Recordings** / 1973-1979 / Fantasy 1012
This gorgeous boxed set is a collection of his '70s selections. It covers everything in all contexts and is a must-have for piano fans. —*Ron Wynn*

Intuition / Nov. 7-8, 1974 / Fantasy 470
This is a wonderful pairing of musically attuned comrades Bill Evans and Eddie Gomez (b). —*Ron Wynn*

Blue in Green / 1974 / Milestone 9185

○ **Tony Bennett/Bill Evans Album, The** / Jun. 10-13, 1975 / Original Jazz Classics 439
Exquisite collaboration between a great romantic vocalist and a tremendous melodic interpreter. Bennett and Evans mesh as though they'd been working together for years, never having any problems with tempo, pacing, or mood. This has been reissued on CD. —*Ron Wynn*

Montreaux—Vol. 3 / Jul. 20, 1975 / Fantasy 644

○ **Alone (Again)** / Dec. 16-18, 1975 / PolyGram 833801
Includes moving, appealing, and expansive solos. The CD issue has two bonus cuts. —*Ron Wynn*

Eloquence / Dec. 16+18, 1975 / Fantasy 9618

Quintessence / May 1976 / Fantasy 698
This album is unhampered by the competitiveness and overplaying too often present in less mature so-called star session men. Bill Evans is ever present, but appropriately follows his soloists, allowing them freedom to fully explore their own creative instincts. Playing brilliantly throughout, pianist Evans joins Ray Brown and Philly Joe Jones to form a rhythm section that could serve as a sterling example for all such aspirants. As a guitarist, Kenny Burrell was not as natural a foil for Evans as Jim Hall. The results are not as gratifying as the classic Hall/Evans duets of some years back, but Burrell is no slouch by any means. At first, Harold Land's tenor seems to be self-effacing, but repeated listenings prove his value to the total sound of the record. Never stepping "outside" even during solos, Land provides unity to the session. —*David Less, Down Beat*

Cross-Currents / Feb. 28, 1977-Mar. 2, 1977 / Fantasy 9568
A change of pace for the Bill Evans trio: the usual threesome is paired with saxophonists Warne Marsh and Lee Konitz on some numbers. There's one excellent duet by Evans and

Konitz on "When I Fall in Love," and one quartet number without Konitz, but otherwise Evans shows he could also head a quintet, play solos, and interact with a combo as effectively as he did his trio. Konitz and Marsh are superb, while bassist Eddie Gomez and drummer Eliot Zigmund work effectively in a different format. —*Ron Wynn*

☆ **You Must Believe in Spring** / Aug. 23-25, 1977 / Warner Brothers 3504
Recorded in the fall of 1977, shortly before bassist Eddie Gomez and drummer Eliot Zigmund left Bill Evans's trio, this posthumous release attests to the continuity and clarity of Evans's musical means and ends. Indeed, much of the trio's work looks backwards to those vintage Riverside sessions, *Moonbeams* and *Sunday at the Village Vanguard*, both impressionistic collections of haunting mood pieces. For example, here Evans's own "B Minor Waltz" simply floats along, interspersed with melodic motifs straight from *Moonbeams*. In the work of lesser players, such deliberate self-quotation lapses easily into self-parody; in the work of a musician of Evans's stature, the melodic permutations of his earlier work simply reaffirms the continuity of his craft and his commitment to it. "You Must Believe in Spring," "We Will Meet Again," and "Sometime Ago" similarly present Evans as a consummate impressionist with his light, thoughtfully voiced iridescent chords and wide, sweeping melodies. His playing on Jimmy Rowles's "The Peacock" is evidence of Evans's darker moods. A languid essay in melancholy, this piece's dissonant melodic leaps and brooding harmonies reminds us of Evans's pensive side and of the depth of his feeling and vision. —*Jon Balleras, Down Beat*

New Conversations / Jan. 26, 1978-Feb. 16, 1978 / Fantasy

Affinity / Oct. 30, 1978-Nov. 30, 1978 / Warner Brothers 3293
With Toots Thielemans (harmonica). A good date from his late-'70s period. —*Ron Wynn*

I Will Say Goodbye (Original Jazz Classics) / May 11-13, 1979 / Original Jazz Classics 761
Nice, occasionally superior late-'70s Evans trio date. Though Evan's impressionistic, shimmering style had been absorbed by countless pianists by this time, he still never failed to provide at least one dazzling solo on every album. For this one, he plays brilliantly on "Dolphin Dance" and reinterprets "A House Is Not a Home." Longtime bassist Eddie Gomez and drummer Eliot Zigmund fit in their respective places perfectly. —*Ron Wynn*

Paris Concert, Edition One / Nov. 26, 1979 / Elektra 60164
On *Paris Concert*, incredibly fluid and romantic solo ruminations roll out of Bill Evans's bottomless wellspring of feelings. Bassist Marc Johnson and drummer Joe LaBarbera, as beautifully as they play, seem an afterthought at times, and come in only halfway (if at all) through most tracks. They are featured in extended solos only on lengthy side-closers, and obtrude only as acolytes on Evans's fantasias. The pianist here is communing in extraordinary intimacy with his music and the audience. His breathless performance, hallowed and hushed as church, rarefied as alpine air with wondrous vistas, clearly captivates the Parisians and stands as one of the most touching and spiritual performances of the latter Evans legacy. —*Fred Bouchard, Down Beat*

○ **Paris Concert, Edition Two** / Nov. 26, 1979 / Elektra 60311
Recorded less than a year before his death (September 1980), this album and its companion volume show us that Evans had at last found a bassist and drummer that fit his particular concept of rhythmic interplay without sacrificing intensity or energy (as seemed to be the case with some of the '70s trios). Marc Johnson (bass), Joe LaBarbera (drums), and Evans collectively demonstrate a wonderful sense of dynamics, and an intuitive sense of musical direction. Johnson, in particular, uses his prodigious technique as a means to an end, playing lines that relate rhythmically and harmonically to Evans's playing, creating a dialogue in the tradition of Scott LaFaro. LaBarbera both blends with and stimulates the other two. The material consists of three pieces from the earliest trio period—"Person I Knew," "34 Skidoo," and

"Nardis"—and three later pieces. On "Nardis," the seven-minute unaccompanied piano solo preceding the theme statement and the entrance of the rhythm sections is worth the price alone. A dark, intensely brooding work, this solo, with its sections of rubato and tempo, redefines the piece in an impressionistic manner, suggesting Evans was finding a different harmonic direction in his last year. . . . Good solos from LaBarbera and Johnson are also featured on this tune. —*Peter Leitch*, Cadence

○ **The Brilliant** / **i.** Aug. 1980-Sep. 1980 / Timeless 329

Nirvana / Rhino 90141
With Dave Pile (vibes) and Herbie Mann (f). A nice date from a surprising team. —*Ron Wynn*

☆ **Conception** / Milestone 47063
This two-record set is most welcome since it combines a reissue of pianist Bill Evans's first trio album released in 1956 with one alternate take and some previously unissued solo tracks from 1958 and 1962. The original album is *New Jazz Conceptions* (Riverside) and is probably the only Evans album that was never recorded in stereo. This trio developed before the idea of interplay with the bassist and before Evans was very much into a bebop bag. Some of it reminds me very much of Dodo Marmarosa, and then I hear traces of Red Garland. There is no doubt that this album adds a bit of underdeveloped polish to the trio sound that had a much rawer approach in those days. "I Got It Bad and That Ain't Good," "My Romance," and the often-heard "Waltz For Debby" are done solo. Even they are somewhat different in approach to his later work. "Displacement" and "Speak Low" have nicely written lines for the bassist (Teddy Kotick), and Tadd Dameron's "Our Delight" never sounded better. "No Cover, No Minimum" is about the most "down-home" blues I ever heard Bill Evans play, and there is even an unissued alternate take of it. The other unissued material consists of a single track, "Some Other Time," done in 1958; it's gorgeous. The other four are "Danny Boy," "Like Someone in Love," "In Your Own Sweet Way," and "Easy to Love." They appear in stereo, and with the exception of the extended length of "Danny Boy," I cannot praise them highly enough. These tracks came during a period of great inactivity by Evans, due mainly to the death of his great bassist, Scott LaFaro. They were done just prior to the formation of the new trio and everybody else seemed to forget about them. This album is certainly both a major reissue and a rediscovery. —*Jerry L. Atkins*, Cadence

☆ **Spring Leaves** / Milestone 47034
The two Bill Evans dates that make up *Spring Leaves* are justly renowned for the excellent bass playing of Scott LaFaro. However, it is up to anyone interested in Evans to decide for themselves whether they can take the hyper-delicate pianist. Paul Bley was into something similar, but was better in albums as far back as 1953-1954. Certainly, Evans fans will find some of his best playing here, along with some remarkable examples of group interplay, including the bass solos on "Autumn Leaves." If only LaFaro had made more records with heavies like alto saxophonist/composer Ornette Coleman and trumpeter Booker Little. —*Martin Davidson*, Cadence

BILL EVANS (SAX)

b. 1958
Saxophone, keyboards / Early jazz-rock, modern creative
Tenor and soprano saxophonist, keyboardist, and composer Bill Evans has made his own mark in the jazz world, though not at the same level as his pianist namesake. But the two musicians share one similarity: both worked for Miles Davis, though saxophonist Evans was actually in Davis's band longer than Evans the pianist. Bill Evans has a tough, taut, and funky/bluesy sound, with a full and authoritative tenor tone, and a thin but assertive soprano style. While he's been associated with jazz-rock, fusion, and instrumental pop, Evans can also play sterling standards and ballads, can

handle himself well on blues, and has written some interesting compositions. He was featured prominently in Davis's early and mid-'80s bands, and was viewed, in many quarters, as the finest instrumentalist in some of those units. Davis himself was once quoted as saying "he's one of the greatest musicians I've ever come upon." Evans was featured with the Davis group on several major American, European, and Japanese tours.

Evans began playing piano as a child, then studied tenor. He had both university and conservatory training before studying privately with David Liebman. He moved to New York in 1978, and joined Davis in 1980, receiving widespread acclaim before going solo in the mid-'80s. Evans recorded with Elements, the band co-led by Mark Egan and Danny Gottlieb in 1982, then debuted as a leader the following year. Evans later worked with the reformed Mahavishnu Orchestra and with John McLaughlin, and played more sessions with Elements, and with Herbie Hancock.

He began studying and playing keyboards in the mid '80s, and his Blue Note album, *The Alternative Man*, featured Evans using multiple synthesizers, drum machines, and signal processors. Since then, he's done several albums for Jazz City, playing with Chuck Loeb, Marc Johnson, Gottlieb, Gil Goldstein, Jim Beard, Mitch Forman, Victor Bailey, Dennis Chambers, and Richie Morales. A pair of these albums was recorded live in Tokyo, and they combine fusion, vintage jazz-rock, and instrumental pop, funk, and rock elements with some straight bebop. Evans also had an early '80s session for the Paddle Wheel label with Hank Jones and Red Mitchell that's almost totally a traditional work, with the trio recording several standards. He was featured on Davis's '80s albums *The Man With the Horn*, *We Want Miles*, and *Star People*. His American label debut as a leader was *Living on the Crest of a Wave* for Elektra/Musician. The Paddle Wheel release preceded the Elektra/Musician release, but was available mainly in Japan. His next release was issued on Blue Note. —*Ron Wynn*

★ **Alternative Man** / Jan. 19, 1985 / Blue Note 46336

GIL EVANS (Ian Ernest Gilmore Green)

b. May 13, 1912, Toronto, Ontario, Canada, **d.** Mar. 20, 1988, Cuernavaca, Mexico
Arranger, composer, piano, bandleader / Cool, progressive big band
A superb arranger and bandleader, Gil Evans rivaled Ellington and Mingus in his ability to provide imaginative frameworks for individual voices within a large orchestra. He wrote elaborate, intricate arrangements that didn't weaken or threaten his band's spontaneity. Evans was hardly a purist; he began using electronics in his bands in the '70s and recorded Jimi Hendrix material, which some people found scandalous. His style got looser in later years, with more space and less precision, but certainly his music remained compelling. Evans's harmonic language, and his compositional and arranging skills were immense, and he was responsible for many masterpieces through his arrangements, his compositions, and his conducting. A self-taught musician, Evans led his own group in California during the mid and late '30s. After Skinnay Ennis became bandleader, Evans remained as the group's arranger, until he joined Claude Thornhill's orchestra in 1941 as an arranger. Evans's arrangements of classical bebop compositions helped shape and make Thornhill's orchestra a topflight band. Except for a stretch in the service during the mid '40s, he stayed with Thornhill until 1948. Evans worked with Miles Davis in the late '40s and early '50s, creating the same magic, but with a smaller combo. He also wrote songs for Peggy Lee, Tony Bennett, and Benny Goodman, while conducting albums for Astrud Gilberto and for Kenny Burrell. Evans generated more fireworks later in the '50s and '60s with Davis, writing spectacular arrangements for the albums *Miles Ahead*, *Porgy and Bess*, and *Sketches of Spain*. Later came *Quiet Nights*. Evans also

played piano on some sessions. These, and the 1958 album *New Bottles, Old Wine*, remain landmark works. His own intriguing releases in the '60s included *Out Of The Cool, Into The Hot*, and *The Individualism of Gil Evans*. Evans did more writing in the '70s, penning works such as "Las Vegas Tango," "Proclamation," and "Anita's Dance." He issued more fine albums, such as the Hendrix projects and *Priestess*. He continued writing, arranging, and recording in the '80s, and, for a lengthy period, his band was the featured attraction at Sweet Basil's in New York on Monday nights. Evans recorded for Enja, Mole, and other import labels in the '80s. His 75th birthday concert was held in London in 1987. Gil Evans died the next year. A representative sampling of his work from the '50s to the '80s remains available on CD from several different labels. —*Ron Wynn*

○ **Gil Evans and Ten** / Sep. 6, 1957-Oct. 10, 1957 / Prestige 346
Excellent arrangements, with a lineup and compositions that are of high quality. —*Ron Wynn*

○ **New Bottle, Old Wine** / Aug. 9, 1958-May 26, 1958 / EMI 46855
Early, intriguing Gil Evans orchestra material, one of the sessions that established his reputation as an arranger and bandleader. The band, which includes Johnny Coles, Cannonball Adderley, Paul Chambers, and Art Blakey, does rousing, fresh versions of vintage songs like the "St. Louis Blues" and "King Porter Stomp." This material has also been issued as a vinyl album and on CD under the title *Pacific Standard Time*. —*Ron Wynn*

○ **Great Jazz Standards** / 1959 / Blue Note 46856

★ **Out of the Cool** / Nov. 18, 1960-Nov. 30, 1960 / MCA 5653
Out of the Cool offers Gil Evans, fresh from triumphs with Miles Davis, pursuing his orchestral muse with a couple of originals, an attractively odd John Benson Brooks song, a Brecht-Weil number from *Happy End*, and a George Russell composition wherein the Lydian concept meets the 12-bar blues. The orchestrations are characteristically rich, layered, and slow to unfold. Johnny Coles assumes the Miles Davis role to some effect, and there are other soloists of interest, foremost of whom is Jimmy Knepper, whose trombone is featured on "Flamingos." Remaining personnel: Phil Sunkel, trumpet; Keg Johnson, trombone; Tony Studd, bass trombone; Bill Barber, tuba; Eddie Caine or Ray Beckenstein, alto sax, flute, piccolo; Budd Johnson, tenor sax, soprano sax; Bob Tricarico, baritone saxophone, flute, piccolo; Evans, piano, arranger; Ray Crawford, guitar; Ron Carter, bass; Charli Persip, Elvin Jones, percussion. The recording date is vague; the LP lists only a year: 1961. Jepsen adds to the confusion by listing November 8, 1960, December 10 and 15, 1960, but indicated these dates as doubtful. . . . Timing: 37:09. —*Alan Bargebuhr, Cadence*

Into the Hot / Oct. 10, 1961 / MCA 39104
The classic early-'60s album that features pianist Cecil Taylor. Gil Evans actually had minimal involvement with the date, letting Taylor and John Carisi record under his name. It was quite controversial, with Taylor already firmly established going his own way. This has been reissued on CD. —*Ron Wynn*

Cannonball Adderley and Gil Evans / i. 1962 / Pacific Jazz 40

★ **Individualism of Gil Evans, The** / Sep. 1963-Apr. 1964 / Verve 833804

Blues in Orbit / 1969 / Enja 79611

Where Flamingos Fly / 1972 / A&M 0831
A transitional album recorded in the early '70s. Evans was beginning a subtle alteration in arranging style and was also investigating rock and electronics. He added Flora Purim on vocals for some tracks, plus Airto on percussion, and recruited emerging stars like tenor saxophonist Billy Harper and Howard Johnson on tuba and baritone. This has been reissued on CD. —*Ron Wynn*

Gil Evans' Orchestra Plays the Music of Jimi Hendrix / Jun. 1974 / Bluebird 8409
A controversial release in its day, this mid-'70s Gil Evans orchestra session has since been recognized by everyone except extreme purists as a vital set and intriguing reinterpretation of Hendrix's work. Such cuts as "Little Wing" and "Angel" convey Hendrix's fiery spirit, yet retain the Evans's orchestra's jazz ties. —*Ron Wynn*

Svengali / 1974 / Atlantic 90048
Another controversial '70s date, this one recorded at Trinity Church. This is an album of original Evans material, and features sections with jagged, almost chaotic passages and animated exchanges and solos. Evans was mixing rock, funk, and contemporary classical influences into his arrangements, and, despite the quality, the results didn't please everyone. —*Ron Wynn*

○ **Live at Sweet Basil—Vols. 1 and 2** / Aug. 20, 1984-Aug. 2, 1984 / Evidence 22026
Gil Evans ran into his share of would-be defenders of his "tradition" when he began experimenting with rock songs and electronic instruments in the '70s and '80s. One of jazz's greatest arrangers was suddenly viewed as a charlatan in certain circles, and a band loaded with great players was being dismissed as a crew of frauds. But the records disprove anyone foolish enough to accept that wisdom. This second volume of songs, done live during the band's long run as Sweet Basil's regular Monday night attraction, proves decisively that neither Evans nor his band lost anything. Their rendition of Hendrix's "Voodoo Chile" includes some riveting tuba and baritone sax work by Howard Johnson, a splintering collective reading of the melody by the band, and strong individual solos all around. The versions of Wayne Shorter's *Parabola* and Herbie Hancock's *Prince of Darkness* are multifaceted and compare favorably with almost anything done by any previous Evans aggregation. Adam Nussbaum proves a solid rhythm asset during his tenure, and the solos of trumpeter Hannibal Marvin Peterson, saxophonists George Adams, Chris Hunter, and Johnson or guitarist Hiram Bullock are always on the money. It may not be "cool," but it is most assuredly great jazz. —*Ron Wynn*

Rhythm-A-Ning / Nov. 2-26, 1987 / EmArcy 836401

Paris Blues / Dec. 1987 / Owl 79247
A new summit of a great arranger and an unorthodox, distinctive soprano saxophonist, Steve Lacy. —*Ron Wynn*

★ **Arrangers' Touch** / Prestige 24049
Here is an excellent reissue from Prestige featuring lesser-known work from two seminal figures in modern jazz: Gil Evans and Tadd Dameron. The Evans material dates from 1957, with Evans as pianist, leader, and arranger heading a medium-sized group filled with outstanding musicians. The beauty of these seven selections is in the balance between ensemble and solo work, all within the boundaries of Evans's disarmingly low-key musical ideas. Tadd Dameron's music *moves* much more than Evans's, although he was concerned with delicacy and musical beauty as much as his colleague. These qualities are better expressed in the four 1956 cuts on the album than in the more promising 1953 sides that include Clifford Brown and Philly Joe Jones. The problem here is that the strident trumpeter and pulsating drummer seem to be carrying the group on their shoulders, and the lack of variation in tonality and musical ideas becomes monotonous. Contrast this to the more subtle and substantial Dameron compositions in the 1956 session, played by a more cohesive group. They create a beautiful mood on "Fontainebleau," provide the framework for Dameron's piano reverie in "Scene Is Clean," and get into a swinging mood on "Delirium." Shadow Wilson's drumming seems much more tasteful than Jones's on the earlier set, and the musicians are obviously more concerned with the group sound than with individual honors. —*Leonard Maltin, Down Beat*

SUE EVANS

b. 1951
Percussion / Progressive big band, modern creative
Sue Evans has provided percussive support for jazz and pop groups, and for instrumentalists and vocalists. She's played conventional trap drums and various percussion instruments. Evans studied with Warren Smith and Sonny Igoe, and graduated from the High School of Music and Art in 1969. She toured Europe and America as a drummer with Judy Collins from the late '60s until the mid '70s, and also toured and recorded as a percussionist with Gil Evans from 1969 until 1982. During the '70s, Evans worked with Steve Kuhn and the Jazz Composer's Orchestra under Roswell Rudd, while she played with Michael Franks, Suzanne Vega, and Tony Bennett in the '80s. She's recorded with Bobby Jones, George Benson, Urbie Green, and Art Farmer in the '70s, and with Morgana King in the '80s. Evans doesn't have any sessions as a leader, but can be heard on many CDs that feature Gil Evans, Benson, Green, Farmer, and King, among others. —*Ron Wynn*

DOUGLAS EWART

b. 1946
Multi-instrumental / Modern creative
Douglas Ewart's a solid multi-instrumentalist who's made his biggest contribution as a sideman. His steady, energetic solos on alto sax, flute, bass clarinet, and bassoon have been heard in the bands of Fred Anderson, George Lewis, Muhal Richard Abrams, Anthony Braxton, and Chico Freeman. A native of Kingston, Jamaica, Ewart moved to Chicago in 1963. He joined the Association for the Advancement of Creative Musicians in 1967, and studied theory and performance with Roscoe Mitchell and Joseph Jarman. He's been featured on several sessions in the '70s, '80s, and '90s, but hasn't issued any releases as a leader. Ewart did record a duo album with George Lewis on Black Saint. It's available on CD. He can also be heard on other discs that feature Freeman, Lewis, Braxton, and Abrams. —*Ron Wynn*

F

JON FADDIS (Jonathan Faddis)

b. Jul. 24, 1953, Oakland, CA
Trumpet, flugelhorn / Bop
Once saddled with the burden of being deemed too close in sound and style to Dizzy Gillespie, Jon Faddis has outlived the charge. Through a successful career that began in the '70s and has continues through the '90s, Faddis has developed his own distinctive musical approach. The closeness and kinship Faddis shared with Gillespie certainly affected his playing; the lines, construction of his solos, phrasing, tone, almost everything in his early years reflected the Gillespie touch. But Faddis evolved and shed his tendency to mimic, even if it took some detractors ages to realize and accept it. He began trumpet studies at age eight and was playing regularly in R&B bands around the San Francisco area at age 13. He moved to New York in the early '70s, playing with Lionel Hampton, Gil Evans, Charles Mingus, and the Thad Jones-Mel Lewis orchestra. Faddis studied at the Manhattan School of Music, and played with Chuck Mangione before he began associating and performing with Gillespie. Gillespie and Faddis toured Europe together in 1977, playing at the Montreux Jazz Festival that year and again in 1983. Faddis made a few recordings as a leader, then retreated to the studios for several years. He formed his own quintet in 1984, then recorded in a group co-led by McCoy Tyner and Jackie McLean in 1985. Faddis reaffirmed the Gillespie legacy during 1993, participating in memorial and retrospective programs that followed his mentor's death. He has recorded as a leader for Pablo, DCC, Concord, and Columbia. Faddis has some sessions available on CD. —*Ron Wynn*

Jon and Billy / Mar. 13, 1974 / Black Hawk 532
Jon Faddis and Billy Harper make an interesting, if, at times, somewhat mismatched team on this 1974 date recently reissued by Evidence. Faddis was then laboring to find his own voice on trumpet; his mentor, Dizzy Gillespie, remained both his predominant influence and his stylistic guiding light. Harper had won critical attention and praise for his work with Lee Morgan, and his robust tenor sax, with its twisting, spurting phrases, is well displayed throughout this date. While Faddis and Harper had differences in volume and approach, they solved things enough to prevent the songs from being ragged or rushed. The times were probably responsible for Sir Roland Hanna sometimes turning to electric piano; his elegant figures, precise melodies, and harmonic interplay are not as expertly articulated on electric as acoustic, which he also plays. Bassist George Mraz and drummer Motohiko Hino do their jobs satisfactorily, though Mraz's work is a bit more distinctive than Hino's. But the date's value is in hearing where Harper and Faddis, as well as jazz itself, were in the mid '70s and then comparing how far they and the music have and have not come since then. Unfortunately, these players are currently in better shape than the idiom. —*Ron Wynn*

★ **Youngblood** / Jan. 8-9, 1976 / Pablo 2310765

   Good and Plenty / Aug. 1978-Sep. 1978 / DRZ 908

☆ **Legacy** / Aug. 1985 / Concord Jazz 4291

A tremendous mainstream session on which Harold Land (ts) and Kenny Barron (p) make excellent contributions. —*Ron Wynn*

Into the Faddisphere / **i.** May 2-8, 1989 / Epic 45266
Check out "Ciribiribin" for a taste of Faddis and his trumpet acrobatics. It also has pianist Renee Rosnes and drummer Ralph Peterson. —*Michael G. Nastos*

○ **Hornucopia** / **i.** 1990 / Epic 46958
This is his best release. He works with his idol, Dizzy Gillespie (tpt), and makes a case for his own voice and style as well. —*Ron Wynn*

CHARLES FAMBROUGH

b. 1950
Bass / Hard bop
A fine bassist who gained notoriety for his contributions to various Art Blakey and the Jazz Messengers sessions in the '80s, Charles Fambrough has recorded as a leader during the early '90s. His huge tone, excellent accompaniment, and tasteful, careful solos have been featured on two CTI albums. Fambrough's played with Grover Washington, Jr., Kenny Garrett, Kenny Kirkland, Wynton Marsalis, Roy Hargrove, Jeff Watts, Abdullah Ibrahim, and others. His sessions are available on CD. —*Ron Wynn*

★ **Proper Angle** / **i.** 1991 / CTI 79476
Excellent bassist Charles Fambrough steps into the spotlight with his debut album as a leader. While his compositions are straightforward hard bop, he's recruited an impressive guest list. The lineup includes both Wynton and Branford Marsalis, Roy Hargrove, Kenny Kirkland, Jeff Watts, Jerry Gonzalez, and Steve Berrios. —*Ron Wynn*

Blues at Bradley's / **i.** 1993 / CTI 67235
Charles Fambrough is a bassist more felt than seen, despite the occasional bass solo. His virtues include a powerful tone, the requisite Scott LaFaroesque solo technique, rock-solid time, and the ability to lock in with different drummers. "Duck Feathers," a Fambrough-Donald Harrison ditty, sets the tone of *Blues;* Ricky Sebastian's second-line drumming leads to a JB Horns-like ensemble and various degrees of funk in solos all around. "Blues For Bu" is churchy, with Steve Turre getting in some juicy wah-wah licks. The trombonist switches to shells near the end of the new-agey "Andrea," another Fambrough original. Turre and guitarist Bobby Broom (shades of B.B. King and Kenny Burrell) are the most consistently rewarding soloists. —*Owen Cordle*, Down Beat

TAL FARLOW (Talmadge Holt Farlow)

b. Jun. 7, 1921, Greensboro, NC
Guitar / Bop, cool
Tal Farlow was a self-taught guitarist whose career began in the early '20s. During the '50s, he emerged as an extremely fast, creative stylist with a highly distinctive style forged partly by using his thumb rather than a pick. Farlow's lines and solos were clean, superbly played, and influential in their harmonic ideas and use of unusual intervals. Farlow was also a skilled inventor. He made a shorter fingerboard to allow looser tuning and a softer sound, and built a divid-

ing device that allowed guitarists to play an extra line while doing single notes. He worked with Marjorie Hyams in 1948, then joined Red Norvo's trio in 1949. When Charles Mingus became a member of the trio, it became an early '50s dynamo. Farlow left in 1953 to join the latest edition of Artie Shaw's Gramercy Five. After six months, Farlow split to form his own combo. He did several recordings in the '50s, some with Eddie Costa. But in 1958, Farlow married and semiretired. He taught, played mostly in private, and made only occasional sessions and club dates. He recorded with Sonny Criss in the late '60s for Prestige. Farlow increased his recording activity in the mid '70s, doing dates for Inner City and Concord. In 1980, he increased his public appearances as well. Farlow helped in the preparation of the documentary film *Talmadge Farlow* in 1981, and reunited with Norvo in another trio. He toured widely both in America and Europe, and was extensively praised for his performance at the 1984 Grande Parade du Jazz in Nice. There were more recordings for Concord, and he's continued with them into the '90s. Farlow material from the '50s on is available through his most recent release, *Sign of the Times*, in 1992. The Norvo trio items are also reissued on CD. — *Ron Wynn and David Nelson McCarthy*

○ **Tal Farlow Album, The** / Apr. 11, 1954-Jul. 5, 1955 / Verve 2584
This album features two groups working with guitarist Tal Farlow: bassist Oscar Pettiford, pianist Barry Galbraith, and drummer Joe Morello are on several numbers, and bassist Red Mitchell and pianist Claude Williamson are on the others. Both it and its companion, *Tal*, are highly recommended. — *Bob Rusch*, Cadence

○ **Fascinating Rhythm** / Jan. 17, 1955 / Norgran 1101

○ **Recital by Tal Farlow, A** / Apr. 25, 1955-May 4, 1955 / Norgran 1030

★ **Tal** / Mar. 1956 / PolyGram 829580
This was recorded in 1956 with Eddie Costa on piano and vibes and Vinnie Burke on drums. Tal Farlow is a most listenable guitarist, accessible without compromising either technical brilliance of depth or content. — *Bob Rusch*, Cadence

○ **Fuerst Set** / Dec. 18, 1956 / Xanadu 109
Recorded in 1956 at the home of Ed Fuerst, this is almost 50 minutes of relaxed jamming. The group was working together at the time and members were obviously comfortable not only in the setting but with themselves. On "Jordu," Farlow sounds way ahead of 1956 guitar. Swing and ideas flow freely. Farlow's voice here is enough reason to get this album, but there is also plenty of the work of Eddie Costa. He provides driving, inventive, futuristic piano work, often dipping down below middle C in a chordal fugal attack, but always swinging. Driving is the best description of Costa's work on these recordings. Vinnie Burke handles the bass with constant drive, making drums unnecessary and unmissed. Gene Williams's vocals appear briefly on "Out of Nowhere" and are pleasant, but neither attract one to nor detract from this exceptional album. — *Bob Rusch*, Cadence

○ **Second Set** / Dec. 18, 1956 / Xanadu 119
Like its predecessor, *Fuerst Set*, this LP of four extended performances recorded in late 1956 at the New York City apartment of jazz fan Ed Fuerst continues the documentation of the remarkable trio Tal Farlow led from 1956 to 1958, which most frequently performed at the Composer in that city. The rapport between the three men—Farlow, pianist Eddie Costa, and bassist Vinnie Burke—was exemplary, and this, coupled with their individual strengths as players, made for performances of great musicality, intelligence, sensitivity, vigorous creativity, and an interactivity of conception and execution that placed the trio among the finest small groups of the period. If it is Farlow's playing that provides the chief impetus for acquiring this album, it is Costa's marvelous, invigorating piano work that will keep the listener coming back to the music. Bassist Burke, now retired from music, proved to be a rock in his handling of the rhythmic-harmonic function

that was his role in the group. His steady, unobtrusively imaginative work is the anchor that permits Farlow's and Costa's more overtly exciting featured playing. — *Pete Welding*, Down Beat

○ **This Is Tal Farlow** / Jun. 1958 / Verve 8289

○ **Guitar Artistry of Tal Farlow, The** / 1959-1968 / Verve 8370

Poppin' and Burnin' / i. 195? / Verve

Guitar Player / Sep. 23, 1969+Oct. 1955 / Prestige 24042
This fine compilation of Farlow's '60s Prestige material is hard to find. — *Ron Wynn*

Tal Farlow Returns / Sep. 23, 1969 / Original Jazz Classics 356

Sign of the Times, A / Aug. 2, 1976 / Concord Jazz 4026

On Stage / Aug. 1976 / Concord Jazz 143
Farlow's reunion with Red Norvo (vib), plus Hank Jones (p) and Ray Brown (b). — *Ron Wynn*

Tal Farlow 1978 / Sep. 15, 1977 / Concord Jazz 57

Chromatic Palette / Jan. 1981 / Concord Jazz 154

Cookin' on All Burners / Aug. 1982 / Concord Jazz 204
Excellent piano from James Williams, plus outstanding guitar by Farlow. — *Ron Wynn*

Legendary, The / i. Sep. 1984 / Concord Jazz 266

ART FARMER (Arthur Stewart Farmer)

b. Aug. 21, 1928, Council Bluffs, IA
Trumpet, flugelhorn / Hard bop
A very lyrical player, Art Farmer popularized the flugelhorn; he has played it extensively since the early '60s, and plays it almost exclusively now. Farmer has made understated, introspective solos his trademark. He's been a member of some memorable bands in different decades. But Art Farmer will be remembered most for his lush, at times sensual, at times haunting flugelhorn playing.

Farmer studied piano, violin, and bass tuba, and turned professional in 1945. He moved with his twin brother, Addison, to Los Angeles in 1945. Farmer played trumpet in the bands of Horace Henderson, Floyd Ray, Benny Carter, Gerald Wilson, and Lionel Hampton. He later worked with Johnny Otis, Joe Turner, Wardell Gray, Hampton Hawes, Teddy Edwards, Sonny Criss, and Frank Morgan before moving to New York in 1953. He recorded some of his finest solos on an album with Quincy Jones, and played in the group New Directions with Charles Mingus, Teo Macero, and Teddy Charles. He was also a member of combos led by Horace Silver and Gerry Mulligan. Farmer co-led a group with Gigi Gryce, and played and recorded with George Russell. He also played in Paris and recorded with Tony Ortega. Farmer made seven albums for Prestige in the mid '50s, playing with Art Taylor, Sonny Rollins, Kenny Clarke, Gryce and others. He recorded with Jones again in 1957, this time for ABC Paramount. There were combo dates on Contemporary in 1958, and both small and large group sessions on United Artists.

Farmer and Benny Golson formed the Jazztet in 1959, a solid group that featured a young McCoy Tyner on piano. They made some first-rate albums for Argo before disbanding in 1962. Farmer did a big-band date on Mercury in 1962 with Oliver Nelson, and co-led a group with Jim Hall until 1964. He gradually adjusted his style, playing in a softer, more lyrical manner.

Farmer began playing more flugelhorn, and finally almost dropped the trumpet. He made three Columbia albums in 1966 and 1967; one with Golson, another recorded live at the Museum of Modern Art, and the third a studio session titled *Plays Great Jazz Hits*. After recording with Golson in 1966, Farmer moved to Vienna in 1968. While in Vienna, he performed with the Clarke-Boland Big Band, with the Osterreichiscer Rundfunk orchestra, and with Peter Herbolzheimer. He stayed in Vienna until 1977.

Farmer stayed busy with sessions for Campi, MPS, Mainstream, Sonet, and Pye throughout the late '60s and early '70s. These were recorded in places such as Rome,

Heidelberg, and Vienna. The 1971 release, *Homecoming*, was with Cedar Walton, with whom he established a profitable musical relationship in the early and mid '70s. The duo made some superb dates for Inner City that also included Sam Jones and Billy Higgins, plus Clifford Jordan for quintet sessions. These were made between 1975 and 1976. Farmer recorded with Art Pepper in 1977, then did five sessions with CTI between 1977 and 1979. He led a quintet and quartet that toured America, Europe, Japan, Austria, Germany, and Switzerland during the late '70s. During the '80s, Farmer maintained his hectic recording pace, cutting sessions for Soul Note, Concord and Contemporary, and for some Japanese labels. There was an excellent tribute album to Billy Strayhorn in 1987 for Soul Note. He and Golson reformed the Jazztet in 1982, touring and recording. Farmer also performed with Chico Freeman in 1983. During the late '80s and early '90s, among his many projects was a reunion album with some survivors of the Central Avenue scene of the '50s. Farmer's still a busy leader and jazz contributor with many dates available on CD. —*Ron Wynn*

○ **Early Art** / Jan. 20, 1954+Nov. 9, 1954 / New Jazz 8258

Art Farmer Quintet, The / May 19, 1954 / Prestige 241

When Farmer Met Gryce / May 19, 1954 / Prestige 072

Two Trumpets / Aug. 3, 1956 / Original Jazz Classics 18

★ **Farmer's Market** / Nov. 23, 1956 / New Jazz 398
Quintet. A top release from the '50s, with precise, deftly played solos, compositions, and arrangements. It has a wonderful all-star lineup, and is one of the rare occasions where Farmer worked on record with his brother Addison. —*Ron Wynn*

Portrait of Art Farmer / Apr. 19, 1958+May 1, 1958 / Contemporary 166

Modern Art / Sep. 10-14, 1958 / Blue Note 84459
An outstanding reissue of late-'50s sessions with Bill Evans (p) and Benny Golson (ts). —*Ron Wynn*

★ **Meet the Jazztet** / Feb. 6-10, 1960 / Chess 91550
With Benny Golson. The first Jazztet recording and definitive ensemble jazz. Featuring McCoy Tyner (p) and Curtis Fuller (t). —*Michael G. Nastos*

☆ **Art** / Sep. 1960 / Argo 678

Live at the Half Note / Dec. 6-7, 1963 / Atlantic 90666

○ **Jazz at the Smithsonian** / i. 1965 / PolyGram 1272

○ **From Vienna with Art** / Sep. 7, 1970 / MPS 741
I find this record to be decidedly superior to Farmer's recently issued effort on the Mainstream label called *Homecoming*.... Thoughtful introspective solos are Farmer's forte, and he gives us some nice ones here that come as an oasis in the desert of free playing and rock-oriented screamers. Jimmy Heath, who'd been a longtime associate of Farmer, completes the frontline. Heath is a solid, mature tenor saxophonist who added the soprano sax and flute to his bag of instruments. He handled both with professional acumen.... I first became aware of the talented Viennese pianist Fritz Pauer from his performance on the Saba recording by Don Menza entitled *Morning Song*.... Those unfamiliar with this imaginative keyboard exponent will discover his abilities on this record.... The rhythm section is completed by Jimmy Woode on bass and newcomer Erich Bachtragl, another musician from Vienna, on drums. They provide a solid foundation. —*Peter Friedman, Coda*

○ **Homecoming** / Jul. 1971 / Mainstream 332

★ **Gentle Rain** / i. 1971-1972 / Mainstream 716

○ **On the Road** / Jul. 26-28, 1976 / Contemporary 478
I have not heard Art Farmer (flugelhorn) play so well and work so hard on a record in many, many years! Comparing this to Farmer's 1979 CTI work, and the like, is similar to listening to Sidney Bechet in the '30s and early '40s, and then later in the '50s, with those French bands. The magic was always somewhere, but it became little more than reflex motion. I could carry on about the Bunny Berigan lineage, the "implied" beat, or Charlie Parker, Art Pepper, and pot, but let

us just call it great creative improvised music: jazz. Forget the era or style for a moment and listen. The message is in the music. —*Bob Rusch, Cadence*

Big Blues / Feb. 1978 / Columbia 45220

Art Farmer Quintet at Boomer's / i. Sep. 1981 / Inner City 6024
Fine small combo jazz by an underrated group. Trumpet and flugelhorn player Art Farmer heads a unit with soulful tenor saxophonist Clifford Jordan, plus an excellent rhythm section featuring pianist Cedar Walton, bassist Sam Jones, and drummer Billy Higgins. They were among the '70s' finest groups, especially those doing mainstream material, but didn't get the recognition they deserved, even from the jazz community. —*Ron Wynn*

Work of Art / Sep. 1981 / Concord Jazz 179

☆ **Maiden Voyage** / Mar. 1983 / Denon 7071

○ **Jazztet, The: Moment to Moment** / i. May 1983 / Soul Note 1066
Two decades (1986) down the road, the reactivated Jazztet still reveres the old values. Would that every hard bop group working now shared this sextet's high level of commitment and aversion to falling into ruts. On *Moment to Moment*, Benny Golson's tenor is particularly arresting, with its post-Lester Young drive, a rapid vibrato under Coleman Hawkins's wing, and a chocolate-syrup tone. He upstages his fellow horn players, even if Curtis Fuller's trombone tone is fat as butter and Art Farmer's flugelhorn's storytelling powers are sharp. Unfailingly tasteful but rarely shy, Ray Drummond shows why he's one of the best mainstream bassists around; drummer Albert Heath came ready to play, keeping up a steady chatter over and above his steady timekeeping. Pianist Mickey Tucker has the chops to hold his own in this company, even on a headily brisk "Farmer's Market." —*Kevin Whitehead, Cadence*

In Concert with Lionel Hampton / i. 1984 / Rhino 79645
With Lionel Hampton. Both have been represented on record with better results, but this is still a good mid-'80s release. —*Ron Wynn*

Back to the City / Feb. 21-22, 1986 / Contemporary 14020
With the Golson Jazztet. This fine update of the vintage Jazztet format has high-quality help from Curtis Fuller (t). —*Ron Wynn*

Real Time / Feb. 1986 / Contemporary 14034

Something to Live for—the Music of Billy Strayhorn / Jan. 14-15, 1987 / Contemporary 14029
The music of Billy Strayhorn. This is a beautiful tribute to Billy Strayhorn. Clifford Jordan (ts) and James Williams (p) are sublime. The CD has a bonus cut. —*Ron Wynn*

☆ **Blame It on My Youth** / Feb. 4-8, 1988 / Contemporary 14042
Sensitivity, subtlety, taste, artistry: all thy names are Art Farmer. The group was no hastily thrown-together unit. Saxophonist Clifford Jordan, a longtime colleague, continued to deepen his expression; James Williams (piano) had long since picked up the jazz torch with skill and authority; Rufus Reid (bass) was the very pillar of swing society (and his notes were so true); and drummer Victor Lewis struck the perfect balance between pulse and volume. His solos are terse, witty, and well-ventilated. The album's repertoire is intelligently varied. The two classic standards that open and close the set are, respectively, Oscar Levant's "Blame It On My Youth" and Alec Wilder's "I'll Be Around," both quartet numbers. The first spotlights Farmer's exquisite muted work, finding those notes that laser through to your heart, unclogging arteries and unlocking feelings. "Around" is a feature for Jordan's self-contained, low-flame tenor. The originals come from Austrian pianist Fritz Pauer in a "Fairytale Countryside," which could serve as part of a film score, but stands nicely on its own. Ex-Messenger pianist Donald Brown plays on "The Smile of the Snake," which is also atmospheric, but evocative of North Africa or the East. Jordan plays on "Third Avenue," a bop anthem that could be prof-

itably picked up by other combos. Jordan is on tenor here, but on "Fairytale" and "Snake" he plays the less-personalized soprano. Benny Carter plays on "Summer Serenade," treated at a mellow tempo that allows Farmer to caress the song. Williams does "Progress Report," a burner on which the composer leads off the soloing. —*Ira Gitler,* Jazz Times

Ph.D / Apr. 3-4, 1989 / Contemporary 14055
Quintet. The follow-up to *Blame It on My Youth,* with Clifford Jordan (sax) and James Williams (p). —*Michael G. Nastos*

Central Avenue Reunion / May 26-27, 1989 / Contemporary 14057
This is an outstanding update of the overlooked West Coast sound by Black jazz players. —*Ron Wynn*

○ **Summer Knows** / Inner City 6004
The Summer Knows is a set of pop tunes that are easy listening in the best sense: soothing and mellow, but never dull or sticky. Art Farmer's understated, almost effortless flugelhorn style blends perfectly with Cedar Walton's more busy, down-to-earth piano approach, and they are both complemented by an adventurous rhythm team. Bassist Sam Jones reaches high on the neck and bends notes at will, while drummer Billy Higgins fires off tom-tom rolls and cymbal flourishes that always fit right in. All four have free reign, but no one is in a hurry, and the set glides smoothly from one number to the next. —*Ben Sandmel,* Down Beat

To Duke with Love / Inner City 6014

JOE FARRELL (Joseph Carl Firrantello)

b. Dec. 16, 1937, Chicago Heights, IL, **d.** Jan. 10, 1986, Los Angeles, CA
Tenor and alto saxophone, flute, oboe / Bop, Latin jazz, early jazz-rock
An all-star caliber session musician, Joe Farrell seldom received the accolades he deserved during his lifetime. He was a vigorous uptempo soloist and an excellent ballad stylist whose sound on any of several instruments he played was always impeccable. Farrell could play anything from a torrid blues lick to a soulful lament or a wailing solo. He was successful playing Afro-Latin jazz, soul, and R&B dates, working in a two- or three-horn frontline for Elvin Jones, or backing Flora Purim or Aretha Franklin. The tenor saxophone was his main horn, but Farrell also played flute, soprano sax, clarinet, and occasionally oboe. Farrell began on clarinet at age 11, and studied music education at the University of Illinois. After graduation in 1959, he moved to New York. He played with Maynard Ferguson and Slide Hampton, and recorded with Charles Mingus and Dizzy Reece in the early '60s. Farrell later played with Jaki Byard, with the Thad Jones-Mel Lewis orchestra, and with Elvin Jones in the late '60s and into the '70s. He cut his debut sessions as a leader in 1970. Farrell was a charter member of Return to Forever in 1971, and split his time between jazz-rock, bebop, hard bop, pop, and soul in the '70s. Farrell joined the Mingus Dynasty in 1979 and toured America and Europe with the group. He co-led a band with Louis Hayes in the mid '80s. Farrell recorded for CTI, Xanadu, Contemporary, and Timeless. He has some sessions available on CD. —*Ron Wynn*

★ **Follow Your Heart** / Jul. 1+2, 1970 / CTI 6003

○ **Joe Farrell Quartet** / i. Jul. 1+2, 1970 / Columbia 40694
Quartet. Early CTI recordings for this West Coast transplant. Farrell's flute and sax are well represented. This must-buy also includes John McLaughlin (g) and Chick Corea (p). Includes "Follow Your Heart." —*Michael G. Nastos*

Outback / Nov. 1971 / CTI 8005
Multi-instrumentalist Joe Farrell was among a select crew of jazz veterans who enjoyed unprecedented attention when they recorded for CTI in the early '70s. This session was his second at the label, and features Farrell playing tenor and soprano sax, flute, alto flute, and piccolo with equal facility. He heads a first-rate band with pianist Chick Corea, guitarist

John McLaughlin, bassist Dave Holland, and drummer Jack DeJohnette. This has been reissued on CD. —*Ron Wynn*

☆ **Moon Germs** / Nov. 21, 1972 / Columbia 40929
Another early CTI recording. Farrell's flute and sax are well represented. A must-buy, though a bit electric. —*Michael G. Nastos*

Benson and Farrell / Mar. 1976-Sep. 1976 / CTI 6069

Skateboard Park / Jan. 29, 1979 / Xanadu

MALACHI FAVORS

b. 1937
Bass / Early free, modern creative
He's well known as a member of the Art Ensemble of Chicago, but Malachi Favors Magostus is also a first-rate bassist outside that organization. He's played with many bebop, hard bop, and free groups, and his rigorous accompaniment is a vital piece of the Art Ensemble puzzle. He also plays zither, melodica, harmonica, banjo, and percussion. Favors has been a bassist since age 15. He worked with Andrew Hill in the mid '50s, and played with Dizzy Gillespie and Freddie Hubbard. Favors joined Muhal Richard Abrams Experimental Band in 1961, and played in Roscoe Mitchell's pre-Art Ensemble quartets and trios. Favors has recorded with Archie Shepp, Sunny Murray, Dewey Redman, Lester Bowie, Abrams, and Mitchell, in addition to the many Art Ensemble releases. He can be heard on all Art Ensemble dates, and on reissues by Bowie, Mitchell, and others. His late '70s unaccompanied solo date is available through mail order; it was issued on the group's own AECO label. —*Ron Wynn*

VICTOR FELDMAN (Victor Stanley Feldman)

b. Apr. 7, 1934, London, England, **d.** May 12, 1987, Los Angeles, CA
Piano, vibes / Cool
A versatile British pianist and vibist, Victor Feldman found a home in America playing effective bebop, cool, swing, big band, and rock, and contributing to several major sessions. Feldman was a fine composer and a classy, often energetic soloist. A self-taught child prodigy, he played with the Glenn Miller band at age ten. Feldman came to America in 1955, then worked with Woody Herman and the Lighthouse All Stars. He played with Cannonball Adderley in 1960 and 1961, backed Peggy Lee in '61, and toured the Soviet Union with Benny Goodman in 1962. Feldman worked with Miles Davis in 1963 and wrote "Seven Steps to Heaven." He turned down Davis's offer of a permanent job because Feldman did not want to hit the road and leave his wife; Herbie Hancock later got the gig. Feldman played with June Christy in 1965, then became a steady session player. He made it into the pop world bigtime in the mid '70s and early '80s working with Steely Dan. Feldman recorded in Britian in the '40s and '50s with John Dankworth, Stan Tracey, Ronnie Scott, and Tubby Hayes, among others. His American label debut was with Keynote, but it was unissued; he later recorded for Mode, Contemporary, Riverside, World Pacific, Concord Jazz, and Palo Alto through the '80s. There are several Feldman titles available on CD. —*Ron Wynn*

Suite Sixteen / Aug. 1955-Sep. 1955 / Original Jazz Classics 1768

With Mallets a Fore Thought / Sep. 1957 / VSOP 13
This very early release, with Feldman's vibes technique emerging, is almost impossible to find. —*Ron Wynn*

★ **Arrival of Victor Feldman, The** / Jan. 1959 / Contemporary 268
This date proclaimed the beginning of Victor Feldman's American recording career as a leader. This January 21 and 22, 1958 recording has some strong jazz performances on its program, but not a particularly strong personality. Feldman reaches back and forth between vibes and piano, making clear, rich, unequivocating pronouncements on both instruments. He is joined by Scott LaFaro (bass) and Stan Levey, who are also effective, particularly LaFaro, whose bass work

is not only very impressive, but so prominent that, without prior knowledge, one might think that this is his session (the vibes-piano trade-off suggests a quartet). The two Feldman originals, "Chasing Shadows" and "Minor Lament," are both catchy, but very derivative of other jazz standards by Milt Jackson and Thelonious Monk. —*Bob Rusch,* Cadence

Merry Olde Soul / Jan. 6+11, 1961 / Riverside 402

Latinsville / Mar. 1961 / Contemporary 580

★ **Artful Dodger** / Jan. 26, 1977 / Concord Jazz 4038
This album brought pianist Victor Feldman back to the recording studio with the standard trio format. His accompanists (Monty Budwig on bass and Colin Barlay on drums) established an easy rapport with the Feldman style, which was very much out front and on top of the beat and just about everything else. On tunes like "Isn't She Lovely," he sounds very much like Ramsey Lewis before he discovered electric. "Agitation," "The Artful Dodger," and "Haunted Ballroom" are interesting lines, but Feldman does not really get an opportunity to stretch out on these tunes because of the inclusion of so many titles on this set. "Sponge Money," which is definitely Sonny Rollins's "St. Thomas," is oddly credited to Feldman; perhaps the title is a double entendre. Be that as it may, this certainly does not indicate too much respect for Rollins's popularization of this basic West Indian folk theme. "Haunted Ballroom," on side one, is interesting because it presents trumpeter/vocalist Jack Sheldon playing the trumpet and singing. Sheldon's appropriately raspy voice fits the mood of this piece, which is dedicated to the swing era big bands. The lyrics make suitable allusions to big bands and the tunes that are associated with them. The record concludes with and old big-band recording of "I've Got Rhythm" on which Feldman, who was still a youngster at the time, takes a Gene Krupa-like drum solo. —*Spencer R. Weston,* Cadence

To Chopin with Love / May 7-8, 1983 / Palo Alto 8056

Fiesta / Jun. 8, 1984-Aug. 1984 / TBA 8066
Good arrangements. Feldman plays with some vigor, though not as strongly as on his more jazz-oriented releases. —*Ron Wynn*

Best of Feldman and the Generation Band / Nova 8922

MAYNARD FERGUSON

b. May 4, 1928, Verdun, Quebec, Canada
Trumpet, bandleader / Cool, progressive big band
A dazzling stylist with an incredible range, Ferguson got notoriety through stints with Boyd Raeburn and Stan Kenton in the late '40s and early '50s. He had his own band from 1957-1965, then began a gradual shift into jazz-rock and pop with the M. F. Horn group. He first increased then shrunk his band, did rock and big-selling film soundtracks, then returned to jazz. At his best, he can blow paint off the roof, then make you sit up and notice his ballad skills. —*Ron Wynn*

○ **Maynard Ferguson Octet** / Apr. 25, 1955 / EmArcy 36021

○ **Birdland Dreamband, The** / i. Sep. 1956 / Bluebird 6455

Message from Newport, A / May 6+8, 1958 / Roulette 59024
Trumpeter Maynard Ferguson leads his big band in a fiery date recorded in 1958, though not at the Newport Festival, but in New York. He was playing no-holds-barred, straighthead jazz at this time, and doing it with gusto. The band includes Bill Chase in his pre-fusion period, Slide Hampton, and Carmen Leggion, and had a good mix between veterans and emerging youngsters. This material has been reissued on Fresh Sound and Roulette CDs. —*Ron Wynn*

★ **Maynard** / Mar. 1961 / Capitol 93900

○ **Blues Roar** / Dec. 1+11, 1964 / Mainstream 717

M.F. Horn/M.F. Horn Two / Feb. 1970-Jan. 1972 / Columbia 33660

○ **Maynard Ferguson's Horn—Vol. 2** / Jan. 1972 / Columbia 31709

○ **Maynard Ferguson's Horn—Vol. 4: Live at Jimmy's** / 1973 / Columbia 32732

○ **Maynard Ferguson's Horn—Vol. 3** / 1973 / Columbia 32403

Carnival / 1978 / Columbia 35480

Conquistador / 1978 / Columbia 34457

○ **Big Bop Nouveau** / 1989-1990 / Intima 73390
Recent session featuring Maynard Ferguson's latest big band. He's returned to conventional jazz material, though the volume remains loud and the mood aggressive. But Ferguson does a wide range of material rather than just earsplitting high-note theatrics, and the band plays the arrangements well. There's no great second soloist, but Ferguson's presence helps compensate. —*Ron Wynn*

MONGEZI FEZA

b. 1945, **d.** 1975
Drums, percussion / World fusion
A marvelous drummer and percussionist and a beloved individual, Mongezi Feza was the anchor for some great international jazz ensembles before his tragic and premature death in the mid '70s. Feza caught the ear of Chris McGregor as a 16-year-old playing with Ronnie Beer's Swinging City Six in Capetown, South Africa. McGregor invited Feza to join his band, the Blue Notes. When they moved to London in 1965, Feza went with them. He subsequently joined McGregor's Brotherhood of Breath, and was a pivotal soloist and rhythm session catalyst. Feza moved to Denmark in 1972, where he played with fellow South African expatriate Johnny Dyani and percussionist Okay Temiz. They recorded in Sweden for Sonet records. He also recorded with Dudu Pukwana in 1973, but died two years later. McGregor recorded the poignant album *Blue Notes for Mongezi* in his honor. Feza did not have any sessions as a leader. —*Ron Wynn*

FIREHOUSE FIVE PLUS TWO (Firehouse Five + Two)

Jazz ensemble / Dixieland
One of the most popular traditional jazz ensembles in the '50s and early '60s, the original Firehouse Five Plus Two was mostly talented players taken from the staff of Walt Disney's animation studios in Hollywood. The ringers were clarinetists Tom Sharpsteen and George Probert, who were respected widely. The band specialized in upbeat, often hilarious traditional numbers, many containing comic vocals and refrains. Trombonist Ward Kimball founded the group in 1949. The ensemble included a bass saxophone or tuba and a washboard, which gave them some instrumental distinction as well as their humorous sound. The group was known for thematic recordings such as *The Firehouse Five Plus Two at Disneyland,* and *The Firehouse Five Plus Two Goes South.* They have several releases available on CD. —*Ron Wynn*

Firehouse Five, The / i. 1953 / Good Time Jazz 16

Dixieland Favorites / Sep. 29, 1958-Mar. 14, 1969 / Good Time Jazz 10040

○ **Firehouse Five Plus Two Crashes a Party** / Sep. 29, 1958-Nov. 10, 1959 / Good Time Jazz 10038

★ **16 Dixieland Favorites** / i. 195z / Good Time Jazz 60008

CLARE FISCHER

b. Oct. 22, 1928, Durand, MI
Keyboards / Progressive big band, Latin jazz
A good pianist and composer, Clare Fischer has succeeded Cal Tjader as the ranking non-Latino bandleader recording Afro-Latin and Latin jazz dates. Fischer's penchant and affinity for Latin rhythms led him to record several compositions with a Latin flavor in the '60s, a trend he's continued into the '90s. He also wrote the widely played "Pensativa" and "Morning." His style influenced Herbie Hancock's. Fischer earned undergraduate and graduate degrees at Michigan State in the '50s, where he also developed an early interest

in Latin music. He wrote arrangements for the West Point band in the early '50s, then served as accompanist and arranger for the Hi-Los. Fischer did the arrangements for Dizzy Gillespie's album, *A Portrait of Duke Ellington,* in 1960, and recorded several compositions with his band in the '60s. He also cut some of the earliest bossa nova material in America during 1962, and began mixing bebop and Latin jazz on his dates. Fischer doubled as an organist. He made an acclaimed duo recording with Gary Foster in 1982, but otherwise has blended bebop and Latin jazz on his sessions for Revelation, Discovery, Pacific Jazz, Trend, and Concord Picante. He has several dates available on CD. — *Ron Wynn*

Salsa Picante / 1963 / Discovery 817
Nice set with Fischer and company in a salsa groove. This is among his hardest, most energetic dates with plenty of strong solos, intense percussive dialogues, and extended jamming. —*Ron Wynn*

☆ **America the Beautiful** / **i.** 1974 / Discovery 786
★ **Machacha** / May 16-17, 1979 / Discovery 835
Salsa picante at its instrumental best. Latin jazz-hots with Rick Zunigar (g), Gary Foster on saxophone and flute, and Alex Acuna and Poncho Sanchez on percussion. —*Michael G. Nastos*

ELLA FITZGERALD

b. Apr. 25, 1918, Newport News, VA
Vocals / Swing, ballads & blues
Ella Fitzgerald stands as the most accomplished jazz singer alive, and is in the pantheon of anyone who has ever performed. Though she has a comparatively small voice, she's compensated for that with a very wide range that she controls expertly and with an amazing ability to swing. She didn't invent "scat" singing, but turned it into an art form as hypnotic and inspiring as any great trumpet, sax, or piano solo. Fitzgerald could have been a professional mimic, and has imitated many famous vocalists flawlessly in concert. She's a tremendous interpreter of prerock pop and show tunes, though she is not as gifted on sad songs. Her influence on numerous singers, from the '40s into the present, has been immense, and she has influenced vocalists in England, Germany, Japan, and Africa.

Fitzgerald was orphaned in early childhood, and moved to New York to attend an orphanage school in Yonkers. She won an amateur contest sponsored by the Apollo Theatre in 1934, which led to an engagement with Chick Webb's band. From 1936 to 1939, Fitzgerald was a celebrity and hit vocalist, especially with the singles "A-Tisket, A-Tasket," and "Undecided." She took over Webb's band following his death in 1939, leading it until 1942 when she went solo. During the '40s, Fitzgerald issued recordings in both jazz and pop settings. Such records as "I'm Making Believe" and "Into Each Life Some Rain Must Fall" with the Ink Spots (one of three duets she did with them) continued her chart run. She sang in the 1942 Abbott & Costello film *Ride 'em Cowboy,* then enjoyed another successful duet in 1946, this time with Louis Jordan on "Stone Cold Dead in the Market." Fitzgerald began working with promoter/producer Norman Granz's Jazz at the Philharmonic in 1946, and the tours and projects won her a huge international following along with a big American audience. Fitzgerald also sang in a group led by her husband at the time, Ray Brown, from 1948 to 1952, and made periodic film appearances. Her biggest appearance was in *Pete Kelly's Blues,* a '55 movie whose soundtrack made the charts (Fitzgerald shared the spotlight with Peggy Lee).

After a decade, Fitzgerald severed her ties with Decca and joined Granz's new company, Verve. One of their first projects was a series of two-record "songbooks" dedicated to the nation's premier songwriters like Cole Porter (the lead release), Rodgers and Hart, and George and Ira Gershwin. Nelson Riddle, among others, provided jazz-tinged arrangements, and these sets enabled Fitzgerald to reach, or cross over, to a general audience. She also had smash albums

singing with Louis Armstrong (with whom she'd make several other successful records), Count Basie, Ellington, Marty Paich, and Riddle. Granz, her manager since the late '40s, kept her very busy, issuing her records regularly and booking constant festival dates, where she'd work with Ellington, Basie, Oscar Peterson, Tommy Flanagan (her regular pianist for many years), and Joe Pass. She kept going into the '70s, expanding her repertoire with an album of Afro-Latin music, *Embraces Antonio Carlos Jobim,* and more projects with Basie, Riddle, Brown, Pass, and Flanagan. Fitzgerald had eye surgery in the early '70s, and has since battled recurring vision problems and illnesses in the '80s. A recognized treasure, she still makes an occasional appearance. Several retrospective sets were issued in 1993 in recognition of Fitzgerald's 75th birthday. –*Ron Wynn with William Ruhlman*

○ **Ella Fitzgerald 1935–1937** / **i.** Jun. 1935-Jan. 1937 / Classics 500

With the Chick Webb Band (1935-1938) / 1935-1938 / Pearl Flapper 9762

○ **Ella Fitzgerald 1937–1938** / **i.** Jan. 1937-May 1938 / Classics 506

○ **Ella Fitzgerald 1938–1939** / **i.** May 1938-Feb. 1939 / Classics 518

○ **Ella Fitzgerald 1939** / **i.** Feb. 1939-Jun. 1939 / Classics 525

○ **Ella Fitzgerald 1939–1940** / **i.** Aug. 1939-May 1940 / Classics 566

○ **Lullabies of Birdland** / Oct. 4, 1945-Mar. 19, 1947 / Decca 8149

Miss Ella Fitzgerald and Mr. Nelson Riddle / Apr. 28, 1949-Sep. 21, 1949 / Decca 8696

Pete Kelly's Blues (Soundtrack) / May 3, 1955 / Decca 8166

★ **Sings the Cole Porter Songbook (Complete)** / Feb. 7, 1956-Mar. 27, 1956 / Verve 821990

Sings Cole Porter / Feb. 7-9, 1956 / Verve 4049

Sings More Cole Porter / Feb. 7, 1956-Mar. 27, 1956 / Verve 4050

Tribute to Cole Porter, A / Feb. 7, 1956-Mar. 27, 1956 / Verve 4066

○ **Ella and Louis Together** / **i.** Aug. 18, 1956 / Laserlight 15706
The master and one of his greatest pupil/trainees, Ella Fitzgerald. –*Ron Wynn*

★ **Sings the Rodgers and Hart Songbook** / Aug. 1956 / Verve
Ella Fitzgerald's *The Rodgers and Hart Songbook* is a winner. A complete musician with the ability to plumb each song's emotional/dramatic core, Fitzgerald forcefully communicates the sophisticated urbanity of Rodgers and Hart. As for the composer and lyricist, a checklist of their many gems should suffice. "Lover," "I Could Write a Book," "Blue Moon," "My Funny Valentine," "Little Girl Blue," "Mountain Greenery,"—they just don't write songs like that anymore. The wit of Larry Hart, the sophistication of Richard Rodgers, the consummate artistry of Ella Fitzgerald: it was a triumvirate that conquered all obstacles. –*Chuck Berg,* Down Beat

○ **Songbooks, The** / **i.** 1956-1964 / Verve 823445

With Louis Armstrong / **i.** 1956 / PolyGram 27176

★ **Ella & Louis Again** / Jul. 22-23, 1957 / Verve 4006
With Louis Armstrong. This is excellent material and wonderful vocals. –*Ron Wynn*

○ **Porgy and Bess** / Aug. 18, 1957-Oct. 15, 1957 / Verve 6040
This version of *Porgy and Bess* (recorded in 1957), with Ella Fitzgerald singing all the female parts and Louis Armstrong singing all the male parts, is as good as any version so far released. But I would rather have had less of the overly long "Overture" and more of Armstrong's trumpet playing (beautiful on "A Woman Is a Sometime Thing"); and I still find it hard to listen to Fitzgerald with her perfect diction sing "Porgy, you is my man." If you're into *Porgy and Bess,* by all

means buy this album, but if you are only interested in Ella Fitzgerald and Louis Armstrong, there is much better material available. — *Carl Brauer*, Cadence

○ **Ella Fitzgerald at the Opera House** / Oct. 19, 1957+Oct. 25, 1957 / Verve 6026

○ **Sings the Irving Berlin Songbook** / Mar. 13+19, 1958 / PolyGram 829534
This was a great period for Ella Fitzgerald; Norman Granz was her producer and she was in great voice and projection. . . . As far as jazz material goes, this songbook is greatly wanting, aside from the occasional brass solo (Harry "Sweets" Edison's patented obligatos sound present) in the Paul Weston orchestrations. It is seamless great American music and well suited to the Fitzgerald ambience. This set (March 13-19, 1958) includes all the 32 titles, in the same sequence, as the original issues. There is, however, one extra track ("Blue Skies") not on my original issues, but which does appear on a "Playboy" collection. — *Bob Rusch*, Cadence

★ **Ella in Rome: The Birthday Concert** / Apr. 1958 / Verve 835454
The singer was in peak form here, in Rome, on her 40th birthday. It's not a birthday ladies usually welcome, but it certainly doesn't seem to have distressed her in the least. After Norman Granz's introduction (in Italian *con dignita*), she comes on with an effervescent "St. Louis Blues," and then offers immediate contrasts with "These Foolish Things" and "Just Squeeze Me." Lengthy public recitals of this kind often compel unwelcome emphasis on variety in programming. But beyond the scatting and hornlike improvising in which she excels, and beyond the humor (as in her affectionate Louis Armstrong salute), her ability to convince and to enchant when singing a lyric straight, with minimal variation of the melody, helps very much to make her the greatest. The supple voice, the attractive vowel sounds (dig "Sophisticated Lady"), the intelligent phrasing, and her infallible gift for swinging at any tempo, all put her in a unique jazz category beyond the reach of tragediennes and operatics. After "Caravan" (no easy number to sing), she takes out with Oscar Peterson (piano) on a long, driving "Stompin' at the Savoy" that leaves the Romans happy, and, to be sure, smiling. That's where she also resembles Armstrong, for she sings in the cause of happiness and leaves her audiences aglow. Her accompanists do well; Gus Johnson's drumming is a big plus throughout. . . . The songs and Billy May's arrangements are superior, and, on the first CD, solos by Benny Carter are like icing on the cake. — *Stanley Dance*, Jazz Times

At the Opera House / Oct. 19, 1958 / Verve 831269
A pair of electric JATP concerts with Ella backed by the crown jewels of swing: Coleman Hawkins (ts), Lester Young (ts), and Roy Eldridge (tpt). — *Ron Wynn*

Ella Swings Lightly / Nov. 22, 1958 / PolyGram 517535
CD reissue featuring Ella Fitzgerald's flowing vocals and Marty Paich's Dek-tette band backing her. This is among several hit albums that Fitzgerald enjoyed in the '50s, when she was reaching the mass audience cutting prerock standards. The CD has three bonus cuts. — *Ron Wynn*

Ella Sings Gershwin / i. 1958 / MCA 215

○ **Sings the George & Ira Gershwin Songbook [box]** / i. 1959 / Verve 825024

Sings the Harold Arlen Songbook / Aug. 1, 1960-Jan. 16, 1961 / Verve 817526
Available for many years only on French Verve, *The Harold Arlen Songbook* appears, at last, on the domestic label and takes its place with Ella Fitzgerald's other remarkable songbooks: Cole Porter, Rodgers and Hart, the Gershwins, and Duke Ellington. If anything, the Arlen set is the most successful of this fine series. But of course, the triumph of the *Arlen Songbook* is mainly Fitzgerald's. Not only warm jazz feeling, but a lyrical restraint characterizes her work here, which is wholly sympathetic to Arlen's strong sentimentality,

but which nevertheless refuses to deliver his compositions as torch songs. "My Shining Hour," for example, is especially vulnerable to the blandishments of the torchbearer. Fitzgerald, however, treats it as a lovingly measured anthem, breathing the melody's long lines with the kind of control for which vintage Sinatra is justly admired. Nothing can be more camp than "The Man That Got Away," but it is heard for the intensely moving claustrophobia of its dead-march cadence and ruthlessy limited melodic range. Fitzgerald reveals the song as an austere masterpiece. — *Alan Axelrod*, Down Beat

In Berlin / i. 1960 / PolyGram 25670
This brings back Ella Fitzgerald's performance of February 13, 1960, with Paul Smith (piano), Jim Hall (guitar), Wilfred Middlebrooks (bass), and Gus Johnson (drums). I've always enjoyed Fitzgerald live, and this program brings together some of her old standbys along with some not-so-typical material. The performance is marked by the usual joie de vivre typical of Fitzgerald, but it fails to reach the exuberant heights that often climax her performances. — *Bob Rusch*, Cadence

○ **Ella Returns to Berlin** / Feb. 1961 / Verve 837758
This is a new release of a concert that Ella Fitzgerald gave on February 11, 1961 in Berlin. This CD has a little of the blues and ballads and a great deal of swinging and scatting on such fare as "Take the 'A' Train." In a strong, girlish voice, as she faced her 43rd birthday, Fitzgerald made a joyful noise on her hits "Rock It for Me Mr. Paganini" and "Mack the Knife" with her unequaled mastery of time. When Fitzgerald lets fly with "Anything Goes," it does. Listen for the strong bass of Wilfred Middlebrooks, and the remarkable accompaniment by Oscar Peterson, whose virtuosity doesn't get in her way, on "This Can't Be Love." — *Leslie Gourse*, Jazz Times

Clap Hands, Here Comes Charlie! / Jun. 22-23, 1961 / Verve 835646

Ella Swings Gently with Nelson / Nov. 13, 1961-Dec. 27, 1961 / Verve 4055
A classic album that matches Nelson Riddle's arrangements and orchestrations with Ella Fitzgerald's soaring, triumphant vocals. Riddle had provided the arrangements for several Fitzgerald songbook projects, and knew the right way to fit the strings behind her. This has not been reissued on CD. — *Ron Wynn*

Ella Swings Brightly with Nelson / Nov. 13, 1961-Dec. 27, 1961 / Verve 4054

★ **Sings the Jerome Kern Songbook** / Jan. 5-7, 1963 / Verve 825669
This double album features the works of two of the greatest composers of the American ballad or song form. Actually, more than two composers, as on the second side side lyricist Johnny Mercer collaborates with such giants as Harold Arlen, Hoagy Carmichael, and Sammy Cahn. Included in the first album are several infrequently heard Jerome Kern pieces, which are minor classics: "I'll Be Hard to Handle," "You Couldn't Be Cuter," and "She Didn't Say Yes." The second album's material is probably better known, and there are some short solo gems from Buddy DeFranco (clarinet) and Willie Smith (alto sax). All the songs are given perfect settings by Nelson Riddle, long a master of orchestration and accompaniment. I know, the writing is kind of stylized. . . . But it is still a pleasure to listen to these arrangements. Fitzgerald doesn't improvise too much here, but the situation doesn't really require stretching out, just great interpretation. Classic songs, great arrangements, and Ella Fitzgerald. Who could ask for anything more? — *Peter Leitch*, Cadence

○ **Sings the Johnny Mercer Songbook** / Oct. 20, 1964 / Verve 823247

○ **Ella Fitzgerald** / i. Jun. 1965 / Living Era 55

○ **Ella at Duke's Place** / Nov. 1965 / Verve 4070

Vocalist Ella Fitzgerald and Duke Ellington collaborated on many occasions.... *Ella at Duke's Place* was recorded in L.A. in October '65 with the full accompaniment of the Ellington band and a full Ellingtonia program. There is some real controlled beauty to some of the performances, but overall, the Ellingtonness of the performance was held somewhat in check and I get the feeling Fitzgerald was also quite aware of a definite predetermined structure to this session. I find few surprises and little sense of inspired ad-libbing. And yet one can not help but enjoy this record; such was the brilliance of its headliners. —*Bob Rusch*, Cadence

Stockholm / Feb. 7, 1966 / Pablo 2308-242

Thirty by Ella / Jul. 1968 / Capitol 48333

○ **Newport Jazz Festival: Live at Carnegie Hall** / Jul. 5, 1973 / Columbia 32557

This two-record set chronicles a series of thoroughly polished vocal performances, ranging in mood from the melancholy "Good Morning Heartbreak" to the ebullient "I've Gotta Be Me." Along the way, Fitzgerald also romps through a wide range of a dozen or so standards, 14 extemporaneous choruses of a blues (post-titled "Any Old Blues"), and a little-known bop classic, George Wallington's "Lemon Drop." The selection of material is judicious, tasteful, and refreshingly free from any jazzed-up versions of current pop tunes that a lesser singer might have been tempted to throw in to please the multitudes. Here, Fitzgerald is backed by musicians in a wide variety of musical contexts, ranging from piano only to quartet to full dance band; this musical variety is one of the album's chief virtues. Flanagan's quartet drives like mad and features some five-star comping by Pass. This guitarist also provides masterful solo accompaniment on "Don't Worry" and "Foolish Things": no fuzz tones, wah-wahs, or other gadgets, just pure, intelligent musicianship. Equal in quality is Ellis Larkins's solo piano backing on "You've Turned the Tables on Me," "Nice Work If You Can Get It," and "I've Got a Crush on You." Roughly a sixth of the concert was devoted to a large dance band's backing of Fitzgerald, which recreated the sound of the band led by her discoverer, Chick Webb. (Actually, only six of the band's members played with the original Webb orchestra.) This segment is a pure nostalgia trip; those cup-muted trumpet fills on "Indian Summer" should send chills up the spines of devotees of middle-'30s dance music. —*Jon Balleras*, Down Beat

Take Love Easy / 1973 / Pablo 2310-702

Fine and Mellow / Jan. 8, 1974 / Pablo 2310-829

Ella in London / Apr. 11, 1974 / Pablo 2310-711

Recorded in 1974 at Ronnie Scott's, this set is pure Ella Fitzgerald. She cooks with happy abandon on uptempo scat tunes like "Happy Blues" and caresses those fine timeless ballads like "The Man I Love" with her distinctive tone and phrasing. Throughout much of the record, Fitzgerald makes use of her "saxophone sound," which is sort of a rough-edged tone that comes across like a calculated hoarseness. She is also fond of dynamically building tunes, beginning easily and in a relaxed style and gradually increasing in intensity and momentum. This technique works especially well on "Sweet Georgia Brown" and "You've Got a Friend." The latter inexplicably started in the middle of a word, the result of sloppy editing, I guess. Backed by an excellent and compatible, though somewhat underrecorded quartet that gives Fitzgerald all the room she requires, she runs through a repertoire of familiar pieces with the kind of spirited joy that usually marked her best performances. —*Herb Nolan*, Down Beat

○ **Montreux '77** / 1977 / Pablo 376

Ella Fitzgerald is in excellent voice in a program of generally blue chip standards. "My Man" is built with the mastery of a great actress. "Billie's Bounce" is a solid scat line from beginning to end. The voice sounds as strong and commanding as ever. No exceptional peaks are struck, but this is satisfying Fitzgerald on stage. —*Douglas Clark*, Down Beat

☆ **Classy Pair, A** / Feb. 15, 1979 / Pablo 2312-132

Ella Abraca Jobim / Sep. 1980 / Pablo 2630-201

Best Is Yet to Come / Feb. 4-5, 1982 / Pablo 2312-138

○ **Early Years—Part 1, The** / i. 1992 / GRP 618

In her first years as a songstress, Ella Fitzgerald projected a sunny, winning personality through clear articulation, flawless intonation, and an assured grasp of swing rhythm. Chick Webbs's utterly professional dance band frames her with attention to the dynamics of its riff-based charts, but Fitzgerald carries the tunes she performed from age 17 on. As for the various tunes themselves, the lyrics Fitzgerald sings are easily as insipid as anything turned out for pop consumption today; for the most part, their melodies share a wearing sameness. Fitzgerald echoes Billie Holiday occasionally, but undercuts any sadder-and-wiser sense with an insouciant bounce. Listen to her vocal quality and forget about meaning. —*Howard Mandel*, Down Beat

75th Birthday Celebration / GRP 619

This is a nice birthday present from Ella, two CDs full of some of the most popular recordings of her Decca years. This package has the novelty hits, beginning with her first record for Decca, "A Tisket, A Tasket." And it has masterpieces from an era when a popular song might also be a musical triumph, as in "Dream a Little Dream of Me" with Louis Armstrong and "Until the Real Thing Comes Along," an exquisite duet with pianist Ellis Larkins. Whether accompanied only by piano, by Louis Jordan's little jump band, or by an elephantine orchestra like that of Gordon Jenkins or Toots Camarata, Ella maintains the artistic level by dint of her taste, purity, tonality, diction, and sovereignty over all aspects of time. On superior material, with Chick Webb, Armstrong, Larkins, Louis Jordan, Benny Carter, Bob Haggart, and Sy Oliver, she is a phenomenon. This collection reminds us that long before Norman Granz started presenting her with the dignity she had earned, she was a vocal artist (in the prehype sense of the word) and hit-maker who set a mark of quality that jazz and popular singers have been shooting for ever since. —*Doug Ramsey*, Jazz Time

TOMMY FLANAGAN (Tommy Lee Flanagan)

b. Mar. 16, 1930, Detroit, MI
Piano / Bop

Tommy Flanagan is a marvelous, often undervalued artist who established his musical reputation quickly as a Detroit teenager. He first recorded in 1945 with Dexter Gordon, moved to New York in 1956, and later worked with Ella Fitzgerald. His tenure with Fitzgerald and with Tony Bennett established the standard for backing vocalists without losing identity as a player. Flanagan is not only one of jazz's finest accompanists, he is an equally amazing bop and blues soloist with a delicate touch that is identifiable immediately. —*Ron Wynn*

○ **Cats, with John Coltrane and Kenny Burrell** / Apr. 18, 1957 / New Jazz 079

Tenor saxophonist John Coltrane was part of a April 18, 1957 blowing session along with Idrees Sulieman (trumpet), Kenny Burrell (guitar), Doug Watkins (bass), Louis Hayes (drums), and the obvious, though uncredited, leader: Tommy Flanagan (piano). This set is also present on a twofer.... Relatively speaking, I don't think it is terribly significant. —*Bob Rusch*, Cadence

○ **Complete 'overseas'** / i. Aug. 1957 / DIW 25004

○ **Jazz . . . Its Magic** / Sep. 5, 1957 / Regent 6055

A late-'50s quintet date, one of the earliest that established pianist Tommy Flanagan as a tremendous soloist and leader. He heads a superior group, with alto saxophonist Sonny Red, bassist George Tucker, trombonist Curtis Fuller, and drummer Louis Hayes. It precedes, by two years, the sessions he'd cut with Coltrane that became the *Giant Steps* album, and was done the same year he and Coltrane recorded for Prestige. Though he wasn't yet as accomplished on ballads, his harmonic brilliance was already evident. —*Ron Wynn*

○ **Plays the Music of Rodgers & Hammerstein** / Sep. 1958 / Savoy 4429

Lonely Town / Mar. 10, 1959 / Blue Note

Moodsville / i. 1960 / Original Jazz Classics 182

Tommy Flanagan Trio / May 18, 1960 / Prestige 182

Tokyo Festival / Feb. 15, 1975 / Pablo 737

Eclypso / Feb. 4, 1977 / Enja 2088
Exceptional late-'70s trio date, with pianist Tommy Flanagan displaying the hard bop proficiency that's been taken for granted because he earned a reputation as a great accompanist backing Tony Bennett and Ella Fitzgerald. His lines, phrasing, and creative solos, plus his interaction with bassist George Mraz and drummer Elvin Jones, won the album rave reviews. —*Ron Wynn*

☆ **Montreux 1977** / Jul. 13, 1977 / Pablo 372
Pianist Tommy Flanagan doesn't suffer in the least from traditionalism; whatever bop's drawbacks may be as a style today (1977), it doesn't yet sound old-fashioned. But then there is an air of skilled conventionalism about this record that makes the contents somewhat passive. The rhythm section (bassist Ketter Betts and drummer Bobby Durham), which had been together for several years as the accompanying pulse of Ella Fitzgerald, serves Flanagan effectively, but without high style. —*Douglas Clark, Down Beat*

★ **Alone Too Long** / Dec. 8, 1977 / Denon 7260

☆ **More Delights with Hank Jones** / Jan. 28, 1978 / Galaxy 5152
These are flawless performances from two absolute masters. This recording consists of alternate takes and other selections recorded at the same session that produced the previously released *Our Delights*. The material is all familiar; Tadd Dameron and Thelonious Monk are treated especially lovingly. Both pianists are part of a great Detroit piano tradition (as are Barry Harris, Sir Roland Hanna, and Kirk Lightsey, among others), and interact beautifully throughout the album. —*Peter Leitch, Cadence*

☆ **Our Delights** / Jan. 28, 1978 / Galaxy 752
Pianists Tommy Flanagan and Hank Jones are not really of the same generation, yet they play so much alike that it is difficult to tell them apart. Flanagan's solo lines tend to be a bit more boppish and convoluted, but there are plenty of passages where even this does not hold true. Jones's accompaniment is smooth and steady, like a guitar quietly strumming along with a walking bass, while Flanagan's accompaniment is choppier, punchier. This music aged well. With "Confirmation," Flanagan takes the lead and the first solo. He plays two spirited choruses while Jones comps gently underneath. The texture immediately thickens with Jones's solo, largely because of Flanagan's busier comp style. The musical energy reaches a peak during the last two choruses when the pianists trade fours, each man pushing the other to dizzier heights. There is nothing fancy about the arrangements, but there is plenty of fancy finger work, and the rapport between the two pianists is remarkable. Like two dazzling dancers, they knew when to step out and when to lend support, when to walk and when to fly. It is a masterful demonstration of mainstream piano. —*Douglas Clark, Down Beat*

Something Borrowed, Something Blue / Jan. 30, 1978 / Galaxy 473

Ballads and Blues / Nov. 15, 1978 / Inner City 3029

Super Jazz Trio / Nov. 21, 1978 / RCA

Together with Kenny Barron / Dec. 6, 1978 / Denon 7263

You're Me / Feb. 24, 1980 / Phontastic

Plays Music of Harold Arlen / 1980 / Inner City 1071

○ **Magnificent Tommy Flanagan** / Jun. 2, 1981 / Progressive 7059
Producer Gus Statiras of Progressive allowed the trio on *The Magnificent Tommy Flanagan* two days to record eight tunes. The extra time and polish is evident with this trio

Jazz Flugelhorn

| Joe Bishop |
| First Introduced in Woody Herman's Band in 1936 |

| Shorty Rogers–early 1950s |

| Miles Davis (1957) on *Miles Ahead* |

After 1970 – Many Players:
Chet Baker – Bill Coleman
Art Farmer – Thad Jones
Clark Terry – Harry Beckett
Kenny Wheeler – Chuck Mangione
Lester Bowie – Woody Shaw
Bobby Shew – Lew Soloff
Johnny Coles – Ian Carr
Donald Byrd – Billy Butterfield
Teddy Buckner – Freddie Hubbard

working on reasonably familiar ground. The two exceptions might be an old Billie Holiday classic "Good Morning Heartache" and Irving Berlin's "Cange Patterns." Both Flanagan's touch and George Mraz's (bass) sound are exceptional, and this entire album was well-planned and tasty beyond just playing choruses and trading fours. —*Jerry L. Atkins, Cadence*

○ **Giant Steps** / Feb. 17+18, 1982 / Enja 79646
Pianist Tommy Flanagan's playing seems to be more direct, edited, and stronger as he gets older; certainly, his reemergence in the mid '70s as a solo artist produced his strongest work. *Giant Steps* is a February 17 and 18, 1982 tribute to John Coltrane with super backing from bassist George Mraz and drummer Al Foster. This is Flanagan's sixth album for Enja, a company whose partnership with the pianist was responsible for some of his best later works. This set is particularly inventive; it is Coltrane's music, but it drinks of its own spirit. You won't listen for the familiar Trane solos, but you will listen! —*Bob Rusch, Cadence*

★ **Thelonica** / Nov. 30, 1982-Dec. 1, 1982 / Enja 79615
Pianist Tommy Flanagan's association with Enja was quite beneficial; Enja produced some of his most adventurous works.... *Thelonica* is again a thematic effort, this time exploring the work of Thelonious Monk. Sandwiched by two takes of the title tracks (10:21) are six Monk originals recorded November 3 and December 1, 1982. As might be expected, this is a reflective/introspective set. That is not to say it is soft or withdrawn. It swings handily and does not remove itself as far from the Monkisms of the music as one might expect. On the other hand, it is obviously not Monk playing, though Flanagan is as comfortable and immediate with the music as if it were his own. Most importantly, inventive spirit and drive pour from the pianist and are picked up by George Mraz (bass) and Art Taylor (drums), are used, and are thrown back. —*Bob Rusch, Cadence*

Blues in the Closet / Jun. 16+17, 1983 / Baybridge

○ **Jazz Poet** / Jan. 1989 / Timeless 301

○ **Beyond the Blue Bird** / Apr. 1990 / Timeless 350
Tommy Flanagan, the gentle genius from Detroit, draws upon boplicity and blues for this effort. Special guest guitar homeboy Kenny Burrell adds his string-proud lilt to the proceedings to turn the corner on what might have been viewed as just another piano date (as if anything Flanagan does is just routine). Burrell's hearty acoustic (which he's

Music Map

Jazz Flute

Little jazz flute before late 1920s

Alberto Soccarras
Bennett's Swamplanders (1930)

First True Jazz flutists
Wayman Carver w/Benny Carter, Chick Webb (from 1932)
Harry Klee w/Ray Linn (1944)
Jimmie Lunceford (1902-1947)

Jazz composers writing for flute (1950s)
Pete Rugolo (1915)
Shorty Rogers (1924)
Marty Paich (1925)

Flute Important Element in Latin American Music
Johnny Pacheco (1935)

1950s–Major Jazz Flutists Emerge
Frank Wess (1922)–Count Basie's band

Also:
Jerome Richardson (1920)
Buddy Collette (1921)
James Moody (1925)
Bud Shank (1926)
Frank Foster (1928)
Eric Dolphy (1928-1964)
Moe Koffman (1928)–Canada
Paul Horn (1930)

Gil Evans began to arrange for flute (1950s)

1956 *Down Beat* Award established for best flutist

More Flutists
Bobby Jaspar (1926-1963)
Herbie Mann (1930)

Jazz/Jazz-Rock
Jeremy Steig (1943)
Dave Valentin
Alexander Zonjic
Bobbi Humphrey

Sing/Hum/Speak into Flute
Sam Most (1930)
Sahib Shihab (1925)
Yusef Lateef (1920)
Rahsaan Roland Kirk (1936-1977)

Major Influence
Rahsaan Roland Kirk (1936-1977)
James Newton (1953)

Saxophone Crossovers
James Moody (1925)
John Coltrane (1926-1967)
Eric Dolphy (1928-1964)
Paul Horn (1930)
Sam Rivers (1930)
Charles Lloyd (1938)
Pharoah Sanders (1940)
Lew Tabackin (1940)

Piccolo
Marshall Allen (1924)
Joseph Jarman (1937)
Hubert Laws (1939)
Roscoe Mitchell (1940)
Anthony Braxton (1945)
Douglas Ewart (1946)

More Major Flutists
Ira Sullivan (1931)
Bob Downes (1937)
Chris Hinze (1938)
Hubert Laws (1939)
A.A. Webb
Simeon Shterev

Ethnic Flutes
Yusef Lateef (1920)–wood/bamboo flutes
Rahsaan Roland Kirk (1936-1977)–nose flute
Don Cherry (1936)
Joseph Jarman (1937)
Roscoe Mitchell (1940)
Douglas Ewart (1946)

Holly Hoffman – Byard Lancaster (1942)

---

said to be turning to with increased frequency these days) provides a lovely tint to Benny Carter's "Blues in My Heart." The thematic core of this timeless Flanagan outing is Charlie Parker's moods, with "Bluebird," and "Barbados" (island blues, if you will) being the centerpieces. Bassist George Mraz and drummer Lewis Nash are locked into Flanagan's muse a la Mraz's uncanny shadow on the first 16 bars of Carter's blues. —*Willard Jenkins*, Jazz Times

Little Pleasure, A / i. Sep. 1990 / Reservoir 109

○ **Trinity** / Inner City 1084

This is a Tommy Flanagan studio date that was produced by CBS/Sony and titled *Positive Intensity* in Japan. Pianist Flanagan never sounded better playing his own material and that of Thelonious Monk, George Gershwin, Benny Carter, Tadd Dameron, and two others that require special

mention. "Hustle Bustle" is a Teo Macero original that produces the best tempo with Ron Carter's bass at its magnificent best. Billy Strayhorn's classic, "Passion Flower," which was once Johnny Hodges's feature, makes itself a magnificent, rarely heard vehicle for Flanagan's unending harmonic ideas. This was all very well rehearsed and tightly played, with only one drummer, Roy Haynes, whose heavy and very busy work sometimes distracts from the good mood transmitted throughout. "Torment" is done solo on a not often heard J.J. Johnson tune, which is more pleasant than its title suggests. —*Jerry L. Atkins*, Cadence

---

BELA FLECK & THE FLECKTONES

Group / Modern creative

A highly original banjo stylist, Bela Fleck has played traditional bluegrass, new grass (with the New Grass Revival), and his own innovative material. Fleck's approach merges improvisational concepts and approaches from both jazz and bluegrass, and his group's concerts feature elements and songs from each genre. Fleck has been in high demand as a session player. —*Ron Wynn and David Vinopal*

○ **Double Time** / **i.** 1984 / Rounder 0181

○ **Inroads** / **i.** 1986 / Rounder 219
Now available for the first time on compact disc, this 1986 release features banjoist Bela Fleck performing an all-instrumental group of original compositions. Fleck is well-known for expanding the horizons of bluegrass, and he creates lots of new sounds here, ably assisted by other talented musicians such as mandolinist Sam Bush, dobroist Jerry Douglas, and violinist Mark O'Connor. Tracks include "Ireland," "Four Wheel Drive," "Perplexed," and "The Old Country." —*Roundup Newsletter*

○ **Crossing the Tracks** / **i.** 1988 / Rounder 0121

○ **Day Break** / **i.** 1988 / Rounder 11518

★ **Bela Fleck & The Flecktones** / **i.** 1990 / Warner Brothers 26124
After disbanding New Grass Revival, Bela Fleck began re-creating the role of the banjo in the same way Charlie Parker redefined the role of the saxophone. But Fleck may be the least innovative member of this quartet: Howard Levy gets chromatics from his blues harp, Victor Wooten picks banjo rolls on his bass, and Roy "Future Man" Wooten plays a Frankenstein-monster drum-machine/guitar synthesizer. For all the flash, there's little pretense; the group's astonishing musicianship keeps an "aw-shucks" accessibility that lets everybody follow the melody while they marvel. —*Brian Mansfield*

BOB FLORENCE (Robert C. Florence)

b. May 20, 1932, Los Angeles, CA
Arranger, piano, bandleader / Swing, big band, bop, cool
Bob Florence is a West Coast studio musician, arranger, pianist, and big-band leader, one of the few still able to record and tour in the '80s and '90s. Florence was a pianist and arranger for Si Zentner from 1959 to 1964, providing a hit for Zentner with his 1960 version of "Up a Lazy River." Florence also provided arrangements for such diverse musicians as Jimmy Witherspoon, Sergio Mendes, Frank Capp, and Bud Shank in the '60s; he played piano in Capp and Shank's bands as well. Florence has led big bands in Los Angeles since 1958, featuring such musicians as Herb Geller, Bill Perkins, Bob Cooper, and Shank. He's also recorded in Dave Pell's octet during the '80s, and has issued recent releases on the Trend and Discovery labels. Currently, Florence has several dates available on CD. —*Ron Wynn*

○ **Westlake** / Mar. 3, 1981 / Musicraft 832

○ **Soaring** / Oct. 1982 / Bosco 3

○ **Magic Time** / Nov. 29+30, 1983 / Trend 536

○ **Trash Can City** / **i.** 1984 / Musicraft 545

★ **State of the Art** / **i.** 1988 / USA Music Group 589
Bob Florence Limited Edition. Five standards, four Florence originals. With a 20-piece big band. Cool as a breeze for these West Coast veterans. —*Michael G. Nastos*

○ **Treasure Chest** / **i.** 1990 / USA Music Group 680

CHRIS FLORY

Guitar / swing
Guitarist Chris Flory is among the generation of contemporary musicians who were drawn to swing rather than bebop and hard bop. His soft, light phrasing, riffs, and steady, relaxed solos aren't so much breezy or passionate as fluid and calming. Flory's played often with Scott Hamilton and has also backed vocalists Rosemary Clooney and Maxine Sullivan. He's recorded as a leader for Concord. Flory has one session available on CD, and also appears on discs by Hamilton, Sullivan, and Clooney. —*Ron Wynn*

★ **For All We Know** / Jan. 1988 / Concord Jazz 4403

City Life / **i.** 1993 / Concord 4589
While he has been on many Concord sessions as a side musician, guitarist Chris Flory's recent CD is only his second as a leader. It has an assured, polished excellence and craftsmanship that show Flory's maturation as a player and his mastery of classic jazz accompaniment and lead playing. The phrasing, timing, and nicely structured solos on such cuts as "My Shining Hour," "S'Posin," and his own "L.A. Blues" and "Drafting" have a swing-era sound, feel, and sensibility but are not merely homage to the old days. Rather, they are a contemporary update, played in a relaxed yet steely manner. The backing rhythm section balances precision and energy; pianist John Bunch, bassist John Webber, and drummer Chuck Riggs do not call attention to themselves or ever get out of sync with Flory. Bunch's flowing melodies and nice accompaniment are a delight, while Webber and Riggs add supple rhythms and support. —*Ron Wynn*

MED FLORY

b. 1926
Bop
Med Flory has enjoyed a profitable music career and successful stints as a television and film writer and actor. His alto sax and clarinet work is influenced heavily by the classic bebop sound, notably the playing of Charlie Parker. Though he doesn't directly emulate Parker, Flory's sound, phrasing, and approach reflect his reverence for Parker's music. He played clarinet and alto with Claude Thornhill in the '50s, and tenor with Woody Herman. Flory formed his own New York band in 1954, then moved to the West Coast two years later. He organized a big band that performed at the inaugural Monterey concert in 1958. Flory played with Terry Gibbs's nonet and orchestra in the late '50s and early '60s, recorded with both units, and also cut sessions with Art Pepper and Herman on baritone. Flory's acting career blossomed in the '60s, as he began appearing on many television shows and in films. He also wrote screenplays and trimmed his playing dates. During Flory's sessions with Pepper, the sax section played arrangements of Parker improvisations. Flory and Joe Maini began transcribing the solos, but after Maini's death in 1964 Flory stopped the process. When Buddy Clark showed interest, Flory began to transcribe again, and coformed a band with Clark to play the material. Supersax began in 1972 and won a Grammy for its debut recording the next year. Flory became the sole leader when Clark departed in 1975, and maintained its operation into the '80s. He also continued to juggle writing and acting. Flory has recorded for Jubille and for World Pacific as a session leader, and for Capitol, MPS, and Columbia with Supersax. Supersax has sessions available on CD. —*Ron Wynn*

RICKY FORD (Richard Allen Ford)

b. Mar. 4, 1954, Boston, MA
Tenor saxophone / Hard bop, modern creative
Ricky Ford had the misfortune to emerge in the '70s, a decade before Dr. George Butler devised his crafty "young lions" marketing scheme. Ford's rich tone and rhythmically slashing tenor style received comparatively little media buildup, but he's maintained his growth and excellence through the '80s and '90s, while still getting far less recognition than his playing has earned. Ford was a drummer as a teen, then began playing tenor at age 15. Ran Blake helped him enter the New England Conservatory at age 17; he studied there with Bill Saxton before leaving in 1974 to join the Duke Ellington Orchestra under Mercer Ellington. Ford replaced George Adams in Charles Mingus's band in 1976, and later helped Mingus with transcriptions. He made his debut as a leader in 1977, featuring an album of only his originals. Ford later played briefly with the Mingus Dynasty and led groups and played with Lionel Hampton and Abdullah Ibrahim in the '80s. He has recorded for New World, Muse, and Candid. Ford has sessions available on CD. —*Ron Wynn*

Loxodonta Africana / Jun. 1977 / New World 204

This is tenor saxophonist Ricky Ford's debut album, done in 1977 as he was just attaining a reputation and name outside the New England area. He'd spent the previous year working with Charles Mingus and helping him transcibe music. The impact is obvious; these are all Ford compositions, and they display pointed Mingus tendencies in the arrangements and structure. —*Ron Wynn*

Flying Colors / Apr. 24, 1980 / Muse 5227

Ricky Ford earned his reputation as a tenor saxophonist with something to say during his tenure in one of Charles Mingus's last bands. Ford is ably backed by a strong rhythm section (bassist Walter Booker, drummer Jimmy Cobb) led by pianist John Hicks. The addition of Ford's saxophone turns this recording unit into a group that has the closeness of a working band. Ford and company range through the saxophonist's original compositions plus the welcomed addition of a rarely done Thelonious Monk masterpiece "Bye-Ya." It is on "Bye-Ya" that Ford distinguishes himself as a superior improviser. He negotiates the angularity and peculiar rhythmic shifts with graceful ease. "Olympic Gaze" brings out Ford's stylistic debt to Sonny Rollins. "Portrait of Mingus" is, as one would expect, a slow dirgelike tribute to the bassist. Ford ranks with the best of the younger (1980) contemporary tenor saxophonists. —*Spencer R. Weston, Cadence*

○ **Tenor for the Times** / Apr. 6, 1981+Jul. 1, 1981 / Muse 5250

Here and there, Ricky Ford's reedy tenor flirts with the standard commercial sax sound, though there isn't a hint of trendiness in the backup. More often, Ford is closer to the languid relaxation of Dexter Gordon. These originals are given mostly laidback renditions, with rare double-timing and John Coltrane flurries from Ford; a bopping uptempo break on "Saxaceous Serenade" breaks up the lazy pattern. The melody of "Christmas Cheer," which sounds like Ford was dipping into the stuff when he wrote it, is a string of repetitive phrases, woefully close to the maudlin pop song "Gentle on My Mind." A few tunes, notably "Orb," are flavored by Latin rhythms from drummer Jimmy Cobb, who takes a nice cooking break under enervated bass and piano on "Hour Samba." Albert Dailey plays twinkling, chromatic, neo-bop piano. Bassist Rufus Reid, of course, walks with style and ease. Jack Walrath cameos with restrained mute trumpet on "Portrait of Love." —*Kevin Whitehead, Cadence*

Interpretations / Feb. 22, 1982 / Muse 5275

○ **Future's Gold** / Feb. 9, 1983 / Muse 5296

Tenor saxophonist Ricky Ford's musical lineage has been traced to Coleman Hawkins, and indeed there's a good helping of Bean's robust tone and extroversion in his playing. But Ford's work also has more than a touch of Sonny Rollins, minus Rollins's sly sarcasm. For instance, on "A-Flat Now," a bright, show-type tune, Ford breezes through the snappy head as his fat tone toys with the opening motif, rippling through nimble runs. His soloing is marked by a feeling of sustained, forward-driving momentum and a seemingly unshakable confidence in the improvisational course he is plotting. Countering Ford's forthright lines are pianist Albert Dailey's facile phrases that verge on hard bop glibness and point up the difference between playing with a kind of forced intensity and playing with conviction. Guitarist Larry Coryell avoids mechanical change-running and holds out for the well-chosen note and nuance. His solo on "Future's Gold," a happy swinger, is gracefully light-fingered, while on "Knowledge," a loping line reminiscent of Thelonious Monk's "Epistrophy," he proffers consistently laidback, thoughtful lines. But the guitar/tenor sonorities blend best on the sentimental "Centenarian Waltz," dedicated to Eubie Blake. Here, as elsewhere, Ford plays without a hint of tentativeness, reminding us what the term straightahead is all about. —*Jon Balleras, Down Beat*

Shorter Ideas / Aug. 28, 1984 / Muse 5314

Ricky Ford's (tenor sax) sixth Muse album explores the music of Wayne Shorter (the first four tunes are by Shorter, the

next two are by Ford, and the last are by Duke Ellington).... Ford's solos are quite good, but as a whole the ensemble doesn't particularly gel. ... I was also surprised that neither Jimmy Knepper (trombone) nor James Spaulding (alto sax, flute) have much solo space.... Obviously, given the material, there is some good music here, but the potential was there for so much more. —*Carl Brauer, Cadence*

Looking Ahead / i. Feb. 14, 1986-Oct. 9, 1986 / Muse 5322

Saxotic Stomp / Sep. 4, 1987 / Muse 5349

★ **Ebony Rhapsody** / Mar. 1989-Jun. 2, 1990 / Candid 79053

Among his most recent, a high-level date with Jaki Byard immense on piano. —*Ron Wynn*

○ **Hard Groovin'** / 1989 / Muse 5373

Drummer Jeff Watts and bassist Robert Hurst animate tenor saxophonist Ricky Ford's *Hard Groovin'.* Ford's fifth Muse release finds him in the company of several distinguished younger peers: Geoff Keezer on piano and Roy Hargrove on trumpet. Hargrove already had his own voice here, but it improved dramatically in three years (1992), as had Keezer's, for they were only 18 when these sides were recorded in 1989. Ford has devoted considerable time to his studies and teaching at Brandeis University in recent years, but his playing continues to maintain a muscular edge. "Minority" marks his recorded debut on alto saxophone, offering a pulsating, energetic approach to the instrument. —*Bret Primack, Jazz Times*

○ **Hot Brass** / i. 1992 / Candid 79518

Nice recent session matching tenor saxophone standout Ricky Ford with a crew of fiery trumpet and trombone players, plus bassist Christian McBride, drummer Carl Allen, and percussionist Danilo Perez. Ford was a young lion back in the '70s when there was no hype. He's now an experienced, skilled veteran, and teams superbly with trumpeters Lew Soloff and Claudio Roditi and trombonist Steve Turre. —*Ron Wynn*

○ **Manhattan Blues** / i. May 11, 1992 / Candid 79036

BRUCE FORMAN

b. 1956

Guitar / Swing, bop

Not a stirring or a dynamic player, guitarist Bruce Forman is a reliable, tasteful musician. His electric solos are thoughtful, well played, and melodically interesting, if not always rhythmically exciting. Forman started on piano, then switched to electric guitar. He moved to San Francisco in the early '70s, then played with local bands. Forman toured and recorded with Richie Cole from 1978 to 1982, then left Cole to lead his own groups. He played with Bobby Hutcherson and recorded with George Cables in the '80s, and did his own sessions as well. Forman's done dates for Muse, Concord, and Kamei. He has a couple of sessions available on CD. —*Ron Wynn and Michael G. Nastos*

○ **Bash, The** / Nov. 2, 1982 / Muse 5315

Good mid-'80s date by guitarist Bruce Forman, with pianist Albert Dailey, bassist Buster Williams, and drummer Eddie Gladden. Forman, a mainstream stylist solidly in the Jim Hall/Herb Ellis/Joe Pass school, plays with a precise, delicate mastery. —*Ron Wynn*

★ **Full Circle** / May 1984 / Concord Jazz 251

Guitarist Bruce Forman has a wealth of major playing experience behind him. While his ability to sustain lengthy single-note guitar lines at top speed is formidable, he is aware of the enhancing effect of restraint. There are a few places where I feel he succumbs to the temptation to fill every hole, but these are few.... The full quintet is present on "Marshall Arts," John Coltrane's "Giant Steps" (taken up with Latin underpinnings), and "Summertime" (in 5/4). "Helen's Song," a George Cables (piano) original, is a Forman-Cables duo. "Sunnyside" is a trio of Forman, bassist Jeff Carney, and drummer Eddie Marshall, and is a particularly impressive example of Forman's facility. "Skylark" is a quartet with vibist Bobby Hutcherson, while "Circular" and

"Desert Rain" are quartets with Cables. Every track on this LP has something of interest, and the entire LP, minor warts and all, repays close study. This is not an "easy" listen, but a rewarding one. —*Shirley Klett*, Cadence

Dynamics with George Cables / Feb. 1985 / Concord Jazz 279
With George Cables. This is Forman's best all-around album: good material and outstanding playing. —*Ron Wynn*

○ **Forman on the Job** / i. 1992 / Kamei 7004
Recent album by guitarist Bruce Forman with his current band. He moves more toward swing, though he also includes some Caribbean flavor on some cuts with guest Andy Narrell on steel drums. Forman uses alternating personnel, and gets great contributions from pianist Mark Levine and saxophonist Joe Henderson, among others. —*Ron Wynn*

20/20 / Muse 5273

JIMMY FORREST (James Robert Forrest)

b. Jan. 24, 1920, St. Louis, MO, **d.** Aug. 26, 1980, Grand Rapids, MI
Tenor saxophone / Swing, big band, blues & jazz, soul-jazz
A first-rate honking tenor saxophonist and an outstanding soul-jazz, blues, and ballad player, Jimmy Forrest was the kind of exuberant, naturally bluesy stylist who inevitably got overlooked and taken for granted. His huge tone and high-voltage, aggressive approach made anything he played memorable, though Forrest could also turn lyrical and inviting on ballads. He played in his mother's orchestra as a child, and with Eddie Johnson, Fate Marable, and the Jeter-Pillars orchestra while still a high school student. Forrest joined Don Albert's touring band in the late '30s, then played with Jay McShann's big band during the era when Charlie Parker was a member in the early '40s. Forrest worked for six years with Andy Kirk, and played briefly with Duke Ellington, then returned to his native St. Louis. His recording of "Night Train," which was based on Ellington's "Happy Go Lucky Local," became his signature song in 1951. Forrest moved back to New York, and worked from the late '50s until the mid '60s with Harry "Sweets" Edison. He recorded as a leader for Prestige in the early '60s, and toured with Count Basie in the early and mid '70s. After leaving the Basie orchestra, Forrest and fellow Basie alumnus Al Grey formed a band. Forrest worked with Grey until Forrest died in 1980. He recorded for United, Delmark, and Prestige. He has a couple of sessions available on CD. —*Ron Wynn*

★ **Night Train** / 1951-1953 / Delmark 435
This is tremendous early-'50s material from Forrest's days on the pioneering United label. The label was owned by a Black postman and was one of the earliest Black-owned record companies in the nation. The title cut was a huge jukebox and R&B hit. —*Ron Wynn*

☆ **All the Gin Is Gone** / Dec. 10-12, 1959 / Delmark 404
An excellent reissue of a wonderful set featuring Grant Green, Harold Mabern, and Elvin Jones (among others). Super work from Forrest. —*Ron Wynn*

☆ **Black Forrest** / Dec. 10-12, 1959 / Delmark 427
Bop. From the same session as *All the Gin Is Gone*. It includes the lovely "But Beautiful," featuring Grant Green (g), with Forrest sitting this tune out. Recorded in Chicago. —*Michael Erlewine*

☆ **Forrest Fire** / Aug. 9, 1960 / Original Jazz Classics 199
This Jimmy Forrest (tenor sax) date from August 9, 1960 is a more common set. Forrest is backed here by Larry Young (organ), Thornel Schwartz (guitar), and Jimmy Smith (drums), all of whom worked quite handily together to produce a solid, blowing sax/organ/guitar date. —*Bob Rusch*, Cadence

○ **Out of the Forrest** / Apr. 18, 1961 / Prestige 097
This is an April 18, 1961 date with Joe Zawinul (piano), Tommy Potter (bass), and Clarence Johnston (drums) backing Jimmy Forrest on eight tracks. This is an honest and re-warding big tenor date with a touch of Lester Young. . . . This is excellent, smoky, soulful tenor playing, which I think has probably been overlooked by many. —*Bob Rusch*, Cadence

○ **Most Much** / Oct. 19, 1961 / Prestige 350

O. D. (Out 'dere) / Jul. 3, 1980 / Greyforrest 1001

SONNY FORTUNE (Cornelius Fortune)

b. May 19, 1939
Alto saxophone, flute, percussion / Hard bop, early jazz-rock
At times as spirited and emphatic as any modern alto or soprano saxophonist, Sonny Fortune hasn't parlayed his considerable skills in the manner one might expect. His whirling soprano sax solos and forceful alto sax playing were featured most impressively on McCoy Tyner's *Sahara* album and in Miles Davis's jazz-rock/funk bands. Fortune began studying music at age 18, and worked in Philadelphia with R&B bands. He backed vocalist Carolyn Harris on her jazz dates, and moved to New York in 1967. Fortune played with Elvin Jones and Mongo Santamaria before joining Tyner in 1971. He led groups in 1973, then began working with Buddy Rich and Davis. Fortune turned to fusion in the mid '70s, cutting more pop-oriented material. He hasn't been as active in the '80s and '90s, at least not in terms of issuing recordings. Fortune has recorded for Strata-East, Horizon, and Atlantic. Currently, he doesn't have any sessions available as a leader. —*Ron Wynn and Michael G. Nastos*

Long Before Our Mothers Cried / Sep. 8+15, 1974 / Strata East 7423
A large-ensemble recording. A fully realized creative album and very listenable as well. With Charles Sullivan (tpt) and Stanley Cowell (p). —*Michael G. Nastos*

Awakening / Aug. 28, 1975 / Horizon 704

★ **Waves of Dreams** / Mar. 22+23, 1976 / Horizon 711
Waves of Dreams is a pleasant, mainstream LP with a definite commercial intent that is slightly alluded to in the liners. It is not a sellout type of trip, as the music really stays in a jazz mold with swinging rhythms and non-poppish tunes, yet the solos and overall drive seem held back. The album lacks guts despite saxophonist and flutist Sonny Fortune's occasionally driving solo work. His main drawback is on the ballad "Space" where he has some real intonation problems with pianist Michael Cochrane. Cochrane, trumpeter Charles Sullivan, and bassist Buster Williams all get solo space, but don't do much with it. A plus for *Waves* is the sensitive use of the synthesizer. It never gets in the way, and is utilized as a textural backdrop rather than another "stop on the organ." —*Milo Fine*, Cadence

☆ **Serengeti Minstrel** / Apr. 6-8, 1977 / Atlantic 18225
A studio date from this virile Philadelphia saxophonist/flutist, who tackles the Coltrane legacy in fine fashion with Woody Shaw (tpt) and Kenny Barron (p). —*Michael G. Nastos*

○ **It Ain't What It Was** / Konnex 5033

FRANK FOSTER (Frank Benjamin, III Foster)

b. Sep. 23, 1928
Saxophone, arranger, composer, bandleader, flute / Swing, big band
An excellent composer, bandleader, and arranger, Frank Foster has been associated with the Count Basie orchestra since 1953, and was the second person in the post-Basie era to lead the band. Foster helped update the orchestra's sound when he joined, bringing a thorough knowledge and mastery of bop technique. His pungent, animated solos were swinging and tasteful, but also reflected, to many Basie fans, what was then still a new sound and style. His arrangements helped to shift the band's focus and to alter subtly, but not distort or pervert, its classic Kansas City foundation. Songs such as "Down for the Count," "Blues Backstage," and his most famous work, "Shiny Stockings," are now as treasured as numbers from the '30s and '40s. Foster played clarinet and alto sax in his youth before switching to tenor. He

played with Snooky Young in Detroit from 1949 until 1951, when he was drafted. After completing his tour of duty, Foster joined Basie's orchestra in 1953, and was a vital soloist and arranger until 1964. He did some sessions in New York, then joined Elvin Jones's band in the late '60s. He appeared on several interesting two- and three-horn albums with Jones, matching solos with such players as Joe Farrell, David Liebman, and Steve Grossman. Foster also continued his big band duties, heading a large ensemble that was known in the early '70s as the Loud Minority. The band's size and personnel alternated, and Foster would occasionally add vocalists or use it to accompany theatrical and spoken word presentations. Foster became the Basie band's nominal leader in 1986, while continuing to compose and arrange for other groups. He's played with some small combos, and his work, "Lake Placid Suite," was commissioned for the 1980 Winter Olympics. Current Basie releases continue to be issued periodically. Basie orchestra reissues that feature Foster, as well as other dates Foster's recorded, are being issued, and many include fellow tenor saxophonist and flutist Frank Wess. —*Ron Wynn*

No Count / **i**. Oct. 31, 1956 / Savoy 12078

★ **Two Franks Please!** / Oct. 13, 1957 / Savoy 2249
High-quality hard bop set with trumpeter Donald Byrd. —*Ron Wynn*

Manhattan Fever / Mar. 21, 1968 / Blue Note 84278

Twelve Shades of Black / Jul. 1978 / Leo 7

Roots, Branches and Dances / Dec. 7, 1978 / Bee Hive 7008

Non-Electric Company / **i**. 1979 / EPM 5501

Two for the Blues / Oct. 11+12, 1983 / Pablo 2310905

★ **Frankly Speaking** / Dec. 1984 / Concord Jazz 4276
One of Foster's many sparkling collaborations with his longtime friend, fellow Basie bandmate Frank Wess. Outstanding rhythm section as well. —*Ron Wynn*

○ **Shiny Stockings** / Denon 8545

POPS FOSTER

b. 1892, **d.** 1969
Bass / New Orleans traditional
George Murphy "Pops" Foster was a dominant bass player, and was one of the earliest to develop and perfect the pizzicato (plucked) style. Foster got an enormous, rich sound from the bass, and his playing had the driving, propulsive component that's now commonplace among bassists. His first instrument was cello, but he soon switched. He began playing with various New Orleans bands in 1906. From 1918 to 1921, Foster worked with Fats Marable's riverboat group, and played some tuba. Foster then played with Kid Ory's band in California, moved to St. Louis and worked with Charlie Creath and Dewey Jackson, then came to New York in 1929 to join Luis Russell. His bass work was an integral ingredient in the band's sound during Russell's prime years (1929-1931), and Foster was still aboard during 1935-1940, when Louis Armstrong headed the band. As the traditional jazz revival flourished, Foster worked with Sidney Bechet, Art Hodes, Mezz Mezzrow, Bob Wilber, and Jimmy Archey from 1945 until 1952. He was a regular participant in the radio series "This Is Jazz" in 1947, and appeared in the 1954 film *Jazz Dance*. Foster toured Europe with Sammy Price in 1955 and 1956, then moved to San Francisco. In the late 1950s and early 1960s, he played with Earl Hines, then did freelance sessions before playing in 1963 and 1964 with Elmer Snowden's trio. Foster's last European tour came in 1966 with the New Orleans All Stars. —*Ron Wynn*

PETE FOUNTAIN (Peter Dewey (Jr) Fountain)

b. Jul. 3, 1930, New Orleans, LA
Clarinet / Dixieland
Clarinetist Pete Fountain goes back to the '40s in New Orleans music, when he worked with Monk Hazel, the Junior Dixieland Band, Phil Zito, and others. While there's a healthy amount of show business gimmickry in Fountain's

music, particularly his post-Lawrence Welk recordings, his style, in its formative years, was an amalgam of things gleaned from Irving Fazola and Benny Goodman, plus his own nuances. Fountain began playing clarinet at age 12, and was in the Junior Dixieland band in New Orleans when he was age 18. He joined Phil Zito's International Dixieland Band in 1949, and made his first recordings with them in 1950. Fountain was a founding member of the Basin Street Six, and spent four years with them. He later formed his own ensemble, Pete Fountain and his Three Coins, in 1955, and played a seven-month engagement in Chicago alongside the Dukes of Dixieland. Fountain returned to New Orleans after that, where he worked with Tony Almerico and Al Hirt. He hit the jackpot in 1957 with Lawrence Welk. Fountain spent two highly visible years with Welk. He was featured on Welk's weekly prime time television show, and made records and other appearances also. Fountain bought a club in New Orleans in 1959, and has since alternated between playing there and appearing at the New Orleans Jazz and Heritage Festival. He was a frequent "Tonight Show" guest during Johnny Carson's long reign, and many people still identify New Orleans music with either Fountain or Al Hirt. While he has undeniable gifts, especially his tone, Fountain doesn't have a formidable recorded legacy that's jazz-based. His finest albums are probably his early '60s releases on Coral, which aren't available on CD. But there are several things on different labels, including a Ranwood date recorded in the summer of '93. —*Ron Wynn*

Lawrence Welk Presents Pete Fountain / 1957 / Coral 57200

Mr. New Orleans / **i**. 1961 / MCA 38021

★ **Best of Pete Fountain—Vols. 1 & 2** / MCA 4032

PANAMA FRANCIS (David Albert Francis)

b. Dec. 21, 1918, Miami, FL
Drums / Swing, big band, bop
A sterling swing drummer who later utilized his skills on blues, gospel, and R&B dates, Panama Francis is famous for sublime accompaniment. He's provided on-the-money fills, driving backbeats, and flashy, yet rhythmically imaginative solos for many combos, big bands, and vocalists. Francis honed his craft playing in a Miami church at revivals before joining George Kelly in the mid '30s, then joining the Florida Collegians. He moved to New York and worked with Tab Smith and Billy Hicks, then played and recorded with Roy Eldridge in 1939. Francis joined Lucky Millinder in 1940, and played with him at the Savoy until 1946. He toured, recorded and was featured on films in the late '40s and early '50s with Cab Calloway. Then Francis became a studio drummer in New York and California during the mid- and late '50s, touring and recording with Ray Charles, Illinois Jacquet, Mahalia Jackson, Buddy Holly, Lionel Hampton, and Jimmy Witherspoon. He was featured in the film *Lady Sings the Blues* in 1972, and formed the Savoy Sultans in 1979. They toured and recorded in Europe and played at the Rainbow Room occasionally in the '80s. Francis played in the reformed Benny Goodman quartet with Teddy Wilson and Lionel Hampton during several festival dates and concert appearances in 1982. He's recorded for Epic, 20th Century Fox, Stash, and the Black and Blue labels, while continuing to perform into the '90s. Currently, Francis has some sessions available on CD. —*Ron Wynn*

★ **All-Stars 1949** / 1949 / Collectables 5313

Battle of Jericho, The / Jan. 16-19, 1962 / Epic 3839

Tough Talk / 1963 / 20th Century 5101

Francis & The Savoy Sultans / **i**. Jan. 31, 1979 / Classic Jazz 150
Panama Francis was one of the great swing era drummers, often playing in the house band at the Savoy. This late-'70s album updates the sound he helped perfect through the heyday of swing and big bands, and on into the early days of R&B. It's dynamic, propulsive, and well played, despite some occasionally sloppy solos. —*Ron Wynn*

○ **Savoy Sultans** / Classic Jazz 149
Drummer Panama Francis is quoted in the liner: "If the spirit hits you and you want to dance, get on up and dance." Fortunately, swing is a sensation even a wallflower like me can experience and endorse, and the Sultans swing with economy and the fierce pride of musicianship. Several of the arrangements of this extremely well-recorded record (licensed from French Black and Blue) reenact Al Cooper's originals; the others are by band members Francis and by tenor saxophonist George Kelly and Norris Turney (alto sax, clarinet). Within their styles, the soloists are all very good, especially Turney, whose lingering pre-Charlie Parker vibrato disguises some surprisingly modern harmonic notions, and Kelly, who is a model of droll virility. The trumpeters form the classic clown (Francis Williams)/crooner (Irv Stokes) opposition; both are expert with mutes. But it is the combined voice of the Sultans that most holds one in sway, and for this praise goes to the rhythm section, the crank of this well-oiled machine. —*Francis Davis*, Cadence

BUD FREEMAN (Lawrence Freeman)

b. Apr. 13, 1906, Chicago, IL, **d.** Mar. 15, 1991
Tenor saxophone / Dixieland
A master of vintage Chicago-style jazz, Freeman was an innovator in his genre. His lush, witty style was absorbed by generations of White tenor players. Freeman began in the '20s with C-melody sax, then switched to tenor in 1925. He spent nine years with the cream of the Chicago-based leaders, including Red Nichols and Eddie Condon. He moved to New York and joined Ray Noble in the '30s, then attained super popularity with Tommy Dorsey. In the late '30s, he appeared on Broadway in a musical with Louis Armstrong and Maxine Sullivan. From the '40s on, through associations with Condon or on his own, Freeman kept the cause of traditional jazz alive. His playing never calcified or lost its charm. He was a founder of the World's Greatest Jazz Band in 1968 and returned to Chicago in 1970. —*Ron Wynn*

★ **Commodore Years (1938–1939), The** / 1938-1939 / Commodore
An anthology/overview of his most influential material from the late '30s. —*Ron Wynn*

Jazz: Chicago Style / i. 1955 / Columbia 2558

Bud Freeman and His All-Star Jazz / Apr. 22, 1957 / Harmony 7046

Bud Freeman and His Summa Cum Laude Trio / Jun. 30, 1958+Jul. 1, 1958 / Dot 25166

★ **All Stars with Shorty Baker** / May 13, 1960 / Prestige 183
Authentic is the word that best describes these musicians. They are among the best of the White mainstream jazz players of the prebop days. Their mixed associates here all represent an era of jazz that wasn't exactly Dixieland and preceded bird (Charlie Parker) and Dizzy (Gillespie). Even after the entry of bop, they continued to do their own thing and almost completely avoided any influence of bebop licks. Bud Freeman had a style and sound on tenor that only a handful of players ever followed, and it leaves you with a feeling that he never tried to alter it. It is yours to accept or to reject. This album represents a style connected with Eddie Condon followers and is very typical of club playing in the early '40s. There is brilliant playing by Tyree Glenn on trombone on "Lonesome Road" and "Crazy Rhythm" where "Red" Allen joins Shorty Baker for a trumpet duo. I can't be too critical of George Wettling's drumming because this was the style before bop and the transition. —*Jerry L. Atkins*, Cadence

○ **Compleat Bud Freeman, The** / Dec. 10+12, 1969 / Monmouth 7022

Joy of Sax, The / Sep. 1974 / Chiaroscuro 135

Song of the Tenor / Nov. 4-5, 1975 / Philips 6308254

○ **Bucky and Bud** / i. 1975 / Flying Dutchman 1378

CHICO FREEMAN (Earl Lavon (Jr) Freeman)

b. Jul. 17, 1949, Chicago, IL

Tenor saxophone, soprano saxophone / Hard bop, modern creative
The son of the great Chicago tenor saxophonist Von Freeman, Chico Freeman has earned praise for his own gritty, exuberant style. Freeman's work mirrors that of both his father and his prime influence, John Coltrane. It's rich, full-toned, and intense, with wide octave leaps, a thorough harmonic intelligence, and swinging solos that have been displayed in bebop, hard bop, and free situations, and on his compositions. Inspired by Miles Davis, Freeman started playing trumpet at age 10. He switched to tenor sax in his third year at Northwestern University, where he studied math and music education. Freeman played in R&B bands, then studied with Muhal Richard Abrams and joined the Association for the Advancement of Creative Musicians (AACM). He played and studied with Fred Anderson, Adegoke Steve Colson, and his uncle, George Freeman. Chico Freeman was a graduate student in composition and performance at Governors State University where he was principle soloist with the university's big band. He toured Brazil with the band in the late '70s. Freeman won awards at the Notre Dame Jazz Festival in 1973. After completing his Masters degree, he moved to New York where he worked with Elvin Jones, Sun Ra, Sam Rivers big band, Jack DeJohnette, and Don Pullen. He began heading his own bands in the late '70s, many including Cecil McBee, and worked with Abrams, John Hicks, Jay Hoggard, Famadou Don Moye, and Steve McCall as well. Freeman's recorded and played in groups with his father, and joined the Leaders in 1984. He's recorded for Dharma, India Navigation, Contemporary, Black Saint, Elektra/Musician, Blackhawk, and Columbia in the '70s, '80s, and '90s. Freeman's played and recorded with Henry Threadgill, Bobby Hutcherson, Wynton Marsalis, Billy Hart, Wallace Roney, Bobby McFerrin, Lester Bowie, Kirk Lightsey, and Kenny Kirkland, among others. He also plays soprano sax and bass clarinet. Freeman has several albums available on CD, from recent sets to '70s reissues. —*Ron Wynn*

Morning Prayer / Sep. 8, 1976 / India Navigation
A tremendous quintet date. Wonderful solos by Freeman, plus a strong supporting cast with Muhal Richard Abrams (p). —*Ron Wynn*

★ **Beyond the Rain** / Jun. 21-23, 1977 / Contemporary 479
With the Hilton Ruiz Trio, featuring the compositions of M. R. Abrams and Freeman's hard-charging playing. —*Michael G. Nastos*

○ **Chico** / 1977 / India Navigation 1031
A standard for creative tenor saxophonists to live up to. With Cecil McBee, Muhal Richard Abrams, and Steve McCall. —*Michael G. Nastos*

Outside Within, The / 1978 / India Navigation 1042

★ **Spirit Sensitive** / Sep. 1979 / India Navigation 1045
On *Spirit Sensitive*, tenor saxophonist Chico Freeman makes a valiant attempt at taking on the standards, something the younger players (other than Arthur Blythe, Air, and Anthony Braxton) have shied away from. (The challenge is *playing the tune* itself without excess additives and passing chords that would arouse the composer's disdain.) "Autumn in New York" is beautifully handled as a Cecil McBee-Freeman bass/tenor duet, but on Horace Silver's "Peace," which is a pace or two slower, the open space and the absence of the upbeat percussion leaves Freeman a bit too out in the open. Freeman is occasionally over-miked, perhaps in an attempt to accomplish that ravishing vibrato characteristic of Ben Webster and the old-style tenor players. (To the guilty parties: all that comes with experience.) The B side does the job of partial vindication: "Don't Get Around Much Anymore" is particularly bouncy and achieves the old style. —*Brent Staples*, Down Beat

○ **Peaceful Heart, Gentle Spirit** / Mar. 6-7, 1980 / Contemporary 14005
On *Peaceful Heart, Gentle Spirit*, good use is made of varied voicings from the various personnel. For example, "Heart and the Gentle Spirit" opens with a bass figure and the other

instruments slowly enter: alto flute, piano, vibes, percussion. The sound remains open and airy, in keeping with the tune's gentle, lilting feel. James Newton (bass flute, C-flute) take flight with a warm, full tone on C-flute, darting through the air. Following a piano solo that brings things back to earth, Chico Freeman tenderly nudges the piece along with his alto flute. "Freedom Swing Song" opens with an angular line played by pizzicato bass and cello, plucked piano strings, and vibes, with drums and Freeman's bass clarinet eventually joining in. Throughout, instrumental colors clash and contrast; such extremes are even found in pianist Kenny Kirkland's piano playing, as a harpsichord-like sound contrasts with crashing chords. Yet despite all the dissonance, the tune still swings, albeit freely, as the title suggests, especially thanks to Billy Hart's cymbal work. The fat, searing tone Freeman employs on "Look Up" is a display of his Chicago tenor school roots. "Morning Prayer" is a gorgeous, plaintive piece that opens with unison arco bass and cello, with C-flute and then bass flute adding additional lines and occasionally harmonizing. Throughout the length of the cut, new material is added, continually exploiting the mournful qualities of the string and woodwind instruments. *—Jerry de Muth*, Down Beat

Destiny's Dance / Oct. 29-30, 1981 / Contemporary 14008

Freeman and Freeman / **i.** 1981 / India Navigation 1070
Father and son make a wonderful team on this release with Von and Chico Freeman. *—Ron Wynn*

Tradition in Transition / **i.** 1982 / Elektra 52412
Superior production values and sound, with excellent playing by Freeman. *—Ron Wynn*

Search, The / 1982 / India Navigation 1059

Pied Piper / Apr. 9, 1984 / Blackhawk 50801
An outstanding mid-'80s date, with Chico Freeman displaying both his strong solo skills and his versatility. He and fellow multi-instrumentalist John Purcell split duties on 12 horns between them. Kenny Kirkland and Mark Thompson admirably divide the piano chores, while bassist Cecil McBee and powerful drummer Elvin Jones nicely handle rhythm section tasks. *—Ron Wynn*

Tales of Ellington / Apr. 1984-Mar. 1987 / Black Hawk 537

Tangents / 1984 / Elektra 9603611
A sometimes-intriguing album, featuring saxophonist Chico Freeman interacting with vocal acrobat Bobby McFerrin on some tracks, otherwise playing standard but inspired hard bop or venturing into free territory. *—Ron Wynn*

Up and Down / Black Saint 120136

RUSS FREEMAN (Russell Donald Freeman)

b. May 28, 1926
Piano / Cool
A compelling soloist, Russ Freeman has also been a good bandleader and a sympathetic accompanist. An accomplished bebop stylist, Freeman executes impressive harmonic maneuvers expertly; his sense of swing is subtle, yet commanding. Freeman studied classical piano as a child, and worked with bebop groups on the West Coast in the late '40s. He played with Howard McGhee and Dexter Gordon, then worked with Art Pepper, Wardell Gray, Shorty Rogers, and Chet Baker in the '50s. He began a longterm relationship with Shelly Manne in the mid-'50s. Freeman toured Europe with Benny Goodman in 1959, and toured the next year with Manne. He formed a publishing company in 1962 to issue his own compositions. Freeman was music director for several nightclubs and played on many film soundtracks. His finest recordings were done with Chet Baker; Mosaic issued *The Complete Pacific Jazz Recordings of the Chet Baker Quartet With Russ Freeman* on a four-album/three-disc set. Freeman also recorded for Contemporary, Brainchild, and Jazz West Coast. Freeman has some sessions available on CD in addition to the Mosaic box. *—Ron Wynn and Michael Erlewine*

Russ Freeman Trio / Oct. 27, 1953+Dec. 28, 1953 / Pacific Jazz 8

★ **Trio with Richard Twardzik** / Oct. 1953-Aug. 1957 / Pacific Jazz 46861

★ **Freeman/Baker Quartet** / Nov. 6, 1956 / Pacific Jazz 1232

VON FREEMAN (Earl Lavon (Sr) Freeman)

b. Oct. 3, 1922, Chicago, IL
Tenor saxophone / Swing, bop
Von Freeman doesn't have an exhaustive discography of recordings, and he has worked mostly in Chicago throughout his career. But tenor saxophonist Von Freeman enjoys widespread respect for his authoritative bebop style on standards, ballads, uptempo tunes, or blues. Freeman played clarinet and C-melody sax at age seven. He attended Du Sable High School (his classmates included Bennie Green and Gene Ammons), and he studied under the famous instructor Walter Dyett. Freeman played in Horace Henderson's group in 1940 and 1941, and in a Navy band from 1941 until 1945. He was in Sun Ra's Arkestra during parts of 1948 and 1949. But his main job was playing in the Pershing Hotel's house band with his brothers, guitarist George and drummer Bruz Freeman. They accompanied Roy Eldridge and Lester Young for nearly four years. Von Freeman also did some private recording dates with Charlie Parker. The Freeman brothers formed a quartet with pianist Ahmad Jamal in the early '50s. Jamal was later replaced by Andrew Hill. Von Freeman worked with some players who eventually helped to found the Association for the Advancement of Creative Musicians (AACM); they included Muhal Richard Abrams, Malachi Favors, and Fred Anderson. In the early '60s, Freeman toured with Chicago blues musicians Jimmy Reed and Otis Rush, and with soul singer Gene Chandler. Freeman was in a show band backing R&B vocalist Milt Trenier from 1966 to 1969, and has since concentrated on jazz. He recorded soul jazz sessions in the late '60s and early '70s with his brother, George, for Delmark, People, and Groove Merchant. Freeman made his own recordings in the '70s for Atlantic, Nessa, Daybreak, and Muse. He played with his son, Chico, on part of a 1981 Columbia album *Fathers and Sons*, and they made complete albums for India Navigation (it's been reissued on CD) and Soul Note. During the '90s, he has continued recording and performing. *—Ron Wynn*

Doin' It Right Now / 1972 / Atlantic 1628

Have No Fear / Jun. 11, 1975 / Nessa 6
Von Freeman's *Have No Fear*, released on the Windy City's Nessa Records, is a madly swinging date. Freeman, a self-described "player of ideas," is a unique stylist with a dry, shallow tone. Joining Freeman within the broad parameters of his imagination is a consistently excellent and challenging Jon Young on piano, solid bassist David Shipp, and the inspiring Wilbur Campbell, an aggressive drummer who'd give Philly Joe Jones more than a few hard sprints around the block. *—Charles Mitchell*, Down Beat

★ **Serenade and Blues** / Jun. 11, 1975 / Nessa 11
To devotees of Ornette Coleman and Albert Ayler, tenor saxophonist Von Freeman's quirky phrasing, rubbery vibrato, microtonal melodies, and abrupt changes of register and timbre raise no hackles, but to some mainstreamers, past revelation becomes present dogma, provoking puzzled reactions that *Serenade & Blues* is "sour," "off key," etc. In this case, Thelonious Monk's dictum that "wrong is right" is precisely applicable, for Freeman projects more creativity and emotional truth through his novel approach to tradition than a whole wax museum full of revivalist clones. There is certainly nothing peculiar in Freeman's choice of material: a Glenn Miller ballad, a Jule Styne/Sammy Cahn standard, and a pair of unpretentious blues. The rhythm section never strays far from orthodox canons, but there is no dearth of swing in the inexhaustible reservoirs of John Young's Art Tatum/Bud Powell piano stylings or Wilbur Campbell's ever-tasty drumming. Freeman's sax, however, is a horn of an-

other color, transmuting familiar melodies into startling, though recognizable abstractions. Although basic chord progressions are left intact, virtually every phrase is permeated with unexpected sharps and flats; not only leading and passing tones, but predictable cadences are warped and bent into brand new configurations. Freeman is one of those rare artists who can expand upon an established idiom without sacrificing authenticity or feeling; *Serenade & Blues* confirms his stature as an improviser of the highest order. — *Larry Birnbaum,* Down Beat

○ **Young and Foolish** / Aug. 12, 1977 / Daybreak 002
Von Freeman's *Young & Foolish*—recorded "live" at Laren in 1977—was probably the best tenor saxophone album issued in 1981. It is another testament to dues-paying, as it is only Freeman's fourth LP in a career even longer than Jimmy Knepper's. Like Knepper, Freeman is a uniquely individual stylist with such a personal way of juxtaposing even the smallest number of notes that he is always instantly recognizable. It says much for the coherence of his invention that the 25-minute "I'll Close My Eyes" (well-chosen, unhackneyed material), which fills side one, rarely falls short of being thoroughly inspired. Unusually for Freeman, there are no blues tunes here, yet they pervade every chorus—in inflection and in mood. They are the unseen hand guiding the unaffected, almost naked emotional directness of his playing, be it on the wailing "Eyes," the singing "Foolish," or the intense "Bye, Bye, Blackbird." His support, too, is exemplary. Inspiration at this level is contagious, infecting pianist John Young's Art Tatum/Bud Powell inventions with quicksilver, and putting even more spring than usual into the rhythmic interplay of bassist Dave Shipp and drummer Charles Walton. It says much for their creativity that even a 52-minute album leaves one wanting more. —*Chris Sheridan,* Down Beat

DON FRIEDMAN (Donald Ernest Friedman)

b. May 4, 1935, San Francisco, CA
Piano, composer / Modern creative
An arresting blend of gifted jazz improviser and contemporary classical and avant-garde experimenter, Don Friedman has demonstrated a fine lyrical touch and style on piano. He has often included classical and free jazz touches in his playing and compositions. Friedman began piano studies at age five, and had classical training. He made his professional debut playing alongside Dexter Gordon, Shorty Rogers, and Buddy Collette. Friedman recorded with Collette, then played with Chet Baker and Ornette Coleman. He moved to New York, and worked with Pepper Adams. Friedman formed his own trio and recorded with Booker Little in the early '60s. He joined the Jimmy Giuffre Three in 1964, then led a quartet with Atilla Zoller. Friedman was in Chuck Wayne's trio in the late '60s, then joined Clark Terry's big band and played with them in a 1970 Carnegie Hall concert. Friedman taught jazz piano at New York University in the '70s, and played with Bob Bodley in the '80s. He continued doing sessions throughout the decade in New York. Friedman has recorded for Owl, Riverside, Progressive, and Lime Tree. He has sessions available on CD. —*Ron Wynn*

★ **Day in the City, A** / Jun. 12, 1961 / Riverside 1775
Don Friedman's June 12, 1961 trio (Friedman, piano; Chuck Israels, bass; Joe Hunt, drums) recording is titled *A Day in the City.* This is six jazz variations on a theme. The theme in this case is "The Minstril Boy," and Friedman uses it as a springboard for each part of the city's day. The mode here is a familiar one and the impressionism in a direction you might expect. . . . But there is nothing predictable about the actual improvised music. Here, Friedman is not afraid to mix his attacks, from Bill Evansish lyricism to dissonant blocks more associated with Cecil Taylor. This is fine, cerebral jazz which remains totally contemporary more than 20 years later. —*Bob Rusch,* Cadence

○ **Dreams and Explorations** / 1964 / Riverside 485

○ **Metamorphosis** / Feb. 22, 1966 / Prestige 7488
Hot Knepper and Pepper / Jun. 26, 1976 / Progressive 7036

DAVID FRIESEN

b. May 6, 1942, Tacoma, WA
Bass / New age, modern creative
A strong, emphatic bassist, David Friesen sometimes uses that talent playing music that's far more introspective and understated than his technique. He's done many almost new age or "chamber" style works, though he's also been a solid contributor on more traditional bebop and hard bop material. Friesen is mainly a self-taught player; he began on bass while stationed in Germany during his years in the service. Friesen later attended the University of Washington. He played with John Handy and Marian McPartland in the '60s, and worked with Joe Henderson in San Francisco. Friesen toured Europe with Billy Harper in the mid '70s, and met Ted Curson in Copenhagen. He later joined Curson's band, and played at the 1977 Monterey Jazz Festival, gaining wide acceptance and fine reviews. He made his recording debut as a leader in 1976, working with John Stowell, a frequent partner on other recording sessions. Friesen also cut sessions with Ricky Ford and Duke Jordan, while playing with Paul Horn and Mal Waldron. He's recorded for Global Pacific, Steeplechase, Golden Flute, Inner City, Palo Alto, and Muse. Friesen sessions are available on CD. —*Ron Wynn*

Star Dance / Nov. 8, 1976 / Inner City 1019
Bassist David Friesen's 1976 debut as a leader remains his finest straight jazz date; it also contains some extraordinary playing, particularly the cut "Duet and Dialogue," where he blends both plucked and bowed work in the same song while using both hands. —*Ron Wynn*

Waterfall Rainbow / Jun. 1977-1977 / Inner City 1027

★ **Amber Skies** / Jan. 1983+Apr. 1983 / Palo Alto 8043
Bassist Dave Friesen has marvelous technical skills, but doesn't always stick to jazz context. This '83 date has him doing quasi-classical, light pop, and more conventional jazz; the compositions are erratic, but his bass solos and skills are consistently impressive. —*Ron Wynn*

Encounters / i. Mar. 18, 1984 / Muse

Departure / i. 1990 / Global Pacific 79338
A good combination of Afro-Latin-jazz and chamber music with guests Airto (per) and Flora Purim (v). —*Ron Wynn*

BILL FRISELL (William Richard Frisell)

b. Mar. 18, 1951, Baltimore, MD
Guitar / Early jazz-rock, modern creative
A stunning, eclectic guitarist who blends the best elements of rock energy and daring with jazz harmonic sophistication and melodic interpretation, Bill Frisell has been a prominent stylist since the early '80s. His playing with the Paul Motian trio (which also included saxophonist Joe Lovano) showed that he was one of the most innovative contemporary jazz guitarists around, as an accompanist and as a soloist. Frisell studied briefly with Jim Hall in the early '70s, and later took composition with Mike Gibbs at Berklee. He toured England with Gibbs's big band in the late '70s, meeting and later recording with Eberhard Weber. Frisell recorded frequently with Jan Garbarek and Paul Motian before cutting his debut as a leader in the early '80s. He's worked often with Tim Berne, and has recorded with John Scofield, Vernon Reid, Arlid Andersen, Kenny Wheeler, Bob Stewart, Dave Hofstra, Wayne Horovitz, and Joey Baron, among others. Frisell's done sessions for ECM, Minor Music, Elektra/Musician, and Elektra/Nonesuch, among others. He has several sessions available on CD. —*Ron Wynn and David Nelson McCarthy*

In Line / Aug. 1982 / ECM 837019

★ **Rambler** / Aug. 1984 / ECM 825234
Guitarist Bill Frisell has created something new and weird out of the modern impressionist's vocabulary: Frisell's swell/volume pedal effects can be traced back to Terje Rypdal's melodramatic style of punctuation, and Frisell's

blurry, wide-open hanging chords to ECM's cloud-chamber theory in general. . . . Frisell's a slick harmonist (more than ever now that he's using a guitar synthesizer), but a playful one, tweaking accepted tonalities. Together, he and the disruptive timekeeper Paul Motian, who's employed the guitarist for years, feed off each other's comic streaks, and that's something the easy-rolling tubaist Bob Stewart readily picks up on playing the tongue-in-cheek march "Music I Heard" (which compares favorably with Pat Metheny's guitar-synth half-time parody "Forward March"). Frisell and Motian also share a fondness for swaying calypsos, which, once Frisell's through with them, usually sound like demented cousins of Chet Atkins's "Yellowbird": "Rambler" and "When We Go" are this LP's entries. Bassist Jerome Harris eases into the Caribbean rhythms; Stewart adds a lazy lope to the title track. . . . Out front, Kenny Wheeler's characteristically warm and economical brass horns, bathed in studio echo, ease the sting of Frisell's spikes, swoops, and metallic whines. Each checks the other from slipping into sentimentality or gaudy excess, notably on the overtly impressionistic rubato tune "Wizard of Odds." Like Motian's recent groups, this is a keenly balanced outfit, providing both surprising jolts and pretty melodies, as they take catchy progressions and contort them every which way. —*Kevin Whitehead*, Cadence

☆ **Lookout for Hope** / Mar. 1987 / ECM 833495
Country and Eastern music with Frisell's distinct guitar sound. Constantly challenging listening. —*Michael G. Nastos*

Works / i. 1989 / ECM 837273
Good representations of creative impulses. Not definitive, but a good point of reference. —*Michael G. Nastos*

Smash and Scatteration / i. 1989 / Rykodisc 10006
Bill Frisell and Vernon Reid were two guitarists on the cutting edge of new sounds when *Smash and Scatteration* was initally recorded. It features the pair on all instruments including guitar synthesizers, banjos, acoustic guitars, and DX drums. "Last Nights of Paris" is a duet with acoustic guitar and banjo that reminded me of the Keystone Kops with its zany humor. "Fr Fr Frisell" features Frisell on a solo number (no overdubs), and with his delay machine, he sounds like several guitarists at once, all on Mars. Reid's best moments come when his guitar synth MIDIs to a keyboard; at times his lead playing is a bit too Jimi Hendrix/'60s-oriented (but it does have soul). Frisell is one of the modern marvels of guitaring. His concept ranges from absolutely free to melodic and everything in between. This is a good album; the two men create a lot of sounds, melodies, and textures to please and challenge. —*Neil Haverstick*, Cadence

Is That You? / Aug. 1989 / Elektra 60956

Before We Were Born / i. 1989 / Elektra 60843
An outstanding example of this guitarist's versatility. There are some sparkling exchanges with the sax section led by Julius Hemphill. —*Ron Wynn*

Have a Little Faith / i. 1993 / Elektra 79301
Have a Little Faith features compositions by everyone from John Phillip Sousa and Charles Ives to Sonny Rollins and Madonna. Bill Frisell describes his approach to the guitar as a combination of Jim Hall and Jimi Hendrix, but there's also a country feeling to his playing, most evident here on Bob Dylan's "Just Like a Woman" and John Hiatt's title track. —*Rick Mitchell*, Request

DAVID FRISHBERG (David L. Frishberg)

b. Mar. 23, 1933, St. Paul, MN
Songwriter, vocals, piano / Blues & jazz, ballads & blues
Other than Mose Allison and perhaps Blossom Dearie, no one has a more unusual act than vocalist Dave Frishberg. He's part philosopher, part comic, part jazz/blues interpreter, part instrumentalist, and a little bit "weary everyman." Frishberg's songs have been recorded by many artists, among them Anita O'Day, Cleo Laine, Al Jarreau, Jackie Cain, and Roy Kral. His wearied, expressive voice and tantalizing piano accompaniment complete his totally individualistic package. Frishberg moved to New York in 1957, where

he did both solo dates and worked with Carmen McRae and Kai Winding. He toured with Gene Krupa in the early '60s, then worked back in New York with Wild Bill Davison, Peanuts Hucko, Bud Freeman, Ben Webster, the Al Cohn/Zoot Sims quartet, Bobby Hackett, and Charlie Shavers. He was the Half Note's resident pianist in the late '60s. Frishberg moved to Los Angeles in the early '70s, performing and recording with his trio, and working with Jack Sheldon, Joe Pass, Bill Berry, and Richie Kamuca. He performed both solo and duo in the '80s. Frishberg's recorded for Fantasy, CTI, Concord, Omnisound and Bloomdido. He has several sessions available on CD. —*Ron Wynn and Michael G. Nastos*

★ **Getting Some Fun out of Life** / Jan. 25-26, 1977 / Concord Jazz 37

You're a Lucky Guy / Jul. 10, 1978 / Concord Jazz 74

○ **Dave Frishberg Classics** / 1982-1983 / Concord Jazz 4462
This hits collection reissues almost all of his most well-known tunes. A must-buy. —*Michael G. Nastos*

★ **Live at Vine Street** / Oct. 1984 / Fantasy 9638
Vocalist/pianist David Frishberg didn't perform this program in anyone's living room or (tee-hee) family room, but he very well could have done just that. Such is the feeling of integral relaxation and informality generated by an artist who makes it all sound deceptively simple, if not easy. Except for the instrumental Johnny Hodges medley, an affectionate tribute which offsets the vocal portion of the program nicely, all the songs are Frishberg's and if some of them aren't particularly brilliant, they are all, at least, good natured and stamped with a certain witty intelligence. . . . Listen closely, however, and you will discern the craftsmanship and craft, if not cunning, of these small musical fables or foibles. . . . Although Frishberg had support from bass and drums on his Songbook LPs, he demonstrates here that he could do it all by himself. —*Alan Bargebuhr*, Cadence

Can't Take You Nowhere / 1986 / Fantasy 9651

Let's Eat Home / Jan. 1989 / Concord Jazz 4402
Good rhythm section and material, plus acceptable vocals. The CD has a bonus cut. —*Ron Wynn*

TONY FRUSCELLA

b. Feb. 4, 1927, **d.** 1969
Trumpet / Swing, bop, cool
A promising trumpeter whose career never had a chance to flourish due to his drug problem, Tony Fruscella had a style close to that of Chet Baker's, though Fruscella developed his style independently. He played in an army band in the '50s, then worked with Lester Young and Gerry Mulligan, and performed and recorded with Stan Getz in 1955. He did some recordings heading his own group that same year, then was basically finished as a prime musician due to his habit. Fruscella did occasional dates with fellow trumpeter Don Joseph, but died in 1969 at the age of 42. His 1955 album on Atlantic, *I'll Be Seeing You*, was an example of his potential. There's a Frusella session available on CD released by Cool N' Blue, *Tony's Blues*, issued in 1992. Fruscella's also featured on a Getz Verve anthology. —*Ron Wynn and Michael Erlewine*

Debut / i. Dec. 1948-1953 / Spotlite 126

Fru 'n Brew / i. 1953 / Spotlite 126

CURTIS FULLER (Curtis Dubois Fuller)

b. Dec. 15, 1934, Detroit, MI
Trombone / Hard bop
Curtis Fuller belongs in the select circle with J.J. Johnson, Kai Winding, and a few others who make the trombone sound fluid and inviting rather than awkward. His ability to make wide octave leaps and to play whiplash phrases in a relaxed, casual manner is a testament to his skill. Fuller's solos and phrases are often ambitious and creative, and he's worked in several fine bands and has participated in numerous great sessions. Fuller studied music in high school, then began de-

veloping his skills in an army band, where he played with Cannonball Adderley. He worked in Detroit with Kenny Burrell and Yusef Lateef, then moved to New York. Fuller made his recording debut as a leader on Transition in 1955, and recorded in the late '50s for Blue Note, Prestige, United Artists, and Savoy. He was a charter member of the Jazztet with Benny Golson and Art Farmer in 1959, then played in Art Blakey's Jazz Messengers from 1961 to 1965. There were additional recording dates for Warwick, Smash/Trip, Epic, and Impulse in the '60s. Fuller toured Europe with Dizzy Gillespie's big band in 1968, then did several sessions in New York. During the '70s, he experimented, for a time, by playing hard bop arrangements in a band that featured electronic instruments, heading a group with guitarist Bill Washer and Stanley Clarke. He concluded that phase with the '73 album *Crankin.'* Fuller toured with the Count Basie band from 1975 to 1977, and did dates for Mainstream, Timeless, and Bee Hive. He co-led the quintet Giant Bones with Winding in 1979 and 1980, and played with Art Blakey, Cedar Walton, and Benny Golson in the late '70s and early '80s. During the '80s, Fuller toured Europe regularly with the Timeless All-Stars, and performed and recorded with the revamped Jazztet. There are a few Fuller sessions available on CD, mostly early dates. —*Ron Wynn*

New Trombone / May 11, 1957 / Prestige 077

Curtis Fuller with Red Garland / May 14, 1957 / New Jazz 8277

With Hampton Hawes / May 18, 1957 / Prestige 5
This is an unorthodox, intriguing date, with Hawes excellent on piano, and Julius Watkins and David Amram on French horns. It's hard to find. —*Ron Wynn*

○ **Opener, The** / Jun. 16, 1957 / Blue Note 1567

Bone and Bari / Aug. 4, 1957 / Blue Note 1572

○ **Blues-Ette** / May 21, 1959 / Savoy Jazz 127
A powerhouse session with Fuller leading a stalwart group. Benny Golson (ts) and Tommy Flanagan (p) are sublime. —*Ron Wynn*

★ **All-Star Sextets** / Aug. 25, 1959+Dec. 17, 1959 / Savoy 2239
Combos led by trombonist Fuller, and members of the Jazztet and the Coltrane ensembles. Essential jazz/post bop. Seminal material from a brilliant trombonist. Features Lee Morgan (tpt), Wynton Kelly (p), McCoy Tyner (p), and others. —*Ron Wynn*

Sliding Easy / Dec. 1959 / United Artists 4041

Boss of the Soul Stream Trombone / Dec. 1960 / Warwick 2038

Magnificent Trombone of Curtis Fuller, The / Feb. 20, 1961 / Epic 16013

Soul Trombone / Nov. 15-16, 1961 / Impulse 13

Cabin in the Sky / Apr. 24, 1962 / Impulse 22

Crankin' / 1973 / MRL 333

○ **Smokin'** / 1974 / Mainstream 370

☆ **Four on the Outside** / Sep. 18, 1978 / Timeless 124
Trombonist Curtis Fuller's LP is nearly stolen by Pepper Adams (baritone sax). Not that Fuller was any slouch in the soloing department, but. . . . Adams romps through several sections of "Suite-Kathy" with particular elan, and has a grand time elsewhere. James Williams (piano) has some excellent solo spots. Most of the originals here seem to be fragments of melody from various standards reworked into a new whole. "Suite-Kathy" is a lengthy example of a reworking using a number of different time signatures and other attractive variations. Everyone bites into "Hello, Young Lovers" and turns this into the highlight of a good album. —*Shirley Klett*, Cadence

G

KENNY G (Kenneth Gorelick)

b. 1959, Seattle, WA
Soprano saxophone, reeds / Instrumental pop
Widely regarded as perhaps the embodiment of everything
wrong with "contemporary" jazz, onetime session player
Kenny Gorelick (a.k.a Kenny G) has become the biggest-selling instrumentalist in history with a series of commercial
hits. Kenny G's sales topped the 17-million mark through
1993. While it's hardly his fault, many have misidentified
Kenny G as a jazz musician, a claim he's never validated. He
plays noodling melodies, simple refrains, and straight instrumental pop tunes, but his music isn't totally devoid of
improvisation. He's backed major pop stars like Smokey
Robinson and Luther Vandross while recording for Arista.
All of his sessions are available on CD. —*Ron Wynn*

Kenny G Live / **i.** 1982 / Arista 8613

Kenny G / **i.** 1982 / Arista 8036

Duotones / **i.** 1986 / Arista 8496

★ **Silhouette** / **i.** 1988 / Arista 8457

STEVE GADD

b. 1945
Drums / Blues & jazz, soul-jazz, contemporary funk
While much of what Steve Gadd has played is either quasi-
jazz or straight pop, R&B, and funk, few question Gadd's
drumming credentials. He's emerged, chronologically after
Billy Cobham and prior to Dave Weckl, as one of the main
drum stylists in jazz-rock, and Gadd's kit tuning and rhyth-
mic approach are widely imitated. Gadd played with Dizzy
Gillespie as an 11-year-old. He studied at the Eastman
school, then later served in the army. After playing in a
Rochester big band, Gadd formed a trio and moved to New
York in the early '70s. He quickly became a prolific presence
in the studios. Gadd played and recorded jazz sessions with
Chick Corea, Al Di Meola, and Carla Bley, and pop and soul
sessions with Aretha Franklin, Barbra Streisand, Stevie
Wonder, Steely Dan, and Paul Simon. His work with David
Sanborn fell into the stylistic cracks. Gadd was a coleader of
the highly touted session band Stuff, with Eric Gale, Cornell
Dupree, and Richard Tee. While all the musicians were ac-
knowledged as studio greats, Stuff's albums stiffed in
America; they did much better in Japan. Gadd later teamed
with Eddie Gomez and Ronnie Cuber to form the Gadd
Gang. They recorded in the late '80s, and cut a date that
mixed Bob Dylan and Bill Doggett compositions. Gadd later
recorded for Projazz with Tee, Cuber, and other guest stars.
His Gadd Gang date for Columbia is available on CD. —*Ron
Wynn*

SLIM GAILLARD (Slim Bulee Gaillard)

b. Jan. 4, 1916, **d.** Feb. 25, 1991
Guitar, vocals / Swing, bop
A versatile musician who played guitar, vibes, and piano,
Slim Gaillard's flair for comedy sometimes overshadowed
his fine gift for playing music. But his mugging and his
asides shouldn't be Gaillard's only claim to fame; he played
mellow, bluesy piano, and was a good guitarist and a com-

petent vibes player. Gaillard developed a solo act in the '30s
where he mixed guitar and tap dancing simultaneously. He
first teamed with bassist Slam Stewart in 1938, and their
"Slim and Slam" musical and verbal patter became a national sensation that was featured on WNEW AM radio in
New York. Gaillard invented "vout," a jive linguistic code
that completed every other word with "oreenee." He wrote
novelty tunes and nonsense numbers like "Avocado Seed
Soup Symphony," "Matzoh Balls," and "Yip Roc Heresy," as
well as the big hit "Flat Foot Floogie." Gaillard would often
stop his songs in mid-stream for a burst of rapid-fire jive
talk. In Los Angeles during the mid '40s, Gaillard was a
popular entertainer who worked with bassist Bam Brown
and, occasionally, with vocalist Leo Watson. He appeared in
the films *Star Spangled Rhythm* and *Hellzapoppin.* Gaillard
had nonmusical gigs as a comedian and emcee for a time in
the '50s, then ran a motel in San Diego in the early '60s. He
also bought an orange farm. Gaillard played guitar, piano,
and sang in the televised miniseries "Roots–The Next
Generation" in 1982. He made some new albums for
Alastair Robertson's Hep label; they reissued some classic
sessions, too. Gaillard was busy through the remainder of
the '80s playing festivals both nationwide and internationally. Gaillard recorded recent sessions with Bucky Pizzarelli
and Major Holley; they're available on CD. —*Ron Wynn and
Michael G. Nastos*

Cement Mixer, Putti, Putti / Jan. 12, 1945 / Folklyric 9038

★ **Opera En Vout** / 1947 / Verve 554
A variety of sessions from 1946, 1947, 1951, and 1952 from
Gaillard. A perfect representation of Gaillard's musical and
comedic mastery. —*Michael G. Nastos*

Gaillard and Gillespie / **i.** 1958 / Ultraphonic 50273

Dot Sessions / Nov. 1959 / MCA 1508

Legendary Mcvouty, The / **i.** Oct. 1982 / Hep 6

○ **Original 1938 Recordings—Vol. 1** / Tax 1

○ **Original 1938 Recordings—Vol. 2** / Tax 2

ERIC GALE

b. Sep. 20, 1938, New York, NY
Guitar / Jazz-rock, Jazz-funk
A first-rate technician, guitarist Eric Gale has played many
bluesy, nicely constructed, and funky solos for various soul
and jazz acts over the years. Gale has fluidity, blues acumen,
and the flair to accompany anyone. —*Ron Wynn*

Forecast / 1975 / Kudu 11

Touch of Silk / 1980 / Columbia 36570

Blue Horizon / Oct. 1981-Nov. 1981 / Elektra 52349
Guitarist Eric Gale has been a regular in the funk, R&B, and
instrumental pop scene since the '70s, and at one time was
part of the supersession group Stuff. His 1982 album *Blue
Horizon*, newly reissued on CD, isn't the crackling funk
he's known for, nor is it smooth fusion or light jazz. It is,
instead, more a multicultural project done long before that
term came into vogue. There are reggae and samba songs,
straight soul and R&B, and Afro-Latin and African rhythms.
Hugh Masekela offers some tart flugelhorn lines in a guest
role, and Gale shows a musical sophistication and ambition

that hadn't been revealed in prior projects, and sadly hasn't been presented much ever since. —*Ron Wynn*

Island Breeze / 1982 / Elektra 7601981

★ **In a Jazz Tradition** / i. Nov. 29-30, 1987 / EmArcy 836369

Resurrection / i. 1988 / Elektra 61083

Let's Stay Together / i. 1989 / Artful Balance 7215

LARRY GALES (Lawrence Bernard Gales)

b. 1936
Bass / Hard bop
Larry Gales, Thelonious Monk's bassist for several years in the '60s, is known for his deep, rich sound and has always been a steady, reliable player. Gales began studying bass at age 11 with George Duvivier. He attended the Manhattan School of Music in 1956, and played four years later with J.C. Heard before joining the Eddie "Lockjaw" Davis-Johnny Griffin quintet. Gales worked with Herbie Mann, Junior Mance's trio, and vocalist Joe Williams in the early '60s before joining Monk. Gales remained with Monk from 1964 until 1969, when he moved to the West Coast and joined Erroll Garner. Gales also made several recordings in the '60s, including sessions with Buddy Tate, Bennnie Green, Charlies Rouse, Sonny Stitt, and Mary Lou Williams. He maintained that pace in the '70s, recording with Blue Mitchell, Jimmy Smith, Sonny Criss, Clark Terry, Dave Frishberg, Joe Turner, and Kenny Burrell. Gales also reteamed with Williams, and played with Willie Bobo, Red Rodney, Harold Land, Harry Edison, and Bill Berry, while also touring Japan and playing on the West Coast with Benny Carter. During the '80s and '90s, Gales has lead his own bands playing Monk-style jazz. In 1990, his band recorded a CD for Candid that is still available. —*Ron Wynn and Michael G. Nastos*

★ **Message from Monk, A** / Jun. 1990 / Candid 79503
Larry Gales, longtime bassist for Thelonious Monk, pays tribute to his former boss, heading a band that includes another Monk veteran in drummer Ben Riley. The other band members are accomplished players, although tenor saxophonist Junior Cook has uneven time. Trombonist Steve Turre and trumpeter Claudio Roditi fill the gap. —*Ron Wynn*

HAL GALPER (Harold Galper)

b. Apr. 18, 1938, Salem, MA
Piano / Bop, modern creative
Pianist Hal Galper has both classical and jazz training, and is one of the finest contemporary bebop-rooted players. His ensemble playing, particularly during his years with the Phil Woods group, was both fluid and invigorating, while his solos are distinguished by their adventurous harmonics and their sophistication. Galper has often written instructional articles for magazines such as *Down Beat* and *Keyboard.* He had classical training as a child, and studied jazz at Berklee from 1955 to 1958. He began working in Boston in 1959 with musicians such as Sam Rivers, Tony Williams, Chet Baker, Stan Getz, the Brecker Brothers, and in Herb Pomeroy's big band. Galper also accompanied vocalists Joe Williams and Anita O'Day. He spent two years playing electric piano in Cannonball Adderley's group in the mid '70s, and also received a grant from the National Endowment for the Arts that allowed him to give three concerts. Galper joined Woods's group in 1981, and played with him until 1990. Galper's also recorded several albums as a leader for various labels, among them Mainstream, Steeplechase, Enja, and Concord. He has several sessions available on CD. —*Ron Wynn and Michael G. Nastos*

Inner Journey / 1973 / Mainstream 398

○ **Now Hear This** / i. Feb. 1977 / Enja 2090
Pianist Hal Galper played churning, high-energy music that sounded quite a bit like McCoy Tyner. Listen to Galper's left hand and you'll see how close to Tyner Galper's playing comes. Two exceptions are "Shadow Waltz," a dreamy ballad, and Thelonious Monk's "Bemsha Swing." Trumpeter Terumasa Hino disappointed me. Having heard him on

other recordings, I know he was capable of more than he does here. On the other hand, bassist Cecil McBee and drummer Williams (whose first name is not listed) don't disappoint, playing with what had become their customary verve and inventiveness. —*Carl Brauer*, Cadence

★ **Speak with a Single Voice** / Feb. 1978 / Enja 4006
The first quintet recording, with the Brecker Brothers, at Rosie's in New Orleans. Essential. —*Michael G. Nastos*

Redux 1978 / 1978 / Concord Jazz 4483
A followup recording to the *Speak with a Single Voice* album. An important document of this great band. The CD has two bonus cuts. —*Michael G. Nastos*

Live at Maybeck Recital Hall—Vol. 6 / Jul. 1990 / Concord Jazz 4438

Invitation to a Concert / i. 1990 / Concord Jazz 4455
Hal Galper Trio. This is one of his most recent. The pianist dominates the session. —*Ron Wynn*

○ **Hal Galper Quartet** / i. Jun. 23, 1992 / Enja 3053

GANELIN TRIO

Modern creative
The premier Soviet free music ensemble, the Ganelin Trio began attracting attention in the '70s. Pianist, percussionist, electric guitarist, and composer Vyacheslav Ganelin (b. 1944), multisaxophonist Vladimir Chekasin (b. 1947), and drummer Vladimir Tarasov (b. 1947) formed the trio in 1971 in Vilnius, which was then in Soviet-controlled Lithuania. They mixed free music with chamber and folk forms, as well as other ethnic styles, and added pop and rock. Their sound is energetic, sometimes comic, sometimes disorganized, but very much their own, though the influences of musicians such as Albert Ayler and Sun Ra can be detected. They began recording on Melodiya in the mid '70s and have recorded several albums since then on England's Leo label. Chekasin has also done solo dates for Leo. Their '80s work has included experiments with drum machines and electronics. They've also recorded for Hat Art in the '80s, and have had some earlier albums issued domestically by Mobile Fidelity. They were featured in Frederick Starr's *Red & Hot: The Fate of Jazz in the Soviet Union* in 1983 and 1985's *Russian Jazz: New Identity*, which was edited by Leo Feigin (the label's head). Currently, the Ganelin Trio has only one album available in the *Spectrum* catalog. —*Ron Wynn and Michael G. Nastos*

Poi Segue / Oct. 25, 1975+Nov. 15, 1975 / Eastwind 20647
Ganelin-Tarasov-Chekasin. More seamless, no-holds-barred free music. —*Michael G. Nastos*

★ **Concerto Grosso** / i. 1978 / Melodiya
Ganelin-Tarasov-Chekasin. Russian trio of wildly pure improvisers. A must-buy for the challengable listener. —*Michael G. Nastos*

JAN GARBAREK

b. Mar. 4, 1947, Mysen, Norway
Tenor and soprano saxophone, flute / New age, modern creative
Norwegian soprano and tenor saxophonist Jan Garbarek has played free, European avant-garde and folk forms, jazz-rock, and George Russell's Lydian chromatic system successfully, and has emerged as one of Europe's finest players. His stark, emphatic soprano style is well respected, particularly his fluid technique, contrasting dynamics, sharp changes in density and mood, and his approach, which is more spacious than the usual dense textures of more urban jazz. Garbarek is a good flutist as well. He has written compositions for television, theater, and film, and incorporates elements of classical music into his playing and writing. Johnny Hodges and John Coltrane were Garbarek's earliest influences; his playing, in that mode, was noticed by both Krzysztof Komeda and Russell. Garbarek made his recording debut in 1966, while also appearing in festivals at Warsaw and Prague. He later recorded and performed with Russell's orchestra and sextet, and studied the Lydian concept with him. Garbarek

formed a quartet with Terje Rypdal that played often with Russell, then began heading a trio in 1973. He toured Europe and America with Keith Jarrett's quartet in 1977. Garbarek subsequently formed a band with Eberhard Weber, David Torn, and Michael Di Pasqua that played in Warsaw and toured Europe, America, Japan, and Norway in the '80s. Garbarek has recorded extensively with ECM; playing in a duo with Ralph Towner, leading bands, working with Jarrett, and playing in Charlie Haden's groups. He has several sessions available as a leader on CD. —*Ron Wynn and David Nelson McCarthy*

Esoteric Circle, The / 1969 / Freedom 741031
The '69 album that introduced the stark, careening soprano sax of Norway's Jan Garbarek to American audiences. Composer and theorist George Russell helped gain Garbarek entry to American recording studios, and the rest is history. —*Ron Wynn*

★ **Afric Pepperbird** / Sep. 22-23, 1970 / ECM 843475

Works / 1970-1980 / ECM 823266

Sart / Apr. 14-15, 1971 / ECM 839305

★ **Witchi-Tai-To** / Nov. 27-28, 1973 / ECM 833330
The Jan Garbarek/Bob Stenson group was certainly one of the most versatile nonelectric ensembles playing anywhere in the world at this time (1973). Frankly, *Witchi-Tai-To*, which was superbly recorded from a technical standpoint, provided a clear, refreshing respite from the surfeit of wah-wahs, electric quirks, and merely funky posturings that were so prevalent on turntables at the time. Each member of this group deserves his own niche in the higher echelons of music polls, and the quartet in toto should have been recognized for its direct blowing, varied and smooth dynamic transitions, and intense emotional fervor. On this album, Garbarek and Stenson perform material by other composers who had strong folk influences. The songs are often based, like John Coltrane's music, on single-chord vamps that are characteristic of the inspiration behind the compositions: Middle-Eastern/Turkish folk music (Carla Bley's "A.I.R."), Spanish flamenco (Carlos Puebla's "Hasta Siempre"), American Indian chant (Jim Pepper's title tune), and Scandinavian folk melody (bassist Palle Danielsson's "Kuka"). Don Cherry's "Desireless" stems more directly from the classic Trane tradition, receiving a majestic, swanlike movement powerfully traced over 20 minutes. Those who think that contemporary music hailing from Europe lacks soulfire are hereby advised to listen to *Witchi-Tai-To*. The Garbarek/Stenson group burned with a brilliant flame, forging a sturdy sound in a classic tradition. —*Charles Mitchell, Down Beat*

Belonging / Apr. 24-25, 1974 / ECM 829115

Luminescence / Apr. 29-30, 1974 / ECM 1049

Dis / Dec. 1976 / ECM 827408

Folk Songs / Nov. 1979 / ECM 8277022
Excellent teaming. Haden and Gismonti awaken the perenially detached Garbarek. —*Ron Wynn*

Paths, Prints / Dec. 1981 / ECM 829377
One of the better, more exciting releases—thanks to Bill Frisell (g). —*Ron Wynn*

Wayfarer / Mar. 1983 / ECM 811968

○ **I Took Up the Runes** / Aug. 1990 / ECM 843850

○ **Star** / Jan. 1991 / ECM 849649
For saxophonist Jan Garbarek, *Star's* approach is jazzier, more ethereal, and less earthy than last year's (1991) *I Took Up the Runes*. There are even instances on three tunes where he somehow uses electronics when stating the melody. The effect is to lift the music heavenward. In an all-originals program (Garbarek penned the lilting title track; bassist Miroslav Vitous wrote four pieces, including the bouncy "Jumper"; drummer Peter Erskine composed two, "Snowman" being a tripartite offering), there is a simple beauty to the melodies. Maybe what makes this album work best for me is its take on the jazz esthetic: the intimate, conversational style that nurtured personal expression, commu-

nication, and spirited improvisation. —*John Ephland*, Down Beat

RED GARLAND (William M. Garland)

b. May 13, 1923, Dallas, TX, **d.** Apr. 23, 1984, Dallas, TX
Piano / Bop, post bop
An outstanding player, Red Garland's style not only reflected the influence of Count Basie and Nat "King" Cole, but also reflected modernists such as Bud Powell and Art Tatum, as well as Erroll Garner and Ahmad Jamal. Garland was noted for his skillful, trademark use of block chords. He played with the great horn players of his era, including Charlie Parker, Coleman Hawkins, and Lester Young. Garland's greatest recognition as a sideman came as part of the famous Miles Davis rhythm section with Paul Chambers and Philly Joe Jones. He also led his own trio, and issued some fine recordings on Prestige, and later on Galaxy. Garland has several sessions available on CD. —*Ron Wynn and David Nelson McCarthy*

Garland of Red / Aug. 17, 1956 / Prestige 126

Dig It! / Feb. 22, 1957-Mar. 26, 1958 / Prestige 392
1989 reissue contains more from the mammoth Garland late-'50s output, with Donald Byrd (tpt), John Coltrane (ts), Paul Chambers (b), Art Taylor (d), and the underrated George Joyner (tpt). —*Ron Wynn*

Groovy / May 24, 1957 / Prestige 061

All Mornin' Long / Nov. 15, 1957 / Prestige 293
Loose, with elements of funk and soul-jazz, plus the usual excellence from Donald Byrd (tpt), Coltrane (ts), and Garland. —*Ron Wynn*

★ **Soul Junction** / Nov. 15, 1957 / Prestige 481
Quintet. More Donald Byrd (tpt), John Coltrane (ts), and Red Garland. Solos from Coltrane and Byrd are better than on *High Pressure*. —*Ron Wynn*

Manteca / Apr. 11, 1958 / Prestige 428
Red Garland Trio. Afro-Latin flavoring from Ray Barretto (per) spices up an otherwise proficient, but musically standard trio date. —*Ron Wynn*

Rojo / Aug. 22, 1958 / Original Jazz Classics 772
Pianist Red Garland's regular trio added Latin jazz great Ray Barretto on congas for this 1958 session, and things were both varied and intensified. Barretto expanded the rhythmic possibilities on both the standards and the songs that had an Afro-Latin foundation. He and drummer Charlie Persip have both their own dialogue and one going with bassist George Joyner, while Garland adds his steady fills, bluesy solos, and rolling phrases. —*Ron Wynn*

Red Garland Trio / Nov. 21, 1958 / Original Jazz Classics 224
First-rate interaction from Garland, Paul Chambers (b), and Art Taylor (d). —*Ron Wynn*

All Kinds of Weather / Nov. 27, 1958 / Prestige 193
Smooth, high-level Garland, with Art Taylor (d) and Paul Chambers (b). —*Ron Wynn*

○ **Red in Bluesville** / Apr. 17, 1959 / Original Jazz Classics 295

○ **Red Garland Live!** / Oct. 2, 1959 / New Jazz 8326

Moodsville—Vol. 1 / Dec. 11, 1959 / Original Jazz Classics 360
Red Garland Trio. As exacting and demanding as any from the combo of Garland, Art Taylor (d), and Paul Chambers (b). —*Ron Wynn*

★ **Red Alone** / Apr. 2, 1960 / Moodsville 3

Bright and Breezy / Jul. 19, 1961 / Original Jazz Classics 265
Red Garland Trio. This 1987 reissue is from a good, though unexceptional, trio date. —*Ron Wynn*

○ **Solar** / Jan. 30, 1962 / Jazzland 755
With Les Spann (g,f), Sam Jones (b), and Frank Gant (d). This is easy-listening, cocktail lounge-style jazz. —*AMG*

Red's Good Groove / Mar. 22, 1962 / Jazzland 87

Large doses of funk and soul-jazz, plus fine baritone from Pepper Adams and Blue Mitchell on trumpet. —*Ron Wynn*

○ **When There Are Grey Skies** / Oct. 9, 1962 / Prestige 704
Good early-'60s standards and originals date featuring pianist Red Garland in a trio with bassist Wendell Marshall and drummer Charlie Persip. Garland roams, explores, and reworks pieces, at times creating alternate melodies, other times working back till he returns to the original. The CD reissue has one bonus cut. —*Ron Wynn*

Red Alert / Dec. 2, 1977 / Galaxy 647
A 1991 issue of an excellent album date with superb Garland piano and top contributions by Nat Adderley (cnt), Harold Land (ts), and Ira Sullivan (tpt). —*Ron Wynn*

★ **Crossings** / Dec. 1977 / Galaxy 472
Tremendous update. An example of Garland's ability to heave and to create in a trio setting, this time with Ron Carter (b) and Philly Joe Jones (d). —*Ron Wynn*

I Left My Heart . . . / **i.** May 1978 / Muse 5311

Strike up the Band / Jul. 11-12, 1979 / Galaxy
Some stunning solos from George Coleman (ts). Garland was still an impressive player in the final stages of his career, though not as much the driving force as in the past. —*Ron Wynn*

Red Garland's Piano / Dec. 30, 1991 / Prestige 073

○ **Jazz Junction** / Prestige 24023

○ **Misty Red** / Timeless 179

ERROLL GARNER (Erroll Louis Garner)

b. Jun. 15, 1921, Pittsburg, PA, **d.** Jan. 2, 1977, Los Angeles, CA
Piano / Swing
He never learned to read music, yet pianist Erroll Garner was a superb player with a completely unique approach. This approach included his use of voicings in the left hand, which is similar to the way guitarists in swing bands play. It also included intentionally lagging behind the beat, and using contrasting textures and dynamics. Garner inserted Latin dance rhythms into his style during the '50s, providing additional rhythmic variety. Garner's elaborate introductions to songs were little masterpieces in themselves. On ballads, he adopted a heavily arpeggiated, romantic method. He made interpretations of pop songs a pianistic adventure, ranging over the keyboard and exploring every available harmonic and melodic option. He was also an excellent composer, creating such recognized classics as "Erroll's Bounce," "Dreamy," "That's My Kick," "Moment's Delight," and his signature piece, "Misty." His songs were featured in the films *A New Kind of Love* and *Play Misty for Me.*
Garner began his professional career in Pittsburgh from 1938 to 1941 with Leroy Brown's orchestra. He moved to New York in 1944, and began playing in clubs and substituting in Art Tatum's trio with Tiny Grimes and Slam Stewart. Garner became the pianist when Slam Stewart took over the trio's leadership in 1945. His first recordings came in the mid '40s. Garner soon formed his own trio; other than playing solo, this was the format he preferred throughout his career. Garner was voted New Star of 1946 in *Esquire's* poll, and became a popular pick in other critics' and reader surveys. He recorded with Charlie Parker in 1947 while in Los Angeles. The group played his tune, "Cool Blues," and also did it at a faster pace and called it "Hot Blues." During the mid and late '40s, there were sessions for Dial and Savoy. He appeared frequently on television in the '50s and '60s, and began touring overseas regularly in 1957. Garner was among the top-selling jazz artists of the decade. *Other Voices* and *Concert By the Sea* on Columbia cracked the Top 20. *Plays Misty, Solitare,* and *Afternoon of an Elf* did well for Mercury, while *Soliloquy, Dreamy, Play It Again, Erroll,* and *Paris Impressions* were big winners for Columbia.
He didn't slow down in the '60s, cutting sessions for his own Octave label, for RCA in France, and for Bulldog in England. He also did domestic dates for ABC Paramount,

Phillips, MGM, Mercury, and EmArcy. Garner began producing his material and showed his versatility. He recorded show tunes, film themes, and originals. There were repertory albums devoted to Gershwin and Kern, live dates, studio sessions, even an album mixing harpsichord and piano. Garner kept working and recording until the late '70s. The last hit version of "Misty" (there have been five since 1959) was done by Ray Stevens, who made it to the number 14 spot on the charts. Garner died in 1977. His work has been reissued steadily, with his earliest material available on a Doctor Jazz compilation. Mercury, Atlantic, Savoy, and Columbia have all rereleased his work. —*Ron Wynn and Dan Morgenstern*

○ **Complete Savoy Sessions—Vol. 1, The** / Jan. 30, 1945 / Savoy 70521

○ **Erroll Garner—Vol. 1** / Feb. 17, 1947+Jun. 10, 1947 / Dial 205

★ **Elf, The** / Mar. 29, 1949 / Savoy 4408
The lion's share of these Erroll Garner recordings was done in 1949. There are also four tunes done in 1945. These earlier recordings are clearly those of a pianist strongly influenced by jazz; but to refer to Garner's playing here as "jazz piano" is simply not correct, or at least not fair to the many keyboardists who were more seriously investigating the resources of the idiom. At this time, Garner was a lush, influential stylist, but a limited improviser. The 1949 tracks loosen up considerably more, but the similar tempos and stylings, while lovely, don't have the lean strength or compelling swing that would emerge a bit later. Everything here is a trio recording, and that, of course, compounds the problem. —*Neil Tesser,* Down Beat

Yesterdays / Mar. 29, 1949 / Savoy 4422

Erroll Garner-Billy Taylor / Mar. 29, 1949+1949 / Savoy 12008

Long Ago and Far Away / Jun. 28, 1950-Jan. 1, 1951 / Columbia 40863
1950-1951. This is great Garner. Unfortunately, the remastering is not as great. —*Michael Erlewine*

○ **Gone-Garner-Gonest** / Jan. 11, 1951-Mar. 30, 1953 / Columbia 617

○ **Gems** / Jan. 11, 1951 / Columbia 6173

○ **Solo Flight** / Feb. 29, 1952 / Columbia 6209

Too Marvelous for Words—Vol. 3 / May 1954 / EmArcy 842419
The third in the Polygram series of overviews. Plenty of majestic performances. —*Ron Wynn*

Mambo Moves Garner / Jul. 27, 1954 / Mercury 834909
A 1988 reissue of a fine session where Garner applied his unforgettable skills to the Afro-Latin arena. —*Ron Wynn*

★ **Erroll Garner Plays Misty** / **i.** 1954 / EmArcy 824892

★ **Original Misty** / **i.** 1954 / Mercury 834910
This is a reissue of the first Garner version of *Misty* made in the early '50s. —*Ron Wynn*

Afternoon of an Elf / Mar. 14, 1955 / Mercury 826457
Spectacular, frenzied solo piano from Erroll Garner, done in 1955. Sometimes he probes, picks apart, then reconstructs standards. Other times, he races through a song, varying the tempo, pulse, and pace with each solo. This has been reissued on CD. —*Ron Wynn*

★ **Concert by the Sea** / Sep. 19, 1955 / Columbia 40589
Concert By the Sea is arguably the finest record pianist Erroll Garner ever made, and he made many recordings—a few outstanding, many good. But this live recording (September 19, 1955) with his trio (Eddie Calhoun, bass; Denzil Best, drums) presents a typical Garner program: a mixture of originals, show biz, and pop standards delivered with his unique delivery and enthusiasm. The rhythms and brilliant use of tension and release are perfectly captured. And while for many jazz listeners Garner's deliberate structures were too orchestrated, there is an equal spontaneity in the propulsion of these orchestrations that swing as

well as anything. Again, on this reissue, original liner notes were deleted, though the memorable comment by Garner at the end of the concert that his voice was "worser than Louis Armstrong's" (misquoted in the new liners) was retained with the entire program. —*Bob Rusch,* Cadence

○ **Most Happy Piano, The** / Jun. 7, 1956-Sep. 11, 1956 / Columbia 939

○ **Paris Impressions—Vol. 1** / Mar. 27, 1958+May 11, 1958 / Sony Special Products 9

This Garner, while not his best, is still fine Garner. The big drawback on this double set is his work on the harpsichord, an instrument which may have knocked him out, but has never adapted well to jazz as far as I know. Garner makes no concessions to the instrument and plays it with the same style he plays the piano, a style that clashes on the harpsichord. Garner fans will be glad to have this back in circulation if they don't already have it. —*Bob Rusch,* Cadence

○ **Paris Impressions—Vol. 2** / Mar. 27, 1958+May 11, 1958 / Columbia 1217

New Kind of Love, A / Jul. 1963 / Mercury 20859

○ **Plays Gershwin and Kern** / Aug. 1964-Feb. 1968 / EmArcy 826224

Erroll Garner Plays Gershwin and Kern is a reissue of material previously issued in Europe on Bulldog, MPS, and Polydor. According to the liners, the bulk of the material comes from two dates: August 19, 1965 and August 5-6, 1964. The Doran Garner discography lists the material as from July 25, 1964 with the exception of "I Got Rhythm" from March 19, 1968. Either way, the material is quite excellent, often adventuresome, and some of his best studio sides. Included here, from February 5, 1968 and never issued before, is a brief (1:05) "Nice Work If You Can Get It" with Garner singing along to himself—it's a wonderful gem of a private moment. Backup is Eddie Calhoun or Ike Isaacs on bass, Kelly Martin or Jimmy Smith on drums, and Jose Mangual on congas. This is the first domestic issue of this material. —*Bob Rusch,* Cadence

That's My Kick / Nov. 1967 / MGM 4463

Hot piano and excellent bass by Milt Hinton, with a guest stint by Johnny Pacheco (f, v, per). —*Ron Wynn*

Up in Erroll's Room / i. 1968 / MPS 29.098

Gemini / i. 1969 / MPS 29.098

○ **Magician** / i. Oct. 1974 / London 640

All of Erroll Garner's familiar trademarks—the thunk-thunk-thunk-thunk chords, the wobbly octave tremolos, the meandering introductions, even the grunts, groans, hums, and yeahs—remain intact here. Added are a couple of new tricks: some funky left-hand rhythms and a rhythm section that plays fluently in straight eighth-note rhythms. The Latin-rock treatments of "Someone to Watch Over Me" and "Yesterdays" owes much to mainstream Ramsey Lewis. But while Garner updates his style in places, his basic style remains intact. And the outlines of Garner's style have more to do with emotion—especially the comic emotions—than with technique. Witness his sly prodding of the sugary-sickly "Close to You"; after a wry, dissonant introduction, he shifts into a tongue-in-cheek backbeat, then doubletimes, and gets down to business. After some excavating into the tune's real possibilities, he effects a real transformation—a saccharin pop tune became a genuine jazz vehicle. In all, this record's virtues far outweigh its defects. And it clearly demonstrates that the truly impressive thing about Erroll Garner was not his idiosyncratic style, but the depth of his wit, verve, and genial good spirits. —*Jon Balleras,* Down Beat

Dancing on the Ceiling / i. 1989 / EmArcy 935

This features Garner at his absolute peak on nine standards, and not once does he let his intensity flag. This music is as alive now as it was a quarter-century ago. Garner fans—rejoice. —*Rich Kienzle,* Rock & Roll Disc

○ **Body and Soul** / i. Mar. 18, 1991 / Columbia 47035

○ **Erroll Garner Collection—Vols. 4 & 5: Solo Time!** / i. Nov. 16, 1992 / Verve 511821

○ **Savoy Sessions** / Savoy 4408

Greatest Garner / Atlantic 1227

KENNY GARRETT

Alto and tenor saxophone, flute / Hard bop, neo-bop

An exciting young saxophonist who emerged in the mid '80s as one of the hottest and freshest talents on the jazz scene. Garrett's tart, bluesy, and emphatic solos on alto sax, as well as his impressive flute work, began to get widespread attention during a short stint he had with Miles Davis. His mid '80s debut on Criss Cross got even more notice, as did subsequent albums on Paddle Wheel, Atlantic, and Warner Bros. Garrett has worked with Woody Shaw, Mulgrew Miller, Charnett Moffett, Tony Reedus, Rudy Bird, Joe Henderson, Kenny Kirkland, Don Alias, and others. Davis made a rare guest appearance on Garrett's Atlantic release, *Prisoner of Love.* All his releases are available on CD. —*Ron Wynn*

Introducing Kenny Garrett / Dec. 1984 / Criss Cross 1014

Prisoner of Love / i. 1989 / Atlantic 782046

An intense, exciting alto saxophonist, Garrett was one of the few musicians old or young favorably mentioned in Miles Davis's recent autobiographical splurge. Results here are mixed; he reaffirms his sax prowess and does a competent job on synthesizers and guitar. —*Ron Wynn,* Rock & Roll Disc

★ **African Exchange Student** / i. 1990 / Atlantic 82156

Black Hope / i. 1992 / Warner Brothers 45017

Alto saxophonist Kenny Garrett hasn't been as heavily publicized as his fellow young lions, but he can play with as much authority, conviction, and sheer energy as anyone. Only some uneven material keeps his '92 album from being exceptional, and even on the weak songs Garrett's playing forces you to pay attention. —*Ron Wynn*

JIMMY GARRISON

b. 1934, d. 1976

Bass / Early free

Jimmy Garrison turned the acoustic bass into a varied, majestic weapon. He provided huge, prominent walking bass lines on standards, blues, and ballads, played some remarkable flamenco figures and patterns on bow, and turned in some astonishing countermelodies during free improvisations. His extensive solo on the album *Live at the Village Vanguard Again* is among the more breathtaking recorded bass improvisations on record. Garrison began playing bass in his youth, and moved to New York from Philadelphia. He'd worked in Philadelphia with Bobby Timmons and Tootie Heath. In New York, Garrison played with many bebop greats, including Philly Joe Jones, Curtis Fuller, Benny Golson, and Lennie Tristano. He worked with Ornette Coleman in the '60s, and had an extensive stint with Coltrane. His playing bridged both the quartet and revised group eras, when Alice Coltrane, Pharoah Sanders, and Rashied Ali, as well as sometime guest Donald Garrett, were included on recording sessions. He stayed with Coltrane from 1961 to 1967, and also worked, for a time, with Alice Coltrane. Garrison then played with Hampton Hawes, and worked with Archie Shepp and Elvin Jones in the '60s and '70s. He also taught at Bennington College at the behest of Bill Dixon, and at Wesleyan. His last stint was with his longtime section mate, Jones, in 1973 and 1974 before Garrison died of lung cancer in 1976. Despite his flamboyant talents, he was the ultimate section man. He does not have any albums listed in Spectrum under his name as a leader, although he co-led a sextet with Jones for the recording date *Illumination* on Impulse. —*Ron Wynn*

CHARLES GAYLE

b. 1939

Tenor saxophone / Modern creative

Certainly one of the most distinctive players among current saxophonists, Charles Gayle's cries, screams, swooping phrases, and tone are a throwback to the sanctified-church and blues-inspired sound of Albert Ayler. It's a raw, on-the-edge, furious approach with little subtlety and often without an identifiable theme, yet his music is undeniably evocative in its intensity. In 1993, Gayle was the subject of some profiles laden with dubious sociopolitical analysis because he's been a street musician and has been homeless for a good part of the '80s and '90s. He recorded for Silkheart in a seven-day span during the late '80s; the recording was made in a manner that was a modern equivalent of Alan Lomax or Victor Peer making a field recording journey. All Gayle's Silkheart sessions are available on CD. —*Ron Wynn*

○ **Spirits Before** / Apr. 1988 / Silkheart 117

○ **Always Born** / i. Apr. 1988 / Silkheart 115

★ **Homeless** / i. Apr. 1988 / Silkheart 116

LARRY GELB

b. 1952
Piano / Post bop, neo-bop
Larry Gelb is a composer/lyricist, a jazz pianist/teacher, and an author. Aside from albums, he has written film scores, off-Broadway musicals, and the book *The Geometry of Melody.*
Gelb began playing piano at age seven, started composing seriously at age 11, and recorded his first album at age 13. At age 14, he won the Yamaha International Young Composer competition. As a teenager, he formed his own trio and toured with Buddy DeFranco and with the Glenn Miller Orchestra. A student of Margaret Chaloff (mother of Serge Chaloff), he attended the Berklee School of Music in Boston, and taught history of jazz at the University of California in the '70s. His first major jazz album, *New Souls,* was released in 1980 establishing a worldwide reputation. His first two albums featured Kim Parker, stepdaughter of Chan Parker. An expert on the pianist Bill Evans, Gelb operates a music publishing company entitled Imagin Action Music. Currently, he doesn't have any sessions available on CD. —*Ron Wynn and Michael G. Nastos*

★ **New Souls** / 1979 / Essene 7001

☆ **Language of Blue, The** / Jun. 1980+Sep. 1, 1981 / Cadence 1012
What a unique record by composer/lyricist/player Larry Gelb featuring the voice of Kim Parker, which seems endlessly flexible. The only completely instrumental track is "Kim, When I Close My Eyes." Everything else was written for Kim, daughter of Chan Parker. You've got to follow the lyrics, which are all included on the back cover, and then you've got to be a bit amazed at how she handles such intervals to match endless and reasonably unfamiliar changes laid down by Gelb (p). The additional bonus is beautiful accompaniment by Doug LeFebvre (sax). He and trumpeter Tiger Okoshi never play on the same tracks, but were probably at the same sessions. Especially dig the soprano sound on "Picasso." You can't just sit down and take this in one dose. Some tracks like "The Record Collector" swing a bit more than most. "Alternate Master" is not another take, but a message. —*Jerry L. Atkins, Cadence*

HERB GELLER (Herbert Geller)

b. Nov. 2, 1928, Los Angeles, CA
Alto saxophone / Cool
Both a tragic story and a tale of perseverance, the Gellers were a successful husband-and-wife alto sax and piano team for a brief moment in the '50s. Herb Geller (b. 1928) had extensive credentials. He'd worked with Joe Venuti in 1946, and performed and recorded with Claude Thornhill in 1949. Lorraine Walsh Geller (1928-1958) had performed with the Sweethearts of Rhythm in New York from 1949 to 1951. She met Geller while he was in New York, and they later married and moved to Los Angeles. Lorraine Geller played with Shorty Rogers, Red Mitchell, Zoot Sims, Stan Getz, Dizzy Gillespie, and Charlie Parker, displaying a vibrant rhythmic sound and extensive harmonic knowledge. Herb Geller played with Billy May's orchestra, and worked with

Maynard Ferguson, Rogers, and Bill Holman. He was a good, steady alto saxophonist; not a particularly intriguing soloist, but a smooth, relaxed player with solid phrasing and technique. Geller formed a quartet with his wife in the mid '50s, and they recorded an album for EmArcy in 1955 with Red Mitchell and Mel Lewis, which wasn't revolutionary, but was nicely played combo material. After making her own album as a leader, playing with Red Mitchell and backing Kay Star, Lorraine Geller died in 1958, one month after her 30th birthday. Herb Geller kept going, playing with Benny Goodman and Louis Bellson in the late '50s and early '60s, and going to Brazil with Goodman at the peak of bossa nova mania. He toured Europe, then moved to Berlin in 1962, where he played in a radio station's jazz orchestra and ran a nightclub. Geller settled in Hamburg, and continued broadcasting, writing arrangements, and playing for Norddeutscher Rundfunk. He was in Friedrich Gulda's Euro-Jazz Orchestra in 1965 and 1966, and in Peter Herbolzheimer's big band through the '70s. Geller headed a bop quartet in 1984. He has recorded for EmArcy, Jubilee, Nova, Circle, Enja, and Discovery. Herb Geller has some sessions available on CD. Lorraine Geller is represented on the Gellers EmArcy date (not currently available), her own solo album (also unavailable) and *Presenting Red Mitchell* on Contemporary, which is on CD. —*Ron Wynn*

Gellers, The / i. 1954 / EmArcy 36024

That Geller Feller / i. Mar. 1957 / Fresh Sound 91

★ **American in Hamburg / View from Here** / i. Jan. 13, 1975 / Nova 28332

Rhyme and Reason / i. Jan. 1975 / Discovery 874
Good quintet sessions, plus (for those who value him) Mark Murphy (v). —*Ron Wynn*

Birdland Stomp / i. Jan. 1986 / Enja 5019

Jazz Song Book / i. Dec. 1988 / Enja 79655
This is much better than you'd expect from the low-key publicity. Geller deserves a wider profile, having been an active player since the '40s. Walter Morris is a prominent figure on the piano. —*Ron Wynn*

Quartet / Fresh Sound

GEORGE GERSHWIN

b. Sep. 26, 1898, **d.** Jul. 11, 1937
Composer, piano / Songwriter
An American composer primarily of musicals and songs (with lyricist brother Ira), Gershwin was famous for "Rhapsody in Blue" (1924), the folk opera *Porgy and Bess* (1935), and the *Piano Concerto in F* (1925). He was probably the first composer of extended musical forms, aside from Scott Joplin in his operas, to embrace fully African-American creative music as a fundamental source of inspiration. Certain works, such as the *I Got Rhythm Variations,* scenes in *Porgy and Bess,* and the *Preludes for Piano,* have a sophistication of variation technique and orchestration comparable to the best of modern French melodists, like Poulenc. (Gershwin applied to study with Ravel and then with Nadia Boulanger, but was turned down by each; they did not want to cramp his natural style.) Gershwin's influence on jazz has been enormous (his harmonic sense studied by bebop composers) and his music continues to have freshness and warmth. —*Blue Gene Tyranny*

★ **Gershwin Performs Gershwin: Rare Recordings . . .** / i. 1931 / Music Masters 5062
1931-1934. A rare treasure, this CD contains two 15-minute episodes of the 1934 "Music by Gershwin" radio program (complete with laxative commercials!), a radio appearance with Rudy Vallee, and rehearsals for the *Second Rhapsody* and *Porgy and Bess* conducted by Gershwin himself. Gives great insight into the personality of one of the century's major composers. —*William Ruhlmann*

Piano Roll Discoveries / i. Aug. 6, 1959 / RCA 2058

Gershwin in Hollywood, The / i. 1991 / Philips 434274

'S Wonderful: The Gershwin Songbook / i. 1992 / Verve 513928

Great Jazz Vocalists Sing the Gershwin, The / i. 1992 / Capitol 80506

Fascinatin' Rhythm–Capitol Sings George Gershwin / i. Feb. 17, 1992 / Capitol 96792

Rhapsody in Blue / i. Apr. 6, 1992 / Biograph 106

'S Wonderful / i. Dec. 2, 1992 / Pro Arte 433

Jazz Album, The / Angel 47991

Gershwin in the Movies / Milan 249

American Songbook Series: George Gershwin / Smithsonian 048

☆ **Columbia Album** / CBS 47862

STAN GETZ (Stanley Getz)

b. Feb. 2, 1927, Philadelphia, PA, d. Jun. 6, 1991
Tenor saxophone / Bop

A truly great tenor saxophonist, Stan Getz's light tone, lush sound, and smoothly swinging solos made him, perhaps, the cool school's most popular player. His approach is largely original, though he owes a partial debt to Lester Young; he parallels Young by retaining his romanticism regardless of tempo. From the '40s until his death in 1991, his body of work contains little that's not first-rate and much that's magnificent.

Getz began playing professionally at age 15 and made his first recordings a year later working with Jack Teagarden. Getz then played in the big bands of Stan Kenton and Benny Goodman during the mid '40s, making his recording debut as a leader in 1946 before joining Woody Herman in 1947. He was part of the Second Herd along with Zoot Sims, Serge Chaloff, and Herbie Steward. They formed the Four Brothers reed section. Getz's solo on "Early Autumn" in 1948 made his reputation. He left Herman in 1949 and began to lead many combos. He became another musician who formed a long and profitable union with Norman Granz in the '50s. Getz recorded frequently for Verve with Oscar Peterson, Gerry Mulligan, J.J. Johnson, and many others, while also touring with Jazz at the Philharmonic revue. Getz spent part of the decade working in Europe and Scandinavia.

When he returned to America in 1961, Getz made a comeback via the album *Focus*, which features Eddie Sauter's arrangements. In that recording, Getz improvises freely over the string section rather than using a preset melody or chord progression. The next year, he and guitarist Charlie Byrd initiated a popular craze when they combined cool jazz and samba to make bossa nova. Their album *Jazz Samba* topped the pop charts in 1962, while *Big Band Bossa Nova* with Gary McFarland reached number 13. *Jazz Samba Encore!* and *Reflections* both made the charts. The *Getz/Gilberto* album with Joao and Astrud Gilberto was number two in 1964, and the single, "The Girl From Ipenema," was number five. *Getz Au Go Go* became his sixth hit album over a two-year span, and reached number 24. Getz even won Grammys in 1962 and 1964.

After the fad cooled, Getz kept making solid albums, working with emerging stars like Gary Burton, Steve Swallow, Chick Corea, Tony Williams, and Airto. *Sweet Rain* with Corea also made the pop charts in 1967. Previously, Getz had made an appearance in *The Benny Goodman Story* film, and he played on the soundtrack for *Mickey One* in 1965. There were other dates in the '60s for Verve, Columbia, and RCA. Getz was featured on a pair of albums recorded in Europe during 1971, *Dynasty* and *Communications. Communications* was recorded in Paris while *Dynasty* was done partially at Ronnie Scott's in London, with other segments recorded at a different location. An album he'd recorded in 1972, *Captain Marvel*, put Getz back on the pop charts when it came out in 1975. He recorded many other albums in the '70s, playing with Albert Dailey, Jimmy Rowles, Joanne Brackeen, and making another album with Joao Gilberto, *The Best of Two Worlds.* During the '80s, Getz toured and recorded often, remaining

true to acoustic, uncompromised jazz. He helped a young vocalist, Dianne Schuur, played frequently with Kenny Barron, and added to his remarkable legacy of great sessions. There are many, many Getz dates available on multiple labels. There's a comprehensive boxed set devoted to his bossa nova material. *—Ron Wynn and Dan Morgenstern*

★ **Complete Recordings of the Stan Getz Quartet with Jimmy Raney** / Yazoo 1082

Early Stan / Apr. 8, 1949+Apr. 23, 1953 / Prestige 654
With Jimmy Raney (g). This is a 1991 reissue of formative material from 1949 1953. Red Mitchell (b) and Shorty Rogers (tpt) occasionally steal the spotlight from the then-emerging Getz. *—Ron Wynn*

Brothers, The / Apr. 1949 / Prestige 008

○ **Quartets** / Jun. 21, 1949-Apr. 14, 1950 / Original Jazz Classics 121
This was Prestige Records' second 12-incher and it presented quartet sides from 6/21/49, 1/6/50, and 4/14/50 with backing from Al Haig or Tony Aless (p), Stan Levey, Roy Haynes, or Don Lamond (d), and Gene Ramey, Tommy Potter, or Percy Heath (b). These are short sides, concisely stated, with Stan Getz (ts) at times as close to Lester Young as he ever got. Some songs were previously issued on twofer sets. — *Bob Rusch*, Cadence

○ **At Carnegie Hall** / i. Dec. 1949-Nov. 1952 / Fresh Sound 1003

Roost Quartets / May 1950-Aug. 1951 / Roulette 96052

○ **Split Kick** / Dec. 10, 1950 / Roost 423

○ **Sounds of Stan Getz, The** / Dec. 10, 1950 / Roost 2207

○ **Chamber Music** / Aug. 15, 1951 / Roost 417

Stan Getz at Storyville—Vols. 1 and 2 / Oct. 28, 1951 / Roulette 94507
Some fierce live Getz with Jimmy Raney (g), Al Haig (p), Teddy Kotick (b), and Tiny Kahn (d). *—Ron Wynn*

○ **Jazz at Storyville—Vol. 3** / Oct. 28, 1951 / Roost 420

○ **Modern World** / Oct. 28, 1951 / Roost 2255

○ **Moonlight in Vermont** / Mar. 11, 1952 / Roost 2251

○ **Birdland Sessions** / i. Apr. 1952-Aug. 1952 / Fresh Sound 149

○ **Getz Age** / Dec. 5, 1952 / Roost 2258

Plays / Dec. 12+29, 1952 / Verve 833535
Recorded in December 1952, *Stan Getz Plays* shows why the group should be considered one of the finest underappreciated jazz ensembles of the '50s. Tenor saxophonist Getz is at absolutely top form in a program consisting largely of the ballad readings at which he always has excelled. At this stage of his development his tone is thinner and airier than it later became and his style much more decorative, making frequent use of appoggiatura, phrase repetition, and a thickened tone for emotional effect. Too, thanks to the lengthy association with guitarist Jimmy Raney, his command of harmony has deepened and, as a result, his playing is not only increasingly confident and assured but charged with considerably greater interest in this area than ever before. Not one of these performances is less than splendid, but even better are the several uptempo selections–notably "Lover, Come Back To Me," "The Way You Look Tonight," and "Hymn Of The Orient"–that indicate the quartet's (pianist Duke Jordan and bassist Bill Crow) marvelously empathic interplay. *—Pete Welding*, Down Beat

○ **Stan Getz and the Cool Sounds** / Apr. 16, 1953-Aug. 19, 1955 / Verve 8200

○ **Stan Getz Plays Blues** / Aug. 15, 1953-Oct. 10, 1957 / Verve 31

★ **Diz and Getz** / Dec. 9, 1953 / Verve 8141
This is prime material with two giants playing bop and old-time standards with characteristic verve and wit. John Lewis (p) and the Oscar Peterson quartet join the masters. *—Michael G. Nastos*

Stan Getz '57 / 1953-1958 / American Recording Society 443
A late-'50s date pairing tenor saxophonist Stan Getz with trombonist J.J. Johnson. Though the two come from different stylistic backgrounds, they find a comfortable meeting place in the middle, with Getz's cool solos and Johnson's hard bop approach proving an ideal team. —*Ron Wynn*

○ **West Coast Jazz** / Aug. 15, 1955 / Norgran 1032

○ **For Musicians Only** / Oct. 16, 1956 / Verve 837435
This has plenty of great players and lots of amazing music. Getz, Dizzy Gillespie (tpt), and Sonny Stitt (as) are great, as are John Lewis (p) and Herb Ellis (g). —*Ron Wynn*

Steamer, The / Nov. 24, 1956 / Verve 8294

○ **And the Oscar Peterson Trio** / Oct. 10, 1957 / Verve 8251
With the Oscar Peterson Trio. Getz shines while Peterson (p) keeps the trio whipped to a frenzy behind him. —*Ron Wynn*

Stan Getz and J.J. Johnson at the Opera House / Oct. 19+25, 1957 / PolyGram 31272
Powerhouse pairing. Explosive music, though the two principals are actually featured in separate concerts. A marvelous teamup between Getz and trombone king J.J. Johnson. —*Ron Wynn*

Meets Gerry Mulligan / Oct. 22, 1957 / Verve 8249

○ **At the Opera House** / Oct. 1957 / Verve 831272

Stan Getz with Cal Tjader / Feb. 8, 1958 / Fantasy 275
With Cal Tjader. 1987 reissue, super Latin-jazz summit. Billy Higgins fits in nicely on drums. —*Ron Wynn*

○ **Jazz Giants '58** / Aug. 1, 1958 / Verve 8248
Tenor saxophonist Stan Getz, baritone saxophonist Gerry Mulligan, and trumpeter Harry Edison headline a 1957 recording called *Jazz Giants '58*. Backing the horns are pianist Oscar Peterson's trio (guitarist Herb Ellis, bassist Ray Brown) plus drummer Louis Bellson. This is a typical Norman Granz super-jazz session. These sessions are rarely "poor" and are occasionally truly outstanding; this is "good." There are no real fireworks. For me, "Woody 'N' You" hits the mark best, though it swings along well as might be expected from the steamroller rhythm section. It's rather even and timeless listening, certainly worth your time and effort, though if you're familiar with the other Verve Getz/Mulligan collaboration, this will seem calmer and less jocular. —*Bob Rusch*, Cadence

★ **Focus** / Jul. 1961-Oct. 1961 / Verve 821982
This 1961 recording put tenor saxophonist Stan Getz in the hired-gun role for an album written and arranged by Eddie Sauter, conducted by Hershy Kay, and originally produced by Creed Taylor. It is a classic example of how successfully inventive pop/semiclassical scoring and jazz horn could be paired. Sure, it is *pretty*, it was meant to be, and the strings and woodwinds ensure that ambience, but it is also imaginative. Getz maneuvers with and in counterpoint to the score; sometimes coy, at other times romantic or challenging. It is a brilliant improvisation. —*Kevin Whitehead*, Cadence

○ **Stan Getz and Bob Brookmeyer** / Sep. 12-13, 1961 / Verve 8418

★ **Jazz Samba** / Feb. 13, 1962 / Verve 810061
This recording is not just a laidback treasure, but a really major milestone: the 1962 album that introduced the bossa nova to the United States. Byrd conceived it, Getz got a Grammy off one cut, "Desafinado." So much silliness ensued that the whole idiom's importance has been downplayed, but it was the beginning of a permanent Brazilian tinge in jazz. —*John Storm Roberts*

Big Band Bossa Nova / Aug. 27-28, 1962 / Verve 825771
This is an essential part of his bossa nova period. With Gary McFarland; this album was one of his biggest sellers. —*Ron Wynn*

☆ **Bossa Nova Years (Girl from Ipanema)** / 1962-1964 / Verve 823611

1962-1964. The five Getz bossa albums in a boxed set: *Jazz Samba*, *Big-Band Bossa Nova*, *Jazz Samba Encore*, *Getz/ Gilberto*, and *Getz/Almeida*. In a word: great music for young and old, even nonjazz buffs. Each of these discs is jam-packed with classic Getz tracks. Highest recommendation. —*Michael Erlewine*

Jazz Samba Encore / Feb. 8-27, 1963 / Verve 823613

○ **Getz and Gilberto Featuring Antonio Carlos Jobim** / Mar. 18-19, 1963 / Verve 810048
Getz/Gilberto & Antonio Carlos Jobim. The huge hit with Getz, Joao (g), and Astrud Gilberto (v). "The Girl From Ipenema" was an international smash. A gold album. —*Ron Wynn*

○ **Stan Getz Years, The** / i. 1964 / Roost 103

○ **Chick Corea / Bill Evans Sessions** / May 5, 1964-Mar. 30, 1967 / Verve 823242
Taken from one session with Evans, and two sessions with Getz and Corea. —*AMG*

Stan Getz and Bill Evans / May 5-6, 1964 / Verve 833802
As musically serene and amazing as you'd expect. Getz and Evans are incredible, while Ron Carter (b), Richard Davis (b), and Elvin Jones (d) aren't too bad either. —*Ron Wynn*

Getz Au Go Go Featuring Astrud Gilberto / Aug. 19, 1964 / Verve 821725
With Joao Gilberto. A landmark release. Getz completed a run of hit albums in 1964 that were both popular and influential. Astrud Gilberto (v) was sensual, dynamic, and unforgettable while with Getz. It will always sound wonderful. Jobim adds extra spice. —*Ron Wynn*

Getz and Gilberto—Vol. 2 / Oct. 9, 1964 / Verve 8623

Song After Sundown, A / Aug. 2-3, 1966 / Bluebird 6284
Getz plays with his usual brilliance on this date, reissued in 1987. With Arthur Fiedler and the Boston Pops. RCA does an excellent remastering job. —*Ron Wynn*

★ **Sweet Rain** / Mar. 30, 1967 / Verve 815054
From someone who made so many classics, this might be his best romantic work overall. —*Ron Wynn*

Dynasty / Jan. 11, 1971-Mar. 17, 1971 / Polydor 839117
Amazing playing from Getz in this date cut in London, partly at Ronnie Scott's. —*Ron Wynn*

Communications '72 / Nov. 1971 / Verve 68807

★ **Captain Marvel** / Mar. 3, 1972 / Columbia 32706
This brilliant mainstream date with Chick Corea (p), Stanley Clarke (b), Tony Williams (d), and Airto (per) got lost in publicity fever over the rise of jazz-rock. It came out three years after it was done in 1972. —*Ron Wynn*

Best of Two Worlds / May 21, 1975 / Columbia 33703
An outstanding set, with Getz doing both mainstream and bop work, then backing Joao Gilberto. —*Ron Wynn*

Master, The / Oct. 1, 1975 / Columbia 38272

Peacocks, The / Oct. 1975 / Columbia 34873
With Jimmy Roules and Jon Hendricks, this includes the "Chess Game" by Wayne Shorter done with Hendricks's lyrics, as precious as anything these jazzmen have done. —*Michael G. Nastos*

Gold / Jan. 27-30, 1977 / Inner City 1040
Recorded for Stan's 50th birthday in 1977 with JoAnne Brackeen on piano and Billy Hart on drums, this album includes two from Getz, Wayne Shorter (sax), and several other single standards. Recorded live at Cafe Montmartre, Copenhagen. A twofer. —*Michael G. Nastos*

Live at Montmartre / Jan. 28-30, 1977 / Steeple Chase 31073

Another World / Sep. 13, 1977 / Columbia
Andy Laverne makes a good impression on the piano. Again, Getz is amazing. —*Ron Wynn*

Dolphin, The / May 10, 1981 / Concord Jazz 4158
An underrated date. Getz is superb, with a sympathetic trio backing him. —*Ron Wynn*

Spring Is Here / May 1981 / Concord Jazz 4500

Super early '80s quartet date with Getz's lyrical, often roaring tenor sax reaffirming the joy inherent in the album title. He's quietly but effectively backed by pianist Lou Levy, bassist Monty Budwigs and drummer Victor Lewis. The CD has one bonus cut. —*Ron Wynn*

Billy Highstreet Samba / Nov. 4, 1981 / EmArcy 838771

Pure Getz / Jan. 29-30, 1982 / Concord Jazz 4188
On this one, "Blood Count" stands out, but this is a good session(s), well programmed, paced, and played. Pianist Jim McNeely is the pleasant surprise here. Furthermore, "On the Up and Up" is a McNeely composition that the group spends better than eight minutes exploring with care. This was done in two recording sessions, one in San Francisco and one in New York. The session in which drummer Billy Hart participated utilized a different technique in picking up Marc Johnson's bass, and this one gave my woofers quite a workout. This is a fine LP. —*Shirley Klett*, Cadence

Poetry / Jan. 12, 1983 / Elektra 60370

Line for Lyons / Feb. 18, 1983 / Gazell 1006
A good collaboration with Chet Baker (tpt) on limited-availability release. —*Ron Wynn*

☆ **Anniversary!** / Jul. 6, 1987 / Polydor 838769
A brilliant, rousing date, with Kenny Barron (p) in peak form. Getz is enthused, animated, and intense. —*Ron Wynn*

Apasionado / 1989-Mar. 2, 1992 / A&M 5297

People Time / Mar. 1991 / Verve 510823
A worthy posthumous set. Two discs of breathtaking songs done with pianist Kenny Barron in the final months of Getz's life. —*Ron Wynn*

Opus de Bop / Savoy Jazz 118

Complete Roost Sessions—Vol. 1, The / Vogue 600128

Complete Roost Sessions—Vol. 2, The / Vogue 600174

Stan the Man / Verve 815239
A wide variety of musicians all play straightahead. Features Duke Jordan, Jimmy Rowles, Bob Brookmeyer, Lionel Hampton, Dizzy Gillespie, Oscar Peterson, Mose Allison, Gerry Mulligan, J.J. Johnson, Victor Feldman, Steve Kuhn, and more. A twofer. All standards. —*Michael G. Nastos*

Desafinado / Polydor 530

TERRY GIBBS (Julius Gubenko)

b. Oct. 13, 1924, New York, NY
Vibes, drums / Bop

Viewed in some circles as a bebop counterpart to Lionel Hampton, Terry Gibbs has forged a successful career as a vibist, a conductor, a composer, and an arranger. He has an energetic style. His playing is well executed and has depth, and can surprise you with its subtlety. His father was a bassist who encouraged Gibbs to study music. He learned drums, timpani, and xylophone and won an amateur contest on xylophone at age 12. Gibbs turned professional as a drummer, then, after serving in the army in World War II, played with Tommy Dorsey, Chubby Jackson, Buddy Rich, and Woody Herman in the late '40s. He also worked with a group co-led by Charlie Shavers and Louis Bellson and with a Benny Goodman combo before beginning his own band. Gibbs led both small combos and large groups in the late '50s, including one 19-piece band with arrangements by Manny Albam and Pete Rugolo. He continued alternating formats into the '60s, then, in the mid '60s, became heavily involved with studio work as a music director on several television shows (one of them Steve Allen's program). Gibbs didn't record for over a decade. He worked with Buddy DeFranco in the '80s and has been active ever since. Gibbs made his recording debut on Savoy in 1949, and has cut sessions on Brunswick, EmArcy, Mercury, Verve, Limelight, Dot, Palo Alto, and Contemporary. Gibbs has several sessions available on CD. —*Ron Wynn*

Mallets A-Plenty / Jun. 15, 1956 / EmArcy 36075

Dream Band—Vol. 1 / **i.** Mar. 17-19, 1959 / Contemporary 7647

Dream Band—Vol. 2 / **i.** 1959 / Contemporary 7652
A 1987 reissue of big-band dates. Nicely played, with excellent arrangements but a low energy level. —*Ron Wynn*

Terry Gibbs Dream Band, Vol. 3—Flying Home / **i.** 1959 / Contemporary 7654

Terry Gibbs Dream Band, Vol. 5—the Big Cat / **i.** 1959 / Contemporary 7657
The last of the quintet, and one of the better volumes in the series. —*Ron Wynn*

★ **El Nutto** / Apr. 15, 1963 / Limelight 82005
From the vibist and quartet with pianist Alice McLeod, featuring all originals. —*Michael G. Nastos*

Air Mail Special / 1964 / Contemporary 14056
Another Gibbs/DeFranco pairing that has some sparks but not enough fire. —*Ron Wynn*

Latin Connection / May 9+10, 1986 / Contemporary 14022
Fine playing by Frank Morgan (sax) and Tito Puente (per). Gibbs handles Afro-Latin rhythms expertly. —*Ron Wynn*

○ **Holiday for Swing** / **i.** Jul. 1987-Aug. 1988 / Contemporary 14047

Chicago Fire / **i.** 1987 / Contemporary 14036
1987 date pairs old friends Gibbs and Buddy DeFranco, whose clarinet sometimes lights things up. —*Ron Wynn*

ASTRUD GILBERTO

b. 1940, Bahia, Brazil
Vocals / World fusion

Before 1963, it's doubtful anyone outside her native city of Rio had ever heard of Astrud Gilberto. Then, in response to a request to sing the English lyrics to a song titled "The Girl From Ipanema," history was made. Despite (or perhaps, in part, because of) her deadpan and childlike vocal style, she and the song were a smash. Gilberto toured frequently through the years with Stan Getz; the 1964 album *Getz Au Go Go* was a chart-topper and has just been reissued. —*Ron Wynn*

Boss of the Bossa Nova, The / **i.** 1963 / Atlantic 8070

Warm World of Astrud Gilberto, The / **i.** 1964 / Atlantic 8076

★ **Look at the Rainbow** / **i.** 1966 / Verve 821556
This is a beautiful bossa nova record of Astrud Gilberto's vocal stylings. All the material here, with the exception of "Learn to Live Alone" and "Pretty Place," which were arranged by Al Cohn, was arranged by Gil Evans. With the exception of a Johnny Coles trumpet solo, the personnel is uncredited on this 1966 recording. Discographies have credited Bob Brookmeyer (vtb), Kenny Burrell (g), and Grady Tate (d), but except for a few bars of sax, there is no solo individualism in this large Creed Taylor-produced orchestra. —*Bob Rusch*, Cadence

Astrud Gilberto with Stanley Turrentine / 1971 / CBS 44168

Astrud Gilberto Plus James Last Orchestra / 1986 / Verve 831123

Silver Collection: The Astrud Gilberto Album, The / Verve 823451

DIZZY GILLESPIE (John Birks Gillespie)

b. Oct. 21, 1917, Cheraw, SC, **d.** Jan. 7, 1993
Trumpet, conga drums, piano, bandleader / Bop

Bop's pioneer trumpet virtuoso, bandleader, and beloved personality, John Birks "Dizzy" Gillespie helped invent and define the musical vocabulary for an entire genre. His role in shaping and popularizing bebop, even coining a lexicon and a temporary fashion line, is legendary. In his early days, Gillespie was basically a Roy Eldridge clone, but Gillespie continued playing trumpet with high drama, amazing speed, and an unequalled harmonic creativity. Only his frequent partner and collaborator, Charlie Parker, ever understood bebop's nuts and bolts as well as Gillespie did. He shattered notions about the trumpet's limitations, and showed that artistry and show business weren't mutually exclusive. A lifelong clown and humorist, Gillespie enjoyed himself on the bandstand. Yet, he was fiercely dedicated to the music and always sought to improve and extend it. Besides his exceptional range, Gillespie played with frightening speed, ripping through lines while playing striking, declarative notes. He'd alternate simple and intricate phrases, and would make dramatic exists and entrances, pauses, bursts, leaps, and jumps. Besides the array of voicelike smears and slurs, Gillespie could shift from playing a poignant melody to an animated one with ease. The Gillespie portrait, puffy cheeks, bulging neck, and upturned horn, was a jazz staple. Gillespie was also a rhythmic, as well as a harmonic and melodic, innovator. Gillespie maintained an active interest in Latin American and Afro-Cuban music from the time he met Mario Bauza (while playing with Cab Calloway) through his entire career. He recorded with Machito, Mongo Santamaria, and Arturo Sandoval, and featured Chano Pozo in his band. Gillespie learned the conga drum, and was competent enough as a pianist and vocalist to record in each context.

Gillespie began teaching himself trombone and trumpet, as well as cornet, as a teen. He attended North Carolina's Laurinburg Institute, a boarding school that was a haven for Blacks seeking a decent education in that part of the South during the '30s. Gillespie wasn't physically able to play football as he desired, and studied both the basic high school curriculum as well as music theory and trumpet lessons. He also played in the band. He left school in 1935 to join his family in Philadelphia. He joined Frankie Fairfax's band, which included Charlie Shavers. Shavers knew several Roy Eldridge solos, so Gillespie learned from Shavers to phrase and play like Eldridge. Gillespie earned his nickname for on- and offstage antics. He moved to New York in 1937. It took several sessions, but he finally earned a job in Teddy Hill's big band, mainly because he sounded so much like their former trumpet player, Eldridge. Hill's band traveled to France and England during Gillespie's first two months. When they returned, he found himself working in various groups, among them Al Cooper's Savoy Sultans and Alberto Socarras's Afro-Cuban band, before rejoining Hill. By 1939, Gillespie had moved to the Cab Calloway big band, one of the era's top attractions. Gillespie developed a friendship with Bauza. Gillespie's trumpet style was evolving and coming out from under the Eldridge shadow. Gillespie met Charlie Parker in 1940 while on tour in Kansas City. They began participating in after-hours jam sessions at various New York sites, among them Minton's Playhouse. Kenny Clarke, Thelonious Monk, and Max Roach were among the other musicians involved in these jam sessions. These young musicians were honing a new approach that would soon be unveiled. Gillespie was bounced from Calloway's band in 1941 over a spitball incident (he was innocent; Jonah Jones actually fired the spitball at Calloway). There were short stints with Ella Fitzgerald, Coleman Hawkins, Benny Carter, Charlie Barnet, Les Hite, Lucky Millinder, Earl Hines, and Duke Ellington.

While with Milinder, Gillespie recorded what many consider to be the first bop solo, though still in a swing context, on "Little John Special" in 1942. Gillespie later reworked the riff the band played following his solo into the song "Salt Peanuts." He co-led a combo with Oscar Pettiford in 1943 and 1944, and later joined Billy Eckstine's big band, eventually becoming its music director. Gillespie recorded the first full-fledged bop session with Coleman Hawkins in 1944 (including Gillespie's composition "Woody 'N You"), then teamed with Charlie Parker in 1945 on a series of classic small group sessions. The songs included "Hot House," "Salt Peanuts," and "Shaw 'Nuff." Gillespie organized a big band in 1945, but it didn't last long. He and Parker formed their own quintet, which later became a sextet, before Gillespie decided to try another big band. This band lasted four years, and experimented with Afro-Cuban and Latin American rhythms. Chano Pozo joined on congas and the band recorded "Cubana Be/Cubana Bop" and "Manteca."

Members of the band, at various times, included Sonny Stitt, James Moody, Jimmy Heath, Paul Gonsalves, and John Coltrane. The rhythm section eventually featured Milt Jackson on vibes, Ray Brown on bass, John Lewis on piano, and Clarke on drums. This core unit eventually regrouped as the Milt Jackson quartet, then the Modern Jazz Quartet. Gillespie disbanded the orchestra in 1950, but, by this time, bop's influence was cemented and the innovations of Gillespie, Parker, Monk, and others were established securely on the jazz horizon.

Gillespie later formed a sextet and started Dee Gee records. It issued some important recordings, but ran into serious financial problems and was short-lived. In 1953, an onstage accident provided a fresh twist (literally) to Gillespie's career. Someone fell on his trumpet, which had been sitting upright on a stand. They bent the bell back, and Gillespie tried playing it that way and discovered he liked it. The upright trumpet became as much a part of his act as "Lucille" is to B. B. King or the violin was to Jack Benny. All future Gillespie trumpets were built with the bell pointing upward at a 45-degree angle. In Toronto that same year, Gillespie participated in a famous concert with Parker, Roach, Charles Mingus, and Bud Powell. The music issued on the album *Jazz at Massey Hall* (also issued as *The Greatest Concert Ever*) was mostly excellent. Gillespie led small groups and combos, and continued recording. His '50s sessions included collaborations with Coltrane, Johnny Richards, Eldridge, Sonny Rollins, and Stan Getz. Gillespie later took a new entertainment role: he became a governmental tour guide. He formed a big band specifically for overseas tours, and went on State Department-sponsored junkets to Yugoslavia and South America. There were visits to Syria, Iran, Lebanon, Pakistan, Turkey, and Greece between 1956 and 1958, then the funding ended. He returned to leading small groups and to making recordings.

Gillespie's achievements in the '60s included cutting some early bossa nova with Lalo Schifrin, working with Moody, Randy Weston, Junior Mance, the Double Six of Paris vocal group, Kenny Clarke, and a big band date in Berlin. The '70s were just as busy; Gillespie toured with an all-star band called the Giants Of Jazz that included Monk, Art Blakey, Stitt, and Al McKibbon. Thanks to a new deal with Norman Granz's Pablo label, Gillespie issued a host of albums. There were fine sessions with Eldridge, Harry Edison, and Clark Terry issued as the Trumpet Kings. There were live dates and studio sessions of Gillespie working with the superb rhythm section of Joe Pass, Brown, and Mickey Roker. He also recorded with Johnny Griffin, Eddie "Lockjaw" Davis, Sandoval, Schifrin, and Santamaria before the Pablo sessions ended in the early '80s. Gillespie's autobiography, *To Be Or Not To Bop*, was published in 1979. The slate of festival appearances, clubs, and cruise ship dates continued. Gillespie went to Cuba on another State Department-sponsored tour in the late '70s, where he met and befriended Sandoval. Gillespie battled illness in the '80s and '90s. There were gala birthday celebrations in 1987 (70th) and 1992 (75th). In 1988, Gillespie lead a star-studded orchestra at the Playboy Festival, then took the United Nations Band to Europe with Moody, Sam Rivers, and Paquito D'Rivera. When he died in 1993, the outpouring of grief from around the world was unprecedented and sustained. His albums are now reappearing at a heavy pace in reissued form. —*Ron Wynn*

★ **Development of an American Artist** / i. 1940-1946 / Smithsonian 004

A thorough compilation of Gillespie's formative '40s dates. Available by mail-order only from the Smithsonian. —*Ron Wynn*

○ **Dizzy Gillespie with Charlie Christian** / May 1941 / Esoteric 4

★ **Shaw 'Nuff** / Feb. 1945-Nov. 1946 / Musicraft 53

Formative sessions cut for the Musicraft label when trumpeter Dizzy Gillespie was just beginning to hone the style that would ultimately emerge as bop. They include one of his earliest hits, plus other solos and vocals. —Ron Wynn

○ **In the Beginning** / May 11, 1945-Nov. 12, 1946 / Prestige 24030
Finally, all the seminal Dizzy Gillespie Musicraft-Guild dates from 1945-46 collected under one roof—and it never rains but it pours! If you consider yourself any sort of jazz person, this album belongs in your collection. The seven pieces with Bird (Charlie Parker) and Dizzy, in particular, are among the key recordings in jazz and, aside from that, just lovely music. The two great cocreators of bebop didn't record together all that much, but every time they did come together, there was fire. The sparks are still flying. Take "Shaw 'Nuff," for instance; at the furious tempo, which scared everybody, the two horns breathe together in perfect unison, as one single-double voice. And the solos! If you want a quick definition of bebop (2:55), this is it. Everything else is commentary. Ralph Gleason's notes are warmly personal, and the sound, despite the poor surfaces of the original 78s, is excellent. —Dan Morgenstern, Down Beat

○ **Modern Trumpets** / Feb. 7, 1946 / Dial 212

One Bass Hit / May 15, 1946 / Musicraft 404
A good reissue spotlighting Gillespie's prime orchestra in the mid '40s. —Ron Wynn

★ **Dizziest** / i. 1946-1949 / Bluebird 5785
The titles on *Dizziest* pretty much speak for themselves. The first four selections are from one of Dizzy Gillespie's most satisfying small-group dates of the '40s despite their briefness (none over 3:04). It's a pity that there wasn't room for the three alternate takes from this session. The remainder is the complete output of Dizzy Gillespie's orchestra for Victor (except the rare alternate of "Dizzier and Dizzier"). Gillespie's big band, after creating quite a stir with its 1946 Musicraft recordings ("One Bass Hit," "Things to Come," "Oop-Bop-Sh'-Bam," etc.), had achieved enough success to be signed to a major company and quickly became the most influential orchestra in American music during the late '40s. Scores of big bands, including those led by Jimmy Dorsey, Gene Krupa, Ziggy Elman ("Boppin' with Zig"), and even Benny Goodman, were soon taking whatever they could steal from Gillespie, turning innovative phrases into cliché. To most collectors, four of the titles ("I Should Care," "That Old Black Magic," "You Go to My Head," and "If Love Is Trouble") will be a bit unfamiliar; these are all ballad features for the smooth baritone of Johnny Hartman and the least exciting tracks of this otherwise essential set. This overflows with classics (especially "Cubana Be/Cubana Bop," "Manteca," "Two Bass Hit," and "Jumpin' with Symphony Sid") that contain plenty of dazzling solos from the leader's trumpet and such players as James Moody, Cecil Payne, J.J. Johnson, the young Yusef Lateef, and Chano Pozo. This orchestra helped alter the course of jazz and arrangments still sound a bit futuristic today, 40 years later (1987). This set belongs in every serious jazz collection. —Scott Yanow, Cadence

○ **Dizzier and Dizzier** / Aug. 22, 1947-Jul. 6, 1949 / Victor 1009

At Salle Pleyel (Paris, France—1948) / Feb. 28, 1948 / Prestige 7818
Trumpeter Dizzy Gillespie dominates the proceedings at this live Paris concert, from cranking out tremendous, octave-leaping solos to heading the big band. They're competent pros but no one else is in Gillespie's class as an improviser. —Ron Wynn

○ **Champ, The** / Apr. 16, 1951+Jul. 18, 1952 / Savoy 12047

★ **Dee Gee Days (The Savoy Sessions)** / i. 1951 / Savoy 4426
Dizzy Gillespie: Dee Gee Days documents the rise and fall of trumpeter Dizzy Gillespie's attempt at producing records for his own company in 1951 and 1952. These sides feature little Gillespie trumpet and lots of vocals, some good by Joe Carroll, some pedestrian by Melvin Moore, a Billy Eckstine imitator. Milt Jackson does a lot of piano work on these sessions, even playing organ and singing on one. For collector

interest, I might note the early appearance of John Coltrane, who has one brief solo betraying his Dexter Gordon and Lester Young roots. Gillespie mostly shucks except on some very nice sides with violinist Stuff Smith (especially two takes of "Caravan" and one of "Stardust"). Jackson comes alive briefly here and there, and saxophonist Budd Johnson makes a couple of flying contributions. —Jon Goldman, Cadence

○ **In Paris** / i. 1952 / Vogue 600047

○ **Dizzy's Diamonds: The Best of Verve Years [box]** / i. 1953-1968 / Verve 513875
Good, multidisc package featuring fine performances by trumpeter Dizzy Gillespie in various decades, situations, and with an assortment of performers. It's not a greatest-hits, more a retrospective collection covering his years on Verve. —Ron Wynn

Dizzy Gillespie with Roy Eldridge / Oct. 29, 1954 / Verve
The Dizzy Gillespie/Roy Eldridge set is joyful and stunning music from beginning to end by two players and trumpeters at the top of their form. The music was recorded at only two sessions and the personnel was constant except for the addition of trumpeter Harry Edison and the substitution of Buddy Rich for Louis Bellson on drums for the final two cuts. Pianist Oscar Peterson, guitarist Herb Ellis, and bassist Ray Brown provide fine and unobtrusive support, and it is fascinating to hear master and pupil side by side, blazing away. This is ferocious and beautiful. —Joel Ray, Cadence

One Night in Washington / Mar. 13, 1955 / Elektra 60300
A superb live date that Elektra reissued for a short while, then deleted. —Ron Wynn

○ **Groovin' High** / 1956 / Savoy Jazz 152
This Dizzy Gillespie disc spans small groups, including a couple of cuts with Bird (Charlie Parker) and big bands featuring the John Lewis/Milt Jackson-led (piano and vibes, respectively) rhythm section that would later mutate into the personnel and format we have known for four decades as the Modern Jazz Quartet. —Gene Santoro, Jazz Times

○ **Modern Jazz Sextet, The** / Jan. 12, 1956 / Verve 12533
There is suave, commanding expertise running throughout this 1956 Norman Granz Verve session featuring trumpeter Dizzy Gillespie, one of the founding fathers of bebop, and Sonny Stitt, the pretender to the throne of Charlie Parker—a title he lived up to nicely over the years while still managing to remain his own man. "Dizzy Meets Sonny" has the speed and urgency of classic bop. There is plenty of wallop in the slashing leaps and dives of Stitt, and the notes fly from Gillespie's horn like rounded brass BBs. Pianist John Lewis plays with spare, laconic one-fingered logic here and throughout the LP, his left hand barely audible. Then there is the funky side of bebop on "Blues for Bird." Lewis seems barely able to shake the notes off his fingertips at some points. But the balance of the album is more or less high-class, if commonplace, stuffing. —John McDonough, Down Beat

○ **Dizzy in Greece** / May 18, 1956-Apr. 8, 1957 / Verve 8017
○ **World Statesman** / May 18-19, 1956 / Norgran 1084
○ **School Days** / i. 1957 / Savoy Jazz 157
○ **Dizzy Gillespie and His Big Band** / i. 1957 / GNP 23
○ **Bird's Works** / Apr. 8, 1957 / Verve 8222
○ **Dizzy Gillespie-Stuff Smith** / Apr. 17, 1957 / Verve 8214
★ **At Newport** / i. Jul. 6, 1957 / PolyGram 513754
Super late '50s set featuring trumpeter Dizzy Gillespie with pianist Wynton Kelly, trumpeter Lee Morgan, trombonist Melba Liston, tenor saxophonist Benny Golson, and pianist Mary Lou Williams at the Newport Jazz Festival in spirited jam session and exchanges. The CD reissue contains three bonus cuts. —Ron Wynn

○ **Dizzy Gillespie at Newport** / Jul. 6, 1957 / Verve 6023
Dizzy Gillespie's "world statesman" big band of the '50s was one of his best and this live set finds the aggregation and its fearless leader at the peak of their creative prowess. With

arrangements by the leader, Quincy Jones, and Ernie Wilkins, played by such rugged individualists as Wynton Kelly (p), Benny Golson (ts), Al Grey (t), Charlie Persip (d), and trumpeter Lee Morgan (at 18, the youngest member), the band absolutely smokes. The emotional range of Gillespie's playing is also astonishing. From a moving rendition of "I Remember Clifford" to the stratospheric "Cool Breeze," Gillespie works that horn. Also included are Gillespie's introductions and musical asides, further evidence of his remarkable gift of showmanship without jive. Lee Morgan's presence is noteworthy because he "arrived" when he played "A Night in Tunisia" with this band at Birdland. Morgan's Clifford Brownie-laced solo is documented for the first time here, thanks to the CD format. The original LP excluded the tracks and two others composed and arranged by Mary Lou Williams. —*Bret Primack*, Jazz Times

○ **For Musicians Only** / Oct. 16, 1957 / Verve 8198

○ **Dizzy Gillespie Duets** / Dec. 11, 1957 / Verve 8260

○ **Sonny Rollins / Sonny Stitt Sessions** / Dec. 11+19, 1957 / Verve 22505

○ **Jazz Portrait of Duke Ellington, The** / Apr. 27+28, 1960 / Verve 8171072

☆ **An Electrifying Evening with the Dizzy Gillespie** / Feb. 9, 1961 / Verve 8401

Perceptions / May 18, 1961 / Verve 8411

Dizzy on the French Riviera / May 1962-Jul. 24, 1962 / Philips 200048

Something Old, Something New / Apr. 23, 1963 / Philips 091

○ **Night in Tunisia** / i. Jun. 1966 / VSP 7

★ **Swing Low Sweet Cadillac** / May 25-26, 1967 / MCA 33121

○ **Reunion Big Band** / Nov. 7, 1968 / MPS 15207
The full range of trumpeter Dizzy Gillespie comes across on *The Dizzy Gillespie Reunion Big Band*, recorded (11/7/68) live at the Berlin Jazz Fest. As one might expect from the title, the music is somewhat familiar; however, it is played with a renewed freshness for its time, in contrast, alas, with many of the post '60s Gillespie recordings. The soloing is strong, the arrangements beautiful, with "Con Alma" particularly rich. As far as the title of this band, it was more a producer's hook than any all-star nostalgia. The band was composed of former and (then) current Gillespieites from the '40s, '50s, and '60s. My only gripe is with Joachim Berendt's perfunctory liners, space which should have included solo identifications—in a day when even the hair stylists are credited on the average trash record, why not give credit to the creative artists. Anyway, creative artistry well done! Thanks—Gillespie, Jimmy Owens, Dizzy Reece, Victor Paz, Curtis Fuller, Tom McIntosh, Ted Kelly, Chris Woods, James Moody, Paul Jeffery, Sahib Shihab, Cecil Payne, Mike Longo, Paul West, and Candy Finch. —*Bob Rusch*, Cadence

Portrait of Jennie / 1970 / Perception 13
This little-known but beautifully played combo session from the '70s seems to have totally vanished from the face of the earth. —*Ron Wynn*

○ **Dizzy Gillespie and the Dwike Mitchell-Willie Ruff Duo** / 1971 / Mainstream 325

Trumpet Kings Meet Joe Turner / Sep. 19, 1974 / Pablo 497
This is an excellent collaboration by three established, outstanding trumpeters, plus rollicking Joe Turner (v) near the end of a wonderful career. With Roy Eldridge and Harry Edison. —*Ron Wynn*

Dizzy Gillespie's Big Four / Dec. 19, 1974 / Original Jazz Classics 443

★ **Afro-Cuban Jazz Moods** / Jun. 4+5, 1975 / Pablo 447
Combining the foremost Afro-Cuban jazz musician, Dizzy Gillespie, with percussionist Machito and his fiery orchestra seems so natural that one wonders why it took so long to do it. Throw in the compositions and arrangements of Chico O'Farrill and you have the makings of a classic album—al-

most. If it weren't for a couple of problems with O'Farrill's compositions, I wouldn't have hesitated to heap plaudits on this record. As it is, the playing of both Gillespie and the orchestra is outstanding. The side-long "Oro, Incienso y Mirra" is worth the price of the album. Here Gillespie gets to display the full range of his trumpeting expertise through a series of shifting rhythms, moods, and instrumental accompaniments. The main shortcoming with the three compositions (the Afro-Cuban Jazz Moods) on side two is that they are more jazz-rock than Afro-Cuban. When one has a rhythm section as multifaceted and dynamic as Machito's, one doesn't waste it by saddling it with relatively simplistic rhythms. Nevertheless, Gillespie is in fine form and when he is, it's easy to overlook any minor quibbles. —*Carl Brauer*, Cadence

Montreux '75 / Jul. 16, 1975 / Pablo 739

Trumpet Kings at Montreux '75, The / i. Jul. 1975 / Original Jazz Classics 445

○ **Bahaina** / Nov. 19+20, 1975 / Pablo 708
The results on this double LP set constitute a respectable entry in the Dizzy Gillespie discography. Gillespie plays with the easy control of one who knows precisely what he's doing and is in complete and unchallenged command. Gillespie fashions some cleverly intricate splashes of invention, but they are little more than dabs of color on a generally monochromatic canvas. Supporting musicians Roger Glenn on flute and vibes and guitarists Mike Howell and Al Gafa provide compatible balance without becoming an opposing center of musical gravity. Drummer Mickey Roker and percussionist Paulinho De Costa are firm but predictable. —*John McDonough*, Down Beat

Dizzy Gillespie Big Seven, The / i. Apr. 1976 / Pablo 2310749

Dizzy's Party / Sep. 15+16, 1976 / Pablo 784

Montreux '77 / Jul. 14, 1977 / Pablo 381
A sextet jam session recorded live at the 1977 Montreux Jazz Festival, with trumpeter Dizzy Gillespie still in explosive form. Though some songs seem to go on forever, Gillespie's theatrics, as well as his incandescent playing, make it worthwhile. —*Ron Wynn*

New Faces / 1984 / GRP 9512
Branford Marsalis (ts) and Kenny Kirkland (p) help out the venerable trumpet giant. —*Ron Wynn*

Dizzy Gillespie Meets Phil Woods Quintet / i. Dec. 1986 / Timeless 250

Paris Concert / i. 1989 / GNP 9006

Live at Royal Festival Hall / Jun. 10, 1989 / Enja 79658
This is a recent all-star effort, with Gillespie exciting and enjoyable. Pacquito D'Rivera burns on alto sax, while longtime friends James Moody (sax) and Slide Hampton (t) are part of the orchestra. —*Ron Wynn*

Bebop and Beyond Plays Dizzy Gillespie / i. May 1991 / Blue Moon 917072

To Diz with Love: Diamond Jubilee Recordings / i. 1992 / Telarc 83307
Nice tribute to the late trumpeter Dizzy Gillespie featuring many who either influenced him or whose style reflects his influence. The list includes Red Rodney, Jon Faddis, Wynton Marsalis, Claudio Roditi, Charlie Sepulveda, and Wallace Roney. The rhythm section contains Junior Mance, Peter Washington, and Kenny Washington. —*Ron Wynn*

JOHN GILMORE (John E. Gilmore)

b. 1931, d. 1991
Tenor saxophone / Early free, modern creative
During the long and glorious run of Sun Ra's Arkestra, there were constant personnel changes, but John Gilmore was a staple. He's a stalwart hard bop tenor and avant-garde improviser who played with the Arkestra from 1953 until the present, and stepped forward in 1993 to assume the leadership mantle following Ra's death. He also doubled on drums for the Arkestra through the '70s and '80s. Gilmore did work

in 1964 and 1965 with Art Blakey's Jazz Messengers, and has done other dates as a sideman, but is almost as much a part of the Arkestra fabric as Ra. His powerful tenor solos, especially the piercing, immediately recognizable upper-register screams and cries, have been heard as both solos and as frenzied extended dialogues with other Arkestra reed and brass members. Gilmore began studying clarinet in Chicago at age 14, and played in bands during his stint in the air force from 1948 to 1951. In 1952, he played tenor sax with Earl Hines in a show organized around a barnstorming tour by the Harlem Globetrotters. He joined Ra the next year. Gilmore briefly co-led bands with Clifford Jordan in the late '50s, and with Dizzy Reece in 1970. He recorded in the '60s with Freddie Hubbard, Elmo Hope, McCoy Tyner, Paul Bley, Andrew Hill, Chick Corea, Pete LaRoca, and Blakey. But otherwise, Gilmore, whose sound influenced John Coltrane, and Sun Ra were constants. Gilmore played on all the big-band, mid-sized combo, and small group sessions for Ra's Saturn company and for many other labels that recorded the band. Presently, there's only one Gilmore title widely available, a quartet date with Paul Bley, Paul Motian, and Gary Peacock made for Savoy in the '60s. —*Ron Wynn*

★ **Blowing in from Chicago** / Mar. 3, 1957 / Blue Note 1549

Dizzy Reece / John Gilmore / i. 1970 / Futura 16

EGBERTO GISMONTI

b. Dec. 5, 1947, Carmo, Brazil
Guitar, composer / World fusion
A marvelous Brazilian guitarist, Egberto Gismonti has blended classical, traditional ethnic, and jazz influences into a distinctive, very personal and alternately lyrical and aggressive style. A self-taught guitarist, Gismonti began on six-string in the '70s, later switched to an eight-stringed instrument, and finally settled on a ten-string with an extended bass range in the early '80s. Gismonti began studying piano at age six, and continued until he journeyed to Paris to study orchestration and composition many years later. His teachers were Nadia Boulanger and Jean Barraque. Gismonti became interested in the choro, a Brazilian variation on African-American funk, when he returned home in 1966. While learning guitar, Gismonti closely examined the music of Baden Powell and flutist Pixinguinha. He toured America with Airto and Flora Purim in the mid '70s, and also with Nana Vasconcelos. Gismonti spent extensive time studying the music of the Xingu Indians in 1977, and later included their compositions on a pair of albums. He's recorded with Paul Horn, Charlie Haden, and Nana Vasconcelos, and has led his own band. Gismonti's done sessions for ECM, EMI, and various Latin labels. He has several sessions available on CD. —*Ron Wynn and Terri Hinte*

○ **Danca Das Cabecas** / i. Nov. 1976 / ECM 827750
The initial American release features extended pieces for guitarist and percussionist Nana Vasconcelos. Side one is a tour de force, with the pieces segueing beautifully. —*Michael G. Nastos*

★ **Sol Do Meio Dia** / Nov. 1977 / ECM 829117
Guitarist Egberto Gismonti's *Sol Do Meio Dia* is very colorful, involved music, quite unlike most ECM recordings. Gismonti, a top figure in the international music scene, was just beginning to make his presence felt in the United States in 1978. The music on this recording is dedicated to the Xingu Indians of the Amazon, and each song is a dedication to the various deities that are a part of the Xingu cosmology. Gismonti's talents gave the folkloric music a deep spiritual quality. —*Spencer R. Weston*, Cadence

Works / i. 1983 / ECM 823269

○ **Solo** / i. 1985 / ECM 827135

JIMMY GIUFFRE (James Peter Giuffre)

b. Apr. 26, 1921, Dallas, TX
Clarinet, tenor and baritone saxophone / Cool
A woodwind specialist who plays brilliantly on any instrument or in any format he chooses, Jimmy Giuffre's tech-

nique grew more ambitious during the '60s, '70s, and '80s. Though he was certainly in the cool mode, Giuffre also utilized bebop; experimented with atonality in the mid '50s; and, by the early '60s, worked in a trio and explored freer music. He began playing with an army band following his graduation from North Texas State Teachers College. Giuffre worked with Boyd Raeburn, Jimmy Dorsey, Buddy Rich, and Woody Herman in the late '40s. Later, he wrote the composition "Four Brothers," which was a featured part of the book for the Four Brothers reed section in Herman's Second Herd. He played Western Swing with Spade Cooley for a short time, then worked with Howard Rumsey's Lighthouse All-Stars and with Shorty Rogers in the early and mid '50s. Giuffre left Rogers's group to form a trio. By 1957, he'd reorganized his group and was working with Bob Brookmeyer, while also teaching at the Lennox School of Jazz. Giuffre performed on the celebrated "Sound of Jazz" television show in 1957, and also appeared on the equally famous 1958 Newport Jazz Festival film *Jazz on a Summer's Day* that was released in 1960. He recorded for Columbia, Atlantic, Capitol, and Verve in the '50s, cutting one session with Lee Konitz. His early '60s trio with Paul Bley and Steve Swallow explored free-form approaches to jazz improvisation. Giuffre led other combos in the '60s, while touring extensively in both America and Europe. He regrouped this innovative ensemble for tours and recordings during the '90s. Giuffre made more recordings for Verve and Columbia, as well as a session for Bley's IAI label with Bill Connors and Bley. He formed another intriguing trio in the '70s; this one mixed African and Asian elements with jazz. Giuffre joined the New England Conservatory of Music's faculty in 1978. He continued cutting sessions, this time for companies such as Choice, DJM, and IAI. Giuffre began playing soprano sax, flute, and bass flute, and headed a quartet. He continued recording through the '80s, playing some excellent dates for Soul Note. Some of his earlier material has been reissued on CD. —*Ron Wynn*

Four Brothers and Tangents in Jazz / Feb. 19, 1954 / Affinity 70

Tangents in Jazz / May 1955 / Capitol 634

★ **Jazzlore: the Jimmy Giuffre Three, Vol. 46** / Dec. 3-24, 1956 / Atlantic 90981

Princess / 1958 / Fini Jazz

○ **Lee Konitz Meets Jimmy Giuffre** / May 12-13, 1959 / Verve 8355
A simply amazing collaboration. Extra spice comes from Hal McKusick (as), Warne Marsh (ts), and Bill Evans (p). —*Ron Wynn*

Easy Way, The / Aug. 6-7, 1959 / Verve 8337

○ **1961** / Mar. 1961-Aug. 1961 / PolyGram 849644
Excellent '92 reissue of a pivotal set featuring multi-instrumentalist Jimmy Giuffre with bassist Steve Swallow and pianist Paul Bley. It's actually two separate, compelling albums issued as one CD, *Fusion* and *Thesis*. The three interact so completely, there is more emphasis on mood, sound, and texture than individual voices. —*Ron Wynn*

Free Fall / Jul. 10, 1962-Nov. 1, 1962 / Columbia 1964

Quiet Song / 1974 / Improvising Artists 37.38.39

○ **Tenors West** / i. Feb. 1978 / GNP 9040
The ensemble passages on this album are very tight, the "Four Brothers" blend is excellent, the arrangements are thoughtful if a little corny. Significantly, the best cuts on the album are Billy Strayhorn's "Take The 'A' Train" and Count Basie's "Shorty George." Marty Paich's best number is the title tune, which is light but swinging. Jimmy Giuffre is the best soloist, naturally, bringing a little personality into an otherwise faceless lineup. The album is best viewed as a historical item, exhibiting Giuffre's tenor style prior to his avant-garde clarinet days. —*Douglas Clark*, Down Beat

IAI Festival / May 19, 1978 / Improvising Artists 37.38.59
First-rate quartet with Lee Konitz (as), Paul Bley (p), and Bill Connors (g). —*Ron Wynn*

★ **Dragonfly** / Jan. 14-15, 1983 / Soul Note 1058
Jimmy Giuffre, he of the intellectual cool and the composer
behind the Four Brothers, goes electric on this album. The
new direction of *Dragonfly* shouldn't have been that startling to anyone who closely followed Giuffre's career.
Beyond his Woody Herman experience, Giuffre took part in
some unique trios ('50s Contemporary dates with Shelly
Manne as a leader and with Shorty Rogers are a personal favorite; they include some stunningly futuristic exercises in
free improvisation that feature drums as a melodic instrument). Yet the dynamics of *Dragonfly* were likely to catch
even longtime Giuffre fans at least a little by surprise. First,
there's the tone on saxes—more sinewy, aided by a slight
electric echo that might be unsettling to fans of Giuffre's
usually spare, dry tone. Giuffre plays off his sidemen much
like he used open spacing on past recordings, melding the
electronically homogenized trio nearly into one polyphonic
foil. It is a strangely bottomless group, since bassist Bob
Nieske has a particularly light and vapory touch. For the
most part, the ensemble is well attuned to Giuffre (longtime
colleague percussionist Randy Kaye is sympathetic to the
moods of the electronics, sometimes shattering the sublime
with chimes or shimmering along with cymbals). Although
Giuffre doesn't use the baritone sax, he adds the spectral
bass flute to his arsenal, using his accompaniment to richly
envelop the instrument on two mystical tone poems, "Sad
Truth" and "Moonlight." They are topped only by "Cool," a
loping blues that most successfully blends the old and new
Giuffre. —*R. Bruce Dold*, Down Beat

Liquid Dancers / Apr. 1989 / Soul Note 1158

GLOBE UNITY ORCHESTRA

Group / Progressive big band, modern creative
Pianist Alexander von Schlippenbach founded the Globe
Unity Orchestra in 1966 to perform his composition "Globe
Unity" at the Berlin Festival. It was a work for 14 players
that had been commissioned for him. The group developed
into an international forum for free jazz musicians, attracting players from Germany, England, Italy, and America. The
roster has included trombonists Albert Mangelsdorff and
Paul Rutherford, trumpeters Kenny Wheeler and Manfred
Schoof, and saxophonist Evan Parker. Globe Unity Orchestra
performed at the World Exhibition in Osaka, Japan in 1970,
but worked mostly in Germany until 1974. It appeared at the
1975 Rheims festival with special guests Anthony Braxton
and Enrico Rava, and made a ten-day tour of England in
1977. The orchestra subsequently appeared at concerts and
festivals in France, Switzerland, India, and the Far East. The
orchestra has made several recordings for the FMP label,
and for Po Torch and Japo. They're available via mail order,
but aren't sold in many record outlets except in big city super stores. —*Ron Wynn*

★ **Live in Wuppertal 73** / i. 1973 / FMP 0160

○ **Evidence—Vol. 1** / i. Mar. 1975 / FMP 0220

Into the Valley—Vol. 2 / i. Mar. 1975 / FMP 0270

○ **Pearls** / Nov. 25+27, 1975 / FMP 0380
Free jazz big band with a cast of stars: Enrico Rava, Albert
Mangelsdorff, Anthony Braxton, and many others. —*AMG*

○ **Hamburg '74** / FMP 0650

BENNY GOLSON

b. Jan. 25, 1929, Philadelphia, PA
Tenor saxophone, composer, arranger / Hard bop
A top arranger and composer, tenor saxophonist Benny
Golson's style and sound reflect strong bebop and some
swing roots, namely the influence of Coleman Hawkins, Don
Byas, and Ben Webster. Golson plays in a soulful, expressive
manner, and is effective especially on ballads, though he is
also able to handle tricky, racing uptempo passages. Golson
compositions such as "Stablemates," "I Remember Clifford,"
"Whisper Not," "Along Came Betty," "Blues March," "Are You
Real," and "Killer Joe" are jazz anthems. He later became
quite successful at composing music for films and television.

Golson studied piano, organ, tenor sax, and clarinet as a
child, and attended Howard University from 1947 to 1950.
He worked in Philadelphia, where some of his friends and
associates included John Coltrane and the Heath brothers. In
1951, Golson joined Bull Moose Jackson's R&B orchestra,
where he met Tadd Dameron. Dameron was a mentor and a
major contributor to Golson's compositional and arranging
style. Golson played in Dameron's band before joining
Lionel Hampton in 1953. There was a brief stint in Johnny
Hodges's band that also included Coltrane, then Golson
played with Earl Bostic from 1954 to 1956. Coltrane took
Golson's composition, "Stablemates," to a Miles Davis session in 1955, and eventually the song was included on albums by Davis and Mal Waldron. Golson joined Dizzy
Gillespie in 1956 and remained with his band until 1958.
While in Gillespie's band, Golson went on extensive tours
for the State Department. Golson's jazz reputation was secured by his writing and by his playing with Gillespie and
with Art Blakey's Jazz Messengers in 1959. He also recorded
for Contemporary, Riverside, and New Jazz in the late '50s.
Golson did freelance work in New York, led his own quintet,
and studied with composer Henry Brant. He cofounded the
Jazztet with Art Farmer and pianist McCoy Tyner in 1959,
and continued with it until 1962. The Jazztet did some sessions on Argo, while Golson recorded as a leader for Audio
Fidelity, Mercury, Argo, and Prestige.
By the late '60s, he'd found a fertile and profitable new
arena: the studios. Golson wrote songs and contributed
arrangements for Peggy Lee, Lou Rawls, Nancy Wilson, and
Sammy Davis, Jr., while composing material for TV shows
such as "Ironside" and for several films. He was away from
the recording and playing scene until 1977, when he made a
quintet date that was not released. Golson's biggest hit was
Quincy Jones's recording of "Killer Joe" that was featured on
his *Walking in Space* album. He made some fine combo sessions for Timeless in the '80s, and Golson and Farmer reunited the Jazztet for periodic appearances with a lineup
that included original trombonist Curtis Fuller. Golson's
1985 appearance leading a quartet at Ronnie Scott's in
London won raves from English jazz critics. He recorded a
1985 tribute album to Clifford Brown with Freddie Hubbard,
Woody Shaw, Kenny Barron, Cecil McBee, and Ben Riley.
Timeless issued that recording in 1990. —*Ron Wynn*

Benny Golson's New York Scene / Oct. 14+17, 1957 /
Contemporary 164
This was one of the first albums to establish Golson's repu-
tation as a soloist and composer. —*Ron Wynn*

Blues on Down / Dec. 19, 1957-Nov. 12, 1958 / Milestone
47048
A good pairing of two fine albums that cemented his sound
and concept. —*Ron Wynn*

○ **Other Side of Benny Golson, The** / i. 1958 / Riverside 1750
This session puts the emphasis on the tenor playing of
Benny Golson as opposed to his writing and arranging
skills (though those are present as well, including a very
nice Golson original, "Are You Real?"). Joining Golson on the
program previously reissued on a twofer is a compatible
group consisting of Curtis Fuller (t), Barry Harris (p), Jymie
Merritt (b), and Philly Joe Jones (d). I've always found this set
a bit of safe, well-put-together music, but built with solos
that don't really grab me or speak of anything more than
professionals going through the motions. Golson is the highlight and he takes a number of nice, steady, slightly John
Coltraneish (or is that Philly-ish?) solos; but as a whole, very
little gets cooking. —*Bob Rusch*, Cadence

Take a Number from 1 to 10 / Dec. 13, 1960-Apr. 11, 1960
/ Argo 681
An often surprising session, with Golson veering between
conventional arrangements and pop/soul-jazz influences. —
Ron Wynn

Turning Point / Oct. 30, 1962-Nov. 1, 1960 / Mercury 20801

○ **Free** / Dec. 26, 1962 / Argo

★ **California Message** / Oct. 20-22, 1980 / Baystate 8013

Here the isolation of instrumental sounds, bass amplification, and an electric piano that oscillates wildly between channels (earphone users should check their Dramamine supplies) conspire against a potentially solid reunion session of the Benny Golson-Curtis Fuller band. Turning hastily to the featured artists, we find trombonist Fuller in gruffer, less fluid form but not substantially changed from his younger self. Golson's case is more interesting, for he's acquired a slight quaver to his tenor tone, and this, coupled with an increased graininess, a burrowing lower register, and a more balanced sense of construction, suggests that the new phase of his development might be quite distinctive. "I Remember Clifford" is a feature for Golson and the most interesting track. — *Terry Martin*, Down Beat

Moment to Moment / **i.** 1983 / Soul Note 1066

Stardust / Jun. 22-23, 1987 / Denon 71838

A high-caliber session, with Golson and Freddie Hubbard (tpt) more than capably splitting the leadership duties. — *Ron Wynn*

EDDIE GOMEZ (Edgar Gomez)

b. Oct. 4, 1944, San Juan, Puerto Rico
Bass / Cool, Latin jazz

A super bassist, Eddie Gomez's brilliant upper-register displays, amazing lines and runs, as well as his adventurous melodics, have been featured in many bands, but they were most notable in the eleven years that he spent backing Bill Evans. Gomez was born in Puerto Rico, but his family came to New York early in his childhood. He started on bass at age 12, and joined the Newport Jazz Festival band at age 14. Gomez attended the High School of Music and Art, then studied with Fred Zimmerman at Juilliard and was in Marshall Brown's International Youth Band. Gomez played with Gary McFarland, Jim Hall, Giuseppi Logan, Rufus Jones, Marian McPartland, Paul Bley, Jeremy Steig, and Gerry Mulligan in the early '60s. The year-long stint with Bley was especially critical; Gomez expanded his ideas about the range and style of his playing, which helped prepare him for the decade-plus experience of working with Evans. He joined Steps Ahead after leaving Evans, and played and recorded with Benny Wallace in the late '70s, and Jack DeJohnette, Hank Jones, and Joanne Brackeen in the '80s. He's recorded as a coleader with Lee Konitz for Milestone, and with Evans for Fantasy. Gomez has also done a session as a leader for Denon; it's the only date that features Gomez that is available on CD. However, he can also be heard on CD reissues by Evans and on more recent dates from Wallace, Jones, Brackeen, and Steps Ahead. — *Ron Wynn*

★ **Gomez** / Jan. 1984-Feb. 1984 / Denon 7189

Street Smart / **i.** 1990 / Columbia 45397

A session with a balance between radio-oriented fusion and more ambitious traditional material. — *Ron Wynn*

PAUL GONSALVES (Paul [Mex] Gonsalves)

b. Jul. 12, 1920, Boston, MA, **d.** May 14, 1974, London, England
Tenor saxophone / Swing, big band

A magnificent ballad player and the king of multiple choruses, tenor saxophonist Paul Gonsalves was one of Duke Ellington's most beloved band boys. His warm, gorgeously expressive tone and his ability to create, in either madcap or achingly slow tempos, was a vital ingredient on numerous Ellington recordings. Gonsalves's tone was similar to that of Ben Webster's, but his long lines and advanced harmonic ideas reflected the influence of Don Byas. He developed a personalized delivery and a unique sound that sometimes seemed like a shimmering, waving sheet, covering flurries of notes. Gonsalves played guitar as well as tenor in his teens, working in the Boston area before joining Count Basie in 1946. He played with Dizzy Gillespie in 1949 and 1950, then, except for a brief period that he spent with Tommy Dorsey in 1953, Gonsalves remained, until his death, with Ellington. Gonsalves admired Dorsey personally,

but he found Dorsey's band to be musically lacking. Gonsalves won international acclaim for his amazing, multichorus solo on "Diminuendo in Blue," and "Crescendo in Blue" at the 1956 Newport Festival. In a driving rainstorm, Gonsalves kept racing through choruses, generating new, fresh frenzies, seldom repeating himself, and never lapsing into cliches. Each round of applause inspired him more and more. The performance got the Ellington orchestra on the cover of *Time* magazine, but it made Gonsalves a legend. But his forte was slow, slithering ballads, on which he would play mournful blues and sentimental melodies, or would wail and honk with abandon. He did occasional sessions outside the orchestra. He recorded with Nat Adderley and Sonny Stitt in the '60s, and with Roy Eldridge in the '70s, while also doing dates with Clark Terry, Dinah Washington, Ray Charles, and Billy Taylor. Usually, he was tabbed for Ellington sideman recordings, working with Lawrence Brown, Ray Nance, and Johnny Hodges. Ellington had such regard for Gonsalves that when Gonsalves died in '74, ten days before Duke, no one had the heart to tell Ellington. — *Ron Wynn*

★ **Cookin'** / Aug. 6, 1957 / Argo 626

Gettin' Together! / Dec. 20, 1960 / Jazzland 203

Tell It the Way It Is / Sep. 4, 1963 / Impulse 55

Salt and Pepper / Sep. 5, 1963 / Jasmine 26

○ **Just A-Sittin' and A-Rockin'** / Aug. 28, 1970+Sep. 3, 1970 / Black Lion 760148

The title here is apt. This is a very relaxed, gently swinging session, almost self-effacing in the musicians' insouciant refusal to call attention to themselves, other than by the obvious merit of their art. It is particularly welcome because we rarely get to hear, on records, Paul Gonsalves outside of the Ellington band or Ray Nance at all. Some highlights: Gonsalves's sensous, breathy, fragile reading on tenor sax of Billy Strayhorn's lovely "Lotus Blossom"; his Ben Websterish blues-building on "Sue"; his conversion of "Tea" into an understated swinger, with a touch of "Peanut Vendor" yet. Then there's Nance's trumpet and vocal on "I'm In The Market For You," both instruments joyously paying tribute to Louis Armstrong; his violin on "Tea for Two"; his simply embellished chorus and a half of "Don't"; his blues playing throughout; and Turney's soulful rendition of "Eyes." The rhythm is discreet, with Jones especially nice on "B.P. Mellow," as they used to say. — *Gary Giddins*, Down Beat

★ **Mexican Bandit Meets Pittsburgh Pirate** / **i.** 1973 / Fantasy 751

While Roy Eldridge (tpt) is in good form on this date, Paul Gonsalves (ts) is not, although choruses reminiscent of his best can be heard on the ballads and "C Jam Blues." He was not in good health in his last years (he died 10 days before Ellington). Despite his poor health and the consequent effect on his solo work, his sense of humor still shines through in appropriate spots. Stanley Dance, who coproduced the album and wrote the liner notes, reports that "It's the Talk of the Town" for just the rhythm section (a nice track—good Sam Jones bass solo as well) was planned for the purpose of resting Gonsalves. Even allowing for the variability in the Gonsalves horn, there are some good turns of phrase from him, very good Eldridge, good support and solo work from the too-seldom recorded Cliff Smalls, and the fine rhythm foundation of Jones and Eddie Locke (d). — *Shirley Klett*, Cadence

Gonsalves, Paul Meets Earl Hines / **i.** 1992 / Black Lion 760177

Paul Gonsalves must share top billing with Earl Hines in an instance of an all-star pairing that works. Everyone here sounds like himself, which ain't bad at all. Gonsalves has the kind of tone (ts) you want to sleep with, and he knows how to bring a solo to its climax. Hines, meanwhile, busies himself with harmonic and metric trickery, and Jo Jones tap-dances on his skins in the background. Bassist Al Hall sounds at home amidst all this. The program reflects Gonsalves's Duke Ellingtonian connection with the medium-tempo "I Got It Bad and That Ain't Good" particularly well. One tune, Hines's "Blue Sands," was recorded two years later without the tenor saxophonist. —*David Dupont*, Cadence

JERRY GONZALEZ

b. 1949
Conga drums, trumpet, bandleader / Latin jazz, world fusion
An outstanding and eclectic percussionist, bandleader, and occasional trumpet player, Jerry Gonzalez has expanded the horizons and scope of contemporary Afro-Latin music. His compositions, especially his sessions for American Clave and with the Fort Apache band, have merged Afro-Latin jazz, salsa, funk, rock, jazz-rock, and other Latin styles seamlessly, combining free-wheeling rhythms, soaring solos, and expressive vocals. A Gonzalez date constantly shifts styles, pace, and mood, with some sections of blistering multirhythmic activity, and others with driving brass or reed solos and stinging guitar interludes. He has recorded for Sunnyside, American Clave, and Enja, among others. Gonzalez has several sessions available on CD. —*Ron Wynn*

○ **Ya Yo Me Cure** / Jul. 1980-Aug. 1980 / Pangaea 6242
An often spectacular, breakout Afro-Latin album by conga player, bandleader, composer, and sometime pianist Jerry Gonzalez. He merges Latin jazz, salsa, and Afro-Cuban rhythms, producing an album that has both multiple textures and plenty of explosive improvising. —*Ron Wynn*

★ **River Is Deep, The** / Nov. 1982 / Enja 79665
Powerhouse group; strong material. A sparkling session that helped cement Gonzalez's status among the new crop of Latin-jazz stars. —*Ron Wynn*

○ **Rhumba Para Monk** / **i.** Oct. 27-28, 1988 / Sunnyside 1036
Great production by Jim Anderson on eight Monk standards. Stripped to quintet with Carter Jefferson, the tenor sax foil. Very intriguing concept, melding Latin rhythms to Monk's off minorisms. —*Michael G. Nastos*

○ **Obatala** / Nov. 6, 1988 / Enja 79665
Explosive Afro-Latin and Latin-jazz with a hard edge. CD bonus cut. —*Ron Wynn*

○ **Earthdance** / **i.** Oct. 2-3, 1990 / Sunnyside 1050
Red-hot modern Afro-Latin and Latin-jazz, with driving grooves, great playing, and up-to-the-minute rhythms. —*Ron Wynn*

BENNY GOODMAN (Benjamin David Goodman)

b. May 30, 1909, **d.** Jun. 13, 1986
Clarinet, composer, bandleader / Swing, big band
Swing's most popular single performer and one of jazz's most complex personalities, Benny Goodman has had controversies rage around and about him seemingly since he began playing. Even his severest critics, however, acknowledge the fluidity, beauty, and majestic quality of his clarinet solos. His sweeping phrases, his ability to extend into the highest reaches of the upper register, his unfailing tone at any speed, and his complete technical command were unequaled. His orchestra was an institution in its heyday, and rightly receives credit for popularizing the swing sound. No one can truly determine if Goodman's band, at its best, was greater than Basie's and Ellington's.

The racial realities of the '40s meant that Goodman's band received far more media exposure and push than Basie's or Ellington's, and the current fractious state of cultural commentary has rendered objective analysis impossible. Goodman was marketed as the "King of Swing," an honor that could have easily been bestowed on Ellington or Basie. Goodman, even more than Paul Whiteman, has been targeted by nationalist and Afrocentric jazz observers. These observers view Goodman as symptomatic of the White media elevating designated White musicians as token players in predominantly Black art forms to keep Black giants from gaining their deserved acclaim. Some Goodman defenders have further inflamed things by insisting there were absolutely no racial motivations involved in anything done on

his behalf by anyone, any record label, any magazine polls, any fans, and so on. But none of this controversy diminishes his legitimate ability, or overshadows Goodman's progressive nature in hiring and featuring seminal Black jazz players, and in using several Fletcher Henderson and Jimmy Mundy arrangements. The Goodman band, both the orchestra and small combos, performed in an uncompromising, pure (if you will, "Black") fashion, and never wavered from it.

Goodman received basic clarinet instruction at the Kehelah Jacob Synagogue in the late 1900s. He joined the boys club band at Jane Addam's Hull House, and received lessons from its director, James Sylvester. For two years, he also studied under classically trained clarinetist Franz Schoepp. Goodman made his professional debut in 1921 at Chicago's Central Park Theater. A member of a large and poor family, Goodman became its sole support in 1926 following the death of his father. While in Harrison High School, he played occasionally with the "Austin High School Gang": Bud Freeman, Dave Tough, and others. The New Orleans traditional jazz style was Goodman's earliest influence, especially clarinetist Leon Roppolo, plus later Joe "King" Oliver, Louis Armstrong, and Bix Beiderbecke. Later, Goodman absorbed and integrated things he'd learned from clarinetists Jimmie Noone, Frank Teschumaker, and Schoepp into his own sound. He left Chicago for Los Angeles in 1926 to join drummer Ben Pollack. A year later, he was back in Chicago with Pollack, where he recorded his first solo. Pollack relocated to New York in 1928, and Goodman played with him until 1929. Over the next five years, he was a busy freelance musician. Goodman did radio programs, worked with Red Nichols, Ben Selvin, Ted Lewis, and Paul Whiteman, and found time to play in Broadway musicals *Strike Up the Band* and *Girl Crazy*. In the early '30s, he also met two people who'd forever have a great impact on his life: John Hammond and Teddy Wilson.

Goodman organized his first big band in 1934, a 12-piece unit. He began recording for Columbia, and had some early success with a Benny Carter arrangement "Take My Word," which featured four saxophones and Goodman, who joined in on tenor. The arrangement was a swing era landmark, and was soon widely imitated. He auditioned in 1934 for the NBC radio program "Let's Dance," and contacted Fletcher Henderson to provide some arrangements. Drummer Gene Krupa joined the band, and Goodman developed the reputation that would make him admired, feared, and hated throughout his career. He demanded unyielding (some called it rigid) performance standards, and insisted on uniform phrasing, accurate intonation, and general precision. Teddy Wilson joined Goodman and Krupa in 1935 for a trio date, doing four sides of exquisite, chamber-oriented material. The Goodman band toured after the radio series ended, closing things in Los Angeles at the Palomar Ballroom. The nationwide broadcast has been cited by many as the start of "swing fever." During a series of appearances at the Congress Hotel in Chicago, Goodman began concert broadcasts. He brought Wilson in from New York for an Easter date. In August of that same year, he expanded the trio to a quartet, adding vibist Lionel Hampton. They made their first recording that month, the song "Moonglow."

The band became a phenomenal success from 1936 to 1939. A series of broadcasts for CBS radio, appearances in the films *The Big Broadcast of 1937* and *Hollywood Hotel*, and a three-week concert series at the Paramount in New York made them national heroes and teen idols. Goodman cemented that fame with his 1938 Carnegie Hall concert, heading a band that included Harry James, Ziggy Elman, Jess Stacy, plus Hampton, Wilson, Krupa, and guests from Duke Ellington's and Count Basie's orchestras. Goodman continued building a parallel classical career, something that dated back to the mid '30s, when he performed Mozart's Clarinet Quintet at John Hammond's home before an invitation-only audience. Goodman recorded the piece with the Budapest String Quartet in 1938, and made his first public classical recital that November. He commissioned Bartok's

"Contrasts" and performed it at Carnegie Hall in 1939. He commissioned clarinet concertos from Copland and Hindemith in 1947, and eventually appeared with several orchestras performing works by Bernstein, Debussy, Stravinsky, and many others. Goodman disbanded his group in 1940 due to illness, then reformed it.

By the early '40s, Krupa, Stacy, James, Wilson, Hampton, and Elman were alumni, replaced by Eddie Sauter, Artie Bernstein, Fletcher Henderson, Johnny Guarnieri, and briefly, Charlie Christian, whose fleeting guitar solos attracted enormous attention before his death in 1942. Goodman made V-discs and transcriptions for the Armed Forces Radio Service during the wartime recording ban. His 1947 band marked the final time Goodman was in the eye of the jazz hurricane. Bop's emergence was forcing career reassessments everywhere, and Goodman's new band played this fresh sound with a roster that included Wardell Gray and Fats Navarro. For two years, they recorded for Capitol. Goodman was usually quite critical of bop. The sessions he made were intriguing in that everyone, except Goodman, played in the genre's faster, harmonically complex style. Goodman soloed in his usual manner. He disbanded the group after the contract ended, and, for the rest of his career, formed bands for specific projects only, rather than as traveling, day-to-day organizations.

Though he was not in the vanguard, Goodman performed regularly throughout the '50s. He did State Department tours, reunited the original Goodman trio in 1951, and was the subject of a Hollywood novelized biography, *The Benny Goodman Story*, in 1956. There were more State Department tours in the '60s and '70s, and he divided his time between those and classical appearances. There was a 40th anniversary concert at Carnegie Hall in 1978 with a specially assembled big band. He cut a fine record with George Benson in 1982, and that same year received a Kennedy Center Honor award. He bequeathed his collection of scores, recordings, and other materials to Yale University. Since his death, Musicmasters has issued periodic releases from the collection, including a comprehensive boxed set in 1993. *—Ron Wynn and Dan Morgenstern*

★ **Complete Capitol Small Group Recordings** / Mosaic

○ **Rare BG** / **i.** Mar. 21, 1928-Dec. 26, 1928 / Sunbeam 112
The collector's label Sunbeam has dedicated half of its releases to documenting Benny Goodman recordings, often rare ones. This LP includes Goodman's first two trio sides (which are from June 13, 1928, not February 1927 as listed), alternate takes of "Jungle Blues" (which has Goodman's only recorded trumpet solo) and "Room 1411," vocal-dominated performances by Johnny Marvin, Irene Beasley, and the great Annette Hanshaw, and sideman appearances by BG with many overlapping groups including those called the All Star Orchestra, the Ipana Troubadours, Mills Musical Clowns, the Lumberjacks, and the Dixie Daisies! Throughout there are many fine examples of jazz and hot dance music from the late '20s. *—Scott Yanow*

Jazz Holiday, A / **i.** 1928-Oct. 23, 1934 / Decca 24018
This two-LP set contains some of Benny Goodman's most interesting preswing recordings. The many highlights include two sides by his very first trio (from 1928!), the satirical "Shirt Tale Stomp," Goodman's only recorded trumpet solo (on "Jungle Blues") and some rare spots on alto and baritone, four classic sides by the Joe Venuti-Eddie Lang All-Star Orchestra (including definitive versions of "Beale Street Blues" and "Farewell Blues" with trombonist-singer Jack Teagarden), and sessions led by Adrian Rollini and Red Nichols (the latter has memorable renditions of "Dinah" and "Indiana" along with a famous version of "The Sheik Of Araby"). These many all-star New York bands are full of young and energetic players with BG only 19 on the earliest of these hot sides. Highly recommended in one form or another; some of the material has since been reissued on CD. *—Scott Yanow*

Benny Goodman on the Side / **i.** Mar. 1929-Apr. 3, 1931 / Sunbeam 107

Although he was a regular member of Ben Pollack's band during the time of these recordings, Benny Goodman (barely out of his teens) quickly earned a strong reputation as a versatile studio musician who could contribute a concise hot jazz solo to what otherwise would be a straight dance band record. This Sunbeam LP finds the clarinetist helping uplift recordings by the likes of the Ten Freshmen, Mills Musical Clowns, Carl Fenton's orchestra, Sammy Fain (The Crooning Composer), light opera singer James Melton, and Art Gillham (The Whispering Pianist). Often intriguing and generally enjoyable music. *—Scott Yanow*

○ **Benny Goodman and the Giants of Swing** / **i.** Apr. 18, 1929-Oct. 23, 1934 / Prestige 7644
This excellent CD collects some of Benny Goodman's best early recordings, all cut at least a few years before he became known as the King of Swing and also costarring the great trombonist-singer Jack Teagarden. BG is heard during 1929-31 with Red Nichols's Five Pennies (whose eight selections include "Indiana," "Dinah," and Teagarden's famous vocal on "The Sheik Of Araby") and on the 1930 session by Irving Mills's Hotsy Totsy Gang that included an ailing Bix Beiderbecke, an Adrian Rollini date from 1934, and four gems by the Joe Venuti-Eddie Lang All-Star Orchestra in 1931. Throughout, Goodman (just barely out of his teens) and Teagarden (along with other talented jazzmen then earning a living as studio musicians) seem overjoyed to be able to play jazz. This is highly enjoyable music that serves as a fine introduction to early preswing jazz. *—Scott Yanow*

○ **B.G. & Big Tea in NYC** / Apr. 1929-Oct. 1934 / GRP 609
CD reissue of some early '30s material that doesn't feature clarinetist Benny Goodman in a leadership role. Instead, he's in bands under the direction of Red Nichols, Arthur Rollini, and Irving Mills. Yet he's the star soloist, along with trombonist Jack Teagarden. *—Ron Wynn*

○ **Benny Goodman—the Early Years, Vol. 1** / **i.** Feb. 9, 1931-Dec. 18, 1933 / Sunbeam 138
Ever since its debut in 1971, Sunbeam has gained a reputation as the most significant Benny Goodman label, particularly in documenting radio broadcasts and early recordings that include Goodman. This LP, the first of three volumes, includes many of Goodman's best jazz recordings from 1931-33, an era when he was a studio musician rather than an orchestra leader. Already a brilliant player, Goodman is heard in fine form throughout these sides, which costar trombonist Jack Teagarden (who has eight vocals including the classic versions of "Basin Street Blues" and "Beale Street Blues" by the Charleston Chasers) and Billie Holiday on her two earliest recordings. *—Scott Yanow*

○ **Benny Goodman—the Early Years, Vol. 2** / **i.** Dec. 18, 1933-Aug. 16, 1934 / Sunbeam 139
The second of three LPs in this valuable series is composed of 16 selections recorded under the leadership of Benny Goodman, most of them before he thought seriously of leading a big band on a regular basis. The fine singer Mildred Bailey has four vocals, trombonist Jack Teagarden helps out on some of the selections, and even the great tenorman Coleman Hawkins is heard on one session. This LP concludes with Benny Goodman's Music Hall Orchestra (his first big band) in 1934 sounding fine (if not distinctive) on five performances including two versions of "Bugle Call Rag." *—Scott Yanow*

○ **Benny Goodman—the Early Years, Vol. 3** / **i.** Nov. 14, 1934-Feb. 19, 1935 / Sunbeam 140
The final of the three volumes in this Sunbeam LP series starts off with four unusual tracks released under the name of Harry Rosenthal's Orchestra. The initial two songs are actually Benny Goodman's band with a string section substituted for the trumpets, while the latter two (which have early vocals by Helen Ward) include some of Goodman's sidemen but not BG himself! After these examples of 1934 dance music, this set picks up momentum with recordings made by Goodman with his orchestra during the period when they were regularly appearing on the "Let's Dance" radio show, just prior to signing a major contract with Victor. Although

these performances are somewhat obscure, they include Gene Krupa's first appearance with Goodman's working band and find the BG sound gradually developing. —*Scott Yanow*

○ **Swinging '34, Volume 1** / i. 1934 / Melodean 7328
These two volumes find Benny Goodman and an impressive nine-piece unit (which includes trumpeter Bunny Berigan, trombonist Jack Jenney, and drummer Gene Krupa) jamming anonymously under the bandname of "Bill Dodge and His All-Star Orchestra" (even though there was no Bill Dodge!). The music, recorded for radio airplay for use between shows, features excellent examples of early swing with plenty of then-recent compositions, and, on the first volume, four vocals by Red McKenzie. Collectors will enjoy comparing these performances to the regular studio versions; both are generally enjoyable. —*Scott Yanow*

○ **Swinging '34, Volume 2** / i. 1934 / Melodean 7329
This is the second of two LPs documenting music recorded for anonymous radio airplay in early 1934 by Benny Goodman and a particularly strong nonet (including trumpeter Bunny Berigan and trombonist Jack Jenney). The results are swing performed a year before it became wildly popular; these performances hold their own against their more familiar studio versions. —*Scott Yanow*

★ **Birth of Swing, The** / Apr. 4, 1935-Nov. 5, 1936 / Bluebird 61038
This three-CD set includes all of the Benny Goodman's big-band recordings from April 1935 through November 1936, a period when the orchestra became the most popular and influential in the world, making both swing and Benny Goodman into household words. Augmented by some alternate takes, this set shows just how solid and musical a unit Goodman had from the start. Key soloists include trumpeters Bunny Berigan and Ziggy Elman, pianist Jess Stacy, and the band's excellent singer Helen Ward, but Goodman usually emerges as the star with the tight and swinging ensembles being a close second. In addition to the hits ("King Porter Stomp," "Sometimes I'm Happy," "When Buddha Smiles," "Stompin' at the Savoy," and "Goody Goody"), even the lesser-known numbers and pop tunes have their strong moments. This music is essential to any serious jazz collection. —*Scott Yanow*

○ **Thesaurus, Vol. 1** / i. Jun. 6, 1935 / Sunbeam 101
June 6, 1935, was a very busy day for Benny Goodman and his big band. The group recorded no fewer than 51 tunes for transcriptions that were leased to NBC radio stations under the pseudonym of the Rhythm Makers orchestra. Recorded shortly before Goodman made it big (otherwise they could not have been disguised as a fictional band), these excellent sides are a fine showcase for Goodman and his sidemen, which at the time included trumpeter Pee Wee Erwin, pianist Frank Froeba, and drummer Gene Krupa. This first of three LP volumes is highlighted by a surprisingly effective swing version of "Yes, We Have No Bananas!" —*Scott Yanow*

○ **Thesaurus, Vol. 2** / i. Jun. 6, 1935 / Sunbeam 102
The second of three LPs documenting one very busy day in the life of Benny Goodman's orchestra, these transcriptions cut for radio are well recorded and consistently swinging even with the presence of a few fluffs (each performance only received one run through). The musicians received just $1 apiece per tune (51 songs were cut that day), so listeners should definitely feel that they've received their money's worth! A fascinating look at the Benny Goodman orchestra just before it became wildly successful. —*Scott Yanow*

○ **Thesaurus, Vol. 3** / i. Jun. 6, 1935 / Sunbeam 103
This is the third and final volume of LPs chronicling the 51 songs recorded by the Benny Goodman orchestra for radio transcriptions in one day. This set includes interesting versions of "King Porter Stomp" and "Sometimes I'm Happy" performed less than a month before the hit studio renditions, and it captures the King of Swing only a short time before he unexpectedly became a household name. —*Scott Yanow*

☆ **Original Benny Goodman Trio and Quartet Sessions—Vol. 1: After You've Gone** / Jul. 13, 1935-Feb. 3, 1937 / Bluebird 5631
Although Benny Goodman came to fame as leader of a big swinging orchestra, from nearly the beginning he always allocated some time to playing with smaller groups. On July 13, 1935, the Benny Goodman Trio debuted (featuring drummer Gene Krupa and pianist Teddy Wilson), and 13 months later vibraphonist Lionel Hampton made the unit a Quartet. The first interracial group to appear regularly in public, this outlet gave BG an opportunity to stretch out and interact with his peers. The CD *After You've Gone* contains the first 10 Trio recordings and the initial 12 studio performances by the Quartet. Helen Ward contributes two fine vocals but the emphasis is on the close interplay between these brilliant players. A gem. —*Scott Yanow*

○ **Stompin' at the Savoy** / Jul. 1935-Feb. 1938 / Bluebird 61067

○ **Complete Benny Goodman—Vol. 2 (1935-1936)** / Nov. 22, 1935-Jun. 16, 1936 / RCA 5562
The second two-LP set in this eight-volume series has all of Benny Goodman's Victor studio sides that were recorded during a seven-month period when the orchestra consolidated and built on its unexpected success. In addition to such popular recordings as "When Buddha Smiles," "Stompin' at the Savoy," and "Goody Goody," there are six selections by the Benny Goodman Trio, many enjoyable vocals from Helen Ward (the best of BG's many singers), and four hot numbers by a combo under Gene Krupa's leadership that matches the clarinetist with trumpeter Roy Eldridge and tenor great Chu Berry. Essential music in one form or another. —*Scott Yanow*

○ **Benny Goodman from the Congress Hotel** / i. Dec. 27, 1935-Jan. 36 0 / Sunbeam 32
This five-LP boxed set houses the same music as the five individual volumes (even including all of the same liner notes) and is overall a gem. Benny Goodman was booked into the Congress Hotel in December 1935 for a one-month stint; the engagement was eventually extended to six months! These well-recorded airchecks are seven separate but continuous broadcasts that contain plenty of strong examples of Goodman's early band. Unlike his 1937 version, this orchestra only had its leader and pianist Jess Stacy as memorable soloists (although trombonist Joe Harris did a good job in a Jack Teagarden vein), but the ensembles are remarkably tight, Helen Ward's vocals are enjoyable, the band always swung (even on the pop tunes), and happily the recording quality is quite good. Highly recommended to those who can find this rare box! —*Scott Yanow*

○ **Swingin' through the Years with Benny Goodman** / i. Dec. 29, 1935-Aug. 21, 1967 / Giants of Jazz 1005
The Giants of Jazz label consistently features very well-recorded airchecks from radio and television shows. This particular LP has 13 examples of Benny Goodman's music from four different decades including a 1935 version of "Alexander's Ragtime Band," a Sextet rendition of "The Sheik of Araby" (with guitarist Charlie Christian), a torrid "Stealin' Apples" from 1943, Goodman guesting with Peggy Lee in 1951, and a reunion by the Benny Goodman Trio in 1967. A nice all-round set of rarities. —*Scott Yanow*

☆ **After You've Gone—Vol. 2** / i. 1935-1957 / RCA/Bluebird 2273
The complete Trio and Quartet sides (along with Volume 1) for Victor. Great sound. —*Cub Koda*

★ **Legendary Performer** / i. 1935-1937 / RCA 2470
A valuable collection of mid-'30s sides, now available in new, better-mastered collections. —*Ron Wynn*

○ **Complete Benny Goodman—Vol. 3 (1936)** / Aug. 13, 1936-Dec. 9, 1936 / RCA 5532
The third of eight two-LP sets reissuing all of Benny Goodman's Victor recordings from the swing era, this twofer has such "killer dillers" as "Down South Camp Meeting," "St. Louis Blues," and two versions of "Bugle Call Rag," in addi-

tion to performances by the Benny Goodman Trio and his new Quartet (with vibraphonist Lionel Hampton), with Ella Fitzgerald as a guest vocalist and trumpeter Ziggy Elman's first recordings with the band. In all there are 32 performances on this set that prove that Benny Goodman really did deserve the title, "The King of Swing." — *Scott Yanow*

○ **Complete Benny Goodman—Vol. 8 (1936-1939)** / Dec. 2, 1936-May 4, 1939 / RCA 5568
The final volume of this definitive series of Benny Goodman's Victor studio recordings not only contains his recordings from April and May 1939 but digs up a variety of alternate takes (most of them previously unissued) from the 1936-39 period. It is fascinating to hear "new" versions of such songs as "Stompin' At The Savoy," "Sing, Sing Sing," "Avalon," and "Sugarfoot Stomp," especially when one is familiar with the original released renditions. In addition, this twofer has the two recordings (and one alternate) cut by the Metronome All-Star Band, which in 1939 (with such musicians as Bunny Berigan, Jack Teagarden, and Tommy Dorsey) allowed Goodman to reunite with some of his associates from the earlier days. A fitting ending to an essential series. — *Scott Yanow*

○ **Complete Benny Goodman—Vol. 4 (1936-1937)** / Dec. 30, 1936-Oct. 22, 1937 / RCA 5537
The fourth of eight volumes (all two-LP sets) documenting Benny Goodman's highly influential Victor studio sides, this covers the 1936-37 period of Goodman's amazing rise in popularity (he was now a household name), with Harry James joining the orchestra and Martha Tilton settling in as the band's regular vocalist. Among the many memorable recordings are "Sing, Sing, Sing," the Benny Goodman Quartet's "Avalon," and "Sugarfoot Stomp." — *Scott Yanow*

★ **On the Air 1937-1938** / **i.** Mar. 25, 1937-Sep. 20, 1938 / Columbia/Legacy 48836
In the early 1950s, after the unexpectedly large sales of Benny Goodman's 1938 Carnegie Hall concert, Columbia came out with a two-LP set of broadcasts from 1937-39 that also sold well. This recent double-CD set not only includes the music on the original LPs but adds 14 tracks only previously put out on collector's labels. After his success with an ensemble-oriented swing band in 1935, Benny Goodman gradually added top soloists to his orchestra including trumpeters Harry James and Ziggy Elman and Vido Musso on tenor. While his studio recordings from 1937 are quite enjoyable, they generally only hint at the excitement that Goodman's ensemble (propelled by an increasingly uninhibited Gene Krupa) could generate before an enthusiastic dancing crowd. *On The Air* captures the Benny Goodman big band (along with some examples of the Trio and Quartet) at its peak and shows why the original swing orchestras (as opposed to the weak nostalgia bands that are currently around) were so popular with younger people in the '30s and '40s. These performances are still exciting! — *Scott Yanow*

○ **Benny Goodman at the Manhattan Room** / **i.** Oct. 13, 1937-Jan. 16, 1938 / Sunbeam 116-127
Available originally as a dozen individual sets, these late 1937 broadcasts of Benny Goodman's orchestra, Trio, and Quartet from the Manhattan Room of the Pennsylvania Hotel in New York were also put out as this 12-LP box, containing exactly the same program and liner notes as the original sets. There are many highlights with strong solos from Goodman and trumpeter Harry James, exuberant backup by Gene Krupa, features for the Trio and Quartet, and plenty of vocals by Martha Tilton. Since this set gives one a valuable look at the Benny Goodman Orchestra as it seems to be counting down to its famous January 1938 Carnegie Hall concert, it seems fitting that the series concludes with two numbers actually from that historic performance that were left out of the Columbia set due to their rough quality. Few bands could withstand the enormous number of recordings, broadcasts, and performances that Benny Goodman's orchestra underwent at the peak of its popularity without losing some of its quality, but the

taskmaster clarinetist kept his troops nearly flawless in their ensemble work and they never failed to swing. This is a great set well worth searching for. — *Scott Yanow*

○ **Complete Benny Goodman—Vol. 5 (1937-1938)** / Oct. 29, 1937-Apr. 8, 1938 / RCA 5557
It was during the period covered by this twofer that Benny Goodman played his famous Carnegie Hall concert and his orchestra reached its peak. This fifth of eight two-LP sets has more than its share of memorable performances including "Don't Be That Way," "One O'Clock Jump," and two versions of "Life Goes to a Party," plus the last recordings of the Benny Goodman Quartet before Gene Krupa (after a dispute with Goodman) left the band to form his own orchestra. Other sessions include an unusual one that finds some of Count Basie's sidemen sitting in (including tenor great Lester Young). There is also a quartet date with Dave Tough sitting and performing ably in the departed Krupa's place. As with all of the twofers in this series, this one is highly recommended and deserves to be reissued in full on CD. — *Scott Yanow*

☆ **Vol. 1—Treasure Chest Series** / **i.** 1937-1938 / MGM 3788
This three-LP series features radio airchecks by the Benny Goodman big band and small groups during 1937-38. Since the producers were quite choosy in designing these programs, there are virtually no weak selections, with the big-band numbers emphasizing middle and uptempo swing and the Trio and Quartet selections up to the level one would expect of Benny Goodman, Lionel Hampton, Teddy Wilson, and Gene Krupa. The first volume contains "When Buddha Smiles," "Dear Old Southland," "Madhouse," and a few quartet performances. The biggest surprise is Lionel Hampton's ad-lib appearance on vibes during the big band's "I Know That You Know." — *Scott Yanow*

☆ **Vol. 2—Treasure Chest Series** / **i.** 1937-1938 / MGM 3789
The second of three LPs in this superior series continues the issuance of rare (and well-chosen) live performances by Benny Goodman's big band and small groups. Virtually every selection is a gem and there are a few surprises. The big band joins the quartet at the end of a rousing "Avalon" while "Space, Man" finds Lionel Hampton and Jess Stacy sharing the same piano. Overall this series finds Goodman and his sidemen at their best — *Scott Yanow*

☆ **Vol. 3—Treasure Chest Series** / **i.** 1937-1939 / MGM 3790
The third and final LP in this wonderful series of radio airchecks once again features Benny Goodman, his big band, and small groups at their best; the producers really cherry-picked the large amount of live documentation to come up with some of the most rewarding performances by Goodman during one of his prime periods. Biggest surprise of Vol. 3 is the addition of Harry James's trumpet to the quartet on "Twilight in Turkey," but even then the selections that should be predictable tend to swing hotter than expected. As a bonus, a 1939 live version of "AC-DC Current" adds a rare performance by guitarist Charlie Christian to his slim discography. Overall, this is a great series that deserves to be reissued on CD. — *Scott Yanow*

☆ **Complete 1937-38 Jazz Concert No. 2** / **i.** 1937-1938 / Columbiua 180
This two-LP series was quickly released after the big success of Benny Goodman's best-selling 1938 Carnegie Hall Concert set. Labeled "No. 2," these excellent aircheck performances have no relation to the Carnegie Hall concert except for the time period. The Benny Goodman orchestra and small groups often sounded much more exciting live in concert than on their studio recordings, and one can really tell from these performances why drummer Gene Krupa was so popular and a thorn in Goodman's side. With Harry James, Ziggy Elman, and Chris Griffin forming a classic trumpet section, the Benny Goodman orchestra (with its clean ensembles and hard-swinging sound) had its own distinctive, well-loved style. This double LP (since reissued with additional tracks on CD) contains essential music; listen to Harry James on "St. Louis Blues" for proof of the band's excitement. — *Scott Yanow*

★ **Benny Goodman Carnegie Hall Jazz Concert** / **i.** Jan. 16, 1938 / Columbia 160

One of the great concerts ever captured on record and in itself a turning point in the way jazz is judged by outsiders. Never before had a full jazz concert been held at Carnegie Hall; it is hard to believe that tapes of this momentous event were kept in a closet, forgotten until rediscovered by accident in 1950! There are many high points including exciting versions of "Don't Be That Way" and "One O'Clock Jump," a tribute to the 20 years of jazz that were then on record, a jam session version of "Honeysuckle Rose" that finds sidemen of the orchestras of Duke Ellington and Count Basie interacting with Goodman's stars, exciting performances by the trio and quartet, and of course "Sing Sing Sing" with Gene Krupa's creative (if not too subtle) drumming and Jess Stacy's remarkable ad-lib piano solo. Fortunately, this program has been reissued in full on CD, and it belongs in every serious music library, capturing Benny Goodman and the swing era in general at its height. — *Scott Yanow*

○ **Benny Goodman Swingtime** / **i.** Jan. 18, 1938-Mar. 18, 1939 / Sunbeam 152

This two-LP set has a variety of 1938-39 performances originally heard on the radio. Some of these performances are a bit unusual, including Benny Goodman playing the classical piece "Quintet For Clarinet & Strings" with the Coolidge String Quartet, a few odd radio interviews, and a trio version of "Tiger Rag" that finds Lionel Hampton on drums. Most of the other tracks (which had never been issued before this set) are more conventional and of consistently high quality. Lots of good music on this twofer. — *Scott Yanow*

○ **Complete Benny Goodman—Vol. 6 (1938)** / Apr. 8, 1938-Oct. 13, 1938 / RCA 5566

This sixth of eight two-LP sets documenting Benny Goodman's Victor studio recordings finds Goodman in his post-Gene Krupa era. The classic trumpet section of Harry James, Ziggy Elman, and Chris Griffin was still intact, but after the Carnegie Hall concert there must have been a feeling of these performances being anticlimactic. Still, there are lots of memorable moments on these big-band and quartet tracks with a liberal number of Martha Tilton vocals, pop tunes (superior ones), and jazz standards. The rhythm was now much more subtle (with Dave Tough on drums) but the Goodman sound in 1938 was not that much different from 1937 and the music is well worth acquiring. — *Scott Yanow*

○ **Best of Newhouse** / **i.** May 10, 1938-Apr. 18, 1939 / Phontastic 26

This two-LP set owes its existence to Jerry Newhouse, in 1938 a young swing fan who had just bought a professional record-cutting machine so as to record his favorite musicians off radio broadcasts. The Swedish Phontastic label wisely went through Newhouse's acetates in 1981 and was able to put together this generous package of timeless swing. Mostly dating from 1938, these well-recorded performances do not necessarily shed new light on Benny Goodman's legacy, but they offer "new" versions of Goodman's standards including a "Sing, Sing, Sing" that lets Lionel Hampton stretch out on drums. — *Scott Yanow*

○ **Complete Benny Goodman—Vol. 7 (1938-1939)** / Oct. 13, 1938-Apr. 7, 1939 / RCA 5567

The seventh two-LP set in this eight-volume series continues the documentation of Benny Goodman's influential studio recordings for Victor in the '30s. High points of this fine twofer include a version of "Ciribiribin" that predates Harry James's famous recording, the unusual "Bach Goes to Town," a memorable "I Cried for You" by Goodman's quintet (with John Kirby on bass), "Sent for You Yesterday" (featuring a Johnny Mercer vocal), and the big Ziggy Elman hit "And the Angels Sing." Recommended. — *Scott Yanow*

○ **Goodman Airchecks/Barnet Rhythmakers** / **i.** Jan. 17, 1939-Jan. 1941 / IAJRC 8

This LP from the collector's label IARC has interesting radio airchecks from both the Benny Goodman and Charlie Barnet orchestras. The Goodman selections, all from January to March 1939, include several oddities such as guest appearances by Billie Holiday (heard on "I Cried For You"). Both trombonist Jack Teagarden and pianist Pete Johnson perform during a rollicking "Roll 'Em," band pianist Jess Stacy gets a rare chance to play with the Benny Goodman trio ("She's Funny That Way"), and Goodman plays the hit song of his chief rival Artie Shaw ("Begin the Beguine"). The Charlie Barnet tracks (two selections from 1938 and the remainder dating from 1941) are more conventional but consistently swing hard; the only vocal is on a hot "I've Got To Be a Rug Cutter." This now hard-to-find LP is worth searching for. — *Scott Yanow*

○ **Legendary Benny Goodman** / **i.** Aug. 10, 1939-Sep. 26, 1951 / Columbia 515536

Put out by Columbia Special Products back in 1981, this five-LP boxed set contains an excellent cross-section of Benny Goodman's recordings for Columbia, dating from 1939-42, 1945-46, and a few tracks from 1950-51. Since CBS has never reissued Goodman's recordings in full, this sampler (which has become hard to find) is the best set from this era, tracing the evolution of Benny Goodman through his second great band (including a few tracks by the Sextet with guitarist Charlie Christian) to some of the clarinetist's first postwar recordings and a few performances where, instead of being the pacesetter, he is looked upon as a nostalgia act. Throughout, Goodman plays quite well and, even with only five selections to a side (for a total of around 150 minutes on the five LPs), this box is worth bidding for. — *Scott Yanow*

○ **Alternate Goodman, Vol. I** / **i.** Aug. 10, 1939-Sep. 13, 1939 / Phontastic 7606

Although Columbia has never fully reissued Benny Goodman's valuable work for the label during 1939-46, the Swedish Phontastic label did come out with no fewer than 12 LPs full of alternate takes and unissued performances from the era, issued chronologically. So, thanks to Phontastic, it is possible to acquire alternate versions of songs while the original takes remain completely unavailable! Volume I contains "new" versions of such classics as "Jumpin' At The Woodside," "Stealin' Apples," "Bolero," and "Boy Meets Horn." With trumpeters Ziggy Elman and Jimmy Maxwell, trombonist Vernon Brown, and tenorman Jerry Jerome among the soloists, it quickly becomes obvious that Benny Goodman (even though his popularity was gradually being exceeded by Glenn Miller) had a great band in 1939. — *Scott Yanow*

○ **Benny Goodman on V-Disc** / **i.** Aug. 11, 1939-Oct. 1948 / Sunbeam 144

Originally released as three separate LPs, this three-LP set is a straight reissue (with the same liner notes) as the individual Sunbeam records. A wonderful acquisition for the true Benny Goodman collector, *Benny Goodman On V-Disc* contains a wide variety of performances that were issued on V-Discs (limited-edition records specially available for servicemen during World War II), and many of the selections were formerly quite rare. Although a few tracks are from 1939-41 and some others date as late as 1948, the bulk of the music is from 1944-46, not one of the King of Swing's better-known periods. Such star soloists as trumpeter Cootie Williams, guitarist Charlie Christian, Gene Krupa, trumpeter Roy Eldridge, vibraphonist Red Norvo, and pianist Mel Powell have their spots, but the clarinetist consistently gets solo honors. Historical and quite enjoyable performances. — *Scott Yanow*

○ **Alternate Goodman, Vol. II** / **i.** Sep. 13, 1939-Nov. 29, 1940 / Phontastic 7610

The second of twelve LPs that chronologically release alternate and rare versions of Benny Goodman's Columbia recordings, this one has quite a bit of variety, including Sextet versions of "Flying Home," "Soft Winds," and "I'm Confessin'," the 1940 Metronome All-Star Band (which is dominated by Goodman alumni) romping through "King Porter Stomp," and a dozen Goodman orchestra performances. Goodman fanatics will want to acquire this entire series. — *Scott Yanow*

○ **Benny Goodman 1939, Volume 2** / **i.** Oct. 20, 1939-Dec. 27, 1939 / Tax 8033

The second of two LPs reissuing Benny Goodman's Columbia big-band recordings of 1939 features charts by Fletcher Henderson and Eddie Sauter, strong solos from trumpeter Ziggy Elman and tenorman Jerry Jerome, eight vocals by guest singer Mildred Bailey, and several instrumental classics including "Honeysuckle Rose", "Zaggin' with Zig," and the original version of "Let's Dance." — *Scott Yanow*

From Spirituals to Swing / **i.** 1939 / Vanguard 47-48

Carnegie Hall concerts featuring five great early Goodman Sextet performances plus a host of jazz greats. — *Cub Koda*

○ **Alternate Goodman, Vol. III** / **i.** Nov. 29, 1940-Jan. 21, 1941 / Phontastic 7612

The third of 12 LPs put out by the Swedish label Phontastic is composed of alternate takes and rare studio recordings by the Benny Goodman orchestra. There are two sextet tracks with trumpeter Cootie Williams, Count Basie, and guitarist Charlie Christian, a few Helen Forrest vocals, and some advanced instrumentals. Most collectors will take an all-or-nothing approach to this important series. — *Scott Yanow*

○ **Eddie Sauter Arrangements** / **i.** Dec. 18, 1940-Mar. 17, 1945 /

Here is an LP crying to be reissued on CD. Eddie Sauter was Benny Goodman's most advanced arranger. His writing for Goodman in the early '40s was much more unpredictable than Fletcher Henderson's and often full of surprises and unusual colors. A dozen of Sauter's greatest arrangements (including "Moonlight on the Ganges," "La Rosita," "Superman," and a remarkable reworking of "Love Walked In") are heard on this set, and they really challenge Benny Goodman to come up with fresh ideas. A classic album. — *Scott Yanow*

Solid Gold Instrumental Hits / **i.** Dec. 18, 1940-Mar. 17, 1945 / Columbia 33405

Despite its dumb title (none of these 20 performances were million sellers), this double LP contains many of the high points of Benny Goodman's most interesting orchestra. The arrangements of Eddie Sauter and Mel Powell in particular challenged Goodman (while giving him an entire new book of material) and led to many classic moments. Highlights include "Air Mail Special," "Clarinet a la King," "Clarinade," "Love Walked In," "String of Pearls," and "Jersey Bounce." — *Scott Yanow*

○ **Swing into Spring** / **i.** Jan. 28, 1941-Feb. 25, 1958 / Columbia 28995

Released to tie in with a television show in the late '50s, this LP features some exciting highlights from Benny Goodman's career, including "Slipped Disc," "The Earl," a hot "Undecided" with vibraphonist Terry Gibbs, and Helen Wardis's rendition of "I'll Never Say 'Never Again' Again." It may be hard to find, but buy this if you see it! — *Scott Yanow*

○ **Alternate Goodman, Vol. IV** / **i.** Jan. 28, 1941-Mar. 27, 1941 / Phontastic 7615

On the fourth of twelve LPs released by the Swedish Phontastic label that issue in chronological order alternate takes and rarities from Benny Goodman's period with Columbia in the 1940s, high points include "Perfidia," "Scarecrow," "Solo Flight" (starring guitarist Charlie Christian), Cootie Williams's feature "Fiesta in Blue," and a sextet version of "Airmail Special." — *Scott Yanow*

○ **Alternate Goodman, Vol. V** / **i.** Mar. 27, 1941-Sep. 25, 1941 / Phontastic 7616

On the fifth volume of a 12-LP series of Benny Goodman alternate takes and rarities, the 1941 orchestra is heard playing "new" versions of such songs as "Don't Be That Way," "Smoke Gets in Your Eyes," "Clarinet A La King," and "The Earl." Also quite interesting (to hear once) is Peggy Lee's debut on the alternate of "Elmer's Tune"; she sounds scared to death! — *Scott Yanow*

○ **Alternate Goodman, Vol. VI** / **i.** Sep. 25, 1941-Nov. 27, 1941 / Phontastic 7617

The sixth of 12 LPs that contain alternate versions of Benny Goodman's recordings from his period on Columbia has several highlights: two versions of "Clarinet A La King," several Peggy Lee vocals (including "Let's Do It"), and two titles ("If I Had You" and "Limehouse Blues") by Goodman's new sextet with trombonist Lou McGarity and pianist Mel Powell. True Benny Goodman collectors are advised to pick up these worthy 12 LPs in a hurry! — *Scott Yanow*

○ **Alternate Goodman, Vol. VII** / **i.** Nov. 27, 1941-Feb. 5, 1942 / Phontastic 7620

Part of a 12-LP series put out by the Swedish label Phontastic, this set (as with the others) is composed of alternate takes and rarities from the Benny Goodman orchestra during his period with Columbia. As interesting as the big-band alternates are (particularly "A String Of Pearls"), it is the two numbers from the Benny Goodman Sextet (which features trombonist Lou McGarity and pianist Mel Powell) and three performances from the 1941 Metronome All-Star Band that are of greatest interest. — *Scott Yanow*

○ **War Years** / **i.** Oct. 19, 1942-Mar. 21, 1945 / Jazz Society 510

Taken from broadcasts of the Benny Goodman orchestra, the emphasis is on hard-driving swing throughout this LP, with some time taken out for vocals by Peggy Lee, Jane Harvey, Mildred Bailey ("Downhearted Blues"), and Goodman himself. Unfortunately, there is no personnel listing given but suffice it to say that Goodman is in brilliant form (really stretching out on "Stealing Apples") during these high-quality performances. — *Scott Yanow*

○ **Way Down Yonder (1943-1944)** / Dec. 9, 1943-Jan. 1946 / Vintage Jazz Classics 1001

This valuable CD contains performances from 1943-46 originally recorded for World War II servicemen. VJC has fleshed out the original recordings with alternate takes and breakdowns, which, due to the high quality of the music, makes this CD even more interesting. Gene Krupa is heard with Goodman's 1943 big band and in a trio with pianist Jess Stacy, while the bulk of this set features the Benny Goodman Quintet with vibraphonist Red Norvo during 1944, including an early version of the classic "Slipped Disc." — *Scott Yanow*

○ **King of Swing** / **i.** Jul. 21, 1944-Jan. 14, 1946 / Giants of Jazz 1017

The Giants of Jazz label consistently released well-recorded LPs of Benny Goodman radio appearances. This one is no exception, giving one a rare (if brief) glance at Goodman's unrecorded big band of 1944 with trumpeter Roy Eldridge along with more extended performances by Goodman's orchestra (which featured trombonist Lou McGarity and a young Stan Getz on tenor) and quintet in January 1946. The vocals of Art Lund and Liz Morrow do not hurt either. Fine swing from the tail-end of the swing era by its King. — *Scott Yanow*

○ **Alternate Goodman, Vol. X** / **i.** Feb. 25, 1945-Jun. 18, 1945 / Phontastic 7650

The tenth of 12 LPs of Benny Goodman alternate takes and rarities from his period with Columbia contains a variety of odds and ends including three "new" versions of "Gotta Be This Or That," two of "Love Walked In," and one apiece of "Clarinade," "Ain't Misbehavin'," and the sextet's "Rachel's Dream." Little did Benny Goodman know that his work in 1945, although hard swinging, was already in danger of slipping behind the times. Despite that, this music is quite enjoyable and timeless. — *Scott Yanow*

○ **Goodman on the Air** / **i.** May 1945-Dec. 23, 1945 / Phontastic 7605

Benny Goodman had one of his great years in 1945 when we was still only 36. Although history looks at him as being a bit old-fashioned musically by this time, especially when compared to Charlie Parker and Dizzy Gillespie, in reality Goodman was still the world's top clarinetist, leader of an exciting (if underrated) big band, and at the peak of his commercial fame. The LP *Goodman on the Air*, released by the Swedish Phontastic label, is composed of radio airchecks from 1945 featuring both the Goodman Sextet (on five numbers) and big band on selections that might be familiar to the clarinetist's fans (such as "Slipped Disc," "Clarinet A La King," and "King Porter Stomp") but actually differ greatly from their studio versions. Worth searching for. *—Scott Yanow*

○ **Alternate Goodman, Vol. XI** / **i.** Aug. 29, 1945-Jan. 30, 1946 / Phontastic 7652
The next-to-last of 12 LPs released by the Swedish label Phontastic continues the documentation of alternate takes and rarities recorded by Benny Goodman during the 1939-46 period. Goodman had an excellent big band in 1945 as one can hear on such selections as "Just You, Just Me," "Give Me The Simple Life," and "Fascinating Rhythm," but it is his sextet (heard here on five performances) that really stars. Vibraphonist Red Norvo, pianist Mel Powell, and bassist Slam Stewart star on such numbers as "Tiger Rag," "Shine," and "China Boy" and really push the clarinetist to some of his best playing. *—Scott Yanow*

○ **Alternate Goodman, Vol. XII** / **i.** Jan. 23, 1946-Aug. 7, 1946 / Phontastic 7654
The twelfth and final of the dozen LPs released by the Swedish label Phontastic completes the issuance of Benny Goodman alternate takes and rarities from his valuable period (1939-46) with Columbia. Although there are some fine big-band performances on this set (particularly a two-part version of "Oh, Baby!") it is the small-group performances (which costar pianist Mel Powell) that are most exciting and foretell Goodman's future. Collectors are well advised to pick up all 12 of these LPs while they can still be found! *—Scott Yanow*

Trios / **i.** Feb. 19, 1947-Nov. 16, 1954 / PA/USA 9031
Benny Goodman was perhaps the top jazz clarinetist of all time, and, although he has always been associated with the swing era, his brilliant playing never declined even after the dominance of the big bands became history. This Pausa LP reissue of some of his Capitol recordings features Goodman mostly in a trio with pianist Teddy Wilson and drummer Jimmy Crawford in 1947 along with a slightly earlier duet with pianist Jess Stacy and a trio track from 1954 with Mel Powell. Throughout, the clarinetist seems inspired, happily stretching out on a variety of standards, most of which were not specifically associated with him. This highly enjoyable music deserves to be reissued on CD. *—Scott Yanow*

○ **Swedish Pastry** / **i.** May 24, 1948-Jun. 5, 1948 / Dragon 16
In 1948, the young Swedish clarinetist Stan Hasselgard so impressed Benny Goodman that Goodman invited him to join his new septet, a unit that also included tenor saxophonist Wardell Gray and pianist Teddy Wilson. Because of the recording strike and Hasselgard's death before year end in a car accident, no commercial recordings were made of the two-clarinet combo. But, luckily, the short-lived septet was captured live at the Cique in Philadelphia during a two-week period. This Dragon LP features 13 selections, and, although Goodman is the dominant soloist, Hasselgard has some solo space and even gets to interact with Goodman. This was one of Goodman's few bop-oriented bands, so this LP fills a major gap in jazz history. *—Scott Yanow*

Sextet / Nov. 24, 1950-Oct. 22, 1952 / Columbia 40379
In 1950, Benny Goodman formed a new sextet and, although he used a big band for some recordings, the small group was his main outlet for the next couple of years. This LP features this somewhat forgotten unit, a hot swing combo featuring vibraphonist Terry Gibbs and usually pianist Teddy Wilson. Rather than repeat his older hits, the clarinetist clearly enoyed playing other standards not generally associated with him. Excellent and easily enjoyable music. *—Scott Yanow*

○ **For the Fletcher Henderson Fund** / **i.** 1954 /

○ **B.G. In Hi/Fi** / **i.** Nov. 8, 1954-Nov. 16, 1954 / Capitol 92864
On this excellent all-round CD, Benny Goodman performs a dozen selections (mostly Fletcher Henderson arrangements) with a big band filled with sympathetic players in 1954 and eight other numbers with a pair of smaller units that also

feature pianist Mel Powell and either Charlie Shavers or Ruby Braff on trumpet. Although the big-band era had been gone for almost a decade, Benny Goodman (then 46) plays these swing classics with enthusiasm and creativity and shows that there was never any reason for anyone to write him off as "behind the times." *—Scott Yanow*

★ **Yale Recordings, Vols. 1-6** / Mar. 26, 1955-Jun. 28, 1967 / Music Masters 5000
In his will, Benny Goodman gave to Yale not only all of his band arrangements (over 1,500) but 400 10-inch master tapes of unreleased studio and concert recordings. Some of the more rewarding sessions have now been issued by Music Masters, and this particular boxed set includes the first five volumes (and a 40-page booklet), six CDs in all (Vol. 5 has two CDs by itself), which are also available separately. The music dates from 1955-84 (the second half of Benny Goodman's career) and is taken from quite a few sessions including a full CD of material by his excellent septet of 1955 (featuring trumpeter Ruby Braff and Paul Quinichette on tenor), big-band performances from 1958 with several vocals by Jimmy Rushing, and many selections from a 1959 engagement with a nonet featuring trumpeter Jack Sheldon, trombonist Bill Harris, and tenorman Flip Phillips. Although no longer a pacesetter, Benny Goodman remained one of the jazz world's most brilliant performers, making this set well worth acquiring. *—Scott Yanow*

○ **Yale Recordings, Vol. 8: Never Before Released Recordings from Benny Goodman's Private** / **i.** May 16, 1957-Jan. 24, 1961 / Music Masters 65093
The eighth volume of previously unreleased material willed by Benny Goodman to Yale continues the series with some very interesting selections. Martha Tilton gets to redo her hit "Bei Mir Bist Du Schon" in 1958 with a big band, Goodman's clarinet is well featured with a quintet that includes pianist Andre Previn on three tracks, and BG has his last musical encounter with pianist Mel Powell on a pair of medleys. But most unusual are eight selections cut with a nine-piece unit in 1961 that are dominated by songs associated with Hawaii including "on The Beach at Waikiki," "Blue Hawaii," "Sweet Leilani," and "My Little Grass Shack"! Bill Stegmeyer's creative arrangements and an all-star lineup actually make this into a highly enjoyable and very surprising session. *—Scott Yanow*

○ **Benny in Brussels, Vol. I** / **i.** May 1958 / Columbia 13502
Benny Goodman's successful stint at the 1958 Brussels World Fair served as an excuse for him to record some albums of his new big band. With tenor saxophonist Zoot Sims, trumpeter Taft Jordan, and Goodman's new discovery, pianist Roland Hanna (then 26) getting some fine solos and Jimmy Rushing taking a personable vocal on "Brussels Blues," Goodman's backup crew was strong. As for the King himself, although no longer thought of as an innovator, he was still at age 49 very much in his prime, and he is in fine form throughout these two volumes. *—Scott Yanow*

○ **Together Again** / **i.** Feb. 13, 1963-Aug. 27, 1963 / RCA 2698
In 1963, Benny Goodman, Gene Krupa, Lionel Hampton, and Teddy Wilson got back together as the Benny Goodman Quartet for the first time in 25 years. This LP contains 10 joyous performances, mostly songs that the Quartet missed the first time around. In addition to being inspired by being in each other's company again, these timeless masters were all still in their prime and their individual styles had not changed much since 1938. The result is a set of musical magic. *—Scott Yanow*

★ **Together Again! (1963 Reunion with Lionel Hampton, Teddy Wilson & Gene Krupa** / Feb. 13, 1963-Aug. 27, 1963 / Bluebird 6283
In 1963, almost exactly 25 years after Gene Krupa left Benny Goodman's orchestra, the Benny Goodman Quartet recorded together again for the first time. This CD, a straight reissue of the original LP, finds BG, Lionel Hampton, Teddy Wilson, and Krupa clearly happy to be back together, not so much revisiting their older "hits" as having a good time playing songs that they missed the first time around. One can feel

the absence of a bass (the more primitive recording quality of the '30s helped cover it up originally), but the music is so joyful and swinging that one doesn't mind. —*Scott Yanow*

Seven Comes Eleven / Sep. 15, 1975-Nov. 14, 1975 / Columbia 38265

Here is an LP full of surprises. Benny Goodman is heard in 1975 playing with four different combos. He performs four songs (including the unfortunate "Send in the Clowns") with a quintet that includes guitarist Bucky Pizzarelli, adds trombonist Al Grey to a similar group for "Sweet Lorraine," and reunites with violinist Joe Venuti (with whom he had last recorded in 1933!) for spirited versions of "Slipped Disc" and "Limehouse Blues." Most noteworthy, though, are the three numbers that find Goodman in a septet that includes guitarist George Benson. Their hot version of "Seven Come Eleven" is memorable. Overall this LP shows that Benny Goodman at 66 remained a force to be reckoned with. —*Scott Yanow*

Yale Recordings—Vol. 7: Florida Sessions / Music Masters 65058

One of the most interesting bands led by Benny Goodman after the end of the swing era was the forgotten septet featured on this CD. It was essentially a sextet co-led by tenor saxophonist Flip Phillips and trombonist Bill Harris that they willingly let Goodman take over. Phillips and Harris were alumni of Woody Herman's First Herd and their constant riffing and well-constructed solos push the competitive clarinetist to play at his best and most fiery. Rather than revisit past glories, during this live date Benny Goodman and his all-stars play infectious arrangements that perfectly set up the solos, creating exciting new music in the swing tradition. Recommended. —*Scott Yanow*

Feat. Helen Forrest / Columbia 48902

Helen Forrest was considered one of the top band singers of the swing era, earning prestigious stints with the orchestras of Artie Shaw, Benny Goodman, and Harry James. Not a jazz singer, she had an appealing voice and attractive phrasing that were considered major assets to any band. This particular CD has 16 of her many recordings with Goodman during 1939-41; Goodman and his star sidemen (including trumpeter Cootie Williams) provide most of the jazz interest. —*Scott Yanow*

Live at Carnegie Hall 1978: 40th Anniversary Concert / London 820349

Live and explosive. Features seven incredible performances from his Trio and Quartet. —*Cub Koda*

MICK GOODRICK

b. Jun. 9, 1945, Sharon, PA
Guitar, instructor / Early jazz-rock, modern creative

A technical genius on guitar, Mick Goodrick's music is well worth studying. Goodrick began playing guitar at age 12 and later attended Stan Kenton's summer camps. A mid-'60s Berklee graduate, Goodrick taught there for four years. He recorded with Woody Herman in 1970, and played in Boston clubs as part of a trio with pianist Alan Broadbent and bassist Rick Laird, while also working in a duo with guitarist Pat Metheny. Goodrick toured and recorded with Gary Burton from 1973 to 1975, and also recorded and played occasionally with Jack DeJohnette, and worked with Joe Williams and Astrud Gilberto. Goodrick recorded with Eddie Gomez, John Surman, and DeJohnette in the late '70s for ECM, and recorded with Charlie Haden in 1982. Goodrick's recorded for CMP in the '90s. His recordings show an individuality that defies easy description and categorization. Goodrick's most recent session is available on CD, and the date with Gomez, Surman, and DeJohnette has been reissued. —*Ron Wynn and Michael G. Nastos*

★ **Biorhythms** / Oct. 1990 / CMP 46

DEXTER GORDON (Dexter Keith Gordon)

b. Feb. 27, 1923, Los Angeles, CA, **d.** Apr. 26, 1990
Tenor saxophone / Bop

Dexter Gordon was a masterful player and the earliest bebop tenor saxophonist. His robust style linked the lyricism of Lester Young with the deep, heavy tone of Dick Wilson and the phrasing of Charlie Parker. Gordon utilized clever quotations of other songs in a manner that influenced Sonny Rollins and, particularly, John Coltrane. Gordon skillfully phrased slightly behind the beat, rather than on top of it. His ballad work was equally superb, and, in tenor battles with artists from Wardell Gray to Jackie McLean, he showed he could hold his own in any jam situation.

Gordon played clarinet at age 13, and studied music with Lloyd Reese. While under Reese's wing, he played in a rehearsal band with other Reese pupils, among them Charles Mingus and Buddy Collette. He worked with Lionel Hampton in the early and mid '40s before making his recording debut as a leader in 1943, working with Nat "King" Cole. Following stints with Lee Young, Jesse Price, Fletcher Henderson, and Louis Armstrong, Gordon moved to New York to play in Billy Eckstine's orchestra in 1944. He began recording with Eckstine, Dizzy Gillespie, and Fats Navarro, and emerged a fine bebop player. He moved to California in 1946, then worked with Cee Pee Johnson for two months. Gordon worked both coasts in the late '40s, playing in New York with Tadd Dameron, then engaging Wardell Gray in some roaring battles out west. The two dueled often in the late '40s and early '50s, and Gordon also battled with Teddy Edwards. Gordon recorded for Dial in 1947. He led a sextet backing Helen Humes in 1950. Gordon worked as an actor, musician and composer for the West Coast version of Jack Gelber's play *The Connection*, and returned to New York in 1962.

A September trip to London and subsequent European tour proved such a hit that Gordon decided to stay overseas. He was in Europe for the next 15 years. Based in Copenhagen, Gordon appeared at the major festivals, toured Japan, cut many superb dates, gave lectures, and taught courses and clinics. He visited New York in 1976, where people lined up in the snow for his return engagements. Amid much fanfare and publicity, Gordon signed with Columbia and came back to America permanently. He was named *Down Beat*'s Musician of the Year in 1976 and 1980, and was elected to the Jazz Hall of Fame in 1980. Gordon received an Oscar nomination for his performance in the 1986 film *Round Midnight*, although the film was based more on the life and turmoil of Bud Powell than Gordon. Having finally gotten some measure of his just due, he died in 1990.

He recorded extensively from the '40s through the '80s. There were sessions for Mercury/Clef, Savoy, Fontana, Swingtime, Trio, Bethlehem, a string of Blue Notes, Storyville, six for Steeple Chase, Black Lion, MPS, Prestige, Columbia, Chiaroscuro, and Prestige. He worked with a host of great musicians over the years. His '70s sessions with Jackie McLean rivaled the battles with Edwards and Gray. Gordon albums are in pretty good supply, especially his Blue Note album. The Black Lion dates, done mostly in Europe, are also around, as are some Fantasy sessions. His earlier Savoy material has been reissued, though they're not available on CD yet. Gordon material is also available on foreign labels, but currently his Columbia material is unavailable. —*Ron Wynn and Dan Morgenstern*

Long Tall Dexter / Oct. 30, 1945-Jan. 29, 1946 / Savoy 2211

Dexter Gordon: Long Tall Dexter from 1945-47 shows tenor saxophonist Gordon's debt to both Lester Young and Charlie Parker. The attack is very staccato but the design is from Young. There is also a (Coleman) Hawkins robustness. The earliest sides have Sadik Hakim's (Argonne Thornton then) eccentric, Thelonious Monkish piano, and they contrast with the very boppish quality of the next session with Bud Powell, which also features Leonard Hawkins's bright but undistinguished trumpet. Powell plays some lovely runs behind Gordon's unusually legato lines on a ballad from this set. Gordon participates in a couple of blowing sessions with baritone saxophonist Leo Parker, which are of little interest due to Parker's lumbering style. Trumpeter Fats Navarro joins Gordon for some Tadd Dameron charts in which

Narvarro is a good foil for Gordon's spirited ballad playing. Also on this album is an unusually long after-hours jam from 1947 that features some humorous Hampton Hawes piano on a slow blues. There are many alternate takes on this set, which is a plus or minus depending on your interest. —*Jon Goldman*, Cadence

○ **Dexter Rides Again** / Oct. 30, 1945-Dec. 11, 1947 / Savoy Jazz 120

○ **Master Takes: The Savoy Recordings** / i. 1945-1947 / Savoy 1154

These are some of tenor saxophonist Dexter Gordon's earliest recordings—he was just 22 to 24 years old at the time of these dates and already a respected and influential stylist on his instrument. This album shows some of his early development. On the 10/30/45 date he still has one foot in swing and the other in bop, whereas by the 12/47 dates he has conquered the newer idiom. Lester Young's influence is there stylistically and tonally, with an Illinois Jacquet hard edge to it (when Gordon was in the Lionel Hampton orchestra in the early '40s, Jacquet was the featured tenor). The fact that 12 of the 15 titles are plays on Gordon's name caused him some embarrassment (they were named by producer Teddy Reig), but the music gives no such cause at all. The album also gives glimpses of other bop stars—pianist Bud Powell's a bit more subdued than usual, but no less inventive. Leo Parker (bs) and Gordon have a battle of the saxes on the two-sided 78 "Settin' The Pace" (a la "The Chase," which Gordon did with Wardell Gray on Dial half a year earlier). Fats Navarro (tpt) has a couple of excellent solos, and Tadd Dameron's arrangements guide most of the album's B side. All these recordings are contained on *Dexter Gordon—Long Tall Dexter*, a two-record set issued in 1976 that also has the alternate takes to these sides, an additional record date, and a live jam session piece. I'd recommend the two-record set first, if you can still find it. If not, this album is still definitely of musical and historical interest. —*Doug Long*, Cadence

Hunt / i. Jun. 12, 1947 / Savoy 2222

The Dexter Gordon/Wardell Gray disc comes from a time when bop was just taking hold in Los Angeles. Recorded in an after-hours club on two direct disc-cutting machines, this is an example of the unconstrained experimenter in a setting conducive to his art. The Gordon/Gray tenor battles were legendary and this album shows why. Gordon's tone is more powerful, and on the surface he is the more aggressive saxophonist. In truth, Wardell Gray's style was more relaxed but no less authoritative. The long fluid lines of Gray contrast with Gordon's big full tone to produce a perfect matchup. The best tune for Gordon is Ray Noble's "Cherokee." Most of the recording is Gordon, with Gray falling in toward the end. Undoubtedly the best tenor battle is on the title cut, "The Hunt." Both men display the intensity and fierce musical exchange that make this record a sterling examples of early bebop. —*David Less*, Down Beat

Dexter Calling . . . / May 9, 1951 / Blue Note 46544

Daddy Plays the Horn / Sep. 18, 1955 / Bethlehem 36

Dexter Blows Hot and Cool / Nov. 11+22, 1955 / Duotone

Resurgence of Dexter Gordon, The / i. Mar. 1961 / Jazzland 29

Doin' Alright / May 6, 1961 / Blue Note 84077

A high-quality Blue Note date with touches of soul-jazz and African-American slang influence in the title. —*Ron Wynn*

○ **Landslide** / May 9, 1961-Jun. 25, 1962 / Blue Note 1051

Landslide is notable for the contributions of Gordon's sidemen, specifically pianists Kenny Drew and Sonny Clark and bassists Paul Chambers and Ron Carter. Unfortunately, though, the trumpeters (Tommy Turrentine and Dave Burns) fare less well, and the over-modulated clattering of the cymbals undoubtedly proves a distraction to many. That shouldn't be a deterrent, however, for Gordon's work alone is ample compensation for these minor flaws. Playing in that lean, brittle manner so long a fabric of his art, he quite literally rises above it all. —*Jack Sohmer*, Down Beat

Go! / Aug. 27, 1962 / Blue Note 46094

With the Sonny Clark (p) Trio. Classic Dexter repertoire includes "Cheese Cake" and "Love for Sale." Rhythm section a monster. —*Michael G. Nastos*

Swingin' Affair, A / Sep. 29, 1962 / Blue Note 84133

○ **Our Man in Paris** / May 23, 1963 / Blue Note 46394

This is a tremendous album done in Paris with Bud Powell (p), Kenny Clarke (d), and Pierre Michelot (b). 1987 reissue, CD version. —*Ron Wynn*

One Flight Up / Jun. 2, 1964 / Blue Note 84176

○ **Cheesecake** / Jun. 1964 / Steeple Chase 6008

Cheesecake, previously unissued, was made in 1964 during Dexter Gordon's three-month stay at Copenhagen's Montmartre Jazzhus. In contrast to his usual reserved studio approach, Gordon plays with a searing intensity, most notably on the title track—an intensity missing in many of his other recordings. The European rhythm section, while lacking the confidence and experience of Blue Note's group, more than makes up for it with their spontaneous enthusiasm and willingness to take liberties with the format at hand. "Second Balcony Jump" shows Gordon's cutting edge. Pianist Tete Montoliu is particularly hot on "Manha De Carnival," taken as a fast bossa. Dynamically, he tends to stay at the same level throughout this recording, but swings as hard as most American pianists, if not harder. —*Arthur Moorehead*, Down Beat

Clubhouse / May 27, 1965 / Blue Note 84445

Gettin' Around / May 28, 1965 / Blue Note 46681

Montmartre Collection / Jul. 20, 1967 / Black Lion

This excellent two-disc sampler is from Gordon's extensive sessions at the famed Montmartre Club. —*Ron Wynn*

Day in Copenhagen / Mar. 10, 1969 / Polydor 821288

This reissue, which originally came out on MPS, contains some inspired blowing from Dexter Gordon (ts). Even more extroverted than usual, his playing on the uptempos is a delight to hear, and at the same time he maintains his firm grasp on the ballad with a tender reading of "The Shadow Of Your Smile." Gordon's strong playing is also a cue to the weak sides of this album. The other soloists (trombonist/arranger Slide Hampton, trumpeter Dizzy Reece, pianist Kenny Drew, bassist Niels-Henning Ørsted-Pedersen, drummer Art Taylor), even if they are not doing a particularly *bad* job, can't help but sound a bit anticlimactic compared to Gordon's statements; particularly so since on many of the numbers everybody solos. Slide Hampton's charts were quite imaginative, even if a certain feeling of "sameness" in sound creeps in after a while. He often uses dissonant voicing to create a "big" ensemble sound, and in "My Blues" the way the inner voices move is quite reminiscent of George Russell's writing for his sextets 20 years earlier. On "Vienna," Gordon sounds more disturbed than inspired by the background figures written for him, however. —*Per Husby*, Cadence

★ **Tower of Power** / Apr. 2+4, 1969 / Prestige 299

With James Moody on tenor as well, the two stretch out on one tune, "Montmartre." Barry Harris Trio shines throughout. —*Michael G. Nastos*

○ **More Power** / Apr. 2+4, 1969 / Prestige 7680

More Power! comes from the same dates (April 2 and 4, 1969) as *The Tower of Power*, and once again James Moody is added on two tracks, although he only solos on Tadd Dameron's lovely "Ladybird." This is a very enjoyable set, and Gordon is comfortable and relaxed. "Meditation," Antonio Carlos Jobim's pretty bossa nova, never sounded better to my ears. Side two consists of three Gordon originals—"Fried Bananas," "Boston Bernie," and "Sticky Wicket," all of which have their asses played off by this very together pickup band. Gordon roars through these catchy pieces literally chewing up the changes. He gets strong support, of course, from Barry Harris (p), Buster Williams (b), and drummer Al "Tootie" Heath (and Moody, in the ensembles only, on "Sticky Wicket"). There is nothing cerebral about this album, but it's head and shoulders above the average blowing session. —*Don Brown*, Coda

Panther, The / Jul. 7, 1970 / Original Jazz Classics 770
In 1970, tenor saxophonist Dexter Gordon returned from Europe, played briefly at the Newport Festival, and then embarked upon a cross-country tour. Tommy Flanagan, Larry Ridley, and Alan Dawson are the compatible, very strong team chosen to work with Gordon at the first of his Prestige sessions. The material consists of three new Gordon originals (one, the title piece, is a forthright exercise in the blues), two excellent ballads ("Body and Soul," "The Christmas Song"), and Clifford Brown's "The Blues Walk." Gordon was a consummate musician equally at home with an uptempo romp through the changes and with embroidering a lyrical piece of music such as "The Christmas Song." The challenge is a little different on "Body and Soul." It's a classic test for any saxophonist and Gordon adds yet another masterful version to a library that began with Coleman Hawkins in 1940. Gordon's version is more oblique, with the rhythm reflecting the more adventurous playing of the '60s. This is true, too, of "The Panther," which provides a nice contrast in blues playing to the more straightahead "Blues Walk." —*John Norris*, Coda

Chase, The / Jul. 26, 1970 / Prestige

Jumpin' Blues / Aug. 27, 1970 / Prestige 10020
On *The Jumpin' Blues* Dexter Gordon is joined by a heavyweight backing trio—pianist Wynton Kelly (his last date), bassist Sam Jones, and drummer Roy Brooks. The tunes are all oldies with the exception of Gordon's own "Evergreenish," a descriptive title of a line that promises to stay as fresh as tomorrow. Gordon's tenor tone is so individual and authoritative that it commands immediate interest and concentration, like the man himself. "Evergreenish" is almost a copybook introduction to his style. His utter assurance and conviction in what he was playing are obvious. His solo unfolds easily, but the development is masterly. There are the quotations (a Gordon trademark), the powerful swing, and harmonic sense, and underlying it all his devotion to melody. Kelly, always an impeccable musician but one who invariably rises to the big occasion with something extra, is in top form with his graceful accompaniment and pithy solo statements always adding to the joyful feeling that permeates the date. In Roy Brooks, Gordon found a drummer of unusual sensitivity and crispness. Brooks came out of the Max Roach school, there could be no doubt about that. What more could one say about Sam Jones? He is a bastion of the beat. Originally this album was to have been titled *Love!* by producer Don Schlitten. That's really what it is—pure love from a master in love with music and his horn. —*Mark Gardner*, Coda

○ **Shadow of Your Smile, The** / Apr. 1971 / Steeple Chase 1206

○ **Generation** / Jul. 22, 1972 / Prestige 10069
Good quintet set, one of three that Gordon recorded in '72. He's ably backed by trumpeter Freddie Hubbard, whose bent notes, slurs, and crackling solos keep the tension going when Gordon's not playing. Gordon mixes things up, sometimes soloing with bluesy force, other times light and easy. —*Ron Wynn*

○ **Ca' Purange** / 1972 / Prestige 10051
The second quintet session that Dexter Gordon cut in '72, this one is probably the most inconsistent. It contains some fabulous Gordon tenor solos, which are then followed with some rather routine compositions. But it's worth getting, though it's proven the least distributed of the three. —*Ron Wynn*

○ **More Than You Know** / Feb. 1975-Mar. 1975 / Steeple Chase 31030
This Dexter Gordon with orchestra session is another one of those albums that does not involve the soloist in the arrangements. The orchestra is merely a backdrop. "Tivoli," though, has Idrees Sulieman (flhn) soloing out of the context of the orchestra, linking tenor saxophonist Gordon

with the orchestra. Both "Tivoli" and "Bernie's Tune" effectively blend in and out the full orchestra with a small group, sometimes only Gordon and bass. "Purple Eyes" is one of those best-forgotten band pieces with repetitious electric bass, fuzz guitar, electric tinkler (aka electric piano), and so on. The remaining tracks all feature lush arrangements, well done, especially "Naima," which includes a lovely floating French horn solo after Gordon's first solo. On this and other tracks arranger and conductor Palle Mikkelborg also makes good use of woodwinds and harp. —*Jerry De Muth*, Cadence

★ **Stable Mable** / Mar. 10, 1975 / Inner City 2040
Dexter Gordon usually managed to put his best foot forward on record dates. *Stable Mable*, his third LP for Steeple Chase, is no exception. Gordon sounds relaxed and slick, blowing nary a line that doesn't make sense. Horace Parlan delivers a typically percussive, yet near-elegant series of performances, and acoustic bassist Niels-Henning Ørsted-Pedersen knows no peer on his instrument. Though the listener will rarely get the impression that any limits are being tested on this collection of tunes by Charlie Parker, Benny Golson, Duke Ellington, Miles Davis, and Erroll Garner (the standard "Just Friends" is also included), taste and swing prevail. —*Charles Mitchell*, Down Beat

○ **Something Different** / Sep. 13, 1975 / Steeple Chase 1136
What makes tenor saxophonist Dexter Gordon's album *Something Different* something special is its lack of *planned* novelty. The album was made in a day, culminating a 22-day, four-album spree for Gordon in 1975. And, title and absence of a piano aside, it showcases the excellence that any great artist must summon under ordinary conditions. More than anything else, *Something Different* presents Gordon the interpreter, the stylist. Rather than accede to a composer's designs, he stamps with suaveness each selection. His urbanity, so typified in long, lush notes, unifies his approach to all the songs. His liberties start with Miles Davis's "Freddie Freeloader." Gordon attacks this staple of starkness with swing and upbeat emotion. He treats the album's two ballads—"Sunny" and "Polkadots"—with judicious evasiveness, for a straight reading of either standard could descend into triteness. While reverting the rhythm and intent of the songs, after the first few bars Gordon abandons the melody, except to touch base every sixth or seventh note. In fiery trombonist Slide Hampton's "Yesterday's Mood," Gordon plays at low volume, letting the changes, rather than the decibels, establish the piece's power. None of this occurs without enviable support. Guitarist Philip Catherine emerges as the "different" element alluded to in the title. He speaks compellingly in two voices: one, the Jim Hall-influenced soloist who hooks the end of each note, letting out solos like lengths of chain; the other, the modern embodiment of Django Reinhardt, a slashing chorder, who supports and even usurps the rhythm. Altogether, his encounter with Gordon equals any guitar-sax match this side of Sonny Rollins's *The Bridge*. Bassist Niels-Henning Ørsted-Pedersen and drummer Billy Higgins, given less solo time, maintain an unbreakable groove. Even when Catherine solos and Gordon lays out, the pace doesn't suffer. —*Sam Freedman*, Down Beat

★ **Bouncin' with Dex** / Sep. 14, 1975 / Inner City 2060
These sides were recorded in Copenhagen in 1975 at a reunion date, the quartet having played together often since the early '60s. The musicians' familiarity with one another is immediately apparent. They have no trouble finding a groove and staying in it. Tete Montoliu is a fine Spanish pianist who was only beginning to become known in this country, although he was well known in Europe. His style draws inspiration from Bud Powell, Thelonious Monk, and McCoy Tyner and is embossed by a touch almost classic in its lightness. Billy Higgins matches Montoliu in lightness, yet his crisp drumming never fails to swing. Niels-Henning Ørsted-Pedersen has as full a sound as any bassist and impeccable time; he is ever solid on these tunes. With such fine sidemen, Gordon was free to enjoy himself. His tenor sax

playing is supremely relaxed but never sloppy, often taking unexpected but fitting turns. —*Douglas Clark*, Down Beat

○ **Lullaby for a Monster** / Jun. 15, 1976 / Steeple Chase 1156
On "Born To Be Blue" Dexter Gordon stretches out his lazy sound even more than usual in a languorous conversational tone. Gordon's familiar fat, rubbery sound and leisurely attacks set a relaxed mood. On his composition "Nursery Blues," which takes children's songs as its compositional springboard, his playing is especially smooth and assured. He mixes cliches and new lines as if embellishing an old story with adventures. The rhythm section does its part and more. Drummer Alex Riel changes character from tune to tune, playing straight on "Green Dolphin Street" and going further afield with polyrhythms and coloristic cymbals a la Elvin Jones on Niels-Henning Ørsted-Pedersen's "Lullaby for a Monster." Pedersen takes a melodic approach to the bass. He changes directions quickly, never settling into any pattern for long. On "Tanya" he lopes along with the spring of a long-distance runner. —*Elaine Guregian*, Down Beat

☆ **Biting the Apple** / Nov. 1976 / Steeple Chase 31080
Even if you obtained tenor saxophonist Dexter Gordon's *Swiss Nights* first, you may want *Bitin' the Apple* because of the presence of pianist Barry Harris and bassist Sam Jones, masterful bop gyrostabilizers who add a timeless performance to the date. Drummer Al Foster does the job but is not a challenging or particularly inventive drummer on this date. This was recorded before the Columbia *Homecoming* and the Al Cohn Xanadu dates. From a standpoint of Gordon, it's about even with the former, superior to the latter. Certainly it beats the *Sophisticated Giant* recording (from June '77) which, from my standpoint, was a bomb. Rarely have I heard Gordon at his best outside of small groups. This is a fine date. —*Bob Rusch*, Cadence

★ **Homecoming—Live at the Village Vanguard** / Dec. 11-12, 1976 / Columbia 46824
This is the set that welcomed Gordon back to the States. His return was a major event in the late '70s, as was his signing to Columbia. In retrospect, this isn't his best work, but it's probably his top Columbia session of the period. —*Ron Wynn*

Sophisticated Giant / Jun. 21-22, 1977 / Columbia 34989
The curtain of Dexter Gordon's uptown show opens on David Raskin's unforgettable "Laura." Gordon's soulful search for the enigmatic lady is propelled along by Slide Hampton's probing bass sonorities, Frank Wess's interrogative flute, and George Cables's questioning piano. Woody Shaw's "Moontrane" is a brilliant roman candle shooting out sparkling modal fireballs by Gordon and Shaw. Gene Ammons's "Red Top" is striped with bright bossa bands whirring with buzzing spins by Gordon, Benny Bailey, vibist Bobby Hutcherson, and Rufus Reid. Aside from the soloists, the extrasensory rhythmic conceptions of Cables, bassist Reid, and drummer Victor Lewis deserve mention. The spirited ensemble work of lead trumpeter Bailey and the rest of the band also merit praise. And then again, so too do the exceptional arrangements of the clever Slide Hampton. —*Chuck Berg*, Down Beat

○ **Swiss Nights—Vol. 1** / i. Nov. 1977 / Inner City 2050
Recorded at the 1975 Zurich Jazz Festival by Steeple Chase and released in America by Inner City, this session finds Dexter Gordon perfectly matched with a rhythm section that fully understands and appreciates the saxophonist's approach. Pianist Kenny Drew, bassist Niels-Henning Ørsted-Pedersen, and drummer Alex Riel listen and respond with faultless supportive commentary. Buoyed by the warm encouragement of the Festival goers, *Swiss Nights* emerges as one of the truly magical efforts in the Gordon discography. —*Chuck Berg*, Down Beat

Nights at the Keystone—Vols. 1-3 / May 13, 1978-Mar. 23, 1979 / Capitol 94848
Nights at the Keystone dates from a couple of years after Dexter Gordon had returned triumphantly to the United States (1978-79). The novelty was beginning to fade, but his

abilities were, if anything, improving with age. He takes strong solos on several lengthy performances. One can fault the occasional excess of song quotes (especially "Laura," which seems to pop up in every solo), but Gordon's authoritative sound, freshness of ideas, and confident explorations easily compensate. Pianist George Cables is often in dazzling form (check out "Tangerine") and continually inventive. Bassist Rufus Reid and drummer Eddie Gladden are perfect in support. In addition, the ambiance of the late, lamented Keystone Korner, San Francisco's top jazz club and possessor of one of the most knowledgeable jazz audiences anywhere, seeps through the vinyl. —*Scott Yanow*, Cadence

Gotham City / 1981 / Columbia 36853
Gotham City is a blues album—a very elegant, sophisticated one, as befits tenor saxophonist Dexter Gordon—but one saturated with blues feeling. The title track is a simple, straightahead 12-bar in B flat: the quintessential blowing tune, the common ground. On this cut, the soloists—Gordon, guitarist George Benson, pianist Cedar Walton, and bassist Percy Heath—all show that they have the emotional chops to carry it off. Drawing inspiration from each other and from Art Blakey's kinetic drumming, they take the ordinary blues form and make it extraordinary. George Benson's playing on "Hi-Fly" and "Gotham City" adds a great deal to the sophisticated feeling of the music. From the piquant bent note that opens the album to his masterfully constructed solo on "Gotham City," which builds from sparse Thelonious Monkish riffs to chopped sliding chords, Benson exhibits the smooth blues/bebop playing that he refined from Charlie Christian's inspiration. Trumpeter Woody Shaw is another welcome guest, adding a strong voice on Clifford Brown's "Blues Walk (Loose Walk)." He blends beautifully with Gordon on the head, balancing the saxophonist's long, flowing lines with his quirky, jagged solo. The tune itself is a classic bop riff over modified blues changes. The album's simple, gimmick-free concept suggests the old production formula that served Prestige and Blue Note so well in the late '50s and early '60s. There is nothing stale or desultory here; there is, in fact, a clear air of excitement. —*Jim Roberts*, Down Beat

American Classic / Mar. 8, 1982 / Elektra 60126
Sometimes unassuming, unpublicized records go unnoticed, despite their quality. That was the case in 1982, when saxophonist Dexter Gordon, in the midst of a resurgence, cut a tight, often delightful record with some excellent players and special guest Grover Washington, Jr., playing soprano and showing he was much more than just another instrumental pop musician. This session has now been reissued, and sounds even more wonderful in digital stereo. It also includes an interview with Gordon, though no extra material. But Gordon, Washington, organist Shirley Scott, pianist Kirk Lightsey, bassist David Eubanks, and drummer Eddie Gladden do their parts and more, helping the album more than live up to its title. —*Ron Wynn*

○ **King Neptune** / i. Jun. 1984 / Steeple Chase 6012

○ **Love for Sale** / i. Jul. 1984 / Steeple Chase 6018

Other Side of 'Round Midnight / Jul. 1987-Feb. 1986 / Blue Note 46397
Outtakes and alternate cuts from the sound track of the film that got him an Oscar nomination. —*Ron Wynn*

○ **Both Sides of Midnight** / i. Jun. 17, 1992 / Black Lion 760103

Dexter Gordon appears with the familiar rhythm section that egged him on for so many years in Copenhagen: pianist Kenny Drew, bassist Niels-Henning Ørsted-Pedersen, and drummer Al "Tootie" Heath. Gordon, somewhere between those rambunctious and full-blooded Blue Note years and the raggedy, slouching postexile decline before his *'Round Midnight* revival, shows the tawny tones of mellowing graciously. His book has that happily well-thumbed look; he is mournful and acerbic at uptempo, and his great ballad ear tenders "For All We Know" with verse and the "voice." Drew

gets good licks throughout, especially on "Doxy" and "Misty."
—*Fred Bouchard,* Jazz Times

○ **Tangerine** / Prestige 10091
Working out of the mainstream tradition of bop and blues, Dexter Gordon spins a set of strong virile performances, which are cushioned by two fine rhythm sections. On the title track, "Tangerine," Gordon deftly mixes cascading sheets of sixteenth notes; notes of longer duration that reveal his potent sound, blending both metallic and woody resonances; and his penchant for dipping back into a tune's melodic contours for slightly shaded variations. As with Gordon's two blues renderings ("August Blues" and "What It Was"), there are tasty, low-key solos by both Thad and Hank Jones and the superb Stanley Clarke. My favorite track, however, is "Days Of Wine and Roses." Gordon beautifully captures the tune's poignant, bittersweet qualities, responding to the challenge of Mancini's harmonic framework with a set of specially inventive choruses. The rhythm section provides a supple, supportive substructure throughout, with tart, pungent solos from pianist Cedar Walton and bassist Buster Williams. —*Chuck Berg,* Down Beat

○ **Apartment, The** / Steeple Chase 1025
While this Steeple Chase reissue doesn't capture the 1977 edition of Dexter Gordon, it certainly captures the inspired, creative genius that was Dexter Gordon. This is, to put it mildly, a marvelous recording. Everyone is "on" for the quartet date ("Old Folks" is a Gordon-bassist Niels-Henning Ørsted-Pedersen duet) with the intensity and inventiveness never flagging. And yet at the same time the music seems too relaxed and unhurried. There is never a hint of unevenness or pressure. And always above everything else soars that warm, rich, broad tenor saxophone of Mr. Gordon. Joyous music. —*Carl Brauer,* Cadence

---

STEPHANE GRAPPELLI (Stephane Grappelly)

b. Jan. 26, 1908, Paris, France
Violin / Swing
Though largely self taught, Stephane Grappelli has helped pioneer the violin as a jazz instrument. His sweeping, jubilant solos and enticing, lovely tone have been extremely influential, plus he's been willing to experiment and expand his style beyond the "hot" swinging mode of the '30s. He has worked with musicians as diverse as Gary Burton, David Grisman, and McCoy Tyner. Grappelli played piano and violin in his formative professional days, working in movie theaters and dance bands. He teamed with guitarist Django Reinhardt in 1934 to form the Quintette of the Hot Club of France, a unit using a three-guitar/violin/bass lineup. They became an international sensation, and Grappelli remained with the group until 1939. Grappelli played piano on a 1937 Paris session with Reinhardt and Coleman Hawkins. He moved to England, then worked with pianist George Shearing. He renewed acquaintances with Reinhardt in 1946, and worked with him back in France in 1947 and 1948, and in Rome in 1949. Grappelli was not as active in the '50s and early '60s, though he did record a fine LP in 1962 with guitarist Pierre Cavalli. Grappelli's career was revived in 1966 with a superb album he recorded with fellow violinists Stuff Smith, Jean Luc-Ponty, and Svend Asmussen, *Violin Summit.* Another marvelous release with a similar title and format that came out later was *Duke Ellington's Jazz Violin Session* with Asmussen and Ray Nance. Grappelli also advised and assisted violinists Didier Lockwood and Ponty. He made his American debut at the 1969 Newport Jazz Festival, and also recorded with Burton and violinist Joe Venuti that year. In 1973, an album he made with classical violinist Yehudi Menuhin was a surprise hit; the two made additional recordings in 1975 and 1977. Grappelli continued a full slate of appearances and sessions in the '70s and '80s, playing with Earl Hines, Philip Catherine, Bill Coleman, Grisman, Teresa Brewer, Barney Kessell, Hank Jones, and pianists Oscar Peterson, Shearing, Martial Solal, and Tyner. —*Ron Wynn and Dan Morgenstern*

Tea for Two / 1928-1930 / Angel 37533

Violins No End / May 4, 1957 / Pablo 2310-907
Although Stephane Grappelli gets top billing, this album is essentially a Stuff Smith session with Grappelli as a guest star. The first four selections are taken from a previously unissued studio date that teamed Grappelli and Smith with the Oscar Peterson trio plus Jo Jones. Oddly enough there is absolutely no interplay between the two violinists. "Don't Get Around Much Anymore," a hard-swinging Smith solo, is followed by a short spot for Ray Brown (b), and then Grappelli leads off and Ellis fills the space before Smith's entrance. On the "I Got Rhythm"-based "No Points Today," although the two violinists are the only soloists, they do not for one second play together. There is no trading off or even a sharing of the melody statement. There is some fine playing on this date despite that oddity. Smith is at his best on "Don't Get Around" and Grappelli is quite creative on a very fast "The Lady Is a Tramp." The remainder of the album is taken from a live concert that does not include Grappelli. Smith plays his most famous composition (a surprisingly rapid "Desert Sands"), a multitempo "How High the Moon," and an overly emotional (and a bit satiric) "Moonlight in Vermont." —*Scott Yanow,* Cadence

Feeling + Finesse = Jazz / Mar. 7-9, 1962 / Atlantic 1391
Fine early-'60s set from violin veteran Stephane Grappelli, who still plays in the "hot" swing style that he championed back in the '30s. This is CD reissue of the album. —*Ron Wynn*

○ **I Remember Django** / Jun. 23-24, 1969 / Black Lion 105
○ **Limehouse Blues** / Jun. 23-24, 1969 / Black Lion 760158
★ **Meets Barney Kessel** / Jun. 23-34, 1969 / Black Lion 760150
○ **Venupelli Blues** / Oct. 22, 1969 / Charly 73

Homage to Django / Jun. 19-22, 1972 / Classic Jazz 23
A nice two-record set, though Grappelli towers over the British session pros. —*Ron Wynn*

○ **Just One of Those Things** / Jul. 4, 1973 / Angel 69172
○ **Parisian Thoroughfare** / Sep. 5+7, 1973 / Black Lion 760132
For *Parisian Thoroughfare,* violinist Stephane Grappelli teams with the 1973 rhythm section of the Thad Jones-Mel Lewis band, pianist Roland Hanna, bassist George Mraz, and, of course, drummer Lewis. It is a magical blend of superb musicianship and sparkling camaraderie. Grappelli's bow/finger coordination is awesome. He skates and slides through the melody and changes on Bud Powell's "Parisian Thoroughfare" with gusto and abandon. Equally impressive is bassist Mraz. His empathy with Grappelli is extraordinary. Listen, for example, to their arco doubling of Hanna's "Perugia" and pizzicato tracing of the pianist's "Too Cute." Hanna, too, is superb. His solo and support work are the ultimate in taste and perception. On drums, Lewis keeps the fire stoked with his characteristic low-key burn. —*Chuck Berg,* Down Beat

○ **Steff and Slam** / Mar. 25, 1975 / Accord 233076
○ **Reunion, with George Shearing, The** / Apr. 11, 1976 / PolyGram 21868
A high-caliber reissue of a delightful date with George Shearing (p). —*Ron Wynn*

○ **Stephane Grappelli / Bill Coleman / i.** Jun. 1977 / Classic Jazz 24
Trumpeter Bill Coleman was 69 when he made these recordings, playing in the same lovely legato style which was his forte for many, many years. Certainly violinist Stephane Grappelli respected him, and his own work accordingly is never crowding and almost always uses the spirit of Coleman's work to develop his own solos. This is a splendid set of swing evergreens that has just enough tartness to avoid the saccharine. A beautiful example is "Stardust," where Coleman follows Grappelli's schmaltzy intro and rearranges the song into a ballad of great inventive warmth. This is a fine recording. —*Geoff Millerman,* Cadence

Live at Carnegie Hall / Apr. 5, 1978 / Doctor Jazz 38727

The combined guitars of featured players Diz Disley and John Ethridge echo Django Reinhardt, who remains violinist Stephane Grappelli's most consistently congenial partner. Disley and Ethridge *echo* Reinhardt; they do not imitate him. The *Live At Carnegie Hall* sides are in fact hotter and more adventurous (but less intimate and ingratiating) than anything issued from the collaboration with Reinhardt in the '30s. Grappelli walks down some new paths here, but they are paths that cross and recross the same old and always-youthful springs that nurtured this violinist's earlier art. —*Alan Axelrod,* Down Beat

★ **Young Django** / Jan. 19-21, 1979 / Verve 815672
Young Django is violinist Stephane Grappelli's album first, guitarist Phillip Catherine's second, and then guitarist Larry Coryell's, but Coryell's role was not inconsiderable. Collecting seven classic Django Reinhardt/Grappelli compositions from the late '30s, plus an original each from the two guitarists, the excellent music here keeps an emphasis on *le jazz hot*. Grappelli, of course, is still in his prime, delivering memorable solos on "Sweet Chorus," "Minor Swing," and elsewhere. But his equally young cohorts manage to keep up with the pace, jumping in together on the skittish "Swing Guitars," doing nice things to "Sweet Chorus," and playing with the whimsical "Are You in the Mood?" The lack of a drummer proves insignificant, as the guitarists share rhythm duties and bassist Niels-Henning Ørsted-Pedersen is super-steady. The older tunes from *Young Django* may recall a bygone style, but they seem far from antiquated in the hands of this amicable foursome. —*Bob Henschen,* Down Beat

Live at Tivoli Gardens, Copenhagen, Denmark / Jul. 6, 1979 / Pablo 441
Guitarist Joe Pass and pianist Oscar Peterson are perfect frames for Stephane Grappelli's sparkling violin work, and these sidemen make *Tivoli* such a choice record. Tapping a keg of vintage compositions, the trio is relaxed and frolicsome from the start. And having added the lessons of bop to his playing since his days with Django Reinhardt, Grappelli constructs his red hot violin solos as only he can—best heard on "Paper Moon" and "Crazy Rhythm." —*Cliff Tinder,* Down Beat

★ **Stephane Grappelli and Hank Jones—a Two-Fer!** / Jul. 20, 1979 / Muse 5287
Don't look for a second record in this folder. *Two-Fer* refers only to the double billing (pianist Hank Jones). In a way, I wish that this review was not mine. I agree that no violinist sounds like Stephane Grappelli and I love to hear him in certain contexts. I'm just not going to be critical of sound, material, or anything except compatibility. His rhythmic sense is adequately described in the notes as "always hearty" and a bit of "boulevard bounce." The record is exactly predictable, so you be the judge as to whether it belongs with you. —*Jerry Atkins,* Cadence

○ **Stephane Grappelli and David Grisman Live** / Sep. 20, 1979 / Warner Brothers 3550
Recorded at the Berklee Center for the Performing Arts in Boston and San Francisco's Great American Music Hall ("Satin Doll"), *Live* is guaranteed to reawaken even the most moribund. Whether because he was surrounded with enthusiastic musicians many years his junior or he just felt inspired, Stephane Grappelli's playing is nothing short of brilliant. Lithe and nimble, Grappelli's violin work shines with class and distinction. Combined with the expert accompaniment of David Grisman (mand) and his quartet (guitarist/violinist Mark O'Connor, bassist Rob Wasserman, electric mandolinist Tiny Moore), this makes for 40 minutes of unadulterated pleasure. True, pieces like "Sweet Georgia Brown" and "Tiger Rag" are standard flag wavers, but the group instills new personality into them; and Sonny Rollins's "Pent-Up House" and Grisman's "Medley" allow for more subtle and intricate interplay. —*Carl Brauer,* Cadence

Happy Reunion, with Martial Solal / Feb. 17-18, 1980 / Rhino 79242

Happy Reunion triumphantly manages what so much postmodern art attempts and achieves only to a limited degree at best: a fertile union of tradition and innovation. "Shine," for instance, is a breathless burst of stride-influenced piano (one that recalls pianist Martial Solal's '50s sides with saxophonist Sidney Bechet) and something that must be called stride violin. "Valsitude," a Solal composition, fuses French impressionism with an ultra-elegant and tonally sophisticated evocation, once again, of the *salon*. "Sing For Your Supper" is a demandingly angular treatment of the Rodgers and Hart standard in the manner of Thelonious Monk and Lennie Tristano. Solal commands several apparently disparate traditions, while Stephane Grappelli is consummate master chiefly of one—an anachronistic one at that. Yet this aging artist almost always succeeds in making anachronism contemporary, imbuing nostalgia with life and youth. —*Alan Axelrod,* Down Beat

At the Winery / Sep. 1980 / Concord Jazz 4139
With Martin Taylor and John Etheridge (g). Recorded live at the Paul Masson Vineyards, Saratoga, CA. Another good Grappelli album. Nice versions of "Willow Weep for Me" and "Minor Swing." —*Michael G. Nastos*

Live in San Francisco / Jul. 1982 / Black Hawk 51601
A good set from '82, with Grappelli leading a two-guitar, drums lineup and coming close to approximating the feel and sound, if not the caliber, of the songs he did with Django Reinhardt. While guitarists Martin Taylor and Diz Disley swap licks and complement or contrast Grappelli, he's freed to take his usual rollicking solos, soar over the arrangements, then return to complete the song. Drummer Jack Sewing isn't a great player, but does a competent job of establishing the backing rhythms. —*Ron Wynn*

○ **Together at Last** / **i.** 1984 / Flying Fish 421

Grappelli Plays Jerome Kern / 1987 / GRP 9542
One would think that the last thing the great swing violinist Stephane Grappelli would need is to be surrounded by a string section. The tendency for any violinist, particularly on a set of mostly ballads, would be to play too sweet, but Grappelli swings consistently and avoids using an excess of vibrato. The two guitarists both get plenty of short solos with Marc Fosset often scatting along with his guitar (like George Benson), a pleasing contrast. The strings (which are absent on the two uptempo tunes "The Way You Look Tonight" and "I Won't Dance") rarely intrude and add to this date's appeal, thanks to the thoughtful arrangements. The ageless Stephane Grappelli has made many enjoyable albums throughout his career, but this set of superb Jerome Kern melodies should not be overlooked. —*Scott Yanow,* Cadence

One on One, with McCoy Tyner / Apr. 18, 1990 / Milestone 9181
With McCoy Tyner. This unlikely pair works well. Very interesting harmonic combinations. —*Michael G. Nastos*

In Tokyo / Oct. 1990 / Denon 9130
Live at Bunkamura Cocoon in Tokyo. Grappelli also plays some piano. One of the violin legend's better albums of the past decade. —*Michael G. Nastos*

Stephane Grappelli Meets Earl Hines / **i.** Nov. 2, 1992 / Black Lion 760168

○ **Paris Encounter** / Atlantic
Thoughtful at times, funky in spots. Gary Burton (vib) proves a fine partner. —*Ron Wynn*

Shades of Django / Verve 825955
A solid tribute piece, one of several that recount the impact and influence of Reinhardt. —*Ron Wynn*

Grappelli, Louis Bellson and Phil Woods / Rushmore 3000

Fascinating Rhythm (Music of the 30's) / Onyx Classix 267329

Menuhin and Grappelli Play "Jalousie" And Other Great Standards / Angel 69220

Menuhin and Grappelli Play Berlin, Kern, Porter And Rodgers & Hart / Angel 69219

Menuhin and Grappelli Play Gershwin / Angel 69218

MILFORD GRAVES

b. Aug. 20, 1941, New York, NY

Drums / Early free, modern creative

Milford Graves has been one of the flashiest drummers in the free mode, known for a skillful inclusion of Asian and African rhythmic ingredients into his solos. His style is extremely fluid and mobile. He's a masterful accompanist who's worked smoothly in many multiple percussion situations. Graves has been one of the most outspoken proponents of performing all jazz, free and other types, in communities rather than in clubs or arenas. He studied Indian music extensively, and learned the tabla from Wasantha Singh. Unfortunately, he has not recorded much in recent years, especially on American labels. Graves played congas as a child, then switched to trap drums at age 17, before his tabla studies with Singh. During the '60s, Graves worked with Giuseppi Logan and the New York Art Quartet. He recorded on ESP in the early '60s with Logan, and was an original member of the Jazz Composers' Orchestra Association. Graves also played with Hugh Masekela and Miriam Makeba in the early '60s. His appearance in the Bill Dixon-sponsored concert series, The October Revolution in Jazz, helped introduce Graves to a wider audience. He did two albums of duets with pianist Don Pullen at Yale in 1966. Graves worked regularly with Albert Ayler in 1967 and 1968, performing at the '67 Newport Festival. He also played with Hugh Glover, and worked in a duo with Andrew Cyrille. During the '70s, Graves participated in a series of mid-'70s concerts with Cyrille and Rashied Ali called "Dialogue of the Drums," which included several shows in Black neighborhoods. Graves taught at Bennington College alongside Bill Dixon in the '70s, and toured Europe and Japan. During the '80s, he played in percussion ensembles with Cyrille, Kenny Clarke, and Don Moye. Philly Joe Jones later replaced Clarke. Graves's only listed in-print date on CD is the quartet percussion session on Soul Note in 1983. —*Ron Wynn*

★ **Graves Pullen Duo, The** / Apr. 30, 1966 / Pullen Graves Music 286

WARDELL GRAY

b. Feb. 13, 1921, Oklahoma City, OK, **d.** May 25, 1955, Las Vegas, NV

Tenor saxophone / Bop

Wardell Gray's swirling, pungent solos and extensive skills enabled him, along with Dexter Gordon, to be one of the earliest and one of the most accomplished bebop tenors. Initially, Gray was influenced heavily by Lester Young, but subsequently incorporated elements of Charlie Parker's playing, as well as his own concepts, into his music. He even played bebop with Benny Goodman in his late '40s group. Gray learned clarinet as a child, then worked in local bands as a teen. He joined Earl Hines's group in 1943, and later recorded with him. After moving to Los Angeles, Gray met promoter Gene Norman. Soon, Norman was spearheading recording sessions and featuring Gray in jam sessions and performances. His duels with Gordon, especially the famous 1947 recording "The Chase," brought Gray widespread fame. He did dates for Dial with Charlie Parker, and sessions for Spotlite and Savoy. Xanadu and Straight Ahead later reissued some Gray recordings as well. While in Goodman's combo, Gray moved to New York, and played at the Royal Roost with Count Basie and Tadd Dameron's band, recording with both groups. He played in Goodman's big band in 1948 and 1949. Gray's solo on "Twisted" was later turned into a "vocalise" epic by Annie Ross, and then became an even bigger hit through Judy Collins's revival. He recorded in Basie's 1950 and 1951 small band, then returned to the West Coast, later working in Las Vegas. Gray recorded with Louis Bellson in 1952 and 1953. There were dates for

Prestige and RCA, and other sessions that have been periodically available on reissues from Top Rank, Onyx, and Polydor. Currently, there are only a couple of Gray sessions available on CD. —*Ron Wynn*

○ **Wardell Gray Tenor Sax** / Nov. 11, 1949+Apr. 25, 1950 / Prestige 115

Wardell Gray Memorial Album / Nov. 11, 1949-Jan. 21, 1952 / Prestige 7343

Most of the tracks on both this and volume two were originally issued in prior Prestige twofer packages. The majority of the cuts are short studio sessions, but 2 of the 20 are extended blowing sessions from 1950 that include Dexter Gordon, Clark Terry, and Sonny Criss. Other participants to these solid sessions include Art Farmer, Hampton Hawes, Frank Morgan, Sonny Clark, Teddy Charles, and Al Haig. Both volumes are lovely. —*Bob Rusch, Cadence*

★ **Central Ave.** / **i.** 1949-1952 / Prestige 24062

Landmark West Coast jazz recordings from a neglected figure who was definitely not part of the dominant cool school. Wardell Gray was a superb soloist, particularly when involved in combative jam sessions with fellow players such as Dexter Gordon. These late '40s and early '50s recordings are among the finest done by Black jazz musicians playing bop in hostile territory. They were rereleased as part of Prestige two-record reissue line in the '70s and are now available on CD. —*Ron Wynn*

○ **Wardell Gray Memorial—Vol. 2** / Aug. 27, 1950+Jan. 21, 1952 / Prestige 051

Both this and the first volume were originally paired in the '60s as one of the first twofers initiated by Prestige (then an independent label). It was a terrific bargain then, a great bargain again almost 10 years later, when it was included in another twofer, and still one now in single-album incarnation. The fine material here all comes from between 11/11/49 and 12/51 and contains almost all of Gray's (ts) Prestige material and some classics. —*Bob Rusch, Cadence*

○ **Wardell Gray's Los Angeles Stars** / Jan. 21, 1952 / Prestige 147

Chase and the Steeplechase, The / **i.** Feb. 2, 1952-Sep. 25, 1953 / Decca 7025

Exuberant romps with fellow tenors Dexter Gordon and Paul Quinichette. Almost impossible to find. —*Ron Wynn*

Live at the Haig / Sep. 9, 1952 / Fresh Sound

A hot 1952 session with an excellent lineup. Previously issued on Xanadu and Straight Ahead with different titles. —*Ron Wynn*

○ **Wardell Gray / Stan Hasselgard** / **i.** Oct. 1978 / Spotlite 134

This album is a mixture of moods. Most satisfying are the three Howard McGhee Sextet concert performances. Wardell Gray is surrounded here by an electrifying Howard McGhee on trumpet and some slashing alto by Sonny Criss ("Bebop"). But his jog through the changes of Cole Porter's "What Is This Thing Called Love" (via "Hot House") is the ultimate marriage of jazz's physical and intellectual elements: swing and ideas. Six Count Basie tracks feature Gray in numbers of varying interest and quality. Tempos are lickety split all the way and the sound is on the murky side, but none is without at least some interesting Gray, especially "The King," a reworking of "Jumpin' at the Woodside." Two cuts that join Gray with clarinetist Stan Hasselgard are pleasant if anticlimactic and are probably included for reasons more historical than musical. —*John McDonough, Down Beat*

BENNIE GREEN (sax)

b. 1923, **d.** 1977

Saxophone, critic / Bop

A capable bebop soloist though his style had firm swing era roots, Bennie Green was a major player and bandleader in the '40s, '50s, and '60s. His sound and tone were large and round, and his approach was influenced heavily by traditionalists like Trummy Young. Green adapted, but was never as ambitious in his playing as latter-day trombonists like J.J.

Johnson or Curtis Fuller. His solos were enjoyable and always well executed. Green had a musical background; one of his brothers played tenor sax with Roy Eldridge's band. He studied at the famous Du Sable High school in Chicago under captain Walt Dyett, then began playing professionally with local groups. Budd Johnson recommended Green to Earl Hines in the early '40s, and he worked with Hines until 1948, except for two years in the Army. Green played with Gene Ammons for a short stint, then with Charlie Ventura in the late '40s and early '50s. He toured with Hines again from 1951 until 1953. Green led his own combo in the '50s and '60s, often playing with either Charlie Rouse or Jimmy Forrest. He also worked with Sonny Clark, Paul Chambers, Sarah Vaughan, Ike Quebec, Booker Ervin, and Elvin Jones. Green performed and recorded with Duke Ellington in 1968, playing on his second sacred concert recording. Green settled in Las Vegas in the late '60s, working in hotel bands. He was also featured on recordings made at the Newport In New York festival in the early '70s. He recorded as a leader for Jubilee, Prestige, Blue Note, Enrica, Time, and Vee Jay. Currently, Green has some dates available on CD. —*Ron Wynn and Michael G. Nastos*

Bennie Green Blows His Horn / Jun. 10+22, 1955 / Prestige 1728

A nice, mainstream showcase for Green's trombone. Charlie Rouse (ts) sparkles outside Monk's group. —*Ron Wynn*

★ **Walkin' Down** / Jun. 29, 1956 / Prestige 1752

Bennie Green and Art Farmer / i. Oct. 31, 1956 / Prestige 7041

Swingin'est, The / Jul. 1958 / Vee Jay 1005

This is an unassuming small-band (Bennie Green, t; Nat Adderley, tpt; Gene Ammons, Frank Foster, ts; Frank Wess, ts, f; Tommy Flanagan, p; Eddie Jones, b; Albert Heath, d) bop date with a predictable Count Basie twinge from 1958. The solos are generally robust and the themes serviceable. The first two numbers are by Foster, with the remaining three by Ammons, Adderley, and Wess, respectively. An additional track ("Swinging for Benny") was added on an Affinity reissue version released in England. —*Alan Bargebuhr, Cadence*

Hornful of Soul / Jul. 1961 / Bethlehem 6054

BENNY GREEN (Piano)

b. 1963
Piano / Neo-bop

Benny Green has drawn critical raves since, at age 20, he joined Betty Carter as her regular pianist in the early '80s. A dashing soloist as equally outstanding on bebop, hard bop, or free tunes as he is in interpreting standards or 12-bar blues, Green spent four years working with Carter, then was in Art Blakey and the Jazz Messengers for another two-and-a-half years. After leaving Blakey, he's divided his time between heading his own trio and touring extensively with Ray Brown in the '90s. Oscar Peterson selected Green to play with him in Toronto in 1992. Peterson had been selected winner of the Glenn Gould award and was asked to name the most promising young pianist as his protege. He selected Green, who later joined him for a concert. Green has been recording for Blue Note since 1990. He's recorded solo and worked with Ray Drummond, Victor Lewis, Christian McBride, and Carl Allen. All of Green's sessions are available on CD. —*Ron Wynn and Michael G. Nastos*

○ **Prelude** / Feb. 1988 / Criss Cross 1036

★ **Lineage** / Jan. 30, 1990-Feb. 1, 1990 / Blue Note 93670
Debut work, with this former Jazz Messenger forging his identity as a leader. —*Ron Wynn*

○ **In This Direction** / Mar. 1990 / Criss Cross 1038
Good set from ranking young jazz lion pianist, along with Geoff Keezer. Green, a former Messenger, plays anything from standards to originals with flair, and his solos are always inventive and nicely crafted. —*Ron Wynn*

Greens / Mar. 1991 / Blue Note 96485
This is the second release from this fine pianist who is destined to be a major keyboard figure. —*Ron Wynn*

○ **Testifyin'!: Live at the Village Vanguard** / i. 1992 / Blue Note 98171
Pianist Benny Green seems intent on continuing the great groove-piano trio tradition in performances such as his title tune, bassist Christian McBride's "McThing," and the traditional "Down By The Riverside." But all is not funk. The ballads—"Beautiful Moons Ago" (by Nat "King" Cole, surely one of Green's models as a trio pianist) and "I Should Care"—illustrate the pianist's ability to embroider a pretty melody. There are also boppish tributes: Green's "Humphrey" for pianist Walter Davis, Jr; his "Blu's March" for former employer Art Blakey; and "Billy Boy," for Ahmad Jamal and Red Garland, who recorded celebrated versions. —*Owen Cordle*, Down Beat

BUNKY GREEN

b. 1935
Saxophone, instructor / Swing, big band, bop

Bunky Green is a fine session player and a good blues and ballad soloist. Due to horrendous management of his catalog at Argo and Vanguard, his output, through much of his career, has disappeared. Since Green was never a big name or a major seller, there has been no rush to crank out obscure dates or albums that feature him. But he's an exuberant bebop, hard bop, soul-jazz, or blues alto player, and is effective, though not as interesting, on soprano. Currently, he has only one CD in print: a fine late '80s date for Delos that was recorded right after the recent deaths of his parents. — *Ron Wynn*

Testifyin' Time / 1965 / Cadet 753

○ **Places We've Never Been** / Feb. 21+22, 1979 / Vanguard 79425
With Randy Brecker (tpt), Al Dailey Trio. Modal "East & West" shows alto saxophonist at his improvisational best. — *Michael G. Nastos*

In Love Again / i. 1987 / Mark 57623
Quintet with trumpeter Willie Thomas. Three by saxophonist Green, one by Thomas, one cowritten by the pair, one standard ("You Stepped Out of a Dream"). —*Michael G. Nastos*

★ **Healing the Pain** / Dec. 1989 / Delos 4020
With Billy Childs Trio, sharp drummer Ralph Penland, and the great bassist Art Davis. All standards save two of Bucky's originals. A bright alto voice shines through. —*Michael G. Nastos*

FREDDIE GREEN (Frederick William Greene)

b. Mar. 31, 1911, Charleston, SC, **d.** Mar. 1, 1987, Las Vegas, NV
Rhythm guitar / Swing, big band

He seldom, if ever, took a solo, yet Freddie Green's importance as a rhythm guitarist surpassed that of many more flamboyant and dynamic lead players. Green's always concise, understated, and perfectly locked seamless alignment with Walter Page's bass and Jo Jones's drums added the final ingredient to the Basie rhythm section. His comping chords squarely on each beat was an anchor, and the way Green managed to make his presence felt without being in the spotlight was sheer artistry. He remained with the Basie band for almost 50 years, leaving it only for brief periods. Like Ellington with Harry Carney, the Basie orchestra without Freddie Green was unthinkable. Green was a self-taught player who started his professional career on banjo before playing guitar in 1936 with Kenny Clarke. John Hammond spotted Green playing at the Black Cat in Greenwich Village. On Hammond's recommendation, Green joined Basie as a replacement for Claude Williams in 1937, after auditioning for Basie in his dressing room. Green contributed an occasional composition to the band's book, among them "Down for Double," "Right On," and "Corner Pocket." Buck Clayton nicknamed Green "Esquire," while Lester Young called him "Pepper." During his lengthy tenure with Basie, Green also found time to record with Clayton, Benny Goodman, Teddy Wilson, Lionel Hampton, Al Cohn and Joe Newman, and Jo Jones, and made an occasional release under his own name. He even cut one vocal on "Them There Eyes" for a 1938 Lester Young session. Green didn't leave when Basie died; he continued with the band under Thad Jones and then Frank Foster's leadership, contributing through the '87 sessions for the album *Diane Schuur & the Count Basie Orchestra*. Only death removed him from the guitar chair. — *Ron Wynn*

★ **Natural Rhythm** / **i**. Dec. 18, 1955-Feb. 3, 1955 / Bluebird 6465
Green's *Mr. Rhythm* and Al Cohn's *Natural Seven* albums combined. A wonderful collaboration between Freddie Green (away from the Basie band) and Al Cohn (ts). — *Ron Wynn*

Mr. Rhythm / Jun. 13, 1956 / Victor 1210

GRANT GREEN

b. Jun. 6, 1931, St. Louis, MO, **d**. Jan. 31, 1979, New York, NY
Guitar / Bop, hard bop, post-bop, blues & jazz, soul-jazz
A severely underrated player during his lifetime, Grant Green had a beautiful sound and excellent guitar skills. He maintained that he listened to horn players rather than other guitarists, and his single-note linearity and style, which avoided chordal playing, was unique. His extensive foundation in R&B combined with a mastery of bebop and simplicity that put expressiveness ahead of technical expertise. Green was a superb blues interpreter, and his later material was predominantly blues and R&B, though he was also a wondrous ballad and standards soloist. He was a particular admirer of Charlie Parker, and his phrasing often reflected it. Green played in the '50s with Jimmy Forrest, Harry Edison, and Lou Donaldson. He also collaborated with many organists, among them Brother Jack McDuff, Sam Lazar, Baby Face Willette, Gloria Coleman, Big John Patton, and Larry Young. During the early '60s, both his fluid, tasteful playing in organ/guitar/drum combos and his other dates for Blue Note established Green as a star, though he seldom got the critical respect that was given to other players. He was off the scene for a bit in the mid '60s, but came back strong in the late '60s and '70s. Green played with Stanley Turrentine, Dave Bailey, Yusef Lateef, Joe Henderson, Hank Mobley, Herbie Hancock, McCoy Tyner, and Elvin Jones. Sadly, drug problems interrupted his career in the '60s, and undoubtedly contributed to the illness he suffered in the late '70s. Green was hospitalized in 1978 and died a year later. Despite some rather uneven LPs near the end of his career, the great body of his work represents marvelous soul-jazz, bebop, and blues. Mosaic, the nation's premier jazz reissue label, issued a wonderful collection, *The Complete Blue Note Recordings With Sonny Clark*, featuring prime early '60s Green albums plus unissued tracks. There are also several Blue Note albums, plus posthumously issued sessions on Muse and Black Lion, available on CD. — *Ron Wynn and Michael Erlewine*

○ **Green Blues** / Mar. 15, 1961 / Muse 5014
This album was released under drummer Dave Bailey's name in 1961 on the Jazztime label. The company and the album quickly disappeared. Now that listener appreciation for this kind of unpretentious modern mainstream music has grown, the tasteful playing of guitarist Grant Green, bassist Ben Tucker, Bailey, and the underappreciated tenor saxophonist Frank Haynes should find a welcome audience. Billy Gardner's piano work is a notch below the general level; his automated comping would be an irritant if there weren't such interesting things going on around him: Bailey's marvelously loose, relaxed, and propulsive drumming, for one, and Green's simple but thoughtful and swinging guitar lines, for another; also, Tucker's big sound and easy drive, and Haynes's round tone and architectural sense of what a solo should be. The saxophonist was a victim of

cancer at the age of 34, and this record is one of very few on which he appeared. This collection, for all practical purposes a new release, is a welcome addition to the discography. — *Doug Ramsey*, Down Beat

Reaching Out / Mar. 15, 1961 / Black Lion 760129
One of four David Bailey-led albums now being released under the guitarist's name. Green is in fine form as is pianist Billy Gardner (better known as an organist), but the album is perhaps most valuable for the contributions of the obscure tenorman Frank Haynes, who died in 1965; his sound will remind some a little of Stanley Turrentine. — *Scott Yanow*, Cadence

Grantstand / Aug. 1, 1961 / Blue Note 46430
This is his third album for Blue Note. A quartet session with Yusef Lateef (ts, f) and vintage Jack McDuff on the Hammond organ. The 15-minute "Blues in Maude's Flat" is very nice indeed, and "My Funny Valentine" (with Lateef on flute) is just plain lovely. No one does standards like Green. — *Michael Erlewine*

○ **Born to Be Blue** / Dec. 11, 1961+Mar. 1, 1962 / Blue Note 84432
Marvelous 1961-62 dates, with splendid playing by Ike Quebec (sax), Sonny Clark (p), and Green. CD has three bonus cuts. — *Ron Wynn*

★ **Complete Blue Note with Sonny Clark** / 1961-1962 / Mosaic 133
With Sonny Clark, 1961-62. Includes Blue Note albums *Gooden's Corner, Nigeria, Oleo, Born To Be Blue* (with Ike Quebec), plus unissued tracks. Some of the best bluesy jazz in existence, with the guitarist at the top of his form. Great liner notes. Just incredible music. — *Michael Erlewine*

○ **Nigeria** / Jan. 13, 1962 / Blue Note 1031
Annotator Ben Sidran perceptively characterizes Green as "kind of corny at times, but very hip." The guitarist's blues-imbued style retains something of a country twang, and, even exploiting the sustain and reflex capacities of his hollow-body electric, he sounds perfectly natural. The familiar tunes all elicit winning solos from Green, but on the sanctified "Necessarily" he is especially good. — *Francis Davis*, Cadence

○ **Latin Bit, The** / Apr. 26, 1962 / Blue Note 4111

○ **Idle Moments** / Nov. 4, 1963+Nov. 11, 1963 / Blue Note 84154
Excellent album, with Green in good form. Bobby Hutcherson (vib) in the group produces a somewhat different sound from the usual Green album, so make a note of that. Joe Henderson (ts) is hot. — *Michael Erlewine*

Solid / Jun. 12, 1964 / Blue Note 990
Green's solos are crisp and clean single-note executions, and Joe Henderson (ts) comes through with some fine moments. What one gets is the by now standard Blue Note recording of that era: solid, straightahead jazz with no frills. — *Carl Brauer*, Cadence

○ **I Want to Hold Your Hand** / Mar. 31, 1965 / Blue Note 4202

★ **Matador** / May 20, 1965 / Blue Note 84442
With Coletrane sidemen McCoy Tyner (p) and Elvin Jones (d)—still with Coltrane at the time. Green tackles the Coltrane hit "My Favorite Things" and pulls it off in his own style. This is a fine album. — *Michael Erlewine*

Iron City / 1967 / Muse 5120

Visions / 1971 / Blue Note 84373

Main Attraction, The / Mar. 1976 / Kudu 29
This dismal reemergence of guitarist Grant Green falls into the laidback, lush CTI [Creed Taylor productions] manufactured formula. It's so formulaic, and that's saying a lot with personnel that includes Joe Farrell, Ronnie Cuber, Mike Brecker, Jon Faddis, and Steve Khan. — *Cadence*

SONNY GREER

b. 1895, **d**. 1982
Drums, percussion / Swing, big band

Sonny Greer was the first great total percussionist. Besides his drum kit, he utilized an array of gongs, skulls, cymbals, and chimes, creating the backdrop for what Duke Ellington called his "jungle" period. He teamed brilliantly with bassist Jimmy Blanton, and was skilled at giving the orchestra subtle rhythm shadings without being overwhelmed or overwhelming. Greer played in various bands around New Jersey, then was in the Howard Theatre orchestra in Washington, D.C. He met Ellington in 1919, and joined his band the next year. Greer became a primary part of Ellington's formula when the orchestra became the Cotton Club's resident band in 1927. Greer remained with Ellington until 1951; after Greer left, precious few drummers approached the rapport they shared. He joined Johnny Hodges's band in 1951, then played with Louis Metcalf, Red Allen, and Tyree Glenn during the '50s. During the '60s, Greer backed Eddie Barefield and J. C. Higginbotham. He appeared in the 1967 film *The Night They Raided Minksy's*, and led a band at the Garden Cafe in New York. He played in Brooks Kerr's trio during the '70s, and worked until a few months before his death. — *Ron Wynn*

AL GREY (Albert Thornton Grey)

b. Jun. 6, 1925, Aldie, VA
Trombone / Big band, swing
Another Basie orchestra mainstay, Al Grey has been a sterling trombonist whose humorous inflections and skill with the plunger have been balanced by his excellent facility and overall technique. He's a reliable, steady type, not the kind to bowl anyone over with multiphonics or circular breathing, but his solos always invoke good feelings from musicians and audiences alike. Grey played in a service band during World War II. He toured with Benny Carter and Jimmie Lunceford in the mid '40s, staying in New York with the Lunceford band after its leader died. He played for a brief time with Lucky Millinder and toured for five years with Lionel Hampton. After working in 1956 with Dizzy Gillespie, Grey joined Count Basie's orchestra. He left in 1961 with Billy Mitchell to form a sextet, which soon disbanded. Grey was unsuccessful heading his group, and returned to the Basie fold in 1964, becoming one of its most popular members in the '60s. He began touring with Jazz at the Philharmonic in 1974, then left the Basie band again in 1977. He worked regularly with Jimmy Forrest through the late '70s. Grey has had periodic reunions and sessions with the Basie band, and has done combo dates in Europe. He's performed frequently with Buddy Tate, and co-led a band with Al Cohn in 1985. — *Ron Wynn*

Al Grey/Billy Mitchell Sextet, The / Jul. 6, 1961 / Argo 689

★ **Having a Ball** / Jan. 29, 1963 / Argo 718

Boss Bone / Feb. 1964 / Argo 731

Grey's Mood / Apr. 3, 1973+Oct. 7, 1975 / Classic Jazz 118

Struttin' and Shoutin' / Aug. 30, 1976 / Columbia 38505
This was fun time for Al Grey (t), who may be remembered best for his long tenure with Count Basie, but he goes back to the Jimmie Lunceford band. Only now, after Jimmy Forrest's death, was this released, and you have to wonder, why so long? The other horn players beside Forrest (ts) generally play only the charts mostly written by Ernie Wilkins; however, Waymon Reed (tpt) does get to play a little on "Struttin' and Shoutin'." The rhythm team of Ray Bryant (p), Milt Hinton (b), and Bobby Durham (d) supplies and personifies all those superlatives such as "rock-solid bottom," "hard and straight 4/4," "walkin', struttin'." Just listen to Hinton throughout if you don't really know what that means. Of course, Grey is one of the masters of the plunger. His playing on "Stardust" and Wilkins's simple written lines are so typical of the Basie approach. Only on "All of Me" do I think Grey plays open, but he has so many ways of playing that plunger that it's really hard to tell for sure. The final track is for Norman Granz. It had to please him. — *Jerry Atkins,* Cadence

○ **Featuring Arnett Cobb and Jimmy Forrest** / Jul. 11, 1977 / Black & Blue 233143

JOHNNY GRIFFIN (John Arnold (III) Griffin)

b. Apr. 24, 1928, Chicago, IL
Tenor saxophone / Bop, hard bop
An exciting, energetic tenor saxophonist, Johnny Griffin is one of the fastest, most charismatic of the funky bop players. His rampaging solos, whether going against another saxophonist in friendly/combative jams or heading a quartet or quintet, are never detached and are seldom predictable or clichéd. He's been able to fit into many diverse situations, whether playing with large orchestras, all-star groups, two-tenor bands, or soul-jazz combos.

Griffin attended Chicago's Du Sable High School and was one of Walter Dyett's pupils. His professional career began in the mid '40s, playing in Lionel Hampton's band from 1945 to 1947. He worked with R&B trumpeter Joe Morris from 1947 to 1950, and also played with Philly Joe Jones, Percy Heath, Papa Jo Jones, Gene Ramey, and Arnett Cobb. Griffin practiced regularly with Thelonious Monk and Bud Powell. He recorded the single "Chicago Riffin'/Flying Home" on Okeh in 1953 under the name Little Johnny Griffin and his Orchestra. Babs Gonzales was the vocalist. After playing for two years with an army band in Hawaii, Griffin moved to Chicago. He joined Art Blakey's Jazz Messengers in 1957 and Monk's quartet in 1958. He appeared on Blakey albums for Bethlehem, RCA, and Atlantic, and had his own sessions for Argo, Blue Note, and Riverside in the '50s. These dates included one jam session with John Coltrane and Hank Mobley, and Griffin also recorded with Wes Montgomery. There were big band and small group recordings for Prestige in the early '60s, and a combo session with trombonist Matthew Gee for Atlantic. Griffin gained the most notoriety in the early '60s for the quintet he co-led with tenor saxophonist Eddie "Lockjaw" Davis. Their group was among the most fiery and dynamic on the scene; the Davis/Griffin battles were magnetic, no-holds-barred affairs, with the two saxophonists sparing nothing on the bandstand.

Tax and personal problems caused Griffin to leave America in 1963. He settled in Paris, where he played with Kenny Clarke, Kenny Drew, Art Taylor, and Powell, often at the Blue Note club. He joined the Clarke-Boland big band in 1967, serving as its principal soloist until 1969, and worked often in groups led by Taylor. Griffin was featured on 13 albums recorded for Japanese and European labels in the '60s and the early and mid '70s. He moved to the Netherlands in 1973, and appeared at several festivals. His playing at the 1975 Montreux and 1976 Tokyo festivals drew widespread praise, as did the *Live in Tokyo* album issued on Inner City with pianist Horace Parlan. Griffin recorded for Pablo, Timeless, Inner City, and Galaxy in the '70s, while touring America in 1978 and 1979. There were albums with Taylor, live dates with Count Basie and with Dizzy Gillespie's Big 7, and combo sessions. The Galaxy recordings were his first American label releases in 15 years.

Griffin has continued touring, recording, and performing in the '80s and '90s. He recorded with Mulgrew Miller in 1983, and led a Paris reunion band with Woody Shaw in 1986. The film *The Jazz Life Featuring Johnny Griffin* was released in 1985, and featured a dynamic concert at the Village Vanguard. He's had two outstanding '90s Antilles releases, *The Cat* in 1991, and *Quartet +3* in 1993. Some of his late '50s Prestige, Riverside, and Blue Note sessions have been reissued on CD, along with some Timeless recordings. The Inner City, Atlantic, and other international material is harder to find, though it's available overseas. — *Ron Wynn*

○ **Chicago Calling** / Apr. 17, 1956 / Blue Note 1533

Introducing Johnny Griffin / Apr. 17, 1956 / Blue Note 46536

○ **A Blowing Session** / Apr. 6, 1957 / Blue Note 1559
This Johnny Griffin date has a young Lee Morgan on trumpet; good, flowing 1957 Hank Mobley; John Coltrane's melodies sometimes even better; and more Art Blakey on

drums. The hero is Griffin, in a ferociously joyous mood, offering a big sound and utterly wild, disorganized, long, gorgeous solos. The chases are outrageous, and "Smoke Stack" is certainly not for the faint of heart. —*John Litweiler,* Down Beat

☆ **Johnny Griffin—Vol. 2: A Blowin' Session** / Apr. 6, 1957 / Blue Note 81559
Half of this session features Griffin. The other half features fellow tenors John Coltrane, Eddie "Lockjaw" Davis, Clifford Jordan, and John Gilmore. —*Michael G. Nastos*

Congregation, The / Oct. 23, 1957 / Blue Note

Little Giant, The / Aug. 4-5, 1959 / Original Jazz Classics 136

Tough Tenors / i. 1960 / Jazzland 31

○ **Tough Tenor Favorites** / i. Jan. 1963 / Jazzland 76

○ **Salt Peanuts** / i. Aug. 1964 / Black Lion 60121

○ **Blues for Harvey** / Jul. 4-5, 1973 / Inner City 2004
On this live session recorded in 1972 at Jazzhus Montmartre, Copenhagen, tenor saxophonist Johnny Griffin plunges into each tune with virtuosic abandon. Griffin's exuberance is obviously contagious for both rhythm section and audience. Pianist Kenny Drew—as in many of Inner City's Steeple Chase releases—comes through in dazzling style. His rich harmonic palette and melodic inventiveness are expressed with a virtually faultless technique. Bassist Mads Vinding commands a large resonant sound, impressive technical facility, and a resilent rhythmic sense. Drummer Ed Thigpen, a master of controlled intensity, drives the proceedings with finesse. —*Chuck Berg,* Down Beat

Jams Are Coming, The / Dec. 1975-Oct. 1977 / Timeless 121

★ **Live in Tokyo** / Apr. 23, 1976 / Inner City 6042
It is an indication of the high level of creativity of Johnny Griffin that one of the long tracks on this two-record set (on which all tunes but the 3:46 "Wee" are between 16:34 and 19:19) is a ballad that's always taken at a slow tempo, and which the saxophonist wrote. Further, although "The Man I Love" is taken at the traditional, for jazz, fast tempo, Griffin slows things down for a long cadenza that captures the wistful sadness of the Gershwin original. It is one of two long cadenzas on this set, and each underlines the effective way Griffin uses both dynamic and rhythmic shading in his phrasing. Griffin's ballad "When We Were One," is filled with sad reminiscence. But the suffering is expressed with beautiful lyricism and strength. His tenor tone is husky, sometimes soft, sometimes forced, but always warm and rich, even when he cries out high notes with painful sharpness. As Griffin ends on this "hurt" mood, pianist Horace Parlan speaks up with bluesy lyricism. His notes are stated with slow insistence, punctuated by steady left-hand chording. Griffin's other original, "Soft And Furry," is a poignant slow blues. The sadness of its first theme is underlined by the unison voicing of tenor sax and arco bass, with Mads Vinding turning to pizzicato accompaniment behind Griffin during a second theme that serves as a bridge for a return to the first. —*Jerry De Muth,* Down Beat

★ **Return of the Griffin** / Oct. 17, 1978 / Galaxy 5117
Return of the Griffin defies notetaking. So much happens so fast and is so good it almost annuls the ability and reason to criticize. *Return* amounts to a history lesson about Johnny Griffin. Start with the standards—"Autumn Leaves" and "I Should Care." Griffin plays the hell out of them, attacking as if he first read them just yesterday. "A Monk's Dream" pays homage to pianist Thelonious, in whose group Griffin replaced John Coltrane. On tenor, Griffin plays both the inscrutable voice of Monk and his own bolting style. The funky "The Way It Is" sounds like an ode to Griffin's barnstorming partner of the early '60s, Eddie "Lockjaw" Davis. But the Griffin of 15 years later leaves space for Ronnie Mathews's tinkling piano, Ray Drummond's extended bass notes, and Keith Copeland's hi-hat pacing. The sound is consummate barroom in the finest jazz definition. —*Sam Freedman,* Down Beat

○ **Bush Dance** / Oct. 18-19, 1978 / Galaxy 5126
Bush Dance was a studio recording with more premeditation. Tenor saxophonist Johnny Griffin heads a sextet—and in addition to sounding somewhat hastily put together, the recording includes studio concessions. This version of "The Jamfs Are Coming" is under seven minutes and stands in sharp contrast to the longer, relaxed segments that show the range of Griffin's strengths and sensibilities. Here, when Griffin loses his roomy spaces, he is greatly restrained. The lead "A Night in Tunisia" is interesting, its intro framed by a pleasant enough African motif, and the head itself extends in a swaggering blues approach. —*Brent Staples,* Down Beat

Meets Dexter Gordon / i. 1981 / Lotus 8247

Call It Whachawana / Jul. 25-26, 1983 / Galaxy 5146
Johnny Griffin in 1983 was playing the upper end of the tenor sax with a heady yet firm tenderness, programming lady-killers instead of lip-busters, and achieving stretches of bittersweet legato lines that yanked instead of kicked the beat. He wasn't snapping off the notes as much, but letting them ring and carry or (as on the last note of "A Waltz with Sweetie") stretch and laze. In fact, Griffin then was sounding a little more like those other members of the classiest expatriate tenor triumvirate: a sinewy Dexter Gordon or a witty Ben Webster. In 1983 tempos were down; there was more relaxed yet never limp phrasing, dense structures, and what may have been the longest and best ballad of his recorded work. The tiptoe "Lover Man" sustains Ben Webster's agony-slow tempo with exceptional performances from all hands, and Griffin squeezes every drop of emotion out of the tune in maybe the sultriest performance since Billie Holiday's. Hear him bleed tears out of that upper register. It's hard to imagine a trio as springy and delightful as Griffin's original comeback band (pianist Ronnie Mathews, bassist Ray Drummond, drummer Keith Copeland) but these copacetic alumni of Betty Carter (pianist Mulgrew Miller, bassist Curtis Lundy, drummer Kenny Washington) fit beautifully here. —*Fred Bouchard,* Down Beat

Paris Reunion Band / i. 1986 / Sonet
Includes some smoking exchanges with Woody Shaw (tpt); steady material. —*Ron Wynn*

○ **Griff and Lock** / i. 1987 / Original Jazz Classics 264
This one presents another two-sax front line, a sometimes working group that made a series of excellent records. *Jaws and Griff* approaches the two-tenor format as a scoring scheme to juxtapose more in harmony than in battle. Both saxmen were *blowers* with personally identifiable styles, and one could rely on a certain level of projection and swing from any of their combined efforts. This Jazzland date (11/4 and 10/60) finds the quintet (Junior Mance, p; Larry Gales, b; Ben Riley, d) at about average form on a program that intrudes little on the open blowing format both tenors seem to enjoy. —*Bob Rusch,* Cadence

Cat, The / Oct. 26-29, 1990 / Antilles 848421

○ **Toughest Tenors** / Milestone 47035
Eddie "Lockjaw" Davis and Johnny Griffin have big fun burning each other up for the most part on these sessions, but there is clearly a sense of kinship within these grooves. It's also good to hear pianist Junior Mance in this context, as these ears haven't heard enough of him in the company of horns; and such horns! Two tough, mean tenor sax styles that playfully nudge each other to stronger degrees of playing than they might have felt alone. The results are gratifying. One side with three Thelonious Monk tunes, kicked off by a medium-tempo romp through "Epistrophy" and ending with a humorous run through of "I Mean You," is highly rewarding. As usual, the Fantasy/Prestige/Milestone packing, liner notes, and recording info are impeccable. —*Willard Jenkins Jr.,* Cadence

HENRY GRIMES (Henry Alonzon Grimes)

b. Nov. 3, 1935, Philadelphia, PA
Bass / Early free

A superb player who simply walked away from music, Henry Grimes was a topflight bassist during the '50s and '60s. He evolved from being a straight bebop stylist who took a mostly supporting role into a freewheeling, driving, and dashing player who mixed stunning arco and plucked solos, and added droning effects and countermelodies. Grimes played violin, tuba, and double bass in his teens, then attended Juilliard. He toured with Arnett Cobb and Willis Jackson. During the '50s, Grimes worked with Bobby Timmons, Lee Morgan, and Tootie Heath, and played in the late '50s with Sonny Rollins, Anita O' Day, Charles Mingus, and Gerry Mulligan in 1957 and 1958. He was featured at the 1958 Newport Jazz Festival working with Lee Konitz, Tony Scott, Thelonious Monk, and Rollins, and later appeared with Monk in the celebrated *Jazz on a Summer's Day* film made of the festival. Grimes played with Lennie Tristano in 1958 and toured Europe with Rollins in 1959. He was among the busiest bassists in free music for a period in the early and mid '60s, recording and playing with Steve Lacy, Cecil Taylor, Perry Robinson, Rollins, Albert Ayler, Archie Shepp, Frank Wright, Mose Allison, and Don Cherry, with whom he made three albums. Then Grimes quit in 1967, for reasons that remain unclear. He appeared on many classic works, among them Taylor's *Unit Structures*. As might be expected, there are no sessions cited anywhere that feature Grimes as a leader. —*Ron Wynn*

★ **Henry Grimes Trio** / **i.** 1965 / ESP 1026

TINY GRIMES (Lloyd Grimes)

b. Jul. 7, 1916, Newport News, VA, **d.** Mar. 4, 1989
Guitar / Bop, blues & jazz
One of the earliest bop guitarists, Tiny Grimes's fleet, darting solos represented his elaborations from the basics provided by Charlie Christian. Grimes worked with Art Tatum and Charlie Parker in the mid '40s, and made excellent recordings with both men. Grimes began as a drummer, dancer, and pianist in Washington, D.C., and in New York. He started playing guitar professionally in 1938, adopting a four-string brand on which he executed some unusual voicings and patterns. He joined the novelty group, The Cats and the Fiddle, in 1940, and began absorbing and adapting Christian's style to his own approach. Tatum tabbed Grimes for his first trio, and they performed through 1943 with Slam Stewart. Charlie Parker played with the Tiny Grimes Quartet in 1944. They recorded four tracks, among them "Romance Without Finance" and "I'll Always Love You Just the Same," which featured Grimes's vocals. He also led the Rocking Highlanders from 1944 to 1947. Grimes did freelance work and tours in the '50s, moving to Philadelphia for a while before returning to New York in 1960. He began to attract new interest in 1971 when he was featured, with several other guitarists, on an anthology called *The Guitar Album*. His '73 Muse release, *Profoundly Blue*, displayed his blues and jazz skills. He also recorded in the '70s with Roy Eldridge and Lloyd Glenn. —*Ron Wynn and Myles Boisen*

Callin' the Blues / Jul. 18, 1958 / Prestige 191
Long, informal, laidback jams. Good guitar, as always, in a jazzier vein than his early work. —*Myles Boisen*

Tiny in Swingsville / Aug. 13, 1959 / Original Jazz Classics 1796

Tiny Grimes and Friends / **i.** 195z / Collectables 5321
Fine '50s and '60s music; very bad production and remastering, though. —*Ron Wynn*

★ **Profoundly Blue** / Mar. 6, 1973 / Muse 5012
The album's title track is a profound dedication by young guitarist Tiny Grimes to Charlie Christian's science of guitar playing. It comes out as a heartfelt tribute because Grimes wasn't as that modern a player—there is nothing in Grimes's work on this track that couldn't have been played by Christian. Other cuts hearken back to Grimes's sessions as a sideman with the late Ike Quebec ("Tiny's Exercise"). Throughout are evidences of the wry humor that marked his work with pianist Art Tatum, though he doesn't go the fa-

mous quotations route the way he did then. Other good things about this album include the drum work of Freddie Waits and the fact that for a change pianist Harold Mabern gets a chance to blow a little. Tenor saxophonist Houston Person is a bit into the soul-jazz bag, but not obnoxiously so. Jimmy Lewis is a fine bassman within the limitations of the Fender electric. Gene Golden's congas hold things together, usually the job of a rhythm guitar. Everybody cooks. —*Joe Klee*, Down Beat

Some Groovy Fours / May 13, 1974 / Classic Jazz 114
Volume 1 and 2 / Collectables 5304
Amazing high-octane R&B from the golden age, with Red Prysock's honkin' tenor sax and Screamin' Jay Hawkins's earliest vocals. —*Myles Boisen*

Tiny Grimes & His Rocking Highlanders Vol. 2 / Collectables 5317

STEVE GROSSMAN (Steven Grossman)

b. Jan. 18, 1951, New York, NY
Tenor and soprano saxophone / Early jazz-rock, modern creative
While many of the saxophonists influenced by John Coltrane turned to hard bop or free jazz, Steve Grossman initially worked in jazz-rock and fusion, though he later played more conventional jazz material. Grossman began studying alto sax in the late '50s, then moved to Pittsburgh from New York in the mid '60s. He returned to New York in 1967, and began playing soprano then tenor sax. Grossman worked with the Jazz Samaritans, which also included Lenny White and George Cables, and led his own bands. He was studying at Juilliard in 1969 when he got the opportunity to record with Miles Davis. A year later, Grossman replaced Wayne Shorter, but only stayed for about six months. He played with Lonnie Liston Smith, Elvin Jones, and Gene Perla's Stone Alliance through the mid '70s. During the '80s and '90s, Grossman's led his own groups, playing with Cedar Walton, Fred Henke, Billy Higgins, Charles Bellonzi, Junie Booth, Joe Chambers, and Gilbert Rovere, among others. He's also worked and recorded with the Jazz Tribe, whose members include Jack Walrath and Bobby Watson. Grossman's recorded for PM, Horo (Italy), Atlantic, Red, Timeless, and DIW. He has several sessions available on CD. —*Ron Wynn*

○ **Steve Grossman Quartet—Vol. 1** / **i.** Nov. 1985 / DIW 8007
○ **Steve Grossman Quartet—Vol. 2** / **i.** Nov. 1985 / DIW 8008
★ **My Second Prime** / **i.** 1990 / Red 123246

GEORGE GRUNTZ (George Paul Gruntz)

b. Jun. 24, 1932, Basel, Switzerland
Piano, composer, arranger, bandleader / Progressive big band
Gruntz is a Swiss-born pianist, composer/arranger, and bandleader. He has worked mostly with extremely large all-star progressive big bands. He makes complex melodic statements, but his harmonic content is most impressive. Gruntz is able to bring the best out of his cohorts. He is a musical contemporary of Gil Evans. —*Michael G. Nastos*

★ **George Gruntz Concert Jazz Band** / **i.** Sep. 22, 1978 / MPS 62305
GG-CJB (George Gruntz Concert Jazz Band). 21-piece band. Stunning music by ensemble. Soloists include Elvin Jones (d), John Scofield (g), and Lew Tabackin (sax). Other players like Woody Shaw (tpt), Jimmy Knepper (t), and Bennie Wallace (ts) make this band special. —*Michael G. Nastos*

Theatre / Jul. 1983 / ECM 815678
This is a 1983 studio date with an 18-piece group. Sheila Jordan singing "No One Can Explain It" is a waterfall of emotion. Lots of Dino Saluzzi on bandoneon, brass-heavy. Operatic and soaring. —*Michael G. Nastos*

○ **Serious Fun** / **i.** Nov. 1, 1991 / Enja 79659
○ **Blues 'n Dues Et Cetera** / **i.** Nov. 17, 1992 / Enja 79673
Blues 'N Dues Et Cetera gets high marks for high-spirited compositions, a high level of musicianship, and sheer enthusiasm. George Gruntz's playfulness erupts in the

Music Map

Jazz Guitar

The Beginning
Lonnie Johnson (1889-1970) (Blues)
Eddie Lang (1902-1933) (Classical)

Early Jazz Guitar
Django Reinhardt (1910-1953)
George VanEps (1913)
Al Casey (1915)
Dick McDonough (1904-1938)
Carl Kress (1907-1965)

Gibson Electric Guitar: 1936
Charlie Christian (1916-1942)
Floyd Smith (1917-1982)
George Barnes (1921-1977)

Brazilian Style Jazz
Laurindo Almeida (1917)
Charlie Byrd (1925)
Luiz Bonfa
Bola Sete (1923-1987)
Baden Powell (1937)
Egberto Gismonti (1947)
João Gilberto (1931)

Cool Jazz
Billy Bauer (1915)

Django Reinhardt Style 1950s/1960s
Les Paul (1915)
Gabor Szabo (1936-1982)
Attila Zoller (1927)
Arthur Smith
Birelli Lagrene (1966)
Phillip Catherine (1942)

Swing & Bop
Oscar Moore (1912-1981)
Tal Farlow (1921)
Herb Ellis (1921)
Barney Kessel (1923)
Jim Hall (1930)
Joe Pass (1929)
Kenny Burrell (1931)
Ed Bickert (1932)
Linc Chamberlain
Joshua Breakstone
Jimmy Raney (1927)

1950s Experimenters
Lou Mecca
Joe Cinderella

1960s Guitar
Wes Montgomery (1923-1968)
Jimmy Raney (1927)
Howard Roberts (1929)
Grant Green (1931-1979)

Acoustic Jazz
Bill Harris (1925)
Ralph Towner (1940)
Lenny Breau (1941-1984)
John McLaughlin (1942)
Larry Coryell (1943)
Earl Klugh (1954)
Al DiMeola (1954)
Paco DeLucia
Gene Bertoncini (1937)
Bucky Pizzarelli (1926)
John Pizzarelli
Howard Alden

Rock: Major Impact
Jimi Hendrix (1942-1970)
Vernon Reid

Keyboard-Like
Stanley Jordan (1959)

Jazz-Fusion
Frank Zappa (1940-1993)
Sonny Sharrock (1940)
John McLaughlin (1942)
Larry Coryell (1943)
George Benson (1943)
John Abercrombie (1944)
Carlos Santana (1947)
Allan Holdsworth (1948)
John Scofield (1951)
Kazumi Watanabe (1953)
Pat Metheny (1954)
Al DiMeola (1954)
Earl Klugh (1954)
Kevin Eubanks (1957)
Mike Stern (1954)
Bill Connors (1949)
John Tropea (1948)
Lee Ritenour (1952)
Larry Carlton

Modern Jazz
Pat Martino (1944) – Emily Remler (1957) – Jack Wilkins

Avant-garde
James Blood Ulmer (1942)
Sonny Sharrock (1940)
Derek Bailey (1932)
Eugene Chadbourne (1954)
Bill Frisell (1951)
Fred Frith
Ted Dunbar (1937)
Raymond Boni
Jean-Paul Bourelly

Soul Guitar
Melvin Sparks
Phil Upchurch (1941)
Wah-wah Watson
Grant Green (1931-1979)
Billy Butler (1924)
Cornell Dupree
Eric Gale (1938)
George Freeman
Freddie Robinson

Steel Guitar
Buddy Emmons – Doug Jernigan

compositions. Who else would let trombonist Ray Anderson "Rap for Nap" (Napolean, that is) or combine guitarist John Scofield, Chris Hunter's Dave-Sanbornish alto, and a scratchin' DJ on a tune called "Q-Base" (a trendy nudge at the M-Basers?). Or weave warm atonal variations around "In a Sentimental Mood"? Soloists like trumpeters Jon Faddis and Wallace Roney and pianist Gruntz himself don't hurt either. —*Art Lange*, Down Beat

Band, The / MPS 60186
Live at Schauspielhaus. 21-piece co-led by the Ambrosettis, drummer Daniel Humair, and Gruntz. "Epitaph" for Ake Persson. No holds barred. —*Michael G. Nastos*

○ **First Prize** / Enja 79606
Live in Zurich. Pianist Gruntz with four compositions, originals by saxophonist Larry Schneider, trumpeters Franco Ambrosetti and Kenny Wheeler and trombonist Ray Anderson. Standout is Gruntz's "Gorby-Chief." 18-piece band, horn- and brass-heavy, with dynamite rhythm section of Gruntz, Mike Richmond (b), Adam Nussbaum (d). —*Michael G. Nastos*

DAVE GRUSIN

b. Jun. 26, 1934, Denver, CO
Piano, arranger, composer, producer / Progressive big band, instrumental pop
Dave Grusin has been a highly successful performer, producer, composer, record label executive, arranger, and bandleader. His piano playing ranges from mildly challenging to competent to routine, but he's an accomplished film and television soundtrack composer. Grusin played with Terry Gibbs and Johnny Smith while studying at the University of Colorado. He was assistant music director and pianist with Andy Williams from 1959 to 1966, and started his television composing career. Grusin recorded with Benny Goodman in 1960, and recorded with a hard bop trio that included Milt Hinton and Don Lamond in the early '60s. He also played and did a session with a quintet including Thad Jones and Frank Foster. Grusin did arrangements and recorded with Sarah Vaughan, Quincy Jones, and Carmen McRae in the early '70s. He played electric keyboards with Gerry Mulligan and Lee Ritenour in the mid '70s, then helped establish GRP Records out of a production company. GRP developed into one of the top contemporary jazz and fusion companies; they were later taken over by Arista, then by MCA. Grusin continued recording through the '80s and '90s, doing numerous projects from fusion to pop to working with symphony orchestras. He's also conducted the GRP big band, scored films such as *The Fabulous Baker Boys*, and done duet sessions with his brother Don, and with Ritenour. Besides his numerous GRP releases, Grusin's also recorded for Columbia, Sheffield Lab, and PolyGram. He has many sessions available on CD. —*Ron Wynn*

Subways are for Sleeping / Nov. 9, 1961 / Epic 3829

★ **Discovered Again** / i. Aug. 1977 / Sheffield Lab 5
○ **Sticks and Stones** / i. 1987 / GRP 9562

Migration / i. 1988 / GRP 9592
○ **Gershwin Collection** / 1991 / GRP 2005

Homage to Duke / i. May 25, 1993 / GRP 9715
Homage To Duke is a pleasantly lukewarm small-band date of Ducal classics. Clark Terry, veteran of Duke's ensembles, provides the spark that ratifies and affirms. Grusin's own piano playing—solos, fills, trios on "Satin Doll" and "Caravan"—is predictably free of Dukish percussion and exclamation but evidently executed with pleasure. These Duke tunes have had a glorious history, and Grusin works hard—with some success—to prove their future can hold more than just business as usual. —*Fred Bouchard*, Down Beat

GIGI GRYCE (Basheer Quism)

b. Nov. 28, 1927, Pensacola, FL, d. Mar. 17, 1983, Pensacola, FL
Alto saxophone, arranger, composer, flute / Bop, hard bop

Gigi Gryce ended a promising playing career in the early '60s to concentrate on teaching music, writing, and composing. A good, though not great, alto saxophonist, he didn't make any more albums after a string of early '60s releases on Mercury/Trip. But he was an excellent composer and arranger, who often wrote tunes that weren't the standard 12 or 32 bars. Gryce's horn voicings reflected the influence of Tadd Damerson. He studied composition in Boston and played with local bands there in the mid '40s. He presented a concert in Hartford with a 23-piece band that included Horace Silver. Gryce won a Fulbright scholarship to Paris in 1952. He later worked with Max Roach and Tadd Dameron, and toured Europe with Lionel Hampton in the early '50s. Gryce wrote and played for Oscar Pettiford, then began leading his own groups. He co-led the Jazz Lab Quintet with Donald Byrd in the mid and late '50s, and arranged sessions for Clifford Brown and Art Farmer. Gryce began recording as a leader for Vogue in the '50s. He recorded with Thelonious Monk, Lee Morgan, and the Lab Quintet, then retired from playing in the early '60s. His best known composition was "Nico's Tempo." There are a few Gryce sessions available on CD. —*Ron Wynn*

Gigi Gryce-Clifford Brown Sextet / Sep. 1953-Oct. 1953 / Vogue 185

Bird Calls 2 / i. Mar. 1955 / Savoy 650111

Gigi Gryce & The Jazz Lab Quintet / Feb. 27, 1957+Mar. 7, 1957 / Riverside 1774
1991 reissue of an intriguing work. Donald Byrd (tpt) and Wade Legge (p) step to the front in this limited-edition offering. —*Ron Wynn*

Modern Jazz Perspective / i. Apr. 1958 / Columbia 1085

Gigi Gryce Quartet / 1958 / Metrojazz 1006

Sayin' Somethin'! / Mar. 11, 1960 / New Jazz 8230

Hap'nin's, The / May 3, 1960 / Prestige

Reminiscin' Gigi Gryce Orch-Tette / Oct. 1961 / Mercury 20628

○ **Gigi Gryce / Donald Byrd** / i. 1963 / Josie 3500
★ **Rat Race Blues, The** / 1984 / New Jazz 081

LARS GULLIN (Gunnar Victor Gullin)

b. May 4, 1928, Visby, Sweden, d. May 17, 1976, Vissefjarda, Sweden
Baritone saxophone, composer, arranger / Swing, big band, bop
The first European performer to win a *Down Beat* New Star poll (in 1954), Swedish baritone saxophonist Lars Gullin was a fine bebop soloist. His smooth yet energized style evolved from a detached, polished orientation in his early years to a more fiery, flamboyant approach. Gullin began playing bugle at age 13, then turned to clarinet and was in a military band. He later studied piano. Gullin played with big bands led by Charlie Redland, Arthur Osterwall, and Seymour Osterwall in the late '40s and early '50s. During the early '50s, he was in Arne Domnerus's orchestra, then began leading his own combos and doing session work. Gullin made several recordings during the '50s and '60s for Metronome, Gazell, Polydor, Sonet, Columbia, and Odeon. He turned to composition in the mid '60s, and scored many works for various European orchestras. Currently, Gullin does not have any sessions as a leader available on CD. —*Ron Wynn*

○ **Great Lars Gullin—Vol. 2, The** / Mar. 1953-Dec. 1953 / Dragon 75

○ **Great Lars Gullin—Vol. 5, The** / i. May 1954-Jan. 1955 / Dragon 181

○ **Great Lars Gullin—Vol. 3, The** / i. Sep. 1954-Jun. 1955 / Dragon 127

★ **Great Lars Gullin—Vol. 1, The** / i. Apr. 1955-May 1956 / Dragon 36

○ **Great Lars Gullin—Vol. 4, The** / i. Jan. 1959-Sep. 1960 / Dragon 156

H

BOBBY HACKETT (Robert Leo Hackett)

b. Jan. 31, 1915, Providence, RI, **d.** Jun. 7, 1976, Chatham, MA
Cornet, trumpet, arranger, bandleader / Dixieland
Bobby Hackett's tone and lyricism were lush, and he was highly respected by many musicians across the stylistic board. Hackett's ringing, striking solos, elegant, sophisticated phrasing, and subtle harmonic skills retained their hook and lure throughout his career. Hackett was a professional at age 14, and played in restaurants and ballrooms. After working in Providence bands, Hackett joined a trio with Pee Wee Russell and Teddy Roy in 1933. He led his own band in 1936, and moved to New York in 1937, playing with Joe Marsala. Hackett was a guest performer at Benny Goodman's 1938 Carnegie Hall concert. He led another band at Nick's in 1938, and a big band at the Famous Door in 1939. Hackett also worked in Boston clubs with Russell, Eddie Condon, and Brad Gowans, recording with them in 1938, and with Bud Freeman's Summa Cum Laude Orchestra in 1939. He also played cornet, trumpet, and guitar with Horace Heidt in '39 and '40. Hackett was in Glenn Miller's orchestra in 1941 and 1942. He played guitar with Miller, but also recorded on "String of Pearls," a notable solo that reflected Beiderbecke's influence. He then joined NBC radio's staff. About two years later, Hackett became a member of the Casa Loma Band, staying with them from 1944 to 1946, after which he signed with ABC. He was a regular at Condon's and served as the music director and second cornetist for Louis Armstrong's historic 1947 Town Hall concert. A jam session with Tony Parenti at the Rustic Lodge Hotel in 1949 was also recorded. During the '50s, Hackett became a well-known personality. He led several groups, among them one at the Henry Hudson Hotel in 1956 and 1957. He played with lyrical flair and beauty on an album series titled *For Lovers Only,* produced by Jackie Gleason. Hackett made television appearances and co-led a sextet with Dick Cary. There was an excellent octet session and another combo date where he was paired with Jack Teagarden in 1955 and 1957, and '50s sessions with Condon. Hackett played with Ray McKinley and Tony Bennett in the '60s, and toured Europe with Bennett in 1966 and 1967. He was in Benny Goodman's band in 1962 and 1963, and was featured on the television show "Just Jazz" with Vic Dickenson in 1971. Hackett toured Japan that year with George Wein, and made frequent guest appearances in the '70s with the World's Greatest Jazz Band and Dave McKenna. A four-volume set featuring Hackett's quintet and another live date, all with Dickenson, was issued by Chiaroscuro. Hackett kept playing until just a few months before his death in 1976. —*Ron Wynn*

★ **Hackett Horn, The** / i. 1930 / Sony Special Products 22003
This set of 16 songs has been reissued intact several times, most notably on this LP. It includes 12 of the first 16 songs cut at dates led by cornetist Bobby Hackett, featuring a pair of hot combos and a larger big band (why are the other four rewarding sides always left out?), along with two Bix-associated songs recorded under the sponsorship of bandleader Horace Heidt and a pair of jams from a set led by critic Leonard Feather. Throughout, Hackett, then barely in

his midtwenties, shows why his original reputation as "the new Bix" never quite fit. Even this early in his career, his pretty tone was distinctive. Among the other stars of these swing/trad performances are trombonists George Brunies and Brad Gowans and clarinetists Pee Wee Russell and Joe Marsala. Fun and still highly enjoyable music. —*Scott Yanow*

Jazz in New York / **i.** 1944 / Commodore 7009
This CD has plenty of hot traditional jazz as played by a variety of top Condonites who were in their prime in the mid '40s. The three separate bands feature overlapping personnel with cornetist Bobby Hackett's octet including trombonist Lou McGarity and the great baritonist Ernie Caceres, trombonist Miff Mole's Nicksielanders also showcasing Hackett and Caceres, and cornetist Muggsy Spanier's Ragtimers featuring Mole. Clarinetist Pee Wee Russell is also heard with all three groups! But even if the individual bands are pickup affairs, a few classic performances result, most notably Mole's version of "Peg Of My Heart," Spanier's "Angry" and "Alice Blue Gown," and Bobby Hackett's "At Sundown" and "Soon." Fun Dixieland from some of the best. —*Scott Yanow*

Live at the Rustic Lodge / **i.** 1949 / Jazz
These radio airchecks feature cornetist Bobby Hackett and clarinetist Tony Parenti sitting in with a fine pickup group in New Jersey for two standards and a lengthy blues medley, the local musicians getting three tunes to themselves, Parenti rejoining them for "That's A Plenty," and the great trumpeter Red Allen dominating "Squeeze Me" and "I Wish I Could Shimmy Like My Sister Kate." Nothing unique occurs but the good feelings generated at the sessions can still be savored (along with the frequently hot music) four decades later. —*Scott Yanow*

Bobby Hackett and His Orchestra / **i.** 194? / Jazzology
Horn a Plenty / **i.** 1951 / Commodore 016

Coast Concert / Oct. 18+19, 1955 / Capitol
In the '50s cornetist Bobby Hackett's pretty tone was often utilized on mood music albums, most notably by Jackie Gleason, but he never lost his ability to play hot jazz. *Coast Concert* finds him leading a particularly strong octet that also features clarinetist Matty Matlock and both Jack Teagarden and Abe Lincoln on trombones. On nine familiar standards (including tunes such as "I Want a Big Butter and Egg Man," "Basin Street Blues," and "Struttin' With Some Barbecue"), the topnotch players inspire each other with some heated ensembles and creative solo work. One of Hackett's best sessions of the decade. —*Scott Yanow*

Live from the Voyager Room / 1956-1957 / Shoestring 108
Cornetist Bobby Hackett is best known for his association with traditional jazz bands, but during 1956-57 he led a surprisingly modern outfit that played everything from Dixie standards to Benny Golson arrangements and Bob Wilber originals. The personnel at various times included Wilber (on clarinet and soprano), baritonist Ernie Caceres doubling on clarinet, Tom Gwaltney on clarinet and vibes, and Dick Cary on piano and alto horn. Although the group did not catch on commercially, its music still sounds quite fresh and unusual today. This LP from the collector's label Shoestring, the first of two, is well worth acquiring. —*Scott Yanow*

Bobby Hackett's Jazz Band—1957 / i. Mar. 30, 1957 / Alamac 2443

The budget LP label Alamac dug up a fine aircheck from Bobby Hackett's unusual sextet of 1957. With Hackett's cornet, Tom Gwaltney on clarinet and vibes, Ernie Caceres doubling on baritone and clarinet, Dick Cary playing piano and E-flat horn, and fine backing from John Dengler's tuba and Nat Ray's drums, the band plays fresh versions of swing standards and a couple of originals from Cary. Music with more than its share of surprises. —*Scott Yanow*

Jazz Ultimate / Sep. 16-17, 1957 / Capitol 933

Bobby Hackett at the Embers / Nov. 1957 / Capitol 1077

Supper club jazz from the Bobby Hackett quartet. The music borders between solid swing and easy listening, with the accent on ballads and mellow sounds from the pretty cornet of Hackett. Nice music but not all that stimulating. —*Scott Yanow*

○ **Live From The Voyager Room, Vol. II.** / i. 1957-1958 / Shoestring SS-113

This second of two Shoestring LPs featuring cornetist Bobby Hackett's unusual group in the mid 50's has a lot of doubling of instruments from the sextet, with the earlier edition finding Bob Wilber playing clarinet, alto, soprano, tenor, and vibes; Dick Hafer switching between tenor and baritone; and Dick Cary heard on piano, alto horn, and trumpet. The later version has Tom Gwaltney on clarinet and vibes and Ernie Caceres switching between baritone and clarinet. But even more impressive than the number of instruments utilized is the range of music performed during these radio airchecks, spanning from Dixieland and some obscure swing tunes to such songs as "Whisper Not," Willie "The Lion" Smith's "Morning Aire," and Duke Ellington's "The Lady With The Lavender Hair." This group never made it commercially. Its music is well worth checking out, if you can find this LP! —*Scott Yanow*

Hawaii Swings / 1959-1960 / Capitol 1316

Because he had a very accessible tone on cornet, Bobby Hackett was in demand during the '50s and '60s for mood music albums in addition to jazz dates. This LP was one of his oddest for Hackett is heard playing a dozen Hawaiian melodies in a band that includes steel guitar, ukulele, guitar, and bongos in addition to a standard rhythm section. Fortunately, the majority of the selections are taken uptempo and Hackett has plenty of solo space to romp over the unusual backing, making this a novelty date well worth picking up. It is doubtful that it will be reissued on CD anytime in the next decade! —*Scott Yanow*

○ **Hello Louis** / Apr. 28, 1964-May 1, 1964 / Epic 26099

This Bobby Hackett album, made in tribute to his idol Louis Armstrong (and obviously recorded after "Hello Dolly" became a huge hit), is somewhat unusual. Marshall Brown's arrangements are a bit modernistic for the concept, soprano saxophonist Steve Lacy (who would soon move permanently to Europe and become a key member of the avant-garde) gets one of his few opportunities to play in a Dixielandish session, and this set of Armstrong compositions contains many obscurities. Not all of the music is successful (and none eclipses Satch's original versions) but, due to the many surprises, this is worth searching for. —*Scott Yanow*

Plays Tony Bennett's Greatest Hits / i. Jun. 22, 1966 / Epic 24220

Throughout his career, Bobby Hackett was in demand due to a wide variety of studio dates due to his highly appealing tone on cornet. He was utilized by Jackie Gleason for a series of commercially successful mood music albums and spent a period touring with Tony Bennett. In tribute to Bennett, Hackett recorded ten songs associated with the singer. Unfortunately, all of these renditions clock in at three minutes or less (making for a 28-minute LP), and none of the performances wander far from the melodies, which include such dubious material as "Put on a Happy Face," "Stranger in Paradise," and of course "I Left My Heart In San Francisco." Pass this one by! —*Scott Yanow*

○ **Creole Cookin'** / Jan. 30, 1967 / Verve 8698

This long out-of-print LP contains one of Bobby Hackett's finest all-round recordings. The cornetist is featured on 11 Dixieland standards and joined by a 15-piece all-star band arranged by Bob Wilber. Wilber and tenor great Zoot Sims also receive some solo space on this essential release which is well deserving of reissue on CD! —*Scott Yanow*

This Is Our Bag / Nov. 1968-Dec. 1968 / Project 3 3PR5034

The only recording by the group Bobby Hackett toured with for several years, this was made in New York, November-December 1968. Here Bobby Hackett presents his whole world in miniature—Dixie, modern, swing, ballad, jazz. You get his unusual choice of tunes, the magnificent palette of cornet tones, open and with various mutes, the convoluted yet graceful ballad-playing that Jackie Gleason Capitolizied, the sprightly Bixian phrasing that was at the heart of his jazz style. Bobby Hackett was at his best when he played with the best jazzmen, and in Vic Dickenson (t) he teams with one of the very best. He plays a great solo on Fats Waller's "Blue, Turning Grey Over You," sliding into notes in a style that makes the most of the slide trombone instead of fighting to be a trumpet. Yet Dickenson was also capable (although he does not do it here) of hitting notes cleanly and in a stacatto fashion that must have been an inspiration to J.J. Johnson. Bobby Hackett was noted for hiring little-known but first-rate musicians, and this version of his quartet (a rather late version) presents a rhythm section of names completely new to me who do a very tasteful job indeed—Lou Forestieri, possessed of a singing piano tone; Tito Russo, an Argentine bassist whom Hackett met in Puerto Rico (the album includes a Puerto Rican tune, "Yellow Days"); and Joe Brancato, the kind of clean, modern drummer that Hackett relished. —*Ron Anger, Coda*

Melody Is a Must: Live at the Roosevelt Grill / i. Mar. 1969-Apr. 1969 / Phontastic 7571

One of Bobby Hackett's favorite groups was the quintet he co-led with trombonist Vic Dickenson during 1969-71. Fortunately, this relatively short-lived unit made more than its share of recordings (all of them live). Hackett and Dickenson both had soft tones and fluent styles that were flexible enough to bring new life and their own brand of sly wit to these veteran songs. This LP does not duplicate any of the Chiaroscuro releases. —*Scott Yanow*

Live from Mannasas / Dec. 7, 1969 / Jazzology

This LP captures a very spirited set starring cornetist Bobby Hackett, trombonist Vic Dickenson, clarinetist Tommy Gwaltney, and singer Maxine Sullivan cut live at a jazz festival. Cornetist Wild Bill Davison and trombonist George Brunies really make the ensembles overcrowded by sitting in unexpectedly during the final two numbers. The good spirits make up for some loose moments. —*Scott Yanow*

Bobby Hackett's Sextet / Feb. 19, 1970 / Storyville 4059

This Storyville LP combines two very different sessions led by cornetist Bobby Hackett. The first side has the soundtrack from a film made for the Goodyear Tire Company in 1962 featuring Hackett, trombonist Urbie Green, clarinetist Bob Wilber, and pianist Dave McKenna in a sextet playing typical Dixieland tunes in spirited if overly concise fashion. The flip side features Hackett with trombonist Vic Dickenson in a quintet in 1970 really pushing themselves on five superior standards, including a version of "String of Pearls" on which Hackett reprises his famous solo of three decades earlier with Glenn Miller. —*Scott Yanow*

Live at Roosevelt Grill / Mar. 1970 / Chiaroscuro 179

Ignoring traditionalist imperatives, the hornmen (cornetist Bobby Hackett, trombonist Vic Dickenson) treat these tunes as they would any others—vehicles for their own unique personalities. The common meeting ground for Hackett and Dickenson was, of course, their mutual love for Louis Armstrong, but the contrast between the two is established by the varying ways they express this love. In tonal approach alone, they constitute a smartly complemented pair: the open-faced, cheerful Hackett and the frowning, sneering

Dickenson. Both were highly personal stylists from whom contemporary players could learn much. Neither has ever been guilty of excessive statement; the well-sculpted phrase, shorn of unnecessary comment, being their preferred mode of expression. Pianist Dave McKenna, bassist Jack Lesenberg, and drummer Cliff Leeman provide perfect support for the hornmen's excursions, and the absence of a reedman is scarely felt at all. —*Jack Sohmer,* Cadence

★ **Featuring Vic Dickenson at the Roosevelt Grill** / **i.** Apr. 1970 / Chiaroscuro CR 161
The Bobby Hackett-Vic Dickenson quintet of 1969-71 was one of Hackett's favorite bands of his career. The cornet-trombone front line worked together very well, as did a rhythm section led by pianist Dave McKenna. This particular LP, released long after the group had become history, differs from the previous releases in that all of the songs are Dixieland (rather than swing) favorites, but no matter; the band's sly wit and subtle creativity remain at a high level. —*Scott Yanow*

○ **Strike Up the Band** / **i.** 1972 / Flying Dutchman 10829
Cornetist Bobby Hackett recorded many excellent performances throughout his life; this LP is one of the more rewarding of his later years. Hackett is teamed successfully with tenor saxophonist Zoot Sims and guitarist Bucky Pizzarelli in a frequently exciting sextet. High points include the uptempo "Strike Up The Band," a revisit to "Embraceable You" (Hackett had cut a famous solo on that standard 34 years earlier!), and a variety of standards and basic originals. A consistently stimulating and enjoyable set well deserving of reissue on CD. —*Scott Yanow*

What a Wonderful World / 1973 / CBS 40234
One of Bobby Hackett's last studio albums. The cornetist is heard in fine form with three different units ranging from 7 to 15 pieces. Teresa Brewer's three vocals are typically unfortunate; but Hackett, trombonist Vic Dickenson, and clarinetist Johnny Mince keep the music (dominated by Dixieland standards) swinging. —*Scott Yanow*

CHARLIE HADEN (Charles Edward Haden)

b. Aug. 6, 1937, Shenandoah, IL
Bass / Early free, modern creative
A great bassist during the '60s whose star shines just as brightly in the '90s, Charlie Haden has been a marvelous player and a committed, articulate champion of social causes and oppressed minorities, musical and otherwise. His technique combines "folk" elements like pedal tones and insistent double-stop chording (similar to country and blues guitarists) with stunning strummed, plucked, and bowed solos. Haden keeps his playing consistently simple, yet creatively stimulating. He can carry, lead, or support a tune with equal flair, and has long been involved in Latin and South American causes. He's also worked with the Jazz Composers Orchestra and other nonprofit musician cooperatives, and has helped expose and publicize great composers and players through his sessions and long-running Liberation Music Orchestra.
Haden got his start playing in a family band in the Midwest, then earned his jazz reputation in Los Angeles working with Art Pepper, Paul Bley, and Hampton Hawes in the late '50s. He moved to New York in 1959 to play with Ornette Coleman. Haden later became a member of Denny Zeitlin's trio, and worked with several free players, among them Archie Shepp. He recorded with Coleman in the '60s, and was part of Keith Jarrett's band with Dewey Redman and Paul Motian that recorded several albums for Impulse. Haden began his Liberation Music Orchestra in 1969, playing and performing revolutionary and freedom songs while integrating jazz elements into their performances. Haden worked with Carla Bley and the Jazz Composers Orchestra in the late '60s, then collaborated and played with Gato Barbieri on the soundtrack for *Last Tango in Paris* in 1972. He played and recorded with Cherry, Bley, and others during the '70s. Haden, Cherry, Dewey Redman, and Edward Blackwell, all former Coleman bandmates, formed Old and

New Dreams in the late '70s. He also made some superb albums for Artists House, cutting duets with Hampton Hawes and Coleman, among others. Haden recorded another duet project with guitarist Christian Escoude on the All Life label, and did other sessions for ECM. He continued performing and recording in the '80s with a new version of the Liberation Music Orchestra. He made trio sessions with Geri Allen and Paul Motian, and Egberto Gismonti and Jan Garbarek. Haden formed a new quartet in 1986 with Billy Higgins, Ernie Watts, and Alan Broadbent. This group has recorded several highly praised albums as Quartet West (Lawrence Marable eventually replaced Higgins). Haden did additional duets in the '90s with Carlos Paraedes, and another trio session, this time with Higgins and Enrico Pieranunzi. Currently, he has several titles available on CD. —*Ron Wynn and Myles Boisen*

★ **Liberation Music Orchestra** / 1969 / MCA 39125
One of the few message/protest jazz vehicles that works on every level. It has brilliant compositions, arrangements, playing, and lineup, plus passionate material. Recently reissued on MCA. —*Ron Wynn*

○ **As Long As There's Music** / Jan. 25, 1976 / Artists House 4
This duo date by bassist Charlie Haden and pianist Hampton Hawes was done in two studio sessions on January 25 and August 21, 1976, when Hawes returned from commercialism. Of course it isn't like the old days, but he has that bluesy feel on "Irene"; and "What Is This Thing" returns him to his bop roots. "Hello/Goodbye" is spontaneous and gives both players complete freedom. With Haden you have to expect much out-of-tempo playing and such harmonic complexity that Hawes seldom plays behind him. There is no real way to predict where he is going. This does require serious listening and if that doesn't bother you, then you'll find a lot of beauty and rapport here. —*Jerry L. Atkins,* Cadence

★ **Closeness** / Jan. 26, 1976+Mar. 21, 1976 / A&M 710
This one is absolutely essential. One duet apiece with Ornette Coleman (sax), Alice Coltrane (p), Keith Jarrett (p), and Paul Motian (d). —*Michael G. Nastos*

Golden Number / Dec. 19, 1976 / A&M 0825
Superb album featuring bassist Charlie Haden in various duet situations, each one a gem. The guest list includes Ornette Coleman, Hampton Hawes, and Don Cherry. It was issued on John Synder's Artist House, a treasured label that went defunct; thus far few CDs have appeared. —*Ron Wynn*

Gitane / Sep. 22, 1978 / ALL LIFE 001
The American bassist meets Gypsy guitarist Christian Escoude. —*Michael G. Nastos*

Magico / Jun. 1979 / ECM 823474
With Egberto Gismonti and Jan Garbarek. Outstanding trio work on this reunion of the group that made the superb *Folk Songs* in 1979. —*Ron Wynn*

Folk Songs / Nov. 1979 / ECM 827705

★ **Quartet West** / **i.** Dec. 22-23, 1986 / Verve 831673
Fine quartet material, with Ernie Watts (d) far more aggressive and animated than usual. —*Ron Wynn*

Etudes / **i.** 1987 / Soul Note 121162

In Angel City / Jun. 1988 / Verve 837031
Charlie Haden Quartet West. This is a solid session, with the undervalued Lawrence Marable on drums. Ernie Watts (reeds) does his best playing with Haden. —*Ron Wynn*

Dream Keeper / Apr. 4-5, 1990 / Blue Note

○ **First Song** / **i.** Apr. 1990 / Soul Note 1222

Dialogues / **i.** 1991 / Antilles 849309
Jazz bassist Haden meets Portuguese guitarist Paredes. Stangely beautiful. —*Michael G. Nastos*

○ **Haunted Heart** / 1992 / Verve 513078
Bassist Charlie Haden, always among the finest accompanists around, has become a first-rate bandleader as well with his Quartet West. The lineup, with tenor saxophonist Ernie Watts, pianist Alan Broadbent, and drummer Lawrence

Marable makes cooperative, stunning sessions in which each player expresses himself fully, yet never destroys the group balance. That's the key on their recent release, which mixes vocal inserts by guest singers taken from classic films and supported by their playing. —*Ron Wynn*

SHAFI HADI (Curtis Porter)

b. 1929
Alto saxophone / Bop
A soulful, solid tenor and alto saxophonist in an R&B, bebop, and hard bop mode, the former Curtis Porter had a brief period in the limelight, primarily when he played with Charles Mingus in the late '50s. His bright, spirited solos, which combined bebop and blues influences, were featured on Mingus releases such as *Tijuana Moods* and *The Clown*, and in the John Cassavetes's film *Shadows*. Hadi also played with Hank Mobley. His earlier career was spent with R&B groups such as the Griffin Brothers, and in a band led by Paul Williams. Hadi studied composition at Howard University and the University of Detroit. He's been inactive since the '60s, but can be heard on Mingus reissues. —*Ron Wynn*

AL HAIG (Allan Warren Haig)

b. Jul. 22, 1924, Newark, NJ, **d.** Nov. 16, 1982, New York, NY
Piano / Bop
A sorely underrated, overlooked pianist for much of his life, Al Haig was one of the earliest players to master bop's techniques and to forge his own style. Though not in Bud Powell's league, Haig had first-rate skills. His flexibility and harmonic knowledge enabled him to respond quickly and inventively regardless of tempo. He was a masterful accompanist, who played with everyone from Charlie Parker to Fats Navarro to Stan Getz. While he seldom got much space, he crammed decisive ideas and statements into concise, crisp solos.

Haig played in coast guard bands during the early '40s, then worked with several Boston groups before joining Dizzy Gillespie's band in 1945. He was soon a fixture on 52nd street, playing in many different groups. Besides Parker and Gillespie, Haig played with Charlie Barnet and Fats Navarro. There were sessions for Prestige, and dates with Stan Getz, Wardell Gray, Coleman Hawkins, John Hardee, Zoot Sims, and Allen Eager. He played with Getz, Gray, and Chet Baker during the '50s, but wound up essentially frozen out of the recording and playing scene in a situation that remains among the most controversial in modern jazz history. Haig is one of the players around whom the "Crow Jim" controversy eventually emerged. As a White player who'd been generally accepted during bebop's early days, Haig found he wasn't able to get opportunities during the '50s and the '60s with many Black bandleaders. Many White critics maintained that this was simply "reverse" racism, while Black observers said these claims were exaggerated and were a move towards racial solidarity and towards ensuring chances for Black musicians in an establishment still totally controlled by Whites.

Regardless of the reasons, Haig's unplanned obscurity robbed him of some productive years, and was a unfortunate, unfair situation out of his control. Happily, when he returned to recording in the mid '70s his skills hadn't diminished. A nice 1974 trio date with Kenny Clarke and guitarist Jimmy Raney, plus a series of records on Trio, Seabreeze, Inner City, Interplay, Musica, and Spotlite reaffirmed Haig's prowess. He cut duets and solos and played acoustic and electric piano, Ellington and Jerome Kern compositions, and bop anthems and originals. There were more Al Haig albums recorded and issued between 1974 and his 1982 death than were recorded during the combined rest of his professional career. Many are still available, while his classic accompaniment on Parker, Gillespie, and Gray albums provides positive proof that excellence has no color. —*Ron Wynn*

○ **Al Haig Meets the Master Saxes—Vol. 1** / **i.** 1948 / Spotlite 139

○ **Al Haig Meets the Master Saxes—Vol. 2** / **i.** 1948 / Spotlite 140

○ **Al Haig Meets the Master Saxes—Vol. 3** / **i.** 1948-1951 / Spotlite 1430

○ **Piano Moderns** / Feb. 27, 1950 / Prestige 175

○ **Al Haig Trio and Quintet** / Mar. 13, 1954 / Prestige 7841
Trio and quartet sessions from the final period before pianist Al Haig would drop out of the jazz scene for several years. These dates are quite uneven, as would be expected, almost mirroring the difference between when Haig was physically functioning and when he wasn't. —*Ron Wynn*

○ **Al Haig Trio** / Mar. 13, 1954 / Esoteric 7

○ **Special Brew** / **i.** Nov. 1974 / Spotlite 8

Strings Attached / May 1976 / Choice 1010
A stalwart early bopper, pianist Al Haig returned to the recording spotlight briefly in the mid '70s with this set that could just as easily have been made in the '40s. Haig's fluidity and ability to navigate blistering passages and make the appropriate chord changes enabled him to survive the turbulent bop era; those skills are now second nature, as he shows with some crisp, rippling solos throughout the album. —*Ron Wynn*

Piano Interpretation / Jun. 21, 1976 / Sea Breeze 1001
A fine solo piano set from 1976, with Al Haig displaying the total technical package on standards and bop anthems. He plays some rapid-fire; others, he slowly, carefully constructs, then tears down and rebuilds the theme, with nicely executed, intricate solos. —*Ron Wynn*

Piano Time / Jun. 21, 1976 / Sea Breeze 1006
The second of two solo piano albums Al Haig made in 1976, both done with exacting precision as well as exuberant force. Haig was disproving the critics who said he was finished, and he shows convincingly that there was still plenty of power in his hands and lots of tricks up his sleeve. —*Ron Wynn*

○ **Interplay** / Nov. 16, 1976 / Sea Breeze 1005
Fine duets featuring pianist Al Haig during a busy period in the mid '70s. He'd overcome personal problems and was cranking out albums left and right for both domestic and foreign labels. These were cut for Interplay, a small West Coast firm, but then were mostly issued in Japan. They are excellent examples of Haig's surging bop style. —*Ron Wynn*

○ **Ornithology** / Jul. 22, 1977 / Progressive 7024

★ **Stablemates** / **i.** Sep. 1977 / Spotlite 11

☆ **I Remember Bebop** / Nov. 3-5, 1977 / Columbia 235381

○ **Expressly Ellington** / **i.** Oct. 1978 / Spotlite 20

Al Haig Plays (Music of Jerome Kern) / 1978 / Inner City 1073
A '78 showpiece for a bop legend. Pianist Al Haig was around during the idiom's early days, playing often with Charlie Parker, Miles Davis, and others, but drug problems reared their head. Haig missed several years during the '50s and '60s but made a stunning return to the playing arena in the '70s. This is one of his most expressive and finely performed sessions among the many he made in the mid and late '70s. —*Ron Wynn*

○ **Bebop Live** / **i.** May 1982 / Spotlite 23

EDMOND HALL

b. May 15, 1901, New Orleans, LA, **d.** Feb. 11, 1967, Boston, MA
Clarinet / New Orleans traditional
An outstanding clarinetist famed for his exuberant, rough-edged solos, Edmond Hall also played baritone sax, and was part of a musical family in New Orleans. His brothers included clarinetist Herbie Hall and saxophonist Clarence Hall, who played, at one time, with Fats Domino. His father, Edward Hall, was a member of the Onward Brass Band. Hall

worked in several New Orleans bands, among them groups led by Jack Carey, Lee Collins, and Kid Thomas, before coming to New York in 1928. He began working with Claude Hopkins in 1930, and remained with him until 1935. Hall joined Red Allen's band in 1940, then played with Teddy Wilson's sextet in 1941 and was featured on their radio broadcasts and recordings of the period. He recorded for Blue Note in the early and mid '40s, and had his own group from 1944 to 1946. This band had a residency at Cafe Society. He later spent four years in Boston before joining Eddie Condon in 1950. Hall played with Condon until 1955, then joined Louis Armstrong's All-Stars, where he worked from 1955 to 1958. He returned to Condon's band in 1960, and stayed with him until his death in 1967. Another in the long line of outstanding Mosaic sets, the four-disc/six album *The Complete Edmond Hall/James P. Johnson/Sidney De Paris/Vic Dickenson Blue Note Sessions* features Hall's finest dates for Blue Note. —*Ron Wynn*

☆ **Complete Edmond Hall/James P. Johnson/Sidney De Paris/Vic Dickenson Blue Note Sessions,** / Mosaic 109

○ **Celestial Express** / Feb. 5, 1941-Jan. 25, 1944 / Blue Note 6505

○ **Jamming in Jazz Hall** / Nov. 29, 1943 / Blue Note 7007

★ **Original Blue Note Jazz—Vol. 1** / Nov. 29, 1943 / Blue Note 6504

○ **Edmond Hall in Copenhagen** / i. Dec. 1966 / Storyville 6022

JIM HALL (James Stanley Hall)

b. Dec. 4, 1930, Buffalo, NY
Guitar / Cool

A sensitive, versatile guitarist equally gifted in solo, trio, or larger combo settings, Jim Hall has been a dynamic jazz contributor since the '50s. His playing reflects the influences of Django Reinhardt and Charlie Christian, and features blues-tinged solos, carefully crafted statements, and a rich, full tone and sound. His harmonic and rhythmic subtlety, achieved without sacrificing swing or intensity, are legendary. Hall began his professional career in as a teen in Cleveland, then attended the Cleveland Institute of Music. After moving to Los Angeles and studying classical guitar with Vincente Gomez, Hall joined Chico Hamilton's quintet in the mid '50s. He was in Jimmy Giuffre's Three from 1956 to 1959, and made his recording debut as a leader in 1957. Hall made several sessions for Pacific Jazz and Pausa in the '60s. He worked extensively in the late '50s and into the mid '60s, though he was also encountering severe problems with alcohol. There were sessions with Ben Webster, the masterpiece *Undercurrents* with Bill Evans, and a stint with Ella Fitzgerald in 1960 and 1961. Hall recorded several frequently with Paul Desmond, and worked with Lee Konitz, Sonny Rollins, and Art Farmer. He played in the "The Merv Griffin Show" studio band, worked with Evans again, and made some excellent duo records with Ron Carter. In the '70s, '80s, and '90s, Hall has divided his time between leading groups and doing sessions. He recorded for CTI, Milestone, Horizon, Artists House, and A&M (Japan) in the '70s, then recorded mostly for Concord in the '80s. He's recorded for MusicMasters in the '90s. Mosaic issued a comprehensive boxed set of his recordings with Desmond in 1987. His early Pacific Jazz recordings, and much of his work with Rollins, has been reissued on CD. Some of the CTI, Fantasy, and Milestone dates have been reissued on CD, too. The Concord and MusicMasters sessions remain in print. —*Ron Wynn and David Nelson McCarthy*

○ **Jazz Guitar** / Jan. 10+24, 1957 / Pacific Jazz 1227
Topflight session. Features a brilliant Carl Perkins (p). Hall is a marvel on guitar. —*Ron Wynn*

Good Friday Blues / Apr. 2, 1960 / Pacific

Guitar Workshop / Nov. 5, 1967 / PA/USA

Where Would I Be? / Jul. 1971 / Milestone 649

★ **Alone Together** / Aug. 4, 1972 / Milestone 467

Concierto / Apr. 1975 / Columbia 40807
A beautiful session, one of the few CTI albums to have a lasting impact. The title cut is a masterpiece. Chet Baker (tpt), Paul Desmond (as), Sir Roland Hanna (p), and Hall are majestic. —*Ron Wynn*

★ **Jim Hall Live!** / Apr. 1976 / Horizon 705
Jim Hall is a musician's musician. His Hall-mark is a terse, witty combination of large chords and pithy single-note lines, given life by an incredibly rich, warm sound. In the company of two fine Canadian musicians—bassist Don Thompson and drummer Terry Clarke—Hall's playing has an exuberance and energy that is somewhat of a departure from his usually more introspective orientation. Listen, for example, to the high intensity of "Scrapple from the Apple." The individual forays meld together in an exciting set of constantly developing episodes. One immediately senses the musicians' warm respect for one another and their desire to communicate with other, the audience at the club, and us. —*Chuck Berg,* Down Beat

Commitment / Jun. 1, 1976-Jul. 1, 1976 / A&M 0811
A sterling reissue of a beautiful album, with only pianist Don Thompson. —*Ron Wynn*

Jim Hall and Red Mitchell / Jan. 20-21, 1978 / Artists House

Concierto De Aranjue / Jan. 18, 1981 / Evidence 22004
Jim Hall's warm, fluid guitar and full tones are the anchor for this good but often unexciting session pairing him with the David Matthews orchestra. Hall has recorded the title track on two other occasions; this third version is nicely orchestrated and produced, and Hall's solo is superbly played but adds little to the earlier interpretations. The other numbers include a fine rendition and arrangement of "El Condor Pasa," a lyrical performance of Hall's "Chorale & Dance," and effective solos on "Red Dragon Fly" and "Summerwaltz." The orchestra is wisely kept from getting in Hall's way, and his guitar lines are bright, sometimes arresting, and frequently dazzling. What is missing is the inventive spark and extra dimension Hall usually injects into his material. When these tracks were originally cut in 1981, Hall had been away from the studio for three years. It took him a while to rediscover the extra dimension that separates a good session from a great one. —*Ron Wynn*

Circles / Mar. 1981 / Concord Jazz 4161

These Rooms / Feb. 1988 / Denon 2297

○ **Live at Town Hall—Vols. 1 and 2** / i. Jun. 26, 1990 / Music Masters 5050

CHICO HAMILTON (Forestorn Hamilton)

b. Sep. 21, 1921, Los Angeles, CA
Drums / Cool

A topflight, innovative accompanist and percussionist, Chico Hamilton has also been an amazing talent scout, and has incorporated unusual instrumentation into his bands. His playing style, with its light accents and less intense, though equally authoritative rhythms, anchored both "chamber" type groups and more emphatic, bluesier ensembles. He often devised totally different rhythms and timbres for each piece.

Hamilton started on clarinet, and played in high school in the Los Angeles area with Buddy Collette, Dexter Gordon, Ernie Royal, Illinois Jacquet, and Charles Mingus. He did his first recording with the duo of Slim Gaillard and Slam Stewart and served as house drummer at Billy Berg's Hollywood club. Following tours with Lionel Hampton and Lester Young, plus studies with Jo Jones and army service, Hamilton became Lena Horne's regular drummer. He played with her from the late '40s into the mid '50s, and was a member of Gerry Mulligan's original "pianoless" quartet in 1952. He did early '50s studio work, playing on the soundtrack for the Bob Hope and Bing Crosby film *The Road To Bali.* Hamilton's own quintets in the '50s and '60s either introduced to the jazz public or helped make stars of such notables as Eric Dolphy, Charles Lloyd, and Larry Coryell. Hamilton used cello extensively, and sometimes pitted a woodwinds/guitar frontline against a bass/drums rhythm section with no brass or piano. He often inserted a cello into this mix as well. The light, lush, and sentimental sound struck a chord with the public, and Hamilton's groups were featured in the films *The Sweet Smell of Success* and the acclaimed *Jazz On A Summer's Day* account of the 1958 Newport Jazz Festival. He recorded for World Pacific and for Warner Brothers in the '50s.

Hamilton revamped his sound in the '60s, replacing the cello with a trombone and playing a harder-edged style. There were sessions for Columbia, Reprise, Impulse, and Solid State in the '60s, and he worked with Lloyd, Gabor Szabo, Coryell, Charlie Mariano, and Carter. Hamilton established a 9-piece band in the late '60s with four trombonists and a vocalist. He entered a new phase in the mid '60s, establishing Chico Hamilton Productions in New York and composing music for advertisements. Hamilton ventured into jazz-rock and fusion in the '70s and '80s, cutting dates for Flying Dutchman, Blue Note, Nautilus, and Elektra. He continued his pattern of helping introduce and/or establish fresh talent, and gave Arthur Blythe (then known as Black Arthur) substantial exposure on *Peregrinations* and *Chico Hamilton And the Players*. His late '80s and '90s Soul Note dates are more in the slashing early-'60s vein, and feature alto saxophonist Eric Person. A moderate amount of Hamilton material from the '50s and '60s is available, along with his newer releases on Soul Note. —*Ron Wynn*

With Gerry Mulligan / i. 1952 / Fantasy 8082

Chico Hamilton Quintet with Buddy Collette / Aug. 4, 1955 / Pacific Jazz 1209

Sweet Smell of Success, The / Jun. 17, 1957 / Decca 8641

○ **The Chico Hamilton Quintet with Strings Attached** / Oct. 26-27, 1958 / Warner Brothers 1245

Gongs East / Dec. 29-30, 1958 / Discovery 831
This Chico Hamilton date, originally released on Warner Bros., has become somewhat of a collector's item because of the presence of Eric Dolphy (as, f, bcl). I am a great fan of Dolphy and to a lesser extent Chico Hamilton (d), but found the recording only of historical interest. I feel Chico Hamilton overreaches a bit, the date seems too calculated, almost an inflexible caricature of the controlled mood jazz he worked successfully at in the early '50s. In addition, the use of gong throughout the date is totally unswinging and ungraceful. Dolphy's role here is mainly on flute and it doesn't show his great individualism, sounding closer to Buddy Collette. The occasional use of bass clarinet will satisfy those looking for (earlier) established Dolphy styles. Dennis Budmir, an exciting guitarist of the time, is also pretty much hobbled by the structure, while Nathan Gershman fills the usual Hamilton cello capacity as expected. —*Bob Rusch*, Cadence

Featuring Eric Dolphy / i. Dec. 1958-May 1959 / Fresh Sound

○ **Chico Hamilton Special, The** / Nov. 29-30, 1960 / Columbia 1619

Drumfusion / Feb. 19, 1962 / Columbia 8607

★ **Passin' Thru** / Sep. 18+20, 1962 / Impulse
One of Hamilton's best groups, with Charles Lloyd (reeds) and Gabor Szabo (g). —*Ron Wynn*

○ **Different Journey, A** / Jan. 19-31, 1963 / Reprise 6078

Man from Two Worlds / Dec. 11, 1963 / GRP 127

El Chico / Aug. 26-27, 1965 / Impulse 9102

Further Adventures of El Chico, The / May 2, 1966 / Impulse

★ **Dealer, The** / Sep. 9, 1966 / MCA 39137
This groundbreaking session heralded the coming of jazz-rock in 1966 and introduced Larry Coryell (g) to the jazz world. —*Ron Wynn*

Peregrinations / 1975 / Blue Note
Not always high-caliber material, but the group gets a boost from then largely unknown Arthur Blythe. —*Ron Wynn*

○ **Reunion** / Jun. 1989 / Soul Note 1191
This 1989 date by the original Chico Hamilton Quintet recreates the unique chemistry of the pianoless quintet Hamilton led from '55 to '61. Fred Katz's bowed cello adds an intriguing texture, while John Pisano, who replaced Jim Hall in the second edition of the original quintet, plays the elegant, fluid plectorist. But the real standout is Buddy Collette, who blows velvety alto ("Ain't Nobody Calling Me"), pungent clarinet ("Delightful, Charming And Cool"), and brisk flute lines ("Magali"). The improvised duets between Hamilton and Collette on "Brushing With B" and "Conversation" are classic examples of listening and reacting. High point is the daring group improv "Five Friends." — *Bill Milkowski*, Down Beat

Arroyo / Dec. 1990 / Soul Note 121241
An excellent recent release for this drummer and the quartet Euphoria, including two standards and four of Hamilton's earthy and electric numbers on the eight cuts. This is easily recommended. —*Michael G. Nastos*

JIMMY HAMILTON (James Hamilton)

b. May 25, 1917, Dillon, SC
Clarinet / Swing, big band
A superb clarinet technician and an excellent soloist, Jimmy Hamilton doesn't use much vibrato but offers cool, beautiful displays in a smooth, sophisticated manner. His approach is the opposite of the intense, vocalized, and exuberant New Orleans clarinet school, but is equally effective. Inspired by Benny Goodman, Hamilton was a principle soloist for the Ellington band, played tenor sax in the ensemble, and was featured on Ellington's Bethlehem and Columbia recordings from 1956 to 1959. Hamilton began as a brass player, then switched to reed instruments. He played with Lucky Millinder and Teddy Wilson before joining Duke Ellington in 1943. Hamilton remained with Ellington for 25 years. He was featured on such numbers as "The Mooche," "V.I.P.'s Boogie," and "Flippant Flurry." When Hamilton left Ellington's band, he led his own group for a while, then relocated to the Virgin Islands. He continued playing and teaching, and worked with Mercer Ellington in the early '80s. Hamilton joined Alvin Batiste, John Carter, and David Murray to form Clarinet Summit, one of the more unusual and exciting units of the '80s. They recorded for India Navigation, and later for Black Saint in the late '80s. Hamilton's own dates were done for Blue Note, Prestige, Urania, and Who's Who, among others. Currently, Hamilton has releases as a leader available on CD. The Clarinet Summit sessions are also available on CD. —*Ron Wynn and Michael G. Nastos*

★ **Benny Morton and Jimmy Hamilton Blue Note Swingtets** / Mosaic

★ **Swing Low Sweet Clarinet** / Jul. 1960 / Everest 5100

SCOTT HAMILTON

b. Sep. 12, 1954, Providence, RI
Tenor saxophone / Swing, bop
Much as Wynton Marsalis captured the imagination of critics and triggered debate about the impact of his looking backward rather than forward, Scott Hamilton generated intense scrutiny and discussion during the late '70s with his vintage swing sound. At first, Hamilton seemed totally under Ben Webster's spell, right down to the formation and choices of notes. But Hamilton slowly and steadily developed his own nuances, phrasing, and mannerisms, and while the Webster influence will always be there, he's much more than a faithful recreation. Stan Getz became one of Hamilton's later inspirations. Hamilton began playing at age 16 and moved to New York in 1976. He played with Chris Flory, Chuck Riggs, Phil Flanigan, John Bunch, and Warren Vache. He and Vache maintained their relationship through the '80s and into the '90s, while Hamilton worked with other musicians on various occasions. Hamilton played with Benny Goodman and Rosemary Clooney in the late '70s and with

Woody Herman in the '80s. He worked with Ruby Braff from the early '80s into the '90s, and also played with the Concord Jazz All-Stars, Concord Superband, and the Newport Jazz Festival All-Stars. Hamilton's recorded as a leader for Progressive and Concord. He has several sessions available on CD. —*Ron Wynn*

○ **Good Wind Who Is Blowing Us No Ill** / Mar. 1, 1977 / Concord Jazz 4042

Tenor saxophonist Scott Hamilton's 1977 debut as a leader astounded the jazz world at the time. Unlike the '80s and '90s generation, whose muses are '50s hard boppers, Hamilton took his inspiration from the lusty swing sound of the '30s, Coleman Hawkins particularly, but also Ben Webster and Lester Young. —*Ron Wynn*

Scott Hamilton / Jan. 7, 1978 / Concord Jazz 61

Good follow-up to his first album as a leader. Another straightahead swing-influenced session, with Hamilton blowing fierce uptempo tunes one minute, then swaggering, soulful ballads the next. He was still heavily under the spell of Coleman Hawkins and Ben Webster at this time but slowly finding his own voice. —*Ron Wynn*

○ **Scott Hamilton and Warren Vache (With Scott's Band in New York)** / Jun. 26, 1978 / Concord Jazz 70

Despite the fact that this is a Scott Hamilton-Warren Vache album, the standouts are trombonist George Masso and Vache (c, flhn). Everyone is given several solo opportunities except Harold Ashby (ts), Phil Flanagan (b), and Chuck Riggs (d). Masso has three turns in the spotlight, all of them outstanding. The best of the three is "Nancy's Fancy," but he is also the standout on "Lightly and Politely" and "Love You Madly." He also contributes three of the arrangements, while Nat Pierce does the remaining in his Count Basieish approach. Warren Vache works himself into a corner on "Cadillac Taxi" but manages to extricate himself at the *nth* instant. He's at his best on "Nancy's Fancy" and "Do It in Blue." Scott Hamilton (tenor) approaches his best on "You Leave Me Breathless" (this one is his alone) and "Lightly and Politely." He is good elsewhere as well, but I've heard him better. The remaining soloists are Joe Temperley (bs), Norman Simmons (p), and Chris Flory (g). All three have their good moments, but none of them match Masso or Vache on this day. —*Shirley Klett*, Cadence

Back to Back / Sep. 1978 / Concord Jazz 85

This session has an excellent "All Of Me" and fine support from pianist Nat Pierce, bassist Monty Budwig, and drummer Chuck Riggs. Chuck Riggs has a particularly good session here. Tenor saxophonists Buddy Tate and Scott Hamilton frequently have appeared together, and it seems to me that a location recording might result in an exceptional LP, as this pair quite frequently catch fire in a personal appearance. At any rate, this is a good album in fine sound—you can even hear Tate urging Hamilton on, here and there, with a well-placed "Yeah!" —*Shirley Klett*, Cadence

★ **Scott's Buddy** / Aug. 1980 / Concord Jazz 148

Tenor saxophonists Scott Hamilton and Buddy Tate played together for several years whenever an engagement came up which both were able to fit into their schedules. This LP was recorded directly after one such engagement in Los Angeles. "Everything Happens to Me" is all Tate's, while "I Want A Little Girl" is all Hamilton's. Tate was still recuperating at this time from severe burns on his hands due to an encounter with excessively hot water, but you wouldn't know it to hear him. Here it sounds like Hamilton had switched to a harder reed and is also experimenting with the use of space. At any rate, this is a good solid session of swing tenor saxophone, with plenty of solo space for both men, plus Nat Pierce's piano, as well as a number of opportunities for chase sequences. One thing which characterized encounters between these two was their sense of fun and good humor, and both are present here in abundance. —*Shirley Klett*, Cadence

Apples and Oranges / Jan. 1981+Aug. 1981 / Concord Jazz 165

Tenor saxophonist Scott Hamilton's work, as effortless as it always sounds, still smacks of midnight oil and preciosity. There is simply too much posture and persona in it to convey all of the truths that the jazz language demands. Certainly his sculpted sound speaks far more in its selectivity of nuance than the roaring bravado of others, but it has never quite encompassed even a small portion of its potential expressiveness. This LP is on a par with his previous ones. The rhythm section (pianist Jimmy Rowles, bassists Bob Maize or George Mraz, drummers Jake Hanna or Joe LaBarbera) is appropriately sympathetic throughout. —*Jack Sohmer*, Cadence

Close Up / Feb. 1982 / Concord Jazz 4197

Scott Hamilton Quintet in Concert / Jun. 1983 / Concord Jazz 4233

Second Set / Jun. 1983 / Concord Jazz 4254

○ **Major League** / May 1986 / Concord Jazz 4305

A baseball motif underlines this good set in which Dave McKenna (p) and Jake Hanna (d) share the spotlight with Hamilton. —*Ron Wynn*

★ **Scott Hamilton Plays Ballads** / Mar. 1989 / Concord Jazz 4386

This is a refreshing album not only for the Scott Hamilton tenor sax, but because the ballads are far from the usual, "In a Sentimental Mood" excepted. Even the latter Duke Ellington title is not recorded all that often. "Two Eighteen" is a Hamilton original, the title referring to his wife's birthday—the liners remark that it is *not* built upon a preexisting chord structure. Nevertheless, listeners may well find the chord structure reminiscent of one well-liked standard. The personnel is Scott's original group plus John Bunch, who has worked with Hamilton group on many occasions. Accordingly, this is a very well knit quintet that works together as one. While the major soloist is the leader, both Bunch and guitarist Chris Flory contribute strong solo statements on more than one title. I found this a most enjoyable album and recommend it without reservation. —*Shirley Klett*, Cadence

Radio City / Feb. 1990 / Concord Jazz 4428

With fine contributions from Dennis Irwin (b). The CD version has two bonus tracks. —*Ron Wynn*

All-Star Tenor Spectacular / Progressive 7019

JAN HAMMER (Jan (Jr) Hammer)

b. Apr. 17, 1948, Prague, Czechoslovakia
Keyboards, composer / Early jazz-rock, world fusion, modern creative

One of the most popular keyboard and synthesizer players during the early days of jazz-rock, Jan Hammer enjoyed fame in a combo and as the primary and theme composer for the television show "Miami Vice." Hammer has shown the ability to turn his electronic instruments into wide-ranging, intriguing, and ambitious musical weapons, rather than merely a collection of knobs and devices. His spiraling solos were a vital part of the original Mahavishnu Orchestra's inspired blend of rock energy and jazz sophistication, as he teamed with Mahavishnu John McLaughlin, Billy Cobham, Rick Laird, and Jerry Goodman in one of the great, pure jazz-rock bands. Originally influenced by Bill Evans, Hammer studied piano and drums as a child, and played in a trio with Alan and Miroslav Vitous during his high school years in Prague. Hammer studied classical composition and piano at the Prague Conservatory and won an international music competition and scholarship to Berklee in 1966. He left Czechoslovakia for America in 1968, following the Soviet invasion. He worked with Sarah Vaughan and Jeremy Steig in the early '70s before meeting McLaughlin. After the original Mahavishnu orchestra disbanded, Hammer played with Cobham's Spectrum band. He began heading his own bands, and co-led a group with Jeff Beck in 1976. Hammer continued working with Beck into the '80s, and toured and recorded with Al Di Meola. He later enjoyed fame as the first composer for the television show "Miami Vice." Hammer's recorded for Nemperor, Miramar, MCA, and Epic as a leader. He has selections available on CD. —*Ron Wynn*

Make Love / **i.** Aug. 30, 1968 / MPS
An album with a wonderful title and an excellent example of real jazz-rock. —*Ron Wynn*

Early Years / **i.** 1974-1979 / Nemperor 40382
A comprehensive compilation of Hammer's best cuts from the '70s. —*Ron Wynn*

Like Children / **i.** 1974 / Atlantic 50092
The keyboardist and violinist Jerry Goodman away from Mahavishnu. They play all instruments (overdubbed). "Country and Eastern Music" and "Steppings Tones" are high-water marks for this new breed (at the time). —*Michael G. Nastos*

★ **Oh Yeah** / **i.** 1976 / Nemperor 50276
This is an album of fusion at its best. "Magical Dog" and "Red & Orange" are definitive statements. This was the first exposure for violinist Steve Kindler. David Earle Johnson is on congas. —*Michael G. Nastos*

Live / **i.** 1977 / Columbia

Escape from Television / **i.** 1986 / MCA 42103
When first seen on TV, "Miami Vice" was known as much for the music as the stylish action-packed plots. The man behind the music was Jan Hammer, a well-established rock and jazz-fusion player with experience that includes Jeff Beck, John McLaughlin, and Jerry Goodman as bandmates and collaborators. On *Escape* a very strong style of current instrumental music can be found, with the edge of rock music and the smooth, spacey appeal of some of the more progressive new age musicians. Two of the cuts ("The Trial and the Search" and "Rum Cay") are often heard on Musical Starstreams. The CD has one extra cut. —*Backroads Music/Heartbeats*

GUNTER HAMPEL (Gunther Hampel)

b. Aug. 31, 1937, Gottingen, Germany
Vibes, clarinet, saxophone, flute, piano, composer / Progressive big band, modern creative
Gunter Hampel is a genuine multi-instrumentalist who plays vibes, clarinet, bass clarinet, flutes, piano, and various saxophones. He's also a composer and bandleader. Hampel's performed numerous free sessions, and has written music for films. He's best known for a series of recordings and duets with musicians including Anthony Braxton and vocalist Jeanne Lee (who is also his wife). His compositions range from introspective and abstract to intense, and usually feature many collectively improvised sections. Hampel studied music and architecture, and began heading his own band in 1958, touring Europe and Germany. During the '60s, he turned to free music almost exclusively, and toured, for the Goethe Institute, in Africa, Asia, and South America. Hampel founded Birth Records in 1969, and started the Galaxie Dreams Band in the early '70s. He performed solo concerts at the 1972 Munich Olympic Games and at that year's Berlin Jazz Festival. Hampel has recorded several albums on Birth, among them sessions with Braxton, Willem Breuker, Enrico Rava, and other European and American free musicians. They can be obtained on CD through mail order or from international sources. —*Ron Wynn*

★ **All the Things You Could Be If Charles Mingus Was Your Daddy** / **i.** Jul. 1980 / Birth 0031

○ **Fresh Heat: Live at Sweet Basil** / Feb. 1985 / Birth 39

LIONEL HAMPTON

b. Apr. 12, 1909, Louisville, KY
Vibes, drums, piano / Swing, big band
Lionel Hampton introduced the vibes as a jazz instrument that could have solo expression or could be the focal point of a group. His percussive approach, coupled with his superior ear and his dexterity, resulted in impressively crafted vibes solos that rival solos on other instruments. He was an extremely versatile musician who also played drums and pi-

ano, and sang. Hampton grew up in Chicago, but was sent to a boys' school in Wisconsin, where he learned to play drums from a nun. When he returned to Chicago, Hampton became a newsboy for the Black newspaper *The Chicago Defender*. The paper had a newsboy band that marched in parades. In that band, Hampton learned to play the marimba.

Hampton's first records were with Paul Howard's Quality Serenaders, with whom he played drums and piano in 1929. Louis Armstrong allowed Hampton to play vibes, and, in 1930, they teamed on the song "Memories of You." Hampton headed a band in Los Angeles, and became famous for a series of film appearances with Les Hite's band. He disbanded his group to join Benny Goodman in 1936, and was a member of Goodman's finest small combos until 1940. At the same time, he was cutting his own small group sessions for Bluebird, was making records for the jukebox market, and was playing with musicians pulled from the Goodman, Ellington, and Basie bands, plus whomever else he could find. Hampton made several fine records in this format, notably "On the Sunny Side of the Street" with Johnny Hodges and Hampton singing. He also did sessions in 1937 and 1939 with Benny Carter, a date that featured one of Dizzy Gillespie's earliest recorded solos, and songs with Ben Webster, Chu Berry, and Coleman Hawkins. Hampton also worked briefly with Nat "King" Cole.

Hampton organized his own big band in 1940, and recorded it for Bluebird while concluding his stint with Goodman. In 1942, a song he cowrote called "Flying Home" had a boisterous, energized Illinois Jacquet solo, and was an early forerunner of swing-based R&B. The big band had a few other successful records, particularly "Down Home Jump," and "Hey Ba-ba-rebop." Hampton kept the big band going until 1965, playing at festivals and recording for Norman Granz's Verve label. He was featured in the 1956 film *The Benny Goodman Story*, and reunited with Goodman for reunion quartet albums in 1963 and 1973. Since 1965, Hampton's led several small groups and big bands. He played and produced a series of records on the Who's Who label. His vibes playing remains vibrant and animated. There's a number of Hampton sessions (covering various eras) available on CD. —*Ron Wynn*

☆ **Complete Lionel Hampton, The** / Feb. 8, 1937-Apr. 8, 1941 / RCA 65536

○ **Stompology** / Feb. 8, 1937 / RCA 575

○ **Lionel Hampton (1937-1938)** / **i.** Feb. 1937-Jan. 1938 / Classics 524

★ **Lionel Hampton's Jumpin' Jive—Vol. 2** / Feb. 1937-Oct. 1939 / Bluebird 2433
The second volume of topflight late '30s material, with exuberant solos from Johnny Hodges (as), Benny Carter (as), and Dizzy Gillespie (tpt). —*Ron Wynn*

Hot Mallets—Vol. 1 / Apr. 1937-Sep. 1939 / Bluebird 6458
Here is sensational late '30s material that forecasts the development of Hampton into a vibes genius. Wonderful swing-era work from Chu Berry (ts), Dizzy Gillespie (tpt), Benny Carter (as), and others, on a great remastering job. —*Ron Wynn*

○ **Lionel Hampton (1938-1939)** / **i.** Jan. 1938-Jun. 1939 / Classics 534

○ **Lionel Hampton (1939-1940)** / **i.** Jun. 1939-May 1940 / Classics 562

○ **Steppin' Out (1942-1944)** / 1942-1944 / MCA 1315

★ **Flyin' Home (1942-1945)** / 1942-1945 / MCA 42349
An excellent compilation of similar material. A great big band, plus some driving vibes solos. —*Ron Wynn*

○ **Jazz Heritage: Steppin' Out (1942-1944)** / 1942-1944 / MCA 1351

○ **Original Stardust, The** / Aug. 4, 1947 / Decca 74194

Just Jazz / Aug. 1947 / MCA 42329
Lionel Hampton All Stars. An erratic but frequently spirited late-'50s reissue. —*Ron Wynn*

Blues Ain't News to Me, The / May 8, 1951+Aug. 3, 1955 / Verve 2543

Despite his long tenure on Verve, this is one of the very few Hampton albums available on that label. —*Ron Wynn*

○ **Lionel Hampton Quartet, The** / Sep. 2, 1953-Apr. 12, 1954 / Clef 142

○ **Air Mail Special** / Sep. 2, 1953-Apr. 13, 1954 / Clef 727

○ **Lionel Hampton Quintet, The** / Apr. 12, 1954 / Clef 628

○ **Swingin' with Hamp** / Apr. 12, 1954+Sep. 15, 1954 / Clef 736

○ **Hamp's Big Four** / Apr. 12, 1954-Sep. 13, 1954 / Clef 744

○ **Tatum-Hampton-Rich . . . Again** / Aug. 1, 1955 / Pablo 775
Missing from the Art Tatum Group Masterpieces set were the previously issued "Body and Soul" from the Tatum-Hampton-Rich date, plus six unissued titles. Here they are at last, with two takes of "Love For Sale" for good measure. This is a fascinating set, at its best fully the equal of the original issue. There are a couple of tracks that sound as though pianist Tatum may have recorded without vibist Hampton present, as happened with the Roy Eldridge-Tatum sides. On others, where Tatum got up a head of steam and kept soloing through Hampton's spot, the recording engineer simply cut off Tatum's mike. However, "Love For Sale," for example, sounds as through Tatum is aware of Hampton's presence and cooperating. Despite the fact that the original issued tracks came out under Hampton's name, this is still a session of Hampton adapting himself to Tatum, and he does it to extraordinarily good effect. This is well worth adding to the other Tatum sides. —*Shirley Klett*, Cadence

★ **Hampton-Tatum-Rich Trio, The** / Aug. 1, 1955 / Clef 709

○ **Hamp in Hi Fi** / May 1-2, 1956 / Harmony 7115

In Paris 1956 / May 13, 1956 / Disques Swing 8415
A good, sometimes insightful pairing of Hampton with Claude Bolling (p). —*Ron Wynn*

Hamp and Getz / i. 1956 / PolyGram 31672

○ **You Better Know It** / Oct. 26-29, 1964 / Impulse 78

Lionel Hampton & Friends—Rare Recordings, Vol. 1 / i. 1965 / Telarc 83318
Anthology covering mid-'40s Lionel Hampton material, both combos and large orchestras. This period is not considered among his prime eras; there are some good songs but also plenty of novelty material and repetitive arrangements, though there's fine playing from Hampton, Illinois Jacquet, and others. —*Ron Wynn*

Where Could I Be? / i. 1971 / Fantasy
A new reissue of this fine date, with some supple, bombastic vibes from Hampton. —*Ron Wynn*

Fiftieth Anniversary Concert Live at Carnegie Hall / Jul. 1, 1978 / Sutra 1106780701
Gala celebration for the fiftieth anniversary of vibist Lionel Hampton. Though this release has lots of show business trappings, Hampton shows he can still rip off marvelous choruses and also has the percussive, energetic attack that made him a legend on his instrument. —*Ron Wynn*

All-Star Band at Newport / Jul. 2, 1978 / Timeless 142
Here is an overlooked live date with ageless Hampton swing and drive. —*Ron Wynn*

Mostly Blues / Mar. 1988-Apr. 1988 / Music Masters 5011
A spry update on the old Hampton swing/drive feeling. A good set of blues cuts. —*Ron Wynn*

Mostly Ballads / Sep. 1989-Nov. 1989 / Music Masters 5044

Just Jazz: Live at the Blue Note / i. 1992 / Telarc 83313

SLIDE HAMPTON (Locksley Wellington Hampton)

b. Apr. 21, 1932, Jeannette, PA
Trombone, tuba, arranger / Hard bop
An excellent composer, bandleader, player, and arranger, Slide Hampton has been a formidable jazz soloist and contributor since the '50s. He's know for his warm, robust, and fast solos, his fine compositions, and his marvelous arrange-

ments. Hampton began playing in a family band at age 14. He worked in the mid '50s with Buddy Johnson's band, writing his first compositions and moving to New York. Hampton spent a year with Lionel Hampton, then played from 1957 to 1959 with Maynard Ferguson before forming his own group. He headed it during much of the '60s. Its members included Freddie Hubbard, George Coleman, Julian Priester, and Booker Little. Hampton recorded in Paris with an octet in 1962, and was also band director for R&B vocalist Lloyd Price. He did several sessions for Atlantic and one for Columbia in the '60s, before going to Europe with Woody Herman in 1968. Hampton stayed in Europe for nearly 10 years. He did solo work and led combos, including one with Joe Haider. He co-led, provided arrangements for, and played with international big bands that featured top expatriate jazz musicians such as Benny Bailey and Johnny Griffin. Hampton did sessions for European labels Supraphon, Carosello, Horo, and MPS. After his return to America in 1977, he worked with many groups, including the nine-member World of Trombones, with whom he's remained involved. He conducted the Collective Black Artists Orchestra, Manhattan Plaza Composers Orchestra, and Continuum, a repertory group that played Tadd Dameron compositions. This group's roster included Jimmy Heath, Kenny Barron, Ron Carter, and Art Taylor. Incredibly, the most recent *Schwann* catalogs do not show any current or reissued Slide Hampton albums available in any configuration. —*Ron Wynn*

★ **His Horn of Plenty** / Oct. 1959 / Strand 1006

★ **World of Trombones** / Jan. 8-9, 1979 / Black Lion 760113
Ambitious project with nine trombonists merging their skills under the leadership of Slide Hampton. The list includes both established veterans like Curtis Fuller and Steve Turre and emerging newcomers Janice Robinson and Afro-Latin star Papo Vasauez. Hampton's arrangements are excellent, but there's more emphasis on performance style than real solo development. Pianist Albert Dailey and bassist Ray Drummond are also outstanding. —*Ron Wynn*

Roots / Apr. 1985 / Criss Cross 1015
Tremendous '85 quintet session with trombonist Slide Hampton heading a distinguished group and nicely teaming with tenor saxophonist Clifford Jordan in a first-rate hard bop front line. The rhythm section's quality isn't far behind, especially pianist Cedar Walton and drummer Billy Higgins. —*Ron Wynn*

Dedicated to Diz / i. 1993 / Telarc 83323
Recorded at the Village Vanguard a month after Dizzy Gillespie's death, this captures the grandeur, exotica, bluesiness, virtuosity, and humor of the late trumpeter. Slide Hampton's arrangements for the 12-piece band are a fertile blend of powerful ensemble passages and creative solo space. And what solos! Trumpeters Roy Hargrove, Claudio Roditi, and Jon Faddis dazzle on Diz's "Tour De Force." Tenorman David Sanchez devours "Bebop" and sectionmate Jimmy Heath is structured and cooking on "Overture," Hampton's vivid mix of several Gillespie themes. Pianist Danilo Perez, bassist George Mraz, drummer Lewis Nash—everyone's inspired. —*Owen Cordle*, Jazz Times

HERBIE HANCOCK (Herbert Jeffrey Hancock)

b. Apr. 12, 1940, Chicago, IL
Keyboards / Hard bop, cool, blues & jazz, early jazz-rock, contemporary funk
If not for the amazing reign of Miles Davis, pianist Herbie Hancock might qualify as jazz's most well-known and popular performer since the '60s. Hancock has eleven albums on the charts during the '70s and had 17 on the charts between 1973 and 1984, including three in 1974. These figures put him well ahead of any other jazz musician in the '70s and beyond. He's also one of jazz's finest eclectic players; he's played everything from bebop to free, jazz-rock, fusion, funk, instrumental pop, dance, hip-hop, and world fusion. Hancock's style, greatly influenced by Bill Evans, mixes in-

trospective and energetic elements, and fuses blues and gospel influences with bebop and classical elements. He's both a great accompanist and an excellent soloist, whose voicings, phrasing, melodic and interpretative skills, and harmonic facility were impressive early in his career, and remain sharp regardless of the style or idiom in which he plays.

Hancock began studying piano at age seven and performed the first movement of a Mozart concerto with the Chicago Symphony Orchestra in a young people's concert at age 11. He formed his own jazz ensemble while attending Hyde Park High School. He was influenced harmonically by the arrangements Clare Fischer provided for the Hi-Los and by Robert Farnon's orchestrations of pop songs. Hancock began working in Chicago jazz clubs with Donald Byrd and Coleman Hawkins upon leaving Grinnel College in 1960. Byrd invited him to join his group and Hancock moved to New York. After Hancock recorded with Byrd's band, Blue Note offered Hancock his own pact. Hancock's debut, *Takin' Off*, was issued in 1962 and yielded a hit with "Watermelon Man."

He joined Miles Davis in 1963. Hancock's solo style became an integral part of Davis's evolving '60s approach. Hancock's interaction with Ron Carter and Tony Williams was at the core of songs that became increasingly more flexible and less fixed. At the same time, Hancock also cut important albums as a leader for Blue Note and gained status as a composer. Some major compositions during the '60s included "Maiden Voyage," "Dolphin Dance," "Speak Like a Child," and "I Have a Dream," which he dedicated to Dr. Martin Luther King, Jr. During the '70s, Hancock led a sextet that merged jazz, rock, African, and Indian musical references and was mostly electric. This band was one of the great jazz-rock groups, though Hancock finally disbanded it due to the group's limited market appeal and limited financial success. The Sextant group sometimes performed in African garb, and Hancock issued the album *Mwandishi* with the African names of the musicians given along with their English names. He played many electronic instruments, and added the Hohner Clavinet, various synthesizers, and Mellotron to his Fender Rhodes.

Hancock disbanded the Sextant in 1973 and formed the Headhunters, a funk, rock, and instrumental pop band that scored a huge crossover hit with the album *Headhunters*. Hancock's records were now being played by the emerging upper- and middle-class Black professionals who, for the most part, had little or no knowledge of his past sound. The single, "Chameleon," which reflected the influence of accompanists in Sly Stone's band, was a club and radio smash in its edited version. Hancock turned more to strict pop music, though he also did an acoustic VSOP tour in the late '70s, and played a series of duo concerts with Chick Corea. He repeatedly defended his right to make any and all kinds of music, and often labeled criticism of his commercial projects as "elitist," an extension of the charge that some Black nationalists leveled against the '60s free players.

During the '80s, Hancock alternated between acoustic and electric material. He had another big hit in 1983 with "Rockit," a song that utilized the scratching technique (and predated the technique's popularity in hip-hop production) and used a multitextured, heavily edited snippet/rhythm framework. The video and single gained Hancock MTV coverage and exposure, and triggered a fresh round of debate over whether or not he was selling out. Hancock spent the next two years doing mostly conventional jazz dates, even winning an Oscar for his score of the film *Round Midnight*. Hancock collaborated with African musician Foday Musa Suso for a fine duet album that made the charts as well. Hancock toured Europe in 1987 with Buster Williams and Al Foster, and did a series of American and Japanese dates with a quartet that included Mike Brecker, Ron Carter, and Tony Williams. Hancock also hosted a variety show on the Showtime cable television network, and did lecture/performances on public television.

Hancock's done numerous albums for Blue Note, Columbia, and Warner Bros. The lengthy list of musicians that Hancock has played with reads like a jazz who's who. It includes Joe Henderson, Freddie Hubbard, Wynton Marsalis, George Coleman, Johnny Coles, Bobby Hutcherson, George Benson, and Paul Desmond, among many others. His versatility and track record ensure Hancock will never have difficulty getting recording opportunities. It would be silly to insist that everything he's done was great, but much of it, even his most commercial and trendy dates, has retained a high level of musicianship and attention to stylistic detail. Hancock has numerous sessions, in each of his genres, available on CD. —*Ron Wynn and William Ruhlmann*

Takin' Off / May 28, 1962 / Blue Note 46506
A prophetic title for this session with Dexter Gordon (ts) and Freddie Hubbard (tpt). —*Ron Wynn*

○ **Best of Herbie Hancock: The Blue Note Years** / May 1962-Mar. 1968 / Blue Note 91142
The Blue Note years. A good compilation to start with. Many of his best works. —*Michael G. Nastos*

○ **My Point of View** / Mar. 19, 1963 / Blue Note 84126
Tremendous compositions and playing in an all-star date that helped make Hancock a star. —*Ron Wynn*

Inventions and Dimensions / Aug. 30, 1963 / Blue Note 84147
First-rate early work. Willie Bobo makes a scintillating percussive contribution. —*Ron Wynn*

○ **Empyrean Isles** / Jun. 17, 1964 / Blue Note 84175
1985 reissue of one of Hancock's seminal releases. Freddie Hubbard (tpt) is daring and aggressive. Ron Carter (b) and Tony Williams (d) are squarely in the pocket. —*Ron Wynn*

★ **Maiden Voyage** / Mar. 17, 1965 / Blue Note 46339
The definitive Blue Note Herbie with an ensemble. You can't go wrong with this one. —*Michael G. Nastos*

○ **Speak Like a Child** / Mar. 9, 1968 / Blue Note 46136
A simply beautiful title cut, plus wondrous arrangements and playing throughout. —*Ron Wynn*

★ **Fat Albert Rotunda** / Mar. 10, 1969+Dec. 8, 1969 / Warner Brothers 1834
Herbie plays Fender Rhodes with Joe Henderson (ts). Featuring "Tell Me A Bedtime Story." —*Michael G. Nastos*

Prisoner, The / Apr. 18-23, 1969 / Blue Note 46845
A poignant tribute to Dr. Martin Luther King, Jr. from pianist Herbie Hancock, whose '69 album features his compositions for large orchestra and is sparked by superb playing from the leader and Joe Henderson on tenor sax. —*Ron Wynn*

★ **Mwandishi** / 1970 / Warner Brothers
A forerunner of Afrocentric sentiment. One of Hancock's finest electric, jazz-rock outings. —*Ron Wynn*

Crossings / Dec. 1971 / Warner Brothers

Sextant / 1972 / Columbia 32212

★ **Headhunters** / 1973 / Columbia 47478

Thrust / Aug. 26, 1974 / Columbia 32965

○ **Live under the Sky** / i. 1976 / Columbia 875
Despite the overwhelming individual virtuosity, these five talents come together as a true *band,* passing the severest test: even their most intricate arrangements (and this is no mere jamming band) sound spontaneous. Consider the wonderful empathy of trumpeter Freddie Hubbard's "One of Another Kind," with its subtle ensemble rubato and tight give and take between soloist and hard-charging accompaniment. And hear the way Hubbard burns and soars, constructing a solo, not merely linking together flashy runs, while Wayne Shorter shows how to handle an inclement weather-affected horn (wet pads, swollen reed, etc.) and still create an intriguing outing through a disintegrating line with shorter and shorter fragments, squeezed and wrung out of a soggy soprano. One is reminded of the Blue Note salad days in any number of ways: the return of Hubbard's chops and his brash, confident yet controlled attitude, Hancock's stylish, intelligent "touch" on acoustic piano, Tony Williams's

propulsive, variegated chattering, and the reckless and excit-ing trumpet/tenor contrapuntal blathering on "Fragile" are held together by Ron Carter's insistent walking. However, it is a bit much to hear the Japanese audience's cheers for each bass glissandi and isolated cymbal crash. —*Art Lange*, Down Beat

○ **V.S.O.P. Quintet** / Jul. 16, 1977-Jul. 18, 1977 / Columbia 34976

This often-stunning quintet set was done live at Newport. Hancock again confounds cynics who insist he's lost his jazz roots. —*Ron Wynn*

○ **Quartet** / i. 1981 / Columbia 38275

A fine mainstream set that shows detractors Hancock hasn't lost his jazz chops. Wynton Marsalis (tpt), then reaping a wave of prodigy/discovery headlines, is in the group. —*Ron Wynn*

Village Life / i. 1985 / Columbia 39870

An arresting mix of Hancock's jazz concept with African Foday Suso's rhythmic innovations. —*Ron Wynn*

○ **V.S.O.P.—Vol. 2** / Columbia 40015

○ **Evening with Chick Corea and Herbie Hancock, An** / Polydor 6238

This double album, recorded in concert, begins with two standards. In "Someday My Prince Will Come" the melody is nearly smothered beneath the garlands of ornaments and runs. Chick Corea and Herbie Hancock did not always main-tain a strict division of labor. In "Someday" there is a won-derful two-chorus embrace where you cannot tell the dancer from the dance. In the other standard, George Gershwin's "Liza," Corea and Hancock trade a few conventional cho-ruses, but then they go loco and take "Liza" to places she had never been before. Sides two and three are taken up by two loosely structured pieces performed with both virtuosity and self-indulgence. Side four is a jewel. On Hancock's clas-sic "Maiden Voyage," both pianists play fine solos to equally fine accompaniment, although the double solo that follows does not fare as well as others on the album. Corea's "La Fiesta" begins with a fiery display of virtuosity, mostly from Corea, who then plays a long imaginative solo. Hancock's splashy solo is driven by Corea's relentless accompaniment to a stunning peak. —*Douglas Clark*, Down Beat

CAP'N JOHN HANDY ("Captain" John Handy)

b. Jun. 24, 1900, Pass Christian, MO, **d.** Jan. 12, 1971, New York, NY

Alto saxophone, clarinet / New Orleans traditional

A fine and intriguing saxophonist whose skills were not ap-preciated by some traditional jazz types in the late '40s, "Cap'n" John Handy was one of the more assertive, bluesy, and imaginative saxophonists of his day. His energetic, often riveting approach reportedly influenced swing and R&B alto players Earl Bostic and Louis Jordan. Handy started on gui-tar, mandolin, and drums. He played in his family's band as a teen, and taught himself clarinet at age 16. Handy worked in jam sessions with Punch Miller, Kid Rena, and Isiah Morgan before moving to New Orleans from Mississippi in 1918. He worked in Tom Albert's band for six years, while also playing with Charlie Love. After a couple of years with Toots Johnson, Handy returned to New Orleans and joined Gus Kelly. He began on alto in 1928, and that became his main instrument. Handy coformed the Louisiana Shakers with his brother, Sylvester, in the early '30s. He later worked with Kid Howard, Jim Robinson, and Lee Collins. Handy played with Charlie Creath in the late '30s, then returned once again to New Orleans, where he played with the Young Tuxedo Brass Band in the '40s, and with Kid Clayton in the '50s. Handy joined Kid Shiek Colar in the early '60s, and fre-quently played clarinet as well as alto sax in this band. He acquired his nickname, Captain, from banjo player Fred Minor due to his take-charge manner in rehearsals. Handy played at Preservation Hall, toured England, Europe, Canada, and Japan in the late '60s, and played at the Newport Jazz Festival in 1970. He made several recordings

for the GHB label, but his best sessions were for Jazz Crusade and RCA in the '60s. Currently, there are a couple of Handy sessions available on CD. —*Ron Wynn*

★ **Capt. John Handy with Geoff Bull and Barry Martyn's Band** / Apr. 12, 1966 / Beautiful Dumaine 001

Introducing Cap'n John Handy / Nov. 15-18, 1966 / RCA 3762

JOHN HANDY (John Richard (III) Handy)

b. Feb. 3, 1933, Dallas, TX

Alto and tenor saxophone, flute / Bop, hard bop

Don't confuse John Handy with the Handy who plays tradi-tional jazz; this Handy is the hard-edged, bluesy, and often blistering alto saxophonist who was featured with Mingus in the late '50s and early '60s. Handy not only played torrid alto, but was a good flutist and one of the first to utilize the saxello. He started on clarinet at age 11. Handy played tenor in blues bands in the San Francisco area, some of which were led by Lowell Fulson. He moved to New York in 1958, where he joined Mingus and also worked with Randy Weston. Handy returned to the West Coast in the early '60s, and studied at San Francisco State College, earning his BA in 1963. Handy formed a ten-piece group, but disbanded it the next year and rejoined Mingus in 1964. He formed an-other group with Michael White in 1965, and recorded its stunning performance at the Monterey Festival. Handy per-formed his *Concerto for Jazz Soloist and Orchestra* with the San Francisco Symphony Orchestra in 1970. He played with sarod player Ali Akbar Khan in 1971. Handy experimented with jazz-rock and fusion in the '70s, but returned to hard bop with the Mingus Dynasty in 1979. Handy worked with Bebop and Beyond in the '80s, and also led an otherwise fe-male band in 1989. He's recorded for Roulette, Columbia, MPS, and Milestone. Handy has only one date currently available on CD. —*Ron Wynn*

○ **No Coast Jazz** / 1961 / Roulette 52058

★ **Live at Monterey** / Sep. 18, 1965 / Columbia 2462

○ **Second John Handy Album, The** / Apr. 27, 1966-Jul. 26, 1966 / Columbia 2567

○ **John Handy** / Sep. 18, 1966 / Columbia

New View / i. 1967 / Columbia

Some shimmering alto sax. Music in the spirit of the im-pending jazz-rock fusion. —*Ron Wynn*

Hard Work / Jan. 1976 / Impulse 9314

JAKE HANNA (John Hanna)

b. Apr. 4, 1931, Boston, MA

Drums / Swing, big band

An adaptable drummer who's worked in bebop, cool, and big-band contexts, Jake Hanna has forged a career as a reli-able accompanist who prefers swing-styled sessions. He's known for tasteful, restrained timekeeping, for carefully pushing the beat and band, and for being a fine, if not fancy, soloist. Hanna was tutored in jazz drumming by Stanley Spector, and painstakingly studied various bands that came through his native Boston. He worked with Woody Herman and Maynard Ferguson in the late '50s, and also served as house drummer at Storyville. Hanna became Marian McPartland's regular drummer in 1959, and remained in her group until 1961. During the remainder of the '60s, Hanna worked with Duke Ellington, Bobby Hackett, Harry James, and Herb Pomeroy. He was the drummer for Merv Griffin's television band from the mid '60s until the mid '70s, and re-located to Los Angeles with the band in 1970. Hanna played with Herman again, with Supersax, and with Herb Ellis in the '70s, while serving as virtual house drummer for Concord, for which he's done dozens of records, both as a leader and sideman. Hanna coformed a band with Carl Fontana in 1975. He can be heard on many Concord sessions currently available on CD. —*Ron Wynn*

★ **Jake Takes Manhattan** / Dec. 14-15, 1976 / Concord Jazz 35

Nice, restrained light swing session led by drummer Jake Hanna with contributions from bassist Mike Moore and pianist John Bunch. Though he's cited as leader, Hanna doesn't dominate, and it's more a cooperative venture than a featured drum date. —*Ron Wynn*

SIR ROLAND HANNA (Sir Roland P. Hanna)

b. Feb. 10, 1932, Detroit, MI
Piano / Bop
Many genres, from stride, swing, bebop, and blues to boogie-woogie and hard bop, can be detected in pianist Sir Roland Hanna's playing. He's one of the most lyrical soloists around, and his touch, phrasing, and pacing are exquisite. Hanna began learning music from his father as a child, and studied classical piano at age 11. Swing and bebop players like Teddy Wilson and Tommy Flanagan were among Hanna's influences. He was in the army during the early '50s, then studied music at Juilliard. He worked with Benny Goodman and then with Charles Mingus in the late '50s before joining Sarah Vaughan in 1960. During the mid '60s, Hanna led a trio at the Five Spot, then joined the Thad Jones-Mel Lewis orchestra in 1966. He played and recorded with them until 1974, and in the process become as well known as any of their saxophone or brass soloists. He also played in the New York Jazz Sextet (later, Quartet) in the '60s and '70s with Frank Wess, Ben Riley, and Ron Carter, among others. A fine composer as well, Hanna's actually the author of *A Child Is Born*, a song mistakenly credited to Thad Jones. Since the mid '70s, Hanna's done many sessions, among them several solo and duo albums for the Freedom, Black & Blue, Black Hawk, DIW, and Enja labels. Unfortunately, the Freedom and Blackhawk labels are now defunct, while Evidence owns the Black & Blue masters. There are only a few Hanna dates available on CD, including a recent session on Music Masters. —*Ron Wynn*

○ **Sir Elf** / Apr. 1974-May 1974 / Choice 1003
Pianist Roland Hanna puts so much music into each song that the listener must be prepared to devote every bit of attention in order to keep up. Art Tatum was like that too, but in the few decades since his recordings were made, listeners learned to follow him. Hanna is much like Tatum in other ways. His similiarities with the master of the solo piano extend beyond the surface trappings of "You Took Advantage of Me," obviously dedicated to Tatum, with its breakaway runs, stop rhythms, and chromatically crawling left-hand chords. Hanna, more than any pianist soloizing in the mainstream (except maybe Billy Taylor) enjoys the ambidextrity that Tatum had, as well as a fistful of knowledge to direct its best use. Hanna also admits his liking for Erroll Garner on "There Is No Greater Love" with shifting focal points on rhythm, staggered chords, and sparkling lines, all taken at that medium drag tempo Garner did so well. Solo piano demands great arrangements as well as great performances, and Hanna's treatments are novel and captivating, although he occasionally tinkles the ivories for one or two choruses too many. But there is plenty of meat on those bone chips, even if my jaws are not always up to tearing in; and *Sir Elf* is definitely a chef's special on the musical menu. —*Neil Tesser*, Down Beat

★ **Perugia** / Jul. 2, 1974 / Freedom 741010
Recorded live at the 1974 Montreux Jazz Festival, this, Sir Roland Hanna's second solo piano album, gives a revealing cross-section of his abilities. Basically a mainstream jazz player in the tradition of Erroll Garner and Oscar Peterson, Hanna opens here with two Ellington-associated tunes, memorializing this bandleader's then-recent death. "Take The 'A' Train," with its gutsy walking bass lines and *verbatim* Oscar Peterson-style licks, seems to please this pianist as much as it does his audience. "I Got It Bad and That Ain't Good," punctuated by some telling grunts and groans in its free-flowing inventive prowess that suggests that anything, just anything, may happen next, is tinged by the spirit of Garner himself. In performing his originals, Hanna comes into his own. "Time Dust Gathered" pulses with high-ten-

sion chords graced by percussive, interlocking keyboard-lines. "Perugia" broods with romanticism and mysticism. His playing is marked with a fine melodic sense throughout, and, as the concert continues, his keyboard textures become more daring and inventive. —*Jon Balleras*, Down Beat

Gift from the Magi, A / Nov. 6-7, 1978 / West 548003
This suitelike program of romantic impressionism, heavily influenced by Debussy, Satie, and Ravel, was, according to one source, "The album Roland always wanted to do." It is beautifully played and very well presented, though for me a bit remote. Within the confines of the general style, however, there is a fairly wide range of moods, from nostalgia to the severity of Charlie Haden's "Silence" (all except "Silence" are Hanna compositions) to an elated passage in "Dee's Unique." The album is an unselfconscious celebration of one branch of Hanna's roots, lovingly done; it is not jazz, nor was it intended to be taken as such. —*Joel Ray*, Cadence

Roland Hanna Plays the Music of Alec Wilder / 1978 / Inner City 1072
Soaring, dramatic interpretations of classic Jerome Kern tunes by pianist Sir Roland Hanna. He plays them with a sophisticated, yet exuberant flair, perfectly executing the basic melodies, then extending and reworking them through often magnificent solos. —*Ron Wynn*

New York Jazz Quartet in Chicago, The / i. Nov. 1984 / Bee Hive 7013
Recorded a scant five months after the late '81 release on Enja, this disc found the group displaying a somewhat more ardent aspect, throwing off—to good purpose—some of the rather tight-lipped, toes-inward mien of their previous recordings. This is not meant, however, to give the impression they bare their souls and play with reckless abandon, but there is about the session a bristling energy I do not recall ever having heard from them. It is not, in other words, my idea of chamber jazz. Despite Sir Roland Hanna's name being the most prominent, this is still a cooperative unit, with no annointed leader. "Four the Hard Way" is a Frank Wess original, the stop/start theme played by unison piano, arco bass, and tenor, with some nicely sculpted solos from the same instruments (but the bass plucked) following. "Wisteria" is George Mraz's lovely ballad, with Wess's tenor in the lead and the sort of empathic instrumental balance for which the Quartet has long been known. "Ruckus" is spirited Roland Hanna line, Thelonious Monkishness noted, with Wess playing tenor on the theme and soloing on flute. So, it is excellent musicianship from start to finish, from four players who obviously know that the whole often exceeds the sum of its parts. —*Alan Bargebuhr*, Cadence

○ **Persia My Dear** / i. Aug. 1987 / DIW 8015

Duke Ellington Piano Solos / i. 1991 / Music Masters 5045
Includes some exquisite solo work—a moving tribute to Duke Ellington. —*Ron Wynn*

JOHN HARDEE

b. 1918, **d.** 1984
Tenor saxophone / Bop, swing
A good swing and bebop tenor saxophonist, John Hardee displayed a robust tone and provided some jubilant solos during sessions in the '40s, '50s, and '60s. Hardee initially played piano, mellophone, C-melody and alto sax before turning to tenor. After graduating from Bishop College in the early '40s, Hardee played clarinet in army bands, and served as a band director. He worked with Tiny Grimes in New York in the mid '40s, then began recording as a leader. Hardee did sessions with Russell Procope, Ike Quebec, Earl Bostic, Billy Kyle, Helen Humes, Billy Taylor, and Lucky Millinder. After moving to Dallas, he worked in clubs there from the early '50s until the early '60s, then led school bands until 1976. Hardee played at the 1975 Nice festival. He's featured prominently on the Mosaic boxed set *The Complete Blue Note Forties Recordings of John Hardee and Ike Quebec*, a four-album/three-disc collection. —*Ron Wynn*

WILBUR HARDEN

b. 1925
Trumpet / Hard bop
Besides being one of the first jazz trumpeters to convert to flugelhorn, Wilbur Harden was also one of hard bop's and bebop's more lyrical, melodic stylists. His flugelhorn solos greatly reflected that tendency; Harden played soothing, lush, middle-register statements, and subtle embellishments and melodic adjustments. He was an R&B player in bands led by Ivory Joe Hunter and Roy Brown during the '50s. Harden played in a navy band before moving to Detroit. His transition to jazz was aided greatly by Yusef Lateef, with whom he played in 1957. He recorded with Lateef on Savoy, then made several marvelous dates with John Coltrane on that same label; though these were Harden's sessions, three of the four were later issued as Coltrane records. Illness ended Harden's active career in 1959. Currently, his albums on Savoy are unavailable on CD under his name; they're available on Coltrane reissues. Harden can also be heard on a Lateef reissue. *—Ron Wynn*

Countdown / **i.** Mar. 1958 / Savoy 650102

★ **Tanganyika Suite** / May 13, 1958 / Savoy 13005

Africa / **i.** May 1958-Jun. 1958 / Savoy 650129

BILL HARDMAN (William Franklin (Jr) Hardman)

b. Apr. 6, 1933, Cleveland, OH, **d.** 1990
Trumpet, flugelhorn / Hard bop
Experience, the assistance of various bandleaders, and his own maturity helped Bill Hardman develop into a confident, aggressive soloist. A Clifford Brown disciple, Hardman's playing always had energy and verve, and he became a top player by the mid '60s. He studied trombone and trumpet as a child, and played with Tadd Dameron while still in high school. Hardman toured with Tiny Bradshaw in the early '50s, then played with Jackie McLean and Charles Mingus before joining Art Blakey in 1956. He worked with Blakey until 1958, then teamed with him again in the late '60s and early '70s. Hardman also played briefly with Horace Silver, played periodically with Lou Donaldson, and played with Lloyd Price and Mingus again in the '60s. He co-led the Brass Company with Bill Lee and Billy Higgins in the '70s, and signaled his ascension in the ranks by winning the *Down Beat* Critics Poll in the mid '70s. Hardman co-led a group with Junior Cook in the late '70s. He has recorded for Savoy, Muse, and Fantasy. Currently, Hardman has some sessions available on CD. *—Ron Wynn*

Home / Jan. 10, 1978 / Muse 5152
Trumpeter Bill Hardman's *Home* is a straightahead bebop session by a journeyman trumpet player, best known for his work with drummer Art Blakey and bassist Charles Mingus. The playing is competent if not exceptional, and anyone who likes bebop will appreciate it. *Home* opens with a Brazilian tune, "Samba Do Brilho," taken at a tempo far too fast for the players. They are so intent on maintaining the tempo that their solos lack a distinctive character. Slide Hampton rushes to push his trombone through the changes, and, while tenor saxophonist Junior Cook is rhythmically perfect, there's no variation in his sound. Hardman does a little better when he drops back to half-time to provide contrast during his improvisation. Mickey Tucker's piano solo is little different from the rhythm changes he plays throughout the tune. "Once I Loved," another Brazilian song, fares better. Hardman is first up, and he begins with slurred notes in the middle range that give way to more distinctly played notes in the upper range. Cook spits out the opening notes of his solo, then pauses before continuing, with occasional slips, into the lower registers of his horn, a change from his middle-register sound. Hampton still pushes through his solo, while Tucker plays percussively and on the beat. "My Pen Is Hot," a Tucker original that opens side two, features a more arranged ensemble passage and more good soloing. Hampton finally settles down and intersperses quarter notes and eighth notes, relieving the tedium of his usual eighth-

note runs. Hardman alternates busy phrases full of slurred notes with less frenetic passages that allow the listener to catch her breath before Hardman's next foray. This is followed by "Rancho Cevarro," another Tucker original and the high point of the album. After another arranged ensemble passage, Hardman enters with jagged, abbreviated phrases that are suggestive instead of declamatory and provide a change of mood. Cook follows this lead and plays longer, smoother phrases while Hampton introduces a lighter, slurring quality to his solo. Completing the sequence, Tucker is less percussive and plays around the beat instead of on it. On Tadd Dameron's ballad "I Remember Love," the band dispenses with the usual bebop treatment for an arrangement that showcases Hardman's trumpet. Hardman's horn has a burnished sound that's all the more eloquent for its understatement as he weaves legato phrases in and out of the textured sound of the ensemble. *—Sam Little*, Cadence

Politely / Jul. 7, 1981 / Muse 5184
This Bill Hardman date is interesting because of his nice trumpet playing, both open and with a mute, and also because he and Junior Cook on tenor sax are such a great team. Hardman's highlight has to be "Love Letters." This was recorded by Rudy Van Gelder at his studio on 7/7/81. *—Jerry Atkins*, Cadence

AL HAREWOOD

b. 1923
Drums / Bop
A fine, but not a showy drummer, Al Harewood has been the epitome of a seasoned, sensitive percussionist since the '50s. He's provided consistent, steady rhythmic support, and can play with force and surprising dexterity when given the spotlight. Harewood began his career in the '50s working with the J.J. Johnson-Kai Winding duo. He later played with Gigi Gryce, Art Farmer, and George Barrow before joining Lou Donaldson in 1959. He recorded in the '50s with David Amram, Curtis Fuller, and Benny Golson as well as Donaldson, and with Horace Parlan, Grant Green, and Donaldson in the '60s. Harewood worked briefly with Mary Lou Williams in 1962, then played with Stan Getz, and later rejoined Amram. Harewood played with Chuck Wayne, Joe Williams, the Newport Jazz Festival All Stars, and Lisle Atkinson in the '70s, recording with Betty Carter, and with Fuller and Parlan once more. He became an instructor at Livingston College in the mid '70s, and played with the descendants of Mike and Phoebe in the late '70s and early '80s. Harewood began playing with Lee Konitz in 1983. He doesn't have any sessions as a leader, but can be heard on reissues by Parlan, Green, Carter, and the Johnson-Winding team. *—Ron Wynn*

ROY HARGROVE

b. 1970
Trumpet / Neo-bop
In the '80s, Roy Hargrove emerged as a leading player among young stylists enamored with the hard bop sound of the '50s. While his early solos seemed overly imitative of Freddie Hubbard, he's become more confident and varied in his approach. Hargrove now pays more attention to colors, tone, and note selection, and is much more effective on uptempo material. His improvement is quite evident from his debut to his most recent release. Hargrove's compositions, notably "Public Eye," contain harmonic twists and melodic surprises, and he's less concerned with flash and fury than with depth and substance. Hargrove won a scholarship to Berklee at age 16, and soon began attracting attention with appearances at local clubs. He hadn't yet turned 20 when his debut album, *Diamond in the Rough*, was issued on RCA/Novus. Since then, he's recorded two other albums as a leader, has done a guest stint with Sonny Rollins, and appeared on the 1993 album *Jazz Futures* with several other Young Lions. Hargrove has expressed interest in doing some jazz/hip-hop sessions and backing vocalists, but has no plans to desert acoustic jazz or hard bop. By his own admis-

sion, he's still an evolving, unfinished player, but each year he gains more stature as a soloist, bandleader, and composer. All Hargrove's sessions are available on CD. —*Ron Wynn*

★ **Diamond in the Rough** / Dec. 1989 / Novus 3082

Public Eye / Oct. 1990 / Novus 3113

Hargrove's second album displays great promise, though things sometimes get ragged. CD has a bonus cut. —*Ron Wynn*

Of Kindred Souls / Jive/Novus 63154

Having begun his apprenticeship with Dizzy Gillespie while still in high school, the 24-year-old trumpeter Roy Hargrove now qualifies as something of a younger Elder Statesman among the new generation of players. On the live *Of Kindred Souls*, his fourth release as a leader, Hargrove refuses to hog the spotlight. His trumpet playing is as sumptuous and darting as ever, yet he allots generous solo space to pianist Marc Carey and saxophonist Ron Blake (who shines on the uptempo "Gentle Wind"). —*James Marcus, Jazz Times*

RUFUS HARLEY

b. 1936
Bagpipes / Bop

One of the great sights and sounds of '60s jazz was Rufus Harley on bagpipes. He sometimes played in kilts, cracked jokes about his ancestry, and made the bagpipes a legitimate jazz instrument, soloing in a vivid, perfectly acceptable hard bop and bebop context. Originally, Harley had played saxophone in high school, then began on bagpipes in the mid '60s, and later formed a band. He cut four Atlantic albums in the late '60s, while he also recorded with Sonny Stitt and Herbie Mann. Harley played at the Montreux International Jazz Festival in the mid '70s with Sonny Rollins. He hasn't been heard from much since then, and his albums aren't currently in print. —*Ron Wynn*

THE HARPER BROTHERS

Neo-bop

Among the big jazz stories of 1993, the breakup of the trumpet/drums duo the Harper Brothers didn't get as much ink as it merited. During the late '80s and early '90s, the Harper Brothers were viewed as some of the more accomplished hard bop players among contemporary jazz musicians. Phillip Harper had played with Art Blakey and the Jazz Messengers during the mid '80s, then teamed with his brother, Winard, and signed with Verve in 1988. They'd done three albums, working with such players as Javon Jackson, Stephen Scott, Justin Robinson, Kiyoshi Kitagawa, and Michael Bowie on the first two releases. They switched direction slightly on the third release, and did more swing and blues material with veterans such as Jimmy McGriff and Harry "Sweets" Edison. In '93, the Harper Brothers went their separate ways. Their three sessions are available on CD. Philip Harper's dates with Art Blakey are available on CD, too. —*Ron Wynn*

Harper Brothers / **i.** Jun. 21, 1988 / PolyGram 837033

The introductory album for the jazz-playing brothers who became staples among mainstream fans in the late '80s and early '90s. Winard and Phillip Harper's music reflects the influence of Art Blakey and Horace Silver, but is played with a youthful zest and individualistic flair. This late '80s release was reissued in '92 on CD with a bonus cut. —*Ron Wynn*

★ **Remembrance** / **i.** Mar. 1990 / Verve 841723

Artistry / **i.** 1991 / Verve 847956

A 1991 session by Winard and Phillip Harper, the brothers whose trumpet/sax sound and conception echoes classic late '50s hard bop material. This, their next-to-last album as a duo, is aided by contributions from Javon Jackson, Kevin Hays, and Nedra Wheeler. —*Ron Wynn*

Jazz Harmonica

Few Early Jazz Harmonica Players

Some Jazz, with Classical & Popular Music
Larry Adler (1914)

Major Player
Toots Thieleman (1922)

Other Players
Sonny Terry (1911-1986) w/Chris Barber Band in 1958
Buddy Lucas – with Thad Jones/Mel Lewis Orchestra 1974
Malachi Favors (1937)–Art Ensemble of Chicago
Rahsaan Roland Kirk (1936-1977)
Whistler
Ron McCroby

BILLY HARPER (Billy R. Harper)

b. Jan. 17, 1943
Saxophone / Hard bop

An animated, slashing player, Billy Harper's cries, angular lines, and phrases demonstrate both his affinity to John Coltrane and Booker Ervin, and his own substantial ability. Harper began tenor sax studies at age 11, while also playing and singing in church. He continued to play and sing while he attended college at North Texas State, where he earned his degree in 1965. Harper moved from Houston to New York in 1966. He toured California with Gil Evans, played in Art Blakey's Jazz Messengers, then worked, for a short time, with Elvin Jones in 1970. Harper played with Max Roach, with the Thad Jones-Mel Lewis orchestra, and with Lee Morgan. He began heading a sextet in 1973, but continued working with Roach until 1978. He's recorded with a quintet that's frequently included Everett Hollins, Gregg Maker, and Malcolm Pinson. He continued working with Evans into the '80s. Harper has recorded for Strata-East, Denon, Black Saint, and Soul Note. He has a couple of sessions available on CD. —*Ron Wynn and Michael G. Nastos*

★ **Black Saint** / Jul. 21-22, 1975 / Black Saint 001

An important document and the first album for the Italian Black Saint label. A potent quartet, with Harper's most familiar themes. This is essential listening in the modal jazz idiom. —*Michael G. Nastos*

Trying to Make Heaven My Home / Mar. 3-4, 1979 / MPS 0068.234

A quintet recording for this incendiary tenor saxophonist. An extended, hard-blowing session. —*Michael G. Nastos*

HERBIE HARPER (Billy Harper)

b. Jul. 2, 1920, Salina, KS
Trombone / Bop, swing

A veteran swing and bebop trombonist who was very active in the West Coast scene, Herbie Harper entered the studios in the mid '50s. He gradually decreased his jazz activity to the point that he seldom did anything outside that environment in the '60s and '70s. Harper was not a star, but a consistently enjoyable, occasionally arresting player who made a good contribution in any situation. Harper had an engineering scholarship, but left college to play with a territory band in Texas. He worked with Johnny "Scat" Davis and Gene Krupa in the early '40s, then toured in the mid '40s with Charlie Spivak. Later, he played in Hollywood with Teddy Edwards. In the late '40s and early '50s, Harper worked in the big bands of Benny Goodman, Charlie Barnet, Stan Kenton, and Jerry Gray, while also playing and recording with Billie Holiday. He led his own groups during the '50s, then joined the NBC orchestra in 1955. While primarily a studio musician from that point into the '80s, Harper also recorded with June Christy, Maynard Ferguson, Ray Brown, Benny Carter, Barnet, and Kenton in the '50s. He did sessions for Nocturne, Bethlehem, Mode, Liberty, and Tampa. He maintained a periodic relationship with big band director Bob Florence, playing with his groups at various points from the late '50s into the early '80s. During the '80s, Harper resumed recording, doing a date for Sea Breeze, and co-forming a band with Bill Perkins. They recorded in 1989 for VSOP. It was issued in 1992. Harper's '80s dates are available on CD. —*Ron Wynn and Michael G. Nastos*

○ **Five Brothers** / Jun. 15, 1955 / VSOP 9
These tracks dating from 1954 are played by a quintet (Herbie Harber, t; Bob Enevoldsen, vtb, ts; Red Mitchell, b; Don Overburg, g; Frank Capp, d) of West Coast pros. They serve up a program that can stand as a good example of the energetic, scrubbed-down, vaguely rococo jazz many were playing on the Pacific shoreline in the '50s. Harper's trombone is brisk and bright and has a sort of repressed integrity all its own, but certainly lacks an emotional charge. Enevoldsen all but dominates with his fluid and attractively grainy tenor playing. —*Alan Bargebuhr*, Cadence

★ **Herbie Harper** / **i**. 1956 / Liberty 6003
A swinging session with Bud Shank (as) and Bob Gordon (bs) from this ex-big-band trombonist. With Charlie Mariano (sax). —*David Szatmary*

TOM HARRELL

b. Jun. 16, 1946, Urbana, IL
Trumpet, flugelhorn / Hard bop
A first-rate soloist who is considered, by many musicians, to be the top hard bop trumpeter of the '80s and '90s, Tom Harrell has performed in a distinguished fashion for several bandleaders. He moved from the Midwest to California, and began playing in small groups at age 13. Harrell played at the Jazz Workshop in San Francisco, then toured with Stan Kenton in 1969 and with Woody Herman in 1970 and 1971. He spent four years in the '70s with Horace Silver, while also performed and recorded with Chuck Israel's National Jazz Ensemble and with Arnie Lawrence. Harrell worked through the '70s with Cecil Payne, Bill Evans, and Lee Konitz's nonet. He played with George Russell in 1982, then joined Phil Woods's quartet in 1983, making it a quintet. Harrell has recorded as a leader for Adamo, Palo Alto, and Contemporary. He has a couple of sessions available on CD. —*Ron Wynn and Michael G. Nastos*

Aurora/Total / **i**. Jun. 24, 1976 / ADAMO 9502
Harrell's first album features choice material and Bob Berg (ts). —*Michael G. Nastos*

Stories / Jan. 1988 / Contemporary 14043
Assisted by Bob Berg (ts), John Scofield (g), Niels Lan Doky (p), Billy Hart (d), and Ray Drummond (b), flugelhornist and trumpeter Harrell charts his way through a solid hour of modern jazz progressions. The CD contains one bonus track. —*Paul Kohler*

★ **Sail Away** / **i**. Mar. 22-23, 1989 / Contemporary 14054
Spirited originals and his best effort to date. Featuring Dave Liebman (ss) and Joe Levano (ts). A must-buy. —*Michael G. Nastos*

Form / Apr. 1990 / Contemporary 14059
On this top quintet session, Joe Lovano (ts) enhances his sizable reputation. CD has a bonus cut. —*Ron Wynn*

Visions / **i**. 1991 / Contemporary 14063

JOE HARRIOTT (Joe Arthurlin Harriott)

b. Jul. 15, 1928, Kingston, Jamaica, **d.** Jan. 2, 1973, London, England
Alto saxophone, clarinet / Hard bop, world fusion

Jamaica's most prominent straight jazz musician until Courtney Pine's arrival, Joe Harriott was a hard-blowing, experimental alto saxophonist. Harriott had the misfortune to begin making his break with traditional bebop and hard bop at the same time that Ornette Coleman's innovations were appearing in England. Those who failed to listen closely pinned the rip-off tag on Harriott, who was actually moving in a different, though related, direction. Harriott's concepts were based on an alternative for ensemble interaction rather than on individual exposition, something that was later recognized by astute critics. Initially, Harriott played in Jamaica with Wilton Gaynair and Dizzy Reece, then came to England in the early '50s. He did sessions and freelance dates until he began working with Pete Pitterson. Harriott played with Tony Kinsey's combo and Ronnie Scott's big band in the mid '50s, then formed his own quintet in 1958. His album, *Southern Horizons*, showed the beginnings of his new notions about playing. Harriott worked on the concepts further while hospitalized in 1960. He continued with his musical ideas on such early '60s LPs as *Abstract* and *Indo-Jazz Fusions*. Harriott later explored other hybrid styles, mixing jazz with poetry and traditional Indian music. He did a duet with Michael Garrick for Argo, *Black Marigolds*, in 1966. Currently, Harriot does not have any sessions as a leader available on CD. —*Ron Wynn*

Southern Horizons / Apr. 21, 1960 / Jazzland 937

Free Forms / 1960 / Jazzland 949

BARRY HARRIS (Barry Doyle Harris)

b. Dec. 15, 1929, Detroit, MI
Piano / Bop
A bebop and hard bop giant, Barry Harris plays every composition with zest, fire, and flair. He's a superb accompanist and an magnificent stylist. Harris's harmonic and melodic gifts have also made him a talented teacher. He's written such works as "Nicaragua" and "Like This!" Harris began studying piano at age 4, and worked extensively in Detroit with Thad Jones, Miles Davis, Max Roach, Sonny Stitt, and Wardell Gray in the '50s. Harris began recording as a leader for Argo/Cadet in the late '50s, then did trio and solo dates for Prestige in the early '60s. He joined Cannonball Adderley's quintet in 1960, and soon moved to New York. Harris worked there with Dexter Gordon, Illinois Jacquet, Yusef Lateef, and Hank Mobley. He played with Coleman Hawkins from 1965 to 1969, while also leading his own bands periodically. He continued recording for Riverside and Prestige in the '60s, doing many trio sets. He also made many recordings for Xanadu in the '70s, including some of his most ambitious, expressive sessions. Harris opened the Jazz Cultural Center in 1982, and has been an active teacher there. He hasn't done much recording in recent years, though he made a strong duet record with saxophonist Charles Davis for the Red label. There's a moderate amount of Harris material from the '60s and '70s available. The Red date is available, too. —*Ron Wynn and Bob Porter*

○ **Barry Harris at the Jazz Workshop** / May 15-16, 1960 / Riverside 208
Pianist Barry Harris has been remarkably consistent over the years. *At the Jazz Workshop* captures him live in 1960 (5/15, 5/16) with Sam Jones (b) and Louis Hayes (d). Adding to the expected pleasures of Harris are the slick work of Jones's active bass and the powerful (as in accomplished) drumming of Hayes. —*Bob Rusch*, Cadence

○ **Preminado** / Dec. 21, 1960+Jan. 19, 1961 / Riverside 486

Listen to Barry Harris / Jul. 4, 1961 / Riverside

○ **Newer Than New** / Sep. 28, 1961 / Riverside 413

○ **Chasin' the Bird** / May 31, 1962+Aug. 23, 1962 / Riverside 9435

○ **Bull's Eye** / Jun. 4, 1968 / Prestige 7600

Barry Harris Plays Tadd Dameron / Jun. 4, 1975 / Xanadu 113

A criminally underrated arranger/composer gets showcase treatment from an equally overlooked pianist. —*Ron Wynn*

★ **Live in Tokyo** / Apr. 1, 1976 / Xanadu

This record of pianist Barry Harris playing five tunes recorded by Bud Powell in his prime, in much the same manner as Powell, simply points out that Harris does not have the urgency that made the best of Powell's work so compelling. As usual, Harris does reveal himself to be an accomplished pianist, but he would have sounded so much better if he had stopped shadowing Powell so closely. He would also have sounded better if he had used a better drummer. After all, Powell's recording of "Un Poco Loco" was assisted by the greatest drummer of them all. —*Martin Davidson*, Cadence

Barry Harris Plays Barry Harris / Jan. 17, 1978 / Xanadu

○ **Bird of Red and Gold, The** / i. Sep. 1989 / Xanadu 213

○ **Live at Maybeck Recital Hall—Vol. 12** / Mar. 1990 / Concord Jazz 4476

In this CD, Barry Harris joins the succession of pianists recorded by Concord in solo performances at Maybeck Recital Hall in Berkeley, California. His leisurely opening piece, "It Could Happen To You," finds him reflecting on Art Tatum, with an incorporation of the master's articulated runs and bursts of swing inside the basic tempo. When Harris is playing, Bud Powell is never far away, and in "All God's Chillum Got Rhythm," after a bow toward Thelonious Monk, the pianist gives the first of several demonstrations in this recital of his absorption of Powell's style into his own. One of the most striking examples of Harris's individuality is in his elliptical interpretation of George Shearing's "She." His performances of "Cherokee" and "Parker's Mood" are ammunition for anyone who might care to argue that he is the pure embodiment of the bebop piano tradition. "It Never Entered My Mind" and the themes from "The Flintstones" and "I Love Lucy" may seem an unlikely medley, but they entered Harris's mind together and he makes them get along. Piano sound, of course, is a matter of taste. Those accustomed to the mellower Steinways and Baldwins may find it difficult to adjust to the glassy upper register of the Yamaha S-400-B used here. But Barry Harris worked it out, so perhaps we listeners can. —*Doug Ramsey*, Jazz Times

---

BEAVER HARRIS (William Godvin Harris)

b. Apr. 20, 1936, Pittsburgh, PA, **d.** Dec. 22, 1991
Drums / Progressive big band, modern creative

A wildly eclectic drummer, Beaver Harris didn't merely know how to play in different styles, he was accomplished in them. He could drive a band in the swing mode, play free, incorporate Caribbean, African, or Afro-Latin rhythms into his group's musical structure, or play in hard bop and bebop fashion. Harris began on drums at age 20. He served in the army during the '50s, then returned to his native Pittsburgh in 1957, where he played with Benny Golson, Slide Hampton, and Horace Silver. Harris moved to New York in 1962, and became active in free and hard bop circles. He played with Sonny Rollins, Marion Brown, Albert Ayler, Roswell Rudd, Steve Lacy, Gato Barieri, Thelonious Monk, and Archie Shepp in the '60s and early '70s. Harris coformed the 360 Degree Music Experience in 1968 with Dave Burrell and Grachan Moncur III. This band continued through the '70s and '80s as a repository of musical genres. Numerous fine players were in and out of the band over the years, including Ken McIntyre, Hamiett Bluiett, Ricky Ford, Cameron Brown, Don Pullen, Rahn Burton, and Francis Haynes. Harris also played with Cecil Taylor in the '70s, and worked with Chet Baker, Al Cohn, and Charlie Rouse during engagements at St. James Infirmary, a New York club co-owned by Hod and Rudd O'Brien. The 360 Degree Experience recorded several albums for Black Saint, Soul Note, Cadence, Shemp, and its own label. The Black Saint and Soul Note dates are available on CD. —*Ron Wynn*

From Ragtime to No Time / Jan. 20, 1975+Feb. 11, 1975 / 360 2001

This record opens with a New Orleans-marchlike drum solo and goes into a ragged solo with piano on Dave Burrell's "A.M. Rag." After a short Roy Haynes-like drum transition, vocalist Maxine Sullivan enters doing "Can There Be Peace." The rest of the ensemble joins in on this dirgelike recitative, and then it's uptempo pleasure on "It's Hard But We Do," featuring clarinetist Herb Hall. A few seconds of drum transition and Sullivan returns in similiar fashion. Bringing this side to an end is one last 23-second drum transition. Side two concerns itself more with explorations of sound and rhythm, shifting position to feature Howard Johnson on tuba and also Burrell. This is all part of "Round Trip Parts 1 & 2" (23 minutes), which covers the second side with music filled with joy. The album in total has a joyful, universal concept about it that I applaud. —*Bob Rusch*, Cadence

★ **In: Sanity** / Mar. 8-9, 1976 / Black Saint 7

Recording with 360 Degree Music Experience. Improvisational music with world music touches from percussionist Harris and pianist Dave Burrell. An essential purchase for the adventurous listener. —*Michael G. Nastos*

○ **Live at Nyon** / Jun. 14, 1979 / Cadence 1002

Drummer Beaver Harris made this date at the Nyon festival in Switzerland with a couple of underexposed horn players with lots of roots. Ken McIntyre, a bookish Bostonian who was a contemporary and associate of Eric Dolphy, grabs honors here as much for unusual compositions full of little tags and twists as well as for his archaic horn styles and pretty, purring alto and slap-tongued, squared-off bass clarinet. Trombonist Grachan Moncur III, a charter member of the 1967 version of the 360 Degree Ensemble, sounds thoughtful if a bit staccato because he is slowed by embouchure problems on "Don't I." He barrels through the very up "High Noon," on which both he and McIntyre sound hamstrung for resources, both inspirational and technical, and shoot far too many courses. This set, recorded by Bob Rusch, editor/publisher of *Cadence* magazine, contains a long swinger, two shorter ballads for quartet and duo, and a long sizzler. Harris, a team player, gives himself little solo space. Yet his ensembles push along the rhythm team joyously, and his mesh with old Army pal pianist Ron Burton, probing and positive throughout, and bassist Cameron Brown cut a clean, happy groove all the way. —*Fred Bouchard*, Down Beat

○ **Negcaumongus** / Dec. 7, 1979 / Cadence 1003

Brilliant septet cuts. Ricky Ford (ts) and Don Pullen (p) are magnificent. —*Ron Wynn*

○ **Well Kept Secret with Don Pullen** / 1984 / Hannibal

This edition of the 360 Degree Experience walks the line between inside and outside playing as well as any unit around at the time; they cover a lot of ground, and swing from a light to heavyhanded approach in no time, rarely letting the transitions and juxtapositions sound forced. The in-out synthesis is most obvious on "Double Arc Jake," a merrily swaggering calypso punctated by hyperactive staccato stomping from the horns. In pianist Don Pullen's solo spot, he displays the sheet-lightning rolling right-hand attack—using the side of the hand rather than the fingers—that makes his piano work so amazing and distinctive. Fittingly, Trinidadian steel drummer Francis Haynes has the last word before the fade. Haynes is not along merely to add exotic color. On the suite "Goree" (named for a slave trade port in Senegal)—which suggests, variously, anger, lamentation, dignity, forebearance, and physical grace—Haynes is often as central to the proceedings as Pullen. Sharon Freeman (French horn) arranged the piece (Harris and Pullen did the remainder), and the peaceful French horn quartet interlude that sets up the last section is an album highlight. "Goree" closes with what could have been a Charles Mingus sanctified prayer, hardly surprising given that half the band worked with Mingus at various times. The jaunty gait and mellow riffs that characterize "Newcomer" smack of Mingus, too. Sound on this studio recording is many times better than on the live *Negcaumongus*, yet for some reason the group fails to attain the same high excitement. Perhaps because the group misses the extra stimulus of a responsive audience. —*Kevin Whitehead*, Cadence

CRAIG HARRIS

b. Sep. 10, 1954, Hempstead, NY
Trombone / Soul jazz, modern creative
A top trombonist, Craig Harris has displayed a robust, heavy sound and has utilized circular breathing and multiphonics creatively. His solos sometimes employ devices from traditional New Orleans jazz; other times, they're raggy and flamboyant, or bluesy and funky. Harris played in R&B bands as a teen, and later studied theory, arranging, and composition with Ken McIntyre at Old Westbury, earning his BA in 1976. Harris played with Sun Ra from 1976 to 1978, then with Abdullah Ibrahim from 1979 to 1981, while also playing in the pit band of Lena Horne's Broadway show *The Lady and Her Music.* Harris played and recorded with David Murray's octet and big band, with Henry Threadgill's sextet, with Olu Dara's Okra Orchestra, and with Charlie Haden's Liberation Music Ensemble. He also played with Lester Bowie's Brass Fantasy, with Jaki Byard's Apollo Stompers, and with the big bands of Muhal Richard Abrams, Cecil Taylor, and Sam Rivers during the '80s. He also led several of his own bands, among them the Aqaustra and Tailgater's Tales. The Aqaustra blended trombone, reeds, violin, cello, horn, tuba, bass, and percussion. Tailgater's Tales mixed trombone, clarinet, trumpet, tuba, and drums. Harris also organized standard quartets and quintets. He collaborated with a dance company, the Urban Bushwomen, on a work titled *Points* in the mid '80s. Harris has recorded as a leader for Soul Note, India Navigation, OTC, and JMT. He has sessions available on CD. —*Ron Wynn*

Black Bone / Jan. 1983 / Soul Note 1055
Outstanding session led by trombonist Craig Harris from '83. His robust, vocalized solos are well supported by an all-star quartet including George Adams on tenor sax, Donald Smith on piano, bassist Fred Hopkins, and drummer Charlie Persip. The pieces range from respectful covers of standards to rousing, spirited originals. —*Ron Wynn*

Aboriginal Affairs / i. 1983 / India Navigation
Craig Harris, a journeyman trombonist, chose the haunting and still mystical native Aboriginal culture of Australia as a filter for his own experiences. It was not that far afield for someone who spent two years in the intergalactic sound laboratories of Sun Ra. Just as Sun Ra's furthest explorations were suffused with his deep understanding of the history and culture of jazz, Harris's ethnological forays are also rooted in American jazz culture. Harris subsumes himself to Aboriginal urges on "Awakening Ancestors." He plays a didjeridu, an Australian wind instrument that is a long tube that rests on the ground and seems to bring its sound straight from the bowels of the earth. Shifting into a Ra-like sonnambulist's rhythm, Ken McIntyre takes his flute in a slow-motion dance across the top, truly in dreamtime. Harris is not pretending to fabricate an Aboriginal artifact here, however, and some of his best playing comes in the swingtime. Donald Smith opens "Dingo" with some blistering Cecil Taylor-ish piano over Strobert's churning percussives and timely cymbal punctuations. Everyone gets in a brief statement before engaging in a free-for-all that reveals Ken McIntyre's roots in the pyromania of '60s jazz avant-garde. His alto exhorts pianist Donald Smith and Harris into a frantic dialog. *Aboriginal Affairs* is an impressive debut from an emerging artist who is looking for some surprising but ultimately right places for his source points. —*John Diliberto*, Down Beat

Shelter / i. 1984 / JMT 870008
With Tailgaters Tales. This is an aggressive, never-dull session that operates in the stylistic middle ground between jazz, R&B, blues, and rock. —*Ron Wynn*

★ **Blackout in the Square Root of Soul** / Dec. 1986-Nov. 1987 / PolyGram 34415

A first-rate example of a fresh direction in jazz that blends improvisatory zeal, funk, and R&B references. —*Ron Wynn*

○ **Cold Sweat Plays J.B.** / i. 1989 / JMT 834426
Great gutbucket R&B and populist jazz played with fire, zeal, and grit. The Godfather would be proud. —*Ron Wynn*, Rock & Roll Disc

EDDIE HARRIS

b. Oct. 20, 1934, Chicago, IL
Tenor and electric saxophone, trumpet, piano / Bop, hard bop, blues & jazz, instrumental pop
A fine modern jazz saxophonist and pianist, Eddie Harris has made some of the best soul-jazz albums of the '60s and '70s. He was one of the earliest jazz-rock fusion players, and combined jazz with funk. He has also proven to be an extremely melodic soloist and improviser. His composition "Freedom Jazz Dance" was a landmark in the '60s, and has been recorded numerous times. He recorded the hit single "Exodus" in a "cool jazz" vein, and has also shown mastery of bebop and post-bop styles. Harris is also an innovative instrument designer, and has shown, with his use of a varitone attachment and signal processors/electronic saxophone, that one can utilize electronics legitimately and creatively within traditional improvisational situations. He also created the reed trumpet, and patented it. The idea of playing trumpet with a reed shocked the audience at the 1970 Newport Jazz Festival. He played some remarkable solos despite the unorthodox sound. Harris later reversed the process and played a saxophone fitted with a brass mouthpiece. Harris has written excellent textbooks about sax playing and composing. His playing has a soulful, bluesy, and fiery quality, and he's shown good range and complete command of the tenor on everything from hard bop and bebop to blues, pop, and soul.

Harris studied piano with a cousin and sang in choirs and gospel groups as a youngster. He played vibes, clarinet, and tenor sax in high school, then made his professional debut as a pianist with Gene Ammons. He toured France and Germany in the '50s with the 7th Army Symphony Orchestra. Harris exploded on the scene in the early '60s with a huge hit version of "Exodus." It was a Top 40 smash in 1961 and eventually sold over a million copies, an incredible figure for a jazz musician at any time. Harris's Vee Jay recordings of the early '60s featured his light-toned tenor solos over a gently funky rhythm section, normally with a guitarist. He signed with Atlantic in 1965, and began cutting basic jazz records before switching to the electronic sax and a funk-dominated style. His single "Listen Here" was another crossover hit in the late '60s, and his album, *The Electrifying Eddie Harris*, was also a success.

Harris's work grew more and more trendy and was dominated by electronics, to the point his mid '70s sessions were basically pop outings with minimal to no jazz links. But a surprise union with pianist Les McCann at the 1969 Montreux Jazz Festival led to another hit album, *Swiss Movement*, which is still one of the most popular, requested albums in the Atlantic catalog. McCann and Harris managed to put aside their stylistic and personal differences long enough to tour and record a sequel, *Second Movement.*

Harris had some uneven albums in the mid and late '70s, then resurfaced in the '80s with more tasteful jazz dates. He's done albums for Enja and Timeless in the '80s and '90s. He also had a set of personal recordings issued in the early '90s as part of the "Radio Nights" series that features songs from the private collections of jazz musicians recorded at concerts. Only a handful of recordings featuring Harris, most of them recent, are available on CD. At the end of 1993, Rhino issued a two-CD set of classic Harris recordings as part of its anthology reissue line with Atlantic. One of his early Vee Jay dates was also reissued in 1993. —*Ron Wynn and Bob Porter*

○ **Exodus to Jazz** / Jan. 17, 1961 / Vee Jay 3016
Once past the phlegmatic movie theme ("Exodus") which was a bit of a hit for Eddie Harris in abbreviated form,

Exodus to Jazz proves to be a surprisingly sturdy LP. It is the tenorist's first and finds him in a somewhat Stan Getzian mood and mode. Joe Diorio's guitar, at the same time, reminded me of Jimmy Raney's. The rhythm trio (Willie Pickens, p; William Yancey, b; Harold Jones, d) is supple and propulsive, and the originals—four by Harris, two by Pickens—are diverse and never less than interesting, with "A.T.C./Velocity/W.P." the clear winners. The recital is topped off by Harris's restrained but fervent reading of Rodgers and Hart's "Little Girl Blue." —*Alan Bargebuhr, Cadence*

○ **Mighty Like a Rose** / Apr. 14, 1961 / Vee Jay 3025

○ **Jazz for "Breakfast at Tiffany's"** / 1961 / Vee Jay 3027

○ **"In" Sound, The** / Aug. 9, 1965 / Atlantic 1448

○ **Best Of, The** / i. Sep. 1965-Dec. 1973 / Atlantic 1545
A skeletal anthology of some of Harris's Atlantic cuts. It leans toward hits, but does contain "Listen Here" and "Theme from Exodus." A good introductory album to his work. —*Ron Wynn*

★ **Electrifying Eddie Harris** / 1967 / Atlantic
The birth and fruition of Harris's use of varitone and electronics on tenor as a legitimate technique. —*Ron Wynn*

★ **Swiss Movement** / Jun. 1969 / Atlantic 50405
With Les McCann. Evergreen! Contains the monster hit "Compared to What." A must-buy, if you don't have it already. —*Michael G. Nastos*

Free Speech / 1970 / Atlantic

☆ **Second Movement** / 1971 / Atlantic 1583
With Les McCann. The follow-up to *Swiss Movement* didn't sell so well, but still has plenty of fine music. —*Ron Wynn*

Live at Newport / i. 1972 / Atlantic

Playing with Myself / 1979 / RCA
The title notwithstanding, this is an intelligent, attention-grabbing solo album. —*Ron Wynn*

Steps Up / Feb. 20, 1981 / Steeple Chase 115

Homecoming / i. 1985 / Spindletop 105
A very nice, underrated teaming of Eddie Harris and Ellis Marsalis (p). It's understated, bluesy, mellow, and sometimes challenging. —*Ron Wynn*

○ **Eddie Who?** / Feb. 1986 / Impulse 33104

Live in Berlin / i. Mar. 24, 1988 / Timeless

○ **There Was a Time (Echo of Harlem)** / May 9, 1990 / Enja 79663
This is a fine retrospective and mainstream date. CD bonus cut. —*Ron Wynn*

For You, for Me, for Everyone / i. Oct. 1992 / Steeple Chase 31322
When the pianist failed to show for a planned duo date in the Copenhagen studio, Eddie Harris decided to accompany himself, and the result is an astonishing tour de force. (Hardly anyone remembers that the tenor sax player with the unique, airy sound was once Billie Holiday's pianist.) Harris first laid down the piano tracks, anticipating his tenor solos and even unison passages, and then wrapped most of the tracks in a first take. Mostly a ballad album, including three sumptuous originals. —*Les Line*

○ **Lost Album Plus the Better Half, The** / i. 1993 / Vee Jay 913
Eddie Harris has been one of jazz's more frustrating and unpredictable musicians since the early '60s. An excellent blues, soul-jazz, and bop player when he exerts himself, Harris has also issued several woeful albums, recording sessions of standup comedy and other filler that wasted his skills. That is not the case on these eight cuts culled from early '60s Vee Jay dates. The first four blend soul-jazz and straight bop with Ira Sullivan sparkling on trumpet and Harris dueling with alto saxophonist Bunky Green. The other two feature Harris wailing the blues alongside organist Melvin Rhyne, Sullivan, Green, and guitarist Joe D'Orio. They recall the glory days of steamy, funky organ combos, with drummer Gerald Donovan keeping the backbeat

steadily in the groove. The other four tracks include a cover of Charlie Parker's "K.C. Blues," a Harris original "Yea, Yea, Yea," a number similar to his hit "Exodus" in *Lawrence of Arabia*, and the decent but uninspired "Half & Half." Harris was just beginning to explode on the jazz scene, and these cuts were recorded when he was an emerging, hungry tenor player. —*Ron Wynn*

○ **Excursions** / Atlantic
An underrated, two-record live set with some of Harris's best acoustic and electric sax solos. —*Ron Wynn*

GENE HARRIS (Eugene Harris)

b. Sep. 1, 1933, Benton Harbor, MI
Piano / Hard bop, blues & jazz
He's not flashy, dazzling, controversial, or unusual; pianist Gene Harris simply plays fluid, bluesy, and entertaining solos whether he's leading trios, working in a large band, or playing with a combo. He's often compared to Ramsey Lewis, Les McCann, or Junior Mance, and does similar material, though he is seldom as pop-oriented as Lewis. Harris taught himself piano after being inspired by boogie-woogie as a child. He played in an army band during the early '50s, then formed a group with Andy Simpkins and Bill Dowdy in 1956 that became the Three Sounds in 1957. They did mostly blues and worked in the Midwest before moving to New York in 1958. In New York, they added show tunes and standards and changed their approach, with Harris showing his bebop and hard bop side along with the blues. The Three Sounds was one of the longest-running combos of its type. Though originals Dowdy and Simpkins departed in the late '60s, Harris maintained a Three Sounds crew into the '70s. He moved to Idaho and turned to more straight jazz. Harris played in Las Vegas with a quartet, and backed Ernestine Anderson in Seattle. He worked with Benny Carter in the mid '80s at the Concord Jazz Festival and played with Ray Brown's trio at the Half Note in New York. Harris continued recording in the '80s and '90s. He was featured on the 23rd volume of Concord's continuing Maybeck Recital Hall solo series in 1993. Harris has done sessions for Blue Note, Verve, and Concord. He has dates available on CD. —*Ron Wynn*

Introducing the Three Sounds / Sep. 16+28, 1958 / Blue Note 1600

★ **Feelin' Good** / i. 1959 / Blue Note
Prototypical Three Sounds release. Elements of funk, soul-jazz, and blues merge into a workable jazz concept. —*Ron Wynn*

The Three Sounds / Oct. 12-15, 1962 / Verve 68514

★ **Live at Otter Crest** / Apr. 24, 1981 / Bosco 4
Underrated latter-period Harris on piano with trio. Great extended "Battle Hymn," Basie's repertoire represented in "Shiny Stockings" and "Ate," and your reliable Harris's "A Little Blues There" included. —*Michael G. Nastos*

Plus One / Nov. 12, 1983 / Concord Jazz 4303
Live at New York City's legendary Blue Note, a great place to hear live music. Ray Brown is a major player on bass and compositionally. Stanley Turrentine (ts) cameos. —*Michael G. Nastos*

Tribute to Count Basie / Mar. 1987-Jun. 1987 / Concord Jazz 4337
An emphatic big-band tribute to the swing master. —*Ron Wynn*

Listen Here! / Mar. 1989 / Concord Jazz 4385
A solid mainstream date with light soul-jazz flavor. CD version has two bonus cuts. —*Ron Wynn*

Live at Town Hall NYC / Sep. 1989 / Concord Jazz 4397
A fine, traditional big-band outing. The song selection is predictably conservative, but there's enough boldness in the arrangements and playing to even things out and make this an above-average entry in a domain screaming for fresh blood. —*Ron Wynn, Rock & Roll Disc*

○ **At Last** / May 1990 / Concord Jazz 4434

A wonderful teamup of Gene Harris with Scott Hamilton's band. CD version has two bonus cuts. —*Ron Wynn*

World Tour 1990 / Oct. 1990 / Concord Jazz 4443

○ **Black and Blue** / **i.** Oct. 25, 1991 / Concord Jazz 4482
Pianist Gene Harris's church-oriented funk and rhythmic stamp is on everything, whether musician's tunes—a half dozen here—or standards. He straight-fours Stevie Wonder's "Another Star" and funk-a-fies the Fats Waller classic "Black and Blue." Guitarist Ron Eschete gets a particularly good airing on "C.C. Rider," the traditional line, done medium up, but no less soulful. On Ralph Flanagan's "Hot Toddy," a guitar-led big-band dance tune, Harris takes on the role of big band, making it sound as smooth as the drink for which it was named. With capable rhythm support from bassist Luther Hughes and drummer Harold Jones, and eschewing the Latin tempo for which it was titled, Kenny Dorham's "Blue Bossa" becomes 4/4 blue with just a hint of bossa. In contrast, Matt Dennis's "Will You Still Be Mine," a popular jazzy vocal standard, is a romantic romp for Harris. Also represented are Jerome Kern, Oscar Hammerstein and Richard Rodgers, and DeSylva, Brown, and Henderson. They wrote the melodies, but it is Harris and company who moves them from standard fare to rarified air. —*Arnold Jay Smith*, Jazz Times

JEROME HARRIS

b. 1953
Bass, guitar / Modern creative
An alternately flashy or reflective player, electric guitarist and bassist Jerome Harris has worked as a session player, sideman, and collaborator with several major players, most notably Sonny Rollins. Harris has been successful playing in many styles, from free to jazz to funk and R&B. He's also recorded as a leader for Minor Music and Muse. Harris has a couple of sessions available as a leader on CD. —*Ron Wynn and Michael G. Nastos*

★ **Algorithms** / **i.** Mar. 1986 / Minor Music 1011
Bassist and guitarist in sympathetic progressive setting. Similiar to Michael Gregory Jackson's *Gifts*, as a companion album with similiar personnel. Highly recommended. —*Michael G. Nastos*

In Passing / **i.** May 23, 1989 / Muse 5386

DONALD HARRISON (Donald "Duck" Harrison)

b. Jun. 23, 1960, New Orleans, LA
Alto and soprano saxophone / Neo-bop
Another member of the second New Orleans group of musicians who became jazz stars in the '80s, alto saxophonist Donald Harrison demonstrated a facility and fluidity that made an instant impact. His solos were fast, sometimes torrid, but were not clichéd nor imitative. Harrison had both a bluesy fervor and solid bebop skills. This was directly attributable to the training he received from Ellis Marsalis while attending the New Orleans Center for the Creative Arts. He'd played there with Terence Blanchard. Harrison later attended Southern University for a year, then went to Berklee College of Music. He led an organ trio in Boston in 1980 with Makoto Ozone, then toured with Roy Haynes in 1980 and 1981. After working the remainder of 1981 with Brother Jack McDuff, Harrison replaced Branford Marsalis in Art Blakey's band just as Blanchard was replacing Wynton Marsalis. A year later the duo made an album for Concord, and shortly afterward left Blakey to form their own band. They made several albums for Concord and Columbia, before disbanding in the early '90s. Harrison has since recorded two albums on the Candid label; one is a quintet hard bop date, the other is an album that mixes the music of the Mardi Gras "Indians" with blues and jazz. His albums with Blanchard, as well as those he did with Blakey and his own sessions, are available on CD. —*Ron Wynn*

★ **For Art's Sake** / Nov. 1990 / Candid 79501
A tribute album to great drummer Art Blakey from one-time Jazz Messenger alto saxophonist Donald Harrison. This is one of Harrison's first sessions after he and longtime partner trumpeter Terence Blanchard went their separate ways, and Harrison is working with new trumpeter Marlon Jordan and other Young Lions: pianist Cyrus Chestnut, bassist Christian McBride, and drummer Carl Allen. The results would have made Blakey smile. —*Ron Wynn*

Indian Blues / May 1991 / Candid 79514
Alto saxophonist Donald Harrison explores another area of his New Orleans heritage, the music of the Mardi Gras "Indians." His solos are more bluesy and R&B-flavored, while the supporting cast includes Dr. John on piano along with Cyrus Chestnut, drummer Carl Allen, bassist Phil Bowler, percussionists Bruce Cox, and Howard Smiley Ricks, plus Harrison's father on vocals. —*Ron Wynn*

ANTONIO HART

Saxophone / Neo-bop
An emerging alto saxophonist who's made three fine albums in the '90s, Antonio Hart has shown a stylistic maturity and versatility that's impressive for someone still in his early twenties. One of the finest disciples of the Cannonball Adderley style, Hart's recorded exclusively for RCA/Novus, and his '93 album included tributes to Adderley and to Charlie Parker. Hart has worked with Gregory Hutchinson, Rodney Whitaker, Gary Bartz, Mulgrew Miller, Christian McBride, Jamal Haynes, Roy Hargrove, and others. All his sessions are available on CD. —*Ron Wynn*

For the First Time / **i.** Oct. 1991 / Novus 3120
Introductory vehicle for yet another Young Lion, alto saxophonist Antonio Hart. The set has the almost obligatory hard bop feel, but Hart's shimmering solos aren't just imitative Charlie Parker licks; he displays sensitivity and style on every selection, and the album demonstrates genuine potential, as well as technical aptitude. —*Ron Wynn*

★ **Don't You Know I Care** / **i.** 1992 / Novus 63142
Some beautiful ballads and surging uptempo songs done by alto saxophonist Antonio Hart on his '92 follow-up release to his '91 debut as a leader. Hart has the tone, style, and skill to be a star and hasn't succumbed to publicity hype. He's aided by cast that blends new players such as Gregory Hutchinson and Rodney Whitaker with veterans like Gary Bartz. —*Ron Wynn*

BILLY HART (William W. Hart)

b. Nov. 29, 1940, Washington, DC
Drums / Hard bop
Drummer Billy Hart can perform in a totally different, yet satisfying manner on jazz-rock, hard bop, and free music. His loosest, most explosive playing comes on freer material, but he's disciplined and on the beat for hard bop, and a relentless basher when he plays rock and funk. Hart taught himself drums, and made his professional debut backing Shirley Horn. He worked with Jimmy Smith, Wes Montgomery, Eddie Harris, Pharoah Sanders, and Marian McPartland in the '60s, then joined Herbie Hancock's band in 1970. He was with Hancock for three turbulent but exciting years in which Hancock experimented with electronic material and on-the-edge jazz-rock. Hart then worked with McCoy Tyner for a year, and played periodically with Stan Getz from the mid '70s until 1980. He did several sessions with Miles Davis, Jimmie Rowles, Niels-Henning Ørsted-Pedersen, Clark Terry, Lee Konitz, Chico Freeman Horn, and James Newton in the '70s and '80s. He also contributed some fine playing to dates by Hal Galper for Inner City. Hart co-formed Colloquium III with fellow drummers Horacee Arnold and Freddie Waits. They led percussive workshops at the New York Drummers' Collective. Hart has recorded as a leader for A&M and Gramavision. Currently, none of his sessions are available on CD. He can be heard on discs by Davis, Terry, Konitz, Freeman, and others. —*Ron Wynn and Michael G. Nastos*

★ **Enchance** / Feb. 24, 1977-Mar. 3, 1977 / A&M 0818

A recording just at the edge of all-out. Powerful, pretty, and potent. All originals. An important document. —*Michael G. Nastos*

Oshumare / 1985 / Gramavision 8502

JOHNNY HARTMAN (John Maurice Hartman)

b. Jul. 3, 1923, Chicago, IL, **d.** Sep. 15, 1983, New York, NY
Vocals / Ballads & blues
A sorely underrated, magical ballad stylist, Johnny Hartman possessed a superb delivery and sound, had remarkable enunciation and had such a rich, evocative voice that it's hard to understand why he wasn't a bigger star. He was subtle, yet swinging on uptempo tunes and commanding on slow numbers. Hartman sang with his high school jazz orchestra in Chicago, later attended Chicago Musical College, then began his professional career, only to have it interrupted by military service. After his discharge, Hartman worked with Earl Hines, Dizzy Gillespie, and Erroll Garner in the late '40s, then became a soloist. He worked in clubs and on television. He recorded for Savoy in the late '40s, and for Bethlehem in the mid '50s. The 1963 Impulse album, *John Coltrane and Johnny Hartman*, electrified people in and out of the jazz world, and remains an endearing session. Hartman sang and recorded in Tokyo with Roland Hanna and George Mraz during the '70s, and received a Grammy nomination for the early '80s album *Once in Every Life*. While he covered everything from standards to pop and country, Hartman's forte was jazz-based compositions and romantic ballads. He recorded for Savoy, Audiophile, Bethlehem, Impulse, Perception, Trio, and Bee Hive. Currently, some of Hartman's sessions are available on CD. —*Ron Wynn*

Songs from the Heart / Nov. 1956 / Bethlehem 43

★ **I Just Dropped by to Say Hello** / Oct. 9, 1963+Oct. 17, 1963 / MCA 39105

Voice That Is, The / Sep. 22, 1964+Sep. 24, 1964 / Impulse 74

Today / 1973 / Perception 30

○ **Once in Every Life** / Aug. 11, 1980 / Bee Hive 7012
Johnny Hartman was the best, or certainly one of the best, mellow jazz singers. Considering all of Hartman's LPs made previous to this Bee Hive recording, he made two great ones: one with John Coltrane for Impulse, and the other for Perception Records called *Today*. This record ranks with his best. It is vocal honey and beyond words. —*Bob Rusch*, Cadence

OTTO HARDWICKE (Otto Hardwick)

b. 1904, **d.** 1970
Alto saxophone / Swing, big band
An outstanding alto saxophonist, Otto Hardwicke (or Hardwick; it's not clear how his name was spelled) was one of the earliest players to give that instrument some identity and to demonstrate its potential for improvisation. He had a consistently swinging, enjoyable style, and provided both sentimental, lyrical refrains on ballads and joyous work on stomps. Hardwicke began as a bassist, then moved to C-melody sax, and finally settled on alto. He was extremely versatile, and, during his first stint in the band, played clarinet and violin as well as baritone and alto. Hardwicke and Ellington were friends for virtually their entire lives, though Hardwicke didn't remain in the band nearly as long as some other musicians. Their friendship began in the early '20s; Hardwicke left the band in 1928 to visit Europe. He played with Noble Sissle and led his own orchestra before returning to New York in 1929. Harwicke worked with a band that included Chu Berry and Fats Waller; this orchestra even bested Ellington in a battle of the bands. But Hardwicke returned to the Ellington orchestra in 1932 following a brief stint with Elmer Snowden, and remained with Ellington until 1946. During this stint, Hardwicke doubled on bass sax. He and Ellington co-composed several pieces, most notably "Sophisticated Lady." He was featured on songs such as

"Jubilee Stomp" and "Got Everything But You." Hardwicke also played lead alto on several pieces in which Johnny Hodges wasn't featured as the principal alto player. After cutting an album in 1947, Hardwick retired from the music business. He can be heard on many Ellington albums reissued on CD from the '20s, '30s, and '40s. —*Ron Wynn*

STAN HASSELGARD

b. Oct. 4, 1922, Sundsvall, Sweden, **d.** Nov. 23, 1948, Decatur, IL
Clarinet / Swing, big band, bop
An outstanding clarinetist in the swing style, Swedish musician Stan Hasselgard moved toward bebop right at the end of his career, but was a first-rate swing soloist in his short prime. Hasselgard played with an amateur group, the Royal Swingers, then began his professional career playing with the bands of Arthur Osterwall, Simon Brehm, Bob Laine, and Gosta Turner in the mid and late '40s. Hasselgard recorded with Brehm, Laine, and Turner. He earned his Masters degree from Uppsala University in 1947, then came to America. Hasselgard played with Johnny White and Count Basie in 1947, while recording four tracks as a leader for Capitol with Barney Kessel and Red Norvo in the band. He joined Benny Goodman's septet at the end of 1947, and stayed with it until it disbanded the next summer. His last band included Max Roach and Barbara Carroll, and was moving toward a more bebop style when Hasselgard died in a car accident in November of 1948. He had turned 26 only a month before the accident. Currently, Hasselgard does not have any sessions available on CD in America. —*Ron Wynn*

★ **Ake 'Stan' Hasselgard (1945-1948)** / i. Oct. 1945-Nov. 1948 / Dragon 25

○ **Jammin' at Jubilee** / i. Jan. 1948-Jul. 1948 / Dragon 29

★ **At Click (1948)** / i. May 1948-Jun. 1948 / Dragon 183

HAMPTON HAWES

b. Nov. 13, 1928, Los Angeles, CA, **d.** May 22, 1977, Los Angeles, CA
Piano / Hard bop
A self-taught pianist, Hampton Hawes was a bellwether on the '50s scene. He was one of bebop's greatest players, and certainly one of the finest bebop players on the West Coast. He was also one of the great uptempo soloists, and displayed a rhythmic intensity and an impressive dexterity on blistering tempos. He later demonstrated that electric keyboards could have a personalized sound. While still a teen, Hawes played with Sonny Criss, Dexter Gordon, Big Jay McNeely, and Wardell Gray. He joined Howard McGhee's band in the early '50s, where he played with Charlie Parker. Parker greatly influenced Hawes's conception. Then came stints with Shorty Rogers and Howard Rumsey, with whom Hawes also recorded, before an army hitch. Hawes played in Japan while in the service, then led a trio with Red Mitchell and Chuck Thompson in 1955 and 1956. He recorded with Wardell Gray in the early '50s, and was featured on half an album with Freddie Redd for Fantasy. He became a prolific session musician, cutting several trio dates for Contemporary, recording on the Trio label with Charles Mingus and Dannie Richmond, and doing quartet sessions with Barney Kessel, Sonny Rollins, and with his own band.

A 1958 arrest and conviction for heroin possession resulted in a 10-year prison sentence for Hawes. A letter Hawes sent to President Kennedy helped to get Hawes pardoned in 1963. He reunited with Mitchell, then led a group with Jimmy Garrison. Hawes continued recording regularly for Contemporary, and also did albums for MPS, Black Lion, Storyville, and others. Though antiquated cabaret card laws prevented Hawes from playing in New York City during the '60s (at the time, any convicted felon couldn't play in a New York club that served liquor), Hawes performed and recorded in Japan and Europe in the late '60s. He began working with Leroy Vinnegar in 1969 and 1970. Hawes also kept busy cutting sessions for Enja, Arista, Prestige,

Concord, and Contemporary. Hawes began using electric keyboards almost exclusively, playing with Carol Kaye and Mario Suraci in the mid '70s. He won a prestigious Deems Taylor award for his autobiography, *Raise Up Off Me*, in 1974. There was one last classic trio date with Ray Brown and Shelley Manne for Contemporary, then Hawes died of a stroke in 1977. After his death, there were some poignant sessions issued on Artists House, which matched Hawes with Charlie Haden. Haden dedicated his own Artists House album, *The Golden Number*, to Hawes. *Hampton Hawes at the Piano* was also released posthumously. There's a surprisingly large number of Hawes releases currently available; they cover the full spectrum of his sessions. —*Ron Wynn*

○ **East/West Controversy, The** / Sep. 22, 1951 / Xanadu 104

Piano: East/West / Dec. 1952 / Original Jazz Classics 1705
Hawes and Freddie Redd (p) split an album, revealing their differing, yet mutually appealing, stylistic tendencies. —*Ron Wynn*

○ **Hampton Hawes—Vol. 1** / Jun. 28, 1955 / Original Jazz Classics 638
Mid '50s trio dates, with pianist Hampton Hawes in peak, robust form. He was then an invigorating soloist, whose runs, phrases, and lines were often remarkable, and whose inventiveness and creativity as a composer were beginning to be noticed. —*Ron Wynn*

Everybody Likes Hampton Hawes—Vols. 1-3: The Trio / Jun. 28, 1956 / Contemporary 316
The Hampton Hawes set is Vol. 3 of "The Trio's" recordings with bassist Red Mitchell and drummer Chuck Thompson in this series for Contemporary. The final volume is again workmanlike, sometimes leaden, and not all that exciting. The catch here, I guess, is that one gets the first album and is so impressed that they get the second and then, well, what the hell, have the set. There are worse sets to have but there is better Hawes piano fare. Do get Vol. 1. —*Bob Rusch, Cadence*

○ **All Night Session!—Vols. 1-3** / Nov. 12-13, 1956 / Contemporary 638
Some wondrous, invigorating playing from everyone included, especially Hawes and Jim Hall (g). —*Ron Wynn*

○ **Four! Hampton Hawes!!!!** / Jan. 27, 1958 / Contemporary 165

Sermon, The / i. 1958 / Contemporary 7653

Green Leaves of Summer / Feb. 7, 1964 / Contemporary 476

Here and Now / May 12, 1965 / Contemporary 178
Adept and nimble work from Hawes. Chuck Israels roams and booms on bass. —*Ron Wynn*

★ **Seance, The** / Apr. 30, 1966-May 1, 1966 / Contemporary 455
There is an uneasy feeling given by pianist Hampton Hawes as he makes little rips in his blues, out of which tumble skittering runs. Hawes's playing here proves more than a backdrop for one's thoughts and action; it draws one's attention to its ideas and body. This set was recorded live over two days at Mitchell's Studio Club, where the group had been gigging for most of a year. Hawes's trio with bassist Red Mitchell and drummer Don Bailey really has everything going for it, including a solid program of standards and excellent originals, superior support, especially from Mitchell, and swinging improvisation that is both inventive and accessible. There is an emotional power here that is subtle but unrelenting, and the tracks seem so arranged that, if played in order, they give the feeling by the end of "My Romance" as though the listener has been part of the music's movement. —*Bob Rusch, Cadence*

★ **Challenge, The** / May 7-12, 1968 / Storyville 1013

☆ **Key for Two** / Jan. 1969 / Affinity

Little Copenhagen Night Music, A / Sep. 2, 1971 / Arista 1043

An album where Hawes adds electric piano and synthesizer to his arsenal. —*Ron Wynn*

○ **Live at the Montmartre** / Sep. 2, 1971 / Arista 1020
What came across when Hampton Hawes played piano was his genuineness. And as this record indicates, he was still vital and changing. He did not create his own language in jazz, but he was a native and fluent speaker of the music, as were bassist Henry Franklin and drummer Michael Carvin. They recorded these five numbers in 1971 at Copenhagen's Cafe Montmartre, and most of it sounds like a conversation in rhythm and melody among three friends. The influence of Coltrane and especially McCoy Tyner is present, but not in a mimicking way. Some of what Hawes was attempting then on acoustic piano oddly presaged what he was soon to implement on the Rhodes. —*Ira Steingroot, Down Beat*

★ **Blues for Walls** / Jan. 16-18, 1973 / Prestige 10060
Good, early '70s set with pianist Hampton Hawes mixing acoustic and electric keyboard numbers, playing with passion, although the material is uneven. He's backed by electric bassist Carol Kaye and tries to find balance between the bop and West Coast-style numbers he'd done in the past and more contemporary material. —*Ron Wynn*

○ **Live at the Jazz Showcase in Chicago** / Jun. 1973 / Enja 3099
As fine as any trio set Hawes ever made, with Cecil McBee (b) and Roy Haynes (d). —*Ron Wynn*

Recorded Live at the Great American Music Hall / Jun. 10, 1975 / Concord Jazz 222
Pianist Hampton Hawes's last live recording presents few critical difficulties. Side one of this release pairs Hawes with bassist Mario Suraci, and the two romp through two time-tested (some might say time-worn) standards. Hawes makes the most of such lightweight material. After a meandering, rubato introduction to "Fly Me to the Moon," Hawes is joined by the bassist and mixes Bird-like phrases with continuous theme and variation improvising peppered with blues licks, a frenzy of runs, and a wringing out of the melody in every possible way. "Sunny" receives an equally elaborate treatment. Opening with churchy chords, Hawes stretches out for some 14 minutes, playfully squeezing every possible melodic nuance out of this vehicle in a series of continuous variational choruses. This release's magnum opus, though, is Hawes's "The Status Of Maceo," a suite for solo piano in three movements. Opening with fluttery chords supporting a lyrical melody backed by a simple bass pattern, Hawes introduces blues motifs over repetitious patterns in the manner of Keith Jarrett. A bossa nova section gives way to a return of the opening motif. Intermixed with this are passages of non-jazz effects, gospel-blues figures, and rolling boogie patterns. —*Jon Balleras, Down Beat*

Killing Me Softly . . . / Aug. 14, 1976 / Contemporary 7637
The swan song for the Hawes trio sessions, with top contributions by Ray Brown (b) and Shelly Manne (d). —*Ron Wynn*

COLEMAN HAWKINS (Coleman Randoph Hawkins)

b. Nov. 21, 1904, St. Joseph, MO, **d.** May 19, 1969, New York, NY

Tenor saxophone / Swing, big band
The popularizer of the tenor saxophone and a true innovator, Coleman Hawkins didn't begin on sax, but started playing it at age nine after first exploring the piano and the cello. He was a professional by the age of 12, playing at school dances. After attending high school in Chicago, Hawkins has said he studied harmony and composition at Washburn College in Topeka, Kansas, for two years. This is not totally clear or verified. Classic blues vocalist Mamie Smith picked Hawkins from a Kansas City theater pit band in 1921 to join her touring Jazz Hounds. He worked with Smith at the Garden of Joy in New York City in 1922, then cut his debut recordings with her, though his contributions were largely negligible except for the song "I'm Gonna Get You."

Hawkins left the Hounds after a 1923 tour, which included an appearance in the revue *Struttin' Along.* Hawkins then freelanced with various musicians in New York. Fletcher Henderson heard him with Wilbur Sweatman's band at the club Connie's Inn and tapped him for a recording session the following August. In the interim, Hawkins worked with pianist Ginger Jones and trumpeter Charlie Gaines at the Garden of Joy, and with Cecil Smith and Lou Hooper at the Renaissance Casino. Both Hawkins and Henderson played under violinist Ralph Jones at the Barnville Club. When Henderson formed a band to play the Club Albam in early 1924, he again contacted Hawkins. Hawkins stayed with the Henderson orchestra for over a decade, making numerous records and cementing his reputation worldwide.

His playing would eventually be influenced by Louis Armstrong and Art Tatum. Hawkins's earliest sax solos featured the heavily articulated slap tonguing that was commonplace; he discarded it later for the legato approach. Armstrong's sense of swing, timing, and smooth melodic lines, plus Tatum's harmonic ideas, was absorbed into Hawkins's approach. The fluidity and rhythmic flexibility in Hawkins's playing—his sensitive, full tone and incorporation of phrases that echoed speechlike patterns—impressed his peers. Hawkins began to play more on the beat and to craft elaborate, artfully constructed solos no matter how fast the tempo. After leaving Henderson, Hawkins was invited to Europe by bandleader and promoter Jack Hylton. He stayed for five years and was an idol to many European musicians. When he returned to America in 1939, Hawkins made history with his recording of "Body and Soul." This was the only best-selling record in jazz history that was comprised primarily of improvisation. Everything, from Hawkins's warm, inviting tenor sound to his harmonic inventiveness and consistent use throughout of double time, established the song as a landmark, and beat back any challenges to his crown as tenor king, something that had been contested by such players as Chu Berry, Herschel Evans, and Lester Young.

Hawkins formed a big band, but it wasn't financially viable, and he soon began heading small combos. Always a step ahead of the pack in his thinking, Hawkins hired several youngsters whose ideas and styles were in conflict with the norm. He employed Dizzy Gillespie, Howard McGhee, Max Roach, and Thelonious Monk before they'd built their reputations, and his 1944 band made recordings now considered the first bop dates. That same year, he introduced Monk to the jazz community. Hawkins spent much of 1945 in California, playing and recording with a band that included McGhee and Oscar Pettiford; they even appeared in the film *The Crimson Canary.*

Hawkins returned to the East Coast briefly, but was back in California in 1946 as part of the Jazz at the Philharmonic tour. He appeared on three tours periodically over the next five years, and went to Europe in 1948 and 1949 (he'd return in 1950 and 1954). Hawkins led recording groups that featured newcomers Fats Navarro, J.J. Johnson, Milt Jackson, and Miles Davis. He also made another masterpiece in 1948, the unaccompanied improvisation "Picasso," which dazzled musicians then and now in its power, structure, and execution. His adaptability kept Hawkins active into the '60s. His '50s dates reflect a harder tone and combative blues style, and he performed a wonderful, updated "Body and Soul" in 1959. Hawkins even plugged into the bossa nova craze of the early '60s, and was comfortable with soul-jazz. He remained a commanding, vital player until his health declined in the late '60s. Regardless of the type of music he played, he's still an inspirational figure to generations of musicians. *—Ron Wynn with Dan Morgenstern*

★ **In Europe 1934/39** / **i.** Nov. 18, 1934-May 26, 1939 / Jazz Up 318-319

In 1934, Coleman Hawkins, after 11 years as the star soloist with Fletcher Henderson's pioneering jazz big band, was looking for other worlds to conquer. To satisfy his curiosity he traveled to Europe and for the next five years was a major celebrity overseas, only returning to the United States

when World War II loomed. This magnificent three-CD set contains every recording that the great tenor saxophonist made in Europe, 71 in all (including alternate takes). Whether featured in London, Switzerland, Paris, or Holland, Hawkins dominates these recordings, which find him in a variety of settings from duets with pianist Freddie Johnson to medium-sized bands. Benny Carter and Django Reinhardt also make a few notable appearances. This perfectly done set is highly recommended. *—Scott Yanow*

○ **Hawk in Holland** / **i.** Feb. 4, 1935-Apr. 26, 1937 / GNP 9003

This enjoyable LP finds Coleman Hawkins guesting with the Ramblers, a fine Dutch swing group, in 1935 and 1937. While pianist Freddie Johnson is the only other distinctive soloist (although Annie de Reuver contributes two haunting vocals), the Ramblers do an excellent job of accompanying their American guest on a variety of standards and a couple of Hawk's originals. The closer, "Something Is Gonna Give Me Away," finds the tenorman romping with just the rhythm section and is quite memorable. This material has since been reissued on CD. *—Scott Yanow*

○ **Coleman Hawkins and Benny Carter** / **i.** Mar. 2, 1935-Aug. 23, 1946 / Disques Swing 8403

This consists of four somewhat familiar but still superb swing sessions. The first date has lots of high-quality Coleman Hawkins on three ballads ("Stardust" has him backed by "only" guitarist Django Reinhardt and Stephane Grappelli's piano) and a hard-driving "Avalon." The second session is quite famous, particularly "Crazy Rhythm," which put Europe's best saxophonists (Andre Ekyan and Alix Combelle) against a couple of not-too-shabby American players (Benny Carter and Hawk). Hawkins played so strongly on this cut that Reinhardt willingly gave up his chorus so Hawkins could continue; he shouts "Go on, go on!" Three selections from 1938 have more good solos from Carter, Combelle, and Reinhardt, while the concluding 1946 date is as strong and swinging as one could expect from a front line of Carter, Al Grey (t), Buck Clayton (tpt), and Ben Webster (ts), a lineup that was taken for granted at the time. Carter's clarinet solo on "Georgia" and Sid Catlett's solo on "Out of My Way" are equal rarities. *—Scott Yanow, Cadence*

★ **Body and Soul** / **i.** Oct. 11, 1939-Jan. 20, 1956 / RCA Bluebird 5658

Much of the material on this two-LP set has been since reissued on CD, but, one way or the other, this music (particularly the first 16 tracks) belongs in every serious jazz collection. In 1939 Coleman Hawkins returned to the United States after five years in Europe, and it took him very little time to reassert his dominance as king of the tenors. This set starts off with the session that resulted in Hawk's classic version of "Body And Soul," teams him with Benny Carter (tpt) for some hot swing (including a memorable rendition of "My Blue Heaven"), and then finds Hawkins using younger musicians (including trumpeter Fats Navarro and trombonist J.J. Johnson) on some advanced bop originals highlighted by "Half Step Down Please." The remainder of this set is also good but less historic with Hawkins well showcased with three larger groups in 1956, culminating in a remake of "Body And Soul." *—Scott Yanow*

○ **Commodore Years: The Tenor Sax** / May 25, 1940-Aug. 12, 1954 / Atlantic 2306

Coleman Hawkins was one of the first great jazz saxophonists and one of the undisputed giants in the music's history, a timeless musical Gibraltar. Hawkins's cuts on this anthology, which also includes a number of tracks by saxophonist/flutist Frank Wess, are never less than excellent and often monumentally great, as on "I Surrender Dear," "I Can't Believe," and "Boff Boff." Everything is in evidence, including Hawkins's big, full tone, his aggressive attack, his harmonic and melodic genius, and his innate sense of structure. In addition, he is surrounded on both sides of this record (the first recorded in 1940, the second three years later) by brilliant sidemen. On side one, the always lyrical Benny Carter alto sax and the slashing, biting Roy Eldridge trumpet complement Hawkins superbly. Eldridge, in fact, achieves the almost-impossible feat of upstaging him during his solo on "I Can't Believe." On side two, pianist Art Tatum shares the limelight with his apt accompaniment and absolutely incredible solos. This collection is well worth owning for the classic Hawkins work it contains. *—Peter Keepnews, Down Beat*

☆ **Classic Tenors—Lester Young & Coleman Hawkins** / i. Dec. 8, 1943-Dec. 23, 1943 / Flying Dutchman 10146
Although this LP is long out of print, its brilliant contents have since been reissued by Bob Thiele on a couple of his labels. Coleman Hawkins is featured on 8 of the 12 selections. Half come from a fine session with trumpeter Bill Coleman, but it is the other four that are of greatest interest for they find tenor saxophonist Hawkins in a quartet with pianist Eddie Heywood, bassist Oscar Pettiford, and drummer Shelly Manne. Their rendition of "The Man I Love" has what is perhaps Heywood's finest solo, preceding a lengthy roaring statement by Hawkins. The other tracks ("Sweet Lorraine," "Get Happy," and "Crazy Rhythm") are almost as special. In addition, this LP finishes off with an excellent session from tenor saxophonist Lester Young, trombonist Dickie Wells, and trumpeter Bill Coleman. Wells's high-note trombone solo on "I'm Fer It Too" is a crackup. Essential music. *—Scott Yanow*

☆ **Big Three, The** / i. 1943-1946 / Doctor Jazz 40950
An album with Lester Young and Ben Webster. This is a 1990 reissue that spotlights classic '40s cuts of the three featured tenor stars. *—Ron Wynn*

★ **Rainbow Mist** / i. Feb. 16, 1944-May 22, 1944 / Delmark 459
Coleman Hawkins was always an open-minded musician. A very advanced player even when he first emerged with Fletcher Henderson's orchestra in the 1920s, by the 1940s he may have been technically middle-aged but remained a young thinker. For his recording session of February 16, 1944, the great tenor invited some of the most promising younger players (including trumpeter Dizzy Gillespie, bassist Oscar Pettiford, and drummer Max Roach), and the result was the very first bebop on records. During their two sessions the large ensemble recorded six selections, including Gillespie's "Woody 'N You," Hawk's "Disorder at the Border," and a new treatment of "Body and Soul" by the tenorman, which he retitled "Rainbow Mist." Also on this highly recommended CD are four titles matching the tenors of Hawkins, Ben Webster, and Georgie Auld (with trumpeter Charlie Shavers included as a bonus) and a session from Auld's big band, highlighted by Sonny Berman's trumpet solo on "Taps Miller." *—Scott Yanow*

○ **Bean's Talking Again** / i. Feb. 16, 1944-Dec. 21, 1949 / Vogue 405
Until the release of *Rainbow Mist*, this French Vogue LP was the most recent issue of the very first bebop sessions, six titles recorded by a 1944 Coleman Hawkins group that included trumpeter Dizzy Gillespie. "Woody 'N You" and "Disorder at the Border" show that change is in the air, while Hawk's new exploration of the chords of "Body and Soul" on *Rainbow Mist* proves that he was still growing as a musician. The second half of this LP finds the tenor saxophonist in Paris, playing stomps and ballads while joined by a fine backup group. *—Scott Yanow*

○ **Thanks for the Memory** / i. May 17, 1944-Dec. 1, 1944 / Xanadu
On this fine LP, Coleman Hawkins is heard on four separate sessions from 1944, only one of which has since been reissued on CD. The latter is his encounter with fellow tenors Georgie Auld and Ben Webster; that date led to the little-known original recording of "Salt Peanuts." In addition, Hawkins is heard with the Esquire All-Stars of 1944 on a date actually led by saxophonist Walter "Foots" Thomas and in a matchup with trumpeter Charlie Shavers and Hawk's greatest disciple, Don Byas. Hot swing that looks forward toward the rapidly emerging bebop. *—Scott Yanow*

○ **Bean and the Boys** / Oct. 19, 1944-Dec. 21, 1949 / Prestige 24124
This Prestige reissue collects Coleman Hawkins sessions from 1944, 1946, and 1959. The first seemingly bids farewell to the swing era with Jonah Jones, Walter Thomas, Hilton Jefferson, and Cozy Cole in a nicely homogeneous group. The second, also made for the Joe Davis label, introduced most of us ancients to Thelonious Monk. The third, originally made for Sonora, puts Hawkins with Fats Navarro, J.J. Johnson, Milt Jackson, and Max Roach. The last was made by the Prestige Blues Swingers, an idiomatically mixed bunch notable for Ray Bryant on piano and, of course, the tenor player. The set is valuable in showing how Hawkins met challenges of the '40s and '50s. *—Stanley Dance, Jazz Times*

★ **Coleman Hawkins on Keynote** / 1944 / PolyGram 830960

○ **Hollywood Stampede** / i. Feb. 23, 1945-Mar. 9, 1945 / Capitol 92596
Coleman Hawkins led one of his finest bands in 1945, a sextet with the fiery trumpeter Howard McGhee that fell somewhere between small-group swing and bebop. This CD contains all of that group's 12 recordings, including memorable versions of "Rifftide" and "Stuffy"; trombonist Vic Dickenson guests on four tracks. This CD concludes with one of Hawkins's rarest sessions, an Aladdin date from 1947 that finds the veteran tenor leading a septet that includes 20-year-old trumpeter Miles Davis. Recommended. *—Scott Yanow*

○ **Coleman Hawkins/Lester Young** / i. Feb. 1945-Apr. 1946 / Spotlite 119
Coleman Hawkins and Lester Young crossed paths constantly throughout their careers but only recorded together on an infrequent basis. This LP from the English Spotlite label features the two great tenors teaming up with trumpeter Buck Clayton for three songs at a jam session; everyone is in fine form. The other side of this set finds Young and Hawkins individually showcased on three numbers apiece. Lester has the benefit of the Nat "King" Cole Trio plus Buddy Rich on two of his songs, while part of Hawkins's miniset is with the great quintet that he led with trumpeter Howard McGhee. Rare broadcasts containing classic music that was fortunately well recorded. *—Scott Yanow*

○ **Hawk Variation** / i. 1945-1957 / Contact 1004
This is an utterly fascinating LP of rare Coleman Hawkins. First the veteran tenor saxophonist is heard on the two-part "Hawk Variation," his initial unaccompanied tenor solo (recorded a couple years before his more famous "Picasso"). Hawkins is also featured backing singer Delores Martin, on two alternate takes from a 1949 Paris session, guest starring with a Danish band, uplifting four so-so songs recorded with a quartet in 1950, on a radio transcription made with Elliot Lawrence's All-Stars, and soloing on two versions of "Walking My Baby Back Home" that were cut with a pickup band that also included cornetist Rex Stewart, trumpeter Cootie Williams, and fellow tenor Bud Freeman. Coleman Hawkins collectors will have to own this set! *—Scott Yanow*

Coleman Hawkins Set, The / i. Sep. 18, 1949-Oct. 19, 1957 / Verve 815148
Coleman Hawkins was frequently featured with Norman Granz's Jazz at the Philharmonic during 1946-59, and Granz usually made sure that Hawk had a special spot in addition to participating in the jam sessions. This LP finds Hawkins showcased with two different quartets from 1949 and 1950 (both recorded live at Carnegie Hall); three of the six selections were not released until the '80s. The repertoire is familiar ("Rifftide," "Stuffy," and ballads including "Body And Soul") but Hawkins's solos are fresh and creative. The second side of this record features the tenor giant matched with trumpeter Roy Eldridge on two jams and a brief ballad medley. The combative Eldridge always brought out the best in Hawkins and this music is quite exciting. *—Scott Yanow*

Favorites / i. Feb. 1951 / Phoenix 22
The collector's label Phoenix has come out with several LPs of rare Coleman Hawkins performances from the 1950s.

This particular one is mostly taken from a period when Hawkins was suffering a bit of critical neglect, overshadowed by Charlie Parker and his disciples despite not having lost any of his creative power. Hawk is heard with an unidentified trio on three selections and in a quintet with trombonist Benny Green for three other songs, all familiar material but with typically explorative solos from the great tenor. Fellow saxophonist Illinois Jacquet sits in on "Bean and the Boys," and there is also a version of "Rifftide" taken from an unknown date (and with personnel long forgotten). A nice set of swinging music, recommended mostly to Coleman Hawkins collectors. —*Scott Yanow*

Body and Soul Revisited / i. Oct. 19, 1951-Oct. 13, 1958 / Decca 627

Coleman Hawkins had been the dominant tenor saxophonist from the mid '20s up until 1940, but, even though he remained a major force, his influence was waning, due to the emergence of first Lester Young and then Charlie Parker. By the early '50s he was only recording on an infrequent basis. But, fortunately, a few years later (partly due to the rise of Sonny Rollins whose original hero was Hawk), his fortunes were on the rise again. This Decca CD contains quite a variety of music. There are 10 selections of melodic "mood" music from 1951-53 in which Hawkins mostly sticks to the melody (an exception is an excellent version of "If I Could Be with You"). Then the great tenor is heard in an occasionally exciting session with Cozy Cole's All-Stars; cornetist Rex Stewart steals the show with a couple of colorful solos. The best music on this CD is taken from a 1955 radio broadcast in which Hawkins plays "Foolin' Around" (based on the chords of "Body and Soul") totally unaccompanied and roars on "The Man I Love." This set concludes with three selections (one previously unissued) from a fine session led by clarinetist Tony Scott. —*Scott Yanow*

Disorder at the Border / i. Sep. 6, 1952-Sep. 13, 1952 / Spotlite 121

Although Coleman Hawkins's studio recordings from this era were relatively few and generally found him restricted to playing commercial mood music, his concert and club appearances showed him to still be in prime form. This enjoyable LP has the great tenor leading two different quintets at Birdland on broadcasts that were aired just a week apart. The rhythm section features the then-unknown pianist Horace Silver, bassist Curly Russell, and either Art Blakey or Connie Kay on drums. More important, trumpeters Roy Eldridge and Howard McGhee (heard separately) inspire the competitive Hawkins to play at his best. A short but very thorough interview wraps up this erratically recorded but very interesting release. —*Scott Yanow*

Masters of Jazz—Vol. 12 / Nov. 8, 1954-Feb. 13, 1968 / Storyville 4112

A very interesting release. This LP has a version of "Honeysuckle Rose" from a 1954 session that usually gets left out of reissues (it was originally released in a sampler), four numbers from a live date in Europe that matches Hawk's tenor with a superb rhythm section (pianist Bud Powell, bassist Oscar Pettiford, and drummer Kenny Clarke), and two songs from what probably was Hawkins's final studio session. On the latter (from February 1968) Coleman Hawkins, despite being very ill, is in surprisingly strong form, easily playing with more fire and strength than he had in 1966 on *Sirius*, his last complete album. —*Scott Yanow*

1954 / i. Nov. 8, 1954 / Jazz Anthology 5186

This relaxed session matches the great tenor Coleman Hawkins with a fine sextet that also includes trumpeter Emmett Berry and trombonist Eddie Bert. Hawk and company sound fine on the nine standards, swinging in a mainstream style that might have been out of fashion at the time but still remains timeless and highly enjoyable. —*Scott Yanow*

○ **Hawk in Paris** / i. Jul. 9, 1956-Jul. 13, 1956 / Bluebird 51059

This CD is a major surprise. Coleman Hawkins had always wanted to record with a large string section and he received

his wish on the majority of these 12 romantic melodies, all of which have some association with Paris. The surprise is that Hawkins plays with a great deal of fire (his double timing on "My Man" is wondrous), and that Manny Albam's arrangements mostly avoid being muzaky and quite often are creative and witty. What could have been a novelty or an insipid affair is actually one of Coleman Hawkins's more memorable albums. Recommended. —*Scott Yanow*

○ **Hawk Flies High, The** / Mar. 12+15, 1957 / Riverside 027

The Hawk Flies High finds tenor saxophonist Coleman Hawkins in the front line company of boppers J.J. Johnson, Idrees Sulieman, Hank Jones, Oscar Pettiford, Jo Jones, and Barry Galbraith. While perhaps not at his most distinctive, he is nevertheless up to any demands and receives from Johnson and Sulieman inspired performances. The entire session was also issued as part of a twofer set. —*Bob Rusch, Cadence*

○ **Think Deep** / i. Mar. 12, 1957-Mar. 15, 1957 / Riverside 3049

This LP has been reissued on CD as *The Hawk Flies High*. Tenor saxophonist Coleman Hawkins, 35 years after his recording debut, was indeed flying high in 1957, a year when he seemed to be rediscovered by the jazz world. He has no difficulty keeping up with the younger players he picked for this date (including trombonist J.J. Johnson and trumpeter Idrees Sulieman) and comes up with a new classic solo on "Sanctity." —*Scott Yanow*

○ **Coleman Hawkins, Roy Eldridge, Pete Brown, Jo Jones, All-Sta** / i. Jul. 5, 1957 / Verve 8829

In 1957, Coleman Hawkins underwent a critical renaissance. Fellow musicians and writers alike finally realized that his style (whether currently in fashion or not) was timeless and that the veteran tenor could still blow most of his competitors away. Hawkins teamed up with trumpeter Roy Eldridge and altoist Pete Brown for what would be a highly successful set at the Newport Jazz Festival. Their first number ("I Can't Believe That You're in Love with Me") was so explosive that it made the rest of the performance (a ballad medley and "Sweet Georgia Brown") anticlimactic. Actually Brown is just okay on "I Can't Believe," but the long solos of Eldridge and Hawkins are among the most exciting of their careers, making this LP well worth searching for. —*Scott Yanow*

Genius of Coleman Hawkins, The / Oct. 16, 1957 / Verve 825673

Genius may not be the right word but "brilliance" certainly fits. At the age of 51 in 1957, Coleman Hawkins had already been on records for 35 years and had been one of the leading tenors for nearly that long. This CD matches him with the Oscar Peterson Trio (plus drummer Alvin Stoller) for a fine runthrough on standards. Hawk plays quite well although the excitement level does not reach the heights of his sessions with trumpeter Roy Eldridge. A nice melodic date. —*Scott Yanow*

○ **High and Mighty Hawk** / i. Feb. 18, 1958-Feb. 19, 1958 / Affinity 163

Although Coleman Hawkins had been a major tenor stylist for over 35 years by the time of this recording, he had never felt all that comfortable playing blues, preferring to dig his harmonic talents into more complicated material. For one of the first times, on the lengthy "Bird of Prey Blues" that opens this LP, Hawkins shows that at last he has mastered the blues. His honking and roaring improvisation, although more sophisticated than the usual solos by R&B tenors, captures their spirit and extroverted emotions perfectly. It is the highlight of this otherwise excellent (if more conventional) quintet session with trumpeter Buck Clayton and pianist Hank Jones. —*Scott Yanow*

Blues Groove / i. Feb. 28, 1958 / Swingville 2035

Strange as it seems, after over 35 years on the scene, Coleman Hawkins seemed to discover the blues in 1958. A harmonic wizard who enjoyed improvising over the most complex chord changes, Hawk finally dug into the blues around this period and learned to emphasize extroverted emotions. This LP finds him jamming happily on two standards and four blues (including the 17-minute "Marchin' Along") with a sextet that also prominently features guitarist Tiny Grimes. Fun music. —*Scott Yanow*

Meets the Sax Section / Apr. 24, 1958 / Savoy 1123
This studio session for Savoy finds the great Coleman Hawkins playing as part of a five-piece sax section. Actually the other saxophonists and part of the rhythm section were taken from the Count Basie orchestra and outfitted with arrangements by Billy Ver Planck. They play a variety of little-known but swinging material; the logical charts and high-quality solos make this LP well worth acquiring. —*Scott Yanow*

Centerpiece / Sep. 1958 / Phoenix 13
Some of the finest Coleman Hawkins anywhere can be found on the *Centerpiece* LP, composed of two live and unissued dates from 1959 and 1962. The '62 material is particularly surprising. His commercial recordings of this period hinted at a slight dissipation. But the rolling, pneumatic momentum generated here shows Hawkins not only in command but at his height. "Bean and the Boys" (or "Lover Come Back") is explosive and irresistible. Side one is nearly as good and also features Benny Golson in some excellent choruses on "Perdido." —*John McDonough,* Down Beat

○ **Coleman Hawkins and His Friends at a Famous Jazz Party** / i. Oct. 16, 1958-Nov. 6, 1958 / Enigma 302
True, this LP looks like a bootleg and it is probably semilegitimate at best, but the music is quite exciting, possibly taken from television shows. Such musicians as tenor great Coleman Hawkins; trumpeters Red Allen, Charlie Shavers, and Rex Stewart; trombonists J.C. Higginbotham and Dickie Wells; and clarinetist Buster Bailey star. And for some reason they seem quite inspired, possibly by each other's presence. "Love Is Just Around the Corner" and a "Bugle Call Rag" that teams Shavers and Stewart are among the high points. Probably difficult to find and not too pretty to look at (with a dumb sketch of Hawkins on the front and a totally blank back cover), this one deserves to be picked up if you see it! —*Scott Yanow*

★ **In a Mellow Tone** / 1958-1961 / Prestige 6001
A superior session with Hawkins, Eddie "Lockjaw" Davis (ts), and others. —*Ron Wynn*

○ **At the Bayou Club** / i. Jan. 1959 / Honeysuckle Rose 5002
Coleman Hawkins teams up with his frequent musical partner, trumpeter Roy Eldridge, for a fairly heated set of music. On the first of two LPs from this particular gig, Hawk and Roy jam on "Bean and the Boys," "How High The Moon," "Basin Street Blues," "Vignette," and a ballad medley. The two veterans always brought out the best in each other and this fine LP has its share of explosive moments. —*Scott Yanow*

○ **At the Bayou Club, Vol. 2** / i. Jan. 1959 / Honeysuckle Rose 5006
The second of two LPs from this particular engagement once again teams the great veterans Coleman Hawkins and trumpeter Roy Eldridge. Tenor legend Hawkins explores "Body And Soul" again (his many interpretations are always different from previous ones), and the duo (backed by a fine local rhythm section) jams happily on such numbers as "Blue Lou," "Soft Winds," and "Just You, Just Me." Although no longer pacesetters, Hawkins and Eldridge remained creative and exciting up until the end; they were still in their prime for this fine session. —*Scott Yanow*

Immortal Coleman Hawkins / i. Jul. 3, 1959-Feb. 1, 1963 / Pumpkin 118
There are quite a few recordings (mostly like this one, on LP) of Coleman Hawkins concert appearances during 1957-65, his final prime period. This Pumpkin set finds Hawk matched with his best partner, trumpeter Roy Eldridge, for fiery versions of "Soft Winds" and "Sweet Sue" in 1959. The second half features the veteran tenor saxophonist with a Swedish rhythm section performing two ballads and the

jumping "Rifftide." A good example of strong late-period Coleman Hawkins. —*Scott Yanow*

○ **Blowin' up a Breeze** / i. Aug. 9, 1959-Jun. 12, 1963 / Spotlite 137
This LP has two excellent concert performances by the great tenor saxophonist Coleman Hawkins. First Hawk is heard at the 1959 Playboy Jazz Festival with a Chicago-based rhythm section performing four standards, including a remake of his old standby "Body And Soul" and a strong version of "Centerpiece." The flip side moves up to 1963 as Hawkins and the Tommy Flanagan trio cover "The Way You Look Tonight" and two ballads. A nice all-round set of strong mainstream jazz from one of its pioneers. —*Scott Yanow*

○ **Dali** / i. 1959-May 1962 / Stash 538
This Stash CD, despite some silly graphics on the liners, has quite a bit of rewarding music. There are three examples of the fireworks that generally occurred when tenor saxophonist Coleman Hawkins and trumpeter Roy Eldridge met up (taken from a live session in 1959), while the remainder of this disc finds Hawk playing in Brussels in 1962. The veteran tenor is particularly strong on "Disorder at the Border" and "Rifftide," but the high point is a rare unaccompanied solo on "Dali," the fourth and final time that Hawkins recorded an improvisation by himself. It is a pity that he never recorded an entire album like that! —*Scott Yanow*

Bean Stalkin' / Oct. 1960-Nov. 1960 / Pablo 2310-933
In contrast to Coleman Hawkins's sometimes sleepy studio albums from this era, his live performances are generally quite exciting. This set features the great tenor at two European concerts in 1960, performing three fairly heated numbers with a four-piece rhythm section, matching wits with trumpeter Roy Eldridge on "Crazy Rhythm," and leading two all-star jams with Eldridge, fellow tenor Don Byas, and altoist Benny Carter. Some of the music is quite fiery, making this a recommended disc. —*Scott Yanow*

Night Hawk / Dec. 30, 1960 / Prestige 420
Coleman Hawkins was one of the main inspirations of his fellow tenor Eddie "Lockjaw" Davis, so it was logical that they would one day meet up in the recording studio. This LP has many fine moments from these two highly competitive jazzmen, particularly the lengthy title cut and a heated trade-off on "In a Mellow Tone," on which Davis goes higher but Hawkins wins on ideas. Recommended. —*Scott Yanow*

European Concert / i. 1960 / Unique 31
Of unknown origin and released on an LP imported from Italy, this set finds Coleman Hawkins, trumpeter Roy Eldridge, and the Tommy Flanagan trio improving on long versions of "Joshua Fit the Battle of Jericho" and "Disorder at the Border" in addition to a ballad medley. Roy and Hawk usually inspired each other and that is certainly true on this rare but frequently exciting session. —*Scott Yanow*

Coleman Hawkins / i. 1960 / Crown 5181
One of two LPs' worth of material that tenor saxophonist Coleman Hawkins recorded in a quintet with trumpeter Thad Jones and pianist Eddie Costa in 1960. The music is reasonably enjoyable if not particularly memorable, but this budget album (which completely lacks liner notes) has since been reissued on CD. —*Scott Yanow*

Hawk Relaxes, The / Feb. 28, 1961 / Prestige 709
While Coleman Hawkins's recordings in the early 1960s for Swingville tended to swing (not too suprisingly!), his Moodsville dates were dominated by overly relaxed treatments of ballads. Such is the case with this CD, which finds the great tenor saxophonist sounding all right on melody statements of such tunes as "When Day Is Done," "More Than You Know," and "Moonglow" but failing to develop his solos very much beyond the opening themes. The sameness of tempos makes this affair chiefly viable as background music, although of a high quality within that genre. —*Scott Yanow*

Body And Soul / i. Jul. 16, 1961 / West Wind 018

Despite the photo of a somewhat decrepit Coleman Hawkins on its back cover, the performances on this LP are actually excellent. Taken from a concert in Brazil in 1961, these selections feature the tenor saxophone pioneer Coleman Hawkins and the combative trumpeter Roy Eldridge on three fairly torrid jams and a ballad medley; pianist Tommy Flanagan is featured with the trio on "Love For Sale." Fine music recommended to true fans of Hawk and Roy. *—Scott Yanow*

○ **Duke Ellington Meets Coleman Hawkins** / Aug. 18, 1962 / Impulse 26

Amid the recent flood of reissues, this is an album to be savored. It took roughly 20 years for jazz giants Duke Ellington and Coleman Hawkins to get into the studio together from the time Ellington first proposed this small-group session until it happened in 1962. It was worth the wait. Hawkins's swinging, full-bodied tenor adds to the Ellington ensemble sound, his distinctive tone fitting like a warm glove. The playing is inspired throughout, particularly the Hawkins solo interpretations on "Mood Indigo," "Wanderlust," and a rollicking head arrangement of "The Jeep Is Jumpin'." His tenor is both knowing and adventuresome. There are also an intriguing, Latinish quintet number, "The Rictic," featuring Ray Nance on violin, Hawkins, and the Ellington rhythm section; an Ellington tribute to his guest, "Self Portrait (of the Bean)"; and a bluesy tip of the Ellington fedora to Ray Charles. *—Ken Franckling, Jazz Times*

★ **Desafinado: Bossa Nova and Jazz Samba** / Sep. 12+16, 1962 / MCA 33118

This set seems to have the word "fad" written all over it, but, surprisingly, it is a major success. During the era when everyone was trying to cash in on the popularity of bossa nova, tenor great Coleman Hawkins recorded eight selections with a group consisting of two guitars, bass, and three percussionists. In addition to a classic version of "O Pato" and such typical songs as "Desafinado" and "One Note Samba," Hawkins and company even turn "I'm Looking Over a Four-Leaf Clover" into a strong bossa. Although this straight CD reissue of a former LP is a bit brief, the music is highly enjoyable. *—Scott Yanow*

○ **Desafinado** / i. Sep. 12, 1962-Sep. 17, 1962 / Impulse 28

In the 1960s, Coleman Hawkins led three sessions for Impulse, a label best known for its recordings of John Coltrane. This particular LP, which has since been reissued on CD, was a real surprise at the time for, at first glance, the concept should not have worked that well. The hard-blowing Hawkins tenor is backed by two guitars, bass, and three percussionists in an attempt to cash in on the bossa-nova fad of the early '60s but, even when the ensemble performs such potentially unsuitable material as "I'm Looking Over a Four Leaf Clover" and "I Remember You" (in addition to "Desafinado" and a classic rendition of "O Pato"), the music is delightful. *—Scott Yanow*

Back in Bean's Bag / Dec. 10, 1962 / Columbia 1991

Tenor great Coleman Hawkins teamed up with the personable trumpeter Clark Terry for this upbeat set of solid swing. Terry in particular is in exuberant form on "Feedin' The Bean" and a delightful version of "Don't Worry About Me," but Hawkins's playing (particularly on the trumpeter's ballad "Michelle") is also in fine form. The Tommy Flanagan trio assists the two classic hornmen on this superior LP. *—Scott Yanow*

Hawkins! Alive! At The Village Gate / i. 1962 / Verve 829 260

The great tenor saxophonist Coleman Hawkins, who had debuted on records 40 years earlier, gets to stretch out on this live outing by his 1962 quartet, which also features pianist Tommy Flanagan. This CD, which as an LP had lengthy versions of "All The Things You Are," "Joshua Fit The Battle Of Jericho," "Mack The Knife," and "Talk Of Town," is augmented by previously unreleased versions of "Bean and the Boys" and "If I Had You," all of which show that Coleman

Hawkins in his late fifties was still a powerful force. *—Scott Yanow*

Portrait Of Coleman Hawkins / i. Mar. 21, 1963-Mar. 25, 1963 / Up Front 119

Of borderline interest to Coleman Hawkins fans, this odd 1963 session surrounds the classic tenor saxophonist with strings arranged (not too creatively) by Frank Hunter. The mood music is instantly forgettable, with Hawk rarely venturing beyond the mundane melodies. *—Scott Yanow*

Today and Now / Sep. 9+11, 1963 / Impulse 34

Of Coleman Hawkins's three sessions for Impulse in the early to mid '60s, this is the most intriguing one due to the unusual repertoire. Included are such songs as "Go Lil Liza," Quincy Jones's ballad "Quintessence," "Put On Your Old Grey Bonnet," "Swingin' Scotch," and "Don't Sit Under the Apple Tree." Despite (or perhaps due to) the strange choice of tunes, Hawkins is in inspired form, taking consistently creative solos on the fresh material. A very enjoyable and somewhat surprising LP. *—Scott Yanow*

○ **Wrapped Tight** / i. Feb. 22, 1965-Mar. 1, 1965 / Impulse 109

Coleman Hawkins's last strong recording finds the veteran tenor saxophonist, 43 years after his recording debut with Mamie Smith's Jazz Hounds, improvising creatively on a wide variety of material on this CD, ranging from "Intermezzo" and "Here's That Rainy Day" to "Red Roses for a Blue Lady" and "Indian Summer." Best is an adventurous version of "Out of Nowhere" that shows that the veteran tenor saxophonist was still coming up with new ideas in 1965. *—Scott Yanow*

Sirius / Dec. 20, 1966 / Pablo 2310-707

Coleman Hawkins's final studio session is rather sad. Due to an excess of drink and his unwillingness to eat, the great tenor saxophonist went steadily downhill between 1965 and his death four years later. Recorded in late 1966, this quartet set finds Hawk constantly short of breath and unable to play long phrases. He is able to get away with this deficiency on the faster pieces, but the ballads are rather painful to hear. Even at this late stage Hawkins still had his majestic tone, but this recording is only of historical interest. *—Scott Yanow*

Rifftide / i. Apr. 1979 / Pumpkin 105

Coleman Hawkins is heard during this concert performance near the end of his career and shortly before the steep decline that resulted in his death. Joined by the Earl Hines trio on this LP from the collector's label Pumpkin, Hawkins is in surprisingly good form on five standards, displaying the tone that had made him the main influence on all saxophonists 40 years earlier. *—Scott Yanow*

Jazz Reunion / i. Sep. 1982 / Jazz Man 5042

The "reunion" in the Pee Wee Russell/Coleman Hawkins date probably refers to an earlier recording they made for the Camden label, *Great Jazz Reeds*. It meshes these two talents as well as valve trombonist Bob Brookmeyer, drummer Joe Jones, trumpeter Emmett Berry, bassist Milt Hinton, and trombonist Nat Pierce in an unlikely combination that succeeds. Russell's low-register clarinet styling, a very linear approach with a strong Dixieland feel, juxtaposed by Hawkins's cutting edge on tenor, furnishes a unique adventure despite the "unmodern" connotations. *—Mike Cornette, Cadence*

Alive! / i. 1992 / PolyGram 513755

From the mid '50s until Coleman Hawkins's death in 1969, the tenor saxophonist frequently teamed up with trumpeter Roy Eldridge. However, Hawkins rarely met altoist Johnny Hodges on the bandstand, making this encounter a special event. Long versions of "Satin Doll," "Perdido," and "The Rabbit In Jazz" give these three classic jazzmen (who are ably assisted by the Tommy Flanagan trio) chances to stretch out and inspire each other. The remainder of this CD has Eldridge and Hodges absent while Coleman Hawkins (on "new" versions of "Mack The Knife," "It's The Talk Of The Town," "Bean and the Boys," and "Caravan") heads the quartet for some excellent playing. Timeless music played by some of the top veteran stylists of the swing era. —*Scott Yanow*

○ **Re-Evaluations: The Impulse Years** / Impulse 9258
Anthology album containing selections by tenor sax great Coleman Hawkins from albums he cut for the Impulse label in the early and mid '60s. It includes performances with Duke Ellington, Oliver Nelson, and Benny Carter, plus Afro-Latin and bossa nova tracks. —*Ron Wynn*

Three Great Swing Saxophones / Bluebird 9683
An album with Ben Webster (ts) and Benny Carter (as). A textbook example of swing sax technique from three of the founding fathers. —*Ron Wynn*

ERSKINE HAWKINS (Erskine Ramsey Hawkins)

b. Jul. 26, 1914, Birmingham, AL, **d.** 1993
Trumpet, bandleader / Swing, big band
Erskine Hawkins was a major bandleader and a good trumpeter who was best known for the 1939 hit recording "Tuxedo Junction." He was especially gifted in the upper register, and often utilized this talent for flamboyant high note displays, earning the nickname "The 20th Century Gabriel." But Hawkins was also a consistently swinging soloist who didn't hesitate to share the spotlight in his band with others such as the Bascomb brothers, Haywood Henry, or Julian Dash. Hawkins began playing drums at age 7, then learned trombone before beginning trumpet at age 13. Hawkins led the Bama State Collegians while at Montgomery State Teachers College. They visited New York twice in the late '30s, the second time with Hawkins as the bandleader. The Hawkins orchestra recorded about 140 songs for Bluebird or Victor in the '30s, '40s, and '50s. They recorded everything from novelty tunes, like "Dolemite," to "Uptown Shuffle" and "Swinging on Lennox." They later did jump blues and swinging R&B-oriented sessions for Coral and King. Hawkins led a smaller combo in the '60s, though he assembled a bigger band on special occasions. He was a guest performer with Sy Oliver at a 1974 Carnegie Hall concert, then was backed at the 1979 Nice festival by the New York Jazz Repertory Orchestra. While Hawkins's sessions are unavailable currently on American labels, they've been reissued on French RCA and on other import labels, like Joyce and First Heard. —*Ron Wynn*

Original Tuxedo Junction, The / **i.** Sep. 1938-Jan. 1945 / Bluebird 90363
These sessions for 14-piece band include pianist Avery Parrish on his immortal "After Hours" and teaming up with the leader for "Swing Out." Several of Hawkins's better selections are included in the 11 tracks. Features tenor Julian Dash, baritonist and clarinetist Haywood Henry, and Hawkins on trumpet. —*Michael G. Nastos*

☆ **Jazz Heritage: Tuxedo Junction** / **i.** 1950-1960 / MCA 1361
This includes 1950 big-band and 1960 quintet recordings. Contrast the title track between the two groups. —*Michael G. Nastos*

LOUIS HAYES (Louis Sedell Hayes)

b. May 31, 1937, Detroit, MI
Drums / Hard bop
A forthright, propulsive drummer, Louis Hayes ranks, after Art Blakey and Philly Joe Jones, as hard bop's top drum stylist. He's anchored many excellent hard bop groups. He doesn't play behind or on the beat, but pushes it. He never hurries or crowds the soloist, but provides fills and interacts nicely with other members in the rhythm section. Hayes was a bandleader in Detroit by the time he was 16. He moved to New York in 1956 to replace Art Taylor in Horace Silver's quintet. He joined the Cannonball Adderley quintet in 1959, remaining until 1965, when he succeeded Ed Thigpen in Oscar Peterson's trio. Hayes stayed with Peterson until 1967, then began heading his own combos. He played with musicians such as Joe Henderson, Freddie Hubbard, and James Spaulding before rejoining Peterson in 1971. Hayes formed a sextet in 1972, which was co-led subsequently by Junior

Cook, then by Woody Shaw (Cook remained in the band until Rene McLean replaced him). The quintet was among the '70s' busiest combos and toured extensively in Europe. They were the host group when Dexter Gordon made his long-anticipated return to America in 1976. Hayes continued leading the group when Shaw departed in 1977. He's also contributed to many bands as a sideman. Only a couple of recent Hayes sessions for Candid and Timeless are available currently on CD. —*Ron Wynn and Michael G. Nastos*

Louis Hayes (Feat. Yusef Lateef & Nat Adderley) / **i.** Apr. 1960 / Vee Jay 906
Drummer Louis Hayes's reputation was partly cemented by his early '60s work with Vee Jay, especially this album that features him propelling a group co-led by Nat Adderley and Yusef Lateef. Hayes was never a flamboyant player; he was a consistent timekeeper and outstanding percussionist, who kept the beat moving and helped push a group, rather than trying to dominate it. Lateef during this period was basically a hard bop player, executing chord changes and blowing with fire, rather than the meditative, reflective soloist he became later. Nat Adderley is just as tart and crisp in his cornet work with this group as with his brother Cannonball, while pianist Barry Harris and bassist Sam Jones mesh with Hayes easily from the opening number. —*Ron Wynn*

Breath of Life / **i.** Feb. 2, 1974 / Muse 5052

Ichi-Ban / May 5, 1976 / Timeless

★ **Real Thing, The** / **i.** May 20, 1977 / Muse 5125
His best band, with Woody Shaw (tpt), Rene McLean (sax), and Slide Hampton (t). All originals, all excellent. —*Michael G. Nastos*

Light and Lively / Apr. 21, 1989 / Steeple Chase 1245
Another good one, with Charles Tolliver (tpt) and Bobby Watson (as). —*Michael G. Nastos*

Crawl, The / Oct. 14, 1989 / Candid 79045
Live at Birdland, with Charles Tolliver (tpt) and Gary Bartz (sax). Very good. —*Michael G. Nastos*

TUBBY HAYES (Edward Brian Hayes)

b. Jan. 30, 1935, London, England, **d.** Jun. 8, 1973, London, England
Tenor saxophone, flute, vibes, composer / Swing, bop
A top English saxophonist, Tubby Hayes was an excellent hard bop stylist whose solos were always dynamic, were expertly articulated and constructed, and were expressive and imaginative. The solos sometimes seemed too jammed full of notes, but Hayes never played himself into a harmonic corner, and finished his statements in a sharp, satisfying manner. Though tenor was his primary instrument, Hayes also played flute, soprano, alto, baritone, and vibes. He began on violin as a child, then switched to tenor at age 12 and was a professional at age 15. He played with the bands of Kenny Baker, Jack Parnell, Bert Ambrose, and Vic Lewis. He had his own octet in the mid '50s, and co-led the Jazz Couriers with Ronnie Scott in the late '50s. Hayes led a big band in the early '60s, and toured America and Europe in the mid '60s, working solo. He played with Duke Ellington at the Royal Festival Hall in 1964. Hayes was also featured with his quintet in the film *Dr. Terror's House of Horrors* in the mid '60s. Hayes began recording as a leader in the late '50s, and did sessions for Tempo, Fontanta, Spotlite, Epic, Smash, and Mole. He also did a date with Dizzy Reece for Blue Note. Hayes died during heart surgery in London in the early '70s. Currently, none of Hayes's sessions are available on CD in America. —*Ron Wynn*

★ **New York Sessions** / Oct. 3-4, 1961 / Columbia 45446
Tubby Hayes blows strong with Clark Terry (tpt). A sleeper. —*Michael G. Nastos*

○ **Tubby the Tenor** / Oct. 3-4, 1961 / Epic 16023

○ **Introducing Tubbs** / **i.** Mar. 1962 / Epic 16019

○ **For Members Only** / **i.** Jan. 1967-Oct. 1967 / Mastermix 10

ROY HAYNES (Roy Owen Haynes)

b. Mar. 13, 1926, Roxbury, MA
Drums / Bop, hard bop
A brilliant combo drummer, Roy Haynes has made supporting and heading small groups an art form since the '40s, and he rivals Max Roach as bebop's most flexible, consistently evolving drummer. Other than a brief stint backing Luis Russell and even shorter periods with Frankie Newton and Pete Brown, Roy Haynes has concentrated on duos, quartets, and quintets, many featuring jazz's greatest players. His taste, timekeeping, harmonic knowledge, and control made him John Coltrane's substitute of choice for Elvin Jones during the '60s, and he's played in swing, free, and even jazz-rock units, providing whatever's needed, while retaining his own sound and style.

Haynes began his career in Boston. During the '40s, he worked with Newton, Brown, and various other groups in the area, before joining Russell's orchestra in 1945. He played with this group during parts of 1946 and 1947. After that, he spent two years with Lester Young, worked briefly in 1949 with Miles Davis and Bud Powell, then was in Charlie Parker's group until 1952. After a summer with Ella Fitzgerald, Haynes was Sarah Vaughan's drummer from 1953 until 1958. He played with Thelonious Monk in 1958, and with Eric Dolphy in 1960. Haynes recorded his first album in Stockholm and Paris in 1954, then made the exceptional 1958 trio release, *We Three*, on Prestige with Joe Benjamin and Phineas Newborn, Jr. During the early '60s, there was considerable recording activity. This included another trio date, *Just Us*, for Prestige, and *Out of the Afternoon* with Rahsaan Roland Kirk and Tommy Flanagan for Impulse in 1962. There were two sessions for New Jazz in 1963, one with Booker Ervin, and another date on Pacific Jazz in 1964. Haynes was regularly on call for Coltrane sessions from 1961 to 1965, and he recorded with Gary Burton, George Shearing, Kenny Burrell, Lambert, Hendricks, and Ross, and Stan Getz. He was featured on the exceptional Chick Corea album, *Now He Sings, Now He Sobs*, in 1968. There was also an award from *Esquire* in the mid '60s; Haynes was named one of the "Best Dressed Men In America." He and Miles Davis were the only jazz musicians so honored that year.

Haynes formed the Hip Ensemble, at the end of the '60s. At various times, the band included trumpeters Charles Sullivan or Hannibal Marvin Peterson, and saxophonist George Adams. They recorded for Mainstream and worked together until 1973. Haynes made an underrated but outstanding jazz-rock album with Larry Coryell for Flying Dutchman in the early '70s. Then came a stint with Duke Jordan in 1975 and 1976, including a recording session and tour of Japan. Haynes became a busy session and studio drummer, recording with Nick Brignola, Burton, Hank Jones, Art Pepper, Ted Curson, Joe Albany, and Horace Tapscott between 1977 and 1979. He also made albums as a leader for Japanese RCA, Horo, Galaxy, and French labels Blue Marge and Freelance. Haynes played with Dizzy Gillespie at the Newport and Monterey festivals in 1979. He joined Chick Corea's Trio music in 1981, while heading his own quartets. There was a fine album called *Blues for Coltrane* for the revived Impulse label.

Haynes moved into the '90s in fine style, playing on Pat Metheny's *Question and Answer* session in 1990. He finally received a just measure of praise when he won the 1994 Jazzpar Prize. This included a $35,000 cash award and a recording deal. At the same time, two classic sessions that Haynes was involved with were reissued in '93: *Newport '63*, with Haynes sparking Coltrane's quartet, and Monk's *At the Five Spot*, which listed him as the drummer, though doubt remains whether Haynes was actually on the date. Coltrane biographer Louis Porter has said, for the record, that he thinks it's Haynes, while session producer Michael Cuscuna is unsure. There's plenty of great Haynes material, however, where it's crystal clear he's the drummer of record. Fantasy has reissued some classic dates. MCA, holders of the Impulse catalog, have issued some classic dates, too. Blue Note's rereleased great sessions with Parker, as well as Discovery sessions with Powell. In 1993, Haynes was profiled heavily in the jazz press both nationally and internationally. —*Ron Wynn*

★ **We Three** / Nov. 14, 1958 / New Jazz 196
A wonderful session, with spectacular piano by Phineas Newborn and great bass from Paul Chambers. —*Ron Wynn*

★ **Out of the Afternoon** / May 16+23, 1962 / Impulse 23
Definitive creative music with Rahsaan Roland Kirk (reeds) and Tommy Flanagan (p). —*Michael G. Nastos*

Cracklin' / Apr. 10, 1963 / New Jazz

★ **Hip Ensemble** / 1971 / Mainstream
This explosive session helped cement the reputations of George Adams (ts) and Hannibal Marvin Peterson (tpt). —*Ron Wynn*

Equipoise / **i.** 1972 / Mainstream 715

Senyah / 1973 / Mainstream
The energetic material continues here, with great Haynes drum support. —*Ron Wynn*

Thank You, Thank You / Jul. 16-20, 1977 / Galaxy
The opening cut of this album is mere pop. It's a simple riff in that light fusion vein of George Benson and others. Side two opens with a George Cables original, "Quiet Fire," a title which, like the closing "Sweet Song," is quite appropriate. Pianist Cables is a fleet improviser at this fast tempo and drummer Roy Haynes solos with more fire than quiet. The gentler Roy Haynes is on display in "Processional," an improvised duet between Haynes's traps and Kenneth Nash's carpetbag full of percussive tricks with congas, bells, and whistles being most prominent. The two percussionists have their ears open. Haynes, using more cymbals here, does not try to outsmash his colleague. The album closes with pianist Stanley Cowell's "Sweet Song." It is a lovely melody that shows the pure, romantic sides of the four involved: Haynes, Cowell, vibist Bobby Hutcherson, and bassist Cecil McBee. —*Lee Jeske, Down Beat*

Vistalite / Jul. 20, 1977 / Galaxy

True or False / **i.** Oct. 30, 1986 / Freelance 007
This live session in Paris with Ralph Moore (ts) is proof that Haynes is a premier jazz drummer. —*Michael G. Nastos*

J. C. HEARD (James Charles Heard)

b. Oct. 8, 1917
Drums / Swing, big band
An influential swing drummer who ranks with the finest in the genre, J.C. Heard filled the percussionist's chair for many of the era's best bands and groups. His playing could be flashy or rock solid, and he could push the band or interact with the rhythm section. Heard did whatever was necessary for the date. He actually started as a dancer in vaudeville shows, then began playing drums in his teens. Heard moved from Detroit to New York in 1919, and joined Teddy Wilson's big band. He later played with Wilson's sextet, and with Benny Carter and Coleman Hawkins. Heard was in Cab Calloway's band in the mid '40s, and participated in some pioneering bebop sessions. He led his own band at Cafe Society in the late '40s, worked with Errol Garner, and participated in Jazz at the Philharmonic sessions. During the '50s, Heard combined drumming, vocals, and dance during performances in Japan and Australia, then worked with Wilson and Hawkins, and toured Europe with Sammy Price. He returned to Detroit in 1966, where he still works, sometimes leading a sextet and other times leading a big band. Heard's also appeared at various festivals. He's made a couple of sessions as a leader for Continental, and can be heard on reissues by Hawkins, Calloway, and Illinois Jacquet, among others. —*Ron Wynn and Michael G. Nastos*

★ **This Is Me, J.C.** / 1958 / Argo 633
○ **Some of This, Some Of That** / **i.** 1986 / Hiroko 187

Master drummer leads 13-piece band. Loads of blues and modern jazz along with some goofy fun and solid musicianship. Fine "Nica's Dream" and "Sweet Love of Mine, Sweet Samantha." Heard vocalizes frequently on this album, which features trumpeter Walt Szymanski. —*Michael G. Nastos*

JIMMY HEATH (James Edward Heath)

b. Oct. 25, 1926
Saxophone, flute / Bop, hard bop
A first-rate player cited by Miles Davis as a favorite ahead of Coltrane, Jimmy Heath has been a sterling soloist and writer since the '40s. Early in his career, his nickname was "Little Bird" as his alto playing was influenced heavily by Charlie Parker. Heath switched to tenor and developed a warm, recognizable, and energetic style. His strong, sturdy tone, and intelligent, robust, and smartly constructed solos are dynamic and striking. He began playing alto sax at age 14, then went to New York in 1947 with his brother, Percy (who played bass). Heath joined Dizzy Gillespie's big band in 1949, and played with both Gillespie's orchestra and his sextet until 1951. Unfortunately, a drug problem grew progressively worse, and Heath was imprisoned in 1955. He was paroled four years later, and played for two months in Miles Davis's band before forming a group. Davis subsequently recorded Heath compositions "C.T.A." and "Gingerbread Boy." Heath's first Riverside album was *The Thumper*, which he made with his brother, Albert. He continued recording on the label until '64, usually with Al and, in 1963, with Percy as well. He co-led some groups with Art Farmer in the mid '60s, then, during the early '70s, Heath recorded for Cobblestone, Muse, CTI, and Xanadu. He teamed with Milt Jackson on some CTI dates. Heath completed *Afro-American Suite of Evolution*, an ambitious work for a 30-piece orchestra, in 1975. That same year, the three Heath Brothers formed an excellent quartet with Stanley Cowell on keyboards. They made tasteful, intelligently produced albums for Columbia in the late '70s, expanding the roster to a quintet when guitarist Tony Purrone joined in 1978. But they were dropped in the early '80s because their albums, which received widespread critical praise, sold poorly. They made other equally fine records for Antilles, which suffered from the same fate as the Columbia albums. In 1987, Jimmy Heath made a superb date for Landmark called *Peer Pleasure*. He remains active as a composer, arranger, and player. —*Ron Wynn*

○ **Nice People** / Dec. 1959-1964 / Riverside 6006

Really Big / Jun. 24, 1960 / Riverside 1799
This is one of Heath's earliest as a leader and showcases his savvy as both a leader and a player. —*Ron Wynn*

Triple Threat / Jan. 4+17, 1962 / Riverside 400

Swamp Seed / Mar. 11, 1963 / Milestone
An early version of the Heath Brothers, with Albert (d) and Percy (b) on board. —*Ron Wynn*

On the Trail / 1964 / Milestone

★ **Gap Sealer, The** / Mar. 1, 1972 / Cobblestone
Some of Heath's finest, most aggressive playing. He is a standout on soprano, flute, and tenor. —*Ron Wynn*

Jimmy / Mar. 1, 1972 / Muse 5138
A typically low-key yet authoritative and impressive session by saxophonist Jimmy Heath from 1972. He's leading a group with pianist Kenny Barron, bassist Bob Cranshaw, his brother Tootie Heath on drums, and son Mtume on congas. They run through mainstream and hard bop, standards, and blues with crisp professionalism. —*Ron Wynn*

Love and Understanding / Jun. 11, 1973 / Muse 5028
An outstanding group buttressed by trombonist Curtis Fuller and Billy Higgins (d). —*Ron Wynn*

Picture of Health / Sep. 22, 1975 / Xanadu
A fine quartet. Super playing by Barry Harris (p), Heath, and Billy Higgins (d). —*Ron Wynn*

Passin' Thru / i. 1978 / Columbia 35573

In Motion / i. 1979 / Columbia 35816

New Picture / Jun. 18-20, 1985 / Landmark 1506
One of Heath's most recent. An assured, consistently productive, and appealing mainstream date, with Tommy Flanagan on piano as a bonus. —*Ron Wynn*

★ **Peer Pleasure** / Feb. 1987 / Landmark 1514
A smooth session with sharp work from Heath. As usual, it has fine compositions. The CD has a bonus cut. —*Ron Wynn*

PERCY HEATH

b. 1923
Bass / Bop, hard bop
Bassist Percy Heath is part of a superb familial unit that was ill-served by record labels. These labels expected the Heaths to match sales figures with flavor-of-the-day bands that played trendy material. Heath played violin in junior high school, then began on bass during his days at the Granoff School of Music. He got a quick education working with local Philadelphia groups, then joined his brother, Jimmy, in Howard McGhee's sextet in 1947. During the '40s and '50s, Percy Heath backed Miles Davis, Fats Navarro, J.J. Johnson, Dizzy Gillespie, Charlie Parker, Thelonious Monk, Clifford Brown, and Horace Silver. He replaced Ray Brown in Milt Jackson's quartet in 1951, and stayed with the group when it was renamed the Modern Jazz Quartet in 1952. Jimmy, Albert, and Percy Heath formed the Heath Brothers band in 1975 when it seemed the Modern Jazz Quartet was history. Percy added piccolo bass to his arsenal, and the Heath Brothers went on to make critically acclaimed, wonderfully played albums for Columbia and Antilles, but never enjoyed label support or understanding. Percy Heath has since worked with both the Modern Jazz Quartet and Heath Brothers, when they've been able to record.

Drummer Albert Heath (b. 1935) followed his older brothers to New York in the late '50s. His sensitive, steadily driving, yet flowing and loose drumming made him a busy session musician. Heath played with J.J. Johnson during the late '50s and early 1960, then with the Jazztet in 1960 and 1961. He later recorded with Nat Adderley, Johnny Griffin, Mal Waldron, Kenny Dorham, and John Coltrane, and Heath also played with his brother, Jimmy, and many others before moving to Scandinavia in 1965. He stayed there for three years, and played with Dexter Gordon and Kenny Drew at the Montmarte, and worked with Tete Montoliu. When he returned to America, Heath played with Cedar Walton, Yusef Lateef, and Billy Taylor's Jazzmobile. During the '70s and '80s, he divided his time between playing in Europe and working with the Heath Brothers band. Heath worked with the revived Jazztet and with Tal Farlow in the early and mid-'80s, and also led his own band.

Percy Heath can be heard on numerous MJQ releases, as well as Gillespie, Davis, Parker, Silver, and Monk reissues. Albert Heath has recorded as a leader for Muse, Strata-East, and Trip; currently, none of these recordings are available on CD, but he can be heard on Coltrane, Johnson, and Gordon reissues, and on his brother Jimmy Heath's recordings. Both Percy and Albert Heath can also be heard with Jimmy on various Heath Brothers discs. —*Ron Wynn and Michael G. Nastos*

NEAL HEFTI

b. Oct. 29, 1922, Hastings, NE
Composer, arranger, trumpet / Swing, big band
An acclaimed arranger, Neal Hefti wrote and/or arranged numerous songs for Count Basie, and for many other bands. He's known for inventive, catchy charts that manage to be both popular and challenging, and that never lose their swinging quality, yet avoid clichés. Hefti wrote his first arrangements in high school, and later worked as both a trumpeter and an arranger for Charlie Barnet, Earl Hines, Charlie Spivak, and Horace Heidt before joining Woody Herman in the mid '40s. He updated their "Woodchopper's Ball" themes, and also arranged "The Good Earth," "Wildroot," and "Northwest Passage," among others. After doing arrangements for Charlie Ventura and Harry James,

Hefti joined Basie in 1950 and remained for over a decade, contributing numerous classic charts. He worked for both the octet and big band; some Hefti gems include "Little Pony," "Lil' Darlin'," "Splanky," and virtually everything from the album *The Atomic Mr. Basie.* Hefti, a trumpeter and pianist in addition being an arranger and composer, led his own bands at times, and served as music director for his wife, Frances Wayne. During the '60s, Hefti did some studio work, contributing to the 1962 Frank Sinatra Reprise sessions, some with Basie. He later became a successful television arranger, writing the TV and film themes for "Barefoot in the Park," and for the "Odd Couple," and the TV theme for "Batman." Hefti toured and gave lectures through the '70s. He recorded a few albums as a leader for Jazz Scene, Coral, and Epic. There are no Hefti albums as a leader on CD, but his arrangements and compositions can be heard on many landmark Count Basie and Woody Herman discs. *—Ron Wynn*

★ **Neil Hefti** / RCA 3573

MARK HELIAS

b. Oct. 1, 1950, Brunswick, NJ
Bass / Modern creative
At one time identified almost exclusively with the free school, Mark Helias has since moved into ethnic, classical, and jazz-rock. With his impressive technique, he's well qualified to perform in any genre. Helias began playing bass at age 20, and studied at Yale, where he earned his degree in 1976. He worked with Anthony Davis, Leo Smith, and Anthony Braxton in the '70s, while recording with Davis, Dewey Redman, and the trio Brahms that included Ray Anderson and Barry Altschul. He and Anderson were in Bass Drum Bone and Slickaphonics in the late '70s and '80s, and recorded in '82 and '83. Helias formed Nu with Ed Blackwell, Don Cherry, Nana Vasconcelos, and Carlos Ward in 1985. They toured Britain in 1987. Helias played with Muhal Richard Abrams, Karl Berger, Julius Hemphill, Oliver Lake, and George Lewis in the '80s, recording with Braxton, Davis, Redman, Altschul, Anderson, and Franco D'Andrea. He has also composed chamber ensemble and theater works. Helias has recorded as a leader for Enja. He has some sessions available on CD. *—Ron Wynn*

Split Image / Aug. 29, 1984 / Enja 4086
With Dewey Redman (ts), Tim Berne (as), Herb Robertson (tpt), and Gerry Hemingway (d). Six more Helias originals. —*Michael G. Nastos*

★ **Current Set, The** / Mar. 4-5, 1987 / Enja 5041
Septet with Tim Berne (as), Robin Eubanks (t), Greg Osby (as), Herb Robertson (tpt), Victor Lewis (d), and Nana Vasconcelos (per). Six originals by leader and bassist, all in strong improvisatory flavor, while keeping rhythm intact. "Greetings from L. C." a fave. *—Michael G. Nastos*

★ **Desert Blue** / Apr. 1-2, 1989 / Enja 79631

JULIUS HEMPHILL

b. 1940, Forth Worth, TX
Alto saxophone / Modern creative
One of the most joyful, exuberant, and masterful saxophonists of the '60s and '70s generation, Julius Hemphill has been a wonderful player and composer whose work blends blues, R&B, bebop, and free elements into a style that's alternately blistering and poignant. Hemphill's sweeping alto and soprano, plus his lyrical flute, have been heard on many albums, as well as in big bands, duos, solo, and with several combos. His screams, cries, squeals, and squiggly lines, plus his frenetic pace and solos, are always enjoyable and expertly played. Hemphill learned clarinet in Fort Worth with the great composer and player, John Carter. He later studied at North Texas State College. Hemphill played in both an army band and with various groups in Texas, among them an R&B unit with Ike Turner. He moved to St. Louis in 1968, where he joined the Black Artists Group (BAG). Hemphill formed his own label in 1972, Mbari. That same year a col-

lection of his works, *The Orientation of Sweet Willie Rollbar* was filmed and he had compositions presented on stage in New York and in Washington, D.C. Hemphill moved to New York in the mid '70s, and began recording with such players as Anthony Braxton and Lester Bowie, as well as on his own and with the funk band Kool and the Gang. He was part of the "loft jazz" movement of the mid and late '70s, but became most famous as a founding member of the World Saxophone Quartet. Hemphill, David Murray, Oliver Lake, and Hamiett Bluiett got together for a New Orleans concert in 1976 and decided to remain as a unit. Hemphill remained with the group for several years, but left recently. He's suffered from severe health problems, including the loss of a leg a few years ago, but has maintained his writing and playing career. Hemphill's worked with such players as Olu Dara, Abdul Wadud, and Warren Smith, and has made many tours of Europe. He began recording for Mbari, and some of those sessions were later reissued on Arista or Sackville. He's issued dates on Arista, Sackville, Black Saint, Red, Elektra/Musician, and Minor Music. Hemphill composed *Long Tongues,* an opera with saxophones as characters, and contributed the composition "Pensive" to the Wildflowers concert series and Douglas recordings. He played there with Wadud, Phillip Wilson, Famodou Don Moye, and Bern Nix. There are a few Hemphill recordings currently available on CD. *—Ron Wynn*

★ **Dogon A.D.** / **i.** Feb. 1972 / Freedom 1028
Between the moment cellist Abdul Wadud and drummer Phillip Wilson interlock to establish the slow, portentous rhythm of "Dogon A.D." and the last fluted notes of the lovely, gravely dancing theme of "The Painter," there are nearly 40 minutes of magical music. Magical because it is at once exhilarating and peaceful. Every bit as remarkable as the compositional synthesis (and related to it) is the merging of these four players into one. Though considerable space is given to the soloing horns, one is always less aware of the individual voice than of the ensemble, and for only four players without the dubious benefit of electronics, the orchestral sound is extremely deep and resonant. It is probably saxophonist/flutist Julius Hemphill's extremely varied use of the cello which is responsible for this, as are Wadud's astute bowing, plucking, and strumming. As thrilling as group improvisation in jazz can be, it too rarely approaches that still center which is one of the fulfilling experiences of *Dogon A.D. —Joel Ray,* Cadence

○ **Coon Bid'ness** / **i.** Jan. 29, 1975 / Freedom 1012
Side one of this album was recorded in 1975 and found Julius Hemphill's interests lying elsewhere, borrowing somewhat from Anthony Braxton. The four tracks actually break quite easily into a pair of two-section pieces, both of which explore the careful dissection of ensemble writing through the gradual prismification of textures and harmonies. Hemphill's major label debut strikes a rich balance between his modern, somewhat academic concepts and the rarefied funk of years past. *—Neil Tesser,* Down Beat

★ **Roi Boye and the Gotham Minstrels** / **i.** Mar. 1, 1977 / Sackville 15
Psychotheater drama in the form of the free African-American creative jazz movement at its height. *—Michael G. Nastos*

Blue Boye / **i.** 1977 / Mbari 1000

○ **Raw Materials and Residuals** / **i.** 1977 / Black Saint 0015

Flat out Jump Suite / Jun. 4-5, 1980 / Black Saint 0040
Quartet with Abdul Wadud on cello, Olu Dara on trumpet, and Warren Smith on percussion. Unabashed free music, at times funky. *—Michael G. Nastos*

○ **Georgia Blues** / Aug. 1984 / Minor Music 003

★ **Julius Hemphill Big Band** / Feb. 1988 / Elektra 60831
A 16-piece progressive big band with lots of saxophones. Good dose of Bill Frisell and Jack Watkins on guitar. Trumpets Rasul Siddik and David Hines are outstanding. —*Michael G. Nastos*

○ **Fat Man and the Hard Blues** / **i.** Jul. 1991 / Black Saint 1201152

Fat Man and The Hard Blues is a selection of sax sextet shorties that includes one piece from *Long Tongues*, Hemphill's saxophone opera, several from a collaboration with choreographer Bill T. Jones, the classic Julius Hemphill gemstone "The Hard Blues," and plenty more. Though their profiles are relatively low, the altoist's five accomplices are outstanding. "Lenny" and "Anchorman" are backdrops for super tenor solos by D.C.-based John Coltrane-scribe Andrew White; young James Carter blows a tongue-chopped tenor solo through the silky "Four Saints"; and the chord progression of "Headlines" gets caught in a revolving door while Hemphill matches alto to Ehrlich's independent but complementary soprano. The group plays the tar out of Hemphill's thick compositions, uniquely arranged with mid-dle-rich (but never muddy) songs. *—John Corbett*, Down Beat

○ **Live from the New Music Cafe** / **i.** 1992 / Music & Arts 731

BILL HENDERSON (William Randall Henderson)

b. Mar. 19, 1930, Chicago, IL
Vocals / Ballads & Blues
For a long time Henderson was one of the best ballad and blues singers. Smooth as any. Can swing with the best. Underappreciated. *—Michael G. Nastos*

○ **Bill Henderson Sings** / Oct. 26-27, 1959 / Vee Jay 1015

Bill Henderson / **i.** 1960 / Vee Jay 1031

Please Send Me Someone to Love / 1961 / Vee Jay 1031

★ **Bill Henderson** / **Oscar Peterson Trio** / May 1963-Jun. 1963 / Verve 837937
Exceptional release from an unsung hero of jazz vocals. Highly recommended. *—Michael G. Nastos*

When My Dreamboat Comes Home / Jan. 25, 1965 / Verve 8619

Live at the Times / Aug. 1975 / Musicraft 779

Something's Gotta Give / **i.** 1979 / Musicraft 932

Tribute to Johnny Mercer / May 5, 1981 / Discovery 846

○ **His Complete Vee-Jay Recordings—Volume One** / **i.** 1993 / Vee-Jay 909

EDDIE HENDERSON (Edward Jackson Henderson)

b. Oct. 26, 1940, New York, NY
Trumpet / Hard bop, early jazz-rock
An assertive, frequently electrifying trumpeter who's strongly influenced by Miles Davis, Eddie Henderson's bristling lines and high-voltage playing have been featured in hard bop and jazz-rock bands. Henderson's family moved from New York to San Francisco when he was 14. He stud-ied trumpet at the San Francisco Conservatory of Music. He combined a musical and medical education, and became a psychiatrist in 1968. While pursuing his medical require-ments, Henderson worked with John Handy during the sum-mers. But on the behest of Miles Davis, Henderson decided to forego being a full-time physician, and concentrated on music instead. He later played with Tyrone Washington and Joe Henderson before forming his own quintet. Henderson was part of Herbie Hancock's jazz-rock and electronic groups in the early '70s, and made his recording debut as a leader. He later toured with Art Blakey, worked with Mike Nock, and recorded with Charles Earland, while he also played with former Hancock mates Julian Priester and Patrick Gleeson. Henderson spearheaded a predominantly rock group in the late '70s, while scoring a pop hit with the song "Prance On" in 1977. He also recorded with Richard Davis, Stanley Cowell, and Pharoah Sanders in the late '70s and early '80s. Henderson recorded with Laurent De Wilde in the '90s. He's done sessions for Capricorn, Blue Note, Capitol, and IDA. Henderson has one date currently available on CD. *—Ron Wynn*

★ **Heritage** / 1975 / Blue Note 636

FLETCHER HENDERSON (Fletcher Hamilton (Jr) Henderson)

b. Dec. 18, 1897, Cuthbert, GA, **d.** Dec. 29, 1952, New York, NY
Bandleader, arranger, piano / Swing, big band
Fletcher Henderson was a superb composer, arranger, and bandleader, and the founder of one of the earliest and best large bands. He had a knack for combining top arrangers and soloists. Henderson earned a degree in chemistry and mathematics from Atlanta University. Though he'd studied European classical music with his mother, who was a piano teacher, Henderson journeyed to New York in 1920 to find work as a chemist. Racial realities reared their head, and in-stead of a job as a chemist Henderson found a job as a song demonstrator with the Pace-Handy music company, a pio-neering Black publishing firm. When Harry Pace founded the Black Swan label, the nation's first African-American recording firm, Henderson became its musical jack-of-all-trades. He organized groups to back their vocalists, and eventually became a bandleader. He obtained work for groups at clubs and dances, and eventually started to per-form at the Club Alabam. When offered a job at the Roseland Ballroom, Henderson accepted, and his band stayed there for over ten years. It was the only way they could get into the Roseland; it was a White-only dance hall. He wasn't a great technical pianist, but learned jazz nuances and techniques successfully as an adult.

Things changed for both Henderson and the orchestra in 1924, when Louis Armstrong, whom Henderson had heard in New Orleans, was hired as a "jazz specialist." Before that, the Henderson orchestra provided lightweight, undistin-guished fare for dancers. It was no different from numerous bands around the nation in style, song selection, or sound. Armstrong's dynamic, individualistic playing galvanized the band, and both band director Don Redman and Henderson smartly adopted it as a signature style for the entire orches-tra. Redman worked out sequences where the brass and reed sections would alternately perform in call-and-response fashion, then one section would play supporting riffs behind the other. Solos were interspersed between these arranged passages. The Paul Whiteman orchestra was also trying this approach, in less complete fashion. In 1924 and 1925, the Henderson band began to use this method extensively. Armstrong's famous solos on "Copenhagen," "Shanghai Shuffle," and "Sugar Foot Stomp," a reworking of King Oliver's "Dippermouth Blues," were huge favorites. "Dippermouth Blues" was their first smash hit.

Armstrong left in 1925, but things were solidified. Redman departed in 1927, putting the arranging burden on the shoulders of both Henderson and his brother, Horace. They responded by writing spare, easy-swinging, delicate arrangements. Horace Henderson provided over 30 arrange-ments for the band and worked in that capacity intermit-tently from 1931 to 1947. "Hot and Anxious/Comin' and Goin'," and "Christopher Columbus" are among his finest arrangements. Other orchestra classics include "King Porter Stomp," "Down South Camp Meeting," and "Wrappin' It Up." Benny Carter gave the band seminal material in 1930 and 1931, while Fletcher Henderson continued writing excellent arrangements and demonstrated a rare knack for spotting talent. Featured in the orchestra were Coleman Hawkins (in the band for a decade), Don Redman, Lester Young, Buster Bailey, Benny Carter, Ben Webster, Chu Berry, John Kirby, Charlie Green, Jimmy Harrison, Dickie Wells, and virtually every top Black trumpeter of the 1925-1940 era, including Louis Armstrong, Joe Smith, Rex Stewart, Tommy Ladnier, Bobby Stark, Cootie Williams, Red Allen, and Roy Eldridge!

A money crunch forced Henderson to sell some arrange-ments to Benny Goodman, who was beginning his own band. These and several other arrangements Henderson pro-vided played a pivotal role in swing's popularity surge. Henderson assembled another fine big band in 1936; his brother wrote several arrangements and doubled as an ex-cellent pianist. Henderson stopped leading bands in 1939 to become Goodman's staff arranger. Goodman always cited Henderson's importance, and in 1941, helped him start another orchestra, which ultimately failed due to budgetary problems. Henderson led a sextet in 1949, but suffered a severe stroke in 1950. He died in 1952. —*Ron Wynn and Dan Morgenstern*

Fletcher Henderson (1923) / **i.** Mar. 1923-Jan. 1924 / BYG 529083
Leader of the first jazz big band, pianist Fletcher Henderson led the finest orchestra in jazz prior to the rise of Duke Ellington in 1927. This European LP (Vol. 33 in the Archive of Jazz series) has 14 early and obscure recordings by Henderson in his formative period. Most of the music (arranged by Don Redman) is closer to dance music than jazz and some of it is rather primitive (especially compared to the contemporary recordings of King Oliver), but, unlike much big-band music of this period, it is quite listenable. A very rare piano solo ("Chimes Blues") by Henderson is a highlight of this interesting set. —*Scott Yanow*

★ **Rarest Fletcher—Vol. 1 (1923-1924)** / Jun. 28, 1923-Mar. 11, 1924 / MCA 1346

★ **Study in Frustration, A** / **i.** Aug. 7, 1923-May 28, 1938 / Columbia
Although still only available as a four-LP set, this is easily the definitive Fletcher Henderson package. Between 1923-38, Henderson's orchestra was one of the finest swing bands in the world, and during 1923-27 (until Duke Ellington's emergence) it was the first and the best. The arrangements of Don Redman in the early days set the pace for jazz; Benny Carter and Horace Henderson also wrote some important charts before Fletcher himself finally developed into a major arranger in 1932. This Columbia set is not "complete," but it includes 64 selections, at least 60 of them gems! Among the remarkable list of sidemen are such masters as tenors Coleman Hawkins, Ben Webster, and Chu Berry; clarinetist Buster Bailey; trombonists Charlie Green, Jimmy Harrison, J.C. Higginbotham, and Dicky Wells; altoist Benny Carter; and Fats Waller on piano. As with Art Blakey three decades later, it seems like Henderson at one time or another employed virtually every top Black trumpeter of the era: Louis Armstrong, Joe Smith, Rex Stewart, Tommy Ladnier, Bobby Stark, Cootie Williams, Red Allen, Roy Eldridge! This essential box (which contains three wonderful versions of "King Porter Stomp") belongs in everyone's jazz collection. —*Scott Yanow*

○ **Pathe Sessions (1923-1925), The** / **i.** Nov. 26, 1923-Jun. 25, 1925 / Swaggie 803
During the year-and-a-half covered by these 19 selections, Fletcher Henderson's orchestra developed from a fine dance band into the first jazz big band. The quick evolution was caused by the addition of a young cornetist whose legato phrases and sense of swing greatly influenced the other members of Henderson's orchestra and eventually all of jazz: Louis Armstrong. While the first 12 selections on this Australian LP have advanced Don Redman arrangements and some interesting moments from the tenor of Coleman Hawkins, the final seven numbers find the band learning to swing. Armstrong's solos sound several years ahead of everyone else but the band was beginning to catch up. —*Scott Yanow*

○ **Henderson Pathes** / **i.** Nov. 1923-Feb. 1925 / Fountain 112

Fletcher Henderson's Orchestra / **i.** 1923 / Biograph 12039

☆ **Fletcher Henderson (1924-1927)** / Jul. 10, 1924-Apr. 24, 1927 / Zeta 753
This French CD contains many of the best recordings from Louis Armstrong's year with Henderson, including such classics as "Copenhagen," "Everybody Loves My Baby," and "Mandy Make Up Your Mind," and "Sugar Foot Stomp." During this time Henderson added other fine soloists (including trombonist Charlie Green and clarinetist Buster Bailey) and Don Redman's arrangements began to swing. The final six numbers from this 22-selection CD are from the Henderson orchestra's zenith in 1927 with "Fidgety Feet" and "Variety

Stomp" featuring brilliant work from tenor great Coleman Hawkins, trombonist Jimmy Harrison, clarinetist Bailey, and trumpeter Tommy Ladnier. A perfect introduction to Fletcher Henderson. —*Scott Yanow*

☆ **Fletcher Henderson and Louis Armstrong** / **i.** Oct. 10, 1924-Oct. 21, 1925 / Timeless 003
This rather unusual CD has 24 selections but most of them are shorter excerpts. The focus is on the brilliant solos that Louis Armstrong took while a member of the Fletcher Henderson orchestra. Since his cornet flights were years ahead of some of the wheezing arrangements and attempts by the other sidemen, the producers simply cut out the more dated segments and sometimes spliced in several of Armstrong's solos from different takes of the same song. Where the producers erred was in not including every Armstrong solo with Henderson and, most important, in not programming the CD in complete chronological order so one could more easily trace the month-by-month growth of this innovative jazzman. Still, this is a historical curiosity, and the music is consistently exciting. —*Scott Yanow*

☆ **Fletcher Henderson (1924-1925)** / Oct. 1924-Feb. 1925 / Jazz Panorama 21
This excellent European LP contains 14 performances (including three alternate takes) from Louis Armstrong's period with Fletcher Henderson's orchestra. Most of these selections are fairly rare (such as "My Rose Marie," "Twelfth Street Blues," and "Me Neenyah") and only one performance is duplicated from the CD *Fletcher Henderson (1924-1927)*. Almost all of these cuts have memorable Louis Armstrong solos that easily take honors and are state of the art for 1925. —*Scott Yanow*

○ **First Impressions (1924-1931)** / 1924-Jul. 17, 1931 / MCA 1310
This Jazz Heritage LP sampler gives a strong overview of the hot big-band music of Fletcher Henderson. Three different periods are represented, with two numbers featuring Louis Armstrong in late 1924, seven mostly heated tracks from Fletcher's prime in 1926-28 (including hot versions of "Clarinet Marmalade," "Fidgety Feet," and "Sensation"), and a few selections (including "Sugar Foot Stomp") from 1931. Not for completists but recommended to general collectors. —*Scott Yanow*

☆ **Fletcher Henderson and the Dixie Stompers 1925-1928** / **i.** Nov. 23, 1925-Apr. 6, 1928 / Swing
One of the main pseudonyms that Fletcher Henderson used while recording illegally for rival record labels was The Dixie Stompers, and all of their 33 recordings are included on this superlative two-LP set. Covering Henderson's prime years (late 1925-28), these very enjoyable performances feature many top soloists (including trumpeters Joe Smith, Tommy Ladnier, and Bobby Stark; trombonists Charlie Green and Jimmy Harrison; and the great Coleman Hawkins), often in small-group settings. Whether explosive numbers like "Oh Baby!" or definitive versions of "Jackass Blues" and "St. Louis Shuffle," these performances are highly recommended. —*Scott Yanow*

○ **Fletcher Henderson (1925-1926)** / Nov. 23, 1925-Apr. 14, 1926 / Classics 610
The Classics series has undergone the admirable task of reissuing on CD in chronological order every selection (although no alternate takes) of Fletcher Henderson's orchestra. This set finds the post-Armstrong edition of this pacesetting big band swinging hard on a variety of standards and obscurities. With cornetist Joe Smith, trombonist Charlie Green, clarinetist Buster Bailey, and tenor great Coleman Hawkins contributing many fine solos, and Don Redman's often-innovative arrangements inspiring the musicians, Fletcher Henderson's orchestra at this period had no close competitors among jazz-oriented big bands. Even the weaker pop tunes (like "I Want To See a Little More of What I Saw in Arkansas") have their strong moments. —*Scott Yanow*

☆ **Fletcher Henderson and the Dixie Stompers (1925-1928)** / 1925-1928 / Disques Swing 6

This duplicates the monumental four-LP set *A Study in Frustration* on 10 of its 33 songs, but the music is of such high quality that it is worth purchasing for the 23 "new" pieces. The program includes all of the titles recorded by Henderson under the band name The Dixie Stompers. The personnel on the inside cover mistakenly lists that of the Chocolate Dandies record. Collectively, the Dixie Stompers consisted of cornetists Tommy Ladnier, Rex Stewart, Joe Smith, Russell Smith, and Bobby Stark (last three titles); trombonists Charlie Green, Benny Morton, and Jimmy Harrison; clarinetist Buster Bailey; Don Redman on clarinet, alto, and (on two songs) vocals; Coleman Hawkins on tenor, clarinet, and bass sax; altoist Don Pasquale; pianist Fletcher Henderson; Charlie Dixon on banjo; June Cole or Ralph Escudero on tuba; and drummer Kaiser Marshall. The music was generally superb and Redman's innovative arrangements made this band often sound futuristic despite the acoustic recordings. The contrast between Ladnier's hot New Orleans cornet and Joe Smith's cool, lyrical style is worth noting, as are the solos by the long-forgotten but very talented Bobby Stark on the final three selections. Buster Bailey plays his usual impossible runs on clarinet, the young Hawkins is still learning at this point, and Charlie Green is in prime form on the early sides. This is a historically significant set and a delight to hear. — *Scott Yanow, Cadence*

☆ **Fletcher Henderson (1926-1927)** / Apr. 14, 1926-Jan. 22, 1927 / Classics 597

This CD, in Classics's chronological series, which captures the Fletcher Henderson orchestra at its peak, is overloaded with classics: "Jackass Blues," "The Stampede" (with a very influential tenor solo by Coleman Hawkins), "Clarinet Marmalade," "Snag It," and "Tozo," among others. In addition to Coleman Hawkins, Tommy Ladnier emerges as a major trumpeter and Fats Waller drops by for his "Henderson . . . Stomp." Eight years before the official beginning of the swing era, Fletcher Henderson's orchestra was outswinging everyone. — *Scott Yanow*

☆ **Complete Fletcher Henderson (1927-1936), The** / Mar. 11, 1927-Aug. 4, 1936 / RCA/Bluebird 5507

"Complete" is in this case a relative term, meaning every recording by Fletcher Henderson's orchestra owned by RCA/Bluebird rather than every record he made during this period. A perfectly done two-LP set, these 34 songs include three from 1927 (featuring trumpeters Tommy Ladnier and Joe Smith at their best), 12 varying sides from 1931-32 (during which tenor saxophonist Coleman Hawkins and trumpeters Rex Stewart and Bobby Stark make even the most commercial material into worthwhile music), a session from 1934 with trumpeter Red Allen, and 15 numbers from 1936 that costar trumpeter Roy Eldridge and Chu Berry on tenor. Throughout, the consistent high quality of the solos and the musicianship (even with some off moments) makes one regret that this classic orchestra was not more commercially successful. — *Scott Yanow*

☆ **Fletcher Henderson (1927)** / Mar. 11, 1927-Oct. 24, 1927 / Classics 580

Fletcher Henderson's orchestra was at the peak of its powers during this period, as can be heard on such torrid recordings as "Fidgety Feet," "Sensation," "St. Louis Shuffle," and "Hop Off"; even the overly complex Don Redman arrangement "Whiteman Stomp" (which Paul Whiteman's musicians apparently had trouble learning) is no problem for this brilliant orchestra. Classics's chronological reissue of Henderson's valuable recordings on this CD covers the many high points of the peak year of 1927; only Duke Ellington's orchestra was on the level of this pacesetting big band. — *Scott Yanow*

○ **Hocus Pocus: Classic Big Band Jazz** / i. Apr. 27, 1927-Aug. 4, 1936 / RCA 9904

High points include "St. Louis Shuffle," "Variety Stomp," "Sugar Foot Stomp," the swinging title cut, examples of early Roy Eldridge trumpet, and "Strangers," which contrasts a

horrendous vocal with some inspired Coleman Hawkins tenor. — *Scott Yanow*

○ **Fletcher Henderson (1927-1931)** / Nov. 4, 1927-Feb. 5, 1931 / Classics 572

With its high musicianship and many talented soloists (including trumpeters Rex Stewart and Bobby Stark, trombonist Jimmy Harrison, Coleman Hawkins on tenor, and altoist Benny Carter), the Fletcher Henderson Orchestra should have prospered during this period, but unaccountably its leader (never a strong businessman) seemed to be losing interest in the band's fortunes and made several bad decisions. The result is that by 1931 Henderson's orchestra was struggling while Duke Ellington's was becoming a household name. This Classics CD, in covering over three years, demonstrates how few recordings this band was making (only four songs apiece in both 1929 and 1930), although the quality largely makes up for the quantity. The original band version of "King Porter Stomp" and an explosive "Oh Baby" are the high points of this satisfying collection. — *Scott Yanow*

○ **Fletcher Henderson (1929-1937)** / i. May 1929-Sep. 1937 / BBC 682

☆ **Fletcher Henderson (1931)** / Feb. 5, 1931-Jul. 31, 1931 / Classics 555

Even with such strong players as trumpeters Bobby Stark and Rex Stewart, trombonist Benny Morton, and tenor saxophonist Coleman Hawkins, the fortunes of Fletcher Henderson's orchestra were slipping during 1931. With the departure of Don Redman several years earlier, the group's arrangements were less innovative, and the pressure was on to perform commercial songs for the Depression audience. Even the jazz standards (such as "Tiger Rag" and "After You've Gone") are less interesting than those of their competitors, although this new version of "Sugar Foot Stomp" is a classic and the strong solos by the all-star cast makes this CD well worth acquiring. — *Scott Yanow*

★ **Crown King of Swing, The** / i. Mar. 1931-Oct. 1931 / Savoy 1152

In 1931, the Fletcher Henderson orchestra recorded 10 titles for the low-budget Crown label. This LP includes all 10 numbers plus two alternate takes, giving Henderson's band a chance to play material generally not associated with its early brand of swing, including such tunes as "After You've Gone," "Stardust," "Tiger Rag," and even "Twelfth Street Rag." Although not essential (only the remake of "Sugar Foot Stomp" is classic), it is interesting to hear trumpeters Bobby Stark and Rex Stewart, trombonist J.C. Higginbotham, and tenorman Coleman Hawkins soloing on this unlikely material. — *Scott Yanow*

☆ **Swing's the Thing (1931-1934)** / 1931-Sep. 25, 1934 / MCA 1318

One of the best collections of the Fletcher Henderson orchestra prior to Louis Armstrong joining up, this Jazz Heritage LP finds the band gradually expanding from 8 to 10 pieces and beginning to come to grips with the emergence in New York of New Orleans jazz brought in by imported players. Evolving from a first-class but dated dance band into a jazz ensemble, Henderson's orchestra was already much more jazz-oriented than the big band led by the "King of Jazz" (Paul Whiteman), but at this point it lacked any great soloists; even 18-year-old Coleman Hawkins, the up-and-coming master of the tenor sax, had a long way to go. — *Scott Yanow*

☆ **Fletcher Henderson (1932-1934)** / Dec. 9, 1932-Sep. 12, 1934 / Classics 535

Although the Fletcher Henderson orchestra was struggling and missing opportunities during this era, its recordings greatly improved from the ones in 1931. Henderson had finally developed into a top arranger (as can be heard on "Honeysuckle Rose" and "Wrappin' It Up"), the band was full of top soloists (trumpeter Bobby Stark has his greatest moments on "The New King Porter Stomp"), and even if Coleman Hawkins chose to move to Europe (after starring on "It's the Talk of the Town") the band should have been poised to flourish in the swing era. These recordings (from Classics's complete chronological program) prove that swing did not begin with Benny Goodman in 1935. —*Scott Yanow*

○ **Big Bands (1933), The** / 1933 / Prestige 7645

○ **Fletcher Henderson (1934-1937)** / Sep. 25, 1934-Mar. 2, 1937 / Classics 527
In early, 1935 Fletcher Henderson broke up his classic orchestra but a year later, with the success of so many other big bands, he formed a new ensemble. This Classics CD includes four songs from 1934, Henderson's entire output from 1936, and his first recording of 1937. The main difference between the two units is that the new ensemble boasted the trumpet of Roy Eldridge and tenor solos from Coleman Hawkins's potential successor Chu Berry. "Christopher Columbus" became a hit as did the band's new theme song ("Stealin' Apples"), but the brief bit of glory would not last. However, Henderson's brand of swing music still sounds fresh today and this CD is easily recommended. —*Scott Yanow*

Fletcher Henderson's Sextet (1950) / i. Dec. 20, 1950-Dec. 21, 1950 / Alamac 2444
Recorded only a day or two before a stroke ended his playing career and soon afterward his life, this LP contains a broadcast that finds Fletcher Henderson playing mostly standards with a fine sextet. Trumpeter Dick Vance and clarinetist Eddie Barefield were alumni of his orchestra but it is tenor saxophonist Lucky Thompson who takes honors on this spirited session of small-group swing. —*Scott Yanow*

☆ **Big Reunion, The** / Nov. 29, 1957-Dec. 2, 1957 / Fresh Sound 44
In 1957 cornetist Rex Stewart gathered together a large group dominated by Fletcher Henderson alumni and the result is this excellent tribute. Not every selection comes from Henderson's book, but the four main jams ("Sugar Foot Stomp," "Honeysuckle Rose," "Wrappin' It Up," and "King Porter Stomp") both revisit past glories and, with the fresh solos of Coleman Hawkins, Ben Webster, Buster Bailey, J.C. Higginbotham, Dickie Wells, and Stewart, among others, create some new history. —*Scott Yanow*

HORACE HENDERSON (Horace W. Henderson)

b. Nov. 22, 1904, Cuthbert, GA
Arranger, piano, bandleader / Swing, big band
While Horace Henderson can't be compared fairly to his brother, Fletcher, in terms of achievement, he has a substantial legacy as an arranger and bandleader. More than 30 Henderson arrangements were incorporated into his brother's band, among them "Hot and Anxious/Comin' and Goin,'" and "Christopher Columbus." He also led a small splinter group in the early '30s that made some fine recordings for Parlophone. Henderson's arrangement of "Hot and Anxious" revised the traditional riff that would eventually be recorded by the Glenn Miller Orchestra on "In the Mood." Henderson also used the melody from the Duke Ellington/Barney Bigard song "Voom" as a reference for his composition "Doin' the Voom." He was an above-average pianist, and more rhythmically intense and varied than his brother. Henderson performed in New York during the mid-'20s while still a student at Wilberforce University. He subsequently toured with his band, the Wilberforce Collegians. The roster included Rex Stewart and Benny Carter. Besides heading bands in the '20s, '30s, and '40s, Henderson also worked in the groups of Don Redman and Vernon Andrae while arranging and playing in his brother's band from 1931 to 1947. Periodically, Henderson also did arrangements for Benny Goodman, Charlie Barnet, Jimmie Lunceford, and Earl Hines, among others. He continued heading bands into the '70s. His work can be heard on Fletcher Henderson reissued CDs. —*Ron Wynn*

★ **Horace Henderson (1940)** / i. Feb. 1940-Oct. 1940 / Tax 8013

JOE HENDERSON (Joseph A. Henderson)

b. Apr. 24, 1937, Lima, OH
Tenor and soprano saxophone, flute, composer / Bop, hard bop
During the early '90s, tenor saxophonist Joe Henderson finally reaped the rewards and widespread recognition he's long deserved. His albums of Billy Strayhorn and Miles Davis compositions have gotten rave reviews in both the jazz and general press; Henderson was profiled during '92 in everything from the *New York Times* to *Newsweek*, and won *Down Beat's* Critics Poll honors for the album and for his tenor playing. He won *Down Beat's* award again in '93. He's back in the public eye in a manner that well exceeds the early '70s, when he was invited to join Blood, Sweat & Tears. Henderson played at the White House jazz concert in '93, and his earlier albums are beginning to resurface. His solos often begin calmly, then their intensity increases with each chorus until Henderson hits a peak. Trills, screams, bursts of notes, swirling lines, and elliptical phrases are among the devices he utilizes, all of them incorporated seamlessly in a fashion that's neither exaggerated nor gimmicky. Except for John Coltrane's and Sonny Rollins's styles, Henderson's style has had the most influence on '70s tenors. Henderson has come closest to free jazz without deserting either preset chords and meter, and his playing is always intelligent and tasteful. It's among the most widely studied and admired by emerging jazz musicians of the '70s.

Henderson studied music at Kentucky State College and Wayne State University in the late '50s and early '60s. His classmates included Curtis Fuller and Yusef Lateef. He played with various Detroit musicians, worked briefly with Sonny Stitt in 1959, then formed his own band in 1960. He toured with an army band from 1960 to 1962, then played with Jack McDuff and co-led a group with Kenny Dorham. Henderson gained critical plaudits during his time with Horace Silver and Herbie Hancock in the '60s. Aside from the brief stint with Blood, Sweat & Tears, Henderson's been a bandleader since the early '70s. He's also worked often with Freddie Hubbard, and played in the band know as Echoes of an Era, then later known as Griffith Park Band and then the Griffith Park Collection. During the '80s and '90s, Henderson's done many concept albums, among them a two-volume set of trio material sans piano for Blue Note, two similar projects for Red in the '80s and '90s, plus the Strayhorn and Davis albums. He also did a New York City concert that featured Kenny Dorham compositions from the early '60s. The Henderson boom is triggering renewed reissue activity at several labels. There's now a fair number of his '60s and '70s dates available. —*Ron Wynn*

★ **Page One** / Jun. 3, 1963 / Blue Note 84140
A 1988 reissue of an outstanding date. Kenny Dorham (tpt) and McCoy Tyner (p) soar; Henderson is frenetic. —*Ron Wynn*

○ **Our Thing** / Sep. 9, 1963 / Blue Note 84152
A wonderful 1986 reissue of a prime 1963 date. The lineup is amazing, with Andrew Hill (p) and Kenny Dorham (tpt). CD has a bonus cut. —*Ron Wynn*

Best of the Blue Note Years / 1963-1985 / Blue Note 95627

○ **In 'n Out** / Apr. 10, 1964 / Blue Note 46510
An early '60s Blue Note classic by tenor saxophonist Joe Henderson. This was one of his first albums as a leader, and it's distinguished by numerous swirling, dynamic solos, the usual first-rate engineering job by Rudy Van Gelder, and fine compositions and arrangements. —*Ron Wynn*

○ **Inner Urge** / Nov. 30, 1964 / Blue Note 84189
A 1989 reissue of another in his line of great Blue Notes from the '60s. —*Ron Wynn*

★ **Mode for Joe** / Jan. 27, 1966 / Blue Note 84227
Kicker, The / Aug. 10, 1967 / Milestone 465
A stormy, dynamic date that teeters on the avant-garde edge, yet holds the bop center. —*Ron Wynn*
Tetragon / Sep. 27, 1967 / Milestone 9017

This strong late '60s release by tenor saxophonist Joe Henderson is squarely in the dynamic groove he'd established by then. The songs are mostly originals and delivered with a crunching power and intense energy that eventually resulted in Joe Henderson becoming a recognized star. — *Ron Wynn*

Power to the People / May 23+29, 1969 / Milestone
An album with Afrocentric flavoring—frenetic and introspective at times. —*Ron Wynn*

If You're Not Part of the Problem . . . / Sep. 24-26, 1970 / Milestone

Live at the Lighthouse / Sep. 24-26, 1970 / Milestone
Firehouse playing from the wonderful team of Henderson and Woody Shaw (tpt). —*Ron Wynn*

In Pursuit of Blackness / May 21, 1971 / Milestone 9034
Dynamite early '70s session by tenor saxophonist Joe Henderson, backed by equally fierce playing from trumpeter Woody Shaw. The date is divided between leftover tracks from a live date and studio sessions with a slightly different band that includes alto saxophonist Pete Yellin. —*Ron Wynn*

Joe Henderson in Japan / Aug. 4, 1971 / Milestone 9047

Black Is the Color / 1972 / Milestone 9040

Multiple / Jan. 30-31, 1973 / Original Jazz Classics 763
Interesting early '70s set by tenor saxophonist Joe Henderson that shows the struggle many veterans faced during that period over whether they should alter their style and hook into the hot jazz-rock format. Henderson on this date changes his approach, using electric piano and bass for one of the few times ever on a session, and even adding some vocals on two cuts. This isn't as bad as some other releases in that period, but stands out today as vastly different from any other Joe Henderson record. —*Ron Wynn*

☆ **Elements, The** / Oct. 15+17, 1973 / Milestone
Ambitious concept work gets an ethereal feeling via Alice Coltrane's harp. —*Ron Wynn*

Canyon Lady / Oct. 1973 / Milestone

Black Narcissus / Oct. 1-6, 1974 / Milestone 9071

Barcelona / Jun. 2, 1977 / Enja 3037
Tremendous, frenzied trio date by tenor saxophonist Joe Henderson with bassist Wayne Darling and drummer Ed Soph. After many years of obscurity, Henderson became famous. But the whirling lines, huge tone, and astonishing solos that he routinely offers on this album have been prized by jazz fans since the early '60s. —*Ron Wynn*

Relaxin' at Camarillo / Aug. 20+29, 1979 / Original Jazz Classics 776
An album of easy and confident yet blistering tenor sax by Henderson. —*Ron Wynn*

○ **Mirror, Mirror** / Jan. 1980 / PA/USA 7075
Even when tenor saxophonist Joe Henderson's approach is low-key, his array of ideas is stunning. Pianist Chick Corea, bassist Ron Carter, and drummer Billy Higgins provide sympathetic support throughout but don't really ignite until "Keystone," Carter's goofy, Thelonious-Monkish blues, and "Bolero." Here Henderson employs one of his favorite effects: a shrieking wall that enchants and distresses simultaneously. The same device in the hands of a less discriminating player usually grates on the nerves. "Mirror, Mirror" shows that Corea was still capable of writing legitimate jazz songs and not just the Mickey Mouse tripe that had plagued so many of his recent (1981) efforts. His solo work with this group is also first-rate. —*Arthur Moorehead*, Down Beat

○ **Live at the Village Vanguard—Vol. 2: State of The Tenor** / Nov. 14-15, 1985 / Blue Note 46296
Comparison with Sonny Rollins's *A Night at the Village Vanguard*," recorded in 1957, is inevitable. Rollins is more melody-oriented, Henderson more rhythm-oriented. Where Rollins bursts into bel canto, Henderson becomes a drummer. There are many rhythm levels—falsetto squeals on top, brusque runs swooping through all registers, low B-flat splats, trills and rolling phrases off to the side. Ron Carter (b)

and Al Foster (d) do not grow conversational in the manner of, say, avant-garde rhythm sections. Henderson is enough by himself up front, with Carter and Foster grooving off that feat. The tunes suit Henderson's convolutions, but Horace Silver's "Soulville," the simplest, comes off best. Henderson's "The Bead Game" is the most outside. This album goes down better in small doses—one tune at a time and then take a break. Otherwise, you could overdose on tedium. It's a heavy album. The state of the tenor is a drum kit. No tenorman matches Henderson's rhythmic variety. —*Owen Cordle*, Jazz Times

○ **Evening With, An** / Jul. 1987 / Red 123215
Recorded at the 1987 Genoa Jazz Festival (and well reproduced on that country's Red Record label), tenor saxophonist Joe Henderson's full-bodied, go-for-broke approach is intact. While I found Sam Rivers's "Beatrice" to be something of a letdown, Henderson's interpretation of Thelonious Monk's "Ask Me Now" is the highlight of this nearly 50-minute recording. Bassist Charlie Haden (Al Foster, drums) gets some marvelously long outings as well and moves things along with finesse and flair. This album makes a fine companion to the Blue Notes and on that basis alone can be recommended. —*Miles Jordan*, Jazz Times

○ **Standard Joe, The** / Mar. 1991 / Red 123248
Joe Henderson breathes new life, ferocity, and humor into the familiar repertorial turf of "Blue Bossa," "Take the 'A' Train," and "'Round Midnight." He serves up 25 minutes' worth of spontaneous observations on that tenor saxist's chestnut "Body and Soul" and realizes the meaning of the title of his own classic "Inner Urge." Henderson shines in a chordless trio setting, and Rufus Reid provides more of a rock-solid brand of bass foundation than Charlie Haden did on Henderson's last trio album on Red, *An Evening With*. — *Josef Woodard*, Down Beat

★ **Lush Life** / i. 1992 / Verve 511779
With his first recording for the Verve label, tenor saxophonist Joe Henderson performs the music of Duke Ellington's composer/collaborator Billy Strayhorn. This date, one of Henderson's best, shows him at his most intimate, virtuosic, and romantic. Henderson, whose style combines the best aspects of John Coltrane, Wayne Shorter, and Sonny Rollins, skillfully navigates through Strayhorn's impressionistic, complex chord changes with a steady pace born of experience and maturity. In "Isfahan" he conjures up the ghost of Johnny Hodes, and in "Blood Count" he evokes the late Stan Getz's sound. Henderson teams with Wynton Marsalis (tpt) on "UMMG" and "A Flower Is . . ." and shows his debt to Sonny Rollins with his "St. Thomas" version of "Rain Check." He closes the album with a haunting solo rendition of "Lush Life" that is so lyrical and impassioned you may be tempted to call him a vocalist. —*Eugene Holley, Jr.*, Jazz Times

○ **So Near, So Far** / i. 1993 / Verve
Discs like *So Near, So Far (Musings For Miles)* shift the focus onto Miles Davis's richly varied compositions. Tenor saxophonist Joe Henderson, a Davis alum by virtue of four weekend gigs in '67, is masterful throughout this well-sequenced program, toasting sublime lyricism on "Miles Ahead," invoking Iberian mysteries on "Flamenco Sketches," and summoning fire on "Side Car." Yet he is not the dominant voice in this quartet. Guitarist John Scofield, bassist Dave Holland, and drummer Al Foster make defining contributions on each track. —*Bill Shoemaker*, Down Beat

---

JON HENDRICKS (John Carl Hendricks)

b. Sep. 16, 1921, Newark, OH
Vocals / Ballads & blues

Jon Hendricks has been a successful vocalist, writer, and critic. He's a master at imitating instrumental sounds, and has performed remarkable vocal accompaniment and harmonies. He's been a historian, a critic for the *San Francisco Chronicle* in 1973 and 1974, and a theatrical director. Hendricks sang on radio in the '30s, after his family moved to Toledo. He sang regularly with pianist Art Tatum at age

14. While attending college in Toledo, Hendricks sang and played drums. He was advised by Charlie Parker to become a professional vocalist, though he was studying literature and had planned to become a lawyer. Hendricks toured Europe before moving to New York in the '50s. He wrote a vocal version of "Four Brothers" in 1955, recording it with Dave Lambert. Then Hendricks recorded "Sing a Song of Basie" with Lambert and Annie Ross in 1958. The trio's performances and practice of putting lyrics to jazz tunes and the improvised solos on classic recordings made them a sensation. Lambert, Hendricks, and Ross stayed together until 1962, when Ross had a child and was replaced by Yolande Bavan. This trio stayed intact until 1964. It made other albums for Columbia, World Pacific, ABC/Impulse, and RCA. Hendricks recorded his own albums for World Pacific, Reprise, and Smash, and recorded with King Pleasure for Prestige. Hendricks wrote lyrics for George Russell's *New York, New York* album in 1959, and wrote and directed the production "Evolution of the Blues Song" for the Modern Jazz Festival at Monterey in 1960. He continued performing as a solo vocalist after the trio disbanded in 1964, and moved to London in 1968. He performed in Europe and Asia for five years before returning to America. Hendricks was a jazz instructor throughout the '70s. He recorded for Arista, Enja, and Pablo during the '70s. He's worked often with his wife, Judith, and children Michelle and Eric. Hendricks has also performed with Bobby McFerrin. During the '80s and '90s, he's recorded for Muse and Denon. The Denon session in 1990 matched him with the Count Basie orchestra, Wynton Marsalis, the Manhattan Transfer, and Stanley Turrentine, among others. His early recordings with Lambert and Ross, and some of his solo dates for Muse and Smash, are being reissued. —*Ron Wynn*

★ **New York, N.Y.** / **i.** Nov. 26, 1959 / Decca 79216

Fast Livin' Blues / Sep. 6, 1961-Sep. 27, 1961 / Columbia 1805

In Person at the Trident / 1963 / Smash 27069

Cloudburst / **i.** Feb. 1972 / Enja

★ **Tell Me the Truth** / 1975 / Arista 4043
Aided by a resurgent interest in the scat vocal styles of Dave Lambert and others, Jon Hendricks took the opportunity to record his first album for an American label in years. Special credit goes to Ben Sidran for sitting back, keeping things clutter-free, and letting Hendricks work his magic. Not surprisingly, that magic comes across better on the uptempo and soulful material, particularly Slim Gaillard's "Flat Foot Floogie" and Hubert Laws's "No More." The selected musicians, particularly Hadley Caliman on sax, perfectly complement Hendricks's pluck and verve. —*Mikal Gilmore*, Down Beat

Love / Aug. 1981-Feb. 1982 / Muse 5258

○ **Freddie Freeloader** / **i.** 1990 / Denon 6302
Tour de force recording with Bobby McFerrin (v), George Benson (g), Al Jarreau (v), and Manhattan Transfer (v). —*Michael G. Nastos*

○ **Jon Hendricks** / Enja 4032

ERNIE HENRY (Ernest Albert Henry)

b. 1926, New York, NY, **d.** Dec. 29, 1957, New York, NY
Alto saxophone / Hard bop
Ernie Henry's is another tragic "what if" jazz story. Alto saxophonist Henry had a blistering, biting style, was remarkably gifted, and seemed on his way to becoming a major star when he died in 1957 at age 31. Henry's phrasing, ideas, technique, and bluesy playing had made its mark in several bands during his brief career. He learned violin as a child, then switched to saxophone at age 12. Henry was assisted by Tadd Dameron, who helped him get started on 52nd street. He worked with Max Roach, Charlie Ventura, Georgie Auld, and Kenny Dorham, as well as with Dameron. Henry played in Dizzy Gillespie's late '40s big band, then joined Illinois Jacquet, with whom he played and recorded

from 1950 to 1952. Henry didn't work much for the next four years, then resurfaced in Thelonious Monk's band. He made some major statements with Monk, offering tremendous, thoughtful, and compelling contrasts to Monk's always engaging, unorthodox piano. Henry recorded with Matthew Gee, played again with Dorham, and led his own sessions for Riverside. He played with Gillespie's reformed big band in 1957, but was dead before the year ended. Henry's few albums as a leader are available on CD; he can also be heard on Monk reissues, and on McGhee recordings. —*Ron Wynn*

○ **Presenting Ernie Henry** / Aug. 23, 1956 / Riverside 102
This presents an artist who died (1957) right at the beginning of his solo career and whose promise has continued to interest listeners ever since. Part of that interest comes from the company he kept on his few recordings; on this (8/23, 8/30) 1956 date it was Kenny Dorham (tpt) and Kenny Drew (p) with Art Taylor and Wilbur Ware on drums and bass respectively. This session is imperfect, and the interplay and exchange between the leader and the group less than smooth, at times almost awkward. Yet there is music here, solos in particular, which is rewarding and plenty of what must be heard as the spontaneous creating of jazz to be enjoyed. This is Young Lion jazz. —*Bob Rusch*, Cadence

★ **Last Chorus** / Aug. 1956-Nov. 1957 / Riverside 086
Last Chorus presents the final (9/57) recordings of Ernie Henry, who died ten months later at the age of 30. Henry's alto playing combines the exigency of the hard alto sound with the big, scooping delivery more associated with the tenor sax and players like Sonny Rollins; a more deliberate sound than fleet register runs. This record, not a totally convincing sample, finds him leading his own groups (Lee Morgan, Melba Liston, Benny Golson, Cecil Payne, Wynton Kelly, Paul Chambers, Art Taylor, Philly Joe Jones, Wilbur Ware, Kenny Dorham, Kenny Drew) or in the company of Kenny Dorham or Thelonious Monk. —*Bob Rusch*, Cadence

Seven Standards and a Blues / Sep. 30, 1957 / Original Jazz Classics 1722
This was recorded 9/30/57, just before Ernie Henry's (as) death and issued posthumously. The main problem is that the leader's alto playing seems to lack any great emotional investment in the music, often seems out of focus, and occasionally seems to make glaring musical missteps which, had his name been Ornette Coleman, would have been in brilliant character but here sound more like unintentional miscues and technical goofs. Wynton Kelly (p), Wilbur Ware (b), and Philly Joe Jones (d) are the rhythm backup. —*Bob Rusch*, Cadence

WOODY HERMAN (Woodrow Charles Herman)

b. May 16, 1913, Milwaukee, WI, **d.** Oct. 29, 1987
Clarinet, alto and soprano saxophone, bandleader / Swing, big band, bop
Over several decades, Woody Herman fought the good fight for big bands. His body of work compares favorably with that of any swing and bop era great. Herman was the supreme organizer, who took fierce, at times almost suicidal pride, in keeping things going regardless of the situation. He was able to incorporate bop into his band brilliantly, and was an incredible talent scout. His clarinet, alto, and soprano sax playing would not put him on anyone's all-time soloist list, but it was efficient within his band's framework, and could frequently surprise with its wit and bite.
Herman had his earliest musical experience when he played in bands led by Tom Gerun and Harry Sosnik. He then toured with Gus Arnheim's band, and tried heading his own group in 1934, but was unsuccessful. He joined Isham Jones's ensemble in 1936. When Jones departed, Herman took his best players and formed another group around them, using the Woodchoppers as a group within an orchestra. Herman cut what would become an anthem in 1939, the first version of "Woodchopper's Ball." The Herman orchestra's greatest period of productivity and public acclaim was from 1937 until 1952. Numerous greats came through the lineup, among them Chubby Jackson, Neal Hefti, Ralph

Burns, Flip Phillips, Bill Harris, Serge Chaloff, Zoot Sims, Al Cohn, and Gene Ammons. Herman started the band as a co-operative venture, but as members were drafted, he bought their shares. Herman was among the earliest of the bandleaders who beat the mid-'40s recording ban, as Decca was one of the first labels to settle with the union. They cut 24 songs in 1944, though only four were issued, prompting a switch, the next year, to Columbia.

Herman disbanded and reformed the band twice in the '40s, in 1947 and in 1949. The '44-'46 edition was called Herman's Herd originally, then was called the First Herd. It was arguably his most joyful, exuberant unit, and contained the Candoli brothers, Ralph Burns, and vibist Margie Hyams, among others. They appeared in such films as *Sensations of 1945* and *Earl Carrol's Vanities*, and had a network radio show sponsored by Wildroot hair oil. By 1946, when they appeared at Carnegie Hall, Shorty Rogers, Sonny Berman, John LaPorta, and Red Norvo were- also on hand, and Herman had formed Woodchoppers II. Classical composer Igor Stravinsky was commissioned to write *Ebony Concerto* for them; it debuted in 1946.

Herman was unafraid to acknowledge the influence of and was afraid to use songs by his supposed competition, Duke Ellington and Count Basie. Burns and Hefti were providing hit arrangements for Herman's band regularly. They had ten Top 10 records in 1945 and 1946, among them a version of Ellington's "Do Nothing till You Hear from Me," Louis Jordan's "Caldonia," and the Sammy Cahn/Jule Styne number "Let It Snow! Let It Snow! Let It Snow!" Hefti provided arrangements for "Jones Beachhead," "The Good Earth," and "Wildroot," among others, and also updated "Woodchopper's Ball." "Bijou" and the four-part "Summer Sequence" (the fourth eventually became "Early Autumn") were among the numbers that Burns arranged.

Herman toured Cuba with a small band in 1947, then reformed his large orchestra. The Second Herd included the famed Four Brothers saxophone section, which was named for a composition by Jimmy Giuffre. They were influenced directly by Charlie Parker and Lester Young, and, in turn, set the stage for the "cool" sound of the '50s. This orchestra made such immortal records as "Early Autumn" and "Lemon Drop."

After leading small combos in 1949 and 1950, Herman formed the Third Herd. They recorded for Capitol and Mars in 1952 and 1953, and enjoyed some success with a reworked "Early Autumn." Nat Pierce, Cohn, and Jake Hanna were some of the musicians in this edition, while Bill Harris had also returned. Herman kept working, touring, and recording through the '50s, '60s, and '70s. Times were perpetually tough for big bands, but he seldom went for long periods without heading a band. They cut a wonderful live album on Atlantic in 1959 at Monterey, and continued recording for Verve, Phillips, and others in the '60s. During the early '60s, Herman's Swinging Herd featured star players such as Bill Chase, Sal Nistico, and Phil Wilson. The orchestra recorded six LPs for Fantasy in the early '70s. These were a decidedly mixed bag, as Herman experimented with electronics, pop, rock, funk, and other genres, though he won a Grammy with the '73 release *Giant Steps*. He got back to basics in the late '70s, recording for Concord. Getz, Dizzy Gillespie, Woody Shaw, Cohn, Flip Phillips, and Rosemary Clooney were among those who appeared on various Concord releases, some done in the studio, others in Japan or at the Concord Festival. Herman continued working, recording, and touring until his death in 1987. He has a substantial amount of material available on CD. —*Ron Wynn*

Blues in the Night / i. Nov. 8, 1936-Sep. 10, 1941 / Sunbeam 206

Woody Herman began his bandleading career on November 8, 1936, making his debut on the radio aircheck on the first half of this LP; this broadcast is from the Roseland Ballroom where Herman would play opposite the fairly new Count Basie orchestra for quite a few months. Isham Jones's fine dance band had broken up shortly before and half of the

musicians reorganized (with some newer players) as a co-op orchestra with the likable Herman as the front man. At 23, Woody Herman was already a fine clarinetist and a good crooner. This very interesting broadcast primarily focuses on standards and Dixieland tunes played in a conventional swing style. The second half of the LP has studio sides mostly dating from 1941 with Bing Crosby heard as a guest singer on "I Ain't Got Nobody," and the Herman band showing that, after five years of existence, they had pretty much developed a style of their own. —*Scott Yanow*

○ **Jukin' with Woody Herman** / i. Apr. 26, 1937-Apr. 2, 1942 / This excellent LP contains 16 studio recordings by Woody Herman's "Band That Plays the Blues," dating from 1937-42. Since most of these selections (other than "Get Your Boots Laced Papa!") are rarely issued and the emphasis here is on jazz rather than Herman's ballad and novelty vocals, this LP is well worth searching for. Next to Herman's clarinet, the top soloists are tenorman Saxie Mansfield and trombonist Neil Reid. —*Scott Yanow*

★ **Blues on Parade** / Apr. 26, 1937-Jul. 24, 1942 / GRP 606
This single CD gives a definitive look at Woody Herman's first orchestra, the Decca ensemble he led during 1936-42 that was billed "The Band That Plays the Blues." Although Herman also recorded many vocal ballads during this era, the emphasis here is on hot swing with such highlights as the original version of "Woodchopper's Ball," "Blue Prelude," "Blue Flame," the humorous "Fan It," and two takes of "Blues On Parade." Also heard are performances by Herman's early small combos (the Woodchoppers and the Four Chips) along with a Dizzy Gillespie composition/arrangement ("Down Under") that hints at Woody Herman's future. Highly recommended. —*Scott Yanow*

Uncollected Woody Herman and His Orchestra (1937) / Sep. 23, 1937-Nov. 1937 / Hindsight 116
These 16 selections are taken from two sessions made for radio transcriptions in 1937; most of the first ten numbers are also included on a Circle LP, although the final six date from two months later. Better than many of Herman's commercial Decca recordings of this period, these 16 jazz-oriented performances are generally quite enjoyable with tenorman Saxie Mansfield, flugelhornist Joe Bishop, and trombonist Neil Reid being the main soloists next to clarinetist Herman (who also takes two vocals). —*Scott Yanow*

○ **Big Band Bounce & Boogie** / i. Apr. 12, 1939-Nov. 8, 1943 /
Prior to the release of *Blues On Parade*, a CD that duplicates 8 of these 16 selections, this LP had been the best all-round set of early Woody Herman available. "The Band That Plays the Blues" did not feature any outstanding virtuosos, but was a versatile and enthusiastic outfit that could swing hard when given a chance. This LP features many of the orchestra's best instrumentals along with a few examples of Woody Herman's crooning style. —*Scott Yanow*

○ **Woody Herman Souvenirs** / May 24, 1939-Dec. 11, 1944 / Coral 56010
This ten-inch LP released in the early '50s contains eight selections: two big-band numbers from 1944 and six more Dixie-oriented performances, mostly from Woody Herman's Woodchoppers (a small group taken out of his orchestra). Since several of the latter have not been reissued in recent times, this one is worth searching for. The versatile Herman proves to be a fine Dixieland clarinetist. —*Scott Yanow*

Best of the Decca Years / i. 1939-1944 / Decca 25195
1939-1944. 1988 issue has some fine cuts. Somewhat supplanted by recent reissue. —*Ron Wynn*

○ **Dance Time—Forty Three** / i. Feb. 1943-Jun. 1943 /
Due to a recording strike by the Musicians Union, very few commercial recordings were made during 1943. First Heard has filled the gap by releasing this LP, which was taken from radio broadcasts aired earlier in the year. Of particular interest in this last version of Woody Herman's "Band That Plays the Blues" are the fine trumpet solos of Billie Rogers, the only female trumpeter to hold a regular position in a major American big band. Novelty aside, she does a fine job

and also takes two good vocals. In addition to Herman's clarinet and alto spots, other key musicians include Vido Musso
on tenor, trombonist Neal Reid, and the young pianist
Jimmy Rowles. A fine set of late swing. Pity that both Billie
Rogers and the big band that she formed in '44 are totally
forgotten today. —*Scott Yanow*

Woodchopper's Ball—Vol. 1 / Aug. 2, 1944-Oct. 18, 1944 /
Jass 621
1944 was a pivotal year in Woody Herman's career, the year
that his orchestra gradually evolved into the First Herd, his
most exciting band. This CD features music from two radio
rehearsals in August plus performances from two prestigious engagements at the Hotel Pennsylvania in August and
the Hollywood Palladium that October. With Flip Phillips's
jump tenor and Bill Harris's expressive trombone already
emerging as the band's top soloists and Francis Wayne contributing a few fine vocals, Ralph Burns and Neal Hefti were
hurriedly putting together colorful arrangements to challenge the young sidemen. The music on this set, which precedes the Herd's first commercial recordings, could be titled
"The Birth of the Herd." Recommended, particularly to serious Woody Herman fans. —*Scott Yanow*

Uncollected Woody Herman and His First Herd / i. 1944
/ Hindsight 134
Hindsight's second LP of Woody Herman broadcasts (the
first volume dates from 1937!) is actually taken exclusively
from rehearsals for radio shows and finds Herman at an important transition in his career. The old "Band That Plays the
Blues" was making way for the First Herd; already tenor
saxophonist Flip Phillips and trombonist Bill Harris were in
place as the key soloists. Other than "Apple Honey," most of
the material heard on this LP was in the earlier band's repertoire, making for very interesting listening for those fans
only familiar with the First Herd's studio recordings. —*Scott
Yanow*

Woody Herman (1944-1946) / 1944-1946 / First Heard 2
Reissue covering mid-'40s Herman orchestra, a period in
which his band had a nationally syndicated radio show and
included such greats as Bill Harris, Flip Phillips, and Neal
Hefti. He also formed a new edition of the Woodchoppers
combo with Red Norvo on vibes and had several hit recordings. —*Ron Wynn*

○ **Thundering Herds 1945-1947** / i. Feb. 19, 1945-Dec. 27,
1947 / Columbia 44108
Since the definitive three-LP boxed set *Thundering Herds* is
out of print, this single CD is the best place for listeners to
go first when starting to explore the music of Woody
Herman. There are 14 selections from what was perhaps
Woody Herman's best band, his First Herd, and two numbers (including the original version of "Four Brothers") by
the Second Herd. A few rarities such as "A Jug of Wine" and
"The Blues Are Brewing" are mixed in with such classics
as "Apple Honey," "Northwest Passage," "Your Father's
Mustache," and a new version of "Woodchopper's Ball," but,
unavoidably, a lot is missing from this single disc, a set
which will have to suffice until a more complete reissue series comes along. —*Scott Yanow*

★ **Thundering Herds** / Feb. 19, 1945-Dec. 27, 1947 / Columbia
44108
This now out-of-print three-LP boxed set is still the best
compilation to date of Woody Herman's First and Second
Herds. These 48 selections (the cream of Herman's Columbia
recordings) include many classics such as "Apple Honey,"
"Caldonia," "Northwest Passage," "Bijou," "Your Father's
Mustache," eight numbers from Woody Herman's
Woodchoppers, "Let It Snow," a new rendition of
"Woodchopper's Ball," the four-part "Summer Sequence,"
and the original version of "Four Brothers." Even the lesser
items on this set are memorable, making this the number-
one Woody Herman release to own. Why hasn't it been reissued in total on CD yet? —*Scott Yanow*

One Night Stand with Woody Herman / i. 1945-1946 /
Joyce 1021

The collector's label Joyce came up with an LP's worth of unreleased radio airchecks from Woody Herman's First Herd.
This release is valuable because that particular band never
commercially recorded most of these songs. Ill-fated trumpeter Sonny Berman (who made relatively few recordings) is
well featured throughout, along with trombonist Bill Harris,
tenor saxophonist Flip Phillips, and vibist Red Norvo. There
is surprisingly little Woody Herman clarinet and alto on this
set, but his sidemen are certainly strong enough to make
this a recommended (if hard-to-find) LP. —*Scott Yanow*

On Keynote / i. 1946 / PolyGram 30968
Outstanding collection of cuts featuring Woody Herman's
"Small Herds" on Keynote. —*Ron Wynn*

○ **Hollywood Palladium 1948** / i. Feb. 12, 1948-Aug. 25, 1948
/ Jazz Anthology 5237
This excellent LP features Woody Herman's Second Herd
(the "Four Brothers" band) caught live during three different
stints at the Hollywood Palladium. Since a strike by the
Musicians Union kept Herman's band off records throughout most of 1948, this album is quite valuable. Solo stars on
these rare sessions include Stan Getz, Al Cohn, and baritonist Serge Chaloff. —*Scott Yanow*

○ **Roadband (1948)** / Mar. 1948-May 12, 1948 / Hep 18
Woody Herman's Second Herd was one of his finest orchestras but, unlike the First Herd, it was a money loser, and the
Musicians Union strike of 1948 kept it off commercial
recordings for much of that important year. Fortunately, a
few LPs of broadcasts (including this one) show just how
strong a unit it was. Solos by the likes of tenors Stan Getz,
Zoot Sims, and Al Cohn and baritonist Serge Caloff (who together formed the "Four Brothers" that year), plus the vocals
of Woody Herman and Mary Ann McCall, make this a memorable outfit that plays at its best on this set imported from
England. It is a particular joy to hear the Second Herd performing so much material that they otherwise never
recorded. Recommended. —*Scott Yanow*

○ **Early Autumn** / i. Dec. 29, 1948-Aug. 9, 1950 / Capitol 1034
Woody Herman's Second Herd was one of his finest orchestras and the last great big band to emerge from the 1940s.
Because its music was bop-oriented and the economic situation made it difficult for any large orchestra to survive, the
Second Herd was history by December 1949. But before its
passing, it created quite a few classics. This LP (whose contents have since been reissued with additional tracks on a
previous album) contains 13 of its best recordings including
"Lemon Drop," "Early Autumn," and "More Moon." With
such tenor soloists as Stan Getz, Zoot Sims, Al Cohn, and
Gene Ammons, the "Four Brothers" band created music that
would be revived often by Woody Herman during the next
three decades. —*Scott Yanow*

Third Herd—Vol. 2 / i. May 30, 1952-Mar. 30, 1954 /
Discovery 845
The second of two LP volumes released by Discovery documents more of the recordings that Woody Herman and his
Third Herd made for their own label, Mars Records, during
1952-54. This melodic but swinging orchestra had its share
of fine soloists (such as trombonist Carl Fontana and tenormen Arno Marsh and Bill Perkins) along with fine arrangements from Nat Pierce and Ralph Burns. Unfortunately, this
LP only has 31 minutes of music and many of Herman's
Mars recordings have been bypassed (they should all be released in chronological order!), but Woody's more devoted
fans will still want it. —*Scott Yanow*

Woody Herman Band, The / Sep. 1954 / Capitol 560
When Woody Herman originally formed his Third Herd in
1950 (after the financial collapse of the Second Herd), he put
the emphasis on music for the dancing public first and the
jazz public second. However, the jazz content was always
strong and by 1954 the band was less shy about swinging
hard. This hard-to-find LP is one of that orchestra's finest
recordings, a strong all-round set highlighted by the flagwa-
ver "Wild Apple Honey," several Ralph Burns arrangements,
and solos by such fine players as tenors Bill Perkins and

Dick Hafer, Cy Touff's bass trumpet, Jack Nimitz's baritone (featured on "Sleep"), and Herman's alto and clarinet. Worth searching for. —*Scott Yanow*

Road Band / Oct. 13, 1954-Jun. 7, 1955 / Capitol 658
This out-of-print LP finds Woody Herman's Third Herd in its prime. Rather than just revisiting his celebrated past, Woody Herman and his orchestra primarily perform then-recent material, much of it arranged by Ralph Burns. Highlights include a big-band version of Horace Silver's "Opus De Funk," Burns's "Cool Cat on a Hot Tin Roof," "I Remember Duke," and Bill Holman's reworking of "Where or When." With tenors Richie Kamuca and Dick Hafer, trumpeter Dick Collins, and bass trumpeter Cy Touff as the main soloists, the Third Herd had developed into a particularly strong unit by the mid '50s. —*Scott Yanow*

Omaha, Nebraska 1954 / i. 1954 / Swing World 4
Imported from England, this LP features Woody Herman's Third Herd heard live in 1954. By then, the big-band era had been gone for almost a decade, but somehow Herman was able to buck the trend, playing swinging music with a young group of musicians willing to constantly travel. On this set half of the repertoire is fairly new, giving such players as trumpeter Dick Collins and tenors Jerry Coker and Bill Perkins some inspiring material to solo over. A good example of the Third Herd. —*Scott Yanow*

○ **Herd Rides Again** / i. Jul. 30, 1958-Aug. 1, 1958 / Evidence 22010
This CD contains a better-than-expected reunion of Woody Herman's First Herd. Actually, many of the key players from that classic band (such as tenorman Flip Phillips and trombonist Bill Harris) are not on this date, while some of the musicians who do participate are Hermanites from a later era or (in the case of trombonist Bob Brookmeyer and tenor saxophonist Sam Donahue) had never been a part of Woody's bands before. Because the music is generally only a decade old, the results are quite satisfying with fresh solos and spirited ensembles giving new life to such numbers as "Northwest Passage," "Caldonia," and "Blowin' Up a Storm," among others. Certainly Brookmeyer's playing on "Bijou" will not remind anyone of Bill Harris. —*Scott Yanow*

○ **Herman's Heat & Puente's Beat** / i. Sep. 1958 / Evidence 22008
By 1958 Woody Herman's Third Herd was history and he was back to working with small groups again. For the sessions that make up this CD, Herman used two separate studio orchestras filled with musicians (and some alumni) familiar with his music. In addition to the fine straightahead charts (which include a new version of "Woodchopper's Ball," "Lullaby of Birdland," and "Midnight Sun"), Woody added Tito Puente's five-piece Latin rhythm section to six selections, bringing variety and strong rhythmic excitement to this fine set. —*Scott Yanow*

○ **Live at Monterey** / Oct. 3, 1959 / Atlantic 90044
Woody Herman returned to the big-band wars in 1959 with these two very successful appearances at the Monterey Jazz Festival. His new band featured such major players as trumpeter Conte Candoli, trombonist Urbie Green, acoustic guitarist Charlie Byrd, and a sax section composed of tenors Zoot Sims, Bill Perkins, and Richie Kamuca, Don Lanphere on alto and tenor, and baritonist Med Flory, in addition to Woody himself. The all-star orchestra romps happily through "Four Brothers," "Monterey Apple Tree" and "Skoobeedoobee," and Urbie Green is well featured on the ballad "Skylark" and "The Magpie." Excellent music that signaled a "comeback" for Woody Herman. —*Scott Yanow*

Swing Low, Sweet Chariot / Jan. 1962 / Philips 600-004
Woody Herman took time off from leading his big band to participate in this unusual quartet session. Sticking exclusively to clarinet, Herman (although never on the same level as Benny Goodman and Artie Shaw) shows himself to be a fine improviser and an expressive player who gives fresh interpretations to a variety of standards, some closely associated with Goodman and Shaw. Nat Pierce leads the fine rhythm section on this out-of-print but worthy LP. —*Scott Yanow*

○ **Woody Herman (1963)** / Oct. 15, 1962-Oct. 16, 1962 / Echo Jazz 17
In 1962, Woody Herman signed a contract with Philips and went on to record some of the finest big-band albums of his long career. Unfortunately, all are currently out of print (none have yet appeared on CD), but most are well worth searching for. This version of Herman's Thundering Herd features high-note trumpet work by Bill Chase, trombonist Phil Wilson, pianist Nat Pierce, and the exciting tenor of Sal Nistico. High points of this fine LP are "Sister Sadie" and "Camel Walk." —*Scott Yanow*

Encore: Woody Herman (1963) / May 19, 1963-May 21, 1963 / Philips 600-092
Woody Herman led one of his finest orchestras during 1962-66, a hard-swinging outfit filled with enthusiastic young players such as high-note trumpeter Bill Chase, trombonist Phil Wilson, and the exciting tenor Sal Nistico. The LP *Encore* has quite a few highlights, including the uptempo blues "That's Where It Is," a Nat Pierce arrangement of Herbie Hancock's "Watermelon Man," Charles Mingus's "Better Git It in Your Soul," and a remake of "Caldonia." Excellent music that deserves to be reissued on CD. —*Scott Yanow*

Woody's Big Band Goodies / May 21, 1963-Sep. 9, 1964 / Philips 600171
Woody Herman's Swingin' Herd of the early to mid 1960s was one of his finest big bands, an ensemble that could compare well with his historic First and Second Herds. Their series of LPs on Philips (all now out of print and well deserving of a complete reissue on CD) are consistently exciting. *Big Band Goodies* consists of some "leftovers" from *Encore* and three newer selections from 1964. Actually the older tracks are on the same high level as those issued previously. No band with such soloists as trumpeters Bill Chase and Dusko Goykovich, trombonist Phil Wilson, and the exciting tenor Sal Nistico, not to mention arrangements by pianist Nat Pierce and a rhythm section propelled by drummer Jake Hanna, should be taken for granted! *Big Band Goodies* finds this orchestra interpreting some older tunes ("Sidewalks Of Cuba," "Bijou," and "Apple Honey"), Thelonious Monk's "Blue Monk," and the well-titled "Wailin' In The Woodshed" with equal success. —*Scott Yanow*

Woody Herman (1964) / i. Nov. 20, 1963-Nov. 23, 1963 / Philips 118
All of Woody Herman's recordings for Philips (which regrettably remain out of print and unissued on CD) are excellent. He was leading one of the finest orchestras of his long career, playing both current and older tunes with creativity (helped out greatly by Nat Pierce's arrangements) and featuring such talented soloists as trumpeter Bill Chase, trombonist Phil Wilson, and tenor great Sal Nistico. *1964* has cuts ranging from "Deep Purple" and "After You've Gone" to Oscar Peterson's "Halleluah Time" and even "A Taste Of Honey"; everything works. Recommended if you can find it. —*Scott Yanow*

Swinging Herman Herd, Recorded Live / Sep. 9, 1964 / Brunswick 54024
Woody Herman's Swingin' Herd of the early to mid 1960s was one of his great orchestras. This live LP, the final one of Herman's consistently exciting Philips releases, has particularly diverse material with many pop tunes of the era represented. Although Joe Carroll's two vocals and "Everybody Loves Somebody Sometime" are not the band's most significant moments, there are other performances on this set (particularly "Bedroom Eyes," "Just Squeeze Me," and "Dr. Wong's Blues") that compensate. —*Scott Yanow*

○ **Woody's Winners** / Jun. 28, 1965-Jun. 30, 1965 / Columbia 2436
Of the many exciting recordings by Woody Herman's Swinging Herd of the '60s, this is the definitive set. With such soloists as trumpeters Bill Chase, Dusko Goykovich, and

Don Rader and tenors Sal Nistico, Andy McGhee, and Gary Klein, this orchestra rarely had any difficulty raising the temperature. Recorded live at Basin Street West in late June of 1965, this set finds the enthusiastic band featuring a three-way trumpet battle on "23 Red," reworking "Northwest Passage" (highlighted by Sal Nistico's long tenor solo), and romping on a lengthy version of "Opus De Funk," in addition to interpreting a few ballads and blues. This is a memorable LP that deserves to be reissued on CD so it can be in every jazz collector's library. —*Scott Yanow*

★ **Concerto for Herd** / Sep. 1967 / Verve 8764

1967 found the Woody Herman orchestra in transition. While tenor saxophonist Sal Nistico and trombonist Carl Fontana were the biggest names, trumpeter Luis Gasca and pianist Albert Daily were up-and-coming players. This LP, recorded live at the 10th annual Monterey Jazz Festival, features the sidelong "Concert For Herd," an adventurous work by Bill Holman. In addition, there are three shorter pieces that find Herman and his musicians exploring a variety of music including a boogaloo and a feature for Herman's soprano sax ("The Horn Of The Fish"). A fine all-round set that has been long out of print. —*Scott Yanow*

Brand New / Mar. 1971 / Fantasy 8414

Of all of the big-band leaders who emerged during the swing era, Woody Herman had always been the most receptive toward keeping his music modern and attuned to the music younger people were listening to. This unusual LP finds Herman welcoming the great electric blues guitarist Mike Bloomfield to the band for three numbers. The other selections include new originals, Ivory Joe Hunter's "I Almost Lost My Mind" and "After Hours." Keyboardist Alan Broadbent arranged most of the material although Nat Pierce's chart on "After Hours" is most memorable. With Woody Herman taking a couple of vocals and soloing on clarinet, soprano, and alto, this early '70s release is a surprise success. —*Scott Yanow*

★ **Giant Steps** / Apr. 9, 1973-Apr. 12, 1973 / Fantasy 344

Woody Herman always went out of his way during his long career to encourage younger players, often persuading them to write arrangements of recent tunes for his orchestra. On this LP, one gets to hear Herman's band interpret such selections as Chick Corea's "La Fiesta," Leon Russell's "A Song For You," "Freedom Jazz Dance," "A Child Is Born," and "Giant Steps"; what other bandleader from the 1930s would have performed such modern material? With strong solo work from tenors Gregory Herbert and Frank Tiberi, trumpeter Bill Stapleton, and Woody himself, this is an impressive effort. —*Scott Yanow*

Thundering Herd / Jan. 2, 1974-Jan. 4, 1974 / Fantasy 9452

Woody Herman always deserved great credit for encouraging his young sidemen to develop their own individual playing and writing styles. Herman kept his own repertoire fresh by having his orchestra perform their own original arrangements. For example, on this LP, Bill Stapleton, Alan Broadbent, and Tony Klatka contribute charts to a wide variety of material that ranges from two John Coltrane tunes ("Naina" and "Lazy Bird") to songs by Stanley Clarke, Frank Zappa, Michel Legrand, and even Carole King! With future leader Frank Tiberi on tenor, trombonist Jim Pugh, and keyboardist Andy Laverne among the key soloists, the Herman legacy continued to grow even as he neared his 40th year as a bandleader. —*Scott Yanow*

King Cobra / Jan. 7, 1975-Jan. 9, 1975 / Fantasy 9499

As the years passed and Woody Herman continued to age, his orchestra's music stayed young and contemporary. Never willing to have a mere nostalgia band, Herman continued looking ahead for new music without lowering his standards. On this LP from 1975, the big band performs an excellent version of Chick Corea's "Spain," explores material by Tom Scott and Stevie Wonder, and sounds fine on "Come Rain Or Come Shine." Herman's vocal on "Jazzman" does not come off so well but occasional misfires are excused

when one considers how many chances he took during his productive career. —*Scott Yanow*

★ **40th Anniversary Carnegie Hall Concert** / Nov. 20, 1976 / Bluebird 6878

Nostalgia is in the ear of the beholder, and this album will send off some honest emotions of remembrance among many who were around for the first flowerings of Herds One and Two. For younger listeners who feel jazz began with John Coltrane in 1960 but who still have open ears, the experience of hearing an earlier generation's view of big-band jazz should be a bracing and rewarding ritual. The rock Herman built his church on in the late '40s produced both material and musicians whose essential qualities not only aged well but were able to bring many latecomers into the fold long after the material ceased to be new and the musicians split for other gigs. Jimmy Giuffre's "Four Brothers" is played by Herman's working band as alums Stan Getz, Zoot Sims, Al Cohn, and Giuffre inject some solo pep. Herman's reed work is pretty much limited to soprano sax, where he plays edgy, nervously contemporary albeit faceless solos on "Penny Arcade" and "Fanfare for the Common Man." —*John McDonough*, Down Beat

Lionel Hampton Presents Woody Herman / 1977 / Who's Who In Jazz 21013

This LP contains a rare small-group session from late in the career of Woody Herman. Switching between clarinet, soprano, and alto, Herman is the lead voice throughout these five extended jams on standards. Joined by a six-piece rhythm section including vibraphonist Lionel Hampton, pianist Roland Hanna, and guitarist Al Caiola, Herman is in fine form on this fun session. —*Scott Yanow*

Woody Herman and Flip Phillips / Jan. 5, 1978 / Century 1090

Over 30 years after the First Herd broke up, Flip Phillips had a reunion with Woody Herman for this LP. The emphasis is on ballads, and Phillips plays beautifully throughout, but this set lacks variety (only "There Is No Greater Love" is taken at a medium pace). Still, within its limitations and with the orchestra itself mostly playing a supporting role, Flip and Woody (the latter particularly on alto) blend very well together on this pretty music. —*Scott Yanow*

☆ **Woody and Friends at the Monterey Jazz Festival** / Sep. 1979 / Concord Jazz 4170

1992 reissue of a fine set with Herman featuring people he seldom played with, such as Woody Shaw (tpt) and Slide Hampton (t). —*Ron Wynn*

Live at Concord Jazz Festival (1981) / Aug. 15, 1981 / Concord Jazz 4191

This is a fine album, from the tenors digging in on "Things Ain't What They Used to Be" with a guest spot by Four Brothers tenorist Al Cohn to the ballroom nostalgia warmth of Gene Smith's trombone on "You Are So Beautiful" to the slugging lift-off of the shout chorus on "John Brown's Other Body." Stan Getz's tenor swimmingly graces "The Dolphin," and elsewhere pianist John Oddo's compositions and arrangements are prominently featured. That beautiful rolling momentum in the drum beat is by Dave Ratajczak, who often recalls one of his predecessors, Jake Hanna. —*Owen Cordle*, Down Beat

World Class / Sep. 1982 / Concord Jazz 4240

As with most of the Woody Herman Orchestra's recordings for Concord, this set (taken from concerts in Japan) welcomes guests from Herman's past. In this case tenors Al Cohn, Med Flory, Sal Nistico, and Flip Phillips get to star on half of the eight selections, including a remake of "Four Brothers" and Phillips's "The Claw." Flip has an opportunity to reprise his famous Jazz at the Philharmonic solo on "Perdido." The regular Herman sidemen do not sound as distinctive in comparison, but they play quite well on these attractive arrangements, four of them by pianist John Oddo. —*Scott Yanow*

★ **Fiftieth Anniversary Tour** / Mar. 1986 / Concord Jazz 4302

This LP, which is the best of the Woody Herman orchestra's Concord recordings, celebrates his 50th year as a bandleader, quite an accomplishment. No guest stars are needed for this set, which shows just how strong a big band Herman still had. With tenor saxophonist Frank Tiberi gradually taking over leadership duties (today he leads the ghost Woody Herman orchestra) and trombonist John Fedchock contributing the arrangements, the band was in fine shape even if the leader was aging. Whether it be "It Don't Mean A Thing," John Coltrane's "Central Park West" (a great arrangement), or Don Grolnick's "Pools," every selection is excellent. Recommended. —Scott Yanow

Woody's Gold Star / Mar. 1987 / Concord Jazz 4330
Woody Herman's final recording, made just weeks before his health began to seriously fail, is actually quite good. With future leader Frank Tiberi contributing some strong tenor solos, John Fedchock writing some colorful arrangements for a varied program (ranging from "Rose Room" and "'Round Midnight" to Chick Corea's "Samba Song"), and three guest percussionists on some of the pieces, this is an enjoyable release. Herman takes short solos on three of the pieces, recorded approximately 50 years after he formed his first successful big band. This serves as a fine closer to a significant career. —Scott Yanow

Concord Years / i. May 1993 / Concord Jazz 4557
Here are the final editions of the Woody Herman band as recorded by Concord beginning in 1979 and ending in March 1987, virtually days before illness finally took him off the road for good. (He died in October 1987.) These selections thankfully avoid the Herman band's various accommodations with pop trends and instead concentrate on its core jazz values. But there are some lively guest appearances, including Woody Shaw and a very strong Dizzy Gillespie on "Woody 'N You," good Flip Phillips on "Perdido," and an appropriately lyrical Stan Getz on "What Are You Doing." Even the old "Four Brothers," performed by the band's resident soloists, sounds marvelous. John Fedchock's charts, for 5 of the 12 cuts here, are well-schooled pieces with a preference for brass colorations over reeds, and his immaculate trombone on "Round Midnight" has a classical stoicism about it. —John McDonough, Down Beat

○ **At Carnegie Hall** / Verve 2317

Greatest Hits / Columbia 09291

○ **Keeper of the Flame: Complete Capitol Recordings** / Blue Note 98453
Subtitled *The Complete Capitol Recordings of the Four Brothers Band*, this CD contains 19 selections from Woody Herman's Second Herd, including three songs never before released. Top-heavy with major soloists (including trumpeters Red Rodney and Shorty Rogers; trombonist Bill Harris; tenors Al Cohn, Zoot Sims, Stan Getz, and Gene Ammons; not to mention vibraphonist Terry Gibbs; not to mention Herman himself) this boppish band may have cost the leader a small fortune, but they created timeless music. Highlights include "Early Autumn," a ballad performance that made Stan Getz a star, the riotous "Lemon Drop," and Gene Ammons's strong solo on "More Moon." A gem. —Scott Yanow

Third Herd—Vol. 1 / Discovery 815
During 1952-53, when Woody Herman's Third Herd had trouble landing a recording contract (big bands were out), he formed his own label, Mars Records. This first of two Discovery LPs contains ten of the Herd's records for Mars, and the music is spirited, swinging, and a bit safer than the sounds created by the first two Herds. Unfortunately, Discovery has thus far not reissued all of Herman's Mars sides and this LP clocks in at under 29 minutes, but the music is excellent and Woody Herman fans will want it anyway. —Scott Yanow

VINCENT HERRING

b. 1964
Alto saxophone, composer / Neo-bop

Here's another new name on the horizon. Vince Herring has already earned praise for good, hard bop compositions and a loose, animated alto sax style that recalls the traditional references of many modern altoists, such as Cannonball and Parker. He has two fine sessions under his own name, plus appearances on other albums, and is gaining stature as a player and leader. —Ron Wynn

★ **Evidence** / i. 1990 / Landmark 1527
A much sharper, clearer statement than his other release. The compositions are better and the music is more dynamic. —Ron Wynn

American Experience / i. Dec. 1990 / Music Masters 5037
The emerging alto saxophonist reveals his debt to Cannonball Adderley and Charlie Parker. Good tone, lots of potential. —Ron Wynn

Secret Love / i. 1993 / Music Masters 65092
There's something downright chilling about an alto sax played with heart and fire, which is the feeling you get from hearing Vincent Herring on *Secret Love*. At 26, Herring has already played with many of the greats—David Murray, Wynton Marsalis, Nat Adderley, and McCoy Tyner among them—yet on his second release as a leader he still sounds like he has something to prove. Though he doesn't, the trying makes for great fun. With a sound somewhere between Johnny Hodges's cream and Bobby Watson's spice, and the sharp-witted rhythm section of pianist Renee Rosnes, bassist Ira Coleman, and drummer Billy Drummond cookin' on all burners, Herring tackles gems like "Chelsea Bridge," "Have You Met Miss Jones," "Autumn Leaves," and Miles Davis's "Solar," and makes them his own. —Bob Young, Jazziz

FRED HERSCH

Piano / Modern creative
A good pianist whose style and approach reflect the influence of Bill Evans, Fred Hersch has made several intriguing dates featuring his originals and probing interpretations of works by composers such as Wayne Shorter and Ornette Coleman. He blends free, contemporary classical, and bebop elements, and has a rhythmically dynamic, lush, and enticing approach. Hersch has worked with Marc Johnson, Joey Baron, Charlie Haden, Mike Formanek, Steve Laspina, and Jeff Hirshfield on his sessions. He's recorded for Chesky, Sunnyside, Concord, Angel, and Red. Hersch has also done a duet project with vocalist Janis Siegel for Atlantic. All Hersch's sessions are available on CD. —Ron Wynn

Horizons / Oct. 1984 / Concord Jazz 267

○ **Heartsongs** / Dec. 1989 / Sunnyside 1047

★ **Forward Motion** / i. 1991 / Chesky 55
This release has components of jazz, chamber, and new age. The playing is better and more consistent than the material. —Ron Wynn

JOHN HICKS

b. 1941, Atlanta, GA
Piano / Hard bop, modern creative
A busy, versatile, and probing pianist, John Hicks has performed with many top musicians, and has demonstrated his craftsmanship and skill repeatedly in hard bop and free sessions. He's done numerous recordings and dates as both a leader and side player, always offering prickly contributions or intriguing melodies and statements. Hicks began on piano at age 6, and later studied music at Lincoln University and Berklee. While attending Berklee, Hicks also played in Boston clubs. He moved to New York in the mid '60s. Hicks worked with Art Blakey, Betty Carter, and Woody Herman from the mid '60s until 1970, then recorded with Oliver Lake. He performed and recorded with Charles Tolliver in the Netherlands, then with Blakey and Carter again from the early '70s until 1980. During that time, Hicks also recorded with Lester Bowie and Chico Freeman, and taught at Southern Illinois University. He led his own trio and played in groups led by Arthur Blythe, David Murray, Hamiett Bluiett, Art Davis, and Pharoah Sanders during the '80s.

Hicks was featured in the seventh volume of Concord's continuing Maybeck Recital Hall series in 1991. He's recorded as a leader for Strata-East, Theresa, Lime Tree, DIW, Timeless, Red Baron, and Concord Jazz, among others. Hicks has some sessions available on CD. —*Ron Wynn*

★ **After the Morning** / Jan. 5-6, 1979 / West 54 8004

Pianist John Hicks hurtles headlong through five of the eight tracks here, slowing long enough to get his teeth into a splendid Tex Allen tune, "Night Journey," with its sinuous vamp and moist minor harmonies, as well as Frieda Herzog's evocative gem "Some Other Spring" and a wisp of Dave Brubeck's "Duke." Sometimes his ideas, usually pretty, florid ones coming from Bill Evans as much as McCoy Tyner, come just a hair too fast for his hands, but he is certainly challenging himself and the listener. Maybe he was nervous; this is his debut as leader on a new label that simultaneously released solo piano albums by the genial Red Richards and the aristocratic Sir Roland Hanna, and Hicks was anxious to show what he could do outside Betty Carter's working group. The tunes themselves are extremely attractive, especially drummer Clifford Barbaro's "Samba" and Hicks's title track. Sometimes I heard gracious rubatos that I associate with the Detroit players Tommy Flanagan and Hank Jones, and I welcomed that relief. Bassist Walter Booker's contributions are selfless and seamless, in such close kin to Hicks's plunging left that at times I had to listen twice for them. —*Fred Bouchard,* Down Beat

Two of a Kind / i. 1980 / Evidence 22017

Pianist John Hicks and bassist Ray Drummond had not worked together often when they recorded the 11 tracks on this '80 session. Neither was the consensus star that they became in the '90s, but they were already accomplished soloists. Their union yields some superb, striking, and distinctive playing on this collection of mostly standards. Hicks nicely outlines the basic melodies on such songs as Ellington's "Take The Coltrane" or Bud Powell's "Parisian Thoroughfare," then begins probing their structure, dissecting, reworking, and restating, finding his own directions and expressing fresh thoughts and statements without distorting the songs. Drummond's heavy yet sometimes barely audible basslines are both supportive and compelling, at times contrasting Hicks and at other times establishing their own direction. The two are a true duo, each player conscious of the other but able to make his own way. It is the kind of outstanding early effort both can now look back on and regard with satisfaction. —*Ron Wynn*

In Concert / i. Aug. 1984 / Evidence 22048

Pianist John Hicks is alternately calm and aggressive, laid-back and attacking on this '84 set newly reissued by Evidence with two bonus cuts. He nicely supports and buttresses Elise Wood's blissful flute tones on "Say It (Over and Over Again)," adding a delicate voice solo. He is animated on "Pas De Trois (Dance Forever)" and "Soul Eyes" and even more energetic on "Take The Coltrane." Bobby Hutcherson's outstanding vibes solo on "Paul's Pal" brings an added bonus while bassist Walter Booker and drummer Idris Muhammad handle their roles with tact and skill, particularly Muhammad, who must sometimes add light textures and touches and at other times must contribute sparks and excitement. —*Ron Wynn*

Naima's Love Song / i. 1988 / DIW 823

Luminous / i. Sep. 1988-Jul. 3, 1985 / Evidence 22033

While regarded as among the finest and most intense jazz pianists currently active, John Hicks is also quite versatile. He is in a reflective, lyrical bent throughout the 11 songs on this '88 date. Flutist Elise Wood's lithe, entrancing, and superbly played solos almost demand things be less vigorous and more introspective, but the session is not devoid of energy. Hicks, rather than ripping or powering his way through, offers soothing melodies, warm and lush solos showing he could be equally outstanding as a complementary/supporting player. The same holds true for bassist Walter Booker, alternating drummers Jimmy Cobb and

Alvin Queen, and special guest tenor saxophonist Clifford Jordan, who plays with warmth, delicacy, and yet plenty of soul on "Luminous," "Yemenja," and "Osaka." The duo numbers between Hicks and Wood are the most sentimental; their concluding version of Strayhorn's "Upper Manhattan Medical Group" puts a poignant cap on what is a thoroughly enjoyable date. —*Ron Wynn*

Is That So? / i. 1990 / Timeless 357

Live at Maybeck Recital Hall—Vol. 7 / i. Aug. 1990 / Concord Jazz 4442

Rollicking, thoughtful, unpredictable, and eclectic solo piano. CD version has two bonus cuts. —*Ron Wynn*

○ **Eastside Blues** / i. 1991 / DIW 828

His most recent excursion into the trio vein, this album is explosive and substantive, with Curtis Lundy and Victor Lewis. —*Ron Wynn*

Crazy for You / i. 1992 / Red Baron 52761

Marvelous piano playing in a trio format by John Hicks, featured on this '92 session with bassist Wilbur Bascomb, Jr. and drummer Kenny Washington. Hicks's solos have feeling, force, and depth, and he's adept at anything from reinterpreting standards to provocative originals, hard bop to swing, blues, spirituals, even ragtime or stride. —*Ron Wynn*

Friends Old and New / i. 1992 / Novus 63141

1992 session with pianist John Hicks playing in various combo settings with some excellent musical associates. Bassist Ron Carter, tenor saxophone dynamo Joshua Redman, trumpeter Clark Terry, trombonist Al Grey, and drummer/vocalist Grady Tate are among the friends who join Hicks for some powerhouse numbers. —*Ron Wynn*

J. C. HIGGINBOTHAM (Jay C. Higginbotham)

b. May 11, 1906, Social Circle, GA, **d.** May 26, 1973
Trombone / New Orleans traditional

An exuberant, entertaining trombonist, J. C. Higginbotham was a delightful soloist whose style included plenty of rough, voicelike smears and slurs, as well as humorous refrains and choruses. He was quite influenced by Jimmy Harrison, but added his own flourishes. Higginbotham played in various southern and midwestern bands as a youngster, then moved to New York in the '20s. He joined Luis Russell in 1928, then worked with Fletcher Henderson, Chick Webb, and Benny Carter during the '30s. His solos in Russell's orchestra, which were featured during the era when Louis Armstrong was also in the band, earned him widespread fame. During the '40s, Higginbotham played with many traditional jazz combos, including groups led by Henry "Red" Allen and by Sidney Bechet, as well as his own group. Higginbotham was part of the excellent trombone section on the Henderson reunion album in the late '50s, teaming with Benny Morton and Dicky Wells. He led groups in the '60s, and appeared at the 1963 Newport Jazz Festival. He recorded for Okeh, Jazzology, and Prestige, and with Bechet, Coleman Hawkins, Carter's Chocolate Dandies, Jelly Roll Morton, and Tiny Grimes. Currently, he has one session available as a leader on CD, and is featured on other reissues by Carter, Bechet, and Hawkins. —*Ron Wynn*

★ **Higgy Comes Home** / i. Nov. 1967 / Cable 126601

BILLY HIGGINS

b. Oct. 11, 1936, Los Angeles, CA
Drums / Hard bop, early free, modern creative

Billy Higgins can fit any role required of a drummer; he can push and drive the beat, play in a swinging, restrained fashion, or provide waves of sound and rhythm. He's been the ultimate eclectic session player since the '50s, and appears on dozens of dates. Everything in Higgins's approach, from his impeccable time to exceptional solos, is flawless. Higgins began playing R&B and rock dates with Amos Milburn and Bo Diddley in Los Angeles, and played jazz with the Jazz Messiahs featuring Don Cherry, James Clay, and Dexter Gordon in the '50s. He started working with Ornette Coleman in rehearsals, and recorded with Coleman and Red

Mitchell in 1958. He played with Coleman's quartet in New York in 1959, then with Thelonious Monk in San Francisco in 1959 and 1960. During the '60s, Higgins recorded with any and everyone, among them Steve Lacy, Sonny Clark, Lee Morgan, Donald Byrd, Jackie McLean, Gordon, and Hank Mobley. He continued the busy pace in the '70s, doing dates with Mal Waldron, Clifford Jordan, Niels-Henning Ørsted-Pedersen, Cedar Walton, Milt Jackson, Art Pepper, and J.J. Johnson. In 1972 and '73, he was a coleader of the Brass Company with Bill Lee and Bill Hardman. Higgins made his own quartet recordings in 1979 and 1980. He was back in the session game in '80, recording with Joe Henderson, Pat Metheny, David Murray's big band, Slide Hampton, and with the Timeless All-Stars. He had a brief role and also played in the film *Round Midnight* in 1986. Higgins had reunions with Coleman in 1977 and 1987. He's also recorded often with Charlie Haden in the '80s and '90s. Higgins does have a couple of albums as a leader listed in the *Schwann* catalog and available on CD. These albums join the many that feature Higgins as a sideman. —*Ron Wynn and Michael G. Nastos*

Soweto / Jan. 21, 1979 / Red
A superior quartet session with some of Bob Berg's best tenor sax work. —*Ron Wynn*

Soldier, The / Dec. 3, 1979 / Timeless 145
This recording with Cedar Walton (p) presents postbop standards, well played. —*Michael G. Nastos*

★ **Bridgework** / Apr. 23, 1980 / Contemporary 14024
A rare Higgins album, with conservative arrangements and compositions, plus outstanding technique and percussive foundations. —*Ron Wynn*

○ **Mr. Billy Higgins** / i. Apr. 12, 1984-May 2, 1984 / RIZA 104
One of jazz's greatest session drummers got a rare date as a leader on this '84 set, yet it's tough to tell that this is Billy Higgins's album. He is in his usual place, driving and pacing the session on drums, while soprano and tenor saxophonist Gary Bias take the spotlight on such songs as "Morning Awakening" and "Humility." Bias worked for many years with the Earth, Wind and Fire horns but shows here with several blistering solos that he is capable of much more than just riffing and playing melodies. William Henderson plays competent piano solos while bassist Tony Dumas provides consistently solid accompaniment and an infrequent solo. The album highlight is the second selection, "John Coltrane," which combines an opening Eastern/Asian passage with some fine hard bop playing by Bias and Henderson's best solo on the date. —*Ron Wynn*

ANDREW HILL

b. Jun. 30, 1937, Port Au Prince, Haiti
Piano / Post bop, early free, modern creative
Andrew Hill has been an underrated composer and an overlooked pianist since the '60s. His unpredictable tempo changes, nicely constructed melodies, and shifting meters are the mark of musical sophistication and expertise. Hill's also among the few jazz musicians who've incorporated Caribbean and Haitian rhythmic and melodic elements successfully into their work. He's one of the more percussive players, good on ballads, but more intriguing and interesting on uptempo material. Though his parents were Haitian, Hill was actually raised in Chicago. He began playing piano at age 13, and studied with Paul Hindemith from 1950 to 1952. In his teens, he worked with Charlie Parker, Miles Davis, Gene Ammons, and Johnny Griffin in Chicago clubs. He played baritone sax briefly in the early '50s, and recorded on the Ping label with Pat Patrick and Wilbur Campbell. Hill had extensive R&B experience before moving to New York in 1961 to be Dinah Washington's accompanist. He played with Rahsaan Roland Kirk in Los Angeles in 1962. Upon returning to New York in 1963, Hill did Blue Note sessions with Joe Henderson, Eric Dolphy, Freddie Hubbard, Woody Shaw, and others through the '60s. These were surging, challenging works, sometimes featuring small combos, other

times elements such as a vocal septet. Hill's compositions were the musical fuel for these engines. He was music coordinator for Amiri Baraka's Black Arts Repertory Theatre in 1965. Hill was composer-in-residence at Colgate from 1970 to 1972, and eventually earned his doctorate. He toured with the Smithsonian Heritage Program from 1972 to 1975, receiving a Smithsonian Fellowship in 1975. Hill kept recording in the '70s for independent labels like Steeple Chase, Arista Freedom, Artists House, and East Wind, and for Soul Note in the '80s. He made a pair of fine albums for Blue Note in the late '80s and early '90s, working with contemporary musicians Greg Osby, Robin Eubanks, Lonnie Plaxico, and Cecil Brooks, plus veterans Bobby Hutcherson, Ben Riley, and Rufus Reid. He's taught in public schools and in prisons, and has toured worldwide. Hill has been active in television, theater, and education. He's published his own music and used the profits to assist other musicians and jazz as a whole. —*Ron Wynn*

☆ **Black Fire** / Nov. 8, 1963 / Blue Note 84151
Haiti's gift to jazz piano of the '50s and now. For adventurous listeners. —*Michael G. Nastos*

☆ **Point of Departure** / i. Mar. 31, 1964 / Capitol 84167
A 1989 reissue of a remarkable session that still has avant-garde quality today. Eric Dolphy (sax) and Joe Henderson (sax) break barriers with their splendid solos. —*Ron Wynn*

○ **Andrew!** / Jun. 25, 1964 / Blue Note 84203

★ **Compulsion** / Oct. 8, 1965 / Blue Note

Involution / Mar. 7, 1966 / Blue Note
Hill splits this two-record set with Sam Rivers (sax). Both are incredible. —*Ron Wynn*

Lift Every Voice / May 16, 1969 / Blue Note
Andrew Hill incorporates vocals into his concept with ease and skill. —*Ron Wynn*

○ **One for One** / Aug. 1, 1969+Jan. 23, 1970 / Blue Note
These are previously unreleased sessions from 1969 and 1970. Group efforts, at times with a string quartet. Hefty solos from Bennie Maupin, Pat Patrick, Joe Henderson, Freddie Hubbard, and Charles Tolliver. —*Michael G. Nastos*

Invitation / Oct. 17, 1974 / Steeple Chase

Spiral / Dec. 20, 1974+Jan. 20, 1975 / Freedom 741007

Live at Montreux / Jul. 1975 / Freedom 741023

★ **From California with Love** / Oct. 12, 1978 / Artists House
This solo piano release contains two long musical epistles, each penned in a stunning variety of moods and techniques. Again, paradox seems one of Andrew Hill's principal organizational strategies. On "California" (20 minutes of thematic variations on a 20-bar theme), crystalline upper-register statements play against cascading runs and pouncing, where-will-the-next-note-clomp? passages. Most striking is Hill's power of invention. A piece like this seems as though it could go on for 40 minutes or two hours, or perhaps even perpetually. "Reverend Du Bop" is even more tightly, thematically developed than "California." Again, Hill mixes delicate rubato with lopsided, pile-driving passages and high-voltage chords. In his dense probing of limited thematic material, this large-form pianist never seems at a loss for a new nuance of expression or for a new twist on an old formula. —*Jon Balleras*, Down Beat

Nefertiti / Jun. 1980 / Inner City 6022
Powerful, outstanding trio session cut in '76 for the East Wind label. Hill was at one time Dinah Washington's pianist, then moved to writing adventurous outside pieces and playing fiery, experimental music. These songs aren't very outside, but they're certainly done in an aggressive, captivating manner. —*Ron Wynn*

Strange Serenade / Jun. 13-14, 1980 / Soul Note

Faces of Hope / Jun. 1980 / Soul Note 1010
Sometimes loping, sometimes soaring solo piano from Andrew Hill, one of several impressive releases he made in the '80s. Hill often used rhythms from his native Haiti in his

compositions. This time, however, it's neither the arrangements nor the songs that score, but Hill's emphatic execution of them. —*Ron Wynn*

Shades / Jul. 3-4, 1986 / Soul Note

★ **Verona Rag** / Jul. 1986 / Soul Note 121110
Pianist Andrew Hill long ago established himself as one of the most creative of postbop improvisors on his instrument. His solo *Verona Rag* richly displays the vast spectrum of sources this gifted artist draws upon, from rags and spirituals to the standard song book to bebop and beyond, not to mention his Caribbean roots. — *W. Royal Stokes, Jazz Times*

Eternal Spirit / Jan. 30-31, 1989 / Blue Note 92051
This newer material showcases Hill's influence on Young Lion Greg Osby (as) and includes a reunion with Bobby Hutcherson (vib). —*Ron Wynn*

But Not Farewell / i. 1991 / Blue Note 94971
A latter-day set with the smouldering Greg Osby on alto sax. Hill updates his sound. —*Ron Wynn*

BUCK HILL (Roger Hill)

b. 1928, Washington, DC
Tenor sax / Swing, big band, post-bop, bop
Hill is a good mainstream tenor saxophonist who has gotten lots of mileage out of the fact he's also a mail carrier. He has recorded infrequently but made a splash with some fiery works in the '80s and '90s. His tenor sax phrasing and tone exemplify the best qualities of the sturdy, robust style of Booker Ervin. Hill is never far from blues and a very solid ballad and standards player. —*Ron Wynn*

This Is Buck Hill / Mar. 20, 1978 / Steeple Chase 1095

★ **Scope** / Jul. 8, 1979 / Steeple Chase 1123

Easy to Love / Jul. 11-12, 1981 / Steeple Chase 1160

○ **Plays Europe** / 1982 / Turning Point 90982

Capital Hill / i. Aug. 7, 1989 / Muse 5384

Buck Stops Here / i. Apr. 13, 1990 / Muse 5416
The Washington, D.C. tenor legend with the big buttery sound gives the warhorse "Harlem Nocturne" one of its most inspired readings. Elsewhere on his third Muse outing he shares the solo spotlight with the rarely recorded Johnny Coles, who seldom plays a superfluous note on his warm-voiced flugelhorn. A nicely balanced set of pretty ballads and jaunty originals like Coles's infectious "Wip Wop." —*Les Line*

I'm Beginning to See the Light / i. 1991 / Muse 5449
The latest entry from this mail carrier turned jazz soloist. Hill's style has soul-jazz seasoning and a bluesy bite. —*Ron Wynn*

EARL HINES (Earl Kenneth Hines)

b. Dec. 28, 1903, Dusquesne, PA, d. Apr. 22, 1983, Oakland, CA
Piano / New Orleans traditional, boogie-woogie, swing
A founding father among pianists, Earl "Fatha" Hines applied the rhythmic and harmonic discoveries of Louis Armstrong in conjunction with his own ideas and changed keyboard thinking and playing. He gave the instrument its own voice within a band, using ringing right-hand octaves and displaying spectacular timing. Unlike many others who'd been soloists first and had to learn how to fit into an ensemble, Hines was an ensemble player from the beginning and his approach continually evolved; he brilliantly incorporated devices such as offbeat accents and strategic pauses. He was also among the earliest of his generation to accept and even champion bop, hiring and showcasing boppers in his bands.

Hines studied trumpet briefly with his father and took his first piano lessons with his mother. He later took additional lessons with other teachers in Pittsburgh. His first professional job was accompanying vocalist Lois Deppe in 1918. He made his debut recordings with Deppe, using the money to study with two local pianists. Hines moved to Chicago in 1923, eventually working with several important city bands.

These bands included Samy Stewart's, Erskine Tate's Vendome Theatre Orchestra, and Carroll Dickerson's. The Dickerson band took over at the Sunset Cafe in 1926, and featured both Hines and Armstrong. Hines became its director a year later, with Armstrong its leader. However, the two went separate ways after a failure to comanage a club. Hines joined Jimmie Noone's band at the Apex club.

In 1928, Hines made seminal recordings with both Noone and Armstrong, particularly the landmark duet "Weather Bird" (Armstrong) and "Apex Blues," plus a group of solos for QRS. He formed his own big band in 1929, which stayed at the Chicago Grand Terrace Ballroom for ten years. Some notable alumni included Omer Simeon, Budd Johnson, Trummy Young, Ray Nance, Billy Eckstine, Dizzy Gillespie, Charlie Parker, and Sarah Vaughan. Hines finally disbanded the orchestra in 1947, but by that time had made several tours and radio broadcasts. He rejoined Armstrong in 1948 in an early, premier edition of the all-star lineup under which Armstrong recorded and toured extensively the latter part of his career. After a three-year stint, Hines headed his own small groups. He settled in San Francisco. A pair of solo New York concerts coproduced by Dan Morgenstern in 1964 led to a fresh wave of publicity and acclaim for Hines, who remained an invigorating, delightful, and unpredictable pianist until his death in 1983. Stanley Dance's book, *The World of Earl Hines*, is invaluable. –*Ron Wynn with Dan Morgenstern*

Harlem Lament / i. 1933-1938 / Portrait 44119
A first-rate compilation of superb '30s cuts with Jimmy Mundy (ts) and Omer Simeon (cl). Stride, rag, and blues elements merge seamlessly. —*Ron Wynn*

★ **Earl Hines (1937-1939)** / i. 1937-1939 / Classics 538

○ **Earl Hines (1939-1940)** / i. Oct. 1939-Dec. 1940 / Classics 567

Piano Man / i. 1939-1942 / Bluebird 6750
Excellent reissue of classic and long-unavailable 1939-42 Hines Bluebird sides including five solo numbers. But the real showpieces are 16 orchestra sides. —*Rich Kienzle*, Rock & Roll Disc

South Side Swing / i. 193? / MCA 1311

○ **Earl Hines Plays Fats Waller** / i. 1953 / Brunswick 58035

★ **Monday Date, A** / i. Sep. 1961 / Riverside 1740

○ **In Concert** / Mar. 7, 1964 / Focus 335

Legendary Little Theater Concert / i. 1964 / Muse 2001
Little Theater Concert consists of two LPs of previously unissued performances from the series of concerts in 1964 that put Earl Hines back in the public eye; thus the "legendary" claim in the title. In 1964, it had been 36 years since Hines had performed as a solo pianist. He was remembered and honored for his work with Louis Armstrong and his own big band, but he was regarded as a symbol of jazz's past and not looked to any longer for great things. The Little Theater concert changed all that. It was as if Jack Dempsey had walked back into the ring in 1964 and reclaimed from Muhammad Ali the title he had lost in 1927 to Gene Tunney. The Hines renaissance was especially exciting because it returned him to the roots of his greatness, not another band but the piano keyboard. One of the greatest pianists in jazz history was playing more piano in 1964 than ever before. The best work here, and it is considerable indeed, is "Brussell's Hustle," a long, medium-fast blues that swings with a relaxed, consistent beat that carries some of Hines's cleanest, most uncluttered playing. The numbers with tenor saxophonist Budd Johnson are outstanding as well, especially "Blues For Jazz Quartet," although Hines takes no solos. And of course the medleys, for all their flashiness, are a patchwork of marvelous Hines gems and trademarks folded within the effects and affectations. —*John McDonough*, Down Beat

○ **Blues in Thirds** / Apr. 1965 / Black Lion 760120
This Black Lion CD has two alternative takes and "Black Lion Blues" added to what was on the original LP. For some-

one who always discounted his own ability as a blues player, Earl Hines had a remarkable gift for coming up with fresh, pleasing blues ideas (remember "Blues for Tatum"?), as he shows in the reworking of his 1928 "Blues in Thirds," in "Blues after Midnight," and "Black Lion Blues." There is a reverse tribute to his friend Nat "King" Cole on "Sweet Lorraine" (which he recorded years before Cole, with Jimmie Noone), where he sings, phrasing neatly in his light voice. And he takes on the characteristics of a whole band on the numbers by Buck Clayton and Frank Foster. In my view, he was the hardest-swingin' pianist in the history of jazz; his time was perfect and his uncanny left hand enabled him to set up counterrhythms whose electrifying, dynamic effect was never equaled by his imitators. Above all, he was a genuine improviser. Alan Bates, in the notes, points out that the 60 minutes of superb music in this set was recorded in an hour and a half! —*Stanley Dance*, Jazz Times

Paris Session / May 27, 1965 / Ducretet Thompson 40262
This Earl Hines session was released by Inner City from Pathe-Marconi and originally issued on Ducretet Thompson with a duplicate release on English Columbia. It had been unavailable for years. Hines made a lengthy concert tour of England and France in April and May of 1965 that resulted in three solo piano albums, of which this is the third. The entire session is excellent, with "Blue Because Of You" and "Sweet Sue" as standouts. There is a good vocal by Hines on "I Can't Give You Anything But Love Baby" and another fine rendition of "Second Balcony Jump". This is recommended. —*Shirley Klett*, Cadence

○ **Once Upon a Time** / Jan. 10-11, 1966 / Impulse 9108
Pianist Earl Hines's *Once Upon A Time* will be great fun for Duke Ellington and Hines fans. The January 10 and 11, 1965 date (reissue) pairs Hines with many Ellingtonians such as Johnny Hodges, Paul Gonsalves, Clark Terry, Larry Brown, Bill Berry, Cat Anderson, Ray Nance, Sonny Greer, Harold Ashby, Jimmy Hamilton, Buster Cooper, and Aaron Bell, along with clarinetist Pee Wee Russell and drummer Elvin Jones. Actually, Hines fans expecting the usual may be surprised to hear how much he remains the pianist here, even on the small-group cuts. For some reason "Black & Tan Fantasy" was omitted from this reissue. Considering brevity here, try to pick up the original Impulse album. — *Bob Rusch*, Cadence

Earl Hines at Home / i. 1969 / Delmark 212

○ **Quintessential Recording Session** / i. Mar. 15, 1970 / Halcyon 101
Pianist Earl Hines's later solo work became even freer of stylistic restriction, and Hines wielded ever-larger palettes with consummate ease, as seen in this version of "Deep Forest," against which earlier versions, however admirable, seem almost incomplete. There were many solo Hines recordings in his later years, but few match this session's dramatic, sweeping statements and none its consistency. It is a highly successful musical autobiography, especially in its reexamination of other early Hines themes, like "Glad Rag Doll," "Down Among The Sheltering Palms," or "Cavernism." If his original intention had been to diverge from the piano's "orchestral" nature to recreate a hornlike persona, then the result at the end of the day was to create a new orchestral persona for the instrument. —*Chris Sheridan*, Cadence

○ **Earl Hines Plays Duke Ellington** / Jun. 1, 1971-Dec. 10, 1971 / Master Jazz 8114
This is the fourth record in a series of unaccompanied Duke Ellington compositions featuring pianist Earl Hines, and, according to the liner notes, Hines did not know any of these tunes before the session. It does not matter; we hear Hines, not Ellington, and each tune becomes a very personal statement. Side one is relaxed and almost subdued, except for that relentless but gentle walking left hand of "Fatha." The "Creole Love Call" of 1927, made famous in the band arrangement by the wordless vocal of Adelaide Hall, and "The Shepherd," a growling Cootie Williams feature, do not

come to mind as Ellington tunes that could be taken out of the band and solo context that Ellington had conceived. Hines plays them with absolutely no indication of the original version; the tune is simply a delicate starting point for Hines's long improvisations, all without a dull or wasted minute. "I Ain't Got Nothin' But the Blues" is taken a bit faster than the above tunes and contains a passing quote of "Shine On Harvest Moon." "Black Butterfly," the longest cut, is much more technical and aggressive than the other compositions, while "The Jeep Is Jumpin'" is a lesson in stride. —*Tom Everett*, Cadence

○ **Hines Plays Hines** / i. Jul. 1972 / Swaggie 1320

Tour De Force / Nov. 1972 / Black Lion 760140
In the opening track, pianist Earl Hines gives us six minutes and 49 seconds of unrelenting passion and drive. Physically, it is a tour de force indeed, with piano playing of a power and freedom matched by no living artist; spiritually, it is a trip to the ultimate heights. And if you want to get a little analytical, Hines does some contrapuntal stuff here that I never heard from him before. That's not all, by any means. "Mack The Knife" offers further surprises with stride and locked hands, bell tones, tremolos, keyboard-wide runs, and a panorama of pianistics with a stomping beat reflected in Fatha's well-recorded foot. "Lonesome Road" is another miracle. No doubt, the very fine and perfectly tuned grand piano and relaxed atmosphere of Hank O'Neal's studio contribute to the heights Hines seems to reach so consistently here. But the essence is in the fingers and mind of Earl Hines, so aptly dubbed "King of Freedom" by Dick Wellstood. Long may he reign! —*Dan Morgenstern*, Down Beat

☆ **Hines Does Hoagy** / i. 1972-1973 / Audiophile 113

★ **Earl Hines at the New School** / Mar. 1973 / Chiaroscuro 157
There is a complex and erratic power in pianist Earl Hines's solo work. His left and right hands hurl fistfuls of notes at each other that weave into splashy plaids right in midair. It is the sort of intricacy that could not be contrived for effect. His left hand works as hard as his right. Sometimes it drops percussive accents between the tiny spaces of time not occupied by his right. But other times it becomes the lead instrument. His slide into "Honeysuckle Rose" is dazzling, starting with a shimmering tremolo on the chords of the bridge and followed by a bass statement of the tune itself. Daring arpeggios swoop about one minute and suddenly alight squarely on a beat and turn into pure swing. Ideas go crashing into each other with disciplined chaos. It is fascinating to hear Hines paint himself into corner after corner. Somtimes he leaps blithely across to the dry areas of order and symmetry. Other times he simply crashes through the wall into another room altogether. —*John McDonough*, Down Beat

Piano Portraits of Australia / Aug. 6, 1974 / Swaggie 1350
Pianist Earl Hines's *Portraits* are all Dave Dallwitz compositions. Dallwitz's music began with 1928-30 Ellington (and Ellington's sources); his compositions were episodic, multithematic, with evocative ambitions that were occasionally even fulfilled. Hines does not interpret Dallwitz any more than he interpreted Ellington, Porter, or Gershwin. But his loving performances discover forgotten or hidden elements of Dallwitz, and the musical result is a kind of round-the-world collaboration. —*John Litweiler*, Down Beat

Solo Walk in Tokyo / i. Jan. 1977 / Biograph 12055
This recording was made in Tokyo in 1972 but not released in the United States until 1978. It is a collection of eight standards, including three by George Gershwin and two by Fats Waller, and two originals. The performances are in the classic Earl Hines style, rich and ornate. Surely Hines had the most interesting left hand in jazz; it switches from walking to stride to chording, stopping along the way for a trill or tremolo. Meanwhile, his right hand spins out arpeggios and single-note lines around the melody. He played the piano orchestrally, using every device in every register. His style was enriched by changes in tempo, meter, and key, by careful dy-

namics and ingenious chord substitutions. This is wonderful, exuberant music. There are a few weak passages and weak cuts ("Embraceable You," for example), but most of them are full of pleasant surprises. —*Douglas Clark*, Down Beat

Earl Hines in New Orleans / Jul. 11, 1977 / Chiaroscuro 200
The Earl Hines studio performances of the New Orleans album are complicated and subjective. In conversation with himself, Hines could be an artist of almost impenetrable perplexity and depth. He built music like the Gothics built cathedrals. —*John McDonough*, Down Beat

Fatha' Plays Hits He Missed / **i.** Jul. 1979 / M&K Real Time 105
This is a direct-to-disc LP, and the quality of the sound is indeed extraordinary. Next to this, an ordinary stereo piano sounds tinny, and the sheer presence of the piano, unamplified bass, and brush-swinging drummer certainly improves on anything you and I are ever likely to hear in person. The lovely, quiet version of "Sophisticated Lady" is precisely the kind of piece to demonstrate the advantages of d-to-d sound even on the most ordinary rig. Earl Hines demonstrates a light touch, and curiously, since this was a most eventful performance, an understated elegance. The rest of the session is circuslike in its extroversion: the delightful kidding of Joe Zawinul's "Birdland," the enlightened honky-tonk of Horace Silver's "The Preacher," the brief looks at Fats Waller, the warmth and, as an alternative, the big repeated chords of "Misty." Any Hines performance is by definition a total transformation of the intent of the given material. The notion of ballads, blues, and sustained moods disappears, for Hines's all-encompassing generosity and quickness of imagination transformed others' vision just as Hines transcended conventions. —*John Litweiler*, Down Beat

★ **Giants of Jazz** / **i.** Mar. 1981 / Time Life 11
The task of paring hundreds of hours of Earl Hines music down to three significant albums for a workable anthology was a prodigious one, and critic Stanley Dance went about it with commendable thoroughness and a dedication that exceeded mere professionalism, going to the source himself, looking over shortlisted tracks, and involving Hines in the decision making. The notes are thus full of Hines's wincing, wonderment, rich anecdotes, and wry asides. The selections included here divide fairly evenly into solo, small-group, and big-band performances. Combo sides include three quintet tracks with Jimmie Noone, four sextet cuts, and the remarkable, groundbreaking duo "Weather Bird" with Louis Armstrong, all from 1928 and perhaps Hines's last adventures working as a sideman. Of the 11 solos, four are from 1928, four from 1939, and one from 1970 with Hank O'Neal revisiting "Blues In Thirds" for an intriguing comparison over 40 years. Dance's order is strictly chronological, which tends to shuffle solos with big-band numbers on four sides, emphasizing the feverish genius's orchestral flair and insuperable headlong swing. Hines often carried the band as easily as he did his solo excursions. This collection is an indispensable document of one of the most formidable American musicians of our century. —*Fred Bouchard*, Down Beat

○ **Earl Hines and Budd Johnson** / Black & Blue 233084

Father Jumps, The / RCA
A good compilation from 1939-1945. The music is now available in other, better remastered reissues. —*Ron Wynn*

★ **Partners in Jazz** / MPS 61172
With Jaki Byard (p). Piano duets from masters of two styles and generations. Definitive. —*Michael G. Nastos*

MILT HINTON (Milton John Hinton)

b. Jun. 23, 1910, Vicksburg, MS
Bass / Swing, bop
A legendary bassist, Milt Hinton has been working in combos, has been making records, and has been touring since the '30s, and remains a formidable figure. As one of the greatest timekeepers ever among bassists who have a huge, magnificent sound, Hinton's worked with numerous vocalists as well as instrumentalists. He's also an outstanding pho-

tographer who's had several exhibitions of his work, and had a book of his jazz photos, *Over Time,* published in 1991. He also conducted several interviews with noted musicians such as Danny Barker, Teddy Wilson, Quentin Jackson, and Jo Jones through National Endowment for the Arts grants during the '70s and '80s. These interviews are now in a collection at the Institute for Jazz Studies at Rutgers. Nicknamed "The Judge," Hinton began playing professionally in Chicago during the '30s with Body Atkins, Tiny Parham, and Jabbo Smith. He also worked with Eddie South, Erskine Tate, and Zutty Singleton, among others, before joining Cab Calloway's band in 1936. He remained with Calloway until 1951, then became a freelancer and, since that time, has remained as a much-in-demand session bassist. Hinton has played with everyone from Bing Crosby to Louis Armstrong and Count Basie, and with Joe Newman, Lionel Hampton, Terry Gibbs, Jimmy Rushing, Branford Marsalis, Buddy DeFranco, and many others. The 1988 book *Bass Line,* cowritten by David Berger and Hinton, covers Hinton's life and times in the jazz world. Hinton's also recorded a few albums as a leader for labels such as Progressive and Chiaroscuro. He has a couple of sessions available on CD. —*Ron Wynn*

★ **Basses Loaded!** / Feb. 1, 1955 / Victor 1107

Rhythm Section, The / **i.** Oct. 31, 1956 / Epic 3271

Trio, The / **i.** 1977 / CR 188

AL HIRT (Alois Maxwell Hirt)

b. Nov. 7, 1922, New Orleans, LA
Trumpet / Dixieland
A classically trained trumpeter, Al Hirt (best known as "Jumbo" to his friends in New Orleans) picked up jazz licks by listening to the recordings of Harry James and Roy Eldridge in the '40s. He began his professional career working with the swing bands of Tommy and Jimmy Dorsey, but when Hirt returned to New Orleans in the latter '40s he gravitated toward the "traditional" jazz format. In 1955 he formed a combo that included Pete Fountain, and, over the next five years, worked on attracting national recognition. His greatest popularity, however, came in the mid '60s, when he had back-to-back hits with "Java" and "Cotton Candy," tunes that were perhaps closer to a popularized country music style than they were to Dixieland. During the '70s, he operated his own nightclub on Bourbon Street. After a hiatus of several years, he returned to Bourbon Street in the early '90s, where he is still active. Al Hirt's substantial popularity stems from his genuine technical virtuosity and powerful delivery. —*Bruce Boyd Raeburn*

★ **That's a Plenty** / **i.** 1988 / Pro Arte 659
Jumbo with Peanuts Hocko, Bobby Breaux, Dalton Hagler, and others pouncing on New Orleans favorites like "Royal Garden Blues," "Bourbon Street Parade," and "Saints." —*Bruce Raeburn*

Best of Al Hirt, The / RCA 1034

Super Jazz—Vol. 1 / Monument 44359
Al Hirt and Pete Fountain's bands play separately and together. This gives an illustration of why these players remain popular and continue to attract new converts to New Orleans jazz. —*Bruce Raeburn*

ART HODES (Arthur W. Hodes)

b. Nov. 14, 1904, Nikoliev, Russia, **d.** Mar. 4, 1993
Piano / New Orleans traditional, blues & jazz
One of the last great traditional jazz and blues pianists, Art Hodes came to America when he was six months old and grew up in Chicago. His rollicking style was honed playing dances at Hull House and working with Chicago bands, as well as playing in New York on 52nd street in the late '30s. Hodes made his recording debut in 1928 with Wingy Manone, and has recorded periodically ever since. Most of his releases are solo, but his activities in music are not limited to the performing arena. Hodes was editor of the magazine *Jazz Record* from 1943-1947. He was a disc jockey and

eventually became an educator and lectured extensively. He moved back to Chicago in 1950, and became a resident at Bob Scobey's nightclub in 1959, while also writing for *Down Beat* and hosting a television series that won him an Emmy. Hodes toured Europe frequently. He resurfaced in New York in the early '80s. His albums are available as reissues from GHB, Delmark, Audiophile, and Jazzology, while his latter-day material has been released on Sackville and Muse. — *Ron Wynn*

★ **Complete Blue Note Art Hodes Sessions** / Mosaic

○ **Art Hodes' Hot Five** / Oct. 12, 1945 / Blue Note 7005

○ **Chicago Rhythm Kings** / i. 1953 / Riverside 1012

★ **Albert Nicholas** / i. Jul. 1959 / Delmark 207

Mama Yancey Sings, Art Hodes Plays Blues / i. 1965 / Verve 9015

○ **Hodes' Art** / Oct. 22, 1968 / Delmark 213
Pianist Art Hodes, at this time 71, not only preserved early jazz piano, but helped keep it alive. Playing in the context of three different groups here, he shows his indebtedness to Jelly Roll Morton and James P. Johnson in his playing as well as in the selection of some tunes by those same greats. On the first three tracks, Hodes plays only with bass (Truck Parham) and drums. Under his fingers, "Winin' Boy Blues" becomes a relaxed, almost pretty blues, while in "Old Fashioned Love," Hodes plays in a busy, hard-driving stride style. However, he never pounds out mushy chords. The slow-tempo "Blues Yesterday" demonstrates his and Duke Ellington's indebtness to Johnson. Hodes, clarinetist Raymond Burke, and bassist Pops Foster make up the group on the second side, and it is a nice relaxed combination. — *Jerry De Muth, Cadence*

Bucket's Got a Hole / 1968 / Delmark 211

○ **Friar's Inn Revisited** / 1968 / Delmark 215
The central idea around which this release was built was that of the New Orleans Rhythm Kings, who played Friar's Inn. Both trombonist George Brunies and clarinetist Volly De Faut were, of course, members of this historic group, Brunies originally, and De Faut later. The titles are also closely associated with or originated by the NORK. One problem is the generally retiring nature of Nappy Trottier's trumpet lead, which might be a result of recording balance. The same thing may apply to the fact that Brunies is over-shadowed throughout by De Faut's clarinet. Even Barrett Deems, generally an especially driving drummer, is relatively restrained on these tracks. Pianist Hodes has an excellent break on "That's A Plenty," and "Tin Roof" is a good track, while Barney Bigard's clarinet is effective on his two appearances and De Faut has some good chalumeau register work. — *Shirley Klett, Cadence*

Funky Piano of Art Hodes, The / i. Jul. 1969 / Blue Note 6502
Pianist Art Hodes was one of the pioneer students of jazz music. Long ago, in Chicago, he absorbed the idiom completely, and, although many people misunderstood his principles, when he is given an opportunity to display his musical ideas, he generally comes through with a brand of jazz full of expression and, dare I say it, full of soul. "M.K. Blues," "Jug Head Boogie," "Eccentric," and "K.M.M. Blues" have some of the best trumpet work Max Kaminsky ever committed to wax. Omer Simeon and trumpeter Oliver Mesheux combine on a sensitive "Blues for Jelly," and then Mezz Mezzrow joins Hodes and Kaminsky in "Shake That Thing." Hodes's reliance on the blues as a vehicle for expression is communicated to his fellow musicians, and they usually adopt a more emotional response to the changes than would be the case in some other company. The Chicagoans' sessions, documented in their entirety on "Sittin' In," are notable for the rock-steady drumming of Danny Alvin, the directness of Kaminsky's trumpet lead, and the generally inspired clarinet work of Rod Cless, a musician who died too soon to receive the credit due him. It is good music played with spirit and drive and Hodes continues to pump out bar-

relhouse blues choruses all over the place. — *John Norris, Coda*

○ **Someone to Watch Over Me** / Feb. 27, 1981 / Muse 5252
Pianist Art Hodes made his recording debut with Wingy Manone back in 1928 and recorded fairly often ever since, but this was his first LP on a widely distributed label in many years. More than many of the crop of '20s White Chicago musicians, he really soaked in the blues but developed a style uniquely his own. This rediscovery LP was well recorded, the piano of high quality and the audience both attentive and appreciative. Hodes favored highly polished black high-topped shoes and you can hear him tapping away, accompanying himself. The title track is outstanding with "St. Louis Blues," "Georgia On My Mind," and "Plain Ol' Blues" the best of the remainder. — *Shirley Klett, Cadence*

○ **Just the Two of Us** / Aug. 26, 1981 / Muse 5279
A bluesman par excellence, Art Hodes could invest even the most tawdry of ballads with a feeling of genuine gut-level involvement. But Hodes was, to boot, a two-fisted stomper as well, one who summoned up, in my memory at least, both Jimmy Blythe and Frank Melrose. Here, the 78-year-old pianist is truly at his best, performing well-honed classics to the accompaniment of the finest traditional bass player still alive. While it is true that the presence of a Baby Dodds, Zutty Singleton, or George Wettling on drums would have added that much more to the overall impact of Hodes and Hinton's music, we must be grateful for what we have. — *Jack Sohmer, Cadence*

★ **Selections from the Gutter** / i. Mar. 1983 / Storyville 4057
Wonderful blues, traditional jazz, and stride numbers by jazz pianist and critic Art Hodes, who cut many superb records for small independents during an extensive career. These were done in mid '80s. — *Ron Wynn*

South Side Memories / Nov. 29, 1983 / Sackville 3032

Blues in the Night / i. Jun. 1985 / Sackville 3039

○ **Live from Toronto's Cafe Des Copains** / i. 1988 / Music & Arts 610

○ **Pagin' Mr. Jelly** / Nov. 198? / Candid 79037

○ **Up in Volly's Room** / Delmark 217

JOHNNY HODGES (John Hodges)

b. Jul. 25, 1907, Cambridge, MA, **d.** May 11, 1970
Alto and soprano saxophone / Swing, big band
Perhaps jazz's most poignant instrumental lyricist, Johnny Hodges's alto sax solos were stunningly beautiful and evocative in the finest blues sense. He had the same knack as Count Basie for knowing what to play and when to play it, and though his improvised solos were often technically simple, they surpassed flurries from less imaginative players. His swing and expressiveness were unmatched. Hodges achieved greatness without having his own forum much of his career; his greatest work came within the Ellington orchestra, though he led many fine combo sessions outside the band and made some good records as a leader.

Hodges played drums and piano before starting saxophone at age 14. He began on soprano, then switched to alto. He received early soprano lessons from Sidney Bechet, an experience he never forgot. Originally, Hodges commuted to New York from Boston in the early '20s, playing with Bobby Sawyer, Lloyd Scott, Chick Webb, and Luckey Roberts. He replaced Bechet in Willie "The Lion" Smith's quartet at the Rhythm Club in 1924, then worked with Bechet at Harlem's Club Basha the next year. He joined Duke Ellington's orchestra in 1928, and was a featured soloist for the next four decades. Hodges also led a small studio band culled from the orchestra, making a series of records with them beginning in 1937. The list of distinguished Hodges performances, in both contexts, was extensive. There were "Jeep's Blues," "Hodge Podge," "The Jeep is Jumpin'," and "Wanderlust," as well as "Things Ain't What They Used to Be" and "Passion Flower." Hodges even cowrote a top-selling Ellington song, "I'm Beginning to See the Light," in 1944, and penned "Good

Queen Bess" for his mother. He put away his soprano sax after he recorded "That's the Blues Old Man." A riff he used in that song became the basis for "Happy-Go-Lucky Local," and subsequently for "Night Train."

Hodges headed his own small group from 1951 to 1955; they often sounded like a Ellington subset. He rejoined Ellington in 1955, and stayed with him until the end, though he'd take periodic breaks. Billy Strayhorn loved Hodges's sound as much as Ellington, and penned some unforgettable pieces that featured Hodges, including "Day Dream" and "Passion Flower." When Strayhorn died, Hodges's solos on the 1967 album, *And His Mother Called Him Bill,* demonstrated his equal affection. Hodges died in 1970, but was featured on the *New Orleans Suite* album. He can be heard on dozens of Ellington sessions on CD. —*Ron Wynn*

★ **On Keynote with Rex Stewart** / i. 1946 / PolyGram 30926
A thorough collection of sides from Keynote, spotlighting Ellingtonians Hodges and Rex Stewart (c). —*Ron Wynn*

★ **Complete Johnny Hodges Sessions (1951-1955)** / 1951-1955 / Mosaic 6126

Jeep Is Jumpin', The / i. 1951 / Verve

Used to Be Duke / Jul. 1954-Aug. 1954 / Verve 849394

★ **Big Sound, The** / Jun. 26, 1957+Sep. 3, 1957 / Verve 8271
The Big Sound by alto saxophonist Johnny Hodges and the Duke Ellington band never has excited me, but it sure has pleased me over the years. No surprises, but the session is as good as one might hope. Gathered here are the Ellington band with Billy Strayhorn at the piano. While it is not an Ellington record, the band brings its solid qualities in backing and the occasional solo to all the fine Hodges features. This is an integrated unit, not some detached studio band for Hodges to blow over, under, around, and through. It is wonderful Hodges and fine Ellington. Nothing more need be said. —*Bob Rusch,* Cadence

Side by Side / Aug. 1958-Feb. 1959 / Verve 821578
Some fine small-group dates with Hodges up front and Duke Ellington around the corner. —*Ron Wynn*

Smooth One, A / Apr. 7, 1959+Sep. 8, 1960 / Verve 2532

Back to Back / i. 1959 / Verve

At Sportpalast, Berlin / i. 1961 / Pablo 2620
Though Duke Ellington wasn't on board for this 1961 concert, his spirit and music certainly influenced the proceedings. Johnny Hodges heads the date, supervising a crew with five other Ellingtonians: Ray Nance on cornet and violin, Harry Carney on baritone sax, and Lawrence Brown on trombone, plus Aaron Bell on bass and Sam Woodyard on drums, with pianist Al Williams acting as substitute Duke in the rhythm section. The floating, mellow, and gorgeous Hodges alto shimmers, sways, and soothes on ballads and longtime Ellington favorites like "Take The 'A' Train" and "C-Jam Blues." The 21 cuts on the two-disc reissue package move so quickly, it's hard to believe the concert lasts over 90 minutes. Hodges and company perform Ellington's music just as brilliantly away from the master as with him. —*Ron Wynn*

Blue Hodges / Aug. 23-24, 1961 / Verve 8406

Johnny Hodges with Billy Strayhorn and the Orchestra / i. Dec. 12, 1961 / Verve 8452

Everybody Knows / Feb. 6, 1964 / GRP 116

In a Mellotone / Sep. 10-11, 1966 / Bluebird 2305

Things Ain't What They Used to Be / i. Oct. 1966 / RCA 533
This Johnny Hodges material contains some classic small-group sides from 1940 and 1941, plus two of the Duke Ellington Orchestra featuring alto saxophonist Hodges's "Mood to be Wooed" (1/4/45) and "Esquire Swank" (9/3/46). The 1940 sides are "Day Dream," "Good Queen Bess," "That's The Blues, Old Man," and "Junior Hop" with, in addition to Hodges, Cootie Williams (tpt), Lawrence Brown (t), Harry Carney (bs), Duke Ellington (p), Jimmy Blanton (b), and Sonny Greer (d). The 1941 sides, "Passion Flower,"

"Things Ain't What They Used To Be," and "Going Out The Back Bay," have the same personnel except that Ray Nance replaces Cootie Williams on trumpet. —*Shirley Klett,* Cadence

Triple Play / Jan. 9-10, 1967 / Bluebird 5903
1987 reissue with Ray Nance (tpt) and Tiny Grimes (g). Small-group Ellingtonia, the first from 1955, the second from 1967. The earlier one has longer and superior performances featuring Harry Carney, Lawrence Brown, and Jimmy Hamilton, while the latter (in stereo) falls just short of the mark. The RCA version will likely appeal to diehard Hodges fans. —*Ron Wynn*

Rabbit in Paris, The / i. May 1980 / Inner City 7003
The Rabbit In Paris puts alto saxophonist Johnny Hodges at the helm of a familiar octet: all Ellingtonians except for pianist Raymond Fol and tenorist Don Byas (Butch Ballard replaces Sonny Greer at the traps about a third of the way through). This is a happy, upbeat blowing session, the tunes mainly Ellington standards or blues riffs. Everybody gets a fair share of blowing space and not even the leader gets too many extra licks. Shorty Baker rips and snorts through his trumpet spots, Butter Jackson earns his monicker well with smooth, greasy trombone solos throughout, and Jimmy Hamilton tosses in some sweet, relaxed clarinet. Hodges's tone is exquisite. His million-dollar glissandi are paraded to fine advantage and his rich vibrato in the belly of the alto on "Mood Indigo" is priceless. And on the uptempo blues numbers Hodges romps and stomps. The solos, however, are 78 rpm length. Hodges is a generous leader, except to Byas, who seems to get short shrift every time he shows up on these Vogues. He also sometimes cuts himself short, as on his superb reading of the melody of "Sweet Lorraine," when he suddenly lets Baker take the bridge. This toe-tapping session would have been better as more of a showcase for its leader. —*Lee Jeske,* Down Beat

Giants of Jazz / i. Jul. 1982 / Time Life 19

Don't Sleep in the Subway / Verve

JAY HOGGARD

b. Sep. 24, 1954, New York, NY
Vibes / Modern creative

Jay Hoggard has a combined African, African-American, and American musical perspective in his approach to vibes, and sometimes plays in a swinging, relaxed and bluesy manner; other times, he increases his rhythmic pace and speed. Also, he has dabbled occasionally in fusion and jazz-rock, and in symphonic and classical music. Initially, Hoggard studied piano and saxophone, then switched to vibes. He had private studies with Lynn Oliver. Though he began at Wesleyan as a philosophy student, Hoggard transferred to the ethnomusicology department. He toured Europe in the early '70s with Jimmy Garrison and Clifford Thornton, and joined a group at Yale with Anthony Davis, Leo Smith, and Pheeroan AkLaff. During the mid '70s, Hoggard studied for a summer in Tanzania learning the balo, a West African xylophone. He taught at the Educational Center for the Arts in New Haven after graduating from Wesleyan, then moved to New York in 1977. He recorded with Chico Freeman in 1978, then did a more pop and fusion-oriented session the next year. Hoggard led his own groups and worked with Davis, Sam Rivers, Cecil Taylor, and James Newton, among others, in the '80s and '90s. He's recorded as a leader for India Navigation, GRP/Arista, Contemporary, and Muse. He has some sessions available on CD. —*Ron Wynn*

Solo Vibraphone / Nov. 18, 1978 / India Navigation 1040
The finest, most complete record released thus far by vibist Jay Hoggard. This solo date puts him alone in the spotlight, and he uses the vehicle to display his total skills, from delicate melodies to aggressive harmonies and expressive solos. —*Ron Wynn*

Rain Forest / Nov. 1980 / Contemporary

Riverside Dance / i. 1985 / India Navigation

Overview / **i.** Jun. 22, 1989 / Muse 5383

○ **Little Tiger, The** / **i.** Jun. 10, 1990 / Muse 5410

An album with the vibist at his best. The title track alone is worth the price. With Benny Green. —*Michael G. Nastos*

○ **Fountain, The** / **i.** 1992 / Muse 5450

The Fountain is a contemporary recording that pairs Jay Hoggard with virtuoso guitarist Kenny Burrell, and their vibes/guitar interplay is superb. Hoggard graces Burrell's *Guiding Spirit* CD and has appeared in concert with Burrell, as has the excellent rhythm section (James Weidman, Marcus McLaurine, and Yoron Israel). It's no surprise that it's a tight and swinging group. The program is rich and varied, showcasing Hoggard's facility with the full range of the tradition, with pieces from Ellington to Monk and Mingus, as well as the "freer" title track. —*Sid Gribetz*, Jazz Times

★ **Mystic Winds, Tropical Breezes** / India Navigation 1049

Strong, freewheeling date by vibist Jay Hoggard, done in the late '70s. He is working with a topflight group, including pianist Anthony Davis, bassist Cecil McBee, drummers Billy Hart and Don Moye, and Dwight Andrews on various saxophones. The compositions are loosely structured and extended, and solos are fierce. —*Ron Wynn*

BILLIE HOLIDAY (Eleanora Fagan)

b. Apr. 7, 1915, Baltimore, MD, **d.** Jul. 17, 1959, New York, NY

Vocals / Swing, big band, ballads & blues

If such a thing as a vocal jazz musician exists, then Billie Holiday rules as the greatest one of all time. She used her voice as an instrument, addressing lyrics, creating and constructing vocal solos, taking lyrics and extending, stretching, and turning them inside out. Her delivery, phrasing, and mannerisms were unique, though she cited Louis Armstrong constantly as a central influence. Holiday was a great singer of blues themes, though hardly a blues singer. She's been a role model to numerous generations of vocalists well outside, as well as inside, the jazz realm.

Holiday's childhood and what she did or did not suffer has been examined rigorously. It's known that her father abandoned the family, and didn't acknowledge Holiday's existence until she became a celebrity. Her mother moved to New York and left her in the care of relatives, whom Holiday said abused her. She sang in Harlem and Brooklyn nightclubs as a teen, and was discovered in Monette's by John Hammond. He arranged two recording sessions for her with Benny Goodman, and found her other engagements in New York clubs. Holiday began recording with studio bands under pianist Teddy Wilson's direction in 1935. These sessions, which continued until 1942, established her as a significant artist, and were among the period's finest. She and Lester Young began an unparalleled musical relationship in 1937, the ideal match of captivating vocalist and remarkable complementary saxophonist. He called her Lady Day, saying her mother must have been a duchess. She named him Prez (for the president). Her light, almost tiny, yet unforgettable voice and his floating, answering or caressing tenor lines were soon enormously popular. Even though they made these records mainly for the Black jukebox audience, the complete music community, particularly singers, was amazed and affected. Some early, ardent admirers included Mildred Bailey (despite some later ugly and ill-timed comments to the contrary), Frank Sinatra, Carmen McRae, and Lena Horne.

Holiday also sang with Count Basie's orchestra in the late '30s, then began working with Artie Shaw in 1938, becoming one of the first Black vocalists featured with a White band. But life on the road in general, and racist incidents in particular, soured her on that job. She began singing at the Cafe Society in 1939; the same year Holiday attracted national attention with the recording of "Strange Fruit" for Commodore. She cut it at Commodore because her employers at the former American Record Company, now a CBS firm, weren't interested in cutting Lewis Allen's anti-lynching song. Holiday eventually scored a two-sided hit, as the flip "Fine and Mellow," with Frankie Newton clicked. She recorded with Paul Whiteman in 1942, her last session be-

fore the musicians union recording ban. After the ban ended in 1944, Holiday began working with Milt Gabler, the former Commodore head now at Decca. He was very supportive, allowing her to do sessions with strings and getting the hit "Lover Man" in return. She began to specialize in slow, at times tortuous, songs about unrequited love or unsuccessful relationships, each sung so movingly they made the hopeless situation depicted even more unbearable. Holiday became a huge attraction; she even appeared in the 1946 film *New Orleans* with Kid Ory and Louis Armstrong, and made her first solo concert appearance at Town Hall.

But Holiday's life soon resembled the dire scenarios in her songs. She'd been introduced to opium by her first husband, James Monroe, and subsequently wound up on heroin. She beat the habit once, but was jailed in 1947, sentenced to a year in the Federal Reformatory for Women at Alderson. Her cabaret card was revoked, as New York City then had a law that would not allow anyone convicted of a felony to work in any establishment that served liquor. She made a triumphant appearance at Carnegie Hall in 1948, where she sang "Don't Explain," a number she'd cowritten with Andy Razaf. The concert was not only sold out, but Holiday did six encores in response to audience reaction.

Holiday's failures at romance have been well chronicled. Her involvement with Joe Guy has been cited as the initial vehicle for her addiction to heroin, which led to her first arrest. Then, while managing to get her jobs at New York clubs though she lacked a cabaret card, Joe Levy diluted the positive impact of that good deed by shorting Holiday on fees. She was arrested on the West Coast in 1949 while in his company. She got out of that situation, but then a tour with Red Norvo and Charles Mingus was a disaster. Levy left her stranded and broke in the mid '50s in the middle of a tour with Gerald Wilson; she made a short film with the Basie Sextet. Through these dispiriting incidents, Holiday kept working, though her voice and health began to crack under the strain.

She performed with Stan Getz at Storyville in 1951, recorded for Aladdin in 1952, then signed with Norman Granz's Verve label in 1953. She toured Europe in 1954 and made her first Newport Festival appearance, where she was surprised by a reunion with Lester Young. Then in 1956, Holiday was arrested once more, this time for drug possession in Philadelphia with Louis McKay. They got married while she was awaiting trial, but the relationship soured. Her trial was postponed indefinitely a year later, and she separated from McKay. Holiday appeared at the 1957 Newport Festival and played concerts in Central Park. She also participated in a landmark television program that year titled "The Sound of Jazz," with Young and several other friends. The album, *Lady in Satin,* appeared on Columbia in 1958, and is both shocking and unforgettable. Her vocal decline was unmistakable, yet she remained a compelling lyric interpreter.

After a European tour was canceled, Holiday became reclusive. She did appear at the first Monterey Festival, but not in good form or voice. In late 1958 and early 1959 she visited Europe, but got bad receptions in Italy and France. Holiday made a television appearance in England, then returned home again, going into virtual isolation. She attended Lester Young's funeral in March of 1959, played at Storyville in April, and went into a coma one month later, entering the hospital with liver and heart trouble. The final indignity came as Holiday lay on a hospital bed suffering from a kidney infection; the police came in to make an arrest for drug possession. Holiday was fingerprinted as she lay dying. By July, she was gone.

Holiday retrospectives, boxed sets, anthologies, and greatest hits packages are available everywhere. Columbia, Verve, and Decca all issued special packages within the last two years (the Columbia and Verve sets are multidisc). There are also many samplers, plus numerous import discs. Both the book *Lady Sings The Blues* and the film of the same name are good entertainment, but are historically worthless. John Chilton's *Billie Blues* is, thus far, the definitive portrait of a tragically magnificent American music great. —*Ron Wynn with William Ruhlman and Dan Morgenstern*

★ **Billie Holiday: The Legacy Box 1933-1958** / 1933-1958 / Columbia 47724
Most welcome; the best overview of her many fine Columbia sessions, from the very first to the last. Great sound quality, high-caliber booklet. —*Ron Wynn*

★ **Quintessential Billie Holiday—Vols. 1—9, The** / i. 1936-1942 / CBS
In-depth material on Columbia. Nine CDs. Excellent. —*Michael Erlewine*

★ **Billie Holiday (1939-1949)** / 1939-1949 /
A European import containing "Strange Fruit" and other recordings made around the same time. —*Bill Ruhlmann*

Billie's Blues / 1942-1954 / Blue Note 48786
1942 Capitol session and 1951 Aladdin session. Billie is a bit rough on the 1951 date. —*Hank Davis*

★ **Complete Decca Recordings** / i. 1944-1950 / GRP 601
An outstanding two-record set of Holiday's Decca cuts from the '40s and '50s. Some of her most pop-oriented dates, but a comprehensive collection with excellent remastering and annotation. —*Ron Wynn*

★ **Complete Billy Holiday on Verve, The** / i. 1945-1959 / Verve 833765
It took the earlier LP version of the 10-CD *The Complete Billie Holiday on Verve 1945-1959* to convince Buck Clayton, who performed with Holiday for both Columbia and Verve, that the Verve recordings were Holiday's greatest. After the 12-hour immersion required to hear this splendidly packaged collection of all-star studio sessions, concert recordings, and revealing rehearsal tapes, it is impossible not to agree. Norman Granz's genius in producing Holiday was returning her to the small-group context. Not only was she inspired by her collaborators, but she also had a minimal load on her shoulders. Granz was wise to surround her frequently with musicians she had known in better times, such as Clayton, Roy Eldridge, and others. The camaraderie of old friends and the energies of younger musicians such as Oscar Peterson, Barney Kessel, and Ray Brown provided the necessary spark for Holiday. —*Bill Shoemaker*, Down Beat

○ **Lady in Autumn: The Best of The Verve Years** / Apr. 1946-Mar. 1959 / Verve 849434
The Best of the Verve Years is a selection of 24 studio sides, plus 11 nondefinitive live takes on Holiday standards like "I Cover The Waterfront," "Strange Fruit," and a '58 "Lover Man." Most are from mid '40s JATP shows, have slightly wobbly sound, and do not measure up to the studio tracks where the sound is okay. In her final decade, Holiday sometimes sounded confident as ever and sometimes winded and pained, as on the barroom lament "One for My Baby," an unlikely vehicle she did not quite make her own. This is a standard, squat double-CD box, about twice as wide as it need be. —*Kevin Whitehead*, Down Beat

☆ **Billie Holiday Sings** / i. 1950 / Columbia 6129

☆ **Favorites** / i. 1950 / Columbia 6163

○ **Billie Holiday at Storyville** / Oct. 1951-Oct. 1953 / Black Lion 760921

Billie Holiday Songbook, The / i. 1952-1958 / Verve 823246
Here's an excellent anthology we've located, which also includes "Strange Fruit" in addition to "Lady Sings the Blues," "Billie's Blues," "Stormy Blues," and six others. Informative notes on each song; clear sound; we recommend this collection highly. —*Ladyslipper*

○ **Jazz at the Philharmonic** / i. 1954 / Clef 169

Lady Sings the Blues / i. 1954-1956 / Verve 833770
Immaculate 1954 and 1956 recordings with an all-star lineup and smashing Holiday cuts. One of her last great dates. CD has three bonus cuts. —*Ron Wynn*

All or Nothing at All / i. 1955 / Verve 827160

Songs for Distinguished Lovers / Jul. 1956 / PolyGram 815055
As was almost always the case, Billie Holiday makes each tune wonderfully hers. Add to this the wondrous backup from Harry "Sweets" Edison (tpt), Ben Webster (ts), and Barney Kessel (g) in particular, with Red Mitchell or Joe Mondragon on bass (Mondragon on some dates), Alvin Stoller or Larry Bunker on drums (Bunker on Jan. 8 cuts), and Jimmy Rowles (p). —*Bob Rusch*, Cadence

Embraceable You / i. Jan. 3-9, 1957 / Verve 817359
Two sessions in 1957. A good two-record set that leans toward ballads and moody material. It's been eclipsed a bit by recent anthologies. —*Ron Wynn*

★ **Lady in Satin** / 1958 / Columbia 40247
An unforgettable date, with Holiday clearly at the end of the line, yet still sounding hypnotic. —*Ron Wynn*

○ **Stay with Me** / i. 1959 / Verve 511523
A '91 reissue from late in vocalist Billie Holiday's career. She was fading but hadn't lost the dramatic quality in her delivery or her ability to project and tell a shattering story. She's backed by trumpeter Charlie Shavers, pianist Oscar Peterson, guitarist Herb Ellis, bassist Ray Brown, and drummer Ed Shaughnessy. The CD reissue has three bonus cuts. —*Ron Wynn*

Last Recordings / Mar. 1959 / Verve 835370
In many ways, a sad event. 1988 reissue of an album with Ray Ellis and his orchestra. It's poignant in a tragic way. —*Ron Wynn*

Story / i. 1959 / MCA 4006

Essential Billie Holiday, The / i. 1961 / Verve 8410

○ **Billie Holiday, Al Hibbler and the Blues** / i. 1962 / Imperial 9185

Commodore Recordings, The / i. 1965 / Mainstream 6000

○ **Giants of Jazz** / i. Mar. 1980 / Time Life 03
For reasons not cheerfully accepted by jazz purists, the Billie Holiday set on Time Life probably enjoyed wider currency than any other in this admirably conceived series. But despite the general public's long-demonstrated indifference to instrumental jazz, there can be no overlooking the consistently high quality of musicianship in this collection. It is not possible to even approach an understanding of this complex and changing artist unless one is first familiar with the entirety of her musical achievements. This set is only a prelude. The first selection in the album, quite logically, reflects Holiday's first experience in a recording studio. She was 18, nervous, and not yet solidified in her style, but she was still able to make her mark, albeit with the help of some never duly credited solo work by Benny Goodman and Jack Teagarden. Recorded less than two years later, the next three titles not only commemorate the beginning of her fruitful partnership with Teddy Wilson, but also reveal for the first time a new, assured woman and artist. When Holiday started recording under her own name one year after her first date under Wilson's leadership, a significant structural change was implemented that, as much as anything else, signaled her arrival as a star. Prior to the session that produced "No Regrets," "Summertime," and "Billie's Blues," Holiday always sang the second chorus much in the manner, if not the style, of band singers everywhere. But leading her own session, she found it just and proper that she should have first and last say on each side. Lester Young makes his first appearance on "This Year's Kisses," heralding the beginning of a musical relationship that to this day remains unmatched in the annals of jazz. Throughout the sides with Young, as well as elsewhere, one can derive an almost equal pleasure from the inspired trumpet work of Buck Clayton, while moments of incontestable superiority are also to be found in the periodic comments of Goodman, Johnny Hodges, Harry Carney, Buster Bailey, Artie Shaw, Charlie Shaver, Benny Morton, Ed Hall, and, of course, Teddy Wilson. —*Jack Sohmer*, Down Beat

☆ **I Like Jazz: The Essence of Billie Holiday** / i. Nov. 21, 1991 / Columbia 47917

○ **Billie's Blues** / i. Aug. 19, 1992 / Bulldog 1007

Golden Years—Vols. 1-2, The / CBS
A pair of three-album boxed sets that at one time were the standard for Holiday reissues. They've since been eclipsed by CD sets, but are still fine. —*Ron Wynn*

Lady Day / Columbia 637
A fine single-disc compilation that has five cuts with Lester Young (ts). —*Ron Wynn*

○ **God Bless the Child** / MCA 60003

☆ **Strange Fruit** / Atlantic 1614

Billie, Ella, Lena, Sarah! / CBS 36811
A collection which has been growing and changing since the release of "Ella, Lena and Billie" in 1956. Some of the most significant recordings by some of the greatest jazz singers ever. Includes Billie's "What a Little Moonlight Can Do," Ella's "My Melancholy Baby," Sarah's "East of the Sun (And West of the Moon)." —*Ladyslipper*

Billie Holiday Collection, The / Deja Vu 5018
Ten golden greats, including one of the very few currently-in-print issues of "Strange Fruit." This song, about lynching, was one of the most political and significant recordings ever made. It was banned officially from British airwaves by the BBC, and unofficially from U.S. radio; even today, it is almost always omitted from anthologies—except occasional European ones, like this release from Italy—to remind us how far our society hasn't come. —*Ladyslipper*

DAVE HOLLAND (David Holland)

b. Oct. 1, 1946, Wolverhampton, England
Bass / Early jazz-rock, modern creative
An amazing, versatile bassist, Dave Holland actually got his biggest break playing in a borderline jazz situation. He appeared on Miles Davis's enormously popular *Bitches Brew*, still one of the biggest-selling jazz albums ever made, and, at the time, a crossover sensation. Holland has been a bass master since the early '70s. His tone, speed, and clean, clear, precise lines are always controlled, yet intense. He's been successful working in combos, duos, large bands, and as a soloist, playing in extremely free or fusion styles. Holland's even done some fine bluegrass sessions. He began playing bass in his teens, and attended the Guildhall School of Music and Drama in London from 1964 to 1968. He played with John Surman, Chris McGregor, Humphrey Lyttelton, Evan Parker, Tubby Hayes, Ronnie Scott, Kenny Wheeler, and the Spontaneous Music Ensemble during this period, and recorded with Wheeler in 1968. He played with Miles Davis in the late '60s and early '70s, gradually phasing out his acoustic bass for an electric as Davis's music headed more in a funk/fusion direction. But in 1970 and 1971, he removed the upright from the closet and headed in a completely different direction, playing almost totally free music in the group Circle with Chick Corea, Anthony Braxton, and Barry Altschul. They made some extraordinary records, but the group had zero commercial potential, and they disbanded in 1971. He began playing cello in the early '70s along with bass. Holland maintained a musical relationship with Braxton until 1976, and made his own stunning record on ECM with Braxton, Sam Rivers, and Altschul in 1972 called *Conference of the Birds*. He worked with Stan Getz from 1973 to 1975, and was in John Abercrombie's trio, Gateway, along with Jack DeJohnette from 1975 to 1977. Holland played and recorded in the '70s with Karl Berger, Joe Henderson, Derek Bailey, Paul Bley, Wheeler, and Altschul, and with Sam Rivers from 1976 to 1980. Holland also issued solo bass and cello albums in the '70s. He formed his own band in 1982. At times, its personnel included Wheeler, Steve Coleman, Marvin Smith, Robin Eubanks, and Julian Priester. Holland's even participated in the hip-hop/jazz and "acid-jazz" furor of the late '80s and '90s, playing with Steve Coleman's Five Elements band. Holland made another solo cello album in 1988. He has a few titles available on CD,

and the magnificent *Conference of the Birds* has been reissued in digital glory. —*Ron Wynn and Myles Boisen*

○ **Music for Two Basses** / Feb. 15, 1971 / ECM 1011

★ **Conference of the Birds** / Nov. 30, 1972 / ECM 829373
This English bassist's finest hour. Definitive progressive music, with Sam Rivers (ts), Anthony Braxton (reeds), and Barry Altschul (d). —*Michael G. Nastos*

○ **Dave Holland—Vol. 1** / Feb. 18, 1976 / Improvising Artists 373848

○ **Dave Holland—Vol. 2** / Feb. 18, 1976 / Improvising Artists

★ **Emerald Tears** / Aug. 1977 / ECM 1109
Bassist Dave Holland's rich, varnished tone and throbbing percussive sensitivity are compounded with keen intelligence and a brooding streak of romantic melancholy. An anxious classicism haunts his somber constructions, but the buoyant pulse of his rhythmic imagination drives him through the abstract, often arid landscape of his intellect. Employing a full panoply of modern effects, Holland pursues his sober visions with masterful deftness and aplomb, occasionally bogging down with portentous weightiness on the bowed material. —*Larry Birnbaum*, Down Beat

Life Cycle / Nov. 1982 / ECM 829200
Wholly original cello solos in jazz and folk flavors. —*Myles Boisen*

Jumpin' In / Oct. 1983 / ECM 817437
On *Jumpin' In*, bassist Dave Holland's bucolic lyricism is most pronounced on "First Snow," a gliding midtempo vehicle for Kenny Wheeler's full-bodied flugelhorn, and on "Sunrise" in the solemn scoring for flute, trumpet, and trombone. Elsewhere, the bassist's consonance is underlined by his propulsive rhythms (drummer Steve Ellington also deserves credit) and his penchant for collective improvisation. Holland favors polyphonous transitions between themes and solos instead of a quick cut; this prompts absorbing banter among trumpeter Kenny Wheeler, alto saxophonist and flutist Steve Coleman, and trombonist Julian Priester on such spirited sprints as "You I Love" and the title composition. Holland's conversant unit gives the music the sharp, hot edge it requires. —*Bill Shoemaker*, Down Beat

☆ **Razor's Edge** / Oct. 1983-Feb. 1987 / ECM 833048
Brisk, edgy work with some top Young Lion types, notably Steve Coleman. —*Ron Wynn*

Seeds of Time / i. Nov. 1984 / ECM 825322
A long album, almost 60 minutes. Holland's group work is substantive. —*Michael G. Nastos*

Triplicate / Mar. 1988 / PolyGram 837113
Trio. The best setting for hearing Holland's bass mastery and compositional logic at work. —*Myles Boisen*

Extensions / Sep. 1989 / ECM 841778
Dave Holland Quartet with Kevin Eubanks (g). This was the 1990 *Down Beat* Critic's Album of the Year. Very good band/album music. Percussionist Smitty Smith is unreal. Recommended. —*Michael G. Nastos*

MAJOR HOLLEY (Major Quincy (Jr) Holley)

b. Jul. 10, 1924, Detroit, MI, **d.** Oct. 25, 1990
Bass / Swing, big band, bop
A fine bassist who's also gifted at accompanying his bowed playing with wordless, bluesy vocalisms, Major Holley was a busy session contributor since 1950. His combination bowing/vocals and his occasional addition of humorous lyrics are now quite familiar, and bolster his tremendous bass playing. Holley began on violin and tuba, then started on bass in the navy. He joined Dexter Gordon after his discharge, then played with Charlie Parker and Ella Fitzgerald before making his recording debut in a duo with Oscar Peterson. Holley moved to London to work as a studio musician with the British Broadcasting Company in the mid-'50s. He joined Woody Herman's orchestra for a South American tour in 1958, then returned to America and worked with the Al Cohn-Zoot Sims band in 1959 and 1960. Holley did many studio sessions in the '60s, and also played

with Kenny Burrell, Coleman Hawkins, and Duke Ellington. He was an instructor at Berklee from 1967 to 1970, then played in New York clubs, toured Europe with Helen Humes and the Kings of Jazz, and recorded with Roy Eldrige, Lee Konitz, and Roland Hanna. During the '80s, Holley made many appearances at European festivals. He recorded on the Black & Blue label as a leader in the mid '70s, and can be heard on CD reissues that feature the Cohn-Sims band, Woody Herman, Teddy Wilson, and Coleman Hawkins. — *Ron Wynn*

★ **Featuring Gerry Wiggins** / Black & Blue 233074

RED HOLLOWAY

b. 1927
Tenor and alto saxophone / Swing, bop, blues & jazz
An energetic, aggressive player with a bright, bluesy, and emphatic style, Red Holloway has played swing, blues, be-bop, and R&B during his lengthy career. His solos are effective, particularly when backing vocalists or on uptempo numbers, while his lyricism and facility are emphasized on ballads. Holloway's father and mother were musicians, and he began on piano. Like several other musicians, Holloway was a student at the legendary Du Sable high school in Chicago. His classmates included Johnny Griffin and Von Freeman. He started playing baritone, then switched to tenor. Holloway worked in Gene Wright's big band for three years before joining the army. He returned to Chicago after his discharge, and worked with Yusef Lateef and Dexter Gordon before joining Roosevelt Sykes's tour in 1948. He played with several blues musicians in the '50s and '60s, among them Willie Dixon, Junior Parker, Bobby "Blue" Bland, Lloyd Price, John Mayall, Muddy Waters, Chuck Berry, and B. B. King. Holloway then moved to New York for a short stay before returning to Chicago. Holloway toured with Lionel Hampton and "Brother" Jack McDuff in the mid '60s, while he also led his own bands. He resettled on the West Coast at the end of the '60s. Holloway teamed with Sonny Stitt in the late '70s, working with him frequently until Stitt's death in the early '80s. After that, Holloway returned to being a solo act, but also played with Jay McShann, Clark Terry, and Carmen McRae. Holloway's recorded several albums as a leader, and has backed jazz greats such as Billie Holiday, Ben Webster, Jimmy Rushing, Sonny Rollins, Red Rodney, Lester Young, and Wardell Gray, as well as the big band Juggernaut. Currently, he has a few dates available on CD. —*Ron Wynn*

Cookin' Together / Feb. 2, 1964 / Prestige 327
With the McDuff Quartet. A 1988 reissue of a textbook soul-jazz date. —*Ron Wynn*

Sax, Strings and Soul / Aug. 1964 / Prestige 7390

Nica's Dream / Jul. 1984 / Steeple Chase 1192

The Late Show—Vol. 2: Live at Maria's Memory Lane Supper Club / i. May 1986 / Fantasy 9655

★ **Locksmith Blues** / i. 1989 / Concord Jazz 4390
Gutbucket blues, stately show tunes, and high-caliber originals from a sextet co-led by two great musicians who don't try to impress anyone with their dexterity, yet dazzle with every effort. — *Ron Wynn*, Rock & Roll Disc

○ **The Early Show—Vol. 1: Blues in the Night** / Fantasy 9647

THE HOLLYDAY BROTHERS

Group / Hard bop
Christoper Hollyday's searing, hard-edged, and biting alto style reflects the influence of Charlie Parker and Phil Woods primarily, and the influence of Jackie McLean, but Hollyday has ripened and grown more into his own voice over the past few years. He began recording for RCA/Novus in the late '80s, and continued into the '90s. He's recorded with Wallace Roney, Cedar Walton, David Williams, Billy Higgins, Scott Coltney, Kenny Werner, Larry Goldings, John Clark, Mark Feldman, and several others. —*Ron Wynn*

★ **Oh, Brother** / i. Jun. 1987 / Jazzbeat 102

GROOVE HOLMES

b. 1931, **d.** 1991
Organ / Blues & jazz, soul-jazz
A great jazz organist, Groove Holmes taught himself to play the organ and developed a strongly swinging style with powerful bass lines and a superb harmonic and melodic edge. Holmes's style reflects his ability to play acoustic bass, and also shows the influence of saxophonists on his approach. He worked in local New Jersey clubs for a number of years. Holmes had successful albums with guests such as Les McCann, Ben Webster, Gene Ammons, and Clifford Scott (using the alias Joe Splink) in the early '60s. Though Holmes played well, these sessions got more exposure due to their illustrious guests. He did more trio settings in the mid '60s, and also got better quality recordings. Holmes scored a huge pop hit with his version of "Misty." His late '60s releases didn't yield hits or memorable efforts, while his early '70s sessions, particularly those with Jimmy McGriff in a pair of organ battles, were good. Holmes turned in several fine efforts from the late '70s on through the late '80s, often working with Houston Person. But Holmes also experimented with various electronic keyboards during the '70s on dates that are short of his best work. He recorded as a leader for Pacific Jazz (twice), Prestige, Groove Merchant, Muse, and Blue Note. Holmes has some sessions available on CD. — *Ron Wynn and Bob Porter*

ELMO HOPE ((St.) Elmo Sylvester Hope)

b. Jun. 27, 1923, New York, NY, **d.** May 19, 1967, New York, NY
Piano / Hard bop
Pianist Elmo Hope forged an original and interesting style with soul and blues influences. He studied classical piano in his youth, and his first major professional job came in R&B trumpeter Joe Morris's orchestra from 1948 to 1951. Hope recorded with him in 1948, and made his own recordings in New York as a leader in the '50s. These included both trio and quintet dates on Blue Note, and other sessions on Prestige with Frank Foster, John Coltrane, and Hank Mobley. Hope later recorded with HiFi Jazz in the late '50s. He worked with Sonny Rollins, Lou Donaldson, and Clifford Brown. Unfortunately, his drug problems led to the revocation of his cabaret card, which shut him out of the New York market. Hope toured with Chet Baker in the late '50s and relocated to Los Angeles. He recorded with Harold Land and Curtis Counce, then performed with Lionel Hampton at the Moulin Rouge. When he returned to New York in 1961, Hope recorded frequently, doing sessions for Riverside, Milestone, VSOP, and recording his last dates for Chiaroscuro and Inner City. He didn't make many public appearances in his final years. A decent number of Hope sessions have been reissued on CD. —*Ron Wynn*

○ **Elmo Hope Trio, The** / May 1953-Jun. 1953 / Contemporary 7620

Trio and Quintet / Jun. 1953-Oct. 1957 / Blue Note 84438
Although a year younger than his friend, Bud Powell was already an established star by the time pianist Elmo Hope made his first leader date, the one in 1953 that opens this album. Following heatedly upon the heels of his impressive contributions to the classic Lou Donaldson/Clifford Brown "10-inch LP," Hope was given this chance to prove his mettle in a trio setting with Percy Heath (b) and Philly Joe Jones (d). The results are fleshed out with an alternate take of "Mo Is On" and a previously unissued, surprisingly hip interpretation of Irving Berlin's rather unhip "It's A Lovely Day Today." One year later, Hope returned to record a quintet session, this time with Art Blakey in place of Jones and a front line composed of trumpeter Freeman Lee and Count Basie's new star tenorman, Frank Foster, who himself was fresh from cutting his own American debut leader date for Blue Note only four days earlier. His playing here is every bit as good as it is on that extremely rare album. Indeed, Foster approaches Hope's program of challenging bop originals with

such easy fluency that one would think that he had composed them rather than the pianist. An alternate take of "Crazy" is added to make the session complete. The album concludes with the three tracks that Hope recorded for Pacific Jazz in 1957 with Harold Land, Stu Williamson, Leroy Vinnegar and Frank Butler. —*Jack Sohmer,* Cadence

☆ **Elmo Hope—Vol. 2** / May 9, 1954 / Blue Note 5044

☆ **New Faces-New Sounds: Elmo Hope Quintet—Vol. 2** / May 9, 1954 / Blue Note 5044

○ **Elmo Hope Memorial Album, The** / Jul. 28, 1955 / Prestige 7675

★ **Hope Meets Foster** / Oct. 1955 / Prestige 1703
This, pianist Elmo Hope's second date as a leader for Prestige, is not one of his quirkier recordings; he plays in a fleet manner very much out of Bud Powell. Three tunes are by a quartet with Frank Foster (ts), John Ore (b), and Art Taylor (d) and three by a quintet with the addition of Foster's Wilberforce University bandmate, the accomplished if little-known trumpeter Freeman Lee. The standout here is "Georgia on My Mind," as it is played at an uncommonly brisk clip.... This is honest, hard-swinging music. —*Kevin Whitehead,* Cadence

Elmo Hope—Vol. 1 / Feb. 8, 1959 / Hi Fi 616

Homecoming / Jun. 22+29, 1961 / Original Jazz Classics 1810
Probing, introspective piano solos from Elmo Hope on this '61 date issued by Riverside. Hope was in a transitional phase, doing more solo dates and also experimenting with two-piano sessions and even electronics. —*Ron Wynn*

○ **High Hope** / 1961 / Beacon 401

Sounds from Riker's Island / Aug. 19, 1963 / Audio Fidelity 6119
Originally produced by vibist Walt Dickerson, this recording was intended to give some lesser-known musicians a chance to present their music to the public. But as it stands, except for pianist Elmo Hope and bassist Ronnie Boykins, none of the other players created anything of lasting beauty. It must be mentioned that tenor saxophonist John Gilmore has a good solo on "A Night In Tunisia," but he is not given much space. Thus, the two trio selections, "Three Silver Quarters" and "Kevin," come off the best. Most of the other tracks are relatively sloppy, and neither trumpeter Lawrence Johnson nor alto saxophonist Eddie Douglas is effective. —*Carl Brauer,* Cadence

Final Sessions—Vol. 1 / Mar. 8, 1966-May 9, 1966 / Specialty 1765
A 1991 reissue of the excellent two-record set that marked the last work of pianist Elmo Hope. —*Ron Wynn*

Final Sessions—Vol. 2 / Mar. 8, 1966-May 9, 1966 / Specialty 1766

○ **All Star Sessions, The** / Feb. 1977 / Fantasy 47037
Includes two sessions, in 1956 and 1961. A gathering of greats, supervised and sparked by Hope on piano. The list includes Coltrane (ts), Donald Byrd (tpt), and Jimmy Heath (sax). —*Ron Wynn*

CLAUDE HOPKINS (Claude Driskett Hopkins)

b. Aug. 24, 1903, Alexandria, VA, **d.** Feb. 19, 1984, New York, NY
Piano, bandleader / Swing, big band, blues & jazz
A rollicking pianist, arranger, and bandleader, Claude Hopkins was an exceptional musician who was underrated due to his success as a conductor and an arranger. He had extensive harmonic knowledge, was a fine melodic interpreter, and played energetic, joyous uptempo tunes and steady blues and ballads. His parents were on the faculty at Howard University, where he studied music and medicine and obtained his degree. Hopkins's bands included players such as Jabbo Smith, Vic Dickenson, and Edmond Hall. He played with Wilber Sweatman in the '30s. Sweatman then led the band that accompanied Josephine Baker on her European tour in the mid-'20s. Hopkins led bands in New

Jersey, New York, and Washington, D.C., then took over the Charlie Skeet band in 1930. The band was featured at the Savoy and Roseland ballrooms, and at the Cotton Club. They also appeared in the films *Dance Team, Wayward, Barber Shop Blues,* and *Broadway Highlights* in the '30s. Orlando Robertsons's vocal on "Trees" turned the song into a huge hit. Hopkins disbanded the orchestra in 1940, and moved to the West Coast. He divided his time between conducting and arranging. He returned to New York in the mid-'40s and formed another band that played at the Zanzibar club. During the '50s, Hopkins led a combo in Boston, then went back to New York and the Zanzibar club in 1951. He worked with groups led by Henry "Red" Allen, Wild Bill Davison, and others. During the '70s, Hopkins made records on the Chiaroscuro and Sackville labels. Currently, there are reissued sessions for Swing Classics and Jazz Archives on CD. —*Ron Wynn*

○ **Singin' in the Rain** / Oct. 18, 1935 / Jazz Archives 27
The Claude Hopkins orchestra's light textures and even-handed attack are tailored for dancing. Solo strength is minor save for Hopkins, whose virtuosity exceeds his originality. His quaint swing has little of the power of Fletcher Henderson or the surprise of Earl Hines and none of the writing innovation of Benny Carter or Duke Ellington. Its pleasant dated sound is strictly for specialists of Harlem, 1935. —*John McDonough,* Down Beat

★ **Soliloquy** / May 13, 1972 / Sackville 3004

FRED HOPKINS

b. 1947
Bass / Hard bop, modern creative
An excellent bassist best known as part of the trios Air and New Air, Fred Hopkins has been a versatile and flexible player who's participated in numerous sessions. His big sound, steady pace, and ability to work with soloists, to help drive or pace a band, and to provide resourceful, exciting solos when necessary have kept him among the bass elite. He's also the consummate contributor; currently, he doesn't have any albums as a leader under his name, though, as a composer, he was a vital contributor to Air and New Air. Hopkins began playing bass as a student at the famed Du Sable High School in Chicago. He joined the Association for the Advancement of Creative Musicians in the late '60s, then played and recorded with Kalaparusha Maurice McIntyre in 1970. Hopkins, Steve McCall, and Henry Threadgill teamed in the trio Reflection, initially to play some Scott Joplin compositions for a concert. They remained together in 1971 and 1972, then they disbanded and McCall went to Europe. Hopkins studied with classical bassist Joseph Guastafeste of the Chicago Symphony Orchestra for three years, while Hopkins also worked in Chicago clubs. He moved to New York in 1975, and rejoined Threadgill and McCall, forming Air. This trio remained together until 1982, when McCall departed. They continued until the mid-'80s as New Air, with Hopkins working alongside Threadgill and Pheeroan AkLaff at first, then with Andrew Cyrille. Air recorded for Nessa, Arista, India Navigation, and Black Saint in the '70s and '80s. Hopkins has also recorded and played with Anthony Braxton and Marion Brown, and with Oliver Lake, David Murray, Hamiet Bluiett, Bobby McFerrin, The World Bass Violin Ensemble, and Craig Harris. He's been part of several Arthur Blythe bands in the '80s and '90s, and continues to work actively with various bands. —*Ron Wynn*

PAUL HORN

b. Mar. 17, 1930, New York, NY
Flute, clarinet, saxophone / World fusion, new age
A classically trained flutist who later emerged as a jazz musician and an environmentalist, Horn, in recent years, has been labelling his material "universal" music. He's recorded sounds made by killer whales, and has taught Transcendental Meditation. His soothing, very lyrical flute reflects his best playing, and though the flute is his finest instrument, he's also a competent tenor saxophonist. Horn's

most jazz-oriented work was done early in his career, and he's done more chamber, new age/ambient, and mood material in recent years than improvisational fare.

Horn started on piano at age four and began playing saxophone at age 12. He studied flute at Oberlin College Conservatory and earned his Bachelor's degree there, then earned a Master's degree at Manhattan School of Music, both in the early '50s. He joined the Sauter-Finegan Orchestra as a tenor saxophone soloist. Horn played in Chico Hamilton's group in the late '50s, then moved into studio work in Hollywood. He won two Grammy awards for his "Jazz Suite on the Mass Texts" in 1965 serving as principal soloist in Lalo Schifrin's band. Horn also played with Tony Bennett in 1966, but departed America for India in 1967 after becoming dissatisfied with commercial music and the Hollywood lifestyle.

He studied Transcendental Meditation (TM) with Maharishi Mahesh Yogi (also the Beatles's guru) and later became a TM teacher. While in India, Horn recorded unaccompanied flute solos in the Taj Mahal at Agra, exploiting the building's famous acoustic properties that provided reverberation time of almost 30 seconds. This album was one of the cornerstones of the then embryonic new age music movement. Horn later recorded in the Great Pyramid of Egypt and in the cathedrals of the former Soviet Union. He collaborated with musicians from China, India, and the Middle East.

In 1970, Horn moved to an island near Victoria, British Columbia, and formed his own quintet. He also had a weekly television show and wrote film scores for the Canadian National Film Board; the Board gave him an award for his music to *Island Eden.* He began his own label in 1981 and has continued performing into the '90s. Horn's recorded as a leader for Epic, RCA, Ovation, Island, Rare Bid, Prestige, Lost Lake Arts, Black Sun, Kuckuck, and his own Golden Flute label. He has many sessions available as a leader. *—Ron Wynn and Linda Kohanov*

Inside the Great Pyramid / i. 1976 / Kuckuck 11060
The flutist continues his travels, arriving in Egypt to record in the Great Pyramid of Giza. The double-CD set features a powerful introspective suite of 40 spontaneously composed "psalms" created by Horn on piccolo, alto, and C flutes. — *Linda Kohanov*

China / i. 1983 / Kuckuck 11080
An exquisite collaboration between Horn and Chinese multi-instrumentalist David Mingyue Liang that captures the timeless elegance of Oriental music. —*Linda Kohanov*

○ **Traveler** / i. 1985 / Kuckuck 11086
Originally released in 1987, this album is a striking summation of Horn's many talents. Reverberant solo instrumental episodes are complemented by evocative original compositions involving synthesizers, a string quartet, even a boys' choir. —*Linda Kohanov*

☆ **Peace Album, The** / i. 1988 / Kuckuck 11083
This holiday release from 1988 is by one of the greatest flutists of our time. The exquisite elegance of the music comes partly from the uniquely conceived "multiflute orchestra," in which Horn is the only musician, adding unusual depth and dimension to the performances of these pieces, ranging from "Silent Night" and "We Three Kings" to "Ave Maria." This Celestial Harmonies release is dedicated to the peace inside each one of us and offers sterling performances throughout. *—Backroads Music/Heartbeats*

Nomad / i. 1990 / Kuckuck 11087
A collection of pieces from eight of Horn's albums, including *Inside the Cathedral, The Peace Album, In Concert, China,* and *Traveler,* among others. —*Linda Kohanov*

★ **Inside the Taj Mahal 2** / i. 1991 / Kuckuck 11085
Horn's most influential album was captured when Horn slipped into the Taj Mahal one night with his flute and a tape recorder. The resulting set of spontaneous solo flute improvisations took full advantage of the magical resonances of India's famous monument. Each tone Horn plays

hangs suspended in space for 28 seconds, and the acoustics are so perfect you can't tell when the original sound stops and the echo takes over. *—Linda Kohanov*

SHIRLEY HORN

b. May 1, 1934, Washington, DC
Vocals, piano, bandleader / Bop, ballads & blues
It's taken a long time, but pianist/vocalist Shirley Horn is finally enjoying the fruits of stardom she should have reaped many years ago. Though she was praised and assisted back in the '60s by Miles Davis, Quincy Jones, and many others, Horn was unknown to even much of the jazz audience until the late '80s. Her understated, subtle yet engaging and harmonically ambitious playing, coupled with her equally capable, delightful vocals, have gained widespread attention. Horn began playing piano at age four, and studied music at Howard University. She started a trio in the mid-'50s, and began recording in the early '60s. Horn did swing and bebop material, recorded with trios, combos, and even made a session with a large orchestra conducted by Jones. But it was a 1987 live date for Verve that proved Horn's breakthrough album. Since then, she's made several acclaimed sessions as a pianist and vocalist, each one getting rave reviews and most also making *Billboard*'s jazz charts. Her '93 release, *Light Out of Darkness,* was a Top-10 seller on the jazz charts. She's recorded for Mercury, Steeplechase, Audiophile, and Verve, among others. Horn has several dates available on CD. — *Ron Wynn*

Live at the Village Vanguard / i. 1961 / CAM-AM
This one is very hard to find. Her first album, it established her skills. —*Ron Wynn*

Loads of Love / i. May 1963 / PolyGram 843454

Travelin' Light / 1965 / Paramount 538

Lazy Afternoon, A / Jul. 9, 1978 / Steeple Chase
Shirley Horn comes up all aces in all categories on *A Lazy Afternoon.* Her sincere, jazz-inflected voice has a delicious purr, her choice of tunes is exemplary, and the spare accompaniment of her own piano, with bassist Buster Williams and drummer Billy Hart, is exquisite. Her dusky, tumbleweed voice is not an emotional one but one that seems to know and can express heartbreak. Her reading of "Why Did I Choose You" is touching and serene, and her workout of the title tune is appropriately humid and sticky, taken at the tempo of a caterpillar crawl. Horn works best in ballad tempo, but her upbeat numbers are solid and display an excellent jazzman's (pardon the expression) use of tempo. — *Lee Jeske,* Down Beat

Garden of the Blues / Nov. 16, 1984 / Steeple Chase

★ **I Thought About You** / 1987 / Verve 833235
The art of comping behind oneself requires a combination of rare skills in a singer/pianist: an unerring sense of time, the ability to fill gaps without disturbing the lyrical flow, and intense concentration. Shirley Horn has mastered the dual role so effectively that she is able to lay back and play "catch up" with herself vocally, reharmonize what she plays creatively, and at times swing so confidently that she manages to goose her rhythm section. It can all be heard on her album *I Thought About You.* The vocal tricks and the freewheeling swing seem to come automatically. The best example of all levels working is "Our Love Is Here To Stay." From the second chorus on, she builds the momentum the way an instrumentalist does when the shackles of the polite, two-beat opening chorus are removed. Incidentally, when she removes her own vocal restraints, as on "Isn't It Romantic," Horn shows she can hold her own against about any combo pianist on the scene today. But "Isn't It Romantic" is the only pure instrumental. Horn is out to sell her voice, and she does it with class and taste. Among the highlights are the moody "Summer (Estate)" which she half talks and half sings with a Nina Simone introspection and "Nice 'N' Easy," taken exactly as the title implies but with her own idea of the changes. She puts "Killer Joe"-type Charleston jabs behind the witty lyrics of "The Great City," and as for the title

tune, she gives it a highly personal treatment, building to a dramatic climax. That tune in particular and the whole album in general is a primer for any lounge singer trying to accompany herself with imagination. —*Harvey Siders*, Jazz Times

Close Enough for Love / Nov. 1988 / Verve 837933
A wonderful release from a surely underrated singer/pianist. CD has two bonus cuts. —*Ron Wynn*

★ **You Won't Forget Me** / Jun. 1990-Aug. 1990 / Verve 847482
The set that finally got her some attention. Miles Davis (tpt) and Wynton (tpt) and Branford Marsalis (ts) are part of the guest cast. Great piano and delightful vocals. —*Ron Wynn*

Here's to Life / i. 1992 / Verve 511879
Recent release by Washington, D.C.-based pianist and vocalist Shirley Horn, who was a local legend for many years but couldn't get any recognition even within jazz circles. This album includes a guest appearance by Wynton Marsalis, plus her regular accompanists Charles Ables and Steve Williams, and she's also backed by a string orchestra. —*Ron Wynn*

LENA HORNE

b. Jun. 30, 1917
Vocals, actress / Swing, big band, ballads & blues
There's so much furor, much of it deserved, over Lena Horne's ageless beauty, that her musical importance has either been obscured or accepted as a given. Her Broadway shows and cast albums have gotten enormous attention. The lion's share of press about her has been devoted to reminiscences about *Stormy Weather*, and to the problems of light-skinned African-American actresses. Horne was a fine, jazz-influenced vocalist who made many outstanding recordings in the swing era. For many years after, she was a solid interpreter of standards and effective with bluesy (though not straight blues) material. She's triumphed as a stylish theatrical performer, a periodic television and film actress, and as a survivor whose prominence as a cultural symbol almost renders the question of her music moot. Horne was performing at age 6, and became a professional singer and dancer at the Cotton Club in 1934. She toured and recorded with Noble Sissle in 1935 and 1936, and was featured in the revue "Blackbirds" during 1939 and 1940. Horne began recording with Teddy Wilson's combos in the '30s, then joined Charlie Barnet's orchestra in 1940 and 1941. She became a favorite in clubs while smashing racial barriers, recording with Barnet and Artie Shaw. Then her film career exploded.

She was featured in *Panama Hattie, Cabin in the Sky, Stormy Weather, Thousands Cheer, I Dood It*, and *Swing Fever* in 1942 and 1943. Between 1944 and 1956, there were several other films, among them *Broadway Rhythm, Two Girls*, and *Words and Music*. Entire books have been devoted to the impact of Horne's roles and to her struggles with stereotyping and rejection on both sides of the color line. She became active on the stage in the '50s, appearing on Broadway in *Jamaica* from 1957 to 1959, and making extensive European tours. But she revived her musical career in the late '50s, recording everything from live sessions to blues-oriented dates, a Porgy and Bess album with Harry Belafonte, and cabaret and supper club fare. She expanded her musical repertoire in the '60s and '70s, making Latin material and doing more cast albums. She published a second autobiography (the first had been released in 1950) and had an extremely successful collaboration with Gabor Szabo in the early '70s. After enduring many professional and personal traumas, Lena Horne emerged triumphant in 1981 with the acclaimed one-woman Broadway show and cast album *The Lady and her Music*. She remains a dignified, outspoken performer whose early musical contributions are now being illuminated through reissues. —*Ron Wynn and Bill Dahl*

★ **Stormy Weather: The Legendary Lena (1941-1958)** /
    1941-1958 / Bluebird 9985

A wonderful anthology covering her '40s and '50s show tunes, blues, and ballads. —*Ron Wynn*

Lena Goes Latin / 1963 / DRG 510
Vintage Lena Horne set from early '60s, with backing from the Lennie Layton Orchestra. Horne makes nice adjustment to Latin tempos and rhythms, though there's lots of show biz touches and flourishes as well. She isn't really doing traditional Latin material, more Latinized pop, but she does it with distinction. —*Ron Wynn*

Men in My Life / i. 1967 / Three Cherries 64411

Lena & Gabor / Oct. 11, 1969 / Gryphon 908
Collaboration between Horne and guitarist Gabor Szabo, who proved one of her most sympathetic accompanists. They make expert duo recordings, with Szabo's delicate, sometimes emphatic playing smoothly accompanying the distinctive Horne vocals. The '69 session has been reissued on CD. —*Ron Wynn*

At Long Last Lena / i. Jul. 1, 1992 / RCA 66021
The most recent Lena Horne reissue, a package of standards and ballads that showcase her less jazz-oriented side. —*Ron Wynn*

★ **Live on Broadway (Lena Horne: The Lady & Her Music)** /
    Qwest 3597
A triumphant cast album from 1981 that effectively captures Lena Horne's acclaimed one-woman Broadway show on a two-record set. The album serves both as a vinyl autobiography and also as a centerpiece to document her rise to symbolic importance for Black performers. —*Ron Wynn*

WAYNE HORVITZ

Piano, keyboards / Modern creative
Pianist and keyboardist Wayne Horvitz has performed and recorded with many major names in free and new music circles, among them William Parker, Butch Morris, John Zorn, and Robert Previte. He's an unpredictable, often intriguing soloist, whose playing ranges from intense, uptempo statements to introspective accompaniment and backgrounds. Horvitz has recorded for Black Saint, Sound Aspects, and Elektra/Nonesuch in the early '80s and '90s. He also teamed with Zorn on various projects with Zorn's Naked City band, and with Bobby Previte and J.F. Jenny-Clark in the Sonny Clark Memorial quartet, a repertory session for Black Saint. Horvitz has several dates available on CD. —*Ron Wynn*

GEORGE HOWARD

Saxophone / Instrumental pop
George Howard is another top instrumental pop and fusion saxophonist, and one of the big sellers of the '80s and '90s. At one time, Howard was on the TBA division of the now defunct Palo Alto label. His thin, light riffs have been heard on several releases for MCA and GRP. Howard does instrumental covers of top urban contemporary and R&B tunes, and his music is heavily produced. It features background vocalists, a dominant backbeat, and minimal improvisation. He has several releases available on CD. —*Ron Wynn*

Do I Ever Cross Your Mind? / i. 1992 / GRP 9669
Unlike most of the soprano blowers out there in the pop-jazz market, Howard avoids the "Fuzak" plague, and keeps a stronghold on his R&B roots. At the same time, Howard's latest stays away from the vocal-dominated tracks, which pop up all the more frequently in this genre. A solid, masterful set of funk-fusion. —*Steve Aldrich*

FREDDIE HUBBARD (Frederick Dewayne Hubbard)

b. Apr. 7, 1938, Indianapolis, IN
Trumpet, flugelhorn, piano, composer / Hard bop
Only occasional lapses in taste and material mar the otherwise glorious reputation and record of Freddie Hubbard, a perennial jazz giant. Hubbard got his start playing with the Montgomery Brothers in Indianapolis, and at a Chicago club with Bunky Green, Frank Strozier, and Booker Little. Hubbard moved to New York in the late '50s and roomed

with Eric Dolphy for 18 months. He worked with Sonny Rollins, Slide Hampton, J.J. Johnson, and Quincy Jones from 1959-1961, when he joined Art Blakey's Jazz Messengers. This stint earned Hubbard widespread recognition, a *Down Beat* New Star award in 1961, and validation of his driving, high-note, and often acrobatic trumpet style. His work with Blakey, his freelance appearances on a host of '60s gems, from Ornette Coleman's *Free Jazz* to Coltrane's *Ascension,* and his own releases show Hubbard's other trumpet gifts. These include a wonderful full tone, extensive range in the upper register and overblowing effects, the ability to play with distinction in structured or free situations, and a dynamic, individualistic approach. Hubbard became a crossover star of sorts in the '70s. His albums, *Red Clay* and *Straight Life,* sold well outside the jazz world and his 1972 album, *First Light,* won a Grammy. Hubbard flirted for a while with fusion and jazz-rock, but he was largely unsuccessful from both an artistic and a financial standpoint. Hubbard reunited with Herbie Hancock, Wayne Shorter, Ron Carter, and Tony Williams in 1977. Calling themselves VSOP, the band had an acclaimed worldwide tour and an equally praised recording. Hubbard was also part of the relaunching of Blue Note Records in 1985. The bulk of his releases in the late '70s and throughout the '80s and '90s have been in the mainstream or hard-bop tradition, though they haven't been on the cutting edge the way his '60s releases were. Hubbard has many sessions available on CD. —*Ron Wynn*

Open Sesame / Jul. 1960 / Blue Note 84040

Hub Cap / Apr. 9, 1961 / Blue Note 84073

★ **Artistry of Freddie Hubbard** / Jul. 2, 1962 / MCA 33111
A misleading title, but a good attempt to compile Hubbard's best cuts from his '60s stint on Impulse. —*Ron Wynn*

○ **Caravan** / Jul. 2, 1962 / Impulse 27

★ **Hub-Tones** / Oct. 10, 1962 / Blue Note 84115

Here to Stay / Dec. 27, 1962 / Blue Note 84135
Half of this package is the long-overdue reissuance of Freddie Hubbard's 1961 classic *Hub Cap,* a work whose intensity paralleled the same blues trail Miles Davis was embarking on and whose instrumentation and break patterns acknowledge a debt to the Jazz Messengers. But Hubbard's hard bop verve rules here in the debut of a 1962 quintet session with saxophonist Wayne Shorter, drummer Philly Joe Jones, pianist Cedar Walton, and bassist Reggie Workman. Hubbard's supple tone, melodic intuitiveness, and interactive capacity point to one of the brightest potentials in the history of jazz trumpeting. —*Mikal Gilmore,* Down Beat

○ **Body and Soul** / Mar. 8+11, 1963 / Impulse 38

Breaking Point / May 7, 1964 / Blue Note 84172
A 1991 reissue. This is prototype Blue Note, with James Spaulding (as) in full gear. —*Ron Wynn*

Blue Spirits / i. Feb. 19-26, 1965 / Blue Note 46545

Night of the Cookers: Live at Club La Marchal–Vols. 1 & 2, The / Apr. 9-10, 1965 / Blue Note
This is an album with Hubbard in the midst of his free-wheeling Blue Note phase. —*Ron Wynn*

Backlash / Oct. 19+24, 1966 / Atlantic 90466
A 1986 reissue of a fine Atlantic date, with none of his stylistic excesses. James Spaulding (as) is fine. —*Ron Wynn*

Black Angel, The / May 16, 1969 / Atlantic 1549

○ **Hub of Hubbard, The** / Dec. 9, 1969 / MPS 15267
Trumpeter Freddie Hubbard had a short stay on Verve Records during the '60s. The songs on this disc are taken from a quintet he led and recorded with in the late '60s. Hubbard works with pianist Roland Hanna, tenor and clarinetist Eddie Daniels, bassist Richard Davis, and drummer Louis Hayes. The date was tightly and professionally produced, and performances are good. —*Ron Wynn*

★ **Red Clay** / Jan. 27+29, 1970 / CBS 40809
With his most well-known composition, it stands the test of time. Done with Joe Henderson (ts). —*Michael G. Nastos*

★ **Straight Life** / Nov. 16, 1970 / CTI 8022

The second of his two best early '70s releases. Joe Henderson (ts) is amazing and Hubbard is in top form, plus George Benson (g). —*Ron Wynn*

Sing Me a Song of Songmy / Jan. 21, 1971 / Atlantic 50235
Intriguing, experimental, sometimes pedantic. Protest lyrics, choir, strings, and electronics. —*Ron Wynn*

○ **First Light** / Sep. 1971 / CBS 40687
This is overarranged (as is usual with CTI), but has wonderful Hubbard solos. —*Ron Wynn*

High Energy / Apr. 29, 1974-May 2, 1974 / Blue Note 80478
High Energy was released almost simultaneously with Freddie Hubbard's final CTI album, a reissue of sides entitled *The Baddest Hubbard.* Compared to the earlier sides, Hubbard seemed to be moving more in the direction of Herbie Hancock's then-recent (1975) work, like the music composed for the film *Death Wish.* Hubbard's use of a large band and heavily orchestrated parts is interesting, especially since the entire LP is recorded "live" without overdubs or effects. "Crisis," for example, sounds similiar to many earlier Hubbard compositions with its medium-tempo and sharp horn riffs. George Cables contributes two fine tunes, "Camel Rise" and "Ebony Moonbeams," the latter a kind of samba-ballad. "Camel Rise" is a nice melodic statement, skillfully enhanced by the orchestrated embellishments. On Stevie Wonder's "Too High," Hubbard takes his biggest steps toward the future. The soloing is opened up, the rhythm undulates more like a Miles Davis LP, a feeling underlined by the wah-wah guitar of Dean Parks and the electronic sounds of the ARP. —*Eric Kriss,* Down Beat

Super Blue / 1978 / Columbia 82866
On the title cut, Ron Carter lays down a funky backbeat on a phase-shifted bass as the horns announce the gentle bluesy theme. It's on the jump numbers "Take It to The Ozone" and "Theme for Kareem" that the listener hears the energy and sincerity of Freddie Hubbard. The stop-and-go theme on "Take It to The Ozone" is redolent of pianist Lamont Johnson's composition "Big Ben's Voice" (from Jackie McLean's '60s recording 'Bout Soul). There's a furious immediacy to Jack DeJohnette's drum breaks and the elastic bass lines of Ron Carter. Kenny Barron (p) is the first to tackle the obstacle course and he builds bright single lines and ringing blues chords into a fine solo. Hubbard follows with a galloping solo: short vulcanized bursts of brass leading to sinuous lines and volleys of notes, concluding in a seam-splitting scream. Joe Henderson's solo reaffirms the conviction that he is one of the great tenor saxophone stylists of our time; his tone is burnished and musical, and he has a loping lyrical conception. Freddie Hubbard the improviser is well represented by *Super Blue.* —*Chip Stern,* Down Beat

Live at the North Sea Jazz Festival / Jul. 12, 1980 / Pablo 113
Triumphant, rousing playing despite lifeless sound production on the recording. —*Ron Wynn*

○ **Live at The Hague (1980)** / 1980 / Pablo 2620113

Little Night Music, A / Nov. 29, 1981 / Fantasy 9626
This date at San Francisco's Keystone Korner with trumpeter Freddie Hubbard's working rhythm section at the time is sturdy but not exciting. Billy Childs comps alertly, his solos are workmanlike, and his incessant chording under Bobby Hutcherson's (chronically) undermiked vibes is gratuitous. The general flow of the music is a little lumpy, like gravy with more flour than juice. But the meat-and-potatoes men out front (catch tenor saxophonist Joe Henderson on "Bird Like" and Hubbard skydiving) still make it a platter fit for famished ears. —*Fred Bouchard,* Down Beat

Born to Be Blue / Dec. 14, 1981 / Pablo 734

Face to Face / May 24, 1982 / Pablo 2310-876
A fine collaboration with Oscar Peterson (p). Neither allows his stylistic excesses to ruin the music. —*Ron Wynn*

Back to Birdland / i. Aug. 1982 / Real Time 305

○ **Sweet Return** / Jun. 13-14, 1983 / Atlantic 80108

Sweet Return is another all-star session, but what a difference! This band, assembled by George Wein to play festival dates in 1983, is simply outstanding. They spur Freddie Hubbard into some of his most inspired and meaningful playing in years, and the result is his best album since *Super Blue* (1978). The key to the success of this album is pianist Joanne Brackeen. She is a vital creative force, and her playing is consistently clear, precise, and devoid of cliches. Bassist Eddie Gomez is familiar with Brackeen's style, having worked extensively with her, and he meshes confidently with her sometimes unorthodox approach. Drummer Haynes, always tasteful, maintains a solid cook and balances Gomez's tendency to rush headlong through the tunes. Lew Tabackin (ts), although he seems like the odd man out in this grouping, is an effective foil for Hubbard. Rather than meeting him head-on (as Joe Henderson might) he works around him. His contrapuntal lines on "Whistling Away The Dark" and "The Night Has A Thousand Eyes" are particularly effective. —*Jim Roberts*, Down Beat

★ **Double Take** / Nov. 21, 1985 / Blue Note 7462942
Other than their joint appearance as sidemen on Benny Golson's *Time Speaks* in 1983, Freddie Hubbard and Woody Shaw had never recorded together before *Double Take*. Because they have similiar sounds and Hubbard preceded Shaw to the jazz major leagues by a few years, Shaw was often unfairly tagged as "Hubbard imitator" in his early years, but actually, due to Hubbard's excursion into commercialism on his Columbia releases, Shaw has had a more consistent career. At this point (1986) in their evolution, Hubbard still gets the edge (his range is wider and he cannot be surpassed technically). Although Shaw tends to play more harmonically sophisticated lines and is remarkably inventive, they are both trumpet masters. Their meeting on *Double Take* is more of a collaboration than a trumpet battle; in fact, the brass giants only trade off briefly on "Lotus Blossom." Each of the tunes is associated with different trumpeters and there are many fine moments from the soloists, particularly on the ballad features (Hubbard's heartfelt "Lament for Booker" and Shaw's "Just a Ballad for Woody.") About the only weak points are that some of the selections would have benefited from longer solos (especially "Sandu" and "Boperation") and altoist Kenny Garrett is sometimes utilized merely as a bridge between trumpeters. —*Scott Yanow*, Cadence

Eternal Triangle with Woody Shaw / Jun. 1987 / Blue Note 48017

Life Flight / i. 1987 / Blue Note 46898

○ **A Hub of Hubbard** / i. 1988 / Polydor 8259562

☆ **Bolivia** / Dec. 1990-Jan. 1991 / Music Masters 5063
A set with good contributions by Ralph Moore (ts), Cedar Walton (p), and Billy Higgins (d). —*Ron Wynn*

○ **Live at Fat Tuesday** / i. 1991 / Music Masters 65075
Recent live date for trumpeter Freddie Hubbard, cut at Fat Tuesday's nightclub in New York. He's got a super group on this session, with pianist Bennie Green, bassist Christian McBride, drummer Tony Reedus, and excellent saxophonist Javon Jackson. The songs are peformed with enthusiasm and solos are torrid. —*Ron Wynn*

HELEN HUMES

b. Jun. 23, 1913, Louisville, KY, **d.** Sep. 9, 1981, Santa Monica, CA

Vocals / Swing, big band, blues & jazz, ballads & blues
Helen Humes was, at various times, a robust, raw blues shouter and a sophisticated, swinging jazz vocalist. She cut songs in vintage style, and made others for jukeboxes. Humes had a high, strong, and dynamic voice, which she adapted to any situation. Humes played piano and organ in church during childhood, and played in the band at the Booker T. Washington Community Center with Jonah Jones and Dicky Wells. She started singing blues for Okeh at age 13 while still in school. She joined the Al Sears band on a trip to Buffalo, then became a permanent member in 1937.

Humes recorded with Harry James in 1937 and 1938, and became another Black artist who broke the color barrier in recording.

Count Basie heard her singing at a club in Cincinnati, and Humes replaced Billie Holiday in his band in 1938. During her three-year tenure, she became known for ballads and pop material. Such songs as "Dark Rapture," "If I Could Be with You One Hour Tonight," "Bolero at the Savoy," and "Between the Devil and the Deep Blue Sea" were some of the smash hits Humes enjoyed while singing with Basie. After leaving his orchestra, she worked in New York clubs from 1941 to 1943. Humes toured with Clarence Love in 1943 and 1944, then moved to Los Angeles. She mixed Jazz at the Philharmonic tours with solo dates.

Humes had a huge jump blues hit in 1945 with Bill Doggett's "Be-ba-ba-le-ba." This enabled her to tap the growing R&B market, and she recorded for Aladdin, Modern, Decca, and Mercury into the early '50s, scoring several hits, notably "Million Dollar Secret" in 1950. Humes sang with Red Norvo in the mid-'50s, and toured Australia in 1956. She contributed songs to the soundtracks for the films *Panic in the Streets* and *My Blue Heaven,* and performed in Hawaii in 1951 and 1952. She was featured in the 1955 syndicated television film *Showtime at the Apollo* with Basie, and was in the show *It's Great to be Alive in Los Angeles* in 1957. Humes sang at the 1959 Newport Jazz Festival. Humes was so beloved in Australia that she made two more appearances there, the last one in 1964. She decided to stay awhile and remained there for ten months. When her mother died in 1967, Humes ended an extensive slate of tours around the world and retired. She was persuaded to sing at a Basie concert in 1973, and a career revival ensued. She appeared at the Montreux Jazz Festival, where a live album was recorded in 1974. There were engagements at the Cookery, and new albums, one with Buddy Tate, for Muse in 1979 and 1980. She died in 1981. —*Ron Wynn*

★ **E-Baba-Le-Ba** / Nov. 20, 1944-Nov. 20, 1950 / Savoy 1159
The rhythm and blues years. 1986 reissue of 1944 and 1950 sessions. Stomping, lusty cuts with Humes at her most down-and-dirty. Though she said she didn't sing blues, this is sure close to it. —*Ron Wynn*

○ **Tain't Nobody's Biz-Ness If I Do** / Jan. 5, 1959-Feb. 10, 1959 / Contemporary 453
This Helen Humes date will lock in your mind because she was one of the immediately identifiable jazz stylists and because it is an excellent example, perhaps one of the best post-Count Basie days examples, of her work. Emotion-open, warm, and swinging-is what you've got here. And the excellent backing gives the set a backroom ambiance; even pianist Andre Previn's contributions are well placed and appropriate. Humes even makes "When The Saints Go Marching In" ring. It's a difficult song to do convincingly, and she succeeds about as well as anyone. "The Saints" is the weak moment, and at the end of side two, one can always end the record before it's played and do an encore for "When I Grow Too Old To Dream," a wonderful, almost-cloying Humes outing. —*Bob Rusch*, Cadence

○ **Helen Humes** / i. Jul. 1960 / Contemporary 3571

Songs I Like to Sing / Sep. 6-8, 1960 / Contemporary 171
Nice, classy set from vocalist Helen Humes, who enjoyed success throughout her career singing everything from classic blues to jazz, gospel to rock. She sticks to jazz on this '60s date, doing both numbers with scat and sophisticated ballads. —*Ron Wynn*

Swingin' with Humes / Jul. 27-29, 1961 / Contemporary 608
An early '60s solid set by vocalist Helen Humes, doing a program of standards with a fine combo sparked by tenor saxophonist Teddy Edwards and trumpeter Joe Gordon. The four-member rhythm section includes pianist Wynton Kelly, guitarist Al Viola, bassist Leroy Vinnegar, and drummer Frank Butler. —*Ron Wynn*

○ **Helen Humes: Talk of the Town** / Feb. 18, 1975 / Columbia 33488

This Columbia session, done in 1975, comes much closer to challenging Helen Humes, due largely to the sensitivity of producer John Hammond who truly understood Humes's musical element. Her "Talk Of The Town" is among the most memorable treatments of the tune since Coleman Hawkins's 1954 version for Vanguard. "Good For Nothing Joe" and "You've Changed" are nearly as impressive. Her renderings are straightforward and totally unaffected, characteristics shared by a handful of great vocalists today. What gives them their unique mark, however, is the lilting innocence with which she graces even the most poignant lyric, lyrics that could sound self-pitying in lesser hands. Support by pianist Ellis Larkins, guitarist George Benson, and saxophonist Buddy Tate is low key but completely sympathetic. All things considered, including the shortcomings, this was one of the most refreshing and satisfying new albums by a vocalist to come along in 1975. —*John McDonough*, Down Beat

Helen Humes with Red Norvo and His Orchestra / **i**. Aug. 1975 / RCA 17018

This RCA LP, originally made in 1958, makes reavailable one of the finest vocal albums ever recorded, by Helen Humes or anyone else. Why is it so remarkable? First, the material is superb, among the finest specimens of American popular music. And second, and most important, the arrangements by Shorty Rogers are among the most perfect matings of vocalist and orchestra ever devised. Norvo's sparkling vibes are the ideal complement to Humes's lithe, light-timbered clarity. Rogers's reed voicings are cool, deft, and softly reminiscent of the Four Brothers' sound. Humes is also in particularly fine voice. In any case, this LP is the perfect Helen Humes session, the ideal marriage of performer, material, and instrumental support. —*John McDonough*, Down Beat

Helen Humes and the Muse All Stars / Oct. 5, 1979+Oct. 8, 1979 / Muse 5473

This album finds Helen Humes collaborating with three saxophonists from the Southwest: Eddie "Cleanhead" Vinson, Arnett Cobb, and Buddy Tate. Each adds spice, grit, and soul to the proceedings. There are a few ill-conceived numbers here—notably "Woe Is Me," a one-joke novelty calypso with no vocal interest, and an uncomfortably slow-paced "These Foolish Things—but these are redeemed by sensitive accounts of "Body and Soul" and "My Old Flame" in the ballad department and a sizzling "Loud Talking Woman," with robust solos from all horns. —*Art Lange*, Down Beat

Sneakin' Around / Apr. 1980 / Classic Jazz 110

Helen Humes did both bawdy, double-entendre-laden blues and R&B numbers and more sophisticated, jazz-tinged pieces during her career. This set done with Gerald Badini, Gerry Wiggins, Major Holley and Ed Thigpen has a little of both, and it's spiced by Humes singing with equal parts sass and grace. It was originally done for the Black and Blue label and recently reissued on CD. —*Ron Wynn*

Helen / Jun. 17-18, 1980 / Muse 5233

The backing group on vocalist Helen Humes's 1980 set includes one of her favorites, tenor saxist Buddy Tate. Mention was made in the liner notes that Tate had just suffered a four-month layoff due to serious burns. What was not mentioned was that the burns included his hands and that, even several months after going back to work, his hands were still so stiff and painful that it required an effort of will to perform. Since this performance was one of his first after the episode, it must have been difficult for him but no such problems are audible. Humes also has the strong support of bassist George Duvivier, with whom she had worked before, and the ideal accompanist in pianist Norman Simmons. Simmons could scarcely be bettered as an accompanist, but he also had the strength of being able to solo to effect as well. Humes flows over the rhythm in her usual effortless

manner and what more could be asked. —*Shirley Klett*, Cadence

ROBERT HURST III

Bass / Neo-bop

Along with Christian McBride, Robert Hurst III has emerged as a prime bassist in the '90s. He joined Wynton Marsalis's band in 1991, and released his debut album as a leader in 1993. His technique, which includes deep, finely articulated phrases, a huge tone, excellent phrasing, and precise accompaniment, was well presented on his debut, which matched him with an all-star ensemble of Branford Marsalis, Marcus Belgrave, Kenny Kirkland, Jeff Watts, and Ralph Miles Jones III. It also highlighted Hurst's compositional abilities, presenting 11 of his songs. It's available on CD. —*Ron Wynn*

BOBBY HUTCHERSON (Robert Hutcherson)

b. Jan. 27, 1941, Los Angeles, CA

Vibes, marimba / Hard bop, modern creative

At one time, Bobby Hutcherson was a daring, radical vibist who expanded the instrument's role. While he's emerged as a great soloist and an established star, Hutcherson's music has moved more to the center and is now expertly played, but nowhere as demanding as his earlier material. His solos in the '60s were full, vibrant, and explosive, with speedy tempos, unusual voicings, and often dazzling harmonic maneuvers with four mallets. He's made many delightful, enjoyable recent albums that have swinging, conservative performances as their hallmark. Hutcherson studied piano as a child, then was inspired to try vibes after hearing a Milt Jackson recording. He studied briefly with Dave Pike. Hutcherson worked with Curtis Amy, Charles Lloyd, and a group co-led by Al Grey and Billy Mitchell before moving, in the early '60s, from the West Coast to New York. During the '60s, his splintering, frequently rampaging style was featured on many Blue Note sessions with Jackie McLean, Grachan Moncur III, Charles Tolliver, Archie Shepp, Eric Dolphy, Hank Mobley, Andrew Hill, Tony Williams, and Herbie Hancock. Hutcherson also played soul-jazz and more mellow material with Grant Green. He worked in the mid-'60s with Gil Fuller's big band at the Monterey Jazz Festival. Hutcherson got a little notoriety in jazz circles for the group he co-led with Harold Land from 1967 to 1971. The group attracted members such as Chick Corea, Stanley Cowell, Joe Sample, Reggie Johnson, Albert Stinson, Donald Bailey, and Billy Higgins. Hutcherson has lived in San Francisco since the early '70s, and has recorded extensively on vibes and marimba. He continued on Blue Note in the '70s doing combo dates, and made occasional albums with vocalists and strings. He moved to the Columbia label in the late '70s, and actually made some of the better jazz albums on that label during that period. One recording was a big band date, another was a quintet session with George Cables. Hutcherson also recorded several dates for Timeless. He has recorded during the '80s and '90s for Contemporary and Landmark, has toured internationally, and has done sessions as a member of the Timeless All-Stars. After Milt Jackson and Gary Burton, Hutcherson remains the leading modern vibes player. There's an ample amount of Hutcherson dates from the '70s, '80s, and '90s available on CD, but very little of his classic '60s sessions are available. —*Ron Wynn*

Farewell to Keystone / Evidence 22018

Vibist Bobby Hutcherson paid the storied Keystone Korner a wonderful tribute by cutting one of the last live record dates done there in July of 1982; the San Francisco club closed almost exactly a year later. Hutcherson's swinging, joyous phrases and bluesy riffs are nicely buttressed by the hard-driving tenor sax of Harold Land, plus excellent rhythm section assistance and textures from the team of pianist Cedar Walton, bassist Buster Williams, and drummer Billy Higgins. Trumpeter Oscar Brashear adds competent solos and meshes smoothly in the ensembles. The concluding *Mapenzi*, a 13-minute-plus hot excursion, puts a nice cap on a strong set. —*Ron Wynn*

★ **Dialogue** / Apr. 3, 1965 / Blue Note 46537
An album that was a landmark work in its time, this still has an edgy, avant-garde feeling, thanks to Sam Rivers (ts) and Andrew Hill (p). —*Ron Wynn*

Components / Jun. 10, 1965 / Blue Note 4213

Happenings / 1966 / Blue Note 46530
Reissue of a fine Blue Note recording when Hutcherson was a dominant force on his instrument. —*Ron Wynn*

Oblique / Jul. 21, 1967 / Blue Note 84444
A Blue Note date reissued. Interesting dialogs with Herbie Hancock (k). —*Ron Wynn*

Total Eclipse / 1968 / Blue Note 84291
The music here is in the mainstream of modern jazz, with a predilection for modal sounds. Occasionally the group goes a bit "out," as on "Pompeian," where there are interludes of so-called free playing. What these really consist of are long static suspensions where sounds are piled on top of one another in layers of increasing density. The sound of the group is ethereal; it floats along in the upper regions, connected to the ground only by the strong, springy bass of Reggie Johnson. In particular, Bobby Hutcherson's vibes have a light, airy sound, quite ephemeral. However, to give the sound a more substantial, durable quality, there is the hard-edged sound of Harold Land's tenor saxophone. In fact, it is Land's presence that much of the success of this record could be attributed to. Land is the anchor that Hutcherson needs. All the musicians play well, with Chick Corea integrating the piano very intelligently into the group—not the easiest thing when vibes are present. Joe Chambers is impressive here, providing all necessary support with restraint, a quality he has lacked in the past. —*Jack McCaffrey*, Coda

Medina / Aug. 11, 1969 / Blue Note 1086
Vibist Bobby Hutcherson's album, recorded in 1969 and containing previously unreleased material, sums up much of the jazz of the 1960s. There are modal-shifitng melodies, an aggressively responsive rhythm section, John Coltrane harmonies and solo patterns, expansive spiritual overtones, and probing ensemble interplay throughout. Hutcherson's commanding technique appears as a vehicle for broader musical statements. Clearly audible are his ringing tones, percussive trills, pentatonic plunges and ascending spirals, drone-hinged melodic buildups, and internal threads of tension and relaxation. But above all, there is a driving, overarching purpose to his solos—and to his writing, represented here by the spikey "Avis" and the music-box ballad "Comes Spring." Pianist Stanley Cowell penned "Dave's Chant," which mixes 6/8 and 4/4, and "Orientale," a stately melody voiced by Harold Land's flute over an irregular stop-time in the rhtyhm section. On tenor, Land is outstanding. Drummer Joe Chambers's "Medina" and "Ungano" boast Land's best playing. Cowell solos with the patented Blue Note, Horace Silver/Herbie Hancock funk-percussive touch and sound. Bassist Reggie Johnson crisscrosses the implied time zones with shadowy runs. —*Owen Cordle*, Down Beat

Blow Up / i. 1969 / Jazz Music Yesterday
This wonderful concert recording of the Hutcherson/Land group never surfaced until now. —*Ron Wynn*

Now / 1969 / Cadet

Head On / 1971 / Cadet
This Bobby Hutcherson album has its moments, but they are few. "At the Source" is the best track, and this time the mood resembles Stravinsky's *The Rite of Spring* (was this intentional?). The piano work of Todd Cochran is outstanding on this track, and he, together with trumpeter/flugelhornist Oscar Brasher, are the only really bright lights on the entire album. —*Garth Jowett*, Coda

★ **San Francisco** / 1971 / Blue Note 84362
Variety seems to be the keynote of this collection of the Bobby Hutcherson-Harold Land quintet. The six compositions, which come from the members of the quintet, range from a fairly heavy rock sound ("Night in Barcelona") to dirty funky bluesy ("Ummh!") to bossa nova to a shimmer-

ing, static reflective effort by pianist Joe Sample. To further extend the range of sounds, the group makes the most of its instrumentation—Sample plays electric as well as acoustic piano (he gets some weird twanging sounds on "Ummh!"); Land plays tenor sax, oboe, and flute; Hutcherson uses vibes and marimba. Though this is a good record, I found that it lacks the excitement and single-minded sense of purpose that the band had in a personal appearance. Nevertheless, *San Francisco* is a good record of honest, uncompromising modern jazz. —*Jack McCaffrey*, Coda

Natural Illusions / Mar. 2+3, 1972 / Blue Note

☆ **Cirrus** / Apr. 17+18, 1974 / Blue Note
On *Cirrus* Bobby Hutcherson often favors the marimba for improvised solos and the vibraphone in the ensemble passages like a second piano. The album itself is one of strong rhythmic melodies laced with a variety of colors. All the music, except "Rosewood," is written and arranged by Hutcherson, and it runs an emotional scale from the tender ballad "Even Later," with its rich flute-trumpet harmonies and blend of acoustic piano and vibes, to the tense and dramatic "Zuri Dance." The rhythm section throughout *Cirrus* is consistently excellent and tight. The arrangements give percussionist Kenneth Nash, keyboardist Bill Henderson, drummer Larry Hancock, and bassist Ray Drummond room to work imaginatively within the framework of each piece, providing depth and diversity. Trumpeter Woody Shaw and tenor saxophonists and flutists Harold Land and Emmanuel Boyd are equally fine. Simply put, *Cirrus* is a musically exciting and emotionally satisfying album. —*Herb Nolan*, Down Beat

Dance of the Sun / i. 1977 / Timeless

★ **Knucklebean** / 1977 / Blue Note 789
For this number vibist Bobby Hutcherson brings in old pal trumpeter Freddie Hubbard, a mate from the Blue Note salad days, whose music at the time (1977) had gone to seed. Fortunately, the huge Hubbard chops were still stimulated by an adventurous romp. He is truly resounding when helping a friend's album, even when giving the listener some sweet mute work on Hutcherson's updated "Little B." "Sundance" finds him opening what becomes a roaring furnace with a beautiful unaccompanied prelude. Elsewhere the leader exhibits scads of his monstrous ability on vibes and the woody marimba. Especially striking are his rapid-fire solo on "Little B" and the joyous groove of the title cut, an Eddie Marshall original. Drummer Marshall is the catalyst, kicking the band with a depth and breadth I find in very few West Coast drummers, no bias intended. This is another winner from jazz's most explosive vibist. —*Willard Jenkins, Jr.*, Cadence

Highway One / May 1978-Jun. 23, 1978 / Columbia
With heavyweight assistance from composer/arranger/pianist George Cables and coproducer/pianist/arranger Cedar Walton, the California malleteer paints a warmly impressionistic canvas with lovely pastel shadings and just the right touch of astringent sophistication to avoid any hint of bathos. "Secrets of Love" features Cables's haunting, Chick Corea-like melody over a shimmering modal vamp while flutist Hubert Laws weaves silken melodic strains through a richly undulating texture. Hutcherson spins filigrees over a repeating motif from Erik Satie's "Trois Gymnopèdies" to achieve an evanescent aura on his own "Bouquet," with Walton supplying a lesson in tasteful string arrangement. Likewise for the added horns on the title track, which gather bouyancy upon an ascending movement of parallel figures before Hutcherson and Cables flesh out the inventive theme with impeccable solo work. Freddie Hubbard adds the understated eloquence of his flugelhorn to the delicate, sinuous lines of Cables's "Sweet Rita Suit." —*Larry Birnbaum*, Down Beat

Un Poco Loco / 1979 / Columbia

○ **Solo / Quartet** / 1981 / Contemporary 425
This was the first record for vibist Bobby Hutcherson in about two years and his first for Contemporary. He left

Columbia along with the Heath Brothers, Dexter Gordon, Woody Shaw, and Freddie Hubbard during a company house cleaning in 1980. This record has a split personality. Besides sharing the same vinyl, one side seems unrelated to the other. On the solo side, Hutcherson plays unaccompanied with some token assistance from producer John Koenig on bells on "The Ice Cream Man." Side two is a quartet (pianist McCoy Tyner, bassist Herbie Lewis, drummer Billy Higgins) featuring the same group that collaborated in 1968 on Hutcherson's Blue Note record Stick Up. On side one Hutcherson sounds like a one-man percussion section. Through the technique of overdubbing and multitrack, Hutcherson is able to fully explore the depth of each instrument independently and collectively (bells, marimba, xylophone, chimbes, and bass marimba besides vibes). He maintains the rhythm with one instrument while he improvises with the other. The quartet side sounds tighter, but it is not as creative as the solo side; it just never emerges from the shadow of the first. This is McCoy Tyner's first sideman appearance in more than 10 years. Drummer Billy Higgins sounds crisp throughout side two and both Tyner and Hutcherson engage him in some interesting dialogs during their solos. It's good to hear Herbie Lewis again. His sound is as distinctive as it was on the Stick Up date. — Gordon F.X. Allen, Cadence

Four Seasons / i. Dec. 11, 1983 / Timeless 210

Good Bait / Aug. 1984 / Landmark 1501

An excellent date with the cream of old and new players. Branford Marsalis (ts) is in top form. — Ron Wynn

Color Schemes / Oct. 1985 / Landmark 1508

On Color Schemes Bobby Hutcherson (vibes) is backed by a top-notch rhythm section for a set of jazz standards and originals. Every selection has its worthwhile points, with the standouts being a bossa nova-flavored version of Joe Henderson's "Recorda-Me." The leader duets with pianist Mulgrew Miller (who continues to move forward as an impressive soloist, gradually discarding the McCoy Tyner influence) on his ballad "Rosemary, Rosemary," an uptempo rendition of "Remember," and on a colorful overdubbed duet with percussionist Airto Moreira ("Color Scheme") that finds Hutcherson blending together vibes, marimba, and orchestra bells. This is an easily recommended album of high-quality, if conservative, music. — Scott Yanow, Cadence

In the Vanguard / Dec. 1986 / Landmark 1513

In the Vanguard shows more fire than vibist Bobby Hutcherson often evinces. To these ears it's the best of his Landmark sets. Where Hutcherson sometimes sounds confined by pianists, he had no such problem here—probably because the pianist is the great Kenny Barron. His harmonic ear, sensitivity, and lightning reflexes allow him to be completely supportive while staying out of the vibist's way. Barron's concentration is facilitated by working with his Sphere buddy Buster Williams (bass). Al Foster's playing is a shade obtrusive, as when his thump-of-doom bass drum draws the slow "Estate" to a close, but it's all the more urgent for that. The band is empathic, with happy consequences for the leader. The fact that a bass drum can be a major distraction at all is a tribute to Tom Mark's exquisitely revealing recording, which does the Vanguard justice. Hutcherson's vibes and marimba have rarely sounded so clear; nuances of touch and long decays survive intact. Likely it is the quality of support that inspires Hutcherson so—which is what makes paying attention worthwhile. "Someday My Prince Will Come" is a textbook example of how to make 3/4 swing, while Randy Weston's "Little Niles"—never recorded often enough—capitalizes on more dramatic use of the same meter. "Well You Needn't" gets out there for a minute; "I Wanna Stand Over Here" is the uptempo romp. — Kevin Whitehead, Cadence

Mirage / 1988 / Landmark 1529

Ambos Mundos / Aug. 1989-Sep. 1989 / Landmark 1522

A fine venture into Afro-Latin and Latin jazz. Hutcherson is tops on vibes and marimba, joined here by three percussionists. — Ron Wynn

---

DICK HYMAN (Richard Roven Hyman)

b. Mar. 8, 1927, New York, NY
Synthesizer, piano, organ, clarinet, composer / Ragtime, stride, boogie-woogie, swing

Dick Hyman has done valuable work on behalf of jazz in several capacities. He collaborated with critic/journalist Leonard Feather on a series of History of Jazz concerts, and, in the '70s, did a series of major historical concerts with the New York Jazz Repertory Company, re-creating the music of Louis Armstrong, James P. Johnson, Jelly Roll Morton, and Scott Joplin. In the '80s, he's done several technically wondrous albums of vintage and classic jazz piano, and has recorded programs for British television. Hyman was an early advocate for expanding the role of synthesizers in jazz, and The Electric Eclectics of Dick Hyman was a '60s sensation. Hyman began studying classical music as a child and, while a student at Columbia, won 12 lessons from Teddy Wilson in a contest sponsored by a radio station. Hyman played both swing and bop after graduating in 1948, and worked with Charlie Parker, Dizzy Gillespie, Lester Young, Red Norvo, and Benny Goodman. Hyman and Goodman worked together infrequently from 1950 into the '80s. Hyman was a studio musician during the '50s. He served as an NBC staff pianist and organist from 1952 to 1957, and was Arthur Godfrey's music director from 1959 to 1962. Hyman did numerous recordings in the '50s and '60s. He headed trios, recorded novelty and country numbers under various aliases, cut ragtime sessions, and made transcriptions of compositions by Jelly Roll Morton, James P. Johnson, Fats Waller, and Louis Armstrong. He played some of these on a mid-'70s tour of the Soviet Union. Hyman formed the Perfect Jazz Repetory Quintet in 1976, which at various times included Pee Wee Russell, Milt Hinton, and Panama Francis. Hyman provided arrangements for several people, including Count Basie, Cozy Cole, the Mills Brothers, and J.J. Johnson. Hyman has several sessions available on CD on various labels. — Ron Wynn

○ **Live at Maybeck Recital Hall–Vol. 3: Music of 1937** / 1937 / Concord Jazz 4415

○ **Some Rags, Some Stomps, and a Little Blues** / Dec. 3, 1973 / Columbia 32587

○ **Satchmo Remembered** / Nov. 8, 1974 / Atlantic 1671

★ **Themes and Variations on "A Child Is Born"** / Oct. 11-12, 1977 / Chiaroscuro 198

Dick Hyman takes "A Child Is Born" and beats it to death by playing it not only in his style, but also in the style of 11 other pianists (Scott Joplin, Jelly Roll Morton, James P. Johnson, Fats Waller, Earl Hines, Teddy Wilson, Erroll Garner, George Shearing, Cecil Taylor, Art Tatum, and Bill Evans). This isn't the first time this sort of thing has been tried and no doubt Hyman is a master mimic (though he misses the point of Cecil Taylor's music completely), but this is more a curiosity item than 46 minutes of fulfilling music. — Bob Rusch, Cadence

○ **Charleston** / i. 1977 / Columbia 33706

A selection of the works of composer James P. Johnson is the focus of this recording issued on Columbia Masterworks. This is not a jazz record, as such. It is too committed to the letter as well as the spirit of the original material to be that. Such a commitment imposes disciplines that replace the cult of personality with the structure and detail of composition. Hyman fashions orchestrations following note for note upon the models of Johnson's piano rolls, recordings, and sheet music. The voicings, which are Hyman's own, are faithful to the period, and the impeccable performances make the music superior to any other modern retrospective of the '20s that comes to mind. — John McDonough, Down Beat

○ **Music of Jelly Roll Morton** / Feb. 26, 1978 / Smithsonian 006

This live recording comes from a concert at the Smithsonian. As the program proceeds, the musicians warm up before an attentive and appreciative audience, and the performances become looser and begin to lose their mechanical quality. "King Porter Stomp" and "Wolverine Blues" (composer/pianist Jelly Roll Morton titled this "Wolverines" and was furious when the publisher changed the name) are scored by James Dapogny rather than pianist Dick Hyman. The former is the only full septet title on side one that achieves some impression of spontaneity. This is an all-star group, and the music is all beautifully played. "Fingerbreaker" and "The Pearls" are Hyman piano solos. "Shreveport Stomp" and "Perfect Rag" are trios (clarinetist Bob Wilber, Hyman, drummer Tommy Benford), and "Mournful Blues" is a quartet made up of the trio plus trombonist Jack Gale. Wilber is particularly good on "Strokin' Away," trumpeter Warren Vache, Jr. has a good solo on "Blue Blood Blues," and Jack Gale lets fly on "Georgia Swing." Major Holley, one of the few modern bassists who doubles on tuba—another was Red Callendar—gets a solo outing on "Strokin' Away." —*Shirley Klett*, Cadence

○ **Manhattan Jazz** / **i.** Dec. 2, 1985 / Music Masters 5031
With Ruby Braff. A wonderful, if very dated, example of vintage swing-era material. It's not traditional, simply a classic approach. —*Ron Wynn*

★ **Blues in the Night** / **i.** 1990 / Music Masters 5021

Plays Fats Waller / **i.** 1990 / Reference 33
Pianist Dick Hyman has mastered reproducing classic songs by jazz masters without losing his identity. That is the case

on this 1990 Fats Waller tribute done directly to disc. Hyman neatly, respectfully, and flawlessly plays such songs as "Honeysuckle Rose" and "Ain't Misbehavin'," captures and reproduces the rhythms and spirit, yet injects enough personal twists and phrases to show he understands he's *not* Fats Waller, just someone who loves his music and wants to convey its importance to the listener. —*Ron Wynn*

○ **Runnin' Ragged** / **i.** 1991 / Pro Arte 652

○ **Stride Piano Summit** / **i.** Nov. 6, 1991 / Milestone 9189

○ **Jelly and James—Music of "Jelly Roll" Morton and James P. Johnson** / **i.** Dec. 22, 1992 / Sony 52552

○ **Face the Music: A Century of Irving Berlin** / Music Masters 5002

Plays Duke Ellington / Reference 50
Hyman's most recent foray into repertory is done with the same ferocity, attention to detail, and reverential qualities as his Fats Waller project, and once more was recorded direct to disc on the amazing Bosendorfer 275SE Reproducing Piano. The instrument's clarity, vivid tuning, and precise pitch make Hyman's solos sound even more striking, and though he doesn't always capture Ellington's stride manner, he's got the pacing and rhythms down. The 14 numbers are wisely chosen; several like "Jubilee Stomp" and "Come Sunday" are piano showcases, while such others as "Echoes of Harlem" and "Prelude to a Kiss" are wonderful works worthy of inclusion on any Ellington set. —*Ron Wynn*

I

ABDULLAH (DOLLAR BRAND) IBRAHIM
(Adolph Johannes Brand)

b. Oct. 9, 1934, Cape Town, South Africa
Piano, flute, composer / World fusion

Abdullah Ibrahim, once known as Dollar Brand, has become a premier musician and pianist. His style mixes traditional South African township music with bebop and free sounds, and is melodically and harmonically compelling, with dense, shifting rhythms. Ibrahim's primary influences are Thelonious Monk and Duke Ellington; Ibrahim's solo works reflect the Monk side with unpredictable, yet satisfying solos and compositions, while his larger band recordings show Ellington's penchant for blending sophisticated arrangements with earthy solos. Ibrahim's an excellent ballad stylist, with a solid left-hand dominated, aggressive approach. He's perfected a breathy flute technique, is an effective soprano saxophonist, and plays cello occasionally.

Ibrahim began on piano at age seven. He was later a member of the Jazz Epistles along with Hugh Masekela, Makaya Ntshoko, Kippie Mocketsi, and Jonas Gwanga. They recorded South Africa's first jazz album, *Jazz Epistles: Verse I*, in 1960. He also played with the groups Tuxedo Slickers, the Streamline Brothers, and the Willie Max big band. Ibrahim recorded some trio albums in South Africa during the early '60s. He and vocalist Sathima Bea Benjamin (his wife) left South Africa for Zurich in 1962. Ellington heard a performance by Ibrahim's trio while on tour and arranged a session for him in 1963. He also sponsored an appearance by Ibrahim at the Newport Jazz Festival. Ibrahim eventually substituted for Ellington on a tour. During the late '60s, Ibrahim worked with Elvin Jones, and toured Europe as both a soloist and in groups with Don Cherry, Gato Barbieri, Ntshoko, and Johnny Gertze. He converted to Islam in 1968, and took his Muslim name in the mid-'70s.

Ibrahim's recording debut on American labels came in the mid-'60s. He was featured on Elvin Jones's Atlantic album *Midnight Walk*, and the session Ellington arranged for him was issued on Reprise in 1963, *Duke Ellington Presents the Dollar Brand Trio*. Since that time, Ibrahim has recorded for Fontana, Black Lion, Arista/Freedom, Enja, and Spectator (Denmark) in the '60s, and Sackville, Phillips (Japan), Denon, East Wind, African Violets, Plane, Baystate, Chiaroscuro, and Blackhawk in the '70s, '80s, and '90s. He's played and recorded with Johnny Dyani, Max Roach, Cecil McBee, Roy Brooks, Cecil Bridgewater, Hamiet Bluiett, Ricky Ford, and Carlos Ward, among others. Ibrahim's cut solo dates and duos, has led septets and large band sessions, and has backed his wife on her albums. He returned to South Africa in 1976 and recorded several albums before going back to New York. During the '80s, Ibrahim performed a multimedia opera, *Kalahari Liberation*, in Europe, and was featured with Ricky Ford and Ben Riley on a television documentary filmed at Sweet Basil's in New York. Ibrahim has many albums from various eras available on CD. *—Ron Wynn and Myles Boisen*

African Sketchbook / 1963 / Enja
While *African Sketchbook* repeats six compositions present on the album *Ancient Africa*, including the flute piece "Air"

(Ibrahim, incidentally, is a competent flutist who produces some intriguing droning and double-time effects), the pianist is presented in a slightly different light. His playing is more dissonant and rhythmically disjointed, his touch more muscular and angry. "Slave Bell," for instance, moves right into the domain of 20th century conservatory music, with its jarring figure in minor seconds and its feeling of random melodic atonality. Also notable is "The Dream," a brooding ballad which reminded me of some of Charles Mingus's rhapsodic solo piano pieces. *—Jon Balleras, Down Beat*

Duke Ellington Presents the Dollar Band Trio / **i.** May 1964 / Reprise 6111
Immaculate, stunning trio work. Ellington knew music and recognized Ibrahim's potential. *—Ron Wynn*

Anatomy of a South African Village / **i.** Jan. 30, 1965 / Black Lion 760172
A sublime, transcendent date. Trio live at Cafe Montmartre in Copenhagen. Rare. *—Michael G. Nastos*

Dream, The / **i.** Jan. 30, 1965 / Freedom

African Piano / Oct. 22, 1969 / ECM 835020
A 1989 reissue of some fine live playing from a 1969 concert in Copenhagen. *—Ron Wynn*

○ **Fats, Duke and The Monk** / **i.** 1973 / Sackville 3048

African Portraits / Feb. 18, 1973 / Sackville

○ **Sangoma** / Feb. 1973 / Sackville 3006
Here Abdullah Ibrahim knits African, Christian, and jazz themes into a cloak of identity that the pianist/composer hasn't before worn on album. Dramatic, somber rubato movements contrast with folkish tunes and stylized single note and stride bass lines. The result is a weave detailing the past times and places of this far-traveled musician. In the classic manner of the keyboard muses he calls on, quotes, and composes from, Ibrahim has as much technique as he needs to accommodate the breadth of his imagination. Occasional rough touches add a primitive strength to the spiny portrait of the jungle lily and rose and add percussive significance to the patchwork he makes from "Single Petal of a Rose," "Honeysuckle Rose," "Think of One," and his own "Ode to Duke," "Monk from Harlem," and "Mumsey Weh." *—Howie Mandel, Down Beat*

○ **African Space Program** / Nov. 7, 1973 / Enja
This is unique, multicultural music. Ibrahim, as his followers know, is a native-born South African who is well-versed both in modern conservatory music and in the music of his native Africa. He's skilled as a pianist, flutist, and composer, and now, with this release of his first recording with a large group, he reveals his talents as an arranger. "Tintiyana, First Part" is enough to establish Ibrahim's credentials as an orchestrator of the first order. He writes in colors, not sections, piling layer upon layer of muted dissonance in a manner worthy of one of his mentors, Duke Ellington. "Tintiyana, Second Part" is mainly a series of remarkably coherent solos by all hands except, unfortunately, Ibrahim himself. (He modestly stays in the background throughout.) His orchestral backgrounds encourage and reinforce the soloists. This passionate, at times violent, music is uncompromisingly per-

sonal, deeply felt, and marked by complete musical integrity. —*Jon Balleras*, Down Beat

Good News from Africa / **i**. Dec. 1973 / Enja 2048
Those not familiar with the probing, soul-cleansing sound of pianist Abdullah Ibrahim would do well to check out any of his solo albums or this fine 1973 effort featuring bassist Johnny Dyani. The fully orchestral and eloquent style of Ibrahim improvising from folk melodies, sometimes dipping into overt jazz colorings, and supported by the sympathetic movements of Dyani speaks much more fully. There is also a lot of coloration with percussion that only occasionally seems to intrude into the mood of the music, and is quite effective on its own. —*Milo Fine*, Cadence

★ **Echoes from Africa** / Sep. 7, 1979 / Enja 79620
Echoes From Africa is, first and foremost, mood music. An atmosphere is immediately established in an African dialect by Abdullah Ibrahim and Johnny Dyani. This leads into a simple, repeated piano vamp, with the voices continuing almost as added instruments. Despite the foreign words, one feels an eloquent story is being told, at times moaning, other times distinctly conversational, and then moving into a crescendo of joy. Ibrahim's piano playing is at its most lyrical and poetic in this music, his right hand delineating his fertile imagination while his left hand keeps up a hypnotic bass line. Dyani is a fellow South African who has lived in Europe and been favored by many American expatriate jazz musicians. "Saud" (dedicated to McCoy Tyner), is also slow and rather introspective, not unlike some of Tyner's best work. Here the pianist and bassist are reading each other's thoughts, a subtle technique one often hears in such sympathetic duo performances. *Echoes Of Africa,* one of a long line of superb works from Ibrahim, comes across as a heartfelt dedication to his and Dyani's homeland, while possessing a strong allegiance to the concepts of their adopted millieu. — *Frankie Nemko-Graham*, Down Beat

○ **African Marketplace** / **i**. Dec. 1979 / Elektra
The title cut on *African Marketplace* is decidedly nonwestern, with African drums rolling through the piece and horn pairings with a Middle Eastern flavor. Except for the drums, this sound depicts a marketplace anywhere in the Third World. Abdullah Ibrahim takes a happy yet restrained soprano sax solo here; it is one of the few chances to hear him on that instrument rather than as a voice in horn pairings. Ironically, the cut is followed by "Mamma," a hymn voiced similiarly to Duke Ellington's "jungle style." Most fascinating is Craig Harris's plunger trombone, which evokes the muted trombone of Joe "Tricky Sam" Nanton and trumpet of Bubber Miley, until Harris sketches higher than Nanton probably ever dared to try. The finest moments on the record are found in those compositions most firmly rooted in the hymns and chants of Ibrahim's social/spiritual background, and it is encouraging to see how that environment more and more dominates his musical conceptions. —*R. Bruce Dold*, Down Beat

Live at Montreux / 1980 / Enja 79623
A 1990 reissue of a tremendous live concert done in 1980. Carlos Ward and Craig Harris star alongside Ibrahim. —*Ron Wynn*

African Dawn / Jun. 7, 1982 / Enja 79621
These are solo versions of his greatest originals, plus Monk tributes. —*Myles Boisen*

☆ **Zimbabwe** / May 29, 1983 / Enja 79632
This is a nicely blended, somewhat mellow, and seemingly quite finished '83 recording by pianist/bandleader/composer Abdullah Ibrahim with Carlos Ward (as, f), Essiet Okun Essiet (b), and Don Mumford (d). Interspaced with nonoriginals are four Ibrahim compositions, most of which were inspired by imagery from Ibrahim's South African roots. Even the Coltrane tribute, with its hammering drum work under Ibrahim's lattice of piano percussion, brings an African imagery as its primary characteristic. On the nonoriginals, the pieces are approached in a rather circuitous fashion, a bit Monkish, and those who regard melodies as a sometimes

necessary vehicle for improvisation will find these performances improvisational delights. Special mention must also be given to Carlos Ward, whose flute playing, heavily featured throughout, is outstanding. —*Bob Rusch*, Cadence

☆ **Ekaya** / Nov. 17, 1983 / Ekapa 005
This studio date with septet is a must-buy. Extraordinary ensemble music. —*Michael G. Nastos*

Water from an Ancient Well / Oct. 1985 / Tiptoe 888812
This second recording by the seven-member ensemble Ekaya was not the masterpiece their debut recording *Ekaya* was. It nevertheless stands as firm testimony to pianist Abdullah Ibrahim's continuing musical conviction. At the heart of Ibrahim's music lies an essential contradiction—instead of unmitigated anger or wallowing self-pity (as one would perhaps expect), there is a quiet and affirmative optimism. Ibrahim's music incorporates diverse elements of Black music (blues, spirituals, Mayan Carnival music, Thelonious Monk, etc.), at times meditative, but not overly solemn. Rather, one is more likely to hear the dark modal lilt of "Tuang Guru" or the crescendo of "Sameeda." Ricky Ford's (ts) playing with Ekaya, both live and on record, is the best I've ever heard—bluesy and infectious with a tone reminiscent of the Chicago tradition of biting and aggressive tenormen. Carlos Ward (as, f) needs little coaxing for his style is based on a propulsive enthusiasm. But the playing of journeymen Dick Griffin on trombone and Charles Davis on baritone sax is a treat. The concise thematic nature of the tunes make excess improbable. David Williams's fat, funky foundation (b) and the always reliable Ben Riley (d) aid the pianist in forming a crack rhythm section. —*Ludwig Van Trikt*, Cadence

☆ **Mantra Mode** / **i**. 1991 / Enja 79671
The sensual, reflective mergings of jazz, gospel, and South African-based music we have come to expect from pianist/composer Abdullah Ibrahim (aka Dollar Brand) over the years are once again in full flower on *Mantra Mode,* recorded in January 1991 after Ibrahim's return to his native Cape Town. *Mantra's* seven selections, recorded with a septet comprising all South African musicians, will not surprise listeners acquainted with Ibrahim's stateside recordings with the aggregation he dubbed *Ekaya* (home). We are once again treated to those warm, Duke Ellington-based reed voicings and the leader's lyrical piano. There are, nonetheless, new melodic treasures to be found in this collection, beginning with "Bayi Lam," a Xhosa folk song whose melody is complemented by the group's unfettered swing and supple, brooding rhythms, and the "Tafelberg Samba/Carnival Samba" medley in which trumpeter Johnny Mekoa and saxophonist Robbie Jansen shine. Ibrahim's "Barakaat," a solo piano vehicle, combines moody bass lines and subtly gorgeous harmonic/melodic patterns to haunting effect. How appropriate for a collection with *Mantra Mode* as its name. —*Reuben Jackson*, Jazz Times

South Africa / **i**. Nov. 4, 1991 / Enja 79618
Abdullah Ibrahim's career has been remarkable both for its consistency and its concerns. *South Africa* has the quiet, meditative lyricism, dancing rhythms, and paradoxical folkish charm that is the essence of his craft and that embodies much of South African music in general. Most of the material on this album is based on the traditional music indigenous to that torn land; and at its heart there is an essential contradiction. There is none of the dead solemnity that one would perhaps expect coming from a people of sorrow. Rather, *South Africa* is representative of a common quality found in much of South African music (from Zulu jive to Ibrahim's), that is, an optimism mixed in amongst the throwaway joy. Add to that a spiritualism that exposes the naked soul. "Siya Hamba Nam Hlanje," which features vocalist Johnny Classens, is soul stirring in the same way that a rural Southern Baptist church choir can send chills down your spine. Classens's voice offeres the memory of an experience that I could never have lived, though the painful rendering of it makes it my own. This is a "live" small-group recording and it gives a good feel for the skill that Ibrahim brings as both programmer and band-

leader. From the brief and largely thematic "Iza-Ne Zembe Gawuale," which is colored by the leader's soprano sax, to "Black and Brown Cherries" with a crazy Carlos Ward alto solo, the mood is upbeat. With the death of the great alto saxophonist Jimmy Lyons, no other altoist has played this long with a pianist. The Ibrahim/Ward association ranks with that of Ellington/Hodges, Taylor/Lyons—both for similiar musical intuitiveness and for the continual way it rewards the listeners. Check out "Our Loving Family" and hear how Ward's anxiety adds the perfect foil to this piece. On this set Ibrahim's austere emotionalism sets the stage for most of what happens. He is helped in no small measure by the firm hand of bassist Essiet Okun Essiet and Don Mumford on drums. — *Ludwig Van Trikt*, Cadence

Desert Flowers / **i.** 1992 / Enja 79680
Recent release by pianist and bandleader Abdullah Ibrahim, combining the sweeping township jive rhythms of his native South Africa, swing and gospel piano riffs, and hard-hitting bop solos and progressions. —*Ron Wynn*

INTERNATIONAL SWEETHEARTS OF RHYTHM

Group / Swing, big band
An outstanding big band whose members were all women, the International Sweethearts of Rhythm began at the Piney Woods Country Life School in Mississippi. International was used in the group's name because the lineup featured members with diverse ethnic and national backgrounds. Vocalist Anna Mae Darden Wilburn was the lead, and among its 18 members were drummer Pauline Braddy, alto saxophonist Roz Cron, tenor saxophonist Viola Burnside, baritone saxophonist Willie Mae Wong, trumpeter Ernestine "Tiny" Davis, trombonist Helen Jones, and bassist Carline Ray. Eddie Durham and Jesse Stone were among the band's arrangers at various times. They debuted at the Howard Theater in Washington, D.C., in 1940, and later performed at the Apollo, and across the country and in Europe through the mid-'40s. The band recorded for Victor in 1946. The original unit disbanded in the late '40s, but Wilburn kept leading various editions of the Sweethearts of Rhythm into the '50s. Greta Schiller and Andrea Weiss made a documentary film about the band, *The International Sweethearts of Rhythm: America's Hottest All-Girl Band*, in the mid '80s. —*Ron Wynn*

CHUCK ISRAELS (Charles H. Israels)

b. Aug. 10, 1936, New York, NY
Bass, educator / Cool
An often stirring, aggressive, and technically wondrous bassist, Chuck Israels was not only an outstanding player in various free situations, but was also a capable and challenging accompanist for Bill Evans. Israels later formed a repertory group that performed and recreated traditional jazz arrangements. He had formal training in both America and Europe before making his jazz recording debut with Cecil Taylor in the late '50s. Israels joined George Russell's sextet in 1959, and recorded with him and also with Eric Dolphy and Paul Horn in the early '60s. He replaced Scott LaFaro in Evans's trio in 1961, and remained with the trio until 1966. Israels also worked and recorded with J.J. Johnson, Herbie Hancock, Gary Burton, Stan Getz, and Hampton Hawes during that period. He formed the National Jazz Ensemble in the mid-'70s. This group recreated and performed arrangements and solos originally done by giants such as Jelly Roll Morton, Louis Armstrong, Duke Ellington, and Thelonious Monk. Tom Harrell, Jimmy Maxwell, Jimmy Knepper, Sal Nistico, and Bill Goodwin were among the ensemble's members during its five-year tenure. They recorded for Chiaroscuro in 1975 and 1976. Israels recorded with Rosemary Clooney in the mid-'80s. Currently, he does not have any sessions available on CD, but can be heard on reissues by Russell, Dolphy, and others. —*Ron Wynn*

★ **National Jazz Ensemble** / **i.** 1976 / Chiaroscuro 151

DAVID IZENZON

b. 1932, **d.** 1979
Bass / Early free, modern creative
One of the great bow soloists among jazz bassists, David Izenzon provided stunning solos and accompaniment in various free jazz bands during the '60s, and did many classical sessions. Izenzon didn't get an early start on bass, but developed into a brilliant player whose booming lines, huge tones, and remarkable bowed solos were highlighted in every band he played with during his relatively brief career. Izenzon was in his mid-twenties when he began studying bass in 1956; shortly afterward, he was playing with musicians such as Dodo Marmarosa. Izenzon moved to New York in the early '60s, and played with Bill Dixon, Sonny Rollins, Archie Shepp, and Paul Bley before joining Coleman's trio in 1961. He recorded with them at a famous Town Hall concert the next year. During the mid- and late '60s, Izenzon worked with Coleman both in America and overseas. After he returned from overseas, he worked with Perry Robinson, Lowell Davidson, Paul Motian, and the New York Philharmonic Orchestra. Izenzon earned a doctorate in psychotherapy in 1973 and started his own practice, splitting his time between his practice and playing with Coleman and Motian. He recorded with Motian in 1977. Izenzon does not have any sessions as a leader available on CD, but he can be heard on Coleman Blue Note CD reissues. —*Ron Wynn*

J

MICHAEL GREGORY JACKSON (Michael Gregory)

b. Aug. 28, 1953, New Haven, CT
Guitar / Ballads, m-base, modern creative, pop
Jackson was an ambitious guitarist who was recording with some of the more experimental, ambitious modern jazz players in the late '70s and early '80s. As an acoustic and electric stylist, he was interested not only in comping behind singers and doing conventional single-line solos, but in sounds, rhythms, and textures. Then he shifted gears abruptly and began doing fusion and R&B songs with quasi-relevant lyrics and lost his jazz focus. —*Ron Wynn*

Karmonic Suite / i. 1978 / Improvising Artists 372857

★ **Gifts / i.** 1979 / Novus 3012
Quintessential group recording for creative guitarist. An important progressive music album, with Jerome Harris, Marty Ehrlich, Baikida Carroll, and Pheeroan AkLaff. —*Michael G. Nastos*

Heart and Center / i. 1979 / Novus 3015

Cowboys, Cartoons and Assorted Candy / i. 1982 / Enja 4026

MILT JACKSON (Milton Jackson)

b. Jan. 1, 1923, Detroit, MI
Vibes, marimba, piano / Bop
Milt Jackson did for the vibes what Dizzy Gillespie did for the trumpet; he revolutionized its approach. Jackson slowed the speed on the instrument's oscillator, changed its vibrato, and perfected slow, cleverly paced blues solos. His floating solos with long, sustained notes and darting rhythms became a bop staple. A former singer, guitarist, and pianist, Jackson has been an extremely versatile player, cutting big band dates, working with orchestras, and fighting to maintain a successful solo career yet retain his ties with the Modern Jazz Quartet, the group he cofounded with pianist John Lewis in 1952.

Jackson started playing guitar and piano as a child, then moved to xylophone and vibraphone as a teen. He made his first public appearances singing in a gospel group. Dizzy Gillespie spotted Jackson playing in a Detroit band in 1945. He hired Jackson to play in his sextet, and later in his big band. Jackson moved to New York and worked with Gillespie from 1946 to 1948. There were stints with Howard McGhee, Thelonious Monk, Charlie Parker, and Woody Herman, plus recording sessions with Galaxy, Savoy, and Gillespie's DeeGee label from 1947 to 1952. Jackson played with Gillespie again from 1950 to 1952, and Jackson recorded for Blue Note with Lewis, Percy Heath, and Kenny Clarke. By the end of 1952, they were renamed the Modern Jazz Quartet. From 1952 to 1974, the MJQ dominated Jackson's life. The group worked steadily for nine months each year. They recorded and toured.

Somehow, during those years, Jackson found time to record on Prestige, Savoy, Atlantic, Riverside, Mercury, Verve, and Impulse. There were seminal albums with John Coltrane, Ray Charles (two albums), Ray Brown, Wes Montgomery, and Quincy Jones, among others. But Jackson became increasingly vocal about his inability to forge a suc-

cessful solo career and about his disenchantment with Lewis and the group's direction. Jackson was widely identified (blamed) as the person responsible for the band's 1974 demise. They issued three albums of goodbye material, and everyone supposedly went on their way forever. Yet, only a few months later, reunion talk began. Soon after that, actual reunions emerged. Jackson did several recordings during the '70s, among them the outstanding CTI session, *Sunflower*. He recorded often for Norman Granz's Pablo label, and worked with Oscar Peterson, with the Monty Alexander trio, and with Count Basie. But by 1982, the MJQ had reformed on a revised, infrequent basis. An impressive boxed set lauding their 40th anniversary was issued by Atlantic in 1992. Jackson's solo career continues, while the MJQ still lives, in some fashion. Jackson shows no signs of slowing down, though he'll celebrate his 71st birthday in 1994. —*Ron Wynn*

In the Beginning / 1947 / Galaxy 1771
With Sonny Stitt (sax). This is a 1991 reissue of superb recordings. Both principals are in top form. Limited-edition recordings. —*Ron Wynn*

Howard McGhee & Milt Jackson / Feb. 1948 / Savoy 12026
Howard McGhee & Milt Jackson offers eight tracks by a sextet with Bags (Jackson), Maggie's wide-open trumpet, and Jimmy Heath playing alto and baritone saxes; plus four tracks by McGhee with Billy Eckstine, tenorist Kenny Mann, Hank Jones, Ray Brown, and J.C. Heard (no Milt Jackson in sight). Both sessions date from February '48. The young vibist's sound is tighter than we've come to expect, but he's pretty fluid. —*Howard Mandel, Down Beat*

○ **Milt Jackson / i.** Jun. 1948-Apr. 1952 / Blue Note 7815092

○ **Milt Jackson / Aug.** 18, 1951 / Blue Note 81509
With Thelonious Monk Quartet, this is the best early Milt away from the Modern Jazz Quartet. —*Michael G. Nastos*

○ **Quartet, The / Aug.** 1951-Apr. 1952 / Savoy 12046

○ **All Star Bags / Apr.** 17, 1952 / Note 590
All Star Bags delineated a crucial transition period in Milt Jackson's journey, when he was converting his bop fluency into a more strident coinage, the reassuring tonal web that has been described as "Bags's Groove." The earliest tracks here, 1952, include pianist John Lewis, drummer Kenny Clarke, and bassist Percy Heath and feature Lou Donaldson's rich tenor foil. The tonal and spiritual catalyst of the saxophone often extracts the most aggressive and inventive sides of Jackson, and these vernal examples bear that out. The subsequent 1957 recordings with saxophonist Hank Mobley, pianist Horace Silver, and drummer Art Blakey are less interactive. Still, one can't help noting the progression in Jackson's style, a steep attack and rhythmic push that matches even Blakey's energy. The closing cuts (with trumpeter Art Farmer, saxophonist Benny Golson, pianist Tommy Flanagan, bassist Paul Chambers, and drummer Connie Kay are a complete turnaround—sparse, stretched, and moody. —*Mikal Gilmore, Down Beat*

○ **First Q, The / Apr.** 1952-Aug. 24, 1952 / Savoy 1106
Very early Milt Jackson material from his formative period, some of it featuring him playing vibes with future Modern

Jazz Quartet colleagues—pianist John Lewis and bassist Percy Heath, plus the Quartet's first drummer Kenny Clarke. These sessions have been reissued on CD. —*Ron Wynn*

Opus De Funk / Jun. 16, 1954-Oct. 31, 1962 / Prestige 24048

Milt Jackson Quartet / May 20, 1955 / Prestige 001

○ **Meet Milt Jackson** / Oct. 28, 1955 / Savoy Jazz 172
Meet Milt Jackson unites cuts from '56 (Wade Legge replacing Hank Jones; best is the lengthy "Soulful"), "Telefunken Blues" from '55 arranged by Ernie Wilkins (Bags is credited for piano and vibes), Bags crooning "I've Lost Your Love" from a '54 session (without the listed horns), and three septet cuts stirred by drummer Roy Haynes from '49. —*Howard Mandel*, Down Beat

Roll 'em Bags / Jan. 5, 1956 / Savoy Jazz 110
Roll 'Em Bags features six cuts by Milt Jackson's '49 sextet fronted by trumpeter Kenny Dorham, French horn player Julius Watkins, and tenor saxist Billy Mitchell and three from the later Jackson/Lucky Thompson/Wade Legge quintet. It doesn't give the bigger group more than three minutes at a stretch, while the small one gets five to six minutes plus. Bags takes credit for almost every song, yet the sextet is more an ensemble than a star turn. Meanwhile, his vibe style is full blown. With age Bags's phrases have gotten longer and more detailed, but the shape's the same. —*Howard Mandel*, Down Beat

○ **Atlantic Years, The** / Jan. 17, 1956-Feb. 24, 1960 / SD 2319

○ **Ballads and Blues** / Jan. 17, 1956 / Atlantic 1242

★ **Jazz Skyline, The** / Jan. 23, 1956 / Savoy 410
This session has interest as an example of Milt Jackson's mid-'50s work in a non-Modern Jazz Quartet context. And despite the many critical assertions that the vibist was restrained by MJQ pianist John Lewis's direction, his playing here reveals no marked changed. The overall feel of the group (Lucky Thompson, tenor sax; Hank Jones, piano; Wendell Marshall, bass; Kenny Clarke, drums; Jackson, vibes) is, however, somewhat more dynamic than that of the MJQ, as Clarke and Jones generally achieve a greater sense of forward momentum than Connie Kay or Lewis. Also, the presence of Thompson's neo-Coleman Hawkins/Ben Webster tenor changes the surface of the music even more. The session obviously found everyone in good form, as the high quality of the music has not diminished with time. —*Bob Rusch*, Cadence

○ **Plenty, Plenty Soul** / Jan. 5, 1957 / Atlantic 1269
This is another of Atlantic's Jazzlore reissues, and it is a welcome return. For not only does it capture vibist Milt Jackson in a straightahead jazz date (some of his Pablo releases treaded the thin line between jazz and pop), but it also offers some fine contributions from the likes of alto saxophonist Cannonball Adderley, tenor saxophonist Frank Foster, pianist Horace Silver, and trumpeter Joe Newman—musicians whose playing sounds almost like a godsend in this era of the cliche. The first side finds Jackson leading a nonet in a set of three jams: a blues, an uptempo number, and a ballad. The second side is a sextet session that evokes the atmosphere of a club performance. All in all there isn't a weak track on this refreshing recording (captured in the full expanse of monaural sound). —*Carl Brauer*, Cadence

Bags & Flute / May 21, 1957-Jun. 1957 / Savoy 1294
With Bobby Jaspar (ts) and Frank Wess (sax). This album is top notch. —*Michael G. Nastos*

Bean Bags / Sep. 12, 1958 / Atlantic 90465

★ **Soul Brothers** / i. 1958 / Atlantic 1279
This Milt Jackson/Ray Charles release is essential. The perfect marriage of blues, jazz, soul, and elegance. —*Ron Wynn*

☆ **Bags and Trane** / Jan. 15, 1959 / Atlantic 1368
Exceptional meeting of minds between Jackson and John Coltrane (ts). —*Ron Wynn*

Statements / Dec. 14-15, 1961 / Impulse 14
Statements finds Milt Jackson in focused combos from '61 and '64: MJQ drummer Connie Kay with Hank Jones and

Paul Chambers (from '61) or Tommy Flanagan and Richard Davis (from '64). Jimmy Heath's on four of the second combo's tracks and there's a rare Flanagan trio track. Telepathically hard-pressing, bluesy, lean, and emphatic, no one wastes a note or misses the groove in a handpicked selection of great songs. Rudy Van Gelder's perfect sound remains intact. —*Howard Mandel*, Down Beat

Bags Meets Wes / Dec. 18+19, 1961 / Riverside 234
His Riverside debut album was a stunner. Wonderful Wes Montgomery guitar. —*Ron Wynn*

Big Bags / Jun. 19, 1962-Jul. 5, 1962 / Riverside 366

Invitation / Aug. 30+31, 1962 / Riverside 260
Milt Jackson Sextet. Second album on Riverside, a crackling sextet date. —*Ron Wynn*

○ **Impulse Years, The** / 1962-1969 / Impulse 92822
Retrospective containing songs cut by vibist Milt Jackson during his tenure at Impulse. He recorded quartet, quintet, sextet and big-band albums between 1962 and 1969, most in the studio, but two recorded live. This release also features several numbers done with non-Modern Jazz Quartet players, among them bassists Paul Chambers and Ray Brown, as well as pianist Hank Jones. —*Ron Wynn*

Live at the Village Gate / Dec. 1963 / Riverside 309

Olinga / Jan. 1974 / Columbia 44174
Olinga, arranged in the distinctive style of Bob James, is a stately introduction to Milt Jackson's new sound. The solos are a bit careful and the group responds like a compact unit, much like the Modern Jazz Quartet did, but somehow the end result is different—more dynamic, perhaps. "Rerev" is a fine showcase for Jackson's single note melodic lines. Tenor and soprano saxophonist Jimmy Heath, pianist Cedar Walton, and bassist Ron Carter all know what Jackson is talking about and embellish the track with tasteful solos of their own. On "Metal Melter," the gospel roots of Jackson take over. With Walton comping on electric piano, Jackson struts through the changes with a delightful grace. Walton follows with a funky solo, much like the early Herbie Hancock playing on *Maiden Voyage*, and then provides solid support for Heath's soprano sax. On all the selections, drummer Mickey Roker adds the rhythmic inspiration that a small group needs to really go somewhere. —*Eric Kriss*, Down Beat

○ **Milt Jackson Big Four, The** / Jul. 17, 1975 / Pablo 2310753

○ **Big Three, The** / Aug. 25, 1975 / Pablo 757
Another entry from the Norman Granz Pablo stable, this is welcome to these ears. Recorded on August 25, 1975, in Los Angeles, this wafer contains some breezy solos that lift the standard of the music above that of run-of-the-mill competence. The program selection varies and the rhythm propels as melodic cohesion. Not being one to take anything away from guitarist Joe Pass and bassist Ray Brown, I must concede that this disc belongs to vibist Milt Jackson—he is remarkably good here. His magnificent solos on the Antonio Carlos Jobim tune "Wave" and the Kenny Dorham composition "Blue Bossa" are of the highest order of musical value. Pass gets in a showcase item on "You Stepped out of a Dream" and "Moonglow," while Brown presents his usual inspired work on "The Pink Panther" and "Wave." —*Bill Gallagher*, Cadence

From Opus De Jazz to Jazz Skyline / i. 1976 / Savoy 70815
A CD reissue from the late '50s, with vibist Jackson perfecting his mix of light blues, relaxed, soulful mainstream cuts, and some hard bop influences. This release combines two albums, *From Opus To Jazz* and *Jazz Skyline*, on one disc. Supporting players include at various times Jackson's Modern Jazz Quartet comrades, pianist John Lewis and bassist Percy Heath. —*Ron Wynn*

At the Kosei Nenkin / Mar. 22+23, 1976 / Pablo 103
Live in Japan with Teddy Edwards (ts) and Cedar Walton (p). Great concert. —*Michael G. Nastos*

Soul Fusion / i. 1977 / Pablo 731

Expert collaboration between vibist Milt Jackson and pianist Monty Alexander's trio recorded in 1977. While bop and the blues are Jackson's focal points, Alexander adds loping Caribbean rhythms and dancing phrases alongside or in contrast to Jackson's lines and solos. —*Ron Wynn*

Live–Montreux 1977 / Jul. 13, 1977 / Original Jazz Classics 375

With Ray Brown (b). Live collaboration between two veterans who are truly in sync. —*Ron Wynn*

Bags' Bag / 1979 / Pablo 2310-842

Relaxed, breezy session from the late '70s with brilliant vibist Milt Jackson leading a crew of veterans through familiar standards and some originals. Besides Jackson's always mellow, soulful vibes solos, other strong players are pianist Cedar Walton, guitarist John Collins. and drummer Billy Higgins. —*Ron Wynn*

All Too Soon–the Duke Ellington Album / Jan. 1980 / Pablo 450

Date in New York, A / **i.** May 1980 / Inner City 7007

Vibist Milt Jackson and trombonist J.J. Johnson would seem a perfect pair; both are consummate bop technicians with deep, sprawling roots in the nuances of the blues. Add the chili pepper of Al Cohn's tenor, the round, cozy pop of Percy Heath's bass, and the cool sizzle of Charlie Smith's drums and you have an ideal session. Right? Well, *A Date in New York* falls just short of the mark on several counts. Most noticeably, Johnson and Jackson could have been in separate studios. There is no trombone/vibes interplay whatsoever—very unusual for two players who have spent a good part of their careers in ensembles where interplay is the keynote. Cohn is atypically dark and dour here, and Henri Renaud's piano (organizer Renaud was ostensibly the date's leader) is choppy and uninspired. Jackson favors us with two piano efforts and a vocal. Jackson is the standard on vibes, Johnson is pure and warm, Heath and Smith are wonderful, and all the above complaints are melted by the glow of Jackson and Johnson. —*Lee Jeske*, Down Beat

○ **Milt Jackson in London (Memories of Thelonious Monk)** / Apr. 28, 1982 / Pablo 235

Commemorative concert for piano great Thelonious Monk done by vibist Milt Jackson in the early '80s. Jackson transferred Monk's intricate, complex compositions to vibes perfectly, getting both the flavor and the difficult harmonic structures down easily. —*Ron Wynn*

★ **Memories of Thelonious Sphere Monk** / Apr. 1982 / Pablo 235

The Thelonious Monk sides on this session are distinctly disappointing, and after listening to the record it seems to me that the "tribute" idea was an afterthought of production rather than a premediated artistic objective. I prefer the non-Monk items. "Django" holds up well for its 10+ minutes; "Groundhog" boasts one of those nice blues grooves that Bags (Jackson) digs into so nicely. One expects a certain standard from these veterans (pianist Monty Alexander, bassist Ray Brown, drummer Mickey Roker) and you get it; look for an average couple of nightclub sets (Ronnie Scott's), don't expect more, and you'll not be disappointed. —*Bob Rusch*, Cadence

Mostly Duke / Apr. 1982 / Pablo 2310-944

Bebop / **i.** Mar. 28-30, 1988 / East West 90991

★ **Harem, The** / **i.** 1991 / Music Masters 5061

Reverence and Compassion / **i.** 1993 / Qwest/Reprise 45204

Reverence And Compassion sets Milt Jackson amid sympatico accompaniment from pianist Cedar Walton, bassist John Clayton, and drummer Billy Hart, with spare horn charts by Clayton. "Reverence" is brisk, showing off Walton on "Y&F." Bags's breaks flow out of unobtrusive horns. Then "Little Girl Blue" brings on an orchestra from a Hollywood soundstage. "J.C." is Bags's major-scale theme, and the bassist/dedicatee bows in an arco-out chorus. "Cedar Lane" and "How Do You Keep the Music Playing" are notable for Bags's con-

versational phrasing, Clayton's deep sound, and Higgins's brushes. Walton's "Newest Blues" frisks at an uptempo, and "Bullet Bag" is Bags's swinging chromatic blues. —*Howard Mandel*, Down Beat

Telefunken Blues / Savoy 106

Telefunken Blues, nominally drummer Kenny Clarke's disc, is titled for the same Ernie Wilkins-charted cut that appears on *Meet Milt Jackson*, with a bluesy sextet featuring Frank Wess on tenor and flute, baritone saxman Charlie Fowlkes, trombonist Henry Coker, and bassist Eddie Jones. A '54 sextet with Klook, Bags, altoist Frank Morgan, tenorist Walter Benton, pianist Gerald Wiggins, and bassist Percy Heath blows four hard bop numbers, too. —*Howard Mandel*, Down Beat

QUENTIN JACKSON

b. 1909, **d.** 1976
Trombone / Swing, big band

One of Ellington's strongest trombone soloists, Quentin "Butter" Jackson displayed a creative, enjoyable style during his years with the orchestra. He was known particularly for his work with the plunger mute, and as an effective section contributor. Jackson began studying piano and violin in his youth, and his brother-in-law, Claude Jones, taught him to play the trombone. Jones was in McKinny's Cotton Pickers. Jackson worked with Zack Whyte in 1930, then was recommended to the McKinny band by Jones. He played with Don Redman from 1932 until the end of the decade, then joined Cab Calloway. Jackson stayed with Calloway from 1940 to 1948, except for one period in 1946 when he toured Europe with Redman. After a short stint with Lucky Millinder, Jackson joined Ellington's band, and remained with the group for 11 years. Jackson toured Europe with Quincy Jones in 1960, and played with Count Basie in 1962 and 1963. He also worked in the '60s with Charles Mingus, Louis Bellson, Gerald Wilson, and Ellington again in 1963. Jackson played in theater bands, and played with Al Cohn and the Thad Jones-Mel Lewis orchestra in the '70s. During the last year of his life, he performed infrequently. Jackson can be heard on many Ellington reissues of the '40s, '50s, and early '60s. —*Ron Wynn*

RONALD SHANNON JACKSON

b. Jan. 12, 1940, Fort Worth, TX
Drums / Early jazz-rock, modern creative

Ronald Shannon Jackson's drum style is too incendiary, too riveting, and too propulsive to be deemed fusion. It reflects R&B, blues, funk, free, and rock influences, and can kick a band ahead, provide brilliant solos, or interact with other instruments in a standard rhythm section role. Jackson hasn't merely played many styles, he's made major contributions to several pivotal groups, and has led the Decoding Society. Jackson began studying drums as a child, and turned professional in his teens playing with James Clay. Jackson did sessions in Dallas with Clay, Ray Charles, and Leroy Cooper. He studied sociology and history in Texas, Missouri, and Connecticut before obtaining a music scholarship to New York in 1966. He played with Charles Mingus, Betty Carter, Stanley Turrentine, Jackie McLean, McCoy Tyner, Kenny Dorham, and with Joe Henderson's big band. He also worked with Albert Ayler in late 1966 and in 1967. Jackson opted to withdraw from active playing for serious study in the first half of the '70s, then resurfaced in Ornette Coleman's "harmolodic" mid-'70s band. He worked with Prime Time from 1975 to 1979, and played with Cecil Taylor in 1978 and 1979. Jackson worked with Blood Ulmer in 1979 and 1980, and formed the Decoding Society in 1979. The group's roster has included current rock star Vernon Reid, Zane Massay, Billy Bang, and Byard Lancaster. Jackson recorded with Albert Mangelsdorff in 1980, and played with the A-1 Jazz Band led by Garrett List in 1982, as well as with Craig Harris and the group Last Exit in the '80s. He hasn't done much recording recently, but *Raven Roc* was issued on

DIW in 1992. There are only a few Jackson dates available on CD. —*Ron Wynn*

Eye on You / 1980 / About Time 1003

On drummer Ronald Shannon Jackson's first record as a bandleader, he picks up the loose threads of funk, free jazz, new wave, trance music, and Ornette Coleman's theories of harmolodics and gathers them all together in a bright and intricate bow of rhythm and dissonance. Jackson solos only once here—a tossing, thrashing break in "Shaman"—but it could be said in praise of him what has often been said in dispraise of free drummers generally: that he is "soloing" continuously, no matter who else is playing. The voices of the saxophonists and the string players rise like vapors from the steaming cauldron he gleefully stirs. Jackson's 11 compositions are expansive miniatures that generate much of their tension by crowding the greatest possible movement within the smallest allowable space—most clock in at around four minutes and "Apache Love Cry," the longest, develops an exhilarating diversity of dynamics and emotions in just over six. It is in the gliding, humorous solos of violinist Billy Bang, the to-and-fro pacing of bassist Melvin Gibbs, and the swelling interplay between the leader and the smoldering, vibrato-heavy, string-bending guitarist Bern Nix that this music comes closest to birthing a new idiom, comes most fully and most frighteningly kicking and screaming to life. —*Francis Davis*, Down Beat

○ **Nasty** / i. Mar. 1981 / Moers 01086

○ **Street Priest** / Jun. 13-16, 1981 / Moers 01906

By the time *Street Priest* was recorded, the aesthetic behind the Decoding Society was in full bloom, and the band had two earlier albums under its belt. Drummer Ronald Shannon Jackson's compositions had jelled; they were more fully realized than on *Eye on You* or *Nasty*. Armed to the teeth with new tunes and a settled lineup, the Decoding Society toured Europe in the early summer of 1981. At the end of the tour Burkhard Hennen recorded the band in a studio in Bremen, Germany, over a period of four days while they were red hot from their performances. Chronologically, *Street Priest* preceded *Man Dance* and differed by the latter in having a wider sonic latitude, as Henry Scott on trumpet replaced Lee Rozie's reeds after the band returned to America. Otherwise, the band personnel remained the same, featuring the two-bass team of Melvin Gibbs and "Rev" Bruce Johnson with guitarist Vernon Reid and saxist Zane Massey alongside the leader's drums. Much of the music enters into the realm of sheer sound, as instruments slip in and out of sync to the beat. Themes are stated, disappear, and resurface again slightly changed. *Street Priest* is a jewel that combines the fire of a live performance and finish of a studio album. —*Jim Brinsfield*, Down Beat

○ **Mandance** / Jun. 1982 / Antilles 846397

Drummer Ronald Shannon Jackson's music, which is based on Ornette Coleman's harmolodic theory, is a pastiche of urban influences—the twanging, booming basses, the loud electric guitar, and the powerful thrust of the horns bleating short riffs. It is all tied down by the tremendous drumming of Jackson. The compositions here, with two exceptions, have a frenetic quality, with the group building a wall of sound that is thick and sometimes impenetrable. Yet there is such a positive feeling to the music, that it does not come off as overkill. The two bassists never clash—Bruce Johnson has a smoother style, accentuated by his use of fretless bass, while Melvin Gibbs has more of a trebly tone. "Spanking" is a hopped-up, heavy metal free-for-all with a flashy guitar solo in the middle. For "Catman," guitarist Vernon Reid switches to a Roland Guitar Synthesizer that acts as both third horn and a string section. Both Zane Massey (sax) and Henry Scott (tpt, flhn) take piercing high-pitched solos, the former on soprano sax. Jackson is the focal point—he directs all the players and controls the fury. —*Richard B. Kamins*, Cadence

★ **Barbeque Dog** / Mar. 1983 / Antilles 848817

What has always been striking about drummer and bandleader Ronald Shannon Jackson and the Decoding Society is their enormous energy, though at this point they were sometimes a free jazz volcano, kept from erupting by the songwriter/drummer's compositional restraints. The layered, skewed-funk title tune is a tour of Jackson's Fort Worth uncle's barbeque kitchen; trumpeter Henry Scott suggests the spicy sauce with his solo, the unison horns are the yams and greens, the basses double for black-eyed peas and corn bread, and Jackson, ambidextrously mixing rhythms, is the master chef. The most memorable songs are "Gossip" and "Harlem Opera." Jackson says the former is "like being in the middle of a New York disco and an African village at the same time." Both places are infested with vicious prattle, and the Decoding Society, with motormouth guitar, brazen horns, and alternating outspoken and private passages, does its damnedest to parody the nuances of idle talk. "Harlem Opera" is an elegy for a fallen cultural center; the blue four-note melodic theme is made all the more dolorous by the inclusion of voices. Saxophonist Zane Massey, who is submerged in the record mix elsewhere, adds some tortured cries. Jackson's songs are infused with intricate rhythmic ideas. African, Central European, and Eastern influences—rhythmic or otherwise—stir drummer and band. —*Frank John Hadley*, Down Beat

Pulse / Jan. 1984 / Celluloid 5011

Furious, classic jazz-rock in the absolute sense of the term, plus some free and R&B influences filtered through the compositions as well. Drummer Ronald Shannon Jackson has played with Ornette Coleman and Cecil Taylor and led his own Decoding Society band. His music rips and roars, while seamlessly moving through multiple idioms, sometimes blurring and combining them as he goes along. —*Ron Wynn*

Live at the Caravan of Dreams / 1986 / Caravan Of Dreams 85005

☆ **Red Warrior** / i. 1990 / Axiom 510149

Sprawling drums and guitar highlight this recent session. Produced by Bill Laswell. —*Ron Wynn*

Taboo / i. 1990 / Venture 1654

Some dynamic adventures with Vernon Reid (g) venturing outside Living Colour arena. —*Ron Wynn*

WILLIS JACKSON (Willis "Gator" Jackson)

b. Apr. 25, 1932, Miami, FL, **d.** Oct. 25, 1987, New York, NY
Saxophone / Swing, blues & jazz, soul-jazz

A great saxophonist in the R&B, blues, and ballad mode, Willis Jackson had an exuberant, alternately explosive and soothing style. Jackson's style was derived from his experiences in swing era bands, from honking and doing short riffs and solos on Atlantic R&B and rock & roll sessions, and from his knowledge of bebop and the blues. He had a huge, robust tone, knew how to pace and build solos, and was a master at generating power and playing in a sturdy, concise fashion, but he also put on a show. Jackson designed a modified saxophone he called the Gator horn, which had a ball-shaped bell with a small opening and was pitched between an alto and soprano, for ballads. He seldom played a bad solo, regardless of the musical style or the quality of the composition.

Jackson began playing in bands around New York in the late '40s, working alongside Blue Mitchell and Cannonball Adderley, among others. He studied theory and harmony at Florida Agricultural and Mechanical University, while playing with Cootie Williams's various bands from the late '40s through the mid-'50s. His composition "Gator Tail" earned Jackson a nickname and Williams's band a hit record. Jackson also had several singles on Apollo, including "Chuck's Chuckles/Dance of the Lady Bug," with Booty Wood, Bill Doggett, and Panama Francis in 1950. He began heading his own band in the early '50s, and recorded for Atlantic, Atco, Deluxe, and Prestige. He backed his wife, Ruth Brown, on Atlantic R&B and early rock & roll sessions in the '50s (they were married for eight years), and worked with Charlie Parker and Dizzy Gillespie. Jackson played everything from urban jazz clubs to chitlin' circuit dives in a touring career that saw him remain on the road from the '50s into the '80s. He began attracting widespread attention and getting heavy response on the soul-jazz circuit with stomping Prestige sessions in the '60s. Jackson recorded with Brother Jack McDuff, Freddie Roach, Kenny Burrell, Tommy Flanagan, Roy Haynes, and others. He did several fine releases for Prestige, Verve, Cadet, and Upfront in the '60s, and for Atlantic, Muse, and Cotillion in the '70s. Jackson kept playing in the '80s, recording with Grove Holmes on Black & Blue, and playing in New York with Sammy Price in 1981 (he had toured France with Price in 1979 and 1980). Like Grant Green, Jackson's considerable skills were sometimes underrated by critics obsessed with flashier, more experimental outside players and bebop veterans. Some of Jackson's albums inevitably became formulaic, but the vast majority had plenty of solid material, and the great ones are soul-jazz classics. Several of his albums are available on CD. In '92, Delmark reissued a collection of his superb Apollo singles from 1949 and 1950. —*Ron Wynn*

On My Own / i. 1950 / Muse

○ **Cool Gator** / May 25, 1959-Nov. 9, 1959 / Prestige 220
Willis Jackson (ts) was one of the prime exploiters of the commercial funk (over)exposure of the late '60s. *Cool Gator*, however, is a reasonably restrained LP made up of three dates: 5/25/59 with Jack McDuff (org), Bill Jennings (g), Tommy Potter (b), Alvin Johnson (d); 11/9/59 with Wendell Marshall substituted on bass; and an unknown date with Milt Hinton taking the bass and Buck Clarke added on congas. This is a credible set of the sax/organ bar jazz genre; nothing particularly memorable, but nothing insulting either. —*Bob Rusch*, Cadence

Please Mr. Jackson / May 25, 1959 / Prestige 321

★ **Together Again** / May 25, 1959-Aug. 16, 1960 / Prestige 7364

○ **Cookin' Sherry** / Nov. 9, 1959-Aug. 16, 1960 / Prestige 7211

Blue Gator / i. Mar. 1961 / Prestige 7183

○ **Thunderbird** / Mar. 31, 1962 / Prestige

★ **Shuckin'** / Oct. 30, 1962 / Prestige
His second great album that year. All-star lineup includes Kenny Burrell (g) and Tommy Flanagan (p). —*Ron Wynn*

Gator Tails / Mar. 18, 1964-Jun. 23, 1964 / Verve

Smokin' with Willis / Nov. 15, 1965 / Cadet

West Africa / Oct. 22, 1973 / Muse 5036
Willis Jackson was a practitioner of the big, full-toned sound who spent considerable time locked into the R&B circuit. But he was a musician whose history dated back to the Cootie Williams band of the 1940s and whose musical heritage and influences were linked closely with people like Ben Webster, Coleman Hawkins, Gene Ammons, and Lester Young. On *West Africa* Jackson almost seems to be exploring this tradition in the way one might sift through some old but not forgotten love letters. There are strong references to Webster, Hawkins, Jug, and Sonny Rollins. One can also detect the presence of Sam "The Man" Taylor. Both the title tune and "Fungii" are similiar pieces using West Indian rhythms; Jackson sounds a lot like Rollins on some of the calypso things he's fond of doing. Three of the six tracks are ballads, which Jackson treats with sensual respect. The accompanying musicians (Mickey Tucker on organ and keyboards, guitarist Ted Dunbar, electric bassist Bob Cranshaw, drummer Freddie Waits, percussionist Sonny Morgan, and Richard Landrum on congas and percussion) are some of the best and most versatile around, and they contribute solid support. —*Herb Nolan*, Down Beat

Headed and Gutted / May 16, 1974 / Muse 5048

○ **In the Alley** / 1976 / Muse 5100
Solid soul-jazz from a tenor sax master of the style. Willis Jackson never tried to play intricate or elaborate solos; he re-

lied on intensity, blues feeling, and simplicity to communicate his soulful messages. —*Ron Wynn*

★ **Bar Wars** / Dec. 1977 / Muse 6011
This Willis Jackson date is solid if unspectacular. Tenor saxophonist Jackson plays assertively and the title track is very fine blues. Guitarist Pat Martino shows himself to be adept as usual. —*Ronald B. Weinstock*, Cadence

○ **Single Action** / Apr. 1978 / Muse 5179
Willis Jackson was one of the most successful tenorists to fill the void Gene Ammons left for big-toned party jazz that was inclined toward R&B. The most glaring problem with this album is the covering of insipid pop material without freshness or imagination. The best piece, six lean and mean minutes of boiling, double-timed blues, features a delightfully frenzied Jackson and the taut Wes Montgomeryisms of guitarist Pat Martino. —*Bill Shoemaker*, Cadence

ILLINOIS JACQUET (Jean Baptiste Illinois Jacquet)

b. Oct. 31, 1922, Boussard, LA
Tenor saxophone, bassoon, clarinet / Swing, big band, bop, soul-jazz
Though he was born in Louisiana, tenor saxophonist Illinois Jacquet was among the foremost practioners of the Texas style of playing, and made the transition from swing to bebop. His dramatic, flamboyant solo on the Lionel Hampton band's single "Flying Home" in 1942 made Jacquet a folk hero. He became famous for high note acrobatics in the tenor's upper register and for putting his teeth on the reed to achieve showy harmonic effects. But as wild as he could be on uptempo tunes or during jam sessions, Jacquet would turn it around and be extremely lyrical and evocative on ballads, and as he became older, his playing mellowed tremendously.

Jacquet's moved from Broussard, Louisiana to Houston, where he grew up. He began playing drums in high school, then learned alto and soprano sax. Before going to the West Coast in the late '30s, Jacquet played with regional groups. He joined Floyd Ray's band in 1941, then became a member of Lionel Hampton's orchestra the next year. He played with Cab Calloway from 1943 to 1944, and appeared in the famous short film Jammin' the Blues along with Lester Young in 1944. Jacquet worked with Count Basie from 1945 to 1946. He became the principal soloist for Jazz at the Philharmonic in 1950, and led his own groups. JATP promoter/organizer Norman Granz signed Jacquet to the Verve label in the '50s, and began recording him regularly with Kenny Burrell, Ben Webster, and Basie, among others.

Jacquet added bassoon in the early '60s, while cutting sessions for Argo. He became one of the rare jazz musicians to play the instrument regularly, live and during recordings. During the '60s, Jacquet recorded some popular soul jazz sessions for Prestige, among them *Bottoms Up, King!, Soul Explosion*, a big-band date, and *Blues: That's Me*. He was a familiar face at festivals and throughout Europe in the '50s and '60s, and appeared often at the Monterey, Nice, and Northsea events. He also toured with the Texas Tenors, a band that included Arnett Cobb and Buddy Tate. He continued recording in the '70s, doing dates with Wild Bill Davis, a Town Hall concert with Cobb and with Panama Francis, and sessions with Gerry Mulligan and James Moody. Jacquet hasn't recorded as often in the '80s and '90s, but played regularly in New York with his big band during the late '80s and early '90s. He made a fine big band date for Atlantic, *Jacquet's Got It!*, in 1988. His vintage sessions for Verve, Prestige, LRC, Black Lion, Black & Blue, and RCA/Bluebird are available currently on compact disc. —*Ron Wynn and Bob Porter*

Flying Home / Dec. 1947-Jul. 1967 / Bluebird 61123

★ **Black Velvet Band** / i. 1947-1950 / Bluebird 6571
Prime 8- and 10-piece group cuts from 1947-50, plus one cut from 1967 Newport Jazz Festival. —*Ron Wynn*

○ **Illinois Jacquet Jam Session** / i. 1951 / Apollo 104

Kid and the Brute, The / Dec. 13, 1954 / Verve 680

○ **Illinois Jacquet** / Sep. 16, 1955 / Clef 676

○ **Port of Rico** / i. 1956 / Clef 701

Swing's the Thing / Jul. 1957 / Verve

Flies Again / Nov. 9, 1959 / Capitol 97272

Banned in Boston / i. Feb. 1962 / Portrait 44391
What a matched pair Illinois Jacquet (ts) and Roy Eldridge (tpt) were! Too bad their pairing does not make for a whole session here. Jacquet takes a decidedly boppish approach to "Indiana," even quoting Charlie Parker in his final chorus. That and Eldridge fanning the flames on "Satin Doll" are about the only really notable moments on this otherwise ho-hum release. — *Willard Jenkins, Jazz Times*

Illinois Jacquet: Illinois Jacquet / May 7-8, 1963 / Argo 722
Illinois Jacquet: Illinois Jacquet is a two-record set bringing together two of Jacquet's Argo/Cadet dates. From 5/7 and 8/63 comes a date with Kenny Burrell or Wally Richardson (g), Ralph Smith (org), Ben Tucker (b), and Willie Rodriquez and Ray Lucas (d) that covers seven tracks. For some reason one track from the original issue ("Wild Man") is not included here. On "Bassoon Blues" Jacquet plays bassoon, but it is Burrell whose solo interests. This session lasts only 26 minutes. The other half of this twofer reissues *Go Power*, a 3/66 date from Lennie's-on-the-Turnpike with the distinctive organ work of Milt Buckner and house drummer Alan Dawson. The material here is more condensed and directly dealt with in terms of both emotional involvement and group interaction. There is also the element here of an appreciative live audience, which, while encouraging some of the more grandstanding moments, also drives the musicians to dig in. This is a date with a party ambiance, but with enough fine improvisatory jazz to please those who wish to listen with both ears. — *Bob Rusch, Cadence*

Message, The / May 7-8, 1963 / Argo
Booming, authoritative soul-jazz, bop, and swing from tenor sax master Illinois Jacquet. He does stomping standards and screaming blues and drives a good combo through a program of routine but enjoyable tunes. — *Ron Wynn*

Bottoms Up / Mar. 26, 1968 / Prestige 417
This is a 1991 reissue of a sterling blues, soul-jazz, and swing date. — *Ron Wynn*

How High the Moon / Mar. 1968-Sep. 1969 / Prestige 24057

○ **King, The** / Aug. 20, 1968 / Prestige 7597

Soul Explosion / Mar. 25, 1969 / Original Jazz Classics 674
This is juicy Illinois Jacquet, piping hot and done to a turn and swimming in good gravy. Here Jacquet rides and rolls in front of a 10-piece keg of a band sporting four brass, two reeds (plus Jacquet who equals three more), and a well-shod rhythm section pumped by Milt Buckner (org) and Wally Richardson (g). Blues are a large part of the menu—"After Hours" and "St. Louis Blues" (both arranged by Buckner) and "The Soul Explosion," charted by Jimmy Mundy, who also scores "The Eighteenth Hole." Jacquet's "After Hours" solo is a masterpiece of slow deliberation within the form. "St. Louis Blues," by contrast, is a fast, tightly controlled sprint down that old familiar road. "Soul Explosion" is rhythm *and* blues. After the ensemble exchanges with organ, Jacquet swoops in like a mighty eagle and indulges in some uninhibited "hounding." Similarly molten solos from Jerome Richardson and Joe Newman and then Jacquet come back hotter than ever. This is a performance that builds up to the feverish as the band punches out great riffs and Newman (or is it Russ Jacquet?) approximates a horse neigh at one point. "After Hours" is a much calmer offering with a near classic introduction by Buckner and some effective work by Richardson. Jacquet, bending and shaping his notes and tone to convey all he feels, is right there, suggesting every after-hours blow there ever was. The ballad is done by Jacquet with the rhythm section. Few soloists could sustain a properly romantic atmosphere for nine minutes. Jacquet and Buckner bring it off convincingly, Jacquet's solo being especially moving. Finally, at "The Eighteenth Hole," a typically swinging Munday effort, Jacquet sinks his putt in a brisk,

brusque manner to set the seal on a fine, aptly named album. — *Mark Gardner*, Coda

Blues–That's Me! / Sep. 16, 1969 / Prestige 614
1991 reissue. A welcome return of this fine blues date, with torrid, lusty Jacquet solos. — *Ron Wynn*

Genius at Work / Apr. 13-14, 1971 / Jzm 5034

Illinois Jacquet with Wild Bill Davis / Jan. 15-16, 1973 / Classic Jazz

★ **Blues from Louisiana** / Jul. 7, 1973 / Classic Jazz
This is an odd record, taken either from different live sessions or part of a bigger all-star bash. Dan Morgenstern's liners say this is from a Newport Town Hall Concert in 1973 put on by Grambling College to honor saxophonist Illinois Jacquet. "On A Clear Day" is open, loose, and swingingly pushed by Jacquet's big throaty vibrato on tenor; "Marlow's La. Blues" is a slow d-r-a-w-n out funky teaser worried to death by organist Milt Buckner and Jacquet. "Hamp's Boogie Woogie" (announced as "Buckner's Boogie Woogie") is Buckner's (bit sloppy) feature—a boogie piece, driving in the manner of jazz organists who used to play organ before Jimmy Smith and the commercialization and formulizing of "funk." "Smooth Sailing" features Arnett Cobb's R&B-ish Texas tenor and obligatory crescendoes (I don't believe Jacquet plays on this). "Flying Home" ends the show, sounding unrehearsed and possibly an encore. While Buckner riffs and Francis bombs, Cobb and Jacquet pull out the stops and jam it off. As for the music, it's rough and ready jazz. — *Bob Rusch*, Cadence

On Jacquet's Street / Jul. 16, 1976 / Classic Jazz 146

★ **Cool Rage, The** / Verve
The Cool Rage reissue by tenor saxophonist Illinois Jacquet was culled from various Verve sessions. The two-record set includes tracks from 4/21/58 with Wild Bill Davis (org), Kenny Burrell (g), and Johnny Williams (d). The rest of the material comes from various early '50s dates. The personnel includes Art Blakey, Hank Jones, Count Basie, Carl Perkins, Sir Charles Thompson, Oscar Moore, Freddie Green, Ben Webster, Leo Parker, and Matthew Gee, among others. The music is a mixture of Jazz at the Philharmonic wailings, after-hour blues, and relaxed Lestorian (Young) blowing. There are some nice tastes of Basie on organ, an organist even for those who do not like organ. This is a good look at '50s Jacquet. — *Bob Rusch*, Cadence

RUSSELL JACQUET (Robert Russell Jacquet)

b. Dec. 4, 1917, Saint Martinville, LA, d. Feb. 28, 1990
Trumpet, vocals / Swing, big band
The older brother of tenor saxophonist Illinois Jacquet, Russell Jacquet was not as flamboyant as his celebrated sibling, and he didn't play the same instrument. A trumpeter, Jacquet was a disciplined, resourceful, and effective player in a swing or bebop mode. Jacquet toured with both Illinois and his even lesser-known brother, Linton, in the California Playboy Band in the mid '30s, then performed in Floyd Ray's orchestra in 1939 and 1940. He studied at Wiley College and led a big band at Texas Southern, then moved with Illinois Jacquet's group to California and participated in two recording sessions. Russell Jacquet's group played at the Hollywood Cotton Club, and he recorded there as a leader between 1945 and 1949. Russell and Illinois toured and performed regularly from the mid-'40s until 1954, when they toured Europe. After that, Russell Jacquet only played with his brother on a couple of other occasions. He recorded with his group in the mid- and late '60s. Russell Jacquet led a band in Houston in the mid-'60s that included Arnett Cobb, and reunited again with Illinois in 1985. Currently, he does not have any albums under his name as a leader, but can be heard on some reissued Illinois Jacquet CDs. — *Ron Wynn*

AHMAD JAMAL (Fritz Jones)

b. Jul. 2, 1930, Pittsburgh, PA
Piano / Bop

Ahmad Jamal's a fine pianist noted for his very melodic improvisations. He parlayed a lean approach that featured an intelligent use of space and an expert sense of pacing, plus simple embellishments, interesting left hand voicings, teasing right hand contrasts, and a liberal dose of block chords. His ensemble was one of the most popular and influential trios of the '50s and '60s. Miles Davis gave him an enormous boost with his open, unqualified praise and by adopting some of Jamal's tunes and concepts in his music.

Jamal worked with vocalist Mary Caldwell Dawson and James Miller in Pittsburgh, where he became a professional at age 11. He left Westinghouse High School in the late '40s to join an orchestra led by George Hudson. Jamal formed his first trio, the Three Strings, in the early '50s. The trio won the attention and support of John Hammond during an appearance at the Embers in New York. Jamal even got an early hit with his arrangement of "Billy Boy." The original trio included guitarist Ray Crawford and bassist Eddie Calhoun. Richard Davis later replaced Calhoun for a short time, then Israel Crosby, the ideal bassist for Jamal's concepts, replaced Davis. Jamal's trio made two albums for Epic, then switched to Argo in 1955. He scored a huge hit album in 1958 with *But Not for Me;* the lineup included Jamal, Crosby, and drummer Vernell Fournier. This album reached the number-three spot on the *Billboard* pop charts, and was the first of five Jamal albums to make that list. It was recorded at the Pershing, and Jamal later made a sequel. Jamal continued at Argo into the '60s, and later recorded for Chess and Cadet. He did dates with string sections, expanded to a quintet with guitarist and violinist, and gradually recorded more trendy projects like *Naked City Theme* and *Roar of the Greasepaint.* He also had the enormous hit single "Poinciana."

Jamal's trio remained a hot item through much of the '60s, and even survived Crosby's death in 1962 (Jamil Sulieman replaced him). Fournier left briefly, then returned in the mid-'60s. Jamal moved to ABC/Impulse in the late '60s, and began playing electric in the early '70s. During the '70s and '80s, he recorded for ABC/Impulse, 20th Century, Kingdom Gate, Motown, Chiaroscuro, Shubra, and Atlantic. Jamal maintained his penchant for experimentation, recording with the Howard Roberts Chorale, adding horn sections, percussionists, overdubbing electric keyboard parts, using string sections, choirs, even working with symphony orchestras. His mid-'80s Atlantic albums were a return to the more jazz-centered pop of his peak years. Jamal has never tried to be pretentious about what he did best, and his finest albums were deservedly popular. He probably exhausted the formula, but has continued working and performing. Jamal has a good amount of recent and vintage material available on CD. —*Ron Wynn*

★ **Poinciana** / **i.** Oct. 25, 1952-1955 / Chess 31266

○ **Chamber Music of New Jazz** / May 23, 1955 / Argo 602

○ **Ahmad Jamal Trio** / Oct. 25, 1955 / Epic 3212

○ **Count 'em–88** / Sep. 27, 1956+Oct. 4, 1956 / Argo 610

★ **At the Pershing** / **But Not for Me** / **i.** Jan. 16, 1958 / Chess 9108
Recorded at the Pershing Club in Chicago. A twofer. Jamal's third album (includes hit "Poinciana") was the turning point in his career. His liberal use of silence influenced many jazz musicians, including Miles Davis. —*Michael Erlewine*

Ahmad Jamal Trio–Vol. 4 / Sep. 5-6, 1958 / Argo 636
One of his most popular albums ever in its original issue. Fine, if a bit to the pop side. —*Ron Wynn*

Ahmad Jamal at the Penthouse / Feb. 22-28, 1959 / Argo 646

○ **Listen to the Ahmad Jamal Quintet** / Aug. 15-16, 1960 / Argo 673

Live at the Alhambra / Jun. 1961 / Vogue

○ **Piano Scene** / **i.** Apr. 1965 / Epic 634

Cry Young / Jun. 1967 / Cadet 792

Tranquility / **i.** 1969 / Impulse

Awakening, The / Feb. 3, 1970 / MCA 5644
This is a 1986 reissue of some of his most beloved trio performances. —*Ron Wynn*

Free Flight / Jun. 17, 1971 / Impulse

Outertimeinnerspace / Jun. 17, 1972 / Impulse

Re-Evaluations: The Impulse Years / **i.** Aug. 1974 / Impulse 9260
Re-Evaluations showcasesd the famous Ahmad Jamal virtues: economy, taste (both in the choice of tunes and their interpretation), and a sensitivity that makes this trio a consistent source of delight. There are also the Jamalian shortcomings, which are nevertheless able to transmute into virtues. One rarely feels that Jamal's bag is an inexhaustible one; he husbands his ideas shrewdly, as on "Wave." There are only three or four figures at work there, sequentially repeated and embellished; but they are good ideas, and three or four of them is two or three more than most other pianists usually came up with. By the way, this is a trio album, and a perfect case study of tripartite musical empathy. Catch bassist Jamil Sulieman on "Dolphin Dance," wailing in harmonics like a prodigious muezzin; and catch Frank Gant throughout. Lots of drummers can play, but not so many can listen. —*Steve Metaliz,* Down Beat

Genetic Walk / 1978 / 20th Century 600
Last of Jamal's albums to enjoy crossover chart activity. Horn section used on some cuts. —*Ron Wynn*

Digital Works / 1985 / Atlantic 81258
Later Jamal, experimenting with digital sound electronics. He remains a gripping player. —*Ron Wynn*

Rossiter Road / 1985 / Atlantic 81645

○ **Live at the Montreux Jazz Festival** / **i.** Feb. 1986 / Atlantic 81699
Shimmering, attacking style at times. Still the master of space and pauses. —*Ron Wynn*

Crystal / **i.** 1987 / Atlantic 81793

Pittsburgh / **i.** 1989 / Atlantic 82029
There are a couple of high points on Jamal's newest venture, as well as some dreary moments, but his flair and style provide far more upbeat sequences than dismal frolics. —*Ron Wynn,* Rock & Roll Disc

☆ **What's New** / Telstar 3604
Giants of Jazz series. Seventeen hits from a variety of his original Chess recordings, including "Poinciana." —*Michael Erlewine*

KHAN JAMAL

b. Jul. 23, 1946, Jacksonville, FL
Vibes / Modern creative
Though not as widely known as some other vibists, Khan Jamal has been a proficient soloist when playing free material, jazz-rock and fusion, hard bop, or bluesy fare. He's also an outstanding marimba player and percussionist. Jamal's mother was a stride pianist, and he began on vibes in the mid-'60s. Jamal was in the Cosmic Forces in the late '60s, then coformed the Sounds of Liberation with Byard Lancaster in the early '70s. He studied vibes and percussion at Combs College of Music, then performed and recorded with Sunny Murray's Untouchable Factor in the late '70s. Jamal played with Ronald Shannon Jackson's Decoding Society, in bands led by Joe Bonner and Billy Bang, and headed his own groups in the '80s and '90s. Jamal has recorded as a leader for Philly Jazz, Steeplechase, Stash, Gazell, and Storyville, among others. He's played with Bill Lewis, Monette Sudler, Dwight James, Jamaaladeen Tacuma, and other musicians. Jamal has some sessions available on CD. —*Ron Wynn*

★ **Infinity** / **i.** Dec. 1982-Mar. 1984 / Stash 278

Dark Warrior / **i.** Sep. 1984 / Steeple Chase 1196

Traveller, The / **i.** Oct. 1985 / Steeple Chase 1217

Speak Easy / Gazell 4001

BOB JAMES (Robert James)

b. Dec. 25, 1939, Marshall, MO
Piano, composer, producer / Early jazz-rock, instrumental pop
Bob James was once nearly as popular an instrumental
crossover star as Kenny G, though James never sold anywhere near as many records. But during the '70s, James's
light, hook-laden pop instrumental sessions were often on
the charts. The songs had minimal improvisation, and were
fortified with either heavy backbeats or were dominated by
strings. They were also tightly produced affairs with background vocalists, and featured simple arrangements or reworkings of urban contemporary and recent pop hits.
James's background as a pianist, composer, and arranger included extensive bebop and free sessions; he even issued an
album of wide-ranging material for ESP. James earned a
masters degree from the University of Michigan in the early
'60s in composition, and recorded albums of bebop and free
music during that time. He was Sarah Vaughan's music director in the mid-'60s, then played with Quincy Jones,
Morgana King, Roberta Flack, and Dionne Warwick as a session player in New York in the late '60s and early '70s. James
joined Creed Taylor's CTI label as an arranger in 1973, and
soon also became a house producer and composer. He
worked with Grover Washington, Jr., Hubert Laws, Ron
Carter, and Eric Gale. In addition, James was a label artist in
1974, but moved to CBS the next year. He worked with Neil
Diamond and Paul Simon before starting his own label,
Tappan Zee, in 1977. Besides working with other artists like
Mongo Santamaria and Richard Tee, James issued his own
hit albums and recorded with Earl Klugh in 1979. He continued making albums through the '80s and '90s, and expanded into television and films. James composed the theme
for "Taxi." He moved to Warner Bros. in the mid-'80s, and
has since issued albums with David Sanborn, with Klugh
again, and has done a classical date as well as his familiar
instrumental pop sessions. James has recorded for ESP and
Mercury, as well as CTI, Columbia/Tappan Zee, and Warner
Bros. He has several sessions available on CD. —*Ron Wynn*

Bold Conceptions / Aug. 13-15, 1962 / Mercury 60768

Bob James Trio / i. 1965 / ESP 1009

One / i. 1974 / Columbia 36835
The first in a string of hugely successful albums from pi-
anist/composer Bob James in the '70s. James joined the CTI
label in 1973 and became its exclusive arranger; the next
year he signed a separate recording deal as an artist. This is
his debut, and he scores a hit with an interpretation of
Mussorgsky's *A Night on Bald Mountain.* —*Ron Wynn*

Lucky Seven / i. 1979 / Columbia 36056
Successful fusion album by a superstar in the genre. James
made an art form of short solos, pop-tinged instrumentals,
multitracked vocals by guest stars, and unchallenging
tracks. This album utilizes all those elements. —*Ron Wynn*

○ **Two of a Kind** / i. 1982 / Capitol 12244

★ **Grand Piano Canyon** / i. 1990 / Tappan Zee 26256

HARRY JAMES (Harry Hagg James)

b. Mar. 15, 1916, Albany, GA, **d.** Jul. 5, 1983, Las Vegas, NV
Trumpet, bandleader / Swing, big band
Harry James had many gifts, including great stamina, a rich
tone, tremendous range, and a willingness to try anything
on stage. Taste and delicacy weren't his strong points, but his
individualism and personality often balanced out lapses in
judgment. James was a fine combo and small band player,
though he enjoyed peak popularity working in big bands
and accompanying sentimental pop singers. Intimate surroundings enabled him to fully display his talents, and
James tended to ditch the show time routines in these settings.
   James started his professional career with his father's circus bands. He was playing drums at age seven, and was
learning trumpet at age ten. He played with different groups

in Texas, then worked with Ben Pollack in 1935 and 1936,
writing "Peckin'," a number that ignited a temporary dance
craze. He joined Benny Goodman in 1937, where his aggressive, animated style got full exposure. The song "Ridin'
High" became his showpiece. James also made some excellent small group recordings with Teddy Wilson, Red Norvo,
and John Simmons in 1937. He left Goodman in 1938 with
the leader's encouragement, forming his own big band,
which became a huge attraction by 1940. An early version of
"One O'clock Jump" and "Ciribiribin," their theme song,
helped launch their success. They did "Ciribiribin" twice in
1939, once with Frank Sinatra. The band had some notable
soloists, among them Vido Musso and Sam Donahue, later
alto saxophonist Willie Smith, and Corky Corcoran's tenor,
plus popular vocalists Sinatra, Dick Haymes, Helen Forrest,
and Kitty Kallen. James even became a film star in the '40s,
appearing, from '42 to '47, in *Syncopation, Best Foot
Forward, Mr. Co-ed, Kitten on the Keys,* and *Carnegie Hall.*
James provided the horn solos for Kirk Douglas in the horrendous 1950 film *Young Man with a Horn,* and was in "The
Benny Goodman Story" in 1955.
   Questionable taste and dubious musical decisions, coupled with the decline of big bands, eventually derailed
James. He added strings to the band, and featured exaggerated trumpet workouts, such as "Flight of the Bumble Bee,"
excessively. The band did enjoy 23 top-10 hits from 1943 to
1947 on the strength of its vocalists, including the songs
"You Made Me Love You" and "I'll Get By." During the late
'40s, James employed Ray Conniff as an arranger, and hired
Juan Tizol, Willie Smith, and Louis Bellson, who all left to
join Duke Ellington in what was called the great James raid
in 1951 (though Tizol and Smith came back in 1954). James
eventually began to organize bands only for tours. He
started hiring better arrangers like Neal Hefti and Ernie
Wilkins, and often used Buddy Rich. He rekindled his ties
with Goodman, touring with the band regularly and going
with them to Europe in 1957. James relocated to Nevada in
the '60s, making frequent appearances in Las Vegas.
Periodically, he traveled to New York. There were European
tours in 1970 and 1971, and a visit to Argentina in 1981.
James headed his band until a few days before his death in
1983. —*Ron Wynn and Dan Morgenstern*

★ **Harry James and Dick Haymes** / 1941 / Circle

○ **Uncollected Harry James & His Orchestra–Vol. 1 (1943-**
   1946) / 1943-1946 / Hindsight 102

○ **Uncollected Harry James & His Orchestra–Vol. 2 (1943-**
   1946) / 1943-1946 / Hindsight 123

○ **Uncollected Harry James & His Orchestra–Vol. 3 (1948-**
   1949) / 1948-1949 / Hindsight 135

○ **Uncollected Harry James & His Orchestra - Vol. 4 (1943-**
   1946) / 1943-1946 / Hindsight 141

○ **Uncollected Harry James & His Orchestra–Vol. 5 (1943-**
   1953) / 1943-1953 / Hindsight 142

○ **Uncollected Harry James & His Orchestra–Vol. 6 (1947-**
   1949) / 1947-1949 / Hindsight 150

○ **Young Man with a Horn** / i. 1950 / Columbia 582
Sound track from a well-intentioned, inaccurate film portrait
of Bix Beiderbecke. —*Ron Wynn*

Man with the Horn, The / i. 1955 / Columbia

Harry James in Hi-Fi / i. 1955 / Capitol 654

More Harry James in Hi-Fi / Nov. 1955-Jan. 1956 / Pasva

Hits of Harry James, The / i. 195? / Capitol 91220

Best of Big Bands / Columbia 45341

Big Band Recordings / Vanguard 406

Golden Trumpet of Harry James, The / London 820178

STAFFORD JAMES (Stafford Louis James)

b. Apr. 24, 1946, Evanston, IL
Bass / Hard bop, modern creative

A gifted and versatile bassist, Stafford James has played be-bop, hard bop, free, and R&B material since he emerged in the late '60s working with Monty Alexander, Albert Ayler, and Sun Ra. He's equally capable on acoustic or electric, and has backed both jazz and R&B singers. James studied at the Chicago Conservatory and Mannes College in the late '60s and early '70s. Following his stints with Alexander, Ayler, and Ra, he played with Melba Moore, Roy Ayers, Garry Bartz, Rashied Ali, Betty Carter, Art Blakey, Al Haig, Barry Harris, Andrew Hill, Andrew Cyrille, and Chico Hamilton at various points during the early and mid-'70s. James appeared with Bartz at the Montreux Jazz Festival. He worked with Dexter Gordon and Woody Shaw in the late '70s, and with John Scofield. James reunited with Shaw in the early '80s, then played with Philly Joe Jones and Dameronia, Slide Hampton, Cecil Payne, and Jimmy Heath. He also recorded as a leader from the mid-'70s through the '80s, heading quartets, quintets, a trio, and a string and percussion ensemble. James has recorded for Horo (Italy) and Red, a subsidiary of Black Saint/Soul Note. Though he does not currently have any dates available on CD, he can be heard on reissues by Ayler, Shaw, and others. James's sessions on Red and Horo are available by import from mail-order sources. —*Ron Wynn*

★ **Stafford James Ensemble** / i. 1978 / Red 142

JOSEPH JARMAN

b. Sep. 14, 1937, Pine Bluff, AK

Reeds, flute, clarinet, piccolo, percussion, composer / Early free, modern creative

Multi-instrumentalist Joseph Jarman hasn't been as prolific as fellow Art Ensemble of Chicago member Lester Bowie outside of the band, but Jarman has his own impressive list of recording and performing credits as a leader. A founding member of the group and of the Association for the Advancement of Creative Musicians (AACM), Jarman's equally as eclectic as Bowie. His style includes several vocal effects in his sax solos such as screams, squeals, squawks, slurs, smears, and twisting, anguished phrases. He plays various saxophones and flutes, and has created many wind instruments, doubling on them and playing percussion items from around the world. Jarman's a published poet and writer who's included poems and readings on his albums and during Art Ensemble concerts. He also utilizes dance and vocals, and is perhaps the Art Ensemble's most theatrical member. Jarman's had several theatrical pieces performed independently of the group or any musical situation. He's supplied many compositions to Art Ensemble albums, among them "Fanfare for the Warriors" and "Ohnedaruth." Jarman studied drums under Walter Dyett, and played in his high school band during the '50s. He later played clarinet and saxophone in army bands. Jarman was in Muhal Richard Abrams Experimental band in the early '60s, and played in Roscoe Mitchell's hard bop group. Besides helping start the AACM, Jarman gave solo concerts and led a free jazz band during the late '70s. But after both his pianist Christopher Gaddy and bassist Charles Clark died, Jarman joined the Art Ensemble in Paris. He'd already recorded with Bowie in 1967. Jarman's done solo dates, worked in a trio with Don Moye and Don Pullen, and played with Anthony Braxton and Oliver Lake. He's recorded in the '60s, '70s, and '80s for Delmark, Nessa, India Navigation, Black Saint, Baybridge (Japan), and the Art Ensemble's own AECO label. Currently, there are only a few Jarman dates available on CD. —*Ron Wynn*

★ **Song For** / Oct. 20, 1966-Dec. 16, 1966 / Delmark 410
The ensemble the criminally underrecorded Joseph Jarman put together for *Song For* is nothing less than legendary: trumpeter Bill Brimfield; tenor godfather Fred Anderson; the late, great drummer Steve McCall and the late, destined-to-be-great bassist Charles Clark; pianist Christopher Gaddy; and drummer Thurman Barker. Additionally, all of the tenets of Jarman's music were already in place, such as fanfares floating over drum swells, elongating into themes

tinged with bop and surrealism, adagios with a hallowed, hymnal feel, catalysing impassioned solos, and a pointed integration of auxiliary percussion and poetry. No wonder, then, that *Song For* has retained its edge and its cogency. —*Bill Shoemaker*, Down Beat

★ **As If It Were the Seasons** / 1968 / Delmark 417
A textbook '60s Chicago free jazz album from a founding member of the AACA, multi-instrumentalist Joseph Jarman. He employs his full array of horns and is joined by several mainstays, among them pianist Muhal Richard Abrams, bassist Charles Clark, drummer Thurman Barker, and tenor saxophonist John Stubblefield. This is not compromising material—songs are long, and everything from bells to whistles to shakers to energized sax screaming makes up the music. —*Ron Wynn*

Together Alone / Dec. 1971 / Delmark 428

Egwu-Anwu / Jan. 8, 1978 / India Navigation 1033
Joseph Jarman and Famoudou Don Moye's collaboration ranges from readings of the gossamer (heaven) to all-out explosions of emotion and longing (earth). *Egwu-Anwu* is a primitive's approach to music, and as such it might not be everyone's cup of tea. There is a lovely Asian flavored dance (the vibes-marimba duet of "Egwu Ping"), Jarman's dark screaming tenor and Moye's lightning drumming on the John Coltrane dedication "Ohnedaruth," a high-stepping African conga dance ("Nke-Ala"), sopranino for belly dancing on "Egwu Ogotemmeli," Moye's three-ring circus of sounds ("Lobo"), the gentle epilogue of "Ekoo-kona-Ye Fai," and much more. *Egwu-Anwu* is a kinetic dialog by musicians who have made a career out of mutual sound sculptures. —*Chip Stern*, Down Beat

○ **Magic Triangle** / Jul. 24-26, 1979 / Black Saint 0038
Though the Magic Triangle is ostensibly equilateral, pianist Don Pullen is the dominant player. Don Moye's "J.F.M. 3-Way Blues" begins with his solo parade drums, soon joined by fellow Chicago Art Ensemblist Joseph Jarman's piccolo for a little Fourth of July fife-and-drum. With the pianist's entrance the piece abruptly changes to a stomping timeless blues, featuring Pullen's boogie-woogie sixths and "Oh baby why did you do" vocal over Jarman's authentic clarinet obbligato and Moye's firm backbeat. Pullen's sing-song "Hippy-Dippy" shows his ability to play independently with each hand—romantic descending chords from the left and crashing density from the right—accompanied by Jarman's tenor squalls; the boys don't wait long to go outside to play. Pullen's saturation bombing attack under Jarman's concluding theme statement is almost incongruous. "Lonely Child" starts with Pullen singing/speaking Jarman's go-with-the-flow lyric poem (hard to believe some people prefer his poetry to his playing) over Moye's timpani roll. With that out of the way, Jarman plays a pastoral flute melody over Pullen's barely restrained web of swelling, inside-the-piano percussion and Moye's congas. The piece begins to grow stronger, like the child addressed in the lyric, as Pullen restrains himself less and less; eventually he emerges in that aforementioned noisy style. Jarman on tenor sounds uncharacteristically John Coltrane-like at times, and Moye propels with his usual zing-around-the-kit busyness. Pullen's "What Was Ain't" (with Jarman on soprano) comes closest to showing his overtly lyrical side but he throws in complex upward runs and has a few banging fits. —*Kevin Whitehead*, Cadence

○ **Black Paladins** / i. Dec. 1979 / Black Saint 0042
The teaming of South African bassist Johnny Dyani with Art Ensemble of Chicago stalwarts Joseph Jarman and Don Moye results here in an absorbing album. This is a program of well-fired, articulate performances, both in individual and collective terms. *Black Paladins* is roughly divided between pieces with a marked Third World flavor and those more squarely implanted in the jazz tradition. "Mama Marimba," "Ginger Song," and "Ode to Wilbur Ware" fall into the former category and are the most buoyant excursions of the set. Percussion figures prominently in each piece, with Moye

handling the hand percussion chores in his exemplary fashion and giving a powerful traps performance on "Ginger Song." Dyani conveys a melodic sense of underpinning whether on bass—his overdubbing of a pizzicato ostinato and an inspired arco solo on "Ode" stand out—or piano, as on "Mama." Jarman rides the current with equal finesse on sopranino and bass clarinet. The remainder of the album combines John Coltranish fervor and Booker Ervinish brawn, digging into the groundswell created by Dyani and Moye and producing a convincingly raw momentum. "In Memory of My Season" is an elastic, balladic structure that enables the trio to pivot about each other, streaming rich hues; the contrast between the warmth of Jarman's bass bamboo flute and Dyani's sparse piano is very engaging. The title piece is a surging tour de force that finds Moye and Dyani in telepathic tandem with Jarman's powerful baritone. —Bill Shoemaker, Cadence

KEITH JARRETT

b. May 8, 1945, Allentown, PA

Piano, composer / Cool, early jazz-rock, world fusion

A gifted pianist who is one of the greatest contemporary players, Keith Jarrett has excelled at bebop, jazz-rock, classical, entrancing duets, and stunning solo dates while heading several fine combos. He is famous for playing frenetic left-hand rhythms, equally intense and linear right-hand runs, subdued blues and swing feeling, and, sometimes, flashy phrases. His solos, particularly when he plays unaccompanied, frequently burst with melodic and harmonic ideas, and are executed with dazzling speed and rhythmic precision. His classical playing doesn't have the emotional impact of his best jazz work, but it is always performed immaculately. He's contributed many compositions to his group projects. Jarrett plays ballads beautifully, but has generated negative critical reaction for his habit of singing and uttering vocal cries while playing (to be fair, this can be extremely irritating, both on record and in live performance). He's outspoken about his disdain for the music business, and wrote a scathing indictment of popular music and general American cultural tastes in *The New York Times* in '93.

Jarrett's work reflects the influence of Bill Evans and Bud Powell, as well as bits of 20th-century classical composers such as Bela Bartok, Alban Berg, Maurice Ravel, and Ornette Coleman, and gospel and country music as well. His style includes what seems like an effortless command of the keyboard, and vamp-based passages with brief accompaniment figures repeating again and again in a manner that's very easy to follow. He's also incorporated world music approaches, group improvisations using rubato, and long, legato lines, which he's mirrored in his soprano sax work. Bobo Stinson, Art Lande, Richard Beirach, and Lyle Mays are among contemporary players who were influenced directly by Jarrett.

Jarrett was a child prodigy who began studying piano at age three and presented a full recital at age seven. He also played drums, vibes, and soprano sax. Jarrett was a professional in elementary school, and toured for a season as piano soloist with Fred Waring's Pennsylvanians while in his teens. He played a two-hour solo concert of his compositions at age 17, and rejected the chance to study privately in Paris with Nadia Boulanger. Jarrett received no training in orchestration or composition, but did take piano lessons. He moved from Pennsylvania to Boston in 1962, and spent a year at Berklee on scholarship before departing to start his own trio, while playing with Tony Scott and Rahsaan Roland Kirk, among others. Jarrett moved to New York in 1965. Art Blakey heard him during a jam session at the Village Vanguard, and Jarrett briefly joined the Messengers in 1965, and made his first recording with a major jazz band. Jarrett joined Charles Lloyd in 1966, and remained with him until 1969. The band attained a huge profile by visiting the Soviet Union (they also recorded there) and by appearing at several rock halls.

Jarrett began playing soprano sax and percussion while in Lloyd's group. He recorded for Atlantic and its subsidiary label, Vortex, in the late '60s. One album, *Restoration Ruin*, featured him on several instruments and on vocals, with an overdubbed string quartet. He joined Miles Davis in 1969, and played on several jazz-rock sessions in the late '60s and early '70s. Jarrett played both electric organ and electric keyboard with Davis, teaming initially with Chick Corea. Jarrett also formed his own band during this period, with Charlie Haden and Paul Motian at first, then adding Dewey Redman later. This unit cut some excellent, though not commercially successful, albums for ABC/Impulse in the '70s.

Jarrett began performing solo concerts in 1972, a practice that's brought him both praise and disdain. His early solos were between 30 and 45 minutes long. The concerts blossomed into a cottage industry that eventually yielded such ECM albums as *The Koln Concert*, a two-album (disc) set, *Solo Concerts*, a three-album (disc) set, and the massive ten-album *Sun Bear Concerts* in 1976. Jarrett recorded for ABC/Impulse, for Columbia and primarily for ECM through the '70s and '80s. Essentially, ECM has given Jarrett a blank check and creative control. He's played with combos, made a duet album with Jack DeJohnette, cut trio sessions, organ dates, and a two-piano session with Dennis Russell Davies. Jarrett had eight albums chart in the '60s and '70s. He's continued to record in the '80s and '90s, but has not maintained such a prolific pace. Jarrett's worked regularly with Jan Garbarek since the '70s, cutting trio projects and recording with symphony orchestras. He's maintained a similar relationship with DeJohnette and bassist Gary Peacock, touring and doing recordings, including a recent tribute to Miles Davis. Jarrett has many titles available on CD from every period; jazz, classical, and others. —Ron Wynn and Michael G. Nastos

☆ **Life Between the Exit Signs** / May 4, 1967 / Vortex 2006

Somewhere Before / Oct. 30, 1968 / Atlantic 8808
A 1968 live trio recording at Shelly's Manne Hole in Hollywood, with Charlie Haden (b), Paul Motian (d). Rare and excellent. —Michael G. Nastos

Mourning of a Star, The / Jul. 9, 1971 / Atlantic 1596
The initial impression of Keith Jarrett's piano playing is one of extreme technical facility—a good start, but unfortunately pyrotechnics or filigree do not of their own accord make an art meaningful. Charlie Haden (b) and Paul Motian (d) both work imaginatively and rewardingly (ultimately, more so than Jarrett) to fill gaps and build ideas under and against the pianist and each other. Jarrett's most considerable recording to date (1970) was still *Life Between the Exit Signs;* everything he had to say on *The Mourning of a Star* had been done much more fulfillingly on the earlier session. —Barry Tepperman, Coda

Birth / Jul. 15-16, 1971 / Atlantic 1612
Very early example of his quirky style, technique. Jarrett is an excellent pianist, but a horrible recorder/soprano saxist. With first-rate personnel: Charlie Haden (b), Paul Motian (d), and Dewey Redman (ts). —Ron Wynn

★ **Expectations** / Oct. 1971 / Columbia 46866
Two-record set with lots of experimental, high-energy moments. 1991 reissue. —Ron Wynn

☆ **Facing You** / Nov. 10, 1971 / ECM 827132
Keith Jarrett, a stunningly original musician, disavows having *any* premeditated approach to improvisation. He has also formulated what amounts to a partially Platonic musical aesthetic, one that suggests he is simply allowing music from a higher source to flow through him. This record is so inspired that it's tempting to believe this was actually happening. Indeed, dividing the music here into eight "tunes" would be highly arbitrary and, in fact, incorrect. What we are listening to is simply the music in Jarrett, whatever its ultimate source. To bring this discussion down to a less mystical level, Jarrett's music here is generally active, rhythmically more so perhaps than *Solo Concert*. Incidentally, label-

ing this music "jazz" would be, I believe, entirely erroneous. Jarrett doesn't swing, he flows. —*Jon Balleras,* Down Beat

Rutya and Daitya / Mar. 1972 / ECM

☆ **Fort Yawuh** / Feb. 1973 / MCA 33122
Pianist Keith Jarrett's biggest contributions on this album come on the two more reflective numbers. The title cut is something of a gem. Jarrett expands his atmospheric (if slightly melodramatic) line with sensitivity and boldness; he, bassist Charlie Haden, and drummer Paul Motian aren't afraid to vary their individual and collective pulses, with some nice results. Dewey Redman on Chinese musette adds a few words, less sweet than pungent, and there is an exquisite bell-like coda. "Still Life" has two sets of romantic feeling to it: the solo piano intro is expressive within a severe, almost metronomic, rhythm, while the tune itself has a looser, lusher ballad sound. Keith Jarrett is one of those musicians whose restlessness and dissatisfaction can be mighty satisfying to hear. —*Steve Metaliz,* Down Beat

In the Light / Feb. 1973 / ECM 835011
In the Light differs so radically from pianist Keith Jarrett's previous works that an instructive comparison is difficult to make. A fundamental change in musical thinking, a shift from the improvisatory world of jazz to the composed control of written music, permeates this record. The traditional jazz rhythm section has been replaced by the Sudfunk Symphony Orchestra; chord progressions have given way to Mahleresque movements of sound; compositions take on the dignified titles of "A Pagan Hymn," "Fughata," or "String Quartet." Of all the material on this release, "A Pagan Hymn" is, I think, the closest to some of Jarrett's previous work. But *In the Light* is a series of contrasts—from the wandering fluid "Hymn" to the strictly rigid "String Quartet," neatly composed in four movements. Nearly everything is new, at least from a jazz perspective; it's quite possible that *In the Light* holds the key to a different, revolutionary view of American music. —*Eric Kriss,* Down Beat

☆ **Solo Concerts–Bremen and Lausanne** / Mar. 20, 1973+Jul. 12, 1973 / ECM 827747
The musical comingling of beauty, strength, and precision can be most elusive. When it is accomplished by one man on one instrument without sacrifice or compromise, it can be an act of total interaction between player and listener. And when it is done by an artist (though he avoids the term) of pianist Keith Jarrett's inventiveness and commitment—and done over the course of a three-record, two hours-plus album—the emotional sharing can be an *incredible* experience. In fact, the word incredible is an understatement here. The music is lyrical without being soft or fragile. It is at once a crystalline and yet flowing beauty, a music with the pastoral grace of Bach and the heart of the blues. It is heart-swelling and head-swinging. And it is totally devoid of vacant impressionism and gushing romanticism. —*Will Smith,* Down Beat

Treasure Island / Feb. 27-28, 1974 / MCA 39106
The Keith Jarrett Quartet's music, as opposed to Jarrett's solo and symphonic LPs, fits more readily into an established jazz format: the selections have clearly stated themes, improvised developments, and predictable conclusions. There is a happiness evident here, expressed by an expansive lyricism that makes the music more like "songs" than anything contained in the *Solo Concerts* album. Technically, Jarrett's playing seems to progress with each recording. The speedy right-hand soloing of *Solo Concerts,* however, is not emphasized on *Treasure Island* because Jarrett is trying to create a subtle group sound. A flashy individual performance might detract from that goal, though I never tire of hearing those magical, unbelievable runs. As always, Dewey Redman, Paul Motian, and Charlie Haden provide a foundation of confidence and solidity. There are few showcase solos; a shyness seems to pervade the sessions exerting a powerful cohesive effect that makes the musicians play as one unit. —*Eric Kriss,* Down Beat

☆ **Belonging** / Apr. 1974 / ECM 829115

"Spiral" is a good introduction to this session, serious but not sober. Keith Jarrett sets up a left-hand drone and plays off right-hand figures against it; the melody—surprisingly, given the drone effect—evokes the days of hard bop. A similiar astonishment surfaces on "Long As." The setting, performed by the piano trio, is nearly gospel, but the melody contains some Caribbean flavoring and some fascinatingly unexpected accents, sliding between bar lines in a most ungospelish manner. But "Blossom" is the best thing on the album, 12 minutes of inspired improvisation. Jarrett begins it unaccompanied, with Jan Garbarek and the rhythm joining for the head, then some gorgeous free form dialog occurs between piano and tenor, with Garbarek leading the way. —*Alan Heineman,* Down Beat

○ **Luminessence** / Apr. 1974 / ECM 839307
Keith Jarrett's *Luminessence* is a musical enterprise that totally transcends the convenient labels used by the music industry, the public, and the critics. Probing deep into his own personal musical cosmos, Jarrett brings back a chilling and singular achievement that stands as a landmark in the musical landscape of the '70s. The musicianship is excellent. Jan Garbarek (ts) shows amazingly harnessed high energy and the superb ensemble playing of the Sudfunk Symphony Orchestra's string section provides an outstanding performance. —*Chuck Berg,* Down Beat

★ **Backhand** / i. Oct. 9-10, 1974 / Impulse 9305
Landmark quintet with Dewey Redman (ts), Charlie Haden (b), Paul Motian (d), and Guilherme Franco (per). Any recording by this band is worthwhile. —*Michael G. Nastos*

☆ **Koln Concert** / Jan. 24, 1975 / ECM 810067
Keith Jarrett recorded this concert in Köln, Germany, and it emerged as the pinnacle of his solo art. Jarrett not only distills and refines the broad concept and specialized technique of his earlier *Solo Concerts;* he also breaks through the potential limitations of the solo idiom—and of his own choices in length and form—to erect magnifying mirrors of his clear vision. The fingers are often startling, the melodies infectious, the piano arranging richly diverse, the self-propulsive rhythmic stomp sections glorious in their vibrancy. And still, the most enduring quality of these performances is their breathtaking intimacy. —*Neil Tesser,* Down Beat

Death and the Flower / i. May 1975 / ABC/Impulse 9301
The title cut, which consumes all of the first side, is a brilliant, flowing construction, the lines of which unfold only during sustained, concentrated listening. Keith Jarrett opens playing an eerie, stately, Chinese-sounding theme on wood flute while drummer Paul Motian and percussionist Guilherme Franco kick in spare percussion comments. Indeed, the entire tune is a study in subtle contrasts as the poignant theme develops into frenzied improvisation (dig Motian's most *insistent* drumming in years) and returns to peaceful resolution. *Death and the Flower* is not music to wash dishes to. While it retains much of the far-famed Keith Jarrett lyricism, it is also far freer, less readily accessible, than much of what the ensemble previously has recorded. —*Bill Adler,* Down Beat

Mysteries / 1975 / MCA 33113

○ **Shades** / 1975 / Impulse 9322
While I can't condone an album with less than 35 minutes of playing time, I can at least condone the music. It is direct and to the point with none of the aimlessness that tended to mar *Death and the Flower* and *Backhand.* Pianist Keith Jarrett and tenor saxophonist Dewey Redman immediately grab the listener on "Shades" with their unison lines. A brisk Jarrett solo follows with him humming along à la Erroll Garner. After Redman's solo and a brief theme restatement, the piece segues into "Southern Smiles," a gospel tune with a calypso-styled beat. Not once is the listener left daydreaming. Unfortunately "Rose Petals" fails to sustain the excitement, but then "Diatribe" rips things apart. It's as avant-garde as Jarrett got during the mid '70s with his dissonant piano chording and a nice arco bass accompaniment from Charlie Haden. —*Carl Brauer,* Cadence

Silence / 1975 / GRP 117

Tremendous mid-'70s quartet session headed by pianist Keith Jarrett. Jarrett was in the midst of an impressive recording and touring string with this group, which included tenor saxophonist Dewey Redman, bassist Charlie Haden, and drummer Paul Motian. Almost every release they issued was superb; this one is no different. It has been reissued on CD. —*Ron Wynn*

Survivor's Suite / Apr. 1976 / ECM 827131

Survivor's Suite, a multifaceted opus, is easily the best of pianist Keith Jarrett's quartet recordings (not surprisingly, it was his regular quartet's first ECM recording). The piece begins evocatively, the mood created by Jarrett's haunting bass recorder, Charlie Haden's bass (recorded beautifully throughout), and the percussion sounds. As the intensity slowly builds, soprano and tenor join together to play a melody line. Dewey Redman takes the first solo followed by Jarrett (on piano) and then Haden (Jarrett's celeste creates background colors). Each gets another solo spot before the side ends on a positive note. The mood is abruptly changed as side two begins. Here everyone gets into some high-energy blowing with Redman's growling tenor the lead instrument. Following a Paul Motian drum solo, the music resolves itself into a joyous and optimistic note. Additional solos follow before the soprano introduces another evocative mood that leads into some powerful and stately ensemble playing, bringing the suite to an end. This is a masterful composition both in terms of Jarrett's writing and the quartet's playing. —*Carl Brauer*, Cadence

Staircase / May 1976 / ECM 827337

Sun Bear Concerts / i. Nov. 5-18, 1976 / PolyGram 843028

Recorded in late 1976, *Sun Bear Concerts* comprises both halves of each of the five solo concerts that made up an extraordinary tour of Japan. A heady encyclopedia of both performance and composition technique, it is not without occasional pretense; but its length is vindicated by the nature and quality of the work. In a way, this album's release represents the boldest act of Keith Jarrett's career, and one of the nerviest in that of ECM's Manfred Eicher as well. Still, the politics pack nowhere near the intrigue of the music itself. Expansive but rarely unwieldy, even the least successful of these musings is a remarkable achievement. The best of them—the entire Kyoto and Nagoya concerts and the first piece from Tokyo—stand with *The Koln Concert* as the apotheosis of this one-man genre. To borrow a phrase from novelist John Cheever, they are the inventions of a giant. —*Neil Tesser*, Down Beat

○ **My Song** / Oct. 31, 1977-Nov. 1, 1977 / ECM 821406

My Song shows Keith Jarrett maximizing his European-Romantic insights at the expense of his incredibly powerful rhythmic and blues roots. Jarrett's focus here seems to be on creating little melodic miniatures and interludes. The playing is refined and the recording is flawless, but at times the concept seems a shade too languid. My favorite selection is "Country," a beautiful pastoral that opens side two with a gently rocking, gospelish theme redolent of some Abdullah Ibrahim compositions. "The Journey Home" is a suite ranging from a slow, brush-colored opening by drummer Jon Christensen to a funky Latin section, images of mosques and evening prayer, and finally a slow R&B beat with pulsing bass work and eloquent spiraling lines by Jarrett. —*Chip Stern*, Down Beat

○ **Nude Ants** / May 1979 / ECM 829119

Nude Ants was the first live album pianist/composer Keith Jarrett made with his quartet featuring the Scandinavian mafia, saxophonist Jan Garbarek, bassist Palle Danielson, and drummer Jon Christensen. It was also the pianist's second in-concert recording at the Village Vanguard. While they are able players—Garbarek's haunting tone and Christensen's subtle backbeats are quite enticing—they were at a disadvantage in dealing with Keith Jarrett, vintage 1980. He was now a star and notoriety had canonized his technique and creative powers. Working with him became a lesson in inhibition. So it was for Garbarek, Danielsson, and Christensen. They play well, but they hold back—Jarrett comes forth, and *Nude Ants* becomes a document of his growth as a composer and pianist since the days of *Fort Yawuh*. These songs are an outgrowth of the on-the-spot compositions Jarrett created for the ECM solo albums *Facing You*, *Solo Concerts*, *The Koln Concert*, and *Sun Bear Concerts*. —*Cliff Tinder*, Down Beat

Concerts / May 28, 1981-Jun. 2, 1981 / ECM 827286

Changes / Jan. 1983 / ECM 817436

Pianist Keith Jarrett's *Changes* was recorded at the same sessions that produced *Standards—Vol. 1*. While that album displayed his trio's readings of other writers' material, this album contains two Jarrett originals. "Flying" is a 30-minute piece that has several distinct sections. The piece starts off slowly with a reflective piano solo spot, then Gary Peacock joins in with an insistent one-note bass line while Jack DeJohnette caresses the cymbals. The work picks up in intensity until a bass solo breaks that feeling up. The melody becomes more formal when the piano returns—the insistent feeling is still prevalent in the rhythm section and the pianist feeds off that for his next solo. "Part 2" gets off on a jaunty foot with a bouncier beat and one of Jarrett's patented solos filled with short, single-note runs. There are solos from everyone involved until the piece simply runs out of steam. "Prism" has a beautiful melody, flawlessly executed by the bass and piano. As opposed to the expansiveness of the opening cut, this piece is more concise. Peacock is impressive in his stateliness—like Charlie Haden, he does not overplay, preferring to follow the melody with well-placed, short phrases. DeJohnette does not display a heavy foot—many times his playing resembles a tap dancer's work, especially when "Prism" opens up. He uses his brushes slyly, to propel the beat. The sound quality is flawless and, once again, Jarrett's voice is evident in the mix. While *Changes* does not show any new directions for Keith Jarrett's music, the interplay of the three musicians makes for a pleasurable experience. —*Richard B. Kamins*, Cadence

○ **Standards—Vol. 1** / Jan. 1983 / ECM 811966

The approach on this record extends the trio concept initiated by pianist Bill Evans, bassist Scott LaFaro, and drummer Paul Motian circa 1960. Keith Jarrett guides, but Gary Peacock and Jack DeJohnette are free to follow their own instincts in pursuing the collective goal. And Jarrett leaves plenty of room for their explorations. The pianist accumulates fragments into longer lines, punctuating with sparsely placed chords. Only "God Bless The Child" receives a different transport—funky, gospel chords and a semi-rock beat. The strength of Jarrett's lines can be measured in terms of momentum, resolution, continuity, direction, and time, and he is absolutely unassailable in these areas. Peacock sets a standard of artistry on the bass—resilient tone, rangy lines, root notes, and inside notes (especially notable on "It Never Entered My Mind"). DeJohnette deserves accolades, too, for his brush and stick fires. He doesn't let Jarrett get complacent. —*Owen Cordle*, Down Beat

○ **Standards—Vol. 2** / Jan. 1983 / ECM 825015

Far better, to these ears, than its acclaimed predecessor, *Vol. 1*, is the second set of Keith Jarrett's *Standards;* it is almost on a par with the freewheeling *Changes* from the same trio sessions. This is one of Jarrett's better trio dates; it's not up to the high-water mark of his Vortex album *Somewhere Before* with Charlie Haden (b) and Paul Motian (d), but then Jarrett was no longer the playfully exuberant pianist he was in 1968. Still, here he neither strains for effect nor attempts to build a cathedral every time out. He settles for prettiness rather than Platonic beauty. His touch is as sensitive as ever, but (as on *Changes*) there is a light breeziness to his lyrical, finespun lines; most every number trails off casually, without a whiff of grand gestures. Jarrett's "So Tender" is the only original, though of a piece with the rest: a pretty tune. Gary Peacock's (b) playing is similarly spacious and airy. His and Jack DeJohnette's (d) nimble dancing are essential to the

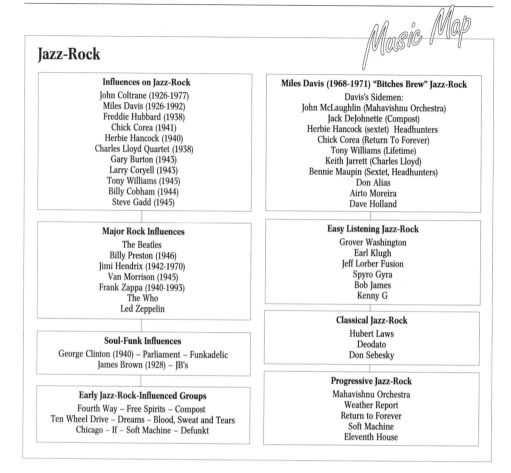

Jazz-Rock

Music Map

Influences on Jazz-Rock
John Coltrane (1926-1977)
Miles Davis (1926-1992)
Freddie Hubbard (1938)
Chick Corea (1941)
Herbie Hancock (1940)
Charles Lloyd Quartet (1938)
Gary Burton (1943)
Larry Coryell (1943)
Tony Williams (1945)
Billy Cobham (1944)
Steve Gadd (1945)

Major Rock Influences
The Beatles
Billy Preston (1946)
Jimi Hendrix (1942-1970)
Van Morrison (1945)
Frank Zappa (1940-1993)
The Who
Led Zeppelin

Soul-Funk Influences
George Clinton (1940) – Parliament – Funkadelic
James Brown (1928) – JB's

Early Jazz-Rock-Influenced Groups
Fourth Way – Free Spirits – Compost
Ten Wheel Drive – Dreams – Blood, Sweat and Tears
Chicago – If – Soft Machine – Defunkt

Miles Davis (1968-1971) "Bitches Brew" Jazz-Rock
Davis's Sidemen:
John McLaughlin (Mahavishnu Orchestra)
Jack DeJohnette (Compost)
Herbie Hancock (sextet) Headhunters
Chick Corea (Return To Forever)
Tony Williams (Lifetime)
Keith Jarrett (Charles Lloyd)
Bennie Maupin (Sextet, Headhunters)
Don Alias
Airto Moreira
Dave Holland

Easy Listening Jazz-Rock
Grover Washington
Earl Klugh
Jeff Lorber Fusion
Spyro Gyra
Bob James
Kenny G

Classical Jazz-Rock
Hubert Laws
Deodato
Don Sebesky

Progressive Jazz-Rock
Mahavishnu Orchestra
Weather Report
Return to Forever
Soft Machine
Eleventh House

---

date's success; their buoyant drive is a particular delight on Jerome Kern's "In Love in Vain." —*Kevin Whitehead*, Cadence

Spirits 1 & 2 / May 1985-Jul. 1985 / ECM 829467

○ **Standards Live** / Jul. 2, 1985 / ECM 827827
Standards Live from 1987 continues at the same high level of previous *Standards–Vol. 1 & 2* with pianist Keith Jarrett often recalling his early influence, Bill Evans. The well-integrated trio (Gary Peacock, bass; Jack DeJohnette, drums) plays three frequently performed tunes and three obscurities (although "Too Young to Go Steady" was also recorded by Pharoah Sanders). The interplay between the players is constantly impressive. Peacock's short bass solos pick up where Jarrett ends his improvisations, and it's barely noticeable when the pianist resumes his role as the lead voice, for the same mood/momentum has been maintained. DeJohnette, who really swings hard on some selections (especially "The Way You Look Tonight" and "Falling in Love with Love"), is a joy throughout, setting a fire under Jarrett. —*Scott Yanow*, Cadence

Still Live / **i.** Jul. 13, 1986 / ECM 835008

Paris Concert / **i.** 1990 / ECM 839173

Vienna Concert / 1992 / PolyGram 513437
Recent Keith Jarrett material. The pianist has come under increasing fire for the sameness of his material and his tendency to sing underneath his piano playing. He doesn't do that this time out, and the piano solos are intense and fre-

quently striking, while ECM's glittering production puts the piano squarely in the spotlight. —*Ron Wynn*

CLIFFORD JARVIS

b. 1941
Drums / Early free, modern creative
A solid drummer in either free or hard bop settings, Clifford Jarvis was featured on several '60s and '70s albums. He proved to be both a consistently engaging, rhythmically diverse and sound drummer and a good percussionist who added textures and colors on African and Latin instruments. Jarvis studied at Berklee with Alan Dawson in the mid- and late '50s, then moved to New York. He recorded with Chet Baker, Randy Weston, Yusef Lateef, Freddie Hubbard, Barry Harris, Jackie McLean, and Elmo Hope from 1959 to 1966, while he also played with Grant Green and Rahsaan Roland Kirk. Jarvis worked with Sun Ra from 1962 to 1976, cutting several records. He also played with Pharoah Sanders, and recorded with Sonny Simmons, Alice Coltrane, and Sanders in the early '70s. Jarvis subsequently recorded with Kenny Drew and Walter Davis in the late '70s, and with Archie Shepp in 1985. He can be heard on reissues by Sanders, Hubbard, and others. —*Ron Wynn*

BOBBY JASPAR (Robert B. Jaspar)

b. Feb. 20, 1926, Liege, Belgium, **d.** Feb. 28, 1963, New York, NY
Tenor saxophone, flute / Post bop

Although his style wasn't the most original, Bobby Jaspar helped debunk the canard that Europeans weren't able to play jazz effectively. His swinging, celebratory tenor and swirling flute solos were as rich, as vividly played, and as harmonically dense and unpredictable as most top American stylists. During his career, Jaspar was highly respected on both sides of the Atlantic. A Belgian who learned piano and clarinet as a child, then moved to alto and tenor, Jaspar was playing in a Dixieland group with Toots Thielemans at age 19. He started on flute in the mid-'50s, and became a professional musician after briefly considering a career as a chemist. Jasper led his own bands and worked with Henri Renaud and Sacha Distel in the '50s; he also recorded with Renaud. Jasper played with visiting Americans Jimmy Raney, Chet Baker, and Blossom Dearie in the mid-'50s, and later married Dearie. He joined J.J. Johnson's quintet in 1956, then left in 1957 and worked briefly with Miles Davis. Jasper played in Donald Byrd's quintet in 1958, then, during 1959 and for the remainder of his career, worked in New York with various musicians, among them Bill Evans, Chris Connor, the International Jazz Quartet, and Raney again. Jasper worked in Europe in 1961 and 1962, and recorded with Baker in Rome while working with various session musicians. He recorded as a leader for Riverside, Barclay (France), EmArcy, and Columbia. Jaspar has some sessions available on CD. —*Ron Wynn*

★ **Bobby Jaspar in Paris / i.** Dec. 27+29, 1955 / Disques Swing 8413
Wonderful 1986 reissue of prime Jaspar small-combo dates from the mid-'50s. Tommy Flanagan (p), Elvin Jones (d), Milt Hinton (b) among the crew. —*Ron Wynn*

○ **Memory of Dick** / Dec. 1955 / Verve 837208

With Friends / 1956-1962 / Fresh Sound

With George Wallington, Idrees Sulieman / May 23+28, 1957 / Original Jazz Classics 1788

Phenil Isopropil Amine / Dec. 1958 / Verve 837207

CARTER JEFFERSON

Tenor saxophone / Hard bop
A good, if at times conservative in tone and style, tenor saxophonist, Carter Jefferson has recorded as a leader for Timeless, and has done sessions with Barbara Donald, Clint Houston, and Jack Walraith, among others. He has a couple of sessions available on CD. —*Ron Wynn*

★ **Rise of Atlantis, The / i.** Apr. 1980 / Muse 309
Carter Jefferson, possibly best known for his association with Woody Shaw (who produced *The Rise of Atlantis*), may not have been an original, but he synthesizes his sources well. The first side of his album takes on an impressionistic hue, especially the mellow sambaish tint of "Why" and "Wind Chimes." Jefferson's soprano articulation and sweet tone are noteworthy, both here and on the vibrant, John Coltrane-styled outing, "Blues For Wood." "Changing Trains," is his stab at a "Giant Steps"-type vehicle, and his fluid, warm work is convincing and dramatic. Jefferson shares his front line alternately with trumpeters Terumasa Hino and Shunzo Ono, both of whom are sparse and unadventurous. —*Art Lange*, Down Beat

EDDIE JEFFERSON (Edgar Jefferson)

b. Aug. 3, 1918, Pittsburgh, PA, **d.** May 9, 1979, Detroit, MI
Vocals / Ballads & blues
Jon Hendricks is better known, and King Pleasure had a bigger hit, but Eddie Jefferson first set lyrics to jazz solos in the late '40s, adding words to Coleman Hawkins's "Body and Soul." Jefferson became more famous in the early '50s, when his version of "Moody's Mood for Love," based on a James Moody sax solo, was turned into a smash by King Pleasure. Before he began doing what some have called jazz "vocalese," Jefferson was primarily a tap dancer. He recorded for Hi-Lo in 1951, then, after "Moody's Mood for Love," joined Moody's combo and remained with him in two stretches that totaled over 20 years. Jefferson combined

singing and managing, and was known for humorous refrains and a gritty, energetic approach. He could be clever, inventive, compelling, or irritating, depending on the song and the night. He and Roy Brooks formed the Artistic Truth combo in 1974. A year later he joined Richie Cole's band, a move that returned him to the spotlight. Cole's bright, torrid alto solos and Jefferson's coarse, bluesy vocals were a perfect match. Jefferson's Muse albums, particularly *Godfather of Vocalese* and *Still on the Planet*, were among his finest. But Jefferson was shotgunned and killed outside a Detroit club in 1979, only two days after he'd completed the film *Eddie Jefferson: Live at the Showcase*. Jefferson's early albums, particularly *Letter From Home*, and other classic '60s sessions have been reissued by Prestige. His late '60s and '70s dates on Prestige and Muse have also been reissued. —*Ron Wynn*

○ **There I Go Again** / Feb. 1953-Aug. 1969 / Original Jazz Classics 503
This material was taken, with the exception of the '53, '54, and '55 tracks, from Eddie Jefferson's releases on Riverside and Prestige. Some of it, especially the Prestige (9/27/68) session, suffers from poor recording sound, balance, and a piano no doubt infamous to the unfortunate pianists made to suffer at its keys. However, this is a most satisfying collection for the joys of jazz singing and Eddie Jefferson. Eddie Jefferson was a distinct and natural jazz vocalist, partly because he had an extremely strong sense of what singing jazz was, for him, all about and the self-confidence to be only himself. Many jazz players found him the easiest of singers to work with, another horn in the ensemble, as it were. This twofer wears well and offers a good look at some of the pre-'70s Jefferson. —*Bob Rusch*, Cadence

Jazz Singer / Jan. 19, 1959-Jul. 1, 1964 / Inner City 1016
Jazz vocalese, the art of putting lyrics to classic instrumental solos, goes back much further than many people think. Indeed, Eddie Jefferson is credited in some circles with inventing the practice in 1939. The 18 selections on this anthology of '50s and '60s tracks include Jefferson's famous "Body and Soul" and "Moody's Mood For Love" numbers, as well as "Honeysuckle Rose," "Night Train," and "Now's The Time." There are times when his lyrics seem a bit on the jive side, but Jefferson had such a good-natured, earnest quality in his singing and projected his words so well that you are willing to forgive occasionally questionable verbal constructions. While I personally prefer hearing Jefferson doing straight jazz singing, these songs are good examples of the underrated art of vocalese. —*Ron Wynn*

☆ **Letter from Home** / Dec. 18, 1961-Feb. 8, 1962 / Riverside 307
1961 and 1962. Definitive vocalese from the man! —*Michael G. Nastos*

★ **Body and Soul** / 1968 / Prestige 396
Body and Soul is an open-hearted loving testament to the greatest tenor saxophonist of the age. It tells about Americans and Europeans. About Coleman Hawkins, born to play the tenor. There are other people: James Moody (reeds), Dave Burns (tpt), Barry Harris (p), Steve Davis (b), and Bill English (d). But there is only one Eddie Jefferson—the composer of "Moody's Mood for Love"; the teacher of bop history; the balladeer of modern jazz. He bridges the gap between music and feeling with meaningful and fanciful lyrics. Eddie Jefferson speaks for himself to anyone who wants to listen. —*Alan Offstein*, Coda

Come Along with Me / Aug. 12, 1969 / Prestige 613

Things Are Getting Better / Mar. 5, 1974 / Muse 5043
Overly optimistic title reflects Jefferson's boundless enthusiasm, energy, wit. —*Ron Wynn*

Still on the Planet / Mar. 17, 1976 / Muse 5063
Eddie Jefferson's voice was in no way polished; some might even call it gruff. I'm more inclined to call his singing delightfully human. The joy he felt in his craft is evident on every tune, and when he had something important to say, as on "Zap! Carniverous!" and "Chameleon" (both commentaries on the deterioration of society), he didn't resort to

melodramatics. My two favorites here are "Pinetop's Boogie" with some nice vocal interplay between Jefferson and Betsy Fesmire and the Charlie Parker classic, "Ornithology." Jefferson's lyrics aren't the greatest on this piece, but hearing his voice scat up, down, and around Bird's solo lines is thrilling. —*Carl Brauer*, Cadence

Godfather of Vocalese / **i.** 1976 / Muse 6013

Main Man / Oct. 9, 1977 / Inner City 1033

For *Main Man* Eddie Jefferson is well served by a challenging set of crisp arrangements from Slide Hampton. The rhythm section of pianist Harold Mabern, bassist George Duvivier, and drummer Billy Hart plus the soloing of trumpeter Charles Sullivan, alto saxophonist Richie Cole, tenorist Junior Cook, and baritonist Hamiett Bluiett are further assets. Among my favorites are a revamped "Moody's Mood For Love" with playful banter between Jefferson and vocalist Janet Lawson, a Latinized "Body And Soul," the still funny "Benny's From Heaven," and the taut and demanding "Freedom Jazz Dance." —*Chuck Berg*, Down Beat

HERB JEFFRIES

b. Sep. 24, 1916, Detroit, MI
Vocals / Ballads & blues
Though he gained plenty of notoriety for appearing in several Oscar Micheaux films as the African-American equivalent to Gene Autry or Roy Rogers, Herb Jeffries has also been a wonderful vocalist since the '30s. In today's market, his good looks would make him a superstar matinee idol and ballad heartthrob, but in the racial environment of the '30s, '40s, and '50s, Jeffries's possibilities were limited. He began his career singing with the Erskine Tate band in Chicago before joining Earl Hines in the early '30s. Jeffries briefly worked with Blanche Calloway, then was featured as a cowboy in a string of late '30s Micheaux films marketed to Black audiences. The most famous was "The Bronze Buckaroo." Jeffries sang with Duke Ellington in the early '40s, and scored a huge hit with "Flamingo." Jeffries also appeared in the original production of "Jump For Joy." He worked in clubs on the West Coast in the '50s, and recorded with Lucky Thompson and Bobby Hackett. Jeffries cashed in on "Flamingo" again, re-recording it in 1957. He continued recording in the '60s, then in the '70s and '80s mixed vocals and acting. He operated his own label, United National records, for a time, and served as master of ceremonies for several Ellington reunion conventions on both sides of the Atlantic. His role in African-American cinema was reaffirmed by an appearance in the Black western *Posse* in 1993. Jeffries can be heard on some Ellington CD reissues. —*Ron Wynn*

★ **Just Jeffries** / **i.** 1951 / Mercury 25091

JOHN JENKINS

b. 1931
Saxophone / Hard bop
A competent journeyman saxophonist, John Jenkins made a handful of good records in the '50s. He was a technically effective soloist, though not an imaginative one. Jenkins played clarinet in high school, then changed to alto sax. He worked with Art Farmer briefly in 1955, and also led his own group. After he moved to New York in 1957, Jenkins played for a short period with Charles Mingus, then recorded a pair of albums for Blue Note with Sonny Clark, Kenny Burrell, Paul Chambers, and Dannie Richmond. He teamed with Jackie McLean and Donald Byrd on another session, and recorded as a sideman with Paul Quinichette, Clifford Jordan, Sahib Shihab, and Wilbur Ware. Jenkins retired from playing in 1965. Currently, he has one session available on CD. —*Ron Wynn*

★ **Jenkins, Jordan and Timmons** / Jul. 26, 1957 / New Jazz 251

1987 reissue of prototype jam session/blowing date with Clifford Jordan (ts), John Jenkins, Bobby Timmons (p). —*Ron Wynn*

LEROY JENKINS

b. Mar. 11, 1932, Chicago, IL
Violin, composer, bandleader / Modern creative
Free jazz's leading violinist, Leroy Jenkins has greatly expanded the options, the range of sounds, and the possibilities for stringed instruments in free music. His techniques have included sawing, string bending, and plucking. Jenkins plays adventurous phrases and distorted solos, while including elements of blues, bebop, and classical in his approach. Jenkins often lists a diverse group of violinists (Eddie South and Jascha Heifetz) and other instrumentalists (Charlie Parker, Ornette Coleman, and John Coltrane, among others) as musical influences.

Jenkins began playing violin at age eight, often at church in Chicago. He was another student of Walter Dyett at Du Sable High, where Jenkins also played alto sax. He graduated from Florida A&M, where he dropped alto and concentrated on violin. He spent about four years teaching stringed instruments in Mobile, Alabama. Jenkins returned to Chicago in the mid-'60s, and divided his time from 1965 to 1969 between teaching in the Chicago public school system and working with the Association for the Advancement of Creative Musicians (AACM). Jenkins was among the AACM musicians who left Chicago for Europe in the late '60s. While in Paris, Jenkins, Anthony Braxton, Leo Smith, and Steve McCall founded the Creative Construction Company. While there, Jenkins also played with Ornette Coleman. Jenkins returned to Chicago in 1970, and moved to New York with Braxton shortly thereafter, living and studying at Coleman's New York home for three months. After working briefly with Cecil Taylor and Braxton, Jenkins played with Albert Ayler, Archie Shepp, Cal Massey, Alice Coltrane, and Rahsaan Roland Kirk. But more importantly, in 1971 Jenkins, Sirone, and Jerome Cooper founded the Revolutionary Ensemble, one of the decade's greatest trios.

The Revolutionary Ensemble was truly a cooperative venture, with each musician contributing compositions. Their performances often resembled works in progress. All three played several instruments during their concerts. The Ensemble maintained its integrity while making albums that were aesthetic triumphs and commercial flops for six years on various labels. After the trio disbanded, Jenkins made several tours of Europe, and led a quintet and a trio featuring Anthony Davis and Andrew Cyrille. During the mid-'80s, he served on the board of directors of the Composers' Forum, and was a member of Cecil Taylor's quintet in 1987. Jenkins has presented many free music performances and has written numerous pieces for soloists, small groups, and large ensembles. A few of his Black Saint and India Navigation sessions are available on CD. —*Ron Wynn*

For Players Only / Jan. 30, 1975 / JCOA 1010
From the opening Middle Eastern flourish through stumpy rhythmic figures and odd instrumental pairings, on into a series of short solos, the Jazz Composer's Orchestra maintains the distinctive style of its contributors while staying close to the leader's conceptions and sensibilities. Leroy Jenkins's violin, starkly emotional and always in touch with classical tradition as much as the jazz background, emerges occasionally—such as in a duet with trumpeter Leo Smith—demonstrating how much amazing music can be conceived on a single instrument. Jenkins's sound is almost painfully clear, yet he creates a shifting field upon which the trumpeter can lay out ideas. —*Howie Mandel*, Down Beat

★ **Solo Concert** / Jan. 11, 1977 / India Navigation

○ **Lifelong Ambitions** / Mar. 11, 1977 / Black Saint 0033
Violinist Leroy Jenkins and pianist Muhal Abrams were recorded in performance at Washington Square Church in 1977 in a half hour-plus duet session. "Happiness" involves inner piano box pluckings, choked string picking, and raspy scratching. "The Blues" is a Jack Benny riff extended by some classical figures and bluesy modulations, mostly at Abrams's insistence. Frenzied bowing describes "The Weird

World," and lengthier lines of the same frenzy characterize "The Father, The Son, The Holy Ghost." —*Howie Mandel*, Down Beat

Legend of Ai Glatson, The / Jul. 1978 / Black Saint 22
Excellent session by dynamic violinist Leroy Jenkins, once part of the wonderful avant-garde trio, the Revolutionary Ensemble. Jenkins cut this session in 1978, shortly after the trio's demise, and it's loaded with great violin solos, as well as some unusual, intriguing arrangements and compositions. —*Ron Wynn*

Space Minds / New Worlds / Survival America / Aug. 1978-Sep. 1978 / Tomato 8001
Music that is dynamic and invigorating, far from hard bop, swing, or traditional styles. —*Ron Wynn*

○ **Mixed Quintet** / Mar. 22-23, 1979 / Black Saint 0060

ANTONIO CARLOS JOBIM

b. 1927
Guitar, piano, composer / World fusion
Without question one of the greatest 20th-century popular music composers in any idiom, Antonio Carlos Brasileiro de Almeida Jobim has had an unprecedented impact on Brazilian, American, and world music. His music mixes the romantic and the ugly, is alternately lyrical, urbane, harmonically and rhythmically sophisticated, and melodically rich and striking. Above all, it's extraordinarily beautiful. His style avoids jarring effects and mixes simple, evocative lyrics with syncopated melodic figures and subtle chord progressions. Jobim persuaded Odeon Records, where he was music director, to record Joao Gilberto performing his composition "Chega de saudade." The recording helped launch a reshaping of the samba into the bossa nova. This was popularized in America by Stan Getz and Charlie Byrd with their 1962 *Jazz Samba* album. The album included Jobim's composition "Desafinado," which was later recorded by Coleman Hawkins. Jobim and Gilberto appeared with Getz, Byrd, and Dizzy Gillespie at a Carnegie Hall concert later in 1962. Astrud Gilberto's recording of Jobim's composition "The Girl from Ipanema" with Stan Getz on tenor sax later was a number-one pop hit. The bossa nova was enormously popular in the '60s, and many other jazz musicians recorded in the style. Jobim recorded as a leader for Verve and A&M in the '60s; for CTI, Discovery, and Columbia in the '70s; for Warner Bros., Verve, and Polydor in the '80s; and for Verve in the '90s. His list of hit compositions includes "Wave," "Corcovado," "Aguas de Marco," "Felicidade," "Once I Loved," "Dindi," "One Note Samba," and "Triste." Vocalist, pianist, and arranger Tom Ze has emerged as one of Jobim's finest interpreters, but many others from Frank Sinatra to Wayne Shorter have recorded his compositions. Jobim's also done albums with Sinatra, Nelson Riddle, and Claus Ogerman's orchestras, and with Gal Costa and Elis Regina, among others. He has several albums available on CD. —*Ron Wynn and Terri Hinte*

Wave / May 22, 1967+Jun. 15, 1967 / A&M 0812

Francis Albert Sinatra / Antonio Carlos Jobim / i. 1967 / Reprise 1021

★ **Elis and Tom** / i. 1974 / Verve 824418
A perfect record: Brazil's beloved cantora Elis Regina singing an all-Jobim program, accompanied by the composer, who also joins her for several duets, notably his masterpiece "Aguas de Marco." —*Terri Hinte*

Terra Brasilis / i. 1980 / Warner Brothers 3409
Once again teaming with arranger Claus Ogerman on this 1980 double album, Jobim reworks many of his classic compositions, including "Dindi," "One Note Samba," and of course "The Girl from Ipanema." —*Terri Hinte*

Passarim / i. 1987 / Verve 833234
Jobim's Banda Nova is a family affair (including wife Ana, daughter Elizabeth, and son Paulo Jobim), which has been touring the world since the mid-'80s. Danilo Caymmi is a featured band member. —*Terri Hinte*

Wonderful World, The / i. 1992 / Discovery 898
'86 reissue featuring noted Brazilian vocalist and composer Antonio Carlos Jobim backed by the Nelson Riddle Orchestra. It's a showcase for Jobim's songs, his sensual style, and charismatic voice, plus Riddle's always impressive arrangements. This was originally issued in 1978. —*Ron Wynn*

☆ **Art Of** / Verve 836253
Recent release covering Jobim material issued on Verve's import label. It includes lush ballads, more-celebratory tunes, and his romantic, poetic love material. —*Ron Wynn*

BUDD JOHNSON (Albert J. Johnson)

b. Dec. 14, 1910, Dallax, TX, **d.** Oct. 20, 1984, Kansas City, MO
Tenor saxophone, arranger / Swing, big band
A fine arranger and multi-instrumentalist, Budd Johnson penned charts for many big bands that were laying the groundwork for bop's emergence. He wrote arrangements for Earl Hines, Billy Eckstine, Woody Herman, and Dizzy Gillespie's big bands, and played with Gillespie in an early bop group. But he also had a firm grounding in traditional and swing music, and was a strong soloist in all three styles. Johnson's best instrument was tenor, but he was an effective alto, baritone, and soprano saxophonist also. He's one of the most prominent figures to bridge the gap between swing and bop.

Johnson began on piano, then turned to drums in 1924, making his professional debut on that instrument. He started playing tenor sax in 1926. Johnson toured with Terrence Holder in 1929, then performed with Jesse Stone and George E. Lee. After moving to Chicago, he played with Louis Armstrong in 1932 and 1933, then with Earl Hines in three periods: 1934, 1936, in 1937, and 1938 to 1942. He did arrangements for Gus Arnheim in 1937, and for both Fletcher and Horace Henderson in 1938, while also providing arrangements for Hines. Johnson remained busy in the '40s, playing and arranging for Don Redman, Al Sears, Gillespie, Georgie Auld, J.C. Heard, Herman, Buddy Rich, Eckstine, Boyd Raeburn, and Sy Oliver. He organized the Coleman Hawkins recording date in 1944, which many claim was the first bop session. Later came sessions with Machito, Bennie Green, and Cab Calloway.

Johnson began heading groups in the '50s, performing in Europe with Snub Mosely in 1952, and in Asia with Benny Goodman in 1957. He cut a septet album, *Blues a la Mode*, in 1958. During the '40s, '50s, and '60s, Johnson crammed several recording sessions into his busy schedule. These included dates with Frankie Laine, Buck Clayton, Jimmy Rushing, Milt Hinton, and Sarah Vaughan. He made *Budd Johnson and the Four Brass Giants* for Riverside. Johnson was Atlantic Records' music director for a while, and had his own publishing company. He worked in the early '60s with Quincy Jones and with Count Basie, then reunited with Hines from 1964 to 1969. They toured America, Europe, the Soviet Union, and South America. He also worked with Gerald Wilson's big band in 1966. Johnson formed the JPJ Quartet in 1969 with Oliver Jackson, Dill Jones, and Bill Pemberton. They made several recordings and tours before disbanding in 1975. Johnson toured Europe with Charlie Shavers in 1970, and did occasional dates with Sy Oliver. He was music director for the New York Jazz Repertory Company's *Musical Life Of Charlie Parker* in 1974, and traveled with the show to Europe. Johnson recorded four jam session albums with Buck Clayton for Chiaroscuro in 1974, and recorded with the Roy Eldridge sextet in 1970. He was featured in the documentary film *Last of the Blue Devils* in 1979, and played many major jazz festivals in the '80s. He also taught at several universities. —*Ron Wynn*

○ **Rock 'n' Roll Stage Show** / May 1954-Jun. 1955 / Mercury 20209

Blues a la Mode / Feb. 1958 / Riverside

○ **And the Four Brass Giants** / Sep. 22, 1960+Sep. 6, 1960 / Riverside 209

This is one of Budd Johnson's (ts) finest leadership moments; he not only wrote charts that do a marvelous job of setting up his gems, but he also makes particularly clever use of four distinctive trumpeters. Cannonball Adderley produced this date; I wonder who was the contractor (Johnson again?). This is a mercurial effort with both the pacing and the talent to make boredom impossible. —*Bob Rusch,* Cadence

★ **Let's Swing** / Dec. 2, 1960 / Prestige 1720

Ya Ya / Jan. 20-21, 1964 / Argo 736

Colorado Jazz Party / i. 197z / MPS

○ **Ole Dude and the Fundance Kid, The** / Feb. 4, 1984 / Uptown 2719

This album is a straightahead swinger, and, unlike some record session pairings, Budd Johnson (ts) and Phil Woods (as) *really do* play together. Not a song goes by that they don't either duet, pass the solo back and forth, or play contrapuntally off each other. Although Johnson was making records two years before Woods was born, they were stylistically compatible. Charlie Parker provided the main stylistic link—an early influence for Woods, a later one for Johnson. At times Johnson's tenor reminds us with a Texas moan that he was born in Dallas, and the influences of Coleman Hawkins, Lester Young, and Bird are still there. But Johnson was no clone; he simply used them to put together his own style, well represented on this album. Similiar things might be said about veteran bassist George Duvivier. And his solo on "After Five" reminds us that a bass player doesn't have to be heavy-handed to be heard. It's easy to overlook pianist Richard Wyands on this album because of his relatively laid-back style, but he provides needed contrast and solid backing to the horns. Bill Goodwin had been Woods's drummer for over a decade. Every track tells a story. —*Doug Long,* Cadence

Buddy Johnson Wails / Mercury 20072

This is first-rate music, but it's really vintage instrumental R&B with a swing foundation. Johnson was a tremendous, energetic saxophonist who had some hit records with his wife, vocalist Ella Johnson, and also had some sessions produced by Quincy Jones. He is a different player from the veteran jazz saxophonist Budd Johnson. —*Ron Wynn*

BUNK JOHNSON (William Geary Johnson)

b. Dec. 27, 1889, New Orleans, LA, **d.** Jul. 7, 1949
Trumpet / New Orleans traditional

Bunk Johnson is another early jazz legend whose achievements are clouded by exaggeration and inaccuracy, much of which must be laid at his own door. Johnson claimed he was born in 1879, but research eventually showed he was much younger than he insisted, which put his contentions that he played with Adam Olivier and Buddy Bolden and that he toured in minstrel shows into the questionable category. Johnson was a skilled ensemble player and an above average soloist. He had a gorgeous tone in his prime, and even his last recordings show he could still play wonderful choruses. Johnson was active in New Orleans bands from 1910 to 1914, working with the Black Eagle Band led by trumpeter Frankie Dusen and others. During a fight, Johnson lost his horn, and soon began having dental trouble. These problems forced him to retire in 1934, and he became a laborer in New Iberia, Louisiana. He was rediscovered there by researchers/writers Bill Russell and Fred Ramsey, who'd been directed to him by Armstrong and Clarence Williams. Johnson got a job as a music teacher in a WPA program, and interest in him soared with the publication of Russell and Ramsey's book, *Jazzmen*, in 1939. Johnson made his first recordings in 1942 with Lu Watters, then cut sessions with Kid Ory in 1944, Bechet in 1945, and others as a leader until 1947. Johnson frustrated musicians and producers by insisting on doing rags and pop tunes rather than blues and traditional New Orleans favorites. He preferred working with trained players and disliked loose jam sessions. By the time he made it to vinyl, Johnson was past his prime. Still, Johnson merits attention for being one of early jazz's vital participants. —*Ron Wynn*

Bunk Johnson and His Superior Jazz Band / Jun. 11, 1942 / Fantasy 12048

'91 reissue of magnificent early '40s traditional jazz album with the great New Orleans trumpeter Bunk Johnson. Johnson didn't make many records, and this was among his greatest. The supporting lineup includes two other Crescent City greats, Jim Robinson and George Lewis. —*Ron Wynn*

★ **Bunk and Lu** / Feb. 1944 / Good Time Jazz 12024

This release puts together two sessions. The first is from 12/19/41 and was recorded on Watters's 30th birthday at a gathering with Bob Scobey (c), Turk Murphy (tb), Ellis Horne (cl), Wally Rose (p), Clancy Hayes, Russ Bennett (bj), Dick Lammi (tba), and Bill Dart (d) to play and pay tribute to the traditional jazz of the "past." Fans will know this material. To those who only know the perversion of the latter revivalists, this may fool you. It's aged well and sounds good. The other session here is from spring of 1944 and features Bunk Johnson's spirited, sometimes sour but strong 66-year-old trumpet with Hayes, Murphy, Horn, Pat Patton (b), Squire Girsback (b), and Sister Lottie Peavey (vocal on two cuts) on eight tracks. The background to both of these sessions and how Johnson came to do the vocal on "Down by the Riverside" is fully covered in interesting liners by Neshui Ertegun and Ralph Gleason. —*Bob Rusch,* Cadence

○ **Bunk Plays the Blues–The Spirituals** / Aug. 2, 1944 / American Music 638

○ **Bunk Johnson (1944)** / 1944 / American Music 3

○ **Bunk Johnson & His New Orleans Jazz Band–New York (1945)** / 1945 / Folklyric 9047

○ **Last Testament of a Great Jazzman** / i. 1947 / Columbia 520

HOWARD JOHNSON (Howard William Johnson)

b. 1941, Boston, MA
Tuba, alto and baritone saxophone / Progressive big band, early jazz-rock, modern creative

Arguably the most influential tuba player to emerge in the modern era, Howard Johnson's fluency, range, and skill on the instrument shattered perceptions about how the tuba could be utilized not only in jazz, but in modern popular music in general. Johnson's also a gifted baritone saxophonist, but has accomplished his greatest feats on tuba. A self-taught musician, Johnson started on baritone at age 13 and moved to tuba at age 14. He was a merchant seaman and met John Surman in England. Johnson came to New York in the mid-'60s, and worked with Charles Mingus, Hank Crawford, and Archie Shepp before meeting Gil Evans in 1966. He and Evans formed a musical bond that was maintained well into the '80s. Johnson formed Substructure in 1966, a band that, at one point, included four tubas and backed Taj Mahal. He wrote arrangements for Maria Muldaur, Paul Butterfield, and B.B. King while working with Mahal. Johnson was conductor of the "Saturday Night Live" band in the late '70s, and formed a second tuba band, Gravity. They performed in New York and toured Europe. Johnson recorded with Jack DeJohnette's Special Edition, and with Jimmy Heath and Crawford again in the '80s, and has continued doing sessions and heading bands into the '90s. Despite his array of credits and sessions, Johnson has no dates available on CD as a leader. But he can be heard on numerous discs of both recent and vintage material by everyone from Mingus to DeJohnette to Gil Evans, Mahal, and Crawford. —*Ron Wynn*

J.J. JOHNSON (James Louis Johnson)

b. Jan. 22, 1924, Indianapolis, IN
Trombone, composer / Hard bop

The first bebop trombonist, a magnificent soloist, and an excellent composer, J.J. Johnson brought a virtuosity to his instrument that was revolutionary and stunning. He displayed such speed and clarity that he was accused of playing the valve trombone. His tone became heavier over the years, and he slowed down from the breakneck pace of his youth, but his solos were no less harmonically sophisticated; they became more melodic. Johnson played intricate bebop and hard bop improvisations easily on the trombone, while incorporating swing and classical influences into his sound and writing.

Johnson studied piano in his childhood with a church organist, then began playing trombone at age 14. He toured with the bands of Clarence Love and Isaac Russell in the early '40s, then joined Benny Carter's orchestra in 1942. He stayed in this band until 1945, playing on radio broadcasts, writing arrangements, and cutting his first recorded solo in 1943. Johnson participated in the initial Jazz at the Philharmonic concert in 1944. He joined Count Basie in 1945, and moved to New York in 1946. Johnson toured with Illinois Jacquet in the late '40s. He played frequently in small combos, working with Bud Powell, Max Roach, Miles Davis, Fats Navarro, Charlie Parker, and Dizzy Gillespie. Johnson began recording as a leader for Savoy and Prestige in the late '40s. He toured Korea, Japan, and the South Pacific in the early '50s with a USO band led by Oscar Pettiford. The next year he worked with another all-star band led by Miles Davis. Johnson semi-retired from music for a period to work as a blueprint inspector for the Sperry Gyroscope Company. He made a couple of recordings, then formed a two-trombone group with Kai Winding in 1954 that proved an inspired pairing.

Jay and Kai played together until 1956, and the union made both highly popular. They'd previously recorded with Charles Mingus and fellow trombonists Bennie Green and Willie Dennis in 1953 on *Four Trombones*. Johnson recorded for several other labels. He made three superb volumes for Blue Note (the first with Clifford Brown), and made many outstanding sessions for Columbia, including a six trombone date. There were also recordings on Bethlehem and RCA. After Jay and Kai disbanded, he led his own quintet until 1960. They reunited for a Newport date, then Johnson toured Europe and composed works for large orchestras. He taught at the Lenox School of Jazz in the summer of 1960, and wrote the major work, *Perceptions*, for Dizzy Gillespie in 1961. He played with Miles Davis in 1961 and 1962, formed new groups, and toured Japan heading a combo with Sonny Stitt and Clark Terry. Johnson continued recording extensively, doing sessions for Verve, Impulse, and RCA. He entered the lucrative studio world in Los Angeles during the '70s, composing several scores for television and film. He did jazz dates in the late '70s, recording for Pablo and Milestone. He did more dates for Pablo in the '80s, and formed a new quintet with Cedar Walton in 1987. Recently, Johnson has been recording for Antilles. A healthy amount of Johnson material from the '50s through the '90s is available on CD. *—Ron Wynn and Michael G. Nastos*

○ **Mad Bebop** / Jun. 26, 1946 / Savoy 2232
Seminal material from 1946-1954. Pivotal dates pairing Johnson with movers and shakers like Sonny Rollins (ts), Charles Mingus (b), Bud Powell (p). *—Ron Wynn*

○ **Early Bones** / May 26, 1949 / Prestige 24067
The groups on this release, especially those led by trombonists J.J. Johnson and Kai Winding, show some of the important writing styles and soloists who were creating new music at the end of the '40s. The most fascinating group, Johnson's 1949 sextet, unfortunately has only four cuts. There is a Miles Davis nonet-influenced composition, "Elysee" by pianist John Lewis and a midtempo bop head by tenor saxophonist Sonny Rollins ("Hilo"). Two excellent tunes come from Johnson, "Fox Hunt" being the classic performance. John Lewis has some extroverted playing, unusual for him, along with his rock solid accompaniment. Young Sonny Rollins does not seem settled yet, but nevertheless reveals the rhythmic approach and sound that were to become his trademarks. Trumpeter Kenny Dorham plays strongly and very sensitively and aggressively. As for Johnson, he retains

that clean, fat, relaxed sound (often helped by playing with cup mute) on all solos. He hadn't reach his peak of creativity and control in 1949 but was playing more trombone in a bop style than anyone. His solos are so well constructed and balanced. Kai Winding, an important but often overrated trombonist of the period, shows roots from swing and mixes bop lines with embellishments (glisses, bends, slips, half-note effects) and vocal effects reminiscent of much earlier, earthier trombonists. Most of the writing in Winding's group was done by baritone saxophonist Gerry Mulligan in typical counter melodies, counterpoint, and sometimes "cuteness" (although "A Night On Bop Mountain" by Kai Winding is a bit too trite). The star here is the exuberant tenor saxophonist Brew Moore. His bright, light sound reminds one of Lester Young or Stan Getz, but the lines are bouncy like Zoot Sims. Pianist George Wallington's playing is intriguing and unpredictable, while Mulligan's technique and playing are not as consistent as they would become in later years. On both the Johnson and Winding sides, the drummers (Max Roach and Roy Haynes—two of my favorites) are very much overbalanced and their unpredictable "bombs" and accentuations most annoying. The Bennie Green sides are split between a blowing section with some distinctive Eddie "Lockjaw" Davis tenor playing and a selection of standards. The charts, most by Green where there is an arrangement, are simple and riff-like. Green, although often associated with the "boppers," was an older-styled player. True, his technical command and harmonic vocabulary permitted him to play with modern players (he earned fame with tenor saxophonist Charlie Ventura's bebop combo), but I think his style and preferences seem closer to Vic Dickenson and Dicky Wells (his consistent individual uses of the gliss and smears) and Lawrence Brown (his uptempo feel as well as that smooth legato at slow tempo) and, I dare say, Bill Harris. Everyone burns on "Whirl-A-Licks" with some fun fours between Green and Lockjaw. The second session features some swinging Green and agile Charlie Rouse (on tenor) with Candido on conga. Cliff Smalls delights with some Erroll Garner-inspired piano "tinkles." *—Tom Everett*, Cadence

○ **Eminent Jay Jay Johnson–Vol. 2, The** / Jun. 1953-Jun. 1955 / Capitol 81506

Four Trombones: The Debut Recordings / i. 1953 / Prestige 24097
With Kai Winding (tb), Willie Dennis (tb), and Bennie Green (tb). Outstanding 1990 reissue of superb 1953 four-trombone summit. *—Ron Wynn*

☆ **Eminent Jay Jay Johnson–Vol. 1, The** / Sep. 24, 1954 / Capitol 81505

○ **Jay and Kai** / Dec. 3, 1954 / Prestige 195

○ **J.J. Johnson, Kai Winding, Bennie Green** / Dec. 3, 1954 / Prestige 7030
All of this album was also issued on a previous twofer set in 1981. The material comes from three dates: 5/26/49, 8/23/49, and 10/5/51. The trombonists are represented this way: Johnson's on the earliest cuts, Winding the middle, and Green the '51 sessions. *—Bob Rusch*, Cadence

★ **Blue Trombone** / i. 1956 / Columbia

Jay and Kai at Newport / Jul. 6, 1956 / Columbia

Live at the Cafe Bohemia / i. Feb. 1957 / Fresh Sound 143

Trombone Master / Apr. 1957-Dec. 1960 / Columbia 44443
1989 compilation of good 1957-1960 Johnson cuts. Mastering is uneven. *—Ron Wynn*

○ **Jay and Kai Octet** / i. 1958 / Columbia

J.J. Inc. / i. Aug. 1, 1960 / Columbia
Fine effort with several Johnson tunes, plus great work by Clifford Jordan (ts), Freddie Hubbard (tpt). *—Ron Wynn*

★ **Great Kai and J.J.** / Oct. 3, 1960-Nov. 9, 1960 / MCA 42012
With Kay Winding. Definitive work for two trombonists, plus Bill Evans (p), Paul Chambers (b), Art Taylor (d). *—Ron Wynn*

Perceptions / **i.** 1961 / Verve

Proof Positive / May 1, 1964 / Impulse

Trombonist J.J. Johnson's playing as such on this session is, as one would expect, quite excellent. But he's best interacting with other horns, and there isn't too much of that here with Harold Mabern (p), Art Harper (b), and Frank Gant (d) over five tracks. On one track ("Lullaby Of Jazzland") Johnson is backed by pianist McCoy Tyner, bassist Richard Davis, drummer Elvin Jones, and guitarist Toots Thielemans. The rolling drums of Jones and Thielemans's guitar solo bridge the trombonist's work into a more complete piece, and a good stride is hit on "Minor Blues," but it falls away when the trombonist lays out. This is nice from the trombone angle, but short in other degrees. —*Bob Rusch,* Cadence

Say When / Dec. 1964-Dec. 1966 / Bluebird 6277

Yokohama Concert / Apr. 20, 1977 / Pablo

This live two-record set, recorded in April 1977 in Japan, is a new testament to the deceptive smoothness of J.J. Johnson's trombone. "Horace" sets the Yokohama stage for hot and cool flashes of postbop brilliance. It begins with a groovy, Horace Silverish ensemble head, followed with Johnson's comfortable solo, and then features trumpeter Nat Adderley, who starts vaguely, heats up, and almost boils over. This blowing pattern, with ample room given to each of the three young accompanists, dominates much of the action ("Walkin'," "Work Song") but generally avoids the mundane effect of solo after solo. Kevin Johnson gets hot on "Jevin," custom-built for his drum spot, but I also like the way he kicks along "Splashes" with big sprays of cymbal work before taking a more frantic solo plunge. Bassist Tony Dumas is the pacemaker on "Walkin'," strolling step for step with the trombonist while the others sit out. Pianist Billy Childs fulfills his support role, comping colorfully on electric piano and turning a dashing solo on "Why Not," though his playing tends toward the standarized. Johnson's performance is rooted in the bop tradition, but his imagination is strongly contemporary. Almost evey solo becomes subtly three dimensional as Johnson interprets the tunes with quiet excitement. —*Bob Henschen,* Down Beat

○ **Pinnacles** / Sep. 17, 1979 / Milestone 9093

Concepts in Blue / Sep. 23-26, 1980 / Original Jazz Classics 735

Concepts lacks the overall tightness and interplay that made the album *J.J. Inc.* so special, although J.J. Johnson, Clark Terry, and Ernie Watts play with an exciting shifting togetherness and there were real joys to be found during this 44 minutes. Trombonist Johnson plays with strength and variety; Terry subdues his humor to play with his old seriousness, his tone and ideas on flugelhorn providing a perfect foil for Johnson's dark, heavy sound; and Watts wails with fiery intensity on alto and wild abandon on tenor, tearing his way forward with wide vibrato. In addition to the exciting horn solos, Ray Brown's flowing, pulsing bass lines, and a nicely varied selection of tunes, a highlight is Johnson's arrangement of John Coltrane's "Village Blues." —*Jerry De Muth,* Down Beat

Things Are Getting Better All the Time / Nov. 28-29, 1983 / Pablo 745

★ **Quintergy–Live at Village Vanguard** / **i.** Jul. 1988-1986 / Antilles 848214

This live album is excellent—top-notch J.J. Highly recommended. —*Michael G. Nastos*

Standards: Live at the Village / **i.** 1991 / Antilles 510059

Vivian / **i.** 1992 / Concord Jazz 4523

1992 date by bop's finest trombonist, J.J. Johnson, featuring a program mixing standards with his originals and arrangements. He heads a quintet with saxophonist Rob Schneiderman, guitarist Ted Dunbar, bassist Rufus Reid, and drummer Akira Tana. Though he's been playing since the '50s, Johnson's trombone solos are still fluid, fast, and impressive. —*Ron Wynn*

JAMES P. JOHNSON (James Price Johnson)

b. Feb. 1, 1894, New Brunswick, NJ, **d.** Nov. 17, 1955, New York, NY

Piano, composer / Stride, boogie-woogie

The "father of stride piano," James P. Johnson was an extensively trained player who still became a great stylist doing the popular music of the era: rags, blues, reels, novelty tunes, and originals. His neatly crafted bass lines, prominent but not rigid rhythms, and sweeping right-hand lines are still masterful. He was a regular in New York by 1912, was cutting piano rolls in 1916, and was recording by 1917. In the '20s he played with a host of famous names, composed scores for a Broadway show, and directed music for Bessie Smith's film short *St. Louis Blues.* He wrote plays and composed a symphony in the '30s. He went back on the circuit playing with bands from 1939 until he became an intermission pianist at Condon's and Pied Piper in Greenwich Village in 1946. There are reissues of classic Johnson material available on CD. —*Ron Wynn*

★ **Carolina Shout** / **i.** 1917-1925 / Biograph 105

James P. Johnson's piano playing here covers an interesting phase from ragtime to stride. The piano roll and the march elements of ragtime seem to have been made for one another, but it is impossible to tell how free to express himself the "first Negro composer to cut his own rags" really was. But on his "Carolina Shout," "Harlem Strut," "Eccentricity," and "Charleston" are routines and ideas that must have influenced many early jazz pianists. His version of "Farewell Blues" is attractive, too. —*Stanley Dance,* Jazz Times

Rare Piano Roll Solos–Vol. 2 / Feb. 1918-Oct. 1921 / Biograph 1003

Vintage James P. Johnson rags and stride material, restored from music rolls to disc by digital technology. Though at times the passages seem more exact than exuberant, Johnson was one of Harlem's legends, a prolific songwriter as well as player. These early cuts show that Johnson was as great as his reputation. —*Ron Wynn*

○ **Snowy Morning Blues** / 1930+1944 / GRP 604

Snowy Morning Blues begins with the very great pianist, composer, *and* songwriter James P. Johnson in his prime in 1930 mixing rhythmic urgency, restless reharmonizing, lacy decoration, and fresh melodies. Some of the intensity, though not the interpretative subtlety, is gone by the 1944 dates that make up the bulk of this disc; by then Johnson had suffered a stroke, and the discreet drumming of Eddie Daugherty proves helpful. Eight 1944 tracks are Johnson originals, including remakes of earlier hits; the other eight are songs by his prize student, Fats Waller, and these prove irresistibly provocative. Here is stride piano with unfailing rocking swing. —*John Litweiler,* Down Beat

○ **James P. Johnson Plays Fats Waller Favorites** / **i.** 1950 / Decca 5228

★ **Giants of Jazz** / **i.** Oct. 1982 / Time Life 18

☆ **Father of the Stride Piano** / Columbia

Piano Solos / Smithsonian/Folkways 40013

Pianist James P. Johnson's first (1918) roll of "Carolina Shout," which sounds like a rough draft of the tune, appears on the track just preceding the more famous 1921 roll version, which contains all the familiar routines. Many of these rolls were recorded under the supervision of J. Lawrence Cook for the now-deleted Riverside Jazz Archives series. —*Tex Wyndham,* Coda

LONNIE JOHNSON (Alonzo Johnson)

b. Feb. 8, 1889, New Orleans, LA, **d.** Jun. 16, 1970, Toronto, Canada

Vocals, guitar, sometimes piano, violin, harmonium / Blues & jazz

An extremely versatile guitarist and an intriguing singer, Lonnie Johnson's jazz importance comes from two equal components: his associations and his technique, though his formative recordings were quite influential. Johnson played with jazz orchestras, recorded with King Oliver as a member of Blind Willie Dunn's (Eddie Lang) Gin Bottle Four, and with Duke Ellington and Louis Armstrong. His "hokum" duets with guitarist Eddie Lang were musically and historically trendsetting because they were some of the earliest collaborations between Black and White musicians. Johnson's touch, phrasing, and intricate patterns, especially on his turnarounds, were studied by jazz and blues players. Johnson's later recordings veered into other areas, but his improvisational flair and swing reflected his mastery of jazz principles. Born into a musical family and the son of a musician, Johnson began playing guitar and violin professionally as a teen in Storyville. He worked on the riverboat St. Paul with Charlie Creath's Jazz-o-Maniacs in 1920, and recorded with them in 1925. Johnson cut numerous sides in the '20s singing blues and accompanying himself on guitar; he was a famous name in the blues world for over 40 years. In 1948, he had an R&B hit with his composition "Tomorrow Night," and, during the '50s and '60s, recorded for blues and folk labels doing his customary mix of styles. Johnson made over 500 recordings over a 40-year span, and left many valuable additions to the American musical legacy. —*Ron Wynn with Cub Koda*

PETE JOHNSON (Peter Johnson)

b. Mar. 25, 1904, Kansas City, MO, **d.** Mar. 23, 1967, Buffalo, NY

Piano / Boogie-woogie

Pete Johnson was another great boogie-woogie pianist whose impact extended beyond his genre. His rumbling, energetic phrases and rollicking rhythms, whether in combative sessions with other players or as accompaniment to his longtime friend and robust shouter Big Joe Turner, were emphatic and majestic. Johnson played drums and piano as a teen in Kansas City. He worked with vocalist Edna Taylor at the Hole in the Wall club and Jazzland, then, while backing Turner at the Sunset Cafe, was heard by John Hammond. Johnson moved to New York in the late '30s, playing in 1936 at the Famous Door. He and Turner joined many other jazz greats at the 1938 Carnegie Hall concert From Spirituals to Swing, which Hammond organized. In December of that year, Johnson played with fellow greats Albert Ammons and Meade "Lux" Lewis in the Boogie-Woogie Trio. The threesome appeared the next year at Cafe Society. Johnson worked regularly with Ammons over the next decade, and made some appearances with Lewis, while also playing as a soloist. Johnson moved to Buffalo in 1950, toured with Lewis, Art Tatum, and Errol Garner in 1952, then toured Europe and performed at the Newport Jazz Festival in 1958. A stroke later that year left him partly paralyzed and virtually ended his career, though he did make a nostalgic appearance at Hammond's Spirituals to Swing concert in 1967. —*Ron Wynn*

☆ **Pete Johnson/Earl Hines/Teddy Bunn Blue Note Sessions, The** / Mosaic 119

★ **Boogie Woogie Boys, The** / **i.** Feb. 1939-Jan. 1953 / Storyville 229

○ **Boogie Woogie Trio** / **i.** Sep. 1939-Oct. 1930 / Storyville 4094

○ **Boogie Woogie Trio–Vol. 3** / **i.** Oct. 1939-Sep. 1954 / Storyville 4006

○ **Pete's Blues** / **i.** 1946 / Savoy 14018

○ **Cozy Cole All Star Swing Groups** / **i.** 1946 / Savoy 2218

Jazz Heritage–Boogie Woogie Mood (1940-1944) / **i.** 1953 / Brunswick 58041

○ **Pete's Blues** / **i.** 1958 / Savoy 414

Master of Blues and Boogie Woogie / **i.** Nov. 1975 / Oldie Blues 2801

○ **All Star Swing Groups** / Savoy 2218

★ **Central Avenue Boogie** / Delmark 656

Pete Johnson's *Central Avenue Boogie* justly celebrates one of the truly authentic barrelhouse pianists, but his 1949-50 output for Apollo was so slender that of his 11 tracks for this CD, three are previously unissued alternate takes of "Hollywood Boogie." Of the remainder, the stride-based "Margie" (*sic*, should read "Marie"), "66 Stomp," and "Minuet Boogie" speak the most, primarily because they disclose another dimension of Johnson's Kansas City roots. Fleshing out the disc are three boogie solos by the obscure Arnold Wiley. —*Jack Sohmer*, Down Beat

PLAS JOHNSON (John (Jr) Johnson)

b. Jul. 21, 1931, Donaldsonville, LA

Tenor saxophone / Bop, soul-jazz

Plas Johnson's not only one of the great honking R&B saxophonists and session musicians, he's a fine bebop and hard bop soloist. Johnson's father was his earliest teacher, and helped him to learn soprano sax, and his brother Ray later recorded with him in the '50s. Johnson was a prolific studio player in the late '50s and through the '60s, working with artists as diverse as Harry Belafonte and Shorty Rogers. He was featured doing breaks, snippets, and short but effective solos on numerous R&B and early rock and roll dates. During the '60s, Johnson was heard on Henry Mancini's *Pink Panther* soundtracks and albums. He also recorded with Red Callender and Earl Palmer in 1960. Johnson was in Merv Griffin's studio band in 1970. His jazz roots and abilities were showcased during the '70s, as Johnson worked with Ray Brown and Herb Ellis, and led his own combos. He did sessions with Brown, Ellis, Bobbie Hall, Jake Hanna, Mike Melvoin, Jimmie Smith, and the Capp-Pierce orchestra. Johnson has recorded for Capitol and Concord, among others. He has a couple of sessions available on CD. —*Ron Wynn*

○ **L.A. (1955)** / 1955 / Carell Music 101

★ **Blues, The** / Sep. 1975 / Concord Jazz 4015

Here is the veteran honking sax star in more conventional jazz setting. —*Ron Wynn*

Positively / May 1976 / Concord Jazz 24

Bop Me Daddy / **i.** 1988 / VSOP 21

Honking sax, instrumental R&B, blues, and boogie from Plas Johnson, among the style's finest tenor players. These cuts are mostly simple, built more on Johnson's robust delivery than any strict chord structure. He blisters through some, slides through others, and keeps the session moving smoothly to its conclusion. —*Ron Wynn*

PETE JOLLY (Peter A. Ceragioli)

b. Jun. 5, 1932, New Haven, CT

Piano, accordion / Cool

A rare jazz accordionist, Pete Jolly achieved much greater fame as a popular pianist. He had a mild hit with "Little Bird" in the '50s. Jolly started accordion and piano studies at age eight. He moved to the East Coast to Los Angeles in the early '50s, and played with Georgie Auld, Shorty Rogers, and Buddy DeFranco before beginning his own groups. Jolly recorded with Red Norvo, Richie Kamuca and Chet Baker, Buddy Collette, DeFranco, Gibbs, Rogers, and Art Pepper in the '50s and early '60s. He also cut sessions for RCA, AVA, Charlie Parker, and Atlas. Jolly's done extensive studio work for films and television since the '60s and '70s, but recorded a quartet album with Pepper in 1980. He has a couple of sessions available on CD. —*Ron Wynn*

Duo, Trio, Quartet / Mar. 7, 1955 / RCA 1125

Little Bird / Nov. 1962+Jan. 1963 / Ava 22

○ **Gems** / **i.** 1990 / Holt 3303

BOBBY JONES

b. Oct. 30, 1928, Louisville, KY, **d.** Mar. 6, 1980, Munich, Germany

Tenor and alto saxophone, flute / Hard bop

Tenor saxophonist and clarinetist Bobby Jones merged a bluesy sensibility with a mastery of bop in a striking and personal fashion through his solos and his playing from the '50s until his death in 1980. His phrases were thoughtful and his solos were lyrical; sometimes heated, other times smooth and relaxed. Jones played with big bands before going into the army in the early '50s. When he was discharged, Jones spent some time working with rockabilly groups before joining the Glenn Miller Orchestra under Ray McKinley's direction in 1959 as a tenor saxophonist. He played with Woody Herman's orchestra in 1963, and also worked with Jack Teagarden as a clarinetist. He returned to his hometown of Louisville to be a teacher, but in 1970 joined Charles Mingus's Jazz Workshop. Jones worked with Mingus until 1972, touring Japan and making two visits to Europe. Jones decided to remain in Europe after the second visit, and eventually decided to live in Munich. But a chronic emphysema problem was aggravated by Munich's climate, and Jones became a nonplaying arranger. During the '70s, he made a handful of fine sessions spotlighting his saxophone and clarinet skills for Cobblestone and Enja. He was also featured on some early '70s Mingus releases, notably *Let My Children Hear Music.* Currently, none of Jones's dates are available on CD. —*Ron Wynn and Michael G. Nastos*

★ **Arrival of Bobby Jones, The** / Jul. 12, 1972 / Cobblestone 9022
This is a studio session from this highly original reed/flute player, plus Charles McPherson (as) and Jaki Byard (p). A must-buy. —*Michael G. Nastos*

Hill Country Suite / Aug. 30, 1972 / Enja 2046
A solid, underrated saxophonist throughout his career, Bobby Jones didn't make a lot of records, but this was a fine one. It's a simple hard bop and mainstream session from '72, with Jones playing furiously on tenor and occasionally flute, while driving a competent band that defers to him on this date. —*Ron Wynn*

CARMELL JONES (William Carmell Jones)

b. Jul. 19, 1936, Kansas City, KS
Trumpet / Bop, hard bop
A most appealing, warm, and inviting soloist, Carmell Jones's trumpet solos were featured in several bands during the '60s, most notably Gerald Wilson's and Horace Silver's bands. Jones was a stirring player though he was not as flashy or flamboyant as some hard bop trumpeters. Jones compensated with an approach and style firmly grounded in bebop fundamentals. He rarely fluffed notes, or rushed or hurried solos. Influenced by Clifford Brown, Jones began on trumpet at age 11, and spent two years at the University of Kansas after he completed his military duty. He participated in the collegiate jazz festival at Notre Dame in 1959. Jones led a group in Kansas City, then moved to California in 1960. He recorded as a leader and played with Bud Shank, Harold Land, Gerald Wilson, and Curtis Amy in the early '60s. Jones toured and recorded with Horace Silver in the mid-'60s, appearing on Silver's popular *Song for My Father* album. Jones moved to Europe in 1965, then joined the SFB orchestra in Berlin. Jones recorded in Europe, but was soon forgotten in America. He returned to the United States in 1980 and two years later turned some heads with an LP recorded for Revelation titled *Carmell Jones Returns.* Currently, that album and other sessions Jones recorded as a leader are unavailable on CD, though Jones can be heard on the CD reissue of *Song for My Father.* —*Ron Wynn and Michael G. Nastos*

○ **Remarkable Carmell Jones, The** / Jun. 1961 / Pacific Jazz 29
The Remarkable Carmell Jones, the 1961 debut for this trumpeter, finds him in the strong company of Harold Land (ts), Frank Strazzeri (p), Gary Peacock (b), and Leon Pettis (d) for six tracks. This is an unspectacular whole with some very nice parts in its program and solos. Jones had a strong Clifford Brown influence, which is very obvious on this date, right down to some of those melodic little quicksilver

phrases Brownie used to tag about with. But Jones was not as quick as Clifford Brown and there are some awkward doubled-up moments where he all but swallows part of his solo. Land is constantly strong and exhibits an authority not always heard on his later recordings. Pianist Frank Strazzeri also has some notable spots, catching this listener off guard with the unusual. Pettis sounds like a poor man's Art Blakey, further giving this date a Jazz Messengerish ambiance (even "Sad March" is reminiscent of "Wail March"). —*Bob Rusch, Cadence*

ELVIN JONES (Elvin Ray Jones)

b. Sep. 9, 1927, Pontiac, MI
Drums, bandleader / Hard bop, early free
A member of the illustrious Jones family from Michigan that also includes trumpeter Thad and pianist Hank, drummer Elvin Jones furthered the percussionist's role in modern jazz. He helped make the drummer an equal contributor to the group's direction. Jones wasn't simply a timekeeper; his interaction with McCoy Tyner and Jimmy Garrison in the Coltrane quartet provided, through subtle percussive density, the balance between Tyner's expansive piano phrases, Garrison's rock-solid bass, and Coltrane's lengthy lines and spiraling solos. Jones inspired the next generation of free players by continuously altering his timekeeping rhythms with his carefully placed accents. He obscured the beat, but seldom abandoned the pulse.

Jones played in local groups around the Detroit area, then in military bands while in the service. After his discharge, he worked in more local groups, some with his brother, Thad. Eventually, he replaced Art Mardigan in Billy Mitchell's quintet; they became the house band at the Bluebird club and accompanied national jazz acts who appeared there. Jones moved to New York in 1956, and soon was working and/or recording with J.J. Johnson, Donald Byrd, Harry Edison, Bud Powell, Sonny Rollins, and Stan Getz. Jones joined John Coltrane's band in 1960, and remained for five pivotal years. He also made his debut as a leader in 1961 for Atlantic, recording with fellow drummer Philly Joe Jones. He continued doing dates in the '60s for Riverside, Impulse, Atlantic, and Blue Note, sometimes with his brothers, other times with section mates Jimmy Garrison or McCoy Tyner. Jones's drumming became more adventurous and ambitious, as well as more rhythmically powerful. Coltrane decided to add a second drummer to the group in 1966, and selected Rashied Ali. Jones left the band shortly after, and briefly played with Duke Ellington's orchestra on a European tour.

After working in Europe for a short period, Jones returned to America and began heading everything from trios to quartets and sextets. He didn't employ pianists too often, and frequently had two or more saxophonists in his groups. Frank Foster, George Coleman, Joe Farrell, David Liebman, and Steve Grossman were among the players he used. During the '70s, Jones continued recording, doing dates on Blue Note, Honeydew, Enja, PM, Vanguard, and MPS/Pausa. He played with a diverse array of musicians, from Art Pepper to James Moody to Chick Corea and Jan Hammer. There were more multiple sax sessions, and other dates with an 11-piece band or with trios. Jones was featured in a 1979 documentary film, *Different Drummer: Elvin Jones,* and also appeared in the 1970 film *Zachariah.* He continued recording during the '80s, doing dates for Denon (Japan), Black Hawk, Palo Alto, and Enja. One of his recent Enja recordings features Ravi Coltrane, one of John's sons, on tenor sax. There are a few Jones sessions available on CD, but nowhere near as many as there should be considering his level of activity. —*Ron Wynn with Myles Boisen*

Elvin! / Jul. 11, 1961-1962 / Original Jazz Classics 259
1987 reissue of fine Riverside set with Thad Jones (cnt), Frank Foster (ts). —*Ron Wynn*

★ **Illumination** / Aug. 8, 1963 / Impulse 49
Sextet with Jimmy Garrison (b), Prince Lasha (as), Sonny Simmons (as), Charles Davis (bs), and McCoy Tyner (p). All

originals in progressive stance. A jewel. Must-find. — *Michael G. Nastos*

★ **Dear John C** / Feb. 23+25, 1965 / Impulse
Drummer Elvin Jones's *Dear John C* with alto saxophonist Charlie Mariano, bassist Richard Davis, and pianists Hank Jones or Roland Hanna is one that does little more than go through the motions of jazz. Jones's star was rising as a celebrity but he hadn't yet gotten a group sound, and I don't believe the group presented here was ever a working unit. There are moments when Jones's drumming actually sounds tentative and one can imagine the players pushing for inspiration but turning in an average, professional date. There is a bit of everything here from the impressionistic title track to Duke Ellington's "Fantazm" and, in between, Charles Mingus's "Reincarnation of a Lovebird" as well as "Smoke Rings," "Feeling Good," "Anthropology," "This Love of Mine," "Ballade," and "Everything Happens To Me." — *Bob Rusch,* Cadence

Puttin' It Together / Apr. 8, 1968 / Blue Note 84282
Solid pianoless trio date; Joe Farrell handles heavy reed load. Jimmy Garrison on bass. — *Ron Wynn*

Heavy Sounds / 1968 / Impulse 9160
One of Elvin Jones lesser-touted albums. A good session co-led by strong bassist Richard Davis. — *Ron Wynn*

○ **Prime Element, The** / Mar. 14, 1969-Jul. 26, 1973 / Blue Note 506
These 1973 sessions place Elvin Jones in the center of an 11-piece ensemble (including saxophonists Frank Foster, Steve Grossman, and Pepper Adams, bassist Gene Perla, guitarist Cornell Dupree and keyboardist Jan Hammer), an uncontainable group with a permutable vocabularly. The sensual horn mating and slight funky and Cubano rhythmic undertow suggest a recasting of Charles Mingus's *Black Saint & the Sinner Lady* in Santana and Frank Zappa settings. The earlier sextet cuts (featuring the horns of George Coleman, Joe Farrell, and Lee Morgan) are a more linear project, although every bit as combustible. The soloists solo rather than mingle, hoot, and banter. Throughout, Jones is typically magnificent, always the consummate percussionist. — *Mikal Gilmore,* Down Beat

Poly-Currents / Sep. 1969 / Blue Note 84331
1986 reissue of Blue Note release. With horn players Joe Farrell, Pepper Adams, George Coleman. Farrell plays English horn on one cut. — *Ron Wynn*

Merry-Go-Round / Dec. 15, 1971 / Blue Note

Genesis / 1971 / Blue Note

Live at the Lighthouse–Vol. 1 / Sep. 9, 1972 / Blue Note 84447
Originally solid twin-record set reissued in separate versions. Strong quartet with saxmen Steve Grossman and Dave Liebman. CD has two bonus cuts. — *Ron Wynn*

○ **Live at the Lighthouse–Vol. 2** / Sep. 9, 1972 / Blue Note 84448

Live at the Village Vanguard / 1973 / Enja 2036

○ **Elvin Jones Is on the Mountain** / 1975 / PM 005
Elvin Jones Is on the Mountain, a keyboard trio date featuring Jan Hammer on electric piano and Moog synthesizer, is quite different from Jones's past recordings. (Hammer plays acoustic piano on "Namuh" and "London Air.") On Gene Perla's "Destiny" there is an intriguing Hammer-Jones duet that is a structural gem. Perla, who along with Hammer wrote all the material for *Mountain* and was Jones's bassist for a number of years, possesses a stalwart style with considerable tonal depth. His work in this trio setting is top-flight. Jones in this somewhat different environment seems subdued—laid back—constructing his rhythmic circle in an almost delicate fashion. — *Herb Nolan,* Down Beat

○ **Elvin Jones Live at the Town Hall** / i. May 1976 / PMR 004
Elvin Jones Live was taken from a John Coltrane memorial concert performed at New York's Town Hall, 9/12/1971, and features his group at that time—Frank Foster on soprano

and tenor saxes, Chick Corea on piano, Joe Farrell on sax and flute, and Gene Perla on bass—on two extended compositions. Side one, "Shinjiju" (identifiably composed by Keiko Jones), opens with a military cadence, which becomes the swirling polyrhythmic base over which Joe Farrell contributes an outstanding, forceful solo on sax. Outstanding solos are also contributed by Foster, Corea, and Jones. Side two is taken up by Frank Foster's composition "Simone," a meandering line again caught up in the swirling rhythm section. Foster turns in his strongest contribution here while Farrell solos on flute; both Perla and Jones contribute long solos. This album shows five strong individual artists giving exceptionally of themselves, bringing forth a record where the dynamics of the whole are equal to the sum of the parts, making for an exceptional and truly beautiful record. — *Bob Rusch,* Cadence

Summit Meeting / Nov. 18, 1976 / Vanguard
These are some top-shelf sessions with James Moody (sax), Clark Terry (tpt). — *Ron Wynn*

Remembrance / Feb. 3-5, 1978 / MPS 7052
Remembrance opens with a medium-tempo tune that spans two styles of John Coltrane's career. While Pat LaBarbera's opening tenor solo recalls Coltrane's late '50s hard, driving sound, Michael Stuart's tenor chorus brings the piece more up to a *Meditations* feel. LaBarbera solos again, then the two tenors combine on a bridge that, before the last, short chorus, reaches out toward the heights of *Ascension.* This is like Coltrane's greatest hits in less than eight minutes. "Section 8," probably the most contemporary-sounding arrangement on the album, swings into a soprano-tenor duet, then breaks for solos by LaBarbera (soprano) and Stuart (tenor). "Little Lady" sounds uncannily Trane-like, with LaBarbera taking a soprano adventure in medium tempo. As for Elvin Jones, he is mixed down on much of the album, so as to drive, but not dominate the hornmen. As if to remind the listener who is the leader, Jones ends each composition with a brief drum roll. His chance to stretch comes on the title piece, which, except for an introduction and closing theme by LaBarbera, is virtually *all* Jones. Here, emphasizing the bass and tom tom, nearly ignoring the cymbals for much of his break, Jones weaves a moody magic. — *R. Bruce Dold,* Down Beat

Very R.A.R.E. / Jun. 13, 1979-Apr. 1978 / Trio 9173
Dynamic drummer Elvin Jones leads two different units on the eight selections (two bonus cuts) featured on this disc of late '70s material. The first six were done in New York during 1978 and include Jones spearheading a great band with Art Pepper spewing and soaring on three selections, backed by outstanding bassist Richard Davis and fine pianist Roland Hanna. This is first-rate quartet material with Pepper surging and the trio challenging him, then contrasting and complementing his solos with their own great work. The other two cuts were recorded in Tokyo and issued on a previous release. They include a turbulent, often evocative version of "A Love Supreme," a 26-minute plus tribute with Jones thrashing and thrusting, driving the band that includes Frank Foster on soprano and tenor, fellow tenor Pat LaBarbera, guitarist Roland Prince, and bassist Any McCloud. With no keyboard to establish a center, Jones and the horns fill the spaces while Prince has a good solo midway through. The other cut is not quite as extensive or intense but has some nice work by Foster. The music is not as special as the title indicates but is well worth hearing. — *Ron Wynn*

Heart to Heart / Aug. 1980 / Denon

Brother John / Oct. 1982 / Quicksilver 4001

Ultimate Elvin Jones, The / Jun. 1990 / Blue Note 84305
The tunes on this second Elvin Jones album for Blue Note (and, incidentally the last for Jimmy Garrison, who then left the trio) are an excursion into pure "hard swing" with more than an ample display of the talent that so rightfully classifies Elvin Jones as the foremost jazz drummer on the scene. The presentation of polyrhythmic measures—by Jones—

sometimes causes the mind to boggle but is handled admirably by its inventor. Side one has a real "sizzler" entitled "In the Truth" and gives its composer Joe Farrell ample scope to speak his mind on tenor. "What Is This?" is a Garrison original that acts more as a showcase for Jones's drums than Garrison's bass. It also is an introduction (in this album) to Farrell's soprano. "Ascendant," the second of three Garrison compositions for this date, again features Farrell on soprano; there is a superb set of exchanges between all concerned in the opening bars that leaves the listener wishing for more! In all probability, this is the best track on the record—a bacchanal of sound, color, and cohesion fills one's ears. Garrison's bass really begins to "warm" from here on in. Side two opens with an old warhorse, "Yesterdays"; Farrell's tenor states the theme in a direct John Coltrane manner, then it's taken up by Garrison, who proceeds to solo in a high register that is pedestrian compared to his other contributions on this album. "Sometimes Jole" is a medium-tempo piece that swings all the way through its 10:35; it also acts as the standard text by which Elvin Jones should be judged (has he really got four hands?). Garrison offers a beautiful solo on unaccompanied bowed bass that shows a conception of beauty and timing that is sadly missing in many a present-day bass player. "We'll Be Together Again" is the closing sermon by the trio and a showcase for Farrell's flute (which is reminiscent of Eric Dolphy's playing). Jones and Garrison keep the background going until a rather abrupt ending. —*Mike Fernades*, Coda

○ **Elvin Jones Jazz Machine in Europe, The** / Jun. 1991 / Enja 79675

HANK JONES (Henry Jones)

b. Jul. 31, 1918, Vicksburg, MS
Piano / Bop
The oldest of the Jones brothers, Hank Jones has been a supreme accompanist and an underrated soloist. He's one of the most accomplished sight readers in jazz, and his flexibility and sensitive style have kept him extremely busy cutting sessions and working in various groups and styles ranging from swing to bebop. He's worked with vocalists, played in big bands, and done many solo, trio, and combo dates.

He studied piano as a child and listened carefully to Art Tatum, Teddy Wilson, Earl Hines, and Fats Waller. He began playing in the Midwest at age 13, and worked in territory bands. Jones met Lucky Thompson in one of these groups, and Thompson invited him to New York in 1944 to work with Hot Lips Page at the Onyx club. Jones worked, for a while, with John Kirby, Howard McGhee, Coleman Hawkins, Andy Kirk, and Billy Eckstine, then began touring in 1947. He worked with Jazz at the Philharmonic, then accompanied Ella Fitzgerald from 1948 to 1953. Jones also cut many sessions for Norman Granz's labels in the late '40s and early '50s, many with Charlie Parker.

He worked and recorded in the '50s with Artie Shaw, Benny Goodman, Lester Young, Milt Jackson, and Cannonball Adderley before joining CBS's staff in 1959. He worked on programs such as "The Ed Sullivan Show" and stayed with CBS until they disbanded the staff in 1976. He recorded several sessions with Savoy in the mid- and late '50s, playing with Donald Byrd, Herbie Mann, Wendell Marshall, and Kenny Clarke, among others. He also recorded solo and quartet dates for Epic. His quartet with Osie Johnson, Barry Galbraith, and Milt Hinton became one of New York's busiest during the early '60s, sometimes doing three dates a day. They cut albums for Capitol and ABC in 1958, though Galbraith missed the ABC sessions.

Jones continued recording at Capitol, Argo, and Impulse in the early '60s, at times working with his brother, Elvin. He made a host of recordings in the '70s: there were solo dates for Trio and Galaxy, and trio sessions for Interface, Trio, Progressive, East Wind, Inner City, Chiaroscuro, Concord, and Muse, among others. There were duo dates with Flanagan for Verve and Galaxy in the late '70s. Jones served as pianist and conductor with the Broadway musical *Ain't*

Misbehavin' in the late '70s. He also played in the Great Jazz Trio, originally with Ron Carter and Tony Williams. Buster Williams replaced Carter on the trio's first recording date. Jones continued with the trio into the '80s, though Eddie Gomez and Al Foster were now his mates. Jimmy Cobb replaced Foster in 1982. The trio also backed Art Farmer, Benny Golson, and Nancy Wilson. Jones was the resident pianist at the Cafe Ziegfeld in the early '80s, and toured Japan with George Duvivier and Sonny Stitt. He kept his recording blitz going in the '80s, cutting sessions for Phonogram, Black and Blue, Timeless, and others. He has a good amount of material available on CD. —*Ron Wynn*

★ **Trio** / Aug. 4, 1955 / Savoy
Seminal stuff from Hank Jones, with Kenny Clarke (d), Wendell Marshall (b). —*Ron Wynn*

○ **Bluebird** / Aug. 1955-Nov. 1955 / Savoy 1193
Kenny Clarke drums with pianist Hank Jones on this satiny trios-plus-guests set, with guests including Donald Byrd and Joe Wilder on trumpets, Herbie Mann on snoozy flute, and Jerome Richardson on better flute and tenor sax. —*John Corbett*, Down Beat

Have You Met Hank Jones? / Jul. 9, 1956-Aug. 20, 1956 / Savoy 12084
Hank Jones's forte is straightahead swing. He loves to get in that groove and let his right hand go. You can tell when he's digging it because he fills out his playing with his own kind of "wordless vocal." The best cuts here are medium-tempo tunes on which Jones can really stretch out. He plays ballads like he's holding a tight rein on a frisky horse. But when he *is* in the groove, few folks swing as well as Hank Jones. —*Douglas Clark*, Down Beat

Relaxin' at Camarillo / **i.** Aug. 21, 1956 / Savoy 1138

Songs from "Porgy and Bess" / 1960 / Capitol

★ **Bop Redux** / Jan. 18-19, 1977 / Muse 5444
This album is unique because pianist Hank Jones plays only Charlie Parker and Thelonious Monk's tunes. His mastery of this material is most evident in the sensitive approach to Monk's ballads, "Ruby My Dear" and "'Round Midnight." His special touches on the Bird material are really a delight to my ears. He has a special finesse and says some really beautiful things. His partners bassist George Duvivier and drummer Ben Riley make this a superior session. —*Jerry L. Atkins*, Cadence

Great Jazz Trio at the Village Vanguard / **i.** Feb. 19-20, 1977 / Vanguard 6013
Stunning and gripping solos, accompaniment. —*Ron Wynn*

Just for Fun / Jun. 27-28, 1977 / Galaxy 471
Includes some good work by this always-insightful, creative soloist. —*Michael G. Nastos*

Tiptoe Tapdance / Jun. 29, 1977-Jan. 21, 1978 / Original Jazz Classics 719
Tiptoe Tapdance is a gentle encounter with lightly swinging grooves and delicate ballads. The mood is relaxed, and pianist Hank Jones's legato touch and firm sense of rhythm are much in evidence. The selections here cover piano styles such as stride ("It's Me Oh Lord"), swing à la Teddy Wilson ("Sweet Lorraine"), and transparent, reflective ballads ("Emily"). Eubie Blake's "Memories of You" is given a rhapsodic treatment, full of lush harmonies and scampering runs. —*Chip Stern*, Down Beat

Solo Piano / **i.** 1978 / All Art Jazz 11003
A well-done, occasionally great solo date by pianist Hank Jones from 1978. Jones was in his busiest period as a leader, juggling trio dates at various studios and also touring and doing session work. But he still turns in a fine series of solos, with only the derivative nature of the material keeping this from being a classic album. —*Ron Wynn*

Groovin' High / Jan. 25, 1978 / Muse 5169
Nicely phrased and played, mellow and memorable. —*Ron Wynn*

Ain't Misbehavin' / **i.** 1978 / Galaxy

In Japan / **i.** May 2, 1979 / All Art Jazz 11001

Hello, Hank Jones / **Clifford Jordan** / **i.** Apr. 1980 / East World 98003

Perhaps tenor saxophonist Clifford Jordan's expansive, serpentine bent prompted pianist Hank Jones into adopting a loose, diffuse approach. Whatever the reason, the result is compelling. On side one of this direct-to-disc recording, the group explores an extended-form version of Jordan's "Vienna," kicked along by bassist Reggie Workman and drummer Freddie Waits. It is an intense performance. Jones's lines become disjunct and tangential. Just as impressively, his solos build seemingly of their own momentum, mixing space with busy, tightly chorded passages. "Bohemia After Dark" continues the group's raw, no-nonsense stance. —*Jon Balleras*, Down Beat

Great Jazz Trio at the Village Vanguard / **i.** 1980 / Inner City 6013

The trio plays with a spirit of empathy and interaction rare in groups with many more years of playing experience. Pianist Hank Jones creates castles of crystal on John Coltrane's "Naima," aided and abetted by bassist Ron Carter's rumbling glissandos and heavy-toned solo spot. Drummer Tony Wiliams times his uncanny rhythmic intrusions with a benign sense of design, and his shift to a Latin tempo adds new dimension to the song. Williams and Carter combine with Jones to create the type of floating time that was the hallmark of Miles Davis's groups of the '60s. "Favors" features more of Jones's elegant swing and another stunning example of Williams's lyrical drumming. "12 + 12" is yet another in a series of fine blues tunes that Ron Carter penned. Jones digs into his wide vocabulary of blues ideas, coming up with lithe, sparkling phrases, and eggs on Williams in a number of exchanges. —*Chip Stern*, Down Beat

Great Jazz Trio at the Village Vanguard: Revisited / **i.** 1980 / East World 9002,9005

★ **Oracle, The** / Mar. 1989-Apr. 1989 / EmArcy 846376

With Dave Holland and Billy Higgins. Includes three different generations of jazzmen. A very nice album. —*Michael G. Nastos*

Lazy Afternoon / Jul. 1989 / Concord Jazz 4391

○ **Live at Maybeck Recital Hall–Vol. 16** / **i.** 1992 / Concord Jazz 4502

A high point in the career of distinguished pianist Hank Jones was joining the artists tabbed for a solo release in the Maybeck series. While he's always been known as a great accompanist and good trio contributor, his solo skills have sometimes been undervalued. But after hearing him work in this unaccompanied setting, there should be no doubt Hank Jones is a superb soloist along with all his other talents. —*Ron Wynn*

I'm All Smiles / Verve

JO JONES (Jonathan Jones)

b. Oct. 7, 1911, Chicago, IL, **d.** Sep. 3, 1985, New York, NY
Drums / Swing, big band

Jonathan "Papa Joe" Jones had the most influential role in the evolution of jazz drum technique. Though he didn't display the flash or the sheer speed of Buddy Rich, or the charisma of Gene Krupa, Jones had arguably more impact on bebop era stylists than either Rich or Krupa. For playing timekeeping rhythms, Jones shifted instruments from the bass drum to the hi-hat cymbal. He let the cymbals ring as much as possible while the hi-hat was opening and closing, thereby producing a legato sound. He rarely stepped into the spotlight, but stayed at the rhythmic center; Jones was famous for strategically inserted rim shots, for bass drum bombs, and for his brilliant brush technique. He helped push the Count Basie rhythm section with guitarist Freddie Greene and bassist Walter Page. When Jones did take a solo, he made every note count with a minimum of flurries.

Jones played piano, trumpet, and reed instruments, as well as drums. He began playing drums at age four. He toured as a tap dancer and instrumentalist with carnival shows in the South before joining Walter Page's Blue Devils in Oklahoma City in the late 1920s. He played with trumpeter Lloyd Hunter in Nebraska before moving to Kansas City in 1933. A year later, he began his long association with Basie. In 1936, he left Basie briefly to join Page in the St. Louis-based Jeter-Pillars Orchestra, but both returned by the end of the year. Green replaced Claude Williams on guitar in 1937, and the rhythm section and orchestra were set.

Jones was featured in the film *Jammin' the Blues* in 1944. He spent two years in the army, but otherwise remained with the Basie orchestra until 1948. Jones made fine records with others during this time, among them Teddy Wilson, Lionel Hampton, and the Benny Goodman sextet. During his career, he also worked with Buck Clayton, Sonny Stitt, Ruby Braff, Paul Quinchette, Coleman Hawkins, Jimmy Rushing, Illinois Jacquet, and Nat Pierce. Jones made his first Jazz at the Philharmonic tour in 1947, then went on several other sojourns to Europe. These trips led to recording projects with Billie Holiday, Wilson, Duke Ellington, Johnny Hodges, Lester Young, Art Tatum, and with Goodman. He worked in several groups doing variations on the Basie beat. Jones later led trios in New York City from 1957 to 1960, then taught and ran a music shop. In the '60s, Jazz Oydessy released an outstanding autobiographical/demonstration record titled *The Drums*, which featured Jones discussing his life, times, and music. Jones continued to record into the '80s, and issued two fine albums late in his career: *The Main Man* on Norman Granz's Pablo label, and *Our Man Papa Jo* with Hank Jones, Major Holley, and Jimmy Oliver in 1982 on Denon. He died in 1985. —*Ron Wynn*

Jo Jones Special / Aug. 11, 1955+Aug. 16, 1955 / Vanguard 8503

This is a first-rate, swing-influenced set, later combined into a second album into the *Essential Jo Jones* package on Vogue. —*Ron Wynn*

★ **Main Man, The** / Nov. 29-30, 1976 / Pablo 799

This date with Harry Edison (tpt), Roy Eldridge (tpt), Vic Dickerson (tb), and others is sterling silver. —*Michael G. Nastos*

Our Man Papa Jo! / Dec. 12, 1977 / Denon 7047

The final session for a jazz legend. Drummer Jo Jones was nearing the end when he got together with old friends pianist Hank Jones and bassist Major Holley for this 1977 session. He still manages to play with some degree of authority and anchors the rhythm section, while saxophonist Jimmy Oliver and Jones take care of solo responsibilites. This has been reissued on CD. —*Ron Wynn*

JONAH JONES (Robert Elliott Jones)

b. Dec. 31, 1909, Louisville, KY
Trumpet / Swing, big band

Both a popular and a talented trumpeter, Jonah Jones could be flashy, spectacular, and sometimes excessive, but he was always a masterful player. Jones played in riverboat bands early in his career, worked with Horace Henderson in the late '20s, then with Stuff Smith and Jimmie Lunceford in the early '30s. Smith and Jones did a combination music/comedy act. Jones worked in Mckinny's Cotton Pickers in the mid '30s, then played with Fletcher Henderson and Benny Carter in the early '40s, before joining Cab Calloway in 1941. He remained with Calloway until 1952. Jones was the culprit in the famous spitball incident that got Dizzy Gillespie tossed from the band. Jones recorded often with Teddy Wilson and Billy Holiday during this period. He played with Earl Hines in the early '50s, and was in the pit band for the Broadway production of *Porgy and Bess*. Jones toured Europe as a solo act, and formed a band to work in clubs. He became a hot property in the '50s, playing muted trumpet and doing vocals. Jones had a string of albums make the Top 20 in the late '50s, among them *Muted Jazz* and *Jumpin' with Jonah* on Capitol. He later recorded for

Decca, Motown, and Chiaroscuro. Currently, he has one reissued session available on a Circle CD. —*Ron Wynn*

○ **Jonah Jones Sextet** / Dec. 9, 1954 / Bethlehem 1014

○ **Jazz Kaleidoscope** / i. 1956 / Bethlehem 4

○ **Jonah Jones at the Embers** / Feb. 14, 1956-Feb. 29, 1956 / Groove 1001

○ **Muted Jazz** / Feb. 22-25, 1957 / Capitol 839

★ **Jazz Legacy** / Inner City 7021

○ **Jonah Jones with Dave Pochonet and His All Stars** / Disques Swing 8408

PHILLY JOE JONES (Joseph Rudolph Jones)

b. Jul. 15, 1923, Philadelphia, PA, **d.** Aug. 30, 1985, Philadelphia, PA

Drums / Hard bop

Along with Art Blakey and Louis Hayes, Philly Joe Jones was hard bop's finest drummer. He was also possibly the most musical and melody-oriented of all the modern drummers to emerge in the '50s. As an accompanist, he combined explosiveness with outstanding imagination and taste. His solos were never excessive or exaggerated, and his technical acumen extended to the crispness of his cymbal playing and to his work with brushes.

Jones began on drums at age four, and studied for three years with Cozy Cole. Max Roach and Big Sid Catlett were among his influences. Jones was in the army in the early '40s, then moved to New York in 1947. He served as the Cafe Society's house drummer, as well as other clubs, where he played with Fats Navarro, Dexter Gordon, Dizzy Gillespie, and others. Jones worked with Ben Webster in Washington, D.C., in 1949, played in an R&B group in the late '40s with Joe Morris and Johnny Grimes, and also played in a band with Lionel Hampton and Tiny Grimes. In the early '50s, Jones became friends with Tadd Dameron, who helped him land some major dates. Jones returned to New York in 1952, and played at the Downbeat club with Miles Davis, Lee Konitz, and Zoot Sims before joining a group led by Dameron. They recorded in 1953. He then joined the Miles Davis quintet. The rhythm section of Jones on drums, pianist Red Garland, and bassist Paul Chambers was one of jazz's greatest rhythm sections ever, and remained intact until 1958. Jones also played at Birdland in the '50s, working with such musicians as John Coltrane, Billie Holiday, and Duke Ellington.

After 1958, Jones became both a bandleader and a session player. He recorded for Riverside in the late '50s and early '60s, then for Atlantic, Black Lion, and Lotus (Italy) in the late '60s. Jones spent much of the late '60s and early '70s in Europe. He lived and taught in London from 1967 to 1969, then in Paris from 1969 to 1972. He returned to Philadelphia and formed a jazz-rock band called Le Grand Prix. He worked with Bill Evans for a year in the late '70s, recording in 1976, and also toured with Garland. There were late '70s sessions for Sonet (Sweden) and Galaxy. Jones formed the repertory band, Dameronia, in 1981. This group played the compositions of Tadd Dameron and included Cecil Payne, Don Sickler, and Frank Wess. They recorded a pair of fine albums for Uptown in the early '80s. Jones played in a 1984 program of jazz and poetry with Archie Shepp and Amiri Baraka. Only a handful of Jones's own dates are available currently on CD. —*Ron Wynn*

★ **Blues for Dracula** / Apr. 2, 1959 / Riverside 230

If you're tuned into the interests of the jazz collector, you know that *Blues for Dracula* has achieved an interest of mythic proportions and many will be glad to have the first Philly Joe Jones date (9/17/58) back in circulation. The program opens with the title track and a too-long and unamusing monolog by the leader spoken in the style of Bela Lugosi and largely borrowed from Lenny Bruce. This, of course, makes the record memorable, but not good. Over the program each member of the sextet (Nat Adderley, Julian Priester, Johnny Griffin, Tommy Flanagan, Jimmy Garrison) has his moments (and this was a prime period for Griffin,

one of the strongest and most distinct bop tenors in the late '50s), but, overall, nothin' happenin'—not for those who *listen.* —*Bob Rusch,* Cadence

Drums Around the World / May 4, 1959 / Riverside 1792

Showcase / Nov. 17, 1959 / Riverside 484

Round Midnight / Jul. 18, 1969 / Lotus

Advance! / Oct. 10-12, 1978 / Galaxy

☆ **Drum Song** / Oct. 10-12, 1978 / Galaxy 5153

There is a definite "Blue Note" ambiance to the music on this session, what with the likes of trumpeter Blue Mitchell (the album is dedicated to him), trombonist Slide Hampton, tenor saxophonist Harold Land, and pianist Cedar Walton being kicked along by the drums of Philly Joe Jones. Not everyone is heard on each track. "I Waited for You" is a ballad feature for Hampton and the rhythm section, while "High Fly" showcases Charles Bowen (ts, ss). Devotees of hard bop should especially enjoy the strong brass and sax frontline on "Our Delight" and "Bird." This is music with no pretense to being anything other than inspired jazz played with skill and feeling by musicians dedicated to their art form. —*Carl Brauer,* Cadence

★ **To Tadd with Love** / Jul. 11, 1982 / Uptown

Dameronia was a working group playing transcriptions of Tadd Dameron's original music and arrangements done by trumpeter Don Sickler and John Oddo, who'd played piano with Woody Herman. All of this became possible when drummer Philly Joe Jones obtained a grant from the National Endowment for the Arts in 1981. The Dameron material contained here differs from the compositions you'd generally hear most and that makes it unique. One of the album's brightest moments is Sickler's great trumpet on "Misty Night." Johnny Coles (trumpet) also plays well on the opener, "Philly Joe." Frank Wess (alto sax) does his chores on "Soultrane," which comes from the record originally done with John Coltrane. Since Wess's sound throughout is more in a Johnny Hodges vein (he plays only alto here), I have to wonder why, since I've never identified him with that mainstream approach. Britt Woodman (trombone) is his true self playing in his Duke Ellington-influenced style, and pianist Walter Davis, Jr. and bassist Larry Ridley do their duty accurately since the material doesn't allow much room for sensational choruses. Jones's drumming is tasteful, and it was natural that he should be the one to fulfill this project. —*Jerry Atkins,* Cadence

Look Stop and Listen / Jun. 1984 / Uptown 2715

With this second release on Uptown Records, drummer Philly Joe Jones and the group Dameronia continue their successful effort to preserve, interpret, and nurture the works of Tadd Dameron. Perhaps the most significant difference from the previous release is the addition of Johnny Griffin (ts) as a featured soloist. Not to take anything away from the other fine soloists, but Griffin has always been a true giant and, as indicated by this and other recent (1984) recordings, is even more of one today. The recording and mastering (an important step in the transfer from tape to disc) by Rudy Van Gelder was superb. The end result was a "hot" master, or a very "live"-sounding recording in which Jones's drums have never sounded more crisp and clean. The same could be said of the ensembles and solos (alto saxophonist Frank Wess, trombonist Benny Powell, and both tenor saxophonist Charles Davis and pianist Walter Davis). The material is familiar to Dameron fans. Three of the pieces ("Choose Now," "Theme of No Repeat," "Dial B for Beauty") are faithfully reproduced, using the same instrumentation as the original '53 Prestige session. Two others ("If You Could See Me Now," "Focus") are effective reductions to smaller orchestrations of Dameron's large orchestra scores (Riverside, 1962). Note: In the arrangement of "If You Could See Me Now," two flutes are heard in the ensemble. As no flute credits are given, we must assume they are played by Wess and probably Charles Davis. In addition, two non-Dameron arrangements are included—Benny Golson's composition "Killer Joe" (arrangement uncredited) and Slide

Hampton's arrangement of Dameron's "Our Delight"—both close to the spirit of Dameronia. —*Peter Leitch, Cadence*

○ **Mean What You Say** / Sonet 735

Drummer Philly Joe Jones leads a quartet (pianist Mickey Tucker, Charles Bowen on soprano and tenor saxes, bassist Mickey Bass) and quintet (add trumpeter Tommy Turrentine) on this April 6 and 7, 1977, date. This is a nice blowing session for Bowen, who at the time had an R&B background and had never before recorded a jazz album. He's a saxman who had obviously listened to John Coltrane and Archie Shepp. Mickey Tucker is very strong on this set and at times almost seems to be the leader with Jones seemingly pushing to assert his position. Still, this is an enjoyable recording with just that little extra added personality to give it an edge. And there are definitely moments of near-perfect realization as on "Jim's Jewel," where Jones is clearly in command and everyone plays with both strength and direction. —*Bob Rusch, Cadence*

QUINCY JONES (Quincy Delight, Jr) Jones)

b. Mar. 14, 1933

Trumpet, composer, arranger / Swing, big band, progressive big band, instrumental pop, contemporary funk

A multifaceted individual, Quincy Jones is one of the top arrangers in jazz history. He's also been a bandleader, arranger, section trumpeter, producer, A&R head, record label executive, record label owner, and film and television soundtrack composer. Currently, he is executive producer of the hit television show "The Fresh Prince of Bel-Air" and president of Qwest Records, and is serving in other capacities for everything from the Montreux festival to *Vibe* magazine, a monthly hip-hop journal. From a jazz perspective, Jones's primary importance isn't as a player. He has been, at best, a serviceable, competent soloist. He has produced and arranged for many legendary figures, and has attained a profile in the music industry approached by only a handful of people, few of them Black. In the '50s and '60s, his compositions and arrangements successfully applied small combo concepts to large orchestras, and got precise, effective results that didn't restrict individual voices, and attained maximum coherence from the whole body.

Jones grew up in Seattle, and began trumpet lessons in 1947. He was tutored by Clark Terry in 1950, and played with Lionel Hampton from 1951 to 1953. The Hampton orchestra recorded in Paris and traveled throughout Europe in the early '50s. Jones began a career as a freelance arranger, providing charts for Oscar Pettiford, Art Farmer, Clifford Brown, Gigi Gryce, Ray Anthony, Tommy Dorsey, Count Basie, George Wallington, Terry, Cannonball Adderley, Jimmy Cleveland, Dinah Washington, Paul Quinchette, and Gene Krupa between 1952 and 1961. He played piano on an Annie Ross session in 1953, and served as trumpeter and band director for Dizzy Gillespie's big band during its 1956 Middle East and South American tour. That year, the album *This Is How I Feel About Jazz* was issued.

Jones signed with Mercury Records in 1957 and went to Paris, where he worked with Barclay for almost two years as a producer, arranger and conductor. He wrote the material for a Count Basie album in 1957. When Jones returned to New York two years later, he didn't remain in America long. After recording sessions for the album *Birth of a Band*, he toured Europe as music director for Harold Arlen's blues opera *Free and Easy*. When the show wrapped in Paris in 1960, Jones toured Europe and the United States with the band that included Benny Bailey, Melba Liston, Phil Woods, and Sahib Shihab. That same year, he arranged the music for a Ray Charles album. In 1961 Jones took the position as head of A&R for Mercury Records, based in New York. He also issued several big band albums in the early '60s, among them *Big Band Bossa Nova, Mode, Quintessence Live at Newport*, and *Great Wide World Live!* By 1964, Jones had become Mercury's first Black vice president, indeed the first Black vice president of any major White-owned and operated label.

Jones began to expand beyond jazz in the early '60s. He produced chart hits for Leslie Gore, and served as Peggy Lee's musical director, occupying that same position for Sarah Vaughan, Billy Eckstine, and even for Frank Sinatra. He was bandleader on Sinatra's mid-'60s album with Basie, and had the same job for Sinatra LPs *It Might As Well Be Spring* and *Sinatra at the Sands*, Sinatra's first concert album. He also began writing film scores and music for television shows in the mid-'60s. Some of his themes included "The Pawnbroker," "In Cold Blood," "Cactus Flower," "The Anderson Tapes," and "In the Heat of the Night." At the same time, Jones maintained a tie with jazz, though his records were becoming more controlled and pop-oriented, and less spontaneous. When he left Mercury for A&M in 1969, Jones promptly won a Grammy for the album *Walking in Space*. He recruited brilliant jazz musicians, then inserted their solos into a montage of light pop, R&B, funk, and quasi-jazz filler, a formula that became one of the best selling in instrumental pop history during the '70s.

His reach secure in the world of films, television, and record label ownership, Jones cemented his status as a dominant personality in the '70s. He was music director for the Oscars in 1971, and scored the films "The Getaway," and "The New Centurions" in 1972. His television themes included "Sanford and Son," the epic "Roots" mini-series in 1977, and even the PBS show "Rebop." Jones supervised the music for a CBS special "Duke Ellington—We Love You Madly!" in 1973, and had his composition "Black Requiem" performed in 1971 by the Houston Symphony Orchestra, with choir and special guest Ray Charles. During the '70s, Quincy Jones also became a superstar R&B and pop producer. He was at the helm for hit albums by Roberta Flack, Aretha Franklin, Al Jarreau, plus, of course, Michael Jackson. While Jackson's *Off the Wall* did well, his *Thriller* established the all-time worldwide album sales record (by 1993, it sold over 22 million copies in the United States alone). Jones was even scoring hit singles, with eight songs reaching the Top 100 between 1970 and 1981, although he never sang. Such albums as *Stuff Like That, Smackwater Jack*, which earned him another Grammy in 1971, *You've Got It Bad, Girl, Mellow Madness*, and *I Heard That* contained Jones's name and production credits. These albums were easy listening/funk/R&B/pop affairs with Chaka Khan, Ashford & Simpson, Stevie Wonder, Donna Summer, and the Brothers Johnson doing vocals over light brass and heavy backbeats. These were staples at urban contemporary radio stations, the emerging new adult contemporary and light jazz outlets, and were ideal for the late night romantic/mood music formats that developed on Black and urban stations in the '80s as an alternative to hip-hop, dancehall, and new jack swing R&B.

Jones's momentum didn't slow during the '80s. *The Dude*, and the singles "Just Once" and "One Hundred Ways" gave him more chart hits. His Qwest label kept rolling with albums by Patti Austin and with Frank Sinatra's '84 LP *L.A. Is My Lady*, which charted as both an album and a single. Jones produced the multiartist "We Are the World" in 1985. He survived serious illnesses and domestic turmoil, and moved into the '90s on new fronts. He became executive producer of the television show "Fresh Prince of Bel-Air" and had his life story told on film/video with *Listen Up*. Jones is part of a combine that started the hip-hop magazine *Vibe* in 1993. His most recent release was a '93 collaboration with Miles Davis, recorded at the 1991 Montreux festival. Generally, his '50s big band albums are available. It's harder to find the early '60s material, but some have been reissued. The late '60s A&M sessions are available again. Jones's pop and R&B hit releases have never been deleted from print. — *Ron Wynn*

Sweden–American All Stars / Nov. 10, 1953 / Prestige 172

This Is How I Feel About Jazz / Sep. 14, 1956 / GRP 115

Arranger Quincy Jones made many excellent straight jazz records in the '50s and '60s, before he began gravitating toward pop and R&B. He assembles a strong cast and makes his arrangements the focal point for *This Is How I Feel About Jazz*, which serves as yardstick for directions that the music was heading in at the time. —*Ron Wynn*

Birth of a Band–Vol. 2, The / May 27, 1959+Jun. 16, 1959 / Mercury 822611

★ **Birth of a Band–Vol. 1, The** / Jun. 16, 1959 / Mercury 8224692

Most of the arranging on this set is Quincy Jones's own and it's pervasively conservative, often resulting in homogenizations of material developed by other groups. Though a far cry from the errantly commercial results of his later labors, this music from the late '50s, taken as a whole, could be seen to lean away from the adventurous or risky and toward the safe and sure. This is not to say that the writing (Melba Liston, Nat Pierce, and Al Cohn contributed) is dull; within the limits observed, it is frequently exciting, certainly always sturdy enough to serve a bevy of first-line horn players (Zoot Sims, Phil Woods, Clark Terry, Harry "Sweets" Edison, Frank Wess, Urbie Green, Jimmy Cleveland, Art Farmer, etc.). Simply on the basis of Jones's commercial visibility and success, this music deserves a place in the present catalog. For those just edging into an interest in jazz, it could serve as an entry window of sorts. —*Alan Bargebuhr,* Cadence

I Dig Dancers / Feb. 27, 1960-Oct. 19, 1960 / Mercury 60612

Live at Newport / Jul. 3, 1961 / Trip 5554

○ **Great Wide World of Quincy Jones: Live!, The** / Nov. 4-9, 1961 / Mercury 822613

Quintessence, The / Nov. 29, 1961-Dec. 18, 1961 / MCA 5728

Listeners only familiar with Quincy Jones's ubiquitous film and TV scores owe it to themselves to investigate these early sides from his formative years. Quincy's orchestrations had become even more polished, lush, and expansive on the 1961 dates, and the cast was filled out to true big-band dimensions with star section men like Clark Terry, Joe Newman, Julius Watkins, Freddie Hubbard, Thad Jones, Oliver Nelson, and Milt Hinton. Whatever hesitancy may have remained in some earlier sessions had vanished and the group performs with a romantic verve that obviates the distinction between mood music and good music—contemporary MOR arrangers take note! The buttery harmonies are slightly overrich but hard to resist and Jones's proclivity for cinematic clichés is held in check, surfacing only in the campy treatment of the theme from "Invitation." —*Larry Birnbaum,* Down Beat

★ **Walking in Space** / 1969 / A&M 0801

A Grammy-winning work that marked the beginning of Jones's shift into R&B and pop. —*Ron Wynn*

○ **Gula Matari** / Mar. 25-26, 1970 / A&M 0820

A superb followup that might have been better than *Walkin' in Space* overall. —*Ron Wynn*

Smackwater Jack / 1971 / Mobile Fidelity 776

Mellow Madness / 1972 / A&M 4526

The first appearance of the Brothers Johnson, with Quincy now a bigtime R&B star. —*Ron Wynn*

Body Heat / 1973 / A&M 3191

Transitional album marking his gradual move toward complete R&B sound, minor jazz influence. —*Ron Wynn*

Roots / 1977 / A&M 4626

Monumental soundtrack for a landmark TV show that eclipses Jones's past film and television work in symbolic impact. —*Ron Wynn*

Sounds & Stuff / 1978 / A&M 3249

Dude, The / i. 1981 / A&M 3248

25th Anniversary Series–Vol. 3 / A&M 6550

SAM JONES (Samuel Jones)

b. Nov. 12, 1924, Jacksonville, FL, **d.** Dec. 15, 1981, New York, NY

Bass, cello / Hard bop, post bop

A wonderful accompanist equally skilled at bass or cello, Jones made being in the rhythm section an art form. He moved from Florida to New York in the '50s, working first with Tiny Bradshaw, then with Illinois Jacquet and Kenny Dorham. His first major impact was as a member of Cannonball Adderley's early quintet from 1956-1957, followed by time with Dizzy Gillespie and Thelonious Monk. Jones stayed in the re-formed Adderley group from 1959-1966, then spent three years in the Oscar Peterson trio. For the rest of his career, Jones was an active session player, and he led a 12-piece band part-time. —*Ron Wynn*

★ **Soul Society, The** / Mar. 8, 1960 / Riverside 1789

☆ **Down Home** / Aug. 15, 1962 / Riverside

○ **Cello Again** / Jan. 5, 1976 / Xanadu

Combining the warmth and guts of a guitar and bass, cellist Sam Jones really puts a splendid session together with everybody concerned, tight, and bending in harmony together. Some of the music here ("In Walked Ray," "Scorpio") sounds very much like the early 1950 recording with Stan Getz and Doug Raney from Storyville. This effect is due to the use of strings (cello and bass) and alto saxophonist Charles McPherson's fluid Getz-like approach, in the confines of basic bop laid down so well by pianist Barry Harris. McPherson comes on more (Charlie Parker) Bird-like on "Angel In The Night," sitting it out on all four other tracks—a wise move, because McPherson's presence on these three might have made Jones's own identity less strong. Jones takes no back seat in this cello-bration, taking long solos on each track, picked for the most part. Jones bows sparingly on some intros and endings. There must have been many smiles on the musicians' faces during this date because throughout the record Jones displays a great warm humor; it's a knowing humor, subtle as he picks around melodies and jumps into solos—there was no holding back his enthusiasm. —*Carol Ober,* Cadence

Something in Common / Sep. 13, 1977 / Muse 5149

Something in Common was done in New York in September 1977, and it is one of two superlative, straightfoward blowing albums produced that month by bassist Sam Jones (the other being *Changes*). *Something* is the more "produced" of the two, having a cleaner, broader sound. The rhythm team of pianist Cedar Walton and drummer Billy Higgins comes through to the ears easily, especially behind the soloists. Compositionally, *Something* is more adventurous than its counterpart, including a tour de force in "Seven Minds," a modal piece that highlights the leader in long, out-of-tempo statements both fore and aft. The opening bass solo goes into a biting ensemble figure that proceeds to spirited playing by all. Also, here are two originals by Walton: the driving "Bolivia" and the title track. —*Zan Stewart,* Down Beat

Bassist, The / Jan. 3, 1979 / Discovery 861

The Bassist is a reissue of a session originally released on Interplay, although I don't remember the record actually existing. This is an outing for a snappy trio. Jones, Kenny Barron (k) and Keith Copeland (d) produce music of subtle but quite unrelenting drive. Even on the slower-tempoed "Lily," the bass and drum work push close up to maintain the swing tension which so marks the entire date. Everybody has some fine moments in a set of demanding protein jazz. Two points of interest: "Rhythm-A-Ning" (5:30) is taken at breakneck tempo and almost seems to get away from the trio, which manages not to stumble, but instead pushes home an exciting foray into Thelonious Monkland. "Hymn Of Scorpio" utilizes electric piano in one of those rare times when it works well (Hank Jones and Tommy Flanagan are two other "traditional" pianists who have succeeded here as well). This is very nice. —*Bob Rusch,* Cadence

○ **Something New** / Jun. 4, 1979 / Sea Breeze 2004

Changes & Things / Dec. 1979 / Xanadu 150

THAD JONES (Thaddeus Joseph Jones)

b. Mar. 28, 1923, Pontiac, MI, **d.** Aug. 20, 1986, Copenhagen, Denmark

Trumpet, cornet, arranger, composer / Bop, hard bop

Thad Jones is hard bop's most harmonically daring trumpeter and is a distinctive stylist, despite Dizzy Gillespie's influence on him. The trumpet-playing member of the Jones family, he's also a first-rate composer, bandleader, and arranger. His writing for the Thad Jones-Mel Lewis big band provided excellent works that were designed to showcase individual orchestra voices. He covered a wide range of styles in his compositions, from swing to Afro-Latin, jazz-rock, bebop, blues, and even waltz rhythms. His horn playing was clean, crisp, direct, and striking, with a full, lyrical touch and a shimmering tone.

Jones began playing trumpet in his teens, and turned professional at age 16, working with his brother Hank and with Sonny Stitt. He spent the mid-'40s playing in army bands, then worked in midwestern show and dance groups. He played with his other brother, Elvin, in Billy Mitchell's band during the early '50s, then worked in 1954 and 1955 with Charles Mingus's Jazz Workshop. Jones joined Count Basie's orchestra in 1954 as well, and remained with the orchestra until 1963. He made his first recording as a leader on Mingus's Debut label. Jones did the writing for a Harry James album in 1963. In 1964 Jones played with Thelonious Monk at Carnegie Hall, worked in a group with Gerry Mulligan, and joined the staff at CBS radio and television in New York. He co-led a quintet with Pepper Adams in 1965 that recorded for Milestone. Mel Lewis was the group's drummer. Near the end of '65, Jones and Lewis organized an 18-piece band. In February of '66, this band started what became a long-running series of Monday night Village Vanguard concerts. The group did club dates, festivals, tours of Europe and Japan, recording sessions, and command performances. Over the years, the roster included Pepper Adams, Richard Davis, Roland Hanna, Joe Farrell, Jerome Richardson, Billy Harper, Jimmy Knepper, Garnett Brown, Jon Faddis, Janice Robinson, Richard Williams, Snooky Young, Cecil Bridgewater, and many others. They recorded mainly for Solid State (the albums were later reissued on Liberty-Blue Note when TransAmerica owned the Solid State masters), but also did two fine albums on Horizon. Jones and Lewis also recorded with the Swedish Radio Jazz Group in 1975.

Jones finally ended his affiliation with the orchestra and with Lewis in the late '70s. In 1977 and 1978, Jones had been the leader of the Radioens Big Band in Denmark, and he relocated there. Jones also injured his lip, but began playing valve trombone. He formed a new big band, the Thad Jones Eclipse, and recorded in 1979 and 1980 for the Metronome (Dutch) label. He also made a quartet date for Steeplechase. Jones returned to America in 1985 to take over the Count Basie Orchestra, and kept that position until February of the next year, when ill health forced him to resign. He played on a Joe Williams session for Delos in 1985. Jones died a few months after leaving the Basie Orchestra. He only has a handful of dates as a leader available on CD, and there's almost nothing on CD that features the Jones-Lewis big band. *—Ron Wynn*

○ **Thad Jones-Billy Mitchell Quintet / i.** 1953 / Dee Gee 4009
★ **Magnificent Thad Jones /** Jul. 14, 1956 / Blue Note 46814
○ **Fabulous Thad Jones /** i. 1958 / Debut 625
○ **After Hours /** i. Mar. 1958 / Prestige 7118
☆ **Mean What You Say /** Apr. 26, 1966-May 9, 1966 / Milestone 464

Monday Night / Dec. 4, 1968 / Solid State 18048
Three years old and already well beyond the toddling stage, the Thad Jones/Mel Lewis Orchestra was here captured at play in its nursery—the Village Vanguard. This album has the band striding eloquently and confidently through five Thad Jones charts—plus a fine Bob Brookmeyer arrangement of "St. Louis Blues." Just how strong and plentiful the band's soloists were is illustrated by the fact Pepper Adams (baritone) is heard only in section on these sides! No single player is relied on and every cat has to take a turn in such

an all-star crew. The titles I enjoy most are the two blues. "St. Louis Blues" gets a great treatment. The pace and intensity gradually increase during a beautiful solo from trombonist Garnett Brown. Jones also blows a nice flugelhorn on this. "Second Race" is a hip, fluid groover spotlighting excellent trumpet by Richard Williams and relaxed tenor work from Sheldon Powell. More tenor—this time from Eddie Daniels—lights up "Mornin' Reverend." The star of "Kids Are Pretty People" is that old "kid" Jimmy Knepper (tb), sounding as brilliant as ever. Jones and Jerry Dodgion (as) are the key voices on "Say It Softly." On "In The Waltz," Jerome Richardson exhibits his polished soprano prowess. Bassist Richard Davis is a gas here, but then he is throughout the set. *—Mark Gardner,* Coda

Central Park North / Jun. 17-18, 1969 / Solid State 18058
This session has good big-band playing, some good dance numbers, and good arranging by Thad Jones that never really comes alive. The one number that gets some blood in its veins is Nat Adderley's "Jive Samba," which really moves rhythmically and cuts loose excellent trumpet solos from Danny Moore and (especially) Richard Williams. Believe it or not, the swingingest solo is a very long one by Jerome Richardson on piccolo! He wails over rhythm and then easily rides over the full powerhouse. Jones's "Big Dipper" provides discouraging evidence that James Nottingham, who used to be one of the great growl trumpeters, seems to have lost it all and descended into cuteness and copying of his onetime section mate in the Charlie Barnet band, Clark Terry. The recorded sound is very full and live. *—Ron Anger,* Coda

Suite for Pops / Jan. 25-31, 1972 / Horizon 701
This could be considered a "concept" album, in which the various moods, textures, and auras of Satchmo's musical personality were combined with tonal character sketches to pay tribute to Louis Armstrong. Most of these pieces were recorded early in 1972, only a few months after Armstrong's death; accordingly, the pall of loss was still manifested in acute pain, which moved coleader and trumpeter Thad Jones to set his personal and professional recollections to staff and chart. Anatomically, the playing was never better. Jon Faddis was barely out of high school on these takes, and the comparisons to Dizzy Gillespie were first being made, initally by the Monday night pilgrims at the Village Vanguard. Here Faddis combines the soul, pacing, and joie de vivre of Armstrong with his admittedly Gillespian flights. Codominating the abundant, yet never indulgent solos is the criminally underrated Jerry Dodgion, fluent on soprano sax and flute. Dee Dee Bridgewater bubbles on "The Great One," a lengthy track where everyone gets a chance to solo. Her Morse code wails, on top of Butter Jackson's muted bone, are designed to create the effect of a eulogy for Satch. *—Arnold Shaw,* Down Beat

Live in Munich / Sep. 9, 1976 / A&M 724
This is not a sole Thad Jones album but one of many outstanding releases featuring the Thad Jones-Mel Lewis orchestra, an 18-piece band that the two had cofounded back in 1965. Jones was the band's principal arranger during the bulk of its tenure, and he supplied several charts for this fine session, their second for the Horizon label. *—Ron Wynn*

★ **Thad Jones and the Mel Lewis Quartet /** i. May 1979 / A&M 0830
Patience and care are the hallmarks of this album. This is evident in the sound, which is clean and live. Most important, it is evident in the music itself. The musicians nurse the tunes lovingly, giving them time to develop. This means that, in spite of a few slow moments, the music is *alive.* The fact that the music was recorded live—at Miami's Airliner Lounge in September 1977—contributes to the organic feeling of this session. "But Not For Me" is a long cut (16 minutes) that introduces each member of the quintet and allows them to limber up. Jones's solo alternates between lyrical sweeps and boppish loop-the-loops. Pianist Harold Danko solos next, locking lines and chords together in a way that

would make Bill Evans smile. Then Rufus Reid plays as fine a straightahead bass solo as you were likely to hear that year (1979). He has it all: good ideas, excellent intonation and execution, and a sound as juicy as a ripe pear. After Mel Lewis trades fours with everyone, the quartet goes into a kind of soft shoe, with Danko strumming the piano strings as though it were a guitar and Jones skipping lightly over the top like a stone over water. —*Douglas Clark*, Down Beat

Three and One / Oct. 4, 1985 / Steeple Chase

SCOTT JOPLIN

b. Nov. 24, 1868, **d.** Apr. 1, 1917
Piano, composer / Ragtime

Scott Joplin was ragtime's greatest composer, and deserves attention for his writing, though he was radically removed from jazz's spirit and sensibility. Improvisation was not a quality he embraced; Joplin wanted to create a body of "serious" music using ragtime as a foundation. He was a stickler for having his rags played at the correct speed, and loathed hearing speeded up versions. But Joplin's attention to detail and line are impressive, as was his ability to express ideas while following extremely rigid compositional and harmonic rules.

Joplin played cornet in the Queen City Negro Band of Sedalia, Missouri, in the 1890s, and appeared at the 1893 World's Fair. He sold his first compositions in 1895, and his first rags in 1899. John Stark, who purchased "Maple Leaf Rag," gave Joplin a royalty agreement, a very uncommon business practice between Whites and Blacks at that time. The song proved to be the genre's biggest hit, and Stark moved his business to St. Louis. Joplin's desire (some would say obsession) to expand ragtime's scope led him to continually try things that weren't commercially viable, and were considered beyond the realm of possibility. "The Ragtime Dance" in 1902 was a 20-minute ballet; Stark published it to meager response and even weaker sales. His 1903 opera, "The Guest of Honor," never appeared and is now considered lost. With his rags being played at faster speeds due to coin-operated player pianos in penny arcades, Joplin kept pushing experimental, extended works. He went to New York in 1910, and a year later debuted the opera *Treemonisha* in Harlem at his own expense. The resounding flop depressed him to the point that Joplin wound up dying in a mental hospital six years later.

He left behind over 50 piano rags that have been revived properly and have been recorded by players such as Max Morath, James Levine, Dick Hyman, Andre Previn, even classical violinist Itzhak Perlman, as well as groups like the New England Conservatory Ragtime Ensemble. The hit film *The Sting* used his tune "The Entertainer" in 1974, introducing ragtime to a new generation (composer Marvin Hamlisch spent considerable time on talk shows explaining that he didn't write the song). *Treemonisha* was revived by the Houston Grand Opera in 1976 with Gunther Schuller conducting, and a two-album (now two-disc) recording was issued. Joplin even received a posthumous Pulitzer for *Treemonisha*, something that outraged many jazz critics and fans who questioned awarding such an honor to Joplin while snubbing Duke Ellington. —*Ron Wynn*

○ **Ragtime–Vol. 2 (1900-1910)** / 1900-1910 / Biograph 1008
Classic Scott Joplin ragtime compositions ranging from early in his career to near the end. Despite the restrictive form (which Joplin rigidly followed), he managed to find ways to creatively rework themes and vary his sound a bit. —*Ron Wynn*

○ **Ragtime–Vol. 3 (Early 1900s)** / 1900 / Biograph 1010
The third volume of digitally remastered classic piano rags by Scott Joplin from the early 1900s. If you're a diehard ragtime lover or piano student, you'll be enthralled by hearing this much ragtime. Others may find it a bit wearing, especially since there's almost no variation in arrangements, pacing, or voicings, only in the player's intensity. —*Ron Wynn*

○ **Joplin, Scott–1916 (Classic Solos from Piano Rolls)** / 1916 / Biograph 1006
More vintage ragtime taken from piano rolls. Scott Joplin was incensed whenever he heard someone playing his rags too fast, so he tried to put them down on piano rolls himself to keep them from being speeded up. These were transferred digitally from rolls. —*Ron Wynn*

Elite Syncopations/The Entertainer / **i.** 1988 / Biograph 101
Digitally recorded from a 1910 Steinway using original piano rolls, these discs boast a superb, natural sound, beautiful packaging, and excellent, informative liner notes. Joplin's classic ragtime influenced any number of pianists who followed him and also started an entire cult among young acoustic guitarists devoted to transcribing his rags for fingerstyle playing. A great representation of the best of the ragtime genre. —*Ralph Stewart Jr.*, Rock & Roll Disc

○ **King of Ragtime Writers** / **i.** Feb. 28, 1992 / Biograph 110

★ **Elite Syncopations: Classic Ragtime from Rare Piano Rolls, The** / Biograph 102
If you want to hear exactly how ragtime should be played, here's the real thing from a founding father. These vintage Scott Joplin rags were transferred to digital from piano rolls, and are played the way he wanted his rags to sound. —*Ron Wynn*

Scott Joplin's Rag Time / Greener Pastures 1

THE JORDAN BROTHERS

Neo bop
Another pair of talented brothers from New Orleans, flutist Kent and trumpeter Marlon Jordan haven't made as much impact or gained as much visibility as the Marsalis brothers. Marlon has issued several releases on Columbia, while Kent demonstrated excellent flute technique on his lone release, though he sometimes squandered it on routine material. Marlon Jordan's sessions remain available on CD, while Kent's only release has since been deleted from print. —*Ron Wynn*

CLIFFORD JORDAN (Clifford Laconia (Jr) Jordan)

b. Sep. 2, 1931, Chicago, IL, **d.** 1993
Tenor saxophone / Hard bop, post bop
Clifford Jordan never attained the widespread exposure he deserved, though he was well-known and highly respected by knowledgeable jazz fans and musicians. He had a warm, exuberant sound and a round, big tone. Jordan was a wonderful blues and ballad player, able to stretch out and swing, then go inside and play with conviction and energy. Jordan started on piano, then switched to tenor sax at age 14. He attended Du Sable High in Chicago, where his classmates included Johnny Griffin, John Gilmore, and Richard Davis. He played in Chicago with both R&B bands and with Max Roach and Sonny Stitt before moving to New York in 1957. He worked again with Roach, then with Horace Silver. Jordan went to the West Coast for a year, then came back to New York and worked with J.J. Johnson. In the early '60s, he played with Kenny Dorham and Andrew Hill. He also worked with Charles Mingus, once more with Roach, and toured Europe, Africa, and the Middle East. Jordan's earliest album was done for Blue Note, working with his old classmate John Gilmore. He did septet and quartet dates for Blue Note in the late '50s. Cannonball Adderley helped him land on Riverside in the '60s, producing his debut for the label in 1960. Jordan later recorded for Jazzland, Atlantic, Vortex, and then the Black-owned label Strata-East in 1969. He continued in the early and mid-'70s on Strata East, leading his Magic Triangle group. Jordan recorded for Steeplechase, Muse, and East World. He played Lester Young in a 1972 theatrical production *Lady Day: A Musical Tragedy* that was performed at the Brooklyn Academy of Music. He also visited Europe often in the '60s and '70s. During the '80s, there were sessions for Soul Note, Criss Cross, Bee Hive, Mapleshade, Jazzline, and others. Jordan recorded for DIW

in the '90s, and led a big band before finally succumbing to cancer in 1992. A fair number of his sessions are available on CD. —*Ron Wynn*

Spellbound / Aug. 10, 1960 / Original Jazz Classics 766
A formative session by tenor saxophonist Clifford Jordan, in 1960 still building his reputation and developing his style. Alto saxophonist Cannonball Adderley not only got Jordan this recording date, he produced it as well. Jordan shows the spry, soulful qualities in his solos that would later become a familiar sound, but his playing doesn't have the harmonic variety or creativity he'd show in subsequent sessions. —*Ron Wynn*

These Are My Roots / Feb. 1, 1965 / Atlantic

○ **Clifford Jordan in the World** / Mar. 1969 / Strata East 19721
Tenor saxophonist Clifford Jordan is impressive here on every count, as composer, soloist, and leader. Pianist Wynton Kelly is heard in a more avant-garde context than customarily. None of his essential qualities are altered, but the high-energy surroundings inspire his solos on "Vienna," "Ouagoudougou," and "Prelude" that are superb even by the standards of his best work. Trumpeter Kenny Dorham has a beautfully developed statement on "Ouagoudougou," the kind of minor key invention at which he was incomparable. It is his only solo on the album and its sense of inevitability and form is in contrast to the playing of trumpeter Don Cherry, whose approach is not architectural but decorative. Cherry's "Vienna" solo is filigree, a series of runs, arabesques, swoops, and nervous jabs. "Vienna" has a two-bass interlude in which Wilbur Ware and Richard Davis complement each other beautifully. Really quite a lovely record, produced, not incidentally, by Jordan. —*Doug Ramsey*, Down Beat

In the World / Mar. 1969 / Strata East

★ **Glass Bead Game** / Oct. 29, 1973+Oct. 29, 1973 / Strata East
Even with two quartets and compositions by each of the six musicians, this set has a unity of conception and feeling that realizes that sense of family that Strata-East recordings often strived for. There is a relaxed easiness among the players and a clear sense of pleasure in playing together. After a year of listening I was still fully charmed by this music, and especially by saxophonist Clifford Jordan's sound, which struck me as among the most beautiful of tenor sounds—warm, rich, and unstrained with a full range and finely controlled vibrato. There are not many long solos here, and yet that hardly seems a deficiency considering the other virtues: simple beguiling tunes, easily remembered, and plenty of tasty interplay. The music is celebratory, but hardly programmatic; wisely there was little effort to imitate those celebrated. Most of the rhythms are taken lightly at medium tempo, which helps to avoid the danger of pretentious solemnity. Pieces like "John Coltrane" and "Prayer to the People," most anthemlike and thus most vulnerable to falseness, come off very well; they lifted my spirits. This is honest, accessible, and lasting music. —*Joel Ray*, Cadence

Night of the Mark VII / Mar. 26, 1975 / Muse 5076

Firm Roots / Apr. 18, 1975 / Steeple Chase
One of Jordan's best releases with the Magic Triangle ensemble of Cedar Walton (p), Sam Jones (b), and Billy Higgins (d). —*Ron Wynn*

Highest Mountain, The / Apr. 18, 1975 / Muse 5445
Tenor saxophonist's Clifford Jordan's *Highest Mountain*, recorded at a Paris club in 1975, has the feel of ongoing evolution rather than retrospection. The opening track, a chanted Coltrane tribute written by Spike Lee's father Bill, sets the mood, followed by a take on "Highest Mountain"—the only Jordan original here—that's much looser and more exploratory than the big-band version on another recent Jordan album. The stellar rhythm trio (pianist Cedar Walton, bassist Sam Jones, drummer Billy Higgins) is likewise laid back, simmering rather than searing, but the empathetic warmth and unfailing good taste of all four players is consistently rewarding. —*Larry Birnbaum*, Down Beat

Adventurer, The / Feb. 9, 1978 / Muse 5163
The Adventurer is a record that stands up to close scrutiny and repeated listening no matter how jaded on modern recreations of the past you may have become. Tenor saxophonist Clifford Jordan is in top form; his solos are superbly constructed, going from one point to another logically, effortlessly, and in the space of only two or three choruses. His flute and alto work ("Blues For Me") is less convincing. As an interpreter of melody, Jordan was among the finest. He went beyond reading a line—he played it. Certainly we can hear the influences of Lester Young (rhythm) and, to a lesser extent, Coleman Hawkins (sound), but Jordan was more than just another disciple. On "I'll Be Around," (another gorgeous Alec Wilder tune) he alternates between lagging behind and jumping ahead of the melody; the chilling, haunting dips into the lower register *ring* with emotion. Pianist Tommy Flanagan, in a somewhat limited role, shines as usual. His accompaniment is first rate (especially on "I'll Be Around" and "No More"), and his solos are brief but interesting. Grady Tate is one of the most consistently interesting drummers around. It's so nice to hear a drummer use even the simplest of contrasting devices—brushes during a bass solo—as on "Quasimodo." Bill Lee, an underrecorded bassist if ever there was one, is solid and tasteful on every tune. —*Arthur Moorehead*, Down Beat

Repetition / Feb. 9, 1984 / Soul Note 1084
Repetition offers monster performances by bassist Walter Booker, who had been under wraps too long. It's always delightful to listen to the attentive drummer Vernel Fournier and pianist Barry Harris, intent on fully being a part of the music (Thelonious Monkishly at times) without getting in the way. The album displays ensemble sensitivity and commitment all the way, with the title tune as the centerpiece. Clifford Jordan solos casually on tenor sax as if to survey the landscape and comment on its many details; his was an ease so magnificent in its big sound it could make you fainthearted. On "Nostalgia/Casbah," the blend of Tadd Dameron and Fats Navarro over "Out of Nowhere," and on Jordan's own "Third Avenue" and "House Call," the collective ensemble mind is heightened as the saxophonist displays his ability to achieve filigree of dynamics, then robust attack, and then float above the energy and foundation he'd empowered. —*Ron Weilburn*, Down Beat

Royal Ballads / Dec. 23, 1986 / Criss Cross 1025

○ **Dr. Chicago** / i. Jan. 1988 / Bee Hive 7018

Four Play / i. Feb. 1991 / DIW 836
Simply magical 1990 quartet date done for a Japanese label. Veteran tenor saxophonist Clifford Jordan teams with another veteran and two young players for the kind of no-frills, dynamic jazz album that seldom gets made anymore by American major labels. Pianist James Williams and drummer Ronnie Burrage bring youthful excitement; bassist Richard Davis and Jordan, seasoning and experience. —*Ron Wynn*

○ **Live at Condon's, New York/Down through the Years** / i. Apr. 24, 1992 / Milestone 9197

Live at Ethell's / Mapleshade 512629
The recent passing of Clifford Jordan was another in a series of irreplaceable jazz greats departing. Jordan was among the finest straightahead soloists, an exceptional ballad interpreter and combative uptempo player who excelled in any situation. This live date, done in 1987 in Baltimore at the club Ethell, is a quartet session, with Jordan handling the front line and repeatedly showing how to craft, develop, and then conclude a solo. He never rushes things or relies on gimmicks or repetition, knowing when and how to end a line or wrap up an idea. —*Ron Wynn*

DUKE JORDAN (Irving Sidney Jordan)

b. Apr. 1, 1922, New York, NY
Piano / Bop, hard bop
An intensely lyrical, enticing pianist who studied classical music and knew it thoroughly, Duke Jordan ranks with the

finest bebop soloists. He is also a topflight accompanist who played frequently with Charlie Parker. Jordan began his classical studies at an early age, then played at the 1939 World's Fair with trombonist Steve Pulliam, winning an amateur contest. He later worked with Al Cooper's Savoy Sultans and with Roy Eldridge's big band. Parker heard him playing at the Three Deuces in New York and invited Jordan to join a new group with Miles Davis, Max Roach, and Tommy Potter. Jordan worked with Parker from late 1946 to 1948, and then would periodically rejoin him. He also played with Sonny Stitt and Gene Ammons in the early '50s, and with Stan Getz in 1949, 1952, and 1953. He began recording as a leader in the mid-'50s for Savoy and Prestige. Jordan teamed with Cecil Payne from the mid-'50s to the early '60s, making several recordings for Muse and Spotlite, among others. The duo played with Rolf Ericson in Sweden in 1956, and toured Europe in the theatrical production of *The Connection*. Using the name Jack Murray, Jordan wrote the music for the French film *Les Liaisons Dangereuses*, and penned the classic composition "Jordu" as well. Jordan recorded for Blue Note and Charlie Parker Records in the '60s, interrupted his musical career in the late '60s, then resumed it in the mid-'70s. Jordan toured Scandinavia in the early and late '70s, and Japan in 1976 and 1982. He's been a resident of Denmark since 1978. During the '70s, he did several dates for Steeplechase, often working with bassist Sam Jones. He contributed to *They All Played Bebop* on Columbia and another Xanadu anthology, and recorded for Baystate (Japan) in the '80s. There are only a couple of Jordan dates currently available on CD. —*Ron Wynn*

★ **Flight to Jordan** / Aug. 4, 1960 / Blue Note 46824
Bucking the Bud Powell tide, Duke Jordan's playing on this disc is subtle and economical. He is nearly flawless in gracefully expressing his melodic feelings, whether with single notes or chorded solos. His roots were in bop and also swing—not surprising, considering that he played for a year with the Savoy Sultans prior to his association with Charlie Parker. Cecil Payne (bs) teamed with Jordan occasionally for several years. He shows why here—his sensitive playing complements Jordan well. Art Blakey's playing here is a fine lesson on the art of jazz percussion. Blakey was just beginning to make a name for himself, with the formation of the Jazz Messengers shortly before these sessions. He not only adapts to the subtlety of the dates in his backing and also accompanies himself during his solo, but he makes the drums melodic by adjusting timbre to create different tones. This is some of the finest percussion work I've heard, done with little fanfare. The music is both relaxed and lively. —*Doug Long*, Cadence

Flight to Denmark / Nov. 25, 1973+Dec. 12, 1973 / Steeple Chase

Lover Man / Aug. 1975 / Steeple Chase 1127
Opening with Miles Davis's "Dig," pianist Duke Jordan channels a vital flow of interesting phrases and flawlessly driving swing into a timeless bop solo. And, because the trio had already warmed up that day by recording the quintet date *Duke's Delight*, the group is highly relaxed, inspired, and lucid. Wryly, Jordan next bounces into the funky offbeat accents of "Dancer's Call," where he proceeds to demonstrate the capsulization of a wide variety of pianistic approaches into one convincing solo. The master bassist Sam Jones shines on "Love Trane," creating a beautiful solo using the rhythmic contours of Jordan's melody for material. In nice contrast to side one, the second side features a more serene aspect of Jordan's music. Bringing the tempos way down, the trio explores the pastoral ballad settings of the title tune and "Wonderful." Majestically supported by Jones and drummer Al Foster, Jordan renders a distinctive version of the standard "Out of Nowhere," taken at a brighter tempo than Charlie Parker's classic interpretation. Jordan's "Lover Man" and "Nowhere" are classics in their own right—two of the best renditions of each I'd ever heard. The bittersweet longing and lush chord voicings conjure "Lover Man" with just the perfect feel for the tune. —*Cliff Tinder*, Down Beat

Duke's Delight / Nov. 18, 1975 / Steeple Chase
Duke's Artistry / Jun. 30, 1978 / Steeple Chase
Great Session, The / Jun. 30, 1978 / Steeple Chase

○ **Thinking of You** / i. Oct. 1979 / Steeple Chase 1165
The Duke Jordan set (pianist Jordan, bassist Niels-Henning Orstead Pedersen, drummer Billy Hart) swings nicely in an underplayed fashion. "Foxie Cakes," taken solo, is interesting for its mix of piano techniques like Thelonious Monk; one begins to hear a more pronounced stride element in Jordan's playing. This is a rather run-of-the-mill outing for him, tasteful, but with few peaks. There is no recording date given, but it probably was done in the fall of '79. —*Bob Rusch*, Cadence

Midnight Moonlight / 1979 / Steeple Chase 1143
Duke Jordan had strong ties with Bud Powell's approach to piano soloing. Jordan's "Yes I Will" (all material here is original) employs several percussive chordal blocks over idiomatic 7ths and 10ths. "Table Chess," the most energetic of these tracks, features dense, serpentine lines. Jordan, however, deftly avoids being locked into one strict idiom. His tastes include the nostalgic, nearly Victorian ballad "Midnight Moonlight" and the musty "Wait and See," both using truncated, nonchalant improvisations. Other curiosities include the aptly titled Scotch-like drone bass of "Dance in Plaid" and "Mellow Mood," a clever reworking of Jordan's most famous composition "Jordu." —*Jon Balleras*, Down Beat

○ **Tivoli One** / i. Oct. 1985 / Steeple Chase 1189
This presents pianist Duke Jordan in a trio setting (Wilbur Little, bass; Dannie Richmond, drums) recorded live. It's an enjoyable session consisting of four Jordan originals and three standards. This is good bop piano from one of its first-generation proponents. —*Peter Leitch*, Cadence

○ **Tivoli Two** / i. Oct. 1985 / Steeple Chase 1193
This recording, like its predecessor *Tivoli One*, documents a performance at Jazzhus Slukefter, Tivoli Gardens, in Copenhagen. Jordan's playing on the album certifies his status as one of the strongest pure bop pianists ever, and accentuates the extent to which his presence on the American jazz scene has been missed. The basic style is still unchanged from the '40s, but the passing years saw the more frequent surfacing of additional influences; alternating with fleet, extended, Bud Powell-like lines would be the almost awkward-sounding angular skips and jagged phrases of a Thelonious Monk. Indeed, a long descending run at the end of "How Deep Is the Ocean" could have been executed by Monk himself. And yet Jordan's lush reading of the melodies of that tune and "I Cover the Waterfront" echo Erroll Garner, with the straight quarter-note chords of the left hand and arpeggiated strums of the right. Drummer Dannie Richmond and bassist Wilbur Little function with the leader as a well-integrated unit. Little's big, solid bass sound and lithe ideas are a natural complement to the drummer's whirlwind of activity. —*A. David Franklin*, Cadence

LOUIS JORDAN

b. Jul. 8, 1908, Brinkley, AR, d. Feb. 4, 1975, Los Angeles, CA
Saxophone, vocals, bandleader / Swing, big band, blues & jazz
Louis Jordan helped create one of biggest alternatives to bop that emerged in the '40s. A onetime Chick Webb orchestra member, alto saxophonist Jordan took conventional swing-era solos and arrangements and wrapped them around short story/songs about neighborhood misadventures, the war between the sexes, and jinxed characters. These tales were filled with humorous quips and clever rejoinders, and were punctuated with a concluding moral. They were fast-paced and played with bustling energy. This sound was the dawn of the R&B era, though other changes would come later.
Jordan learned clarinet and sax from his father, who'd led the touring band for the Rabbit Foot Minstrels. Jordan toured with them while in high school. He debuted professionally with Jimmy Pryor's band in 1929, then played with

other Arkansas groups, among them Ruby Williams's, before joining Jim Winters's band in Philadelphia during 1932. He later worked for Charlie Gaines and Leroy Smith before joining Chick Webb in 1936, remaining with him until 1938.

There were brief stints with Fats Waller and Kaiser Marshall, then Jordan formed a band in 1939. He called them the Tympany Five, though they were actually a small swing orchestra. The group, with Jordan doing lead vocals and most alto sax solos, perfected a seamless swing/jump blues hybrid, and, from 1944 to 1949, had 19 chart hits. "G.I. Jive/Is You Is Or Is You Ain't (My Baby)" and "Choo Choo Ch'boogie" were million sellers in the mid-'40s. Jordan had smash duets with Bing Crosby and Ella Fitzgerald, and his songs were recorded by Woody Herman and the team of Pearl Bailey and Moms Mabley. The group also appeared in several films, among them *Follow the Boys, Meet Miss Bobby Sox, Beware, "Swing Parade of 1946, Reet, Petite and Gone*, and *Look Out Sister* from 1944 to 1948. The Jordan formula was subsequently modified and turned into rock & roll. His fortunes began to dip in the '50s. He briefly led a big band, and returned to leading combos. Jordan left Decca, where he'd been dominant, but never achieved identical success recutting his hits for Mercury. He recorded for Ray Charles's Tangerine label in the '60s, and kept touring until he suffered a heart attack in 1974. Jordan died a year later. A 1992 Broadway play based on his life and music, *Five Guys Named Moe*, rekindled interest in Jordan. His songs have been recorded by everyone from B.B. King to Asleep at the Wheel to Joe Jackson. *—Ron Wynn and Dan Morgenstern*

○ **At the Swing Cats' Ball** / i. Jan. 1937-Nov. 1939 / JSP 330

○ **Let the Good Times Roll: The Complete Decca Recordings 1938-54** / i. 1938-1954 / Bear Family 15557
With nine CDs and a 48-page color bio/discography full of fabulous photographs, this boxed set of *all* of Louis Jordan's Decca recordings asks the musical question, "How much jive can the human body stand?" Plenty! The collection chronicles Jordan's career from his first jokey swing novelties of 1939 to wartime smash hits like "What's the Use of Gettin' Sober" and "Is You Is Or Is You Ain't (My Baby)." From there, Jordan picked up speed, delivering one of the most productive, influential, and successful careers in American popular music. It's hard to imagine another artist of Jordan's commercial stature with so few duds in his past. The big hits like "Caldonia" came for nearly a decade until rock & roll pushed him into dabbling with larger bands and ballads. For the most part, however, he stuck with a manager's advice elucidated in a 1946 cartoon history of his career: "Make 'em laugh and they'll love you." He kept 'em dancing, too, with everything from calypsos to hard rockin' jump swing. A great mimic and comedian, he kept the level of musicianship high in his bands and grabbed a good song wherever he found one. He acted and wrote tunes for "Black Hollywood" soundtracks. He sang duets with Louis Armstrong, Bing Crosby, and Ella Fitzgerald (whose seven tracks make up the ninth CD, for contractual reasons). Among the 215 cuts here, there are fewer than a handful of alternate take overlaps. The smattering of previously unreleased tunes are all musically strong and include gems like the devastatingly dark but hilarious "If You've Got Someplace to Go." Most of this timely retrospective shows Jordan thriving in his irreverent cosmos of good food, barnyard animals, slippery money, fast trains, leeches of both genders, memorable parties, and unforgettable characters, some of whom have moved beyond the hit parade into the realm of folklore. Sure, it was a formula, but Jordan worked it better and hipper than most entertainers before him or since. The enclosed book is a classy, sympathetic measure of both the man and his career. Highest recommendation—big fun for hepcats of all ages. *— Tom Smith*, Roundup Newsletter

○ **Five Guys Named Moe: Original Decca Recordings, Vol. 2** / i. 1939-1955 / MCA 10503
Eighteen Decca sides, 1942-52, from the king of jump 'n' jive. Ten of the selections are used in the Broadway revue

about Jordan, *Five Guys Named Moe*. (The other ten songs used in the show—and several other tracks as well—can be found on *The Best of Louis Jordan*, MCA CD-4079.) This set includes Jordan's biggest hit (number one on both the R&B and pop charts) "G.I. Jive," as well as other hits "Boogie Woogie Blue Plate," "Open the Door Richard," and more. — Roundup Newsletter

Jazz Heritage: Greatest Hits–Vol. 2 (1941-1947) / 1941-1947 / MCA 1337
Another package of Louis Jordan's R&B hits, this one covering the early and mid-'40s. Jordan was among the biggest stars in the nation during this period, and not only did he have smash songs for himself, but others like Woody Herman, Ella Fitzgerald, and even Pearl Bailey and Moms Mabley covered his material. *—Ron Wynn*

☆ **Best of Louis Jordan, The** / 1942-1945 / MCA 4079
This is the best domestic collection of seminal Jordan cuts. In many ways, it's foundation music for the creation of R&B and can be linked to rap as well. Funny lyrics, superior arrangements, amazing material from the '40s and '50s. *—Ron Wynn*

★ **Louis Jordan and His Tympany Five** / i. 1944 / Circle
Wondrous cuts that combine hip vocals, robust solos, and inventive lyrics into a sound that was later called R&B. These are also available in other collections on Charly and Jukebox Lil. *—Ron Wynn*

Five Guys Named Moe, Vol. II / 1948-1949 / Decca 10503
The second volume of '40s hits featuring R&B legend Louis Jordan. Jordan, formerly in Chick Webb's band, took the swing principles he'd learned there and mixed them with comedic energy and wit. The results helped fuel a musical revolution, and these are among the songs that played a vital role in it. *—Ron Wynn*

○ **One Guy Named Louis** / i. 1954 / Blue Note 96804
Twenty-one tracks recorded for the Aladdin label in 1954, nearly three years after the end of Jordan's hit-making decade with Decca. The first single from these sessions—"Whiskey, Do Your Stuff"—was penned by bass player Shifty Henry, who was later immortalized in song by Leiber and Stoller ("Jailhouse Rock"). More fine jump blues and novelty tunes include "Dad Gum Ya Hide, Boy" and "Fat Back and Corn Liquor." *— Roundup Newsletter*

○ **Complete Aladdin Sessions, The** / i. Jan. 1954 / EMI 7965672

○ **I Believe in Music** / Nov. 6, 1973 / Evidence 26006
Nice early '70s date with alto saxophonist and vocalist Louis Jordan doing more conventional blues and jazz material, very few comedy routines. Jordan's instrumental prowess took a back seat as he became a celebrity to his quips and monolog. But this time, the music reigned. *—Ron Wynn*

○ **Reed Petite and Gone** / i. 1983 / Krazy Kat 414

Live Jive / Magic DATOM-4
Nice jive and R&B numbers from Louis Jordan, recorded in live performance. Jordan is at his witty, mischievous best, while his tight combo adds the right blend of supporting riffs and catchy arrangements. *—Ron Wynn*

★ **Look Out!** / Charly

Just Say Moe! Mo' Best of Louis / Rhino 71144
Rhino's *Just Say Moe!* covers Jordan's entire career, including some material from his peak years at Decca and a song from the Broadway musical, *Five Guys Named Moe*, based on his life. A good complement to MCA's *Best of Louis Jordan*. *—Ron Wynn*

SHEILA JORDAN (Sheila Jeanette Jordan)

b. Nov. 18, 1928, Detroit, MI
Vocals, songwriter / Ballads & blues, modern creative
There are several outstanding vocal improvisers, but few are as versatile and striking as Sheila Jordan. Jordan consistently varies the timbre, dynamics, and timing of melody lines, producing remarkable results. She's equally accomplished at

bebop, free, Afro-Latin, scatting, or ballads, standards, and show tunes. Jordan has one of the most personal, intense, and energetic vocal styles in the genre, and never substitutes glibness or technical gimmicks for intensity and conviction. She's also gifted with a quirky sense of humor. A multiple winner of the *Down Beat* Critics Poll Talent Deserving Wider Recognition honors, Jordan's never recorded as frequently as she should have recorded, but hasn't made any safe or predictable releases. She studied piano at age 11, and began singing jazz during her teens. Jordan was entranced by bebop, especially the sound of Charlie Parker. She was a member of a vocal ensemble in the '40s that sang vocalese using Parker's melodies and solos. Jordan moved to New York from Detroit in the '50s. She met and later married Duke Jordan, while working extensively in the New York bebop scene. She studied jazz theory with Lennie Tristano in the mid-'50s, then sang regularly in Greenwich Village in the early '60s. George Russell recommended Jordan to Blue Note, and wrote an arrangement of "You Are My Sunshine" for her, which she later did on his album *The Outer View*. She did many American and European tours in the '60s and '70s. Jordan sang in the chorus on Carla Bley's *Escalator Over the Hill* album in the early '70s, and recorded the soundtrack for a CBS television show "Look Up and Live" with Don Heckman. She sang on two mid-'70s Roswell Rudd albums and co-led a band with Steve Kuhn in the late '70s, while recording with Steve Swallow. Jordan was in a duo with Harvie Swartz in the '80s, and also sang on '80s albums by Kuhn, George Gruntz, and Aki Takase. Jordan did her own albums for Blue Note in the '60s, Arista and Steeplechase in the '70s, and Palo Alto, Blackhawk, and Muse in the '80s. Presently, she has only a couple of titles available on CD. —*Ron Wynn and Richard Lieberson*

○ **Portrait of Sheila Jordan** / Sep. 1962-Oct. 1962 / Blue Note 89002
Innovative date with Barry Galbraith (g), Steve Swallow (b), and Denzil Best (d). The one to get. —*Richard Lieberson*

Sheila / Aug. 27-28, 1977 / Steeple Chase 1081
Vocalist Shelia Jordan makes the tunes on *Sheila* all her own, with personal, almost prayerlike readings of tales of personal devotion ("What Are You Doing," "Don't Explain"), ebullient celebration ("Better Than Anything"), childlike, singsong mockery ("Please Don't Talk About Me When I'm Gone"), and the close-to-home alcoholic readings ("Hold Out Your Hand," "Lush Life"). Her patented scat ("day-to-to-gong"), heard only on "Hold Out Your Hand" and "On Green Dolphin Street" can really make you believe in the gift of tongues. —*Fred Bouchard*, Down Beat

○ **Playground** / Jul. 1979 / ECM 1159
A studio date with the Steve Kuhn Trio. The most distinctive voice in modern jazz. Some of Jordan's best work. —*Michael G. Nastos*

Old Time Feeling / Oct. 15, 1982 / Muse 5366
Palo Alto 1982. Wonderful leads. Good duo date with Harvie Swartz (b). —*Ron Wynn*

Crossing, The / Oct. 1-2, 1984 / Blackhawk 505

Outstanding sessions with brilliant–often breathtaking–lead vocals. —*Ron Wynn*

Lost and Found / 1989 / Muse 5390

★ **Last Year's Waltz** / ECM 1213
Live at Fat Tuesdays in New York City with the Steve Kuhn Trio. Sheila at her best. —*Michael G. Nastos*

STANLEY JORDAN

b. Jul. 31, 1959, Chicago, IL
Guitar / Instrumental pop, neo bop, contemporary funk
Guitarist Jordan was an '80s sensation. His background as a pianist has certainly played a role in his revolutionary guitar technique. He is famous for the "hammering-on" technique, a method in which he plays the guitar like a keyboard, with both hands playing melody lines by tapping the strings rather than strumming or using a pick. He also uses different tuning, getting a much different sound, one that his detractors say sounds too much like a thin piano instead of a guitar, although they acknowledge that he's been able to do some amazing things like playing melodies in the right hand and doing chords and bass lines in the left. Though he was discovered playing guitar on the streets, no one should confuse Jordan with a vagrant prodigy. He began playing piano at age six, was playing guitar at age 11, and earned a music degree from Princeton. He also spent parts of those years practicing and playing in clubs. He moved to New York in 1984 and, shortly thereafter, got an invitation to play the Kool Jazz Festival. That was followed by an appearance at Montreux and a recording contract. —*Ron Wynn*

Touch Sensitive / i. 1982 / Tangent 1001
Rare independent release on which he first featured the two-handed touch style which he has perfected. —*Paul Kohler*

★ **Magic Touch** / 1985 / Blue Note 46092
The debut album by a musician who helped to redefine how a guitar is played. A must! —*Paul Kohler*

Standards–Vol. 1 / 1986 / Blue Note 46333
A stunning collection of jazz standards done to perfection by a superb guitarist. —*Paul Kohler*

Flying Home / 1988 / EMI 48682
Recent album from contemporary guitar hero who sometimes justifies his reputation, particularly when he stretches out on standards or jazz anthems and showcases his unique way of playing guitar. Jordan's strumming technique enables him to present unusual chords, phrases and statements. When done in a nongimmicky manner, it offers a genuine alternative to traditional and fusion guitar vocabulary. —*Ron Wynn*

○ **Stolen Moments** / i. 1991 / Somethin' Else 97159
Guitarist Stanley Jordan's acclaimed technique, in which he roams over the fretboard strumming and gliding rather than picking, has earned him both plaudits and brickbats. His albums have been inconsistent affairs, but he quieted critics with this '91 session. He takes standards and anthems that have been done to death and makes them sound fresh through invigorating, explosive guitar solos. —*Ron Wynn*

K

MAX KAMINSKY

b. Sep. 7, 1908, Brockton, MA
Trumpet / Dixieland

An assertive, often delightful trumpeter, Max Kaminsky is one of the more concise, swinging traditional players whose tone and style echo the influence of King Oliver, Freddy Keppard, and Louis Armstrong. He's performed since the late '20s, and has done both swing and traditional jazz. Kaminsky worked in Boston in the '20s before moving to Chicago in 1928. He played with George Wettling and Frank Teschemaker at the Cinderella Ballroom, then played with Red Nichols in New York for a short stint in 1929. During the '30s, Kaminsky played with dance bands, while recording with Eddie Condon, Benny Carter, and Mezz Mezzrow. He worked with Tommy Dorsey and Artie Shaw in the late '30s, and recorded with Bud Freeman in both 1939 and 1940. Kaminsky teamed with Shaw again from 1941 to 1943, playing in Shaw's navy band that toured the South Pacific. He later participated in early '40s New York concerts at Carnegie Hall and Town Hall organized by Condon, and played traditional jazz in the '40s with Sidney Bechet, Georg Brunis, Art Hodes, Joe Marsala, Willie "the Lion" Smith, and Jack Teagarden. Kaminsky toured Europe with Teagarden and Earl Hines's All Stars in the late '50s, and played at Ryan's periodically from the late '60s until 1983. He also made appearances at the Newport Jazz Festival and at the New York World's Fair in the mid-'60s. Kaminsky recorded some fine material for Commodore in the '40s, then did some stellar material in the '70s for the Fat Cat's Jazz label. Presently, he has no sessions available on CD. *—Ron Wynn*

★ **Chicago Style** / 1954 / Jazztone 1208

RICHIE KAMUCA (Richard Kamuca)

b. Jul. 23, 1930, Philadelphia, PA, **d.** Jul. 22, 1977, Los Angeles, CA
Tenor saxophone / Cool

One of the true ballad artisans and an ardent Lester Young disciple, Richie Kamuca played with a rounded, light quality and a sturdy tone. His style grew more impressive until he had his own sound, though he still paid homage to Young with every solo. Kamuca met and worked with Roy Eldridge while a teen, and then played in Stan Kenton's orchestra in the early '50s, making an early reputation. He was principal soloist for Woody Herman from 1954 to 1956. In the '50s and early '60s, Kamuca played with Cy Touff, Chet Baker, Art Pepper, and Shelly Manne before moving from California to New York. He reunited with Eldridge and recorded with him, and also played in the Merv Griffin television show orchestra, returning to the West Coast when Griffin moved there in 1970. Kamuca recorded with Bill Berry's L.A. Big Band in the mid- and late '70s, but his career was cut short by cancer. He has a couple of sessions available on CD. *—Ron Wynn and Michael G. Nastos*

○ **Tenors Head On** / Jul. 1956 / Liberty 3051

Brothers, The / i. 1956 / RCA 1162

Jazz Erotica / 1959 / Hi Fi 604

★ **West Coast Jazz in Hi Fi** / 1959 / Hi Fi 1760

A worthy reissue. A good West Coast-style effort. Limited-edition release. *—Ron Wynn*

○ **Richard Kamuca (1976)** / 1976 / Jazz 104

○ **Richie** / 1977 / Concord Jazz 41

It still hurts to realize tenor saxophonist Richie Kamuca left us in July of 1977. The word emotion will always relate to his playing but it was strong controlled emotion and never "raw." According to his conception of sound, his instrument was meant to sound beautiful in all registers at all times. This is not so easy to do and it's a lesson that many players just can't learn. I'll always be in agreement with Kamuca's ideas and his playing here is some of his best on record. The choice of tunes is as pleasing as his companions on this date (guitarist Mundell Lowe, bassist Monty Budwig, drummer Nick Ceroli). His ballads "Some Other Spring," "Say It Isn't So," and "Tis Autumn" are all essential to lovers of the tenor saxophone and it's comforting to have his vocal interpretations preserved on the final track. The other tunes are done at relaxed and easy tempos and fit Kamuca's playing so well that there's no way to be critical. I think you'll enjoy the use of guitar in lieu of piano when it's in the capable hands of Lowe. *—Jerry L. Atkins, Cadence*

○ **Charlie** / 1978 / Concord Jazz 96

A little-known facet of tenorman Richie Kamuca's musical personality was his love for the alto, an instrument he associated almost exclusively with Charlie Parker and which he himself enjoyed playing, but only "for fun." Alternatively, had he devoted more of his time to the smaller horn, his chops would have been in better shape for this date. But as it was, ill-aligned mouthpiece grip and all, he does surpassingly well. His equally pronounced admiration for Lester Young is apparent in his poignant, touching tone, a fragile/firm reminder of Bird's in the old McShann days. But the flow of Kamuca's ideas, the patterns, even the interstitial filigrees come directly out of classic bop. Trumpeter Blue Mitchell makes an ideal teammate for Kamuca, but it is pianist Jimmy Rowles who stands out as the soloist of the day. The repertoire consists almost entirely of Parker compositions or tunes he was fond of playing. And while the master never recorded "If You Could," he most certainly did record a few "Blues In B Flat." However, the blues so entitled on this record is not one of Parker's lines, although he is credited with its composition; clearly, it is the well-known "Tiny's Tempo," a swing/bop riff by Tiny Grimes and Clyde Hart, the guitarist/leader and pianist on the record Bird made so famous. *—Jack Sohmer, Cadence*

CONNIE KAY

b. 1927
Drums / Cool

He's best known in his long-running role as drummer for the Modern Jazz Quartet, but Connie Kay was also an innovator in the use of percussion instruments. He was one of the first drummers since Sonny Greer to utilize the triangle, chimes, timpani, and finger cymbals regularly and creatively, in addition to the standard drum kit. MJQ co-leader John Lewis wrote sections in compositions that took advantage of Kay's ability on these instruments. The MJQ's "chamber jazz" reputation has resulted in an underrating of Kay's rhythmic abilities; he's not expected or asked for great displays of polyrhythmic technique, but contributes to the tightly controlled, relaxed ensemble sound instead. He does this with precision and style. He seldom solos and is often barely audible, but he embellishes and keeps a steady pace. Kay studied piano with his mother from the age of six, and taught himself drums. He worked with Sir Charles Thompson and Miles Davis in the mid-'40s at Minton's Playhouse, and with Cat Anderson. They recorded together in the late '40s. Kay toured the South in an R&B show, then joined Lester Young's band, and played with him periodically until 1955. He also worked with Beryl Booker, Stan Getz, Coleman Hawkins, and Charlie Parker. Kay recorded with Getz and Hawkins in 1952. He joined Lewis, Milt Jackson, and Percy Heath in 1955 as Kenny Clarke's replacement. Kay's been in the MJQ drum chair since then, and weathered the storm during their temporary disbanding in 1974. Over the years, Kay has recorded with Chet Baker, Cannonball Adderley, and Jimmy Heath. He worked extensively with Paul Desmond from 1963 to 1974. Kay has also worked and recorded with Tommy Flanagan, John Lewis, Soprano Summit, and Benny Goodman. He was house drummer at Eddie Condon's in the mid-'70s, then rejoined the MJQ once they regrouped permanently. He can be heard on numerous MJQ sessions on CD, and on other dates by Young, Desmond, Goodman, Flanagan, and others. —Ron Wynn

GEOFF KEEZER

b. 1970
Piano / Neo bop
A pianist and close associate of fellow keyboard artist James Williams, Geoff Keezer generated great response with his contributions to sessions by Roy Hargrove and Antonio Hart. His own debut as a leader also elicited strong critical support, and Keezer's phrasing, speed, facility, range, and harmonic knowledge are remarkable at his young age. His only solo date thus far is available on CD. —Ron Wynn

Waiting in the Wings / **i.** Sep. 1988 / Sunnyside 1035
The impressive debut for the acclaimed young pianist Geoff Keezer, whose name had been mentioned in New York jazz circles for many months before this release appeared in 1988. He quickly justified the advance notices; his facility, solo flair, and harmonic knowledge are quite impressive. He plays with a strong band that includes vibist Steve Nelson, tenor saxophonist Billy Pierce, and bassist Rufus Reid. —Ron Wynn

○ **Curveball** / Jun. 1989 / Sunnyside 1045
★ **Here and Now** / Oct. 1990 / Blue Note 96691
Best album from Wisconsin pianist. More to come from Keezer. With Steve Nelson on vibes. Excellent version of Harold Mabern's "There But for the Grace of . . ." —Michael G. Nastos

○ **World Music** / **i.** 1992 / Columbia 52958
The most recent release by critically acclaimed pianist Geoff Keezer. Despite the title, there's as much American hard bop as anything, but the set also shows Keezer's knowledge of Afro-Latin rhythms and pulse. He's working with a new group featuring James Genus, Tony Reedus, and Rudy Bird. —Ron Wynn

ROGER KELLAWAY

b. Nov. 1, 1939, Newton, MA
Piano, composer, arranger / Bop
While pianist, arranger, and composer Roger Kellaway includes several non-jazz elements into his playing style, he's never far away from improvisation or swing. Kellaway's utilized electronics and bitonality into his compositions, but also plays delightful, jaunty solos, boogie tunes, and bop numbers. He's written scores for such films as *Paper Lion, A Star Is Born,* and *Breathless;* had the ballet *PAMTGG* commissioned by George Balanchine in 1971; and the orchestral

work "Portraits of Time" commissioned by the Los Angeles Philharmonic in 1983. For many years, Kellaway's piano playing was featured weekly on the television program "All in the Family." Kellaway studied piano as a child, and taught himself bass. He later studied piano, bass, and composition at the New England Conservatory before leaving to play bass with Jimmy McPartland and Ralph Marterie in 1959. He worked briefly as a pianist in Kai Winding's band in New York, then played in the mid-'60s with a quintet co-led by Al Cohn and Zoot Sims (in 1963). From 1963 to 1965, he played in a group co-led by Clark Terry and Bob Brookmeyer. Kellaway recorded with Ben Webster, Maynard Ferguson, Wes Montgomery, and Sonny Rollins from 1964 to 1966, then moved to Los Angeles to join Don Ellis's big band. He became music director for Bobby Darin in 1967, and remained in that position for two years. Kellaway became a busy and prolific composer, arranger, and occasional performer in the television studios. At the same time in the late '60s and early '70s, he recorded and performed with Tom Scott, Mundell Lowe, and Carmen McCrae, and toured with Joni Mitchell. Later in the '70s, Kellaway worked with Jimmy Knepper and with a quintet co-led by Sims and Harry Edison. He returned to New York in 1984 and frequently worked in a duo with Dick Hyman at Michael's Pub. Kellaway has recorded as a leader for such labels as Prestige, A&M, Dobre, Concord, All Art, Voss, Regina, and Stash. He has several sessions available as a leader. —Ron Wynn and Michael G. Nastos

Roger Kellaway Trio / **i.** May 11, 1965 / Prestige 7399
Trio. This superb session date includes originals and a Beatles tune. Creative work. —Hank Davis

Stride! / **i.** 1966 / World Pacific 21861
Spirit Feel / Jun. 1967 / Pacific Jazz
Cello Quartet / **i.** Jul. 1971 / A&M 3034
Keyboardist Roger Kellaway has specialized in both classic prejazz and pop music and has also done some classical arrangements and conducting. This early '70s record features Kellaway serving as arranger/conductor for a cello quartet and is not a jazz date. It's also out of print. —Ron Wynn

○ **Ain't Misbehavin'** / **i.** 1986 / Bainbridge 6833
After suffering through an overly precious version of "A Time for Love" and noticing the same style developing on "Here's That Rainy Day," I was nearly ready to write off this album as technically impressive background music. But then the tempo doubled, Kellaway began to cook, and the record came alive. The title cut is surprisingly adventurous with the pianist hinting at a variety of possible approaches before settling into an eccentric stride while switching keys constantly with his right hand, an odd but interesting performance. Kellaway shows off his command of the piano on a medium-tempo "How Deep Is the Ocean." Although "Blue in Green" wanders a bit, "Skylark" is very explorative, almost atonal in spots. Despite its weak beginning, *Ain't Misbehavin'* is one of Kellaway's best jazz records to date. —Scott Yanow, Cadence

Fifty-Fifty / **i.** 1987 / Stash
★ **Live at Maybeck Recital Hall–Vol. 11** / Mar. 1991 / Concord Jazz 4470
Recent view of Kellaway's style. Melodic yet driving. Strong stride piano influence. —Hank Davis

○ **Roger Kellaway Meets Gene Bertoncini and Michael . . .** / Chiaroscuro 315

WYNTON KELLY

b. Dec. 2, 1931, Jamaica, **d.** Apr. 12, 1971, Toronto, Canada
Piano / Hard bop, post bop, soul-jazz
Wynton Kelly's seamless blend of blues and bebop made him one of the '50s and '60s premier pianists. His solos were infectious and swinging; he played with warmth, flair, and conviction. Nat "King" Cole and Bud Powell were his original influences, while both Miles Davis and Cannonball

Adderley ranked him among premier accompanists. Kelly's family moved to America from Jamaica when he was four. His early training came in R&B bands, and that aspect was also a major influence. Kelly worked with Eddie "Lockjaw" Davis in the late '40s, then with Dinah Washington. He played for a short time with Lester Young, then worked with Dizzy Gillespie twice in the early '50s, the stints sandwiched around military duty. Kelly recorded with Ernie Henry, Blue Mitchell, Clark Terry, and Nat Adderley before cutting his own sessions for Blue Note in the early '50s. He later recorded for Riverside, Vee Jay, Verve, Xanadu, and Milestone, and also made sessions with John Coltrane and Adderley. Kelly became one of the busiest session pianists in New York in the '50s, leading many trios, but earned his highest acclaim with Miles Davis's quintet from 1959 to 1963. Kelly's best trio included former Davis band members Paul Chambers and Jimmy Cobb. They played and recorded with Wes Montgomery before disbanding due to the health problems of various members. Kelly didn't have a lengthy career. But his sound can be heard in the work of many among the '60s generation, especially Herbie Hancock and McCoy Tyner. Any Kelly session done with Chambers or with a good drummer, such as Blakey or Cobb, is a listener's delight. There's a fair amount of Kelly material currently available on CD. —*Ron Wynn and Bob Porter*

Piano Interpretations / Jul. 25, 1951-Aug. 1951 / Blue Note 84456
Recorded at WOR Studios in New York. Trio. His first solo recording sessions. Even the uptempo pieces have a gentle quality. Very nice mainstream jazz. —*Michael Erlewine*

○ **Wynton Kelly** / i. Jan. 31, 1958 / Riverside 1540
This is a satisfyingly low-keyed trio date from June 1961, with Paul Chambers and Sam Jones alternating on bass and Jimmy Cobb on drums. Yes (in anticipation of the next question), with Chambers on bass, this trio was the Miles Davis rhythm section of the time. Two fine Kelly originals are offset by six standards. Throughout the set, Kelly's uncluttered melodic swing holds sway. —*Alan Bargebuhr, Cadence*

★ **Kelly Blue** / Feb. 19, 1959-Mar. 1959 / Riverside 033
Recorded at Reeves Sound Studios, New York City. Small Group. Classic Kelly. Bluesy, bright, nice. There is magic in this album. —*Michael Erlewine*

☆ **Kelly Great** / Aug. 12, 1959 / Vee Jay 907
This presents pianist Wynton Kelly from 2/19/59 and 3/10/59 with trumpeter Nat Adderley, saxophonists Bobby Jaspar and Benny Golson, bassist Paul Chambers, and drummers Jimmy Cobb. Adderley, Jaspar, and Golson play only on the two 2/19/59 tracks, and Kelly is accompanied by just the rhythm trio on the remaining four cuts. The sides with horns are the best; Nat Adderley is in especially good form. The trio sides are solid, if not particularly explosive or individualistic. The entire LP was also issued as part of a twofer. —*Bob Rusch, Cadence*

☆ **Best of Wynton Kelly, The** / i. 1963 / Vee Jay 1086

○ **Blues on Purpose** / Jun. 25, 1965+Aug. 17, 1965 / Xanadu
Listeners familiar with the work of pianist Wynton Kelly will find no surprises in his set, which stems from a string of engagements at the Half Note, when the trio functioned as three-fourths of the Wes Montgomery quartet. These tracks find Kelly and cohorts (bassist Paul Chambers, drummer Jimmy Cobb) in fine form. They were recorded variously on 6/25/65, 7/2/65, and 8/17/65. Fidelity may not be as high as some may wish on this mono disc, but the level of playing *is*, and the sound is quite good enough to document the bristling excitement these three soulmates could generate, whether playing the blues at various tempos (medium: "Somebody's Blues"; fast: "Blues on Purpose"; faster: "Another Blues") or giving Tadd Dameron's "If You Could See Me Now" an elegantly burnished treatment. "Milestones" is a fleet backward look at the days with Miles Davis. Chambers and Cobb are with Kelly every step of the way, as the trio's "oneness" is a wonder to behold. —*Bob Rusch*, Cadence

★ **Smokin' at the Half Note** / Jun. 1965+Sep. 22, 1965 / Verve 829578
Some recorded Sept 22, 1965, at Englewood Cliffs, New Jersey. Wynton Kelly Trio with Wes Montgomery (g). Slow to midtempos and very listenable. Both Wynton and Wes are in fine form. A rare chance to hear Montgomery in a small-group setting. —*Michael Erlewine*

Full View / 1966 / Milestone 9004

Last Trio Session / Aug. 4, 1968 / Delmark 441
Recorded at P.S. Recording Studios in Chicago. The last trio work by Wynton Kelly. An album of mostly pop tunes, "Light My Fire," "Say A Little Prayer For Me," plus a nice blues by Kelly. Great players working off lighter material, but there are plenty of fine moments. Or, just nice listening. —*Michael Erlewine*

In Concert / i. Sep. 22, 1988 / Vee Jay 3071
Nearing the end. Ron McClure brings new sound and fresh direction on bass. —*Ron Wynn*

☆ **Someday My Prince Will Come** / Vee Jay 902
Wynton Kelly was perhaps the most rhythmically energetic and intense soloist among those who were in demand during the '50s. He and Red Garland did numerous dates, with Garland's block chords and relaxed pacing the stylistic opposite of Kelly's faster, more linear approach. This 15-cut session contains four bonus cuts, one number with Wayne Shorter and Lee Morgan, and the other tunes trio dates with Kelly's often-raging piano contrasted by Paul Chambers' strong, big-toned bass and Philly Joe Jones's resolute fills. —*Ron Wynn*

STAN KENTON (Stanley Newcomb Kenton)

b. Dec. 15, 1911, Wichita, KS, d. Aug. 25, 1979, Los Angeles, CA

Piano, arranger, composer / Cool, progressive big band
There have been few in jazz history who've generated as much discussion and controversy as Stan Kenton. He was a good composer/arranger and a competent pianist who, to his credit, tried to do something distinctive and different. Kenton experimented with huge groups, and demanded an extremely precise sound. He started what he deemed "Progressive Jazz," and worked with Afro-Latin rhythms and 40-plus member groups while mixing symphonic elements with jazz. Kenton's orchestras were quite popular for many years, and his best bands displayed an impressive, polished sound (Jimmie Lunceford's orchestra was a prime influence). But there were times when Kenton's music seemed more form than substance, and substituted bombast for swing.

Kenton played piano and wrote arrangements for various theater and dance bands in the '30s, among them Benny Goodman's, Vido Musso's, and Gus Arnheim's. He formed his 14-piece Artistry in Rhythm Orchestra in 1941. The orchestra quickly became a popular attraction, and, in the mid-'40s, were regular winners in polls, thanks partly to Pete Rugolo's arrangements. Kenton did his first recordings for Decca in 1941 and 1942. They cut their theme, "Artistry in Rhythm," in 1943, and also cut the song "Eager Beaver." Some of the great soloists that came through Kenton bands included Stan Getz, Conte Candoli, Lennie Niehaus, Kai Winding, Bob Cooper, Art Pepper, Maynard Ferguson, and Lucky Thompson. He also had Anita O'Day, June Christy, and Chris Connor as vocalists. Kenton enjoyed six Top 10 hits in the mid '40s, among them "And Her Tears Flowed Like Wine" with O'Day, and "How High the Moon" with Christy.

Kenton came to Carnegie Hall in 1949 with a 20-piece orchestra called Progressive Jazz, the same name he gave to music. He retired briefly for health reasons, then returned with a 49-piece Innovations in Modern Music orchestra, complete with strings and an enlarged wind section. They toured nationally in 1950 and 1951, but cost factors forced Kenton to abandon the concept. Kenton continued touring, but with more conventional-sized big bands. When Kenton's band went to the United Kingdom in 1956, they were the first American act to play there since 1937. Kenton helped English musicians end some union restrictions. He had more chart hits in the '50s, among them "September Song" and "Delicado."

Kenton was active in jazz education, establishing clinics at Midwest universities in 1959, and appearing and performing regularly on campuses. He launched the Los Angeles Neophonic orchestra in 1965, a 23-piece concert jazz band with symphonic components. It lasted for two years. Kenton formed recording and publishing firms, Creative World Records and Creative World Music in 1970, to release both reissues and current material. He received numerous honorary doctorates. Kenton recorded prodigiously for many labels, among them Decca, Capitol, and Balboa. He leased his old master tapes after he left Capitol and reissued much of his early material long before the majors figured out that old music sells. A pair of books by Carol Easton and William F. Lee offer varying portraits of Kenton. Easton's work spotlights his personality, while Lee's examines his music and is also heavily documented. There's a multitude of Kenton music available, most on Creative World, though Capitol has also begun issuing early dates. *The Kenton Era*, a four-disc set on Capitol, will more than satisfy those for whom a little Kenton goes a long way. —*Ron Wynn*

★ **Complete Capitol Recordings of the Bill Holman and Bill Russo Charts** / Mosaic

○ **Kenton Era** / 1941-1955 / Creative World 1030
A limited-edition four-record set that covers the Stan Kenton orchestra in its formative period from 1941 to 1955. It includes a four-page booklet with Kenton biography and shows how the controversial composer moved from being strictly a swing-era leader into his wide-ranging blend of jazz, Afro-Latin, and classical. —*Ron Wynn*

○ **Christy Years** / May 4, 1945-1947 / Creative World 1035
A 1977 anthology covering hits turned out when June Christy was the Kenton Orchestra's lead vocalist from 1945 to 1947. There's also some material with Pied Pipers vocal group. —*Ron Wynn*

○ **Innovations in Modern Music** / Feb. 3-4, 1950 / Creative World 1009
A pivotal Kenton album from 1950, one of the first in which he displays the controversial unorthodox time signatures, huge brass sections, and bombastic sound. —*Ron Wynn*

○ **Artistry in Rhythm** / Sep. 4, 1950 / Creative World 1043
Probably Stan Kenton's most jumping band was this mid-'40s group. Anita O'Day not only established the style in which June Christy and Chris Connor followed less successfully, but she practically marked the way for every female jazz singer to come along in the '40s and '50s. Eddie Sofranski's bass reflected Jimmy Blanton, as did Gene Englund's on "5 O'Clock Drag." "Southern Scandal," "Painted Rhythm" (with Vido Musso), and "Artistry Jumps" are all fairly standard late-swing-era pieces. —*John McDonough, Down Beat*

★ **New Concepts of Artistry in Rhythm** / Sep. 8-10, 1952 / Capitol 386

○ **Kenton Showcase** / 1953 / Creative World 1026
1966 release of material that was originally recorded in '53 and '54. This was among Kenton's finest bands ever, especially due to such soloists as Frank Rosolino, Lee Konitz, and both Conte Candoli and Maynard Ferguson in the trumpet section. —*Ron Wynn*

○ **By Request–Vol. 2 (1953-1960)** / 1953-1960 / Creative World 1040
The second of what was a series by the Kenton orchestra doing everything from standards to originals. This covered the period from 1953 to 1960, the first of two devoted to this time frame. —*Ron Wynn*

○ **By Request–Vol. 5 (1953-1960)** / 1953-1960 / Creative World 1066
The fifth volume in the series dedicated to the Kenton orchestra cutting a variety of material, some of it their own,

some their interpretations and reworkings. This one covered the mid '50s to 1960. —*Ron Wynn*

○ **Kenton in Hi-Fi** / Feb. 11-12, 1956 / Blue Note 98451
1992 reissue of a '56 album that was an early Kenton orchestra release in stereo. It's otherwise a pretty routine release, but it's interesting to hear imbalance as engineers had a difficult time balancing the huge Kenton brass section. —*Ron Wynn*

○ **Cuban Fire–Vol. 1** / May 22-24, 1956 / Blue Note 96260

○ **Cuban Fire–Vol. 2** / May 22-24, 1956 / Creative World 1008

Jazz Compositions of Stan Kenton / 1956-1973 / Creative World 1078
Good, comprehensive anthology covering Kenton compositions from 1956 to 1973. It shows chronologically how Kenton's experiments with voices, rhythms, time signatures, and brass configurations evolved over a 17-year period; also how he incorporated Afro-Latin and classical influences into his work. —*Ron Wynn*

Road Show–Vol. 1 / Oct. 10, 1959 / Capitol 96328
With June Christy and the Four Freshmen. Fine live recording from 1959. June Christy is a bit below par due to a cold on the day of the recording. —*Kenneth M. Cassidy*

Road Show–Vol. 2 / Creative World 1020
The second volume featuring the Kenton orchestra recorded live at various locations during the late '50s. This was the era when Kenton had his finest brass soloists; thus every album done has value. —*Ron Wynn*

West Side Story / Mar. 15+20, 1961 / Creative World 1007

Adventures in Blues / Dec. 7, 1961-Dec. 14, 1961 / Creative World 1012

Adventures in Jazz / Dec. 12, 1961 / Capitol 1796

Artistry in Bossa Nova / Apr. 1772, 1963 / Creative World 1045
The 1963 album that marked Kenton's entry into the then-booming bossa nova market. It features the usual bombastic arrangements, with Afro-Latin seasoning. The vocals are not as enticing as those on the Getz albums, but full brass backdrop proves interesting. —*Ron Wynn*

Artistry in Voices and Brass / Apr. 19, 1963 / Creative World 1038
Another in series of intricate, unorthodox, and controversial Kenton albums issued in the mid '60s on his Creative World label. This one matches his usual array of horns with multiple voices. The resulting wave is sometimes arresting, sometimes chaotic, and still seems both advanced and bizarre 30 years later. —*Ron Wynn*

○ **Kenton / Wagner** / Sep. 16-24, 1964 / Creative World 1024
Among his least jazz-oriented albums. The Kenton orchestra offers his take on works and compositions written by classical and operatic figure Richard Wagner. Strictly for Kenton fans. —*Ron Wynn*

○ **Live at Butler University (1972)** / 1972 / Creative 1058
A mixed bag by the Kenton orchestra, as they try to juggle the past and present during an early '70s concert. They do Beach Boys material one moment, then come back with a nostalgic venture featuring the Four Freshman. —*Ron Wynn*

○ **Stan Kenton and His Innovations Orchestra** / i. 1992 / Laserlight 15770
A 1992 anthology featuring bandleader Stan Kenton and his orchestra from 1951, with their experimental orchestral recordings. Kenton's unorthodox time signatures and rhythms were always controversial, and never more so than on these recordings, which present even more unusual orchestrations. —*Ron Wynn*

★ **Retrospective** / i. 1992 / Blue Note 97350
Anthology covering the Kenton orchestra from its early years into the '70s. A good introduction or sampler, though not really a greatest-hits presentation. —*Ron Wynn*

☆ **Comprehensive Kenton** / Capitol 12016

☆ **Stan Kenton** / Mosaic 136

The Holman and Russo charts. Four-CD set contains all 72 works that Russo and Holman wrote and/or arranged for Kenton. Long unavailable. This is the high-water mark of Kenton's career as one of the chief innovators in experimental big-band jazz. —*Michael Erlewine*

ROBIN KENYATTA (Prince Roland Haynes)

b. Mar. 6, 1942, Moncks Corner, SC
Alto saxophone, bandleader / Hard bop, blues & jazz, soul-jazz

Though an often fierce and spirited alto saxophonist, Robin Kenyatta has enjoyed a rather uneven career, particularly in terms of recordings. His best material has been in the hard bop and free vein, where his solos have been both intense and imaginative. At other times, he's done more contemporary material that's been overproduced and not very memorable. Kenyatta played with Bill Dixon in the mid-'60s, and was featured during a series of New York concerts Dixon co-sponsored called The October Revolution in Jazz. He recorded with the Jazz Composer's Orchestra, Roswell Rudd, Sonny Stitt, Dixon, Archie Shepp, and Barry Miles in the mid- and late '60s, before heading his own bands. Kenyatta recorded with Alan Silva and Andrew Hill in the '70s. During the late '70s, he had a dismal flirtation with instrumental pop. In the '80s and '90s, he has tried to find a comfortable middle ground between fusion, instrumental pop, and his hard bop and free music roots. Kenyatta has recorded for Vortex/Atlantic, ECM, ITM, and Jazz Dance. Currently, he does not have any sessions as a leader available on CD. —*Ron Wynn*

FREDDIE KEPPARD

b. Feb. 27, 1890, New Orleans, LA, **d.** Jul. 15, 1933, Chicago, IL
Cornet / New Orleans traditional

A lack of recorded evidence hasn't diminished Freddie Keppard's reputation among musicians and critics who heard him validate his skills. Keppard's approach was quite close to ragtime in its staccato style, but his few recordings (only one as a leader) show a soaring melodic quality and sound. Unfortunately, by the time he got a chance to record professionally, his health was failing. Keppard studied mandolin, violin, and accordion, and began playing professionally as a cornetist in 1906 with his band the Olympia Orchestra and with other New Orleans groups. Keppard became a national sensation in 1914, when he went to California to join the Original Creole Band. The band did a "white-tie, all-musical act" sans blackface mugging and comedic quips. They were so beloved that Keppard had a chance to record with Victor in 1916, but turned it down because he didn't want other bands copying the group's style. They toured the Orpheum vaudeville circuit, then Keppard settled in Chicago after a brief period with King Oliver. In Chicago, he played with his own groups and with those of Doc Cook, Erskine Tate, Ollie Powers, and Charlie Elgar. Keppard's lone date as leader had him heading a quintet with Johnny Dodds and with trombonist Eddie Vincent. He also recorded with Doc Cook's Dreamland Orchestra and with Erskine Tate. —*Ron Wynn*

BARNEY KESSEL

b. Oct. 17, 1923, Muskogee, OK
Guitar / Bop, cool

A polished, smooth guitarist who is also able to swing and play the blues, Barney Kessel has been the ultimate ensemble player. He's been in big bands, acclaimed trios, combos, and duos, and has done numerous studio dates. His sound and style are flexible and fit any situation without becoming so generic that they lose individuality. He's mastered both the single-string and chord-melody approaches. Kessel played for Ben Pollack in the Chico Marx Orchestra during the early '40s, and appeared in the Lester Young short film *Jammin' the Blues* in 1944. He also played with Artie Shaw's Orchestra and Gramercy Five in 1946. He cut some singles on the

Atomic label in the mid-'40s, and later led a sextet whose personnel included Dodo Marmarosa. He became a freelance player in Los Angeles, then attracted widespread attention for his role in Oscar Peterson's trio in 1952 and 1953. He recorded for Verve and especially for Contemporary, cutting several albums for them in the '50s and '60s. Kessel even worked in Verve's A&R department on the pop side, helping oversee some Elvis Presley films. His albums with bassist Ray Brown and drummer Shelly Manne helped popularize the guitar trio format in the '50s. He began playing club dates with his own groups in the '60s. Kessel did sessions for Reprise, Emerald, Saba, Black Lion, Polydor, Contemporary, RCA (Italy), and Mercury in the '60s. He worked with Paul Horn, Bud Shank, Jim Hall, Bobby Hutcherson, and Elvin Jones, led his own bands, and recorded with big bands. Kessel toured Europe with George Wein's Newport All Stars in 1968, then lived in London in 1969 and 1970. He co-formed the Great Guitars with Charlie Byrd and Herb Ellis in the mid-'70s. They recorded some albums for Concord and toured Australia and New Zealand. There were solo, duo, quintet, and quartet sessions for Sonet, Black Lion, and Concord. Kessel's groups continued performing into the '90s. He's done many workshops, seminars, and lectures, and has published instruction manuals, among them the widely distributed *Guitar: A Tutor* in 1967. He's well-represented on other people's sessions, and has a fair amount of his own material available on CD. —*Ron Wynn and Richard Lieberson*

○ **Easy Like** / Nov. 14, 1953-Dec. 19, 1953 / Original Jazz Classics 153

This presents the first two sessions guitarist Barney Kessel recorded for Contemporary: 11/14/53 and 12/19/53. These are pleasant, somewhat easy-swinging dates with backing from Bud Shank (as, f), Arnold Ross (p), Harry Babasin (b), and Shelly Manne (d). Originally released as a 10-incher, they blend well with the 2/23/56 date that fills out the 12-inch LP. For that session, the instrumentation remained the same, but the personnel was Buddy Collette (reeds), Claude Williamson (p), Red Mitchell (b), and Manne. —*Bob Rusch, Cadence*

○ **Kessel Plays Standards** / Jun. 4, 1954-Jul. 1, 1954 / Contemporary 238

Guitarist Barney Kessel and the great American standard are the program on *Plays Standards*, the ringer being "Barney's Blues," the one Kessel original. Recorded between June 4, 1954, and Sept. 12, 1955, the three sessions include Bob Cooper, Claude Williamson, Monty Budwig, Shelly Manne, Hampton Hawes, Red Mitchell, and Chuck Thompson. —*Bob Rusch*, Cadence

○ **Music to Listen to Barney Kessel By** / Aug. 6, 1956-Oct. 15, 1956 / Contemporary 160

Kessel's guitar with five woodwinds and a rhythm section. Twelve songs with Buddy Collette (f), Andre Previn (p), Shelly Manne (d), Jimmy Rowles (p), Red Mitchell (b), Buddy Clark (b), and others. This CD is 42 minutes in length. —AMG

★ **Poll Winners with Ray Brown and Shelly Manne** / Mar. 18-19, 1957 / Contemporary 156

This was a 3/18 and 19/57 trio session with bassist Ray Brown and drummer Shelly Manne. These Poll Winners' concepts were at one time quite popular, especially with Contemporary. They were a throwback to the Metronome All Stars concept, which was pretty much left along with the concentration of recording coming from a handful of jazz independents and the general decentralization of jazz—both in geographical and stylistic terms. Back in the '50s, jazz was basically American, bop, or prebop. While this release isn't as powerful as *Feeling Free*, it does succeed, and again, the drummer must get equal credit. There is a comfortable, conversational tone about this recording, a fact mentioned by Nat Hentoff in his liners. This kind of effort will always sound good, familiar, yet with enough meat and thinking to sustain concentrated listening. One large annoyance is the clipped ending on "Jordu," and a fair amount of hiss is present. —*Bob Rusch,* Cadence

Let's Cook / Aug. 6, 1957+Nov. 11, 1957 / Contemporary 7603
A good reissue of prime cuts originally on a 10-inch album. Two cuts with Ben Webster (ts). —*Ron Wynn*

★ **Poll Winners Ride Again, The** / Aug. 1958 / Contemporary 607

Barney Kessel Plays *Carmen* / Dec. 19+23, 1958 / Original Jazz Classics 269

★ **Some Like It Hot** / Mar. 30-31, 1959 / Contemporary 168
Here is one of two sessions guitarist Barney Kessel recorded in the middle of his 10-year exclusive Contemporary period ('53-'62). This is a 1959 (3/30-31, 4/3) date that includes Art Pepper (cl, as), Joe Gordon (tpt), Jimmy Rowles (p), Jack Marshall (rhythm guitar), Monty Budwig (b), and Shelly Manne (d). It is somewhat contained by 10 air-play-length cuts. This has moments from the leader, Pepper, and Gordon, but it really only visits the listener. —*Bob Rusch,* Cadence

○ **Guitar Workshop** / Nov. 5, 1967 / Saba

Blue Soul / i. 1967 / Black Lion

Feeling Free / Mar. 12, 1969 / Original Jazz Classics 179
The last date (3/12/69) guitarist Barney Kessel led for Contemporary Records, this was recorded 13 long years after his initial sessions for the company and features a quartet with Bobby Hutcherson, Chuck Domanico, and Elvin Jones stretching out over six tracks. The title, "Feeling Free," could be interpreted in different ways, but would seem mainly to deal with Kessel's decision to abandon the studio work on the West Coast and move to England. But it's also obvious that the guitarist kept in touch with post-Charlie Parker music (I hear some Wes Montgomery influence at this time, also), and, while still in honest touch with the blues, he now took so many more chances, digging in and challenging the listener and the quartet. A great deal of credit must go to Elvin Jones (d)—his support, base, and encouragement are brilliant. Bobby Hutcherson offers an interesting soft, contrasting coloring to the often-locked sounds of Kessel and Jones. This group, though brought together just for this session, was obviously hot to play—even the two standards quickly shed their themes to open up to hard-working creative interpretations. —*Bob Rusch,* Cadence

Reflections in Rome / May 7, 1969 / RCA

☆ **Straight Ahead** / i. 1975 / Contemporary 7635

Jellybeans / Apr. 1981 / Concord Jazz 164

Solo / i. Apr. 1981 / Concord Jazz 221

Artistry of Barney Kessel / i. 1984 / Fantasy 021

Spontaneous Combustion / i. 1987 / Contemporary 14033

○ **Red Hot and Blues** / Contemporary 14044
We have long contended that Barney Kessel is one of the hottest guitarists picking today. His roots are in his native Oklahoma and he comes from two Charlies: Christian and Parker. Kessel is at his best on *Red Hot and Blues* for which he was joined by an all-star cast of vibraphonist Bobby Hutcherson, pianist Kenny Barron, bassist Rufus Reid, and drummer Ben Riley. —*W. Royal Stokes,* Jazz Times

Red White and Hot / Contemporary 14044
With Bobby Hutcherson (vib) and the Kenny Barron trio. Three original tunes. —*Michael G. Nastos*

STEVE KHAN

b. Apr. 28, 1947, Los Angeles, CA
Guitar / Early jazz-rock, neo-bop
Steve Khan, son of Sammy Cahn, is a well-known session guitarist who has amassed a large number of credits doing mainly fusion-style material, though he's a good straighthead jazz player. He has been ranked alongside Cornell Dupree and Eric Gale as one of the most versatile studio players around, but he doesn't have the blues facility of the other two musicians. He has made some records as a leader,

but has done better as accompanist to a host of pop/R&B big names, among them Sheila Jordan, Chaka Khan, Bob James, and Grover Washington, Jr. —*Ron Wynn*

Blue Man, The / **i.** Nov. 1978 / Columbia 35539
The guitar sound on this album is broad, slightly distorted, and played with a hornlike fluidity, a stylistic criterion for Steve Khan, who mastered the feedback technique to perfection. On "Daily Valley" he carries the weight of the full orchestra behind his dubbed-in acoustic solo; on "An Eye Over Autumn" his chase with Michael Brecker comes off at times like a sax duel; and throughout the horn tracks his sweeping yet pliant phrasing is always the immaculately proportioned foil for the peppery Brecker licks. The musicianship, of course, is top notch on all accounts, performed with the professional sideman's instrumental acumen and empathy (drummer Steve Gadd strikes me as particularly enjoyable here). *The Blue Man* is one strong effort from a group that isn't ashamed to be entertaining. —*Lars Gabel,* Down Beat

★ **Evidence** / Jul. 1980 / Novus 3074

○ **Eyewitness** / **i.** 1981 / Antilles 848821
Eyewitness is a straightforward, simple yet challenging LP. The guitarist changes his compositional approach from earlier albums like *Arrows* and *Tightrope.* No more playing the head, soloing over the changes, repeating the head, and out. Khan allows much of the music here to happen as it would. There's very little flaunting of chops here. Khan leaves a lot of space for his bandmates (bassist Anthony Jackson, drummer Steve Jordan, percussionist Manolo Badrena) and uses his guitar to suggest ideas and textures for the band to explore and to create unusual washes. "Guy LaFleur" showcases not only Khan's fluid delay sound, but the togetherness of this rhythm section. Jackson sets some rich tones ringing, Badrena steadies it with shakers, and Jordan gets in his whacks grooving. —*Robin Tolleson,* Down Beat

Local Colour / Apr. 1983-May 1987 / Denon 1840
Good '87 duo session, in which session and studio ace guitarist Steve Khan went against his reputation and did an album of duets with keyboardist and vocalist Rob Mounsey that aren't just funk and fusion, but mostly jazz-tinged instrumentals. —*Ron Wynn*

Casa Loco / May 21-22, 1983 / Antilles 848822
Mid-'80s session that blends funk, fusion, and occasional mainstream work by guitarist Steve Khan. Nice production, decent arrangements, and generally fine playing by Khan, though he does few solos. —*Ron Wynn*

☆ **Let's Call This** / Blue Moon 79168
This tenacious trio of jazz heavyweights puts together a fine compilation of tunes—spontaneous, yet relaxed with that nightclub feel. Throughout, guitarist Steve Khan offers his smooth and silky feather-light fingerwork on the frets. On the title cut, a Thelonious Monk tune, Khan is complemented by the seasoned rhythm section of Ron Carter (b) and Al Foster (d). Regardless of who takes the solo, the other musicians fill the background with style and grace. The infectious bassline of "Masquelero" spotlights Carter's expertise, while "Backup" is bluesy and loose with Foster exhibiting a soft snare and sizzling cymbals. Khan heads south of the border with earthy Latin rhythms on "Out of This World" and moves into the bright and boppy "Played Twice" (another Monk contribution). Other highlights find the trio conjuring magic with Freddie Hubbard's "Little Sunflower," Lee Morgan's "Mr. Kenyatta," and Khan's own "Buddy System." —*Scott Thompson,* Jazz Times

JOHN KIRBY

b. Dec. 31, 1908, Baltimore, MD, **d.** Jun. 14, 1952, Hollywood, CA
Bass, tuba, bandleader, arranger / Swing
John Kirby led one of the finest small combos of the '30s and '40s. He was a disciplined, technically proficient bassist and leader whose band played a popular brand of jazz that came close to being a forerunner of the "lite" music currently favored on adult contemporary radio stations. They were a fi-

nesse group that avoided exuberant displays and hard-hitting, bluesy solos for melodically enchanting, swinging music that lacked fire, but was brilliantly played. The group was known for "jazzin' the classics." Kirby had earlier played trombone and tuba, before settling on bass. He played with Fletcher Henderson in the early '30s, then joined Chick Webb in the mid '30s, and returned to Henderson again. After a stint with Lucky Millinder, Kirby began his own band. Saxophonist Pete Brown and trumpeter Frankie Newton were originals. The group's popularity zoomed when it settled on the lineup of trumpeter Charlie Shavers, clarinetist Buster Bailey, saxophonist Russell Procope, pianist Billy Kyle, and drummer O'Neill Spencer. Shavers contributed arrangements and played lots of muted trumpet, while Kirby's wife at the time, Maxine Sullivan, did vocals. They did dates at Whites-only hotels and even were featured on a 1940 radio show, "Flow Gently, Sweet Rhythm." But when Sullivan left to go solo, Shavers joined Tommy Dorsey and Kyle in the army, and the group eventually disbanded. A Carnegie Hall reunion concert with Big Sid Catlett on drums was a commercial failure. Kirby later died of diabetes. The survivors staged a quasi-reunion on the Bethlehem date *The Complete Charlie Shavers with Maxine Sullivan* in 1953. Their finest work was reissued on a Smithsonian collection *John Kirby: The Biggest Little Band 1937-1941.* There are also reissued CDs on Circle and Classic Jazz. —*Ron Wynn*

○ **John Kirby** / i. 1938 / Columbia 502

★ **Biggest Little Band, The** / Oct. 28, 1938-Jan. 15, 1941 / Smithsonian 013

Boss of the Bass / i. Apr. 1977 / Columbia 33557
In the history of jazz very few bassists have remained in the consciousness of both listeners and historians. This set shows the progression of John Kirby from sideman to leader of one of the more well-known chamber jazz groups of the '40s. We hear him first as a tubaist with the Chocolate Dandies and then with Fletcher Henderson, Chick Webb, Teddy Wilson, and other bands. Then, as part of small accompanying groups, he supports singers like Maxine Sullivan, Mildred Bailey, and Midge Williams. If this was merely an excuse to get some of these excellent sides back in circulation then it was worth it. The second disc is a collection of Kirby Sextet pieces that largely avoid the usual renditions of classical melodies. There is one unissued piece ("Jumpin' in the Pump Room") and another that only previously appeared on an LP ("Beethoven Riffs On"). This is a pleasant selection of the groups' sides featuring the muted trumpet of Charlie Shavers, the liquid and bouncy alto sax of Russell Procope, Buster Bailey's clarinet, and Billy Kyle's elegant piano styling. Their tightly arranged music still sounds relaxed and continues to evolve the atmosphere of cafe society. They are having fun and this ebullient sensibility is communicated well over 35 years later. —*Jon Goldman*, Cadence

ANDY KIRK (Andrew Dewey Kirk)

b. May 28, 1898, Newport, KY, **d.** 1992
Baritone saxophone, bass, bandleader / Swing, big band
Andy Kirk was a major bandleader whose greatest skills were his leadership of a successful orchestra and his ability to find talented people to showcase. He was a decent, though far from great, saxophonist and tuba player. He was one of the rare bass sax players before he opted for full-time conducting status. One of Kirk's early teachers was Paul Whiteman's father, Wilberforce. He studied piano, vocals, alto and tenor sax, and music theory with Whiteman. Kirk began playing bass sax and tuba in violinist George Morrison's orchestra in 1918, and moved to Dallas in 1925. He joined Terrence Holder's band and assumed its leadership in 1929. Kirk spent ten years as a postman, but also toured and recorded with an 11-piece band led by vocalist George Morrison. He later joined Terrence Holder's band in Dallas, and became its leader in 1929. They attained national attention in 1936, thanks to the high-note vocals of Pha Terrell. They were buoyant and bright, and Kirk proved

a good bandleader. The band remained intact for 12 years. Kirk's group included, at various times, Mary Lou Williams, Terrell, Dick Wilson, Henry Wells, Fats Navarro, Don Byas, and Howard McGhee. They had enormous success from 1936 to 1938, with such songs as "Christopher Columbus," "Until the Real Thing Comes Along/Cloudy," "Dedicated to You," "Skies Are Blues," and "What Will I Tell My Heart," among others. They scored two more hits in the '40s, "Now I Lay Me Down to Dream" in 1940 and "I Know" in 1946 with the Jubilaires. Kirk occasionally led a West Coast band, managed a New York City hotel, and formed a band for special dates in 1955. He toured Europe throughout the '60s, and was greeted with open arms. —*Ron Wynn and Michael G. Nastos*

○ **March 1936** / Mar. 1936 / Mainstream 399
A neat bonus, this: five Mary Lou Williams solo pieces and 13 tracks by what proved the most commercially successful of the legendary Kansas City bands, nicely packaged and with useful Charles Fox liners. These were the Decca recordings that began Andy Kirk's most popular period, and if you missed the deleted Kirk reissue on Decca, you'll find six of the best pieces here. Mary Lou Williams's solo tracks are mainly in a Fats Waller vein, and, while her approach to the style is slightly more conscientiously detailed than Waller's, she quite lacked the main quality that so frequently made Fats viable. "Swingin' For Joy" is the best of the five. And there's one hilarious track, "Until the Real Thing Comes Along," the ultimate Depression-era masochism song, with an outrageous vocal; it was Kirk's theme song, far more dated than most of Kirk's dance band principles. —*John Litweiler*, Down Beat

○ **Jazz Heritage: Instrumentally Speaking (1936-1942)** / 1936-1942 / Decca 9232

○ **Jazz Heritage–Lady Who Swings the Band (1936-1938)** / 1936-1938 / MCA 1343

★ **Andy Kirk (1944)** / 1944 / Hindsight 227

RAHSAAN ROLAND KIRK (Ronald T. Kirk)

b. May 15, 1936, Columbus, OH, **d.** Dec. 5, 1977
Tenor saxophone, multi-reeds / Bop, hard bop
Sometimes, musicians use flamboyance to mask deficiencies in talent. But at other times, a talented player's willingness to have a good time results in his skills being downplayed. That was the case with Rahsaan Roland Kirk, who loved clowning, telling outrageous jokes, and enjoying himself in concert. That, coupled with his penchant for playing three horns at once and playing homemade instruments, convinced some individuals that he was more sideshow than legitimately superb soloist. But Kirk's playing three horns was done through skillful use of false fingerings. He modified the keys of his tenor, using the left hand to cover the tenor's range and his right to play the manzello and stritch. It was an incredible combination of musical knowledge and physical dexterity, made even more amazing because the individual doing it had been blind since age two. Kirk was a master of circular breathing, another practice that led him to be accused of gimmickry. He could hold and sustain notes for what seemed like hours. Kirk used a siren whistle to punctuate key moments in his solos. He discovered the long forgotten manzello and stritch, a pair of saxophones used in turn-of-the-century Spanish marching bands, in a music store. He made alterations to the instruments with rubber bands and tape, and turned them into part of his performing arsenal.

Rahsaan Roland Kirk was an amazing musician and personality, who could play lightning fast bebop, outrageous free solos, heartfelt 12-bar blues, and any and everything in between. He played over 40 instruments, many of his own making. At his concerts, it seemed he'd raided a music store; there were so many horns, flutes, and devices on stage. His homemade instruments included the trumpophone (trumpet with soprano sax mouthpiece), slidesophone (miniature trombone resembling Snub Mosley's slide saxophone), black puzzle flute, and black mystery pipes. He used flutes like microphones, speaking and sending messages with them. Kirk was one of the funniest people of all time on or back stage, but he didn't find anything humorous about the music business or the treatment jazz musicians received from the general media. He was the leader of the early '70s Jazz and People's Movement, another of those worthy causes that later degenerates into a mutually unproductive series of confrontations. Kirk and Lee Morgan got nationwide press, little of it favorable, in 1970 when they disrupted the taping of a "Merv Griffin" show to protest the lack of African-American musicians and the absence of Black music and compositions from most radio and television shows. The Jazz and People's Movement had a legitimate beef; unfortunately, they were bogged down by publicity-seeking ringers in the ranks, and their tactic of disrupting television tapings cost them points with many of the people they were trying to reach. That was probably the low point of Kirk's great career.

He began playing bugle and trumpet as a child, and later started on clarinet and C-melody saxophone. He was a professional at age 15, working in R&B bands. He moved from Louisville to Chicago in 1960. Ira Sullivan played on Kirk's second album. Kirk toured Germany in the early '60s, and later played briefly with Charles Mingus. Then he led his own bands exclusively, playing a wide variety of styles and mainly originals while fronting his "Vibration Society." Kirk made his first album for King in 1956, then moved to Argo. He recorded in the '60s and '70s for Argo/Cadet, Prestige, Mercury, Verve, Atlantic, and Warner Bros. Before becoming a leader, Kirk played with Brother Jack McDuff and Jaki Byard. He took the name "Rahsaan" after having a vision during a dream. Such albums as *Volunteered Slavery*, *Natural Black Inventions*, and *Bright Moments* packed musical and philosophical/political punch. Kirk worked with guests on his albums such as Horace Parlan, Quincy Jones, Al Hibbler, and Leon Thomas. He suffered a stroke in 1975, but continued playing for two more years. Kirk founded the Vibration School of Music in 1977 to help saxophonists. It was one of his final acts. Mercury issued a two-record compilation of his early '60s work immediately after his death, then did Kirk justice with a boxed set compilation of his sessions, *The Complete Roland Kirk on Mercury*. There are several Kirk dates available on CD, and Rhino issued an anthology of Kirk Atlantic cuts in '93. Warner Bros. released a compilation of his final sessions in 1978. —*Ron Wynn*

Does Your House Have Lions: The Rahsaan Roland Kirk Anthology / Rhino R2-71406
The Atlantic/Rhino anthology line has delighted novices and angered purists who have balked at what they deem questionable inclusions and exclusions, plus nonchronological sequencing and liners with plenty of personal anecdotes but limited musical analysis. None of these things are corrected with this CD of Rahsaan Roland Kirk material, which does raise the question: who are these intended for anyhow? If they are designed to interest a newcomer in the artist, they do the job. The 31 selections range from 1961 to 1976 and cover Kirk originals, covers, straight jazz, pop/soul, gospel-backed, and hard bop workouts and feature both live and studio segments. While it is a bit jarring to hop from the early '60s to the '70s and back, series compiler Joel Dorn opted for stylistic organization rather than session exactness. It is not the way I would personally do it, but it is not the hanging crime some imply. Since no one is claiming that this series is supposed to resemble Mosaic's climactic boxed line, it is hard to understand what the fuss is all about. Any hardcore Kirk fan will want the individual albums the label is reissuing. Otherwise, the anthology serves its purpose, which is to spotlight a brilliant player and make you want to hear more. —*Ron Wynn*

Early Roots / 1956 / Bethlehem 6064
Rahsaan Roland Kirk's *Early Roots* is one of the most sought-after and elusive of Bethlehem's harvest. Kirk had just turned 20 when he entered the Cincinnati studios in

1956 to make this debut album, basically an R&B affair with strong bop leanings. Even on this maiden occasion, most of his stylistic traits were in ample supply, including his celebrated multi-instrumental technique. Kirk, apparently, had been sharpening his multi-instrumental maneuvers for several years before committing the idea to vinyl, because it comes off here with commanding finesse. He extracts a sweet, thin, milky tone from the altolike manzello that melds in a pleasing, insinuating way with his sopranolike stritch, or assumes its own full-bodied character on solo lines, as in the Ellington-inflected "Slow Groove" blues. Later, in the brooding "Easy Living," the multiple-reed harmonies dovetail and breath lightly with the late-night, slurry wit of a vintage horn duo, then knock back into the hard-bent bop blues of "Triple Threat." Kirk's rhythmic support is nicely lean and itchy, responsive to his every turn without usurping his direction, as if they could. —*Mikal Gilmore, Down Beat*

Introducing Roland Kirk / Feb. 1961 / Chess 91551

★ **Rahsaan–Complete on Mercury** / 1961-1964 / Mercury 846630

Kirk's Work / Mar. 1962 / Prestige 459
With Jack McDuff. This is a fine reissue of Kirk in a soul-jazz and mainstream vein. —*Ron Wynn*

☆ **We Free Kings** / Apr. 1962 / Mercury 826455

○ **Reeds & Deeds** / Aug. 1963 / Mercury 20800

○ **Rip, Rig and Panic / Now Please Don't . . .** / Jan. 13, 1965-Apr. 1967 / EmArcy 832164
1965 and 1967. Also *Now Please Don't You Cry, Beautiful Edith*. A couple of Kirk's more popular '60s albums combined. —*Ron Wynn*

○ **Now Please Don't You Cry, Beautiful Edith** / Jul. 1968 / Verve 68709
This has been reissued in a single-fold jacket, minus the original Billy Taylor liners. This April 1967 recording with Lonnie Smith (p), Ronnie Boykins (b), and Grady Tate (d) presents a solid display of Rahsaan Roland Kirk's talents on tenor, manzello, whistle, stritch, and flute in what was perhaps typical of the cornucopia of musical roots and messages that became part of his statements from the '60s up until his death. A Creed Taylor production, this is Kirk's only session for Verve—but as was usually the case, this is Rahsaan Roland Kirk's session, not a particular record company or producer's. —*Bob Rusch, Cadence*

Inflated Tear, The / Nov. 1968 / Atlantic 90045
Recorded in November 1967 with pianist Ron Burton, bassist Steve Novosel, drummer Jimmy Hopps, and trombonist Dick Griffin, this is in many ways a typically planned date to display the 360 degrees of Rahsaan Roland Kirk. I remember my reaction at the time was one of anticlimax—simply because no recording ever managed to really capture all the magic of Kirk at his best. But now I can't catch Kirk live and this record brings back memories with its good jazz and the hints of his unique personality. What a wonderful fruitcake—I am glad for all his recordings; this was Kirk in the fall of '67. —*Bob Rusch, Cadence*

★ **Volunteered Slavery** / Jan. 1970 / Atlantic 1534
There seems to be no expression which Rahsaan Roland Kirk couldn't elicit from his arsenal of horns, individually or in multiples. "A short medley of tunes that John Coltrane left here for us to learn" is eight minutes of pure devotion and love. Kirk plays "Lush Life," "Afro Blue," and "Bessie's Blues." "Three for the Festival" is just wild grunts, groans, shouts, smashings, whistles, and did I hear "We Shall Overcome" in the melee? It sounds like a coda for "One Ton" and takes the record out the same way it came in. Side two was recorded at the Newport Jazz Festival in 1968. Kirk delights the audience and the crowd. This portion of the disc is a really powerful side of Kirk's unique personality. The Newport episodes are entertaining enough to warrant purchasing the album for the studio cuts. —*Alan Offstein, Coda*

☆ **Rahsaan / Rahsaan** / May 11-12, 1970 / Atlantic 1575

This session consists of a repetition of Rahsaan Roland Kirk's nightclub patter, a medley of references to jazz history—Charlie Parker, New Orleans, Duke Ellington—and a couple of new items of minimal interest. The sidemen include Howard Johnson on tuba; Dick Griffin's trombone is also good and adds quite a bit of presence to the orchestra. Leroy Jenkins does a violin solo that stands him in good stead on "The Seeker." The rhythm section of Ron Burton (p), Vernon Martin (b), and James Madison (d) is augmented by Alvern Bunn and Joe Texidor (miscellaneous percussion). The second medley finds Kirk soloing on a new saxophone that allows him to play two melody lines simultaneously. The effect is one of two melodies being played simultaneously. —*Alan Offstein*, Coda

Natural Black Inventions: Root Strata / Jan. 26, 1971-Feb. 4, 1971 / Atlantic 1578

☆ **Bright Moments** / Jun. 8-9, 1973 / Atlantic 907
Rahsaan Roland Kirk was a trip in himself, and this live recording, done at Todd Barkan's Keystone Korner, shows why. Whether stretching into well-used solo space or spinning out his handwoven, Rahsaanicized philosophy, he gripped an audience via the sincerity and exuberance of his sayings and playings. Kirk was a modern master with awesome technique, and he was so versatile that the word cannot fully apply to anyone else. The audience was ready for him this night, and Kirk was as "on" as they were. That was why *Bright Moments* is so engrossing and absorbing: Kirk's musical fanaticism and sheer joy drew you into the world seen only by his inner eye, and when you left, you were exhausted but fulfilled. He took you on the trip he promised—and then some. —*Neil Tesser*, Down Beat

Kirkatron / Jul. 18, 1975-1976 / Warner Brothers 2982

Case of the 3-Sided Dream in Audio Color, The / Nov. 1975 / Atlantic 1674
This album is a self-examination of Rahsaan Roland Kirk's waking and sleeping dreams. The six *Dream* episodes interspersed among the album's three sides are sound collages of recurring aural stimuli—thunder, the tinkling of a ragtime piano, an altoist playing "Just Friends" (Bird?), a female voice singing "God Bless The Child" (Billie?), a chugging steam locomotive, glass breaking, exploding cannons, etc.—which derive from Kirk's childhood experiences in Ohio. The dream concept extends to the music as well. "Echoes of Primitive Ohio and Chili Dogs," for example, gets a low-key blues, back-room, summer-in-the-country treatment. The circular, repetitive structure of the album itself is a further extension of dream phenomena. Variations of the same tunes, as with the *Dream* motifs, make kaleidoscopic, elliptical returns. And like dreams, the repetitions are never quite the same. —*Chuck Berg*, Down Beat

Boogie Woogie String Along for Real / 1975-1976 / Warner Brothers 3085
Boogie Woogie String Along for Real was Rahsaan Roland Kirk's last recording, made after he taught himself to play his instruments one-handed to foil his disabling stroke. The improvisations here are not as sustained as Kirk, their creator, intended—but his spirit was ever buoyant. The support of an orchestra on the title track, of his last working band on "Dorhaan's Walk" and (with ringer Percy Heath on cello) "Hey Babebips" and "Watergate Blues," and of a swinging quartet of veterans on "Make Me a Pallet on the Floor" and "In a Mellow Tone" relieves Kirk of some of the responsibility for virtuosity. But his raucous horn is still the motivating force behind "Boogie Woogie," his easy singing belies the problematic clarinet work on "Pallet," he urges everyone on "Walk," and gruffly decides "Watergate" ("Take 'em away. Don't give 'em no break"). —*Howie Mandel*, Down Beat

○ **Vibration Continues, The** / Atlantic 1003
This is a compilation from 1968-1974. Excellent introduction to a virtuoso. —*Michael G. Nastos*

KENNY KIRKLAND (Kenneth David Kirkland)

b. Sep. 28, 1955, Newport, NY

Piano, synthesizer / Postbop, neo-bop
Currently, Kenny Kirkland can be seen on weeknights at his position behind an array of keyboards on the "Tonight Show." He displays his versatility to millions, backing everything from lounge lizards to blues and jazz greats, while interacting with the rhythm section and occasionally having a composition featured during a band segment. Kenny Kirkland has hit the big time, and he's merited it through his outstanding work with several groups. Kirkland's equally solid on acoustic or electric keyboards, and shows his grounding in bebop through an energetic, swinging style. He's worked with several rockers and adjusts easily to rock's bombastic qualities or to jazz's harmonic demands. He cites Herbie Hancock as a prime influence, and his work has a similar easy, relaxed, yet prickly edge. Kirkland began playing piano at age six, and took saxophone lessons in high school. He graduated from the Manhattan School of Music in 1977, then toured with Michael Urbaniak. Kirkland played with Miroslav Vitous in 1979, and also worked with Don Alias. He toured Japan with Terumasa Hino, played with Elvin Jones, and was in Wynton Marsalis's early and mid-'80s quartet. Kirkland was later featured on Sting's concert album and video along with Branford Marsalis. Kirkland subsequently went on to do more session work, before landing his high-profile position with the "Tonight Show" band. He's also recorded with Dizzy Gillespie, Chico Freeman, and Crosby, Stills, and Nash. He currently has one GRP session available on CD. —*Ron Wynn*

★ **Kenny Kirkland** / i. 1991 / GRP 9657
This is a good set with Afro-Latin and hard bop influences mixed. —*Ron Wynn*

JOHN KLEMMER

b. Jul. 3, 1946, Chicago, IL
Saxophone / Bop, early jazz-rock
John Klemmer's tenor playing has a pronounced Coltrane influence. On his best '70s recordings, Klemmer soloed with energy, drive, and harmonic inventiveness. He skillfully utilized the echoplex and wah-wah on such recordings as *Waterfulls* and *Intensity*. He started on piano at age seven, then switched to alto at age 11 and to tenor by his first year in high school. Klemmer studied with Joe Daley, conducted his school's concert band, and led the stage band. He toured with Ted Weems's dance band at age 16. Klemmer worked with the orchestras of Les Elgart and Ralph Marterie, while attending several Stan Kenton summer workshops and the Interlochen Arts Festival. He made his recording debut for Cadet in the late '60s, and moved west to work with Don Ellis's band in 1968. Klemmer remained with the band until 1970, while he also participated in a State Department-sponsored African tour with Oliver Nelson's sextet, and played with Alice Coltrane and the Crusaders. He began heading his own groups in the '70s. Klemmer's recorded as a leader for Cadet, ABC/Impulse, Arista/Novus, and Elektra/Musician, among others. He has a few dates available on CD. —*Ron Wynn*

★ **Waterfalls** / Jun. 17+22, 1972 / MCA 33123

Intensity / Feb. 23, 1973 / Impulse 9244
Tenor saxophonist John Klemmer is an energy player. There are times here—notably moments of "Rapture" and the completely spontaneous "Spell"—when he seems to fall back on energy as a substitute for ideas, but more often than not he knows how to use his energy in the service of his excellent musicianship. "Love Song" and the easy-on-the-ears "Play" give him a chance to display a warmth and lyricism that I found totally convincing. Electric pianist Tom Canning has a pretty, bittersweet solo spot, "Prayer," which is actually the introduction to "Waltz." The team of electric pianist Todd Cochran, bassist James Leary, and drummer Woody Theus, heard on the album's two live cuts, plays with a little more fire than the other tandem, and Cochran is outstanding on the sometimes chaotic, sometimes melodic "Spell." Although he is prone to occasional excesses that don't hit my ears right, Klemmer is a player of much spirit and imagination,

and *Intensity* is an exciting and pleasurable recording. — *Peter Keepnews*, Down Beat

Touch / **i.** 1976 / Mobile Fidelity 522
Better solos and higher energy level than most of Klemmer's albums. This is the best-sounding version. —*Ron Wynn*

☆ **Nexus for Duo and Trio** / **i.** 1978 / Novus 23500
Nexus is a return for tenor saxophonist John Klemmer to the solid jazz he was weaned on long ago. The shadows of John Coltrane and Sonny Rollins loom over a highly spontaneous session that was recorded live (unoverdubbed) in the studio with, Klemmer relates, no preparation or prior discussion of the music to be played. Carl Burnett is particularly noteworthy in both the trio (first two sides) and sax-drums duo format. He is a dynamo of energy, but like Elvin Jones with Trane, his polyrhythmic subtleties offer an impressive range of color and constant change. "Misty" opens and closes with Burnett totally on his own, very casual and free, playing with his hands and even fingernails on the cymbals. "Softly" and "Impressions," of course, are totally on fire in the finest Coltrane tradition. Likewise, Klemmer is completely uncompromising, wide open to blowing free jazz, and his chops are up. And the hot, lively, modal exploration of the finishing title track shows that Klemmer can still *write* substantial progressive compositions when he wants to. —*Bob Henschen*, Down Beat

○ **Solo Saxophone II: Life** / 1981 / Elektra 566
This album is almost totally echoplexed—the gadget is used on all tracks except for the two short versions of "Life," where John Klemmer plays kalimba (African thumb piano), and the vocal tracks where he plays the Fender burdened with a quite annoyingly heavy stereo vibrato. Klemmer's extreme mastery of his tenor sax often turns into glibness, rhythmic ideas lose impact, and much musical personality is lost in a dreamy whole. Closer listening reveals that Klemmer is a talented player with a lot to say on his own. There are moments on this record where truly original and creative passages manage to cut through the seemingly endless sea of reverberation and echo, like on "The Journey" and "The Celebration." —*Per Husby*, Cadence

ERIC KLOSS

b. Apr. 3, 1949, Greenville, PA
Alto saxophone / Bop, hard bop, postbop, neo-bop
Eclecticism has its good and bad points, and examples of each are presented in the music of Eric Kloss. A blind alto saxophonist, Kloss has turned in some outstanding solos, has made fine hard bop albums, and has even successfully included free jazz and contemporary classical elements. But he's also made some dreary works loaded with mundane pop, rock, and funk filler. Kloss studied alto, tenor, and soprano at the Western Pennsylvania School for Blind Children, and began his professional career in the early '60s. He played with Pat Martino in the mid-'60s, and was the featured subject of a 1966 television documentary aired on local television in Philadelphia. Kloss was recording sessions at age 16, and has played with Jimmy Owens, Booker Ervin, Cedar Walton, Leroy Vinnegar, Billy Higgins, Kenny Barron, Bob Cranshaw, Alan Dawson, Chick Corea, Dave Holland, Jack DeJohnette, and Martino. He also studied with Lee Konitz, Sonny Stitt, and James Moody. Kloss has earned advanced degrees in math and philosophy. He's recorded as a leader for Prestige, Muse, and Omnisound, and has some sessions available on CD. —*Ron Wynn*

And the Rhythm Section / **i.** 1969-1970 / Fantasy/Original 24125
Eric Kloss is a consistent journeyman saxophonist who usually makes enjoyable, if unmemorable, albums with nice songs. But he is much more than that on the two sessions captured on the single-disc reissue *Eric Kloss and the Rhythm Section.* Working with a great rhythm section of pianist Chick Corea, bassist Dave Holland, and drummer Jack DeJohnette, accompanied up front by guitarist Pat Martino, Kloss soars on alto and tenor, playing with a fury, precision,

and excellence he never again attained. Martino's tingling runs and octave dances are just as masterful, while the rhythm section stars more than fulfill their glittering reputations. —*Ron Wynn*

One, Two, Free / Aug. 28, 1972 / Muse 5019
The best album to date from alto saxophonist Eric Kloss, thanks in part to guest stars guitarist Pat Martino and bassist Dave Holland, plus his own explosive playing and better compositions than usual. —*Ron Wynn*

★ **Celebration** / Jan. 6-7, 1979 / Muse 5196
Good, sometimes strong alto sax solos by Eric Kloss are the lure for this otherwise routine blend of fusion, soul-jazz, and funk with decent production, arrangements, and compositions. —*Ron Wynn*

EARL KLUGH

b. Sep. 16, 1954, Detroit, MI
Guitar / Early jazz-rock, new age, instrumental pop, contemporary funk
Self-taught guitarist Earl Klugh claims to have been inspired by Chet Atkins, George Van Eps, and Laurindo Almeida. Klugh recorded with Yusef Lateef at the age of 15. He worked with George Benson and Chick Corea's Return to Forever, and was selected by George Shearing for one of Shearing's famous tours. Klugh plays acoustic nylon-stringed guitar, and has resisted efforts to go electric. Although not strictly jazz, almost all of his albums have found commercial success in the pop-instrumental market. He is noted for his deft solos and subtle phrasing. —*Ron Wynn and Michael Erlewine*

★ **Earl Klugh** / **i.** 1976 / EMI 46553

Living Inside Your Love / 1977 / Capitol 48385

○ **Heart String / Late Night Guitar** / **i.** 1983 / Liberty 183439
Heart String offers a round of friendly little Earl Klugh originals that all stay within a slow to medium tempo range and all feature the guitarist's fluently melodic style. Stripped of extremities and intensities, the album's sound is as mood-controlled and mood-conducive as a piece of muzak, but it is saved from being entirely a commodity article by Klugh's quiet yet engaging warmth and by the swinging pulse of the backing. —*Lars Gabel*, Down Beat

Wishful Thinking / 1983 / Capitol 46030
Recorded at Media Sound in New York and A&M Studios in Los Angeles. Jazz light. With some heavyweight sidemen mixed in, the sound is light, relaxing jazz-space music. Pleasant stuff. —*Michael Erlewine*

Soda Fountain Shuffle / 1984 / Warner Bros. 25262
Recorded at A&M Recording Studios in Hollywood. Synthesizer, drum machine backgrounds. Easy-listening programmed light jazz with a touch of space music. One of his most popular. —*Michael Erlewine*

○ **Solo Guitar** / **i.** 1989 / Warner Bros. 26018
Earl Klugh's long-awaited solo album showcases his pretty sound on the acoustic guitar, giving two to three minute melodic readings of superior standards. Some of the pieces (notably "I'm Confessin'") find Klugh playing a relaxed "stride" similiar to some of the guitarists of the '30s. I would have preferred that Klugh really dig into some of these tunes (a little more like Joe Pass) rather than treating the melodies with such overwhelming respect, but this ballad session is quite enjoyable; it's Earl Klugh's most rewarding album to date (1990). —*Scott Yanow*, Cadence

Whispers and Promises / **i.** 1989 / Warner Bros. 25902

○ **Earl Klugh Trio—Vol. 1, The** / **i.** 1991 / Warner Bros. 26750

JIMMY KNEPPER (James M. Knepper)

b. Nov. 22, 1927, Los Angeles, CA
Trombone, arranger / Bop, hard bop
Trombonist Jimmy Knepper forged his own sound independent of the enormous impact J.J. Johnson made on players of his generation. He's considered jazz's finest modern trombonist after Johnson and Carl Fontana. His playing blends

modern and vintage elements. It contains the slurs, growls, and smears of "tailgate" players, plus the speed and harmonic complexity of beboppers. Knepper's phrasing, sound, and carefully constructed solos avoid excess and are always played superbly. Knepper played alto horn before starting on trombone at age nine. He studied formally later in college in Los Angeles. He began to play professionally at age 15, working in several big bands. During the '40s, he played with a band co-led by Dean Benedetti and Chuck Cascales, then toured with Freddie Slack in 1947 and Johnny Bothwell in 1948. Knepper worked in Roy Porter's big band in 1948 and 1949, playing alongside Eric Dolphy. He also played, on occasion, with Charlie Parker. During the '50s, Knepper worked in the big bands of Charlie Spivak, Charlie Barnet, Woody Herman, Claude Thornhill, Tony Scott, and Stan Kenton. He played in Charles Mingus's bands in the late '50s and early '60s. Knepper and Mingus had a turbulent relationship, though the stint with Mingus got him his major attention. Knepper was featured on several Mingus records from 1957 to 1962, until Mingus ended their relationship by punching Knepper in the mouth. Knepper recorded with Pepper Adams in 1959 on MGM, then did his own recordings on Mingus's Debut label and on Bethlehem. Knepper toured Africa with Herbie Mann in 1960, and toured the Soviet Union with Benny Goodman in 1962. He worked periodically with Gil Evans from 1960 to 1977, and was in the Thad Jones-Mel Lewis orchestra from 1968 to 1974. He also played in the *Funny Girl* pit band on Broadway from 1964 to 1966. Knepper played in and wrote arrangements for Lee Konitz's nonet from 1975 to 1981. He's toured and recorded with the Mingus Dynasty repertory band since the late '70s. He's served as music director for the Dynasty on occasion. During the '70s, Knepper began recording again as a leader after a two-decade absence from the studios. He did sessions on Steeplechase, Inner City, Hep, Daybreak (Holland), and for Soul Note in the '80s. Currently, there are no Knepper sessions listed as available in any configuration, though some can be obtained from mail-order sources. —*Ron Wynn*

○ **Idol of the Flies** / Sep. 1957 / Bethlehem

Idol of the Flies is trombonist Jimmy Knepper's second album, and it features a surprisingly reticent drummer Danny Richmond and a still-verdant pianist Bill Evans. Evans's formative subtlety is notable for the fine tension between his percussive propensities and his ruminative, dissonant breaks. Like Donald Byrd, Knepper's solo style favors "vocalisms" (another trumpet trait) with wry, rolling intonations. Tellingly, he relaxes and flaunts his lyricism more readily in the presence of trumpeter Gene Roland, particularly on "Gee Baby, Ain't I Good To You," featuring Roland's riveting, ghostly vocal. Not until the wanton bop of "Avid Admirer" does the Charlie Parker image loom, with Knepper spewing taut interrogative clips in a staccato fashion. — *Mikal Gilmore*, Down Beat

★ **Pepper-Knepper Quintet** / i. 1958 / MGM

★ **Cunningbird** / Nov. 8, 1976 / Steeple Chase
Quintet with Al Cohn (ts), Sir Roland Hanna (p), George Mraz (b), Dannie Richmond (d). A tremendous date. —*Ron Wynn*

Jimmy Knepper in L.A. / Sep. 8-9, 1977 / Inner City 6047
Trombonist Jimmy Knepper is supported here by tenor saxophonist Lew Tabackin along with a West Coast rhythm section that includes pianist Roger Kellaway, bassist Monty Budwig, and drummer Shelly Manne. The quintet romps through a couple of original tunes based on traditional chord sequences and jazz classics. Trombonist Knepper reveals his debt to Duke Ellington's trombonist Lawrence Brown as well as the impact of his Charles Mingus experience. Tenorman Tabackin rips and tears through the material with a joie de vivre reminiscent of Eddie "Lockjaw" Davis and Johnny Griffin. He plays with a surging hard-charging style. The material used on this date seems to deny Tabackin the opportunity to display originality. In contrast, pianist Kellaway takes advantage of things to play several solos that

display his individual approach. —*Spencer R. Weston*, Cadence

○ **Tell Me . . .** / Aug. 14, 1979 / Daybreak 001
Tell Me was only the fifth LP under trombonist Jimmy Knepper's name in a 25-year period, and it made an auspicious start for the then-new Dutch Daybreak label. Knepper's neglect is extraordinary when each successive recording (whether under his own or Charles Mingus's name) reaffirmed his stature as the most creative post-J.J. Johnson trombonist until George Lewis's emergence. Knepper's is a uniquely conversational style, full of asides, questions, and a witty rhetoric that is never empty. It is expressed in a gruff, opaque tone whose vocal nature is obtained by subtle variations of inflection and timbre. Though the other players on this date are all Europeans (Eddie Engles, tpt/flhn; Dick Vennik, ts; Nico Bunink, p; Harry Emmery, b; John Engels, d), they play with assurance and fire, using imagination to prevent received ideas from becoming anticlimactic. The album is nevertheless dominated by Knepper's rubbery lyricism, with its surprising twists and turns—nowhere better demonstrated than on his former employer's "Ecclesiastics" or on the duet with piano, dedicated to Billie Holiday, "I Thought About You." His work on "Home," the impishly titled "Nearer My God In C," and the title track are of an equally high standard, so comparison becomes sterile. —*Chris Sheridan*, Down Beat

○ **Dream Dancing** / i. Apr. 1986 / Criss Cross 1024
My initial impression of this album as the opening track began was not too favorable: Jimmy Knepper's trombone tone seemed tentative. But soon I was caught up in the spirit of the session as the quintet dug into the tune's hard bop heritage. What really won me over, though, was the next piece, an excellent ballad performance spotlighting Knepper's considerable improvisatory talents. He truly digs into the emotional core of the song. (And he repeats this intensity on another excellent ballad, "Of Things Past".) Tenor sax player Ralph Moore has played with Horace Silver, and his contribution to this date is mostly to provide additional color since his solo work is relatively limited. Truthfully, his best moments come when he's providing counterpoint, floating in and around Knepper's solos. Dick Katz (p), George Mraz (b), and Mel Lewis (d) provide all the support that Knepper could want accentuating the floating quality of the music. — *Carl Brauer*, Cadence

LEE KONITZ

b. Oct. 13, 1927, Chicago, IL
Alto saxophone / Postbop, cool
Lee Konitz became, perhaps, the most important cool saxophonist. He emphasized a smooth sound with no vibrato and few overtones. He played in an even manner without bebop's jagged, jutting accents, cross-rhythms, or inflections. His lines were lengthy, and he could execute masterful harmonic maneuvers in a tight, precise fashion. This style didn't lack swing, as some detractors claimed, but it wasn't the bobbing up and down flow of bebop. It was very much a cerebral method, so much so that it was written off in some circles as overly intellectual. Konitz's later playing wasn't quite as crisp or densely packed as his formative work.

Konitz studied clarinet with a member of the Chicago Symphony Orchestra in his early days, then played briefly with Jerry Wald after he started on alto sax. Konitz joined Claude Thornhill's band in 1947. Through Thornhill, he met Miles Davis, and later played on the "Birth of the Cool" sessions. By this time, he had also met Tristano. Konitz studied extensively under Tristano, and, at one point, taught at Tristano's private school. Konitz recorded with Tristano in 1949, and also began recording that year as a leader for Prestige. When he broke from Tristano in the early '50s, Konitz toured Scandinavia and worked in Kenton's big band in 1952 and 1953. He recorded again with Tristano in 1954 and 1955. He also did sessions for World Pacific with Gerry Mulligan, led his own quartet dates for Storyville, and later recorded with Hans Koller, Lars Gullin, and other European musicians for the Carish (Italian) label. There were other '50s dates for Atlantic and Verve, notably the excellent *Motion* album with Elvin Jones and Sonny Dallas.

Konitz had difficulty getting jobs in the early '60s and, essentially, was almost retired. He returned in the mid-'60s working with Paul and Carla Bley on more experimental material. He soon returned to his cool style, and became involved in teaching. Konitz conducted lessons with students worldwide through tapes, and started a duet series for Music Minus One. He continued recording for Verve in the early '60s, then for Limelight in the mid-'60s. He overdubbed duets with himself for a Milestone project in 1967, and recorded with Atilla Zoller for MPS. He joined fellow Tristano student Warne Marsh in the early '70s for some intriguing duets, and formed his own nonet modeled after the Birth of the Cool sessions lineup. There were albums for Phillips (Japan), Steeplechase, Milestone, Horo, MPS, Pausa, Choice, Improvising Artists, Chiaroscuro, and other import/foreign labels. These included duets with Hal Galper, Martial Solal, and Harold Danko. Konitz did several festivals and clubs in the '80s, and continued recording with Enja, Soul Note, and others. He was a Jazzpar prize winner in 1992, receiving $300,000 and worldwide attention. A moderate amount of Konitz material from his various eras is available on CD. —*Ron Wynn and Dan Morgenstern*

Subconscious-Lee / Jan. 11, 1949-Apr. 7, 1950 / Prestige 186

1949-1950. Intriguing material with oracle Lennie Tristano (p), plus Warne Marsh (ts). —*Ron Wynn*

★ **Konitz Meets Mulligan** / i. 1953 / Capitol 46847
With Gerry Mulligan Quartet. A simply wonderful pairing of idiosyncratic talents. —*Ron Wynn*

○ **Inside Hi-Fi** / Sep. 26, 1956+Oct. 16, 1956 / Atlantic 90669

★ **Motion** / Aug. 29, 1961 / Verve 2563
Alto saxophonist Lee Konitz's August 29, 1961, set with Elvin Jones (d) and Sonny Dallas (b) was not overall a superb example of the Konitz art, but like almost all of his recordings, the music is of interest and certainly deserving of reissue every decade or so. The trio had not played together before the session. If Jones seems a bit heavy for a Konitz drummer, the contrast is interesting and probably forces a unity of projected swing that might have eluded an average unrehearsed rhythm section working with Konitz. Repeated listenings make obvious how attentive Elvin Jones was to both the swing and intellectual nuances of the session. This was not a prolific recording period for Lee Konitz, but this session would suggest it wasn't for want of ideas or skill. —*Bob Rusch*, Cadence

Lee Konitz Duets / Sep. 25, 1967 / Milestone 466
Tremendous late '60s session, with alto saxophonist Lee Konitz matching his jagged, introspective style against that of several partners, among them tenor saxophonists Joe Henderson and Richie Kamuca, vibists Karl Berger and Marshall Brown, violinst Ray Nance, and guitarist Jim Hall. This is available on CD. —*Ron Wynn*

○ **Peacemeal** / Mar. 20-21, 1969 / Milestone 9025
The music on this session is much less cerebral than one might expect. This, of course, is due to the quiet simplicity and relaxed personalities of the players on this particular date. Lee Konitz's (as) touch is masterful. His tone is pure and ideally suited to the lyrical nature of the Béla Bartók numbers. Marshall Brown (arranger/bassist) is careful and selective, a calm and flawless musician whose easy approach molds well to the others. Eddie Gomez (pizzicato bass) provides some outstanding moments in his turns on "Village Joke" and "Peasant Dance," the sound of his responsive bass playing warm and pleasant. Jack DeJohnette's (d) playing reveals the careful, learned musician in firm possession of his instrument and its capabilities of a wide range of nuance. A very high standard of musicianship was set and maintained throughout this mature and satisfying LP. —*Alan Offstein*, Coda

★ **Altissimo** / Jul. 15, 1973 / West Wind 2019

Alto Summit / **i.** 1973 / Verve 843139
This is an outstanding LP, a reissue of a fine 1968 MPS recording from Germany. Aside from the unusual joining of four altos, which produces some very interesting ensemble moments, the individual playing is first-rate, and there's a splendid range of compositions and a judicious balance of time among the four principals. Clearly more than just a blowing session, this project was conceived and executed with a lot of care. There is one minor flaw, when all four horns obliterate the ballad medley with a chaotic free ending—but the medley itself is superb. Somewhat bemusing also is Konitz's "Tribute," which joins together a grave Bach hymn and a fast unison version of a Charlie Parker solo; so beguiling is the alto choir's sound here that the seam between the two sections is a bit of a jolt. —*Joel Ray*, Cadence

I Concentrate on You / Jul. 30, 1974 / Steeple Chase 1018

Satori / Sep. 30, 1974 / Milestone 9060

Windows / Nov. 6, 1975 / Steeple Chase 1057

Lee Konitz Meets Warne Marsh Again / May 21, 1976 / PA/USA 72

○ **Figure and Spirit** / Oct. 20, 1976 / Progressive 7003
Alto and soprano saxophonist Lee Konitz sounds very good on this date and it's good to hear pianist Albert Dailey and tenor saxophonist Ted Brown, two talents that were underrecorded and overlooked. Brown sounds a bit like Konitz on tenor, and more than once the flow of the record distinctly reminded me of the Stan Getz-Gerry Mulligan Verve date. However, this is no nostalgia trip, but vital and lasting music of the moment. —*Bob Rusch*, Cadence

Lee Konitz Nonet, The / Sep. 20-21, 1977 / Chiaroscuro 186
This band's sound, reflecting its leader's impeccably fine musicianship and penchant for understatement, is fresh. Instead of blowing us away with overinflated barn burners and athletic exhibitions, the nonet fixes on such time-honored artistic tenets as balance, form, and proportion. Consequently, the music possesses an uncommon degree of emotional and intellectual maturity. Aside from Konitz, the nonet boasts a roster of outstanding players whose ability to function in widely varied contexts is exemplary. Also integral is the band's book. Drawing on traditional and contemporary tunes, arrangers Sy Johnson and Kenny Berger crafted charts that perfectly mesh talents and textures. "If Dreams Come True" is a leisurely paced outing with a nod to Basie. Konitz's solid soprano, trombonist Jimmy Knepper's slippery slides, and the band's relaxed rhythmic flow are outstanding. Johnson's excellent arrangements of "A Pretty Girl Is Like a Melody" and "Tea For Two" bring new life to these usually dusty clichés. The other standard, "Without a Song," is one of the best performances of Vincent Youman's classic since Sonny Rollins's definitive essay in *The Bridge. —Chuck Berg*, Down Beat

Lee Konitz Quintet / Sep. 1977 / Verve
This version of the Lee Konitz quintet features the alto flights of Konitz and Bob Mover. Backed by the supple rhythmic support of pianist Ben Aranov, bassist Mike Moole, and drummer Jimmy Madison, the hornmen bring out the best in each other's playing. Though the two altoists share many stylistic characteristics, Mover emerges the more vital. Employing broad emotional and dynamic ranges, Mover drives with muscle and sails with lyric abandon. His solos are an effective blend of conceptual and dramatic vigor. Though most of the space is reserved for the saxes and Ben Aranov's crisp piano work, there are spots for the energetic work of Moole and Madison. The tunes themselves present challenging chordal frameworks that fully test the players' harmonic dexterity. —*Chuck Berg*, Down Beat

Live at Laren / Aug. 12, 1979 / Soul Note 1069
1979 version of his nonet. Extended examples of Chick Corea's "Matrix" and "Times Lie." —*Michael G. Nastos*

☆ **Seasons Change** / Oct. 29, 1979 / Circle 291079

Ideal Scene / Jul. 1986 / Soul Note

Lee Konitz: Round and Round / **i.** Aug. 1989 / Music Masters 60167

The fertile musical imagination of Lee Konitz (as), whose saxophonic voice is immediately identifiable, is showcased on *Round and Round* with nine tunes that includes Sonny Rollins's "Valse Hot," John Coltrane's "Giant Steps," and originals. Fred Hersch's piano, diamond bright here, softly kneaded there, is the perfect complement to Lee's delicious timbre. Bassist Mike Richmond and drummer Adam Nussbaum are the icing on the cake. — *W. Royal Stokes,* Jazz Times

○ **First Sessions (1949-1950)** / Prestige 24081

First Sessions is a collection of early sessions from the New Jazz, Birdland, and Prestige labels. The first session features a quintet that includes pianist Lennie Tristano, alto saxophonist Lee Konitz, and guitarist Billy Bauer. The four cuts by this group transcend time; when you listen to them, there are few clues that they were recorded in 1949, so fresh and bright is the sound. Tristano's piano style concentrates on the melody and his playing is generous, inviting and complementing the contributions of Konitz and Bauer. Konitz and Bauer, in turn, work off Tristano's melodic ideas, producing a flowing tapestry of sound, woven out of the subtle shadings of piano, alto sax, and guitar. The balance of side one is taken up by another quintet led by Konitz and tenor saxophonist Warne Marsh. Tristano's influence is heard in the melodic interplay of the two horns and in the piano playing of Sal Mosca, a Tristano disciple. On each of the four tunes Konitz and Marsh, whether trading choruses and fours or playing in unison, exhibit an uncanny sympathy for both the melody and each other's improvisations. This is another excellent session. Side two opens with two throwaway cuts by tenor player Don Lanphere. Only the presence of pianist Duke Jordan on "Strike Up the Band" rescues this from obscurity. Next, two alternate takes from a Kai Winding (tb) sextet are marred by the "bombs" of Roy Haynes's drumming, with Brew Moore's tenor the only light on an otherwise foggy recording. Four tunes by Don Lanphere's quintet featuring trumpeter Fats Navarro close side two. Here Lanphere has to compete with another horn and as a result his playing is stronger than on the earlier session. Sadly, Navarro never hits his stride, so this session adds little to his legacy. Pianist Al Haig and Tommy Potter on bass shine on one tune, "Go." Four alternate takes from a J.J. Johnson (tb) session, which open side three, are notable for the playing of saxophonist Sonny Stitt. His deep, full tone is coupled with a swinging attack. On "Elora," Johnson overcomes the sometimes ponderous sound of the trombone to follow Stitt's lead. Pianist John Lewis sounds out of place with a stiff manner that cuts across the horns' rocking rhythm, particularly on "Blue Mode." Tenor saxophonist Wardell Gray is represented by one track that didn't fit on his *Central Avenue* reissue. It is a fine example of the graceful and sophisticated style Gray embodied. Another single track, an alternate take of a Sonny Stitt session, follows. This time the pianist is Bud Powell, and the tune swings throughout. Side three closes with two tracks from an Eddie "Lockjaw" Davis session. Davis walks through both tunes with a raucous R&B feel, while pianist Wynton Kelly solos nicely on "Squattin'." Side four contains ephemeral sessions by Al Haig and baritone saxophonist Leo Parker. Haig is best on "Opus Caprice," but otherwise he sounds too much like a cocktail pianist; Roy Haynes drops more bombs. Parker plays with a healthy tone, but he has little to say. Only on the blues "Who's Mad" does he produce any excitement. — *Sam Little,* Cadence

Ezz-Thetic / Prestige 7827

Early Lee Konitz from late '40s and early '50s, when he was establishing his sound and style. A superb date with Miles Davis on trumpet and the band still doing "cool" material but expanding beyond the genre, this has unfortunately been deleted and thus far is not available on either album or disc. — *Ron Wynn*

○ **Jazzlore: Lee Konitz** / **Warne Marsh** / Atlantic 90050

TEDDY KOTICK

b. 1928, **d.** 1986
Bass / Bop
The prototype bassist and a favorite of Charlie Parker, Teddy Kotick preferred supporting the frontline and interacting in the rhythm section to displaying his considerable skills on solos. Despite his substantial ability, he had to be prodded into the spotlight by bandleaders such as Bill Evans and Horace Silver. Kotick was one of the most reliable accompanists of his day, a player whose timing was impeccable and whose tone was huge and assertive. He was always an in-demand bassist who remained busy throughout most of his career. Kotick began studying guitar at age six, then turned to bass in high school. He worked in New England before moving to New York in 1948. Kotick played with Johnny Bothwell, Buddy Rich, Tony Pastor, Buddy DeFranco, Artie Shaw, Stan Getz, and Charlie Parker from 1948 to 1954. He then worked with Bill Evans, George Wallington, and Horace Silver, and recorded with Rene Thomas, Martial Solal, and Teddy Charles. After a long period of inactivity, Kotick returned to playing in the late '70s with J.R. Monterose. He didn't make any sessions as a leader, but can be heard on reissues by Getz, Parker, Wallington, Evans, Silver, and Monterose. — *Ron Wynn*

DAVE KOZ

Alto saxophone, flute / Instrumental pop
The latest contender for the instrumental pop saxophone throne, Dave Koz came out of nowhere after his self-titled 1990 release made it onto the *Billboard* Contemporary Jazz charts and stayed there for several weeks. He has more fire and intensity in his work than Kenny G, and often sounds like a reworked David Sanborn. Koz also played on Arsenio Hall's show, which increased his popularity among the urban contemporary, light jazz, and pop audiences. Koz plays instrumental pop covers and some upbeat tunes, and generally sticks to the fusion production formula: background vocalists, synthesizers, drum machines, a minimum amount of solo space, and so on. His sessions are available on CD. — *Ron Wynn*

ROY KRAL AND JACKIE CAIN

b. 1921 and 1928
Ballads & blues
The duo of Roy Kral (b. 1921) and Jackie Cain (b. 1928) were particularly popular in the '40s and '50s. They mixed vocalese, humor, and show business patter. Cain was also a good ballad and interpretative vocalist. Kral met Cain in Chicago while Kral was playing piano in a quartet. They worked with Charlie Ventura in the late '40s, with Kral doubling as Ventura's pianist, and also supplying some arrangements. The duo left Ventura, married each other in 1949, and began a sextet. They had their own television show temporarily in Chicago in the early '50s. They played with Ventura again briefly in the mid-'50s, then became a successful nightclub act in the late '50s and early '60s, playing in New York, Los Angeles, and Las Vegas. They moved to New York in 1963. Kral penned several commercials featuring the duo in the '60s, among them a famous Plymouth ad, and they've continued recording and performing into the '90s. They've recorded for Brunswick, Storyville, ABC-Paramount, Columbia, Audiophile, Discovery, Fantasy, Verve, CTI, and Concord. They have several dates available on CD. — *Ron Wynn*

★ **Jackie and Roy in the Spotlight** / **i.** May 14, 1959 / Paramount 267

KRONOS QUARTET

Modern creative
It's unclear whether they're a classical group with jazz and populist leanings, or a populist band with classical expertise. Whatever their motivation, the Kronos Quartet has been blurring categories and attracting interest from audiences

that are normally unaware that string quartets even exist. A superb ensemble, they began in 1974 when violinist David Harrington founded the quartet at Mills College in Oakland. Hank Dutt on viola, John Sherba on violin, and cellist Joan Jeanrenaud gradually became the quartet's other regulars in the late '70s. They made a quick impression with guest stints on recordings by Warren Benson, Dane Rudhyar, and David Grisman, before cutting their own debut on the Sounds Wonderful label in 1982 (on cassette only). They've since covered everything from standard classical compositions to bebop while they've also included international strains, rock, avant-garde, and pop. They recorded *Monk Suite* in 1984 with Ron Carter and *Music of Bill Evans* in 1986 with Eddie Gomez and Jim Hall; both were produced by Orrin Keepnews. They've also done a two-album set of compositions by noted new music composer Terry Riley, and recorded songs by Phillip Glass and Colin Nancarrow, Jimi Hendrix, Astor Piazzolla, and Alfred Schnittke. The Quartet has championed the work of Ornette Coleman, Webern, and James Brown. They've been profiled on CBS' "Sunday Morning" program, and have had their own syndicated radio program that combined interview and performance segments. Their albums continue (correctly) to be listed in classical guides rather than pop supplements, but their work deserves scrutiny by any serious music fan. Along with the Uptown String Quartet and String Trio of New York, the Kronos Quartet are changing lots of people's minds about what can and can't be played on stringed instruments. — *Ron Wynn*

Monk Suite / 1984 / Landmark 1505
The first thing you notice, hearing Thelonious Monk's piano music adapted (by Tom Darter) for string quartet—for many of these string parts were lifted straight off Monk's keyboard—is how astonishingly modern his characteristic harmonies sound, his clunky minor seconds in particular. Monk's compositions spring so clearly from his individualistic piano style, one doesn't usually think of his works in the context of midcentury composition, yet here he sounds very much like a *serious* composer of his time: hat and beard holds his own among the tuxes. A few of these string settings sound most appropriate: Monk's keyboard-climbing "broken field runs" introducing "Round Midnight" translate perfectly into romantic violin flourishes. For a fresh perspective on Monk, this LP is valuable. It may be of greater interest to "classical" music listeners, listeners notoriously deaf to jazz musicians' and composers' contributions to contemporary music. Maybe the only way to catch their ears is to put Monk's music in an instrumental setting they can understand. —*Kevin Whitehead*, Cadence

○ **Music of Bill Evans** / 1985 / Landmark 1510
Eclectic string quartet that operates from a classical base, then expands to include everything from jazz to rock. They pay tribute to Bill Evans with some spirited remakes of his classics. They don't swing much, but they do communicate a good sense of his brilliance. —*Ron Wynn*

★ **Pieces of Africa** / i. Sep. 10, 1992 / Nonesuch 79275
Kronos Quartet is a one-woman, three-man classically trained string quartet (two violins, viola, and cello) from the United States, known for their interpretations of world folk music. Here they perform songs by African composers, most with the composers also contributing musically to the performances, vocally and instrumentally. The sounds are stunning blends of cultures, or perhaps the creation of something new from traditional elements—much like the patchwork quilt design suggested by the cover art. Commentary from the composers is included. —Ladyslipper

GENE KRUPA

b. Jan. 15, 1909, Chicago, IL, **d.** Oct. 16, 1973, Yonkers, NY
Drums, bandleader / Swing, big band
One of the swing era's most charismatic figures, Gene Krupa is alternately hailed and denigrated. Goodman detractors rip him for his role as the band's rhythmic foundation, accusing Krupa of lacking subtlety (true) and confusing bombastic

presence with percussive dynamics (debatable). What Krupa did accomplish was dramatizing the drummer; no longer was he the guy with sticks bashing away behind everyone. Krupa made drummers stars, with his kit, looks, and undeniable ability to create excitement. He was a good drummer who got better over the years, and pushed the Goodman band far more aggressively than some will admit.

Krupa began playing in Chicago with the Benison Orchestra, then made his first records in 1927 with Mckenzie-Condon's Chicagoans. These sessions are some of the earliest that involve a drummer with a full kit. Krupa worked with Red Nichols and Irving Aaronson before making his first records in Chicago in November of 1935. The band was called Gene Krupa and His Chicagoans, an octet with Benny Goodman and Jess Stacy, among others. Once the Goodman band exploded, Krupa became a pop idol. He was a featured attraction in Goodman's combos, and Krupa was shown in filmed shorts with his hair flying one way, his drum sticks flying the other way, chomping on gum and generally enjoying life. Krupa stayed with Goodman from 1935 to 1938, then led his own bands from 1938 to 1943 and 1945 to 1951. His peak period was between 1938 and 1943; the band had such hits as "Let Me Off Uptown," with shared vocals by Anita O'Day and Roy Eldridge, and "Knock Me a Kiss," with lead singer Eldridge and other vocalists Irene Daye and Johnny Desmond. They appeared in the films *Some Like It Hot* in 1939 and *Ball of Fire* in 1941, but then the Krupa train nearly derailed. In 1943, he was arrested on a marijuana charge (the story goes he refused to pay crooked cops and was framed) and served time, returning to the Goodman orchestra later that year.

He moved to Tommy Dorsey's band in 1944, then re-formed his band and led it until 1951. There were more film appearances in the mid-'40s, *George White's Scandals* in 1945, *Meet the Band* in 1947, and *Make Believe Ballroom* in 1949. Krupa's band had more hits, most novelty tunes like "Chickery Chick," and "Boogie Blues." Musicians in that band included Charlie Ventura, with Gerry Mulligan supplying some arrangements, plus vocalists Buddy Stewart, Bobby Scots, and O'Day. Krupa toured with Jazz at the Philharmonic in the early '50s, then ran a drum school with Cozy Cole in New York during the mid-'50s. He led some combos, and appeared in two Hollywood quasi-biographies *The Glenn Miller Story* and *The Benny Goodman Story* in 1954 and 1956, also playing on the Goodman soundtrack. His own cinematic fantasy, *The Gene Krupa Story* in 1959, made the Miller and Goodman movies appear authenticated masterpieces by comparison. Krupa made some studio big band dates during the '50s and early '60s, and toured with JATP again in 1959. He reunited with Goodman once more for a quartet album in 1963, and did yet another reunion date, this time with Ventura in 1964. He died in 1973. —*Ron Wynn and Bob Porter*

★ **Drummer Man** / i. 1956 / Verve 827843
Roy Eldridge (tpt) gets the featured billing (along with vocalist Anita O'Day) he deserves on *Drummer Man*, a 2/12/56 date featuring Gene Krupa (d) fronting a big band. This was a reunion of sorts, but one that worked well, better in some cases than the original. The title's a bit misleading, for although Krupa's propulsions are clearly heard, his soloing is limited to a few features. Still, any drummer or fan of drumming will respond to the ambiance of this date. The featured soloist on all the tracks except one ("Wire Brush Stomp") is Roy Eldridge, and he blows powerfully with fine form and a reserve of ideas. Anita O'Day sings on six tracks and she is also in top form: warm, inviting, and buttery. Arrangements are by Quincy Jones, Manny Albam, Nat Pierce, and Billy Byers and they knew how to give body without interference. The band is composed of all-stars, but only on "Leave Us Leap" do they really get to step out and solo (Eddie Shu, Jimmy Cleveland, Dave McKenna, Aaron Sacks), and members like J.J. Johnson, Kai Winding, and Hal McKusick do no soloing at all. —*Bob Rusch*, Cadence

☆ **Gene Krupa, His Orchestra and Anita O'Day** / i. Apr. 1974 / Columbia 32663

○ **That Drummer's Band** / i. 1985 / Columbia 22027
Anthology from 1988 featuring the biggest hits by drummer Gene Krupa heading his own band in 1940. This was the period directly after Krupa left the Benny Goodman orchestra and formed his own big band, which included tenor saxophonist Charlie Ventura and used arrangements from a young baritone saxophonist named Gerry Mulligan. *—Ron Wynn*

○ **Gene Krupa and Buddy Rich** / Echo Jazz 14
On the title track the two drummers square off in somewhat contrived fashion, and, as the sound is original mono, the spatial dimension is totally lost. Buddy Rich's playing throughout is all speed and precision–but I'd still rather hear the elegant Baby Dodds playing a quarter as many notes, or at least Dodds as echoed in Gene Krupa's more formally coherent style. Krupa was a more subtle drummer than Rich by a mile, and that's never been more clear than here. Typically, each track features a hot horn solo or two as a setup for a freight-train drum segment. Before Krupa turns loose on "Drum Boogie," Tab Smith plays alto with a big, tenory conception (mirroring the official JATP tenor style), followed by Hank Jones, who implies stride feeling in the opening measures of his piano solo. Rich's "Flying Home" (the ringer here, recorded in Hartford, 9/17/54) features Buddy DeFranco's pipsqueak/teakettle clarinet; "Perdido," with both drummers, showcases the real star of JATP, the booting tenorist Flip Phillips, who as usual combines Coleman Hawkins's verticality with a hefty dollop of R&B. Duke Ellington's "Cottontail" with Rich is one of those curious swing/bop hybrids these concerts sometimes produced. (Other personnel on "Cottontail" and "Perdido": Roy Eldridge, Charlie Shavers (tpt); Benny Carter (as); Lester Young, Flip Phillips (ts); Oscar Peterson (p); Barney Kessel (g); Ray Brown (b). "Flying Home" also has Lionel Hampton (vibes, d) and the same rhythm section. *—Kevin Whitehead,* Cadence

Drum Battle: Jazz at the Philharmonic / Verve 815146
Jazz at the Philharmonic appearances by various performers (together on the title track), with emphasis on drum solos. Certain to excite drum fanatics. *—Bob Porter*

STEVE KUHN (Stephen Lewis Kuhn)

b. Mar. 24, 1938, Brooklyn, NY
Keyboards, piano, composer / Postbop, neo-bop
Steve Kuhn often gets more attention for being one of the pianists to precede McCoy Tyner in John Coltrane's group than for his own fine playing and writing abilities. Kuhn began taking lessons at age five, and by 1959 he was accomplished enough to earn stints with Coltrane, Kenny Dorham, and Stan Getz. He was a member of the Art Farmer Quartet from 1964 to 1966. Kuhn moved to Sweden in 1967 and lived there until 1971, heading his trio throughout Europe from his Stockholm base. He returned to New York that year and headed a quartet. Since then, he has recorded and toured frequently, appearing at festivals throughout America and Europe. *—Ron Wynn*

○ **October Suite** / Nov. 1, 1967 / Impulse 9136

Raindrops (Steve Kuhn Live in New York) / Nov. 1972 / Muse 5106
A good quartet date from 1984, cut live in New York. Pianist Steve Kuhn's greatest attributes are his steady, sometimes impressive phrasing and interpretative ability; his weak links are a less than intense rhythmic capability and a derivative style. That's overcome on this session mainly because he's playing with a sympathetic rhythm section, and bassist George Mraz in particular helps push the music and increase the energy level. *—Ron Wynn*

Ecstasy / Nov. 1974 / ECM 1058
The five Steve Kuhn compositions that make up *Ecstasy* represent a thoroughly personal journey through the pianist's uncluttered world of melody, dynamics, and color. More than anything, this is an album dominated by an intense sensitivity and tumbling emotions, with Kuhn's work moving from the darkly austere to the brightly romantic. His playing can be deceptively simple as well as churning and complex. There is no paradox here, just the pianist using the instrument's full range of percussive dynamics and color. Kuhn is continuously building, the left hand often rumbling over bass chords while the right explores a simple figure; then he backs off, leaving moments of space and silence embroidered sparsely with one or two chords. If one wanted to classify Kuhn's work on this recording, it would have to be said that the dominant influence was European classical as opposed to, say, blues or contemporary jazz. But beyond any consideration of derivative style, there remains a strong, satisfying expression of Kuhn's mature musical personality. *—Herb Nolan,* Down Beat

★ **Playground** / Jul. 1979 / ECM 1059
With Sheila Jordan (v), Harvie Swartz (b), Bob Moses (d). Intense group interplay with Jordan's deep tones. Very emotional music, especially "The Zoo" and "Deep Tango." A record for the ages. *—Michael G. Nastos*

Last Year's Waltz / Apr. 1981 / ECM 1213
Live at Fat Tuesday's in New York City. "Turn To Gold" an absolute tearjerker. *—Michael G. Nastos*

Mostly Ballads / Jan. 3, 1984 / New World 351
The title tells all; pianist Steve Kuhn's menu of mostly standards and ballads, with the occasional original, is well played and recorded. Kuhn's a good, lyrical soloist, who's not among the more intense or aggressive players, instead relying on his harmonic and interpretative skills. *—Ron Wynn*

Life's Magic / Mar. 28-30, 1986 /
Live at New York City's Village Vanguard. With Ron Carter (b), Al Foster (d). Four Kuhn originals, three standards. Pristine quality of Kuhn's playing shines. *—Michael G. Nastos*

○ **Porgy** / i. Dec. 1988 / Jazz City 66053012

Looking Back / Oct. 1990 / Concord Jazz 4446

Oceans in the Sky / i. 1991 / Owl 79232

○ **Live at Maybeck Recital Hall–Vol. 13** / i. Oct. 25, 1991 / Concord Jazz 4484

L

STEVE LACY (Steven Morman Lackritz)

b. Jul. 23, 1934

Soprano saxophone, composer / Dixieland, postbop, early free, modern creative

Steve Lacy has made a career out of specializing on an instrument that, for many years, was almost completely ignored by most jazz musicians. Outside of Sidney Bechet, and, in his early days, Johnny Hodges, and until John Coltrane picked up the soprano and popularized it in the '60s, the instrument was played almost as infrequently as the cumbersome bass sax. Indeed, it was Bechet who inspired Lacy to begin playing the soprano sax. Lacy has become celebrated for his unorthodox, but compelling approach. He does everything from suck air out of the instrument to screeches, screams, squeals, irregular phrases, and swirling phrases. He began as a Dixieland player but hasn't done that for years. At one time, he and trombonist Roswell Rudd co-led a group playing almost exclusively Thelonious Monk's music, but now Lacy mainly plays originals. He's known as a free player, but has also done rock, jazz-rock, electronic music, and a combination of all the above. His concerts have increasingly mixed poetry and dramatic readings, vocal improvisations by his wife, Irene Aebi, and other things such as Japanese Kabuki and traditional Indian music.

Lacy began his professional career playing Dixieland as Steven Lackritz. He was working with much older musicians like Cecil Scott and Rex Stewart. Stewart renamed him Lacy in 1952. About three years later, Lacy moved to the opposite end of the musical spectrum. He began playing with Cecil Taylor, working in a quartet with him from 1955 to 1957. Taylor's work wasn't as completely outside then as it became, but it was heading in that direction. After Taylor, Lacy performed and recorded with Gil Evans in 1957, beginning a relationship that would see them work together periodically into the '80s. Lacy worked twice with Thelonious Monk in the early '60s, and, with Rudd, co-led a Monk repertory quartet from 1961 to 1964. Lacy did free music with a variety of artists, among them Don Cherry and Carla Bley. He toured South America with Enrico Rava, Johnny Dyani, and Louis Moholo, and moved to Rome in 1967. While there, Lacy played free, jazz-rock, electronic, and classical music, working with various Italian jazz and rock players and the Musica Elettronica Viva. He relocated to Paris in 1970.

Gradually, alto saxophonist Steve Potts, Lacy's wife Aebi on vocals and cello, bassist Ken Carter, and drummer Oliver Johnson became Lacy's working ensemble, and Aebi's wordless vocals steadily emerged as one of their trademarks. During the '80s, Lacy co-led bands with Misha Mengelberg. His recording career began with some mid-'50s dates on the Jaguar label that were straight Dixieland. He later recorded for Prestige, working with Wynton Kelly, Buell Neidlinger, Elvin Jones, and Mal Waldron. During the '60s, he recorded for European labels like Emanem, BYG, and Vik, plus American companies Atlantic, Prestige, and Candid. His mates included Rudd, Charlie Rouse, Cherry, and various French players, while one release was a solo date. His '70s sessions were recorded for Emanem, Saravah (French), Red

(Italian), Quark (Canadian), and other assorted French, Japanese, and Swedish labels. In the '80s, he continued on various foreign labels until late in the decade, when he made his return to major label RCA Novus. He also did some sessions for Silkheart. The bulk of these sessions featured his regular sextet. There's plenty of Lacy available on CD. —*Ron Wynn*

Complete Steve Lacy, The / i. Aug. 8, 1954-Nov. 24, 1954 / Fresco 1

Twofer of "progressive" Dixieland with Dick Sutton sextet. Lacy on soprano and clarinet. Interesting, considering where Lacy's music was headed. —*Michael G. Nastos*

○ **Soprano Sax / i.** Apr. 1958 / Prestige 7125
The first of three recordings soprano saxophonist Steve Lacy made for Prestige, this 11/1/57 session marks his first as a leader. There is a controlled tension to this date, like everybody's trying to play, carefully, to a common goal. Dennis Charles's drumming is metronomic, tiresome, and undaring. Buell Neidlinger (b) is in lockstep with Charles, and things really seem more at home when Lacy sits out and it becomes the Wynton Kelly (p) trio. It's hard to project back to the state of the art in 1957—but it seems in many ways that Lacy's playing here has the same spirit of freeness that Ornette Coleman had (Coleman's first revolutionary recordings were in 1958!). The two big differences here are Coleman's group was *with* him spiritually/musically, and he was playing original music. How illuminating it would have been to hear this same session with original music. Anyway, I find this music quite provocative historically, and I suspect if I had heard it in 1958 it would have seemed provocative, albeit for different reasons. Recommended in particular for the student of Lacy and/or postbop. —*Bob Rusch,* Cadence

★ **Reflections: Steve Lacy Plays Thelonious Monk / Oct. 17,** 1958 / New Jazz 063
Enamored of Thelonious Monk, Lacy stretches out on challenging harmonic material with the Mal Waldron trio. —*Michael G. Nastos*

○ **Evidence / Nov. 14, 1961 / New Jazz 1755**
Evidence finds soprano saxophonist Steve Lacy in nettle fettle with Ornetteans—incisive, prancing, right on Thelonious Monk's funny money. Every note is just ducky, each rest neatly timed, phrase after lucid phrase precisely right. Trumpeter Don Cherry, too, is in wryly inspired form, his chicken-scratching approach containing a quivering fullness vis-à-vis Lacy's limpid fishhorn. Bassist Carl Brown is light and sure, drummer Billy Higgins a bounty of good time (check "Let's Cool's" accents). Lacy's phase of preoccupation with distillations of Monk hit, for me, the peak of his checkered, often obscure career, and his music remains one of the freshest outpourings (include here dates like *School Days* on Emanem and *Straight Horn* on Barnaby/Candid) of the '60s. —*Fred Bouchard,* Down Beat

★ **Straight Horn of Steve Lacy, The / i.** Aug. 1962 / Candid 8007
Soprano saxophonist Steve Lacy, who now works exclusively in a free jazz context, was at the time of this recording heavily involved with pianist Thelonious Monk and his music. Though there are two tunes of pianist Cecil Taylor and

Charlie Parker's "Donna Lee," it is the Monk themes that are the meat and potatoes of this session. It's a real pleasure to hear "Played Twice" and "Criss Cross" executed so easily by Lacy and baritone saxist Charles Davis. This is a pianoless group in which there is a lot of spaciousness, so much in fact, one wishes to hear a pianist at times—perhaps, Monk himself. Drummer Roy Haynes and bassist John Ore, who were Monk's rhythm section at the time, play so well together that they bring to mind Monk's apparent absence from this date. Retrospectively, this is a good example of a soprano saxophonist who mastered the instrument before John Coltrane and his legion of followers. And Charles Davis displays a surprisingly fluent understanding of the vagaries of Monk's music. —*Spencer R. Weston*, Cadence

School Days / Mar. 1963 / Emanem 3316

○ **Forest and the Zoo** / i. 1966 / ESP 1060
A brilliant mid-'60s album by soprano saxophonist Steve Lacy that's textbook free work; virtually no structure; roaring, screaming solos from Lacy and comrades, including trombonist Roswell Rudd. This was poorly recorded, but the playing more than compensates for the sonic flaws. —*Ron Wynn*

○ **Scraps** / Feb. 18+21, 1974 / Sravah 10049
This sextet set is an import from France. Its finest single track is "Torments," Steve Potts's unaccompanied alto sax solo. He features an unusually full, resonant tone throughout all ranges, particularly noticeable in the lower octaves. It augments a rather Roscoe Mitchell-like sensitivity to sound detail and timing, and indeed, Potts's sense of structure and linear purpose sustain tension throughout this work's five minutes. "Obituary" is an instance of Dada wedged between two long and uneventful communal blow-outs, though a third collective improvisation, "The Wire," is nicely done, with a sounds-against-silence sequence. The group behind Steve Lacy's only solo—organette, strings, marching drums—is interesting and compensates for the quite ordinary sax. —*John Litweiler*, Down Beat

Saxophone Special / Dec. 19, 1974 / Emanem 3310

Trickles / Mar. 11+14, 1976 / Black Saint 8

○ **Sidelines** / Sep. 1, 1976 / Improvising Artists 123847
Soprano saxophonist Steve Lacy and pianist Michael Smith work well together and no doubt succeed admirably in what they set out to do, but the controlled, deliberate manner in which they play gets oppressive after two whole sides. All but two of the compositions are Lacy's, so the blame must fall on him. Certainly his playing can't be faulted—his command of the full range of the soprano sax is outstanding. Smith is a pianist who continues to intrigue me with his personal approach. His two pieces, "Austin Stream" and "Time 2," are more successful mainly due to their brevity. It's unfortunate that these two fine musicians decided to play "heavy" music without lightening it up here and there. —*Carl Brauer*, Cadence

Raps / Jan. 29, 1977 / Adelphi 5004
This is a quirky, explosive date with coconspirator Steve Potts (as). —*Ron Wynn*

Clinkers / Jun. 9, 1977 / Hat Hut CH-F
Clinkers is a solo soprano sax session in which repetition and slight variation intersect in geometric designs, with a bare minimum of rhythmic variety, all but the theme in an unstated medium four time. The softness of Steve Lacy's sound is absolutely necessary in order that this LP not be a collection of blares and screeches—the soprano sax is a singularly unlovely instrument. As a matter of fact, the warmth of his music derives directly from his soft sound and his masterful integration of inside and outside sounds: very often I couldn't be sure which notes were false in this recital. —*John Litweiler*, Down Beat

Way, The / Jan. 23, 1979 / Hat Hut 32R03
The Way is a six-piece cycle based on a Chinese text attributed to Lao Tzu. It was written by soprano saxophonist Steve Lacy and includes pieces (dedicated, variously, to John

Coltrane, Charlie Parker, Duke Ellington, and others) for each time of day: dawn, morning, noon, afternoon, evening, and night. Besides her bravura strength, vocalist Irene Aebi's most important contribution is her understanding of stress and phrasing. The ensemble solves the matters of phrasing and forward momentum in several ways, all successful. On "Raps," set in duple meter, a bass ostinato anchors the tune while Lacy solos. "Dreams," atonal and set in free time, is more difficult to absorb. Unlike "Raps," no one element is structural; responsiblity is shared by the ensemble. The group is stronger melodically (mostly because of Lacy) than rhythmically; at times the rhythm section (bassist Kent Carter and drummer Oliver Johnson) isn't tight enough to structure the music as it should. Still the ambitious mixing of styles works well, and this tune is, for the most part, a good example of how two large problems of playing new music can be solved. —*Elaine Guregian*, Down Beat

Troubles / May 24-25, 1979 / Black Saint 35

Capers / Dec. 29, 1979 / Hat Hut 142R14
Capers has four 26-minute sides dimly recorded live at the European/American Music Festival (NYC, 12/29/79), where a more playful Steve Lacy works over repeated idea kernels as intensely (and even more horizontally) as he dissected Thelonious Monk two decades earlier. Fully half of each track is given over to the "rhythm," though drummer Dennis Charles stays ever mindful of the themes (cf. "The Crunch") and excitingly dances on toms, and bassist Ronnie Boykins (on perhaps his final recording) exerts deep sympathy for the linearity that spins even these blowing tracks a bit thin. The new Lacy often restricts his shorthand lyricism to the curly heads, and his tone is usually drier and more rarefied (except on "Kitty Malone" and "Capers"). If Lacy's singing is austere, his wit is still at least as nimble as his fingers; his sopranino bestiary fascinates (rooster to puppy to hog on "Bud's Brother II"); and his wild, rarefied statements, now cut of a querulous loquacity rather than placid reserve, still place him *sui generis* on soprano. —*Fred Bouchard*, Down Beat

○ **Stamps** / Feb. 22, 1981 / Hat Hut
One disc of *Stamps* was recorded at the jazz festival in Willisau in 1977, the other at Jazz au Totem in Paris in 1978. Soprano saxophonist Steve Lacy's timbral effects are as important as the melodic and rhythmic styles in giving the music a contemporary feel. In "Names," Lacy's tone is Eastern in color: nasal and turgid, like a primitive oboe, a drone in the bass circles with a ringing pulsation. The bass's (Kent Carter) timbre is raw with overtones and well-matched to Lacy's, as is Steve Potts's saxophone sound. Lacy is just as comfortable here as he is running changes or squealing. —*Elaine Guregian*, Down Beat

Snake Out / Aug. 14, 1981 / Hat Music 3501
This is an excellent record that captures a live performance in Paris. Steve Lacy (soprano sax) and Mal Waldron (piano) make an almost perfect duo, and, even without the propulsion of a rhythm section, their music takes off. Because of their excellent organic sense of form, they create cohesive performances out of these fairly simple compositions. Lacy and Waldron blend together well yet retain their strong individual characters. Lacy's humor, knack for the unexpected, and oblique phrasing are distinctive. Waldron uses rhythmically repeated chords and gets a sound of great weight and density like no one else. Both are among the best improvisers I've heard at using repetition effectively. —*Paul Roger Barnes*, Cadence

○ **Flame, the** / i. Jan. 1982 / Soul Note 1035
The Flame was recorded in January 1982. This Steve Lacy conversation brings together Bobby Few (p) and Dennis Charles (d). "Wet Spot" is a solo spot for Few and "Gusts" and "Licks" are solo outings for Lacy (soprano sax). Lacy is a great conversationalist. I find his overall style appealing, but on this record I didn't find all that he had to say very interesting, and on repeated listenings things began to drag, particularly through "Licks" and "Flames," tracks that make up

the whole of side two. Of course, this is relative to a Lacy standard. I admit I entered into this listening relationship with expectations perhaps higher than normal—such are the burdens of being a master. I recommend one track, "The Match," a very powerful performance with both the group and individuals within the group moving/playing in-out, out-in, and exchanging leading roles with a naturalness and freedom that transcend a leadership position. This one track presents a strong statement out of proportion with the rest of the music. —*Bob Rusch, Cadence*

○ **Regeneration** / **i.** 1982 / Soul Note 1054
The consensus album of the year in 1983, it includes one side of Monk and the other of Herbie Nichols's music. Includes Roswell Rudd (tb), Misha Mengleberg (p), Kent Carter (b), and Hans Bennik (d). —*Michael G. Nastos*

Change of Season / **i.** Jul. 2-3, 1984 / Soul Note 1104
The follow-up to *Regeneration*, this features George Lewis (tb) and Anjen Garter (b). All material by Herbie Nichols. —*Michael G. Nastos*

Only Monk / 1986 / Soul Note 1160

★ **Momentum** / May 1987 / Novus 3021
This record, soprano saxophonist Steve Lacy's first on an American label in a decade (1987), is surprisingly lyrical. Only the title cut, an accelerating three-note motif based on the syllables and intervals of the word *momentum,* is dissonant. Drummer Oliver Johnson stars in this tribute to the late Kenny Clarke. "Momentum" and Lacy's other compositions stick in one's mind. "Art" and "The Song" are sung by Irene Aebi, whose austere, art-song voice remains an acquired taste. The words are by Herman Melville and Brion Gysin, respectively. "The Bath," a languid melody, is my favorite. Lacy describes the music perfectly in the liner notes: "In this scene, Henry Miller allows his favorite bum to bathe and change in his Paris flat." Lacy's Paris-based sextet is perfect for the imagery of his compositions. Bobby Few's piano is like a darker Bill Evans or a less dense Cecil Taylor, Steve Potts' alto sax echoes Lacy's intervallic approach, Jacquines Avinel's bass occupies both foreground and background, Johnson's drums are free and colorful, yet grooving, and Aebi's violin adds a mysterious European and Asian quality. The group interacts like minimalists at times, poring over each detail. But then it opens up and liberation music follows from logic. —*Owen Cordle,* Jazz Times

○ **Window, The** / Jul. 1987 / Soul Note 121185
This purified distillation of soprano saxophonist Steve Lacy's extensive improvisational experience emits a cool, yet warm glow nourishing body and soul as well as mind. Shedding his usual sextet format for the intimacy of a trio, Lacy and his soprano weave their way through sensitive backdrops spun by bassist Jean-Jacques Avenel and drummer Oliver Johnson. The view from Lacy's "window" is constantly shifting. In "Twilight" for example, we glimpse boppish romps as well as cerebral, rubatoesque meditations. "The Gleam," a celebration of good times with good companions, sparkles with spirited give-and-take dialogs covering a gamut of moods and atmospheres. Lacy is phenomenal in a kind of quirky and understated way. A sense of swing permeates everything, even in the broken-time episodes. And his unique sound is something of a cross between the visceral palpitations of Sidney Bechet and the steel edginess of John Coltrane. Lacy's control of the soprano's difficult upper range and harmonics is also notable. He never sounds as if he's pressing. It all flows. Reflecting years of collective experimentation as collaborators in Lacy's larger group, Lacy's trio offers inspired interactions that are simultaneously ethereal and earthy. —*Chuck Berg,* Jazz Times

Super Quartet Live at Sweet Basil, The / **i.** Aug. 28, 1987-Aug. 2, 1987 / Evidence 22032
Mal Waldron and Steve Lacy reunited on this four-track set recorded live at Sweet Basil's in 1987. The usually undulating, highly unorthodox Lacy sounds at times almost self-effacing, though his playing retains its sharpness and harmonic edge. But he has played looser, more quirky versions

of "Evidence" and "Let's Call This." He seems more in a commemorative than a freewheeling mood. Waldron's snaking, ripping chords and angular piano solos are more aggressive, while bassist Reggie Workman and drummer Eddie Moore alternate between providing concise support and taking their own strong solos. It is a fine date, just not as electrifying as some of Lacy's studio and independent sessions. —*Ron Wynn*

Door, The / Jul. 1988 / Novus 3049

☆ **Live at Sweet Basil** / **i.** 1991 / Novus 63128
Recorded live in a New York club with a sextet. Includes many familiar themes. Soprano saxophonist with regular working band: Steve Potts on alto and soprano sax, Irene Aebi on violin and vocal, Jean Jacques Avenel on bass, Bobby Few on piano, and John Betsch on drums. —*Michael G. Nastos*

TOMMY LADNIER (Thomas J. Ladnier)

b. May 28, 1900, Florence, LA, **d.** Jun. 4, 1939, Geneva, NY
Trumpet / New Orleans traditional

Though he didn't have a lengthy career, Tommy Ladnier made some important contributions as a trumpeter in the '20s and '30s. An excellent swinging soloist, Ladnier was a melodic conservative, but brilliantly used the cackling muted timbre that was in vogue at the time. He was influenced strongly by King Oliver's phrasing, and often adapted musical elements that are similar to the ones used by blues pianists, such as double time. Ladnier blended compelling energy with lyrical, relaxed precision. He moved to Chicago from Louisiana in 1917, and worked with such bandleaders as Ollie Powers, Fate Marable, and Oliver in the early '20s. Ladnier recorded with several blues vocalists, among them Ma Rainey. He toured Europe with Sam Wooding and worked with Billy Fowler before becoming Fletcher Henderson's principal soloist in the mid-'20s. Ladnier returned to Europe with Wooding in 1928 and 1929, also working there with Benny Peyton, heading his own band, and playing with Noble Sissle in 1930 and 1931. Ladnier worked with Sissle in both Europe and America, then became a coleader with Sidney Bechet of the New Orleans Feetwarmers in the early '30s. They briefly ran a tailor shop in New York, then Ladnier led his own group in New Jersey, worked and taught in Connecticut, and played in New York State. He recorded with Bechet and Mezz Mezzrow in 1938. Ladnier had a heart attack in Mezzrow's apartment in 1939. His work with Rainey, Henderson, and Bechet was often magnificent. He made no sessions as a leader for Bluebird, but one date he did with Mezzrow later had four songs split off and released as *Tommy Ladnier and his Orchestra.* He has no sessions available on CD. —*Ron Wynn*

★ **Tommy Ladnier** / **i.** 1954 / 'X' 3027

SCOTT LAFARO

b. 1936, **d.** 1961
Bass / Early free

A technically wondrous bassist, Scott LaFaro's contributions include being an exceptional soloist who created an original, nonbebop melodic style. His accompaniment offered rhythms that weren't timekeeping but contrapuntal, though LaFaro also played both decorative and walking-style lines. His fluid, impressive work in the Bill Evans trio and with Ornette Coleman in the early '60s was legendary. LaFaro began playing clarinet at age 14, then played tenor in high school before studying bass at Ithaca Conservatory and at Syracuse. LaFaro traveled with Buddy Morrow's band to Los Angeles. His professional career started in Chet Baker's group in the mid-'50s. He worked briefly with Ira Sullivan in Chicago, then worked in San Francisco with Sonny Rollins and Harold Land, and played with Barney Kessel. LaFaro worked, for a time, in a group that played at the Lighthouse. He moved to New York in 1959 and, after touring for a short time with Benny Goodman, joined the Bill Evans trio with Paul Motian. He played in the trio with Coleman and Stan

Getz, and also lead his own trio until he was killed in a car accident in 1961. LaFaro was 25 when he died. Though he doesn't have any recordings available on CD (or otherwise) as a leader, he can be heard on some seminal dates by Evans and Coleman including Evans's *Portrait in Jazz, Waltz for Debby*, and *Sunday at the Village Vanguard*, and on Coleman's *Free Jazz* and *Ornette.* —*Ron Wynn*

BIRELI LAGRENE

b. Sep. 4, 1966, Saverene, France
Guitar / Early jazz-rock, world fusion, modern creative
Once overly flashy and prone to fits of gimmickry, French guitarist Bireli Lagrene has learned discipline and restraint. He's harnessed his remarkable skills, and while he still plays with speed and flamboyance, he doesn't zip aimlessly across the frets, but displays ideas and substance. Lagrene has been playing guitar since childhood, and was improvising in a Django Reinhardt mode at age seven. The Reinhardt influence remains embedded in his style, but Lagrene has developed his own voicings, patterns, and approach. Both his father and grandfather were guitarists, and Lagrene's technique was fortified early in his career. He began recording for Antilles in 1980, and has since done sessions for Jazzpoint and Blue Note. Lagrene's worked with Larry Coryell, Miroslav Vitous, and Jaco Pastorius, among others. He has sessions available on CD. —*Ron Wynn and Michael G. Nastos*

Routes to Django–Live / i. 1980 / Jazz Point
Guitarist Lagrene turns in a stunning live performance on this recording, which, as the title implies, is an homage to the great guitarist Django Reinhardt. Perhaps the most extraordinary thing about this recording is the fact that Bireli is a mere 13 years old! Recommended. —*Paul Kohler*

○ **Fifteen / i.** Feb. 1982 / Antilles 848814
An early, inconsistent album by guitarist Bireli Lagrene that, despite its problems, still shows his enormous potential. At this stage, Lagrene is so intent on displaying his complete arsenal that he roams all over the fretboard on every song, throwing in extraneous lines and elaborate licks where they aren't necessary. But the album presents an early portrait of a player who's gone on to fulfill his promise. —*Ron Wynn*

★ **Foreign Affairs / Aug. 1988 / Blue Note 90967**
From the gentle opening tune, "Timothee" (to whom the album is dedicated), to the cool and mysterious "Josef," to the blistering "Senegal," the listener just keeps getting more facets of this jewel. Guitarist Bireli Lagrene demonstrates some remarkable versatility here. On Herbie Hancock's "Jack Rabbit" he plays some thrilling acoustic leads. On "Foreign Affairs" he is a rock/fusion stylist of the highest degree. On "Passing Through the Night" he even runs his lead through a voicebox gadget and manages to make it sound tasteful. At each turn, the music is riveting, fun, and even pleasant. The tunes, mostly by Lagrene, show him to be a fine writer and arranger. And he certainly knows how to assemble a crackerjack band (Koono, k; Jeff Andrews, b; Jurgen Attig, bass on "Josef"; Dennis Chambers, d; Cafe, per). On the rock-solid foundation of Chambers's and Cafe's outstanding percussion, the band rolls along like a finely tuned engine. —*Denny Townsend, Jazz Times*

Standards / i. 1992 / Blue Note
Changing his direction once again Lagrene heads full-steam into the realm of pure jazz standards. Assisted by Niels-Henning Ørsted-Pedersen (b) and Andre Ceccarelli (d), Lagrene caresses each and every song as if he himself had written it. Several Charlie Parker tunes are performed. An excellent recording–top of the pile! —*Paul Kohler*

Jazz Piano Lineage / DMP
Featured here on solo piano, Lagrene displays a vast harmonic sensibility by arranging several well-known jazz tunes into almost brand new songs. Superb recording. —*Paul Kohler*

OLIVER LAKE (Oliver Eugene Lake)

b. 1942, Marianna, AR
Alto and soprano saxophone, flute, synthesizer / Early free, world fusion, contemporary funk, modern creative
A expressive, energetic alto, tenor, and soprano saxophonist and flutist who's led free, hard bop, and reggae bands, Oliver Lake has been a consistently outstanding soloist, composer, and bandleader since the early '70s. His solos, especially on alto, have a pungent, bluesy edge that reflects Lake's bebop and R&B background. He's accomplished on tenor, soprano, and flute, but alto is his best instrument. Lake began playing drums as a child, then turned to alto sax at age 18, and to flute later. He graduated from Lincoln University in 1968, then taught for a while in public schools and played in R&B bands around the St. Louis area, while also serving as a leader in the Black Artists Group (BAG). Lake played in Paris with a quintet of BAG members from 1972 to 1974. He then moved to New York, where he played both free jazz and classical music with combos and as a soloist. With Hamiett Bluiett, David Murray, and Julius Hemphill he was a founding member of the World Saxophone Quartet in 1976, and played in a New Orleans concert. That same year Lake began a trio with Michael Gregory Jackson and Pheeroan AkLaff. In 1977, he staged the theatrical presentation *The Life Dance of Is*, for which he also wrote the music and poetry. Lake presented a program of compositions for string quartet at Carnegie Hall in 1979. Then he switched gears in the early '80s, and formed a reggae/funk/fusion unit called Jump Up. They played into the mid-'80s and recorded for Gramavision. Lake recorded in Italy in 1984 and 1985, and performed in New York with a free jazz band that included Kevin Eubanks and AkLaff. He recorded with Fred Hopkins, Geri Allen, AkLaff, and Rasul Sidik on Gramavision in 1987, and did another session in '88. Lake began recording as a leader in the '70s, and has done sessions for Arista, Sackville, Black Saint, Gramavision, Blue Heron, and Gazell. There are only a few Lake sessions currently available on CD. —*Ron Wynn*

○ **Ntu: The Point from Which Freedom Begins / 1971 / Arista 1024**
This group shows its roots in the Albert Aylerish number, "Zip," with its brief introductory fragment and coherent free solos. However, other pieces are so loosely structured as to be dull except for brief, but intelligent trumpet solos (Baikida E.J. Carroll). Oliver Lake himself solos little, sputtering out rather quickly on alto in "Africa." There is one pleasant theme "Tse'lane," a modal piece with a nice brass arrangement, a swinging piano solo by John Hicks, and a rather tentative guitar solo by Richard Martin. Drummer Charles Bobo Shaw is excellent throughout, but electric bassist Don Officier gets in the way when he tries to play straight rhythm. They were still learning here. —*Jon Goldman*, Cadence

Heavy Spirits / Jan. 1975 / Freedom
The three brief pieces by the New England Conservatory Oliver Lake Ensemble and the following solo (a Julius Hemphill song) are beautifully performed, with such clarity of harmony and dynamics that this presentation was among the year's major events (1976). The genuine beauty of the strings' sounds, harmonies, and melodies in "Movement Equals Creation"—and the remarkable lack of resemblance to any other avant-garde composer I've heard—make the work special. But the rhythmic contrasts in "Altoviolin," and particularly the contrasts of agitation and flow, project Lake's sense of drama, for the sardonic stresses verge on wicked irony. "Intensity" finds marvelous sounds in the strings' long tones, then Lake makes long tones while the fiddles play a dance. The pastoral-mourning theme of "Lonely Blacks" completes the sequence. It is broken briefly into rugged phrases, and there's a fine instant near the end when firmly stated long tones are broken by a pianissimo objection in the low register. The remainder of the disc presents Lake in more familiar surroundings, with concepts

nowhere near as ambitious. His alto style derives from several sources, and he absorbed the dramatic quality of the younger Archie Shepp as well as aspects of the far less eclectic Roscoe Mitchell. —*John Litweiler,* Down Beat

Holding Together / Mar. 1976 / Black Saint 9
Holding Together (recorded in 1976) gives us intimate miniatures on "Trailway Shake," postbop unison lines on "Hasan" that walk into a sultry Latin vamp, echoplex flute on the title tune's intro, and a tiny, farewell "Ballad." Though sharp tempo shifts and peppery unisons crop up, the main thrust is good old, brisk, and fruitful improvisatory interaction. Michael Gregory Jackson is a supple, intriguing guitarist, making unusual choices that always seem just right. Paul Maddox is a challenging drummer who knows when to lay out; his understated solo on "Macine Wing" is gripping. —*Fred Bouchard,* Down Beat

Buster Bee / Mar. 1, 1978 / Sackville 3018
These duets are not for casual listening: they demand the listener's whole attention. By far, most of the album is two alto saxes improvising; despite sometime adventures incorporating "outside" sounds, there is no harshness of sound or emotion. Bright, vivid lyrical melody leads to a sense of sunny day music, unforced, moving freely in time and space. There is more hot sax blowing in the blues "A Stand"; in the twining of lines, the shared inspiration inspires the listener in turn. The differences between the players are modified, but the act of creating together brings forth grace, respect, easy humor. Again and again each man's sensitivity to the other is tangible: here are two outstanding jazzmen renewing the discoveries of their many years' association. —*John Litweiler,* Down Beat

★ **Shine!** / Oct. 30-31, 1978 / Novus 3010
Shine! is a sort of Oliver Lake sampler: on side one, which focuses on his composing, Lake uses his version of a string quartet (three violins and a cello and no basses at all) to augment his regular trio; the remaining two pieces were recorded at a concert by that energetic threesome in late 1978. It is here that Lake's broad and authoritative instrumental saxophone vocabularly is heard to best advantage; his sound alone, be it one or three dimensional, gutturally rough or Parker-pretty, helps him mold a conversational style of great virtuosity. —*Neil Tesser,* Down Beat

Clevont Fitzhubert / Apr. 13-14, 1981 / Black Saint
Oliver Lake's (as, ss, f) *Clevont Fitshubert (A Good Friend Of Mine)* by his (1982) regular group (Bakida Carroll, tpt; Donald Smith, p; Pheeroan AkLaff, d) is refreshing, though his description of the music being mainly "collective improvisation" is misleading. Rather, the music is quite structural with members of the band improvising accompaniment within the structures, usually underneath a soloist, or, at times, a duet. Make no mistake, this is solid contemporary jazz, with open-ended expression, but it is not "group music" per se. Structures range from the Thelonious Monk-like "November '80" with strong solos from everyone to the marching "Sop" (which features some group improvisations around the sprightly melodic line and over Laff's march variations) to the slightly funky (only slightly thanks to Laff's loose fluid stylings with mallets) title cut, which includes some strong dueting from the horns, to the building free ballad "King" to the medium swing "Tap Dancer," featuring some extended work from Laff on brushes, to the melodic invocation with rolling accompaniment of "Hmbay," which conjures up images of older Pharoah Sanders music (here, though, one waits for the ostinato bass pattern that never comes). All solo and support is quite strong (with Smith's often-startling subtle juxtapositions being particularly interesting), making for a solid album. —*Bob Rusch,* Cadence

★ **Expandable Language** / Sep. 17-20, 1984 / Black Saint
Oliver Lake (as, ss, f) is one of the few postfree structuralists to record much with electric guitarists. Kevin Eubanks is the picker on *Expandable Language.* Here his tone is a compromise between rock distortion and mainstream jazz muffling,

and he doesn't bring the same assurance to Lake's roving interplay that Michael Gregory Jackson did. Obviously Lake was looking for a guitarist who thinks harmonically, not harmolodically, but on the more energetic jams (like the title track), the rest of the quintet wends its way into free territory where Eubanks seems to lose his bearings. He does play a few nice, wacky licks on the free-blowing "Comous," and he is sure-fingered and lyrical on the peppy flute feature "N.S.," where the harmonic progression is always clearly defined. Still, given pianist Geri Allen's penchant for tight, dense chords, there may be one too many rhythm instruments on hand—there are more rough edges here than on any other of Lake's freebop records. Lake's own solos are full of coiled tension, and his tunes are sleek, despite their Eric Dolphian angles. ("Soon" sounds like his cubist recasting of "The Love Boat.") Bassist Fred Hopkins and drummer Pheeroan AkLaff are typically, pleasantly loose. Lake and Allen duet on the closely plotted art song "Everybody Knows That"; "Page Four" and "Expandable Language" round out the program. —*Kevin Whitehead,* Cadence

○ **Gallery** / Jul. 1986 / Gramavision 8609
This quartet recording features pianist Geri Allen. An A+ album of angular saxophony. The cover artwork is as fascinating as the music. —*Michael G. Nastos*

○ **Boston Duets** / i. 1989 / Music & Arts 732
Here Oliver Lake works in a duet with a classically trained pianist, Donal Fox, trying out some fascinating improvisational ideas. Fox's spartan playing can run along the keyboard in the customary post-Cecil Taylor fashion, but he never aims for Taylor's critical mass. Instead, he resolves into stabbing chords and ominous vamps that often approach Ran Blake territory. He is very interesting, but his partner is brilliant. For me, the freer Lake plays, the better he sounds. Whether blowing long, serpentine melody lines or squalling and squeaking like Jimmy Lyons, he and Fox have a grand time. The Thelonious Monk "variants" are really a fragment of "I Mean You," worried by Fox's brusque stabbing and pulled to shreds by Lake's soul-based overblowing. Fox's skipping vamp on "No V.T." is countered by Lake's heated soprano, which wails on and on before turning into a nagging rhythm and blues motif that is then handed back to Fox for a pumping and gliding solo. Lake gets to recite his own poem "Tone Clone" as part of the propulsive "Segue Blues" and Fox gets his own dissonant and sinister piano solo on "Intermezzo." This is an exhausting and stunning CD. It is a dazzling workout even for Oliver Lake and I hope Donal Fox continues to find time to work in improvised music. —*Jerome Wilson,* Cadence

○ **Again and Again** / Apr. 1991 / Rhino 79468
Again and Again, a collection of eight original ballads, might be the perfect gift for that cynical friend who considers the World Saxophone Quartet, of which Oliver Lake is a member, little more than a collection of aural anarchists committed to razing the more traditional approaches to the music. *Again's* titles are—at their finest—a sublime mix of light and shadow. The leader is joined (along with drummer Pheeroan AkLaff and bassist Reggie Workman) by one of the greatest living interpreters of the ballad form—pianist John Hicks, whose subdued but sensual accompaniment and solo work on "Touch" both complement and substantially contribute to Lake's consistently bittersweet saxophone. Even so, these aren't predictable compositions. In fact, several of *Again's* themes are as difficult to gauge as love itself. —*Reuben Jackson,* Jazz Times

DONALD LAMBERT

b. 1904, **d.** 1962
Piano, vocals / Stride
Donald Lambert was a strong stride pianist who didn't make many dates, but played in such a prominent left-handed style that reportedly even the great Art Tatum wouldn't follow him. Lambert and Paul Seminole had a double piano act, but Lambert disliked playing in New York so he confined the act to bars in New Jersey. Lambert didn't do

much recording; he cut some material for Bluebird in the early '40s, and later recorded in the late '50s and early '60s for Jazzology. His reluctance to do anything except what he wanted, his penchant for show business "jazzing the classics," and the general unavailability of most of his material has led to Lambert's low profile in most jazz circles. However, pianists who've heard any of his work attest to the power, facility, and imagination his stride solos display. As would be expected, Lambert has no CDs represented currently in Spectrum. —*Ron Wynn*

BYARD LANCASTER (William Byard Lancaster)

b. Aug. 6, 1942, Philadelphia, PA
Saxophone, flute / Hard bop, early free, modern creative
An expressive alto saxophonist and bass clarinetist who mixes honking R&B and funky soul licks with searing free statements, Byard Lancaster made his mark playing blues and rock as well as animated jazz. He studied piano and saxophone as a child, then worked as a teen with J.R. Mitchell. Lancaster studied music at Troy University, Boston Conservatory, Berklee, and Howard University. He played and recorded with Sunny Murray periodically in both America and Europe from the mid-'60s until the '80s. Lancaster played with Bill Dixon and Sun Ra in the '60s, and with McCoy Tyner, Dixon, and Ra in the '70s. He also worked with Memphis Slim in Paris in the late '70s. Lancaster hasn't recorded often as a leader, but did sessions for Vortex/Atlantic and Bellows. Currently, none of his releases are available on CD. —*Ron Wynn and Michael G. Nastos*

★ **It's Not up to Us** / Dec. 19, 1966 / Vortex 2003
Byard Lancaster plays both flute and alto on this album, and the flute tracks, for me, are the more interesting. His shrill sound is quite attractive, but for depth and any fulfilled creative improvisation, jazz lovers will have to look elsewhere. Sonny Sharrock (g) has little of the solo space. This was a good buy for the jazz fringe audience but of little use to any serious collector. —*Bill Smith, Coda*

HAROLD LAND (Harold de Vance Land)

b. Dec. 18, 1928, Houston, TX
Tenor saxophone, flute, oboe / Hard bop, postbop
Harold Land was a member of the Max Roach-Clifford Brown quintet in the '50s, and co-led another quintet with Bobby Hutcherson in the late '60s and early '70s. Early in his career, he was noted for a dry tone and a rather individualistic approach. During the '60s, Land's tone became harder and his phrasing and style became more intense as he incorporated elements of John Coltrane's approach into his style. But Land was first and foremost a hard bop stylist. He began playing sax at age 16, after his interest in music increased during high school. Initially, he played in San Diego bands, then moved to Los Angeles. Land's earliest recording experience was for Savoy in 1949, when he cut four tracks with Leon Petties, Froebel Brigham, and others leading the Harold Land All Stars. He joined the Max Roach-Clifford Brown quintet in the early '50s, replacing Teddy Edwards. Land stayed in the group for about 18 months, recording with them for EmArcy, then left to play with Curtis Counce. He played with Counce from 1956 to 1958, appearing on Counce dates for Contemporary and Dootoo. He also recorded with Frank Rosolino on a Specialty date that didn't surface until the late '80s, though it was originally done in 1959. Land recorded as a leader on Contemporary in the late '50s, making one of his finest albums, *The Fox*, with Elmo Hope. He worked often with Gerald Wilson in both the '50s and '60s. During these decades, Land also divided his time between heading groups and playing with Red Mitchell. He and Mitchell recorded an album for Atlantic in 1961. There were also dates with Wes Montgomery and Kenny Dorham for Jazzland, and sessions for Imperial and Pacific Jazz. Land played with Carmell Jones, Bud Shank, Leroy Vinnegar, Gary Peacock, Thelonius Monk, and Wilson, among others. He and Hutcherson coformed a quintet in 1967, and contin-

ued until 1971. They recorded for Cadet, Mainstream, and Blue Note. Land and Blue Mitchell co-led a quintet from 1975 to 1978, recording for Concord, Impulse, and RCA. Land worked with his son, Harold Land, Jr., in Wilson's orchestra, and reunited with Hutcherson for a Muse session in the '80s. He's continued working and performing into the '90s. There are a few early Land titles, as well as a couple of more recent dates, available on CD. —*Ron Wynn*

Harold in the Land of Jazz / Jan. 14, 1958 / Contemporary 162

Grooveyard / Jan. 14, 1959 / Contemporary 7550

★ **Fox, The** / Aug. 1959 / Contemporary 343
This Harold Land session, originally issued in 1960, has four Elmo Hope tunes (only "Little Chris" and "The Fox" are by the leader) and all except for "Mirror-Mind Rose" are up-tempo. Pianist Hope's ascending ("Rose") and descending ("One Down") chord changes help shape the solos, and he plays in his quirky, modernist style. Dupree Bolton's trumpet is fleet and strident; drummer Frank Butler rides the cymbals, punctuating with odd—often heavy—snare accents; on "One Down" his tonal tom work recalls Max Roach. Land's tenor, as with the Clifford Brown/Roach band, is an interesting amalgam of bop and swing styles. —*Kevin Whitehead*, Cadence

West Coast Blues! / May 17-18, 1960 / Jazzland 146
Recorded with Wes Montgomery (g), this is another of many excellent Land albums. —*Michael G. Nastos*

Eastward Ho! Harold Land in New York / Jul. 5, 1960 / Jazzland 493

Choma / 1971 / Mainstream 344
Solid early '70s date with tenor saxophonist Harold Land, his then-musical partner vibist Bobby Hutcherson and cast that includes Land's son Harold C. on keyboards. Land is a bluesy, steady soloist whose rich sound makes a fine contrast to the fluid, energetic solos by Hutcherson. —*Ron Wynn*

Damisi / 1971-1974 / Mainstream 714
An excellent date with a touch of funk. Listen to the elegant "Pakistan." —*Michael G. Nastos*

☆ **Mapenzi** / Apr. 14, 1977 / Concord Jazz 4044
With Mitchell Quintet. With Kirk Lightsey (p), Blue Mitchell (tpt). Near essential album. —*Michael G. Nastos*

Xocia's Dance (Sue-Sha's Dance) / Oct. 22, 1981 / Muse 5272
An early '80s reunion between tenor saxophonist Harold Land and vibist Bobby Hutcherson, who co-led some vital West Coast combos in the late '60s and early '70s. Their cohesion and interaction remains intact, as does their solo prowess. Pianist George Cables and drummer Billy Higgins are also terrific. —*Ron Wynn*

EDDIE LANG (Salvatore Massaro; Blind Willie Dunn)

b. Oct. 25, 1902, Philadelphia, PA, **d.** Mar. 26, 1933, New York, NY
Guitar / Blues & jazz
Guitarist Eddie Lang ignored social conventions and made musical and cultural history in the process. He became not only the first well-known solo jazz guitarist, but also became one of the first to record with groups that featured interracial lineups. Lang's single-string solos, interspersed chords, and accompaniment using single-string lines in the middle register were quite influential, as was his rhythm playing. Lang formally studied violin for 11 years, and learned guitar from his father, who was an instrument maker as well as a guitarist. Lang had a successful partnership with violinist Joe Venuti in the early '20s, then recorded with the Mound City Blue Blowers after moving to New York in 1924. He played with Red Nichols, Jean Goldkette, Frankie Trumbauer, the Dorsey Brothers, and Paul Whiteman, and cut a series of duets with Venuti from 1926 to 1928, among them "Stringing the Blues." In 1928 and 1929 he recorded with guitarist Lonnie Johnson, using the pseudonym Blind

Willie Dunn. He recorded with the Gin Bottle Four, whose roster included Johnson and King Oliver. He played for Whiteman in 1929 and 1930, then became Bing Crosby's accompanist. Though his output and life span were short, Eddie Lang's contributions were considerable. —*Ron Wynn and Richard Lieberson*

★ **Jazz Guitar** / 1925-1932 / Yazoo 1059
Lang's solo features, plus duets with guitarists Lonnie Johnson and Carl Kress. To get the complete picture of Lang this recording should be heard in conjunction with the Joe Venuti/Eddie Lang duets (*see* Joe Venuti). —*Richard Lieberson*

☆ **Stringing the Blues** / i. Mar. 1963 / Columbia 2124

JOHN LAPORTA (John D. LaPorta)

b. Apr. 1, 1920, Philadelphia, PA
Tenor and alto saxophone, clarinet, teacher / Cool
A good clarinetist and an outstanding alto saxophonist, John LaPorta made contributions to groups led by two of jazz's most mercurial composer/performers: Lennie Tristano and Charles Mingus. His clarinet solos for Tristano and Mingus were expressive, searching, and intense. LaPorta played in the Bob Chester and Woody Herman big bands in the '40s, and began studies with Tristano and other teachers. He recorded with Tristano in 1947, and was a founding member, with Mingus, Teo Macero, and others, of the Jazz Composers' Workshop in New York in 1953. He later began teaching at the Manhattan School of Music, and has been on the faculty at Berklee since the late '50s. LaPorta recorded for Fantasy and Everest. He's been featured recently on a new recording, but none of his older sessions are available currently on CD. LaPorta can be heard on Tristano and Mingus reissues. —*Ron Wynn*

Clarinet Artistry of John LaPorta, The / Jan. 30, 1957 / Fantasy 3248

ELLIS LARKINS (Ellis Lane Larkins)

b. May 15, 1923, Baltimore, MD
Piano / Stride, boogie-woogie, swing
Few have attained as much fame for accompaniment as pianist Ellis Larkins, the player of choice for numerous singers. Blessed with an impeccable ear and an ability to provide absolutely perfect support for any vocalist, Larkins has done numerous recordings and sessions. Larkins's father was a janitor and a part-time violinist who played in a local Baltimore orchestra. Larkins studied at the Peabody Conservatory and at Juilliard, and worked in New York clubs in the '40s and '50s. He debuted in a trio led by Billy Moore at Cafe Society in New York. Larkins worked sporadically in New York at the Blue Angel in the '40s and '50s, and played at Cafe Society in Edmond Hall's sextet in the mid-'40s. He accompanied Mildred Bailey on a Majestic recording session, then worked with Coleman Hawkins and Dickey Wells at Signature. He accompanied Joe Williams, Larry Adler, and Chris Connor in the '50s, as well as Ruby Braff on sessions for Vanguard and Bethlehem. Larkins began recording for Decca, but took time off from performing to concentrate on studio duties. He returned in the '70s doing several dates on Antilles, Chiaroscuro, Classic Jazz, and Concord. He also recorded with Braff, Sylvia Sims, and Ella Fitzgerald. Larkins performed at Town Hall in 1973, and toured South America with Marian McPartland, Teddy Wilson, and Earl Hines in 1973 and 1974. Larkins worked in the late '70s and through the '80s at New York clubs, among them Gregory's, Michael's Pub, the Cookery, and Carnegie Tavern. Larkins was featured in Concord's acclaimed *Live at Maybeck Hall Series* in 1992. He also has a session available on an Audiophile CD. —*Ron Wynn*

★ **Blues in the Night** / Jun. 21, 1951-Jan. 9, 1952 / Decca 5391
Stomping blues, charming ballads, and dazzling interpretations of standards by pianist Ellis Larkins, one of the most underrated players from the swing era still active. This al-

bum was done in early '50s, when Larkins was making more-animated releases than he does today. —*Ron Wynn*

○ **Live at Maybeck Recital Hall–Vol. 22** / i. 1992 / Concord Jazz 4533

PETE LAROCA (Peter Sims)

b. Apr. 7, 1938
Drums / Hard bop, Latin jazz
Pete LaRoca was an excellent player who stopped playing when he was unable to find enough regular dates. Though he was among the more advanced drummers of his day, gifted at providing rhythmic variety, texture, shifts, and tempo changes, LaRoca wasn't interested in the emerging jazz-rock sound of the '60s. He decided to become an attorney and left jazz behind. LaRoca returned to music in 1979, and has worked periodically since. He studied classical percussion at the High School of Music and Art and the Manhattan School of Music. He changed his name from Pete Sims to Pete LaRoca when he played timbales in various Latin groups. LaRoca worked with Sonny Rollins in the late '50s, then played with Jackie McLean, Slide Hampton, Tony Scott, John Coltrane, Marian McPartland, Art Farmer, Charles Lloyd, Paul Bley, and Steve Kuhn. He led his own groups and was house drummer at Boston's Jazz Workshop club in 1963 and 1964. LaRoca made a couple of recordings for Blue Note and Douglas in the '60s. He can be heard on many reissues featuring Rollins, McLean, Bley, Kuhn, and others. —*Ron Wynn and Michael G. Nastos*

★ **Basra** / May 19, 1965 / Blue Note 84205

PRINCE LASHA (William B. Lawsha)

b. Sep. 10, 1929, Fort Worth, TX
Saxophone, flute / Early free, modern creative
A Texas alto saxophonist and flutist, Prince Lasha definitely doesn't fit the pattern of a classic honking R&B stylist. Instead, he played in many free bands during the '60s, and worked, at one time, with Eric Dolphy. Lasha's solos are often furious and energized; not as harmonically creative or inventive as Dolphy's, but almost as aggressive. Lasha worked with Ornette Coleman in a local band during the early '50s. He moved to California after touring the South with territory bands in 1954. Lasha recorded two exciting, if uneven, albums with Sonny Simmons in the early '60s. He returned to New York, leading a band at Birdland, while playing and recording with Eric Dolphy and a group co-led by Elvin Jones and Jimmy Garrison. Lasha headed his own band in the mid-'60s, recorded an album, then moved to Europe. He made another album there in 1966, then returned to California. Lasha has recorded with his own groups at various intervals in the '60s, '70s, and '80s. He's also done sessions with Harold Land, Bobby Hutcherson, Charles Moffett, and Michael White. Currently, none of his releases are available on CD. —*Ron Wynn and Michael G. Nastos*

★ **Cry, The** / Nov. 21, 1962 / Contemporary 7610

Firebirds Live–Vol. 1-3 / May 1974 / Birdseye Series 99001
Vol. 1, recorded at the Fifth Avenue Garde festival at U.C. Berkeley, is characterized by what Nat Hentoff once called the "affirmative lyricism" of multi-instrumentalist Prince Lawsha (Lasha). It is free jazz—free rhythms rather than meter, free polyphony rather than a chart with changes—but it is accessible free jazz. Lawsha leads the way on alto, flute, and clarinet. His lines have an unmistakable boppish bent; his speed ccn be dazzling, but his articulation is always as clean as jewels on a chain. In comparison, tenor saxophonist Hadley Caliman has more blues in his music and less ingenuity. Vibist Bobby Hutcherson is in top form. Drummer Charles Moffett plays colorfully and always musically, freely mixing the crack of sticks, the pat and taps of brushes, and the shimmer of cymbals. The jazz on *Vol. II*, recorded at the 1974 Berkeley Jazz Festival, is much closer to the mainstream. The tunes are all played in regular meters, pinned down nicely by Ron Carter's walking bass, Hubert Eaves's pi-

ano comping, and Roy McCurdy's cymbal-dominated drumming. Above this conventional rhythm section, Lawsha runs free. He hovers around the groove constantly, but only occasionally slips into it. His baritone playing is relaxed but not as fresh as his alto work. Coming from the stage of the 1975 Monterey Jazz Festival, *Vol. III* was better recorded than the first two volumes. It is also the most intense of the three volumes, and overall it contains the most consistent performances. *Vol. III* is also noteworthy because it reunites the original Firebirds, one of the most creative if unsung groups of the '60s, who recorded twice, with slight personnel shifts, for Contemporary. "Scarlet Ibis Birds" is a forceful 17-minute opus, thick with sounds but never impenetrable. Lawsha's Islamic leanings are most pronounced here, especially when he plays in a Middle Eastern-flavored mode while Moffett strikes the tambourine, Sonny Simmons calls on English horn, and Buster Williams drones on bass. Buster Williams performs beautifully throughout the album, playing not only with accuracy and resonance but always with appropriateness—walking, droning, sliding, bowing at just the right times. Hutcherson has less room to stretch out here than on *Vol. I*, which is a disappointment, but he is an integral part of the music's varied and vivid coloring. —*Douglas Clark*, Down Beat

BILL LASWELL

b. 1950

Bass, producer / Early jazz-rock, M-Base, modern creative
Bassist/producer Bill Laswell has made important contributions to many jazz, jazz-rock, and pop sessions as a performer and behind the scenes. As a bassist, he played with Material, Curlew, and Last Exit, where his pounding riffs and accompaniment were a good match for the slashing riffs of Sonny Sharrock, Peter Brotzmann's outside playing, and Ronald Shannon's drumming. Laswell also helped to establish record labels OAO and Celluloid. He produced sessions for Herbie Hancock, Material, Curlew, James "Blood" Ulmer, Manu Dibango, Fela Kuti, and pop/rock performers Iggy Pop, Motorhead, Laurie Anderson, Gil Scott-Heron, Yoko Ono, Public Image Limited, Mick Jagger, and Nona Hendryx. Some of his productions have been controversial; Gil Scott-Heron expressed disdain with Laswell's method of stripping away a lot of his vocals, while his decision to eliminate Fela Kuti's sax solos and substitute others triggered negative comments. Laswell's best playing may be on the album *Basslines* with John Zorn. He has several sessions available on CD both as a performer and producer. —*Ron Wynn*

★ **Hear No Evil** / **i.** 1988 / Venture 90888

YUSEF LATEEF (William Evans)

b. Oct. 9, 1920, Chatanooga, TN
Reeds, composer / Hard bop, world fusion, new age
Yusef Lateef was exploring fusions of jazz with Asian and Middle Eastern rhythms, instruments, and concepts without fanfare long before "world beat" or world fusion was in vogue. A hard-blowing bebop and hard bop tenor saxophonist, Lateef expanded his stylistic menu, doubling on many non-Western instruments and moving beyond straight jazz into a wide range of styles and sounds. A gifted player, Lateef's tenor had a hard, full, and robust sound. His flute playing was lyrical, moving, and fluid. Lateef mastered such unconventional instruments as the argol (double clarinet that sounds similar to a bassoon), shanai (a North Indian oboe), algaita (West African oboe), and many flutes, among them the homemade bamboo and pneumatic bamboo. Lateef added the regular oboe and bassoon. Lateef has published technical playing manuals, and has been a painter. He has written compositions for everything from jazz combos to chamber ensembles.

His family moved from Chattanooga to Detroit when Lateef was five. He began playing tenor at age 18, and studied with Teddy Buckner. During the mid-'40s, Lateef worked with Lucky Millinder, Hot Lips Page, Roy Eldridge, and Herbie Fields. Following a move to Chicago, Lateef worked

with Dizzy Gillespie in 1949 and 1950. He then returned to Detroit, where he studied flute and composition at Wayne State University. He changed his name from Bill Evans to Yusef Lateef in the mid-'50s, and co-led quintets with Curtis Fuller and Wilbur Harden in the mid- and late '50s. In 1958, he also worked with Kenny Burrell, who encouraged him to play flute more often. Lateef moved to New York in 1959, where he played and recorded with Charles Mingus, Grant Green, and Donald Byrd. Lateef joined Cannonball Adderley's band in 1962, and remained with the band until 1964.

He performed as a leader into the '80s, when he left America temporarily to teach in Nigeria. Lateef's recording career as a leader began with a session for Savoy in 1957. He continued on Prestige/New Jazz, Argo, and Savoy in the late '50s. Lateef co-led quintets for Vee Jay sessions in the '60s, and recorded on the Charlie Parker label. Later came dates for Riverside, Prestige, Impulse, and Atlantic. Lateef continued on Atlantic and CTI in the '70s, before taking a hiatus from the studio. He returned in 1983 with the album *In Nigeria* on Landmark. Lateef again recorded on Atlantic in the late '80s, and has issued a pair of sessions in the '90s. He has a good selection of recent dates and classic reissues on CD. The holder of an MA and a doctorate in education, Lateef once taught at CUNY until New York City went bankrupt. Currently, he's an instructor at the University of Massachusetts in Amherst. —*Ron Wynn*

○ **Morning** / Apr. 5, 1957 / Savoy 2205
This collection compresses the material originally issued on three Savoy LPs onto two records—modern technology, etc.—but would be well worth the price even if it didn't. Yusef's quintet stars Curtis Fuller, fleet and driving on trombone; Hugh Lawson on piano; Louis Hayes on drums; and Ernie Farrow on bass and rabat, a one-stringed Eastern axe that appears only once. Another bassist, the redoubtable Doug Watkins, plays "finger cymbals and miscellaneous percussion." By the time of this date (1957), Lateef's interest in the music of the Middle and Far East had already led him to skirt with modality; his flute work, making its debut on these sessions, is generally considered to have helped pioneer that instrument's jazz development; and "Happyology" is alive with Lateef's stylized African vocalizations. Yet on "Yusef's Mood" he cooks on tenor through a jump band riff-jam. This set is panoramic and an important part of an unusual musician's past. —*Neil Tesser*, Down Beat

○ **Prayer to the East** / Oct. 10, 1957 / Savoy 12117

○ **Yusef Lateef** / Oct. 11, 1957-Dec. 29, 1961 / Prestige 24007
This double-record set is a reissue of selected material originally found on three New Jazz albums entitled *Other Sounds, Cry Tender,* and *Into Something.* The music on these sides was recorded between 1957 and 1961 and I consider that a rich period for jazz music. Lateef's main appeal seems to be his use of instruments such as the flute, oboe, and argol as well as his Eastern-influenced compositions. It is his full-bodied straightahead tenor saxophone blowing that I personally consider his chief asset. This man swings so naturally and with such warmth that I would place him among the ranks of my favorite tenor saxophonists. Lateef's playing is imbued with his individual character and is readily identifiable. The sidemen here are all solid players in their own right, though overlooked ones. Hugh Lawson comes out of the Detroit tradition of piano players headed by the two masters Barry Harris and Tommy Flanagan. Lawson has been a long-ignored musician but is a highly consistent performer who exhibits a swinging, fluent keyboard always in the best of taste. Harris himself appears on two tracks and as always shows why he deserves the acclaim such writers as Mark Gardner and Ira Gitler bestow upon him. Wilbur Harden on flugelhorn and Lonnie Hillyer on trumpet both make effective contributions in their Milesian stylistic bags. Herman Wright and Ernie Farrow provide stellar support, as do drummers Oliver Jackson, Frank Gant, and Elvin Jones. —*Peter Friedman*, Coda

Latin Jazz

W.C. Handy employs "tango" elements in St. Louis Blues

The 1930s Latin Dance Bandleaders:
Don Azpiazu (popularized rumba)
Xavier Cugat
Noro Morales
Prez Prado

1930s-1940s
1929   Juan Tizol (1900-1984) w/Duke Ellington
1930s   Noro Morales (1911-1964)
1940s   Cuban Instrument, players
        Machito's (1912-1984) Afro-Cubans
1947   Dizzy Gillespie's Afro-Cuban Jazz Orchestra
        Chano Pozo (1915-1948)–conga
        Stan Kenton (1911-1979)
        Brazilian Laurino Almeida (1917)–guitarist
        Jack Costanzo (1922)–bongos
        Tito Rodriquez (1923-1973)
        Benny More (1924-1963)

1950s Latin Dances
Mambo
Merengue
Cha Cha Cha

Jazz Musicians into Latin Sounds
Charlie Parker (1920-1955)
George Shearing (1919)
Cal Tjader (1925-1982)
Horace Silver (1928)
Sonny Rollins (1930)
Herbie Mann (1930)
Dizzy Gillespie (1917-1993)
Stan Getz (1927-1991)
Terry Gibbs (1924)

Main Jazz/Latin Influence
Tito Puente (1923)
Mario Bauza (1911-1993)
Arsenio Rodriquez (1930)

The 1960s
Brazilian Influence
   Samba
   Bossa Nova
      Charlie Byrd (1925)
      Stan Getz (1927-1991)
      Astrud Gilberto (1940)
      Antonio Carlos Jobim (1927)
Cuban Influence
   Mongo Santamaria (1922)
   Ray Barretto (1929)
   Willie Bobo (1934-1983)
   Eddie Palmieri (1936)
   Jerry Gonzalez
   Charlie Palmeri (1927-1988)
   Fania All Stars
Brazilian (second round–1970s)
   Airto Moreira (1941)
   Weather Report (1970-1988)
   Flora Purim (1942)
   Gilberto Gil (1942)
   Milton Nascimento (1942)
   Djavan (1950)
   Tom Ze
   Margareth Menzies
   Joyce
   Elis Regina (1945-1982)
   Caetano Veloso (1942)
   Eliane Elias
   Azymuth

1970s & 1980s
Arturo Sandoval (1949)
Johnny Pacheco (1935)
Reuben Blades (1948)
Willie Colon (1950)
Celia Cruz
Nana Vasconcelos w/Pat Metheny's jazz-rock groups
Paquito D'Rivera (1948) (Afro-Cuban jazz)
Francisco Mora
Victor Para – Milton Cardona
Sonora Mantacera – Hermeto Pascoal
Irakere (1973) – Los Van Van

Yusef Lateef Plays for Lovers / Oct. 11, 1957+Dec. 29, 1961 / Prestige 7447

Blues for the Orient / Oct. 1957-Sep. 1961 / Prestige 24035
Fine compilation that combines late '50s and early '60s sessions by multi-instrumentalist Yusef Lateef. He's in the midst of a transition that would soon see him exploring an African/Asian/African-American musical mix. But he's still doing mostly hard bop on this session, backed by a lineup that includes Wilbur Harden on flugelhorn, pianist Barry Harris, bassist Ernie Farrow, and drummers Lex Humphries or Oliver Jackson. Farrow doubles on rabat. —*Ron Wynn*

☆ **Angel Eyes** / Jun. 11, 1959 / Savoy 2238
Outstanding late '50s jazz with Lateef not yet in his pioneering worldbeat/international music phase. —*Ron Wynn*

★ **Cry! / Tender** / Oct. 16, 1959 / Prestige 482
First-rate '50s work covers a diversity of jazz standards, European folk, and blues, with Yusef on tenor, flute, and oboe fronting a midsized group. —*Myles Boisen*

Centaur and the Phoenix, The / Oct. 4+6, 1960 / Riverside 337
Rare 1960 session with multi-instrumentalist Yusef Lateef featured playing with a large orchestra. This is a concept album and was one of the last times that Latef played almost totally Western instruments. He did do other large group recordings later, but they weren't strictly jazz like this one. —*Ron Wynn*

○ **Many Faces of Yusef Lateef, The** / May 1961-Jun. 1961 / Milestone 47009

☆ **Eastern Sounds** / Sep. 5, 1961 / Prestige 612
Asian sounds abound here, as well as a couple of movie themes, with accompaniment by Barry Harris on piano and bass and drums. —*Myles Boisen*

○ **Into Something** / Dec. 29, 1961 / New Jazz 700

○ **Live at Pep's** / Jun. 29, 1964 / Impulse

A Flat, G Flat and C / Mar. 8, 1966 / Impulse 9117

☆ **Golden Flute, The** / Jun. 15-16, 1966 / Impulse

★ **Blue Yusef Lateef, The** / 1968 / Atlantic 82270

○ **Re-Evaluations: The Impulse Years** / **i.** Jun. 1974 / Impulse 92592
Spanning the years 1963-1966, these cuts find Yusef Lateef working out on several different instruments, most of which were simply unheard of in the jazz world at the time. And if, consequently, the recordings at hand don't sound revolutionary today, it's probably because they didn't really sound that way then, either. Lateef shared with a handful of other musicians the gift of transmuting standard sows' ears into silken purses of jazz. His selections ranged from the exotic to the excruciatingly familiar, while his compositions (over half of these tunes are originals) combined theories native to jazz—bop, ballad form, and lots and lots of blues—with just enough atonality, Orientalisms, and rhythmic experimentation to produce an alloy both scintillating and durable. — *Steve Metaliz*, Down Beat

Gentle Giant / Jul. 5-6, 1974 / Atlantic 1602

In Nigeria / **i.** 1983 / Landmark 502
In this 1983 session, Lateef plays with more vigor and fire than on most of his recent sessions. —*Ron Wynn*

○ **1984** / 1984 / Impulse 84

Nocturnes / Feb. 1989 / Atlantic 81977
A sizable improvement over his last, although it still doesn't approach the levels of his past Impulse and Atlantic albums. —*Ron Wynn*, Rock & Roll Disc

Meditations / **i.** 1990 / Atlantic 82093

AZAR LAWRENCE

b. Nov. 3, 1953, Los Angeles, CA
Tenor and soprano saxophone / Hard bop, neo-bop
A prominent John Coltrane disciple, Azar Lawrence exploded on the jazz scene in the '70s during a stint with McCoy Tyner. His powerful, rippling tenor solos were featured on several Tyner albums, but his star has diminished since then. Lawrence started studying piano and violin at age five, then turned to tenor and soprano late in his teens. He worked with Horace Tapscott and studied informally with Arthur Blyth. Lawrence toured Europe with Clark Terry and worked with Ike and Tina Turner, the Watts 103rd Street Rhythm Band, and Elvin Jones before joining Tyner in 1973. He spent four years with Tyner, and provided some exciting moments while also playing with Miles Davis and making his recording debut as a leader. Lawrence's first post-Tyner album was a fusion date. He's recorded as a leader for Prestige, but currently none of his sessions are listed as available on CD. —*Ron Wynn*

★ **Bridge into the New Age** / May 1974+Sep. 1974 / Prestige 10086
As builders, tenor and soprano saxophonist Azar Lawrence and his producers (Orrin Keepnews and Jim Stern) laid a sturdy foundation with Lawrence's recording debut as a leader. Marshaling fine sidemen, finding a suitable and sensitive lyricist (Ray Straugher) and the perfect corresponding vocalist (Jean Carn), coming up with fresh material and arrangements to showcase his talents as a saxist and composer, Lawrence made all the right choices. The title cut features traditional African sounds and an invitation feelingly sung by Jean Carn to enter "the land where children dance," while drummer Billy Hart and bassist Clint Houston spread rhythms like chasms for Lawrence to leap. Trumpeter Woody Shaw's solo is surefooted, alternately smoky and piercing. The age Lawrence is building toward is the future, of course, and he starts well with distinctive melodies, rhythmic complexities, and energetic, emotional blowing, offering joyful and affirmative sensuality in sounds. —*Howie Mandel*, Down Beat

Summer Solstice / Mar. 29, 1975+May 1, 1975 / Prestige 10097
This is a mellow, controlled chaos, threatening to break its melodious bounds but never quite taking that giant step. Azar Lawrence's perceptions are his own. Both pianist Albert

Daily and guitarist Amaury Tristao are blessed with splendid chops, yet they stay in the background. The best keyboard solo, Dailey's excursion on "Point Of Love," is quite accessible, and Lawrence's soprano sings along in crystal clarity. Lawrence's tone throughout is pure, and given the foible of sporadic predictability, still quite inventive. Unencumbered by stock funkisms, such compositions as "Highway" and "Novo Ano" are greatly aided by the stellar work of Raul de Souza on trombone. True teamwork is the keynote here. Ron Carter's tasteful underpinning on bass is no surprise. Drummer Billy Hart stimulates Lawrence to new heights on "Summer Solstice." And buried deep in the mix are the percussive tools of Guilherme Franco. Sparingly used, their collective rings and clanks never take center stage but lurk in the background, the rhythmic strikes of their master another propulsive device. —*Arnold Shaw*, Down Beat

HUBERT LAWS

b. Nov. 10, 1939, Houston, TX
Flute, tenor saxophone / Postbop, early jazz-rock, instrumental pop
While he's a virtuoso flutist, Hubert Laws hasn't always displayed or taxed that skill. His flute solos are played with an impressive tone and sound, but other than his classical sessions they've often been featured on lightweight instrumental pop dates. Laws is also a competent saxophonist. He took a hiatus from recording in the late '80s, but returned with a new project in 1993. Laws was a member of the Jazz Crusaders at age 15, playing with childhood friends Joe Sample, Wilton Felder, Stix Hooper, and Wayne Henderson. He also studied and played classical music in Houston. Laws recorded for Atlantic and CTI in the '60s and '70s, and also played in the New York Jazz Sextet for several years. He was a member of the Metropolitan Opera Orchestra and played with the New York Philharmonic. Laws's CTI album, *Afro-Classic*, was a huge hit, and he also enjoyed success with *Morning Star*. During the '80s, Laws worked with Jean-Pierre Rampal and cut some instrumental pop dates for Columbia before his hiatus. He has recorded as a leader for Atlantic, CTI, and Columbia. Laws has several sessions available on CD. —*Ron Wynn*

★ **Afro-Classic** / Dec. 1970 / Columbia 44172
This is by far the best solo work Laws has on record. He sets the standard for classical-influenced modern jazz. —*Ron Wynn*

Best of Hubert Laws / **i.** 1970-1975 / Columbia 45479

○ **Rite of Spring** / Jun. 1971 / Columbia 40693

○ **Wild Flower** / Jan. 27, 1972 / Atlantic 1624
A nice date from an earlier Laws period with a harder tone and more traditional jazz direction. —*Ron Wynn*

○ **In the Beginning** / **i.** Sep. 1974 / CTI 3+3
The amazing thing about flutist Hubert Laws's music is that it can appeal to a broad range of musical tastes without making any sort of commercial concessions. How does Laws accomplish this? First, he gathers together a crack rhythm section as tight and well-balanced as any I've heard. Ron Carter's time and giantic tone probably need little description, but the playing of drummer Steve Gadd might. His accents uncannily anticipate and complement Carter's bass lines; his bass drum patterns are incredible (check the cooker "Airegin"); he seems comfortable in everything from free music to sanctified 12/8; and if this isn't enough, he's a master of the declining art of brush playing (note "Reconciliation"). Bob James, who does most of the keyboard work on the album, is another musician to watch for. He contributes several cohesive, facile, and well-structured solos. Laws himself is in little danger of being upstaged by his sidemen. He's become a master improviser who weaves logical musical statements while never sounding mathematical or premeditated. At times, especially during his extended duet with Gadd on Sonny Rollins's "Airegin," Laws

comes close to matching Rollins's own virtuosity. —*Jon Balleras,* Down Beat

San Francisco Concert / Oct. 4, 1975 / Columbia 40819

HUGH LAWSON (Richard Hugh Jerome Lawson)

b. Mar. 12, 1935, Detroit, MI
Piano, composer, arranger / Bop, hard bop
A compelling bebop piano stylist, especially on standards, Hugh Lawson has played quietly, but superbly on many topflight sessions since the mid-'50s. Despite being an excellent soloist and possessing skills the equal of anyone currently active, Lawson doesn't have as much name recognition as several other equally worthy, but not superior stylists. He was very influenced by Bud Powell, but has developed his own voicings, phrasing, and approach. Lawson worked with Yusef Lateef in the mid-'50s and '60s, both in Detroit and in New York. He also recorded with Harry Edison and Roy Brooks in the '60s, and with Lateef again. Lawson continued recording in the '70s, this time with Kenny Burrell and Brooks again. He gained some fame for his role in helping form the Piano Choir, a group of seven keyboardists that recorded for Strata East. Lawson toured Europe with Charles Mingus in the mid- and late '70s, then made his own Middle East tour in the early '80s. Lawson recorded with Charlie Rouse and cut trio sessions in the late '70s and early '80s, then worked with former Mingus group members George Adams and Dannie Richmond in Italy. He taught composition and jazz improvisation at the Henry Street Settlement in New York. Lawson's done sessions for Soul Note and Storyville, and currently has a couple of dates available on CD. —*Ron Wynn*

JANET LAWSON

b. Nov. 13, 1940, Baltimore, MD
Vocals / Postbop, ballads, neo-bop
An intriguing vocalist who creates new nuances that others will not attempt, Lawson can swoop and soar or sing a straight lyric with her pliant, resounding voice. —*Michael G. Nastos*

☆ **Janet Lawson Quintet** / Mar. 28, 1980 / Inner City 1116
Features the same band as *Dreams Can Be.* Tunes are by Fats Waller, Bob Dorough, Thelonious Monk, Blossom Dearie, and Sam Brown. Lawson's creative voice comes through and the bandmates are locked in. This is artistry on such a high level that it may take some getting used to. —*Michael G. Nastos*

○ **Dreams Can Be** / May 1983 / Omnisound 1052
Lawson, called "the dream jazz voice," is a wise and wondrous improviser. She can scat, whir, and whisper with inventive and singular purpose. Noncompromising. —*Michael G. Nastos*

YANK LAWSON (John Rhea Lawson)

b. May 3, 1911, Trenton, MO
Trumpet / Dixieland
A stalwart veteran, trumpeter Yank Lawson's played both pop and jazz classics with flair, wit, and a sophisticated, classy edge since the '20s. His swinging tone, evocative blues, and accomplished technique have made Lawson's solos delightful on uptempo numbers, rags, ballads, or originals. He turned to trumpet as a teen after taking piano and saxophone lessons as a child. Lawson studied at the University of Missouri and worked with Wingy Manone in the '30s. He joined Ben Pollack in the mid-'30s, playing with his band until 1934. Lawson was a cofounder of Bob Crosby's orchestra with several Pollack band members in 1935. His skills, plus the composition "Five Point Blues," helped build Lawson's reputation. He worked with Tommy Dorsey in the late '30s, and was featured on such hits as "Milenberg Joys" and "Hawaiian War Chant." Lawson returned to Crosby briefly in the early '40s, then joined Benny Goodman. After leaving Goodman, Lawson did various radio, recording, and, later, television dates. He was featured

on a great Frank Sinatra version of "Stormy Weather" in the '40s, and led a recording band with Bob Haggart in the '50s and early '60s. Louis Armstrong tabbed Lawson to play the role of King Oliver on his album "A Musical Autobiography." Lawson worked with Armstrong again in the early '60s at the Newport Jazz Festival, then played at Condon's in New York. Those performances, plus stints with the Greats of Jazz from 1965 to 1969, and in Crosby band reunions led to the formation of the World's Greatest Jazz Band with Haggart in 1968. The group lasted for over a decade; Haggart and Lawson continue to play together periodically. Lawson's led his own band and has appeared at various Crosby reunions. He's recorded for the Riverside, Decca, Signature, ABC-Paramount, and Project labels, among others. Currently, Lawson has a few sessions available on CD. —*Ron Wynn*

World's Greatest Jazz Band—Vol. 1 / **i.** 1968 / Project 3 5033

World's Greatest Jazz Band—Vol. 2 / **i.** 1968 / Project 3 5039

★ **Live** / **i.** 1970 / Atlantic 90982

JEANNE LEE

b. Jan. 29, 1939, New York, NY
Vocals / Early free, modern creative
Jeanne Lee combines acrobatic vocal maneuvers with a deeply moving sound and quality that allows her to alternate between soaring, upper-register flights and piercing, emotive interpretations. She's extremely precise and flexible, and moves from a song or solo's top end to its middle and bottom, accompanying an instrument with a stunning ease. Though many critics have cited Lee as creating free jazz's most innovative vocal approach, she's done very little recording, almost none of it as a leader and even less on American labels. She's best known for her many sessions with Gunther Hampel. Lee studied dance rather than music at Bard College, and met Ran Blake while she was a student there. They formed a duo, and she did her first recordings with him, which excited many critics. They toured Europe in 1963. Lee moved to California in 1964, and worked with Ian Underwood and sound poet David Hazelton, whom she later married. She and Hampel established their musical relationship while Lee was in Europe in 1967. Lee recorded with Archie Shepp, Sunny Murray, and Hampel in the late '60s, and with Marion Brown, Anthony Braxton, Enrico Rava, and Andrew Cyrille in the '70s, while working with Cecil Taylor. She began composing extensively in the '80s, and, in recent years, has concentrated on performing her original material, which frequently includes poetic and dance components. Lee's written five- and ten-part extended works. Most of her recordings have been done for either European labels or for small independents. Only a couple of Lee's sessions, one a reissue of early duets with Blake, are available on CD. —*Ron Wynn*

★ **Legendary Duets** / Nov. 15, 1961-Nov. 16, 1961 / Bluebird 6461
With Ran Blake. It's an appropriate title. A must-buy for creative music listeners. Jeanne Lee does vocals; Ran Blake is on piano. —*Ron Wynn*

MICHEL LEGRAND

b. Feb. 24, 1932, Paris, France
Arranger, composer / Progressive big band, instrumental pop
Michel Legrand is a well-known pop music composer. He works with symphonies and does not have much connection to jazz, but jazz players appreciate his melodies. —*Michael G. Nastos*

○ **I Love Paris (Features Miles Davis)** / **i.** 1954 / Columbia 555

★ **Legrand Jazz** / 1957-1958 / Philips 830074
Michel Legrand's "Southern Routes" on *Legrand Jazz* is a suite based on his sound track for the film "Les Routes de la Sud"—a work of evolving lines and shifting moods with fine

solos by alto saxophonist Phil Woods, baritone saxophonist Gerry Mulligan, and trumpeter Jon Faddis backed by a 16-piece band whose sounds range from driving brass to delicate harp. Sometimes harp strings are stroked in a series of breaks during blazing trumpet, alto, and baritone solos. Legrand's orchestrations make effective use of his forces, from a single instrument to a full brass section. While Legrand is a real talent as composer and arranger, as a jazz pianist he relies on dragging out clichés, rather than playing fresh ideas that relate to the written music and what the soloists are doing—Woods and Mulligan burning at fast tempos and Faddis playing a slow blues, alternately bright and sad. —*Jerry de Muth*, Down Beat

○ **I Love Paris (Features Miles Davis)** / **i.** 1960 / Columbia 8237

○ **Michel Legrand at Shelly Manne's Hole** / Jan. 1968 / PolyGram 834827
A good upbeat mainstream session. Legrand shines as an improviser. —*Ron Wynn*

○ **After the Rain** / May 28, 1982 / Pablo 139

Compact Jazz: Michel Legrand / **i.** Jan. 8, 1991 / PolyGram 840944

○ **Castles in Spain** / Columbia 888
Finely produced, orchestrated, and arranged work by a master of moods and textures. It's doubtful that much of what Michel Legrand does could really be deemed jazz in terms of improvisational content or playing style, but it is attractive and striking in other ways. —*Ron Wynn*

Sarah Vaughan/Michel Legrand / Mainstream 361
A meeting that works better than anyone might have expected. Vaughan is still her dynamic, charismatic vocal self, while Legrand doesn't obscure or dilute her singing and also effectively supports her in his own way. —*Ron Wynn*

GEORGE LEWIS

b. 1952, Chicago, IL
Trombone, electronics
Though he's dropped off some from the hectic recording pace he set in the '70s, trombonist George Lewis remains as a most intriguing composer and player. While he knows and respects many jazz traditions and has worked in many styles, including free, Lewis shuns the word jazz, and in interviews has denied repeatedly that he's a jazz musician. His playing incorporates long lines, phrasing, and voice-like effects commonplace among jazz trombonists. He's also an exceptional soloist who is able to improvise cleanly and fluidly at blistering tempos and can play with warmth, humor, and originality. Lewis is as equally comfortable in the electronic and symphonic worlds as he is at improvisation. He's worked frequently with electronic keyboardist Richard Teitelbaum, has written works for multiple synthesizers, has used computers, electronic sounds, tapes, and other signal processing devices not normally associated with jazz composition and performance. Lewis began studying trombone at age nine, and at age 12 was transcribing Lester Young solos for trombone. He studied theory with Muhal Richard Abrams through a program of the Artists for the Advancement of Creative Music (AACM) in the early '70s, and played in Douglas Ewart's band Elements. Lewis attended Yale, where he earned a philosophy degree, and studied privately with Anthony Davis and Fred Anderson. He toured with Count Basie's orchestra briefly in 1976, then joined Anthony Braxton's group that same year. He played in the brass quartet Quadrisect with Ewart in the mid-'70s, and from 1980 to 1982 served as the director of the Kitchen, New York's avant-garde cultural center. Lewis recorded and played in the '70s with Lester Bowie, Carla Bley, Roscoe Mitchell, and Derek Bailey while cutting his own sessions for Black Saint, Sackville, Hat Art, Incus, and Moers. He continued recording in the '80s, but hasn't been featured as prominently. Lewis has recorded solo trombone sessions, multiple brass dates, albums featuring electric keyboards, orchestral dates, and combo works. His work remains com-

pelling, if at times quite removed from jazz ties. He only has a couple of sessions available on CD. —*Ron Wynn*

★ **Solo Trombone Album** / **i.** 1976 / Sackville 3012

Homage to Charles Parker / 1979 / Black Saint 29

HERBIE LEWIS

b. 1941
Bass / Hard bop
A good bassist and a strong accompanist, Herbie Lewis has never been a star or a bandleader, but is simply a reliable session contributor and an occasional soloist. Lewis recorded with Lennie McBrowne, Harold Land, and Les McCann in the late '50s and early '60s. He moved from California to New York in 1961, and played and recorded again with McCann. Lewis also recorded with Dave Pike, Stanley Turrentine, and Jackie McLean before returning to California. He and McCann recorded together again under the leadership of Clifford Scott, and Lewis did a session with Gerald Wilson in the mid-'60s. By the late '60s, Lewis had moved back to New York again, where he recorded with Sam Rivers, Bobby Hutcherson, and Freddie Hubbard. He played in Cannonball Adderley's ensemble in 1966, and played and recorded with McCoy Tyner from 1967 to 1970. During the '70s and '80s, Lewis recorded with Tete Montoliu, Chico Freeman, Bobby Hutcherson, and Archie Shepp, among others. He doesn't have any sessions available as a leader on CD, but can be heard on recent discs by Montoliu, Shepp, Freeman, and others, and on reissues of Tyner, McLean, and others. —*Ron Wynn*

JOHN LEWIS (John Aaron Lewis)

b. May 3, 1920, La Grange, IL
Piano, composer, arranger / Bop, cool
It has been said that John Lewis is one of the few people who really understands the similarities between jazz and classical music, and helps bridge gaps between these disciplines. Lewis was Kenny Clarke's recommendation to replace Thelonious Monk in Dizzy Gillespie's band in the late '40s. After the band's demise, Lewis and Clarke stayed in Paris. Lewis was a steady freelance player and arranger in the late '40s and early '50s, working with Illinois Jacquet, Charlie Parker, Miles Davis, and Lester Young. The longtime Modern Jazz Quartet had its beginnings in the Milt Jackson quartet of the early '50s. The MJQ emerged in 1954 and was augmented in 1955 when Connie Kay replaced Kenny Clarke. That's been the main vehicle for Lewis ever since, though he's done film soundtrack work, has been a professor of music at City College since 1977, was the cofounder of the American Jazz Orchestra and has been its conductor since the late '80s. What either delights or irritates fans about Lewis is the sparseness of his playing; there's none of the volume, power, or rhythmic intensity normally associated with jazz. Instead, he ambles along, seeming to prefer subtlety and suggestion to energy or verve. But some of his compositions (notably "Django") are legends, and his contrast with Milt Jackson's bluesy, often funky, vibes make the MJQ sound a jazz staple. —*Ron Wynn*

○ **Afternoon in Paris** / Dec. 4, 1956 / Atlantic 1267

Wonderful World of Jazz / Jul. 1960-Sep. 1960 / Atlantic 90979

European Encounter / Jul. 2-3, 1962 / Atlantic 90533
A 1986 reissue of a sublime meeting between Lewis and violinist Svend Asmussen. —*Ron Wynn*

★ **Kansas City Breaks** / **i.** May 25+26, 1982 / Disques Swing 8430
Has the interesting instrumentation of a flute, violin, guitar, and piano trio. All selections are Lewis originals, including the especially famous "Django," "Milano," and "Sacha's Mardi." A sweet session. —*Michael G. Nastos*

Bach Preludes and Fugues—Vol. 2 / Jan. 16, 1984-Sep. 25, 1984 / Verve 826698

Bach Preludes and Fugues–Vol. 3 (Well-Tempered Clavier) / Jan. 16, 1984-Sep. 25, 1984 / Verve 836821
Another foray into Lewis's penchant for classical and third-stream concept pieces. —*Ron Wynn*

★ **Chess Game–Vols. 1 & 2, The** / i. 1987-1988 / Verve 832015

Midnight in Paris / Dec. 1988 / EmArcy 838036

MEADE "LUX" LEWIS (Meade Anderson Lewis)

b. Sep. 4, 1905, Chicago, IL, d. Jun. 7, 1964, Minneapolis, MN
Piano, composer / Boogie-woogie
The third member of the great triumvirate of the '30s and '40s, Meade "Lux" Lewis may have been the most captivating of the boogie-woogie pianists from a rhythmic standpoint. His cross-rhythms were dynamic and invigorating, and he was a gifted all-around player who chafed at being regarded as only a boogie-woogie and a blues practitioner. His solos were remarkable for their speed and for his ability to create at will. His playing reflected his admiration for Jimmy Yancey and Fats Waller, but was hardly imitative. Lewis played at Chicago bars and clubs before he cut the classic "Honky Tonk Train Blues." Lewis recorded the song in 1927, but it wasn't issued until 18 months later. Still, it wasn't until 1935, when John Hammond found him and Lewis re-recorded "Honky Tonk Train Blues," that he gained his deserved recognition. Lewis was part of a short-lived boogie-woogie trio with Albert Ammons and Pete Johnson in 1938 and 1939, but when they disbanded, he returned to solo dates at clubs in New York and California. He and Ammons made occasional appearances together, and Lewis also played with Sidney Bechet. His desire to display other facets of his playing led to recordings with celesta and harpsichord. Lewis's later sessions were often disappointing, but they don't diminish his great earlier work. —*Ron Wynn*

★ **Complete Blue Note Recordings** / Jan. 6, 1939-Aug. 22, 1944 / Mosaic
1939-1944. A wonderful, comprehensive compilation of stamping, romping boogie-woogie piano by the masters. —*Ron Wynn*

1939-1954 / i. 1939-1954 / Story of Blues 3506
Vintage recordings from premier boogie-woogie stylist detailing evolution and fruition of his great style. This release features recordings done in the '30s, '40s, and '50s and sessions for various labels—solos, duets with Albert Ammons, and some combo dates. —*Ron Wynn*

Cat House Piano / i. 194z / Verve

Blues Piano Artistry of Meade Lux Lewis / Nov. 1, 1961 / Riverside 1759

MEL LEWIS (Melvin Sokoloff)

b. May 10, 1929, Buffalo, NY, d. 1990
Drums / Big band, bop, postbop, progressive big band
An immaculate timekeeper, Mel Lewis is one of jazz's finest drummers. Whether anchoring a big band or a small combo, he provides exactly what's necessary, from steady beats to bombastic support, ideal shading, texture, and foundation. He's not a dominant soloist, but can provide sterling solos when in the spotlight. Lewis's father was a drummer, and Lewis turned professional at age 15. He worked in several dance bands early in his career. These included Boyd Raeburn's, Alvino Rey's, Ray Anthony's, and Tex Beneke's in the '40s and early '50s. He played with Stan Kenton in the mid- and late '50s, also working with Frank Rosolino and Hampton Hawes. He recorded for San Francisco Jazz Records in 1956, for Mode in 1957, and for Andex in 1958. Lewis became a Los Angeles resident in 1957, and co-led a quintet with Bill Holman in 1958. He did extensive studio work, cutting sessions with Art Pepper, Pepper Adams, and Gerry Mulligan. Lewis also played and recorded with Gerald Wilson's and Terry Gibbs's big bands. He began commuting to New York in 1960 for engagements with Mulligan's Concert Band. Lewis toured Europe with Dizzy Gillespie in 1961, and toured the Soviet Union with Benny Goodman the

next year, while serving as house drummer for the Monterey Jazz Festival from 1959 to 1962. He resettled in New York a year later, then helped form the Thad Jones-Mel Lewis Orchestra in 1965. This became the premier big band of the '60s and '70s; for many years, they were the featured attraction Monday nights at the Village Vanguard. The Orchestra made numerous recordings and toured extensively until Jones departed in 1979. Lewis remained as sole leader until Bob Brookmeyer assumed the duties of composer, arranger, and music director, functions that Jones had done previously. Lewis's recording career gained prominence in the '70s. He recorded for A&M, then for Telarc, Gryphon, MPS/Pausa, Finesse, and Atlantic in the '80s. Surprisingly, there are more Mel Lewis dates available than Thad Jones-Mel Lewis big band sessions. Only a couple of their dates have been reissued on CD. —*Ron Wynn*

Greetings and Salutations / i. 1975 / Biograph

★ **Suite for Pops** / i. 1975 / A&M
An album of spry, invigorating, and memorable Jones-Lewis recordings. —*Ron Wynn*

○ **Mel Lewis and Friends** / Jun. 8-9, 1976 / A&M 0823
This is a fine straightahead blowing bop date, with the only electricity being that produced by the players themselves. This is trumpeter Freddie Hubbard's best recorded effort in nearly five years, and he deserves support for his work here, especially on "Nu" and "A Child Is Born." "Child" is his masterpiece, here a showcase for Hubbard's flugelhorn backed sympathetically by just the rhythm trio (pianist Hank Jones, bassist Ron Carter, drummer/bandleader Mel Lewis). The trio also shines on "Wind Flower," a John Lewis-type loper by Sarah Cassey on which the horns sit out; Jones, Carter, and Lewis all have outstanding feature spots. "Sho' Nuff" is another Thad Jones original and the longest track. It's a midtempo, openly structured piece that features workmanlike solos from alto saxophonist Greg Herbert and trumpeter Cecil Bridgewater with the meat supplied by tenor saxophonist Mike Brecker and Hubbard (flugelhorn). "De Samba" is a pleasant samba played unobtrusively but with few highlights of inspiration. Charlie Parker's "Moose The Mooche" is jammed with Hubbard (trumpet) taking the opening solo, picked up and followed immediately by a Brecker John Coltrane-inspired solo; Hank Jones follows with his best work before it is again tossed back to Hubbard, who trades with Lewis, who in turn trades with Brecker and then Ron Carter, before returning to the theme, and everyone taking it out. This is a faultless date with many high moments of musical substance. —*Bob Rusch*, Cadence

Naturally / Mar. 20, 1979 / Telarc 83301

Live at Village Vanguard / Feb. 1980 / Dcc 616
A 1991 reissue of prime sessions, with Lewis at the helm of his longtime big band. High-octane solos and energetic compositions. —*Ron Wynn*

★ **Mel Lewis Plays Herbie Hancock** / Jul. 16, 1980 / MPS

20 Years at the Village Vanguard / i. 1985 / Atlantic 81655

Soft Lights and Hot Music / i. Feb. 11-15, 1988 / Music Masters 5012
Here are some excellent big-band tracks, with fine solos by Joe Lovano (ts). —*Ron Wynn*

Definitive Thad Jones–Vol. 1 and 2 / i. 1988 / Music Masters 5024
The Mel Lewis Jazz Orchestra playing from the book of longtime coleader Thad Jones. —*Ron Wynn*

○ **Lost Art, The** / Apr. 11-12, 1989 / Music Masters 5023
Sextet. This is the definitive small-group album, with pianist Ken Werner. —*Michael G. Nastos*

Central Park North / Solid State

Consummation / Blue Note

Live in Munich / A&M

Monday Night / Solid State

To You: A Tribute to Mel Lewis / Music Masters 5054

RAMSEY LEWIS (Ramsey Emmanuel (Jr) Lewis)

b. May 27, 1935, Chicago, IL
Piano, keyboards, synthesizer, composer / Soul-jazz, instrumental pop

A survivor who is highly controversial in some quarters and is currently an influential host on Black Entertainment Television (BET), pianist Ramsey Lewis has blended populist and traditional styles since the late '50s. The top-selling jazz artist between 1955 and 1981, Lewis is a good bebop and hard bop soloist, but a better blues and funk stylist. Lewis's pleasant, entertaining melodies and breezy solos have been the subject of bitter tirades and equally exuberant praise; he's often responded to critical attacks with dismissals of detractors as rigid purists out of touch with Black community taste and lifestyles.

Lewis began studying piano at age six, and attended Chicago Music College and DePaul University. He formed his first trio in 1956 with Eldee Young and Red Holt. They worked together for a decade, then Young and Holt left and were replaced by Cleveland Eaton and Maurice White; Maurice Jennings took White's place in 1970. Lewis cut nearly 30 albums for Cadet or Argo from 1956 to 1971; he included vocals or strings on some, and many featured reworkings of pop hits. He began hitting the charts with his 1962 Christmas LP; then *Back to the Blues* and *Live at the Bohemian Caverns* also made the Top 200. Then came *The In Crowd* in 1965; the title track was a number-five pop single and the album reached the number-two spot overall. Lewis eventually landed 30 albums on the charts from 1962 to 1984, and was one of the rare jazz musicians to have albums and hit singles in the '60s, '70s, and '80s. He had 13 Hot 100 singles between 1964 and 1969 alone, all instrumental covers like "Hi-Heel Sneakers" and "Hang on Sloopy." Lewis LPs *Hang on Ramsey!, Wade in the Water*, and *Sun Goddess* were Top 20 sellers in the '60s and '70s. Lewis also played with Max Roach on an Argo session and made more conventional jazz dates as well as recording with Nancy Wilson in the '80s.

He's not as complete a pianist as Junior Mance, Gene Harris, or Ahmad Jamal, though he does similar material. Lewis is closer in spirit to Les McCann, though he's not a vocalist and isn't as funky or exuberant a performer as McCann. The fact that he's sold more records than all four of these individuals grates on many critics. Lewis hosts BET's weekly "On Jazz" program and was slated for greater involvement in the network's all-jazz channel that was earmarked to start in 1994. He has recorded for Cadet, Argo, Columbia, and GRP. Lewis has many sessions available on CD. *—Ron Wynn*

○ **Lem Winchester and the Ramsey Lewis Trio** / Oct. 1958 / Argo 642

★ **In Crowd, The** / 1965 / Chess 9185
The In Crowd was the Ramsey Lewis Trio's (Ramsey Lewis, piano; Eldee Young, bass, cello; Red Holt, drums) big hit of the time. The title track typified part of the Lewis style, but helped commercially lock it in to a narrow style. Recorded in May 1965 at the once-hip Bohemian Caverns in Washington, D.C., it remains a pleasant easy listen; it will never be more. Cover graphics and liners remain exactly the same as on the original except the producers have deleted the personnel identification, recording info, dates, and production, design, and photo credits. In their place sits the *new* producer's name along with new credits for "art" production. And this sets the pattern for all the reissues in this set (1985). For shame! *—Bob Rusch, Cadence*

Wade in the Water / 1966 / Garland 004
A major hit in its time, but of dubious quality from a re-mastering standpoint. *—Ron Wynn*

○ **Upendo Ni Pamoja** / 1972 / CBS 31096

★ **Sun Goddess** / 1974 / Columbia 33194
Teo Macero and Maurice White (of Earth, Wind and Fire) did an excellent job in putting together this package of a dozen-odd musicians whom they called in to supplement and perhaps rejuvenate the Ramsey Lewis Trio. Richard Evans's string and brass arrangements provide pretty background filler, and the whole thing clicks along as precisely as a Swiss timepiece. The musical content here is naturally quite predictable. There is the obligatory Stevie Wonder remake and the usual pretty Latin piece, this time a Lewis original, "Love Song." And, as on "Solar Wind," Lewis throws in a touch of honest straightahead jazz, presumably just to show his fans that he could still get do it if he chose. Parts of "Gemini Rising," granted, do cook. *—Jon Balleras*, Down Beat

Live at the Savoy / 1982 / CBS 85502

Two of Us, The / i. 1984 / Columbia 39326

Keys to the City / i. 1987 / Columbia 40677

We Meet Again / i. 1990 / CBS 44941
Billy Taylor (p) takes the date, but Lewis shows chops he seldom taps these days. *—Ron Wynn*

Best of Ramsey Lewis, The / Columbia 36364

Electric Collection / Columbia 46822

DAVID LIEBMAN

b. Sep. 4, 1946, New York, NY
Tenor and soprano saxophone, flute, piano, drums / Postbop, early jazz-rock, neo-bop, modern creative

Another versatile musician who's worked in jazz and pop contexts, David Liebman has been a successful bebop, hard bop, R&B/funk, and jazz-rock soloist on tenor and soprano sax and on flute. Liebman mixes jazz improvisation, African and Asian scales and rhythm elements, as well as funk, pop, blues, and even Caribbean and European symphonic influences. He's absorbed the music of John Coltrane and his tone and approach reflect the impact of Coltrane and Wayne Shorter, but Liebman has developed his own angular voice and plays in both an earthy, animated fashion on tenor, and a lyrical, more meditative manner on soprano and flute.

He took piano lessons as a child, then began playing clarinet and, later, saxophone. Liebman started working in bands at age 14, and was aided and inspired by drummer Bob Moses. He studied privately with Joe Allard, Charles Lloyd, and Lennie Tristano. Liebman graduated from New York University with a degree in American history and a teaching diploma in the late '60s. His first engagement was with the jazz-rock band Ten Wheel Drive in 1970. A year later, he joined Elvin Jones's band, and was featured on some freewheeling two- and three-sax recording sessions. Liebman played with Miles Davis in 1973 and 1974, doing more jazz-rock and funk material. He formed his own band, Lookout Farm, in 1974, cutting some fine recordings for ECM, touring and playing festivals both in America and Europe. He also worked in the trio Open Sky with Moses and Gene Perla, and made some outstanding sessions for PM. Liebman did several sessions in the '70s, among them a heralded date with John McLaughlin, as well as several duo and trio recordings. He worked with Richie Beirarch, Bill Goodwin, Steve Gilmore, Gil Goldstein, and Dave Love, among others. He also became active in jazz education during the '70s, conducting workshops and clinics and giving private instruction.

Liebman's next group was in the late '70s and early '80s, with Terumasa Hino, John Scofield, Ron McClure, and Adam Nussbaum. They toured Europe in '79 and '80. Liebman worked as a soloist in the '80s, and played at various European festivals. Liebman worked with Albert Mangelsdorff and played the Berlin Festival with Franco Ambrosetti in 1985. Liebman's worked frequently with the Jamey Aebersold organization. He's recorded for several labels, among them ECM, Red, Soul Note, Heads Up, CMP, Storyville, Timeless, and Candid. Liebman, who now concentrates almost exclusively on soprano sax, has many titles available on CD. *—Ron Wynn*

Open Sky / May 1, 1972-Jun. 10, 1972 / PM

Adventurous pieces. A triumphant exhibition of multireed versatility. Tremendous work in a small-combo format. — *Ron Wynn*

★ **Lookout Farm** / Jun. 12, 1975 / Jugoton 6132
Lookout Farm has Dave Liebman's working quartet augmented by a percussion ensemble, voice, and the omnipresence of John Abercrombie's guitar. "Pablo's Story" begins with Abercrombie's Spanish moss-flavored classical guitar. Alto flute weaves in along with a multitude of bells, tambourine, and castinets. Soon, a "Granada"-groove is established, with Liebman's soprano coolly melodic in the world of restrained intensity fashioned by Miles Davis. Richie Beirach takes the first solo, weaving an electric pattern through varying tempo and rhythm changes. His left hand chords strongly in a staggered manner as his right hand searches for the proper melodic fragment. Liebman restates the theme as the tune imperceptibly picks up to where an entire samba school of percussion is boiling under his smooth Joe Farrellish soprano. Only, unlike Farrell, Liebman is willing to test the instrument's more-dissonant overtones, which allows him a freedom of expression more closely aligned to John Coltrane's soprano playing. "M.D." is closer to Davis's *Kind Of Blue* phase than to his later postures. Beirach on acoustic piano sounds like a serious Bill Evans, though with more rhythmic verve. Liebman handles the tenor like an early Trane or a Cannonball Adderley playing alto on the historic session. Signatures take root and then are broken up. No firm melodic line is sustained. An exquisite mood is established by Don Alias on congas and Badal Roy on tablas. Beirach plays around with the strings of his piano, and then Liebman returns, only this time with the full, commanding tone associated with Gato Barbieri. —*Ray Townley*, Down Beat

○ **Forgotten Fantasies** / Nov. 18-20, 1975 / Horizon 709

Quest / i. Dec. 28-29, 1981 / Palo Alto 8061
Quartet with Liebman, Beirach (p), George Mraz (b), and Al Foster (d). They hit hard and heavy, or at times mournfully wistful. An excellent document of this all-world group. — *Michael G. Nastos*

○ **Loneliness of a Long-Distance Runner, the** / Nov. 11-12, 1985 / CMP 24
David Liebman does it alone (solo and ensemble multidubbing) on *The Loneliness of a Long-Distance Runner*. The "distance" on this very personal program conception is that of one's lifespan, with Liebman viewing the importance of the race as not the finality but the process of the experience. Included with this work are notes by the artist, which may or may not help the listener relate to the music by the suggested imagery of the notes or titles. The multiple overdubs are particularly well integrated, giving much of this a World Saxophone Quartet-like texture under Liebman's bluesy Ornette Coleman-like lines (a lonely woman-like phrase recurs throughout). The overdubbing adds a great textural emotion and conveys the involvement and harmony one expects from a group. Over this the soprano saxman involves himself in some outstanding improvisations, maintaining a tension, passion, and involvement that are unfaltering. — *Bob Rusch*, Cadence

○ **Quest II / i.** Apr. 17, 1986 / Storyville
Quartet set with Liebman, Richie Beirach (p), Ron McClure (b), and Billy Hart (d). —*Ron Wynn*

Homage to John Coltrane / Jan. 27-28, 1987 / Owl 79245
1991 reissue. An intense tribute to one of Liebman's prime influences. —*Ron Wynn*

Trio + One / May 1988 / Owl 380051
Soprano master doing variation of familiar themes and out-and-out original material. With Dave Holland (b) and Jack DeJohnette (d). Very worthwhile new music. —*Michael G. Nastos*

○ **Tree, The** / Apr. 1990 / Soul Note 121195
The Tree is the best David Liebman record I've heard, a strong set of solo free improvisations on loosely predetermined material relating to a (very loose) arborescent theme.

Each piece is announced unceremoniously by Liebman, the entire suite played frontward, then back. Following his woody concept, I find the juiciest bits those furthest "out on a limb," namely toward the middle of the disc. The two takes of harsh, multiphonic "Leaves" are great, and both "Twigs" are fine, static studies in breath and trill, riding close to the line of intonation and occasionally dropping out into the toneless zone. Liebman owes much to the two solo soprano masters, Steve Lacy and Evan Parker. His tone is dry and thin, not especially resonant, and the pieces at either end of the disc seem somewhat aimless. —*John Corbett*, Down Beat

KIRK LIGHTSEY

b. Feb. 15, 1937, Detroit, MI
Piano / Hard bop, modern creative
A tremendous soloist, Kirk Lightsey plays with verve, style, and zeal, and demonstrates extensive harmonic knowledge and rhythmic drive without ever seeming rushed or harried. Lightsey doesn't get extensive coverage, in part because he records for small independent labels and because his music doesn't follow any particular trend other than being uniformly excellent. Lightsey started on piano at age five and later played clarinet in high school and in the army. He played in the early '60s with Melba Liston and Ernestine Anderson in New York. He worked with other vocalists for several years in Detroit and California, among them Damita Jo, O.C. Smith, and Lovelace Watkins. He recorded with Sonny Stitt in 1965, and cut five albums that year with Chet Baker. He got his first substantial exposure playing with Dexter Gordon in the late '70s and early '80s, and recorded with Jimmy Raney and Clifford Jordan in the mid-'80s. Lightsey played at the Jazzfest Berlin with Jabbo Smith and Don Cherry in 1986, and has worked with the Leaders in the late '80s and early '90s. He's recorded his own sessions for Sunnyside, Criss Cross, and Lime Tree, and with the Leaders for Blackhawk, Sunnyside, and Black Saint. Lightsey has sessions, both solo and in the group, available on CD. —*Ron Wynn and Michael G. Nastos*

○ **Isotope / i.** Feb. 1983 / Criss Cross 1003

○ **Lightsey Live** / Jun. 28, 1985 / Sunnyside 1014
Lightsey Live is a program recorded 6/28/85 at the Smithsonian Institution. For this solo concert Lightsey plays one original along with works by Tony Williams, Thelonious Monk, Rodgers & Hart, Wayne Shorter, and Cole Porter, a rather distinct group of composers. Even so, all the music here became a collaboration with the pianist whose individual style composes itself on the music as well. Lightsey is not a direct stylist attacking melody and rhythm in a direct manner. Rather, he pulls his punches and wanders, touching the perimeters of the musical core. He is the most direct on a delightful interpretation of "Trinkle Tinkle" where he maintains a Monkian stride essence with a suggestion of Teddy Wilson. This is immediately followed by a flowery "Spring is Here" adorned with Gershwinesque arabesques that suggest the technique of Tatum and Oscar Peterson, but without the ordered rhythm. One does not get the feeling the pianist is playing the lyrics. It's a lovely interpretation, but instead of a sense of traveling movement one is left more with a sense of seeing anew that which surrounds you: fresh views of the obvious. In total, this is a fine, introspective, and highly inventive set of improvisatory interpretation. —*Bob Rusch*, Cadence

★ **Everything Is Changed** / Jun. 4-5, 1986 / Sunnyside 1020
This is pianist Kirk Lightsey's fourth album for Sunnyside, but his first as a group leader for the label. And what a group he chose. Eddie Gladden (d) was Lightsey's partner in the Dexter Gordon rhythm section of the early '80s. Santi Wilson DiBriano (b) is a solid resilient anchor. But the real standout on this LP is trumpeter Jerry Gonzalez. His ballad artistry is well showcased, especially on the title track, and his muted trumpet recalls Miles Davis of the late '50s (a comparison that's hard to avoid). The Davis influence is particularly felt since he uses a mute on four of the six tracks. But Gonzalez isn't just aping Davis's licks, and in addition to

great ballad work, his uptempo work is strong and assured as well. As a "leader," Lightsey doesn't just present a blowing session, although freewheeling spirit comes through on the uptempo tracks. He harmonizes "Billie's Bounce" thoroughly. DiBriano's "Nandi" adds a French horn, and the soft brass front line gives the music some nice warm hues. Although the piece was inspired by a trip to Africa, it has an almost Brazilian feel to it. "Evidence" is played over a bed of bubbling percussion. About the only negative on this LP is the distracting tick of the claves on this track. Lightsey's piano playing demonstrates why he was chosen as the pianist for the Leaders. His playing is particularly notable on the ballad tracks (the title cut and "Estate"), where it is pure crystalline elegance. One gets the impression that he enjoys ballad playing best of all. —*Robert Iannapollo*, Cadence

○ **From Kirk to Nat** / Nov. 1990 / Criss Cross 1050
That Detroit native Kirk Lightsey chose to utilize a trio format in tribute to the very same elegant and subtly swinging facet of the late Nat "King" Cole's career should not trouble listeners. *From Kirk To Nat* is not some ideal well-meaning replication of Cole favorites like "Sweet Lorraine." For one thing, the pianist/leader's choice of personnel (bassist Rufus Reid, guitarist Kevin Eubanks) practically guarantees a healthy technique/feeling ratio, and in an appropriately low-key sort of way they deliver urgency when they dig into "Appointment in the North Country." One will enjoy the sojourn. Invent a scenario (probably romantic) and kiss the city goodbye. —*Reuben Jackson*, Jazz Times

ABBEY LINCOLN (Anna Marie Wooldridge)

b. Aug. 6, 1930, Chicago, IL
Vocals / Ballads & blues, modern creative
Abbey Lincoln has enjoyed a career revival in the late '80s and '90s after years of undeserved obscurity. She altered and expanded her style in the '60s, becoming a genuine vocal improviser who experimented with rhythms, explored lyrics, and sang about social and political issues. Her voice grew bolder, and her approach became more aggressive and animated than it had been before. Lincoln began her career in the '50s, using such names as Gaby Lee and Anna Marie. She moved to Los Angeles from Chicago. At first, Lincoln was marketed as a vamp, and even briefly billed as "the Black Marilyn Monroe," appearing in the 1957 film *The Girl Can't Help It*. She took the name Abbey Lincoln for a 1956 recording date with the Benny Carter band. Once she met and began working with Max Roach, Lincoln changed even more. She cut some intriguing dates in the late '50s, where her phrasing, dramatic delivery, and unusual sound attracted attention. She and Roach recorded together during the early '60s, and were married in 1962. His influence, plus that of Charles Mingus and Thelonious Monk, among others, radically reshaped Lincoln's attitude. Roach and Lincoln's *Freedom Now Suite* album, released in 1960, was quite revolutionary in its message and tone. They did other albums for Candid, Impulse, and Liberty; some of these albums conveyed similar ideas. In the mid- and late '60s, Lincoln began to do more acting than music, as some club owners and record labels shied away from her and from Roach because of their "militant" posture. She did some sessions for European labels in the early '70s, and changed her name to Aminata Moseka in 1975. Lincoln appeared in the films *Nothing But a Man* and *For the Love of Ivy*, visited Africa, and conferred with political leaders in such nations as Guinea and Zaire. She taught drama at Cal State University, and did some guest stints on television shows. Things began to pick up for her musically in the '80s. She recorded for Enja, doing some superb tribute albums to Billie Holiday in 1987. Her acclaimed Verve albums in the '90s led to a public television special and renewed interest by the music media. Some classic Lincoln sessions, as well as her '90s albums for Verve, are available on CD. —*Ron Wynn*

☆ **Freedom Now Suite** / **i.** 1960 / Candid

Definitive social protest and jazz. Lincoln and her then-husband Max Roach are a great team. —*Ron Wynn*

★ **Straight Ahead** / Feb. 22, 1961 / Barnaby 31037
Vocalist Abbey Lincoln has been too forthright and hard-hitting a performer through her long career to gain establishment acceptance and fame, but time heals most wounds. In what is for me perhaps her very finest date, Lincoln wrenches out her tough soul in her steadfast, determined way with an all-star cast led by her then-husband drummer Max Roach. "All-star" is not used loosely here: Coleman Hawkins (ts) intones gruffly in measured authority on the title track, Eric Dolphy (as) and Mal Waldron (p) are superb in support, and trumpeter Booker Little, whose brilliant candle was snuffed much too soon, plays bittersweet throughout. The charts, many by Little, are a total gas. "When Malindy Sings," with its tune by Oscar Brown, Jr., text by poet/novelist Paul Laurance Dunbar (1872-1906), and arrangement by Little, may be one of the most complete jazz vocals on record. —*Fred Bouchard*, Jazz Times

Sounds as a Roach / **i.** 1968 / Lotus

★ **People in Me** / Jun. 23, 1973 / Inner City 6040
As good as she gets on this recording. A perennial favorite for many. With David Liebman (ss, ts, f), Al Foster (d), James Mtume (per), Kunimitsu Inaba (b), and Hiromasa Suzuki (p). "Living Room," "Africa," "Naturally," and the title track stand out. Proud music. —*Michael G. Nastos*

○ **Golden Lady** / **i.** Mar. 1982 / Inner City 1117
Early '80s material by the neglected vocalist Abbey Lincoln. Her intonation, delivery, phrasing, and style are unique and sometimes so distinctive they seem wrong for a song. But Lincoln makes every number come alive, giving even overly familiar lyrics fresh, vibrant treatments. —*Ron Wynn*

Abbey Sings Billie—Vol. 1 / **i.** Nov. 6-7, 1987 / Enja 79633
Interesting concept. In many ways, Lincoln is much closer to Holiday than many think. —*Ron Wynn*

○ **You Gotta Pay the Band** / 1991 / Verve 511110
Studio date featuring Stan Getz one last time and the Hank Jones Trio. Maxine Roach plays viola for two cuts. Six cuts feature either words and/or music written by Moseka. She has lost absolutely none of her brilliance or passion for singing, interpreting, and creating. —*Michael G. Nastos*

○ **Abbey Sings Billie—Vol. 2** / **i.** 1992 / Enja 7037
This Billie Holiday disc was recorded live in New York in 1987, featuring a strong rhythm section and tenorman Harold Vick. In fact, the two concerts took place just a few days before the saxophonist died. Like Stanley Turrentine, who plays sensitive tenor on *Devil's Got Your Tongue*, Vick was a seasoned, supportive accompanist and his *Stepping Out* ('60s Blue Note) is a rare prize. There's no better place to observe the differences and likenesses of Billie Holiday and Abbey Lincoln than on Lincoln's less eerie "Don't Explain," or her lovely version of "For All We Know." —*John Corbett*, Down Beat

JOHN LINDBERG (John Arthur (III) Lindberg)

b. Mar. 16, 1959, Royal Oak, MI
Bass / Modern creative
A steady, sympathetic accompanist and a solid soloist, bassist John Lindberg's best known for his work in the String Trio of New York. Lindberg studied music in Ann Arbor, Michigan before moving to New York in 1977. He played and recorded in the Human Arts Ensemble with Joseph Bowie and Bobo Shaw in the late '70s, and worked with Anthony Braxton from 1978 to 1985. They performed in both Europe and America. Lindberg was a founding member of the String Trio of New York in 1979, and currently remains with the ensemble. He also worked in a trio with Jimmy Lyons and Sunny Murray in 1980. Lindberg lived and worked in Paris from 1980 to 1983, leading small combos, playing solo, and working in a group led by Murray that also featured John Tchicai. Lindberg has recorded as a leader for Cecma, Black Saint, West Wind, ITM, and Sound

Aspects. He has some sessions available as a leader. —*Ron Wynn*

★ **Trilogy of Works for Eleven Instrumentalists / i.** Sep. 1984 / Black Saint 0082

MELBA LISTON (Melba Doretta Liston)

b. Jan. 13, 1926, Kansas City, MO
Trombone, arranger / Bop, hard bop, progressive big band
Melba Liston has achieved double fame in the jazz world; she's both a fine trombonist and a heralded arranger. Her range, huge sound, flexibility, and speed established Liston as an important trombone voice since the '40s. Her creative, often challenging arrangements have been featured with many bands, from Quincy Jones's to Randy Weston's. Liston moved from Kansas City to California with her family at age 11. She played with youth bands, then began playing professionally in a pit orchestra. Liston joined Gerald Wilson's big band in 1943, and began writing arrangements. She also recorded with Dexter Gordon. After Gordon's orchestra disbanded on the East Coast in the midst of a tour, Liston remained there and took a job with Dizzy Gillespie. She toured with Billie Holiday, but grew disgusted with the politics and turmoil of the jazz life. Liston quit music and took a clerical job. She was an extra in the films *The Prodigal* and *The Ten Commandments* during the mid-'50s, then rejoined Gillespie for State Department tours in 1956 and '57. Liston also visited Europe for the show *Free and Easy*, playing in Jones's band (he was the project's music director). During the '60s, Liston worked for several leaders, among them Weston. She taught at the Jamaica School of Music for six years in the '70s, then returned to America to lead her own bands. She continues to arrange and compose with Weston, though lately she's been battling illness. Sadly, there are no Liston sessions as a leader currently available on CD. —*Ron Wynn*

★ **And Her Bones** / Dec. 22-24, 1958 / Metrojazz 1013

BOOKER LITTLE (Booker (Jr) Little)

b. Apr. 2, 1938, Memphis, TN, **d.** Oct. 5, 1961
Trumpet / Hard bop
Among the many cases of jazz musicians' premature deaths, trumpeter Booker Little's ranks as one of the most tragic. Little had emerged as a majestic player whose solos were fierce and impeccably executed, and whose imaginative use of dissonance was particularly impressive. His style was rooted in hard bop, but he played with such intensity, speed, and flair that he constantly stretched the harmonic fabric of any piece that featured his work. His collaborations with Eric Dolphy, from the riveting ensemble lines to the dazzling exchanges and individual solos, were hypnotic and entrancing. But Little only lived to age 23, dying of uremia. He came from a musical family, and Little played clarinet before switching to trumpet at age 12. He worked around Memphis with Phineas Newborn while still a teenager. Little played with Johnny Griffin and Walter Perkins's MJT + 3 while attending the Chicago Conservatory. He played with Max Roach after his graduation in 1958 and 1959, then did freelance sessions in New York with Mal Waldron and others before returning to play with Roach in 1960. He worked with Eric Dolphy in 1961, coleading a great quintet and cutting some sensational records at the Five Spot. These were made in July 1961. By October, Little was dead. He'd also done sessions as a leader for United Artists, Bainbridge, Candid, and Bethlehem. Most of Little's dates, including the sessions with Dolphy, are available on CD. —*Ron Wynn*

☆ **Booker Little 4 and Max Roach** / 1958 / Bainbridge 1041
A tremendous showcase of early '60s sessions that has exceptional musicians and wonderful compositions. Everyone from Phineas and Calvin Newborn to George Coleman and Max Roach. —*Ron Wynn*

○ **Out Front** / Mar. 1961-Apr. 1961 / Candid 79027
Trumpeter Booker Little is the principal soloist on this date. He plays a trumpet that is sometimes as sweet as Clifford Brown's but often tinged with acidity. Undoubtedly, if Little

had survived, he would have been a major trumpet voice. His style was characterized by extended tones which he was able to bend in much the way Thelonious Monk did piano notes. He used sonority and harmonic intervals that also bring to mind Monk. Little's tunes here are filled with thoughtfulness and seem to suggest moving objects. Often, the arrangements are suggestive of antiphonal chants. The use of colorations such as the timpani and vibes of Max Roach as well as the changes in tempo and mood impart a natural fluidity of development and conclusion. The compositional work of both Duke Ellington and Charles Mingus comes to mind in these unorthdox lines. Max Roach is a powerful force throughout, as are the bassist Ron Carter and Art Davis, with whom Roach is able to parlay rhythmic variations that converge with harmonic variants. —*Spencer R. Weston*, Cadence

★ **Victory and Sorrow** / Aug. 9, 1961 / Affinity 124
Booker Little's *Victory and Sorrow* was the last statement of an auspicious vision in midbloom, recorded approximately one month before his death in the fall of 1961. Like Clifford Brown (his major influence), Little was an astonishingly protean stylist and composer who reconciled the structures and temperament of bop to fit his own pointedly lyrical vistas. This final winging offers Little at his most assertive and museful, careening generally in a supple, honeyed voice, but rising up hard on the right occasion for a metal-line exclamation. In one of his most reflective performances of the set, the doleful "If I Should Love You," he revels in the quality of delay, petting each note with full sweeps and resting on the beauteous support of the band. Leading a horn trio that includes saxophonist George Coleman and trombonist Julian Priester, Little contrives a tonal fabric that seems broader than possible, while maintaining close harmonic formations. This is a music of symmetry and sympathy, a gentle, inviting music that invites those who perceive the active force in fertility. —*Mikal Gilmore*, Down Beat

CHARLES LLOYD

b. Mar. 15, 1938, Memphis, TN
Tenor saxophone, flute / Hard bop, early jazz-rock, world fusion
One of the more engaging tenor saxophonists and daring flutists, Charles Lloyd played in R&B and blues bands with B.B. King and Bobby "Blue" Bland before moving from Memphis to the West Coast in 1956. He later worked with Chico Hamilton and Gerald Wilson, and toured with Cannonball Adderley before forming his own group in the mid '60s. His late '60s group, which also included pianist Keith Jarrett, enjoyed both jazz and pop notoriety, thanks to a 1967 concert his quartet played at the Fillmore. His tenor has the warm, bluesy sound associated with Southern and Southwestern stylists, although Lloyd also weaves vocal effects, honks, and upper-register careening into his solos. His flute lines, wavery phrases, and over-blowing are more energetic. —*Ron Wynn*

★ **Forest Flower** / Sep. 8, 1966+Sep. 18, 1966 / Atlantic 1473
In the Soviet Union / May 14, 1967 / Atlantic 1571
This album was recorded at the 14th International Jazz Festival at Tallinn, the capital of Estonia, in May of 1967. The performances of these four tunes and the enthusiastic responses to them show that it was a rewarding experience for Charles Lloyd and the members of his quartet: pianist Keith Jarrett, bassist Ron McClure, and drummer Jack DeJohnette. By 1967, this group was really together. They had been almost constantly on the road for two years, and the festival at Tallinn was their fourth overseas tour in 13 months. Some of the best moments on the record are a direct consequence of their time together. Probably no amount of rehearsal in a studio could have produced McClure and Jarrett's interplay immediately before Lloyd restates the head at the end of "Days and Nights Waiting," or Jarrett's upper register responses to Lloyd's flute in "Love Song to a Baby." Looking back at this group, it's a little hard to fathom that they used to be considered avant-garde. True, they occasionally suspend the chord structure to allow some free blowing, as they

do here on the uptempo tunes "Sweet Georgia Bright" and "Tribal Dance." But these are only interludes, and the group essentially adheres to the pattern of stating the head, standing in the line for solos, and restating the head. What distinguishes it from a lot of other groups is that each member is a virtuoso. Their imaginations are never checked by merely technical limitations, either their own or somebody else's. — *Jack McCaffrey*, Coda

Fish out of Water / Jul. 1989 / ECM 841088
This new release offers quasi-mystical themes, shimmering horn riffs, and flute melodies plus fine keyboard contributions from Bob Stenson and decent, though hardly aggressive, rhythm section work by bassist Palle Danielsson and drummer Jon Christensen. —*Ron Wynn,* Rock & Roll Disc

Dream Weaver / Mar. 20, 1996 / Atlantic
Sweeping flute, craggy tenor sax solos, and fine piano by Keith Jarrett. —*Ron Wynn*

MIKE LONGO (Michael Joseph Longo)

b. Mar. 19, 1939, Cincinnati, OH
Piano, composer / Bop
A good bebop pianist and accompanist, Mike Longo's style has been influenced greatly by Oscar Peterson and Bud Powell. His phrasing and his solos aren't flashy, but are expressive and well played. Longo began piano lessons at age three, and was playing professionally at age 15. He played with Cannonball Adderley while still in high school. He graduated from Western Kentucky in 1959, where he earned a Bachelors degree in music. Longo was also a *Down Beat* Hall of Fame scholarship winner that year. He played at the Metropole in New York with Red Allen, Coleman Hawkins, and George Wettling in 1960. Longo moved to Toronto in 1961, where he studied with Peterson, and also led a trio. After returning to New York in 1962, Longo spent the next four years doing freelance dates backing singers. He joined Dizzy Gillespie in 1966, and remained with him until 1973. During that time, Longo became Gillespie's music director and arranger. While still in the group, Longo took lessons in counterpoint from Hall Overton. He began recording as a leader in the '70s, cutting sessions for Mainstream and Pablo, and cutting a 1981 solo album for Consolidated Artists. Currently, none of these dates are available on CD, but Longo can be heard on Gillespie CD reissues. —*Ron Wynn*

★ **Awakening, The** / **i.** Oct. 1972 / Mainstream 357

JOE LOVANO

b. 1952
Tenor saxophone / Postbop, neo-bop, modern creative
Joe Lovano's become one of the most familiar names on the '90s jazz scene. He's been featured in the bands of John Scofield and Bass Desires, and has lead his own group on some acclaimed albums. Lovano has emerged as a prime player through his ability to play "outside" (or in an avant-garde style) without abandoning meter or chord progressions. He's developed an approach that mixes elements gleaned from players such as Dewey Redman, John Coltrane, Wayne Shorter, and Joe Henderson, and has now been cited by musicians such as Joshua Redman as an as an influence on their playing. Lovano's father was a saxophonist, and he helped introduce Lovano to jazz through his playing and records. Lovano attended Berklee in the early '70s, studying with Gary Burton and meeting Bill Frisell and John Scofield. He later returned to his native Ohio, where he played with Lonnie Liston Smith, making his recording debut on a mid-'70s Smith album. Lovano later toured with Brother Jack McDuff. He moved to New York in 1976, and, following stints with Albert Dailey and Chet Baker, joined the Woody Herman Orchestra. Lovano played with them until 1979, then joined Mel Lewis's big band. Lovano began working with Paul Motian in the early '80s, and they've maintained a working relationship that's seen them appear regularly on each other's albums. Lovano's also maintained

a similar relationship with Frisell. He toured Europe with Elvin Jones in 1987, and participated in the recording sessions for Charlie Haden's revived Liberation Music Orchestra. He later toured with them. After doing a duo album with Aldo Romano, Lovano appeared on John Scofield's debut for Blue Note Records. He signed with the label in 1991. Lovano has also recorded for Soul Note and Enja, working with Michel Pertucciani, Dave Holland, Edward Blackwell, John Abercrombie, Kenny Werner, Marc Johnson, Bill Stewart, and Anthony Cox, among others. Currently, Lovano has five albums available on CD. —*Ron Wynn*

○ **One Time Out** / **i.** Sep. 1987 / Soul Note 1224

★ **Village Rhythm** / Jun. 7-9, 1988 / Soul Note 182.1
Quintet with Tom Harrell (tpt) and Ken Werner (p). This Cleveland saxophonist at his best. —*Michael G. Nastos*

○ **From the Soul** / **i.** 1992 / Blue Note 98636
A 1992 release by acclaimed tenor saxophonist Joe Lovano. He's heading a different lineup here from his most recent releases, with pianist Michel Petrucciani, bassist Dave Holland, and the late drummer Ed Blackwell. It's hard-edged, explosive playing all around, with Blackwell laying down his patented bombs while Petrucciani and Holland converge behind Lovano's dynamic solos. —*Ron Wynn*

Universal Language / Capitol 99830
Joe Lovano's *Universal Language* is a picaresque collage of epic tales based on the saxophonist's variegated musical and biographical roots. It's an open-ended affair where individual and ensemble adventures unfold with audacity. That it works so well is a credit to Lovano's bold vision and to the empathic talents of vocalist Judi Silvano, trumpeter Tom Hagans, pianist Kenny Werner, drummer Jack DeJohnette, and bassists Steve Swallow, Scott Lee, and Charlie Haden. — *Chuck Berg,* Jazz Times

FRANK LOWE

b. Jun. 24, 1943, Memphis, TN
Tenor saxophone / Early free, modern creative
Another saxophonist who is forging an alliance of R&B, soul, and free music, Frank Lowe's high-energy style has been heard on '60s and '70s sessions. Though his tone seems to flatten out sometimes, his array of screams, shrieks, octave leaps, and bursts is always attention-grabbing, if occasionally chaotic. Lowe began on tenor at age 12, then studied briefly at the University of Kansas and with Donald Garrett in San Francisco. He played with Sun Ra in New York during the late '60s, returned to study classical music at San Francisco Conservatory, then played with Alice Coltrane, Rashied Ali, Archie Shepp, Milford Graves, and Don Cherry in New York in the early '70s. He's been a leader since the mid-'70s, recording on Survival, ESP, Cadence Jazz, Musicworks, and Soul Note, among others. Lowe has played with Lester Bowie, Bobo Shaw, Joseph Bowie, Anthony Braxton, and many others. Currently, he has several dates available on CD. —*Ron Wynn*

★ **Fresh** / **i.** Apr. 1976 / Arista 1015
The album's title, *Fresh,* aptly describes the music. Instead of focusing on improvisations based on the traditions of Western harmonic practice, Frank Lowe's group centers on the emotive ramifications of color and texture. Regarding color, the substitution of Abdul Wadud's cello for bass is brilliant. The crystal warmth of his cleanly articulated, plucked, strummed, and bowed figures is awesome. Lowe and both trumpeter Lester and trombonist Joseph Bowie produce an incredible array of sound which, in the manner of John Cage's prepared piano, extends the boundaries of their respective instruments past the canons of conventional technique and taste. An additional accent is Selene Fung's cheng, a Chinese string instrument. With its broad polychromatic palette and fluid approach to meter and tempo, the ensemble freely oscillates from one textural web to the next. — *Chuck Berg,* Down Beat

○ **Skizoke** / **i.** Nov. 1982 / Cadence CJR

This is an enjoyable album documenting tenor saxophonist Frank Lowe's conception of the mainstream, which appears to be a very fertile place for him. All the tunes save "Close to the Soul" are in a medium tempo bag (though the title cut and "Some Do, Some Don't" feature heads that move from medium to slow tempo and then back again). Vibist Damon Choice and guitarist Larry Simon are mainly on hand for inventive coloration—backdrop for the soloists (either together, alone, or in flux). Bassist Wilbur Morris and drummer Tim Pleasant support the proceedings well, though the drummer seems to have a bit of trouble fitting into the ballad's ("Close To The Soul") rhythmic head before it enters the floating free space where the majority of playing takes place. Lowe's solo work here is quite original—oddly spaced lines and fragments, much of it overtly referring to the composed material. He gets into some more obviously robust playing on "Some Do, Some Don't" and "Close To The Soul." Cornetist Butch Morris is quite solid throughout, but he's especially interesting on "Soul," where he toys with the mute and amplification getting some very distinct effects. —Milo Fine, Cadence

○ **Decision in Paradise** / Sep. 24+28, 1984 / Soul Note 1082
Tenorist Frank Lowe's Decision in Paradise is a meeting of first, second, and fourth wave avant-gardists: Don Cherry, pocket trumpet; Grachan Moncur III, trombone; Geri Allen, piano, ringer; Charnette Moffett, bass; Charles Moffett, drums. If the music's not quite as explosive as the lineup promises, it's still quite fine—robust, sinewy blowing music in a relatively straightahead vein. Just the idea of a father-son rhythm team is appealing, and the Moffetts do have a nimble rapport and a mutual buoyancy which, if not born of blood, is certainly much in evidence. They have a mirror image at the group's top end, for Cherry is something of a musical mentor to Lowe; both bring a rough and burly grace to their improvising. Lowe doesn't sound like Ben Webster, but his style, as on the title track, is a paradoxical blend of tenderness and bluster. (Butch Morris's ballad "I'll Whistle Your Name" is a soLowe.) Cherry, a giant of the music, is in excellent form; his curling, muted lines on "Lowe-ologie" recall his early '60s work, further evoked by "Cherryco," which he recorded with John Coltrane in 1960. There's nothing really radical about Allen's playing, except that she eschews the normal McCoy Tyner or Cecil Taylor tendencies you might expect in this context. Her clipped sound and hornlike conception have their origins in older styles, and her pre-Bud Powell intro to the charmingly jaunty "You Dig!" (featuring a shouting solo by composer Moncur) is delightfully, respectfully old-fashioned. Lowe's "Dues and Don'ts"—aka "Some Do, Some Don't"—is a fetching riff reprised from Skizoke. —Kevin Whitehead, Cadence

Flam, The / Black Saint 120005
Frank Lowe is a tenor saxophonist with some interesting ideas, but he too often lapses into a formula in his solos: scalar runs followed by growls, shrieks, and overtones. What makes this album of interest is not so much Lowe's playing but the playing of trumpeter Leo Smith and trombonist Joseph Bowie. Both approach their instruments as sources of sound rather than notes per se, and this results in many interesting textures and colors. Smith, one of the few trumpet players who charts new frontiers for that instrument, utilizes all the resources of his instrument and himself, pinching notes here, blowing through his horn there. Bowie uses his instrument mostly for vocal-style effects. Rounding out the group are bassist Alex Blake and drummer Charles Bobo Shaw. —Carl Brauer, Cadence

MUNDELL LOWE (James Mundell Lowe)

b. Apr. 21, 1922, Laurel, MS
Guitar, arranger, composer / Swing, big band, bop
A steady, smooth, and understated guitarist and composer, Mundell Lowe's style has moved from traditional jazz early in his career to swing and cool. Lowe played traditional jazz around New Orleans from 1936 to 1940, and also did some country sessions in Nashville. He played in swing bands led

by Jan Savitt, Ray McKinley, Mary Lou Williams, Red Norvo, and Ellis Larkins from 1942 until 1950. Lowe studied composition with Hall Overton from 1948 to 1952, and became a staff musician at NBC in 1950. Besides an occasional acting stint, Lowe composed scores for several television shows. He was a member of the Sauter-Finegan Orchestra in 1952 and 1953, and worked with Benny Goodman in 1952. That began an association that continued periodically until 1984. Lowe began heading a quartet in the '50s that he led intermittently until the '80s. He moved to California in 1965 and started to emphasize composition ahead of playing. But he also worked with Richie Kamuca in Los Angeles, and toured Europe with Betty Bennett in 1974 and 1975, and toured Japan with Benny Carter in 1977, 1978, and 1983. He became background guitarist at the Monterey Jazz Festival in 1970, and finally became the Festival's music director in 1983. Lowe taught film composition at the Dick Grove School of Music in Los Angeles from 1979 to 1985. He didn't make many recordings, but did some sessions for Riverside in the '50s and for Famous Door in the '70s. Recently, The Mundell Lowe Quartet, a 1955 date, was reissued by Fantasy on CD, and a '92 date on the Jazz Alliance label is also available. —Ron Wynn and Michael G. Nastos

★ **Mundell Lowe Quartet** / Aug. 27, 1955-Oct. 4, 1955 / Riverside 1773

California Guitar / i. 1974 / Famous Door
Classy, sophisticated fare with some funk supplied by Irving Ashby (g). —Ron Wynn

○ **Souvenirs** / i. 1992 / Jazz Alliance 10011
A nice tribute album to Nick Ceroli by guitarist Mundell Lowe. Drummer Ceroli also plays on the album, along with saxophonist Bob Magnusson and drummer Mike Wofford. The mood's both cool and cagey, with no one trying to take the spotlight but contributing some fervent solos when the spotlight shines. —Ron Wynn

JIMMIE LUNCEFORD (James Melvin Lunceford)

b. Jun. 6, 1902, Fulton, MS, d. Jul. 12, 1947, Seaside, OR
Reeds, conductor, arranger / Swing, big band
Jimmy Lunceford's orchestra played a pivotal role among swing era bands. They perfected ensemble interaction, especially on the arrangements that featured two-beat swing at medium tempos. They were flamboyant showmen without being clowns. They were influenced by Alphonso Trent and the Casa Lama Orchestra, but the key figure in the band's distinctive sound was trumpeter and arranger Sy Oliver. He was a master at incorporating unusual elements into an arrangement. His "Organ Grinder Swing" included woodblocks, celeste, and saxes playing in an exaggerated, vocal-like manner. Oliver was known for his imaginative interplay between soloists, brass, and reed sections. While the arrangements were intricate, Oliver always left plenty of room for the soloists, and concluded songs with an impressive flourish.

Jimmy Lunceford learned several instruments during his childhood, and studied under Paul Whiteman's father, Wilburforce J. Whiteman. Lunceford graduated from Fisk University, and later taught at Manassas High in Memphis after working for Elmer Snowden and Wilbur Sweatman. Lunceford organized a student band in 1927, the Chicksaw Syncopators. They turned professional in 1929, and issued their first recordings in 1930. Though proficient on several saxophones, Lunceford was strictly a bandleader, except for his flute solo on the song "Liza." He insisted on precision in performance, excellence in dress, and a sophisticated, though humorous, stage show. At various times, the Lunceford band included Willie Smith, Jimmy Crawford, Trummy Young, Joe Thomas, Eddie Durhan, and Tommy Stevenson. They've been credited with having 22 hits between 1934 and 1946, more than any other Black swing band except Duke Ellington's and Cab Calloway's. These hits included "Rhythm Is Our Business" in 1935, "Blues in the Night" in 1942, and "I'm Gonna Move to the Outskirts of Town." Their masterpiece was "For Dancers Only," though

"Tain't What You Do (It's the Way That You Do It)" in 1939 and "Organ Grinder's Swing" were also exceptional. They played many engagements in the Midwest during the early '30s before coming to New York and to the Cotton Club in 1934. A pair of songs, "Jazznocracy" and "White Heat," had arrangements by Will Hudson and won national attention; the group's reputation was cemented by 1935.

The Lunceford Orchestra recorded for nearly a decade for Decca, except for one year they recorded for Columbia. They did some broadcasting, but opportunities were limited by racial barriers. Lunceford died suddenly on the road in 1947; a rumor persists he was poisoned by a racist restaurant owner after Lunceford insisted that he feed the band, but this has not been verified. The band continued for a short period under the leadership of Joe Thomas and pianist Eddie Wilcox, but eventually disbanded. A Lunceford reunion album was recorded for Capitol in the mid-'50s. —*Ron Wynn*

○ **Jimmie Lunceford (1930-1934)** / **i.** Jun. 1930-Nov. 1934 / Classics

○ **Stomp It Off** / **i.** Sep. 1934-May 1935 / MCA 16082
If craftsmanship is its own reward, then there is much to admire in this Decca set, which collects Jimmie Lunceford's early 1934-1935 recordings in chronological order, skipping a half-dozen mediocrities and some alternates. Reed players Willie Smith and Joe Thomas deliver smart solo work. And the ensembles are precise, sometimes to the point of pickiness, not just in their attacks but in the shadings and dynamics that only a leader's vision can bring to a score. You'll find all this summarized in a remarkable reed passage on "Sleepy-Time Gal." —*John McDonough*, Down Beat

○ **Jazz Heritage–Jimmie's Legacy (1934-1937)** / 1934-1937 / MCA 1320
A detailed anthology covering the mid-'30s Jimmie Lunceford band. It's more detailed and annotated, as well as better remastered and sequenced than most other Lunceford sets. The three years covered (1934-1937) were pivotal, as Lunceford's whole conception of light, bouncy blues swing was honed during this time. —*Ron Wynn*

○ **Jazz Heritage–Harlem Shout (1935-1936)** / 1935-1936 / MCA 1305
Unlike Fletcher Henderson's band, Jimmie Lunceford's did not have the all-star lineup, alto saxophonist Willie Smith being a notable exception, but the almost instant polish and advanced sophisticated arrangements certainly made this a modern hip band of its day. It was also, to a great extent, the base upon which many of the jazzy dance bands that were to come along, even into the '70s, were built upon. There were some commercial clinkers sewn along the tracks. Lunceford, like Henderson, Duke Ellington, Count Basie, and most other great bandleaders, built upon a base of strength: distinctive arrangements (Sy Oliver, Ed Wilcox) laced with solid solos. But Lunceford more than the others played toward the commercial dance crowd. —*Bob Rusch*, Cadence

○ **Jazz Heritage–For Dancers Only (1936-1937)** / 1936-1937 / MCA 1307
The first in a series dedicated to the late '30s recordings of the Jimmie Lunceford orchestra, among the greatest swing bands ever. It covers 1936 and 1937, their earliest years on Decca, and predates most of their big hits. It's a nicely packaged collection, and remains one of the better Lunceford anthologies. —*Ron Wynn*

★ **Jazz Heritage–Last Sparks (1941-1944)** / **i.** 1941-1942 / MCA 1321
Recorded 1941-1944. Arrangements here are by Ed Wilcox, Horace Henderson, Roger Segure, Tadd Dameron, Pee Wee Jackson, and Billy Moore Jr. These are another twelve great tracks. —*Michael G. Nastos*

Harlem Shout / **i.** May 1969 / Decca 79238

Margie / Savoy 1209

○ **Rhythm Is Our Business** / Living Era 5091

This is the earliest of several Jimmie Lunceford MCA reissues from the early '80s. These sessions cover the period from 9/4/34 to 12/17/34 and include "Rose Room," "Black and Tan Fantasy," "Stomp It Off," and the title track. The six Lunceford albums originally issued in the set covered 80 tracks over a 10-year stretch. —Cadence

JIMMY LYONS

b. Dec. 1, 1933, Jersey City, NJ, **d.** May 19, 1986, New York, NY
Alto and soprano saxophone / *Early free, modern creative*
He was known mainly for his long and fertile association with Cecil Taylor, but Jimmy Lyons deserved just as much praise for his abilities as an alto saxophonist outside of that union. A bebop player who juxtaposed bepop with Taylor's avant-garde works, Lyons had a dynamic, energetic, and searing style, which was necessary considering the aggressive quality of Taylor's music. But there was also a lyrical, introspective air in Lyons solos, a softness that balanced the fury. Lyons was given an alto sax by Buster Bailey as a teen, and was aided musically by Elmo Hope, Bud Powell, and Thelonious Monk. He studied with Rudy Rutherford, then began his long tenure with Taylor in the early '60s. Lyons sometimes did other jobs. For a while in the '70s he taught music at a New York drug treatment center. He was an artist-in-residence with Taylor and Andrew Cyrille at Antioch College and served with Bill Dixon as director of the Black Music Ensemble at Bennington College in 1975. But until the late '70s, Lyons's poignant, fiery alto solos were the other familiar part of Taylor's music. Lyons and Taylor recorded for many labels, and Lyons adjusted to constant personnel changes, sometimes playing with other saxophonists like Sam Rivers, other times with violinists, multiple drummers, or trumpeters. Lyons and Taylor made their recording debut in 1962, and Lyons was on every Taylor record until Lyons began heading his own bands. His late '70s and '80s groups usually included his wife, bassoonist Karen Borca, and drummer Paul Murphy, and assorted guest stars. Lyons also worked in a trio with vocalist Jeanne Lee and Andrew Cyrille, and in duos with Cyrille and Sunny Murray. Lyons recorded for Byg, Hat Hut, and Black Saint. Only a few of his sessions are available on CD. —*Ron Wynn*

★ **Jump Up / What to Do About** / Aug. 30, 1980 / Hat Hut 21
Alto saxophonist Jimmy Lyons's trio recording with Sunny Murray (d) and John Lindberg (the bassist in the String Trio of New York and the Anthony Braxton quartet) is a real gem. Lyons's prior Hat Hut three-record set, *Push Pull*, with his regular group, suffered from poor recording quality, but this performance at the 1980 Willisau Jazz Festival was very well recorded. If one word could be used to describe the playing it would be "hot." Like his recordings with pianist Cecil Taylor, Jimmy Lyons maintains a high level of intensity and inspiration from the first note to the last. Murray and Lindberg are more than equal to the task in this cooperative effort. —*Carl Brauer*, Cadence

○ **Something in Return** / 1981 / Black Saint 120125

○ **Burnt Offering** / **i.** 1982 / Black Saint 120130

Wee Sneezawee / Sep. 26-27, 1983 / Black Saint 0067
Altoist Jimmy Lyons on *Wee Sneezawee* continues to blend Ornette Coleman and Charlie Parker conceptions into a most productive mix of overt passion and fleet phrasing. Yet this session with his "bassoon quintet" (Raphe Malik, trumpet; Karen Borca, bassoon; William Parker, bass; Paul Murphy, drums) sounds rather stiff. Borca in particular seems to struggle with her very difficult double-reed axe; she rarely matches Lyons's mesmerizing facility on his horn (though there are moments on "Gossip" when Borca does get remarkably close to the leader's conception). Then too, a string of solos format seems strangely restrictive here. Presumably Lyons wanted to get away from the dense interplay he got working with Cecil Taylor, but Taylor's sense of compressed urgency would have been welcome here, as it was such a natural complement to Lyons's own tightly wound sound. As it is, nearly all of the best moments come when he solos; elsewhere, the excitement lags. —*Kevin Whitehead*, Cadence

M

M'BOOM

Group / World fusion, modern creative

Max Roach established M'Boom (the full name is M'Boom Re) in 1972. The group was a rhythm ensemble whose members played only percussion instruments: trap drums, marimba, xylophone, timpani, woodblocks, orchestral bells, gongs, vibes, congas, and other assorted African and Latin devices. Its members play over 100 instruments. Roach, Ray Mantilla, Joe Chambers, Freddy Waits, Roy Brooks, Warren Smith, Omar Clay, and Fred King were the original members. The group has maintained a periodic performance and recording schedule over the years, doing albums for Baystate, Soul Note, Mesa, and Columbia. While their albums, particularly the 1992 *Live at S.O.B.'s*, have been excellent their live performances are sensational. The array of colors, rhythms, and sounds, unencumbered by studio demands, are among the most amazing in any style, and are reminiscent of West African or Cuban drumming ensemble performances. *—Ron Wynn*

Re: Percussion / i. Aug. 25, 1973 / Baystate 2604
Max Roach's percussion sextet. Two extended compositions by Joe Chambers. Excellent. *—Michael G. Nastos*

○ **Live at S.O.B.'s New / i.** 1992 / Blue Moon 79182
Exciting percussion duels, multiple rhythms, and teeming arrangements and performances by the conglomeration of drummers known as M'Boom. This recent release included founding member Max Roach, plus Roy Brooks, Joe Chambers, Omar Clay, Fred King, Ray Mantilla, Warren Smith, and Freddy Waits performing live at celebrated New York club S.O.B.'s. *—Ron Wynn*

★ **M'Boom** / Columbia 36247

HAROLD MABERN (Harold (Jr) Mabern)

b. Mar. 20, 1936, Memphis, TN

Piano / Hard bop

One of jazz's great melodic interpreters, Harold Mabern's taken his place among the ranks of first-rate Memphis pianists who've attained international stature as solid soloists and fine composers. At home with the blues, bebop, hard bop, and swing, Mabern's fleeting chordal style and driving approach were influenced by Phineas Newborn, and by John Coltrane and George Coleman. His composition, "Blues for Phineas," acknowledged his debt to Newborn, while the composition "Rakin' and Scrapin'" may be his finest. Mabern taught himself piano as a teenager, then studied harmony with Ahmad Jamal after moving from Memphis to Chicago in the mid-'50s. He was in Walter Perkins's MJT + 3 group, then moved to New York in 1959. Mabern played with Lionel Hampton, Art Farmer and Benny Golson's Jazztet, Donald Byrd, Miles Davis, and J.J. Johnson in the early and mid-'60s. He was then an accompanist for vocalists Joe Williams, Sarah Vaughan, and Arthur Prysock, while also playing with Sonny Rollins, Freddie Hubbard, and Wes Montgomery. Mabern was in the Piano Choir with Stanley Cowell and several others, cutting some critically praised, but poorly distributed albums for Strata-East. Mabern played in Walter Bolden's trio, recorded with Billy Harper,

and performed in England. He worked extensively with Lee Morgan in the early '70s, playing on his final Blue Note dates. Mabern doesn't have a hefty number of sessions as a leader. He recorded some nice soul jazz, blues, and hard bop dates for Prestige in the late '60s, and was featured on a strong Sony/DIW date with Ron Carter and Jack DeJohnette in 1992. He did a live date at the Cafe Des Copains for Sackville. Currently, Mabern has only three sessions available as a leader on CD; his sessions with others are available also. *—Ron Wynn and Michael G. Nastos*

★ **Rakin' & Scrapin'** / Dec. 23, 1968 / Prestige 330
Any old Mabern album is great. The Memphis pianist is now in New York City. *—Michael G. Nastos*

Live at Cafe Des Copains / Sackville

TEO MACERO

b. Oct. 30, 1925

Tenor saxophone, arranger, bandleader, producer / Cool

A wide-ranging individual who's been a saxophonist, a bandleader, a composer, a producer, and an arranger, Teo Macero's impact has been multifaceted. Many remember him as Miles Davis's producer during most of his Columbia tenure, the "Teo" whom Davis often referred to at the end of takes. But Macero was also a distinctive, original, and experimental saxophone player. Macero studied at Juilliard in the late '40s and early '50s, and recorded on Mingus's Debut label. He had one of the more ambitious dates of the '50s; the album *Explorations* featured him playing two tenors and two altos via multitracking, an unusual practice for the time. Macero headed dance bands, won Guggenheim grants, and had his composition, "Fusion," performed by the New York Philharmonic Orchestra and conducted by Leonard Bernstein. He also recorded for Columbia, and composed a ballet suite with a chamber orchestra that was recorded and was issued by a Swedish label. Macero joined Columbia in 1957 as a music editor, then became a producer. Besides Davis's recordings, Macero also produced several great Mingus records, among them *Mingus Dynasty* and *Mingus Ah Um*. He also produced Thelonious Monk albums, and Monk wrote and recorded "Theo" for him in 1964. Macero took over George Avakian's job and began producing Miles Davis with *Kind of Blue*. Macero took as much, if not more, of the heat when Davis moved into jazz-rock, funk, R&B, and instrumental pop. Macero recorded his own album for American Clave in 1980, produced an anthology, *Portrait of Charles Mingus*, for Palo Alto in 1983, and produced a Loose Tubes date in 1987. He has a couple of sessions as a leader available on CD; Davis, Mingus, and Monk productions are available, too. *—Ron Wynn and Michael G. Nastos*

Time + 7 / i. 1965 / Finnadar 9024
This album was way ahead of its time. A reissue with Art Farmer (tpt), John La Porta (reeds), Ed Shaughnessy (d), and Mal Waldron (p). *—Michael G. Nastos*

★ **Acoustical Suspension / i.** 1984 / Doctor Jazz 40111
Teo Macero's *Acoustical Suspension* has a ton of great players on it, but seems to suffer from a lack of creative songwriting and arranging. On "The Man with the Horn," for instance, Gato Barbieri's solo goes on way too long for such a

simple rhythmic backup, and "Summer Rain" is dangerously close to being elevator music, saved only by Dave Liebman's soaring soprano sax. Liebman also blows hard on "Acoustical Suspension," but the guitar solo is choppy and nervous. *—Neil Haverstick, Cadence*

○ **Best of Teo Macero, The** / **i.** Aug. 1990 / Stash 527
Interesting anthology with superproducer Teo Macero presented during his playing days in various lineups. Guests include Art Farmer, Bill Evans, Lee Konitz, Ed Shaughnessy, Mal Waldron, Al Cohn, and Charles Mingus. *—Ron Wynn*

MACHITO (Frank Grillo)

b. 1912, Havana, Cuba, **d.** London, England
Vocals / Latin jazz, world fusion
An institution in Latin jazz and international music, Machito (Frank Raul Grillo) was a fixture from the early '40s till the mid-'80s. Thanks to the innovations of brother-in-law and longtime musical director Mario Bauza, Machito's bands blended excellent jazz arrangements with frenetic Cuban rhythms, creating a sound that was fresh and intriguing. Bauza called it Afro-Cuban music, while others labeled it "Cubop." Machito was the leader, vocalist, and maracas player.

The son of a cigar manufacturer, he sang and danced with his father's employees as a child, and later sang in the group Jovenes de Rendicion. He worked with several Cuban bands in the late '20s and '30s before coming to America in 1937 as a vocalist with the group La Estrella Habanera. Machito recorded with Alfredito Valdez, El Quarteto Caney, El Conjunto Moderno, and La Orchestra Hatuey while working with other groups in the late '30s. He and Bauza formed a band, but disbanded it shortly afterwards. Machito worked with the Orchestra Siboney and recorded with Xavier Cugat before forming the Afro-Cubans in 1940. The next year Bauza joined this band, and remained until they had another conflict in 1976, one that couldn't be resolved. The band made its first recordings for Decca. Machito's sister, Graciela, was bandleader while he was in the army in the mid-'40s.

The Afro-Cubans became immensely popular. They appeared with Stan Kenton's big band in the late '40s, and played several concerts with jazz groups. Bauza's idea that they employ top non-Latin jazz stars as special guests led to players such as Charlie Parker, Dizzy Gillespie, Flip Phillips, Howard McGhee, Brew Moore, Buddy Rich, Harry Edison, Cannonball Adderley, Curtis Fuller, Herbie Mann, Johnny Griffin, Eddie Bert, and Aaron Sachs working and recording with the band from the late '40s through the '60s.

They maintained their popularity through the mambo era of the '50s and early '60s, and were a staple when salsa surged in popularity during the '70s and '80s. The Afro-Cubans kept busy on both the jazz and salsa circuits, and were featured in Carlos Ortiz's 1987 documentary film *Machito: A Jazz Legacy*. They recorded for Verve, Roulette, Trip, Tico, Secco, Forum, Coral, RCA, Pablo, and Timeless. Machito's 1982 LP, *Machito and His Salsa Big Band*, won a Grammy. Only a couple of Machito albums, reissues of classic dates from the late '40s and early '50s, are currently available on CD, according to *Schwann*. But like other great Latin stars, Machito's albums remain in circulation on the Latin music circuit. *—Ron Wynn and Michael G. Nastos*

○ **Dizzy Gillespie/Charlie Parker** / **i.** 1948 / Verve
A selection of prime Latin jazz cuts with both Parker and Diz plus Machito. *—Ron Wynn*

Afro-Cuban Jazz / Dec. 20, 1948-Jan. 1949 / Verve 2522
Late '40s and early to mid-'50s pivotal sessions with Chano Pozo, Chico O'Farrill, Dizzy Gillespie (tpt), Charlie Parker (as), Mario Bauza, Flip Phillips (ts), and Buddy Rich (d). A must-buy. *—Michael G. Nastos*

★ **Machito and His Afro-Cuban Salseros** / **i.** 1948 / Pablo

○ **Afro-Cuban Jazz Suite** / Dec. 21, 1950 / Clef 505

★ **Latin Soul Plus Jazz** / 1957 / Charly 149

This band, under Machito's sizzling baton, blows up a storm that could wipe Cuba right off the map! Sitting in are jazz heavyweights Cannonball Adderly, Curtis Fuller, Joe Newman, Herbie Mann, Johnny Griffin, Candido Camero, and others. The year is 1957. Twelve sizzlin' sides, digitally remastered. *—Myles Boisen, Roots & Rhythm*

○ **Machito at the Crescendo** / 1960 / GNP 58
Excellent 1960 sessions made in Hollywood with a great dance and Latin-jazz band. *—Ron Wynn*

World's Greatest Latin Band / **i.** 1960 / GNP 72

★ **Afro-Cuban Jazz Moods** / **i.** Jun. 4-5, 1975 / Pablo

○ **Machito and His Salsa Big Band** / **i.** 1982 / Impulse 33106
This was the recording that won Machito a Grammy in 1983. A dynamite band with Chocolate Armenteros in the trumpet section and Macho's daughter as lead female vocalist, and a fine mix of well-known and less-familiar numbers including "El Manicero" and a Machito warhorse, "Quimbombo." A worthy memorial indeed. *—John Storm Roberts*

Live at North Sea / Jul. 18, 1982 / Timeless

Machito! / Jul. 16, 1983 / Timeless

☆ **1983 Grammy Award Winner** / **i.** 1983 / MCA 33106
Machito and His Salsa Big Band. Showing the band is still vital, this live recording in Holland is hot. *—Michael G. Nastos*

ADAM MAKOWICZ (Adam Matyszkowicz)

b. Aug. 18, 1940, Cesky Tesin, Czechoslovakia
Piano / Bop
He began playing professionally in 1962 in Kracöw, then moved to Warsaw in 1965. Makowicz's voicings, phrasing, and approach, while certainly his own, also shows the heavy influence of Art Tatum. Makowicz headed his own trio and toured extensively through Europe, Cuba, India, and around the world. Makowicz began writing both music and music criticism, as well as arrangements, in 1971. He joined violinist Michael Urbaniak's group the same year, spending three years with Urbaniak and his wife, Urzula. He began working with the Tomasz Stanko trio and later formed a band with Stanko in 1975. Makowicz's reputation in Europe eventually spread to America, where critics began to recognize his fluency, rhythmic verve, and dazzling technique. *—Ron Wynn*

★ **Adam** / 1977 / Columbia 35320
Polish pianist Adam Makowicz's debut American release is definitely a tour de force from a traditional/technical point of view. The variety of colors in his improvisations as well as the cliché hook of pure speed in his runs make this an enjoyable album. *—Milo Fine, Cadence*

Classic Jazz Duets / 1979 / Stash 216

Name is Makowicz (Ma-Ko-Vitch) / Apr. 25-29, 1983 / Sheffield Lab 21

○ **Naughty Baby** / **i.** 1987 / Novus 3022
An all-Gershwin program with two bassists, Dave Holland and Charlie Haden. Essential. *—Michael G. Nastos*

JUNIOR MANCE (Julian Clifford (Jr) Mance)

b. Oct. 10, 1928, Chicago, IL
Piano / Hard bop, blues & jazz, soul-jazz
Junior Mance has maintained his integrity expertly while inserting large doses of funk, blues, soul, and gospel influences into his piano style. The results are a loose, often exciting and energetic approach with nifty runs, clever phrases, and soulful choruses, yet it is an approach that's also thoroughly grounded in bebop fundamentals. Mance can execute tricky harmonic maneuvers, rhythmic licks, or melodic turns, then play passages that are simple and compelling. As a leader, he's never attained the chart success of Ramsey Lewis, Ahmad Jamal, or Les McCann, though Mance operates in similar territory. His father was a stride and boogie-woogie player, and Mance learned piano from him. He also studied formally, including two years at Roosevelt College. Mance was playing professionally at age ten, and worked

with Gene Ammons in the late '40s. He spent a year with Lester Young, then rejoined Ammons. Mance played in an army band at Fort Knox in 1951, along with the Adderley brothers and Curtis Fuller. He honed his skills during a stint as house pianist at the Beehive; he worked with many visiting jazz stars. Mance later spent a year and a half accompanying Dinah Washington. He was the pianist for the first edition of the Adderley brothers band in the mid-'50s, then played with Dizzy Gillespie from 1958 to 1960. Mance was in the two-tenor band co-led by Eddie "Lockjaw" Davis and Johnny Griffin in the early '60s, then headed his own trio at the Village Vanguard in 1961. Since then, Mance has led his own bands, and has worked with players such as Billy Cobham, Shelly Manne, and Pet Candoli. His trio and combos were a popular attraction at several major jazz clubs in the '70s and '80s. Mance recorded with Aretha Franklin on her *Soul '69* album. His own recording career began in the early '60s, when he made several trio albums for Verve, Jazzland, Ozone, and Riverside. He's recorded for Capitol, Atlantic, Milestone, Polydor, East Wind/Inner City, Flying Disc (Japan), JSP, Sackville, and Beehive. Some of his recording partners have included David "Fathead" Newman, Martin Rivera, and Walt Bolden. Currently, Mance only has a few titles available on CD. —*Ron Wynn*

○ **Junior Mance Trio at the Village Vanguard** / Feb. 22-23, 1961 / Jazzland 204
This session presents the Junior Mance trio (Ben Riley, drums; Larry Gales, bass) in a live program from 2/22-23/61. Mance was one of the first crop of funk cum soul cum funky pianists of the '60s to follow in the lineage developed by Horace Silver in the '50s. And, like his West Coast contemporary Les McCann, he made his best records at a time before commercial considerations put his playing under the looking glass and a purity and naturalness were lost. When this record was cut, funk was merely hip, not yet hype. Mance is a great player of the blues; check out his work with Dizzy Gillespie or "63rd St. Theme" and "Smokey Blues" on this record." If latter-day Mance has not gotten to you, try this one from those past days when even the Vanguard had a hip hiring policy—but that's another story. —*Bob Rusch, Cadence*

★ **Truckin' & Trakin'** / Dec. 13, 1983 / Bee Hive 7015
Recorded by a quartet with pianist Mance and saxophonist David Newman. Produced by Bob Porter. Includes one Mance original, Hank Crawford's "Truckin'", and four standards. The group really comes together for the blues/jazz legend. —*Michael G. Nastos*

Tender Touch Of, The / 1984 / Nilva 3405
Produced by Alvin Queen, this album features duets between Mance and bassist Martin Rivera, a reprise of George Harrison's "Something," and five standards. They create their own subtle rhythms nicely. —*Michael G. Nastos*

○ **Mance's Special** / Sep. 1986-Nov. 1988 / Sackville 3043
Fine '86 set with pianist Junior Mance running through romping blues, intricate originals, and moving standards and ballads in a solo set. While he's best at blues-tinged material, Mance shows the versatility necessary to do other material, and doesn't substitute clichés and gimmicks for ideas and substance. —*Ron Wynn*

ALBERT MANGELSDORFF

b. Sep. 5, 1928, Frankfurt, Germany
Trombone, composer / Early free, progressive big band, modern creative
Mangelsdorff is the master of multiphonics: the trombone technique of playing more than one note simultaneously. He's also among the prime veterans in the European free-improvisation school, though his roots date back to the late '40s when he was playing bop. He appeared in America in 1958 as a member of the Newport International Band. He then played with a specially organized group called the European All Stars, and toured Western Europe and Yugoslavia with his own band in the early '60s. He recorded

with pianist John Lewis in 1962, then toured Asia in 1964. At one early point in his career, Mangelsdorff's music had a slight cool influence from his admiration for Lennie Tristano. Later, enchanted by the sound of Indian music, Mangelsdorff began to work some ragas into his own music and recorded a song by Ravi Shankar. Subsequent visits to Japan and Eastern and Western Europe, plus his involvement with the Globe Unity Orchestra beginning in the '60s, moved Mangelsdorff into free improvisation. Through the '70s, '80s, and '90s, Mangelsdorff has recorded with symphony orchestras, has done solo concerts, and has worked with trios and duos. He has been voted Europe's "Musician of the Year" many times. —*Ron Wynn*

○ **Tromboneliness** / Jan. 1976-Mar. 1976 / Sackville 2011
Tromboneliness comes on like a swarm of boppish bees—buzz, flying, aerobatics, focus, sting—but underlying all is as strong a sense of form and organization as a hive, and as much care and workmanship as a honeycomb. Forty-four minutes of raw trombone—with Creole plunger mute and mute I detected—may sound insufferable, but Albert Mangelsdorff blows miracles: he swings, sighs, structures, and sustains with little *sturm und drang* and plenty *gemut-lichkeit*. Here Mangelsdorff utilizes his chordal capabilities nearly all the time for haunting motifs ("For Peter"), basslines ("Mark Suetterlyn's Boogie," under his sped-up flugelly overdub), whole pieces ("Questions To Come"), call-and-response to single lines ("Creole Love Call"), and dazzlingly quick display (title track). Mangelsdorff's timing is as varied and on-the-spot as a standup comic's, as is his ability to shift voice and expression. He yodels, yawps, blares, warbles, moans—growls from time to time—even imitates Echoplex on "Brief Inventions." But melody and form always come first. A landmark album for solo trombone. —*Fred Bouchard, Down Beat*

★ **Trilogue** / Nov. 6, 1976 / PA/USA 7055
Live trio recording for virtuoso German trombonist. Startling sounds! With Jaco Pastorius (b). —*Michael G. Nastos*

CHUCK MANGIONE

b. Nov. 29, 1940, Rochester, NY
Trumpet, flugelhorn, keyboards, composer / Early jazz-rock, instrumental pop
Flugelhorn player and trumpeter Chuck Mangione hasn't been in the limelight as much in the '80s and '90s as he was in the '70s. His light, mildly entertaining instrumental pop was dominant in that era. Mangione helped to popularize the flugelhorn by featuring it on his biggest hits. He never claimed that much of what he played was anything other than trendy sounds for a mass audience. As a teen, Mangione played in Rochester with Dizzy Gillespie, Jimmy Cobb, Ron Carter, Sam Jones, and Kai Winding. He earned his bachelor's degree from the Eastman School in 1963, and led a hard bop group with his brother, Gap, in the mid-'60s after moving to New York. Mangione played with Woody Herman, Maynard Ferguson, and Art Blakey in the mid- and late '60s, then formed a quartet with Gerry Niewood in 1968. During the '70s, Mangione's songs "Feels So Good" and "Land of Make Believe" enjoyed wide crossover appeal. The LP *Feels So Good* eventually sold more than two million copies. Mangione also toured extensively and provided the music for the Olympics held in Los Angeles. His '78 album, *Children of Sanchez*, was also quite popular. Mangione became involved in jazz education during the late '60s and was on the Eastman faculty from 1968 to 1972. He organized a jazz program at the Hochstein School of Music in Rochester and remains an active instructor. Mangione's recorded as a leader for Riverside, Mercury, A&M, and Columbia. He has several sessions available on CD. —*Ron Wynn*

○ **Recuerdo** / Jul. 31, 1962 / Jazzland 495
With Wynton Kelly (p), Sam Jones (b), Lou Hayes (d), and Joe Romano (f, as). This is the real jazz Mangione. Recommended. —*Michael G. Nastos*

○ **Alive!** / Aug. 1972 / Mercury 1650

○ **Together** / 1972 / Mercury 7501

  Land of Make Believe / i. 1973 / Mercury 822539

★ **Bellavia** / 1975 / A&M 3172
Bellavia follows the same popular formula Chuck Mangione adopted for his *Chase the Clouds Away*: a warm phase-shifted electric piano lightly outlines the chords, the rhythm section and orchestra form sweeping underlayers for the horn vamps, and the brass section immodestly punctuates the break points, which serve as transitions for the soloing instrument. By far the most exciting element in the Mangione quartet is the rhythm section, composed of Joe LaBarbera on drums and Chip Jackson on bass. Together they form an attentive, empathetic, and sinewy union that sustains the otherwise monotonous flow of things. Mangione's proficiency for powerhouse arrangements is truly staggering and his music undeniably friendly. —*Mikal Gilmore*, Down Beat

Feels So Good / 1977 / A&M 3219
Recorded at Kendun Recorders, Burbank, California. Small group. Pop/jazz yes, but it is too pretty to not enjoy. Platinum album. —*Michael Erlewine*

○ **An Evening of Magic, Live at the Hollywood Bowl** / Jul. 16, 1978 / A&M 66701
An extremely popular late '70s date done at the Hollywood Bowl by trumpeter Chuck Mangione. At that time Mangione was enjoying success similar to Kenny G's in the '90s and wasn't doing much straight jazz. These are sometimes entertaining, usually well-produced, but very lightweight tracks, with the production dominating rather than the musicians. —*Ron Wynn*

  Children of Sanchez / 1978 / A&M 66700

HERBIE MANN (Herbert Jay Solomon)

b. Apr. 16, 1930, New York, NY
Flute, tenor saxophone, bass clarinet / Bop, early jazz-rock, world fusion, instrumental pop

Herbie Mann enjoyed great popularity during the '60s. He played flute on several hit recordings, but it wasn't his first instrument. Early in his career, Mann played tenor sax and bass clarinet, and was a conventional bebop stylist with a light, "cool" sound that reflected the influence of Lester Young. But when he began emphasizing flute and mixing jazz-rock, Afro-Latin, pop, blues, soul, funk, disco, and reggae, Mann attained crossover success. He dominated jazz polls for years. Mann played simple, funky melodies and blues riffs, and became popular enough to be placed in charge of producing sessions on a subsidiary Atlantic label. Mann recorded such things as Turkish folk and Japanese court music, and also covered many other ethnic styles as well as rock, pop, soul, funk, and disco.

Mann studied clarinet at age nine, and later played flute and tenor sax. He spent three years in the army in Italy, then began playing and recording with Mat Mathews and Pete Rugolo in the early '50s. Mann toured France and Scandinavia in 1956, then toured 15 African nations on a State Department-sponsored sojourn, heading his own band. He also visited Brazil twice in the early '60s and became enamored of the bossa nova. He started a steady string of hit singles with the tune "Coming Home Baby," which was featured on his *Herbie Mann at the Village Gate* album in 1961. Mann toured Japan in 1964, then formed a big band featuring himself on tenor sax. It played at the Newport Jazz Festival in 1965. His biggest album was *Memphis Underground* in 1968.

The next year Mann became the owner/producer for the Embryo label. They issued some great sessions by Miroslav Vitous, Ron Carter, Atilla Zoller, and Sonny Sharrock before folding. Mann continued dabbling in various styles during the '70s, cutting disco and reggae albums, scoring a club hit with the single "Hijack," and forming the Family of Mann in 1973, a band that also spanned the musical gamut. Mann finally tired of doing everything but jazz; he returned to an

acoustic format, then was bumped from the Atlantic roster in 1979. He began his own label, Herbie Mann Music, in 1981.

Mann's list of recording labels and credits is extensive. He did sessions for Bethlehem, Prestige, Savoy, Riverside, Epic, and Verve in the '50s. Mann began his nearly 20-year association with Atlantic in 1960. Through the '60s and '70s, he had 25 albums make the pop charts. Mann was an extremely savvy judge of talent, and the list of people who played with him is amazing. It includes Willie Bobo, Patato Valdes, Johnny Pacheco, Ahmed Abdul-Malik, Antonio Carlos Jobim, Roy Ayers, Larry Coryell, Sonny Sharrock, David "Fathead" Newman, Albert Lee, Tommy McCook, Stephane Grappelli, Cissy Houston, Bill Evans (piano), Duane Allman, and John Abercrombie. Mann issued several albums on his own label in the '80s. During the '90s, he's recorded for GRP with Dave Valentin, and for Chesky. Despite Mann's prodigious output, few of his titles are available currently on CD. Some early dates, a few big Atlantic sessions, and his most recent Chesky and GRP material are available. —*Ron Wynn*

○ **Yardbird Suite** / Nov. 14, 1957 / Savoy 12108

★ **Nirvana** / Dec. 8, 1961 / Atlantic 1426

  At the Village Gate / i. Jul. 1962 / Atlantic 1380

○ **Impressions of the Middle East** / Mar. 7, 1966-Nov. 9, 1966 / Atlantic 1475

★ **Memphis Underground** / Aug. 21-23, 1968 / Atlantic 1522
Mann's best pop/R&B recording has been enormously popular and is still somewhat influential. With Roy Ayers (vib), Larry Coryell (g), and Sonny Sharrock (g). —*Ron Wynn*

  Live at the Whisky / Jun. 7, 1969 / Atlantic 1536

  Memphis Two Step / i. 1971 / Embryo 531

  Push Push / Jul. 1, 1971 / Atlantic 532

  Gagaku and Beyond / i. 1976 / Finnadar 9014

  Herbie Mann with Joao Gilberto & Antonio Carlos Jobim / i. 1977 / Atlantic 8105
Nice, though more light than empathic, Afro-Latin and jazz mixture by flutist Herbie Mann and composer/vocalist Joao Gilberto from 1977. The two make an effective team, with Gilberto's sometimes sentimental, sometimes impressionistic works effectively supported by Mann's lithe flute solos. —*Ron Wynn*

SHELLY MANNE (Sheldon Manne)

b. Jun. 11, 1920, New York, NY, **d.** Sep. 26, 1984, Los Angeles, CA
Drums / Cool

Though his background was swing, Shelly Manne epitomizes the cool school more than any drummer, including Chico Hamilton. The most recorded drummer on the West Coast during the '50s and '60s, Manne was opposed to lashing, showy, or dominating drumming styles, and preferred a subdued, consistent percussive approach, one that buttresses a group's melodic development and offers a generous, but very much in the background, boost.

With a father and two uncles who were also drummers, Manne was originally a saxophonist, then became a drummer at age 18. He substituted for Dave Tough in Benny Goodman's band, then replaced him in Joe Marsala's group. Manne recorded with Marsala in 1941, then later in the '40s played in bands led by Will Bradley, Raymond Scott, and Les Brown. He was on Coleman Hawkins's famous "The Man I Love" recording in 1943. He worked in the late '40s and early '50s with Stan Kenton. Manne also played with Johnny Bothwell, George Shearing, Charlie Ventura, Bill Harris, and Woody Herman, and toured with Jazz at the Philharmonic. He moved to Los Angeles from New York, and in the mid-'50s became an important bandleader and session musician. He led many combos and played with Stu Williamson, Russ Freeman, Leroy Vinnegar, Charlie Mariano, Joe Gordon, Richie Kamuca, Monty Budwig, Conte Candoli, and many others. He led the Poll-Winners trio with Ray Brown and

Barney Kessell; a popular, influential guitar/bass/drums trio in the late '50s. Manne appeared in the film *Man With the Golden Arm* in 1956, and played on Henry Mancini's hit television soundtrack, *Peter Gunn*. Both Mancini and Manne made sequel recordings. But for all Manne's traditionalism and restraint, he played in 1959 with Ornette Coleman on Coleman's second Contemporary album *Tomorrow Is the Question*. This was a polar opposite to everything else Manne had done. He was a member of Andre Previn's trio, and played on instrumental versions of songs from *My Fair Lady* in 1956. The album was a smash, and the trio did other treatments for such plays as *Lil' Abner, West Side Story,* and *Pal Joey*.

Manne worked extensively for Contemporary in the '50s and early '60s. He entered the nightclub business in 1960, successfully presenting concerts (some of which were later recorded and issued) until 1974. He recorded for Impulse, Verve, Capitol, Concord, and Contemporary in the '60s, then for Mainstream, Discovery, Pausa, East Wind, and Galaxy in the '70s. Manne was in the L.A. Four in the mid-'70s, led a quartet including Lew Tabackin, and re-recorded with the Poll-Winners trio. He toured Japan in 1980 with the Gentlemen of Swing, which included Benny Carter, Teddy Wilson, and Milt Hinton. Manne was extremely busy doing percussion parts in film scores and television background work throughout the time he lived and worked in California. There were more dates for Trend, Atlas, Jazzizz, and Concord. Shelly Manne sessions, as a leader and with various groups and combos, are widely available on CD. —*Ron Wynn and Michael G. Nastos*

○ **Here's That Manne** / Nov. 12, 1951 / Dee Gee 1003

○ **Shelly Manne and His Men** / i. 1953 / Contemporary 2503

Volume 1–The West Coast Sound / Sep. 1953 / Contemporary 152
With His Men. A nice larger group recording with Art Pepper (as) as a standout. —*Ron Wynn*

○ **Shelly Manne–Vol. 2** / Dec. 8, 1953-May 17, 1954 / Contemporary 2511

○ **Shelly Manne–Vol. 3** / Sep. 10, 1954 / Contemporary 2516

Three and "The Two", The / Sep. 10, 1954 / Contemporary 172
A first-rate reissue. Shorty Rogers (tpt) and Jimmy Giuffre (sax) are tremendous. —*Ron Wynn*

Swinging Sounds–Vol. 4 / 1956 / Contemporary 267
Shelly Manne and His Men. The fourth in a good series, though solidly in the style that by then was established. —*Ron Wynn*

Shelly Manne & His Friends / i. Feb. 11, 1956 / Doctor Jazz 38728

○ **Shelly Manne & His Friends–Vol. 1** / Feb. 1956 / Contemporary 240
From the sometimes torturous testifying of the Jazz Workshop to the mercurial music of André Previn (p), Leroy Vinnegar (b), and Shelly Manne (d), this date provides plenty of contrast. Not much can be said about this 2/11/56 session that hasn't been said about most other Shelly Manne and His Friends' dates with Previn. The program is neither the epitome of hip jazz that the socialites of the upper middle class would have you believe, nor the epitome of sterile jazz cliché that the elitists would have you believe. It is just light, unpretentious, and swinging music. —*Bob Rusch, Cadence*

More Swinging Sounds / Jul. 16, 1956-1956 / Contemporary 320

My Fair Lady / Aug. 17, 1956 / Contemporary 336

★ **At the Blackhawk–Vols. 1-5** / Sep. 22-24, 1959 / Contemporary 660
This series was taped at San Francisco's now-defunct Black Hawk club in September 1959 under the direction of Lester Koenig, Contemporary's founder and guiding light. The five artists play extensively and with intensity, feeling, and thought on a tasteful variety of material. Shelly Manne is su-

perb throughout, revealing Jo Jones and Max Roach influences with his drive and musicality, feeding the band both rhythmically and melodically, pushing hard to brazen crescendoes, then dropping back down to whisper levels, leading by supporting rather dominating. Joe Gordon, a trumpet wizard who died in 1963 at the age of 35, is also stunning, brandishing an energized, shimmering sound not unlike Clifford Brown's. His unflagging creativity continually enlivens the performances. Tenor saxophonist Richie Kamuca, whom illness claimed in 1977 when he was 47, is more low-keyed than Gordon, developing his solos with subtle rhythmic interplay, using a light, yet expansive tone and a supple technique on several first-rate outings. Pianist Victor Feldman, whose handsome linear ease reminds one of Tommy Flanagan, is most expressive, offering percussive accompaniment and delivering penetrating solos. Monty Budwig's walking bass provides an ever-steady buoyancy to the proceedings. —*Zan Stewart*, Down Beat

○ **Essence** / Jul. 5-6, 1977 / Galaxy 5101
This Shelly Manne album is a straightahead session featuring Lew Tabackin's strong tenor saxophone and liquid flute, with material by Duke Ellington, Jerome Kern, and George Gershwin. With strong support from pianist Mike Wofford and bassist Chuck Domanico, Manne and Tabackin get down to some hard swinging on tunes like "What Am I Here For?" and "Take the Coltrane." On the other hand, "Yesterdays" and "Essence" involve a probing interplay between Manne and Tabackin's flute, highlighting the drummer's special sense of percussion color. —*Herb Nolan*, Down Beat

☆ **Double Piano Jazz Quartet at Carmelo's–Vol. 1** / Sep. 12-13, 1980 / Trend 526
An unusual 1980 session with drummer Shelly Manne heading a group that includes pianists Bill May and Alan Broadbent and bassist Chuck Domanico but no brass, reeds, or woodwinds. Manne's crisp, steady drumming teams with Domanico's consistent bass to set the rhythmic foundation, while pianists Mays and Broadbent alternate solos and either interact, complement, or contrast Manne and Domancio. —*Ron Wynn*

☆ **Double Piano Jazz Quartet at Carmelo's–Vol. 2** / Sep. 12-13, 1980 / Trend 527
Drummer Shelly Manne's *Double Piano Jazz Quartet*, recorded in performance at a California club, is headed by a competent piano duo. Alan Broadbent and bassist Bill Mays have little trouble in negotiating tunes like "The Night Has a Thousand Eyes" and that musical obstacle course "Lennie's Pennies." There is a happy, kicky version of Horace Silver's "Strollin'," as well as a casually interwining reading of "Sweet and Lovely." —*Jon Balleras*, Down Beat

★ **At the Manne-Hole–Vols. 1 and 2** / Contemporary
1992 reissue of a '61 live release by drummer Shelly Manne's quintet. Trumpeter Conte Candoli, tenor saxophonist Richie Kamuca, pianist Russ Freeman, and bassist Chuck Berghofer join Manne for program of swing, cool, and mainstream fare that's nicely played. —*Ron Wynn*

WINGY MANONE (Joseph Matthews Manone)

b. Feb. 13, 1900, New Orleans, LA, **d.** Jul. 9, 1982, Las Vegas, NV

Trumpet, vocals, bandleader / Dixieland

A good traditional jazz trumpeter with an assertive tone and an accomplished style, Wingy Manone overcame the loss of his right arm, which occurred during a childhood accident. While his use of humor could be exaggerated, Manone wasn't simply a campy performer; he was a solid contributor to many important jazz and pop sessions. Manone played trumpets on riverboats at age 17, then worked in Chicago and New York, for a short time, before he joined the Crescent City Jazzers in Alabama. Manone traveled with the group to St. Louis, then worked with various bands in Texas, and began recording as a leader. Manone toured with Jack Teagarden in a band led by Doc Ross that toured New Mexico, Texas, and California. He later led a band in

Mississippi, recorded in New York and New Orleans, then worked in Chicago. Manone's 1930 number, "Tar Paper Stomp," issued by Barbecue Joe and His Hot Dogs, was also known as "Wingy's Stomp." The riff later appeared in "Hot and Anxious" by Horace Henderson, and was featured on "In the Mood" by Glenn Miller. Manone did recording sessions with Benny Goodman, then became involved with theatrical companies. He led bands in the late '30s and '40s in New York, scoring a hit with the single "The Isle of Capri." Other successful singles were "Nickel In the Slot," his rendition of "Flat Foot Floogie," and "Limehouse Blues." Manone moved to Hollywood in 1940, and appeared in the film *Rhythm on the River*. He was a regular on radio with Bing Crosby, and settled in Las Vegas in 1954. Manone worked there into the '70s. He was featured on recordings issued by Columbia, Champion, Vocalion, and Brunswick. Currently, Manone doesn't have any releases available on CD. —*Ron Wynn*

○ **Wingy Manone / Papa Bue's Viking Jazzband** / Storyville 4066

MICHAEL MANTLER

b. Aug. 10, 1943, Vienna, Austria
Composer, trumpet, bandleader / Progressive big band, modern creative
Michael Mantler has been equally prominent in the performing and the business ends of the improvisational world. He was part of the original group that formed the Jazz Composer's Guild, which hoped to improve the lot of jazz musicians. This was the forerunner to the Jazz Composers Orchestra and Jazz Composers Orchestra Association (JCOA), a nonprofit cooperative conceived to commission, perform, and record original compositions for jazz orchestras in the '60s. The JCOA eventually started a record company, JCOA Records, and a distribution outlet, the New Music Distribution Service (NMDS). Mantler and Carla Bley, whom he later married, also formed, in '73, Watt Works, a publishing company to issue their compositions, and Watt Records, a recording label. As a trumpeter, Mantler's a steady, occasionally outstanding, but not innovative or influential player. He's better known for his compositions and collaborations with Bley, which have often been recorded by either the JCOA or its members.

Mantler began playing trumpet at age 12, and attended the Akademie in Vienna. He studied trumpet and musicology before moving to America in 1962, and settling in Boston. He studied at Berklee, then moved to New York in 1964, working with Lowell Davidson. They played at places such as the Cellar Cafe and Town Hall. Mantler also played trumpet with Cecil Taylor's group. After meeting Bley, the two became involved in various JCOA groups and organizations. They traveled to Europe in 1965, where they formed the quintet Jazz Realities with Steve Lacy, and toured Germany and Austria. On their return to America in 1966, Mantler composed a number of rather bleak orchestral works noteworthy for their slow tempos. He played trumpet on Bley's "A Genuine Tong Funeral" composition for Gary Burton's album with orchestra, then did his own double album on the JCOA label in 1968, working with Taylor, Don Cherry, Rosewell Rudd, Pharoah Sanders, and many others. The album won several international awards including the "Grand Prix, Academie, Charles Cros, France." Mantler joined Charlie Haden's Liberation Music Orchestra in 1969 and recorded it for Impulse. He also conducted performances of his original pieces by the orchestra and soloists at the Electric Circus in New York. With Bley, Mantler coordinated the recording of her *Escalator Over the Hill* in 1970 and 1971, and worked on a JCOA triple album with guest soloists Jack Bruce, John McLaughlin, Linda Ronstadt, Gato Barbieri, and Cherry.

He started the NMDS in 1972, then he and Bley began Watt Works and Records in 1973. Mantler built a recording studio near Woodstock, New York, in 1975, and received composition grants from the Creative Artists Program Service and from the National Endowment for the Arts.

These and a Ford Foundation grant enabled Mantler to record *13*, a work for two orchestras and piano. He later recorded six more albums of his originals featuring Bley, Jack DeJohnette, Steve Swallow, Ron McClure, Larry Coryell, and Terje Rypdal. Mantler eventually became the executive director of JCOA/NMDS. Later, he worked, performed, and recorded with Bley's big band. In the '80s, Mantler's new orchestral suite, "Twenty Five," was premiered in Cologne by the West German Radio Orchestra. He also continued recording on Watt, which secured a distribution deal with ECM, through the '80s. There are only a few Mantler sessions available on CD, all of them on Watt/ECM. —*Ron Wynn*

No Answer / Jul. 1973-Nov. 1973 / Virgin 2
Music by Mantler, Don Cherry, Carla Bley, and Jack Bruce with words from Samuel Beckett. —*Michael G. Nastos*

★ **Live** / Feb. 1987 / ECM 833384
Performance art at its heights, with Jack Bruce (b), Don Preston (synth), and Pink Floyd drummer Nick Mason. —*Michael G. Nastos*

Many Have No Speech / Apr. 1987-Dec. 1987 / ECM 835580
An intriguing concept with 42-piece Danish Radio Concert Orchestra, rockers, and jazz elements. Not for all tastes. —*Ron Wynn*

LAWRENCE MARABLE (Larance Norman Marable)

b. May 21, 1929, Los Angeles, CA
Drums / Hard bop, modern creative
A highly respected drummer who's proven himself in bebop, hard bop, and cool situations over the years, Lawrence Marable has been quite active on the West Coast since the early '50s. Not a smashing soloist and not as inventive as veterans like Billy Higgins or Elvin Jones, Marable has nevertheless shown that he's an adaptable, sympathetic drummer who doesn't draw attention to himself, but never fails to keep the pace moving and the beat driving. Marable was mainly self-taught on drums. He played bebop in 1950 with Stan Getz, Hampton Hawes, Zoot Sims, and Charlie Parker, among others. Marable did recording sessions with Hawes, Wardell Gray, Dexter Gordon, Chet Baker, Sonny Stitt, Wes Montgomery, and Victor Feldman in the '50s and '60s. He also made a fine album of blues and soul-jazz with James Clay for Jazz West. Marable had a period of inactivity in the '60s, then toured in 1976 with Supersax and in 1979 to 1980 with Bobby Hutcherson. He reteamed with Milt Jackson in 1980, also recording with him. Marable toured with Supersax again in 1986, and worked with Johnny Griffin on the West Coast. He remains active as a session musician and is a regular member of both the revived Lighthouse All-Stars and Charlie Haden's Quartet West. He has one date as a leader, *Tenorman*, available on CD. —*Ron Wynn*

★ **Tenorman** / Sep. 1956 / Blue Note 84440
A truly great disc from a driving, exciting percussionist who never enjoyed marginal stardom. —*Ron Wynn*, Rock & Roll Disc

STEVE MARCUS (Stephen Marcus)

b. Sep. 18, 1939, New York, NY
Tenor and soprano saxophone / Progressive big band, early jazz-rock, modern creative
Steve Marcus is a sometimes fiery player who has worked in contemporary jazz ensembles, in big bands, and in jazz-rock groups. He attended Berklee in the late '50s and early '60s, then joined Stan Kenton as a tenor saxophonist in 1963. Marcus enjoyed great visibility with Herbie Mann from 1967 to 1970; he also worked with Woody Herman periodically. Marcus recorded with Gary Burton, with the Jazz Composers' Orchestra, and with his own band in the late '60s and early '70s. He recorded with Larry Coryell in the early '70s before beginning the Count's Rock Band. Marcus toured and recorded with Buddy Rich in the mid- and late '70s, and in the '80s, too. Marcus issued a new album in 1992

for the Red Baron label. It's currently his only date available on CD. —*Ron Wynn*

★ **Steve Marcus and 201** / i. Nov. 24, 1992 / Red Baron 52908

CHARLIE MARIANO (Charles Hugolie Mariano)

b. Nov. 12, 1923, Boston, MA

Alto saxophone / Bop, Postbop, early jazz-rock, world fusion

A stirring, explosive alto saxophonist with substantial roots in bebop, Charlie Mariano has enjoyed success over several decades. He expanded his musical frontiers in the '60s, experimenting with jazz-rock and fusion, and mixing Asian influences, Indian instruments, and American rhythmic and melodic elements. While some purists were turned off by this experimentation, it expanded Mariano's audience.

Mariano started on sax at age 17. He studied at Berklee for three years and also played in an army band. He worked in the late '40s with Shorty Sherock, Larry Clinton, and Nat Pierce, while doing some recording for the Motif label. Mariano began leading a quintet in 1950 and 1951, then worked in a group co-led by Chubby Jackson and Bill Harris. He spent two years with Stan Kenton's orchestra in the mid-'50s, then moved to Los Angeles in 1956. He worked with Shelly Manne's group, then returned to Boston in 1958. Mariano played with Herb Pomeroy and taught at Berklee. He did sessions in the '50s for Imperial, Prestige, Fantasy, Bethlehem, and World Pacific, among others. In 1959, he began working again with Kenton, and married Toshiko Akiyoshi. They formed a band in 1960, and did quartet sessions for Candid in 1960 and in Tokyo in 1963. The band lasted for about seven years, and Mariano spent much of that time in Japan, though he worked in a ten-member band led by Charles Mingus in 1962 and 1963, and recorded with Mingus on Impulse in 1963.

There were additional teaching stints at Berklee in the mid- and late '60s, and also in 1975. Marino formed Osmosis, an early jazz-rock band, in 1967, and later traveled and worked in India and the Far East, studying Asian music. Mariano spent several months with the Radio Malaysia orchestra and learned to play the nadaswaram, a South Indian double-reed instrument with a sound and properties similar to the Chinese musette. He settled in Europe during the early '70s, leading the group Pork Pie with Phillip Catherine and Jasper van't Hof. He was a founding member of the United Jazz and Rock Ensemble in 1975, and played with them into the '80s. Mariano also recorded with Eberhard Weber's Colours in the mid-'70s and early '80s. He teamed with Kenton alumni for a concert in England in 1987. There were sessions for RCA (Finland), MPS, and CMP in the '70s, and for Leo (Finland), Calig (Germany), ECM, and Mood in the '80s. Mariano sessions from the '50s, '60s, and '70s, mostly domestic material, are available on CD. —*Ron Wynn*

○ **Boston All Stars** / 1951-1953 / Prestige 1745

Bethlehem Years, The / i. 1953-1954 / Fresh Sound

★ **Helen 12 Trees** / May 6-8, 1976 / BASF 22941

In *Helen 12 Trees* one hears an amalgam of Charlie Mariano's varied experiences—the bop inflections of the Charlie Parker school, the Indian/Asian overtones, and the driving pulse of rock. Because of Mariano's unifying and uncompromising musical vision, the synthesis works well. Also in Mariano's favor is his fine supporting cast; violinist Zgigniew Siefert, keyboardist Jan Hammer, bassist Jack Bruce, drummer John Marshall, and percussionist Nippy Noya bring a compelling elan and vigor. —*Chuck Berg, Down Beat*

Reflections / i. Jun. 1978 / Catalyst 7915

With Finnish musicians, particularly saxophonist Eero Koivistoinen. —*Michael G. Nastos*

Crystal Bells / Dec. 1979 / CMP 10

Jyothi / Feb. 1983 / ECM 811548

Mariano wails, winds, and experiments with Karnataka College of Percussionists. —*Ron Wynn*

Jazz Marimba

Red Norvo (1908) soloed in 1933

Major Players
Mike Mainieri (1938)–Steps Ahead
Bobby Hutcherson (1941)
Gary Burton (1943)
Dave Samuels (1948)–Spyro Gyra 1979

Unaccompanied Soloist
Sun Ra (on Heliocentric World of Sun Ra) 1965

Drummer Doubles
Max Roach (1924)
Joe Chambers (1942)

Free Jazz
Joseph Jarman (1937)
(w/Art Ensemble of Chicago 1969 and 1972)
Tony Vaccha

Warren Smith (1908-1975)
Thurman Barker (1948) w/Cecil Taylor
M'Boom Re:Percussion (formed by Max Roach in 1970)

Standard Time–Vols. 1 and 2 / i. Apr. 1989 / Fresh Sound 97

Charlie Mariano Group, The / Mood

DODO MARMAROSA (Michael Marmarosa)

b. Dec. 12, 1925, Pittsburgh, PA

Piano / Bop

A wonderful melodic interpreter and soloist, Dodo Marmarosa was one of a handful of important White bop pianists. He was a gifted rhythmic improviser who skillfully adapted swing elements for bop tunes, and proved to be a reliable and engaging ensemble contributor. Marmarosa's style was derived partly from contemporary classical music in the mid- and late '40s. Because of a lack of available material and an illness that took him off the scene in his prime, he has been forgotten. Marmarosa retired in the early '60s. Though he started studying classical piano, Marmarosa was interested in the keyboard techniques of Art Tatum and Teddy Wilson. He joined Gene Krupa's band in 1942 after playing in Pittsburgh groups. Marmarosa worked with Tommy Dorsey for part of 1944, then worked with Artie Shaw for the remainder of that year and the next, and cut some outstanding records with Shaw's big band and quintet. A 1946 move to Los Angeles, coupled with his growing interest in the new bop sounds, resulted in an evolution in Marmarosa's style. He became house pianist for Atomic Records, and recorded with Boyd Raeburn, but the pivotal event in his musical life was meeting and playing with Charlie Parker. These sessions won Marmarosa widespread acclaim. In 1948, an illness took Marmarosa away from clubs and studios for nearly ten years, though he did tour briefly with vocalist Johnny "Scat" Davis and Shaw during this time. Marmarosa made a nice comeback album in 1961, *Dodo's Back*, and also recorded with Gene Ammons around that same time. The following year he appeared in concert at the University of Chicago. But that was it for his return. Marmarosa retired to Pittsburgh and hasn't recorded since. Very little of his fine work is in print, though one album,

Dodo's Bounce, was reissued by Fresh Sound in 1992. —*Ron Wynn*

★ **Dodo's Back** / May 9-10, 1961 / Argo 4012

BRANFORD MARSALIS

b. Aug. 26, 1960, Breaux Bridge, LA
Tenor, soprano, and alto saxophone / Post bop, neo bop
Branford Marsalis is an outstanding tenor, soprano, and alto saxophonist who's become extremely well-known in the '90s for heading the "Tonight Show" orchestra and for hosting a weekly program on National Public Radio. A first-rate soloist whose tenor sax playing, in particular, has matured, and whose soprano is becoming steadily more impressive, Marsalis's recent pianoless trio albums feature many solos that were constructed carefully and creatively. They contain interesting harmonic ideas, excellent tone, and powerful phrasing. One of many talented sons, Branford and his brothers Wynton, Delfeayo, and Jason were well schooled by their father, the distinguished pianist Ellis Marsalis. Branford joined Art Blakey's Jazz Messengers shortly after Wynton in 1981, replacing Bobby Watson. A year later, he left to join Wynton's band, which quickly became the talk of the '80s in jazz circles. While playing with Wynton, Branford Marsalis also played on Miles Davis's album, *Decoy,* and did a variety of session work. He left his brother's band in the mid-'80s, shortly after Branford toured with Sting. Marsalis continued cutting his own albums for Columbia through the '80s and '90s, while also recording with Bruce Hornsby, Tina Turner, Teena Marie, Gangstarr, and many others. He also played with Dizzy Gillespie, subbed for David Murray in the World Saxophone Quartet, and appeared in the films *School Daze* and *Throw Mama From the Train.* Branford Marsalis has also recorded blues and classical albums. It was this eclecticism and enhanced public profile that helped him get the "Tonight Show" job. Marsalis has several albums available on CD, including the recent *Bloomington.* —*Ron Wynn*

★ **Scenes in the City** / Apr. 18, 1983-Nov. 29, 1983 / Columbia 38951
The title cut of this album is a well-staged, smoothly narrated bit of Charles Mingus theater, older than most of these musicians. The remaining material is mainstream modern: three tunes in the John Coltrane/McCoy Tyner mold, a run at Sonny Rollins ("No Backstage Pass"), and a piece ("Parable") on pensive it almost disappears. The material may be routine; the playing isn't. The album is an exposition of Young Lions that augurs health for the decade (the '80s). The various rhythm sections hunker down and fire. Pianists Mulgrew Miller and Kenny Kirkland are exceptional whether comping or soloing. Bassist Charnett Moffett offers the most impressive bass work of the album on "Waiting For Tain." Drummers Smitty Smith and "Tain" Watts are a joy—deft, exuberant, expressive—so bodacious I want to call them the best drummers to come along in 15 years. —*J.B. Figi,* Down Beat

Royal Garden Blues / Mar. 1986-Jul. 1986 / Columbia 40363
Quartet sessions that feature some outstanding piano by Kenny Kirkland. —*Ron Wynn*

○ **Renaissance** / i. 1987 / Columbia 40711
Marsalis's best ensemble with Kenny Kirkland (p), Bob Hurst, and Tony Williams (d). Four standards, two of Tony's originals, and one of Branford's. A very solid album. —*Michael G. Nastos*

Trio Jeepy / 1989 / Columbia 44199
His exhaustive, well-conceived, and impressive tenor solos, plus the nimble bass work and always consistent drumming provide a variation on the theme. —*Ron Wynn,* Rock & Roll Disc

Beautyful Ones Are Not Yet Born / 1991 / Columbia 46990
Trio. An exciting pianoless session, plus a cut with guest star British tenor saxophonist Courtney Pine. Intense, deeply personal, and searing pianoless trio sessions for the '90s. —*Ron Wynn,* Rock & Roll Disc

I Heard You Twice the First Time / i. 1992 / Columbia 46083
A first-rate recent release by tenor saxophonist Branford Marsalis. This is his "blues" date, and it includes songs and/or performances by B.B. King, Joe Louis Walker, Linda Hopkins, and John Lee Hooker, plus a guest stint by Wynton Marsalis and contributions from Kenny Kirkland, Jeff Watts, Robert Hurst III, and, of course, Branford Marsalis on tenor and soprano. He and the rest of the cast fill their roles well, but it's the least self-conscious performers like vocalist Linda Hopkins who steal the show. —*Ron Wynn*

DELFEAYO MARSALIS

Trombone, producer / Postbop, neo-bop
One of jazz's busiest producers, Delfeayo Marsalis has only recently started to make his mark as a trombonist. His style is still developing, but on his debut session he sounded aggressive and animated, reflecting the influence of a J.J. Johnson in his tone and phrasing, especially on uptempo tunes. Marsalis has produced over 30 albums since the late '80s, including most of the releases by Branford and Wynton Marsalis. A former Berklee student, Marsalis attended several classes conducted by the institution's then fledgling engineering department. He later began producing albums for Branford, and expanded his activities to include the other family members and occasional outside assignments in both jazz and classical music. Marsalis's first session as a leader, *Pontius Pilate's Decision,* is still available on CD. —*Ron Wynn*

★ **Pontius Pilate's Decision** / i. 1992 / Novus 63134
The debut major label project by longtime producer and trombonist Delfeayo Marsalis. It's a concept work based on an instrumental interpretation about events behind Christ being crucified. Marsalis, who plays some long and harmonically impressive trombone solos, is joined by his brothers Wynton, Branford, and the newest prodigy Jason, plus pianists Kenny Kirkland and Marcus Roberts. —*Ron Wynn*

ELLIS MARSALIS

b. Nov. 14, 1934
Piano / New Orleans traditional, Postbop
It's rather inconceivable and incredible that the father of the talented Marsalis clan gets such little respect and recognition, but many publications that wax so eloquently about Branford and Wynton don't even bother to list their father. A distinguished pianist, educator, and bandleader, his impact has not only registered among his famous sons (whose ranks also include producer/trombonist Delfeayo and drummer Jason) but has also registered among former pupils Terence Blanchard, Donald Harrison, Harry Connick, Jr., and Kent Jordan, to cite only a few. Marsalis's carefully built, bluesy, and harmonically rich solos showcase his knowledge of multiple genres and his accomplished technique. He played in a Marine Corps band, worked with Al Hirt, and did some recording for the AFO label. He also played with musicians such as James Clay, Eddie Harris, and David Newman. Marsalis has recorded for Columbia/Sony, Spindletop, ELM, Blue Note, and Rounder in the '80s and '90s. He has some sessions available on CD. —*Ron Wynn*

★ **Father and Sons** / i. 1982 / CBS
The side with sons Wynton and Branford is worth the price. They swing very hard. —*Michael G. Nastos*

☆ **Piano in E-Solo Piano** / 1984 / Rounder 2100

○ **Heart of Gold** / 1991 / Columbia 47509
Of his few recordings, this is a gem. With Ray Brown (b) and Billy Higgins (d)—none finer for rhythm mates. All standards save one by Ellis, two by his son and producer Delfeayo. This album shows the pianist's depth in perception of the entire jazz spectrum. —*Michael G. Nastos*

WYNTON MARSALIS

b. Oct. 18, 1961, New Orleans, LA
Trumpet, flugelhorn / Postbop, neo-bop

Wynton Marsalis has earned public relations honors for jazz during the '80s. No single player has won more awards, has created more controversy, and has also sold tons of records in the process, though not as many records as some pop instrumentalists and fusion musicians. He's celebrated in some quarters as the voice of integrity and honor; he's viewed in others as the leader of jazz's flat earth society. He has been accused of ripping those who dare to try and move the music forward, and of reproducing second-rate Miles Davis solos to high praise from uninformed elitists supporting his pedantic positions. But even his most ardent critics can't begrudge his growth on trumpet. Marsalis's tone, attack, phrasing, choices of notes, range, compositional skill, and general technique have improved remarkably from his early '80s records. By his own admission, he has not been an innovator. Whether he places too much value on jazz's past at the expense of its future remains open for debate. But he's certainly advanced the cause by using his celebrity status to speak on behalf of the music, whether's he's on NBC, ESPN, National Public Radio, or is doing a local interview for a 1,000-circulation weekly.

His path to stardom was a bit different from his brother Branford's. The word about his prowess began circulating when he was a youngster. Given his first horn at age six by Al Hirt, Marsalis was studying both jazz and classical at age 12. He played in marching bands and went to high school with Terence Blanchard and Donald Harrison. Marsalis attended Juilliard and was in the pit band for *Sweeny Todd* before joining Art Blakey. He toured with Herbie Hancock in 1981 and appeared on a two-album (disc) Columbia recording of the band. Marsalis was featured on the *Young Lions* album for Elektra in 1982, but made his debut as a leader the year before on Columbia. *Think of One* subsequently won a Grammy. Marsalis became the first musician to win Grammy awards as best jazz and classical soloist in the same year, then later repeated the trick.

He eventually stopped playing classical music, saying he wanted to concentrate on jazz, though he's recently recorded with opera star Kathleen Battle. His face made the cover of numerous magazines throughout the '80s. Marsalis interviews were always good for at least one eye-popping quote, many of which he would later charge were taken out of context. His contention that Miles Davis was engaging in minstrel show antics during the late '80s triggered wholesale critical backlash, and many have never forgiven him for that one. Marsalis has moderated, but has not backed down from dismissals of many other musical styles from free to rap, though he has recanted his early statements deriding the blues. He's headed the Lincoln Center jazz series for the past few years, and drew charges of racism from White jazz critics in the summer of '93 because the Center has never had a retrospective or concert that features music by a White bandleader or composer (of course, most of the publications where these charges appear have few, if any, nonwhite writers). As a superb player still in his '30s, it's far too early to either anoint Wynton Marsalis as the messiah who saved jazz, or to assume that he's gone as far as he can go. The best way to assess Marsalis is to survey his Columbia records over the past decade; there's much to admire, and yes, there's also room for criticism. *—Ron Wynn*

★ **Wynton Marsalis** / **i.** Oct. 11, 1980 / Columbia 37574
Wynton Marsalis's eagerly awaited debut recording finds him in fine form and in fine company. He digs in on "Father Time"; his sure-toned trumpet comments with authority while following the tune's metrical shifts. Marsalis's cannily shaped phrases (reference point: Miles Davis) are buoyed by his brother Branford's saxophone—when the older Marsalis blows we hear the influence of Wayne Shorter. Wynton Marsalis produces a dark mood on "Twilight," his mix of long tones and spurts of notes proceeding on top of ominous repeating bass and restless cymbals. Agitated solos by Branford and pianist Kenny Kirkland add to the piece's somber mystery. On these tracks pianist Kirkland, drummer Jeff Watts, and alternately Charles Fambrough or Clarence

Seay on bass—all impressive young players—aid and abet the brothers with active concern. Venerable Miles Davis alumni Herbie Hancock, Ron Carter, and Tony Williams (with whom Wynton Marsalis toured in 1981) are on hand for several numbers. The Marsalis brothers aren't the least bit intimidated, playing with the same poise they display with the other musicians. *—Frank-John Hadley,* Down Beat

○ **Think of One** / 1983 / Columbia 38641
Think Of One is Wynton Marsalis's second Columbia effort as leader—the first to use only the Marsalis brothers' working band. From "Knozz-Moe-King" (no smoking?), which opens side one, through pianist Kenny Kirkland's "Fuchsia," the standard "My Ideal," bassist Ray Drummond's "What Is Happening Here (Now)?," the title track by Thelonius Monk, Wynton Marsalis's two originals ("The Bell Ringer" and "Later"), and Duke Ellington's "Melancholia," the Marsalis quintet appropriates with little embellishment the sophisticated and occasionally explosive sound of Miles Davis's mid-'60s combo. Drummer Jeff Watts has good command of Tony Williams's ability to expand and contract the rhythms across his kit; both Ray Drummond and Phil Bowler, the bassist on six of the eight cuts, have the dark, rubbery tone, fast walk, and accuracy Ron Carter made standard for bassist. Of the whole band, Branford Marsalis's voice is most distinctly his own. Influenced though he is by Wayne Shorter, Branford blows soprano on "The Bell Ringer" as though in pursuit of a passionate impulse of his own. *—Howard Mandel,* Down Beat

Hot House Flowers / Mar. 30-31, 1984 / Columbia 39530

Black Codes (from the Underground) / Jan. 11-14, 1985 / Columbia 40009

J Mood / Dec. 1985 / Columbia 40308

Standard Time–Vol. 1 / May 1986-Sep. 1986 / Columbia 40461

○ **Live at Blues Alley** / Dec. 1986 / Columbia 40675
This offering by the brilliant Wynton Marsalis quartet, recorded several months after *Marsalis Standard Time–Vol. 1,* bolstered the case of those who at the time held Marsalis to be one of the most important young musicians in jazz. Although it remained to be seen in 1988 whether he would eventually pioneer novel approaches or processes, he is without doubt as well prepared for such a role on the basis of technical mastery and historical awareness as anyone of his generation. There is nothing he cannot do on his horn, and his understanding of his predecessors' music is all-encompassing. But regardless of the future, he is playing as well today as anybody. For those observers who still wonder whether Marsalis can loosen his tie and play some blues, this record can put their minds at ease. He can and he does, on several occasions, combining earthiness and warmth and wit and playfulness with high seriousness and invention. And although he often shows a Milesian gift for intuiting just the right note to play, perhaps the most significant aspect of his work is its rhythmic daring. Disarming at first to the unsuspecting listener, his unorthodox manipulation of normal flow by forcing accents on other-than-expected beats, all the while keeping his place in the form, and, most important, maintaining the swing, is masterful and arresting. Such adventurousness requires the kind of strong support this rhythm section provides. Drummer Jeff Watts and bassist Robert Hurst, who appeared on the previous two albums but have since left the band, are powerful, sensitive, and fully compatible with the other musicians. *—David Franklin,* Jazz Times

○ **Carnival** / **i.** 1987 / CBS 42137
This is a dandy on which a maturing Wynton Marsalis trades his trumpet for cornet and pays homage to some of the great music made and popularized by wind bands throughout the United States from the 1860s through the 1930s. Marsalis's tone and coloring are impeccable here. This performance is highlighted by a fast and dazzling rendition of Rimsky-Korsakov's "The Flight of the Bumblebee," thanks to circular breathing, and a soulful interpretation of

"Sometimes I Feel Like a Motherless Child." The only fault, admittedly a minor point, is that the Eastman Wind Ensemble, composed of undergraduate and graduate students at the Eastman School of Music in Rochester, New York, gets little room to showcase its fine artists. Nearly all of the focus here is on Marsalis's cornet solos. *—Ken Franckling, Jazz Times*

Standard Time–Vol. 2: Intimacy Calling / Sep. 1987-Aug. 1990 / Columbia 47346

○ **Majesty of the Blues, The** / 1989 / Columbia 45091
A more appropriate title for this album would be one word: homecoming. Wynton Marsalis returns to his New Orleans roots in this album. Yet, it's a homecoming with a difference, with an appreciation for where he's been and all of those values along with those he'd carried from home. Marsalis has matured. He appreciates what Louis Armstrong was doing; his solo efforts are more concise and lyrical here than ever—with the *Hot House Flowers* ballads as exceptions. He's learned the value of what Jelly Roll Morton did as an orchestrator; his voicings on side B reflect that appreciation. And pervading this whole album is the spirit of Duke Ellington and Charles Mingus. Marsalis incorporates all of these kindred spiritualists into this *album*. And it is an *album*, not a collection of disparate pieces. It is a unit, and should be listened to as such. Marsalis gathers new and old New Orleans musicians here and the superb liner notes give the genealogy. All acquit themselves superbly, especially alto saxophonist Wes Anderson (an adopted Southern University Alvin Batiste-taught Orleansian) and Dr. Michael White, the head of the Spanish Department at a local university who didn't play traditional jazz until he was in his twenties. Marsalis in the past showed his speed, his technique, his fleetness. He showed he could play ballads. Here he shows appreciation for roots, for dynamics, and for programmatic orchestration for a small group (at which Tadd Dameron excelled). *—Rhodes J. Spedale, Jr., Jazz Times*

Standard Time–Vol. 3 / 1990 / CBS 46143
1987-1990. Subtitled: *The Resolution Of Romance*. Wynton, with his father Ellis on the piano. Very traditional and very nice listening. *—Michael Erlewine*

Thick in the South–Soul Gestures in Southern Blue, Vol. 1 / **i.** 1991 / Columbia 47977
The best of the three-part series, with Joe Henderson (ts) dead center. *—Ron Wynn*

Uptown Ruler–Soul Gestures in Southern Blue, Vol. 2 / **i.** 1991 / Columbia 47976

Levee Low Moan–Soul Gestures in Southern Blue, Vol. 3 / **i.** Nov. 1991 / Columbia 47975

○ **Blue Interlude** / **i.** 1992 / Columbia 48729
Good '92 session with trumpeter Wynton Marsalis's latest combo doing his hard bop and mainstream compositions. The lineup includes pianist Marcus Roberts, saxophonists Wessell Anderson and Todd Williams, bassists Reginald Veal or Herlin Riley, plus drummer Wycliffe Gordon. *—Ron Wynn*

○ **Citi Movement** / **i.** Dec. 18, 1992 / Columbia 53324
Written for Wynton Marsalis's septet as the score for Garth Fagen's Bucket Dance Theater's modern ballet, *Griot New York*, this collection tells a story—of the history of humanity, of life in the teeming metropolis, of the tenacity of the human spirit—through music that is intricately written and expertly performed. The best sections occur when the band is swinging, as it does mightily and joyfully throughout a broad range of expressions: traditional New Orleans brass band, '60s modal jazz, big-band swing, calypso, even circus music. Within those sections (especially "Some Present Moments of the Future"), the band's solos and Marsalis's evocative voicings conjure Jimmie Lunceford, Duke Ellington, Count Basie, Fletcher Henderson, and Charles Mingus. In all, Marsalis's brilliant orchestration stands on its own. *—Suzanne McElfresh, Down Beat*

WARNE MARSH

b. Oct. 26, 1927, Los Angeles, CA, **d.** Dec. 18, 1987, Hollywood, CA
Tenor saxophone / Cool
A star pupil of Lennie Tristano, Warne Marsh forged a style and an approach that have been praised highly by numerous musicians. He played solos that were clear and concise, and was a gifted melodic and harmonic creator. Marsh began playing professionally in the mid-'40s, and worked with Hoagy Carmichael's Teenagers in 1945. Marsh served in the army and was exposed to Tristano when stationed near New York in the last part of his stretch. He did some work in Los Angeles and played with Buddy Rich, then moved to New York in 1948. He became one of Tristano's best pupils in the late '40s and into the '50s, then left the academy Tristano founded. For a short time, he worked with fellow pupil Lee Konitz, then worked as a leader briefly in California. Marsh recorded with Hampton Hawes in the early '50s, then for Riverside with Joe Albany in 1957. He did other albums for Imperial, Kapp, Mode, Atlantic, Verve, and Revelation in the '50s. Marsh returned to New York, then moved back to the West Coast in 1966 and became an instructor. He joined Supersax in 1972 and played with them until 1977. Marsh toured Europe and recorded with Supersax in 1975. When he returned to New York, he continued teaching. Marsh did several live dates in the '70s, including three with Konitz at the Montmarte club for Storyville, and a duo date with Red Mitchell. There were two other sessions with Konitz at the Half Note, and other dates on Nessa, Interplay, Discovery, and Criss Cross in the '70s and '80s. Marsh collapsed and died on stage at Donte's jazz club while playing "Out of Nowhere" in 1987. There's a fair amount of his early and recent material available on CD. *—Ron Wynn*

○ **Live in Hollywood** / **i.** Dec. 1952 / Xanadu 151
About three years had passed since tenor saxophonist Warne Marsh had recorded those famous Capitols with alto saxophonist Lee Konitz and pianist Lennie Tristano when he cut this date. His sound here is much the same and his amazing ideas are a pleasing contrast to pianist Hampton Hawes's bebop phrases. Most of the material is standard repertoire for the Tristano school and Marsh is magnificent with his ever-changing ideas and phrasing. "All The Things You Are" shows Hawes at his best with many "Bird-Like" (Charlie Parker) references. There is a bit of "toying" around on "I'll Remember April," but it really gets moving. Drummer Shelly Manne's breaks are recorded well and are not overpowering. It's unfortunate bassist Joe Mondragon can't be heard as easily. This unusual meeting date is essential listening for me. I'm grateful it was preserved. *—Jerry Atkins, Cadence*

○ **Warne Marsh Quintet** / **i.** 1956 / Storyville 4001

Jazz of Two Cities / Sep. 1956 / Imperial 9027

Winds of Marsh / Oct. 3, 1956 / Imperial 12013

★ **Music for Prancing** / Sep. 1957 / Mode 125

Jazz from the East Village / Aug. 9, 1960 / Wave 10

★ **Warne Marsh & Lee Konitz (Live at Club Montmartre)** / Dec. 1975 / Storyville 4026
State of the art throughout. Blues, ballads, uptempo, and standards. *—Ron Wynn*

○ **Warne Marsh and Lee Konitz–Vol. 3** / **i.** Dec. 1975 / Storyville 4096

○ **How Deep, How High** / Apr. 25, 1977-Aug. 8, 1979 / Discovery 863

Warne Out / May 15, 1977-Jun. 5, 1977 / Interplay
An album where wit and inventiveness are the theme, from the title to the leads. *—Ron Wynn*

Star Highs / Aug. 1982 / Criss Cross 1002
A recent indication of this tenor's considerable and continued talent. With Hank Jones (p). *—David Szatmary*

○ **Warne Marsh Meets Gary Foster** / **i.** 1982 / Ewd 90024

EDDIE MARSHALL

b. 1938

Drums / Bop, early jazz-rock, modern creative

Both a dependable session player and an occasional band-leader, Eddie Marshall has played and recorded in free, hard bop, and jazz-rock situations in the '60s, '70s, '80s, and '90s. Marshall moved to New York from Springfield, Massachusetts, in the early '60s, and played with Sam Rivers and Stan Getz. He recorded with Charlie Mariano and Toshiko Akiyoshi. He worked in the jazz-rock bands Almanac and Fourth Way with Mike Nock in the late '60s and early '70s, then was house drummer at the Keystone Korner from 1971 to 1980, playing with Dexter Gordon, George Benson, and many others who appeared at the venue. Marshall recorded extensively with Bobby Hutcherson in the '70s, and with John Klemmer, Kenny Burrell, and Jon Hendricks. He recorded with Larry Vukovich, Bruce Forman, and as a leader with the group Bebop and Beyond. Marshall did his own session as a leader for Timeless in the late '70s, but it is not available currently on CD. *—Ron Wynn*

PAT MARTINO (Pat Azzara)

b. Aug. 25, 1944, Philadelphia, PA

Guitar / Postbop, early jazz-rock, neo-bop

Pat Martino's speed, voicings, harmonic knowledge, phrasing, and all-around technical abilities have made him one of the most respected and critically admired guitarists of the '60s. Martino played impressively in bebop, hard bop, or soul-jazz settings, and was making a name for himself in the classical field studying the work of Stockhausen and Elliott Carter. He was an expressive, tasty soloist who worked in the familiar octave style of Wes Montgomery, but without the same stylistic compromises. In 1980, surgery to correct an aneurysm caused Martino to suffer from a temporary loss of memory. He taught himself to play guitar again, which took nearly four years, then resurfaced as a fine stylist once more. Martino began playing professionally at age 15. He worked with Willis Jackson and Red Holloway, then later performed in soul-jazz groups led by Don Patterson, Jimmy Smith, Brother Jack McDuff, Groove Holmes, and Jimmy McGriff. He worked in John Handy's mid-'60s band, then began heading his own groups. Martino made several fine recordings for Muse in the '60s and '70s, but was off the scene while recovering. He currently has several titles from the '60s and '70s available on CD. *—Ron Wynn and David Nelson McCarthy*

○ **East!** / Jan. 1968 / Prestige 248

East! was a thematic production and also somewhat reflected a period (1/8/68) of growing interest in the East. The title track is a lengthy (12:40) piece for which the quartet (Eddie Green, p; Ben Tucker, b; Lenny McBrown, d) is augmented by bassist Tyrone Brown (Tucker moves to tambourine for this piece). The mood here is meditative, circular, and repetitive with lengthy solos by Pat Martino (g) and Eddie Green. The rest of the program is more idiomatically bop, quite nice, but exposing both the piano's and Green's limitations. *—Bob Rusch, Cadence*

○ **Live!** / Sep. 1972 / Muse 5026

★ **Consciousness** / Oct. 7, 1974 / Muse 5039

Martino on the way up. Mostly quartet recordings for the brilliant guitarist. "Willow," a dark, understated gem. Contains seven tracks, three by Martino, three standards, and Joni Mitchell's "Both Sides Now." Guitar students should study this one. *—Michael G. Nastos*

○ **We'll Be Together Again** / Feb. 13-17, 1976 / Muse 5090

HUGH MASEKELA (Hugh Ramopolo Masekela)

b. Apr. 4, 1939

Trumpet, flugelhorn, vocals / World fusion

Hugh Masekela has an extensive jazz background and credentials, but has enjoyed major success as one of the earliest leaders in the world fusion mode. Masekela's vibrant trumpet and flugelhorn solos have been featured in pop, R&B, disco, Afropop, and jazz contexts. He's had American and international hits, has worked with bands around the world, and has played with African, African-American, European, and various American musicians during a stellar career. His style, especially on flugelhorn, is a charismatic blend of striking upper-register lines, half valve effects, repetitive figures and phrases with some note bending, slurs, and tonal colors. Though he's often simplified his playing to fit into restrictive pop formulas, Masekela's capable of outstanding ballad and bebop work.

He began singing and playing piano as a child, influenced, at age 13, by the film *Young Man With a Horn*. Masekela started playing trumpet at age 14. He played in the Huddleston Jazz Band, which was led by anti-apartheid crusader and group head Trevor Huddleston. Eventually, Huddleston was deported, and Masekela cofounded the Merry Makers of Springs along with Jonas Gwangwa. He later joined Alfred Herbert's Jazz Revue, and played in studio bands backing popular singers. Masekela was in the orchestra for the musical *King Kong*, whose cast included Miriam Makeba. He was also in the Jazz Epistles with Abdullah Ibrahim, Makaya Ntshoko, Gwanga, and Kippie Moeketsi. Masekela and Makeba, his wife at that time, left South Africa in 1961, one year before Ibrahim and Sathima Bea Benjamin. Musicians such as Dizzy Gillespie, John Dankworth, and Harry Belafonte assisted Masekela. He studied at the Royal Academy of Music, then at the Manhattan School of Music.

During the early '60s, his career began to explode. He recorded for MGM, Mercury, and Verve, developing his hybrid African/pop/jazz style. Masekela moved to California and started his own record label, Chisa. He cut several albums, which expanded his formula, and began to score pop success. The song "Grazing in the Grass" topped the charts in 1968 and eventually sold four million copies worldwide. That year, Masekela sold out arenas nationwide, including Carnegie Hall, during his tour. He recorded in the early '70s with Monk Montgomery and the Crusaders.

Masekela moved in a more ethnic direction during the '70s. He traveled to London to play with Nigerian Afrobeat great Fela Kuti and his Africa '70; then came a session with Dudu Pukwana, Eddie Gomez, and Ntshoko, among others, that resulted in his finest jazz/African album, *Home Is Where the Music Is*. Masekela toured Guinea with the Ghanian Afropop band Hedzollah Zoundz, then recorded a series of albums with them both in California and in Africa that featured guest stints from the Crusaders, Patti Austin, and others. Masekela alternated between America and Africa, and cut a successful pop/dance album with Herb Alpert in the late '70s. During the '80s, Masekela returned to South Africa. He visited Zimbabwe and Botswana, and recorded two albums with the Kalahari Band that once more merged jazz-rock, funk, and pop. Masekela was part of Paul Simon's Graceland tour in the mid-'80s, while he continued recording and producing sessions by Makeba. Though the jazz content of his work has varied over the years, Hugh Masekela has far more material on the plus side than the negative. Assuming recent *Schwann* listings are accurate (a major assumption), there aren't that many Masekela albums available on CD. Fortunately, some of the Jazz Epistles tracks have been reissued on CD. *—Ron Wynn*

Trumpet African / i. 1962 / Mercury

24 Karat Hits / i. 1966 / Verve 651

Promise of a Future, The / 1968 / One Way 22077

★ **Masekela** / i. 1969 / UNI 73041

It all comes together here. Magic synthesis of trumpet-led African sounds, jazz, and R&B. *—Hank Davis*

○ **Grrr** / Mercury 61109

Masekela as a young trumpeter from the mid '60s. Rare, but clearly his best format and playing. *—Michael G. Nastos*

★ **Home Is Where the Music Is** / Jan. 1972 / Blue Thumb

An outstanding blend of Afropop and jazz with strong work by Dudu Pukwana (as). —*Ron Wynn*

Uptownship / **i.** 197z / Novus 3070

CAL MASSEY

b. 1928, d. 1972
Keyboards, composer / Hard bop, progressive big band
There's some doubt about the birthdate of composer and trumpeter Cal Massey; some accounts claim he was born in 1928. But there's no question about his ability as a composer. Massey wrote some poignant and compelling material, and had works recorded by John Coltrane, Freddie Hubbard, Jackie McLean, Lee Morgan, Philly Joe Jones, and Archie Shepp, among others. Some Massey numbers that were cut include "Bakai," by Coltrane, "Fiesta" by Jones, "Assunta, Father and Son" by Hubbard, "Message from Trane" by McLean, and "Cry of My People" by Shepp. Massey studied trumpet with Freddie Webster and worked in big bands led by Jay McShann, Jimmy Heath, and Billie Holiday. Massey then opted to concentrate on composing and didn't do much playing for the rest of his career, though he did lead an ensemble that included Jimmy Garrison, McCoy Tyner, and Tootie Heath in the late '50s. This group played Massey's compositions, and had periodic guest appearances from Coltrane and Donald Byrd. Massey worked and toured with Archie Shepp from 1969 until Massey's death in 1972. He also worked with Romulus Francechini, cofounding the Romas Orchestra, which also performed Massey compositions. His musical play, *Lady Day: A Musical Tragedy*, was Massey's final work. The Shepp albums *Attica Blues, Things Have Got to Change*, and *Cry of My People* contain several Massey compositions. There is also a Candid CD that features rare examples of Massey's fine trumpet playing. —*Ron Wynn*

★ **Blues to Coltrane** / Jan. 1961 / Candid 79029

BENNIE MAUPIN

b. Aug. 29, 1940, Detroit, MI
Saxophone, flute, bass clarinet / Hard bop, soul-jazz, early jazz-rock
A powerful tenor sax soloist who has also played flute, soprano sax, bass, and alto clarinet, Bennie Maupin contributed to some landmark groups and recordings during the '70s, but hasn't been as active since. Maupin began on tenor in high school, and attended the Detroit Institute for Musical Arts. He played with Yusef Lateef, Alice McLeod (Coltrane), Hugh Lawson, and Barry Harris before moving from Detroit to New York in 1963. Maupin played and recorded with Marion Brown, worked with Pharoah Sanders, and did sessions with organ combos, soul vocalists and bands, rock, and calypso ensembles. He played with Roy Haynes and Horace Silver in the late '60s, before joining Miles Davis on *Bitches Brew*. Maupin recorded with McCoy Tyner, Chick Corea, Jack DeJohnette, and Lee Morgan in the late '60s and early '70s, then joined Herbie Hancock as Joe Henderson's replacement. He was on board during Hancock's electric "Sextant" period and was among the only holdovers of Hancock's transition from jazz-rock to funk with the "Headhunters" band. Maupin also recorded with Woody Shaw in the early '70s and Sonny Rollins in the mid-'70s. He did his own sessions for ECM and Mercury in the mid- and late '70s. Currently, Maupin has no dates as a leader available on CD, but he can be heard on reissues by Davis, Corea, Hancock, Morgan, and others. —*Ron Wynn*

Almanac / **i.** 1967 / Improvising Artists 373851
Hard-edged swing and improvisations with Mike Nock, Cecil McBee, and Eddie Marshall. —*Michael G. Nastos*

★ **Jewel in the Lotus, The** / Mar. 1974 / ECM 1043
Detroit multi-instrumentalist with other members of Herbie Hancock's Mwandishi. Early-period progressive fusion. —*Michael G. Nastos*

LYLE MAYS (Lyle David Mays)

b. 1953
Keyboards / Early jazz-rock, modern creative
Best known for a long musical relationship with Pat Metheny, Mays won prior acclaim for composing and notating an album for the North Texas State University Lab Band. In 1975, that album became the first by a college band to get a Grammy nomination. That same year, he met Pat Metheny, and began their association. Through the '70s and early '80s, Mays worked exclusively with Metheny. Mays's background was in classic bop, and his occasional forays on acoustic piano reveal those roots, but it's his array of colors, sounds, textures, and electronic support on synthesizer that has earned him respect with Metheny. Mays has released recordings as a leader on ECM since the mid-'80s. —*Ron Wynn*

★ **Lyle Mays** / **i.** 1986 / David Geffen Co. 24097
His best as a leader. Contemporary multi-keyboardist, with an original concept. —*Michael G. Nastos*

Street Dreams / **i.** 1988 / David Geffen Co. 24204
This is more to the fusion side but has lots of exceptional playing. —*Ron Wynn*

Fictionary / **i.** 1993 / Geffen 24521
Because of his long association with guitarist Pat Metheny, pianist Lyle Mays is often tagged as a fusion artist, but his playing has more substance than that suggests. You can hear it in *Fictionary*, Mays's third album as a leader. Produced by Metheny, this is an impressive set of trio performances that owes much to the superb rhythmic support of bassist Marc Johnson and drummer Jack DeJohnette. Two selections, "Trio #1" and "Trio #2," are freely improvised by the three players; another one, "Falling Grace," was written by bassist Steve Swallow, and the rest are Mays's own. They include the aptly named "Bill Evans," an introspective, delicate solo number called "On the Other Hand," and the title tune, a clear floor-stroking bow to Chick Corea. —*Chris Albertson, Stereo Review*

CECIL MCBEE

b. May 19, 1935, Tulsa, OK
Bass / Modern creative
A powerful, though not flashy, bassist, Cecil McBee has been one of the most prolific players since the '60s. He's a highly talented accompanist whose rich, superb lines and strong tone make their presence felt, though he usually stays in the background. When McBee does take the spotlight, he offers an amazing array of speedy licks, bowed or plucked lines, and furious tones. McBee played clarinet before turning to bass at age 17. He attended Central State University, but at various times in both the '50s and '60s, sandwiched this around a two-year stretch in the service from 1959 to 1961 and a stint with Dinah Washington in 1959. While in the army, McBee played in a trio with Kirk Lightsey and Rudy Johnson, and also conducted the Fort Knox band. He moved to Detroit in 1962, where he played with Paul Winter, then moved to New York in 1964. McBee's schedule was full through the '60s. It included performances and/or recording sessions with Grachan Moncur III, Jackie McLean, Wayne Shorter, Charles Tolliver, Charles Lloyd, Yusef Lateef, Sam Rivers, Pharoah Sanders, and Alice Coltrane. During the '70s, McBee had extended stints with Abdullah Ibrahim and Chico Freeman that lasted into the '80s. He worked with Ibrahim in combo and large band settings, and when McBee started doing his own recordings in the mid-'70s they usually included Freeman. He also worked in the '70s with Sanders, Coltrane, Sonny Rollins, and Art Pepper. His own sessions were for Strata-East, Enja, and India Navigation. In the '80s, McBee worked with McCoy Tyner, Mal Waldron, James Newton, and Joanne Brackeen before joining the Leaders in 1984, with whom he's continued playing into the '90s. He played at the 1985 Kool Jazz Festival with Harry Edison and Buddy Tate. A couple of McBee's own albums are

available on CD, along with several others that feature him. —*Ron Wynn*

★ **Mutima** / May 8, 1974 / Strata East 7417

CHRISTIAN MCBRIDE

b. 1973
Bass / Neo-bop
Despite his youthful age, McBride rates as the '90s busiest bassist. He's done acclaimed sessions with Joe Henderson, Joshua Redman, Stephen Scott, Antonio Hart, and numerous others. McBride was voted top bassist by *Rolling Stone* in 1992 and 1993, and has been featured on so many sessions during the '90s he hasn't had time to cut one as a leader. McBride can be heard on almost any recent topflight date on CD. —*Ron Wynn*

STEVE MCCALL

b. 1933, **d.** 1989
Percussion / Early free, modern creative
A major percussionist whose dynamic drumming was featured in many free ensembles during the '60s, '70s, and '80s, Steve McCall's probably best known for his years in the tremendous trio, Air. He was extremely sensitive in his accompaniment and interaction within bands, and was also an individualistic, confident player whose rhythms could shape a group's musical direction. McCall had conservatory musical training, but got his early professional grounding playing blues with Lucky Carmichael. He met Muhal Richard Abrams in the early '60s, and both he and Abrams were founding members of the Association for the Advancement of Creative Musicians (AACM) in 1965. McCall worked with Chicago bebop bands, while he also played with Fred Anderson, Anthony Braxton, Joseph Jarman, Leroy Jenkins, Roscoe Mitchell, and Leo Smith. He lived in Paris during the late '60s and early '70s, recording with Maron Brown and Braxton. In the early '70s, McCall returned to Chicago. He did sessions with Dexter Gordon and Gene Ammons while forming a trio, Reflection, with Henry Threadgill and Fred Hopkins. They disbanded when McCall returned to Europe, then regrouped in the mid-'70s as the original Air. McCall toured and recorded extensively with them until he returned to Chicago. He also recorded with Chico Freeman, Arthur Blythe, and David Murray in the late '70s and early '80s. McCall joined Cecil Taylor's band in 1985, and also gave solo concerts and occasionally led a sextet. He can be heard on Air CD reissues, on releases by Murray and Blythe, and on Jarman reissues. —*Ron Wynn*

PAUL MCCANDLESS

b. 1947
English horn / World fusion, new age
An excellent multi-instrumentalist who plays the oboe, the English horn, the bass clarinet, and the soprano saxophone with passion and distinction, Paul McCandless is a fine improviser even though much of what he's done with various groups is not considered jazz. He's worked with the Winter Consort, Gallery, and Oregon, each a band with as much, if not more, classical, ethnic, and even new-age influence as jazz and blues links. McCandless began studying clarinet at age nine, and moved from Pennsylvania to New York in the late '60s. He studied oboe at the Manhattan School of Music, working with Robert Bloom. He played in Paul Winter's band, the Winter Consort, from 1968 to 1973, and was a co-founder, with Ralph Towner, Glen Moore, and Collin Walcott, of Oregon. McCandless led his own octet in 1979, and played with Gallery in the '80s. He continued recording in the '80s and '90s. McCandless has done sessions as a leader for Elektra and Windham Hill. He has some dates available on CD, many with Oregon. —*Ron Wynn and Michael G. Nastos*

All the Mornings Bring / Jan. 1979 / Elektra 196
★ **Navigator** / Feb. 1981 / Landslide 1005

Group includes McCandless (on his usual soprano sax, English horn, oboe, bass clarinet), vocalist Jay Clayton, and vibist David Samuels plus Steve Rodby (b). His best album. —*Michael G. Nastos*

○ **Heresay** / i. 1988 / Windham Hill 1075
This is a studio date with Art Lande (p) and Trilok Gurtu (per). Atmospheric without being dissipated. Very good record. —*Michael G. Nastos*

LES MCCANN (Leslie Coleman McCann)

b. Sep. 23, 1935, Lexington, KY
Piano, vocals / Blues & jazz, soul-jazz
A prime player in the soul-jazz and pop jazz arenas, McCann got his first major exposure as a member of the Gene McDaniels backing band in 1959, following a stint in the navy. He formed his own trio in 1960 and has been consistently popular ever since that time. A fine, earthy singer who has also done well with romantic ballads and occasional protest songs, McCann has done a lot with limited instrumental gifts. A dependable player in terms of establishing grooves or setting up rhythms, he is not renowned as a great soloist or technician. Instead, he lets others—like the Jazz Crusaders, Eddie Harris, or Rahsaan Roland Kirk—do the work when they collaborate. —*Ron Wynn*

○ **The Les McCann Anthology** / i. 1960-1971 / Rhino/Atlantic 271279
Keyboardist/vocalist Les McCann ranked among jazz's more successful populists, injecting healthy doses of blues, soul, and R&B vocals and feeling into his work, without neglecting the improvisational end. McCann made hits, but didn't plug into any formula, moving back and forth between short, pop-centered arrangements and longer, looser funk jams. The 21 tracks on this twin-CD set range from trio works to complex, multi-artist suites and include two songs from his tenure with Eddie Harris, plus collaborations with the Jazz Crusaders, Groove Holmes, Ben Webster, the Gerald Wilson orchestra, Stanley Turrentine, and Lou Rawls. The most ambitious piece, the layered, ethereal "The Lovers," offers a fitting climax to a set showcasing an undervalued, underrated performer. —*Ron Wynn*

★ **Les McCann Sings** / Aug. 1961 / Pacific Jazz
A super set with Ben Webster (ts) and Groove Holmes on organ. Soul-jazz and blues at their best. —*Ron Wynn*

Les is More / i. 1967 / Capitol 86201
A tremendous soul-jazz date composed of cuts previously in McCann's vaults. —*Ron Wynn*

Comment / Aug. 19, 1969-Oct. 22, 1969 / Atlantic 1547

Live at Montreux / Jun. 24, 1972 / Atlantic 312
A good two-disc date, with two hot stints by Rahsaan Roland Kirk (reeds). —*Ron Wynn*

★ **Invitation to Openness** / Nov. 1972 / Atlantic 1603
Hustle to Survive / 1975 / Atlantic 1679

RON MCCLURE (Ronald Dix McClure)

b. Nov. 22, 1941, New Haven, CT
Bass, composer / Modern creative
A resourceful and flexible bassist, Ron McClure has thrived in hard bop, jazz-rock, free, and bebop sessions and bands. One of the finest upper-register players around on either acoustic or electric, his rhythmic skills are tremendous. McClure's also been an active educator since the early '70s, teaching at Berklee and at Long Island University, and doing workshops both nationally and internationally. He started on piano at age five, and later played accordion and bass. McClure studied privately with Joseph Iadone and attended the Hartt School of Music, graduating in 1963. He later studied composition with Hall Overton and Don Sebesky. McClure played with Buddy Rich in the mid-'60s, and worked and recorded with Marian McPartland, Herbie Mann, and Maynard Ferguson during that same period. McClure played in Wyton Kelly's band in 1966, then joined Charles Lloyd in 1967. The Lloyd group also included Keith

Jarrett and Jack DeJohnette, and enjoyed unusual popularity and publicity for a late '60s jazz band. They were the first American group to play at a Soviet jazz festival, and were also one of the few jazz acts that played at the Fillmore. In 1968, McClure was a founding member of the ahead-of-its-time jazz-rock band the Fourth Way, with Michael White, Mike Nock, and Eddie Marshall. They got a good response at the Newport and Montreux festivals in 1970, but disbanded in 1971 after a three-year stint. During the '70s, McClure played with Joe Henderson, Gary Burton, Mose Allison, Jack DeJohnette, Dave Liebman, Thelonious Monk, Tony Bennett, and Jarrett. He recorded with Jerry Hahn, Julian Priester, Cal Tjader, and the Pointer Sisters, and spent three years with Blood, Sweat & Tears in the mid-'70s. McClure played and recorded with George Russell, Tom Harrell, John Scofield, John Abercrombie, Mark Gray, Jimmy Madison, Adam Nussbaum, Richie Bierarch, Vincent Herring, Kevin Hayes, Bill Stewart, and Michel Petrucciani in the '80s and '90s. McClure has done sessions as a leader for Ode, Bellaphon, EPC, Steeplechase, and Ken Music. He has a few dates available on CD. —*Ron Wynn and Michael G. Nastos*

★ **Tonight Only** / **i.** 1991 / Steeple Chase 31288
After decades as a sideman, the bassist leads a truly first-rate album. With Randy Brecker (tpt), John Abercrombie (g), and Adam Nussbaum (d). Five McClure originals, mostly in postbop/neo-contemporary vein, and three nice standards. A great record. —*Michael G. Nastos*

Inspiration / Ken Music 015
Stellar trio with McClure, Richard Beirach (p), and Adam Nussbaum (d). Strong statement. Good on repeated listenings. Two originals by bassist and three by pianist. Also Gordon Jenkins, Cole Porter, Miles Davis, and Wayne Shorter standards. —*Michael G. Nastos*

ROB MCCONNELL (Robert Murray Gordon McConnell)

b. Feb. 14, 1935, London, Ontario, Canada
Trombone, bandleader / *Swing, big band, progressive big band*
Canadian trombonist, bandleader, arranger, and composer Rob McConnell has ignored the warnings and conventional wisdom that the popularity of big bands is confined to "ghost" organizations and nostalgia shows. One of the most widely respected arrangers in the field, McConnell's led the Boss Brass for over 25 years, and has helped it to evolve from a pop organization with no reed section to a large orchestra (over 20 members) that plays both jazz standards and originals. The orchestra is well disciplined and is expert at what it does. It plays big band material at its most conservative, but the music is presented, performed, arranged, and recorded excellently. McConnell played valve trombone in Toronto during the '50s and early '60s, and studied with Gordon Delamont while working in various dance bands. He worked and recorded with Maynard Ferguson in New York during the mid-'60s, then played with Phil Nimmons's group, Nimmons 'n' Nine Plus Six, in Toronto from 1965 to 1969. McConnell also worked as a studio musician. His original pop ensemble Boss Brass added a horn section in 1971, and five years later swelled to over 20 members. They've toured and recorded during the '80s and '90s, and McConnell won a 1984 Grammy for the '83 release *All in Good Time*. The band's done sessions for Sea Breeze, Unisson, and Concord. They've also backed Mel Tormé on a mid-'80s date. McConnell and the band have several sessions available on CD. —*Ron Wynn and Michael G. Nastos*

★ **Boss Brass & Woods** / Mar. 11-12, 1985 / MCA 5982
Rob McConnell & Boss Brass. Potent solos by Phil Woods (as), excellent playing by Canada's premier big band. Four standards, one each by saxophonist Rick Wilkins and Quincy Jones, two by the leader. Twenty-three pieces working as one. Great solos from Guido Basso, Jan McDougal, and Ed Bickert. —*Michael G. Nastos*

Jive 5 / Aug. 1990 / Concord Jazz 4437

Brass is Back / Jan. 1991 / Concord Jazz 4458

More emphasis on postbop from composers Horace Silver and Kai Winding. Tunes from Don Thompson, R. Wilkins, Roger Kellaway, and McConnell. Two standards. Lots of music (over an hour) on this CD (2 bonus cuts). —*Michael G. Nastos*

SUSANNAH MCCORKLE

Vocals / *Ballads & blues*
An exuberant, sparkling, and articulate vocalist, Susannah McCorkle has been delighting critics and audiences since the early '70s. Her voice has a clear, striking sound, and timbre and tone that are equal parts alluring, sensitive, vulnerable, and commanding. She's also a fine writer who's had short stories and pieces published in many places, including the *New Yorker*. McCorkle moved to England from Paris shortly after her first encounter with Billie Holiday's music in the early '70s. She worked with Bruce Turner, Keith Nichols, Dick Sudhalter, and Keith Ingram, and also with visiting jazz musicians like Ben Webster, Dexter Gordon, and Bobby Hackett. McCorkle performed for a year at the Riverboat jazz room in Manhattan in the mid-'70s, and earned critical praise. She spent another year in England, where she cut two albums of repertory material featuring vintage prerock popular music. McCorkle returned to America in the late '70s, and cut an album of Johnny Mercer material in 1977. During the '80s and '90s, McCorkle has recorded for Concord. She has some sessions available on CD.

○ **Over the Rainbow** / Jan. 11, 1980-Feb. 19, 1980 / Inner City 1131
More classy standards and prerock pop from jazz vocalist Susannah McCorkle, whose rendition of the title track wisely doesn't try to imitate other, higher-pitched vocalists, but instead works off her strengths: pacing, enunciation, dramatic tension, and delivery. —*Ron Wynn*

○ **Songs of Johnny Mercer, The** / **i.** Aug. 1981 / Inner City 1101
A first-rate interpretive and standards vocalist tackles the classic songs written by a compositional master. The results are just what you'd expect: magical and outstanding. McCorkle's timing, instincts, and lyric readings are exceptional, as are her choices of Mercer material. —*Ron Wynn*

★ **No More Blues** / Nov. 1988 / Concord Jazz 4370

Sabia / Feb. 1990 / Concord Jazz 4418
Here are some good arrangements and cuts. CD version: three bonus cuts. —*Ron Wynn*

I'll Take Romance / Sep. 1991 / Concord Jazz 4491

○ **How Do You Keep the Music Playing?** / PA/USA 7195
The lightweight title song aside, here's another expertly done album showcasing the swinging skills of jazz vocalist Susannah McCorkle, among the finest contemporary singers around. Her timing, delivery, and sound, even on disposable fodder, are consistently impressive, and she's an outstanding lyric interpreter as well. —*Ron Wynn*

○ **Thanks for the Memory (Songs of Leo Robin)** / PA/USA 7175
While several of these songs aren't strictly jazz or even necessarily pop, Susannah McCorkle makes them all worth hearing. That's because she's a marvelous lyric interpreter, who also has an easy, swinging style and excellent delivery. She makes you pay attention to whatever she's singing, whether you understand it or not (or even care about it). —*Ron Wynn*

ROY MCCURDY

b. 1936
Drums / *Hard bop*
A fine hard bop and soul-jazz drummer, Roy McCurdy rose to fame during his decade-long stint with Cannonball Adderley. His ability to maintain the groove or stretch out and extend the rhythm was a vital part of the Adderley populist equation. McCurdy developed a fresh drumming style

that bridged the gap between hard bop, funk, and the innovations ushered in by Elvin Jones. The approach was very active, and spread timekeeping rhythms around the drums in a dense, turbulent fashion, as presented on the compositions "Fun" and "Games" featured on the Adderley brothers album *Mercy, Mercy, Mercy*. McCurdy played with the Mangione's Jazz Brothers band in the early '60s. He then worked in the Art Farmer-Benny Golson Jazztet, the Ruff-Mitchell trio, and the groups of Bobby Timmons, Betty Carter, and Sonny Rollins during the mid-'60s. McCurdy toured Japan with Rollins, then joined Adderley in 1965 and remained in the band until Cannonball's death in 1975. He played and toured with rock/pop vocalist Kenny Rankin in the mid- and late '70s, then turned to television and recording studio work. McCurdy played periodically with Golson, Jerome Richardson, and Nancy Wilson in the '80s. He does not have any sessions available as a leader, but can be heard at his peak on numerous Adderley mid- and late '60s, and early and mid-'70s CD reissues. —*Ron Wynn*

JACK MCDUFF (Eugene McDuffy)

b. Sep. 17, 1926, Champaign, IL
Organ / Blues & jazz, soul-jazz
A marvelous bandleader and organist and a capable arranger, "Brother" Jack McDuff has one of the funkiest, most soulful styles of all time on the Hammond B-3. His rock-solid bass lines and blues-drenched solos are balanced by clever, almost pianistic melodies and interesting progressions and phrases. McDuff began on bass playing with Denny Zeitlin and Joe Farrell. He studied privately in Cincinnati and worked with Johnny Griffin in Chicago. He taught himself organ and piano in the mid-'50s, and began gaining attention working with Willis Jackson in the late '50s and early '60s, cutting high-caliber soul-jazz dates for Prestige. McDuff made his recording debut as a leader for Prestige in 1960, playing in a studio pickup band with Jimmy Forrest. They made a pair of outstanding albums, *Tough 'Duff* and *The Honeydripper*. McDuff organized his own band the next year, which featured Harold Vick and drummer Joe Dukes. Things took off when McDuff hired a young guitarist named George Benson. They were among the most popular combos of the mid-'60s, and made several excellent albums. McDuff's later groups at Atlantic and Cadet didn't equal the level of the Benson band, while later dates for Verve and Cadet were uneven, though generally good. McDuff experimented with electronic keyboards and fusion during the '70s. In the '80s, he got back in the groove with the Muse session *Cap'n Jack*. Other musicians McDuff played with in the '60s and '70s include Joe Henderson, Pat Martino, Jimmy Witherspoon, David "Fathead" Newman, Rahsaan Roland Kirk, Sonny Stitt, and Gene Ammons. There are only a few McDuff sessions available on CD, though they include the fine sessions with Forrest. His work with Benson has also been reissued on CD. —*Ron Wynn and Bob Porter*

Tough 'Duff / Jul. 12, 1960 / Prestige 324
Funk, soul-jazz. McDuff's second lead session for Prestige. Good small-group Hammond organ funk—provided you like vibes, which is not a usual funk instrument. The title cut is excellent. Jimmy Forrest (ts) is in top form here. With Lem Winchester (vib). —*Michael Erlewine*

Honeydripper, The / Feb. 3, 1961 / Prestige 222
Soul-jazz/funk. This is first-rate jazz-funk, perhaps a little more bluesy than average, which is nice. His third album, with Grant Green (g). Excellent. —*Michael Erlewine*

★ Brother Jack Meets the Boss / Jan. 23, 1962 / Prestige 326
With Gene Ammons. Exceptional organ/tenor sax meetings from the early '60s. A looser, more relaxed McDuff than his subsequent Prestige recordings, yet equally good. With Harold Vick (ts). —*Bob Porter*

Mellow Gravy / Jan. 23, 1962 / Prestige

Screamin' / Oct. 23, 1962 / Prestige 7259

○ Live! / i. Jun. 5, 1963 / Prestige 7274

Moon Rappin' / Dec. 3-11, 1969 / Blue Note

★ Heating System, The / i. 1972 / Cadet

Re-Entry / 1988 / Muse 5361
A late '80s return to the sound of earlier recordings, featuring Houston Person (ts). Not inspired, but a solid performance all around. —*Bob Porter*

BOBBY MCFERRIN

b. Mar. 11, 1950, New York, NY
Vocals, piano / Ballads & blues, early jazz-rock
Bobby McFerrin is a true vocal improviser. His ability to stretch and strain his voice, to produce rhythmic patterns, to use his entire body like a drum, and to make notes by breathing in and out has made McFerrin an '80s pop icon. Jon Hendricks saw McFerrin, encouraged him, and later sang some duets with him. McFerrin began doing solo performances in 1983. He later scored a huge pop hit with "Don't Worry, Be Happy" and became a huge attraction. Over the years, his song content and performance approach have veered away from jazz, but he's an awesome stylist and a compelling vocalist. —*Ron Wynn*

Bobby McFerrin / 1982 / Elektra 60023
McFerrin's debut, which shocked, rocked, and amazed everyone. He's more of a vocal improviser than a performer of strictly jazz. —*Ron Wynn*

★ Voice, The / Mar. 17-26, 1984 / Elektra 60366
The Voice is a milestone in jazz history; it marks the first time a jazz singer has recorded an entire album solo, without accompaniment or overdubbing, for a major label. Bobby McFerrin's amazing ability to switch back and forth between bass notes and falsetto, along with his talent for jumping octaves, makes this record quite a virtuoso showcase. Taken from concerts in Germany. McFerrin's creativity keeps one's interest; the medley is certainly one of the high points. After scatting the melody of "Donna Lee" and improvising a bop solo for a few choruses, McFerrin gradually picks up a new rhythm, one that sounds like a musical washing machine. He answers himself while continuing the bass line, at several points having three lines on at once. After sounding like he's singing underwater, McFerrin concludes by imitating a trumpet on "We're in the Money." Other highlights include his philosophical "I'm My Own Walkman" (which asks why listen to the radio when one can sing?) and "Music Box," on which McFerrin imitates a child's toy, spinning fast semi-classical melodies. Now granted, a full album of McFerrin's voice isn't for everyone, but then again neither is Ornette Coleman or even Charlie Johnson's Paradise 10. For those interested in the potential of the human voice and in an important jazz talent, *The Voice* is recommended without reservations. —*Scott Yanow*, Cadence

Spontaneous Inventions / 1986 / Blue Note 46298
More superb vocal gymnastics. Takes on everyone from the Beatles to Dizzy Gillespie. —*Hank Davis*

★ Simple Pleasures / 1988 / EMI 48059
The breakthrough album. Contains the megahit "Don't Worry, Be Happy" and other gems like "Drive My Car." Platinum album. —*Hank Davis*

HOWARD MCGHEE (Howard B. McGhee)

b. 1918, d. 1987
Trumpet, composer / Bop, hard bop, postbop
A first-rate trumpet soloist who's equally solid on uptempo numbers and on ballads, Howard McGhee was one of the few players to make a successful transition from a swing style to a bebop style as an improviser. He gained recognition for his performances in Jazz at the Philharmonic revues, but was inactive during much of the '50s before making a heralded return in the '60s. McGhee played briefly with Duke Ellington during the mid-'60s. He was one of the most principled of all jazz musicians, and refused to cut corners or to make records based on any dictate except good music. In the latter part of his career, McGhee's ideals increasingly limited his opportunities.

McGhee played clarinet and tenor sax before starting on trumpet in 1935. He worked in territory bands in the Midwest and Northwest during the late '30s, then joined Lionel Hampton in 1941. He became Andy Kirk's principal soloist that same year, and remained with him until 1942. McGhee also wrote arrangements and compositions for Kirk, among them "McGhee Special" in 1942. He played often at Minton's Playhouse in 1942, and also at Monroe's Uptown House. McGhee worked with Charlie Barnet, Kirk (again), Georgie Auld, and Count Basie from 1942 to 1945, before going to Los Angeles with Coleman Hawkins. He made his debut recordings for Modern in 1945, and stayed in Los Angeles for two years. McGhee recorded with Jazz at the Philharmonic and with Charlie Parker in the late '40s. Some of the *Lover Man* sessions, slated to be Parker's date, became McGhee's when Parker appeared unable to play. Originally, these were issued under McGhee's name. He also played on the *Relaxin' at Camarillo* album. McGhee recorded for Savoy and Blue Note in the late '40s, playing with Milt Jackson, the Heath Brothers, and Fats Navarro. He also toured frequently, and acquired a reputation as a top player, winning *Down Beat*'s 1949 Best Trumpeter honors. There were additional sessions in the early '50s for Blue Note, plus quintet and ten-piece group dates for Bethlehem. But McGhee became inactive through much of the '50s. He formed a big band in the '60s and played in jazz services at St. Peter's Lutheran Church in New York. There was a flurry of recording sessions for Bethlehem, Felsted, Contemporary, Fontana, Argo, United Artists, and Hep/Zim. He played with Pepper Adams, Bennie Green, Ron Carter, Tommy Flanagan, Tina Brooks, Milt Hinton, Freddie Redd, and a big band. — *Ron Wynn*

○ **Howard McGhee's All Stars** / Oct. 11, 1948-Jan. 23, 1950 / Blue Note 5012

★ **Maggie** / i. 1948-1952 / Savoy 2219
Maggie is a two-disc set of trumpeter Howard McGhee's work during the late '40s and early '50s. McGhee, who gained attention with Andy Kirk's band during the early '40s, also gigged with Coleman Hawkins, Charlie Parker, and Norman Granz's Jazz at the Philharmonic. Then, in 1948, he put together a sextet with alto/baritone saxophonist Jimmy Heath, vibist Milt Jackson, pianist Will Davis, bassist Percy Heath, and drummer Joe Harris. The 1948 session was a bop-inspired unit of considerable energy. Here Maggie (McGhee) is a gutsy, full-toned player whose innate sense of lyrical swing enables him to extract the best from ballads, standards, and burning blues. Jimmy Heath, however, is still a struggling youngster whose baritone efforts are firmer than his tentative outings on alto. The second session from 1948 has an unidentified tenorist in for Heath, and Billy Eckstine on valve trombone, in place of Jackson. The tenor player, an aggressive Lesterite, and Maggie shine on otherwise undistinguished performances. The McGhee dates of 1952 include trombonist J.J. Johnson, tenorist Rudy Williams, guitarist Skeeter Best, bassist Oscar Pettiford, and drummer Charlie Rice. This is a group that toured U.S. military bases in Asia presenting programs on the evolution of jazz. Consequently, the repertory embraces everything from "Royal Garden Blues," "Mood Indigo," "12th Street Rag," and "Stompin' at the Savoy" to "How High the Moon." There are some inspired moments, but for the most part the renditions are routine. — *Chuck Berg*, Down Beat

○ **McGhee-Navarro Sextet (With Fats Navarro), The** / i. 1952 /

○ **Return of Howard McGhee, The** / Oct. 22, 1955 / Bethlehem 42

★ **Maggie's Back in Town** / Jun. 26, 1961 / Contemporary 693
Trumpeter Howard McGhee's date is a rather common outing made interesting because of the quality of the individuals. Maggie (McGhee) is in good command; his rumpled style of playing always seems to have direction and purpose and rarely dips into predictable phrasing. Bassist Leroy Vinnegar and drummer Shelly Manne are as you would ex-

pect—solid. The added plus is pianist Phineas Newborn, whose quixotic playing provides a strong second voice adding unexpected zing. — *Bob Rusch*, Cadence

Cookin' Time / Sep. 22, 1966 / Zim

Here Comes Freddy / Mar. 30, 1976 / Sonet

Jazz Brothers / Oct. 19, 1977 / Storyville 4077

Live at Emerson's / Mar. 10-11, 1978 / Zim

Home Run / Oct. 11, 1978 / Jazzcraft 5

Young at Heart / Oct. 4-6, 1979 / Storyville

CHRIS MCGREGOR

b. Dec. 24, 1936, Umtata, South Africa, d. May 26, 1990
Piano, bandleader / Progressive big band, world fusion
A revered and respected bandleader and pianist, South African Chris McGregor's life was changed forever when he heard the hymns of the Xhosa people in his father's Church of Scotland mission. Eventually, he left his South African homeland in protest against apartheid, and led several seminal ensembles of expatriate South Africans. At the 1962 Johannesburg Jazz Festival, McGregor selected many great players to be in a new band, among them Mongezi Fesa, Dudu Pukwana, and Johnny Dyani. As an integrated band, The Blue Notes were anathema in '60s South Africa, which was ruled by strict apartheid. They left the country in the early '60s on a European tour and never returned. They remained in Switzerland for a year, then moved to London. At various times, McGregor led the Chris McGregor Group and the Brotherhood of Breath. This was an African version of Sun Ra's Arkestra or Cecil Taylor's large orchestra, and mixed free and avant-garde arrangements with township jive and other African styles. The Brotherhood of Breath developed out of a series of big band concerts McGregor had been presenting weekly at Ronnie Scott's club. McGregor moved to France in the mid-'70s, and did solo dates, but revived the Brotherhood of Breath periodically. At one time, the groups' ranks included Pukwana, Fezi, Dyani, and Louis Moholo. McGregor died in 1990 of lung cancer. Currently, none of his sessions are available on CD in America. — *Ron Wynn*

★ **And the Brotherhood of Breath** / i. 1971 / Neon 2
Studio release with excellent compositions, particularly "The Bride." — *Michael G. Nastos*

○ **Live at Willisau** / i. 1974 / Ogun 100
The pianist/leader with an 11-piece band of South African expatriates and English free jazz musicians. Explosive. — *Michael G. Nastos*

Live at Toulouse / i. 1977 / Ogun 524

☆ **Country Cooking** / Venture 90998

JIMMY MCGRIFF (James Harrell (Jr) McGriff)

b. Apr. 3, 1936, Philadelphia, PA
Organ, bandleader / Blues & jazz, soul-jazz
The finest blues soloist among organists, Jimmy McGriff can also play superb soul jazz, though he's turned in dreary performances on fusion and pop dates in the '70s. McGriff studied bass, drums, tenor sax, and vibes in his teens, and attended Combe College of Music in Philadelphia and Juilliard. McGriff later studied electric organ with Jimmy Smith, Milt Buckner, and Groove Holmes. His debut record on Sue, *I Got a Woman*, was a Top 20 hit in 1962, and he followed it with *All About My Girl* and *Kiko* in 1963 and 1964. McGriff began a long relationship with producer Sonny Lester in 1966, when McGriff joined Solid State Records. The two later teamed at Blue Note, Capitol, Groove Merchant, and LRC. McGriff recorded many fine organ combo sides while also cutting R&B-tinged work during the '60s. He had a huge hit with "The Worm" in '68/'69, but also made the LP *The Big Band*, a stirring tribute to Count Basie. During the '70s, McGriff made more solid small combo jazz dates, including some organ battles with Groove Holmes. But he also did trendy material that utilized multiple elec-

tronic keyboards. He didn't distinguish himself on several later LRC sessions. McGriff's earlier Groove Merchant recordings were his best in this period. McGriff, like Hank Crawford, got back to basics when he signed with Milestone in 1980. He's done several dates with Hank Crawford, and has played with Al Grey. McGriff's early '90s Headfirst sessions mix electronic fusion material with organ jazz. Most of the McGriff available on CD is recent Milestone and Headfirst dates. None of the Groove Merchant, Sue, or LRC dates are listed as available currently on CD, according to *Schwann*. —*Ron Wynn and Bob Porter*

★ **At the Apollo** / **i.** 1963 / Collectables 5126

☆ **I've Got a Woman** / 1963 / Collectables 3062

Blues for Mister Jimmy / 1965 / Collectables 5147

Worm, The / Sep. 1968 / Solid State 18045

○ **Movin' Upside the Blues** / **i.** Apr. 1982 / Jazz America 005
Few better combinations exist for producing after-hours funk than organist Jimmy McGriff and guitarist Jimmy Ponder. Irrepressibly swinging McGriff is always in spitting distance of those down-home or South Side blues. Ponder complements with a lightness that brings an appealing optimism to the realities. This is McGriff's second JAM release and it's good to see he's found a producer who realizes that he is a great funk organist with commercial appeal without trying to exploit him in any type of commercial setting, depending on the winds of the day. McGriff is an original. I wouldn't want to see a return of the organ/sax/guitar funk blitz that strangled or at least crowded out so much of the other jazz activities of the mid- to late '60s, but it has its place. This genre, with the exception of an odd Muse release, almost disappeared during the '70s. If you haven't had a taste yet, start here; if you have had a taste and have room for more in your diet, this is a savory dish. —*Bob Rusch*, Cadence

Countdown / Apr. 27-28, 1983 / Milestone 9116

Skywalk / Mar. 19-20, 1984 / Milestone 9126
McGriff sometimes veers away from his soul-jazz strength, but it's still a fine set overall. —*Ron Wynn*

★ **Starting Five, The** / 1986 / Milestone 9148
Best of the last decade for one of the better Hammond B-3 organists. —*Michael G. Nastos*

Blue to the Bone / Jul. 19-20, 1988 / Milestone 9163

○ **State of the Art** / **i.** 198z / Milestone 9135
Organist Jimmy McGriff's *State of the Art* is, according to the liner notes, an attempt to "bring the sound of the organ group into today." Actually, this is a fairly self-conscious effort to graft "new" sounds, meaning synthesizers, onto an "old" sound, meaning the organ trio. Does it work? I don't feel a sweaty atmosphere on this record; it feels clean and spruced up, and it does not feel like an '80s organ trio. —*Neil Haverstick*, Cadence

○ **On the Blue Side** / **i.** May 1990 / Milestone 9177
An updated version of the vintage McGriff formula; bluesy, soulful organ fare with a balance struck between jazz sensibility and a funk/R&B groove. McGriff has wisely decided to play more organ and less synthesizer and has also mostly scrapped the quasi-fusion and gone back to pretty straight soul-jazz. —*Ron Wynn*

○ **Toast to Golden Classics** / Collectables 5125

KALAPARUSHA MAURICE MCINTYRE
(Maurice McIntyre)

b. 1936
Saxophone / Early free, modern creative
An animated, intense saxophonist whose work can feature penetrating screams and cries, soulful blues, honking R&B thrusts, or poignant melodies, Kalaparusha Maurice McIntyre hasn't gotten as much attention as many of his Chicago comrades or his fellow members of the Association for the Advancement of Creative Musicians (AACM). Part of this lack of attention is due to the paucity of his albums; he's

only done a scant handful since his 1969 debut. But it's not due to any lack of ability; he's just as versatile and invigorating a soloist as Roscoe Mitchell, Joseph Jarman, or any other AACM saxophonist. McIntyre began playing drums at age seven, then switched to clarinet and sax when he was nine. McIntyre was an AACM founding member in 1965, and made his recording debut with Mitchell on the album *Sound* in 1966. He played and recorded with other AACM members, like Muhal Richard Abrams, and worked with Jerome Cooper in 1968. His debut album as a leader, *Humility in the Light of the Creator,* was issued in 1969. McIntyre took his Muslim name, moved to New York, and began playing with Warren Smith. He returned to Chicago in 1970, but went back to New York in 1974. He worked with Cooper again, and continued playing and recording with him into the '80s. He led a quartet with Warren Smith, Sonelius Smith, and Wilber Morris. McIntyre recorded albums in the '70s and '80s for Trio, Black Saint, and Cadence, and with Cooper on Karma in 1977. A couple of McIntyre releases on Delmark and Black Saint are available on CD. —*Ron Wynn*

Humility in the Light of the Creator / **i.** Apr. 1970 / Delmark 419
Superb album by multi-instrumental McIntyre, one of the lesser-known Chicago musicians who helped form the AACM and has participated in the city's avant-garde jazz movement since its inception. This is his finest album, a work with sweeping, complex, yet also invigorating and visceral compositions. It features dazzling playing from McIntyre and his associates. —*Ron Wynn*

★ **Ram's Run** / **i.** 1981 / Cadence 1009
Ram's Run documents a concert at New York's Soundscape, capturing the spontaneity of a live performance at some cost to its recorded presence. Malachi Thompson's agile, flat-toned trumpeting complement Maurice McIntyre's grainy tenor contortions, but Julius Hemphill's alto, distinguishable by its smoother contours, is largely overhadowed. Drummer J.R. Mitchell lays down an appropriately open-ended barrage, but the absence of a bass imparts a slightly arid quality to the set. —*Larry Birnbaum*, Down Beat

KEN MCINTYRE (Kenneth Arthur McIntyre)

b. Sep. 7, 1931, Boston, MA
Alto saxophone, piano, instructor / Postbop, early free
Ken McIntyre has moved from playing to teaching and back to playing, demonstrating, in the process, great flexibility, diversity, and ability. A multi-instrumentalist who plays alto sax, oboe, flute, and bass clarinet, McIntyre has demonstrated a strong, robust tone, good range, interesting harmonic ideas, and a willingness to experiment in his playing. But he left the music scene in both the '60s and '70s for long stretches to devote himself to teaching. Recently, McIntyre returned again, recording in the early '90s. His father was a mandolin player, and McIntyre took lessons in classical piano as a child. He began on alto sax at age 19, studying with Andrew McGhee, Gigi Gryce, and Charlie Mariano. He attended Boston Conservatory and eventually earned an MA in composition. McIntyre studied for two more years at Brandeis, then formed his own band in Boston and released his debut album for Prestige. He moved to New York and met Eric Dolphy in 1960. They later recorded together, then McIntyre opted for a full-time teaching career and part-time recording work. He continued doing sessions as both a leader and with Bill Dixon, with the Jazz Composers Guild Orchestra, and with Cecil Taylor in the '60s, and on Steeplechase in the '70s. McIntyre also recorded with Charlie Haden's Liberation Music Orchestra. He's headed the African-American Music and Dance department at Old Westbury since the early '70s. McIntyre recorded a tribute album to Dolphy in 1991 with French reed player Thierry Bruneau. He has a couple of sessions available on CD. —*Ron Wynn and Michael G. Nastos*

★ **Looking Ahead** / Jun. 28, 1960 / New Jazz 252

Eric Dolphy (as, bcl, fl) has a featured role on Ken McIntyre's date *Looking Ahead* (6/28/60), which also includes Walter Bishop (p), Sam Jones (b), and Art Taylor (d). Ken McIntyre's alto playing is marked by an original tone (sort of an unresolved thrust that seems bent on trailing away into the outward bounds). The program here sports some nice solos but seems restrained in a rather perfunctory structure. At times things turn loose (best on "George's Tune," McIntyre's original written for dancer George Howard), and then the music most succeeds in reaching this listener. A somewhat dead-pan delivery on "They All Laughed" reminded me a bit of the Bob Wilber/Kenny Davern team. The record is worth a listen as one of the early and too-few examples of Ken McIntyre and, of course, for Dolphy, who steals the spotlight, it seems, with ease. —*Bob Rusch,* Cadence

Year of the Iron Sheep / Jun. 1962 / United Artists 15015

Way Way Out / **i.** 1963 / United Artists 6336

Tribute / Serene

DAVE MCKENNA (David McKenna)

b. May 30, 1930, Woonsocket, RI
Piano / Stride, swing, bop

A veteran pianist, McKenna is especially appealing in solo format because of his ability to utilize both classic and contemporary keyboard styles. McKenna can play "stride," blues, or conventional bop, and is known for brisk, romping solos that include aggressive passages, strong right-hand rhythmic accompaniment, excellent statements, and quick, unpredictable harmonies. He's also well-known for playing walking bass lines with his left hand. McKenna began working with Charlie Ventura in 1949, then spent 1950-1951 with Woody Herman. McKenna worked with Gene Krupa, Stan Getz, Zoot Sims, and Ventura during the '60s, then started a string of club dates in Cape Cod in 1967. He returned to the touring circuit in the '70s and began a run on Concord in the '80s. Since then, he's worked with small combos, done several solo releases, and appeared with the label's big Superband. During the early '70s, McKenna led a quartet with Zoot Sims, Major Holley, and Ray Mosca, whose 1974 album was reissued last year by the Chiaroscuro label. —*Ron Wynn*

○ **This is the Moment** / **i.** 1959 / Portrait 44091

○ **Dave McKenna Quartet Featuring Zoot Sims** / Oct. 1974 / Chiaroscuro 136
With Zoot Sims. Quartet. A 1990 reissue of a delightful date that's hotter than usual, thanks to Zoot Sims (ts) and Major Holley (b). —*Ron Wynn*

○ **Giant Strides** / May 1979 / Concord Jazz 99
There is a single-mindness to Dave McKenna's piano playing that is unique. The engine that powers it is his right hand, which flicks off long, assertive strings of eighth notes in an immaculate pulsation of even accents. The pattern is uninterrupted by arpeggios, frills, triplets, octaves, chords, silences, and dynamic variations. Tunes like "Dreams Come True" and "Lulu" from the *Giant Strides* solo album are typical. McKenna underpins himself with a rolling 4/4 pulse for a chorus or two before falling suddenly into an almost cathartic two-beat stride gait. And if Charlie Parker boptized swing staples like "I Got Rhythm" and "Honeysuckle Rose," McKenna reverses the process just as effectively by recasting a bebop anthem like "Yardbird Suite" in a pure swing idiom. —*John McDonough,* Down Beat

○ **Left Handed Complement** / Dec. 1979 / Concord Jazz 4123
Look again at the title of pianist Dave McKenna's album. That's not "compliment," but "complement," as in McKenna's left hand acts as an entire rhythm section (i. e., "a full complement of rhythm") or as in McKenna's left hand complements what the right is doing. I swear at times ("Miss Jones," "Splendid Splinter") the man must have not only three hands but two independently functioning yet interconnected brains. There are at least three, often four levels of activity going on at any given time—melody, right-hand comping,

left-hand bass line, and/or left-hand comping. Add to that fills and embellishments from either hand, and you've got incredible amounts of piano playing and musical thinking from two hands and one brain! Even the ballads, which don't have as forceful a bass line, have an awful lot going on. McKenna is relatively restrained here in that there were fewer out-and-out stompers on the album, which is dominated by easy-going midtempo numbers (of which "Thanks for the Memory" is a standard). But fast, slow, in-between, there is so much good stuff on this record, no self-respecting piano fan will want to pass this by. —*Tom Bingham,* Cadence

★ **No Bass Hit** / 1979 / Concord Jazz 4097
The bassless trio with Scott Hamilton on tenor sax and Jake Hanna on drums is a nice idea. All selections are early period standards. McKenna is an undisputed master. —*Michael G. Nastos*

○ **Piano Mover** / Apr. 1980 / Concord Jazz 146
On this session, recorded in April 1980, the best of Dave McKenna's piano is heard on "Cottontail," where McKenna throws caution to the winds and ignores the presence of bassist Bob Maize, while producing a roaring and furious solo. Elsewhere, the presence of Maize takes a little something away from the McKenna style. "Nobody Else But Me" illustrates the results of putting a bass with McKenna, as Maize attempts to stay out of McKenna's way, while McKenna simplifies his left hand in order to give the bassist some room. This Jerome Kern composition, thought to be his last, is based on sixths, which Dick Johnson on alto is able to explore nicely. "Cottontail" is fast and furious and brings out the best in both McKenna and Johnson, the latter on alto again. Johnson takes to the flute on his waltz, while "Star Eyes," as might be expected, is all Bird feathers. Johnson goes back to alto on Clare Fischer's introspective "Morning," and does some nice clarinet work on his other composition, "A Spider Sat Down Beside Her." The remaining two titles are taken on alto, with "In Love In Vain" especially good. Through the entire LP, McKenna's piano work is never less than fine, but for the essence of McKenna, try one of the several solo piano LPs available or any of the LPs which have no bass. —*Shirley Klett,* Cadence

○ **Dave McKenna Trio Plays Music of Harry Warren** / Aug. 1981 / Concord Jazz 174

○ **Celebration of Hoagy Carmichael** / May 1983 / Concord Jazz 227

○ **Keyman, The** / Aug. 1984 / Concord Jazz 261
This LP by Dave McKenna is recommended to all lovers of good piano. All musicians, or their producers, are hard put to find material that is new to their recorded works and provides variety and interest. This particular program is an excellent example of a successful solution to this problem. Where McKenna is concerned, no rhythm section assistance is needed; in fact, it would detract from the enjoyment. This is an exceptional issue. —*Shirley Klett,* Cadence

○ **Dancing in the Dark** / Aug. 1985 / Concord Jazz 4292
Here is still another fine album from pianist Dave McKenna. All the compositions are by Arthur Schwartz and pianist Marian McPartland wrote excellent liner notes in praise of both McKenna and composer Schwartz. McKenna's unique pianistics have one feature that can be very prominent on occasion. The beat does not constitute one fixed point in time. Charles Mingus once characterized a beat as having an oval shape and, as long as you placed your note within that oval, you were keeping time. Dave McKenna has a tendency to shrink that oval down so small as to approach the fixed point in time, with the result that he can frequently sound metronomic, even though he may accelerate and decelerate for some particular effect within one performance. He is particularly metronomic on several titles here. In the event that this bothers you upon first hearing, persevere. The beauties of this LP will grow upon you on replays. —*Shirley Klett,* Cadence

○ **My Friend the Piano** / Aug. 1986 / Concord Jazz 4313

Pianist Dave McKenna fills *My Friend the Piano* with constant surprises; rhythm, tempo, and key changes somehow seem logical after the fact. There is a slight emphasis on ballads, but one's attention rarely wanders, for the music, although tasteful, is never entirely predictable. Naming one example, it is not unusual for a pianist to start a tune such as "This is Always" as a waltz during its verse and then shift to 4/4 for the chorus. McKenna instead plays several choruses in 3/4 and then, when he decides to turn the piece into an uptempo stomp, he initiates the change by roaring through the verse! It's moments like that that make Dave McKenna's albums particularly enjoyable listening experiences. —*Scott Yanow*, Cadence

○ **No More Ouzo for Puzo** / Jun. 1988 / Concord Jazz 4365
Recorded by a quartet with guitarist Gray Sargent. The title piece was written by McKenna, the rest are all standards treated with tender loving care. —*Michael G. Nastos*

○ **Live at Maybeck Recital Hall–Vol. 2** / Nov. 1989 / Concord Jazz 4410

○ **Shadows 'N Dreams** / i. 1990 / Concord Jazz 4467
As usual, McKenna's playing ranges from good to great. CD version has two bonus cuts. —*Ron Wynn*

RED MCKENZIE

b. 1899, **d.** 1948
Swing, big band
A true character, Red McKenzie played a comb with tissue paper, which made a sound that resembled that of a kazoo. That was his "instrument." He was not a compelling vocalist; he was barely marginal as a singer. But McKenzie was an ace judge of talent, and helped Bix Beiderbecke, The Chicago Rhythm Kings, the New Orleans Rhythm Kings, the Spirits of Rhythm, and many others obtain recording contracts. He formed the Mound City Blue Blowers in the '20s with Jack Bland and Dick Slevin, and his composition "Hello Lola" did well, though the group did even better with "Darktown Strutter's Ball." Frankie Trumbauer guested on some of the early Blue Blowers sides. McKenzie also recorded with Red Nichols, Adrian Rollini, and Paul Whiteman in the late '20s and '30s, using musicians such as Jack Teagarden, Eddie Condon, Bunny Berigan, and Muggsy Spanier. McKenzie even had a hit in 1929 with "(If I Could Be With You) One Hour," which featured a tremendous solo by Coleman Hawkins. McKenzie later led a band with Mike Riley and Eddie Parley, temporarily revived the Mound City Blue Blowers, and recorded with the Bob Crosby band. McKenzie had a club on 52nd street in New York. He retired from 1939 to 1944, then returned to New York and sang with Condon at Town Hall, while he also recorded for Commodore. McKenzie has some sessions available on Jazzology CDs. —*Ron Wynn*

AL MCKIBBON

b. 1919
Bass / Bop
A versatile, veteran bassist, Al McKibbon has been a prominent contributor to bebop, Latin, and hard bop groups, but began his career working in swing orchestras. His authoritative, steady bass work has never made him a star, but he's made his presence felt in every recording session and in any group he's joined. McKibbon worked with local Detroit bands in the '30s, then moved to New York in the mid-'40s. He cemented his reputation there, playing with Lucky Millinder, Tab Smith, J.C. Heard, and Coleman Hawkins. He replaced Ray Brown in Dizzy Gillespie's band in 1947, and worked with Gillespie periodically until 1950. McKibbon was also featured with Miles Davis's nonet on the cool sessions. He played with Thelonious Monk at Minton's in the '50s, and recorded with Earl Hines, Count Basie, Johnny Hodges, and Monk. McKibbon was also part of the Afro-Latin explosion; he played with George Shearing through most of the decade, and spent two years with Cal Tjader's group. McKibbon initially spurred Tjader's interest in Latin

music. He also recorded with Herbie Nichols and with Coleman Hawkins at the Newport Jazz Festival in 1957. McKibbon did session work on the West Coast in the '60s, then played on the final Monk album in 1971. He was a member of the Giants of Jazz in 1971 and 1972, recorded with Benny Carter in 1976, and has remained active on the West Coast in the '80s and '90s. He doesn't have any albums as a leader, but can be heard on many reissues by Gillespie, Davis, Carter, Tjader, and the Giants of Jazz. —*Ron Wynn*

MCKINNEY'S COTTON PICKERS

b. Sep. 17, 1895, **d.** Oct. 14, 1969
Swing, big band
McKinney's Cotton Pickers, fronted by Bill McKinney, was one of the first swinging big bands (although it predated swing) under the direction of the great arranger Don Redman. It hit number one with "If I Could Be With You One Hour Tonight" in 1930, and disbanded in 1935. —*Ron Wynn and William Ruhlmann*

★ **Band Don Redman Built, The** / Jun. 1928-Nov. 1930 / Bluebird 2275
McKinney's Cotton Pickers were among the most forward-looking big jazz bands of the late '20s, clearly anticipating the swing era that arrived in the mid-'30s. These recordings, some of which feature Benny Carter, Coleman Hawkins, and Fats Waller, show the band emerging from a Dixieland style into what can only be called swing. —*William Ruhlmann*

HAL MCKUSICK (Harold Wlldred McKusick)

b. Jun. 1, 1924, Medford, MA
Alto saxophone / Swing, big band, cool
An early experimenter with time signatures and counterpoint, Hal McKusick enjoyed some notoriety for these tactics in the '50s. He also enjoyed fame for his light, delicate tone and phrasing on alto sax, which was featured on several sessions for Decca, RCA, Bethlehem, Prestige, and Fantasy. McKusick played for several big bands in the '40s, including the bands of Les Brown, Woody Herman, Boyd Raeburn, Alvino Rey, Al Donahue, Buddy Rich, and Claude Thornhill. He played with Terry Gibbs, Bill Harris, and Elliot Lawrence in the '50s, and was also a studio musician and bandleader. McKusick joined CBS's staff in 1958, and mixed studio dates with jazz sessions. He's now retired. Fantasy reissued a 1957 McKusick date in 1993, *Triple Exposure*, that features three bonus tracks, and also spotlights McKusick on tenor and clarinet as well as alto. He has one other session currently available on CD. —*Ron Wynn*

Triple Exposure / i. 1957 / Original/Fantasy 1811
Hal McKusick was a well-respected multi-instrumentalist who made a string of fine albums in the mid-'50s that unfortunately didn't attract much attention from anyone except musicians and attentive jazz fans. One of these was *Triple Exposure*, a 1957 date that's mainly a hard-blowing date but still has some coherence and organization. This CD reissue includes three bonus tracks that weren't included on the original album, though they came from the same session. McKusick fares best on clarinet, though his alto and tenor work isn't shameful either. But his clarinet offers an alternative approach to either swing/big band, Dixieland/New Orleans revival or free/avant-garde extensions. Bassist Paul Chambers is exceptional, and trombonist Billy Byers makes a interesting second solo voice, while pianist Eddie Costa and drummer Charlie Persip handle their duties expertly. —*Ron Wynn*

★ **Jazz Heritage: Hal McKusick Quintet with Art Farmer (1957)** / 1957 / MCA 1379

JOHN MCLAUGHLIN

b. Jan. 4, 1942, Yorkshire, England
Guitar, bandleader / Early jazz-rock, world fusion
A great player and easily the finest guitarist to emerge from the jazz-rock movement, England's John McLaughlin has played spectacularly on electric and acoustic through the

late '60s, '70s, '80s, and '90s. His solos are explosive and daz-zling, and feature long passages, bent notes, jagged lines, highly melodic and rhythmic phrases, a splendid mix of vir-tuoso technique, and an alternately lyrical/animated sensi-bility. McLaughlin has played free, has incorporated Asian scales, has done straight rock and blues solos, has blended acoustic and electric, and has rotated between spontaneous, improvised material and intricately notated compositions. He was one of the individuals on the ground floor of the jazz-rock movement.

Though he took piano lessons at age nine, McLaughlin's essentially a self-taught guitarist. He played blues and jazz records, teaching himself from the sound and style of Django Reinhardt and Muddy Waters, among others. McLaughlin was active in the '60s London rock scene, and played with Jack Bruce, Mick Jagger, and Eric Clapton before moving to America in 1969. He joined Tony Williams's pio-neering Lifetime band, and also recorded with John Surman and Buddy Miles. McLaughlin played with Miles Davis and appeared on several influential sessions: *In a Silent Way*, *Bitches Brew*, and *Jack Johnson*.

He became a disciple of Sri Chinmoy in 1970, and formed the Mahavishnu Orchestra a year later. The group proved to be the finest in jazz-rock history; they blended furious rock energy with first-rate improvising and were also influenced by Indian music. The original unit of McLaughlin, Jan Hammer, Jerry Goodman, Rick Laird, and Billy Cobham made some stunning albums for Columbia. The second ver-sion wasn't as anthemic, and the orchestra disbanded in the mid-'70s. McLaughlin worked with the acoustic group, Shakti, until he settled in Paris in the late '70s and returned to electric. But he switched again to acoustic in the '80s, cut-ting trio and duo dates with Paco De Lucia, Al Di Meola, Larry Coryell, and Christian Escoude. He led a third Mahavishnu Orchestra in 1984, touring and recording with them. McLaughlin also wrote a guitar concerto that was pre-miered by the Los Angeles Philharmonic in 1985. He's made numerous recordings since the late '60s for Douglas, Columbia, Polydor, Warner Bros., and recently, Verve. He's played with Carlos Santana, Stanley Clarke, Chick Corea, L. Shankar, and Trilok Gurtu, among others. McLaughlin has several recent and reissued titles available on CD. —*Ron Wynn and Stephen Aldrich*

★ **Extrapolation** / Jan. 18, 1969 / Polydor 841598
The success of this album is very hard to separate into nice neat clichéd boxes, but a good deal of it has to do with the extraordinary talents of John Surman. Surman plays bari-tone and soprano sax on this recording, but it's more than apparent that baritone is his horn. He appears to have re-jected the premise that the baritone is an unwieldy instru-ment and just plays it however he wants. His control, from the conventional range of the horn to the several false oc-taves, is all done with apparent ease. And he swings like hell. Surman, John McLaughlin (g), Brian Odges (b), and Tony Oxley (per) succeed in completely molding together all their independent talents into one large collective one. —*Bill Smith*, Coda

☆ **Devotion** / 1970 / Restless 72656
John McLaughlin's *Devotion* may very well have been to Jimi Hendrix on this reissue of a Douglas recording of 1970. Along with the Band of Gypsies rhythm section (Billy Cox, b; Buddy Miles, d), organist Larry Young is added. McLaughlin is at his rawest, blues-rock-oriented state, much different from his work on, say, *My Goals Beyond*, the Mahavishnu Orchestra, or much later Shakti. The music is more reminis-cent of his work with Tony Williams's Lifetime. It has a real '60s psychedelic/garage band feel to it and puts McLaughlin into perspective in terms of his gravitation to more refined modal reflections of North and South Indian classical music. The players work well together. Especially noteworthy is the playing of Larry Young (Khalid Yasin) who has developed a timelessly modern approach to the organ. —*Brian Auerbach*, Cadence

★ **My Goals Beyond** / 1970 / Rykodisc 10051

A reissue of an original Douglas/CBS album. A landmark recording. One side is solo guitar, the other is the first Mahavishnu Orchestra. A must-buy. —*Michael G. Nastos*

Where Fortune Smiles / i. 1970 / Dawn 3018

Between Nothingness and Eternity / Aug. 1973 / Columbia 32766

★ **Shakti with John McLaughlin** / Jul. 5, 1975 / CBS 46868

○ **Passion, Grace and Fire** / 1983 / CBS 38645
There's a lot to be said for athletic muscle, and on *Passion, Grace and Fire*, guitarists John McLaughlin, Paco De Lucia and Al Di Meola flex a lot of it. Every solo has an edge of danger here, a sense that the artist is putting himself on the line. And they communicate that danger with a reckless pas-sion, carrying you to the edge with them. McLaughlin cen-ters the trio with solos that are miniature excursions into a detailed world full of sharp angles and intricate bas-reliefs. Di Meola takes his steel-strung acoustic on the heroic route, trying to find the quickest way to the top of his high E string. The flamenco-based arrangements that dominate this album are De Lucia's home turf. He milks all his notes, tweaking them with worry on "Aspan" and giving them wry slants on "Orient Blues Suite." —*John Diliberto*, Down Beat

Live at the Royal Festival Hall / i. Nov. 27, 1989 / JMT 834436
Trio recording with Kai Eckhart (b) and Trilok Gurtu (per). His best of the last decade. —*Michael G. Nastos*

○ **Jazz—Vol. 2** / i. 1991 / Rhino 270722
It certainly has no shortage of amazing playing—amazing just from a physical standpoint, let alone an artistic one. But that's also the volume's main problem. It leaves out the myr-iad shades and styles that have colored jazz besides the sim-ple fret speed. —*Dan Heilman*, Rock & Roll Disc

---

JACKIE MCLEAN (John Lenwood (Jr) McLean)

b. May 17, 1932, New York, NY
Alto saxophone / Hard bop
Jackie McLean's style rivals almost any alto player for sheer intensity and urgency. He played hard bop with a vivid tone and a surging, emphatic approach in the '50s and '60s. His early '60s solos reflected the influence of Ornette Coleman. McLean's father played in Tiny Bradshaw's orchestra, and McLean started on alto at age 15. He studied, for a short time, with Foots Thomas and Cecil Scott, then began work-ing with Sonny Rollins in 1948 and 1949. He made his recording debut with Miles Davis in 1951 and 1952, then worked in the mid-'50s with Paul Bley and George Wallington, and with Charles Mingus in the late '50s. He played on classic Mingus albums *Pithecanthropus Erectus* and *Blues & Roots*. He was in Art Blakey's Jazz Messengers in 1956, '57, and '58, then began leading a quintet in 1959. McLean made his recording debut as a leader in 1955, work-ing with Mal Waldron. He made some fine sessions for Prestige and for subsidiary labels Status and New Jazz, with Waldron, Elmo Hope, Paul Chambers, and others. He made several recordings for Blue Note, about 20 releases from 1959 to 1967, most of them quintets. McLean played with Tina Brooks, Cecil McBee, and even Ornette Coleman. The list of seminal sessions includes *A Fickle Sonance* and *Action*. McLean toured Japan in 1965, and joined the faculty at the Hartt School of Music in Hartford in 1968. For several years during the summer, McLean toured and taught in Europe. He made some superb releases for Steeplechase in the early '70s; a couple that matched him with Dexter Gordon in spirited dialogues, another with a group that in-cluded his son, Rene, and a duet session with Michael Garvin. McLean was featured on a '74 session with Lee Konitz, Gary Bartz, and Charlie Mariano (it was Konitz's date), and on a good quartet set with Hank Jones, Ron Carter, and Tony Williams for East Wind/Inner City. He was featured recently on a new Antilles album, where he played with young lions Roy Hargrove and Steve Nelson. He recorded again with his son on Triloka. McLean was fea-tured in the 1980 Ken Levis documentary film *Jackie*

McLean on Mars, in which he was shown teaching, playing, and talking about life and music. Several classic McLean Blue Note and Prestige sessions have been reissued; his recent Triloka and Antilles releases are available also. The Steeplechase releases aren't in print in America. —*Ron Wynn*

★ **Complete Blue Note 1964-1966** / Mosaic

○ **Jackie McLean Quintet, The** / **i.** 1956 / Jubilee 1064

Lights Out / Jan. 27, 1956 / Prestige 426
Super quintet date. Elmo Hope is breezy and understated on piano and Donald Byrd is dynamic on trumpet. —*Ron Wynn*

★ **Jackie's Pal** / Aug. 31, 1956 / Original Jazz Classics 1714
Jackie's Pal here was Bill Hardman (trumpet), who he introduced into a quintet with Mal Waldron (piano), Paul Chambers (bass) and Philly Joe Jones (drums). Hardman's hot breaking tone sounds a bit less forceful than on his (soon-to-be) later work with the Messengers, but it was already identifiable. Chambers has some exciting bowed spots, Mal Waldron was a bit bland and while Jones' drumming fills the role, it missed the push Art Taylor's drumming seemed to invite so often with McLean. So, not as I might have planned it, but I wouldn't change a note on this program which aged so well. —*Bob Rusch*, Cadence

★ **Alto Madness** / **i.** May 3, 1957 / Prestige 1733
All of this material except "Bird Feathers" was originally issued on Prestige and later reissued on Status. For the first time, McLean's entire session with fellow alto saxman John Jenkins is available on one LP. Ira Gitler's original notes from 1957 and 1958 appear as well as an update. The music is what you would expect from the two altoists, since Bird (Charlie Parker) had only been dead a couple of years. The performances are rather raw, using Bird's many inflections, licks, and other creations, which were also being used by almost everybody. "Alto Madness" is blues; "Windy City" is hard blowing with lots of exchanges. Drummer Art Taylor is always very busy, while pianist Wade Legge is very much into Bud Powell's bag. "Pondering" is soulful playing by John Jenkins, while "Easy Living" is almost all Jackie McLean's vehicle. The 10+ minutes of "Bird Feathers" has some 24 choruses by the altoists before the exchanges start again. The sound of bassist Doug Watkins is neglected, so if you want this one just expect it to be fully concentrated on two of Bird's better followers. —*Jerry L. Atkins*, Cadence

Long Drink of the Blues, A / Aug. 1957 / New Jazz 253

McLean's Scene / +14 / New Jazz 098
This excellent McLean hard bop date from the late '50s features the masterly Red Garland (p), Paul Chambers (b), and Arthur Taylor (d) in the rhythm section. —*Ron Wynn*

○ **Jackie's Bag** / Jan. 18, 1959-Sep. 1960 / Blue Note 46142

New Soil / May 2, 1959 / Blue Note 84013

Bluesnik / Oct. 8, 1961 / Blue Note 84067

★ **Fickle Sonance, A** / Oct. 26, 1961 / Blue Note 84089
A remarkable merger of new-thing/avant-garde leanings and hard bop fluidity and feelings. —*Ron Wynn*

Let Freedom Ring / Mar. 19, 1962 / Blue Note 46527
The outer limits of the music is in good hands. Also look for *Destination Out*. —*Michael G. Nastos*

Tippin' the Scales / Sep. 28, 1962 / Blue Note 84427

One Step Beyond / Apr. 30, 1963 / Blue Note 46821
Terse, extensive solos are part of McLean's free/avant-garde-influenced Blue Note sessions from the early and mid-'60s. —*Ron Wynn*

Destination Out / Sep. 20, 1963 / Blue Note 4165

○ **It's Time** / Aug. 5, 1964 / Blue Note 4179

Action / Sep. 16, 1964 / Blue Note
Blistering sessions spiced by the tremendous bass playing of Cecil McBee. —*Ron Wynn*

Right Now / Jan. 29, 1965 / Blue Note 84215

With pronounced Black liberation and civil rights undercurrents, this album is not so strong musically as others in the same period. —*Ron Wynn*

○ **Jacknife** / Apr. 12, 1966 / Blue Note 457
A twofer with Lee Morgan (tpt), Charles Tolliver (tpt), Larry Willis (p), and Jack DeJohnette (d). Potent. —*Michael G. Nastos*

Hipnosis / 1967 / Blue Note
McLean steps away from the Parker influence and makes his own sound and statement in this gem. —*Ron Wynn*

★ **New and Old Gospel** / Mar. 24, 1967 / Blue Note 84262

○ **Demon's Dance** / Dec. 22, 1967 / Blue Note 84345

★ **Meeting, The** / Jul. 20+23, 1973 / Steeple Chase 31006
This set with tenor saxophonist Dexter Gordon and alto saxophonist Jackie McLean is less a "meeting" than a date on which both appear and solo. There is little sign of having worked anything out in advance. When they simultaneously play the intros and endings on tunes they are not together. Their timing is sometimes different and one of the two frequently holds back, not sure of what to do. When they play separate lines, the lines don't weave around each other. When they play the same lines together, the heavy vibrato of both saxes prevents their playing from blending. They only trade choruses on "All Clean," but do it well. Although McLean worshipped Gordon, or perhaps because of it, his weakest solo is on "All Clean," the only tune on which he follows Gordon. Gordon's solo on this tune also lacks the drive found in his other solos, especially "Trail," on which he charges through a well-developed solo. But the 13-minute "Trail" packs a wallop and "Sunset" is a nice warm ballad. This is generally good Gordon, but not much of a meeting. —*Jerry De Muth*, Cadence

☆ **Source, The** / **i.** Jul. 20+23, 1973 / Steeple Chase
The feeling that alto saxophonist Jackie McLean had for tenor saxophonist Dexter Gordon is warmly stated in McLean's closing remarks on this, the second volume of the McLean/Gordon Montmarte recordings (Vol. 1 was *The Meeting*). What is captured on this recording is the essence of jazz: the instantaneous creation of moving and stimulating music. You can hear ideas being developed and cast off, and new ones forming. Sure, there are those moments when the creative process seems to be struggling and searching (most notably on "Another Hair-do"), but it's just those moments that make jazz so vibrant. For when the soloist eventually finds his inspiration and takes off, the effect is cathartic. There is some sloppy playing here and there, and I found drummer Alex Riel to be rather insensitive, but you would be hard pressed to find music any more exciting or emotionally charged than this. —*Carl Brauer*, Cadence

New York Calling / Oct. 30, 1974 / Steeple Chase
A wonderful session that helped introduce McLean's then-26-year-old son Rene to the jazz audience. —*Ron Wynn*

Altissimo 1974 / 1974 / Philips
This is a great summit meeting with McLean and fellow horn players Lee Konitz, Gary Bartz, and Charlie Mariano, plus a piano trio. —*Ron Wynn*

☆ **New Wine, Old Bottles** / Apr. 6-7, 1978 / Inner City 6029
A superb quartet date with Hank Jones (p), Ron Carter (b), and Tony Williams (d). —*Ron Wynn*

Dynasty / Nov. 5, 1988 / Triloka 181
Quintet. This album marks McLean's return to the recording scene in the '90s after a lengthy sabbatical. It features him alongside his son Rene (sax, f). —*Ron Wynn*

RENE MCLEAN

b. 1946
Saxophone, flute / Hard bop, world fusion
In Rene McLean's case, there's been no struggle with his father's legacy. Though the elder Jackie McLean was and is a living legend and is one of the greatest alto players of the post-Parker era, the younger McLean has proven to be neither a slouch nor an imitator. His skills extend not only to

alto, but to tenor, soprano, baritone and flute. He's played African, Afro-Latin, and Caribbean music as well as jazz, and his sound, tone, phrasing, and direction are his own. Rene McLean had private studies with Sonny Rollins and his father, then played baritone and alto sax with Tito Puente for three years during the early '70s. McLean worked with Sam Rivers, Lionel Hampton, and Doug Carn, and recorded with Carn in 1973. He and his father co-led the Cosmic Brotherhood, and McLean recorded with them in 1974. McLean also did sessions with Tyrone Washington, and was in a quintet co-led by Woody Shaw and Louis Hayes. He recorded separately with Shaw and Hayes. McLean led his own bands in the early '80s, and co-led a hard bop sextet with his father. He's recorded as a leader for Steeplechase and Triloka, among others, but currently has no sessions as a leader available on CD. —*Ron Wynn and Michael G. Nastos*

★ **Watch Out** / Jul. 9, 1975 / Inner City 2037
Jackie McLean's then-30-year-old son (1976) appears as a leader himself on *Watch Out* with a hard-driving, Art Blakeyesque sextet. The group includes trumpeter Danny Coleman, who doesn't get much room to blow; versatile guitarist Nathan Page; and one of the more propulsive recent rhythm combinations—pianist Hubert Eaves, an imaginative accompanist with an indomitable left hand; the redoubtable bassist Buster Williams once again; and Freddie Waits, a consistent, critically ignored drummer. Despite the solid support and big sound, it is McLean's show all the way. He is a forceful, mature instrumentalist of excellent taste and convincing expressive range on the three upper-register saxes and flute. —*Charles Mitchell*, Down Beat

BIG JAY MCNEELY

b. Apr. 29, 1928
Tenor saxophone / Blues & jazz, soul-jazz
A tenor sax giant of the honking sax school, McNeely mixed flamboyant onstage antics with a simplistic, volcanic sax style. His robust, huge tone and vocal effects were an extension of the swing-era technique into the R&B/blues market. His penchants for rolling on the floor, playing on his back, or walking out into the audience were crowd-pleasing maneuvers commonplace on the R&B scene in the '40s and '50s, but were incorporated so flawlessly into his act that some thought he invented them. McNeely remains active on the California oldies and R&B circuit, and cut some new recordings on his own label in the late '80s. —*Ron Wynn*

★ **Swingin'** / Collectables 5133

Deacon Rides Again, The / Marconi
Hot tenor licks, sweltering vocals from Jesse Belvin, and bluesy inflections courtesy of Mercy Dee. —*Ron Wynn*

From Harlem to Camden / ACE

Meets the Penguins / ACE
This reissue of raucous, upbeat R&B cuts also includes the doo-wop harmony ensemble The Penguins. —*Ron Wynn*

○ **Big Jay in 3-D** / Federal 530

JIMMY MCPARTLAND (James Douglas McPartland)

b. Mar. 15, 1907, Chicago, IL, **d.** Mar. 13, 1991
Cornet / Dixieland
One of the most lyrical, concise, and stately trumpeters in the early jazz scene, Jimmy McPartland made his mark in the Chicago jazz scene of the late '20s and '30s, and was one of the celebrated Austin High Gang. McPartland's solos balanced a sophisticated sound with an energetic edge; he was one of the finest ballad players of his day. As a 17-year-old, McPartland replaced Bix Beiderbecke in the Wolverines, and he was greatly influenced by Beiderbecke's phrasing. He later worked with Ben Pollack, Roger Wolfe Kahn, Russ Columbo, and Smith Ballew. McPartland joined his brother Dick's Embassy Four in Chicago in the mid-'30s, then formed his own band. McPartland was in the military during World War II, and met his wife, pianist Marian McPartland, in Belgium. He led bands in the Midwest in the late '40s and the '50s before working at Nick's in New York. McPartland also played at a 50th anniversary party for the Austin High School Gang in 1965. McPartland worked with Bud Freeman in the '60s, and appeared with his now ex-wife, Marian, at the Newport Jazz Festival in 1978. He continued working into the '80s. McPartland recorded for several labels, among them Decca, Brunswick, Epic, Jazzology, MCA, and Marian McPartland's label, Halcyon. He currently has a couple of recordings available on CD. —*Ron Wynn*

○ **Meet Me in Chicago** / i. Dec. 1960 / Mercury 20460

McPartlands Live at the Monticello / Nov. 1972 / Halcyon 107

★ **Shades of Bix** / i. Oct. 1977 / Brunswick 58049
This Jimmy McPartland set begins with some fine 1953 reworkings of a dozen Bix Beiderbecke pieces. The personnel are all from the Eddie Condon stock company (Peanuts Hucko, George Wettling, Ernie Caceres, Bud Freeman, etc.) and bite into things with exhilaration if not inspiration. McPartland's horn is a commanding surrogate for Beiderbecke. Except for "In a Mist," the spirit of the original generally prevails. Side three has two peppy sessions that look back to the Chicago days. And side four features Beiderbecke's other disciple, Bobby Hackett, in pretty, though routine, ballads. —*John McDonough*, Down Beat

☆ **At the Festival** / i. 1979 / Concord Jazz 118
This nice small-group session accents McPartland's fortes: touch, delicacy, and melodic interpretation. —*Ron Wynn*

MARIAN MCPARTLAND (Marian Margaret McPartland)

b. Mar. 20, 1920, Windsor, England
Piano / Swing, bop
Pianist Marian McPartland has combined playing, broadcasting, recording, and teaching in a distinguished manner. Her playing style fuses swing and bebop elements, and is both sophisticated and earthy. She studied at London's Guildhall School of Music, but left to join a vaudeville piano act. She performed for British and American troops during World War II, using the name Marian Page. She met Jimmy McPartland in Belgium. They were married and came to America in the late '40s. McPartland established her own trio in the early '50s, playing at the Embers Club and Hickory House in New York, recording at the Hickory House for Savoy. Her compositions began to attract attention, with Sarah Vaughan recording "There'll Be Other Times" and with Doc Severinsen, Tony Bennett, and the Thad Jones-Mel Lewis big band also cutting her songs. McPartland recorded for Savoy and RCA in the '50s, and began teaching jazz history to school children in the mid-'50s. She established the Halcyon record label in 1959, which issued albums by Jimmy McPartland and other artists, as well as her own releases. Eventually, the McPartlands were divorced, but they performed together occasionally in the '70s, and appeared at the 1978 Newport Jazz Festival. They remarried before Jimmy McPartland's death. She began the syndicated program "Marian McPartland's Piano Jazz" on National Public Radio in 1979 and eventually won a Peabody award. She recorded heavily for Concord in the '70s and '80s, making duo dates, repertory albums, and live and studio sessions, mostly with small combos. A collection of her essays on jazz musicians, *All in Good Time*, was published in 1987. Her early Savoy material has been reissued, while her Concord albums from the '70s, '80s, and '90s are available on compact discs. —*Ron Wynn*

○ **Great Britain's Marian McPartland / George Shearing** / Dec. 22, 1952 / Savoy 12016

Plays Alec Wilder / 1973 / Halcyon 109
McPartland plays sharp, arresting versions of songs by a preeminent composer. —*Ron Wynn*

○ **Solo Concert at Haverford** / Apr. 12, 1974 / Halcyon 111
Marian McPartland's LP is as sophisticated and stimulating a piano record as I've heard. It is a credit to McPartland's en-

ergy and imagination that she adds enough dimension to her piano sound to overcome the dismal tone given her instrument by the Halcyon Records tape machines. Wide in stylistic scope, her program begins with a trenchant, tone-setting blues, running a conventional pattern with most unconventional chord substitutions, melodic digressions of singular eloquence, strong basslines, and smoothly flowing rhythm shifts. On ballads such as "Send In the Clowns" and "Killing Me Softly With His Song," McPartland lets her melodies stand with little embellishment; she prefers instead to employ advanced chord support and unexpected turns of rhythm. Yet she doesn't come off as fickle; each mood and tempo is thoroughly established before new changes set in. —*Charles Mitchell*, Down Beat

○ **Concert in Argentina** / Nov. 1974 / Jazz Alliance 10008
This document of a 1974 concert in Buenos Aires showcases four wonderfully personable piano stylists in solo recital. Marian McPartland's portion of the show is highlighted by a reverent, if reserved, medley of Ellingtonia, though she does pick up steam and take a few more chances on "It Don't Mean a Thing." Teddy Wilson puts his graceful stamp on a Gershwin medley, then trots out a delightful stride version of "Body and Soul" before "Flying Home" in swinging fashion. Ellis Larkins opens with a slow, luxuriant take on "Perfidia," then can be heard scatting along with "Blues In My Heart" and humming wistfully behind "Ill Wind." Of the four pianists, Earl Hines turns in the most rhythmically compelling, unpredictable performance. He injects a jaunty stride sensibility into corn, like Burt Bacharach's "Close to You," and on "Girl From Ipanema" he leaps all over the keyboard with stop-time breaks, brief double-time figures, and flowery right-hand embellishments, while varying the dynamics from a whisper to a shout. He brings a Lisztian kind of flamboyance to "Bluesette" and pulls out all the stops on "Tea For Two." —*Bill Milkowski*, Down Beat

Maestro and Friend / i. 1974 / Halcyon

From This Moment On / Dec. 1978 / Concord Jazz 4086

Let It Happen / i. 1978 / RCA
An immaculate piano quartet session with guests Dick Hyman, Hank Jones, and Roland Hanna. —*Ron Wynn*

○ **Willow Creek and Other Ballads** / Jan. 1985 / Concord Jazz 4272
The exemplary solo playing on this album helped embellish her new-star status won through her "Piano Jazz" series on National Public Radio. —*Ron Wynn*

Music of Billy Strayhorn, The / Mar. 1987 / Concord Jazz 4326
This is a solid tribute to Strayhorn, whose compositions are a perfect fit for McPartland. —*Ron Wynn*

★ **Marian McPartland Plays the Benny Carter Songbook** / i. Oct. 1990 / Concord Jazz 4412
This is McPartland's finest work in quite some time and includes wonderful interpretations of great compositions by Benny Carter—a spry, exciting alto soloist, in his eighth decade as a player! CD has two bonus cuts. Good support comes from John Clayton and Harold Jones. —*Ron Wynn*

Live at Maybeck Recital Hall Volume 9 / Jan. 1991 / Concord Jazz 4460
Great solos, with strong rhythmic work and phrasing. CD version has two bonus cuts. —*Ron Wynn*

JOE MCPHEE

b. Nov. 3, 1939, Miami, FL
Alto, soprano, and tenor saxophone, leader / Modern creative
An interesting player, composer, and critic whose commentaries and reviews often appear in *Cadence* magazine, Joe McPhee has never followed any set trend. His trumpet, cornet, and saxophone solos could be categorized as free, though they're also influenced by hard bop, R&B, blues, and gospel. He's a self-taught saxophonist, and his jagged lines and bluesy phrases are arresting on all of the instruments he

plays. McPhee made his recording debut in the late '60s with Clifford Thornton. He began recording his own albums in the late '60s, and has continued recording on labels such as Hat Hut, Hat Art, and Sackville. McPhee has added other wind instruments and percussion to his arsenal, and lectured on jazz at Vassar in the late '60s and early '70s. He worked in New York with Don Cherry, and lived in Europe from 1975 to 1977. His albums are not available on CD, but can be obtained through mail-order sources. —*Ron Wynn*

★ **Willisau Concert, The** / Oct. 11, 1975 / Hat Hut
Joe McPhee teams with synthesist John Syndor and drummer Makaya Ntshoko on *The Willisau Concert*, for problematic results. McPhee could have employed the synthesizer to texturally extend his highly unconventional, even courageous, rhythmic and melodic sense—instead Syndor plays the offbeat counterpoint of the "sound" of McPhee's tenor and soprano, and actually seems to little serve the tonally distorted lyricism of McPhee's best music. "Voices," the most complete piece of the concert, has McPhee and Syndor achieving a very attractive, mournful texture. The brief lead bids homage to one of Ornette Coleman's lesser-known themes. The remainder of the LP is noteworthy for the pleasant Caribbean flavor of "Bahamian Folksong," spotlighting McPhee's unique minimalism. —*Roger Riggins*, Down Beat

○ **Variations on a Blue Line 'Round Midnight** / Oct. 11, 1977 / Hat Hut
Variations On A Blue Line: 'Round Midnight, taped live in Paris, a few months after *Graphics (Vol. I & II)*, makes clear how Joe McPhee solves the tonal problems he makes for himself. The performance showcases an "artistic" attempt at solving technical ambiguities. "Beanstalk," side one, is an abstract improv off a simple blues, not explicit in the piece's beginning, which emerges later. "Motian Studies" is a discourse for soprano, in much the same strained areas of sound. More microtonally and spatially arranged, it features a gorgeously obtuse episode that is masterfully employed. Also quite attractive is its lyrical sequence slowly progressing toward an elusive, almost unobtainable melodic setting. "'Round Midnight," Thelonious Monk's classic, the closing work, is given a sensitive, nearly sentimental reading that retains an armed guard at the gates of romanticism. —*Roger Riggins*, Down Beat

○ **Old Eyes and Mysteries** / i. May 1979 / Hat Art 6047

○ **Po Music: Oleo** / Mar. 24-25, 1984 / Hat Music 3514
Po Music: Oleo ranked as one of the most referential records of its day. Dedications to seven people—including Pablo Picasso, Neruda, and Casals—are made for the same number of tunes. On top of that, numerous musical homages are paid to past styles and performers. Moving out from under this weight of influence is a tricky proposition, but these players do it. They write new texts instead of just annotating old ones. In their versions of Sonny Rollins's "Oleo" and Benny Golson's "I Remember Clifford," the musicians rework the tunes according to updated principles. The two takes of "Oleo" are faster and harder swinging, less offhand, than the recording headed by the composer along with Miles Davis, Horace Silver, Percy Heath, and Kenny Clarke in 1954. Raymond Boni's guitar tremolos wash over the melody, while underneath Francois Mechali keeps a swinging bassline going. With the help of resonant engineering, they achieve a multidimensional layered effect that is quite different from the flatter finish of 30 years ago. —*Elaine Guregian*, Down Beat

○ **Visitation** / i. May 1987 / Sackville 3036
Despite unequal billing and misleading packaging, *Visitation* is an equal collaboration between the pride of Poughkeepsie, Joe McPhee (flhn, pkt-t, ts, ss), and Toronto's Bill Smith (sno, ss, as) Ensemble, and the Canadians coax McPhee into some areas he might not have gotten into on his own, with mixed results. The best is Smith's angular fanfare "Home at Last." The unison theme statement by two sopranos is a lovely, coolly glowing blur, and the two leaders'

excited straight-horn chatter/sputter, over a hotly grumbling rhythm section, is reason enough for this album's existence. Violinist David Prentice's appealing "If I Don't Fall," with its pointillistic intro, constructivist springboard figure, and free interplay, recalls the increasingly influential co-op Circle— the rhythm section's particularly indebted to bassist Dave Holland and drummer Barry Altschul—which like Albert Ayler seems to have had a delayed-reaction effect on other improvisers (McPhee plays pocket trumpet here). "Exuma" is a trio track, on which Richard Bannard's restructured-Max Roach rim clatter suggests the piece is a cubist version of a Sonny Rollins calypso; McPhee shows off his facility and Don Cherry-like, attractively raw sound on flugelhorn. — *Kevin Whitehead*, Cadence

CHARLES MCPHERSON

b. Jul. 24, 1939, Joplin, MO
Alto and tenor saxophone / Bop, hard bop
Alto saxophonist Charles McPherson's combination of lyrical beauty and aggressive, spirited expressiveness reflects attributes of his two prime influences, Johnny Hodges and Charlie Parker. Like Phil Woods and Frank Morgan, McPherson's sound and style embody the best aspects of the Parker legacy, and he has maintained his commitment to bebop throughout his career. McPherson became a professional at age 17, working in Detroit with groups and players such as Barry Harris and Lonnie Hillyer. He moved to New York in 1959, and periodically worked with Charles Mingus's Jazz Workshop groups until 1974. McPherson was featured on some seminal Mingus albums, among them *Blue Bird*. He co-led a quintet with Hillyer in the mid-'60s that eventually took the place of Mingus's group at the Five Spot. He recorded for Prestige in the mid-'60s, and appeared in the 1968 documentary film *Mingus*. He moved to San Diego in 1970. During the '70s and '80s, he was a freelancer on the West Coast, heading his own groups and playing regularly with Harris and Billy Higgins. McPherson also recorded for Mainstream in the early '70s, and then for Xanadu in the mid-'70s. In addition to his festival appearances and tour dates, McPherson worked with a quintet called Uptown Express in the late '80s. The personnel included his son, Chuck, and Tom Harrell. He also recorded for Discovery. Some of McPherson's '60s sessions have been reissued on CD, and some of his Xanadu dates are still available. —*Ron Wynn and Michael G. Nastos*

○ **Be-Bop Revisited** / Nov. 20, 1964 / Prestige 710
This is one of his first strong dates as a leader outside the Charles Mingus Jazz Workshop fold. Includes fine contributions from Barry Harris on piano and Carmell Jones on trumpet. —*Ron Wynn*

Con Alma / Aug. 6, 1965 / Prestige 7427
Good follow-up to *Be-Bop Revisited*, though the playing is a step below. —*Ron Wynn*

○ **Charles McPherson Quintet Live!, The** / Oct. 13, 1966 / Original Jazz Classics 1804
Some frenetic trumpet solos from Lonnie Hillyer, recorded live at the immortal Five Spot. —*Ron Wynn*

○ **Live in Tokyo** / Apr. 14, 1976 / Xanadu
I don't know if the tunes on alto saxophonist Charles McPherson's album are in the order of the concert program, but there is a distinct improvement in the playing as things proceed. "Tokyo Blues" is a perfunctory blues with everyone (pianist Barry Harris, bassist Sam Jones, drummer Leroy Williams) feeling things out. McPherson is the lone soloist on "East of the Sun," where he begins extending himself. When he lets loose on "Desafinado," all the cobwebs have been totally eradicated. From there on the music sparkles. "Orient Express" burns with a vitality and imaginative soloing; "These Foolish Things" is a gorgeous mood-changer; and "Bouncing With Bud" is the kind of set-closer guaranteed to leave the audience spellbound. —*Carl Brauer*, Cadence

★ **Free Bop!** / Oct. 23, 1978 / Xanadu

There are some good moments, especially Charles McPherson's tenor on "Chuck-A Luck" and "Estrellita." Charles McPherson, Jr. (d) plays extremely well, but he and Kevin Jones (per) put forth an awfully busy backing. My first hearing of guitarist Peter Sprague left me wanting to hear more. "Free Bop" is his best, but he has some great solos on "A Day in Rio" and "Si Si." In fact the best straightahead playing by all is on that latter track with Lou Levy (p) more into his own bag. "Come Sunday" is only McPherson (as) and Levy with a brief intro by Sprague. The introduction to Sprague and McPherson's good tenor are the highlights. — *Jerry Atkins*, Cadence

Siku Ya Bibi / Mainstream 713
A CD reissue of a 1972 tribute album to Billie Holiday suffers a bit from overproduction and glossy orchestrations, but alto saxophonist Charles McPherson's passionate playing, along with that of pianist Barry Harris and trumpeter Lonnie Hillyer, helps overcome the sappiness and at least bring home the point of Holiday's poignancy as a vocalist. — *Ron Wynn*

CARMEN MCRAE

b. Apr. 8, 1920, New York, NY, **d.** Nov. 10, 1994
Vocals / Ballads & blues
Carmen McRae ranks among the greatest of the bebop vocalists; she's a singer with comprehensive musical knowledge and training who's applied the genre's harmonic rigors to her vocal approach. Whether doing originals, standards, pop, or ballads, McRae's sound, phrasing, delivery, and inflections are rousing and impressive. She's a good pianist; her early days playing in clubs helped her develop extraordinary timing and pace. McRae's a first-rate scat singer and as rhythmically accomplished as any jazz vocalist. McRae studied piano before joining Benny Carter's orchestra in 1944. She sang with Mercer Ellington and Count Basie's bands in the late '40s, and also worked at Minton's Playhouse as an intermission singer and pianist. During the '50s, McRae made her first recordings and won *Down Beat*'s Best New Female Singer award. McRae even had chart singles with the songs "The Next Time It Happens," from the Broadway musical *Pipe Dream*, and "Skyliner." She recorded with Decca and began forging a reputation for distinctive vocals. McRae toured Europe and Japan often from the '60s through the '80s, though she settled in Los Angeles in 1967. She also recorded extensively for several labels, among them Atlantic, Mainstream, Pausa, Concord, Buddah, Trio, Dunhill, and Denon. Some of the people she recorded with include George Shearing and Dave Brubeck. McRae has done albums dedicated to Nat "King" Cole and Sarah Vaughan, and also did a stunning late '80s work *Carmen Sings Monk*. Her dismay over not winning a Grammy for that date has led to some blistering interviews and comments about the music business and about phony jazz vocalists in various articles. Only a few of McRae's classic albums have been reissued, though Atlantic now has *The Great American Songbook* on CD. Some of her early Decca dates were reissued in '92, while more recent Concord and RCA/Novus sessions are available currently. —*Ron Wynn*

By Special Request / Jun. 14, 1955+Jun. 16, 1955 / Decca 8173

○ **Lover Man** / 1962 / Columbia 8530

Ultimate Carmen McRae / 1964-1972 / Mainstream 705

Live–Take Five / i. 1965 / Columbia Special Products 9116
A very good meeting of the minds. Dave Brubeck (p) gets comfortable behind McRae. —*Ron Wynn*

Just a Little Lovin' / i. Mar. 1970 / Atlantic 1568
Sophisticated yet exuberant. A great version of the title cut, plus both jazz and American popular tunes. —*Ron Wynn*

★ **Great American Songbook, The** / i. Oct. 1972 / Atlantic 904
A wonderful two-disc set, with McRae showing her complete music vocabulary and interpretive talents. —*Ron Wynn*

I Am Music / Apr. 1975 / Blue Note

You Can't Hide Love / **i.** 1976 / PA/USA

○ **Greatest of Carmen McRae, The** / **i.** Oct. 1977 / MCA 24111
A misnomer, but a decent attempt at presenting '60s and
'70s Carmen McRae material. It is impossible to cover such
a varied career in one record, and this one is even more limited since it doesn't extend to her formative years in the '50s.
—*Ron Wynn*

Live at Bubba's / Jan. 17, 1981 / Who's Who In Jazz 21020

★ **You're Lookin' at Me (A Collection of Nat King Cole
Songs)** / Nov. 1983 / Concord Jazz 4235
The title of this album has a subtitle—*A Collection of Nat
King Cole Songs*—and Carmen McRae adds John Collins (g)
to her regular supporting trio to enhance the tribute to Cole
(Collins was Nat Cole's regular guitarist from 1951 on). What
appears to happen is that McRae loses her natural sense of
phrasing but comes nowhere near Cole's either, and the result, in several cases, is notably unswinging. This is most noticeable on "If I Had You," and I fidget impatiently through
this every time I play the LP. The first five titles are, generally, more successful than the remainder, although "Just You,
Just Me" allows John Collins to come front and center and
also has pianist Marshall Otwell in good form on some solo
work. As a minor point, McRae sings "Sweet Lorraine" with
no change in the lyrics, resulting in some eyebrow lifting for
those of you who pay attention to lyrics. —*Shirley Klett,*
Cadence

Duets with Carter / **i.** Jan. 30-31, 1987 / Great American
Music Hall 2706
With Benny Carter (sax). The music is superb. The two find
ways to link dissimilar styles. —*Ron Wynn*

Fine and Mellow: Live at Birdland West / Dec. 1987 /
Concord Jazz 4342
An excellent live set. McRae handles uptempo and ballads
with ease. CD has one bonus cut. —*Ron Wynn*

★ **Carmen Sings Monk** / Jan. 30, 1988-Feb. 1, 1988 / Novus
3086

Sarah–Dedicated to You / Oct. 1990 / Novus 3110

It Takes a Lot of Human Feelings / Groove

Setting Standards / Pair 1182

Sound of Jazz / Masters 5009

JAY MCSHANN (James Columbus McShann)

b. Jan. 12, 1916, Muskogee, OK
Piano / Boogie-woogie, swing, big band, blues & jazz
While he enjoys substantial and deserved recognition for his
role in bringing alto saxophonist Charlie Parker to the forefront, Jay McShann should be lauded for being a consistently enjoyable, rollicking pianist, composer, vocalist, and
bandleader. During swing's heyday, McShann's early '40s orchestra ranked just behind the Basie machine for providing
propulsive, steady grooves and bluesy, compelling solos. His
driving boogie-woogie and blues licks, riffs, and solos seldom fail to ignite any musical situation.
McShann's primarily a self-taught pianist. He attended
Tuskegee Institute in the '30s, at one time working with Don
Byas. He later played in Arkansas and Oklahoma, before
teaming with Oliver Todd and Elmer Hopkins in a Kansas
City trio during 1936. He was later in a group with Buster
Smith and trumpeter Dee Stewart before forming his own
band in 1937. By late 1939, McShann had expanded this
group into a big band, and performed in the Century Room
and Fairyland Park in 1940. They recorded with Decca in
1941, with a lineup that included vocalist Walter Brown,
Parker, Gene Ramey, Gus Johnson, Buddy Anderson, and
Orville Minor. The band made its New York debut at the
Savoy in 1942, and both Jimmy Forrest and Paul Quinchette
became members that same year, and remained until 1943.
During this stretch, they enjoyed such hits as "Confessin' the
Blues," a song cowritten by McShann and Brown with
Brown's vocal, and "Get Me On Your Mind" in 1943 with vo-
calist Al Hibbler.

McShann spent 1943 and 1944 in the army, then reformed
the band. But they broke up in 1944, and McShann performed at various New York clubs, and later, in California
with small combos. While on the West Coast, McShann
recorded at various times for Philo/Alladin, Mercury,
Capitol, and Downbeat/Swingtime. His late '40s group featured Jimmy Witherspoon. McShann returned to the
Midwest in the '50s, going back to Kansas City in 1951. They
had another hit in 1955, with "Hands Off," which featured
vocalist Priscilla Bowman. He became a regular at festivals
both in America and overseas in the '60s, '70s, and '80s, dividing his time between leading a trio and recordings.
During the '70s, McShann cut several excellent independent
label sessions. These included a quartet date with violinist
Claude Williams and a duet session with Tate, plus a respectable major label effort on Atlantic. There were also several solo piano releases. McShann was also featured in two
films at the end of the '70s, *Hootie's Blues* by Bart Becker
and Michael Farrell, and the documentary *The Last of the
Blue Devils. —Ron Wynn and Barry Pearson*

★ **Early Bird–Charlie Parker, The** / Nov. 30, 1940-Mar. 27,
1944 / Spotlite 120
1940-1944 airchecks. With Charlie Parker (as), Paul
Quinichette, and Gus Johnson. —*Michael Erlewine*

○ **Jazz Heritage–Early Bird Charlie Parker (1941-1943)** /
1941-1943 / MCA 1338
Until the '92 release of another, better-prepared reissue
package, this single-album reissue was the only domestic Jay
McShann covering this vital early '40s period in print. As
such, if you can't find or don't want the more recent release,
it's worth having. It is inexpensive and reasonably comprehensive for the times, though it's not as well engineered as
the current material. —*Ron Wynn*

○ **Confessin' the Blues** / Mar. 28, 1969 / Classic Jazz 128
Pianist Jay McShann is perhaps best known as the bandleader with whom Charlie Parker first recorded. In his own
right, McShann is a competent blues player having impressive blues lore under his fingertips. *Confessin' the Blues,*
recorded in 1971 and first issued on the European Black
and Blue label, pairs McShann with a small jump band containing two adequate accompanists and an outstanding one,
T-Bone Walker. "Our Kinda Blues" is a slow-bounce kicker
with laidback triples and some fresh guitar/piano interplay.
In the teasing "Stompin' In K.C.," a slow blues, interlacing
piano treble figures give way to tight, taut runs and block
chords à la Red Garland, and there is a snappy "After
Hours" with bouncing chordal punctuation. Wynton Kelly
couldn't have put it better. —*Jon Balleras,* Down Beat

○ **Big Apple Bash, The** / Aug. 3-10, 1971 / New World 358
Most of this all-star get-together is more mainstream oriented than the opener ("Crazy Legs and Friday Strut"). Still,
this is primarily the jazz Jay McShann rather than the blues
McShann, though the latter does get his licks in. Alto saxophonist Earle Warren, trombonist Dicky Wells, and trumpeter Doc Cheatham all play beautifully on their four
"purist" cuts. Herbie Mann's tenor fits in surprisingly well,
though his solos aren't exactly supremely inspired, and his
clarinet work is stiff. Guitarist John Scofield's ideas are a
touch too "modern" harmonically to blend in perfectly.
McShann's piano is solid, good natured and consistently inventive, while his singing is cozy and amiable. "Ain't
Misbehavin'," though, finds him in vocal mismatch with the
Manhattan Transfer's Janis Siegel, whose neo-band-singer
phrasing is as stylized as McShann's is unaffected. As a
whole, however, *Big Apple Bash* is far less disastrous than it
could have been. That it works at all says a lot about
McShann's versatility, as well as his willingness to risk the
wrath of those hardcore supporters whose image of what he
should do clashes with his own inclinations. —*Tom
Bingham,* Cadence

○ **Man from Muskogee** / Jun. 24, 1972 / Sackville S3005
One of McShann's finest recordings. With Claude Williams
(violin). —*Michael Erlewine*

○ **Crazy Legs and Friday Strut** / Jul. 1, 1976 / Sackville 3001
On this recording pianist Jay McShann's playing is closer in many ways to Earl Hines and Teddy Wilson than to what I know as McShann. McShann is even a little Erroll Garnerish on "Crazy Legs" with touches of Randy Weston and Mal Waldron. Certainly McShann's work on "Crazy Legs" will fascinate his fans. With further listenings I began to detect a detachment between saxophonist Buddy Tate and the rest of the group (McShann). This is least noticeable on "Melancholy Baby" and the Ellington medley ("I Got It Bad and That Ain't Good," "Sentimental Mood," "Sophisticated Lady") where they both seem to be listening to each other, more so McShann. But on the majority of these tracks Tate seems quite apart, playing as a soloist in a larger group, not as part of a duo with its special demands. —*Bob Rusch*, Cadence

○ **Paris All-Star Blues–A Tribute** / i. 1979 / Music Masters 5052
A '91 tribute album (recorded in '89) to Charlie Parker by a great cast of veteran and recent jazz musicians, under leadership of pianist Jay McShann, who conducted the band that gave Parker his start. The lineup runs from Benny Carter, Al Grey, and James Moody to Terence Blanchard. —*Ron Wynn*

○ **Swingmatism** / Oct. 1982 / Sackville 3046

DON MENZA

b. Apr. 22, 1936, Buffalo, NY
Tenor saxophone / Big band, bop
Don Menza is an intense, big-toned tenor saxophonist, composer, and flutist who's one of the better soloists and section players. Menza's neither relaxed nor detached in his approach or sound; his surging, fiery solos are constructed carefully, but are also dense and emphatic. Menza began playing tenor at age 15, and taught himself composition and arranging in army bands. He toured with Maynard Ferguson in the early '60s, then played with Stan Kenton before returning to his native Buffalo. Menza lived in Munich from 1964 to 1968, and worked in clubs while serving as a studio musician. He also learned to play flute and other saxophones. When he returned, Menza joined Buddy Rich's band. He settled on the West Coast, played briefly with Elvin Jones, then worked for a decade as a player and composer for Louis Bellson. Menza toured Scandinavia and England during the '80s, and played flute in the orchestra for the play *Cats*. Currently, he has one session available on CD. —*Ron Wynn and Michael G. Nastos*

★ **Horn of Plenty** / May 1-2, 1979 / Voss 72931

JOHNNY MERCER

b. Nov. 18, 1909, Savannah, GA, **d.** Jun. 25, 1976, Los Angeles, CA
Lyricist, vocals / Ballads & blues
A marvelous lyricist and multifaceted composer, talent scout, and recording artist, Johnny Mercer truly did it all. He wrote, or co-wrote, more than 1,000 songs, and his compositions have been played and sung by numerous jazz greats and many pop stars. As a vocalist, Mercer lacked great technique or tools, but performed many hits from the late '30s into the early '50s in a relaxed, easygoing style. He teamed with Bing Crosby on Decca from 1938 to 1940, then had 25 hits on Capitol over a ten-year period, including chart toppers "Candy" with Jo Stafford, "Ac-Cent-Tchu-Ate the Positive," and "On the Atchinson, Topeka and the Santa Fe." Mercer won multiple Oscars, cofounded Capitol Records, signed Nat "King" Cole and Peggy Lee, was a cofounder and president of the Songwriters Hall of Fame, and was a director of ASCAP in 1940 and 1941. His lyrics were unfailingly upbeat and optimistic; by today's cynical standards he'd be deemed not just a hopeless romantic, but a foolish one. Mercer gems include "I'm an Old Cowhand," "Dream (When You're Feelin' Blue)," "That Old Black Magic," "One for My Baby," "Lazy Bones," and numerous others. He collaborated on masterpieces with Henry Mancini, Harold Arlen, Hoagy Carmichael, Harry Warren, Billy Strayhorn and Duke Ellington, Ralph Burns, Jerome Kern, Gordon Jenkins, and Rube Bloom, among others. Mercer sang with Benny Goodman on radio, hosted his own shows with Paul Whiteman as music director, contributed to films and plays, and recorded duets with Bobby Darin. There's almost no facet of American popular entertainment Mercer didn't affect positively. Compilations of various singers doing his compositions have recently been issued on Rhino, and are available on other labels like RCA. Mercer's vocals are featured on CD compilations by Capitol, Hindsight, and other labels. —*Ron Wynn and Kenneth M. Cassidy*

★ **Capitol Collectors Series** / i. Jul. 26, 1989 / Capitol 92125
Mercer was one of America's great lyricists, whose understanding of mainstream American life and vernacular was matched only by Hoagy Carmichael or, later on, Hank Williams, Chuck Berry, or Smokey Robinson. Mercer was also a tremendous and swinging vocalist and proved it with a solid string of hit records in the '40s. Ironically, many of Mercer's own hits (and most of the songs on this disc) were written by others. This set is a treasure. —*Rich Kienzle*, Rock & Roll Disc

HELEN MERRILL (Helen Milcetic)

b. Jul. 21, 1930
Vocals / Ballads, bop
Helen Merrill was a successful jazz singer in the '50s and '60s who then opted for a long break from the recording scene. She became a professional in 1945 and sang in Earl Hines's sextet in 1952. Merrill had four prolific years in 1954-1958 and made one album featuring Quincy Jones arrangements and Clifford Brown's extraordinary trumpet solos. In 1959 she made an album for Atlantic and went to England that same year. She became a big name overseas and moved to Japan in 1967, then returned to America in 1972 and has made infrequent albums ever since. She reunited with Gil Evans, whom she'd worked with in the '50s, for an album shortly before his death in 1988. Merrill has always been a charmingly enjoyable singer with good articulation. —*Ron Wynn*

★ **Complete Helen Merrill on Mercury (1954-1958)** / 1954-1958 / Mercury 826340

○ **Helen Merrill with Clifford Brown** / i. 1955 / PolyGram 814643
This has arrangements by Quincy Jones and trumpet by Clifford Brown. It is a wonderfully emotive session, perfect for Merrill's serenely confident tones. All are standards. —*Michael G. Nastos*

Dream of You / i. 1956 / PolyGram 514074

Merrill at Midnight / i. 1957 / EmArcy 36107

Nearness of You, The / i. 1957 / EmArcy 1018
With small-ensemble accompaniment. Soloists include Bill Evans (p), Oscar Pettiford (b), George Russell (g), Jo Jones (d), and John Frigo (b). —*Michael G. Nastos*

Helen Merrill in Italy / i. 1959-1962 / Liuto 5

Artistry of Helen Merrill, The / i. 1965 / Mainstream 6014

○ **Shade of Difference, A** / Jul. 1968 / Landmark 1308

Sposin' / Oct. 21-25, 1971 / RCA 10132

Helen Merill / John Lewis / May 17, 1976+Sep. 8, 1976 / Mercury 11150

○ **Chasin' the Bird** / Mar. 6+9, 1979 / Inner City 1080

Helen Sings, Teddy Swings / i. 197z / Catalyst 7903
All standards. The combination works well. Some tracks have a Japanese rhythm section, but the bulk are with Teddy Wilson (p), Larry Ridley (b), and Lennie McBrown (d). —*Michael G. Nastos*

Rodgers & Hammerstein Album / Jan. 1982+Mar. 1982 / DRG 5104

Music Makers / Mar. 1986 / Owl 79226

○ **Collaboration** / i. 1987 / EmArcy 834205

○ **Alone Together** / i. Sep. 1989 / EmArcy 16000

Duets / **i**. Nov. 1990 / EmArcy 838097
Carter's dense, sparkling bass accompaniment lifts and caresses Merrill's vocals. *—Ron Wynn*

No Tears, No Goodbyes / 1991 / Owl 79227

Clear Out of This World / **i**. 1992 / Antilles 512654
A '92 session with jazz vocalist Helen Merrill's smoky, sometimes sensual, sometimes piercing singing supported by a group including pianist Roger Kellaway, bassist Red Mitchell, and drummer Terry Clarke. It's carefully crafted, finely executed standards and ballads for adult audiences. *—Ron Wynn*

Just Friends / **i**. Aug. 4, 1992 / EmArcy 842007

Something Special / Inner City 1060

Sings Cole Porter / Pro Arte 709

Sings Irving Berlin / Pro Arte 710

○ **You've Got a Date with the Blues** / Verve 837936

JYMIE MERRITT

b. 1926
Hard bop
A classically trained player with a surging style characterized by the frequent use of triplet figures and by putting notes ahead of the beat, Jymie Merritt made a successful switch from jazz to R&B and blues, and back to jazz again, in the '50s. Merritt played with John Coltrane, Benny Golson, and Philly Joe Jones in 1949, but worked with Bull Moose Jackson and B.B. King playing electric bass in the early and mid-'50s. Merritt returned to jazz when he joined Art Blakey's Jazz Messengers in the late '50s, and also went back to the acoustic. He later invented his own instrument, the Ampeg, sort of a modification hybrid of both electric bass and acoustic. Merritt stayed with Blakey until 1962, then recorded with Chet Baker in 1964. Merritt played with Max Roach, Dizzy Gillespie, and Lee Morgan from the mid-'60s to the early '70s. In 1962, he helped form an organization comprised of musicians and performers from other disciplines known as the Forerunners. This became Forerunner, a cooperative organization that was active in Philadelphia's cultural and community activities into the late '80s. He's never recorded as a leader, but Merritt can be heard on CD reissues by Morgan, Roach, and others. *—Ron Wynn*

PAT METHENY (Patrick Bruce Metheny)

b. Aug. 2, 1954, Lees Summit, MO
Guitar / Early jazz-rock, modern creative
Pat Metheny has achieved the best of both worlds. He's an extremely popular guitarist on the fusion circuit, and has enjoyed top-selling albums and packed concert halls coast-to-coast and around the world. He's attained enough clout and the skill to record with Ornette Coleman, Dewey Redman, and new sensation Joshua Redman on major label projects. Multinational conglomerates put enough publicity muscle behind these sessions to ensure widespread audiences and response. It's hard not to root for Metheny, who's never made any album that scraped the bottom of the lowest common denominator barrel. He has speed, a fleeting touch, and lyrical style that makes his solos instantly identifiable and never abrasive. He's smart enough to strike a balance between a light sound and an emaciated one, and never allows his playing to lack drive or ideas. He stresses simplicity rather than complexity, and tastefully uses chorus boxes, fuzz tones, wah-wah pedals, echoplexes, and guitar synthesizers. Metheny has incorporated Caribbean and Latin elements into his music, has done film work such as the theme to "The Falcon and the Snowman" with David Bowie, and has refused to sit still or coast.

He played French horn in school, and began guitar at age 13. Metheny gave lessons while still in his teens. He formed an early and long-lasting relationship with Gary Burton; recording three albums with him in the mid-'70s and reuniting with him in the '90s. Metheny studied and taught at Berklee and the University of Miami. He formed his own

group in the late '70s and began recording for ECM. Though he didn't have huge crossover hits, Metheny attracted a wide audience and enjoyed consistent sales throughout the '70s and '80s. Those who dismissed him as a lightweight were caught by surprise when he issued *80/81* with Dewey Redman in 1980. The album also included Charlie Haden and Michael Brecker, and was one of the most exuberant albums ever issued on ECM. Those who dismissed it as a fluke were even more astonished when Metheny cut *Song X* with Ornette Coleman on Geffen, probably the least likely label in America to issue an Ornette Coleman record, in 1986. Metheny co-wrote much of the music and sounded right at home. He's continued to record for Geffen, doing fine trio and combo material. Metheny scored a number-one jazz album with *Still Life (Talking)* in 1987. Recently, he's toured and recorded with Joshua Redman, son of Dewey Redman and jazz's hottest new saxophonist in '93. He has many titles available on CD. *—Ron Wynn and David Nelson McCarthy*

Bright Size Life / Dec. 1975 / ECM 827133
First album, with Jaco Pastorius (b) and Bob Moses (d). Excellent original material. *—Michael G. Nastos*

Watercolors / Feb. 1977 / ECM 827409
Reissue. The group's second album; important since it shows Metheny breaking away from the style he'd honed with Gary Burton. *—Ron Wynn*

★ **Pat Metheny Group** / Jan. 1978 / ECM 825593
Here Pat Metheny plays a 12-string and six-string guitar with what was then his regular band: Lyle Mays on piano, autoharp, and Oberheim synthesizer; Mark Egan on bass; and Dan Gottlieb on drums. Metheny's guitars and the synthesizer give this music a decidedly electric feel. The rhythm section keeps a sprightly bouncing beat but the music does not swing in the true jazz sense. I was reminded of Chick Corea's old Return to Forever group, which seems to be the stylistic model on which Metheny bases his music. This recording appeals mainly to listeners who are youthful and new to jazz. *—Spencer R. Weston*, Cadence

New Chautauqua / Aug. 1978 / ECM 825471
Among his formative albums: he was still trying to find the right blend of rock, pop, fusion, and jazz elements. *—Ron Wynn*

American Garage / Jun. 1979 / ECM 827134
This is the session that marked Metheny's coming of age; better songs, more intense playing, and more variety in arrangements. *—Ron Wynn*

★ **80/81** / May 1980-1981 / ECM 843169
The album that showed jazz purists Metheny's guitar chops extended beyond fusion rock. Extensive crisp performances. The CD issue contains two bonus cuts. *—Ron Wynn*

As Falls Wichita, So Falls Wichita Falls / Sep. 1980 / ECM 821416
Intelligent, thoughtful compositions, with excellent solos and ensemble work. Billboard #50. *—Ron Wynn*

Offramp / Oct. 1981 / ECM 817138
This 1982 date is the successor to *Wichita Falls* but lacks that album's charm and flair. *—Ron Wynn*

○ **Rejoicing** / Nov. 29-30, 1983 / ECM 817795
This trio setting harkens back to guitarist Pat Metheny's first album as a leader, *Bright Size Life*, recorded in 1976 when he was still a member of the Gary Burton Quartet. That impressive debut featured sensitive support from drummer Bob Moses and bassist Jaco Pastorius. *Rejoicing* shows the gifted guitarist playing with a scope and maturity only hinted at on *Bright Size Life*. Backed by the sublime accompaniment of bassist Charlie Haden and drummer Billy Higgins, kindred spirits from their days together in the revolutionary Ornette Coleman Quartet of the late '50s, Metheny seems especially inspired on this outing. Throughout side one the guitarist's playing is imbued with the spirit of Wes Montgomery and Jim Hall. His tone is warmer than usual, à la Hall, and he swings furiously in ways that he rarely could with his own electrified group. The

centerpiece of side one is the Coleman composition "Humpty Dumpty," where Haden and Higgins break away from the chord changes and indulge in more personal expression. Side two is a whole other story. After a mournful acoustic guitar ballad, Metheny's "Story from a Stranger," he pulls out the high-technology weapons and launches into a frenzied 10-minute manifesto for the guitar synthesizer. This triumphant freak-out session, entitled "The Calling," is as daring and full of tension as anything he'd recorded (to that point)—an extension of his dissonant excursions on the title cut from *Offramp*, (then) his group's last studio album. —*Bill Milkowski*, Down Beat

First Circle / Feb. 15-19, 1984 / ECM 823342

★ **Song X** / Dec. 1985 / David Geffen Co. 24096
With Ornette Coleman. Metheny pays tribute to a surprising influence, teaming with Ornette Coleman in a collaboration that shocked everyone with its musical effectiveness. —*Ron Wynn*

Still Life (Talking) / i. 1987 / David Geffen Co. 24145
A standard Metheny session from 1987; he now has the formula down pat. It is well-played and well-recorded. —*Ron Wynn*

☆ **Question and Answer** / Dec. 1989 / David Geffen Co. 24293
A great trio. Metheny stretches out. This is highly recommended. —*Michael G. Nastos*

Secret Story / i. 1992 / David Geffen Co. 24468
Assisted by the London Symphony Orchestra on several selections, guitarist/composer Metheny displays a true understanding of life's joys and sorrows by letting his music tell the tale of a deep love relationship between a man and a woman. This record is without a doubt his most sensitive and sincere work to date. Compositionally this record will set new standards. —*Paul Kohler*

Letter from Home / 1989 / David Geffen Co. 24245
Continuing in the steps of his previous release, *Still Life (Talking)*, Metheny's band continues to explore the use of Brazilian rhythms in their music with excellent results. —*Paul Kohler*

MEZZ MEZZROW (Milton Mesirow)

b. Oct. 9, 1899, Chicago, IL, **d.** Aug. 5, 1972, Paris, France
Clarinet, soprano saxophone, author / Dixieland
While Norman Mailer probably didn't have Mezz Mezzrow in mind when he wrote his famous essay *The White Negro* (referring to white people who so identified with black culture they considered themselves black), Mezzrow was filling that bill for many years before Mailer wrote the essay. Either the ultimate hipster or a complete fraud, depending on your perspective, Mezz Mezzrow rivaled Eddie Condon as a jazz advocate, personality, insider, and confidant, and was also one of the all-time greatest drug connections. All these things can't completely compensate for the fact that he was marginally talented; his clarinet solos were often hideous and, at best, were barely listenable. Probably no one realized this more than he did; therefore, he worked intensely on behalf of genuinely gifted musicians, and organized many vital sessions, including a number that were integrated. Mezzrow played in the '20s with the Austin High School Gang comprised of White jazz musicians in Chicago. He was in Ben Pollack's band in 1928, and recorded playing C-melody sax with Eddie Condon in 1929. After some freelance sessions in New York, he began to organize recording dates in the '30s and '40s. Teddy Wilson, Benny Carter, Max Kaminsky, Bud Freeman, Willie "The Lion" Smith, John Kirby, Chick Webb, Frankie Newton, Sy Oliver, and J.C. Higginbotham were among the people he spearheaded dates for between 1933 and 1937. He co-led a quintet with Tommy Ladnier in 1938, and participated in the famous sessions organized by Hughes Panassie. During the mid-'40s, Mezzrow began his own record company, the King Jazz label. He recorded many sessions featuring Sidney Bechet, and published the book *Really the Blues* with Bernard Wolfe that purported to tell the real jazz story, but was fleshed out with embellished

yarns and outright myths. He made his first visit to Paris in 1948, and returned in 1951. He gradually spent more and more time there in the latter stages of his life. Mezzrow's fame as a supplier of marijuana was supposedly unmatched in his day. He carried around a shoe box full of the drug at all times, and would call a particularly potent joint a "meziroll" or "mighty mezz." The 1943 hit "The Reefer Song" by Fats Waller was an ode to his productivity. But Mezzrow's activism and advocacy on behalf of neglected musicians, particularly Black musicians (he often got arguments going that still rage today over authenticity and race), should be remembered more than his ability to supply joints. —*Ron Wynn*

★ **Masters of Jazz: Sidney Bechet** / i. Jul. 1945-Dec. 1947 / Storyville 4104

○ **Mezz Mezzrow** / Disques Swing 8409

PALLE MIKKELBORG

b. Mar. 6, 1941, Copenhagen, Denmark
Trumpet, flugelhorn, leader, composer / World fusion, new age, modern creative
An introspective Danish trumpeter, flugelhorn player, composer, and bandleader, Palle Mikkelborg's style combines cool, bebop, and classical influences. Mikkelborg's solos are sometimes brooding, sparse statements; at other times, they are lyrical, fleeting phrases. A self-taught player, Mikkelborg's worked with combos, big bands, and orchestras. He joined the Danish Radiojazzgruppen in 1963, and served as its leader from 1967 to 1972. Mikkelborg also belonged to the Radioens Big Band from 1964 to 1971, and led it on several occasions. He co-led both the V8 octet and a quintet with Alex Riel that played at the Newport and Montreux Jazz festivals in the late '60s and '70s. Mikkelborg headed the group, Entrance, in the '70s and '80s, and led a trio with Thomas Clausen and Niels-Henning Ørsted-Pedersen in the mid-'80s. He toured and recorded with the big bands of Peter Herbolzheimer and George Grunz, worked with Terje Rypdal, and played with Ørsted-Pedersen and Kenneth Knudsen in the '80s. Mikkelborg's done compositions and arrangements for film, television, and radio. He's worked with Abdullah Ibrahim, Jan Garbarek, Gil Evans, Eje Thelin, Karin Krog, and Bill Evans. Mikkelborg's suite, *Aura*, was part of one of the last enchanting Miles Davis albums of the '80s. He's recorded for Debut, Metronome, Sonet, and ECM. Mikkelborg has sessions available on CD. —*Ron Wynn*

BUBBER MILEY

b. 1903, **d.** 1932
Trumpet / Swing, big band
One of the great growling trumpeters in jazz history, Bubber Miley created a resonant, gripping sound with the mute that has seldom been equalled. It became a cornerstone of Ellington's celebrated "jungle" band in the '20s, and was imitated subsequently by many others, including Cootie Williams. Ellington credited Miley with being the person who changed the orchestra's direction, and Miley was featured on classics such as "Flaming Youth," "Creole Love Call," and "East St. Louis Toodle-oo" (which he co-wrote), among many other songs. "Black and Tan Fantasy" and "Doin' the Voom-voom" are also thought to be Miley compositions. Miley's sisters worked as the South Carolina Trio, and he played with Mamie Smith before he joined Elmer Snowden's Washingtonians in the early '20s in New York. Miley was in Ellington's Orchestra from 1924 until 1929. Sadly, he had an alcohol problem that worsened to the point where he became quite unreliable. After leaving Ellington, Miley played with Noble Sissle in France, then recorded with Jelly Roll Morton, King Oliver, and Leo Reisman before forming his own band. Miley and his Mileage Makers recorded eight numbers for the Victor label in 1930. He was soon forced to retire due to tuberculosis, and died in 1932. Miley's glorious sound can be heard on several anthologies that feature Ellington's '20s bands. —*Ron Wynn*

GLENN MILLER (Alton Glenn Miller)

b. Mar. 1, 1904, Clarinda, IA, **d.** Dec. 15, 1944, English Channel

Bandleader, trombone / Swing, big band, instrumental pop

Few names can generate more comment, pro and con, than Glenn Miller, a trombonist and the most popular bandleader from the last part of the swing era. Miller detractors simply dismiss him as the ultimate lightweight. His defenders insist that he didn't regard what he was playing as jazz (it wasn't), but insisted that his period pieces and simple fare be extremely well played. Miller had done arrangements for Ben Pollack in the late '20s, and studied music while playing in pit bands on Broadway. He toured with Smith Ballew, and worked for the Dorsey Brothers, Ray Noble, Glen Gray, and Ozzie Nelson before forming his own band. The band was a flop the first time out, and Miller tried again in 1938. Miller's band emerged as a hit act through radio broadcasts. They included vocalists Ray Eberle, Marion Hutton, and the Modernaires. His band's strengths were consistent section playing, the trademark clarinet lead over a saxophone section, and Miller's savvy choice of material. Their most famous selection, "In the Mood," was an update of a riff that had been played by Black swing bands for years. Joe Garland provided a new arrangement of "Hot and Anxious," previously credited to Horace Henderson. It was first played by Edgar Hayes and became popular after the band played it regularly during a three-month engagement at the Glen Island Casino on Long Island in 1939. Their theme was "Moonlight Serenade," which Miller composed and which eventually became a two-sided hit when it was backed by Frankie Carle's "Sunrise Serenade." Miller's band attained over 40 Top 10 records in a three-year period according to *Billboard*, which began keeping pop charts in 1940. They had hits when they slowed down Erskine Hawkins's "Tuxedo Junction" and Luckey Roberts's piano rag on "Moonlight Cocktail." "Chattanooga Choo Choo" was featured in the band's first film, *Sun Valley Serenade*. Miller joined the army in 1942, formed an all star service personnel band, and was sent to England in 1944. Miller got the chance to play for American troops on what was to be a concert broadcast on Armed Forces Radio. The band was sent to France, but Miller's plane never arrived and was never found. His records remain available constantly. There are numerous compilations of studio, concert, and broadcast releases in any and every configuration. —*Ron Wynn and William Ruhlmann*

★ **Popular Recordings (1938-1942), The** / 1938-1942 / Bluebird 9785

This is a three-CD (or four-LP) set containing 60 of Glenn Miller's studio recordings, and, although a few of the more popular numbers are missing ("To You," "My Prayer," "Johnson Rag," and "Song of the Volga Boatman"), it does an excellent job of collecting together highlights from Miller's career. For some odd reason the music is not programmed in strict chronological order. This is a fine set for those listeners who do not already possess many of these recordings, some of which are very jazz-oriented. The sessions run from 1938-1942. The total time is 183:29. —*Scott Yanow, Cadence*

○ **Legendary Performer** / i. 1939-1942 / Bluebird 0693

The 22 live performances found here, taken from 1939-1942 airchecks, demonstrate that, in performance, the Miller band's notorious precision could give way (slightly) to electric excitement. If any demonstration were needed for the band's success, these tracks provide it. —*William Ruhlmann*

Glenn Miller in Hollywood / i. 1941 / PolyGram 826635

Major Glenn Miller & the Army-Air Force Band (1943-1944) / 1943-1944 / Bluebird 6360

Recorded 1943-1944 with the Army-Air Force Band. At what turned out to be the end of his career, Glenn Miller led a very big band, playing martial arrangements of often military-oriented material at bond rallies around the country. This collection preserves the gaudy, uplifting style of Miller's last music. —*William Ruhlmann*

○ **Memorial 1944-1969** / 1944-1969 / Bluebird 55103

★ **Chattanooga Choo Choo–#1 Hits** / Bluebird 3102

Collector's Choice/Vintage Glenn Miller / Columbia 11393

☆ **Complete Glenn Miller–Vols. 1-13** / Bluebird 61015

☆ **Moonlight Serenade and Other Hits** / RCA 2168

☆ **Pure Gold** / Bluebird 3666

MULGREW MILLER

b. Aug. 13, 1955, Greenwood, MS

Piano / Postbop, neo-bop

An excellent soloist and one of the most in-demand jazz pianists of the '80s and '90s, Mulgrew Miller has blended bebop and hard bop masterfully. His solos are energetic and rigorous, and are flawlessly played with surprising twists and turns, shifts, and changes. He's equally outstanding at interpreting standards and at playing originals. He's seldom done any free-form dates, at least on record, but has been a top contributor to large bands and has backed vocalists, and has headed or played in trios and combos. Miller played in gospel and R&B groups in Memphis, and later attended Memphis State University. He played in the late '70s in Mercer Ellington's orchestra, touring Europe with them in 1977. Miller then played with Betty Carter in 1980, worked with Woody Shaw in 1981 and 1982, and played in Art Blakey's Messengers from 1983 to 1986. Since then, he's led his own groups and has also done numerous recording sessions. Miller's worked with Johnny Griffin, Branford Marsalis, Terence Blanchard and Donald Harrison, John Stubblefield, and Bobby Hutcherson, and, for the past few years, has been a regular member Tony Williams's band. He's issued several trio dates for Landmark, all of which are available on CD. —*Ron Wynn*

Keys to the City / Jun. 1985 / Landmark 1507

Trio session. Marvin "Smitty" Smith's drumming and Miller's solos give this one some clout. —*Ron Wynn*

★ **Work** / Apr. 1986 / Landmark 1511

Memphis pianist Miller with trio (Teri Lyne Carrington on drums). Excellent. —*Michael G. Nastos*

Wingspan / 1987 / Landmark 1515

Fine group jazz, with saxophonist Kenny Garrett. Bonus cut on CD. —*Michael G. Nastos*

Countdown, The / Aug. 1988 / Landmark 1519

A sparkling release that boasts standout writing and exacting interaction between Joe Henderson (ts), Ron Carter (b), and Tony Williams (d). —*Ron Wynn*

From Day to Day / Mar. 14-15, 1990 / Landmark 1525

Miller takes center stage and shows his Memphis roots in blues and gospel throughout, plus a good touch on the occasional standard. —*Ron Wynn*

○ **Time and Again** / i. 1992 / Landmark 1532

A recent release by pianist Mulgrew Miller, this time featuring him in a trio format playing primarily his own compositions from '91. He's backed by bassist Peter Washington and drummer Tony Reedus, and this constitutes his most intimate, distinctive set as a leader. —*Ron Wynn*

○ **Landmarks** / i. Feb. 12, 1992 / Landmark 1311

Hand In Hand / i. 1993 / Jive/Novus 63153

Hand In Hand is first and foremost a showcase for the compositions of Mulgrew Miller. These range from the pensive balladry of "Like the Morning" to the plush septet harmonies of "Grew's Tune" to the Monkish workout on "Neither Here Nor There." The superb band he's assembled includes Kenny Garrett on alto and soprano saxes, Steve Nelson on vibes, Christian McBride on bass, and Lewis Nash on drums. Eddie Henderson joins the quintet on several cuts on trumpet, as does saxophonist Joe Henderson (no relation). —*James Marcus, Jazz Times*

○ **Trio Transition** / DIW 808

LUCKY MILLINDER (Lucius Venable Millinder)

b. Aug. 8, 1900, Anniston, AL, **d.** Sep. 28, 1966, New York, NY
Bandleader / Swing, big band
Lucky Millinder was a big-band leader of the '30s. His bands spawned Sweets Edison, Tab Smith, Bill Doggett, Wynonie Harris, and countless others. Millinder was active until the early '50s. —*Michael G. Nastos*

○ **Jazz Heritage–Lucky Days (1941-1945)** / 1941-1945 / MCA 1319

★ **1942** / **i.** 1942 / Hindsight 233

○ **Jazz Heritage–Let It Roll** / **i.** 1972 / MCA 1357
Vintage swing and transitional material by the Lucky Millinder orchestra. His band was among the earliest to shift its focus toward upbeat, hard-driving arrangements, vocal numbers, and instrumentals that laid the groundwork for the coming of R&B. These cuts were reissued by MCA on vinyl in the '70s. —*Ron Wynn*

IRVING MILLS

b. Jan. 16, 1884, New York, NY, **d.** Apr. 21, 1985, Palm Springs, CA
Impressario, music publisher, composer, vocals
A valued associate of and advocate for Duke Ellington, Irving Mills published Ellington's music, aided him in getting better contracts and improved concerts, and worked to ensure that the Ellington band received the treatment it merited. He wasn't always successful, but battled for the band through the '20s and '30s. Mills also managed Cab Calloway, Benny Carter, Fletcher Henderson, Jimmie Lunceford, Don Redman, and other acts, while serving as a lyricist, occasional bandleader, and singer. In 1919, Mills and his brother, Jack, established Jack Mills, Inc., a music publishing business that specialized in the work of Black artists. They renamed it Mills Music, Inc., the next year. Mills wrote the lyrics for songs such as "I Let a Song Go Out of My Heart" and "It Don't Mean a Thing If It Ain't Got That Swing." He assembled bands for recording sessions to promote the music he published. As leader of the Hotsy-Totsy Gang, Mills had a 1929 hit with Bill "Bojangles" Robinson doing "Ain't Misbehavin'." The next year, "Stardust," featuring composer Hoagy Carmichael on piano and Jimmy Dorsey on sax, was also a hit. Mills backed the Bubber Miley band in 1930, and led what was originally the Coconut Grove Orchestra, a relief band at the Cotton Club that played when Ellington and Calloway were on tour. The Coconut Grove Orchestra became the Mills Blue Rhythm Band, and was also known as the Harlem Hot Shots, Earl Jackson and His Musical Champions, and had various other identities. It included vocalist Chuck Bullock, Billy Banks, plus Sheldon Hemphill, Hayes Alvis, Edgar Hayes, and Joe Garland. Mills and Ellington finally split in 1939. Mills's labels, Master and Variety, eventually went broke. But Mills rebounded in 1943, when he assembled the cast for the film *Stormy Weather*, and also wrote some of the film's music. He remained active in management and music publishing into the '60s. —*Ron Wynn*

★ **Irving Mills and His Hotsy Totsy Gang–Vol. 1** / **i.** Jul. 1928-May 1929 / Retrieval 122

○ **Irving Mills and His Hotsy Totsy Gang–Vol. 2** / **i.** Jul. 1929-Jan. 1930 / Retrieval 123

○ **Irving Mills and His Hotsy Totsy Gang–Vol. 3** / **i.** Feb. 1930-May 1931 / Retrieval 127

ROY MILTON

b. Jul. 31, 1907, Wynnewood, OK, **d.** Sep. 1983, Canoga Park, CA
Vocals, drums / Blues & jazz
Roy Milton's jazz connections are tenuous, but they do exist. Influenced by swing, he's most famous for leading one of the hottest R&B bands of the '40s and '50s. Milton was a vocalist and bandleader who formed combos in the '20s to play dances in Oklahoma. He moved to California in the mid-

'30s. Milton formed his Solid Senders orchestra and mixed big band swing with gospel and blues; the results were a vibrant, romping genre with just enough instrumental acumen to display jazz roots, and more than enough vocal force and celebratory fervor to reflect gospel and blues ties. Milton issued his early records on his own label, then began on Hamp-Tone. He joined Specialty in 1947 and remained there until 1954, scoring ten R&B hits between 1949 and 1952. His single, "R.M. Blues," was a Top 20 smash in 1949. Other singles include his version of "The Hucklebuck" in 1949, "Information Blue" in 1950, and "Best Wishes" in 1951. Milton later recorded for Dootone, King, Warwick, and Kent. He appeared at the Monterey Jazz Festival in 1980. In its prime, Milton's band was one of the few that could match the swinging fire and entertainment values of Louis Jordan's. Fantasy has been reissuing vintage Milton singles on CD for several years. —*Ron Wynn*

★ **Roy Milton & Solid Senders** / **i.** 1977 / Sonet 5019

○ **Groovy Blues, Vol.2** / **i.** 1992 / Specialty 7024

CHARLES MINGUS (Charles (Jr) Mingus)

b. Apr. 22, 1922, Nogales, AZ, **d.** Jan. 5, 1979, Cuernavaca, Mexico
Bass, composer, bandleader, piano / Bop, hard bop, post-bop, early free, progressive big band
Charles Mingus's accomplishments and stature merit their own category. He was an awesome bassist, a phenomenal composer, and an irascible, beloved, hated, and celebrated personality. His music combined numerous influences; gospel, blues, traditional New Orleans, swing, bebop, Afro-Latin, and symphonic. He turned the bass into a percussive, harmonic, melodic, rhythm and lead instrument. Only Ellington and Monk rivaled his creativity; his use of shifting tempos and alternating meters, and use of trombones, tuba, and baritone sax in his arrangements was inspired. He insisted on individuality among his players, but would also assign parts and time improvisations in rehearsals. Mingus's knowledge of and ability on the piano led him, at one point, to hire separate bassists and to play piano himself at Jazz Workshop concerts. His legendary temper caused many confrontations on and off the bandstand, and often lead to musicians being fired in mid-performance, or concerts being halted so reprimands could be given immediately. His ire would even extend to audiences that he felt were inattentive.

Mingus's sisters studied classical violin and piano, but his stepmother only allowed religious music in the house. She took the young Mingus to church meetings where the moans, groans, and hollers, as well as pastor/congregation interaction, proved ultimately influential. He studied trombone and cello, then switched to bass partly due to his exasperation over poor teachers, but also because a classmate, Buddy Collette, informed him that the high school band needed a bassist. Others in this band included Chico Hamilton, Dexter Gordon, and Ernie Royal. Mingus later studied with Joe Comfort and Red Callender, plus classical player H. Reinschagen, and took composition lessons with Lloyd Reese. Mingus wrote "What Love" in 1939 and "Half-Mast Inhibitions" in 1940 while working with Reese; these were recorded in the '60s. He played in Barney Bigard's band in 1942 along with Kid Ory, then joined Louis Armstrong in 1943. While in Armstrong's band, some transcription sessions for broadcast became Mingus's first recordings. Mingus briefly replaced Callender in Lee Young's band. There were stints with Howard McGhee, Illinois Jacquet, Dinah Washington, and Ivie Anderson, plus a few engagements heading groups.

In 1946 and 1947, Mingus worked with Lionel Hampton, and made jazz and R&B recordings, becoming known as "Baron Von Mingus." But his major jazz attention came in the early '50s. Mingus left a post office gig to join Red Norvo's trio with Tal Farlow. He exited the ensemble a year later after an incident in which he was displaced temporarily by a White bassist on a New York television show. This ugliness was caused by a combination of union and racial politics. Mingus worked with Billy Taylor, Lennie Tristano, Duke Ellington, Stan Getz, Art Tatum, and Bud Powell in the early and mid-'50s. His stint with Ellington ended on a downbeat; Mingus's legendary temper erupted during a dispute with trombonist Juan Tizol, and he joined the short list of musicians who were fired openly by Duke. Mingus participated in the landmark 1953 Massey Hall concert in Canada with Charlie Parker, Dizzy Gillespie, Bud Powell, and Max Roach. He began his own record company, Debut, in partnership with Roach in 1952. It lasted until 1955, issuing recordings by Teo Macero, Kenny Dorham, Paul Bley, John La Porta, and Sam Most, among others. One Debut release, *Four Trombones*, led to Mingus cutting a Savoy session with J.J. Johnson and Kai Winding. He also worked with Thad Jones, Eddie Bert, Willie Jones, George Barrow, and many others. From 1953 to 1955, he was one of several musicians who contributed pieces to a Jazz Composers' Workshop. Mingus founded his own Jazz Workshop in 1955, turning it into a top repertory company. He would present his pieces to musicians partly by dictating their lines to them. The personnel ranged from a low of four to a high of 11, and included, over the years, Eric Dolphy, Booker Ervin, Jackie McLean, Shafi Hadi, John Handy, Rahsaan Roland Kirk, Jaki Byard, Jimmy Knepper, and longtime drummer Dannie Richmond.

Mingus's unprecedented compositional skills flourished from the mid-'50s through the '60s. He wrote extended suites, open-ended jams, "free" selections, songs with collectively improvised sections colliding with chaotic dialogues, works for large orchestra, tributes, socio-political anthems, and songs with Afro-Latin and African rhythms. The list of brilliant compositions included "My Jelly Roll Soul," "Jelly Roll," "Fables of Faubus," "Orange Was the Color of Her Dress," "Goodbye Pork Pie Hat," "Meditations on Integration," and "Wednesday Night Prayer Meeting." There were others, like "Epitaph," that were never completely performed or perfected during his lifetime. This proved an equally productive period for albums. Seminal works issued included *Pithecanthropus Erectus*, *The Clown*, *East Coasting*, *Scenes in the City*, *Tijuana Moods*, and *Wonderland*. There were also remarkable dates for Columbia with Mingus leading a superb eight- to ten-piece unit and cutting unforgettable versions of "Goodbye Pork Pie Hat" and "Fables of Faubus."

His early '60s groups with Dolphy may have been his finest; they were certainly among his most dynamic performance bands. There were artistic triumphs, but sales failures for Candid, ambitious dates for Impulse, including one where he played unaccompanied solo piano throughout, and more financially successful works for Atlantic. His acclaimed early and mid-'60s European tours with the Dolphy group were later issued on Atlantic and Prestige recordings. Earlier in his career, Mingus had expressed outrage over the treatment and inequities musicians faced. He'd tried to change things before with his record label. He tried again in 1960, organizing a series of concerts to compete with the Newport Jazz Festival. This effort led to the formation of the short-lived Jazz Artists Guild, an organization that was conceived to assist musicians in promoting and controlling their work. Unfortunately, it collapsed in a wave of rancor and discord, and a financially disastrous 1962 Town Hall concert virtually ended his promotional ventures. Mingus tried to start another record company, but the Charles Mingus label issued few titles and made even less money in its brief existence during 1964 and 1965. He stormed off the Monterey Festival stage in 1965, and, broke and embittered, he eventually withdrew from performing. A 1968 film, *Mingus*, which was directed by Thomas Reichman, got lots of attention for showing Mingus being booted out of his New York apartment.

Mingus resumed his performing career in 1969. Fantasy purchased the Debut masters and provided him with vital funds. Early '70s albums on Columbia and Atlantic, including a live sold-out date at Avery Fisher Hall, rekindled public attention. He received a well-deserved Guggenheim fellowship in composition. Mingus's controversial autobiography,

Beneath the Underdog, which had been rejected for publication nearly ten years earlier, was published and triggered widespread discussion and evaluation (though many raised doubts about various chapters and incidents). Sadly, Mingus's health was fading; he had developed amyotrophic lateral schlerosis (ALS), better known as Lou Gehrig's disease. He composed more big band music, including the wonderful *Cumbia and Jazz Fusion* in 1977, and led one last great combo before becoming physically unable to play. This group, with tenor saxophonist George Adams, trumpeter Jack Walrath, pianist Don Pullen, and drummer Dannie Richmond, issued superb albums in the early '70s: *Mingus Moves*, *Changes One*, and *Changes Two*. Mingus collaborated on an album with folk and rock vocalist Joni Mitchell, and directed his bands from a wheelchair. His last session came in January of 1978, though he did live long enough to be recognized at the White House by President Carter, a truly poignant moment.

Charles Mingus's work lives on via reissues galore. Mosaic has reissued both his Candid output and his amazing 1959 Columbia releases. Prestige has issued the complete Debut masters. In 1993, Atlantic issued the Mingus anthology *Thirteen Pictures*, and reissued *Mingus Moves*, and *Changes One & Two*. His piano album and other Impulse recordings are being reissued by MCA. England's Affinity has reissued some of his great late '50s albums. "Epitaph" was finally performed by an orchestra in 1991, and an album that features it has also been released. The Mingus Dynasty repertory band has recorded and toured to various editions. Brian Priestly's fine 1982 book, *Mingus*, provides a scholarly and comprehensive view of his achievements. —*Ron Wynn and Mike Katz*

Thirteen Pictures / i. 1952-1977 / Atlantic/Rhino 271402

Even on a loving two-disc anthology, it's impossible to accurately or fully convey the accomplishments of Charles Mingus, jazz's finest modern bassist/composer. *Thirteen Pictures* tries to outline his career achievements by spotlighting his most famous works and also showcase his abilities. But the set does it in a curious manner; the sequencing is particularly odd, with songs hopping all over the place from decade to decade and the older things coming near the end rather than beginning. They also jump from intricate suites with huge groups to solo works to combo dates. Still, there are many essential Mingus pieces here, from the sprawling "Cumbia & Jazz Fusion" to seminal "Goodbye Pork Pie Hat," "Pithecanthropus Erectus," and "Better Git It in Your Soul." The absence of "Fables of Faubus" is puzzling, and the inclusion of only one track featuring Eric Dolphy bizarre, but for the Mingus newcomer to whom this set is obviously directed, it fulfills its basic goal of introducing a genius's work. —*Ron Wynn*

○ **Mingus at the Bohemia** / Dec. 23, 1955 / Debut 045
This date comes from a particularly fertile period for bassist/bandleader/composer Charles Mingus (the whole session was on a previous Prestige twofer set). The music here is not as dynamic as the soon-to-come Atlantic recordings, but Eddie Bert (tb) and George Barrow (ts) are more pastel players and closer to some of the chamber jazz which seemed to interest Mingus during the period just prior to this. This is adventuresome music and Mingus is heard to good advantage (he overdubs cello on "Percussion Discussion," a piece which has drummer Max Roach as guest). The remaining members of the workshop are Mal Waldron (p) and Willie Jones (d). —*Bob Rusch, Cadence*

○ **Plus Max Roach** / Dec. 23, 1955 / Fantasy 440
The Mingus/Roach/Mal Waldron dialogs overcome the ordinary stylings of Eddie Bert and George Barrow. —*Ron Wynn*

○ **Charles Mingus** / Dec. 23, 1955 / Prestige 24010

★ **Pithecanthropus Erectus** / Jan. 30, 1956 / Atlantic 8809
The year was 1956 and Dwight Eisenhower *was* president, but bassist/composer/bandleader Charles Mingus, like the musical revolutionary and visionary he was, was forecasting—still reachin', still teachin'. This is music that gets in yo'

soul. This is a historic recording, an essential! —*Bob Rusch, Cadence*

☆ **Clown, The** / Feb. 13, 1957 / Atlantic 90142
A wonderful date that has bitter, reflective, and poignant Mingus compositions. The album marked the first appearance on vinyl of trombonist Jimmy Knepper. —*Ron Wynn*

★ **New Tijuana Moods** / Jul. 18, 1957-Aug. 6, 1957 / Bluebird 5644
It has never been explained, at least publicly, why the *Tijuana Moods* tapes languished in RCA's vaults from 1957, when they were recorded, to 1962. Thanks to RCA's revitalized Bluebird reissue program, not only is the *Tijuana Moods* album available again, it is accompanied by a second LP of alternate takes. More accurately, producer Ed Michel has used base takes to carry previously unissued solos. When the solos are of the quality of those recorded in two eventual days by Clarence Shaw (tpt), Shafi Hadi (as), Jimmy Knepper (tb), Bill Triglia (p), and Charles Mingus (b), there is reason to celebrate. The combination of raw rhythmic passion and lyrical improvisation is all but unequaled in the work of Mingus or anyone else. He called it "the best record I ever made." In each of the five alternate performances, the restoration of unused material from the session results in a longer track than that in the original release. In nearly every case, the "new" solos match the "old" in quality and dramatically differ from them in content. Knepper, Triglia, and Porter/Hadi are consistently inspired. This is unquestionably some of Knepper's best work. The fluidity of Shaw's expression, which occasionally stops just short of sloppiness in execution, is stunning on the alternate of "Los Mariachis." He dallies with a phrase from "For All We Know" in the opening bars of his solo on the alternate take of "Dizzy Moods," taking an approach to the piece that is totally different from his work on the original issue. The astonishing beauty of Shaw's famous solo on "Flamingo" is not matched on the alternate. But a lovely one by Knepper is added. We now get all of Danny Richmond's (d) solo in "Dizzy Moods," rather than just the snippet left in for the original album. The quality of Richmond's playing throughout is amazing in light of the fact that Mingus had converted him to drummer from tenor saxophonist only a few weeks earlier. But, then, this is amazing music in every respect. By the way, it is not monaural, as the record labels announce. It is in excellent two-channel stereo. —*Doug Ramsey*, Jazz Times

○ **East Coasting** / Aug. 6, 1957 / BCP 6019
Same group as in *Tijuana Moods*. Really a Clarence Shaw session. Cool jazz that sounds like Miles Davis in spots. Easy listening. With Bill Evans (p). —*Michael Katz*

★ **Complete 1959 CBS Charles Mingus Sessions** / i. 1959 / Mosaic 143
Charles Mingus turned the jazz world upside down when he signed with Columbia in 1959. Once Atlantic learned that he had made a deal with a major label, the company temporarily withheld release of the stunning *Blues And Roots*. RCA had already delayed *Tijuana Moods* and it would not be issued until 1962, though it had been recorded in 1957. Mingus was in the midst of a creative explosion; he was working with small and large bands, mixing symphonic influences with gospel and blues, experimenting with time signatures and odd rhythms. He insisted on both spontaneity and rigorous memorization of compositions from his musicians. Mingus assembled powerhouse bands for the Columbia sessions, but in true clueless fashion the label never issued the music in the manner his bands recorded it. They released *Mingus Ah Um* in 1959, *Mingus Dynasty* in 1960, then issued *Better Git It In Your Soul* as a double album and *Nostalgia In Times Square* as a reissued special, never bothering to explain what they were doing. Mosaic has finally issued the music the right way on this wonderful four-album (no CDs) boxed set, intact and in chronological order. The songs were recorded during sessions on May 5, May 12, November 1, and November 13, 1959. The lineup for the May dates was John Handy on alto and tenor saxes

and clarinet, Booker Ervin on tenor, Shafi Hadi on alto or tenor sax, either Jimmy Knepper or Willie Dennis on trombone, pianist Horace Parlan, and drummer Dannie Richmond. They romp, strut, clash, and soar on such classics as "Better Git It In Your Soul," "Fables of Faubus," "Jelly Roll," and the complete "Goodbye Pork Pie Hat," which had never been available in its full glory. Only Ellington and perhaps Gil Evans compared with Mingus in crafting works for individual musicians' voices; Ervin's soulful, bluesy refrains, Handy's vibrant alto, and Richmond's steady, careful drumming are vividly expressed, as are the leader's shouts and resourceful bass, interacting with Parlan's sparkling riffs and accompaniment. The November session has an expanded lineup, personnel changes, and intriguing instrumentation. Mingus features as many as four saxophones on some pieces, adding Jerome Richardson on baritone or flute and Benny Golson on tenor. He also recruited Richard Williams on trumpet and Teddy Charles on vibes. They cover Ellington classics "Mood Indigo" and "Don't Get Around Much Anymore," and Mingus-penned "Gunslinging Bird" in tribute to Charlie Parker. There is a swing feel and a swaying, cohesive group sound. But things are no less intense, particularly in the exchanges between Ervin, Handy, Richardson, and Golson. Hanna adds tantalizing solos on "Gunslinging Bird" and "Song with Orange," while Mingus is again authoritative, both on bass and leading the band. This set is exquisitely mastered, and Mingus biographer Brian Priestly provides background and historical information while Sy Johnson gives a musical analysis of the sessions. The original liner notes from *Mingus Ah Um* by Diane Dorr-Dorynek and *Mingus Dynasty* by Mingus himself are included. Grab this quickly; there is no telling how long Columbia will let Mosaic retain the license once they realize how dumb they were to not issue this boxed set from the start. —*Ron Wynn*

☆ **Blues and Roots** / Feb. 4, 1959 / Atlantic 1305
A great Mingus album of gospel church music. Exciting, high-energy music. —*Michael Katz*

☆ **Mingus Ah Um** / May 5, 1959 / Columbia 40648
Many think this is Mingus's best studio album. All the selections are top-notch: there are no letdowns on this album. Similar in feel to *Blues and Roots*, but more fully realized. If you could have only two Mingus albums, this and *Mingus at Antibes* would be the two. —*Michael Katz*

★ **Mingus at Antibes** / Jul. 13, 1960 / Atlantic 90532
This never-before-heard two-record set of performances was recorded live at the Antibes Jazz Festival on July 13, 1960, just a scant three months before the classic Candid session *Charles Mingus Presents Charles Mingus*, which utilized the same personnel (minus saxophonist Booker Ervin and pianist Bud Powell, of course). Two works from that date, "What Love" and "Folk Forms I," appear in still-formulating arrangements here, though trumpeter Ted Curson's long, tumbling, rhapsodically reflective solo in the former is easily one of the concert's high points. And while any chance to hear Mingus and Eric Dolphy in collaboration is one to be cherished, the presence of Booker Ervin's booting Texas tenor attack seems to inspire Dolphy even more, as in "Wednesday Night Prayer Meeting," where Ervin's aggressive cosmopolitan preaching kicks Dolphy into overdrive for a bubbling, boiling testimonial. Or consider "I'll Remember April," where the pair trade fours energetically, and Dolphy's typically unique, jaggedly chromatic intervals infect Ervin, who reacts with some abstractly angular phrasing of his own, fed by the exquisitely timed, confident comping from Bud Powell's piano. —*Art Lange*, Down Beat

Charles Mingus Presents Charles Mingus / Oct. 20, 1960 / Candid 79005
A roaring, magnificent session from '60 with bass legend Charles Mingus heading a band that included Booker Ervin and Eric Dolphy playing complex, intricately layered, yet also soulful and animated compositions. This was reissued

on vinyl in the '70s and then issued on CD in '90. —*Ron Wynn*

★ **Complete Candid Recordings** / Oct. 20, 1960-Nov. 11, 1960 / Mosaic 111
Studio sessions with a particularly strong group that had been playing at the same club together for a year. Mingus at his most avant-garde. Beautiful solo work by all throughout. Many Mingus standards. Incredible packaging (always the case with Mosaic). Limited edition, so *buy it while you can!* —*Michael Katz*

○ **Reincarnation of a Lovebird** / Oct. 31, 1960-Nov. 27, 1960 / Candid 79026
A vastly different counterpoint was happening in the music of Charles Mingus in 1960, as demonstrated by *Reincarnation of a Lovebird*, which contains four reissued performances and one previously undiscovered alternate take. It shows the stylistic counterpoint of swing era veterans Roy Eldridge and Jo Jones, boppers Jimmy Knepper and Tommy Flanagan, and bop extenders Eric Dolphy and Mingus and the blues-rooted, Ellington-like, jazzed orchestral development of the title cut and "Bugs." Dolphy's alto solo, threatening to fly apart with odd intervals, is brilliant on "Body and Soul," one example that shows that the parts are greater than the sum on this CD. —*Owen Cordle*, Jazz Times

☆ **Oh Yeah** / Nov. 6, 1961 / Atlantic 90667
This album has a bluesy, New Orleans feel. Mingus plays piano and sings (no bass). Roland Kirk is featured on the siren and other instruments. A spirited, fun album. Very droll. There is a bonus 25-minute interview of Mingus by Nesuhi Ertegun that makes this a must-have for the Mingus fan. — *Michael Katz*

○ **Money Jungle** / **i.** 1962 / United Artists 15017

Mingus Plays Piano / **i.** 1963 / Mobile Fidelity 783
Mingus's range, ideas, touch, and technique are sonically outlined to their untimate glory. — *Ron Wynn*, Rock & Roll Disc

☆ **Black Saint and the Sinner Lady** / Jan. 20, 1963 / MCA 5649
A remarkable work that showcases both Mingus the composer and Mingus the bandleader. A six-piece suite, the session shows the influence and impact of Ellington on Mingus as an arranger. —*Ron Wynn*

☆ **Mingus, Mingus, Mingus** / Jan. 1963-Sep. 20, 1963 / MCA 39119
Somewhat similar in feel to *Black Saint and the Sinner Lady*. More driving and spontaneous sounding, without the pervading sound of Charles Mariano's sax. A solid album, worth owning. —*Michael Katz*

Paris 1964 / **i.** 1964 / Lejazz/Charly 19
Bassist Charles Mingus is back in the limelight. Mosaic and Rhino have recently issued nice sets, with Mosaic finally putting out his late '50s Columbia material in the fashion in which it was originally recorded. This '64 concert date featured one of his greatest bands; it had two saxophonists in Eric Dolphy and Clifford Jordan, plus pianist Jaki Byard and drummer Dannie Richmond. There are only four songs on the disc, with the shortest one over 11 minutes and both "Meditations for Integration" and "Fables of Faubus" 20 minutes plus. Mingus created expansive, works-in-progress compositions, letting his band react, interact, develop, tear apart, and reconstruct his music. Dolphy and Jordan play intense, animated, surging solos, and Dolphy's alto sax and bass clarinet fury is contrasted by an evocative lyricism on flute with Jordan struggling to avoid being obliterated by Dolphy's brilliance. Byard was both a strong traditionalist well schooled in stride and ragtime and a humorous progressive capably working in the gaps provided by Mingus and reliable drummer Dannie Richmond. While the ethics of some Charly projects remain highly debatable (nonpayment of royalties, release of sessions without permission, etc.) there is nothing to question about this disc; the sound quality is great and the performances unforgettable. —*Ron Wynn*

○ **Mingus in Europe–Vol. 1** / Apr. 26, 1964 / Enja 3049
The tour from which this album was drawn was Eric Dolphy's last with Charles Mingus—Dolphy stayed in Europe and was dead two months later. Mingus and drummer Dannie Richmond were telepathic musical blood brothers, and the greatest joys here are their playing together and their obvious pleasure in driving Dolphy to his limits. The album contains a 38-minute "Fables of Faubus" and a Mingus/Dolphy duet on "I Can't Get Started." Mingus is particularly light in his long exploration, but doesn't seem to catch fire until Dolphy dances in for one of his famous conversations with the leader. They have their little chat—like two old, wizened friends in a Cairo coffeehouse—and it is a pleasure to listen in. The album ends with the retitled "Started"—Dolphy, on flute, sends cascades, flutters, and twitters around Mingus. —*Lee Jeske*, Down Beat

○ **Mingus in Europe–Vol. 2** / Apr. 26, 1964 / Enja 3077
This album opens with "Orange Was the Color of Her Dress Then Blue Silk." Pianist Jaki Byard is the lead-off hitter, and, rather than driving for the fences, he settles for a bloop single. Tenor saxophonist Clifford Jordan is tough and strong with Charles Mingus hard driving on the bottom but, again, it is Eric Dolphy's bass clarinet that picks things up. Dolphy plays a no-nonsense solo that's short and to the point. A hard-working Mingus then checks in with a solo "Sophisticated Lady" (save for a note here and a chord there from Byard) that is quite forward and musical, if less than explosive. Byard then unleashes a solo piece of his own—striding and romping with enthusiasm. The album ends with Mingus's lovely "Peggy's Blue Sunlight" which, thanks to his confusing introduction, is renamed "Charlemagne" here and credited to Clifford Jordan. This is, perhaps, the best track on both volumes. Byard plays a little Thelonious Monk in his comping, and everybody seems to latch onto Dannie Richmond's glistening cymbal work. Byard hands Mingus his solo space with some roof-raising gospel playing, and the bassist takes off with a short, effusive spot that leads into a cyclonic Dolphy, this time on alto. —*Lee Jeske*, Down Beat

Right Now–Live at Jazz Workshop / Jun. 23, 1964 / Debut 237
Funky and vibrant material, with sterling work from Clifford Jordan (ts), John Handy (as), Jane Getz (p), and Dannie Richmond (p). —*Ron Wynn*

Mingus at Monterey / Sep. 20, 1964 / VDJ 1572
At the Monterey Jazz Festival. Has attained legendary status. Some of his other live performances seem stronger. Good performance of his and Ellington's material. —*Michael Katz*

○ **Great Concert of Charles Mingus, The** / **i.** 1964 / Prestige 34001

Let My Children Hear Music / Sep. 23, 1971 / Columbia 48910
Some of his strongest later compositions. Can get a little tedious at times ("The Chill of Death"), but Mingus merely follows his muse. If you weren't told this was jazz, you might think it was modern classical music. —*Michael Katz*

Shoes of the Fisherman's Wife . . . / **i.** Sep. 23, 1971-Nov. 1, 1959 / Columbia 44050
The Shoes of the Fisherman's Wife Are Some Jive Ass Slippers. Most of the *Mingus Dynasty*, which features the same lineup as *Mingus Ah Um* and has a similar feel but is less driving. Inexplicable inclusion of "Shoes of the . . . . " from *Let My Children Hear Music*, recorded twelve years later. All great music. —*Michael Katz*

Mingus Moves / Oct. 29-31, 1973 / Atlantic 1653
It took forever, but Atlantic (through Rhino) has finally had the good sense to reissue on CD the outstanding sessions of Charles Mingus's last great Jazz Workshop band, his early '70s unit. Pianist Don Pullen, the twisting, swaying tenor saxophonist and flutist George Adams, and drummer Dannie Richmond subsequently formed three-fourths of the Pullen/Adams quartet, a powerhouse late '70s and early '80s combo. While Rhino previously rereleased *Changes One* and *Changes Two*, here is the fiery, and slightly better, date that

preceded them. That is due to the propulsive solos of Adams and Pullen, each percussive, angular, and dynamic as they construct remarkable solos on "Wee," "Opus 4," and the title cut. Richmond had just returned to jazz drumming but has no trouble getting back in stride. His cymbal and drums interplay, teaming with Mingus's still-dominant bass lines and rumbling tones, anchor everything capably within the rhythm section. There is even the bonus of two extra cuts, both as charged and invigorating as the main menu. Thank goodness for Rhino's reissue campaign; let us hope Atlantic extends its licensing life. —*Ron Wynn*

Mingus at Carnegie Hall / Jan. 19, 1974 / Atlantic 1667
A live set with only two compositions. Rahsaan Roland Kirk steals the show with explosive, extensive tenor sax solos. —*Ron Wynn*

★ **Changes One** / Dec. 27-30, 1974 / Atlantic 1677
Spotlighting the last of his great small bands, heralding the forerunner of the George Adams/Don Pullen quartet that became a preeminent '80s jazz quartet. —*Ron Wynn*

○ **Changes Two** / Dec. 27-30, 1974 / Atlantic 1678
The second of a pair that heralded the forerunner of the George Adams/Don Pullen quartet that became a preeminent '80s jazz quartet. —*Ron Wynn*

Cumbia and Jazz Fusion / Mar. 31, 1976+Apr. 1, 1976 / Atlantic 8801
Japanese issue. His strongest late recording. Somewhat of a departure for him. Big ensemble, exotic sound effects. Worthwhile. —*Michael Katz*

Three or Four Shades of Blues / Mar. 9, 1977 / Atlantic 1700
Many rock types first learned of Mingus from this 1977 session that guest-shots everyone from Larry Coryell to Phillip Catherine. The date is uneven, with Mingus in his late stages of ALS, but it's still worth having. —*Ron Wynn*

Me, Myself an Eye / Jan. 19, 1978 / Atlantic 8803

Nostalgia in Times Square / i. Mar. 1980 / Columbia 35717

☆ **Epitaph** / i. 1990 / Columbia 45428
A tribute. Memorial orchestra directed by Gunther Schuller playing the late bassist's works. A magnum opus. —*Michael G. Nastos*

Next Generation Performs . . . / i. 1991 / Columbia 47405
Next Generation Performs Charles Mingus's Brand New Compositions. Spirited repertoire and tribute efforts from past Mingus sidemen like George Adams (ts). Two Mingus siblings, Charles and Eric, are along as well. —*Ron Wynn*

★ **Complete Debut Recordings** / Debut 4402
1951-1958. Early recordings. All of the sessions on which Mingus played for the label he and Max Roach founded. If you are a Mingus student, you need this set to trace his development. If not, you can get the highlights by getting *Mingus at the Bohemia* and *Jazz at Massey Hall.* —*Michael Katz*

Better Git It in Your Soul / Columbia 30628

Debut Rarities–Vol. 1 / Original Jazz Classics 1807
The Charles Mingus Octet cuts from '53 that make up the first half of *Debut Rarities, Volume 1* are ambitious but polite by Mingus's later standards, particularly the impressionistic balladry of "Blue Tide" and cool-hued bop of "Pink Topsy" and "Miss Bliss." Only "Eclipse," which features singer Janet Thurlow, has the provocative edge of Mingus's mature work, as the svelte lyricism of the song collides with the bold orchestral interludes scored by the date's arranger, pianist Spaulding Givens (aka Nadi Qamar). "Eclipse" fully utilizes the tandem work of Mingus and cellist Jackson Wiley, the fluid front line of Willie Dennis, trumpeter Ernie Royal, and wind players John Caine and Teo Macero, as well as the sensitivity of John Lewis and Kenny Clarke. The remainder of the disc features a robust Jimmy Knepper-led quintet, with Mingus, Richmond, altoist Joe Maini, and pianist Bill Triglia. —*Bill Shoemaker*, Down Beat

Debut Rarities–Vol. 2 / Original Jazz Classics 1808

Debut Rarities, Volume 2 features Charles Mingus in '51 duets with Spaulding Givens, a florid, facile pianist, and in '53 trios rounded out by Max Roach. This is a comparatively soporific collection, though Mingus's numerous solos make it suggested listening for students of Mingus the virtuoso. —*Bill Shoemaker*, Down Beat

BOB MINTZER

b. 1953
Tenor saxophone / Progressive big band, early jazz-rock, neo-bop
A good soloist in several genres, from bebop to jazz-rock, Afro-Latin, and fusion, Bob Mintzer has compiled some impressive credits in a short time. He's not a particularly dynamic player, but offers exuberant and competent solos that are influenced very much by Mike Brecker, who, in turn, was influenced by mid- and late period John Coltrane. Mintzer attended Interlochen Arts Academy in the early '70s, as well as Hartt College of Music and Manhattan School of Music. He worked in the '70s with Deodato, Tito Puente, Buddy Rich, Hubert Laws, the Thad Jones-Mel Lewis band, Sam Jones, and Eddie Palmieri. Mintzer also wrote for the Jones/Lewis band. During the '80s, Mintzer played with Ray Mantilla and with Lewis, and led his own band. He also worked with Jaco Pastorius, Mike Manieri, Louis Bellson, and Joe Chambers. He spent the early part of the '80s dividing his time between Bob Moses's band, the New York and Brooklyn Philharmonics, the American Ballet Theater, and his own big band and quintet. Mintzer also played with Liza Minnelli and the American Saxophone Quartet. He worked as a soloist and a composer with the Radio bands of Rome, Helsinki, and Hamburg. He's recorded for Canyon, CBS/Sony, and DMP. Mintzer has several selections available on CD. —*Ron Wynn and Michael G. Nastos*

Camouflage / Jun. 1986 / Digital Music 456
Good '86 big-band set led by tenor saxophonist and bass clarinetist Bob Mintzer, a fine player and arranger. These recordings are in conventional format, with polished ensemble sections and good, occasionally great, solos. They are well produced and mastered, but material and style tend to be conservative. —*Ron Wynn*

★ **Spectrum** / Jan. 1988 / Digital Music 461
Quartet, quintet, orchestra, and solo performance make up the dozen selections for Bob Mintzer's debut release, *Spectrum.* Mintzer, who's gigged with Peter Erskine and was on the drummer's *Transition* album and has been heard in tandem with fellow tenorist Joe Lovano, has one of the gutsier and meatier sounds for an instrument of his generation. He particularly impresses one with knowing the necessity of space and variably paced rhythmic phrasing. Mintzer is firmly rooted in the tenor sax tradition that savors standards like the Rodgers and Hart exemplified in his leisurely yet sure-footed reading of "My Romance." But Mintzer's own writing demonstrates his attempt to avoid becoming anachronistic while, within his structures, he finds ways to reconcile hard jazz with the modern sound. Although Lincoln Goines plays acoustic bass on most selections, Mintzer still finds the electric textures suitable for some ensemble themes while he charts territory for solos through the bopper's imagination. Taking pride in the acoustical recording technique, the leader concentrates on subtle dynamics to buoy both the punch of his orchestral writing and the off-time jerky themes written for combo. Aptly named, the album offers a spectrum of settings where Mintzer can test the waters of harmonic and rhythmic interest. "Hanky-Panky" features the full orchestra in a very today frame of mind beatwise, while "Mr. Funk" may surprise less as a "now" type of performance than a swinger à la Count Basie-Woody Herman, with Dave Bargeron and Don Grolnick strutting their stuff with elan on trombone and piano, respectively. For "Heart of the Matter," Mintzer comes up with one of those ballads we hear today whose melody is tailor-made for lots of modal improvising. "Frankie's Tune" is the most attractive of the large-scale arrangements, for though Mintzer tends to write choppy melody figures, this one

emerges as an orchestral fanfare of sorts in hocket style over the congas of Frankie Malabe. "Mine is Yours" and "Cowboys and Indians" are by a quintet including Randy Brecker. On flugelhorn Brecker is also present on the scene-stealing tune, "The Reunion," an intriguing work that uses "I Got Rhythm" changes in minor for its theme and first chorus before brightening into two choruses in harmonic major. Fortunately, Mintzer gives baritonist Roger Rosenberg a solo on "I Hear a Rhapsody" and Rosenberg, long in the studios and once in a while appearing in a salsa band, plays with admirable strength and facility. —*Ron Weilburn, Jazz Times*

Urban Contours / Mar. 2+5, 1989 / Digital Music 467

Art of the Big Band / Sep. 22-23, 1990 / Digital Music 479

○ **One Music** / 1991 / DMP 488
This saxophonist's best small-group work, with fellow Yellowjackets. The best cuts are the title and "Look Around." Ventures funky and creative into neo-bop modes. —*Michael G. Nastos*

BILLY MITCHELL

b. Nov. 3, 1926, Kansas City, MO
Tenor saxophone / Hard bop, bop, postbop
A big-toned, soulful tenor saxophonist whose style combines equal parts bluesy fervor and sophisticated phrasing, Billy Mitchell has successfully melded bebop and hard bop elements into a personable, appealing style. Mitchell worked with Nat Towles in Detroit before moving to New York in the late '40s with Lucky Millinder's orchestra. He recorded with Milt Jackson in 1949, then worked with Milt Buckner and Gil Fuller's big bands, and spent a brief period in Woody Herman's second Herd. He returned to Detroit in 1950, and led a quintet containing both Thad and Elvin Jones until 1953. Mitchell toured in the late '50s with Dizzy Gillespie, then joined Count Basie's orchestra, making several recordings with them before leaving in the early '60s. Mitchell and longtime Basie trombonist Al Grey formed a band that offered a downsized musical version of the Basie formula in the early '60s. He recorded with the Kenny Clarke-Francy Boland big band in the mid-'60s, and again in the early '70s. Mitchell played and taught in New York during the '70s, and recorded with the Xanadu All Stars in 1978. He recorded as a leader in the '80s and '90s. Mitchell's done sessions for Dee Gee, Argo, Smash, and Xanadu. Currently, he doesn't have any sessions as a leader available on CD, though Mitchell can be heard on Basie and Thad Jones reissues, and on the reissue of Ray Charles's *Soul Brothers*. His best playing's probably on Thad Jones's Blue Note LPs. —*Ron Wynn*

★ **Colossus of Detroit** / Apr. 18, 1978 / Xanadu
The feel of the Barry Harris/Sam Jones/Walter Bolden rhythm combination (piano/bass/drums) on Billy Mitchell's *Colossus of Detroit* session is alone almost worth the price of the record (veterans usually come through in the clutch). Harris's nutshell introductions rarely fail to put a tune in its proper frame of reference (check out "'Round Midnight" on his own *Tokyo Live* date). Jones's tone is so rich, and his sense of swing so relaxed! But the tenor saxophonist remains at the center of attention; while he experiences occasional intonation problems, he constructs thoughtful, sincere solos on this LP, which is superior to his first date for Xanadu. Mitchell alludes to Don Byas and Sonny Rollins but doesn't stay in the same bag, tune to tune. The quartet seems most comfortable on "I Should Care," and Mitchell is particularly inspired in duet with Harris on "How Am I to Know." —*Arthur Moorhead, Down Beat*

De Lawd's Blues / Jun. 26, 1980 / Xanadu
Rare appearance from expatriate trumpeter Benny Bailey and declarative tenor sax by Mitchell. —*Ron Wynn*

BLUE MITCHELL (Richard Allen Mitchell)

b. Mar. 13, 1930, Miami, FL, **d.** May 21, 1979, Los Angeles, CA
Trumpet / Hard bop, blues & jazz

A wonderful hard bop, blues, and ballad player, Blue Mitchell was the kind of hard-working, consistent player who gets overlooked because he's not a star or an innovator. Mitchell's lyrical sound and luminous timbre were presented superbly in some fine groups and as a leader in his own combos. He began playing trumpet in high school, acquiring both a good reputation and his nickname. Mitchell toured with the R&B bands of Paul Williams, Earl Bostic, and Chuck Willis in the early '50s. He returned from the road to his hometown, Miami, in the late '50s, and Cannonball Adderley heard him playing at a club. Adderley took Mitchell with him to New York and they recorded for Riverside in 1958. Mitchell joined Horace Silver's quintet that same year and remained with the group until 1964, participating in some invigorating dates. When Silver disbanded the ensemble, its members stayed together. The original band was Mitchell, Junior Cook, Gene Taylor, and Roy Brooks. Later, Chick Corea and Al Foster replaced Taylor and Brooks, with Mitchell and Cook dividing leadership duties. Subsequently, Harold Mabern and Billy Higgins replaced Corea and Foster. Mitchell became a prolific pop and soul session player in the late '60s, recording instrumental pop LPs, and touring with Ray Charles and John Mayall. During the mid-'70s, Mitchell did various dates in Los Angeles, while often serving as principle soloist for Tony Bennett and Lena Horne. He played in the big bands of Louis Bellson, Bill Holman, and Bill Berry, and worked in several bebop bands, including a quintet with Richie Kamauca. From 1975 to 1978, Mitchell was also in a quintet with Harold Land, while cutting more instrumental pop and disco albums in the late '70s. His career was cut short at age 49 by his death from cancer. He has only a few dates available on CD. —*Ron Wynn*

Blue Soul / Sep. 28, 1950 / Original Jazz Classics 765
Nice late '50s sextet session by underrated trumpeter Blue Mitchell. Mitchell was better known for his work with Horace Silver than anything he did as a leader, but this is excellently played, steady soul-jazz and hard bop. Jimmy Heath provides some outstanding tenor sax solos, while trombonist Curtis Fuller, pianist Wynton Kelly, bassist Sam Jones, and drummer Philly Joe Jones are all in top form. —*Ron Wynn*

○ **Big Six** / Jul. 2, 1958-Apr. 2, 1959 / Riverside 615
An outstanding date, with above-average solos from Johnny Griffin (ts), Curtis Fuller (tb), and Mitchell. The rhythm section of Wynton Kelly (p), Wilbur Ware (b), and Philly Joe Jones (d) doesn't slouch, either. —*Ron Wynn*

Blues on My Mind / Jul. 1958-Sep. 1959 / Riverside 6009
An all-star lineup of mainstream/bop greats. Mitchell holds his own against sax greats Jimmy Heath, Benny Golson, and Johnny Griffin. —*Ron Wynn*

Blue's Moods / Aug. 24-25, 1960 / Riverside 138
Smooth 1960 session that blends romantic pieces, soul-jazz, and mainstream. —*Ron Wynn*

★ **Thing to Do, The** / Jul. 30, 1964 / Blue Note 84178
With Chick Corea, Junior Cook (ts), and Al Foster (d). Recommended for jazz/trumpet lovers. —*Michael G. Nastos*

○ **Down with It** / Jul. 14, 1965 / Blue Note
One of Mitchell's least-recognized sessions, this has some fervent trumpet pieces, plus nice piano from a then-still-emerging Chick Corea. —*Ron Wynn*

Blue's Blues / 1972-1974 / Mainstream 374
A fine mainstream/bop date that includes some arresting Mitchell trumpet work on ballads. —*Ron Wynn*

RED MITCHELL (Keith Moore Mitchell)

b. Sep. 20, 1927, New York, NY, **d.** 1992
Bass / Cool
Red Mitchell has been a prolific bassist, session musician, and bandleader since the late '40s. His facility, range, and percussive, dashing style have made him a premier player. Mitchell's phrasing and huge, full tones, as well as his ability to make the bass a lead melodic instrument, are a testa-

ment to his immense talents. He studied piano for nine years before switching to bass while in an army band stationed in Germany. Mitchell worked with Jackie Paris and Mundell Lowe in the late '40s, then joined Chubby Jackson's big band, playing both piano and bass. Mitchell played with Charlie Ventura, and toured and recorded with Woody Herman in the late '40s and early '50s, and with Red Norvo's trio in the early '50s. He recorded with Billie Holiday and Jimmy Raney while in the Norvo trio, then joined Gerry Mulligan in the mid-'50s. Mitchell performed and recorded with Hampton Hawes during the '50s and '60s, worked again with Holiday in 1956 and 1957, and recorded with Ornette Coleman's band in 1959. He also did many film and television soundtracks while serving as the main bassist in MGM's studio band from 1959 to 1968. He led his own quintet in 1957, then co-led a group in 1961 and 1962 with Harold Land. Mitchell moved to Stockholm in 1966, and played in Europe for ten years. He worked with touring musicians like Dizzy Gillespie and Phil Woods, while also playing with the Swedish Radiojazzgruppen and with pianist Guido Manusardi. He formed the group Communication in 1976, with both top European musicians and American expatriates like Horace Parlan. He worked with this band into the '80s, and made occasional return visits to America. He recorded with Jim Hall in 1978 and toured with Communication in 1979. Mitchell recorded with Tommy Flanagan and Jimmie Rowles in the '80s. He also did sessions in the '80s and '90s for Capri and Sunnyside. There's a moderate amount of Mitchell material available on CD. — *Ron Wynn*

Presenting Red Mitchell / Mar. 26, 1957 / Contemporary 158

One of the earliest sessions for this bassist, pianist, and singer from New York City; it helped launch his career. Recently reissued. — *Ron Wynn*

Five Brothers / i. Apr. 4, 1957 / Tampa 25

○ **Hear Ye!** / 1989 / Atlantic 1376

★ **Talking** / i. 1989 / Capri 74016
A piano/drum/bass date with Kenny Barron and Ben Riley, Red Mitchell's *Talking* is especially companionable. On the deepest level, you'd be hard-pressed to find a trio swing with more conviction or spirited interplay than these old mates from Bradley's (University Place, Manhattan). They speak with warmth, pointedness, and occasional hilarity ("Locomotive"). Their swing, more often implied than bared, gets around to all sorts of cutting, curving, joshing. — *Fred Bouchard*, Down Beat

ROSCOE MITCHELL (Roscoe Edward (Jr) Mitchell)

b. Aug. 3, 1940, Chicago, IL
Reeds, composer / Early free, modern creative
A multi-instrumentalist and a wild eclectic player, Roscoe Mitchell willingly blurs the lines between free and structured music, jazz, and pop. He's a composer who's penned exacting works for solo sax, orchestras, and electronic instruments. He's also played explosive free works, particularly with his Art Ensemble of Chicago colleague Joseph Jarman, and with Anthony Braxton. Mitchell was a charter member of the Art Ensemble in 1969, along with Jarman, Lester Bowie, and Malachi Favors Magostus. He plays alto, soprano, baritone, and bass saxophones, several flutes, and percussion instruments, and adds vocal effects on both his horns and through the singing/yelling/chanting in his compositions. Mitchell's swirling flute solos offer another side of his personality, the lyrical alternative to the bleats, squawks, booms, and screams featured during his extended sax solos. Mitchell played clarinet, baritone, and alto sax in high school and army bands before leading a hard bop sextet in Chicago that included Jarman and Henry Threadgill. He also played in a free jazz group with Jack DeJohnette, and was in Muhal Richard Abrams Experimental Band. Mitchell was a founding member of the Association for the Advancement of Creative Musicians (AACM) and led a sextet, quartet, and

trio composed of various AACM members. Mitchell, Favors, Bowie, and Phillip Wilson recorded as the Roscoe Mitchell Art Ensemble in 1967 on Delmark. Jarman replaced Wilson when the group moved to Paris and was renamed the Art Ensemble of Chicago. Mitchell performed solo from 1967 until the Art Ensemble's origin. He played briefly in St. Louis when the Art Ensemble returned to America in the early '70s, before returning to Chicago. He established the Creative Arts Collective in East Lansing, Michigan, in 1974, modeling it after the AACM. Several of its members later joined his Sound Ensemble (since expanded to the Sight and Sound Ensemble), which recorded in Chicago in 1980 and in Milan in 1981. Mitchell's albums as a leader have included combo dates on Delmark in the '60s, solo sessions for Sackville, a duet with Anthony Braxton, and combo dates for Nessa, Moers, Black Saint, Silkheart, and Cecma in the '70s, '80s, and '90s. He also did a solo date for Cecma in 1987. A few Mitchell sessions are available on CD. — *Ron Wynn*

○ **Sound** / 1966 / Delmark 408
Mitchell's first significant statement as a leader has ambitious pieces, amazing solos, and unorthodox arrangements. — *Ron Wynn*

★ **Old / Quartet** / May 18-19, 1967 / Nessa 5

Congliptious / i. 1968 / Nessa
Simply a standout quartet date. Mitchell honks, bleats, and dashes full steam ahead. Issued as Roscoe Mitchell and Ensemble. — *Ron Wynn*

○ **Roscoe Mitchell Solo Saxophone Concerts, The** / Oct. 22, 1973+Nov. 2, 1973 / Sackville 2006
Roscoe Mitchell's solo work has often been ignored, which makes this brilliantly vigorous Sackville LP all the more welcome. Like Cecil Taylor, Mitchell here thinks in highly structured outlines, though his extraordinary concept of rhythm often makes for delightfully odd forms. Note the twining of theme and supporting lines in "Eeltwo I" and "II," a work as consciously disturbed and extremely organized as any of Taylor's. "Ttum" is wilder and even more complex, with contrasts of dirge and happiness revealed early, the opposites creating a centrifugal force that eventually yields extremes, the work ending on a question. Why solo? Because here Mitchell communicates absolutely. Nobody else hears rhythm as such a flexible element. — *John Litweiler*, Down Beat

Quartet / Oct. 4-5, 1975 / Sackville 2009
With pianist Muhal Abrahms, trombonist George Lewis, and guitarist A. Spencer Barefield. Very challenging listening. — *Michael G. Nastos*

★ **Nonaah** / Aug. 23, 1976-Feb. 22, 1977 / Nessa 10
1976-1977. This is perhaps Mitchell's best solo statement. It includes a full-side treatment of the title cut, solo works, duos, and an incredible alto number with Mitchell, Henry Threadgill (as), Joseph Jarman (reeds), and the undervalued Wallace McMillan (b). — *Ron Wynn*

Duets with Anthony Braxton / Dec. 13, 1977 / Sackville 3016

L-R-G / The Maze / SII Examples / Jul. 27, 1978-Aug. 17, 1978 / Nessa 15
Free improvisation. Definitive statement from Art Ensemble saxophonist and composer. One piece is all horns, another all percussion, and one is solo. This one is for open ears only. — *Michael G. Nastos*

3x4 Eye / Feb. 18-19, 1981 / Black Saint 0050

○ **Snurdy McGurdy and Her Dancin' Shoes** / Jun. 1982 / Nessa 20
This album is more upbeat and humorous, less dense and intense than some past Mitchell dates, but the music's just as ferocious. — *Ron Wynn*

Flow of Things, The / Jun. 1986-Sep. 1986 / Black Saint 0090
High-energy, kinetic pieces. Jodie Christian (p) opens the eyes of doubters. — *Ron Wynn*

BILL MOBLEY

Trumpet / Neo-bop
A Memphis-based trumpeter and a contemporary of players such as James Williams, Mulgrew Miller, and Donald Brown, Mobley's reputation and profile aren't as large as his contemporaries'. But he's a strong, often stirring lead trumpeter with excellent range. He can be heard on Bill Easley's *First Call* album, issued in 1991. *—Ron Wynn*

HANK MOBLEY (Henry Mobley)

b. Jul. 7, 1930, Eastman, GA, **d.** May 30, 1986, Philadelphia, PA
Tenor saxophone / Hard bop
Hank Mobley was one of the great journeyman players. He was a consistently swinging hard bop stylist who crafted precise solos with a steady rhythmic vigor, relaxed pace, and subtle harmonic creativity that included great lyricism and a strong swing feeling. He maintained those qualities despite his refusal to stray far away from any composition's beat. Mobley played in the R&B band of Paul Gayten in the early '50s, then worked with Max Roach and Dizzy Gillespie. He was a founding member of Art Blakey's Jazz Messengers in 1954, and remained with them until 1956. Mobley played with Silver's quintet, worked again with Blakey, and then played with Dizzy Reece. He was in Miles Davis's band in the early '60s, but Davis was not a fan of Mobley's playing, though Mobley worked much more effectively in Davis's rhythm section on such albums as *Someday My Prince Will Come* and *Friday and Saturday Night at the Blackhawk*. Mobley recorded several times as a leader in the '50s and '60s, playing with John Coltrane, Johnny Griffin, Paul Chambers, Blue Mitchell, Jackie McLean, Cedar Walton, Donald Byrd, Ron Carter, Wynton Kelly, Philly Joe Jones, Lee Morgan, and Billy Higgins, among others. He did sessions for Blue Note, Savoy, and Prestige, but Blue Note was his primary vehicle. Mobley toured Europe in the late '60s and early '70s, but encountered health problems. He finally had to abandon music in the mid-'70s. He made a nonplaying appearance at the 1985 concert that relaunched Blue Note, and did a short playing date with Duke Jordan in 1986; shortly thereafter, Mobley died from double pneumonia. He has several classic sessions available on CD reissues. *—Ron Wynn*

Hank Mobley Quartet / Mar. 27, 1955 / Blue Note 46816
This debut of Mobley on Blue Note includes Horace Silver on piano and Doug Watkins on bass, plus someone named Art Blakey on drums. *—Ron Wynn*

Hank Mobley's Message / Jul. 20, 1956 / Prestige 7661

Hard Bop / Jul. 23, 1956 / Savoy 1125

Tenor Conclave / Sep. 7, 1956 / Prestige 127
With Al Cohn, John Coltrane, Zoot Sims. A hard-blowing, straightahead jam session that matches four identifiable and individualistic voices. All can be heard elsewhere to greater glory, but it's still interesting. *—Ron Wynn*

Hank Mobley and His All-Stars / Jan. 13, 1957 / Blue Note 1544
This is great Mobley with Milt Jackson (vib) and Horace Silver (p). *—David Szatmary*

Hank Mobley Quintet / Mar. 9, 1957 / Blue Note 81550
Quintet. A classic date with Art Farmer (tpt), Art Blakey (d), and Horace Silver (p). *—David Szatmary*

☆ **Peckin' Time** / Feb. 9, 1958 / Blue Note 81574
One of the best by this prolific yet underrated tenor. With Lee Morgan (tpt) and Wynton Kelly (p). *—David Szatmary*

★ **Soul Station** / Feb. 7, 1960 / Blue Note 46528
Another good Blue Note date that languished until its reissue in 1987. *—Ron Wynn*

○ **Roll Call** / Nov. 13, 1960 / Blue Note 46823

○ **Workout** / Mar. 26, 1961 / Blue Note 84080

★ **Another Workout** / Mar. 1961-Dec. 1961 / Blue Note 84431
A wonderful session that remained in the Blue Note vaults until 1985. *—Ron Wynn*

○ **Straight No Filter** / Jul. 7, 1963-Feb. 4, 1965 / Blue Note 84435
Straight No Filter consists of the last remaining unissued Hank Mobley-led Blue Note recordings. The first half of this disc is often superb with several brilliant solos from Mobley, McCoy Tyner (p), and the still-underrated Lee Morgan (tpt). The oddest part about this date lies in the song titles. "Soft Impressions" is a blues while "Chain Reaction" utilizes the "Impressions" chord changes with eight bars added to the bridge; were these titles reversed in error? The Lee Morgan improvisations alone make this album valuable, especially his solo on "Chain Reaction." A pair of fine selections with the young brash trumpet of Freddie Hubbard and Barry Harris (p) include the 20-bar "Third Time Around" and a happy blues waltz. In his liner notes, Bob Blumenthal mentions a Larry Ridley bass solo on "Third Time," yet the personnel listing has Paul Chambers; if forced to guess I'd say the former was correct. Donald Byrd sounds a little weak on the funky "The Feeling's Good" but Hancock's strong comping and Mobley's inventive tenor compensate. Discographical quirks aside, *Straight No Filter* (a smokin' album?) is a worthy addition to the seemingly endless Blue Note archives. *—Scott Yanow, Cadence*

No Room for Squares / Oct. 2, 1963 / Blue Note 84149
This is an interesting session with Lee Morgan (tpt) and Andrew Hill (p). *—David Szatmary*

Turnaround, The / Feb. 5, 1965 / Blue Note 84186

Dippin' / Jun. 18, 1965 / Blue Note 46511

Caddy for Daddy, A / Dec. 18, 1965 / Blue Note 84230
One of Mobley's best, with Lee Morgan (tpt) and Curtis Fuller (tb). *—David Szatmary*

Far Away Lands / May 26, 1967 / Blue Note 84425
With high-octane trumpet work by Donald Byrd and excellent tenor sax from Mobley. Cedar Walton (p), Ron Carter (b), and Billy Higgins (d) uphold the rhythm section with distinction. *—Ron Wynn*

Hi Voltage / 1967 / Blue Note 84273
Later Mobley, backed by Jackie McLean (as) and Blue Mitchell (tpt). *—David Szatmary*

○ **Flip, The** / Jul. 12, 1969 / Blue Note 84329
This collection was recorded in Paris on July 12, 1969, with young Vince Benedetti (p), Frenchman Alby Cullaz (b), Philly Joe Jones (d), Dizzy Reece (tpt), and Slide Hampton (tb). The five tunes are all Hank Mobley originals and serve their purpose as springboards for explosive jazz excitement. "The Flip" is a 40-bar vamp number on which Jones bears down heavily, a trifle too heavily, on the soloists. All three horns and Benedetti are featured and Dizzy Reece takes an outstanding solo. "Feelin' Folksy" is a minor key melody. Mobley (tenor) blows with considerable aggression and power as does Hampton, who may well have helped arrange this and some of the other numbers. But Reece again steals the spotlight with one of his more characteristic, long-lined statements. Benedetti copes very well in this fast company and is reminiscent of Kenny Drew at times. Indications that all was not well in the studio are provided by the fact that the balance on "Folksy" is highly variable and that *after* Rudy Van Gelder had rerecorded the original tapes. There are no slow ballads on this fiery set, which goes out with a blazing "Early Morning Stroll" (trot would seem to be more appropriate). Once more Jones appears to be challenging Mobley to let go—if he dares! He pushes the soloists and makes all of them move. In this mood Jones is a complete rhythm section and woe betide the slouchers. This is a really good blowing session in the best tradition of Blue Note. *—Mark Gardner, Coda*

MODERN JAZZ QUARTET

b. 1951
Cool
The Modern Jazz Quartet has survived for 40 years with a fine blend of jazz originals, nicely crafted pop tunes, and a thoroughly rehearsed, yet relaxed and loose group sound

that has a spontaneous sensibility. The band's light swinging, sophisticated sound with its classical influences definitely puts them in the cool category, but vibist Milt Jackson can play smokey blues, and pianist John Lewis has even been known to cut loose with some stomping numbers. The original group began in 1951 when Lewis, Jackson, bassist Percy Heath, and Kenny Clarke, all alumni of Dizzy Gillespie's mid-'40s big band, recorded together. Clarke was supplanted by Connie Kay in 1955; otherwise, the group has remained intact. Lewis met Clarke in the army, and played on Miles Davis's *Birth of the Cool* sessions. Lewis, Jackson, and Clarke previously worked together as part of the Milt Jackson Quartet with Ray Brown, recording on Gillespie's Dee Gee label in the early '50s. Then, they worked with Heath and Lou Donaldson as the Milt Jackson Quintet on Blue Note. Prestige reissued several tracks that the group recorded from 1952 through 1955, including the albums *Django* with Clarke and *Concorde* with Kay on Fantasy. From 1956 until 1974 they recorded mostly on Atlantic, cutting albums that blended a symphonic sensibility with a jazz flavor. They covered the stylistic gamut, doing concept albums, playing live with Sonny Rollins, doing chamber and "Third Stream" works with orchestras, and collaborating with guitarist Laurindo Almeida. They disbanded in 1974, with the superb two-record set *The Last Concert* supposedly the final straw. Shortly after its release, reunion talk began. They recorded as a unit again in 1982 and in 1984, and have maintained an active, though nowhere near as intense, pace ever since. Atlantic released a gala MJQ 40th anniversary boxed set in 1991, and there's plenty of their previous material available on CD. *—Ron Wynn and William Ruhlmann*

○ **Modern Jazz Quartet Plays Jazz Classics, The** / Dec. 22, 1952-Jul. 2, 1955 / Prestige 7425
An early work that lays out the essence of the Modern Jazz Quartet: a unit that brings both jazz sensibility and classical precision to anything they play. This time they perform classical material with improvisational backdrop, something that pianist John Lewis particularly loved. Vibist Milt Jackson also executes his parts smoothly, while bassist Percy Heath and drummer Connie Kay are consistently supportive and steady. *—Ron Wynn*

○ **Modern Jazz Quartet** / Dec. 22, 1952-Jul. 2, 1955 / Savoy Jazz 111
First works from early '50s with drummer Kenny Clark. Quintessential MJQ. Rare Prestige recordings. *—Michael G. Nastos*

★ **MJQ–40 years [Boxed Set]** / 1952-Feb. 3, 1988 / Atlantic 82330
Recent set gathers a variety of styles from 40 years of recording. *—Michael Erlewine*

Django / 1953-1955 / Prestige 057
Their signature song and the last call for Kenny Clarke as the group's drummer. *—Ron Wynn*

Concorde / Jul. 2, 1955 / Prestige 002
A bit of blues, a little third stream, and lots in between. The Gershwin medley is recommended. *—Ron Wynn*

★ **No Sun in Venice** / Apr. 4, 1957 / Atlantic 1284
An adventurous John Lewis score for the Roger Vadim film of the same name. *—Ron Wynn*

Pyramid / Aug. 1959-Jan. 1960 / Atlantic 1325

Odds Against Tomorrow / i. Oct. 9, 1959 / Blue Note 93415

Modern Jazz Quartet with Milt Jackson Quintet / Dec. 22, 1959 / Prestige 7059

European Concert / Apr. 11-12, 1960 / Atlantic 603
This double-set pairing of two single albums marks the MJQ's visit to Europe. *—Ron Wynn*

Comedy / Jan. 1962 / Atlantic 1390
Not for all tastes. Includes one vocal from Diahann Carroll. Lacks improvisational punch, but has solid playing. *—Ron Wynn*

Lonely Woman / 1962 / Atlantic 90665

○ **Collaboration with Almeida** / Jul. 21, 1964 / Atlantic 1429
With Laurindo Almeida. Lush and romatic, very much a product of the early '60s Latin craze. Almeida makes a sympathetic collaborator. *—Ron Wynn*

Blues at Carnegie Hall / Apr. 27, 1966 / Atlantic 1468
A fine live set with first-rate Milt Jackson vibes solos and good ensemble pieces. *—Ron Wynn*

Place Vendome / Sep. 27, 1966-Oct. 30, 1966 / PolyGram 24545
With The Swingle Singers. This is a good departure for MJQ. Swingle Singers are a fine unit. *—Ron Wynn*

Plastic Dreams / May 1971 / Atlantic 1589
It's sassy, bluesy cute at times. John Lewis is on harpsichord for a few tracks. *—Ron Wynn*

★ **Complete Last Concert** / Nov. 25, 1974 / Atlantic 81976
At the time, this two-record set was viewed as the end of an era. Now it only represents the climax of phase one. It's an excellent set, though—among their best live efforts. *—Ron Wynn*

○ **More from the Last Concert** / Nov. 25, 1974 / Atlantic 8806
When the Modern Jazz Quartet got together in 1974 to do what was thought to be their final recording, it was a historic occasion. So much worthwhile material was done, there was enough for a second album. Fortunately, it turned out not to be the end for the band, but this second album from the '74 date is still well worth hearing. *—Ron Wynn*

Together Again at Montreux Jazz / Jul. 25, 1982 / Pablo 2308-244
The session that marked the group's return to active touring and performing. *—Ron Wynn*

Echoes / Together Again 1984 / Mar. 6, 1984 / Pablo 2312-142
Their second "return" album has typically bright and glossy playing, but it lacks the quality and power of their Atlantic releases. *—Ron Wynn*

Three Windows / 1987 / Atlantic 81761

○ **For Ellington** / Feb. 1988 / East West 90026
For Ellington is a salute to Duke's genius, but it seems to tightrope the effete and tepid in the Modern Jazz Quartet's response with moments of musical excitement. This happens with their reading of "Come Sunday," which seems languorous in its spiritualist evocations and on "Prelude to a Kiss". But this collection does have its moments of brilliance and glory. Even "Prelude" is full of tenderness, and on "Ko-Ko" pianist John Lewis plays Harry Carney's figure to vibist Milt Jackson's response with the melody—Ellington would have appreciated Lewis's percussive texture on the solo here. It is perhaps the album's strongest performance. "Rockin' In Rhythm" is quite dramatic, with perfectly elucidated individual roles, and Ellington's one-time theme, Billy Strayhorn's "Sepia Panorama," is a blues given a groove for leisurely swing arranged to project the eminence of Percy Heath (b). Jackson composed "Maestro E.K.E.," with its resonant melody deftly voiced by the quartet. This is the kind of work one would think had been in the orchestra's repertory for years, so filled is it with the spirit of Ellington and his veterans. But for "It Don't Mean a Thing If It Ain't Got That Swing," the showcase intended for Connie Kay's cymbal work, not even Jackson's solo can lift it out of the chamber music doldrums. This musical penchant is just enough to make one wonder, or continue wondering after all these years, how the success of the group's measured moods is also so incomparable. *—Ron Weilburn, Jazz Times*

○ **Modern Jazz Quartet with Sonny Rollins, The** / Atlantic 1299

Best of the Modern Jazz Quartet / Atlantic 1546
Grab-bag single-album set of their '50s and '60s cuts, worth very little now. *—Ron Wynn*

CHARLES MOFFETT

b. 1929

Drums / Modern creative

A solid drummer in either an R&B, hard bop, or free jazz mode, Charles Moffett's best known for his mid-'60s recording sessions with Ornette Coleman. In these sessions, Moffett's loose, frenetic playing provided ideal rhythmic underpinning for Coleman's alto sax thrusts and for David Izenon's equally individualistic bass lines and phrases. Moffett was a trumpeter as a teen, and worked with Jimmy Witherspoon and other R&B and blues bands around his Fort Worth home area. Moffett switched to drums in college, and, following his discharge from the navy, finally earned his degree in music education. He was a high school teacher in Texas from 1953 to 1961, but found time to play with jazz bands and to back Little Richard for one year. Moffett joined Coleman in New York in '61, and worked with him during the years Coleman shunned public performances, then toured and recorded with Coleman and Izenon from 1965 to 1967. Moffett played with Sonny Rollins in 1963, and led a group with Pharoah Sanders, Alan Shorter, and Carla Bley in 1964. He moved to Oakland in 1970, where he directed a music school and led two bands: a family unit with his children, and another band comprised of his students. Moffett played with Steve Turre, Keshavan Maslak, and Prince Lasha before returning to New York. In the '80s and '90s, he's divided his time between teaching and playing with Frank Lowe, Maslak, and others. His son, Charnett, has recorded as a leader with Blue Note. The album *Nettwork* united Moffett with both his son and daughter. Moffett has recorded for Savoy and Lester Recording Society as a leader; currently, his dates are unavailable on CD. —*Ron Wynn*

CHARNETT MOFFETT (Charnet Moffett)

Bass / Instrumental pop, contemporary funk, modern creative

The son of drummer Charles Moffett, Charnett Moffett's bass skills have never been questioned. His only problem has been taste; his sessions as a leader have been uneven, and littered with disposable fusion filler. When he's chosen to play jazz, or even more intense instrumental pop, Moffett's demonstrated first-rate solo and accompanist skills. He recorded with Branford Marsalis and Stanley Jordan in the mid-'80s, then began recording as a leader for Blue Note in the late '80s, and continued for them and for Manhattan into the '90s. He's recorded with Kenny Garrett, Kenny Kirkland, Don Alias, Barry Lynn Stemley, Bernard Wright, Jordan, and Kenny Drew. His early '90s release, *Nettwork*, included appearances from his father and from his sister, Charisse Moffett. He's also recorded with his brother, Cody. All Moffett's sessions are available on CD. —*Ron Wynn*

Beauty Within / **i.** 1957 / Blue Note 91650

★ **Nettwork** / **i.** 1957 / Blue Note 96109

LOUIS MOHOLO (Louis T. Moholo)

b. Mar. 10, 1940, Cape Town, South Africa
Drums, cello, percussion, vocals / World fusion

A riveting, constantly charging drummer, Louis Moholo blends the precision and textural subtlety of jazz with the rippling rhythms and multiple beats of African music. A self-taught drummer, Moholo founded the Chordettes, a big band, in 1956. He later joined the Blue Notes, an integrated jazz band led by Chris McGregor. Moholo left South Africa with the rest of the band, settling first in Switzerland, then moving to London. Moholo toured for a year with Steve Lacy, performing throughout South America. He also worked with Rosewell Rudd, Archie Shepp, and John Tchicai. He returned to England in 1967, played with McGregor's Brotherhood of Breath, and with groups led by European musicians Peter Brotzmann and Mike Osborne. He's done extensive recording in the '70s and '80s, while heading such bands as Moholo's Unit, Spirits Rejoice, Culture Shock, and the African Drum Ensemble. Moholo's recorded as a leader principally for Ogun. Currently, none of his sessions as a leader are available on CD in America. —*Ron Wynn*

★ **Spirits Rejoice** / Jan. 24, 1978 / Ogun 520
The South African drummer with the Blue Notes and Brotherhood of Breath leads an octet. This is a great album– a must-buy. —*Michael G. Nastos*

Vive La Black / **i.** 1988 / Ogun 533
London studio date with a sextet featuring Sean Bergin and Steve Williamson on saxes. Excellent modern music. —*Michael G. Nastos*

MONCUR III, GRACHAN

b. 1937
Trombone / Early free, modern creative

A fine trombonist who can contribute effectively to combos or to large orchestras, Grachan Moncur III was a freewheeling participant on some pivotal '60s sessions, and was a busy session player who worked with everyone from the Jazz Composers Orchestra Association (JCOA) to the cast of a James Baldwin play. In recent years he hasn't been as active, at least in terms of recording, but has an impressive body of work that displays his strong tone, steady sound, and harmonically and melodically rich, imaginative style.

The son of swing-era bassist Grachan Moncur, he began playing piano and cello as a child before beginning on trombone at age 11. He played in an orchestra led by Nat Phipps in Newark that also included Wayne Shorter. Moncur briefly attended both the Manhattan School of Music and Juilliard, then worked with Ray Charles in the late '50s and early '60s. He was in the Jazztet for a short time in 1962 and served as Charles's music director. Moncur was in Jackie McLean's excellent mid-'60s group that merged hard bop and free elements. He began heading his own groups, while he also worked and recorded with Shorter, Herbie Hancock, Tony Williams, and Bobby Hutcherson. He did some acting in 1964 and 1965, appearing in the New York and London productions of Baldwin's *Blues for Mr. Charlie*, and wrote some music for the play.

Moncur toured with Sonny Rollins in 1964, then played and recorded with Marion Brown and Joe Henderson. He coformed the 360 Degree Music Experience with Beaver Harris and Dave Burrell in 1968, and served as its music director. Moncur performed in Europe with Archie Shepp at the Actuel and Donaueschingen festivals in 1969. He received a grant from the National Education Association's jazz program in 1970. He composed and participated in the JCOA recording, *Echoes of Prayer*, in 1974, a work the JCOA commissioned that merged Caribbean, Latin, and classical music elements. Moncur worked with choreographer Keith Lee in 1978, and won the Mason Gross Award from the New Jersey Council for the Arts. He rejoined the 360 Degree Music Experience in 1979, and became composer-in-residence at the Newark Community School of the Arts in 1983. During the remainder of the '80s, Moncur toured with Blue Ark and poet Amiri Baraka, and recorded and toured with Frank Lowe, Cassandra Wilson, and Nathan Davis's Reunion Band. There's currently an absence of available Moncur titles on CD, at least according to the *Schwann* catalog. —*Ron Wynn*

○ **Evolution** / Nov. 21, 1963 / Blue Note 84153
Easily recommended Blue Note date from the '60s with Lee Morgan (tpt) and Jackie McLean (as). —*Michael G. Nastos*

New Africa / Aug. 11, 1969 / Actuel 529321
The trombonist in a modal setting with Archie Shepp (sax), Roscoe Mitchell (reeds), and Dave Burrell (p) in a Paris studio. —*Michael G. Nastos*

○ **Echoes of Prayer** / Apr. 11, 1974 / JCOA 1009
The 1974 *Melody Maker* Jazz Album of the Year. Progressive and thought-provoking. A legendary recording, with the Jazz Composers Orchestra. —*Michael G. Nastos*

THELONIOUS MONK (Thelonious Sphere Monk)

b. Oct. 10, 1917, Rocky Mount, NC, **d.** Feb. 17, 1982, Weehawken, NJ
Piano, composer, bandleader / Bop, postbop

A brilliant composer and a criminally underrated pianist, Thelonious Sphere Monk unfortunately received as much, if not more, ink during his lifetime for his eccentric behavior as he did for his astonishing talent. His playing took classic stride to an almost unrecognizable, yet effective level. His approach included melodic alterations, unexpected and unorthodox rhythm changes, and sweeping harmonic substitutions. No one made better use of "wrong" notes, and his solos, which eschewed normal patterns, always worked. His compositions utilized the same technique; Monk was interested in ideas rather than formulas. His greatest songs, such as "'Round Midnight," "Brilliant Corners," or "Pannonica," weren't seamless, flowing works; they had sections that sounded disjointed, but when performed by musicians willing to stick them out to the end, revealed the subtle beauty and exacting structure Monk devised. His songs required complete instrumental mastery and supreme personal confidence from musicians.

Monk began playing piano at age 11. He accompanied his mother in church, then began to play professionally in 1939. Monk worked with various New York groups in the early '40s, and served as house pianist at Minton's Playhouse. Monk was first recorded playing at Minton's in 1941 with special guest Charlie Christian. He was a major influence on the early playing of Bud Powell. Monk played with Charlie Christian, Don Byas, Roy Eldridge, and Helen Humes during Minton's stints. After hours, he'd gather with Charlie Parker, Dizzy Gillespie, Kenny Clarke, and others to experiment with new directions. Monk made his studio recording debut in 1944 as a member of the Coleman Hawkins's quartet. Cootie Williams recorded "'Round Midnight" that same year. Monk also played on 52nd Street at the Spotlite Club with Gillespie's orchestra from 1944 until 1947, then made his first recording as a leader for Blue Note. Monk recorded from '47 until '52, cutting early versions of "Evidence," "Criss Cross," and "Thelonious." He also recorded with Charlie Parker in 1950.

Monk encountered problems finding work in New York during the '50s due to a previous arrest and conviction. At that time, New York's infamous "cabaret card" law stated that anyone convicted of a felony couldn't work in a place that sold liquor (because they couldn't get a card). He was prohibited from playing in most significant jazz clubs from 1951 until 1957. Monk signed with Prestige in 1952, staying with them for three years. During this stretch, there were sessions with Miles Davis and Sonny Rollins, plus a solo date for the Swing label in Paris, which he recorded in 1954. Prestige sold his contract to Riverside in 1955; he stayed with Riverside until 1961.

Despite lukewarm audience and critical response, Monk continued making fine records. He recorded "Gallop's Gallop" for Signal with Gigi Gyrce, and worked with Art Blakey for Atlantic. The critics and public alike were caught short by three marvelous late '50s albums: *Brilliant Corners*, *Thelonious Himself*, and *Thelonious Monk with John Coltrane*. Suddenly, Monk was being praised as an overnight compositional star. He made regular appearances at the Five Spot with Coltrane. Roy Haynes, Johnny Griffin, and Charlie Rouse, who'd become his comrade-in-arms, worked with him, and his bands received extensive tour and performance opportunities. There were visits to Europe, and a highly covered 1959 Town Hall concert with an orchestra playing Hall Overton arrangements of Monk's works. By the early '60s, tales of Monk's greatness and eccentricity filled journals, newspapers, and magazines. Columbia signed him after the Prestige deal expired, and he was on the cover of *Time* magazine in 1964. Unfortunately, once Columbia signed him they mishandled his contract. The company wanted him to record Beatles' tunes, and eventually withheld much of his greatest work from release until after he had left the label. What did get issued between 1962 and 1967 often came out with minimal or no track and musician information. *Monk's Dream, Criss-Cross, Monk, Straight, No Chaser,* and *Underground* were superb records. Monk did

make several European tours, as well as visits to Japan and Mexico.

He got some exposure and attention from his participation in the Giants of Jazz group from 1970 to 1972. This band included Gillespie, Sonny Stitt, Kai Winding, Al McKibbon, and Blakey, and recorded for Atlantic in addition to touring. English labels Black Lion and Vogue recorded Monk playing solo and in a trio. Then, without fanfare or announcement, the great Thelonious Monk simply quit. He made three appearances with an orchestra at Carnegie Hall, and with a quartet at the 1975 and 1976 Newport Jazz Festivals in New York. But from 1976 until his death in 1982, Monk remained mostly in seclusion at the home of his longtime friend, the Baroness Pannonica de Koenigswarter, in New Jersey. There was one moving moment in 1978, when Monk was honored at the White House Jazz Party by President Carter.

Several labels have issued significant Monk reissue packages. Mosaic has issued complete sets of the Blue Note, Vogue, and Black Lion recordings, while Prestige (actually Fantasy/Milestone) issued the Complete Riverside recordings. An international competition in his honor has yielded some impressive stars, among them outstanding saxophonist Joshua Redman. The repertory group Sphere, with old friend and companion Charlie Rouse, recorded some wonderful tribute albums in the '80s, and in 1984 an all-star lineup of jazz and rock players cut *That's the Way I Feel Now*, a two-record set honoring his compositions. Both Steve Lacy and Buell Neidlinger have led Monk repertory groups. Monk's son, T.S. Monk, made a few R&B and urban contemporary recordings, but is currently playing jazz and is working as a jazz advocate in broadcasting and media. He hosted a 1993 jazz concert at the White House that aired nationally on public television. —*Ron Wynn*

○ **Complete Genius, The** / Oct. 15, 1947-May 30, 1952 / Blue Note 579

For some time I had been hoping that Blue Note would get around to reissuing all of their 1947-1952 Thelonious Monk tracks on a double album, and it's happened at last. It's no longer necessary to grope around the random selections of Monk tracks on Blue Note's various albums because they are all collected on this double LP (including the two issued alternate takes). And if that's not enough, there are also two items that were previously only on a 78. For some strange reason, they are not presented in chronological order, but all the pieces from each session are grouped together, and that's the most important thing on such a reissue. This reissue includes superlative examples of Monk *the* pianist (if he didn't have technique as has been claimed, how come no one could imitate him?), Monk *the* composer (22 of his best tunes are performed), and the lesser-known Monk *the* arranger (hear especially how he transforms the hypermaudlin "Carolina Moon" into a masterpiece for jazz quintet). As an integral bonus, most of the performances are booted along stupendously by Art Blakey at his very best—those that do not feature some fine drumming by Max Roach or Shadow Wilson. The horns on the two 1947 quintet dates leave a lot to be desired, but one can always listen to Monk and Blakey instead. Things get better on the 1951-52 sessions with good work by trumpeter Kenny Dorham and saxophonists Lucky Thompson and Sahib Shihab (who was rather dubious on a 1947 date). Special mention should be made of vibist Milt Jackson whose playing on two sessions fits right in with Monk's like a glove on a hand—if only Monk had been the pianist with the MJQ! Finally, for the first time on microgroove, there are the 1948 "I Should Care" and "All The Things You Are," which feature the absurd deadpan operatics of Kenny Hagood. Try and forget him and listen to Monk and Jackson lay down what must be the strangest (and strongest) accompaniment to a vocal on record. (To Hagood's credit, he does not get thrown off his chosen course, though it might have been as well if he had been.) —*Martin Davidson*, Cadence

○ **Genius of Modern Music—Vol. 1** / Oct. 15, 1947-Nov. 21, 1947 / Capitol 81510

★ **Complete Blue Note Recordings** / 1947-1952 / Mosaic 101
Here's everything you ever wanted to know about pianist/composer/bandleader Thelonious Monk's Blue Note recordings. These 1947 through 1952 sessions were his first as a leader and prime mover. Replete with alternate takes, they show him to have been an iconoclast from the start, a unique jazz composer with such a special sense of accent, rhythm, and dour melody that his compositions, even when under hands other than his, always bear his distinctive stamp. With this box of four LPs, which holds a contiguous record of his earliest works, we are able to discover (or rediscover) and explore the very foundations of his canon. Eleven previously unreleased alternate takes are made available that offer insight into Monk's methodology. Most surprising of all, a previously unissued Monk tune, "Sixteen," is herewith presented in two takes (from the 5/30/52 session), and—from the same session—we get a previously unreleased standard, "I'll Follow You," never again recorded by Monk. The accompanying large booklet contains a complete Monk discography of authorized recordings and a fascinating essay by Michael Cuscuna (who produced this set for release) that takes you through the individual recording sessions one by one. High-quality pressings in rice paper sleeves only confirm the high production values evident in all aspects of this historically essential compendium of early Monk. —*Alan Bargebur,* Cadence

○ **Genius of Modern Music–Vol. 2** / Jul. 23, 1951-May 30, 1952 / Capitol 81511

Thelonious Monk Trio / Oct. 15, 1952+Dec. 18, 1952 / Prestige 010
Wonderful trio recordings. The difference between the Max Roach (d) and Art Blakey (d) cuts is quite instructive. These are some of Monk's more captivating solos from the '50s. —*Ron Wynn*

Monk / Nov. 13, 1953-May 11, 1954 / Prestige 016
These fine '50s quintet dates include particularly strong solos from tenors Sonny Rollins and Frank Foster, plus typically unusual and odd Monk piano solos. —*Ron Wynn*

★ **Thelonious Monk and Sonny Rollins** / 1953 / Original Jazz Classics 59
This date contains "The Way You Look Tonight" from the *Moving Out* session, plus titles from 11/13/53 (Friday the 13th) and 9/22/54. The latter two were pianist Thelonious Monk's dates with tenor saxophonist Sonny Rollins, Julius Watkins (frhn), Percy Heath (b) and Willie Jones (d) or Heath and Art Blakey (drums on the 9/22/54 cuts). For me, the standout here is the wonderfully effervescent handling of "The Way You Look Tonight." Rollins attacks it with a *major* spirit and plays with a euphoria rarely matched in recorded jazz. It is just one of the fine elements on the record, but one I'd alone recommend the record for, and, in fact, have many times. —*Bob Rusch,* Cadence

★ **Complete Black Lion and Vogue** / 1954-1971 / Mosaic
This release serves two important purposes. It cleans up the mess that had been made of the 1954 Paris session, which had been sloppily reissued on a variety of irresponsible labels. Tunes had been mislabeled and the session as a whole had been generally overlooked because of poor pressings and the blatant casualness of these misguided reissues. This Thelonious Monk box also offers what turned out to be the pianist's last recordings as a leader. This was a marathon session, held some 17 years after Paris in another European capital, London. The Paris tracks are all solo piano, as are roughly half those from London. Al McKibbon (b) and Art Blakey (d), on tour with Monk as members of the Giants of Jazz package, join to make it a trio at some point, but the emphasis falls throughout on Monk's piano and the fascinating process of his musical thought transmogrified into the music that was so uniquely his. There is much to enjoy and study here, the opportunity to compare the Paris material with its Blue Note and Prestige forerunners, even the opportunity to make comparisons between the Paris and London sessions. Unissued material surfaces to complete the

London picture, and detailed notes on the recordings by Brian Priestly serve to guide you through the Monkian forest. You will hear for yourself that in 1971 Thelonious Monk was still the master of his muse. —*Alan Bargebuhr,* Cadence

Plays Duke Ellington / Jul. 21+27, 1955 / Riverside 024
One genius tackles the music of another. Superb trio recordings spiced by Oscar Pettiford (b) and Kenny Clarke (d). —*Ron Wynn*

Unique Thelonious Monk / Mar. 17, 1956+Apr. 3, 1956 / Riverside 064
The trio with Oscar Pettiford (b) and Art Blakey (d). Plays standards, no originals. —*Hank Davis*

☆ **Brilliant Corners** / Dec. 17-25, 1956 / Riverside 026
A recording feat. Clark Terry (tpt), Sonny Rollins (ts), and Max Roach (d). Excellent version of the title tune. —*Hank Davis*

★ **Complete Riverside Recordings** / 1956-1960 / Riverside 022
1955-1960. Priceless Monk, 15 CDs and worth every cent. Essential. —*Michael Erlewine*

Thelonious Himself / Apr. 5-16, 1957 / Riverside 254
These are mostly solo with one cut adding Coltrane (ts) and Wilbur Ware (b). —*Ron Wynn*

○ **'Round Midnight** / Apr. 5, 1957 / Milestone 47067
'Round Midnight contains all the complete takes from the two-day session for *Mulligan Meets Monk.* There are two takes each of two tunes, and three—a full side—of "I Mean You." The three versions differ in detail but not in overall feel, as the quartet tinkers with the tempo, and Gerry Mulligan looks for unobtrusive things to do when he is not soloing. Any one of these takes could have been a master; in some ways, the originally issued take is the roughest. The Mulligan/Monk collaboration works well most of the time. The baritonist's laidback, easy swing, particularly on the first "Straight, No Chaser" is a suitable complement to Monk's subtractive philosophy: "if you can't play something that's better than playing nothing, don't play it." Only on the quick "Rhythm-a-ning" does Mulligan commit the cardinal sin of the Monk canon. In his prolix solo, he is running the changes, not playing the tune. He really digs into the melody of "'Round Midnight," included at his request. Monk on his part audibly responds to the challenge of a new tune—Mulligan's "Decidedly," based on "Undecided"—on the first full take. Side four contains raw material: Monk at the piano musing over "Round Midnight" through six fragmentary takes, through to a complete but still ruminative seventh solo take (also reissued on *Pure Monk*). The fumbling, false starts and studio chatter clearly weren't intended for release, and I'm undecided as to the ethics of releasing it all now. At any rate, one could argue that Monk thinking aloud at the keys is more interesting than some solo piano ramblings intended for waxing. But like a full side of "I Mean You," it seems aimed more at a specialty audience than at casual listeners. —*Kevin Whitehead,* Cadence

○ **Art Blakey's Jazz Messengers with Thelonious Monk** / May 14-15, 1957 / Atlantic

○ **New York with Johnny Griffin** / May 14-15, 1957 / Atlantic

☆ **Monk's Music** / Jun. 25-26, 1957 / Riverside 084
Superb septet with tenor greats John Coltrane and Coleman Hawkins. A five-star album in *Down Beat.* —*Hank Davis*

★ **Thelonious with John Coltrane** / Jun. 25-26, 1957 / Original Jazz Classics 39
Tenor saxophonist John Coltrane was present on a spring of '58 date as part of the Thelonious Monk quartet (bassist Wilbur Ware, drummer Shadow Wilson) on a session that makes up half of *Thelonious Monk with John Coltrane.* The remainder is a 6/12/57 date with Trane, Coleman Hawkins, Gigi Gryce, Ray Copeland, Ware, and Art Blakey with Monk solo piano on "Functional." The material has been scattered around; most of it was on a previous twofer. It is great music—Trane, Hawk, Blakey; Blakey, I think, was the drummer

best suited to Monk. This presents classic encounters and lasting music. —*Bob Rusch*, Cadence

Mulligan Meets Monk / Aug. 12-13, 1957 / Riverside 301
With Gerry Mulligan. What seemed like a mismatch proved superb. The Wilbur Ware-Shadow Wilson (d) rhythm section clicks as well. —*Ron Wynn*

☆ **At the Five Spot** / Aug. 7, 1958 / Milestone 47043
A landmark live date by a legendary pianist and composer. Monk was just starting to emerge as a dynamic, highly distinctive, and unorthodox player, while his compositions were getting equal acclaim both for their unusual structure and their overall brilliance. He headed a group that included at various times tenor saxophonist John Coltrane, drummer Shadow Wilson, and bassist Wilbur Ware. —*Ron Wynn*

Mysterioso / Aug. 7, 1958 / Riverside 206
Additional sessions with the Johnny Griffin (sax), Ahmed Abdul-Malik (b), Roy Haynes (d) group. —*Ron Wynn*

○ **In Person** / Feb. 28, 1959 / Milestone 47033
This Thelonious Monk session is a reissue of his Riverside "Town Hall" (February 1958) and "Black Hawk" (April 1960) albums with an additional previously unissued version of "Little Rootie Tootie" added. The dilution of the jazz group into larger ensembles usually results in very dull music. However, the strength of Monk's compositions and the ideal arrangements that he put together shed a new light on the material without either really adding or detracting anything. Even the dubious gimmick of orchestrating previously recorded sides here becomes great music as the seven horns play Monk's 1952 "Little Rootie Tootie" solo—what a glorious sound. (The 1963 Columbia big-band version contains an equally exhilarating orchestration of Monk's "Four In One" solo contained on the other half of this double album.) The only drawback to both sessions on this reissue is that while all the horn soloists play well, none of them has the strength to make the most of Monk's music in the way that, say, tenor saxophonist Sonny Rollins or soprano saxophonist Steve Lacy have. Even so, this makes for essential listening (unlike many of Monk's subsequent records) since the general standard is very high—not, however, as high as on other Monk reissues on Milestone, Prestige, and Blue Note. —*Martin Davidson*, Cadence

Five by Monk by Five / Jun. 1-2, 1959 / Riverside 362
Quintet. The music proves as intriguing as the title. Excellent trumpet solos from Thad Jones. CD has bonus cuts. —*Ron Wynn*

Alone in San Francisco / Oct. 21, 1959 / Original Jazz Classics 231
Solo piano. Exacting, distinctive renditions of such Monk classics as "Blue Monk," "Pannonica," and "Reflections." Bonus CD cuts. —*Ron Wynn*

At the Blackhawk / Apr. 29, 1960 / Riverside 305
Special guests Harold Land (ts) and Joe Gordon (tpt) make this a great sextet. Monk's playing is daring and energized. The CD version includes the complete "Epistrophy." —*Ron Wynn*

○ **Two Hours with Thelonious Monk–Vol. 1** / Apr. 18+21, 1961 / Riverside 9460

○ **Two Hours with Thelonious Monk–Vol. 2** / Apr. 18+21, 1961 / Riverside 9461

○ **April in Paris** / Apr. 18, 1961 / Milestone 47060
This was originally a Riverside limited-edition (so it is claimed), two-record set called *Two Hours with Thelonious* and made up of concert material (April 1961) from Italy and France. On this reissue, Milestone cuts it down to 82:17 with pianist Thelonious Monk and quartet (tenor saxophonist Charlie Rouse, bassist John Ore, and drummer Frankie Dunlop) by eliminating the Italian concert material. Relative to the Monk available today (1981) this is super; relative to the Monk available through reissue, it is still only a workmanlike set. Orrin Keepnews's notes are an insightful plus on this reissue, but there is a noticeable fallout of volume

during Monk's solo on "Well, You Needn't." —*Bob Rusch*, Cadence

Thelonious Monk in Italy / Apr. 21, 1961 / Original Jazz Classics 488
A good quartet date, with tremendous work from Charlie Rouse (ts) and Monk. —*Ron Wynn*

Monk's Dream / Oct. 1962-Nov. 1962 / Columbia 40786
Quartet with Charlie Rouse (ts). Monk is in superb form on his debut Columbia album. —*Hank Davis*

Criss-Cross / Feb. 26-28, 1963 / CBS 48823
This is as fine a quartet recording of Monk's early '60s work as exists in the Columbia catalog. —*Ron Wynn*

Tokyo Concerts / May 21, 1963 / Columbia 38510
Live quartet date with Charlie Rouse (ts). Excellent version of "Pannonica." —*Hank Davis*

Solo Monk / Oct. 31, 1964 / CBS 47854

○ **Live at the Jazz Workshop** / Nov. 3, 1964 / Columbia 238269
We realize Thelonious Monk's gang of four was having an off night at the Jazz Workshop through the false starts and endings, botched cues, samey tempos, and routine play of tenor saxophonist Charlie Rouse, bassist Larry Gales, and drummer Ben Riley. The combo gets warmed up by side three, following an unaccompanied piano rendition of "Memories of You" that sounds like a retired entertainer reflecting wryly on his surviving skills, and leaps into "Just You Just Me." A smooth "Hackensack," a rare, rambunctious "Bright Mississippi" (based on "Sweet Georgia Brown"), and a truly strong "Epistrophy," with Rouse alluding to Middle Eastern harmonies and wailing like a muscular sephardic with Monk in complementary stride, justify the album—but it might have been better as an edited-down single LP. —*Howard Mandell*, Down Beat

Straight, No Chaser / Nov. 14, 1966-Jan. 10, 1967 / Columbia 9451
Charlie Rouse (ts) and Monk's magic are the highlights of this 1966 set. —*Ron Wynn*

★ **Underground** / Dec. 14, 1967-Feb. 14, 1968 / Columbia 40785
An excellent latter-period Monk group. "Green Chimneys" is a prime cut. Charlie Rouse is on tenor sax. —*Michael G. Nastos*

☆ **London Collection–Vol. 1, The** / Nov. 15, 1971 / Black Lion 760101
Stride, boogie, bebop—all of these styles were encapsulated and embodied into Thelonious Monk's piano individualism. This 1971 London recording is a delightful collection of his singularity. There are extended incursions into Monkland as well as introspective, brief commentaries on other vistas of his original compositions ("Trinkle Tinkle," "Crepuscle with Nellie," "Little Rootie Tootie," and "Jackieing"). The blues ("Blue Sphere") sound like James P. Johnson in spots. The ballads are some of Monk's finest later ruminations, especially the seven-minute previously unreleased "Lover Man." This is a well-recorded and reproduced CD. —*Rhodes Spedale*, Jazz Times

And the Jazz Giants / Fantasy 60018
Interesting dialogs between Monk and various greats among saxmen: John Coltrane, Sonny Rollins, and Coleman Hawkins. —*Ron Wynn*

Standards / Columbia 45148
A sparkling solo and good quartet performances culled from Columbia dates. —*Ron Wynn*

J.R. MONTEROSE (Frank Anthony (Jr) Monterose)

b. 1927, d. 1993
Saxophone / Bop, hard bop, postbop
One of the more fluid, swinging, but lightly regarded bebop saxophonists, J.R. Monterose seldom made great solos, but hardly ever played poor ones. He crafted efficient, solid statements that displayed his substantial skills without being

flashy or showy. Monterose played in territory bands in the Midwest during the '40s, then moved to New York. He worked with Buddy Rich and Claude Thornhill in the early and mid-'50s, then recorded in bands led by Teddy Charles, Jon Eardley, Ralph Sharon, and Eddie Bert in 1955. Monterose joined Charles Mingus's Jazz Workshop in 1956 and Kenny Dorham's Jazz Prophets. He began recording as a leader that same year, and also did sessions with Sharon and George Wallington in the '50s, Rene Thomas in the '60s, and Rein De Graaff in the '70s. Monterose recorded for labels such as Jaro, Uptown, and Xanadu. Monterose died in 1993, and retrospectives were cranked out immediately by publications that ignored him through much of his recent career. He has a few reissues available on CD. —*Ron Wynn*

○ **J.R. Monterose** / Oct. 21, 1956 / Blue Note 1536

★ **Message, The** / Nov. 24, 1959 / Jaro 5004

○ **Straight Ahead / i.** Nov. 24, 1959 / Xanadu 126
Nobody's going to have to convince J.R. Monterose (ts) fans about this release. Even though the music is magnificent, it wouldn't matter to Monterose fanatics. The added treat is the liner notes that fill us in on where Monterose had been (Europe) and what he was into (playing sax and guitar). This record is a reissue of the phantom Jaro disc, *The Message*, recorded on November 24, 1959. "Straight Ahead" is just that: driving, staccato, with a brilliant stop-time exchange with Pete LaRoca's drums. "Violets" and "I Remember Clifford" are warm ballads that reflect the man (Monterose) whose aquaintance I made on a few occasions between 1954-1963: serious, almost withdrawn, and a bit sad. "Chafic" is a waltz, with Monterose hugging close to the inside of the melody and rhythm. "Greenstreet Scene" is a riffing blues that includes a nice bowed Jimmy Garrison bass solo and sharp trading between LaRoca and Monterose. "You Know That" is an "Aregin"-like piece; "Short Bridges" also employs Sonny Rollins-like figures and strong playing. Throughout this set Monterose plays with great ease and authority. Certainly there is never a played-out quality in the improvised work, which comes with an ease of breath, nor does the improvising become static. It is always inventive and warm. —*Bob Rusch*, Cadence

In Action with the Joe Abodeely Trio / Nov. 1964 / Bainbridge 503
Good, nicely played mid '60s cool and mainstream session with underrated saxophonist J.R. Monterose running through standards, blues, and originals backed by low-key trio with pianist Joe Abodeely and friends assisting. Monterose plays everything so fluidly and smoothly it seems he's hardly expending energy, but his solos and phrases are often impressive. —*Ron Wynn*

○ **A Little Pleasure** / Apr. 6-7, 1981 / Uptown 2706
This is intimate and somewhat stimulating quiet clublike music. Pianist Tommy Flanagan's fluency as he spreads improvised melodic lines effortlessly over the bar lines is a wonder to hear as are his lush chordal voicings. Tenor and soprano saxophonist J.R. Monterose is more noteworthy for the sincere feeling inherent in his playing than for technical skills. Together they are an interesting pair, playing off one another with sensitivity and grace. —*Milo Fine*, Cadence

MONTGOMERY BROTHERS

b. 1930
Postbop, soul-jazz
Buddy and Monk Montgomery, along with their more celebrated brother, Wes, rival the Heath family as jazz's most prolific family act. Pianist/vibraphonist Buddy Montgomery (b. 1930), bassist Monk (1921-1982) and guitarist Wes (see separate entry) played together in two well-known, and other lesser-known groups. Monk was the first jazz musician to specialize on and record with the electric bass, which began playing in the early '50s when he was on tour with Lionel Hampton's big band. Buddy is a soulful, underrated pianist and vibist who's effective in bebop, hard bop, blues, or soul-jazz situations. The three brothers worked together

in the Montgomery-Johnson quintet with Alonzo Johnson and Robert Johnson in the mid-'50s, and then as the Mastersounds from 1957 to 1960, and the Montgomery Brothers in 1960 and 1961. Monk returned to acoustic bass, but then went back to electric in the mid-'60s playing with Cal Tjader. He settled in Las Vegas in 1970, and played with Red Norvo until 1972. He worked as a disc jockey and started the Las Vegas Jazz Society, while also visiting South Africa as the leader of an African-American jazz group in the mid-'70s.

Buddy Montgomery played piano in a group with Slide Hampton during the early '50s, then worked with Roy Johnson in a quartet in 1954, prior to the formation of the Montgomery-Johnson quintet. After the other groups with his brothers disbanded, Buddy divided his time on the two instruments until 1969, then chose piano full time. Buddy remained in Milwaukee, playing with area soul-jazz and bebop bands and doing solo dates. He moved to Oakland in the early '80s, playing in the Bay Area and touring with vocalist Marlena Shaw. He organized the first Oakland Festival in 1987, bringing acts such as Kenny Burrell, Ron Carter, Junior Cook, and Hampton to Oakland. He also began recording for Landmark in the '80s, then was tabbed as a contributor to Concord's prestigious solo piano series in 1992. His recordings were the 15th volume in the line. Buddy Montgomery has a few sessions available as a leader, and both brothers can be heard on CD reissues featuring the Mastersounds and Montgomery Brothers. —*Ron Wynn*

★ **Groove Yard** / Jan. 3, 1961 / Riverside 9362
Indianapolis brothers in their heyday together. Essential listening. —*Michael G. Nastos*

Montgomery Brothers in Canada, The / Dec. 1961 / Fantasy 8066

WES MONTGOMERY (John Leslie Montgomery)

b. Mar. 6, 1925, Indianapolis, IN, **d.** Jun. 15, 1968, Indianapolis, IN
Guitar / Hard bop, instrumental pop
A story that's made the rounds in jazz circles is that in the last part of his life, Wes Montgomery refused to listen to or to let his friends hear his albums when they visited his home because he was ashamed of the music. Whether that's true or not, the creative sacrifices Wes Montgomery made for commercial success almost rival those made by Nat "King" Cole. But when Cole stopped playing piano almost completely, he attained plaudits singing with gusto and quality; Montgomery had to downshift his playing to a level that didn't begin to approximate his brilliance. He'd achieved greatness playing with his thumb rather than with a pick. His sound was warm, carefully controlled, melodic, and accessible with fluid voicings and easy, relaxed progressions. He mastered the parallel-octave style, giving his solos a thick edge and a bluesy underpinning. Prior to the hit releases, Montgomery became the single most influential modern guitarist of the '60s.

Montgomery's brothers were musicians, and he began teaching himself the guitar at age 15 and was soon playing in local Indianapolis bands. He toured and recorded with Lionel Hampton from 1948 until early 1950, playing brief solos on live broadcasts. Montgomery also recorded with Gene Morris and Sonny Parker, one of Hampton's vocalists. Montgomery returned to Indianapolis later in the '50s, then joined the Montgomery-Johnson Quintet in 1955. He played his first extended solos working in his brothers' bands. Montgomery organized his own trio in 1959, featuring organ and drums, and recorded for Riverside. That began a series of Montgomery's finest recordings. He worked with Tommy Flanagan, Hank Jones, Ron Carter, Tootie Heath, and Louis Hayes, and began to be a popular winner of *Down Beat* and *Playboy* polls. Among his string of fine LPs, arguably the finest was *West Coast Blues*, which was done under the leadership of tenor saxophonist Harold Land for Jazzland. Montgomery moved to San Francisco in 1960, where he continued working with his brothers, and also appeared with John Coltrane in 1961 and 1962. He returned to Indianapolis in 1962, and resumed touring in 1963 with a trio.

Montgomery started recording for Verve in 1964, and the label developed Creed Taylor's formula that featured Don Sebesky's string-laden arrangements and large, faceless jazz bands. These albums turned Montgomery into a celebrity, and he won a Grammy for his rendition of "Goin' Out of My Head" in 1965. The 1967 album, *A Day in the Life,* on A&M was the year's best-selling jazz release. Montgomery appeared on television with A&M founder and trumpeter Herb Alpert. He maintained a creative balance by doing live dates with small groups, among them the Wynton Kelly trio and a quintet with his brothers. But in the midst of this popularity and fame, Wes Montgomery suffered a heart attack in 1968 and died at age 43. Fantasy recently issued a huge boxed set containing Montgomery's complete Riverside Recordings, which is, without a doubt, the real recorded measure of his skills. A host of his recordings are available on CD. —*Ron Wynn and David Nelson McCarthy*

○ **Beginnings** / Apr. 18-22, 1958 / Blue Note 531
This Wes Montgomery grouping is a hodgepodge of early groups, in a period when he was at his best. Gifted at blues and bop, his reputation rests on such works as "Montgomeryland Funk." Certainly his rhythmic vigor was distinctive in a period of less-forceful guitarists. His mastery of construction in those days was his most noted feature: he built his forms in a classic way, with a deceptively relaxed versatility and an attractive tone. Harold Land appears on seven of these tracks to make the point: the tenorist lacked many of Montgomery's virtues, yet here he is joyously articulate, playing lovely arpeggios, the best music on the records. —*John Litweiler,* Down Beat

Far Wes / Apr. 18, 1958-Oct. 6, 1959 / Pacific Jazz 94475
1958 and 1959. With Harold Land (ts) and the Montgomery Brothers. —*Michael G. Nastos*

★ **Complete Riverside Recordings [Box Set], The** / Oct. 5, 1959-Nov. 27, 1963 / Fantasy 4408

Wes Montgomery Trio / Oct. 5-6, 1959 / Riverside 034

○ **Yesterdays** / Oct. 5-6, 1959 / Milestone 47057
Compilation from *Wes Montgomery Trio* (six cuts), *Boss Guitar* (five cuts), *Portrait of Wes* (three cuts), and four cuts previously unissued. —*Michael Erlewine*

Portrait of Wes / Oct. 10, 1959-Oct. 10, 1963 / Riverside 144

○ **Pretty Blue** / 1959-1963 / Milestone 47030
1959-1963. A double album that includes the complete *Fusion* album, plus cuts from *Wes Montgomery Trio* (3), *Boss Guitar* (2), *Portrait of Wes* (3), and *Guitar on the Go* (2). —*Michael Erlewine*

★ **Incredible Jazz Guitar of Wes Montgomery** / Jan. 26+28, 1960 / Riverside 036
Considered by many to be his best album. "West Coast Blues" is considered a classic jazz guitar piece. This album resulted in Montgomery winning the 1960 *Down Beat* Critic's New Star award. Recorded in New York City. —*Michael Erlewine*

○ **Groove Brothers** / Oct. 11, 1960-Dec. 1961 / Milestone 47051
A compilation from *The Montgomery Brothers* (three cuts), *The Montgomery Brothers in Canada* (four cuts), and *Groove Yard* (eight cuts—whole album). —*Michael Erlewine*

Movin' Along / Oct. 11, 1960 / Riverside 089
This is especially noteworthy for the presence of James Clay (ts). Solid Montgomery guitar. —*Ron Wynn*

Alternative Wes Montgomery / 1960-1963 / Milestone 47065
1960-1963. This is a nice two-record set of early '60s Montgomery (14 previously unissued tracks) with a host of great players including Wynton Kelly (p), Paul Chambers (b), Milt Jackson (vib), and Johnny Griffin (ts). —*Ron Wynn*

So Much Guitar / Aug. 4, 1961 / Riverside 233

Includes an unaccompanied guitar solo on "While We're Young" in a chordal style, and the down-home "One for My Baby." —*Michael Erlewine*

Full House / Jun. 25, 1962 / Riverside 106
Ranks with *Incredible Jazz Guitar of Wes Montgomery* as one of Montgomery's best albums. —*Michael Erlewine*

Movin' / Jun. 25, 1962 / Milestone 47040
This is a two-LP set containing the Montgomery albums *Movin' Along* and *Full House.* —*Michael Erlewine*

★ **Boss Guitar** / Apr. 27, 1963 / Riverside 261
Tart, stinging Montgomery guitar and good support from Jimmy Cobb on drums. —*Ron Wynn*

Guitar on the Go / Oct. 10, 1963+Nov. 27, 1963 / Riverside 489
One of his last two albums on the Riverside label (the other being *A Portrait of Wes*) that were released without the artist's approval. —*Michael Erlewine*

Plays the Blues / Nov. 11, 1964-Sep. 28, 1966 / PolyGram 835318
A grab-bag set from past efforts. It's good for its mix of sessions pitting Montgomery with Jimmy Smith (org) but has somewhat of a slapdash quality. —*Ron Wynn*

Bumpin' / May 1965 / Verve 821985
It's light on the compositions, but plenty of substance in Montgomery's lines. —*Ron Wynn*

○ **Small Group Recordings** / Jun. 1965-Sep. 22, 1965 / Verve 833555
1965-1966. A compilation of cuts from *Smokin' at the Half Note, Further Adventures of Jimmy [Smith] and Wes,* and *Willow Weep for Me* (cuts released in original form, without orchestration). —*Michael Erlewine*

★ **Smokin' at the Half Note** / Jun. 1965-Sep. 22, 1965 / Verve 829578

Goin' Out of My Head / Dec. 7-22, 1965 / Verve 825676
This is standard mid '60s pop fare. —*Ron Wynn*
Creed Taylor-produced album and Grammy Award winner that marked the beginning of Montgomery's pop success. Large band with arrangements by Oliver Nelson. —*Michael Erlewine.*

Tequila / Mar. 17, 1966-May 18, 1966 / Verve 831671
Produced by Creed Taylor. With Ron Carter (b), Grady Tate (d), Ray Baretto (conga) and strings. The title track has real jazz content. —*Michael Erlewine*

Down Here on the Ground / Jan. 20, 1967-Jan. 26, 1968 / A&M 0802

Day in the Life, A / Jun. 6-26, 1967 / A&M 0816
One of Montgomery's biggest pop-hit albums. His playing is excellent. It's the inspiration behind similar George Benson efforts. Gold album. —*Ron Wynn*

Road Song / May 7-10, 1968 / A&M 0822
Creed Taylor produced. Although it's pop-oriented, it still offers plenty of fine Montgomery. —*Ron Wynn*

TETE MONTOLIU (Vincente Montoliu)

b. Mar. 28, 1933, Barcelona, Spain
Piano / Bop, world fusion
One of the fastest and most compelling of all European pianists, Montoliu has become an international star without resettling permanently in America. Blind since birth, Montoliu became interested in jazz by hearing Duke Ellington records. A native of Catalonia, He accompanied many visiting American musicians, recording with Lionel Hampton, Rahsaan Roland Kirk, and Anthony Braxton, among others, in the '50s, '60s, and '70s. He's made many outstanding releases on European and independent labels, with his best work coming in either solo or trio settings. —*Ron Wynn*

○ **That's All** / i. Sep. 1971 / Steeple Chase 1199
Pianist Tete Montoliu is a brilliant technician at the keyboard, yet he never overpowers or bores, probably due to his tone and the uniqueness of his rhythmic and harmonic

ideas, which, while remaining within the mainstream, are nevertheless quite personal. He ranges from the mainly right-handed, horn-influenced bop idiom (Bud Powell) to a more two-handed approach (coming out of Art Tatum or Oscar Peterson), but with his own unique voicings, updating these two harmonically with slight touches of McCoy Tyner and Bill Evans. The program consists of very well known pieces and he makes them all come alive and maintains interest. —*Peter Leitch*, Cadence

○ **Lush Life** / **i.** Sep. 1971 / Steeple Chase 1216

○ **Tete!** / May 28, 1974 / Inner City 2029
On this trio disc (bassist Niels-Henning Ørsted-Pedersen and drummer Albert Heath), Tete Montoliu demonstrates a tradition in stride piano that is almost lost in the contemporary jazz scene. The sound here owes more to a slightly later school that includes Bud Powell, Oscar Peterson, and Wynton Kelly, yet it possesses a more modern sense of tonality. Heath and Ørsted-Pedersen help propel this record to a status somewhat above a tribute to any one album. The album contains spirited versions of John Coltrane's "Giant Steps," Tadd Dameron's "Hot House," and the standard "Body and Soul." —*David Less*, Down Beat

Catalonian Nights–Vol. 1 / **i.** May 1980 / Timeless 1148

Catalonian Nights–Vol. 2 / **i.** May 1980 / Steeple Chase 1241

★ **Lunch in L.A.** / Oct. 22, 1980 / Contemporary 14004
Fine two-piano set from the early '80s, with the flamboyant Spanish pianist Tete Montoliu dueting with fellow pianist Chick Corea. Their exchanges, sometimes combative, sometimes complementary and always engaging and gripping, are brilliant. —*Ron Wynn*

○ **Music I Like to Play–Vol. 1, The** / Dec. 1986 / Soul Note 121180
The first in a four-part series that features pianist Tete Montliu doing his favorite material, much of it standards, but also bop and mainstream pieces, ballads, and an occasional blues. —*Ron Wynn*

○ **Music I Like to Play–Vol. 2, The** / **i.** Dec. 1986 / Soul Note 1200

JACK MONTROSE

b. Dec. 30, 1928, Detroit, MI
Saxophone / Cool
A talented West Coast-style arranger in the 1950s and a fine tenor soloist, Jack Montrose displayed a flowing, concise style and a solid, big sound, but found opportunities limited during the '60s. He was a prototype West Coast/cool saxophonist in a period when audience demand was perceived as limited for that style, and when recording company interest was really light. Montrose, a talented alto and tenor saxophonist and clarinetist, ended up working in Los Angeles strip joints and doing rock sessions. He moved to Nevada in the mid-'60s and backed vocalists and show business types at casinos. Montrose emerged from the abyss in the mid-'80s, working with a group that included Pete Jolly. He's continued in his second stint as an active jazz musician into the '90s, playing the same way that he did in the '60s. Montrose has a couple of dates available on CD. —*Ron Wynn and Michael G. Nastos*

★ **With Bob Gordon** / Mar. 7, 1956 / Atlantic 1223

JAMES MOODY

b. Mar. 26, 1925, Savannah, GA
Alto and tenor saxophone, flute / Bop
The longtime playing partner of Dizzy Gillespie, James Moody was one of the first saxophonists to play bebop extensively on tenor. An extremely versatile stylist, Moody has played superb blues and bebop, effective R&B-influenced material and soul-jazz, and first-rate ballads. He's an accomplished player on alto as well as tenor, and was also one of the earliest jazz musicians to become a tremendous flutist. Moody began playing alto at age 16, then switched to tenor.

He played in a military band while in the air force, and had one engagement with Dizzy Gillespie's orchestra. After his discharge, Moody joined Gillespie, playing tenor until leaving in 1948. He traveled to Europe, touring France, Scandinavia, and Sweden, and playing alto. Moody made his recording debut as a leader for Blue Note in 1948, leading an octet that included Cecil Payne, Art Blakey, and Chano Pozo. He recorded "I'm in the Mood for Love" in 1949, and it became a hit three years later, thanks to Eddie Jefferson's lyrics and King Pleasure's vocals. During the '50s, Moody led a septet that played R&B-tinged material, made several excellent dates for Argo, and, playing mainly flute, led another group. During the '60s, he played in a three-tenor band with Sonny Stitt and Gene Ammons. Moody cut many '50s albums for Prestige and Argo, and continued recording for Prestige in the '60s, as well for DJM. He rejoined Gillespie from 1963 to 1968, then worked in Las Vegas during the late '70s. There were '70s sessions on MPS/Pausa, Muse, and Vanguard. Moody continued visiting Europe and heading bands, and played occasional reunions with Gillespie. They toured in 1980. Moody resurfaced in the late '80s recording for RCA/Novus, and has made some fine albums for that label. His early Blue Note and some '50s Prestige sets have been reissued on CD, as have some '70s Muse releases. Currently, his RCA/Novus dates, including *Honey* from '91, are available. —*Ron Wynn*

○ **New Sounds** / **i.** 1948 / Blue Note 84436

○ **Beginning and End of Bop, The** / Oct. 19, 1948 / Blue Note 6503
This James Moody recording basically presents two different groups. The first five selections on side one find Moody (ts) with Max Roach (d), Kenny Dorham (tpt), Al Haig (p), and Tommy Potter (b) (Moody is absent on "Ham and Haig"). While the recording quality leaves something to be desired, the music itself is hot and often inspired. The selections on side two were recorded in Switzerland and played by Moody with a group of musicians who were in the army at that time. (The notes state that "Trummie" Young was not "Trummy" Young, and that Red Allen was in actuality Marshall Allen best known as a member of the various Sun Ra "Arkestras.") The music here in no way matches the playing from side one, but Moody is quite good. —*Carl Brauer*, Cadence

○ **Moodsville** / May 21, 1951-Jan. 8, 1954 / EmArcy 26040

James Moody's Moods / Sep. 1954-Dec. 1955 / Prestige 188
An excellent reissue of mid-'50s sessions, with some strong Moody solos. —*Ron Wynn*

Wail, Moody, Wail / Dec. 12, 1955 / Riverside 1791
A tremendous late '50s workout, featuring fine blues and expressive Moody. —*Ron Wynn*

★ **Moody's Mood for Love** / Dec. 14, 1956 / Argo
A strong version of "Moody's Mood for Love," with a vocal by the late Eddie Jefferson. —*Ron Wynn*

○ **Great Day** / Jun. 17-18, 1963 / Chess 91522
Some good, sometimes excellent sax and flute work from the always reliable James Moody. This was a period in which he was dabbling sometimes in soul-jazz, other times hard bop, but here he mostly plays mainstream, straightahead originals, standards, and ballads. —*Ron Wynn*

★ **Don't Look Away Now** / Feb. 14, 1969 / Prestige

Too Heavy for Words / Aug. 12, 1971 / PA/USA

★ **Everything You've Always Wanted to Know About Sax** / **i.** Mar. 1972 / Cadet 60010
Twofer date with Eddie Jefferson (v) on some tracks. Also with Tom McIntosh (tb), Howard McGhee (tpt), Hank Jones (p), and Kiane Zawadi (euph/tb). —*Michael G. Nastos*

○ **Jazz Legacy** / **i.** 1980 / Inner City 7020

Moving Forward / Nov. 1987 / Novus 3026
Excellent Kenny Barron piano. It's decent major-label material, with a good menu of standards. —*Ron Wynn*

○ **Sweet and Lovely** / Mar. 1989 / Novus 3063

Saxophone veteran James Moody stages impromptu re-union with his longtime friend and one-time leader Dizzy Gillespie on this '89 session. Their interaction hasn't been dulled by their time apart; they still anticipate each other and mesh effectively. Moody's own solos are mellow, well constructed, and superbly played. The backing band wisely defers to the giants, though keyboardist Marc Cohen has a few good passages. —*Ron Wynn*

○ **Honey** / Oct. 1990 / Jive/Novus 3111
The selections on this recent album are erratic, but he and veteran Kenny Barron (p) uphold things. It is certainly not a classic but is worth having. —*Ron Wynn*

JEMEEL MOONDOC

b. 1951
Alto and tenor saxophone / Modern creative
Though he hails from Chicago and shares their same in-spired love of traditional and progressive sounds, alto saxo-phonist Jemeel Moondoc never joined forces with the Association for the Advancement of Creative Musicians (AACM) crew. Instead, he studied with Ran Blake in Boston, played in the James Tatum Blues band, and followed Cecil Taylor to Wisconsin University and to Antioch, where he played in Taylor's student orchestras. His ability to move from moving, down-home blues to outrageous, explosive free solos has made Moondoc's appearances on sessions quite memorable. He moved to New York in the early '70s, where he worked with William Parker and Roy Campbell. Moondoc formed the Ensemble Munta, a band he main-tained for over a decade. He toured Poland and recorded for the Polijazz label in 1981, then formed the 15-piece Jus Grew Orchestra in 1984. They were the resident band at the Neither/Nor club on New York's Lower East side. Moondoc also recorded with Bern Nix, Parker, and Dennis Charles. He's recorded for Soul Note and Cadence Jazz, among others. Moondoc has some sessions available on CD. —*Ron Wynn*

★ **Nostalgia in Times Square** / Soul Note 1141
Cut off from the social and music milieu of the New York club scene, Jemeel Moondoc's music rings with a raw vital-ity. As this recording reveals, Moondoc is still a technically primitive altoist, but it is this very quality that gives his ver-sion of "Nostaglia in Times Square" its charm. With Bern Nix on guitar, Moondoc's playing is very much like his odd-ball appearance (he resembles a cross between Humpty Dumpty, Buddha, and a Black Mongolian king)—weird, yet dignified. William Parker is simply a great bassist who re-stores the fine art of "walking" to its grandeur, providing a history lesson on "Nostalgia." This version of "Nostalgia" never betrays the lyrical beginnings of the theme; Moondoc is at once playful and astringent. The straight interpretation in the first part changes to a twisted ending. The ballad "Flora" finds Moondoc on soprano and he thankfully avoids the Eastern nasal sound most saxophonists bring to this axe. "Flora" drips with Sidney Bechet sweetness by the sopra-noist and a quick-witted Rahn Burton solo (p) that never loses its momentum. "In Walked Monk" captures the hat and beard quality of Thelonious Monk, while "Dance of the Clowns" is a march anthem where the merits of this group ring out without question. Moondoc, the primitive altoist, is complemented by a composer who is a great storyteller, much like the great Black novelist Ishmael Reed. Both men are idiosyncratic, using a language that has a vibrant street pulse and a dynamic emotional sweep. —*Ludwig Van Trikt,* Cadence

BREW MOORE (Milton Aubrey (Jr) Moore)

b. Mar. 26, 1924, Indianola, MS, **d.** Aug. 19, 1973, Copenhagen, Denmark
Tenor saxophone / Bop, postbop
A stalwart swing stylist, Brew Moore found the going rough for a few years in the '40s as styles were changing and he was caught in the transition. He was the archetype surging, swing era tenor soloist, and was deemed old fashioned. Moore finally found a role in Claude Thornhill's 1948 and 1949 band, as well as in Afro-Latin bands. He played clarinet and trombone from the age of 12, then changed to tenor sax in high school. Moore was unable to find much work in the South during the '40s due to his style. After moving to New York and working with Thornhill, Moore was a soloist with Machito and played in Kai Winding's band. He also recorded with Stan Getz's Five Brothers, in a kind of ahead-of-their-time Supersax, only they were five tenor saxophonists who displayed smooth tones and their allegiance to Lester Young rather than Charlie Parker. Moore moved to San Francisco in the mid-'50s, and worked and played with Cal Tjader. He traveled to Paris in 1961 to play with Kenny Clarke, then set-tled in Copenhagen. Moore returned to America periodically in the mid- and late '60s and early '70s. He recorded for Savoy, Black Lion, Fantasy, Jazz Mark, and Sonet, among others. Currently, Moore has a few sessions available on CD. —*Ron Wynn and Michael G. Nastos*

○ **Brothers and Other Mothers–Vol. 2** / May 21, 1949 / Savoy 2236
This Savoy collection of Lester Young apostles should please any listener with a preference for the semi-sheer spindrift sound of early Young. Alan Eager and Brew Moore have a lovely rolling attack that catches the subtle slopes and rises of the Young dialect well. They glide from bar to bar like a couple of deluxe baby buggies, occasionally hitting a note or phrase with a little extra weight or chewing it for a bar or two. Although they add little except for a certain period fla-vor of bop to the original substance of the Young testament, they are nice to hear, like a slightly out-of-register reflection from a pond of water. Side one offers two takes of each of four titles by a Brew Moore group; side two, the same by an Allen Eager contingent. In each group the tenor is the main focus, although baritone saxophonist Gerry Mulligan is in ample evidence in the Moore unit, both as soloist and as bot-tom rung of the ensembles, which are thick but rather dry and even drab at times. Eager swings with gentle decisive-ness but Doug Mettome's trumpet is standarized bebop. Eager continues on side three in league with trombonist Kai Winding. Drummer Shelly Manne lends extra power to Eager's lines. By the time the Phil Urso records were made in the mid-'50s, the direct link to Young was weakening. Tenor saxophonist Urso seems to have come to Young through Zoot Sims. His quartet sides are routine. Somewhat more lively are the four final tracks with valve trombonist Bob Brookmeyer, pianist Horace Silver, and drummer Kenny Clarke. Thus a nice album ends on a solid note. — *John McDonough,* Down Beat

★ **Brew Moore Quintet** / Feb. 1955-Feb. 1956 / Original Jazz Classics 100
Unsung tenor saxophonist with pianist and composer John Marabuto. A good bet. —*Michael G. Nastos*

Brew Moore / Nov. 1957-1958 / Fantasy 049
A good late '50s hard-blowing session from an underrated saxophonist. —*Ron Wynn*

○ **If I Had You** / i. Apr. 1965 / Steeple Chase 6016

GLEN MOORE (Glen R. Moore)

b. Oct. 28, 1941, Portland, OR
Bass / World fusion, new age, modern creative
Glen Moore is another player whose normal approach and style aren't always jazz-oriented, but whose influences and experiences include several jazz dates. Glen Moore can play with authority in a straight jazz setting, but is better known for his complimentary/interactive role in groups such as the Paul Winter Consort and Oregon. The musical mix of these groups includes as much, if not more, ethnic, folk, and clas-sical strains as jazz. Moore began on piano, then started on bass at age 13. He was a professional at age 14, and studied in Copenhagen before moving to New York. Moore played with Ted Curson, Jake Hanna, and Zoot Sims, recorded with Nick Brignola in 1967, and played periodically with Paul Bley's Synthesizer Show in the late '60s and early '70s. Moore joined the Paul Winter Consort in 1970, and co-

founded Oregon with Ralph Towner, Collin Walcott, and Paul McCandless a year later. Besides his work with Oregon, Moore recorded with Tim Hardin and Cyrus in the early '70s. He did sessions with Annette Peacock, Larry Coryell, and Towner in the '70s, and with Zbigniew Seifert in the '80s. Moore recorded with several other bassists on the Enja session *Bass Is* in 1970, and did a solo date for Elektra in 1979. *Bass Is* is available on CD. —*Ron Wynn*

○ **Mokave–Vol. 1** / Audioquest 1006

MICHAEL MOORE (Michael Watson Moore)

b. May 16, 1945, Glen Este, OH
Bass / Swing
Though he's a musical arch-conservative, Michael Moore is an impressive, capable bassist noted for his restraint and support in small group settings. He has few peers for tasteful, lyrical playing, and has constantly drawn raves for his work in New York clubs. Moore began playing bass at age 15, and worked with his guitarist father in Cincinnati clubs. He studied at the Cincinnati College Conservatory and played at the local Playboy club with Cal Collins and Woody Evans. Moore toured Africa and Eastern Europe on a State Department-sponsored junket with Woody Herman's band in 1966, and recorded with Herman in New York and with Dusko Goykovich in Belgrade. Moore played with Marian McPartland, Freddie Hubbard, Jim Hall, and Benny Goodman in the '70s, and with quartets led by the duos of Ruby Braff and George Barnes, and Chet Baker and Lee Konitz. Moore teamed with Gene Bertoncini in the late '70s, and continued their association through the '80s into the '90s. He also recorded with Jake Hanna, Warren Vache, Herb Ellis, and Zoot Sims in the '70s, and Kenny Barron, Michael Urbaniak, and Sims in the '80s. Moore and Bertoncini have recorded for OmniSound, Stash, and Chiaroscuro. They have a few sessions available on CD. —*Ron Wynn*

RALPH MOORE

b. Dec. 24, 1956
Tenor saxophone / Neo-bop
A solid, sometimes exceptional tenor saxophonist, Ralph Moore hasn't gotten the headlines given to some other contemporary players, and isn't quite "young lion" age. But his solos have a jagged, striking character and are attractive without lacking either substance or strength. He's solid on bebop and hard bop, but can also play delightful ballads, fine blues, and masterful standards. In 1972, Moore emigrated to America from England to join his father. He attended Berklee in 1975, and became one of the school's finest pupils. Moore moved to New York in 1981, and worked with Horace Silver, Roy Haynes, Dizzy Gillespie, Freddie Hubbard, Jimmy Knepper, J.J. Johnson, Bobby Hutcherson, and Kenny Barron. Moore's debut album in 1985, which included Kevin Eubanks and Benny Green, won him substantial respect and exposure. Moore has continued recording into the '90s, and has done several albums for the Landmark label. He's another player still developing who's expected to be a standard bearer in the next century. Unfortunately, at present only two of Moore's recordings are available on CD. —*Ron Wynn*

Round Trip / Dec. 1985 / Reservoir 104
First date from British tenor saxophonist. Some great playing here, in the mainstream bag with Brian Lynch (tpt). —*Michael G. Nastos*

Images / i. 1988 / Landmark 1520
This is a well-done 1988 set with Terence Blanchard (tpt) and Benny Green (tb). —*Ron Wynn*

★ **Furthermore** / Mar. 3-5, 1990 / Landmark 1526
One of the best among the Young Lion tenor saxophonists makes an aggressive, explosive statement. —*Ron Wynn*

AIRTO MOREIRA (Airto Guimorva Moreira)

b. Aug. 5, 1941, Itaiopolis, Brazil
Percussion, vocals / Latin jazz, early jazz-rock, world fusion

Brazil's most famous percussionist, Airto Moreira became a jazz superstar during the '70s, and has remained a prominent session contributor into the '90s. He introduced instruments such as the cuica and berimbau to jazz audiences, and when he toured with Miles Davis, his array of odd-looking instruments were often as discussed as the band's music. Moreira provided a wealth of colors, tones, sounds, and rhythmic embellishments for Davis's band and for other bands. He's best known for his percussion arsenal, but also plays conventional trap drums, tambourine, and bongos effectively. Moreira began playing tambourine and singing as a child, and was featured on Brazilian radio at age six. He studied piano and guitar in the late '40s, then led a quartet in the mid-'60s that also included Hermeto Pascoal. Moreira moved to Los Angeles with his wife, Flora Purim, in the late '60s. The couple relocated to New York in 1970. He joined Miles Davis, and was featured on several of his famous jazz-rock recordings. He also played on Weather Report's debut album, and was Return to Forever's first percussionist. Later, he played in sessions with Lee Morgan, Stan Getz, Cannonball Adderley, Gato Barbieri, Al Di Meola, and others. Moreira began heading his own bands in the mid-'70s, which usually featured Purim, as well as Stanley Clarke, George Duke, Keith Jarrett, and others. He recorded for CTI, Salvation, and Accord in the '70s, and for Venture/Caroline in the '80s. His most recent session was recorded for Rykodisc. Airto's solo releases have been uneven affairs, but his performances on other sessions are uniformly impressive. He has a few dates available on CD. —*Ron Wynn*

○ **Seeds to the Ground** / i. 1970 / Buddah 5085

★ **Free** / Apr. 1972-May 1972 / Columbia 40927
Includes first version of "Return To Forever." With Chick Corea (k), Keith Jarrett (p), Stanley Clarke (b), and Joe Farrell (ts). A great album. —*Michael G. Nastos*

JOE MORELLO (Joseph A. Morello)

b. Jul. 17, 1928, Springfield, MA
Drums, composer, arranger, bandleader / Cool
The qualities sensitive, clear, and disciplined are always associated with drummer Joe Morello, best known for his lengthy tenure with Dave Brubeck. Morello wouldn't impress many people in a cutting contest, but for years he was outstanding playing Brubeck's unorthodox, seemingly arhythmic compositions and showing they could swing despite their structure. Morello studied violin in his childhood, then changed to drums in high school. He played as a teen with Phil Woods and Sal Salvador. After moving to New York in 1952, Morello worked with Johnny Smith and Stan Kenton, and recorded and played with Gil Melle. He played in Marian McPartland's trio in the mid-'50s, and also recorded with Tal Farlow, John Mehegan, Jimmy Raney, Jackie Cain and Roy Kral, Woods, and Salvador. He joined Brubeck in 1956, and remained with the group until 1967. He became an instructor for the Ludwig drum company, and made international tours for them. Morello periodically plays, usually doing reunions with Brubeck or McPartland. He recorded with Salvador again in the late '70s, and has also led his own group for club dates in New York. Morello's done private tutoring. One of his star pupils was Danny Gottlieb. Morello can be heard on many Brubeck or McPartland CD reissues. —*Ron Wynn and Michael G. Nastos*

★ **Joe Morello Sextet** / Jan. 3, 1956 / Intro 608

○ **Joe Morello** / i. 1961 / Bluebird 9784
In 1961, Joe Morello, drummer with the Dave Brubeck quartet for the past six years (with six more years to go), received an opportunity to lead his own album. Originally released as *It's About Time*, the album features 10 songs with the word "time" in their title. Of these, five of the six quintet selections (starring Phil Woods and a young Gary Burton) and two of the four other songs (with the quintet augmented by a brass section) are on this issue, along with a totally unreleased big-band session from the following year. A powerful drum-

mer with impressive technique, Morello is also a master of subtlety and, although an important part of this set, does not dominate the music. With Manny Albam contributing the arrangements, *It's About Time* was a happy surprise, a hard-driving set of swinging music. The personnel on the 6/6 & 15/61 selections are Morello, drums; Woods, alto sax; Burton, vibes; John Bunch, piano; Gene Cherico, bass. It's the same personnel with Ernie Royal, Doc Severinsen, Nick Travis, Clark Terry, trumpets; Bob Brookmeyer, Urbie Green, Richard Hixson, trombones; Harvey Phillips, tuba on the 6/7 & 9/61 cuts. On the Aug. 30, Nov. 12 & 13, 1962 tracks, the collective personnel includes Morello, drums; Woods, Phil Bodner, alto sax; Al Cohn, Frank Socolow, tenor sax; Sol Schlinger, baritone sax; Jimmy Maxwell, Al DeRisi, Bernie Glow, Doc Severinsen, Nick Travis, Clark Terry, trumpets; Bob Brookmeyer, Willie Dennis, Wayne Andre, Alan Ralph, Richard Hixson, Bill Byers, trombones; Hank Jones or John Bunch, piano; Gary Burton, vibes; Bill Crow, bass; Phil Krus, percussion. —*Scott Yanow*, Cadence

FRANK MORGAN

b. Dec. 23, 1933, Minneapolis, MN
Alto saxophone / Bop

Alto saxophonist Frank Morgan became one of jazz's, indeed one of America's, success stories in the mid-'80s. Morgan, along with Phil Woods, is the greatest living exponent of the Charlie Parker legacy. Morgan overcame years of drug addiction and turned his life around after getting out of prison. He was profiled in numerous music and general circulation magazines and on television. Morgan finally grew tired of the constant attention focused on his past. His biting, driving style, facility, and fluidity are compelling whether he's playing bebop anthems, originals, blues, standards, or ballads. Morgan has fulfilled the promise he showed as a youngster. He began playing clarinet at age seven, then alto sax at age ten. He won a talent contest in the late '40s in Los Angeles, where his family had moved. He recorded a solo with Freddie Martin at age 15, and during the mid-'50s played with Teddy Charles and Kenny Clarke before cutting his own album in 1955. Unfortunately, his drug problem soon led to his imprisonment. He did do some sessions for Savoy and GNP in the early '50s. During one stretch at San Quentin, Morgan was in a band that also included Art Pepper. But when his albums began appearing in 1985 for Contemporary, Morgan's vibrant solos offered clear proof he had triumphed over his demons. He recorded often in the '80s, switching to Antilles in 1989. Though quite uneven, his early material for Savoy and GNP Crescendo displays the potential and the Parker influence. All of his Contemporary and Antilles dates are available. —*Ron Wynn*

○ **Frank Morgan / i.** 1955 / GNP 12
Recorded in 1955, this reissue is more than another period piece. For one thing, it marks the rediscovery of a very talented alto player in Frank Morgan. For another, it gives us Wardell Gray's last recording. Moreover, it is a worthwhile period piece because it catches so many of the currents swirling through jazz in 1955. Morgan was 22 at the time of this recording. Most glorious of all is his golden tone, which shines through on every cut. Scarcely less lustrous are Morgan's deft, yet soulful solos. Four cuts are backed by the rhythm section of the Machito Orchestra, providing an Afro-Cuban flavor which had become a bebop substyle. The best of these is "Bernie's Tune." Wild Bill Davis pulls thick swooping sounds from the organ, and Conte Candoli, at his keenest here, sometimes sounds like Dizzy Gillespie himself. The material is remarkably well balanced, including blues, ballads, standards, and originals. In spite of many boppish traits, the overall impression is clearly postbop. With slower tempos and fewer notes, the music is not as hyper as bop. —*Douglas Clark*, Down Beat

○ **Introducing Frank Morgan** / 1955 / GNP 904

Easy Living / Jun. 1985 / Contemporary 14013

Double Image / May 21-22, 1986 / Contemporary 14035

With George Cables. An excellent collaboration, pairing a great old veteran and a relatively youthful one on piano in Cables. —*Ron Wynn*

○ **Bebop Lives!** / Dec. 1986 / Contemporary 14026
Live date at the Village Vanguard in New York City, with this veteran alto saxophonist on top of things. Prime bop, not to be missed. —*Michael G. Nastos*

★ **Yardbird Suite** / Nov. 1988 / Contemporary 14045
Excellent piano from Mulgrew Miller, bass from Ron Carter, and drums from Al Foster. Morgan is sharp and authoritative as a leader and player. —*Ron Wynn*

Reflections / 1988 / Contemporary 14052
Frank Morgan all-stars. Studio date with Joe Henderson (sax). Recommended. —*Michael G. Nastos*

Mood Indigo / i. 1989 / Antilles 791320
Morgan's finest album since he became a jazz icon fortifies the wisdom of his recent label switch to Antilles. Besides Morgan's sparkling alto sax is trumpeter Wynton Marsalis. Seldom has he been recorded in sharper, more incisive or soulful form. —*Ron Wynn*, Rock & Roll Disc

You Must Believe in Spring / i. 1992 / Antilles 512570
A '92 release by the marvelous alto saxophonist Frank Morgan, whose life story and triumph over heroin addiction and imprisonment was one of the '80s great success tales. Morgan's biting, yet sensitive and rich alto has rightly been traced to Charlie Parker, but Morgan long ago rid his style of any imitative excesses. He is excellently supported on this program of duets by an amazing rotating lineup of pianists: Kenny Barron, Tommy Flanagan, Barry Harris, Roland Hanna, and Hank Jones. —*Ron Wynn*

○ **A Lonesome Thing / i.** 1992 / Antilles
Displays the other side of Morgan's personality, as he turns to sentimental numbers and old favorites like "When You Wish Upon a Star" and "Ten Cents a Dance." There's also the demanding "Pannonica," where Morgan gets to stretch out a bit more, but mostly he's doing light, impressionistic fare here, albeit doing it with his customary flair and fire. —*Ron Wynn*, Rock & Roll Disc

LEE MORGAN

b. Jul. 10, 1938, Philadelphia, PA, **d.** Feb. 19, 1972, New York, NY
Trumpet / Hard bop

A virtuoso trumpeter, Lee Morgan made an immediate and lasting impact on the jazz and hard bop scene. His blistering, acrobatic forays were nicely contrasted by equally lyrical, sensitive ballad solos. Morgan was a great accompanist and a magnetic soloist, and his technique evolved from its early debt to Clifford Brown into a style and flavor all his own. Morgan was a master of irregular phrases and half-valve effects.

He began his professional career in Philadelphia at age 15. He joined Dizzy Gillespie's orchestra in 1956, and began his recording career as a leader for Savoy. Morgan remained with Gillespie until 1958, then became a member of the Jazz Messengers. He also recorded with John Coltrane in 1958, appearing on the marvelous *Blue Train* album. Blakey's band made many majestic records during Morgan's tenure (Mosaic recently issued a boxed set just covering the 1960 band with Morgan and Shorter). He began recording for Vee Jay/Trip and Prestige in the early '60s. Morgan left the Messengers in 1961, spent a couple of years in Philadelphia, then returned to New York. He scored the biggest hit of his career in 1963, when *The Sidewinder* became a soul-jazz anthem. Eventually, the song was used in '70s television commercials, was reissued as a 12-inch single in England during the mid-'80s, and is now a staple of "acid" jazz bands. Morgan recorded prolifically for Blue Note from 1963 until his death. He enjoyed more chart success with *Search for the New Land* and *Caramba!* Morgan had another stint with Blakey in 1964 and 1965, while heading his own groups.

His '60s and early '70s sessions were sizzling affairs, and brilliantly mixed soul-jazz and hard bop. He even attracted attention from some corners of the R&B and pop spectrum, though he didn't embrace or record fusion. His 1970 album, *Live at the Lighthouse*, was quite popular on college campuses, and Morgan became active in the early '70s Jazz and People's Movement. He was one of the musicians who appeared on the "Dick Cavett" show to protest media booking practices. Morgan was killed at Slugs in 1972 in a wild incident that still hasn't been resolved or explained fully. He was shot by a woman who may or may not have been his mistress, and who later said she'd shot Morgan by mistake. A posthumously issued two-record set, *Lee Morgan*, garnered sizable attention. Blue Note has kept some Morgan albums in print and has reissued several, while Prestige and Fresh Sound have issued classic sessions. His early Savoy material is not yet available on CD. —*Ron Wynn*

○ **Introducing Lee Morgan** / Nov. 5, 1956 / Savoy 12091
Even at 19, on *Introducing Lee Morgan*, trumpeter Morgan was astounding. He hadn't completely honed the trademark slurs, but his remarkable control and bright, inventive phrasing make this a great listen—not to mention tenor saxophonist Hank Mobley, pianist Hank Jones, bassist Doug Watkins, and drummer Art Taylor, all playing in top form. —*John Corbett*, Down Beat

○ **Cooker, The** / Sep. 29, 1957 / Blue Note 1578

★ **Best of Lee Morgan** / 1957-1965 / Blue Note 91138

Candy / Feb. 2, 1958 / Blue Note 46508

☆ **A-1** / **i.** 195z / Savoy 1104
A collection of cuts from the group Morgan co-led with Hank Mobley (sax) in the '50s. —*Ron Wynn*

Young Lions, The / Apr. 25, 1960 / Vee Jay 3013

Expoobident / Oct. 13, 1960 / Vee Jay 901
Lee Morgan's '60s releases crackle with intensity and abandon, as he was stretching out and testing his range and limits. He never wavers throughout *Expoobident*, offering first-rate solos throughout and driving a fine band that includes tenor saxophonist Clifford Jordan, pianist Eddie Higgins, bassist Art Davis, and drummer Art Blakey. There are four bonus cuts, all of them excellent, and the Morgan/Jordan front line is one that should have lasted longer than it did. —*Ron Wynn*

Take Twelve / Jan. 24, 1962 / Jazzland 310

★ **Sidewinder, The** / Dec. 21, 1963 / Blue Note 84157

★ **Search for the New Land** / Feb. 15, 1964 / Blue Note 84169
With Grant Green. Absolutely gorgeous compositional jazz. Near essential. —*Michael G. Nastos*

Tom Cat / Aug. 11, 1964 / Blue Note 84446

Rumproller / Apr. 21, 1965 / Blue Note 46428
Anything but standard, thanks to Joe Henderson (sax) plus dynamic drums by Billy Higgins. —*Ron Wynn*

Gigolo, The / Jun. 25, 1965-Jul. 1, 1965 / Blue Note 84212
Here is first-rate, outstanding tenor sax work by Wayne Shorter, with a wonderful rhythm section. —*Ron Wynn*

Cornbread / Sep. 8, 1965 / Blue Note 84222
You can't go wrong with Morgan matching phrases with Jackie McLean (sax) and Hank Mobley (ts), plus Herbie Hancock on piano. —*Ron Wynn*

Delightfulee / Apr. 8, 1966 / Blue Note 84243
This is a slightly below par Blue Note date, though Morgan is on fire. —*Ron Wynn*

Rajah, The / Nov. 29, 1966 / Blue Note 84426

Procrastinator, The / Jul. 14, 1967 / Blue Note 582
Featuring Wayne Shorter (sax), George Coleman (ts), and Bobby Hutcherson (vib). —*Michael G. Nastos*

★ **Live at the Lighthouse** / Jul. 10-12, 1970 / Blue Note 89906
Twofer of great live club date with extended versions and Bennie Maupin (sax), Harold Mabern (p), Jymie Merritt (b), and Mickey Roker (d). —*Michael G. Nastos*

Lee Morgan / Sep. 17-18, 1971 / Blue Note 84901

Studio date. Some of his last sessions and going progressive. A great band featuring Harold Mabern (p), Billy Harper (ts), Jymie Merritt (b), and Freddie Waits (d). —*Michael G. Nastos*

Dizzy Atmosphere / Specialty 1762
This is an excellent match between Lee Morgan and Wynton Kelly (p), plus stirring tenor from Billy Mitchell and rollicking trombone from Al Grey. Bonus cuts on CD. —*Ron Wynn*

BUTCH MORRIS (Lawrence Morris)

b. 1940, Los Angeles, CA
Cornet, composer, conductor / Progressive big band, modern creative

Once an emerging star on cornet, Butch Morris has concentrated on conducting and composing in recent years, working often with David Murray. He played with J.R. Monterose, George Morrow, Frank Lowe, and Don Moye on the West Coast, then moved to New York in the mid-'70s. Morris worked there with Charles Tyler, Hamiett Bluiett, Murray, Stanley Crouch, and Lowe. He lived in Paris in 1976 and 1977, recording with Steve Lacy, Jef Gilson, and Lowe, and playing with Alan Silva. Morris did sessions heading his own group in the late '70s, '80s, and '90s for Black Saint, New World/Countercurrents, and DIW, while serving as a conductor and arranger for Murray's large orchestra. He also recorded with Lowe again, and led a trio. Morris has some sessions available on CD. —*Ron Wynn*

○ **Current Trends in Racism in Modern America** / **i.** Feb. 1985 / Sound Aspects 4010
The significant question in this case is not whether the sanctity of free improvisation is violated, but whether in a free-improvised format, a conductor serves a useful purpose. There are overemphasized, rather-too-sharp turns in direction (dynamics, time, texture) during *Current Trends* that suggest cues from the conductor; often they sound more jarring than organically developed. Left to their own devices, these New York art players, more or less familiar with each other's m.o.'s, would surely have produced something much different. Morris does exercise real control; he may not call individual notes, but he shapes the performance in a real if not always desirable way. The piece has textural sweep, but sometimes the results are ambiguous: the singsong rhythm at the start of side two is amusing, yet also kind of crude. But there are also obvious fruits of conduction—like the descending cascades that precede Christian Marclay's heavy rap-record cameo—that sound okay. —*Kevin Whitehead*, Cadence

★ **Dust to Dust** / **i.** Nov. 18-20, 1990 / New World 80408
A fine large-group recording. The ensemble has several top players, including Wayne Horvitz (k), Marty Ehrlich (reeds), and John Purcell (reeds). Morris conducts and supervises with his usual skill. —*Ron Wynn*

JELLY ROLL MORTON (Ferdinand Joseph Lemott)

b. Oct. 20, 1890, New Orleans, LA, **d.** Jul. 10, 1941, Los Angeles, CA
Piano, composer / New Orleans traditional

His penchant for exaggeration, distortion, and, in some instances, fabrication, turned many in the jazz community against flamboyant Jelly Roll Morton, while others have had a hard time determining his value against this backdrop of hyperbole and legend. But Morton truly ranked among jazz's first great composers, and was also an outstanding bandleader and pianist. Morton's compositions featured advanced ensemble and solo writing; he traveled extensively and heard numerous musical styles. Ragtime, spirituals and hymns, field songs, riverboat melodies, Tin Pan Alley, and Afro-Latin rhythms all influenced his writing. His works were carefully rehearsed, and were structured to give each player a substantial solo that usually climaxed in an exuberant two-bar break, yet didn't destroy the song's cohesion. He judiciously balanced ensemble interaction and freedom for the soloist, while inserting piano solos that sometimes exploded, and other times laid down soothing counter-melodies.

Morton grew up in New Orleans, and started piano lessons at age ten. He was very proud of his Creole background and French heritage, and earned family disapproval by playing in Storyville bordellos in the early 1900s. Morton reportedly earned $100 a night playing in places such as the Hilma Burt House while he was not yet drinking age. He spent many years traveling, both solo and with tent shows and vaudeville troupes, which enabled him to hear numerous regional sounds. He led a colorful life as a gambler, pool player, and procurer, experiences that were so embellished later in his stories that few knew where myth ended and reality began.

Morton visited both New York and Los Angeles during this time. James P. Johnson heard him playing "Jelly Roll Blues" in 1911, and Morton arrived in California in 1917. He stayed in Los Angeles until 1922, then moved to Chicago. He cut his first recordings in Richmond, Indiana, in 1923, two with a White group called the New Orleans Rhythm Kings (NORK) and the others solo. Morton cut these sessions in a well-known Ku Klux Klan stronghold, passing as a Spaniard. Over the next five years, Morton toured with several groups while using Chicago as home base. This included stints with Fate Marable and W.C. Handy and the Alabamians. He was a staff writer for the Melrose Publishing House, which covered many of his most famous compositions. Most importantly, he recruited many famous New Orleans sidemen and formed the Red Hot Peppers. The roster included Omer Simeon, Kid Ory, and Johnny and Baby Dodds. They issued numerous wonderful recordings, among them "Grandpa's Spells," "Black Bottom Stomp," and "The Pearls."

Morton moved to New York in 1928, and recorded both nontraditional and traditional New Orleans pieces. His work began to place more emphasis on extended solo improvisation and to branch away from strict New Orleans style, though he never deserted his beloved sound.

By 1930, swing's innovations had shifted the music in a different direction, and Morton's approach was dated. Yet his compositions retained their appeal; "Wolverine Blues," "Milenberg Joys," and "King Porter Stomp" were swing era staples, and Fletcher Henderson's updated arrangement of "King Porter Stomp" for Benny Goodman became a big band anthem. Morton moved to Washington, and was deemed missing in action by the jazz audience until 1938, when Alan Lomax recorded an extensive series of interviews at the Library of Congress. These were issued on an album in 1948, and were reissued in 1957. Though the albums came out posthumously, the interviews generated tremendous new interest in Morton's life and music. There were recording sessions in 1939 and 1940, and Morton's career began to regain momentum due to the New Orleans revival. Unfortunately, his health faded and Morton died in 1940. While his incessant claims that he "invented" jazz triggered resentment and backlash (Morton's among the few musicians Duke Ellington supposedly criticized publicly) he certainly belonged among early jazz's elite composers, players, and bandleaders. —*Ron Wynn with Bruce Boyd Raeburn*

○ **Jelly Roll Morton (1917-1921)** / 1917-1921 / Biograph 1003

○ **Jelly Roll Morton (1923-1924)** / Apr. 1923-Jun. 1924 / Milestone 47018
Landmark stomps, blues, Afro-Latin-tinged romps and early versions of anthems "King Porter Stomp" and "Wolverine Blues" make this pivotal work essential by a jazz legend. Morton probably didn't invent jazz as he claimed, but he certainly had a lot to do with it. This material was issued on two-record vinyl set in '75, and sound quality is dubious. This set has been supplanted by CD reissues on both domestic and import labels. —*Ron Wynn*

★ **Piano Solos (1923-1924), The** / i. Jul. 1923-Jun. 1924 / Fountain 104
Pianist/composer/bandleader Jelly Roll Morton's crucial years were 1923 to 1928. They see him in the process of putting spring in his slightly stiff step of formal piano rag-time, synthesizing it orchestrally to the point of becoming preeminent as a bandleader in 1926, before taking his first steps toward becoming an anachronism. The piano solos here demonstrate that Morton was by no means a faultless technician—he sometimes rushed tempos and stiffened under pressure at speed. He preferred a medium tempo, which gave him the freedom to swagger spryly and the space to deploy those personal pianistic characteristics he added to the piano's vocabulary. Among these were ever-shifting rhythms, presaging Earl Hines, as on "Perfect Rag"; four-bar tag endings; syncopated alterations of the major and minor third; and his love of a stressed off beat. It was partly by "inverting" that last device that "stride" piano emerged in New York during the '20s. Morton maintained his lilting swing by playing a single bass note on the "on" beat, followed by a chord below it, putting the stress on beats 2 and 4. It was a simple matter to place the chord on the "off" beat and higher up the scale, and thus it was that Morton's stomps and rags became the "stride" man's "shouts." "Kansas City Stomp" provides a particularly interesting example, both of his "off" beat syncopation, and of his alternation of thirds. The type of ragtime that pervaded New Orleans at the turn of the century is mirrored in the jaunty "King Porter Stomp," while "Perfect Rag," with its constant thematic development, is more directly linked with the classic ragtime of Missouri and hence Scott Joplin. "The Pearls," another gem of variation, also bears witness to the fact that Morton was harmonically advanced for his time. —*Chris Sheridan*, Cadence

Pianist and Composer–Vol. 1 / i. 1923-1926 / Smithsonian 043

Blues and Stomps: Rare Piano Rolls / Sep. 1924-Dec. 1924 / Biograph 111
1924-1926. These are just immaculate classic rolls, seminal piano cuts. —*Ron Wynn*

☆ **Jelly Roll Morton** / i. 1926-1938 / Bluebird 6588
A more manageable selection of Morton's Red Hot Peppers, well suited to the beginner. —*Bruce Raeburn*

★ **Jelly Roll Morton Centennial: His Complete Victor Recording** / 1926-1939 / Bluebird 2361
1926-1929. The ultimate Morton collection for the specialist, although not all possible Victor takes are included and some appear twice. Even so, a splendid range of Mortonia from the Red Hot Peppers through Jelly Roll Morton and his New Orleans Jazzmen. —*Bruce Raeburn*

○ **Library of Congress Recordings Vol. 1, The** / i. May 1938-Jun. 1938 / Classic Jazz 1
A fascinating mixture of music and reminiscence. Jazz history from the Morton perspective. —*Bruce Raeburn*

○ **Library of Congress Recordings Vol. 2, The** / i. May 1938-Jun. 1938 / Classic Jazz 2

○ **Library of Congress Recordings Vol. 3, The** / i. May 1938-Jun. 1938 / Classic Jazz 3

○ **Library of Congress Recordings Vol. 4, The** / i. May 1938-Jun. 1938 / Classic Jazz 4

○ **Library of Congress Recordings Vol. 5, The** / i. May 1938-Jun. 1938 / Classic Jazz 5

○ **Library of Congress Recordings Vol. 6, The** / i. May 1938-Jun. 1938 / Classic Jazz 6

○ **Library of Congress Recordings Vol. 7, The** / i. May 1938-Jun. 1938 / Classic Jazz 7

○ **Library of Congress Recordings Vol. 8, The** / i. May 1938-Jun. 1938 / Classic Jazz 8

New Orleans Memories Plus Two / i. 1939 / Commodore 624062
Piano solos from Jelly just before his death, some with vocals, make for interesting comparisons with his first recordings. —*Bruce Raeburn*

○ **Jelly Roll Morton: Rediscovered Solos** / i. 1953 / Riverside 1018

○ **Mr. Jelly Lord** / i. 1956 / Tomato 70384

★ **Complete Vols. 1 and 2, The** / i. Jun. 1980 / RCA 42405
This double album contains—chronologically for the first
time—all the pianist/composer/bandleader's Chicago recordings of 1926-27. Their importance as initial organizing and
formalizing instruments, creating structure within the music, has often been stressed, though this emphasis neglects
the extent to which they formed the basis for future developments. In "Black Bottom Stomp," the first, and ironically,
unsurpassed Morton masterpiece, we have a pre-echo, not
merely of Kansas City swing, but of later methods like
Horace Silver's brand of hard bop. Time and again, in performances like "Dead Man Blues," "Steamboat Stomp,"
"Grandpa's Spells," "Doctor Jazz," "The Pearls," or "Wolverine
Blues," we are given evidence of Morton's ability to vary
rhythm or to spin secondary and tertiary themes from the
material as a means of unifying the improvisations. And
even in a saccharine piece like "Someday Sweetheart" there
is a concern for texture that, albeit comparatively unsophis-
ticated, remained neglected outside the Ellington milieu until modern times, finding sympathy in such diverse am-
biances as those of Charles Mingus, the Art Ensemble of
Chicago, and Air. One final point is that "Dead Man Blues"
appears for the first time on LP in unexpurgated form. —
Chris Sheridan, Down Beat

BOB MOSES (Robert Laurence Moses)

b. Jan. 28, 1948, New York, NY
Drums, percussion, composer / Modern creative
A crafty, humorous drummer, Bob Moses combines Afro-
Latin, funk, and African elements in his playing. His style is
loose and propulsive, and can be consistently swinging and
driving or more restrained
and understated. Moses played vibes in Latin bands around
New York as a teen, and coformed the Free Spirits with
Larry Coryell in 1966. He worked briefly the next year with
Rahsaan Roland Kirk, then joined Gary Burton and played
with him until 1968. Moses was in Jack DeJohnette's jazz-
rock group Compost, and did sessions in New York. He
played in David Liebman's trio Open Sky in the '70s and
'80s. Moses toured and recorded with Burton in the mid-'70s,
while doing sessions with Mike Gibbs and Pat Metheny. He
rejoined Burton in the late '70s, and also recorded with Hal
Galper, Gil Goldstein, and Steve Swallow. Moses worked
and recorded with Steve Kuhn's band featuring Sheila
Jordan from 1979 to 1982. He did sessions with George
Gruntz's Concert Jazz Band, with Emily Remler, and with
Mister Spats in the '80s. Moses recorded as a leader for
Mozown and Gramavision records. He has one date avail-
able on CD. —*Ron Wynn*

○ **Bittersuite in the Ozone** / i. Oct. 1975 / Mozown 001
This is true soul music, with the soul of Bob Moses shining
forth from every facet of this production. Though much of
the music on *Bittersuite in the Ozone* is indeed funny and
free, one shouldn't think for a moment that this is merely a
loose blowing session, flirting with the borders of the chaos
that has so often passed for musical freedom. Everything
here is extremely well ordered; the players are free enough
to travel inside and out with complete confidence. The areas
defined by Moses's compositional approach are wide, yet
clearly etched. The measure of pleasure and insight one derives from *Bittersuite in the Ozone* in large part depends on
the openness of one's own ears, mind, and soul. —*Charles
Mitchell*, Down Beat

○ **Family** / 1980 / Sutra 1003
Family is a light, well-constructed album of straightahead
but very contemporary jazz. Drummer Bob Moses, who
wrote three of the five tunes, selected players who were old
musical friends, and arranged the music to showcase their
talents as well as his own. There is a warm, comfortable atmosphere on the album—a feeling of mutual enjoyment and
support (hence the title). Dave Liebman seems to benefit
most from this atmosphere. For this session, he passes up
his trademark soprano sax and concentrates on the tenor.
Although he can still tear off phrases in a hard-edged John

Coltrane style—he does so on Steve Swallow's "Portsmouth
Figurations"—he also shows a breadth on this album not often heard. Terumasa Hino, while not quite as strong a voice
as Liebman, is also in fine form. His cornet playing evokes
Miles Davis—long lines of fuzzy-edged notes, broken by
rests in unusual places and sharp punctuations. But he
clearly has some ideas all his own, which he demonstrates
on "Devotion," the modal vamp tune that closes the album.
Steve Kuhn and Steve Swallow are fine complements to
Moses's light, fluid drumming. Kuhn's piano comping is per-
sistent without being intrusive, and his solos show excellent
range and the ability to respond to different material within
his style. For example, he breaks up his long phrases on
"Heaven" with sharp, percussive interjections that are definitely Dukish. Swallow is impeccably solid and consistent,
as he continues his quiet demonstration of what an effective
instrument the electric bass can be in jazz (why didn't he get
a solo?). —*Robin Tolleson*, Down Beat

★ **Visit with the Great Spirit** / 1983 / Gramavision 8307
This is another ambitious outing from Bob Moses, a musician's drummer if ever there was one. As on his Gramavision
release, *When Elephants Dream of Music*, Moses uses an
outstanding group of musicians, and uses them well. The
leader lays down a loose tom-tom groove on "Fat Man,"
sneaking talking drums in and out of the percussion collage.
He is soon greeted by some frenetic guitar and sax squalling,
a crisp, punchy bass slightly out of phase, and a horn section
that punctuates and fills out the holes in the original drum
beat. Moses dedicates this album to Hermeto Pascoal, and
he shows his love of Brazilian and African rhythms on this
cut. —*Robin Tolleson*, Down Beat

SAM MOST (Samuel Most)

b. Dec. 16, 1930, Atlantic City, NJ
Saxophone, flute / Bop
Flutist, clarinetist, and alto saxophonist Sam Most was bebop's first significant flute soloist. He switched to flute after
working, in the late '40s and early '50s, with Tommy Dorsey,
Boyd Raeburn, and Don Redman, among others. Most's
1953 LP, *Undercurrent Blues*, helped him build a new identity on flute, and he was voted *Down Beat*'s New Star in the
1954 Critics Poll. Most, the brother of clarinetist Abe Most,
later played with Calvin Jackson, Paul Quinichette, and
Teddy Wilson, and backed vocalist Chris Connor. He was a
member of Buddy Rich's orchestra from 1959 to 1961, and
toured India, the Far East, and South America with Rich's
band. He later joined his brother in Los Angeles and, at that
point, played mostly alto sax with Louis Bellson. Most
worked with Red Norvo in Las Vegas and did session work
on the West Coast before cutting some recordings in the late
'70s for Xanadu. Aside from his albums on Prestige, all of
Most's albums on the Xanadu label are worth hearing. Thus
far, none are available on CD. —*Ron Wynn and Michael G.
Nastos*

Introducing a New Star / Jan. 20, 1953 / Prestige 1322

○ **Bebop Revisited–Vol. 3** / i. Dec. 1953 / Xanadu 172
This album presents a nice cross-section of known and unknown artists—a second generation of bop. All account for
themselves well, with Tony Fruscella's trumpeting being a
real ear-opener and the arrangements for most selections
clearly charting ideas/forms for the future. The music
swings in that traditional manner and Mark Gardner's comprehensive notes complement the aural experience very
well. —*Milo Fine*, Cadence

I'm Nuts About the Most: East Coast Jazz Series–Vol. 9 /
Mar. 29, 1955 / Bethlehem 18

★ **Mostly Flute** / May 27, 1976 / Xanadu
With Duke Jordan Trio and Tal Farlow on guitar. Two Sam
Most originals, five standards. Great interplay between Most
and Farlow. —*Michael G. Nastos*

○ **Flute Flight** / i. Dec. 1976 / Xanadu 141
Flutist Sam Most's beautiful vibrato and duo with pianist
Lou Levy on "It Might As Well Be Spring" make this a great

track. The album surprise comes in the last three tracks. "Last Night When We Were Young" is a magnificent tune, and this has to be a classic rendition. I'd always dug the changes in "It Happened in Monterey," and Most turns this into a great blowing vehicle with little rhythmic influence from below. I read about his reluctance to play clarinet and thought the final tune selected to use that horn was pretty poor, but I was wrong! He explores this old tune ("Am I Blue") with a blues feel that left me smiling and playing the track again. —*Jerry Atkins*, Cadence

○ **But Beautiful** / 1976 / Catalyst 7609

Sam Most was among the early exponents of the jazz flute. He played with people as diverse as Henry Mancini, Charles Mingus, and Oscar Pettiford, occasionally wandering off into the wilderness of Las Vegas, Palm Springs, and Los Angeles. With a subdued rhythm section here of drummer Will Bradley, George Muribus on piano, and Patrick "Putter" Smith on bass, Most drifts through standards like "But Beautiful" and "There Is No Greater Love." His interpretation of "I've Grown Accustomed to Your Face," featuring a passage with flute and bass, is stunning. Most also plays some tenor sax on this date, but his flute is the most compelling component. —*Herb Nolan*, Down Beat

★ **From the Attic of My Mind** / Apr. 25, 1978 / Xanadu

Flutist Sam Most has it all here: a distinctively dark, breathy tone, technique to spare, a varied batch of original tunes, an able backup crew, even a hilarious album title. Most's clean, expressive articulation recalls Rahsaan Roland Kirk (who of course followed Most onto the scene); he explicitly evokes Kirk on the hum-and-blow choruses of the irresistibly danceable "Keep Moving," which features some gracefully choppy funk from pianist Kenny Barron, Most's most consistently sympathetic sideman. (Bassist George Mraz and drummer Walter Bolden opt for unobtrusive but admirably assured timekeeping; percussionist Warren Smith makes occasional discreet appearances). Most's compositions cover a wide range: three blues, ranging from "Keep Moving" to the cool-school "Blue Hue"; a ballad lively ("You are Always the One") and reflective ("Yesterdays," a duet for Most and Barron); serviceable blowers ("What Is, Is" and "Child of the Forest"). Even on the mellow samba "Breath of Love," on which Most's delicate alto flute work has an Asian flavor, he resists the temptation to lay back and take it easy; he never seems at a loss for something to say or the means to say it. —*Kevin Whitehead*, Cadence

○ **Flute Talk** / Jan. 23-24, 1979 / Xanadu 173

Sam Most's *Flute Talk* breaks no new ground in the sense of setting standards by which all jazz flutists are judged. Primarily a high-spirited straightahead session, this record nevertheless fills the void for those who like the sound of jazz flute yet are disenchanted with the peppy Muzak of Herbie Mann, Dave Valentin, and Hubert Laws. Most provides some interesting originals for coleader Joe Farrell and him to blow on, as well as clever arrangements of Charlie Parker's "Kim" and the Disney standard "When You Wish Upon a Star." Generally, both flutists contrast each other effectively; one picks up ideas logically where the other left off, eschewing jagged, misplaced bursts of individual inspiration. Most has a raspy jazz tone, and, although his technique isn't as focused as Farrell's, his phrasing is more relaxed, his sound more distinctive. Farrell's rhythmic concept is more symmetrical in approach and his tone more "legit"—the Hubert Laws influence abounds. Pianist Mike Wofford's one chorus solo on "Love Season" alone is almost worth the price of the record. He is also a sincere accompanist, as best demonstrated on "Hot House" and "Kim." Bassist Bob Magnusson possesses a glowing, resonant sound and swings impeccably. Drummer Roy McCurdy and percussionist Jerry Steinholtz perform solidly, although McCurdy seems uncharacteristically subdued (perhaps for the better). —*Arthur Moorehead*, Down Beat

BENNIE MOTEN (Benjamin Moten)

b. Nov. 13, 1894, Kansas City, MO, **d.** Apr. 2, 1935, Kansas City, MO
Piano, bandleader / Swing
Bennie Moten laid the foundation for the band that became a swing institution: the Count Basie orchestra. His territory bands grew from five pieces to a large orchestra during the '20s, and included many musicians who emerged as stars in the big bands' heyday. Though not a great player or arranger, Moten was a visionary leader and a savvy judge of talent. His bands helped create and hone the classic Kansas City swing style; flexible, floating four-beat rhythmic patterns, blues chord sequences, instrumental riffs, and sharp ensemble interaction, with everything connected by well-crafted arrangements that balanced ripping uptempo passages with smooth transitional sections and first-rate solos. Moten recorded for Okeh in 1923 with a sextet. Their songs "South" and "Vine Street Blues" were issued in 1924, and "South" became a huge hit in 1925. Moten switched labels to Victor, and, in 1927, had another hit with "Kansas City Shuffle." At that point, he was developing a cohesive sound with a steady, blues-rooted backbeat underneath. Eddie Durham and Count Basie joined Moten in 1929. Moten switched to full-time conducting, letting Basie have piano duties. Durham, Basie, and Eddie Barefield provided arrangements. By 1932, Moten's band included Ben Webster, Hot Lips Page, Jack Washington, Dan Minor, Walter Page, Jimmy Rushing, and Basie. But the Depression had taken the wind out of the recording industry's sails, and they had their last session that year. Moten died in 1935 following a tonsillectomy. Basie took this band's nucleus and made history, but never forgot his boss. The Basie orchestra did a reverent tribute in 1947, updating "South." —*Ron Wynn*

○ **Bennie Moten Complete–Vols. 1 and 2** / i. 1926 / RCA 42410
1926-1928. Chicago recordings for pianist's Kansas City orchestra. —*Michael G. Nastos*

★ **Basie Beginnings (1929-1932)** / 1929-1932 / Bluebird 9768
Bennie Moten's orchestra, perhaps the top territory band at the time Count Basie joined as second pianist in 1929, has been reasonably well-represented on records since 1923. All of their Victor recordings are available on the three twofers released in the French RCA Jazz Tribune series, the best source of their music. This release does have the cream of Moten's 1929 and 1930 sessions, plus seven of the ten songs cut at their superb December 13, 1932, date. Moten himself never again appeared on records after Basie joined. Basie was an excellent stride pianist strongly influenced by Fats Waller, sounding on "Lafayette" like Waller did on his "The Minor Drag." The 1929 band had a spirited ensemble sound and during the next year they added the trumpet of Hot Lips Page and vocalist Jimmy Rushing (who on 1930's "That Too Do Blues" sings lyrics that would eventually become "Sent for You Yesterday and Here You Come Today"). The 1932 session, the last for Moten's orchestra, features a particularly strong unit with Page, Eddie Durham (tb, g), trombonist Dan Minor, and Ben Webster all getting solo space. Even at this late date, Moten's band never really sounds like Basie's would five years later (the fast riffing seems more influenced by the Casa Loma Orchestra), but it does stand out as one of the early swing bands. This is valuable music—don't miss Basie's scat vocal on "Somebody Stole My Gal." Selections were recorded on 10/23, 24, and 27/29, 10/29 and 10/30/30, 10/31/30, and 12/13/32. Total time is 66:24. —*Scott Yanow*, Cadence

PAUL MOTIAN (Stephen Paul Motian)

b. Mar. 25, 1931, Philadelphia, PA
Drums, percussion, composer / Cool, modern creative
One of jazz's most spontaneous, interactive drummers, Paul Motian seldom employs steady, on-the-beat percussive techniques. His groups use varied sound textures and a wide range of concepts. Motian divides the beat, interacts with

group members, and has a cerebral, abstract approach, though he can swing when the need arises. An Armenian, Motian was fascinated by Turkish music as a child, as well as cowboy movies. He began on guitar, then switched to drums at age 12. After serving in the navy, Motian recorded on the Progressive label in the mid-'50s with pianist and vocalist Bob Dorough. He moved to New York from Philadelphia in the mid-'50s, and played with a diverse group of musicians. They included Gil Evans, George Russell, Stan Getz, Lennie Tristano, Thelonious Monk, Coleman Hawkins, and Roy Eldridge. Motian was part of Bill Evans's superb trio in the late '50s and early '60s, which included working with Scott LaFaro in 1960 and 1961. Motian's leaving triggered a rift with Evans that wasn't healed until a few months before Evans's death. Motian then played with Paul Bley for a year, and appeared on his album, *Turning Point*, before beginning a long-term collaboration with Keith Jarrett. He was with Jarrett for two stretches that ranged from the mid-'60s to the mid-'70s and included a few outstanding Impulse recordings. He also worked with Mose Allison, Charles Lloyd, and Arlo Guthrie, recorded with Lennie Tristano, and played in the original Liberation Music Ensemble in 1969. Besides the stints with Jarrett, Motian was active in the Jazz Composers Orchestra Association (JCOA), and appeared on Carla Bley's albums *Escalator Over the Hill* and *Tropic Appetites*. He made his recording debut as a leader in 1972 on ECM, heading a group with Charlie Haden, Sam Brown, and special guest Jarrett. Motian led small combos in the '70s and '80s, while cutting albums with musicians such as Charles Brackeen, David Izenon, Jean-Francois Jenny-Clark, John Surman, Ed Schuller, Jim Pepper, Joe Lovano, and Bill Frisell. He recorded primarily for ECM and Soul Note. Motian reunited with Bley for a pair of excellent late '80s releases, and has been part of Charlie Haden's outstanding '80s and '90s quartet. He has a good selection of releases as a leader available on CD. —*Ron Wynn*

○ **Conception Vessel** / Nov. 25-26, 1972 / ECM
This is Motian's debut as a leader. It includes ambitious cuts with guitarist Sam Brown and also features pianist Keith Jarrett. —*Ron Wynn*

Tribute / May 1974 / ECM 1048
Quintet with guitarist Sam Brown, Charlie Haden (b), early work of saxophonist Carlos Ward. Ornette's "War Orphans" and Haden's immortal "Song for Che" are included. —*Michael G. Nastos*

★ **Dance** / Sep. 1977 / ECM
Excellent solos by saxophonist Charles Brackeen and above-average writing and ensemble work. —*Ron Wynn*

Jack of Clubs / Mar. 26-28, 1984 / Soul Note 1124
A quintet with Jim Pepper (ts), Joe Lovano (ts), Bill Frisell (g), and Ed Schuller (b) plays seven pieces, all by Motian. This is very intense yet lyrical. Pepper and Lovano are excellent sax foils. —*Michael G. Nastos*

It Should Have Happened a Long Time Ago / Jul. 1984 / ECM 823641
Trio. A capable trio set. Motian is both a good percussionist and a fine bandleader. —*Ron Wynn*

☆ **Monk in Motian** / Mar. 1988 / JMT 834421
A top tribute, with sterling work by Frisell (g) and Dewey Redman (ts). —*Ron Wynn*

★ **Paul Motian on Broadway–Vol. 1 (with Bill Frisell, Charlie Haden, Joe Lovano & Paul Motian)** / Nov. 1988-Sep. 1989 / JMT 834430

○ **Paul Motian on Broadway–Vol. 2** / Nov. 1988-Sep. 1989 / JMT 834440

○ **Bill Evans: Tribute to the Great Post-Bop Pianist** / May 1990z zz / JMT 834445
An excellent quartet date featuring sensational guitar by Bill Frisell and nice tenor sax from Joe Lovano. —*Ron Wynn*

ALPHONSE MOUZON

b. Nov. 21, 1948, Charleston, SC

Drums / Early jazz-rock, instrumental pop
Alphonse Mouzon is a premier fusion/funk drummer whose flashy clothes and startling technique have made him a star. He is a busy sideman, too. —*Michael G. Nastos*

★ **Funky Snakefoot** / Dec. 10-12, 1973 / Blue Note 222
Within a framework of tight melodies and a pervasive rhythmic orientation—slight harmonic depth—drummer/vocalist Alphonze Mouzon hones a distinctive style. The instrumentals are excellent and his percussive virtuosity evident throughout, whether supplying funky R&B accompaniment or, as in "Where I'm Drumming From" and "Ism," ferocious, freewheeling jazz-rock lead. —*Ray Townley*, Down Beat

Essence of Mystery, The / i. 1973 / Blue Note 059
Some frenetic drumming and good jazz-rock arrangments lift this far above many of the later Mouzon releases. —*Ron Wynn*

BOB MOVER (Robert Alan Mover)

b. Mar. 22, 1952, Boston, MA
Alto and soprano saxophone / Bop
A fierce defender of the bebop tradition and one of the lesser publicized modern boppers, Bob Mover has played with fire and consistency since the '70s. His tone, approach, lines, and phrasing reflect the Parker lineage, as well as the influence of Lee Konitz, with Mover's own inflections and flourishes added. Mover began working with Ira Sullivan at age 16. When his family moved to New York in 1969, Mover began studying with Richie Kamuca, and worked informally with Roy Eldridge and Brew Moore. Following a brief stint with Charles Mingus, he began playing with Chet Baker in 1973, and played with Baker until 1975. He's led his own groups since '76, recording in the '70s and '80s. Perhaps his most controversial record was 1981's *In the True Tradition*, a session that seemed to be Mover's answer to Anthony Braxton's two volumes of bebop done his way, *In the Tradition, Vols. 1 & 2*. Mover also recorded with Lee Konitz in 1977, and rejoined Baker for a European tour and recording date in 1981, one of Baker's last. He's recorded for Xanadu, Vanguard, and Jazz City. Currently, Mover does not have any sessions available on CD. —*Ron Wynn*

★ **In the True Tradition** / i. Jun. 1981 / Xanadu 187
Forget about extravagant arrangements, just turn Bob Mover and his associates loose. The originals and classics ("Poinciana" and "Evidence") are equally outstanding with Mover's gritty, sometimes abrasive alto tone riding high. Bassist Rufus Reid and drummer Bobby Ward are excellent accompanists and listeners won't miss the absence of a piano in the least. This is great jazz. —*Carl Brauer*, Cadence

○ **Things Unseen!** / i. Jun. 1981-Dec. 1982 / Xanadu 194
Alto saxophonist Bob Mover's album is a good record. The quartet tracks glimmer with creativity. Pianist Albert Dailey, though saddled with an inferior instrument and under-recorded to boot, is a lively accompanist and a stellar soloist. Bassist Ray Drummond dips and dances, his thick, booming sound filling the middle of the mix. Drummer Bobby Ward, a Bostonian who preferred to stay put, is extremely sympathetic, never flailing, always swinging. Tenor saxophonist Steve Hall plays on one track, "Twardzik," which is noteworthy for its mazelike theme and Hall's prancing solo. Another track, "Jimmy Garrison's Blues," is from the 2/82 session that produced Mover's first Xanadu LP. The tune swings lazily in the style of *Coltrane Plays the Blues* and features some excellent arco work from Rufus Reid. The album's material is a nice blend of lesser-known works of well-known composers with the aforementioned "Twardzik" the only original. Perhaps the best known of the standards is Jerome Kern's "Yesterdays," which is performed as a piano-alto sax duet. Mover weaves the melody in and out of his solo, imbuing it with a bittersweet feeling. Daily not only keeps the tempo, but also elaborates on what the saxophonist is doing. The album closer, "Busy Day," is a solo piece with a wistful melody that Mover stays close to throughout his reading. The rest of the tracks are fairly straightahead with strong so-

los from Mover and Dailey (Drummond and Ward get several short solo spots). —*Richard B. Kamins*, Cadence

FAMOUDOU DON MOYE

b. May 23, 1946, Rochester, NY
Drums, percussion / Early free, modern creative
Famoudou Don Moye's masterful rhythms, expert solo and accompaniment skills, and personality have been a vital part of the Art Ensemble of Chicago since the group's second year of existence. He's also done several fine dates with other groups, including sessions with Steve Lacy, Sonny Sharrock, Dave Burrell, Gato Barbieri, and Pharoah Sanders, and with trumpeter Alan Shorter. Moye studied percussion at Wayne State University and played in the group Detroit Free Jazz, touring Europe in 1968 and 1969. He played with Lacy in Rome before joining the Art Ensemble in Paris in 1970. Moye recorded and performed with members of the St. Louis-based Black Artists Group (BAG) in the early '70s, and played at the Montreux Festival with Randy Weston in 1974. He was also in a duo with Steve McCall and the Association for the Advancement of Creative Musicians' big band, while also leading the rhythm group Malinke Rhythm. Moye added Famoudou to his name in the mid-'70s. He recorded a solo date, and played with Joseph Jarman and Don Pullen in various trio and quartet settings. Moye also worked and recorded with Cecil McBee, Hamiett Bluiett, Julius Hemphill, Chico Freeman, and Jay Hoggard in the late '70s and early '80s, then joined the Leaders in the mid-'80s. Moye has sessions as a leader available on CD, and can be heard on many Art Ensemble sessions as well. —*Ron Wynn*

○ **Sun Percussion / i.** Jan. 1979 / AECO 001
Quintessential solo recording (all percussion) from an Art Ensemble standout. —*Michael G. Nastos*

Earth Passage / Density / i. Feb. 16-17, 1981 / Black Saint
First-rate compositions, solos, and thematic execution. Moye is especially noteworthy in a fine rhythm section. —*Ron Wynn*

★ **Black Paladins / i.** 1981 / Black Saint
Adventurous concept pieces, excellent percussive foundations, and adept playing. —*Ron Wynn*

MTUME

Group / Early jazz-rock, instrumental pop, modern creative
James "Mtume" Heath, the son of the great tenor saxophonist Jimmy Heath, was once an excellent conga player and percussionist who played jazz and even recorded as a leader for Strata-East. But he departed the jazz world for funk, soul, and urban contemporary production and performance in the '70s. Mtume and Reggie Lucas were a successful production team for several years, working with Stephanie Mills, Phyllis Hyman, and Norman Connors, among others. Mtume recorded hits heading a funk band in the '80s. Prior to moving into pop, Mtume played congas and percussion for Miles Davis, Sonny Rollins, Art Farmer, McCoy Tyner, the Heath Brothers, and many other musicians. His Strata-East sessions included the LP *Land of the Blacks*. Mtume's dates as a leader are not available on CD, but he can be heard on reissued discs by Davis, Rollins, Tyner, and others. —*Ron Wynn*

★ **In Search of the Rainbow Seekers / i.** 1980 / Epic 36017

IDRIS MUHAMMAD (Leo Morris)

b. Nov. 13, 1939, New Orleans, LA
Drums / Hard bop, soul-jazz, contemporary funk, modern creative
Though consistency has not been his strong point, drummer Idris Muhammad has turned in some outstanding performances on hard bop and soul-jazz dates. His own albums as a leader have been another matter; at best and for the most part, they have been undistinguished. Muhammad's strengths include his ability to provide rhythmically dynamic backgrounds and to smoothly vary a session's tempo and pace. Muhammad began playing drums at age eight,

and worked in jazz groups at age 16. He backed soul vocalists Sam Cooke and Jerry Butler in the early and mid-'60s, and also backed the Impressions. Muhammad played with Lou Donaldson in the mid- and late '60s, and was in the pit band for the musical *Hair* from 1969 to 1973. He was Prestige's house drummer in the early '70s, and anchored several rocking soul-jazz dates, while cutting some not-so-rocking dates as a leader. He played with Roberta Flack in the early '70s, led his own bands and played with Johnny Griffin in 1978 and 1979, and played with Pharoah Sanders in 1980. Muhammad's continued his odd recording pattern in the '80s and '90s with such tepid releases as *Black Rhythm Revolution* and *My Turn*. He's recorded as a leader for Prestige, Theresa, and Lipstick, among others. Muhammad has a couple of sessions available on CD. —*Ron Wynn*

Black Rhythm Revolution / i. 1970 / BGP 46
The well-known session drummer steps out front with a session that's funk and soul-jazz oriented. There's minimal solo space, but some expert production and competent playing. —*Ron Wynn*

★ **Kabsha / i.** Nov. 1981 / Theresa 110
Much more jazz oriented than some of the session drummer's releases, this '81 date includes a guest stint by Pharoah Sanders and has Muhammad playing far more aggressively and anchoring the date. —*Ron Wynn*

GERRY MULLIGAN (Gerald Joseph Mulligan)

b. Apr. 6, 1927, New York, NY
Baritone saxophone, arranger / Cool
Gerry Mulligan's fluidity on the baritone sax and his ability to play with speed and lyricism, to execute in the upper and lower registers, and to display bluesy skill on ballads, stamp him as a marvelous improviser. He's also versatile; he has recorded bebop, traditional jazz, and swing, and has backed singers such as Judy Holliday and Annie Ross. He's made exceptional albums with musicians as diverse as Chet Baker and Thelonious Monk. His arrangements are famous for their low dynamics, carefully balanced timbres, and subtle, yet forceful swinging quality.

Mulligan began playing piano, and while still a teen, wrote arrangements for Johnny Warrington's radio band during the mid-'40s. He moved to New York from Philadelphia in 1946, and joined Gene Krupa's band as a staff arranger. Mulligan was involved with Miles Davis's cool nonet in 1949 and 1950. He also contributed arrangements and scores to Elliot Lawrence's and Claude Thornhill's bands. He played with Kai Winding and wrote scores for Stan Kenton's band in the late '40s and early '50s, while recording with his own tenet modeled after the Davis nonet. His debut album was on Prestige in 1951. Mulligan formed his first "pianoless" quartet in 1952 with trumpeter Chet Baker. This group was enormously popular for a short period. Mulligan led a new tenet and various quartets in the mid-'50s, recording for Prestige, EmArcy, Columbia, and Pacific Jazz. He began working with Bob Brookmeyer in the mid-'50s, and maintained a continuing musical relationship with him. Mulligan appeared on the acclaimed "The Sound of Jazz" television show in 1957 and in the movie *Jazz on a Summer's Day* that was filmed at the 1958 Newport Jazz Festival and released in 1960. He recorded the soundtrack for the Susan Hayward film *I Want to Live*, and played and recorded with Duke Ellington and Ben Webster. He had an acting role in the 1960 release *The Subterraneans*.

Mulligan organized a 13-piece concert band in 1960, and toured Europe and, in 1964, Japan. Mulligan underwent a drug ordeal in the '60s, and finally beat his addiction in 1965. He became a busy session and studio musician after disbanding the concert band, playing with Dave Brubeck from the late '60s to the early '70s, and doing freelance arrangements. Mulligan recorded in the '60s for Columbia, Verve, Mercury, Limelight, and Phillips, including a session with Johnny Hodges. He formed a new 14-piece big band, the Age of Steam, in 1972, and was Miami University's artist in residence in 1974. There was a reunion with Baker in 1974. Mulligan led another sextet in the mid- and late '70s with vibist Dave Samuels, worked in New York and Italy, and added soprano sax to his repertoire. He formed a 14-piece concert band in 1978. Mulligan experimented with a 20-piece big band and electronic instruments in the early '80s, then returned to a quintet with Scott Hamiliton and Grady Tate, among others, in the late '80s, while also leading a big band. There were many more sessions in the '70s and '80s for A&M, CTI, Chiaroscuro, Who's Who, DRG, GRP, and PAR. He had wanted to do a reunion session with Miles Davis and cut new *Birth of the Cool* sessions, but Davis died in 1992 before the date. *Rebirth of the Cool* featured Wallace Roney in his spot. Mulligan's early '50s work with Baker has been reissued in a superb Mosaic set. There are numerous Mulligan albums, early and recent, available on CD. —*Ron Wynn*

○ **Mulligan Plays Mulligan** / Sep. 27, 1951 / Prestige 003
A standout date, with Mulligan doing his own songs and top-echelon playing by Allen Eager (ts). —*Ron Wynn*

★ **Pacific Jazz and Capitol Recordings** / Jun. 10, 1952-May 20, 1953 / Mosaic 203(I)
Complete Pacific Jazz and Capitol Recordings of the Original Gerry Mulligan Quartet and Tentette with Chet Baker. Virtually the entire '50s output of the superb Mulligan/Baker small and large groups (except their Fantasy dates). —*Ron Wynn*

Best of Gerry Mulligan Quartet with Chet Baker / Aug. 16, 1952-Dec. 17, 1957 / Pacific Jazz 95481
A good anthology presenting a sampling of cuts linking Chet Baker (tpt) and Mulligan, but far from comprehensive. —*Ron Wynn*

Gerry Mulligan with Paul Chambers / Sep. 2, 1952-Sep. 1954 / Original Jazz Classics 73
With Paul Desmond; 1952 and 1954 dates. This is a sparkling blend of alto and baritone horns. —*Ron Wynn*

○ **Lee Konitz Plays with the Gerry Mulligan Quartet** / Jan. 30, 1953-Feb. 24, 1953 / Pacific Jazz 2

○ **Pleyel Concert (June 1954)** / Jun. 1-7, 1954 / Vogue 655610
Recorded at the Third Paris Jazz Festival, the album captures this particular Gerry Mulligan unit on an inspired occasion. The main attraction of the music is the interplay between Mulligan (bs) and Bob Brookmeyer (vtb), which gives the music substantial depth. The uptempo numbers like "I May Be Wrong" and "Gold Rush" are not merely flag-wavers used to show off prodigious technique but instead allow for some marvelous counterpoint. This is excellent jazz. —*Carl Brauer*, Cadence

California Concerts–Vols. 1 and 2 / Nov. 12, 1954 / Pacific Jazz 46860
A top reissue of the opening volume of a Mulligan live date with Chico Hamilton (d) and Red Mitchell (b). The second volume has eight fresh tracks, with great cuts from tenor saxophonist Zoot Sims, Red Mitchell (b), and Bob Brookmeyer (tb). —*Ron Wynn*

At Storyville / Dec. 1-6, 1956 / Pacific Jazz 94472

○ **Arranger, The** / 1957 / Columbia 34803
As the title announces, this is a notable attempt at documenting the status and evolution of Gerry Mulligan's first love: orchestral arrangement. It makes available for the first time a handful of Mulligan's primal, formative arrangements for Gene Krupa and Elliot Lawrence's orchestras, as well as several extensive blowing sessions from his own late '50s orchestra with Bob Brookmeyer, Lee Konitz, and Zoot Sims, predating his imperial Concert Jazz Band. Actually, the signature of Mulligan's style changed little over the 11 years documented here. He consistently favored a seamless themeline underscored with a smooth sax bedding, stated often in terms of simple counterpoint and gentle contrary sweeps. But it was from the timing of those lines, the way they stretched around and overlapped one another, and the percussive texture of whole sections, that he derived his re-

silent and elegant sense of tension. —*Mikal Gilmore*, Down Beat

○ **Mulligan Meets Monk** / Aug. 12-13, 1957 / Riverside 12247

○ **Gerry Mulligan Meets Stan Getz** / Oct. 22, 1957 / Verve 8535

★ **Gerry Mulligan Meets Ben Webster** / Nov. 3, 1959-Dec. 2, 1959 / PolyGram 841661
Gerry Mulligan Meets Ben Webster is a classic confrontation of two of the mellowest, most virile, and most expressive of saxophonists. Recorded when Mulligan was 32 and Webster 50 (Los Angeles, November 1959), this is my personal favorite of several meetings Norman Granz set up for Mulligan in Verve's heyday (including Johnny Hodges, Stan Getz, Paul Desmond, and Orrin Keepnews's Monk encounter). Mulligan's renowned adaptability complements rather than idolizes Webster, and the two prove boon companions (like genial sumo wrestlers sparring), blowing heads at full sail or cracking fours with drummer Mel Lewis. Mutual respect inspires them and never fades into obeisance, and the rhythm supports admirably (keyed by the sprightly, canny Jimmy Rowles on piano) with never a thought to obtruding on the dialog—practically unimaginable today! Mulligan beauties—blues, ballad, blues—take it out nice and easy. No rush, but timing everywhere is perfection. —*Fred Bouchard*, Down Beat

☆ **Holliday with Mulligan** / Apr. 10-17, 1961 / DRG 5191
Here is a previously unreleased set by the Gerry Mulligan band in a unique setting—backup to a singer. The main problem here is not with the material, including four Mulligan-Judy Holliday collaborations, or the arrangements by Ralph Burns, Bill Finegan, Al Cohn, Bob Brookmeyer, or Mulligan. The problem is that this is first and foremost a singer's date and Holliday was not a jazz singer. She had a flat, deadpan singing voice with a limited range; no doubt it will be described as "poignant" and "charming." If that is the case, this record is heavy on charm, light on jazz, but still a very interesting footnote. —*Bob Rusch*, Cadence

☆ **Jeru** / Jun. 8, 1962-Aug. 13, 1962 / RCA Victor 2624

Night Lights / Sep. 12, 1963-Oct. 3, 1963 / Verve 818271
Has class and charm. Art Farmer shines on trumpet and meshes well with Mulligan. —*Ron Wynn*

Age of Steam / Feb. 1971-Jul. 17, 1971 / A&M 0804
This large orchestral work marked the start of Mulligan's post-Brubeck period. —*Ron Wynn*

Walk on the Water / Sep. 1980 / DRG 5194

Soft Lights and Sweet Music / Jan. 1986 / Concord Jazz 4300

Symphonic Dreams / Feb. 6-7, 1987 / Pro Arte 703

★ **Lonesome Boulevard** / i. 1990 / A&M 5326

○ **Rebirth of the Cool** / Jan. 1992 / GRP 9679
Baritone saxophonist Gerry Mulligan fulfilled a long dream in '92 with a rerecording of the late '40s sessions that launched the "cool" era. He'd wanted to do it with trumpeter Miles Davis, but Davis died before the project could reach fruition. So trumpeter Wallace Roney took his spot, and he does an admirable job. Gil Evans is the other principal who'd died, but pianist John Lewis, alto saxophonist Phil Woods, and vocalist Mel Tormé help rekindle the original feeling. —*Ron Wynn*

Meets the Saxophonists / PolyGram 827436
A cross-section of cuts matching Mulligan with most of the great sax players, among them Ben Webster, Paul Desmond, Stan Getz, Johnny Hodges, and Zoot Sims. —*Ron Wynn*

JIMMY MUNDY (James Mundy)

b. Jun. 28, 1907, Cincinnati, OH, **d.** Apr. 24, 1983, New York, NY

Arranger, tenor saxophone / Swing, big band
A superb arranger, one of the swing era's finest, Jimmy Mundy was a vital contributor to sessions by everyone from Earl Hines to Count Basie in the '30s and '40s. Mundy

trained as a classical violinist and toured with an evange-list's orchestra while a teen, playing violin and tenor sax. He developed his arranging skill working in Washington during the mid-'20s. Mundy worked for Earl Hines in the early and mid-'30s, providing arrangements of "Cavernism" and "Copenhagen," among others, for Hines. Mundy also played tenor sax and recorded while with Hines. Mundy arranged "Swingtime in the Rockies," "Jumpin' at the Woodside," "Solo Flight," and "Air Mail Special" while serving as staff arranger for Benny Goodman in the mid-'30s. "Swingtime in the Rockies" and "Solo Flight" were also Mundy composi-tions. Gene Krupa recorded Mundy arrangements in the '30s. Mundy recorded for Varsity in 1937, and led his own big band briefly in 1939. He supplied several arrangements to Count Basie in the '40s, among them "Super Chief," "Queer Street," and "Blue Skies." He also had arrangements recorded by Dizzy Gillespie in the '40s. Mundy didn't do much in jazz from the '50s on, though he occasionally wrote arrangements for and led studio orchestras that backed var-ious jazz and pop musicians. He served as music director for Barclay Records in France in the late '50s and early '60s, then returned to New York and provided more freelance studio arrangements. Vintage Basie and Goodman reissues feature stunning Mundy arrangements and compositions. —*Ron Wynn*

MARK MURPHY (Mark Howe Murphy)

b. Mar. 14, 1932, Syracuse, NY
Vocals / Ballads & blues
A truly great scat singer, an inventive and humorous vocal-ist, and a witty and outspoken individual, Mark Murphy has been a jazz artist for his entire career. He hasn't expanded into more lucrative areas, and hasn't tried "lite" jazz or fu-sion. Instead, he's played animated standards, surging origi-nals, sensitive ballads, and he's done his characteristic scat-ting. Murphy began performing at age 16. He toured and recorded in the late '50s and early '60s, earning some fame by appearing on Steve Allen's "Jazz Scene USA." Allen pro-vided the title track of Murphy's album *This Could Be the Start of Something*. He began recording on Decca, then turned to Capitol and Riverside, with Al Cohn serving as arranger and director for *That's How I Love the Blues*. He moved to London in the mid-'60s, and toured Europe, mak-ing periodic radio and television broadcasts and recordings. He recorded *Midnight Mood* in Germany. Murphy returned to America in 1973. Since then, he's recorded exclusively for Muse, except for one Audiophile session. Murphy works for a fee rather than royalties, and retains creative control. He's continued recording throughout the '80s and into the '90s. Many Murphy sessions are available on CD. —*Ron Wynn and Michael G. Nastos*

Rah / Sep. 1961-Oct. 1961 / Riverside 9395
○ **That's How I Love the Blues** / 1962 / Riverside 367
☆ **Bop for Kerouac** / Mar. 12, 1981 / Muse 5253
On *Bop For Kerouac*, alto saxophonist Richie Cole plays Charlie Parker to vocalist Mark Murphy's Miles Davis. You get the vividly hot and detached cool intensity of the music. Kerouac captures the feeling in his writing, which is charted lovingly here in keyboarder Bill Mays's nostalgic yet exul-tantly contemporary settings. The makeup inspires solos that are on target and dancing. The singer's thoroughly mas-culine timbre coarsens or cracks for dramatic emphasis. His vibrato swaggers or glides. *Bop For Kerouac* is a great al-bum for romance. —*Owen Cordle*, Down Beat

★ **Artistry of Mark Murphy** / Apr. 2-3, 1982 / Muse 5286
Includes a stunning medley of "Babe's Blue/Little Niles/Dat Dere." Recorded with Tom Harrell (tpt), Gene Bertoncini (g), and Ben Aranov (p) in a larger-group setting. —*Michael G. Nastos*
☆ **Beauty and the Beast** / 1983-1986 / Muse 5355
This is really good Murphy, arranged by Bill Mays. McCoy Tyner's "Effendi" is a highlight, as are "Doxy" and "I Can't Get Started." —*Michael G. Nastos*
☆ **Kerouac Then and Now** / Nov. 1986 / Muse 5359

September Ballads / Sep. 15, 1987-Nov. 22, 1987 / Milestone 9154
Includes some beautiful playing from Larry Coryell (g) and Art Farmer (tpt). —*Ron Wynn*
What a Way to Go / Nov. 1990 / Muse 5419

TURK MURPHY (Melvin Edward Alton Murphy)

b. Dec. 16, 1915, Palermo, CA, **d.** May 30, 1987, San Francisco, CA
Trombone, bandleader / New Orleans traditional
A major force in the '40s traditional jazz movement, Turk Murphy helped popularize the genre in San Francisco dur-ing World War II. He was among the more colorful players, and utilized the full array of "tailgate" effects, achieving moods ranging from humor to pathos. His solos were robust, and he mixed period pieces with familiar ballads and origi-nals. Murphy was in Lu Watters's early '40s band before forming his own group in 1947. This band recorded from the '50s to the '80s. They were based in San Francisco, and were the resident band at Earthquake McGoon's, a night club that Murphy and Pete Clute (his pianist) co-owned for many years. They also did some East Coast dates, toured Australia and Europe in the '70s, and played in the Netherlands dur-ing the '80s. The San Francisco Traditional Jazz Foundation opened a museum honoring Turk Murphy in the Front Page in San Francisco in 1986. Despite a lengthy illness, Murphy continued playing until his final days. Several Murphy ses-sions on the Good Time Jazz, GHB, Sonic, and Verve labels are available on CD. —*Ron Wynn and Bruce Boyd Raeburn*

Turk Murphy-Vol. 1 / May 31, 1949-Jan. 19, 1950 / Good Time Jazz 12026
Turk Murphy Jazz Band, 1949 and 1950. Murphy with Bob Scobey (tpt), Burt Bales (p), Bob Helm (cl), and others doing what comes naturally on "Struttin' with Some Barbecue," "New Orleans Stomp," "1919 Rag," and other favorites. —*Bruce Raeburn*
○ **Favorites** / i. 1949-1951 / Good Time Jazz 60011
Turk Murphy Jazz Band. A good introduction to the Turk Murphy style. —*Bruce Raeburn*
○ **San Francisco Jazz-Vol. 1** / Jan. 19, 1950 / Good Time Jazz 12026
★ **Turk Murphy's Jazz Band** / May 8, 1950 / Good Time Jazz
Turk Murphy is a Kid Ory-inspired trombonist featured prominently in the revivalist era. This record (and Vol. 2) is a classic of sorts (historical more than musical). It rates high in enthusiasm and for Bob Scobey's trumpet, but low for fi-nesse and subtlety; repeated and extended listenings be-come a bit weary. —*Bob Rusch,* Cadence
○ **San Francisco Jazz-Vol. 2** / May 8, 1950-Jul. 10, 1951 / Good Time Jazz
○ **Music of Jelly Roll Morton** / Aug. 29, 1953-Sep. 14, 1953 / Columbia 559
Concert in the Park / Aug. 10, 1986 / Merry Makers 117
A rarity—Turk Murphy recorded live. A classic performance of "Weary Blues" closes the set. —*Bruce Raeburn*

DAVID MURRAY (David Keith Murray)

b. Feb. 19, 1955, Berkeley, CA
Tenor saxophone, bass clarinet, bandleader / Early free, modern creative
David Murray may be the most recorded jazz musician in modern music history. If it's true that Duke Ellington recorded almost everything he ever did, Murray must come close to doing the same thing. His output has included solo dates and sessions with quartets, quintets, octets, big bands, and duos. Murray's recorded for numerous foreign labels, plus various Columbia/Sony custom and subsidiary compa-nies. He's now one of the artists featured on the Sony/DIW joint venture. That's not counting the sessions Murray's done with the World Saxophone Quartet, Clarinet Summit, Jack DeJohnette's Special Edition, and other dates that may not have even been publicized in America. Murray has achieved

a distinctive synthesis of classic and contemporary influences. His tenor sax blends the sanctified gospel/voice-like effects of free era players like Albert Ayler with the soulful, huge-toned, swinging approach of Coleman Hawkins and the bebop/hard bop mode of Sonny Rollins. Murray's octave leaps, upper-register squeals and screams, and shuddering and explosive phrases are always employed intelligently, even though his solos sometimes seem to burst with tension and energy. He's overcome a tendency, in his early years, to substitute volume and effect for ideas, and his ballads are played as impressively as his originals and uptempo tunes. Murray's bass clarinet has the rumbling, boisterous elements of Eric Dolphy, plus Harry Carney's lyrical, reflective qualities and Murray's stately touches.

He grew up on the West Coast and began taking piano lessons as a child, playing stride and ragtime, before beginning on alto sax at age nine. He played with his mother, a famous gospel singer, in their Berkeley church. Murray played in a soul group as a teen, and also played in bebop and swing bands. He studied and played at Pomona College with Stanley Crouch, Bobby Bradford, and Arthur Blythe, who helped introduce him to free jazz in the mid-'70s. Murray, along with Crouch, Blythe, and James Newton, moved to New York in the '70s. In 1976, Murray was a cofounder of the World Saxophone Quartet with Oliver Lake, Julius Hemphill, and Hamiet Bluiett. He's since led other bands, working with Olu Dara, Lawrence "Butch" Morris, Art Davis, Anthony Braxton, Don Cherry, Edward Blackwell, Air and Henry Threadgill, Sunny Murray, James "Blood" Ulmer, and many others. Murray was part of the "loft jazz" movement in the mid-'70s, played in the Wildflowers concert, and was featured on the album series. He was once touted by *Village Voice* critic Gary Giddins as one of the few players in the loft jazz movement worthy of unqualified praise. Murray began recording in the mid-'70s on Adelphi, and has since cranked out many sessions for India Navigation, Circle, Red, Marge, Black Saint, DIW, Palm, Horo, Cecma, Hat Hut, Hat Art, Columbia/Portrait, Red Baron, and Sony/DIW. There are numerous Murray sessions available on CD, but he's done many more. —*Ron Wynn and Stephen Aldrich*

Low Class Conspiracy / May 14, 1976 / Adelphi 5002
This is one of his earliest albums to make an impact on the general jazz audience. Fred Hopkins (b) and Phillip Wilson (d) excel. —*Ron Wynn*

★ **Flowers for Albert** / Jun. 26, 1976 / India Navigation
Twenty-one-year-old tenor saxophonist David Murray (1976) personifies the new generation of jazz musicians—a forward-looking artist steeped in the whole history and tradition of jazz from Louis Armstrong to Albert Ayler. As far as the tenor sax is concerned, Murray lists Coleman Hawkins, Lester Young, John Coltrane, Sonny Rollins, Archie Shepp, Roscoe Mitchell, and Dewey Redman as influences in one way or another. Listening to him play, one is immediately struck by his control, flexibility, and range. He can play with a bluesy brashness or delicate wistfulness. A technique of his I'm especially fond of is his use of an airy, ethereal intonation that appears as fragile as a spider's web but has the same inner strength. A common link to all four pieces of this live recording from the Ladies' Fort in New York City is a relaxed restraint. Nobody is trying to dazzle the listener with speed or technique; there are no ego trips. Drummer Phillip Wilson is so unobtrusive that one might overlook his importance to the overall mood and sound. At times, such as on parts of "Roscoe," a Murray/Wilson duet, he lays out completely. "Ballad for a Decomposed Beauty" is another duet, this time with Murray and bassist Fred Hopkins, whose arco playing will dazzle you. Olu Dara's bright trumpet can be heard on the two quartet pieces, "Joanne's Green Satin Dress" and "Flowers for Albert," the latter my personal favorite with its engaging melody line. Maybe after hearing Murray, the "jazz-is-dead-or-dying" crowd will finally be silenced. —*Carl Brauer*, Cadence

Solomon's Sons / Jan. 16, 1977 / Circle 5

○ **Live at the Lower Manhattan Ocean Club–Vols. 1 & 2** / Dec. 31, 1977 / India Navigation 1032
In his discursive, two-volume concert with trumpeter Lester Bowie at the Lower Manhattan Ocean Club, David Murray seems to have stretched out beyond the limits of his improvisatory resources, often resorting to baldly imitative borrowings from Ornette Coleman, Albert Ayler, and Archie Shepp. Bowie frequently dominates the *Live* sessions, but he too rambles on at length, falling back on his familiar repertoire of half-valve squawks and smears. The rhythm duo of bassist Fred Hopkins and drummer Phillip Wilson, far more effective on Murray's debut, *Low Class Conspiracy*, is largely at fault. Surely, the two sets could have been packaged together or condensed into one, avoiding the awkward sequencing of two long pieces on the second volume, following the four shorter ones, including the apparent finale, on the first. —*Larry Birnbaum*, Down Beat

Interboogieology / Feb. 1978 / Black Saint 0018
More rousing quartet material. Murray emerges as a standout with singular style. —*Ron Wynn*

○ **Murray's 3D Family** / Sep. 3, 1978 / Hat Art 6020
This particular two-record set captures tenor saxophonist David Murray and his trio in performance at the '78 Willisau Jazz Festival. From the opening high-energy tenor exorcisms of "In Memory of Jomo Kenyatta" to the final quiet ending of "Shout Song" this trio is in total command of its music. Murray's most outside playing is found on the opening track, but he never falls over into random noise or the trap of running out of ideas. I was particularly struck by how close to the blues Murray's music is. Both "3D Family" and "P.O. In Cairo" are heavily laden with the feeling of the blues, albeit a kind of inside-out blues. Murray's vocalizations on tenor are also well documented on each of the pieces. "Shout Song" has some semi-whispering passages, while "P.O." gets into a more overt style. There is also an example of Murray's down-and-out romantic lyricism in the lovely "Patricia." Both bassist Johnny Dyani and drummer Andrew Cyrille are major contributors to the album's success, particularly Dyani, whose arco harmonics on "Shout Song" are breathtaking. Cyrille has a couple of minor solo gems on "3D Family" and "Patricia." —*Carl Brauer*, Cadence

Sweet Lovely / Dec. 4-5, 1979 / Brass Star 0039

★ **Ming** / Jul. 25+28, 1980 / Black Saint 120045
Saxophonist David Murray is at his best when his protean technique is prodded beyond an emulative mode by lean material and taxing company. These conditions figure more prominently on this octet outing than on any recording that had been issued under Murray's leadership to that point (1980). Murray rises so impressively to the occasion as a triple-threat composer, arranger, and soloist that his budding legend gains new credibility. Confirming Murray's importance as a post-Ayler traditionalist, *Ming* may very well prove to be his first indispensable recording. Murray galvanizes this sterling unit with a diverse program culled, in large measure, from previously recorded material. Earlier versions of "Dewey's Circle" and "The Fast Life" had not been fully fleshed in comparison to the rich, close-order arrangements given here. Spliced in the rapid fire of "Dewey's Circle" is a hip-shaking strut that prompts neo-New Orleans polyphony, highlighted by trumpeter Olu Dara's heralding of Louis Armstrong. Formerly a launching pad of boppish flash, "The Fast Life" gains heft from a tight weave of brass and reeds; barreling unaccompanied four-bar exchanges from the horns; and pummeling solos from Murray, cornetist Butch Morris, pianist Anthony Davis, and drummer Steve McCall. Murray's orchestration of "The Hill" fowards an emotional duality more clearly than do the solo or quartet versions currently available. With the title piece and "Jasvan," Murray taps the torchy essence of the ballad and the sleek syncopations of the waltz without a trace of overt influence. His tenor slipknots a few wisps of melody in the title piece to create a romantic atmosphere that is emphatic but not overbearing. —*Bill Shoemaker*, Down Beat

○ **Home** / Oct. 31, 1981+Nov. 1, 1981 / Brass Star 0055
Tenor saxophonist David Murray regrouped the same octet (Henry Threadgill/Olu Dara/Butch and Wilber Morris/Steve McCall/Anthony Davis/George Lewis) that recorded *Ming* on this 1981 recording. This LP seems to bring greater emphasis to arrangement, with mixed results. Employing a Charles Mingus-like ersatz free ensemble confusion on "Santa Barbara and Crenshaw Follies" is most effective, but I found the moody pastels of the title track (5:58) little more than exercise. On "Last of the Hipmen" (9:12) the arrangement is more open, but still effective and important in giving impetus to the strong solo workings. Actually, there is not a weak solo moment on the set, and that combination of arrangements and ensemble strength makes this more than just another date. —*Bob Rusch*, Cadence

☆ **Murray's Steps** / Jul. 19, 1982 / Black Saint 120065
David Murray's octet stands as the premier ensemble in contemporary jazz, and this, their third album, is an effervescent, swinging, joyous piece of work. Henry Threadgill, Butch Morris, Steve McCall, and Wilber Morris are still in tow from previous Murray Octet albums, with Craig Harris (tb), Bobby Bradford (tpt), and Curtis Clark (p) replacing, respectively, George Lewis, Olu Dara, and Anthony Davis. It's hard to single out soloists or solos here. Threadgill's foray on the title tune is a fiery alto turn, while his flute work on "Sing-Song" is colorful and pretty; Murray is soulful throughout, whether on tenor or, as on "Sweet Lovely," a soft, vocal bass clarinet; Craig Harris is typically nimble and sly on each of his turns; the two trumpeters, Bradford and Butch Morris (actually on cornet) are a delightful study in contrasts—the former aggressive and witty, the latter spare and lovely; Clark is a jagged soloist and full, generous comper; bassist Morris and drummer McCall are gloriously tight in providing the backbone. This is a group effort, but the combined voice is very much that of David Murray. He's proven himself, at age 27, a fully developed writer and bandleader and a still-growing soloist. —*Lee Jeske*, Down Beat

Morning Song / Sep. 25, 1983 / Black Saint 120075
Tenor saxophonist and bass clarinetist David Murray has seldom recorded a bad album, no matter what the label or the configuration. This is a straightahead quartet set, with lengthy, tartly played originals and some high-register wailing by Murray on tenor and bass clarinet. —*Ron Wynn*

○ **Live at Sweet Basil–Vol. 1** / Aug. 24-26, 1984 / Black Saint 0085

○ **Live at Sweet Basil–Vol. 2** / Aug. 24-26, 1984 / Black Saint 95
The second of two marvelous big-band dates featuring the Murray big band recorded at Sweet Basil's. The band includes the cream of '70s and '80s jazz, with Murray roaring and spearheading things on tenor and bass clarinet, and Butch Morris conducting. —*Ron Wynn*

Hope Scope / May 1987 / Black Saint 120139

Healers, The / Sep. 1987 / Brass Star 120118

Ming's Samba / i. Jul. 20, 1988 / Portrait 44432
Recorded at CBS Studios in New York City, this album is named after David Murray's wife Ming. It includes some nice work, in particular the very lovely cut "Spooning." —*Michael Erlewine*

○ **Special Quartet** / 1990 / Columbia 52955
A simply magnificent Murray quartet session from '90, among the first issued under a joint Columbia/DIW deal. His roaring tenor sax is the focal point for some excellent compositions that are punctuated by pianist McCoy Tyner, bassist Fred Hopkins, and drummer Elvin Jones. Here's one group that most definitely should record again. —*Ron Wynn*

Shakill's Warrior / Mar. 1991 / Columbia 48963

○ **David Murray Big Band, Conducted by Lawrence "Butch" Morris** / Mar. 1991 / Columbia 48964
The triptych of tenor homages (Ben Webster, Lester Young, Paul Gonsalves) is an invigorating reassessment of David Murray's roots, with an unavoidable touch of Duke Ellington

and Charles Mingus in the orchestration. Nice solos sliced in by the likes of trumpeter Hugh Ragin, trombonist Craig Harris, clarinetist Don Byron, and alto saxophonist James Spaulding, too. Conductor Butch Morris's "Calling Steve McCall," for the late AACM drummer, acts as a memorial coda. High spirits are represented by Harris's "Lovejoy," another sizzler with surprising interludes, while Murray's "Istanbul" is a fragrant whiff of exotic spices, and "David's Tune" swaggers in on a backbeat and a bad attitude. —*Art Lange*, Down Beat

Spirituals / i. Apr. 1991 / DIW 841

Black and Black / i. 1992 / Red Baron 48852
A powerhouse '92 session by the prolific tenor saxophonist and bass clarinetist David Murray. He heads a strong quintet with trumpeter Marcus Belgrave, pianist Kirk Lightsey, bassist Santi Debriano, and drummer Roy Haynes through some bristling uptempo originals, mixed with a couple of nice midtempo and ballad pieces for contrast. —*Ron Wynn*

○ **MX** / i. Dec. 21, 1992 / Red Baron 53274
MX takes David Murray about as far inside as he goes. Dedicated to Malcolm X, *MX* is no dirge. Murray contributes three memorable new tunes, ranging from an exotic processional ("Icarus") to uptown R&B ("Harlemite"). Murray shares solo space with John Hicks, Bobby Bradford, and Ravi Coltrane on tenor. The kid competently handles everything thrown at him, including Murray's high-speed blues, "El Hajj Malik El-Shabazz." —*Jon Andrews*, Down Beat

Body and Soul / i. 1993 / Black Saint 120155-2
The prolific David Murray manages an impressive feat: no matter how many albums he issues, he never coasts or goes through the motions. This is mainly a quartet date, though Murray shows on the title track his ability to back a singer and play in a conventional, restrained mode as Taana Running gives a moving vocal, complete with her original lyrics. Otherwise these are either spirited uptempo numbers or equally energized ballads. Murray's riveting, undulating lines and sweeping tenor sound remain a marvel no matter how often you hear them, and few can match him in controlling his drive, pitch, and volume. Murray has picked some fine players who do not get much exposure in pianist Sonelius Smith and bassist Wilber Morris; they show their selection was not simply a favor from a friend. Drummer Rashied Ali has not lost the rippling intensity from his days with John Coltrane; he and Murray conclude things in a dazzling duo performance on "Cuttin' Corners" that is deliberately intended to evoke memories of the Coltrane/Ali album *Interstellar Space*. It does, but it also shows that time does not stand still and that Ali has grown as a player. Do not neglect this date thinking it is merely one more David Murray album; all his sessions are special. —*Ron Wynn*

SUNNY MURRAY (James Marcellus Arthur Murray)

b. Sep. 21, 1937, Idabel, OK
Drums, percussion / Early free, modern creative
An animated and energetic drummer, Sunny Murray is known for his slashing cymbals, pronounced emphasis on the bass drum and tom toms, and swirling, driving style that's both fluid and fully percussive. His approach furthered the cause of rhythmic freedom in the '60s, as he explored multiple pitches and various timbres on drums, changing the tone and pace of a group's music rather than simply meshing with the rhythm section or pushing the group from the background. He began playing drums at age nine, and moved to New York in the late '50s. Murray worked with Red Allen, Willie "The Lion" Smith, Jackie McLean, and Ted Curson before meeting Cecil Taylor in 1959. He traveled to Europe with Taylor and Jimmy Lyons in 1963. While with Taylor, Murray's style evolved dramatically, and it continued changing after he played with John Coltrane's quartet in an informal situation. Murray worked periodically with Albert Ayler during the mid-'60s, usually in a trio situation with Gary Peacock, while making his recording debut as a leader. He worked with Don Cherry and Archie Shepp before re-

turning to Europe in 1968. In Europe, he played with Shepp, Moncur, and with other American and European musicians. Most of Murray's '60s albums were for Byg, though he also made sessions that were unreleased; one for Columbia, and one session narrated by Amiri Baraka. Murray altered his playing slightly during the late '70s, switching to a more conventional rhythmic approach. His group, the Untouchable Factor, appeared at the mid-'70s Wildflowers concerts that spotlighted bands playing in New York City lofts (also known as "loft jazz" bands). Murray recorded for the Philly Jazz label in 1978 with Don Pullen, Cecil McBee, and Frank Foster, and made other '70s dates on Moers and Circle, a pair of foreign labels. He led a quintet in the '80s that included Grachan Moncur III, Steve Coleman, Curtis Clark, and Williams Parker, and led another more unorthodox group with two violins and two tenors, while maintaining his relationship with Untouchable Factor. Murray recorded again with Taylor in 1980 and with David Eyges. Currently, there are no Murray titles available on CD, at least according to the *Schwann* catalog. —*Ron Wynn*

Sunny Murray Quintet / Jul. 23, 1966 / ESP
Dynamic, slashing, left-field jazz, both free form and more traditional hard bop. —*Ron Wynn*

○ **Hard Cores** / i. 1968 / Philly Jazz

Homage to Africa / Aug. 15, 1969 / BYG
If you can find it, this is a celebratory blend of nationalism, avant-garde fire, and spectacular drumming. —*Ron Wynn*

★ **Never Give a Sucker an Even Break** / Nov. 22, 1969 / Affinity
This recording from 11/22/69 featuring drummer Sunny Murray was revolutionary music of the period. Free rhythm, resuscitations, and spiritual quaverings make up an LP of music that sprang directly from the Albert Ayler/John

Coltrane roots. It's a solid effort in structured freedom, rather even-handed, and with no great peaks or insights revealed. —*Bob Rusch*, Cadence

Applecores / 1978-1979 / Philly Jazz 1004

AMINA CLAUDINE MYERS

b. Mar. 1943, Blackwell, AR
Piano, organ, vocals / Modern creative
Both a fine instrumentalist and a vocalist, Amina Claudine Myers has displayed an individualistic, sparkling approach on organ, piano, and various synthesizers and keyboards when playing free music or wailing the blues. She began formal music studies at age seven, and directed and sang in gospel groups throughout her childhood and through high school. Myers played in jazz and rock groups in Arkansas, then moved to Chicago, where she became a public school teacher. Myers became a member of the Association for the Advancement of Creative Musicians (AACM) and worked with Sonny Stitt and Gene Ammons. She commuted between New York and Chicago during the mid-'70s, working with AACM members. Myers moved to Europe in 1980 and remained there for several years before returning to New York. She did free sessions with Lester Bowie, Muhal Richard Abrams, and Frank Lowe in the late '70s and early '80s, plus gospel with Martha Bass, David Peaston, and Fontella Bass in 1980. Myers has recorded as a leader for Sweet Earth, Leo, Minor Music, and Black Saint. She has a couple of sessions available on CD. —*Ron Wynn and Michael G. Nastos*

★ **Song for Mother E** / i. 1979 / Leo 100
Duets with percussionist Pheeroan AkLaff. Sounds like a bigger group. Excellent. —*Michael G. Nastos*

☆ **Salutes Bessie Smith** / i. 1980 / Leo 103

N

NAJEE

Tenor and soprano saxophone / Instrumental pop
Najee is a popular multi-instrumentalist whose style is very
similar to Kenny G's, Dave Koz's, and George Howard's. His
releases feature heavily produced, tightly arranged covers of
urban contemporary songs, often include appearances by
R&B vocalists, and have very limited solos and improvisational space. A saxophonist, flutist, and occasional keyboardist, Najee makes no claims to being a jazz musician,
but his releases are marketed as "contemporary" jazz, and
he's aired on "lite" jazz stations. He's recorded several sessions for EMI and Manhattan; all are available on CD. —*Ron
Wynn*

RAY NANCE (Ray Willis Nance)

b. Dec. 10, 1913, Chicago, IL, **d.** Jan. 28, 1976, New York, NY
Trumpet, cornet, violin, vocals / Swing, big band
A versatile trumpeter, violinist, vocalist, and dancer, Ray
Nance brought both high artistic and great entertainment
values to the Duke Ellington orchestra. His violin solos, replete with plucked string segments, broken lines, and bluesy
phrases, were crowd pleasers, while his ringing, superbly
played trumpet solos and occasional vocals were equally
well appreciated. Nance wasn't as accomplished on mutes as
predecessor Bubber Miley, but could provide exaggerated,
voice-like effects and tonal colors. Nance even sometimes
added some dance excitement. He began on piano at age six,
and took lessons on violin while teaching himself trumpet.
Nance was a drum major in high school, then led a sextet in
Chicago in the early and mid-'30s. He worked with Earl
Hines and Horace Henderson, mostly as a trumpeter, in the
late '30s. Nance performed solo for a few months in 1940,
then joined the Ellington orchestra, where he was free to
showcase his entire repertoire. Nance remained with
Ellington until 1963, taking only a few brief periods off dur-
ing the 23-year run. His violin was featured on such cuts as
"Moon Mist" and "Come Sunday," while his wah-wah trumpet embellished an early '40s version of "Take the A-Train."
Nance later switched to cornet in the '60s. After leaving the
Ellington orchestra, Nance played at the mid-'60s World's
Fair with Paul Lavelle's orchestra, and with Sol Yaged in the
late '60s and Brooks Kerr in 1973. He toured England with
Chris Barber in 1974, then worked New York clubs. Nance
can be heard on numerous Ellington recordings. He also
recorded with Paul Gonsalves on Solid State, Black Lion,
and MPS/BASF. Except for Black Lion, these recordings are
not available on CD. —*Ron Wynn*
★ **Body and Soul** / **i.** Apr. 1969 / Solid State 18062

SAM NANTON

b. 1904, **d.** 1946
Trombone / Swing, big band
"Tricky" Sam Nanton was one of the most compelling trombonists in the Ellington orchestra. The emotional directness
and intensity of his playing, coupled with his ability on the
plunger, made every Nanton solo memorable. His growls
and humorous choruses were often featured during
Ellington's "jungle" period, and after it. In the early '20s,

Nanton played with Cliff Jackson and Elmer Snowden before joining Ellington in the mid-'20s. Nanton was featured
on songs such as "East St. Louis Toodle-oo," "Harlem Flat
Blues," and "A Portrait of Bert Williams." He also recorded
with Cootie Williams on Varsity, and with Rex Stewart on
Vocalion. Unfortunately, Nanton didn't have a long life, but
he made sizable contributions to Ellington and to jazz in
those short years. He can be heard on many Ellington reissues. —*Ron Wynn*

MARTY NAPOLEON (Matthew Napoli Napoleon)

b. Jun. 2, 1921, New York, NY
Piano / New Orleans traditional
Pianist Marty Napoleon actually preferred bebop to traditional jazz, but because of his famous uncle (Phil Napoleon),
he was always placed in the early camp. Napoleon had good
touch, fine phrasing and range, and displayed flexibility and
fluidity in his solos. He effectively moved back and forth between the two styles. Napoleon started as a trumpeter, but a
heart attack caused him to switch to piano. He worked in the
big bands of Chico Marx, Joe Venuti, Lee Castle, and Charlie
Barnet in the early '40s, then replaced his brother, Teddy, in
Gene Krupa's band in 1945. He joined his uncle's Memphis
Five band in 1950, where he got his traditional jazz initia-
tion. The next year, Napoleon played in Charlie Ventura's Big
Four. He later worked with Louis Armstrong's All-Stars, then
co-led a quartet with his brother. Napoleon ended the '50s
working with Coleman Hawkins and Charlie Shavers, then
led his own trios and played solo in the '60s. Napoleon
would reunite periodically with Armstrong in the late '60s.
He continued working into the '80s, recording with Peanuts
Hucko in 1983 and appearing at an Armstrong memorial
concert in New York in 1986. Napoleon recorded with
Ventura, Krupa, Armstrong, Ruby Braff, and Red Allen,
among others, on Manor, Columbia, Clef, Decca, Concert
Hall, RCA, Mercury, and Brunswick. He has no albums listed
under his name as a leader on CD. —*Ron Wynn*

PHIL NAPOLEON

b. Sep. 2, 1901, Boston, MA, **d.** Oct. 1, 1990
Trumpet / New Orleans traditional
The leader of the original Memphis Five, Phil Napoleon was
a competent, though unimaginative trumpeter whose greatest value was the many recording sessions he led that
helped increase jazz's popularity in the mid-'20s. Napoleon
was part of the huge musical family that also included saxophonists George and Joe, drummer Ted, guitarist Matthew,
and pianist Marty, the best player in the family. Phil
Napoleon also played with the Cotton Pickers and
Charleston Chasers, then led his own bands in the '30s. He
worked with the Dorsey brothers, with Joe Venuti and Eddie
Lang, then played in radio orchestras. Napoleon briefly led a
big band later in the '30s, then entered the instrument business. He returned to playing in 1949, and appeared at Nick's
until he moved to Florida in 1956. Napoleon played at the
1959 Newport Jazz Festival, and opened a club in Miami,
Napoleon's Retreat, in 1966. He remained active into the
'80s. Napoleon recorded for labels such as Arto, Paramount,
Vocalion, and Columbia leading the Memphis Five, and

Edison, Victor, Swan, Decca, Capitol, and Okeh, among others, as a leader. Search out import and specialty stores for his recordings. —*Ron Wynn*

JAMIL NASSER

b. 1932
Bass / Modern creative
A topflight hard bop and bebop bassist, Jamil Nasser has also played blues and R&B, and has doubled on tuba. Nasser studied piano with his mother, then began on bass at age 16. He led the band during his student days at Arkansas State University in the late '40s and early '50s, then played bass and tuba while in the army. After his discharge, Nasser worked on electric bass with B.B. King in 1955 and 1956, then moved to New York. He played and recorded with Phineas Newborn in 1956 and 1958, while working with Sonny Rollins. He toured Europe and North Africa with Idrees Sulieman in 1959, and recorded with Lester Young in Paris. Nasser lived in Italy in 1961, then returned to America the next year and formed a trio that he led until 1964. He worked with Ahmad Jamal for eight years from the mid-'60s until 1972, then played periodically with Al Haig through the late '70s. Nasser did sessions during the '80s and '90s, working with Clifford Jordan, among others. He doesn't have any dates as a leader, but can be heard on several early '70s Jamal CD reissues. —*Ron Wynn*

FATS NAVARRO (Theodore Navarro)

b. Sep. 24, 1923, Key West, FL, **d.** Jul. 7, 1960, New York, NY
Trumpet / Bop
Fats Navarro was an outstanding soloist and trumpeter who had a short, but distinguished career. His playing established him as one of Dizzy Gillespie's few rivals among the bebop players of the late '40s and early '50s, and he was a major influence on Clifford Brown. Navarro had a lighter, less harsh tone than Gillespie, though it was also full and beautiful. He didn't use as many upper-register notes and didn't play as fast as Gillespie, but could produce stunning solos with surprising harmonic twists and wonderful melodic elaborations. He was also known for his use of Spanish-tinged phrases. Navarro played piano and tenor sax before turning to the trumpet in his late teens. He toured with dance bands at age 17, then joined Andy Kirk's band in 1943. Navarro replaced Gillespie in Billy Eckstine's band in 1945, and became its principal soloist. He left the band in 1946, then worked in small combos for the remainder of his career. Navarro recorded extensively in the groups of Kenny Clarke, Coleman Hawkins, Bud Powell, Charlie Parker, and Tadd Dameron, making many radio broadcasts as well as studio dates. Navarro died of tuberculosis, which was no doubt exacerbated by his heroin addiction. His sessions have been compiled in various packages. There are two-disc sets of Savoy and Milestone material; the Milestone dates feature him with Dameron. There were also a pair of single albums on Blue Note that were later issued as a double album, and some other tracks compiled and released as a memorial album. Navarro was also included on a Metronome All Stars session for RCA and on a Capitol recording where he plays the song "Stealin' Apples" with Benny Goodman. Only a couple of Navarro dates are available on CD at the moment. —*Ron Wynn and Michael G. Nastos*

☆ **Fat Girl** / Sep. 6, 1946-Dec. 5, 1947 / Savoy 2216
Landmark Navarro Savoy sessions with Howard McGhee (tpt), Ernie Henry (as), and others. —*Ron Wynn*

☆ **Fabulous Fats Navarro–Vol. 1, The** / Jan. 29, 1947-Nov. 29, 1948 / Blue Note 81531
1947-1948. Here are brilliant trumpet solos from the sadly neglected trumpet master Navarro. Blue Note may have deleted this completely by now. It has six bonus cuts featuring the equally undervalued Tadd Dameron. —*Ron Wynn*

○ **Fats Navarro with Tadd Dameron** / **i.** Jan. 29, 1947 / Milestone 47041

1989 reissue. Simply sublime sessions spotlighting the radical innovations of the great Fats Navarro, plus Tadd Dameron's creative arrangements. —*Ron Wynn*

★ **Prime Source** / Sep. 26, 1947-Aug. 9, 1949 / Blue Note
1947, 1948, and 1949 recording dates. Navarro as featured soloist with the Tadd Dameron Sextet and Septet, the Howard McGhee/Navarro Boptet, and Bud Powell's Modernists. Reissue compilation of Navarro's prime early work. —*Michael G. Nastos*

○ **Fabulous Fats Navarro–Vol. 2, The** / Sep. 1947-Aug. 1949 / Blue Note 81532
The importance of this follow-up volume is equal to that of the first one. —*Ron Wynn*

NDUGU (Ndugu Chancler)

b. 1952
Drums / Early jazz-rock, instrumental pop
An excellent pop and funk drummer, Ndugu Chancler also played on many jazz dates, particularly early in his career. His rhythmic aggressiveness and vitality distinguishes anything he plays, regardless of context. Chancler began playing drums at age 12, and studied music in high school. His family moved from Louisiana to Los Angeles when he was eight years old. As a high school student, Chancler played with Willie Bobo and Gerald Wilson. After two years at a state college, Chancler began playing with Hugh Masekela, and also worked with Herbie Hancock, Eddie Harris, and Thelonious Monk. He had brief stints with Miles Davis and Freddie Hubbard, then joined George Duke. Chancler played with Duke periodically from 1972 to 1980, while he recorded and performed with Harris, Julian Priester, Weather Report, and Duke. He toured with Santana in the mid-'70s, and formed the band Chocolate Jam Co. in 1978. Chancler was a prominent producer in the '80s, spearheading sessions for Kenny Rogers and Michael Jackson, while he also did several dates as a session player. He was in the Crusaders briefly in 1983. Chancler does not have any sessions available as a leader, but can be heard on discs by Harris, Duke, Weather Report, and others. —*Ron Wynn*

BUELL NEIDLINGER

b. Mar. 2, 1936, New York, NY
Bass / Early free, modern creative
An accomplished jazz, symphonic, and bluegrass bassist, Buell Neidlinger has made the unusual routine during his career. He's played in Dixieland groups, in adventurous free bands, and in orchestras, and has appeared at bluegrass festivals. His broad, robust tone, virtuoso skills with either bow or plucking strings, and harmonic knowledge and skill have enabled him to thrive in this eclectic atmosphere. Neidlinger established his own record label rather than deal with major company politics. He studied cello with Luigi Silva and Gregor Piatigorsky, and won a competition to play with the New York Philharmonic at age 12. He also studied trumpet and piano. As a teen, Neidlinger was playing both Dixieland and swing with Vic Dickenson, Ben Webster, Joe Sullivan, and Billie Holiday. Then he joined Cecil Taylor in 1955, making another huge stylistic leap. He remained with Taylor until the early '60s, helping influence and shape the style that ultimately became one of the free school's dominant voices. Neidlinger and Taylor did their most intriguing dates for the Candid label. Neidlinger also recorded with Steve Lacy in 1957. He played in several symphony orchestras during the mid-'60s, while working with Van Dyke Parks, Andrew White, and Robert Ceecly. Neidlinger traveled to Los Angeles in 1969 to record jazz-rock with Jean-Luc Ponty and Frank Zappa. Neidlinger was a teacher at the California Institute for the Arts in the '70s and '80s, while he served as a studio musician on acoustic and electric bass. He also served as principal bassist for the Los Angeles Chamber Orchestra from 1972 to 1978. Neidlinger and Marty Krystall have collaborated since the late '70s in various jazz-rock bands, and Neidlinger has also led his own bluegrass ensemble, Buellgrass, that's appeared at many national festi-

vals. He and Krystall coformed the K2B2 label in the '70s and have issued several albums of everything from jazz to bluegrass. Neidlinger has done a few sessions for Antilles and Black Saint, as well as his K2B2 dates. He has only three sessions available on CD, though Mosaic issued a marvelous boxed set containing the complete Taylor Candid recordings in 1992. —*Ron Wynn*

○ **New York City R&B** / **i.** Jan. 9+10, 1961 / Candid 79017
With Cecil Taylor. This is actually Neidlinger's date, though it is currently issued under Cecil Taylor's name. —*Ron Wynn*

○ **Buellgrass (Swingrass)** / **i.** 1980 / KZBZ
Ready for the '90s / 1980 / KZBZ

★ **Locomotive** / Jun. 1987 / Sound Note 121161
Virtuoso bassist and Marty Krystall on tenor sax. Fine music written by Monk and Ellington. —*Michael G. Nastos*

OLIVER NELSON (Oliver Edward Nelson)

b. Jun. 4, 1932, St. Louis, MO, **d.** Oct. 27, 1975, Los Angeles, CA
Composer, arranger, alto and tenor saxophone, flute / Postbop, soul-jazz, progressive big band
Oliver Nelson was a remarkable saxophonist who played with fire, speed, and creativity in a variety of styles, including bebop, hard bop, soul-jazz, instrumental R&B, and blues. He was also a good composer, though his works for larger groups were sometimes pretentious. He wrote ambitious pieces such as "Afro/American Sketches," which effectively merged blues, swing, alto and tenor sax solos, West African drumming and polyrhythms, and a brass chorale. He began on piano as a child, playing public recitals at a young age. Nelson studied piano and sax before joining the Jeter-Pillars Orchestra in the late '40s, becoming their lead alto saxophonist. He later played in big bands led by George Hudson and Nat Towles. Nelson worked with Louis Jordan's band in New York, completed his army service, then studied composition and theory at Washington University and Lincoln University, earning bachelor's and master's degrees before returning to New York. He played and recorded with Louis Bellson, Eddie "Lockjaw" Davis, and Duke Ellington's bands in the late '50s and early '60s, while also leading combos and writing several compositions. He played briefly with Erskine Hawkins and Wild Bill Davis, as well as Quincy Jones in 1960 and 1961. Nelson made several superb dates for various labels in the '60s. These included soul-jazz sessions with Johnny Smith, Jimmy Forrest, and King Curtis for Prestige, and big band recordings and combo sessions featuring players such as Eric Dolphy, Bill Evans, and Phil Woods. Nelson also did arrangements for Jimmy Smith, Billy Taylor, and Wes Montgomery. He trimmed his performance schedule during the mid-'60s, preferring to concentrate on teaching, arranging, bandleading, composing for films and television, and working on large-scale pieces that mixed improvisational and symphonic concepts. But Nelson still found time to record for Argo and Impulse, including a tribute album to the slain John F. Kennedy. He moved to Los Angeles in 1967 and toured Africa in 1969 with a septet. During the '70s, Nelson continued a heavy recording pace, doing dates for Flying Dutchman with Johnny Hodges and Leon Thomas, plus Verve and Inner City sessions. He died suddenly of a heart attack in 1975. There's a good cross section of Nelson's classic material for several labels available on CD. —*Ron Wynn*

Meet Oliver Nelson / Oct. 30, 1959 / Original Jazz Classics 227
This dynamic session pairs Nelson with Kenny Dorham (tpt), Art Taylor (d), and others. —*Ron Wynn*

○ **Screamin' the Blues** / May 27, 1960 / New Jazz 080
Alto saxophonist/bandleader/arranger and composer Oliver Nelson and Eric Dolphy (as, bcl, f) collaborate on some classic material and while *Screamin' the Blues* may not be classic, it does have bite and excellent solos from a band that includes Richard Williams (once again producing stronger trumpet work as a sideman than as a leader), Richard

Wyands (p), George Duvivier (b), and Roy Haynes (d). But the mark here is Dolphy; this is another of the sessions he made for Prestige as a featured sideman who steals the show. This 5/27/60 date was half of a twofer that put together both LPs by this group. —*Bob Rusch*, Cadence

★ **Soul Battle** / Sep. 9, 1960 / Prestige 325
Recorded at Englewood Cliffs, New Jersey. Oliver Nelson with King Curtis and Jimmy Forrest engage in a *Soul Battle* that's really just a straightahead blowing date by three saxmen with distinct styles representative of different eras and/or genres. None of the saxes concedes or compromises. This is King Curtis's most compelling jazz work and makes one wonder just how big his talent was—a stimulating session. —*Bob Rusch*, Cadence

★ **Blues and the Abstract Truth** / 1961 / MCA 5659
This LP offers six substantial Oliver Nelson-conducted and arranged originals that allow for exciting solo work by young Freddie Hubbard (tpt), Eric Dolphy (as, f), and Nelson himself (ts, as). Bill Evans (p) solos but not with the impact of the horns noted. The ensemble is completed by George Barrow (bs), Paul Chambers (b), and Roy Haynes (d). This is inventive jazz that still sounds fresh 25 years after it was recorded (1961). —*Alan Bargebuhr*, Cadence

○ **Straight Ahead** / Mar. 1, 1961 / New Jazz 099
Oliver Nelson and Eric Dolphy are a formidable pair, but this isn't my favorite collaboration, maybe because it's too *straightahead* rather than letting the muses go where they might naturally take themselves at this point (3/1/61). However, as usual, Dolphy's playing (as, bcl) is rewarding. The program has Richard Wyands (p), George Duvivier (b), and Roy Haynes (d) as the rhythm section. This date was also issued on another twofer. —*Bob Rusch*, Cadence

☆ **Main Stem** / Aug. 25, 1961 / Prestige 1803
This is a laudable small-group date with solid piano by Hank Jones. With Joe Newman (tpt). —*Ron Wynn*

More Blues and the Abstract Truth / Apr. 1965 / MCA 5888

Sound Pieces / 1966 / GRP 103
This is slightly mannered, but Nelson's biting phrases cut through to the quick. —*Ron Wynn*

Black, Brown and Beautiful / 1969 / Bluebird 6993

Swiss Suite / Jun. 18, 1971 / Flying Dutchman
Gato Barbieri (ts) almost steals the show on tenor; Eddie "Cleanhead" Vinson (sax) also sparkles in a guest stint. —*Ron Wynn*

☆ **Stolen Moments** / Mar. 6, 1975 / Inner City 6008

○ **More Blues and the Abstract Truth** / Impulse
Unlike his *Blues and the Abstract Truth* from a few years earlier, *More Blues and the Abstract Truth* does not feature Oliver Nelson's fine saxophone playing. Here he restricts himself to arranging and conducting the all-star unit. Although Nelson's solo talents are not really missed on a date that features the likes of Thad Jones, Phil Woods, Pepper Adams, and (on two tracks) Ben Webster, there is certainly room for him to join in. It is a tragedy that Nelson deemphasized his own strong voice during his last years while mostly concentrating on arranging for studios. Anyway, *More Blues and the Abstract Truth* is far from a tragedy; it's an excellent blues-oriented date that includes plenty of bright moments, both from the colorful charts and the soloists, especially Adams and Roger Kellaway (p). —*Scott Yanow*, Cadence

---

STEVE NELSON

Vibes / Modern creative
Steve Nelson has developed into a consistently outstanding vibes soloist and session musician. He's recorded as a leader for Sunnyside and Red, and has played with musicians such as Mulgrew Miller, Bobby Watson, Kirk Lightsey, Ray Drummond, Donald Brown, Victor Lewis, and others. Nelson has also backed vocalists, worked in large and small com-

bos, and played in hard bop, bebop, blues, and free settings. He has some sessions available on CD. —*Ron Wynn*

★ **Communications** / Oct. 1989 / Criss Cross 1034

CALVIN NEWBORN

b. 1933
Guitar / Blues & jazz
The often overlooked brother of Phineas Newborn, guitarist Calvin Newborn has almost as much command of his instrument as his pianist sibling. He's an excellent melodic interpreter who plays with great fluidity and blues sensibility, and he can execute complex chord progressions smoothly, or can accompany vocalists subtly. Newborn's problem has been a lack of a recorded legacy and his desire to remain in Memphis, where he's played in local clubs and with various groups in the '70s, '80s, and '90s. Newborn worked and recorded with his brother from 1953 to 1958, and joined up with Earl Hines a year later. Newborn recorded with Hines in 1960, and toured and recorded with Lionel Hampton in both New York and Paris. Newborn also toured and recorded with Jimmy Forrest, Wild Bill Davis, Al Grey, and Freddie Roach in the early '60s. Newborn did his own date for Rooster in the '70s. Unfortunately, virtually everything he's done is no longer available, and hasn't been reissued on disc. —*Ron Wynn*

PHINEAS NEWBORN (Phineas (Jr) Newborn)

b. Dec. 14, 1931, Whiteville, TN, **d.** 1989
Piano / Hard bop, postbop
Despite severe personal and mental problems that plagued him for most of his career, Phineas Newborn, Jr. was one of jazz's most accomplished, technically brilliant pianists. Many compared his incredible speed, harmonic knowledge, dexterity, and rhythmic facility with that of Tatum and Bud Powell. But a combination of being repeatedly off the scene due to illness and spending much of his life in the South rather than on the East or West Coast, prevented Newborn from attaining his rightful place in jazz history during his lifetime. He studied piano, theory, alto sax, and various brass instruments while in high school. Both his father and brother were musicians, and Newborn played in various Memphis bands during the '40s until he joined Lionel Hampton in the early '50s. He played with Hampton in 1950 and 1952. Newborn was in the service during 1953, '54, and '55, then moved to New York in 1956. He had a duo with Charles Mingus in 1958, and toured Europe in '58 and '59. Newborn made some highly praised records for Atlantic, RCA, and United Artists in the late '50s, gaining enormous respect from critics and musicians alike. He continued recording on Prestige and Roulette through the late '50s, doing a trio date with Roy Haynes and Paul Chambers for Prestige. He moved to Los Angeles in 1960, and made more outstanding trio sessions for Contemporary in the '60s. But his illness, coupled with a hand injury, led to infrequent appearances, at best, and long absences from playing, touring, or recordings. Newborn was hospitalized in Memphis for a time. He returned to a limited schedule of performances and recordings in the early and mid-'70s. His album *Solo Piano* for Atlantic was a brilliant exposition of gospel and blues-tinged modern playing. Newborn made an acclaimed appearance at a 1975 concert sponsored by the World Jazz Association in Los Angeles. There were other sessions for Pablo and some foreign labels. During the '80s, Newborn was a familiar sight at Memphis clubs, and he recorded sonatas by Alexander Scriabin for VSOP in 1987. Newborn died in Memphis in 1989. There are several Newborn '50s and '60s dates that have been reissued on CD within the last couple of years. —*Ron Wynn*

Piano Artistry Of / **i.** 1955 / Atlantic 90534
Brilliant Memphis pianist with phenomenal technique. Can't go wrong. —*Michael G. Nastos*

○ **Here Is Phineas** / May 3-4, 1956 / Atlantic 1235

○ **While My Lady Sleeps** / 1957-1958 / Bluebird 61100

Some late '50s cuts by piano great Phineas Newborn, then at the peak of his powers. Newborn could totally pick apart and rework any standard, while his own works were often so full of tricky phrases and dazzling devices they astonished even other great players. These were done in 1957 and 1958; the CD features two bonus cuts. —*Ron Wynn*

★ **Great Jazz Piano of Phineas Newborn Jr, The** / Nov. 21, 1961-Sep. 12, 1962 / Contemporary 388
Pianist Phineas Newborn, Jr. can hardly restrain himself on this trio disc. Both rhythm sections (bassist Leroy Vinnegar, drummer Milt Turner on the first five songs; bassist Sam Jones, drummer Louis Hayes on the last four) are at his service and don't get a chance to step out; Newborn has so many ideas there is hardly room for anyone else; even when he's comping he's in a hurry, and he shifts between left-hand chording and two-handed octave unison work without apparent effort. Miles Davis's "Four" and Bud Powell's "Celia" are uptempo displays. Bobby Timmons's "This Here" is funky (Horace Silver) blues, while "New Blues" is the old melancholy heartfelt slow variety. On Thelonious Monk's "Well You Needn't" Newborn demonstrates two ways to state a melody, first with embellishment, Art Tatum-style, and then Monk's plain way, before getting down to the razzle-dazzle: the left-handed sixths on the out-chorus allude to "Misterioso." Somehow on "Prelude" Newborn suggests stride style while playing left-hand chords. His taste rarely fails him; only Sonny Rollins's "Way Out West" gets too cute. This is great piano. —*Kevin Whitehead, Cadence*

○ **Newborn Touch** / Apr. 1, 1964 / Contemporary 270
This 4/1/64 date features the Phineas Newborn trio (Leroy Vinnegar, b; Frank Butler, d; Newborn, p) on a program of compositions by Benny Carter, Russ Freeman, Hampton Hawes, Art Pepper, Ornette Coleman, Carl Perkins, Frank Rosolino, Leroy Vinnegar, Jimmy Woods, and Barney Kessel. There are a few problems with this date, but the main one is that it gets very little past exposition. The concept seems the *thing*, whereas we all know the *thing* should be the playing. Very little feeling comes across past the perfunctory. —*Bob Rusch, Cadence*

○ **Harlem Blues** / Feb. 12-13, 1969 / Contemporary 662
In 1969, when this date was recorded, Phineas Newborn was an awesome pianist, having combined the dark, mahogany rich sound and dazzling technique of Art Tatum with the fertile linear imagination of Bud Powell into an individual style that was passionate and explosive. There was nothing in jazz beyond his reach: His uptempos were full of vivid, polished ideas, brought off with the utmost confidence; he could swing hard enough to make you put your foot through the floor; and his ballad renditions evoked images of quietude and grandeur. Although Newborn has most of the solo space here, *Harlem Blues* comes off as an integrated trio date (not just two jazz giants making a third sound good). These men (bassist Ray Brown and drummer Elvin Jones) had never played together as a unit before the date, but you couldn't tell by listening to this album. —*Zan Stewart, Down Beat*

○ **Please Send Me Someone to Love** / Feb. 12-13, 1969 / Contemporary 7622
Fabulous piano technique by the late Phineas Newborn, one of jazz's finest pure soloists. His amazing harmonic knowledge and masterful playing were ideal for the standards he performed on this album, especially the title track. —*Ron Wynn*

★ **Back Home** / 1976 / Contemporary 57648

○ **Look Out–Phineas Is Back** / Dec. 7-8, 1976 / Pablo 801
Pianist Phineas Newborn's playing twists in new directions on each tune, such as the touch of stride in "Salt Peanuts" that suddenly leads into runs in octaves. His various influences—James P. Johnson, Art Tatum, Bud Powell—were well knitted together with his own brilliant ideas and approaches. "The Man I Love" most strongly shows his debt to Tatum with its many runs, but in addition to breaking a phrase for a run, Newborn sometimes plays a run with one hand while carrying on the melody with his other hand.

Newborn, however, is not just a technical display, and he really gets going on Stevie Wonder's "You Are the Sunshine of My Life." Playing at a fast tempo, he breaks into joyous improvisation after the opening chorus. And on bassist Ray Brown's Bud Powellish "Abbers Song," Newborn shows that he can simultaneously display his fantastic technique and swing like mad. Another source—Meade Lux Lewis—is demonstrated on his own funky "Tamarind Blues," which reminded one of Newborn's R&B roots. Although drummer Jimmy Smith is perhaps too steady in his support, Brown does some nice soloing and sensitive backing. Also worthy of mention is the piano, which has a nice rich sound and was well-recorded with all the resonance captured. —*Jerry De Muth*, Cadence

DAVID "FATHEAD" NEWMAN

b. Feb. 24, 1933, Dallas, TX
Tenor saxophone, flute / Blues & jazz, soul-jazz
A first-rate soul-jazz, blues, R&B, and funk saxophonist and flutist, David "Fathead" Newman has been a star in seminal bands, has issued excellent recordings, and has been featured on several fine sessions. He can certainly play bebop and has shown surprising chops when so inclined, but that's not his strength. One of jazz's and popular music's great pleasures is to hear, during a vocalist's break, the gorgeous, huge Newman tones filling the space left by a singer laying out; sax solos ripping through a 12-bar blues, interacting with an organist or guitarist, or just embellishing a melody. His taste has sometimes deserted him, but when working in the right arena Newman's a wonderful player and bandleader. He got his "Fathead" nickname from a music teacher as a child. He began playing with local bands in Dallas, and later toured with Lowell Fulson and T-Bone Walker. Newman became a star while working with Ray Charles. He stayed with Charles for a full decade in the '50s and '60s, and was a pivotal part of many landmark R&B dates. The sounds he made with Charles still guide Newman's music. He later worked with King Curtis in the mid-'60s. Newman began recording as a leader for Atlantic in the late '50s. He did several small combo sessions, then later worked with larger bands. Newman played with Blue Mitchell, Roy Ayers, Dr. John, and Ron Carter, among others. Things began to go astray in the mid-'70s; there were some experiments with overdubbed strings and horns. But Newman returned to soul-jazz and blues basics on Prestige, Muse, and Atlantic in the '80s. He's recorded for Milestone in the late '80s and '90s, still doing reliable blues and soul-jazz, with an occasional bebop date. He's also recorded for Candid and Timeless, and has worked with Cornell Dupree and Ellis Marsalis on a fine session for Amazing Records. Newman has a fair number of titles available on CD. In '93, Rhino issued a CD anthology of some earlier Atlantic dates. —*Ron Wynn*

Fathead: Ray Charles Presents David Newman / Nov. 5, 1958 / Atlantic 1304

★ **Lonely Avenue** / Nov. 2-4, 1971 / Atlantic

Resurgence / Sep. 1980 / Muse 5234
Newman shows bop talents heading a fine ensemble and supported by Cedar Walton on piano. —*Ron Wynn*

○ **Still Hard Times** / Apr. 1982 / Muse 5283
The original intent of the David "Fathead" Newman (ts, as, ss, f) session was to recreate a Ray Charles reunion band, but scheduling conflicts prevented that. Nevertheless, this septet admirably captures the spirit of the Charles band even if solos are relatively straightforward. —*Carl Brauer*, Cadence

Fire! Live at the Village Vanguard / Dec. 22-23, 1988 / Atlantic 81965
A nice outing that matches Newman with Stanley Turrentine (ts) and Hank Crawford (as). —*Ron Wynn*

○ **Blue Head** / Sep. 1989 / Candid 79041
An excellent '90 session by tenor saxophonist and flutist David Newman, done without fanfare or flash. Newman plays big-toned, bluesy tenor and more introspective flute. He's backed by some top players, among them guitarist Ted

Dunbar, tenor saxophonist Clifford Jordan, and Buddy Montgomery on piano. —*Ron Wynn*

○ **House of David Newman–David "Fathead" Anthology / i.** 1993 / Rhino 271452
There have not been many saxophonists and flutists more naturally soulful than David "Fathead" Newman. His tenor has honking resiliency, a deep, mournful tone, and the compelling qualities that define soul, plus he knows the blues inside out. Newman's playing in Ray Charles's great combos with such leaders as Herbie Mann, and either as a lead act or with James Clay, was both simple and shattering. This two-disc set may be the best of all Rhino's anthologies, for it does capture Newman at his best. He has never really been an album artist, though he has done lots of LPs. Each one has had its nuggets and this release captures them. It is almost a greatest hits record. There is Newman wailing the blues, then stretching out in the Charles band. He covers a Beatles number, then an Aaron Neville number. He backs Aretha Franklin and pays homage to the great Buster Cooper. The sound, as on all the Rhino sets, is breathtaking, as is Newman's shimmering sax and flute. Here is one anthology that can be recommended without hesitation, because you are not going to get many complete Newman albums coming down the reissue pike. —*Ron Wynn*

JOE NEWMAN (Joseph Dwight Newman)

b. Sep. 7, 1922, New Orleans, LA, **d.** Jul. 5, 1992
Trumpet / Swing, big band
Joe Newman was a superb, exciting trumpeter whose style echoed the best of Harry Edison, Dizzy Gillespie, and Thad Jones, seasoned with his own flavoring. He was among a select corps who not only enjoyed playing, but communicated that joy and exuberance in every solo. He provided high-note and upper-register antics, but functioned best doing soft, enticing melodies or engaging in mildly combative jam sessions. He was also an accomplished player in the traditional New Orleans style. Newman began his professional career with Lionel Hampton in 1942 and 1943, joining Hampton after touring with the Alabama State Teachers College band. Newman became a member of the Count Basie orchestra in 1943, and remained until 1947. He co-led groups with Illinois Jacquet and J.C. Heard before returning to the Basie band for a great run from 1952 to 1961. During that time, there were periodic outside recording sessions. Newman did sessions for Savoy, Vanguard, and RCA in the '50s, most of them small-combo and tasteful, enjoyable outings. The 1956 album *Salute to Satch* was with a big band. *The Happy Cats* was a sextet date. There was a quintet session with Zoot Sims on Roulette, and another Roulette recording with an 11-piece band. Newman toured Europe with the Basie band in 1954. During the early '60s, he continued recording and touring with Basie and making other sides on his own. These included sessions with Tommy Flanagan for Prestige and a quartet set for Stash. There was a 1962 Russian tour with Benny Goodman. Newman became involved with Jazz Interaction, an organization that promoted awareness and jazz education in the early '60s, and soon became a tireless advocate. He assumed the organization's presidency in 1967. Newman also wrote compositions for their organization. He began playing with the New York Repertory Orchestra in 1974, and toured Europe and the Soviet Union with them in 1975. During the '70s, '80s, and '90s, Newman juggled educating, recording, and an infrequent reunion with the Basie orchestra. He made nice sessions with Ruby Braff and Jimmy Rowles in the '70s, and with Joe Wilder and Hank Jones in the '80s. —*Ron Wynn*

Salute to Satch / Mar. 4, 1956 / RCA
Quintet. Newman makes a keen tribute to his mentor, featuring a tart big band. —*Ron Wynn*

Jive at Five / May 4, 1960 / Prestige 419
A hot quintet date sparked by Newman's interaction with Frank Wess (f, sax). —*Ron Wynn*

★ **Good'n'Groovy** / Mar. 17, 1961 / Prestige 185

This was the second of three dates Joe Newman (tpt) led under the Swingville banner. For this 3/17/61 session he was in the very fine company of Frank Foster (ts), Tommy Flanagan (p), Eddie Jones (b), and Bill English (d). The two hornmen have had their share of recorded mismatches, but on this set they play in the vernacular in which they both excel. This was more or less a working group at the time with Flanagan and English, and there is a good sense of cohesion (the liners imply the dates were more arranged than listening suggests) and the soloing from the horns is prime in this Count Basie-boppish mainstream. —*Bob Rusch*, Cadence

In a Mellow Mood / 1962 / Stash 219

Hangin' Out / May 1984 / Concord Jazz 4262
This relaxed, jovial session is co-led by Joe Wilder (tpt). "Smitty" Smith adds fire on drums. —*Ron Wynn*

○ **Featuring Shirley Scott** / MCA 1380

FRANKIE NEWTON (William Frank Newton)

b. Jan. 4, 1906, Emory, VA, **d.** Mar. 11, 1954, New York, NY
Trumpet / New Orleans traditional
A fine trumpeter who often used a buzz-wow mute for contrast, Frankie Newton had a singular, entertaining approach and was a highly respected player. Though his career was repeatedly interrupted by illness, he made a sizable impact during those periods when he was active. Newton moved to New York after he toured the West Coast in the early and mid-'20s. He played with Cecil Scott, Chick Webb, Elmer Snowden, Charlie Johnson, Garland Wilson, and Sam Wooding in the late '20s and early '30s, then recorded with Bessie Smith and Mezz Mezzrow in the '30s. Newton was in John Kirby's small group in 1937, and with Lucky Millinder in both 1937 and 1938. He formed a band in 1939 that played at the Cafe Society, Kelly's Stable, and other clubs. Newton continued heading both large bands and small combos in the '40s. He also worked with players such as James P. Johnson in the mid-'40s. Except for occasional appearances, Newton eventually stopped playing and devoted himself to painting. He made some recordings for Vocalion and other labels, but is probably better known for his solos on Bessie Smith's "Gimme a Pigfoot" or on Mezz Mezzrow's "Mutiny in the Parlor." Currently, Newton is not represented as a leader on CD, but can be heard on anthologies that feature Smith, Mezzrow, and Johnson. —*Ron Wynn*

★ **At the Onyx Club** / **i.** Mar. 1937-Oct. 1937 / Tax 8017
William Frank Newton (tpt) seemed preoccupied with tone itself—as color and as the dominant means of expression. Like many of his contemporaries he found himself in recording situations that, given the commercial considerations of the period, teamed him with singers who were rarely better than second rate—often not as good as that. This circumstance has lent his surroundings a somewhat dated air, disguising the more lasting value of his own work, and that of certain key associates: the altoists Pete Brown and Tab Smith, and the clarinetist William "Buster" Bailey. Though a fine melodist, Newton also uses often-sharp variation in timbre that catches the ear and seems to direct the emotional expressiveness of a performance. Against the third-rate joviality of singer Clarence Palmer on "You Showed Me the Way," he weaves a totally independent solo of slightly darker edge, the terpsichorean steps of his line colored by a gauzy tone. On the subsequent "Who's Sorry Now?," the tone is decidedly more umbrous, and his note placement more emphatic. In contrast, "Frankie's Jump" features a bitingly brassy tone on an optimistic line of admirable melodic coherence. Here and there, the shadow of Louis Armstrong looms, but, on "Where or When," the steepling creation is also imbued with an entirely personal plaintiveness. In general, though, the influence seems to be the more interesting combination of Jabbo and Joe Smith. And, when using the cup mute, as on "Jam Fever," Newton produces an exquisitely personal singing tone. This performance also reveals one of his remarkably few musical mannerisms—a galloping percussive four-note figure used to

generate momentum at uptempo. Throughout, Newton demonstrates immense skill in tonal variation, but of a kind that eschews use of growl effects and makes only sparing use of half-valving. It is a subtle thing but, in the manner of something original, capable of making a personal mark in a few short bars. At the time of these recordings his effective career had only seven to nine years left—after 1946 he never recorded again and died virtually forgotten in 1954. —*Chris Sheridan*, Cadence

JAMES NEWTON

b. May 1, 1953, Los Angeles, CA
Flute / Modern creative
James Newton comes closest of any contemporary flutist to invoking the spirit of Eric Dolphy. His soaring, beautiful tones have that same evocative, bird-like quality, and he's nearly as accomplished as Dolphy with his armada of trills, vocal effects, swirling phrases, flutter tonguing, humming, glissandos, and overblowing. Newton once played alto and tenor saxophones, but gave them up to concentrate on flute. He has a classical timbre, but a jazz musician's heart and that's enabled him to execute solos that are astonishing in their harmonic brilliance and are performed with what seems a minimum of effort. Newton played electric bass, alto and tenor sax, bass clarinet, and flute in high school, oddly picking up flute last. He attended a California junior college, majored in music, and studied under Buddy Collette. Newton played flute and sax in a funk band, and performed with Arthur Blythe, David Murray, and others in Stanley Crouch's Black Music Infinity in the early '70s. He became a flutist exclusively in the late '70s, and joined the exodus of West Coast musicians to New York. He co-led an ensemble with Anthony Davis, and performed in a trio with a Japanese koto player, a flute quartet with Frank Wess, and a woodwind quintet. He began recording as a leader on India Navigation in the late '70s, and continued on Circle, ECM, Gramavision, BVHaast, Celestial Harmonies, and Blue Note in the '80s. Newton's also remained active in the classical music community. Presently, he has only a few titles available on CD. —*Ron Wynn*

From Inside / Jul. 27-29, 1978 / BVHaast

○ **Crystal Texts** / **i.** Nov. 1978 / Moers 01048

Paseo Del Mar / 1978 / India Navigation 1037

★ **Mystery School** / 1979 / India Navigation
James Newton, who composed these three pieces for wind quintet, is a talented flutist, and he has assembled a team of skilled players who have no trouble making the transitions from composed to improvised sections and back again. "The Wake" (written in tribute to the late composer Dr. Howard Swanson) strings together some pretty phrases in a loose counterpoint that shows Newton's classical orientation. But since the phrases are much longer than is normal in classical music, the ensemble work still sounds like a collection of jazz riffs. John Carter and John Nunez weave a clever, graceful clarinet and bassoon duo, however, and Newton serves up elegant flights of fancy in his duet with tuba player Red Callendar. In addition, Charles Owens's oboe solo in the "dirge" section has a pleasingly dark, piquant flavor. More than either of its companion pieces, "Past Spirits" utilizes the full palette of colors that can be obtained by blending the timbres of five different wind instruments. There are links here to the coloristic tendencies of composers like Alan Hovhaness and John Corigliano, and the multiphonics employed in one section parallel the "extended techniques" of modern classical composers. —*Joel Rothstein*, Down Beat

○ **James Newton** / Oct. 1982 / Gramavision 8205
Features three Newton originals for pianists Anthony Davis and Billy Strayhorn. With Jay Hoggard (vib) and Slide Hampton (tb). Excellent, creative music. —*Michael G. Nastos*

○ **Portraits** / 1982 / India Navigation
The opener is a duet for flutist James Newton and Abdul Wadud, who whips all around his cello both with bow and fingers, with seemingly little effort. It begins with quick in-

teractive lines having a distinct avant-classical feel. It ends up in a unison line that harmonizes in the last notes. From this line are built longer tones via improvisation. This sensitive interplay builds in terms of animation and also touches quite heavily on blues inflections. The second side features the bass/drums/flute (bassist Cecil McBee, drummer Phillip Wilson) trio. "Portrait of David Murray" is a loose, open medium-swinging tribute. "Laff" starts as a ballad and erupts into some intense flute/arco bass harmonic interplay that is audially breathtaking (Wilson colors softly behind the high tones with some sparse cymbal explorations). —*Milo Fine*, Cadence

○ **Luella** / 1983 / Gramavision 8304
An ambitious, intricately composed and structured album from flutist James Newton that blends improvised and set pieces played by an eight-piece group. The lineup includes vibist Jay Hoggard, pianist Kenny Kirkland, violinists John Blake and Gayle Dixon, cellist Abdul Wadud, bassist Cecil McBee, and drummer Billy Hart. —*Ron Wynn*

Echo Canyon / i. 1984 / Celestial Harmonies 13012

○ **Water Mystery** / Jan. 1985 / Gramavision 8407
Some soothing, some entrancing, and some astonishing flute performances from James Newton on this album—one of his finest ever from both a performance and compositional standpoint. —*Ron Wynn*

○ **African Flower, The** / Jun. 1985 / Blue Note 46292
On *The African Flower* flutist James Newton explores the music of Billy Strayhorn and his mentor Duke Ellington; the results are a fresh reappraisal of timeless music. "Black and Tan Fantasy" has Olu Dara's wah-wah cornet recalling Cootie Williams, some stride from Roland Hanna, and Newton singing through his flute. "Virgin Jungle" is of more recent vintage; it was part of Ellington's 1965 Virgin Island suite. The African rhythms of Billy Higgins and Anthony Brown, along with the talking drum of Pheeroan AkLaff, set the mood for contrasting solos by Jay Hoggard (vib), John Blake (vn), Newton, Arthur Blythe (as), and Dara, while the riffing and percussion give this piece much urgency. The dissonant "Strange Feeling" is mostly a feature for Milt Grayson's deep baritone. while "Fleurette Africaine" showcases Newton. "Cottontail" allows straightahead blowing from a roaring Arthur Blythe, some trading off between Hoggard and Hanna, and a chance for Newton to blow over the chord changes. "Sophisticated Lady" will be remembered as one of the high spots of Newton's recording career; it has two choruses of beautiful unaccompanied flute that tastefully embellish the classic melody. "Passion Flower" closes this varied album with some impassioned Blythe alto. —*Scott Yanow*, Cadence

○ **Romance and Revolution** / i. 1987 / Blue Note 46431
Flutist James Newton's brilliantly written and performed pieces for octet are featured on this '87 session. Trombonists Steve Turre and Robin Eubanks, vibist Jay Hoggard, and pianist Geri Allen along with Newton are among solo stars. —*Ron Wynn*

ALBERT NICHOLAS (Albert [Nick] Nicholas)

b. May 27, 1900, New Orleans, LA, **d.** Sep. 3, 1973, Basel, Switzerland
Clarinet, saxophone / New Orleans traditional
A remarkable clarinetist and one of the great blues improvisers, Albert Nicholas played wonderful low register tunes, offering rich, gritty inflections and phrases during his solos. A nephew of Wooden Joe Nicholas, he studied with Lorenzo Tio, Jr. Nicholas played with Buddy Petit, King Oliver, and Manuel Perez while still a teenager. He spent three years in the merchant marine, then joined Perez's band in 1922. Nicholas led his own group at Tom Anderson's New Cabaret and Restaurant in 1923, then worked with Oliver in Chicago for two years. He toured internationally with various groups, appearing in China, Egypt, and Paris from 1926 to 1928 before returning and joining Luis Russell's orchestra. He stayed with Russell until the early '30s, then spent the next several

years playing with several major figures. These included Rex Stewart, Chick Webb, John Kirby, and Louis Armstrong. Periodically, Nicholas also led his own bands. He lived and toured in Europe from 1953 until his death in 1973, returning to America in 1959 and 1960 for recording sessions and concerts. Nicholas appeared on Vocalion, Jazztet, and Okeh records as a sideman, and on Circle and Delmark as a leader. He can be heard on anthologies featuring Oliver, Stewart, and Russell. —*Ron Wynn*

○ **Albert Nicholas Quartet, The** / Jul. 19, 1959+Jul. 27, 1959 / Delmark 207
The Albert Nicholas Quartet is part of the venerable and diversified Chicago label Delmark's *Art Hodes Notebook* series. While clarinetist Nicholas and pianist Hodes come from different regions, cliques, and cultures, they're delightfully and effortlessly compatible, finding common home ground in the blues. Hodes's style is distinguished by agreeable relaxation. So is Nicholas's—high notes and low float from his horn with equal ease. His sound is not as haunting as George Lewis's but it is prettier. The good vibes coming from this record stem mostly from its casual polish; everyone sounds at home and comfy. In quartet—joined by Earl Brown, bass, and Freddy Kohlman, drums—Nicholas and Hodes reflect the tight-knit cohesion of bop and small-group swing, not the rowdy individualism of Dixie—even as harmony and rhythmic emphases declare trad loyalties. No one would mistake Kohlman's heavy foot for a bopper's. As usual when the pianist is cooking, any ingredients will do. The crop is a typical Hodes mix of classics and enduring corn—revivalism at its best. —*Kevin Whitehead*, Cadence

★ **All Star Stompers** / Jul. 30-31, 1959 / Delmark 209

BIG NICK NICHOLAS (George Walker)

b. 1922
Vocal / Swing, big band, bop, blues & jazz
George Walker, aka "Big Nick" Nicholas, is both a rousing, heavy-voiced vocalist and a robust instrumentalist. He's been unable to get steady work except for a brief period in the mid-'80s when he was a near celebrity thanks to a pair of India Navigation albums. Nicholas studied piano and clarinet as a child, and played sax with Hank and Thad Jones while a teen. He played in the early '40s with Earl Hines and Tiny Bradshaw, then went into the army. After his discharge, Nicholas played with Sabby Lewis, J.C. Heard, and Lucky Millinder. He began playing with Hot Lips Page in 1947, and worked with him until 1954. Nicholas also played in Dizzy Gillespie's big band in 1947. He became celebrated for his role in a series of Harlem jam sessions in 1950 and 1951 at the Paradise Club, where his shouting vocal style emerged. He played with vocalist Timmie Rogers's band with Jonah Jones in 1953, and with Buck Clayton in 1955. Coltrane recorded "Big Nick" in 1962, but it didn't generate much improvement in Nicholas's career. Then, in 1984, the album *Big and Warm* was issued by India Navigation, and Nicholas was in the limelight briefly. The follow-up album, *Big Nick*, was equally outstanding, but neither album generated much sales force, and Nicholas was soon in the background again. Currently, both albums are unavailable on CD. —*Ron Wynn*

★ **Big Nick** / i. Jul. 1986 / India Navigation 1066

HERBIE NICHOLS (Herbert Horatio Nichols)

b. Dec. 3, 1919, New York, NY, **d.** Apr. 12, 1963, New York, NY
Piano, composer / Bop
Although he was involved in bebop's beginnings, pianist/composer Herbie Nichols shied away from the attendant scene and spent his time in the '40s and mid-'50s playing swing and Dixieland. He made only a handful of recording sessions in his lifetime. There were three remarkable recordings for Blue Note in 1955 and 1956, and some quartet dates for Savoy in 1952. These quartet dates include a pair of vocals by bassist Chocolate Williams plus Shadow Wilson on drums, and a guitarist. There was also a session

with George Duvivier and Dannie Richmond that surfaced briefly on Bethlehem, and later resurfaced briefly on Affinity (Britain), dates with Rex Stewart on Jazztone, and an Atlantic date with Vic Dickenson and Dicky Wells, among others. Nichols's music was enticing, enjoyable, and listenable, yet also abstract and penetrating; it echoed both Thelonious Monk and modern European classical artists like Erik Satie. Nichols utilized unusual rhythms and voicings, and borrowed freely from swing and Dixieland. A highly intelligent player and composer whose occasional writings on jazz were concise, analytical, and critical without being petty or personal, Nichols simply couldn't accept the nonsense that came with "the jazz scene" of his (or anyone else's) day. He preferred instead to play with musicians he felt didn't fear or distrust him for nonmusical reasons. It's impossible to judge whether Nichols's fears were accurate or were based on perceptions that may have been as questionable as the prejudices he felt were directed at him. Nichols studied piano starting at age nine, and attended City College of New York. After playing at Monroe's Uptown House, Nichols worked with Danny Barker, Illinois Jacquet, John Kirby, Snub Moseley, Edgar Sampson, Lucky Thompson, Arnett Cobb, and Wilbur DeParis while bebop was beginning to explode. He didn't have a single composition recorded until Mary Lou Williams included "Stennell" (retitled "Opus Z") on her *Mary Lou Williams Trio* Atlantic album. Nichols died of leukemia in 1963. Mosaic released an essential boxed set, *The Complete Herbie Nichols Blue Note Recordings*, in 1987. The Savoy and Bethlehem albums are the type of records collectors willingly pay ultrapremium prices to own. —*Ron Wynn and Michael Erlewine*

○ **Third World, The** / May 6, 1955-Apr. 19, 1956 / Blue Note 142
1955 and 1956 trio session. Many of his best numbers. Part of the Mosaic box. —*Michael G. Nastos*

○ **Art of Herbie Nichols, The** / 1955-1956 / Blue Note 99176
An anthology collecting some pieces by the neglected and overlooked pianist Herbie Nichols. Nichols had one of the truly unique styles in all jazz piano history, and didn't really borrow from or imitate anyone. This single disc doesn't match either an earlier Blue Note two-record set, now deleted, or the outstanding Mosaic set, but it's a fine introduction to Nichols's music. —*Ron Wynn*

★ **Complete Blue Note** / 1955-1956 / Mosaic 118
1955-1956. This is just great stuff, desert island material. The notes are informative, the sound superb, but it is the music that will make you return time and again. This material is best described as intelligent yet emotional music. It has its roots in the blues and postbop—truly timeless. —*Richard B. Kamins*, Cadence

○ **Thelonious Monk and Herbie Nichols** / i. 1956 / Savoy 1166
Nichols is like a bridge from the outside world to Monk. His dissonance is not as stark as Monk's, nor does he rely on it as much. And those who find Monk's technical abilities limited will find Nichols much more impressive. A thoughtful and unique musician. —*Doug Long*, Cadence

○ **Bethlehem Sessions, The** / Nov. 1957 / Affinity 759
This latest reissue should open even more ears. In short, Nichols was an unrequited master who was pitifully underrecorded and overlooked while alive. —*Williard Jenkins*, Cadence

RED NICHOLS (Ernest Loring Nichols)

b. Aug. 5, 1905, d. Jun. 28, 1965
Cornet / Dixieland
Overrated in Europe in the early 1930's when his records (but not those of his Black contemporaries) were widely available, then underrated later and often unfairly called a Bix imitator, Red Nichols was actually one of the finest cornetists to emerge from the 1920's. An expert improviser whose emotional depth did not reach as deep as Bix's or Louis Armstrong's, Nichols was, in many ways, a hustler,

who participated in as many recording sessions (often under pseudonyms) as any other horn player of the era, and who cut sessions as Red Nichols and his Five Pennies, as the Arkansas Travelers, as the Red Heads, as the Louisiana Rhythm Kings, and as the Charleston Chasers, among others, usually with similar personnel!

Nichols studied cornet with his father, a college music teacher. After moving from Utah to New York in 1923, Nichols, an excellent sightreader who could always be relied upon to add a bit of jazz to a dance band recording, was quickly in great demand. At first, his own sessions, featuring trombonist Miff Mole and Jimmy Dorsey on alto and clarinet, played advanced music that utilized unusual intervals, whole tone scales, and often the timpani of Vic Berton along with hot ensembles. Later on in the decade his sidemen included young greats such as Benny Goodman, Glenn Miller, Jack Teagarden, Pee Wee Russell, Joe Venuti, Eddie Lang, Adrian Rollini, Gene Krupa, and the wonderful mellophone specialist, Dudley Fosdick, among others; their version of "Ida" was a surprise hit.

Although still using the main name of The Five Pennies, Nichols's bands were often quite a bit larger and, by 1929, he was alternating sessions that featured bigger commercial orchestras with small combos. At first, Nichols weathered the Depression well by working in shows, but by 1932 his long string of recordings came to an end. He headed a so-so swing band up until 1942, left music for a couple of years, and, for a few months in 1944, was with Glen Gray's Casa Loma orchestra. Later that year, he reformed the Five Pennies as a Dixieland sextet and it became one of the finer traditional jazz bands of the next 20 years, particularly after bass-saxophonist Joe Rushton became a permanent member. Nichols recorded several memorable hot versions of "Battle Hymn of the Republic" (the best version was done in 1959). That same year, a highly enjoyable, if rather fictional, Hollywood movie called *The Five Pennies*, which featured Nichols's cornet solos and Danny Kaye's acting, made Red into a national celebrity at the twilight of his long career. Nichols's earlier sessions are just now being reissued on CD in piecemeal fashion, but none of his later albums are in print yet. —*Scott Yanow*

★ **Red Nichols 1925-28** / i. Nov. 1925-Sep. 1928 / Fountain 110

○ **Jazz Classics (1925-1930)** / 1925-1930 / Mobile Fidelity 00664

○ **Red Nichols–Vol. 2** / i. Jun. 1927-Mar. 1928 / Classic Jazz 25

○ **Red Nichols–Vol. 3** / i. Mar. 1928-May 1928 / Classic Jazz 27

○ **Red Nichols–Vol. 4** / i. Jun. 1928-Jan. 1929 / Classic Jazz 28

○ **Red Nichols–Vol. 5** / i. Feb. 1929-Apr. 1929 / Classic Jazz 30

○ **Syncopated Chamber Music–Vol. 1** / i. 1953 / Audiophile 7

LENNIE NIEHAUS (Leonard Niehaus)

b. Jun. 1, 1929, Saint Louis, MO
Alto saxophone, composer, arranger / Cool
Though he's won a lot of contemporary notice for his work on Clint Eastwood films, Lennie Niehaus was one of the finest West Coast saxophonists to emerge in the '50s. Though his sound was relaxed and his solos smooth rather than intense, his phrasing, technique, and swing were reminiscent of players such as Benny Carter and Charlie Parker. But Niehaus's primary influence was Lee Konitz. Niehaus worked with Jerry Wald in the early '50s, then joined Stan Kenton. After an army stint, Niehaus rejoined Kenton, where he won praise and fame for his playing on several sessions through the '50s. He then moved into film and television work, and has remained there. Niehaus has appeared on Eastwood films such as *Bird, Unforgiven*, and *Play Misty For Me*. A few of Niehaus's Contemporary albums have been reissued on CD. —*Ron Wynn*

★ **Lennie Niehaus—Vol. 1: The Quintet** / Nov. 17, 1954 / Contemporary 2513

○ **Lennie Niehaus—Vol. 2: The Octet—Part 1** / 1954 / Contemporary 2517

○ **Lennie Niehaus—Vol. 3: The Octet—Part 2** / Jan. 11, 1955-Feb. 1, 1955 / Contemporary 1767

This music stretches, squeezes, and in general turns figure eights on itself and glides through the whole like a well-oiled eel. —*Bob Rusch*, Cadence

SAL NISTICO (Salvatore Nistico)

b. Apr. 12, 1940, Syracuse, NY, **d.** 1991
Tenor saxophone / Bop

A powerful, aggressive soloist, Sal Nistico has demonstrated his fiery bebop skills many times with Woody Herman. His playing has energy and soulfulness, as well as harmonic invention and rhythmic vitality. Nistico began playing alto at the end of the '40s, then switched to tenor in the mid-'50s. He worked in Syracuse R&B bands until the late '50s, then played in the Jazz Brothers group co-led by the Mangione Brothers. Nistico made his first recordings with them. He made his first stop with Herman in the mid-'60s, and continued to work with him periodically into the '80s. Nistico played briefly with Count Basie in 1965, then moved to Sweden. Nistico returned to Herman's band for a 1966 African tour. He worked with Herman again in the late '60s, and also in 1971. Nistico lived in Los Angeles briefly, and played briefly with Don Ellis. Following another short stint in Boston, Nistico moved to New York. He played with Buddy Rich in 1974, with the National Jazz Ensemble under Chuck Israels in the mid- and late '70s, and headed his own groups. Nistico had his final stint with Herman in the early '80s. He's recorded a couple of sessions for Jazzland and Bee Hive. Currently, Nistico does not have any dates as a leader available on CD, but can be heard on Herman reissues. — *Ron Wynn*

★ **Empty Room** / **i.** 1988 / Red 123222

RAY NOBLE (Raymond Stanley Noble)

b. Dec. 17, 1903, Brighton, England, **d.** Apr. 2, 1978, London, England
Bandleader, arranger, composer / Swing, big band

An arranging and compositional mainstay, as well as a good pianist and a top bandleader, England's Ray Noble enjoyed great popularity in both America and Europe. He cleverly infused his songs with jazz, swing, and pop influences, creating numbers that were both popular and artistic successes. Noble was HMV's music director in the late '20s and early '30s, and wrote early '30s hits such as "Love Is the Sweetest Thing," "The Very Thought of You," "The Touch of Your Lips," and the instrumental anthem "Cherokee." Charlie Barnet had a hit with "Cherokee" in 1938, and Charlie Parker was quoted as saying that it was improvising on that song that let him play the music he'd been hearing in his mind. Noble scored four number-one hits in 1933 and 1934, among them "Isle of Capri" and "The Old Spinning Wheel." Noble came to America in 1934 with Al Bowlly and drummer/manager Bill Harty. Glenn Miller assembled a band for him that included Bud Freeman, Claude Thornhill and Will Bradley. The results were songs such as "Paris in the Spring" and "Let's Swing It" in 1935. Noble backed Fred Astaire on the hit songs "Nice Work If You Can Get It," "A Foggy Day," and "Change Partners" in the late '30s on Brunswick. He signed to the label as an artist, then moved to Columbia in 1940. The song "By the Light of the Silvery Moon" was on the charts in 1941 and 1944. Noble's last number-one hit was "Linda" in 1947. He recorded for Victor in America, and also for Sunbeam, Aircheck, and Monmouth Evergreen, among others. Import and jazz specialty stores are the place to consult for Noble CDs. —*Ron Wynn*

★ **1935-1936** / **i.** 1976 / Jazz Band 2112

MIKE NOCK (Michael Anthony Nock)

b. Sep. 27, 1940, Christchurch, New Zealand
Piano / Postbop, early jazz-rock, new age, neo-bop

Mike Nock was one of the early jazz converts to synthesizers and electric keyboards, and has labored to make his sound and solos as personalized on these instruments as they sound on acoustic. While he's proficient at bebop and hard bop, Nock was a pioneer in jazz-rock, and remains one of that idiom's best improvisers. Nock's also played free and ethnic music. He began taking piano lessons at age 11, and was a professional at age 15. Nock moved from his native New Zealand to Australia at age 18, and formed a hard bop trio. The three moved to England in 1961. Nock departed for America, and attended Berklee in 1962. He left Berklee in 1963 to work at a Boston club as house pianist, then toured with Yusef Lateef for two years. Nock worked briefly with Art Blakey, then moved to San Francisco. He helped form the adventurous group the Fourth Way with Michael White in 1968. They disbanded in the early '70s. Nock composed and recorded film soundtracks until he returned to New York in 1975. Nock played sessions there until he returned to Australia in 1985, where he composed and taught at New South Wales State Conservatorium in Sydney. Nock has recorded as a leader for IAI, Laurie, ECM, Timeless, Tomato, VeraBra, Mainstream, and Enja. At present, he has only one date available on CD. —*Ron Wynn*

★ **Ondas** / Nov. 1981 / ECM 829161

A good trio date. Eddie Gomez on bass tends to be a more interesting improviser than Nock or Jon Christensen (d.). —*Ron Wynn*

WALTER NORRIS

b. Dec. 27, 1931, Little Rock, AR
Piano / Early free, modern creative

A resourceful pianist and composer, Walter Norris has been a prominent player in both America and Europe since the '50s. He's a vigorous, excellent improviser, whose solos are expertly played and smartly constructed, and are full of harmonic surprises and melodic twists. Norris studied piano as a child. He worked in Little Rock with Howard Williams in the mid-'40s and early '50s, worked with Jimmy Ford in Houston in the early '50s, and worked in Las Vegas with his own trio in the mid-'50s. He moved to Los Angeles in 1954. Norris recorded with Jack Sheldon, Frank Rosolino, Herb Geller, and Ornette Coleman in the late '50s. After moving to New York, Norris split his time between studying at the Manhattan School of Music and being music director of the Playboy Club between 1963 and 1970. He joined the Thad Jones-Mel Lewis Orchestra in 1974, played at the Village Vanguard regularly on Monday nights, and toured Europe and Japan in the mid-'70s. Norris recorded with Klaus Weiss and Pepper Adams in Europe, and with Frank Foster in Japan. He left the orchestra in 1976, and played in Scandinavia for seven months with Red Mitchell and groups led by Dexter Gordon and Red Rodney. He then returned to New York, where he worked briefly with Charles Mingus before moving to Berlin. Norris played in the orchestra of Sender Freies Berlin from 1977 to 1980. He joined the faculty of the Hoshschule in 1984, and taught piano improvisation. Norris also played throughout Europe with Aladar Pege, and made annual visits to America. He's recorded as a leader for Enja, Shiah, Progressive, and Concord in the '70s, '80s, and '90s. Norris has a few sessions available on CD. —*Ron Wynn*

★ **Live at Maybeck Recital Hall—Vol. 4** / **i.** 1990 / Concord Jazz 4425

Here is another solid entry in this solo series. Norris is an underrecorded, daring pianist who also writes distinctive pieces and is good on standards as well. The CD version has three bonus cuts. —*Ron Wynn*

○ **Sunburst** / **i.** 1991 / Concord Jazz 4486

After struggling for years to get some exposure, pianist Walter Norris made a critically acclaimed solo release for

Concord and suddenly found himself in demand. This '92 date has the added bonus of superb tenor solos from the great Joe Henderson. He and Norris threaten but don't totally overwhelm bassist Larry Grenadier and drummer Mike Heyman. —*Ron Wynn*

BOB NORTHERN

French horn / Modern creative

A rare jazz French horn player and soloist, Bob Northern (aka Brother Anhh) was one of the busiest session musicians in the '50s and '60s. He worked and recorded with numerous jazz stars including Donald Byrd, John Coltrane, Gil Evans, Sun Ra, Gil Evans, McCoy Tyner, Rahsaan Roland Kirk, and with the Jazz Composers Orchestra. He did some recording for small independents as Brother Anhh in the '70s. None of those dates are available, but he can be heard on reissues by Evans, Kirk, Ra, and others. —*Ron Wynn*

RED NORVO (Kenneth Norville)

b. Mar. 31, 1908, Beardstown, IL
Vibes / Swing, big band

A master at playing intense, yet disciplined, subtle and swinging solos on vibes and xylophone, Red Norvo might have been the swing era's greatest player on these instruments if not for Lionel Hampton. Norvo moved away from elaborate, brassy arrangements and embraced a more intimate, quieter, and refined style, making inroads with this alternative direction. Norvo's approach often faltered on material with rapid tempos, but was ideal for slow ballads because of his emphasis on clarity and sophistication. Norvo usually played vibes without vibrato, which generated some interesting reactions. He was arguably even better on xylophone, turning what's usually considered a child's toy into an impressive instrument.

Norvo began on marimba at age 14, then went on to xylophone. He moved to Chicago at age 17, and toured with a marimba band in the late '20s. He became a vaudevillian, and did a solo act that included a tap-dance routine. He had a short stint as a bandleader, and a period with NBC as a staff musician before he joined Paul Whiteman. Norvo later married Mildred Bailey, who was singing in the orchestra. He did freelance work in New York during the early '30s while coleading a group with Charlie Barnet in 1935 and 1936 on 52nd Street. Norvo recorded with Teddy Wilson, Benny Goodman, Jimmy Dorsey, Artie Shaw, Gene Krupa, Bunny Berigan, Chu Berry, and Jack Jenney, among others. He and Bailey teamed to head a band from 1936 to 1939, and earned the nicknames "Mr. and Mrs. Swing." Norvo experimented in the '30s with a sextet minus a drummer, and his 1936 and 1937 orchestra dates with Eddie Sauter's arrangements were critically praised.

While he led big bands in the early '40s, Norvo was far more suited to the sextet Benny Goodman formed in 1944. He switched permanently to vibes at that point. Norvo conceived and selected the musicians for an unusual project in 1945: an octet date that blended swing and bop, and included Charlie Parker and Dizzy Gillespie playing alongside Wilson and Norvo. Norvo also recorded with Slam Stewart in 1945: He toured with Billie Holiday and joined Woody Herman in 1946, and was part of Herman's first Herd. Norvo recorded with Stan Hasselgard in 1948, then returned to the East Coast in 1949, leading a sextet with Tony Scott and Dick Hyman.

He opted to lead trios in the '50s, most of them featuring guitar and bass. His 1950 and 1951 unit with Tal Farlow and Charles Mingus was exceptional, as was a later edition with Red Mitchell and Jimmy Raney. Norvo made his first overseas visit in 1954, and appeared on a television show with Benny Goodman in 1958. They continued working together in 1959, going to Europe and playing an engagement on Basin street with a ten-piece group. They had another reunion in 1961, but it was cut short when Norvo underwent a serious ear operation. He later toured Europe as a solo act in 1968, and worked with George Wein's All Stars in 1969.

Norvo spent much of the '60s and '70s in California and Nevada. There were plenty of television engagements with stars such as Frank Sinatra and Dinah Shore, plus festival dates. He returned to international touring in the '70s and '80s, visited Europe often, and reformed his trio with Farlow. Norvo recorded with Scott Hamilton and Ross Tompkins in 1977 and Bucky Pizzarelli's trio in 1983. He joined Benny Carter and Louis Bellson for a gala concert in New York in 1985. —*Ron Wynn and Dan Morgenstern*

★ **Featuring Mildred Bailey** / **i.** 1933 / Portrait 44118
1933-1938. This neglected gem features Norvo with Mildred Bailey (v), Bunny Berigan (tpt), and Charlie Barnet (sax) on superb '30s swing cuts with excellent mastering. It's probably deleted by now. —*Ron Wynn*

○ **Time in His Hands** / **i.** May 1945-Aug. 1945 / Xanadu 199
During that marvelous jazz year of 1945, when Dizzy Gillespie and Charlie Parker were causing most swing musicians to reassess their musical values, Red Norvo was one of the first veteran players to encourage and record with exponents of the new music. The music on *Time in His Hands* is definitely in the swing category but tinged with the influence of bop. Actually none of these sessions was led by Norvo; the first two showcase bassist Slam Stewart, and the August 22 sides were put together by entrepreneur Timmie Rosenkrantz. At the time, Norvo, Stewart, and drummer Morey Feld were all members of the Benny Goodman sextet. Stewart's trademark of humming an octave above his bowed bass is well featured and still quite enjoyable. Stewart also takes an excellent pizzicato solo on "Jingle Bells." Bill DeArango, one of the most advanced guitarists of the time, is a joy to hear. He would become known for appearing on a Gillespie small-group date in '46 and then disappear into obscurity by the end of the decade. Norvo, by virtue of the instrumentation, emerges as the main voice, in his usual impeccable form. Johnny Guarnieri offers several examples of stride piano, and on "Honeysuckle Rose" he does a humorous imitation of Fats Waller's vocal style—only a slightly higher voice gives him away. The second date, with the more conventional but talented Chuck Wayne in DeArango's spot, took place a month after Norvo's Dial session and is more boppish. The Rosencratz combo has a strong Dukish flavor and is highlighted by some strong Harry Carney baritone (what a talent!), Johnny Bothwell's Johnny Hodges-inspired alto, and Charlie Ventura's tough tenor (at its best on the first take of "Bouncy"). It's a pity that the legendary altoist Otto Hardwicke is only heard from in the ensembles. Although this is not an essential album, the music is flawless, swinging, and really beyond any serious criticism. —*Scott Yanow*, Cadence

○ **Fabulous Jam Session** / Jun. 1945 / Spotlite 127
Cream-of-the-crop recordings pairing this vibes great with Charlie Parker (as), Dizzy Gillespie (tpt), and friends. A high-caliber reissue. —*Ron Wynn*

Improvisations on Keynote / **i.** 194z / Mercury 830966
As nice a cross-section of mid-'40s Norvo cuts as is available. It was culled from the massive Keynote box. —*Ron Wynn*

★ **Red Norvo Trio with Tal Farlow and Charles Mingus at the Savoy** / 1950-1951 / Savoy 2212
Trio. This excellent two-record set highlights Norvo in peak playing form with Tal Farlow (g) and Charles Mingus (b). Thoughtful yet aggressive playing. —*Ron Wynn*

○ **Fabulous Jazz Session** / **i.** 1951 / Dial 903

○ **Move! (With Tal Farlow and Charles Mingus)** / **i.** 1951 / Savoy 12088

○ **Red Norvo Trios, The** / 1953-1955 / Prestige 24108
Fine two-record set from the mid-'50s featuring sessions led by vibist Red Norvo, with trio members guitarists Jimmy Raney or Tal Farlow and bassist Red Mitchell. They made both chamber jazz and light swing recordings. —*Ron Wynn*

Just a Mood / Aug. 1954-Jan. 18, 1957 / Bluebird 6278

With Jimmy Raney and Red Mitchell / **i.** 1954 / Original Jazz Classics 641

Forward Look, The / **i.** 1957 / Reference 8

Red Norvo showed in the '40s and '50s that the vibes could be a legitimate jazz instrument. He was among the first to successfully duplicate bop's intricate chord changes and rhythms on vibes, and his solos swung, yet were cleverly constructed and performed. By the time of this recording in 1957, Norvo wasn't at his peak, but could still play with intensity and delight audiences. He heads a group with saxophonist Jerry Dodgion, guitarist Jimmy Wyble, bassist Red Wootten, and drummer John Markham doing a blend of original pieces such as "For Lena and Lennie," hot numbers like "Cookin' at the Continental," and old favorites "I'm Beginning to See the Light" and "My Funny Valentine." Not essential, but very enjoyable; the digital sound is remarkable. —*Ron Wynn*

☆ **Red Plays the Blues** / Jan. 28, 1958+Mar. 6, 1958 / RCA 1792

○ **Live at Rick's Cafe Americaine** / 1978 / Flying Fish 079

A joyful, exuberant, and loose session led by vibist Red Norvo and recorded in 1978 at Rick's. Besides Norvo's swinging, propulsive vibes there's also Buddy Tate's lusty tenor and Urbie Green's resilient trombone, with pianist Dave McKenna adding his own stride and boogie riffs. The four are so relentless it's easy to forget about the absence of bass and drums. —*Ron Wynn*

SAM NOTO

b. Apr. 17, 1930, Buffalo, NY

Trumpet, flugelhorn / Bop

A stirring trumpeter whose crackling lines and slashing phrases echo the influence of Dizzy Gillespie and Clifford Brown, Sam Noto has shown his mettle as a soloist and composer. He began playing with Stan Kenton in the mid-'50s, and worked with him again in 1960. Noto also played with Louis Bellson in 1959, and with Count Basie in 1964, 1965, and 1967. After leaving Basie, Noto coformed a quintet in 1976 with Joe Romano in Noto's native Buffalo. Noto worked in Las Vegas from 1969 to 1975, and made his first recording for Don Schlitten's Xanadu label. He made several other Xanadu dates in the '70s. Noto moved to Toronto in 1975, and worked there in studios and clubs until 1980. He played and wrote material for Rob McConnell's Boss Brass; they recorded about 20 Noto compositions. Noto also recorded with Blue Mitchell, Al Cohn, and Dexter Gordon at the Montreux Festival in 1978. Noto operated a club in Buffalo during the early '80s, then began working with Toronto show bands in the mid-'80s. Currently, none of Noto's Xanadu albums are available on CD. —*Ron Wynn*

★ **Notes to You** / **i.** May 1977 / Xanadu 144

○ **Act One** / **i.** Jun. 1977 / Xanadu 127

○ **Noto-Riety** / **i.** Oct. 1978 / Xanadu 168

All of this material is attributed to pianist Dolo Coker although the title of "To Me Everything Happens" naturally brings to mind an old challenging standard. That graceful tune belongs to trumpeter Sam Noto and Coker, who give it some real lyricism. The rest of the material contains great blowing space for the adventuresome Noto and the enviable technique of flutist Sam Most. The many unison passages deserve praise well beyond Most's remark, "we played a few times together." The blend is so good that it sometimes appears to be only Most playing, even Noto using a mute. It's good to have a rhythm section (bassist Monty Budwig, drummer Frank Butler) that had spent a lot of time together and Dolo Coker seems to be constantly growing. —*Jerry L. Atkins*, Cadence

○ **2-4-5** / **i.** Nov. 1986 / Unisson 1007

ADAM NUSSBAUM

b. 1955

Drums / Early jazz-rock, new age, modern creative

Both a prolific contributor and a fiery drummer, Adam Nussbaum's one of the most in-demand percussionists currently active. He's a passionate soloist and an ideal accompanist who is able to play with combos, trios, or large bands, and to contribute effectively in hard bop, free, swing, jazz-rock, or even new age/contemporary instrumental contexts. Nussbaum studied drumming with Charli Persip, and worked at New York clubs with Monty Waters, Albert Dailey, and Nina Sheldon in the mid-'70s. He also worked with David Liebman in Washington. Nussbaum played with John Scofield in the late '70s and early '80s, performing and recording with Scofield in both America and Europe. He also did sessions with Hal Galper. Nussbaum and Scofield played and recorded with Liebman and with Steve Swallow in the early '80s. He played with the Gil Evans orchestra through the '80s, touring Europe and Japan in 1985. Nussbaum also recorded with Bill Evans (saxophonist), Bobby Watson, and Art Farmer in the mid-'80s, and worked with Eddie Gomez and Gary Burton. Nussbaum's extensive list of late '80s and '90s sessions include dates with Jerry Bergonzini, Mike Brecker, Richie Bierarch, Joey Calderazzo, Eddie Daniels, Christian Minh Doky, Marc Ducret, Evans, Lee Konitz, Rick Margitza, Ron McClure, Mark Murphy, Mike Richmond, and Glenn Wilson. Though he doesn't have any sessions as a leader, Nussbaum's well-represented on an array of current discs, and on many done earlier in the '80s. —*Ron Wynn*

O

ANITA O'DAY (Anita Belle Colton)

b. Oct. 18, 1919, Kansas City, MO

Vocals / Big band, bop

Along with Billie Holiday and Mildred Bailey, Anita O'Day was one of the fine pure jazz vocalists of the swing era. She had superb timing and excellent phrasing, and conquered anything from uptempo numbers to standards, slow laments, novelty, and comic bits. O'Day's also an excellent scat singer and a marvelous interpretative artist. She overcame severe drug problems in mid-career and has even served as a record executive, operating her own label.

O'Day got her start competing in dance marathons as a teen. After singing with the Max Miller combo in Chicago during the late '30s, O'Day joined Gene Krupa's band. Between 1941 and 1943 she enjoyed sizable popularity as the vocalist on such hits as "Just a Little Bit South of North Carolina," "Georgia on My Mind," "Let Me Off Uptown" and "The Walls Keep Talking" (both with Roy Eldridge), "Thanks for the Boogie Ride," "Bolero at the Savoy," and "Two in Love" with Johnny Desmond. She later joined Stan Kenton, and was featured on his first big hit in 1944, "And Her Tears Flowed Like Wine." After leaving Kenton, O'Day recommended a replacement named Shirley Luster, whom Kenton renamed June Christy. She returned to Krupa's band and enjoyed more success with "Chickery Chick" and "Boogie Blues."

O'Day then began her solo career. There were guest spots with Duke Ellington and Benny Goodman, plus recording sessions with Will Bradley, Ralph Burns, Benny Carter, and Alvy West with the Little Band. O'Day had more hits: "Hi Ho Trails Boot Whip" in 1947, and "Tennessee Waltz" in 1951. She began a long, profitable association with Norman Granz in 1952. O'Day cut many types of albums for Verve in the '50s; there were sessions of Cole Porter and other standards, albums headlining her originals, and even a reunion project with Krupa and Eldridge in 1956. She appeared in the 1959 film *The Gene Krupa Story* and in 1960 performed in the acclaimed *Jazz on a Summer's Day*, a film of the 1958 Newport Festival. O'Day did sessions with arrangers Marty Paich, Billy May and Rus Garcia, and kept this frantic pace into the early '60s, working with Cal Tjader, Johnny Mandel, and the Three Sounds. But her frequent drinking, compounded by an even more severe heroin problem, kept O'Day inactive throughout much of the mid- and late '60s. She returned strong with a 1970 live album recorded at the Berlin Festival. That year, she played a singer in the film *Zigzag* (aka *False Witness*). From 1975 to 1978, O'Day recorded and performed extensively in Japan; this activity resulted in the release of several albums, many of which she issued in America on her own Emily label. O'Day kept recording through the '70s and into the '80s, making combo and big-band sessions on labels such as Dobre, GNP, and Emily. She had another film appearance, once more as a singer, in the 1974 film *The Outfit*. O'Day's 1981 autobiography *High Times Hard Times* was brutally frank and honest, and interviews she's given to music publications in recent years have been similarly direct and blunt. In 1985, her 50th anniversary as a jazz artist was celebrated at Carnegie Hall.

Increasingly, her great material from the '50s is being reissued. —*Ron Wynn*

Anita O'Day Sings Jazz / Jul. 1952-Dec. 1952 / Norgran 1049

Authoritative, commanding, excellent vocals. Later reissued under a different title. —*Ron Wynn*

Songs by Anita O'Day / **i.** 1954 / Norgran 30

Anita / **i.** Apr. 18, 1956 / PolyGram 829261

Good, if conservative, set of standards, jazz-based pop by Anita O'Day from the mid-'50s. Her voice is in solid shape, and her technique, particularly her delivery, timing, and sense of swing, puts her at the forefront of vocalists in the era. —*Ron Wynn*

Anita Sings the Most / Jan. 31, 1957 / Verve 829577

1987 reissue of prime cuts, with Oscar Peterson (p) heading the backing combo. —*Ron Wynn*

Anita O'Day Swings Cole Porter with Billy May / Apr. 2, 1959+Apr. 9, 1959 / Verve 849266

A most appropriate title, since that's just what she does on the Cole Porter menu. Nice reissue. —*Ron Wynn*

★ **Cool Heat** / Apr. 6-8, 1959 / Verve

○ **Jimmy Giuffre Arrangements** / Apr. 6-8, 1959 / Verve 8312

★ **Anita O'Day and the Three Sounds** / Oct. 12-15, 1962 / Verve 8514

In Berlin / Nov. 7, 1970 / PA/USA 7092

Mello Day / Nov. 1978 / GNP 2126

A better production and performance than most of what O'Day put on her own label in the '70s. —*Ron Wynn*

S' Wonderful (Big Band Concert–1985) / 1985 / EMI 92685

○ **In a Mellow Tone** / **i.** 1989 / DRG 5209

A good '89 session with singer Anita O'Day doing her familiar jazz-based prerock standards and ballads, backed by a quintet with some different names. A particular change is the appearance of harpist Corky Hale, plus Pete Jolly (p) and Gordon Brisker (ts, f). —*Ron Wynn*

○ **At Vine St.–Live** / Sep. 1991 / DRG 8435

Recent live recordings by vocalist Anita O'Day done in an intimate setting as part of the Vine Street series. O'Day's voice has lost some luster and shine over the years, but she compensates with great timing, delivery, and tone that help overcome some loss of range. —*Ron Wynn*

CHICO O'FARRILL (Arturo O'Farrill)

b. Oct. 28, 1921, Havana, Cuba

Arranger / Latin jazz, world fusion

Chico O'Farrill is a pivotal composer, arranger, and trumpeter who was highly visible during the Afro-Latin and Latin jazz revolution of the '40s and '50s as a writer and bandleader. His compositions were recorded by Benny Goodman, Stan Kenton, Machito, and Dizzy Gillespie. They include "Undercurrent Blues" and "Shishka-Bop" for Goodman, and "Cuban Suite" for Kenton. He provided other arrangements of "Cuban Suite" for Machito and various bands. O'Farrill studied composition in Havana and played with Armando Romeu's band, as well as his own group, in the '40s. He

moved to New York in 1948, and began writing compositions for Goodman, Kenton, Machito, Gillespie, and Charlie
Parker. O'Farrill formed his own band in 1950, appeared at
Birdland, and recorded for Clef. He moved to Mexico City at
the end of the '50s, and performed concerts there in the early
'60s. O'Farrill returned to New York in the mid-'60s, and
worked as an arranger and music director on the CBS show
"Festival of the Lively Arts." Gillespie, Count Basie, Gerry
Mulligan, and Stan Getz were some of the musicians who
participated in the program. He wrote arrangements of pop
tunes for Basie in the mid-'60s, and composed songs for
Gato Barbieri, Kenton and a band co-led by Gillespie and
Machito in the '70s. O'Farrill tunes were included on a
Candido LP in the '70s, and on a Frank Wess date. He also
had a symphony premiered in Mexico City in 1972. O'Farrill's
own albums are scarce, but include sessions for Verve and
Impulse, and for Clef. O'Farrill was profiled in Ira Gitler's
book *From Swing to Bop* in the mid-'80s. Presently, there are
no O'Farrill albums listed in the *Schwann* catalog. —*Ron
Wynn and Michael G. Nastos*

★ **Chico O'Farrill Jazz** / Aug. 7, 1951-Mar. 24, 1952 / Clef 132
Chico with Flip Phillips (ts), Nick Travis (tpt), and Roy
Eldridge (tpt). —*Michael G. Nastos*

Jazz North of the Border and South of the Border / Aug. 7,
1951-Mar. 22, 1954 / Verve 8083

○ **Afro-Cuban** / 1951 / Clef 131

BABATUNDE OLATUNJI

Percussion / World fusion
Babatunde Olatunji was a virtuoso drummer who became a
sensation in the '60s with his albums of traditional Nigerian
drumming and chanting. If Olatunji debuted in today's environment, he would be subjected to much tougher scrutiny
and evaluation regarding "authenticity" than he received in
the '60s. His heralded albums, particularly *Drums of
Passion*, weren't quite the innovative event some claimed.
They were fine LPs, but also contained a heavy dose of show
business and sanitized playing that would be duly noted today, particularly in the specialist press. Still, his albums reportedly were very influential on John Coltrane. They were
among the few international releases to make the charts and
remain on them for years. Olatunji didn't make many albums in his prime. From 1964 until 1967, he had four hit
LPs. He originally came to America in the early '60s to study
medicine. Olatunji formed a band of African expatriates
mainly as an exercise and as a way to help each other avoid
being homesick. The ensemble scored a hit record and he
became a musician. The popularity of *Drums of Passion* and
More Drums of Passion predated the '60s Black Nationalist
movement and Afrocentricity of the '80s and '90s. They also
had some impact in jazz circles, though they weren't as significant as the Afro-Latin revolution initiated by Mario
Bauza, Machito, and Chano Pozo. Olatunji resurfaced in the
late '80s on the Blue Heron label with *The Beat of My Drum*,
a release featuring a 17-piece band that included Carlos
Santana and Airto Moreira. He subsequently recorded more
sessions for Rykodisc, including a digital remix of "Drums of
Passion." A few of his albums are available on CD. —*Ron
Wynn with J. Poet*

★ **Drums of Passion** / i. 1959 / CBS 8210
This set came out on vinyl in 1959 and stayed on the charts
for several years, an amazing feat for a record of traditional
chanting and drumming. Olatunji's success allegedly sparked
John Coltrane's interest in African culture, and the music
has lost none of its power over the years. —*J. Poet*

Drums of Passion: The Beat / i. 1989 / Rykodisc 10107
Babatunde Olatunji has been active as a tireless ambassador
of Nigerian drum music to the West for over twenty years.
The Beat, recorded in 1986, is a collection of songs that celebrates the evocative power of the drum, with Olatunji's massive bass drums leading a fiery percussion assault of djembe,
agogo, talking drums, and other West African instruments.
Impassioned call and response vocals give melodic shape to

Music Map

Jazz Oboe

First used in 1920s to add tone-color in bands, symphonic jazz

Don Redman (1900-1964)
w/ Fletcher Henderson (1924)

Whitman's orchestra (included oboe parts)

Mitch Miller (1911) in Alec Wilder's band (octets)

First Solo Instrument (improvisation) 1950s
Bob Cooper (1925)
Cool West Coast Jazz

1950s Yusef Lateef (1920)
("The Complete Yusef Lateef")

Marshall Allen (1924)
(on Sun Ra's "Cosmic Tones for Mental Therapy")

Paul McCandles (1947)
(Oregon, 1976s "Together")

Charlie Mariano (1923)
(Coltrane style)

Mainstream
Harold Land (1928)

Jazz-Rock
Andrew White (1942)–Weather Report 1971
(*I Sing The Body Electric*)

Free-Jazz
Karen Borca
Ken McIntyre (1931)

Brazilian
Janet Grice

the intense rhythms, while bass, guitars, guitar synthesizer,
and some wailing electric lead from guest musician Carlos
Santana add spice to the brew. The furious pace is only temporarily slowed midway by a smooth 1:40-minute a cappella
choral song in praise of a legendary Nigerian train conductor. Produced by Mickey Hart as part of his World series on
the Ryko label, *The Beat* more than delivers on the promise
of its title. —*Backroads Music/Heartbeats*

OLD AND NEW DREAMS

Group / Modern creative
Though they didn't make many records, the late '80s quartet
Old and New Dreams was one of finest of the decade. The
lineup included trumpeter Don Cherry, tenor saxophonist
Dewey Redman, bassist Charlie Haden, and drummer
Edward Blackwell. They were veterans of Ornette Coleman
bands, and united to celebrate his music. They made their
first album for ECM in 1978, a self-titled release. They followed it with another wonderful ECM session, *Playing*, in
1980. The group reunited for a third album for Black Saint,
One for Blackwell, seven years later in 1987. The first two al-

bums were superbly produced and engineered, with ECM's customary high-quality sound making their interactions and solos even more resplendent. As with Coleman's groups, this was a cooperative venture. Redman soloed on both tenor and musette, while Cherry played more conventional trumpet and didn't have any intonation problems on either album. The quartet regrouped in 1987 at a Blackwell festival in Atlanta. Though not in the best of health, Blackwell provided fiery rhythmic support, mixing New Orleans marching band beats with African talking drum rhythms and multiple accents and textures. Cherry and Redman were excellent again, as was Haden. Why this band only recorded three albums is anyone's guess, but they joined the Mingus Dynasty, Sphere, and Dameronia as bands that weren't simply repertory units, but evolving groups that used a great composer's material as a starting point for their own peerless interpretations. —Ron Wynn

○ **Old and New Dreams** / Oct. 1976 / ECM 829379
Debut. Fully realized. Quintessential. Modern jazz supreme from Don Cherry (cnt), Dewey Redman (ts), Charlie Haden (b), and Ed Blackwell (d). —Michael G. Nastos

★ **Old and New Dreams** / Aug. 1979 / ECM 1154
Great music from Ornette Coleman's band, playing with his verve and creative spirit. —Michael G. Nastos

Playing / Jun. 1980 / ECM 829123

One for Blackwell / i. Nov. 1987 / Black Saint 120113

KING OLIVER (Joe Oliver)

b. May 11, 1885, New Orleans, LA, **d.** Apr. 8, 1938, Savannah, GA

Cornet, bandleader / New Orleans traditional
Joe "King" Oliver may or may not have been the greatest traditional New Orleans player ever, but he deserved his royal title. His influence on many aspiring players, especially Louis Armstrong, cannot be denied. His flair for voice-like effects was unsurpassed; his clipped melodic style, vivid pitch changes, use of blues, and wah-wah technique were absorbed eagerly. Oliver's solo on "Dipper Mouth Blues" in 1923 was required learning during the era; it was later reworked into the anthem "Sugar Foot Stomp."

Initially, Oliver studied music as a trombonist. He got some early cornet training from Bunk Johnson. Oliver began playing in brass and dance bands and various small New Orleans groups in 1907. He worked twice with Kid Ory in this period before moving to Chicago in 1918, and heading his own bands beginning in 1920. A trip to California gained Oliver some national fame and he returned to Chicago in 1921. A year later, he started an engagement at Lincoln Garden heading King Oliver's Creole Jazz Band. Armstrong arrived in Chicago a month later to join the band. The group, boasting a two-cornet lineup, plus Johnny Dodds, Honore Dutrey, Lil Hardin Armstrong, Baby Dodds, and Bill Johnson began recording in April 1923. Their sessions and live performances influenced countless musicians across the color line. Oliver instilled a precise, disciplined quality into their performances, perfecting the balance between ensemble interaction and solo expressiveness. Oliver reorganized the band in late 1924, following tours of the Midwest and Pennsylvania. Now it included either two or three saxophones and was called the Dixie Syncopators.

Oliver began to move slightly away from the strict New Orleans format in the late '20s, but still made many stunning recordings. Among the other great players who passed through Oliver's bands in the '20s and '30s were Red Allen, Bubber Miley, Barney Bigard, Albert Nicholas, Hilton Jefferson, and later, Lester Young. The band began to break up after a successful engagement at the Savoy Ballroom in New York, and disbanded by the fall of 1927. During the '20s, Oliver also recorded with Jelly Roll Morton, Clarence Williams, Butter Beans & Susie, and many blues vocalists. These included Katherine Henderson, Eva Taylor, Victoria Spivey, Hazel Smith, Elizabeth Johnson, Lizzie Miles, Sippie Wallace, and Texas Alexander.

Oliver started touring with pickup bands once the orchestra disbanded. From 1930 to 1935 he toured throughout the Midwest and upper South with different ten- to 12-piece bands. But Oliver stopped playing in 1931. He was already suffering from severe dental trouble. Pyorrhea forced him to have most of his teeth removed, and he was plagued with bleeding gums for the rest of his life. A horrendous Southern tour in 1935 ended his music career. King Oliver died destitute, unable to obtain medical treatment due to bureaucratic red tape at the Savannah welfare department. —Ron Wynn and Bruce Boyd Raeburn

☆ **King Oliver–Vol. 1 (1923-1929)** / **i.** Apr. 1923-May 1929 / BBC 787

★ **King Oliver-Louis Armstrong** / **i.** 1923-1924 / Milestone 47017
1923-1924. Classic renditions of "Snake Rag," "Dipper Mouth Blues," and "Canal Street Blues" by the hottest band of its day—Oliver's Creole Jazz Band. Also includes Oliver duets with Jelly Roll Morton. —Bruce Raeburn

○ **King Oliver (1926-1928)** / **i.** Mar. 1926-Jun. 1928 / Classics 618

○ **Jazz Heritage: Papa Joe (1926-1928)** / 1926-1928 / Affinity 1025
And His Dixie Syncopators. Recorded from 1926 to 1928. Mid-'20s jazz with Oliver leading a coterie of New Orleans stars like Omer Simeon (cl), Kid Ory (tb), Barney Bigard (cl), Luis Russell (p), and Paul Barbarin (d) on tunes such as "Snag It," "Sugar Foot Stomp," and "Farewell Blues." —Bruce Raeburn

○ **Sugar Foot Stomp** / **i.** 1926-1927 / GRP 616
Vintage, historically vital early jazz featuring the King Oliver orchestra that also included Kid Ory, Albert Nicholas, Luis Russell, and Barney Bigard. The title track later became a swing-era staple when it was adapted by the Fletcher Henderson orchestra. This is the first time these sessions have been available on a domestic release, and the mastering makes it possible to hear them better than ever before. —Ron Wynn

★ **New York Sessions (1929-1930)** / **i.** 1929-1930 / RCA 9903
1929 and 1930. The King in the final chapter of his recording career with an excellent selection of titles, showcasing his abilities as a bandleader more than as a soloist. —Bruce Raeburn

○ **King Oliver's Jazz Band** / **i.** May 1976 / Smithsonian 001
It seems to me that it's particularly easy to overrate the King Oliver sides with Louis Armstrong. Certainly cornerstone recordings in any jazz collection, they are among the most finished and polished specimens of a form that was quickly becoming obsolete even as they were being made. That and the fact they were the first important Black jazz records make it very easy to lose perspective. There are masterpieces here ("Chattanooga Stomp," "Dipper Mouth Blues," "I Ain't Gonna Tell Nobody") that derive primarily from the perfection of the ensembles. But the word is somewhat devalued when used to describe music of such limited horizons. The changes are simple and rather repetitious, and Oliver's playing is impressive only when viewed in the context of 1923. And even then, we are not dealing with the work of an innovator but rather a talented working musician. Armstrong is already a commanding force here. His lead is strong on "Tears," and smoulders in several breaks with Oliver. But if Armstrong had stopped recording at the end of this series, he would not have been long remembered. His work was immature in the light of what we know was yet to come. We can hear an identifiable tone, but not the conceptual originality that would reach its heights in the early '30s. These may not be the greatest recordings ever made, but they are certainly among the most important. In addition to bringing together all the Okeh and Columbia Olivers, the program is filled out by several Oliver accompaniments to blues singers. He is heard to best advantage on "Empty Bed Blues," both in terms of sound quality and Elizabeth Johnson's singing. If I have reservations about the

music, I have no reservations about the wonderful way in which it is assembled in this beautifully annotated (by Lawrence Gushee) album. It's a credit to the Smithsonian series. —*John McDonough*, Down Beat

SY OLIVER (Melvin James Oliver)

b. Dec. 17, 1910, Battle Creek, MI, **d.** May 28, 1988, New York, NY

Arranger, trumpet / Swing, big band

Sy Oliver's arrangements for the Jimmie Lunceford band blended simplicity and sophistication with exuberance, which helped Lunceford's orchestra to temporarily challenge giants like Ellington, Basie, and Goodman, for whom Oliver also did arrangements. Oliver learned trumpet and played in local bands in Ohio. He worked with Zack Whyte's Chocolate Beau Brummels in the late '20s and early '30s, and played, for a short time, with Alphonso Trent. He moved to Columbus and worked as a freelance arranger and teacher. Oliver joined Lunceford in 1933, and remained until 1939. He wrote arrangements and compositions, played trumpet, and sometimes sang. Tunes such as "Stomp It Off/My Blue Heaven," "Organ Grinder's Swing," and "On the Beach at Bali-Bali" were hits for the Lunceford orchestra thanks to Oliver. He also wrote arrangements for Goodman from 1934 until 1939, then joined Tommy Dorsey as a vocalist and arranger. After completing his army service, Oliver led his own band for a time, served as a music director and supervisor to various record labels, then led his own band again. Oliver toured extensively during the '60s and '70s, directing a band in Paris during 1968 and 1969. He resumed playing trumpet and led a nonet that played at several New York clubs. Oliver worked with Money Johnson, Bobby Jones, Mousey Alexander, and Chris Woods, among others. They played Oliver's arrangements, and worked into the '80s. Oliver also recorded for the Black and Blue label in 1973. Recent Lunceford and Goodman reissues spotlight several Oliver arrangements and compositions. —*Ron Wynn*

OREGON

Jazz chamber ensemble / World fusion, modern creative, new age

Oregon emerged in 1970 as a splinter band from the Paul Winter Consort. Its members each had experience in jazz, classical, and a variety of nonwestern musical styles, and were also multi-instrumentalists. Ralph Towner played standard acoustic and 12-string guitar, piano, a variety of electric keyboards, trumpet, and flugelhorn. Paul McCandless's instrumental arsenal included oboe, English horn, soprano sax, bass clarinet, the musette, and tin flute. Collin Walcott handled most of the percussion duties on tabla and various African and Latin rhythm instruments, plus sitar, dulcimer, clarinet, and violin. Glen Moore was the bassist, and also played clarinet, viola, piano, and flute. They suffered from some snide comments, which labelled them as the "Modern Jazz Quartet of the '70s" or "a White, European imitation of the Art Ensemble of Chicago." In truth, they were an excellent ensemble playing a hybrid style that wasn't exactly jazz, certainly wasn't rock, but liberally quoted and borrowed from free jazz, Asian, African, European, and pop music sources. They began on Vanguard, later moved to ECM, and also issued albums on Elektra and Portrait/Columbia. The group survived Collin Walcott's death, and replaced him with Trilok Gurtu in the late '80s. They've also worked with guest stars such as Zgigniew Seifert, David Earle Johnson, and Nancy King. Their Elektra albums have been reissued on Discovery CDs, while many of their Vanguard and ECM albums are available on CD also. —*Ron Wynn*

★ **Distant Hills** / Jul. 2-5, 1973 / Vanguard 79341

This is one of the first releases to click from this group that knows how to make soothing, acoustic fare without becoming boring or wimpy. —*Ron Wynn*

☆ **Music of Another Present Era** / 1973 / Vanguard 79326

A 1989 reissue of an outstanding release that blows most similar ECM albums out of the water. —*Ron Wynn*

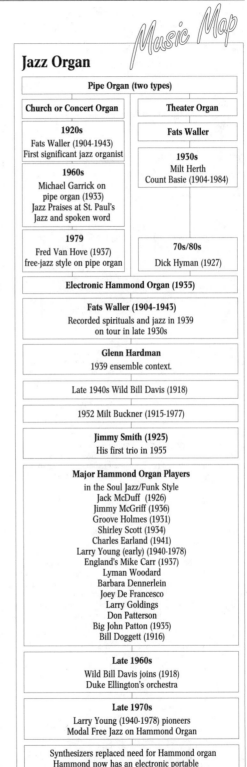

Jazz Organ   *Music Map*

Pipe Organ (two types)	
Church or Concert Organ	**Theater Organ**
1920s Fats Waller (1904-1943) First significant jazz organist	**Fats Waller**
1960s Michael Garrick on pipe organ (1933) Jazz Praises at St. Paul's Jazz and spoken word	**1930s** Milt Herth Count Basie (1904-1984)
1979 Fred Van Hove (1937) free-jazz style on pipe organ	**70s/80s** Dick Hyman (1927)

Electronic Hammond Organ (1935)

Fats Waller (1904-1943) Recorded spirituals and jazz in 1939 on tour in late 1930s

Glenn Hardman 1939 ensemble context.

Late 1940s Wild Bill Davis (1918)

1952 Milt Buckner (1915-1977)

Jimmy Smith (1925) His first trio in 1955

Major Hammond Organ Players in the Soul Jazz/Funk Style Jack McDuff (1926) Jimmy McGriff (1936) Groove Holmes (1931) Shirley Scott (1934) Charles Earland (1941) Larry Young (early) (1940-1978) England's Mike Carr (1937) Lyman Woodard Barbara Dennerlein Joey De Francesco Larry Goldings Don Patterson Big John Patton (1935) Bill Doggett (1916)

Late 1960s Wild Bill Davis joins (1918) Duke Ellington's orchestra

Late 1970s Larry Young (1940-1978) pioneers Modal Free Jazz on Hammond Organ

Synthesizers replaced need for Hammond organ Hammond now has an electronic portable

☆ **Winter Light** / Jul. 16, 1974-Aug. 7, 1974 / Vanguard 79350
Here are some simply brilliant, feathery compositions.
Marvelous playing. —*Ron Wynn*

Moon and Mind / 1978 / Vanguard 79419

Roots in the Sky / i. 1992 / Musicraft 71005
A '92 CD reissue of their '79 album, among their only releases ever issued by a major label. It is characteristically
freewheeling and eclectic, with long stretches of classical,
Asian, African, and jazz things coming together. The group
mixes structured ensemble work with surging free solos. —
Ron Wynn

Essential / Vanguard 109-110

ORIGINAL DIXIELAND JAZZ BAND

Group / Dixieland
In many ways, the Original Dixieland Jazz Band (ODJB) was
at the foundation of a long-running, still-simmering feud in
jazz over origins and authenticity. The Original Dixieland
Jazz Band was a five-member, five-piece White New Orleans
ensemble. They played in Chicago in 1916, then moved to
New York. They received a great reception for their appearances at Reeisenweber's Restaurant in 1917, and, because
they were the first jazz band to make phonograph recordings, they had enormous exposure and gained a reputation
that their skills didn't merit. They disbanded in the mid-'20s,
then regrouped briefly in 1936. Because they were the first
band to record for the phonograph, the historical importance of cornetist Nick LaRocca, clarinetist Larry Shields,
trombonist Eddie Edwards, drummer Tony Sbarbaro, and pianist Henry Ragas (later replaced by J. Russel Robinson) cannot be denied. But it must also be noted that, in 1917, a
White jazz band certainly would have been picked ahead of
any Black jazz band to cut the first recordings. When Black
jazz bands got their shot, it was evident immediately that
the ODJB was outclassed. Some see this as the first example
of White imitators capitalizing on Black innovations, though
the ODJB's sound was radically different from anything else
on record. The band's defenders argue that the group provided a service by exposing the music to audiences who
would never have heard it otherwise, and that the group
also spurred interest in the genuine item (a familiar argument still recycled in other jazz, blues, R&B, and even reggae and Latin situations). LaRocca further inflamed things
by insisting his band played a vital role in "inventing" jazz
during the early 1900s, a claim that thus far lacks either
hard or soft evidence. They were responsible for popularizing the Dixieland style in parts of Europe and America. —
Ron Wynn

★ **Original Dixieland Jazz Band** / **Louisiana Five** / **i.** Aug.
1917 / Retrieval 101
As Black musicians in New Orleans took steps to instru-
mentalize the blues over martial and ragtime syncopations,
White musicians there also began to recognize the possiblities. But the blues were not an integral part of White culture,
so, inevitably, the music of White bands emerging during the
first two decades of the 20th century leaned more heavily on
ragtime and marching band idioms. The founder of this side
of the "jazz" tradition was undoubtedly Jack "Papa" Laine,
who was leading marching bands in New Orleans before the
turn of the century. But it was the young members of Laine's
various bands who were to consolidate this tradition into an
idiom whose perfection forestalled further development.
They included Nick LaRocca, who boasted that he invented
jazz when his Original Dixieland Jazz Band cut the first-ever
"jass" records for Columbia in 1917. Their music reflected
Blacks' more colorful work without being directly influenced
by it. The latter (the music of the Black groups they imitated)
made its mark tonally, rather than structurally, for the form
Black players used was purely ragtime with its secondary,
even tertiary themes. Thus "Dixie Jazz Band One-Step" is
largely Joe Jordon's "Teasing Rag," while "Tiger Rag" is
based on Laine fare like "Praline" and "Sendation Rag" (the
ODJB's best sides), jazz-tinged rags for dancing.

Rhythmically, the pulse was syncopated march time—two-
beat, but more enervating than the work of Sousa, which it
reflected. But, melodically, the ODJB's music was crammed
with activity to the point of being hectic, even hasty. And a
misunderstanding of instrumental blues "vocalese" led to
the use of novelty effects like crowing clarinet, whinnying
cornet, and neighing trombone of "Livery Stable Blues," a
Victor remake five weeks after Columbia had shelved the
band's original version. Larry Shields reached furthest into
the Blacks' bag, and was clearly one of the finest early White
clarinetists—there was none better until the emergence of
Frank Teschemacher. Shields's agitated, reedy work on "Lazy
Daddy" and "Clarinet Marmalade" shows a flair for melody
that underlines the band's dance origins as much as his
grasp of Black style. Trombonist Edwards's uncanny sense of
dynamics plays an important part in his success in assimi-
lating the Black "tailgate" style, giving the band lift, even if
his playing is more energetic than adventurous. And
LaRocca's light, dancing cornet was to be echoed time and
again in the work of the "Chicago School" of the later '20s
and on into the swing era of the '30s. Not the least of his pro-
teges was Bix Beiderbecke, and the lineage is not difficult to
trace when listening to LaRocca's lead in "Clarinet
Marmalade," his breaks in "Jazz Me Blues," or his closing
chorus in "Marge." —*Chris Sheridan*, Cadence

KID ORY (Edward Ory)

b. Dec. 25, 1890, La Place, LA, **d.** Jan. 23, 1973, Honolulu,
Hawaii
Trumpet, bandleader, trombone / New Orleans traditional
A gifted multi-instrumentalist whose favorite and best instrument was trombone, Edward "Kid" Ory reigned supreme
as the greatest of the "tailgate" players and as an inspirational figure to generations. The tailgate style featured trombonists who played rhythmic bass parts in the "front line"
while they soloed in a personable, humorous, and exuberant
manner. When performing on streets, trombonists would
carefully aim their slides over wagon "tails" to avoid knock-
ing anyone's hat off.
Ory began on banjo at age ten, and organized a band playing homemade instruments. He played with Buddy Bolden,
then later organized his own New Orleans group in 1911. At
various times, this ensemble included Mutt Carey, Louis
Armstrong, King Oliver, Johnny Dodds, Jimmie Noone,
Sidney Bechet, and George Lewis. Ory was also a Creole and
part of the last generation that maintained their customs
and language, and incorporated them into the period's music. Ory sang vocals in patois along with trombone solos and
accompaniment. He formed the first Black jazz band to
record in California in 1922 along with Carey and others,
Spikes' Seven Pods of Pepper. On doctor's orders, Ory temporarily went to the West Coast, but, in 1925, Ory turned the
group over to Carey and moved to Chicago to record with
Armstrong. He participated in the Hot Five sessions, and
contributed the composition "Muskrat Ramble," which became a traditional jazz anthem. Ory played alto sax and
trombone with King Oliver from 1925 to 1927, then worked
with other groups before returning to the West Coast in
1930. For much of the '30s, Ory ran a chicken farm with his
brother.
Ory got back into the national spotlight during the early
'40s traditional jazz revival, and joined Barney Bigard's band
in 1942 on bass, alto sax, and cornet. During an Orson Wells
radio program about jazz history in 1944, Ory returned to
the trombone. He recorded with Carey, Omer Simeon, Bud
Scott, Minor Hall, and Darnell Howard as Kid Ory's Jazz
Band 1944-1945, and appeared in the films *New Orleans* in
1946 along with Armstrong, and *Crossfire* in 1947. Ory also
recorded with Armstrong in the mid-'40s. He headed several
bands throughout the '50s, and was often a featured attraction at Disneyland and on overseas tours. He made more
film appearances in *Mahogany Magic* and *The Benny
Goodman Story*, and cut albums on the Good Time Jazz
Label. Ory retired and moved to Hawaii in 1966, but resur-

faced at a New Orleans festival in 1971. He died two years later. His greatest composition, "Muskrat Ramble," got fresh exposure when it was reworked by Country Joe MacDonald into a protest number titled "Feel Like I'm Fixin' to Die." — *Ron Wynn with Bruce Boyd Raeburn*

○ **Kid Ory (1944-1945)** / 1944-1945 / Good Time Jazz 12022
Mid-'40s traditional jazz by trombonist Kid Ory, a New Orleans legend. Ory's trombone mastery was second only to Jack Teagarden's among traditional players, so his solos and sound provide the album's hook. The material for the most part is well played but very similiar throughout. — *Ron Wynn*

★ **Creole Jazz Band at Club Hangover** / May 9-16, 1953 / Storyville 4070
The Kid with Don Ewell (p), Albert Burbank (cl), Ed "Montudie" Garland (b), and others, captured in remote broadcast. Specialties include "South Rampart Street Parade," "High Society," and "Milneberg Joys." Ewell and Burbank offer some inspired soloing and ensemble work. — *Bruce Raeburn*

○ **Legendary Kid** / Nov. 22-25, 1955 / Good Time Jazz 12016
Ory's Creole Jazz Band delivering traditional favorites such as "Mahogany Hall Stomp," "Snag It," and "Pallet," with sidemen Alvin Alcorn (tpt), Phil Gomez (cl), Wellman Braud (b), and Minor Hall (d). — *Bruce Raeburn*

○ **This Kid's the Greatest!** / i. 195? / Good Time Jazz 12045
This is a collection of Kid Ory (tb) cuts from 7/17/53, 12/1/53, 12/1/54, and 6/18/56. The lineup includes Teddy Buckner, Al Alcorn, Pud Brown, Lloyd Glenn, Julian Davidson, Ed Garland, Minor Hall, Bob McCracken, Don Ewell, Morty Corb, and Barney Kessel. If you have a lot of Ory, this will not be a pressing need. It's consistent with his other numerous '50s sessions. There are a couple of nice vocals, but for the most part it is more of the same. — *Bob Rusch*, Cadence

Kid Ory Favorites! / i. Aug. 1961 / Good Time Jazz 60-009
A compilation of various Ory bands, this CD gives a useful overview of the typical Creole Jazz Band repertoire. — *Bruce Raeburn*

GREG OSBY

Alto saxophone / Modern creative
A fiery, outspoken alto and soprano saxophonist, flutist, and keyboard player, Greg Osby has been highly critical of many of his contemporaries who, he claims, are retarding jazz's progress. Though he's a first-rate bebop and hard bop soloist, Osby has avoided, for the most part, doing standard jazz repertory except on other people's dates. His own albums have included funk tracks, both electric and acoustic instrumentation, lots of original material, and recently, guest stints by rappers. Long before jazz/hip-hop was the in thing, Osby was seeking a stylistic blend of the two. He's recorded sessions for JMT and Blue Note. His albums are usually uneven affairs, mainly because he's trying so many different things; some work, others don't, but no Osby album is predictable. He's also done sessions with Andrew Hill, Jack DeJohnette, Steve Coleman, Cassandra Wilson, and other M-Base and Black Rock Coalition members. His dates are all available on CD. — *Ron Wynn*

★ **Greg Osby and the Sound Theatre** / Jun. 1987 / JMT 834411
This is Osby's most accomplished ensemble, especially with Michele Rosewoman on piano. — *Ron Wynn*

Season of Renewal / Jul. 1989 / JMT 834435

Man-Talk for Moderns–Vol. 10 / Oct. -Nov. 1990 / Blue Note 95414
Osby is among the top players in the emerging new jazz movement. Hip-hop, funk, R&B, and bop intersect, not always smoothly but never predictably. — *Ron Wynn*

3-D Lifestyles / Capitol 98635
From the opening track of this cutting-edge album, it's apparent that Greg Osby is making more than just a token gesture toward hip-hop. Not only does the jazz-trained saxo-

phonist understand and respect the rhythmic virtuosity of hardcore rappers, but he seems to genuinely enjoy playing in these slamming surroundings. The material is worked up organically with coproducers Lee Johnson, Eric Sadlerr of Public Enemy, and Ali Shaheed Muhammad of A Tribe Called Quest providing the earthy street-funk base. Osby exchanges phrases like a vocalist with members of the audacious Philadelphia rap crew 100X. The most intriguing track is "Honor the Example," an homage to Osby's jazz heroes. In this typically hard-hitting piece, the names of Trane, Dizzy, Monk, and Bird are uttered on top of the monstrous groove. There is a reference to Billie Holiday, and Duke Ellington is referred to as "the educator, piano player, no other man played it greater." — *Bill Milkowski*, Jazz Times

HAROLD OUSLEY (Harold Lomax Ousley)

b. Jan. 1929, Chicago, IL
Saxophone, flute / Swing, blues & jazz, soul-jazz
A competent funk and soul-jazz saxophonist and flutist, Harold Ousley's bluesy playing on organ combo dates, on rock and roll tunes, and when backing vocalists was stronger than much of what he did when leading groups. His albums were often uneven, both in terms of compositional quality and playing. Ousley began his professional career in the '40s, and at one point backed Billie Holiday. During the '50s, he played with King Kolax and Gene Ammons and worked in circus bands. Ousley backed Dinah Washington at the 1958 Newport Jazz Festival, an engagement that led to him winning a recording deal. He traveled to Paris the next year with a song revue, then worked with Clark Terry, Howard McGhee, Machito, and Joe Newman in the '60s. Ousely began leading his own groups and recording with organ combos, notably Brother Jack McDuff, in the mid-'60s. He worked with Lionel Hampton and Count Basie in the '70s. Currently, Ousley has no releases available on CD. — *Ron Wynn*

★ **People's Groove, The** / 1972 / Muse 5107
Saxophonist who worked with Dinah Washington. The all-star cast includes Ray McKinney (b), Bobby Rose (g), and Norman Simmons (p). — *Michael G. Nastos*

JIMMY OWENS (James Robert Owens)

b. Dec. 9, 1943, New York, NY
Trumpet, flugelhorn, composer, instructor / Hard bop
A fine trumpeter and flugelhorn player, especially on up-tempo tunes, Jimmy Owens doesn't have an extensive amount of recordings as a leader. But he's distinguished himself through session work with numerous bandleaders and groups. Owens played with Miles Davis's band in the late '50s, but didn't record with them. He studied with Donald Byrd in 1959, and was in Marshall Brown's Newport Youth Band in 1959 and 1960. During the '60s, Owens worked with Slide Hampton, Lionel Hampton, Maynard Ferguson, Gerry Mulligan, Charles Mingus, Hank Crawford, Herbie Mann, and Max Roach. He was a founding member of the Thad Jones-Mel Lewis orchestra in 1966, and played with the New York Jazz sextet from 1966 to 1968. Owens was also in Clark Terry's big band, and performed in Billy Taylor's orchestra for David Frost's television show. He toured Europe with Dizzy Gillespie's band in 1968, then played and recorded with Duke Ellington and worked with Count Basie. He was one of the founders of the Collective Black Artists organization in 1969, and worked with the Jazzmobile as a teacher and performer in the late '60s and early '70s. Owens toured Europe with the Young Giants of Jazz in 1971, and led his group, the Jimmy Owens Quartet Plus One. He performed with radio orchestras in Germany and Holland and played with Chuck Israels's National Jazz Ensemble. Owens recorded with the Mingus Dynasty in 1979, and with Errol Parker in 1980. He's done sessions as a leader for Atlantic, Polydor, and Horizon. Currently, Owens doesn't have any sessions available on CD. — *Ron Wynn*

TONY OXLEY (Tony [Oxo] Oxley)

b. Jun. 15, 1938, Sheffield, England
Drums / Modern creative
One of the loosest, truly "free" European drummers, Tony Oxley works percussive wonders playing on or off the beat. He's a good conventional player, but is far more arresting when he varies the time, changes the pace, and influences the musical dialogue. The English drummer and percussionist played in military bands before he began working with Derek Bailey and Gavin Byars in the '60s. He moved from Sheffield to London in 1967, where he became resident drummer at Ronnie Scott's nightclub. This position won Oxley international acclaim, and a late '60s recording invitation. He experimented with amplified percussion, and later helped found Incus, a label devoted to recording noncommercial British and European improvisers. Oxley joined the London Jazz Composers Orchestra and later formed SOH with Alan Skidmore and Ali Haurand. He moved to Germany in 1979, and led his Celebration Orchestra throughout the '80s. Currently, Oxley doesn't have any sessions available on CD in America. *—Ron Wynn*

★ **Live in Berlin (1985)** / 1985 /
Sixteen-piece free jazz ensemble led by drummer Oxley. Three pieces written by Oxley and played with wild abandon. With saxes G. Dudek, E.L. Petrowsky, and Larry Stabbins, Marcio Mattos (b), Barry Guy (b), and five drummers. *—Michael G. Nastos*

MAKOTO OZONE

b. Mar. 25, 1961, Kobe, Japan
Piano / World fusion, modern creative
A good, occasionally exceptional pianist whose albums have not adequately reflected his evolution and growth, Makoto Ozone is still maturing as a pianist. His solos in live performance have been sharper, more creative, and more invigorating than those on his albums, which have leaned toward the introspective and polite. Ozone began teaching himself piano at age five, then started formal studies at age 12. He attended Berklee in the early '80s, worked closely with Gary Burton, and thoroughly studied Chick Corea's music. He joined Burton's band after graduation, and also did solo concerts. He made his Columbia debut playing with Burton and Eddie Gomez in the mid-'80s. Ozone's since recorded for GRP. He has sessions available on CD. *—Ron Wynn*

○ **Makoto Ozone** / Jun. 23-24, 1981 / CBS 26198
Produced by Gary Burton. Solo piano in light jazz to edges of new age. Bright, but not shining. *—Michael G. Nastos*

★ **Starlight** / 1990 / JVC 3323

HOT LIPS PAGE (Oran Thaddeus Page)

b. Jan. 27, 1908, Dallas, TX, **d.** Nov. 5, 1954, New York, NY
Trumpet, vocals / Swing, big band
Oran "Hot Lips" Page loved jam sessions. He thrived in the competitive, unpredictable heat of battle, where his on-the-edge style was at its best. Page could ad lib, construct marvelous hot blues, or begin ripping through fiery phrases. He was an excellent blues vocalist, though he sometimes put so much intensity into his singing that it became overbearing. Page made a tactical error in the late '30s, leaving the Basie orchestra to go out on his own at a time when Page was principal soloist. He took the advice of Louis Armstrong's manager, Joe Glaser; he enjoyed a good career, but his decision still doesn't seem like a wise choice. Page was a professional musician as a teen in Texas during the '20s, and was part of Ma Rainey's backing band on the old chitlin' circuit. They also accompanied Bessie Smith and Ida Cox, and Page maintained this was where he learned how to sing the blues. He worked with Walter Page's Blue Devils in the late '20s and early '30s, then joined Bennie Moten's band in Kansas City. Page led his own band in New York in 1937, then worked with Artie Shaw in 1941 and 1942. He worked in combos in the mid- and late '40s, then became mainly a solo act after 1950. Page made a number of recordings from the late '30s until the mid-'50s, working with Earl Bostic, Ben Webster, Don Byas, and J.C. Higginbotham, among others. He recorded for Savoy, Bluebird, and on V-discs. Page has some sessions available on CD. *—Ron Wynn*

☆ **Chronological Hot Lips Page (1938-1940), The** / **i.** Mar. 1938-Dec. 1940 / Classics 561

★ **After Hours in Harlem** / **i.** Oct. 1973 / Onyx 307

P

WALTER PAGE

b. 1900, **d.** 1957

Bass / Swing, big band

He didn't single-handedly invent it, but Walter Page played a major part in creating swing's loping, hypnotic beat. He was one of the earliest bassists to adopt a new style; he played four beats to a measure rather than the customary two, which was the preferred New Orleans style. Page has been credited with developing the "walking effect," which is when a bassist ranges far up the instrument, then gradually comes back down. Page on bass, Basie on piano, Freddie Green on guitar, and Jo Jones on drums was a smooth, stylish, but not a slick rhythm machine that kept the Basie band locked into a groove, one loose enough to insert soaring, gliding horn solos and bluesy, enticing melodies easily. Page's fluid, definitive bass work let Jones ditch more rigid stride patterns and shift the pulse to the hi-hat cymbals. Page joined Bennie Moten in 1918, and remained with him until 1923. He left to join a road show, but returned when the show folded. Page eventually became a bandleader, renaming the group Walter Page's Blue Devils. They worked from Oklahoma City from 1925 to 1931, and cut a couple of songs for Vocalion in 1929 with Hot Lips Page, Buster Smith, and Jimmy Rushing, among others. Page left his band in 1931 to rejoin Moten, and stayed, this time, until 1934. After a year of freelance sessions, Page became a member of the Count Basie Orchestra in 1935, and was part of its rhythm section until 1942. His solo on "Pagin' the Devil," done with a spin-off Basie unit called the Kansas City Six, was one of the earliest solo bass numbers. He rejoined Basie in 1946, and remained with Basie until 1948. Page worked in 1949 with Hot Lips Page, then freelanced with various New York musicians. He did one final recording session with Basie before Page died of pneumonia in 1957. —*Ron Wynn*

MARTY PAICH (Martin Louis Paich)

b. Jan. 23, 1925, Oakland, CA

Arranger, bandleader, composer / Cool, progressive big band

Marty Paich is an arranger, big-band leader, and composer who's been involved in different capacities with several fine jazz and jazz-based recordings since the '50s. At one time, Paich led a band that included Art Pepper and Russ Freeman. He later became a successful studio and session musician, and also did television and film soundtrack work. Paich was featured on a number of recordings as a pianist, playing with Shelly Manne and Shorty Rogers. But he's much better known for his arrangements for many groups and artists, among them his own Dek-tette, the Dave Pell Octet, Mel Tormé, and Art Pepper. Paich has also written music for artists such as Ella Fitzgerald, Anita O'Day, Chet Baker, Ray Brown, Buddy Rich, and Stan Kenton, and remains very active in contemporary music. He was one of the arrangers who worked on Natalie Cole's *Take a Look* session in 1993. Paich has many arrangements and compositions featured on CDs that are available currently. —*Ron Wynn*

★ **Picasso of Big Band Jazz** / **i.** Jun. 7-8, 1957 / Candid 79031

West Coast mainstream. These arrangements create a light, airy feeling punctuated by a crisp (Mel Lewis) beat. —*Paul B. Matthews*, Cadence

○ **Moanin'** / **i.** Jul. 22, 1992 / Discovery 962

CHARLIE PALMIERI

b. 1927, New York, NY, **d.** 1988

Piano / Latin-jazz

Charlie Palmieri was a child prodigy pianist and was among Latin-jazz's flashiest, most flamboyant stylists. His playing was alternately aggressive and mellow, percussive, then very supportive and low-key. He began studying piano at age seven, and eventually attended Juilliard. Palmieri played dances at age 14, and turned professional at age 16. He started his group, El Conjunto Pin Pin, in 1948, and played piano for Pupi Campo, Tito Puente, Tito Rodriquez, Bicentico Valdes, and Pete Terrace before forming his Charanga Dubonney group in 1958. They recorded in the '60s for United Artists and Alegre.

Palmieri helped initiate the charanga (flute and violin band) explosion of the early '60s. He was music director for the Alegre All Stars on a series of descarga (jam session) albums, working with stars such as Johnny Pacheco, Willie Rosario, and Cheo Feliciano. They spawned a growth industry as other Latin labels, like Tico and Fania, established their own all-star groups to compete. Palmieri formed the Duboney Orchestra in the mid-'60s, replacing the violin and flute with three trumpets and two trombones. He temporarily moved to RCA from Alegre, but returned and recorded some albums in the popular R&B/Latin "boogaloo" style. One such album was produced for Atlantic by Herbie Mann. Palmieri survived a near mental breakdown in 1969, and was hired by Tito Puente to be musical director for his "El Mambo de Tito Puente" television program.

In the '70s, Palmieri began a parallel career as a cultural historian and a lecturer on Latin music and history, and subsequently taught courses at various New York institutions. He added organ to his band in the '70s, and continued recording on Alegre before switching to Coco. There were subsequent albums on Tipica, Cotique, then Alegre again. He was featured on the 1979 British television film *Salsa*. Palmieri moved to Puerto Rico in 1980, and remained there until 1983. He'd planned a concert in Puerto Rico with his brother, Eddie, but suffered a severe heart attack and stroke while back in New York organizing the event. After his recovery, Palmieri returned to the Latin music wars with a small combo in 1984. He played with Ralphy Marzan and with Joe Quijano, and co-led the band Combo Gigante with Jimmy Sabater. Palmieri made his first trip to England in 1988, but suffered another heart attack when he returned to New York. This time he didn't recover. Charlie Palmieri left a legacy of masterful albums in various Latin pop and jazz styles. Unfortunately, most of them aren't available on CD, except through Latin or international music specialty stores. —*Ron Wynn and Max Salazar*

○ **Tribute to Noro Morales** / **i.** 1965 / Alegre

○ **Giant of the Keyboard, The** / **i.** 1972 / Alegre

★ **Giant Step, A** / **i.** 1988 / Tropical Budda

○ **Adelante Gigante** / Alegre 7013
Eddie Palmieri always said his elder brother was the better
player, and by the time of his death, Charlie Palmieri was
well enough known outside the barrio to get an obituary in
the *New York Times*. This classic mid-'70s album has all his
usual taste, talent, and classic piano (and in a couple of
places organ) along with his favorite lead singer, Vitin
Aviles, and a tight band. —*John Storm Roberts*

EDDIE PALMIERI

b. Dec. 15, 1936, New York, NY
Vocals, piano / Latin-jazz
A sometimes dazzling pianist whose technique incorporates
bits and pieces of everyone from McCoy Tyner to Herbie
Hancock and recycles their styles through a dynamic Latin
groove, Eddie Palmieri has been a Latin-jazz and salsa master since the '50s. His approach can be compared to
Thelonious Monk's in its unorthodox patterns, odd rhythms,
sometimes disjointed phrases, and percussive effects played
in a manner that seems frazzled, but is always successfully
resolved. It's a free/bebop/Latin blend, with keyboard solos
that are never predictable, but always stimulating.

Palmieri started as a vocalist, but his elder brother,
Charlie, influenced him to become a pianist. Eddie began
with the neighborhood band of Orlando Marin, then made
his professional debut in 1955 with Johnny Sequi's orchestra. Following stints with Vicentico Valdes, Pete Terrace, and
Tito Rodriguez, Palmieri formed Conjunto La Perfecta in
1962. The group included Barry Rogers, Johnny Pacheco,
Manny Oquendo, and George Castro. With Rogers, Palmieri
developed a two-trombone/flute frontline that was a variation on the charanga (flute and violin) style that Palmieri
dubbed "trombanga." Initially, the group recorded for Alegre,
then switched to Tico. They made several albums in the '60s,
including two with Cal Tjader, before disbanding, due to
money problems, in 1968. Palmieri worked with the Tico
All-Stars and appeared on the Fania All-Stars debut album.
He continued recording, working with such players as
Alfredo "Chocolate" Armenteros, Israel "Cachao" Lopez, and
Justo Betancourt. He made some R&B/Latin "boogaloo"
dates, and, in the early '70s, attracted some R&B and funk interest working with the band Harlem River Drive. Palmieri
held concerts at Sing Sing and at the University of Puerto
Rico.

Palmieri began recording for Coco in the mid-'70s, and
eventually amassed five Grammy awards in the '70s and
'80s. His productions were elaborate combinations of contemporary Latin, pop, rock and soul, jazz improvisation,
Spanish vocals, and Afro-Latin rhythms. He became so popular that even albums he didn't like personally, such as
1976's *Unfinished Masterpiece* on Coco, won Grammys.
Every album he issued between 1978 and 1987 was nominated for a Grammy. But Palmieri didn't fare as well with
record labels. His superb late '70s album recorded for
Columbia, *Lucumi Macumba Voodoo*, was a sales flop despite its huge publicity campaign. Palmieri was later quoted
as saying that joining Columbia had been a major mistake.
He also said the same thing about his affiliation with Fania,
even though he won a fifth Grammy for the album *La
Verdad/The Truth*. Palmieri suffered yet another label disappointment with 1989's *Sueno* on Capitol that included special guest Dave Sanborn. It flopped sales-wise and aesthetically, as Capitol sought some Latin instrumental filler to
plug into the Kenny G/Najee urban contemporary/quiet
storm market. Palmieri eventually issued another album on
Fania in 1990, *EP*. Despite his failure to attain major label
success, Eddie Palmieri's artistic triumphs have cemented
his place in the Latin-jazz, salsa, and international arena. He
has very few albums available anywhere on CD, except
through the specialist and mail-order route. —*Ron Wynn
and Max Salazar*

○ **Sin Sabor Nada, Cafe, Si Hecho Palante** / i. 1964 / Tico

Mozambique / i. 1965 / Tico 1126

Eddie Palmieri first hit in the '60s with his classic two-trombone sound. This is one of his finest albums; unassuming,
joyous, punchy, and sharp, with the outstanding Ismael
Quintana on vocals and Manny Oquendo on timbales. —
John Storm Roberts

★ **Sun of Latin Music** / i. 1973 / Coco 3109
This album almost perfectly combines Palmieri's experi-
mentalism with the devastating swing that kept him ahead
on the street. The "Un Dia Bonito" suite got the most attention, but "Una Rosa Española," a one-cut mini-history of
salsa, is enchanting. —*John Storm Roberts*

○ **Lucumi, Macumba, Voodoo** / i. Jan. 1979 / Epic 35523

Sueno / i. Mar. 1990 / Intuition 3011
The master of Latin-jazz and dazzling piano licks in a salsa
context makes his major label debut in style. —*Ron Wynn*,
Rock & Roll Disc

Rey De Las Blancas Y Las Negras, El / Sony 80651

★ **Unfinished Masterpiece** / Coco 3120
The late '70s *Unfinished Masterpiece* caused a huge quarrel
because Eddie couldn't or wouldn't get it done to his own
satisfaction (Coco finally put it out anyway, thus the title).
Unfinished or no, it's classic Palmieri from his late golden
age and long unavailable. —*John Storm Roberts*

○ **Sentido** / Mpl 3103
The Coco Records-era *Sentido*, regarded by some as his
greatest album ever. "Puerto Rico" alone would put it hors
concours, even without the version of that piano intro in
"Adoracion" and the bicultural funk of "Condiciones." A one-
man avant-garde who did it all while still preserving his
street cred! What a family! Pa and Ma Palmieri, we thank
you! —*John Storm Roberts*

CHARLIE PARKER (Charles (Jr) Parker)

b. Apr. 29, 1920, Kansas City, **d.** Mar. 12, 1955, New York, NY
Alto and tenor saxophone, composer / Bop
Charlie Parker radically reshaped jazz, and changed the way
musicians, fans, and critics approached it. If Dizzy Gillespie
was bop's patron saint, Parker was its founding elder. He
was an amazing improviser who used a slow, thin vibrato,
astonishing harmonic knowledge, and total technical command to recast songs via his solos. He usually ignored the
melody and went instead to the harmonic structure. By
breaking the pulse, varying the rhythm, experimenting with
pitch, and, in short, doing any and everything possible,
Parker created solos that were fresh, radical, and totally distinctive, yet were related to the original and didn't destroy
its organization. He knew thousands of tunes, and freely incorporated snatches of Tin Pan Alley, blues, hillbilly, and
classical music into other tunes. But these weren't randomly
inserted; they were included in ways that fit the moment.
These snippets were both humorous and relevant. Parker
did this while playing at either rapid-fire tempos or while
doing slow, agonizing 12-bar wailers. He emerged as the
most imitated and admired saxophonist of his day, and
though his influence eventually waned, his impact remains
substantial. There aren't many alto saxophonists, especially
those playing bebop or related styles, that haven't closely
studied his work and haven't committed many Parker solos
to memory. He's responsible for numerous American music
classics, among them "Confirmation," "Yardbird Suite,"
"Relaxin' at Camarillo," "Ornithology," "Scrapple from the
Apple," "Parker's Mood," and "Now's the Time," which was
later reworked into an R&B sensation "The Hucklebuck."

Parker got his first music lessons in Kansas City public
schools. His father was a vaudevillian. He began playing alto
sax in 1931, and worked infrequently before dropping out in
1935 to become a full-time player. Sadly, his involvement
with drugs started almost as soon as he began playing professionally. He worked mainly in Kansas City until 1939,
playing with jazz and blues groups, and honing his craft in
legendary Kansas City jam sessions. One incident during
this period stands out: Jo Jones reportedly fired a cymbal at
Parker one night in a rage over Parker's playing. Parker's as-

tonishing harmonic skills were developed during this time; eventually, he was able to modulate from any key to any other key. Local musicians Buster Smith and the great Lester Young were major influences on Parker's early style. Initially, Parker played with Jay McShann in 1937, and also with Harlan Leonard. While in Leonard's band, he met Tadd Dameron, a superb arranger. Parker began developing his lifelong reputation for unpredictability. He visited New York in 1939, and stayed until 1940. He participated in some jam sessions, and was a dishwasher for three months at a club where Art Tatum was playing. He started his harmonic experiments one night at a Harlem club, improvising on the chord's upper intervals, rather than its lower ones, on "Cherokee." But his first visit to New York didn't make much impact.

Parker met Gillespie in 1940, when Gillespie came through on tour. Parker joined McShann's big band in 1940, and remained until 1942. They toured the Southwest, Midwest, and New York, recording in 1941 in Dallas. These were Parker's first sessions. He was beginning to become famous for brilliant solos, though he still worked in strict swing style. There was a short stint with Noble Sissle's band, then he joined Earl Hines in 1942, reuniting with Gillespie. By 1944, he, Gillespie, and many other top young players were in Billy Eckstine's big band. Parker had been participating nightly in after-hours jam sessions since 1942. These sessions were held at various locations, among them Minton's Playhouse and Monroe's Uptown House. He began recording after the war-related recording ban ended in 1944 (though there are some acetates from '43 with Parker on tenor), cutting songs with Tiny Grimes. He began heading his own band in 1945, while working with Gillespie in combos. The two took their group to Hollywood in December of that year, playing a six-week engagement at various clubs. These were historic gigs; both club audiences and musical lineups included a good mix of Blacks and Whites.

Parker remained in Los Angeles, recording for Ross Russell's Dial label and performing until he suffered a nervous breakdown in 1946. His mental and physical condition (he suffered from heroin and alcohol addiction) caused him to be confined at the Camarillo State Hospital. After his release in 1947, Parker continued working in Los Angeles, making more fine records for Dial. He came back to New York in April of 1947, forming a quintet with Miles Davis, Duke Jordan, Tommy Potter, and Max Roach, and cutting several seminal dates. Roy Haynes and Lucky Thompson also worked with this band occasionally, as did Red Rodney and Kenny Dorham.

Parker became a larger-than-life celebrity from 1947 to 1951. He played in clubs, did concerts and broadcast performances, toured with Jazz at the Philharmonic, worked in Afro-Latin bands with Gillespie, and visited Europe in 1949 and 1950. He did a controversial session with strings in 1950 that became as popular as anything he ever recorded. At the same time, in the midst of this celebrity status, Parker's drug addiction worsened. He became just as famous for no-shows, for pawnshop incidents with his saxophone, and for irrational behavior as he was for his matchless tone and soaring solos. Parker's cabaret license was revoked in 1951 at the behest of the city's narcotics squad. It was reinstated two years later, but by that time the damage had been done. Parker did appear at the 1953 Massey Hall concert in Canada with Gillespie, Roach, Charles Mingus, and Bud Powell, and cut both a wonderful big-band release in Washington, D.C., and a combo session at Storyville in Boston that same year. But the end was nearing. Prevented from working in nightclubs, Parker's health declined steadily while his habit grew worse. He twice attempted suicide before committing himself to Bellevue in 1954. His last public appearance came at Birdland, the club named in his honor, in March of 1955. Parker died seven days later, at the Manhattan apartment of the Baroness Pannonica de Koenigswarter, the same place where Thelonious Monk would eventually die.

Fortunately, Parker reissues are widely available. His early work with McShann has been reissued by domestic and import labels. His Verve output has been reissued twice on mammoth sets; once on a ten-album box, and recently on a ten-CD set with many additional tracks. There have been two-record and two-disc "best of" anthologies. His Dial material has been reissued haphazardly, but there are complete import collections available. Some Prestige material is available, and his landmark Savoy sessions are coming out in separate editions. Previously, they were reissued in two-album "best ofs" and complete boxed editions. Hopefully, the handful of Columbia Parker sessions that were available in the '70s on vinyl will reappear. Blue Note has reissued the Storyville session. Elektra had reissued the Washington, D.C. date on vinyl, but it was deleted. Mosaic has issued a mammoth boxed set of Parker recordings made by fanatical follower Dean Benedetti, who took a portable recorder to countless Parker performances, concerts, and sessions, faithfully copying every Parker solo. This is the only collection in the company's illustrious history that they personally own. Stash has issued the '43 Parker sessions on tenor, and also has issued a two-disc "best of" Dial package. There's lots of transcription, bootleg, and broadcast items available. Ross Russell's self-serving book, *Bird Lives!*, irritated many by its slant, as did Robert Reisner's *Bird—The Legend of Charlie Parker*. Gary Giddins's *Celebrating Bird—The Triumph of Charlie Parker* is the best combination of scholarship, commentary, and analysis. There are also many accounts available in anthologies. Clint Eastwood valiantly attempted to get Parker's life on the screen in the 1986 film *Bird*. The results were quite mixed. —*Ron Wynn*

○ **Complete "Birth of Bebop," The** / May 1940-Nov. 1953 / Stash 535

A more comprehensive '91 CD update of formative Charlie Parker sessions from the label that originally issued an edited version in the '80s. Stash reworked this compilation, including more alternate takes and also more complete liner notes. As a result, while the original release was vital, this new one is essential. —*Ron Wynn*

○ **Early Bird (1940-1944)** / 1940-1044 / Stash 542

Bird—The Savoy Recordings (master takes) / i. 1944-1948 / Savoy 8801

Foundation recordings by alto sax giant Charlie Parker, which have been reissued in many other forms. These are remastered versions taken directly from the master tapes. Parker was making history at this point, playing with a speed, harmonic brilliance, and creativity that hadn't been imagined before, particularly on alto sax. —*Ron Wynn*

○ **Charlie Parker on Dial—Vol. 5** / Jun. 1945-Nov. 1947 / Spotlite 105

On Volume 5, pianist Duke Jordan is in a better mood, Miles Davis, open horn for a change, is more coherent, and drummer Max Roach is at his best. "Bird Feathers" is excellent for everyone. In "Scrapple from the Apple," C, Charlie Parker is fluent, straightening out the awkward pause that mars B, Roach in stimulating interplay with Davis. Bird's wealth of emotion extends far beyond the pretty confines of "Don't Blame Me"; the opening four measures of his bridge are incredible—and maybe the only reason he made momentary "Don't Blame Me" theme fragments was to show how his rhythmic and tonal variety completely transcend the original. Three versions of "Out of Nowhere" seem preoccupied with where to place a slurred descending decorative phrase, A a bit disjointed, B expansive, taking off from the theme, highly decorated, C with more brittle, spaced phrases at the beginning. —*John Litweiler*, Down Beat

★ **Complete Studio Sessions, The** / i. 1945-1948 / Savoy 5500

A three-disc compendium of virtually everything Charlie Parker did for Savoy. It includes a 24-page booklet with specific compositions transcribed, breakdowns of individual solos and collective instrumentation, interviews, and commentary. The discs cover his 1944 sessions with the Tiny Grimes Quintet and continue through dates with Parker's groups the

Reboppers and All-Stars, and his work with the Miles Davis All-Stars. Savoy Jazz's painstaking care and diligence in compiling the whole of Parker's work, rather than making assumptions about what should and should not be inserted, provide a service to the music and one of its most important participants. — *Ron Wynn*, Rock & Roll Disc

○ **At the 1946 JATP Concert** / May 27, 1946 / Verve 513756
A no-holds-barred, exciting jam session with several all-time greats going after each other in instrumental battle. This 1946 date featured Charlie Parker, Lester Young, Dizzy Gillespie, Coleman Hawkins, Buck Clayton, and Buddy Rich among others taking turns showing their mettle. The '92 CD reissue brings things up front with some glorious remastering. —*Ron Wynn*

☆ **Bird & Pres** / i. 1946 / Verve 2518
Jazz at the Philharmonic. More in Los Angeles from Lester and Lee Young, Dizzy Gillespie, Charlie Parker, Buck Clayton, Willie Smith, Mel Powell, Howard McGhee, and Charlie Ventura. It is the ultimate melding of swing-era and bop musicians. —*Michael G. Nastos*

★ **Bird: Complete on Verve** / 1946-1954 / PolyGram 837141
If you want one good boxed set, get this one. It contains 51 unissued selections—over 11 hours of engrossing, majestic music thematically and chronologically assembled to reflect Parker's peak 1946-1954 period on Verve. An exhaustive 36-page booklet is included. —*Ron Wynn*

○ **Charlie Parker on Dial—Vol. 1: The West Coast Days** / i. 1947 / Stash 23

☆ **Charlie Parker on Dial—Vol. 2: The New York Days** / i. 1947 / Stash 25

○ **Charlie Parker on Dial—Vol. 3** / Feb. 1947 / Spotlite 103
Volume 3, recorded only a week after Volume 2, is curious. Parker is extremely relaxed, not at all inclined to smash bar lines or chord barriers, expansive or decorative or powerfully expressive phrases absent, each improvised strain beginning on the beat or laid back. The result is, as the liners say, "floods of melody," the very lyrical, happy Bird at work: light in "Relaxin' At Camarillo," E, lovely in "Cheers," B, and especially C and D, smoking tenorist Wardell Gray in "Chasin' The Bird," both takes making love to the "Stupendous" changes. Again, trumpeter Howard McGhee is hip throughout, though certainly less high-tensioned than on Volume 1. Pianist Dodo Marmarosa and Wardell Gray are also generally appealing. Throughout, the high tenor sound and Lester Young-derived lines are superficially related to this once-in-a-lifetime Parker style, but even at Gray's best ("Cheers," D) he is emotionally limited. The "Home Cooking" tracks are jam session Parker with the occasional carelessness and cliché that implies, excellent in the first chorus of "III" and all of "II" (where, in the bridge, he implies—for the only time on the LP—the vastness of his emotional range). —*John Litweiler*, Down Beat

★ **Dean Benedetti Recordings of Charlie Parker, The** / Mar. 1947-Jul. 1948 / Mosaic 129

○ **Charlie Parker on Dial—Vol. 4** / Oct. 1947 / Spotlite 104
Volume 4 is New York Charlie Parker, eight months after recording Volume 3, and the change is terrific. "Dexterity," B, is the great Parker, the virtuoso of structured emotion. "Bongo Bop," A, is remarkable for the satiric quality inherent in the bold staging of his blues phrases, and the staged quality persists in the first chorus of B, pain, then sorrow emerging as the work progresses (note the easy, flowing Miles Davis). Three takes of "Dewey Square" are terrifically dramatic, A strongly structured, B including some high notes in the bridge that hint at an imagined joy quite incompatible with the grim reality outlined in the rest of the solo, C expanding—at moments, explosively—on the extremes of contrast. Two versions of "Embraceable You" are acknowledged masterpieces. A is the one with the opening phrase repeated five times and no hint of the original theme except a crying reference near the end. B opens in an entirely different mood and flows into emotions equally complex, the feelings, questions, conflicts, dismissals as perfectly

defined as they ever have been in the recorded history of jazz. Throughout the LP, Miles Davis's evolving style hints at individuality in medium tempos, still in Dizzy Gillespie's shadow at fast and slow, irritatingly frivolous on "Embraceable You," A. All of pianist Duke Jordan's brief solos seem to be random excerpts from a longer (unheard) solo. —*John Litweiler*, Down Beat

★ **Dial Masters—Vol. 1** / i. Dec. 1947 / Stash 23
This contains 25 of the master takes from Charlie Parker's Dial sessions. The Dials have always been a bit underrated compared to the better-distributed Savoys, but they are of equal value with Miles Davis, Lucky Thompson, Dodo Marmarosa, Howard McGhee, Erroll Garner, Wardell Gray, and J.J. Johnson making important contributions. Dizzy Gillespie is on "Diggin' Diz." These are ideal for general listeners and CD collectors. The sessions on this disc are from 1946-1947. The disc's total time is 75:25. —*Scott Yanow*, Cadence

★ **Dial Masters—Vol. 2** / i. Dec. 1947 / Stash 25
This contains the remaining 10 masters from Charlie Parker's Dial sessions (25 were on Vol. 1), 9 of the 57 alternate takes, and the complete *Home Cooking* private session, including a pair of poorly recorded (but previously unissued) minute-long blues. These cuts run from 2/19/47 to 11/17/47. The disc's total time is 69:29. —*Scott Yanow*, Cadence

○ **Charlie Parker on Dial—Vol. 6** / Dec. 1947 / Spotlite 106
Volume 6 highlights Charlie Parker's new Selmer saxophone with a richer sound and a super blues solo, especially "Bongo Beep," C, with the legendary firecracker up his ass. "Quasimodo," A, reflects a bit of "Embraceable You" a month later, but B is more vigorous and emotionally contained. His "Charlie's Wig," B, solo, is perhaps the best of the three here, though a wonderful phrase enters his improvised bit in the theme of D. The two complete "Crazelogys" offer a more emotionally complex Parker, while the final, more somber "How Deep is the Ocean" is weaker than the first take, with lovely phrasing. These volumes come from the peak of Parker's career, chronologically simultaneous with Savoy and JATP Parker. —*John Litweiler*, Down Beat

Charlie Parker on Dial—Vol. 7 / i. 1947 / Spotlite 107

Bird on 52nd Street / Jul. 1948 / Original Jazz Classics 114
An excellent 1948 date, with formative Miles Davis (tpt) solos, good Duke Jordan (p), and brilliant Parker. —*Ron Wynn*

○ **Bird at the Roost—Savoy Years** / i. Sep. 4, 1948-1949 / Savoy 4411
Volumes 1-4, 1948-1949. Absolute must-buys, every volume. Live at the Royal Roost in the late '40s. —*Michael G. Nastos*

○ **Live at Carnegie Hall** / i. 1949 / CP 2

One Night in Chicago / i. 1950 / Savoy 4423
A magnificent '50 concert by Charlie Parker that was previously available for only a short time on a domestic vinyl album. This demolishes the myth that by 1950 Parker was already in decline. Furious alto solos on some tracks, simmering, poignant ballads on others. —*Ron Wynn*

Bird at St. Nick's / Feb. 18, 1950 / Original Jazz Classics 41
In this top-shelf session, Red Rodney shines on trumpet and Al Haig stars on piano. —*Ron Wynn*

○ **Genius of Charlie Parker—Vol. 4: Bird and Diz, The** / Jun. 6, 1950 / PolyGram 831133
Sharp date with Thelonious Monk (p) and Buddy Rich (d) is a nice introductory vehicle for Parker novices. It has three bonus cuts on disc. —*Ron Wynn*

Verve Years (1950-1951) / 1950-1951 / Verve 821684
This authoritative twin set nicely compiles and covers two prime Parker years. —*Ron Wynn*

Inglewood Jam / i. Jun. 16, 1952 / Time Is 9801
With Chet Baker. A superior 1990 reissue of an almost forgotten early '50s concert with both Baker and Parker on file. —*Ron Wynn*

Verve Years (1952-1954) / 1952-1954 / Verve 827154

1952-1954. This is the continuation of twin anthologies covering the Verve years. —*Ron Wynn*

○ **One Night in Washington** / **i.** 1953 / Elektra 60019
Starting in 1951, Voice of America's Willis Conover, then a local jazz disc jockey, began functioning as host and producer for a series of Washington, D.C. concerts designed to feature resident big-band players working from a book of original charts by such well-known writers as Al Cohn, Johnny Mandel, and Gerry Mulligan, as well as other less-renowned local musicians. Guest artists of national reputation were also brought in as featured soloists, and these included Cohn, Zoot Sims, Lee Konitz, Warne Marsh, Dizzy Gillespie, Stan Getz, and on Febuary 22, 1953, Charlie Parker. In spectacular form, even by his own amazingly high standards, Parker is almost everywhere in evidence. Obviously eschewing the need for any lead sheet cues that might have been provided for him, he plays wherever and whenever he wants, searing, soaring, and literally ripping asunder any preconceived notions some may have entertained as regards the proper role of a big-band soloist. In the words of Bill Potts, "Bird plays straight through sectional solis, full band tuttis, and even the modulations. Some of the key changes are abrupt and without a modulation but this bothered him none." —*Jack Sohmer*, Down Beat

Charlie Parker at Storyville / Mar. 1953-Sep. 1953 / Blue Note 85108
This spirited session from Boston only appeared in 1985. It has fiery Parker alto, inspired piano by Red Garland, and some surprise guests, including Boston hero Herb Pomeroy (tpt). —*Ron Wynn*

○ **Jazz at Massey Hall** / **i.** May 15, 1953 / Original Jazz Classics 044
This is a Charlie Parker (as) and Dizzy Gillespie (tpt) album, with Charles Mingus on bass. —*Michael Katz*

Bird at the Hi-Hat / **i.** 1954 / Capitol 99787
First released in the 1950s on a 10-inch LP on the Phoenix label, this aircheck recording had restricted distribution and disappeared almost immediately into the vaults of collectors. Reissued by Blue Note on CD and cassette, it catches Parker in good form with a pickup band about 14 months before his death. The looseness and relaxation of his playing and the extracurricular banter and carrying on make it clear that Bird was having fun on this engagement at Boston's Hi-Hat club. On some pieces, notably the first run at "My Little Suede Shoes," he can be heard working toward new ways of manipulating the interior time of his phrases with an elasticity of meter unlike that of any other jazz musician before or since; the extremities of Thelonious Monk's playing lags behind the beat, the recent explorations of Wynton Marsalis notwithstanding. The only familiar name among Parker's Hi-Hat colleagues is that of 25-year-old bassist Jimmy Woode, who went on to become a prominent member of Duke Ellington's rhythm section. Trumpeter Herbie Williams, pianist Rollins Griffith, and drummer Marquis Foster are bebop journeymen. Their work here indicates a high level of competence, despite Williams's struggle through the fast tempo of "Groovin' High." The recording is reasonably good broadcast quality for the period, although on a couple of numbers the microphone is not in the vicinity of the piano. This is Charlie Parker comfortable in the complexities of a language he largely invented but still capable of electrifying listeners with his audacity. —*Doug Ramsey*, Jazz Times

★ **Live at Carnegie Hall** / **i.** Mar. 27, 1965 / PolyGram 26985
Tenth Memorial concert. Not Parker himself. Immortal sessions with various artists celebrating the Bird. —*Michael G. Nastos*

Bird with Strings / **i.** Feb. 1978 / Columbia 34832

One Night at Birdland / **i.** Feb. 1978 / Columbia 34808

○ **Summit Meeting at Birdland** / **i.** Feb. 1978 / Columbia 34831

Here Charlie Parker, Dizzy Gillespie, and Bud Powell were heard in their only recorded meeting aside from the Massey Hall concert. The time was 1951. The place, Birdland. The sound quality, sparkling. Everything fell into place flawlessly. The music rolls with a smooth, well-oiled sense of control. Even at such triphammer tempos as "Anthropology," no detail or nuance is lost. Bird's third chorus is a marvel as he whirls about weaving familiar quotations from "Tenderly" and "Temptation" into his fabric. Drummer Roy Haynes's ability to accent precisely the right notes as they fly by is dazzling. Side two moves ahead two years to 1953. Parker is still the complete genius and musician. Drummer Kenny Clarke and pianist John Lewis make a fine rhythm team, although Don Young's engineering allows Curley Russell's bass to swamp them out a bit. —*John McDonough*, Down Beat

Cole Porter Songbook / Verve 823250
Bird takes Porter's songs and extends them to glorious heights. A fine reissue. —*Ron Wynn*

☆ **Very Best Bird, The** / Warner Brothers 3198
Despite a confusing and misleading title, this is a good two-record set of Parker cuts, covering songs he is best known for. It's not comprehensive, but a good introduction. —*Ron Wynn*

EVAN PARKER (Evan Shaw Parker)

b. Apr. 5, 1944, Bristol, England
Tenor and soprano saxophone / Early free, modern creative
One of Europe's most innovative and intriguing saxophonists, Evan Parker's solos and playing style are distinguished by his creative use of circular breathing and false fingering. Parker can generate furious bursts, screeches, bleats, honks, and spiraling lines and phrases, and his solo sax work isn't for the squeamish. He's one of the few players who's not only willing but anxious to demonstrate his affinity for late-period John Coltrane. Parker worked with a Coltrane-influenced quartet in Birmingham in the early '60s. After resettling in London in 1965, Parker began playing with Spontaneous Music Ensemble. He joined them in 1967 and remained until 1969. Parker met guitarist Derek Bailey while in the group, and the duo formed the Music Improvisation Company in 1968. Parker played with them until 1971, and also began working with the Tony Oxley Sextet in the late '60s. Parker started playing extensively with other European free music groups in the '70s, notably the Globe Unity Orchestra as well as its founder Alexander von Schlippenbach's trio and quartet. Parker, Bailey, and Oxley coformed Incus Records in 1970 and continued operating it through the '80s. Parker also played with Chris McGregor's Brotherhood of Breath, in other groups with Bailey, and did duet sessions with John Stevens and Paul Lytton, as well as giving several solo concerts. Parker's albums as a leader and his collaborations are all on various foreign labels; they can be obtained through diligent effort and mail-order catalogs. —*Ron Wynn*

Saxophone Solos / Jun. 17, 1975 / Incus 19

○ **Process and Reality** / **i.** 1991 / FMP 37

LEO PARKER

b. Apr. 18, 1925, Washington, DC, **d.** Feb. 11, 1962, New York, NY
Baritone saxophone / Hard bop
Leo Parker was one of the most soulful and skilled jazz baritonists around; unfortunately, he didn't make many albums and didn't have a lengthy career. But he displayed a sustained excellence and intensity that made his baritone solos memorable. Parker blended the flamboyance and downhome simplicity of blues and R&B with the sophistication of bebop. Initially, he recorded on alto sax with Coleman Hawkins in 1944. While playing with Billy Eckstine's orchestra in 1944, '45, and '46, Parker switched to baritone. He worked in a group led by Dizzy Gillespie on 52nd Street in 1946, and played briefly in Gillespie's big band. A 1947

recording with Sir Charles Thompson, "Mad Lad," brought Parker some fame and notoriety. He played with Fats Navarro and in Illinois Jacquet's group from 1947 into the '50s, while making his recording debut as a leader for Savoy in 1947. He was most famous for his late '50s Blue Note albums, but also did sessions for Columbia and Chess. Parker died of a heart attack in 1962 at age 37. There's actually quite a bit of Parker's output available on CD, considering the brevity of his career. —Ron Wynn

○ Back to Back Baritones / i. 1948-1950 / Collectables 5329
1948-1950 recordings. Baritone sax work in early R&B honker style with some jazz leanings. Small-combo backing. Album's use of multiple and alternate takes will be of particular interest to musicians and collectors. —Hank Davis

★ Baritone Great (1951-1953), The / 1951-1953 / Chess 413
His best, with Sahib Shihab (f, sax) and Red Saunders (d). One to seek. —Michael G. Nastos

Let Me Tell You 'Bout It / Sep. 9, 1961 / Blue Note 84087

○ Rollin' with Leo / Oct. 12+20, 1961 / Blue Note 84095
Rollin' with Leo was the better-late-than-never first release for the baritone saxophonist. A typical Parker date, it finds him in the company of hard-working journeymen, improvising on blue minor ballads and jump tunes based on the hoariest of riffs—precisely the kind of surrounding where he emerges transcendent by rolling up his sleeves and pitching in. A braying, yawping player whose solos head first for the feet and for the heart, he wields his big horn with such fluid grace and constructs his statements with such passion and compressed logic that they continue to unfold in the mind long after the record is over, the foot has stopped tapping, the heart stopped thumping. Parker's influences were Charlie Parker, the outhouse tenors, and, on his ballads, the black-tie vocal phrasing of Billy Eckstine; posthumously, he has become a major influence on baritonists like Nick Brignola and Ronnie Cuber. Like that other seminal baritonist of his era, Serge Chaloff, he is pitifully underrepresented in the current catalogs, and so this release would be most welcome even if it were not so very good as it is. —Francis Davis, Cadence

HORACE PARLAN (Horace Louis Parlan)

b. Jan. 19, 1931, Pittsburgh, PA
Piano / Hard bop
Horace Parlan has overcome physical disability and has thrived as a pianist. His right hand was partially crippled by polio in his childhood, but Parlan's made frenetic, highly rhythmic, right-hand phrases part of his characteristic style, contrasting them with striking left-hand chords. He's also infused blues and R&B influences into his style, playing in a stark, sometimes somber fashion. Parlan has always cited Ahmad Jamal and Bud Powell as prime influences. He began playing in R&B bands during the '50s, and joined Charles Mingus's group from 1957 to 1959 following a move from Pittsburgh to New York. Mingus aided his career enormously, both through his recordings and his influence. Parlan played with Booker Ervin in 1960 and 1961, then in the Eddie "Lockjaw" Davis-Johnny Griffin quintet in 1962. Parlan played with Rahsaan Roland Kirk from 1963 to 1966, and had a strong series of Blue Note recordings in the '60s. He left America for Copenhagen in 1973, and gained international recognition for some stunning albums on Steeplechase, including a pair of superb duet sessions with Archie Shepp. He also recorded with Dexter Gordon, Red Mitchell, and, in the '80s, with Frank Foster and Michael Urbaniak. He's done sessions in the '80s on Enja and Timeless. Currently, only a few Parlan sessions are available on CD. —Ron Wynn

Movin' and Groovin' / Feb. 29, 1960 / Blue Note

Up and Down / Jun. 18, 1961 / Blue Note
Tremendous solos from Booker Ervin (ts) and Grant Green (g), with dynamic and bluesy Parlan piano. —Ron Wynn

○ Back from the Gig / Feb. 15, 1963 / Blue Note

This was later issued under Booker Ervin's name, but it is truly Parlan's date. Ervin's lusty tenor and Parlan's shimmering piano are impressive. —Ron Wynn

★ Happy Frame of Mind / Feb. 15, 1963 / Blue Note 84134
Expatriate pianist on a reissue of one of his best albums, with Booker Ervin (ts). Search for others. —Michael G. Nastos

No Blues / Dec. 10, 1975 / Steeple Chase

Blue Parlan / Nov. 13, 1978 / Steeple Chase

★ Going Home / i. Apr. 25, 1979 / Steeple Chase

○ Pannonica / Feb. 11, 1981 / Enja 4076
Good early '80s trio session with pianist Horace Parlan working alongside bassist Reggie Johnson and drummer Alvin Queen. The material, mostly standards, some originals and ballads, isn't overly ambitious, but Parlan's dense, strong blues-influenced solos and good interaction among the three principals keeps things moving. —Ron Wynn

J.D. PARRAN

Multi-instruments / Modern creative
A stirring multi-instrumentalist, J.D. Parran hasn't done sessions as a leader and lacks name recognition, but has contributed quite effectively to some outstanding free dates. Parran plays a wide range of clarinets, from soprano to contralto, as well as soprano, bass and tenor saxophone, flute, and others. He's recorded with Leroy Jenkins, Hamiet Bluiett, John Lindberg, Peter Brotzmann, and the group Company, which included Derek Bailey, Jon Corbett, Hugh Davies, Jamie Muir, Evan Parker, Vinko Globokar, and Joelle Leandre. Parran does not have any sessions available on CD, but can be heard on reissued discs by Jenkins, Bluiett, Hemphill, and others. —Ron Wynn

JOE PASS (Joseph Anthony Passalaqua)

b. Jan. 13, 1929, New Brunswick, NJ, d. 1994
Guitar / Bop, cool
A master of guitar technique, Joe Pass ranks among the great finger pickers and is a brilliant soloist. His phrasing, speed, note selection, harmonic and interpretative skills, flair, swing, and feel for the blues is awesome. He's in the select circle of players who've recorded so much that they have a signature sound, yet seldom become locked into rote, clichéd, or gimmicky playing styles. He worked with Tony Pastor during his high school days, then served a year in the marines. Pass, like far too many other greats of his generation, had his career interrupted by drug problems. But he was able to deal with his problems in a quicker, more decisive fashion than many others. He was imprisoned and hospitalized before entering Synanon in 1961. Pass and other musicians confined there issued an album in 1962, Sounds of Synanon, that helped Pass professionally and medically. He licked his habit, won Down Beat's New Star award in 1963, and became a busy studio player in the '60s. He made several albums for Pacific Jazz and World Pacific in the '60s, with both quartet and larger group sessions. He played with Les McCann, Gerald Wilson, and Julie London, and toured with George Shearing in the mid-'60s and Benny Goodman in 1973. He was signed by Norman Granz to the Pablo label. His first solo album, Virtuoso, was an affirmation of Pass's majestic abilities. He recorded prolifically for Pablo in the '70s, accompanying Ella Fitzgerald, Count Basie, Duke Ellington, and Sarah Vaughan, playing with Oscar Peterson's trio, and touring with Dizzy Gillespie. Pass did several solo albums and played in various ensembles in the '80s. He's made a number of sessions for Concord, and has continued recording for the revived Pablo label. His current and many of his '70s Pablo dates are available widely. Unfortunately, there's not much other material in print. —Ron Wynn and David Nelson McCarthy

Virtuoso–Vol. 1 / Dec. 1973 / Pablo 2310-708

Best of Joe Pass / i. 1973-1982 / Pablo 2405-419

The title is a misnomer, but there are good '70s and early '80s cuts from his Pablo sessions. —*Ron Wynn*

○ **Joe Pass at Akron University** / **i.** 1974 / Pablo 2308-249
Unlike Stanley Jordan, whose dazzling technique makes most guitarists sound one-handed, Joe Pass's solo style sounds like a logical extension of past greats. His ability to play both melody and chords together is still very impressive and there are times during his solo concerts when you would swear you heard a bass. Most of the material on this concert is familiar, but remains fresh. Of the newer work, "Bridgework" is a blues with a bridge, "Tarde" a Milton Nascimento ballad, and "Time In," a key-switching blues. Joe Pass retains his position as one of the masters of the jazz guitar with this album. —*Scott Yanow*, Cadence

Portraits of Duke Ellington / Jun. 21, 1974 / Pablo 2310-716

○ **Live at Dante's** / Dec. 1974 / Pablo 114
Over the four sides of this set guitarist Joe Pass treats us to some stunning playing. Despite being a regularly working group, Pass, bassist Jim Hughart, and drummer Frank Severino achieve a more prosaic type of interaction here. If the bassist and drummer had risen to the soaring levels of Pass's playing, the results would have been spectacular. As it is, they are merely excellent. The guitarist plays marvelously, close to and often at peak ability, never holding back or letting facility carry the day but always digging in, stretching, challenging himself to extract as much from his material as he can. More often than not, he succeeds, with the result that there is plenty of fiery, inventive, surprise-filled, and occasionally astonishing guitar playing all through the recital. The set is worth acquiring if only for the breathtakingly exciting version of "Secret Love," which finds Pass framing his gripping statement of the theme and many of his variations antiphonally, in effect dueting with himself. "Milestones" is treated similiarly. —*Pete Welding*, Down Beat

★ **Virtuoso–Vol. 2** / Sep. 14-Oct. 26, 1976 / Pablo 2310-788
Guitarist Joe Pass deals with material ranging from Chick Corea's near-standard "Miles High" to everybody's pop hit "Feelings" with that impeccable tone and warm approach that have made him worthy of the mantle "Virtuoso." The music is played at an easy pace that makes it especially great late-night music. Pass's treatment of "Miles High" is particularly tasty as is his humor-filled blues "O.P." There aren't many guitarists who can handle the solo idiom as well as Joe Pass. —*Willard Jenkins, Jr.*, Cadence

Virtuoso–Vol. 3 / May 2-Jun. 1, 1977 / Pablo 684
A '92 CD reissue of the third in a series recorded in 1977. Guitarist Joe Pass, whose talent is often taken for granted due to the introspective, relaxed nature of his sessions, displays his full range and technical skills on a three-volume set designed to highlight those abilities. This third volume is no less a standout than the previous two. —*Ron Wynn*

★ **I Remember Charlie Parker** / Feb. 17, 1979 / Original Jazz Classics 602
This is a worthy reissue of Pass's late '70s tribute to Charlie Parker. —*Ron Wynn*

○ **Northsea Nights** / Jul. 1979 / Pablo 221
These are not really duets; the guitarist and bassist embrace but never entwine. No, this live concert is all solo plus rhythm, with Pass chording for the bassist and Niels-Henning Ørsted-Pedersen often achieving behind Pass the status of a rhythm guitar. The limber bassist underlines Pass with such good-natured force that he often seems like a gallant dandy coaxing a wallflower to the heart of a crowded dance floor. Obviously indebted to Wes Montgomery and Jim Hall, Pass lacks their pulsation, though there is a dazzling single-string passage on "Stella By Starlight" that builds its own momentum. On an up or medium blues, his choice of which notes to flat is not always judicious, and such factors should really come into play in defining technique. But one would have to be coldhearted indeed to question the authenticity of depth of his feeling on "Stella" or "'Round Midnight." I wouldn't change a hair of those Pass so-

los simply to see a hair out of place. —*Francis Davis*, Cadence

Quadrant Toasts Duke Ellington / Feb. 21, 1980 / Original Jazz Classics 498
There's a bit more intensity here, thanks to the presence of Milt Jackson (vib), Ray Brown (b), and Mickey Roker (d). —*Ron Wynn*

Whitestone / Feb. 28-Mar. 1, 1985 / Pablo 2310-912

Blues for Fred / Feb. 2, 1988 / Pablo 2310-931
The Pass guitar is impressive as always, though the songs are erratic. —*Ron Wynn*

One for My Baby / Apr. 1988 / Pablo 2310-936
Plas Johnson (ts) sounds a bit out of place in a 1988 recording; Pass is uniformly excellent. —*Ron Wynn*

Summer Nights / Dec. 1989 / Pablo 2310-939
This recent Pass boasts impeccable guitar but sometimes undistinguished cuts. —*Ron Wynn*

○ **Virtuoso–Live!** / **i.** 1991 / Pablo 2310948
A continuation of the virtuoso series spotlighting guitarist Joe Pass's skills differs from the others in that this time he is recorded live. The extra ingredient seems to make Pass play with even more brilliance. He executes difficult runs, octave jumps and phrases with verve, while his interpretations of standards and harmonic maneuvers are often amazing. —*Ron Wynn*

Live at Yoshi's / **i.** Jan. 1992 / Pablo 951
An inspired and exciting set by jazz's guitarist nonpareil, ranging from a blistering race through Sonny Rollins's "Oleo" to the gentle duet with Pass's longtime partner Pisano on "Alone Together." "Swingin' Till the Girls Come Home" is a feature for Monty Budwig, the great West Coast bass player who died shortly after this set. One of the best of the many Joe Pass albums. —*Les Line*

○ **All Too Soon** / Original Jazz Classics 450
Solid, nicely played standards, originals, blues, and ballads by guitarist Joe Pass. He seldom plays in exuberant fashion, preferring a smooth, relaxed, yet also intricately crafted solo approach. His full notes and elaborate voicings are technically impressive, though sometimes a lack of thematic variety results in his albums all sounding the same. —*Ron Wynn*

○ **Virtuoso–Vol. 4** / Pablo 102
The fourth in the series that gives guitarist Joe Pass a forum to show things that aren't always evident on his many studio dates. Everything from the elaborate and sophisticated solos to his choice of material reflects his commitment to excellence, and every release he made for the line is superb. —*Ron Wynn*

JACO PASTORIUS (John Francis Pastorius)

b. Dec. 1, 1951, Norristown, PA, **d.** Sep. 21, 1987, Fort Lauderdale, FL
Bass / Early jazz-rock
The Jaco Pastorius story is a tragedy in a type of music that is littered with far too many tragedies, each frustrating and maddening. Pastorius was simply the greatest electric bassist of the jazz-rock/fusion era; an incredibly fast, imaginative, and brilliant musician and technician, who not only conceived possibilities on the instrument that no one else considered, but executed them flawlessly. He considered the electric bass a bass guitar and lead rather than a rhythm/support instrument; even as an accompanist his lines and phrases had so much depth and form they stood out within the arrangement. His solos were adventures, performed with a fluidity and harmonic elan that remain unbelievable no matter how many times they're heard. Pastorius also knew how good he was, and his personality, coupled with repeated drug and alcohol problems, no doubt hastened his demise. "I'm Jaco f-ing Pastorius," was heard far too often at his concerts or in response to questions from admiring fans about his facility. But there was no faulting his tone or talents.

While in his teens, Pastorius accompanied visiting R&B and pop musicians who came to his native Fort Lauderdale. He emerged quickly as a major electric bassist by the mid-'70s, and his work with Pat Metheny attracted so much notice that he was tabbed to join Weather Report in 1976. That long-term role, plus many other sessions, cemented Pastorius's stature within the jazz and rock/pop world. He played with Blood, Sweat & Tears in 1975, and their drummer, Bobby Colomby, helped arrange the session that led to Pastorius's Epic debut as a leader. Pastorius recorded with Ira Sullivan, Paul Bley, Joni Mitchell, Metheny, and Bireli Lagrene in the '70s and '80s, in addition to his Weather Report duties. He toured with his own group, Word of Mouth, from 1980 to 1983, recording in 1980 with various jazz musicians and, in 1982, with a big band. Pastorius recorded an album in 1983 and 1984 with Brian Melvin. Then he suffered a series of personal reversals and problems that were as monumental as his musical talents. There were repeated rumors of sightings in drug-infested inner city hangouts. Pastorius died as a result of injuries suffered during a brawl at the Midnight Club in Fort Lauderdale in 1987. His death remains as mysterious as those of Albert Ayler and Wardell Gray, since motivations and exact events are still hazy, though the club manager was arrested eventually for assault. A battle has since raged between his estate and various bootleg companies over poorly recorded Pastorius concert discs and albums that have surfaced since his death. A handful of Pastorius recordings are available on CD from sessions on DIW, IAI, Columbia, and other labels. —Ron Wynn

★ **Jaco Pastorius** / **i.** Aug. 1976 / Epic 33949
Studio group date and first album from this late electric bass guitar genius. A must-buy. —Michael G. Nastos

○ **Jaco** / **i.** 1978 / Improvising Artists 373846
This was the recording debut for both electric bassist Jaco Pastorius and electric guitarist Pat Metheny and not too surprisingly, the biggest seller in IAI's history. An electric session with creative but dated-sounding keyboards (Paul Bley), Metheny searching for his sound, and an already very distinctive bassist; the music rewards repeated listening. Bruce Ditmas is the drummer. After Jaco was released in 1976, Bley gave up electronics. —Scott Yanow, Coda

○ **Word of Mouth** / **i.** Dec. 1981 / Warner Brothers 3535
Word of Mouth was Jaco Pastorius's first release under his own name since his Epic debut, Jaco Pastorius, in 1976. After Jaco, Pastorius became a progressively important member of Weather Report and eventually a coproducer of the group's albums and contributor of much of its repertoire. On one hand, this album is largely derivative and unresolved; on the other, it boasts some overwhelming and amazing moments. The opener, "Crisis," is a powerful futuristic piece. Recalling John Coltrane's "Countdown," "Crisis" starts in medias res and, whipped along by an incredibly percussionistic bass guitar, races forward in collectively improvised cacophony. "Three Views," which appeared in a different form on Weather Report's Night Passage, is a gesture in the opposite direction, wrapping Toots Thielemans's professional harmonica nostalgia in a sugary arrangement of equal parts Ray Conniff and Jerry Goldsmith. Side two opens with Bach's "Chromatic Fantasy" performed on bass guitar by Pastorius with a trace of Wendy Carlos. An ultra-brief but full-sounding orchestra statement (Word of Mouth has a staggering amount of puzzle pieces, excerpts, and other edited elements) marks the transition to a mix of flutes, voices, and percussion instruments, which, upon repeated listening, form an intriguing overture to Thielemans's and Pastorius's virtuoso dueling on a very fast "Blackbird." A segue to the title track paves the way for a complete montage of vertiginous bass guitar solos, booming drums, and a Jackson Pollock portrait in sound effects. —Lars Gabel, Down Beat

PAT PATRICK

b. 1929, **d.** 1989

Saxophone, flute / Early free, progressive big band, modern creative
After John Gilmore, Pat Patrick's name was synonymous with Sun Ra's Arkestra. While Patrick studied other instruments and doubled on various saxophones, flutes, bass, and percussion, the baritone was his stock-in-trade. His rumbling, lusty sound frequently dominated the bottom of Arkestra reed section dialogues. Patrick did for Ra what Harry Carney did for Ellington; he provided a consistently dependable voice at the other end of the musical spectrum that could be isolated, combined, or complemented in any composition. Patrick studied piano and drums as a child, and took trumpet lessons from his father and from jazz great Clark Terry. He studied at the famous Du Sable High School in Chicago along with John Gilmore, Clifford Jordan, and Richard Davis. Patrick played with Sun Ra periodically from 1954 well into the '80s. He also worked with James Moody, John Coltrane, Cootie Williams, Duke Ellington, Thelonious Monk, and the Jazz Composer's Orchestra under the direction of Clifford Thornton and Grachan Moncur III. But Pat Patrick's claim to fame came from being Sun Ra Arkestra's baritone saxophonist. He appeared on countless dates. Patrick doesn't have any sessions listed under his own name in various catalogs. —Ron Wynn

DON PATTERSON (Donald B. Patterson)

b. Jul. 22, 1936, Columbus, OH, **d.** Feb. 10, 1988
Organ / Blues & jazz, soul-jazz
A solid soul-jazz, blues, and hard bop organist with a pianistic background, Don Patterson didn't utilize the pedals or play with as much rhythmic drive as some other stylists, but developed a satisfactory alternative approach. Patterson's organ solos were played smartly, and were more melodic than explosive. He switched from piano after hearing Jimmy Smith. Patterson made his organ debut in 1959, and worked with Sonny Stitt, Eddie "Lockjaw" Davis, Gene Ammons, and Wes Montgomery in the early '60s. He recorded with Ammons, Stitt, and Eric Kloss in the early and mid-'60s. Patterson worked often in a duo with Billy James, and made several recordings as a leader in the '60s and '70s. He and Al Grey worked together extensively in the '80s. Patterson recorded as a leader for Prestige and Muse. He has one session available on CD. —Ron Wynn and Michael G. Nastos

○ **Exciting New Organ of Don Patterson, The** / Dec. 1964 / Prestige 7331

Return Of . . . , The / Oct. 30, 1972 / Muse 5005
Quartet with Eddie Daniels (ts), Ted Dunbar (g), and Freddie Waits (d). Any Don Patterson album is worthwhile. — Michael G. Nastos

○ **Genius of the B-3, The** / Oct. 30, 1972 / Muse 5443
A fine album (fast and slow) with Patterson in excellent form. There is some very nice music here. CD clocks out at 43 minutes. —Michael Erlewine

★ **These Are Soulful Days** / Sep. 17, 1973 / Muse 5032
Quartet with this great Hammond B-3 organist, Jimmy Heath (sax), Pat Martino (g), and Albert "Tootie" Heath (d). — Michael G. Nastos

JOHN PATTON (Big John Patton)

b. Jul. 12, 1935, Kansas City, MO
Organ / Blues & jazz, soul-jazz
A first-rate soul-jazz and blues organist, Big John Patton's dates are among the most danceable, funky, and exuberant ever done at Blue Note. He wasn't as adventurous as Larry Young, but matched any organist for sheer energy and rousing fervor. Patton played piano in the late '40s, and toured with Lloyd Price in the mid- and late '50s. He began playing organ in the '60s, and recorded with Lou Donaldson from 1962 to 1964. Patton also did sessions with Harold Vick, Johnny Griffin, Grant Green, and Clifford Jordan in the '60s, while doing his own dates with a trio. At various times, Clifford Jarvis and James "Blood" Ulmer were members of Patton's trio. Bobby Hutcherson, Junior Cook, Blue Mitchell,

and Richard Williams, as well as Vick, served as special guests on different sessions. Patton recorded with Johnny Lytle in 1977 and 1983. He's done sessions for Blue Note and Nilva, among others. Currently, Patton has some sessions available on CD. —*Ron Wynn*

★ **Blue John** / Jul. 11, 1963 / Blue Note 84143
Recording from "Big John," another Hammond heavyweight. With George Braithwaite (sax), Grant Green (g), and Tommy Turrentine (tpt). —*Michael G. Nastos*

CECIL PAYNE (Cecil McKenzie Payne)

b. Dec. 14, 1922, Brooklyn, NY
Baritone and alto saxophone, flute / Bop, hard bop
A fluid, soulful, and excellent baritone saxophonist, Cecil Payne has been a top player since the '40s when his work in Dizzy Gillespie's big band established his credentials. He has a softer, lighter sound than on his earlier recordings, but hasn't sacrificed any power or authority. Payne's emotional intensity and natural bluesy qualities enabled him to do some R&B and rock & roll dates in the '50s, and his rumbling baritone navigates a steady middle ground between earthiness and a smooth, polished approach. Initially, Payne played guitar and then alto sax, and played clarinet in army bands from 1943 to 1946. He began on baritone while in Clarence Biggs's big band in 1946. Payne made his recording debut on alto sax that same year with J.J. Johnson on Savoy. After a brief stint with Roy Eldridge, Payne played in Gillespie's big band from 1946 until 1949. He worked for Tadd Dameron and James Moody in New York, before becoming a freelancer from 1949 until 1952, and also doing some Atlantic sessions. Payne toured with Illinois Jacquet from 1952 to 1954, while doing numerous recording dates with players such as Duke Jordan and Randy Weston. Payne played on Tadd Dameron's *Fontainebleau*, and on John Coltrane's *Dakar*, while doing two albums with Jordan on Savoy. He left the music world temporarily in the '50s, then returned to both act and write songs for Jack Gelber's play *The Connection* in 1961 and 1962. Payne teamed with Jordan again for two sessions on Charlie Parker Records in 1961 and 1962. He was a soloist in Machito's band, the Afro-Cubans, in 1963 and 1964, while also playing in Lucky Thompson's octet and touring Europe with Lionel Hampton in 1964. He worked with Jordan again on a 1966 date for Spotlite. Payne left music for a second time in the mid-'60s, then returned to work with Weston, Woody Herman, and Gillespie in the late '60s. He played with Count Basie in 1969, 1970, and 1971, and also led a quartet. Payne recorded with Kenny Dorham in 1969 for Strata-East, and headed a combo. In the '70s, he recorded on Muse and on Spotlite, with Nick Brignola and also with Jordan again, and accompanied Bill Hardman and Richard Wyands's trio in 1986. There's only a few Payne sessions available on CD. —*Ron Wynn*

Night at the Five Spot / Aug. 12, 1955 / Signal 1204

○ **Patterns** / May 1956 / Savoy 1167
Fine late '50s hard bop session featuring baritone saxophonist Cecil Payne. This was one of two strong albums that matched Payne with pianist Duke Jordan, who was then establishing his own reputation as an aggressive soloist and good accompanist. These are mostly short, tartly played, and well-written and arranged pieces. —*Ron Wynn*

★ **Zodiac** / i. 1969 / Strata East
Outstanding quintet date featuring Kenny Dorham (tpt), but hard to find. —*Ron Wynn*

○ **Brooklyn Brothers** / Mar. 16, 1973 / Muse 5015
Thanks to Muse producer Don Schlitten, veteran beboppers baritone saxophonist and flutist Cecil Payne and pianist Duke Jordan were given the opportunity of recording a program of their music their way with, apparently, no restrictions imposed upon them. *Brooklyn Brothers* is a pleasant, unpretentious set of performances notable mainly for the craftsmanlike consistency and easy familarity the coleaders bring to the assignment. Payne and Jordan work well in tan-

dem and the music courses along effortlessly if unadventurously, the two winding their solo ways through the changes with the practiced ease and agility of past masters running through their paces on home ground. Don't expect any great depths of improvisatory inventiveness, for there aren't any here. What there is, though, is plenty of skill and sensitivity and unfeigned affection for this musical idiom. Enjoyable, naturally, but surprising, never. —*Pete Welding, Down Beat*

☆ **Bird Gets the Worm** / Feb. 2, 1976 / Muse 5061
Some of Payne's most vibrant, expressive playing. Good ensemble and compositions. —*Ron Wynn*

Bright Moments / Jul. 19+20, 1979 / Spotlite

GARY PEACOCK

b. May 12, 1935, Burley, ID
Bass / Modern creative
An adventurous and explosive bassist, Gary Peacock has been a topflight player since the '60s. He worked with different and dynamic personalities such as Bill Evans, Jimmy Giuffre, George Russell, and Albert Ayler, and with Miles Davis. His tone, timing, and skills have enabled Peacock to thrive in any situation. He began playing piano and drums at age 13, then started on bass in 1956 while stationed in Germany during his time in the army. Peacock worked with musicians such as Bud Shank, Atilla Zoller, Bob Cooper, and Albert Mangelsdorff after his discharge, then moved to Los Angeles in 1958. He played and recorded there with Barney Kessel, Clare Fischer, Don Ellis, and Paul Bley. Peacock moved to New York in the early '60s, and joined Evans's trio in 1962. He played with Evans in '62 and '63, then rejoined Paul Bley for a time, and also played with Giuffre and George Russell. Peacock toured and played with Davis and Ayler in 1964, and recorded frequently through the remainder of the '60s with Ayler, while also working briefly again with Davis, and recording with Bley in 1967 and 1970. Peacock moved to Japan in 1969, and recorded with Sadao Watanabe, Masabumi Kikuchi, and various visiting American musicians. He came back to America in 1972, and studied biology at the University of Washington from 1972 to 1976. Peacock made a return visit to Japan in 1976 touring with Bley and Barry Altschul, then began recording as a leader in 1977. He did several dates for ECM, and has been a prolific sideman in the '80s and '90s. Peacock's been part of Keith Jarrett's regular trio throughout the '80s and '90s, and has recorded a number of sessions including 1993's *Bye Bye Blackbird: A Tribute to Miles Davis*. Peacock's also featured on recent CDs by Paul Bley, and has a couple of his own dates available as well. —*Ron Wynn and Michael G. Nastos*

★ **Tales of Another** / Feb. 1977 / ECM 827418
With Keith Jarrett (p) and Jack DeJohnette (d). Their playing interweaves tightly, with many lines going on at once. Each musician strengthens rather than just supports the other. —*Jerry De Muth, Cadence*

Shift in the Wind / Feb. 1980 / ECM 829159
With Art Lande (p) and Elliot Zigmund (d). This recording is a beautiful example of three musicians blending together to create outstanding music. —*Carl Brauer, Cadence*

DUKE PEARSON (Columbus Calvin (Jr) Pearson)

b. Aug. 17, 1932, Atlanta, GA, **d.** Aug. 4, 1980, Atlanta, GA
Piano, composer, arranger / Bop, hard bop
A good pianist who later became a producer and A&R assistant, Duke Pearson was a fine bebop player during the '50s and early '60s, providing nicely constructed solos on many dates. He was a crafty rather than dazzling player, and a fine composer and arranger. Jordan studied piano and several brass instruments in his youth, then chose piano because problems with his teeth eliminated the trumpet. He worked in the South as a pianist during the mid- and late '50s, then moved to New York. Pearson worked regularly with Donald Byrd and Pepper Adams, and Byrd recorded Pearson's seminal compositions "Cristo Redentor" and "Jeannine." He was briefly in the Jazztet in 1960, and served as Nancy Wilson's

accompanist in 1961. Pearson produced many sessions for Blue Note from 1963 to 1970, and coformed a big band with Byrd. He soon had sole leadership duties, and the Duke Pearson Big Band dueled the Thad Jones-Mel Lewis Orchestra from the late '60s until 1970. Adams, Lew Tabackin, Randy Brecker, Joe Shepley, and Garnett Brown were regular members, and the band provided a forum for Pearson's compositions. He taught at Clark in 1971, then reformed the big band in 1972. Pearson toured with Carmen McRae in 1972 and 1973; he battled multiple sclerosis in the late '70s, which severely limited his playing. The former husband of jazz vocalist Sheila Jordan, Pearson also accompanied Dakota Staton and Joe Williams. He recorded for Prestige, Polydor, and Atlantic, in addition to Blue Note. Pearson recorded with Freddie Hubbard, Airto, and Flora Purim, and with the members of his big band. Currently, there are no Pearson sessions available on CD. —*Ron Wynn and Michael G. Nastos*

★ **Dedication** / Aug. 2, 1961 / Prestige
This is among Pearson's finest '60s sessions. Includes sterling solos by Freddie Hubbard (tpt) and Pepper Adams (sax). —*Ron Wynn*

○ **Wahoo** / Nov. 24, 1964 / Blue Note 84191
From this late pianist/composer/arranger and A&R man. Many others by him are as excellent. Find this one and as many others as you can. —*Michael G. Nastos*

☆ **Introducing Duke Pearson's Big Band** / Dec. 1967 / Blue Note 84276

☆ **Now Hear This!** / Dec. 2-3, 1968 / Blue Note
The music on this session is pleasant, though a bit on the bland side. Here and there one hears some nice touches; but rarely is there any real bite or excitement. With ballads, especially, pianist Duke Pearson's approach tends to be deadly. For big-band fans who prefer something not too challenging, this would be fine. —*Jack McCaffrey, Coda*

NIELS-HENNING ØRSTED-PEDERSEN

b. May 27, 1946, Osted, Denmark
Bass / Swing, modern creative
Along with Eberhard Weber, Miroslav Vitous, and Palle Danielsson, Denmark's Niels-Henning Ørsted-Pedersen is a premier European bassist who's played superbly in free, bebop, or swing situations. Pedersen's tone, bow or plucked skills, counterpoint, and accompaniment, as well as his solo talents, are at the virtuoso level, and have been that way since he was a teen. Pedersen has won numerous European magazine polls as the continent's top bassist, and has done well in similar polls conducted by American music publications. His mother was a church organist, and Pedersen studied piano, but was such a great bassist he began playing with groups at age 14. Count Basie wanted to recruit him at age 17. Pedersen was the house bassist at the Club Montmarte, and was a member of the Danish Radio Orchestra. He worked with numerous musicians during the '60s and '70s, among them Sonny Rollins, Bill Evans, Rahsaan Roland Kirk, Albert Ayler, Dexter Gordon, Anthony Braxon, and many others. Pedersen recorded two duo albums with Kenny Drew, was featured on many Pablo sessions recorded at the 1975 Montreux Festival, and was a regular member of the Oscar Peterson Trio for many years. He hosted a British jazz show in the early '80s. Pedersen has recorded in groups with Monty Alexander and Grady Tate and Claudio Fasoli, and with Drew and Barry Altschul. He currently has a couple of sessions as a leader available on CD, and is featured on records by numerous jazz musicians. —*Ron Wynn*

★ **Jaywalkin'** / i. Sep. 1975+Dec. 1975 / Steeple Chase 1041

KEN PEPLOWSKI

b. 1959
Saxophone, clarinet / Swing
A swing-influenced clarinetist and alto and tenor saxophonist, Ken Peplowski plays nicely and pays great attention to the nuances and sound of earlier eras. His solos are well done and often quite lyrical. Peplowski began on clarinet as child, playing his debut professional gig at age ten. He later had formal music studies and played both jazz and classical music, appearing on radio and television as well as in local clubs in his native Cleveland. Peplowski's quartet played opposite a late '70s edition of the Tommy Dorsey orchestra led by Buddy Morrow, who offered Peplowski a spot. He toured with this band throughout America and Europe, spending nearly three years with them before departing. Peplowski settled in New York, where he worked in everything from symphony orchestras to a touring company of *Annie*. He also did studio work for both films and records, and worked with various groups. Peplowski did one television session and two recordings with Benny Goodman. He recorded during the '80s backing Mel Tormé, Peggy Lee, and Rosemary Clooney, and played with Hank Jones, George Shearing, Dan Barrett, Scott Hamilton, and Howard Alden. He's recorded as a leader in the '80s and '90s for Concord. Peplowski has several sessions available on CD. —*Ron Wynn and Michael G. Nastos*

○ **Double Exposure** / Dec. 1987 / Concord Jazz 4344
Good swing-influenced small combo set by alto, tenor sax, and clarinetist Ken Peplowski. While Peplowski's solos are conservative in their range and style, they're well-played and done with good taste. He's backed by a group whose members all reflect his values in their own playing: guitarist Ed Bickert, pianist John Bunch, bassist John Goldsby, and drummer Terry Clarke. —*Ron Wynn*

○ **Sonnyside** / Jan. 1989 / Concord Jazz 4376
Quintet. Another tasteful, restrained mainstream date, though Dave Frishberg (p) isn't for everyone. Extra cut on CD issue. —*Ron Wynn*

★ **Mr. Gentle and Mr. Cool** / Feb. 1990 / Concord Jazz 4419
Quintet. This tasty swing/mainstream date has exciting piano by Hank Jones and excellent drumming from Alan Dawson. The CD boasts two bonus cuts. —*Ron Wynn*

○ **Illuminations** / Nov. 20-21, 1990 / Concord Jazz 4449
Quintet. A conservative but well-played small-combo set with swing influences. Junior Mance brings some blues fervor on piano. The CD has two bonus cuts. —*Ron Wynn*

○ **Natural Touch, The** / i. 1992 / Concord Jazz 4517
A '92 session done in saxophonist Ken Peplowski's usually restrained, sophisticated fashion. His material, solo approach, and ensemble style can be called either conservative or derivative, depending on one's slant. He picks supporting players who also don't get overly aggressive or animated in either their solos or their reponses. The CD has three bonus cuts. —*Ron Wynn*

ART PEPPER (Arthur Edward (Jr) Pepper)

b. Sep. 1, 1925, Gardenia, CA, **d.** Jun. 1, 1982
Alto saxophone / Cool
Alto saxophonist Art Pepper combined the best elements of two supposedly divergent styles; he had the light, clear tone and sound that exemplified the cool school, but played with the intensity and harmonic excellence usually associated with bebop. He displayed influences from Charlie Parker, Lester Young, and Lee Konitz, and his best alto solos were searing, searching statements, though he could also produce choruses that were incredibly poignant and beautiful.

Pepper played with Gus Arnheim as a teen, then worked on Central Avenue in Los Angeles. He played in the big bands of Benny Carter and Stan Kenton during the early '40s, and toured with Kenton's band as their primary soloist from the late '40s until the early '50s. He also did various sessions in Los Angeles. Pepper battled drug addiction throughout the '50s and '60s; he made many superb recordings during that time despite those problems. There were sessions with Shelly Manne, Chet Baker, Mel Tormé, and Carl Perkins during the '50s, and with Hampton Hawes, Sonny Clark, Russ Freeman, Warne Marsh, and Marty Paich. He worked in Jack Montrose's quintet in 1956. There were many exceptional sessions for Contemporary that began the next year and continued until 1960. Pepper played with Howard Rumsey's Lighthouse All-Stars in 1960, then began playing tenor in the mid-'60s, during a time that he was strongly influenced by John Coltrane. Pepper even experimented with free jazz, but by 1968 Pepper had returned to conventional material, working in Buddy Rich's band. Physical problems forced him to leave Rich's organization in 1969. In addition, Pepper's continuing addiction led to periods of confinement until he finally spent three years in Synanon. He held a job as a bookkeeper until he returned to music, demonstrating instruments for Buffett.

Pepper did a big-band album on a Japanese label, then joined Don Ellis's band in 1975. He made numerous great recordings for Contemporary, Interplay, and Galaxy in the '70s and early '80s, working with Hawes, Charlie Haden, Manne, George Cables, and many others. He performed extensively in Japan and at festivals until his sudden death in 1982. There were brilliant solos in such film soundtracks as *The Enforcer* and *HeartBeat*. Pepper was the subject of the documentary *Art Pepper: Notes from a Jazz Survivor* directed by Don McGlynn in 1981. His autobiography, *Straight Life*, was written with his wife Laurie, and is a brutally frank, open work that discusses his life, problems, and disillusionment with the jazz scene, particularly his inability to understand the Black militancy of the '60s and '70s. Many Pepper albums have been reissued from the '50s and '60s. A comprehensive boxed set that contains all of his Galaxy sessions has also been reissued. —*Ron Wynn*

☆ **Complete Pacific Jazz Small Group Recordings of Art Pepper, The** / Mosaic 105

Vol. 1–With Sonny Clark Trio / **i.** 1953 / Time Is
Quartet. This is not one of the more intelligently compiled reissues, but it does have some nice Sonny Clark piano. —*Ron Wynn*

Discoveries / Mar. 29, 1953-Aug. 25, 1954 / Savoy 2217
Some early Art Pepper done for the Savoy label. At this point (1953/1954) Pepper was still heavily under Charlie Parker's influence and was also filtering Lester Young elements through his style. He was also entrenched in the "cool" sound and wasn't playing with the spark or ambitiousness that marked his later work in the '50s or his comeback sessions in the '70s and '80s. This was issued as a two-record set on vinyl in the '70s. —*Ron Wynn*

Early Art / Aug. 1956-Jan. 14, 1957 / Blue Note 591

○ **Way It Was, The** / Nov. 1956-Nov. 1960 / Contemporary 389
The first four tracks on this album are from Art Pepper's first Contemporary date, November 1956; three include an ideal partner, Warne Marsh. The others are additions from the famous 1957 to 1960 Pepper dates. The saxophone playing is beautiful throughout, almost as fine as on Pepper's great *Smack Up*. Pepper and Marsh are an even hipper team than the classic Marsh-Lee Konitz pairings, and it's a sin they didn't work together frequently. Their rhythmic and harmonic bases are fairly similiar (both swing era), and their art is defined by inflection, accent, tonal variation, and nuance. They share the Lennie Tristano ideas of heavy swing and total improvisation, and they are immense emotionalists; otherwise, no two musicians could be more different. Pepper's perfect formalism is totally complemented by Marsh's romantic sensibility; the granite alto structures meet the emotionally spontaneous tenor's eternal search for the beautiful melody, the perfect phrase. The Ronnie Ball (p), Ben Tucker (b), Gary Frommer (d) rhythm section is the best on this record, and, contrary to Pepper's own opinion, probably the most empathic he ever used. —*John Litweiler,* Down Beat

Modern Art / Dec. 28, 1956-Apr. 1957 / Blue Note 46848
Complete Aladdin Recordings, Vol. 1. This 1988 reissue is slightly altered from the original Omega release. It has five cuts added from Omega sessions. —*Ron Wynn*

★ **Meets the Rhythm Section** / Jan. 19, 1957 / Original Jazz Classics 338

This Art Pepper album was, according to producer Lester Koenig, beset with problems, but the results are a marvel of inventive blowing. The rhythm section of course was Miles Davis's (pianist Red Garland, bassist Paul Chambers, drummer Philly Joe Jones), and they are so hip that I suspect they could have even made Mezz Mezzrow swing. As a unit they had a great gift. This is one of Pepper's finest mid-'50s efforts; it came at the end of a period when Paul Desmond, Lee Konitz, and Pepper had pretty much established the West Coast alto sound. Pepper had the hardest tone, and, as one can hear, it was brilliantly imaginative. Pepper's was a sad tale but Pepper, like Charlie Parker, seemed to surmount all those earthly burdens when playing. His music can do the same for the listener. —*Bob Rusch,* Cadence

★ **Smack Up** / Oct. 24-25, 1960 / Contemporary 176
By 1960 alto saxophonist Art Pepper had picked up on Ornette Coleman, the composer, and on *Smack Up* he includes Coleman's "Tears Inside" as part of the program—recorded 10/24-25/60. On this record, Pepper is backed by Jack Sheldon (tpt), Pete Jolly (p), Jimmy Bond (b), and Frank Butler (d). —*Bob Rusch,* Cadence

Intensity / Nov. 23-25, 1960 / Contemporary 387
Although not Pepper's greatest release from the standpoint of lineup, Dolo Coker has several good moments on piano. Pepper is at his usual best. —*Ron Wynn*

○ **Living Legend** / Aug. 9, 1975 / Contemporary 408
This session features an excellent rhythm section with alto saxophonist Art Pepper out in front for a whole LP. Art Pepper has a piercing quality in his playing (as does Jackie McLean) that breaks the surface and attacks the absolute heart of the music. An excellent illustration of what I mean can be heard on the ballad "Here's That Rainy Day." Dig Pepper's stark and direct but powerfully beautiful performance. Thank goodness pianist Hampton Hawes returns on this date to the type of straightahead jazz playing that he seemed to have forsaken during the '70s. He also thankfully plays the acoustic piano on four of the six tracks. Bassist Charlie Haden and drummer Shelly Manne merge drive and taste in just the right proportions. So while by no means is this Art Pepper's best album, it remains a damn fine one nonetheless. —*Peter S. Friedman,* Cadence

○ **Trip, The** / Sep. 15+16, 1976 / Contemporary 410
With the George Cables Trio and Elvin Jones (d). One of his strongest quartet efforts in his final ten years. —*Michael G. Nastos*

○ **No Limit** / Mar. 1977 / Contemporary 411
No Limit was recorded during a March 1977 session and was, in fact, less successful than its predecessors, but it nonetheless remains an essential item for Art Pepper devotees. The reasons for this are both on the second side of the album. The high point of the record is the modal ballad "My Laurie," which is a superb example of the dialectics of grace and pain typical of Pepper's post-1960 style. The sober line is broken by Jackie McLean-like shrieks (the McLean of *Let Freedom Ring* and *Right Now*); there are also of course those entirely distinctive marks of Pepper's personality in the abundance of timbral alterations, provocative silences, and control of time. The rhythm section (pianist George Cables, blitz bassist Tony Dumas, drummer Carl Burnett) is merely a presence rather than a contributor to these explorations, and Pepper's is the only solo voice of substance to be heard on the album. A positive feature of the production is Pepper's own liner notes, which pay tribute to his friend Lester Koenig of Contemporary Records, who died shortly after this session. —*Terry Martin,* Down Beat

○ **Live at the Village Vanguard** / Jul. 28, 1977 / Contemporary 400-7642-3
Alto saxophonist Art Pepper recorded several albums during an extended stint at the Village Vanguard in 1977. They were originallly issued as *Live At The Vanguard* Volumes 1-4, then reissued using various weeknights as the reference. Either way, all are exceptional, with burning Pepper solos, outstanding secondary solos by pianist George Cables, and

equally fine work from bassist George Mraz and drummer Elvin Jones. This was rereleased on CD as *Thursday Night At The Village Vanguard. —Ron Wynn*

More for Less / Jul. 28-30, 1977 / Contemporary 697
This fourth volume of Village Vanguard sessions is no leftover item. Pepper is masterly, as are George Cables (p), George Mraz (b), and Elvin Jones (d). *—Ron Wynn*

○ **Friday Night at the Village Vanguard** / Jul. 29, 1977 / Contemporary 695
1992 CD reissue of one among several superb sets done live at the Village Vanguard in the late '70s. Pepper plays furious, twisting, and energized alto sax solos, while pianist George Cables shows his empathy with Pepper's style, and bassist George Mraz and drummer Elvin Jones find a way to fit themselves into the dialogs. The CD has one bonus cut. *—Ron Wynn*

○ **Saturday Night at the Village Vanguard** / Jul. 30, 1977 / Contemporary 696
The fourth and final release in the series recorded at the Village Vanguard in 1977. It was issued originally as *Live At The Village Vanguard, Vol. 4* on vinyl, then reissued on CD under the *Saturday Night* title. But no matter, it is riveting material, keyed by the surging Pepper alto sax. Pianist George Cables, bassist George Mraz, and drummer Elvin Jones are just as remarkable. *—Ron Wynn*

★ **Complete Galaxy Recordings** / 1977-1982 / Galaxy 1016
This massive 16-disc set covers almost everything in the last phase of Pepper's career. Exquisite piano throughout by George Cables; invaluable liner notes by Gary Giddins. It has 58 unissued tracks, plus alternate takes. *—Ron Wynn*

Art Pepper Today / Dec. 1+2, 1978 / Galaxy 5119

Birds and Ballads / i. Dec. 1+2, 1978 / Galaxy 1573
Good duels of three headliners. Pepper and Joe Henderson (sax) make an interesting contrast, but Joe Farrell (ts) is not so impressive. *—Ron Wynn*

Ballads by Four / Dec. 2-5, 1978 / Galaxy 5133

New York Album / Feb. 1979 / Galaxy 5154

○ **Artworks** / Mar. 1979 / Galaxy 5148
An exceptional quartet date from '79, with Pepper having just established what became a regular working relationship with pianist George Cables, who plays with passion and conviction. He hadn't yet hired a bassist and drummer, so for the occasion Charlie Haden and Billy Higgins were used. Pepper was certainly inspired by what they contributed; his alto sax solos are intense and often jubilant. *—Ron Wynn*

★ **Straight Life** / Sep. 1979 / Galaxy 475
Authoritative, statesmanlike Pepper on alto, while Tommy Flanagan proves a distinguished second soloist on piano. *—Ron Wynn*

☆ **Winter Moon** / Sep. 3-4, 1980 / Galaxy 677
Art Pepper's *Winter Moon* features a full complement of strings plus guitarist Howard Roberts, in addition to the usual rhythm trio. The combo, including bassist Cecil McBee and pianist Stanley Cowell, provide firm but understated support, which cannot be said for the often obtrusive fiddles. Still, as string productions go, this one is a success; the dreamy charts of Bill Holman and Jimmy Bond enhance the altoist's accessibility at not too great a cost to his bittersweet purity. "Blues In the Night," however shopworn, is an effective vehicle for Pepper's rich and distinctive clarinet work; no doubt his voice would be as instantly recognizable even on a harmonica. *—Larry Birnbaum, Down Beat*

○ **One September Afternoon** / Sep. 5, 1980 / Galaxy 678
Yet another first-rate early '80s Art Pepper album, this one featuring pianist Stanley Cowell, guitarist Howard Roberts, bassist Cecil McBee, and drummer Carl Burnett. It has a few more midtempo numbers and a generally more upbeat feel than most Pepper sessions from this period. The CD reissue contains two bonus cuts. *—Ron Wynn*

○ **So In Love** / i. Jul. 1981 / Artists House 9412

Of the new releases issued under Art Pepper's name in 1980, *So In Love* was overall the finest. The altoist stretches out here on a program of standards and blues, backed by alternating rhythm sections from the East and West coasts. Pianist Hank Jones is all one could ask for in an accompanist, and his aching solo on "Diane" sustains perfectly the restive mood of Pepper's opening choruses. But on the Thelonious Monk tune ("Straight No Chaser"), bassist Ron Carter and drummer Al Foster seem startled at first by the brevity and bark of Pepper's phrases, and overall the West Coast team (pianist George Cables, bassist Charlie Haden, drummer Billy Higgins) achieves a higher level of involvement with the leader and a greater degree of unity behind him. Cables isn't in Jones's league as a pianist, but his rapport with Pepper is even greater than the veteran's, and Haden and Higgins power the music along with great care and economy. Pepper had climbed to such a plateau of individuality that he seems often here to be drawing his unconscious influences into the light and remembering what it was he loved about them in the first place. On a leisurely "Stardust," he daffodils his sentiments with the grace and cunning of a Lester Young. The title track, a Cole Porter waltz that agitates into a collective improvisation by its climax, offers the best illustration of the wondrous use Pepper makes of John Coltrane. It isn't in this case a matter of piling up chords or of playing more notes, as it is with so many others, but rather of drawing on extreme registers of the horn to express more conflicting emotions, to reach deeper and higher recesses of the viscera and the psyche. *—Francis Davis, Cadence*

Maiden Voyage Sessions / Aug. 13-15, 1981 / Galaxy 5151

○ **Art Lives** / Aug. 1981 / Galaxy 5145
Nice live '81 set from alto saxophonist Art Pepper, who was still playing with fire and fury despite being in poor health. Pianist George Cables had become a Pepper favorite by this time, and he offers some sparkling solos, while bassist David Williams and drummer Carl Burnett give the duo the room and space to roam, then deliver when they are called to take the spotlight. *—Ron Wynn*

Goin' Home / May 1982 / Galaxy 679
Vibrant interaction between Pepper and George Cables (p), plus fine renditions of bop standards. CD has two extra cuts. *—Ron Wynn*

○ **Rediscoveries** / i. Mar. 1987 / Savoy 1170
More early '50s Pepper material culled from Savoy's vaults and issued in the late '80s as part of what was at the time the most recent Savoy reissue series. Since Denon now owns the label, the listener can hope that at some point they will put all the Pepper tracks into one well-done package, rather than have them floating all over the place. *—Ron Wynn*

○ **Among Friends** / Musicraft 837
Excellent late '70s set by alto saxophonist Art Pepper, one of several that made this as productive a period for Pepper as the early '50s. He works here with longtime friend and associate pianist Russ Freeman, plus bassist Bob Magnusson and drummer Frank Butler on some vigorous, dynamic numbers. *—Ron Wynn*

○ **Modern Jazz Classics** / Mobile Fidelity 805
Another outstanding Art Pepper late '50s album, though in a different style. Pepper is backed by an 11-piece orchestra and applies his torrid solos to works arranged by Marty Paich. This has been issued both as *Modern Jazz Classics* on CD and as *Modern Jazz Classics: Art Pepper Plus Eleven* on vinyl. *—Ron Wynn*

BILL PERKINS (William Reese Perkins)

b. Jul. 22, 1924, San Francisco, CA
Tenor saxophone, bandleader / Cool
A good multi-instrumentalist whose playing has broadened and changed direction slightly over the years, Bill Perkins has played tenor and baritone saxophone, flute, and clarinet. He was a proud member of the Lester Young-influenced school early in his career, and displayed a light tone and a

requisite floating style. But his '70s and '80s sessions have seen Perkins play with more force and a harder tone. Though still not an intense player, his approach seems more energetic. Perkins was born in San Francisco, but grew up in Chile. He later moved to Santa Barbara. Perkins spent time in the army, then studied music and engineering in California. He played in the early '50s with Jerry Wald and Woody Herman. He later worked with Stan Kenton, then rejoined Herman, this time as a principal soloist. Perkins recorded in the mid-'50s with John Lewis, and also with Richie Kamuca and Art Pepper. He became a prominent studio musician and engineer in the '60s; Perkins occasionally played in the "Tonight Show" orchestra. He performed and recorded in the mid- and late '70s with the Toshiko Akiyoshi-Lew Tabackin Big Band. Perkins played in England with Tommy Whittle in the '80s, and continued recording. He coformed a group with Herbie Harper. They recorded for VSOP in 1989, and their recording was released in 1992. Perkins has also recorded for Interplay, Storyville, Candid, Contemporary, Seabreeze, Jazz Mark, Fantasy, and Pacific Jazz, among others. Currently, he has several dates available on CD. —Ron Wynn

○ Jazz Origin–2 Degrees East, 3 Degrees West / i. 1956 / PA/USA 9019

★ Quietly There / Nov. 23-30, 1966 / Riverside 1776
Quintet. A very overlooked West Coast saxophonist in one of his better sessions. Reissue of 1966 album on compact disc. —Ron Wynn

CARL PERKINS (Jazz)

b. 1928, d. 1958
Piano
Not the rockabilly/rock star, but a fine pianist whose potentially great career was cut short by drug problems. Carl Perkins's left hand was slightly crippled by polio, but he overcame that and inserted superb blues inflections into his work with that same hand. An excellent bebop and hard bop soloist, Perkins initially worked with Tiny Bradshaw and Big Jay McNeely. After moving from the Midwest to the West Coast, Perkins was in an early edition of the Max Roach-Clifford Brown quintet. Later, Perkins was in the Clifford Counce quintet, and played and recorded with Harold Land, Art Pepper, Chet Baker, and Jim Hall, among others. He began recording for Savoy as a leader in 1949, then issued the outstanding Introducing Carl Perkins on Dootone in 1956. He made another session the next year with Red Mitchell and Hall; drum tracks were later overdubbed. Sadly, Perkins was dead at age 29. His composition, "Grooveyard," remains a jazz anthem. Perkins has a couple of sessions available on CD. —Ron Wynn

CHARLIE PERSIP (Charles Lawrence Persip, Charli Persip)

b. Jul. 26, 1929, Morristown, NJ
Drums / Swing, big band, bop, progressive big band
Though it seems like a contradiction, drummer Charlie Persip actually prefers playing bebop and hard bop in a big band setting as opposed to a combo situation. His slashing style and percussive abilities are more evident heading large groups, but Persip has also proven himself well working in small bands. Persip played with Tadd Dameron in the early '50s, then toured and recorded with Dizzy Gillespie in the mid- and late '50s. He joined Harry Edison's group and worked for a sort time with Harry James before forming the Jazz Statesmen with Freddie Hubbard and Ron Carter in 1960. Persip was a busy session player in the '50s and '60s; he worked and/or recorded with Lee Morgan, Dinah Washington, Kenny Dorham, Zoot Sims, Red Garland, Gil Evans, Don Ellis, Eric Dolphy, Rashaan Roland Kirk, and Gene Ammons. He toured with Billy Eckstine, serving as drummer and conductor from the mid-'60s to the early '70s. Persip was the Jazzmobile's principal drum instructor in the mid-'70s, and he played and recorded with Archie Shepp, Frank Foster, and Kirk in the late '70s. He co-led the Superband with trumpeter Gary La Furn in the early '80s,

worked in a trio with Eddie Gomez and Jack DeJohnette (piano) in the mid-'80s, then later re-formed, led, and recorded with Superband (II). Persip's done sessions for Bethlehem, Stash, and Soul Note. Some of his dates are available currently on CD. —Ron Wynn and Michael G. Nastos

★ Charles Persip and the Jazz Statesmen / Mar. 1961 / Bethlehem 6046
At the time of this recording, most of this group's members were in their early twenties, except for the leader, drummer Charlie Persip, who was a relative veteran at 31. This probably explains a certain air of immaturity that this record has. The good moments belong mostly to Persip and trumpeter Freddie Hubbard, who was already at this stage a quite personal soloist. Persip's drumming is crisply swinging and inventive throughout, although the 10-minute version of "The Champ" (subtitled "Suite in Five Movements" on the original issue), which is for the most part a drum feature with short solos by the others thrown in for contrast, wears a little long. I especially dug Persip's drumming on the theme statement of the "The Song is You." Hubbard also plays well on this tune, as he does on "Soul March," a very Art Blakey-ish thing alternating between 12/8 and 4/4 that comes off as the most satisfying track of the record. The rhythm section of bassist Ron Carter and Persip works well, if a bit hurried on the uptempo things, and Carter has a nice bass spot on "The Champ." —Per Husby, Cadence

○ Superband / Jul. 1982 / Stash 209

HOUSTON PERSON

b. Nov. 10, 1934, Florence, SC
Tenor saxophone / Blues & jazz, soul-jazz
A rock-solid, full-toned tenor saxophonist, Houston Person plays ballads and blues with a flair and with expressive ardor and power, while he also plays well on uptempo material, bebop, and hard bop. But it's on standards, ballads, and blues, whether backing vocalists or playing in groups, that Person shines. His mother taught him piano, but Person's interest in jazz emerged when he began collecting records as a teen. He started on tenor at age 17, and worked with groups that also included Eddie Harris, Lanny Morgan, Leo Wright, Cedar Walton, and Lex Humphries while stationed in Germany during army service. Person attended the Hartt School of Music, and toured with Johnny Hammond. He formed his own band after leaving Hammond, and did several recordings with various personnel. Person and Etta Jones did sessions and concerts together periodically in the late '60s and the '70s. He also played with Charles Earland, Groove Holmes, and in a duo with Ran Blake. Person appeared in Nice at the 1984 Grande Parade du Jazz. Person has recorded as a leader for Prestige and Muse. He has a few sessions as a leader available on CD. —Ron Wynn

★ Goodness! / Aug. 25, 1969 / Prestige 332
This is the first album of Person's that was a real hit. Here is one of the best examples of his late '60s/early '70s style. Small organ combo with that funky sound. Perhaps too formulaic, but still nice. Includes the hypnotic tune "Jamilah." —Michael Erlewine

○ Stolen Sweets / Apr. 29, 1976 / Muse 5110
First-rate soul-jazz, funk, blues, and ballads by tenor saxophonist Houston Person. Vocalist Etta Jones wasn't on this session, so things are mostly uptempo and cooking, with plenty of robust tenor from Person, tasty guitar by Jimmy Ponder, swirling organ riffs and support from Sonny Phillips, and percussion and rhythmic assistance from Frankie Jones and Buddy Caldwell. —Ron Wynn

○ Big Horn / May 20, 1976 / Muse 5136
Reliable soul-jazz, nicely played ballads, and good standards are tenor saxophonist Houston Person's forte, as he demonstrates repeatedly on this '76 set. Pianist Cedar Walton's the type of no-nonsense, consistent player whose skills are often taken for granted, while bassist Buster Williams, and drummer Grady Tate are equally unassuming veterans. —Ron Wynn

Talk of the Town / **i.** 1987 / Muse 5331
Marvelous standards and ballads, with excellent trumpet solos by Cecil Bridgewater. —*Ron Wynn*

Basics / **i.** Oct. 12, 1987 / Muse 5344

Something in Common / Feb. 1989 / Muse 5376
Person shows his more adventurous side in duels with bass great Ron Carter. No funk or blues or soul-jazz licks to hide behind. —*Ron Wynn*

○ **Party, The** / Nov. 1989 / Muse 5451
Good recent soul-jazz and blues session, with Young Lion organist Joey DeFrancesco providing the funky undercurrent to tenor saxophonist Houston Person's thick, authoritative solos and Randy Johnston and Bertell Knox filling the spaces on bass and drums, plus Sammy Figueroa adding some Afro-Latin fiber for additional support. —*Ron Wynn*

○ **Why Not!** / Oct. 5, 1990 / Muse 5433
Organ-tenor-trumpet session. Person's most recent album includes hot contributions by Young Lions Philip (tpt) and Winard Harper (d). With Joey DeFrancesco on the Hammond organ. —*Ron Wynn*

AKE PERSSON

b. Feb. 25, 1932, Hassleholm, Sweden, **d.** Feb. 5, 1975, Stockholm, Sweden
Trombone / Swing, big band
An effective swing and big band trombonist, Swedish player Ake Persson didn't have an exceptionally long career, but crammed plenty of fine playing into several memorable sessions in the '50s, '60s, and '70s. He recorded and played with Simon Brehm in the early '50s, and with Arnie Domnerus in the '50s and '60s. Persson also recorded and worked with Hacke Bjorksten, with Harry Arnold's Radio Band, and with Lars Gullin, George Wallington, Roy Haynes, Benny Bailey, and Joe Harris in the '50s and early '60s. Persson worked briefly with Quincy Jones's orchestra, then joined the Rias, a Berlin band, in 1961. He stayed with them until 1975, while he also played and recorded with the Kenny Clarke-Francy Boland big band in the early and late '60s and early '70s, and played with Count Basie, Duke Ellington, and Dizzy Gillespie. Persson recorded with Basie in 1962. He did not do any sessions as a leader, but can be heard on Clarke-Boland band reissues. —*Ron Wynn*

★ **Ake Persson Swedish All Stars** / Apr. 21, 1954 / Prestige 173

MARVIN HANNIBAL PETERSON

b. Nov. 11, 1948, Smithville, TX
Trumpet, composer / Progressive big band, modern creative
Able to blend a lyrical, careful approach with sweeping, snapping upper-register solos, Marvin Hannibal Peterson's style is an intriguing mix of hard bop and free influences. He learned drums and cornet as a child, then played trumpet in the North Texas State University band in the late '60s. Peterson moved to New York in 1970, and toured the East Coast with Rahsaan Roland Kirk. He began playing with the Gil Evans orchestra in 1971, and remained with them until 1980. Peterson worked and recorded with Pharoah Sanders, Roy Haynes, and Elvin Jones in the early '70s, then formed his own band. He's led the Sunrise Orchestra with Diedre Murray and other small combos. Peterson headed a free group in the late '70s with Ken McIntyre, Pat Patrick, Enrico Rava, and Roswell Rudd. He has recorded as a leader for Sunrise, MPS, EMI, Ear Rational, and Enja. Currently, there are no Peterson sessions available on CD. —*Ron Wynn*

○ **Hannibal** / Jul. 1-2, 1975 / MPS 22669
Trumpeter Marvin "Hannibal" Peterson's musical vocabularly ranges from the sharp staccato runs of Clifford Brown to a breathy impreciseness like Miles Davis, each used in the appropriate setting. The compositions here provide varied formats in which the musicians solo, from the slow changes of "Misty" to the modal repetition of "Revelation." "The Voyage," Hannibal's tribute to Africa, is the weakest cut, adding nothing to the jazz or African tradition.

Accompanying Peterson is a standard rhythm trio (bassist Stafford James, pianist Michael Cochrane, drummer and percussionist Michael Carvin, plus percussionist Chris Hart on "The Voyage"), presumably elevated to the stature of orchestra with the (welcomed) addition of cellist Diedre Murray. The cello stands out on most of the pieces as an exciting sound, used more texturally than as a melodic element (as in Ron Carter's recordings). Like his "orchestra," Hannibal plays with a vitality and intensity that make this album a worthwhile experience. —*Kevin Yatarola*, Cadence

★ **In Antibes** / Jul. 20, 1977 / Inner City 3020
Marvin "Hannibal" Peterson combines superior technique with emotional intensity to produce a sound totally satisfying to anyone even remotely attracted to the trumpet. While this album doesn't showcase Peterson at his best, it is sufficient to whet the listener's appetite for this remarkable musician. Hannibal and George Adams are both superb soloists, although Adams's forte is really tenor, which he plays on "Ro." His flute solo on "Swing Low Sweet Chariot" is very bluesy but generally less satisfying than earlier recordings made with Charles Mingus. Diedre Murray (cello) and Makaya Ntshoko (d) are competent despite the technical problems with the recording mix. —*David Less*, Down Beat

★ **Visions of a New World** / **i.** 1989 / Atlantic 781973
High-note hijinks, verbal forays, superb percussion, and alternately gripping and confusing lyrics combine to keep things unpredictable, intense, and sometimes infuriating. —*Ron Wynn*, Rock & Roll Disc.

☆ **Kiss on the Bridge** / **i.** 1990 / Ear Rational 882454909

OSCAR PETERSON (Oscar Emmanuel Peterson)

b. Aug. 15, 1925, Montreal, Quebec, Canada
Piano / Swing, bop, hard bop
Thanks to Norman Granz, Oscar Peterson ranks as one of the most extensively recorded jazz pianists in history. He's also been more harshly criticized than many who aren't nearly as gifted a stylist. Peterson's technique comes close to, though isn't as awesome as, Art Tatum's; Peterson's phrasing, facility, speed, harmonic knowledge, ideas, and style are dazzling. But he's been accused of lacking soul, being unable to play the blues (which is questionable), and making too many records that sound the same (which is fair criticism). His early work reflected the influence of Teddy Wilson, Earl Hines, and Nat King Cole, but he's long since developed his own recognizable, compelling approach. The elegant lines, flashy, yet intricate phrases, and teeming solos represent the work of a genuine piano master, though he does recycle overly familiar standards and ballads. He works best in a trio setting, where he gets the space to create freely.

Peterson studied classical piano at the age of six, and won a local talent contest in Montreal at age 14. He was a regular on a weekly radio program during his late teens, and played with the Johnny Holmes Orchestra throughout the mid-'40s. Granz invited him to appear at a 1949 Carnegie Hall Jazz at the Philharmonic concert, and shortly after became Peterson's manager. When Granz founded Verve in the '50s, Peterson became their house pianist. He also became the house pianist for subsidiaries Norgran, Clef, and Mercury, and in the '70s, for Pablo, which Granz formed. The bulk of Peterson's nearly 100 albums as a leader have been made on Granz labels. While on Verve, Peterson recorded with Billie Holiday, Lester Young, Louis Armstrong, Ella Fitzgerald, Coleman Hawkins, Fred Astaire, Benny Carter, Roy Eldridge, Buddy DeFranco, Nelson Riddle, and Milt Jackson. He traveled with the JATP revue through the early '50s, and formed a trio patterned after the Cole ensemble; guitar, piano, and bass. From 1953 until 1958, the Oscar Peterson Trio, with guitarist Herb Ellis and bassist Ray Brown, was a popular attraction. When Ellis left, drummer Ed Thigpen replaced him, and this trio stayed intact from 1959 until 1965. Peterson, Brown, Thigpen, and Phil Nimmons established the Advanced School of Contemporary Music in Toronto in 1960. Peterson kept things going for three years. He recorded for the MPS/BASF label in the late

'60s and early '70s. He rejoined Granz on Pablo in the '70s, and decided to concentrate on solo recordings, issuing a number of often astonishing, if thematically similar, releases.

Peterson began branching out by mid-decade, working with orchestras and playing with veterans like Gillespie, Terry, Joe Pass, Eddie "Lockjaw" Davis, Count Basie, and Niels-Henning Ørsted-Pedersen. Peterson has steadily continued touring and recording in the '80s and '90s, making mainly dull dates, and some dates for independent labels like Telarc. Prestige has reissued many of the Pablo's, and several Verve dates are available also. Gene Lee's biography, *Oscar Peterson: The Will to Swing*, was published in 1988, and is mandatory reading for Peterson fans. —*Ron Wynn and Michael Erlewine*

○ **Oscar Peterson Plays Cole Porter** / Nov. 25, 1951-Dec. 1952 / Mercury 603
This is one in a series of recordings pianist Oscar Peterson did showcasing the music of particular American composers. It's hard to get up great enthusiasm for this set with bassist Ray Brown and drummer Ed Thigpen because there's so much superior Peterson available. An easy ballad approach mixes with the usual Peterson panache on the swingers. The relative quality of Peterson's playing is high and this session reaches that minimum. This is a "good" set of Cole Porter; there are many better Oscar Peterson outings. —*Bob Rusch*, Cadence

George Gershwin Songbook / Nov. 1952-Dec. 1952 / Verve 823249

○ **Oscar Peterson Plays the Jerome Kern Songbook** / Dec. 1952-Dec. 31, 1953 / Clef 623
Oscar Peterson Plays the Jerome Kern Songbook comes from the same recording period (7/21-8/1/59) that produced not only the *Oscar Peterson, A Jazz Portrait of Frank Sinatra* set, but also about 10 other recordings. By and large, this kind of marathon studio effort rarely produces extraordinary results even from an artist with Peterson's consistency. The material put together to form this release, then, is like the rest from this session: reasonably brief. While this keeps the program shifting, there was relatively little stretching out and digging into the meat beyond the surface. —*Bob Rusch*, Cadence

○ **Oscar Peterson Plays Duke Ellington** / Dec. 1952 / Mercury 606

○ **Oscar Peterson Plays George Gershwin** / Dec. 1952 / Mercury 605

Roy Eldridge and Jo Jones at Newport / i. 1958 /

○ **Oscar Peterson Trio at the Concertgebouw, The** / Apr. 12, 1958 / Verve 8268

★ **Very Tall** / Sep. 1961 / Verve 827821

West Side Story / Jan. 24-25, 1962 / Verve 821575
Trio. Peterson does a wonderful job of bringing a jazz edge to the show-tune arena. —*Ron Wynn*

Bursting Out with the All Star Big Band / Jun. 13, 1962 / Verve 821986
Peterson shows he can fit into the big-band context. The lineup includes Cannonball Adderley (as), James Moody (sax), and Ray Brown (b). —*Ron Wynn*

☆ **Night Train—Vol. 1** / Dec. 15-16, 1962 / PolyGram 821724

○ **We Get Requests** / Oct. 19, 1963 / Verve 810047
We Get Requests is a 1964 (10/19-20 and 11/19) date with the Oscar Peterson (p) Trio (Ray Brown, b; Ed Thigpen, d). Relative to the dozens and dozens of Peterson issues and reissues available, this material is low-priority, mediocre Peterson. —*Bob Rusch*, Cadence

○ **Oscar Peterson Trio Plus One** / i. Nov. 1964 / Mercury 20975
A first-rate early '60s release in which the usual Oscar Peterson trio gets a nice addition via trumpeter Clark Terry. Terry's humor, tart trumpet solos, and general upbeat personality help pump some life into Peterson and his crew,

and he also gives a contrasting solo voice and options to the selections. This has been reissued on CD. —*Ron Wynn*

Eloquence / May 29, 1965 / Limelight 818842

Blues Etude / Dec. 3, 1965 / Verve 818844

Tristeza on Piano / 1970 / PolyGram 817489

Tracks / Nov. 1970 / Verve 821849

○ **Reunion Blues** / Jul. 1971 / PolyGram 817490
Fine early '70s set with pianist Oscar Peterson working in alternative situation from his characteristic trios or solos or duos. He's featured in a quartet with vibist Milt Jackson, bassist Ray Brown, and drummer Louis Hayes, who's much more wide open and groove-oriented than most who've worked with Peterson. The results are looser, with more blues sensibility and rhythmic punch. —*Ron Wynn*

○ **History of an Artist—Vol. 1** / Dec. 27, 1972 / Pablo 702
The first of a two-part anthology collecting Peterson material from his years on Verve. It has solo, trio, and combo sessions with numerous interpretations of standards, blues, ballads, and various other things. Excellent playing throughout. The only problem is that if you're not a piano lover, the lack of diversity can become troubling. —*Ron Wynn*

○ **Oscar Peterson Featuring Stephane Grappelli** / Feb. 22+23, 1973 / Prestige 24041

Good Life / May 16-19, 1973 / Pablo 627

★ **Trio, The** / May 16-19, 1973 / Pablo 2310-70
The Nat Cole piano/guitar/bass lineup Oscar Peterson uses here represents not a departure for him, but a somewhat nostalgic return to the format he perfected in the company of such musicians as Ray Brown, Barney Kessel, and Herb Ellis. The result, recorded live at Chicago's London House, is gratifying. Peterson is as loquacious and polished as ever; only a cursory listening to, say, "Blues Etude" (a kind of microhistory of blues piano from barrelhouse to stride to bop) confirms that Peterson can effortlessly realize just about everything on piano. And he swings so hard that adding a drummer to this record would have been a redundancy. Joe Pass and Niels-Henning Ørsted-Pedersen are cast in minor roles. Aside from Pass's delicate a cappella cameo appearance on Ellington's "Come Sunday," he remains hidden in the background, stepping stage center only briefly. When he is spotlighted, he's worth listening to carefully. On "Chicago Blues," for example, he effortlessly blends Charlie Parkeresque double-time licks with relaxed phrases reminiscent of Charlie Christian. Ørsted-Pedersen's clean, thoughtful, precisely articulated lines and brief solos likewise confirm that his lofty reputation is well deserved. —*Jon Balleras*, Down Beat

Oscar Peterson with Harry Edison & Eddie Vinson / i. 1974 / Pablo 2310-927
Good change-of-pace date; pianist Oscar Peterson isn't doing the standard elegant trio material or solo recitals, but interacting with swing-era trumpeter Harry Edison. Far more energy, variety, and unpredictability on this date than on many other Peterson sessions. —*Ron Wynn*

Oscar Peterson & Dizzy Gillespie / Nov. 1974 / Pablo 2310-740
With Dizzy Gillespie. Well done. It's restrained but has moments of brilliance. —*Ron Wynn*

○ **Oscar Peterson and Roy Eldridge** / Dec. 8, 1974 / Pablo 739
This is generally a good Eldridge album, considering his limitations at the time (1975). He acquits himself well indeed on less frantic pieces such as "Little Jazz," "Sunday" (with a walking bass line by Oscar Peterson on organ), and "Blues For Chu," in which a few brief high-note thrusts are brought off nicely. When muted (on more than half the LP), he is incisive and reasonably articulate. His open horn is clean, round, and characteristically rugged. If it isn't a landmark record, it's far from being a disappointment. —*John McDonough*, Down Beat

At Salle Pleyel / Mar. 17, 1975 / Pablo 705

○ **Oscar Peterson & Jon Faddis** / Jun. 5, 1975 / Pablo 743

Jon Faddis starts off this album with a sullen "Things Ain't What They Used To Be," which growls through several muted choruses and climaxes with rounds of economical high-note work that suggest Harry Edison more than Dizzy Gillespie, who is considered Faddis's mentor. The energy level is high throughout this LP, as high as the keys in most cases. Faddis appears to be completely comfortable in the upper register and succeeds in working out intelligent ideas without hesitation or strain. "Blues for Birks" recalls Gillespie's more flamboyant days, but it is no imitation of the master. Oscar Peterson's piano seems particularly inspired. But the most satisfying tract is "Lester Leaps In," simply because it is the most swinging. There is a lot of playing at the top of the register here, and it's a little hard on the ear after a while without an ensemble to balance things out. —*John McDonough*, Down Beat

○ **Oscar Peterson Big Six, The** / Jul. 16, 1975 / Original Jazz Classics 496
Fine live set with piano wizard Oscar Peterson leading a sextet at the 1975 Montreux Festival. Peterson is a longtime favorite of Norman Granz, who's issued numerous Peterson recordings over the years on many labels. The piano solos are rigorous and intricately constructed and executed, while the ensemble work and solos from other participants are equally impressive, especially those from guitarist Joe Pass and vibist Milt Jackson. —*Ron Wynn*

○ **Oscar Peterson and Clark Terry** / i. 1975 / Pablo 742
Pianist Oscar Peterson is in excellent company with Clark Terry on what was the first of the Pablo label's piano-trumpet records. Terry's nimble attack serves him well, even though neither musician really rises to any unexpected heights. "Slow Boat to China" provides a particularly attractive set of changes, while "Shaw Nuff" locks both into a high-speed duel of runs. "Chops" is a slow blues of considerable beauty, almost Ellingtonian in character with Peterson's sensitive support. —*John McDonough*, Down Beat

○ **Montreux (1977)** / Jul. 15, 1977 / Original Jazz Classics 385
Peterson takes the harmonic and solo spotlight. Nice assistance by Ray Brown (b) and Niels-Henning Ørsted-Pedersen (b). —*Ron Wynn*

Silent Partner / Mar. 14, 1979 / Pablo 103
A simply wonderful date, with special solos from Zoot Sims (ts), Clark Terry (tpt), Eddie Davis (sax), and company. —*Ron Wynn*

Live / i. Nov. 12-14, 1980 / Pablo 2310940

Nigerian Marketplace / Jul. 16, 1981 / Pablo 2308-231

Tribute to My Friends / i. Nov. 8, 1983 / Pablo 2310902

Saturday Night at the Blue Note / i. Mar. 16, 1990 / Telarc 83306

○ **Exclusively for My Friends [Boxed Set]** / i. 1992 / PolyGram 513830
The music here, originally released on six MPS LPs, has been reissued as *Exclusively for My Firends*, a four-CD set that awesomely reconfirms the opinion expressed by Oscar Peterson that these were the best recordings he ever made. Of criticism leveled at Peterson in the past—empty virtuosity, a mechanical approach to swing, lack of originality (with too much reliance on Art Tatum), inability to play the blues honestly—this set stands in defiance. Peterson controls his vast technique at all times. The earliest tracks were recorded with bassist Ray Brown and drummer Ed Thigpen in 1963. However, the majority of the trio tracks include Sam Jones on bass and Bobby Durham on drums, with Louis Hayes in for Durham on two tracks. Brown's walking bass is exemplary on Billy Taylor's "Easy Walker," as is Jones's on "In a Mellotone." Volume 4, recorded in 1968, is all solo piano. —*Owen Cordle*, Down Beat

RALPH PETERSON

Drums / Neo-bop
A fine hard bop drummer, Ralph Peterson plays with a precise, driving intensity that provides energetic fills and slashing accents and texture. He's led both trios and large groups, and has been recording since the late '80s for Blue Note. Peterson's played with Geri Allen, Terence Blanchard, David Murray, Don Byron, Frank Lacy, Phil Bowler, and several others. All his sessions are available on CD. —*Ron Wynn*

★ **Triangular** / Aug. 21-22, 1988 / Blue Note 92750

○ **Volition** / Feb. 1989 / Blue Note 93894
Quintet. Excellent session and wondrous lineup. Pianist Geri Allen and trumpeter Terence Blanchard are masterly. —*Ron Wynn*

Ralph Peterson Introduces the Fo'tet / Dec. 22-23, 1989 / Capitol 95475
An album where this tremendous young drummer unveils a strong lineup of contemporary talent and turns it loose on a hard bop menu. —*Ron Wynn*

○ **Fo'tet Ornettology** / Aug. 1990 / Somethin' Else 98290
An outstanding hard bop session by drummer Ralph Peterson. He heads a band that includes many top modern players, among them Don Byron on clarinet, plus Melissa Slocum and Bryan Carroll. The compositions are mostly originals, and though arranged in a vintage style they have a contemporary flavor. —*Ron Wynn*

MICHEL PETRUCCIANI

b. Dec. 28, 1962, Orange, France
Piano / Cool, neo-bop
Michel Petrucciani is a French pianist who's made some technically impressive, very lyrical recordings in the '80s and '90s. His harmonic, rhythmic, and melodic excellence has sometimes led to the criticism that he puts too much emphasis on keyboard skills and not enough emotion and individual flavor into his style. Petrucciani is a masterful ballad player, and some of the things he executes during his solos are astonishing, even if he's not the most energetic or bluesy pianist. His father was a jazz guitarist, and Petrucciani studied classical piano for seven years, giving his first concert as a teen. He played with Clark Terry and Kenny Clarke at age 15. Petrucciani moved to Paris at age 17, and cut his first album. He also began working with Lee Konitz. Petrucciani travelled to California in the early '80s and started playing with Charles Lloyd. An appearance at the Kool Jazz Festival in the mid-'80s, in addition to his playing on Lloyd's comeback album for Elektra, stimulated interest in Petrucciani. He worked and recorded with John Abercrombie, Jim Hall, Wayne Shorter, Mike Zwerin, Aldo Romano, Eliot Zigmund, J.F. Jenny Clark, Konitz, Lloyd, and Jack DeJohnette in the '80s, while recording for Owl, Concord, EPM. George W., and Blue Note. Petrucciani has continued recording for Owl and Blue Note in the '90s. He has several sessions available on CD. —*Ron Wynn*

Oracle's Destiny / Oct. 18, 1982 / Owl 79229

○ **100 Hearts** / Jun. 1983 / George Wein Collection 3001
If it's possible to fault pianist Michel Petrucciani's playing, his considerable technique and expansive imagination do sometimes lead him to pack too much into one piece, to journey down every possible improvisational byway, to sometimes play more than necessary. But such exuberance is nonetheless fascinating to contemplate. Consider the approach Petrucciani takes to Ornette Coleman's "Turn Around". He addresses this gutsy, side-slipping blues line with brittle excursions into inside and outside tonalities supported by a hefty walking bassline spiced with witty twists. Sonny Rollins's "St. Thomas" similiarly bursts at the seams as Petrucciani scampers through a nonstop grab bag of pianistic devices and pounces into unexpected tonalities, again creating the impression that his powers of invention range too widely to be contained in one tune. In light of Petrucciani's active imagination, a piece like the aptly titled "Pot Pourri" should be no surprise. Here, Petrucciani blends five different vehicles, but the result is by no means a straightforward medley. Instead, it is a freely associative evocation of the mood of these pieces, with themes fragmented and extended, linked with rapid-fire, Bud Powellian lines,

bits of blues funk, and countless transitional permutations of the Charlie Parker/Dizzy Gillespie introduction to "All the Things You Are." A flat-out showpiece, like Petrucciani's "St. Thomas" variations, it verges on the brink of flamboyancy, yet is saved by the aplomb with which Petrucciani ties the pieces together. —*Jon Balleras,* Down Beat

○ **Live at the Village Vanguard** / Mar. 16, 1984 / George Wein Collection 43006
Comparisons to the great Bill Evans trios may seem premature; they are not unwarranted. More than the setting, format, and drummer Eliot Zigmund's presence suggest them. Michel Petrucciani's sure-handed swing and soft lyricism, the balance of interpretations and original material, and, most of all, the interplay between him, bassist Palle Danielsson, and Zigmund recall another set of trio performances recorded at the Vanguard. The trio plays long—only "Le Bricoleur" is under six minutes on this double album—but never appears to coast. Petrucciani uses standard devices of shifting tempos, dynamics, and solo spaces in ways that are not surprising or new but are always notable for their control and sense of proportion. —*Eric Shepard,* Cadence

○ **Cold Blues** / Jan. 1985 / Owl 79224
A '91 CD reissue featuring the outstanding pianist Michel Petrucciani in duets with bassist Ron McClure. While some accuse Petrucciani of too much flash and not enough soul, his expressive phrasing and often dazzling solos reflect a complete knowledge and mastery of the keyboard, while bassist McClure adds enough depth and bottom to keep things from getting too spacy. —*Ron Wynn*

★ **Pianism** / Dec. 20, 1985 / Blue Note 46295
The virtuosic pianist Michel Petrucciani is at his best throughout this dazzling set. Although frequently recorded in recent years, Petrucciani can point to *Pianism* as one of his most satisfying releases because he emphasizes emotion over his remarkable technique. Petrucciani's style, an extension of his idol Bill Evans, also included his own blend of passion and playfulness; the latter is strongest on "Our Tune." The interplay of the leader with Palle Danielsson (b) and Eliot Zigmund (d) on Petrucciani's four originals and the two standards is quite impressive. —*Scott Yanow,* Cadence

☆ **Power of Three** / Jul. 14, 1986 / Blue Note 46427
It is logical that Michel Petrucciani (p) and Jim Hall (g) would eventually play together. Both are masters of chordal improvisation and possessors of harmonically rich and introverted styles. In addition, Hall recorded two superb duet albums with Bill Evans, Petrucciani's idol and main influence. At the 1986 Montreux Jazz Festival the pair work together perfectly, sounding as one on the altered blues "Careful" (where their comping behind each other's solos is exquisite) and on a lengthy and well-constructed version of "In a Sentimental Mood." A special treat of this album is the inclusion of Wayne Shorter on three selections. Whether playing tenor on a revival of his obscure "Limbo" and the calypso "Bimini" or switching to soprano for Petrucciani's ballad "Morning Blues," Shorter shows much more passion and creativity before the appreciative crowd than at any point on his late '80s Columbia albums. —*Scott Yanow,* Cadence

Michel Plays Petrucciani / Sep. 1987-Dec. 1987 / Blue Note 48679
The frequently arresting player tackles his own work. His solos outstrip his writing. —*Ron Wynn*

Playground / 1990 / Blue Note 95480
In his most recent set, he dominates as soloist. Omar Hakim provides welcome energy on drums. —*Ron Wynn*

OSCAR PETTIFORD

b. Sep. 30, 1922, Okmulgee, OK, **d.** Sep. 8, 1960, Copenhagen, Denmark
Bass, cello / Bop
Pettiford is one of the most exemplary bassists and cellists of the '50s. He was born on a Native American reservation. Along with ten of his musical siblings, he played in a family band that was quite popular in the Midwest. He worked with

Charlie Barnet in 1942, then went to New York and joined Roy Eldridge in 1943. He did several sessions in the mid-'40s with Coleman Hawkins, Earl Hines, and Ben Webster. He co-led a group with Dizzy Gillespie in 1944, then had his own combos and big band in 1945. Pettiford relocated on the West Coast to work with Hawkins in 1945, then spent three years with Duke Ellington's orchestra. After that, he usually led his own bands, with the exception of a year with Woody Herman in 1949, and another year with Charlie Shavers and Louie Bellson's band in 1950. Pettiford was a marvelous improviser, and pioneered the art of playing the pizzicato style on cello. His technique and intonation have been absorbed by nearly every bassist from the early '50s on, and pieces such as "Bohemia After Dark" and "Laverne Walk" are modern masterpieces. —*Ron Wynn*

○ **Oscar Pettiford Memorial Album** / Mar. 10, 1949+Mar. 13, 1954 / Prestige 7813
Stunning bass and cello playing from Oscar Pettiford (the bass parts are multitracked) showing his technical prowess both with bow and plucked. Phenomenal showcase for Pettiford's work and for bass and cello in general. —*Ron Wynn*

○ **Discoveries** / Feb. 21, 1952-Oct. 1957 / Savoy 1172
1952-1957. A stunning early work by the bass and cello great. Has some duets with Charles Mingus (b), plus other examples of his stirring cello technique. —*Ron Wynn*

★ **New Oscar Pettiford Trio, The** / Dec. 29, 1953 / Debut 112
A wonderful set. Pettiford is in prime form as a bassist and composer. —*Ron Wynn*

○ **O.P.'s Jazz Men (The Oscar Pettiford Orchestra)** / i. 1958 / Paramount 227

Vienna Blues–The Complete Sessions / Jan. 9, 1959 / Black Lion 760104
Tremendous sessions featuring bass and cello giant Oscar Pettiford heading an unusual group with tenor saxophonist Hans Koller, guitarist Atilla Zoller, and drummer Jimmy Pratt. These were recorded near the end of Pettiford's career but are first-rate, especially Pettiford's cello solos and Koller's tenor. —*Ron Wynn*

○ **Montmartre Blues** / Black Lion 760124

FLIP PHILLIPS (Joseph Edward Filipelli)

b. Mar. 26, 1915, New York, NY
Tenor saxophone / Swing, bop
Though he's approaching his eighties, a still spry Flip Phillips hasn't stopped recording or performing. He's a consummate player, who's most famous for holding his own in freewheeling jam sessions, but is also a wonderful ballad and standards interpreter, and a good blues and bop artist. He's no innovator, but is one of the reliable foot soldiers who plugs away in the jazz infantry. Phillips played in New York with various groups before joining Frankie Newton in 1940. He played clarinet while in this group, before switching to tenor. Phillips joined Benny Goodman in 1942, then worked with Wingy Manone and Red Norvo in 1943. From 1944 to 1946, Phillips played with Woody Herman, before beginning the association that made him an international favorite. He started touring with Jazz at the Philharmonic in 1946, and over the next ten years engaged in numerous honking, screaming, and emphatic jam sessions and cutting contests with fellow stars from Coleman Hawkins to Charlie Parker to Lester Young, and all comers in between. Phillips toured Europe with Benny Goodman in 1959, then settled in Florida, becoming a part-time player and full-time apartment building manager. He did some work with Bill Harris and Herman, and headed bands when he felt like playing. A 1970 appearance at the Colorado Jazz Party, followed by a 1972 Newport Jazz Festival concert date, rekindled his interest, and Phillips returned to music exclusively in 1975. He recorded for Signature in the mid-'40s with various sidemen from Herman's orchestra. Phillips made several albums for Verve and Clef in the late '40s and early '50s, then did sessions with Oscar Peterson, Herb Ellis, and Ray Brown, and

Music Map

Jazz Piano

Keyboards from Europe

Ragtime
Scott Joplin (1868-1917)
Joe Lamb (1887-1960)

Early Jazz Piano
Eubie Blake (1883-1983)
Jelly Roll Morton (1890-1941)
Earl Hines (1903-1983)

Stride Piano
Lucky Roberts (1887-1968)
Willie "The Lion" Smith (1897-1973)
James P. Johnson (1894-1955)
Fats Waller (1904-19430)

Major Influence
Art Tatum (1909-1956)

Boogie-Woogie
Jimmy Yancey (1898-1951)
Pinetop Smith (1904-1929)
Pete Johnson (1904-1967)
Meade Lux Lewis (1905-1964)
Little Brother Montgomery (1906-1985)
Albert Ammons (1907-1949)
Memphis Slim (1915)
Art Hodes (1904)

1930s Experimental
Clarence Profit (1912-1944)

Swing Piano
Count Basie (1904-1986)
Jess Stacy (1904)
Teddy Wilson (1912-1986)
Erroll Garner (1921-1977)
Ralph Sutton (1922)

Transition to Bop
Thelonious Monk (1917-1982)

Bop Piano
Mary Lou Williams (1910-1981)
Lennie Tristano (1919-1978)
Bud Powell (1924-1966)
Al Haig (1924)
Oscar Peterson (1925)
Barry Harris (1929)
Hank Jones (1918)
Tommy Flanagan (1930)
Duke Jordan (1922)
Walter Bishop, Jr. (1927)
Elmo Hope (1923-1967)
Kenny Drew (1928)
Dodo Marmarosa (1925)

Cool Piano
Lennie Tristano (1919-1978) – John Lewis (1920)
Bill Evans (1929-1980) – Dave Brubeck (1920)

Post Bop
Herbie Nichols (1919-1963)
Red Garland (1923-1984)
Randy Weston (1926)
Horace Silver (1928)
Phineas Newborn (1931)
Wynton Kelly (1931-1971)
Bobby Timmons (1935-1974)
McCoy Tyner (1938)
Hal Galper (1938)
George Cables (1944)
Horace Parlan (1931)
Hugh Lawson (1935)
Joanne Brackeen (1938)
Sonny Clark (1931-1963)

Free Style
Sun Ra (1915)
Cecil Taylor (1929)
Alex Von Schilippenbach (1938)
Yosuke Yamashita (1942)
Marilyn Crispell (1947)
Don Pullen (1944)
Horace Tapscott (1934)
Muhal Richard Abrams (1930)
Dave Burrell (1940)

Experimental
Mal Waldron (1926)
Andrew Hill (1937)

Keith Jarrett (1945)
Michel Petrucciani (1962)
Hilton Ruiz (1952)
Tete Montoliu (1933)

Electric
Joe Zawinul (1932)
Herbie Hancock (1940)
Chick Corea (1941)
Lonnie Liston Smith (1940)

Soul and R&B Piano
Ramsey Lewis (1935)
Junior Mance (1928)
Gene Harris (1933)
Joe Sample (1939)
Les McCann (1935)

Revival
Jim Dapogny (1940)
Judy Carmichael
Mr. B.
Dick Wellstood (1927-1987)
Dick Hyman (1927)
Roger Kellaway (1939)
Reginald Robinson

New Players
Mulgrew Miller (1955)
Renee Rosnes
Geri Allen (1957)
Marcus Roberts (1963)
Michele Rosewoman(1953)
Stephen Scott
Kenny Kirkland (1957)
James Williams
Donald Brown
Kenny Drew, Jr.
Geoff Keezer
Benny Green

Jacki Byard (1922), Marian McPartland (1926), Ellis Larkins (1923)

recorded an album with Buddy Rich. During the '60s, he added bass clarinet and alto sax to his arsenal, while recording quartet sessions for Sue and Onyx. Phillips reunited with Herman's orchestra for a 1978 date, and headed quartets and quintets for sessions on Phillips, Progressive, PHM, Concord, and MPS through the '70s and into the '80s. He toured Europe again in 1982. —*Ron Wynn*

★ **Melody from the Sky, A** / **i**. 1944-1945 / Doctor Jazz 39419
An album of 1944-1945 sessions from New York City with a good, swinging sound. —*Michael G. Nastos*

○ **Rock with Flip** / Sep. 13, 1954 / Clef 740

○ **Flip in Florida** / **i**. May 1974 / Onyx 214
This recording, made in 1963 and issued briefly, shows Flip Phillips in familiar territory. The tenor saxophonist and bass clarinetist plays a program of standards ("Sweet Georgia Brown,"), jazz classics ("'Round Midnight"), Ellingtunes ("Satin Doll"), and lovely ballads ("Nuages") backed by a rhythm section. The experiments on bass clarinet are fine examples of what can be done to bring instruments normally considered outside the scope of jazz into the idiom. —*Joe Klee*, Down Beat

Flipenstein / Jul. 20, 1981 / Progressive 7063

○ **Claw—Live at the Floating Jazz Festival, The** / **i**. 1986 / Chiaroscuro 314
According to producer Hank O'Neal's notes to *The Claw*, this CD is a complete and unedited record of a concert that took place on a jazz cruise aboard the S.S. *Norway* heading toward St. Thomas in the Caribbean Sea. We are also told that the concert was recorded on VHS videotape and that, once transferred to DAT, only a small amount of enhancing was done to bring out certain instruments. Certainly there is nothing wrong with the fidelity of this CD nor with the immediacy of a group of seasoned professionals playing to the delight of a live audience. What the liner notes do not tell us is the order of the solos. Unless you can always tell Flip Phillips from Scott Hamilton from Buddy Tate (all tenor sax), you simply hear one feverish tenor solo after another. Thus you miss what must have pleased the crowd in the Caribbean that day: the sight of four veterans (Hamilton ceased to be an ingenue some years ago) going at each other in the old, crowd-pleasing tradition of the Savoy and JATP. While this CD cannot show us the musicians, it would have been nice to have known who was playing what. —*Krin Gabbard*, Cadence

○ **Sound Investment, A** / Mar. 1987 / Concord Jazz 4334
With Scott Hamilton (ts). An excellent, sympathetic collaboration. A standout pairing of this top swing-era stylist and a modern disciple. —*Ron Wynn*

★ **Real Swinger** / May 1988-Jun. 1988 / Concord Jazz 4358
With Howard Alden (g), Butch Miles (d), and this veteran saxophonist on his most recent album. Still swinging after all these years. Highly recommended. —*Michael G. Nastos*

○ **Small Herd on Keynote** / **i**. Aug. 15, 1991 / Verve 830968

BILL PIERCE (William Pierce)

b. Sep. 25, 1948, Hampton, VA
Multi-instruments / Hard bop, postbop, neo-bop
Bill Pierce is a good tenor and soprano saxophonist whose style matured during his years with Art Blakey in the early '80s. Pierce began his professional career in Boston during the '70s, playing in clubs and backing such R&B and soul stars as Stevie Wonder and Marvin Gaye. He played and recorded with fellow Messenger James Williams in both the '70s and '80s. Pierce later returned to Boston from New York after leaving Blakey, continued performing, and also began to teach privately. He's been a key member of Tony Williams's quintet of the late '80s and early '90s. He's recorded for Sunnyside in both the '80s and '90s, playing with Hank Jones, Roy Haynes, Terence Blanchard, Mulgrew Miller, Ira Coleman, Keith Copeland, Alan Dawson, and others. His sessions are all available on CD. —*Ron Wynn*

★ **William the Conqueror** / May 29-30, 1985 / Sunnyside 1013
It is the powerful tenor of Billy Pierce that makes this a highly recommended album. —*Scott Yanow*, Cadence

DAVE PIKE (David Samuel Pike)

b. Mar. 23, 1938, Detroit, MI
Vibes / Latin jazz, early jazz-rock
A good, if sometimes rather bland vibist, Dave Pike's enjoyed some successful dates and has been in high-profile bands. His playing has some moments of vitality and depth, but overall has more pretty melodies and light vamps than substantial solos. Pike began playing drums at age eight, then taught himself vibes. His family moved from Detroit to Los Angeles in the early '50s, and Pike played in the mid-'50s with Curtis Counce, Harold Land, Elmo Hope, and Dexter Gordon. He worked and recorded with Paul Bley, and briefly led his own quartet. Pike added marimba to his arsenal in the late '50s. He moved to New York in 1960 and put an amplifier on his vibes from that point. He toured with Herbie Mann in the early and mid-'60s, scoring some crossover attention with renditions of bossa nova. Pike played at the Berliner Jazztage in 1968, and decided to remain in Europe for a while. He formed the Dave Pike set with Volker Kriegel and J.A. Rettenbacher. They played at festivals and clubs all over Europe until the early '70s. Pike recorded with the Kenny Clarke-Francy Boland big band in 1968. He returned to America and moved to Southern California, forming a group that played at Hungry Joe's club during the '70s. Pike has recorded as a leader for Riverside, Muse, Criss Cross, and Timeless. He has a couple of sessions available on CD. —*Ron Wynn*

★ **Pike's Groove** / Feb. 1986 / Criss Cross 1021

COURTNEY PINE

b. Mar. 18, 1964, London, England
Tenor and soprano saxophone / Hard bop, world fusion
England's reigning jazz star, Courtney Pine has made some interesting, sometimes controversial decisions. He's done as much reggae, pop, funk, and jazz-rock as jazz, and has run into a critical backlash regarding the closeness of his soprano style to Wayne Shorter's, and his tenor style's similarity to that of middle-period John Coltrane's. Pine has demonstrated significant ability, and a soulful, exuberant style, but has also run into compositional and content difficulties. But he remains arguably the best of England's contemporary saxophonists. Pine began on clarinet, then turned to sax. He played hard bop in his teens, forming a group called Dwarf Steps, and also played with funk and reggae bands. Pine participated in John Stevens's workshops and occasionally played in his band, Freebop. He formed Abibi Jazz Arts in 1984. This organization was intended to be an advocacy group to promote jazz interest in Black British musicians. It led to the formation of the Jazz Warriors big band in 1985, which combined jazz with other musical styles in performance and on album. Pine also headed his own groups, among them the World's First Saxophone Posse. He made his debut as a leader for Antilles/Island in 1986 with *Journey to the Urge Within*. Pine also worked with Grand Union, and with Art Blakey's Jazz Messengers during a London visit. Pine toured with Elvin Jones, George Russell, and Charlie Watts's big band. He's continued recorded for Island/Antilles into the '90s. Pine has several sessions available on CD. —*Ron Wynn*

○ **Journey to the Urge Within** / Jul. 1986-Aug. 1986 / Antilles 842687
Courtney Pine's singing soprano may echo Wayne Shorter (on Shorter's "Delores") or Jane Ira Bloom, and his tenor's indebted to John Coltrane and Sonny Rollins. But then Pine was only 22 at the time of this release and already reaching beyond his models. His orderly bass clarinet is distinctive on a freebopping "C.G.C." with bass and Cleveland Watkiss's Bobby McFerrin-like vocal and on a dancing pianoless quartet ("As We Would Say") with Harmon-muted trumpeter

Kevin Robinson. Pine is consistently strong in a loose foursome with pianist Julian Joseph, bassist Gary Crosby, and drummer Mark Mondesir. (Auxilary players are Ray Carless, bs; Orphy Robinson, tb; Roy Carter, k; Martin Taylor, g; Ian Mussington, per.) London-born but Jamaica-bred and with reggae experience, Pine doesn't push the island "riddims" that snagged Oliver Lake; he plays mostly pretty ballads or alert, slightly outward-moving postbop that betrays subtle Latin tinges. He wrote most of these serviceable vehicles too. —*Kevin Whitehead*, Cadence

★ **Destiny's Song and the Image of Pursuance** / **i.** 1988 / Antilles 842772
English Young Lion Courtney Pine has heart and soul, but sometimes lacks ideas and taste. —*Ron Wynn*

Vision's Tale, The / **i.** 1990 / Antilles 91334
Pine has upgraded his tenor sax talents. A lot more personalized playing appears on his third Island disc. The alternation of bop classics with intriguing new works doesn't hurt matters either. — *Ron Wynn*, Rock & Roll Disc

Within the Realms of Our Dream / Jan. 20-21, 1990 / Antilles 848244

BUCKY PIZZARELLI (John Paul (Sr) Pizzarelli)

b. Jan. 9, 1926, Paterson, NJ
Guitar / Swing, big band
A father and son guitar team known for expressive, if at times introspective, acoustic and electric playing, Bucky and John Pizzarelli (Jr.) are successful apart and together. Bucky Pizzarelli (b. 1926) plays a seven-string guitar with the extra string tuned to allow him to play a bass line to his own solos. He's also a first-rate classical guitarist and a good, though conservative, electric stylist. John Pizzarelli (b. 1960) began working with his father in 1980. He also plays a seven-string, and the similarities between the two men's voicing and phrasing often makes it seem like they're both playing the same instrument when they work together. Bucky Pizzarelli played banjo and guitar as a child, and toured with Vaughn Monroe's band at age 17. He rejoined Monroe after completing army service in the mid-'40s, recorded with him for RCA, and did radio broadcasts. Pizzarelli joined NBC in 1952. He toured with the Three Sounds in 1956 and 1957, then did freelance studio work in New York. Pizzarelli toured with Benny Goodman, led his own trio, and recorded with Zoot Sims, Bud Freeman, and Stephane Grappelli in the '70s. He began working with his son, John, in the '80s, and has continued playing with him into the '90s. John Pizzarelli joined Tony Monte's trio in 1986, has performed and recorded as a leader, and has recorded several vocals. The Pizzarellis have recorded as a duo for Stash. Bucky Pizzarelli records as a solo artist on Stash, while John records as a leader for RCA/Novus. They have sessions available on CD separately and as a duo. — *Ron Wynn*

○ **Buck and Bud** / **i.** Feb. 1977 / Flying Dutchman 11378

★ **Complete Guitar Duos** / 1991 / Stash 536
Fine guitar vehicle for Bucky (John) Pizzarelli and John, Jr. They team on both uptempo and slow tunes, some originals, mostly interpretations of both jazz and nonjazz items. This is wonderful for guitar devotees; others may have problems with the lack of variety and generally sedate production and sound. —*Ron Wynn*

○ **Rhythm Encounters with Red Norvo and Slam Stewart** / Stash 18

LONNIE PLAXICO (Lonnie Luvell Plaxico)

b. Sep. 4, 1960, Chicago, IL
Bass / M-Base, modern creative
A very fine accompanist and a good soloist, Lonnie Plaxico was an important contributor to several combos in the '80s. Before joining Wynton Marsalis's band in 1982, Plaxico played with Chet Baker, Sonny Stitt, and Junior Cook, among others. The following year, he worked with Dexter Gordon and Hank Jones, then became part of Art Blakey's

Jazz Messengers. Plaxico played with the regular band, and also played with a special edition that toured and recorded in Japan that same year. Plaxico did sessions with Dizzy Gillespie and David Murray, and with Blakey, and later recorded with fellow Messengers Terence Blanchard and Donald Harrison for Concord. He made his recording debut for Muse in the late '80s, and continued doing sessions for them in the '90s. Plaxico has recorded with Steve Coleman, Greg Osby, Robin Eubanks, Geri Allen, Mike Cain, Kenny Davis, and David Gilmore, among others. Both his sessions are available on CD. —*Ron Wynn*

★ **Plaxico** / **i.** 1991 / Muse 5389
This fine young bassist makes a good though derivative hard bop and mainstream statement. —*Ron Wynn*

KING PLEASURE (Clarence Beeks)

b. Mar. 24, 1922, Oakdale, TN, **d.** Mar. 21, 1981, Los Angeles, CA
Vocals / Bop, ballads & blues
Regardless of whether Eddie Jefferson or King Pleasure invented "vocalese," the art of putting lyrics to jazz solos, Pleasure (aka Clarence Beeks) had the first huge hit. His version of "Moody's Mood for Love" on Prestige with Jefferson's lyrics did so well in 1952 that it landed Pleasure a label deal. He also had success with "Red Top" and "Parker's Mood." Though he continued recording for Prestige, Jubilee, and Aladdin, and for HiFi Jazz and United Artists, Pleasure did not enjoy sustained success. His style influenced the team of Lambert, Hendricks, and Ross as well as more contemporary performers like Al Jarreau and Manhattan Transfer. He and Ross, as well as Hendricks, subsequently recorded together. Several vintage Pleasure sessions have been reissued. —*Ron Wynn and Bob Porter*

★ **Source** / Feb. 19, 1952-Dec. 7, 1954 / Prestige 24017
1952-1960. A twofer of essential material from the essential master of vocalese. —*Michael G. Nastos*

○ **King Pleasure Sings with Annie Ross** / 1952-1954 / Prestige 217

○ **Moody's Mood for Love** / **i.** 1992 / Blue Note 84463

DANIEL PONCE

b. 1953
Percussion / Latin jazz, world fusion
One of the finest star percussionists to come from Cuba since the heyday of Chano Pozo, Candido Cameron, and Armanda Peraza, Daniel Ponce displays rhythmic mastery of both traditional Cuban sounds and contemporary African-American rhythms. Ponce's grandfather was a famous bata drum player and gave his grandson his earliest training. Ponce played cowbell with Los Brillantes in Havana at age 11. He switched to congas as a teen, and played with Comparso Federacion Estuniantil Universitario. He came to America in 1980, and soon moved to New York. Andy and Jerry Gonzales invited Ponce to sit in at the Village Gate, where he met saxophonist Paquito D'Rivera. He later played on a pair of D'Rivera albums, and did sessions for Eddie Palmieri. But producer/bassist Bill Laswell really aided Ponce. He landed him a session with Herbie Hancock that led to the critically and commercially successful release, *Future Shock*, in the mid-'80s. Ponce did several sessions for OAO and Celluloid, and issued his first session as a leader, *New York Now*, in 1984. He's also led a pair of New York groups: New York Now and Jazzbata. Unfortunately, Ponce's session is no longer available on CD. —*Ron Wynn and Michael G. Nasto*

★ **Arawe** / **i.** 1987 / Antilles 842659
Ponce is a charismatic conga player as hot as any. There are six pieces here, five written by Ponce, played by mostly nine-to ten-piece bands with one quintet cut. Ponce gets help from notables Yomo Toro, Nicky Marrero, Steve Turre, Isidro Bobadilla, Law Soloff, and Vernon Reid. —*Michael G. Nastos*

○ **Chango Te Llama** / **i.** 1991 / Mango 9877

The large ensemble is burning hot. This is an excellent companion to *Arawe*. Ponce wrote three selections. There is lots of vocalist Tito Allen and saxophonists Mario Rivera and Dave Snachez. —*Michael G. Nastos*

JEAN-LUC PONTY

b. Sep. 29, 1942, Avranches, France
Violin / Early jazz-rock

A wide-ranging violinist and one of the finest soloists in the instrument's history, French musician Jean-Luc Ponty helped popularize the use of electronics among string players. He also developed a style that mixed swing, bebop, free, and modal jazz, as well as jazz-rock and pop. He sometimes plays dynamic, intricately constructed, harmonically surprising solos; other times, he offers simple, bluesy statements with a prominent rhythmic focus. Ponty moved from amplifying an acoustic violin to using electric violins exclusively. He also began playing a violectra (an electric instrument tuned an octave below the violin). Ponty utilized wah-wah pedals, fuzztone, echoplex, and phase shifters creatively, sometimes using an electronic device with a conventional mute. He later began using a five-string electric violin, with the lowest string tuned to C. Ponty alternated between acoustic and electric in his '70s bands and added synthesizer.

Ponty's father was a violin teacher and director of the music school in Avranches, France, while his mother taught piano. Ponty began playing piano and violin at age five, and clarinet at age 11. He left school at age 13, opting to become a concert violinist. He studied for two years at the Paris Conservatory, winning the Premier prix at age 17. Ponty played for three years with the Concerts Lamoureux orchestra, where he was introduced to jazz. He started improvising on clarinet and tenor sax, and doing violin duets with Jef Gilson. Ponty was in the army during the early '60s, then turned to jazz exclusively. He appeared at the 1964 Antibes-Juan-les-Pins Jazz Festival leading a quartet. Ponty played and recorded in quartets and trios with Eddy Louis and Daniel Humair in the '60s, and also headed a quartet with Wolfgang Dauner, Niels-Henning Ørsted-Pedersen, and Humair. Ponty paid his first visit to America in the late '60s, and played at a violin workshop at the Monterey Jazz Festival. His quartet went to England in February of 1969. Ponty went to Los Angeles in March where he played and recorded with Frank Zappa, cutting the album *King Kong*. Later that year, Ponty joined George Duke's trio. Ponty returned to France and lead a free jazz band, the Jean-Luc Ponty Experience, in the early '70s. He returned to America in 1973, and toured with Zappa's Mothers of Invention band. He worked in 1974 and 1975 with the second edition of the Mahavishnu Orchestra.

Ponty began heading his own bands in 1975. He started recording for European labels in the mid-'60s, cutting sessions for Palm, Phillips, Saba/Pausa, and Electrola, before making his American recording debut on Pacific Jazz with Duke in 1969. Ponty has subsequently recorded for Blue Note, Pausa, MPS/BASF, Inner City, Atlantic, Columbia, Prestige, and Verve in the '70s and '80s. He's recorded with George Benson, Chick Corea, and Giorgio Gaslini, while doing a violin summit LP with Stuff Smith, Svend Asmussen, and Stephane Grappelli. Ponty has also included solo tracks on several albums. Currently, he has several titles, most of them Atlantic dates from the '70s, available on CD. —*Ron Wynn and Michael G. Nastos*

★ **Violin Summit** / **i.** Sep. 30, 1966 / Verve 821303
Violin Summit features Stuff Smith, Stephane Grappelli, Svend Asmussen, and Jean-Luc Ponty (with pianist Kenny Drew, bassist Niels-Henning Ørsted-Pedersen, and drummer Alex Riel) in concert (9/30/66). It was previously issued in America in 1969 by Prestige as part of its MPS series. The music comes off quite well, in large part probably because the four violinists are paired in different sets with all four actually featured together on only one take, "It Don't Mean a Thing If It Ain't Got That Swing." There is also a compatability within the various styles, all quite obvious, and nice

pacing along with a good standard of improvisation. This is a welcome reissue. —*Bob Rusch*, Cadence

○ **Canteloupe Island** / Mar. 1969 / Blue Note 632
The late '60s experiments that violinist Jean-Luc Ponty recorded with Frank Zappa are resurrected here. Thematically, it's Zappa's show, from compositions to arrangements, but Ponty plays with a fervor and imagination fresh to the rock idiom, if that generic term can be applied here. An outgrowth of Zappa's brilliant *Uncle Meat* and *Hot Rats*, this is a brave vista indeed, blending structural disciplines and rhythmic complexities with rock dynamics and jazz improvisations. Tracks like "King Kong" and "Twenty Small Cigars" have as much to do with shaping musical growth patterns in the last decade as *Bitches Brew*, which is no more a qualitative comparison than it is a rhetorical one. The tracks with George Duke are equally inquisitive, but more intimate and spontaneous. —*Mikal Gilmore*, Down Beat

○ **New Violin Summit** / **i.** 1972 / MPS 8

○ **Upon the Wings of Music** / Jan. 1975 / Atlantic 18138
Violinist Jean-Luc Ponty put together a well-paced, unified, and sweet-tempered LP in the high-energy vein, and it is eminently listenable. Although planned and recorded while Ponty was still playing in the Mahavishnu Orchestra, *Upon the Wings of Music* serves nonetheless as a sort of declaration of independence for the French fiddler, who, after detours with Frank Zappa and Mahavishnu, finally hits the open road with his own listenable concept. Like the recent work of his former employers, this is not a blowing date. Rather, it reflects Ponty's penchant for writing and his desire to play music more structured than that of the European free scene, which he left in 1972. Ponty, in fact, plays intelligently throughout, with authority and grace, but not always with excitement. When he does, as on the album's finale, he is a corker. The other main soloist is Patrice Rushen, then 21. Her synthesizer break on "Bowing" is an object lesson in how to match melody contours to timbre. Drummer Ndugu brings a heavier touch, and a more African rhythmic drive, to the contemporary drum style than most of his fusion colleagues, yet it prevents him from attaining that light speed exemplified by Billy Cobham. —*Neil Tesser*, Down Beat

Jean-Luc Ponty and Stephane Grappelli / Verve 835320
With Stephane Grappelli. This is a good combination. Two generations of jazz violin virtuosos. —*Michael G. Nastos*

ODEON POPE

b. Oct. 24, 1938, Ninety Six, SC
Trumpet, bandleader / Hard bop

A dynamic, hard-driving tenor sax soloist noted for his work with Max Roach, Odean Pope is one of the most fiery contemporary players around. His muscular tone, thrusts, honks, and vocal cries make every Pope solo memorable. He learned saxophone and harmony from Ray Bryant while growing up in Philadelphia. Jymie Merrit introduced Pope to Roach, and Pope toured Europe with Roach's quartet in the late '60s, and also accompanied Vi Redd during a London recording session. He formed Catalyst in 1971, a band that made four good jazz-rock and hard bop albums in the early '70s. Pope organized the Saxophone Choir in 1977, a band that featured eight saxes and a rhythm section. He headed the group until 1979, when he rejoined Roach for another European tour. Pope made four recordings with the Roach band in the '80s. He also led the Saxophone Choir again and recorded with a trio. Pope has a couple of dates available on CD. —*Ron Wynn*

○ **Saxophone Shop, The** / **i.** Sep. 1987 / Soul Note 1129
The Saxophone Choir is distinct from the World Saxophone Quartet or the 29th Street Saxophone Quartet in that the reeds (outside of Odean Pope's lead voice) are used primarily for embellishment. Pope surrounds himself with this cadre of mass saxes composed of barroom jam session survivors (Bootise Barnes), young upstarts (Joe Sudler, whose name is misspelled on the album jacket, is a Philadelphia big-band leader in his own right), and session men (Julian

Priestly). The other saxes never sound too charty, which can be a problem since there is little interwining amongst the horns. Pope is one of the few saxophonists to use multiphonics without sounding self-conscious. It is, in fact, the basis of his style, as "Elixir" and "Almost Like Me, Part 2" demonstrate. Philadelphia composers have always been deft musical portraitists. The vibrancy and edge of the streets can be heard in McCoy Tyner's "Blues on the Corner" or Lee Morgan's "The Rump Roller." With the exception of the two lovely ballads, "Cis" and "Doug's Prelude," there is a pulse here that could only be from Philadelphia. —*Ludwig Van Trikt, Cadence*

★ **Out for a Walk** / **i.** Oct. 1990 / Moers 02072

○ **Ponderer, The** / **i.** May 19, 1992 / Soul Note 121229

COLE PORTER

b. 1891, **d.** Oct. 15, 1964
Composer / Ballads & blues
Many arguments could be generated over whether Cole Porter or Irving Berlin should be considered America's greatest tunesmith. Both wrote music and lyrics; it's clearly a pick 'em situation. Porter had violin and piano lessons as a child, and studied law and music at Harvard, courtesy of a rich grandfather. His grandfather was appalled that Porter would consider music as a career and never forgave him. Porter was in the French army during World War I, and spent the '20s in Paris as the husband of a wealthy woman. He began scoring hits in that decade, though "I'm in Love Again," which Porter wrote in 1924, didn't click until 1929. The list of Porter shows and films is immense; his lyrics were literate, sophisticated, yet could be charming, suggestive, and even naughty. His first show was *Paris* in 1928; it included "Let's Do It." That was followed by *Frenchmen* in 1929, which contained "You Do Something to Me." Porter returned to New York in 1930, but was a lifelong Parisian in his heart. *Wake Up and Dream, The New Yorkers, The Gay Divorcee, Jubilee, Leave it to Me,* and *Kiss Me Kate* are only a few of his marvelous shows. The song list is just as impressive: "What Is This Thing Called Love," "Love For Sale," "Anything Goes," "You're the Top," "Begin the Beguine," and "Count Your Blessings," for starters. There were also films such as *Silk Stockings, Born to Dance, Broadway Melody of 1940, High Society,* and *Night and Day.* Porter's legs were crushed by a horse in 1937, and he became a semi-invalid who endured numerous operations for the rest of his life. He finally lost his right leg in 1958, only four years after his wife died. But his songs live on; numerous anthologies and songbooks devoted to his music have been issued and are available on CD, including the recent Smithsonian four-disc set issued in 1993. —*Ron Wynn*

★ **Cole Porter Collection** / **i.** 1926-1941 / Jass 632
A delightful 25-song anthology of vintage (1928-1941) recordings of obscure but equally arch Porter songs. Performers include Ethel Waters, the Dorsey Brothers, the Paul Whiteman Orchestra, and others. —*Mark A. Humphrey*

BUD POWELL (Earl Powell)

b. Sep. 27, 1924, New York, NY, **d.** Jul. 31, 1966, New York, NY
Piano, composer / Bop
Bop's tragic, remarkable piano genius, Bud Powell made amazing stylistic inroads while battling severe illness during his entire career. His approach of playing quick, fast melody lines with the right hand and oddly spaced, dissonant chords with the left became the standard bop approach from the mid-'40s on. Powell's ability to invent and rework melodies was unsurpassed; he was amazing also at changing and varying his phrasing, moving from short, choppy statements to lengthy, flowing lines at will. Powell, like Oscar Peterson, was at his best in the trio setting. He could work off a bassist and drummer, and could compliment, compete with, or elevate them. He was one pianist who could hold his own with any saxophonist or trumpeter on any song (at least when lu-

cid). He was also an underrated composer; Powell numbers like "Dance of the Infidels," "Tempus Fugit," and "Bouncing with Bud" became anthems.

Powell began to make his reputation in early '40s jam sessions in New York. Thelonious Monk was his mentor; he took the young Powell under his wing and carefully instructed him. Powell played in Cootie Williams's (who was Powell's guardian) band, but, in 1945, suffered a severe head injury (Williams said he was beaten by police). This occurred in the midst of an ugly racial incident, and triggered what would be a recurring series of nervous breakdowns and frightening incidents that plagued Powell for the rest of his life. Of course, his extensive use of drugs and alcohol didn't help matters either. Powell had to return to the hospital in 1948 and 1951, and was subjected periodically to electroshock treatments. Whenever he could play during the late '40s and early '50s, Powell astonished audiences and musicians alike. There were wonderful late '40s and early '50s sessions on Blue Note. Powell recorded with Max Roach, Curley Russell, George Duvivier, Art Taylor, Fats Navarro, Sonny Rollins, Roy Haynes, Tommy Potter, and Curtis Fuller, among others. There were some trio sessions and one solo session for Clef, Norgran, and Verve. But Powell began to cut back his appearances in the late '50s, and his mental health went steadily downhill.

In 1953, he played at the famous Massey Hall Concert with Charlie Parker and Dizzy Gillespie, among others, and a separate, first-rate trio session was made during the concert. But two years later, during a reunion concert, Powell had to be helped off the stage as both his and Parker's behavior degenerated into a sad and bizarre spectacle. He did some uneven trio dates for RCA in 1956 and 1957. Powell moved to Paris in 1959, and played in a trio with Kenny Clarke for three years. They backed Dexter Gordon on a 1963 session, and they recorded for Xanadu in 1960. Powell recorded for ESP, Black Lion, Columbia, Steeplechase, and others while in Paris. He returned to America in 1964, but a disastrous Carnegie Hall concert in 1965 led him to quit music altogether. Powell was dead by August of the next year. His fantastic Blue Note material has been reissued by Mosaic on a comprehensive boxed set. This is the finest Powell set available. There are single-disc reissues on several import labels; all five Steeplechase volumes are available, as are the Black Lion and Vogue sessions. Other import companies, such as Royal Jazz, Jazz Door, and Mythic Sound, have '50s and '60s Powell trio, combo, and large band reissues in circulation. —*Ron Wynn*

★ **Complete Bud Powell Blue Note Recordings** / Mosaic 116

○ **Shaw Nuff** / **i.** 1945-1960 / EPM 5167
An anthology with performances by pianist Bud Powell from three periods. Some songs were done in 1945 (the best), others in 1959 and 1960. Powell's work was in its formative stages in the '40s but was exploding and maturing. He'd become an established star in the late '50s, and on the '59 and '60 tracks he plays with an easy confidence and relentless skill that's technically superior to the '40s material, but lacks the same passion. —*Ron Wynn*

○ **Alternate Takes** / Aug. 9, 1949-May 23, 1963 / Mainstream 724
Various alternate or unissued takes by the great hard bop pianist Bud Powell recorded in the late '40s. These were gathered on an album and issued by Blue Note in the late '60s. While the playing's mostly excellent, there's really nothing here that hasn't been surpassed on other Powell releases. However, it's still good to hear almost any Powell piano. —*Ron Wynn*

★ **Amazing Bud Powell–Vol. 1** / 1949-1953 / Blue Note 81503
Vol. 1: You don't need these two volumes if you get the full set; otherwise, these are seminal late '40s sessions. CD bonus cuts. —*Ron Wynn*

★ **Amazing Bud Powell–Vol. 2, The** / May 1951-Aug. 1953 / Blue Note 81504

☆ **Bud Powell's Moods** / Jul. 1950-Feb. 1951 / Mercury 610

★ **Genius of Bud Powell–Vol. 1, The** / Jul. 1950-Feb. 1951 / PolyGram 827901

These trio sides represent pianist Bud Powell at his very best. Particularly stunning are the uptempo tracks such as "Tempus Fugit," "Sweet Georgia Brown," and "Just One of Those Things," in which he creates a continuously brilliant yet highly emotional line that moves at breathtaking speed. But then some of the medium tempo swingers like "Celia" and "Parisian Thoroughfare" make for equally strong music even if they are not so obviously stunning. Even about half of the slow ballads maintain this high standard, notably the powerfully muscular "I'll Keep Loving You," one of several of Powell's fine original tunes included here. Other ballad performances such as "Body and Soul" tend to suffer from the blandness that mars much of Powell's later work and the work of his disciples. In taking certain aspects of Art Tatum and adding some emotional spice from Thelonious Monk, then simplifying it all down into a line of single notes, Powell creates some fine music that isn't, however, as satisfying as that of either of his main influences. This can be ascertained by listening to the Tatumesque "Yesterdays" and the Monkish "Last Time I Saw Paris." But his playing here is far superior to that of his multitude of followers, who jumped onto his easy way out (just as saxophonists have since been doing with John Coltrane). What most of his followers, with a few exceptions like Barry Harris and Elmo Hope, forgot to include was the most important ingredient of all—the emotional content—hence their evaporation into utter blandness. In a sense, Powell was no longer a pianist since his single-handed lines could just as well have been those of a horn player—no doubt Charlie Parker was another important influence. Just as Tatum's orchestral style virtually demanded that he play unaccompanied, so Powell's linear approach was designed to be filled out by bass and drums. It is therefore particularly interesting to hear the unique unaccompanied fast and medium tracks in this collection, like "The Fruit" and "Just One of Those Things." On these there is a curious tension between the continually forward-driving right hand and the occasional staccato stop/go chords on the left. —*Martin Davidson, Cadence*

★ **Genius of Bud Powell–Vol. 2, The** / Jul. 1950-Feb. 1951 / Verve 827901

○ **Charles Mingus Trios** / i. Mar. 1953 / Jazz Door 1213

○ **Legacy, The** / i. Mar. 1953-1964 / Jazz Door 1204

○ **Jazz at Massey Hall–Vol. 1** / May 15, 1953 / Original Jazz Classics

○ **Jazz at Massey Hall–Vol. 2** / May 15, 1953 / Debut

This is the less famous half of the 5/15/53 Massey Hall concert. These are the trio (Charles Mingus, bass; Max Roach, drums) sides that also appeared on a prior Prestige twofer. Also on this LP are four tracks with pianist Powell, George Duvivier (b), and Art Taylor (d) and one track ("Bass-Ically Speaking") which, though not credited as such, has Billy Taylor (p), Mingus, and Taylor. This last track contains a miserably recorded though interesting exploration by Mingus on fingered and bowed bass. However, on the record as a whole, the brilliance comes overwhelmingly from Powell. —*Bob Rusch, Cadence*

★ **Amazing Bud Powell–Vol. 3, The** / 1956 / Blue Note 81571

○ **Groovin' at the Blue Note (1959-1961)** / i. 1957-Jan. 1961 / Mythic Sound 6005

○ **Amazing Bud Powell–Vol. 4: Time Waits** / May 1958 / Blue Note 46820

The fourth volume in a series featuring hard bop piano legend Bud Powell during an extensive series of recordings for Blue Note in the early '50s. These are items that weren't included in any of the first three volumes or the CD reissue that covered them. —*Ron Wynn*

Scene Changes / Dec. 29, 1958 / Blue Note 46529

This late '80s Blue Note reissue is uneven but has plenty of Powell fireworks. —*Ron Wynn*

Time Waits / May 25, 1959 / Blue Note 46820

A bonus cut in the 1987 reissue. Good sound and exceptional Powell solos. —*Ron Wynn*

○ **Cookin' at Saint Germain (1957-1959)** / i. Nov. 1959 / Mythic Sound 6003

○ **Bud in Paris** / Jun. 15, 1960 / Xanadu 102

Pianist Bud Powell had his on and off moments during his last years, but on this recording, recorded 3½ years before his death, he is very much *on*, lucid and direct. The tormented brilliance that became characteristic of his later work is not present here; here is a young, alert, and futuristic personality. A fine set of music with Gilbert Rovere (b) and Kansas Fields (d) completing the trio. —*Bob Rusch, Cadence*

○ **Relaxin' at Home (1961-1964)** / i. 1961-1964 / Mythic Sound 6004

Bouncing with Bud / Apr. 1962 / Delmark 406

1987 reissue of a good set. Delmark deserves kudos for putting this out again. —*Ron Wynn*

○ **Return to Birdland (1964)** / i. Sep. 1964 / Mythic Sound 6009

○ **Award at Birdland (1964)** / i. Oct. 1964 / Mythic Sound 6010

○ **Invisible Cage, The** / i. Sep. 1974 / Black Lion 153

Recorded in Paris in July 1964, two years to the day before Bud Powell's death and only several weeks before what was to be his last return from Europe to the States, this album gives us a sober picture of the artist in his declining years. Some brighter spots come on the delightful "Like Someone In Love." After an Art Tatumesque opening, Powell slides into a relaxed, medium-groove tempo and renders a chorus in effortless, swinging George Shearing-style block chords. This is easily the album's most relaxed and successful track. "Una Noche Con Francis," named for Francis Paudras, the French commercial artist who befriended Powell and accompanied him when he returned to work at Birdland, is a bright calypso tune, which except for a few fluffed notes is largely successful. Given the adverse circumstances of the later years of this artist's life—the tuberculosis and schizophrenia, perhaps even his uneasiness about returning to meet the test of working at Birdland—I suppose the surprising thing is that Powell fares as well as he does here. —*Jon Balleras, Down Beat*

○ **Bud Powell Trio at the Golden Circle, Vol. 1** / i. Jan. 1980 / Steeple Chase 6001

For students and serious collectors of pianist Bud Powell recordings, this first volume of previously unissued masters is a must. These sessions were recorded when Powell's loneliness and depression seemed to blossom as in a garden of moonless, windless darkness. The importance of these sides lies in the fact that they are "living transcriptions" of Powell's music, vintage bop in slow motion. What we find on these sides are the roots and foundations of the bop idiom, via Powell, at a tempo that makes it possible to hear better what he is doing. His "terrace effect" of running two distinct harmonies, with right and left hands playing rhythmic and harmonic lines in alternating keys, is explored to its fullest in the classic "Cherokee" and can be heard in "Star Eyes" from this date. —*Bradley Parker-Sparrow, Down Beat*

Best of Bud Powell, The / Blue Note 93204

MEL POWELL (Melvin Epstein)

b. Feb. 12, 1923, New York, NY
Piano, composer / Swing

A former Pulitzer Prize winner, composer, pianist, and arranger, Mel Powell doesn't play much jazz these days, and hasn't played any for a long time. But in the '40s, he was a prime player, composer, and arranger. His playing was unpredictable, challenging, and impressive, though not flashy or bluesy. Powell led a traditional jazz band at age 12. He joined Benny Goodman at age 19, and was a member of the CBS orchestra under Raymond Scott. His military service included a tour and recording session with Glen Miller's Air Force band. Powell also recorded with the Jazz Club

American Hot Band in Paris in the mid-'40s that included Django Reinhardt and Ray McKinley. After his discharge in 1945, Powell recorded with Goodman, then went to Los Angeles, where he worked with studios and recorded with Jazz at the Philharmonic. He worked periodically with Goodman, and also led groups in the late '40s. Powell then decided to study composition with Paul Hindemith in the early '50s; he quit film and studio work. Powell had composed pieces such as "The Earl" and "Mission to Moscow" for Goodman. Powell worked with Goodman again in the mid- and late '50s, and worked with Bobby Hackett in the mid-'60s. But Powell decided to become a contemporary classical composer, and became heavily involved in serial and electronic music. Powell was a teacher at Queens College and at Yale from the mid-'50s to the end of the '60s. He became Dean of Music at the California Institute of Arts in Valencia in 1969, and became a fellow in 1976. Powell surprised many observers by playing on the SS *Norway's* Floating Jazz Festival out of Miami with Ruby Braff, Mel Lewis, Bob Wilber, Warren Vache, and Svend Asmussen in 1986. In 1987, he surprised even more observers with the *The Return of Mel Powell* on Chiaroscuro with Benny Carter, Howard Alden, Milt Hinton, and Louis Bellson. Powell's been battling a muscular disease in his legs for the last few years. He won a Pulitzer for composition in the early '90s. Powell began recording on Commodore with Joe Bushkin in the '40s, and did other sessions on Pausa, Vogue, Chiaroscuro, and Vanguard. He has a couple of dates available on CD. —*Ron Wynn*

★ **World is Waiting, The** / Feb. 4, 1942 / Commodore 543
The Mel Powell-Joe Bushkin album contains the Powell session of 2/4/42 with Powell (p), Billy Butterfield (tpt), Lou McGarity (tb), Al Morgan (b), and Kansas Fields (d). The titles are "When Did You Leave Heaven," "The World is Waiting for the Sunrise," "Blue Skies," and "Mood at Twilight." In addition, there is Powell's big-band experimental session of 6/3/46 with "Lover Man" and two takes of "Avalon." The Bushkin session of 5/24/44 comprises Bushkin (p), Ernie Figueroa (tpt), Bill Harris (tb), Zoot Sims (ts), Sid Weiss (b), and Specs Powell (d). The tracks include "Fade Out," plus both regular and alternate takes of "Pickin'" at the Pic," "Oh, Lady Be Good," and "Georgia On My Mind." — *Shirley Klett*, Cadence

Unavailable Mel Powell / Dec. 10, 1947-Dec. 31, 1947 / PA/USA 9023
Late '40s. Some of his top compositions from a peak period as a jazz writer and player. —*Ron Wynn*

○ **Columbia Special Products** / i. Dec. 1979 / XFL 14943
Return of Mel Powell / i. 1987 / Chiaroscuro 301
This Pulitzer Prize winner returns to his jazz roots. Benny Carter (as) makes this session shine. —*Ron Wynn*

SELDON POWELL

b. Nov. 15, 1928, Lawrenceville, VA
Tenor saxophone, flute / Swing, big band, soul-jazz, progressive big band
A veteran tenor saxophonist and flutist, Seldon Powell has adjusted and honed his style over the years, and is flexible enough to play anything from swing to hard bop and anything in between. He's not a great soloist, an ambitious composer, or a spectacular arranger; he's simply a good, consistent player who's survived many changes and trends to remain active from the late '40s until the '90s. Powell was classically trained in New York, then worked briefly with Tab Smith in 1949 before joining Lucky Millinder and recording with him in 1950. Powell was in the military in 1950 and 1951, then became a studio musician in New York. He worked and recorded with Louis Bellson, Neal Hefti, Friedrich Gulda, Johnny Richards, and Billy Ver Planck in the mid and late '50s. Powell also played with Sy Oliver and Erskine Hawkins, and studied at Juilliard. He traveled to Europe with Benny Goodman's band in 1958, and worked briefly with Woody Herman. Powell was a staff player for

ABC television in the '60s, and also played and recorded with Buddy Rich, Bellson, Clark Terry, and Ahmed Abdul-Malik. He did a number of soul-jazz and pop dates in the late '60s and early '70s, including a session with Groove Holmes and big band dates backing Gato Barbieri and Dizzy Gillespie. Powell was principal soloist in Gerry Mulligan's 16-piece band at the JVC Jazz Festival in New York in 1987. He has recorded as a leader for Roost and for Epic. Currently, Powell does not have any sessions available on CD. —*Ron Wynn*

★ **Seldon Powell Sextet** / 1956 / Roost 2220

CHANO POZO

b. 1915, d. 1948
Percussion / Latin jazz
Despite his short career, percussionist Chano Pozo played a pivotal role in expanding the rhythmic profile of Latin music in jazz. His playing and vocals came directly from the Cuban Lucumi faith, which is derived from West African practices and rhythmic tradition. When Pozo and bongo player Chiquitico performed at a 1947 Carnegie Hall concert with Dizzy Gillespie, their interaction, rhythms, and energy opened eyes to the prospects for Jazz and Latin music to mate successfully. Though Machito's band with Mario Bauza proved the same thing, this was the first time an ostensibly straight jazz band had made the mixture work. Unfortunately, Pozo made his debut in 1947 and was killed in December of 1948. During that period, he did appear on the Gillespie albums *Dizzy Goes to College, Afro-Cuban Suite,* and *Melodic Revolution.* Pozo also played with Milt Jackson and Tadd Dameron. He didn't record any albums on his own as a leader. Reissues featuring Pozo include *Dizzy Gillespie Big Band, Afro-Cuban Suite,* and *Melodic Revolution.* —*Ron Wynn*

ANDRE PREVIN (Andreas Ludwig Priwin)

b. Apr. 6, 1929, Berlin, Germany
Piano, conductor / Cool, swing, bop
A conductor and classical pianist of immense standing, André Previn has also amassed some impressive jazz credentials. While he's not one of the most spectacular or dazzling stylists and is certainly not a great soloist, Previn has made many creditable recordings and has enjoyed major crossover success. He started piano lessons as a child in his native Berlin, and later was booted out of the Conservatory in a blatant anti-Semitic incident. His family immediately went to Paris, and then to Los Angeles after they received their visas. Previn played piano and did the score for a Jose Iturbi film at age 16. He split time between classical, film, and jazz material until he was drafted in the early '50s, and was stationed in San Francisco. Previn scored numerous films in the '50s, '60s, and early '70s, among them Oscar winners *Gigi, Porgy and Bess, Irma La Douce,* and *My Fair Lady.* During the '40s, '50s, and '60s, Previn made over 20 trio albums that ranged from Fats Waller material to jazz versions of Broadway shows. The trio of Previn, Leroy Vinnegar, and Shelly Manne struck commercial gold with *My Fair Lady* in 1956. Previn had a string of albums make the charts in the '60s, among them *Like Love, A Touch of Elegance, André Previn in Hollywood,* and a remake of *My Fair Lady.* He concentrated on conducting and classical music during much of the mid- and late '60s, and through the '70s. But Previn returned to jazz in the early '80s, working with Manne and Monty Budwig, cutting an album of rags with Itzhak Perlmann, and working in a quintet with Perlmann, Red Mitchell, Manne, and Jim Hall on the session *A Different Kind of Blue* that again resulted in a Previn date making the pop charts. This group did another album in 1981, and Previn recorded with Ella Fitzgerald and Niels-Henning Ørsted-Pedersen in 1983. He teamed up with Ray Brown and Mundell Lowe for a jazz date, and with Thomas Stevens for a repertory set of prerock standards in the '90s. Previn has many dates available on CD. —*Ron Wynn with Michael G. Nastos*

★ **Double Play!** / May 11, 1957 / Original Jazz Classics 157
This is a two-piano (André Previn and Russ Freeman) with rhythm (drummer Shelly Manne) date (4/30, 5/11/57) with a baseball theme. The thematic perspective doesn't get in the way of the music, and the two pianists work more in harmony and counterpoint than in juxtaposition to each other. Together they bring on a reflective whimsy somewhat reminiscent of Vince Guaraldi. It is a rather containable date, but quite nice on an easy level. —*Bob Rusch*, Cadence

Pal Joey / Oct. 28-29, 1957 / Contemporary 637
Shelly Manne (d) and Red Mitchell (b) put some snap into Previn's musical menu. —*Ron Wynn*

Gigi / Apr. 7-8, 1958 / Contemporary 407
The Shelly Manne (d)/ Red Mitchell (b) duo helps lift the session's energy level. —*Ron Wynn*

Like Previn! / Feb. 20-Mar. 1, 1960 / Contemporary 170
Before he became a famous maestro, Previn was a decent, sometimes superior, jazz pianist. This is solid, occasionally excellent, mainstream material. —*Ron Wynn*

After Hours / Mar. 29, 1989 / Telarc 83302

Uptown / Mar. 9-10, 1990 / Telarc 83303
This recent Previn is nicely done but doesn't have the sparkle of his Prestige sessions. —*Ron Wynn*

○ **Old Friends** / Aug. 1991 / Telarc 83309
Superb trio recordings that marked the return of well-known classical conductor André Previn to intimate jazz recording. He teams with bassist Ray Brown and guitarist Mundell Lowe, and the three complement each other expertly, while their solos are tasteful and concise. —*Ron Wynn*

BOBBY PREVITE

Drums, bandleader / Modern creative
A freewheeling drummer and percussionist whose compositions and sessions range from jazz-rock, fusion, and new age to free and blues, Bobby Previte has played with several of the "downtown" performers, including Wayne Horovitz and John Zorn. He began recording as a leader in the mid-'80s, and has done sessions for Sound Aspects, Gramavision, and Enja. Previte's done sessions with Robin Eubanks, Marty Erhlich, Tom Varner, Jerome Harris, and Elliot Sharp, among others. All his dates are available on CD. —*Ron Wynn*

Music of the Moscow Circus / i. 1984 / Rhino 79466

★ **Claude's Late Morning** / i. 1989 / Gramavision 79448
The daring drummer doesn't tailor his work to conventional jazz tastes. Excellent playing, erratic compositions. —*Ron Wynn*

Empty Suits / May 1990 / Gramavision 79447
○ **Weather Clear Track Fast** / i. 1991 / Enja 79667
○ **Pushing the Envelope** / Mesa Blue Moon 79449

SAMMY PRICE (Samuel Blythe Price)

b. Oct. 6, 1908, Honey Grove, Texas, d. Apr. 14, 1992
piano, leader / Stride, swing, boogie-woogie
Among the last of the vintage stomping barrelhouse, blues, and boogie pianists, Sammy Price actually got his start professionally as a singer and dancer with Alphonso Trent's band in the late '20s. He arrived in Kansas City in 1930 and spent three years immersing himself in the swing sound of Count Basie and Pete Johnson before moving to Chicago and later Detroit. Price moved to New York in 1938, becoming house pianist for American Decca and providing the pianistic foundation for great sessions featuring such vocalists as Trixie Smith and Sister Rosetta Tharpe. He subsequently worked on 52nd Street, appearing at such clubs as the Famous Door and Cafe Society. Price organized the first jazz festival supervised and administered by African Americans in Philadelphia in 1946 and later appeared at the Nice Festival with Mezz Mezzrow. Price worked a decade with Red Allen, until the latter's death in 1967. —*Ron Wynn*

○ **Blues and Boogies** / Nov. 14, 1955 / Black & Blue 33.040

Price is heard here on solo piano and vocal, playing eight Price originals and "See See Rider." It is good to hear him alone on this rare solo album, recorded in France. —*Michael G. Nastos*

☆ **In Paris** / i. 1956 / Brunswick 54037
With Sidney Bechet (ss), Price's "Bluesicians" hit on old-time and good-time standards—Bechet, as always, in good tune. —*Michael G. Nastos*

Rock with Sam Price / i. 1956 / Savoy 14004

Price Is Right, The / Feb. 21, 1956-Feb. 22, 1956 / Jazztone 1260

Midnight Boogie / i. Nov. 1969 / Black & Blue 59.025

Barrelhouse and Blues / Dec. 4, 1969 / Black Lion 760159

★ **Fire** / May 1, 1975 / Black & Blue 233079
The Texas blues and jazz pianist plays in good-time and old-time format with the basic trio of J.C. Heard (d), Carl Pruitt (b), and guests Ted Buckner (tpt), The Mighty Flea (Gene Connors, tb), and Doc Cheatham (tpt). Includes ten Price originals. —*Michael G. Nastos*

Boogie & Jazz Classics / i. May 1975 / Black & Blue 59.111
Price, delightful, romping pianist in vintage barrelhouse and boogie-woogie genres, interpreted, reworked, and remade a series of traditional blues and jazz tunes on this fine 1975 release. Everything, from song selection to solos, is wonderful. —*Ron Wynn*

Just Right / Nov. 2, 1977 / Black & Blue 33.154
A sextet with George Kelly (sax) and Freddie Lonzo (tb) plays two of Price's tunes, five standards (two by W.C. Handy), and one by trumpeter Johnny Lettman. —*Michael G. Nastos*

Sweet Substitute / Nov. 1, 1979 / Sackville 3024

○ **Paradise Valley Duets** / i. Feb. 26-Feb. 28, 1988 / Parkwood 112
Recorded live in Windsor, Ontario, this album features J.C. Heard (d), George Benson (g), and Marcus Belgrave (tpt) playing nine standards and one blues from Price and Belgrave. This is a delight. One whole side features Price and the legendary drummer Heard. Precious Texas piano stomps and jazz. —*Michael G. Nastos*

○ **And the Blues Singers** / Wolf 007
○ **Rib Joint/Roots of Rock & Roll** / Savoy 4417

JULIAN PRIESTER (Julian Anthony Priester)

b. Jun. 29, 1935, Chicago, IL
Trombone, synthesizer / Hard bop, modern creative
A good, sometimes outstanding trombonist who's also dabbled in electronics, Julian Priester has played blues, hard bop, jazz-rock, and free music, has done studio and session work, and has led his own band. His range and facility on trombone are excellent, even if his taste and compositions are sometimes questionable. Priester studied piano as a child, played euphonium in his teens, then changed to trombone. He played with Muddy Waters and Bo Diddley in the early '50s, then worked with Sun Ra's Arkestra from 1954 to 1956. Priester worked with Dinah Washington in 1957, then joined Max Roach's band that, at various times, also included Eric Dolphy, Booker Little, and Clifford Jordan. Priester also recorded with Abby Lincoln. He departed Roach's band to do studio and session work in New York, and later joined Duke Ellington's orchestra in 1969 and 1970. Priester joined Herbie Hancock's electric group in 1970, and remained with him until 1973, when Hancock made the switch to funk. He recorded with Stanley Cowell and Red Garland's quintet in the late '70s, and with Dave Holland and George Gruntz's big band in the '80s. He has recorded as a leader for Jazzland and ECM. Currently, Priester does not have any sessions available on CD, but can be heard on reissued discs by Ra, Roach, Hancock, and others. —*Ron Wynn*

○ **Keep Swinging** / Jan. 11, 1960 / Riverside 316

Quintet. With Jimmy Heath (sax), Tommy Flanagan (p), and Elvin Jones (d). Excellent. —*Michael G. Nastos*

Spiritsville / Jul. 12, 1960 / Jazzland 925

★ **Love, Love** / Jun. 28, 1974-Sep. 12, 1974 / ECM 1044
Trombonist Priester is electrified; setting is extended. Hardhitting. —*Michael G. Nastos*

Polarization / Jan. 1977 / ECM 1098
More power to Priester. Ambitious music with Ray Obiedo (g) and Curtis Clark (p). —*Michael G. Nastos*

RUSSELL PROCOPE

b. Aug. 11, 1908, New York, NY, **d.** Jan. 21, 1981, New York, NY
Alto saxophone, clarinet / Swing, big band
A consistently solid section contributor and a dependable, if not intriguing, soloist, Russell Procope was a longtime Ellingtonian. He was also part of the John Kirby band of the '30s, one of the more popular small combos with whom he displayed a vital and highly original alto sax style. Procope studied violin for eight years before turning to clarinet and alto sax as a teenager. He played clarinet with Jelly Roll Morton in the late '20s, then worked with the big bands of Benny Carter, Chick Webb, Fletcher Henderson, and Teddy Hill in the late '20s and the '30s, touring Europe with the Hill orchestra. Procope enjoyed stardom in the Kirby band from 1938 to 1943. He played in shows while stationed in New York during his army tour of duty. He rejoined Kirby in 1945, then joined Ellington the next year. He remained with Ellington until 1974; he was never a star, but was someone who could be counted on, night after night, to play the music with energy and accuracy. Following Ellington's death, Procope worked in New York with Brooks Kerr in the musical *Ain't Misbehavin'.* He also led the group Ellingtonia. Procope can be heard playing on countless Ellington dates from the mid-'40s until the '70s. —*Ron Wynn*

★ **Persuasive Sax of Russell Procope, The** / **i.** 1956 / Dot 3010

ARTHUR PRYSOCK

b. Jan. 2, 1929
Vocals / Blues & jazz, ballads & blues
Arthur Prysock's commanding, robust, and deep baritone voice have made a huge impression through smash R&B, blues, and jazz-flavored recordings, and through commercials and radio spots. Arthur Prysock became famous in Buddy Johnson's band in 1944-1952. Prysock had a number of big R&B hits; his sister, Ella Johnson, had a number of big hits, too. He gained even more notoriety as a romantic ballad specialist in the '50s and '60s. During the '70s, Prysock did mainly club dates, but resurfaced as a recording artist in 1985 with some superb recordings. —*Ron Wynn*

○ **Like Who? Like Basie** / **i.** 1959 / United Artists 5024

○ **Basie Reunion (With Buck Clayton)** / **i.** 1962 / Swingville 2037

★ **Arthur Prysock and Count Basie** / **i.** Dec. 13-21, 1965 / Verve 827011
Seven saxes are led by Lockjaw Davis in a big band that drives Prysock. Eleven songs, the best of which are, "I Could Write a Book" and "Don't Go Fo' Strangers." —*Michael G. Nastos*

A Double Header with Arthur Prysock / **i.** 1965 / Old Town 2009

24 Karat Hits (2 LPs) / Sep. 21, 1966 / Verve 650

This Is My Beloved / Dec. 16, 1968 / PolyGram 827012

★ **Rockin' Good Way** / Jul. 29, 1985-Aug. 2, 1985 / Milestone 9139
Great comeback on records that helped reestablish Prysock among some who'd forgotten his '50s and '60s material. —*Ron Wynn*

This Guy's in Love with You / Aug. 1986 / Milestone 9146

Today's Love Songs Tomorrow / **i.** 1987-1988 / Milestone 9157
1988 release of some lush 1987 and 1988 sessions. Arthur Prysock sings wonderful ballads, backed by brother Red's good band. —*Ron Wynn*

○ **Silk and Satin** / Polydor 28901

Best Of / Verve 827013

☆ **Songs That Made Him Famous** / Decca
Good compilation of R&B and jukebox hits from '40s and '50s, some featuring Prysock's sister Ella Johnson. —*Ron Wynn*

TITO PUENTE

b. Apr. 20, 1923, New York, NY
Percussion, piano, vibraphone, timbales / Latin-jazz
Mario Bauza's death in 1993 left Tito Puente as the elder, reigning leader of Latin-jazz, salsa, and Afro-Cuban/Afro-Latin music. A magnificent timbales player, great bandleader, flamboyant entertainer, underrated vibes soloist, and a competent saxophonist, pianist, conga, and bongos player, Puente has done everything in Latin music. His original intention was to be a dancer, but that dream was ruined by a torn ankle tendon he suffered in an accident. Puente got early lessons in composition from Charlie Spivak, whom he met aboard the USS *Santee* in World War II. Puente later got formal training at Juilliard, which he attended after his discharge.

He worked in the bands of Noro Morales, Machito, and Pupi Campo before forming the Piccadilly Boys in the late '40s; they eventually became the Tito Puente Orchestra. With lead vocalist Vincentico Valdes, Puente's group made its recording debut on Secco. Puente was the first signee on Tico, then a new Latin label, in the late '40s. He made several albums for them in the late '40s and '50s, and helped popularize the "mambo" rage. His hit "Abaniquito" was a crossover smash, and RCA lured Puente from Tico for a string of albums in the '50s that mixed spicy dance beats and red-hot jam sessions. His single, "Para los Rumberos," was later covered by Santana, and his late '50s singles and albums were prominent in the rise of the chachacha sound. Puente took vintage Cuban chachacha songs and transferred them from the violin/flute charanga format to a brass and reeds, big band context.

His '50s bands included several major stars like Ray Barretto, Mongo Santamaria, Willie Bobo, and Johnny Pacheco. Puente enjoyed more crossover success in the early '60s for GNP, with albums combining Latin interpretations of Broadway shows, bossa nova, and big band dates. He returned to Tico and stayed there until the '80s, cutting numerous records in the Latin-jazz, Afro-Cuban, and Afro-Latin vein. Puente recorded with Santamaria, Bobo, and Carlos "Patato" Valdez; did a live date in Puerto Rico; played with the Tico All Stars and Fania All Stars; backed vocalists such as Manny Roman, Rolando Le Series, and Celia Cruz; cut "boogaloo" and pop dates; and recorded salsa and big band albums. Santana enjoyed a huge hit with a cover of his single "Oye Como Va."

Puente's bands and albums were the source for hearing the greatest Latin musicians and vocalists of the '70s. Puente was one of the artists featured in Jeremy Marre's television film, *Salsa '79.* Puente made several tours of Europe with the Latin Percussion Jazz Ensemble. They became an octet in the early '80s, and the album *Tito Puente and His Latin Ensemble on Broadway* won a Grammy in 1983 and gained credibility and exposure for Concord's Picante Latin line.

Puente has continued recording for Concord/Picante, and won another Grammy in 1985 for the album *Mambo Diablo* that included special guest George Shearing on "Lullaby of Birdland." Puente also did guest stints with Cal Tjader and Ray Barretto for '70s albums on Fantasy and Atlantic, and another guest stint with Barretto on an '81 CTI album. He's also recorded for Timeless, and was featured in the 1992 film *The Mambo Kings.* Some of his classic RCA dates are being reissued on CD by RCA/Bluebird, and his recent

Concord and Timeless material is also available on CD. Several of his numerous Tico releases are available on CD from Latin music stores. —*Ron Wynn and Michael G. Nastos*

Puente Goes Jazz / 1956 / RCA 66148
On this mid-'50s reissue, the king of Latin music strays into the realm of straightahead big-band jazz. These guys swing hard! With the full dynamic range you'd expect from the best big band. —*Len Paterson, Roots & Rhythm*

○ **Top Percussion** / i. 1957 / Bmgi 3264
A stunner from Puente's golden age, this 1957 recording brings together Tito, Mongo Santamaria, Willie Bobo, Aguabella, and Julito Collazo on percussion with vocalists that include Mercedita Valdez, in seven wonderful cuts of traditional and (then) contemporary Afro-Cuban skin-on-skin. Then as an unexpected gift, there is a seven-minute Latin-jazz suite featuring Puente's considerable jazz-arranger head and a powerful band with (Ripley, though, should still be living at this hour) Doc Severinson on lead trumpet. —*John Storm Roberts*

Let's Cha Cha with Puente / i. 1957 / RCA 1392

★ **Dance Mania** / i. 1958 / BMG 72252
What a treasure! We'd long despaired of finding anything from the days of Puente's young prime, and here's one of his two best albums reissued in CD! This is Puente's big band at the height of its powers, one of the great documents of New York Latin music and the sort of thing that established the man's claim to be one of the creators of big-band mambo. — *John Storm Roberts*

○ **On Broadway** / Jul. 1982 / Concord Jazz 4207
Among the various Latin groups, that of vibist/percussionist/bandleader Tito Puente has generally been more accessible to jazz fans than many of the others because he plays a hybrid form of Latin music that is readily recognized as jazz played over Latin-influenced rhythms. On this LP in Concord's Picante series, Ray Gonzales (tpt) is added to the regular group and enhances it to good effect in several places, notably as an echo to Jimmy Frisaura (tpt, tb) on "First Light," a feature for the latter trumpeter. The title piece features the guitar of Edgardo Miranda and Mario Riveria's flute (also tenor, soprano sax) while "Maria Cervantes" and "Sophisticated Lady" feature Puente's vibes. The program is well-varied in material, featured soloists, and rhythmically, and the recorded quality is fine. This makes a well-done release within this specialized field. —*Shirley Klett, Cadence*

★ **El Rey** / May 1984 / Concord Jazz 4250

Mambo Diablo / Dec. 1985 / Concord Jazz 4283

☆ **Un Poco Loco** / i. Jan. 1987 / Concord Jazz 4329
One of his best for the label. Puente's playing in both large and small contexts. —*Ron Wynn*

○ **Salsa Meets Jazz** / i. 1988 / Concord Jazz 4354
Excellent, maybe his best on the label. Phil Woods (as) joins the party and soars. —*Ron Wynn*

○ **Goza Me Timbal** / i. 1990 / Concord Jazz 4399
1990 release with extended timbales solos. The songs mix Sonny Rollins and Miles Davis landmarks with topical Puente numbers, extending both bop and Latin horizons. —*Ron Wynn, Rock & Roll Disc*

○ **Mambo King, The** / i. 1991 / RMM 80680
Puente's 100th album is a celebration of that fact, with a procession of vocalists, most of whom—like Celia Cruz—were professionally associated with him at one time or another. That doesn't make for a very tight concept, but recordings by musicians of Tito's generation didn't have concepts, they had music. So does this one, including a minor riot with Celia Cruz riding a big, burly mambo arrangement by a band full of just everybody, and a wonderful "El Bribon del Aguacero" with Chocolate Armenteros on trumpet. —*John Storm Roberts*

Out of This World / i. 1991 / Concord Jazz 4448

○ **Mambo of the Times** / i. 1992 / Concord Jazz 4499

A '92 CD session showing that the great Afro-Latin and Latin-jazz master Tito Puente continues to churn out tremendous music. This is his current band, and they're all first-rate jazz players and execute the tricky Latin clave beat easily. The CD version contains two bonus cuts. —*Ron Wynn*

Royal T / i. May 1993 / COJ
Timbale titan Tito Puente remains as much a force in Latin-jazz today as at any time in his astounding five decade-long career. *Royal T,* featuring a full Latin rhythm section and six horns, throbs with the energy of a big band but dances as lightly as the most quick-footed jazz combo. *Royal T* is notable for the fiery solo work of brass players like trombonist Art Velasco and trumpeter Tony Lujan and the choice of material. "Mambo Gallego," a Puente original, is a synthesis of salsa and flamenco that's among the leader's all-time best work. His choice of jazz standards like Charlie Parker's "Donna Lee" and Horace Silver's "Tokyo Blues" reflects Puente's genius at knowing just what non-Latin fare will adapt best to an Afro-Cuban treatment. —*Mark Holston, Jazziz*

Hits Candentes / RCA 8349

DUDU PUKWANA

b. Jul. 18, 1938, Port Elizabeth, South Africa, **d.** 1990
Piano, saxophone / World fusion
A fiery, inspirational alto saxophonist, Dudu Pukwana's wailing leads and indomitable spirit brilliantly fused township jive, free music, and honking R&B. Pukwana actually began on piano, taking lessons from his father at age ten. He joined Tete Mbambisa's Four Yanks as a teen in the late '50s after the family moved from Port Elizabeth to Cape Town, South Africa. He learned saxophone from Nick Moyake, and listened to imported American jazz and R&B records. Chris McGregor invited Pukwana to join the Blue Notes, an integrated band in the early '60s. Pukwana eventually left his homeland with the rest of the band, settled temporarily in Switzerland, then later moved to London. Pukwana stayed with McGregor's groups until 1969, when he joined Hugh Masekela's Union of South Africa in America. After they disbanded in 1970, Pukwana returned to England and formed his own band. They were initially called Spear, and later called Assegai. Pukwana also worked with Keith Tippett's Centipede, Jonas Gwangwa, Traffic, the Incredible String Band, Gwigwi Mrwebi, Sebothane Bahula's Jabula, Harry Miller's Isipingo, and the Louis Moholo Unit. Pukwana recorded with Mrwebi in 1970, and made two albums with Assegai before founding a new edition of Spear in 1972. He also played that year on Masekela's *Home Is Where the Music Is* Chisa session. The new Spear, which included Mongezi Feza, Moholo, and Miller, plus Bixo Mngqikana, made some excellent albums, among them *In the Townships* and *Flute Music,* before they disbanded in 1978. Pukwana formed the big band, Zila, recorded with them, and continued heading the group until his death from liver failure in 1990. Sadly, none of Pukwana's sessions are available in America on CD. —*Ron Wynn*

In the Township / i. 1973 / Earthworks 90884
An excellent recording with Mongezi Feza, Louis Moholo, and Harry Miller. —*Michael G. Nastos*

★ **Diamond Express** / i. Oct. 1978 / Freedom 41044
An early '70s recording of this saxophonist, with the late trumpeter Mongezi Feza, in their last meeting before Feza died of pneumonia. Squeaky sax and ensemble in an unabashed mood. South African free jazz. —*Michael G. Nastos*

DON PULLEN (Don Gabriel Pullen)

b. 1941, Roanoke, VA
Piano, organ, composer / Hard bop, modern creative
Don Pullen rivals Cecil Taylor in his percussive approach to the piano. Pullen incorporates free, blues, and bebop elements into his solos, and features tone clusters, funk, and R&B backbeats and rhythms, glissandos, and dense, rigor-

ous right-hand lines. Pullen's also an accomplished organist; his bass pedal work, accompaniment, and soulful melodies and riffs are reminiscent of classic soul-jazz combo dates. Pullen began playing gospel in church, and played R&B in clubs in his youth. He turned to jazz in his teens. Pullen played in Muhal Richard Abrams's Experimental Band during the mid-'60s in Chicago, and Giuseppi Logan's quartet in New York. He also played on R&B sessions backing Big Maybelle, Ruth Brown, and Arthur Prysock, and played organ with soul-jazz groups. Pullen led a group in the '60s and early '70s that included Roland Prince, Tina Brooks, and Al Dreares. He worked in a duo with Milford Graves in the mid-'60s. Pullen was in Charles Mingus's last great '70s combo along with George Adams and Dannie Richmond. After that experience, Pullen went solo. He worked with Sam Rivers, David Murray, Hamiet Bluiett, and various Art Ensemble of Chicago members before coforming a quartet with Adams in the '70s that also included Richmond and Cameron Brown. The Don Pullen/George Adams quartet was a super band whose only failing was recording their finest work for an independent label; they never enjoyed the exposure available only through a conglomerate's publicity machine. Pullen also played with Beaver Harris's 360 Degree Music Experience, and in the Mingus Dynasty. Since the quartet disbanded, Pullen has led his own bands and currently records for Blue Note. His recent *Ode to Life* has been highly praised in the mainstream jazz press, in hip-hop magazines like *Vibe*, and even in international publications such as *Latin Beat*. Pullen has recorded for Atlantic, Horo, Timeless, Black Saint, Sackville, and DIW, among others. He's played with Eddie Gomez, Nina Simone, Bobby Battle, Fred Hopkins, Olu Dara, Donald Harrison, Alex Blake, Gary Peacock, Tony Williams, and Chico Freeman, among others. Currently, Pullen has several recent and reissued titles available on CD. —*Ron Wynn*

○ **Jazz a Confonto** / Mar. 21, 1975 / Horo 21

○ **Tomorrow's Promises** / 1976-1977 / Atlantic 1699
A certain hesitancy and stodginess aside, the fine moments here are fine indeed. "Autumn Song," a George Adams composition that finds the protean saxophonist playing in a nicely slumberous, John Klemmerian voice over a martial cadence, is a winsome moment. In a livelier vein, the Afro-Cuban "Kadji" is effervescent, as explosive—and as pretty—as this album gets, while "Last Year's Lies and Promises" weaves Adams's breathy, romantic bass clarinet in an alternating fashion with some truly jarring soprano sax shrills and Don Pullen's multidirectional support. The tension and erratic moods are engulfing, making it the album's most potent and heady performance. —*Mikal Gilmore*, Down Beat

★ **Earth Beams with George Adams Quartet** / i. 1980 / Timeless

Decisions / i. 1984 / Timeless
With George Adams Quartet. Earthy, roaring hard bop from a superb, disciplined combo. Newly reissued on CD. —*Ron Wynn*

★ **Sixth Sense, The** / Jun. 1985 / Black Saint 0088
Don Pullen's singular warp-speed keyboard blurs—again on display here—can make one forget how deep his soul-jazz roots are. *The Sixth Sense* is a refresher course. The cooking Latin-funk 5/4 title track could well occupy the kickoff spot on a late '60s Blue Note LP; the joyful dance "All is Well" demonstrates the continuing influence of Abdullah Ibrahim's writing on Pullen's. And the duet "Gratitude" is as pretty a gospel hymn as you'll hear these days—especially as filtered through Donald Harrison's gorgeously mobile alto. The presence of (then) Jazz Messenger Harrison would appear to bolster the music's straightforward character. But here—on "In the Beginning" in particular—Harrison unexpectedly emerges as a successor to Jimmy Lyons's frenetic offshoot of Charlie Parker orthodoxy. The typical track here floats easily between inside and outside playing. "In the Beginning" sounds like a harsh but vital caricature of a hard bop tune. The straightforward melody in "Sixth Sense"

doesn't prepare you for the feverish solos to come, prodded along by some of the most delightfully talky drumming heard in years. (Arthur Blythe sideman Bobby Battle is an old cohort of Pullen's.) Fred Hopkins (b) and "super-bugler" Olu Dara excel at this sort of pan-stylistic swing. The end result is one of those rare albums with genuine appeal to listeners in more than one camp (as opposed to the many eclectic albums that try and fail to attain it). —*Kevin Whitehead*, Cadence

☆ **Breakthrough** / i. Apr. 30, 1986 / Blue Note 46314
With George Adams Quartet. Pianist Don Pullen and sax/flute/vocalist George Adams (both ex-Mingus players) with drummer Dan Richmond at their creative zenith. —*Michael G. Nastos*

Song Everlasting / i. 1987 / Blue Note 46907
With George Adams Quartet. Another in a series of exceptional Pullen/George Adams dates. This was a superb small combo, one of the best and most popular in the '80s. —*Ron Wynn*

Random Thoughts / Mar. 23, 1990 / Blue Note 94347

○ **Kele Mou Bana** / i. May 7, 1992 / Blue Note 98166
On *Kele Mou Bana*, pianist Don Pullen's third release as a leader for Blue Note, his percussive tendencies culminate in an album of Afro-Brazilian tunes. Pullen has gathered an authentic, high-powered ensemble, the African-Brazilian Connection, starting with his percussionists, Brazilian Guilherme Franco and Senegalese Mor Thiam. These two provide clatter and beat out an insistent, colorful foundation for the band, which responds in turn. Carlos Ward's alto floats over, jabs at, or edges into the pulse, pushing the band ever forward as he digs deep and plays hard. And Brazilian Nilson Matta, a powerhouse of a bassist, infers a whole range of rhythms in every bassline, such as swinging and funking an Afrobeat all at once. —*Suzanne McElfresh*, Down Beat

Ode to Life / i. 1993 / Blue Note 89233
Ode to Life is the second showcase for Don Pullen's new African-Brazilian Connection, a quintet that places Pullen in the company of musicians (read: rhythms) from the cultures in the group's title. Those ringing upper-end runs and clusters we normally associate with Pullen are scarce; what replaces them is generally rhapsodic and reflective—most assuredly in remembrance of George Adams. Consequently, the ensuing silkiness is by turns harmonically accessible (Pullen's own "Ah George, We Hardly Knew Ya"), danceably placid (Carlos Ward's "Anastasia/Pyramid"), and pleasantly exotic (Mor Thiam's "Aseeko!"). —*K. Leander Williams*, Down Beat

JOHN PURCELL

Reeds / Modern creative
Though he hasn't recorded as a leader yet, multi-instrumentalist John Purcell has won praise and recognition for his playing on several sessions, most notably his work with Jack DeJohnette's Special Edition. He's an excellent soprano sax player, and an effective soloist on several other reed instruments and on flute. Purcell can be heard on DeJohnette's *Album Album*. —*Ron Wynn*

★ **Third Kind of Blue** / Minor Music 8006

BERNARD PURDIE

b. Jun. 11, 1939, Elkton, MD
Drums / Blues & jazz, soul-jazz, contemporary funk
An all-time great soul, R&B, funk, and pop drummer, Bernard Purdie's jazz connections aren't as well known, but they're solid, if thin. Purdie's impeccable timing and mastery of backbeats and grooves are celebrated. He moved to New York from Maryland in 1960, and recorded with James Brown, King Curtis, and many others. He was CTI's house drummer in the late '60s and early '70s, and worked with Grover Washington, Jr. and with George Benson, and with several other musicians. Purdie toured with Curtis and Aretha Franklin in 1970, and was Franklin's music director

until 1975. During his studio days in the early '70s, Purdie recorded with Louis Armstrong and Gato Barbieri, and with numerous rock, pop, and soul sessions. He recorded with Dizzy Gillespie in 1980 at the Montreux Jazz Festival and toured with him in 1983. Purdie recorded with Hank Crawford during the early '80s, and has continued working steadily into the '90s. In '93, he generated a fire storm of reaction when he charged that it was his uncredited drumming, rather than Ringo Starr's, on some Beatles tracks. Purdie claimed proof was forthcoming, but, by the end of '93, no evidence had been presented. He made a rare date as a leader for Flying Dutchman, *Pretty Purdie*, in 1972, that has long since disappeared. But Purdie can be heard on countless discs by Brown, Franklin, Curtis, Gillespie, and Crawford, among many others. —*Ron Wynn*

○ **Soul Drums** / **i.** 1968 / Direction 863290

★ **Soul Is . . . Pretty Purdie** / **i.** 1972 / Fly 10154

FLORA PURIM

b. Mar. 6, 1942, Rio de Janeiro, Brazil

Vocals, guitar, percussion / Latin-jazz, early jazz-rock, world fusion

Since her husband, Airto Moreira, ranks as Brazil's most famous percussionist, it's only fitting that Flora Purim qualifies as that nation's most celebrated jazz vocalist, though she's never had a huge hit like Astrud Gilberto's "The Girl from Impanema." While Purim's thunder has been stolen in the '80s and '90s by newer, more invigorating, progressive types like Margareth Menezes and Tania Maria, Purim was a revelation in the '70s. With a voice that, at one time, could range over six octaves, a soothing, alluring sound, and superb timing and delivery, she thrilled audiences with her vocals as a leader, and on the debut Return to Forever album. The daughter of professional musicians, Purim studied piano and guitar, and performed in Sao Paulo and Rio de Janeiro with Moreira. They moved to Los Angeles in the late '60s, then to New York. While Moreira worked with Miles Davis, Purim joined Stan Getz's band. She recorded with Duke Pearson, then with Return to Forever and Moreira. The duo left Return to Forever in the mid-'70s to form their own band, but Purim's career was derailed by an arrest for cocaine possession. She was imprisoned in 1974 and 1975, then resumed her career. In the late '70s, Purim's records were more pop- and light-jazz oriented. She started her own band in 1978, as her career and Moreira's seemed headed in opposite stylistic directions. But they reteamed in the mid-'80s, and are still working together. Purim recorded in the '70s for Milestone, then for Concord/Crossover, Sobocode, Venture, and Reference with Mickey Hart in the '80s. She's recorded for Fantasy in the '90s. Most of Purim's own dates, and her dates with Airto, are available on CD. —*Ron Wynn*

★ **Butterfly Dreams** / Dec. 1973 / Milestone 315

The influences on this album are derived from Flora Purim's native Brazil, and the music of Chick Corea's early Return To Forever, which included Stanley Clarke, Airto Moreira, and Purim and added greatly to the continuing popularity of blended Brazilian and American music. Stanley Clarke had a good deal to do with the contents of this recording, arranging most of it and contributing several compositions of his own. George Duke also contributed, as did Purim with her arrangement of Antonio Carlos Jobim's "Dindi," which she sings in Portugese. Flora Purim uses her voice as a delicate, highly controlled instrument. Whether doing wordless vocals or lyrics, it is light and sensitive, yet capable of being flung into stratospheric free flights of sound, as on "Dr. Jive (Part 1)." She also tracks over her own voice, creating subtle harmonies and counterpoint with splendid results. The addition of Joe Henderson on tenor sax adds a kind of strength that complements the electric and acoustic string instruments, thereby avoiding a redundancy in tone and flavor. —*Herb Nolan*, Down Beat

Love Reborn / **i.** 1973-1976 / Milestone 9095

Stories to Tell / **i.** 1974 / Milestone 619

○ **500 Miles High** / Jul. 6, 1974 / Milestone 9070
Fine album by Purim from the period when she was a dominant Afro-Latin vocalist. She cut this with husband Airto Moreira; it's a blend of light romantic songs, Afro-Latin tunes, and easy-listening instrumentals. Purim's singing, which grew in range, depth, and impact during this period, keeps things interesting, as does the presence of Milton Nascimento. —*Ron Wynn*

○ **Open Your Eyes You Can Fly** / 1976 / Milestone 9065
Flora Purim emerged from imprisonment in the mid-'70s with a renewed vision, an undaunted resolve, and an unblemished vision. *Open Your Eyes You Can Fly* is proclaimed as her "freedom album." All involved sought to make it Purim's strongest entry to that date, and it is just that, a remarkably cohesive, impressively passionate set of performances. The arrangements, shaped largely by Purim, Airto Moreira, Hermeto Pascoal, and George Duke, sharply freshen the delivery of the songs, effectively varying the dynamics, tempo, and voicings. —*Mikal Gilmore*, Down Beat

Nothing Will Be as It Was . . . Tomorrow / **i.** 1977 / Warner Brothers 2985
With lots of string, synth, and vocal arrangements, this includes classics such as the title track, "You Love Me Only," and "Bridges" (written by Milton Nascimento). Support comes from keyboardists Patrice Rushen and George Duke, and Airto Moreira (per). —*Michael G. Nastos*

○ **Humble People** / 1985 / George Wein Collection 43007
An all-star band supports Flora and Airto Moreira (per) through jazz, funk, and Latin pop. Guests include David Sanborn (as), Joe Farrell (ts), Milton Cardona (per), and Jerry Gonzalez (per). This is one of Purim's better later-period albums. —*Michael G. Nastos*

Q

IKE QUEBEC (Ike Abrams Quebec)

b. Aug. 17, 1918, Newark, NJ, **d.** Jan. 16, 1963, New York, NY
Tenor saxophone / Swing, hard bop, soul-jazz

A magnificent "populist" saxophonist whose abilities were undervalued by many critics during his lifetime, Ike Quebec showed that simple, compelling music didn't have to be played in a simplistic manner. He had a pronounced swing bent in his style and tone, particularly the sound of Coleman Hawkins. But Quebec didn't simply parrot Hawkins; he displayed a huge, bluesy tone, and swooping, jubilant phrases, and played joyous uptempo tunes and evocative, slow blues and ballads. There were no false fingerings, or anything intricate; it was just direct, heartfelt solos. Quebec was once a pianist and part-time soft shoe artist, but switched to tenor in the '40s, playing with the Barons of Rhythm. He worked with several New York bands, including groups led by Kenny Clarke, Benny Carter, and Roy Eldridge. He cowrote the song "Mop Mop" with Clarke, which was later recorded by Coleman Hawkins during one of the earliest bebop sessions. Quebec played from the mid-'40s into the early '50s with Cab Calloway's orchestra and also Calloway's spin-off unit, the Cab Jivers. Quebec cut one of Blue Note's rare 78 albums in the '40s, and also recorded for Savoy. His song "Blue Harlem" became a huge hit. Quebec also worked with Lucky Millinder and recorded with Calloway. Alfred Lion made Quebec Blue Note's A&R man in the late '40s, after Quebec repeatedly informed him about talented prospective signees. Quebec doubled for a while as a bandleader, but, until the late '50s, concentrated on recording and finding acts for the label. Some of the people he brought to Lion included Thelonious Monk and Bud Powell. Quebec wrote "Suburban Eyes" for Monk's label debut. He began playing again in the late '50s, doing Blue Note sessions with Sonny Clark, Jimmy Smith, singer Dodo Green, and Stanley Turrentine, and doing his own dates. Just as he was attracting renewed attention and some appreciation from critics who'd previously dismissed him as another honking R&B type, Quebec died of lung cancer in 1963. Mosaic has issued some superb Quebec boxed sets, *The Complete Blue Note Forties Recordings of Ike Quebec and John Hardee* and *The Complete Blue Note 45 Sessions*. A few individual Quebec Blue Note sessions are also available on CD. —*Ron Wynn*

○ **Tenor Sax Album: The Savoy Sessions, The** / **i.** Aug. 1945 / Savoy 70812

★ **Complete Blue Note 45 Sessions** / 1959-1962 / Mosaic
A wonderful three-disc collection of Quebec's 1959-1962 songs that pack jazz punch, have R&B appeal, and were originally recorded for and designed as singles for jukeboxes. —*Ron Wynn*

○ **Blue and Sentimental** / Dec. 1961 / Blue Note 84098
Hot, lusty, and wonderful. Quebec was a rare jazz musician who never lost his appeal in the R&B community. With Sonny Clark (p), Grant Green (g), Paul Chambers (b), and Philly Joe Jones (d). —*Ron Wynn*

Congo Lament / Jan. 20, 1962 / Blue Note 1089

Easy Living / **i.** 1962 / Blue Note 46846

★ **Complete Blue Note Recordings** / Mosaic

This is an essential compilation of virtually all the laudable Quebec jazz dates. —*Ron Wynn*

ALVIN QUEEN

b. Aug. 16, 1950, New York, NY
Drums / Hard bop

A crisp, powerful, and swinging drummer, Alvin Queen hasn't recorded as often as his talents merit, but what he's done is consistently engaging and demanding. Queen worked with George Benson and Stanley Turrentine, then traveled to Europe with Charles Tolliver's quartet. During the '70s, he worked with the group Music Inc. co-led by Tolliver and Stanley Cowell. Queen departed America in 1979 for Switzerland, and established Nilva Records. Queen toured France with Plas Johnson and Harry Edison. He recorded with John Collins and Junior Mance in the '80s, while working in Zurich with a trio led by Wild Bill Davis and recording with another led by Lonnie Smith. He also did his own dates. Currently, there are no Queen sessions available on CD, but he can be heard on reissues by Music Inc. —*Ron Wynn and Michael G. Nastos*

★ **In Europe** / **i.** 1980 / Nilva 3401
Quintet with drummer Queen at the helm. Mainstream, bordering on progressive. —*Michael G. Nastos*

GENE QUILL (Daniel Eugene Quill)

b. Dec. 15, 1927, Atlantic City, NJ
Alto saxophone, clarinet / Bop, cool

A consistent alto saxophonist whose style changed from straight bebop to a milder, more mellow sound, Gene Quill initially played with fire and exacting fluidity. He gradually smoothed the edges off his solos, and opted for a relaxed, introspective approach. Quill started on saxophone in his childhood, and was a professional at age 13. He worked in big bands during the '50s and '60s, playing and recording with Buddy DeFranco, Claude Thornhill, Gene Krupa, Quincy Jones, Johnny Richards, Manny Albam, Johnny Carisi, Bill Potts, and Gerry Mulligan. Quill also played in the combos of Mundell Lowe and Jimmy Knepper, led his own bands, and teamed memorably with Phil Woods. He did some session work, but tragically his career was cut short when he suffered partial paralysis following brain damage. Quill's sessions with Woods for Prestige and RCA have been reissued on CD, but their Epic dates have not be reissued. His own dates for labels such as Dawn and Roost haven't been reissued on CD. —*Ron Wynn*

★ **Three Bones and a Quill** / 1958 / Roost 2229

PAUL QUINICHETTE

b. May 17, 1916, Denver, CO, **d.** Jun. 2, 1983, New York, NY
Tenor saxophone / Swing, big band

A robust, energetic tenor saxophonist, Paul Quinichette was among the purest swinging players of his generation. He earned the nickname "Vice Pres" because he sounded so close in both style and sound to Lester Young. But Quinichette could also play bebop, honking R&B, blues, or traditional jazz. He began on clarinet and alto sax in his childhood, then switched to tenor. Quinichette toured with

Nat Towles and Lloyd Hunter in the early '30s, then worked with Shorty Sherock. During the early '40s, he played in the bands of Ernie Fields, Jay McShann, Johnny Otis, Benny Carter, and Sid Catlett. He moved to New York, and played there with Louis Jordan, Lucky Millinder, J.C. Heard, Henry "Red" Allen, Eddie Wilcox, Dinah Washington, and Hot Lips Page. He played with Count Basie from 1951 to 1953. Quinichette recorded with a Basie small combo for Verve in the early '50s, and cut his own combo dates for Fantasy and Prestige. He led Basie reunion sessions in 1957 and 1958. There were later dates with Benny Goodman, Nat Pierce, John Coltrane, Bob Brookmeyer, Woody Herman, Lavern Baker, Washington, and Billie Holiday. Quinichette took a break from music to work as an electrical engineer in the '60s, but returned in the '70s. He played with pianist Brooks Kerr in New York, worked in Two Tenor Boogie with either Harold Ashby or Buddy Tate, and recorded for Famous Door and Master Jazz. There's very little vintage Quinichette available, at least on the American market. —*Ron Wynn*

★ **Pres Meets Vice-Pres** / **i.** 1954 / EmArcy 26021

Vice-Pres / **i.** 1954 / EmArcy 26022

★ **On the Sunny Side** / May 1957 / Original Jazz Classics 76

A standout late '50s blowing date led by tenor saxophonist Paul Quinichette with trombonist Curtis Fuller, alto saxophonists John Jenkins and Sonny Red, pianist Mal Waldron, bassist Doug Watkins, and drummer Ed Thigpen. This is simply straightahead blues, ballads, and standards, with Jenkins in particular taking some torrid solos. —*Ron Wynn*

Chase is On, The / Aug. 29, 1957+Sep. 8, 1957 / Bethlehem 6038

With fellow tenor Charlie Rouse and the Wynton Kelly Trio, this is a nice mix of standards and tunes by Rouse and Carmen McRae. Two tracks are with Hank Jones (p) and Freddie Green (g). —*Michael G. Nastos*

Cattin' / **i.** 1958 / Prestige 7158

R

CHUCK RAINEY (Charles W. (III) Rainey)

b. Jun. 17, 1940, Youngstown, OH
Bass, guitar / Blues & jazz, soul-jazz, contemporary funk
Another instrumentalist widely associated with soul, pop, funk, and R&B, yet highly respected by jazz musicians, Chuck Rainey's been a star electric bassist since the '60s. While Jaco Pastorius and Stanley Clarke featured flashy, blistering playing and approached electric bass as if they were improvising on a guitar, Rainey's bass has been a heavy, steady pulse and vigorous support, fitting into a rhythm section and locking onto a groove with a vengeance. Rainey studied violin, piano, and trumpet in his youth, then moved from Youngstown to Cleveland at age 21. He played electric guitar and bass in various R&B bands, then joined King Curtis's group in New York during 1964. Rainey's done hundreds of recording sessions since then, but has also done a fair number of jazz dates. He played with Jerome Richardson, Grady Tate, Mose Allison, Gato Barbieri, and Gene Ammons in the late '60s and early '70s, and with Eddie "Cleanhead" Vinson at the 1971 Montreux Festival. That same year, Rainey toured and played with Aretha Franklin. He moved to Los Angeles in 1972 and worked there with the Crusaders and with Hampton Hawes, and recorded with Donald Byrd, Sonny Rollins, and John Handy in the mid-'70s. Rainey recorded in Japan with Hiroshi Fukumura in 1978. He's made two rare dates as a leader; for Cobblestone in 1971, and for Hammer n' Nails in 1981. Neither of these recordings are around today, but Rainey can be heard on many discs by Franklin, Curtis, Rollins, and others. —*Ron Wynn*

GENE RAMEY

b. 1913, **d.** 1984
Bass / Swing, bop
A masterful swing and bebop bassist, Gene Ramey was a propulsive, dependable contributor to many fine sessions from the '30s to the '80s. He seldom soloed, but provided reliable support and meshed effectively with drummers and pianists in ideal replications of the classic Basie rhythm section. Ramey's technique was shaped by lessons he took from Walter Page in the early '30s. From Page, Ramey learned the value of precise timekeeping and of interacting with section members, something Ramey excelled at throughout his career. Initially, he played trumpet, then sousaphone, which was his first professional instrument. When he moved to Kansas City in the early '30s and switched to bass, Page helped him make the transition. He led his own bands and played with local groups before joining Jay McShann in 1938. He remained with him until 1943, when McShann joined the army. Ramey then moved to New York, where he played with Ben Webster, Coleman Hawkins, Charlie Parker, Eddie "Lockjaw" Davis, Miles Davis, and Lester Young. Ramey worked with Art Blakey in the mid-'50s, then, in the late '50s and throughout the '60s and '70s, played with Buck Clayton, Muggsy Spanier, Teddy Wilson, and McShann. He toured Europe with Clayton twice in the late '50s and early '60s. Ramey reunited with McShann in 1969 and 1979, and returned to Texas in 1976. He worked regularly into the '80s.

Ramey did not make any sessions as a leader, but can be heard on McShann, Basie, and Young reissues. —*Ron Wynn*

DOUG RANEY

b. 1957
Guitar / Bop
The son of legendary guitarist Jimmy Raney, it's understandable that Doug Raney has been influenced heavily by his father. Doug is an impressive soloist, and utilizes full tones, crisp chording, and fluid voicings that are almost identical to his father's. He made his first recording with his father and Al Haig in the mid-'70s, then did duo dates with his dad in the late '70s. Raney recorded for Steeplechase in the '70s and '80s, and for Criss Cross in the '80s. He has recorded with Chet Baker and Bernt Rosegren, and played in Horace Parlan's band. Raney has a couple of sessions available on CD. —*Ron Wynn*

★ **Meeting the Tenors** / Apr. 29, 1983 / Criss Cross 1006

JIMMY RANEY (James Elbert Raney)

b. Aug. 20, 1927, Lousiville, KY
Guitar / Bop
A superb accompanist and an outstanding player who, originally, was greatly influenced by Charlie Christian, Jimmy Raney emerged as one of bebop's greatest players. He utilized long, brilliantly played lines and subdued, yet emphatic rhythms. Raney's mother also played guitar, and he studied with another player, Hayden Causey. Raney later replaced Causey in Jerry Wald's band. He played in Chicago with Lou Levy in the mid-'40s, and worked in New York before joining Woody Herman in 1948, and also recording with Stan Getz. During the late '40s and '50s, Raney worked with Al Haig, Buddy DeFranco, Artie Shaw, and Terry Gibbs before joining a quintet led by Getz. Raney's solos and accompaniment in this band won him widespread acclaim. He later worked with Red Norvo and Les Elgart, and played extensively at the Blue Angel working with Jimmy Lyon's trio. Raney and Getz reteamed in 1962, but Raney left the next year. He became an active session musician on radio broadcasts and television shows in New York. Raney returned to his native Louisville in the late '60s, but returned to play New York clubs in the '70s. He gave a recital at Carnegie Hall with Al Haig in 1974, and toured with his son, Doug, and with Haig. Raney and Doug have recorded and toured in the '80s. Raney's also led groups, both with and without his son. He has several sessions available on CD. —*Ron Wynn*

○ **Introducing Phil Woods** / **i.** 1953 /

Jimmy Raney Plays / Aug. 26, 1953 / Prestige 156

Quartet / May 28, 1954 / New Jazz 1101

○ **A** / Feb. 18, 1955 / Original Jazz Classics 1706
This session presents three dates from 5/28/54, 2/18/55, and 3/8/55 with guitarist Jimmy Raney in quartet and quintet groups. The '54 sides with Hal Overton (p), Teddy Kotick (b), and Art Madigan (d) are brilliant. On parts Raney overdubs himself and in effect becomes Stan Getz to his own Raney. The music is smooth, hip, felt, and swinging. On the later dates Nick Stabular replaces Madigan and John Wilson's

trumpet is added. Wilson's dry trumpet counterpoints well with the guitarist's lines, but it is used mostly in themes. The show is all Raney's and things move wonderfully when he solos. This is great guitar—recommended. —*Jimmy Raney*, Cadence

○ **Jimmy Raney Featuring Bob Brookmeyer** / Dec. 12, 1956 / Paramount 129

★ **Two Jims and Zoot** / Sep. 1964 / Mobile Fidelity 833

○ **Complete Jimmy Raney in Tokyo, The** / Apr. 12+14, 1976 / Xanadu 5157
Guitarist Jimmy Raney's album is brilliant from start to finish. While I don't usually quote from liner notes, I think Don Schlitten's notes express as well as possible Raney's virtuosity: "creatively brilliant mind," "amazing technical skill," "rhythmically and harmonically adventurous," "highest melodic order," "never boring." That was Jimmy Raney and the proof is in this recording. You can listen to "Darn That Dream" (Raney said it was "the best thing I've ever done"), "Anthropology" (probably my personal favorite), "Stella By Starlight" (unaccompanied Raney), and the rest over and over, and each time hear nuances that might have been overlooked previously. —*Carl Brauer*, Cadence

○ **Jimmy and Doug Raney Quartet** / Apr. 19, 1979 / Steeple Chase 31118

○ **Wisteria** / Dec. 1985 / Criss Cross 1019

ENRICO RAVA

b. Aug. 20, 1943, Trieste, Italy
Trumpet, flugelhorn / World fusion, modern creative
Perhaps Italy's finest native trumpeter, Enrico Rava has been a prolific contributor to many free and avant-garde sessions since the mid-'60s. He's demonstrated a strong tone and solid style, though he's not one of the great soloists. He plays effectively and has worked well with some exacting bandleaders. Rava's mother was a classical pianist, and he began playing traditional New Orleans jazz on trombone before moving to trumpet. Rava studied with Carmine Caruso in New York, then joined Gato Barbieri in the mid-'60s. He toured with Steve Lacy in the late '60s, then played with Roswell Rudd until 1972. Rava also worked with the Jazz Composers Orchestra and with Bill Dixon. During the '70s, he played with Abdullah Ibrahim, Giorgio Gaslini, and the Globe Unity Orchestra. He coformed a group with John Abercrombie in the mid-'70s, while he also led his own bands. Rudd rejoined him in 1978 and 1979. Rava collaborated with classical composer Morton Feldman and visual artist Michelangeo Pistoletto for a project in Atlanta. He played with Gil Evans and toured with Cecil Taylor in the '80s, and with Tony Oxley in the mid-'80s. He reteamed with Taylor in the late '80s. Rava's recorded for ECM, Soul Note, and Adda. He has several dates available on CD. —*Ron Wynn*

★ **Il Giro Del Giorno in 80 Mondi** / Feb. 1972 / Black Saint 0011
A recording that is "out" and sometimes funky, with guitarist Bruce Johnson. —*Michael G. Nastos*

○ **Pilgrim and the Stars, The** / Jun. 1975 / ECM 1063
As a trumpeter, Enrico Rava reveals the omnipresent influence of Miles Davis. He is fond, for example, of rapid upward glissandi, frozen single-note stabs suspended in space, and a dark brooding sound. Rava also expresses a warm lyricism and a spatial sparseness reminiscent of early Davis. Among the most impressive of Rava's originals is "Parks," a deceptively simple duet built around Rava's mellow smoke-toned trumpet and Abercrombie's subtle fluctuations between Barney Kessel and samba-comping styles. This brief duet (1:45) effectively captures the open and expansive qualities we associate with parks. Also striking is "By the Sea." It creates a sultry, low-burn atmosphere charged with a tense sensuality due to the careful placement of Abercrombie's high-pitched erotic jabs in the background. —*Chuck Berg*, Down Beat

○ **Plot, The** / Aug. 1976 / ECM 1078

Ragtime

Ragtime
A piano-based music style that is classically derived and rhythmically bouncy. Main proponents: Scott Joplin, Eubie Blake, Joe Lamb.

Piano Origins

1890s Ragtime Composers/Notators
Scott Joplin (1868-1917)
Tom Turpin (1873-1922)
James Scott (1886-1938)
Artie Matthews (1888-1958)

Novelty Piano
George Botsford's (1874-1949) "Black and White Rag" (1908)
Charles Johnson's (1876-1950) "Dill Pickles Rag" (1906)
Henry Lodge's (1884-1933) "Temptation Rag" (1909)
Adeline Shepard's (1885-1950) "Pickles and Peppers" (1908)

Jazz-Oriented Ragtime
Eubie Blake (1883-1983)
Jelly Roll Morton (1890-1941)

Ragtime Composers
James P. Johnson (1894-1955)
Fats Waller (1904-1943)
Willie "The Lion" Smith (1897-1973)
Luckey Roberts (1887-1968)

Late 1940s–Ragtime Revival
Max Morath (1926)
Ralph Sutton (1922)
Joshua Rifkin (1944)

1950s and beyond
Dick Hyman (1927)
Joe Fingers Carr (1910-1979)
Movie *The Sting* (1973)
Gunther Schuller (1925)
Scott Kirby (c. 1965)

Enrico Rava's trumpet tone and technique are straighter and cleaner than Miles Davis's. With the exception of the pensive "On the Red Side of the Street," a kind of anatomy of morosity, Rava's stance is less oblique and introverted, more fluid and impressionistically romantic. Rava's quartet's density is open, thinner, with ample breathing space for all. This aura of collective, sometimes meandering invention is keynoted by John Abercrombie; instead of cluttering the middle register with full chords, he restricts himself to oblique fills and sparse solos emanating from the guitar's highest positions. At their best, on "Tribe" for instance, Rava and Abercrombie interact in a freely associative, loosely contrapuntal, stream-of-conscious dialog. —*Jon Balleras*, Down Beat

Quartet / Mar. 1978 / ECM 1122

ANDY RAZAF

b. 1895, **d.** 1973
Ballads & blues
A descendant of the royal family of Madagascar, Andy Razaf's lyrics were certainly high class. He was involved

with many of the biggest hit songs and shows in early American popular music, as either the lyricist or as the writer of words and music. Razaf wrote the lyrics for *Keep Shufflin*, *Hot Chocolates*, and *Blackbirds of 1930*. None of these shows would be cause for jubilation in the '90s, but they were major achievements in the '20s and '30s. He collaborated with Fats Waller on many epic hits, including "Honeysuckle Rose," "Ain't Misbehavin'," "How Can You Face Me," and "The Joint Is Jumpin'." He also worked with Don Redman, Paul Denniker, James P. Johnson, Eubie Blake, and William Weldon. Razaf wrote the big novelty smash, "That's What I Like About the South," for Phil Harris. Razaf added lyrics to instrumentals such as "Reefer Man," "Knock Me a Kiss" and "Christopher Columbus," which Waller turned into a novelty hit. Razaf sometimes used an alias to record as a singer. He cut "Back in Your Own Backyard" and "Nobody Knows How Much I Love You" as Tommy Thompson with Waller on piano. A stroke made Razaf an invalid for much of his life. His collaborations with Waller and others are available on many CD reissues. —*Ron Wynn*

JASON REBELLO (Jason Rebellio)

b. 1969
Piano / Neo-bop
English pianist Jason Rebello generated lots of interest and discussion when his debut album appeared in late 1990. Rebello had already gotten raves among international critics for his flashy mix of stride and boogie with bebop and blues. Rebello studied both classical and jazz, attended Guildhall School of Music, and later worked with fellow British performers Courtney Pine, Jean Toussaint, Steve Williamson, and Cleveland Watkiss. His playing in Steve Smith's late '80s band was the most daring and jazz-based of anyone in the group except Smith, and the added bonus of having Wayne Shorter produce his debut garnered Rebello even more attention. The session is still available on CD. —*Ron Wynn*

★ **Clearer View** / 1991 / Novus 63000

SONNY RED (Sylvester Kyner)

b. Dec. 17, 1932, Detroit, MI, **d.** Mar. 20, 1981, Detroit, MI
Alto saxophone, bandleader / Hard bop
Sonny Red Kyner was a wailing, emphatic alto saxophonist who had one of the most evocative tones and spirited styles on the instrument among hard bop players. He made his first impact with Barry Harris in the late '40s and early '50s, then played tenor with Frank Rosolino in 1954, but soon returned to alto. He joined Art Blakey later that year. Red moved to New York with Curtis Fuller in 1957, and settled there in 1959. He recorded with Paul Quinichette and Fuller in 1957, then did his own albums in the late '50s and early '60s, mostly for Prestige and Blue Note. He worked in the '60s and '70s with Donald Byrd and Kenny Dorham, and recorded with Clifford Jordan, Pony Poindexter, Yusef Lateef, Howard McGhee, and Byrd. Red has a couple of dates available as a leader on CD. —*Ron Wynn*

Out of the Blue / Dec. 5, 1959 / Blue Note 4032

○ **Two Altos** / **i.** 1959 / Blue Note 6069

★ **Images** / Jul. 1961 / Jazzland 148
These tracks were recorded in June and December of 1961. The leader, Sonny Red Kyner (as), never really became the individual strong player that his playing hinted he might develop into. Basically he was in the Charlie Parker-Jackie McLean tradition, and the material here has that spirit, but little punch. Others involved are Grant Green (g), Barry Harris (p), George Tucker, (b), and Lex Humphries or Jimmy Cobb (d). Trumpeter Blue Mitchell is also featured on three cuts. —*Bob Rusch*, Cadence

☆ **Sonny Red** / **i.** 197? / Mainstream 324

FREDDIE REDD

b. May 29, 1927, New York, NY
Piano, composer / Hard bop

Freddie Redd has blended the rough, furious rhythmic pace of early blues and barrelhouse playing with bebop's voicings and structures. The results are a sound that's both dense and sprawling, and is energetic, yet is never clichéd or simplistic. Redd's largely a self-taught player. He began working in New York and Syracuse clubs after his discharge from the army in 1949. He was in a small group led by Johnny Miller, then recorded in the early '50s with Tiny Grimes, and toured the South with Cootie Williams. Redd returned to New York in 1952, and worked for a brief period with Oscar Pettiford and Charles Mingus in 1953. Redd played in the Jive Bombers, and recorded with Art Farmer and Gigi Gryce's quintet, plus the Gene Ammons all-stars. He toured Sweden with Ernestine Anderson and Rolf Ericson in 1956, recording with Ericson and Tommy Potter and cutting trio sessions. He moved to San Francisco when he returned to America, working for a short time at the Black Hawk club with Mingus, and serving as house pianist at Bop City. Redd wrote most of the music for Jack Gelber's play, *The Connection*, and participated in the New York performances in 1959 and 1960, and in London and Paris performances in 1961. Redd also played on the soundtrack for the film version. He lived and performed in Europe during the '60s and early '70s, working and playing in Paris, Denmark, and the Netherlands. Redd returned to America in 1974, and settled in Los Angeles. He recorded a new trio album in 1977, and did more work in the '80s, but didn't maintain a hectic schedule. He recorded new sessions for Triloka in 1988 and Milestone in 1990. Only a couple of his early dates, along with his recent releases, are available on CD. —*Ron Wynn*

☆ **Piano East–Piano West** / Feb. 1955 / Prestige 7067
A deluxe session with Redd and Hampton Hawes dominating the piano. Limited-edition set. —*Ron Wynn*

○ **San Francisco Suite for Jazz Trio** / Oct. 2, 1957 / Riverside 1748

★ **Complete Blue Note Freddie Redd, The** / Feb. 15, 1960-Jan. 17, 1961 / Mosaic 124
Freddie Redd has been recording since 1951, but his works have been conspicuously absent from the bins and displays of most record and/or CD stores, for some time. This is a three-LP Blue Note blast from the past by Mosaic. Redd's splayed angularity and percussive drive place him solidly on the Thelonious Monk to Bud Powell continuum. The first disc in this set is his music for Jack Gelber's play about heroin addicts *The Connection*, in which the quartet members performed both as musicians and actors. Despite a bassist (Michael Mattos) who sometimes fails to thwart the thwack of the band's hurtling attack, this is a search-and-destroy bop mission, music that speaks to the abandonment of the emotive moment while maintaining a coherence of form. Jackie McLean (as) and Redd solo with a vehemence that could be borne only of conviction. McLean was in his late twenties and Redd in his early thirties. Only in "Smile" is there anything approaching a letdown in the urgent impetus of this session. Redd follows up with another hard-edged date (*Shades of Redd* on Blue Note), adding Tina Brooks's tenor to the front line and improving the bass position with 25-year-old Paul Chambers, who had already established preeminence on his instrument with the Miles Davis quintet. Brooks had been McLean's *Connection* understudy and shows that he is familiar with the group's febrile gestalt. His anguished lucidity jostles against McLean's chafing querulousness to produce stingingly snappish bop. The alternates of "Ole" and "Melanie" are credible additions to the date that are issued here for the first time. Blue Note issued the date, inexplicably, in mono only. (The preceding *Connection* had been issued in stereo.) Mosaic has put things right by finally issuing this second Redd rumble in stereo. The final third of the set is the unissued session about whose omission I complained when Mosaic issued their Tina Brooks box. Benny Bailey (tpt) joins the front line of McLean and Brooks and plays with bristling buoyancy. As far as I can determine, this is Bailey's only appearance under the Blue Note escutcheon, and he makes it a decisive one, as

if to show us how well he might have adapted to life in the Lion and Wolff's den. His muted solo on "Spice" is a model of control and detail and his open horn on "Lost" is a model of the sort of vicissitudinous romanticism one hears after the hipsters go home and bop gears down into sad time. McLean glows with his usual gemlike flame, while Brooks confuses tenor history by suggesting a short cut from Lester Young to John Coltrane. Chambers is his usual strong and supple self, and the obscure Sir John Godfrey avoids calling attention to himself in disporting the drum duties with, perhaps, just a slightly tentative grace. By the time you reach the third and last of Freddie's Blue Note sessions, you may have the feeling you've heard it all before, and that's quite possibly how it would've been received by the 1961 critics who were spoiled rotten by what must have seemed like an endless feast of hard bop from Blue Note. Freddie Redd wrote all the tunes for all three dates, and plays with a brittle, bustling, assertive lyricism from start to finish. He drew his inspiration from Powell and Monk and Horace Silver and others, so I measure his contribution in terms of the use he made of those influences. Yes, it's probably too easy to hear this music as derivative. What lifts it is its honesty and authenticity, which are unmistakable. —*Alan Bargebuhr,* Cadence

☆ **Shades of Redd** / Aug. 13, 1960 / Blue Note 4045
Quintet with Tina Brooks on tenor sax and Jackie McLean on alto sax plays all Redd originals with flair and bluesy poignancy. —*Michael G. Nastos*

Live at the Studio Grill / May 19-26, 1988 / Triloka 182

○ **Everybody Loves a Winner** / 1990 / Milestone 9187
Pianist Freddie Redd created his own prodigal son image by dropping out here and turning up there, always to raves. Redd was seen and heard to great effect in New York City's off-Broadway hit, *The Connection,* in which Jackie McLean and later Dexter Gordon in Los Angeles played and acted (Gordon's prelude to *'Round Midnight?).* Redd composed, conducted, played and acted in the 1960s show and film. West coasting, East coasting, Europe, in and out he went until recently (1992), when he appeared with a trio to considerable fanfare at Birdland in New York City. There is a sextet on *Winner,* but it is not a matter of the individual performances contained here. Redd composed and arranged all the tracks and he *plays* the arrangements. They are not head-solos-lines. The chart is adhered to with under-solo riffing. That is not to say the horns are not exemplary nor does the rhythm simply support. It is just that you get a feeling of unity, a sense of beginning-middle-end. Here come two infrequently heard jazz friends, Teddy Edwards and Curtis Peagler, on tenor and alto saxes respectively, plus Redd's personal friend, trombonist Phil Ranelin, with bassist Bill Langlois and drummer Larry Hancock listening, in the tradition of jazz, to each other. —*Arnold Jay Smith,* Jazz Times

○ **Lonely City** / Uptown 2730
Freddie Redd, an aggressive, emphatic hard bop pianist, has had an erratic recording career due to personal and drug problems that forced him off the scene. He shows on this session the swinging style, distinctive phrasing, and consistently impressive solo skills that made his Blue Note and Prestige dates so popular during the late '50s. —*Ron Wynn*

DEWEY REDMAN (Walter Dewey Redman)

b. May 17, 1931, Fort Worth, TX
Reeds, composer / Early free, modern creative
A shattering, slashing, bluesy tenor saxophonist who doubles on musette, Dewey Redman's twisting forays and voice-like solos are expressed masterfully whether he's working with longtime musical companions Ornette Coleman and Don Cherry, is heading his own band, or is contributing to someone's session. Redman is a powerhouse artist capable of downshifting to a poignant, anguished style for ballads, doing bebop changes in rigorous fashion during standards, or playing snaking, eerie lines on the Chinese double-reed musette.

Redman studied clarinet at age 13, then began on alto sax before switching to tenor while attending Prairie View Agricultural and Mechanical University. He graduated in 1953. Redman played in a high school marching band with Coleman, Charles Moffett, and Prince Lasha. He was a high school teacher in the '50s and early 1960, and also played professionally and attended North Texas State. Redman earned his Masters degree in 1959. Then he moved to California, where he began playing with Donald Garrett, and worked with Pharoah Sanders, and with Wes Montgomery. Redman moved to New York and played with Coleman from 1967 to 1974, while working in Charlie Haden's Liberation Music Orchestra in 1969 and Keith Jarrett's group in the early and mid-'70s. Redman also played with Carla Bley and Roswell Rudd, and even found time to lead his own bands. He began recording as a leader in 1966 for the Freedom label (later released on Arista in America), and continued in 1969 on Byg. He also had a Blue Note session in 1969 that was never released, and continued recording in the '70s for Impulse and Galaxy. Redman, Cherry, Haden, and Edward Blackwell formed Old and New Dreams in 1976, touring, performing, and recording on ECM into the '80s. They weren't exclusively a Coleman repertory group, but did several of his compositions.

Redman continued leading his own bands in the '80s and '90s, cutting sessions for Black Saint and ECM in the '80s, and Enja and Black Saint in the '90s. His son, Joshua Redman, emerged as a huge star in 1993, following a large media blitz that ensued after Joshua won the Thelonious Monk International Saxophone Competition a couple of years ago. Joshua has already issued two critically praised albums on the Warner Bros. label, and has recorded and played with his father. Presently, Dewey Redman has only three sessions listed as available on CD; two of them were done in the '90s. —*Ron Wynn*

★ **Look for the Black Star** / i. Jan. 4, 1966 / Arista
This album full of intensity, humor, and excess was the earmark (literally) of the New Music—a music in its fullest flower in 1966 when this was recorded. Its most immediate quality is its rawness. There are large sections of sweet anarchy here ("Seven and One," "Spur of the Moment"). Redman himself simply isn't as mature a player at the time as he later became. But there is a delightfully raucous, happy feeling that informs all. Redman had only recently discovered his wildly touching technique of singing and screaming through his horn, and bassist Donald Garrett can't help but join him vocally sometimes. Drummer Eddie Moore is a source of power and invention throughout, combining elements of the playing of Ed Blackwell and Elvin Jones in his stew. The title cut, calypso-based, bubbles over with this good feeling. "For Eldon," cooks relatively straight-ahead and is a showcase for Redman's John Coltranish tenor. "Of Love" gives us a taste of the distinctive, lush pianist Jym Young. —*Bill Adler,* Down Beat

Tarik / i. Oct. 1, 1969 / Affinity 42

★ **Ear of the Behearer, The** / i. Jan. 1974 / Impulse
Much of the music here (or "sounds" if you prefer) is difficult to get into at first. One must decide to take that extra effort needed to realize Dewey Redman's brooding, dark world. For, despite the melodic similiarities to Ornette Coleman, the music contains little of Coleman's lyrical brightness. Perhaps the most successful compositions are "Boody" and "Images (In Disguise)." The first is an avant-gardist's interpretation of a 12-bar blues, or, in this case, Redman's Texas roots. Over 12 minutes, it spans the gamut of blues styles, and, most important, it has feeling, a heart of warmth that the other tunes lack. "Images" has Redman featured on the double-reed musette, an instrument that goes back as far as 800 B.C. Ted Daniel joins in on the Moroccan bugle. Redman codas the album with a screeching, upper-register chorus that sounds like multiple instruments in ultraviolet harmony. I found bassist Sirone (then of the Revolutionary Ensemble) extremely inventive and appealing. Eddie Moore (d, per) adds the right amount of percussion at the right mo-

ments. And I was particularly glad to see Jane Robertson engaging in some serious musical endeavors; her cello definitely adds to the textures and colorations of the ensemble. —*Ray Townley,* Down Beat

Coincide / **i.** Sep. 9, 1974 / Impulse 9300
Debut for this exciting saxophonist in a progressive setting, leaning toward avant-garde. —*Michael G. Nastos*

○ **Musics** / **i.** Mar. 1980 / Galaxy 5118
Though on *Musics* tenor saxophonist Dewey Redman sacrifices much of his expansive instrumental palette, he gains a measure of warmth and lyrical understatement, especially evident on his sentimental but uncloying version of "Alone Again (Naturally)." The balance of the album's first side remains in a mainstream mood, featuring Redman's Sonny Rollins-tinged tenor dancing over "Need To Be's" bossa nova changes and the quirky "Virgin Strike (March)," which begins with an out-of-step parade rhythm and slides into a boppish bridge and subsequent solo of "Giant Steps" vintage. Though not the most viscerally exciting of Dewey Redman's recordings, *Musics* is a solid, satisfying tour through Dewey Redman's musical landscape, aided masterfully by Fred Simmon's tasteful piano arabesques, bassist Mark Helias's heroic solidity and tone, and Eddie Moore's unobtrusive, propulsive drumming. Well worth the trip. — *Art Lange,* Down Beat

Redman and Blackwell in Willisau / Aug. 1980 / Black Saint 93

○ **Struggle Continues, The** / Jan. 1982 / ECM
His best. Shows great teamwork from bassist Mark Helias, drummer Ed Blackwell, and pianist Charles Eubanks. It's a record to make you say "wow." "Turn Over Baby" is a good boogie and "Joie de Vivre" one of Redman's best vehicles for improv. —*Michael G. Nastos*

☆ **Living on the Edge** / Sep. 1989 / Black Saint 120123
A first-rate late '80s date by tenor saxophonist Dewey Redman. He's working alongside the excellent pianist Geri Allen, and the compositions are rigorously played. Redman as the only horn player gets extensive space and offers his patented twisting, slashing solos. Bassist Cameron Brown and drummer Eddie Moore prove equally adept at adjusting to the Redman/Allen team. —*Ron Wynn*

DON REDMAN

b. 1900, **d.** 1964
Bandleader, tenor saxophone / Swing, big band
A pioneer arranger, many of the things Don Redman premiered in the Fletcher Henderson orchestra became established procedures. His first arrangements mixed ensemble passages with solos in an improvised manner, and incorporated breaks, horn chases, and call-and-response patterns between sections or individual players into arrangements. Redman was a child prodigy who eventually mastered nearly every instrument. As a high school senior, he was already writing arrangements. He graduated from Storer College at age 20 with a music degree. He worked in Piedmont for a year, then worked with Billy Paige's Broadway Syncopators, a Pittsburgh band. Redman played clarinet and saxophones, and wrote arrangements. He met Henderson while on tour in New York. Redman joined him on recording sessions. When Henderson formed his orchestra, Redman was one of its first members. He played clarinet, saxophones, and wrote arrangements. When Armstrong joined as their jazz specialist, Redman made the arrangements increasingly more imaginative and loose to reflect Armstrong's impact. Henderson's orchestra moved away from rigidly structured dance music and into hot jazz. Redman left Henderson to join McKinney's Cotton Pickers in 1927. His influence transformed the group into a topflight jazz orchestra. Redman's arrangements were more sophisticated than the group's previous ones, and he also played alto sax solos and sang. Redman formed his own band in 1931, with Benny Morton and Harlan Lattimore, among others. His song "Chant of the Weed" was a major work. The band

was quite popular at the start of the '40s. It appeared on radio and made several records for Victor and for Brunswick, among others. Redman later composed and wrote arrangements for radio, television, and big bands in the '40s. He provided scores for Count Basie and Jimmy Dorsey. Redman led a big band on an post-World War II European tour, and became Pearl Bailey's music director in 1951. He issued a few recordings at the end of the '50s, but during his final years, didn't do much playing, preferring to write. Redman's arrangements can be heard on CD reissues of the Henderson band. —*Ron Wynn*

○ **Shakin' the African** / **i.** Sep. 1931+Oct. 1931 / Hep 1001

○ **Doin' the New Low Down** / **i.** Sep. 1931-Apr. 1933 / Hep 1004

○ **For Europeans Only** / **i.** Sep. 1946 / Steeple Chase 6020

★ **Chronological Don Redman, 1931-1933, The** / Classics 543

DIZZY REECE (Alphonso Son Reece)

b. Jan. 5, 1931, Kingston, Jamaica
Trumpet / Bop, world fusion
An outstanding, but little-noticed trumpeter, Dizzy Reece has a sparkling, ringing style ideal for driving bebop and hard bop, but flexible enough for blues or pop. Reece worked in Jamaica as a teen, then moved to England in 1948. He became well known throughout Europe in the '50s, and worked with Kenny Graham, Victor Feldman, and Tubby Hayes, and with Don Byas. He moved to America at the end of the '50s, and played with Duke Jordan, Philly Joe Jones, and Dizzy Gillespie and the Paris Reunion Band. He's made periodic return trips to Europe, but has yet to make the impact he merits. Reece has recorded for Tempo, Blue Note, Bee Hive, Interplay, and Discovery, both in America and Europe. He's done sessions with Ronnie Scott, Hank Mobley, Donald Byrd, Joe Farrell, Cecil Payne, John Gilmore, Clifford Jordan, Ted Curson, and others. Currently, there are no Reece sessions available on CD in America. —*Ron Wynn*

○ **Asia Minor** / 1958 / New Jazz 1806
With Cecil Payne (bs), Hank Jones (p) Trio. Fine document. — *Michael G. Nastos*

★ **Blues in Trinity** / Aug. 24, 1958 / Blue Note 84006

Manhattan Project / Jan. 17, 1978 / Bee Hive 7001

WAYMON REED

b. Jan. 10, 1940, Fayetteville, NC, **d.** Nov. 25, 1983, Nashville, TN
Trumpet, flugelhorn / Hard bop, soul-jazz
Both a crackling R&B player and a strong jazz soloist, trumpeter Waymon Reed got more publicity from his tenure with James Brown than from his crisp solos and heady playing in big-band horn sections as a leader, or backing his wife, Sarah Vaughan. Reed played trumpet in school bands before attending the Eastman School of Music for one year. He toured with carnival and R&B bands before settling in Miami. Reed worked with Ira Sullivan and Pee Wee Ellis, while also heading his own groups. He played with James Brown from 1965 to 1969, appearing on some seminal Brown hits. Reed did some session work in New York after leaving Brown and before joining Count Basie. He remained with Basie from 1969 to 1973. Reed recorded with big bands led by Frank Foster, Thad Jones, and Mel Lewis, and Basie in the mid- and late '70s, and also had his own bebop quintet. He toured with Vaughan from 1978 to 1980. Reed continued doing session work in the early '80s. He made an outstanding LP for the now-defunct Artists House label in 1977, *46th and 8th.* It's not currently available on CD, but Reed can be heard on reissues by Basie and Vaughan, among others. — *Ron Wynn and Michael G. Nastos*

★ **46th and 8th** / **i.** Apr. 1980 / Artists House 10
While unknown to most jazz listeners, trumpeter Waymon Reed is a superior bebop-oriented instrumentalist. A veteran of the Count Basie and Thad Jones-Mel Lewis big bands as

well as other ensembles, he also collaborated with his wife, singer Sarah Vaughan. For his debut recording as a leader Reed chooses musicians and a program to complement his dark-toned sound and communicative style. Jimmy Forrest, a hard-swinging saxophonist who was the trumpeter's colleague in the Basie band, shares the front line, while Ella Fitzgerald's former rhythm section of pianist Tommy Flanagan, bassist Ketter Betts, and drummer Bobby Durham provides smooth, integrated accompaniment. Reed's choice of compositions consists mainly of popular standards—"But Beautiful"–and pieces from the jazz tradition—"Don't Get Around Much," "Au Privave," and "Blue Monk." Even his own tune—"46th and 8th"—uses the popular 12-bar blues form, although there is a rhythmic surprise in the sixth measure. Reed usually makes the most of his solo spots, although "But Beautiful" is particularly inspired. The trumpeter's tone, inflections, and use of grace notes lend a warm feeling to everything he plays, reminiscent of Clark Terry without being derivative. Forrest also contributes several effective improvisations. Backing and complementing the horn players' considerable contributions, Flanagan is impressive both in his soloing and accompanying roles. —Clifford Jay Safane, Down Beat

TONY REEDUS

b. 1959
Drums / Neo-bop
A dynamic, very aggressive, and animated, yet disciplined drummer, Tony Reedus gained initial attention as a member of Woody Shaw's early '80s band. Since then, he's done other session work with players such as James Williams and Mulgrew Miller, and has also led sessions for Jazz City and Enja in the '80s and '90s. His dates are still available on CD. —Ron Wynn

★ **Incognito** / Dec. 1989 / Enja 6058

RUFUS REID (Rufus L. Reid)

b. Feb. 10, 1944, Sacramento, CA
Bass / Bop
A prolific bassist who is, it seems, always in the recording studio, Rufus Reid's name appears on countless hard bop, bebop, swing, and even on some pop sessions. His restrained, yet emphatic and pungent tone, timing, harmonic sensibility, and discernible, if understated, swing are welcome on any session. Trumpet was Reid's first love, but he switched to bass while in the air force. He played with Buddy Montgomery in Sacramento, then studied music in Seattle and Chicago in the late '60s and early '70s. Reid worked in Chicago with Sonny Stitt, James Moody, Milt Jackson, Curtis Fuller, and Dizzy Gillespie, and recorded with Kenny Dorham, Dexter Gordon, Lee Konitz, and Howard McGhee in 1970. He toured internationally several times with the Bobby Hutcherson-Harold Land quintet, and with Freddie Hubbard, Nancy Wilson, Eddie Harris, and Gordon through the '70s. Reid moved to New York in 1976, played and recorded with a quartet co-led by Thad Jones and Mel Lewis, and, beginning in 1979, taught at William Patterson College in Wayne, New Jersey. He recorded with Konitz, Ricky Ford, Jack DeJohnette's Special Edition with Kenny Burrell, with a quintet co-led by Frank Wess and Art Farmer, and in duos with Kenny Burrell and Harold Danko in the '80s. Reid also did sessions with Art Farmer and Jimmy Heath. He has co-led a group with drummer and longtime musical confidant Akira Tana in the late '80s and '90s. Reid has recorded as a leader for Theresa and Sunnyside. He has some dates available as a leader. —Ron Wynn

★ **Perpetual Stroll** / Jan. 27, 1980 / Theresa 111
Rufus Reid's album represents a logical modern extension of the classic jazz piano trio—a format that flourished in the 1950s and reached a pinnacle in the work of Bill Evans, Scott LaFaro, and Paul Motian. The music here swings hard, and the compositions (three of them written by Reid) are firmly rooted in bebop harmonies. This is no surprise—Reid,

pianist Kirk Lightsey, and drummer Eddie Gladden spent a couple of years working as Dexter Gordon's rhythm section. Although both Lightsey and Gladden are heard to excellent advantage, the album is clearly a showcase for the superb playing of Rufus Reid. His work here is a virtual catalog of modern bass technique, tempered by his infallible musicians. Like Charlie Haden, Reid has mastered the art of packing tremendous intensity into a few well-chosen notes. All of Reid's solos begin with articulate melodic statements that are logically developed and extended. His rhythm and intonation are nearly flawless, and he draws a sound from his instrument that is consistently full. He closes the album with a solo interpretation of Oscar Pettiford's "Tricotism," a tune originally recorded by O.P. in 1956 with the Lucky Thompson Trio. Reid gives the tune an inventive updating, using well-placed chords and harmonics to fill out the sound, while remaining faithful to the impeccable rhythm and deep feeling that characterized Pettiford's work. —Jim Roberts, Down Beat

○ **Seven Minds** / **i.** 1984 / Sunnyside 1010
Live at William Patterson College, New Jersey. Premier bassist Reid with pianist Jim McNeely and drummer Teri Lyne Carrington. Extraordinary playing, approaching telepathic. —Michael G. Nastos

Corridor to the Limits / **i.** May 5, 1989 / Sunnyside 1043
Recent Reid, featuring Harold Land (ts) plus excellent Reid compositions and playing. —Ron Wynn

☆ **Yours and Mine** / **i.** Sep. 1990 / Concord Jazz 4440
Rufus Reid (b) and Akira Tana (d). Effective session with strong help from Young Lions Ralph Moore (ts) and Jesse Davis (as). CD version has two bonus cuts. 1991 release. —Ron Wynn

DJANGO REINHARDT (Jean Baptiste Reinhardt)

b. Jan. 23, 1910, Liberchies, Belgium, **d.** May 16, 1953
Guitar / Swing
Europe's first influential jazz figure, Django Reinhardt's melodic and harmonic ideas, solo style, and general technique have been recycled, absorbed, and spread by generations of jazz and blues guitarists. A 1928 fire cost him two fingers on his fret hand. Reinhardt developed a new fingering system and switched from banjo to guitar. He was a spectacular soloist, able to play with furious intensity or incredible sensitivity, and a remarkable accompanist who could complement and support any musician. His switch to electric guitar in the '40s made him even more influential, as he tackled and mastered issues of amplification and volume. Reinhardt wandered through Belgium and France as a gypsy, playing mostly violin and banjo, plus a little guitar. He was already an adult and professional musician when he discovered jazz. Working with vocalist Jean Sablon, Reinhardt synthesized jazz and traditional gypsy music, and developed an approach that borrowed from both musical styles, but wasn't defined totally by either style. He formed the Hot Club of France in 1934 with violinist Stephane Grappelli and two other guitarists and a bassist. One original guitarist was his brother, Joseph. The Hot Club recorded over 200 songs and was a sensation on both sides of the Atlantic. Such Reinhardt compositions as "Love's Melody," "Stomping at Decca," "Djangology," and "Nocturne" became an established part of the jazz vocabulary. Reinhardt recorded with Coleman Hawkins, Benny Carter, Dicky Wells, Rex Stewart, and Barney Bigard between 1937 and 1939, then the quintet recorded in London in 1939. Reinhardt's "Nuages" was a fan favorite during World War II. He began experiments with a big band, while he also formed a quintet with clarinetist Hubert Rostaing. The Nazis banned jazz in France and murdered 500,000 gypsies, but Reinhardt continued playing. The quintet was recreated for a 1946 recording session, and Reinhardt arranged the music for the film *Le Village de la Colere* with Andre Hodeir. Later that year, Reinhardt journeyed to America to tour with Duke Ellington, but the tour was unsuccessful, in part due to Reinhardt's penchant for disappearing. He began to appreci-

ate, then play bop and adapt its lines on guitar. There were occasional reunions with Grappelli before Reinhardt died of a stroke in 1953. A documentary film about his life was made by Paul Paviot in 1958 —*Ron Wynn and Dan Morgenstern*

☆ **Djangologie–Vol. 2** / **i.** 1930 / Disques Swing 8424-26
A terrific two-CD set of '30s sides. Django is heard in small groups with Rex Stewart (cnt), Benny Carter (as), Eddie South (violin), as well as with Stephane Grappelli (violin) and The Hot Club Quintet. —*Richard Lieberson*

○ **Django '35-'39** / 1935-1939 / GNP 9019

○ **Djangologie–Vol. 1** / **i.** 1935-1938 / Disques Swing 8421-23
The first volume in a comprehensive seven-disc set of Reinhardt's great music. If you can afford it, get it. —*Ron Wynn*

Swingin' with Django / **i.** 1935-1940 / Pro Arte 549

○ **Swing Guitar** / Oct. 1945-Mar. 1946 / Vintage Jazz 628
A '91 CD reissue featuring mid-'40s material with guitarist Django Reinhardt and his American Swing Big Band. This was the guitarist's attempt at expanding his frontiers, and it worked fairly well considering Reinhardt was much more comfortable in small surroundings. This was an experiment that didn't totally work, but wasn't a complete failure either. —*Ron Wynn*

Swing de Paris / Jul. 1947-Nov. 1947 / Arco 110

★ **Quintette of the Hot Club of France, The** / **i.** 1947 / GNP 9053
A new set featuring his mid and late '40s dates with the Hot Club. Wondrous playing by Reinhardt and Grappelli (violin). —*Ron Wynn*

Djangology (1949) / Jan. 1949-Feb. 1949 / Bluebird 9988
Django and Stephane Grappelli (violin) with an Italian rhythm section in 1949. A cooler, more harmonically advanced Django with a pronounced bop influence. —*Richard Lieberson*

○ **Django Reinhardt and the American Jazz Giants** / **i.** 1969 / Prestige 7633
Here's one Django Reinhardt package that's *not* like all the others. Reinhardt got together during the '30s with some major American jazz stars for some special sessions. The roster included both Benny Carter and Coleman Hawkins and the resulting material ranks alongside the quintet dates Reinhardt did with violinist Stephane Grappelli. Prestige put this out on vinyl in 1969; unfortunately it's still available only that way. —*Ron Wynn*

★ **Djangologie/USA–Vols. 1-7** / **i.** Jun. 1988 / Swing 842026
To detail all the titles and personnel relevant to this handsome box would require too much space. This is a definitive collection that contains a high and truly representative proportion of Django Reinhardt's greatest music. The really dedicated Reinhardt fan will, of course, know of still other admirable performances on labels not available to EMI, but the essence of the guitarist's art is here. "Art" is not used lightly, for Reinhardt was the first non-American to astound and delight American jazz musicians, and to a degree subsequently reached by no one else. The set has a 46-page "Complete Discography" and excellent notes by Charles Fox. It includes many of the best performances by the Quintet of the Hot Club of France (Stephane Grappelli on violin), and the first record amusingly illustrates Reinhardt's beginnings with singers like Jean and Germaine and some pretty weird bands. Then there is that peak year of 1937 when Hughes Panassie recorded the classic sessions with Coleman Hawkins and Benny Carter, with Dicky Wells, Eddie South, and Bill Coleman. From the following year comes another fine Benny Carter date, and from 1939 the remarkable quartet session with Rex Stewart. All these are indispensable recordings in any serious collection, and they are very conveniently gathered together in this box. —*Stanley Dance, Jazz Times*

○ **First Recordings** / Prestige 7614

Exactly what the title says, sessions done in the very earliest stages of guitarist Django Reinhardt's career. This album's value has been reduced by the release of a boxed set by Affinity that includes 144 Reinhardt tracks over the years 1936-1940. It has most of this release and with more information. —*Ron Wynn*

○ **Legendary Django** / GNP 9039
A decent, though not comprehensive, anthology of '30s and '40s cuts by Django Reinhardt. It tries to cover every aspect and doesn't aim to be anything except a sampler. In that regard, it accomplishes its goal. —*Ron Wynn*

○ **Parisian Swing** / GNP 9002
Delightful, often energetic session with the great guitarist Djano Reinhardt displaying his jam session and combative nature. Reinhardt plays with force, joy, and creativity, while incorporating some blues licks and feeling into his fleeting solos. —*Ron Wynn*

○ **Solos/Duets/Trios** / Inner City 1105
An interesting concept work: pulling and issuing selected sessions from guitarist Django Reinhardt either alone or playing with just a bassist or a drummer. His solos are striking in their simplicity and beauty, while his duets are intimate and attractive; the trio sessions are faster, more competitive, and among the least satisfying, at least on this release. —*Ron Wynn*

EMILY REMLER

b. Sep. 18, 1957, New York, NY, **d.** 1990
Guitar / Postbop, neo-bop
One of the sadder cases in the '80s, guitarist Emily Remler had established herself as an outstanding soloist and versatile player who was at home with bebop, jazz-rock, pop, blues, and Afro-Latin. She utilized some of the same stylistic devices as Wes Montgomery, right down to playing without a pick, at times, and to playing with the same fluidity and phrasing as Montgomery. Remler began playing guitar at age ten, and later attended Berklee. She was house guitarist at the Fairmont Hotel in New Orleans, where she accompanied such guests as Nancy Wilson, Michel Legrand, and Robert Goulet. Herb Ellis introduced her at the 1978 Concord Jazz Festival and also aided her career. Remler worked with Astrud Gilberto in the early '80s, and did an album of duets with Larry Coryell in the mid '80s. She also worked with the group Great Guitars that included Charlie Byrd, Barney Kessel, and Ellis, and in a quartet with Bob Moses, Eddie Gomez, and John D'Earth. Remley recorded as a leader for Concord and Justice in the '80s. Sadly, Remler had a longtime problem with heroin addiction. She died at age 32 while on tour. Remler has several sessions available on CD. —*Ron Wynn and Dan Morgenstern*

★ **Firefly** / Apr. 1981 / Concord Jazz 4162
Guitarist Emily Remler's album starts slowly with the first three cuts presenting little more than perfunctory albeit quality playing. However, starting with the title cut, things really pick up and remain on a solid level for the second side. For example, there is the solid octave work on "Inception" and "Movin'" (the latter and the title cut featuring her most invigorating solos), the subtle fluttering attack surfacing a few times on "In a Sentimental Mood," and the accompanying effects during the bass solo on "Inception," to say nothing of her solid use of interlocking over-the-bar phrasing and the casual fluff-like way that she sometimes ends lines or phrases. Special mention also goes to her a cappella "A Taste of Honey"—an effective and brief study in understatement. Pianist Hank Jones is his usual tasty self, complete with rolling, engratiating long solos, and drummer Jake Hanna and bassist Bob Maize provide good support with above-average solo contributions. —*Milo Fine, Cadence*

Retrospective–Vol. 1: Standards / 1981-1988 / Concord Jazz 4453

☆ **Retrospective–Vol. 2** / 1981-1988 / Concord Jazz 4463
Excellent compositions from this late guitarist. You don't want to miss this. —*Michael G. Nastos*

Take Two / Jun. 1982 / Concord Jazz 4195

Transitions / Oct. 1983 / Concord Jazz 4236

○ **Catwalk** / Aug. 1984 / Concord Jazz 4265

Guitarist Emily Remler at the time of *Catwalk* (1984) was rapidly developing her chordal style to add to her single string work, and the variety achieved here, when combined with her fertile imagination, enhances her solos and comping even more. As usual, bassist Eddie Gomez complements her work beautifully, trumpeter John D'Earth adds solo and atmospheric interest, and the ever-reliable Bob Moses (per) provides a springy foundation. —*Shirley Klett, Cadence*

East to West / May 1988 / Concord Jazz 4356

REVOLUTIONARY ENSEMBLE

Drums / Early free, modern creative

The Revolutionary Ensemble was one of the greatest free music trios ever assembled, though they were never able to turn even a modest profit. The unit was formed in 1971 and included violinist Leroy Jenkins, bassist Sirone (Norris Jones), and drummer Frank Clayton. They were a smaller version of the Art Ensemble of Chicago, with each musician doubling on several instruments and all of them doing occasional vocals and contributing compositions. Clayton was replaced by Jerome Cooper in September of '71. Their concerts and albums reflected the trio's ability to anticipate each other's direction, and reflected the brilliance of their union. But none of their critically acclaimed albums for ESP, India Navigation, A&M, or Enja ever came close to earning enough to keep the group going. They tried to make ends meet through festival and concert appearances, but finally had to give up the ghost in 1977. Only their debut release on ESP is available currently on CD. —*Ron Wynn with Myles Boisen*

Vietnam / 1972 / ESP 3007

★ **People's Republic, The** / Dec. 4-6, 1975 / A&M 708

Recorded beautifully, more resonant and full than I thought technically possible, *The People's Republic* is a powerful argument for group improvisation. The trio shifts through textures with individual brilliance while retaining the ensemble blend. Horizon thankfully includes some of the scores, providing the listeners with the material from which the artists (violinist Leroy Jenkins, bassist Sirone, percussionist Jerome Cooper) worked. Very free and musically intricate, *The People's Republic* is a cornucopia for the involved listener. —*Kevin Yatarola, Cadence*

Psyche, The / i. 1975 / RE 3117

BUDDY RICH (Bernard Rich)

b. Sep. 30, 1917, New York, NY, **d.** Apr. 2, 1987, Los Angeles, CA

Drums, vocals, bandleader / Swing, big band

A flamboyant character, a snappy dresser, an accomplished marital arts fighter, and a preferred guest on the "Tonight Show" with Johnny Carson throughout the '70s and early '80s, Buddy Rich was above all a magnificent drummer. There was almost universal respect among Black drummers for his skills. Max Roach, Art Blakey, and Jo and Philly Joe Jones spoke glowingly in various forums about Rich, and he and Roach even staged their version of famous gunfighters going at each other on album (a friendly battle). Rich was arguably Roach's only rival among modern drummers for definitive unaccompanied solos; Rich's array of accents, crossrhythms, patterns, and licks, all played at faster and faster speed until a show-stopping conclusion, were free of gimmicks and clichés until the latter part of his career, when his solos became a show business ritual. Rich was an underrated vocalist who made some respectable albums as a singer, and could play with restraint when necessary. But at his best, he drove and pushed a band with flair and fire. Rich was also brutally outspoken, unafraid to make enemies or outrageous quotes. He made no secret of his dislike for Tommy Dorsey, and wasn't that fond of Frank Sinatra despite the fact that they became friends and toured together.

His longtime friend, vocalist Mel Tormé, cited an impressive enemies list in his Rich biography.

As a baby, Rich worked with his parents on stage, and used the tag "Baby Traps." He played on Broadway at age four and was leading bands at age 11. Rich played with Joe Marsala in 1937 and 1938, then worked with Bunny Berigan, Harry James, Artie Shaw, Tommy Dorsey, and Benny Carter from 1938 to 1942. Rich had two years of military service, then rejoined Dorsey in 1944 and 1945. He started his own band in 1945, then joined Jazz at the Philharmonic in 1947. His rollicking drum solos were as much a crowd pleaser as the various honkers and wailers. But Rich switched gears and joined Les Brown in 1949. During the '50s, Rich was in the Big Four with Charlie Ventura, Chubby Jackson, and Marty Napoleon. He worked once more with James and Dorsey, led combos, and recorded as a bandleader, sideman, and singer. He was featured on many impressive sessions with the era's leading musicians: Flip Phillips, Dizzy Gillespie, Gene Krupa, Harry Edison, Art Tatum, and Lionel Hampton. The famous *Rich Versus Roach* battle was recorded in 1959. Rich made some surprising vocal albums, one that featured Johnny Mercer tunes. After a heart attack, Rich began practicing martial arts, and eventually acquired a black belt in karate.

He worked with James again in 1961, then formed a big band in 1966 when industry consensus was that large groups were dinosaurs. Rich kept the band going in the '60s and into the '70s, cutting albums and touring extensively. He did everything, and made some stylistic concessions on records that rubbed some people the wrong way. These concessions included cutting Beatles and Paul Simon songs. Rich used arrangers like Bill Holman and Don Sebesky, hired Art Pepper (briefly), and featured Steve Marcus and Pat Labarbera. He even got his own television show in 1968. Rich trimmed the band down to a combo in 1974, and lent his name to a club the next year. He reformed the big band in 1975, and cranked out more recordings. He was back at work two weeks after bypass surgery in 1983, and toured nine months a year right up to a few months before his death in 1987. His work remains alive thanks to Tormé's comprehensive (though insider and celebrity-oriented) biography, and to numerous reissues that bear Rich's name. —*Ron Wynn and Buz Overbeck*

And His Legendary '47-'48 Orchestra / 1947-1948 / Hep 12

Swinging Count / i. 1952 / Verve

Sings Johnny Mercer / Jan. 5-6, 1956 / Verve

★ **This One's for Basie** / Aug. 18+25, 1956 / Verve 817788

A classic! Marty Paich, Buddy, and top Los Angeles studio musicians play Basie. —*Buz Overbeck*

Just Sings / Jan. 31, 1957 / Verve

★ **Rich Versus Roach** / Apr. 1959 / Mercury 826987

Definitive battle of the drummers from 1959. CD has four bonus cuts. —*Ron Wynn*

Buddy & Soul / Jan. 3, 1969-Jun. 22, 1969 / PA/USA 9004

Different Drummer / Jul. 14-16, 1971 / RCA

★ **Rich in London** / Dec. 6-8, 1971 / RCA

Buddy Rich and His Orchestra / i. Oct. 1973 / Laserlight 15758

A good solid collection of Buddy's 1973 band. Great studio recordings. —*Buz Overbeck*

Sound of Jazz / i. Sep. 1977 / CLCD 65010

Best Band I Ever Had / i. Oct. 1977 / Dcc 606

Great direct-to-disc recording of an exciting, driving, contemporary big band. No drum solos. —*Buz Overbeck*

Live at King Street Cafe / Apr. 3, 1985 / Pacific Jazz

☆ **Swings and Swings and Swings** / RCA

Textbook album by drummer Buddy Rich. It features the characteristic uptempo arrangements and sweeping ballad treatments. The horn and brass solos are good, the rhythm section competent, and Rich, as usual, dominates from the drum position. —*Ron Wynn*

JEROME RICHARDSON (Jerome C. Richardson)

b. Nov. 15, 1920, Sealy, TX

Saxophone, flute / Big band, bop, hard bop, postbop, progressive big band

Jerome Richardson was once a notable, versatile jazz saxophonist. He remains quite versatile, but his visibility has been limited for years due to his heavy studio output. Since the early '70s, Richardson's often robust saxophone and tart flute have been heard mostly on film and television soundtracks. Richardson began playing alto at age eight, and was a professional at age 14. He worked with Texas dance bands until 1941, then was in Jimmie Lunceford's band briefly before joining the navy. He worked in a band led by Marshall Royal in the service. Richardson toured with Lionel Hampton after his discharge in the late '40s, then played with Earl Hines in the early '50s. Richardson moved to New York in 1953, led his own band at Minton's, and worked with Oscar Pettiford in 1956 and 1957. He did sessions with Lucky Millinder, Cootie Williams, Chico Hamilton, Johnny Richards, Gerry Mulligan, and Gerald Wilson, then joined Quincy Jones's orchestra in 1959. He was part of the band for the show *Free and Easy*, which toured Europe, and he performed in Paris. Richardson played in bands backing several singers in the '60s, among them Peggy Lee, Billy Eckstine, Brook Benton, and Julie London. He was a founding member of the Thad Jones-Mel Lewis orchestra in the mid-'60s, and was its lead alto saxophonist until 1970. Then Richardson moved to Hollywood, and since that time has collaborated with Jones frequently, doing albums and touring Japan three times together. He toured Europe with Nat Adderley in 1980. Richardson recorded in the '60s as a leader for New Jazz and United Artists, among others. Currently, he doesn't have any sessions available as a leader, but can be heard on CD reissues by Jones and the Thad Jones-Mel Lewis orchestra. *—Ron Wynn*

○ **Midnight Oil** / i. 1958 / Original Jazz Classics 1815

★ **Roamin' with Richardson** / Oct. 21, 1959 / New Jazz 8226

Going to the Movies / Apr. 1962 / United Artists 15006

DANNIE RICHMOND (Charles D. Richmond)

b. Dec. 15, 1935, New York, NY, **d.** Mar. 15, 1988, New York, NY

Drums, tenor saxophone / Bop, hard bop, progressive big band, early jazz-rock

He began as a saxophonist, but Dannie Richmond was Charles Mingus's faithful drumming companion for many years. Richmond was both an unpredictable and a consistent player, who alternated between loose, extremely free, and very structured, disciplined playing. He'd shift between these extremes, often in the same composition. His affinity with Mingus's music and his role in pacing and building his compositions was vital to the success of numerous Jazz Workshop performances and recording sessions. Richmond could play in the heavy backbeat, blues/R&B mode, could let things hang out in a swing-tinged jam session, or could play crisp, furious bebop. He was an R&B tenor saxophonist in his teens, then switched to drums. He took over drum duties for Mingus in 1956, and retained that position until 1970. He handled any and every situation, from tight combos to chaotic big bands and in-between. Richmond did a trio date with Hampton Hawes in 1957 for Atlantic, and later did sessions with Chet Baker for Riverside, and with Jimmy Knepper and Herbie Nichols for Bethlehem. He recorded his own albums for Impulse in the '60s, for Horo, Steeplechase, and Soul Note in the '70s, and for Gatemouth and Red in the '80s. Richmond played jazz-rock in the '70s with the Mark-Almond band, backed Joe Cocker, and toured with Elton John and Johnny Taylor. He gave drum clinics when he wasn't touring, and published a method book in Germany in 1964. Richmond had a brief stint with Chet Baker, then rejoined Mingus in 1974. When Mingus died in 1979, Richmond helped form the Mingus Dynasty repertory band, and served as musical director for a time. He was also a

founding member of one of the late '70s and early '80s great combos, the Don Pullen-George Adams quartet. Richmond continued recording as a leader after the Pullen/Adams group disbanded, until his death in 1988. He has a few releases available on CD. *—Ron Wynn*

★ **In Jazz for the Culture Set** / 1965 / Impulse 98

With pianist Jaki Byard and harmonicist Toots Thielemans. Andy Warhol soup can cover art. Great record. *—Michael G. Nastos*

☆ **Ode to Mingus** / Nov. 23-24, 1979 / Soul Note 1005

A super tribute to his longtime employer and musical comrade. The set should have made the jazz world notice Bill Saxton on tenor sax. *—Ron Wynn*

○ **Quintet** / Sep. 24, 1980 / Gatemouth 1004

It came as no surprise that it would ultimately take Charles Mingus's right-hand man to take up the torch where others stumbled. Projecting an insight that only Mingus's closest musical associate could possess, drummer Dannie Richmond captures more of the Mingus gift and genius than all the Dynasties (even those he was a part of) or Joni Mitchells put together, and in addition offers an entire side of rich material composed by band members. Reviving the last working band Mingus personally put together and placing in the bass spot Cameron Brown—one of the few bassists who wouldn't pale in the awesome light of Mingus's own bass playing—Richmond starts off on the right foot. Adding his own strengths as a bandleader, Richmond cuts this record solidly in the Mingus groove. Featuring a pared-down orchestration of "Cumbia and Jazz Fusion" (recorded by Mingus on the classic album of the same name), the quintet captures more than its share of the exotic space Mingus wrote into the piece. The ensemble work simply sparkles with vitality. With his crystal-sharp tenor conception, Ricky Ford delivers solos that Mingus would have been pleased with—which says a lot. Wisely avoiding an attempt to top the first side with more Mingus, trumpeter Jack Walrath and Richmond show just how well they can fuse what they learned about composing at Mingus University with their own burgeoning styles, and pianist Bob Neloms rolls up a funky hard bop number for the band to take on. *—Cliff Tinder,* Down Beat

☆ **Dionysius** / May 30, 1983 / Red Record

An album played by ex-Mingusites, this is one side originals and one side of Charles Mingus's music. Features Jack Walrath (tpt), Ricky Ford (ts), Bob Neloms (p), and Cameron Brown (b). *—Michael G. Nastos*

Gentleman's Agreement / i. 1983 / Soul Note

Sizzling cuts, with old pros Jimmy Knepper on trombone and Hugh Lawson on piano taking care of business. *—Ron Wynn*

LARRY RIDLEY

b. 1937

Bass / Hard bop

A consistently propulsive, aggressive player, bassist Larry Ridley's one of the more energized players in bebop and hard bop circles. His tone isn't as pronounced as some other tones, but he compensates with strong support and a steady rhythmic intensity. Ridley began on violin as a child, then later turned to bass. He worked with longtime friend Freddie Hubbard in Indianapolis as a teen, then got his first professional job with Wes Montgomery. Ridley changed from violin to bass studies at Indiana University, and later was tutored by Percy Heath at the Lenox School of Jazz. He worked briefly with Hubbard in New York in 1959, then toured the next year with Slide Hampton. Ridley worked with Max Roach, Philly Joe Jones, Roy Haynes, and Horace Silver in the '60s, then recorded in Europe with George Wein's Newport All Stars in 1969. He toured with Thelonious Monk in 1970, and played with him until 1973. After obtaining a degree in music education from New York University in 1971, Ridley eventually became head of the jazz program and chairman of the music department at Livingston College (Rutgers). He was in Jones's group

Dameronia in the '80s, and served on the executive committee of the National Jazz Service Organization. Ridley recorded as a leader for Strata-East in the '70s, and with Hampton, Lee Morgan, Silver, Stephane Grappelli and Joe Venuti, James Moody, and Teddy Edwards in the '60s and '70s. His lone album has not been reissued on CD, but he can be heard on reissues by Morgan, Silver, and others. — Ron Wynn

BEN RILEY

b. 1933
Drums / Hard bop
One of the top swinging, supportive drummers in jazz, Ben Riley's famous for his ability to add exactly the right background and textures to a date. He worked in the late '50s and early '60s with Randy Weston, Sonny Stitt, Stan Getz, Woody Herman, Junior Mance, Kenny Burrell, Eddie "Lockjaw" Davis, and Johnny Griffin. Riley recorded with Paul Winter, Jeremy Steig, Ray Bryant, and Junior Mance, and worked with Ahmad Jamal, Roland Hanna, Billy Taylor, Walter Bishop, Jr., and Kai Winding during that same period. He was Thelonious Monk's regular drummer from 1964 to 1967, and toured extensively. Riley recorded with Alice Coltrane from 1968 to 1975, and began performing with her in 1971. He also joined the New York Jazz Quartet, playing and recording periodically with them into the '80s. Riley played with Toots Thielemans, Milt Jackson, and Bob James in the Soviet Union, played and recorded with Ron Carter's group in the mid-'70s, and worked briefly with Jim Hall's trio in 1981. He was a founding member of Sphere with Charlie Rouse, Buster Williams, and Kenny Barron in the early '80s, and toured Africa and America with Abdullah Ibrahim in the mid-'80s. Riley has recorded as a leader for Musician/Elektra. His dates with Sphere are available on CD. —Ron Wynn

HERLIN RILEY

Drums / Neo-bop
One of the newest members of the Wynton Marsalis band, Herlin Riley hasn't recorded as a leader yet, but has grown and matured as a drummer. He took over in a difficult spot when he replaced the outstanding Jeff Watts in the late '80s. Riley's improved his playing on Marsalis's albums, not yet as steady or as assertive as Watts, but influencing the music more than Watts does on releases such as *The Majesty of the Blues* and *Uptown Ruler*. Riley can also be heard on the soundtrack *Tune in Tomorrow, Levee Low Moan,* and *Standard Time, Volume Three—The Resolution of Romance.* All are still available on CD. —Ron Wynn

LEE RITENOUR (Lee Mack [Captain Fingers] Ritenour)

b. Nov. 1, 1952, Hollywood, CA
Guitar, banjo, mandolin / Early jazz-rock, instrumental pop, contemporary funk
Ritenour taught classical guitar at USC and has been a premier Los Angeles studio player since the mid-'70s. Ritenour's knowledge of jazz, international, and pop styles is impressive, and his speed, facility, phrasing, and technique are always flawless. Sometimes, he's been criticized for his choice of material and his penchant for fusion and commercial music. He has issued rock-dominated, instrumental pop, and light Brazilian releases, and film soundtracks, plus one or two rare sets where he's been able to stretch out and play with flair, distinction, and individuality. —Ron Wynn

Captain Fingers / i. 1977 / Epic 34426
A great player shows how easily he can handle trite pop. Wonderful Mobile Fidelity mastering job. —Ron Wynn

Captain's Journey / i. 1978 / Elektra 136
Guitarist Lee Ritenour had just switched labels from Epic to Elektra when he cut *Captain's Journey* in 1978. It was a follow-up to the successful crossover work *Captain Fingers* and uses a similiar strategy: tight, hook-laden arrangements, polished production, and minimal solo space. What individual

things it has are dominated by Ritenour, a supremely talented guitarist who doesn't display that much of it with these arrangements. —Ron Wynn

Rio / Aug. 1979 / GRP 9524

Feel the Night / i. 1979 / Elektra 192

Rit—Vol. 1 / i. 1985 / Elektra 331

Portrait / Jan. 1987 / GRP 9553

Color Rit / Mar. 1989 / GRP 9594

Stolen Moments / Dec. 1989 / GRP 9615

★ **Wes Bound** / i. 1993 / GRP 9697
On *Wes Bound*, Lee Ritenour pays homage to Wes Montgomery, the last great jazz guitarist of the prefusion era. Ritenour does an uncanny job of recreating Montgomery's hollow-body Gibson L-5 sound and flowing octave melody lines on standards such as "Road Song" and "West Coast Blues." Ronnie Foster takes Jimmy Smith's role on a cookin' organ-trio arrangement of "4 on 6," and Maxi Priest handles the vocal on a surprisingly effective version of Bob Marley's "Waiting in Vain." —Rick Mitchell, Request

SAM RIVERS (Samuel Carthorne Rivers)

b. Sep. 25, 1930, El Reno, OK
Tenor and soprano saxophone, flute, composer / Early free, modern creative
Perhaps the greatest musician and composer that no one's ever heard (or heard about), Sam Rivers has battled gamely through his entire career in virtual anonymity. That doesn't mean he hasn't had high-profile gigs; he worked once with Miles Davis, has recorded with Cecil Taylor, and even had albums released by a major label (ABC) in the '70s. But Rivers's sound and style are so resolutely original and uncompromising that he hasn't found a way to even break out into the jazz mainstream. He's a versatile artist who plays frenetic, smashing tenor sax, equally aggressive soprano and piano, and flute.

His father was a member of the Fisk Jubilee Singers and Silvertone Quartet. Rivers studied piano, reed instruments, and viola in Little Rock, Arkansas, and in Chicago, and attended Boston Conservatory of Music in the late '40s and early '50s. He played regularly in Boston with musicians such as Jaki Byard, Gigi Gryce, and Herb Pomeroy until the mid-'60s, then attracted some critical attention (pro and con) when he worked with the Miles Davis quintet in 1964. He left Boston for New York that year, and also played and recorded with the band in Japan. He began recording on Blue Note, playing with Bobby Hutcherson, helping to introduce Tony Williams, and featuring his originals. Rivers worked with Taylor in the late '60s and joined him as artist-in-residence at the Foundation Maeght in France. A series of concerts Rivers did with Taylor for the Shandar label (issued domestically as a three-record set by Prestige and long ago consigned to history's bin) features some of the freest, most personal, over-the-edge music issued on album since John Coltrane's final days. He taught in Harlem and played and recorded again with Taylor.

Rivers and his wife, Bea, established Studio Rivea in Soho during the early '70s. It became a prime forum for new and free music, and was considered the foundation home of the "loft jazz" movement. Rivers continued recording, doing some outstanding, poor-selling records for ABC/Impulse, cutting brilliant duets with Dave Holland, and getting some measure of recognition for his appearance on Holland's seminal *Conference of the Birds* ECM date in 1972. The loft jazz movement seemed to peak with the mid-'70s Wildflowers concert series, which was later featured on several albums. Rivers continued recording on Horo, Red, Black Saint, and Blue Marge in the '70s and '80s. He played with Holland, Barry Altschul, the Tuba Trio, which featured Joe Daley, George Lewis, and Thurman Barker and his 11-piece Winds of Manhattan orchestra. Rivers recently recorded for Timeless. He has a scant few titles available on CD, though the two fine duet albums he did with Holland have been reissued. —*Ron Wynn*

○ **Fuschia Swing Song** / Dec. 11, 1964 / Blue Note 84184
Mid-'60s date with Jaki Byard (p). All Rivers originals and his best period album. —*Michael G. Nastos*

★ **Contours** / May 21, 1965 / Blue Note

○ **New Conception, A** / Oct. 11, 1966 / Blue Note 4249

○ **Involution** / Mar. 17, 1967 / Blue Note 4261
Six emotion-titled pieces from a session led by pianist Andrew Hill are included on Sam Rivers's *Involution* (Rivers played as part of Hill's quartet), along with a major and truly remarkable sextet session Rivers led in 1967. Hill's playing at this time is forcefully directed. His compositions, though, stem from different sources than on earlier releases: "Lust" and "Desire" are less lyrical in any traditional sense, and the aptly named "Violence" is an uncompromised avant-garde performance owing at least something to Cecil Taylor. And the main event on most of the tracks is Sam Rivers, virtually unrecognized in 1966. This material thrust his individuality under our noses. For even then he was one of the New Music's most fascinating players, ranging freely with intense imagination and order. A year and a half after the Hill recording, Rivers led James Spaulding, Donald Byrd, Julian Priester, Cecil McBee, and Steve Ellington in a session that should be ranked among the key events in Rivers's career. Preceding his startling big-band LP *Crystals* by some seven years, Rivers's linear compositional style is shown here in full, if miniaturized, bloom. The resulting tracks offer stupendous charts and clear, adventurous performances by a group that deserved to be recorded more than once. —*Neil Tesser*, Down Beat

Dimensions and Extensions / i. Mar. 17, 1967 / Blue Note 84261
Here are stinging, expansive solos with one foot in avant-garde, one in hard bop. —*Ron Wynn*

★ **Streams–Live at Montreux** / Jul. 6, 1973 / MCA 39120
Streams features Sam Rivers as the lead voice on the album-long "Streams," a lengthy (59:56) multisectioned free improvisation recorded at the Montreux Jazz Festival (7/6/73). With support from the brilliant bassist Cecil McBee and subtle drumming from the predisco Norman Connors, Rivers takes a powerful solo on tenor, sings through his flute, rambles a bit on piano, and concludes with a strong dosage of his soprano. Rivers's vocal shouting acts as a segue between his subtle shifts of instruments and the momentum never slows during his set. *Streams* remains one of Sam Rivers's strongest recordings. —*Scott Yanow*, Cadence

○ **Crystals** / 1974 / Impulse 9286

Sizzle / 1975 / Impulse 9316
Trio with Barry Altschul (d) and Dave Holland (b). Funky with electric touches. Fierce. —*Michael G. Nastos*

☆ **Sam Rivers and Dave Holland** / Feb. 18, 1976 / Improvising Artists 373843
Vols. 1 & 2. Excellent, experimental duets between a great bassist and a superior improviser. Unfortunately, it's hard to find. —*Ron Wynn*

○ **Sam Rivers–Vol. 2** / Feb. 18, 1976 / Improvising Artists 373843
"Ripples" finds Sam Rivers on flute, along with the tenor saxophone, the instrument on which I find him most satisfying. The music proceeds along a multitude of paths: there is a swinging, bluesy section; a *muy rapido* section with a maniacal walking pattern from bassist Dave Holland; an Eastern-tinged section with a rhythm-guitar-like ostinato pattern from Holland; and a free-form section with Holland simultaneously bowing and plucking his bass. This is a classic performance. "Deluge" is the more abstract of the two pieces due to Rivers's piano stylings. He seems intent on playing every note on the piano, leaving as few spaces as possible. The title pretty much describes his approach to the piano. Nevertheless, repeated listenings found this performance nearly as stunning as "Ripples." And that's how I

would approach this music: get rid of all distractions, sit down, and concentrate on the music produced by this musical fellowship. —*Carl Brauer*, Cadence

Paragon / Apr. 18, 1977 / Fluid 101

Colours / Sep. 13, 1982 / Black Saint
Stomping, swinging arrangements. Exuberant 11-piece orchestra supervised and spurred by Rivers. —*Ron Wynn*

MAX ROACH (Maxwell Roach)

b. Jan. 10, 1924, New Land, NC
Drums, marimba, composer, bandleader / Bop
On the basis of his persistence, adaptability, and symbolic importance, Max Roach would merit inclusion in jazz's pantheon of special performers. But he's done more than outlive many of his contemporaries; Roach, along with Kenny Clarke, changed the direction of drummers in the bop revolution. He shifted the rhythmic focus from the bass drum to the ride cymbal, a move that gave drummers more freedom. He emerged as arguably bebop's greatest drum soloist. Roach didn't simply drop bombs and blast away. He told a complete story, varying his pitch, tuning, patterns, and volume. He was a brilliant brush player, and could push, redirect, or break up the beat. Roach has never stood still musically, though the links between what he played in the '40s and today aren't that far apart. He's worked with pianoless trios, has played with symphony orchestras, has done duos with free and avant-garde musicians, has backed gospel choirs, and has even played with a rapper long before the jazz/hip-hop thing became a media event. He was outspoken about social injustices in the pre-civil rights era, and recorded powerful, undiluted protest material.

His mother sang gospel, and Roach began playing drums in gospel bands at age ten. He had formal studies at the Manhattan School of Music, then started playing with Charlie Parker, Dizzy Gillespie, and others at Minton's Playhouse in 1942. He was house drummer and a frequent participant in after-hours jam sessions. One of the other participants was Kenny Clarke. Roach had brief stints with Benny Carter, with Duke Ellington's band, then joined Gillespie's quintet in 1943 and was in Parker-led bands in 1945, 1947 to 1949, and 1951 to 1953. He made his recording debut with Coleman Hawkins in 1943, then recorded with Miles Davis and Parker in the late '40s. Roach traveled to Paris with Parker in 1949, and recorded there with him and with others, including Kenny Dorham. He also played with Louis Jordan, Red Allen, and Coleman Hawkins, and participated in the *Birth of the Cool* sessions in 1948-1950. During the early '50s, Roach toured with the Jazz at the Philharmonic revue, played at Massey Hall in an all-star concert with Parker, Gillespie, Charles Mingus, and Bud Powell, and recorded with Howard Rumsey's Lighthouse All-Stars. During the mid-'50s, he co-led the Max Roach/Clifford Brown orchestra with Powell's brother, Richie, on piano, and with saxophonists Harold Land and Sonny Rollins. His frenetic, yet precise drumming laid the foundation for Brown's amazing trumpet solos. This group made some landmark records in its short tenure, among them *Study in Brown* and *At Basin Street*.

After Brown and Powell were killed tragically in a car crash in 1956, Roach tried to keep the group going using Dorham and Rollins. He became involved in a record label partnership with Charles Mingus as well, and formed Debut Records in the mid-'50s. Later, Roach led another influential band, this time with trumpeters Dorham or Booker Little, tenor saxophonist George Coleman, trombonist Julian Priester, and sometimes Ray Draper on tuba. They cut seminal dates for Riverside and EmArcy, among them *On the Chicago Scene*, and *Deeds Not Words*. The Max Roach Plus Four became a prototype hard bop unit.

Then, during the early '60s, Roach composed multifaceted suites, and wrote openly political, confrontational material that featured his wife, Abbey Lincoln, criticizing American racial injustices. He dispensed with the piano on occasion, and experimented with solo drum compositions as wholly independent pieces. There were more albums for Atlantic and Impulse. The list included *Freedom Now Suite*, *Percussion Bitter Sweet*, *It's Time*, *Speak, Brother, Speak*, *The Legendary Hassan*, *Lift Every Voice and Sing*, and *Members, Don't Get Weary*. There was also the brilliant *Drums Unlimited* in 1965. The *Freedom Now Suite* was made into a film by Gianni Amici in 1966, but Roach and Lincoln maintain they suffered severe career reprisals as a result.

During the '70s, Roach continued recording prolifically for various labels, though most were for import companies like Denon and Soul Note. Roach founded M'Boom Re: Percussion in 1970, a cooperative group of ten percussionists who performed works written for them. The group still records and performs 23 years later. He recorded with Cecil Taylor, Anthony Braxton, Archie Shepp, and Abdullah Ibrahim, while he maintained his own bands. Roach also began a career in education; he became a professor at the University of Massachusetts at Amherst, and later held a position at the Lennox School of Jazz. In the '80s and '90s, he has led, at various times, a regular quartet, a double quartet (an acoustic and string quartet together), and M-Boom, and he continues to lecture, to perform, and to exemplify the real meaning of jazz. —*Ron Wynn*

Max Roach Quartet, Featuring Hank Mobley, The / Apr. 10-21, 1953 / Original Jazz Classics 202

In Concert / Apr. 1954-Aug. 30, 1954 / GNP 18

★ **Max Roach Plus Four** / Oct. 12, 1956 / EmArcy 36098
This is great. Max Roach with Sonny Rollins (ts), Kenny Dorham (tpt), Hank Mobley (ts), and more. —*Ron Wynn*

☆ **Jazz in 3/4 Time** / Mar. 18-21, 1957 / Mercury 826456

Percussion Discussion / i. 1958 / Chess 92511

○ **Max Roach Plus Four on the Chicago Scene** / Jun. 1958 / EmArcy 36132

○ **Max Roach Plus Four at Newport** / Jul. 6, 1959 / EmArcy 80010

Deeds, Not Words / Sep. 4, 1959 / Riverside 304
A late '50s classic, one of many that Roach released in this period with some pointed sociopolitical album titles. This was cut for Riverside with a group that included Ray Draper on tuba, George Coleman on tenor sax, and Booker Little on trumpet. There's a brilliant, incendiary drum solo to conclude the set. —*Ron Wynn*

★ **Freedom Now Suite** / Aug. 31+Sep. 6, 1960 / Columbia 36390
Like tenor saxophonist Coleman Hawkins, who appears on the reissued *Freedom Now Suite*, drummer Max Roach spans several musical generations and, in middle age here, was still showing the capacity to assimiliate newer styles without compromising his personal approach. As Hawkins adapted to bop, Roach embraced free rhythms as a natural outgrowth of the odd time signatures he himself pioneered. The *Freedom Now Suite* dates from 1960, just as the first sit-in demonstrations ushered in a decade of racial upheaval. Abbey Lincoln, then Roach's wife, gives voice to the lyrics of Oscar Brown, Jr., articulating concerns that Roach would continue to espouse: African-American heritage, pan-African musical culture, the travails of slavery and discrimination, and the ongoing liberation struggles in Southern Africa. Roach's Charles Mingus-like compositions represent the culmination of the new musical revolution then waiting in the wings. Coleman Hawkins delivers a brilliantly resonant and moving solo on "Driva Man," while Booker Little burns on trumpet and Julian Priester outdoes himself on trombone. Roach was quite a "driva man" himself, and when he is joined by percussionists Olatunji, Ray Mantilla, and Tomas du Vall, the smoking rhythms burst into flame. Abbey Lincoln's literal screaming anticipates the shrieking saxophonics yet to come, but overall her singing is the weakest link in the suite, more appropriate to the original theatrical conception of the work than to a recorded presentation. —*Larry Birnbaum, Down Beat*

Max Roach, Sonny Clark, George Duvivier / i. 1962 / Bainbridge
This is really more of a Sonny Clark (p) recording, and it serves to show how tragic his death at such an early age (27) was. All eight selections are Clark originals showcasing his formidable composing talents. With its trio format (George Duvivier as bassist) the music takes on a lean and intimate quality drawing the listener into the center. "Blues Blue" is a Clark-Duvivier duet (one of the album's highlights), and "My Conception" is a solo piano feature. —*Bob Rusch, Cadence*

○ **Max Roach Trio, Featuring the Legendary Hassan, The** / Dec. 4+7, 1964 / Atlantic 82273
This album for many years seemed to be only legend until it recently resurfaced on the reissue trail. Hassan was an East Coast pianist reputed to be among the greatest pure technicians. He made precious few recordings and disappeared from the jazz world long ago. Max Roach was among the few to ever perform with him, and this session verifies Hassan's credentials while also showing how masterful a percussionist and combo leader Max Roach always has been. —*Ron Wynn*

Drums Unlimited / Oct. 14, 1965-Nov. 12, 1966 / Rhino 1467

○ **Force—Sweet Mao—Suid Africa '76** / Jul. 1976 / BASE 28976
Duets with Archie Shepp (sax). Extended pieces from two virtuosos. Quintessential. —*Michael G. Nastos*

Loadstar, The / Jul. 27, 1977 / Horo 10
Quartet twofer (one piece per album) with Billy Harper (ts), Cecil Bridgewater (tpt), Reggie Workman (b). This is powerful music. —*Michael G. Nastos*

Birth and Rebirth / Sep. 1978 / Black Saint 0024

○ **Long March, The** / Aug. 30, 1979 / Hat Hut 2R13
The Long March finds its antecedent in earlier pairings of drummer Max Roach with Anthony Braxton. Roach's approach is by no means trendy; he merely carries the best of "old" stylings to the *nth* degree. He constructs the entire 26-minute title selection around a series of drum rolls so fast and focused as to evoke in sound, blurred vision. Not simply a showcase for his virtuosity, a typical Roach solo builds like a deliberate, spontaneous argument, both felt and reasoned. On "U-Jaa-Ma," he beats separate pulses on the hi-hat, toms, and bass drum without raising any voice's dynamic level; his rhythms, it seems, could percolate endlessly. "South Africa Goddam" shows Roach to be as strong a conceptualist as musician. This work harkens back to Roach's controversial *Freedom Now Suite*, and successfully integretates three separate elements: an ominously regular heartbeat, light tom-tom work as if passing messages from village to village, and a rumbling turbulence of violence ready to burst forth. The selection also culls tenor saxophonist Archie Shepp's best work on the entire album—long, curving notes dipping to breathy lows and rising to chromatic peaks. —*Sam Freedman, Down Beat*

○ **Historic Concerts** / Dec. 15, 1979 / Soul Note 11001
This 80-minute portion of drummer Max Roach and multi-instrumentalist Anthony Braxton's 1979 duet concert bears out the press's initial lionizing of Roach for his magnetolike role. Taylor proves himself to be an especially responsive pianist, employing Bud Powell-like sprinting when Roach quickens the pulse or laying into tangy left-hand figures when Roach coaxes a Latin tinge from his toms. Conversely, Taylor elicits from Roach a daring departure from his usually classic narrative style. Roach's extended, nonmetric tangents and his willingness not to deliberate every concept to the *nth* degree (he quickly dispenses with hand percussion late in the piece) contribute greatly to the dynamic asymmetry of the piece. The net result is a music much more overtly linked to Taylor than to Roach, though one should not underestimate the firm, subtle grip Roach has on the reins. It is this relationship that was the crux of the cross-generational new deal, a radically different proposition from the "in the tradition" rites of the post-Albert Ayler genera-

tion or the intern programs Art Blakey and others have sponsored in recent years. *Historic Concerts* is a stunning affirmation that yesterday's innovations are today's traditions, and that the innovations of today are the traditions of tomorrow. —*Bill Shoemaker,* Down Beat

○ **Scott Free** / May 1984 / Soul Note 1103
Steady, consistently urgent mid-'80s quartet session by drummer Max Roach, who was regularly recording, thanks to foreign labels that recognized and welcomed his talent. This one isn't much different from others he did for the Soul Note/Black Saint label; the arrangements and songs are tight, the solos are expressive, and his drumming is always crackling and intense. —*Ron Wynn*

○ **Bright Moments** / **i.** Sep. 1987 / Soul Note 1159
A great late '80s album as drummer Max Roach, with roots going back to the bop days, keeps growing and changing with the times. He uses the double quartet: his regular group with longtime trumpeter Cecil Bridgewater plus the explosive saxophonist Odean Pope paired with a string quartet that includes his daughter Maxine on viola. The results are stimulating, unpredictable, and exciting. —*Ron Wynn*

Max & Dizzy–Paris 1989 / **i.** 1989-1977 / A&M 6404
With Dizzy Gillespie. This recent summit meeting of founding bop fathers shows both are still in shape. —*Ron Wynn*

★ **To the Max** / 1991 / Blue Moon 79164
Showcases Roach working solo, with his own quartet and double quartet, with the M'Boom percussion delegation, and with a string section, singers, and full orchestra. It's a great two-disc set, one that highlights Roach's percussive talents and versatility, plus his compositional verve. At 68, he's still an invigorating, amazing player. —*Ron Wynn,* Rock & Roll Disc

HANK ROBERTS

Cello / World fusion, neo-bop, modern creative, avant-garde, contemporary
A cellist who plays creative improvised music, with an occasional foray into commercial funk, Hank Roberts is a unique artist. —*Michael G. Nastos*

☆ **Black Pastels** / Nov. 1987-Dec. 1988 / Polydor 834416

Birds of Prey / Jan.-Feb. 1990 / Verve 834437
This music crosses pop/funk/jazz/third world parameters. Roberts is an excellent cellist. The music is progressive at times and too commercial at others. His best work lies ahead. —*Michael G. Nastos*

Little Motor People / **i.** Dec. 1992 / Jmt 514005-2

MARCUS ROBERTS

b. 1963
Piano / Neo-bop
Marcus Roberts has begun to get some of the attacks normally reserved for Wynton Marsalis and others who are regarded as reactionaries by some members of the jazz press. Roberts's seeming obsession with vintage styles, notably stride, and his willingness to speak openly and voice his disdain of contemporary music has not been well accepted in some circles. A notorious *Down Beat* blindfold test in which Roberts casually ripped some major players for an alleged lack of swing also generated heated replies via letters to the editor. But Roberts must be credited with going his own way; he's one of the few contemporary pianists with little or no ties to McCoy Tyner, Ahmad Jamal, or Bill Evans. He has some Thelonious Monk influence, especially in his phrasing, but Roberts's models, at least in the last few years, have been Jelly Roll Morton and Fats Waller. While his earlier work reflected pronounced gospel and blues ties, mixed with bebop, Roberts has now devoted himself to stride and ragtime, a tactical decision wide open to intense scrutiny and second guessing. He hasn't mastered either form, but continues cutting solo piano albums that feature these styles. Roberts studied piano at Florida State after beginning on the instrument in his youth. He won several competitions in the mid-

'80s, then joined Wynton Marsalis's band as Marsalis's first regular pianist since Kenny Kirkland. Roberts emerged as the Marsalis band's second prime soloist, and the hub of its rhythm section. His swing kept the group focused, and prevented Marsalis's music from getting too stiff or introspective. Roberts's own late '80s and '90s albums for RCA/Novus, particularly the 1990 release *Alone with Three Giants,* detail his commitment to classic music. Whether that makes him a dedicated preservationist or a hopeless nostalgia buff remains open to debate. All his albums are available on CD. —*Ron Wynn*

Truth is Spoken Here, The / Jul. 26-27, 1988 / Novus 3051

○ **Deep in the Shed** / Aug. 9-Dec. 10, 1989 / Jive/Novus 3078
His second solo project accents the blues, with nicely arranged compositions and a full band that sometimes swells to include alto and tenor sax, trumpet, and trombone, plus bass and drums. —*Ron Wynn,* Rock & Roll Disc

★ **Alone with Three Giants** / Jun. 3-Sep. 22, 1990 / Novus 3109
Fifteen tracks of solo piano from a young, blind pianist from Jacksonville, Florida. Repertoire of Monk, Ellington, and Jelly Roll Morton. Fares best on the Monk pieces, and there are five of them. —*Michael G. Nastos*

○ **Prayer for Peace** / **i.** 1991 / Jive/Novus 63124
Outstanding piano solos, so good that even those who loathe holiday music might find it hard to ignore if they give it a listen. Roberts's solo dates have moved more and more back to early styles like stride, ragtime, and boogie-woogie, but here he's more contemporary and introspective than reflective. —*Ron Wynn*

○ **As Serenity Approaches** / **i.** Dec. 18, 1991 / Novus 63130
Pianist Marcus Roberts's penchant for florid blues-ragtime and/or stride variations isn't what's so enticing about *Serenity.* His pensive collaborations with tenor saxophonist/clarinetist Todd Williams, trumpeter Wynton Marsalis, and trombonist Ronald Westray are. The first and last of these collaborations, "Nigh Eve," a Roberts composition, and Duke Ellington's "Creole Blues," highlight less showy, more effective examples of the leader's command of the music's evolution than much of the collection's breakneck (primarily) solo piano fare. They also showcase Roberts's evolving yet attractive artistry. Wynton Marsalis's contribution to their reading of Jelly Roll Morton's "King Porter Stomp" is infinitely wittier and more emotional than what's heard on most of his recordings; I hope this means his heart is beginning to catch up to his ravishing technique. As for Roberts, his most successful solo outings include an exuberant romp through "Cherokee," in which he includes harmonic alterations, and a thoughtful, discreet yet urbanely emotional stroll through Rodgers and Hart's "Where or When." —*Reuben Jackson,* Jazz Times

○ **If I Could Be with You** / **i.** Dec. 21, 1992 / Novus 63149

PERRY ROBINSON (Perry Morris Robinson)

b. Aug. 17, 1938, New York, NY
Clarinet / Early free, modern creative
Prior to Don Byron, the clarinetist most associated with free-wheeling, unpredictable music was Perry Robinson. His solos, with their upper-register squeals and furious sound, were featured on albums for tiny independent labels. Robinson also led groups with unusual configurations, notably Pipe Dreams with its clarinet/guitar/twin vocal lineup. Robinson, whose father was the songwriter Earl Robinson, began studying piano, but switched to clarinet at age nine. He attended the High School of Music and Art, then the Manhattan School of Music in 1958. He met Ornette Coleman while studying at the Lennox School of Jazz in 1959. Robinson played with Chuck Israels and Tete Montoliu in Spain in 1960, then worked in Europe with Don Friedman, Archie Shepp, and Bill Dixon. Robinson formed a group with Bill Folwell and Tom Price while in a navy band. After his discharge, Robinson worked in New York with Sunny Murray, Roswell Rudd, Charlie Haden, and the Jazz

Composers Guild. He recorded with Henry Grimes in 1965, participated in the *Escalator Over the Hill* sessions from 1968 to 1971, and played with both Gunther Hampel in the Galaxie Dream Band and with Darius Brubeck in the early '70s. He remained with Hampel's band into the '80s. He also recorded infrequently as a leader for Improvising Artists and Jazzmania. The IAI session is available on CD. —*Ron Wynn and Michael G. Nastos*

★ **Funk Dumpling** / 1962 / Savoy 1180

○ **Traveler, The** / 1978 / Chiaroscuro 190

Here one has a fairly light yet completely enjoyable album from one of the contemporary heavyweights of the clarinet. But make no mistake, *The Traveler* is an honest effort and not some kind of commercial token. It's a freewheeling, rough-edged reflection of Perry Robinson's multifaceted abilities and wry sense of humor. More open sonorities can be found on "The Call," "Mordechai's Blues," and "Feud." Serene pictures can be felt in "You Are Too Good" and "How Can I Keep From Singing" (the latter penned by Robinson's father). And just plain fun is the recipe for "Henry's Dance," "Atomic Twist" (inspired by Chubby Checker), and Willem Breuker's "Ham and Eggs" (done as a duet by Robinson and pianist Hilly Dolganes). As usual, Robinson is all over his horn, from breathy, melodic passages to controlled screams and intricate lines. Bassist Frank Luther and drummer Phillip Wilson are excellent foils for the clarinetist with the former's contributions being particularly outstanding. (Check out his creative and fleet solo on "Henry's Dance," the harmonics at the beginning of "You Are Too Good," as well as his legato strumming techniques and inventive pizzicato throughout the LP.) And while Dolganes does not really have any memorable moments, his playing is nonetheless sustaining and integral to the overall sound. —*Milo Fine,* Cadence

---

BETTY ROCHE (Mary Elizabeth Roche)

b. Jan. 9, 1920, Wilmington, DE
Vocals / Ballads & blues

Betty Roche had a short stay in the spotlight, but, during her stints with Ellington, made an immediate impact with her strong, declarative vocals. Roche won an amateur contest at the Apollo, and later sang with the Savoy Sultans in 1941 and 1942, then with Hot Lips Page and Lester Young before joining Duke Ellington in 1943. She was the first to sing the "Blues" sequence of Ellington's *Black, Brown and Beige* suite, performing at Carnegie Hall in 1943. She left Ellington in 1944, and joined Earl Hines. Then came a long period of inactivity before she rejoined Ellington in 1952 and cut a celebrated version of "Take the A-Train." Roche made a few albums as a solo act in the late '50s and early '60s. One Roche album from '60, *Singin' & Swingin',* is now available on CD. —*Ron Wynn*

★ **Singin' & Swingin'** / Mar. 1961 / Prestige 1718

Backed soulfully by a quintet, her free use of tempos and warm, distinct sound is nicely captured on this record. —*Bob Rusch,* Cadence

---

RED RODNEY (Robert Chudnick)

b. Sep. 27, 1927
Trumpet / Bop

Red Rodney has had two careers, and though his '70s comeback was less publicized it was almost as remarkable as Frank Morgan's in the '80s. In his early years, Rodney was a gifted, fiery trumpeter who played with bebop's greats and more than held his own. His solos, harmonic imagination, and melodic ability established his stardom. Sadly, Rodney emulated his heroes in both positive and negative ways, developing a drug habit that eventually interrupted his career.

Rodney began playing trumpet in his early teens, and toured in Jimmy Wald's big band at age 15. He later had short stints with several bands, among them Jimmy Dorsey's, Elliot Lawrence's, Georgie Auld's, Benny Goodman's and Les Brown's. Rodney changed his approach after hearing Dizzy Gillespie and Charlie Parker, and adopted bebop rather than

the swing style he'd previously championed. He began building his reputation with Gene Krupa, Claude Thornhill, and Woody Herman in the mid- and late '40s. He recorded heading Red Rodney's Be-Boppers for Mercury, EmArcy, and Keynote. Then he joined Parker in 1949, and stayed with him until 1951. Rodney had reached bebop's summit. The group's Carnegie Hall concert indicated he was at his playing peak.

Though he continued working in the '50s, Rodney's drug habit was wreaking havoc. He played with Charlie Ventura in 1950 and 1951, and recorded for Prestige, Okeh, Fantasy, Signal, and Cadet. But his habit resulted in periods of imprisonment and in beatings from police. Rodney's fortunes were also affected by the rise of Black power and Afrocentric sentiments in the '60s; some Black bandleaders that he knew did not hire him because they wanted to provide opportunities for Black musicians. Rodney moved to the West Coast, played in Las Vegas, and even started a scam where he impersonated an air force officer and cashed forged checks on bases, which resulted in a 27-month prison term. Rodney kicked his drug habit, graduated from college, and even earned a law degree, though his felony conviction kept him from taking the California bar. He suffered a stroke in the early '70s, and medical expenses zapped the money he'd earned from Las Vegas and show biz dates. Rodney returned to bebop and began turning heads with blistering solos and fine albums on Muse, Spotlite, and Storyville. A chance meeting with fellow trumpeter Ira Sullivan led to them performing and recording together in the early '80s and making more celebrated albums. Rodney toured with Australian trumpeter and trombonist James Morrison in the late '80s, and has continued recording in the '90s. Despite a recent flirtation with fusion, Red Rodney remains a victorious bebop survivor. Some early tracks with the Be-Boppers have been reissued on CD. Rodney sessions from the '70s and '80s, plus his recent *Then and Now,* are also available. —*Ron Wynn*

★ **Early Bebop on Keynote** / Jan. 29, 1947 / Mercury 830922

With Hefti. A good 20-track overview of Rodney's mid-'40s cuts on Keynote. Both his own band and his stints with others are covered. —*Ron Wynn*

Modern Music from Chicago / Jun. 20, 1955 / Fantasy 048

This nice reissue features the famous white trumpeter who once passed for both Black and Native American! —*Ron Wynn*

☆ **Red Arrow, The** / i. 1957 / Onyx 204

With Ira Sullivan (tpt, sax) and Tommy Flanagan Trio. Historic early meeting between Rodney and Sullivan. Two by Rodney, one by bassist Oscar Pettiford, three standards. —*Michael G. Nastos*

Bird Lives! / Jul. 1973 / Muse 5371

Quintet with Roy Brooks (d), Charles McPherson (as), Barry Harris (p), and Sam Jones (b). Three Bird compositions, Monk's rousing "52nd St. Theme," "'Round Midnight," and one standard. This is one great band for Red to blow with. —*Michael G. Nastos*

○ **Live at the Village Vanguard** / May 8, 1980-Jul. 7, 190 / Muse 5209

With Ira Sullivan (tpt, sax) and quintet. Three Jack Walrath originals, three standouts. This is one of the most together jazz bands of the '80s. A perfect vehicle for Red and Ira to blow. Sullivan plays saxs, flute, and flugelhorn. —*Michael G. Nastos*

○ **Night and Day** / Jun. 15-16, 1981 / Muse 5274

Trumpeter Red Rodney has worked with multi-instrumentalist Ira Sullivan since the '50s. Their friendship carries over into their musical relationship. This '81 date sometimes has Rodney dominating a song with Sullivan supporting him; then they switch roles, and sometimes they're dueling or complementing each other. They carry the album, for everything else, from backing musicians to songs and production, is competent but nothing more. —*Ron Wynn*

Sprint / Nov. 3-4, 1982 / Elektra 60261

Recorded live at New York City's Jazz Forum. Three by pianist Garry Dial, two standards. More hot stuff. The Red-Sullivan show shines. —*Michael G. Nastos*

Red Alert! / i. 1990 / Continuum 19101

○ **Spirit Within** / Elektra 60020
The first of two early '80s albums reuniting frequent collaborators trumpeter Red Rodney and multi-instrumentalist Ira Sullivan. Sullivan plays second trumpet and a variety of saxophones and provides a challenging and complementary presence to Rodney, who sometimes plays in restrained, easy fashion, then other times turns up his own playing a notch in response to Sullivan. —*Ron Wynn*

SHORTY ROGERS (Milton M. Rajonsky)

b. Apr. 14, 1924, Great Barrington, MA
Trumpet, composer, arranger, bandleader / Cool
A fine writer and a good trumpet player, Rogers began with Will Bradley, Red Norvo, and Woody Herman in the '40s, and penned "Keen and Peachy" for Herman's band before joining Stan Kenton in 1950-1951. He become a prominent member of the White West Coast school during the '50s, recording and touring with Art Pepper, Jimmy Giuffre, Shelly Manne, and others. He wrote some invigorating arrangements for both big bands and small combos in the '50s and '60s, and turned increasingly to film and television, giving up playing completely from the '60s to the early '80s. His compositions and arrangements merged the best of cool era discipline, precision, and subdued tones with the swing period's organization and sound. His pieces for nonet were especially inspired. —*Ron Wynn*

Big Band—Vol. 1 / Jul. 11, 1953 / Time Is 9804

★ **Short Stops** / 1953-1954 / Bluebird 5917
1953-1954. A thorough reissue that covers his first three RCA albums. For some strange reason, the CD only has 20 of 32 cuts. —*Ron Wynn*

○ **Martians, Stay Home** / Nov. 3, 1955 / Atlantic 50714
The quintet for this trumpeter from the West Coast via Massachusetts and New York includes Jimmy Giuffre (cl), Pete Jolly (p), Curtis Counce (b), Shelly Manne (d), and others. There are six Shorty originals and three standards. These are nice groups with Rogers's sensitive trumpet leading in a nonthreatening, mainstream groove. —*Michael G. Nastos*

○ **Afro Cuban Influence** / Jun. 19, 1958 / RCA 1763

Swings / Dec. 1958-Dec. 1959 / Bluebird 3012

Jazz Waltz / Dec. 1962 / Discovery 843
This is a big band (28 different players at one time or another) of all-stars too numerous to mention. Songs are by Shorty and Duke Ellington, and there are four other standards. —*Michael G. Nastos*

Yesterday, Today and Forever / Jun. 1983 / Concord Jazz 4223
This quintet, with Bud Shank on flute and alto sax, plays three Shorty tunes and four standards. They perform fine readings of Tiny Kahn's "TNT" and Bud Powell's "Budo." —*Michael G. Nastos*

○ **Jazz Origin: Shorty Rogers / Stan Kenton / June Christy** / i. Mar. 1984 / PA/USA 9016

★ **Complete Atlantic and EMI Jazz Recordings, The** / i. Aug. 1989 / Mosaic 6125
Another exhaustive Mosaic boxed set, this one devoted to the complete material trumpeter Shorty Rogers cut for EMI and Atlantic in the '50s, including both cool-influenced material and concept *Martians* albums. Art Pepper is featured on some cuts on alto sax, also Shelly Manne, Jimmy Giuffre, and Curtis Counce. —*Ron Wynn*

SONNY ROLLINS (Theodore Walter [Newk] Rollins)

b. Sep. 7, 1930, New York, NY
Tenor and soprano saxophone, composer / Hard bop, bop

Sonny Rollins is the man most often deemed the greatest living saxophonist, and with good reason. He has been a dominant player since the early '50s, and has made, note-for-note, as many unforgettable solos and recordings as any musician active in any idiom. His tone is among jazz's most vivid and full ever; his ability to create, recycle, and rework melodies constantly, and to incorporate fragments into his solos is both instructive and amazing. He's also the master of the calypso jazz mode. He switched from alto to tenor and made his first recordings with Babs Gonzales in 1948. He subsequently worked with J.J. Johnson, Thelonious Monk, Art Blakey, Bud Powell, Tadd Dameron, and Miles Davis. Rollins's reputation soared when he joined the Clifford Brown/Max Roach quintet in 1955. When that group disbanded following Brown's death, Rollins began heading his own bands, which he's done ever since. He made numerous fantastic releases in the '50s and '60s, including the famous pianoless trio dates, plus sessions with Monk and a guest stint on a Modern Jazz Quartet release. In the mid-'60s he flirted with free playing, but returned to a mainstream framework shortly after that, though he's always out on the edge in his playing. In the '70s, he began playing soprano. —*Ron Wynn*

★ **Complete Prestige Recordings** / 1949-1956 / Prestige 4407
Sonny Rollins on Prestige—a seven-CD boxed set covering the years 1949-1956 (90 selections). Includes his early work as a sideman plus all of his solo albums for Prestige. About every jazz great appears somewhere in this compilation, from Charlie Parker and Miles Davis to Clifford Brown and John Coltrane. The liner notes are superb. This set is a treasure. —*Michael Erlewine*

Sonny Rollins with the Modern Jazz Quartet / Jan. 17, 1951-Oct. 7, 1953 / Prestige 7029
1951-1953. Fire meets cool in this excellent reissue of their early '50s collaboration. —*Ron Wynn*

Moving Out / Aug.-Oct. 1954 / Prestige 058

○ **Work Time** / Dec. 2, 1955 / Prestige 007
Worktime presents an entire Sonny Rollins (ts) session from 12/2/55 with pianist Ray Bryant, drummer Max Roach, and bassist George Morrow. There is nothing tentative about this performance, and fans of Rollins and Roach should find many joyful encounters with it. Morrow and Roach are a great combination and while Bryant's playing is not poor, he is really not needed for this music. —*Bob Rusch, Cadence*

Sonny Rollins Plus 4 / Mar. 22, 1956 / Prestige 7038
A wonderful outing that was among the last for the Clifford Brown/Max Roach group. —*Ron Wynn*

☆ **Tenor Madness** / May 24, 1956 / Prestige 124
Just a gigantic session with the Miles Davis rhythm section and a wonderful duet with John Coltrane (ts) on the title cut. Rollins emerges as his own man in style. —*Ron Wynn*

★ **Saxophone Colossus and More** / Jun. 22, 1956 / Original Jazz Classics 291
Superb. Reissue of a seminal late '50s Rollins session. Max Roach crackles on drums. —*Ron Wynn*

Best of Sonny Rollins / 1956 / Blue Note 93203
Title is wholly misleading. Everything here is wonderful, but it's impossible to collect his best songs on one set. —*Ron Wynn*

★ **Way out West** / Mar. 7, 1957 / Contemporary 337
A remarkable masterpiece. Explosive Rollins gets steady support from Ray Brown (b) and Shelly Manne (d). —*Ron Wynn*

★ **Newk's Time** / Sep. 22, 1957 / Blue Note 84001
With Wynton Kelly (p) and Philly Joe Jones (d). Blue Note. Just a super quartet date; excellent reissue with original cover and notes. —*Ron Wynn*

More from the Vanguard / Nov. 3, 1957 / Blue Note 475

☆ **Night at the Village Vanguard—Vol. 1** / Nov. 3, 1957 / Blue Note 46517

One of two incendiary live dates from Vanguard in the late '50s. The pianoless trio steps forth and claims its fame. — *Ron Wynn*

☆ **Night at the Village Vanguard–Vol. 2** / Nov. 3, 1957 / Blue Note 46518

○ **Freedom Suite** / Feb. 11+Mar. 7, 1958 / Riverside 067
By the time *Freedom Suite* was recorded (February 1958), Sonny Rollins's influences were well integrated into a mature, individual style. *Freedom Suite* was much heralded and the title can be interpreted both musically and socially. An extended piece (19:17), not yet usual then for jazz recordings, it holds up well over its entire run. This is a tribute not only to tenor Rollins's technical and imaginative power, but also to Oscar Pettiford (b) and Max Roach (d), who completed the trio and were "up" for the entire 19 minutes. The other side has never grabbed me with the same demand as the title track. Even so, Rollins makes each tune his, and it all belongs with the best of his work. This was also issued on a Milestone twofer. — *Bob Rusch, Cadence*

★ **Bridge, The** / Jan. 30, 1962-Apr. 5, 1962 / Bluebird 61061
Rollins makes a shattering return from sabbatical. He's joined by the youthful Jim Hall (g), who makes a great partner. — *Ron Wynn*

○ **What's New?** / Apr. 25-May 14, 1962 / RCA
Some early '60s cuts featuring tenor saxophonist Sonny Rollins leading a pianoless quartet with Jim Hall on guitar. These are songs taken from the landmark session on RCA that marked Rollins's return from a sabbatical in 1962. They weren't included on *The Bridge* album but were done by the same personnel. — *Ron Wynn*

All the Things You Are / Jul. 15, 1963-Jul. 2, 1964 / Bluebird 2179
1963-1964. Super 1990 reissue. It includes stints by Coleman Hawkins (ts) and Herbie Hancock (k). — *Ron Wynn*

Sonny Meets Hawk! / Jul. 15+Jul. 18, 1963 / RCA
With Coleman Hawkins (ts). The grand master teams with the still relatively young master for a moving, evocative session. Available mainly in a two-record reissue with *The Bridge* by French RCA. — *Ron Wynn*

Sonny Rollins on Impulse! / Jul. 8, 1965 / MCA 5655

Alfie / Jan. 26, 1966 / MCA 39107

★ **East Broadway Run Down** / May 9, 1966 / MCA 33120
The title cut is exceptional. Freddie Hubbard (tpt) is also great, as are Elvin Jones (d) and Jimmy Garrison (b). — *Ron Wynn*

Next Album / Jul. 1972 / Milestone 312
Rollins makes another incredible return in this 1972 album, now available in a 1988 reissue. — *Ron Wynn*

Horn Culture / Jun.-Jul. 1973 / Original Jazz Classics 314

In Japan / Sep. 30, 1973 / JVC

☆ **Cutting Edge, The** / Jul. 6, 1974 / Milestone 468
"The Cutting Edge" and "First Moves" have Sonny Rollins improvising on the rhythmic character of the themes, the latter being a very good Rollins tune. The best part, though, and the most significant moment on the record, is Rollins playing "To a Wild Rose" unaccompanied, breaking time, dissecting the theme and lightly embellishing it, adding cadenzas and bits of extraneous material—it isn't quite the spiritual freedom he often proves in his a cappella works, but it is certainly engaging. — *John Litweiler, Down Beat*

Nucleus / Sep. 2-5, 1975 / Milestone 620

Don't Stop the Carnival / Apr. 1978 / Milestone 55005
Majestic. A fiery calypso beat on the title track and first-rate Rollins throughout. — *Ron Wynn*

Milestone Jazzstars in Concert / i. Sep. 1978-Oct. 1978 / Milestone 55006

Sunny Days, Starry Nights / Jan. 23-27, 1984 / Milestone 9122

Solo Album, The / Jul. 19, 1985 / Milestone 9137

Long moments of aimless noodling are balanced by stretches of awesome improvising. To get the full effect, listen to it all the way through. — *Ron Wynn*

G-Man / Aug. 16, 1986 / Milestone 9150

Falling in Love with Jazz / i. Aug. 5, 1989-Sep. 9, 1989 / Milestone 9179

Old Flames / i. 1993 / Milestone 9215
When you are acknowledged as the greatest tenor saxophonist in the world and you have conquered every challenge, there is really little left to do except to keep playing. That is what Sonny Rollins does; he makes good albums that occasionally suggest his greatness but seldom seem to really stimulate him. This latest, recorded in the summer of '93, features Rollins covering such standards as "Darn That Dream," "My Old Flame," and Ellington's "Prelude to a Kiss" backed by such great musicians as pianist Tommy Flanagan and drummer Jack DeJohnette, plus regulars trombonist Clifton Anderson and bassist Bob Cranshaw. Jimmy Heath conducted and arranged the supporting horns, whose lineup includes Jon Faddis on flugelhorn and Bob Stewart on tuba. Everything is highly professional, and Rollins offers enough swirling phrases, loops, dips, and extrapolations to make things entertaining. But the relaxed mood sometimes comes close to being a stupor, and you cannot help feeling Rollins has done this before; in fact, he is probably thinking the same thing during his solos. — *Ron Wynn*

○ **Vintage Sessions** / Prestige 24096
Early '50s sessions featuring the formative Sonny Rollins tenor style, which at this point is still emerging from a synthesis of Coleman Hawkins, Lester Young, and Charlie Parker, plus his own contributions. — *Ron Wynn*

WALLACE RONEY

b. 1960
Trumpet / Neo-bop
Wallace Roney's dilemma recalls Sonny Stitt's dilemma in the '50s and '60s: Roney's trumpet tone, timbre, approach, phrasing, and sound so closely mirror Miles Davis's pre-jazz/rock phase that Roney's been savaged for being a clone and an unrepentant imitator. Stitt stopped playing alto for years because of his disdain with being labeled a Charlie Parker clone. Roney, on the other hand, played many of Miles Davis's parts on the 1992 tribute to the *Birth of the Cool* sessions, which was issued in 1993 as *Miles Davis and Quincy Jones at Montreux*. Roney even addressed the situation in the publication *Jazz Times* in 1993, blasting what he saw as unfair critical obsession with his stylistic similarity to Davis. It's a classic no-win situation; Roney does sound tremendously like Davis and can't be completely absolved from critical charges of imitation. But he's also a fine, evocative player on ballads, and can be fiery and explosive on uptempo tunes. Roney put in his stint in Art Blakey's Jazz Messengers, and was in one of the last editions of that famous group. He began recording as a leader in the late '80s, and has since done several sessions for Muse in a primarily hard bop mode, many pairing him with equally energized saxophonists Gary Thomas or Kenny Garrett. They're all available on CD. — *Ron Wynn*

Verses / Feb. 19, 1987 / Muse 5335
Aggressive, attacking material with fiery exchanges between Gary Thomas (reeds) and Roney. Top front line of young talent. — *Ron Wynn*

Intuition / Jan. 1988 / Muse 5346
This is a stirring set from one of the best Young Lion trumpeters. Very dynamic hard bop line with superior alto and tenor sax by Kenny Garret (as, ts) and Gary Thomas (ts). Roney is great. — *Ron Wynn*

★ **Obsession** / 1990 / Muse 5423
The latest from this trumpet whiz boasts excellent songs supplied by both Roney and pianist Donald Brown. — *Ron Wynn*

○ **Seth Air** / i. Oct. 14, 1992 / Muse 5441

Seth Air is not only Wallace Roney's first recording after his 1991 Montreux gig with Miles Davis and tour with Davis's '60s quintet, but it was recorded on the day Davis passed, the news of which reportedly reached the musicians in midsession. It's a solid album, leavening the muscular modal blowing and vaguely Wayne Shorteresque expositions with engaging interpretations of Gershwin's "Gone," which is hinged on nimble trumpet-drums exchanges, and Burt Bacharach's loopy waltz, "Wives and Lovers." Roney's brother, Antone, has a sleek sense of form and a burnished tone. The rhythm section of pianist Jacky Terrason, whose originals blend well with the Roneys', heavy-lifter bassist Peter Washington, and drummer Eric Allen is fluent and flexible. Like a glowing coal, all heat with little flame. —*Bill Shoemaker,* Down Beat

Crunchin' / i. 1993 / Muse 5518
Trumpeter Wallace Roney has taken so much grief over his alleged Miles Davis imitations that he recently struck back with a bitter interview in *Jazz Times.* Fortunately, Roney's anger has not hindered his playing. He sounds poignant and fabulous throughout the eight tracks on his latest release. His lines on "What's New" and "You Stepped Out of a Dream" are full and gorgeous, while his soloing on "Woody'n You" and "Time After Time" has warmth, intensity, and edge. Alto saxophonist Antonio Hart chimes in with equal facility and spark, while Geri Allen shows that she is just as outstanding as an accompanist on standards and hard bop as in trios or as a leader. When you add the longtime, always impressive rhythm section collaborators bassist Ron Carter and drummer Kenny Washington, you have got a great band and a marvelous date. Roney need not worry about detractors as long as he keeps on making sessions like this one. —*Ron Wynn*

Standard Bearer / Muse 5372
High-flying mainstream from a strong Young Lion. The firebrand trumpeter displays his sentimental side on a collection of six show tunes and jazz anthems, with one drum/trumpet duet original. There's no place for gimmicks or fancy tricks, and Roney shows he knows the difference between technique and style. —*Ron Wynn,* Rock & Roll Disc

MICHELE ROSEWOMAN

b. 1953
Piano / World fusion, neo-bop
An exciting, ambitious pianist particularly effective with Afro-Latin rhythms, Michele Rosewoman has been in the forefront of jazz composers and performers anxious to find new frontiers. But instead of fusion or hip-hop, Rosewoman chose Afro-Cuban music. With parents who owned a record store in Oakland and an older brother who's a musician, Rosewoman began playing piano at age six and took lessons at age 17 from Edwin Kelly. She studied Cuban percussion with Orlando Rios, and also studied traditional Shona and Yoruba African music. Rosewoman later worked with members of both the Black Artists Group and Association for the Advancement of Creative Musicians. She moved to New York in 1978, and played with Oliver Lake at a Carnegie Hall concert. Rosewoman worked with Billy Bang in the early '80s, and also recorded with Los Kimy, a contemporary Cuban band. She formed the 15-piece New Yor-Uba in the mid-'80s, and later premiered the production "New Yor-Uba: A Music Celebration of Cuba in America" at the Public Theatre. Rosewoman began recording as a leader for Soul Note in the mid-'80s, and formed the quintet Quintessence in 1986. She toured with Carlos Ward in the early '90s, and later did a trio date with Rufus Reid and Ralph Peterson, Jr. Rosewoman's sessions are available on CD. —*Ron Wynn and Michael G. Nastos*

★ **Contrast High** / Jul. 1988 / Enja 79607

RENEE ROSNES

b. 1962
Piano / Neo-bop

Canadian pianist Renee Rosnes gained some initial attention when she was part of Joe Henderson's exclusively female rhythm section. That didn't get as much coverage as might be expected given the run of articles in the '80s and '90s that have rained down on jazz for sexist practices, but Rosnes's excellent solos, with their rich harmonic and melodic variations, have continued to be featured in Henderson bands on a regular basis. She has also led sessions for Blue Note since the late '80s, and recorded with O.T.B. in 1989. Rosnes has played with Branford Marsalis, Wayne Shorter, Ralph Bowen, Herbie Hancock, Ira Coleman, Ron Carter, Steve Wilson, and Lewis Nash, among others. Her sessions are available on CD. —*Ron Wynn*

★ **Renee Rosnes** / Apr. 18, 1988-Feb. 4, 1989 / Blue Note 93561
High-caliber duet and quartet sessions. Rosnes proves captivating in any context. Guests include Wayne Shorter (sax) and Branford Marsalis (sax). —*Ron Wynn*

○ **For the Moment** / Feb. 15-16, 1990 / Blue Note 94859
The better of her two albums. Four Rosnes originals, four others from Monk, Woody Shaw, Walt Weiskopf, and the Warren/Dubin team. Joe Henderson featured on seven of the eight cuts. —*Michael G. Nastos*

○ **Without Words / i.** 1993 / Blue Note 98168

FRANK ROSOLINO

b. Aug. 20, 1926, Detroit, MI, **d.** Nov. 26, 1978, Los Angeles, CA
Trombone / Bop, big band
Trombonist Frank Rosolino matched any of the idiom's giants in fluidity, technique, and imagination. He was a comic vocalist, but there was nothing funny about his solos. They were delivered with ease, and were precise, smooth, and dazzling. Rosolino began as a guitarist at age ten, then played trombone in his teens. He joined the army at age 18, and played with service bands both in America and in the Philippines. He played in several big bands after his discharge, among them Bob Chester's, Glen Gray's, Gene Krupa's, Tony Pastor's, Herbie Fields's, and Georgie Auld's. Rosolino began leading his own group in Detroit, then joined Stan Kenton's orchestra in late 1952. He spent his latter career in California, playing with Howard Rumsey's Lighthouse All-Stars from 1954 to 1960, and with Donn Trenner's band for Steve Allen's television show from 1962 to 1964. Rosolino did several studio dates in Hollywood, then worked in Europe with Conte Candoli during the '70s. He toured with Benny Carter in 1974, and worked with Supersax and Quincy Jones in Japan, appearing often on recording sessions and film soundtracks. Rosolino committed suicide in 1978. Only a couple of his sessions as a leader are available, though he can be heard on many Quincy Jones sessions. —*Ron Wynn and Michael G. Nastos*

Kenton Presents Jazz: Frank Rosolino / Mar. 12-16, 1954 / Capitol 6507

○ **Frankly Speaking** / May 4-5, 1955 / Affinity

○ **I Play Trombone** / May 1956 / Bethlehem 26

★ **Frank Rosolino Quintet** / Jun. 1957 / VSOP 107
This brilliant trombonist, with a quintet including Richie Kamuca (sax) and Vince Guaraldi (p), plays three Rosolino originals and five standards including Bill Holman's "Fallout." A beautiful charcoal portrait of Rosolino by Eve Diana is on the front cover. —*Michael G. Nastos*

☆ **Free for All / i.** Dec. 22, 1958 / Specialty 1763
Top Rosolino session with Harold Land (ts) and Leroy Vinnegar (b). Outstanding CD reissue is a limited edition. —*Ron Wynn*

☆ **Thinking About You** / Apr. 21+23, 1976 / Sackville 2014
Recorded live at Bourbon Street in Toronto with Ed Bickert (g), Don Thompson (b), and Terry Clarke (d), this album includes four long standards. With room to stretch, the whole band is up to the task. This is on the mellow side. There is a

cover painting of the trombonist by Jerry Lazare. —*Michael G. Nastos*

CHARLIE ROUSE (Charles Rouse)

b. Apr. 6, 1924, Washington, DC, **d.** Dec. 1988
Tenor saxophone / Bop

Charlie Rouse filled one of jazz's toughest jobs with distinction; he was Thelonious Monk's playing partner. He established an affinity and had an understanding of Monk's complex, often irregular compositions. His solos were constructed carefully, and were slowly delivered statements that perfectly contrasted and complimented Monk's equally deliberate, unorthodox playing. Rouse had a fluid, full tone and an understated sense of swing. He'd often restate the melody repeatedly, before eventually creating a strong, emphatic statement. Rouse studied clarinet before moving to tenor sax. He played in Billy Eckstine's and Dizzy Gillespie's mid-'40s big bands, then made his recording debut as a soloist in 1947 with Tadd Dameron and Fats Navarro. He played with R&B groups in Washington and New York before joining the Duke Ellington Orchestra in 1949 and 1950. Rouse played in Count Basie's octet in 1950, and was on Clifford Brown's first recordings in 1953. He played with Bennie Green and Oscar Pettiford in 1955. Rouse led the group Les Modes (later the Jazz Modes) with French horn player Julius Watkins from 1956 to 1959. He recorded for Seeco and for Atlantic, and with Paul Quinichette for Bethlehem. After a brief stint with Buddy Rich, Rouse joined Monk in 1959. He stayed with him until 1970, playing in many contexts and on various labels. He also made his own albums for Jazzland, Epic, and Blue Note in the '60s. During the '70s, Rouse recorded for Strata-East, Casablanca, and Storyville, while doing many sessions. For a short time, he worked with Mal Waldron, then cofounded and served as the leader of Sphere in 1980. They began as a repertory group playing Monk's music, though they later also included originals. He recorded on Enja, Uptown, and Steam in the '80s. Rouse played in Wynton Marsalis's group at the 1987 Concord Jazz Festival, and recorded with Carmen McRae on her seminal 1988 album *Carmen Sings Monk*. A few Rouse sessions are available on CD. —*Ron Wynn*

○ **Chase Is On, The** / i. 1957 / Bethlehem 6021
If you associate the term "chase" with a cutting contest, this album has quite a misleading title. The character of the session is rather that of friendly interplay, and the result is a thoroughly relaxed and enjoyable affair. All hands work well, in a mood that is kind of low-keyed Al Cohn and Zoot Simsish, with a sprinkle of Count Basie added for taste. The two tenor saxophone soloists (Charlie Rouse, Paul Quinichette) contrast each other quite effectively; the Lesterish (Young) sound of Quinichette and Rouse's characteristically staccato phrasing make for a very well-balanced pair. On many of the numbers Rouse is actually so relaxed that Quinichette emerges as the more aggressive, even diggin' into some unexpected preachin' in his solo on "Knittin." —*Per Husby, Cadence*

Takin' Care of Business / May 11, 1960 / Jazzland 491
Quintet with Blue Mitchell (tpt) and the Walter Bishop (p) Trio plays two numbers penned by Randy Weston, one apiece by Kenny Drew and Rouse, and two standards. This is a supremely confident group that plays strong music in a somewhat cool mood. —*Michael G. Nastos*

Unsung Hero / Dec. 1960-Jul. 1961 / Epic 46181

★ **Two Is One** / 1974 / Strata-East

Cinnamon Flower / 1976 / Rykodisc 10053
A fine big-band date led by Rouse. A topflight reissue courtesy of Rykodisc. —*Ron Wynn*

○ **Moment's Notice** / Oct. 1977 / Storyville 4079
This quartet features pianist Hugh Lawson, bassist Bob Cranshaw, and drummer Ben Riley. Rouse, a model tenor saxaphonist, plays with melodic wit and sense of purpose throughout. —*Michael G. Nastos*

Social Call / Jan. 21-22, 1984 / Uptown
This studio session with Red Rodney and the Albert Dailey Trio consists of all postbop standards save Rouse's "Little Chico." Arrangements are by Don Sickler. The front line of Rodney and Rouse comes up all aces. —*Michael G. Nastos*

Epistrophy / Oct. 10, 1988 / Landmark 1521
An adventurous late '80s date, with Rouse stepping out and handling the challenge posed by Don Cherry (cnt), Buddy Montgomery (p), and George Cables (p). —*Ron Wynn*

JIMMY ROWLES (James George Rowles)

b. Aug. 19, 1918, Spokane, WA
Piano / Swing

A prime accompanist for vocalists, Jimmie Rowles's piano style blends swing, bebop, and cool elements. He's largely a self-taught musician, and an underrated composer. Rowles played in Seattle groups during his days at the University of Washington. He moved to Los Angeles and joined Lester Young's band in 1942. He played with Benny Goodman and Woody Herman in the '40s, but gained his greatest fame backing Billie Holiday and Peggy Lee. This led to later sessions backing Julie London, Carmen McRae, and Sarah Vaughan. Rowles also worked with Slim Gaillard, and recorded with Buddy DeFranco. He played on film soundtracks and did studio work during much of the '50s. Rowles settled in New York after playing at the 1973 Newport Jazz Festival. He played in clubs and worked with Zoot Sims, George Mraz, and Buster Williams. He didn't do much recording in the '60s, but stayed busy in the '70s. There were sessions with Benny Carter, Sims, Bob Brookmeyer, and Barney Kessel, plus his own dates on Halcyon, Choice, Columbia, Xanadu, Progressive, and Sonet. Rowles toured for two years with Ella Fitzgerald, then returned to the West Coast. He recorded for Contemporary with Red Mitchell in 1985, and for Capri with Mitchell and Donald Bailey. His song "The Peacocks" was included in the soundtrack to the 1986 film 'Round Midnight. Rowles recorded with his daughter, Stacy, for Concord and Delos in the '80s, and also recorded for Contemporary. A fair amount of Rowles recent and earlier dates are available on CD. —*Ron Wynn*

☆ **Special Magic of Jimmy Rowles, The** / Apr. 7, 1974 / Halcyon 110
This album includes duets with Rusty Gilder on bass. Solo, Rowles shows he can do it alone, and with Gilder, sparks occasionally fly. Mostly, this is laidback. They play lots of Duke Ellington, and there is a good version of Carl Perkin's "Grooveyard." —*Michael G. Nastos*

★ **Grandpaws** / Mar. 1976 / Choice 1014
The trio for this pianist includes Buster Williams on bass and Billy Hart on drums. They play two by Rowles; the others are standards. They do an exquisite medley of "Lush Life / A Train / I Love You / I Hadn't Anyone 'Till You / Margie / Chicago / Desert Fire." Rowles shows his ballad skills best. —*Michael G. Nastos*

○ **Plays Ellington and Billy Strayhorn** / Jun. 1981 / Columbia
Jimmie Rowles divides this entry in half, with side one devoted to compositions by Duke Ellington (although "Jumpin' Punkins" was actually written by his son, Mercer) and side two to some of Billy Strayhorn's less frequently heard tunes. There are well-worn items on both sides, to be sure, but in Rowles's hands they take on a freshness only in part due to the pianist's deep understanding of the various compositional methods involved. Far from being mere stylistic replications, Rowles's interpretations are wholly his own; but at the same time, they are also well within the scope of authentic Ellingtonia. While sharp ears will also discern the odd nod in the direction of Thelonious Monk, the major influence on Rowles's pianistic style is clearly Rowles himself. —*Jack Sohmer, Cadence*

With the Red Mitchell Trio / Mar. 18-19, 1985 / Contemporary 14016

Jimmy Rowles—Vol. 2 / 1985 / Contemporary 14032

Although done in 1985, this set wasn't released until 1988. It is well done by Rowles, Red Mitchell (b), Rowles's daughter Stacy (tpt, flhn, v), and Colin Bailey (d). —*Ron Wynn*
Trio / Aug. 1990 / Capri 74009

STACY ROWLES

b. Sep. 11, 1955
Trumpet / Swing
A steadily improving trumpeter, Stacy Rowles has worked to build her own reputation and niche independent of her famous father, though she's often recorded and worked with him. Rowles has also done session work and recorded with Nels Cline. She has done a session as a leader in a duo with her father for Delos. Currently, it's available on CD. —*Ron Wynn*

★ **Tell It Like It Is** / Mar. 1984 / Concord Jazz 249
This is a debut album for Stacy Rowles (tpt, flhn) and one that grows on you. Leonard Feather was responsible for pushing Stacy and her father Jimmy Rowles into doing an album, and he produced it and wrote the liners. Feather remarks that this was a first for a father-daughter jazz team. Stacy Rowles's first inspiration was Freddie Hubbard. Although there are many points of interest on this debut album, the best illustration to my ears is her extended work on "Old Folks." "Lotus Blossom" is a fine duo track, while Herman Riley (ts, f) contributes strongly elsewhere, particularly in providing imaginative background and fills. This is well worth a listen. —*Shirley Klett*, Cadence

BADAL ROY

b. 1945
Tabla / Early jazz-rock, world fusion
No one's done more to popularize the tabla in jazz circles than Badal Roy. He moved to America from Pakistan in the late '60s, and since then has appeared in almost every conceivable jazz circumstance, and has also worked in many world music situations. Roy played jazz-rock in New York clubs with John McLaughlin, and recorded with him in 1970. He toured and recorded with Miles Davis in the early '70s, and recorded with Pharoah Sanders and Lonnie Liston Smith. Roy was part of David Liebman's Lookout Farm in the mid-'70s, and toured Europe, India, and Japan with them. When that group disbanded, Roy recorded on other Liebman albums. He later worked with Frank Tusa and Ryo Kawasaki in the late '70s. Roy's continued to record and perform in the '80s and '90s, but did not make any sessions as a leader. He can be heard on numerous CD reissues by Davis, McLaughlin, Liebman, and others. —*Ron Wynn*

GONZALO RUBALCABA

Piano / Bop, Latin-jazz, world fusion
A fiery, rhythmically assertive Cuban pianist, Gonzalo Rubalcaba has alternately excited some observers and alienated others with his sometimes chaotic piano solos. Charlie Haden was an early booster, and the head of Blue Note went to Rubalcaba's aid and helped him to get a visa to play at the Newport in New York Festival in 1992. As of '93, Rubalcaba hadn't defected to America, and was still playing under the auspices of the Cuban government. He's recorded for Blue Note since the early '90s, and also has earlier material on Messidor. Rubalcaba has several sessions available on CD. —*Ron Wynn*

★ **Blessing** / Blue Note 97197
Pianist Gonzalo Rubalcaba is capable of playing a flurry of notes and he does so on the opening tune "Circuito." The surprise of where he will go next is what holds the interest of the listener and not his virtuosity. He can suggest influences from Cecil Taylor on "Circuito" to Bill Evans on "Blue in Green." What impresses me most is that he can take the hoary Latin chestnut "Besame Mucho" and a standard like Miles Davis's "Blue in Green" and dare to play them differently from the almost expected standard improvisation and interpretation that show up in recordings. Of course one cannot underestimate the playing and the presence of his mentor bassist Charlie Haden, who has championed Rubalcaba's recordings, nor the very inventive drumming of Jack DeJohnette. —*Shaukat Husain*, Coda

○ **Mi Gran Pasion** / **i.** Apr. 1989 / Messidor 15999
Cuba's most celebrated musical prodigy, Rubalcaba, is presently busy becoming a major jazz pianist, having expanded his activities well outside Cuba. This album, recorded in Germany with a Cuban band, is a masterpiece: his salute to *danzon*, the music Rubalcaba's father (Guillermo Rubalcaba) still plays in Havana. Modernist and at the same time an elegant essay on how to play this most decorous of musical forms. —*Ned Sublette*

○ **Discovery—Live at Montreux** / Apr. 1991 / Blue Note 95478

○ **Images: Live at Mt. Fuji** / **i.** 1992 / Somethin' Else 99492
A powerhouse live session from the dynamic Cuban pianist Gonzalo Rubalcaba. Recorded live for Blue Note, this is a trio date with bassist John Patitucci and drummer Jack DeJohnette. Patitucci, normally heard in either a fusion or an instrumental pop setting, shows his facility and versatility as he smoothly adjusts to Rubalcaba's upbeat, unorthodox style and meshes with DeJohnette. —*Ron Wynn*

Suite 4 y 20 / **i.** 1993 / Blue Note 80054
Pianist Gonzalo Rubalcaba's fourth Blue Note album, *Suite 4 y 20*, displays range and erudition. The selections include Cuban standards, original compositions, Lennon-McCartney's "Here, There and Everywhere," and Heyman-Young's "Love Letters." Joined by electric bassist Felipe Cabrera, drummer Julio Barreto, trumpeter Reynaldo Mellian, and Charlie Haden on bass (on "Love Letters," "Perfidia," "Transparence," and his own composition "Our Spanish Love Song"), Rubalcaba indulges a meditative side. He remains a very proficient pianist, but the revelation here is that he can also be a moving one. —*Marcela Breton*, Jazz Times

ROSWELL RUDD (Roswell Hopkins (Jr) Rudd)

b. Nov. 17, 1935, Sharon, CT
Trombone / Early free, modern creative
If Jack Teagarden or Kid Ory had been free musicians, they would have sounded like Roswell Rudd. One of the most imaginative, stimulating players around, Rudd brings to the free arena a full slate of tricks from the traditional jazz/Dixieland era. These include growls, a rich, earthy tone, humorous licks, and a superb rhythmic touch. Rudd began studying French horn at age 11, and taught himself trombone while a teen. He was a member of Eli's Chosen Six in the late '50s when he attended Yale. Rudd worked in the early '60s with Herbie Nichols, and played in a quartet with Steve Lacy and Dennis Charles that performed Thelonious Monk compositions exclusively. He joined Bill Dixon's free jazz band in 1962, then, with John Tchicai and Milford Graves, was a founding member of the New York Art Quartet in 1964. Rudd wrote arrangements and compositions for the group and participated in Dixon's historic concert series, the October Revolution in Jazz. He joined Shepp's band in 1965, played with them in London, and recorded at the Donaueschingen Musiktage in 1967. Rudd began recording as a leader with Tchicai in '65. He did an album for Impulse with Charlie Haden in '66. Rudd formed the Primordial Quartet with Robin Kenyatta in 1968. He also worked with Haden's Liberation Music Orchestra in 1969, then joined and recorded with Gato Barbieri's band with Haden, Beaver Harris, and Lonnie Liston Smith. Rudd disbanded the Primordial Quartet in 1970 and wrote compositions for the Jazz Composer's Orchestra. His *Numatik Swing Band* was issued on the JCOA label in 1973. Rudd also recorded for Arista, Phillips (Japan), Bv Haast (Holland), and Horo in the '70s. Rudd taught at Bard College and the University of Maine, and worked as a musicologist with Alan Lomax. He recorded for Soul Note in the early '80s. Rudd currently has only two sessions available on CD. —*Ron Wynn with Michael G. Nastos*

★ **Everywhere** / Sep. 1966 / Impulse 9126
With legendary flutist/bass clarinetist Giuseppi Logan and
two bass players. All originals. —*Michael G. Nastos*

Numatik Swing Band / Jul. 6, 1973 / JCOA 1007

○ **Flexible Flyer** / Mar. 1974 / Freedom 1006
Date for creative trombonist who fell in the cracks when Ray
Anderson arrived. A solid album, with Sheila Jordan (v). —
Michael G. Nastos

Inside Job / May 21, 1976 / Arista

★ **Regeneration** / Jun. 25-26, 1982 / Soul Note 1054
One of many intriguing collaborations pairing Rudd and
Steve Lacy (ss). —*Ron Wynn*

WILLIE RUFF

b. 1931
French horn / Bop
A dynamic French horn player and an excellent teacher and
linguist who's fluent in eight languages, Willie Ruff ranks
alongside Julius Watkins and Robert Northern for mastering
and adapting the French horn to a jazz context. Ruff's also a
good bassist. He studied French horn in the army, and
played in bands at the Lockbourne Air Force base in Ohio,
where he met longtime partner Dwike Mitchell in 1947. Ruff
continued his education at Yale, where he studied orchestral
horn. He was one of Paul Hindemith's pupils, and earned his
Masters degree in 1954. Ruff joined Lionel Hampton's band,
and reunited with Mitchell, who was already a member.
They began working as a duo in 1955. They lectured and
performed all over the world during their lengthy association. They toured with the Yale Russian chorus in 1959, and
were the first American musicians to perform in the Soviet
Union after World War II. They accompanied President
Johnson to Mexico in 1966, and made a film in Brazil tracing the African roots of Brazilian music in 1967. Ruff became a music professor at Yale, and inaugurated the Duke
Ellington Fellowship Program in 1972. The duo played in
China in 1981, and Ruff recorded solo in St. Mark's basilica
in 1983. They've recorded for Roulette, Atlantic, Epic,
Mainstream, Kepler, and even the Book-of-the-Month Club.
But despite their exploits, the duo currently does not have
any sessions available as either a unit or as separate performers, which is a deplorable situation. —*Ron Wynn*

HILTON RUIZ

b. May 29, 1952, New York, NY
Piano / Bop, Latin-jazz, world fusion
An inventive, delightful pianist, Hilton Ruiz's is one of the
best Afro-Latin and Latin-jazz bandleaders and players
around, and is also a good hard bop and bebop soloist. He
began studying piano at an early age, and gave recitals as a
child. Ruiz turned professional as a teen, playing in bands
doing South American music, then turned to jazz in the
early '70s. He studied with Mary Lou Williams, then began
appearing on record dates with Joe Newman, Freddie
Hubbard, Clark Terry, Charles Mingus, Rahsaan Roland
Kirk, Chico Freeman, Betty Carter, and Archie Shepp. Ruiz
worked in Terry's all-star band in the '80s, and recorded with
Marion Brown. He began recording as a leader in the '70s,
and continued in the '80s and '90s. He's done dates for
Steeplechase, Denon, Stash, and RCA/Novus. He currently
has sessions available on CD. —*Ron Wynn and Michael G.
Nastos*

○ **Piano Man** / Jul. 10, 1975 / Inner City 2036
Pianist Hilton Ruiz gets a rhythmic boost from the ever-reliable bassist Buster Williams and the ever-impeccable drummer Billy Higgins on this interesting selection of tunes, including two originals and pieces by Duke Jordan, John
Coltrane, Mary Lou Williams, and Charlie Parker (an unfortunately awkward, overlong "Big Foot.") —*Charles Mitchell,
Down Beat*

★ **Cross Currents** / Nov. 1984 / Vintage Jazz 19

These trio and quintet performances helped cement Ruiz's
status in the Afro-Latin and jazz communities. —*Ron Wynn*

Something Grand / i. Oct. 14-15, 1986 / Novus 3011
Fine Afro-Latin jazz excursion by this solid pianist. Sensational trombone by Steve Turre. Sam Rivers (sax) is also in
the ensemble. —*Ron Wynn*

Strut / Nov. 9-11, 1989 / Novus 3053

○ **Moment's Notice, A** / Feb.Mar. 1991 / Novus 3123
Pianist Hilton Ruiz mixes Afro-Latin, Latin-jazz, and bop on
this '91 session. Flutist Dave Valentin has stronger, more dynamic solos here than on his own records, while saxophonists George Coleman and Kenny Garrett are hot and consistently outstanding. —*Ron Wynn*

○ **Manhattan Mambo** / i. Jul. 30, 1992 / Telarc 83322
Pianist Hilton Ruiz emphasizes his Latin roots on this one.
Working with a nonet (three horns, six rhythm), he ranges
from a Perez Prado mambo of the '50s to a Horace Silver-
tinged original called "Home Cookin'" to John Coltrane's
"Impressions." He's a firm, rhythmically enticing pianist, and
when he breaks loose, as he does on "Impressions," he can
dazzle. Tenorman David Sanchez, who recalls Ralph Moore,
is also heavily featured. In the writing department, trombonist Papo Vazquez scores with his "Overtime Mambo,"
which superimposes a tricky jazz line over the mambo
rhythm. In percussionists Ignacio Berroa and Steve Berrios,
Ruiz has two of the best for his chosen idiom. —*Owen
Cordle, Jazz Times*

HOWARD RUMSEY

b. Nov. 7, 1917, Brawley, CA
Bass, piano, drums / Cool
Bassist Howard Rumsey started on piano, then switched to
drums before settling on bass while in college. He began
work in Vido Musso's band with pianist Stan Kenton, and
was later a founding member of Kenton's first big band.
Rumsey did a lot of freelance work in West Coast groups in
the '40s, and started some jam sessions at the Lighthouse in
Hermosa Beach, California, in 1949. The sessions evolved
into a who's who of West Coast jazz, and Contemporary began recording a series of albums done at the Lighthouse.
Rumsey was a steady presence and a unifying figure who
was able to get contrasting, sometimes vastly different personalities to mesh smoothly in a studio/jam environment.
The All-Stars series was a profitable one for Contemporary
in the '50s, and some six volumes have been reissued by
Fantasy. Rumsey went on to head various combos and big
bands and spearhead a *Concerts By the Sea* series in the '60s
and '70s. —*Ron Wynn*

★ **Sunday Jazz á la Jazzhouse** / Feb. 21, 1953 / Original Jazz
Classics 151
This was a varying group—Shorty Rogers, Maynard
Ferguson, Jimmy Giuffre, Milt Bernhart, Bob Cooper, Shelly
Manne, Carlos Vidal (congas), Frank Patchen (p), Hampton
Hawes—collectively known as the Howard Rumsey (b)
Lighthouse All-Stars. Rumsey made numerous LPs for
Contemporary in the '50s and this was the first (2/21/53).
This is live and captures the hip jams that took place every
Sunday from noon till night. People would sit in and drop
out and the changing personnel reflects that. The playing is
intense and enthusiastic though imperfect, and at times ill
constructed; the frontier ambiance comes through. There are
some notable parts (the piano sounds almost beaten into
tack), the highlight being Giuffre's Lester Young-inspired
solo work. —*Bob Rusch, Cadence*

Sunday Jazz á la Lighthouse—Vol. 2 / i. Oct. 7, 1953 /
Original Jazz Classics 151
Another in a series of sessions done at the Lighthouse fea-
turing Howard Rumsey and various musicians. These are
loosely organized blowing dates with Lighthouse, West
Coast, and special guests getting together and playing.
Rumsey serves as both quasi-leader and also house pianist.
—*Ron Wynn*

○ **Howard Rumsey's Lighthouse All-Stars—Vol. 3** / Oct. 20, 1953 / Contemporary 266

This is a set of three dates put together by entrepreneur and bassist Howard Rumsey. The 7/22/52 session (Shorty Rogers, Milt Bernhardt, Jimmy Giuffre, Bob Cooper, pianist Frank Patchen, Shelly Manne, and percussionist Carlos Vidal) on four tracks boasts crowded arrangements and not very distinct solos. On "Big Girl" there is a deep bow to the R&B sax honkers that is more imitative than parody. The 10/20/53 date produced songs by a group with Rolf Ericson, Herb Geller, Bob Cooper, Bud Shank, Claude Williamson, Max Roach, Milt Bernhardt, and Jack Costanzo. There is a heavy Latin tinge to some of this music, but, overall, it is largely undistinguished. The last date opens things up a bit more with a smaller group (Shank, Cooper, Williamson, Stan Levey, Frank Rosolino) on three tracks and has the most extended blowing and clearest projection along with some nice solos from Shank and Rosolino in particular. —*Bob Rusch*, Cadence

Oboe/Flute / 1954-1956 / Contemporary 154
Lighthouse All-Stars. Sonny Clark (p) and Max Roach (d) are standouts. —*Ron Wynn*

Lighthouse at Laguna / Jun. 20, 1955 / Contemporary 406
Lighthouse All-Stars. Trombonist Frank Rosolino is a standout on this otherwise routine set. —*Ron Wynn*

○ **In the Solo Spotlight—Vol. 5** / Mar. 12, 1956 / Contemporary 3517

Music for Lighthousekeeping / i. Oct. 2-16, 1956 / Contemporary 636

The title of this Howard Rumsey date refers to the Lighthouse jazz club where Rumsey (b) was a regular with his various Lighthouse All-Stars. The only time I was grabbed here was by trumpeter Conte Candoli's solo on "Latin for Lovers." Perhaps it is the leader's logy rhythm that weighs this set down. —*Bob Rusch*, Cadence

★ **In the Solo Spotlight** / Mar. 12, 1957 / Contemporary 451
Lighthouse All-Stars, 1954 and 1957. This large-group date has its moments, but not enough to make it fully successful. —*Ron Wynn*

Jazz Rolls-Royce / Oct. 28, 1957 / Lighthouse 300

○ **Jazz Invention** / i. Feb. 12, 1989 / Contemporary 14051
If you're sentimental about what used to be called "West Coast Jazz," the cover will bring a little moisture to your eyes. William Claxton restaged his famous band-on-the-beach cover for the first 12-inch Contemporary LP. Not all the faces are the same—for one, Shelly Manne's gone, alas—but those that are have weathered well. Alto saxophonist Bud Shank's the youngest of the old-timers and he looks it—the beard and shades and curls are a long way from the crewcut look of yore. The altoist is also, willy-nilly, the star of this reunion concert, playing with a sometimes fierce intensity that is anything but "cool," though it is definitely cool to play like that. His feature, "Lover Man," a tune that certainly has both West Coast and alto-sax associations, is state-of-the-art ballad jazz, a lesson in how to both respect a great melody and put your own stamp on it. Shank shines elsewhere as well, not least on the duet with Bob Cooper (ts), "Softly." Cooper's showcase, "Gee Baby," is fine, honest blowing. He treats this ageless goodie (past 60—thank you, Don Redman) with passion, bringing to mind Al Cohn, who liked to play this one, too. There is no feature for the trumpet, but the younger of the Candoli Brothers (Conte) makes his presence felt in lead and solo on the ensemble numbers—the title tune (nice writing by Cooper, with a bit of fugueing but straightahead changes); Dizzy Gillespie's "Woody 'n' You" (the most boppish of these performances); "Bernie's Tune," almost the national anthem of West Coast jazz; and "Broadway." "Feeling" is Bob Enevoidsen's (valve trombone). One of the handful of valve trombone specialists (Juan Tizol, Bob Brookmeyer, Brad Gowans, Frank Orchard, Marshal Brown, John Sanders—who else?) and a neat tenorman, at times, he, too, is playing more robustly than in the '50s and

does his best to circumvent the on-the-beat phrasing inherent to that horn. —*Dan Morgenstern*, Jazz Times

JIMMY RUSHING (James Andrew Rushing)

b. Aug. 26, 1903, Oklahoma City, OK, **d.** Jun. 8, 1972, New York, NY
Vocals / Swing, big band, blues & jazz

A huge, striking artist, Jimmy Rushing defined and transcended jazz-based blues shouting. His immense voice was dominating and was intricately linked to the beat. He could maintain his intonation regardless of volume, and could sing sensitively one moment, then bellow and yell in almost frightening fashion the next, making both styles sound convincing.

Rushing's parents were musicians, and he studied music theory in high school. He attended Wilberforce University, but dropped out. He moved to the West Coast, and had odd jobs while sometimes singing at house parties. Composer and pianist Jelly Roll Morton was among the people he met while making these appearances. Rushing joined Walter Page's Blue Devils in the late '20s. He left them to work in his father's cafe in Oklahoma City, but returned to Page's group in 1928. He made his first records with the Blue Devils in 1929. Rushing toured with Bennie Moten from 1929 to 1935, recording with Moten in 1931, then joined Count Basie in 1936. Basie has credited Rushing with helping hold things together when times got tough. At an early 1936 session that John Hammond produced, things came together. This marked Lester Young's debut with the band. The songs "Boogie-Woogie" (better known as "I May Be Wrong") and "Evenin'" were instant classics.

Rushing's booming voice and the Basie orchestra proved to be a perfect fit until 1950; they recorded for Columbia and RCA, and cut everything from steamy blues to joyous stomps and novelty tunes like "Did You See Jackie Robinson Hit that Ball." When Basie disbanded the orchestra in 1950, Rushing tried retirement briefly. He ended his retirement a short time later, and formed his own band. He'd made some solo recordings in 1945, and continued in the mid-'50s and early '60s, this time for Vanguard. Rushing recreated Basie classics, worked with some of his sidemen, and even accompanied himself on piano. He cut other sessions with Buck Clayton, Dave Brubeck, and Earl Hines, and frequently had reunions with Basie and/or his sidemen. Rushing appeared in both film shorts and features between 1941 and 1943, among them *Take Me Back, Baby Air Mail Special, Choo Choo Swing,* and *Funzapoppin'.* He participated in the historic 1957 television show "The Sound of Jazz," and was featured on the sixth episode of a 13-part 1958 series called "The Subject is Jazz." He was also in the 1973 film *Monterey Jazz,* which profiled the '70 festival. Rushing also had a singing and acting role in the '69 film *The Learning Tree.* He died three years later. —*Ron Wynn and Bob Porter*

★ **Essential Jimmy Rushing, The** / 1954-1957 / Vanguard 65-66
Fine anthology collecting material done by the great blues shouter for Vanguard during the mid '50s. Songs include a remake of "Going to Chicago" plus other combo dates. He is backed by such Basie comrades as Jo Jones and Buddy Tate. This has been reissued on CD. —*Ron Wynn*

Jazz Odyssey of James Rushing, Esq., The / i. May 30, 1957 / Columbia

☆ **And the Big Brass** / i. 1958 / Columbia 1152

Rushing Lullabies / i. Mar. 1960 / Columbia Special Products 8196
An album from 1960 with stalwart blues shouter Jimmy Rushing doing more intimate material, though he still displays his powerful sound and explosive qualities. But this session also requires Rushing to show more versatility, control of dynamics, and his ballad touches. —*Ron Wynn*

○ **Dave Brubeck and Jimmy Rushing** / i. 1961 / Atlantic

○ **Blues and Things** / i. 1967 / Master Jazz

Blues and Things is a remarkable collection. Combining vocalist Jimmy Rushing with the Earl Hines quartet (Budd Johnson, Bill Pemberton, and Oliver Jackson) was a stroke of genius and the empathy between all concerned is marvelous to hear. This particular version of the Hines quartet was a landmark in the pianist's career. Here Hines the pianist is able to extend his improvisations at will, firm in the knowledge that both Pemberton and Jackson will be with him all the way. It also gives Budd Johnson a real chance to demonstrate his excellent solo powers in a disciplined and well-directioned manner. Jimmy Rushing joins the quartet for four tunes. The perfect choice of tempo, just the right support from Hines, and the inspiration gained from working with musicians of the same stature in full command of their musical faculties let Rushing sound relaxed and unhurried. There is no necessity for him to fight, lead, or direct the music—everyone simply fits in together. —*John Norris,* Coda

○ **Gee, Baby, Ain't I Good to You** / i. Jan. 1969 / Master Jazz 8104
This certainly looks good on paper—the accompanying musicians are Buck Clayton, Julian Dash, Dickie Wells, Sir Charles Thompson, Gene Ramey, and Jo Jones. On top of that, the session took place in a recording studio (which means good sound) but was turned into a jazz party—the idea being to remove the clinical sterility of most studio sessions. The results are somewhat less exciting than the promise. The main problem is that the years have blunted the sharp edges of the musicians' sensitivities. Individually, there are good solos, but rough edges creep in too often. There are occasional bum notes and consistent inspiration is lacking, but no one can substitute for these musicians when it comes to this style—they bring authenticity to their role. They back Jimmy Rushing in fine fashion and coordinate their efforts with grace despite some awkward moments in the rhythm section where considerable stress can be felt. Swing-era addicts will more than enjoy this casually put together session, but a little more care and preparation could have made it that much better an example of the musicians' work and Jimmy Rushing's singing. —*John Norris,* Coda

Who Was It Sang That Song / i. Sep. 1973 / Master Jazz 8120

Mr. Five by Five / i. Aug. 1981 / Columbia 36419

Jimmy Rushing and the Smith Girls / Columbia 1605
The amazing, powerful blues shouter Jimmy Rushing tackles songs done by Bessie, Clara, Mamie, and Trixie Smith backed by a fine studio band led by trumpeter Buck Clayton with a blend of Basie alumni and mainstream jazz greats. —*Ron Wynn*

GEORGE RUSSELL (George Allan Russell)

b. Jun. 23, 1923, Cincinnati, OH
Composer, piano, theorist, drums / Progressive big band, modern creative
George Russell's "Lydian Concept," which he began working on in the '40s, has evolved into one of jazz's major advances. Russell, whose father was a professor of music at Oberlin, derived a system that graded intervals by how far their pitches were from a central note. This theory provided musicians with a wider choice of notes by making the tonal center of a piece also its center of gravity. He linked the ancient Lydian mode with modern uses of chromaticism. Russell developed this into his "Lydian Chromatic concept of Tonal Organization," and his work was hailed as a historical breakthrough. He was among the first to combine Afro-Latin influences and jazz elements such as "Cubana Be/Cubana Bop." Russell studied composition with Stefan Wolpe. He taught at the Lenox School of Jazz, Lund University in Sweden, and at the New England Conservatory. Russell also published several papers and two volumes on the Lydian Chromatic Concept.
He began playing drums in Cincinnati clubs while attending Wilberforce University High School, to which he'd won a scholarship. Russell played briefly in Benny Carter's band,

but was replaced by Max Roach and turned to composing and arranging. He sold his first big band arrangement to Carter and Dizzy Gillespie in the mid-'40s. Russell later wrote for Earl Hines. He moved to New York and wanted to play drums in Charlie Parker's group, but became ill. Russell worked on his Lydian theories during a lengthy recovery period in the mid-'40s. Later, he wrote several pieces for Dizzy Gillespie, including "Cubana Be/Cubana Bop," and also wrote compositions for Buddy DeFranco and Lee Konitz. He wrote for Charlie Ventura, Artie Shaw, and Claude Thornhill as well. In addition to his teaching stints in the '50s, Russell also made his recording debut as a leader on RCA and Decca. He turned to piano, and formed a group in the early '60s. Its members included Don Ellis, Eric Dolphy, Chuck Israels, and Steve Swallow. There were sessions for Riverside, Decca, MPS, and Flying Dutchman. He also played at the landmark 1962 Washington, D.C. Jazz Festival.
Russell moved to Europe in the mid-'60s, and spent six years there teaching at various institutions and recording before returning to America in 1969, where he joined the faculty at the New England Conservatory. During the '70s and '80s, he recorded for Soul Note, Blue Note, and ECM. Russell stopped composing in the mid-'70s to finish the second volume of the "Lydian Chromatic Concept." He recorded albums in the late '70s and '80s with the Swedish Radiojazzgruppen and with big bands in New York. Russell's compositions have earned him many honors, among them composer awards from *Metronome* and *Down Beat* magazines, a pair of Guggenheim fellowships, the National Music Award, three grants from the National Education Association, and the Oscar du Disque de Jazz. Among his discoveries were vocalist Sheila Jordan, and he was also an early champion of European saxophonist Jan Garbarek. His 1985 *African Game* album was one of the first albums issued on the revived Blue Note label, and included Russell's compositions inspired by African drum choirs. He toured England in the late '80s and worked with Courtney Pine and Kenny Wheeler, and with other British jazz and rock musicians. —*Ron Wynn*

○ **Jazz Workshop** / Dec. 1956 / Bluebird 6467
A CD reissue of an intriguing release from 1956 by conductor/composer/arranger/pianist George Russell. This is a superb late '50s album, marked by brilliant playing and provocative compositions. Russell spearheads everything and occasionally helps out on piano. The band includes another brilliant player in pianist Bill Evans, plus Hal McKusick on alto sax and flute, Art Farmer on trumpet, guitarist Barry Galbraith, bassists Milt Hinton and Teddy Kotick, and Joe Harris, Osie Johnson, or Paul Motian on drums. —*Ron Wynn*

★ **New York, New York** / 1959 / MCA 31371
This is a landmark of conceptual, arranging, production, and playing magnificence. John Coltrane (ts), Max Roach (d), Bill Evans (p), and Jon Hendricks (v) all soar. —*Ron Wynn*

Jazz in the Space Age / May 1960 / Decca 9219

George Russell at the Five Spot / Sep. 20, 1960 / Decca 9220

Stratusphunk / Oct. 18, 1960 / Riverside 232

☆ **George Russell in Kansas City** / Feb. 1961 / Decca 74183

☆ **Ezz-Thetic** / 1962 / Riverside 070
The sextet on this 1961 Riverside date—pianist/leader George Russell; Eric Dolphy, whose "'Round Midnight" solo alone is worth the album price; trumpeter Don Ellis; Dave Baker on trombone; bassist Steve Swallow (this was his first record session); drummer Joe Hunt—links Russell's compositional concepts and the brand of on-top-of-the-chords improvisation he traced to Lester Young. —*Bill Shoemaker,* Cadence

Stratus Seekers / Jan. 31, 1962 / Riverside 365
Septet. Fine example of Russell's inside/outside arranging style. Dave Baker (tb) is impressive. —*Ron Wynn*

Outer Thoughts / Jan.-Aug. 1962 / Milestone 47027

A great release, one of the best from George Russell's early phase. It combines material recorded from 1960 to 1962 and includes Eric Dolphy on alto sax and bass clarinet, Dave Baker and Garnett Brown on trombones, trumpeters Don Ellis and Alan Kiger, bassists Steve Swallow and Chuck Israels, and drummers Pete LaRoca and Joe Hunt, with vocalist Sheila Jordan. The songs are unpredictable, the arrangements excellent, and the album includes some pivotal Russell compositions in "Ezz-thetic" and "Stratusphunk." —*Ron Wynn*

Outer View / Aug. 27, 1962 / Riverside 616
Sextet. Ensemble with progressive pianist. Excellent reissue. —*Michael G. Nastos*

Othello Ballet Suite and Electronic Sonata No.1 / Jan. 1967 / Flying Dutchman 122
An uneven, but compelling work by George Russell that combines jazz, classical, and Shakespeare. The results range from magnificent to chaotic; there's a large band that includes mostly obscure foreign musicians. This marks one of the first times that Norway's Jan Garbarek appeared playing tenor sax on a major label. It has been reissued on CD. —*Ron Wynn*

Vertical Form VI / Mar. 1977 / Soul Note 1019
A magnificent and critically acclaimed large-band recording with arrangements by George Russell, who also conducted. His compositions with their intricate, unpredictable, and keenly structured pace, textures, and layers are expertly played by an international orchestra. This '77 release was unfortunately poorly distributed in America since it was on a foreign label. —*Ron Wynn*

New York Big Band / 1977-1978 / Soul Note 1039

★ **Electronic Sonata for Souls Loved by Nature 1968** / i. Apr. 1982 / Soul Note 1009
Electronic Sonata for Souls Loved by Nature covers more than 50 minutes, filling an entire album. The sextet consists of composer/pianist George Russell, tenor saxophonist Jan Garbarek, guitarist Terje Rypdal, drummer Jon Christensen, bassist Red Mitchell, and German trumpeter Manfred Schoof, plus an electronically treated tape with fragments of different styles of music. The performance, recorded live in concert, is powerful. Russell's compositional genius shines through the freedom of the performers and the catalytic inclusion of the prerecorded tape. Schoof, who seems unfamiliar with the music and the concept, falls short of his brilliant capabilities, but acquits himself sensitively and handsomely nonetheless. —*Michael Cuscuna,* Down Beat

African Game / Jun. 18, 1983 / Blue Note 46335
Fine recent material, Russell still an aggressive, dynamic arranger/composer. —*Ron Wynn*

So What / 1986 / Blue Note 46391

HAL RUSSELL

b. 1926, **d.** 1992
Piano, composer / Modern creative
Composer and instrumentalist Hal Russell was an ardent free music participant and booster, though he also played every other kind of music, from traditional jazz to blues. Russell's NRG Ensemble, which he assembled in the late '70s, was the ideal forum for his songs, which ranged from comedic and simple to intricate and intense. Russell's prime instruments were drums and vibes, though he also played trumpet, C-melody and tenor sax, cornet, and various percussion devices. He moved to Chicago from Detroit as a teen, and majored in trumpet at the University of Illinois. He played with Woody Herman and Boyd Raeburn in the '40s. Russell once sat in with Duke Ellington and a Benny Goodman combo, and played with Miles Davis, Sonny Rollins, and Stan Getz in Chicago clubs. He played in a band led by Joe Daley in the '50s, then turned to free music in the early '60s. Russell later rejoined Daley in a trio with Russell Thorne. They recorded an album for RCA in 1963. During the '70s, Russell led various experimental and free groups in Chicago, including the Chemical Feast, before finally assem-

bling his NRG Ensemble in 1978. He led different editions of the ensemble until his death, and recorded occasionally for Nessa. The final Russell album, *Hal's Bells,* issued in 1992, is available on CD. —*Ron Wynn*

○ **Conserving NRG** / Mar. 15-16, 1984 / Principally Jazz 02
Like good Chicagoans, the NRG Ensemble's members are multi-instrumentalists, but each limits himself to one axe per track, yielding various combinations. The switch-hitting yields surprises, too: nothing in the first three tracks prepares one for the blend of crunching horn clusters and dirty electric guitar on "Pontiac," ostensibly inspired by the Sonny Boy Williamson II tune of the same name. Brian Sandstrom's trumpet here and Hal Russell's cornet ("Blue Over You") have a raw, eager edge that grabs attention. They seem to be playing at the limits of their abilities, rather like early Don Cherry; they don't have the polish to shuck, but they do have the musical instincts to make their cliffhanger primitivism work. One key to NRG's success: they transcend individual instruments to always sound like a band. Their attitude gives them continuity—that, and the reliable rolling rhythms of bassist Curt Bley (a constant) and pulse-keeper Steve Hunt (who drums on all but one track). —*Kevin Whitehead,* Cadence

★ **Hal's Bells** / i. 1992 / PolyGram 513781

LUIS RUSSELL (Luis Carl Russell)

b. Aug. 6, 1902, Careening Clay, Panama, **d.** Dec. 11, 1963, New York, NY
Bandleader, arranger, piano / New Orleans traditional
Luis Russell led some outstanding big bands in the late '20s and early '30s, though he was overshadowed by the Ellington and Basie orchestras. His bands mixed comic vocals, stomping arrangements, and elements of traditional New Orleans with swing, making delightful and popular tunes while enabling some emerging players to sharpen their skills. Russell was born in Panama, and used the winnings from a lottery ticket to move his mother and sister with him to New Orleans. He played with King Oliver in New York, then, after working with some other groups, formed a band in Chicago. They recorded four songs in 1926. The Heebie Jeebie Stompers included Darnell Howard and Barney Bigard. They appeared at Harlem's Saratoga Club with a lineup that included Henry Allen, Bill Coleman, Albert Nicholas, Charlie Holmes, and Paul Barbarin. J.C. Higginbotham, Dicky Wells, and Teddy Hill were added to the group later. The band recorded more than 30 songs between 1929 and 1934 for various labels, and backed Louis Armstrong on "Song of the Islands" in 1930. They made such popular tunes as "Call of the Freaks," "Saratoga Shout," "Jersey Lightning," and, with songwriter Andy Razaf doing lead vocals,"On Revival Day." Louis Armstrong's manager, Joe Glaser, took the group over in 1935, after two days of the group supporting Armstrong at the Savoy. This move effectively destroyed the band's identity. Russell served as Armstrong's musical director until 1943. The coming of bop drove Russell, unable to make the adjustment, out of music. He was a businessman for a time, then became a piano teacher, and, later, a chauffeur. Russell died in 1963. As yet, his work has not gotten the widespread exposure it merits through reissue mania. —*Ron Wynn*

★ **Luis Russell Collection (1926-1934), The** / 1926-1934 / Collector's Classics 7

○ **Luis Russell and His Louisiana Swing Orchestra** / i. Apr. 1974 / Columbia 32338
Forgotten by all but specialists and collectors, the Luis Russell band in its prime (1929-1931) was one of the greatest of pre-swing-era big bands. A compact 10 pieces, with musicians from New Orleans in key positions (Russell himself was Panamanian-born but cut his musical eyeteeth in the Crescent City), the band combined the looseness and flexibility of the parent style with the drive and swing of the evolving big-band language. Russell, also the band's chief arranger, knew how to give his soloists maximum freedom,

and he had some great ones, chiefly the magnificent Henry "Red" Allen and J.C. Higginbotham on trumpet and trombone. Allen, just up from New Orleans, was perhaps the first trumpeter to truly absorb Louis Armstrong's message, and the freshness, directness, and exuberance of his work with Russell remains a high point in a long and fruitful career. On this generous sampling of the band's growth, development, and beginning decline, the great stuff is on tracks 10 through 26. What comes before is mainly of historical interest, and the last six sides, without Allen or Higginbotham, reflect the waning of the band's intrinsic style in favor of the pervasive Casa Loma approach. Of the masterpieces from the important period, "Jersey Lightning" is perhaps the most perfect; it could be by Jelly Roll Morton, certainly Russell's chief influence, both as pianist and arranger, but is more successful than Morton's own attempts to adapt to the larger instrumentation. Nearly as fine are "Panama," "Doctor Blues," "Saratoga Shout" (an interesting combination of the "The Saints" and the minor blues), "High Tension," and "Feelin' the Spirit." Along with the dozen or so great works recorded by the band for Victor under Red Allen's name, these are the Luis Russell legacy of Louisiana Swing. The well-conceived two-record set (with eight tracks per side) contains several rare alternate takes, and has informative notes by producer Frank Driggs. —*Dan Morgenstern, Down Beat*

PEE WEE RUSSELL (Charles Ellsworth Russell)

b. Mar. 27, 1906, St. Louis, MO, **d.** Feb. 15, 1969, Alexandria, VA

Clarinet / Dixieland

Born in Oklahoma, Russell played piano and violin before taking up clarinet; he was a pro at age 15. In 1924, he worked with the legendary pianist Peck Kelly in a band that also included Jack Teagarden, who became his lifelong friend. In 1925, he played with Bix Beiderbecke in Frank Trumbauer's band. In 1927, he settled in New York and recorded frequently in all-star groups assembled by Red Nichols, but also worked in dance bands, and doubled on tenor, alto, and soprano. In 1935 he joined Louis Prima's band on 52nd Street and went to California with the trumpeter. Back in New York, he was a key member of the musical fraternity around Eddie Condon; with Condon, he was a fixture at Nick's, and was later a fixture at Condon's clubs. He played in an always unclassifiable and totally original style, with a tonal palette that ranged from whispers to raspy shouts. Near death in 1951, he recovered and began to lead his own groups, mostly made up of young musicians, such as Ruby Braff. In 1963, he formed a quartet with valve trombonist Marshall Brown that featured a repertoire including pieces by John Coltrane and Ornette Coleman. In that same year, Russell performed with Thelonious Monk at Newport and finally began to receive the critical attention he'd so long deserved. Late in life, he took up painting, and showed as natural a gift for art as he showed for music, though he didn't develop his talent for painting. —*Ron Wynn and Dan Morgenstern*

○ **Chronological Remembrance, A** / **i.** Sep. 6, 1927-Sep. 4, 1965 / IAJRC 28
IAJRC, the superb collector's label, issued this single LP, which is full of rare studio recordings and concert performances from a wide assortment of groups, all of them featuring the distinctive clarinet of Pee Wee Russell. Whether heard with the Charleston Chasers in 1927, with Red McKenzie, Louis Prima, Bobby Hackett, and Teddy Wilson, or "in concert" with Eddie Condon, Russell is in fine form. An extra bonus is an ad-lib blues from the 1964 Monterey Jazz Festival that is shared with baritonist Gerry Mulligan. Recommended. —*Scott Yanow*

And Rhythmakers / 1938 / Atlantic 126
Top date with octet, now available as half of two-record set along with good Jack Teagarden (tb) session. —*Ron Wynn*

○ **Jack Teagarden / Pee Wee Russell** / **i.** Aug. 1938 / Original Jazz Classics 1708

This limited-edition reissue combines two very successful sessions. The great trombonist Jack Teagarden heads up an all-star swing octet in 1940 that includes cornetist Rex Stewart, clarinetist Barney Bigard, and Ben Webster on tenor for three standards and a blues. Clarinetist Pee Wee Russell is heard on a pair of trio sides with pianist James P. Johnson and drummer Zutty Singleton, along with four of his own octet performances, which also feature trumpeter Max Kaminsky and trombonist Dicky Wells, from 1938. In all cases the music swings hard and is filled with colorful solos from these classic jazzmen. —*Scott Yanow*

★ **Individualism of Pee Wee Russell, The** / **i.** 1952 / Savoy
In December 1950 clarinetist Pee Wee Russell nearly died from the effects of years of excessive drinking and limited eating. By the time of the Boston engagement that resulted in this double LP, Russell was 90% recovered. Leading a strong sextet that boasts fine solos from trombonist Eph Resnick and the great young trumpeter Ruby Braff, Russell mostly performs veteran, Dixieland standards during these extended workouts, avoiding clichés and playing his typically unique ideas with spirit and enthusiasm. —*Scott Yanow*

○ **We're in the Money** / 1953-Oct. 2, 1954 / Black Lion 70909
The unique clarinet style of Pee Wee Russell is featured on this CD with two overlapping groups, both of which include trombonist Vic Dickenson and pianist George Wein. One band has Pee Wee matching wits with the brilliant trumpet of Wild Bill Davison while the other date showcases the more mellow horn of Doc Cheatham, heard in a rare solo spot in the mid '50s. This music mostly avoids the old warhorses and features superior swing standards by some of the top Condonites. —*Scott Yanow*

Over the Rainbow / Feb. 18-19, 1958 / Xanadu 192
With the exception of a 1965 version of "I'm in the Market For You," which has a few notes at its close by cornetist Bobby Hackett, this LP finds clarinetist Pee Wee Russell (normally heard in Dixieland bands) showcased as the only horn. The other selections (taken from two sessions in 1958) feature Pee Wee and one of two rhythm sections playing some of his favorite songs including "I Would Do Anything For You," "I'd Climb The Highest Mountain," and "If I Had You." Russell, always a modern player although usually confined to more traditional settings, is heard at his most lyrical throughout this very interesting set. Three of these performances are also included on *Portrait of Pee Wee.* —*Scott Yanow*

Portrait of Pee Wee / **i.** Feb. 18, 1958-Feb. 19, 1958 / DCC Compact Classics 611
Issued originally on Counterpoint and reissued many times since by budget labels like Everest, this CD version has superior sound. From 1958, this set matches the great clarinetist Pee Wee Pussell with an all-star horn section (trumpeter Ruby Braff, trombonist Vic Dickenson, and tenor saxophonist Bud Freeman) on a program of swing standards along with "Pee Wee Blues." Russell, a bit weary of playing Dixieland by this time, was starting to look toward more modern eras of music, although in reality his own playing was always beyond categorization. —*Scott Yanow*

Ji Grandi Di Del Jazz / **i.** 1958-1962 / Fabbri Editori 17
CBS recordings from 1958 and 1962. Package is stunning from an artwork and liner note standpoint. Music shows the clarinetist turning the corner. With Ruby Braff (cnt), Bud Freeman (ts), Vic Dickenson (tb), and Nat Pierce (p). Liners by John Lewis. —*Michael G. Nastos*

○ **Jazz Reunion** / Feb. 23-Mar. 8, 1961 / Candid 79020
The reunion that took place in this 1961 session was between clarinetist Pee Wee Russell and tenor great Coleman Hawkins; they had first recorded one of the songs, "If I Could Be With You," back in 1929! Both Hawk and Pee Wee had remained modern soloists and on this unusual but very satisfying date (which also features trumpeter Emmett Berry and trombonist Bob Brookmeyer) they explore such numbers as a pair of Ellington classics ("All Too Soon" and "What Am I

Hear For"), two Pee Wee originals, and even the boppish "Tin Tin Deo." Timeless music. —*Scott Yanow*

Hot Licorice / i. 1964 / Honey Dew 6614
In 1964, clarinet great Pee Wee Russell was caught live jamming through some Dixieland standards with a pickup group of New England musicians. Only trombonist Porky Cohen (who later played with Roomful of Blues) is slightly known, although trumpeter Tony Tomasso acquits himself well on this decent outing. Pee Wee Russell fans will want to search for this now-rare LP, the first of two Honeydews from this gig. —*Scott Yanow*

Gumbo / i. 1964 / Honey Dew 6616
The second of two LPs taken from a pickup date in 1964, this album finds veteran clarinetist Pee Wee Russell jamming Dixieland standards with some local musicians from New England; trumpeter Tony Tomasso and trombonist Porky Cohen keep up with Russell on this happy if somewhat predictable session. —*Scott Yanow*

○ **Ask Me Now! / i.** May 1966 / Impulse 96
After a lifetime spent playing unusual and unpredictable clarinet solos in Dixieland settings, Pee Wee Russell late in life broke out of the stereotype and played in more modern settings. This Impulse LP (which is begging to be reissued on CD) has Russell's clarinet placed in a pianoless quartet with valve trombonist Marshall Brown, playing tunes by John Coltrane, Thelonious Monk, and Ornette Coleman along with some classic ballads. It is a remarkable, lyrical date that briefly rejuvenated the career of this veteran individualist. A classic of its kind. —*Scott Yanow*

○ **Spirit of '67, The** / 1967 / Impulse 9147

College Concert of Pee Wee Russell and Henry Red / i. Jan. 1968 / Impulse 9137
Although trumpeter Red Allen (heard In his final recording) and clarinetist Pee Wee Russell had recorded back in 1932, their paths only crossed on an infrequent basis through the years. For this LP, the two veteran modernists (who spent much of their careers in Dixieland settings) are joined by a young rhythm section of pianist Steve Kuhn, bassist Charlie Haden, and drummer Marty Morell. The music is generally relaxed with an emphasis on blues and a fine feature for Red on "Body and Soul." —*Scott Yanow*

★ **Memorial Album / i.** 1969 / Prestige 7672
Teaming together trumpeter Buck Clayton with clarinetist Pee Wee Russell in 1960 was a logical move. Both of these individual stylists had been stuck often in Dixieland settings in the '50s yet they were really highly distinctive swing soloists. Joined by a modern rhythm section led by pianist Tommy Flanagan, Buck and Pee Wee are in top form on six fine standards, making one wish that they had teamed up in this type of setting more often. —*Scott Yanow*

Salute to Newport / i. Apr. 1979 / IA 93592
This out-of-print double LP reissues Pee Wee Russell's 1959 Dot album with trumpeter Buck Clayton, trombonist Vic Dickenson, and veteran tenor Bud Freeman along with a particularly hot 1962 session from Impulse by George Wein's Newport All-Stars, which also includes Freeman along with cornetist Ruby Braff and trombonist Marshall Brown. The earlier record is fine but the Newport All-Stars (whose exciting performance is highlighted by such tunes as "At the Jazz Band Ball," Freeman's feature on "Crazy Rhythm," and Russell's "The Bends Blues") is the reason to search for this set. —*Scott Yanow*

○ **Giants of Jazz / i.** Jan. 1982 / Time Life 18
This three-LP box set is regrettably out of print for it serves as a fine introduction to the unique clarinetist Pee Wee Russell. The 40 selections that are included here span a 35-year period and are highlighted by early sides with Red Nichols, many encounters with Eddie Condon's bands (including some real classic performances), a few numbers from Russell's mid-'30s association with Louis Prima and later recordings with his own pickup groups. Along with an excellent booklet, this box is a fine tribute to a truly individual stylist. —*Scott Yanow*

○ **Pied Piper of Jazz, The / i.** Sep. 1982 / Commodore 16440
Now here's some cooking music. I'd recommend this record just for the seven trio tracks; the added quartet tracks are a good bonus, but clearly of a more common cloth, though Pee Wee Russell was never really common. Surprisingly, to me, these sessions are rather overlooked by annotations of Russell's music, but then again Zutty Singleton (d) and Joe Sullivan (p) are often overlooked in favor of derivative or lesser talent. Sullivan was a great two-fisted pianist, and Singleton, along with Baby Dodds, a great stylist and father of traditional jazz whose influence could probably be traced right up to Ed Blackwell through Gene Krupa and Art Blakey. It is absolutely fitting that he be the drummer on this trio date, because with Singleton at the drums you really never need a bass. On this record one gets to hear some prime playing from the clarinetist, but pay attention to the rhythm, particularly Sullivan and Singleton. —*Bob Rusch*, Cadence

PAUL RUTHERFORD (Paul William Rutherford)

b. Feb. 29, 1940, London, England
Trombone / Modern creative
An experimental, unpredictable player who also has a good sense of humor, English trombonist Paul Rutherford's worked in many seminal free bands since the '60s. He started on saxophone in the mid-'50s, then switched to trombone and played that instrument in Royal Air Force (RAF) bands from 1958 to 1963. He met John Stevens and Trevor Watts in the RAF, and they coformed the Spontaneous Music Ensemble in 1965. Rutherford studied during the day at the Guildhall School of Music in London, and played free sessions at night during the mid- and late '60s. He began working regularly with Mike Westbrook in 1967, and formed his own group, Iskra 1903, with Derek Bailey and Barry Guy in the early '70s. Rutherford also played with the London Jazz Composers Orchestra, with the Globe Unity Orchestra, with the Tony Oxley septet, and with Evan Parker and Paul Lovens. He began developing an unusual trombone language in the mid-'70s, mixing electronics, vocal effects, traditional jazz devices, and intriguing sounds and voicings. Rutherford issued some compelling solo sessions in the '70s, then formed a new edition of Iskra 1903 with Guy and Phil Wachsmann in the '80s. He also continued working with the London Jazz Composers Orchestra, played in the Free Jazz Quartet, and recorded duos with George Haslam. Currently, Rutherford does not have any sessions available on CD in America. —*Ron Wynn*

★ **Gentle Harm of the Bourgeoisie / i.** 1974 / Emanem 3305
Recording of solo trombone. One of the most revered avant-garde statements. —*Michael G. Nastos*

TERJE RYPDAL

b. Aug. 23, 1947, Oslo, Norway
Guitar, flute, soprano saxophone, composer / Early jazz-rock, world fusion, new age, modern creative
A flexible Norwegian guitarist and composer, Terje Rypdal's blended rock and jazz elements, as well as contemporary classic and even New Age ingredients into his solos. He adds an unusual touch, sometimes playing electric guitar with a violin bow, and utilizes synthesizers and electronic attachments. Rydal's a self-taught guitarist who studied classical piano. He attended Oslo University, studied composition with Finn Mortensen, and learned the Lydian chromatic concept from its creator, George Russell. Rypdal worked with Jan Garbarek from the late '60s into the '70s, and gained significant attention for his performance at the 1969 New Jazz Meeting in Baden-Baden, Germany. He formed the group Odyssey in the early '70s, and visited London and America with them. Rypdal recorded with Palle Mikkelborg at the Festpill in Norway in 1978. He led a trio with Audun Kleive and Bjorn Kjellemyr that toured Eastern Europe and England in the mid-'80s. Rypdal played in a duo with Mikkelborg in 1986. He's recorded often as a leader for ECM

in the '70s, '80s, and '90s. Rypdal has several sessions as a leader available on CD. —*Ron Wynn*

Waves / Aug. 1973-Sep. 1977 / ECM 827419

Contains some of Rypdal's jazziest music—"Per Ulv" even verges on bebop, despite its chattering rhythm box—alongside the more characteristic free-fall rhapsodies. —*Michael P. Dawson*

★ **Works** / 1974-1981 / ECM 825428

Excellent sampler of Rypdal's music, including two cuts from his superb (but currently unavailable) early '70s albums. —*Michael P. Dawson*

○ **Odyssey** / Aug. 1975 / ECM 835355

Most the cuts on this album are lengthened beyond what they deserve. The compositions are pleasant, but there's not enough material to warrant making half the songs last over 10 minutes. On the plus side, guitarist Terje Rypdal masters the lyrical beauty of Carlos Santana, whose solid intonation most certainly influenced Rypdal. More important, Rypdal is able to inform this style with an individualism that identifies him as a musician. While not to be rated as the most influential of guitarists, he is a competent craftsman who plays with conviction and taste. Ironically, the most expressive and successful cuts are the shorter ones, especially "Darkness Fall" and "Better Off Without You," where the music is compact and to the point. —*Kevin Yatarola*, Cadence

Descendre / Mar. 1979 / ECM 829118

The unusual trio form of guitar, trumpet, and drums makes for some gorgeous floating sounds. —*Michael P. Dawson*

Eos / May 1983 / ECM 815333

Probably Rypdal's most experimental release, a set of heavily electronic duets with cellist David Darling. —*Michael P. Dawson*

Undisonus / i. 1990 / ECM 837755

None of Rypdal's haunting guitar here: this is an album of his purely orchestral compositions. —*Michael P. Dawson*

S

EDDIE SAFRANSKI

b. 1918, **d.** 1974
Bass / Swing, big band
A very effective swing or bebop bassist, Eddie Safranski was known for very precisely articulated lines, a good tone, and an aggressively swinging sound that served him well in Stan Kenton's band and in other bands. He studied violin in his childhood, then played bass in high school. Safranski joined Hal McIntyre in the early '40s, played with him until 1945, and also wrote arrangements. He later worked with Miff Mole, Kenton, and Charlie Barnet in the late '40s. Safranski moved to New York, and became a staff musician at NBC in the early '50s. He worked with Benny Goodman in 1951 and 1952. Safranski did studio work until the late '60s, then became a representative for a bass company. He also gave workshops and taught, while playing traditional jazz and bebop with various Los Angeles groups. Safranski recorded for Atlantic and Savoy as a leader, but these are currently unavailable on CD. He can be heard on CD reissues by Kenton, Goodman, and Don Byas. —*Ron Wynn*

SAL SALVADOR

b. Nov. 21, 1925, Monson, MA
Guitar / Bop
A versatile guitarist and the recent head of the guitar department at the University of Bridgeport, Sal Salvador has been a capable soloist and accompanist since the late '40s. His single string style, shaped by his early interest in the music of Charlie Christian, has been augmented by extensive studies of guitar technique. Salvador's years of research, playing, and analysis eventually led to his writing guitar methodology books in the '50s and '60s, among them *Sal Salvador's Chord Method for Guitar* and *Sal Salvador's Single String Studies for Guitar*. He became interested in jazz during his teens, and began playing professionally in Springfield, Massachusetts in 1945. He worked with Terry Gibbs and Mundell Lowe in New York at the end of the '40s, then joined Stan Kenton's orchestra in 1952. Salvador worked with Kenton until the end of 1953, and appeared on the *New Concepts of Artistry in Rhythm* album. He led bebop bands that featured Eddie Costa and Phil Woods. Salvador was featured in the film *Jazz on a Summer's Day*, and headed a big band in the late '50s and early '60s. He worked in a guitar duo with Alan Hanlon in the early '70s, and began recording again as a leader later in the decade. He reformed his big band in the '80s, and was named to his position at the University of Bridgeport. Salvador has recorded for Bee Hive and Stash, among others. Currently, he has a few sessions as a leader available on CD. —*Ron Wynn*

Kenton Presents Jazz: Sal Salvador / Jul. 21, 1954 / Capitol 6505

○ **World's Greatest Jazz Standards** / Nov. 1983 / Stash 234
As guitarist Sal Salvador points out in the liner notes, the idea of this session was to do an album of songs that had been overplayed in the past. A better idea would have been to "stretch out" a little more on these pieces, since everyone (musicians and listeners) knows them extremely well. There are a few twists here—"Misty" as a waltz, "Cherokee" as a samba—but the program is basically straightahead. Salvador is a good soloist in an older bebop style, and he has the lion's share of the solo space. This album is another example of using vibraphone to serve the harmonic/melodic function often assigned to guitar or piano. Paul Johnson is a much more interesting and adventurous soloist than is evidenced here, given the limited solo space. The quartet works well together, but I'd just prefer to hear more extended explorations of these pieces. —*Peter Leitch,* Cadence

★ **Sal Salvador and Crystal Image** / Stash 17
With Teo Macero (s), Barbara Oakes (v). Very enjoyable and unusual in its instrumentation and approach. —*Shirley Klett,* Cadence

JOE SAMPLE (Joseph Leslie Sample)

b. Feb. 1, 1939, Houston, TX
Piano, composer / Blues & jazz, soul-jazz, instrumental pop, contemporary funk
In the late '50s, pianist Sample formed a group with some Texas comrades that played an aggressive brand of funky blues, and instrumental R&B with jazz touches that they called the "Gulf Coast Sound." When the group moved to Los Angeles in 1960 they changed their name to the Jazz Crusaders. Though he also worked with some other musicians in the '60s, among them Tom Scott and the Harold Land/Bobby Hutcherson group, the main unit (Sample on keyboards, Wayne Henderson on trombone, Wilton Felder on tenor sax, and Stix Hooper on drums) was unparalleled at playing R&B-infused soul-jazz. The group dropped the Jazz surname in the '70s, became the Crusaders, and gradually began doing less ambitious, markedly lighter material without the strong blues and R&B backing. Sample got more involved in the production in '70s and '80s. His most recent releases have been heavy on studio touches and weaker on content. —*Ron Wynn*

○ **Fancy Dance** / Apr. 1969 / Gazell 1016
A different, and rather strong session for keyboardist Joe Sample from '69. Rather than the fusion, blues, and funky instrumentals he's done both with and without his fellow Crusaders, this is a mainstream trio session with Sample, bassist Red Mitchell, and drummer J.C. Moses. While there are two spry blues pieces, some demanding bop and standards let Sample show he can execute the chord changes and perform conventional jazz with conviction, even if it's not what he does today. —*Ron Wynn*

○ **Rainbow Seeker** / 1978 / MCA 31067
Joe Sample's solo effort *Rainbow Seeker* epitomizes some of the strengths and weaknesses of contemporary fusion. At the core of Sample's music is still a deep gospel resonance. "In All My Wildest Dreams" has a gentle churchy ambiance, and Sample's transparent electric piano has a sing-song blues quality. Bassist Robert Popwell and drummer Stix Hooper provide the rhythmic punch, as on "There are Many Stops Along the Way." Hooper's reading of funk beats is more loose-limbed than that of some disco computers; the bass drum is insistent but not predominant, and he provides a shifting canvas of cymbal and snare accents over Popwell's

solid bottom. On "As Long as it Lasts" guitarist Ray Parker lays down some choppy chords for Popwell and Hooper to groove on, as Sample creates a lilting melody on top. "Islands in the Rain" is a Latin cooker that showcases Sample's acoustic piano talents, while the unaccompanied "Together We'll Find a Way" finds him involved in more reflective musings that mix '50s-style block chords with romantic melodies. —*Chip Stern*, Down Beat

★ **Carmel** / 1979-1981 / MCA 37210

EDGAR SAMPSON (Edgar Melvin Sampson)

b. Aug. 31, 1907, New York, NY, **d.** Jan. 16, 1973, Englewood, NJ

Saxophone, violin, composer, arranger / Swing, big band
While he was a first-rate violinist and a versatile saxophonist, Edgar Sampson's greatness came as a composer and an arranger. His greatest works include "Stompin' at the Savoy," "Don't Be That Way," "Blue Minor," "If Dreams Come True," "Blue Lou," "Lullaby in Rhythm," and many others, plus numerous arrangements. He began playing violin as a child, then played alto sax as a teen. He started his professional career with Joe Coleman in 1924, then worked with Duke Ellington in 1925. Later came stints with Bingie Madison, Billy Fowler, Arthur Gibbs, Charlie Johnson, and Alex Jackson. Sampson joined Fletcher Henderson in 1931, and remained with him until 1933. He played with Chick Webb from '33 until '37, and began writing arrangements with Rex Stewart while in Webb's band. Sampson was a prolific freelance arranger during the swing era's heyday, providing arrangements for Webb, Benny Goodman, Artie Shaw, Red Norvo, and Teddy Wilson. He played the baritone sax with Lionel Hampton in 1938, then became Ella Fitzgerald's music director in 1939. Sampson played alto and baritone sax for Al Sears in 1943, then started his own bands. During the late '40s and '50s, Sampson played in many Afro-Latin bands, including those of Marcellino Guerra, Tito Puente, and Tito Rodriquez. He continued heading bands through the '60s, and died in 1973. —*Ron Wynn*

★ **Jazz Heritage: Sampson Swings Again** / MCA 1354

DAVE SAMUELS

b. Oct. 9, 1948, Waukegan, IL
Vibes / Modern creative
A vibist and marimba player whose records run the gamut from exacting and ambitious to impressionistic and tedious, Dave Samuels can sometimes be more technically impressive than musically enticing. He studied with Gary Burton at Berklee, and later became an instructor there in jazz improvisation and percussion. Samuels moved to New York in 1974, and recorded for three years with Gerry Mulligan while he also toured internationally. Samuels played and recorded with Carla Bley and Gerry Niewood. He formed a duo with fellow vibist, marimba player, and percussionist Dave Friedman. They recorded with Harvie Swartz and Hubert Laws under Friedman's name in 1975, then called themselves Double Image for sessions with Michael Di Pasqua and Swartz from 1977 to 1980. Double Image toured Europe, taught at workshops, and were on the faculty at the Manhattan School of Music for a time. Samuels worked and recorded with Double Image in 1985, and also played with the group Gallery. He began to work with Spyro Gyra in 1979, and continued to play with them until he joined full time in 1986. Samuels recorded with Paul McCandless, Art Lande, Anthony Davis, and Bobby McFerrin in the late '70s and '80s, and did a solo date in 1981. He's recorded with his own group in the late '80s and '90s. Samuels has several sessions available on CD. —*Ron Wynn*

DAVID SANBORN (David William Sanborn)

b. Jul. 30, 1945, Tampa, FL
Alto saxophone / Blues & jazz, instrumental pop
Without question a versatile, technically superior alto saxophonist, Dave Sanborn has alternately delighted and frus-

trated the jazz community. He's alternated between making mildly competent, commercially profitable records and doing dates that more closely reveal his skills. He has one of the most striking, pure alto sounds since the late Cannonball Adderley, and he's among the few players who truly understand the blues and can also play bebop and free styles brilliantly. Over the years, Sanborn has worked with Paul Butterfield, David Bowie, Stevie Wonder, James Taylor, and Albert King, and has led his own bands. While growing up in St. Louis, he played with many Chicago blues greats and became a skilled saxophonist despite battling polio in his youth. Sanborn began recording as a leader in the mid '70s and racked up a string of pop successes with works that have more instrumental integrity than standard Kenny G/ Dave Koz fluff, but still don't represent a test of his abilities. But Sanborn's balanced the scales by cutting such sessions as *Another Hand*, an excellent hard bop and bebop date, and turning in a superb guest stint with Tim Berne on a '93 album that features the compositions of Julius Hemphill. Sanborn was host of one of the all-time great music shows, the syndicated "Night Music." It was truly an eclectic program in the best and broadest sense, and featured everyone from Sun Ra to heavy metal, reggae, blues, rock, funk, punk, and other types of music. Sanborn interviewed and played with the performers. Sadly, it was canceled after two years for lack of sponsorship. Sanborn also did a syndicated radio program earlier in the '90s. All his sessions are available on CD. —*Ron Wynn and William Ruhlmann*

★ **Taking Off** / 1975 / Warner Brothers 2873
Alto saxophonist David Sanborn's debut album for Warner Bros. is a polished, toe-tappin', finger-poppin', jazz-flavored rhythm and blues outing, infectious in nature. Working out of the tradition of such R&B saxophonists as Junior Walker and King Curtis, Sanborn convincingly engages the tight, funky charts of David Matthews, Howard Johnson, Don Grolnick, and Randy Brecker. —*Chuck Berg*, Down Beat

David Sanborn / i. Feb. 1976 / Warner Brothers 2957

Heart to Heart / Jan. 1978 / Warner Brothers 3189

○ **Another Hand** / 1990 / Elektra 61088
Return by Sanborn to his real, true love: unadorned (or only partly adorned) jazz. —*Ron Wynn*

○ **Upfront** / 1991 / Elektra 61272
Despite an array of session musicians and some heavily arranged material, alto saxophonist Dave Sanborn cuts long with his most expressive, joyous playing in many years. That's partly due to Marcus Miller's bass work, which is fluid and backbeat-oriented, while others like trumpeter Herb Robertson and organist Richard Tee lay in some perfect riffs in support of Sanborn's earnest solos. —*Ron Wynn*

PONCHO SANCHEZ

b. Oct. 30, 1951, Laredo, TX
Flute, guitar, percussion / Latin-jazz
A bandleader and conga player, Poncho Sanchez has made several sessions in the '80s and '90s for Concord and Concord Picante. He's recorded with Clare Fischer, Freddie Hubbard, Gary Foster, and many others. Sanchez has several sessions available as a bandleader. —*Ron Wynn*

★ **Gauiota** / i. 1980 / Discovery

○ **Papa Gato** / i. 1986 / Concord Jazz 4310
Poncho Sanchez continues to turn out fine recordings. Justo Almario takes over the reeds (as, ts, f) with the remaining personnel veterans of this popular group. Almario has a good showcase (along with pianist Charlie Otwell) on the title song, but is, of course, much in evidence elsewhere. Here, I most enjoyed the title number and "Senor Blues." —*Shirley Klett*, Cadence

○ **Fuerte** / i. 1987 / Concord Jazz 4340
Features an octet with standout pianist/composer Charlie Otwell, who wrote the title track and two other cookers. Saxophonist Ken Goldberg wrote two others. Because of

these two, this stands as a prime Sanchez album, aside from the group's hot playing. —*Michael G. Nastos*

☆ **Night at Kimball's East, A / i.** 1990 / Concord Jazz 4472
Recorded at Kimball's East, this live performance starts out warm and finishes smoking. The final cut, Charlie Otwell's "La Familia," is a pulsating show stopper with everyone doing something to blow the roof off. The "Tito Puente Medley" of "El Cayuco," "Oye Como Va," and "Claveltos" delivers as well, with Sal Cracchiolo's trumpet work a model of Latin-style blowing, bursting high notes articulated with piercing clarity. On "Bien Sabroso," Cracchiolo is again exemplary, while "Papo" Rodriguez's bongo solo and the precision ensemble playing live up to the tune's title, very tasty. "Alafia" showcases the tenor work of Gene Burket while Sanchez opens up on congas. West Coast-based Sanchez is a conguero with Mexican roots, whose influences include Puente and Mongo Santamaria. The Pozo/Gillespie classic "Manteca" is given a mellow treatment with Art Velasco leading the way on trombone. "Sonando" has a dazzling solo by Cracchiolo and Papo Rodriguez's high-energy percolation on bongos. This was clearly a night to remember. —*Marcela Breton*, Jazz Times

PHAROAH SANDERS (Farrell Sanders)

b. Oct. 13, 1940, Little Rock, AR
Tenor saxophone / Early free, modern creative
He's a respected, established figure today, but in the '60s Pharoah Sanders was viewed in some quarters as a talentless upstart who had helped to shatter the greatest quartet in modern jazz history. John Coltrane saw both a kindred spirit and an important voice in Sanders, and made the unknown, inexperienced player an equal in his group. While working alongside Coltrane, Sanders perfected the long, linear solos, jagged phrases, and trilling, bird-like lines that were so controversial. The Coltrane/Sanders dialogues were so fierce, stark, and naked that many in the jazz world just couldn't cope. Their screams, shrieks, lengthy solos, and blistering exchanges eliminated the restrictions imposed by bebop, hard bop, cool, swing, and any other term anyone could suggest. Their detractors suggested that this music ended any chance for jazz to become a popular sound. They called the Coltrane/Sanders music hopelessly esoteric and utterly self-indulgent.

Since those years, Sanders has made calmer, gentler music at times, though he's never completely forsaken the turbulent '60s. He began playing professionally in high school, experimenting with various instruments before settling on tenor. Sanders played both R&B and jazz in San Francisco after graduation. He moved to New York in 1962, where he played with Billy Higgins, Don Cherry, Sun Ra, and Rashied Ali. From 1965 to 1967, Sanders played with Coltrane. He remained with Alice briefly after John Coltrane's death. Sanders recorded one album for Strata-East, then led a group in the late '60s and early '70s with Leon Thomas. Thomas's yodeling and vocal acrobatics were the centerpiece for another series of remarkable, controversial Impulse albums, and, as the leader, Sanders got the heat for the album. But these albums ran out of steam in the mid-'70s, and Sanders turned to pop, R&B, funk, and even disco, for a time, in the late '70s. He worked with people like Phyllis Hyman, and even got songs aired on urban contemporary stations. During the '80s, Sanders tried a variety of approaches. He cut sessions on Teresa, Timeless, and Dr. Jazz. Some featured vocalists like Bobby McFerrin; others used ethnic reggae or African elements. Sanders also did conventional hard bop with Bobby Hutcherson and Elvin Jones. None of these recordings had the impact of his earlier material, but they kept his career going. Recently, Sanders recorded new sessions for Timeless. Some of his earlier Impulse albums have been reissued on CD by MCA; Evidence is reissuing his Theresa sessions, and his newer dates are available also. —*Ron Wynn and Myles Boisen*

○ **Journey to the One** / Evidence 22016

Journey to the One confirms that Pharoah Sanders continues to command one of the richest, loveliest, and fiercest tenor sax sounds in all of jazz. The immediacy and almost tactile intimacy of his tone and intonation again are stunningly employed to serve the awesome emotional power that is Sanders's ultimate contribution. *Journey* also confirms, however, the static nature of the saxophonist's musical concept built on religious mysticism and his somewhat banal sense of dynamics, which constantly balance fervor against lyricism. As a whole, this double album represents a more traditionalist approach for Sanders. Most compositions are relatively tightly arranged and performed, with a few ("Greetings," "Freedom," and "Bedria") displaying that "rollicking" jam session quality that used to inform Sanders's uptempo pieces. Others go even further back: "Doktor Pitt" is straight bebop, and "After the Rain" and "Easy to Remember" are virtual John Coltrane ballad impersonations with a possible difference noticeable between Sanders's romanticism and Coltrane's melancholy. The absolute highlight of *Journey* is the Eastern-flavored "Kazuko," whose stark and stagnant setting provides the saxophonist with a lean, crisp backdrop for a dramatic tonal improvisation. —*Lars Gabel*, Down Beat

Rejoice / Evidence 22020
Pharoah Sanders again offers something new on this album. "Nigerian JuJu HiLife" is a presentation of a quasi-African pop song, though more pop than African. "Lights are Low" and "Farah" are mellow, reflective numbers, while "Rejoice" is a celebratory outing. But on "Central Park West" and "Origin," Sanders plays with the ferocity, vocal effects, and intensity that mark his finest work. He enlists some outstanding musicians, including vibist Bobby Hutcherson, drummer Elvin Jones, trombonist Steve Turre, bassist Art Davis, drummer Billy Higgins, and pianist John Hicks. As is the case on every Sanders Theresa session, this is uneven but the good moments outweigh the bad. —*Ron Wynn*

Izipho Zam / Jan. 14, 1969 / Strata-East 19733

★ **Karma** / Feb. 14-Oct. 20, 1969 / MCA 39122
Karma is a real rarity, an avant-garde "hit." One could almost call it "free jazz for the masses." Pharoah Sanders, who in 1966 would have easily won a poll for "least likely to succeed commercially," by 1969 was out on his own featuring his Jekyll and Hyde tenor (alternately peaceful and screaming) over rhythmic vamps. With Leon Thomas singing and yodeling, the 33-minute atmospheric "The Creator Has a Master Plan" caught on and received quite a bit of airplay on jazz stations at the time. Nostalgia aside, this jam (overlong by 10 minutes) still sounds good and the all-star personnel doesn't hurt (Sanders, ts; Leon Thomas, v, per; James Spaulding, f; Julius Watkins, French horn; Lonnie Liston Smith, p; Richard Davis, Reggie Workman, b; Billy Hart, d; Nathaniel Bettis, per), although Sanders at his most violent is unintentionally humorous. The ballad "Colors" continues the same pseudo-sacred mood, wrapping up this historic LP. (Sanders, ts; Thomas, v, per; Watkins, French horn; Smith, p; Workman, Ron Carter, b; Freddie Waits, d). —*Scott Yanow*, Cadence

Tauhid / Sep. 10, 1969 / Impulse

Sumnen, Bukmen, Umyun / **i.** 1970 / Impulse

Jewels of Thought / **i.** 1971 / Impulse

Thembi / Nov. 25, 1971-Jan. 1, 1972 / MCA 5860

Black Unity / Dec. 8, 1971 / Impulse

★ **Love in Us All** / Sep. 13-14, 1973 / ASD 9280
Side one, "Love is Everywhere," which Pharoah Sanders does regularly in concert in foot-stomping style, is here a crudely spliced, 20-minute exercise in rhythmic entropy where Sanders is heard just once, very briefly, on soprano sax. To be just, side two, "To John," is music high as an elephant's eye, as Sanders, an anonymous trumpet player, and another anonymous tenor player all conspire to make this an intensely gratifying tribute. —*Bill Adler*, Down Beat

Beyond a Dream / Jul. 22, 1978 / Arista

Oh Lord, Let Me Do No Wrong / i. Jul. 17, 1987 / Doctor Jazz 40952

Good use of reggae beat on title cut. Fair set that splits contemporary production with traditional energy. —*Ron Wynn*

Quartet Africa / i. 1987 / Timeless

ARTURO SANDOVAL

b. Nov. 6, 1949, Artemisa, Cuba

Trumpet, piano, composer / Latin-jazz, world fusion

Arturo Sandoval is an energetic, often exciting trumpeter whose flashing phrases, high note acrobatics, and dynamic, charismatic playing style was first noticed in the group Irakere. As a leader, Sandoval hasn't made the great records that many anticipated he would make, but he displays such potential as a soloist that it seems only a matter of time before his definitive recording will be made. His timing, range, timbre, and approach are solid, as are his ballad skills. The only thing lacking has been consistency, particularly on record. Sandoval was one of the founding members in the Orquesta Cubana de Musica Moderna in Havana during the '70s, along with Paquito D'Rivera. Various members of this band later formed Irakere. The group recorded with David Amram in 1977. Sandoval left the group in 1981, toured internationally with his own band, and recorded in Cuba. He met his idol, Dizzy Gillespie, in the '70s, and played with him in Cuba, America, Puerto Rico, and England. They recorded together in Finland for Pablo in the early '80s. Sandoval defected to America during the '80s, and has since recorded for Messidor and GRP. He and D'Rivera played together on a recent Messidor release. Sandoval has a few sessions available on CD. —*Ron Wynn*

★ **To a Finland Station** / i. 1982 / Pablo 889

With Dizzy Gillespie (tpt) in Helsinki. Excellent interplay. Lots of good feeling on this session. —*Michael G. Nastos*

○ **Breaking the Sound Barrier** / i. 1983 / CCAA 8301

Live date in Chicago from Cuban trumpeter, playing it straight in jazz and Latin veins. No funk. His best. —*Michael G. Nastos*

○ **Tumbaito** / Messidor 15974

A tremendous session with dynamic trumpeter Arturo Sandoval mixing things up with an all-star lineup. It was originally available only overseas, but has now been issued in the United States through Messidor. —*Ron Wynn*

MONGO SANTAMARIA

b. Apr. 7, 1922, Jesus Maria, Havana, Cuba

Percussion / Latin-jazz

Arguably the greatest Cuban percussionist of his generation and, outside of Chano Pozo, the most influential in jazz history, Mongo Santamaria's astonishing musical ability remains impressive, even when's he is featured on albums far below his abilities. No one's been more dominant on congas and bongos for as long as Santamaria, who's played in bebop, hard bop, big bands, Latin-jazz combos, dance bands, and pop groups. He's recorded for major labels, for independents, and for tiny Latin companies. There aren't many musicians who are more intense, or as blazingly fast, as Santamaria doing a conga solo.

Originally, he studied violin, but then switched to drums. Santamaria dropped out of school in Cuba to become a professional conguero. He was an established star in Havana prior to Castro's takeover. Santamaria left Cuba for Mexico City with his cousin, Armanda Peraza, in 1948. They arrived in New York City in 1950 and were billed as the Black Cuban Diamonds. Santamaria made his American debut with Perez Prado; he played with him for three years, then spent seven fabulous years with Tito Puente. Their multiple percussion barrages and rhythmic assaults were historic in Latin-jazz and jazz circles. Santamaria made several first-rate albums of traditional African and Afro-Cuban music in the early '50s, taking the music directly from Cuban religious practices and ceremonies. He began playing Latin-jazz with George Shearing in the early '50s; the group also included Willie Bobo on timbales, Peraza on bongos, and Cal Tjader on vibes. Santamaria and Bobo joined Tjader's group in 1958. Santamaria made several fine albums with Tjader for three years, then played with Dizzy Gillespie and Brother Jack McDuff. He began recording for Fantasy in the late '50s.

Santamaria's '60s and early '70s releases blended pop, fusion, rock, jazz, and R&B with Latin arrangements and rhythms. He had a Top 10 hit with his cover of Herbie Hancock's "Watermelon Man" in 1963, and employed jazz stars such as Chick Corea and Hubert Laws in various bands. Santamaria's LPs on the Battle and Riverside labels were extremely popular, and eventually led to a contract with Columbia. Santamaria recorded several albums on Columbia between 1965 and 1970; many of them made the pop LP charts. His cover of the Temptations' "Cloud Nine" single also made the Top 40. Santamaria made "boogaloo" recordings, and crossover releases such as "Soul Bag," "Stone Soul," "La Bamba," and "Workin' on a Groovy Thing." He continued cutting fusion material in the early '70s for Atlantic, though his band, at this time, included Israel "Cachao" Lopez and Peraza. He soon returned to more traditional Latin music. The LP *Up From the Roots* blended Afro-Cuban and conjunto. He signed with Vaya in the early '70s, shared a Yankee Stadium bill with the Fania All Stars, and did a guest stint with the group.

Santamaria cut a Latin-jazz date live at Montreux for Pablo in the '80s with Dizzy Gillespie and Toots Thielemans. There were also sessions for Roulette, Tropical Buddah, and a reunion date with the Fania All Stars. Santamaria was featured in the documentary film *Salsa*, and teamed with Charlie Palmieri on a sensational late '80s session for Concord Picante, one of Palmieri's final albums. Santamaria has continued to play in the '90s, recording a new album of Latin music for Chesky in 1993. Several classic Santamaria sessions have been reissued on CD, and he also has current releases available. His recordings on Latin labels can be obtained from specialty stores. —*Ron Wynn*

○ **Afro-Roots** / i. 1958-1959 / Prestige 24018

Mongo Santamaria made a pair of superb Latin-jazz albums for Fantasy in the late '50s. These were subsequently reissued on a two-record set on vinyl in the '70s, then repackaged again for CD. The disc contains the full albums *Yambu* and *Mongo*, each one brilliant. —*Ron Wynn*

○ **Skins** / 1962 / Milestone 47038

This twofer (originally *So Mongo* and *Mongo Explodes* on Riverside) includes many compositions by trumpeter Marty Sheller. Guests include Hubert Laws, Chick Corea, and Jimmy Cobb. Every track is vital. —*Michael G. Nastos*

★ **Mongo at the Village Gate** / i. 1963 / Riverside 490

This is a nonet with Pat Patrick, Bobby Capers, Marty Sheller, and Chihuahua Martinez—a Latin, jazz, and soul combo. Emceed by Symphony Sid, it is startlingly fresh for its era. It still sounds fresh. —*Michael G. Nastos*

○ **Bravo, El** / i. 1966 / CBS

○ **Mongo at Montreux** / i. 1971 / Atlantic

○ **Amanecer, Gabrielle** / i. 1977 / Vaya

○ **Bomboro, Asiha, Guajiro, Nada Mas** / i. 1978 / Vaya

Free Spirit / i. 1985 / Buddah

Soca Me Nice / i. May 1988 / Concord Jazz 4362

Another good date with his '80s band, though more Afro-Cuban jazz than Soca. —*Ron Wynn*

★ **Live at Jazz Alley** / i. 1990 / Concord Jazz 4427

SAHEB SARBIB

Bass, keyboards / Hard bop

A contemporary bassist, as well as a keyboardist and an occasional shenai player, Saheb Sarbib has recorded for Cadence and Soul Note. He's a good, though not spectacular or challenging bassist, but has assembled some impressive talent for his albums. Sarbib's recorded in a variety of styles: hard bop, big band, outside, almost new age, and bebop.

Jazz Saxophone

1900: Classical sax players
Little Jazz Influence

1916 Vaudeville
Rudy Wiedoeft used the C-melody sax in vaudeville
performances.

1920s Jazz and Commercial Dance Music

1930s Jazz Instrument Ensembles

Most Significant Soloists
Sidney Bechet (1897-1959)–soprano
Coleman Hawkins (1904-1969)–tenor
Lester Young (1909-1959)–tenor
Johnny Hodges (1907-1970)–alto, soprano
Charlie Parker (1920-1955)–alto
John Coltrane (1926-1967)–tenor and soprano
Sonny Rollins (1930)–tenor
Ornette Coleman (1930)–alto, tenor
Harry Carney (1910-1974)–baritone
Adrian Rollini (1904-1956)–bass

Players such as Mark Whitecage, Jack Walraith, Kirk Lightsey, Joe Ford, and Rashied Ali (in one of his few sessions during the '80s) have appeared on a Sarbib date. Sarbib currently has several sessions available on CD. —*Ron Wynn*

○ **UFO! Live on Tour** / Mar. 1979 / Cadence 1008
○ **Live at the Public Theater** / Oct. 1980 / Cadence 1001
★ **Aisha** / i. Jul.-Aug. 1981 / Cadence 1010
○ **Seasons** / i. Nov. 1981 / Soul Note 1048
Seasons is a live recording from 1981. With a dueling sax front line—often tangling in tandem—and drummer Paul Motian in the driver's seat, Saheb Sarbib's quartet is sharp-edged, energy-oriented, and openly bluesy, though it has a well-formed sense of syncretism and temporal flexibility that binds the group. Pianist and bassist Sarbib is no showboater, but lays down solidly underneath, grooving hard on "Nymph of Darkness" and matching Motian's sure swing on Ornette Coleman's "Round Trip." —*John Corbett,* Down Beat
○ **It Couldn't Happen Without You** / Jan.-Feb. 1984 / Soul Note 1098
Bassist Saheb Sarbib heads a group with piano and two saxes on *It Couldn't Happen Without You.* The success of the session rests on the band's cohesiveness, Sarbib's familiar-sounding themes, and a pair of well-chosen interpretations. Sarbib doesn't throw his quintet any impossible curves. He does test their soloing and supporting capabilities equally, calling on the musicians to freshen up a romantic ballad, a waltz, a few scorchers, and some modern lyricism. Everyone comes through, but Joe Ford (as, ss) with particular distinction. The ensemble charges through "East 11th Street" and "Watchmacallit" as confidently as it glides through "Sasa's Groove," sounding throughout like a regular working band. While the uptempo tracks have the most immediate appeal, it is at the slower tempos that the quintet reveals its depth and commitment to the project. For "You Don't Know What Love Is," Ford fills tartly behind Joe Lovano's (ts) straightfoward rendering before stepping in briefly with his own, telling statement. The saxophonists close the tune, intertwining their lines, taking the performance beyond just another ballad reading. "Crescent" is a

bit eerie, and equally effective. Everyone gets a chance to pay tribute to Coltrane, Lovano approximating the familiar tenor sound, Ford interpreting on soprano, and drummer Rashied Ali recalling his work with Coltrane. *It Couldn't Happen Without You* mines the vein of uncompromising accessibility. —*Eric Shepard,* Cadence

BILL SAXTON

Tenor saxophone / Hard bop
Tenor saxophonist Bill Saxton is still developing an identity, mostly due to sparse recording opportunities and/or sessions. He first attracted attention recording and playing with Dannie Richmond in 1979, and has since worked with Charli Persip's big band, and with Errol Parker. His playing has been strong and confident, but is also essentially standard hard bop in a Wayne Shorter/John Coltrane mode. Since there's relatively little of his music in the public domain, it's probably too early to make any judgment. Currently, Saxton does not have any sessions available on CD. —*Ron Wynn*
★ **Beneath the Surface** / i. Jan. 1986 / Nilva 3408

ALEX SCHLIPPENBACH (Alexander von Schlippenbach)

b. Apr. 7, 1938, Berlin, Germany
Piano, composer, bandleader / Early free, progressive big band, modern creative
One of Europe's premier free jazz bandleaders and a pianist as well, Alexander von Schlippenbach's music mixes free and contemporary classical elements, and his slashing solos often form the link between the two genres in his compositions. Schlippenbach formed the Globe Unity Orchestra in 1966 to perform the piece "Globe Unity," which had been commissioned by the Berliner Jazztage. With the exception of one period from 1971 to 1972, he remained involved with the orchestra into the '80s. Schlippenbach began taking lessons at age eight, and studied at the Staatliche Hochschule for Musik in Cologne with composers Bernd Alois Zimmermann and Rudolf Petzold. He played with Gunther Hampel in 1963, and was in Manfred Schoof's quintet from 1964 to 1967. Schlippenbach began leading various bands after 1967, among them a 1970 trio with Evan Parker and Paul Lovens, and a duo with drummer/vocalist Sven-Ake Johansson, which they coformed in 1976. Schlippenbach has also given many solo performances. He's recorded for the FMP, Japo, Saba, and Po Torch labels, both as a leader and with the Globe Unity Orchestra. These CDs can be obtained through diligent searches and through mail order. —*Ron Wynn*
★ **Globe Unity** / i. 1966 / Saba 15109

DAVID SCHNITTER (David Bertram Schnitter)

b. Mar. 19, 1948, Newark, NJ
Tenor saxophone / Hard bop
If someone was asked to suggest an example of a textbook hard bop player, they wouldn't go wrong naming Dave Schnitter. Here's one saxophonist who's most certainly not an eclectic; the fierce, driving, big-toned Schnitter sound is definitely in the hard bop camp. He studied clarinet as a child, then switched to tenor sax at age 15. Schnitter worked in rock bands and played at weddings before forming his own group in the early '70s. He worked with Ted Dunbar in 1973, then played with Art Blakey's Jazz Messengers from 1974 to 1979. Schnitter worked with Freddie Hubbard from 1979 to 1981, and recorded with him in '80 and '81. Schnitter played with Frank Foster, Charles Earland, Groove Holmes, and Johnny Lytle in the '80s. He recorded with Sonny Stitt and Blakey in the '70s, and did several sessions as a leader for Muse in the late '70s. Currently, none of Schnitter's dates are available on CD. —*Ron Wynn and Michael G. Nastos*
★ **Invitation** / 1976 / Muse 5108
David Schnitter proves on this debut album that he is not fully in command of the tenor saxophone, though he is to-

The Tenor Saxophone

Tenor Sax Early Influences
Prince Robinson (1902-1960)
Happy Caldwell (1903-1978)
Stump Evans (1904-1928)

Coleman Hawkins (1901-1969)
First Major Early Tenor Soloist

Major influence on:
Charlie Barnet (1913-1991)
Tex Beneke (1914)
Chu Berry (1908-1941)
Vido Musso (1913-1982)
Ben Webster (1909-1973)
Herschel Evans (1909-1939)
Dick Wilson (1911-1941)

Bud Freeman (1906-1991)–First Major White Tenor Player
Eddie Miller (1911-1991)
Babe Russin (1911-1984)
Boomie Richman (1921)

Arnett Cobb (1918-1990)
Illinois Jacquet (1922)
Ike Quebec (1918-1963)
Jimmy Forrest (1920-1980)
Hal Singer (1919)
Buddy Tate (1915)
Don Byas (1912-1972)

Lester Young influenced by:
Frank Trumbauer

Lester Young (1909-1959)
Major Saxophone Soloist

Influenced:
Budd Johnson (1910-1984)
Jerry Jerome (1912)
Paul Quinichelte (1916-1983) – Al Klink (1915-1991)
Charlie Parker (1920-1955)

Later influence on:
Gene Ammons	Jackie McLean
Al Cohn	Warne Marsh
John Coltrane	James Moody
Allen Eager	Art Pepper
Stan Getz	Herbie Stewart
Wardell Gray	Zoot Sims
Lee Konitz	Sonny Stitt
Dexter Gordon	

Sonny Rollins influenced by
Charlie Parker
Coleman Hawkins
Dexter Gordon

Sonny Rollins (1930)
Major Saxophone Soloist

Influenced:
Joe Henderson (1937)
Rahsaan Roland Kirk (1936-1977)
Yusef Lateef (1920)
Barney Wilen (1937)
Branford Marsalis(1961)
Ricky Ford (1954)
David Murray (1955)
Junior Cook (1934-1992)

John Coltrane Influenced by:
Earl Bostic (1913-1965)
Big Nick Nicholas (1922)
John Gilmore (1931) w/Sun Ra
Dexter Gordon (1923-1990)
Stan Getz (1927-1991)

John Coltrane (1926-1967)
Major Saxophone Soloist

Influenced:
Mike Brecker (1949)	Dave Young (1912)
Bob Berg (1951)	George Coleman (1935)
Steve Grossman (1951)	Joe Farrell (1937-1986)
John Klemmer (1946)	Charles Lloyd (1938)
Booker Ervin (1930-1970)	Sonny Fortune (1939)
Bill Evans (1957)	Pharoah Sanders (1940)
Azar Lawrence (1953)	Dave Liebman (1946)

Wayne Shorter (1953)

Free Jazz
Albert Ayler (1936-1970)

Other Free Jazz:
David Murray (1955) – Joseph Jarman (1937)
Archie Shepp (1937) – Frank Lowe (1943)
Willem Breuker (1944) – Rev. Frank Wright (1935)
Peter Brotzmann (1941) – Jan Garbarek (1947)
Sam Rivers (1930) – Gato Barbieri (1934)
Kalaparusha Maurie McIntyre (1936)
George Adams (1940-1993)

tally aware of the literature of the postbop era. While nothing new is being done here, something more interesting is happening. These young musicians are creating lively and stimulating lines within an established framework. Schnitter and pianist Mickey Tucker have both studied in the Art Blakey school of music and their contributions to the most recent (1976) edition of the Jazz Messengers are worthy of recognition. Here they deal in four standards and an original blues. Schnitter's hard-edged sound comes out of Sonny Rollins and John Coltrane, yet, unlike his contemporaries,

Schnitter is no slavish Coltrane imitator and is in the process of finding his own voice. He told me that Dexter Gordon (one of Coltrane's influences) continues to inspire him. Schnitter soars on "Body and Soul," which he has all to himself and in which he uses Rollins for guidance. All this music is chordally based on changes rather than modes, thus requiring a knowledge of harmony and the use of rhythmic punctuation. On this score Schnitter and Tucker (a straightahead bopper) are much in command. *—Jon Goldman,* Cadence

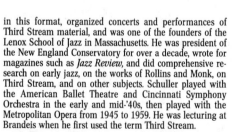

The Alto Saxophone

Early Alto Players:
Otto Hardwick (1904-1970) w/Duke Ellington
Johnny Hodges (1907-1970) w/Duke Ellington
Charles Holmes (1910-1985) w/Luis Russell
Earl Warren (1914) w/Count Basie – Benny Carter (1907)

Alto Players of the 1920s
Jimmy Dorsey (1904-1957) – Frank Trumbauer (1901)

Influenced: Lester Young (1909-1959)

Alto Players of the 1930s
Hilton Jefferson (1903-1968) – Woody Herman (1913-1987)
Buster Smith (1904) – Pete Brown (1906-1963)
Tab Smith (1909-1971) – Eddie Barefield (1909)
Earl Bostic (1913-1965) – Don Stovall (1913-1970)
Louis Jordan (1908-1975) – Scoops Carry (1915-1970)
Willie Smith (1910-1967) – Benny Carter (1907)

Bop Alto Sax Players
Charlie Parker (1920-1955)

Influenced:
Charlie Mariano (1923) – Sonny Stitt (1924-1982)
Lou Donaldson (1926) – Sonny Criss (1927-1977)
Eric Dolphy (1928-1964) – John Jenkins (1931-1994)
Ornette Coleman (1930) – Jackie McLean (1932)
Cannonball Adderley (1928-1975) – Phil Woods (1931)
Sonny Red (1932-1981) – Gene Quill (1927)
Charles McPherson (1939)

Lester Young's Influence on Alto Players:
Lee Konitz (1927)
Art Pepper (1925-1982)
Paul Desmond (1924-1977)

Free Jazz Alto Saxophone Player
Ornette Coleman (1930)

Influenced:
John Tchicai (1936)
Marion Brown (1935)
Roscoe Mitchell (1940)
Henry Threadgill (1944)
Anthony Braxton (1945)
Vladimir Chekasin (1947)
Ray Nathanson
John Zorn (1953)

Free Jazz Players
Jimmy Lyons (1933-1986)
Gary Bartz (1940)
Roscoe Mitchell (1940)
Julius Hemphill (1940)
Oliver Lake (1944)
Arthur Blythe (1940)
Marshall Allen (1924)
James Spaulding (1937)
Ken McIntyre (1931)
Greg Osby
Ken McIntyre (1931)
Sonny Simmons (1933)

LOREN SCHOENBERG

b. 1958
Bandleader / Hard bop
A prolific swing and big band historian, as well as a bandleader and a radio personality, Loren Schoenberg has raised eyebrows in the '80s and '90s with some interesting sessions for Musicmasters and Stash. He's led vintage swing-styled orchestras, and spearheaded a quartet date with Adam Nussbaum, John Goldsby, and Kenny Werner. But the session that's truly raised some questions was a '92 date that featured Schoenberg with David Murray and Doc Cheatham playing classic Louis Armstrong tunes with a host of lesser-known names usually associated with vastly different material. Schoenberg has several sessions available on CD. —*Ron Wynn and Michael G. Nastos*

Solid Ground / **i**. 1988 / Music Masters 5014
○ **Time Waits for No One** / **i**. 1989 / Music Masters 5032
★ **Just A-Settin' and A-Rockin'** / **i**. 1990 / Music Masters 5039
More interesting and entertaining, familiar agenda. —*Ron Wynn*

GUNTHER SCHULLER (Gunther Alexander Schuller)

b. Nov. 11, 1925, Jackson Heights, NY
French horn, composer, author / Early free, progressive big band
Gunther Schuller has made major inroads in jazz and classical music as a theorist, author, and performer. The son of a former New York Philharmonic violinist, Schuller helped popularize the term "Third Stream," a hybrid of symphonic and improvisational strains. He wrote several compositions

in this format, organized concerts and performances of Third Stream material, and was one of the founders of the Lenox School of Jazz in Massachusetts. He was president of the New England Conservatory for over a decade, wrote for magazines such as *Jazz Review*, and did comprehensive research on early jazz, on the works of Rollins and Monk, on Third Stream, and on other subjects. Schuller played with the American Ballet Theatre and Cincinnati Symphony Orchestra in the early and mid-'40s, then played with the Metropolitan Opera from 1945 to 1959. He was lecturing at Brandeis when he first used the term Third Stream.

Schuller composed works such as "Transformation," "Concertino," and "Abstraction" for jazz ensemble, quartet, and orchestra, respectively, and later wrote a piece for 13 instruments that was recorded by Ornette Coleman, Eric Dolphy, and Bill Evans. Schuller played French horn on Miles Davis's *Birth of the Cool* sessions in 1949 and 1950. Schuller recorded on Columbia and Verve in the '50s. He and John Lewis formed a close bond, and the Modern Jazz Quartet performed and recorded several Schuller pieces in the late '50s and early '60s, and even made an album titled *Third Stream Music*. His ballet, "Variants," was choreographed in 1961 by George Balanchine, he participated in the Montreux festivals in 1959 and 1961, and he presented the first jazz concert held at Tanglewood in 1963. Schuller, Lewis, and Harold Farberman led Orchestra U.S.A. from 1962 to 1965, and Lewis assisted in establishing the Lennox School. Schuller was an instructor there. In the mid-'60s, he toured Eastern Europe lecturing for the State Department. While at the New England Conservatory, Schuller prepared editions, did transcriptions, and gave performances of works by Scott Joplin, Jelly Roll Morton, Paul Whiteman, and Duke

The Soprano Saxophone

Music Map

The Baritone Saxophone

Older Sax Players
Dexter Gordon (1923-1989)
Budd Johnson (1910-1984)
Oliver Nelson (1932-1975)
Jerome Richardson (1920)
Sam Rivers (1930)
Lucky Thompson (1924)
Cannonball Adderley (1928-1975)
Sonny Rollins (1930)
Zoot Sims (1925-1985)

Soprano Saxophone
Sidney Bechet (1897-1959)

Influenced:
Bob Wilber (1928) – Johnny Hodges (1907-1970)
Don Redman (1900-1964) – Charlie Barnet (1913)
Woody Herman (1913-1987)
Emmett Mathews (1902)

European Soprano Players inspired by Sidney Bechet
Jeann-Pierre Bonnel
Claude Luter (1923)
Wally Fawkes (1924)

Free Jazz Soprano Sax
Steve Lacy (1934)
Evan Parker (1944)
Jan Ira Bloom (1953)

Early Baritone Sax
Harry Carney (1910-1974)
Jack Washington (1910-1964)
Ernie Caceres (1911-1971)

1950s
Bob Gordon (1928-1955)
Gerry Mulligan (1927)
Lars Gullin (1928-1976)

Also:
Serge Chaloff (1923-1957)
Leo Parker (1925-1962)
Cecil Payne (1922)
Doc Holladay
Pepper Adams (1930-1987)
Nick Brignola (1936)

Coltrane's Influence
Charles Davis (1933)
Hamiet Bluiett (1940)
John Surman (1944)
Pat Patrick (1929)
Ronnie Cuber (1941)
Charles Tyler (1941)

1960s Dixieland
John Barnes (1932)

Ellington. As a performer, he formed the New England Conservatory's Ragtime Ensemble, which had a hit album called *Scott Joplin: The Red Back Book,* that made it to number 65 on the pop charts in '73. Later, the arrangements were incorporated into the film *The Sting.* Schuller also began the New England Conservatory Jazz Repertory Orchestra, which played vintage early jazz pieces. He started the firms Margun Music and Gunmar Music in the '70s to publish works by Charles Mingus, George Russell, Johnny Carisi, Ran Blake, and Jimmy Giuffre, and founded the GM record label in 1980. GM releases have included previously unissued Eric Dolphy recordings and big-band sessions of Schuller compositions from the '40s to the '60s that had never been recorded. Schuller's seminal books, particularly *Early Jazz* and *The Swing Era,* remain in print. —*Ron Wynn*

Jazz Abstractions / Dec. 19, 1960 / Atlantic

★ **John Lewis Presents** / 1960 / Atlantic 1365

○ **Jumpin' in the Future** / i. May 1990 / GM 3010CD43:5
A historic big-band session led by composer/conductor Gunther Schuller. The band performs Schuller compositions that had never been recorded, covering the years 1947-1966. The band includes such musicians as Howard Johnson. —*Ron Wynn*

DIANE SCHUUR

Vocals / Ballads & blues
Another artist for whom there seems to be no middle ground, Diane Schuur has been praised heavily in some quarters and dismissed vigorously in others. Her sometimes overly loud, brassy style and wide range of material have led to some serious over-singing during earlier albums. She has curbed that tendency and, on recent releases, her vocals

have been more restrained, expressive, and centered. Schuur's delivery and timing have also improved, and she now seems to be developing the potential Stan Getz saw in her when he played with her earlier in her career. She began recording for GRP in the mid-'80s, and has several sessions available on CD. —*Ron Wynn and Richard Skelly*

○ **Timeless** / i. 1986 / GRP 9540
★ **Collection** / i. 1986-1989 / GRP 9591
○ **And the Count Basie Orchestra** / i. 1987 / GRP 1039

BOB SCOBEY (Robert Alexander Scobey)

b. Dec. 9, 1916, Tuumcari, NM, **d.** 1963
Trumpet / Dixieland
Energetic and always crowd-pleasing, trumpeter Bob Scobey was one of the most popular players in the '50s and '60s traditional jazz school. He played in pit bands, dance orchestras, and clubs during the '30s, and met Lu Watters in 1938. He spent most of the '40s playing second trumpet to Watters's first in the Yerba Buena Jazz Band, but took four years off for army duty. Scobey left Watters's band in '49 and formed his own band, and was a beloved leader, soloist, and performer for the rest of his life. His group made many recordings on the Good Time Life label, were headliners at most traditional festivals, and had a three-year residency at two clubs in Oakland. Scobey opened his own club in Chicago in 1959, but made regular trips to New York, Las Vegas, and San Francisco with his group on off weeks. —*Ron Wynn*

Bob Scobey's Frisco Band—Vol. 1 / Sep. 23, 1950-Apr. 12, 1952 / Good Time Jazz

★ **Scobey's Story—Vols. 1 and 2** / Nov. 6, 1951-Apr. 12, 1952 / Good Time Jazz

Bob Scobey Frisco Band. First-rate traditional date with veterans like Albert Nicholas (cl) and George Probert (sax) in lineup. —*Ron Wynn*

○ **Scobey and Clancy** / Jul. 6-7, 1955 / Good Time Jazz 12009

Direct from San Francisco / **i.** 1956 / Good Time Jazz 12023

Frisco Band Fav / Fantasy 010
A protype traditional jazz/Dixieland record featuring Bob Scobey and his Frisco Band. It includes Clancy Hayes on banjo and vocals, plus Wally Rose on piano. Scobey's trumpet solos are authentic, exuberant, and enjoyable, as is the music. —*Ron Wynn*

JOHN SCOFIELD

b. Dec. 26, 1951, Dayton, OH
Guitar / Early jazz-rock, modern creative
An often dazzling, accomplished guitarist with a flexible style that's equally at home in bebop, jazz-rock, free, rock, R&B, or country music, John Scofield has been a familiar face on the jazz scene since the early '70s. His sophisticated voicings, tasteful accompaniment, intelligent and imaginative use of electronics within a mainstream context, and sophisticated blending of blues and bebop have kept Scofield busy doing numerous recording dates, sessions, and concert assignments. A devotee of blues, R&B, and rock in his childhood, he later attended Berklee and studied with Mick Goodrick and Gary Burton. Following a performance with a band at Carnegie Hall that featured Gerry Mulligan and Chet Baker, Scofield joined a group co-led by George Duke and Billy Cobham. He later worked with Gary Burton, Charles Mingus, Jay McShann, Ron Carter, Dave Liebman, the Don Pullen/George Adams quartet, and Lee Konitz in the '70s, while he formed his own band. This group toured Europe and was featured on his debut live album. Scofield formed a new trio in 1980, working with Adam Nussbaum and Steve Swallow. He joined Miles Davis in the early '80s, and teamed, for a while, with fellow guitarist Mike Stern, then played alone. In the '80s and '90s, he's played in Bass Desires and has led his own groups. Scofield has recorded for Enja, Arista/Novus, Gramavision, and Blue Note. Some other people he's recorded with include Charlie Haden, Jack DeJohnette, Joe Lovano, Bill Stewart, and Dennis Irwin. There are several Scofield titles available on CD. —*Ron Wynn and Michael G. Nastos*

Rough House / Nov. 27, 1978 / Enja 79657

Who's Who? / 1979-1980 / Novus 3071

○ **Shinola** / Dec. 12-13, 1981 / Enja 79656
Trio set reissued in 1991. Dense, prickly, and lots of space for guitar work. —*Ron Wynn*

Still Warm / Jun. 1986 / Gramavision 79401

Blue Matter / Sep. 1986 / Gramavision 79403

Pick Hits Live / Oct. 1987 / Gramavision 79405

Loud Jazz / Dec. 1987 / Gramavision 79402

○ **Time on My Hands** / Nov. 1989 / Blue Note 92894
His best contemporary album. Excellent playing and writing. A must-buy for jazz/contemporary music listeners. —*Michael G. Nastos*

★ **Meant to Be** / Dec. 1990 / Blue Note 95479
Quartet. Just about as good as *Time on My Hands,* maybe a little better in terms of composition. —*Michael G. Nastos*

○ **Grace under Pressure** / Dec. 1991 / Blue Note 98167
Guitarist John Scofield leads a topnotch group on this '91 session. It's a pianoless band, with Scofield's nimble guitar lines contrasted by those of second guitarist Bill Frisell. They team with trombonist Jim Pugh, bassist Charlie Haden, and drummer Joey Baron, plus Randy Brecker on flugelhorn and John Clark on French horn. —*Ron Wynn*

Slo Sco: Best of Ballads / Gramavision 79430
1990 reissue of slow cuts. Good showcase for the other side of Scofield as improviser. —*Ron Wynn*

BOBBY SCOTT

b. 1937, **d.** 1990
Bandleader / Ballads & blues
Though he left performing for composing at the end of the '50s and stayed away for many years before returning to performing and recording, Bobby Scott made some entertaining, delightful music. He was a good pianist, an effective vocalist, and an above-average vibist. Scott also played accordion, bass, cello, and clarinet. He studied at the La Follette School of Music in New York City in 1945 with Edvard Moritz, who was taught by Debussy as a child, and was a professional at age 11. Scott played with Louis Prima and travelled with veteran musicians at age 15. He worked with Gene Krupa and Tony Scott (no relation) in the mid-'50s, and had a pop hit with his version of "Chain Gang." Scott worked at the Cafe Bohemia, and appeared at the Great South Bay Jazz Festival in 1958 and the New Haven Festival of Arts in 1959. He became a teacher of theory and harmony and resumed his studies with Moritz. But Scott gradually returned to performing and recording. He issued a Nat "King" Cole tribute album in the '80s. Scott recorded as a leader for Verve, ABC-Paramount, Bethlehem, and Musicmasters. He has a couple of sessions available on CD. —*Ron Wynn*

★ **Slowly** / Oct. 20+25, 1960 / Music Masters 5053
An album that is smooth, sometimes sentimental. For the supper-club crowd. —*Ron Wynn*

For Sentimental Reasons / **i.** 1989 / Music Masters 5025

HAZEL SCOTT (Hazel Dorothy Scott)

b. Jun. 11, 1920, Port of Spain, Trinidad, **d.** 1981
Piano, vocals / Postbop, cool
Though she didn't call it "Third Stream," and it wasn't associated with the genre, Hazel Scott was another musician who found a successful way to blend jazz and classical influences. Scott took classical selections and improvised on them, a practice dating back to the ragtime era. Numbers such as "Hungarian Rhapsody no. 2" (Liszt) backed by "Valse in D Flat Major" (Chopin, opus 64, no. 1) were audience favorites, even if some critics suggested they smacked of gimmickry (which they sometimes did). Scott was also a good bebop soloist, a nice ballad interpreter, a fair blues player, and an underrated vocalist. Her nightclub act was often more appealing than her albums; on her recordings, the absence of mitigating circumstances, like an audience and a club setting, meant that her compositions received more scrutiny than they could stand. Scott studied classical piano at Juilliard from the age of eight, while playing jazz in clubs. She became an attraction at downtown and uptown branches of Cafe Society in the late '30s and early '40s. Scott had her own radio show in 1936, appeared on Broadway in 1938, and was in five films during the '40s, among them *Rhapsody in Blue*. She wrote songs such as "Love Comes Softly" and "Nightmare Blues." Scott later had her own television show and was married to Adam Clayton Powell, Jr. Their highly visible, high-profile relationship degenerated under the heat of a nationwide obsession with Powell's activities, influence, and behavior, and the marriage ended in divorce. Scott recorded for Decca, Signature, Tioch, and Columbia, but made her finest jazz album, *Relaxed Piano Moods*, in 1955 for Charles Mingus's Debut label. Mingus and Max Roach joined Scott on this session. It's her only date currently available on CD. —*Ron Wynn and Michael G. Nastos*

★ **Late Show** / May 6, 1953 / Capitol 364

○ **Relaxed Piano Moods** / Jan. 21, 1955 / Debut 1702
Definitive piano trio with Charles Mingus (b) and Max Roach (d). A must-buy. Three bonus tracks on the CD. —*Michael G. Nastos*

Afterthoughts / **i.** 1980 / Tioch
Last known recorded work of Hazel Scott, still an intriguing pianist. —*Ron Wynn*

SHIRLEY SCOTT

b. Mar. 14, 1934, Philadelphia, PA
Organ / Blues & jazz, soul-jazz

Shirley Scott surprised many people in 1992 when she appeared on Bill Cosby's reprise of the Groucho Marx game and personality show "You Bet Your Life." That Cosby had picked her to be his music director was not surprising; it was surprising that Scott was playing piano. During the '60s, Scott's reputation was cemented on several superb, soulful organ/soul-jazz dates where she demonstrated an aggressive, highly rhythmic attack that blended intricate bebop harmonies with bluesy melodies and a gospel influence. She punctuated everything with a great use of the bass pedals. But Scott demonstrated an equal flair and facility on piano, and often incorporated snatches of anthemic jazz compositions while noodling in the background. The show was a bore, but it was great to see Scott back in the spotlight. She began playing piano as a child, then played trumpet in high school. Scott was working a club date in the mid-'50s in Philadelphia when the owner rented her a Hammond B-3. She learned quickly, and was soon leading both popular and artistically superior trios that featured either Eddie "Lockjaw" Davis or her husband at the time, Stanley Turrentine, on tenor sax. The Scott/Turrentine union lasted until the early '70s, and their musical collaborations in the '60s were among the finest in the field. Scott continued recording in the '70s, working with Harold Vick and Jimmy Forrest, then, in the early '80s, with Dexter Gordon. She also made a lot of appearances on television in New York and Philadelphia. Scott recorded prolifically for Prestige in the '50s and '60s, then for Impulse in the mid-'60s and Atlantic in the late '60s. She moved to Chess/Cadet in the early '70s, and also did sessions for Strata-East. In recent years, Scott has recorded for Muse and Candid. Her later material wasn't as consistent as her best work for Prestige and Impulse. She only has a few dates available currently on CD. —*Ron Wynn and Bob Porter*

★ **Great Scott! / For Members Only** / May 27, 1958-1963 / MCA 33115
Compilation blends two prime Scott albums (1958 and 1963); some cuts arranged and conducted by Oliver Nelson. —*Ron Wynn*

Soul Sisters / Jun. 23, 1960 / Prestige 7392

Like Cozy / Sep. 27, 1960 / Moodsville 19

Satin Doll / Mar. 7, 1961 / Prestige 7283

Hip Soul / Jun. 2, 1961 / Prestige 7205

Blue Seven / Aug. 22, 1961 / Prestige 7376
A quintet with Roy Brooks (d), Oliver Nelson (ts), and Joe Newman (tpt) plays one Scott original, the title song by Sonny Rollins, and an excellent "Wagon Wheels." —*Michael G. Nastos*

Hip Twist / Nov. 17, 1961 / Prestige 7226

★ **Sweet Soul** / Dec. 5, 1962 / Prestige 7360
Reissued from the *Happy Talk* session, this features Earl May on bass and Roy Brooks on drums. It includes a nice "Jitterbug Waltz." All are standards. —*Michael G. Nastos*

Soul Shoutin' / Oct. 15, 1963 / Prestige 7312

☆ **Blue Flames** / Mar. 31, 1964 / Prestige 328
Recorded at Englewood Cliffs, New Jersey with Stanley Turrentine. This is exactly the kind of straightahead funky music you would expect from the Scott/Turrentine combination. No disappointments. —*Michael Erlewine*

○ **Great Live Sessions, The** / Sep. 23, 1964 / ABC/Impulse 9341
Double-record live date from the '60s, with Scott's then-husband Stanley Turrentine, is impressive in its solid tasty swing and Scott's restraint in building a burning intensity. Turrentine's tenor is brimming with confidence and is wonderful to hear in such a sparse setting. Scott hasn't been exactly overrecorded in recent years and her playing here is stunning in its logic and swing. —*Ronald B. Weinstock, Cadence*

○ **Queen of the Organ** / Dec. 2, 1964 / GRP 123
A steamy, hot mid-'60s soul-jazz session with the soulful, bluesy organist Shirley Scott providing some booming, funky solos. This is one of several combo works she cut, usually with saxophonist Stanley Turrentine, who was her husband at the time. Anything Scott recorded from this period is worth hearing. —*Ron Wynn*

Girl Talk / 1967 / Impulse 9141
Trio. Album includes one Scott original. The rest, including the classic title track, are standards. A bit sweet. —*Michael G. Nastos*

○ **One for Me** / Nov. 1974 / Strata-East 7430
The record is a beauty with Harold Vick, perhaps the most suited and sensitive horn player Scott has worked with. Among her best recordings, this is a thoroughly enjoyable album of bop stream music, and, while it is nothing overly heavy or deep, it's thoughtfully and sensitively produced and of its kind an almost perfect album. —*Bob Rusch, Cadence*

STEPHEN SCOTT

Piano / Neo-bop

Stephen Scott is another highly publicized "young lion" pianist from New York. Recently, he worked with Joe Henderson on Henderson's acclaimed album, "Lush Life," and has also released his own debut session. A captivating soloist who is only in his twenties, his debut reveals considerable expertise as a composer. He is certainly still in the developmental stage, but is someone to watch in the '90s. —*Ron Wynn*

★ **Something to Consider** / i. 1991 / Verve 849557
Young Lion roars out of the box with impressive piano debut, aided by both old stars like Joe Henderson (sax) and fellow brats like Roy Hargrove (tpt). —*Ron Wynn*

Aminah's Dream / i. 1993 / PolyGram 517996
Great touch, super pacing, mature humor, polished writing— at the quarter-century mark, pianist Stephen Scott is showing himself to be a real wowser. The trio tracks are best on his second lead date; they show Scott can launch a blithe legato over steaming veterans bassist Ron Carter and drummer Elvin Jones ("Young Confucius"), spin a pretty ballad ("You are Too Beautiful"), and rattle the blues loosely while on the mark. Four tracks that add four nonsoloing horns, reminiscent of Herbie Hancock (*Speak Like A Child*, not *The Prisoner*), exhibit no great sense of original melody, but rather Scott's dense, occasionally somber, harmonic palette. Lotsa talent and sincere intentions from this emerging youngster. —*Fred Bouchard, Jazz Times*

TOM SCOTT (Thomas Wright Scott)

b. May 19, 1948, Los Angeles, CA
Tenor, alto, soprano sax, flute, composer / Fusion, contemporary funk, neo-bop

Multireed player and composer, Scott was among the most high-profile pop and rock session players and bandleaders on the West Coast in the '70s and '80s. While still in his teens, Scott was playing with Oliver Nelson and Don Ellis and appearing in bands for television shows. At 19 he was a featured soloist in Roger Kellaway's quartet and in his early twenties Scott was writing extensively for film and television. An excellent technical player with extensive range, superb tone and facility, plus the flexibility to fit into blues, rock, pop, and fusion contexts as well as standard jazz, Scott became a crossover success with the formation of the LA Express in the '70s. Scott's own albums have tended to be fusion/pop endeavors, and seldom adequate showcases for his skills. He's done better in his stints providing solos for sessions by Carole King, Joni Mitchell, and others. —*Ron Wynn*

Rural Still Life / i. 1967 / Impulse 9171

Hair to Jazz / i. Jan. 1969 / Flying Dutchman 106

★ **Tom Scott & LA Express** / 1973 / Epic 34952

Great Scott / **i.** 1973 / A&M 4330

Blow It Out / 1976 / Epic 46108

Street Beat / **i.** 1979 / Columbia 36437

Foundations / **i.** Apr. 1979 / IA 93542

Best of Tom Scott / **i.** 1980 / Columbia 36352

Apple Juice / Jan. 15-17, 1981 / Columbia 37419

Desire / Jul. 23-24, 1982 / Elektra 60162

Target / Jul. 23-24, 1983 / Atlantic 80106

Streamlines / Jul. 1987 / GRP 9555

Flashpoint / 1988 / GRP 9571

Keep This Love Alive / **i.** 1991 / GRP 9646

○ **Born Again** / **i.** 1992 / GRP 9675
The longtime session and studio saxophonist Tom Scott surprised many inside and outside the jazz community in '92
when he made this nonfusion, mainstream, and straightahead session. It shows he can still play strong, undiluted
tenor sax solos and also fit in with a group that includes
such distinguished players as pianist Kenny Kirkland, trumpeter Randy Brecker, and trombonist George Bohannon.
Bassist John Patitucci and drummer Will Kennedy are the fusion stars who round out the date. —*Ron Wynn*

Tom Cat / Ode 77029

Intimate Strangers / Columbia 35705

One Night . . . One Day / Soundwings 2102

TONY SCOTT

b. Jun. 17, 1921, Morristown, NJ
Clarinet / Cool, big band, postbop
A bebop lover often unable to play the music he preferred
due to his instrument of choice (clarinet), Tony Scott has experimented with other styles and situations. He's worked in
big bands, combos, and trios, has played Asian, Latin, and
Indian music, and has led his own groups that have drawn
on everything from traditional to swing to bebop to free.
He's an outstanding soloist in any style, with extensive range
and a full, rousing tone. Scott studied at the Institute of
Musical Art in the early '40s, attended Julliard, and participated in Minton's Playhouse jam sessions. He was in the
army from 1942 to 1945, and was stationed in the New York
area. He played alto sax in big bands, tenor in traditional
and Dixieland groups, and clarinet and piano in swing combos. Scott played clarinet with Ben Webster, Sid Catlett,
Trummy Young, and Earl Bostic in the mid- and late '40s,
and led his own groups. He recorded as a leader on Gotham
with Sarah Vaughan in 1946, and with Dizzy Gillespie and
others for Brunswick in 1953. There were stints with Buddy
Rich, Tommy Dorsey, Claude Thornhill, and Duke Ellington
in the '40s and '50s. He was also an arranger for Billie
Holiday and Sarah Vaughan. Scott recorded for RCA, Secco,
ABC-Paramount, Dot, Coral, Signature, and Muse in the '50s.
He was pianist and music director for Harry Belafonte in
1955, toured Europe in 1957, and traveled and studied in the
Far East from 1959 to 1965. Scott closely examined and
played Indonesian, Asian, and Indian music. His two albums
for Verve, which centered around meditation, were done in
the '60s. He also did a date with Indonesian All Stars for
MPS in the '60s. Scott gave a concert of Indian, Asian, and
jazz material at New York City's Museum of Modern Art in
1967. He's lived in Italy since 1970, though he visited
America periodically in the '70s doing club dates. Scott
works mostly in Europe now. He recorded in Stockholm in
the early '70s, and in England and Italy in the '80s. He did
sessions for Sonet, Polydor, Supraphon (Czechoslovakia),
and Soul Note in the '70s and '80s. A handful of Scott sessions from the '50s and '60s, plus his more recent '80s material, are available currently. —*Ron Wynn*

○ **Scott's Fling** / **i.** 1955 / RCA

★ **Complete Tony Scott, The** / **i.** Oct. 3, 1957 / RCA Victor
1452

Best from a series of mid '50s recordings showcasing Scott
in quartet, big band, and combo situations. —*Ron Wynn*

Modern Art of Jazz, The / Dec. 1958 / Seeco
Beautiful, accomplished, and distinctive solos from Scott.
Very hard to find. —*Ron Wynn*

★ **Golden Moments** / 1959 / Muse 5230
Recorded in 1959, just after pianist Bill Evans had finished a
stint with Miles Davis, this record shows Evans with his Bud
Powell influences intact. The pianist had worked with clarinetist Tony Scott several times over the prior two years and
was accustomed to his freewheeling style. The tape, recorded
by Scott, is a decent one with only a few problems. The major one, however, is the nearly total exclusion of bassist
Jimmy Garrison, who is constantly drowned out by the
drummer. Pete LaRoca both hold the bottom together nicely,
giving good support. Scott's playing is a revelation—here is a
player who has gone beyond the stylistic influences of
Benny Goodman and Pee Wee Russell and forged his own
sound out of bebop. Scott sounds more like Charlie Parker
and Lester Young, two musicians to whom he listened and
from whom he learned. His phrasing is entirely modern for
the time (and not so bad for today)—his execution is deft, the
lines flowing freely and swiftly. On the 12-minute "My
Melancholy Baby," Scott blows chorus after chorus, shedding
the original melody and forming long sweeping improvisations. Evans is the perfect foil, laying down quiet chords. The
rest of the record has some excellent interplay between Scott
and the group—he leaves the other players plenty of space
with which to develop their own ideas. *Golden Moments* is
a solid recording. —*Richard B. Kamins*, Cadence

I'll Remember / Aug. 1+9, 1959 / Muse 5266

Sung Heroes / **i.** 1959 / Sunnyside
Nice 1959 date, with Scott taking turns on guitar and piano
plus baritone. —*Ron Wynn*

○ **Music For Zen Meditation (and Other Joys)** / **i.** 1964 /
Verve
This elegant, contemplative set of pieces was conceived during one of the artist's trips to Japan when Scott had the opportunity to record with a shakuhachi flutist and a koto
player. Though ears unaccustomed to Oriental styles might
assume it's a performance of traditional Japanese music, the
album is actually a set of finely wrought improvisations
merging Eastern and Western sensibilities. —*Linda
Kohanov*

Prism / Jun. 17, 1977 / Polydor

○ **African Bird: Come Back! Mother Africa** / 1981-1984 /
Soul Note 1083
Clarinetist as a world music pacemaker. Removed from his
early jazz and meditative phases, while combining aspects
of both with African rhythms and Charlie Parker inflections.
"African Bird Suite" is a modal stunner. —*Michael G. Nastos*

AL SEARS (Albert Omega Sears)

b. Feb. 21, 1910, Macomb, IL, **d.** Mar. 23, 1990
Tenor saxophone, composer / Swing, big band
A huge sound and flamboyant style were tenor saxophonist
Al Sears's stock-in-trade. He had the big swing era tone, and
was featured prominently on many Duke Ellington selections during the '40s. Sears also worked with Johnny Hodges
in the early '50s, then switched to R&B publishing. He
played with Chick Webb and Zack Whyte in the late '20s,
then with Elmer Snowden in the early '30s, and led his own
bands during the '30s. Sears worked in Andy Kirk's orchestra in 1941 and 1942, then joined Ellington in 1944, replacing Ben Webster. He was featured on such classic numbers
as "I Ain't Got Nothing But the Blues," and "It Don't Mean a
Thing (If It Ain't Got That Swing)." Sears remained until
1949, then worked with a Hodges combo in the early '50s.
Hodges recorded Sears's tune "Castle Rock," and scored a hit.
Sears formed a publishing company, Sylvia Music Inc., and
turned to R&B. He recorded for Swingville in 1960. Sears
can be heard on CD reissues by Ellington and Hodges. —
Ron Wynn

Dance Music with a Swing Beat / i. 1959 / Audio Lab 1540
★ **Swing's the Thing** / Nov. 29, 1960 / Swingville 2018

DOC SEVERINSEN

b. Jul. 7, 1927, Arlington, OR
Trumpet, bandleader / Big band, bop, progressive big band
Though faithful watchers of the "Tonight Show" with Johnny
Carson and most of the '70s-and-beyond generation identify
Doc Severinsen as a garish dresser and a psuedo-hip bandleader with minimal ability, Severinsen has a substantial bebop heritage. He's also a much better trumpeter than was
usually shown during his television years, and is gifted with
a great range and excellent timbre and tone. Judging from
recent records, issues of taste are another matter, but
Severinsen has shown his skill on past sessions. He was a
soloist in Tommy Dorsey's big band in the late '40s and early
'50s, and had brief stints with Charlie Barnet and Benny
Goodman. Severinsen joined NBC in 1949, and 13 years
later was assistant leader of the orchestra, with Skitch
Henderson running the band. Henderson left in 1967 for
reasons that, as of 1993, had never been fully explained (no
one, from Henderson to Severinsen to Johnny Carson, will
address the situation for the record) and Severinsen took
over. He lasted until 1992, when Carson retired and Jay Leno
brought in a new band. Though it seems like 43 years at one
place and 25 years heading a band would be a great run,
there were rumors that everyone, including Severinsen, got
pushed rather than voluntarily left their post. He's led brass
workshops for years, has conducted the Phoenix Pops, and
has played with other orchestras and led various groups,
among them the unctuous Xebron. Severinsen took "Tonight
Show" alumni around the nation on a farewell tour in '93.
He has many sessions available on CD, but you'd be better
off getting Barnet and Dorsey reissues from the late '40s. His
own albums, particularly recent releases, have minimal jazz
content at best. *—Ron Wynn*

★ **Once More, With Feeling!** / Amherst 94405

BUD SHANK (Clifford Everett (Jr) Shank)

b. May 27, 1926, Dayton, OH
Alto saxophone, flute / Cool
Alto saxophonist and flutist Bud Shank was a major player
in '50s West Coast circles, and has continued as an active
contributor into the '90s. His light, steady, yet confident and
assured style has been featured on bebop, cool, big band,
and Latin dates, and Shank was one of the earliest, most accomplished jazz flutists. He studied clarinet, alto, tenor
saxes, and flute, and attended the University of North
Carolina in the mid-'40s. Shank studied with Shorty Rogers
on the West Coast in 1947. He began to specialize on alto in
the late '40s, playing with Charlie Barnet, then added flute
while with Stan Kenton in 1950 and 1951. Shank played and
recorded with Howard Rumsey's Lighthouse All-Stars, and
with Laurindo Almeida and Bob Cooper in the '50s, as well
as with Kenton, Rogers, Jimmy Giuffre, Gerald Wilson, and
many others. Shank also recorded extensively for World
Pacific as a leader in the '50s and '60s, most of the time
working with a combo. He appeared at several festivals in
Europe and South America in the '60s. Shank became
mainly a studio musician during the '60s, playing on film
scores and soundtracks such as *Slippery When Wet, Barefoot
Adventure, War Hunt, Assault on a Queen*, and *The Thomas
Crown Affair*. He recorded with Sergio Mendes for Capitol in
1965, and with Chet Baker on World Pacific a year later.
Their album, *Michelle*, reached number 56 on the pop
charts. Shank formed the L.A. Four along with Almeida, Ray
Brown, and Chuck Flores in 1974. Flores was later replaced
by Shelly Manne, then by Jeff Hamilton. Shank toured in the
'80s with Shorty Rogers and in a duo with Almeida. He severed ties with Almeida and the L.A. Four in the mid-'80s.
There were several dates for Concord in the '70s and early
'80s, for Muse, Capri, and Contemporary in the mid- and late
'80s, and for the newly revived Candid label in the '90s.
Shank sessions from the '70s, '80s, and '90s are in abun-

dance, while there are a couple of things available from the
'50s on Bainbridge and Fresh Sound. *—Ron Wynn*

Crystal Comments / i. Oct. 1979 / Concord Jazz 126
Good trio outing, though no one takes it beyond a merely
enjoyable level. *—Ron Wynn*

○ **This Bud's for You** / Nov. 11, 1984 / Muse 5309
Probably his best quartet date ever, and certainly among the
top three. Alto saxophonist Bud Shank takes a page from
Art Pepper's book, and decides to work with a set rhythm
section. Bassist Ron Carter, pianist Kenny Baron, and drummer Al Foster kick into gear on the opening song and never
falter. Shank soars, playing more aggressively and showing
more conviction in his solos than at any time since the '50s.
—Ron Wynn

★ **Serious Swingers / i.** Feb. 2-4, 1986 / Contemporary 14031
○ **That Old Feeling** / Feb. 1986 / Contemporary 14019
The presence on this session of George Cables (p) suggests
that Bud Shank had the feel of a latter-day Art Pepper session in mind, and the playing exhibits a Pepper date's energy
and fleet fecundity. Shank doesn't attempt to steal Pepper's
sound, but the similiarities are there: the once-wispy West
Coast alto now shouts. The lovely "Cabin in the Sky" preserves the fine art of the bebop ballad; alternate fingerings
and raspy emphases make it sound particularly vital. (But I
could live without another "As Time Goes By," valiantly as
Shank tries to find something new in this overworked item.)
The backing (John Heard, b; Albert Heath, d) is usually as
aggressive as the alto work, but this bopper's delight is
Shank's show all the way. *—Kevin Whitehead*, Cadence

At Jazz Alley / Oct. 1986 / Contemporary 14027

Tomorrow's Rainbow / i. Sep. 2-3, 1988 / Contemporary
14048

Drifting Timelessly / i. 1990 / Capri 75001
☆ **Doctor Is In, The / i.** 1991 / Candid 79520
Good '91 session featuring the steady cool and bop-tinged
alto sax solos of Bud Shank in a combo setting. He's backed
by pianist Mike Wofford, bassist Bob Magnusson, and drummer Sherman Ferguson. They tackle familiar standards and
a few originals, and make satisfying, if unchallenging, music. *—Ron Wynn*

ELLIOTT SHARP

b. 1951
Guitar, electronics / Modern creative
Perhaps the most eclectic and outrageous member of the
'90s "downtown" group (next to John Zorn), Elliot Sharp
plays free, ethnic, rock, and a wild mixture of everything else
in the musical spectrum. The composer/performer plays
electric and steel guitar, electric bass, soprano sax, bass clarinet, and many other instruments. With his band, Carbon, he
brings a spirit of adventure, bizarre antics, and rampaging
musical experimentation to his dates, which makes it difficult to assess much of his material. It may be improvisational, but it's also deliberately chaotic, sometimes horrendous, and other times quite insightful. He's recorded for the
Enemy label, and has been featured on Knitting Factory sessions. Sharp's one musician who's truly not for all, or even
most, tastes. *—Ron Wynn*

★ **In the Land of Yahoos / i.** 1987 / SST 128
Elliott's "pop" album, made as sort of a joke, features lots of
sampled vocals on top of dance-club beats. It's certainly his
most accessible: his other recordings have more of his
trademark guitar turbulence and mathematically oriented
compositional style. *—Myles Boisen*

○ **Datacide / i.** 1990 / Enemy 116

AVERY SHARPE

Bass / Hard bop, neo-bop
A strong bassist with a compelling tone and fine technique,
Avery Sharpe has been featured prominently with McCoy
Tyner for several years. Sharpe began recording with Tyner

in the mid-'80s, and has remained with him through the '90s. He can be heard on several Tyner CDs that are available currently, including the most recent *Remembering John*. —*Ron Wynn*

LINDA SHARROCK

Vocals / Early jazz-rock, modern creative
While not as well known or as extensively recorded as other vocal improvisers like Jeanne Lee, Irene Abei, or even Urzula Dudziak, Linda Sharrock's soaring, swelling sound is just as penetrating and striking. She was featured with her former husband, Sonny, on the classic Atlantic album *Black Woman* (sadly out of print), in which her screams, yelps, cries, and calls were punctuated by Sharrock's splintering riffs, dissonant lines, and slamming, percussive phrases. It was a jarring experience even for listeners who'd heard late-period Coltrane and were still dealing with Albert Ayler. Linda Sharrock later parted musical company with Sonny, then resurfaced on a 1986 album by a group called the Pat Brothers. On this recording, she did a quasi-'50s cool narratives/vocals, while the trio of Wolfgang Puschning, Wolfgang Mitterer, and Wolfgang Reising meshed an array of alto sax screams and bleats, flute lines, synthesizer noodling, sampled snippets, and crashing drum beats. Sharrock was the calming influence on that album. She certainly hasn't been a straight singer. —*Ron Wynn*

SONNY SHARROCK (Warren Harding Sharrock)

b. Aug. 27, 1940, Ossining, NY
Guitar, slide guitar / Early jazz-rock, modern creative
It would be a mistake to call Sonny Sharrock a jazz artist, though he's certainly an improviser. There's a jazz link in much of his work, though he also has ties to blues, rock, and ethnic styles. Sharrock is a free player, though that freedom doesn't necessarily mean the same thing to him as other, more jazz-rooted artists. Sharrock's an American equivalent of British guitarist Derek Bailey; but while Bailey is a sound merchant, Sharrock's more a riff and rhythm merchant. His solos seldom obey the tenets of swing and bebop established by Django Reinhardt and Charlie Christian. They're not smooth, fluid, and linear, and they are not devoted to faithful chordal accompaniment. Sharrock works in a relentless, galvanizing, and charismatic manner, effectively uses distortion and the slide, playing in a flailing, splintering fashion that can get chaotic, but is never gimmicky. Sharrock will use drones and gospel riffs, and will attack the guitar, but he'll also display impressive technique and intriguing ideas. Sharrock sang in a doo-wop band called the Echoes in the '50s. He began playing guitar in 1959, and was largely self-taught. Sharrock attended Berklee for one semester in 1961, then moved to New York in 1965. He played free jazz with Byard Lancaster and Marzette Watts. At various times in the '60s and '70s, Sharrock worked with Herbie Mann, while he also played with Don Cherry, Wayne Shorter, and Milford Graves. He began working as a leader in 1969, recording with his wife Linda. Sharrock had a dry spell in the mid '70s, but in the early '80s became a celebrity and guru to emerging guitarists like Vernon Reid. He recorded with Material in 1982, and performed with Last Exit in 1986. This group included Peter Brotzmann and Ronald Shannon Jackson. Sharrock then formed two bands. One was a quartet with guitar, electric bass, and two drummers, the other featured guitar, trumpet, and synthesizers. Sharrock has continued in the '90s recording wildly eclectic albums for Enemy and Axiom, and doing sessions. Unfortunately, only the '91 date, *Ask the Ages*, on Axiom is available on CD under his name. —*Ron Wynn*

Black Woman / May 16, 1969 / Vortex 2014

Highlife / Oct. 1990 / Enemy 119
More rock, pop, and blues elements, but superbly crafted and employed. —*Ron Wynn*

★ **Ask the Ages** / 1991 / Axiom 848957

Across-the-board acclaim for this splendid power-drunk band. Sharrock's guitar still exposes new and fresh sounds. With Pharoah Sanders (ts) and Elvin Jones (d). Six pieces written by Sharrock. Need wide-open ears, and they may implode. Revolutionary and revelationary. —*Michael G. Nastos*

CHARLIE SHAVERS (Charles James Shavers)

b. Aug. 3, 1917, New York, NY, **d.** Aug. 8, 1971, New York, NY
Trumpet / Swing, big band
Charlie Shavers was a topflight trumpeter, particularly effective with high-note flurries. He was extremely fluid and flexible, and provided memorable, exciting solos at impressive tempos. His tone was warm, rich, and inviting, and he often elevated routine, below-par music through his playing. Shavers's father was also a trumpeter and a distant relative of Fats Navarro. But Shavers initially played piano and banjo. He started in the bands of Tiny Bradshaw and Lucky Millinder, then earned his reputation during a lengthy stint with the John Kirby sextet. This was the premier "chamber" and small jazz combo of the day, and Shavers's compositions "Pastel Blue" and "Undecided" earned him additional fame. "Undecided" became a hit for Ella Fitzgerald, Benny Goodman, and the Ames Brothers. Shavers stayed with Kirby until 1944. He later played with Tommy Dorsey and co-led a sextet with Terry Gibbs and Louis Bellson. Later, Shavers toured with Jazz at the Philharmonic (where he had some exciting trumpet battles with Roy Eldridge), but he stayed mostly buried in Tommy Dorsey's orchestra where he was well treated and occasionally featured. He stayed with the orchestra even after Dorsey's death. He had recording sessions with Coleman Hawkins, Bellson, Goodman, Georgie Auld, Charlie Ventura, and Lionel Hampton. A mid-'50s album he made with vocalist Maxine Sullivan for Bethlehem rekindled interest in the Kirby band. His only fault was unfailing loyalty. He worked for years with a Dorsey ghost band fronted by Sam Donahue, and eventually toured with it as a vocalist; by this time, the name had been changed to the Frank Sinatra, Jr. show. Fortunately, his earlier work more than overwhelms this period and material. —*Ron Wynn*

★ **Girl of My Dreams** / Oct. 10, 1959 / Everest 1070

○ **Here Comes Charlie** / Jul. 1960 / Everest 108

○ **Like Charlie** / Oct.-Nov. 1960 / Everest 1127

○ **Charlie Shavers at Le Crazy Horse** / Jun. 1964 / Everest 5225

ARTIE SHAW (Arthur Jacob Arshawsky)

b. May 23, 1910, New York, NY
Clarinet, bandleader, composer, arranger / Swing, big band
One of jazz's finest clarinetists, Artie Shaw never seemed fully satisfied with his musical life; he constantly broke up successful bands and ran away from success. While Count Basie and Duke Ellington were satisfied to lead just one orchestra during the swing era, and Benny Goodman (due to illness) had two, Shaw led five, all of them distinctive and memorable.

Shaw grew up in New Haven, Connecticut, and played clarinet and alto locally. He spent part of 1925 with Johnny Cavallaro's dance band, then played off and on with Austin Wylie's band in Cleveland during 1927-29 before joining Irving Aaronson's Commanders. After moving to New York, Shaw became a close associate of Willie "the Lion" Smith at jam sessions, and, by 1931, was a busy studio musician. He retired from music for the first time in 1934 in hopes of writing a book, but when his money started running out, Shaw returned to New York. A major turning point occurred when he performed at an all-star big-band concert at the Imperial Theatre in May 1936, surprising the audience by performing with a string quartet and a rhythm section. He used a similar concept when he put together his first orchestra, and added a Dixieland-type frontline and a vocalist while retaining the strings. Despite some fine recordings, that particular group disbanded in early 1937, and Shaw put together a more conventional big band.

The surprise success of his 1938 recording of "Begin the Beguine" made the clarinetist into a superstar and his orchestra (which featured the tenor of Georgie Auld, vocals by Helen Forrest and Tony Pastor and, by 1939, Buddy Rich's drumming) became one of the most popular in the world. Billie Holiday was with the band for a few months although only one recording ("Any Old Time") resulted. Shaw found the pressure of the band business difficult to deal with, and, in November 1939, he suddenly left the bandstand and moved to Mexico for two months. When Shaw returned, his first session, which utilized a large string section, resulted in another major hit, "Frenesi." It seemed that no matter what Shaw did he could not escape from success!

Shaw's third regular orchestra, which had a string section and star soloists such as trumpeter Billy Butterfield and pianist Johnny Guarnieri, was one of his finest, and waxed perhaps the greatest version of "Stardust" along with the memorable "Concerto for Clarinet." The Gramercy Five, a small group out of the band (using Guarnieri on harpsichord), also scored with the million-selling "Summit Ridge Drive." Despite all this success, Shaw broke up the orchestra in 1941, only to reform an even larger one later in the year. The latter group featured Hot Lips Page along with Auld and Guarnieri.

After Pearl Harbor, Shaw enlisted and led a navy band before getting a medical discharge in February 1944. Later in the year, Shaw started a new orchestra that featured Roy Eldridge, Dodo Marmarosa, and Barney Kessel. Shaw's style, with this orchestra, had become quite modern, almost boppish. But, with the end of the swing era, Shaw again broke up his band in early 1946 and was semi-retired for several years, and played classical music as much as he played jazz. His last attempt at a big band was a short-lived. It was a boppish unit that lasted for a few months in 1949 and included Zoot Sims, Al Cohn, and Don Fagerquist; its modern music was a commercial flop. After a few years of only limited musical activity, Shaw returned one last time, and recorded extensively with a version of the Gramercy Five that featured Tal Farlow or Joe Puma on guitar along with Hank Jones. Then, in 1955, Artie Shaw permanently gave up the clarinet to pursue his dream of being a writer. Although he served as frontman (with Dick Johnson playing the clarinet solos) for a reorganized Artie Shaw orchestra in 1983, Shaw never played again. Although he received plenty of publicity for his six marriages (including marriages to Lana Turner, Ava Gardner, and Evelyn Keyes) and his odd autobiography, *The Trouble With Cinderella,* (which barely touches on the music business or his wives!), the still-outspoken Artie Shaw deserves to be best remembered as one of the great clarinetists. His recordings are available in piecemeal fashion on Bluebird. — *Scott Yanow*

One-Night Stand with Artie Shaw at the Steel Pier / **i.** Apr. 8, 1936-Apr. 8, 1945 / Joyce 1148

Half of this LP from the collector's label Joyce features the 1941 Artie Shaw orchestra during a broadcast that is highlighted by "Frenesi" and Hot Lips Page singing and playing on a Bill Challis arrangement of "Blues in the Night." Also included on this set are a few numbers from Shaw's orchestra in 1940 and two cuts from 1945 featuring trumpeter Roy Eldridge on "Little Jazz." But the most significant selection is the earliest: Artie Shaw's historic 1936 performance of "Interlude" (here mistitled "Blues in B Flat") with a string quartet. The acclaim received from the latter inspired the clarinetist to form his first big band. Overall this is a varied and continually interesting set. — *Scott Yanow*

Early Artie Shaw, Vol. 1 / **i.** Jun. 11, 1936-Oct. 30, 1936 / Columbia/Legacy CK 53423

This second of two CDs released by Columbia traces the development of Artie Shaw's first big band, an innovative but short-lived unit that died after eight months. The first 15 selections (highlighted by "Sobbin' Blues," "Copenhagen," and "My Blue Heaven") are by this very interesting band, which,

by including a string quartet in its instrumentation, had a unique sound. The final three numbers (listed as by "Art Shaw & His New Music) feature the clarinetist's second orchestra, a more conventional band that within a year (with "Begin the Beguine") would be the surprise success of 1938. Fine swing music. — *Scott Yanow*

Early Artie Shaw, Vol. 3 / **i.** Feb. 15, 1937-Jul. 22, 1937 / Ajazz 270

Clarinetist Artie Shaw's first orchestra (heard on the opening two numbers in the third volume of this five-LP series) was an admirable but commercially unsuccessful venture which incorporated a string quartet as part of a swing band. When that folded, Shaw returned with a more conventional and louder orchestra, a band that would soon be a major success (perhaps because it was less unusual). This LP contains that orchestra's first dozen recordings and, although it had not caught on yet, one can hear (in Tony Pastor's vocals, Shaw's superb clarinet and the tightness of the ensembles) the beginnings of his "Begin the Beguine" band. Most of this material has not yet been reissued on CD. — *Scott Yanow*

○ **Artie Shaw and the Rhythmakers, Volume One** / **i.** Feb. 19, 1937-Apr. 29, 1937 / Swingdom 7001/2

Although heard here a year or so before his orchestra hit it big with "Begin the Beguine," Shaw was already leading a band with an easily recognizable sound. Singers Dorothy Howe and Peg LaCentra would not last, and, surprisingly, Tony Pastor sticks to playing tenor, but otherwise the orchestra's style was quickly being formed. Artie Shaw fans should particularly enjoy hearing these rare sides on this two-LP set, for many of the selections were not otherwise recorded by the great clarinetist. — *Scott Yanow*

○ **Early Artie Shaw, Vol. 5** / **i.** Apr. 29-Dec. 30, 1937 / Ajazz 283

The fifth and final LP in this collector's series concludes the documentation of the pre-"Begin the Beguine" Artie Shaw orchestra. In addition to four numbers taken from broadcasts, the final ten selections cut by Shaw in 1937 are included with "Just You, Just Me," "Free For All," and "Non-Stop Flight" being the hottest numbers. A struggle still lay ahead for Artie Shaw because it would be over seven months before his orchestra entered the recording studio again, but from then on Shaw would be a household name. This valuable early music has not yet appeared on CD. — *Scott Yanow*

○ **Artie Shaw and The Rhythmakers, Volumes Five Through Eight** / **i.** Jul. 13, 1937-Feb. 15, 1938 / Swingdom 7005-4

During 1937-38 the then-fairly unknown Artie Shaw orchestra participated in six marathon recording sessions in which they cut 127 selections for radio transcriptions. The Artie Shaw success story really began in 1938 with his signing to Victor. Between then and 1945, Shaw would lead and break up four separate orchestras, but his artistic and commercial success would be consistently phenomenal. Fortunately, RCA in its Bluebird series of two-LP sets released every Shaw recording in its vaults on eight volumes; unfortunately, much of this music (outside of the better-known hits) has not yet appeared in coherent fashion on CD, so I would advise searching for (and treasuring) the LPs. The first volume finds Shaw debuting on Victor with his giant hit "Begin the Beguine" and continuing with such classics as "Back Bay Shuffle," "Any Old Time" (Billie Holiday's only recording with Shaw), his theme "Nightmare," "Softly, As in a Morning Sunrise," "They Say" (featuring Helen Forrest's vocal), and "Carioca," among many others. It is no wonder that by 1939 Artie Shaw led the most popular big band in jazz and popular music. — *Scott Yanow*

★ **Free for All** / **i.** 1937 / Portrait 44090

22 Original Big / **i.** 1938 / Hindsight 401

Hindsight specializes in reissuing radio broadcast performances and transcriptions from most of the main swing bands. This fine CD features Artie Shaw's most famous orchestra, his 1938-39 band with tenor Georgie Auld, Tony Pastor, singer Helen Forrest, and (in '39) Buddy Rich. There is no version of "Begin the Beguine" (their big hit) on this CD, but there are many superior examples of the band's music with solos always differing from their studio records. — *Scott Yanow*

Begin the Beguine / i. 1938-1941 / Bluebird 6274
Since Artie Shaw's Victor recordings have not been reissued in full on CD, this sampler serves as a fine place for swing beginners to start. Included are many of the more popular recordings of his second and third orchestras including the title cut, "Frenesi," "Star Dust," and "Summit Ridge Drive," giving a good idea as to why Artie Shaw was so popular and still remains highly rated as a clarinetist today, decades after his retirement. — *Scott Yanow*

☆ **Complete Artie Shaw—Vol. 1 (1938-39)** / 1938-1939 / RCA 5517
This two-record set contains, in chronological order, all the titles that clarinetist and bandleader Artie Shaw recorded for Victor between July 24, 1938, and January 23, 1939, commencing with "Begin the Beguine" and continuing through "Carioca." When Shaw signed with Victor, prior to the "Beguine" date (flip side "Indian Love Call"), his reputation as a big-band leader was at a low ebb. But with this release the Shaw fortunes drastically changed, and he found himself challenging Benny Goodman for the title "King of Swing," for the release propelled him into the national limelight. It was during this period that the band found itself, due in large measure to the playing of Johnny Best, Claude Bowen, and Bernie Priven (tpt); George Arus and Les Jenkins (tb); and the tenor sax solos/antics of Tony Pastor. This group was further strengthened in late '38 with the addition of George Auld (ts) and again in early '39 with the addition of Buddy Rich on drums. Helen Forrest handled all the female vocals during this period with one exception—Billie Holiday slipped in for a dandy vocal on "Any Old Time." — *Bill Gallagher*, Cadence

Personal Best / i. 1938-1945 / Bluebird 61099
This is a rather odd but intriguing collection of Artie Shaw featuring Buddy Rich. All of this material has since been reissued elsewhere but, if one runs across this set, it is worth picking up. — *Scott Yanow*

Broadcast Years / i. Nov. 1939 / Sounds of Swing 126
This LP features Artie Shaw's very popular 1939 orchestra playing live shortly before its leader chose to flee the pressure and run off to Mexico. With Buddy Rich propelling the rhythm section and Georgie Auld and Bernie Previn providing solos, Shaw and his band perform 10 instrumentals among the 16 selections; Tony Pastor and Helen Forrest have three fine vocals apiece. Easily enjoyable swing music. — *Scott Yanow*

☆ **Complete Artie Shaw—Vol. 2 (1939)** / 1939 / RCA 5533
The second of seven two-LP sets released by RCA Bluebird in the late '70s (still the best Artie Shaw series ever) traces Shaw's orchestra throughout 1939, the year that they were the most popular in the land. Among the 32 studio sides are "Deep Purple," "One Night Stand," and "Traffic Jam." In addition to the leader-clarinetist, the main soloists include Georgie Auld on tenor, trumpeter Bernie Privin, and pianist Bob Kitsis, while Helen Forrest and Tony Pastor provide vocals on half of the songs. Shaw would lead stronger orchestras but this band remains the best loved. — *Scott Yanow*

☆ **Complete Artie Shaw—Vol. 3 (1939-1940)** / 1939-1934 / RCA
The third of seven two-LP sets in Bluebird's definitive Artie Shaw series consists of the last 18 recordings by his very popular 1939 orchestra (riding on the success of "Begin the Beguine"), Shaw's two orchestral sessions of 1940 (recorded after the clarinetist's return from his celebrated flight to Mexico), and three of the four selections performed by his new small group, the Gramercy Five, in September 1940. The 1939 orchestra (featuring Georgie Auld's tenor, Buddy Rich's drums, and vocals from Helen Forrest and Tony Pastor) is at its best on "Lady Be Good" and "I Surrender Dear." Artie Shaw's first session after his return yielded his

second-biggest hit ("Frenesi") and some fascinating classical-influenced pieces with a full string section. The initial Gramercy Five date included yet another major best-seller in "Summit Ridge Drive." Artie Shaw just could not avoid success at this time despite his best efforts! — *Scott Yanow*

☆ **Complete Artie Shaw—Vol. 7 (1939-1945)** / 1939-1945 / RCA 5580
The final volume in this definitive series of two-LP sets covers Artie Shaw's 1945 orchestra, a band that boasted the playing of trumpeter Roy Eldridge, pianist Dodo Marmarosa, and guitarist Barney Kessel; all three also joined Shaw and the rhythm section in his Gramercy Five. The band often hints strongly at bop and has moments of excitement, but the end of the swing era brought its demise. All seven volumes in this series should be acquired if they can still be found! — *Scott Yanow*

Artie Shaw at the Hollywood Palladium / i. Oct. 26, 1940-Sep. 6, 1941 / Hep 19
Although there are many releases featuring radio broadcasts from Artie Shaw's very popular 1939 orchestra, relatively few exist from his next two bands, the outfits from 1940 and 1941. This particular LP shows just how creative the writing was for Shaw's string orchestras. Billy Butterfield, Hot Lips Page, Jack Jenney, and Georgie Auld are among the many soloists, and there is one rare small-group live version of "Dr. Livingstone I Presume." Excellent music. — *Scott Yanow*

★ **Complete Gramercy Five Sessions, The** / 1940-1945 / Bluebird 7637
This set marks the first time in at least 20 years that the classic small-group Gramercy Five material has been available. The playful, sophisticated, and hot interplay between Shaw and his sidemen made this what it is. — *Rich Kienzle*, Rock & Roll Disc

☆ **Complete Artie Shaw—Vol. 4 (1940-1941)** / 1940-1941 / RCA 5572
Of the six main orchestras that Artie Shaw formed and broke up during 1936-49 his third, the "Stardust" band, was possibly his greatest. He had a strong variety of soloists in trumpeter Billy Butterfield, trombonist Jack Jenney, tenor-saxophonist Jerry Jerome, and pianist Johnny Guarnieri in addition to a string section. Such arrangers as William Grant Still, Lennie Hayton, Jerry Gray, and Ray Conniff were employed, and the writing was as creative as the solos, with the string section really uplifting the music instead of weighing it down. The results, as heard on this twofer, include such classics as "Temptation," "Prelude in C Major," "Moonglow," "Love of My Life," and particularly "Concerto for Clarinet" and the best-ever version of "Stardust." As a bonus, this set also has five of the eight recordings made by Shaw's original Gramercy Five (with Johnny Guarnieri heard on harpsichord). — *Scott Yanow*

Blues in the Night / Sep. 1941-Jul. 1945 / RCA 2432
While Bluebird in the late 1970s released all of Artie Shaw's recordings in chronological order on a series of two-LP sets, its CD reissues have thus far been samplers. *Blues in the Night* has ten selections from the 1941 string orchestra that featured trumpeter-singer Hot Lips Page in addition to 11 by the 1945 big band that showcased trumpeter Roy Eldridge. Filled with such memorable performances as "Blues in the Night," "St. James Infirmary," "Lady Day," "Little Jazz," and a classic Eddie Sauter arrangement of "Summertime," this excellent CD is recommended to those not already possessing the twofers. — *Scott Yanow*

☆ **Complete Artie Shaw—Vol. 5 (1941-1942)** / 1941-1942 / RCA 5576
Despite his success with his "Stardust" band, Artie Shaw broke up the orchestra and took time off in early 1941. This fifth in a highly recommended (but increasingly hard to find) series of two-LP sets documents Shaw's activity during the remainder of 1941. The clarinetist led a very successful if unusual orchestral session with such guests as trumpeter Red Allen, trombonist J.C. Higginbotham, altoist Benny Carter, and singer Lena Horne, and then later in the year

formed his fourth big band. The new orchestra had an even larger string section than its predecessor, and boasted such alumni as trombonist Jack Jenney, Georgie Auld on tenor, and pianist Johnny Guarnieri in addition to the great trumpeter-singer Hot Lips Page. Unfortunately, Shaw impulsively broke it up shortly after Pearl Harbor but, as can be heard on this very enjoyable set, the band had a personality of its own. High points include "Blues in the Night," "Beyond the Blue Horizon," "St. James Infirmary Blues," and several classical-oriented pieces. Fascinating if relatively obscure recordings from another of Artie Shaw's great orchestras. —Scott Yanow

☆ **Complete Artie Shaw—Vol. 6 (1942-1945)** / 1942-1945 / RCA 5579

The sixth in a seven-volume set of twofer LPs that reissues all of clarinetist Artie Shaw's recordings for Victor during 1938-45 includes the last session by his fourth orchestra, then concentrates on his fifth big band, a modern swing outfit from 1944-45 that featured trumpeter Roy Eldridge, pianist Dodo Marmarosa, and guitarist Barney Kessel. Quite a few of the arrangements are memorable; among the classics are Jimmy Mundy's "Lady Day," Eddie Sauter's "Summertime," Buster Harding's "Little Jazz," and Ray Conniff's "'S Wonderful." It is difficult to believe that, with one brief exception, this was Artie Shaw's last regularly working big band. Recommended. —Scott Yanow

Spotlight On Artie Shaw—1945 / i. Sep. 12-Sep. 26, 1945 / Joyce 1003

This collector's LP contains three rare broadcasts from September 1945 by Artie Shaw's fifth big band, a unit featuring trumpeter Roy Eldridge. Three performances by Shaw's Gramercy Five and two vocals from Imogene Lynn add variety to this fine set, recorded shortly before the clarinetist gave up the big band business altogether. —Scott Yanow

○ **Later Artie Shaw, Vol. 1** / i. May 31, 1949-Apr. 4, 1950 / Ajazz 291

Artie Shaw's recordings of 1949-52 remain his rarest, last issued on this collector's LP series. Having largely given up the band business by mid-1946, the clarinetist came out of semiretirement in 1949 to lead his sixth and final regularly working orchestra, but that modern bop group was a quick flop and left few recordings. Volume 1 (out of seven) in the Later Artie Shaw series has a wide variety of recordings including two with a studio orchestra; a pair of intriguing items in which the clarinetist fronts a quartet consisting of cello, piano, bass, and drums; six titles with his short-lived orchestra; and two with a new Gramercy Five (featuring vocalist Mary Ann McCall and trumpeter Don Fagerquist). Although Artie Shaw's career had become directionless, his playing remained in its prime. This "lost" music deserves to be reissued on CD. —Scott Yanow

Pied Piper / i. Dec. 1949 / First Heard 105

In 1949, Artie Shaw put together what would be his last regularly working orchestra, a modern outfit featuring such younger players as trumpeter Don Fagerquist, the tenors of Al Cohn and Zoot Sims, pianist Dodo Marmarosa, and guitarist Jimmy Raney. Striking a balance between his earlier swing hits and the new bop music, Artie Shaw's new orchestra had a great deal of potential and seemed like a perfect outlet for his always-modern playing. But it stood little chance in 1949 when the big-band era was gone and his older fans wanted Shaw to put on a nostalgic show. The orchestra flopped commercially. This LP of live performances shows that the music of Artie Shaw's last big band was excellent, swinging and well worth remembering. —Scott Yanow

○ **1949** / 1949 / Music Masters 65026

In 1949, the swing era was already in the past and the public's enthusiasm for bebop was quickly receding. No matter, Artie Shaw decided that it was time to put together a modern big band. The venture only lasted three months, but the largely forgotten music that it performed was quite rewarding. This Musicmasters CD consists of private recordings of the barely documented orchestra, valuable performances that feature the always-modern clarinetist with an outfit that included trumpeter Don Fagerquist, a great saxophone section with the tenors of Al Cohn and Zoot Sims, and guitarist Jimmy Raney. It is a real pleasure to hear Artie Shaw stretching out in this setting and a real pity that this band could not have lasted! —Scott Yanow

For You, For Me, Forever / i. 194? / Musicraft

On the second of two LPs of Artie Shaw's recordings for Musicraft, the great clarinetist is heard with studio musicians playing superior standards and obscurities in 1946. Mel Tormé and/or his Mel-Tones are actually the stars on nine of these fifteen selections including a spirited "What is This Thing Called Love." The clarinetist plays well enough but often sounds as if his heart is not really in the music; at this point it was just a day's work for him. —Scott Yanow

With Strings / i. 194? / Musicraft

By the end of 1945, Artie Shaw was ready to leave the big-band business and become semiretired musically. He recorded his fifth big band (which by this time no longer had trumpeter Roy Eldridge) and then broke it up. This Musicraft LP, the first of two, features Shaw with his modern swing band of 1945 (Ray Linn takes the trumpet solos) and then on some less significant dance sides from 1946. A young Mel Tormé sings two numbers, his Mel-Tones romp on "I Got the Sun in the Morning," and the clarinetist himself is in generally good form, but one senses by the later sessions that his heart is not always in the music he's playing anymore. —Scott Yanow

Later Artie Shaw, Vol. 2 / i. Apr. 4-Jul. 19, 1950 / Ajazz 298

With the collapse of his short-lived bop big band in early 1950, Artie Shaw went back into semiretirement. His recordings heard on this LP (the second in a valuable seven-volume series) find him with studio groups ranging from a standard big band to ballads with string sections and two jazz performances with a new Gramercy Five (this time featuring Lee Castle's trumpet and Don Lanphere's tenor). Most of these performances, however, have Shaw merely backing up commercial vocalists including Dick Haymes, Don Cherry (no relation to the trumpeter), and the Chelsea Three. —Scott Yanow

Later Artie Shaw, Vol. 3 / i. Sep. 14, 1950-Jul. 2, 1953 / Ajazz 426

The third volume in this seven-LP series by the collector's label Ajazz (a subsidiary of Joyce) has some real Artie Shaw rarities, taken from a period of time when he was barely active in music. Shaw is heard with studio big bands on such songs as "Jingle Bells," "White Christmas," and "In the Still of the Night," backing singer Trudy Richards and with two versions of the Gramercy Five (but somewhat confined to accompanying vocals by June Hutton and Connie Boswell). True Artie Shaw collectors will have to get this intriguing set but more general listeners are advised to acquire his earlier recordings instead. —Scott Yanow

Later Artie Shaw, Vol. 4 / i. Jul. 2, 1953-Feb. 1954 / Ajazz 431

The fourth in a seven-LP series documenting Artie Shaw's little-known "later" recordings has six selections featuring the clarinetist with a studio orchestra and strings, and seven more rewarding performances with his final Gramercy Five, a sextet featuring pianist Hank Jones, guitarist Tal Farlow, and vibraphonist Joe Roland. Shaw had listened closely to bebop and had subtly modernized his style; now he was fully prepared to stretch out with younger players. Most of this material has not been reissued on CD. —Scott Yanow

○ **More Last Recordings** / i. Feb.-Mar. 1954 / Music Masters 65101

The second two-CD set of recordings by Artie Shaw's final Gramercy Five is comparable to the first. Shaw would give up his clarinet for good shortly after this band broke up, but the musical evidence shows that he was still very much in his prime and growing as an improviser, making his retirement a tragedy for jazz. With pianist Hank Jones, vibraphonist Joe Roland, and guitarist Tal Farlow contributing strong solos and inspiration for Shaw, this cool bop music (which even has updated performances of "Begin the Beguine," "Frenesi," and "Stardust" that owe surprisingly little to the original hit versions) is quite enjoyable and creative. —*Scott Yanow*

Later Artie Shaw, Vol. 5 / i. Feb. 1954 / Ajazz 440
The fifth of seven LPs in this collector's series of Artie Shaw recordings from the post-swing era features seven lengthy performances from the clarinetist's last Gramercy Five, a boppish unit with guitarist Tal Farlow, pianist Hank Jones, and vibraphonist Joe Roland that served as a perfect outlet for Shaw's creativity. It is a real shame that he did not have the willpower to keep similar groups in existence for the remainder of the decade, instead choosing to quit altogether the year after this session. —*Scott Yanow*

Later Artie Shaw, Vol. 6 / i. Feb. 1954 / Ajazz 446
The sixth in a valuable seven-LP series put out by the collector's label Ajazz focuses on Artie Shaw's final working band, a version of the Gramercy Five that also boasts solos by pianist Hank Jones, guitarist Tal Farlow, and vibraphonist Joe Roland. On such songs as "Besame Mucho," "The Grabtown Grapple," "Stop and Go Mambo," and "Love of My Life," Artie Shaw shows that he never did decline and that there was no musical reason (except his own boredom) why he chose to quit playing clarinet shortly after this band broke up. All of the entries in this series are worth searching for. —*Scott Yanow*

Later Artie Shaw, Vol. 7 / i. Jun. 1954-Nov. 21, 1955 / Ajazz 451
The seventh and final volume in this valuable LP series completes the Artie Shaw story only 19 years after his first recording session as a leader. There are five lengthy performances with his final Gramercy Five in June 1954 (featuring solos from pianist Hank Jones and guitarist Joe Puma) and three final performances with a string orchestra in November 1955. Artie Shaw then became one of the very few major jazz figures to retire at his prime, a major loss to the music. This LP shows that he pretty much went out on top, still sounding quite modern. —*Scott Yanow*

○ **Last Recordings—Vol. 1: Rare and Unreleased, The** / 1954 / Music Masters 65071
The first of two double-CD sets contains a healthy share of the recordings that clarinetist Artie Shaw made with his final Gramercy Five, a unit that included pianist Hank Jones, either Tal Farlow or Joe Puma on guitar, and usually Joe Roland's vibes. Unlike his longtime competitor Benny Goodman, Artie Shaw felt perfectly comfortable with younger modernists. In fact his own clarinet playing had evolved through the years and sometimes he hints strongly at Buddy DeFranco without losing his own musical personality during these 20 performances. This is very rewarding music that makes one especially regret that Artie Shaw chose to give up the clarinet after this band ran its course. —*Scott Yanow*

Begin the Beguine / i. Oct. 19, 1992 / Pro Arte 3405

Beat of the Big Bands / Columbia 32021
Artie Shaw's first big band was quite unusual, originally composed of four horns, a string quartet, and a four-piece rhythm section. This unimaginatively titled CD (whose chatty liner notes unfortunately do not include personnel and date information!) has the first 16 recordings by this fine orchestra, featuring vocals by the forgettable Wesley Vaughn, Peg LaCentra, and the young Tony Pastor, but, more important, successfully matching the horns with the strings on such enjoyable numbers as "Japanese Sandman," "Sugar Foot Stomp," and "The Skeleton in the Closet." Pity that this potentially great orchestra did not catch on! —*Scott Yanow*

○ **This is Artie Shaw—Vols. 1 and 2** / RCA 5096
Fine introductory volume to his RCA/Bluebird output. —*Ron Wynn*

CHARLES "BOBO" SHAW

b. Sep. 5, 1947, Pope, MS
Drums, leader / Modern creative
An outstanding free drummer who's also able and willing to get funky at any time, Charles "Bobo" Shaw's playing is rhythmically diverse and alternately intense or relaxed, frenetic or steady. Shaw studied drums with Ben Thigpen, and briefly doubled on trombone and bass. He was one of the founders of the St. Louis-based Black Artists Group in the '60s. Shaw and other BAG members went to Europe later in the '60s, and Shaw played free jazz in Paris for a year with Anthony Braxton, Steve Lacy, Frank Wright, Alan Silva, and Michel Portal. He returned to St. Louis in the '70s, and recorded there with Oliver Lake in 1971. He led the Human Arts Ensemble in the mid-'70s, recording with Lester and Joseph Bowie, Julius Hemphill, Lake, and others. Shaw worked and did sessions with Lester Bowie, Frank Lowe, Hamiet Bluiett, and Lake in the mid-'60s. After touring with the Human Arts Ensemble in Europe during the late '70s, Shaw recorded with Billy Bang in the mid-'80s. He's recorded as a leader for Moers and Black Saint, among others. Shaw currently has one session available on CD. —*Ron Wynn*

★ **Bugle Boy Bop** / Feb. 5, 1977 / Muse 5268

WOODY SHAW (Woody Herman (II) Shaw)

b. Dec. 24, 1944, Laurinburg, BC, Canada, **d.** 1989
Trumpet / Hard bop
A wonderfully lyrical, delightful, and intense trumpeter who always seemed on the verge of stardom, Woody Shaw was among the finest hard bop players of the '60, '70s, and '80s. He was influenced heavily by Clifford Brown, and often soloed in a similar, attacking fashion, but there was also a sensitive, almost innocent quality in his ballad playing. There were also stylistic similarities in the playing of Shaw and Freddie Hubbard, which were especially noticeable when the duo recorded together, though Shaw always denied he'd been influenced by Hubbard. Shaw didn't waste energy; his lines and phrases were precise, often sparkling, and vibrant.

His father sang with the Diamond Jubilee Singers, a gospel group. Shaw began on bugle, then switched to trumpet at age 11. In the early '60s, he worked with Willie Bobo and Chick Corea, while he played and recorded with Eric Dolphy. Dolphy invited Shaw to join him in Paris during 1964, but died before Shaw could leave. Shaw went to Paris anyway, and worked regularly with Nathan Davis, Bud Powell, Johnny Griffin, Kenny Clarke, and Art Taylor. Shaw also worked in Berlin and London, and recorded with Davis and Larry Young in London. When he returned to America, Shaw played with Horace Silver in 1965 and 1966, and recorded with Corea, Jackie McLean, McCoy Tyner, and Andrew Hill. He worked periodically with Max Roach in 1968 and 1969, and also did some playing in Broadway pit orchestras and New York studios.

He formed a quintet with Joe Henderson in 1970 that made some furious combo dates. Shaw made his recording debut for Contemporary in 1970, and later did dates for Muse. Columbia signed him on Miles Davis's recommendation, then, incredibly, dumped him after three great albums because they didn't sell in large quantities. Shaw played in Art Blakey's Jazz Messengers in 1971 and 1972 before settling in San Francisco and leading a group with Bobby Hutcherson for a while. He returned to New York in 1975, playing in the Louis Hayes-Junior Cook Quintet. When Cook left, Shaw became coleader with Hayes. Dexter Gordon used the band when he made his historic return to America in 1976. Shaw's combos of the late '70s and early '80s included many top young and/or emerging jazz players, among them Mulgrew Miller, Carter Jefferson, Victor Lewis, Tony Reedus, Stafford James, David Williams, and Teri Lyne Carrington. He recorded for Red, Enja, Elektra, Timeless, and Muse in the '80s. Mosaic compiled the Columbia sessions into a superb boxed set in 1993; Many of Shaw's Muse sets, and some of the Timeless dates, have been reissued on CD. —*Ron Wynn*

★ **Complete CBS Studio Recordings of Woody Shaw, The** / Mosaic 142
Woody Shaw was among the finest trumpeters in the hard bop tradition, yet he never attained the recognition he earned or deserved. The bulk of his great sessions were recorded for small jazz independents, ensuring them widespread critical evaluation but little audience except with the hardcore faithful. But things seemed about to change in the late '70s when Miles Davis suggested to Columbia that they record Shaw's group. The company actually took his suggestion and signed Shaw. He issued a string of remarkable but low-selling records, and Columbia cut him loose after four years and four albums, an eternity for a conglomerate such as Columbia, which compounded the crime by deleting the records shortly after Shaw departed. Mosaic has corrected that slight with another of their marvelously produced and comprehensively notated and packaged boxed sets. This three-disc collection covers Shaw's Columbia sessions. They begin with December 15, 1977, dates and conclude with songs recorded March 17, 1981. Shaw works with a quintet, sextet, septet, and large band, string sections, and a vocalist. There are also dates featuring him on cornet, an instrument Shaw played beautifully but not nearly often enough.

Shaw's approach is original and thoroughly infused with jazz tradition. His solos are never flashy, derivative, or tainted with gimmicks. He plays wonderful, evocative melodies, improvises with clarity, precision, and flair and offers chorus after chorus of blistering, cleanly articulated brass magic. The roster of guests ranges from the spiraling fury of tenor saxophonist Joe Henderson to the more blues-drenched tenor sound of Carter Jefferson, James Spaulding's controlled but striking flute and alto sax, and excellent trombone contributions from Curtis Fuller and Steve Turre.

While it is sad that Shaw's stay at Columbia was not more personally beneficial, it was musically productive. Thanks to Mosaic for returning into circulation great music that its first label could not or would not give the treatment it merited. —*Ron Wynn*

○ **In the Beginning . . .** / i. 1965 / Muse 5298
Some interesting, uneven, but worth-hearing '65 material from trumpeter Woody Shaw. He was then still fresh on the jazz scene, and had only recently recovered from the death of mentor Eric Dolphy. Shaw teamed with tenor saxophonist Joe Henderson, pianist Herbie Hancock, and bassists Ron Carter or Paul Chambers on these cuts. His potential certainly emerges, as does the fact he was a tentative, unsure soloist at this juncture. —*Ron Wynn*

☆ **Blackstone Legacy** / Dec. 8-9, 1970 / Contemporary
There is a good amount of passion here, but it falls flat as the group never manages to ignite beyond the basic professionalism that one might expect from any set of seven accomplished improvising artists. —*Bob Rusch*, Cadence

Moontrane, The / Dec. 11+18, 1974 / Muse 5058

Love Dance / 1975 / Muse 5074

☆ **Little Red's Fantasy** / Jun. 29, 1976 / Muse 5103
Little Red's Fantasy was recorded in June, 1976. That's when Shaw was an underdog, a scrappy talent deserving wider recognition, a veteran of stints with Eric Dolphy, McCoy Tyner, Art Blakey, and Horace Silver. It was also a period when Shaw was scuffling for a place in the sun as coleader of a solid neo-bop quintet with drummer Louis Hayes. Shaw is at the top of his game for this '76 Muse date. His tone is rounder, his ideas more developed, his involvement total. This is the real Woody Shaw. Shaw's foil up front is Frank Strozier, a remarkable altoist who deserves to be heard more often. In back, pianist Ronnie Matthews, bassist Stafford James, and drummer Eddie Moore listen and support with tasteful zest. Whether a tough burner like "Tomorrow's Destiny," a gritty bossa nova like "Sashianova," or a reflective outing like "Jean Marie," the ensemble and so-

los here crackle with emotion, drama, and virtuosity. —*Chuck Berg*, Down Beat

○ **Woody Shaw Concert Ensemble at the Berliner Jazztage** / Nov. 6, 1976 / Muse 5139
Trumpeter Woody Shaw and drummer Louis Hayes worked together in a dynamic quintet during the mid-'70s that also included the considerable talents of reedman Rene McLean, pianist Ronnie Mathews, and bassist Stafford James. For the 1976 Berlin Jazz Festival, however, Shaw augmented the quintet by adding the voices of saxophonist Frank Foster and trombonist Slide Hampton. The result is a dynamic set of performances that attests to Shaw's growth as both a player and arranger. "Hello to the Wind" by Joe Chambers stretches brooding chords and McLean's lithe flute over a medium 4/4 charged with sambalike inflections. As with the other tracks, the supple rhythm carpet of Mathews, James, and Hayes supplies the right support for the solos and ensembles. —*Chuck Berg*, Down Beat

★ **Rosewood** / Dec. 15-19, 1977 / CBS
This album offers the two presentational modes Woody Shaw worked with for four years during the '70s. The first of these is the quintet. This one, however, is the *new* five-piece dynamo featuring saxophonist Carter Jefferson, pianist Onaje Allan Gumbs, bassist Clint Houston, and drummer Victor Lewis. Their compact intensity makes the brisk "Rahsaan's Run" and tasty "Theme for Maxine" tautly coiled forays. The other tracks feature the Woody Shaw Concert Ensemble. Beyond the personnel of the quintet and saxophonist Joe Henderson are reedmen James Vass, Frank Foster, and Art Webb, plus trombonists Steve Turre and Janice Robinson. Additional musicians, such as harpist Lois Colin, are called in as needed. The great advantage of the ensemble was that it gave Shaw the best of both big-band and small-group worlds. With Victor Lewis's "The Legend of Cheops," for instance, flutes, harp, and percussion are deftly employed to create pungent shifts in texture and timbre. For Gumbs's "Every Time I See You," rich woodwind sonorities frame poignant trumpet and piano essays. Overall, *Rosewood* presents contemporary acoustic playing at its best. —*Chuck Berg*, Down Beat

Stepping Stones / Aug. 5-6, 1978 / Columbia
This is as fine a major-label jazz album as possible in the late '70s. —*Ron Wynn*

Woody III / 1978 / Columbia
Third consecutive wonderful album for Columbia, which responded by cutting him loose. —*Ron Wynn*

Lotus Flower / Jan. 7, 1982 / Enja 79637

☆ **Night Music** / i. 1984 / Elektra 60299
This album is the second one culled from a 1982 recording session at the Jazz Forum in New York City, with Bobby Hutcherson featured as a "guest artist." Trumpeter Woody Shaw's distinctive music mixes elements of bebop and modal playing into a style that might be called "modern mainstream." The three originals here—one each by Shaw, trombonist Steve Turre, and pianist Mulgrew Miller—are all taken at somewhat relentless tempos, and the solos sound like a relay race after a while. "All the Things You Are" finally slows the pace and gives Shaw a chance to develop some of his darkly glowing, lyrical lines. —*Jim Roberts*, Down Beat

Imagination / Jun. 1987 / Muse 5338

GEORGE SHEARING (George Albert Shearing)

b. Aug. 13, 1919, London, England
Piano / Bop, cool, Latin-jazz
Pianist George Shearing, who was influenced by Errol Garner, popularized a unique jazz sound in 1949 with a quintet that featured piano, vibes, guitar, bass, and drums. Shearing used a block chord approach, which he probably got from Lennie Tristano, that combined techniques dating back to Milt Buckner. Shearing mixed this with the chordal playing style of the Glenn Miller orchestra, whose records

he'd closely examined. His sound and touch have been greatly admired by various musicians. Shearing's ensemble sound, especially the piano/vibes interplay, attracted widespread attention. He later performed classical concertos with orchestras during his concerts, including orchestrations that featured his quintet. Talents such as Cal Tjader, Gary Burton, Toots Thielemans, Joe Pass, Israel Crosby, and Vernel Fournier passed through the Shearing group.

Shearing began playing piano at age three, but had only limited musical training at the Linden Lodge School for the Blind in London, which he attended from ages 12 to 16. Through records, he absorbed the techniques and influence of boogie-woogie and blues pianists, and of Fats Waller, Teddy Wilson, and Art Tatum, among others. He played on British Broadcasting Company broadcasts, which included appearances with Ambrose. An accomplished jazz accordionist as well as a fine boogie-woogie player, Shearing once played for the King of England. He began recording in 1936, then came to America in 1947 with Leonard Feather's assistance, and settled in New York where he immersed himself in bebop. Shearing replaced Erroll Garner in the Oscar Pettiford trio, then led a quartet with Buddy DeFranco in 1948, before forming his famous quintet in 1949. The original members included Marjorie Hyams on vibes, Chuck Wayne on guitar, John Levy on bass, and Denzil Best on drums. Shearing compositions "Conception" (which was recorded by Miles Davis as "Deception") and "Consternation" were recorded eventually by one of Shearing's idols, Bud Powell.

Shearing recorded for Discovery, Savoy, and MGM in the late '40s and early '50s. He wrote "Lullaby of Birdland" in 1952 as a theme for both the club and the radio shows that were from broadcast there. He switched to Capitol and remained with that label into the early '70s, and enjoyed substantial chart success in the late '50s and early '60s. Shearing made albums with Peggy Lee, Nancy Wilson, Dakota Staton, and Nat King Cole, and later with Stephane Grappelli and the Robert Farnon Orchestra. He started his own label, Sheba records, for a brief period, then, in the '70s, signed with Concord. He earned critical plaudits and Grammy awards for dates with Mel Tormé. Shearing also worked with Carmen McRae, Jim Hall, and Marian McPartland, among others, in the '70s and '80s. Currently, he records for the Telarc label. Pianists such as Bill Evans and Herbie Hancock are among the many who've been influenced by Shearing. His material from the late '40s to the '90s is available on CD. —*Ron Wynn*

So Rare / 1947-1949 / Savoy 1117

○ **Lullaby of Birdland** / i. 194z / Polydor 827977
His classic and best-known cuts, plus lots of other seminal music in this 1986 reissue of late '40s and '50s material. —*Ron Wynn*

★ **I Hear Music** / i. 1952 / Metro 534

Evening with George Shearing, An / i. 1954 / MGM 252

Latin Escapade / i. 1956 / Capitol

Black Satin / White Satin / i. 1956-1959 / Capitol 92089

Burnished Brass / i. 1958 / Capitol 1038

Swinging's Mutual, The / i. 1960 / Blue Note 99190

★ **George Shearing and the Montgomery Brothers** / Oct. 9-10, 1961 / Original Jazz Classics 40
Recorded 10/9-10/61, this session has pianist George Shearing joining the Montgomery Brothers (guitarist Wes, vibist Buddy, and bassist Monk) and Walter Perkins (drums, plus Latin percussion). The music never really flows as a whole, but is more a set of parts; some of them are very fine, but it does not hold together well as a whole. It is Wes, but in frustratingly brief doses. The whole date was also issued as part of a twofer. —*Bob Rusch*, Cadence

★ **Nat King Cole Sings / Shearing Plays** / i. 1961 / Capitol

My Ship / Jun. 25, 1974 / Polydor 821664

○ **Reunion, The** / Apr. 11, 1976 / PA/USA 7049

A wonderful duo release from '76 with pianist George Shearing collaborating with violinist Stephane Grappelli. Shearing's sessions are usually more introspective and light than upbeat and hot, but Grappelli's soaring, exuberant violin solos seem to put a charge into Shearing, who responds with some of his hottest playing in many years. —*Ron Wynn*

Blues Alley and Jazz / Oct. 1979 / Concord Jazz 4110
With Brian Torft (b). Shearing is immaculate as usual, but material is slim. —*Ron Wynn*

○ **Two for the Road** / Jun. 1980 / Concord Jazz 4128
With George Shearing. Shearing (p) is smooth. McRae's hot at times and reflective or probing at others. —*Ron Wynn*

On a Clear Day / Aug. 1980 / Concord Jazz 132

★ **Alone Together** / Mar. 1981 / Concord Jazz 4171
With these two players it should be almost unnecessary to say that this album represents a thoroughly relaxed, tasteful, and professionally executed set. Like the liner notes, the music bears the air of a slightly formal tea time conversation between two impeccable musical minds. There were few musical surprises, apparently no musical chances are taken, and the treatment of each song is very natural but hardly ever surprising. It might be fair to say that it scores higher as hip supper club music than as a straightahead jazz date. And that, after all, might very well be what the players set out for in the first place. —*Per Husby*, Cadence

First Edition / Sep. 1981 / Concord Jazz 4177

Top Drawer / Mar. 1983 / Concord Jazz 4219
Grammy-winning combination with Mel Tormé (v), one of several sparkling cuts featuring the duo. —*Ron Wynn*

Live at the Cafe Carlyle / Jan. 1984 / Concord Jazz 4246
Typically clean, vibrant Shearing. Solid team effort. Shearing more animated than usual. —*Ron Wynn*

Grand Piano / May 1985 / Concord Jazz 4281

Plays Music of Cole Porter / Jan. 1986 / Concord Jazz 42010

More Grand Piano / Oct. 1986 / Concord Jazz 4318

☆ **Breakin' Out** / May 1987 / Concord Jazz 4335
Marvin "Smitty" Smith's chuckling drums bring out fresh qualities and rhythmic verve in old master Shearing. —*Ron Wynn*

Dexterity / Nov. 1987 / Concord Jazz 4346
This is a concert in Japan; usual brisk, delightful solos by Shearing, fine vocals by Ernestine Anderson. CD has three bonus cuts. —*Ron Wynn*

Spirit of 1776 / Mar. 1988 / Concord Jazz 4371

Perfect Match / May 1988 / Concord Jazz 4357
Topflight collaboration between Shearing and Ernestine Anderson (v). —*Ron Wynn*

George Shearing in Dixieland / Feb. 1989 / Concord Jazz 4388
Authentic New Orleans-style; Kenny Davern (cl) nearly steals the show. Shearing is impressive. CD version has bonus solo piano cuts. —*Ron Wynn*

Piano / i. May 1989 / Concord Jazz 4400

○ **I Hear a Rhapsody—Live at the Blue Note** / i. 1992 / Telarc 83310

In the Mind / Capitol

JACK SHELDON

b. Nov. 30, 1931, Jacksonville, FL
Trumpet, bandleader, comedian / Bop, cool
Trumpeter Jack Sheldon got more general audience recognition for his years in the Merv Griffin studio orchestra and a short-lived stint on a television show than for his lyrical, middle-register style, which is quite similar to '50s and early '60s Miles Davis in tone and conception. Sheldon studied trumpet in Detroit at age 12, and played professionally the next year. He moved to Los Angeles in 1947 and attended Los Angeles City College. He played in military bands in Texas and California in the early '50s, then formed his own

quintet after his discharge. Sheldon also worked with Jimmy Giuffre, Herb Geller, Wardell Gray, Stan Kenton, Benny Goodman, and Curtis Counce. He recorded with Dave Pell and Art Pepper in the '50s and '60s. Sheldon portrayed a jazz musician on a television series in the mid-'60s, and recorded with Gary Burton. He was highly visible in the "Merv Griffin Show" band, a sort of lesser-known Doc Severinsen. Sheldon also played with the big bands of Bill Berry, Goodman, and Woody Herman in the '70s and '80s, and recorded with June Christy in 1977. Sheldon's worked steadily playing on film and television soundtracks and on jingles, as well as heading small groups in Los Angeles. Sheldon has recorded for GNP, Reprise, and Concord. He has several sessions as a leader available on CD. —*Ron Wynn*

Oooo, But It's Good / Dec. 1962 / Capitol 1963

★ **Stand by for Jack Sheldon** / Mar. 1983 / Concord Jazz 229
This is a very fine Jack Sheldon (tpt, v) LP. Listeners to this recording may perhaps discern some "Chet Baker" in the way of a wistful tone (or some early Miles Davis, for that matter), but they would be hard pressed to find other comparisons except with Sheldon's own work. My picks here are "Daydream" (good vocal by Sheldon, with a very nice fill from bassist Ray Brown), "Cherry" taken at medium tempo, and "Bye, Bye Blackbird," which has an out chorus of Ross Tompkins's piano with Sheldon riding over it in tandem that bears repeated hearing. I liked the entire album, even the sour touch engendered by a possibly deliberate flatness on "The Shadow of Your Smile." Sheldon's singing voice is not memorable, but it's fully up to the job and used with great skill. —*Shirley Klett*, Cadence

Hollywood Heroes / Sep. 1987 / Concord Jazz 4339
A quintet of fairly undistinguished sidemen provides good support for Sheldon. Mostly they play early-period swing-era music bordering on bop. —*Michael G. Nastos*

MARTY SHELLER

Trumpet, arranger / Bop, Latin-jazz
A veteran trumpeter and arranger, Marty Sheller's best known for his work with Mongo Santamaria. He's done arrangements and played in various bands with Santamaria since the '70s. Sheller's worked with other Afro-Latin and Latin-jazz groups. His composition, "Marvellous Marvin," was recorded by a number of bands, including Don Sickler's group Superblue. —*Ron Wynn*

ARCHIE SHEPP (Archie Vernon Shepp)

b. May 24, 1937, Fort Lauderdale, FL
Saxophone / Hard bop, early free, modern creative
At various times, Archie Shepp has been a feared firebrand and radical, a soulful throwback, and a contemplative veteran. In the '60s, he was viewed as perhaps the most articulate and disturbing member of the free generation, a published playwright willing to speak on the record in unsparing, explicit fashion about social injustice and the anger and rage he felt. His tenor sax solos were searing, harsh, and unrelenting, and were played with a vivid intensity. But in the '70s, Shepp employed a fatback/swing-based R&B approach, and in the '80s he mixed straight bebop, ballads, and blues pieces, and displayed little of the fury and fire from his earlier days. Shepp studied dramatic literature at Goddard College, and earned his degree in 1959. He played alto sax in dance bands and sought theatrical work in New York. But Shepp switched to tenor, and played it in several free jazz bands. He worked with Cecil Taylor, co-led groups with Bill Dixon, and played in the New York Contemporary Five with Don Cherry and John Tchicai. He led his own bands in the mid-'60s with Roswell Rudd, Bobby Hutcherson, Beaver Harris, and Grachan Moncur III. His Impulse albums included poetry readings and quotes from James Baldwin and Malcolm X. Shepp's releases sought to paint an aural picture of African-American life, and included compositions based on incidents like Attica or folk sayings. He also produced plays in New York, among them The

Communist in 1965, and *Lady Day: A Musical Tragedy* in 1972 with trumpeter/composer Cal Massey. But starting in the late '60s, the rhetoric was toned down and the anger began to disappear from Shepp's albums. He substituted a more celebratory, and, at times, reflective attitude. Shepp turned to academia in the late '60s, and taught at SUNY-Buffalo, then at the University of Massachusetts (he was named an associate professor there in 1978). Shepp toured and recorded extensively in Europe during the '80s, and cut some fine albums with Horace Parlan, Niels-Henning Ørsted-Pedersen, and Jasper van't Hof. Over the years, he has recorded extensively for Impulse, Byg, Arista/Freedom, Phonogram, Steeplechase, Denon, Enja, EPM, and Soul Note, among others. Shepp currently has a healthy amount of recent and vintage sessions available on CD. —*Ron Wynn*

○ **New York Contemporary Five in Europe** / i. 1967 / Delmark 9409
Originally released by Delmark in 1967, this recording came about from an agreement with Sonet Records (1979), which recorded the New York Contemporary Five in 1962 at the Jazzhus Montmarte. I suppose it was because tenor saxophonist Archie Shepp had the "biggest" name, but there really was no call for releasing this under his name, for he has no more solo space than anyone else. Besides, the NYCF was a cooperative unit in the strictest sense of the term. Terry Martin's usual well-thought-out and informative liner notes place this short-lived group in the proper historical perspective while giving the music a brief interpretation. At turns the music is sloppy, powerful, imperfect, moving, irritating—but always alive and distinctly human. Regarding soloists, I find Don Cherry (cnt) to be the most consistent in terms of fashioning an effective statement. John Tchicai (as) also comes across quite well. Shepp doesn't come across for me on this date; he doesn't sound like he has things together. The rhythm section (bassist Don Moore, drummer J.C. Moses) serves its function although Moses could have learned a little subtlety in certain passages. —*Carl Brauer*, Cadence

★ **Four for Trane** / Aug. 10, 1964 / Impulse 71

Fire Music / Feb. 16, 1965 / MCA 39121

New Thing at Newport / Jul. 2, 1965 / Impulse 97

Live in San Francisco / Feb. 19, 1966 / Impulse
Includes some wonderful trombone by Roswell Redd, intense Shepp solos. —*Ron Wynn*

Mama Too Tight / Aug. 1966 / Impulse

On This Night / i. 1966 / GRP 125

★ **Magic of Ju-Ju** / Apr. 26, 1967 / Impulse

○ **Live at the Donaueschingen Music Festival** / Oct. 21, 1967 / Saba 15148

○ **In Europe** / i. Jun. 1968 / Delmark 409
Some brilliant moments and some uncertain, tentative sections on this late '60s work by tenor saxophonist Archie Shepp, recorded in Europe. He was working with the New York Contemporary Five, a brilliant band that didn't stay together long due to having absolutely no commercial future. The songs are played with fire and intensity. Besides Shepp, trumpeter Don Cherry and alto saxophonist John Tchicai are outstanding. This was reissued in '90 on cassette. —*Ron Wynn*

Yasmina: A Black Woman / Aug. 12, 1969 / Affinity 771

Blase / Aug. 16, 1969 / Charly 77

○ **Three for a Quarter: One for a Dime** / i. Sep. 1969 / Impulse 9162

○ **Live at the Pan-African Festival** / i. 196? / Affinity
Tenor and soprano saxophonist Archie Shepp probably led more BYG recordings than anyone else. The first of his BYGs has been reissued as *Live at the Pan-African Festival*. The Pan-African Festival in Algiers served as a great realization of art and culture for many of the participants, and on this recording we hear Shepp, Clifford Thornton, and Grachan Moncur III in an impromptu jam ("Brotherhood at Ketcha")

with various native Algerian percussionists and "horn" men. The other piece on the record, recorded 7/30/69 (a day later) in formal concert, is "We Have Come Back." The title is taken from a Ted Joans poem, which serves to open the piece that has Clifford Thornton, Dave Burrell, Alan Silva, and Sunny Murray along with some Algerian and Tuareg musicians joining Shepp. Shepp was recording during this period for Impulse in the States, but nothing ever reached the raw excitement, inspiration, and nakedness of statement that his BYG recordings managed. This is not to say that the BYGs are perfect; they are far from it, but they capture the jazz—free jazz if you will—mood of the time like few other recordings. Any study of Shepp makes listening to all of his BYG recordings essential. —*Bob Rusch,* Cadence

Attica Blues / **i.** Jan. 24-26, 1972 / Impulse

○ **Kwanza** / **i.** 1974 / Impulse 9262
This album shows once again why tenor saxophonist Archie Shepp deserves to be regarded as one of the leaders of the avant-garde. The beat on all these compositions is distinctively and repetitively enunciated in a manner that is often rocklike. In fact, until Shepp solos you'd swear you were listening to yet another anonymous jazz-rock band. Despite the dangers inherent in heavy and repetitious beat enunciation, Shepp and his partners make that element a *constituent* part of the compositions. And their solos as well as the ensemble section are as "out" as if they were played on top of beats only arbitrarily insinuated. Shepp's solos are always recognizably Shepp: the guttural, raspy vocal tone; yelps in the middle of a scale; melodic all the time. "Vocal" or songlike, in fact, best typifies not only Shepp's solo style but also his loosely structured compositions. Like songs, they are concrete and melodic. *Kwanza* shows too a variety uncommon in avant-garde enterprises. There are changes of pace, instrumentation, and mood that make this a thoughtful as well as expressive album. —*Gordon Kopulous,* Down Beat

There's a Trumpet in My Soul / Apr. 12, 1975 / Freedom 741016

Montreux—Vols. 1 and 2 / Jul. 18, 1975 / Arista

Sea of Faces, A / Jul. 18, 1975 / Black Saint 0002

Steam / May 14, 1976 / Enja

★ **Goin' Home** / Apr. 25, 1977 / Steeple Chase
Tenor and soprano saxophonist Archie Shepp and pianist Horace Parlan recorded this selection of traditional spirituals in a reverential yet contemporary context. The repertoire is a familiar one, as familiar as "Swing Low, Sweet Chariot" and "Go Down Moses," but Archie Shepp does his best to kindle the spark of spontaneity, even in the hoariest classics. Shepp's burred and husky intonation here frequently suggests Ben Webster, but as always he returns to the sound of his principal mentor, John Coltrane, particularly in his soprano work on such pieces as "My Lord What a Morning" and "Sometimes I Feel Like a Motherless Child," where his singing radiance reflects Trane's own debt to the spiritual. Parlan's wonderfully spare and dignified accompaniment serves to leaven Shepp's more fanciful excursions with a genuinely churchy sensibility, but on the whole this is less a devotional album than a jazzman's homage to the gospel tradition. —*Larry Birnbaum,* Down Beat

Ballads for Trane / May 7, 1977 / Denon 8570

On Green Dolphin Street / Nov. 28, 1977 / Denon 7262

Duet with Dollar Brand / Jun. 5, 1978 / Denon 7008

Duo Reunion / **i.** 1979 / L & R Music 5003
With Horace Parlan. One of the better, more moving sax/piano duos of the '70s reunites effectively. —*Ron Wynn*

☆ **Attica Big Band** / **i.** 1979 / Inner City 1001

☆ **Trouble in Mind** / Feb. 6, 1980 / Steeple Chase 31139
It seems to me that neither Archie Shepp (ts, ss) nor pianist Horace Parlan is completely comfortable with the material for this session in the sense that both are very conscious of various classic performances and find it difficult to find their

own individual expression. Nevertheless, I would agree with Spencer Weston's summation that both "retain the feeling and the rich melody along with the pathos and hope which is the unique quality of this musical source." —*Shirley Klett,* Cadence

Looking at Bird / Feb. 7, 1980 / Steeple Chase 31149

Soul Song / Dec. 1, 1982 / Enja 4050
With Ken Werner (p), Santi Di Briano (b), and Smitty Smith (d). Powerful statement. —*Michael G. Nastos*

Down Home New York / Feb. 5-8, 1984 / Soul Note 1102

Splashes (Tribute to Wilbur Little) / May 1987 / L & R Music 5005
Bluesy, aggressive, typically expressive. With Horace Parlan (p), Harry Emmery (b), and Clifford Jarvis (d). —*Ron Wynn*

BOBBY SHEW (Robert Joratz)

b. Mar. 4, 1941, Albuquerque, NM
Trumpet / Swing, big band, progressive big band
A fine technical trumpeter, Bobby Shew works well in brass sections and in big bands. As a soloist, his soft tone and striking, but derivative style don't always result in memorable statements. But he's a highly competent player, with good facility and command of the horn. Shew began working professionally at age 13 at dances in New Mexico. He played in bands during his years in the service, then joined the Tommy Dorsey Orchestra under Sam Donahue in the mid-'60s. Later came stints with Woody Herman and Buddy Rich. Shew was Rich's lead trumpeter during one stretch. During the '60s and '70s, he worked in Las Vegas for nine years backing singers, playing in show bands, and playing on film and television shows. Shew moved to Los Angeles in the '70s, and divided his time between studio work and jazz dates. He played with the Akiyoshi-Tabackin big band in the late '70s, and worked in bands led by Don Menza, Frank Capp, Nat Pierce, and Louis Bellson. Shew moved from big bands to small combos in the '80s, recording and performing, heading a quintet, and playing in bands led by Art Pepper and Bud Shank. He's done workshops nationally and internationally. Shew's recorded for Delos, Pausa, and Inner City. He has some dates available on CD. —*Ron Wynn and Michael G. Nastos*

★ **'Round Midnight** / **i.** Dec. 17-19, 1984 / Mo Pro 111
All standards, all vital, from this trumpeter and the Steve Schmidt Trio. —*Michael G. Nastos*

○ **Shewhorn** / PA/USA 7198

SAHIB SHIHAB (Edmund Gregory)

b. Jun. 23, 1925, Savannah, GA
Alto, baritone, and soprano saxophone, flute / Bop
A compelling baritone saxophonist and an above-average alto saxophonist who's added soprano and flute in recent years, Sahib has a sturdy tone, great range, and facility in the upper and lower register, and plays with warmth, flair, and conviction at any tempo. Sahib, then known as Edmund Gregory, gained his earliest experience in territory bands. He journeyed to Boston in 1941 from Georgia for music studies. Shihab toured with Fletcher Henderson in the mid-'40s playing alto, then joined Roy Eldridge's big band in 1946. He moved to New York in 1947, and worked with Art Blakey, Thelonious Monk, and Tadd Dameron for the remainder of the '40s and into the early '50s. He joined Dizzy Gillespie in 1953 playing baritone. Shihab played with Illinois Jacquet in the '50s, with Oscar Pettiford's big band, accompanied Dakota Staton, and played in Quincy Jones's orchestra. He also led his own group. Shihab also became famous for his playing on several Thelonious Monk Blue Note sessions. He settled in Europe after a Jones tour in 1959 and 1960, and remained there 12 years. Shihab was a regular member of the Clarke-Boland big band from 1961 to 1972. Currently, there are only a couple of Shihab sessions available on CD. —*Ron Wynn*

★ **All Star Sextets** / Jul. 11-Sep. 7, 1957 / Savoy 2245

This excellent reissue spotlights great groups Sahib worked with in the late '50s. Phil Woods (as), Bill Evans (p), others on hand. —*Ron Wynn*

Summer Dawn / **i.** May 8-9, 1964 / Chess 91563

Sentiments / Mar. 1971 / Storyville

BOBBY SHORT

b. Sep. 15, 1926

Vocals, piano / Ballads & blues

Vocalist and pianist Bobby Short is a one-of-a-kind entertainer, and is, perhaps, the finest male cabaret vocalist and performer around. With his mother's permission, Short left home at age 11 to perform in Chicago. He has made singing the material of Cole Porter, Rodgers and Hart, and other classic composers of the pre-rock era a genuine art form. His diction, delivery, performance style, personality, and act charm even those who are usually bored to tears by the stiff, proper cabaret environment and attitudes. In the '40s, he worked the Midwest circuit, where he met Nat "King" Cole and Art Tatum, as well as prime influences Hildegarde and Mabel Mercer. He survived a slump in the club business during the mid-'60s, then, on a recommendation from the Erteguns at Atlantic, Short replaced pianist George Feyer at the Cafe Carlyle in 1968 and has become an institution there, working eight months a year. His finest, highly stylized releases for Atlantic are now all available on CD reissues, including a wonderful pairing with Mabel Mercer. —*Ron Wynn*

○ **Bobby Short** / Sep. 15-16, 1955 / Atlantic 1230

○ **Bobby Short Loves Cole Porter** / **i.** 1971 / Atlantic 606
An album in which one of the great cabaret singers tackles a ready-made menu. —*Ron Wynn*

○ **Bobby Short Is K-RA-ZY for Gershwin** / 1973 / Atlantic 608
On these two albums (discs) Bobby Short gives us 35 Gershwin tunes in one form or another. They range from "I Was So Young (You Were So Beautiful)" from the 1919 musical *Good Morning Judge*, to several selections from the score of the film *Goldwyn Follies*, including the final "Love Walked In." No attempt is made at chronology. Songs are just programmed however the performer thinks they fit. There are even a few songs that never did get into the film for which they were intended ("Hi-Ho") or were dropped from a show before it hit Broadway ("Feeling Sentimental"). —*Joe Klee*, Down Beat

★ **Celebrates Rodgers & Hart** / **i.** Oct. 1975 / Atlantic 610

Guess Who's in Town, the Songs of Andy Razaf / **i.** 1988 / Atlantic 81778
Release in which Short interprets Andy Razaf's lyrics. Outstanding arrangements and vocals. —*Ron Wynn*

Bobby, Noel & Cole (Loves Cole Porter/ Is Mad About Noel Coward) / **i.** May 16, 1990 / Atlantic 82062
Great pairing of material from a pair of two-record sets devoted to Noel Coward and Cole Porter. Brilliant performances. —*Ron Wynn*

★ **50 by Bobby Short** / Atlantic 81715
The premier collection from a giant of cabaret music. For those who'd like one comprehensive batch of his music. —*Ron Wynn*

WAYNE SHORTER

b. Aug. 25, 1933, Newark, NJ

Tenor and soprano saxophone, composer / Bop

It's possible to measure the tenure of some who follow jazz and popular music by how they recognize Wayne Shorter. There are many who remember him only as the soprano saxophonist in Miles Davis's jazz-rock bands, and as co-leader of Weather Report. Those with longer memories harken back to his days as a Young Lion on Vee Jay and with Art Blakey. On tenor and soprano sax, Shorter has perfected the same evolving, eclectic approach as his longtime friend and musical comrade Herbie Hancock has perfected on pi-

ano. Shorter's combined hard bop and modal elements in his solos, and plays with an intense and original style that includes a biting, terse attack and soulfulness. His soprano has one of the most elastic, wondrous tones ever; its beauty and lyricism is unparalleled. Since 1969, Shorter has been better known for soprano than tenor, and, during the Weather Report era, played it about twice as often as he did tenor. He's also an excellent composer who was once Blakey's music director and provided compositions to Miles Davis such as "E.S.P.," "Pinocchio," "Nefertiti," and "Sanctuary." His writing was altered and simplified for Weather Report, and consisted mainly of lyrical melodies and heavily syncopated funk backbeats.

Shorter began playing clarinet at age 16, then switched to tenor sax. He studied music at New York University in the '50s, and graduated in 1956. After working in a local band, Shorter joined Horace Silver for a short time before being drafted. After his discharge, he joined Maynard Ferguson in 1958, and met Joe Zawinul while in this group. Shorter began working with Art Blakey in 1959, and was in the Messengers until 1963. He made his recording debut as a leader on Vee Jay, and made several recordings for Blue Note in the mid '60s, working with many top musicians, including his latter-day Miles Davis comrades, as well as Freddie Hubbard, James Spaulding, and others. Shorter joined Davis's band in 1964, finally filling the seat and vacuum left after John Coltrane's departure. He stayed with the band until 1970, playing in two critical eras: the looser, freer work of the mid '60s and the jazz-rock of the late '60s and early '70s, during which time Shorter began playing soprano. He recorded in the late '60s and '70s with Davis's comrade John McLaughlin, and with Sonny Sharrock, Miroslav Vitous, and others like Chick Corea and Jack DeJohnette who had also played jazz-rock with Davis.

Shorter experimented with Latin and rock on Blue Note albums such as *Super Nova* and *Odyssey of Iska*. Shorter and Zawinul cofounded Weather Report in 1970, and continued with the group until 1985. The band began as a jazz-rock group, but gradually enjoyed so much success as a funk/rock/fusion outfit that they grew stagnant churning out albums filled with conservative, trendy material and less open-ended, aggressive playing. Outside of working with Weather Report, Shorter was relatively inactive in the '70s, but recorded a Brazilian album (*Native Dancer*) with Milton Nascimento early in the decade that made the *Billboard* charts. He toured with Hancock and other Davis alumni on the VSOP acoustic jazz tour in the late '70s, and also recorded for Columbia. Shorter did sessions with Joni Mitchell and Steely Dan.

Shorter and Zawinul disbanded Weather Report in 1985. Shorter started a new group in 1986, but overloaded it with electronics and generic compositions and arrangements. The results were poorly received albums such as *Atlantis* and *Phantom Navigator*, although the band's tours were more successful in eliciting audience response and reaction. Shorter presented a promising discovery in his group, drummer Terri Lyne Carrington. She parlayed the exposure into a contract with talk show host Arsenio Hall's first "posse," and into her own album deal. Shorter performed in the film *'Round Midnight* in 1986, and played on the *Power of Three* album with Michel Petrucciani and Jim Hall. He co-led a Latin jazz-rock group with Carlos Santana in 1988, and toured internationally with them. His '88 Columbia album, *Joy Ryder*, didn't recapture past glories. But Wayne Shorter's list of achievements are so long that fans anxiously anticipate new developments from him in the '90s. There's a fair amount of Shorter sessions available on CD. In 1993, Mosaic issued a wonderful six-disc boxed set that features the complete Blue Note recordings of the 1960 Art Blakey Jazz Messengers with Shorter. —*Ron Wynn*

☆ **Blues á la Carte** / **i.** Nov. 10, 1959 / Affinity

Wayning Moments / **i.** 1960 / Vee-Jay 900
Wayne Shorter's second Vee Jay date is as explosive and invigorating as his debut; he and trumpeter Freddie Hubbard

were then Young Lions building their reputations and playing every cut with abandon and fire. This session reminds us that the young Wayne Shorter was tabbed the up-and-coming tenorman in jazz circles, and that he could wail and handle driving hard bop with as much skill and ease as he later did playing jazz-rock solos for Miles Davis or fitting into the electronic jungle of Weather Report. The 15-cut package includes plenty of alternate takes and bonus cuts. —*Ron Wynn*

Second Genesis / **i.** Oct. 11, 1960 / Vee Jay 2014

★ **Some Other Stuff** / Jul. 6, 1964 / Blue Note 84177
Red-hot dates, with Moncur and Wayne Shorter (sax) swapping licks and keying the session. —*Ron Wynn*

○ **JuJu** / Aug. 3, 1964 / Blue Note 46514
His best single album composition. The playing is extraordinary. With McCoy Tyner (p). —*Michael G. Nastos*

Night Dreamer / Aug. 3, 1964 / Blue Note 84173
1988 reissue of prime '60s lineup: Lee Morgan (tpt), McCoy Tyner (p), Reggie Workman (b), and Elvin Jones (d). —*Ron Wynn*

☆ **Speak No Evil** / Dec. 24, 1964 / Blue Note 46509

○ **Best of Wayne Shorter** / 1964-1967 / Blue Note 91141
A very well done compilation. Good for beginners and aficionados. —*Michael G. Nastos*

☆ **Etcetera** / **i.** Jun. 4, 1965 / Blue Note 1056
As with so many of these Blue Note discoveries, the question naturally arises: Why wasn't this music issued soon after it was recorded in 1964? No doubt the answer lies in Wayne Shorter's prolificacy back then, for he led one fine recording session after another and, particularly in Grachan Moncur III's *Some Other Stuff* (recorded soon after *Etcetera*), tested again the limits of his mastery.

Here these musicians experience twofold triumph. First, this postbop rhythm section's (pianist Herbie Hancock, bassist Cecil McBee, drummer Joe Chambers) self-discovery; as they join Shorter in ensemble creation, they assert their independence from traditional solo-accompaniment relationships—at a time when their "outside" peers were seeking parallel freedom. Second, Shorter's improvising, for while the conflicts in style are not resolved, they are reconciled in a program that is unique for the sustained depth and sensitivity of his tenor saxophone solos. Crucially, this is an ensemble performance; these tenor solos would be inconceivable without the incisive participation of the rhythm section. True, bassist Cecil McBee's part is secondary, laying out for much of *Etcetera*, supplying vamps for the last two tracks. Herbie Hancock's solos, particularly in "Barracudas" and "Etcetera," are created with a fine intelligence, with a nervous harmonic movement to complement Shorter's rhythmic intensity. Joe Chambers's fierce performance—the power of Art Blakey and the explosiveness of Tony Williams—is inspiring throughout; he is the most essential man of this unit. —*John Litweiler*, Down Beat

★ **Adam's Apple** / Feb. 24, 1966 / Blue Note 46403
This is a galloping romp, one of Shorter's best '60s dates. Great record. —*Ron Wynn*

Schizophrenia / Mar. 20, 1967 / Blue Note

Super Nova / Aug. 29+Sep. 2, 1969 / Blue Note 84332
1988 reissue of careening, eventful date; has Chick Corea (k), John McLaughlin (g), Jack DeJohnette (d). —*Ron Wynn*

Moto Grosso Feio / Aug. 26, 1970 / Blue Note

☆ **Odyssey of Iska** / Aug. 26, 1970 / Blue Note 84363
An album that is alternately daring and sentimental. Wonderful soprano solos. —*Ron Wynn*

★ **Native Dancer** / Dec. 1974 / Columbia 46159

Joy Ryder / **i.** 1988 / Columbia 44110

Wayne Shorter / GNP 2-2075

ALAN SILVA

b. 1939
Bass, cello / Early free, modern creative

A consistently strong accompanist and bassist, Alan Silva played on several recordings during the '60s and '70s, and worked with many top groups and players. He's a strong soloist, particularly with the bow, and is an assertive stylist. Silva studied piano and violin in his youth, and later attended the New York College of Music. He began playing bass in the early '60s. Silva teamed with Burton Greene in the Free Form Improvisation Ensemble, and participated in the October Revolution in Jazz concert series. He played with Cecil Taylor, Sun Ra, Albert Ayler, Sunny Murray, and Archie Shepp in the late '60s and early '70s before settling in Europe. Silva formed the Celestrial Communication Orchestra, a group with rotating personnel, and also played with Frank Wright, Bobby Few, and Muhammad Ali (drums). He lived and worked in both Paris and New York during the '70s and '80s, and played and recorded with Taylor, Bill Dixon, Andrew Hill, and the Globe Unity Orchestra. He recorded as a leader for BYG and Sun. Silva doesn't have any sessions available as a leader, but can be heard on Taylor and Ayler CD reissues. —*Ron Wynn*

★ **Seasons** / Dec. 29, 1970 / BYG 529342

Solos, Duets / **i.** 1975 / Sun 3

HORACE SILVER (Horace Ward Martin Tavares Silver)

b. Sep. 2, 1928, Norwalk, CT
Piano, bandleader, composer / Hard bop
The leading hard bop composer and pioneer, Horace Silver's piano solos have been a jazz force since the early '50s. He blended vintage R&B, bebop, gospel, blues, and Caribbean elements into jazz in an inspired manner, writing and playing works that were rhythmically and melodically simple, yet gripping and compelling. His work has harmonic sophistication, but seldom loses its earthiness and grit. He's been among the rare jazz musicians who've composed the bulk of their material. Silver's written equally well for combos and vocalists, and has even, on many occasions, provided lyrics to accompany his instrumental pieces. Silver was a founding member of the original Jazz Messengers, and his ensembles have helped introduce and/or nurture quite a few careers as well, including the careers of Donald Byrd, Art Farmer, Woody Shaw, Tom Harrell, the Brecker Brothers, and Blue Mitchell.

Silver began studying saxophone and piano in high school; he listened often to the blues and to boogie-woogie. He later mixed those genres with the Cape Verdean folk music he'd heard as a child. Silver worked in 1950 on a date with Stan Getz, who'd come to make a guest appearance in Hartford. Getz tabbed Silver to work with him, and Silver stayed for a year. Getz cut three of Silver's compositions: "Penny," "Potter's Luck," and "Split Kick." Silver moved to New York the next year, where he worked with Coleman Hawkins, Lester Young, Oscar Pettiford, and with Art Blakey. He recorded with Lou Donaldson for Blue Note in 1954, and subsequently cut his own trio sessions for the label shortly afterwards, working with bassists Gene Ramey, Percy Heath or Curley Russell, and Blakey on drums. This began an association with Blue Note that lasted nearly 30 years. From 1953 to 1955, Silver was coleader of a band with Blakey known as the Jazz Messengers. When Silver departed in 1956, Blakey took over the leadership role.

Silver's groups became quite popular in the '50s and '60s. Numbers such as "The Preacher," "Doodlin'," "Sister Sadie," and "Song for My Father" became jazz classics, and Silver's albums often crossed over to R&B, soul, and blues audiences. Ray Charles covered "Doodlin'," and Silver band members Mitchell, Joe Henderson, Kenny Dorham, Clifford Jordan, and Hank Mobley went on to lead their own bands. Silver's forays into hard bop, soul-jazz, and funk made Blue Note both an artistic and commercial juggernaut. "Song for My Father" and "Cape Verdean Blues" both charted in the mid-'60s. Silver began to experiment with concept albums in the '70s, and made a trilogy he called "The United States of Mind." The jazz content of some of this was minimal, but Silver experimented with strings, African and Indian percussion, and multiple vocalists. Silver left Blue Note at the end of the '70s, formed his own label, and issued recordings he called "Holistic Metaphysical Music." Much of Silver's late '70s and early '80s material was in a quasi-religious bent, but he also established Emerald, a subsidiary of Silveto, and issued vintage dates like *Horace Silver-Live 1964*, which had unreleased versions of "Senor Blues" and "Filthy McNasty." A new Silver album was released in 1993 by Columbia, *It's Got to Be Funky*. There's plenty of classic Silver sessions available on CD. —*Ron Wynn*

Horace Silver Trio—Vol. 1: Spotlight on Drums / Oct. 23, 1952 / Capitol 81520

Most Silver albums are with a mid-'60s combo (quintet, etc.). It is refreshing and clarifying to listen to his trio work. Includes the classic "Opus De Funk." —*Michael Erlewine*

Horace Silver Trio—Vol. 2: Spotlight on Drums / Oct. 23, 1952 / Blue Note 5034

★ **Best of Horace Silver—Vol. 1** / 1953-1959 / Blue Note 91143

The Blue Note Years Vol. 1 & 2. Excellent compilation on CD. Two volumes. —*Michael G. Nastos*

○ **Horace Silver and the Jazz Messengers** / Nov. 13, 1954 / Capitol 46140

Horace Silver and the Jazz Messengers contains a lot of memorable music. Some of the melodies here have been overdone ("Doodlin'," "The Preacher"), while some others ("Room 608," Hank Mobley's "Hippy") deserve wider exposure. Yet this tight-knit quintet of stars sounds *so* good on almost everything! Kenny Dorham (tpt), Hank Mobley (ts), Horace Silver (p), and Doug Watkins (b) all benefit substantially from the association. It's rather curious that Art Blakey (d) barely acknowledged this band and probably didn't play any of these tunes for 25 (or more) years. It's not to be missed. —*Bob Porter, Jazz Times*

Silver's Blue / Jul. 2, 1956-Jul. 19, 1956 / Epic 5106

One of Silver's most obscure sessions, this set of mostly new boppish tunes with attractive chord changes features his quintet in its initial recording. This early quintet is heard in the process of forming its own identity, while the leader's piano is already quite distinctive. —*Scott Yanow, Cadence*

★ **Six Pieces of Silver** / Nov. 10, 1956 / Blue Note 81539

Quintet. Hard bop, gospel-tinged jazz gem. 1988 reissue; CD has three bonus cuts. —*Ron Wynn*

○ **Sterling Silver** / Nov. 10, 1956-Jan. 28, 1964 / Blue Note 945

Sterling Silver is a classic compilation of previously unissued (at least on LP) material from the period 1956 through 1964, selected by Horace Silver himself. Featuring mainly the Blue Mitchell/Junior Cook/Gene Taylor/Roy Brooks quintet, the album spotlights Silver on piano, demonstrating again that feeling and taste need not take a back seat to technical bravura. Silver's breezy pianistics shine on Musa Kaleem's "Sanctimonious Sam," as his right hand paints deceptively simple gospel figures over the peerlessly swinging punctuation of his left. Silver's own standard "Que Pasa" is heard in a brilliant unreleased trio version; Silver makes every note count in a shimmering blue texture that floats over the Afro-throb of a characteristic one-chord Latin vamp. "Sighin' and Cryin'" is another gorgeous original, again sans horns solos, with Silver displaying the effortless, soul-strutting elegance that makes his work so timelessly contemporary. Don Newey's "How Did it Happen" demonstrates Silver's masterfully rhythmic comping abilities, but the inclusion of a shortened alternative take of the classic "*Señor Blues*" from 1956 is the real treat of the album. Originally released on a 45, it features Silver and drummer Louis Hayes along with original Jazz Messengers' tenor saxophonist Hank Mobley, trumpeter Donald Byrd, and bassist Doug Watkins in an unforgettable rendition of the Caribbean-inflected gem whose vibrant sonorities have echoed down through endless jazz and pop variations to this day. —*Larry Birnbaum*, Down Beat

Finger Poppin' with the Horace Silver Quintet / Feb. 1, 1959 / Blue Note 84008

With the Horace Silver Quintet. State-of-the-art late '50s Silver gospel, Caribbean-influenced jazz. —*Ron Wynn*

Blowin' the Blues Away / Aug. 10, 1959 / Blue Note 46526

Standout Silver jazz *cum* blues and gospel from late '50s, 1985 reissue. —*Ron Wynn*

Horace-Scope / Jul. 9, 1960 / Blue Note 84042

Quintet. 1990 reissue of another Silver masterpiece. Includes the famous piece "Nica's Dream." —*Ron Wynn*

Doin' the Thing (At the Village Gate) / May 19-20, 1961 / Blue Note 84076

Quintet. 1989 reissue of standard live set with Silver super, Blue Mitchell (tpt), Junior Cook (ts) in the groove. —*Ron Wynn*

★ **Song for My Father** / Oct. 26, 1963+Oct. 1964 / Blue Note 84185

Silver's most successful and popular album. Includes three additional tracks. Two sessions, two different bands. Aside from the famous title track, this includes the quintet and trio versions of "Que Pasa." Essential. —*Michael Erlewine*

Horace Silver Live—1964 / Jun. 6, 1964 / Emerald

Subsidiary label established to reissue selected dates leads off with very nice hard bop set. Joe Henderson (sax) solid. —*Ron Wynn*

★ **Cape Verdean Blues** / Oct. 1-22, 1965 / Blue Note 84220

Jody Grind, The / Nov. 2-23, 1966 / Blue Note 84250

☆ **Serenade to a Soul Sister** / Feb. 23+Apr. 29, 1968 / Blue Note 84277

This 1968 reissue is typical of the then-fashionable genre that Blue Note was churning out in those desperate, red ink days. Quite simply, there was just no way of competing with rock. Record companies, as always, had to either go with the flow or drop by the wayside. Horace Silver's record provides a good example of just what was happening then. There isn't a musician on either of the two dates represented here who wasn't a pure jazz player—at least when he or she first entered the field as a professional. But even getting on a so-called jazz record date in those years meant doing something that would, at the very least, pay the bills for the session! By jazz standards, this album is better than many that followed it, largely because the patterns had not yet become so formulaic as they would a few years hence. But to judge it fairly, one should not compare it to the far purer efforts of the '50s, when the exciting, turbulently creative pianist/composer had not yet been sobered by perusals of the debit columns. Actually, there is a lot of competent playing here by Stanley Turrentine (ts), Charles Tolliver (tpt), and the somewhat more modern Bennie Maupin (ts). But, frankly, I would have preferred hearing Silver and a rhythm team back up Clara Ward and her gospel singers. Now, that would have been a record! —*Jack Sohmer*, Jazz Times

That Healin' Feelin' / Apr. 8-Jun. 18, 1970 / Blue Note

☆ **In Pursuit of the 27th Man** / Oct. 6+Nov. 10, 1972 / Blue Note 054

Quintet. recording with the Brecker brothers (sax and tpt). Very good. —*Michael G. Nastos*

Silver 'n Brass / Jan. 10+17, 1975 / Blue Note

Silver 'n Wood / Nov. 7, 1975-Jan. 3, 1976 / Blue Note

Silver 'n Voices / Oct. 19+22, 1976 / Blue Note 7086

Followers of Horace Silver from the '50s aren't going to like this blowing quintet sharing time with voices singing poetic lyrics, but at least Horace has again assembled a good quintet. Horace's piano playing has changed somewhat from the "funky" days. —*Jerry Atkins, Cadence*

☆ **Silver 'n Percussion** / Nov. 12-30, 1977 / Blue Note 853

On this album pianist/composer Horace Silver mixes African and Native American chants with his own distinctive sound and style. It is a highly successful mix, coupling jazz, the American folk form, with the stylized folk traditions of tribal music. The voices establish theme and feeling for each piece, but it is the playing of tenor saxophonist Larry Schneider, trumpet and flugelhorn player Tom Harrell, Silver, bassist Ron Carter, and drummer Al Foster that is the dominant factor. This is music of exceptional quality and imagination, another variation on the Horace Silver style—straightahead, cooking, and occasionally funky. —*Herb Nolan,* Down Beat

Spiritualizing the Senses / i. Jan. 19, 1983 / Silveto

There's No Need to Struggle / i. Aug. 25-Sep. 1, 1983 / Silveto

OMER SIMEON (Omer Victor Simeon)

b. Jul. 21, 1902, New Orleans, LA, **d.** Sep. 17, 1959, New York, NY

Clarinet / New Orleans traditional

Omer Simeon was another early clarinetist skilled in lower-register solos, and was a warm, often delightful improviser in the traditional style. Simeon began to play clarinet when his family moved from New Orleans to Chicago in 1914. Lorenzo Tio, Jr. gave him lessons from 1918 to 1920. Simeon played briefly in his brother Al's band, then worked with Charlie Elgar's Creole Orchestra in Chicago and Milwaukee in the mid- and late '20s. Simeon recorded with Jelly Roll Morton in 1926, and was featured on "Black Bottom Stomp." Simeon joined King Oliver in 1927, touring with him in St. Louis and New York. He also worked with Luis Russell in New York, and recorded with Morton again in 1928. Simeon worked in Chicago with Erskine Tate in the late '20s and early '30s, then with Earl Hines in the early and mid-'30s, Horace Henderson in 1938, Walter Fuller in 1940, and Coleman Hawkins in 1941. Simeon became a member of Jimmie Lunceford's orchestra in 1942. Simeon also recorded with Kid Ory in 1944 and 1945 in Hollywood. After Lunceford's death, Simeon stayed with the Lunceford band until 1950, then worked in New York for the remainder of his life. Simeon played and recorded with Wilbur de Paris from 1951 until 1959. He made a few recordings, mostly for Brunswick as a leader. Simeon was featured on Victor, Crescent, and Atlantic working with Morton, Jimmie Noone, and de Paris, among others. He has one CD of vintage recordings available, though others can probably be obtained via imports. Simeon can also be heard on Morton reissues. —*Ron Wynn*

★ **Omer Simeon Trio with James P. Johnson** / i. 195? / Disc 748

SONNY SIMMONS (Huey Simmons)

b. Aug. 4, 1933, Sicily Island, LA

Alto sax / Early free, jazz-rock, modern creative, avant-garde

A solid saxophonist who made some interesting records in the late '60s, Simmons then seemed to disappear. His best date, *Burning Spirits,* has long since been deleted, but the equally good *Manhattan Egos* is now available on compact disc. For a time he was married to trumpeter Barbara Donald, and the two recorded together. —*Ron Wynn*

On the Watch / i. 1966 / ESP 1030

Staying on the Watch / i. 1966 / ESP 1030

★ **Manhattan Egos** / i. 1969 / Arhoolie

○ **Music from the Spheres** / i. 1969 / ESP 1043
Free jazz gem from this saxophonist with trumpeter Barbara Donald. —*Michael G. Nastos*

Rumasuma / i. Oct. 1970 / Contemporary 3623

Burning Spirits / i. Dec. 1971 / Contemporary 7625
A twofer with Barbara Donald (tpt), Cecil McBee (b), and Richard Davis (d). Simmons is also known as "Huey Simmons." —*Michael G. Nastos*

Backwoods Suite / i. Jan. 1982 / West Wind 2074

NINA SIMONE

b. Feb. 21, 1933

Vocals / Ballads & blues

An amazing performer and writer, Nina Simone's popularity endures even though her behavior could alienate her most faithful fan. Her parents were both involved in the Methodist Church. All seven of her brothers and sisters worked in the music industry; her youngest brother served as her manager at one time. Simone moved to Philadelphia at age 17, and eventually went to New York, where she attended Juilliard. Her late '50s debut on Bethlehem was a major event; its single, "My Baby Just Cares for Me," was an advertising staple for years. Simone has done every type of song feasible, from jazz to folk to gospel to blues to covers of Beatles and Broadway tunes. She left America in the late '60s, initially going to Barbados and Liberia, then to France and England. Her 1969 composition, "Young, Gifted & Black," is among the anthems of Black America. Many of her other albums are classics, while some of her protest work, especially "Mississippi Goddam," has earned her both plaudits and long stretches of limited employment opportunity. Unfortunately, Simone also has a long history of missed engagements, conflicts with promoters and fans, and periods of announced retirement. Her autobiography has just been released. —*Ron Wynn*

☆ **Nina Simone and Her Friends** / 1957 / Bethlehem 6041

☆ **Little Girl Blue** / 1957 / Bethlehem 6028

My Baby Just Cares for Me / i. 1959 / Happy Days 4374
Nina has a lot of fun with this live recording. Her charm and energy come through loud and clear on songs as lovesick as "Do What You Got to Do" and as unique as "You Took My Teeth." It also includes an audience-assisted version of the title cut and the rollicking "Pirate Jenny," as well as "Mississippi Goddam," "Four Women," "Sugar in My Bowl," and more. —*Ladyslipper*

○ **At the Village Gate** / i. 1961 / Roulette 95058

☆ **Best of Nina Simone, The** / i. 1962-1967 / PolyGram 22846
The Best of Nina Simone presents 10 tracks taken from the many recordings Simone did for Phillips in the '60s. As is often noted, Simone is a dynamic and powerful vocal interpreter who often brings her social consciousness directly into her artistry. Some of the material on this record would have been considered topical for the period when it was first issued. Twenty years later (1985) much of it retains the emotional power of its original time. Ignore the liner note hyperbole; this is, in fact, certainly some of the *best* of Simone. There's a universality to the emotion and text of this theatrical music—any doubts, just substitute the name "South Africa" for "Mississippi" in "...Goddamn." Too removed? Try your own locale. —*Bob Rusch,* Cadence

○ **Nina Simone at Carnegie Hall** / 1963 / Colpix 455

★ **Silk & Soul** / 1967 / RCA 3837
There is quite a variety with this program ranging from the gospel-flavored "I Wish I Knew How it Would Feel to be Free" to the ingenuous "Turning Point" to the rock-flavored "Some Say" to the straight pop of "The Look of Love." Not surprisingly, the weakest moments come when Simone sings rock and pop. She does not sound nearly as committed on those pieces as she does on "I Wish" or "Go to Hell." —*Carl Brauer,* Cadence

★ **High Priestess of Soul** / 1967 / Philips 600219

Here Comes the Sun / i. 1971 / RCA Victor 4536

Baltimore / i. 1978 / CTI
Includes an evocative rendition of the Randy Newman title composition. —*Ron Wynn*

ZOOT SIMS (John Haley Sims)

b. Oct. 29, 1925, Inglewood, CA, **d.** 1985, New York, NY

Tenor saxophone, bandleader / Cool

Zoot Sims was a tenor sax stylist who was associated with the cool era and whose sound had an exuberant, swinging energy and bluesy zeal, though it maintained a smooth, relaxed feel. Sims was particularly outstanding in a combo setting, though he could also soar in jam sessions, with a large orchestra, or when accompanying vocalists. Though inspired by Lester Young, Sims was far from a slavish imitator. Indeed, near the final portion of his career, Sims reverted back to playing in a Ben Webster mode rather than either a Lester Young or a bop-influenced approach.

Sims's family were vaudeville artists, and he began playing drums and clarinet as a child, then moved to tenor sax at age 13. He was a professional two years later, and began touring in dance bands. He played with Bobby Sherwood in the early '40s before joining Benny Goodman in 1943, beginning a prominent association that would remain into the '70s. Sims played at Cafe Society in New York during 1944 with Bill Harris, and recorded with the group under Joe Bushkin's leadership. Then he went to California, and performed with Big Sid Catlett. Following army service, Sims worked again with Goodman in 1946 and 1947, and with Gene Roland. Sims played in Woody Herman's big band from 1947 to 1949, and it was Roland's compositions for four saxes that led to the creation of the Four Brothers section. Sims played with Stan Getz, Jimmy Giuffre, and Herbie Steward. After leaving Herman, Sims spent a brief period with Buddy Rich, had another stint with Goodman in 1950, and had an even shorter stay with Chubby Jackson. He then worked with Elliot Lawrence in 1951. Sims debuted as a leader on Prestige in the early '50s, and played in Stan Kenton's group for a while in 1953. He toured Europe and played in Gerry Mulligan's bands from 1954 to 1956, and was later a soloist in Mulligan's Concert Band. Sims began a long-term musical collaboration with Al Cohn in the '50s; the two had a friendly, yet mildly combative relationship and made some marvelous twin sax recordings. They toured Scandinavia and Japan in the '70s.

Some sessions Sims did in a quintet with Bob Brookmeyer eventually found their way to five different labels. Sims recorded on United Artists, on Riverside, and on ABC-Paramount in the '50s. Sims visited England and Europe with Jazz at the Philharmonic in 1967 and 1975, and performed at the Grande Parade du Jazz in Nice with various ensembles. He also toured the Soviet Union with Goodman in the early '60s, and played with John Coltrane, Sonny Rollins, and Coleman Hawkins at a 1966 Titans of the Tenor concert in New York City. Sims began playing soprano sax in the '70s, and recorded an excellent Pablo album playing soprano exclusively. He remained busy in the '60s and '70s, recording for Pumpkin, Impulse, Sonet, Argo, RCA, Pacific Jazz, Colpix, Famous Door, Choice, Groove Merchant, Ahead, and Pablo. He continued into the mid '80s, mostly on Pablo. There's lots of Sims available, including many sessions that feature his groups, and others that match him with Cohn, Brookmeyer, Harry Edison, Jimmy Rowles, and Joe Pass. —*Ron Wynn and Dan Morgenstern*

★ **Brother in Swing** / Jun. 26, 1950 / Inner City 7005

This was a Jazz Legacy album in 1950, recorded by a quartet with Gerald Wiggins on piano, Pierre Michelot on bass, and Kenny Clarke on drums. A great rhythm section stokes the Sims fire. The album includes five Sims originals, some with alternate takes. It was recorded in Paris, and the liner notes by Herb Wong are very informative. —*Michael G. Nastos*

Quartets / Sep. 16, 1950 / Original Jazz Classics 242

○ **Zootcase** / Sep. 16, 1950+Jul. 16, 1954 / Prestige 24061

This is a set in which historical factors clearly outweigh aesthetic ones. It offers us the music of the first Prestige LP with liner notes (a modest historical advance indeed), chronological space in which to listen for tenor saxophonist Zoot Sims's development (1951-1954), East and West Coast settings, and two tunes described by Ira Gitler as bearing clearly heard evidence of the new freedom afforded soloists by the LP record. And of course early Zoot Sims. While not greatly exciting, these sessions do swing well throughout, and the variety of groups backing Sims (there are four) makes for some useful comparisons. —*Joel Ray, Cadence*

☆ **Zoot!** / Oct. 12, 1956 / Riverside 228

The arrangements of George Handy made their mark on *Zoot!*, a December (13/18) 1956 recording under the leadership of Zoot Sims and also nicely featuring the reaching trumpet work of Nick Travis. Unfortunately, here the arrangements tend to diminish and hold in check the essential *Zootness*, which Sims blew so well. In addition, the rhythm section (Handy, p; Wilbur Ware, b; Osie Johnson, d) seems a bit flat-footed and restrained. —*Bob Rusch, Cadence*

○ **Zoot Sims Plays Four Altos** / Jan. 11, 1957 / Paramount 198

Zoot Sims Plays Four Altos is not from the Impulse catalog but a multitracked ABC date of 1/11/57. The material here is all by George Handy and its construction is very similiar to another Handy-Sims collaboration of November 1956. To further confuse things, MCA put the liners, personnel, and dates to that record on this record. Both dates have Knobby Totah (b), while the '57 date has Handy (p) and Nick Stabulas (d) rounding out the quartet. The novelty to this date is the multitracking of Sims on four altos; the earlier date had him on tenors and baritone as well. Don't expect to hear the four Brothers; it sounds more like Supersax. This swings as one would expect from any Sims date, but in strictly musical terms I suspect everyone would agree, four heads would have been better than one. —*Bob Rusch, Cadence*

Happy Over There / i. 1957-1958 / Jass 12

1957-1958. Septet with Al Cohn on baritone sax, Jimmy Cleveland on trombone, and session leader Elliot Lawrence. All tunes are the music of Hoagy Carmichael. Cute album cover. Also with Milt Hinton (b), Osie Johnson (d). Arrangements by Bill Elton. —*Michael G. Nastos*

One to Blow On / i. 1958 / Biograph 12062

★ **Down Home** / Jul. 1960 / Bethlehem 6051

Zoot Sims's *Down Home*, recorded in 1960 with bassist George Tucker and drummer Dannie Richmond as well as pianist Dave McKenna, is widely considered to be one of his strongest efforts. He is in a jouncier swing of mind here than on the Booker Ervin *The Book Cooks* album, shaking the tail of his notes firmly but lovingly, and emoting hardest in his gossamer upper range, where he pushes his tone as close as one could get to brittle and still stay safe. Sims's style, honed in big-band congregations, was so predisposed and attuned to ensemble textures that he could convincingly manage a section-like warmth and breadth in a tight quartet setting. His springing legatos, not surprisingly, recall Lester Young, as do several of the selections here, including "Jive at Five" and "Dogging Around," from Count Basie's repertoire, and "I Cried for You," a Billie Holiday signature tune. The ubiquitous Richmond pushes and slugs the rhythm with his characterstic high quota of resiliency, McKenna's blues-voiced excursions are sentiently sparse and coy, and Tucker's bass is melodically robust and revelatory. —*Mikal Gilmore, Down Beat*

Live at Ronnie Scott's / Nov. 14-15, 1961 / Fontana 123

Zoot Sims and the Gershwin Brothers / Jun. 6, 1975 / Pablo 444

Marvelous Sims solos, great assistance from Oscar Peterson (p). Timeless Gershwin songs. —*Ron Wynn*

○ **Zoot Plays Soprano** / Jan. 8-9, 1976 / Pablo 770

A masterpiece, perhaps the best single record Zoot Sims made for Pablo. He'd never done a full record on soprano only, so the idea resulted in him really extending himself and exploring the instrument rather than just treating it as an alternative voice. His rhythm section, with pianist Ray Bryant, bassist George Mraz and drummer Grady Tate, responds as well. —*Ron Wynn*

○ **Hawthorne Nights** / Sep. 20-21, 1976 / Pablo 783

Tenor saxophonist Zoot Sims recorded almost constantly for the Pablo label in the '70s, the final phase of his career. This is a pleasant session with Sims heading a midsized band playing charts provided by Bill Holman. There aren't any fireworks, but Sims plays with his usual mix of blues and swing, and the backing band gives him enough support to keep things interesting. —*Ron Wynn*

If I'm Lucky / Oct. 27-28, 1977 / Pablo 683

For Lady Day / Apr. 1978 / Pablo 2310-942

★ **Just Friends** / Dec. 18+20, 1978 / Pablo 499

Passion Flower / Aug. 14+Dec. 11, 1979 / Pablo 120

I Wish I Were Twins / Jul. 6, 1981 / Pablo 868

Blues for Two / Mar. 6+Jun. 23, 1982 / Pablo 635

Quietly There—Zoot Sims Plays Johnny Mandel / Mar. 20-21, 1984 / Pablo 2310903

With the Mike Wofford Quartet. Easy-does-it program focusing on many great compositions of the legendary Johnny Mandel. For those special moments. *—Michael G. Nastos*

In a Sentimental Mood / Nov. 21, 1984 / Sonet

Best of Zoot Sims, The / Pablo 2405-406

Modern Art of Jazz, The / Fresh Sound

FRANK SINATRA (Francis Albert Sinatra)

b. Dec. 12, 1915, Hoboken, NJ
Vocals / Ballads & blues

A certified (some say he should have been certified years ago) American music legend, Francis Albert Sinatra represents the ultimate male romantic vocalist to many people. A huge argument starter, as the 20th century ends, is who's America's premier singer: Armstrong, Holiday, Sinatra, or Presley? Aside from the fact that several other singers could legitimately be named to this list, a serious case can be made for Sinatra. As a relaxed, yet swinging stylist, he was magnificent in his prime, and this quality has slipped more dramatically than anything else in his arsenal. Though he's not a good scatter or a great vocal improviser, Sinatra helped expand Crosby's breakthroughs with microphone singing, achieved a wide range of dynamics, and displayed a delivery and crystal-clear enunciation that projected any and every possible nuance or emotional shade in a lyric. Until age turned his act into a parody, Sinatra was among the most convincing singers ever; the sincerity he expressed frequently fooled people into thinking his offstage character was as innocent and good-natured as the onstage persona. Indeed, Sinatra's rocky personal life, which is not plagued with public drug incidents outside of alcohol, still makes many jazz and popular music bad boys (and girls) look like candidates for sainthood. Still, Sinatra's had enormous impact on prerock era vocalists, and has never hesitated to say how much Billie Holiday influenced his style.

Sinatra's parents were Italian immigrants. He quit school at age 16 to sing anywhere he could get an audience. He was in the Hoboken Four singing group when they won the Major Bowes Amateur Hour talent show on radio in 1935. This quartet toured with Bowes and had the dubious distinction of being caught on film performing as blackface minstrels. They sang from 1937 to 1939 at the Rustic Cabin roadhouse in New Jersey, with Sinatra doubling as head waiter. He started singing, sans fee, on a WNEW radio program "Dance Parade" in 1939. Harry James was starting a band after leaving Benny Goodman and quickly contacted Sinatra. A song that Sinatra recorded with James in the summer of '39, "All or Nothing at All," sold 8,000 copies when initially issued with Sinatra uncredited; it topped the charts when Columbia reissued it in 1943. On the recommendation of a Columbia executive, Tommy Dorsey went to hear Sinatra sing. James let Sinatra leave to join Dorsey and Sinatra's ascension to icon status began.

He recorded with Dorsey in 1940 backed by a vocal quartet with Jo Stafford and Connie Hines called the Pied Pipers. Sinatra made his first film appearance in 1940 with the band; *Las Vegas Nights* didn't win anyone any Oscars, but Sinatra soon became a commercial juggernaut. "I'll Never Smile Again," "Delores," "There are Such Things," and "In the Blue of the Evening" all topped the charts between 1940 and 1943. Sinatra bought out his contract with Dorsey in 1942. He appeared for a month at the Paramount Theatre in 1942 with Benny Goodman, and the screams and yells from girls (it was rumored that some were paid for their trouble)

are considered the beginning of modern pop idolatry and/or groupies. A Sinatra return engagement in 1944 resulted in 25,000 teenagers blocking the streets. He cut his first solo dates for Columbia in 1943, and had 86 hit records for them from 1943 1952, 33 in the Top 10.

Sinatra began to appear frequently in films, and in gossip columns, after he left his wife, Nancy, to marry actress Ava Gardner in 1951. He was even targeted for accusations of communism. His support for Franklin D. Roosevelt and his winning a special Oscar in 1946 for his efforts on behalf of religious and racial tolerance established Sinatra's reputation as a liberal, progressive-minded individual (at least in public). He held this reputation well into the '60s, before switching allegiances to the Republican party.

Sinatra rebounded from a slump in the mid-'50s, winning an Oscar for his film role in *From Here to Eternity* in 1954. He cut several tremendous records for Capitol with arrangers like Billy May and Nelson Riddle. He was remarketed successfully as a seasoned vocalist who sang adult love songs for older audiences. He made 13 enormously profitable albums for Capitol from 1954 to 1961. Some, like *Songs for Swingin' Lovers* in 1956, used creative big-band arrangements and support; others, such as *In the Wee Small Hours* in 1955, featured him doing songs around a singular concept or developing themes and moods with related tunes throughout an album. Sinatra reaffirmed his jazz credentials in the '60s, with albums that had arrangements from Don Costa and Neal Hefti, collaborations with Count Basie, and albums that featured Quincy Jones arrangements. He even tackled the bossa nova. But decline and exhaustion began to set in, and there were unfortunate flirtations with dubious material like Rod McKuen poetry. Sinatra did land another number-one hit in 1966, "Strangers in the Night," but the '60s established that he needed the right material, producers, and arrangers. He could no longer survive just by being Sinatra, at least not in the creative arena. The '70s would clearly prove that.

He retired for a while, but the '73 comeback album, *Ol' Blue Eyes is Back*, reached the number 15 spot on the charts. He remained in the Top 40 with the next album, *Sinatra: The Main Event*, even though the two-record set was littered with painful material. Sinatra returned to the charts in 1980 with *Trilogy: Past, Present, Future*, thanks to arrangements from May, Riddle, and others. Jones arranged and released "L.A. is My Lady" on his own album in 1984.

Sinatra kept touring and performing into the '90s and issued an album of duets in the fall of '93 featuring collaborations with U2's Bono, Tony Bennett, and Aretha Franklin, among others. It also topped the charts and closed out 1993 among the Top 10 best-selling pop releases. The list of horrendous Sinatra marriages, ugly affairs, hotel and nightclub incidents, rumors of reprisals against club owners, performers, critics, and managers, and supposed gangster links, filled several magazines long before Kitty Kelley's infamous biography. But none of that deserves equal billing with Frank Sinatra's achievements. Even if you feel some Sinatra boosters think he invented music, there's no denying he earned his spurs many years ago. *—Ron Wynn and John Floyd*

★ **Voice—the Columbia Years (1943-1952), The** / 1943-1952 / Columbia 40343

An exhaustive six-disc presentation of his formative years, divided into six themes: saloon songs, standards, screen, love songs, swing, and stage. It might be too much for skeptical novices, but this is a marvelous set. *—John Floyd*

☆ **Songs for Young Lovers/Swing Easy** / i. 1955 / Capitol 48470

This brings together Sinatra's first two 10-inch releases for Capitol, with zesty arrangements by Nelson Riddle and a newfound bounce and confidence in Sinatra's vocals. *—John Floyd*

☆ **In the Wee Small Hours** / i. 1955 / Capitol 96826

His first full-blown concept album (from 1955) is a gut-wrenching collection of maudlin ballads, including definitive readings of "I'll Be Around," "Ill Wind," and "Dancing on the Ceiling," with Nelson Riddle's most beautiful soundscapes. —*John Floyd*

★ **Songs for Swingin' Lovers! / i.** 1956 / Capitol 46570
The title says it all. Soaring big-band arrangements and the best set of songs Sinatra's ever had make this release the best introduction to Sinatra's swinging world. —*John Floyd*

○ **Frank Sinatra Story in Music, The / i.** 1958 / Sony 20709
A stunning two-disc collection of Sinatra's early years. His nickname at the time was "The Voice," and you can hear why: if you could "hear" velvet, it would sound like Sinatra's vocals on "I Concentrate on You" and "I've Got a Crush on You." —*John Floyd*

○ **Come Fly with Me / i.** 1958 / Capitol 48469
Sinatra's persona as a wanderlust romantic was introduced on this Billy May-arranged set of travel-oriented swingers and crooners that charts our hero all over the globe in his quest for perfect love. —*John Floyd*

○ **Come Dance with Me! / i.** 1959 / Capitol 48468
A bright, splashy set of hard-thumping dance-floor invitations. Sinatra's voice is showing signs of wear, but Billy May's arrangements make them easy to ignore. —*John Floyd*

○ **It Might As Well Be Swing / i.** Dec. 1964 / Reprise 1012

○ **September of My Years / i.** 1965 / Reprise 1014
After four years of duds on his own label, Sinatra and Gordon Jenkins bounced back with a set that examines the meaning of life, confronting both the ghosts of the past and the spectre of old age. —*John Floyd*

Sinatra at the Sands / i. 1966 / Reprise 1019

Sinatra Rarities—the Columbia Years / i. 1988 / Columbia 44236
Don't let the title fool you; this batch of overlooked material (which includes a breathtaking version of "Why Shouldn't I?") is all grade-A Sinatra. —*John Floyd*

★ **Capitol Years / i.** 1990 / Capitol 94777
A well-selected three-disc set that contains the high marks of his Capitol era, but you really should hear them in their original contexts. —*John Floyd*

★ **Reprise Collection, The / i.** 1990 / Reprise 26340
A lavishly packaged four-disc hodgepodge of later years. For fanatics it's essential, but it unintentionally documents the demise of Sinatra's talents. —*John Floyd*

Capitol Collectors Series / i. 1990 / Capitol 92160
Rounding up the best material from otherwise mediocre albums like *This is Sinatra, Nice and Easy,* and *All the Way.* —*John Floyd*

○ **Sinatra Reprise—The Very Good Years / i.** Mar. 26, 1991 / Warner Brothers 26501
This contains the worthwhile material from *The Reprise Collection* in a less cumbersome single-disc package. A necessary addition to your Sinatra collection. —*John Floyd*

○ **Come Fly with Me (Cema) /** CEMA 9190

HAL SINGER (Harold Singer)

b. Oct. 8, 1919, Tulsa, OK
Tenor saxophone, bandleader / Blues & jazz, swing, big band
A fine swing-era tenor saxophonist who later became an equally first-rate R&B honker, Hal Singer was a master of expressive, upper-register, exuberant playing. He was also a wonderful ballad and blues stylist. Singer began playing violin, then switched to clarinet and alto as a teen. He was on tenor by the time he joined Ernie Fields in 1938. Singer later played with Lloyd Hunter, Nat Towles, and Tommy Douglas before moving to New York with the Jay McShann orchestra. He played with Hot Lips Page, Roy Eldridge, Don Byas, Red Allen, Sid Catlett, Lucky Millinder, and Duke Ellington in the '40s. One of his first recordings as a leader was the immortal "Corn Bread," which gave him both a hit and a nickname in 1948. Singer toured with his own band for over a decade, and was in the Metrople house band from 1958 to

1961. He toured with a trio and led a band in New York during the early '60s, before settling in Paris in 1965. Singer kept performing and recording into the '80s. Unfortunately, he doesn't have any sessions as a leader available on CD. —*Ron Wynn*

★ **Rent Party / i.** 1984 / Savoy 1147

SIRONE

b. 1940
Bass / Early free, modern creative
An excellent technician and underrated composer, Sirone was part of the great Revolutionary Ensemble trio in the '70s, and also worked with many free bandleaders and groups. His prominent tone and decisive playing meshed expertly with Leroy Jenkins's and Jerome Cooper's on Ensemble recordings and in concert. Sirone worked in Atlanta with a band called The Group in the late '50s and early '60s. George Adams was among the players in this ensemble. Sirone moved to New York in the mid-'60s, and helped form the Untraditional Jazz Improvisational Team with Dave Burrell. He did sessions with Marion Brown, Gato Barbieri, Pharoah Sanders, Noah Howard, and Sonny Sharrock in the late '60s, and also played with Sunny Murray, Albert Ayler, Archie Shepp, Sun Ra, and many others. Sirone spent six years with the Revolutionary Ensemble, originally forming it with Jenkins and Frank Clayton (later replaced by Cooper). He recorded with Clifford Thornton, Roswell Rudd, Dewey Redman, Cecil Taylor, and Walt Dickerson in the '70s and early '80s. The trio date with Sirone, Dickerson, and Andrew Cyrille is available on CD, as are some earlier dates that feature Sirone with Taylor, Redman, and others. —*Ron Wynn*

○ **Artistry / Jul.** 5, 1978 / Of The Cosmos 801
On this, his first recording since the dissolution of the Revolutionary Ensemble, bassist Sirone attempts to surround himself with a familiarly constructed ensemble consisting of a companion string instrument and experienced members of the new musicianship. The other strings are provided by Muneer Bernard Fennell on cello; the greatest depth of musicianship is lent by Art Ensemble drummer Don Moye. Though flutist James Newton is not without considerable talents, here he is caught in a contest not totally sympathetic to his skills. From the outset a peculiar set of alliances is set up; Sirone interlaces with cellist Fennell, and the peppery Moye is, perhaps by necessity, left to interact with Newton. The session has this somewhat divided character throughout. It is clear that Sirone is in search of another string partner with whom to renew the empathic relationship he had with RE violinist Leroy Jenkins—the comparison is unfortunate, but unavoidable—and his dialog with Fennell's cello has its moments, but more often than not the two are searching for the right wavelength. —*Brent Staples,* Down Beat

★ **Live / Jul.** 11, 1980 / Serious 1000

NOBLE SISSLE

b. 1899, **d.** 1975
Composer, bandleader / Ballads & blues
Noble Sissle was one of the nation's premier composers and bandleaders, particularly in the early days of American popular song and theatre. He worked in a band with Eubie Blake in Baltimore as early in 1915; Luckey Roberts sometimes played piano. The Sissle/Blake team scored an early hit with "It's All Your Fault," which Sophie Tucker performed in her act. Sissle later teamed with James Europe from 1916 until Europe's death in 1919. They co-wrote and produced with Blake the historic shows *Shuffle Along* and *Chocolate Dandies.* Sissle recorded over 30 vocals during the early and mid-'20s, many times accompanied by Blake. They also appeared in some pioneering sound film shorts in 1930. Sissle led several bands and visited Europe often; his traveling ways led to a split with Blake, who preferred staying in America. Sissle's circle of friends also included Cole Porter

and Fred Waring, and the Prince of Wales was a guest drummer at one of his concerts in 1930. When Sissle returned to America, he was featured on a broadcast from the Park Central Hotel in 1931, effectively breaking that establishment's color barrier. Lena Horne sang with his band in the mid-'30s; Nat "King" Cole was reportedly among the cast of *Shuffle Along of 1933*, which didn't enjoy the success of its predecessor. Sissle's band included Buster Bailey, Tommy Ladnier, and Sidney Bechet. Except for the times Sissle's orchestra made USO tours during World War II, his group was a featured attraction at Billy Rose's Diamond Horseshoe club from 1938 to 1950. Sissle succeeded Bill "Bojangles" Robinson as honorary mayor of Harlem in 1950, and played at Eisenhower's inaugural in 1953. He was WMGM's first Black disc jockey in 1960, ran his own publishing company, and owned a club. But repeated muggings led him to close the club, and to retire to Florida to spend time with his son. The 1973 book *Reminiscing with Sissle and Blake* detailed his varied experiences. Sissle's music is featured on import CDs and anthologies of early stage, show, and popular music. —*Ron Wynn*

CAROL SLOANE

b. 1937
Vocals / Ballads, bop
Contemporary jazz vocalist and Concord recording artist, Sloane began to attract some attention in the '70s and blossomed in the '80s. Adept at standards and a good interpreter, she sings melody lines well and shies away from scat. Well worth hearing. —*Ron Wynn*

Out of the Blue / Dec. 1961 / Columbia 1766

Carol Sloane Live at 30th Street / 1963 / Columbia 1923

○ **Cotton Tail** / Nov. 12, 1978 / Choice 1025
Classy, late '70s session by vocalist Carol Sloane. She sings sophisticated ballads, reworks standards, and does prerock pop, all of it in a polished, entertaining manner. Sloane isn't quite as accomplished on lowdown or bluesy material, but does it well enough not to destroy any credibility. —*Ron Wynn*

Carol Sings / Oct. 28-29, 1979 / Progressive 7047
One of the first albums by vocalist Carol Sloane to enjoy widespread acclaim and critical praises. She shows her ability to swing without overpowering lyrics or losing the tempo, while her ballads and slow songs are done with a modicum of gimmicks and plenty of real soul and depth. —*Ron Wynn*

○ **As Time Goes By** / Aug. 29, 1982 / Eastwind 706
An early '80s session highlighted by the clean, confident vocals of Carol Sloane. Though she's more jazz-influenced than anything, her understated delivery and surprising range give her renditions of prerock standards and pop flavor, depth, and character. —*Ron Wynn*

★ **Love You Madly** / i. Oct. 6-28, 1988 / Contemporary 14049

Real Thing / i. May 24-25, 1990 / Contemporary 14060

○ **Heart's Desire** / i. 1992 / Concord Jazz 4503
A '92 release from vocalist Carol Sloane that's in the mode of her previous releases. She's backed by a trio and does the usual uptempo jazz-tinged ballads, prerock pop, an occasional original or two, and even some more contemporary material. She sings any and everything well, displaying the delivery, lyric command, and style that's won critical acclaim. The CD has two bonus cuts. —*Ron Wynn*

Sweet & Slow / i. Apr. 1993 / Concord Jazz CCD-4564

BUSTER SMITH (Henry Smith)

b. Aug. 24, 1904, Ennis, TX, **d.** Aug. 10, 1991
Alto saxophone, clarinet, arranger / Swing, big band
Though he was a good arranger who is credited with arranging "One O'Clock Jump," Buster Smith's influence on Charlie Parker, at an early stage in Parker's development, was vital. Smith's spry, fluid, and warm sound, as well as his phrasing and subtle use of blues inflections, certainly influ-

enced Parker's style, though Parker took these sounds, phrasings, and inflections to a different level. Smith played alongside a 17-year-old Parker in the late '30s, and served as both his playing and general mentor. Some of Smith's techniques, notably his biting tone and crisp articulation, as well as some of his phrases, were particularly influential, as was Smith's method of moving through chord progressions. He taught himself clarinet, and played in the '20s with local Dallas groups. He began on alto sax in 1925, when he joined Walter Page's Blue Devils. Jimmy Rushing, Hot Lips Page, Count Basie, and Eddie Durham had all joined the group by 1928, but they soon departed to join Bennie Moten's band. Smith took over the Blue Devils in 1931. The group now included Lester Young, and was called the 13 Original Blue Devils. When they disbanded in 1933, Smith settled in Kansas City and joined Moten's band. The group disbanded when Moten died in 1935. Smith joined a band Basie was leading with other former Moten players, but he stayed in Kansas City when Basie took the band to New York. Smith played with Claude Hopkins and Andy Kirk, and wrote arrangements for Nat Towles. He formed a group in 1937 with Jay McShann, Fred Beckett, and Parker. Smith took the band to New York the next year, but couldn't land engagements as a leader. He became an arranger for Basie, Benny Carter, and Snub Mosley, and played with Don Redman. Smith moved to Dallas in 1942, and led groups at clubs and hotels. He stopped playing sax in 1959, but kept going on piano, bass, and guitar until he retired in 1980. Currently, there aren't any Buster Smith albums available on CD. —*Ron Wynn*

★ **Legendary Buster Smith, The** / Jun. 17, 1959 / Atlantic 1323

JABBO SMITH (Cladys Smith)

b. Dec. 24, 1908, Pembroke, GA, **d.** Jan. 16, 1991
Trumpet, trombone / Swing, big band
One of the '20s greatest and most exceptional trumpeters who was gifted with exemplary all-around skills, Jabbo Smith possessed great range and wonderful tone. He was a fine singer and could play both striking uptempo tunes and nicely evocative ballads. Smith played longer and more complex lines than most trumpeters played during the late '20s, and was one of the most advanced musicians of his day. He was also a decent trombonist and pianist. Smith learned music at Jenkins's Orphanage in Charleston. He was a professional at age 16, and worked in Charlie Johnson's band in the mid- and late '20s. He recorded with Duke Ellington's orchestra in 1927, soloing on "Black and Tan Fantasy." Smith toured with James P. Johnson in "Keep Shufflin'" in 1928, then worked in Chicago during the late '20s and early '30s with Carroll Dickerson, Earl Hines, Erskine Tate, Charlie Elgar, Tiny Parham, and Fess Williams. He also led his own bands in the Midwest. Smith played with Claude Hopkins's band in the late '30s, then led his own groups in the '40s. After that, he cut his appearances back to only part-time, but received universally positive notices for his appearance in the show *One Mo' Time* during the '70s. He continued to appear as a vocalist in the '80s, despite erratic health problems. He appeared at festivals in 1983 and 1986. Currently, Smith has only one selection available on CD. —*Ron Wynn*

★ **Jabbo Smith—Vol. 1** / i. Mar. 1928-Feb. 1929 / Retrieval 131
☆ **Jabbo Smith—Vol. 2** / i. Mar. 1929-Feb. 1938 / Retrieval 132
○ **Jazz Heritage—Ace of Rhythm** / 1929 / MCA 1347
○ **Sweet 'n' Lowdown** / i. Mar. 1987 / Affinity 1029

JIMMY SMITH (James Oscar Smith)

b. Dec. 8, 1925, Norristown, PA
Organ / Postbop, soul-jazz
Though he never received any exaggerated title like the king of soul-jazz, Jimmy Smith certainly ruled the Hammond organ in the '50s and '60s. He revolutionized the instrument, and showed it could be used creatively in a jazz context, and could be popularized in the process. His Blue Note sessions from 1956 to 1963 were extremely influential and are highly

recommended. Smith turned the organ almost into an ensemble. He provided walking bass lines with his feet, left hand chordal accompaniment, solo lines in the right, and a booming, funky presence that punctuated every song, particularly the uptempo cuts. Smith turned the fusion of R&B, blues, and gospel influences with bebop references and devices into a jubilant, attractive sound that many others immediately absorbed before following in his footsteps. Initially, Smith learned piano, from his parents and on his own. He attended the Hamilton School of Music in 1948, and Ornstein School of Music in 1949 and 1950 in Philadelphia. Smith began playing the Hammond in 1951, and soon earned a great reputation that followed him to New York, where he debuted at the Cafe Bohemia. A Birdland date and 1957 Newport Jazz Festival appearance launched Smith's career. He toured extensively through the '60s and '70s. His Blue Note recordings included superb collaborations with Kenny Burrell, Lee Morgan, Lou Donaldson, Tina Brooks, Jackie McLean, Ike Quebec, and Stanley Turrentine, among others. He also did several trio recordings, some of which were a little bogged down by the excess length of some selections. Smith scored more hit albums on Verve from 1963 to 1972, many of them featuring big bands and using fine arrangements from Oliver Nelson. These included the excellent *Walk on the Wild Side.* But Verve went to the well once too often seeking crossover dollars, and loaded Smith's late '60s album down with hack rock covers. His '70s output was quite spotty, though Smith didn't stop touring, and visited Israel and Europe in 1974 and 1975. He and his wife opened a club in Los Angeles in the mid-'70s. Smith resumed touring in the early '80s, and returned to New York in 1982 and 1983. He resigned with Blue Note in 1985, and has done more representative dates for them and Milestone in the '90s. Smith has a good supply of sessions from both the past and present available on CD. *—Ron Wynn and Bob Porter*

New Sound, A New Star, A / Feb. 13+18, 1956 / Blue Note 1512
Recorded in New York City. This is his debut album with his original trio. *—Michael Erlewine*

☆ **Greatest Hits—Vol. 1** / Mar. 27, 1956-Feb. 8, 1963 / Blue Note 89901

Jimmy Smith at the Organ—Vol. 1: All Day Long / Feb. 12, 1957 / Blue Note 81551
With Kenny Burrell (g), Art Blakey (d), and Lou Donaldson (as). Bluesy, yet driving. *—Hank Davis*

○ **Best of Jimmy Smith, The** / Feb. 12, 1957-Jan. 3, 1986 / Blue Note 91140
1958-1986. Small-group setting. Selections from some of Smith's best Blue Note albums, such as *The Sermon, Go for Whatcha Know, Midnight Special, Back at the Chicken Shack, A New Sound,* and *At the Organ. —Michael Erlewine*

Jimmy Smith at the Organ—Vol. 2 / Feb. 13, 1957 / Blue Note 1552

Confirmation / Aug. 25, 1957+Feb. 25, 1958 / Blue Note 992
Smith has the best playing companions. Art Blakey (d) contains himself, playing a subdued and excellent supportive role. Kenny Burrell's (g) solo work on "Cherokee" is a highlight. Lee Morgan (tpt) makes this album essential—bop lovers have to have this. *—Jerry L. Atkins, Cadence*

○ **House Party** / Aug. 25, 1957 / Blue Note 46546
With Tina Brooks (ts), Lee Morgan (tpt), Kenny Burrell (g), Art Blakey (d). Mid-sized band plays all uptempo pieces. Studio jam session for nonregular sidemen. With this many sidemen, the group is a little too large for that classic Smith sound. *—Michael Erlewine*

Special Guests / Aug. 25, 1957 / Blue Note 50101
Recorded at Hackensack, New Jersey. Some nice jam session/blowing date cuts. *—Ron Wynn*

★ **Groovin' at Small's Paradise—Vols. 1 and 2** / Nov. 14+18, 1957 / Blue Note 1586

★ **Sermon** / Feb. 25, 1958 / Blue Note 46097

Recorded in Manhattan Towers, New York. Small-group studio jam sessions (also two from August 25, 1957) featuring Lou Donaldson (sax), Lee Morgan (tpt), Kenny Burrell (g). *—Michael Erlewine*

Softly as a Summer Breeze / Feb. 26, 1958 / Blue Note 4200
Recorded at Englewood Cliffs, New Jersey. Nice title cut, some good moments. *—Ron Wynn*

☆ **Cool Blues** / Apr. 7, 1958 / Blue Note 84441
Live album at the legendary Harlem club Small's Paradise, where Smith was first discovered by Blue Note in 1956. Mono recordings with Tina Brooks (ts) and Lou Donaldson (sax).*—Michael Erlewine*

Home Cookin' / 1958-1959 / Blue Note 84050
Recorded at Hackensack, New Jersey. Bluesy, intense trio recording. Nice title track, good soul-jazz set. *—Ron Wynn*

☆ **Crazy! Baby** / Jan. 4, 1960 / Blue Note 84030
Recorded at Englewood Cliffs, New Jersey. Classic Smith trio includes the hit single "When Johnny Comes Marching Home." *—Michael Erlewine*

Open House / Plain Talk / Mar. 22, 1960 / Blue Note 84269
Recorded at Hackensack, New Jersey. Studio session featuring Blue Mitchell (tpt), Ike Quebec (ts), and Jackie McClean (as). This is essentially a jam session without Smith's regular sidemen. More mainstream than most, but very nice tracks—fast and slow. This is an excellent album. *—Michael Erlewine*

★ **Back at the Chicken Shack** / Apr. 25, 1960 / Blue Note 46402

○ **Midnight Special** / Apr. 25, 1960 / Blue Note 84078
Recorded at Englewood Cliffs, New Jersey. Small-groups recording from the same session as *Back at the Chicken Shack,* and it is almost as fine—that is: magical! This is a must-have for jazz organ fans. With Stanley Turrentine (ts). *—Michael Erlewine*

Bashin' the Unpredictable Jimmy Smith / Mar. 26+28, 1962 / Verve 823308
Debut session for Verve, his first with big-band backing. Featuring Oliver Nelson, his orchestra, and "Walk on the Wild Side" (a hit single). Smith's first album with a bass player! Three cuts are with small combo. *—Michael Erlewine*

☆ **Prayer Meetin'** / Feb. 8, 1963 / Blue Note 84164
A fine small-group album with Stanley Turrentine. Smith's last Blue Note album until 1986 (*Go for Whatcha Know*). Also, last two cuts from June 13, 1960, were released in Japan on an album, *Special Guests. —Michael Erlewine*

Live at the Village Gate / May 31, 1963 / Metro 521
Recorded at the Village Gate, New York City. Smith in a trio setting. Plenty of fine playing. *—Ron Wynn*

Blue Bash / Jul. 16-29, 1963 / Verve 8553

Who's Afraid of Virginia Woolf? / Jan. 20, 1964 / Verve 8583

Cat, The / Apr. 27-29, 1964 / Verve 810046
Recorded at Englewood Cliffs, New Jersey. A large band conducted and arranged by Lalo Schifrin. This is perhaps his best-known album featuring the big-band sound. A Grammy Award winner. *—Michael Erlewine*

Monster / Jan. 19-20, 1965 / Verve 8618
Recorded at Englewood Cliffs, New Jersey. Oliver Nelson conducts his large band with Smith. Blistering organ solos. *—Ron Wynn*

In Hamburg Live / May 27, 1965 / Metro 607
Recorded in Hamburg, Germany. Jimmy Smith with a trio as part of a European tour in 1965. Latter-day sessions, Smith still plays torrid organ. *—Ron Wynn*

☆ **Organ Grinder Swing** / Jun. 14-15, 1965 / Verve 825675
Recorded at Englewood Cliffs, New Jersey with Kenny Burrell (g). Trio album by Smith after much big-band success. This is reminiscent of Smith's early small-combo work. In other words, he cooks on this one. *—Michael Erlewine*

Got My Mojo Workin' / Dec. 16-17, 1965 / Verve 8641
Recorded at Englewood Cliffs, New Jersey. Smith in his large-band context with Oliver Nelson and his orchestra. — *Michael Erlewine*

★ **Dynamic Duo, The** / Sep. 21+28, 1966 / Verve 821577
This may or may not have needed the big-band setting for some of the tracks, but Oliver Nelson's tight, hard arranging and conducting give the music the same added attraction he gave to Sonny Rollins's *Alfie* date. This is a pairing of giants and, while the music is broadly accessible, it needs no apology. Good listening. —*Bob Rusch, Cadence*

○ **Further Adventures of Jimmy and Wes** / Sep. 21+28, 1966 / Verve 68766

Respect / Jun. 2+14, 1967 / Verve 8705
Recorded in New York City. Superb solos, soul-jazz with class. Prototype Smith. —*Ron Wynn*

Boss, The / Nov. 20, 1968 / Verve 8779
Recorded at Paschal's La Carousel, Atlanta, Georgia. Lots of fine solos. George Benson (g) does his best soul-jazz work since McDuff days. —*Ron Wynn*

○ **Bluesmith** / 1972 / Verve 8809

☆ **Fourmost** / Nov. 16-17, 1990 / Milestone 9184
Recent material, Smith still wails on the organ. Stanley Turrentine (ts) and Kenny Burrell (g) in top form. —*Ron Wynn*

Greatest Hits—Vol. 2 / Blue Note 83367

It's Necessary / Mercury 1-1189

JOHNNY SMITH (John Henry (Jr.) Smith)

b. 1922
Guitar/bop, cool
Best known for his huge hit "Moonlight in Vermont," Johnny Smith has been a nice, occasionally inspired guitarist who's made pleasant, charming, but not especially memorable records. His playing is equally consistent and steady; it's not that exciting, but it's technically fine. Smith taught himself trumpet, violin, and viola before turning to electric guitar. He was an NBC studio musician in the late '40s and early '50s, playing trumpet and guitar. Smith led his own group in 1952, and *Down Beat* selected "Moonlight in Vermont" as Record of the Year. Smith played with Bennie Green, Hank Jones, and Kenny Clarke on a 1953 Decca session using the alias of Sir Jonathan Gasser. He did several sessions in the '50s, then moved to Colorado in the '60s. Smith opened a music store, performed, and taught. He recorded in New York until the late '60s, then toured England with Bing Crosby in the late '70s. Smith has one session currently available on CD; appropriately, it's *Moonlight in Vermont.* —*Ron Wynn*

Opus De Funk / May 12, 1961 / Prestige 7420

★ **Soul Talk** / May 19, 1969 / Prestige 7681

LEO SMITH

b. Dec. 18, 1941, Leland, MS
Trumpet, flugelhorn / Modern creative
While he is an ambitious, unpredictable composer, Leo Smith's trumpet playing leans more toward the reflective, introspective side. His tone, approach, and sound emphasize lyricism and a calm, pleasing style rather than an energized, exuberant approach. Smith began on mellophone and French horn before turning to trumpet. He played in R&B bands and in the service following his high school graduation. He became a member of the Association for the Advancement of Creative Musicians (AACM) in 1967, and co-founded the Creative Construction Company with Leroy Jenkins and Anthony Braxton later that year. They played and recorded in Europe and with other AACM members in New York during the late '60s before disbanding in 1970. Smith teamed with Marion Brown to make the documentary film *See the Music* in 1970, then formed the New Delta Ahkri in New Haven. The group's personnel ranged from two to five members, and included, at various times, Henry

Threadgill, Anthony Davis, Oliver Lake, and Dwight Andrews. Smith began the Kabell record label in 1971, and studied ethnomusicology in the mid-'70s at Wesleyan. He played with Braxton again in the late '70s, and recorded with Derek Bailey's group, Company, in London. Smith also led a trio with Peter Kowald and Gunther Sommer. He's recorded for Kabell, Moers, ECM, Nessa, Black Saint, and Sackville in the '70s and '80s. Smith has a couple of sessions available on CD. —*Ron Wynn*

★ **Rastafari** / i. Feb. 1985 / Sackville 3030
Here is American trumpeter Leo Smith in Canada with the Bill Smith group. In free improvisation, smallest ensembles are best, otherwise lines and textures become obscured and direction dispersed. On *Rastafari,* the problem generally gets solved by one or more players dropping out of the ensemble from passage to passage. Extensive, very sober improvisation is the content of three tracks—the trumpeter providing the music's warmth. I especially liked the first half of "Madder Lake," in which a quiet, languid mystery is sustained over a dark and mobile bass while Smith, remarkably, extends the others' isolated fragmentary ideas into satisfying moods. —*John Litweiler, Down Beat*

Reflectativity / Kabell 2

LONNIE SMITH (Organ)

Organ / Blues & jazz, soul-jazz
Not to be confused with Lonnie Liston Smith, organist Lonnie Smith has been on the soul-jazz and jazz scene since the '60s. He's worked often with Lou Donaldson, and has done sessions on his own. He's not a great organist, but can play the requisite bluesy licks, can work the bass pedal, and can offer good stomping numbers. Though he's recorded as a leader for Blue Note, CTI, and other labels, and has done sessions with Donaldson, George Benson, Hank Crawford, and many other notables, currently Smith has no sessions available on CD. He isn't even cited in many major jazz publications. —*Ron Wynn*

★ **Mama Wailer** / Jul. 14-15, 1971 / Kudu

○ **Think** / i. 1986 / Blue Note 84290
With Lee Morgan (tpt). This is an excellent 1986 reissue of a fine soul-jazz Blue Note date by organist Lonnie Smith. — *Ron Wynn*

LONNIE LISTON SMITH (Lonnie Liston (Jr) Smith)

b. Dec. 28, 1940, Richmond, VA
Keyboard / Early jazz-rock, instrumental pop, modern creative
Pianist Lonnie Liston Smith underwent a great stylistic change during the '70s. At one point, he worked with Pharoah Sanders and Gato Barbieri and provided keyboard interludes for their highly charged, explosive settings. Then Smith played with Miles Davis, and plugged into electric funk. When he formed the Cosmic Echoes with his brother, Donald, things were radically different. Smith presented low-key arrangements, with Donald singing psuedo-mystic laments and pontifications, and with minimal improvisation and solo space. But these albums put Lonnie Liston Smith on the fusion and crossover map; he enjoyed great sales for a string of releases in this pattern that continued through the '80s and into the '90s. He established himself as one of the more popular acts on the Black upper middle class professional circuit, playing college campuses and appearing in several cities with heavy African-American populations and high-profile urban contemporary radio stations. Prior to his stylistic change, Lonnie Liston Smith had graduated from Morgan State in 1961 in music education, then moved to New York. He had played with Betty Carter, Rahsaan Roland Kirk, Art Blakey, Joe Williams, and Sanders. Smith has recorded as a leader for Flying Dutchman, Doctor Jazz, and Signature. He has several sessions available on CD. —*Ron Wynn*

○ **Astral Traveling** / 1973 / Flying Dutchman 0163

★ **Expansions** / i. 1975 / Flying Dutchman 0934

☆ **Reflections of a Golden Dream** / Sep. 1976 / RCA 1460
There is an innate sensuality here, with the haunting echoes of electric piano, the mooing vocals of Lonnie Liston and Don Smith, and the weird melange of space sounds. — *Arnold Shaw,* Down Beat

MARVIN SMITH (Marvin "Smitty" Smith)

b. Jun. 24, 1961, Waukegan, IL
Drums, percussion / Hard bop
A prolific, constantly in-demand drummer whose sensitive, yet authoritative playing has been heard on dozens of '80s and '90s sessions, Marvin "Smitty" Smith seems to live in the studio. A one-time Berklee student, he played with Jon Hendricks's band in New York during the early '80s, then worked with John Hicks, Bobby Watson, and Slide Hampton. Smith later recorded with Archie Shepp, then with a quintet co-led by Frank Wess and Frank Foster. He did sessions with Hamiet Bluiett, Kevin Eubanks, and David Murray, and played with Ray Brown, Dave Holland, Ron Carter, Hank Jones, and the Jazztet. Smith made his recording debut as a leader in 1987, and also recorded with Sonny Rollins that year, and toured with Sting. Since then, Smith's been featured constantly on sessions, and has often paired with Ray Drummond. He has a couple of Concord dates available on CD, and can also be heard on numerous releases by other musicians. —*Ron Wynn*

○ **Keeper of the Drums** / Mar. 1987 / Concord Jazz 4325
☆ **Road Less Traveled** / Feb. 1989 / Concord Jazz 4379
Fine 1989 date with strong piano from James Williams. CD version has two bonus cuts. —*Ron Wynn*
★ **Carryin' On** / Concord Jazz 325
Good, nicely played date with a harder edge than usual for Concord material. —*Ron Wynn*

STUFF SMITH (Hezekiah Leroy Gordon Smith)

b. Aug. 14, 1909, Portsmouth, OH, **d.** Sep. 25, 1967, Munich, Germany
Violin / Swing
Violinist Stuff Smith was an extraordinary player, who had, among other things, the opportunity to record with Nat "King" Cole. His wide vibrato, frenetic rhythmic sense, unique intonation, and ambitious style are only part of the story; he was one of the best at inspiring other musicians during a performance, and Dizzy Gillespie has often credited Smith with showing him that artistry and entertainment could be combined. Smith studied music with his father and performed with the family band as a child, eventually winning a scholarship to Johnson C. Smith University. Then, at age 15, Smith joined a touring revue. He performed for two years with Alphonso Trent, and briefly with Jelly Roll Morton, but returned to Trent because he felt he couldn't be heard in Morton's band. After spending several years in Buffalo, Smith moved to New York in 1936. He led a quintet at the Onyx Club with Jonah Jones and Cozy Cole, and began playing an amplified violin there. His group mixed music and comedy performances, sometimes nearly crossing the line between risque humor and lamentable stereotype. They recorded a novelty song "I'se a Muggin'" in 1936. They did 15 more songs for Vocalion and five for Decca. Smith added clarinetist Buster Bailey and pianist Clyde Hart for the Decca sessions, then recorded with a group he called Stuff Smith and His Orchestra in 1939 and 1940 for the Varsity label. When Fats Waller died in 1943, Smith was chosen to lead his band. Norman Granz recorded several exceptional sessions with Smith on Verve in the late '50s, and Smith toured extensively in the '60s. During that decade, he recorded with Nat King Cole, Dizzy Gillespie, Ella Fitzgerald, Stephane Grappelli, Svend Asmussen, and the Oscar Peterson Trio. Smith resettled in Copenhagen in 1965, and died there two years later. —*Ron Wynn*

○ **Swingin' Stuff** / Mar. 23, 1956 / Storyville 4087
One of two mid-'60s sessions that violinist Stuff Smith recorded with a mostly foreign band, plus expatriate pianist Kenny Drew. He plays with his characteristic fervor, punctuating his rippling phrases with blues licks, smears, and slurs, plus some dazzling phrases. Bassist Niels-Henning Ørsted-Pedersen emerges as the dominant rhythm section member besides Drew, while drummer Alex Riel mainly follows their lead. —*Ron Wynn*

Stephane Grappelli with Stuff Smith / May 1957 / Verve 8270
★ **Live at the Montmartre** / Mar. 1965 / Storyville 4142

TAB SMITH (Talmadge Smith)

b. Jan. 11, 1909, Kinston, NC, **d.** Sep. 17, 1971, St. Louis, MO
Saxophone, alto saxophone / Swing, big band, blues & jazz
A honking R&B/swing sax master, Tab Smith began on the C-melody, then switched to alto and eventually became a giant within his genre. Smith, who also played extensively on tenor later in his career, had lots of experience in territory bands during the '30s, but achieved his first real fame with Lucky Millinder from 1936 to 1939. Later came stints with Frankie Newton, Red Allen, Teddy Wilson, and Eddie Durham, before Smith joined Count Basie in 1940. He returned to Millinder in 1942 and stayed until 1944, then led his own groups, sometimes with singer Wynonie Harris. His explosive, torrid solos were tailor-made for the swing-derived, jumping material that comprised vintage R&B. During the '50s, Smith cut many songs that were huge hits in the Black community on jukeboxes for tiny independent labels. He retired from the music business in the '60s and became involved in real estate, often playing the organ in clubs for fun. His finest sessions are now reappearing on both domestic and import reissue packages. —*Ron Wynn*

★ **I Don't Want to Play . . .** / **i.** 1944-1945 / Saxophonograph 1944-1945. *I Don't Want To Play in the Kitchen.* Great honking sax, swing-inflected solos. —*Ron Wynn*

Joy at the Savoy / 1944-1954 / Saxophonograph 509
☆ **Because of You** / 1951-1957 / Delmark 429
Tab Smith, a reedman with Lucky Millinder and Count Basie, had a hit with the title tune of this collection. A very sweet ballad, it oozes from Smith's sax to drench the laid-back band support. So the cry of Smith's alto is urbane, rather than raunchy, and some of the material he chose reflects overly cautious taste. While the organ fills strive for the roller rink, couples could dance cheek to cheek to Smith's efforts; when the organist remembers the chitlin circuit, Smith's bounce becomes a bit lighter and the jitterbuggers take over. And though the tight ensembles don't offer much stretching space to anyone else in Smith's band, Walter Johnson's drumming, much of it simply brushes, is classic, much more difficult than it sounds. —*Howie Mandel,* Down Beat

○ **Jump Time** / 1951-1952 / Delmark 447
Alto and tenor saxophonist Tab Smith recorded several dozen tunes for United between '51 and '57, 20 of which (including five hitherto unreleased) show up in this Delmark collection. They're a mixed bunch, reflecting the practice then of appeasing buyers by placing sweet numbers back-to-back with swinging ones. Hearts-and-flowers ballads, typically featuring Smith's saxes cooing endearments, are deadly, but most of the jump and slow blues selections are plenty pleasurable. A proficient soloist, he shakes and bounces over his fit little band without going over the top, ennobling "Slow Motion," "Dee Jay Special," "Wig Song," and "Boogie Joogie." Good fun. —*Frank-John Hadley,* Down Beat

WILLIE SMITH (William McLeish Smith)

b. Nov. 25, 1910, Charleston, SC, **d.** Mar. 7, 1967, Los Angeles, CA
Alto saxophone, clarinet / Swing, big band
The alto saxophone stylist who is generally considered the finest swing performer after Johnny Hodges and Benny Carter, Willie Smith was an accomplished section leader and soloist in the Lunceford Orchestra in the '20s, '30s, and '40s.

He also wrote first-rate arrangements of "Sophisticated Lady" and "Rose Room," and sometimes doubled as a vocalist. Smith attended Fisk University where Lunceford heard him and invited him to join the orchestra. Smith stayed from 1929 until 1942, then worked in 1942 and 1943 with Charlie Spivak. He played in Harry James's band for two extended tours, from 1944 to 1951 and from 1954 to 1964. He briefly replaced Johnny Hodges in the Duke Ellington orchestra, toured with Jazz at the Philharmonic, and led R&B and jazz groups in Los Angeles. Unfortunately, Smith has no albums to provide a fuller portrait of his skills, but he can be heard on Lunceford reissues and early '50s Ellington sessions. —*Ron Wynn*

WILLIE "THE LION" SMITH (William Henry Joseph Bonaparte Bertholoff Smith)

b. Nov. 25, 1897, **d.** Apr. 18, 1973
Piano, composer, vocals / Stride

A great musician and an equally flamboyant character, Willie "The Lion" Smith covered numerous jazz eras in his piano playing in the same way that Doc Cheatham currently covers many eras with his trumpet solos. Smith's mother was an organist and pianist, and Smith began in the ragtime era. He played on Mamie Smith's first blues recording in the '20s, and was a cohort and keyboard jouster with Eubie Blake, Luckey Roberts, Fats Waller, and James P. Johnson. Smith directly influenced Duke Ellington, and tutored Mel Powell, Joe Bushkin, and Artie Shaw, among many others. The Lion was a match for Jelly Roll Morton in the exaggeration/embellishment category, though Smith did it in such a gregarious manner that he didn't create anywhere near as many enemies. He traced his nickname back to both his family heritage (one of his parents was Jewish) and his alleged prowess as a soldier in World War I. Smith was a native New Yorker, and spent virtually his entire professional life there; he'd brag often about his preference for playing free in Harlem rather than earning millions anywhere else. Smith's impressive legacy includes writing over 70 compositions and playing with a host of bands and performers from the '20s to the '70s. The list includes Mezz Mezzrow, Milt Herth, O'Neill Spencer, Joe Bushkin, Jess Stacy, Sidney Bechet, Max Kaminsky, Lucille Hegamin, and Don Ewell. Among seminal Smith compositions and songs were "Echo of Spring," "Portrait of the Duke," "The Stuff is Here and It's Mellow," and "Sweeter than the Sweetest." He collaborated with Walter Bishop, Andy Razaf, and Jack Lawrence, and made commanding solo records in the '30s, '40s, '50s, '60s, and '70s. The 1949 album *Reminiscing the Piano Giants* featured Smith in interview and performance segments, while his 1965 autobiography with George Hoefer, *Music on My Mind,* put Smith's vivid story in print (Ellington contributed a foreword). The cigar-chomping, derby hat wearing keyboard giant finally passed away in 1973, a few months short of his 76th birthday. —*Ron Wynn*

★ **Snooty Fruity** / **i.** 1944-1955 / Columbia 45447
Hot Willie "The Lion" Smith. 1944-1955. Nice collaboration with Harry James that has more form than many of James's cuts. —*Ron Wynn*

Reminiscing the Piano Greats / 1949 / Vogue 008
Extremely rare date with Smith stomping and romping for Dial USA label. —*Ron Wynn*

☆ **Willie The Lion Smith** / Dec. 1, 1949-Jan. 29, 1950 / Inner City 7015
Part of the Jazz Legacy series, these 1949-1950 sessions with Wallace Bishop on drums include some solos and some combo efforts with Buck Clayton on trumpet, Claude Luter on clarinet, and Bishop on drums. Ten Smith numbers and eight standards. Includes Smith's classic "Echoes of Spring." —*Michael G. Nastos*

Compositions of James P. Johnson / **i.** 1953 / Blue Circle

○ **Relaxin' After Hours** / **i.** 1954 / EmArcy 26000
The material on this album was recorded a short time after the sessions that produced *Live at Blues Alley* and, except

for the addition of a drummer, little was changed. Smith's piano work is as infectious as ever. He struts and stomps his way through the equivalent of two sets, granting solo space to the drummer, and above all, conveying a spirit of good times. Smith's harmonic conception was unique among stride pianists, for the most distinctive of his compositions recall more strikingly the gentle piano works of Debussy and Bix Beiderbecke than they do the rowdiness and bravado generally associated with rent party piano. But there is less of the strictly meditative and reflective here than one has come to expect from Smith. Perhaps because Chiaroscuro had only a limited amount of material from which to select, his most perfectly realized piece, "Echoes of Spring," is absent, liner note assertions to the contrary. However, his playing on the selections that were released only adds to his reputation. —*Jack Sohmer*, Cadence

★ **Legend of Willie Smith, The** / Aug. 21+Sep. 19, 1957 / Grand Award 368

Lion Roars / Nov. 8, 1957 / Dot 3094

Songs We Taught Your Mother / **i.** 1961 / Prestige

Grand Piano / Feb. 20, 1967 / Sackville 2004

○ **Memoirs of Willie "The Lion" Smith** / Apr. 25-28, 1967 / RCA 6016
Mike Lipskin had a good idea here that doesn't quite come off, but we should have more failures like this. Willie "The Lion" Smith was a great pianist, an excellent composer, a very good raconteur with a memory to go with his talent, and a godawful singer. Smith was one of the last of the magnificent Harlem pianists, a school perhaps more pianistic than anything done in jazz since their time. The Lion illustrates the style perfectly by playing Scott Joplin's "Maple Leaf Rag" and then showing how a Harlem pianist would change the stiff rhythms and set phrases of "classical" ragtime into loose, driving "stride." He reminisces in talk and music about the pre- and post-World War I scene in New York City, the pop music, the Clef club, vaudeville, the nightclub shows of the '20s, Louis Armstrong with King Oliver, etc., but the real nub is the Harlem pianists. His versions of the music of Eubie Blake, James P. Johnson, Fats Waller, and Duke Ellington are very much his own, but they also bear unmistakable touches of each of these men as well. Only a player who understood their music from the inside could do as he does here. His spoken commentary about each of them is also very personal and interesting. This album is not a very good representation of what The Lion could do at the piano. Yet, this is Willie The Lion Smith and, therefore, the greatness of the man has to be there, too, and it is. Your eyes will be opened by what he does with "Alexander's Ragtime Band," "Blue Skies," "Charleston," "Ain't Misbehavin'," "Sophisticated Lady," and "Satin Doll." He takes them over, reharmonizes them, rephrases them, alters their usual tempo, creates new melodies on their familiar chords. Then there is the ebullient stride of "Diga Diga Do," "A Porter's Love Song to a Chambermaid," and "Keeping Out of Mischief Now." Flawed and incomplete though some of these performances are, what is there is still great. His long version of Eubie Blake's "Memories of You" is a masterpiece, as good as anything Lion ever recorded, played with love and appreciation for beauty that comes across superbly. There have been many fine recordings of this haunting tune, but the one on this album is the best I've heard and ranks with the best jazz piano. —*Ron Anger,* Coda

Live at Blues Alley / Jun. 11, 1970 / Chiaroscuro 104

Relaxin' / 1970-1971 / Chiaroscuro 159

ELMER SNOWDEN (Elmer Chester Snowden)

b. Oct. 9, 1900, Baltimore, MD, **d.** May 14, 1973, Philadelphia, PA
Guitar, banjo, saxophone, bandleader / Swing, big band

A great banjo player and a versatile musician who could also play excellent sax and guitar, Elmer Snowden was a rarity in the early jazz era: he was a trained player who could read in any key, and he was also a smart businessman.

Snowden played banjo and guitar as a child, and worked with Eubie Blake in a dance school in 1915, then played in a trio with Duke Ellington in 1919. Snowden took a band to New York from Washington in 1923, planning to use Fats Waller. When that didn't materialize, Snowden sent for Ellington, and the group became the Washingtonians. Snowden ran several bands in the mid- and late '20s and early 30s. He headed his own bands for three decades, before moving to California in 1963 to teach at Berkeley. He toured Europe for George Wein in 1967. Snowden declined an offer to rejoin Ellington's orchestra in late '60s. A fine quartet album he recorded for Fantasy in 1960 has been reissued recently. —*Ron Wynn*

★ **Harlem Banjo** / Dec. 9, 1960 / Riverside 1756
Legendary banjo player Elmer Snowden, with the Cliff Jackson (p) Trio, plays standards with the emphasis on old-time swing, including some Ellington. This is a unique album, one every jazz fan should get to know. —*Michael G. Nastos*

MARTIAL SOLAL

b. Aug. 23, 1927, Algiers
Piano, composer / Postbop
Any player with remarkable prowess and technical talents who is prone to utilize and display them on record runs the risk of critical displeasure, and that's been the case with Martial Solal. His vast harmonic knowledge, tendency to literally assault the listener with rippling phrases and complex passages, and he sometimes relentless pacing, turn off as many people as they impress. Solal settled in Paris in the late '40s, worked with expatriate American musicians like Kenny Clarke and Don Byas, and recorded with Sidney Bechet, Lee Konitz, and Hampton Hawes. He's led his own trios, done extensive session work since 1959, and became internationally famous through a 1963 visit to New York and subsequent Newport festival appearances. He's also done substantial film score work in Europe. Solal doesn't have an overabundance of available recordings in print, but just recently issued a session with a European sax group. —*Ron Wynn*

Happy Reunion / i. 1956 / Vogue
1990 reissue of a session with Solal playing with a group of one-time Stan Kenton luminaries. —*Ron Wynn*

★ **Martial Solal** / i. 1961 / Blue Note 10261

○ **Trio in Concert** / i. 1962 / Liberty 3335
Paris concert by this Algerian pianist, with Guy Pederson on bass and Damiel Humaia on drums. An excellent album to find. —*Michael G. Nastos*

☆ **Four Keys** / May 1979 / PA/USA 7061
This Lee Konitz/Martial Solal disc is rewarding, due primarily to Konitz's increasingly refined approach to organization in his solos and Solal's carefully constructed arrangements and means of presentation. There is a particularly attractive balance to the material, too: the first side features some programmatic, chamberlike pieces, and the accompaniment seems more designed and less felt. Here, alto saxophonist Konitz is at his best, as Solal and guitarist John Scofield take turns supporting. Solal, the real leader of the date, underplays his role throughout, it seems, but contributes some fine solos, especially on "Brain Stream." The second side is more adventurous, yet only partially successful. There are moments of spirited group improvisation and others seemingly cluttered by overenthusiastic comping on the part of Solal and Scofield. Throughout, everyone receives adequate solo space, and the date taken overall is a refreshing alternative to just another run-of-the-mill blowing session. —*Arthur Moorehead, Down Beat*

Big Band / i. 1981 / Gaumont

Bluesine / Jan. 18-19, 1983 / Soul Note 1060

Triptyque / i. 1991 / Adda

☆ **Live** / Stefanotis 239214

Comprehensive four-disc set of his material from 1959-1985 in every context. —*Ron Wynn*

☆ **Martial Solal** / I Grandi Del Jazz 97
Italian release with fabulous graphics and liner notes. The music is also first rate. —*Michael G. Nastos*

LEW SOLOFF (Lewis Michael Soloff)

b. Jan. 20, 1944, New York, NY
Trumpet, flugelhorn, piccolo, trumpet / Swing, progressive big band, early jazz-rock, Latin-jazz
Although he's a brilliant, flexible trumpeter, Lew Soloff has probably garnered more fame for his longtime membership in the Gil Evans Orchestra, and for working with Blood, Sweat & Tears in the '70s, than for being a first-rate soloist and accompanist. Soloff had formal studies at Juilliard Preparatory from 1961 to 1965; he later completed his music education at Eastman School and did supplemental studies at Julliard in 1965-1966. He got experience doing Latin-jazz in 1967-1968, then did freelance sessions with Maynard Ferguson, Joe Henderson, Clark Terry, and many others before joining Blood, Sweat & Tears from 1968 to 1973. While Wynton Marsalis won many classical Grammys in the '80s, Soloff was a featured soloist on many classical pieces in the '70s. He joined the Evans orchestra in 1973, and continued playing with Evans extensively during that decade and beyond. Soloff also formed a quintet with Jon Faddis in 1975. He headed a trio in 1977, then did sessions and worked with Evans in the '80s. —*Ron Wynn*

○ **But Beautiful** / Jun. 29-Jun. 3, 1987 / Evidence 22005
Longtime session and section trumpeter Lew Soloff steps into the spotlight on this '87 date, his third as a leader. Soloff chose a quartet context with no second reed or brass player, putting the melodic and harmonic focus squarely on himself. The results are good but sometimes a bit subdued. Soloff's tone, phrasing, and attack are solid, and his playing on such cuts as "Stella by Starlight," "Speak Low," and the title cut is striking. But there is also a low-key feeling, as if Soloff would rather gamble on things being too cool than overly intense. As a result, a fantastic rhythm section that includes pianist Kenny Kirkland, bassist Richard Davis, and drummer Elvin Jones lays back rather than surges ahead. If you like overly calm, reflective, and mellow material, this one is for you, but it would have been interesting to hear what might have happened had Soloff stepped things up a bit. —*Ron Wynn*

★ **Speak Low** / i. Jun. 29-30, 1987 / Projazz 656

EDDIE SOUTH

b. Nov. 27, 1904, Louisiana, MO, **d.** Apr. 25, 1962, Chicago, IL
Violin / Swing
Classical training and swing in his soul made Eddie South a jazz giant on violin. South's tremendous technique and riveting, left-hand playing style was supported by strong, aggressive bowing and a commanding approach on either up-tempo or slow material. His rich, dreamy tone earned him the nickname "Dark Angel," and he was hypnotic and moving on ballads. South could also blaze and delight on fast-paced material. He was a child prodigy who was coached in jazz by Darnell Howard. Following his studies, which included some time at the Chicago Musical College, South became music director for Jimmy Wade's Syncopators in the mid-'20s. He played in Europe during the late '20s, touring and studying in Paris and Hungary. South also recorded with his group the Alabamians for HMV in Paris. He returned to Chicago in the early '30s, and co-led a band with Everett Barksdale and Milt Hinton that recorded for Victor. He returned to Paris in the late '30s, and made seminal recordings with Django Reinhardt and Stephane Grappelli. South later worked in New York, Chicago, and Los Angeles at the end of the decade. He recorded with a West Coast quintet that included Tommy Benford. South led his own groups through the '40s and '50s, mostly combos, but occasionally a big band. He did several radio and television pro-

grams, and spent his final years in Chicago. Besides his sessions for HMV and Victor, South also recorded for Okeh, Columbia, and Mercury, and some of his early material was reissued in Europe on Swing. Some South sessions have been reissued on DRG CDs. —*Ron Wynn and Michael Erlewine*

Dark Angel of the Fiddle, The / i. 1958 / Trip 5803

★ **In Paris** / DRG 8405

Rare cuts from the late '30s featuring violinist Eddie South, whose beautiful, swinging solos were unfortunately seldom recorded. These songs were cut when South was living in Paris and playing with such European jazz greats as Django Reinhardt and Stephane Grappelli. —*Ron Wynn*

○ **Eddie South** / DRG 8405

This is one of the very few Eddie South albums available. The talented violinist made comparatively few recordings for a player of his stature, and he suffered quite a bit of criticism because some jazz critics felt his tone was a bit too "legitimate." Well, South's talents should be beyond dispute by now, and in case proof is needed, this date will suffice. The first two selections, poorly recorded and highlighted by Clifford King's atmospheric bass clarinet, are merely a prelude to the real meat of the album, South's 1937 Paris sessions. Backed by the remarkable guitarist Django Reinhardt in settings ranging from duets to a sextet, South both displays his virtuostic technique and swings inventively. He is joined by his admirer and fellow violinist Stephane Grappelli on six cuts, including two interpretations of a Bach melody. "Lady Be Good" also has a third string player, the excellent Michel Warlop, and although Reinhardt takes solo honors, the contrast and similarities between the three violinists is worth repeated listenings. —*Scott Yanow*, Cadence

MUGGSY SPANIER (Francis Joseph Spanier)

b. Nov. 9, 1906, Chicago, IL, **d.** Feb. 12, 1967, Sausalito, CA
Cornet / Dixieland

Spanier was more of a soul mate with King Oliver than with Louis Armstrong, but didn't match either musician's cornet skills. But Spanier's simple, though effective, lead playing made him a popular figure in the New Orleans revival movement, and a role model for Dixieland stylists. Spanier started on drums, then switched to cornet at age 13. He began his professional career with Elmer Schoebel's band, and made his first recordings in 1924. After working with various Chicago dance bands, Spanier joined Ted Lewis's orchestra in 1929, and remained with him until 1936. During that time, he appeared in two films. Spanier joined Ben Pollack's orchestra in 1936, but an alcohol-triggered illness forced him to leave in 1938. When he recovered, Spanier organized his Ragtime Band, an eight-piece unit that included Georg Brunis and Rod Cless. They made a string of 16 recordings that helped fuel both the New Orleans traditional revival and the emergence of the Dixieland circuit. They played in Chicago and in New York, but disbanded due to financial problems. Spanier rejoined Lewis for a brief period, led a recording unit with Sidney Bechet titled the Big Four, and spent a year with Bob Crosby's big band. He led his own big band patterned after Crosby's from 1941 to 1943, then played and recorded exclusively in small Dixieland combos while working frequently in the '50s with Earl Hines. Spanier toured Europe in 1960, then retired in 1964. —*Ron Wynn*

○ **Muggsy Spanier (1924-1928)** / i. Feb. 1924-Apr. 1928 / Retrieval 108

The music of the two earliest groups on Muggsy Spanier's LP—the Bucktown Five (1924) and the Stomp Six (1925)—was peculiarly transitional. While the ensemble work owes its structure largely to the approach of the Original Dixieland Jazz Band, Spanier's cornet playing was significantly influenced by King Oliver and Louis Armstrong. From the Bucktown Five to the Stomp Six, however, the ensembles became increasingly loose-limbed, as Spanier mirrored Armstrong's gradual relegation of the ensemble to the

stature of a framework for solo performance. Spanier used a plunger mute—referred to as "Muggsy's cocktail unit"—with great skill to achieve the necessary vocalization, and he provided a heated lead, driving a band to stroll, strut, or stomp at will. Yet he was also a limited soloist, his reputation based on that strong, clear lead and the conciseness of his breaks. The waspish, angular clarinet (or white-hot alto) of Frank Teschemacher was another no-holds-barred ingredient of this breezy music. Tesch died young—in a car crash in 1932—but not before he demonstrated promise of great individuality. Taking Johnny Dodds as his point of departure ("Bullfrog Blues," which, incidentally, later became famous in Charlie Parker's hands as a basis for "Now's the Time"), he became influential himself before long. In "Friar's Point Shuffle," he began replacing the New Orleans arpeggiated ensemble and solo style by an angular, legato line which became a "blueprint" for many Chicagoans. —*Chris Sheridan*, Cadence

Muggsy Spanier (1931+1939) / Mar. 1931-Dec. 1939 / BBC 687

Brand new reissues of super '30s dates with Spanier and Fats Waller (p), Benny Goodman (cl), and Joe Bushkin (p). —*Ron Wynn*

○ **Great Sixteen, The** / i. 1939 / RCA 1295

○ **Muggsy Spanier** / i. Oct. 1944-Oct. 1945 / Everybody's 1020

Originally released in 1945 on the Manhattan label in three three-record albums and sold only at Nick's and the Commodore Music Shop, these timeless remembrances of the Eddie Condon era had never been reissued in their entirety. Even on this stateside version of the Danish Storyville, cognoscenti will regretfully note the continued absence of four titles: "Miff's Blues," "That's a Plenty," "Clarinet Marmalade," and "Mam's in the Groove." Additionally, one may also wonder why Storyville chose to package the lot under Muggsy Spanier's name, when it all could have just as logically been attributed to Pee Wee Russell, who, like Spanier, was present on all sides in his customary outrageous splendor. These sides easily rank with the best of the mid-'40s Commodores, with top-grade solo work emanating from each of the three "leaders," as well as from sidemen Lou McGarity (tb) and Ernie Caceres (bs). But, expectedly, it is Russell (cl) who emerges as the most genuinely inspired and creative throughout. Those familiar with the wars of the period will catch the irony inherent in Spanier's retitling of his famous "Touro" routine as "Feather Brain Blues," a then quite-obvious reference to the vitriolic antitraditionalist of *Metronome* notoriety, Leonard Feather. At the time, *Down Beat* leaned more favorably in the direction of the Condonites, while *Metronome* opted for the boppers. Friendships were made and lost simply on the basis of jazz partisanship, but, happily, today most of our sanity has been restored. Now we can enjoy the best of both worlds. —*Jack Sohmer*, Cadence

Relaxin' at the Touro / 1952 / Jazzology 115

★ **Columbia, the Gem of the Ocean** / Jun. 13-14, 1962 / Mobile Fidelity 857

Excellent recording of a fine '50s date. —*Ron Wynn*

MELVIN SPARKS

Guitar / Blues & jazz, soul-jazz

A good soul-jazz and organ combo guitarist, Melvin Sparks has recorded and performed with musicians such as Hank Crawford, Rusty Bryant, and Johnny Lytle. His solos are usually soulful, funky, and nicely played, with fluid phrases, quirky lines, strumming effects, and tasty riffs. Sparks does not have any selections available as a leader. —*Ron Wynn*

JAMES SPAULDING (James Ralph (Jr) Spaulding)

b. Jul. 30, 1937, Indianapolis, IN
Alto saxophone, flute / Hard bop, progressive big band, modern creative

Spaulding is a tremendous alto sax and flute player with one of jazz's slimmest profiles. He came to prominence during the '60s and '70s as a stirring alto soloist with one foot in bop and one foot in the free, expressive style that was being pioneered by Ornette Coleman. He was also one of the best flute players of the period and was able to play lengthy lines and swirling solos, to play sweetly, or to play with funk and bite. Spaulding recorded quite frequently with Sun Ra's Arkestra in the late '50s and early '60s, then moved to New York in 1962. He began heading his own bands, while also working and recording through the '60s with Freddie Hubbard, Max Roach, Randy Weston, and Art Blakey, among others. He did numerous dates in the '70s, and played with Horace Silver, Bobby Hutcherson, Budd Johnson, Milt Jackson, and Bob Wilber, while he continued to head his own combos periodically. Spaulding earned his BA from Livingston College, Rutgers, in the mid-'70s, but wasn't heard from much during the late '70s. He resurfaced on the '81 Alvin Queen LP *Ashanti*, and since then has been featured on both his own dates and other sessions. Spaulding has some '80s and '90s dates available on CD, and can also be heard on Blue Note CD reissues of '60s sessions with Hubbard. —*Ron Wynn*

○ **Gotstabe a Better Way** / May 31, 1988 / Muse 5413
★ **Brilliant Corners** / Nov. 25, 1988 / Muse 5369

LOUIS SPEARS

Bass, cello / Hard bop
He doesn't have an extensive list of credits, but bassist/cellist Louis Spears has played acoustic bass with Eddie Harris and Billy Harper, and cello with Horace Tapscott. He's demonstrated good ability in his sessions; nothing extraordinary, but good timing, technique, and tone. —*Ron Wynn*

SPYRO GYRA

Group / Early jazz-rock, instrumental pop
Spyro Gyra is, perhaps, the best-selling and most popular fusion group ever. They were started in the mid '70s by saxophonist Jay Beckenstein and pianist Jeremy Wall. Initially, the group was primarily a studio band that cut faceless instrumentals. Then their 1979 album, *Morning Dance*, went gold and they became an international success. During the '80s and '90s, they've had a string of similar-sounding recordings, have been derided repeatedly by many jazz critics, and have become a staple on adult contemporary, new age, and easy listening stations. —*Ron Wynn*

Morning Dance / Aug. 1979 / MCA 37148
★ **Access All Areas** / Nov. 17+19, 1983 / MCA 6893
An excellent double album that includes live versions of songs from early albums. —*Paul Kohler*
Alternating Currents / i. 1985 / MCA 5606
Great songwriting and playing, and nice work by keyboardist Tom Schuman. —*Paul Kohler*
Breakout / 1986 / MCA 5753
An album with more midtempo jazz-style tunes and nice arrangements, with Julio Fernandez. Synths programmed by Eddie Jobson. —*Paul Kohler*
Stories Without Words / i. Jan. 1988 / MCA 42046
A nice mix of jazz, with tenor and soprano sax melodies that really sing. —*Paul Kohler*
○ **Collection** / GRP 9642

JOHNNY ST. CYR

b. 1889, **d.** 1966
Banjo / New Orleans traditional
A tremendous banjoist and star in traditional jazz, Johnny St. Cyr was a fine accompanist who offered interesting, sometimes humorous counterpoint and support. St. Cyr led his band, the Young Men of New Orleans, on the miniature river steamer Mark Twain at Disneyland in the '60s. St. Cyr worked with Armand Piron in 1917. In 1925, he was tabbed by Armstrong to join the Hot Five and Hot Seven recording sessions. He later played with King Oliver, Jelly Roll Morton, Polo Barnes, Paul Barbarin, and many other greats. He was

extremely busy during the late '40s traditional revival. St. Cyr will be heard forever on the Hot Five and Hot Seven cuts, and is featured on other reissues by Oliver and Morton. —*Ron Wynn*

★ **Blues Suite** / i. 1958 / Savoy 13001

JESS STACY (Alexandria Stacy)

b. Aug. 11, 1904, Bird's Point, MO
Piano / Swing, big band
Jess Stacy was one of jazz's and swing's great pianists, and his gifted right-hand forays and stomping phrases were featured in many bands, notably Benny Goodman's. While Stacy incorporated devices and figures from the styles of Earl Hines and Teddy Wilson, he added his own elegant, yet energetic harmonic touches and phrasing. His solos were never too long or overly exaggerated, and seldom failed to inject additional punch into a song or arrangement. Stacy was essentially self-taught, and got his professional start on riverboats as a teen. He worked with several combos before joining Goodman in the mid-'30s. His unscheduled, but spectacular solo on the song "Sing, Sing, Sing" at the 1938 Benny Goodman concert helped cement Stacy's reputation. During the '40s, Stacy played with Bob Crosby, Horace Heidt, and Goodman at two different intervals. He was married to Lee Wiley during this period, and served as bandleader for her backing group. Among the songs they cut for Victor were "It's Only a Paper Moon." Stacy later moved to the West Coast where he worked in piano bars through the '50s. After a lengthy sabbatical, Stacy returned to music in the mid-'70s, recording for Chiaroscuro and playing at Carnegie Hall for a Newport in New York concert. He recorded more Chiaroscuro dates through the '70s. Stacy also did sessions for Paramount, Commodore, Esquire, and Columbia, among others. His sessions have been reissued on CD by Aircheck, Jazzology, Swaggie, and Chiaroscuro. —*Ron Wynn*

○ **Piano Solos** / Nov. 16, 1935-Mar. 3, 1959 / Swaggie 1248
1935-1956. Includes a nice cross-section of influential, fine Stacy cuts. —*Ron Wynn*
★ **Jess Stacy and Friends** / Apr. 30, 1938-Nov. 25, 1944 / Commodore 7008
Blue Notion / Oct. 6, 1944 / Jazzology 90
Stacy's Still Swinging / Sep. 1974 / Chiaroscuro 133

MARVIN STAMM (Marvin Louis Stamm)

b. May 23, 1939, Memphis, TN
Trumpet / Postbop, Neo-bop
A prolific trumpeter and busy session player noted especially for his range, talent in the upper register, and flexibility, Stamm has played in big bands and combos, recorded with Gil Evans's orchestra, and worked in pit bands for Broadway shows and television studios. —*Ron Wynn*

Machinations / Apr. 16-24, 1968 / Verve 8759
Stampede / 1982 / Palo Alto 8022
★ **Bop Boy** / i. 1991 / Music Masters 65065
This trumpeter's first album in a long time as a leader. Spirited playing. —*Michael G. Nastos*
Mystery Man /

DAKOTA STATON (Aliyah Rabia)

b. Jun. 3, 1931, Pittsburg, PA
Vocals / Ballads
A good jazz and blues singer who made a big impact in the mid '50s and early '60s, Staton was named by *Down Beat* most promising newcomer in 1955. Her releases, especially *The Late, Late Show*, were popular as well as enhancing her reputation as a vocalist who could swing, interpret standards, and sing convincing, pulsating blues tunes. She recorded with George Shearing in 1958 and also did one of the most successful vocal versions of "Misty." —*Ron Wynn*

★ **Late, Late Show, The** / Feb. 28+Mar. 2, 1957 / Capitol 876

Crazy He Calls Me / Feb. 2-Nov. 12, 1958 / Capitol 1170

Dynamic! / Feb. 2-Nov. 12, 1958 / Capitol 1054

Ballads and the Blues / Oct. 10-Dec. 22, 1959 / Capitol 1387

Time to Swing / 1959 / Capitol 1241

Dakota / Jun. 1960 / Capitol 1490

Softly / Dec. 1960 / Capitol 1427

☆ **Dakota at Storyville** / Mar. 1962 / Capitol 1649

Live and Swinging / Jul. 7, 1963 / United Artists 3312

Dakota Staton with Strings / i. 1964 / United Artists 3355

From Dakota with Love / i. 1970 / United Artists 3292

In the Night / i. 1976 / Capitol 1003

Dakota Staton / i. 1990 / Muse 5401

A 1990 session with vocalist Dakota Staton, who's recorded everything in her career, going back to the combo jazz she made in the '50s and '60s. Her husky, authoritative voice has gotten stronger and deeper with age. She's backed by tenor saxophonist Houston Person and cuts some fine soul-jazz, blues, and standards. There are two bonus cuts on the CD and cassette. —*Ron Wynn*

Moonglow / LRC Jazz Classics 9036

My Funny Valentine / Capitol 6168

Manny Albam Big Band / LRC Jazz Classics 9017

JEREMY STEIG

b. Sep. 23, 1943, New York, NY

Flute / Early jazz-rock

One of the earliest and finest jazz-rock flutists, Jeremy Steig's an outstanding soloist. He's mastered the entire flute family, including bass, and also plays piccolo well. He has a similarly rich, classically pure tone and timbre like James Newton's or Hubert Laws's, and uses almost as many devices, such as tongue fluttering, humming, and swirling lines, as Newton and Laws. But Steig's not as blues- or swing-oriented, and his associations include working with Richie Havens in the early '60s, and heading Jeremy and the Satyrs in 1967. Steig's father was the famous artist William Steig. He began playing recorder at age six and took flute lessons at age 11. Steig attended the High School of Music and Art. He played with Gary Peacock and Paul Bley in the early '60s, then led a jazz-rock combo in 1967 that backed Tim Hardin before Steig headed his own groups. He played with Mike Manieri and Eddie Gomez in the '60s, and with Jan Hammer in 1970. He began using electronics and synthesizers in the '70s, and toured Europe both as a soloist and heading quartets and quintets. He recorded with Gomez and Joe Chambers in the late '70s, and did sessions with Mike Nock, Karl Ratzer, Nana Vasconcelos, Ray Baretto, Steve Gadd, and Jack DeJohnette in the '80s. Steig currently has a couple of sessions available on CD. —*Ron Wynn*

★ **Flute Fever** / i. 1963 / Columbia

Jeremy and the Satyrs / i. 1967 / Reprise

○ **This Is Jeremy Steig** / 1969 / Solid State 18059

Lend Me Your Ears / Jun. 3-4, 1978 / CMP 3

○ **Music for Flute & Double Bass** / Dec. 1978 / Creative Music Prod.

☆ **Rain Forest** / Feb.-Mar. 1980 / CMP 12

Virtuoso flute player. An improvisational tradition of various groupings. With Eddie Gomez (b), Jack DeJohnette (d), Mike Nock (k), and Nana Vasconcelos (per). —*Michael G. Nastos*

MIKE STERN (Michael Stern)

b. Jan. 10, 1954, Boston, MA

Guitar / Early jazz-rock, instrumental pop, modern creative

A rocking, experimental guitarist who rose to fame playing in a pair of Miles Davis bands, Mike Stern's a competent be-bop and hard bop player, but an excellent fusion and jazz-rock musician. He's provided some wondrous riffs, blistering lines, complex voicings, and dynamite phrases doing fusion, playing with much more force and vigor than on more con-

ventional jazz. Stern attended Berklee in the early '70s, where he studied with Pat Metheny and Mick Goodrick. Metheny recommended him for a vacancy with Blood, Sweat & Tears, and Stern played with them for two years. He later worked with Billy Cobham, then joined Davis's band in 1981. Stern stayed with Davis for two years, then played with Jaco Pastorius's group Word of Mouth. Stern made his recording debut as a leader in 1985. He later toured with Davis again, played with Steps Ahead, and worked in bands led by Mike Brecker and Harvie Swartz. Stern's recorded as a leader for Atlantic in the '80s and '90s. He has several sessions available as a leader. —*Ron Wynn with Michael G. Nastos*

Upside Downside / Mar.-Apr. 1986 / Atlantic 81656

Time in Place / Dec. 1987 / Atlantic 81840

With Michael Brecker (sax) and Bob Berg (ts). "Gossip" a good opening track. —*Michael G. Nastos*

○ **Standards (and Other Songs)** / i. Sep. 23, 1992 / Atlantic 82419

Just as the title implies, this is an album of mostly jazz standards augmented by several of Stern's own original compositions. Also featured are Jay Anderson (b), Randy Brecker (tpt), and Bob Berg (ts). This is perhaps Stern's finest recording. —*Paul Kohler*

BOB STEWART

b. Feb. 3, 1945, Sioux Falls, SD

Tuba / Modern creative

A virtuoso tuba player, Bob Stewart's solos explore the instrument's full range and show its ability to serve as both a lead and support instrument within a jazz ensemble. He rivals Howard Johnson in terms of demonstrating depth, facility, and imagination on tuba. Stewart began playing trumpet at age ten, and studied trumpet and tuba at the Philadelphia College of the Performing Arts. He taught in the public school system in Pennsylvania, then later played in a traditional jazz band at a Philadelphia club. Stewart moved to New York in the late '60s, and joined the tuba ensemble Gravity. He played with Carla Bley, Frank Foster's Loud Minority, and the orchestras of Sam Rivers and Gil Evans in the late '60s. Stewart was a featured member of Arthur Blythe's mid-'70s band that recorded for Columbia, and also worked with the Globe Unity Orchestra, and with Charles Mingus and McCoy Tyner. Stewart played with David Murray's Big band, Lester Bowie's Brass Fantasy, and Henry Threadgill's orchestra in the '80s and into the '90s. He currently teaches at LaGuardia High School for the Performing Arts in New York City, the same school showcased in the film and television series "Fame." Stewart has not recorded as a leader, but can be heard on many CDs by Blythe, Murray, Threadgill, and many others. —*Ron Wynn*

★ **First Line** / i. Nov. 1987 / Verve 834414

Bob Stewart's simple variation on the role of the bass in the small group results in music that is sparklingly fresh, yet comfortably familiar. To begin with, he plays the tuba, rather than bass violin or bass guitar. And he plays it well, with a clear, focused technique that is surprisingly agile for such an elephantine instrument. Then, instead of the expected beat or rhythmically free melodic line as a harmonic and rhythmic foundation, he generally supplies short, repeated, riff-like figures. Those highly charged lines, coordinated with the infectious patterns of drummer Idris Muhammad and percussionist Arto Tuncboyaci, give the music an engaging vitality. Although Stewart carries the melodic line on occasion, and sometimes constructs solos from his ostinato figures, he seems mostly content with his role as an anchor, and never improvises in the conventional, straightahead bop/postbop manner of his excellent colleagues (Steve Turre, tb, Haitian shell; Stanton Davis, tpt; Kelvyn Bell electric guitar; Muhammad; and Tuncboyaci), all of whom acquit themselves well. Half the tunes are Stewart originals, three others are traditional songs, and a pair were written by "Black" Arthur Blythe. Although it includes the wistful "C.J."

and the quietly reflective "Sometimes I Feel Like a Motherless Child," this music is essentially vigorous and vivacious. Some of it is Latin-derived, but its dominant spirit is one of gritty earthiness, often reinforced by a heavy-handed backbeat, the jaunty "second line" parade-style drumming on "Hey Mama," "Hambone," and to some extent the title track (a play on words?) being obvious examples. And every one of the original melodies, either Stewart's or Blythe's, is adventurous and full of the pleasingly unpredictable. —*David Franklin*, Jazz Times

☆ **Goin' Home** / **i.** 1988 / Verve 834427
Premier tuba player Bob Stewart with quintet. One side is originals and the other is standards and traditional fare. Highly recommended. —*Michael G. Nastos*

REX STEWART (William (Jr) Stewart)

b. Feb. 22, 1907, Philadelphia, PA, **d.** Sep. 7, 1967, Los Angeles, CA
Cornet / Swing, big band
Rex Stewart achieved his greatest glory in a subsidiary role, playing cornet for 11 years in the Duke Ellington Orchestra. His famous "talking" style and half-valve effects were exploited brilliantly by countless Ellington pieces that contained passages perfectly tailored to showcase Stewart's sound. He played in a forceful, gripping manner that reflected the influence of Louis Armstrong, Bubber Miley, and Bix Beiderbecke, whose solos he once reproduced on record. Stewart played on Potomac riverboats before moving to Philadelphia. He went to New York in 1921. Stewart worked with Elmer Snowden in 1925, then joined Fletcher Henderson a year later. But he felt his talents were not at the necessary level, and departed Henderson's band, then joined his brother Horace's band at Wilberforce College. Stewart returned to Henderson's band in 1928. He remained for five years and contributed many memorable solos. There was also a brief period in McKinney's Cotton Pickers in 1931, a stint heading his own band, and another short stay with Luis Russell before Stewart joined the Ellington Orchestra in 1934. He was a star throughout his tenure, co-writing classics like "Boy Meets Horn" and "Morning Glory." He also supervised many outside recording sessions using Ellingtonians. After leaving Ellington's band, Stewart led various combos, and performed throughout Europe and Australia on an extensive Jazz at the Philharmonic tour from 1947 to 1951. He lectured at the Paris Conservatory in 1948. Stewart settled in New Jersey to run a farm in the early '50s. He was semiretired, but found new success in the media. He worked in local radio and television, while leading a band part time in Boston. Stewart led the Fletcher Henderson reunion band in 1957 and 1958, and recorded with them. He played at Eddie Condon's club in 1958 and 1959, then moved to the West Coast. Stewart again worked as a disc jockey and became a critic. While he published many excellent pieces, a collection containing many of his best reviews, called *Jazz Masters of the Thirties*, came out posthumously. There's also a Stewart autobiography available. —*Ron Wynn*

○ **Rex Stewart and the Ellingtonians** / Jul. 23, 1940-1946 / Riverside 1710
This brings together three HRS dates: 7/23/40 with Rex Stewart, Lawrence Brown, Barney Bigard, Billy Kyle, Brick Fleasle, Wellman Bruad, and Dave Tough; the fall of '46 with Stewart, Kyle, John Levy, and Cozy Cole; and 1/10/46 with Joe Thomas (tpt), Lawrence Brown, Otto Hardwick (as), Ted Nash (ts), Harry Carney, Jimmy Jones, Billy Taylor (b), and Shelly Manne (d). The '40 date lacks a depth and bottom to its Dixieish feel. The '46 quartet sides give a full spotlight on Stewart's special trumpet playing, always a pleasure for me, but the group lacks a cohesive intimacy. At times the leader's solo development transcends that and his challenging bursts of fire and brimstone on "Loopin' Lobi'" please as much as remind me of the potential. The last two tracks are under Jimmy Jones's name and do not include Stewart. —*Bob Rusch*, Cadence

○ **Big Reunion, The** / Nov.-Dec. 2, 1957 / Jazztone 1285

○ **Henderson Homecoming** / Aug. 1, 1958 / United Artists 4009

○ **Rendezvous with Rex** / Jan. 28+Jan. 31, 1958 / Felsted 7001
Rendezvous with Rex brings together two Rex Stewart dates: 1/28/58 and 1/31/58. Stewart will inevitably be tagged an Ellingtonite. That is understandable as it was with Ellington where he was most magnificent. That said, then note that this is not a recording in the Ellington genre, except for a little of the harmonic ensemble blending that might suggest that association. Stewart was in some ways a progressive musician in that he valued the tradition and was also open to expanding it. Here we have a masters' showcase, not just for the leader's cornet, but also nice spots for Hilton Jefferson, Haywood Henry, George Stevenson, and Everett Barksdale in a combined personnel that also includes George Kelly, Willie "The Lion" Smith, Dick Cary, Garvin Bushnell, Leonard Gaskin, Art Tappier, Joe Benjamin, and Mickey Sheen. There are many faces on this program of chamber mainstream jazz; it romps, stomps, swaggers and carefully caresses the blues and grows in depth with repeated listenings. Rex Stewart may have been the leader, but his role was managing team player; this has no grandstanding or twisting egos—even the great personality of Willie The Lion becomes a part, not the focus, of this team for the two tracks he is aboard. —*Bob Rusch*, Cadence

★ **With Henri Chase** / Jun. 12, 1966 / Polydor 623234

Trumpet Jive / **i.** 1971 / Prestige 24119

SLAM STEWART (Leroy Elliot Stewart)

b. Sep. 21, 1914, Englewood, NJ, **d.** Dec. 10, 1987, Binghamton, NY
Bass / Swing
Just as the ignorant occasionally dismiss Clark Terry's great talent because of his on-stage antics, Slam Stewart's bass skill was sometimes undervalued because of the success of his bowing/humming act. Stewart used the bow and sang the melody simultaneously at an octave's interval. It was a delightful act, but it was sometimes regarded as close to a reincarnated minstrel routine by the purist/nationalist sect who overlooked Stewart's outstanding solos and his great skill in constructing them. Stewart was a tremendous bassist, able to accompany anyone regardless of tempo, and to play magnificent "straight" solos. He studied at the Boston Conservatory, and, in the late '30s, developed a novelty act with guitarist Slim Galliard called "Slim and Slam." Their signature song, "The Flat Floot Floogie," remained popular throughout both their careers. They had other hits, among them "Tutti Frutti," "Jump Session," and "Buck Dance Rhythm." Stewart was in the film *Stormy Weather*. He worked with Red Norvo and Benny Goodman, and played with Art Tatum from the mid-'40s to the early '50s. He also worked in a trio with Billy Taylor, and recorded with the Lester Young Quartet. Stewart and Don Byas teamed on some stunning sax/bass duets in 1945. He later worked with Roy Eldridge, Beryl Booker, and Rose Murphy in the '50s and '60s. Stewart taught music in New York in the '70s, and toured with Goodman. He formed a partnership with Bucky Pizzarelli in 1978. Stewart played with Illinois Jacquet in London in the '80s, and recorded with bassist Major Holley in a bass/vocal duo setting. Stewart recorded for Savoy, United Artists, Stash, Delos, and Black & Blue, among others. He has a few dates available on CD. —*Ron Wynn*

○ **Two Big Mice** / Jul. 14, 1977 / Black & Blue 59124

○ **Dialogue** / 1978 / Stash 201
Individually, bassist Slam Stewart and guitarist Bucky Pizzarelli had both been part of very successful partnerships in the past. Stewart and Pizzarelli don't necessarily hit a home run here, but it's at least a double. I think Stewart fans will be the greater satisfied, as Stewart is featured more. Still to be developed between these two is a loose swing with each other that's more intuitive than planned, a greater dialog. The weakest moment is "Masquerade," which does little

more than genuflect to Leon Russell's melody and George Benson's instrumentation. —*Bob Rusch*, Cadence

★ **Shut Yo' Mouth!** / Dec. 6, 1981 / Delos 1024
With Major Holley. Two great bassists get together for a good time. Highly recommended. —*Michael G. Nastos*

ALBERT STINSON

b. 1944, **d.** 1969
Bass / Cool
Albert Stinson's promising career ended abruptly in the late '60s. A prodigious bassist with a huge tone and a sharp attack, Stinson had distinguished himself through his work with Chico Hamilton and Terry Gibbs. Stinson played piano, trombone, and tuba as a child before turning to bass at age 14. He worked with Gibbs and Hamilton in the early and mid-'60s, then was Charles Lloyd's first bassist in 1965. Stinson did sessions on the West Coast in 1966, then worked and toured with John Handy and Larry Coryell. He didn't do any dates as a leader, but can be heard on Hamilton CD reissues. —*Ron Wynn*

SONNY STITT (Edward Stitt)

b. Feb. 2, 1924, Boston, MA, **d.** Jul. 22, 1982, Washington, DC
Saxophone / Bop, hard bop
Charlie Parker has had many admirers and his influence can be detected in numerous styles, but few disciples have been as avid as Sonny Stitt. There was almost note-for-note imitation in several early Stitt solos, and the closeness in style remained until Stitt began to de-emphasize the alto in favor of the tenor, on which he artfully combined the influences of Parker and Lester Young. Stitt gradually developed his own sound and style, though he was never far from Parker on any alto solo. A wonderful blues and ballad player whose approach was one of the influences on John Coltrane, Stitt could rip through an uptempo bebop stanza, then turn around and play a shivering, captivating ballad. He was an alto saxophonist in Tiny Bradshaw's band during the early '40s, then joined Billy Eckstine's seminal big band in 1945, playing alongside other emerging bebop stars like Gene Ammons and Dexter Gordon. Later, Stitt played in Dizzy Gillespie's big band and sextet. He began on tenor and baritone in 1949, and at times was in a two-tenor unit with Ammons. He recorded with Bud Powell and J.J. Johnson for Prestige in 1949, then did several albums on Prestige, Argo, and Verve in the '50s and '60s. Stitt led many combos in the '50s, and rejoined Gillespie for a short period in the late '50s. After a brief stint with Miles Davis in 1960, Stitt reunited with Ammons and, for a while, was in a three-tenor lineup with James Moody. During the '60s, Stitt also recorded for Atlantic, and cut the transcendent *Stitt Plays Bird*, which finally addressed the Parker question in epic fashion. He continued heading bands, though he joined the Giants of Jazz in the early '70s. This group included Gillespie, Art Blakey, Kai Winding, Thelonious Monk, and Al McKibbon. Stitt did some sessions in the '70s for Cobblestone, Muse, and others, among them another definitive date, *Tune-Up!* He continued playing and recording in the early '80s, recording for Muse, Sonet, and Who's Who in Jazz. He suffered a heart attack and died in 1982. There's plenty of old and more recent Stitt available on the reissue market. This includes several Prestige and Muse sessions, as well as material on Delmark, Fresh Sound, Gazell, and Polydor. Sadly, his fine dates on Atlantic and Argo/Chess aren't available currently on American labels. —*Ron Wynn and Bob Porter*

○ **Sonny Stitt with Bud Powell and J.J. Johnson** / Oct. 17, 1949-Dec. 11, 1949 / Prestige 009

Kaleidoscope / 1950-1952 / Prestige 060
Five dates from 1950-1952. Fine reissue that features early '50s Stitt. —*Ron Wynn*

Symphony Hall Swing / i. 1952 / Savoy 1165

○ **Sonny Stitt Plays Arrangements of Quincy Jones** / Oct. 17, 1955 / Roost 2204

○ **New York Jazz** / Sep. 14, 1956 / Verve 8219

When Sonny Stitt was hot and had a mind to, he could play most inspired music. *New York Jazz* was recorded with Jimmy Jones (p), Ray Brown (b), and Jo Jones (d), and it is a serious but average (good) session. Dividing himself between tenor and alto, Stitt blows 10 tracks, some of which run long on flash but short of depth. Where Stitt excels here is on the medium to slow tempos and on tenor—though on "12th Street Rag" he transcends someone's banal idea of repertoire. Perhaps the work point here is the backup, which rather falls away on its own. This is stronger on individual parts than overall but gets a qualified recommendation. —*Bob Rusch*, Cadence

Sonny Stitt Sits in with the Oscar Peterson Trio / Oct. 1957-May 1958 / Verve 849396

○ **Burnin'** / Aug. 1, 1958 / Argo 661

○ **Sonny Stitt and the Top Brass** / Jul. 16-17, 1962 / Atlantic 90139
Some wonderful Sonny Stitt alto solos, both in collaboration with the brass section and as a soloist. This early '60s release matches Stitt with a full brass section playing the customary blues, ballads, and standards. His soaring, exuberant playing never overwhelms the accompaniment but sometimes transcends it, other times elevates it. —*Ron Wynn*

Autumn in New York / i. 1962-1963 / Black Lion 760130
Some top '60s sessions with Kenny Clarke (d), Walter Bishop, Jr. (p), and Tommy Potter (b). —*Ron Wynn*

☆ **Soul Classics** / i. 1962-1972 / Prestige 6003
Fine playing, frequently galvanizing solos. 1988 reissue of cuts from 1962-1972. —*Ron Wynn*

★ **Stitt Plays Bird** / Jan. 29, 1963 / Atlantic 1418
Logging in at 45:08, this CD reissue exceeds its LP predecessor by some eight minutes because of its first-time presentation of the only previously unreleased titles from Sonny Stitt's January 29, 1963, session, "Now's the Time" and "Yardbird Suite." Of course, Stitt fanciers will be grateful for this long-overdue act of completion, if not contrition, by the powers that be; but it still seems somewhat odd, especially in light of the fact that the quality of these performances varies not a whit from that of the more familiar bulk, why Atlantic elected to release a 37-minute LP in the first place. Stitt was not a perfectionist in the sense that he would have been overly distraught had he missed a note, fumbled a phrase, or even played out of tune. Indeed, these very characteristics were hallmarks of his stylistic persona, and this is not to denigrate his very real stature as a blowing jazzman. At his best, Stitt had an intense driving swing, a limitless reservoir of ideas, many of which were admittedly not his own, and an almost compulsive need to compete. He was, in short, a jammer to the manner born. But such puristic virtues, as breathtaking as they are in the flesh, do not always come across, especially in settings provided by such comparatively conservative players as the ones here (John Lewis, p; Jim Hall, g; Richard Davis, b; Connie Kay, d). With all due credit to the rhythm players concerned, Stitt sounds unduly constrained and, most sadly of all, as if he is not having the fun he should have been having on this occasion, namely, a tribute to his favorite spiritual brother. —*Jack Sohmer*, Jazz Times

☆ **My Mother's Eyes** / May 1963 / Pacific Jazz 71

○ **Salt and Pepper** / Sep. 5, 1963 / Impulse 52

Soul People / Aug. 1964 / Fantasy 24127

★ **Tune-Up!** / Feb. 1972 / Muse 5334
Sonny Stitt was more respected than loved. He epitomized bebop as contest. Stitt's work, even at its hard-driving best like this, appears as a routine reissue. Routine or not, this reissue will be welcomed. Musicians and critics respected him, and with his smoothed-out bop horn style, he exerted a strong influence on younger players. Supported by a sympathetic rhythm section of Barry Harris (p), Sam Jones (b), and Alan Dawson (d), Stitt works out on both alto and tenor saxophone a program of the usual suspects. Though the notes indicate other takes for "I Can't Get Started," "Just Friends,"

and "Groovin' High," none are included. What is here, though, is classic Sonny Stitt. —*David Dupont*, Cadence

★ **Constellation** / Jun. 27, 1972 / Muse 5323
On February 8, 1972, Sonny Stitt recorded what I rate as his finest album of his last decade, *Tune-Up!* His followup session *Constellation*, a close second, is happily available again. Sonny Stitt's style features a complete mastery of the bop language, the ability to think and play very fast, and an individual sound on both alto and tenor. At one time castigated because of his similiarity in tone to Charlie Parker on alto, Stitt was later recognized as an original who explored a similiar terrain as Bird. All eight cuts on *Constellation* are excellent, highlighted by the ridiculous tempo of the title cut, Stitt's enthusiastic melody reading of "Ray's Idea," his ballad rendition of "It's Magic," and the fast "Blues By Accident." Stitt could not have wished for a more suitable rhythm section (Sam Jones, b; Roy Brooks, d); Barry Harris's playing (p) is a particular delight throughout. Sonny Stitt led over 150 recording sessions in his career, but few are more consistently exciting than the brilliant *Constellation*. —*Scott Yanow*, Cadence

Champ, The / Apr. 1973 / Muse 5429

Mellow / Feb. 14, 1975 / Muse 5067

In Walked Sonny / May 16, 1975 / Sonet

○ **My Buddy: Stitt Plays for Gene Ammons** / Jul. 2, 1975 / Muse 5091
On this album alto and tenor saxophonist Sonny Stitt starts off well on the opening track ("You Can Depend on Me"). Stitt turns to alto only on the Charlie Parker tune ("Confirmation"), and I wish he had stuck to tenor, where at least his tone is rich and strong, although it occasionally gets shrieky and shaky in the upper register. But his alto tone is thin—unpleasant to listen to. Things brighten up a bit with the blues ("Blues for Brad and Kola"), smoothly and warmly played in a slow tempo. The tempo alone is a welcome relief since all other tunes are uptempo. Stitt isn't inspired here but pleasant and fun to hear. The best aspect of this release is pianist Barry Harris. Bassist Sam Jones takes a few good solos but his sound is marred by that dull flatness too many bassists in this day of electric pickups seem to prefer to the full acoustic sound. The recorded sound is good, although there is little stereo separation. —*Jerry De Muth*, Cadence

☆ **Blues for Duke** / Dec. 3-4, 1975 / Muse 5129

Moonlight in Vermont / Nov. 23, 1977 / Denon 7046

☆ **I Remember Bird** / 1977 / Catalyst 7616
I Remember Bird features the fine trombonist Frank Rosolino, who also appeared on several Catalyst dates, and a rhythm section of Dolo Coker, piano, Allen Jackson, bass, and Clarence Johnston, drums. This is essentially Sonny Stitt playing Sonny Stitt; he works his patented Stitt licks, turns those familiar phrases, and always makes them sound new. He runs through a diverse collection of material including "Body and Soul," "Jeepers Creepers," Michel Legrand's "Watch What Happens," and the traditional "Yes Jesus Loves Me." —*Herb Nolan*, Down Beat

○ **Sonny Stitt with Strings** / 1977 / Catalyst 7620
Sonny Stitt with Strings is dedicated entirely to the music of Duke Ellington and covers some of Ellington's most famous melodies like "Take the 'A' Train," "Cotton Tail," "Sentimental Mood," and so on. Among the more refreshing aspects of this album are Bill Finegan's string arrangements, which are often coarse, subtle, and filled with spaces for Stitt to play around and through. His writing is devoid of the sweet syrupy string sound that tends to pour over the featured player whether the sound is compatible or not. Finegan's strings have a strong similarity to what Eddie Sauter produced for Stan Getz's album *Focus*, which came out in 1962, probably because Finegan and Sauter co-led a band in the early 1950s. *Sonny Stitt with Strings* is easy-listening jazz that emerges a cut above background dinner music. —*Herb Nolan*, Down Beat

Sonny's Back / Apr. 7-Jul. 14, 1980 / Muse 5204

In Style / Mar. 18, 1981 / Muse 5228

○ **Last Stitt Sessions—Vols. 1 & 2** / Jun. 1982 / Muse 6003
Some early '80s dates by saxophonist Sonny Stitt, which were issued in single-album form shortly after his death. They've been combined and reissued in one two-disc package and are also available in single-disc fashion. Though Stitt is on his last legs, he summons enough energy and strength to play some booming blues and intense uptempo originals and standards. He is backed on both albums by bassist George Duvivier and drummer Jimmy Cobb. Junior Mance plays piano on the first volume, Walter Davis on the second. Trumpeter Bill Hardman appears only on volume two. —*Ron Wynn*

○ **Last Stitt Sessions—Vol. 1** / Jun. 1982 / Muse 5269
This Muse album is another in the series of good solid Sonny Stitt (as, ts) sessions for that label, with pianist Junior Mance (George Duvivier, bass, Jimmy Cobb, drums) adding an extra filip to the session. The outstanding track here is "Angel Eyes," but the session as a whole is successful—not the equal of his most outstanding Prestige and Verve sessions of earlier years, but certainly well worth having. —*Shirley Klett*, Cadence

With Art Blakey / Gazell

BILLY STRAYHORN (William [Swee' Pea] Strayhorn)

b. Nov. 29, 1915, Dayton, OH, **d.** May 31, 1967, New York, NY
Piano, arranger, composer / Swing, big band
Billy Strayhorn made collaboration an art form; he combined with Duke Ellington on more than 200 numbers in the orchestra's book, and enjoyed a creative empathy with him that has been alternately described as spooky, remarkable, and magic. From the time he submitted a piece to Ellington in 1938 and was contacted three months later, until his death in 1967, Strayhorn functioned as coleader, arranger, pianist, confidant, and muse. Among his gems are "Take the 'A' Train," "Lush Life," "Something to Live for," "Day Dream," "After All," "Passion Flower," "Lotus Blossom," "Johnny Come Lately," "U.M.M.G.," and "Blood Count." Strayhorn found time to write, to arrange, and to participate in many extra-Ellington sessions with such sidemen as Cootie Williams, Barney Bigard, Johnny Hodges, Louie Bellson, The Coronets and Ellingtonians, Ben Webster, and Clark Terry, plus duos and trios with Ellington and an occasional album of his own. Strayhorn received extensive musical training, and the piece he submitted to Ellington surprised Ellington by its depth and structure. The first Strayhorn number they cut was "Something to Live for" in 1939, with Jean Eldridge on the vocals. They did more Strayhorn that year, including "I'm Checkin' Out," "Goo'm Bye," and "Grievin'," which were co-written with Ellington, "Lost in Two Flats" by Barney Bigard, and an Ellington tribute to Strayhorn, "Weely (A Portrait of Billy Strayhorn)." He served briefly as pianist in Mercer Ellington's Orchestra before officially becoming Ellington's associate arranger and second pianist. Strayhorn helped with both ambitious pieces and with pop material; these included "The Perfume Suite," "A Drum is a Woman," and "Such Sweet Thunder." He directed the band for Ellington's '63 production "My People." His final composition, "Blood Count," was sent to the band from the hospital where he died of cancer. The Ellington orchestra cut one of its most poignant albums in tribute, *And His Mother Called Him Bill.* Ellington played "Lotus Blossom" solo at the end of the session while the musicians packed their gear. Other Strayhorn tributes have been recorded by several musicians, including Art Farmer and Marian McPartland. Joe Henderson won widespread acclaim for his '92 Strayhorn tribute album, and Strayhorn was a prominent influence on Tadd Dameron. —*Ron Wynn*

Trio / Oct. 3-Nov. 1950 / Mercer 1001

○ **Billy Strayhorn Septet** / i. 1958 / Felsted 2008

★ **Cue for Saxophone** / Apr. 14, 1958 / Verve 820604

Billy Strayhorn Sextet. Fine Strayhorn arrangements for session of topflight Ellingtonians. Johnny Hodges (sax) takes honors. Reissue of 1959 date. —*Ron Wynn*

Peaceful Side, The / i. Mar. 1963 / United Artists
Billy Strayhorn Sextet. Superb arrangements, vocals, and orchestrations. Made in Paris. —*Ron Wynn*

○ **Lush Life** / i. 1967 / Red Baron 52760
A '92 reissue of a rare session issued under the name of noted arranger/composer Billy Strayhorn, providing the inspiration and material for a combo with Duke Ellington, trumpeters Cootie Williams and Cat Anderson, drummer Sam Woodyard, etc., and featuring his most famous compositions. —*Ron Wynn*

FRANK STRAZZERI (Frank John Strazzeri)

b. Apr. 24, 1930, New York, NY
Piano, composer / Bop, hard bop, postbop, cool
A polished, disciplined, and fluid pianist, Frank Strazzeri has been successful at playing everything from traditional New Orleans to cool and bebop. Not an exciting soloist or a dazzling stylist, he can provide unobtrusive accompaniment, plus good, if not great, individual contributions. Strazzeri began on tenor and clarinet during the early '40s, and then switched to piano. He studied piano at the Eastman school. During the early '50s, Strazzeri worked with Roy Eldridge, J.J. Johnson, and others serving as house pianist for a Rochester club. He eventually played in New Orleans with Sharkey Bonano and Al Hirt, and worked with Charlie Ventura and Woody Herman. Strazzeri moved to the West Coast in the '60s, and became a studio musician. He recorded for several labels and played with Herb Ellis and Carmell Jones, among other others, while also touring with Joe Williams, Maynard Ferguson, and Howard Rumsey's Lighthouse All-Stars. During the '70s, Strazzeri worked with Les Brown and Cal Tjader, then began heading his own combos. He recorded with Bellson and Tal Farlow in the '80s. Strazzeri has done sessions for Glendale, Fresh Sound, Sea Breeze, and Catalyst. Currently, he has some sessions available on CD. —*Ron Wynn*

★ **Frank's Blues** / Night Life 3008
A '92 release with pianist Frank Strazzeri playing his own and other composers' blues pieces, doing them nicely, with a modicum of passion and energy. He's assisted by a quintet of mostly faceless players, flute and saxophonist Sam Most excepted. —*Ron Wynn*

STRING TRIO OF NEW YORK

Group / Modern creative
Violinist Billy Bang, guitarist James Emery, and bassist John Lindberg were the original members of the String Trio of New York. They made complimentary music, and worked as a tight-knit, yet freewheeling trio playing music that maximized intra-group harmony, but also spotlighted each player's own unusual style. The group began recording in 1979; Bang departed in the late '80s, and was replaced by Charles Burnham. Things changed again in '93, when Regina Carter recorded with holdovers Emery and John Lindberg. They've done sessions for Black Saint, Stash, and Arabesque. The String Trio has some sessions available on CD. —*Ron Wynn*

★ **Area Code 212** / i. Nov. 1980 / Black Saint 0048
○ **As Tears Go By** / i. Dec. 1987 / ITM 0029
○ **Ascendant** / Jun. 1990 / Vintage Jazz 532

FRANK STROZIER (Frank R. Strozier)

b. Jun. 13, 1937, Memphis, TN
Alto saxophone / Postbop
An adventurous alto saxophonist, Frank Strozier became a prominent hard bop player in the late '50s and '60s. He displayed some of the same biting, animated tendencies as fellow altoists James Spaulding and Jackie McLean, with a furious intensity on uptempo tunes and a poignant quality on

ballads. His style built from the classic Charlie Parker foundation, with some blues elements. Strozier studied piano during his younger days in Memphis, then moved to Chicago in 1954 where he played with fellow transplanted Memphians Harold Mabern, George Coleman, and Booker Little. He worked in the group MJT + 3 with Walker Perkins in 1959 and 1960, and moved to New York in 1959. Strozier recorded for Vee Jay in the early '60s, and later played briefly with Miles Davis alongside Mabern and Coleman. He also worked in Roy Haynes's group. He spent six years in Los Angeles, where his associates included Chet Baker, Shelly Manne, and Don Ellis. Strozier returned to New York in the early '70s, joining Keno Duke's Jazz Contemporaries. This group recorded for Strata-East, a Black-owned musicians cooperative. Strozier also played in the New York Jazz Repertory Company, and recorded his own albums in the late '70s for mostly independent and/or import labels, such as Steeplechase. He also worked with Horace Parlan. At present, Strozier doesn't have any current or vintage titles listed in the *Schwann* catalog, though two of his early '60s Vee Jay dates were reissued on CD in 1993. —*Ron Wynn*

Fantastic Frank Strozier / Jan. 1961 / Vee Jay 3005
Classic hard bop by this Chicago alto saxophonist, with help from Booker Little (tpt) and Wynton Kelly (p). —*David Szatmary*

Long Night / Sep. 12, 1961 / Jazzland 56

★ **March of the Siamese Children** / Mar. 28, 1962 / Jazzland 70

Remember Me / Nov. 10, 1976 / Steeple Chase 1066

JOHN STUBBLEFIELD (John (IV) Stubblefield)

b. Feb. 4, 1945, Little Rock, AR
Saxophone, flute / Postbop, neo-bop
Not as heralded as some fellow members of the Association for the Advancement of Creative Musicians (AACM), John Stubblefield's made some excellent hard bop, bebop, and free sessions. He's also an in-demand teacher who has lectured, led seminars, and organized workshops at many universities and colleges, and has worked with the Jazzmobile. Stubblefield joined the AACM after moving to Chicago from Arkansas. He studied with Muhal Richard Abrams and George Coleman, then recorded with Joseph Jarman in 1968. Stubblefield moved to New York in 1971, and played with the Collective Black Artists big band and Mary Lou Williams. He was also in groups led by Charles Mingus, the Thad Jones-Mel Lewis orchestra, and Tito Puente's orchestra. Stubblefield switched gears in 1972 and played a free jazz concert at Town Hall with Anthony Braxton; he was also featured with Braxton on an album of the same name. He recorded with Abdullah Ibrahim and worked with Miles Davis in 1973. Stubblefield recorded with McCoy Tyner, Gil Evans, Lester Bowie, Nat Adderley, and Sonny Phillips in the '70s, and with Kenny Barron and Teo Macero in the '80s. He also recorded as a leader in the '70s and '80s. Stubblefield's done sessions for Soul Note and Enja, among others. He has some dates available on CD. —*Ron Wynn*

○ **Prelude** / i. 1976 / Storyville 4011
John Stubblefield (ts, ss) plays "freebop," the final confluence of mainstream hard bop. The value of the form is to review which elements of the '60s avant-garde the mainstream could absorb (modal structures, approximate harmonies, saxophone glossolalia, the sixteenth note as the basic unit, the use of auxiliary percussion and once "exotic" horns—John Coltrane, in other words) and which it perhaps wanted to but could not (variable pitch, free time, collective improvisation—Ornette Coleman, Albert Ayler, Cecil Taylor). Those like me who think the latter the greater direction are likely to find this music very conservative, an impression reinforced by the absorption of other '60s elements as well (Onaje Allen Gumbs's vibelike electric piano on several numbers and the obligatory bossa nova "If You Only Knew"). Regardless, the leader's tenor is spirited throughout, and he plays his weaker soprano only on one cut. Trumpeter Cecil

Bridgewater, though, is ragged in places and merely dull in others, and Gumbs sinks fast in the vortex of McCoy Tyner. Bassist Cecil McBee is solid as always, but Joe Chambers, for whatever reason, is not so lively a drummer now (1980) as he was 10 years ago. —*Francis Davis*, Cadence

★ **Bushman Song** / Apr. 22-23, 1986 / Enja 79660
On the surface, John Stubblefield and his compatriots offer a number of approaches (funk-fusion, Latin, calypso, swing) *creatively* rendered. But careful listening reveals an all-too-telling commercial underbelly that puts subtle though damaging constraints on the music. So while the leader has a passionate tenor outing (shades of the Pharoah Sanders of yesteryear) on the Trane-influenced "East," and plays some sinewy soprano on the Weather Report-like title cut and "Things," keyboardist Geri Allen spotlights her adept skills at imaginatively convoluting phrases over and around stated and implied bar lines (to say nothing of her solid chops overall), and the whole band illustrates solid facility as a group as well as individuals, overall the album doesn't reach the heights to which it aspires. —*Milo Fine*, Cadence

L. SUBRAMANIAM (Lakshiminarayana Subramaniam)

b. Jul. 23, 1947, Madras, India
Violin / World fusion
An excellent violinist in traditional Asian, jazz, or jazz-rock/fusion circles, L. Subramaniam has been mixing the improvisational concepts of America and India since the '70s. He learned violin and played classical concerts as a child. Subramaniam studied medicine, then came to America to pursue a graduate degree in Western music, which he earned from the California Institute for the Arts. He toured America and Europe with George Harrison and Ravi Shanker in the mid-'70s, then composed for and recorded with Stu Goldberg, and, in 1978, with Larry Coryell, and made his recording debut as a leader that same year. Subramaniam was later part of John Handy's group, Rainbow, with Ali Akbar Khan in the late '70s. During the '80s, he led a group with Coryell, George Duke, and Tom Scott, then co-led another band with Stephane Grappelli. Subramaniam's recorded for Milestone in the '80s, and has some sessions available on CD. —*Ron Wynn*

★ **Spanish Wave** / i. 1983 / Milestone 9114
The earliest and most satisfying of his classical/jazz-fusion albums for Milestone, with top jazz and Indian musicians mixing it up. —*Myles Boisen*

IDREES SULIEMAN (Idrees Dawud ibn Sulieman)

b. Aug. 7, 1923, St. Petersburg, FL
Trombone, flugelhorn / Bop
Idress Sulieman was one of the earliest trumpeters to fully embrace bebop, and has played it with passion and fire since the '40s. Because he left America for Sweden in the early '60s, Sulieman is not well known. He played with the Carolina Cotton Pickers in the early and mid-'40s before joining Thelonious Monk in 1947. He worked with Cab Calloway in 1948, then played with Count Basie, Lionel Hampton, and Dizzy Gillespie. Sulieman was in Friedrich Gulda's ensemble of American players in the mid-'50s, then worked with Randy Weston in 1958 and 1959. He toured Europe with a group led by Oscar Dennard, then settled in Stockholm in 1961. He also began playing alto sax. Sulieman was a principal soloist with the Kenny Clarke-Francy Boland big band from the mid-'60s until 1973. He moved to Copenhagen in 1964, and since that time, has played mainly in Denmark, and has worked with the Radioens Big Band since the early '70s. He recorded as a leader for Steeplechase in the mid-'70s, and as a sideman with Monk, Mal Waldron, the Radioens Big Band, and Horace Parlan, among others. Currently, he does not have any sessions available on CD, but can be heard on Monk reissues. —*Ron Wynn*

★ **Coolin'** / Apr. 14, 1957 / New Jazz 8216

CHARLES SULLIVAN (Charles Henry Sullivan)

b. Nov. 8, 1944, New York, NY
Trumpet, flugelhorn, bandleader / Bop
A most underrated trumpeter, Charles Sullivan has excellent technique, fine tone, a bright, shimmering sound, and is effective in hard bop, free, big band, or bebop contexts. Although he doesn't have a large legacy of recordings to tout, he simply hasn't gotten the credit he deserves. Sullivan studied at the Manhattan School of Music in the '60s, and worked for Off-Broadway productions. He played with Lionel Hampton and Roy Haynes's Hip Ensemble in the late '60s, then toured briefly as Count Basie's lead trumpeter in 1970, and toured with Lonnie Liston Smith in 1971. He played with Sy Oliver in 1972, and with Norman Connors in 1973. Sullivan toured Europe and recorded with Abdullah Ibrahim in 1973 as well, then worked and recorded with Sonny Fortune, Carlos Garnett, Bennie Maupin, Ricky Ford, Eddie Jefferson, and Woody Shaw, and cut his own records through the remainder of the '70s. Despite all that activity, Sullivan couldn't expand his audience and gain more recognition. He began heading the band Black Legacy in the late '70s, and continued into the '80s. Sullivan doesn't have any sessions currently available on CD, but can be heard on reissues by Shaw, Jefferson, Fortune, and others. —*Ron Wynn*

★ **Genesis** / Jun. 20-Jun. 21, 1974 / Inner City 1012
Charles Sullivan deserves full honors for this lyrical debut album. Though his liner notes refer to a Scorpio's need to be reborn phoenixlike from the ashes of his own existence, the trumpeter's style is so warm and creative it's difficult to believe he had to negate himself to arrive at such celebratory and stimulating music. Each of the compositions is Sullivan's own, as are the simple but effective arrangements that forge a collection of talented sidemen into an inspired ensemble. Most of the blowing is also Sullivan's; not a showboater, he seems nonetheless to command the focus of each selection. Sonny Fortune spins through "Genesis" like a whirlwind clearing a path through the desert with percussive rushes from percussionist Lawrence Killian's fingertips right behind him. Fortune, Sullivan, pianist Stanley Cowell, drummer Billy Hart, and bassist Alex Blake work from the theme toward unaccompanied free-style solo climaxes, returning in an almost revolutionary process; they go out, but they come back, and the song's movement is reenergized. Sullivan creates a satisfying aural experience, an acoustic set electrified with feeling, alternating blue and brightly burning. —*Howie Mandel*, Down Beat

IRA SULLIVAN (Ira Brevard (Jr) Sullivan)

b. May 1, 1931, Washington, DC
Winds, trumpet, saxophone / Bop
Ira Sullivan is one of the great multi-instrumentalists of modern jazz. Long associated with the Chicago modern jazz scene, Sullivan moved to Florida in the mid-'60s, and has remained there for most of his career. Fluent on trumpet, flugelhorn, flute, and all the saxophones, Sullivan has almost always been involved with small groups. He has made a dozen or so albums under his own leadership and all are challenging, inspired modern jazz. His work with Red Rodney in a co-led group delighted fans in the early and mid-'80s, and the albums they recorded for Muse and Elektra/Musician are well worth seeking out. —*Ron Wynn and Bob Porter*

○ **Nicky's Tune** / Dec. 24, 1958 / Delmark 422
Some stirring solos by trumpeter and saxophonist Ira Sullivan make this late '50s session delightful. There's also excellent piano from the sadly neglected pianist Jodie Christian. Sullivan was soon to take a long hiatus from the music business but at this juncture was playing with flair and conviction. —*Ron Wynn*

Ira Sullivan Quintet: Blue Stroll / Jul. 26, 1959 / Delmark 402
In Chicago with Johnny Griffin (sax) and Jodie Christian (p). Excellent. —*Michael G. Nastos*

★ **Ira Sullivan** / Dec. 9, 1976-Mar. 9, 1976 / A&M 706
This record offers no sensational performances. Indeed, with the exception of the uniformly high quality of the playing throughout, there is nothing spectacular about it at all. Understandably, the focus of attention is on multi-instrumentalist (tpt, fltn, ss, f) Ira Sullivan, but not at the expense of his companions. Simon Salz, a dexterous and thoughtful guitarist, is also heavily featured, his preferred acoustic instrument and classical technique affording a luxurious complement to the diverse sounds created by Sullivan. Also heard in solo is Jodie Christian, who directs his crisp touch with equal intensity to both acoustic and electric pianos. Though not showcased, the roles played by bassist Dan Shapera and drummer Wilbur Campbell deserve commensurate praise as well. Sullivan plays accessible contemporary jazz that accomplishes its purposes without benefit of the fusion clichés elsewhere so abundant. —*Jack Sohmer,* Down Beat

Ira Sullivan / i. 1977 / Flying Fish 075

Peace / Sep. 20+21, 1978 / Galaxy 5114

○ **Incredible, The** / Stash 208
Multi-instrumentalist Ira Sullivan puts on an impressive display of technique as he plays several saxes, plus trumpet and flutes. His facility, solos, and spirit are what make this album interesting. The backing band, arrangements, and production are rather routine, but Sullivan's domination keeps it from bogging down. —*Ron Wynn*

MAXINE SULLIVAN (Marietta Williams)

b. May 13, 1911, Homestead, PA, **d.** Apr. 7, 1987, New York, NY

Vocals, trombone, flugelhorn / Swing, ballads & blues
A great singer and an engaging performer, Maxine Sullivan parlayed a subtle, yet undeniable sense of swing with distinctive phrasing and excellent interpretative qualities to become a fine jazz, standards, and pre-rock pop vocalist. She enjoyed success in the swing era, then repeated that success several eras later. Sullivan sang in clubs in Pittsburgh and on radio broadcasts. In 1937, her vocals and Claude Thornhill's arrangement of "Loch Lomond" resulted in her first hit. That was followed by a series of folk novelty numbers like "Cockles and Mussels" and "If I Had a Rainbow Bow." Sullivan landed a nationwide radio program with her husband at the time, John Kirby. "Flow Gently Sweet Rhythm" aired Sunday afternoons in 1940, and was the only coast-to-coast radio show that featured Black performers. Sullivan even did some acting, and appeared on stage in *Swinging the Dream* and in the films *Goin' Places* and *St. Louis Blues.* She toured with Benny Carter in 1941, then retired in 1942. Sullivan returned in the mid-'40s. After tours of England in 1948 and 1954, and another stage appearance in the 1953 play *Take a Giant Step,* Sullivan retired once more. She became a nurse, but came back again in 1958, this time both singing and playing valve trombone and flugelhorn. She appeared at several festivals, then did sessions with the World's Greatest Jazz Band, Earl Hines, Ike Isaacs, Bob Wilber, and Dick Hyman. In the '80s, Sullivan recorded classic pre-rock pop, and worked with Scott Hamilton. She wanted to win a Grammy, but missed out in 1986 with the album *The Great Songs from the Cotton Club.* It was one of three unsuccessful nominations. Sullivan's fine 1987 LP of Jule Syne songs was her final studio date. —*Ron Wynn*

Maxine Sullivan and John Kirby / i. 1940-1941 / Circle

○ **Biggest Little Band in the Land, The** / i. 1941 / Circle 125

Complete Charlie Shavers with Maxine Sullivan, The / i. 1956 / Bethlehem 67

★ **Tribute to Andy Razaf** / i. 1956 / DCC 610
This Maxine Sullivan CD is a release of a 1956 session for Period that has been virtually impossible to find for 30 years or so. The album concept was in honor of Andy Razaf, one of the great lyricists. Inevitably, it also honors Fats Waller, who wrote so much of the music to which Razaf put words.

And the collection is a delightful reminder of Sullivan's ability, without strain or pretense, to interpret a song with feeling, sensitivity, and swing. The septet led by trumpeter Charlie Shavers plays arrangements by Dick Hyman, with contributions by producer Leonard Feather. The charts have the sound and spirit of the John Kirby band, with which Sullivan first made her mark. Thirty-five years ago (1992) Hyman was already an astonishing Waller interpreter. Shavers is magnificient in his solos; Buster Bailey solos on clarinet, Jerome Richardson on alto. The songs include "Honeysuckle Rose," "Ain't Misbehavin'," and other well-known Waller/Razaf collaborations, as well as the undeservedly obscure "How Can You Face Me." There are also songs Razaf wrote with Feather, Eubie Blake, Luckey Roberts, and Paul Denniker. Maxine Sullivan sings them all beautifully. —*Doug Ramsey,* Jazz Times

Maxine / i. 1975 / Audiophile

Good Morning, Life! / Nov. 13-14, 1983 / Audiophile

It Was Great Fun / 1983 / Audiophile

Swingin' Sweet / Sep. 1986 / Concord Jazz 4351
With Scott Hamilton Quintet. Successful meeting with Scott Hamilton (ts) Quintet. —*Ron Wynn*

Together / i. 1987 / Atlantic 81783
1987 release. Fine merger between Sullivan and Keith Ingram's (p) group. —*Ron Wynn*

★ **Sings the Music of Burton Lane** / i. 1991 / Mobile Fidelity 773

☆ **Maxine Sullivan** / Riff 659004

SUN RA (Herman "Sonny" Blount)

b. May 22, 1914, Birmingham, AL, **d.** May 30, 1993, Birmingham, AL

Piano, bandleader, composer / Big band, postbop, early free, progressive big band, modern creative
Sun Ra was a much-maligned bandleader, composer, and pianist until his death in 1993, when he was canonized immediately and was recognized by many institutions that ignored him throughout his lifetime. The former Herman "Sonny" Blount had gotten plenty of ink for his tongue-in-cheek views on the solar origins of African-Americans, and for his own otherworldly residence. But behind the complicated mythology was one of the more remarkable family/band/combine/record label enterprises in modern American music.
Sun Ra's keyboard work alternated between free improvisation and swing-based accompaniment and solos, electronic textures and synthesized coloration, and straight bebop chord changes. He shrewdly mixed these approaches, and never produced what would be expected in a given situation. His band was similarly eclectic; they would play standard swing numbers, then would improvise collectively. Ra would break quartets, quintets, soloists, or duos from the total band. Sun Ra's revue included dancers, vocalists, a slide show, and a personnel roster that could be as few as ten people or as many as 30, or any other configuration equal to or less than either extreme.
Ra was a pioneer on electronic instruments in the mid-'50s, and invented the rocksichord; a keyboard that blended properties of the harpsichord and electric piano. His playing on clavoline, celeste, Moog, and organ ranged from cute to aggressive and animated. Ra gathered superb players; his ranks included, at various times, Marshall Allen, Craig Harris, John Gilmore, Pat Patrick, Clifford Jarvis, Julian Priester, and Lex Humphries. Because major labels didn't have a clue about Ra's music and weren't very interested in it much of the time, he recorded prolifically on his own labels. There's no way to know how much material has been accumulated in his archives because detailed, systematic organization wasn't Ra's strong point. His concerts included buying sessions during intermissions, where fans rummaged through unmarked, unlabeled recordings in boxes. When they got home with their purchase, they might or might not have what they expected.

Sun Ra played piano in Fletcher Henderson's orchestra in the late '40s, reportedly using the names Herman "Sonny" Blount and Le Sony'r Ra. He began to get attention as an arranger, penning charts at the Club DeLisa in the late '40s. After leaving Henderson, Ra formed a trio, and built it into a rehearsal band. He played piano with Eugene Wright and his Dukes of Swing on the Aristocrat label in 1948, with a group that included Hobart Dotson and Yusef Lateef. Ra was also featured on a Chess single with Red Saunders in 1954.

He began recording as a leader with Stuff Smith in the early '50s. His group, the Myth-Science (or Solar) Arkestra, was gradually shortened to the Arkestra. Ra became a prominent part of Chicago's growing free jazz scene in the '50s, and even did the score for a 1959 documentary *The Cry of Jazz*. He began cutting his own records in the mid-'50s for his Saturn label, and also recorded for Transition (later reissued by Delmark) and Savoy. During the '60s, Ra continued recording both for his own label and for ESP, MPS, Savoy, Impulse, Black Lion, and BYG. He moved to New York in 1960, then settled in Philadelphia ten years later.

During the '70s, Sun Ra began to get much-deserved and wider exposure. The Arkestra played at many college campuses, performed throughout Europe, and appeared on "Saturday Night Live" in 1976. There were also recordings for Actuel, Inner City, Philly Jazz, and Sweet Earth. Ra did two fine albums of solo piano for Paul Bley's Improvising Artists Incorporated label, and made fine duo and quartet albums with vibist Walt Dickerson for Steeplechase and MGM. Filmmaker Robert Mugge's acclaimed 1980 film, *A Joyful Noise*, was a comprehensive portrait of the artist at work and play. Sun Ra and his band continued recording for Hat Art, Rounder/Virgin, Praxis (Greece), Leo (England), and Black Saint. Ra continued into the '90s, but became quite ill in late 1991 and didn't work that often in 1992. There's plenty of Sun Ra available on both domestic and foreign label CDs. Evidence has been reissuing the Saturn catalog, while many other sessions are now reappearing because labels scrambled to get his material back in circulation while interest was red hot. —*Ron Wynn and Stephen Aldrich*

○ **Sun Song** / i. Jul. 12, 1956 / Delmark 411

○ **We Travel the Spaceways / Bad and Beautiful** / i. 1956-1960 / Evidence 22038
Sun Ra was preparing to exit Chicago and head for New York as the first seven selections on this disc were being recorded. The other seven were cut by a sextet edition of the Arkestra in New York during 1961. The opening numbers range from the humorous and futuristic bent of *Interplanetary Music* and *We Travel the Spaceways* to the more musically expansive *New Horizons* and *Space Loneliness*. Trumpeter Phil Cohran plus the superb horn section of Marshall Allen, John Gilmore, and Pat Patrick sometimes remain in the maze, other times explode with short but peppery solos. The other songs mix bop and swing tunes with more experimental fare like "Ankh" and "Exotic Two," where Patrick, Gilmore, Ra, and Allen soar while bassist Ronnie Boykins and drummer Tommy Hunter maintain the rhythmic center. Their versions of "Just In Time" and "And This Is My Beloved" show Ra's penchant for inspired, zany, yet faithful recreations of pop and show tunes, something he did throughout his career. These mark his introduction to New York; it would prove a most intriguing stay. —*Ron Wynn*

○ **Sound Sun Pleasure** / 1955-1960 / Evidence 22014
Sun Ra's kaleidoscope of sounds was just taking shape in the '50s and early '60s when the 13 tracks making up this CD were recorded. His Astro-Infinity Arkestra included several emerging musicians who would later become major stars like baritone saxophonist Charles Davis, Bob Northern on flugelhorn, and James Spaulding, who is featured on various reeds. The great jazz violinist Stuff Smith is even along on "Deep Purple," providing a dazzling, bluesy solo that is right at home in the Ra mix. The final five cuts, recorded in 1955, are particularly instructive, from the short yet compelling "Piano Interlude" to the haunting original "Dreams

Come True" and enticing remakes of "'S' Wonderful" and "Lover Come Back to Me." It shows Sun Ra had solved the dilemma of interpreting the past without being dominated by it back in the '50s. It is a lesson many '90s stars have yet to learn. —*Ron Wynn*

★ **Nubians of Plutonia, The** / i. 1959 / Impulse 9242
By the time of *The Nubians of Plutonia* session (1959), the strongly rhythmic undercurrent of Sun Ra's hard bop band had developed into his heavy percussion period. Three events on the LP are of special interest. The brief "Watusa" is two themes that begin in 6/4, like Mongo Santamaria, then grow increasingly strong as they ascend and the tempo speeds. There is alto saxophonist Marshall Allen's 40-measure solo on "Star," a curious collection of phrases marked by original accenting and a raw Jackie McLean-like sound, not really a prediction of his free style, but, my God! *The Magic City* was recorded the next year (1960). And notice the tonality of "Nubia," for Ra already is moving into poly-tonal/atonal areas, while completely isolated from the evolution of Ornette Coleman and Cecil Taylor. In fact, in "Nubia" he is moved by no real influence besides the vigor of his own rhythm section. —*John Litweiler, Down Beat*

We are in the Future / i. Oct. 10, 1961 / Savoy 1141

○ **Cosmic Tones for Mental Therapy / Art Forms of . . .** / i. 1963 / Evidence 22036
Controversy has always revolved around Sun Ra, but few of his albums ever generated more discussion than *Cosmic Tones for Mental Therapy*, which covers half the 12 numbers on this two-LP, single-disc outing. Ra plays "astro space organ," and the array of swirling tones, funky licks, and smashing rhythms—aided and abetted by John Gilmore on bass clarinet, Marshall Allen flailing in the stratosphere on oboe, and arrangements that sometimes had multiple horns dueling in the upper register and other times pivoting off careening beats—outraged those in the jazz community who thought Eric Dolphy and John Coltrane had already taken things too far. The other numbers were done in the early '60s but are no less futuristic. The extended, heated instrumental dialogs, Ra's spinning piano, and the Arkestra's blend of fervent and controlled fury, are equally impressive. —*Ron Wynn*

★ **Heliocentric Worlds of Sun Ra—Vols. 1 and 2, The** / Apr. 20, 1965 / ESP 1017
The Heliocentric Worlds of Sun Ra, Vol. 1 made Sun Ra's cult reputation in 1965; and though it's no longer shocking, it still has the power to unsettle. The tightly plotted compositions rumble with ominous percussion, creak with haunted-house horns, and shiver with the spooky timbres of Ra's marimba and celeste. Robert Cummings's deep-throat bass clarinet solo on "Outer Nothingness" harks back to Stravinsky, but John Gilmore's high-energy tenor on "Other Worlds" rages straight into the future. Ronnie Boykins's arco bass sets the elegiac tone as Ra's clavoline buzzes like a tuned electric razor on "The Sun Myth," the first of only three pieces on *The Heliocentric Worlds of Sun Ra, Vol 2*. On these loosely structured jams, the modern classical ingredients blend inconspicuously into the astral gumbo. Marshall Allen's piccolo agitates a "House of Beauty," working up to the extended saxophone squealathon of "Cosmic Chaos," where Ra's bongo playing serves almost as comic relief. —*Larry Birnbaum, Down Beat*

○ **Monorails and Satellites** / 1966 / Evidence 22013
Although he did not record nearly as much solo piano as he should have, whenever Sun Ra did take the keyboard spotlight the results were memorable. That was certainly the case on this 1966 date with Ra showing the complete range of his styles and influences. There are rumbling boogie progressions and angular bop harmonies, bluesy passages, free sections, and even stride and Afro-Latin references. Though no song is longer than six and a half minutes, Ra's short tunes like "The Galaxy Way" and "Space Towers" grab listeners quickly, hold them transfixed, then conclude with a flourish. It is beautiful, expressive yet forceful piano work,

just one more indicator of Sun Ra's multiple skills. —*Ron Wynn*

Atlantis / 1967-1969 / Saturn
Sun Ra soars far and wide on these late '60s sessions, most notably the 20-minute-plus title cut. This is one of his earliest dates on nothing but electric keyboards, and his manipulation of sounds, noise, whirling phrases, and rhythms is creative and innovative. The other shorter pieces move from somber, almost morose arrangements on "Mu" to the teeming beats of "Bimini" and the otherworldliness of both the Saturn and Impulse versions of "Yucatan." As usual, Ra's band meshes hard bop, bebop, cool, free, and swing elements, with John Gilmore, Marshall Allen, and company alternately wailing, colliding, and complementing the master's dashing clavinet, synthesizer, and organ journeys. An essential and excellent set. —*Ron Wynn*

○ **Holiday for Soul Dance** / 1968-1969 / Evidence 22011
Sun Ra never concerned himself with the issues of innovation vs. preservation that seem to be the rage in current jazz circles. Instead, his music was both futuristic and classic, embracing the past and anticipating the future. A prime example is this fine eight-track collection of prerock standards done in 1968 and 1969, long before the debate about what is and what is not "in the tradition" ever began. But of course Ra would not simply cover these numbers in a reverential manner; instead, he and the Astro-Infinity Arkestra stomp, romp, twist, strut, and cut through a collection ranging from "But Not for Me" through "Early Autumn" and "Body and Soul." They invert and rework, embellish and extend but never fail to retain the flow and beauty of the original. With John Gilmore and Marshall Allen getting the bulk of the solo space, they demonstrate their mastery of the mainstream. Ra's playing on "Holiday for Strings" is intriguing and dashing, while the lyrics on "You're the Cream In My Coffee" are his own impish touch. —*Ron Wynn*

Pictures of Infinity / 1968 / Black Lion

○ **My Brother the Wind—Vol. 2** / 1969-1970 / Evidence 22040
Sun Ra's synthesizer, organ, and electric keyboard playing is probably the most underrated element of his arsenal. Even those who do not understand them acknowledge that his compositions are special, and few detractors would dismiss the capabilities of his band members. But Ra's piano and electronic keyboard journeys are often viewed as gimmicky, clowning, or musically illiterate ramblings. Sadly, this ignorance was the prevailing view for much of his career. Now, in retrospect, Ra's playing is being celebrated. The remarkable phrases, rhythms, progressions, statements, and solos he offers throughout this 11-cut late '60s and early '70s session are a tribute to his understanding of the Moog synthesizer's possiblities and options. While others were noodling and nibbling, Ra was soaring, extending, and stretching out in his inimitable fashion. The Arkestra here is missing Ronnie Boykins's supple bass playing but is otherwise in good hands. The reliables John Gilmore, Pat Patrick, and Marshall Allen are on hand, along with some newer names like Alejandro Blake, Kwame Hadi, and Nimrod Hunt. Ra's inclusion of soulful themes, vocals, and African and Afro-Latin rhythms along with arrangements that sometimes swing and other times jut or slash is once more compelling, unpredictable, and wonderful. —*Ron Wynn*

Solar Myth Approach—Vol. 1, The / 1970-1971 / Affinity 10

Solar Myth Approach—Vol. 2, The / 1970-1971 / Affinity 76

My Brother the Wind—Vol. 1 / i. Apr. 1971 / Saturn 521

Astro-Black / May 7, 1972 / Saturn

★ **Space Is the Place** / 1972 / Blue Thumb
Here is a genuine bonus, some previously unissued cuts. *Space is the Place* is the soundtrack to a film that was made but never released, and the tunes are among Sun Ra's most ambitious, unorthodox, and compelling compositions. Between June Tyson's declarative vocals, chants, and dialog and Ra's crashing, flailing, and emphatic synthesizer and organ fills and with such songs as "Blackman/Love in Outer Space," "It's After the End of the World," and "I Am the Brother of the Wind," this disc offers aggressive, energized, and uncompromising material. As the saxophone/flute section of Marshall Allen, John Gilmore, Eloe Omoe, Danny Thompson, Larry Northington, and Danny Davis along with trumpeter Kwame Hadi plays, Wayne Harris wails, screams, roars, and bleats in both the ensemble sections and during solos. Tyson is a wonderful singer whose appealing vocals were often underrated; likewise, Ra's pianistic forays, phrases, and textures were sometimes dismissed as mere noodling when they were part of a well-constructed multimedia package. This comes as close as any of Ra's releases to being not only a concept work but a blueprint for his live shows from the early '70s until the end of his career. —*Ron Wynn*

○ **Live at Montreux** / Jul. 1976 / Inner City 1039
For Sun Ra, space was not a void. It was a place where sound floated free from the gravity of specific jazz styles. Likewise, the soloists are not bound by standard techniques. Altoist Marshall Allen speaks in flurries of notes and in altissimo bird cries. On trumpet, Ahmed Abdullah smears, whinnies, and bends his way toward new sonorities. John Gilmore pushes his tenor higher and higher, then honks out a low tone or a boppish line, slightly awry. But the most dazzling soloist is Sun Ra himself. He could play the piano like a harp, full of ripples and waves, or he could play percussively, with thunderous rumblings in the bass and staccato attacks all around. All but one of the cuts here are Sun Ra compositions. Each is a series of moments that dissolve into one another. A swinging dance band passage melts into an Arkestral free-for-all; a French horn rips repeatedly up to the same note; suddenly everything stops except for one horn that solos alone, unmetered and unafraid of taking risks. These moments may be wild, comic, serious, lyrical, hip. Some sections are pure noise, almost unbearable; all involve the most direct kind of musical expression. —*Douglas Clark, Down Beat*

Solo Piano—Vol. 1 / May 20, 1977 / Improvising Artists 373850

○ **Unity** / i. Oct. 24+29, 1977 / Horo 20
Live at the Storyville, New York City. The Arkestra's best live album. Loaded with standards. Incredible musicianship. —*Michael G. Nastos*

○ **Solo Piano—Vol. 2** / i. 1978 / Improvising Artists 373858

Visions / i. Jul. 11, 1978 / Steeple Chase

Lanquidity / i. Jul. 17, 1978 / Philly Jazz

Sunrise in Different Dimensions / Feb. 1980 / Hat Art 6099

★ **Strange Celestial Road** / i. 1980 / Rounder 3035

○ **Of Mythic Worlds** / i. Jun. 1981 / Philly Jazz 1007
This release was Sun Ra's second for Philly Jazz. Taken from a performance in Chicago (I assume this was in 1979) the album largely highlights Sun Ra's keyboard work along with the solo skills of saxophonists John Gilmore and Marshall Allen. By and large, the ensemble interplay of the entire Arkestra is ignored. The opening piece, a dirgelike processional, makes effective use of flutes and percussion. But the established mood is broken by the next two tracks which are features for Ra's individualistic piano style. Following a cacophonious horn fanfare, he gradually explores a favorite tune, "Over the Rainbow," first solo and then with a swinging bass and drums accompaniment. This same format is used for "Inside the Blues," the album's best moment. The two tracks on the second side are largely given over to Ra's idiosyncratic organ, some unimaginative percussion, and solos by Gilmore on tenor and Allen on alto. —*Carl Brauer, Cadence*

Reflections in Blue / i. Dec. 18-19, 1986 / Black Saint 0101

Hours After / Dec. 1986 / Black Saint 111

Live at Pit-In / i. 1988 / DIW 824

Out There a Minute / i. 1990 / Blast First 71427

Destination Unknown / i. 1992 / Enja 7071

○ **Sun Ra Visits Planet Earth / Interstellar Low Ways /** Evidence 22039

Fondation Maeght Nights—Vol. 1 / Jazz View 006

Fondation Maeght Nights—Vol. 2 / Jazz View 007

JOHN SURMAN (John Douglas Surman)

b. Aug. 30, 1944, Tavistock, England
Baritone and soprano saxophone, clarinet, synthesizer, electronics / Early jazz-rock, modern creative
A marvelous baritone saxophonist and a good soprano player who's added electronics and bass clarinet in recent years, John Surman has thrived in free, jazz-rock, big band, and varied musical situations since the '60s. His baritone playing has richness and great range. A prominent Coltrane disciple, Surman utilizes a full array of tonal colors, and is equally effective in the instrument's upper and lower registers. He combines smashing intensity and soft lyricism. Surman's mastery of electronics and his application of synthesizers and keyboards into his compositions has expanded his options as a songwriter and arranger. He's blended European folk, classical, and religious sounds into his music, particularly those of England. Surman played in jazz workshops while still in high school. He studied at the London College of Music and London University Institute of Education in the mid-'60s. Surman played with Alexis Korner, worked with Mike Westbrook until the late '60s, and recorded with him until the mid-'70s. He was voted best soloist at the 1968 Montreux Festival while heading his band. Surman worked with Graham Collier, Mike Gibbs, Dave Holland, Chris McGregor, and John McLaughlin in the '60s, and toured Europe with the Kenny Clarke-Francy Boland big band in 1970. Surman toured and recorded with Barre Phillips and Stu Martin in the late '60s and early '70s, and again in the late '70s, adding Albert Mangelsdorff to the group. They called themselves the Trio, then Mumps. Surman played with Mike Osborne and Alan Skidmore in the sax trio SOS in the mid-'70s. He also collaborated with the Carolyn Carlson dance company at the Paris Opera through the mid- and late '70s. Surman recorded with Stan Tracey and Karin Krog, while working with Miroslav Vitous and Azimuth. He led the Brass Project in the early '80s, and played in Collier's big band and Gil Evans's British orchestra. Surman toured with Evans again in the late '80s. He began recording as a leader for Pye in the early '70s, and did sessions for Ogun and ECM. Surman continued recording in the '80s, mostly for ECM. He worked with Terje Rypdal, Jack DeJohnette, Pierre Favre, Bengt Hallberg, Archie Shepp, Warne Marsh, and Red Mitchell, an also cut a solo session. Surman recorded for ECM again in 1992 with Paul Bley, Gary Peacock, and Tony Oxley. He has recent and reissued sessions available on CD. —*Ron Wynn*

Anglo Sax / 1969 / Deram 18027

Road to Saint Ives / **i.** 1970 / ECM 843849

★ **Westering Home** / 1972 / Island 10

○ **Morning Glory** / **i.** 1973 / Island

☆ **S.O.S.** / Jul. 27-28, 1974 / Ogun

☆ **Upon Reflection** / May 1979 / ECM 825472

Amazing Adventures of Simon Simon / Jan. 1981 / ECM 829160

Such Winters of Memory / Dec. 1982 / ECM 23795

Private City / **i.** Dec. 1987 / PolyGram 835780

RALPH SUTTON (Ralph Earl Sutton)

b. Nov. 4, 1922, St. Louis, MO
Piano / Stride, boogie-woogie, swing
Among the last of the classic New York stride pianists, Ralph Sutton was a contemporary of Fats Waller and James P. Johnson. His playing combines a lusty, exuberant quality with a concise, carefully controlled touch and approach. Sutton's rhythms blend precision with alacrity and verve. He played in St. Louis during the '30s, then worked with Jack

Teagarden before and after serving in the army. Sutton moved to New York in the late '40s, and became intermission pianist at Eddie Condon's club. He later moved to the West Coast, and replaced Earl Hines at the Hangover Club in San Francisco while Hines went on tour in 1957. Sutton relocated to Aspen in the mid-'60s, and worked in a supper club. He began playing and recording with a group known as the Ten Giants of Jazz in 1965. They were later renamed the World's Greatest Jazz Band, and Sutton recorded many albums with them. He's recorded for Commodore, Audiophile, Storyville (England), Flyright (England), Ace of Hearts, and Chiaroscuro, among many other labels. He currently has sessions reissued on Chiaroscuro, Aircheck, and Jazzology. —*Ron Wynn*

○ **Ralph Sutton** / **i.** Jun. 15, 1951 / Commodore 30001
Sutton is one of last great stride pianists whose style directly reflects the Fats Waller and James P. Johnson influence. This early '50s date offers marvelous stride solos and rollicking rhythms and was among the best releases in this vein done during the decade. —*Ron Wynn*

★ **Last of the Whorehouse Piano Players** / 1969 / Chiaroscuro 306

○ **Ralph Sutton Quartet, The** / 1969 / Storyville 4013
Long respected as a master of Fats Wallerian stride piano, Ralph Sutton is captured here in a setting rather unlike those of more recent American vintage. The rhythm section (guitarist Lars Black, bassist Hugo Rasmussen, drummer Svend Erik Norregard) play in an appropriately mainstream groove, with the guitarist and bassist each contributing well-paced solos when the moment calls. The drummer lays out on four titles ("Crazy," "At Sundown," "I Want to be Happy," and "If I Could Be with You"), while Sutton plays Bix Beiderbecke's "In the Dark" and his own "Worrying the Life Out Of Me" as unaccompanied solos. —*Jack Sohmer, Cadence*

○ **At Cafe Des Copains** / **i.** Jun. 1983-Jan. 1987 / Sackville 2019

NEIL SWAINSON

b. 1955
Bass / Modern creative
A consistently effective swing and bebop bassist, Neil Swainson has worked with hard bopper Woody Shaw and with milder trumpeter Sam Noto, but is better known for his dates with swing and big band musicians like Jay McShann, Ed Bickert, Doc Cheatham, Rob McConnell, and Pat Labarbera. He's also worked with Jon Ballantyne. Swainson has not done any sessions as a leader, but can be heard on discs by McShann, Bickert, McConnell, and others. —*Ron Wynn*

★ **49th Parallel** / **i.** 1990 / Concord Jazz 4396
Bassist Swainson fulfills the first mandate of the jazz rhythm section—anchor the music and fortify the front line. —*Ron Wynn*, Rock & Roll Disc

STEVE SWALLOW (Stephen W. Swallow)

b. Oct. 4, 1940, Fair Lawn, NJ
Bass, composer / Postbop, early jazz-rock, modern creative
Swallow ranks as one of the innovators on the electric bass, someone who's redefined the instrument and has actually approached it as a totally different animal from its acoustic counterpart. Swallow changed the fingering system and played it like a guitar, and also sought out situations and songs where the electric bass was the requisite instrument. He joined Paul Bley's trio in the '60s, then worked with George Russell, Jimmy Giuffre, and Art Farmer before joining Stan Getz's group from 1965 to 1967. After that, he participated in Gary Burton's radical ensemble from 1967 to 1970. This quartet was a forerunner of a true fusion group, and played jazz, rock, and country in a seamless mix that emphasized electric, rather than acoustic, contexts. This experience led Swallow to give up the acoustic bass. He's worked extensively with Mike Gibbs and Carla Bley in the '70s and '80s, and has also become a prolific composer; his

Music Map

Jazz Synthesizer

Prior to 1970–Pioneers
Robert Moog (1934)
Karl Heinz Stockahusen (1928)

Modular Moog (Studio)
Sun Ra (1914-1993)
Jon Appleton
Dick Hyman (1927)
Richard Teitelbaum (1939)
Paul Bley (1932)

Other early synths:
ARP 2500 modular
Buchla
Synket
Minimoog (portable)

Minimoog (Portable) 1970
Sun Ra (1914-1993)
Mike Nock (1940)
George Duke (1946)
Jan Hammer (1948)

Other Early Monophonics:
ARP's Odyssey and 2600

Electric Pianists (by 1970)
Gil Evans (1912) arrangements
Joe Zawinul (1932)
Quincy Jones (1933) from mid '70s
Ramsey Lewis (1935)
Herbie Hancock (1940)
Chick Corea (1941)
Brian Eno (1948)

1975 – Bob James adopted synthesizer

Free Jazz:
Gordon Beck – George Gruntz
Jasper Van't Hof – Stan Tracey
Michael Waisvisz – John Taylor
Wolfgang Dauner

Synth Players
Neil Ardley (1937)
Alvin Curran
Tangerine Dream
Joseph Jarman (1937) – Art Ensemble of Chicago
George Lewis (1952)
Richard Teitelbaum (1939)
George Duke (1946)
Dr. Patrick Gleeson

The Oberheim (1974) – First Available Polyphonic
Chick Corea
Joe Zawinul
Lyle Mays – Jan Hammer

First Real Polyphonic
Polymoog (1976)
Sequential Circuit Prophet
Korg
Oberheim
Roland
Yamaha

Computer-based Synthesizers
PPG Wave Computer:
  Jasper Van't Hof
  Oscar Peterson
Fairlight CMI:
  Herbie Hancock
  Jan Hammer

Synclavier:
  Chick Corea
  Duke Pearson
  Jean-Luc Ponty
  Lyle Mays

1980s Inexpensive Digital Synths: Yamaha DX-7
Sun Ra
Miles Davis
John Surman
Django Bates

Drum Synthesizers
Moog Drum:
  Billy Cobham
  Joe Gallivan in Gil Evans's orchestra

Simmons Set:
  Billy Cobham
  Jon Hiseman
  Bill Bruford
  Steve Smith
  Tony Williams

Rhythmic Drum machine:
  Herbie Hancock
  Bill Evans (III)
  Miles Davis

Wind Controllers
Lyricon:
  Wayne Shorter
  Sonny Rollins
  Michael Urbaniak
  Bennie Maupin
  Klaus Doldinger
Electronic Valve Instrument (EVI):
  Sun Ra
Akai Electronic Wind Instrument (EWI):
  Michael Brecker

Guitar Controllers
Roland in 1977
ARP Avatar in 1978:
  Pat Metheny
  John Abercrombie
  Bill Frisell
  Trje Rypdal
  David Torn
  Mike Stern
  John McLaughlin
Synth-axe:
  Lee Ritenour
  Allan Holdsworth

Now synthesizers are widely used, especially in the studio.

works have been recorded by Bley, Burton, Gibbs, and Chick Corea, among others. —*Ron Wynn*

Home / Sep. 1979 / PolyGram 513424

Carla / 1986-1987 / ECM 833492
This is a sextet with a three-piece string ensemble playing eight cuts with a progressive focus. All are originals by Steve Swallow. —*Michael G. Nastos*

★ **Swallow** / Sep. 1991-Nov. 1991 / ECM 511960
Bassist Steve Swallow's current work is as far removed from the asceticism of Jimmy Giuffre's *1961* as Club Med is from a monastery. *Swallow* rarely departs from the recipe used in the bassist's 1987 *Carla* and in recent small-group Carla Bley records (with similiar personnel). Cushy arrangements padded with multiple keyboards frame springy stop-and-go rhythms. Bley's three-chord organ vamps set up Swallow's

lead bass and solos from former employers vibist Gary Burton and guitarist John Scofield. Grooves (fast and slow) are everything here. Sweet, frothy, and vaguely tropical, *Swallow* is the musical equivalent of a banana daiquiri. It's lightweight fun, if not completely satisfying. —*Jon Andrews*, Down Beat

HARVIE SWARTZ

b. Dec. 6, 1948, Chelsea, MA
Bass / Early jazz-rock, modern creative
His duets with the redoubtable Sheila Jordan have been a delight, but bassist Harvie Swartz's skillful accompaniment and propulsive lines aren't limited to that role. He's played in many diverse settings, from bebop to large orchestra, hard bop to cool, jazz, and pop vocals. Swartz began playing bass at age 19, and worked in Boston with Mose Allison, Chris Connor, and the duo of Al Cohn and Zoot Sims. He moved to New York in 1972 and worked in tandem with Mike Abene backing such vocalists as Jackie Cain and Roy Kral, Jackie Paris, and Connor. Swartz recorded with Jackie and Roy in 1973. He also played with the Thad Jones-Mel Lewis and Gil Evans orchestras. Swartz was a regular at Richard's Lounge in New Jersey during the mid-'70s, where he sometimes backed Lee Konitz, Jan Hammer, and John Abercrombie. He played in Barry Miles's Silverlight from 1974 to 1976, doubling on electric bass. Swartz also worked with different editions of groups led by David Friedman, recording with them from 1975 to 1981. He was in a trio with Eddie Daniels, and also played with Dave Matthews's big band. Swartz recorded with Friedman's bands between 1975 and 1978, and worked for four years with Steve Kuhn. Besides the duo with Jordan, Swartz's groups and collaborations in the '80s have included heading an ensemble of bass, piano, flugelhorn, cello, percussion, and drums. He led the Harvie Swartz String Ensemble in 1982 and 1983. Swartz has recorded as a leader for Gramavision and Bluemoon on his own, and with Jordan for Muse. He has sessions available on CD as a leader and with Jordan. —*Ron Wynn*

★ **Underneath It All** / Mar. 1-2, 1980 / Gramavision 8202
This bassist's debut album is with Ben Aranov on piano and John D'Earth on trumpet. This is challenging music, approaching fusion. All selections are Swartz's originals. His later albums don't quite match up, but this is virtuoso. His best is on the way. —*Michael G. Nastos*

○ **Full Moon Dancer** / **i.** 1991 / Blue Moon 79150

SYLVIA SYMS

d. 1992

Vocals / Ballads & blues
Sylvia Syms was a vocalist who performed cabaret music, standards, and light-jazz. She was a very stylized vocalist who shone on older prerock material. She had releases on DRG, Bainbridge, and other independent labels. —*Ron Wynn*

○ **Fabulous Sylvia Syms, The** / Nov. 1964 / 20th Century 4123

★ **Then Along Came Bill: A Tribute to Bill Evans** / DRG 91402

GABOR SZABO

b. Mar. 8, 1936, Budapest, Hungary, **d.** Mar. 1, 1982, Budapest, Hunagary
Guitar, composer / Cool, early jazz-rock
Though he didn't come to America until he was nearly twenty, Hungarian guitarist Gabor Szabo was still a successful contributor to several jazz groups and sessions. He made his first impact as a member of Chico Hamilton's groups, and later worked with Gary McFarland and Charles Lloyd. He co-led a group with Cal Tjader and McFarland in 1968-1969, then did some recording in which Lena Horne was the featured vocalist. Szabo led other West Coast bands in the '70s, among them a fusion/jazz-rock unit called Perfect Circle in 1975. He later recorded with Chick Corea. —*Ron Wynn*

○ **Gypsy '66** / 1965 / Impulse 9105

○ **Spellbinder** / May 6, 1966 / Impulse 9123

○ **Sorcerer, The** / Apr. 14-15, 1967 / MCA 33117

★ **Greatest Hits** / MCA
This is a combination of tracks that guitarist Gabor Szabo recorded over a three-year period (1965-1967) plus a pair of tracks from his earlier association with drummer Chico Hamilton's group. The 18 cuts literally range from the sublime to the ridiculous. The Hamilton cuts are long improvisational romps; the fluffy little "pop" tunes ("Twelve Thirty" and "White Rabbit") are replete with electric sitars and singers. Several of Gary McFarland's arrangements bury the poor guitarist under a landslide of horns and rhythm instruments. Still, Szabo's tone is unabrasive and many of his riffs have a nice fluid motion. There are also a great number of notables on these four sides: Charles Lloyd, Tom Scott, Richard Davis, Phil Woods, Zoot Sims, Emil Richards, Ron Carter, Willie Bobo, and more; all these talented people squandered on the limp material. The album was originally released around 1971. —*Richard B. Kamins*, Cadence

T

LEW TABACKIN (Lewis Barry Tabackin)

b. May 26, 1940, Philadelphia, PA
Tenor saxophone, flute / Bop, postbop, progressive big band
Lew Tabackin's flute playing is so distinguished that his tenor work sometimes gets ignored. His flute solos incorporate both an Asian influence and a rich, classical style, while he's a rugged tenor soloist with a smooth, relaxed, yet energetic approach. His tenor style is influenced by both John Coltrane and Ben Webster. Tabackin began on flute, then started playing tenor in high school. He attended the Philadelphia Conservatory of Music in the early '60s, while studying privately with composer Vincent Persichetti. He also studied with Julius Baker, the principal flutist for the Philadelphia Symphony Orchestra. After serving in the army, Tabackin played with Tal Farlow and Don Friedman before moving from New Jersey to New York. He worked in the big bands of Les and Larry Elgart, Cab Calloway, Buddy Morrow, Maynard Ferguson, and Thad Jones and Mel Lewis, while also playing with Clark Terry, Duke Pearson, Chuck Israels, and Joe Henderson. He recorded with Ferguson and Pearson. Tabackin led his own trio in Philadelphia in the late '60s, and worked in combos with Elvin Jones, Donald Byrd, Atilla Zoller, and Roland Hanna. He worked in Bobby Rosengarden's band in 1969, and worked in the "Tonight Show" band in both New York and Los Angeles until he voluntarily left and was replaced by Pete Christlieb. Tabackin also played with Dick Cavett's studio band. He was a soloist in Europe with the Hamburg Jazz Workshop, the Danish Radiojazzgruppen, and the International Jazz Quintet. Tabackin played extensively with Toshiko Akiyoshi (whom he also married) in the '70s. They formed a quartet and toured Japan, and appeared at the Expo '70 jazz festival. Then they co-led a big band in Los Angeles from 1973 until the mid-'80s. Tabackin served as principal soloist, and the band recorded often for RCA and import labels. The duo returned to New York in 1983. Tabackin also played and recorded with the big bands of Louis Bellson and Bill Berry in the late '70s. He recorded for Inner City as a leader in the '70s, and for Concord in the '80s and '90s. —*Ron Wynn*

Tabackin / 1974 / Inner City 1038
Recorded in Japan with bass and drums only, this album includes four standards and one apiece from leader, Toshiko Akiyoshi, and Sir Roland Hanna (p). Without a piano, Tabackin has more room to breathe. —*Michael G. Nastos*

★ **Dual Nature** / Aug. 31, 1976+Sep. 3, 1976 / Inner City 1028
Tabackin on flute (he is unbelievable), alto, and tenor sax, with the Don Friedman Trio. Tunes are from Tabackin, Toshiko Akiyoshi, and Bill Mays. Also included are three standards. Tabackin is on sax on one side and flute on the other. There is some astounding musicianship from all. —*Michael G. Nastos*

○ **Tenor Gladness** / Oct. 13-14, 1976 / Inner City 6048
Dueling tenors with Warne Marsh. Six originals were written by the principles or Toshiko Akiyoshi. It is a bit progressive and a thoroughly satisfying date from two virtuosos. —*Michael G. Nastos*

☆ **Rites of Pan** / 1977 / Inner City 6052

Tabackin here is on flute alone with the Toshiko Trio. This is deep harmonic music from the participants' pens as well as some from Dizzy Gillespie, Fats Waller, and Kurt Weill. The flute is startling, but for open ears. —*Michael G. Nastos*

Desert Lady / Dec. 1989 / Concord Jazz 4411
Quartet. Better-known as coleader of Akiyoshi/Tabackin big band; Lew Tabackin (sax) shows he's a fine soloist as well. 1989 session. CD version has two bonus cuts. —*Ron Wynn*

○ **I'll Be Seeing You** / **i.** 1992 / Concord Jazz 4528
Lew Tabackin's is an arpeggiated tenor sax approach, chords up and down, with a throaty attack made up of equal parts cataclysmic slurs and staccato runs. His vibrato is a broad swipe: horse laugh meets a slow, hot wind. He likes to decorate a melody, as Thelonius Monk's "Ruby, My Dear" and Duke Ellington's "Isfahan" make clear. There are three flute pieces here, too, which he plunges into with the same passion that he exercises on tenor. Pianist Benny Green (more and more like a Red Garland or Wynton Kelly of the '90s), bassist Peter Washington, and drummer Lewis Nash also show respect for the jazz tradition of swing and soulful investment. A Tabackin-Nash duet on Monk's "In Walked Bud" brings out the drummer's bopping beat. The pianist's block chords on "Lost in Meditation," another Ellington tune, are divine. —*Owen Cordle, Down Beat*

Let the Tape Roll / RCA
Quartet. Excellent (very-hard-to-find) date with Donald Byrd (tpt) and Duke Pearson (p). —*Ron Wynn*

TANI TABBAL

Drums / World fusion, modern creative
He's best known as the drummer for Roscoe Mitchell's Sight and Sound Ensemble, but Tani Tabbal has also added percussive support to David Murray's big band, and to various combos and sessions featuring A. Spencer Barefield and Cassandra Wilson. Tabbal's a well-drilled, frenetic, and aggressive player who's never failed to keep Mitchell's uptempo material soaring forward, and to provide whatever changes are needed in rhythmic pace and direction. He doesn't have any sessions available as a leader, but can be heard on several Mitchell discs, and on dates by Murray, Wilson, and Barefield. —*Ron Wynn*

JAMAALADEEN TACUMA (Rudy McDaniel)

b. Jun. 11, 1956, Hempstead, NY
Bass / Early jazz-rock, instrumental pop, modern creative
In the wake of Stanley Clarke and Jaco Pastorius, a number of stunning electric bassists have emerged who approach the instrument as a bass guitar and are more intrigued by its potential as a lead then as a support/rhythm vehicle. Jamaaladeen Tacuma is among the finest in this class; he zips over the bass executing amazing lines, getting a huge tone and as distinctive and unconventional a sound as any guitarist. Unfortunately, he's yet to demonstrate an equal capability as a composer or bandleader; his releases are dominated by great playing expended on routine fusion filler and unfocused free exchanges. Originally named Rudy McDaniel (before converting to Islam), Tacuma sang in a doo-wop group as a teen in Philadelphia. He started on bass at age 13,

and later played in area R&B bands. He made his professional debut with Charles Earland as Rudy McDaniel, and later played with Edwin Birdsong. Tacuma joined Ornette Coleman's Prime Time band in 1975, and recorded with them in Paris. While there, he converted to Islam. Tacuma was on board for some superb, if poor-selling, Coleman albums, and for some triumphant concerts. After he left the band, Tacuma began recording for Gramavision, billing his concept as a mix of Coleman's "harmolodic" theories and progressive R&B/fusion. His debut featured contributions from American, European, and Asian musicians; some labeled it multicultural muzak. Tacuma has also played with Jeff Beck, James "Blood" Ulmer, Olu Dara, Coleman, Julius Hemphill, David Murray, Vernon Reid, and the Ebony String Quartet. He reteamed with the Prime Time Band for another stint in the '80s, and did more recording for Gramavision and New Artists. His '93 date, *Boss of the Bass*, and one other session for New Artists are currently the only Tacuma dates in print. —*Ron Wynn*

○ **Show Stopper** / 1982-1983 / Gramavision 79435
1982-1983. The five-piece electric band for this electric bassist shows many positive and eclectic forces rooted in jazz but not stuck in the past. Includes "Bird of Paradise" with the Ebony String Quartet. Title track with Olu Dara and Julius Hemphill is a treat of all-out contempo-bop. Other cameos are by Blood Ulmer on guitar and Cornell Rochester on drums. This is a fun album. —*Michael G. Nastos*

★ **Music World** / 1986 / Gramavision 79437
1990 reissue that again shows Tacuma cannot harness his great talent into an effective showpiece. —*Ron Wynn*

HORACE TAPSCOTT

b. Apr. 6, 1934, Houston, TX
Piano / Postbop, early free, progressive big band, neo-bop, modern creative
Horace Tapscott has spent his career on the West Coast, and is highly respected by many musicians, but unknown to the mainstream jazz audience. He's aided and worked with many musicians who've later become stars, has been praised often in interviews, and has recorded principally for the tiny Nimbus label. He's a fine composer and a carefully controlled, sparse pianist with a style that's not flashy, but is powerful, with rumbling bass lines, percussive phrases, and moving statements. Tapscott's family moved from Houston to Los Angeles in the '40s. He began as a trombonist, then added piano in the early '50s while in an Air Force band. Tapscott turned to piano full-time after suffering injuries in an auto accident. He worked with Eric Dolphy and Don Cherry in a school band during the late '40s and early '50s, and with Gerald Wilson's orchestra. He began groups in 1958, and toured with Lionel Hampton in 1959 and the early '60s. Tapscott formed the Pan Afrikan Peoples Arkestra in 1961. At various times, the group included Arthur Blythe, Azar Lawrence, and Jimmy Woods. Tapscott recorded with Leon Thomas, Lou Blackburn, Lorez Alexandria, and Charles Lloyd, and composed songs for a late '60s Sonny Criss LP, *Sonny's Dream*. He recorded with Blythe in 1969, then began cutting a series of albums for Nimbus in the '70s and '80s. Tapscott led his own Arkestra, a West Coast variation on Sun Ra's great groups. They recorded in 1978 and 1979. Tapscott did solo works on Nimbus in 1978, 1982, and 1983, a trio session in 1979, and recorded at the 1981 Lobero Festival in Italy. In 1980 he did a duo date with drummer Everett Brown, Jr., and also did some recording for Flying Dutchman. Forget about trying to obtain Tapscott sessions through conventional channels. His name isn't even in the last two *Schwann* catalogs, and isn't cited in several jazz anthologies and encyclopedias. —*Ron Wynn and Michael G. Nastos*

○ **Giant is Awakened, The** / **i.** May 1970 / Flying Dutchman 107

★ **Dark Tree—Vol. 1, The** / Dec. 14-17, 1989 / Hat Art 6053

Pianist and bandleader Horace Tapscott has defied easy categorization for over 20 years. His compositions are as likely to be hinged on waltz time or melodies tinged with sentiment as they are on propulsive vamps and jagged themes. Stylistically, his playing is all over the map—from Mal Waldron-like distillations to McCoy Tyneresque power. He tenaciously anchors tempo and form, often with elemental left-hand ostinatos, and often for far longer than it takes to make the point. His best work pivots on sudden, exciting transitions in technique and mood. "Giant" is usually cited for debuting altoist Arthur Blythe, whose already matured, hard-edged tone and contoured lines are constantly engaging. But a second reason for "Giant's" legendary status is the polyrhythmic fireworks of longtime Tapscott drummer Everett Brown, Jr., who would receive worldwide attention if he ventured out of Los Angeles. Another distinctive aspect is the use of two bassists, David Bryant and Walter Savage, Jr., who supply plenty of textured counterpoint. The club recordings also feature bassist Cecil McBee and drummer Andrew Cyrille, and clarinetist John Carter appears on every track. —*Bill Shoemaker*, Down Beat

○ **Dark Tree—Vol. 2, The** / **i.** Dec. 1989 / Hat Art 6083
The Dark Tree, Volume 2 includes club recordings featuring clarinetist John Carter done by pianist/bandleader Horace Tapscott in 1989. The recordings, which also feature bassist Cecil McBee and drummer Andrew Cyrille, include long stretches of inspired improvisational interplay. Carter appears on only two out of five selections, including another version of the title composition, which opens the first disc. He is simply masterful throughout, woody and throaty in the low and mid registers, and utterly piercing in his extraordinary high register. —*Bill Shoemaker*, Down Beat

BUDDY TATE (George Holmes Tate)

b. Feb. 22, 1913, Sherman, TX
Tenor saxophone / Swing, big band, blues & jazz
A prototype Texas tenor saxophonist with a huge tone, a fine command of the instrument in every register, and an outstanding blues sensibility, Buddy Tate has been an active player since the '20s. He's done swing, soul-jazz, R&B, rock and roll, traditional jazz, big band, and blues, among other styles. He began playing professionally in the late '20s, and worked with Terrence Holder, Count Basie, and Andy Kirk in the early and mid-'30s. He spent nearly five years with Nat Towles's band, then rejoined Basie in 1939. Tate replaced Herschel Evans, and remained for a decade. During the early '50s, he played with Hot Lips Page, Lucky Millinder, and Jimmy Rushing. Tate recorded for Columbia and Vanguard in the '50s, and formed his own band in 1953. This became the resident group at the Celebrity Club in New York for over 20 years. Occasionally, Tate would reunite with Basie, while working with others like Buck Clayton, with whom he toured Europe in the late '50s and early '60s. There was a session for Candid with Nancy Harrow in 1960, and another for Columbia in 1962. Tate led a group on his own European tour in the late '60s, and played in Saints and Sinners. The '70s were a busy period, as Tate made recordings for Muse, MJR, Chiaroscuro, Black Lion, and Sackville. He co-led a band with Paul Quinichette at the West End cafe in 1975, and played in Canada with Jay McShann and Jim Galloway. He also co-led a group with Al Grey. Tate toured with the Texas Tenors in the early '80s, and played at the Newport and Cork festivals. He was a regular at the Grande Parade du Jazz in Nice. Tate kept busy recording in the '80s, cutting sessions for Open Sky, Sackville, and Concord. Tate dates from the '60s, '70s, and '80s are available on CD. —*Ron Wynn*

★ **Swinging Like Tate** / Feb. 12+Feb. 26, 1958 / Verve 820599
Prototype Kansas City stomping set with Papa Jo Jones on drums. Dynamic, hot solos. —*Ron Wynn*

○ **Tate-A-Tate** / Oct. 18, 1960 / Prestige 184
Bubbly modern mainstream is found on *Tate-A-Tate*, a 10/18/60 date with Buddy Tate (ts) leading a group (Clark Terry, tpt; Tommy Flanagan, p; Larry Gates, b; Art Taylor, d)

on six tracks. Over the years I've found much of Tate's output to be somewhat anticlimactic, but this combines fine spirit with a fluidity of ideas. In addition, Clark Terry is right on the money and sounding '60s fresh. The only drawback is Art Taylor's drumming, which sounds uncharacteristically unchallenging. —*Bob Rusch*, Cadence

And His Buddies / Jun. 3, 1973 / Chiaroscuro 123

Kansas City Woman / Jul. 3, 1974 / Black Lion 312

Meets Dollar Brand / Aug. 25, 1977 / Chiaroscuro 165

○ **Sherman Shuff** / Jan. 29, 1978 / Sackville 3017
This Canadian Sackville recording stemmed from an ingenious New York mating of mainstream saxists Buddy Tate and Bob Wilber with modernist bassist Sam Jones and drummer Leroy Williams. While the tenorman's sustained excellence should surprise no one familiar with his current work, many will note approvingly Bob Wilber's progress on alto sax, an instrument he associates almost exclusively with Johnny Hodges. Wilber's soprano and Tate's clarinet are voiced together for the serenely romantic "Curtains of the Night" (one more of the gifted sopranist/composer's highly personal melodies), while the looser combination of clarinet and tenor is used for "Back Yard" and "Best Things." With the exception of Duke Ellington's "Sherman Shuffle," a feature for Tate's gruff, barking baritone, the remainder of the numbers find Wilber on alto and Tate on tenor. At his best on the ballad medley's opener, "Lover Man," Tate is followed by Jones, whose "Body and Soul" paves the way for Wilber's masterly reading of the Hodges anthem, "Warm Valley." "Potentate," one of the tenorman's many heads on "I Got Rhythm," offers driving, inventive solos by both saxmen, with Wilber quite effectively evoking images of a '30s Pres (Lester Young) on alto. —*Jack Sohmer*, Down Beat

★ **Hard Blowin'** / Aug. 25-26, 1978 / Muse 5249
This is the sixth Muse LP from the Sandy's Jazz Revival venue, taped during two days when the machine must have been allowed to run around the clock, and the second of the six to appear under tenor saxophonist Buddy Tate's name. The other horn players involved in that session (Arnet Cobb and Eddie Vinson) do not appear on even one track of this latest release. So what we have here is Tate's puissant tenor in front of a dynamic rhythm section. You won't have to listen with any amount of concentration (this LP, after all, is not *hard listenin'*) to hear allusions to some of the tenor's past greats—Lester Young, Coleman Hawkins, Ben Webster—but that shouldn't be surprising, because Tate has been on the scene since the late '20s. And he's still playing with power and punch! "Sweet Georgia Brown" and "Undecided" stomp and steam along, powered smoothly by Ray Bryant (p), George Duviver (b) and Alan Dawson (d). "Summertime" is somewhat of a bravura performance as Tate and Bryant both give it solo fervor. The track is vitiated, unfortunately, when Tate reaches for his relatively lightweight flute. "Body and Soul" flows with melodic ardor, receiving a stately, almost reverent reading, and the program closes with its intensely sculpted coda. All in all, one of Tate's tastiest and best. —*Alan Bargebuhr*, Cadence

○ **Live at Sandy's** / Aug. 25-26, 1978 / Muse 5198
It's obvious this is tenor saxophonist Buddy Tate's gig since the other two saxophonists only play on "She's Got It" and I think the great rhythm section is the major contributor to that track—especially bassist George Duvivier. Since Eddie "Cleanhead" Vinson and Arnett Cobb come from Houston and Tate is from Sherman (more than two hundred miles north), it's no surprise that he and Vinson had never played together before. There is a "Texas Tenor Sound," and no doubt about it, this is exactly the way dozens of tenor players sounded in the very early '40s. Tate plays clarinet blues on "Blue Creek" with simple construction and much the way Lester Young sounded on that horn, but his tenor on "Jumpin' at the Woodside" and "Tangerine" is heavy, broad, and not always distinct. There's much of the Hawk (Coleman Hawkins) in him on "Candy" and it's hard to believe this is not Cobb. Drummer Alan Dawson and pianist Ray Bryant,

who are almost another generation, adapt well to this style of jamming and the pianist plays blues as you would expect to hear it from an early era. There is lots of left hand and even some shuffle behind Cobb's only two choruses. Taping this live was a good idea, but it could have been a lot better if all six musicians had appeared on all the tracks. —*Jerry L. Atkins*, Cadence

Muse All-Stars / Aug. 25-26, 1978 / Muse
This is a great jumping set with Arnett Cobb (sax) and Eddie Vinson (tpt). —*Ron Wynn*

☆ **Ballad Artistry of Buddy Tate** / Jun. 12-13, 1981 / Sackville 3034
The name of guitarist Ed Bickert could easily be substituted for Buddy Tate's in the title of this album. For while Tate plays well, Bickert steals the show. Aside from "B.T. Blues" and a mildly swinging version of "A Foggy Day," this is an album of ballads, something of a switch for Tate. His strong points are usually his bluesy and hard-swinging characteristics, which are set aside for these ballads. Instead, his playing here is mostly restrained, sticking close to the melody, adding appropriate embellishments here and there. Occasionally, he seems to be chafing at the bit. But if Tate is not outstanding, he doesn't falter, either. He masterfully sculpts a solo from the melody of "Darn That Dream," and it's nice to hear his wonderfully woody-toned clarinet on "Cry Me a River." He finally gets to cut loose on "B.T. Blues," an offshoot of another blues with a bridge, Lester Young's "D.B. Blues." But I found it hard not to give primary attention to Ed Bickert, even when he was backing a soloist. His backing is not obtrusive, but the chords he plays are so pretty it would be hard for a soloist to top them. It often sounds like he's playing a duet with Tate. Bickert gets his share of solos, too, and whether they are chorded or single stringed, he is as clean and mellow-toned a guitarist as I have heard. His laidback style fits well with the album's focus. —*Doug Long*, Cadence

For Sentimental Reasons / i. 1982 / Open Sky

GRADY TATE

b. Jan. 14, 1932, Durham, NC
Drums, vocals / Bop, ballads & blues
Grady Tate has gained as much fame and recognition as a drummer as he could have gained as a star vocalist. He's equally effective pushing and driving the beat or providing shading and subdued rhythms. Tate's recorded bebop, hard bop, swing, big band, and soul-jazz, as well as his ability as a singer, make him the ideal drummer to accompany vocalists. He began playing drums at age five, and initially taught himself. Tate later learned more fundamentals and nuances while in the Air Force during the '50s. He returned to his North Carolina home after his discharge, and studied literature, theater, and psychology at North Carolina College while working part-time as a musician. Tate moved to Washington in 1959, where he played with Wild Bill Davis. He moved to New York two years later, where he played in Quincy Jones's big band and with Jerome Richardson. Tate has worked with Duke Ellington, Count Basie, Jimmy Smith, Wes Montgomery, Rahsaan Roland Kirk, and many others. He's also backed vocalists Peggy Lee, Sarah Vaughan, Ella Fitzgerald, Astrud Gilberto, Chris Connor, Ray Charles, Blossom Dearie, and Lena Horne. Tate's albums for Skye, Impluse, Milestone, and other labels have emphasized his vocals as much, if not more, than his drumming. But his drumming is well represented on sessions. Tate has a couple of dates available currently on CD. —*Ron Wynn*

★ **By Special Request** / i. Apr. 1975 / Buddah 5623
This album represents Grady Tate the vocalist rather than Tate the percussionist. As such it has primarily pop/soul performances wrapped around Tate's sensual voice. *By Special Request*, which is based on the theory that everybody wants to hear those popular tunes just one more time, succeeds moderately well, with adequate, though occasionally pretentious arrangements. —*Herb Nolan*, Down Beat

ART TATUM (Arthur (Jr) Tatum)

b. 1909, Toledo, OH, **d.** Nov. 5, 1956, Los Angeles, CA
Piano / Swing

Art Tatum literally defined solo piano improvisation, transporting it to unforeseen heights. His touch, technical command, harmonic and melodic knowledge, and rhythmic imagination were extraordinary. Tatum's ability to substitute harmonies during a solo were unequalled, and he turned simple statements into sweeping, majestic movements. He combined elements of both stride and swing playing, sometimes using techniques from each genre in a single solo, juxtaposing them in movements. He wasn't much of a composer, but his variations on pop tunes, light classical, and, occasionally, the blues, created and recreated so many alternatives to the original that it was as if he'd written new material. Tatum had a superb sense of swing and timing; he never prematurely concluded a solo and seldom fluffed any notes. Numerous pianists in various genres studied and memorized Tatum solos note for note.

As a teenager, Tatum received some formal training at the Toledo School of Music, though he was blind in one eye and seriously impaired in the other. He learned to read sheet music in Braille and with glasses, but essentially taught himself, learning from piano rolls, records, and broadcasts. He began playing professionally in Toledo in the mid-'20s, and appeared on broadcasts in 1929 and 1930. He accompanied vocalist Adelaide Hall in 1932, and traveled with her to New York, where he made his solo recording debut in 1933. Tatum recorded for Brunswick, Columbia, and Decca into the '40s, doing many solo and a few combo dates. One 1937 recording included a remarkable version of "Body and Soul" that was a top-selling single. He repeated that success in 1939 with "Tea for Two." Tatum also played in Cleveland and Chicago from 1934 to 1936. By the late '30s, his reputation had grown, thanks to appearances on radio shows, and to recordings and club dates. He toured England in 1938, and became a regular in New York and Los Angeles prime spots in 1939 and 1940.

Tatum founded a trio patterned after the Nat "King" Cole group in 1943, with guitarist Tiny Grimes and bassist Slam Stewart. When Grimes left in 1944, Tatum continued the trio with Everett Barksdale as the most prominent of the replacement guitarists. During the mid- and late '40s, Tatum continued recording and making club and radio appearances. He appeared briefly in the 1947 film *The Fabulous Dorseys*, and was featured in a 1944 concert at the Metropolitan Opera House. He recorded for Dial and Capitol. But much of his fame came in the '50s, thanks to his association with Norman Granz. Granz recorded Tatum throughout the '50s in solo and group settings with Benny Carter, Roy Eldridge, and Ben Webster. These recordings have since been reissued in boxed set form and in separate volumes; the Tatum recordings on Decca and Verve, and on many import labels, have also been reissued. Though he died in 1956, the Tatum legacy continues thanks to reissues and the reverent accounts of jazz musicians and fans who were astonished by his skills. —*Ron Wynn and Dan Morgenstern*

Masters of Jazz—Vol. 8 / Aug. 1932-Jan. 1946 / Storyville 4108

The Swedish label Storyville's "Masters of Jazz" LP series released a dozen volumes of mostly rare music by swing-era greats. Art Tatum's set is primarily composed of selections cut in 1935 for radio airplay, giving listeners a chance to hear the young genius perform some songs that he never recorded otherwise. In addition, there are two selections from 1945-46 along with Tatum's earliest recording, a broadcast version of "Tiger Rag." —*Scott Yanow*

★ **Piano Starts Here** / Mar. 21, 1933-Apr. 2, 1949 / Columbia 9655

Piano also ends here. This LP contains more than its share of stunning performances, consisting of Art Tatum's first recording date (which is highlighted by an incredible version of "Tiger Rag") and a 1949 concert. From the latter, Tatum's reworking of "Yesterdays" and blinding stride on "I Know That You Know" will make many amateur pianists look for day jobs. The studio date has since been reissued on CD, but the live performance remains unavailable. —*Scott Yanow*

○ **Art Tatum (1932-1934)** / **i.** Mar. 1933-Oct. 1934 / Classics 507

This comprehensive CD contains Art Tatum's very first recording (a broadcast version of "Tiger Rag"), four selections in which he accompanies singer Adelaide Hall (along with a second pianist!), and then his first 20 solo sides. To call Tatum's virtuosic piano style remarkable would be a major understatement; he has to be heard to be believed. His studio version of "Tiger Rag" may very well be Tatum's most incredible recording; he sounds like three pianists at once! —*Scott Yanow*

○ **Pure Genius** / **i.** Feb. 27, 1934-1945 / Atlantis 3

This English LP contains some rare solo performances by Art Tatum that his fans will want to get. A Cleveland broadcast from 1934 (less than a year after his initial recordings) features Tatum performing some rare material, particularly "Young & Healthy" and "Morning, Noon & Night". He is also heard in duet with bassist Junior Raglin (1945's "The Man I Love") and on an extensive solo broadcast from the same year. Art Tatum was an amazing pianist and no jazz collection is complete without a few of his recordings. —*Scott Yanow*

○ **Masterpieces** / Aug. 22, 1934-Nov. 29, 1937 / MCA 4112

This double LP from the late '70s brings together many valuable recordings from two of the master pianists. The incredible Art Tatum is featured on nine piano solos from 1934 and 1937 and on a four-song session with a sextet in 1937. James P. Johnson, the king of stride piano, pays tribute to his student Fats Waller with a dozen songs associated with Fats. This set is rounded off with James P. guesting with Eddie Condon's band on a rousing "Just You, Just Me." Classic jazz. —*Scott Yanow*

★ **Classic Piano Solos (1934-39)** / 1934-1939 / GRP 607

This excellent CD reissues all of Art Tatum's early Decca piano solos cut at three sessions in 1934 and one in 1937. Tatum was decades ahead of his contemporaries not only in technique but in harmonic ideas. Highlights of this very impressive set include "Emaline," "After You've Gone," "The Shout," two versions of "Liza," and "The Sheik of Araby." —*Scott Yanow*

○ **Standard Transcriptions** / 1935-1943 / Music & Arts 673

In 1935, 1939, and 1943 Art Tatum recorded an extensive series of piano solos (163 in all) for radio airplay; these were not available commercially until long after the LP era was under way, and then only piecemeal. Music & Arts on this two-CD set gives listeners all of the remarkable music together for the first time. Tatum fans only familiar with his commercial recordings will find much to marvel at during this recommended set. —*Scott Yanow*

○ **Art Tatum Masterpieces, The** / Nov. 29, 1937-Jan. 5, 1944 / MCA 4019

This excellent two-LP set was the best all-round set of Art Tatum's Decca years prior to the advent of the CD. Included are 16 Tatum piano solos, the eight selections from 1941 that he cut with a group featuring blues singer Joe Turner, and seven numbers from his 1944 trio with guitarist Tiny Grimes and bassist Slam Stewart. Highly recommended to those listeners who do not have this material on CD. —*Scott Yanow*

○ **Standards** / 1938-1939 / Black Lion 760143

This Black Lion CD features brilliant piano solos from Art Tatum that were originally cut as noncommercial radio transcriptions during 1938-39. Duplicating part of Tatum's Music & Arts double CD, *Standards* features a great deal of magic from the remarkable virtuoso. —*Scott Yanow*

○ **Solos (1940)** / 1940 / MCA 42327

MCA's short-lived Decca CD reissue program put out this gem, all of Art Tatum's piano solos from 1940, including two versions of the previously unknown "Sweet Emalina, My Gal." Some of the routines on these standards had become a bit familiar by now (this "Tiger Rag" pales next to his 1933 version) but are no less exciting and still sound seemingly impossible to play. Well worth picking up. —*Scott Yanow*

Remarkable Art of Tatum, The / **i.** Jan. 5, 1944 / Audiophile 88

After years of appearing almost exclusively as a piano soloist, Art Tatum formed a trio in the mid '40s with guitarist Tiny Grimes and bassist Slam Stewart. Fortunately Grimes and Stewart were quick thinkers and witty improvisers, for they needed all of their creativity in order to keep up with the astounding pianist. All 11 of the performances (including one alternate take) that they cut for World Broadcasting transcriptions are included on this rather brief (under 27 minutes) LP. Their magical interplay is consistently memorable. —*Scott Yanow*

○ **V-Discs, The** / 1944-1946 / Black Lion 760114
This Black Lion CD mostly features the phenomenal Art Tatum playing solo during 1945-46, really digging into a variety of standards. A rare version of "Sweet Lorraine" (with bassist Oscar Pettiford and drummer Sid Catlett in 1944) and two numbers with his 1945 trio (featuring guitarist Tiny Grimes and bassist Slam Stewart) round out this excellent CD. —*Scott Yanow*

In Private / **i.** 1948 / Fresh Sound 127
This collector's LP features the amazing Art Tatum playing solo piano at a private party. Although the recording quality is not flawless, Tatum's melodic interpretations of 11 standards are typically virtuosic and fascinating; he was always well worth hearing. —*Scott Yanow*

Art Tatum at His Piano, Vol. 1 / 1950 / GNP 9025
On the first of two LPs featuring Art Tatum live at the Crescendo Club in 1950, the great pianist interprets a dozen standards in familiar but impressive fashion. His routines on some tunes became set pieces but still were quite remarkable as evidenced by this fine performance. —*Scott Yanow*

Art Tatum at His Piano—Vol. 2 / 1950 / GNP 9026
In this second of two LPs taken from a 1950 Los Angeles concert, Art Tatum performs concise melodic variations on another dozen standards. Although not his most adventurous set, Tatum was definitely in fine form that day. —*Scott Yanow*

Complete Capitol Recordings—Vol. 1 / Jul.-Dec. 1952 / Capitol 92866
Art Tatum recorded 20 piano solos in 1949 and eight selections with his 1952 trio, with guitarist Everett Barksdale and bassist Slam Stewart, for Capitol. Ten solos and four trios are included on each of the two CDs in this "complete" series. Tatum can be heard here at the height of his powers (he never did decline) creating miraculous variations of standards that still amaze today's pianists. —*Scott Yanow*

Complete Capitol Recordings—Vol. 2 / Sep.-Dec. 1952 / Capitol 92867
On the second of two CDs, Art Tatum is heard playing solo in 1949 on 10 standards and interacting with his 1952 trio, including guitarist Everett Barksdale and bassist Slam Stewart, during four numbers. Tatum always had the ability to amaze fellow pianists (not to mention fans) and there are plenty of remarkable moments in this fine set. —*Scott Yanow*

★ **Complete Pablo Solo Masterpieces, The** / Dec. 28, 1953-Jan. 19, 1955 / Pablo 4404
During four marathon recording sessions in 1953-55, Norman Granz recorded Art Tatum playing 119 standards, enough music for a dozen LPs. The results have been recently reissued separately on eight CDs and on this very full seven-CD box set. Frankly, Tatum did no real advance preparation for this massive project, sticking mostly to concise melodic variations of standards, some of them virtual set pieces formed over the past two decades. Since there are few

uptempo performances, the music in this series has a certain sameness after a while but, heard in small doses, it is quite enjoyable. A special bonus on this box (and not on the individual volumes) are four numbers taken from a 1956 Hollywood Bowl concert. —*Scott Yanow*

○ **Tatum Solo Masterpieces—Vol. 1** / 1953-1955 / Pablo 2405-432
The first of eight CDs reissuing the 119 piano solo performances that Art Tatum recorded for Norman Granz during four marathon record sessions has its moments, but in general this series lacks the excitement of Tatum's earliest recordings. On this first volume the pianist interprets such standards as "Body and Soul," "It's Only a Paper Moon," and "Willow Weep for Me." —*Scott Yanow*

○ **Art Tatum Solo Masterpieces—Vol. 2** / 1953-1955 / Pablo 2405-433
The second of eight CDs in this series of Art Tatum solo performances taken from four marathon record sessions has among its highlights "Elegy," "This Can't Be Love," and "Tea for Two," but in general this series lacks the excitement of Tatum's earliest recordings. Excellent but somewhat predictable performances by the classic virtuoso. —*Scott Yanow*

○ **Art Tatum Solo Masterpieces—Vol. 3** / 1953-1955 / Pablo 2405-434
The third of eight CDs in the Norman Granz series of Art Tatum piano solos is highlighted by "Yesterdays," "Prisoner of Love," and "Begin the Beguine," among others. Tatum did little prior preparation for the four marathon sessions that resulted in a dozen LPs (now reissued as eight CDs), so this series lacks the excitement and adventure of Tatum's earliest recordings, although it is still enjoyable in its own right. —*Scott Yanow*

○ **Art Tatum Solo Masterpieces—Vol. 4** / 1953-1955 / Pablo 2405-435
On the fourth volume in this eight CD-series, Art Tatum sounds at his best on "Ill Wind" and "The Man I Love." Taken from the 119 piano solos that Tatum cut for Norman Granz in four lengthy recording sessions during 1953-55, these performances are concise, relaxed, and surprisingly predictable if virtuosic. —*Scott Yanow*

○ **Art Tatum Solo Masterpieces—Vol. 5** / 1953-1955 / Pablo 2405-436
Volume five of this eight-CD series features Art Tatum interpreting 15 of the 119 standards that he recorded during four marathon solo recording sessions for Norman Granz. Tatum sounds typically wondrous in spots even though there are few surprises throughout this generally relaxed set. —*Scott Yanow*

○ **Art Tatum Solo Masterpieces—Vol. 6** / 1953-1955 / Pablo 2405-437
Volume six of this eight CD-series features Art Tatum interpreting such standards as "Night and Day," "Cherokee," "Happy Feet," and "Someone to Watch over Me" with taste and melodic creativity. There are no real barn-burners or new revelations on this generally relaxed set but the music should please Tatum's fans. —*Scott Yanow*

○ **Art Tatum Solo Masterpieces—Vol. 7** / 1953-1955 / Pablo 2405-438
The next-to-last volume in this eight CD-series features Art Tatum interpreting a variety of standards including "Moon Song," "Japanese Sandman," "Moonlight on The Ganges," and even "Mighty Like a Rose." Taken from the 119 numbers that Tatum recorded for Norman Granz during four marathon sessions, the music is pleasing if at times a bit too relaxed for those who would like to hear the virtuoso really tear into these pieces. —*Scott Yanow*

○ **Art Tatum Solo Masterpieces—Vol. 8** / 1953-1955 / Pablo 2405-439
The final volume of this eight-CD (and originally 12-LP) series is similar to the first seven in that Art Tatum melodically improvises on a variety of standards, in this case such tunes as "She's Funny That Way," "I Won't Dance," "Begin the

Beguine," and "Humoresque." Few revelations occur (most of the interpretations are in the same relaxed medium tempo), but the music is typically well-played and generally quite enjoyable. —*Scott Yanow*

★ **Complete Pablo Group Masterpieces, The** / Jun. 1954-Aug. 1956 / Pablo 4401

Art Tatum spent most of his career as a solo pianist; in fact, it was often said that he was such an unpredictable virtuoso that it would be difficult for other musicians to play with him. Producer Norman Granz sought to prove that theory false, so between 1954 and 1956 he extensively recorded Tatum with a variety of other classic jazz players, resulting originally in nine LPs of material that is now available separately as eight CDs and on this very full six-CD box set. In contrast to the massive solo Tatum sessions that Granz also recorded during this period, the group sides have plenty of variety and exciting moments, which is not surprising when one considers that Tatum was teamed in a trio with altoist Benny Carter and drummer Louie Bellson; with trumpeter Roy Eldridge, clarinetist Buddy DeFranco, and tenor-saxophonist Ben Webster in separate quartets; in an explosive trio with vibraphonist Lionel Hampton and drummer Buddy Rich; with a sextet including Hampton, Rich, and trumpeter Harry "Sweets" Edison; and on a standard trio session. Highly recommended. —*Scott Yanow*

Tatum Group Masterpieces—Vol. 1 / Jun. 25, 1954 / Pablo 2405-424

This is an absolute essential. Since Tatum was well-recorded solo, his group efforts are all that much more important. All here are standards (80 cuts), some of them alternate and previously unissued takes. Mates include Louis Bellson, Red Callender, Buddy DeFranco, Harry Edison, and Roy Eldridge. Comprehensive six-disc set: lots of unreleased performances and everything is glorious. —*Ron Wynn*

Tatum Group Masterpieces—Vol. 2 / Aug. 1955 / Pablo 2405-425

The second of eight CDs teaming the amazing pianist Art Tatum with a variety of his contemporaries finds Tatum sharing the stage with trumpeter Roy Eldridge, bassist John Simmons, and drummer Alvin Stoller. Eldridge, normally a very combative player, knows better than to directly challenge Tatum and instead is surprisingly restrained and muted on this enjoyable set of swing standards. —*Scott Yanow*

Tatum Group Masterpieces—Vol. 3 / Aug. 1955 / Pablo 2405-426

The third of eight CDs matching the great Art Tatum piano with a variety of classic jazz artists is the first of two that finds him in a trio with vibraphonist Lionel Hampton and drummer Buddy Rich; no wet spots in that group! Much of this music really burns. —*Scott Yanow*

Tatum Group Masterpieces—Vol. 4 / Aug. 1955 / Pablo 2405-427

The fourth of eight CDs featuring pianist Art Tatum interacting with some of his most notable musical contemporaries is the second to match his virtuosity with that of vibraphonist Lionel Hampton and drummer Buddy Rich. The three immortals really challenge each other during this frequently heated jam session. —*Scott Yanow*

Tatum Group Masterpieces—Vol. 5 / Aug. 1955 / Pablo 2405-428

The fifth of eight CDs in this recommended series (which is also available complete as a six-CD box set) features the largest band in this program, a sextet with Tatum, vibraphonist Lionel Hampton, trumpeter Harry "Sweets" Edison, guitarist Barney Kessel, bassist Red Callender, and drummer Buddy Rich. Their treatment of blues and standards is as exciting as one would expect from this all-star lineup. —*Scott Yanow*

Tatum Group Masterpieces—Vol. 7 / Aug. 1955 / Pablo 2405-430

The seventh of eight CDs in this valuable series matches the remarkable piano of Art Tatum in a quartet with clarinetist

Buddy DeFranco. DeFranco, no slouch himself, directly challenges Tatum and their uptempo romps are often quite wondrous. —*Scott Yanow*

Tatum Group Masterpieces—Vol. 8 / Aug. 1955 / Pablo 2405-431

The final volume in this very worthy series that features Art Tatum (who spent most of his life as a solo pianist) musically interacting with some of his greatest contemporaries is a comparatively relaxed affair, a quartet set with tenor saxophonist Ben Webster. Webster lets Tatum fill the background with an infinite number of notes while emphasizing his warm tenor tone in the forefront on a variety of melodic ballads and standards. The combination works very well. —*Scott Yanow*

20th Century Piano Genius / i. 1955 / Verve 826129

With the exception of two numbers recorded in 1950, all of the contents on this double LP were taped at a private party in 1955, featuring the amazing Art Tatum on solo piano. Tatum, who died the following year, never did decline and he is in prime form throughout this highly enjoyable and frequently exciting set of standards. There are no real romps à la "Tiger Rag" but the 27 performances contain plenty of remarkable moments. —*Scott Yanow*

Art Tatum Trio, The / Jan. 27, 1956 / Verve 8118

Art Tatum spent most of his career playing solo in night clubs, which makes his mid-'40s trio with guitarist Tiny Grimes and bassist Slam Stewart a real delight, offering the opportunity to hear Tatum interact with witty and alert players. Their recordings have long been difficult to acquire; this hard-to-find Tulip LP contains virtually all of their studio recordings, 10 delightful performances. —*Scott Yanow*

★ **God is in the House** / Polydor

A real historical curiosity, this out-of-print LP features Art Tatum playing in nightclubs and in apartments, sometimes with a bassist. Privately recorded (and not of digital quality), the music is still utterly fascinating, particularly a pair of jams with trumpeter Frankie Newton and bassist Ebenezer Paul and two surprise blues vocals by Tatum himself. —*Scott Yanow*

ART TAYLOR (Arthur S. (Jr) Taylor)

b. Apr. 6, 1929, New York, NY
Drums / Bop, hard bop

A great drummer and an impressive, occasionally controversial author, Art Taylor has an authoritative, crisp, and crackling style that's enlivened dozens of bebop and hard bop sessions. He's a disciplined accompanist and an excellent soloist. Taylor got his grounding when he worked in Harlem with Sonny Rollins and Jackie McLean. He played with Howard McHee in 1948, then performed and recorded with Coleman Hawkins, Buddy DeFranco, and Bud Powell in the '50s. Taylor later did sessions with Art Farmer, George Wallington, and Miles Davis, while leading his own band, Taylor's Wailers. Taylor made his first European trip with Donald Byrd and Bobby Jaspar in 1958, then played with Thelonious Monk in 1959. He lived in France and Belgium during the '60s and '70s, played frequently with Johnny Griffin, and toured America. Taylor recorded many candid interviews with musicians during these years. His book, *Notes and Tones*, presented these interviews in a no-holds-barred form in 1977. Taylor returned to New York in 1984, and hosted an interview program on WKCR. He's one of the most in-demand drummers in history, and was incredibly busy during the '50s and '60s. Taylor has appeared on an estimated 300 recordings. He's worked with John Coltrane, Mal Waldron, Red Garland, Gigi Gryce, Thelonious Monk, Gene Ammons, and Dexter Gordon, to name only a few. Taylor can be heard on many reissues by any of those musicians. His own sessions are also available on CD, including a 1992 Enja date. *Notes and Tones* was re-released in 1993 with new interviews added. —*Ron Wynn*

○ **Taylor's Wailers** / Feb. 25, 1956-Mar. 22, 1957 / Prestige 094

This is typical of the recorded jams that regularly flowed from the Prestige-Rudy Van Gelder connection. It was issued under drummer Art Taylor's name and came from two dates: a 2/25/56 session with Donald Byrd (tpt), Jackie McLean (as), Charlie Rouse (ts), Ray Bryant (p), and Wendell Marshall (b); and a 3/22/57 session (*C.T.A.*) with John Coltrane (ts), Mal Waldron (p), and Paul Chambers (b). This LP lists Red Garland on piano, but it is clearly not him, and usual credit goes to Mal Waldron, who hadn't yet become the highly identifiable pianist of the '70s (and '80s), nor had he developed the definition found in a stylist like Garland. This is fine Prestige bop of the period. —*Bob Rusch*, Cadence

○ **Taylor's Tenors** / Jun. 3, 1959 / New Jazz 8219

★ **Art Taylor's Delight** / i. Aug. 6, 1960 / Blue Note 84047
Early '60s definitive sides from this drummer and group known as Taylor's Wailers. —*Michael G. Nastos*

○ **Mr. A. T.** / 1991 / Enja 79677
Mr. A. T. reaffirms the jazz values of the '50s and '60s: bebop, hard bop, and the postbop experimentation of John Coltrane (with whom Art Taylor recorded). Taylor is a bop drummer in the Max Roach, Art Blakey, and Philly Joe Jones style. Tenor saxophonist Willie Williams suggests John Coltrane, Sonny Rollins, and Hank Mobley, and alto saxophonist Abraham Burton has the hard edge and firm note placement of Jackie McLean, his teacher. Pianist Marc Cary is a more mature soloist who gravitates toward energetic lines and Red Garland-like block chords. —*Owen Cordle*, Down Beat

---

BILLY TAYLOR (William Billy Taylor)

b. Jul. 21, 1921, Washington, DC
Piano, educator / Bop
Dr. Billy Taylor's activities on behalf of jazz education and his profiles of jazz musicians on CBS's "Sunday Morning" television program have sometimes overshadowed his considerable piano skills. But Taylor was once house pianist at Birdland, and his fluidity, flexibility, and technical excellence are noticeable on several recordings. He displays a light touch, features long lines, and has performed some intriguing contrapuntal works. Taylor's knowledge of jazz history and keyboard technique have distinguished his scholarly works. Taylor studied music at Virginia State College. He graduated in 1942, and moved to New York. He played with Ben Webster, and worked in the '40s with Dizzy Gillespie, Eddie South, Stuff Smith, Cozy Cole, Machito, Slam Stewart, Don Redman, and Charlie Parker. He led his own quartet in 1949 and 1950, then, after being Birdland's house pianist in 1951, formed a trio. He's continued leading trios at various intervals. Taylor made history in 1969 when he became the first Black band director for a daily, syndicated, or network talk show: "The David Frost Show." He later founded and served as director for the radio program "Jazz Alive." Previously, he had helped found the Jazzmobile in 1965. After printing four brief primers on jazz piano styles, Taylor earned his doctorate in 1975 at the University of Massachusetts. His dissertation was on jazz piano history and stylistic development. He later published a further work, *Jazz Piano: History and Development*, in 1982. Taylor joined "Sunday Morning" in 1981 and continues to air periodic interviews and performance segments with jazz greats. All these achievements aside, he has an extensive series of recordings. These date back to the '50s, and include sessions on Argo, Atlantic, Capitol, Mercury, Savoy, ABC-Paramount, Prestige, Pausa, and Concord. Some early Taylor dates are available via reissue, while his latest, *Dr. T*, is on GRP. —*Ron Wynn*

Cross Section / May 7, 1953-Jul. 30, 1954 / Prestige 1730

With Candido / Sep. 7, 1954 / Prestige 7051

★ **Billy Taylor Touch, The** / Oct. 28, 1957 / Atlantic 1277

☆ **Billy Taylor with Four Flutes** / Jul. 20, 1959 / Riverside 1151
With Frank Wess, Herbie Mann, Jerome Richardson, and Phil Bodner. —*Michael G. Nastos*

○ **Wish I Knew How it Would Feel to be Free** / 196? / Tower 5111
Recorded with a trio, this features Taylor's immortal song bearing the title of the album, several pop and jazz standards, Clare Fischer's "Morning" and "Pensativa," and Taylor's "CAG." Bandmates featured are Ben Tucker (b) and Grady Tates (d). —*Michael G. Nastos*

★ **Live at Storyville** / Dec. 2-3, 1977 / West 54
Recorded in New York City with drummer Grady Tate and bassist Victor Gaskin, this album includes classic standards and three Taylor originals including "I Wish I Knew . . .". It ranges from modern to bop to ballads. This is standard virtuosity from Taylor—you expect nothing less. —*Michael G. Nastos*

You Tempt Me / Jun. 1981 / Taylor Made 1004
Trio. Not as good as some of his other material. Fine melodies, nice solos. —*Ron Wynn*

White Nights and Jazz in Leningrad / Jun. 13-14, 1988 / Taylor Made 1001

Solo / Aug. 1988 / Taylor Made 1002

○ **Jazzmobile All Stars** / Apr. 1989 / Taylor Made 1003

CECIL TAYLOR (Cecil Percival Taylor)

b. Mar. 15, 1929, New York, NY
Piano, composer / Early free, modern creative
Pianist Cecil Taylor's approach disturbs as many, if not more, people than Ornette Coleman's on alto sax. Taylor has suffered an equal amount of critical abuse, and has had as much trouble as Coleman did getting his work recorded by major labels since it's probably the least commercially viable music made in America. Taylor approaches the piano as an extension of dance and drums; his work emphasizes chordal clusters and percussive patterns, and he plays it not only with his hands, but, at times, with open palms, fists, and elbows. There are often huge leaps and odd rests and breaks in his solos; other times he seems to be ripping across the keyboard as though he's attacking it.

While Taylor's earlier material had its share of single-note melodies and standard jazz rhythmic and harmonic maneuvers, by the early '60s he had almost eliminated these melodies and maneuvers from his menu. Without question, there's a healthy dose of European avant-garde and classical influence in his work, but Taylor also cites Fats Waller and James Brown as favorites along with Dave Brubeck. His stylistic influences include Duke Ellington, Thelonius Monk, and Lennie Tristano. He abhors stereotypes, and has upbraided interviewers for assumptions he feels they've made. Taylor's also a fine poet, and many recent concerts have combined martial arts demonstrations, dance, and poetry.

Taylor was encouraged by his mother to begin piano lessons at age five, and he later studied percussion with a timpanist. He entered the New England Conservatory in 1952, and studied piano and theory. Taylor began recording in 1956, working with Steve Lacy, Buell Neidlinger, and Dennis Charles. He also had an extended, six-week engagement at the Five Spot, and made an appearance at the Newport Jazz Festival, which Verve recorded in 1957. Taylor recorded with Earl Griffith, Charles, and Neidlinger for Contemporary, and with John Coltrane for United Artists. He also made his own date for the label in 1959. That same year, Taylor recorded with Gil Evans. There were more Candid sessions in 1960, one a Neidlinger date that was not issued for 11 years before it was partially released under Taylor's name (until 1987, the other part was only issued in Japan). Taylor then went to Europe and Scandinavia with Jimmy Lyons and Sunny Murray, and recorded at the Cafe Montmartre in late 1962. This recording later appeared on Arista/Freedom. Albert Ayler worked with the trio during their European swing.

Though Taylor won *Down Beat's* New Star award in 1962, offers weren't that plentiful in the early '60s, especially from club owners who worried about both the condition of their pianos after a Taylor performance, and the fact that his music wasn't exactly conducive to buying drinks and food. Taylor continued recording, and worked with Bill Dixon in the short-lived Jazz Composers Guild. He cut two ahead-of-their time albums for Blue Note in the mid-'60s, *Conquistador!* and *Unit Structures*. He was back in Europe by the mid-'60s, recording on the Freedom label, appearing on French Radio, and eventually working and recording with the Jazz Composers Orchestra in 1968.

Taylor turned to academia during the early '70s, and taught at the University of Wisconsin in Madison. He resigned after a controversy involving several students that he failed who were passed despite his protests; Taylor's administrative skills and lecture techniques were also questioned during the dispute. He later taught at Antioch College, with Lyons and Cyrille joining him. Bassist Sirone made it a quartet in 1973.

Taylor did many sessions in the '70s for Arista/Freedom, Enja, MPS, Hat Art, New World, and Soul Note. These included a 50-minute solo piano foray, duets with Mary Lou Williams and Max Roach, plus sextet and combo sessions. Taylor won a Guggenheim fellowship in 1972, and brought his act to the White House in 1979, playing at a jazz concert with featured attractions that ranged from Eubie Blake to Dizzy Gillespie. He stayed just as busy in the '80s, recording for Pausa, Hat Art, Praxis, Soul Note, Black Lion, and Leo. Taylor remains an uncompromising iconoclast in the '90s, and was featured in 1992 on an album with the Art Ensemble of Chicago. Since the album was dedicated to Thelonious Monk, Taylor, in typical fashion, didn't play on the cuts that featured Monk's compositions. Mosaic collected the compete Taylor Candid sessions on a magnificent four-disc boxed set in 1992. That's as good a starting point as any for someone seeking an introduction to his music. There's a good amount of Taylor titles available on CD. *—Ron Wynn and Michael G. Nastos*

Jazz Advance / Sep. 1956 / Blue Note 84462
1991 reissue of super set, one of Taylor's best groups with Steve Lacy (sax). *—Ron Wynn*

Looking Ahead / Jun. 9, 1958 / Contemporary 452
Quartet. Prophetic title; Taylor, Earl Griffith (vib), and comrades beckon to the future. *—Ron Wynn*

○ **New York City R&B** / Jan. 1961 / Candid 79017
This was a Buell Neidlinger (b) session that was originally to be issued on Candid Records in 1961. It wasn't released until 1971 and then was billed as a co-led session with Cecil Taylor (p). Taylor's presence does initially overshadow the participation of everyone. And the quartet of Taylor, Neidlinger, Dennis Charles (d), and Archie Shepp (ts) recorded one of Taylor's greatest early pieces at these sessions, "Cell Walk for Celeste." (It's right up there with "Mixed" and "Air" as one of Taylor's best compositions. Some enterprising Young Lion would do well to give these pieces a contemporary reassessment.) But clearly the date is Neidlinger's. His presence should not be underestimated. It was Neidlinger and trombonist Roswell Rudd who coarranged Ellington's "Things Ain't What they Used to Be" (a track that augments the basic trio of Neidlinger, Taylor, and Billy Higgins on drums with Rudd, Steve Lacy on soprano sax, Charles Davis on baritone, and Clark Terry on trumpet, a last-minute replacement for Don Cherry). Neidlinger arranged "O.P." as a 12-bar blues feature for Taylor. It's his all-out assault on the form that makes the impression, but it's Neidlinger's rock-solid bass playing that holds the piece together. "O.P." sports one of the all-time great walking bass intros. "Cindy's Main Mood" is one of the earliest recorded examples of free improvisation and the situation is clearly directed by Neidlinger. But *New York City R&B* isn't perfect music. The ensemble playing on the Ellington tune is scrappy. The playing and development of "Cindy's Main Mood" is tentative. It's searching music and that type of playing always has its risks (particularly in 1961). But it is also satisfying music, particularly "O.P." and "Cell Walk for Celeste." Be forewarned, the sound on this issue is much hissier than the recently issued Mosaic release

of this complete session. And the time of the CD is 36:24 (recorded 1/9-10/61, New York City). *—Robert Iannapollo,* Cadence

★ **Unit Structures** / May 19, 1966 / Blue Note 84237

Conquistador / Oct. 6, 1966 / Blue Note 84260

○ **Student Studies** / Nov. 30, 1966 / Affinity 770
Student Studies by the Cecil Taylor Unit (alto saxophonist Jimmy Lyons, bassist Alan Silva, drummer Andrew Cyrille) is a BYG date I believe was only previously issued in Japan. The music on this two-record set was recorded in concert in Paris. As usual, the whole is much larger than the parts and I found there is enough inspired listening here to easily recommend the music. *Student Studies* tells some good tales and is full of the Taylor (piano) dynamics and at the same time quite accessible. *—Bob Rusch,* Cadence

○ **Great Paris Concert** / i. 1966 / Freedom 10
This three-record set contains a 90-minute performance entitled "Second Act of A" and a 20-minute encore. The main work—consisting of quartets, trios, duets, and solo passages—proceeds with almost unrelieved intensity. Even the few lyrical segments, arcane and shimmering, ache under the strain. There is only one dynamic level—loud—occasionally broken by bursts of volume or sudden lulls. Harmony, rhythm, and melody are absent in any conventional sense. The music is more heterophonic than harmonic. Taylor's performance is stunning. Volcanic rumblings in the lower register erupt into unbelievably fast single-note lines or dancing patterns of tone clusters in the middle and upper registers. Drummer Andrew Cyrille responds to this virtuosity with dense and complex workings. Yet his texture is surprisingly static and conventional. Jimmy Lyons's alto sax playing is a free mixture of blues inflections, boppish flurries, and birdlike flights through the harmonics of his horn. Traditional jazz elements are less apparent in the playing of Sam Rivers. His leaps and trills are as akin to contemporary chamber music as they are to jazz. *—Douglas Clark,* Down Beat

★ **Great Concert of Cecil Taylor** / i. Jul. 29, 1969 / Prestige 34003
Boxed set with Taylor in searing live concert alongside Sam Rivers (sax) and Jimmy Lyons (as). Three discs of amazing playing. *—Ron Wynn*

○ **Fondation Maeght Nights—Vol. 1, 2 & 3** / i. Jul. 1969 / Jazzview 001
Originally issued in separate volumes, this classic live recording of the Cecil Taylor Unit at Saint-Paul-de-Vence, France, has been made available as a boxed, three-record set. The music is gloriously alive with a depth and richness that grows with each new listening. "Second Act of A" begins with the piano and horns in a semi-unison "theme statement." This builds up to Taylor's first solo which takes up the remainder of side one. He begins with an almost deliberate-sounding style of picking out notes. And soon he is off into an exploration of the higher timbres of the keyboard. Alto saxophonist Jimmy Lyons and Sam Rivers (ts, ss) return on side two for an extended dialog before Lyons takes over for a first-rate solo. And, as always, drummer Andrew Cyrille is a whirling dervish. Rivers (on tenor) has a short solo at the beginning of side three before Lyons rejoins the proceedings. Here Lyons solos with inspired abandonment. Taylor then takes an unaccompanied solo that is my favorite part of the performance. Cyrille returns to complement Taylor with spicy percussion work. The horns return (Rivers on soprano) on side four, and it is here that I found the weakest part of the album. But once Taylor takes over for another bravura solo, the music is back on the right track. Rivers is back on tenor for side five with much more satisfactory results. He and Lyons get into some stunning interchanges and conversations before the piece concludes rather abruptly. Side six appears to be an encore performance of the same piece here refined into a polished gem. *—Carl Brauer,* Cadence

Akisakila / i. May 22, 1973 / Trio 5

○ **Spring of Two Blue Jays** / **i.** 1973 / Unit Core
It's impossible to be indifferent to Cecil Taylor's music; one
either loves it or hates it. Taylor, it seems to me, has essentially forged a revolutionary approach to jazz piano. Sections
of *Spring of Two Blue Jays* sound as if they were recorded at
half speed and then accelerated, such is the velocity and brilliance of Taylor's upper register work. As a pianist, Taylor
uses more of the whole keyboard than most other players;
deep galumping bass figures pitted against slashing upper
register dissonances. Mind-splitting percussive sections balance lightly textured lyrical interludes. Taylor is Monk plus
complete structural, metrical, and harmonic freedom. Yes,
on first hearing, Taylor's Unit may seem to encapsulate the
whole history of contemporary music rum amok. But the incredible thing is that somehow it works. A moving performance. —*Jon Balleras*, Down Beat

Silent Tongues / Jul. 2, 1974 / Freedom 741005

Air Above Mountains . . . / 1976 / Enja 3005
Air Above Mountains (Buildings Within). Bursting, dynamic
piano solos. —*Ron Wynn*

☆ **Unit** / Apr. 3-6, 1978 / New World 201
The inclusion here of Ramsey Ameen's violin alongside the
familiar trumpet and sax completes the full symphonic tonal
palette in miniature, rounding out a rich timbral blend that
augures possible larger-scaled projects. On the other hand,
the intimacy of the quintet permits a degree of spontaneous
interplay impossible in larger formats, a responsiveness
quite remarkably illustrated in this tour de force of empathic
improvisation. This beautifully packaged and annotated album captures pianist Cecil Taylor at the peak of his maturity, employing essentially the same conceptual group
framework he has utilized at least since *Unit Structures*. —
Larry Birnbaum, Down Beat

Three Phasis / Apr. 1978 / New World 303
The follow-up to *Unit*, this is one long piece of improv over
two sides (57:12) with the same sextet. This unit is a glorious
monster. —*Michael G. Nastos*

Live in the Black Forest / Jun. 3, 1978 / PA/USA 7053

○ **One Too Many Salty Swifty and Not Goodbye** / Jun. 4,
1978 / Hat Hut 3R02
With drummer Ronald Shannon Jackson in peak rhythmic
form, the group that made *One Too Many Salty Swift and
Not Goodbye* in 1978 was perhaps the finest larger Cecil
Taylor Unit to date. Recorded shortly after the landmark studio sessions for New World Records, this is the sextet's epic
final concert, restored to its entirety on two CDs with the addition of three Taylor-less stage warmers. Without all that
bothersome flipping, the CD format makes the big adventure more approachable. To suggest the magnitude of the
journey, intrepid altoist Jimmy Lyons hardly appears for the
first hour and a half (CD 2, track 4). Of course, the infernal
pianist is present all along, growing especially tempestous
when others drop out. —*John Corbett*, Down Beat

★ **Historic Concerts** / **i.** 1979 / Soul Note

○ **It Is in the Brewing Luminous** / Feb. 8-9, 1980 / Hat Art
6012

○ **Fly, Fly, Fly, Fly, Fly** / Sep. 14, 1980 / MPS 7108
A solo piano album that defines Taylor's individuality and
does indeed fly. Diamond Award Winner in 1981. —*Michael
G. Nastos*

○ **Eighth, The** / Nov. 1981 / Hat Art 6036
The chemistry of this group combined with pianist Cecil
Taylor's structural landmarks and the *drive* are the essence
of this music. Some of Taylor's work with just the bass and
drums (William Parker, Rashid Bakr) during sections missing from the original release spotlight an attractive rough,
ragged approach, where he chops at the piano in flurried
and/or pounded fragments. This belies the more overt feeling of direct structural adherence one got from the former
edition and adds to the performance overall. And, of course,
it is good to hear Jimmy Lyons's (as) full contribution to this
piece. He plays excellently throughout. Indeed, listening to

the "complete unedited performance" (as it states clearly on
the jacket), one can understand why Hat Hut wanted to release it. It's just a shame that it wasn't done originally. —
Milo Fine, Cadence

In Florescence / Jun. 1989 / A&M 5286
Taylor remains as unbowed and unpredictable as ever. This
is music as sound, rather than structured patterns, easily discernible melodies, or simple backbeats. The 60-minute-plus
date sways between snippets, extensive dialogs, and tunes
with vocalisms and hollers. —*Ron Wynn*, Rock & Roll Disc

★ **Complete Candid Recordings of Cecil Taylor** / **i.** Jun. 1990
/ Mosaic 127
Cecil Taylor plays piano like no one inside or outside jazz.
His highly percussive, animated approach mixes drum and
dance influences with keyboard technique. He has played
with his arms and feet, produced galvanizing rhythms, odd
tonal clusters, furious octaves of sound, and teeming harmonies. Reponse to Taylor's music is either fiercely positive
or harshly negative. It is probably the least commercially viable music made in America. That, coupled with Taylor's uncompromising attitude, has resulted in very little of his work
being done for American labels and even less of it staying in
print.
    The sessions that make up the four discs on this first-rate
Mosaic boxed set were done in 1960 and 1961 for the short-
lived Candid label. Taylor's concept had not yet evolved into
a finished package. If one impression dominates these discs,
it is that Taylor himself was not always sure where he was
going. There are solos that begin in one direction, break in
the middle, and conclude in another. Tenor saxophonist
Archie Shepp often sounds unsure about what to play—
whether to try and interact or establish his own direction.
    At the same time, there is plenty of exceptional playing
from Taylor, Shepp, and the drum/bass combination of Buell
Neidlinger and Dennis Charles. These are Neidlinger's dates
as much as Taylor's, and it is his harmonic and rhythmic
skill, along with Charles's, that often rescues things. There
are quartet, trio, and large-band dates. The large-band numbers add baritone saxophonist Charles Davis, trombonist
Roswell Rudd, and ringer Clark Terry on trumpet, who fits
in despite being an established swing/bebop artist.
    You cannot honestly say everything works on these four
discs, but there is never a dull moment. It will not please
everyone, but listeners ready for a challenge should step
right up and take on this set. —*Ron Wynn*

SAM TAYLOR

b. 1916
Saxophone / Blues & jazz, soul-jazz
A certified honking sax legend, Sam "The Man" Taylor's nonstop drive and power worked perfectly in swing, blues, and
R&B sessions. He had a huge tone, perfect timing, and a
sense of drama, as well as relentless energy and spirit. An
argument could be advanced, certainly among jazz musicians, that Teagarden was actually the greatest White blues
singer. Taylor began working with Scat Man Crothers and
the Sunset Royal Orchestra in the late '30s. He played with
Cootie Williams and Lucky Millinder in the early '40s, then
worked with Cab Calloway for six years. Taylor toured
South America and the Caribbean during his tenure with
Calloway. Then Taylor became the saxophonist of choice for
many R&B dates through the '50s, recording with Ray
Charles, Buddy Johnson, Louis Jordan, and Big Joe Turner,
among others. He also did sessions with Ella Fitzgerald and
Sy Oliver. During the '60s, Taylor led his own bands and
recorded in a quintet called the Blues Chasers. Currently,
Taylor has one session available on CD recorded in the late
'50s with Charlie Shavers and Urbie Green. —*Ron Wynn*

JOHN TCHICAI (John Martin Tchicai)

b. Apr. 28, 1936, Copenhagen, Denmark
Saxophone, bandleader / Early free, modern creative
Alto, soprano, and bass clarinetist John Tchicai will probably
always be remembered for his alto playing on John

Coltrane's *Ascension* recording, but he's actually spent most of his life in Europe playing tenor sax. During the free period of the '60s, his style had a dry tone and featured a staccato attack; his later material has a fuller, more soulful and earthy sound. Tchicai began playing violin at age 10, then played clarinet and alto sax at age 16. He studied saxophone for three years at the Royal Conservatory in Copenhagen. Tchicai met Archie Shepp at a festival in Helsinki in 1962. That same year, he made his recording debut in Warsaw leading a quintet. Tchicai moved to New York in 1963. He played with Shepp and Don Cherry in the New York Contemporary Five, and with Roswell Rudd and Milford Graves in the New York Art Quartet in 1964 and 1965. Both bands toured Europe and recorded. Tchicai also recorded with the Jazz Composers Guild and with Shepp, John Coltrane, and Albert Ayler. He returned to Denmark in 1966, and led the workshop ensemble, Cadentia nova danica, from 1967 to 1971, performing with them in London in 1968. Tchicai cut back on his playing and began teaching full-time in 1972, then resumed active playing in 1977. He joined Pier Dorge's New Jungle Orchestra and appeared with them at the 1986 Chicago Jazz Festival. Tchicai began recording as a leader in the '60s for MPS. He's done other dates for FMP, Steeplechase, Black Saint, and Enja. He has a couple of sessions available on CD, and is on reissues with other artists like Shepp and Coltrane. —*Ron Wynn*

★ **John Tchicai and the Strange Brothers** / Oct. 9, 1977 / FMP 15

JACK TEAGARDEN (Weldon Leo Teagarden)

b. Jul. 19, 1905, Vernon, TX, **d.** Jan. 15, 1964, New Orleans, LA

Trombone, vocals / Dixieland

The king of early jazz trombone, Jack Teagarden towered over his contemporaries, even such greats as Kid Ory. Teagarden's father was an engineer, and Teagarden had an extraordinary mechanical mind. He once rebuilt a Stanley Steamer, and was an accomplished auto mechanic. He took a similar approach to the trombone; Teagarden had played the peck horn, a valve instrument, and perfected his technique to the point that he never moved his slide more than 18 inches. He redesigned his equipment until he had the ideal mouthpieces and mutes. Teagarden was almost as gifted as a vocalist as he was an instrumentalist; he sang in a charming, humorous, yet appealing and moving manner. Everything he played or sung was done smoothly, but never in detached or rote fashion (except when he was bored with the material or situation).

He was part of a musical family, and had a sister and two brothers who were professionals. Teagarden began on piano at age five, then baritone horn at age seven, and trombone at age 10. He turned professional at age 15, and played with territory bands such as Peck Kelley's Bad Boys. Teagarden did his first recording in 1927, then divided his time between heading pickup bands for sessions and working with Ben Pollack from 1928 to 1933, and with Paul Whiteman from 1933-1938, though he professed to have little respect for Whiteman's music. Teagarden made some brilliant records with Eddie Condon in 1929. The song "That's a Serious Thing" contained solos by pianist Joe Sullivan and saxophonist Happy Cauldwell using the tenor before it was fashionable, while "I'm Gonna Stomp Mr. Henry Lee" featured Teagarden vocals and trombone solos. He worked with Fats Waller in 1931, and cut "You Rascal You" and "That's What I Like About You." "Someone Stole Gabriel's Horn" and "I've Got It" in 1933 and 1934, and "The Sheik of Araby," "Cinderella," and "Stay in My Arms" with Charlie Spivak in the late '30s, were hit recordings. He worked on several of these with his brother, Charlie, then played with his other brother, Cub, backing Hoagy Carmichael for a film short in 1939. Teagarden, Charlie and Frankie Trumbauer also worked together in New York in 1936 as the Three Ts, and had mild success with the Victor recording "Tse a Muggin."

Teagarden led other bands from 1939 to 1946, but encountered little financial success. He did appear in the 1941 film *Birth of the Blues*. For a time, Teagarden did a radio series at the Roseland in Boston, but the coming of World War II ended that and several other opportunities. Through all this, Teagarden continued to make brilliant records. In the early '40s, he recorded with vocalist Kitty Kallen, David Allyn, and Jack and Marianne Dunne. The song "A Hundred Years From Today" became a Teagarden staple, while Bing Crosby, Mary Martin, and Teagarden turned the novelty song "The Waiter and the Porter and the Upstairs Maid" into a smash. After heading a sextet, Teagarden joined Louis Armstrong's All-Stars from 1947 to 1951, and helped to make it the best Armstrong all-star unit. He and Armstrong teamed on the duet "Rockin' Chair" at the All-Stars 1947 Town Hall concert, and the group's RCA and Decca recordings were superb. Teagarden began making more acclaimed records as a leader after departing the All-Stars. There were spectacular dates on Bethlehem, Verve, Roulette, and Capitol. He did many sessions in the '50s, and worked with such players as Bobby Hackett, Peanuts Hucko, and Billy Bauer. Jay D. Smith and Len Guttridge did a definitive biography in 1960 titled *Jack Teagarden*. —*Ron Wynn*

☆ **That's a Serious Thing** / Mar. 1928-Jul. 1957 / Bluebird 9986

★ **King of the Blues Trombone** / i. 1928-1940 / Sony Special Products 6044

○ **I Gotta Right to Sing the Blues** / Feb. 1929-Oct. 1934 / ASV 5059

○ **Indispensable, The** / i. 1929-1933 / RCA 45695
1929-1933. With a wide variety of bands—Eddie Condon, Ben Pollack, Paul Whiteman, Budd Freeman, and others—this is a great overview of the trombonist's career. There are several vocals on the 31 cuts and four alternate takes. —*Michael G. Nastos*

○ **100 Years From Today** / i. 1931 / Grudge 4523

○ **Jack Teagarden's Big Eight / Pee Wee Russell's Rhythmakers** / Aug. 31, 1938-Dec. 15, 1940 / Riverside 1708
With Pee Wee Russell (cl). 1938 & 1940. Two titans of classic New Orleans style make a great match. —*Ron Wynn*

Varsity Drags / Feb.-Jul. 1940 / Savoy 1162
Material not previously issued on any album. Originally from Varsity Label 78s. Features vocalists David Allyn, Kitty Kallen, and Marianne Dunne. —*Michael G. Nastos*

☆ **Meet Me Where They Play the Blues** / Nov. 1954 / Bethlehem 6040
The 12 tracks from these 1954 sessions were issued by the Jazztone Society in the '50s, and the serious record buyer would do well to keep searching the bargain bins for the reissue of that five-star LP. This more expensive LP has only 10 titles, and the long "Blue Funk," by far the best performance from the Leonard Feather date, is among the missing. The remarkable similarity between Jack Teagarden and baritone crooner Hoagy Carmichael has been remarked upon—but Carmichael had the advantage of singing his own songs, whereas Teagarden, alas, was all too inclined to sing trash like "Meet Me Where They Play the Blues" and "Music to Love By." Indeed, it is a bonus that "Misery and the Blues" is such a good song; "Bad Acting Woman," a blues, is less suited to his ballad vocal strengths. The selection of instrumental titles, however, is superb. The organization and high melodic content of these trombone solos are among the most sophisticated elements of Teagarden's multifaceted art. Everyone plays well on "Woman," but the leader's solos at the beginning and end are models of his style. The beauty of his opening phrase, its conclusion in decorative detail, and the avant-garde harmony of the answer phrase outline the chorus' shape, its final phrase being a perfect summary. In the last chorus, the theme phrase, with heavy emphasis of the beat, has its elaborate tag, to again stage-set the rest of the 12 bars, the sum being a wonderful tribute to the blues,

rich, earthy, with a summer kind of elegance. —*John Litweiler,* Down Beat

☆ **Columbia Special Products / i.** Dec. 1979 / XFL 14940
This Jack Teagarden set is three discs (boxed) containing a total of 48 tracks, covering a period from Nov. 27, 1928 ("Whoopee Stomp") to July 23, 1940 ("Shi-Me-Sha-Wabble"). The only real gaps are from mid 1936 to mid 1939, a Paul Whiteman period (Decca and RCA), and considering what usually surrounded his work with this orchestra, their exclusion is of little loss. There are some cornball tracks in the Teagarden set, but not the music from Teagarden's horn. The individuals making up the discography of these sides reads like a Who's Who of Chicago jazz (chronologically and intelligently printed in the liners). —*Bob Rusch,* Cadence

Giants of Jazz / i. Jan. 1981 / Time Life 08

★ **Accent on Sound** / Fresh Sound

Tribute to Teagarden / PA/USA 9026

CLARK TERRY (Clark [Mumbles] Terry)

b. Dec. 14, 1920, St. Louis, MO
Trumpet, flugelhorn, vocals / Big band, bop, progressive big band

No one could ever accuse Clark Terry of solemnity or detachment; his penchant for humor in his music, especially in his scat singing and "mumbles" routine, often trigger accusations of silliness. But Terry's an excellent modern trumpeter who's perfected, among many other things, "dialogues" with himself, sometimes playing different instruments and other times alternating between mute and unmuted passages. His tone, range, and solo technique are superb, and he's equally proficient at swing or bebop. Terry worked in local groups around the St. Louis area, then was in a navy band during World War II with Willie Smith. After his discharge, he played with Charlie Barnet in 1947, and with Count Basie's small and large groups during the late '40s and early '50s. Terry played with Duke Ellington into the late '50s, and appeared on several suites and extended pieces. He worked with Quincy Jones, then was recommended by Ray Copeland for a staff position at NBC after Copeland had to turn it down. Terry worked at NBC through the '60s and early '70s. He appeared regularly on the "Tonight Show," while doing jazz dates with J.J. Johnson and Oscar Peterson, and coleading a group with Bob Brookmeyer that became popular in the early '60s. There were sessions on Mainstream, Vanguard, Big Bear, Mercury, Impulse, and Riverside in the '50s and '60s. Terry began playing flugelhorn in the '50s while in the Ellington orchestra. He included more flugelhorn solos in his repertoire during the '70s, and recorded often for Pablo, and for MPS/BASF and Pausa. He's maintained his activity in the '80s and '90s. Some of Terry's best recorded work can be heard on the Ellington album *Cosmic Scene,* while classic Terry dates from the '50s and '60s, plus more recent '70s and '80s cuts, are available on CD. —*Ron Wynn*

☆ **Clark Terry** / Jan. 3-4, 1955 / EmArcy 36007

○ **Serenade to a Bus Seat** / Apr. 17, 1957 / Original Jazz Classics 66
Why it took so long for Clark Terry to be recognized for his fine stylized trumpet work is hard to understand, as even by the time of this date (4/57) he had quite well established himself as a capable individual voice. The '50s were a great period for Clark Terry, as I think it was then that he recorded his best work; his puckery sound had a particular lyricism to it which in later years seems to have become self-conscious. He is joined here by Johnny Griffin (ts), just beginning to come into his own as a major voice and heard to good advantage. The rhythm is Wynton Kelly (p), Paul Chambers (b), and Philly Joe Jones (d). This was fresh, working jazz when it was first released and the program remains ever fresh. —*Bob Rusch,* Cadence

Duke with a Difference / Jul. 29-Sep. 6, 1957 / Riverside 229

★ **In Orbit** / May 7+12, 1958 / Riverside 302
Quartet with Thelonious Monk. Terry shows he can fit into any setting, even with Monk's always arresting, unorthodox piano style. Date also has Sam Jones (b) and Philly Joe Jones (d). CD has bonus cut, 1988 reissue. —*Ron Wynn*

Paris (1960) / Jan. 2, 1960 / Swing SW8406

Color Changes / Nov. 19, 1960 / Candid 79009

★ **New York Sessions / i.** Oct. 3-4, 1961 / Fontana

☆ **Gingerbread Men** / 1966 / Mainstream 373
With Bob Brookmeyer (tb) Quintet. This is a fine set, reissued recently. —*Ron Wynn*

It's What's Happenin' / Jul. 24, 1967 / Impulse 9157
Good mix of topicality, humor, and fine playing. MCA reissue a bit questionable. —*Ron Wynn*

★ **Clark Terry's Big B-A-D-Band Live at the Wichita Jazz Festival** / Apr. 21, 1974 / Vanguard 79355
The fact that this band didn't work steadily makes its performance here even more remarkable. Much credit has to go to the unit's arrangers, especially to Phil Woods and Ernie Wilkins. Note Wilkins's now-revised "Take the 'A' Train" chart, a masterpiece of ensemble writing and reed voicings. Even more impressive is Woods's ballad "Randy." It's impossible to imagine this chart played better—perfect articulation, perfect intonation, perfect balance. Woods has become a consumate saxophonist of the stature of Stan Getz or Sonny Rollins. Two fun pieces, "Mumbles" and "Cold 'Tater Stomp," are exhilarating outings. The latter of these features a strong trombone solo by Janice Robinson, the first woman bone soloist since Melba Liston. But check all solos. With the exception of Duke Jordan's slightly confused "A Train" intro, they are all impressive. —*Jon Balleras,* Down Beat

○ **Clark Terry and His Jolly Giants** / 1975 / Vanguard 79365
Clark Terry has his thing down pat; a small group drawn from his active big band records a lighthearted selection of tunes, either familiar or blues-based. Uptempos alternate with medium speeds, and there isn't one sloppy moment. Vic Spriles is a handy bassman, Ronnie Matthews a tasty accompanist, Ernie Wilkins a smooth sax player. Terry cites his predecessors—quotes from Clifford Brown, Fats Navarro, and Dizzy Gillespie abound. And he tosses in hints of other, familiar tunes: a bit of "My Blue Heaven" shows up, and "People" ends "Somewhere Over the Rainbow." —*Howie Mandel,* Down Beat

○ **Ain't Misbehavin'** / Mar. 15-16, 1976 / Pablo 105
This serves as a sprightly showcase for tunes either written or associated with Fats Waller. Outstanding in his role as front-line mate is the underappreciated alto saxophonist Chris Woods. Clark Terry's (flugelhorn) unforced humor is evident throughout the 45:00 of this 3/15-16/76 session, but be advised that the current (1986) pressing is not up to the standard of the original Pablo. Also present are Johnny Hartman (v), Oscar Peterson (p), Vic Sproles (b), and Billy Hart (d). —*Bob Rusch,* Cadence

☆ **Big Bad Band Live at Buddy's Place** / 1976 / Vanguard 79373
What we really get for our money on this album is an assortment of fine soloists working out with an alternately conventional and funky rhythm section with a few big-band punctuations dropped in like cameos. Not surprisingly, the best sounds are rooted in a time when giants wrote big-band music. Duke Ellington's "Come Sunday" and especially "Jeeps Blues," with Chris Woods's sumptuous alto, are the album's high points, followed very closely by Walt Levinsky's sax writing on "Sugar Cubes." More of such quality and this would be a real big-band session. —*John McDonough,* Down Beat

Out of Nowhere / Jul. 20, 1978 / Bingow 3101

Funk Dumplin's / Aug. 21, 1978 / Matrix 100

Mother . . . ! Mother . . . ! / Feb. 2, 1979 / Pablo 115

Memories of Duke / Mar. 11, 1980 / Pablo 604

To Duke and Basie / Jan. 28, 1986 / Rhino 79627

○ **Jive at Five** / **i.** Feb. 1986+Jul. 1988 / Enja 6042

This is a wondrous combination. Trumpeter/flugelhornist Clark Terry and bassist/pianist Red Mitchell represent the apogee of the mainstream meld where bebop meets swing. Recorded in "Red's Flat, Stockholm," according to the liners, this 1988 meeting is a meditation on the powers of positive swing. It's also out-and-out great music played by two inventive masters at the height of their powers. The repertoire includes Harry Edison's poppin' "Jive at Five," Neal Hefti's "Late Date" and "Cute," Ellington's "Sophisticated Lady," "Love You Madly," "Cottontail," and "Prelude to a Kiss," Lester Young's "Lester Leaps In," and Mitchell's engaging romp, "Big'n The Bear." It's a warm embrace of great music and life! —*Chuck Berg, Jazz Times*

Portraits / Dec. 1988 / Chesky 2

Having Fun / Apr. 11-12, 1990 / Delos 4021

Live from the Village Gate / Nov. 1990 / Chesky 49

Some very fine recent Terry with excellent Jimmy Heath (d), good Pacquito D'Rivera (as). —*Ron Wynn*

Live on 57th Street / Big Bear

WOODY THEUS

Drums / Early jazz-rock, modern creative

Confusion reigns in the case of drummer Woody Theus, who's also recorded as Son Ship Theus and as Woodrow Theus. Theus's playing hasn't changed as much as his name; it's rooted in hard bop and blues, and has a strong backbeat. He's provided good rhythmic assistance and support when working with Curtis Clark, Harold Land, Charles Lloyd, and Woody Shaw. Theus does not have any sessions available as a leader on CD. —*Ron Wynn*

JEAN TOOTS THIELEMANS (Jean Baptiste Thielemans)

b. Apr. 29, 1922, Brussels, Belgium

Harmonica, guitar / Swing, bop, Latin-jazz

Though he's a good guitarist, Toots Thielemans is much better known for his whistling and for his harmonica playing. His chromatic harmonic solos are exceptional, and only Larry Adler has adopted the harmonica more effectively to jazz situations. Thielemans has recorded extensively as a whistler, and has made several appearances on popular Quincy Jones albums. His guitar work is solid, but not exceptional. Thielemans played accordion at age three, and began playing chromatic harmonica at age 17. He taught himself to play guitar in the early '40s, and was influenced heavily by Django Reinhardt. He visited America in 1947, and played with Charlie Parker in 1949. Thielemans toured Europe with Benny Goodman in 1950, then came to America in 1951. He worked in the '50s with George Shearing. Thielemans commuted for years between Sweden and America, and cut his best known composition, "Bluesette," in Stockholm in 1961. He began recording as a leader in the late '50s for Riverside. There were several dates with Jones in the late '60s and early '70s, plus an appearance on the *Midnight Cowboy* soundtrack. Thielemans began making trips to Brussels in the '70s, and started heading swing and bebop quartets. He recorded at the Montreux International Jazz Festival with Dizzy Gillespie in 1975, and with Paquito D'Rivera in 1984. He's recorded for Verve, Columbia, Polydor, A&M, Pablo, Choice, Jeton, Stash, EmArcy, Private Music, Concord, and Soul Note. Thielemans has done high-profile pop and R&B sessions with Jones, Aretha Franklin, and Billy Joel. During the '90s, he's recorded two volumes of Afro-Latin material, *The Brasil Project, Vols. 1 & 2.* A little of his early material, and quite a bit of the more contemporary dates, are available on CD. —*Ron Wynn and Michael G. Nastos*

★ **Man Bites Harmonica** / Dec. 30, 1957+Jan. 7, 1958 / Riverside 1738

Early period. Definitive harmonicist from Belgium. With Pepper Adams, Kenny Drew, Wilbur Ware, and Art Taylor. —*Michael G. Nastos*

Toots and Svend / Nov. 22-23, 1972 / Sonet 253

☆ **Silver Collection** / Apr. 1974-Apr. 1975 / Verve 825086

○ **Captured Alive** / Sep. 1974 / Choice 1007

There is a decidedly schizophrenic quality to the music here—the feeling of split personality runs all through the performances—that results from very real conceptual differences at the core of Toots Thielemans's playing and that of the rhythm section. Coming from basically the same place, pianist JoAnne Brackeen, bassist Cecil McBee, and drummer Freddie Waits work well together, playing a hard, tight, sinewy modernized bebop of an absolute pared-to-the-bone economy. It is Thielemans on harmonica who is the odd man out, his broadly romantic, frequently florid approach to this music very much at variance with the no-nonsense muscularity of the trio. It's as though Thielemans viewed this as something on the order of a mood jazz date, while the others saw themselves as participating in, say, the Miles Davis *Cooking'* and *Relaxin'* sessions. Were Thielemans in more of a boppish mood, he would have set much better with them. —*Pete Welding, Down Beat*

Apple Dimple / Nov. 1979 / Denon 7578

Aquarela Do Brasil / **i.** 1987 / Verve 830391

☆ **Only Trust Your Heart** / Apr. 1988-May 1988 / Concord Jazz 4355

Bit to sentimental side, good playing. CD version has two prime cuts. —*Ron Wynn*

Footprints / **i.** Dec. 19-20, 1989 / Verve 846650

Autumn Leaves / **i.** 198? / Soul Note

ED THIGPEN (Edmund Leonard Thigpen)

b. Dec. 28, 1930, Chicago, IL

Drums / Bop

Ed Thigpen's highly respected, seasoned drummer and percussionist with great skills in every phase of his craft. Thigpen plays with sensitivity and swing; he uses brushes as expertly as sticks, can provide a driving, steady beat, can vary the pulse, and can solo with flair or remain anchored in the background. He's also written several books on drumming and has led international workshops. Thigpen worked with Cootie Williams, Dinah Washington, Johnny Hodges, Lennie Tristano, Bud Powell, Jutta Hipp, and Billy Taylor in the '50s. He played in Oscar Peterson's trio with Ray Brown from 1959 to 1965, then joined Ella Fitzgerald's backup band. He moved to Los Angeles in 1967, and rejoined Fitzgerald from 1968 to 1972. Thigpen relocated to Copenhagen in 1972, and taught at the Malmo Conservatory in Sweden while forming the group Action-re-action. He's worked with numerous players in the '70s and '80s, among them Monty Alexander, the Berlin Contemporary Jazz Orchestra, Kenny Drew, Art Farmer, Dexter Gordon, Lionel Hampton, Boulou and Elios Ferre, and Johnny Griffin. Thigpen has recorded as a leader for Verve, GNP Crescendo, Reckless, Timeless, and Justin Time. He has a couple of sessions as a leader available on CD. —*Ron Wynn*

★ **Mr. Taste** / Apr. 1991-Jul. 1991 / JustIn Time 79379

GARY THOMAS

b. 1962

Saxophone / Neo-bop, modern creative

As arresting and animated as any tenor saxophonist in his generation, Gary Thomas has alternated between dashing hard bop, jazz-rock, and funk, and some things in between the extremes on his sessions. He's been recording as a leader since the late '80s, and has also recorded with Greg Osby, Geri Allen, and Kevin Eubanks, among others. He has several sessions available on CD. —*Ron Wynn*

★ **While the Gate is Open** / 1986 / Verve 834439

Despite some rough moments in his solos, this is worth checking out. Emblematic of the new wave of '90s jazz types with one foot in other camps. —*Ron Wynn*

Code Violations / Jul. 1988 / Enja 79604

Striking 1988 session; Thomas can be exciting one cut, exasperating the next. —*Ron Wynn*

○ **By Any Means Necessary** / May 1989 / JMT 834432
Aggressive, Young Lion-led session with R&B, electronic elements. Thomas is an explosive, constantly growing improviser. —*Ron Wynn*

JOE THOMAS

b. Jun. 16, 1933, Newark, NJ, **d.** Feb. 18, 1981
Tenor saxophone / Swing, big band
Joe Thomas was a fine swing-era player whose sound and style emphasized rhythmic invention rather than melodic or harmonic development. He was a flashy player who doubled as a vocalist, and was a star in the Lunceford band of the '30s and '40s. He started as an alto saxophonist playing in the bands of Earl Hood and Horace Henderson in the early '30s, then switched to tenor sax and played with Stuff Smith and Guy Jackson before joining Lunceford in 1933. He remained in the Lunceford orchestra until 1947. Thomas became coleader with Eddie Wilcox before leaving to form his own band. He led this band until the early '50s, then temporarily retired to join his father's undertaking business. Thomas continued to play periodically, appeared at the 1970 Newport Jazz Festival, and recorded with a quartet featuring Jimmie Rowles in 1979. He only made a few sessions as a leader for labels such as Melodisc and Uptown. Thomas can be heard on various Lunceford orchestra reissued CDs. —*Ron Wynn*

★ **Blowin' in from K.C.** / Dec. 9, 1982 / Uptown 2712

LEON THOMAS (Amos Leone (Jr) Thomas)

b. Oct. 4, 1937, St. Louis, IL
Vocals / Ballads & blues, early free
Before Bobby McFerrin, Al Jarreau, and others came along and turned vocal improvising into a lucrative urban contemporary pastime, Leon Thomas was yodeling, doing vocal fills, scatting, and singing on some seminal free jazz dates. Thomas's cries, calls, yelps, and wailing, coupled with Pharoah Sanders's equally arresting tenor sax, were a highlight of many early and mid-'70s Impulse sessions, but Thomas's career has been spotty since then. He studied music at Tennessee State and also played in a Nashville group with Hank Crawford. Thomas moved to New York in 1958, and performed at the Apollo before touring with an all-star show that worked the TOBA circuit. Thomas had a pair of brief stints with Count Basie, and also worked with Mary Lou Williams, Randy Weston, Joe Newman, Rahsaan Roland Kirk, Benny Powell, Oliver Nelson, and Tony Scott in the '60s before meeting and working with Pharoah Sanders. Their run of fine albums extended through to the mid-'70s. Nelson also began recording as a leader in 1969. He sang with Carlos Santana, Oliver Nelson, Louis Armstrong, and Freddie Hubbard in the '70s. Thomas has recorded with Gary Bartz, Malachi Thompson, and Sanders during the '80s. He has one session available on CD. —*Ron Wynn and Michael G. Nastos*

○ **In Berlin** / Nov. 6, 1970 / Flying Dutchman 10142

★ **Blues and the Soulful Truth** / i. Aug. 1973 / Flying Dutchman 10155
This is his best studio album. Contains many of his best numbers. —*Michael G. Nastos*

○ **Facets** / Flying Dutchman 10164
A compilation of late '60s and early '70s material that is well put together. —*Michael G. Nastos*

LUCKY THOMPSON (Lucky [Eli] Thompson)

b. Jun. 14, 1924, Columbia, SC
Tenor and soprano saxophone / Bop
A masterful soloist who finally got disgusted with the perils of being a jazz musician, Lucky Thompson was a topflight player in the '40s, '50s, and '60s. He was one of the first great soprano saxophonists, and with his fleeting, energetic style and approach, made several memorable recorded solos

while playing with many top bop leaders. Thompson demonstrated that a soft tone need not be a weak one; he was most strongly influenced by Don Byas's approach. Thompson toured with the Bama State Collegians in the early '40s, before moving to New York. He spent six months with Lionel Hampton, then played in Billy Eckstine's bebop orchestra, and later, in 1944 and 1945, played with Count Basie. After moving to Los Angeles, Thompson was in great demand as a session player, and appeared on more than 100 records as either a leader or sideman over a two-year period. He recorded for Dial with Charlie Parker and Dizzy Gillespie in 1946, then played with Parker's septet, and later played with Boyd Raeburn. Thompson returned to New York in 1948, and led his own band at the Savoy in the early '50s. Thompson also became involved in the growing R&B field, and did some recording, song writing, and publishing. But he came back to jazz in the mid-'50s, playing on the Miles Davis's *Walkin'* sessions in 1954. He recorded for Vanguard, Atlantic, and Savoy in the '50s, then did several recordings in Paris during 1956. He made another session for Atlantic in 1957 with Milt Jackson. Thompson toured Europe and America with Stan Kenton's orchestra, and was featured on the Kenton LP *Cuban Fire.* He lived in France during the late '50s and early '60s, mastering the soprano sax and playing steadily in Europe. Thompson made some superb albums for Prestige in the early '60s, among them the seminal *Lucky Strikes!* He went back to France from 1968 to 1971, and recorded for MPS and Nessa. After teaching at Dartmouth in 1973 and 1974, then cutting two albums for Groove Merchant, Thompson left the music business. There are precious few Lucky Thompson dates available via reissue. There are some on Fresh Sound, and others on Xanadu and Fantasy. —*Ron Wynn*

○ **Lucky Thompson** / Jan. 27-Feb. 1956 / Paramount 111

★ **Lucky Thompson Featuring Oscar Pettiford** / Jan. 27-Feb. 1956 / Jasmine
Very neglected tenor on a super album, backed by great Pettiford (b). —*Ron Wynn*

☆ **Paris (1956)** / Mar. 12+14, 1956 / Swing 30030
This Lucky Thompson recording is composed of two sessions with the only change in personnel being the replacement of bassist Pierre Michelot with Benoit Querson. Given the paucity of Thompson recordings, one can't really complain about the rerelease of this one. For the most part, his dry and fleet tenor is the centerpiece on these standards, but pianist Martial Solal does have some good moments as well. —*Carl Brauer,* Cadence

Brown Rose / Mar. 29, 1956 / Xanadu 204

★ **Lucky Strikes!** / Sep. 15, 1964 / Prestige 194
Lucky Thompson brings along Hank Jones (p), Richard Davis (b), and Connie Kay (d) to back him on two standards and six originals. The program here is quite strong and the leader, on both tenor and soprano, brings a soulful and personal approach to his playing. And in case anyone still thinks that the soprano only sounds like John Coltrane, here is another of those handful of artists to have an individual touch. —*Bob Rusch,* Cadence

Lucky Meets Tommy / i. 1965 / Fresh Sound 199
There are far too few Lucky Thompson records; in part because the legendary sax player had a reputation of being "difficult." These rare 1965 sessions with the great Tommy Flanagan on piano (on all but three tracks) produced 70 minutes of relaxed jazz that are a superb introduction to Lucky's tenor stylings, out of Coleman Hawkins and Don Byas, and his soft, airy sound on the soprano. —*Les Line*

Body and Soul / May 1-2, 1970 / Nessa

Lullaby in Rhythm / i. Oct. 1980 / Biograph 12061

MALACHI THOMPSON

Trumpet / Modern creative
A veteran Chicago trumpeter who's worked with many of the city's famous players, Malachi Thompson's never been

able to break through for himself. He's recorded a number of albums for Delmark. Thompson finally got some attention in the late '80s with an album for Delmark that also featured vocals by Leon Thomas. He made an even better follow-up album with Carter Jefferson, Harrison Bankhead, and some other solid, but lesser-known, players, and displayed a pungent tone, a good command in every register, and some intriguing solos. Unfortunately, neither release got widespread coverage. Thompson's also been a member of Lester Bowie's Brass Fantasy, the Ra Ensemble, and the Association for the Advancement of Creative Musicians (AACM). He has two sessions available on CD. —*Ron Wynn and Michael G. Nastos*

★ **Seventh Son, The** / May 1972 / RA 102

Trumpeter Malachi Thompson, who's formerly worked with the AACM Big Band, calls his work "freebop," but it isn't, as I understand the term. Rather, it's an elementary jazz-fusion graft with rock/Latin/funk from the rhythm section (though sometimes drummer Billy Salter kicks the groove around more than one might suspect), jazzy soloing over the top, with a heavy dousing of insistent electric pianos in between. Exploratory, perhaps, at the time of these recordings (though similiar ground had been trod previously), but not now (1980). The soloing is quite competent but mostly undistinguished, excepting the leader's fine wah-wah mute work on "Kirk's Tune" (as opposed to his typical modern bop open horn work) and the nicely sculpted beginning of tenorist Jesse Taylor's spot on "Two Nights in Malakai." John Thomas plays an almost hilariously aggressive guitar solo on the blues-based "West Side Stomp." Aaron Dodd's tuba, too often restricted to doubling Curtis Robinson's electric bass on two numbers, adds a bit of a distinctive edge but alas not enough: a freer rein might have helped. —*Kevin Whitehead, Cadence*

○ **Spirit** / Delmark 442

SIR CHARLES THOMPSON (Charles Phillip Thompson)

b. Mar. 12, 1918, Springfield, OH
Piano / Bop, soul-jazz
An excellent pianist and organist, Sir Charles Thompson has been a successful swing and bebop player. His organ-playing style showed that this instrument could effectively play bebop. On either instrument, his style is light and bluesy, but his solos aren't clichéd, dependent on gimmicks, or bereft of ideas. After working in territory bands, Thompson began playing for Lionel Hampton in 1940. He worked with Coleman Hawkins in the mid-'40s, and played with him on the outstanding *Hollywood Stampede* sessions for Capitol in 1945. Thompson then worked with Illinois Jacquet in 1947 and 1948. His composition "Robbins Nest," a tribute to disc jockey Fred Robbins, became both a huge hit for Jacquet and a jazz anthem. Bob Russell recorded a vocal version titled "Just When We're Falling in Love." Thompson often worked with Buck Clayton in the '50s, and appeared on a famous series of jam sessions on Columbia. He recorded as a leader for Vanguard in the '50s, and as a sideman with Clayton and Jimmy Rushing. Later, he made albums for Black and Blue, for Prestige, and some tracks for Master Jazz. Thompson toured Europe with Clayton in 1961, and toured America, Canada, and Puerto Rico leading groups. After working in Pennsylvania during the early '70s, he had some health problems, but bounced back in the mid-'70s. His seminal dates with Coleman Hawkins, and some cuts with Charlie Parker, were reissued recently by Delmark. Mosaic has reissued the Clayton jam sessions. A little Thompson material is also available on Sackville. —*Ron Wynn*

○ **Takin' Off** / **i.** 1945-1947 / Delmark 450
This is a reissue of the classic Apollo series. The 1945 and 1947 sessions feature legendary bands with Charlie Parker, Dexter Gordon, Buck Clayton, Danny Barker, J.C. Heard, Joe Newman, Freddie Green, Pete Brown, and Shadow Wilson playing sixteen cuts, seven previously unissued. This is prime bop. —*Michael G. Nastos*

★ **And His All Stars** / **i.** 1950 / Apollo 103
With Charlie Parker (as), Dexter Gordon (ts), and Leo Parker (bs). —*Michael G. Nastos*

○ **Sir Charles Thompson Sextet** / **i.** 1953 / Vanguard 8003

○ **Sir Charles Thompson Quartet** / **i.** 1954 / Vanguard 8006
With Coleman Hawkins / **i.** 1954 / Vanguard 8009

○ **Sir Charles Thompson Trio** / **i.** 1955 / Vanguard 8018

CLAUDE THORNHILL

b. Aug. 10, 1909, Terre Haute, IN, **d.** Jul. 1, 1965, New York, NY
Piano, arranger / Swing, big band, progressive big band
A swing big band leader and pianist who was influenced by Claude Debussy, Claude Thornhill's ideas influenced Gil Evans, Gerry Mulligan, Lee Konitz, and Miles Davis, among others. The Thornhill sound featured big bands that played static textures in the lower registers without vibrato or vocal-like effects, and got support, colors, and textures from the tuba, bass clarinet, and French horn, instruments that weren't normally heard in jazz settings. It was certainly an original sound, though also softer and less forceful than much of the jazz of the time. Thornhill worked for Paul Whiteman, Benny Goodman, and Ray Noble in the mid-'30s. His arrangement of "Loch Lomond" for Maxine Sullivan led to a hit recording and the start of her solo career in 1937. Thornhill recorded as a leader in 1937, and led a band from 1940 to 1942, reforming it in 1946. Thornhill also wrote arrangements for radio orchestras and jazz bands, among them groups led by Benny Goodman and Skinny Ennis. Thornhill's group included Charlie Spivak, Manny Klein, and Conrad Gozzo, but was a straight dance band. Thornhill experimented with band instrumentation in the early '40s, sometimes using a reed section with clarinet, saxophones doubling on clarinet, and two French horns. At times, the Thornhill orchestra featuring six clarinets at once. He played in Artie Shaw's Navy Band, then regrouped after his discharge. At that time, Thornhill's included Red Rodney and Lee Konitz. In the '50s, Thornhill served as Tony Bennett's music director, and led a small combo. A prime influence on Stan Kenton, Thornhill's work has been reissued on CD, and is often listed in pop, rather than jazz, sections in catalogs. —*Ron Wynn*

★ **Claude Thornhill and His Orchestra** / 1947 / Hindsight 108

○ **Real Birth of the Cool** / **i.** 194? / Columbia
A formative date featuring Thornhill's band doing "cool" arrangements back in early and mid '40s. Has never been widely available in America, even the import. —*Ron Wynn*

Best of Big Bands / Columbia 46152

☆ **Tapestries** / Affinity
A comprehensive, two-disc set of his prime cuts, with 17 arranged by Gil Evans. —*Ron Wynn*

CLIFFORD THORNTON (Clifford Edward (III) Thornton)

b. Sep. 6, 1936, Philadelphia, PA, **d.** 1989
Trumpet, trombone / Modern creative
An entertaining, unorthodox, and often delightful trombonist, trumpeter, and bandleader, Clifford Thornton's music blended free arrangements, humorous refrains, African, Caribbean, and Latin rhythms, and elements of blues, soul, and funk. Thornton was a better trombonist than trumpeter or cornetist, but played effectively on all three instruments. He worked with Ray Draper in the late '50s, and studied with Donald Byrd. Thornton toured Korea and Japan with an army band in the late '50s and early '60s, then performed and recorded in New York with Sun Ra. He also played with Pharoah Sanders and John Tchicai, and recorded with Marzette Watts. Thornton formed the New Arts Ensemble and recorded with them in 1967, played at a Belgian jazz festival, and recorded in Paris with Dave Burrell, Sunny Murray, Archie Shepp, and his own bands in 1969 and 1970. He also recorded with Shepp at the Antibes Festival.

Thornton was on the Wesleyan faculty from 1969 to 1975, while recording with Shepp again, writing compositions, and leading bands. He became an educational counselor at the African American Institute in 1976, an organization with United Nations (UNESCO) sponsorship. Thornton recorded for the Jazz Composers Orchestra Association (JCOA), BYG, and Thirdworld. Currently, Thornton doesn't have any sessions available on CD. —*Ron Wynn and Michael G. Nastos*

○ **Freedom and Unity** / Jul. 22, 1967 / Third World 9636

★ **Ketchaoua** / Aug. 18, 1969 / BYG 529.323
Paris studio date with firebreathers Archie Shepp (sax), Grachan Moncur III (tb), Dave Burrell (p), and Sonny Murray (d). —*Michael G. Nastos*

○ **Gardens of Harlem, The** / Apr. 1974 / JCOA 1008
Definitive, brilliant creative statement from visionary trombonist with the Jazz Composers Orchestra. A must-have for progressive music listeners. —*Michael G. Nastos*

HENRY THREADGILL (Henry Luther Threadgill)

b. Feb. 15, 1944, Chicago, IL
Alto saxophone, composer / Modern creative
While his initial fame came from his role as a composer and a member of the marvelous trio Air, Henry Threadgill's importance as a leader, arranger, writer, and player shouldn't be minimized. He's one of the more careful, yet creative alto and baritone saxophonists. He plays in a concise, yet urgent and animated manner. Threadgill mixes harsh, cutting lines with lyrical cries and bluesy refrains. He blends swing, be-bop, stride, traditional jazz, and free influences in his compositions, using offbeat rhythms, time signatures, and tempos. No Threadgill album or song ever falls under the heading of predictable. Threadgill was a percussionist in street marching bands as a child in Chicago. He started on baritone and clarinet in high school. Threadgill played hard bop and free jazz in a sextet with Joseph Jarman and Roscoe Mitchell in the early '60s, and was in Muhal Richard Abrams's Experimental Band, and in Phil Cohran's Heritage Ensemble. Threadgill later became a member of The Association for the Advancement of Creative Musicians (AACM), and toured with gospel singer Jo Jo Morris. Following a stint in the army in which he played in a rock band, Threadgill worked in the house band at a Chicago blues club and recorded with Abrams. He studied flute, piano, and composition at the American Conservatory of Music, earning his degree, and at Governors State University. Threadgill formed the cooperative trio Reflection with Steve McCall and Fred Hopkins in 1971 to perform Scott Joplin compositions for an assignment. This trio later reformed as Air in 1975. They toured and recorded regularly with each member providing compositions. Threadgill moved to New York in the mid-'70s, where he began leading various groups once Air and New Air disbanded. One was the Windstring Ensemble; others included the Society Situation Orchestra, and Very Very Circus. He also recorded with Mitchell, Olu Dara, and David Murray, and did albums with Murray from 1980 to 1982. Threadgill continued recording in the '80s with his sextet and large band, and has recorded for the Axiom label in the '90s. Threadgill's albums as a leader for Axiom and other labels are available on CD; some of the Air and New Air sessions are available on CD, too. —*Ron Wynn*

X-75—Vol. 1 / Jan. 13, 1979 / Novus 3013
Four bassists predominate (Fred Hopkins, Rufus Reid, Brian Smith, and Leonard Jones) in this pre-sextet recording. Amina Myers (p) and Joseph Jarmen (reeds) also show. Unrestrained freedom and beauty. —*Michael G. Nastos*

★ **Just the Facts and Pass the Bucket** / 1983 / About Time 1005
Sextet (actually seven pieces). Dynamite open-ended compositions, especially the surly "Black Blues" and the determined "Man Called Trinity Deliverance." Features Olu Dara, Pheeroan AkLaff, John Betsch, and bassist Fred Hopkins. All pungently original material. —*Michael G. Nastos*

☆ **When Was That?** / i. 1983 / About Time
Same band as 1983 except bassist Brian Smith. The title track is a riot on record. Some extraordinary improvising and spontaneous combustion going on here. Landmark recording. —*Michael G. Nastos*

Subject to Change / Dec. 1984 / About Time

☆ **You Know the Number** / Oct. 1986 / Novus 3013
A wonderful release with quirky, jerky cuts; resolute, superb solos. —*Ron Wynn*

Easily Slip into Another World / Sep. 1987 / Novus 3025

☆ **Rag, Bush and All** / Dec. 1988 / Novus 3052
Ted Daniel (tpt), Bill Lowe (bass tb), and Newman Baker (per) are in. "Off the Rag" and "The Devil is Loose" and "Dance with a Monkey" are on. —*Michael G. Nastos*

★ **Spirit of Nuff . . . Nuff** / Nov. 1990 / Black Saint 120134
The latest Threadgill armada proves every bit as appealing as his past brigades. —*Ron Wynn*

○ **Too Much Sugar for a Dime** / i. 1993 / PolyGram 514258
When it comes to compostional cunning, Henry Threadgill is hard to beat. Yet the sheer eccentricity of Very Very Circus, which includes two tubas, two electric guitars, trap set, and an alto-and-French-horn front line, might well stump a less ambitious composer. Not this one. Just listen to "Little Pocket Size Demons," for example, in which Threadgill's alto and Mark Taylor's French horn declaim over a bed of guitar noise and tuba riffs. "Try Some Ammonia" is my own favorite, alternating delirious polyrhythms, a Latin-tinged melody, a shrewd solo by Mark Taylor, and several high-pitched, marvelously grainy choruses from the leader. Every single cut, however, testifies to Threadgill's talent for creating intricate, abrasive, and downright exhilarating music. —*James Marcus, Jazz Times*

BOBBY TIMMONS (Robert Henry Timmons)

b. Dec. 19, 1935, Philadelphia, PA, **d.** Mar. 1, 1974, New York, NY
Piano / Hard bop
Pianist Bobby Timmons became so famous for the gospel and funky blues presence in his solos and the compositions that he wrote in that vein that his skill as a bebop player was nearly forgotten. Timmons composed three soul-jazz classics, "Moanin'," "This Here," and "Dat Dere." These were great, but their success put Timmons in the position of being a "hit" artist, and labels wanted him to reproduce the formula ad infinitum. Timmons's earlier '60s albums displayed more variety and contained more challenging playing than his later dates. He studied piano from the age of six. Timmons moved to New York from Philadelphia in 1954, and played with Kenny Dorham's Jazz Prophets, and with Chet Baker, Sonny Stitt, and Maynard Ferguson in the late '50s. He joined Art Blakey's Jazz Messengers in 1958 and 1959, and toured Europe with them. "Moaning'" later became a regular number in the Blakey book; it was played at numerous concerts and was recorded frequently. He worked with Cannonball Adderley in 1959 and 1960 and wrote other successful compositions. Timmons rejoined Blakey briefly in 1960. During the '60s, Timmons led several trios, and even began playing vibes in 1966. But his health degenerated, and Timmons died in 1974. He made several albums on Riverside and Milestone. Timmons's frequent playing partners were Sam Jones and Jimmy Cobb. He only has a couple of dates available currently on CD. —*Ron Wynn*

○ **This Here is Bobby Timmons** / Jan. 13-14, 1960 / Riverside 104
Trio with Sam Jones (b) and Jimmy Cobb (d). This is the pianist's single best album. —*Michael G. Nastos*

★ **Moanin'** / Aug. 12, 1960-Sep. 10, 1963 / Milestone 47031
Compilation of five different albums 1960-63. Great collection and collectible. —*Michael G. Nastos*

☆ **Workin' Out** / Oct. 21, 1964 / Prestige 7387

Soul Man, The / Jan. 20, 1966 / Prestige

☆ **Live at the Connecticut Jazz Party** / 1981 / Early Bird 104
Pianist Bobby Timmons had the good fortune to get visibility with drummer Art Blakey and later with alto saxophonist Cannonball Adderley. And, of course, as a composer—"Moanin'" is his credit. Sonny Red did not get the same visibility. A hard player, out of the Jackie McLean alto sax school, he had a personal, almost sour tone to his playing. Here Red is in good passion, and Sam Jones (b) has a nice solo on "Here's that Rainy Day." Timmons moved me on "Prelude to a Kiss" and works hard through the din of cocktail chit chat on "Theme"; perhaps because of that, the trio (Red is out on "Prelude") is playing for themselves. "Now the Time" and "Moanin'" move along well, but contain no memorable moments. These are workmanlike performances, which won't waste your time or insult your mind. This is an album of interest. —*Bob Rusch*, Cadence

KEITH AND JULIE TIPPETT (Keith Graham Tippett)

b. Aug. 25, 1947
Keith and Julie (b. Jun. 8, 1947) Tippett are a British husband and wife performing team who've recorded with both jazz and rock groups. Keith Tippett led a sextet in the '60s and wrote a piece, "Septober Energy," that was performed by the 50-piece orchestra Centipede. He later led a free ensemble called Ovary Lodge, worked in piano duos with Stan Tracey and Howard Riley, and toured with a septet. Julie worked with Keith in Ovary Lodge, sang in Brian Auger's rock and jazz-rock group, and has recorded with John Stevens and Bobby Bradford, as well as with Keith. —*Ron Wynn*

○ **Sunset Glow** / i. 1975 / Utopia 1248
Exploratory vocalist at her best and most accessible. With English and South African musicians. —*Michael G. Nastos*

★ **Frames** / May 22-24, 1978 / Ogun 004
A tour de force project with Ark Big Band, strings, horns, and vocals. —*Michael G. Nastos*

JUAN TIZOL

b. 1900, **d.** 1984
Trombone / Swing, big band
Though he seldom soloed, valve trombonist Juan Tizol played a pivotal role in the Ellington orchestra in three different periods: from the late '20s to the mid-'40s, from 1951 to 1953, and from 1960 to 1961. An arranger and copyist as well as instrumentalist, he contributed compositions such as "Perdido," "Moonlight Fiesta," and "Caravan," and added a Latin melodic and rhythmic element into the Ellington compositional mix. With his large tone and flexible style and sound, he was a valued member of the trombone section. Tizol worked in an orchestra in San Juan, Puerto Rico, before moving to America in 1920. He met Ellington while working at the Howard Theatre in Washington, D.C. Tizol worked briefly with Bobby Lee's Cotton Pickers and with the White Brothers Band, then joined Ellington in 1929. He left in 1944 to work with Harry James and alternated between the two groups for several years, and also played with Louis Bellson and Pearl Bailey. After his last stint with Ellington, Tizol retired in California, and later moved to Las Vegas. Tizol can be heard on many Ellington CD reissues. —*Ron Wynn*

CAL TJADER (Callen Radcliffe (Jr) Tjader)

b. Jul. 16, 1925, St. Louis, MO, **d.** May 5, 1982, Manila, Philippines
Vibes / Cool, Latin-jazz
The greatest non-Latin bandleader in Latin-jazz history, Cal Tjader's early interest in the music blossomed into a lifelong love affair. While he wasn't the fastest vibes player, his style matured to the point that he could provide efficient, effective solos while his band maintained the groove. Tjader also played piano and bongos. He studied music at San Francisco State University and began as a drummer with Dave Brubeck's trio in the late '40s and early '50s. He worked with Alvino Rey before beginning his own band. Tjader joined George Shearing in 1953; Shearing's band eventually had Tjader playing vibes and percussion with Willie Bobo, Mongo Santamaria, and Armanda Peraza. Shearing's bassist, Al McKibbon, helped stimulate Tjader's love affair with Latin-jazz and Afro-Latin music. When Tjader left Shearing, he started his own groups, which mixed Latin-jazz, Afro-Cuban, and jazz. Bobo and Santamaria joined Tjader later in the '50s, and he led fine bands in the '60s, '70s, and '80s. He recorded for Fantasy from the '50s to the mid-'60s, then switched to Verve. Tjader's Verve sessions included Lalo Schifrin, Bobo, Donald Byrd, and Kenny Burrell, and the albums *Several Shades of Jade*, and *Soul Sauce* made the pop albums chart. He recorded with Eddie Palmieri on Verve and Tico, and with Charlie Palmieri on Fantasy. Tjader continued on Fantasy in the '70s, and worked with Stan Getz, Charlie Byrd, Hank Jones, and Clare Fischer. He also began recording for Concord in the '70s, and cut both straight jazz sessions with Scott Hamilton and Jones and Latin dates, one that included Carmen McRae. He won a Grammy for the 1980 release *La Onda Va Bien*, and continued on Concord until his death in 1982. Tjader has many sessions available on CD. —*Ron Wynn*

★ **Tjader Plays Mambo** / Aug.-Sep. 1954 / Fantasy 3221
Tjader Plays Mambo and *Mambo with Tjader* feature three fall 1954 sessions with vibist/pianist Tjader playing two dozen Latinized standards. Four of the tracks find Tjader in the company of a small orchestra (Dick Collins, John Howell, Al Porcino, Charlie Walp, trumpets; Manuel Duran, piano; Carlo Duran, bass; and Ed Rosalies, Edward Verlardi, percussion) for added brass accents. The remainder of the tracks are without the horns and with Verlardi added as a third Latin percussionist. On "Sonny Boy," Tjader croons the opening vocal, which then breaks into an uptempo Spanish chant, an improvement on this song of questionable jazz interest. —*Bob Rusch*, Cadence

Latin Kick / Nov. 1956 / Fantasy 642

Jazz at the Blackhawk / Jan. 20, 1957 / Fantasy 436
Quartet. Expressive playing, pretty basic Afro-Latin Tjader groove. With Vince Guaraldi (p), Gene Wright (b), and Al Torre (d). —*Ron Wynn*

Mas Ritmo Caliente / Nov. 20, 1957 / Fantasy

Concert by the Sea—Vols. 1 and 2 / Apr. 20, 1959 / Fantasy 8038

☆ **Monterey Concerts** / Apr. 20, 1959 / Prestige 24026
Outstanding combination of his sessions with Willie Bobo and Mongo Santamaria plus *Concerts by the Sea* LP linked in two-record package. —*Ron Wynn*

☆ **Night at the Blackhawk, A** / 1959 / Fantasy 278
A Night at the Blackhawk stretches out even further and offers up a program that includes some of Cal Tjader's stronger jazz material. Along on board is Vince Guaraldi (p), who builds some fine solos and should impress the listener with his inspiration, and Joe Silva, whose Getzian/Hawkish tenor adds some nice touches, though he seems reticent to really assert his playing. The best work here is on "Bill B," a blues stretcher. —*Bob Rusch*, Cadence

Sona Libre / Jan. 28+30, 1963 / Verve 815058

★ **Soul Sauce** / Nov. 20, 1964 / PolyGram 27756
One of his most influential '60s releases with Willie Bobo, Donaly Byrd, and Kenny Burrell. —*Ron Wynn*

○ **El Sonid Nuevo (The New Soul Sound)** / i. May 24-26, 1966 / Verve

☆ **Primo** / i. 1970 / Original Jazz Classics 762

Breathe Easy / Sep. 1977 / Fantasy

○ **La Onda Va Bien** / Jul. 1979 / Concord Jazz 4113
This was the debut album for Concord Jazz Picante, an offshoot of Concord Jazz dedicated to recording Latin-jazz. Cal Tjader's style to these ears is a fairly watered-down version of Latin-jazz. For while the music is exciting from a rhythmic point of view (provided mainly by drummer/percussionist Vince Lateano and percussionist/conguero Poncho

Sanchez), there is no deeper spirit to the music. As a soloist, Tjader (vibes) is relatively lightweight, and Roger Glenn's flute work isn't much stronger. The listener isn't challenged by the music or uplifted. But it makes for a pleasant enough party record. —*Carl Brauer,* Cadence

Gozame! Pero Ya / Jun. 1980 / Concord Jazz 4133

Shining Sea / Mar. 1981 / Concord Jazz 4159

Heat Wave / Jan. 1982 / Concord Jazz 4189

Good Vibes / 1983 / Concord Jazz 4247

☆ **Bamboleate** / Tico

○ **Greatest Hits—Vols. 1 and 2** / Fantasy 4527

Latin + Jazz Equals / Dcc 604

Tambu / Fantasy 9453

With Donald Byrd (tpt). Fine collaboration between two prominent Latin-jazz players. —*Ron Wynn*

CHARLES TOLLIVER

b. Mar. 6, 1942, Jacksonville, FL
Trumpet / Hard bop

Charles Tolliver is a durable, consistently fine trumpeter who has contributed to several fine groups, and has been a combo leader and a record label co-owner. The Strata-East company was another in a line of musician-owned-and-operated ventures that were designed to let players control the rights to their recordings and to participate more equitably in the proceeds. The label began in 1971 and issued some outstanding recordings until the late '70s. It was reactivated in the late '80s. Tolliver's playing strengths include a firm, bright tone and timbre, an engaging, inventive approach, and an understated, yet swinging solo style. Clifford Brown and Freddie Hubbard are among his prime influences. Though Tolliver attended Howard University for three years before returning to New York in the early '60s, he is primarily self-taught. He performed and recorded with Jackie McLean in the mid-'60s, and appeared on and provided some songs for McLean's Blue Note album *It's Time.* He worked for a short time with Art Blakey and Sonny Rollins, and did recording sessions and performances with Gerald Wilson, Booker Ervin, Roy Ayers, Horace Silver, and McCoy Tyner. Tolliver played in Gerald Wilson's big band in 1966 and 1967 while in California. He was a member of Max Roach's quintet from 1967 to 1969, and appeared on some superb combo dates for Atlantic. Tolliver formed Music, Inc., a quartet that sometimes expanded to become a big band, in 1969. Stanley Cowell, John Hicks, Cecil McBee, Reggie Workman, Clint Houston, Jimmy Hopps, and Clifford Barbaro were some of the players in the group, which performed and recorded until the late '70s. Music, Inc. was also one of the acts on the Strata-East label, along with The Piano Choir, Clifford Jordan, Cecil Payne, Pharoah Sanders, and Keno Duke's Jazz Contemporaries. Tolliver made several records in the late '60s and the '70s, primarily for Strata-East. There were also sessions on Polydor, Black Lion, and Arista/Freedom. After both Music, Inc. and Stata-East encountered difficulties in the '70s, Tolliver went to Europe where he led a quartet. He's still active, and, in 1990, a new Tolliver quartet recording was issued on the Strata-East label and featured his European band playing live in Berlin. It's one of only a couple of Tolliver sessions that are available currently on CD. —*Ron Wynn and Michael G. Nastos*

○ **Ringer, The** / Jun. 2, 1969 / Freedom 1017
Includes five Tolliver originals with the Stanley Cowell Trio. All the cuts are important, but "Plight" and "On the Nile" are particularly gripping. Cowell solos marvelously. —*Michael G. Nastos*

★ **Live at Slugs—Vols. 1 and 2** / May 1, 1970 / Strata East 1972
These four sides are part of a live session done in the intimate East Village club Slugs on May Day, 1970. While a certain sameness tends to envelop the two volumes, the improvisational strength of the artists keeps the session on such a high level that the music consistently sounds fresh and

spontaneous. Tolliver's horn style isn't revolutionary but possesses a melodic warmth and compactness of expression shared by few other trumpeters. Traces of the old Chet Baker, or better, '50s Miles; snatches of Freddie Hubbard played straight (with no chaser). Neither dispassionate nor pretentious, Tolliver's blowing is, rather, quite poignant. On "Orientaale," an Eastern mode is struck, accented by Cecil McBee's bowed bass and Tolliver's romantic fanfares. "Our Second Father" is uptempo and rumbles along freely, each member of the ensemble keenly attuned to the advancing ideas of the others. McBee's "Felicite" is a soft tone poem with brushes and a long, introspective piano solo by Stanley Cowell, played in subdued shades of blue and red. McBee steps in for a few loping configurations on the upright, and Tolliver takes it home with soothing, globular notes. —*Ray Townley,* Down Beat

☆ **Grand Max** / i. 1972 / Black Lion 760145
A brilliant showcase for Charles Tolliver with a superb rhythm section—makes one realize how underrated he has consistently been. —*Bob Rusch,* Cadence

○ **Live at Loosdrecht Jazz Festival** / Dec. 1973 / Strata East 19470
This two-record set from Strata-East, recorded in 1972 at the Loosdrecht Jazz Festival in Holland, is an exquisite Charles Tolliver showcase. On four sides there are just five compositions, giving everybody plenty of room to play. As a matter of fact, it is a great date for everybody; pianist John Hicks, bassist Reggie Workman, and drummer Alvin Queen work together beautifully. Charles Tolliver's trumpet player of the Clifford Brown lineage by way of Freddie Hubbard, and at 31 (when this recording was made) ranked among the finest players of the day. Here he shows power and imagination, wrapped in a kind of electric excitement generated by all four superb musicians meeting the music head on and cooking. —*Herb Nolan,* Down Beat

☆ **Impact** / Jan. 17, 1975 / Strata East 51-004
Six spectacular performances from trumpeters and a 23-piece (plus eight-piece string section) orchestra. Great solos from Tolliver and pianist Stanley Cowell on "Plight" and throughout by James Spaulding (as), George Coleman (ts), Charles McPherson (sax), and Harold Vick (ts). As powerful a record as you're likely to hear. —*Michael G. Nastos*

☆ **Live in Berlin at the Quasimodo—Vol. 1** / i. 1988 / Strata East 9003
A quartet recording from 1988, this features a stunning elongated version of "Ruthie's Heart" among four originals. There is great group interplay. —*Michael G. Nastos*

MEL TORMÉ (Melvin Howard Tormé)

b. Sep. 13, 1925, Chicago, IL
Vocals / Ballads & blues

At the age of three, Mel Tormé was singing in public; at age four, he was on the radio; at age nine, he was acting professionally; and at age 15, he published his first composition—an instrumental. After playing drums and singing in Chico Marx's band (1942 to 1943), he formed a vocal ensemble, the Mel-Tones, for which he wrote exceptional arrangements; the group performed with Artie Shaw's band. From the late '40s on, Tormé has pursued a consistently successful career as a solo singer, has acted in films and on television, and has written songs ("The Christmas Song" and "Born to be Blue") have become standards. He has published a novel, a reminiscence of Judy Garland, an autobiography, and a biography of his friend and frequent coworker, Buddy Rich. Tormé is clearly a man of exceptional gifts; his voice has remained an astonishingly consistent and accurate instrument, and his upper range, always a special feature of his style, remains intact in his seventh decade of performing. He has few peers as an interpreter of the great American songbooks. —*Ron Wynn and Dan Morgenstern*

○ **Gone with the Wind** / i. 1946 / Musicraft
Momentous 1946 and 1947 cuts that indicate Tormé's something special. —*Ron Wynn*

It Happened in Monterey / i. 1946 / Musicraft

Sings His California Suite / i. 1949 / Discovery
Seminal 1949 cuts. Tormé wrote all songs, harmonizes with the Mel-Tones. —*Ron Wynn*

Sings Fred Astaire / i. Nov. 1956 / Affinity

Live at the Crescendo / i. 1956-Feb. 22, 1957 / Charly 60

Sings About Love / i. 1958 / Audiophile

Tormé / i. 1958 / PolyGram 23010
Outstanding session. Tormé singing expressively backed by Marty Paich (p) orchestra. —*Ron Wynn*

Back in Town / Apr. 23-Apr. 29, 1959 / Verve 511522

☆ **Mel Tormé Swings Schubert Alley** / Jan. 21-Feb. 11, 1960 / Verve 821581
This Mel Tormé set comes from around 1959 and presents the carefully controlled and complementary West Coast backing of Marty Paich's Orchestra (Al Porcino, Stu Williamson, Frank Rosolino, Vince DeRosa, Red Callender, Art Pepper, Bill Perkins, Bill Hood, Joe Mondragon, Mel Lewis), which when called upon offers a solo or two of substance (yes, Pepper does solo). This is prime "fog" as Tormé hiply handles 12 pieces ("Too Close for Comfort," "Once In Love with Amy," "Sleepin' Bee," "The Street Where You Live," "All I Need is a Girl," "Just in Time," "Hello Young Lovers," "Surrey with the Fringe on Top," "Old Devil Moon," "What Ever Lola Wants," "Too Darn Hot," and "Lonely Town") of American stage music. He never sounded in better voice. —*Bob Rusch*, Cadence

★ **Duke Ellington and Count Basie Songbooks** / Dec. 12, 1960+Feb. 2, 1961 / Concord Jazz 4382
Recorded with the Johnny Mandel Orchestra at sessions in Los Angeles, it includes half Duke Ellington and half Count Basie plus Leroy Carr's "In the Evening (When the Sun Goes Down)." With all these things going for it, how can Tormé do wrong? —*Michael G. Nastos*

Comin' Home, Baby / Jul. 11, 1962-Sep. 13, 1962 / Atlantic 8069
One of his biggest hits ever, though Tormé loathes both the song and his Atlantic Records period. —*Ron Wynn*

Songs of New York / Dec. 2-Dec. 7, 1963 / Atlantic 80078

At Maisonette / Sep. 1974 / Atlantic 18129

○ **New Album, A** / Jun. 1977 / Gryphon 916
If vocalist Mel Tormé's fine 1975 album *Live at the Masionette* got a Grammy Award nomination, then *A New Album* should be in line for a Nobel Prize. It's a winner, with few serious weaknesses and at least one track that is a masterpiece of lyric, arrangement, and performance. Here he takes on Billy Joel ("NY State of Mind"), Janis Ian, Stevie Wonder ("All In Love Is Fair"), and Paul Williams ("Ordinary Fool"), bringing out the qualities in their work that are likely to survive. And because he does, they are all that much closer to comparison with the ranks of Jerome Kern, George Gershwin, Irvin Berlin, and other masters. There are some remarkably good lyrics here, and Tormé doesn't let a syllable slip by that isn't well thought out. Janis Ian's "Stars" is an extraordinary achievement, a sort of "No Business Like Show Business" for the '70s. Chris Gunning's arrangement, with its soft strings and woodwinds, brings a profundity to the words that is equal to the finest work Gordon Jenkins ever did for Frank Sinatra. And Tormé handles the whole piece not only with impeccable craftsmanship, but with a moving emotional resonance that should duly lay to rest any thought that he is nothing more than an excellent technician. There's an authority to his words that is convincing. —*John McDonough*, Down Beat

London Sessions / i. 1977 / Dcc 608
Tormé with the London Symphony and jazz soloists like Phil Woods (ts), Barry Miles, Vic Juris and Gordon Beck. Includes "Send in the Clowns," "New York State of Mind," and "When the World was Young." This is a good compilation of cuts done in London. —*Ron Wynn*

Together Again—For the First Time / i. 1978 / Gryphon 903
Recorded with Buddy Rich (d) and Orchestra and special guests Steve Marcus (sax), Phil Woods (sax), and Hank Jones (p). "Blues in the Night" and "Bluesette" stand out. —*Michael G. Nastos*

☆ **Live at Marty's** / i. 1981 / Finesse 37484
Trio sessions with guests Cy Coleman (p), Gerry Mulligan (sax), and Jonathan Schwartz (p); these are Tormé's finest live dates, a twofer loaded with standards and fun. Everyone really enjoys this one, and Tormé's voice is unfettered. —*Michael G. Nastos*

Evening with George Shearing / Apr. 15, 1982 / Concord Jazz 190

Top Drawer / Mar. 1983 / Concord Jazz 219

○ **Evening at Charlie's** / Oct. 1983 / Concord Jazz 4248

○ **Elegant Evening** / May 1985 / Concord Jazz 294
By the choice of material and tempos, this LP is ideal for romantic evenings. The music is redolent of late at night and warm of heart. Engineer Edwards, no doubt in consultation with Tormé, has even added a whiff of mist to the traditional English song "Brigg Fair." In all fairness, this album should have been billed as a Mel Tormé LP with Shearing in accompaniment as that is essentially what it is. Contrary to most of their collaborations, this has no extensive Shearing solo work nor any solo titles by him, perhaps because Shearing recorded a solo album of his own at or near the same time (2/86). —*Shirley Klett*, Cadence

○ **And Rob McConnell's Boss Brass** / May 20, 1986 / Concord Jazz 306
With Rob McConnell's Canadian big band. Pop to swing, including a monster Ellington medley and the spirited "Cow Cow Boogie." —*Michael G. Nastos*

Vintage Year / Aug. 1987 / Concord Jazz 4341

Reunion / Aug. 1988 / Concord Jazz 4360
Marty Paich Dek-Tette. Tight arrangements; Tormé is lush and enchanting. —*Ron Wynn*

In Concert in Tokyo / Dec. 1988 / Concord Jazz 382

○ **Mel and George Do World War II** / 1990 / Concord Jazz 4471

Night at the Concord Pavilion / Aug. 1990 / Concord Jazz 4433

JEAN TOUSSAINT

Saxophone / Neo-bop
One of England's finest young jazz musicians and strongly influenced by Wayne Shorter, saxophonist Jean Toussaint began winning converts in America during his stint with Art Blakey's Jazz Messengers in the early and mid-'80s. Toussaint has also played with other British artists like Jason Rebello, Courtney Pine, Steve Williamson, and Andy Sheppard. He doesn't have any albums as a leader, but can be heard on Blakey albums such as *Blue Night* and *Hard Champion*. —*Ron Wynn*

RALPH TOWNER (Ralph N. Towner)

b. Mar. 1, 1940, Chehalis, WA
Guitar, piano / World fusion, modern creative
Besides his impressive work as a founding member of Oregon, Ralph Towner has been featured as a leader on many important sessions outside the group. One of the few topflight contemporary guitarists who've focused exclusively on acoustic, Towner utilizes the instrument's total range; sometimes playing vividly expressionistic solos, other times playing very rhythmically and aggressively. He doesn't consider himself a jazz musician, but sees himself as an improviser, which is an accurate appraisal. There's much Asian/Indian influence in his style, and there are also European symphonic and chamber elements. He seldom swings in either a blues or jazz sense, but what he plays is always memorable, regardless of context. Towner studied

trumpet and is a self-taught pianist. He earned a BA in composition from the University of Oregon in 1963. Towner studied classical guitar technique with Karl Scheit in Vienna in the mid- and late '60s. After returning to New York, he began working in combos playing mainly piano. Towner was a member of Oregon from the group's inception and has played on every album over the years. He got his first taste of crossover stardom when he did a guest stint on 12-string guitar for Weather Report's *I Sing the Body Electric* album on Columbia in 1971. Towner has done numerous duet and solo albums for ECM in the '70s, '80s, and '90s. He's often worked with Gary Burton, Kenny Wheeler, Jan Garbarek, Eberhard Weber, and Jon Christensen, among others. He has several titles available on CD. —*Ron Wynn*

Trios / Solos / Nov. 27-28, 1972 / ECM 833328

☆ **Diary** / Apr. 4-5, 1973 / ECM 829157
Solo guitar and piano. Quintessential melodic content is like no other. —*Michael G. Nastos*

★ **Matchbook** / Jul. 26-27, 1974 / ECM 835014
Definitive duet with vibist Gary Burton and Ralph Towner (g). Buy it on CD. —*Michael G. Nastos*

○ **Solstice** / Dec. 1974 / PolyGram 825458
Those who waited to hear guitarist Ralph Towner in a rhythmic environment more highly charged than the gossamer wings giving flight to the group Oregon are no doubt pleased with polyrhythmist drummer Jon Christensen. His restless, clean attack underscores Towner's tendency to peculiar turns of rhythm, fleshing out in bold relief a cragginess often smoothed by the rolling tablas of Oregon's Collin Walcott. Eberhard Weber, a skilled, mournful countermelodist, gets the action and some of the tone of an electric bass on his peculiarly rebuilt acoustic instrument, which seems to be neither yin nor yang in the bass department, but is obviously ideal for his concept. Jan Garbarek has developed from a talented post-John Coltraner, retaining some of the master's tonal qualities but now constructing leaner solos, fervently blown, possessed of a lyricism with hoarfrost. A very complete Ralph Towner is in evidence here; we sample his classical guitar skills ("Winter Solstice") and several sides of his 12-string playing. Among these are a rockish, rippling duet with Christensen ("Piscean Dance") that is almost Leo Kottkesque; a brief, dissonant "Red and Black" on which abstracted single voicings stand out as severely as a stone circle on the Cornish moors—with, I might add, similar enigmatic presence; and more characteristically rich and flowing instances, such as "Oceanus," where the pianistic conceptions of his solo and accompanying techniques are most apparent. —*Charles Mitchell*, Down Beat

Sounds and Shadows / Dec. 1974-Feb. 1977 / ECM 829386

○ **Old Friends, New Friends** / Jul. 1979 / ECM 829196

○ **Solo Concert** / Oct. 1979 / ECM 827268
Comprising excerpts from live recorded dates in Zurich and Munich during the fall of '79, Ralph Towner's *Solo Concert* is most impressive and again demonstrates that one needn't be electric to be electrifying. "Spirit Lake" opens on a 12-string with a short series of vibrant, chordal harmonics interchanged with free linear inventions in the major mode. Two fluid themes unfold in a quasi-rondo form, which the guitarist delicately embellishes, while he keenly dovetails a drone with one of his strings, producing a blissful tambura effect. Towner demonstrates equally rich chops on the nylon string classical guitar (Towner's "Piano Waltz"). However, it is his 12-string offerings that are most impressive. A good example is "Timeless," where the guitarist takes the John Abercrombie tune and handles it with bejeweled sensitivity. Special credit should be given to recording engineer Martin Welland for the exceptional sonic quality of this live set. Audience applause and clamors are audible only between tracks, and even the most delicate musical passages are heard with a crystalline clarity and ultraspaciousness—a perfect mesh of studio-produced accuracy and concert hall excitement. —*Stephen Mamula*, Down Beat

Blue Sun / Dec. 1982 / ECM 829162

City of Eyes / i. 1989 / ECM 837754

LENNIE TRISTANO (Leonard Joseph Tristano)

b. Mar. 19, 1919, Chicago, IL, d. Nov. 18, 1978, New York, NY
Piano / Postbop, cool, early free
There aren't many mavericks in any musical form, and even fewer people whose work represents a legitimate alternative. Pianist Lennie Tristano's playing took a definite departure from established jazz tradition. It emphasized the same instrumental and harmonic mastery as bebop, but included many other unrelated elements. These elements included complex time signature changes, even rhythmic backgrounds rather than irregular cross-accents, carefully measured dissonance, and quite jarring polytonal effects. Tristano's music even veered into what would later be considered "free" collective improvisation, and he was also a pioneer in multitrack dubbing and recording. Tristano insisted that his students, who included everyone from Bud Freeman to Art Pepper, thoroughly investigate the work of jazz greats from Louis Armstrong to Parker, and he put a premium on advanced ear training.

Tristano's mother was an amateur pianist and opera singer, and he first studied music with her. He continued his studies at a school for the blind, and spent ten years there learning piano, wind instruments, and music theory. Tristano then entered the American Conservatory in Chicago, and graduated in 1943. He played piano and various instruments in jazz contexts, and taught privately on the side while he attended the Conservatory. By the mid '40s, Tristano was attracting musicians such as Billy Bauer, Lee Konitz, and Bill Russo. He made his first solo and trio recordings during this period. He moved to New York, performed with Charlie Parker and Dizzy Gillespie in concerts and on broadcasts, and did arrangements for the Metronome All Stars. He was *Metronome*'s Musician of the Year in 1947 and occasionally wrote for the magazine. Warne Marsh became his pupil in 1948, then Konitz and Bauer returned and helped to form a sextet. This group recorded in 1949. Tristano founded a school in 1951, and hired his pupils, such as Konitz, Marsh, and Sal Mosca, as teachers. He steadily withdrew from public view, sporadically issuing some recordings. Various pupils and teachers left the fold. Tristano closed the school in 1956, and became a private teacher on Long Island. He made periodic appearances at the Half Note between 1958 and 1965, had a European tour in 1965, then made his last American public appearance in 1968. There was a French documentary interview about his life, times, and work in 1973. After his death in 1978, there was a deluge of reissued and newly released Tristano recordings. There are a few Tristano sessions from the '40s and '50s available on CD. —*Ron Wynn and Dan Morgenstern*

○ **Continuity** / i. 1952 / PolyGram 830921
This album consists of two live sessions recorded six years apart at the Half Note in New York, featuring the pianist with his two best known disciples, alto saxophonist Lee Konitz and tenor saxophonist Warne Marsh. The first rhythm section here (Henry Grimes, bass, and Paul Motian, drums) is one of Tristano's better ones. Motian keeps good time and accents fairly freely within the limitations, and Grimes—one of the better bassists of the late '50s and early '60s—has a good, strong sound and sequences notes beautifully within the walking line. Marsh, who grew into one of the great improvisers, had not at this time developed the fuller tone that he later obtained, but his work is always interesting rhythmically and harmonically. Tristano's best outing here is the ballad "She's Funny That Way." At faster tempos, the pianist's concept of the eighth-note line has often seemed to me to be strangely out of sync within the rhythm section. By the way, on Marsh's tune, "Background Music," Tristano plays a descending cycle of fifths figure several times that comes directly from Thelonious Monk. The second group features, in addition to Marsh, Lee Konitz and a more typical Tristano rhythm section (Sonny Dallas, bass, and Nick Stabulus, drums). Konitz, too, has developed his

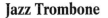

Jazz Trombone

Parade Bands–c. 1900

1920s
Increase of Trombones in Large Bands
Fletcher Henderson & Duke Ellington

Early Trombonists
Ike Rodgers (Rec. 1929-1934)
Jim Robinson (1892-1976) w/Sam Morgan 1927
George Lewis (1900-1968)
Charles Irvis (1899-1939)
Charlie Green (1900-1936)

Major Early Players
George Brunies (1902-1974)
Kid Ory (1890-1973)

Miff Mole (1898-1961)
Influence on trombonists, bandleaders:
Glenn Miller (1904-1944)
Jack Teagarden (1905-1964)
Tommy Dorsey (1905-1956)

Trummy Young (1912-1984)
Jimmy Harrison (1900-1931)

Duke Ellington's Trombonists:
Juan Tizol (1900-1984)
Tricky Sam Nanton (1904-1946) (w/Ellington from 1926)
Lawrence Brown (1907)
Quentin Jackson (1909-1976)
Britt Woodman (1920)
Buster Cooper (1929)

Swing-Era Trombonists
Tommy Dorsey (1905-1956)
Jack Teagarden (1905-1964)
Vic Dickenson (1906-1984)
J.C. Higginbotham (1906-1973)
Benny Morton (1907-1985)
Al Grey (1925)
Fred Beckett (1917-1946)

Humor associated with
Dicky Wells (1907-1985)
Trummy Young (1912-1984)

Traditional Jazz Revival in late 1930s

Bop Trombonists
Bill Harris (1916-1973)
Lou McGarity (1917-1971)
Kai Winding (1922-1983)
Bennie Green (1923-1977)
J.J. Johnson (1924)
Frank Rosolino (1926-1978)
Carl Fontana (1928)
Bill Watrous (1939)
Curtis Fuller (1934)

Bob Brookmeyer (1929) (valve trombone)
George Roberts (bass)

Slide Hampton (1932)–circular breathing
Jimmy Knepper (1927)–w/Charles Mingus

Multiphonics
Dick Griffin
Ray Anderson (1952)
Phil Wilson (1937)
George Lewis (1952)
Albert Mangelsdorff (1928)

European Free Jazz
Eje Thelin (1938)
Paul Rutherford (1940)
Albert Mangelsdorff (1928)

American Free Jazz
Roswell Rudd (1935)
Ray Anderson (1952)
George Lewis (1952)
Craig Harris (1954)
Grachan Moncur III (1937)
Julian Priester (1935)
Steve Turre (1948)

Trombone in Jazz-Rock
Chicago – Tower of Power – Blood, Sweat and Tears

Modern Big-Band Use
Gil Evans (1912-1988)
Thad Jones (1923-1986)
Maynard Ferguson (1928)
Mel Lewis (1929)
Toshiko Akiyoshi (1929)
Lew Tabackin (1940)

R&B Influence
Fred Wesley

Fusion
Wayne Henderson (1939) (Crusaders) – Bill Watrous (1939)

---

tone and broadened his concepts since this recording. Here he (and Marsh as well) repeat often several Tristanoite rhythmic melodic clichés, which I have always found annoying. The material consists of disguised standards— "Continuity" was "I'll Remember April," "My Baby" was "Melancholy Baby," "Subconscious-Lee" was "What Is This Thing Called Love," "East 32nd Street" was "Out of Nowhere," and "Background Music" was "All of Me." The recorded sound is not state of the art, the bass is indistinct at times, and recording levels change during the course of several pieces. —*Peter Leitch*, Cadence

★ **Descent into the Maelstrom** / 1952-1966 / Inner City 6002

Scarcity alone makes *Descent into the Maelstrom* valuable, but it is also a magnificent potpourri of bits and pieces recorded from 1952 through 1966. Side one is solo Tristano. The title cut, inspired by Edgar Allan Poe's short story of a mariner being driven by a hurricane into an obliterating whirlpool, is simply one of the most amazing bits of program music ever recorded. Furiously double, perhaps triple tracked, it is a relentlessly atonal crosscurrent of sound waves. Done in 1953, long before the popularization of synthesizers and sequencers or, for that matter, the legitimization of tape manipulation, it is a reminder not only of Tristano's liberating penchant for unorthodox experimentation but also of his rubric that music should "flow from the id." Side two finds Tristano in the company of two pairings of drummers and bassists, not surprisingly a generally unhappy marriage in light of Tristano's avowed disdain for the way these instruments are played. Further, the miking and mixing are bad, particularly on Nick Stabulas's drum kit. The result: boomy, clattery, bebop drumming, an unfitting counterpoint to Tristano's intricate piano inventions. And yet, with the subtle accompaniment of Roy Haynes's brushes, a track like the allegedly overdubbed "Pastime" shimmers with layer upon layer of dense, successful, multiline improvisations. —*Jon Balleras*, Down Beat

○ **Lennie Tristano Quartet** / Jun. 11, 1955 / Atlantic 1224
These are previously unreleased performances from the Sing Song Room date. Several things struck me about this really delightful two-record set. Perhaps first is a feeling of gratefulness that Atlantic was there originally with interest to record the date. Second, that the tapes survived and, finally, that Atlantic issued them. Here pianist Tristano presents his music in more refined terms with alto saxophonist Lee Konitz's interplay both in the Tristano tradition and on his own personal terms. This is a set of excellent vintage that remains remarkably stimulating.   —*Bob Rusch*, Cadence

○ **Requiem** / Jul. 1955-Aug. 1962 / Atlantic 7003
This two-record set represents pianist and composer Lennie Tristano's last outings for Atlantic, two sessions spanning 1955 to 1962. They came out at a time when his reputation was at its highest in decades. Were it rereleased while he was alive, it might have precipitated a return to public activity. Tristano was a bit of a visionary and as such he seemed to accept ultimate posthumous acceptance. The first four pieces, from the summer of 1955, are all examples of multitracking, for which Tristano drew heavy criticism. The important point is that he did it not to disguise a technical deficiency, but to extend the rhythmic and linear boundaries of the music. The remaining five tracks come from a live date featuring alto saxophonist Lee Konitz and a couple of unlikely Tristanoites: bassist Gene Ramey and drummer Art Taylor. Standard tunes were always fodder for Tristano's recompositional efforts, and the reharmonizations in this case are very impressionistic. Konitz is in fine form, and his lines on "These Foolish Things" and "All the Things You Are" are both lovely and vital. The second LP has solo Tristano with no overdubbing. Although most the titles are attributed to Tristano, five of the pieces are thoroughly reworked standards. The three miniatures in "Scene and Variation" are portraits of Tristano's children and all based on "Melancholy Baby." "G Minor Complex" is a stripped-down and rebuilt "You'd Be So Nice to Come Home To." Like all the other solo pieces, it gives a clear, unadorned look at Tristano's conception of structural modification and variation. The bass is steady and functional, walking through and around the changes at the same time, while the right hand is free to embroider single-note and chordal baroqueisms. —*Kirk Silsbee*, Down Beat

★ **Complete Lennie Tristano on Keynote** / Mercury 830921

BIG JOE TURNER (Joseph Vernon Turner)

b. May 18, 1911, Kansas City, MO, **d.** Nov. 24, 1985, Inglewood, CA
Vocals / Swing, blues & jazz

Big Joe Turner enjoyed stardom in two related, but quite different, eras. The Big Chill generation appreciates Turner for his contribution to rock and roll; those who know prerock history cherish his vocal contributions to the boogie-woogie and Kansas City jazz eras. He was one of the greatest, most vociferous shouters ever, and was able to holler and roar above a striding big band, yet also fit his huge sound into situations with boogie-woogie players who relied on timing and pace. Turner was tending bar and singing in Kansas City at age 14. Known as the "singing bandleader," the youth attracted the attention of bandleaders such as Bennie Moten, Andy Kirk, and Count Basie. He and pianist Pete Johnson became great friends and a popular touring act in the late '30s and the '40s. After his appearance with Johnson at the Spirituals to Swing Carnegie Hall concert in 1938, Turner made his first recordings, notably the spectacular "Roll 'Em Pete." Turner's huge voice half shouted and half sang; he built the piece's tension superbly using repeated phrases and Johnson's rumbling, churning riffs and accompaniment. Turner was an equally gifted slow blues and ballad stylist, and his work with pianists and bands reflected his fluidity, knowledge of inflections, and ability to develop themes and embellish lyrics. He recorded with Joe Sullivan, Benny Carter, and Art Tatum, among others. But his early '50s R&B hits "Still in the Dark," "Chains of Love," and "Sweet Sixteen" were forerunners of a new era. "Honey Hush" and "Shake, Rattle and Roll" marked Joe Turner's move to the pop arena, even though cover versions of both songs had better sales than his originals. After his rock success ebbed, Turner returned to the jazzy blues he'd always done. He made fine dates in the '70s with Count Basie, the Trumpet Kings, Eddie "Cleanhead" Vinson, and Jimmy Witherspoon. In 1983, two years before his death, Turner recorded with Roomful of Blues. —*Ron Wynn and John Floyd*

○ **Joe Turner Sings Kansas City Jazz** / i. 1953 / Decca 8044

★ **Boss of the Blues** / i. Sep. 19, 1956 / Atlantic 8812
This Big Joe Turner set is a good one, particularly since, at the time, Turner was being successfully packaged and pushed into an R&B cum rock & roll *sensation*. Here he is backed by a compatible and sympathetic group. Turner is in good voice and there's the added plus of Pete Johnson on piano, a legendary Kansas City artist in his own right, and other capable soloists—particularly tenor saxophonist Frank Wess and alto saxophonist Ray Brown. Ernie Wilkins's arrangements are a perfect match for the music and open, rolling shouts of Turner. —*Bob Rusch*, Cadence

○ **Jumpin' the Blues** / i. Oct. 1962 / Arhoolie 2004

○ **Best of Joe Turner, The** / i. 1982 / Atlantic 8081

○ **Have No Fear, Big Joe Turner Is Here** / i. 1982 / Savoy 2223

☆ **Greatest Hits** / i. 1987 / Atlantic 81752
These are Turner's finest early-rock-era recordings, including his best (and best-known) hits and some tasty obscurities. A must-have. —*John Floyd*

★ **Complete 1940-1944** / i. 1990 / Official 80001
Between 1940 and 1944, Turner recorded 25 songs for Decca. His Decca sides are jazz of a blue shade, moody and expansive, street poetry framed by expressive pianists (Pete Johnson, Willie "The Lion" Smith, Sam Price, Freddie Slack, and Art Tatum) and small combos. This music charts an important chapter in the saga of a stentorian voice that thundered across five decades and nearly as many phases of American popular music. —*Mark A. Humphrey*, Rock & Roll Disc

○ **Rhythm & Blues Years** / Atlantic 81663
Big Joe Turner, who started out as a singing bartender in 1930s Kansas City, is best known to jazz listeners for his early dates with the Boogie Woogie trio, his collaborations with Pete Johnson ("Roll 'Em Pete") and his much later albums for Pablo in the '70s. But the general public best remembers the shouting blues singer for his string of Atlantic

Music Map

Jazz Trumpet

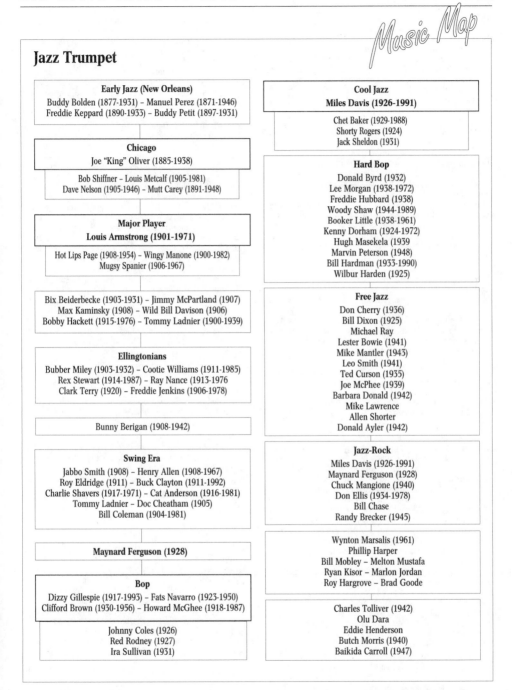

Early Jazz (New Orleans)
Buddy Bolden (1877-1931) – Manuel Perez (1871-1946)
Freddie Keppard (1890-1933) – Buddy Petit (1897-1931)

Chicago
Joe "King" Oliver (1885-1938)

Bob Shiffner – Louis Metcalf (1905-1981)
Dave Nelson (1905-1946) – Mutt Carey (1891-1948)

Major Player
Louis Armstrong (1901-1971)

Hot Lips Page (1908-1954) – Wingy Manone (1900-1982)
Mugsy Spanier (1906-1967)

Bix Beiderbecke (1903-1931) – Jimmy McPartland (1907)
Max Kaminsky (1908) – Wild Bill Davison (1906)
Bobby Hackett (1915-1976) – Tommy Ladnier (1900-1939)

Ellingtonians
Bubber Miley (1903-1932) – Cootie Williams (1911-1985)
Rex Stewart (1914-1987) – Ray Nance (1913-1976)
Clark Terry (1920) – Freddie Jenkins (1906-1978)

Bunny Berigan (1908-1942)

Swing Era
Jabbo Smith (1908) – Henry Allen (1908-1967)
Roy Eldridge (1911) – Buck Clayton (1911-1992)
Charlie Shavers (1917-1971) – Cat Anderson (1916-1981)
Tommy Ladnier – Doc Cheatham (1905)
Bill Coleman (1904-1981)

Maynard Ferguson (1928)

Bop
Dizzy Gillespie (1917-1993) – Fats Navarro (1923-1950)
Clifford Brown (1930-1956) – Howard McGhee (1918-1987)

Johnny Coles (1926)
Red Rodney (1927)
Ira Sullivan (1931)

Cool Jazz
Miles Davis (1926-1991)

Chet Baker (1929-1988)
Shorty Rogers (1924)
Jack Sheldon (1931)

Hard Bop
Donald Byrd (1932)
Lee Morgan (1938-1972)
Freddie Hubbard (1938)
Woody Shaw (1944-1989)
Booker Little (1938-1961)
Kenny Dorham (1924-1972)
Hugh Masekela (1939)
Marvin Peterson (1948)
Bill Hardman (1933-1990)
Wilbur Harden (1925)

Free Jazz
Don Cherry (1936)
Bill Dixon (1925)
Michael Ray
Lester Bowie (1941)
Mike Mantler (1943)
Leo Smith (1941)
Ted Curson (1935)
Joe McPhee (1939)
Barbara Donald (1942)
Mike Lawrence
Allen Shorter
Donald Ayler (1942)

Jazz-Rock
Miles Davis (1926-1991)
Maynard Ferguson (1928)
Chuck Mangione (1940)
Don Ellis (1934-1978)
Bill Chase
Randy Brecker (1945)

Wynton Marsalis (1961)
Phillip Harper
Bill Mobley – Melton Mustafa
Ryan Kisor – Marlon Jordan
Roy Hargrove – Brad Goode

Charles Tolliver (1942)
Olu Dara
Eddie Henderson
Butch Morris (1940)
Baikida Carroll (1947)

hits ("Shake, Rattle and Roll," "Corrine Corrina" and others) in the 1950s. The twofer *Rhythm & Blues Years* does not include the biggest sellers, but features selections from some of the same sessions, 32 cuts in all. Turner sings in a timeless blues style that dominates these performances and easily communicates to a large audience during this period. The backup is generally pretty anonymous with the brief tenor solos all sounding a bit like Gene Ammons and the accompanying pianists emphasizing triplets. There are some familiar names in the groups (including Budd Johnson, Taft Jordan, Al Sears, Red Tyler, Sam The Man Taylor, Earle Warren, Jerome Richardson, Hilton Jefferson, King Curtis, Jesse Stone, George Barnes, Panama Francis, and even Connie Kay) but they are virtually unrecognizable in this setting. Ray Charles sits in on piano for "Wee Baby Blues." — *Scott Yanow*, Cadence

NORRIS TURNEY

b. 1921
Alto saxophone / Swing, big band
One of Ellington's most lyrical soloists, Norris Turney has a fine sound and style on alto sax, flute, and clarinet. His alto combines swing era urgency and fluidity with bebop era exactness and technical expertise. Turnery played with A.B. Townsend in Ohio before working with the Jeter-Pillars orchestra in the '40s. He later played with Tiny Bradshaw. Turney was in Billy Eckstine's orchestra in 1945 and 1946, then returned to Ohio. He moved to Philadelphia and played with Elmer Snowden in 1951, and toured Australia with the Ray Charles orchestra in the late '60s. Turney joined Ellington as a substitute for Johnny Hodges in 1969, then became a full-time member of the group the next year. He remained until 1973, then worked in pit orchestras in New York for the remainder of the decade. Turney joined Panama Francis's Savoy Sultans in 1980, and also toured and recorded with George Wein's Newport All Stars in the '80s and '90s. Turney can be heard on several '70s Ellington reissued CDs, and on '80s and '90s discs by the Savoy Sultans and the Newport All Stars. —*Ron Wynn*

STEVE TURRE

b. Sep. 12, 1948, Omaha, NB
Trombone / Neo-bop, modern creative
Steve Turre is a dynamic trombonist who is equally versed in hard bop, mainstream, and Latin-jazz. He is currently a member of the "Saturday Night Live" pit band. Turre got his start playing with Woody Shaw. In recent years, has been an active bandleader and one of the premier trombone soloists among the contemporary generation. He's gaining recognition as a composer as well. He can play brisk uptempo pieces, slow ballads, or funk and R&B-flavored tunes. His latest release includes a song where he displays a facility with mutes and a knowledge of plunger and wah-wah techniques that are reminiscent of jazz greats like Tricky Sam Nanton and Al Grey. —*Ron Wynn*

○ **Viewpoint** / Feb. 7-8, 1987 / Stash 270
Viewpoint affords trombonist Steve Turre and his guest sidemen a chance to bring great texture to the jazz tradition and the many swinging styles he has played, from hard swing to bebop, from New Orleans to the avant-garde, from the blues to salsa. One of the most imaginative offerings is his version of the Miles Davis classic "All Blues (Flamenco Sketches)." Turre lays aside his trombone and plays a series of ethereal-sounding conch shells. Another to savor is his plunger mute version of the Duke Ellington standard "In a Sentimental Mood," which Turre calls a tribute to the 'bone players of the Ellington generation: Lawrence Brown, Dickie Wells, Tricky Sam Nanton, Vic Dickenson, Trummy Young, and Quentin Jackson. The title track, "Viewpoint," is an A-flat blues Turre wrote to a scale provided by Dizzy Gillespie. The result is a rollicking tribute to the bop tradition. The most spirited performances come on "Midnight Montuno," a Latin tune on which Turre plays both trombone and his shell collection. It's a toe-tapper on which the ensemble playing is tight and whimsical (note Jon Faddis's "Mona Lisa" quote). *Viewpoint* is a dandy debut and one long overdue. —*Ken Franckling*, Jazz Times

★ **Fire and Ice** / **i.** Feb. 5-6, 1988 / Stash 7
Steve Turre has been steadily gathering together all the major strands of the jazz trombone tradition, weaving in the process a musical fabric that bears his imprint. On *Fire and Ice* Turre is in the cooking company of pianist Cedar Walton, bassist Buster Williams, and drummer Billy Higgins and, on half of the selections, the string quartet Indigo, with John Blake and Gayle Dixon on violins. —*W. Royal Stokes*, Jazz Times

☆ **Right There** / Mar. 1991 / Antilles 510040

STANLEY TURRENTINE (Stanley William Turrentine)

b. Apr. 5, 1934, Pittsburgh, PA
Tenor saxophone / Blues & jazz, soul-jazz

While highly regarded in soul-jazz circles, Stanley Turrentine is one of the finest tenor saxophonists in any style in modern times. He excels at uptempo compositions, in jam sessions, at interpreting standards, at playing the blues, or on ballads. His rich, booming, and huge tone, with its strong swing influence, is one of the most striking of any tenor stylist, and, during the '70s and '80s, made otherwise horrendous mood music worth enduring. Turrentine toured with R&B and blues bands led by Ray Charles, Lowell Fulson, and Earl Bostic in the early '50s; he replaced John Coltrane in Bostic's band. He later played with Max Roach in 1959 and 1960, and cut his first recordings with him. Turrentine started recording as a leader on Blue Note in 1959 and 1960, while he also participated in some landmark Jimmy Smith sessions such as *Midnight Special, Back at the Chicken Shack*, and *Prayer Meeting*. His decade-plus association with Shirley Scott was both professional and personal; they were married for most of the time that they played together. They frequently recorded together, and the featured leader's name often depended on the session's label affiliation. When they divorced and split musically in the early '70s, Turrentine became a crossover star on CTI. Several of his CTI, Fantasy, Elektra, and Blue Note albums in the '70s and '80s made the charts. Though the jazz content of his music became proportionally lower, Turrentine's playing remained consistently superb. He returned to straightahead and soul-jazz in the '80s, cut more albums for Fantasy and Elektra, then returned to Blue Note. He's currently on the Musicmasters label. Almost anything Turrentine's recorded, even albums with Stevie Wonder cover songs, are worth hearing for his solos. Many of his classic dates and his recent material are available on CD. —*Ron Wynn and Bob Porter*

Look Out / Jun. 18, 1960 / Blue Note 46543
Small group recorded at Englewood Cliffs, New Jersey. 1987 reissue of excellent soul-jazz. —*Ron Wynn*

○ **Blue Hour** / Dec. 16, 1960 / Blue Note 84057
Recorded at Englewood Cliffs, New Jersey, with the Three Sounds. Small group. A beautiful album of relaxed, bluesy sound. —*Michael Erlewine*

★ **Comin' Your Way** / Jan. 20, 1961 / Blue Note 84065
Small group recorded at Englewood Cliffs, New Jersey. 1988 reissue of sumptuous '60s soul-jazz date. Horace Parlan (p) at his bluesy best. —*Ron Wynn*

○ **Up at Minton's—Vol. 1** / Feb. 23, 1961 / Blue Note 4069

○ **Up at Minton's—Vol. 2** / Feb. 23, 1961 / Blue Note 84070

Z.T.'s Blues / Sep. 13, 1961 / Blue Note 84424
Recorded at Englewood Cliffs, New Jersey. Small group. 1985 reissue of good, steady material. —*Ron Wynn*

That's Where It's At / Jan. 2, 1962 / Blue Note 84096

○ **Jubilee Shout** / Oct. 18, 1962 / Blue Note 84122
This long-awaited (1979) twofer is as much brother Tommy Turrentine's as it is its leader's, raising the question of why he never made it big like Donald Byrd or Freddie Hubbard, who were hardly fit to even mooch Tommy Turrentine's valve oil. A dramatic style and ever-dependable sense of melody instead of vacuous technical displays characterize Turrentine's art: a simplification of Clifford Brown, incapable of any falsehood; generally light-hearted but with never a frivolous moment. On song after song, on 9 of these 11 tracks, Tommy Turrentine's long, singing tones add grace and creativity in a rewarding way. The '61 date is one of the very finest of Stanley Turrentine's career, and pianist Horace Parlan excellently captures and returns the brothers' mood. Sonny Clark in the next year's sextet is even better, an unfailingly supportive and imaginative accompanist, flowing in solo. Also in the sextet, the self-effacing guitarist Kenny Burrell is at his melodically most rewarding; to select one of six fine solos, he is the centerpiece of "Cotton Walk," a perfectly typical Burrell blues—but with just that touch of inspiration that places it above the others. Stanley Turrentine plays outstanding tenor sax with the quintet, and almost as well with the sextet. His big sound booms the accented notes of his heavily inflected lines; because his

style is less concentrated in effect and a bit older in inspiration than Gene Ammons's, he achieves a warmth even Ammons's best lacks. The lack of artifice in these bands' music distinguishes the overtly soulful material of the sextet, of which only "My Ship" is unsatisfying. —*John Litweiler,* Down Beat

Joyride / Apr. 14, 1965 / Blue Note 46100
Recorded at Englewood Cliffs, New Jersey. Large group. Throbbing tenor solos, big-band backing. —*Ron Wynn*

○ **Let It Go** / Apr. 15, 1966 / GRP 104
Recorded at Englewood Cliffs, New Jersey. Small group. Some recorded on September 21, 1964. Husband and wife team Turrentine and Shirley Scott (organ) produce one lovely album—blues/jazz, funky. —*Michael Erlewine*

Rough 'n Tumble / Jul. 1, 1966 / Blue Note 84240
Recorded at New York City. One of his most popular, tightest soul-jazz releases. —*Ron Wynn*

Look of Love / Sep. 29-Oct. 6, 1968 / Blue Note 84286
Recorded at Englewood Cliffs, New Jersey. Both romantic and lusty, nice sessions. —*Ron Wynn*

★ **Sugar** / Nov. 1970 / Columbia 40811
Recorded at Englewood Cliffs, New Jersey. Larger group. By far the best thing he ever made on CTI. Among the handful of genuine jazz albums that were cut on that label. —*Ron Wynn*

Sugar Man, The / Feb.-Mar. 1971 / CTI 6052

○ **Cherry** / May 17, 1972 / Columbia 40936
Recorded at Englewood Cliffs, New Jersey. Small group. Lush, wonderful playing by Turrentine, Jackson, despite very uneven material. —*Ron Wynn*

○ **Don't Mess with Mister T.** / Jun. 7, 1973 / Columbia 44173

○ **Wonderland** / 1987 / Blue Note 46762
The music of Stevie Wonder. Recorded at Yamaha Studios, Glendale, California. —AMG

○ **La Place** / 1989 / Blue Note 90261

○ **More Than a Mood** / i. 1992 / Music Masters 65079
More Than a Mood has the effect of a big, cheerful pinch, delivered just in time to wake up those who were dozing off from all the copycat jazz that's around these days. These guys don't need to borrow nostalgia; they know whereof they play. After a three-year gap in recording, tenor saxophonist Stanley Turrentine has come back with a winner. His playing on *More Than a Mood* swings with the kind of sophistication it takes years to develop and with none of the mannerisms that sometimes cавор along the way. Turrentine gets an unusually sweet, honed sound for a tenor player. The crisp, economical pianism of Cedar Walton, the discreet but always firmly guiding bass of Ron Carter, and the time press rolls and delicate brushwork of Billy Higgins highlight Turrentine's considerable talents. Trumpeter Freddie Hubbard's presence is limited to two cuts, but his flugelhorn makes "Spirits Up Above" soar. —*Elaine Guregian,* Down Beat

TOMMY TURRENTINE (Thomas Walter (Jr) Turrentine)

b. 1928
Trumpet / Bop
Despite his crisp, crackling style and his fine lyrical playing, trumpeter Tommy Turrentine never got his career in gear like Stanley, his famous brother, did. Tommy's been in virtual retirement since the early '70s. He made only one album as a leader; it was briefly reissued, but isn't on CD. Turrentine's father played tenor sax with Al Cooper's Savoy Sultans, and he started on trumpet as a teen. He worked with Benny Carter in the '40s, and with Earl Bostic, Charles Mingus, and Max Roach in the '50s and early '60s. Turrentine also performed in big bands led by Billy Eckstine, Dizzy Gillespie, and Count Basie. He did several sessions in New York during the early '60s, playing with Horace Parlan, Jackie McLean, Sonny Clark, Lou Donaldson, and his brother. But then he seems to have disappeared from the jazz performing and recording scene. He can be heard on reissues such as McLean's *A Fickle Sonance* and Clark's *Leapin' and Lopin'.* —*Ron Wynn*

★ **Tommy Turrentine** / i. Jun. 1960 / Bainbridge 1047
A good bop date led by trumpeter Turrentine joined by brother Stanley on tenor, trombonist Julian Priester, pianist Horace Parlan, bassist Bob Boswell, and drummer Max Roach. —*Carl Brauer,* Cadence

CHARLES TYLER (Charles Lacy Tyler)

b. Jul. 20, 1941, Cadiz, KY, **d.** Jun. 27, 1992
Baritone and alto saxophone, teacher / Early free, progressive big band, modern creative
One of the freer, more flamboyant baritone saxophonists, as well as a capable alto stylist, Charles Tyler unfortunately never attained widespread recognition. He had complete command of the baritone, was expressive in every register, and played with speed, lyricism, or energy. Tyler studied clarinet and alto sax as a child before playing baritone in an army band. He moved to Cleveland in 1960, where he played with Albert Ayler. Tyler later moved to New York, where he became involved in the city's free jazz scene, recording and working extensively with Ayler. He was featured on the albums *Bells* and *Spirits Rejoice*, and also played C-melody sax on a bootleg album with Ayler and Ornette Coleman on trumpet. He made his recording debut as a leader on ESP in the late '60s. Tyler also played with Sunny Murray and others. He moved to California, taught music for four years at Merritt College, and worked with Arthur Blythe, David Murray, and Bobby Bradford. Tyler was featured on a Stanley Crouch album in 1973. When he returned to New York in 1976, Tyler began leading his own groups. He recorded for Ak-Ba, Nessa, and Adelphi in the '70s, and for Sonet, Storyville, Silkheart, Mustevic, and Nessa in the '80s. He worked with Dave Baker, Dewey Redman, Frank Lowe, Steve Reid, and Cecil Taylor, and recorded and played with the Billy Bang Ensemble in 1981 and 1982. Only a couple of Tyler's sessions are available on CD. —*Ron Wynn*

★ **Definite** / i. Oct. 1981 / Storyville 4099
This session takes the sax into the Ornette Coleman and post-Coleman era with Charles Tyler's alto and baritone joined by trumpeter Earl Cross, bassist Kevin Ross, and drummer Steve Reid. Side one features Tyler's alto sax, which combined with Cross's Don Cherry-like bit and the floating rhythm of Ross and Reid gives the music a strong Coleman sense. "Cadiz," the longest track (13:55) moves for most of its time until it breaks away for a bass solo and a certain pressurized spirit fails to maintain itself. A similiar break in atmosphere occurs also on "Just for Two." However, both pieces are very strong examples of fluent freebop. The passion and involvement continue on side two, though at a slower pace as here Tyler plays the baritone sax. With Ross bowing the bass and each member of the group working an area of free improvisation, the piece becomes impressionistic, and one can see the imagery of New York City's South Bronx by which it was inspired and to which it is dedicated. The final track builds off a line that sounds like "16 Tons." Its structure is quite simple, but the exploration doesn't really hold strong over its 10+ minutes, and only Cross manages to extend his improvisation beyond the limitations of the rhythm melody. Both sides (41:40) were recorded live at the Fasching Club and present the kind of visceral free jazz not so often heard anymore (1983)—it may not be perfect, but you know communication and expression are going on. —*Kevin Whitehead,* Cadence

○ **Autumn in Paris** / i. Jun. 1988 / Silkheart 118

MCCOY TYNER (Alfred McCoy [Saud, Sulaimon] Tyner)

b. Dec. 11, 1938, Philadelphia, PA
Piano / Postbop, neo-bop
Pianist McCoy Tyner's inventive, two-handed forays, extensive modal solos, dashing phrases, and dense, explosive right-hand chording were as vital an ingredient in the classic sound of the '60s John Coltrane quartet as the leader's roaring tenor and soprano sax. In both his solo playing and his accompaniment, Tyner is the creator of a striking, immediately recognizable style. He is a familiar, welcome pres-

ence on the improvisational scene, heading combos, doing big band and orchestral dates, playing solo sessions, or doing an occasional unusual collaboration with someone like Stephane Grappelli or with an unnamed rapper in a forthcoming planned date. He has also influenced vast numbers of pianists, including Chick Corea, Hal Galper, Hilton Ruiz, and Alice Coltrane, among others. Tyner began studying piano at age 13, and took theory lessons at the Granoff School of Music. His first major engagement came when he joined the Benny Golson-Art Farmer Jazztet at age 20 in 1959. A year later, he was in Coltrane's band, where he remained an integral member until 1965. As a leader for Impulse and Blue Note, Tyner also made his own striking albums. He led a trio in 1966, then led a quartet. Earlier in his career, Tyner did unlikely things such as work with the Ike and Tina Turner band, and with Jimmy Witherspoon. He continued recording excellent albums for Blue Note in the late '60s and early '70s, before joining Milestone in 1972. He remained on the label through much of the decade, made stunning albums such as *Sahara*, and did a variety of things from trios to solo and quartet dates. Tyner also did sessions for Columbia and Elektra. During the '80s, he recorded for Blackhawk, Palo Alto, Blue Note, Denon, and Milestone again. He's worked with musicians such as Azar Lawrence, John Blake, Ron Carter, Joe Henderson, Ron Carter, Cecil McBee, Pharoah Sanders, his Coltrane comrade Elvin Jones, Hubert Laws, and Billy Cobham. Tyner's remained active in the '90s, and recently recorded for Red Baron and Verve with both a big band and a combo that included David Murray and Arthur Blythe. A healthy amount of Tyner sessions are available on CD. —*Ron Wynn and Myles Boisen*

Inception / Jan. 10, 1962 / MCA 42233

★ Inception / Nights of Ballads and Blues / Jan. 10, 1962-Apr. 4, 1963 / MCA 42000

Nights of Ballads and Blues / Mar. 4, 1963 / Impulse 39

Today and Tomorrow / Jun. 4, 1963 / GRP 106
1991 release, reissue from limited Jazz Masters Series of '70s reissues. Superb music throughout. —*Ron Wynn*

○ McCoy Tyner Live at Newport / Jul. 5, 1963 / Impulse 48

Mccoy Tyner Plays Ellington / Oct. 1965 / MCA 33124

○ McCoy Tyner: The Early Trios—Vol. 6 / i. 1966-1968 / ABC/Impulse 9338
Adherents of McCoy Tyner's current emotive pedal style may be surprised at the dry sophistication he brought to his early '60s trio work with members of various Coltrane rhythm sections. Although the composer he favored most often was Duke Ellington, his pianistic inspiration clearly derived from Bud Powell, with the decorative proclivites of Art Tatum much in evidence. Breezing swiftly through thematic statements, Tyner jumps into complex streams of improvisation, investing the mostly rapid-tempo exercises with dramatic tension and subtle irony. Already his chordal voicings are distinctive and original, and with masterful technical command he refutes the contention of early critics that he was initially a mere cocktail pianist. The accompaniment, especially by drummer Elvin Jones and bassist Jimmy Garrison, throbs with controlled energy, and Jones's solo spots are marvels of compressed intensity. —*Larry Birnbaum*, Down Beat

★ Real McCoy, The / Apr. 21, 1967 / Blue Note 46512

○ Tender Moments / Dec. 1, 1967 / Blue Note 84275

Time for Tyner / May 17, 1968 / Blue Note 84307
1987 reissue of dense session. Tyner and Bobby Hutcherson (vib) have some sparkling exchanges and dialogs. —*Ron Wynn*

Expansions / Aug. 23, 1968 / Capitol 84338

○ Reflections: A Retrospective (1972-1975) / Jan. 1972-Apr. 9, 1975 / Milestone 47062
When pianist McCoy Tyner moved to CBS in the early '80s, Milestone released *Reflections*, a two-record retrospective of Tyner's recordings from 1972 to 1975. The selections were taken from the following albums: *Sahara, Song for My Lady,*

Echoes of a Friend, Song of the New World, Enlightenment, Sama Layuca, Atlantis, and *Trident,* and involved groupings from solo piano to large band. What they all have in common is an uncompromising commitment to good music. —*Bob Rusch*, Cadence

★ Sahara / Jan. 1972 / Milestone 311

★ Echoes of a Friend / Nov. 11, 1972 / Milestone 650

Song for My Lady / Nov. 27, 1972 / Milestone 313

○ Song of the New World / Apr. 6-9, 1973 / Milestone 618
Pianist McCoy Tyner takes a number of his most attractive themes, as well as Mongo Santamaria's "Afro Blue," and provides them large orchestral settings using two groups, one a bank of strings and woodwinds, the other brass and reeds. His ensemble writing is rich and assured, not particularly adventurous but quite attractive and effective. Certainly it leads to no lessening of the power of Tyner's music or of his playing (which is vigorous and imaginative on most of the cuts), and in fact the added instrumentation lends a real dimension of excitement as well as a broadening of the music's colors and textures. —*Pete Welding*, Down Beat

○ Enlightenment / Jul. 7, 1973 / Milestone 55001
This is, above all, a *piano* album. McCoy Tyner's work adds support to the idea that, since the death of Coltrane, it's been the pianists who've been on the cutting edge of the music's development and who will be remembered as the seminal artists of the '70s. Unlike most of his fellow keyboard trendsetters, however, Tyner eschews the electric instruments and devotes himself to an exploration of the frontiers of acoustic piano sound. *Enlightenment* testifies to the brilliant sound of his endeavors. Tyner's *inside* the instrument, as Coltrane was with the sax, drawing from it colors, textures, and intensities unprecedented in jazz. No wonder the sidemen tend to get lost in the shuffle a bit. Tenor saxophonist Azar Lawrence in particular sometimes seems overwhelmed by the energy emanating from the keyboard; but on the whole he acquits himself well in a role in which it was understandably difficult to retain a distinctive voice. Drummer Al Mouzon deserves special note; his crisp drumming is a good foil for Tyner's shattering polyphony. *Enlightenment* is a celebration of the epoch of the pianists and also of a musician who has never ceased to grow. —*Steve Metaliz*, Down Beat

○ Sama Layuca / Mar. 26-28, 1974 / Milestone 9056
Sama Layuca has much of the feeling and direction of *Song of the New World*, recorded with a large orchestra. The album also represents the sum total of where McCoy Tyner's musical mind was heading at that point—his blending of instruments and his concept of rhythm and melody. The group assembled for *Layuca* was Tyner's then-current band (soprano and tenor saxophonist Azar Lawrence, bassist Buster Williams, drummer Billy Hart, percussionist Guillermi Franco) augmented by John Stubblefield on oboe and flute, Mtume on percussion and congas, alto saxophonist Gary Bartz, and Bobby Hutcherson on vibes and marimba. The addition of vibes and flute, which Tyner lets dominate the group sound, gives the music a melodic quality that balances Lawrence's strong, John Coltrane-ish tenor and, naturally, Tyner's thundering power with its tendency to overshadow everything. "Desert Cry," for example, is a mood piece. With Stubblefield's oboe setting a North African tone, and the percussive imagination of Franco and Mtume adding texture, the piece teases the brain with images of Alexandria or an isolated desert caravan. "Above the Rainbow," performed simply by Tyner and Hutcherson, has the same quality. Both "La Cubana" and "Sama Layuca" are based on simple rhythmic melodies and are typically Tyner. On "Cubana" Bartz comes up with an exceptionally strong solo and Hutcherson plays marimba with a speed that parallels Tyner's right hand. Both Williams and Hart work beautifully with Tyner. In many ways, Hart is a more suited drummer for Tyner, his playing broader and more flexible than was former drummer Alphonze Mouzon's in the same context. —*Herb Nolan*, Down Beat

○ Asante / i. Jun. 1974 / Blue Note 223

Recorded in 1970, pianist McCoy Tyner's music here, as we've come to expect, is vibrant and cohesive, the kind of music that resists conventional terminology and categories. This is almost entirely an excursion in group improvisation. Tyner himself stays mostly in the background, emerging to solo only occasionally. When he does, it's usually in an up-tempo section. And as we would expect, his playing is marked by long, deft lines, rhythmic excitement, and harmonic density. Its roots are in both the old and new worlds. And like the joyous face of the African dancer who graces the album's cover, it too is confidently exuberant. *—Jon Balleras*, Down Beat

Atlantis / Aug. 31+Sep. 1, 1974 / Milestone 55002

☆ **Trident** / Feb. 18-19, 1975 / Original Jazz Classics 720
McCoy Tyner's rolls of exploratory thunder, always virtuosic but occasionally overgymnastic, are controlled here through the presence of some sobering influences. Yet these elements do not restrain creativity. As all constructive input should and does, they enhance, they broaden, and they perfect. The choices and departures, taken at Tyner's volition, impose a kind of savage grace that is the persona of *Trident*. Ron Carter, of course, is as precise as an alarm clock on bass. Carter's fascination with Latin and Brazilian rhythms is well known, leading to the supposition that Antonio Carlos Jobim's "Once I Loved" was included at his suggestion. Even Elvin Jones has the perfect beat on "Once I Loved." Yet more welcome is the fact he actually solos on "Land of the Lonely." With all these elements combined, *Trident* is a true connubial synthesis. *—Arnold Shaw*, Down Beat

○ **Fly with the Wind** / Jan. 19-21, 1976 / Milestone 699

○ **Supertrios** / Apr. 9-10, 1977 / Milestone 55003
In formulating *Supertrios*, producer Orrin Keepnews decided to pair McCoy Tyner with two diverse and potentially heady rhythm sections, the teams of bassist Ron Carter/drummer Tony Williams and bassist Eddie Gomez/drummer Jack DeJohnette. In particular, the Tyner-Williams-Carter sessions are effusively expressive without being thoughtfully reactive. Tyner is typically romantic and dramatic, his percussive left-hand ostinatos melding effectively with his lucid right-hand exercises, an always interesting blend of bluster and blues. Still, tracks like "Waves" and "The Greeting" are undeniably visceral, fully realized fusions of muscular passion with form, which was probably the worthy intent behind this session all along. By comparison, the sides with Gomez and DeJohnette are more resilient and pensive. DeJohnette makes the notable difference, opting to play in a tight spectrum, as concisely as possible, only occasionally reaching for flourishes of color and depth. We hear a gentler style of tension at work here, evident in Tyner's mutable temperament and deft chord transpositions. Gomez favors high staccato streams, just a shade more aggressive than his work with the Bill Evans trio of recent years. *—Mikal Gilmore*, Down Beat

Inner Voices / Sep. 1-8, 1977 / Milestone 9079

Passion Dance / Jul. 28, 1978 / Milestone 9091

★ **4 X 4** / Mar. 3-May 29, 1980 / Milestone 550072
4 X 4 may not have appeased all of McCoy Tyner's recent critics. It certainly doesn't open any untamed territory for this seminal pianist. But it does offer some of the variety everyone had been screaming for at that time, and is yet another solid addition to Tyner's impressively consistent discography. At first glance, Tyner's collaborations with guitarist John Abercrombie and alto saxophonist Arthur Blythe seem to hold the brightest prospects for brave new music. But of the two, only Blythe proves capable of substantially matching Tyner's energy. The young turks aside, Tyner's master contemporaries, trumpeter Freddie Hubbard and vibist Bobby Hutcherson, get yet another chance with the pianist. Hubbard is somewhat disappointing. Of course he is technically masterful as always, but he seems to struggle to come up with novel ideas on the uptempo numbers, "Inner Glimpse" and "Paradox," relying instead on his all-too-familiar stock licks for the majority of his solos. Hutcherson's side

is another story altogether. Tyner and Hutcherson interact with immense sensitivity and love for each other's music. There is no sense of rivalry here, just respect and joy. *—Cliff Tinder*, Down Beat

13th House / 1981 / Milestone 9102

☆ **La Leyenda De La Hora** / i. 1981 / Columbia 37375
For *La Leyenda*, his Columbia debut date, McCoy Tyner chose to use a nonet, plus a string section, to play five originals, four of them in an Afro-Cuban vein. The opening "Vida" is a complex tune with unexpected melodic and rhythmic shifts. Taken medium-up with an Afro-bossa flavor, the melody is played by horns and rhythm section interweaving with piano, vibes, and flute. Bobby Hutcherson and Chico Freeman both solo enthusiastically, the hornman getting a light, pleasing tone as he scrambles amidst the changes. Tyner shows again that he is a constantly improving pianist, dashing out rock-hard bass notes and effortless-sounding right-hand lines, propelled by Ignacio Berroa's bracing trap work—which is excellent throughout the session. "Ja'Cara" is a warm, pretty tune played by piano, rhythm, and strings echoing some of the piano lines. "Habana," based around four propulsive rhythmic figures, is highlighted by the leader's rippling lines and Paquito D'Rivera's bristling alto. The only non-Afro-Cuban piece is "Walk Spirit, Talk Spirit," a 12-bar tune that alternates between minor chords a whole step apart. While Tyner has produced more memorable musical moments, *La Leyenda* is still a rewarding listening experience. *—Zan Stewart*, Down Beat

Dimensions / Oct. 1983 / Elektra 60350

It's About Time / Apr. 6-7, 1985 / Blue Note 46291

Double Trios / Jun. 7+9, 1986 / Denon 1128

Revelations / Oct. 1988 / Blue Note 91651

○ **Uptown-Downtown** / Nov. 1988 / Milestone 9167
Live date at the Blue Note in New York City. Quintessential Tyner big band. You can't live without this one. *—Michael G. Nastos*

Things Ain't What They Used to Be / 1989 / Blue Note 93598
Upbeat attitude, with struttin' solos from John Scofield (g), George Drams. *—Ron Wynn*

New York Reunion / Apr. 1990 / Chesky 51
Quartet with Joe Henderson (sax). A great idea to bring them back together. *—Michael G. Nastos*

44th St. Suite / May 1991 / Red Baron 48630
Recent date, slashing solos from David Murray (ts), Arthur Blythe (as). Fine Tyner. *—Ron Wynn*

Remembering John / i. 1991 / Enja 79668
A trio session that's mainly Tyner extrapolations on Coltrane compositions; matches his peerless keyboard improvisation with the equally adventurous bass work of Avery Sharpe and good, though not exceptional, drum support from Aaron Scott. *—Ron Wynn*, Rock & Roll Disc

○ **Turning Point, The** / i. 1992 / Verve 513573
The 15-piece ensemble, heavier on brass than reeds, is a modal juggernaut that possesses the uncommon ability to inspire us in both musical and emotional terms. McCoy Tyner's revival of "Passion Dance," immortalized by his ace quartet in the Blue Note late '60s, is intelligent excitement typified: Avery Sharpe's fleet bass serves as the mooring for sinewy solos and onslaughts of reactive sectional work. The writing for orchestra is stellar, audacious, and productive in its formation of textures and colors. Arrangers Tyner, trombonist Steve Turre, tuba player Howard Johnson, Denis Mackrel (d), and the estimable trombonist Slide Hampton understand how to capture the exultant or thoughtful tone of the songs; they fit together solo instruments and sections with apparent ease. Bob Belden is the able director of the band. *—Frank-John Hadley*, Down Beat

Double Exposure / Lester Recording Catalog 9040

U

JAMES "BLOOD" ULMER

b. Feb. 1942, St. Matthews, SC
Guitar, vocals / Early free, early jazz-rock, contemporary funk
James "Blood" Ulmer's a slashing, blues and rock-tinged guitarist and vocalist, and one of the most influential to emerge
in the '70s. Ulmer's jagged chords, and his adaptation of
Ornette Coleman's "harmolodic" concept to the guitar, have
been honed into an individualistic mode that merges funk
and hard rock as well as jazz. Ulmer sang gospel and
learned guitar as a child, then moved to Philadelphia as a
professional in 1960 and worked with organ funk bands. He
came to New York in 1971 and worked at Minton's for several months. Ulmer played with Paul Bley, Art Blakey, and
others in the early '70s before studying with Ornette
Coleman. Ulmer was in Coleman's band in the late '70s, and
appeared at the Ann Arbor Jazz and Blues Festival. He
recorded with Joe Henderson and Arthur Blythe, and cut his
own session on Artists House. During the '80s, he recorded
for Rough Trade, Columbia, the Caravan of Dreams, and
Blue Note. He was in the group Phalanax with George
Adams, and has recorded on DIW with David Murray. *—Ron
Wynn*

★ **Tales of Captain Black** / Dec. 5, 1978 / Artists House
Tales of Captain Black, the first release by guitarist James
Blood Ulmer, represents a greenhouse for his artistic intuition. Here Ulmer is joined by alto saxophonist Ornette and
drummer Denardo Coleman and the highly gifted bassist
Jaamaladeen Tacuma. Each player comfortably coexists with
the others, though a generation separates the soloists from
the rhythm section. The band operates within three improvisational systems—ensemble, reed soloist/trio accompaniment, and guitar soloist/rhythm accompaniment—with a
freedom that beguiles each song's formal construction.
There is dissonance, as you might expect, explored in each
musician's individual sound and in the harmonic overtones
of the guitar/saxophone pairings that are delightful in their
fragile opulence. *—Jim Brinsfield,* Down Beat

○ **Are You Glad to Be In America** / i. 1980 / Rough Trade 16
America isn't really a jazz record, but James Blood Ulmer's
no one-chord guitar player. *America,* recorded in 1980, was
first released on England's Rough Trade label and later issued on Artists House. On these jams, Ulmer allows himself
free rein. Here, too, the horns are used prominently and to
great advantage. On "Layout," one of Ulmer's more delightful melodies, tenor saxophonist David Murray meets him on
his own turf—though there are times on this LP when Ulmer
leaves the horns in the dust. The nexus of horns on
"Pressure" almost perfectly complements the guitarist's jit-
tery business. Ulmer's tunes, like his playing, move at a gallop. There are two vocals: "Jazz is the Teacher (Funk is the
Preacher)" is groove-based (testifying in the James Brown
vein. The title track, with its delightfully sour horn riffs,
should be declared the national anthem. Ulmer's a slinky,
compelling singer, and yes, he absorbed a lot of Jimi
Hendrix's crooning. So, with all this rock in his roots, can
Ulmer flourish in the hot house of improvisers? Yes. He has
Ornette Coleman to thank for the blues-drenched harmonic
unpredictability of his lines, but Ulmer has found his own

voice on the instrument. *America* is no jazz player's get-rich-
quick record like Oliver Lake's lame reggae LP *Jump Up;* this
was the real stuff. *—Kevin Whitehead,* Cadence

☆ **Freelancing** / 1981 / Columbia 37493
Freelancing, Ulmer's first major-label release, is also his
most eclectic. Columbia appeared to be hedging a bit, eager
to display its Great Black Hope as both spacey conceptualist
and post-Jimi Hendrix funkster, à la the *No Wave* and
America albums, respectively. Accordingly, Ulmer's basic
power trio featuring drummer G. Calvin Weston and bassist
Amin Ali (drummer Rashied's son) is displayed in three settings; alone, with a rock-oriented chorus, and with the neo-
jazz horns of David Murray, Oliver Lake, and Olu Dara.
Ulmer's reference points are myriad; Elmore James and
James Brown, Ornette Coleman's *Dancing in Your Head* and
Miles Davis's *On the Corner,* the Art Ensemble and Weather
Report, Jimi Hendrix and James Chance. Notions of spaced-
out rhythm & blues have been around at least since Captain
Beefheart, but Ulmer transfuses the vanguard genre with a
stunningly percussive attack; at times his flailings suggest
an electrified banjo. Ulmer spurts forth with adrenaline-
charged velocity, as Weston's drums set the rampaging pace
and Ali slaps a churning maelstrom out of his electric bass.
The horn section lasers through the heavy metal barrage in
blue unison, intoning fractured Horace Silver melodies at furious tempos. Solos are infrequent, but tenorman Murray
(the guitarist's most usual foil) spars and jabs with bluff urgency on "Rush Hour," and trumpeter Dara blows a fat and
sassy tribute to Miles Davis on "Hijack." His singing and guitar work on these tracks recall both Hendrix and Richie
Havens, but his wrenching sincerity and gut-rock prowess
distinguish him from such crossover candidates as the cynical Defunkt and the scatologically posturing George
Clinton. *—Larry Birnbaum,* Down Beat

America: Do You Remember . . . / 1986 / Blue Note 46755
America: Do You Remember The Love. 1987 release, uneven
but lots of excitement. *—Ron Wynn*

Original Phalanx / i. Mar. 1989 / DIW 8013

MICHAEL URBANIAK (Michal Urbaniak)

b. Jan. 22, 1943, Warsaw, Poland
*Violin, tenor saxophone, bandleader / Early jazz-rock, world
fusion, instrumental pop*
Polish violinist, tenor saxophonist, and bandleader Michael
Urbaniak was a breath of fresh air when he first appeared
on the American music scene in the mid-'70s. His violin
playing had warmth, wit, and flair, and Urbaniak's electric
violin, and violectra (an electronic bowed string instrument
with a sound an octave lower than the violin's) were both a
curiosity and a different sound and voice. His sawing, bluesy
phrases and interesting, if at times, raw sax playing, coupled
with his wife Urzula Dudziak's scatting and vocal gymnastics, added welcome unpredictability and edge to what was
already becoming a dreary landscape as jazz-rock's promise
was fading into fusion's profitability. But Urbaniak never fulfilled that initial potential, and has enjoyed a very successful,
but aesthetically uneven career. He studied violin, as well as
soprano sax, as a child, and later played tenor. He experi-

mented with traditional jazz and swing, then concentrated on bebop. He played with Zbignew Namyslowski, Andrzej Trzaskowski, and Krzysztof Komeda in the early and mid-'60s, while working as a classical violinist. Urbaniak led a group in Scandinavia with Dudziak in 1965, then returned to Poland in 1969. He formed Constellation with Dudziak, Adam Makowicz, Czeslaw Bartkowski, and Pawel Jarzebski (later Roman Dylag). Urbaniak and Dudziak came to America in 1974, and he formed Fusion. They performed and recorded some compelling albums blending Dudziak's vocals and vocal effects, Polish folk melodies, and irregular meters, plus Urbaniak's scintillating violin solos. Urbaniak worked and recorded with Larry Coryell and Dudziak in the '80s, and also led his own bands. His albums became less freewheeling and more restrained and overproduced. Urbaniak also did sessions with Archie Shepp. He recorded as a leader for Columbia, Muza, Jazz America Marketing, Milan, Rykodisc, and Steeplechase. Urbaniak has a couple of sessions available on CD. —*Ron Wynn*

★ **Fusion** / **i.** 1975 / Columbia 32852

Cinemode / **i.** 1988 / Rykodisc 10037
Polish violinist and saxophonist Michael Urbaniak was a fresh voice on the horizon when he arrived here in the early '70s and began recording. Unfortunately, Urbaniak's once-vital sound was quickly absorbed into the trendy fabric of fusion, and his music diluted to the point it was undistinguished and empty. This 1988 solo set, with Urbaniak free from commercial pressures and considerations, ranks as his most accomplished, intriguing release. He plays violin, saxes, and keyboards, and his solos are fierce, extensive, and joyous. —*Ron Wynn*

PHIL URSO (Philip Urso)

b. Oct. 2, 1925, Jersey City, NJ
Saxophone / Big band, cool
A no-frills, almost prototype cool tenor saxophonist, Phil Urso's never modified his original Lester Young-influenced sound. His tone, style, phrasing, and approach are his own, but they reflect the floating tone and lush, striding Young sound. Urso played clarinet at age 13, then studied tenor sax in high school. He moved to New York in the late '40s, and played with Elliot Lawrence and Woody Herman until the early '50s. Urso played with many leaders during the '50s, among them Jimmy Dorsey and Miles Davis. He recorded with Don Elliott, Terry Gibbs, and Oscar Pettiford, while leading his own bands. Urso co-led a band with Bob Brookmeyer that also included Horace Silver, Kenny Clarke, and Percy Heath. He played with Chet Baker in 1955, and recorded with him in 1956 and again in 1965. Urso moved back to Denver in the late '50s, and continued to play in Denver during the '70s and '80s. Currently, Urso does not have any sessions as a leader available on CD. —*Ron Wynn and Michael G. Nastos*

Philosophy of Urso / Apr. 14, 1953 / Savoy 12056

Sentimental Journey / Feb. 18, 1954 / Regent 6003

★ **Urso-Brookmeyer Quintet** / **i.** 1954 / Savoy 15041

V

WARREN VACHE (Warren (Jr) Vaché)

b. Feb. 21, 1951, Rahway, NJ
Cornet, flugelhorn / Swing, big band, cool

Relatively youthful cornetist and trumpeter who prefers the swing-era sound, prerock standards to hard-bop. Heavily influenced by Bobby Hackett and Ruby Braff, Vaché plays with the vibrato of a vocalist and has a beautiful sound and extensive range. He was a student of Pee Wee Ervin and Jim Fitzpatrick and began working with Benny Goodman after he earned his music degree, also playing at Eddie Condon's in New York with Vic Dickenson and Bob Wilber. Vaché played with his father's group as well before issuing his debut release in 1976. His albums, whether collaborations with like-minded players like Dan Barrett or with longtime veterans like Hank Jones and George Duvivier, are always nice, sometimes dazzling, and usually conservative from the standpoint of the material. —*Ron Wynn*

Jersey Jazz at Midnight / Dec. 31, 1975 / Concord Jazz 1002
Blues Walk / Nov. 1977 / Dreamstreet 101
○ **Jillian** / Nov. 1978 / Concord Jazz 87
In New York City / i. 1978 / Concord Jazz 70
★ **Polished Brass** / 1979 / Concord Jazz 98
Iridescence / Jan. 1981 / Concord Jazz 153
Midtown Jazz / Feb. 1982 / Concord Jazz 4203
Easy Going / Dec. 1986 / Concord Jazz 4323
☆ **Warm Evenings** / 1989 / Concord Jazz 4392
Wonderful sound quality, production, and solos. Good production and arrangements, strings kept in right balance with Vaché's trumpet. —*Ron Wynn*

DAVE VALENTIN

Flute / Latin-jazz, instrumental pop

Dave Valentin is an Afro-Latin and Latin-jazz flutist who's recorded mainly for GRP. His albums have been nice, middle-of-the-road affairs. One, with Herbie Mann, is quite substantial. —*Ron Wynn*

★ **Live at the Blue Note** / i. 1988 / GRP 9568
Mind Time / i. 1988 / GRP 9554
Two Amigos / i. 1990 / GRP 9606

TOM VARNER

French horn / Postbop, Early free, Neo-bop, Modern creative

Varner's French horn is his axe. He plays neo-bop or creative music, more swinging than free, but he's able to do both. Varner's recorded output thus far has substance and quality. —*Michael G. Nastos*

○ **Tom Varner Quartet** / i. Aug. 1980 / Soul Note 1017
Motion / Stillness / i. Mar. 1982 / Soul Note 1067
Long Night Big Day / 1985 / New World 80410
★ **Jazz French Horn** / Oct. 1985 / New Note 1004
Debut with quintet. Contains the parody on "What is This Thing Called Love" titled "What is This Thing Called First Strike Capability." Uplifting jazz. —*Michael G. Nastos*
Covert Action / i. Jan. 1987 / New Note 1009

Mystery of Compassion, The / i. Mar. 1992 / Soul Note 121217

NANA VASCONCELOS

b. 1945, Recife, Brazil
Percussion / World fusion

An excellent percussionist known for creating amazing melodies and rhythms, Brazilian ace Nana Vasconcelos had the misfortune to make his American debut in the same era as Airto Moreira. Moreira has had a larger profile, but Vasconcelos need not take a back seat to anyone. His playing on the berimbau and cuica can be mesmerizing in its beauty and flair, and Vasconcelos can also dazzle on bongos, maracas, and drums. He played bongos and maracas in his father's band at age 12. Vasconcelos was later a drummer in Rio de Janeiro, and mastered several traditional Brazilian rhythm instruments while playing with Milton Nascimento. He came to America with Gato Barbieri in the early '70s, and went to Argentina and Europe as well. His berimbau playing and percussive support were featured on several Barbieri Flying Dutchman albums. Vasconcelos later lived in Paris for two years, working primarily with handicapped children and doing some dates in Sweden with Don Cherry. He toured and co-led a group with Egberto Gismonti in the mid-'70s, then cofounded the trio Codona with Don Cherry and Collin Walcott in the late '70s. This group combined African, Asian, and South American ethnic styles, and played them in an improvisational, but not necessarily jazz-based manner. They disbanded after Walcott's death in 1984, but made some fine ECM albums during their tenure. Vasconcelos also played with Pat Metheny's band in the early '80s, and was in Don Cherry's group, Mu, in 1984. In the late '80s, Vasconcelos recorded with the Bushdancers and made duet sessions with Gismonti for ECM and Antonello Salis for Soul Note. His albums with Codona, and the duets with Gismonti and Salis, are available on CD, as are his earlier dates with Gismonti. Currently, the early '70s Flying Dutchman albums with Barbieri are not unavailable. —*Ron Wynn*

○ **Saudades** / Mar. 1979 / ECM 829380
If a solo by percussionist Nana Vasconcelos is provocative, on *Saudades*, Vasconcelos plus guitarist Egberto Gismonti plus strings plus voices is awesome and utterly disarming. The berimbau, on whose one string slides a pitch-altering resonating gourd, is wonderfully suited as a solo improvising instrument, and with Vasconcelos in control, its music is remarkably rich in texture and tone. "O Berimbau" begins with Vasconcelos alone, working through round, ringing single tones whose presence swells as if absorbing all the air around them. He moves on to rapid-fire triplets and beyond, modulating the pitch subtly at first, then drastically changing keys with rapid, unpredictable gourd movements. With all this going on, one is hardly ready for the strings that creep into "O Berimbau" just after Vasconcelos begins his breathy singing. The strings, written by Gismonti and conducted by Mladen Gutesha (who worked on Keith Jarrett's *In the Light*, *Luminessence*, and *Arbour Zena* projects), drop out, then soon return in an odd, almost implied swing rhythm, rising and falling comically. Even this doesn't

prepare the listener for the onslaught of echoing and over-lapping voices that is "Vozes." Beginning with chantlike incessance and building to an almost psychotic density, Vasconcelos's voices begin to, not surprisingly, resemble the sound of his berimbau—but as if 10 or 20 lines were simultaneously punched onto a player piano roll, and played back at four or five times normal speed. There is also a marvelous duet between Vasconcelos and Gismonti on "super eight-string guitar," which recalls the excitement of "Dancas." The wandering Gismonti plays with such amazing presence and texture it sounds like he was double-tracked, but one suspects not. This is a very special record, with sounds and shapes you've probably never experienced before. *—Michael Zipkin*, Down Beat

★ **Bush Dance** / 1986 / Antilles 842897

The singer and master of the musical-bow berimbau plays percussion, synthesizer (and other keyboards), and is occasionally joined by Arto Lindsay or Mario Toledo (electric guitar) or Peter Scherer (k). Mr. Rhythm Machine plays drums on most tracks, and, as on any album where he appears, the beat is as stiff as a clergyman's collar; where Vasconcelos's chants and vocal colorations are recognizably Brazilian, the results support an incongruous rain forest dance party. At best, Vasconcelos blends ethnic percussion with Weather Report synth lines ("Estrela Brilhante"). *— Kevin Whitehead*, Cadence

Rain Dance / i. 1989 / Antilles 842416

1989 release spotlighting Vasconcelos band the Bush-dancers. Mixed results. *—Ron Wynn*

SARAH VAUGHAN (Sarah Lois Vaughan)

b. Mar. 27, 1924, Newark, NJ, **d.** Apr. 3, 1990

Vocals / Bop, ballads & blues

Bop's greatest diva, Sarah Vaughan was one of jazz's and popular music's supreme vocalists. She treated her voice as an instrument, improvising melodic and rhythmic embellishments, using her contralto range to make leaps and jumps, changing a song's mood or direction by enunciation and delivery, and altering her timbre. She turned sappy novelty tunes and light pop into definitive, jazz-based treatments. She had a distinctive swinging quality and intensity in her style, and was also a great scat singer. Vaughan was a dominant performer from the late '40s until the '80s, when illness forced her to cut back her appearances. Vaughan's recorded legacy stands with anyone else's in modern jazz history.

She sang in the Mt. Zion Baptist Church choir as a child, and became its organist at age 12. Vaughan won the famous Amateur Night at the Apollo talent contest in 1942, and, by April of the next year, had joined Earl Hines's band as a second pianist and vocalist. When Billy Eckstine left Hines and formed his own band in 1944, Vaughan soon joined Eckstine's band and made her recording debut with his orchestra at the end of December. She went solo a year later, and remained that way for the rest of her career, except for a brief stint with John Kirby in 1945 and 1946. She became a star by performing pop ballads and show tunes, though she made numerous jazz anthems. Eckstine was a frequent duet partner, and the two collaborated on a fine Irving Berlin repertory record in the mid-'50s.

Vaughan showed her jazz capabilities early in her solo career, recording a remarkable version of "Lover Man" with Dizzy Gillespie and Charlie Parker in 1945. But from 1949 to 1954, when she was with Columbia, she made hit albums with studio orchestras and cut only one jazz date with Miles Davis and Budd Johnson. When Vaughan switched labels to Mercury in 1954, she won the right to make light pop and straight jazz recordings. She did jazz material for EmArcy, recording with Clifford Brown, Cannonball Adderley, and Count Basie's sidemen, while cutting pop tracks for Mercury. These included the 1958 smash "Broken-Hearted Melody." Vaughan maintained similar relationships with Roulette, Mercury, and Columbia from 1960 to 1967.

After a five-year break, she returned to recording in 1971, this time with Norman Granz's Pablo label. Granz made many sessions with Vaughan through the '70s; some were excellent, others were not so good. She made a Duke Ellington Songbook, worked with Count Basie and Oscar Peterson, and even did an album of Afro-Latin and Brazilian material. There was a marvelous two-record live set recorded in Japan. Her health worsened in the '80s, but she recorded an album of Gershwin songs with the Los Angeles Philharmonic in 1982, and an interesting concept/vocal album, *The Planet Is Alive . . . Let It Live!*, in 1985 on Gene Lees's Jazzletter label. This was an album of poems by Pope John Paul II adapted by Lees with music by Tito Fontana and Sante Palumbo. It featured Vaughan's vocals backed by an orchestra that included jazz veterans such as Art Farmer, Benny Bailey, and Sahib Shihab.

When Vaughan died in 1990, there were tributes and worldwide outpourings of grief. Her albums are being steadily reissued, from the formative '40s dates to the '70s sets. Mercury has issued the mammoth *Complete Sarah Vaughan on Mercury* collection, which breaks down her career at the label into eras with multidisc packages for each period. The songbooks have been reissued, and Columbia has a two-disc package of material from the late '40s and early '50s. Single album reissues are also available from the '50s, '60s, and '70s. *—Ron Wynn and Dan Morgenstern*

○ **It's You or No One** / May 1946-Apr. 1948 / Musicraft 55

★ **Columbia Years (1949-1953)** / 1949-1953 / CBS 44165

In Hi-Fi / i. May 1950 / Columbia Special Products 13084

★ **With Clifford Brown** / Dec. 1954 / EmArcy 814641

★ **Gershwin Songbook** / i. 1954-1957 / Mercury 814187

The tracks here are around three minutes apiece, so there is little time for Sarah Vaughan to get sidetracked. There are occasional lapses into operatic excess and vibrato abuse, but in general she puts the melody and Ira Gershwin's wonderfully urbane lyrics first, letting the songs sell themselves. Oddly enough, I prefer Hal Mooney's orchestrations when they're heavy on the strings than when he gets into big-band bombast in the Nelson Riddle/Frank Sinatra vein; the charts are way too busy on a crawling "The Man I Love." But the band sound on "Stairway to Paradise" is just about right. This is a great refresher course for people who are cynical about the Gershwin brothers' achievements—and Vaughan's. Some cuts include Jimmy Jones (p), Joe Benjamin (b), and Roy Haynes (d). The rest of them are with the Hal Mooney Orchestra and Jones. Most were recorded in 1957; "But Not for Me" was recorded 11/56. *—Kevin Whitehead*, Cadence

Great Jazz Years (1954-1956)—Vol. 1 / i. 1954-1956 / PolyGram 26320

Great Show on Stage / i. 1954-1956 / PolyGram 26333

1954-1956. Another concept work. These are excellent songs and lead vocals, available elsewhere in original context. *— Ron Wynn*

Rodgers & Hart Songbook / 1954-1958 / EmArcy 824864

Sarah Vaughan in the Land of Hi Fi / i. 1955 / EmArcy 36058

○ **Sassy** / Apr. 1, 1956-Apr. 8, 1956 / EmArcy 36089

Linger Awhile / i. 1956 / Sony Special Products 14364

★ **Irving Berlin Songbook** / 1957 / EmArcy 822526

Misty / Jul. 1958 / Mercury 846488

Actually two great albums on one disc, the other being *Vaughan and Voices*. *—Ron Wynn*

At Mister Kelly's / i. 1958 / PolyGram 832791

First-rate, long-unavailable live club date with great rhythm section. *—Ron Wynn*

No Count Sarah / i. 1959 / EmArcy 824057

Roulette Years / 1960-1964 / Roulette 94983

Singles Sessions / 1960-1962 / Roulette 95331

After Hours / Jun. 1961 / Sony Special Products 660

Excellent early '50s cuts that haven't always been available domestically. —*Ron Wynn*

Sarah Slightly Classical / May 1963-Jul. 1963 / Roulette 95977

Again, its value is in relation to appreciation of the concept. She sings wonderfully. 1991 CD reissue has six bonus cuts. —*Ron Wynn*

★ **Sassy Swings the Tivoli** / Jul. 18, 1963 / Mercury 832788
Sassy Swings the Tivoli is an even, swinging live jazz set with backing by Kirk Stuart (p), Charles Williams (b), and George Hughes (d). Stuart joins Vaughan briefly on vocals, but besides that this is not all that unusual a date for the singer. It is, however, one of her *jazz* dates. Part of this was reissued on the Mercury twofer *Record Live*. —*Bob Rusch*, Cadence

Sassy Swings Again / Jan. 1967 / Mercury 814587

○ **Jazz Fest Masters** / i. 1969 / Jazz Masters 75244

★ **Complete—Live in Japan** / i. 1974 / Mobile Fidelity 844
This is the first Sarah Vaughan album to knock me out since those early Continental and Musicaft 78s. She gives the string section time off and works with a cooking rhythm trio. Especially interesting is the piano of Carl Schroeder, who has been a favorite of mine from his days with the Roy Haynes Hip Ensemble. Jimmy Cobb plays the drums well and John Gianelli would have been a fine bassist if he hadn't been so far up on the mix. Vaughan's good taste in tunes, which brings us such fine oldies as "Mean to Me" and "My Kinda Love," is shown in her selection of such fine current material as "Singing Off" and "If You Could See Me Now." Such gems as "Foggy Day," "Funny Valentine," and "Over the Rainbow" speak well for her ability to size up tunes that wear well, but haven't been done to death. If this album has a high point, it is Vaughan's scat singing of "Willow Weep for Me," because she claims to have forgotten the lyric. Vaughan's way is a vast improvement over the original. Still, in any way, shape, or form, it's good to have Sarah Vaughan back as a jazz singer. The pop world had her for far too long without sharing her with us. —*Joe Klee*, Down Beat

Duke Ellington Songbook—Vol. 1 / Aug. 15-Sep. 12, 1979 / Pablo 2312-111

Nice '70s update on Songbook concept. Some of her last truly great singing. —*Ron Wynn*

Duke Ellington Songbook—Vol. 2 / Aug. 15-Sep. 12, 1979 / Pablo 2312-116

○ **Send in the Clowns** / Feb.-May 1981 / Pablo 2312-130
Vaughan in a less distinguished phase of her career, but maintains her dignity. This collaboration with the Basie orchestra isn't what it would have been in the '50s or '60s, but it's still nice. —*Ron Wynn*

Brazilian Romance / i. 1987 / Columbia 42519

Sassy Sings and Swings / i. 1992 / CEMA 57591

☆ **Sarah Vaughan on Mercury** / Mercury
Complete on Mercury. Monumental six-disc set that covers her extensive and exhaustive Mercury career. Of course, the company has also hacked this up into multiple packages to get separate profits off each. You can get it either way; I prefer the boxed set. —*Ron Wynn*

REGINALD VEAL

Bass / Neo-bop
Another relative newcomer, bassist Reginald Veal has alternated with Robert Leslie Hurst III on recent Wynton Marsalis dates and tours. Veal began recording with Marsalis in the mid-'80s, and has appeared on *Standard Time, Volumes Two and Three, The Majesty of the Blues, Crescent City Christmas, Uptown Ruler, Levee Low Moan, Tune in Tomorrow, Blue Interlude,* and *Citi Movement*. —*Ron Wynn*

CHARLIE VENTURA (Charles Venturo)

b. Dec. 2, 1916, Philadelphia, PA, **d.** Jan. 17, 1992

Saxophone / Swing, bop
A definite entertainer and a flamboyant personality, bebop tenor saxophonist Charlie Ventura enjoyed great popularity in the '40s and '50s. A disciple of Ben Webster, his style was directly influenced by the swing-derived, jump blues, boogie, and R&B approach of Louis Jordan and Illinois Jacquet. Ventura couldn't quite match them in sheer power, but was almost as explosive and animated in his solos. He started on C-melody sax and then played alto before turning to tenor. Ventura was featured in the Gene Krupa band of the early and mid-'40s, as well as with Teddy Powell, and also led his own groups. He began recording for Phoenix in the mid-'40s. Ventura started his own big band in 1946, and also had a sextet that included Bill Harris, Buddy Stewart, Kai Winding, Jackie Cain, and Roy Kral. He formed a big band in 1948 with his younger brothers, then paired it down to an octet. His band featured gimmicks such as having voices and instruments perform bebop themes in unison. Ventura tried again to form a profitable big band in the early '50s, then created the Big Four with Marty Napoleon, Chubby Jackson, and Buddy Rich. He also reteamed with Krupa, Cain, and Kral. He and Krupa worked periodically until the end of the '60s. Ventura led small groups in various cities, but he worked regularly in Connecticut through the '70s. He recorded sessions for Sunset, National, Victor, Zim, Savoy, Harlequin, and Famous Door, among others. Ventura has some reissued sessions currently available on CD. —*Ron Wynn and Michael G. Nastos*

○ **Euphoria** / Aug. 28, 1945 / Savoy 2243
While no claim is being made that Charlie Ventura (tenor, soprano and bass saxes) was an "important" tenorman, he did enjoy a period of celebrity during the '40s; but it was one that unfortunately owed as much to his shameless grandstanding as it did to his very real musical abilities. At the start, Ventura was a better-than-average dance-band tenorman, with roots in Coleman Hawkins, Ben Webster, and Chu Berry; but his later associations with drummer Gene Krupa, JATP, and other excesses of the time soon worked to undermine his chances for serious consideration. However, "Dark Eyes" and other abominations aside, he did manage to record some creditable sessions in the '40s, and most of these make up *Euphoria*. The best comes first. Flanked by that paragon of taste, trumpeter Buck Clayton, Ventura turns in some of the most convincing playing of his career, his sumptuous tone and technical ease for once an actual aid rather than ends in themselves. He is equally good on the quartet date with pianist Arnold Ross, but after he jumped on the bop bandwagon something happened. Despite his eagerness to embrace the newer concept, he just never quite got beyond the superficialities. Bebop was a language Ventura could never learn to speak without an accent, so it is in the statements of his sidemen that modernists will find the greater interest. On the later tracks, there are good solos by trumpeter Charlie Shavers and trombonists Bill Harris, Kai Winding, and Bennie Green, as well as period flavor bopperies by vocalists Buddy Stewart, Roy Kral, and Jackie Cain. But however popular these National 78s were at the time of their original release, the passing years have done nothing to augment their value. —*Jack Sohmer*, Cadence

★ **Charlie Ventura and His Sextet** / May 1946 / Imperial 3002

Charlie Boy / i. 1946 / Phoenix

In Chicago / i. 1947 / Zim
Some hot work from Ventura, plus Kai Winding (tb), Shelly Manne (d). —*Ron Wynn*

Charlie Ventura Concert Featuring the Charlie Ventura Septet / i. 1949 / MCA 42330
Septet. Good high-energy concert reissue with Jackie & Roy, Bennie Green (tb). —*Ron Wynn*

In a Jazz Mood / Mar. 7, 1951-Dec. 22, 1952 / Norgran 1073

Charlie Ventura Quintet in Hi-Fi / i. 1956 / Harlequin

East of Suez / i. 1958 / Regent 6064

Chazz / 1977 / Famous Door

In Concert / GNP 001

JOE VENUTI (Giuseppi Venuti)

b. Sep. 16, 1903, Philadelphia, PA, **d.** Aug. 14, 1978
Violin / Dixieland, swing

An excellent soloist with an exuberant style and a driving, rhythmic approach, violinist Joe Venuti had success before, during, and after the swing era, and was equally outstanding in small combos or heading a big band. He was also one of jazz's greatest practical jokers, whose stunts were legendary. The same playful spirit that led Venuti to throw pianos out of hotel rooms or to put jello into Bix Beiderbecke's bath water was exemplified in his solos and choruses. Venuti grew up in Philadelphia, and was a childhood friend of guitarist Eddie Lang. They formed an early, highly influential partnership. After moving to New York in 1925, they played with Red Nichols, Frankie Trumbauer, Benny Goodman, and Jack Teagarden, among others. Their violin/guitar recordings were the blueprint for the Django Reinhardt/Stephane Grappelli "hot" quintet in Paris. Venuti and Lang led the Blue Four from 1927 until the early '30s, and cut some tracks with Trumbauer and Lennie Hayton. They appeared as special attractions with Paul Whiteman, and Venuti even appeared in the 1930 film *King of Jazz*. Venuti made the transition to swing in the '30s. He and Lang co-led an all star band that included both Jack and Charlie Teagarden, plus Goodman in 1931. Lang's sudden death in 1933 left Venuti devastated, but he bounced back to lead his own big band, with Kay Starr as featured vocalist at one point. Venuti toured Europe in 1934, and did sessions with Jimmy Dorsey, Adrian Rollini, Jean Goldkette, Red McKenzie, and Roger Wolfe Kahn. Venuti settled in Hollywood in 1944 to do film work, but was drafted during World War II. During the early '50s, he was featured on radio with Bing Crosby, and began to play amplified violin. He had some alcohol problems, and disappeared into obscurity for several years. But Venuti made a triumphant comeback in 1967 when he appeared at Dick Gibson's Colorado Jazz Party, then followed that with an even more spectacular appearance at the 1968 Newport Festival. Though battling cancer much of the '70s, Venuti recorded with Zoot Sims, Marian McPartland, Earl Hines, Ellis Larkins, George Barnes, Grappelli, and Bucky Pizzarelli, and played with the Detroit Symphony Orchestra, before finally succumbing to the disease in 1978. —*Ron Wynn and Dan Morgenstern*

★ **Joe Venuti with Eddie Lang—Vols. 1 & 2** / i. 1926-1927 / JSP 10
In at least one respect, the Joe Venuti-Eddie Lang set sounds very up to date; there are a lot of funny instruments—bass sax, comb, kazoo, hot fountain pen, bassoon, and, of course, Frankie Trumbauer's C-melody sax. For good measure, Tommy Dorsey plays exciting trumpet on "Hot Heels," Jimmy Dorsey not-so-good trumpet (according to Robert Parker), and Venuti bass on "Vibraphonia." There was much talent and playful inventiveness among these New Yorkers, but they lacked swinging rhythm sections until the Chicagoans came to their rescue. —*Stanley Dance*, Jazz Times

☆ **Violin Jazz 1927-1934** / 1927-1934 / Yazoo 1062
The 14 selections on this disc include several marvelous examples of the close communication Joe Venuti had with guitarist Eddie Lang. Anyone seeking a clue to the roots of the swing era will hear it clearly on these songs; this is danceable, joyful jazz from an era when rhythm, rather than harmony, was king. —*Ron Wynn*, Rock & Roll Disc

Stringin' the Blues / i. 192?-193? / Sony Special Products 24

Mad Fiddler from Philly, The / i. 1952-1953 / Shoestring

Joe Venuti Plays Jerome Kern / 1960 / Golden Crest 3101

○ **Venupelli Blues** / i. 1969 / BYG 529122

Daddy of the Violin, The / Mar. 29, 1971 / MPS 5050

○ **Joe and Zoot** / 1973-1974 / Chiaroscuro 128

Music Map

Jazz Vibraphone (Vibes)

Introduced USA in 1916 as "Steel Marimba"

Early Players
Adrian Rollini (1904-1956)
Lionel Hampton (1909-1930)
Red Norvo (1908-1944)

First Major Soloists
Milt Jackson (1923)–from 1945
Lionel Hampton (1909)
Red Norvo (1908)

Major Players in the 1950s
Margie Myams (w/George Shearing)
Teddy Charles (1928)
Lem Winchester
Bobby Hutcherson (1941)
Terry Gibbs (1924)

1960s Doubling Instrument
Victor Feldman (1934-1987)–piano
Alice Coltrane (1937)–piano
Tubby Hayes (1935-1973)–tenor sax, flute, alto, baritone
Dusko Goycovitch (1931) (Trumpet)

New levels of technical virtuosity
Gary Burton (1943)

1960s-1970s-1980s
Walter Dickerson
Darwin Gross (Darji)

Free Jazz
Walt Dickerson(1931)
Gunter Hampel (1937)
Karl Berger (1935)
Khan Jamal (1946)
Jay Hoggard (1954)

1970s Jazz-Rock
Electric Vibes–Synthivibe
Mike Mainieri (1938)
Roy Ayers (1940)
Dave Pike (1938)

Young Vibists
Joe Locke
Rob Pipho
Steve Nelson
Warren Smith, Jr. (1932)
Monte Croft

In 1964, Dick Gibson got violinist Joe Venuti and tenor/soprano saxophonist Zoot Sims together on stage, and the music that culminated in this recording began. Maybe Sims was not familiar with some of the older numbers like Venuti's "Wild Cat" or "It's the Girl," which hadn't been heard since the Boswell Sisters recorded them. And maybe the more recent material, like "My One and Only Love," wasn't the best vehicle for Venuti. But if anybody was uncomfortable with the repertoire, they sure didn't let on. Whether stompin' through

"Oh Lady Be Good" or essaying a pretty ballad like "Small Hotel," everybody is right on target. —*Joe Klee*, Down Beat

○ **Blue Four** / **i.** Jun. 1974 / Chiaroscuro 134
There is nothing but warmth and happiness here, with wily old master violinist Joe Venuti conducting a magical history tour of some classic music. "Blue Too," "Lady Be Good," and "String the Blues," for example, are duo tracks using just violin and acoustic guitar (Bucky Pizzarelli), while "Diga Diga Doo" and "Blue Room" find Venuti with Spencer Clark's bass sax, pianist Dill Jones, and Pizzarelli. Besides the overall good feeling this album conveys, there is a joyous bounce that never fades. —*Herb Nolan*, Down Beat

Hot Sonatas / Oct. 1975 / Chiaroscuro 145

Sliding By / Apr. 15, 1977 / Gazell 1014

Joe in Chicago / 1978 / Flying Fish 077

HAROLD VICK (Harold Edward Vick)

b. Apr. 3, 1936, Rocky Mount, NC, **d.** 1987
Saxophone / Postbop, soul-jazz, progressive big band
A topflight blues improviser, Harold Vick also played with passion and strength on bebop, hard bop, and especially on soul-jazz music, where his rippling tone and hard-hitting phrases were perfectly punctuated by the organ support of Brother Jack McDuff and Jimmy McGriff, among others. Vick got started on clarinet at age 13 after his uncle, Prince Robinson, gave him a clarinet as a gift. He began on tenor three years later, and performed with R&B groups while attending Howard University as a psychology student. Vick rose to prominence cutting soul-jazz and organ combo dates in the early and mid-'60s. He worked with McDuff, McGriff, and Big John Patton in the '60s, with Shirley Scott in the '70s, and with McGriff again in the '80s. He began recording as a leader in the mid-'60s, and was a star soloist in Jack DeJohnette's ahead-of-its time jazz-rock group, Compost, in the early '70s. Vick recorded as a leader for Blue Note, RCA, Strata-East, Black Jazz, and Muse. Currently, Vick doesn't have any dates available on CD. —*Ron Wynn and Michael G. Nastos*

★ **Steppin' Out** / May 21, 1963 / Blue Note 84138

LEROY VINNEGAR

b. Jul. 13, 1928, Indianapolis, IN
Bass / Postbop, cool
A great, self-taught "walking" bassist, Leroy Vinnegar was a prolific player on the '50s and '60s West Coast recording scene, and he remains active. He's most famous for his dynamic accompaniment and "walking" lines. Vinnegar plucked open strings with his left hand, adding heavier accents. He doesn't take that many solos, but the ones he delivers are outstanding. Vinnegar and pianist Carl Perkins attended school together in Indianapolis, and later became colleagues on the West Coast. Vinnegar worked in Chicago during the early '50s, serving as house bassist at the Beehive, and playing with Sonny Stitt and Charlie Parker. He moved to Los Angeles in 1954, and eventually recorded with Stan Getz, Shorty Rogers, Herb Geller, Chet Baker, Gerald Wilson, and Serge Chaloff. Vinnegar, Shelly Manne, and André Previn formed a popular trio that did jazz adaptions of Broadway songs and scores. They enjoyed a huge hit album with *My Fair Lady* in 1956. Vinnegar began to cut his own recordings in 1957, and his "walking" trademark was featured on the Contemporary albums *Leroy Walks!* and *Leroy Walks Again*. He worked often with Joe Castro and Teddy Edwards, coleading groups and even touring Europe with them. Vinnegar made some seminal recordings with Sonny Rollins, Phineas Newborn, the Jazz Crusaders, and Kenny Dorham. He remained in demand during the '60s, doing several sessions. Perhaps the most successful session was another smash album, *Swiss Movement*, with Les McCann and Eddie Harris in 1969. Vinnegar was in a quintet co-led by Howard McGhee and Edwards in the '70s, and worked in the Panama Hats, a quasi-Dixieland band that backed actor George Segal, and often appeared on late night television

during the '80s. At present, only his two best-known titles, the "walks" albums, are available on CD. —*Ron Wynn*

★ **Leroy Walks!** / Jul. 15-Sep. 16, 1957 / Contemporary 160
This date from 1957 features bassist Leroy Vinnegar's sextet (Vic Feldman, Gerald Wilson, Teddy Edwards, Carl Perkins, Tony Bazley). It isn't Vinnegar's best. —*Bob Rusch*, Cadence

○ **Leroy Walks Again** / Aug. 1, 1962-Mar. 5, 1963 / Contemporary 454
Bassist Leroy Vinnegar's date comes from two sessions: one from 8/1/62 with Victor Feldman (p, vib), Ron Jefferson (d), Teddy Edwards (ts) and Freddy Hill (tpt); and the other from 3/5/63 with Edwards, Hill, and Mike Melvoin (p), Roy Ayers (vib), and Milt Turner (d). This is a bop release that has, for the most part, music of the moment, good but not lasting. It's notable for being Freddy Hill's recorded debut (at 28 years old) and for the solid solos of Roy Ayers, another jazz talent lost to fusion. The date was, I believe, only the second recording for both Melvoin and Ayers. —*Bob Rusch*, Cadence

☆ **Jazz's Great Walker** / 1964 / Vee Jay 2502

EDDIE "CLEANHEAD" VINSON

b. Dec. 18, 1917, Houston, TX, **d.** Jul. 2, 1988, Los Angeles, CA
Alto saxophone, vocals / Bop, blues & jazz, soul-jazz
Eddie "Cleanhead" Vinson combined bop and blues vocals in a completely unique manner. Influenced by Johnny Hodges, Vinson's alto sax work with its spiraling lines, intense tone, and forceful sound were delivered with a searing intensity. His blues singing had a jagged, animated edge, but also had a tender underpinning, and was performed with a mix of earthy humor and resigned irony. The actual composer of both "Tune Up" and "Four" (Miles Davis was incorrectly credited), Vinson performed his bop/blues hybrid from the '30s to the '80s. He joined Arnett Cobb and Illinois Jacquet in Chester Boone's big band one year after he'd begun playing alto sax. He stayed in the band from 1935 until 1941, while it changed its leaders to Milt Larkin in 1936, and to Floyd Ray in 1940. Vinson toured the South with blues vocalists Big Bill Broonzy and Lil Green, then went to New York, joining Cootie Williams's band. He had a huge hit in 1944 with "Cherry Red Blues." He recorded with Williams's band on Okeh, Hit, and Capitol. Vinson led a big band in 1946 and 1947, and a septet with John Coltrane, Red Garland, and Johnny Coles in 1948. There were sessions with Mercury and King in the late '40s and early '50s, and there were later sessions for labels such as Bethlehem, Riverside, Delmark, and Blues Way. He kept working and recording, but didn't enjoy renewed popularity until 1969, when a European tour with Jay McShann and a recording of "Wee Baby Blues" alerted old and new generations about Vinson. This band also recorded for Black & Blue. Vinson played and recorded frequently in the '70s and '80s, working with Count Basie, Johnny Otis, Arnett Cobb, and Buddy Tate, and even with Roomful of Blues. He did sessions in the '70s and '80s for Muse, Fantasy, Circle, and Pablo. Vinson's playing strongly influenced Cannonball Adderley. A healthy amount of Vinson dates are available on CD, including much of the Muse and Pablo sessions, as well as material on Black & Blue, Delmark, Fantasy, Bluebird, and Landmark. Currently, his King sessions are unavailable on a domestic label. —*Ron Wynn*

○ **Eddie Cleanhead Vinson Sings** / **i.** 195? / Bethlehem 5005

○ **Cherry Red** / Mar. 1967 / Bluesway 6007

★ **Kidney Stew** / Mar. 26+28, 1969 / Black & Blue 233021

○ **Hold It Right There!** / Aug. 25-Aug. 26, 1978 / Muse 5243
Eddie "Cleanhead" Vinson (as, v), Arnett Cobb, and Buddy Tate (ts), together with a top-drawer rhythm section made a fine group for an engagement in August 1978 at Sandy's Jazz Revival in Beverly, Massachusetts, and Bob Porter was on hand to record the event. Porter sorted out the performances according to the featured musician and several LPs on the Muse label were issued. This is the second volume of the

Vinson specialties. Vinson has vocals on "Cherry Red" and the title piece. Cobb and Tate are present only on the title number and "Take the 'A' Train," while the rhythm section (pianist Ray Bryant, bassist George Duvivier, drummer Alan Dawson) purrs along in firm support and adds solo work of its own. —*Shirley Klett*, Cadence

○ **Live at Sandy's** / Aug. 25-Aug. 26, 1978 / Muse 5208
Here, in one of several LPs from a historic confrontation of three top-ranking Texas saxmen in a popular Massachusetts jazz club, Eddie "Cleanhead" Vinson has the stage almost entirely to himself. And, because of the heady atmosphere that was most certainly engendered by the uniqueness of the situation, he succeeds in registering what was perhaps his best work on record to date (1981). He sings on four of the titles, "Cleanhead Blues," "Railroad Porter Blues," "High Class Baby," and "Things Ain't What They Used to Be," with the two titans of Texas tenor (Buddy Tate and Arnett Cobb) making valuable and extended appearances on the third and fourth. But he plays alto on all but the second. And how he plays! Ripe and juicy, his tone suggests a combination Charlie Parker/Earl Bostic/Louis Jordan, and while his concern for intonation is casual at best, the resultant sound nevertheless strikes far closer to the core of jazz than any of the glib posturings of his many stylistic inheritors. Of special interest is the way-up version of the boogie classic "Tune Up." Along with its companion vintage standard, "Four," this number has, for almost 30 years, been considered a Miles Davis composition. But according to Fred Bouchard's notes, obviously gleaned directly from source information, both were originally penned by Vinson! Another purely instrumental gem is "My Man Sandy." Again an upper, this boasts a seldom-used structure of AABC, with the first repeated section being a 12-bar blues, this is followed by an "I Got Rhythm" bridge (eight bars) and the final 10 bars of the original "I Got Rhythm," inclusive of tag. It makes for a healthy concentration while playing, and, happily, no one goofs. —*Jack Sohmer*, Cadence

○ **I Want a Little Girl** / Feb. 10, 1981 / Pablo 866
Eddie "Cleanhead" Vinson's '80s albums tended to concentrate more on his boppish alto than on the blues-singing "Mr. Cleanhead," but this digital recording tips the scales in favor of the blues. The title track is a gem, soulfully sung over Art Hillery's pre-Jimmy Smith organ colorations, supple rhythm work, and breathy Jamal Ali tenor, with space left open for a smoothly nuanced Vinson alto solo. More finely phrased alto opens "Somebody's Got to Go," with a gutsily determined vocal over a firm, astute John Heard bassline. At 10:50, "Stormy Monday" gives the soloists room to stretch out. Hillery, on organ, links familiar blues licks with a refreshingly light touch reminiscent of Booker T. Jones. Vinson's expressive alto gives way to an unhurried and mournful vocal, the tremulous wobble in his voice seeming especially appropriate here. Guitarist Cal Green's spot is his most fully realized of the date. "Worried Mind Blues" has a jaunty riff arrangement, but the horns' execution is ragged; this is nice Vinson in any event. —*Tom Bingham*, Cadence

★ **And Roomful of Blues** / Jan. 27, 1982 / Muse 5282
Pairing Eddie "Cleanhead" Vinson with Roomful of Blues is one of those ideas that seems so natural one wonders why it wasn't done sooner. Listeners shouldn't expect any great revelations, but they can hear hard, swinging jazz and blues that would make Count Basie proud. Vinson's alto solos have great spirit, but aren't really anything out of the ordinary. In fact, the solos by the various members of Roomful of Blues (alto saxophonist Rich Latallie on "Movin' with Lester," tenor saxophonist Greg Piccolo on "That's the Groovy Thing," baritone saxophonist Doug James on "Movin' with Lester") come across stronger. Vinson's three vocals ("Friend of Mine," "Past Sixty Blues," "Farmer's Daughter Blues") are typical Vinson, which means a delight. What we have here is a great party record. —*Carl Brauer*, Cadence

○ **Cleanhead & Cannonball** / 1988 / Landmark 1309

Jazz Violin

Solo Instrument in Ragtime Orchestras (c.1915)

Territory Bands
Andy Kirk (1898-??) Band
Alphonso Trent (1905-1959) Band

Soloist Claude Williams (1908)

Matty Malneck (1903-1981) w/Paul Whitman's band
Erskine Tate (1895-1978)

Great Soloists
Joe Venuti (1903-1978) (w/Eddie Lang)
Stephane Grappelli (1908) (w/Django Reinhardt)
Stuff Smith (1909-1967)

Swing-Era Violinists
Svend Asmussen (1916)
Eddie South (1904-1962)–recorded with Grappelli/Reinhardt
Ray Nance (w/Duke Ellington)

Experimental, Free Jazz Players
Zbigniew Seifert (1946-1979)
Jean-Luc Ponty (1942)
John Blake
Didier Lockwood (1956)

Fusion
John Blake
Michael White (1933)
Sugarcane Harris
Papa John Creach

Avant-Garde
Ornette Coleman (1930)
Leroy Jenkins (1932)
Billy Bang (1947)
Charles Burnham
Michael White (1933)

Violectra
Jean-Luc Ponty (1942)
Micha Urbaniak (1943)

Viola
Maxine Roach

○ **Bosses of the Blues—Vol. 2** / Bluebird 8312

MIROSLAV VITOUS (Miroslav Ladislav Vitous)

b. Dec. 6, 1947, Prague, Czechoslovakia
Bass, guitar, composer, educator / Early jazz-rock, world fusion, modern creative
Czechoslovakian bassist Miroslav Vitous is one of the greatest European players in modern jazz history. Besides being a magnificent bowed player, Vitous has the ability and flair to make the bass a lead rather than a support instrument. He has flourished in bebop, hard bop, free, jazz-rock, pop, classical, and international sessions, and displayed stunning tone, and solo and accompaniment abilities. Vitous studied

violin and piano before turning to bass; his father was a saxophonist. Vitous won a scholarship to Berklee while studying at the Prague Conservatory in the '60s. He moved to
New York in 1967, and played with Art Farmer, Freddie
Hubbard, and the Clark Terry-Bob Brookmeyer quintet. He
later worked with two extremely popular jazz-rock groups
of the late '60s and early '70s; Miles Davis's and Herbie
Mann's. Vitous recorded with Donald Byrd, Chick Corea,
Jack DeJohnette, Wayne Shorter, and Larry Coryell in the
'60s and early '70s. He toured with Stan Getz in the early
'70s, played with Mann again, and was a founding member
of Weather Report with Shorter and Joe Zawinul. He left
Weather Report in the mid-'70s, and, for a time in the '70s,
experimented with electric guitar. He returned to the bass
and joined the faculty of the New England Conservatory in
1979. Vitous headed its jazz department during the mid-'80s.
He also lead a group with John Surman, either Kenny
Kirkland or John Taylor, and Jon Christensen in the late '70s
and early '80s, and played in Chick Corea's Trio music with
Roy Haynes in the '80s. Vitous recorded the majestic *Infinite
Search* in 1969 with Herbie Hancock, Joe Henderson, and
several others for Embryo, a division of Atlantic. It was temporarily reissued as *Mountain in the Clouds* then was fool-

ishly deleted from print. He's also recorded for Storyville,
ECM, and Freedom. He has a few sessions available on CD.
—*Ron Wynn*

★ **Mountain in the Clouds** / i. 1973 / Atlantic
A groundbreaking LP for fusioneers—pre-Weather Report—
with John McLaughlin, Joe Henderson, Herbie Hancock, Jack
DeJonette, and Joe Chambers. All Vitous originals except
"Freedom Jazz Dance," clocking in at 11 minutes. Originally
Infinite Search. —Michael G. Nastos

○ **Miroslav** / Dec. 1976-Jul. 1977 / Freedom 741040
1976-77 sessions with Don Alias and Armen Halburian on
percussion. Vitous overdubs bass and keyboards. A stunning
musical trip through Afro-jazz texture music. "Tiger in the
Rain" is absolutely captivating. —*Michael G. Nastos*

☆ **First Meeting** / May 1979 / ECM 1145
Seven pieces written by Vitous. With John Surman (sax, b,
cl), a very young Kenny Kirkland (p), and stellar Jon
Christenson (d). This is very listenable music, rooted in freedom of expression. —*Michael G. Nastos*

Journey's End / Jul. 1982 / ECM 843171

Emergence / Sep. 1985 / ECM 827855

W

ABDUL WADUD (Abdul Khabir Wadud)

b. Apr. 30, 1947, Cleveland, OH
Cello / Modern creative
An outstanding cellist, Abdul Wadud has concentrated solely on the instrument since the age of nine, and never decided to double on bass. His plucking and bowed solos have been featured in jazz and symphonic/classical settings, and Wadud is easily the finest cellist to emerge from the '60s and '70s generation. He studied at Youngstown State and Oberlin in the late '60s and early '70s. He played in the Black Unity Trio at Oberlin and met Julius Hemphill; the two subsequently worked together well into the '80s. Wadud played in the New Jersey Symphony Orchestra in the '70s, and earned his Masters degree in 1972. He played with Arthur Blythe for the first time in '76, and has since maintained a working relationship with him. He also worked and recorded with Frank Lowe, George Lewis, Oliver Lake, Sam Rivers, Cecil Taylor, David Murray, Chico Freeman, Anthony Davis, and James Newton in the '70s and '80s. Wadud, Newton, and Davis were in the octet Episteme and were in a trio from 1982 to 1984. Wadud recorded as a leader for Bishara and Gramavision in the '70s and '80s, and in a duo with Jenkins for Red in the '70s. He has one session currently available on CD. —*Ron Wynn*

FREDDIE WAITS

b. 1943
Drums / Hard bop
He began playing blues and soul, but Freddy Waits eventually became an excellent hard bop, bebop, and free jazz drummer, as well as a charter member of the percussive group M'Boom Re. Waits worked with Memphis Slim and John Lee Hooker, and with Motown vocalists, in the late '50s and early '60s. He then moved from Mississippi to New York. Waits recorded and played with Ray Bryant, Johnny Hodges, Andrew Hill, and McCoy Tyner during the '60s, with Richard Davis, Ella Fitzgerald, Lee Morgan, Bennie Maupin, Teddy Edwards, Curtis Fuller, and Tyner during the '70s, and with Bill Dixon in the '80s. Waits, Horace Arnold, and Billy Hart formed Colloquium III in the late '70s. He played with Cecil Taylor in the late '80s. Waits hasn't led any sessions, but can be heard on recent discs by M'Boom Re and on reissues by Hill, Tyner, Morgan, Dixon, and others. —*Ron Wynn*

COLLIN WALCOTT

b. Apr. 24, 1945, New York, NY, **d.** Nov. 8, 1984, Magdeburg, Germany
Percussion, sitar / World fusion
One of the first Western musicians to master both sitar and tabla, Collin Walcott also played violin, snare drum, and timpani. He was one of the most gifted and knowledgeable percussionists in recent jazz history. Walcott studied sitar with Ravi Shankar, and tabla with Alla Rakha. As a teen, he was resident percussionist at the Yale Summer School of Music in Norfolk, Connecticut. Walcott graduated from Indiana University in 1966, and later traveled to Los Angeles. After moving to New York, he worked and recorded with Tony Scott in the late '60s; they played bebop and a wide range of ethnic musics. Walcott played sitar on a recording with Miles Davis in 1972. He played with the Paul Winter Consort in the early '70s, then with Oregon and Codona in the mid-'70s and the '80s. Walcott was killed in an accident in what was then East Germany while on tour with Oregon. He recorded as a leader for ECM. Walcott has a compilation, *Works*, available, and also can be heard on various discs by Oregon and Codona. —*Ron Wynn and David Nelson McCarthy*

○ **Cloud Dance** / Mar. 1975 / ECM 825469
Collin Walcott's effective *Cloud Dance* produces a series of life-giving musical showers. Taking the form of intimate conversations among musical friends, these protean exploratory dialogs radiate warmth, trust, and adventure. As a trio, Walcott's sitar and John Abercrombie's guitar mingle above Dave Holland's bass in an open terrain of infinite dimensions. In "Night Glider," for example, shafts of moonlight extend outward to provide a mystically shrouded roadway for Walcott's phantasmagoric lunar voyage. "Padma" is a lyric melding of sitar and guitar while "Scimitar" pits Abercrombie's flesh-rending slashes against Walcott's tense tabla textures. Bass and tabla are energetic partners in "Prancing," whereas "Easter Song" presents the fugal interwinings of Holland's bass and Walcott's sitar. —*Chuck Berg, Down Beat*

★ **Works** / 1975-1984 / ECM 837276

☆ **Grazing Dreams** / Feb. 1977 / ECM 827866
With Don Cherry and John Abercrombie. His glory. Group music based around Walcott's sitar and tabla work. —*Michael G. Nastos*

Codona—Vol. 1 / i. Sep. 1980 / ECM 829371

Codona—Vol. 2 / i. May 1980 / ECM 833332
With Don Cherry and Nana Vasconcelos. Excellent playing, varying quality of material. —*Ron Wynn*

Codona—Vol. 3 / i. Sep. 1982 / ECM 827420

MAL WALDRON (Malcolm Earl Waldron)

b. Aug. 16, 1926, New York, NY
Piano, composer / Hard bop
Mal Waldron's piano playing has a pinched, angular sound. He's one of the artists who was not simply influenced by Thelonious Monk's unorthodox style, but was able to incorporate it into his own work in an individualized way. Waldron isn't quite as idiosyncratic and scattershot as Monk, but utilizes the identical sparse approach, and unusual voicings and rhythms. He's written compositions for large and small groups, has backed vocalists, and has done film and ballet scores. Originally, Waldron only played jazz on alto sax, and preferred to play classical on piano, but switched while at Queens College. Waldron earned his degree in composition, then worked with various New York bands. He made his recording debut in the late '40s with Ike Quebec. Waldron played with Della Reese, then joined Charles Mingus in 1954, and played at the Newport Jazz Festival in 1955 and 1956. He then formed his own group with Gigi Gryce and Idrees Sulieman. Waldron functioned as quasi-house pianist for Prestige in the late '50s. He was Billie Holiday's accompanist from 1957 until her death in 1959,

then worked with Abbey Lincoln and did studio dates. Waldron was part of the remarkable Eric Dolphy quintet with Booker Little that played at the Five Spot in 1961. He also did a studio session with Dolphy. Waldron composed the film scores "The Cool World" in 1963, "Three Bedrooms in Manhattan," and "Sweet Love Bitter" in 1965. But he had to relearn the piano after suffering a nervous breakdown in the mid-'60s. Waldron learned to play again partly by listening to his own recordings. He moved to Europe in 1965 to do more film work, and settled in Munich in 1967. A trio album Waldron recorded was one of the first issued on the then new ECM label. He recorded and worked frequently with Steve Lacy and Archie Shepp in the '70s, toured Japan, and began making return visits to America in 1975. Waldron was featured on numerous Enja releases in the '70s with trios, with quartets, and solo. He continued recording in the '80s on Enja, Palo Alto, Muse, Projazz, Hat Art, and Soul Note. Waldron has a full slate of past and present sessions available on CD. —*Ron Wynn*

★ **Mal—Vols. 1 and 2** / Nov. 9, 1956-Apr. 19, 1957 / Prestige 611

On these early dates, the first under pianist Mal Waldron's leadership, he had not developed the strength that characterized his later work on Prestige—both as a sideman with Eric Dolphy and Steve Lacy and as a trio leader on his *Impressions*. His best contributions to this reissue are the haunting, stark arrangements of "Don't Explain" and "Yesterdays." The first date in particular is generally rather dull with only trumpeter Idrees Sulieman coming up with anything of interest to say. Things get better on the second half with an improvement in the piano solos as well as an overall high standard of horn soloing. The best solos are those of Sahib Shihab (on alto rather than baritone, fortunately), while John Coltrane sounds rather stiff in this setting on tenor. Not bad music by any means, but not remarkable either—suitable for hard bop combers. —*Martin Davidson, Down Beat*

○ **Wheelin' / i.** Apr. 1957+Sep. 1957 / Prestige 24069

Impressions / Mar. 20, 1959 / New Jazz 132

Set Me Free / Oct. 1969 / Affinity 116

Free at Last / Nov. 24, 1969 / ECM 831332

Black Glory / Jun. 29, 1971 / Enja 2004
One among many superb trio dates. Waldron's playing is alternately expressive, bluesy, and exacting. —*Ron Wynn*

Blues for Lady Day / Feb. 5, 1972 / Black Lion 30142

○ **Up Popped the Devil** / Dec. 28, 1973 / Enja 2034
Pianist Mal Waldron's music is characterized by a heavily brooding rhythmic quality, with the left hand usually carrying the theme at one repetitious tempo while the right hammers away in juxtaposition with a countertempo (usually faster). Such is the case with "Up Popped the Devil," "Snake Out," and "Changachangachang," three very Waldronian pieces in both structure and execution, the latter deriving its melody from the whole-tone scale. Aside from Waldron, the record's strongest points are bassist Reggie Workman and drummer Billy Higgins, their work being sensitive and supportive throughout. —*Bob Rusch, Down Beat*

★ **Hard Talk** / May 4, 1974 / Enja 2050
Mal Waldron, the pianist who accompanied Lady Day (Billie Holiday) during her last years and worked with Charles Mingus and others during his lengthy stay in Europe, comes to grips with free jazz. He doesn't try to emulate players like Cecil Taylor but, rather, fuses his somewhat stiff but recognizable and immensely enjoyable style with players of the modern school. Soprano saxophonist Steve Lacy and trumpeter Manfred Schoof make up the front line on *Hard Talk* with able support coming from drummer Allen Blairman and bassist Isla Eckinger. The two cooking tunes, the title cut and "Snake Out," provide the most excitement. From the traditional side, all the tunes feature a head-solo-head format; but, in adhering to the free school, the solos are wide open, with room allowed for pure sound exploration, irregular

pulse, etc. The rhythm section is liquid enough to keep things cooking in a traditional sense, while not becoming overbearing for the soloist. Most amusing is what the group does when Lacy solos. When he solos, the rhythm section starts to break down and get free to support him. Lacy, no young pup to the potentials and traps of "freedom," does a turnaround and plays some of the most melodic lines he has recorded in years. It's only when the band starts to cook again in 4/4 that he steps outside to the farthest perimeter, illustrating he is the most powerful and individualistic player in free jazz. —*Milo Fine*, Cadence

Moods / May 6+8, 1978 / Enja 23
1990 reissue of a solid set. Wonderful sextet with Steve Lacy (sax) and Cameron Brown (b). —*Ron Wynn*

Call, The / i. 1979 / ECM

Herbe de L'oubli / Aug. 13-15, 1981 / Hat Art 2015

What It Is / Nov. 15, 1981 / Enja 4010

You and the Night and the Music / Dec. 9, 1983 / Projazz 617

Encounters / Mar. 18, 1984 / Muse 5305
Though not with enough jazz edge, first-rate duets with David Friesen. —*Ron Wynn*

Live at the Village Vanguard / Sep. 16, 1986 / Soul Note 1118
This is a high-caliber quartet set, with Woody Shaw (tpt). Triumphant. —*Ron Wynn*

Our Colline's a Treasure / Apr. 1987 / Soul Note 1198

○ **Crowd Scene / i.** 1989 / Soul Note 121218
Mal Waldron can sound miraculous in the right environment, but he is just a little off this time around. One of Waldron's customary devices in group sessions is to write a fairly simple line and let his musicians improvise on it for a long time. This particular group (Waldron, piano; Sonny Fortune, alto sax; Ricky Ford, tenor sax; Reggie Workman, bass; Eddie Moore, drums) works on "Crowd Scene" and "Yin and Yang" for over 20 minutes each. "Scene" is a bustling minor vamp that sounds like the music for the chase scenes in a TV police show. "Yin and Yang" is an interesting multipart piece with touches of the Orient, Latin music, and an uptempo section with a definite whiff of *Milestones* to it. The rhythm section, Waldron, Reggie Workman, and the late Eddie Moore, is consistently brilliant on both charts, but Ricky Ford and Sonny Fortune, though both excellent players, sound uncomfortable. Their solos start well but become repetitive and climax in high-pitched squeaks that seem to be there because there was nothing else to do at the time. They do not match any of the magic that Steve Lacy and Enrico Rava or Charlie Rouse and Woody Shaw created in earlier Waldron quintets. There are moments of glory. Waldron helps himself out with an insistent blues solo on "Scene" and Workman plays with outstanding virtuosity in his solos. A trio session might have been magical. —*Jerome Wilson*, Cadence

FATS WALLER (Thomas Wright Waller)

b. May 21, 1904, New York, NY, **d.** Dec. 15, 1943, Kansas City, MO

Piano, organ, vocals, bandleader, composer / Stride, boogie-woogie

Thomas Wright "Fats" Waller belongs in a select circle of performers who are virtuosos with their technical gifts and with their show business skills. Waller's love for sheer entertainment didn't dilute his musical brilliance, but has led some to downgrade his impact and importance inaccurately. His piano work, particularly in the late '20s and early '30s, was intricately constructed and beautifully crafted; he had a wide dynamic range and created rich, imaginative voicings and chord structures. His stride rhythms were emphatic and full, while he was jazz's first great organist, and one of the first to include the celeste in his arsenal and play it in conjunction with the piano. His vocals were underrated; he tastefully employed vibrato, and his insertion of comedic chants and clever quips and dialogues were witty, but seldom overdone.

Waller's skill as a melodic creator was unmatched, and he collaborated with lyricist partner Andy Razaf on dozens of classics, among them "Ain't Misbehavin'," "Honeysuckle Rose," and "Black and Blue." He was the first pianist to swing in the light, graceful fashion that's now associated with modern jazz. Waller influenced pianists such as Count Basie, Art Tatum, and Dave Brubeck. He made hundreds of records, had his own radio programs, and appeared in three films, plus a handful of shorts. His father was a Baptist preacher who conducted open air religious services in Harlem at which the young Waller played reed organ. He played piano at school and, by age 15, was house organist at Lincoln Theatre. After his mother died in 1920, Waller moved in with pianist Russell Brooks's family, dashing his father's hopes that Waller would become a religious organist. Brooks introduced Waller to James P. Johnson, who became a tutor and mentor.

Waller began making piano rolls in 1922, and made his recording debut as a soloist for the Okeh label, cutting "Muscle Shoals Blues" and "Birmingham Blues." Waller has claimed he studied piano with Leopold Godowsky and composition with Carl Bohm at the Juilliard School during this early period; this has not been fully verified. During the early '20s, Waller recorded with blues vocalists such as Sara Martin, Alberta Hunter, and Maude Mills. He collaborated with Clarence Williams in 1923, an effort that led to his song, "Wild Cat Blues," being published and recorded by Williams's Blue Five with Sidney Bechet. This song, and the composition "Squeeze Me" issued that same year, helped make Waller's initial reputation as a songwriter. He made his radio debut in 1923 on a local Newark station, then began regular appearances on WHN in New York, while still playing organ regularly at both the Lincoln and Lafayette theaters. He began recording with the Victor company in 1926, cutting the organ solos "St. Louis Blues" and "Lenox Avenue Blues;" he did most of his sessions for the label for the rest of his career. Waller recorded his song "Whiteman Stomp" with Fletcher Henderson's orchestra in 1927; Henderson added other Waller songs like "Crazy 'Bout My Baby" and "Stealin' Apples" to the band's book. While working with other groups like Morris's Hot Babes, McKinney's Cotton Pickers, and his own Fats Waller's Buddies (one of the earliest interracial groups to record), Waller turned heads with a string of marvelous solo recordings in 1929; these included "Handful of Keys," "Smashing Thirds," "Numb Fumblin'" and "Valentine Stomp."

But he attained equal fame for his collaborations with lyricists. He and Razaf did much of the music for the 1928 Black Broadway musical *Keep Shufflin',* and a year later did songs for the shows *Load of Coal* and *Hot Chocolates,* which marked the debut of "Ain't Misbehavin'." Waller made his own Carnegie Hall in 1928, when he served as piano soloist in Johnson's *Yamekraw,* a fantasy for piano and orchestra. In the '30s, Waller did sessions with Ted Lewis, Jack Teagarden, and Billy Banks Rhythmakers, before starting a lengthy recording series with the six-piece group Fats Waller and his Rhythm. Participants included Al Casey, Gene Sedric or Rudy Powell, and either Herman Autrey, Bill Coleman, or John Hamilton. Waller appeared in the films *Hooray for Love!* and *King of Burlesque* in 1935, while on the West Coast with Les Hite's band. Waller soon formed his own big band, and recorded with a unit that mixed some members of the Rhythm with additional personnel. Waller toured Europe in 1938 and 1939, and cut solo pipe organ tracks for HMV. He recorded "London Suite," an extended series of six related solo piano pieces, during his '39 London visit. This was his longest single composition.

Waller returned to Hollywood in 1943, and made the film *Stormy Weather* with Lena Horne and Bill Robinson. He led an all-star unit for the movie that included Benny Carter and Zutty Singleton. Waller also toured extensively that year, and collaborated with lyricist George Marion, Jr. on the score for

the theatrical production *Early to Bed* that had its Boston opening on May 24, 1943. A lifetime of overeating and alcohol abuse, plus financial pressures from many years of legal controversy over alimony payments, took its toll. Waller became ill during another visit to the West Coast where he was solo pianist at the Zanzibar room in Hollywood. He died of pneumonia while returning to New York with his manager, Ed Kirkeby. A volume of articles, plus several books, have been written about Waller; there are many valuable reissues of his work available, while "Ain't Misbehavin'" has become an oft-recorded classic, cut by everyone from Nell Carter to Hank Williams, Jr. —*Ron Wynn and Dan Morgenstern*

○ **Fats Plays, Sings, Alone and with Various Groups** / **i.** Oct. 21, 1922-Jul. 26, 1932 / CBS 63366
This out-of-print LP contains many of Fats Waller's most enjoyable pre-Rhythm recordings. In addition to his first two piano solos, Waller sings and plays delightful solo versions of "I'm Crazy About My Baby" and "Draggin' My Heart Around" and jams with the Little Chocolate Dandies, Red McKenzie's Mound City Blue Blowers, the Rhythmakers, Jack Teagarden, and even Ted Lewis! This is a strong LP of Waller rarities, many of which do not get reissued very often. —*Scott Yanow*

★ **Giants of Jazz** / **i.** Oct. 21, 1922-Jan. 23, 1943 / Time Life 15
Although now difficult to find, this three-LP boxed set gives listeners a perfect summation of Fats Waller's career and hits most of the high points. Starting with his very first piano solo and progressing to "Ain't Misbehavin'" from the 1943 sound track of *Stormy Weather,* this well-conceived package covers most of the talents of the multifaceted Fats Waller. There are classic piano and organ solos, a guest appearance with Fletcher Henderson's orchestra ("Henderson Stomp"), a chance to be Alberta Hunter's accompaniment on "Beale Street Blues," jams with Fats's Buddies in the 1920s and his Rhythm in the '30s, some jiving around with Jack Teagarden, examples of Waller's occasional big band, and guest appearances with Eddie Condon and an all-star group with Bunny Berigan and Tommy Dorsey. Waller excels in every setting. While some of the complete reissues of Fats Waller's 1930s recordings can be a bit repetitious, this sampler has virtually no slow moments. It needs to be reissued on CD! —*Scott Yanow*

Fats Waller in London / **i.** Oct. 21, 1922-Jun. 13, 1939 / Disques Swing 8442
Other than Fats Waller's first two recorded piano solos (from 1922), this double LP concentrates on the recordings that he made while in London during 1938-39. Doubling on piano and organ, Waller romps and sings with a fine English octet, takes six comparatively somber organ solos (featuring Black spirituals), and backs singer Adelaide Hall on a delightful version of "I Can't Give You Anything But Love." In addition, Waller (backed by drummer Max Lewin) performs one of his few long works, the six-part "London Suite." Excellent music with plenty of variety on this fine twofer. —*Scott Yanow*

Rare Piano Roll Solos—Vol. 1 / **i.** 1923-1924 / Biograph 1002

Rare Piano Roll Solos—Vol. 2 / **i.** 1924-1931 / Biograph 1005

★ **Turn on the Heat: The Fats Waller Piano Solos** / Feb. 16, 1927-May 13, 1941 / Bluebird 2482
With the exception of a third take of "I've Got a Feeling I'm Falling" and his two earliest records from 1922, all of Fats Waller's recorded piano solos are on this superior double-CD set. Over half of these recordings are from 1929 but fortunately Fats also cut three sessions of piano solos after he became much more famous as a comedy personality with his Rhythm sides. Highlights include the virtuosic "Handful of Keys," the earliest version of "Ain't Misbehavin'," "Clothes Line Ballet," "I Ain't Got Nobody," and "Honeysuckle Rose." A special bonus is a pair of piano duets with Bennie Payne ("St. Louis Blues" and "After You've Gone"). Classic music. —*Scott Yanow*

○ **Fats Waller—1927-1929** / **i.** May 20, 1927-Dec. 18, 1929 / Swaggie 850

This Swaggie CD has many of Fats Waller's hotter band sides from the 1920s. Waller is heard playing piano and pipe organ with cornetist Thomas Morris's Hot Babies (making the other musicians sound old-fashioned in comparison). There are a couple of his solo pipe organ recordings from 1927, and Fats takes his first recorded vocal, scatting on "Red Hot Dan." The second side of this LP has the classic Fats Waller and His Buddies recordings of 1929; best are "The Minor Drag" and "Harlem Fuss." Classic early jazz (much of which has since been reissued on CD) from the masterful stride pianist before he became famous. *—Scott Yanow*

★ **Fats Waller and His Buddies** / May 20, 1927-Dec. 18, 1929 / Bluebird 61005

This CD has most of Fats Waller's best band recordings of the 1920s including eight selections by his "Buddies" (highlighted by "The Minor Drag" and "Harlem Fuss"), six (counting two alternate takes) from the Louisiana Sugar Babes (an odd quartet featuring Fats's organ and James P. Johnson's piano), and seven selections on which Waller sits in with cornetist Thomas Morris's Hot Babies in 1927. Surprisingly, other than his scat vocal on "Red Hot Dan," Fats Waller is heard strictly as a pianist, but his talents are so giant as an instrumentalist that one never minds. With trombonists Charlie Irvis and Jack Teagarden and trumpeters Red Allen and Jabbo Smith among the strong supporting cast, the one word for this superior CD is hot! *—Scott Yanow*

○ **Here 'Tis** / **i.** Oct. 14, 1929-Dec. 1943 / Jazz Archives 7

This long-out-of-print LP is a real collector's item, featuring seven rare alternate takes and a few real Fats Waller oddities. Among the latter is an excerpt from the legendary production "Hot Chocolate" in 1929; Waller backs some of the dialog. In addition, this LP has Fats's final recordings, a broadcast from Los Angeles in December 1943 with the pianist-singer performing "Your Feet's Too Big" and "Handful of Keys" one last time just a short while before his premature death. This LP is well worth acquiring but will take a long search! *—Scott Yanow*

★ **Complete Fats Waller—Vol. 1** / **i.** May 16, 1934-Mar. 6, 1935 / RCA 5511

This double LP was the first in a planned series of reissues that would document all of Fats Waller's popular Rhythm recordings. Lack of corporate interest and the rise of CDs led to this particular series stopping after the fourth volume but these are all worth acquiring. Starting in 1934, Fats Waller, then best known as a pianist and a composer, began recording with a two-horn sextet called his "Rhythm." Fats from the start of this series emerges as a superior jazz vocalist and an often-hilarious personality, generally satirizing the lyrics of the inferior material his band was often given to record. One can fully understand his great popularity from hearing the recordings on this initial volume, particularly such tunes as "A Porter's Love Song to a Chambermaid," "How Can You Face Me," "You're Not the Only Oyster in the Stew," and "Honeysuckle Rose." Recommended. *—Scott Yanow*

○ **Complete Fats Waller—Vol. 2 (1935)** / Mar. 6, 1935-Aug. 20, 1935 / RCA 5575

Although this double-LP series was originally planned to reissue all of Fats Waller's Rhythm recordings, it only made it to the fourth volume. Vol. 2 has 32 exciting examples of his band's music, featuring solos from trumpeter Herman Autrey, Rudy Powell's clarinet and alto, and the leader's powerful stride piano. However, it is Waller's humorous and often-satirical vocals that really sell these hot recordings. Among the classics on this set are "What's the Reason I'm Not Pleasin' You," "Oh Suzanna Dust Off That Old Pianna," "You've Been Taking Lessons in Love from Somebody New," "My Very Good Friend the Milkman," and the touching (and relatively straightforward) hit version of "I'm Gonna Sit Right Down and Write Myself a Letter." *—Scott Yanow*

○ **Definitive Fats Waller—Vol. 1: His Piano His Rhythm, The** / Mar. 11, 1935-Aug. 7, 1939 / Stash 528

In addition to his many studio recordings for Victor, the popular pianist/singer/composer Fats Waller recorded two extensive sessions of radio transcriptions which could be used to fill in time between radio shows. These have now been reissued in full on two CDs. The first volume finds Waller performing seven songs in 1935 (two duets with the reeds of Rudy Powell and five solos with some vocals) in addition to 23 performances from 1939 (17 with his Rhythm, an excerpt from an organ solo, and five unaccompanied piano solos). Throughout, Fats Waller, who never really needed an audience, is in exuberant form, playing material that is generally superior to the dog tunes he was often handed at recording sessions. A fun set. *—Scott Yanow*

○ **Definitive Fats Waller—Vol. 2: Hallelujah, The** / **i.** Mar. 11, 1935-Apr. 3, 1939 / Stash 539

This second volume of rare Fats Waller items includes 24 selections performed at a marathon radio transcription session in 1935 (there were actually 31 pieces played, seven of which are on Volume 1!). Waller is heard solo, singing and playing piano without the assistance of his sidemen, and he is in top form on a wide variety of material. This CD concludes with previously unreleased items from three different occasions: a 1936 solo broadcast from Bluefield, West Virginia; two selections privately recorded in London in 1939; and Waller's appearance on the George Jessel Show during the same year. A superior release from the great stride pianist, vocalist, composer, and personality. *—Scott Yanow*

○ **Complete Fats Waller—Vol. 3 (1935-1936)** / Aug. 20, 1935-Jun. 5, 1936 / RCA 5583

Although this "complete" reissue of Fats Waller's Rhythm sides was never finished (it only made it to four volumes), each of the four twofers that did get released are perfectly done. The third volume features many fine solos by trumpeter Herman Autrey and Gene Sedric on tenor and clarinet, has three examples of Fats Waller's exciting big band (which on "I Got Rhythm" finds Waller "battling" fellow pianist Henry Duncan), and contains quite a few memorable recordings including "Got a Bran' New Suit," "I've Got My Fingers Crossed," and "All My Life." Throughout even the weakest selection, Fats Waller's powerful stride piano and verbal interjections really drive the ensembles. *—Scott Yanow*

○ **Complete Fats Waller—Vol. 4** / **i.** Jun. 5-Nov. 29, 1936 / Bluebird 5905

The fourth and unfortunately final twofer from this "complete" series of Fats Waller Rhythm recordings brings the program up to near the end of 1936. With a sextet that also features solos from trumpeter Herman Autrey, Gene Sedric on clarinet and tenor, and guitarist Al Casey, Fats Waller romps through most of these 28 performances. Highlights include "Black Raspberry Jam," "I'm Crazy 'Bout My Baby," "The Curse of an Aching Heart," the somewhat hilarious "Floatin' Down to Cotton Town," and two versions of "Swingin' Them Jingle Bells." All four volumes of this series are highly recommended, at least until the music eventually resurfaces on CD. *—Scott Yanow*

○ **Fats Waller and His Rhythm: The Middle Years, Pt. 1 (1936-1938)** / **i.** Dec. 24, 1936-Apr. 12, 1938 / Bluebird 66083

Since virtually all other Fats Waller and his Rhythm reissue programs have started out with his first Victor recordings from 1934 and then have petered out before reaching the end of the huge quantity, the new Bluebird Bluebird series starts with Waller's final studio recordings and works its way backwards! This particular three-CD set (which follows *The Last Years*) picks up around where Vol. 4 of the *Complete* LP series ended and includes no less than 70 recordings from Fats Waller's "Middle Years." With spirited solos from trumpeter Herman Autrey, Gene Sedric (on clarinet and tenor), and acoustic guitarist Al Casey, not to mention the leader's powerful stride piano, Waller's Rhythm was one of the hottest sextets in jazz. Fats's satirical vocals could be a bit tiring if this entire set were heard in one sitting (some of this material could not be saved even by Waller) but, taken an hour or less at a time, these recordings are highly enjoyable. There are more highpoints than one can name but just to mention a few: "I'm Sorry I Made You Cry," "Nero," an instrumental version of "Honeysuckle Rose" (even if drummer Slick Jones proves that he could not play vibes!), "The Joint Is Jumpin'," and a rare Waller big-band session. Highly recommended. — *Scott Yanow*

○ **Jugglin' Jive of Fats Waller and his Orchestra** / **i**. Jul. 16-Oct. 18, 1938 / Sandy Hook 2097
This very enjoyable CD contains three radio broadcasts featuring Fats Waller and his Rhythm in 1938. Despite some dated chatter (and not so subtle racism) from a radio announcer, the music on these live performances is quite spirited with Waller singing and playing heated stride piano with his sextet. While trumpeter Herman Autrey and Gene Sedric's reeds are major assets, Fats is virtually the whole show, really driving his sidemen and stimulating both a memorable party atmosphere and creative swinging jazz. — *Scott Yanow*

Fine Arabian Stuff / **i**. Nov. 20, 1939 / Muse 601
The music on this LP was all recorded in one day and finds an unaccompanied Fats Waller dealing with a variety of folk songs and spirituals, much of it out of character with the stereotype of Fats as a happy-go-lucky partying extrovert. Waller plays piano on the first six numbers while performing in a much more somber mood on organ for the last seven songs. Not essential music but Fats Waller collectors will want this unusual set. — *Scott Yanow*

African Ripples / RCA 562

GEORGE WALLINGTON (Giacinto Figlia)

b. Oct. 27, 1924, Palermo, Sicily, Italy, **d**. Feb. 15, 1993
Piano, composer / Bop
For sheer speed and harmonic dexterity, there haven't been many bebop pianists who've played better than George Wallington. Other musicians might have been superior in terms of melodic interpretation or rhythmic intensity, but Wallington's blazing single-note lines, precisely and cleanly played, rivaled Bud Powell's, though the two men didn't meet until after Wallington joined Dizzy Gillespie in the mid-'40s. Wallington's family came to America from Sicily, Italy, in 1925. He played in New York during the early '40s, and worked with Charlie Parker, Max Roach, Gillespie, Don Byas, and Oscar Pettiford. Wallington was a member of the first bop band on 52nd Street in 1943 and 1944. He played swing with Joe Marsala, then worked in bebop bands led by Parker, Serge Chaloff, Alan Eager, Kai Winding, Terry Giggs, Brew Moore, Al Cohn, Gerry Mulligan, Zoot Sims, and Red Rodney from 1946 until 1952. In his only big band dates, Wallington toured Europe with Lionel Hampton in 1953. He led groups in New York from 1954 to 1960, playing with Donald Byrd and Phil Woods. Then Wallington left the music world and joined his family's air conditioning business. He returned to music in the '80s, and recorded a solo date in 1984 for Interface. He recorded the interesting *The Pleasure of a Jazz Inspiration* in 1985. Wallington recorded for Verve, Prestige, Savoy, Norgran, Atlantic, and Interface. VSOP reissued the *Jazz Inspiration* session on CD in 1992. There are other Wallington dates on CD. — *Ron Wynn and Michael G. Nastos*

George Wallington Trios / **i**. 1952-1953 / Prestige 1754
Charles Mingus (b) and Oscar Pettiford (b) soar in these 1952 and 1953 trio dates. Wallington plays well, though not in either's class as a soloist. — *Ron Wynn*

★ **Jazz for the Carriage Trade** / Jan. 20, 1956 / Prestige 1704
This is a 1/20/56 date with Donald Byrd (tpt), Phil Woods (as), Teddy Kotick (b), and Art Taylor (d) that has also been reissued as part of a twofer. The session has a lasting hard bop edge and closely parallels what the Messengers were sounding like at the time. An exemplary sample of New

York style bop, the program is a mixture of standards and originals (by Foster and Woods). The leader pianist George Wallington, a Bud Powell devotee, has his share of solo space (I think of him more often as a composer and catalyst) but solo honors go to the hornmen, with Woods particularly brilliant and daring on his own "Together We Wait." — *Bob Rusch,* Cadence

○ **Dance of the Infidels** / Nov. 14, 1957 / Savoy 1122
Pianist George Wallington had his critics, but I jump to everything he did; his groups (on this session trumpeter Donald Byrd, alto saxophonist Phil Woods, bassist Knobby Totah, drummer Nick Stabulas) produced some of Phil Woods's greatest playing. — *Jerry L. Atkins,* Cadence

The Pleasure of a Jazz Inspiration / **i**. 1985 / V.S.O.P. #84
George Wallington was one of the original young bop lions, a pianist whose speed and phrasing set him apart from all but a handful of players. This 1985 solo set, done when he was 68 years old, might surprise those unaware of Wallington's prowess. He rips through the blues, shifts back to delicate voicings, then opens up and leaps over octaves, spins out lines, then connects everything effectively, turning the piano into a communicative device telling a marvelous harmonic and rhythmic story. — *Ron Wynn*

JACK WALRATH (Jack Arthur Walrath)

b. May 5, 1946, Stuart, FL
Trumpet / Postbop, progressive big band, neo-bop
An often exciting, thoughtful trumpeter and a good arranger, Jack Walrath has gained attention and exposure steadily through his contributions to outstanding sessions. Walrath began playing trumpet at age nine, and studied at Berklee in the mid- and late '60s while working with other students and backing up R&B vocalists. He moved to the West Coast in 1969, and co-led the bands Change with Gary Peacock and Revival with Glenn Ferris. Walrath also toured with Ray Charles for a year. Walrath relocated to New York in the mid-'70s, and worked with Latin bands while playing with Charles Mingus from 1974 to 1978. Walrath contributed some arrangements and orchestrations to Mingus's final recordings. In the '80s and '90s, he's led his own bands, and has toured Europe with Dannie Richmond and the British band Spirit Level. Walrath's most recent group, the Masters of Suspense, includes Carter Jefferson, Mike Cochrane, Anthony Cox, and Ronnie Burrage. He's recorded as a leader for Gatemouth, Stash, Blue Note, and Muse. Walrath has sessions available on CD. — *Ron Wynn*

○ **Demons in Pursuit** / Aug. 21-22, 1979 / Gatemouth 1002
As far as I can gather, this is trumpeter Jack Walrath's debut album as a leader, and a pretty good one indeed. The music in general lies within the stylistic area explored by Freddie Hubbard (tpt) and Wayne Shorter (ts) in their mid-'60s Blue Note recordings, but it manages to achieve a character quite its own. The main credit for this must go to Walrath's compositions (all the tunes on the album are his originals), his writing being very imaginative, both melodically and in construction, without ever sounding deliberately "fancy." Also, the combination of Walrath with John Scofield's guitar makes for a nice, unusual ensemble sound. There is a lot of high-quality soloing to be heard, with Scofield maybe taking top honors; he shows us how a rock background can positively influence a jazz guitar-playing style. The weak spots of the album for me are the two tracks with organ ("Ray Charles on Mars" and "Demons in Pursuit"). Here, the stylistical unity of the rest of the album seems to be broken, and the results aren't too successful either. On "Mars," both piano and organ (via overdub) are comping at the same time, which gives a very cluttered and almost corny rhythm section sound. Also, the organ registration could have been better, the sound here being all too close to a "cheap" combo organ sound. And again Ray Drummond has this strangely "electrical" acoustic bass sound. These are minor objections, however, to an album that as a whole provides a very stimulating listening experience. — *Per Husby,* Cadence

Plea for Sanity, A / **i**. Sep. 1982 / Stash 223
Drummerless trio with pianist Michael Cochran and bassist Anthony Cox. All originals. A delight. —*Michael G. Nastos*

○ **Master of Suspense** / **i**. 1987 / Blue Note 46905
Septet cuts with exceptional playing by Walrath, Steve Torre (tb), and James Williams (p). —*Ron Wynn*

★ **Neohippus** / **i**. Aug. 19+21, 1988 / Blue Note 91101
John Abercrombie slashes away on guitar. Rick Margitza (reeds), saxophonist for Miles Davis at the time, is an effective soloist. CD has two bonus cuts. —*Ron Wynn*

CEDAR WALTON (Cedar Anthony (Jr) Walton)

b. Jan. 17, 1934, Dallas, TX
Piano / Postbop

A classy, sophisticated, but also expressive and skilled hard bop pianist, Cedar Walton has proved to be the ideal accompanist for numerous combos. He's never been a star, but has provided tasteful, challenging backing and concise, impressive solos in many situations. Walton learned piano from his mother, and later studied music at the University of Denver in the early '50s. He went to New York in 1955, but was drafted by the army. He played with Leo Wright, Don Ellis, and Eddie Harris while stationed in Germany. Walton recorded with Kenny Dorham after returning to New York, then played in J.J. Johnson's group from 1958 to 1960. He took McCoy Tyner's place in the Jazztet from 1960 to 1961, and continued recording with Art Farmer in 1965. Walton played in Art Blakey's Jazz Messengers during a peak period, 1961 to 1964. He replaced Bobby Timmons, and was in the group with Wayne Shorter and Freddie Hubbard. He was Abbey Lincoln's accompanist in 1965 and 1966, recorded with Lee Morgan in 1966, '67, and '68, then was Prestige's house pianist from 1967 to 1969. Walton played in a group with Hank Mobley in the early '70s, then rejoined Blakey in the mid-'70s for a tour of Japan. He began a quartet that continued evolving and recording through the '70s and into the '80s. Walton first played with Clifford Jordan, and has since co-led this band with George Coleman, Bob Berg, and fellow rhythm section mates Sam Jones and Billy Higgins. The group took the name Eastern Rebellion in 1975. Walton had a brief fling with fusion and jazz-rock in the early '70s, heading a group called Soundscapes that featured electric instrumentation, funk, fusion, and rock rhythms and compositions. He also did some dates for RCA under the label of Mobius. Walton toured Europe, Japan, and the United States in the late '70s in a trio with Higgins. Since the '80s, Walton has been a member of the Timeless All-Stars. He's played with Johnson's new quintet since 1987. Walton's also done many duo performances and sessions with various bassists. Walton's recorded in the '60s, '70s, '80s, and '90s for Blue Note, Prestige, Muse, Timeless, Steeplechase, CBS, Clean Cuts, and Red, among others. Several Walton sessions from the '70s and '80s, plus recent material from the '90s, are available on CD. —*Ron Wynn*

Among Friends / Evidence 22023
Cedar Walton is one of jazz's great accompanists and session pianists, able to adjust to and interact with any bassist and drummer. He constructs and presents glorious melodies and creates delightful solos. But he is even more accomplished in trio situations, where he gets the space to fully develop ideas, demonstrate his facility and offer insightful interpretations. This set includes superb Walton reworkings of Thelonious Monk classics "Ruby My Dear" and "Off Minor" plus his own midtempo gem "Midnight Waltz" and a lushly performed "My Foolish Heart" that includes a nice vibes solo from special guest Bobby Hutcherson. Walton works with a thoroughly experienced rhythm section in bassist Buster Williams and drummer Billy Higgins. Walton's solos on "Midnight Waltz" are carefully crafted with little fanfare or flash, just thoughtful, marvelous playing. That is the tone struck throughout this date: three longtime musical associates demonstrating what polished, yet distinctive, jazz is all about. —*Ron Wynn*

Cedar! / Jul. 10, 1967 / Prestige 462
Excellent 1967 session with Kenny Dorham (tpt) and Junior Cook (ts). Released in 1991. Typically no-frills, emphatic pieces and solos. —*Ron Wynn*

○ **Plays Cedar Walton** / Jul. 10, 1967-Jan. 14, 1969 / Prestige 6002
1967-1969. 1988 reissue of Walton giving his own work a showcase. Host of great players, among them Kenny Dorham (tpt) and Clifford Jordan (ts). CD has bonus cut. —*Ron Wynn*

★ **Breakthrough** / Feb. 22, 1972 / Muse 5132
This is a reissue of an album originally minted in 1972. It was, in fact, a classic all-star session with all personnel playing at or near the peak of their prowess. Tenor saxophonist Hank Mobley particularly sounds better than he had since his brilliant salad days in the 1950s. "Breakthrough" by Mobley features a sax battle between Hank and Charles Davis on baritone in vintage hard bop fashion with pianist Cedar Walton comping up a storm. Comparisons seem irrelevant—Mobley's tone is sharper than Rollins or Stitt, and Davis is a perfect foil in the lower register as they proceed to worry the sketchy tune into exhaustion. Bassist Sam Jones and drummer Billy Higgins are strong on the rhythm as the members take turns strutting their stuff. The blowing is about as far out on the edges of "inside" music as the changes could bear without spilling over into free form—a tour de force. —*Larry Birnbaum*, Down Beat

★ **Night at Boomer's—Vol. 1, A** / Jan. 4, 1973 / Muse 5010
The late tenor saxophonist Clifford Jordan meets the mainstream requirements of this occasion with aplomb and, obviously, pleasure. The way pianist Cedar Walton, bassist Sam Jones, and drummer Louis Hayes empathize on "This Guy's in Love with You" is something approaching a working definition of jazz. Jones provides rhythmic thrust up a hacienda in "Down in Brazil" and "St. Thomas" to the enthusiastic accompaniment of Hayes's cymbals and traps. This is a happy record, full of the good feeling that became all too rare in jazz for awhile there during a general and frantic search for "freedom." —*Doug Ramsey*, Down Beat

★ **Night at Boomer's—Vol. 2, A** / Jan. 4, 1973 / Muse 5022
January 4, 1973, was a doubly fortuitous night at Boomer's, for it produced not one but two excellent recordings. To my ears, Cedar Walton's piano style blends Bud Powell's forceful, percussive touch with Bill Evans's style of linear melodic invention, sprinkled with the slightest bit of current McCoy Tyner. This eclectic mixture produces an entirely transparent style, never obscuring the music itself. Tenor saxophonist Clifford Jordan is equally fascinating. Primarily a lyrical player whose tenor sounds almost like a Paul Desmondesque alto at times, he, like Walton, is mainly a linear improviser. Yet his playing has a subtle sense of form: in a typical solo he starts in his axe's lower register and gradually ascends to its heights, roughening his tone as he goes along and ending with a minor flurry of light cries, an approach with its own kind of organic logic. Three tunes here, "Stella by Starlight," "I'll Remember April," and "Blue Monk," are in the area of 11 minutes each, and because of this extended space (which for once is really *used*), these tracks were my favorites. All tracks, though, are clearly above average, and none of them seem too long. —*Jon Balleras*, Down Beat

☆ **Eastern Rebellion—Vol. 1** / **i**. 1975 / Timeless
Recorded slightly more than a year apart, these quartet dates are welcome additions to the discography of one of the consistently fine jazz composer/performers active over the last several decades. Each set features a different tenor player, George Coleman having just succeeded Clifford Jordan when the first album was recorded in 1975, Bob Berg replacing Coleman for the second, taped early in 1977. Thanks largely to Walton's forceful shaping of the group's music and the longstanding participation of bassist Sam Jones and drummer Billy Higgins, no less than the quite similiar approaches of the saxophonists, the two sets possess a strong cohesiveness of conception and execution that comes as no

surprise to those familiar with Walton's music. These albums maintain his standards of creativity and musicianship within the bebop rubric to which he held steadfast. —*Pete Welding,* Down Beat

○ **Eastern Rebellion—Vol. 2** / **i**. 1975 / Timeless

CARLOS WARD (Carlos Nathaneil Ward)

b. May 1, 1940, Ancon, Panama Canal Zone
Saxophone / Postbop, world fusion, neo-bop, modern creative

A versatile tenor saxophonist and flutist, Carlos Ward's played African music, hard bop, disco, and R&B with fine jazz bands and chart-topping funk groups. He moved from the Panama Canal Zone, where he was born, to Seattle in the '50s, and began playing clarinet. Ward switched to sax in the mid-'50s, and worked in various rock bands. He played in a military band during army service in the early '60s, and was stationed, at one point, in Germany. Ward remained in Europe after his discharge, and worked with Abdullah Ibrahim, Don Cherry, and Karl Berger. He returned to Seattle in 1965, and worked with John Coltrane in concert that fall. He moved to New York, and played with Coltrane again, and with Sunny Murray and Sam Rivers. Ward traveled to the West Coast with Murray in 1967, and settled in San Francisco. He came back to New York in 1969, and recorded with B.T. Express, while also playing with Murray at the Newport Jazz Festival, and working with Rashied Ali. He later joined the Jazz Composer's Orchestra Association and worked with a group that included David Izenzon, Berger, Gato Barbieri, and Barry Altschul. Ward played in bands led by Carla Bley, Ibrahim, and Cherry in the '80s. He and Ibraham recorded as a duo for Ekapa in 1983; this recording is unavailable currently on CD. But Ward can be heard on reissues by Ibrahim, Cherry, and B.T. Express, among others. —*Ron Wynn and Michael G. Nastos*

★ **Lito** / Jul. 1988 / Leo 166
Live date at the North Sea Jazz Festival for saxophonist/flutist with quartet featuring trumpeter Woody Shaw. Extended work. Excellent. —*Michael G. Nastos*

DAVID S. WARE (David Spencer Ware)

b. Nov. 7, 1949, Plainfield, NJ
Tenor saxophone / Modern creative

A powerhouse tenor saxophonist, David S. Ware's swirling solos, with their overblowing, energized screams and intensity, make him one of the few current players willing to display ties to the '60s free style. Ware also smartly employs multiphonics and false fingerings. He played baritone, alto, and tenor sax as a teen, and attended Berklee from 1967 to 1969. Ware formed the group, Apogee, in 1970, and played in Boston until they relocated to New York. Ware played in Cecil Taylor's orchestra during his 1974 Carnegie Hall concert. He spent two years with Andrew Cyrille in the mid-'70s, while he also worked in a trio with trumpeter Ralphe Malik and toured Europe with Taylor. Ware and Barry Harris made a duet album in 1977, and Ware and Cyrille rejoined forces, recording in 1978 and 1980. Ware has recorded as a leader in the '80s and '90s. He's done sessions for DIW/Columbia and Silkheart. Ware has a couple of dates available. —*Ron Wynn*

○ **Great Bliss, Vol. 1** / **i**. Jan. 1990 / Silkheart 127
Great Bliss, Vol. 1 is David S. Ware's statement of purpose, a bold, sometimes chaotic, always gripping excursion. The young pianist Matthew Shipp is especially inspiring in his grasp of the free tradition. The tunes are long, the structure expendable, dictated by the spirit of the moment. But lyricism is not lost: "Bliss Theme" has a different sort of gospel luster. "Saxelloscape" is a pensive solo for that obscure member of the sax family. —*Josef Woodard,* Down Beat

★ **Flight of I** / Dec. 1991 / Columbia 52956
Flight of I, recorded a year after David S. Ware's *Great Bliss, Vol. I,* combines fiercely original pieces with two standards. The blend is beguiling. Ware finds a wholly new way to say

"There Will Never Be Another You," checking in with the chord changes and the melodic chassis only peripherally. He plays the head to "Yesterdays" with a fluttering, beehivelike quality. Ware's quavering, Albert Ayleresque vibrato, split tones, and general-action painting approach to the tune, against the rhythm section's rumbling backdrop, are evident on the title cut, as the band lays out a looping, sententious chordal statement. Ware enters the fray with a long-winded, scabrous tone, a wail from the depths. The effect is at once anthemic and cathartic. —*Josef Woodard,* Down Beat

WILBUR WARE (Wilbur Bernard Ware)

b. Sep. 8, 1923, Chicago, IL, **d.** Sep. 9, 1979, Philadelphia, PA
Bass / Bop, hard bop, postbop

An exciting, first-rate bassist, Wilbur Ware was noted for a percussive approach with a heavy tone. He broke up beats and substituted tones and notes in his solos. This could cause confusion and chaos on the bandstand, but Ware always resolved things thematically. He had great touch and tone, but preferred emphasizing the bass's lower end. A self-taught banjo player, Ware's father made him a bass. He worked in Chicago string bands, then played with groups led by Stuff Smith, Roy Eldridge, and Sonny Stitt in the late '40s. Ware led his own groups in the '50s, and worked and/or recorded with Eddie "Cleanhead" Vinson, Art Blakey, Buddy DeFranco, Johnny Griffin, Thelonious Monk, and J.R. Monterose. Ware played at the Five Spot with Monk and John Coltrane in 1957, and in Sonny Rollins's trio at the Village Vanguard. He returned to Chicago from New York due to illness. Ware was inactive in the mid-'60s until joining Archie Shepp in 1968. He played with Clifford Jordan, Blue Mitchell, Elvin Jones, and Sonny Rollins in 1969, and with Shepp in 1970. Ware worked with Monk again in 1970, and with Sun Ra in 1973. He has one session currently available on CD. —*Ron Wynn*

★ **Chicago Sound** / Oct.+Nov. 1957 / Riverside 1737
Quintet. Legendary bassist. With Johnny Griffin (ts) and John Jenkins (as). A classic. —*Michael G. Nastos*

TIM WARFIELD

Saxophone / Neo-bop
Tenor saxophonist Tim Warfield, Jr. has begun to make his mark in the '90s. He's demonstrated a swaggering, soulful tone and emphatic style during his solos on the anthology *Tough Young Tenors,* and will no doubt begin to display his talents in a leadership role soon. —*Ron Wynn*

BUTCH WARREN

b. 1939
Bass / Bop, hard bop

A prolific bassist who began his career at age 14, Butch Warren has played in swing, bebop, and hard bop sessions, working with musicians as diverse as Gene Ammons and Thelonious Monk. He's one of the great accompanists, known for his creative use of walking lines and tight, bluesy phrases, as well as his nicely placed accents. Warren played bass in his father's band as a teen, then worked in the Washington, D.C. area with Gene Ammons and Stuff Smith in the late '50s. He moved to New York to play with Kenny Dorham in 1958, and served as house musician at Blue Note in the early '60s. Warren recorded with Jackie McLean, Donald Byrd, Herbie Hancock, Joe Henderson, Sonny Clark, and Dexter Gordon, while he also played in New York clubs. He was Monk's bassist in 1963 and 1964, appearing on various Monk recordings and touring Japan and Europe with him. After Warren returned from touring, he appeared on television in Washington, and backed R&B vocal groups like the Platters. Illness forced a temporary retirement in the late '60s and early '70s, but he returned in the mid-'70s, playing with Howard McGhee and Richie Cole, and continued to play part-time. Warren's bass can be heard on CD reissues of classics such as *Miles and Monk at Newport, It's Monk's Time,* Sonny Clark's *Leapin' and Lopin',* and Herbie Hancock's *Takin' Off.* —*Ron Wynn*

EARLE WARREN (Earl Ronalde Warren)

b. Jul. 1, 1914, Springfield, OH
Alto saxophone / Swing, big band

Earle Warren helped bring some attention to the alto sax through his playing in the Count Basie band of the late '30s and '40s. While seldom a soloist with Basie, Warren played melodic lead on many superb recordings. He later provided some hot solos and swinging statements on albums with Buck Clayton and as the head of the Countsmen. Warren played piano, banjo, and ukulele in a family band, then turned to C-melody and tenor saxophones before finally settling on the alto. He added an E to his name in 1930, and led his own groups that toured the Midwest with various bands before he joined Basie in 1937. He moved from sharing baritone and lead alto duties to being a principal alto player, as well as a vocalist and clarinetist, in 1938. After leaving Basie's band in 1945, Warren reteamed with Basie periodically while leading his own bands. He recorded and toured extensively with Clayton in the late '50s, and toured Europe as a solo act in 1967. Warren performed in the '70s film *Born to Swing*, then formed the Countsmen in 1973. They played regularly at the West End Club throughout the '70s. He moved to Geneva in the early '80s, and played at various international festivals. Warren has recorded for RCA as a soloist, and can be heard on Basie Decca/MCA CD reissues, and on Buck Clayton reissues. *—Ron Wynn*

★ **Count's Men, The** / Jul. 9, 1985 / Muse 5312
As producer Phil Schaap writes in this album's liner notes, the Countsmen first performed at a Spring 1972 concert that he produced at CCNY in New York City. The Countsmen were conceived as and essentially were a Count Basie alumni band that had as its focal point the repertoire of the original Basie band. The Basie book was supplemented on live performances and on this record by some ballads such as "White Christmas" and "Body and Soul." This album is in fact the second by the Countsmen, the first being a release for RCA-England, probably long out of print. The leader of the Countsmen is alto saxophonist Earle Warren, who after replacing Caughey Roberts, was the leader of the Count Basie band's saxophone section and sometimes vocalist with the band. This is a nice set of swinging jazz, though there is nothing spectacular here, just some Basie standards and some ballads performed with feeling and panache. Trombonist Eddie Durham and Warren take much of the spotlight and play capably. Warren is not a great singer, but his sense of timing and phrasing invests his vocals with a certain charm. Pianist Don Coates is consistently tasty and the rhythm section of Tootsie Bean (d) and Jimmy Lewis (b) is solid with the exception of Bean's somewhat overbearing drumming on "The Blues I Like to Hear" (this may be as much a consequence of the recording—I found that this album sounded better when I listened to it through speakers and not headphones). The version of "Jumping at the Woodside" is also somewhat lackluster. High points include a bouncy "Swinging the Blues," the classic stomp "Doggin' Around" with some meaty playing, and a lovely "Sweet Lorraine." There is generous playing time and this record is an enjoyable, if not earthshaking, set of swinging jazz. *—Ronald B. Weinstock, Cadence*

DINAH WASHINGTON (Ruth Lee Jones)

b. Aug. 29, 1924, Tuscaloosa, AL, **d.** Dec. 14, 1963, Detroit, MI
Vocals / Ballads & blues

One of the most versatile and gifted vocalists in American popular music history, Dinah Washington made extraordinary recordings in jazz, blues, R&B, and light pop contexts, and could have done the same in gospel had she chosen to record in that mode. But the former Ruth Jones didn't believe in mixing the secular and the spiritual, and once she'd professionally entered the nonreligious music world she refused to include gospel in her repertoire. Washington's penetrating, high-pitched voice, incredible sense of drama and

timing, crystal clear enunciation, and equal facility with sad, bawdy, celebratory, or rousing material enabled her to sing any and everything with distinction.

Washington played piano and directed her church choir growing up in Chicago. For a while, she did split her time between clubs and singing and playing piano in Salle Martin's gospel choir under the name of Ruth Jones. There's some dispute about the origin of her name. Some sources say the manager of the Garrick Stage Bar gave her the name Dinah Washington; others say it was Hampton who selected it. However, no one disputes that Hampton heard and was impressed by Washington, who'd been discovered by manager Joe Glaser. She worked in Hampton's band from 1943 to 1946. Some of her biggest R&B hits were written by Leonard Feather, the distinguished critic who was a successful composer in the '40s. Washington dominated the R&B charts in the late '40s and '50s, but also did straight jazz sessions for EmArcy and Mercury, with horn accompanists Clifford Brown, Clark Terry, and Maynard Ferguson, and pianists Wynton Kelly, a young Joe Zawinul, and Andrew Hill. She wanted to record what she liked, regardless of whether it was considered suitable, and would be a crossover superstar in today's market.

Songs such as "Harbor Lights," "Unforgettable," and "What a Difference a Day Makes," a hit that stemmed from a rare Washington misreading of a lyric, and duet this she had with Brook Benton demonstrated her abilities as a pop interpreter. Unfortunately, Washington had an obsession with her appearance and frequently took diet pills, as well as sleeping pills. She mixed pills and alcohol one time too many, and, in 1963, died from an accidental overdose exacerbated by alcohol. After her death, Washington received tributes from many vocalists, from Ruth Brown to Aretha Franklin, who recorded a tribute album to her. Her sound lives on in the work of Nancy Wilson and the records of Esther Phillips. Washington's music has been anthologized frequently. Polygram reissued her complete output in a series of multidisc packages that cover specific years. There are also plenty of single-disc anthologies. *—Ron Wynn and Dan Morgenstern*

Slick Chick—R&B Years / i. 1943-1954 / EmArcy 814184

★ **Mellow Mama** / Dec. 1945 / Delmark 451
Recorded in Los Angeles in 1945, shortly after she had left Lionel Hampton's band, Dinah Washington's 12 classic blues performances, which include "Rich Man's Blues," "My Voot is Really Vout," "No Voot No Boot," and "My Lovin' Papa," are now available for the first time in one package. For pure jazz fans, the best news is that the young, salty mama's accompaniment is provided by tenor great Lucky Thompson and a carefully assembled combo of then-L.A. residents, including Milt Jackson and Charles Mingus. *—Jack Sohmer, Down Beat*

★ **Complete Dinah Washington on Mercury—Vols. 1-7, The** / i. 1946-1963 / Mercury 832444
If you buy one, you'll want them all. Important musical documents. *—Michael G. Nastos*

○ **Wise Woman Blues** / i. 1949-1963 / Rosetta 1313
"Miss D was a witch and didn't hesitate to use her witchcraft, shouting unadulterated incantations to cast a magic spell." This compilation contains both blues and jazz tunes, genres which the artist helped bridge, combining the best of both Bessie and Billie, while making the music her own. This volume, part of the *Foremothers* series, includes some great tunes. In addition to the title track: "Mellow Mama Blues," "My Voot Is Really Vout," "Shoo Shoo Baby" (play this one at your next jitterbug party). Most songs recorded 1943-45; one in 1963. *—Ladyslipper*

○ **Dinah Jams** / Aug. 1954 / EmArcy 814639

★ **Jazz Sides** / i. 1954-1958 / EmArcy 824883
1954-1958. Great two-record set that accents her mid-'50s jazz cuts. Until recently, that was about all the jazz of Dinah's that was in print. *—Ron Wynn*

In the Land of Hi-Fi / Apr. 1956 / EmArcy 826453

Swingin' Miss D, The / i. 1956 / EmArcy 36104

Fats Waller Songbook / Oct. 1957 / EmArcy 818930

★ **Bessie Smith Songbook** / 1957-1958 / EmArcy 826663
Recorded in three sessions (12/30/57, 1/7 and 20/58), this release has Dinah Washington in fine, full voice handling the material in her own fashion and style. The weakness is in the setting, not the singer. Washington was both a great soul singer and a great jazz singer, as her more open jam session for EmArcy will attest. Here she is dealing with material very well suited to her strengths, but instead of being an instrument among other instruments, reflecting and improvising on a theme, she is placed above the pack and backed by some corny Mickey Mouse arrangements which are both limiting and clichéd. There is very little individual identity or interaction from the band, which includes Eddie Chamblee (ts), Flip Ricard (tpt), Charles Davis (bs), Julian Priester (tb), Jack Wilson (p), Robert Wilson (b), James Slaughter (d), Clark Terry (tpt), McKinley Easton (bs), Quentin Jackson (tb), James Graig (p), and Robare Edmonson (b), in various combinations. —*Bob Rusch,* Cadence

What a Diff'rence a Day Makes! / 1959 / Mercury 818815
Title cut is one of her biggest hits ever. Everything else is a bit overarranged, but she sounds great. Billboard #34. —*Ron Wynn*

Best of Dinah Washington, The / 1962-1963 / Roulette 52289

Dinah '63 / 1963 / Capitol 94576

○ **Unforgettable** / i. 1963 / Mercury 510602
Here we get the incredible voice and spirit of Dinah Washington with the pop confectionary sweetings of a sumptuous studio orchestra in a reissue of material from 1959. In addition to the heartfelt title track, there is a vibrant duo with the great pop baritone Brook Benton and a host of other melodramatically presented ballads such as "This Love of Mine." Still, Washington's incredible musicianship and three-hankie dramaturgy command attention. —*Chuck Berg,* Jazz Times

Essential Dinah Washington: the Great Songs, The / i. Dec. 11, 1992 / Verve 512905

☆ **Back to the Blues** / Roulette 25189
Washington, known as the "Queen of the Blues," shows how she earned the nickname with this marvelous set of basic 12-bar compositions. She'd moved away from this style by the early '60s, but proves immediately and often here that she hadn't lost the ability to sing these kinds of songs better than anyone else. —*Ron Wynn*

After Hours with Miss D / EmArcy 36028

Original Queen of Soul, The / Mercury 121

GROVER WASHINGTON, JR. (Washington Jr., Grover)

b. Dec. 12, 1943, Buffalo, NY
Saxophone / Soul-jazz, instrumental pop, contemporary funk
Grover Washington, Jr. is one of the most commercially successful saxophonists in jazz history. A versatile reed specialist, Washington is equally at home on soprano, alto, or tenor sax, and has recorded on flute and baritone sax. A much more creative improviser than his hit-making saxophone competitors, Washington has had hits with almost everything he has done since his first album, *Inner City Blues,* for Kudu in 1971. His biggest albums, *Mr. Magic* (Kudu) and *Winelight* (Elektra), have also spawned hit singles. His recordings for Kudu, Motown, Elektra, and Columbia are mostly commercial in content, but Washington's saxophone work is always first rate and a good distance in front of his closest fusion rivals. —*Bob Porter*

★ **Inner City Blues** / i. 1972 / Motown 5189
Definitive early '70s soul-jazz date. Washington has seldom been more convincing. Ron Carter is stalwart on bass. With

Bob James (p), Eric Gale (g), Airto Moreira (per), and Thad Jones (tpt). —*Ron Wynn*

★ **Mister Magic** / Nov. 1974 / Motown 5027

Feels So Good / May+Jul. 1975 / Motown 5177

Secret Place / All the King's Horses / i. 1977 / Motown 8130

Live at the Bijou / i. 1978 / Motown 0239

Reed Seed / i. 1979 / Motown 5236

☆ **Winelight** / i. Jun. 1980 / Elektra 305
Winelight combines total commerciality with unfailing good taste. Saxophonist Grover Washington, Jr. has hit on a sure-fire funk success formula, and en route to the bank he blows some very pleasant stuff. Washington extends the soul-jazz set tradition of Arnett Cobb, Gene Ammons, Stanley Turrentine, and others. Within that middle-of-the-road entertainment contest—always responsive to popular trends—he does indeed get down. Essentially *Winelight* is top-of-the-line mood music, soothing, relaxing, and eminently danceable. Drummer Steve Gadd and bassist Marcus Miller keep a fresh, spontaneous pocket, while guitarist Eric Gale, keyboardist Richard Tee, and Paul Griffin and the rest chord with intelligent variety. The unobtrusive strings are subtly effective throughout, and Washington himself plays with exquisite tone, range, and dexterity, firing or caressing with equal aplomb and grooving always. In urgent moments he recalls the R&B "honkers." —*Ben Sandmel,* Down Beat

Anthology / i. 1982 / Motown 6015

☆ **Then and Now** / i. 1988 / Columbia 44256
We are pleased to observe that Grover Washington, Jr. has—at least for the moment (1988)—returned to the fold, eschewing gimmickry and the trappings of pop, with the no-nonsense, straightahead *Then and Now,* a nice balance of ballads and uptempos, standards and originals, and the leader's tenor, alto, and soprano. His companions include tenorist Igor Butman, pianists Tommy Flanagan or Herbie Hancock, bassist Ron Carter, and drummers Grady Tate or Marvin "Smitty" Smith. —*W. Royal Stokes,* Jazz Times

KENNY WASHINGTON

b. 1958
Drums / Neo-bop
Kenny Washington is a concise, very steady drummer who's not flashy or spectacular, but has been an effective session and studio player. Washington's played with Lee Konitz and Betty Carter in the '70s, and with Johnny Griffin in the '80s. His studio work has resulted in recording sessions with Kenny Burrell, Carter, Frank Wess, Milt Jackson, George Coleman, Johnny Griffin, and Cedar Walton, among others. He can be heard on CDs by Burrell, Carter, Wess, and many others. —*Ron Wynn*

KAZUMI WATANABE

b. Oct. 14, 1953, Tokyo, Japan
Guitar / World fusion, instrumental pop, contemporary funk
A skilled guitarist, Kazumi Watanabe has moved more toward jazz-rock and fusion as his sound of choice than toward hard bop, bebop, or free music. His style, approach, use of electronics, and orientation have seen him include rock, pop, and funk licks liberally in his solos and compositions. Watanabe took guitar studies at Tokyo's Yamaha Music School, and was performing and recording as a teen. He formed the group Kylyn in 1979, and formed the Mobo Band with Mitsuru Sawamura, Ichiko Hasimoto, Gregg Lee, Shuichi Murakami, and Koyohiko Senba in 1983. He's recorded for Toshiba Express, Teichiku, Columbia, Trio, Denon, and Gramavision. Watanabe has some sessions available on CD. —*Ron Wynn*

○ **Mobo—Vols. 1 and 2** / Aug. 14-Sep. 9, 1983 / Gramavision 79417
Guitarist and keyboardist Kazumi Watanabe is one of the more acclaimed and experienced jazz musicians in Japan. He's a clean, technically adept player with quite a bit of skill

in using electronic effects. Watanabe tends to be self-effacing to a fault, soloing for a few bars before fading back into the musical wallpaper. He does get untracked on "Half Blood," playing a long, rapid-fire solo that sounds a bit like Larry Carlton. His best work is probably on "Yenshu Tsubame Gaeshi" (Vol. 1), which is the most imaginative tune, a juxtaposition of bebop and funk. The bridge—a cut-and-paste surprise à la Miles Davis—is one of the few truly engaging moments on the album. —*Jim Roberts*, Down Beat

★ **To Chi Ka** / i. 1984 / Denon 7136
A great album featuring Kenny Kirkland (k), Mike Manieri (vib), and Warren Bernhardt (p). —*Paul Kohler*

☆ **Spice of Life** / i. 1987 / Gramavision 79420
This album is a fusion-lover's dream. Bill Bruford (d) and Jeff Berlin (b) drive Watanabe. —*Paul Kohler*

Spice of Life Too / i. 1988 / Gramavision 79416
A continuation of *Spice of Life* with stronger compositions and a hint of softer tones. Very nice! —*Paul Kohler*

Kilowatt / i. 1989 / Gramavision 79415
This release picks up where *Spice of Life Too* left off. Bunny Brunel's bass work shines. —*Paul Kohler*

SADAO WATANABE

b. Feb. 1, 1933, Utsunomiya, Japan
Alto and soprano saxophone, flute / Bop, world fusion, instrumental pop, contemporary funk
A player who's advanced from being essentially a mimic into a solid, often interesting improviser, Sadao Watanabe's solos now contain growls, smears, and a driving, striking energy that he lacked when he first began recording in the '60s and '70s. Watanabe's father was a professional musician who played the biwa and sang. Watanabe learned clarinet and alto saxophone in high school. He moved to Tokyo in the early '50s, and began flute studies with Ririko Hayashi of the Tokyo Philharmonic Orchestra. Watanabe joined Toshiko Akiyoshi's bop quartet, and became its leader when she moved to America in the mid-'50s. He attended Berklee in the early '60s, and played and wrote arrangements for the school's Jazz in the Classroom series. He also worked with Gary McFarland, Chico Hamilton, and Gabor Szabo. Watanabe was appointed director of the Yamaha Institute of Popular Music when he returned to Tokyo in 1966. He presented concerts there and also toured with his quartet, which played a blend of bebop, jazz-rock, pop, R&B, and funk material. Watanabe recorded with Chick Corea in New York during 1970, and with the Galaxy All Stars in Tokyo in 1978. He's issued several releases as a leader. Watanabe became the first jazz musician to win the annual Grand Prix award from the Japanese government, which he received in 1976. He's primarily recorded for Elektra and Elektra/Musician during his American tenure. Watanabe has several sessions available as a leader. —*Ron Wynn and Michael G. Nastos*

Nabasada and Charlie / Jun. 27, 1967 / Catalyst 7911
An excellent date with fellow saxophonist Charlie Mariano. Standards played with verve. —*Michael G. Nastos*

★ **Dedicated to Charlie Parker** / Mar. 15, 1969 / Denon 7689

Round Trip / Jul. 15, 1974 / Vanguard 79344
More-progressive setting with Chick Corea (k), Miroslav Vitous (b), and Jack DeJohnette (d). —*Michael G. Nastos*

☆ **Bird of Paradise** / May 4, 1977 / Elektra 60748
Just looking at the cover photos of alto saxophonist Sadao Watanabe and Bird and reading Watanabe with the Great Jazz Trio (pianist Hank Jones, bassist Ron Carter, drummer Tony Williams) immediately evokes the question: how well does Japan's best saxophonist play Charlie Parker's best material? To these ears, as well as anybody could no matter where they came from. The entire group has played and recorded together before. The precision, sound, and inventiveness are all there. Watanabe has the fire to play "Donna Lee" and the emotion to play "Embraceable You." Even though all of this has been done many times before, there is still something refreshing to hear. —*Jerry L. Atkins*, Cadence

○ **I'm Old Fashioned** / May 22, 1976 / Inner City 6015
This (1976) session predates much of alto saxophonist and flutist Sadao Watanabe's available recordings. This is a brilliant recording opening with Bird's (Charlie Parker) "Confirmation" and the altoist very much in Bird's groove. This rhythm section is something to hear and pianist Hank Jones places a magnificent lingering chord on the end. "Gary," "Episode," and "One for C." are all Watanabe compositions, and the latter has Jones by himself in a beautiful mood. "Gary" undoubtedly was written for composer/bandleader Gary McFarland whom Watanabe once enjoyed as a musical companion. It has a beautiful alto sound and could also be a link with Gary Foster. "3:10 Blues" is both funky and refreshing. "Chelsea" is one of the most beautiful harmonically constructed tunes ever written and Watanabe plays the Billy Strayhorn classic as if he knew its creator and interpreter. Bassist Ron Carter's half chorus further enhances a lovely track. The blowing sides are "I Concentrate on You" and "I'm Old Fashioned." The first really cooks, especially on the out chorus, but Watanabe's five or six choruses on "Old Fashioned" display a drive and technique that I didn't know he had. Jones has three great ones, drummer Tony Williams has his longest solo, Carter's contribution is unpredictably imaginative and the surprise of no tag on the end makes this a masterful track of improvisation. This is superb alto and a rhythm section that is rarely equaled in this vein of jazz. —*Jerry L. Atkins*, Cadence

Parker's Mood / Jul. 13, 1986 / Elektra 60475
Close to his best, both on his merit and thanks to aid from James Williams (p) and Jeff Watts (d). 1986 date. —*Ron Wynn*

Jazz and Bossa / Nov. 25, 1986-Dec. 1986 / Denon 7870

Elis / Feb. 1988 / Elektra 60816

BENNY WATERS (Benjamin Waters)

b. Jan. 23, 1902, Brighton, MD
Alto saxophone, clarinet, arranger / New Orleans traditional, swing, big band
A superb tenor saxophonist and a fine clarinetist and alto player, Benny Waters's career spans the growth and development of jazz and American popular music. His huge tone and swaggering tenor style were honed in the swing era, as was his darting clarinet and tart alto approaches. Waters played piano and reed instruments as a child, then worked with Charlie Miller from 1918 to 1921. He studied at the New England Conservatory and later became a teacher (one of his pupils was Harry Carney). Waters recorded with King Oliver and Clarence Williams in the '20s and '30s, while writing arrangements for Charlie Johnson. For a few months, he also played with Fletcher Henderson, then rejoined Johnson in the mid-'30s. He worked with Hot Lips Page, Claude Hopkins, and Jimmie Lunceford in the '40s, and recorded with Hopkins and Lunceford. Waters led his own band for four years, then played in Roy Milton's R&B orchestra. Waters worked with traditional jazz leader Jimmy Archey in 1949, and opted to stay in Europe during a group tour. He settled in Paris and remained there until the end of the '60s. He was a regular at the club La Cigale. Waters was a festival favorite throughout Europe in the '70s and '80s, and paid some visits to New York in the '80s. Currently, he has a few dates available on CD. —*Ron Wynn*

★ **From Paradise (Small's) to Shangrila** / i. Jun. 26, 1987 / Muse 5340

○ **Memories of the Twenties, Stomp Off** / i. 1988 / Southern Studios 1210

ETHEL WATERS (Ethel [Née Howard] Waters)

b. Oct. 31, 1896, Chester, PA, **d.** Sep. 1, 1977, Chatsworth, CA
Vocals / Blues & jazz, ballads & blues
A well-known vaudeville and Cotton Club diva, Waters became famous recording "St. Louis Blues," "Stormy Weather," and "Cabin in the Sky." She worked with Duke Ellington,

Benny Goodman, and many Black theater troupes. —
Michael G. Nastos

○ **Jazzin' Babies Blues—Vol. 2 (1921-1927)** / 1921-1927 /
Biograph 12026

Cabin in the Sky / i. 1923-1955 / Milan 35626

○ **Legendary Performer** / i. 1974 / RCA 3370

★ **Ethel Waters on Stage/Screen (1925-1940)** / Sony Special
Products 2792

DOUG WATKINS (Douglas Watkins)

b. Mar. 2, 1934, Detroit, MI, **d.** Feb. 5, 1962, Holbrook, AZ
Bass / Hard bop, postbop
A topflight bassist who was extremely active during the '50s,
Doug Watkins established himself as a first-rate accompa-
nist and a tasteful soloist on several recordings with
Prestige, and through many associations with major players.
His career was cut short by an automobile accident in 1962.
In the early '50s, Watkins worked with James Moody, then
came back to his native Detroit to play with Barry Harris's
trio. In that role, Watkins worked with Stan Getz, Charlie
Parker, and Coleman Hawkins. He moved to New York in
1954, and, during the remainder of the decade, played with
Horace Silver, Kenny Dorham, and Hank Mobley, worked at
Minton's, and was an original member of Art Blakey's Jazz
Messengers. He began doing sessions with Prestige in the
mid-'50s, and appeared on recordings by Gene Ammons,
Sonny Rollins, Phil Woods, Art Farmer, Donald Byrd, Kenny
Burrell, and Mobley. He substituted for Charles Mingus
when Mingus moved to piano on Jazz Workshop perfor-
mances and recording sessions in 1960 and 1961. Watkins
also did a couple of recordings as a leader for Transition and
New Jazz. These recordings are not available on CD, but
Watkins can be heard on reissues by Blakey, Rollins,
Ammons, Mingus, and others. —*Ron Wynn*

★ **Watkins at Large** / Dec. 8, 1956 / Transition 20

○ **Soulnik** / May 17, 1960 / New Jazz 8238

JULIUS WATKINS

b. Oct. 10, 1921, Detroit, MI, **d.** Apr. 4, 1977, Short Hills, NJ
French horn / Hard bop, postbop, progressive big band
Julius Watkins was one of the first and remains one of the
few musicians to play French horn in a jazz context. His solos and mastery of intricate compositions, particularly the
unorthodox songs of Thelonious Monk, which he recorded,
showed Watkins's harmonic mettle. Watkins began playing
French horn at age nine, and in the '40s and early '50s was
featured on trumpet when he worked in the bands of Ernie
Fields and Milt Buckner. He switched to French horn exclusively in the '50s. Watkins studied for three years at the
Manhattan School of Music, then did recording sessions
with Pete Rugolo and Charlie Rouse before joining Oscar
Pettiford's sextet. He, Rouse, Guildo Mahones, Pettiford, and
Ron Jefferson formed Les Modes in 1956. Later, the group
became the Jazz Modes, and alternated between being a
quintet and a larger band with vocalist Eileen Gilbert, saxophonist Sahib Shihab, and percussionist Chano Pozo. But
the Jazz Modes found regular dates hard to obtain, and finally disbanded in the late '50s. Watkins played with George
Shearing in 1959 and with Quincy Jones in 1961. He worked
on several Broadway shows in the early '60s, while recording with John Coltrane, Tadd Dameron, Milt Jackson,
Freddie Hubbard, and the Jazz Composer's Orchestra. In the
late '50s and mid-'60s, Watkins often worked with Gil Evans,
and worked with him again in 1969. Currently, there are no
Watkins titles, as a leader or with the Jazz Modes, available
on CD, at least according to the *Schwann* catalog. —*Ron
Wynn and Michael G. Nastos*

★ **Julius Watkins Sextet—Vol. 2** / Mar. 19, 1954 / Blue Note
5064

○ **New Faces–New Sounds: Julius Watkins Sextet** / 1954 /
Blue Note 5053

Jazz Modes, The / Oct. 28, 1958 / Atlantic 1306

BILL WATROUS (William Russell (II) Watrous)

b. Jun. 8, 1939, Middletown, CT
Trombone / Hard bop, early jazz-rock
Though he's possibly the most skilled and facile trombone
technician and stylist of any trombonist in the modern era,
Watrous has become increasingly irrelevant, from a recording standpoint. His late '80s sessions were routine mood music, and he's had only one recent release, a '92 GRP outing.
But his beautiful tone, command, and fluidity with the slide
were impressive and remain impressive. His father was also
a trombonist, and introduced his son to music. Watrous is
largely self-taught, though he took a few lessons and played
in traditional jazz bands as a youngster. He studied with
Herbie Nichols during his military stint, and then made his
professional debut with Billy Butterfield. Watrous worked
with Kai Winding's various groups from 1962 to 1967. He
also did many studio sessions, working and recording with
Quincy Jones, Maynard Ferguson, Johnny Richards, and
Woody Herman. Watrous was in Merv Griffin's studio band
from 1965 to 1968, and was on the CBS staff from 1967 to
1969. He joined the jazz-rock band Ten Wheel Drive in the
early '70s, then led his own group, Manhattan Wildlife
Refuge, in the mid- and late '70s, and gained critical praise
for his playing and arrangements. Joe Beck, Dick Hyman, Ed
Soph, Danny Stiles, and Ed Xiques were some of the musicians in his group. Watrous moved to Los Angeles in the late
'70s, where he continued recording and heading bands. He
played throughout Germany with Albert Mangelsdorff and
Winding in 1980 in the group Trombone Summit, and
played in London in 1982. Watrous has recorded as a leader
for Famous Door, Columbia, Soundwings, and GRP. He has
some sessions available on CD. —*Ron Wynn*

Manhattan Wildlife Refuge / May 1+3, 1974 / Columbia
33090

★ **Tiger of San Pedro** / 1975 / Columbia 33701
Second albums, like second novels, are harder to bring off
than firsts, but the Manhattan Wildlife Refuge manages to
improve on its excellent debut LP with this superior effort.
The music here is more varied, the ensemble playing more
secure and relaxed, and the soloists in as good or better
form. There are a few changes in personnel, but the only
truly significant ones are in the rhythm section, which has
become the band's regular team rather than a star-studded
studio lineup. What stands out about this band is its mellow
ensemble quality. Even when it shouts—and it can shout
plenty—it doesn't become strident. The music is contemporary in flavor and rhythm, but does not commit the cardinal
contemporary sin of loudness. It is a pleasure to hear a band
that understands the importance of dynamics and shading.
—*Dan Morgenstern, Down Beat*

Bone-Ified / i. 1992 / GNP 2211

Trombone Summit / PA/USA 7111

BOBBY WATSON (Robert Michael (Jr) Watson)

b. Aug. 23, 1953, Lawrence, KS
Alto saxophone / Hard bop, postbop, neo-bop
One of the great jazz events of the '90s occurred when
Bobby Watson got a chance to record for a major label
(Sony/Columbia). The promise he showed in the early '80s
with Art Blakey's Jazz Messengers, and his torrid playing
with various groups and for independents finally paid off.
Watson earned a degree from the University of Miami in
theory and composition, then moved to New York. He was in
the Messengers from 1977 to 1981, and served as music director for two years. He composed and arranged several
pieces during his tenure. Watson played with George
Coleman and Louis Hayes in the early '80s, while recording
with Ricky Ford and Sam Rivers. With Curtis Lundy and another business partner, he formed the New Note record label
in 1983. Watson toured Europe, led and recorded with a hard
bop band, and also did arrangements and played with the
29th Street Saxophone Quartet. He recorded with Charli

Persip in 1984, and played in London in 1987. Watson's led and recorded with Horizon in the '90s. He's done sessions for Enja, Red, Blue Note, and Columbia. Watson has several dates available on CD. —*Ron Wynn*

○ E.T.A. / 1977 / Roulette 5009

★ Advance / i. Aug. 8, 1984 / Enja 79653
1991 reissue that heralded the arrival of former Jazz Messenger Bobby Watson as a major figure in 1984. —*Ron Wynn*

Round Trip / i. Mar. 1988 / Red 187

No Question About It / i. 1988 / Blue Note 90262
Watson heads two groups. Many of the best players around, including John Hicks (p) and Roy Hargrove (tpt). —*Ron Wynn*

☆ Post-Motown Bop / i. Sep. 17-18, 1990 / Blue Note 95148
Despite the title, this is an excellent and traditional set. Watson is sparkling. —*Ron Wynn*

Inventor, The / i. 1990 / Blue Note 91915

ERNIE WATTS (Ernest James Watts)

b. Oct. 23, 1945, Norfolk, VA
Tenor and soprano saxophone / Hard bop, progressive big band, early jazz-rock
Though you wouldn't know it from hearing him on some recent laid-back, overproduced instrumental pop dates, Ernie Watts is a fine, frequently exciting tenor saxophonist. He's played swing, bebop, hard bop, blues, funk, and soul-jazz, and can still provide some glorious moments when so inspired. Watts attended Berklee in the '60s before joining Buddy Rich in 1966. He moved to Los Angeles in 1968, shortly after leaving the Rich orchestra. He was a studio musician and NBC staffer in the early '70s, and also played with Gerald Wilson. Watkins toured Africa with Oliver Nelson in 1969. He recorded with Bobby Bryant and Jean-Luc Ponty in 1969, with Cannonball Adderley in 1972, and with writer/historian Leonard Feather on his *Night Blooming Jazzmen* project in 1975. He was in Lee Ritenour's group in 1977. Watts recorded with Sadao Watanabe, Anita O' Day, J.J. Johnson, and Wilson in the late '70s and early '80s. He won a Grammy for his performance on the *Chariots of Fire* soundtrack in 1982. Watts recorded with Tom Scott, Stanley Clarke, and Ritenour in the early and mid-'80s, has worked with his own jazz-rock and fusion group, and has been a soloist with Charlie Haden's Liberation Music Orchestra. Watts continued steady session work into the '90s. He's been featured in Charlie Haden's Quartet West band since 1987, and appeared on several of their acclaimed recordings. Watts has recorded as a leader for CTI, JVC, and Amherst. He has some sessions available on CD. —*Ron Wynn*

★ Ernie Watts Quartet / Dec. 1987 / JVC 3309
This is a delightful disc: crisp and sophisticated, rich with emotion and craftsmanship. Ernie Watts, an alumnus of dozens of groups ranging from Buddy Rich's band to the Tonight Show Orchestra to Wayne Henderson's group, is a highly listenable saxophonist. Watts's style is one that bespeaks years of honing and polish, and he has chosen an absolutely flawless rhythm section here to grace his playing. It is hard to name any one song in this collection as being the best, as all are superb, but among my favorites is "Echoes," which finds bassist Joel Dibartolo doubling the melody with Watts, creating a compelling mystical mood. Pat Coil plays a rollicking piano solo here with nods toward McCoy Tyner. Coil also shines in the group's graceful rendition of the classic "My One and Only Love." "On the Border" features some dazzling soprano work, and "Chelsea" is a beautiful little waltz played by Watts with heart-tugging tenderness. —*Denny Townsend, Jazz Times*

JEFF WATTS

Drums / Neo-bop
A marvelous drummer, Jeff Watts was the rhythm anchor for Wynton Marsalis's group from its beginnings until the

celebrated departure of Watts, Kenny Kirkland, and Branford Marsalis. Watts found a suitable replacement gig; he's now in the "Tonight Show" orchestra alongside Branford Marsalis and Kirkland. Watts can also be heard on all of the early Wynton Marsalis sessions on CD. —*Ron Wynn*

CHUCK WAYNE (Charles Jagelka)

b. Feb. 27, 1923, New York, NY
Guitar / Bop
A guitarist whose style is classic bebop, Chuck Wayne was involved in the genre's formative period of the early '40s; he has never taken his mellow, fluid, and inventive style into other arenas. Wayne's tasteful accompaniment and concise, tight solos were featured on seminal recordings. He was a mandolin player originally, then switched to guitar and worked with Clarence Profit in the early '40s. Following an army stint, Wayne played with Joe Marsala on 52nd Street. He worked with Dizzy Gillespie and Benny Harris, and was in Woody Herman's orchestra in the mid '40s. Wayne played with George Shearing from 1949 to 1952, and did sessions in New York during the '50s. Wayne also played and toured with Tony Bennett from 1954 to 1957. He wrote the music and compositions for the Broadway play *Orpheus Descending* in 1957. Wayne became a CBS staffer in 1959, and did many television shows, as well as occasional club dates. He performed and recorded with Joe Puma in the '70s, and became a teacher at Westchester Conservatory of Music in White Plains in the '80s. He has a couple of sessions available on CD. —*Ron Wynn*

★ Tapestry / 1963 / Focus 333

WEATHER REPORT

b. 1971, d. 1986
Early jazz-rock, world fusion
Weather Report was one of the earliest and most influential of all jazz-rock bands. The original unit was cofounded by Wayne Shorter and Joe Zawinul in the early '70s. Like the original Mahavishnu Orchestra, Tony Williams Lifetime, the original Return to Forever, and Dreams (minus vocals), Weather Report was a band that stretched the boundaries and created a fresh hybrid that really blended jazz and rock. From years of playing with Miles Davis, Shorter and Zawinul had learned how to combine rock energy, funk rhythms, and a jazz sensibility. The group's early lineup included bassist Miroslav Vitous and drummer Alphonze Mouzon. Their self-titled debut and second release, *I Sing the Body Electric*, remain as seminal jazz-rock classics. Even as they began the game of rotating personnel that would be continue until they disbanded in 1986, they continued to make intriguing releases into the early '80s. Dom Um Romao, Eric Gravitt, and Alphonso Johnson were in the band during the mid-'70s. But its greatest lineup was the late '70s contingent that included Jaco Pastorius and Peter Erskine. These men were virtuosos on their instruments, and were excellent contributors who were able to hold their own in any situation. They were also superb accompanists. The last great Weather Report albums were issued by this configuration of players, and included *Black Market, Heavy Weather*, and *Mr. Gone*. But things deteriorated when Pastorius, then Erskine left in the early '80s. Their replacements, Victor Bailey and Omar Hakim, were excellent musicians, but were not flamboyant soloists or imaginative thinkers like their predecessors. Shorter and Zawinul began to coast and grew tired of working in the group concept. The final albums were the detached, polished, and extremely professional output of topflight musicians who were anxious to finish the gig and move on. Percussionists Jose Rossey, then Mino Cineliu, were in and out of the band, and Erskine returned from Steps Ahead for their final dates. Shorter first took an extended leave of absence, then he and Zawinul called it quits. The Weather Report legacy is impressive, but sad. They had probably gone as far as they could go, but it's a shame they're remembered more for the trendy flash of the single "Birdland" than for many monumental sessions

that were the best of jazz-rock. Virtually every Weather Report album is available on CD. —*Ron Wynn and Stephen Aldrich*

Weather Report / i. 1971 / Columbia 37616
Jaco Pastorius (b) rules the day. The 1971 release that heralded their coming. At the time they were a breath of fresh life, with sterling compositions and great solos from Wayne Shorter (sax), Joe Zawinul (k), and Miroslav Vitous (b). —*Ron Wynn*

★ **I Sing the Body Electric** / Nov. 1971 / Columbia 46107
A great record from the days when they were still a serious jazz band. —*Ron Wynn*

Sweetnighter / 1972-1973 / Columbia 32210

★ **Mysterious Traveller** / 1973-1974 / Columbia 32494
Soprano and tenor saxophonist Wayne Shorter is less in the spotlight on the fourth Weather Report outing, primarily because *Mysterious Traveller* shows a preponderance of Joe Zawinul influence. Rousing synthesizer and crowd yells usher in Zawinul's "Nubian Sundance," a frisky African celebration possessing an automated eeriness as well as jungle playfulness. Shorter appears sparingly on the 10-minute cut, as the percussionists reign over the latter half. The effervescent "American Tango" sports Zawinul on Fender Rhodes in addition to synthesizer. Bassist Alphonso Johnson co-penned "Cucumber Slumber" with Zawinul, and it is here that Shorter finds ample breathing space. —*Marv Hohman*, Down Beat

Tale Spinnin' / 1974 / Columbia 33417

Black Market / 1976 / Columbia 34099

Heavy Weather / 1976 / Columbia 47481

○ **Live in Tokyo / i.** 1977 / Columbia 1213

Mr. Gone / i. 1978 / Columbia 46869

○ **8:30 / i.** Dec. 1979 / Columbia 83670
Weather Report live at last! Famous for their meticulously produced albums—one a year since 1971 (throughout their tenure)—the once and future fusion band comes out of the studio with three sides that strike the color and power of an electrical storm (side four contains four new studio cuts). The curtain opens on a jumping "Black Market." Drummer Peter Erskine plunges right in; keyboardist Joe Zawinul and bassist Jaco Pastorius hustle along beside him, and Zawinul plays the tune. A cheer goes up when saxophonist Wayne Shorter comes out to play the second strain. Suddenly Pastorius and Zawinul drop out, and Shorter plays a marvelous duet with Erskine, the tenor swinging high and loose above the chattering patter of tight skins. Back to the top for a catlike Zawinul thought. This is *wonderful* music. Zawinul plays a quiet, foreboding sci-fi intro to the next number. Bass and drums begin the mysterious march of "Scarlet Woman." "Teen Town" is very uptempo, Pastorius playing his own melody at lightning speed without any loss of precision as Shorter's soprano gets a test. "A Remark You Made" is most remarkable for Shorter's open-heart expression of Zawinul's lovely melancholy strains. "Slang" is a bass solo." "Birdland" is greeted with cheers and applause, as it should have been. Could it have been a coincidence that "Birdland" is followed by Shorter's solo interpretation of the 1937 standard "Thanks for the Memory"—especially with rumors flying that the band had been bickering? In any case, Shorter plays a stunning tenor solo, chopping up the melody and tossing the pieces into a chef's salad of low honks, high squeals, and melodic swirls. A panting "Badia/Boogie Woogie Waltz" ends the concert. Back in the studio, the band spins out an odd assortment of new tunes. This side comes off as filler and is only mildly interesting compared to the exciting set that precedes it. —*Douglas Clark*, Down Beat

---

CHICK WEBB (William Henry Webb)

b. Feb. 10, 1909, Baltimore, MD, **d.** Jun. 16, 1939, Baltimore, MD
Bandleader, drums / Swing, big band

His career was short, and Chick Webb seemed cursed with only bad luck. He was a hunchback and died at age 30 from tuberculosis of the spine. But during his short lifetime, Webb was a propulsive, dominating figure behind the drums. He was a dynamo, whose speed, power, and rhythmic skills were never fully captured on record, according to many who saw him triumph repeatedly in head-to-head battles with swing-era royalty. Reportedly, Gene Krupa was in awe of Webb, and spoke in shell-shocked tones after being blown away at the Savoy in legendary combat that occurred only a few months before Webb died. Webb overcame his inability to read music by memorizing the arrangements. He led the band from a raised platform in the center, cueing sections via his drumming. He ranged over a huge kit with specially constructed pedals and cymbal holders, and was an imaginative stylist who shoved drum technique ahead through dashing fills and crashing cymbals. He came to New York in 1924, and formed a band two years later. Webb cut his first record in 1927. By the early '30s, he'd recruited Hilton Jefferson, Jimmy Harrison, John Trueheart, and Benny Carter. Later came Mario Bauza, Taft Jordan, John Kirby, and Edgar Sampson. Louis Jordan was another luminary in the band. They recorded for Decca, and later for ARC. Sampson's "Stompin' at the Savoy" became a hit for Webb's orchestra in 1934. The next year, Webb discovered Ella Fitzgerald, and she helped the orchestra score 11 hits between 1934 and 1939. "A-Tisket, A-Tasket" topped the charts in 1938. Goodman also had a hit with his version of "Stomping at the Savoy" in 1936. Webb's illness worsened in 1938, and he was gone by the summer of 1939. Fitzgerald sang "My Buddy" at his funeral, and kept the band together for two more years. Webb had adopted Fitzgerald when her mother died. —*Ron Wynn*

★ **Chick Webb (1929-1934) / i.** Jun. 1929-Nov. 1934 / Classics 502

○ **Jazz Heritage: A Legend (1929-1936)** / 1929-1936 / MCA 1303

☆ **Jazz Heritage: Princess of the Savoy (1934-1939)** / 1934-1939 / MCA 1348

○ **Ella Swings the Band (1936-1939)** / 1936-1939 / MCA 1327

○ **Immortal Chick Webb, The / i.** 1967 / Columbia 9439

○ **Immortal Chick Webb: Stompin' at the Savoy / i.** Jun. 1967 / Columbia 2639

EBERHARD WEBER

b. Jan. 22, 1940, Stuttgart, Germany
Bass, cello, composer / World fusion, new age, modern creative

Though not strictly a jazz bassist and certainly one of the least flamboyant improvisers, Eberhard Weber is one of Europe's finest bassists. His style doesn't embrace either a bluesy orientation or an animated, energetic approach. Weber's influences are primarily European, notably contemporary classical and new music. His technique of using contrasting ostinato patterns in different voices was taken from composer Steve Reich. He's also made innovations in bass design. Weber added an extra string to the top of his electric bass in the early '70s; this extended its range and gave it a deeper, more striking sound. He added yet another string above that in the late '70s. Weber once doubled on cello, but dropped it to concentrate on acoustic and electric bass. Weber's father taught him cello at age six, and he began to play bass at age 16. He worked in school orchestras, dance bands, and local jazz groups. He met Wolfgang Dauner while participating in the Dusseldorf Amateur Jazz Festival in the early '60s; they worked together over the next eight years, both as a duo and in the group Et Cetera. Weber worked with Dave Pike in the early '70s, and co-led the band Spectrum with Volker Kriegel. His early '70s album, *The Colours of Chloe*, was one of ECM's most acclaimed albums. He formed the group Colours in 1974, headed it until 1981, and toured America in 1976, '78, and '79. From the mid-'70s to the early '80s, Weber also played with the United Jazz and Rock Ensemble. During the '80s, Weber worked and recorded with Jan Garbarek, wrote film scores, and gave solo concerts. He continued recording with ECM, both with his group and with other musicians, such as Gary Burton. Weber has several ECM titles available on CD. —*Ron Wynn*

★ **Colours of Chloe, The** / Dec. 1973 / ECM 833331
The abilities bassist Eberhard Weber bring to this date are formidable. He is a more than capable player, a gifted lyricist (catch the line of the title cut, before it etches itself indelibly in your mind's ear), an effective if monochromatic orchestrator. All that's missing is a sense of freedom. Possibly that illustrates one difference between our side (historically improvised) and their side (historically precomposed) of the pond. —*Steve Metaliz*, Down Beat

☆ **Works** / ECM 825429

BEN WEBSTER (Benjamin Francis Webster)

b. Mar. 27, 1909, Kansas City, MO, **d.** Sep. 20, 1973, Amsterdam, Holland
Tenor saxophone / Swing, big band
The master of rumbling, evocative tenor sax ballads, Ben Webster rose to fame in Duke Ellington's Orchestra, then continued as a striking soloist and interpreter through many other jazz eras. His huge tone, distinctive timbre, control, and versatility (he was featured on several R&B and rock and roll sessions in the '50s) enabled Webster to adapt during changing times and tastes. Like Lester Young, he was influenced by Frankie Trumbauer, especially Trumbauer's solo on "Singin' the Blues." He also admired Budd Johnson (he learned a scale from him at one point), and was influenced directly by Coleman Hawkins. The composer of the classic work "Cottontail," Webster began on violin as a child, and had formal studies at Wilberforce University. His earliest professional work came as a pianist; Webster had learned piano from Pete Johnson, and played in silent cinemas. He turned to the tenor in 1930, and played with Jap Allen, Blanche Calloway, Bennie Moten, and Andy Kirk in the early '30s. Webster moved to New York in 1934, and joined Fletcher Henderson's band. He worked with several other bands in the mid- and late '30s, among them Benny Carter's, Cab Calloway's, and Teddy Wilson's. He had short stints with Ellington in 1935 and 1936 before he was offered a permanent position in 1940. From 1940 to 1943, Webster solidified his style and approach, and was featured on several magnificent compositions including "All Too Soon" and "Stardust." Webster recorded with Big Sid Catlett in 1944, and rejoined the Ellington Orchestra in 1948 and 1949. Webster toured frequently with Jazz at the Philharmonic in the '50s, and also accompanied Billie Holiday, Ella Fitzgerald, and Carmen McRae. There were sessions with Coleman Hawkins, Gerry Mulligan, Illinois Jacquet, and Roy Eldridge. He left America for Copenhagen in 1964, and played frequently in European clubs and at festivals with expatriate American and local musicians. There were sessions in the '60s and '70s with Hank Jones, Don Byas, Tete Montoliu, and Junior Mance. Webster's sound and influence echoes in the work of many tenor saxophonists, among them Archie Shepp, Charlie Ventura, Scott Hamilton, and Lew Tabackin. He can be heard on several of his own CD reissues, and with the Ellington Orchestra and other musicians. —*Ron Wynn and Dan Morgenstern*

★ **Complete Ben Webster on EmArcy (1951-1953), The** / 1951-1953 / EmArcy 824836
This is two records, with fine program notes by Dan Morgenstern, full discographical information, nicely packaged, wonderful music and all at a special twofer price. My only gripe is noisy pressings. The program has six fine tracks of territorial jazz with Jay McShann's band of 10/27/51; nine tracks of territorial jazz once removed from Johnny Otis's band from 12/26/51. Here Ben Webster increases the vibrato and upper register work. The music is solid, spirited, honestly rhythm and blued, most of which has been previously unissued. The same is true for the 10

tracks from the 12/27/51 session led by Webster in the company of Maynard Ferguson, Benny Carter, Gerald Wiggins, John Kirby, and George Jenkins. This is a modern-mainstream date and the group works well and reminds one how exciting a trumpeter Ferguson used to be. The alternate takes here are all interesting. The remaining sides cover four dates made over the next 14 months. "Trouble in Mind" (2:48) with Dinah Washington from 1/18/52 includes Wardell Gray, Wynton Kelly, Jimmy Cobb, and unidentified others. "I'll Be Back" and "Don't Mention My Name" (5:38) from 1/18/52 are a couple of tunes with the Ravens with Webster doing the R&B tenor thang. "Hoot," "Pouting," "The Iron Hat"—two tracks (11:46) are from a Webster-led date (1/23/53) with Johnny Richards's Orchestra (Eddie Bert, tb; Sam Rubinowitch, reeds; Billy Taylor, p; Milt Hinton, b; Jo Jones, d). It is mostly Webster features but is missing the relaxed group groove the 12/27/51 date maintained. The final track is "S' Wonderful" (2:50), a 4/7/53 date with Webster guesting with Marshall Royal's Quartet (Bobby Tucker, p; Milt Hinton, b; Jo Jones, d). —*Bob Rusch*, Cadence

○ **King of the Tenors** / Dec. 8, 1953 / Norgran 1089

Ballads / Mar. 30+May 28, 1954 / Verve 833550

○ **Ben Webster / i.** Jul. 14, 1954 / Norgran 1001

Soulville / Oct. 15, 1957 / Verve 833551

Ben Webster Meets Oscar Peterson / Nov. 6, 1959 / Verve 829167

○ **Ben Webster and Associates / i.** 1959 / Verve 835254
You can't go wrong with Webster, Coleman Hawkins (sax), Budd Jones (b), and many other masters of ballads, blues, and standards. —*Ron Wynn*

At the Renaissance / Oct. 1960 / Contemporary 390

Ben and Sweets / Jun. 1962 / Columbia 40853
1987 release of super date. Harry Edison (tpt) is dynamic, Webster his usual impressive self. —*Ron Wynn*

○ **Trav'lin Light** / Sep. 20+Oct. 14, 1963 / Milestone 47056
In 1956, a year after tenor saxophonist Ben Webster's sessions with Art Tatum, one of these four sides was recorded; the others come from 1963 sessions by these once roommates, Webster and pianist Joe Zawinul—long before the latter became known for the various electronica that he made famous with Weather Report. Sides one and two are set up for collectors. There are three sets of double takes: "Too Late Now," "Come Sunday," and "Frog Legs"—every second worthwhile. The quartet cuts are spacious enough for Webster to employ his casual bests, and on "Trav'lin Light," "Like Someone in Love," "Too Late Now," and "Come Sunday," Webster's warm and provocative solos are rocked gently (but firmly) in the hands of bassist Richard Davis and drummer Philly Joe Jones. On the title cut, Zawinul's extraordinary solo resolution smacks of Tommy Flanagan or Hank Jones. The extraordinary value of these recordings lies not only in their reiteration of Webster's mastery of soft vehicles, but also in their presentation of Webster's relationship to Coleman Hawkins, in whose shadow he stood for most of his early career. This twofer provides more documentation of the stylist who not only absorbed the prime elements of Hawkins, but those of Lester Young and Johnny Hodges as well. —*Brent Staples*, Down Beat

See You at the Fair / Mar. 11+Mar. 25, 1964 / GRP 121

○ **Stormy Weather** / Jan. 1965 / Black Lion 760108
The first seven selections on *Stormy Weather* were originally issued on Black Lion in 1974 under the title *Saturday Night At The Montmarte*, that particular occasion being January 30, 1965, in Copenhagen. However, added to the CD release are the three final tracks, which bring the total time up to an almost respectable 55:47. Tenor saxist Ben Webster had only moved to Europe one month before this date and this may very well have been his first appearance at the famed Jazzhus, home to many a visiting American hornman and where pianist Kenny Drew had been leading the house rhythm section (Niels-Henning Ørsted-Pedersen, b; Alex Riel, d) for about a year. The ambiance of the room, as well

as the charm of the city itself, must have seemed very inviting to Webster, for one quickly senses in his playing the relief he most likely felt upon being liberated from the American rat race. There is lacking, however, that spirit of restless, searing intensity that had always characterized his best stateside work; but, then again, at the time this was recorded, he was probably still in a holiday frame of mind. For those who may pass this album because they already own the LP version, let it be mentioned that "Friskin' the Frog" (7:16) and "Stormy Weather" (7:21) alone could easily justify the purchase of the CD. *—Jack Sohmer,* Jazz Times

○ **Meets Bill Coleman** / Apr. 27, 1967 / Black Lion 760141

★ **Ben Meets Don Byas** / Feb. 1-2, 1968 / Verve 827920
Both Ben Webster and Don Byas stemmed from Coleman Hawkins, and Byas was Webster's junior by a mere four years. Nevertheless, by the time of this recording (1968) Byas had begun to move into his final, somewhat unfortunate stylistic phase. Hitherto, his melodic sense had never betrayed him, but now he was beginning, in a desire to remain "modern," to adopt some surface aspects of Sonny Rollins and John Coltrane. Webster, on the other hand, remained wholly himself to the end, and his simpler, more direct style and brilliant use of space wore better. Both men produced beautiful sounds, and sometimes sound alone seemed enough. And Byas, slight disorientation notwithstanding, was a supreme master of the saxophone, always instructive to hear. The blues and standards here are dialogs, but each man has a ballad feature to himself. Byas's "Lullabye to Dottie Mae" is beautifully played and harmonically challenging, but Webster's "When Ash Meets Henry," though the album's shortest track, is also its high point. The rhythm section (pianist Tete Montoliu, bassist Peter Trunk, drummer Albert Heath) is adequate, but not ideal. Montoliu, the gifted Spanish (Catalonia) pianist, has some good moments. *—Dan Morgenstern,* Down Beat

○ **For the Guv'nor (Tribute to Duke Ellington)** / May 26, 1969 / Charly 15

○ **At Work in Europe** / May 26, 1969 / Prestige 24031
Ben Webster was, and almost always has been, considered one of the leading tenor saxophonists, and while the Black Lion 1965 dates were probably by far the finest results of his last years in Europe, there remains precious little in today's record racks by which to judge this master's value. The soul LP on this Prestige twofer package is *Blow Ben Blow,* from a Scandinavian label; the Ellington tribute is from a Dutch label; both LPs are from '69. Like his stylistic mentor, Johnny Hodges, Webster toward the end of his career was highly variable, and on these 10 songs he tends to rely on his big, lovely sound (guaranteed to melt a cold heart at 50 paces). Other familiar Webster-Hodges techniques include the dramatic attack, the perfectly timed upper-register phrase, the minute decoration, and Webster's patented solo-ending trills. If the soul LP has shorter ideas, the second is more mellowed-out—"I Got it Bad (And That Ain't Good)" and the jaunty relaxation of "Rockin' in Rhythm." On the whole, however, the soul set is a better. Among his accompaniments, pianist Kenny Drew and Frans Wieringa alternate solos in each song, and the usually admirable former is not at his best. Drummer John Engels's nervous energy conflicts with a basically poised percussion style, while bassist Niels-Henning Ørsted-Pedersen again proves he's one of the most genuinely musical bassists in today's jazz. *—John Litweiler,* Down Beat

○ **Live at the Haarlemse Jazzclub** / May 9, 1972 / Cat 11
The unmistakable tenor "whoose" that announces the first tune of *Live at the Haarlemse Jazzclub* tips the listener off to the identity of the saxophonist. Captured on the bandstand of a nitery in Haarlem, Holland, is yet another late period (5/9/72) sampling of Ben Webster doing his wonderful thing with a pickup trio (Tete Montoliu, p; Bob Langeris, b; Tony Inzalaco, d) over a set of standards (55:28), the last of which, "Perdido," did not appear on the original issue. Webster is in fine form, investing the medium swingers with physical

drive, literally pulling the bassist along at times and touching the hearts of the ballads with his inimitable tender gruffness. Montoliu helps him carry the load and you can hear Webster in the background digging his solo work and uttering encouragement. *—Larry Hollis,* Cadence

Did You Call / i. 1972 / Nessa

○ **My Man** / Jan. 11-19, 1973 / Steeple Chase 1008
This session was taken from a series of recorded nights live at the Montmarte, and tenor saxophonist Ben Webster, whether relaxed or jumping, is on the money. The top moment for me comes on a 10-minute beautifully sustained "Old Folks." Webster really sings it, and Billie Holiday comes to mind the way he phrases. Pianist Ole Hansen also does a beautiful job of bridging Webster's two solos. Recorded just a bit before Webster's death, this is no second-best tribute. *—Bob Rusch,* Cadence

○ **Ben and the Boys** / i. Apr. 1977 / Jazz Archives 35
This covers tenor saxophonist Ben Webster betwixt and between. On "Tea for Two" we have the rough Webster, on the next track the mellow warmth more closely associated with his later work and I think really his forte. For the most part it's the mellow Webster on the 1944 radio transcriptions (excellent sound). Evidently this was Webster's date as he dominates. Trumpeter Hot Lips Page is most interesting on "Woke Up Clipped" where he sounds more like Cootie Williams. Of the three uptempo pieces ("Tea," "The Horn," "Teezol"), only on "Teezol" does Webster show an independence from Coleman Hawkins. Even on the 1958 date he has a tendency to fall into the leathery Hawkins style, although it is more assuredly Ben Webster on this rather cold TV taping. In fact, it isn't until guitarist Mundell Lowe solos, after choruses from Webster and trumpeter Buck Clayton, that things begin to warm up a bit. The two dates with Duke Ellington suffer from the worst sound and are obviously from a dance or private party. Buster Bailey takes a rather inspired solo, uncharacteristically vibrant but a bit shrill (possibly the reproducing system). Ellington's work is drowned out by the sound. Tenor saxophonist Don Byas takes the best solo; in fact it really belongs on a Byas anthology, especially since Webster's solo following a bit of Ellington is rather sloppy, and again heavily dependent on Hawkins, sounding a bit forced. This is the longest track, lasting about 13 minutes and really of note only for Byas's work. "Honeysuckle" has the same atmosphere, opening midway into Stuff Smith's solo riffs; Webster forces while Herbie Fields struggles in their respective tenor solos. The piece ends during Dexter Gordon's lengthy tenor solo, but I suspect not much was lost—certainly not much was gained. The Woody Herman date is from a V-disc and largely dominated by Herman's period vocal. Trombonist Bill Harris solos, then Flip Phillips on tenor with Webster coming in so closely after Phillips's solo that for the few bars he sounds like Phillips. While side two has interest, this record could be recommended for the eight 1944 sides by themselves. *—Geoff Millerman,* Cadence

○ **Saturday Night at the Montmartre** / i. 1987 / JZM 5029

○ **Plays Duke Ellington** / Storyville 4133

Giants of Tenor Sax / Commodore 7005

Kid and the Brute, The / Verve
Here is another excellent pairing, this time with Illinois Jacquet (ts). *—Ron Wynn*

FREDDIE WEBSTER

b. 1916, d. 1947
Swing, big band, bop
Miles Davis's unqualified praise of Freddie Webster, and his adaption of several of Webster's stylistic tendencies, coupled with Webster's brief career, have made Freddie Webster a legendary figure. He recorded only a few solos, which definitely have a poignant, compelling sound. Dizzy Gillespie was quoted as saying that Webster had the best sound of anyone since the horn was invented, certainly a staggering

statement. But close listening to his few recorded solos shows that Webster had a huge, gorgeous tone and was quite melodically inventive. He led his own band as a teen, and worked with Earl Hines and Erskine Tate in the late '30s. Webster moved to New York in 1939; for the remainder of his life, he worked with Benny Carter, Eddie Durham, Lucky Millinder, Jimmie Lunceford, Sarah Vaughan, Cab Calloway, John Kirby, Dizzy Gillespie's big band, and Sonny Stitt. The limited amount of Webster's music available on record makes it difficult to assess the accuracy of his reputation, but it's hard to go against musicians the caliber of Dizzy Gillespie and Miles Davis. Webster's playing on songs by Sarah Vaughan and Millinder supports Gillespie's contention. —*Ron Wynn*

DICKY WELLS (William Wells)

b. Jun. 10, 1907, Centerville, TN, **d.** Nov. 12, 1985, New York, NY

Trombone / Swing, big band

Dicky Wells numbers among swing's most admired, influential trombonists. His playing balanced comedy with sophistication, could be bluesy or harsh, and was often dazzling and fluid. He had a rich, expressive and flashy approach, and cleverly utilized growls and smears. Wells solos were characterized by superb melodic skills and expert pacing and note selection. He played in local bands as a teen in Louisville, where he first encountered the music of a player who was a lifelong influence, Jimmy Harrison. Wells moved to New York in 1926. During the early '30s, he worked in the bands of Fletcher Henderson, Benny Carter, Spike Hughes, and Teddy Hill, then earned national acclaim during his first stint with Count Basie. He played with Basie from 1938 to 1945, and penned "After Theatre Jump" during this tenure. He played with Sy Oliver in 1946 and 1947, then returned to Basie from 1947 to 1950. Wells played with Jimmy Rushing in the early '50s, and toured Europe with Buck Clayton in 1959 and 1961. He spent 1961, '62, and '63 in the Ray Charles Orchestra, and also worked in the '60s for B.B. King. Wells did freelance recording and touring for the remainder of his career, and occasionally cut sessions with various Basie sidemen and alumni under the banner the Countsmen. He made a fine album in 1981 with Buddy Tate. Wells's autobiography, *Night People*, was both hilarious and informative. —*Ron Wynn*

★ **Dickie Wells in Paris** / Jul. 7-Jul. 12, 1937 / Prestige 7593

○ **Bones for the King** / Feb. 3-4, 1958 / Felsted 2006
This LP comprises two different dates, 2/3/58 and 2/4/58. The 2/3 date finds Wells in a trombone choir with Vic Dickenson, Benny Morton, and George Matthews backed by Skip Hall (o), Major Holley (b), and Jo Jones (d). It's a very nicely arranged session, though still relaxed and open with some nice jive bantering on "Sweet Daddy." The next day's session has a more jamming ambiance with Skip Hall, now on piano, Jones, and Holley now joined by Buck Clayton (tpt), Rudy Rutherford (cl, bs), and an effective Everett Barksdale on guitar. There is some fine riff and chorus material here as you'd expect, but it is also good to hear Rudy Rutherford exposed so well, his clarinet sounding like a mix of Pee Wee Russell and Tony Scott, on an attractive mix of mainstream and modern. —*Bob Rusch*, Cadence

○ **Trombone Four in Hand** / Apr. 21, 1959 / Felsted 2009

○ **Lonesome Road** / **i.** Oct. 1982 / Uptown 2707
This was Dicky Wells's first LP in over 20 years and a remarkable achievement in view of the fact that he suffered a savage beating during the course of a robbery in 1975 and spent most of that year and 1976 in and out of the hospital. A layoff of this length when you are in your mid-sixties would be difficult for any musician, but particularly so for a trombonist. Indeed, Wells starts off the very first track out of tune, which gives a poor initial impression. On the blues, he uses most of his space for ingratiating vocals and contents himself with a short solo staying fairly close to the tune on most of the remainder. However, on "Dicky's Famous

Break," he concentrates all his resources and produces a fine example of trombone playing. Buddy Tate (ts, c) also takes little solo space, leaving more than usual room to stretch out and display the skills of the rhythm section led by reliable pianist Dick Katz and with the two premier bassists, George Duvivier and Michael Moore. —*Shirley Klett*, Cadence

DICK WELLSTOOD (Richard McQueen Wellstood)

b. Nov. 25, 1927, Greenwich, CT, **d.** Jul. 24, 1987, Palo Alto, CA

Piano

A gifted, aggressive pianist who choose to play mostly traditional styles rather than contemporary material, Dick Wellstood excelled at boogie-woogie, stride, and ragtime, as well as traditional jazz and swing, since the mid-'40s. One of the most knowledgeable harmonic technicians, Wellstood also mastered bebop, and included songs such as "Giant Steps" in his concerts, along with the music of Fats Waller and Scott Joplin. His playing wasn't simply repertory, but blossomed and featured his own distinctive sound and flair, no matter what style. Wellstood played with Bob Wilber in the mid-'40s, then worked with Sidney Bechet in Chicago. He later played with Rex Stewart and Charlie Shavers at Nick's in New York. Wellstood toured with the World's Greatest Jazz Band, and, in the '80s, played with the Blue Three featuring Kenny Davern and Bobby Rosengarden. He did numerous dates for Chiaroscuro, as well as sessions for Jazzology, Swingtime, and Statiris, among others. Wellstood's list of musical associates included Roy Eldridge, Conrad Janis, Henry "Red" Allen, Coleman Hawkins, Wild Bill Davison, Vic Dickenson, Buster Bailey, Gene Krupa, and society orchestra bandleader Paul Hoffman. He's well represented on CD. —*Ron Wynn*

○ **Dick Wellstood Alone** / Nov. 1970-Mar. 1971 / Jazzology 73

★ **Dick Wellstood and His Famous Orchestra Featuring Kenny Davern** / Jul. 1973-Dec. 1973 / Chiaroscuro 129
The album's title is a put-on; Dick Wellstood and Kenny Davern are the only two members of this "orchestra," and their mood is equally lighthearted. The feeling is unabashedly retrospective as these men nostalgically glance at the Chicago jazz scene of the '20s. The spirit of good clean fun is especially evident in Wellstood's playing. Davern is easier to take seriously. A loose, metallic-toned saxophonist fond of long, high, held notes laden with vibrato, he is never guilty of Wellstood's occasional lapses of taste. He peaks on his original "Cashmir and Togas," which he plays unaccompanied. His playing, always idiomatically correct, is frequently quite exciting. —*Jon Balleras*, Down Beat

○ **Live at Hanratty's** / 1981 / Chaz Jazz 108
The choice of tunes here—and there are nearly two dozen of them—was excellent. It is a canny mixture of less-often-heard standards (though the required "Ain't MisBehavin'" is included) and jazz and blues tidbits. Basically, this is an album of one of our finest solo pianists, playing on a piano of his own choosing in a relaxed club atmosphere that inspires him to various heights without causing him to reach for flashy effects. It swings mighily and packs an inordinate amount of joy into each side. —*Lee Jeske*, Down Beat

○ **I Wish I Were Twins** / **i.** Mar. 1983 / Swingtime 8204

○ **Plus the Blue Three** / **i.** 1992 / Chi-Sound 129

FRANK WESS (Frank Wellington Wess)

b. Jan. 4, 1922, Kansas City, MO

Flute, tenor and alto saxophone / Bop, postbop, progressive big band

A pioneering jazz flutist, Frank Wess has blended a swinging style with bebop influences and nuances. He was an ideal partner to Frank Foster in the Basie band of the mid-'50s and early '60s, and played a softer, smoother, and lighter sound with Foster's harder and more aggressive mode. Wess's flute work, with its full, upbeat lines and expressive tones, upgraded the instrument's role in jazz. Wess began on alto sax and even played some alto solos with Count Basie, but became better known for his playing on tenor. He worked with Blanche Calloway before World War II, then served in army bands. After his discharge, Wess had a brief stint in Billy Eckstine's band, and worked for short periods with Eddie Heywood, Lucky Millinder, and Bull Moose Jackson. Wess began playing flute in 1949, then joined Count Basie in 1953. He remained with Basie until 1964. At Basie's request, Wess played alto with the band from the late '50s until the mid-'60s. He became active doing commercials and playing in pit and studio bands for plays and television shows. Wess was in the New York Jazz Quartet during the '70s, and was in the repertory group, Dameronia, in the '80s. He was also in the Toshiko Akiyoshi and the Woody Herman big bands. He's performed and recorded with old friend Frank Foster in the '80s and '90s. Some recent Wess dates on Concord and Progressive are available on CD, while earlier material has been reissued on Savoy and Fresh Sound. — *Ron Wynn and Michael G. Nastos*

Commodore Years / i. 1954 / Atlantic

○ **Flutes and Reeds** / Aug. 2, 1955 / Savoy 12022

Opus De Jazz / Oct. 28, 1955 / Savoy 12036

○ **Jazz for Playboys** / Jan. 5, 1957 / Savoy 412

★ **I Hear Ya' Talkin'** / i. Dec. 8, 1959 / Savoy 1136
This is the initial release of the '59 Savoy recording by tenor saxophonist/flutist Frank Wess. It comes as a surprise, mainly for Thad Jones's three arrangements (in light of his later big-band charts and success). He composed and arranged "Liz," "Opus," and "Struttin." Two of these employ Wess's flute in ensemble and solo; the third, "Struttin,'" is a fast vehicle for Wess's early Sonny Rollins-like tenor. The session is oriented toward Basie and the blues (Wess, Thad, bassist Eddie Jones, and baritone saxophonist Charlie Fowlkes were members of the Basie band then; drummer Gus Johnson had departed that band in 1954). Thad Jones had come under the influence of Clark Terry and the diminished scale at the time. His trumpet strikes with arrowlike precision. Pianist Hank Jones's solos flash a Cheshire smile and move lightly. — *Owen Cordle,* Down Beat

Wess to Memphis / 1971 / Enterprise

☆ **Flute Juice** / Apr. 8, 1981 / Progressive

○ **Flute Talk** / i. 1981 / Progressive
With Tommy Flanagan Trio and guitarist Chuck Wayne, Wess is unbelievable. Includes four standards and two Wess originals. This might be tricky to locate, but dig for it. It is a great album. — *Michael G. Nastos*

Two at the Top / Jun. 8-9, 1983 / Uptown 27.14
With Johnny Coles on trumpet and the Kenny Barron Trio, these are all standards with the emphasis on hard and cool bop from Kenny Dorham (tpt), Gigi Gryce (as), and Benny Golson (ts). Wess plays alto and tenor sax only. The arrangements are by Don Sickler. — *Michael G. Nastos*

Entre Nous / Nov. 1990 / Concord Jazz 4456
Frank Wess Orchestra. Very nice 1990 date, with longtime swing veterans showing the way it's done. CD version has two bonus tracks. — *Ron Wynn*

HAROLD WEST

b. 1915, d. 1951
Drums / Swing, big band, bop
A tasty, versatile drummer who functioned equally well in swing or bebop situations, Harold "Doc" West worked in many fine combos and subbed for Jo Jones in Count Basie's band during the early '40s. West provided steady, on-the-beat timekeeping for numerous bands, and never failed to keep things moving. Initially, he was a pianist and cellist before switching to drums. West played with Tiny Parham in the early '30s, then worked with Erskine Tate and Roy Eldridge. West later subbed for Chick Webb during his orchestra's Texas tour in the late '30s. West played periodically with Hot Lips Page in the late '30s and early '40s, and participated in jam sessions at Minton's Playhouse along with his occasional work in the Basie Orchestra. He recorded with

Sammy Price, Una Mae Carlisle, Roy Eldridge, Slam Stewart, Joe Turner, Leo Watson, and Wardell Gray in the '40s. He also played on a great mid-'40s session that features Charlie Parker and Tiny Grimes, and was in Errol Garner's trio in 1945 and 1950. West died while touring with Eldridge in 1951. He can be heard on various CD reissues by Billie Holiday, Grimes, Don Byas, and Garner. — *Ron Wynn*

RANDY WESTON (Randolphe E. Weston)

b. Apr. 6, 1926, Brooklyn, NY
Piano, composer, bandleader / Postbop, progressive big band, world fusion, neo-bop, modern creative
Randy Weston has pioneered a compositional and playing style that merges the influence of Thelonious Monk's unconventional concepts with the multiple rhythms and accents of African music. Weston's also utilized bebop, blues, and funk, and has mixed all this into an arresting, energetic style with simple melodies and creative uses of dissonance, Caribbean themes, and gospel/blues riffs. Monk's impact on Weston extends to Weston's early years, when Monk informally trained Weston on piano during visits to his apartment. Weston started playing professionally in R&B bands, then worked in bebop groups with Kenny Dorham and Cecil Payne. He played with Art Blakey in the late '40s, and became Riverside's first bebop signee in 1954. Weston began leading bands with Ahmed Abdul-Malik, Ray Copeland, Payne, Booker Ervin, and Melba Liston in the late '50s. He also gained fame as a composer, with works such as "Hi-Fly," "Little Niles," and "African Cookbook." Weston worked on the West Coast before heading to Nigeria in the early '60s. He returned to Africa on a tour in 1967, then settled in Morocco and remained there until the early '70s. Weston established a nightclub and led a trio. He continued traveling in the early '70s, appearing at the 1974 Montreux Jazz Festival. Weston started recording in the '50s, and has been featured on sessions for United Artists, Jubilee, Dawn, Roulette, Bakton (his own label), Riverside, Trip, Arista/Freedom, Polydor, CTI, Atlantic, Owl, Inner City, Enja, Verve, and Antilles. After a recording drought in the early '80s, there's now an ample amount of Weston sessions available on CD. — *Ron Wynn*

Jazz à la Bohemia / Oct. 14, 1956 / Riverside 1747

How High the Moon / i. Nov. 21-22, 1956 / Biograph 12065

Live at the Five Spot / Oct. 26, 1959 / United Artists 4066

★ **Uhuru Africa** / Highlife / i. 1961 / Roulette 94510
Futuristic exploration of link between Africa and jazz, done in 1961 and 1964. Great players, and both traditional jazz and African and Latin. Reissue with many of this pianist's best compositions. — *Michael G. Nastos*

○ **Blue Moses** / Mar.-Apr. 1972 / CTI
Very rare date on CTI, one of the few that wasn't geared to pop/R&B public but was ambitious and aggressive. — *Ron Wynn*

★ **African Cookbook** / i. 1972 / Atlantic

Carnival / Jul. 5, 1974 / Freedom 741004

Blues to Africa / Aug. 14, 1974 / Freedom 741014

African Nite / Sep. 21, 1975 / Inner City 1013

○ **Little Niles** / i. Aug. 1977 / United Artists 4011
Little Niles gathers three long-unavailable late '50s Randy Weston sessions under the same title. The first, the entire reissue of the 1958 *Little Niles*, is probably the most opulent and fulfilling Weston work readily available, an intricate fabric of charging percussive layers and tight performances, underscored with a sprawling sensuality. Like Duke Ellington and Charles Mingus's boldest music, *Little Niles* is elegant, patient, and mystically urbanized in spite of its pastoral influences. The remaining sessions, an interpretative sampling of *Destry Rides Again* and a *Live at the Five Spot* album, are similarly magnetic and progressively looser. — *Mikal Gilmore,* Down Beat

Portraits of Duke Ellington / i. 1990 / Verve 841312

Topflight set by Weston, paying his homage to Duke in a very distinctive fashion. —*Ron Wynn*

Portraits of Monk / **i.** 1990 / Verve 841313

Self Portraits / **i.** 1990 / Verve 841314

☆ **Spirits of Our Ancestors** / **i.** 1991 / Antilles 511896
Weston with 11-piece band and guests Pharoah Sanders and Dizzy Gillespie. The stellar arrangements are by Melba Liston. Familiar themes are "The Healers," "Blue Moses," "African Cookbook," and "African Village/Bedford Stuyvesant." Most of the ten tracks are extended on this two-CD set. This has album of the year potential. —*Michael G. Nastos*

☆ **African Sunrise—Selections from "The Spirits . . ."** / **i.** 1992 / Antilles 517177

○ **Perspective** / Denon 8554

Zulu / Milestone

GEORGE WETTLING (George Godfrey Wettling)

b. Nov. 28, 1907, Topeka, KS, **d.** Jun. 6, 1968, New York, NY
Drums, author / Dixieland, swing, big band
A remarkably flexible drummer, George Wettling played in traditional New Orleans, swing, and Dixieland bands during his lengthy career. He was also a critic who contributed to *Down Beat*, and an artist whose work was featured on album sleeves of sessions by Eddie Condon and Joe Sullivan. Wettling was known for inventive breaks and a declarative, striking sound, plus sympathetic accompaniment and exuberant solos in those rare times he got the spotlight. Wettling worked in several Chicago bands during the '20s, then played and recorded with Paul Mares in the mid-'30s. He toured with Jack Hylton's band, and played in several cities with Wingy Manone. Wettling recorded with Jimmy McPartland in 1936 and with Manone, then worked in the orchestras of Artie Shaw, Bunny Berigan, Red Norvo, and Paul Whiteman in the late '30s and early '40s. He recorded frequently with groups assembled and/or led by Condon. During the '40s, Wettling played with Bobby Hackett and Muggsy Spanier, and with Benny Goodman, Miff Mole, and Chico Marx, and with McPartland as well. He was an ABC staff musician in the '40s and early '50s, and made regular appearances at Condon's club. Wettling made numerous recordings in the '40s and '50s with Yank Lawson, Dick Cary, Billie Holiday, Pee Wee Russell, Jack Teagarden, Hackett, Spanier, Bud Freeman, Joe Sullivan, Sidney Bechet, and Ralph Sutton. He led his own band in the mid-'50s, and played throughout the decade with McPartland, Condon, and Spanier. He kept working with Condon in the '60s, and worked with Clarence Hutchenrider. Wettling recorded as a leader for Decca, Keynote, Commodore, World Pacific, and Weathers Industries. He can be heard on CD reissues by McPartland, Holiday, Lawson, Bechet, and several others, and on the Keynote Collection. —*Ron Wynn*

★ **George Wettling's Jazz Band** / **i.** 1951 / Columbia 6189

KIRK WHALUM

Saxophone / Instrumental pop, contemporary funk
Kirk Whalum is a Memphis-born saxophonist who worked, at one time, with Arnett Cobb, and who ranks alongside George Howard and Najee as the current rage of the urban/Quiet Storm set. He's had several popular albums, and occasionally displays the kind of bombastic attack and sense of swing one would associate with a straightahead player. But most of Whalum's recordings have been rather standard fusion/instrumental pop music. —*Ron Wynn*

KENNY WHEELER (Kenneth Vincent John Wheeler)

b. Jan. 14, 1930, Toronto, Canada
Trumpet, flugelhorn / World fusion, modern creative
A Canadian-born British resident, Kenny Wheeler plays trumpet and flugelhorn. He has worked in traditional and progressive big bands, and in free music ensembles. Like his personal sound, his own group has an atmospheric, intro-

spective quality. Hard to categorize, Wheeler is an improviser and melodicist first. —*Michael G. Nastos*

○ **Gnu High** / Jun. 1975 / ECM 825591
This is long-winded and worthwhile, with the Keith Jarrett (p) Trio. —*Michael G. Nastos*

★ **Deer Wan** / Jul. 1977 / ECM 829385
For *Deer Wan*, Kenny Wheeler emerges a romanticist in the grand heroic mode. His compositions and trumpeting suggest an Olympic majesty. There is grace and eloquence, as well as a purity of sound and purpose. The players share Wheeler's point of view and also have a history of past playing experiences. This helps give the music coherence and unity. Of course, players like tenor and soprano saxophonist Jan Garbarek, guitarist John Abercrombie, bassist Dave Holland, drummer Jack DeJohnette, and guitarist Ralph Towner intrinsically shape their statements around each composition's general context. Conceptually, the players flow with and cut across Wheeler's mellow yet provocative romantic grain. In all, *Deer Wan* presents a set of impassioned lyrical sketches that effectively exploit the warm empathy of six outstanding musicians who trust and respect each other's work. —*Chuck Berg*, Down Beat

Double, Double You / May 1983 / ECM 815675

Music for Large and Small Ensembles / Jan. 1990 / ECM 843152

Widow in the Window / Feb. 1990 / ECM 843198
Quintet. Among his best, thanks to John Abercrombie (g) and Peter Erskine (d). —*Ron Wynn*

ARTHUR WHETSOL

b. 1905, **d.** 1940
Trumpet / Swing
A wonderful lead trumpeter and a remarkable soloist, Arthur Whetsol was a star in the early editions of Duke Ellington's orchestra. He had both great skills and the ability to utilize them tastefully without losing any fire or flamboyance. Whetsol was an extremely lyrical player who was gifted with one of the most touching tones of any jazz trumpeter in any era. A childhood friend of Duke Ellington, Whetsol moved to New York while playing in Elmer Snowden's band, the Washingtonians, but returned to Washington, D.C. in 1924 to study medicine at Howard University. He rejoined the band, which had become the Ellington Orchestra, in 1928. Whetsol was featured on selections such as "Black Beauty," "The Dicty Glide," "Stevedore Stomp," and "Jungle Jamboree," and on "Mood Indigo" and "Black and Tan Fantasy" as well. Whetsol played Ellington's "sweet chair" in the trumpet section, and remained an orchestra member until he was forced to retire in 1936 due to ill health. Whetsol never fully recovered, and was unable to become an effective player again. He died at age 35. Whetsol can be heard on many Ellington CD reissues of the '20s and '30s. —*Ron Wynn*

ANDREW WHITE (Andrew Nathaniel (III) White)

b. Sep. 6, 1942, Washington, DC
Saxophone, educator, transcriber / Postbop, early free, modern creative
While he is a multi-instrumentalist of some note, Andrew White's also a dedicated transcriber of John Coltrane's solos. He formed Andrew's Music in Washington, D.C. in 1971, and has published volumes of transcriptions. White's not only done hundreds of Coltrane solos in painstaking detail, but has also transcribed Charlie Parker's and Eric Dolphy's music. White's own playing, particularly on soprano and oboe, has some of the Coltrane fervor and Eastern sensibility. White also plays alto, English horn, and electric bass. He began on soprano as a child, then moved to alto before beginning on oboe as a teen. White earned his Bachelors degree at Howard University, where he studied oboe and theory. He attended Dartmouth, the Conservatoire in Paris, and SUNY-Buffalo during the mid- and late '60s. White was principal oboist with the orchestra of the American Ballet Theatre in

New York from 1968 to 1970, and played electric bass with Stevie Wonder and the Fifth Dimension from 1969 to 1970. He recorded on English horn and electric bass with Weather Report in the early '70s. White arranged and conducted music for a Coltrane big band tribute at the 1976 Newport Jazz Festival in New York. During the '80s, White led a quartet and played alto and soprano saxophones. Mal Waldron was among the musicians who played in the group. White also played in combos led by Elvin Jones and Beaver Harris. White has published books on music production and retailing in the '80s, and has also published several volumes of X-rated road stories. He's recorded many sessions on his Andrew's Music label, but none of them are available currently on CD. —*Ron Wynn and Michael G. Nastos*

Seven Giant Steps for Coltrane / Mar. 1974-Nov. 1976 / Andrew's Music 30

★ **Maxine Spotts and Brown** / i. Nov. 9, 1975 / Andrew's Music 24

Live recording at Top o' the Foolery with quartet. Includes the lengthy "Dizzy Atmosphere." Very good. —*Michael G. Nastos*

Andrew White Live in New York at the Ladies Fort / Jun. 24-25, 1977 / Andrew's Music 32

Fonk Update / Oct. 12-14, 1979 / Andrew's Music 37

Another solid statement, including the delightfully delirious "Who Got De Fonk?" —*Michael G. Nastos*

○ **I Love Japan** / Oct. 12-14, 1979 / Andrew's Music 38

Live recording at the One Step Down with quartet and this D.C. historian/transcriber/progressive saxophonist. — *Michael G. Nastos*

PAUL WHITEMAN

b. Mar. 28, 1890, Denver, CO, d. Dec. 29, 1967, Doylestown, PA

Bandleader / Big band, instrumental pop

Paul Whiteman was enormously popular in the '20s, pioneered the concept of "symphonic jazz," and was eventually tabbed "King of Jazz." That has generated a fire storm of revisionist criticism and equally spirited defense through the years, but in Whiteman's day, jazz referred only to popular, snappy, dance-based fare, not to the music of Louis Armstrong and Duke Ellington. Whiteman's father was supervisor of school music in Denver, and though Whiteman was in the local symphony, he also was interested in the fresh sound of dance rhythms. He formed a band in San Francisco, and an Atlantic City engagement won him a contract with Victor. The band had a smash in 1920 with "Whispering." They used original scores rather than stock arrangements, an innovation courtesy of pianist/composer Ferde Grofe. This helped Whiteman's orchestra became the front-runner among similar bands. Whiteman expanded into popular concert music and presented his "symphonic concert" in New York in the mid-'20s. A youthful George Gershwin was commissioned to write "Rhapsody In Blue" for the occasion. Whiteman became the most acclaimed, highest paid band leader in the world. He toured Europe in the late '20s, then opted for true jazz musicians by dismissing most of his band and hiring the greatest players from the bankrupt, disbanded Jean Goldkette orchestra. These included Bix Beiderbecke, Frankie Trumbauer, and arranger Bill Challis. A new singer named Bing Crosby was creating a stir; Whiteman later featured him in the Whiteman Rhythm Boys trio. He also headlined Jack Teagarden and Bunny Berigan in later editions, and, in the late '20s and early '30s, hired arrangers such as William Grant Still, Lennie Hayton, Challis, and Tom Satterfield. Whiteman was an astute judge of talent, and a generous employer. Like Benny Goodman, Whiteman's been judged guilty for faulty, exaggerated assessments made by others, and has not been credited fairly for his real contribution: helping to create higher performance standards in jazz-based popular music. One of his final dates spotlighted Billie Holiday. Though he retired in 1943, Whiteman was heard often on radio and

television shows, and hosted popular music programs. His huge library of arrangements was given to Williams College. Whiteman has a few reissued sessions available on CD. — *Ron Wynn and Dan Morgenstern*

☆ **Paul Whiteman and His Orchestra with Bing Crosby** / i. 192?-193? / Columbia 2830

This set, along with the two-record albums produced by Epic and Columbia and the early '30s set (*Ace of Hearts*), provides a bounty for the Crosbian, old or new; the new collector will find a great deal of jazz on these tracks, perhaps much that they were heretofore unaware of. Crosby, either solo or in section, sings on every track save one. Bix Beiderbecke gets special liner credit for his work on five of the other tracks. My copy is monaural, but this record may have been issued in "stereo" also, and I hardly need mention that the former is preferable in every respect. Too, this is one of the first reissues to utilize Columbia's new filter, which supposedly enhanced the original recordings without messing them up. The transfers are very good, but seem less lively in comparison to the three-record Beiderbecke Story discs or other Columbia reissue LPs from that general period. The notes, by Miles Kreuger, are lightly authoritative and consist largely of Whiteman's biographical details. Just as well, for there isn't much to say about most of these recordings. — *Wayne Jones*, Coda

Bix Beiderbecke Legend / i. 196? / RCA

★ **Victor Masters** / RCA 9678

Some fine sessions. Regardless of anyone's feeling about whether or not he was overrated due to racial politics, Whiteman's music was very influential on a certain level. Some fine sessions. —*Ron Wynn*

GERALD WIGGINS (Gerald Foster (Sr) Wiggins)

b. May 12, 1922, New York, NY

Piano, arranger, organ / Bop, postbop

A veteran pianist who's backed many extraordinary performers, Gerald Wiggins has a swinging style and an accomplished technique that's enabled him to adjust in swing, bebop, blues, and hard bop situations, as well as with different vocalists. Wiggins toured with comedian Stepin Fechit in the early '40s, then worked in Les Hite's orchestra and with Louis Armstrong and Benny Carter. He moved to the West Coast in the early '50s where he backed Lena Horne, and accompanied Kay Starr, Eartha Kitt, and Helen Humes. He was a music director and film coach in the studios during the '60s, while leading and recording with various trios. During the '70s, '80s, and '90s, Wiggins has done sessions for Muse, Hemisphere, Trend, Palo Alto, Specialty, Challenge, Black and Blue, and Concord. He has several dates available on CD. —*Ron Wynn and Michael G. Nastos*

Around the World in 80 Days / i. 1957 / Original Jazz Classics 1761

Wiggin' Out / Sep. 1960 / Hi Fi 618

○ **Relax and Enjoy It** / i. May 1962 / Contemporary 3595

Pianist Gerald Wiggins led this trio date (1961) with Joe Comfort (b) and Jackie Mills (d). While most people have probably heard Wiggins in support, here is a record that spotlights him (he's made numerous recordings under his name but most for very obscure labels). The playing is light swing and not terribly memorable—if there is an individual style, it's part Count Basie, Bud Powell, Art Tatum, Oscar Peterson, and some others. Ralph Gleason's liner appreciation uses the word "unspectacular" to describe Wiggins and I have no reason to suggest otherwise; it is unspectacular but pleasant basic jazz piano. —*Bob Rusch*, Cadence

★ **Live at Maybeck Recital Hall—Vol. 8** / Aug. 1990 / Concord Jazz 4450

Outstanding solo set shows Wiggins in more straight jazz setting. CD version has three bonus cuts. —*Ron Wynn*

BOB WILBER (Robert Sage Wilber)

b. Mar. 15, 1928, New York, NY

Soprano saxophone / Dixieland, swing

An excellent soprano and alto saxophonist, and a clarinetist as well as an arranger and composer, Bob Wilber has remained dedicated to classic jazz, as a player and as an educator. His shuddering soprano and woody clarinet solos as a leader, as a member of the World's Greatest Jazz Band, or with Kenny Davern, have made him a perennial favorite among traditional and nontraditional fans. Wilber's maintained his integrity and has never allowed his music to degenerate into camp or parody. He studied with Sidney Bechet in the late '40s, then, heading his band, the Wildcats, helped to bring the West Coast traditional revival to the East Coast. Wilber played with Mezz Mezzrow at the 1948 Nice Jazz Festival. He served in the army during the early '50s, then formed the Six, a group that blended traditional and bebop styles. Wilber played in the '50s with Bechet again, and with Bobby Hackett, Benny Goodman, Jack Teagarden, and Eddie Condon. He was a founding member of the World's Greatest Jazz Band in 1969, then co-led Soprano Summit with Kenny Davern from 1974 to 1979. He also began leading the Smithsonian Jazz Repertory Ensemble in the late '70s, and founded his own label, Bodeswell. Wilber led the Bechet Legacy from 1980 to 1983, and became director of jazz studies at Wilkes College in 1982. His musical arrangements for the film *The Cotton Club* won a Grammy in 1986. Wilber's recorded for Jazzology, Project 3, Monmouth-Evergreen, World Jazz, Chiaroscuro, Concord, Phonotastic (Swedish), Bodeswell, and Circle. He recreated Goodman's Carnegie Hall concert on January 19, 1988, its 50th anniversary. He's done repertory albums of Gershwin, Cole Porter, Rodgers & Hart, and Ellington music. Wilber has albums on CD that feature him as a leader, and also has dates with the Bodeswell Strings, Davern, and Pug Horton with the Crescent City Cats. *—Ron Wynn*

○ **New Clarinet in Town** / 1960 / Classic Editions 8

○ **Music of Hoagy Carmichael, The** / Jun. 1969 / Monmouth 6917

○ **Soprano Summit** / i. 1973 / World Jazz 5

This was a pleasant collection of songs, quite well done, and how good it is to hear the soprano played in an old-fashioned, big, "pretty" manner! I prefer their "Song of Songs" tempo to Sidney Bechet's, but eek, that riff in "The Mooche"! Swing players both, they are most comfortable with Bechet. *—John Litweiler*, Down Beat

○ **Chalumeau Blue** / i. Apr. 1977 / Chiaroscuro 148

Soprano saxophonist Bob Wilber has good taste, swings, is rewarding and exciting. This is another fine Hank O'Neal production with good tunes ("Black and Tan" would make Duke Ellington smile), good performances, an interesting cover, and necessary liner notes. The sound is all right, though I'd rather hear George Duvivier's bass gutsier and Fred Stoll's drumming crisper. I agree with Don Lass who states in the liners that *Soprano Summit* contains "individual voices that understand the riches of the jazz tradition and express them in modern terms." And perhaps most important, *Soprano Summit* produces music that anyone could enjoy. Certainly a change of pace for Miles Davis followers! Seriously, this is a pleasant, tasteful dish that could be placed on your (turn) table and taken away with many rich, pleasing helpings. *—Dennis R. Hendley*, Cadence

★ **Soprano Summit in Concert** / i. 1990 / Concord Jazz 4029

Soprano Summit in Concert takes a moment or two to get off the ground, with Kenny Davern providing the lift in "Stompy Jones." But once they're up they don't come down until the teasing final bars of "Swing that Music." This one is carefully crafted and balanced with lots of solo room for everyone (even drummer Jake Hanna takes one), a good mix of swingers, stompers, and ballads, canny planning in the solo order, a Duke Ellington intro, and a Louis Armstrong finale, and witty updating throughout. Bassist Ray Brown and Hanna seem very comfortable propelling the older styles, and are modern and up front in their soloing. Brown switches from two to four after the opening theme of "Swing

that Music," then back to two for guitarist Marty Groz's solo, then back again to four, intensifying the drive by matching Groz's accompaniment. Groz's Django Reinhardt-style acoustic playing has a freshness and energy most welcome after all the years of uninterrupted electric players—no mean task to bring that style back to life against such cultural resistance. As for the leaders, Bob Wilber and Davern have distinct styles and yet mesh perfectly in counterpoint. Wilbur is drier of wit and hews more closely to the idiom of the tune than Davern, whose playing is both less involved and quirkier, more piquant. On both "Stompy Jones" and "The Grapes are Ready" (the latter especially) these differences are quite clear; generally I found Davern more appealing because he is less intellectual, readier to risk a broad effect and usually able to bring it off. But, then again, Wilbur's playing on "The Golden Rooster," his own ballad, has a palpable tenderness and warmth. One shouldn't have to choose, really, between two such fine musicians—anyway when they play together you can't tell them apart. *—Joel Ray*, Cadence

LEE WILEY

b. Oct. 9, 1915, Fort Gibson, OK, **d.** Dec. 11, 1975, New York, NY

Vocals / Ballads & blues

A top jazz vocalist with a distinctive vibrato, a husky voice, and a progressive style, Lee Wiley was one of the earliest White singers to utilize the rhythmic innovations of Ethel Waters and other classic blues singers. Her sound contained a sensual quality, and wasn't detached despite the light, "little girl" quality she sometimes invoked. She was also an outstanding lyrical interpreter. Wiley sang in the bands of Johnny Green and Eddie Condon during the '30s, and was married to Benny Goodman's pianist, Jess Stacy. She had a hit with "It's Only a Paper Moon" while touring and playing with Stacy's band. Wiley was most active in the '30s and '40s, recording with Condon, Joe Bushkin, Max Kaminsky, Bunny Berigan, Bud Freeman, Pee Wee Russell, and Fats Waller, among others. She did sessions for Totem, Decca, Storyville, Liberty Music Shop, Columbia, and RCA, and other labels. Wiley's finest songs were interpretations of compositions by Harold Arlen, George Gershwin, Cole Porter, and Richard Rodgers/Lorenz Hart. She appeared at several Condon Town Hall concerts, and recorded periodically into the '70s. Wiley has several sessions available on RCA, Black Lion, Jass, Totem, Audiophile, and VJC CDs. *—Ron Wynn*

○ **Complete Young Lee Wiley (1931-37)** / 1931-1937 / Vintage Jazz Classics 1023

★ **Sings the Songs of Rodgers and Hart & Harold Arlen** / Audiophile 10

☆ **Sings the Songs of Ira and George Gershwin . . .** / Audiophile 1

☆ **As Time Goes By** / Bluebird 3138

ERNIE WILKINS (Ernest Brooks Wilkins)

b. Jul. 20, 1922, St. Louis, MO

Composer, arranger, tenor saxophone / Swing, big band, progressive big band

A good saxophonist, but a better arranger and composer, Ernie Wilkins has been providing fine compositions and arrangements for big bands since the early '50s. He learned piano and violin in his youth, then studied music at Wilberforce University. Wilkins played in a military band under Willie Smith's leadership in the service, then worked in the late '40s with the Jeters-Pillars Orchestra, and with Earl Hines's final big band. He joined Count Basie in the early '50s, playing alto and tenor and supplying compositions and arrangements. Wilkins also wrote tunes and arrangements for Dizzy Gillespie's mid-'50s band that toured the Middle East and South America. He later wrote arrangements for Tommy Dorsey, was a staff composer for Harry James in the early '60s, and wrote pieces for his brother Jimmy Wilkins's band. Wilkins joined Clark Terry's

B-A-D band in the late '60s as music director and principal composer, but left to form his own band after they appeared at the Montreux Jazz Festival. He supplied more compositions to Count Basie, then became head of Mainstream Records' A&R department in the early '70s. Wilkins toured Europe with Terry in the late '70s, and settled in Copenhagen in 1979. He organized the Almost Big Band in 1980. Currently, Wilkins does not have any sessions listed as available on CD, but his music can be heard on any Basie reissue after 1951. —*Ron Wynn*

○ **Trumpet Album** / **i**. 1955 / Savoy 2237
A veteran swing-era tenor saxophonist, Wilkins turns to trumpet for this occasion, with mixed results. His solos aren't embarrasing, but he is clearly working with a different instrument he hasn't fully mastered. The arrangements are good, and the overall playing fine. —*Ron Wynn*

○ **Flutes and Reeds** / Jul. 1955 / Savoy 12022

★ **Here Comes the Swingin' Mr. Wilkins** / Dec. 9, 1959 / Everest 1077

○ **Big New Band of the '60s, The** / Apr. 4+28, 1960 / Everest 1104

JACK WILKINS

b. Jun. 3, 1944
Guitar / Postbop
A masterful, in-demand guitarist, Jack Wilkins might be the finest mainstream player on the New York scene. A New York native, Wilkins has an expressive, light style with great warmth and melodic integrity. He's famous for using classical guitar techniques in his playing, and for achieving an approach similar to a pianist's in his chording. But he's also a superb blues player. Wilkins had formal training with jazz education pioneer John Mehegan, and also studied vibes, piano, and classical guitar. He's toured and recorded with Buddy Rich, and performed in concert with Stan Getz, Dizzy Gillespie, Morgana King, and Pearl Bailey. Wilkins has recorded with Jack DeJohnette, Eddie Gomez, Randy Brecker, Phil Woods, and Harvie Swartz. He currently has several sessions available on CD. —*Ron Wynn and David Nelson McCarthy*

★ **Windows** / 1973 / Mainstream 396
Among the influences guitarist Jack Wilkins cites on this album are Johnny Smith and Barney Kessel, both guitarists' guitarists, and Wilkins is a worthy successor: technically immaculate, fast, agile, and smooth. His solo on the first cut, "Windows," is representative—long, fluid, and pretty. As Chick Corea composed and performs the tune, it is full of exciting harmonic and rhythmic possibilities, none of which Wilkins exploits. The best thing on the track is the exchange and duet between bassist Mike Moore and drummer Bill Goodwin. "Red Clay" and "Last Act" are both well conceived, the former a medium-tempo march, the latter an acoustic foray for Wilkins with a bolero introduction. —*Alan Heineman,* Down Beat

○ **Call Him Reckless** / **i**. 1988 / Music Masters 5019

Alien Army / **i**. 1991 / Music Masters 5049

BUSTER WILLIAMS (Charles Anthony Williams)

b. Apr. 17, 1942, Camden, NJ
Bass / Postbop, neo-bop
Here's one bassist who prefers the background to the spotlight, and sees himself in a supportive rather than starring role. Buster Williams has made subtle swing, precise rhythms, a startling tone, and impeccable technique the hallmark of his playing with numerous bands since the early '60s. He learned both bass and drums from his father, opting for bass after he was impressed by recordings featuring Oscar Pettiford solos. Williams studied harmony, composition, and theory at Combs College of Music in Philadelphia in the late '50s, then worked with Jimmy Heath. He toured and recorded with the Gene Ammons/Sonny Stitt quintet in 1960 and 1961. Williams played with vocalists Dakota

Staton, Betty Carter, Sarah Vaughan, and Nancy Wilson in the mid- and late '60s, recording with Vaughan and Wilson. Williams moved to Los Angeles while with Wilson, and played and recorded with the Jazz Crusaders, Prince Lasha, and the Bobby Hutcherson-Harold Land quintet while he also worked with Miles Davis. He moved to New York in 1969 and joined Herbie Hancock, playing with him until 1972. Williams also recorded with Dexter Gordon and Mary Lou Williams in the late '60s and early '70s. He worked with Ron Carter in Carter's group during the late '70s, and did some rare sessions as a leader for Muse and Buddah. Williams worked with Kenny Barron, the Timeless All-Stars, and Sphere in the '80s. Unfortunately, at present there's only one Williams session available on CD, a '76 date on Muse. — *Ron Wynn*

○ **Crystal Reflections** / Aug. 1976 / Muse 5430
Excellent set. No reed or brass soloist but Kenny Barron (p) and Jimmy Rowles (p) are super. One of the last times Roy Ayers plays vibes in a jazz context on record. —*Ron Wynn*

★ **Heartbeat** / Mar. 28-Apr. 3, 1978 / Muse 5171
A diverse session of jazz touches by pop guests on the four originals by bassist Williams, one standard, and one by Jimmy Rowles. Includes Rowles (p), Kenny Barron (p), Ben Riley (d), and vocalist Suzanne Klewan, and strings from Pat and Gayle Dixon. —*Michael G. Nastos*

CLARENCE WILLIAMS

b. 1893, Plaquemine, LA, **d.** Nov. 6, 1965, New York, NY
Piano, vocals / New Orleans traditional
Organization and consistency were what made Clarence Williams a key figure among early jazz musicians. He rivaled Fletcher Henderson as one of the most recorded Black performers during the '20s, and published and promoted the work of seminal stars such as Fats Waller, James P. Johnson, Willie "The Lion" Smith, and Spencer Williams, while co-writing major songs like "Royal Garden Blues," "Squeeze Me," "Baby, Won't You Please Come Home" and "Taint Nobody's Business If I Do." In addition, his groups, especially The Blue Five, were an important repertory ensemble and backing band for several vocalists. Williams's piano playing and vocals were merely effective at best, but the 300 Williams songs issued between 1921 and 1938 included many extraordinary performances.

Williams was part Creole and part Choctaw. At one time, both his widow and his death certificate gave Williams's birth date as 1898, but further research now shows it was 1893. His childhood included periods where he worked in a hotel and sang in a street band. He came to New Orleans in 1906, and traveled with a minstrel show as an emcee, singer, and dancer until 1911. Williams began managing a cabaret in 1913, then started a music publishing venture with A.J. Piron. Williams moved to Chicago later in the decade, before relocating permanently to New York City in 1920. Prior to going to Chicago, he toured with Piron. Williams cut his first records in 1921, singing with a White band. By 1923, he'd become Okeh's "race music" A&R director, and in that capacity, along with being a bandleader, he became a conduit for the jazz community.

The careers of Louis Armstrong, Sidney Bechet, Buster Bailey, King Oliver, Don Redman, Coleman Hawkins, Lonnie Johnson, Bubber Miley, Tommy Ladnier, and Jimmy Harrison were aided by Williams, who either employed them or got them recording sessions. Williams played on Bessie Smith sessions, and she cut several of his songs. He also backed vocalists Butterbeans & Susie, Sara Martin, Sippie Wallace, and Eva Taylor (whom he married in 1921). The original Blue Five included Thomas Morris, Charlie Irvis or John Mayfield, Sticky Elliott or Bechet, and Buddy Christian. Armstrong was a member of the Blue Five in 1924 and 1925, and Bailey, Aaron Thompson, Hawkins, Redman, and Miley later became members. They continued recording through 1927. Williams later made nearly 100 recordings for Okeh, Vocalion, and Victor from 1927 to 1939 with "washboard" bands that included Ed Allen, Bailey or

Cecil Scott, and Floyd Casey. Williams concentrated on writing after the late '30s, but led a final Blue Five session in 1941 with James P. Johnson, Wellman Braud, and Taylor doing vocals, then sold his catalog to Decca in 1943. He was a shop owner in Harlem, but went blind after he was hit by a taxi in 1956. Nearly 11 years after his death, a comprehensive bio-discography by Tom Lord called *Clarence Williams* put his accomplishments into perspective. —*Ron Wynn*

○ **Complete Sessions—Vol. 1 (1923-1926), The** / Jul. 30, 1923-Nov. 14, 1923 / EPM 5107

○ **Complete Sessions—Vol. 2 (1923-1931), The** / Nov. 1923-Mar. 1925 / EPM 5109

★ **Clarence Williams (1927-1934)** / 1927-1934 / DRG 36829

○ **Jazz Heritage: Music Man (1929-1934)** / 1929-1934 / MCA 1349

COOTIE WILLIAMS (Charles Melvin Williams)

b. Jul. 10, 1911, Mobile, AL, **d.** Sep. 15, 1985, New York, NY
Trumpet, bandleader / Swing, big band
A majestic soloist, Cootie Williams turned the trumpet into a sonic weapon. Whether he played open or muted, Williams performed ringing anthems that could sear paint off the walls or reduce listeners to tears with their shimmering beauty. He was just as masterful accompanying singers, and rivaled any Delta or gutbucket vocalist in his blues interpretations. Duke Ellington's "Concerto for Cootie" and "New Concerto for Cootie," done 23 years apart, are clinical workouts that reflect trumpet greatness, and experience.

Williams played in his school band on Long Island. At age 14, he played one summer with the Young Family band, and met Lester Young in the process. Williams toured Florida with Edd Hall, and worked in Eagle Eye Shields's band before going to New York with Alonzo Ross's Dixie Syncopators. He worked briefly with Chick Webb and Fletcher Henderson before replacing Bubber Miley in the Ellington Orchestra in 1929. Besides being featured on several combo sessions with Ellingtonians outside the orchestra, Williams amazed the jazz world with marvelous solos on "Echoes of Harlem" in 1936 and "Concerto for Cootie" in 1940. Williams made his own outside sessions from 1937 to 1940, heading a combo billed as the Gotham Stompers. It blended Ellington and Webb band personnel, plus vocalist Ivie Anderson. Williams also recorded with Lionel Hampton, Teddy Wilson, and Billie Holiday during this period. He left Ellington to join the Benny Goodman orchestra in 1940, and was featured on some impressive recordings. These included "Breakfast Feud," "Wholly Cats," and "Royal Garden Blues."

After a year, Williams left to form his own band, which he led for most of the '40s. At various times, the group included Charlie Parker, Eddie Davis, Ben Thigpen, Kenny Clarke, and Bud Powell, but they never achieved much success. They recorded an early version of Thelonious Monk's "Epistrophy" under the name "Fly Right." The band scored its biggest hits in the mid-'40s with "Tess Torch Song," which featured vocalist Pearl Bailey, and "Cherry Red Blues" with lead singer Eddie Vinson. After more tours, Williams served as a session musician on various R&B dates in the early '50s. He continued leading groups, and teamed with Rex Stewart on some studio dates in 1957 and 1958. He rejoined Ellington in 1962. Illness began to affect his playing, and Ellington featured him primarily as a soloist in the '70s rather than with the trumpet section. He remained in the band after Duke died, and played with it into the late '70s. He died in 1985. —*Ron Wynn*

★ **Sextet And Orchestra: 1944 Recordings** / Jan. 6-Aug. 22, 1944 / Phoenix 1

○ **Big Challenge, The** / i. Apr.+May 1957 / Jazztone 77

○ **Cootie and Rex** / i. Dec. 12, 1957 / Jazztone 1268

JAMES WILLIAMS

b. Mar. 8, 1951, Memphis, TN
Piano / Neo-bop

A dynamic rhythm player and perhaps jazz's best gospel-tinged pianist since Bobby Timmons, James Williams has been an important contributor to many groups and has issued several good recordings. Red Garland, Herbie Hancock, and Ahmad Jamal are mentioned prominently as Williams's influences, though he's never recorded in Jamal's pop style. His voicings and phrasing are quite reminiscent of Phineas Newborn, though he's not as imaginative a harmonic stylist nor as emphatic a soloist. Williams's playing has gained sophistication steadily, and his most recent release, *James Williams Meets the Saxophone Masters*, demonstrates his heightened leadership and solo prowess. He played gospel and R&B in Memphis, and started on piano at age 13. Williams became interested in jazz after attending Memphis State University. Following his graduation, he taught at Berklee in the mid-'70s. Williams also worked with several area groups and played with Joe Henderson, Alan Dawson, Woody Shaw, Milt Jackson, and Clark Terry. He joined Art Blakey's Jazz Messengers in 1977, and remained until 1981. Williams began leading bands in the mid-'80s, and played with Sonny Stitt, Louis Hayes, and Slide Hampton. He began recording for Concord, and has also done dates for Sunnyside, DIW, Red, and EmArcy. Williams has recorded with Bill Easley, Kevin Eubanks, Rufus Reid, Tony Reedus, Jerry Gonzales, Richard Davis, Ronnie Burrage, Charnett Moffett, Jeff Watts, Ray Brown, Elvin Jones, George Coleman, and Blakey, among others. He has several releases available on CD. —*Ron Wynn*

Everything I Love / Apr. 17, 1979 / Concord Jazz 104
Nice touch by Williams on everything. Billy Pierce (sax) front and center. —*Ron Wynn*

Arioso Touch / Feb. 1982 / Concord Jazz 192
Wonderful 1982 date; great solos, blues influences. Buster Williams (b) and Billy Higgins (d) are great. —*Ron Wynn*

○ **Alter Ego** / Jul. 19+20, 1984 / Sunnyside 1007
This reissue, recorded in 1984, is notable for Williams's writing and engaging piano solos. With a front line of Bill Easley (sax, f, cl), Billy Pierce (ts, ss), and Kevin Eubanks (whose guitar often functions like a third horn), Williams fashions several attractive ensemble combinations. With Ray Drummond on bass and Tony Reedus on drums, the beat stays on an exciting edge. As a pianist, Williams demonstrates a bright, insistent, two-handed firmness. Thad Jones's "Yours and Mine," an unaccompanied piano solo added to this reissue, shows his harmonic richness. And Donald Brown's "Waltz for Monk" gives us his sparkling, chops-laden runs. The clarinet-tenor-guitar blend on Williams's "Black Scholars" is one example of the voicings here. This is one of Williams's six originals on the albums. Nine years later, this set more than endures; it still sounds hip. —*Owen Cordle*, Jazz Times

★ **Progress Report** / 1985 / Sunnyside 1012
Progress Report features three Art Blakey alumni: James Williams (k), Billy Pierce (reeds), and guitarist Kevin Eubanks (a member of Blakey's short-lived 1980 big band). None of the six originals (half by the leader, one from Eubanks, and a pair by Donald Brown, Williams's successor with Blakey) has a memorable melody, but all contain plenty of room for explorative chord-based improvisations. Bill Easley plays some hot modern clarinet on "Progress Report," Billy Pierce is heard throughout in top form on both tenor and soprano, and James Williams continues to display his growing mastery of the piano. The biggest surprise of the date is Kevin Eubanks who, although well recorded previously, here moves a giant step forward. His electric sound on the guitar is quite original and even if his choice of notes is more conventional, he emerges as one of the stars of this excellent date. —*Scott Yanow*, Cadence

☆ **Magical Trio 1** / i. 1987 / PolyGram 832859

Meet the Magical Trio / i. Sep. 2, 1988 / EmArcy 838653

Magical Trio 2 / i. 1989 / EmArcy 834368
Date that's just as great as its predecessor. Elvin Jones in drummer's chair this time. —*Ron Wynn*

I Remember Clifford / DIW 601

JOE WILLIAMS (Joseph Goreed)

b. Dec. 12, 1928, Cordele, GA

Vocals / Big band, blues & jazz, ballads & blues

The consummate big band vocalist, Joe Williams broadened and greatly expanded the profile of singing with large orchestras. Though his earliest influence was gospel music, Williams parlayed a rich, demonstrative bass/baritone voice and a swinging, passionate flair into stardom. He proved equally gifted at singing lush, sentimental fare, as he was at singing lowdown, gutbucket blues, or roaring, uptempo tunes. Williams was born in Georgia, but grew up in Chicago. He sang in a gospel quartet, then began performing secular music in 1937. He occasionally sang in bands led by Jimmie Noone, Coleman Hawkins, Lionel Hampton, Andy Kirk (with whom he made his first records), Hot Lips Page, and with Red Saunders (three different times) in the years prior to 1954 when he joined Count Basie. He stayed with Basie until 1961, cutting and performing many exceptional numbers and turning "Every Day I Have the Blues," which he'd initially recorded in 1951 with the King Kolax R&B band, into a definitive signature song. Williams toured with Harry Edison in 1961 and 1962, then sang with Junior Mance until 1964. In the '70s, he worked with George Shearing and Cannonball Adderley, and also had periodic reunion appearances and recording dates with Basie. After Basie died, Williams toured with the band in 1983 under Thad Jones's direction. An album Williams cut that year with Jack McDuff, Eddie Vinson, and Ray Brown got rave reviews, as did an '87 live date with the Norman Simmons quartet. He's maintained a prolific schedule, and for a few years had a recurring role on the Cosby television show. In 1993, he was one of several jazz artists who appeared at the White House. *—Ron Wynn*

☆ **Every Day I Have the Blues** / i. 1951-Sep. 28, 1953 / Savoy 1140

From the Roulette catalog, this superior Joe Williams/Count Basie collaboration finds the singer concentrating on the blues with consistently excellent results. In addition to a remake of the title cut, Williams is heard at his best on the classic "Goin' to Chicago" and such numbers as "Just a Dream," "Cherry Red," and "Good Mornin' Blues." This LP is well worth searching for. *—Scott Yanow*

★ **Count Basie Swings / Joe Williams Sings** / i. Jul. 17-Jul. 26, 1955 / Verve 825770

This is the definitive Joe Williams record, cut shortly after he joined Count Basie's orchestra. Included are his classic versions of "Every Day I Have the Blues," "The Comeback," "Alright, Okay, You Win," "In the Evening," and "Teach Me Tonight." Williams's popularity was a major asset to Basie and getting to sing with that swinging big band on a nightly basis certainly did not harm the singer! This gem belongs in everyone's jazz collection. *—Scott Yanow*

☆ **A Swingin' Night at Birdland** / Jun. 1962 / Roulette 52085

In 1961, after six years as one of the main attractions of Count Basie's orchestra, Williams (with Count's blessing) went out on his own. One of his first sessions was this live recording cut at Birdland with a strong quintet that featured trumpeter Harry "Sweets" Edison and Jimmy Forrest on tenor. Williams mostly sings standards and ballads but also tosses in a few of his popular blues (including "Well Alright, Okay, You Win" and "Goin' to Chicago") during a well-rounded and thoroughly enjoyable set. *—Scott Yanow*

☆ **Overwhelmin', The** / i. 1963-1965 / Bluebird 6464

A CD sampler drawn from five former LPs, this fine CD features Joe Williams doing three songs from Duke Ellington's play *Jump for Joy*, five numbers at the 1963 Newport Jazz Festival (joined by trumpeters Clark Terry and Howard McGhee and tenor greats Coleman Hawkins, Zoot Sims, and Ben Webster), four blues backed by an all-star jazz group, and five ballads in front of an orchestra. Although it would be preferable to have each of the five original albums intact,

this superb collection features Joe Williams on a wide variety of material and he is heard close to his peak throughout. *—Scott Yanow*

☆ **Presenting Joe Williams and Thad Jones-Mel Lewis** / Sep. 30, 1966 / Solid State 18008

This was a logical matchup. The Thad Jones-Mel Lewis orchestra, heard during its first year in existence when it was really an all-star ensemble, does an excellent job of accompanying Joe Williams on a few of his standards (including "Gee Baby, Ain't I Good to You," "Come Sunday," and "Smack Dab in the Middle") and a few more-obscure tunes. Even though Thad Jones's charts allocate little solo space to the many great sidemen, Williams is in such fine form on this out-of-print LP that one barely notices. *—Scott Yanow*

Music Is to Hear: Joe Williams / Mar. 12, 1971 / Sheba
The Heart and Soul of Joe Williams. Impossible to find, but well worth the hunt. *—Ron Wynn*

★ **Joe Williams Live** / i. 1978 / Fantasy 438

Williams meets the Cannonball Adderley septet on this rather interesting session. The expanded rhythm section, which includes keyboardist George Duke and both acoustic bassist Walter Booker and the electric bass of Carol Kaye, gives funky accompaniment to Williams while altoist Cannonball and cornetist Nat have some solo space. Actually, the singer easily steals the show on a rather searing version of "Goin' to Chicago Blues," his own "Who She Do," and a few unusual songs including Duke Ellington's "Heritage." *—Scott Yanow*

☆ **Every Night—Live at Vine St.** / i. 1979 / Verve 833236

The focus is entirely on Joe Williams (who is backed by a standard four-piece rhythm section) during this live session from Vine Street. Then 69, Williams had not lost a thing and his voice has rarely sounded stronger. This version of "Every Day I Have the Blues" is transformed into Miles Davis's "All Blues." Williams revives Eubie Blake's "A Dollar for a Dime" and sounds wonderful on such songs as "Too Marvelous for Words," "I Want a Little Girl," and "Roll 'Em Pete." The best of Joe Williams's records from the 1980s. *—Scott Yanow*

○ **Prez Conference** / i. 1979 / GNP 2124

Dave Pell's Prez Conference was to Lester Young what Supersax was to Charlie Parker. Pell's short-lived group featured harmonized Lester Young solos recreated by three tenors and a baritone; their matchup with singer Joe Williams is quite enjoyable. Since Young was in Count Basie's orchestra when Jimmy Rushing was the vocalist, Joe Williams has a rare opportunity here to give his own interpretation to Rushing and Billie Holiday classics like "I May Be Wrong," "You Can Depend on Me," "If Dreams Come True," and "Easy Living." A delightful and swinging date. *—Scott Yanow*

○ **Nothin' But the Blues** / i. Mar. 1983 / Delos 4001

Sticking to blues, Joe Williams is in prime form on this special session. His backup crew includes such all-stars as tenor saxophonist Red Holloway, organist Brother Jack McDuff, and (on alto and one lone vocal) the great Eddie "Cleanhead" Vinson. The many blues standards are familiar, but these versions are lively and fresh. *—Scott Yanow*

○ **Every Day I Have the Blues** / i. Mar. 1985 / Roulette 52033

☆ **I Just Wanna Sing** / i. 1987 / Delos 4004

For this session, Joe Williams is backed by such master jazzmen as trumpeter Thad Jones, the contrasting tenors of Eddie "Lockjaw" Davis and Benny Golson, and guitarist John Collins. The material varies from the dated humor of "It's Not Easy Being White" to classic versions of "Until I Met You" and "I Got It Bad." Joe Williams is in prime form and this is one of his better sessions from his later years. *—Scott Yanow*

○ **Ballad and Blues Master** / i. May 7-8, 1987 / Verve 511354

Taken from the same sessions that had previously resulted in *Every Night*, the identical adjectives apply. Joe Williams is in superior form on this live date, putting a lot of feeling into such songs as "You Can Depend on Me," "When Sunny Gets

Blue," and "Dinner for One Please, James." A closing blues medley is particularly enjoyable, and the backup by a quartet that includes pianist Morman Simmons and guitarist Henry Johnson is tasteful and swinging. —*Scott Yanow*

☆ **In Good Company** / **i**. 1989 / PolyGram 837932
A bit of a grab bag, this CD finds Joe Williams joined by Supersax on two numbers, doing a pair of vocal duets with Marlena Shaw ("Is You Is or Is You Ain't My Baby" is excellent), teaming up with vocalist-pianist Shirley Horn for two ballads, and being joined by the Norman Simmons quartet for the remainder. Sticking mostly to standards, Joe Williams shows that at 70 he still had the magic. —*Scott Yanow*

○ **Jump for Joy** / RCA 2713

MARY LOU WILLIAMS (Mary Lou [Née Scruggs, Mary Elfrieda] Williams)

b. May 8, 1910, Atlanta, GA, **d**. May 28, 1981, Durham, NC
Piano, composer, arranger / Swing, big band
A superb pianist, Mary Lou Williams was one of jazz's more progressive and forward-looking stylists. Her early playing fused stride and boogie-woogie elements; she adapted to bop, and by the '60s, her solos had become more complex, and creatively incorporated dissonance without sacrificing blues feeling or emotional intensity. She was a vital composer and arranger whose work included pivotal music for Andy Kirk's swing band in the '30s, 1946's "Waltz Boogie" in which Williams adapted jazz to non-duple meters, and her sacred works of the '60s and '70s, masses and a cantata.

Williams grew up in Pittsburgh, where she was playing by ear at age six, and worked in carnival and vaudeville shows at age 13. She started performing as Mary Lou Burley, and joined a group led by John Williams in 1925. The two married shortly afterward. She became Andy Kirk's deputy pianist and arranger in 1929, after he took over Terrence Holden's band, of which Williams was a member. By 1930, she was a full member. Her arrangements, compositions, and outstanding solos helped make the Kirk band one of the decade's finest. At the time, she was also writing arrangements for Benny Goodman, Earl Hines, and Tommy Dorsey. "Froggy Bottom," "Walkin' and Swingin'," and "Little Joe from Chicago" were among the songs she wrote for Kirk's orchestra, while she penned "Camel Hop" and "Roll 'Em" for Goodman.

Williams stayed with Kirk until 1942, then formed her own band in New York with trumpeter Shorty Baker, who became her second husband. There was a brief stint as a staff arranger for Duke Ellington in the '40s, and she contributed "Trumpet No End" to his orchestra's book in 1946. One year after Williams played "Zodiac Suite" at Town Hall, the New York Philharmonic performed three movements from it at Carnegie Hall, one of the first times a major symphony orchestra recognized a jazz composer's works. Williams contributed scores to Dizzy Gillespie's big band, and continued writing influential songs. "In the Land of Oo-Bla-Dee," which she co-wrote and recorded for King with Pancho Hagood's vocals in 1949, was subsequently recorded by Gillespie. The 1947 song "Satchel-Mouth Baby" on Asch was turned into "Pretty Eyed Baby" for Frankie Laine and Jo Stafford in 1951. She played briefly with Goodman in 1948, then moved to Europe from 1952 to 1954. She left the music world in 1954, became a Catholic, and formed a foundation to help musicians with personal problems.

Williams returned to playing music in 1957, and played with Gillespie at the Newport Festival. In the '60s and '70s, she divided her time between leading groups in New York clubs and recording and composing sacred pieces for jazz orchestras and voices. These included "Black Christ of the Andes" in 1963, and "Mary Lou's Mass" in 1970, which Alvin Ailey later choreographed. There were memorable '70s albums with Buster Williams, Mickey Roker, Buddy Tate, and the controversial, sometimes compelling, but ultimately uneven *Embraced* in 1977, which paired her with Cecil Taylor. Williams also became a busy educator. She recorded *The History of Jazz* in 1970, an elaborate project featuring her

solo piano and commentary. After getting several honorary doctorates, Williams joined Duke University's faculty in 1977, and stayed at the university until her death in 1981. —*Ron Wynn and Dan Morgenstern*

★ **Roll 'Em** / **i**. 1944 / Audiophile
Good 1988 reissue of Williams doing boogie, swing, and blues from the '40s. —*Ron Wynn*

Asch Recordings / Mar. 12, 1944-1947 / Smithsonian/Folkways 2966

Town Hall (1945): The Zodiac Suite / Jun. 29, 1945 / Vintage Jazz Classics 1035

First Lady of the Piano, The / Jan. 23, 1953 / Inner City 7006
Exceptional pieces, with Coleman Hawkins (sax), Don Byas (ts), and other swing lords. —*Ron Wynn*

In London / Jan. 23, 1953 / GNP 9029

Zoning / 1974 / Smithsonian/Folkways 40811

Free Spirits / Jul. 8, 1975 / Steeple Chase 104
Includes great trio cuts with Buster Williams (b) and Mickey Roker (d). —*Ron Wynn*

★ **Live at the Cookery** / Oct. 1975 / Chiaroscuro 146
Mary Lou Williams could, without a doubt, handle solo piano. Here she plays with rhythm (b) and leaves space to be filled by rhythm. Only at times is it filled fully by the bass, the result being that on some of the uptempos ("Praise the Lord," "Grand Night," and "Surrey with Fringe on Top" in particular) there is an imbalance, openings alluded to, but not fully filled by Brian Torff. In such a duo setting the bassist must not only maintain or imply the rhythm, but add the accent as well. Here I think Torff follows too closely to Williams's own bass lead. The music would perhaps sound fuller had he taken more of the shared role and exerted his own lead more. Aside from this, and this is an aside and not omnipresent, there is some exceptionally fine music with "Roll 'Em" covering about 20 years of jazz style. Williams is particularly inventive throughout and it makes the 20 minutes move exceptionally fast. —*Carol Boer*, Cadence

☆ **Embraced** / Apr. 17, 1977 / Pablo 108
This record documents one of 1977's "big events," the meeting of pianist Mary Lou Williams and Cecil Taylor at Carnegie Hall, on April 17, 1988, a get-together mounted with much pomp and circumstance. Most of the music consists of superimpositions of Williams's traditional blues-based approach and Taylor's volcanic eruptions of multinoted flurries. —*Chuck Berg*, Down Beat

My Mama Pinned a Rose on Me / Dec. 27, 1977 / Pablo 819

○ **Mary Lou Williams Solo Recital** / Jul. 16, 1978 / Pablo 2308218
On this live recording from the Montreux Jazz Festival of 1978, pianist Mary Lou Williams's musical pictures include forms that go back as far as ragtime, boogie, and early swing. The mastery of so many diverse styles became the foundation of her recent compositions and the heart of her multisided improvisation. Softly, the way fingers tease a silk stocking, melodic lines spin from her right hand. At other times bold clusters and percussive basslines reveal one of the best-developed left hands in modern jazz. These melodic-harmonic extremes create a profound tension that keeps the listener and musician on the edge of their chairs, lost in the power, grace, and technique. —*Bradley Parker-Sparrow*, Down Beat

Solo Recital (Montreux Jazz Festival 1978) / Jul. 16, 1978 / Pablo 218

RICHARD WILLIAMS (Richard Gene Williams)

b. May 4, 1931, Galveston, TX, **d**. 1985
Trumpet / Hard bop
A sorely neglected, underrated trumpet, Richard Williams was an excellent hard bop player. His playing, particularly on uptempo tunes, reflected the influence of Fats Navarro, but had its own twists and peculiarities. Williams's lines, so-

los, phrasing, and tone were authoritative, and were articulated cleanly and executed with depth and intensity. Yet he actually started on saxophone as a child, before switching to trumpet in his teens. Evans received a degree in music from Wiley College, then served in the Air Force for four years. After his discharge in 1956, Williams joined Lionel Hampton's big band, and toured Europe as its principal trumpeter. Evans earned his Masters degree from the Manhattan School of Music after returning to America. He played and recorded with Gigi Gryce in the late '50s and early '60s, and with Charles Mingus, Lou Donaldson, Quincy Jones, Slide Hampton, and Duke Ellington between 1959 and 1965. Williams recorded with Ellington again in 1971. He toured Europe and Japan with the Thad Jones-Mel Lewis orchestra in the late '60s, and played with Gil Evans's band, with Broadway pit orchestras, and with Hampton again in the '70s. Williams led his own band in Europe during the '70s, and recorded with Duke Jordan and Sam Jones in the late '70s. Williams was a member of the Mingus Dynasty in 1982. He recorded as a leader for Candid in 1960; it's available on CD. —*Ron Wynn and Michael G. Nastos*

★ **New Horn in Town** / Nov. 1960 / Candid 79003
Richard Williams's *New Horn in Town* joined trumpeter Williams with the later expatriate altoist/flutist Leo Wright along with a typical hard bop rhythm section including pianist Richard Wyands and bassist Reggie Workman. Much of the music contained on this record reflects that genre of music that was being exemplified by the Horace Silver Quintet and the Jazz Messengers. Tunes such as "Blues in a Quandry" and "Renita's Bounce" have that good bluesy feeling of hard bop swing at its best. Williams's trumpet is showcased on "I Remember Clifford" and "Somewhere Over the Rainbow." His tone is very dark and he's able to exploit the deeply felt respect of Clifford Brown's elegy as well as the sing-song quality of "Somewhere Over the Rainbow." Leo Wright contributes some good alto spots and Wyands, the pianist, displays a subtle touch and rhythm magic. —*Spencer R. Weston, Cadence*

ROD WILLIAMS

b. 1954
Piano / Neo-bop
Rod Williams is a pianist and bandleader who's recorded one session for Muse with Marty Erlich, Graham Haynes, and Charnett Moffett in the late '80s. Williams is still developing a sound and style, but has shown good skills on previous sessions playing with Eddie Harris, David Murray, and Cassandra Wilson. He's been a solid soloist and effective accompanist in large bands or small combo situations. Williams's session as a leader is available on CD, and he can be heard on recent dates by Murray and Wilson. —*Ron Wynn*

★ **Hanging in the Balance** / i. 1989 / Muse 5380
Debut for this Detroit pianist and sextet. This is exploratory jazz. —*Michael G. Nastos*

RUDY WILLIAMS

b. 1909, **d.** 1954
Alto saxophone / Swing, big band
A hard-blowing alto saxophonist, Rudy Williams made many records with combos and big bands in the '30s, '40s, and '50s. He was best known for his tenure in the Savoy Sultans. Williams began playing saxophone at age 12, and eventually emphasized alto, though he also played baritone and tenor. He joined Al Cooper's Savoy Sultans in 1937, and was featured on many recordings, including the 1939 hit "Little Sally Water." He played with Hot Lips Page, Luis Russell, Chris Columbus, and John Kirby in the '40s, and led bands in the mid- and late '40s in Boston and New York. Williams played with Tadd Dameron in 1948, then led bands in Boston in the late '40s and early '50s. He worked with Illinois Jacquet and Gene Ammons in California, later toured the Far East with Oscar Pettiford's band, and recorded in Howard McGhee's group. After returning to America,

Williams led bands, and recorded with Dud Bascomb and Don Byas, with Babs Gonzales, with Dameron and Eddie "Lockjaw" Davis, Eddie "Cleanhead" Vinson, with Gene Ammons and Bennie Green, and with Johnny Hodges. He doesn't have any sessions under his own name available on CD, but can be heard on various discs that feature Jacquet, McGhee, Ammons, and others. —*Ron Wynn*

TONY WILLIAMS (Anthony Williams)

b. Dec. 12, 1945, Chicago, IL
Drums, bandleader / Postbop, early jazz-rock, neo-bop, modern creative
It seems as though drummer Tony Williams has been around forever, yet he's still only in his forties. Williams was at the rhythmic center of some intriguing events in recent jazz and popular music, including Miles Davis's mid-'60s band, and his own late '60s jazz-rock groups. His solos are a superb combination of a light, delicate style with relaxed, crisply played accents and unpredictable rhythmic patterns. On fusion numbers, his trademark is closing the cymbal on every beat. He's been a successful drummer in high-voltage rock and jazz-rock bands, free combos, bebop ensembles, and large groups, and arguably ranks as the '60s and '70s most influential stylist on his instrument.

Influenced by Pete LaRoca, Williams's father was a saxophonist who took his son to various clubs that would let the young Williams sit in; this enabled him to start appearing at these places by himself at age 11. Williams had private drum studies with Alan Dawson, and played with influential figures, such as Max Roach and Art Blakey, in his childhood. Williams was a prolific contributor to various Boston jam sessions at age 15. He began working with Sam Rivers in 1959 and 1960, and Rivers gave him valuable advice and counsel. Williams worked with Jackie McLean in 1962, and was invited to join his group. Miles Davis heard him, and recruited Williams for his band in 1963. He remained with Davis's band until 1969, and gained widespread recognition and critical praise. Williams also worked with other groups led by Eric Dolphy, Herbie Hancock, and Rivers. Rivers appeared on some early Williams Blue Note recordings in the '60s.

The influence of Davis's jazz-rock group led Williams to form his own group in a similar vein. The group, Lifetime, featured musicians such as Jack Bruce, John McLaughlin, and Larry Young, and was one of the greatest jazz-rock combos of all time. Unfortunately, that didn't translate into sales, and Lifetime had internal conflicts and constantly shifting personnel before it disbanded in the early '70s. Williams tried several new groups, but albums such as *Ego*, *The Old Bum's Rush*, and *Million Dollar Legs* flopped, even with players such as ex-Gong saxophonist Allan Holdsworth. Williams returned to acoustic jazz in the late '70s, touring and recording with Davis alumni mates Hancock, Wayne Shorter, and others on the VSOP dates. Williams worked with Sonny Rollins, Hank Jones, Stan Getz, and Wynton Marsalis in the late '70s and '80s. He made a Columbia session in 1979, *The Joy of Flying*, that included contributions from Hancock, Jan Hammer, George Benson, and Cecil Taylor. The album actually made the charts. During the '80s, he's led one of the better jazz combos, cutting nice albums for Blue Note with a group that's included Mulgrew Miller, Wallace Roney, Billy Pierce, and Charnett Moffett. Williams, Carter, and Hancock also did a trio session for a French label in 1987. Only a few titles featuring Williams as a leader, most of them recent Blue Note dates, are available on CD. A collection of selections from his light-selling early '70s Columbia albums were issued on an anthology in 1992. An earlier Polygram anthology of material by the Lifetime bands has also been reissued on CD. —*Ron Wynn and Stephen Aldrich*

★ **Life Time** / Aug. 21, 1964 / Blue Note 84180
○ **Spring** / Aug. 12, 1965 / Blue Note 46135
Early period Blue Note recording with Sam Rivers (sax). Powerful music. —*Michael G. Nastos*

★ **Emergency** / May 26+28, 1969 / Polydor 849068

☆ **Tony Williams Lifetime, The** / Jan. 17, 1970 / Polydor 244021
Groundbreaking early fusion in the late '60s with Jack Bruce (b), Larry Young (o), and John McLaughlin (g). *—Michael G. Nastos*

○ **Ego** / 1970 / Polydor 2425070

Believe It / 1975 / CBS 33836
This is a hard-edged fusion quartet with guitarist Allan Holdsworth. *—Michael G. Nastos*

★ **Joy of Flying, The** / 1979 / CBS 35705
There are three quartet alignments at work here, plus a minus a few studio extras, and two more potent duets. Jan Hammer, then (1979) leading a Jimi Hendrix-influenced rock group and wearing a portable keyboard strapped across his shoulders, supplies the strongest fusion clout on the album. Weakest of the two near-jazz groupings is guitarist George Jackson/bassist Paul Jackson with a partially shackled Hammer and some glossy horns. Pianist Herbie Hancock fares better with Tom Scott and Stanley Clarke, his warm synthesizer mix announcing "Hittin' on 6"—then he throws a funky clavinet into gear. And yet the album's closing duet with Cecil Taylor caused the greatest critical stir. Only drums and piano are featured on "Morgan's Motion," but it is sheer molten explosiveness between these two volatile jazz giants. Williams's empathy for Taylor's brand of convoluted soloing is both surprising and impressive, and, by keeping his usual cymbal flash in reserve, Williams is able to play the skins for their darker tonalities. It is a remarkably cohesive duet, with potent internal dynamics. *—Bob Henschen*, Down Beat

○ **Foreign Intrigue** / Jun. 18-19, 1985 / Blue Note 46289
There are three basic points to make about this album. First, there is the matter about the electronic drum and drum machine. Tony Williams only employs these devices during a few ensembles and, although they do sound a bit silly there (especially the drum machine), it's about as effective a use for these unnecessary inventions that I've heard, short of satire. Second, the melodies are all quite appealing and several deserve to become standards. "Sister Cheryl" is already well known, thanks to Wynton Marsalis; other musicians would be well advised to pick up on "Life of the Party" (great Latin dance music) and "My Michele." Williams has really developed over the years into a talented composer—all seven tunes are his. Third, despite some excellent solos by all concerned, especially the young turks Donald Harrison (as), Wallace Roney (tpt), and pianist Mulgrew Miller, the real star of this date is the leader. Williams had never led a straightahead recording session before and is a little higher in the mix than drummers usually rate. But despite the fact that he almost drowns out Bobby Hutcherson's vibes at times, Williams playing is consistently colorful and would hold one's interest even if he were underrecorded. *—Scott Yanow*, Cadence

Civilization / 1986 / Blue Note 46757
Good set, with Williams serving as mentor and leader for a good crop of Young Lions. *—Ron Wynn*

Third Plane / i. 1987 / Carrere
Super trio date with Herbie Hancock (k) and Ron Carter (b). Available only as French import. *—Ron Wynn*

○ **Angel Street** / Nov. 1986-Apr. 1988 / Blue Note 48494
First-class lineup of Young Lions fueled by red-hot Williams drumming. *—Ron Wynn*

Native Heart / Sep. 1989 / Blue Note 93170
Leading his by now familiar band with Wallace Roney (tpt), Bill Pierce (reeds), and Mulgrew Miller (p). *—Ron Wynn*

○ **Story of Neptune** / i. 1992 / Blue Note 98169
The Tony Williams quintet has two obvious assets that put it ahead of most acoustic jazz bands: Williams's powerful and consistently creative drumming and his compositional talents. On this group's fifth Blue Note recording, the drummer contributes the three-part "Neptune," essentially a feature

for his drums; a more memorable original, "Crime Scene"; and arrangements of three standards. "Poinciana" has some superlative muted Wallace Roney in the manner of Miles Davis but with a bit of his own personality; new life is discovered in the Beatles' "Blackbird"; and Freddie Hubbard's "Birdlike" (or should it be "Byrdlike"?) is a short but rousing closer. Bill Pierce (ts, ss), Mulgrew Miller (p), and Ira Coleman (b) are excellent as supportive players, but Tony Williams emerges as the top star of this fine modern hard bop date. *—Scott Yanow*, Cadence

Tokyo Live / i. 1993 / Capitol 99031
Tony Williams introduced this aggregation in 1986 and six recordings have documented its authoritative ascendancy. This February, 1992, Tokyo date provides a rare opportunity to experience, in an extended manner, the power and passion of five eminently individualistic improvisers. Wallace Roney may have been lost in the New Orleans shuffle but when the Miles reunion band assembles, it is Roney who occupies the trumpet chair. With stylistic ties to Davis, Roney's fluid, probing extemporizations are a testament to the same rugged lyrical individualism epitomized by our departed Prince of Darkness. Bill Pierce is another vastly underrated saxophone sovereign. His emotional tenor and sinewy soprano electrify and assuage. Not unexpectedly, Mulgrew Miller is tasteful, resourceful, and invigorating. At the multiple percussion kit, Tony Williams wields the sort of power reserved for Greek gods. However, he's anything but imperious. His benevolent command of the drums serves to both coalesce and aggrandize these proceedings. And except for "Blackbird," his compositions and arrangements are featured. *—Bret Primack*, Jazz Times

○ **His Greatest Hits** / Reprise 6006

CLAUDE WILLIAMSON (Claude Berkeley Williamson)

b. Nov. 18, 1926, Brattleboro, VT
Piano / Swing, bop
A classically trained pianist who became one of the most prolific and recorded players among '50s West Coast stylists, Claude Williamson began in the swing era. He later embraced bebop under the spell of Bud Powell. His swing playing was entertaining and enjoyable, but his bebop was stronger and more compelling, though he was more polished and elegant than the soloists he admired. Williamson worked in the late '40s with Charlie Barnet, and played briefly with Red Norvo. He led his own trio in the '50s, then toured and recorded with Bud Shank, playing in Africa and Europe in 1958. Williamson worked in Hollywood for over 20 years, mostly with trios. He recorded for Capitol, Bethlehem, Criterion, Broadway International, and Eastworld, among others. Williamson currently has a few sessions available on Fresh Sound and on Discovery CDs. *—Ron Wynn*

★ **Kenton Presents Jazz: Claude Williamson** / Jun. 26, 1954 / Capitol 6502

Fabulous Claude Williamson Trio, The / 1961 / Contract 15001

All God's Chillun Got Rhythm / Flying Fish 358

LARRY WILLIS (Lawrence Elliott Willis)

b. Dec. 20, 1940, New York, NY
Piano / Postbop, soul-jazz, progressive big band, Latin-jazz, early jazz-rock, neo-bop
Once identified with on-the-edge free music, keyboardist Larry Willis had a profitable flirtation with fusion in the '70s, then moved to hard bop in the '80s and '90s. Willis's playing has been frenetic, ambitious, and interesting, but during his jazz-rock and fusion days, was funky, but greatly restrained and simplistic. A devotee of Herbie Hancock, Willis has found a good balance between formalism and freedom, with expertly constructed modal solos and also lyrical, relaxed statements. Willis graduated from the Manhattan School of Music in the early '60s, then played with Jackie McLean and Hugh Masekela. He recorded with Lee Morgan and McLean

in the mid-'60s, worked with Kai Winding and Stan Getz, and recorded with Robin Kenyatta in 1969. Willis turned to synthesizer and electric piano in the '70s, doing sessions with Cannonball Adderley, Earl May, Joe Henderson, Groove Holmes, and Masekela again. He joined Blood, Sweat & Tears in 1972, recorded with Alphonze Mouzon in both 1972 and 1973, and did dates as a leader and freelance session musician. Willis also recorded with Ryo Kawasaki and Sonny Fortune in the late '70s, and with David "Fathead" Newman and Carla Bley in the '80s. Willis toured and recorded with Nat Adderley in the '80s, and joined Woody Shaw's quintet in 1986. He's done sessions as a leader for Groove Merchant, Steeplechase, Audioquest, and Brunswick, among others. Willis has one date available on CD. —*Ron Wynn and Michael G. Nastos*

★ **Inner Crisis** / **i.** 1973 / Groove Merchant 514
Willis plays acoustic and electric. Two different ensembles. Good compositional jazz. —*Michael G. Nastos*

○ **Just in Time** / **i.** 1989 / Steeple Chase 1251
Here is trio jazz from a veteran pianist, one of the best in America. —*Michael G. Nastos*

☆ **New Kind of Soul, A** / Brunswick 754181
More funky. With viable jazz horn sound for support. Easy to like. Three flugelhorns (Joe Newman, Jimmy Owens, Marvin Stamm). —*Michael G. Nastos*

CASSANDRA WILSON

b. 1955
Vocals / Ballads & blues, neo-bop, M-Base
Cassandra Wilson has generally been regarded as the finest vocalist in the current class of contemporary jazz performers, though she has, at times, gone out of her way to sing everything but jazz. Still, her glorious voice, timing, delivery, and flexibility have been almost universally praised. There are a few detractors, the most notable being the outstanding critic Francis Davis, who's found Wilson's skills lacking. Others have come close to calling her the next Ella Fitzgerald or Betty Carter. Wilson certainly can improvise, scat, sing on or off the beat, interpret standards, and punctuate lyrics. What distresses even her admirers has been a tendency to use her excellent skills and husky voice on second-rate material, a jazz version of the Jackie Wilson syndrome. Wilson began piano and guitar lessons at age nine, and began singing folk, blues, pop, and rock as a professional in the mid-'70s. She began singing jazz while studying with Alvin Fielder and singing with the Black Arts Music Society in Jackson, Mississippi. She moved to New Orleans in 1981, where she studied with Earl Rubinton. Wilson moved to New York in 1982 at the behest of Woody Shaw, and began working with Dave Holland and Abbey Lincoln. She met Steve Coleman, and became actively involved in helping to establish his M-Base collective. After a guest appearance on Coleman's *Motherland Pulse* LP, JMT invited her to do her own album. *Point of View* featured soaring vocals, Coleman's torrid alto licks, and Jean-Paul Bourelly's amazing guitar accompaniment and solos. Wilson was soon in demand; she worked with Henry Threadgill and with New Air; Threadgill provided arrangements for her second album. Wilson's third album, a standards collection called *Blue Skies,* was widely viewed as an epic achievement. Some critics jumped off the bandwagon when her next album featured rock, funk, blues, and hip-hop, with only a slight jazz tinge. She kept the same approach on her next album in 1991, though the ratio of jazz to pop was much higher. Wilson has done sessions with other musicians, has continued appearing on Coleman's albums, and was the subject of a major marketing push in the fall of 1993, which celebrated her switch to Blue Note. All of Wilson's previous albums are available on CD. —*Ron Wynn*

Point of View / Dec. 1985 / JMT 834404

Days Aweigh / May 1987 / JMT 834412

○ **Blue Skies** / Feb. 1988 / JMT 834419

Vocalist Cassandra Wilson does not accomplish the integration of her voice into the fabric of the music by assuming the improvisational role of a horn; there is only one, most judicious, instance of scatting in the entire 51 minutes of the CD. She does it, rather, by singing these 10 superb examples of American popular song with understanding of their nature and with respect for their integrity, and yet by transforming them through masterful phrasing, intonation, and command of time. Her vehicle is a smoky contralto, slightly veiled, with a hint of great power in reserve. The voice is governed by intelligence and taste. In "Polka Dots and Moonbeams," as an example, Wilson treats the line "I held my breath and said 'May I have the next one?'" with rare dramatic understatement, enhancing the lyric's point of view—youthful infatuation overcoming youthful shyness. In "I've Grown Accustomed to His Face," she bends the notes almost into quarter tones when she sings "like breathing out and breathing in," so that the phrase implies a sigh without the singer using the obvious and corny device of actually sighing. In the same song, there is a marvelous example of musicality when she ends the phrase, "something in the air" a step above the written note (C rather than B-flat in the home key of E-flat), giving it an aspect of joy. All of this, and a great deal more, is done with supreme relaxation, confidence, and in some cases, as in "Gee Baby, Ain't I Good to You," a sardonic edge. And all of it is performed by Wilson as a member of the band, with absolute musical validity. When she reenters after a solo by pianist Mulgrew Miller, bassist Lonnie Plaxico, or drummer Terri Lyne Carrington, she has listened closely and responds to their ideas and moods. Correspondingly, Miller's solos seem to grow out of the vocal choruses. The pianist's work on this album is spare, lyrical, and warm. Miller accompanies beautifully. Plaxico, impressive in any context, is extremely supportive and has a witty bowed solo on "Gee, Baby." Carrington's playing throughout the album is marked by versatility, subtlety, dash, and an attribute she shares with Wilson, taste. —*Doug Ramsey, Jazz Times*

Jumpworld / Jul.-Aug. 1989 / JMT 834434

★ **She Who Weeps** / Nov.-Dec. 1990 / JMT 834443
Very good album, with Rod Williams on piano and Tani Tabbal on drums. —*Michael G. Nastos*

Live / Aug. 5, 1992 / PolyGram 849149

Blue Light Til Dawn / **i.** 1993 / Blue Note 81357 2 2
Cassandra Wilson has steadfastly refused to be pigeonholed or confined to any stylistic formula. She has done conventional jazz singing and standards, vocal improvisations, and "outside" material as well as rock, pop, funk, and blues. Now her highly anticipated Blue Note debut may stir renewed controversy, as she is once again all over the stylistic ballpark. She begins the set with her intriguing version of "You Don't Know What Love Is." Then she moves from vintage delta blues (Robert Johnson's "Come on in My Kitchen" and "Hellhound on My Trail") to rock compositions from Van Morrison and Joni Mitchell, then to her own title track and blues cut "Redbone" and a piercing version of "I Can't Stand The Rain" that can hold up to comparisons with Ann Peebles's classic. It will be interesting to hear how the blues purists react to hearing her Robert Johnson songs; she does not have his menacing quality (who does?) but does invoke an equally compelling air. Wilson has great timing, pacing, and delivery and certainly has blues sensibility in her sound. She will never be a prototype jazz singer in the strictest sense; her background is not the swing era, and she will not confine herself to doing brassy vehicles and interpreting pre-rock pop. But she is without question a superb vocalist, and her opening Blue Note album should satisfy both those who carp she is overrated and those who feel she can do no wrong. —*Ron Wynn*

GERALD WILSON (Gerald Stanley Wilson)

b. Sep. 4, 1918, Shelby, MS
Trumpet, arranger / Hard bop, progressive big band

An outstanding bandleader and arranger as well as a good trumpeter and composer, Gerald Wilson has updated and evolved his approach to big bands from the swing era to the present. His bands have been heralded for their topflight, well-drilled musicians who presented immaculately played, superbly written and arranged material. Wilson studied music in high school after his family moved from Memphis to Detroit. He worked with Jimmie Lunceford's band from 1939 to 1942, where he replaced Sy Oliver and learned how to combine precision and flair in his roles as soloist, composer, and arranger. Wilson moved to Los Angeles in the early '40s, and played with Benny Carter and Les Hite. He later worked with Clark Terry and Ernie Royal in Willie Smith's navy band, then organized his own big band. This intriguing group included Melba Liston and Snooky Young, and played an aggressive, forward-looking blend of swing and bebop. Wilson kept it going from 1944 to 1947. He was off the scene for part of the '50s, then returned with a new band in 1952 in San Francisco. Among Wilson's studio duties in the '50s were sessions for Larry Williams on Specialty. He made several albums for World Pacific in the '60s that were highly successful, most notably *Moment of Truth* that featured Mel Lewis, Carmell Jones, Harold Land, and Joe Pass. His band played at the 1963 Monterey Festival, and its roster included Land, Teddy Edwards, and Pass. Wilson also did song arrangements on albums by Buddy Collette, Johnny Hartman, Nancy Wilson, Ella Fitzgerald, Al Hibbler, Julie London, and Bobby Darin, and played trumpet solos on Leroy Vinnegar's LP *Leroy Walks!* on Contemporary. He had a regular radio program, wrote for the symphony, and did film and television scores. A little tune Wilson penned in 1970 titled "Viva Tirado" became a huge pop hit when recorded by the band El Chicano. He continued recording in the '80s for Discovery, World Pacific, and Trend, and ran the house band for Redd Foxx's NBC shows. Currently, Wilson has recent and reissued sessions available on CD. *—Ron Wynn*

Portraits / 1963 / Pacific Jazz 93414
Wonderful large-group recordings made in the '60s for Pacific Jazz. A 1992 reissue. *—Ron Wynn*

★ **Golden Sword, The** / **i.** 1966 / Discovery 901
○ **Eternal Equinox** / 1969 / Pacific Jazz 10160
Gerald Wilson's disc *Eternal Equinox* dresses in the trendy gear of the East Village (dig the jacket design), talks hip (titles like "Aquarius," "Scorpio Rising," "Celestial Soul"), and absurdly salutes the Mississippi Delta. The tunes were all written by Wilson except for "Baby, Baby, Don't Cry," "Equinox" (John Coltrane), and "Aquarius," and they all sound the same. Tempo is the only recognizable difference, and that doesn't count for much. Slow or fast, they all have that ethereal quality associated with zodiacal imagery. Arrangements proceed in predictable linear progression: melody built by reeds; colors provided by expert brass; highlights supplied by lonely, echoing vibes. "Bluesnee" is the most successful and unstrained piece among the collection, because of its full blowing spirit in the solo department. Tenorman Hadley Caliman lays it down very nicely here. *— Alan Offstein, Coda*

Lomelin / May 13-14, 1981 / Discovery
○ **Jessica** / Nov. 29+Dec. 6, 1982 / Trend 531
○ **Orchestra of the '80s** / **i.** 1983 / Trend 537
Calafia / Nov. 29-30, 1984 / Trend
○ **Jenna** / **i.** Jul. 22, 1992 / Discovery 964

JOE LEE WILSON (Joseph Lee Wilson)

b. Dec. 22, 1935, Bristow, OK
Vocals, leader / Ballads & blues
One of the '70s most striking jazz vocalists, Joe Lee Wilson blended a strong, stirring baritone voice and good delivery with a swinging style and savvy selection of material. The results made him quite popular for a few years, especially on college campuses in the Northeast. Wilson studied classi-

cal singing, and attended Los Angeles City College in the '50s, where he studied jazz. He toured the West Coast and Mexico as a jazz vocalist in the late '50s, and moved to New York in 1962. Wilson worked with Sonny Rollins, Lee Morgan, Miles Davis, Pharoah Sanders, and Jackie McLean in the '60s, then sang with Archie Shepp in 1971 and 1972. His dynamic lead vocals on Shepp albums such as *Things Have Got to Change*, and *Attica Blues* won Wilson recognition. Wilson also won recognition for his recordings as a leader, and for performances with Sunny Murray, Mtume, and Billy Gault. Wilson operated a loft in New York, the Ladies Fort, from 1973 to 1978, and appeared at the 1973 Newport in New York and 1975 Live Loft festivals. He recorded with Clifford Jordan in 1977, then moved to London in 1978. Wilson toured Europe, performed in London clubs, and did some periodic New York dates, but never regained his earlier momentum. Currently, none of Wilson's albums are available on CD, though Shepp's *Attica Blues* was reissued in 1993. *—Ron Wynn*

★ **Livin' High off Nickels and Dimes** / Jul. 16, 1972 / Oblivion 5
Joe Lee Wilson uses his dramatic voice and range with strength and flexibility on his first recording in front of his working group, making personal though careful readings of ballads like "It's Nice or No One" and "God Bless the Child." Wilson has been heard with large ensembles led by the likes of Archie Shepp, and he seems one of the few young singers who could give a convincing and meaningful reading to slower, serious works. But the vibrant energy he releases on the other four numbers! Through these live broadcast tapes it is easy to imagine Wilson singing "Strollin'" atop a Central Park statue, or running through Manhattan streets with "You Make Me Want to Dance" on his lips. "Jazz Ain't Nothin' But Soul" also gets an enthusiastic, heartfelt belting out; showy as his voice is, Wilson almost overwhelms his colleagues, and saxist Bob Ralston, especially, seems to have trouble finding something to play as clear and swinging as the vocalist's statements. *—Howie Mandel,* Down Beat

○ **Secrets from the Sun** / Inner City 1042

NANCY WILSON

b. Feb. 20, 1937, Chillicothe, OH
Vocals / Blues & jazz, ballads & blues
Wilson made her national debut in 1959, fronting the Billy May Orchestra. She has been a huge influence on a variety of singers, including Anita Baker and Regina Belle. Wilson's crisp, articulate, intricate jazz phrasing distinguishes her 53 albums, which encompass standards, Broadway, blues, jazz, pop, and contemporary soul. *—Bil Carpenter*

○ **Greatest Hits** / **i.** 1959-1977 / CEMA 9449
★ **Nancy Wilson and Cannonball Adderley** / 1961-Mar. 1962 / Capitol 48455
○ **Forbidden Lover** / 1987 / Columbia 40787
○ **With My Lover Beside** / **i.** 1991 / Columbia 48665
A superbly arranged, produced, and mastered session from a wonderful vocalist. Wilson's singing, delivery, and tone are enticing and sensual throughout, even when the songs threaten to get overly sentimental or just sappy. Though the album was aimed at the Adult Contemporary audience, Wilson never coasts through any number, and this is about as polished and effective as this kind of session could get. *— Ron Wynn*

SHADOW WILSON

b. 1919, **d.** 1959
Drums / Swing, big band
A colorful, propulsive drummer, Shadow Wilson worked with many major bands during his career. He was both a sensitive and an exciting stylist, and could provide rhythmically dynamic and softly sympathetic accompaniment using sticks or brushes. He began playing with Lucky Millinder in 1939, then worked with Benny Carter, Tiny Bradshaw, Lionel Hampton, Earl Hines, Count Basie, and Woody

Herman. Wilson later worked in the combos of Illinois Jacquet, Erroll Garner, and Thelonious Monk, and played with Ella Fitzgerald. He worked frequently with Sonny Stitt in the '50s, and recorded with Basie, Joe Newman, Monk, and Lee Konitz. Wilson didn't record any albums as a leader, but can be heard on CD reissues by Basie, Phil Woods and Gene Quill, Tadd Dameron, and Monk. —*Ron Wynn*

TEDDY WILSON (Theodore Shaw Wilson)

b. Nov. 24, 1912, Austin, TX, **d.** Jul. 31, 1986, New Britain, CT
Piano / Swing

One of the swing era's greatest pianists, Teddy Wilson's restrained, sophisticated approach moved the instrument into fresh territory. He used the piano's full range, fashioning a legato style that was fluid and expressive. His single-note lines reflected Earl Hines's and Art Tatum's influence, but were executed in far less flashy and understated fashion, a stylistic preference that sometimes resulted in an underrating of Wilson's harmonic skills. His accompaniment, riffs, and solos were never less than inspired, and were often sensational.

Wilson grew up in Tuskegee, Alabama, and studied, for a short time, at Talladega College. He worked in Chicago with Jimmie Noone and Louis Armstrong, among others, before moving to New York in 1933 to join Benny Carter's band. Wilson was featured on some Chocolate Dandies sessions in 1933. He played informally with Benny Goodman and Gene Krupa in 1935. Goodman wanted Wilson for an Easter radio concert. He officially joined Goodman's orchestra that year, and became one of the first Black musicians featured with a White band. When Lionel Hampton joined, Wilson, Hampton, Krupa, and Goodman made quartet recordings, while Wilson, Goodman, and Krupa formed the trio. Wilson remained in Goodman's orchestra until 1939, while he made his own recordings with other musicians and backed several vocalists. These included Billie Holiday, Lena Horne, Helen Ward, Thelma Carpenter, Sally Gooding, Nan Wynn, and Jean Eldridge. "Carelessly," "Where the Lazy River Goes," "My Melancholy Baby" with Ella Fitzgerald, and "Remember Me" were hits that featured Wilson with various singers, while the instrumental "You Can't Stop Me From Dreaming" topped the charts. Wilson also recorded with Red Norvo, Harry James, and John Simmons, an unusual trumpet/vibes/piano/bass quartet. He cut 19 piano solos in 1938 and 1939.

Wilson briefly led a big band in 1939 and 1940, then concentrated on solo and ensemble work. He led a sextet from 1940 to 1944 in New York, and taught at Juilliard, during the summers, from 1945 to 1952. During the '40s, Wilson played with Maxine Sullivan and Sarah Vaughan while he also did some solo dates. He had his own radio show and was on staff at CBS radio in the mid-'50s. Wilson recorded with Lester Young, Vic Dickenson, Roy Eldridge, and various Basie sidemen in 1956, and did many trio and solo sessions in the '60s and '70s. There were periodic reunions with Goodman throughout his career. These included the Broadway production *Seven Lively Arts* in 1945, a tour of the Soviet Union in 1962, a Newport Festival date in 1973, and a Carnegie Hall concert in 1982. He died in 1986. Numerous Wilson works remain in print, or have been reissued. —*Ron Wynn with Michael G. Nastos*

★ **Statements and Improvisations (1932-1934)** / 1932-1934 / Smithsonian 13708

When these recordings were made, pianist Teddy Wilson was still in his twenties and somewhat of a sensation. Listening, it was no wonder. Here the cadenzas, harmonics, technics, and sensitivities are all jazz; Wilson had not yet to contend with the cocktail element. All the recordings were done under Wilson's name except "I Surrender Dear" under Red Norvo and "Someday Sweetheart" under Mildred Bailey, the latter featuring a very fine vocal by Bailey. —*Bob Rusch*, Cadence

○ **Teddy Wilson (1935-1936)** / **i.** Dec. 1935-Aug. 1936 / Classics 511

○ **Teddy Wilson (1936-1937)** / **i.** Aug. 1936-Feb. 1937 / Classics 521

○ **Teddy Wilson (1937)** / **i.** Mar-Aug. 1937 / Classics 531

○ **Teddy Wilson (1937-1938)** / **i.** Sep. 1937-Apr. 1938 / Classics 548

○ **Teddy Wilson (1938)** / **i.** Apr-Nov. 1938 / Classics 556

○ **Teddy Wilson (1939)** / **i.** Jan.-Sep. 1939 / Classics 571

★ **And His All-Stars** / **i.** 193?-1940 / Columbia

This is a blowing ensemble. There's a collective intimacy achieved here that is both soothing and stimulating. Trumpeter Harry Edison, trombonist Vic Dickenson, and soprano saxophonist and clarinetist Bob Wilber make a marvelously liquid blend to which pianist Teddy Wilson adds the carbonation ("June Night," "I'll Get By," "Lonesome and Sorry"). "Miss You" borrows the bristling abruptness of the John Kirby sound to good effect. The looser style of the '30s surfaces on "I'll Get By," "Just Friends," and "Blues in D Flat." Wilson's piano work is full of gentle detail. This album, more than any other in recent years, reestablishes his preeminence among contemporary pianists. "Blues in D Flat" is a moving transposition of Wilson's classic "Blues in C Sharp Minor." The logic and economy are totally disarming. —*John McDonough*, Down Beat

Sunny Morning / **i.** 1946 / Musicraft 2008

○ **Central Avenue Blues** / 1948 / Vintage Jazz Classics 1013

○ **Teddy Wilson Featuring Billie Holiday** / **i.** 1949 / Columbia 6040

Time After Time / **i.** 194? / Musicraft

For Quiet Lovers / **i.** 1956 / Verve

Impeccable Mr. Wilson, The / **i.** Oct. 1958 / Verve

Gypsy and Mr. Wilson / **i.** 1959 / Columbia

Elegant Piano / **i.** 195? / Halcyon

★ **I Got Rhythm** / **i.** 195? / Verve

Air Mail Special / Jun. 1967 / Black Lion 760115

Trio in Europe / **i.** 1968 / Fantasy

Stomping at the Savoy / **i.** 1969 / Black Lion 760152

○ **With Billie in Mind** / May 1972 / Chiaroscuro 111
Elegant, superior swing and mainstream material, fine tribute to Lady Day. 1990 reissue of 1972 set. —*Ron Wynn*

○ **Piano Solos** / **i.** 1973 / Affinity 1016

Blues for Thomas Waller / Jan. 1974 / Black Lion 760131

Swingin's Mutual / **i.** 1992 / Capitol 99190

Mr. Gershwin / Columbia

Prez and Teddy / Verve

LEM WINCHESTER

b. 1928
Tenor saxophone, vibes / Postbop

One of the more intriguing vibes players of the '50s, Lem Winchester displayed an inventive style that featured creative phrasing and rhythms and adventurous solos, and also reflected the blues sensibility and leanings of Milt Jackson. He made several albums in the late '50s and early '60s. His grandfather was a drummer for Bert Williams and other early comedians in the '20s. Winchester studied piccolo in high school, and later played tenor, baritone sax, and piano before turning to vibes. In the '50s, he split his time between being a police officer in Wilmington, Delaware, and playing in area bands. Winchester appeared at the 1958 Newport Jazz Festival in the Critics Choice concert, picked by Leonard Feather. He also recorded for Argo and New Jazz, playing with Oliver Nelson, Curtis Peagler, Benny Golson, Wendell Marshall, Roy Johnson, Tommy Flanagan, and Art Taylor. Winchester has several sessions currently available on CD. —*Ron Wynn*

Lem Winchester and the Ramsey Lewis Trio / Oct. 9, 1958 / Argo

Tribute to Clifford Brown / **i.** 1958 / Argo

★ **Winchester Special** / Sep. 25, 1959 / New Jazz 1719
Lem's Beat / 1960 / New Jazz 1785

KAI WINDING (Kai Chresten Winding)

b. May 18, 1922, Aarhus, Denmark, **d.** May 6, 1983, Yonkers, NY
Trombone / Bop

Kai Winding achieved significant fame in the '50s as an excellent trombonist in the Stan Kenton orchestra. He had a rough, biting tone initially, but smoothed it out and became a more restrained, though just as effective, soloist who was able to play difficult passages with ease and speed. He persuaded other trombonists in the Kenton section to produce a vibrato with the lip rather than the slide, and revolutionized the section's sound. Winding teamed with J.J. Johnson to create one of jazz's finest brass teams. The two seemed to bond into one horn; their lines, playing styles, and phrasing were so similar that, at times, it was almost impossible to tell them apart. Winding moved with his family from Denmark to America when he was age 12; he began playing trombone later in his teens, and was largely self-taught. He played with the big bands of Alvino Rey and Sonny Dunham, then played for three years in a service band while in the coast guard. Winding participated in several early bebop sessions at Minton's Playhouse and Monroe's Uptown House. He was also in Benny Goodman's, Stan Kenton's, and Charlie Ventura's big bands in the mid- and later '40s, while he worked at tunes with Charlie Parker. Winding played on Miles Davis's *Birth of the Cool* sessions in 1948. He and Johnson formed their quintet in 1954, and worked together until 1956. They reunited in 1958 and, for a time, were part of a four-trombone septet. Winding was music director for the Playboy clubs in New York during the '60s, and later toured with the Giants of Jazz. He joined Gillespie, Thelonious Monk, Al McKibbon, and Max Roach in 1971 and 1972. He co-led the group Giant Bones with Curtis Fuller in 1979 and 1980. Winding moved to California in 1969, then went to Spain in 1977. He appeared at the Aurex Jazz Festival in Japan with Johnson in 1982, and at the Kool Jazz Festival in New York. Winding recorded for Impulse, Black & Blue, Verve, Cobblestone, MPS, Hall of Fame Jazz, A&M, Gateway, Glendale, Red, and Who's Who in the '50s, '60s, '70s, and '80s. Winding has very few titles currently available; only a little of the Glendale material and a recent session on Red out of Italy. —*Ron Wynn*

★ **Kai Winding, J.J. Johnson and Bennie Green with Strings** / Dec. 3, 1954 / Original Jazz Classics 1727
This is an outstanding three-trombone lineup, with understated arrangements. —*Ron Wynn*

Brass Fever / **i.** 1956 / Impulse

○ **Incredible Kai Winding Trombones, The** / Nov. 17-Dec. 13, 1960 / Impulse 3

PAUL WINTER (Paul Theodore (Jr) Winter)

b. Aug. 31, 1939, Altoona, PA
Soprano and alto saxophone, bandleader / World fusion, new age

Environmental causes have been Paul Winter's concern as much, if not more, than music since the '70s. Winter has joined Greenpeace expeditions, has recorded music that is accompanied by whales and wolves, and formed an organization that links environmental issues with musical concerns. Winter has never been one of the more soulful, hard-edged, funky, or bluesy players; he's utilized improvisation, but has also incorporated elements from ethnic, European folk, symphonic/classical, and other sounds that gradually became known as new age (and is now called contemporary instrumental in some circles). His alto and soprano sax playing is melodically enticing, but is seldom harmonically or rhythmically challenging. Winter founded the Paul Winter sextet while a Northwestern University student. This group was a winner at the 1961 Intercollegiate Jazz Festival held at Notre Dame (John Hammond and Dizzy Gillespie were some of the judges on the panel). Hammond got the sextet onto Columbia. They proved quite popular, and the State Department sponsored a Latin American tour for the band in 1962. But five years later, Winter broke from a strict jazz sound with the Winter Consort, a band that blended ethnic influences from Africa and Latin America, as well as Europe and America. At one time, Ralph Towner, Glen Moore, Collin Walcott, Paul McCandless, and David Darling were all members, and the instrumentation included acoustic guitar, sitar, bass, cello, and oboe. But the Consort eventually disbanded, with its core members forming a similar, even more successful band, Oregon. Winter has blended music and environmental politics throughout the '80s and '90s. He's recorded as a leader for Columbia, A&M, Epic, and Living Music. Winter has several sessions available on CD. —*Ron Wynn and Linda Kohanov*

☆ **Icarus** / **i.** 1972 / Epic 31643
This, a reissue of saxophonist Paul Winter's finest album, marks a transitional point in his career from jazz to his own brand of contemporary instrumental. But one can simply revel in the lovely melodies, the contemplative sounds, and the tasteful production of George Martin, especially on the justly famous title track by Ralph Towner. —*William Ruhlmann*

BOOTY WOOD (Mitchell W. Bootie)

b. Dec. 27, 1919, Dayton, OH, **d.** Jun. 10, 1987, Dayton, OH
Trombone / Swing, big band

Another one of the musicians who excelled on mutes in the Ellington band, Booty Wood provided humorous, effective, and exuberant trombone solos with the plunger, and several solid unmuted solos as well. He began his professional career in the late '30s, and worked with Tiny Bradshaw and Lionel Hampton in the early '40s. Wood played in a navy band with Clark Terry, Willie Smith, and Gerald Wilson, then reteamed with Hampton after his discharge. He joined Arnett Cobb's small band in 1947 and 1948, played with Erskine Hawkins from 1948 to 1950, and with Count Basie in 1951. Wood left music for a while before joining Ellington in 1959 and working with him until 1960. He rejoined Ellington's band in 1963, but stayed only briefly. Wood returned to the band for a third time in the early '70s. He also worked with Earl Hines in 1968, and with Mercer Ellington in the '70s. Wood recorded with the Count Basie orchestra from 1979 to the mid-'80s. He can be heard on Ellington and Basie reissued CDs, and on some Hampton discs. —*Ron Wynn*

Hang in There / **i.** Nov. 1968 / Master Jazz 8102

RICKY WOODYARD

b. 1956
Saxophone / Neo-bop

A Nashville saxophonist who moved to the West Coast in the '80s, Ricky Woodard made an acclaimed guest appearance with the Frank Capp band, then made his debut as a leader with a '91 session for Candid that features him with Dwight Dickerson, Tony Dumas, and Harold Mason. Woodard plays alto and tenor, and displays an acerbic soul-jazz style on alto and a more bebop and hard bop approach on tenor. He has a good range and tone in every register. His session is still available on CD; his guest stints with Capp are available, too. —*Ron Wynn*

JIMMY WOODE (James Bryant Woode)

b. Sep. 23, 1928, Philadelphia, PA
Bass / Swing, big band

A prolific session player and an occasional bandleader, Jimmy Woode has worked with numerous bands since the late '40s. He played in combos and orchestras, led trios, and backed everyone from Duke Ellington to Eric Dolphy, and always provided intelligent, first-rate accompaniment. Woode played baritone horn and studied piano and bass as a child. He formed a trio after leaving the service in 1946.

Woode toured with Flip Phillips in 1949, then recorded with Zoot Sims and Toots Thielemans. He later worked with Sarah Vaughan, Ella Fitzgerald, and Nat Pierce in the early '50s. Woode served as house bassist at Storyville in Boston for two years, recording with Sidney Bechet and Billie Holiday. He worked with Duke Ellington in the mid-'50s, recorded as a leader in 1957, and played with Johnny Hodges and Clark Terry. After moving to Sweden in 1960, Woode joined the Kenny Clarke-Francy Boland Big Band, and remained with them until they disbanded in 1973. He moved to Germany and managed his own publishing firm, then lived in the Netherlands and Munich. Woode played often for radio and television broadcasts, and on film soundtracks as well. He appeared at festivals, and recorded with Don Byas, Albert Nicholas, Johnny Griffin, Sahib Shihab, Ted Curson and Booker Ervin, Milt Buckner, Benny Bailey, Mal Waldron, and Helen Humes. Woode lived in Vienna during the '80s, and worked periodically with Nathan Davis's Paris Reunion Band. He can be heard on CD reissues of the Ellington mid-'50s band, on Mal Waldron's *Oneupmanship* session on Enja, and on Johnny Hodges reissues. —*Ron Wynn*

BRITT WOODMAN

b. 1920

Trombone / Swing, big band

An extremely versatile trombone soloist, Britt Woodman led Duke Ellington's section in the '50s, and was flexible enough to record with Charles Mingus and Miles Davis. Woodman had range, fire, and the harmonic knowledge to handle sophisticated big band and swing dates, as well as Mingus's futuristic, challenging arrangements. Woodman and Mingus were boyhood friends and longtime musical associates. Woodman played with Phil Moore and Les Hite in the '30s, then with Boyd Raeburn and Eddie Heywood in the mid-'40s before joining Lionel Hampton in 1946. He studied music at Westlake College in Los Angeles from 1948 to 1950, then joined Ellington. Woodman replaced Lawrence Brown and remained with Ellington until 1960. In 1955 he also recorded in a band led by Davis that included Mingus. Woodman worked in several Broadway shows in the '60s, and also recorded with Mingus on three sessions ranging from 1960 to 1963. He then returned to California in 1970, where he recorded, leading an octet, and played with the Akiyoshi-Tabackin, Capp-Pierce, and Bill Berry bands. Woodman toured Japan twice with Benny Carter in the late '70s, then returned to New York in the '80s, where he played with swing and bebop bands. Woodman can be heard on reissued Ellington and Mingus CDs, on recent Capp-Pierce sessions, and on reissued Akiyoshi-Tabackin band discs. — *Ron Wynn*

CHRIS WOODS (Christopher Columbus Woods)

b. Dec. 25, 1925, Memphis, TN, **d.** Jul. 4, 1985, New York, NY

Alto saxophone / Bop, blues & jazz

A hard-blowing, evocative alto saxophonist with a great flair for the blues, Chris Woods was great playing in a combo, behind a singer, or featured in a large orchestra. He didn't make an overwhelming number of recordings, but anything he recorded was memorable. Woods worked in Memphis before moving to St. Louis, where he played with the Jeter-Pillars orchestra and with George Hudson. He also recorded as a leader in the '50s and '60s. Woods moved to New York in 1962, where he played, worked, and recorded with Dizzy Gillespie and Clark Terry in the '60s. He played with Sy Oliver from 1970 to 1972, then did various sessions, including a tremendous album with Ted Curson. Woods played in the Count Basie orchestra in 1983. He recorded as a leader for Delmark and Futura. Currently, Woods doesn't have any sessions available on CD. —*Ron Wynn*

★ **Somebody Done Stole My Blues** / **i.** Dec. 23, 1991 / Delmark 434

JIMMY WOODS

b. 1934

Alto saxophone / Cool, progressive big band

An often fiery, animated alto saxophonist, Jimmy Woods made some fine recordings in the '60s on the West Coast. He studied clarinet at age 13, and made his first recording in the early '60s with Joe Gordon. Woods later recorded two albums for Contemporary, heading his own group. He played in Gerald Wilson's orchestra in the '60s, and with Chico Hamilton. He has not made any records as a leader since the Contemporary dates, which are not available on CD. —*Ron Wynn*

Conflict / **i.** Nov. 1963 / Contemporary 3612

PHIL WOODS (Philip Wells Woods)

b. Nov. 2, 1931, Springfield, MA

Alto saxophone, bandleader, clarinet / Bop

One of bebop's most outspoken advocates and an admired alto saxophonist among numerous musicians, Phil Woods has fought the good fight since the '50s, even though he began playing in a time when other styles were challenging bebop's hegemony. Perhaps the fastest alto saxophonist currently active, Woods's technique, from its bright, shimmering tone to his dynamic interpretative abilities and insertion of humorous musical quotations into solos, is textbook bebop. He rivals Frank Morgan as the closest thing going to Charlie Parker in terms of sound and approach, and probably plays better in-tune than virtually any other modern jazz alto stylist. He could be considered a hard bopper, but his reverence for Parker makes it difficult not to associate Woods with this genre.

He began playing sax at age 12, and later attended Juilliard. While there, he played briefly with Charlie Barnet. Woods then worked with George Wallington, Kenny Dorham, and Friedrich Gulda, recorded with George Russell, and toured the Near East and South America with Dizzy Gillespie during the mid-'50s. He began heading combos in the late '50s, while playing in Buddy Rich's band, toured Europe with Quincy Jones in 1959 and 1960 (he was a founding member of the big band), and toured the Soviet Union with Benny Goodman in 1962. There were sessions for Prestige in the late '50s, and for Candid in the early '60s, some with fellow saxophonist Gene Quill. *Phil & Quill* and *Phil Talks with Quill* were the sax equivalent of the J.J. Johnson and Kai Winding collaborations. The 1960 *Rights of Swing* for Candid showcased his extended compositions. Woods turned to studio work for a while in the '60s, and played on several commercial, television, and film dates. He played on the soundtracks for *The Hustler* and *Blow Up*. He recorded with Benny Carter in 1961, appearing on the *Further Definitions* album. During the summers from 1964 to 1967, he taught at the Ramblerny performing arts camp in Pennsylvania.

Woods moved to France in 1968, and returned to straight jazz. He formed a combo called the European Rhythm Machine with pianist George Gruntz, bassist Henri Texler, and drummer Daniel Humair. They remained intact until 1972. Woods moved to Los Angeles and formed an electronic quartet that met with criticism and audience displeasure, and soon disbanded. He relocated to the East Coast, and, in 1973, started an acoustic group with pianist Mike Melillo, bassist Steve Gilmore, and drummer Bill Goodwin. This band was critically acclaimed, and Woods won three Grammy awards in the mid-'70s on the strength of albums such as *Images* and *Live from the Showboat*. He also was recognized for his work with pop and soul musicians; he did solos on vocal recordings by Billy Joel and Aretha Franklin, among others. He made fine albums for Muse, Testament, Adelphi, and Clean Cuts. Woods made personnel changes in the '80s, as Hal Galper replaced Melillo in 1981 and trumpeter Tom Harrell came on board in 1983. There were more solid dates for Palo Alto, Red Record, Blackhawk, Denon, Omnisound, and Antilles. Galper and Harrell eventually moved on to form their own bands, but Woods has continued recording and performing into the '90s. He's playing more clarinet and occasionally uses synthesizer in his recordings. Woods's earlier albums have been reissued steadily, and he keeps making uncompromising music that reflects the influence of mentor Charlie Parker. He's also among the small corps of jazz saxophonists who continue to tour regularly. —*Ron Wynn*

Woodlore / Nov. 25, 1955 / Prestige 052

Altology / Jun. 15, 1956-Mar. 29, 1957 / Prestige 24065

★ **Pairing Off** / Jun. 1956 / Prestige 092
Septet. First-rate '80s reissue of an excellent 1956 date with lots of heavy hitters—Kenny Dorham (tpt), Donald Byrd (tpt), Tommy Flanagan (p), and Woods. —*Ron Wynn*

Young Bloods / Nov. 2, 1956 / Prestige 1732
Fine reissue taken from days when Woods, Donald Byrd (tpt), and Teddy Kotick (b) were rising stars. —*Ron Wynn*

○ **Four Altos** / Feb. 9, 1957 / Prestige 1734
Familiarity with Phil Woods's later work is all that distinguishes his solos on this Prestige session from the solos of lesser lights like Gene Quill, Sahib Shihab, and Hal Stein. Each of the *Four Altos* plays well enough, but each sounds so much like the others—sounds, that is, so much but not *quite* like Charlie Parker, even to the deftly interpolated nursery rhymes—that you need a scorecard to tell them apart (and the sleeve of this no-frills budget-priced LP doesn't give you one). Ironically, the Parker influence is even more noticeable on the set's standard ballad, where the players are presumably speaking from their hearts, than on the "Cherokee" derivative, where they are more single-mindedly chasing the Bird. There is plenty of good music here—needling piano solos and accompaniment by Mal Waldron, surprisingly detailed arrangements (probably by Waldron and/or Teddy Charles) on which the altoists blend well as a section, and a remarkable consistency in the alto solos—but the ear wants greater contrast. —*Francis Davis*, Down Beat

Bird Feathers / Mar. 29, 1957 / New Jazz 1735
With fellow altoists Jackie McLean, John Jenkins, and Hal McKusick. High-flying blowing/jam session from the '50s. —*Ron Wynn*

☆ **Phil and Quill with Prestige** / Mar. 29, 1957 / Original Jazz Classics 215

Warm Woods / Sep. 11+Nov. 8, 1957 / Portrait 44408

★ **Rights of Swing** / Jan. 26, 1960 / Candid 79016
Rights of Swing, composed and arranged by Grammy-winning altoist Phil Woods, is his first major compositional work. Though the work has five parts, each part works just as well separately as together. Woods appears with musicians such as trumpeter Benny Bailey, trombonists Curtis Fuller and Willie Dennis, baritone saxophonist Sahib Shihab, Julius Watkins on French horn, pianist Tommy Flanagan, and drummers Osie Johnson or Mickey Roker. The album brings together a good sampling of musicians and contains a major contribution from Woods's alto, as the principal soloist. —*Spencer R. Weston*, Cadence

○ **At the Frankfurt Jazz Festival** / 1970 / Embryo 530

★ **Musique Du Bois** / Jan. 14, 1974 / Muse 5037
Don Schlitten first assembled the trio of pianist Jaki Byard, bassist Richard Davis, and drummer Richard Dawson for some Booker Ervin dates in the '60s that remain minor masterpieces (they're on Prestige), and the passing years have scarcely tarnished the ensemble's sheen. *Musique Du Bois* also demonstrates, for the umpteenth time, that each is a more than worthy soloist. And then there is Phil Woods. Woods, of course, has a lot of Charlie Parker's *sound*, but even more of Bird's spirit. It's pointless to run down the soloist's performances on this set (a balanced and conventional one—two originals, two ballads, two modern standards) because Woods masters them all. But the overriding impression simply is of being in the presence of a superior improviser, who restlessly and inexhaustibly creates melodies, explores them, embellishes them, discards and re-

turns to them, and forges the whole venture into something lucid, coherent, and satisfying. —*Steve Metaliz*, Down Beat

Phil Woods Quartet, Live—Vol. 1 / i. 1975 / Clean Cuts 702

Live from the Showboat / Nov. 1976 / RCA

More Live / May 23, 1978-May 26, 1979 / Mobile Fidelity 755

Phil Woods / Lew Tabackin / Dec. 10, 1980 / Omnisound 1033

Three for All / Jan. 6-7, 1981 / Rhino 79614
1990 reissue. This is an excellent trio date. With Tommy Flanagan (p). —*Ron Wynn*

☆ **Phil Talks with Quill** / i. Oct. 1981 / Columbia 36808
In *Phil Talks with Quill* alto saxophonists Phil Woods and Gene Quill are given more of the stretch-out room young players seem to need, and they strike a good balance between competition and cooperation. This is a working band brought into the studio exactly at the point at which night after night on the bandstand had tightened its loose head arrangements just enough. The best track is the one Woods original, "Hymn For Kim," which features a haunting solo by its composer and lightly swinging work by the obscure Bud Powell- and George Wallington-styled pianist Bob Corwin, though Quill sounds more comfortable on "Scrapple from the Apple" and "A Night in Tunisia," where the going is more breathless. There is a strident Hotspur quality to Quill's solos that sometimes proves his downfall—he often seems to be giving the chords a fast shuffle in a desperate attempt to come up aces—but this same quality is what enables him to egg Woods on to some of the latter's best work of the period. —*Francis Davis*, Down Beat

At the Vanguard / Oct. 2, 1982 / Antilles 846396

Integrity / Apr. 1984 / Red 123177

Bop Stew / Nov. 1987 / Concord Jazz 4345
Quintet. First in a series of live dates from 1987 Concord Festival in Japan. Tom Harrell (tpt) and Woods emphatic. CD version has bonus track. —*Ron Wynn*

Bouquet / i. 1987 / Concord Jazz 4377

Little Big Band / i. 1988 / Concord Jazz 4361

Evolution / May 1988 / Concord Jazz 361
Strong swing, bop cuts from ensemble that's neither traditional big band or small combo. —*Ron Wynn*

Here's to My Lady / Dec. 1988 / Chesky 3
First-rate 1988 date released in 1989. Woods is invigorating, as is Tommy Flanagan (p). —*Ron Wynn*

Flash / Apr. 1989 / Concord Jazz 4408

All Bird's Children / Jun. 1990 / Concord Jazz 4441
Quintet. One of Charlie Parker's forthright disciples shows where he got his inspiration. CD version has two bonus cuts. —*Ron Wynn*

Real Life / Sep. 1990 / Chesky 47
1991 release of a good combo date. Larger group than on most of his recordings. —*Ron Wynn*

Live / i. 1991 / Novus 3104

Live from New York / i. 1991 / Quicksilver 4011
Poor recording but excellent solos, especially Woods and Hal Galper (p). —*Ron Wynn*

REGGIE WORKMAN (Reginald Workman)

b. Jun. 26, 1937, Philadelphia, PA
Bass / Hard bop, early free
Reggie Workman became a star during the '60s when he established his reputation through his ability to thrive in either free or hard bop settings, and to work with musicians such as John Coltrane. Since then, he's faithfully survived in the jazz jungle; he's seldom out front, but always makes his presence felt with steady, masterfully played bass lines, a solid tone, and brilliantly articulated, impressive solos. Workman's proven himself repeatedly as a strong melodic and rhythmic improviser. He played piano, tuba, and euphonium in his youth, and settled on bass in the mid-'50s when

he was working in R&B bands. Workman began playing with Gigi Gryce in the late '50s, then with Red Garland and Roy Haynes. He started with Coltrane in the early '60s, and played with James Moody, Art Blakey's Jazz Messengers, Tootie Heath, Yusef Lateef, Herbie Mann, and Thelonius Monk later in that decade. His recording sessions were no less impressive; they included albums with Coltrane, Freddie Hubbard, Archie Shepp, Lee Morgan, and Cedar Walton. Workman also taught at the New Muse Community Museum of Brooklyn, and was eventually appointed director of the music workshop in 1975. He's also taught at several colleges and universities. He remained busy in the '70s, playing with Max Roach, and recording with Charles Tolliver, Billy Harper, Shepp, Art Farmer, and many others. His '80s associations have been with Jubani Aaltonen, Mal Waldron, and David Murray. Presently, he has only one session as a leader available on CD, an '89 date for the Music and Arts label with Jeanne Lee, Marilyn Crispell, Michelle Navazio, Don Byron, and Gerry Hemingway. —*Ron Wynn*

★ **Synthesis** / Jun. 1986 / Leo 131

WORLD SAXOPHONE QUARTET

Group / Modern creative
The World Saxophone Quartet is one of the finest small combos to emerge in jazz during the '80s. They are a foursome of sax players who, until their last release, recorded and performed all their music without any other accompanists. The original quartet consisted of David Murray, Julius Hemphill, Oliver Lake, and Hamiet Blueitt. Hemphill left in 1993 and was replaced by Arthur Blythe. They began splitting the material between driving originals, avant-garde blowing, and more hard-bop and mainstream pieces. In recent years, they've expanded the repertoire to include an Ellington tribute, an album of classic R&B, and their latest effort, a date with African percussionists. —*Ron Wynn*

○ **Steppin' With** / Dec. 1978 / Black Saint 0027
Steppin' With was the long-awaited first LP by the sort of group that succeeds so well in theory but only sometimes in practice: four of the very best modernists with shared principles of harmony and free melodic motion. The players' differences are distinctive, too, for previous LPs by each showed dissimilar attitudes to line, space, and expression. They play elaborate scores and the four Julius Hemphill pieces each achieves distinction—"Steppin'" through no more than a bass clarinet vamp. "Hearts" is a near ballad, no improvising, an archetypical Hemphill melody. "Dream" is certainly the best of these realizations. Improvised snips of sound and melodic snatches evoke the imperfect glimpses and changing images of the dreaming state, with clever themes to clarify the dream's movement. The characteristic Hemphill care for detail in melody and orchestration and, of course, the responses of four outstanding saxophonists (the flutes and bass clarinets are largely peripheral), make the album valuable. —*John Litweiler,* Down Beat

W.S.Q. / Mar. 1980 / Black Saint 0046

Revue / Oct. 14, 1980 / Black Saint 0056

Live in Zurich / Nov. 6, 1981 / Black Saint 0077

Live at Brooklyn Academy of Music / Dec. 6-7, 1985 / Black Saint 0096

★ **Plays Duke Ellington** / Apr. 1986 / Nonesuch 79137

Dances and Ballads / Apr. 1987 / Nonesuch 79164
The Quartet extends its reach and scope to include danceable material. —*Ron Wynn*

Rhythm & Blues / 1989 / Elektra 60864
Smashing update of traditional R&B. The masterful ensemble turns R&B and soul classics into dynamic portraits of sax brilliance. The WSQ's inspired playing transcends idiomatic considerations; they're an institution and the greatest small combo inside or outside jazz. —*Ron Wynn,* Rock & Roll Disc

Metamorphosis / i. 1991 / Nonesuch 79258

Amazing mix of African rhythms, African-American harmonies, and solos. Spectacular solos augmented by thrilling African percussion. —*Ron Wynn,* Rock & Roll Disc

WORLD'S GREATEST JAZZ BAND

Group / Dixieland
The finest "trad"/swing group of modern times, the World's Greatest Jazz Band grew out of jazz fan and millionaire Dick Gibson's annual jazz parties. After his sixth celebration in 1968, a group featuring Yank Lawson, Bob Haggart, Bob Wilber, Ralph Sutton, and Billy Butterfield was tagged by Gibson as "The World's Greatest Jazz Band." They played together for ten years, stressed the collective style of vintage New Orleans music, but were distinguished both by the caliber of players and their unwillingness to stagnate and become a camp Dixieland outfit. Their albums surpass anything else remotely associated with "trad" or Dixieland material. —*Ron Wynn*

○ **World's Greatest Jazz Band of Yank Lawson and Bob Haggart** / Dec. 10, 1968 / Project 3 3PR5033

★ **At Massey Hall** / Dec. 4, 1972 / World Jazz 3
Anything from this delightful traditional jazz group is worth hearing. —*Ron Wynn*

EUGENE WRIGHT

b. 1923
Bass / Swing, cool
Best known for his steady, concise contributions to the Dave Brubeck quartet for a decade in the '50s and '60s, Eugene Wright was a dependable, never flamboyant bassist. He was mostly self-taught on bass, but took a few lessons late in his career from Paul Gregory. Wright studied cornet in high school. He led a 16-piece band, the Dukes of Swing, in the mid and late '40s. Wright played with Gene Ammons, Count Basie, and Arnett Cobb in the late '40s and early '50s, then worked with Buddy DeFranco from 1952 to 1955, touring Europe with him. He played in the Red Norvo trio in 1955, and toured Australia with the group. Wright was featured in a film short with Charlie Barnet, then joined Brubeck in 1958 and remained with him until 1968. He led his own ensemble on a tour of Black colleges in 1969 and 1970, then played with Monty Alexander's trio from 1971 to 1974. Wright worked in television studios and did film soundtrack work, and played in clubs during the '70s. He also taught privately, and became head of the advisory board in the jazz division of the International Society of Bassists, and head of the University of Cincinnati's jazz department. Though he doesn't have any sessions of his own as a leader, Wright can be heard on numerous Brubeck CD reissues, and on sessions by Paul Desmond. —*Ron Wynn*

FRANK WRIGHT

b. Jul. 9, 1935, Grenada, MS, d. 1990
Tenor saxophone / Early free
As animated and energized as any saxophonist in the free style, Frank Wright triggered a lot of debate over whether his approach was legitimate expression or self-indulgent noise. His solos often seemed to be almost pure sound, though they weren't quite as devoid of harmonic concept as some critics claimed. Wright had as many defenders as detractors, and remains one of the saxophonists around whom arguments for and against free music seem to center. He's also one of the rare free jazz musicians who's also an ordained minister. Before meeting Albert Ayler in Cleveland, Wright was an electric bassist who played R&B, soul, and funk in Memphis and Cleveland. But Wright switched to tenor sax after hearing and meeting Ayler, and played with Larry Young, Noah Howard, and Sunny Murray after moving to New York in the early '60s. He had brief stints with John Coltrane and Cecil Taylor, then recorded as a leader for ESP in 1967 and 1969. Wright moved to France in 1969, and led a quartet with Bobby Few, Muhammad Ali, and Howard, who was later replaced by Alan Silva. They recorded in 1969

and 1970. Wright briefly returned to America in 1971, then went back to France. He toured Europe and continued recording in the early '70s. Wright played and recorded with Taylor in the mid '80s. Currently, he does not have any sessions available on CD. —*Ron Wynn and Michael G. Nastos*

Trio / Nov. 16, 1965 / ESP 1023
With Henry Grimes on bass, Tony Price on drums. Unafraid to explore new terrain. —*Michael G. Nastos*

Your Prayer / May 1967 / ESP
Quintet. More groundbreaking avant-garde music. Lengthy improvs and counterpoint. —*Michael G. Nastos*

★ **Stove Man, Love Is the Word** / May 22, 1979 / Sandra 2106
Live at The Loft in Munich, Germany, with sextet. Rev. Wright is on the edge. This is an extension of Eric Dolphy. Must have open ears. —*Michael G. Nastos*

RICHARD WYANDS

b. Jul. 2, 1928, Oakland, CA
Piano / Bop
A fine ballad and standards player, Richard Wyands is such a strong accompanist that his abilities as a soloist are overlooked. However, he plays with taste, delicacy, and sophistication, but doesn't ignore the blues or lack intensity in his solos. Wyands began playing professionally in the '40s, working with Oakland groups. He backed Ella Fitzgerald and Carmen McRae in the mid '50s, then moved to New York. Wyands played with Roy Haynes, Charles Mingus, Jerome Richardson, and Gigi Gryce in the late '50s, then was extremely active in the early '60s. He was featured on recordings by Oliver Nelson, Etta Jones, Eddie "Lockjaw" Davis, Lem Winchester, Gene Ammons, Willis Jackson, Taft Jordan, and Gryce. Wyands toured and recorded with Kenny Burrell from 1965 to 1974, visiting England in 1969 and Japan in 1971. He also recorded with Freddie Hubbard in 1971. Wyands joined Budd Johnson's JPJ quartet in 1974, and recorded with Benny Bailey in 1978 and Zoot Sims in 1982. He has continued recording and touring through the '80s and '90s, but has done few recordings as a leader. Currently, there are no Wyands sessions available on CD, but he can be heard on reissued discs by Burrell, Ammons, Hubbard, and many others. —*Ron Wynn*

★ **Then, Here and Now** / **i.** Oct. 1978 / Storyville 4083

ALBERT WYNN

b. 1907, **d.** 1973
Trombone / New Orleans traditional
A first-rate blues and stomp trombonist who could also hold his own in jam sessions, Albert Wynn was quite active from the '20s until the '60s. He was well schooled in the "tailgate" style, but was also adept at low-down ballads. Wynn toured with Ma Rainey and led his own band in Chicago in the late '20s; he recorded and worked with Charlie Creath in St. Louis in 1927. He moved to Europe in 1928, and worked in 1929 with Sam Wooding and Harry Flemming. After returning to America, Wynn worked in New York with the New Orleans Feetwarmers and with Jesse Stone, Jimmie Noone, Richard M. Jones, and Earl Hines in Chicago. He played with Fletcher Henderson in the late '30s, then joined Noone's big band. Wynn worked in Chicago with various musicians in the '40s and '50s, among them Floyd Campbell, Baby Dodds, and Lil Armstrong. He later played with Franz Jackson and the Gold Coast Jazz Band in the late '50s and early '60s. He recorded for Riverside in the early '60s as part of their Living Legends series. But illness greatly restricted his playing from the mid '60s until his death in 1973. Fantasy reissued his Riverside date in 1993 as part of a traditional reissue line. —*Ron Wynn*

Chicago: The Living Legends / **i.** 1961 / Fantasy/Original 1826
Trombonist Albert Wynn's 1961 return to traditional jazz recording was a high point that year for New Orleans fans. He had not made a record in 33 years, yet his playing on the album *Chicago: The Living Legends*, is joyous, vibrant, and exciting. Wynn also assembled a great group for the date, led by the outstanding clarinetist Darnell Howard. This long out-of-print date, newly reissued with two fine bonus cuts added, is a primer for the joys of traditional jazz and blues music. —*Ron Wynn*

★ **Al Wynn and His Gutbucket Seven** / Sep. 5, 1961 / Riverside 426

Y

YOSUKE YAMASHITA

b. Feb. 26, 1942, Tokyo, Japan
Piano / Modern creative
A Japanese pianist very much in the Cecil Taylor school, Yamashita is a wildly unabashed improviser, all dense chords and slam-bang pyrotechnics. Great rewards for the listener willing to be challenged. —*Michael G. Nastos*

Concert in Jazz / Sep. 21, 1969 / Union 4

Ghosts by Albert Ayler / **i.** Jun. 1974+May 1977 / West Wind 2050

Frozen Days / Sep. 24-28, 1974 / Crown 6

★ **Chiasma** / Jun. 6, 1975 / MPS 68.115
Trio recording. Influenced by Cecil Taylor. For special tastes only. —*Michael G. Nastos*

Breath Take / Jul. 1975 / West 54 8009

Banslikana / **i.** Jul. 1976 / Enja 2080

Arashi / Sep. 29, 1976 / Frasco 20

Inner Space / **i.** Jun. 1977 / Enja 3001

Jugenmu / Feb. 17-18, 1981 / Frasco 28PJ1005

Live and then Picasso / **i.** 1982 / Panja 7070

In Europe (1983) / 1983 / Panja 7079

Sentimental / Aug. 28, 1985 / 33K20018

Sakura (Cherry) / **i.** 1990 / Antilles 849141

Kurdish Dance / **i.** 1993 / PolyGram 511708
Pianist and composer Yosuke Yamashita has made several smart moves on this disc, starting with his choice of bassist Cecil McBee and drummer Pheeroan Aklaff as sparring partners. Augmenting this champion rhythm section with Joe Lovano's tenor was another inspiration. When the quartet leans into the minor-keyed title cut, or when Lovano works his chocked upper register over McBee's bowed bass in "Tiny Square," there's no question that the leader's choices are paying off. His solo performance on "Subway Gig" shows him harnessing his style to better effect. And the disc's two ballads, "Tiny Square" and "K's Gift," point Yamashita the composer in a highly promising (and highly pleasurable) direction. —*James Marcus, Jazz Times*

Kodo Vs. Yosuke Yamashita in Live / Denon 7900

JIMMY YANCEY (James Edward Yancey)

b. Feb. 20, 1898, Chicago, IL, **d.** Sep. 17, 1951, Chicago, IL
Vocals, piano, harmonium / Boogie-woogie
Though he's the pianist who chronologically preceded Albert Ammons and Meade Lux Lewis, Jimmy Yancey is more often placed into the blues category than either of these men. Yancey was a boogie-woogie giant, perhaps the most inventive of all the players in the genre. He frequently created moving, gripping music. Yancey often changed his bass patterns in response to the right hand movements, producing shifting polyrhythms and arresting bass lines. He provided stunning accompaniment for both his own vocals and for those of his wife, Mama Yancey. Yancey was a professional from the age of six, and toured both America and Europe as a singer and tap dancer in vaudeville shows. He came off the

road in 1915 and settled in Chicago. His "day" job, for many years, was groundskeeper at Comiskey Park for the Chicago White Sox. Yancey would play informally at clubs and rent parties, and became known as a boogie-woogie champion. He was heard by both Ammons and Lewis. Lewis cut the "Yancey Special" in 1936, which generated some notoriety for the composer. Yancey then made his own recordings in 1939 and 1940, which featured many songs he'd written years earlier. He and Mama Yancey appeared at Carnegie Hall in 1948; Yancey died three years later. His work, especially its rhythmic variations, has since gotten much acclaim, and he's been recognized as a vital early influence. —*Ron Wynn and Cub Koda*

○ **In the Beginning** / **i.** 1939 / Solo Art 1

○ **Blues and Boogie** / Oct. 25, 1939-Sep. 6, 1940 / X 3000

○ **Yancey-Lofton Sessions—Vol. 1, The** / **i.** 1943 / Storyville 238

○ **Yancey-Lofton Sessions—Vol. 2, The** / **i.** 1943 / Storyville 239

★ **Yancey Special** / **i.** 1950 / Atlantic 103

○ **Lost Recording Date** / **i.** Apr. 7, 1954 / Riverside 1028

○ **Yancey's Getaway** / **i.** 1956 / Riverside 12-124

○ **Chicago Piano Vol. 1** / **i.** 1972 / Atlantic 82368
This reissue of a 1951 Yancey session that briefly surfaced in 1959 and 1972 is fine hard-yet-delicate piano soul. Jimmy cut this after his stints with Bluebird, Victor, and Vocalion, but these duets (Israel Crosby plays bass) are prime boogie-woogie, a spirited middle ground between Meade Lux Lewis and Jerry Lee Lewis. The final 5 of these 14 tracks feature vocals by Jimmy's wife Estelle ("Mama"), and her contributions are intense. *Chicago Piano Vol. 1* is almost defiantly low-key, but the modest, spare settings allow everyone to shine. Highly recommended, and kudos to Atlantic for rescuing this from obscurity. (Note: four of these tracks appear on the *Atlantic Piano* collection and *Atlantic Blues* box.) —*Jimmy Guterman, Roundup Newsletter*

★ **Volume 1 (1939-1940)** / Document 5041
Yancey's earliest and best sides for the Solo Art label. Beautiful and sensitive performances. (Import) —*Cub Koda*

○ **Volume 2 (1939-1950)** / Document 5042

○ **Volume 3 (1943-1950)** / Document 5043

PETE YELLIN

b. 1941
Alto saxophone / Postbop, neo-bop
His father was a pianist and an NBC staffer, and Pete Yellin has recorded as a leader and was also part of Joe Henderson's early '70s band. Yellin is a solid, sometimes exuberant player with extensive range, and is also a decent flutist. Yellin studied sax with Joe Alldard and flute with Harold Bennett. He earned his degree from Juilliard, and entertained thoughts of basketball stardom at one point. As a freshman, Yellin had an athletic scholarship to the University of Denver, but then turned professional as a musician. He played with Lionel Hampton in the early '60s, then with Buddy Rich and Tito Puente. Yellin joined Joe

Henderson's band in 1970, and remained until 1973. He formed his own band the next year, and played at the Newport Jazz Festival in New York. He returned to play with Puente in 1974. Yellen worked in Rich's and Bob Mintzer's horn sections during the '80s. He recorded for Mainstream, but the session is currently unavailable on CD. —*Ron Wynn*

★ **It's the Right Thing** / **i.** Feb. 1974 / Mainstream 397

YELLOWJACKETS

Fusion
Though now known for increasingly sophisticated and polished studio albums with diverse influences, including jazz, world music, and pop, the Yellowjackets started in 1981 as an R&B-oriented band with guitarist Robben Ford. Russel Ferrante (keyboards) and Jimmy Haslip (bass) are the remaining original members, joined by drummer William Kennedy in the most recent lineup. Originally, the idea was that they were studio musicians who wanted to play "real music," and they have crafted a string of very listenable and successful releases. Despite some harping by critics who can't quite find the right label to stick on them and at least one rather forgettable album (*Shades*), the band has enjoyed well-deserved success behind fine compositions (notably by Ferrante), excellent musicality, and very professional production work in the studio. Their most recent album, *Greenhouse*, received four stars from *Down Beat*, no small feat for a band in their genre. —*David Nelson McCarthy*

Yellowjackets / **i.** 1981 / Warner Brothers 3573

Mirage a Trois / **i.** 1983 / Warner Brothers 23813

○ **Shades** / 1986 / MCA 5752

○ **Four Corners** / **i.** 1987 / MCA 5994

Politics / **i.** 1988 / MCA 6236
Features appealing sax of Marc Russo, compositions of Russel Ferrante. Unpretentious, melodic, memorable. Fine studio sound. —*David Nelson McCarthy*

★ **Spin, The** / **i.** 1989 / MCA 6304

Green House / **i.** 1991 / GRP 9630
Guest sax by Bob Mintzer, with fine orchestration for a real live string ensemble by Vince Mendoza. High level of musicianship all around. Very accessible. —*David Nelson McCarthy*

Live Wires / **i.** 1992 / GRP 9667

Like a River / GRP 9689

GEORGE YOUNG

Tenor saxophone / Progressive big band, neo-bop
An often dashing, animated tenor saxophonist, George Young doesn't display that fire consistently. At times, his polished, smooth tone can sound detached, and he has sometimes been overshadowed on recording sessions by musicians such as Ron Carter, Jack DeJohnette, Dave Holland, and Toots Thielemans. But Young's alto and tenor style has been flexible enough for him to make creditable contributions to swing, to fusion, and to bebop sessions since the '60s. He's recorded in the big bands of Louis Bellson and Benny Goodman, and in the combos of Steve Gadd, Jay Leonhart, and John Tropea. Young has recorded as a leader for Chiaroscuro and Paddle Wheel. He has one session available as a leader. —*Ron Wynn*

LARRY YOUNG (Khalid Yasin Abdul Aziz)

b. Oct. 7, 1940, Newark, NJ, **d.** Mar. 30, 1978, New York, NY
Organ / Postbop, soul-jazz, early jazz-rock
Larry Young, also known as Khalid Yasin, offered as radical an approach on organ in the '60s as Jimmy Smith posed in the '50s. Young's free, swirling chords, surging lines, and rock-influenced improvisations were an alternative to the groove-centered blues and soul-jazz sound that had become the organ's dominant direction. He brought John Coltrane's late '60s approach to the organ, generating waves of sound and greatly influencing any session he participated in dur-

ing the '60s and '70s. Young studied piano rather than organ, and began playing organ in R&B bands in the '50s. He recorded in 1960 with Jimmy Forrest, and then did his first session for Blue Note as a leader. He worked and recorded in a hard bop vein with Grant Green in the mid '60s, though, and he was beginning his experiments at that point. Young worked with Joe Henderson, Lee Morgan, Donald Byrd, and Tommy Turrentine, and toured Europe in 1964. His 1965 album, *Into Somethin'*, alerted his listeners that he was heading a different direction. He played with Coltrane, recorded with Woody Shaw and Elvin Jones, then joined Miles Davis's band in 1969. Young worked with John McLaughlin in 1970, and was in Tony Williams's Lifetime with McLaughlin and Jack Bruce, among others, in the early '70s. He only made a couple of other records for Perception and Arista; both of them were uneven, but had some intriguing moments. Neither label had the vaguest idea what Young was trying to do, or how they could sell it. Sadly, he died in 1978 at age 38. He'd only made a handful of recordings, and his labels never knew what to make of his music. Mosaic issued a superb boxed set of Young's Blue Note recordings, a six-CD (nine-album) collection, *The Complete Blue Note Recordings of Larry Young*. A very early session, *Testifying*, on New Jazz, was reissued by Fantasy in a limited edition in '92. Blue Note has an anthology package available, *The Art of Larry Young*, as well. —*Ron Wynn*

☆ **Testifying** / Aug. 2, 1960 / New Jazz 1793
With Joe Holiday (ts), Thornel Schwartz (g), and Jimmie Smith (d). —*Michael G. Nastos*

Groove Street / Feb. 27, 1962 / Prestige 7237

★ **Complete Blue Note Recordings** / Sep. 11, 1964-Feb. 7, 1969 / Mosaic
Definitive boxed set of visionary organist's work. A must-buy. Set includes the first three Grant Green (g) albums. —*Michael G. Nastos*

☆ **Into Somethin'** / Oct. 12, 1964 / Blue Note 4187

★ **Unity** / Nov. 10, 1965 / Blue Note 84221
Recorded at Englewood Cliffs, New Jersey. Innovative, far-reaching organist. —*Ron Wynn*

○ **Heaven on Earth** / Feb. 9, 1968 / Blue Note 84304
Of all the organists around, Larry Young was probably the one with the most ambitious musical outlook. Only occasionally does Young's talent emerge above the surface on this release, for funk was the order of the day. Byard Lancaster's presence doesn't help much except on "The Hereafter." Althea Young's interpretation of "My Funny Valentine," strangely enough, is the most enjoyable part of this repetitious release. —*John Norris*, Coda

○ **Contrasts** / 1968 / Blue Note 84266

Lawrence of Newark / 1973 / Perception 34

Spaceball / **i.** 1975 / Arista 4072

Fuel / 1975 / Arista 4051

LESTER YOUNG (Lester Willis Young)

b. Aug. 27, 1909, Woodville, MS, **d.** Mar. 15, 1959, New York, NY
Tenor saxophone / Swing
A dashing soloist and an equally gifted quipster and conversationalist, Lester Young's one of those select artists whose impact extends far beyond his years in the spotlight. He loved the light, dry sound of saxophonists Jimmy Dorsey and Frankie Trumbauer, and combined it with timbral effects like honks and alternative fingerings. He gradually adopted a darker, heavier tone, a wider vibrato, and more wails and blue notes in later years, but was most famous for his immaculate phrasing and solo construction. His approach of playing slightly behind the beat instead of aggressively pushing it forward, of emphasizing melodic development rather than chord changes in his solos, and his generally radical approach for the era initially outraged some musicians and observers.

But no one told a story better, from opening note to concluding phrase, and his accompaniment behind Billie Holiday was so magical that it was sometimes difficult to determine which was more moving, her singing or his support. Eventually, Young's floating, breezy approach was not just accepted, it was embraced; virtually the entire generation that comprised the "cool" school echoed it; and bebop, in turn, was partly founded on it through Charlie Parker's emulation of Young. Young invented his own language, and was a master of the casual put-on; it's been suggested that this device was a defense mechanism to conceal his extreme shyness.

Young grew up near New Orleans, but by 1920 had moved to Minneapolis. His father was a versatile musician who taught his children to play instruments and formed a family band that toured with carnivals and various shows. Young studied violin, trumpet, and drums, then concentrated on alto sax at age 13. He left the family band in 1927, allegedly because he refused to tour in the South. Young toured for a year with Art Bronson's Bostonians, where he began to play tenor. Young returned to the family group in 1929, but remained behind when they moved to California. He played briefly with Walter Page's Blue Devils in 1930, then reunited with Bronson and settled in Minneapolis. Young played with Eddie Barefield in 1931, and worked at the Nest Club with different bandleaders. He joined the Thirteen Original Blue Devils in 1932, and met Charlie Christian while touring in Oklahoma City. Young made Kansas City his base after the Blue Devils disbanded in 1933. He played that year with the Bennie Moten-George E. Lee Band, with Clarence Love, with King Oliver, and, for one night, with Fletcher Henderson, whose star at that time was Coleman Hawkins.

Young joined Count Basie in 1934, but left shortly after to replace Hawkins in Henderson's band. This proved to be a disastrous experience, since Henderson expected Young to play in a style similar to Hawkins's rather than in Young's own lighter approach. He soon left, and joined Andy Kirk's band while en route to Kansas City. After more brief stints with Body Atkins and Rook Ganz, plus other freelance jobs, Young was back with Basie in 1936, where he became a star this time. Early recordings with the band featured the songs "Lady Be Good" and "Shoe Shine Boy," and became required listening for numerous musicians. Young headlined Basie radio broadcasts and recordings. He and fellow saxophonist Herschel Evans had some famous battles; songs such as "Every Tub," "Doggin' Around," "Jumpin' at the Woodside" with Evans on clarinet, and "Texas Shuffle," where they exchanged roles with Young on clarinet and Evans on tenor, were outstanding. Songs that featured landmark Young solos included "Taxi War Dance," "Rock-a-Bye Basie," and "Lester Leaps In," an anthem that allegedly developed from Young walking in during a take and "leaping in."

Young made celebrated small-group recordings outside the Basie band. Many were small-group sessions with pianist Teddy Wilson and vocalist Billie Holiday, who nicknamed him Pres. He returned the favor by crowning her "Lady Day." Young made a guest appearance at Benny Goodman's 1938 Carnegie Hall concert, and did a masterful date for Commodore with various Basie sidemen that same year. He went solo in 1940. Young moved to Los Angeles in 1941 to lead a band with his brother Lee. They returned to New York in 1942 to play at the Café Society, but disbanded the following year. Young did freelance sessions with Al Sears, Basie, and Dizzy Gillespie, and toured with a USO band before rejoining Basie in 1943. Once more, Young was a star, with an appearance in the 1944 film *Jammin' the Blues*. Such up-and-coming saxophonists as Stan Getz, John Coltrane, and Sonny Rollins studied every Young solo closely. Young also made small-group sessions for Commodore, Signature, and Keynote.

Then an epic disaster occurred. Young was drafted in September of 1944. He was isolated and cut off from his friends and music. Young ended up with a 1945 court martial for drug use, served several months in a Georgia detention center, then was released. He resumed recording and performing in Los Angeles, and at his first session produced the glorious "These Foolish Things." He began touring with Jazz at the Philharmonic in 1946, and divided his duties between those tours and small-combo sessions. In the late '40s, Young remained a vital force, tutoring and assisting many young musicians. He recorded from 1945 to 1948 for Aladdin and Savoy. But what had once been a troublesome alcohol problem mushroomed into a catastrophic one.

Though he made many fine records in the '50s, from 1953 on his health degenerated. Young made guest appearances with the Basie band from 1952 to 1954. There were some remarkable dates at a club in Washington, D.C. in 1956 (which were later reissued on both vinyl and CD), plus a session with Wilson, Vic Dickenson, Roy Eldridge, and a classic Basie-styled rhythm section with old comrades Jo Jones and Freddie Green. Young appeared at the Newport Festival in 1957, and participated in the landmark "The Sound of Jazz" television program. There were frequent hospital stays, and in 1959 Young began an extended appearance at the Blue Note in Paris. He cut his last sessions there in March, then became severely ill. He returned to New York, and died shortly thereafter. In 1986, a feature film, 'Round Midnight, premiered. It was dedicated to Young and Bud Powell, and was largely (though not totally) based on his life. Tenor saxophonist Dexter Gordon, a Young devotee, received an Oscar nomination for his performance. The comprehensive book *Lester Young*, by Lewis Porter, was published in 1986. —*Ron Wynn and Dan Morgenstern*

★ **Complete Lester Young on Keynote** / i. 1944 / Mercury 830920

○ **Master Takes** / i. May 1, 1944 / Savoy 4419
The release of this Lester Young album is questionable, as all the material here is also contained on a double album featuring the complete Savoy recordings of Young, including alternate takes of various tunes. A careful reading of the liner notes reveals that the notion behind this release is to introduce Young to the generally uninformed listener who wants to hear him without digging through alternate takes of the previous release. That's a reasonable enough intent, but one that should have been more obviously stated on the cover. — *Milo Fine*, Cadence

★ **Pres: The Complete Savoy Recordings** / i. 1944-1949 / Savoy 70819
The method of including master and alternates—thus allowing the listener to hear a piece develop through several recorded attempts—is tried-and-true scholarship, and it helps make the Lester Young collection an excellent experience. There are 25 tracks, but only 15 titles are covered, and there is joy and wonder in hearing Pres treat each of 3 or 4 takes as a new piece, creating totally different solos at each opportunity. In some cases, each succeeding take provides a solo extended from the one taken before in overall concept. Pres's Savoy recordings—everything he did for the label is included here—were undertaken in 1944 and again in 1949, with a highly charged bop ensemble. Eight tracks, by the way, are released here for the first time; they add nothing startling to the legacy, but help complete the picture, as do J.R. Taylor's notes. —*Neil Tesser*, Down Beat

○ **Prez Conferences (1946-1958)** / Mar. 1946-1958 / Jass 18

☆ **Carnegie Blues** / i. 1946-1957 / Verve 825101
All the material here, with the exception of three tracks from 9/19/53 with Lester Young (ts) backed by the Oscar Peterson trio (Herb Ellis (g), Ray Brown (b), Peterson (p)), plus J.C. Heard (d), was previously unissued. The title track (11:02) is from 5/27/46 and has Young, Coleman Hawkins, and Illinois Jacquet as a tenor troika with Buck Clayton (tpt), Ken Kersey (p), Al McKibbon (b), and Heard filling out the group. It is not terribly distinguished and actually shows Hawkins off to better advantage. "Tea for Two" (7:20) brings in Joe Guy (tpt) and drops the other two hornmen. The performance here is perfunctory, Young sounding rather unPresish. Side one ends with two fragments, "Blues" (2:15) and "I Got Rhythm"

(3:12), featuring Young's solos. In the company are Clayton, Trummy Young (tb), Kersey, John Collins (g), McKibbon, and Heard. For me, Young's best work on the side is his short solo on "Rhythm." The remaining unissued material follows the previously issued 9/19 material (some fine Young) and is a medley with Jacquet, Flip Phillips, Peterson, Ellis, Brown, and Jo Jones (d). Each tenor has a featured solo; in the medley it is Jacquet, Young, then Phillips, and it is quite nice, though not particularly a "Pres item." —*Bob Rusch*, Cadence

☆ **Lester Young Quartet and Count Basie Seven** / i. 1950 / Mercury 25015

○ **Lester Swings** / i. 1951 / Verve 22516
Lester Swings consists of five dates with four rhythm sections. Far and away the best of these is the 1945 material with tenor saxophonist Lester Young playing with a sense of adventure, sympathetically backed by pianist Nat Cole and drummer Buddy Rich. The March 1950 session is the worst, as Pres has intonation problems and solos with little imagination. Pianist Hank Jones is no relief (Ray Brown is the bassist and Buddy Rich the drummer). John Lewis, the pianist on the July 1950 date as well as the two dates from 1951, is an improvement over Jones but not by much. Bassist John Schulman and drummer Bill Clarke are on the July date. The final two sessions are much better mainly due to the drumming of Jo Jones. —*Carl Brauer*, Cadence

☆ **Kansas City Style** / i. Jun. 4, 1952 / Commodore 20021

○ **Pres and Sweets** / i. 1955 / Verve 849391
With Harry Edison. Brilliant duo work with Lester Young and "Sweets" Edison. —*Ron Wynn*

○ **Nat "King" Cole-Buddy Rich Trio** / i. 1956 /

Lester Young & Piano Giants / Mar. 1956-Jan. 1956 / Verve 835316
Dynamite Young encounters with Nat "King" Cole (p), Teddy Wilson (p), and others. —*Ron Wynn*

○ **Lester Young in Washington, D.C., 1956—Vol. 2** / Dec. 1956 / Pablo 225

○ **Lester Young in Washington, D.C., 1956—Vol. 3** / Dec. 1956 / Pablo 228
Though much younger than he, Lester Young's accompanists (pianist Bill Potts, bassist Norman Williams, drummer Jim Lucht) on this date at Olivia's Patio Lounge do not seem to share their peers' disdain of earlier styles and stylists. Indeed, they are actually in awe of Young's very presence, but not so much they could not give him the type of support he wanted. Instead, they treat him with all the loving care and respect a master of his venerable stature deserved. As a consequence, Young plays the best he has in years. His tone full and confident, his ideas almost as freely flowing as ever, the prematurely aged tenorman seems as though he has finally grasped a new lease on life. But club gigs being what they always have been, this one, too, had to end. Later recordings showed Young in the company of musicians closer to his own age and experience; however, the feeling and drive that came to him so effortlessly at Olivia's never, to our present knowledge, surfaced again. —*Jack Sohmer*, Down Beat

○ **Lester Young in Washington, D.C., 1956—Vol. 4** / Dec. 1956 / Pablo 230

○ **Lester Young in Washington, D.C., 1956—Vol. 1** / Dec. 1956 / Pablo 2308-219
Collectors who were amazed at "These Foolish Things," "Jumpin' With Symphony Sid," and "Three Little Words" on a mysterious Lester Young Queen-Disc LP will be delighted to hear this entire Pablo album from the same 1956 nightclub sessions. This rhythm section (pianist Bill Potts, bassist Norman "Willie" Williams, drummer Jim Lucht) is highly active, capturing Young's high spirits without intruding, thereby fulfilling one of his own ideals—indeed, there is a special atmosphere of relaxed intensity, confident mastery, and straightforward creation about the entire date, and bassist Williams deserves particular credit for inspiring the band's high level of swing. The result is the kind of inner ex-

citement, so different from bombast or high volume, that distinguishes the best jazz combo records. —*John Litweiler*, Down Beat

Jazz Giants '56 / 1956 / Verve 825672

Pres in Washington D.C. (1956) / 1956 / Pablo 2308

With the Oscar Peterson Trio / i. 1957 /

★ **Lester Young-Buddy Rich Trio** / i. 1957 / Verve 8164

○ **Lester Young-Nat "King" Cole Trio** / i. 1958 / Score 4019

Giants of Jazz / i. Oct. 1958 / American Recording Society 444

Giants of Tenor Sax / i. 1958 / Commodore 7002

☆ **Pres at His Very Best** / i. Jan. 1966 / EmArcy 26010
These are among the greatest performances Lester Young ever cut. If I had to pick one record with which to spend the rest of my days, it would be this one. —*Don DeMicheal*, Down Beat

Newly Discovered Performances—Vol. 1 / i. May 1975 / ESP 3017

○ **Coleman Hawkins & Lester Young** / i. Nov. 1975 / Zim 1000
This is extraordinary music beautifully reproduced. Every airy puff from Lester Young's tenor comes over with sumptuous depth and presence. His work on "I Got Rhythm," "Lady Be Good," and "Sweet Georgia Brown" soars from its first unearthly notes in a tone so sheer you can almost see through it. Buck Clayton is in fabulous form, and Coleman Hawkins performs at his typical high level. But Young's unique tone and his instinct for the surprising turn of phrase steal the ear away from Bean's rolling aggressiveness. Hawkins is heard in a small-group framework on side one in two compelling renditions of "Body and Soul." Young is heard in a marvelous "Lester Leaps In" and a definitive "D.B. Blues." All the material was recorded in 1946, not normally considered an important year for either Young or Bean. But don't let that fool you. This is a great LP that swings like hell. —*John McDonough*, Down Beat

○ **Pres and Teddy and Oscar** / i. Oct. 1976 / Verve 22502

○ **Lester Young Story—Vol. 3, The** / i. Jan. 1978 / Columbia 34840
Although it was the same Count Basie orchestra, the sound and character of Basie's Columbias are oddly different from his Deccas. Lester Young is more heavily featured, and the entire band comes to sound more and more like a small group, so perfect in its balance and cohesiveness. This is readily apparent on "Taxie War Dance #1," the exquisite "Miss Thing," and "Pound Cake." As for Young, his statements on these tracks are profoundly iconoclasic, particularly the dark, brooding drive of "Pound Cake." So perfect is his sense of form on "Taxie #1" that hearing the alternate, on LP for the first time is like hearing "Moonlight Sonata" played without the black keys. The Basie band sounds so intimate and chamberlike, in fact, that one hardly notices a difference in character when the performances are actually by a small group. "Love Me or Leave Me" and "Nobody" each contain perfectly sculptured full choruses by Young. "China Boy" (from a later session) is taken at a brisk clip, but Young slides along with a glancing attack, digging in hard only when in dialog with trumpeter Lee Castle. Even when working over something as alien as "12th Street," Young achieves remarkable things. He simply discards the rigid rhythmic patterns of the tune and plays as he would do "Shoe Shine Boy." —*John McDonough*, Down Beat

Evening of a Basie-Ite / i. Nov. 1980 / Columbia 234849

○ **Giants of Jazz** / i. Apr. 1981 / Time-Life 13
The pleasant surprise of this Time-Life *Giants of Jazz* offering is the 52-page booklet included with the three-record set, half Lester Young biography and half commentary on the album's recordings. Particularly interesting are the efforts of biographer John McDonough to document the foggy years before and after Young's first stay with the Count Basie band. The strength of the recordings chosen here is that they

present Pres in several different dimensions. To better illustrate his ability as an improviser, the set offers alternate takes of "When You're Smiling" (with Billie Holiday) and "I Want a Little Girl" (Kansas City 6). Young's talents as a soloist tended to overshadow the fact that he provided the finest backing for vocalists in the '30s and '40s of any tenor saxophonist. In "I Left My Baby" (no solo) he backs Jimmy Rushing, and Billie Holiday is the beneficiary on "A Sailboat in the Moonlight," one of Young's favorites from his own recordings. Pres's ballad style is demonstrated on "I Can't Get Started," sometimes thought of as the beginning of his postwar sound (due to the smokier tone he employs here), although it was recorded in 1942. The shortage of post-World War II material in the album (only "Fine and Mellow" and "D.B. Blues") does little to counter the erroneous idea that Young said all he had to say prior to his military time. The prewar selections are largely on target. Exceptions include the two recordings taken from the Kansas City 7 session of 1944, "Lester Leaps Again" and "Destination K.C.," which combined do not match the haunting beauty of another 1944 piece, "Midnight Symphony," recorded as part of the movie short *Jammin' The Blues* sound track shortly before Young entered the army. —*Doug Long,* Down Beat

★ **Lester Young Story—Vols. 1-3, The** / Columbia
Tremendous set that compiles Young's top work for Columbia label. —*Ron Wynn*

SNOOKY YOUNG

b. Feb. 3, 1919, Dayton, OH
Trumpet / Swing, big band, progressive big band
If it's possible to be a star in the background, then Snooky Young has been that kind of star. He's one of the most famous section and session trumpeters, and has been a valued player in that role since his days with the Jimmie Lunceford orchestra. While he's able to play effectively in any situation, Young can provide dazzling high-note solos and blazing tempos, poignant ballads, and outstanding blues interpretations. He was lead trumpeter in the Lunceford orchestra from 1939 to 1942. Young was featured on the soundtrack for the film *Blues in the Night.* He worked with Count Basie in 1942, and with Lionel Hampton in 1942 and 1943. Young played in California with Les Hite and Benny Carter, then joined Gerald Wilson's big band. He played with Basie again in the mid '40s, and once more from 1957 to 1962, when he teamed with Wendell Culley and Thad Jones in a marvelous trumpet section. Young became a studio trumpeter with NBC in 1962, and was a founding member of the Thad Jones-Mel Lewis orchestra. He divided his time between that band and the "Tonight Show" orchestra until 1972, when he moved to California with the "Tonight Show" band. Young toured with the Basie Alumni band in 1981, and played on the "Tonight Show" until Carson left in '92 and the band was replaced. Young also did studio work in Los Angeles. Recently, he's played some dates with Doc Severinsen's orchestra. Young can be heard on many reissued Count Basie CDs. —*Ron Wynn*

★ **Horn of Plenty** / Mar. 1979 / Concord Jazz 91
Trumpet and flugelhorn player Snooky Young's horn is showcased here against a quartet (pianist Ross Tompkins, guitarist John Collins, bassist Ray Brown, drummer Jake

Hanna). The style is middle-of-the-road mainstream. Perhaps the very laidback atmosphere of the date is meant to be, or perhaps it is just a tribute to the professional quality of the musicians. Young has an excellent tone and exercises discipline and control over the music. He has a good sense of improvisational composition. "Bad News," "Lady Be Good," and "My Buddy" are worthy. *Horn of Plenty* didn't send shock waves through the world of jazz; however, it did make small ripples of comment about the tastiness of Young's horn. —*Spencer R. Weston,* Cadence

TRUMMY YOUNG

b. 1912, **d.** 1984
Trombone / New Orleans traditional, swing, big band
A master musician whose style evolved until he could play the cumbersome trombone as though it were a trumpet or a saxophone, Trummy Young was a great instrumentalist and a fine vocalist. He matured from being mainly a functional player to an outstanding talent; Young gained total control of the trombone's upper register, expanded his tone, and incorporated a harmonic and melodic sophistication in his playing that highlighted the trombone's possibilities as a lead instrument. Only a handful of others in the pre-bebop era rank alongside Young as a soloist and a technician. He began on trumpet, but soon switched to trombone. Young's professional career began with Booker Coleman and his Hot Chocolates in the late '20s. He joined Earl Hines's orchestra in the '30s. Young's skills flourished in the Jimmie Lunceford Orchestra of the mid '30s, where he had more solo space and freedom. Lunceford's arranger, Sy Oliver, wrote pieces that spotlighted Young's rich sound. Young also added several "jive" vocals. He led his own band after leaving Lunceford in the mid '40s, then worked with Roy Eldridge, Claude Hopkins, and Benny Goodman, while touring with Jazz at the Philharmonic. Young moved to Hawaii in the late '40s, then joined Louis Armstrong's All-Stars in 1952. He found ways to play stimulating, intriguing solos even though he was working in a restrictive, quasi-show business format. Young stayed with the All-Stars until 1964, then returned to Hawaii. He toured as a solo act and played with Chris Barber. Young appeared at the Grande Parade du Jazz in Nice, France in the 1980s. He can be heard on reissued Lunceford and Armstrong CDs. —*Ron Wynn*

WEBSTER YOUNG

b. Dec. 3, 1932
Cornet, trumpet / Postbop, Cool
Columbia, South Carolina, native Young is a cornet and trumpet player who played in army bands in Washington, D.C., played with Hampton Hawes in 1956, and collaborated with John Coltrane in 1957. He plays in the style of Miles Davis and was championed by Billie Holiday. His smooth, lyrical lines are a model for young brass students. —*Michael G. Nastos*

★ **For Lady** / Jun. 14, 1957 / Prestige 1716
Five of Billie Holiday's most famous tunes done instrumentally, plus the title track written by oft-neglected Young. With Paul Quinichette (ts), Joe Puma (g), and the Mal Waldron Trio. Every young brass player should study Young's absolute lyricism and straight, strong tone. —*Michael G. Nastos*

Z

KIANE ZAWADI (Bernard McKinney)

b. 1932

Euphonium / Hard bop, early free, progressive big band

An excellent player on the seldom-heard euphonium and also a good trombonist, Kiane Zawadi has been a first-rate hard bop and free soloist and accompanist since the early '50s in Detroit. That's when he began playing with Barry Harris and Sonny Stitt as Bernard McKinney, which is Zawadi's original name. Zawadi joined Art Blakey in 1954, then recorded with Donald Byrd in 1955. He played with Yusef Lateef, then relocated to New York. Zawadi worked with Illinois Jacquet and Slide Hampton, and recorded with Pepper Adams, Curtis Fuller, and Hampton at the end of the '50s. He recorded in the '60s with James Moody, Sun Ra, Freddie Hubbard, and Hampton, and changed his name in 1965. Zawadi played both free and hard bop in the '70s, recording with Archie Shepp, McCoy Tyner, Abdullah Ibrahim, Charles Tolliver, Carlos Garnett, and Frank Foster. He recorded with and was a member of Harold Vick's octet in 1974. Zawadi participated in a Charlie Parker tribute concert in 1985. He doesn't have any current sessions available as a leader, but can be heard on reissues by Adams, Lateef, Fuller, Ra, and others. —*Ron Wynn*

JOE ZAWINUL

b. Jul. 7, 1932, Vienna, Austria

Piano, keyboards, synthesizer, composer / Hard bop, early jazz-rock, world fusion

No one has ever been able to get a more human, funky sound out of electric keyboards and synthesizers than Joe Zawinul, Vienna's gift to the improvisational world. Zawinul began playing the accordion at age six, and started studying classical music a year later at the Vienna Conservatory. He worked with Austrian jazz saxophonist Hans Koller in 1952, then with various Austrian groups in the mid and late '50s, while also playing in France and Germany with his own trio. Zawinul won a scholarship to Berklee in 1959, and after coming to America, spent only a week at Berklee before joining Maynard Ferguson and touring with him for eight months. He became Dinah Washington's pianist after a brief stint with Slide Hampton in 1959, and stayed with her until 1961. After a month in Harry Edison's group, he joined Cannonball Adderley and remained with his band until 1970. There, Zawinul's skills flourished, and he become a sturdy blues player, good soloist, and excellent accompanist. In 1969 and throughout 1970, he worked in Miles Davis's electric units, gradually moving away from acoustic and concentrating on electric instruments. He cofounded Weather Report in 1971 with Wayne Shorter, and, through the '70s and '80s, made many influential recordings. Weather Report, especially in its early years, was a true jazz-rock band, able to make appealing, seminal work that had loose, adventurous foundations and energetic solos. Zawinul's synthesizer solos were never dry or dependent on gimmicks, but showed that it was possible to play with individuality and distinction on what many regarded as simply a technological tool. He and Shorter finally went their separate ways

in 1986; since then, Zawinul has worked with his own bands. —*Ron Wynn*

Money in the Pocket / Feb. 7, 1966 / Atco 3003

Rise and Fall of the Third Stream, The / Oct. 16-Dec. 12, 1967 / Vortex 2002

○ **Zawinul** / **i.** 1971 / Atlantic 1579

★ **Immigrants** / **i.** 1984 / Columbia 40969
Again, a wildly eclectic menu. Interest depends on how much you enjoy improvisatory music filtered through lots of styles rather than the straight jazz approach. —*Ron Wynn*

Black Water / **i.** 1989 / Columbia 44316
His recent band has some strong players. This session is uneven by design, with Zawinul and crew going through many styles. —*Ron Wynn*

Lost Tribes / **i.** 1992 / CBS 46057

DENNY ZEITLIN (Dennis Jay Zeitlin)

b. Apr. 10, 1938, Chicago, IL

Piano / Post-bop, Cool, Early free, Early creative

Chicago-born pianist Zeitlin formed a trio in 1964 after receiving his M.D. in psychotherapy at Johns Hopkins. His early period groups are quite stimulating. Newer material is also intriguing, a little more free-floating. All are excellent documents of his search for individualistic expression. He succeeds on all fronts, modern and creative. —*Michael G. Nastos*

Cathexis / **i.** 1964 / Columbia 8982

Carnival / Oct. 28-Oct. 30, 1964 / Columbia 9140

★ **Live at the Trident** / 1966 / Columbia 2463

☆ **Shining Hour** / **i.** 1966 / Columbia 9263

Zeitgeist / Apr. 11, 1966-Mar. 18, 1967 / Columbia 2748

Expansion / 1973 / Arch 1758

Syzygy / 1977 / Arch 1759

Soundings / **i.** 1978 / Arch 1770

○ **Time Remembers One Time Once** / Jul. 1981 / ECM 1239
Live date at Keystone Korner in San Francisco with bassist Charlie Haden. Extraordinary recording of compositions by Ornette Coleman, Coltrane, and the participants. —*Michael G. Nastos*

Tidal Wave / Jan.-Mar. 1983 / Quicksilver 4007

Homecoming / **i.** 1986 / Living Music 11

Homecoming / **i.** 1986 / Living Music 0011

Trio / **i.** 1988 / Windham Hill 0112
1988 release containing five Zeitlin originals, plus standards by Mingus, Ornette Coleman, J.J. Johnson, and Kern/Hammerstein. Quite enjoyable. —*Michael G. Nastos*

In the Moment / **i.** 1989 / Windham Hill 0121

Live at Maybeck Recital Hall—Vol. 27 (Denny Zeitlin At Maybeck) / **i.** Oct. 1992 / Concord Jazz CCD-4572

JOHN ZORN

b. 1953, New York, NY

Alto saxophone, duck calls, composer / Modern creative

The term avant-garde truly fits John Zorn; he falls into no easily definable category or school of playing or composition. His splaying, screaming alto sax solos; use of duck calls; fondness for film soundtracks; and mixing of rock, free, pop, and bop settings confound foes and friends alike. He's been identified with the New York "downtown" crowd, a tag he disdains. Zorn's work began to get wide attention in the mid '80s, particularly the *Cobra '86* album on Hat Art with its molecular system for 13 players, and Zorn's live act, which has included him blowing a mouthpiece under water. He's also worked with rockers the Golden Palaminos and with the Kronos Quartet. He has been featured on tribute albums to Thelonious Monk and Sonny Clark; has done solo, trio, duo, and combo recordings; and has utilized studio technology, like multitrack dubbing, quite creatively. Among more recent Zorn projects is an album that mixes Klezmer and free jazz, plus sessions of pop and rock covers, and thrash/avant-garde material with the Naked City band. Zorn has many sessions in all styles available on CD. —*Ron Wynn*

Pool / Mar. 1+4, 1980 / Parachute
An album that is anarchic, chaotic at times. Gripping and emphatic always. —*Ron Wynn*

Archery / 1981 / Parachute

Big Gundown / Sep. 1984-Sep. 1985 / Elektra 79139
Music of Ennio Morricone. 1984-1985. Ambitious, rambling, and reflective of Zorn's flirtations with rock and the New York downtown scene. —*Ron Wynn*

Yankees / **i.** 1984 / Celluloid
Far, far afield with ear-splitting exchanges between Zorn, George Lewis (tb), and string-breaker Derek Bailey (g). —*Ron Wynn*

Cobra / Oct. 21, 1985 / Hat Art 26040
Not sure if this is "jazz" in the strictest sense. Zorn leads a 13-piece group through songs based on a "molecular" system and doesn't play himself. Still, it's as interesting as it sounds. —*Ron Wynn*

Spillane / Aug. 1986-Sep. 1987 / Elektra 79172
An album of nice, dense, and foreboding concept work, with everything from shuffle guitar by Albert Collins to the Kronos Quartet. —*Ron Wynn*

★ **Voodoo: The Music of Sonny Clark** / **i.** 1987 / Black Saint 0109
This is not an album by Sonny Clark, but a tribute to him by John Zorn. Essential Clark repertoire played by progressivists, with John Zorn on alto sax and Wayne Horvitz on piano. —*Michael G. Nastos*

More News for Lulu / Jul. 1987+Jan. 1989 / Hat Art 6055

○ **News for Lulu** / **i.** Aug. 1987 / Hat Art 6005
This is a great power trio with George Lewis (tb), and Bill Frisell (g). —*Ron Wynn*

★ **Spy vs. Spy: The Music of Ornette Coleman** / **i.** Aug. 1989 / Elektra 60844
On *Spy vs. Spy* (a title that is never explained although it probably alludes to the cartoon in *Mad* magazine), John Zorn and his quintet play 17 Ornette Coleman tunes ranging chronologically from 1958's "Disguise" to four selections from 1987's *In All Languages.* The performances are concise with all but four songs being under three minutes and seven under two, but there is absolutely no variety in moods or routines. Virtually every song has a rapid melody statement followed by an extremely intense group improvisation and finishes with a second dash through the melody. Most of the performances are so violent as to be humorous, with Mark Dresser's bass generally being inaudible behind the pairs of screaming altos and thunderous drums. —*Scott Yanow, Cadence*

★ **Naked City** / **i.** 1990 / Nonesuch 79238
His most intriguing, nicely conceived and executed date, with sparkling solos by Bill Frisell (g), Wayne Horvitz (k), and Joey Baron (d). CD has three bonus cuts. —*Ron Wynn*

☆ **Heretic: Jeux Des Dames Cruelles** / Avant Garde 01

MIKE ZWERIN

b. 1930
Trombone / Cool
Now best known as a columnist and a contributor to *Jazz Journal,* Mike Zwerin missed out on history during his days as a trombonist. He played with the Miles Davis Birth of the Cool group during their residency at the Royal Roost in the late '40s, but missed the recording sessions and doesn't appear on the date. He studied violin and attended the High School of Music and Art. Zwerin spent several years in Paris before returning to America in 1958. He played with Claude Thornhill, Maynard Ferguson, and Bill Russo in the early '60s, then played with Orchestra USA, and served as musical director and arranger for a sextet culled from the orchestra's ranks. He worked in various combos and toured the Soviet Union with Earl Hines in 1966. Zwerin contributed jazz articles to *The Village Voice, Rolling Stone* and *Down Beat* in the '60s, but quit playing at the end of the decade. He returned to France and wrote novels and nonfiction. Zwerin moved to Paris in the late '70s, and did some occasional playing while contributing to publications such as the *International Herald Tribune* and *Jazz Journal.* He's recently done some articles for *Spin.* Zwerin's 1983 autobiography, *Too Close for Jazz,* has some provocative things to say. —*Ron Wynn*

VARIOUS ARTISTS

○ **1930s: Singers–Columbia Jazz Masterpieces, The** / 193? / Columbia 40847

○ **1930s: Small Combos, The** / 193? / Columbia 40833

○ **1940s: Big Bands, The** / 194? / Columbia 38574

★ **1940s: Singers–Columbia Jazz Masterpieces, The** / 194? / Columbia 40652

○ **1940s: Bebop–Columbia Jazz Masterpieces, The** / 194? / Columbia 38575

○ **1950s: Singers–Columbia Jazz Masterpiece, The** / 1950 / Columbia 40799

○ **1960s: Singers–Columbia Jazz Masterpieces, The** / 196? / Columbia 38579

○ **40 Years of Women in Jazz: Feminist Retrospective** / Jass 9/10

○ **40s–Volume 2** / 1940 / RCA 9864
Another in an extensive series covering historical recordings from the RCA family of labels. This second volume continues on the trail of its predecessor, covering material from varied lineups including Glenn Miller, Frank Sinatra, and Artie Shaw. It includes mostly swing era, pre-rock, novelty, and jazzy pop material. —*Ron Wynn*

○ **50 Years of Jazz Guitar** / Apr. 1977 / Sony Special Products 33566

50th Anniversary Box / 1942 / Blue Note 98931
Comprehensive boxed set showcasing the complete range of Capitol as a jazz label. The set includes intimate piano trio work, big bands, cool jazz, torch and nightclub singers, even some hard bop and a little free music, plus fusion. —*Ron Wynn*

★ **Ahmet Ertegun's Cabaret Music** / Atlantic 81817

○ **Americans in Europe–Vol. 1** / Aug. 1963 / Impulse 36

○ **Americans in Europe–Vol. 2** / Aug. 1963 / Impulse 37

Atlantic Jazz 12 Vol. Box Set / 1947 / Atlantic 81712

Atlantic Jazz: Boxed Set / 1947 / Atlantic 81712
This entire series is worth having and can be purchased in one 12-volume disc set or one 15-LP/cassette set. In compiling the discs, Atlantic for some reason omitted some cuts, making the vinyl a better buy. Of course, the vinyl is now deleted. —*Ron Wynn*

○ **Bass Is** / May 18, 1992 / Enja 2018

○ **Be Bop Era, The** / Sep. 1965 / RCA 519

○ **Bebop Revolution, The** / Bluebird 2177
A 1990 reissue. Nice formative cuts from the '40s. With Dizzy Gillespie, Kenny Clarke, Coleman Hawkins, Lucky Thompson, and Allen Eager. —*Ron Wynn*

★ **Best of Blue Note–Vol. 1 & 2** / Blue Note B2-96110
Japanese import. An incredible (just the best!) collection of the very best cuts from the Blue Note label. A perfect introduction to hard bop and soul-jazz, if you can find it. —*Michael Erlewine*

★ **Best of Chess Jazz** / MCA 6025
This is actually a nice package of cuts pulled from various Argo sessions. —*Ron Wynn*

Best of the Big Bands / Madacy 2308

This offers a nice cross-section of Decca sets, especially Woody Herman. —*Ron Wynn*

Best of the Jazz Saxophones / Lester Recording Catalog 9025

Best of the Swing Bands / Vanguard 311
A good cross-section, heavy on big names. —*Ron Wynn*

Bethlehem's Best (3 Albums) / Mar. 7, 1956 / Bethlehem EXLP 6

Big Band Jazz: Various / Delmark 439

Big Band Sampler: Best of the Big Bands / Columbia 45476
A nice overview of the big-band era. —*Ron Wynn*

Big Band's Greatest Hits: Volume 1 / Columbia 30009
Well-known, easily obtainable swing era material. —*Ron Wynn*

★ **Big Bands of the Swinging Year–Vol. 1** / Collectables 5096

○ **Big Bands of the Swinging Year: Vol. 2** / Collectables 5097

☆ **Bird & Pres: The '46 Concerts** / 1946 / Verve 833565-1
Jazz at the Philharmonic (JATP). Bird/Pres 1946 concert. Great session with Charlie Parker (as), Dizzy Gillespie (tpt), and Lester Young (ts). Ultimate melding of swing era and bop musicians. —*Michael G. Nastos*

○ **Birdology** / Oct. 1990 / Verve 841 132
Sampler with various alto saxophonists doing Charlie Parker tunes or otherwise showing their stylistic debt to his approach. Another concept album aimed at what major labels see as an increasingly profitable new young audience interested in learning about jazz and purchasing these grab-bag anthologies. —*Ron Wynn*

○ **Birth of Bop–Vol. 1, The** / 1953 / Savoy 9022

○ **Birth of Bop–Volume 2, The** / 1953 / Savoy 9023

○ **Birth of Bop–Volume 3, The** / 1953 / Savoy 9024

○ **Birth of Bop–Volume 4, The** / 1953 / Savoy 9025

○ **Birth of Bop–Volume 5, The** / 1953 / Savoy 9026

○ **Black Jazz & Blues: First Sound Films** / Sandy Hook 2068

○ **Black Jazz in Europe 1926-1930** / Dec. 1926-Dec. 1930 / EMI Pathe/Jazztime 252714-2

○ **Black Lion at Montreux** / Mar. 1975 / Black Lion 213

○ **Blue Montreux: 1978 Montreux Jazz Festival** / Bluebird 6573

Blue Note 50th Anniversary Collection–Vol. 1–1939-1956–From Boogie to Bop / Dec. 9, 1991 / Blue Note 92465
Parts of the 50th Anniversary boxed set. This volume features formative label sessions with boogie-woogie piano up to hard bop. —*Ron Wynn*

Blue Note 50th Anniversary Collection–Vol. 2–1956-1965–The Jazz Message / Aug. 5, 1991 / Blue Note 92468
Dynamic cuts, hard bop, and avant-garde. —*Ron Wynn*

Blue Note 50th Anniversary Collection–Vol. 3–1956-1967–Funk & Blues / Dec. 9, 1991 / Blue Note 92471
The birth of soul-jazz. —*Ron Wynn*

Blue Note 50th Anniversary Collection–Vol 4–Outside in 1964-1989 / 1964-1989 / Blue Note 92474
Avant-garde, explosive cuts. —*Ron Wynn*

Blue Note 50th Anniversary Collection–Vol 5–Lighting the Fuse 1970-1989 / 1970-1989 / Blue Note 92477

Bluebird Sampler / RCA 6389

Bluebird Sampler 1990 / 1990 / Bluebird 2192-2-RB11

Blues for Coltrane–A tribute to John Coltrane / MCA 42122

○ Boogie Woogie Masters / Black & Blue 590632

○ Bop Session, The / Apr. 1978 / Sonet 692

★ Candid Jazz / 1988 / Candid 79000

○ Charlie Parker 10th Memorial Concert 3/27/65 / Mar. 27, 1965 / PolyGram 826985

★ Chicago Boogie / May 1977 / Barrelhouse 04

★ Chicago Jazz (1923-1929)–Vol. 1 / 1923-1929 / Biograph 12005

★ Chicago Jazz (1925-1929)–Vol. 2 / 1925-1929 / Biograph 12043

Chicago Jazz Summit / Atlantic 81844-2
A 1988 release of some nice cuts done by Chicago jazz veterans at the 1986 JUC festival. —*Ron Wynn*

○ Chicago South Side Vol. 2 / Jun. 1969 / Historical 30

Chicago: At the Jazz Band Ball / RCA 6752

Chicago: The Living Legends–Volume 1 / Sep. 1-8, 1961 / Riverside 12-389

Chicago: The Living Legends–Volume 2 / 1960 / Riverside 12-390

★ Clarinet Summit–Volumes 1 & 2 / 1984 / India Navigation 1062

Classic Female Jazz Artists / RCA 6755
1939-1952. Despite a dubious title, this is a worthwhile anthology of both blues and jazz artists. —*Ron Wynn*

★ Classic Jazz Piano / Jun. 1927-Feb. 1966 / RCA 6754
1927-1957. An excellent compilation of some seminal players and styles. CD has three bonus cuts. —*Ron Wynn*

★ Classic Jazz Piano Styles / Oct. 1967 / RCA 543

★ Classic Jazz: Vol. 1–5 / Smithsonian 331
The Smithsonian Collection of Classic Jazz is itself somewhat of a classic, referred to in many books and used as the main learning source in at least one. If you don't know what you like in jazz and are looking for a well-put-together introduction, this set is a good bet. It starts with ragtime's Scott Joplin and proceeds through Bessie Smith, Louis Armstrong, Art Tatum, Duke Ellington . . . all the way up to and including the free jazz of Ornette Coleman and even the World Saxophone Quartet. Of course John Coltrane, Thelonious Monk, Miles Davis, and all the other big guns are here—even Horace Silver and Lennie Tristano. This 5-CD set (94 tracks) contains classic cuts in most cases. This set is a great place to begin. —*Michael Erlewine*

☆ Cole Porter: A Centennial Celebration / RCA 3090
This master of the urbane lyric and chic tune is himself heard here singing demos of three of his standards. Includes 20 performances from the '30s to the '80s, featuring Fred Astaire, Artie Shaw, Lena Horne, and others. This is the cornerstone of 20th-century music. —*Mark A. Humphrey*

Columbia Jazz Masterpiece Series / CBS 40799
A good starter collection spotlighting jazz in the period when it still had some pop influence. This is a recent cross-section of jazz-based, scat, and popular song stylists. —*Ron Wynn*

Columbia Jazz Masterpiece Series: 1930s Big Band / 193? / CBS 40651
An excellent single-disc overview of '30s bands, both big names and obscure groups. —*Ron Wynn*

Columbia Jazz Masterpieces: 1940s–the Singers / 194? / CBS 40652

Columbia Jazz Masterpieces: Sampler–Vol. 1 / Columbia 40474

Columbia Jazz Masterpieces: Sampler–Vol. 2 / Dec. 20, 1991 / CBS 40798

Columbia Jazz Masterpieces: Sampler–Vol. 6 / Columbia 45146

○ Commodore Jazz Sampler–Classics in Swing, The / 1988 / Commodore 7000

★ Complete Blue Note Recordings of Hall/Johnson/Deparis/Dick / Apr. 1986 / Mosaic 6 109

★ Complete Commodore Jazz Recordings Vol. 1 / Dec. 1988 / Mosaic 123

★ Complete Commodore Jazz Recordings Vol. 2 / Feb. 1990 / Mosaic 128

★ Complete Commodore Jazz Recordings Vol. 3 / Feb. 1990 / Mosaic 134

★ Complete Master Jazz Piano Series, The / Mosaic 140

★ Dancing Twenties / Smithsonian/Folkways RF-27

○ Dixieland Jazz Gems / 1950 / Commodore 20010

☆ Dixieland's Greatest Hits / Pro Arte 8018

Down Yonder / 1989 / Rounder 11562
A 1989 anthology featuring current New Orleans brass bands. The roster includes Dejan's Olympic Brass Band, the Chosen Few, the Rebirth Marching Jazz Band, and the Dirty Dozen Band. —*Ron Wynn*

○ Early and Rare: Classic Jazz Collectors Items / Oct. 1960 / Riverside 12 134

★ Early Black Swing–the Birth of Big Band Jazz: 1927-1934 / 1927-1934 / Bluebird 9583-2-RB11
Valuable, timeless tunes from jazz pioneers, swing, and classic New Orleans jazz. First-rate examples of vintage swing from the '20s and '30s. Plenty of examples from the cream of the crop, including Louis Armstrong, Duke Ellington, Fletcher Henderson. Great introductory item. —*Ron Wynn*

★ Earthy / Jan. 25, 1957 / Prestige 1707-2
Dazzling stints by Kenny Burrell (g), Art Farmer (tpt), and Mal Waldron (p) on otherwise standard cuts. Limited edition release. —*Ron Wynn*

○ Exciting Battle / Pablo
Frenetic jam session date done in 1955 in Stockholm with an all-out tenor battle between Illinois Jacquet, Flip Phillips, and many others. This has been reissued on CD. —*Ron Wynn*

○ Exciting Battle: JATP Stockholm '55 / 1955 / Pablo 2310713

○ Fabulous Ellingtonians on Keynote, The / 1987 / Mercury 830 926

○ First Esquire Concert, The / 1944 / Laserlight 15723
January 18, 1944, was definitely the night to be at the Metropolitan Opera House. It was the night Louis Armstrong, Art Tatum, Coleman Hawkins, and some equally famous colleagues—all winners in *Esquire* magazine's first annual jazz poll—made their Met debuts. Recordings of that evening were originally issued by the U.S. Government on V-Discs for distribution to GIs overseas, but the concert was also broadcast live. A handful of small labels have made this astonishing event available to collectors over the years, but this CD release offers the best technical quality I have heard so far. Mildred Bailey's inimitable version of "Honeysuckle Rose" and interacts with the audience to turn "Squeeze Me" into the kind of performance one could never get in a studio. Billie Holiday was still in top form, and we hear it on "I'll Get By" and "Billie's Bounce," both of which are enhanced by Roy Eldridge. There are several superb instrumental performances featuring Barney Bigard, Bailey's husband Red Norvo, Lionel Hampton, Jack Teagarden, and the entire cast. —*Chris Albertson*, Stereo Review

○ First Sessions 1949-1950 / 1949-1950 / Prestige 24081

★ Footnotes to Jazz–Vol. 2: / Smithsonian/Folkways 31

★ **Footnotes to Jazz–Vol. 3:** / Smithsonian/Folkways 32

★ **Four Giants of Swing: S'wonderful** / Flying Fish 900035

○ **Free Music One and Two** / Jun. 1971 / ESP 1083

★ **From Spirituals to Swing–Carnegie Hall Concerts, 1938-1939** / May 1974 / Vanguard 2-47/48

★ **Fun on the Frets: Early Jazz Guitar** / Yazoo 1061
A companion volume to Yazoo Records' *Pioneers of the Jazz Guitar*. This compilation (1939-1949) features George Van Eps, Carl Kress, and Tony Mottola. —*Richard Lieberson*

★ **Giants of Funk Tenor Sax** / Prestige 2302
A great two-disc introduction to both honking blues and funk (soul-jazz) tenor saxophone. Great for beginners but should be in any collection. Over three hours of blues/funk greats like Arnett Cob, Eddie "Lockjaw" Davis, Sonny Stitt, Willis Jackson, Houston Person, Stanley Turrentine, Rusty Bryant, and Gene Ammons. A classic collection. —*Michael Erlewine*

○ **Giants of Jazz, The** / Apr. 1973 / Atlantic 2 905

★ **Giants of Small Band Swing–Vol. 1** / 1946 / Riverside 1723
Fine combo dates, mostly bop, plus occasional classic New Orleans style. A tremendous 1990 reissue of 1946 recordings featuring various small combos in vintage swing style. —*Ron Wynn*

★ **Giants of Small Band Swing–Vol. 2** / 1945-1946 / Riverside 1724

○ **Giants of Traditional Jazz** / Savoy 2251

☆ **Great Ladies of Jazz** / K-Tel 539

○ **Great Ladies of Jazz–Vol. II** / K-Tel 6023

Great Trumpets (Classic Jazz to Swing) / Feb. 1927-May 1954 / Bluebird 6753

★ **Greatest Jazz Concert in the World, The** / Nov. 1975 / Pablo 2625 704

GRP Super Live in Concert / GRP 1650
A live 2-CD set of Lee Ritenour, Dave Grusin, Tom Scott, and 60 minutes of the Chick Corea Elektric Band. An excellent performance and a fantastic digital recording. —*Paul Kohler*

Guitar Workshop in L.A. / 1988 / JVC 3314
Nice jazz-fusion guitar work featuring Jeff Baxter and Buzzy Feiten. —*Paul Kohler*

★ **Hal Willner Presents Weird Nightmare: Meditations on Mingus** / Nov. 12, 1992 / Columbia 52739
Another installment in Hal Willner's series of tribute albums. This time, Willner assembled a house band for his guests (including Keith Richards, Chuck D, Elvis Costello, Bill Frisell, Vernon Reid, Charlie Watts, Gary Lucas, Leonard Cohen, and Henry Rollins) to sit in with. *Weird Nightmare: Meditations on Mingus* is predictably uneven and wildly entertaining; it is a fitting tribute to the genius of Charles Mingus. —AMG

Happy over Hoagy/We Dig Cole / Jass 5

○ **Hipsters' Holiday: Vocal Jazz & R&B Classics** / Rhino 70910
Typical of Rhino releases, *Hipster's Holiday* has very well laid-out annotation and pictures. This collection covers tracks from 1946 to 1988. Eartha Kitt's "material girl" ode, "Santa Baby," is here, along with its antithesis, the Miles Davis "Blue Xmas (To Whom It May Concern)." The hyper-scat singing of Leo Watson and Lambert, Hendricks & Ross are also on the CBS *Jingle Bell Jazz* collection, but they sound better here. As with the Jass and Savoy discs, Rhino has drawn from some performances of off-vinyl sources. All in all, this disc sounds cleaner and more detailed than those two releases, primarily due to the more recent vintage of recordings. —*Rick Clark*

★ **Honkers & Bar Walkers–Vol.1** / Delmark 438
1952. A blasting R&B sax anthology consisting of early '50s tracks from the Regal and United labels. —*Michael G. Nastos*

Hot Jazz for Cool Nights / 1992 / Music Masters 65089
Anthology featuring vintage performers doing classic traditional jazz cuts. Earl Hines, Charlie Johnson, Tiny Parham, The Missourians, The Jungletown Stompers, and Musical Stevedores are the acts presented. —*Ron Wynn*

Illuminations / 1989 / Axiom 422-848958
Compilation featuring cuts from Axiom artists on the stylistic cutting edge. The list includes Sonny Sharrock, Bill Laswell, Ronald Shannon Jackson, and Shankar. It covers jazz, African and Caribbean styles, and fusion and dance-rock. —*Ron Wynn*

Impulse Collection: Best of–Vol. 1 / MCA 8026
Cross-section of good performances from the larger set. —*Ron Wynn*

Impulse! Jazz–a 30 Year Celebration / 1991 / GRP 101
A two-record set that has many fine cuts celebrating this distinguished label's three decades. —*Ron Wynn*

★ **In Berlin 1971** / 1971 / PolyGram 834567
Fine supergroup matchup with Dizzy Gillespie, Thelonius Monk, Sonny Stitt, Kai Winding, Art Blakey, and Al McKibbon. The all-star lineup unites and makes quality music. —*Ron Wynn*

In Concert at the Public Theater / Innovative 1062
Wondrous performances by the outstanding Clarinet Summit at Public Theater. Includes the late John Carter (cl). —*Ron Wynn*

★ **JATP: Historic Recordings** / 1944 1946 / Verve 2-2504

★ **JATP: Tokyo–Live** / Nov. 18, 1953 / Pablo

Jazz 'Round Midnight / 1992 / PolyGram 513462
Anthology presenting various ballads by jazz greats such as Billie Holiday, Ella Fitzgerald, Sarah Vaughan, Shirley Horn, Mel Torme, Dinah Washington, and others. Strictly for newcomers; the tracks are great but can all be found elsewhere, for the most part on recently or newly issued discs. —*Ron Wynn*

★ **Jazz–Vol. 1: The South** / 1951 / Smithsonian/Folkways 53/4

★ **Jazz–Vol. 2: The Blues** / 1951 / Smithsonian/Folkways 55/6

★ **Jazz–Vol. 3: New Orleans** / 1951 / Smithsonian/Folkways 57/8

★ **Jazz–Vol. 4: Jazz Singers** / 1951 / Smithsonian/Folkways 59/60

★ **Jazz–Vol. 5: Chicago** / 1951 / Smithsonian/Folkways 63/4

★ **Jazz–Vol. 6: Chicago #2** / 1951 / Smithsonian/Folkways 65/6

★ **Jazz–Vol. 7** / 1951 / Smithsonian/Folkways 66/8

★ **Jazz–Vol. 8** / 1951 / Smithsonian/Folkways 69/70

★ **Jazz–Vol. 9** / 1951 / Smithsonian/Folkways 71/2

★ **Jazz–Vol. 10** / 1951 / Smithsonian/Folkways 73/4

★ **Jazz–Vol. 11** / 1951 / Smithsonian/Folkways 75/6

★ **Jazz at Santa Monica Civic '72** / 1972 / Pablo 2625701
JATP-styled blowing date with well-known Pablo acts. A three-record set from 1972. —*Ron Wynn*

○ **Jazz at the Hollywood Bowl (2 Lps)** / 1958 / Verve 8231

★ **Jazz at the Philharmonic: Hartford, 1953** / 1953 / Pablo 2308-240
Includes a fifteen-minute jam on "Cottontail," an Oscar Peterson Quartet set with Lester Young (ts). J.C. Heard and Gene Krupa are on drums with Ben Webster (ts), Flip Phillips (ts), Benny Carter (as/tpt), and Roy Eldridge (tpt) as jammers. —*Michael G. Nastos*

Jazz at the Philharmonic: London (1969) / 1969 / Pablo 2620-119
London 1969. This is a nice two-record set. More intensity than usual. —*Ron Wynn*

★ **Jazz at the Philharmonic: Stockholm (1955), The** / Feb. 2, 1955 / Pablo 2310-713

○ **Jazz Band Ball** / Fantasy 12005

Jazz Club: Alto Sax / PolyGram 40036

Jazz Club: Alto Sax Clarinet & Flute / PolyGram 45145

Jazz Club: Bass / PolyGram 40037
A fine addition in a rare worthwhile compilation series. CD has one bonus cut. —*Ron Wynn*

Jazz Club: Big Band / PolyGram 40030

Jazz Club: Drums / PolyGram 40033

Jazz Club: Guitar / PolyGram 40035

Jazz Club: Guitar & Bass / PolyGram 45150

Jazz Club: Piano / PolyGram 40032

Jazz Club: Tenor & Baritone Sax / PolyGram 45146

Jazz Club: Tenor Sax / PolyGram 40031

Jazz Club: Trombone, Mainstream / 1991 / Polydor 845 144

Jazz Club: Trumpet / PolyGram 40038

Jazz Club: Vibraphone / PolyGram 40034

○ **Jazz Guitar Classics (1953-1974)** / Dec. 1953-Feb. 1974 / Original Jazz Classics 6012

○ **Jazz Heritage–Big Bands Uptown** / MCA 1323

○ **Jazz Heritage–Blues & All That Jazz** / MCA 1353

○ **Jazz in a Vertical Groove** / May 31, 1991 / Biograph 12057

★ **Jazz in the Thirties** / Disques Swing 8457
A very nice anthology with lots of cuts from underrated performers. —*Ron Wynn*

○ **Jazz in the USSR** / Mobile Fidelity 21-00890
Wonderfully recorded collection spotlights Soviet artists. —*Ron Wynn*

Jazz Loves Paris / Speed Record 5002
A Buddy Collette session with wonderful arrangements and nice solos. It's available once more after a long absence. —*Ron Wynn*

★ **Jazz Men Detroit** / 1955 / Savoy 12083

Jazz Piano / Smithsonian
Four discs—68 cuts and over 40 artists—all the way from Jelly Roll Morton through Teddy Wilson, Art Tatum, Erroll Garner, Bud Powell, Thelonious Monk, Tommy Flanagan, and Bill Evans up to Chick Corea, Keith Jarrett, and Herbie Hancock—a great survey of piano styles. This collection focuses on piano solos, and most are unaccompanied. Overall, a very nice collection. —*Michael Erlewine*

Jazz Piano, Smithsonian Collection 1924-1977 / 1924-1977 / Smithsonian 039

★ **Jazz Sampler: Classics in Swing 1938-1944** / 1938-1944 / Commodore 7000

★ **Jazz Singers** / Prestige 24113
Good range of featured artists aimed at novices and new fans. Very fine two-record set with an extensive cross-section from early Armstrong to Flora Purim. This is worth having, regardless of your jazz knowledge. —*Ron Wynn*

★ **Jazz Singers: Vocals by Great Instrumentalists, The** / Oct. 23, 1992 / Bluebird 3137

★ **Jazz Tribe, The** / 1990 / Red 123254

Jazz Trumpet: Classic Jazz to Swing / Prestige 2301
Vol. 1. An excellent anthology covering a range of trumpet styles in the first phase of jazz. —*Ron Wynn*

Jazz Years, The / Nov. 1973 / Atlantic 2 316

○ **Jazzin' Baby Blues: Hot Piano Roll Solos** / Biograph 117

★ **Jazzmen: Detroit** / 1956 / Savoy 12083

○ **Jazzology Poll Winners** / Aug. 1965 / Jazz Crusade 2004

☆ **Jingle Bell Jazz** / 1989 / CBS 40166
Jingle Bell Jazz is a single-CD compilation of two previously released CBS holiday jazz albums, *Jingle Bell Jazz* (1974) and *God Rest Ye Merry Jazzmen* (1985). This disc is loaded with strong performances by Herbie Hancock, McCoy Tyner, Dexter Gordon, Wynton Marsalis, Duke Ellington, Lionel

Hampton, Miles Davis, and more. —*Rick Clark*, Rock & Roll Disc

Just Friends–Gathering in Tribute to Emily Remler–Vol. 1 / 1992 / Justice 0502-2
The first album of two all-star tributes to guitarist Emily Remler by her distinguished friends. They got together in 1989 and cut these sessions for the Austin, Texas, Justice label, with all proceeds going to Remler's Jazz For Kids fund in Pittsburgh. There are no stars or supporting musicians here, just several great musicians saying good-bye to their friend. —*Ron Wynn*

Just Friends–Tribute to Emily Remler–Vol. 2 / 1992 / Justice 503
This is the second of a pair of albums done by an all-star lineup assembled to record two tribute albums following guitarist Emily Remler's death in 1989, with all proceeds going to her Jazz For Kids fund in Pittsburgh. The roster includes Herb Ellis, Bill O'Connell, Eddie Gomez, Marvin "Smitty" Smith, and David Benoit. They made a reverential, yet loving and energetically played, tribute. —*Ron Wynn*

★ **Kings of Ragtime Banjo** / Yazoo 1044

Legends of Guitar: Jazz–Vol 1 / Rhino 70717

Legends of Guitar: Jazz–Vol 2 / Rhino 70722

★ **Manhattan Project, The** / 1990 / Blue Note 94204
Much of this sounds wonderful, especially in comparison with recent releases, but it still lacks some of the crispness, flair, and fire that they achieved in days past. —*Ron Wynn*, Rock & Roll Disc

○ **Memorable 1957 Telecast** / 1957 / CBS 45234

★ **Mercury 40th Anniversary** / 1985 / PolyGram 24116

○ **Metronome All Stars, The** / 1949 / Columbia 2528

○ **Metronome All-Star Bands** / Apr. 24, 1991 / Bluebird 7636-2-RB11

★ **Modern Art of Jazz: Modern Art of Jazz** / Biograph 120
A nice 1991 sampler with collected performances showing the growth of bop and hard bop. —*Ron Wynn*

Modern New Orleans Masters / Rounder 11514
Excellent current music by well-known New Orleans performers. —*Ron Wynn*

More Best Dixie: Compact Jazz / PolyGram 38347
Another decent compilation drawing from various traditional performances. —*Ron Wynn*

Music of the Brazilian Masters / 1989 / Concord Jazz 4389

Musicmasters Jazz Sampler / Music Masters 5022

New Orleans Brass Bands: Down Yonder / Rounder 11562
An eclectic sampler of some of New Orleans' best: the Dirty Dozen, Dejan's Olympic Brass Band, the Rebirth, and the Chosen Few. —*Bruce Boyd Raeburn*

★ **New Orleans Jazz & Heritage Festival** / Nov. 1977 / Island 9424

★ **New Orleans Jazz & Heritage Festival** / Jun. 1979 / Flying Fish 099

New Orleans Jazz & Heritage Festival (1976) / 1976 / Rhino 271111
Includes great live action from Professor Longhair, five tunes from the renowned piano-playing producer Allen Toussaint, a gritty selection of hits by Ernie K-Doe and Robert Palmer, blues from Earl King and Lightnin' Hopkins, and classic R&B belting by Irma Thomas. —*J. Poet*, Rock & Roll Disc

★ **New Orleans Jazz/Heritage Fest: 10th Anniversary** / Flying Fish 99

○ **New Orleans Jazz–Vol. 1 (1942-1955)** / 1942-1955 / Wolf 1001

○ **New Orleans Jazz–Vol. 2 (1926-1951)** / 1926-1951 / Wolf 1002

○ **New Orleans, Chicago, New York** / Jul. 1918-Sep. 1934 / BBC 3CD 821

○ **Newport Festival All Stars** / Oct. 1960 / Atlantic 1331

Newport Jazz Festival All Stars / Jul. 1985 / Concord Jazz 4260

Nice, loose date with a specially assembled group of mostly veterans plus one or two younger players performing in vintage jam session style. This is modeled after the old Jazz at the Philharmonic dates, and the atmosphere and musical performances come close to equaling that fervor. —*Ron Wynn*

○ **Newport Rebels** / Dec. 1978 / Candid 79022

○ **Nipper's Greatest Hits: 30s–Volume 1** / 1930 / RCA 9971

○ **On the Edge–Progressive Music Pushing The** . . . / 1991 / Antilles 848 210

○ **On-The-Road Jazz** / 1957 / Riverside 12-127

○ **Opus De Bop** / 1957 / Savoy 12114

○ **Opus in Swing** / 1956 / Savoy Jazz 144

○ **Paris All-Stars: Homage to Charlie Parker** / A&M 5300

★ **Parlor Piano** / Apr. 1971 / Biograph 1001Q

Piano Giants / Prestige 24052

A two-record anthology featuring vintage performances by various piano greats taken from Prestige sessions. The styles range from updated stride to hard bop, mainstream, and soul-jazz. Featured artists include Duke Ellington, Chick Corea, Keith Jarrett, McCoy Tyner, Red Garland, Earl Hines, and Art Tatum. —*Ron Wynn*

★ **Picante** / Concord Jazz 295

An anthology featuring cuts from various Afro-Latin and Latin jazz artists. The roster includes Cal Tjader, Poncho Sanchez, Tania Maria, Tito Puente, Laurindo Almeida and Charlie Byrd, and Monty Alexander. —*Ron Wynn*

○ **Pioneers of Boogie Woogie** / 1953 / Riverside 1009

★ **Pioneers of the Jazz Guitar** / Yazoo 1057

Terrific compilation of '20s and '30s acoustic jazz guitar music featuring Eddie Lang, Carl Kress, Lonnie Johnson, Dick McDonough, and others. Yes, Virginia, there was jazz guitar before Charlie Christian. This volume is preferable to Yazoo's companion, *Fun On The Frets.* —*Richard Lieberson*

Prestige 1st Sessions–Vol. 1–Various / 1949 / Prestige 24224

Early material from artists who cut dates that were among the first issued by the Prestige label. Performers include Roy Haynes, Don Lanphere, Fats Navarro, Duke Jordan, Al Haig, and Oscar Pettiford. —*Ron Wynn*

Prestige 1st Sessions–Vol. 2–Various / 1949 / Prestige 24115

The second volume in the series devoted to the early recordings issued on the Prestige label in 1949 and 1950. More from Don Lanphere, Leo Parker, Tubby Phillips, Al Haig, and Max Roach, among others. —*Ron Wynn*

Prestige 1st Sessions–Vol. 3–Various / 1950 / Paris 24116

The third volume in the series covering early sessions issued on the Prestige label, this one moving into the '50s. Eddie "Lockjaw" Davis, Dizzy Gillespie, Red Rodney, and Bennie Green are among the artists presented on this release. —*Ron Wynn*

☆ **Prestige Soul Masterpieces** / Original Jazz Classics 1201

Fine intro to funk or soul-jazz on the Hammond organ. Fifteen cuts from classic funk albums by Charles Earland, Billy Butler, Jack McDuff, Gene Ammons, Charles Kynard, Oliver Nelson, King Curtis, Jimmy Forrest, Rusty Bryant, Shirley Scott, Stanley Turrentine, Willis Jackson, Houston Person, Harold Mabern, Eddie Davis, Red Holloway, Arnett Cobb, Richard Holmes, and many featured soloists. This is the real stuff. —*Michael Erlewine*

★ **Ragtime Piano Origionals** / Oct. 1974 / Smithsonian/Folkways 23

○ **RCA Victor Jazz Workshop: the Arrangers** / Bluebird 6471

○ **Real Sound of Jazz, The** / Dec. 1985 / Pumpkin 116

★ **Rhythm & Blues Sax Anthology** / Atlantic 81666

Riverside Presents . . . : **History of Classic Jazz** / Riverside 1575

Roots / Oct. 25, 1957 Dec. 6, 1957 / Prestige 062

More big-band bop with a stellar cast that includes Cecil Payne, Pepper Adams, and Idrees Sulieman on saxes and Bill Evans on piano. —*David Szatmary*

★ **Smithsonian Collection–Jazz Piano Vol. 1** / Smithsonian 0391

★ **Smithsonian Collection–Jazz Piano Vol. 2** / Smithsonian 0392

★ **Smithsonian Collection–Jazz Piano Vol. 3** / Smithsonian 0393

★ **Smithsonian Collection–Jazz Piano Vol. 4** / Smithsonian 0394

★ **Smithsonian Collection of Classic Jazz–Vol. 1** / 1991 / Smithsonian 0331

★ **Smithsonian Collection of Classic Jazz–Vol. 2** / 1991 / Smithsonian 0332

★ **Smithsonian Collection of Classic Jazz–Vol. 3** / 1991 / Smithsonian 0333

★ **Smithsonian Collection of Classic Jazz–Vol. 4** / 1991 / Smithsonian 0334

★ **Smithsonian Collection of Classic Jazz–Vol. 5** / 1991 / Smithsonian 0335

☆ **Sound of Chicago: Jazz Odyssey–Vol.2** / Nov. 1964 / Columbia 32

☆ **Sound of Chicago: Jazz Odyssey–Vol.3** / Nov. 1964 / Columbia 33

○ **Sound of Jazz, The** / May 1958 / Columbia 1098

○ **Southern Bells** / Mar. 29, 1987 / Black Saint 0107

Specialty Legends of Boogie Woogie / Oct. 30, 1992 / Specialty 7019

Art Rupe's Specialty label had its heyday around 1956 when one Little Richard tune after another sold a million copies. The current series of reissues proves, however, that Specialty was far more than a one-trick enterprise. Rupe had been making records since the mid '40s, and many of his early productions are collected in the *Legends of Boogie Woogie,* which shows that the pounding piano and driving beat of Little Richard and labelmate Larry Williams were nothing new to Rupe. The earliest number, vocalist Roy Milton's "Milton's Boogie" from 1945, is a spirited steal of Joe Turner and Pete Johnson's "Roll 'Em Pete." Milton's pianist, Camille Howard, would become one of Specialty's first stars. The eight Howard tunes begin with her biggest hit—the straight-ahead "X-Temporaneous Boogie," which despite its title sounds rehearsed, or at least worked out. Her numbers are loaded with flying fingers and occasionally have a jazzing-the-classics feel, as on "Barcarolle Boogie." The most modern and rocking of the half-dozen other pianists is probably Jo Jo Jackson, whose "Boogie in the Groove" (1951) hints at things to come. Early sparks of rock & roll can also be heard on Nelson Alexander's "Rock That Voot" from 1947. The 21 tracks are nice reminders that 40 years ago, the guitar hadn't quite dominated blues and rock music.

While Rupe supervised the boogie-woogie sessions himself, he purchased his John Lee Hooker cuts from Bernie Besman. They're part of Hooker's huge 1948-1952 output that's been issued, reissued, and issued again in so many forms. Rupe was said to be less than keen on Hooker and most of these 20 songs were kept in the can for a long time. A second volume of them is supposed to be released in fall 1994. This is Hooker at his most primitive and off-the-cuff, so it's not hard to see why a craftsman like Rupe may have found it outdated or uncommercial. "Henry's Swing Club," "Boogie Chillen #2," and "Momma Poppa Boogie" are all variations on Hooker's hit "Boogie Chillen." A few other songs display Hooker's sources—"Sailing Blues" is a clone of Charles Brown's "Drifting Blues"; "Alberta" uses the melody of "Catfish Blues"; and "Hastings Street Boogie" is a foot-stomping instrumental that may have been inspired by

Blind Blake's ode to the same Detroit street. Standouts include "Burnin' Hell," on which Hooker is joined by Eddie Burns on harmonica. The result is similar to the rendition with Canned Heat's Al Wilson 20 years later. "War Is Over (Goodbye California)" catches well the late '40s, a time when defense plants were closing and many blacks sank back into hard times. Also topical is "Build Myself a Cave," a song about being drafted. Hooker even whistles on "Goin' Down Highway 51," a tune resurrected on his *Mr. Lucky* album.

For evil, nasty guitar, not even Hooker could match Frankie Lee Sims, a cousin of Lightnin' Hopkins. Twenty of Sims's 1953-1954 songs are on *Lucy Mae Blues*. Sims might have recorded more for Specialty, but he left with his producer, Johnny Vincent, when Vincent split with Rupe and formed Ace Records. Believe me, there's no fooling around on Sims's records, no John Lee laidback rambling, no piano grace notes. Sims can be weird, as on "Rhumba My Boogie," surely the oddest version ever done of "South of the Border." He can sound almost pretty, as on "Frankie's Blues," and he can recycle traditional material, as on "I'm So Glad," which uses "Grinnin' in Your Face" lines. More often, he's violent and threatening, as on "I Done Talked," or sounds distorted and mean, as on "Married Woman." His guitar solo almost careens out of control on "Ragged and Dirty," making even a blues historian forget the tune is derived from Blind Lemon Jefferson. "Long Gone" is a marvelous rocking rendition of a number that most performers have countrified. Nowhere, though, is Sims better than on the title tune, "Lucy Mae Blues," a ten-star classic. —*John Douglas*, Blues Access

★ **Spirituals to Swing** / Feb. 1973 / Columbia 30776

★ **St. Louis Barrelhouse Piano (1929-1934)** / 1929-1934 / Document 5104

○ **Stride Piano Summit: a Celebration of Harlem . . .** / 1990 / Milestone 9189

Sullivan Years: Louie Armstrong, The / Tee Vee Toons 9427
An anthology from the recent collection featuring material recorded on the long-running Ed Sullivan television show. This contains selections from the many times Louis Armstrong appeared on the program. Some marvelous play-ing and singing, juxtaposed with the usual large amounts of show business. —*Ron Wynn*

Swing (4 CD Box Set) / MCA 80724

Swing Time! (1925-1955) / 1925 / Columbia 52862
Extensive multidisc set that presents an overview of the swing and big-band era with performances from numerous bands in hot, sweet, and pop contexts. The anthology hasn't been weighted toward any one period or style, and it doesn't necessarily offer all the genre's finest works. But it does give a thorough presentation of what defined the period and its appeal. —*Ron Wynn*

○ **This Is Acid Jazz** / Jan. 1991 / Instinct 2250

○ **Timeless All Stars: Time for the Timeless All Star** / Early Bird 101

○ **Town Hall Concert 1945** / 1945 / Commodore 7006

○ **Township Swing Jazz Vol. 1** / Harlequin 8

★ **Tribute to Duke, A** / Concord Jazz 4050

Tribute to John Coltrane–Live under the Sky / Dec. 20, 1991 / Columbia 45136

Vocal Jazz / Adventures in Music 53

Vocalists / Jul. 31, 1992 / RCA 66072
A 1992 anthology that spotlights vocal numbers done by both instrumentalists and singers. The list includes Lionel Hampton, Fats Waller, Mildred Bailey, Jack Teagarden, Lee Wiley, Dave Lambert, Jon Hendricks, Joe Williams, and Nina Simone. —*Ron Wynn*

Vol. 3–Various / DRG 6182
The third in the Robert Parker import series featuring vintage early jazz performers. This set includes selections by Bessie Smith, Fletcher Henderson, Duke Ellington, Louis Armstrong, and Benny Goodman. —*Ron Wynn*

★ **Women (Classic Female Jazz Artists: 1939-1952), The** / 1939-1952 / RCA 6755

Yazoo's History of Jazz / Yazoo 1070
In an interesting approach, this focuses on some of the label's quirkier, expressive artists from the '20s and '30s. —*Ron Wynn*

Young Lions, The / May 25, 1960 / Vee Jay 3013

LABELS

Aladdin

Jim and Edward Mesner formed Aladdin Records in Los Angeles in the mid '40s. The company's original name was actually Philco, and the first sessions were issued under that name in 1946. The name changed shortly after to eliminate confusion with Philco products. Aladdin's early importance was as a jazz and blues label, though it subsequently became among the most prominent R&B companies in operation during the '50s and also had some major gospel releases. Lester Young, Illinois Jacquet, Billie Holiday, Louis Jordan, Art Pepper, Lawrence Marable, Harry Edison, Helen Humes, Howard McGhee, and Jay McShann were among the jazz artists who recorded for Aladdin and its late '50s subsidiary operation Jazz West (1956-1957). The company also leased some jazz masters by Erroll Garner and Howard McGhee from the Black and White label. Aladdin jazz sessions by Young, Pepper, and a few other artists have been reissued by United Artists and EMI. Aladdin's masters were purchased by Imperial in 1961 and were passed on to the Minit label in 1963. Liberty eventually purchased Aladdin as well as Imperial and Minit. Liberty was in turn absorbed in 1969 by United Artists, which later became part of EMI, the current holders of the Aladdin masters.

American

Bill Russell founded the American Music company in the early '40s, operating it at various times from homes in Pittsburgh, Chicago, New Orleans, and Canton, Missouri. Bunk Johnson was first featured recording artist with the initial sessions issued in 1944. George Lewis, Dink Johnson, and Wooden Joe Nicholas were among the artists spotlighted by the label. It issued over 50 records on 78 rpm and continued into the 12-inch LP era of the '50s, finally ceasing production in 1957. The company also reissued Paramount blues and jazz dates from the '20s. Storyville reissued American sessions, and the Japanese label Dan started a reissue line in 1973.

Argo/Cadet

The jazz wing of the Chess empire, Argo was established by Leonard and Phil Chess in the mid '50s as a separate division. It represented an expansion into jazz by a company that up to that point was almost exclusively known for blues and R&B. Chess had previously recorded a few sessions by Leo Parker, Gene Ammons, and Al Hibbler, but now Argo signed James Moody, Ahmad Jamal, and Ramsey Lewis. Lewis's dates were among the best-selling in jazz history, though with controversial jazz output. Barry Harris and Ira Sullivan made their debuts on Argo, and Illinois Jacquet, Budd Johnson, Kenny Burrell, Max Roach, and Red Rodney were other label artists. Argo's name was changed to Cadet in 1965, after the Argo company in England raised objections and pointed to its longer history with the name. After Leonard Chess died in 1971, a series of misadventures with the total Chess catalog affected Argo/Cadet. It was bought and mismanaged by GRT, which sold it to All Platinum in 1975. It was then bought by Sugar Hill. MCA now owns all Chess, Checker, and Argo/Cadet material but has not been as exhaustive in mining its jazz resources as it has been with Chess blues and R&B material. MCA has reissued specific titles by Jamal, Lewis, and a few others.

Arista

Clive Davis, who had formerly been with many other labels including Columbia, formed Arista in New York in 1974. The company had three jazz divisions with Steve Backer directing each one and issuing material on separate labels. The Arista/Freedom wing reissued free jazz originally released on the labels Freedom, Black Lion, Fontana, Polydor, and Debut as well as new sessions. Anthony Braxton, Albert Ayler, Charles Tolliver, Cecil Taylor, Randy Weston, Archie Shepp, and Oliver Lake were among artists with titles on this label. Arista/Novus began in 1978 with new material by free jazz players like Air, Muhal Richard Abrams, and Henry Threadgill. The company also acquired the rights to the Savoy catalog and started a reissue series from its masters. Backer even began issuing jazz-rock dates from the GRP catalog. But everything crumbled in the '80s. New recording ended, Arista sold Savoy to Muse in 1985, and RCA acquired the Novus line along with Backer's services. MCA eventually purchased GRP. Arista has kept its foot in the jazz market, albeit in the fusion/contemporary pop category, thanks to Kenny G.

Artists House

John Snyder established Artists House in the late '70s and modeled it after his previously acclaimed Horizon operation. He signed Ornette Coleman, Paul Desmond, Charlie Haden, Jim Hall, Thad Jones, and Mel Lewis. Artists House was also the company that issued James "Blood" Ulmer's debut jazz session. Snyder allowed musicians maximum creative input and quality control and once again included extensive biographical and musical information with each release as well as exhaustive liner notes. The featured musicians also retained ownership of the rights to the music, giving musicians a chance to earn much more than was usual in the standard contract and royalty percentage. Sadly, this label did not last any longer than Horizon. Snyder issued about 10 albums over a two-year period and nothing was recorded after 1978.

Atlantic

The Atlantic legacy in R&B and jazz is unsurpassed among American labels, though a few others have been its equal. Herb Abramson and Ahmet Ertegun founded Atlantic in 1947, with Tiny Grimes and Erroll Garner among their earliest signees. They leased sessions from the French company Blue Star for Wilbur de Paris, Jimmy Yancey, Sidney Bechet, Don Byas, and Dizzy Gillespie in the early '50s. While Jerry Wexler became justifiably famous for his production work with Joe Turner, Ray Charles, and Aretha Franklin, Ertegun's brother

Nesuhi became just as prominent for his efforts in the jazz division. As head of Artists and Repertory (A&R) for the album catalog, he was responsible for sessions by Lennie Tristano, Lee Konitz, Charles Mingus, the Modern Jazz Quartet, Ornette Coleman, John Coltrane, Phineas Newborn, Eddie Harris, Charles Lloyd, Yusef Lateef, Herbie Mann, and Rahsaan Roland Kirk among many others. Mann's sessions in the '60s were often pop/crossover hits. The company established some subsidiary operations in the '50s and '60s that issued many notable jazz dates. Atco (1955) featured sessions by Herb Geller, Helen Merrill, Betty Carter, Vi Redd, and Roland Hanna. It also distributed the Flying Dutchman label in the mid '70s. Vortex (1966) was a jazz operation that issued the recording debuts of Keith Jarrett and Chick Corea and released albums by Robin Kenyatta, Dave Pike, Byard Lancaster, Von Freeman, and Clifford Jordan. For a brief time in the late '60s and early '70s Herbie Mann served as a producer and operated Embryo Records, which issued albums by Ron Carter, Sonny Sharrock, Miroslav Vitous, and Attila Zoller.

Atlantic was purchased by Warner Bros. in 1967 and is now part of the Warner/Elektra/Atlantic combine within the greater Warner Communications conglomerate. Things got a bit bleak from a cutting-edge and jazz standpoint in the late '70s and early '80s, as fusion and instrumental pop artists dominated. But Atlantic initiated a "Just Jazz" reissue campaign in 1986 and began an ambitious cross-company reissue campaign with Rhino Records in 1993. The results were impressive: two-disc anthologies by Les McCann, Coltrane, Kirk, Mingus, David Newman, and Eddie Harris; single re-issues of prime Mingus, McCann, and Newman dates; and the four-disc gem *The Complete Recordings of Ornette Coleman* were among '93 releases. The company also hired Michele Taylor with great fanfare at the end of '93 to oversee the revamping of its jazz division.

Bethlehem

Though it was absorbed by King in the early '60s, Bethlehem was a prominent label through the '50s. It began operations in 1953 and issued albums in the 10-inch format during its first two years before converting to 12-inch in 1955. Carmen McRae made her debut for Bethlehem, while Chris Connor was the first artist to record for it in 1953. The label had a diverse catalog of hard bop and cool West Coast performers, among them Dexter Gordon, Frank Rosolino, Charlie Mariano, Duke Ellington, Oscar Pettiford, Art Blakey, Booker Ervin, Herbie Nichols, Claude Williamson, Conte Candoli, Johnny Hartman, and Mel Torme. By having both New York and Hollywood offices, Bethlehem was able to line up prime talent on both coasts. Creed Taylor and Teddy Charles were among its producers. The company's original jazz sessions came to a standstill after the purchase by King. Bethlehem reissue campaigns have been conducted frequently in the '70s, '80s, and '90s. Some Bethlehem sessions have been reissued by Affinity in England, and others are currently coming via Evidence.

Black & Blue

This was a French company that began operations in 1968 and focused on blues and jazz. Black & Blue started as a reissue company but soon started recording original sessions as well. Buddy Tate, Papa Jo Jones, Milt Buckner, Sammy Price, Jay McShann, Illinois Jacquet, and Ray Bryant were among the jazz acts that recorded for Black & Blue. The label finally ceased operation in the late '80s. Evidence now owns the catalog and has been reissuing selected titles since 1992.

Black Jazz

Producer and musician Gene Russell started Black Jazz in Glenview, Illinois, in 1971. It was one of the rare companies

owned and operated by African Americans that specialized in jazz during the '70s. The roster included Doug and Jean Carn, Walter Bishop, Jr., Harold Vick, and a group called the Awakening. It unfortunately had a short life, ending operations before the end of the decade. But in December 1993, former Arista Artist and Repertory (A&R) representative Erik Nuri bought the Black Jazz holdings and announced plans to both start a reissue campaign and issue new releases in the mainstream, contemporary/fusion, and acid-jazz mode using the original Black Jazz title and logo.

Black Lion

Alan Bates started Black Lion in 1968. The London-based label issued new material by a diverse roster that ranged from Stephane Grappelli and Barney Kessel to Philly Joe Jones, Abdullah Ibrahim (then known as Dollar Brand), Thelonious Monk, and even Sun Ra. It reissued recordings originally released on the Sunset label, V-discs from Art Tatum, and European dates recorded by American jazz artists like Ben Webster, Earl Hines, Bud Freeman, and Bud Powell. Black Lion also issued sessions by British musicians such as Chris Barber, Freddy Randall, and Humphrey Lyttelton. It had a subsidiary wing, Freedom, that concentrated on free jazz and was purchased in 1975 by Arista, which also bought some Black Lion dates as well. DA music currently owns and distributes Black Lion reissues.

Black Saint

A critically acclaimed label that has emerged as perhaps the finest foreign jazz outlet, Black Saint began in 1975. Giacomo Pellicciotti started the company in Milan and established its prime concentration on free jazz. In 1978 Giovanni Bonandrini became executive producer and helped expand the operation. Soul Note was established for recordings by bebop and hard bop musicians. The releases were distributed in America by many companies, among them Rounder, but are now part of the Sphere marketing group, along with Red, DIW, Avant, and others. David Murray, Air, Anthony Braxton, the World Saxophone Quartet, Old and New Dreams, Max Roach, the String Trio of New York, Muhal Richard Abrams, Julius Hemphill, Oliver Lake, Hamiet Bluiett, the Saxophone Choir, and many others are among the wide array of artists recording for the Black Saint/Soul Note family.

Black Swan

Black Swan, the nation's first record label owned and operated by African Americans, began in 1921. It was part of the Pace Phonograph Corporation, with president and general manager Harry H. Pace, the former partner of W. C. Handy in the music publishing firm Pace & Handy. The company took its name from opera singer Elizabeth Taylor Greenfield, nicknamed "The Black Swan." Fletcher Henderson was house accompanist, and he not only backed vocalists like Ethel Waters and Trixie Smith and led his own band but also played with and for classical musicians as the label issued jazz, blues, and classical works. Pace bought the Olympic Disc Record Corporation in 1922 with John Fletcher, reorganized it as the Fletcher Record Corporation and made its Brooklyn plant a pressing and production outlet of Black Swan. Black Swan got lots of mileage by claiming loudly and often that they were run solely by Blacks and only issued recordings by race artists, but they fudged those claims by issuing sessions by such white bands as the Original Memphis Five and others from the Olympic catalog, trying to mask this practice by releasing them as "Henderson's Dance Orchestra." The Pace Phonograph Corporation was renamed the Black Swan Phonograph Company in 1923. By May of 1924, Pace and Paramount had made an arrangement:

Paramount would reissue Black Swan dates with the company logo on the records as part of Paramount's race line. Paramount absorbed Black Swan's artist contracts and made monthly payments to the musicians. This arrangement lasted until 1926, with Black Swan then getting back its masters but going out of business. Jazzology started a Black Swan reissue series in the late '80s, featuring previously issued material from Paramount.

Blue Note

The company many consider the greatest modern jazz label began in 1939. Alfred Lion established Blue Note Records and subsequently teamed with childhood friend Francis Wolff to make it a prime player in traditional jazz, swing, hard bop, and soul jazz, making later forays into free music, jazz-rock, and fusion. Blue Note was among the earliest labels to move to the 12-inch format for 78 rpm discs, providing additional recording space. Sidney Bechet, Earl Hines, Albert Ammons, Meade "Lux" Lewis, James P. Johnson, Art Hodes, and Edmond Hall were some early Blue Note artists. Lion and Wolff made Blue Note famous for everything from sound, with engineering great Rudy Van Gelder, to album cover art, thanks to the designs of Paul Bacon, Gil Melle, and John Hermansader. Under the direction of A&R heads and musicians Ike Quebec and Duke Pearson, Blue Note expanded into bebop, hard bop, and soul jazz. Thelonious Monk, Jimmy Smith, Grant Green, Stanley Turrentine, Jackie McLean, Lou Donaldson, Hank Mobley, Lee Morgan, Miles Davis, Sonny Rollins, Art Blakey & The Jazz Messengers, Freddie Hubbard, and Horace Silver, who recorded for the label over 25 years, were among the stars of the second wave. Artists who made Blue Note dates in the '60s included Bobby Hutcherson, Andrew Hill, Herbie Hancock, Joe Henderson, Wayne Shorter, McCoy Tyner, and even Ornette Coleman.

Things changed in the '70s as jazz-rock, fusion, and instrumental pop were produced under the influence of George Butler with Larry Mizell, Wayne Henderson, and the Dave Grusin-Larry Rosen team. Donald Byrd's *Black Byrd* was a milestone. It was the company's best-selling record of all time but one that was markedly different from those it had become famous for making. Noel Pointer, Bobbi Humphrey, Byrd, Ronnie Foster, and Ronnie Laws were among the artists during this period. The team of Michael Cuscuna and Charlie Lourie began a reissue program in 1975, and their efforts would lead to the creation of the ultimate reissue company Mosaic in the '80s. Blue Note was sold to Liberty in 1967. EMI distributed Liberty at that time, and Blue Note reissue lines appeared throughout Europe and Japan. EMI then purchased Liberty in 1980 and passed Blue Note on to Manhattan in 1985. The label was reactivated that year with a gala series of events and later commemorative album reissues and concert recordings. The current Blue Note includes contemporary names like the newly signed Cassandra Wilson, Benny Green, Kevin Eubanks, Bobby McFerrin, Stanley Jordan, Don Pullen, and Michel Petrucciani. Mosaic continues to issue the best of the classic items, and Blue Note has also been reissuing many titles itself, from single sessions to anthologies, compilations, and boxed sets.

Bluebird

RCA Victor established the subsidiary label Bluebird in 1932 to issue 8-inch discs that were first sold in drugstores. The next year it began releasing 10-inch discs and continued until 1950. Bluebird was the company's "race" label in the '30s, with discs numbered differently from those on RCA Victor. Earl Hines, Fats Waller, Jelly Roll Morton, and Artie Shaw, as well as blues, folk, and gospel acts, recorded on Bluebird. It was also used to reissue some traditional jazz material and sessions not originally issued. RCA revived

Bluebird in the late '70s for reissues and has since periodically released several classics on Bluebird.

Cadence

Writer/historian Bob Rusch started Cadence Jazz Records in 1980. The record label is still in operation, with sessions by such artists as Bill Dixon, Chet Baker, and Beaver Harris. Cadence Distribution distributes recordings by hundreds of small jazz and blues independents.

Candid

This company has had a distinctive history. Originally owned and operated by Nat Hentoff in the early '60s, it issued recordings by Charles Mingus, Cecil Taylor, Abbey Lincoln, Lightnin' Hopkins, Otis Spann, Steve Lacy, and the Newport Rebels among others. The company was later purchased by Andy Williams, and there was a Candid reissue series in the '70s that was operated by his Barnaby label. Candid albums were also reissued in Japan and Europe. Mosaic has compiled deluxe boxed sets of classic Candid dates by Mingus, Taylor, Hopkins, and Spann. Candid currently operates as a contemporary jazz label under DA Music and has issued recordings by Gary Bartz, Larry Gales, Greg Abate, and many others.

Capitol

A team consisting of songwriting great Johnny Mercer, record store executive Glenn Wallichs, and Paramount Pictures representative Buddy de Sylva began Capitol in Los Angeles in 1942. Originally called Liberty, the label changed its name to Capitol in two months. Under the Artists and Repertory (A&R) direction of Dave Dexter, Capitol's jazz importance zoomed. Nat "King" Cole's trio, Stan Kenton, Benny Goodman, Marian McPartland, George Shearing, Jonah Jone, and Miles Davis were among the acts who recorded for Capitol in the '40s, '50s, and '60s. But in the '70s the company's prominence and jazz activity diminished. Capitol was purchased by EMI in 1979 and has been reissuing several classic sessions since the '80s. A 40th anniversary boxed set was issued in 1992.

Charlie Parker

Doris Parker, the widow of Charlie Parker, and Aubrey Mayhew founded Charlie Parker Records in 1961 in New York. They intended to issue previously unreleased Parker dates and did release two albums of new Parker as well as three albums initially released by Le Jazz Cool. They also reissued a Red Norvo record originally made for Comet and put into circulation for the first time air checks of sessions by Lester Young and Billie Holiday. The company cut new recordings by Cecil Payne, Duke Jordan, Sadik Hakim, Joe Carroll, Barry Miles, Mundell Lowe, Teddy Wilson, and Slide Hampton. Charlie Parker Records only lasted a couple of years; Audiofidelity Enterprises purchased the masters and began reissuing some dates in 1981 for a brief period.

Chiaroscuro

Hank O'Neal started Chiaroscuro in New York in 1970. The label emphasized mostly bebop and swing sessions, with Joe Venuti, Teddy Wilson, Mary Lou Williams, and Earl Hines among its roster. But in 1976 and 1977 it also issued compelling free and more adventurous material by Hamiet Bluiett, Abdullah Ibrahim, Perry Robinson, and others. O'Neal was the primary producer, coproducing the first album with John Hammond in 1969. He sold the label in 1978 to Audiophile, which issued original albums using the Chiaroscuro banner and also reissued material by Louis Armstrong, Elmo Hope, and others. O'Neal and Andrew Sordoni formed SOS Productions in Pennsylvania in 1987 and reacquired the Chiaroscuro catalog. They are currently issuing new and reissued material.

Circle

Rudi Blesh and Harriet Janis began Circle in 1946. They recorded more than 500 masters over a six-year span in several cities, featuring such artists as Baby Dodds, Chippie Hill, George Lewis, and Albert Nicholas, and also issued recordings from Blesh's radio series "This Is Jazz" in 1947. Circle was the first label to issue Jelly Roll Morton's Library of Congress sessions on 12 albums of 78 rpm discs. The label blended old and new material in 1951 and 1952. Riverside had the Circle catalog for a while, then it was sold to George H. Buck's Jazzology label in the mid '60s. Some reissues were released on the GHB label.

Columbia

A legendary label and recording company, Columbia counted among its innovations the first LPs in the late '40s, subsidiaries in various European companies to issue Columbia material available in America, and reissues in the '60s. Columbia actually recorded the Original Dixieland Jazz Band before Victor in 1917 but did not issue the sessions until after Victor. It also recorded W.C. Handy's Orchestra of Memphis, Wilbur Sweatman's Original Jazz Band, the Louisiana Five, and other dance bands before starting a "race" series in the early '20s. The first recordings of Bessie Smith, Clara Smith, and Johnny Dunn's Original Jazz Hounds were not among "race" entries, but were part of Columbia's general catalog. The company went into receivership in 1922, then started its "race" line in 1923. Four Bessie Smith titles and one by King Oliver appeared among the initial eight issued. The line started again later in the year with material from Bessie and Clara Smith and Ethel Waters. This time Columbia maintained it with a series of recordings by Clarence Williams and New Orleans dates from Oscar Celestin and Sam Morgan. There were also sessions by Paul Whiteman, Jack Teagarden, and Red Norvo in the general line, along with Atlanta recordings by white territory bands. The company was owned for a time by British interests in the mid '20s and acquired Okeh in 1926.

By the early '30s, through various worldwide financial machinations, Victor ended up owning the American branch of Columbia. Fearing antitrust action, the owners shuffled Columbia around, and, when the maneuvering ended, the American Record Company and Brunswick (ARC-BRC) were its owners in 1933. For a time during the mid '30s, no American branch of Columbia existed—it was operated overseas. The Columbia Broadcasting System purchased ARC-BRC in 1938 and revived Columbia in 1939. Operations at Brunswick ceased in 1940. George Avakian and John Hammond became production heads, and Columbia emerged as one of the nation's finest jazz labels. Benny Goodman, Count Basie, Woody Herman, and Duke Ellington were among acts creating classics during the '40s, while the company reinstituted a "race" line in 1945 that continued into the '50s. CBS severed its affiliation with the non-American branches of Columbia in the mid '50s due to these companies' reluctance to enter the album market. Columbia inked an agreement with the Dutch company Phillips and its subsidiaries to sell its records in Europe and overseas.

Meanwhile, the company continued to grow in scope with Dave Brubeck, Louis Armstrong, Miles Davis, Ellington, Charles Mingus, and others joining in. Unfortunately, as it grew so did its reputation for artistic mismanagement. The experiences of Thelonious Monk, Mingus, Ornette Coleman, and many others were not positive; Mingus's late '50s sessions were not properly released, while much of Monk's best music in the '60s was not issued until he had left the company. There were more misadventures in the '70s and '80s: mass firings of such acts as the Heath Brothers and Coleman, incredible hype centered around Arthur Blythe that hindered every Columbia release he made in the '80s, and controversial reissues of seminal dates like *Miles Ahead* by their premier modern artist, Miles Davis. Dr. George Butler's coming in the '80s and the signing of Wynton Marsalis helped trigger the "young lions" and "neobeop/neoconservative" controversies of the '80s and '90s. Columbia has tried to reclaim some luster with extensive reissue programs, and its Jazz Masterpieces line has helped ease some image problems, as has its 1993 "Pioneers of Jazz" line. But the company's legacy was hurt by the '60s, '70s, and '80s fiascos (another was the sabotaging of the Portrait label), and it has not been completely forgiven by knowledgeable jazz fans.

Commodore

Milt Gabler began Commodore in 1938 from his New York Commodore Music Shop. Commodore was the label that issued some of Jelly Roll Morton's final dates and was also one of the pioneers in 12-inch 78 rpm discs. It released plenty of swing material by such acts as Coleman Hawkins and Hot Lips Page and was the label that issued Billie Holiday's "Strange Fruit" composition. Commodore has been reissued many times by Mainstream, Columbia, and PPI in America and by London and Telefunken in Germany. Mosaic reissued the entire Commodore catalog in three huge boxed sets during the early '90s.

Concord

Carl Jefferson established Concord in 1973 in Concord, California. The label was initially and is still primarily an outlet for swing and veteran bebop players, though it has also issued recordings by Marvin "Smitty" Smith and Jesse Davis. It was the label that helped make media sensations out of young swing-influenced types like Scott Hamilton and Warren Vaché in the '70s, but it has grown into a multifaceted operation with separate divisions for Latin (Concord Picante), fusion/jazz-rock (Concord Crossover) and classical (Concord Concerto). The company is also famous for a solo piano series recorded at the Maybeck Recital Hall; the 30th volume in this line appeared in 1993.

Debut

A company established jointly by musicians Charles Mingus and Max Roach, Debut was intended to give jazz greats an alternative to the major labels. Debut began in 1952 and continued until 1955. Many of the early sessions by Mingus's Jazz Workshop were issued by Debut, as well as the first releases by Teo Macero, Kenny Dorham, Paul Bley, John LaPorta, and Sam Most. In 1992 Fantasy issued a 16-disc set, *The Complete Debut Sessions*, that featured virtually the entire output of the label.

Decca

Decca was begun in England in 1929 by Edward Lewis, and he soon acquired British rights to recordings by the American Record Company (ARC) and issued them on the subsidiary Brunswick label. Jack Kapp helped establish an American branch in 1934, and soon it began issuing "race" records. J. Mayo Williams served as a talent scout, and the company purchased part of Gennett's catalog plus the Champion label in 1935. Decca bought the early catalogs of Brunswick and Vocalion from CBS in 1938 and was soon reissuing classic titles plus new dates from Louis Armstrong, Woody Herman, Andy Kirk, Billie Holiday, Johnny Dodds, Count Basie, Louis Jordan, and Lionel Hampton through the '40s and '50s. The American branch of Decca split from its British counterpart in the '40s. It was affiliated with Coral and Brunswick in the '40s and '50s but was acquired in 1959 by the Music Corporation of America (MCA). MCA has since reissued many Decca titles.

Delmark

Bob Koester established Delmark in 1953 in St. Louis. He originally named it Delmar after the street where the company was located and began issuing 10-inch LPs of traditional jazz by local musicians. When Delmar moved to Chicago in 1959 the name was changed to Delmark. The company's roster included urban and traditional blues musicians ranging from Junior Wells and Magic Sam to Big Joe Williams and Sleepy John Estes; free jazz types like the Art Ensemble of Chicago, Anthony Braxton, and Muhal Richard Abrams; and traditional jazz musicians George Lewis and Earl Hines. Delmark also released the earliest material by Ira Sullivan, had soul jazz from Jimmy Forrest and Sonny Stitt, and even issued some Sun Ra dates. It acquired the masters from the United, States, Pearl, and Apollo labels in the '70s, '80s, and '90s and has reissued several titles. The company has also released new jazz dates by Jodie Christian, Malachi Thompson, Brad Goode, and others.

Dial

Ross Russell founded Dial Records in Hollywood in 1946. Russell owned the Tempo Music Shop and received financial support from Marvin Freeman. When Dial recorded Charlie Parker, its status within the jazz world zoomed. Parker did seven sessions for Dial in the late '40s, and the company also recorded dates by Dizzy Gillespie, Howard McGhee, Dodo Marmarosa, Dexter Gordon, James Moody, Erroll Garner, and Don Lanphere. It acquired a Red Norvo session with Gillespie and Parker from Comet, recordings by Art Tatum, and sessions from Woody Herman's sidemen. The company shifted locales to New York in 1947 and released more dates by Parker and McGhee. Dial scored with tenor sax "battle" sessions matching Dexter Gordon/Wardell Gray on *The Chase* and Gordon/Teddy Edwards on *The Duel*. It also had recordings by Earl Hines, Sidney Bechet, Roy Eldridge, and Willie "The Lion" Smith in its "historical jazz" catalog and issued dates that were fragments, such as Parker's "The Famous Alto Break" in 1946. Dial innovations included being among the earliest companies to issue 33⅓ rpm recordings and pioneering in the 12-inch album format. Dial recorded most of its releases on pure vinyl and cut jazz sessions on 16-inch lacquer discs, producing masters from these and keeping a second set for protection in the pretape era. Russell ended jazz production in 1949 and sold some Dial masters to Concert Hall in 1955. Other items were sporadically reissued by various labels until the late '60s when Russell helped English owner Tony Williams initiate a coherent Dial reissue series on vinyl for his Spotlite label in the late '60s. Warner Bros. briefly released an unimpressive Parker Dial "best of" reissue in the late '80s. Stash reissued the full Parker Dial sessions on CD in 1993.

EmArcy

Longtime jazz producer and Artists and Repertory (A&R) head Bob Shad launched the EmArcy division of Mercury in 1954 as the company's prime jazz wing. Shad produced dates by the Clifford Brown/Max Roach quintet, Dinah Washington, Cannonball Adderley, Rahsaan Roland Kirk, and Sarah Vaughan, among others. Jack Tracy replaced Shad as EmArcy's head in 1958 but was unable to keep it active as Mercury began funneling jazz talent to the main label. EmArcy folded altogether in the early '60s, though there was a reissue series in the '80s.

FMP

Free Music Production (FMP) Records emerged from the brief New Artists Guild organization, a group of European musicians that included Manfred Schoof, Alex Von Schlippenbach, Peter Brotzmann, and Peter Kowald. In Berlin in 1968 the guild sponsored an alternative festival to the Berliner Jazztage that featured free performers. The next year the organization took the name FMP and began recording free sessions, notably by the Globe Unity Orchestra. It has continued issuing them into the '90s with two types of sessions. Those produced by individual musicians remain their property. Others that are produced in collaboration with other participating labels, such as Bvhaast or Claxion, remain the properties of those companies with the musicians being paid only once for the recording, as on a session.

Fantasy

Max and Sol Weiss established Fantasy in 1949. Some of its earliest artists were Dave Brubeck, Gerry Mulligan, Cal Tjader, Vince Guaraldi, and Earl Hines. Later came Duke Ellington, Cannonball Adderley, Kenny Burrell, Bill Evans, and Flora Purim. The label also issued comedy recordings by Lenny Bruce in the late '50s and reaped dividends in the pop/rock market of the '60s and '70s with Creedence Clearwater Revival. But Fantasy's greatest role was as a pioneer in the reissue field. Saul Zaentz joined the company in 1955. He was a co-owner of Debut with his wife, Charles Mingus, and Max Roach. Fantasy soon acquired the Debut catalog, and Zaentz eventually became head of Fantasy in 1967 after he formed an investment team that purchased it and the Galaxy subsidiary label it had started in 1964.

Fantasy purchased Prestige and Riverside in 1971 and 1972 and bought Milestone in 1973. The company has since acquired Contemporary, Good Time Jazz, and Stax. Orrin Keepnews, who was formerly the sole owner of Milestone and a joint owner of Riverside, became head of jazz productions for Fantasy in 1972. He began a series of double and occasionally triple reissue albums spotlighting classic titles and artists. The success of this venture led to the establishment of the Original Jazz Classics series in 1983. This series presented reissues of vintage titles but reproduced the original cover art and liner notes. It supplanted the "twofer" line and sparked a reissue boom that has yet to subside through the '90s. It also spawned the subsidiary lines, Original Blues Classics and Limited Edition. Fantasy has not only reissued Stax items but has also reactivated the Volt division and released new albums by the Dramatics and Dorothy Moore. It has also issued deluxe boxed sets featuring complete Prestige, Milestone, or Riverside recordings by John Coltrane, Miles Davis, Thelonious Monk, Bill Evans, and Wes Montgomery.

Flying Dutchman

One of Bob Thiele's many labels, Flying Dutchman began operation in 1969 and continued until 1975. Thiele had a roster ranging from Gato Barbieri, Leon Thomas, and Oliver Nelson to Bobby Hackett, Groove Holmes, Shelly Manne, and the World's Greatest Jazz Band. Flying Dutchman issued some of Louis Armstrong's final recordings and helped launch the career of poet/musician Gil Scott-Heron. Atco acquired the label in 1971, then RCA distributed and issued material from Flying Dutchman sessions until 1984.

GNP Crescendo

GNP Crescendo was founded by West Coast producer and promoter Gene Norman in 1947. He had organized a series of concerts called Just Jazz, and that was the company's original focus. It expanded into regular studio sessions in the '50s, featuring dates by Dizzy Gillespie, Charlie Ventura, Lionel

Hampton, Gerry Mulligan, Teddy Buckner, and Frank Morgan. The label was the earliest to record the Clifford Brown/Max Roach quintet. GNP Crescendo also issued recordings by Cajun and Afro-Latin artists such as Bobby Enriquez and Queen Ida in the '60s and '70s. GNP Crescendo releases are currently available via reissue.

GRP

Pianist, film score composer, and bandleader Dave Grusin teamed with producer Larry Rosen to form the GRP record label in the early '70s. The label quickly established its reputation as the company of choice for jazz-rock, instrumental pop, and fusion. Arista began issuing GRP sessions in the late '70s but then severed the arrangement in the '80s. MCA now owns GRP and has continued its jazz-rock and fusion practice but also used GRP to oversee and maintain its Impulse reissue line. GRP's most popular acts include Chick Corea's Elektric Band, Eric Marienthal, David Benoit, and Grusin.

Hat Hut/Hat Art

Werner Uehlinger established the Hat Hut label in 1974 in Therwil, Switzerland. Hat Hut featured free jazz by such musicians as Cecil Taylor, Anthony Braxton, the Vienna Art Orchestra, and, most notably, Steve Lacy and Joe McPhee. Uehlinger expanded the operation during the '80s, adding Hat Art and Hat Musics. Max Roach also made a pair of two-record duo recordings with Braxton and Archie Shepp. The older dates, as well as new sessions, are now being issued on CD.

Horizon

Horizon was among the finest '70s labels. It was a subsidiary of A&M and established by producer John Snyder in 1975. Snyder's roster had a good mixture of styles and artists, with Ornette Coleman and Charlie Haden representing more outside material; Dave Brubeck, Paul Desmond, and the Thad Jones/Mel Lewis orchestra holding down the mainstream; and Andrew Hill and Hampton Hawes somewhere between the poles. Snyder divided settings between studio and live dates, and each release included comprehensive information about musical compositions, solo transcriptions, and other discographical material. Recordings were also issued in gatefold packages with elaborate designs and photographs and extensive liner notes. Horizon albums were famous for high-quality sound and were pressed on virgin vinyl. Unfortunately, the label lasted only two years, after which Snyder left A&M.

Improvising Artists

Pianist Paul Bley along with artist Carol Goss founded Improvising Artists Incorporated in 1974. The company issued recordings by such artists as Dave Holland and Sam Rivers, Sun Ra playing solo piano, Lee Konitz, and Bley. Emphasizing mainly acoustic free dates, it continued through the '70s and into the early '80s before folding. But it resurfaced in 1993 as a CD-reissue label.

Impulse

Creed Taylor helped create Impulse as a subsidiary outlet of ABC-Paramount in 1960. An album by the duo of Kai Winding and J.J. Johnson officially launched the label in 1961, and Taylor signed John Coltrane and produced the *Africa/Brass* album before departing. Bob Thiele became major producer and Impulse became the voice of the new jazz sound, recording releases by Archie Shepp, Cecil Taylor, Marion Brown, and Coltrane. But the label did not restrict itself to free material; it issued albums by Coleman Hawkins, Gil Evans, Duke Ellington, Oliver Nelson, Gary McFarland, Paul Gonsalves, Curtis Fuller, Terry Gibbs, and many others. The label was active into the '70s, with several posthumous Coltrane recordings

coming in its last years. Impulse material was reissued haphazardly for several years by both domestic and foreign companies; MCA's recent decision to put the Impulse reissue campaign in the hands of its GRP subsidiary has resulted in the albums finally being reissued the right way.

Incus

Musicians Derek Bailey, Evan Parker, and Tony Oxley started Incus in London in 1970. They have primarily issued dates by English free jazz players, particularly Bailey and Parker, but also have issued dates by Alan Skidmore, John Surman, and others, plus sessions with American and international guest stars.

Jazzology

George H. Buck owned and operated Jazzology, which was initially conceived in 1949 solely to issue sessions by Tony Parenti. Nothing further came of Jazzology for several years. In 1954 Buck started GHB, a label for traditional New Orleans music. Jazzology was later activated, at first as a label for vintage Chicago-style jazz, but it began purchasing and reissuing dates from other labels in the '60s. Jazzology bought the catalogs of Icon, Mono, Southland, Jazz Crusade, and Circle. It soon revived Circle to reissue swing and big band dates from the World label and items from the Lang-Worth catalog. Jazzology took over Paramount in 1970 but was inactive from 1973 to 1975 as it moved from South Carolina to Atlanta. A debacle occurred when RCA, in the midst of shutting down its pressing plant, destroyed Jazzology's masters. While recovering from that disaster, Jazzology purchased Audiophile's catalog but then used the label to issue more popular music rather than jazz. The company also acquired the Jazz Record and Lang-Worth catalogs in the early '80s and took over Bob Wilber's Bodeswell company and Monmouth-Evergreen in the mid '80s. It purchased Progressive from Gus Statiras in 1984. GHB currently reissues numerous materials.

Keynote

When Eric Bernay, a record store owner, founded Keynote in 1940, it was a folk music label. Paul Robeson and the Almanac Singers were some of the early artists. But when Harry Lim began recording artists in 1943, the focus shifted to jazz. Lester Young, Count Basie, Coleman Hawkins, Nat "King" Cole, and many others were recorded on Keynote. The company suffered through problems getting quality pressings after Capitol became too busy to continue with them. Mercury took over the label in 1948 but soon closed it down. A spectacular 21-album boxed set was issued in 1986 featuring over 330 tracks, among them 115 previously unissued cuts plus booklets with notes by Bob Porter, Dan Morgenstern, and Lim, plus rare photographs. Special sets have since been culled from this massive reissue.

Leo

Leo Feigin began Leo in London in 1980. Feigin had emigrated to England from Russia in 1973. His catalog has become one of Europe's finest for free jazz, featuring both American and international musicians like Anthony Braxton, Sun Ra, and Marilyn Crispell, and also 20 albums of the Russian trio the Ganelin Ensemble.

Limelight

Limelight replaced EmArcy as the jazz subsidiary of Mercury in 1962 with Jack Tracy as its main producer and head. The company featured Dizzy Gillespie, Art Blakey, Earl Hines, Milt Jackson, Rahsaan Roland Kirk, Gerry Mulligan, and Oscar Peterson among its artists. Limelight albums also contained expensively produced, elaborate folds and cuts plus odd liners. The label only made new recordings from 1962 to

1966, though there were albums issued until 1970. Polydor and Trip reissued Limelight dates in the '70s, and an '80s line appeared in Japan under the original company name.

Mercury

A premier label for both jazz and popular music, Mercury began operation in 1945 with Irv Green as president. Erroll Garner and both Albert and Gene Ammons were among early company signees. Mercury distributed recordings by Norman Granz's Clef label in the '40s and early '50s and acquired the Keynote label in 1948. Bob Shad began the EmArcy division, which was devoted to jazz, in 1954, but there was no rigid separation between the labels. Only Sarah Vaughan was contractually bound to do pop for Mercury and jazz for EmArcy. Quincy Jones came on board as a staff arranger, composer, bandleader, and producer in 1956 and remained 10 years. He became head of Artists and Repertory (A&R) in 1961. Ernestine Anderson, Al Cohn, Buddy Rich, and Cannonball Adderley and Dinah Washington from EmArcy were among jazz acts on Mercury. EmArcy folded in the early '60s, replaced by Limelight, but that did not last long either. Mercury was acquired by Polydor in the '70s, with Trip reissuing much of its catalog. *Mercury 40th Anniversary V.S.O.P.* was issued in 1985.

Metronome

Sweden's major source for jazz in the '50s, Metronome was started by Lars Burman, Borje Ekberg, and Anders Burman. It issued both 78 rpm releases and EPs, drawing some material from Prestige and Atlantic but also recording several of Sweden's top stars. Arne Domnerus, Bengt Hallberg, Lars Gullin, Rolf Ericson, Jan Johansson, and Eje Thelin recorded for Metronome as well as Zoot Sims, Toots Thielemans, Alice Babs, Svend Asmussen, and Stephane Grappelli. It continued until the mid '60s.

Mosaic

The greatest American reissue company in recent history evolved from the efforts of veteran producers Charlie Lourie and Michael Cuscuna to maintain Blue Note's heritage and tradition. Cuscuna and Lourie had jointly spearheaded a Blue Note reissue series from the mid '70s until 1981, issuing two-album sets by artists from the Jazz Crusaders to Art Pepper, Herbie Nichols, and Thelonious Monk. They designed an operation that differed in many ways from the conventional record company, making albums available only by mail order and only producing a certain number and only one edition. Each boxed set contained an expertly annotated, comprehensively prepared booklet with exacting discographical and personnel information. Mosaic spotlighted many deserving artists deemed of little or no importance by their original labels, though it also presented major names like Charles Mingus, Thelonious Monk, Count Basie, Art Blakey, Chet Baker, Gerry Mulligan, Nat "King" Cole, and T-Bone Walker. The company issued magnificent sets by Tina Brooks, Larry Young, Buddy DeFranco, Ike Quebec and John Hardee, Freddie Redd, and Shorty Rogers. It released the complete output of the Commodore label in three volumes and the full Nat "King" Cole trio sessions.

Though it began in Santa Monica, California, Mosaic has been located for several years at 35 Melrose Place, Stamford, Connecticut. Unfortunately, some of the earlier sets are now out of print and others are soon slated to disappear. In addition, major labels that once sat by and gladly made material available to Mosaic with a "good riddance" attitude are now being much tougher about what they will issue and how long they will allow it to be licensed. But Mosaic continues fighting the good fight; its most recent series in 1993 included superb sets from Jackie McLean, Benny Goodman, and Count Basie.

Norgran

Norman Granz established Norgran in Los Angeles in the early '50s and used it to both reissue and issue new material. He rereleased some Clef dates on Norgran and also new sessions by swing and bebop players, among them Johnny Hodges, Louis Bellson, Benny Carter, and Ben Webster. Granz absorbed both Norgran and Clef into Verve in 1956.

Okeh

The General Photograph Corporation founded Okeh in 1916 to manage the American holdings of Carl Lindstrom's German company. It began releasing recordings two years later. The New Orleans Jazz Band was the first group to begin recording for Okeh, but it was Mamie Smith's "Crazy Blues" that made the label a power in the newly evolving "race" recordings market. Okeh established a line originally called "The Colored Catalog," then the "race" series. Clarence Williams handled the Artists and Repertory (A&R) duties in New York and Richard M. Jones in Chicago. Williams and His Blue Five, King Oliver, Louis Armstrong's Hot Five and Hot Seven, Bennie Moten, Bix Beiderbecke, Eddie Lang, and Lonnie Johnson were among the groups and musicians who recorded for Okeh. Columbia began operating Okeh in 1926. By the mid '30s, ARC-BRC had acquired Okeh and dropped the "race" series and the name. Columbia purchased the company and revived it in 1938, using the vintage 8,000 "race" series designation and Okeh labels for Vocalion material. When Danny Kessler became head of A&R in 1950, Okeh's direction became predominantly R&B, though it maintained a jazz catalog as well. A two-record reissue, *Okeh Jazz*, was released in the '80s.

Prestige

Bob Weinstock founded Prestige Records in 1949. The original offices were at 446 West 50th Street in New York, and the company used several New York studios for sessions, though most recordings were done during the '50s at Rudy Van Gelder's studios in Hackensack, New Jersey. The label moved to Bergenfield, New Jersey, in 1967. It was sold in 1971 to Fantasy, a San Francisco Bay Area company. Everything moved to Berkeley, California. Prestige continued recording new dates until the late '70s, then began reissuing classic items in two-album sets. In the label's heyday, the roster included Lennie Tristano, Lee Konitz, Stan Getz, Thelonious Monk, Miles Davis, John Coltrane, Art Farmer, Red Garland, Jackie McLean, Sonny Rollins, Booker Ervin, and many others. Prestige issued cool, hard bop, and soul jazz dates and also maintained subsidiary operations Bluesville, Swingville, and Moodsville in the '60s. All the masters on Prestige and its subsidiary labels are now property of Fantasy.

Progressive

Gus Statiras started Progressive in New York in 1950. It has had a spotty history, issuing dates by Al Cohn and George Wallington in the '50s, then closing up shop in 1955. Several Progressive masters were sold to Savoy, which reissued many dates in the '60s. Prestige issued a Cohn session from 1954 in 1970, then a George Wallington date was reissued in the late '70s through the Japanese company Baybridge with some bonus unissued cuts from the original mid '50s date. J.R. Monterose, Al Haig, and Tommy Flanagan were among artists who cut new sessions for the temporarily revived Progressive. Statiras did the productions, wrote the liners, and took the photographs, using the original '50s cover art and logs for the new dates. There are currently Progressive sessions being reissued through the Collector's Record Club (CRC) of the GHB Music Foundation.

RCA Victor

Eldridge R. Johnson founded the Victor Talking Machine Corporation in Camden, New Jersey, in 1901. It was initially linked with Emile Berliner's Gramophone Company and shared the rights to use the dog-and-gramophone logo that became the trademark of His Master's Voice. The company issued recordings of James Reese Europe's Society Orchestra in 1913 and 1914 and released the first jazz record, which was recorded by the Original Dixieland Jazz Band. But Victor abandoned both jazz and the emerging "race" market during the Artists and Repertory (A&R) reign of Edward T. King. Victor tried a "race" series in the '20s, but it lapsed after a few releases by such performers as Lizzie Miles and Rosa Henderson. It did issue sessions by Paul Whiteman and A.J. Piron's New Orleans orchestra. When Nat Shikret took over, the company began emphasizing jazz and became a force in the late '20s and the '30s. Jelly Roll Morton, Bennie Moten, Duke Ellington, and King Oliver and the Missourians were pivotal in establishing Victor's jazz line. It also did extensive recordings of the Memphis Jug Band and restarted a "race" series in 1929. Victor soon split the series into vocal and instrumental divisions.

The Radio Corporation of America (RCA) bought Victor in 1932 and while it initially trimmed recording activity, the company was soon back at full strength in both the jazz and "race" markets. Fats Waller, Lionel Hampton, and Benny Goodman were among big sellers in the '30s and '40s. It also established subsidiary labels for cheap releases, like the short-lived Elektradisk and Sunrise and far more substantial Bluebird. During the '40s, Sidney Bechet and Ellington were among the prime sellers. Victor began using vinyl rather than shellac in the mid '40s and issued the first 45 rpm single in 1949. The company name was officially changed that year to RCA Victor. The label has consistently maintained its jazz interest since then, and has reissued through its French RCA wing material on the Black & White and Treasury of Jazz labels. The main company briefly ran a reissue label, X, in the early '50s for traditional jazz. During the mid '70s it distributed and manufactured Flying Dutchman releases and in the late '80s revived the Novus label. RCA Victor has issued new titles by James Moody, Antonio Hart, Chris Hollyday, and others on Novus in the '80s and '90s.

Riverside

Orrin Keepnews and Bill Grauer, Jr., established Riverside in 1953 in New York. They began issuing classic sessions from the Paramount catalog as well as recordings from Champion, Gennett, the Hot Record Society, QRS, Circle, and others. Randy Weston was the company's first contemporary artist; a pair of 10-inch albums featuring Weston was released in 1954. Keepnews was the main producer, and the Riverside roster included Thelonious Monk, Bill Evans, Cannonball Adderley, Johnny Griffin, Wes Montgomery, and Barry Harris among its main stars. Riverside began the subsidiary labels Judson and Jazzland in the late '50s and early '60s. It started a Living Legends series of traditional artists in the early '60s, recording Lil Hardin Armstrong, Albert Wynn, and others in either New Orleans or Chicago. Grauer died in 1963 and Riverside went bankrupt in 1964. Keepnews eventually resurfaced at Fantasy, and the current Riverside holdings are now part of the Fantasy empire. Many Riverside sessions, including most of the Living Legends series as well as various Judson and Jazzland dates, have been reissued on CD as part of Fantasy's Original Jazz Classics line.

Roulette

Morris Levy was the head of a group of directors that founded Roulette Records in New York in 1957. The most significant jazz releases were issued on the Birdland series. These included sessions from Count Basie, Joe Williams, Maynard Ferguson, Harry Edison, Jack Teagarden, Randy Weston, and Sarah Vaughan in the late '50s and early and mid '60s. Many were produced by Teddy Reig, who signed several of the premier artists at Roulette in its prime period. The company continued recording into the '70s with Betty Carter, Art Blakey, and Lee Konitz performing on some of its final new dates. Currently, CEMA is reissuing Roulette material via Blue Note, while Mosaic issued the complete studio and live Roulette recordings of Count Basie in two massive boxed-set packages in 1993.

Sackville

John Norris and Bill Smith, the editor and publisher of *Coda* magazine, Canada's finest jazz publication, started Sackville in Toronto in 1968. The company has issued both sessions by Canadian musicians and dates recorded there by American players. Ralph Sutton, Sir Charles Thompson, Sammy Price, Jay McShann, and Willie "The Lion" Smith are among pianists who have done Sackville dates, and it has also issued sessions by Frank Rosolino, Buddy Tate, Doc Cheatham, Archie Shepp, and Bill Holman's big band. Sackville's recordings can also be ordered through *Coda*, as well as found in stores.

Saturn

Herman "Sonny" Blount, aka Sun Ra, operated the Saturn label as a conduit for his recordings in the '50s, '60s, and early '70s. It was one of many labels Sun Ra recorded on; other labels include Transition, Delmark, Steeplechase, ESP, Inner City, Improvising Artists Incorporated, Savoy, ABC/Impulse, BASF/MPS, Actuel/BYG, and Black Saint/Soul Note. Evidence acquired the Saturn masters in 1992 and reissued 15 CDs through 1993. Most were two-in-one discs covering studio and live material recorded in both Chicago and New York.

Savoy

Herman Lubinsky founded the Savoy label in Newark, New Jersey, in 1942. Its first releases were 1939 sessions recorded by the Savoy Dictators. Artists and Repertory (A&R) head Teddy Reig arranged, recorded, and/or produced releases by Charlie Parker, Dexter Gordon, Miles Davis, Fats Navarro, J.J. Johnson, and others in the mid and late '40s and early '50s, making the company one of the strongest in bebop. It also issued swing and early R&B. Ralph Bass would become a legendary R&B producer and A&R head, but he was also the person who signed Erroll Garner to Savoy. Savoy purchased Regent from Fred Mendelsohn in 1948, getting subsidiary labels National, Bop, and Discovery in the process. The company leased material from Century and Crown and reissued recordings from Jewell. While Lee Magid turned Savoy's focus more toward R&B during his A&R tenure, Ozzie Cadena put renewed focus on jazz in the mid and late '50s. He signed Kenny Clarke, Cannonball Adderley, Yusef Lateef, and Hank Jones, and Savoy established the subsidiary label Worldwide in 1958. It also did some free dates by Sun Ra, Bill Dixon, and Archie Shepp in the '60s. After Lubinsky's death in 1974, Arista purchased the Savoy catalog in 1975. Muse bought it 10 years later; both companies maintained reissue lines while they owned the masters. The current holder, Denon, started a reissue campaign in 1993.

Signal

The team of Don Schlitten, Jules Colomby, and Harold Goldberg established Signal Records in New York in 1955. The company issued dates by Duke Jordan, Cecil Payne, Red Rodney, and Gigi Gryce, plus an all-star sextet that recorded a Charlie Parker tribute at the Five Spot. Signal also started a Jazz Laboratory series with particular albums featuring music by quartets with a saxophonist and rhythm section on one side and rhythm section sans sax on the other. Savoy purchased part of the Signal catalog in the mid '50s and issued several titles. Shortly after that operations ceased.

Signature

The Signature label was the very first company started by longtime producer and label executive Bob Thiele, in 1939. Erroll Garner made his recording debut on Signature, and the company also had Coleman Hawkins, Lester Young, Julian Dash, Flip Phillips, Anita O'Day, and Eddie "Lockjaw" Davis on its roster. Thiele operated Signature until 1948. He later reissued vintage Signature sessions on his Dr. Jazz label in the '80s and temporarily revived Signature as well.

Strata-East

Trumpeter Charles Tolliver and pianist Stanley Cowell founded the Strata-East record label in 1971. Amid much publicity about being owned and operated by African Americans, Strata-East was designed to be a cooperative venture, with musicians getting larger shares of royalties and maintaining part ownership of publishing and copyrights. Some Strata-East artists included Cecil Payne, Charles Brackeen, the Piano Choir, Pharoah Sanders, Keno Duke, Mtume, and the co-owners themselves. The label continued until near the end of the decade, then ran into financial problems and ceased production. A reissue campaign has recently begun.

Timeless

Wim Wigt founded Timeless in the Netherlands in 1975 as a label devoted mainly to hard bop. The company has also recorded Lionel Hampton and Machito but has been an outlet for such players as Cedar Walton, Curtis Fuller, Buster Williams, Harold Land, and Bobby Hutcherson. It issued many remarkable sessions by the George Adams/Don Pullen combo in the late '70s and early '80s and also some of the final recordings by Art Blakey and the Jazz Messengers. Timeless has also regularly recorded and released sessions by a group known as the Timeless All-Stars that includes Walton, Land, Fuller, Hutcherson, Williams, and Billy Higgins. It has a subsidiary line devoted to traditional jazz by such acts as Chris Barber and Peanuts Hucko.

United Artists

United Artists Records was established as a subsidiary of the United Artists film company in 1958. The label was one of the finest of its time with such individuals as George Wein, Jack Lewis, Tom Wilson, and Alan Douglas serving as producers. Duke Ellington, Charles Mingus, Max Roach, Art Blakey, Count Basie, Ruby Braff, Gerry Mulligan, Betty Carter, the Modern Jazz Quartet, Booker Little, Oliver Nelson, Teddy Charles, Zoot Sims, and Bud Freeman were among those who recorded for United Artists. A subsidiary company, Solid State, was formed in 1966 and was the label that issued many fine Thad Jones-Mel Lewis dates. EMI took over United Artists in the '80s and has subsequently reissued much of its catalog.

United/States

United and States were co-owned by African-American postman Leonard Allen and Lew Simpkins in Chicago during the early '50s. These two labels issued a wide range of sessions, many of them R&B and blues, but they also featured jazz dates by Tab Smith, Paul Bascomb, and Jimmy Forrest. Forrest's initial recording of "Night Train" was the company's biggest hit in 1951. Simpkins died in 1953, but Allen maintained the labels until 1957. Delmark acquired the

masters in 1975 and initiated a combination reissue and new release program of classic material.

Vee Jay

Vivian and James Bracken, along with Calvin Carter, started Vee Jay Records in Chicago as a gospel operation in 1952. Maceo Smith and the Staples Singers were their first artists. They were best known for extraordinary R&B, blues, and gospel, but Vee Jay also had an active jazz division. Lee Morgan, Wynton Kelly, Eddie Harris, Wayne Shorter, Frank Strozier, Bill Henderson, Ira Sullivan, Louis Hayes, and many others recorded for Vee Jay from the late '50s to the mid '60s. Big Sid McCoy, who later became famous as a disc jockey and then as the voice introducing Don Cornelius on "Soul Train," produced many of the sessions. Vee Jay was among the premier labels owned and operated by African Americans in the '50s and '60s until it ran into money problems. The company also produced hits by the Four Seasons and, indeed, was the first American company to issue material by the Beatles. That coup probably hastened Vee Jay's demise, as it was unable to come up with the pressings required to meet the demand the recordings generated, due to slow pay from distributors.

Verve

Norman Granz established Verve in 1956 after having purchased the rights to all the recordings he had previously issued on prior labels Norgran and Clef. Granz folded these into Verve and also issued new recordings of swing and bebop, though what the label issued was solely dependent on Granz's taste. Ella Fitzgerald, Louis Armstrong, Duke Ellington, Count Basie, Sarah Vaughan, and many other major names appeared on Verve. Granz sold the company to MGM in 1960, but it continued issuing new material through 1967 while also having sessions issued in England by Columbia and HMV and in France by Barclay and Blue Star. Polydor purchased Verve from MGM in 1967 and it ceased operation. Polydor reissued many dates through the '70s and into the '80s, then reactivated Verve, both in its domestic and foreign operations, for new dates in the '80s and '90s as well as continuing reissues.

Vocalion

Vocalion was part of the Aeolian Company, a piano manufacturing firm in New York. It began releasing records in 1916 and released a series by the Original Dixieland Jazz Band in 1917. These were vertically cut releases; the company switched to lateral-cut discs in 1920 and dropped the Aeolian part of the name in 1924. (In early recordings sounds were directed into a large horn, which was connected to a cutting stylus at its tapered end. This stylus cut a spiral groove in the thick wax coating of a cylinder or disc in response to the vibrations af air in the horn. The stylus was rotated by a crank. If the stylus moved up and down in the cutting process it was termed "vertical-cut"; if the stylus moved side to side, it was termed "lateral-cut.") Vocalion was sold that same year to Brunswick, and the Brunswick-Balke-Callendar firm that owned both labels operated them separately but intermingled personnel and material. Vocalion started a formal "race" series in 1926 with Jack Kapp serving as producer and issued sessions by King Oliver, Jimmy Noone, and Duke Ellington. Warner Bros. took over Vocalion in 1930, then sold it to Consolidated Film Industries in 1931. It temporarily stopped marketing "race" records but resumed in 1933. Billie Holiday and Duke Ellington's combos recorded on Vocalion in the early '30s. CBS eventually purchased Vocalion as well as ARC and Brunswick. Vocalion kept issuing dates until 1940. Then it was phased out in favor of the Okeh name and logo, with many Vocalion dates being reissued as Okeh but with their original Vocalion numbers.

Vogue

This label began in France in 1948, with Charles Delaunay in charge of its Artists and Repertory (A&R). Henri Renaud, Sidney Bechet, Clifford Brown, Bobby Jaspar, and Art Farmer were among the acts who recorded on Vogue, which also reissued American dates. It distributed recordings in France from the King, Coral, Contemporary, Good Time Jazz, Hot Record Society, Blue Note, and Fantasy labels. In 1951 a subsidiary Vogue branch in Britain began, which England's Decca took over in 1956. The Vogue trademark reverted to the parent company in 1962. Decca absorbed the label, and French Vogue found a new British subsidiary via the Pye companies. Vogue has continued issuing jazz in France and had a reissue series called Jazz Legacy in the '80s. It has also periodically reissued blues and gospel titles from American labels.

Xanadu

Veteran producer Don Schlitten started Xanadu in the mid '70s, shortly after a dispute with Joe Fields at Muse led to a dissolution of their partnership agreement. Schlitten made Xanadu one of the finest bebop, cool, hard bop, and mainstream labels of the '70s and '80s, issuing over 200 albums by such artists as Al Cohn, Dolo Coker, Barry Harris, Sonny Criss, Bob Mover, and Frank Butler, among others. He also issued a series of live dates recorded at the 1978 Montreux International Jazz Festival and a reissue line that included the first recordings by Billy Eckstine and vintage dates from the '30s. Xanadu sponsored tours of Japan and West Africa in the late '70s and early '80s, respectively, and was among the first to feature American jazz acts in Africa and also to record African jazz performers for distribution and sales overseas. Xanadu has not been active since the late '80s, but its catalog remains in print. However, it had not entered the reissue market as of 1993.

—Ron Wynn

PRODUCERS

Steve Backer

Steve Backer moved from the unemployment line to the jazz front line in the late '60s. Backer had a business degree from Hofstra and at one point was running a travel firm in France. When the business went under, Backer turned toward music, having once entertained a desire to be a jazz musician. He initially worked for MGM and Verve as a promotion executive and later for Elektra, where he helped start the Elektra/Musician series in the early '70s. Then Backer moved to Impulse where he served as the label's general manager from 1971 to 1974. He put several marquee label artists on tour and introduced Alice Coltrane, Sam Rivers, Pharoah Sanders, Keith Jarrett, and others to new and larger-than-usual audiences before he departed for Arista in 1974. There, Backer got the chance to run three different labels: one division reissued classic free jazz material from several labels as well as some new dates; another issued exclusively new free jazz; a third issued jazz-rock, fusion, and instrumental pop. Backer was even able to land the GRP label and for a while issued its recordings, coordinating and spearheading the efforts of four operations. But the wheels came off the entire automobile in 1980, and Backer soon left the company. He is currently at RCA, working with the Novus label that he previously founded at Arista.

Rudi Blesh

(1899-1985) Rudi Blesh's interest in jazz began when he was a Dartmouth College student. He became jazz critic for the *San Francisco Chronicle* in the early '40s, then for the *New York Herald Tribune* when he moved to New York in the mid '40s. Blesh promoted concerts while on the West Coast, presenting events featuring New Orleans veterans Bunk Johnson and Kid Ory, among others. He wrote one of the first comprehensive jazz histories, *Shining Trumpets*, in 1946 and cowrote with Harriet Janis in 1950 *They All Played Ragtime*, that music's first legitimate history. Blesh and Janis cofounded Circle Records, the first label to issue Jelly Roll Morton's Library of Congress recordings. He wrote and narrated a series of radio broadcasts on jazz and American vernacular music, "This Is Jazz," from 1947 to 1950 and in 1964. Blesh was an instructor in jazz history during the '50s at Queens College and New York University and contributed liner notes for ragtime recordings in the '70s while helping to rediscover ragtime musicians Eubie Blake and Joseph Lamb and compiling ragtime collections. Blesh was also an art and film critic.

Richard Bock

(1927-1988) Richard Bock was among the early producers and record company owners to fully exploit the roster of available talent on the West Coast, along with Lester Koenig of Contemporary. Bock coformed Pacific Jazz in 1952 with drummer Roy Harte. He eventually became its sole owner and built the label through astute signings even though many of the artists he inked eventually left for bigger companies. Bock signed and produced some of the earliest dates by Chet Baker, Clare Fischer, Jim Hall, Art Pepper, Les McCann, and many others. He also started World Pacific in 1958, recording Indian sitar master Ravi Shankar. Bock began this subsidiary label feeling Shankar's music did not fit on Pacific Jazz. He would later issue other types of jazz on World Pacific, but it was a short-lived label. Bock sold it and Pacific to Liberty in 1965. He remained as an advisor until 1970, when he left music production completely and entered the world of film. But Bock later become a producer for Koenig's Contemporary label after it had been acquired by Fantasy and produced sessions by George Cables, Bud Shank, Frank Morgan, Art Farmer, and Barney Kessel until his death in 1988.

Dr. George Butler

The current head of jazz at Columbia Records and the person credited (or blamed) in many circles for instituting the "Young Lions" furor of the '80s through his signing and promotion of Wynton Marsalis, Dr. George Butler has been a controversial figure since his days at Blue Note. He was the impetus behind such albums as Donald Byrd's *Ethiopian Nights* and *Black Byrd*. *Black Byrd* became the biggest-selling album in Blue Note history, and the former bastion of traditionalism subsequently issued pop-oriented dates by Bobbi Humphrey, Ronnie Foster, Noel Pointer, Ronnie Laws, Alphonse Mouzon, and Earl Klugh. Butler moved to Columbia in the '80s and was the person who signed Wynton and Branford Marsalis to the label and helped drum up the publicity for a "Young Lions" movement (though Butler denies ever using that term). Columbia also inked deals with Marlon and Kent Jordan, Monte Croft, Terence Blanchard, and Ryan Kisor, among others in the 20-30 age group. Butler eventually rose to become head of the jazz division and has generated equal furor in the other direction during the '90s launching of a "Pioneers of Jazz" series. Some signings include Doc Cheatham and Alvin Batiste. Butler is also a trustee at LeMoyne-Owen University in Memphis.

Ozzie Cadena

The head of jazz Artists and Repertory (A&R) at Savoy in the mid and late '50s, Ozzie Cadena oversaw the debut sessions of Cannonball Adderley, Donald Byrd, Yusef Lateef, and Charlie Byrd and produced dates by Hank Jones, Kenny Clarke, and Milt Jackson. Cadena left Savoy in 1959 and later produced dates at Prestige for Brother Jack McDuff, Eddie "Lockjaw" Davis, Etta Jones, Shirley Scott, Willis Jackson, Frank Wess, and many others.

Willis Conover

(b. 1920) A voice better known to generations of foreign listeners than to many Americans, Willis Conover began broadcasting both jazz and classical music in Washington, D.C., and Manhattan in 1939. He started doing jazz worldwide via the Voice of America in 1954 and traveled to more than 40 countries. Conover presented concerts at Washington, D.C., nightclubs and insisted on integrated seating in the '40s at a time when segregation was not merely policy but actual law. He also instituted a midnight concert series on Saturday nights at the Howard Theater. Conover served as emcee of the Newport Jazz Festival for over 10 years in the '50s and '60s and produced and narrated the New Orleans International Jazz Festival in 1969. He produced and narrated Duke Ellington's 70th birthday concert at the White House in 1969 and established and chaired the jazz panel for the National Endowment for the Arts, raising the annual allotment to $250,000 in the early '70s. Conover also taught summer courses in jazz appreciation for elementary and secondary school teachers at the University of Maryland in the '70s and '80s.

Michael Cuscuna

(b. 1948) Currently the co-owner with Charlie Lourie and executive producer of the fantastic Mosaic reissue label, Michael Cuscuna began playing drums at 12 and, later, sax and flute. He attended the Wharton School at the University of Pennsylvania in the mid '60s with an eye on eventually establishing a jazz label. Soon he had a nightly jazz program on radio station WXPN and later worked part-time for ESP-Disk. Cuscuna was a critic for *Jazz and Pop* and *Down Beat* magazines and later produced a date by guitarist George Freeman that was issued by Delmark. He was a disc jockey for stations in Philadelphia and New York and helped launch a mixed musical approach that was eventually known as "progressive" rock, sans playlists and restrictive formats. Cuscuna left radio in the early '70s subsequent to the institution of demographic charting, consultants, and rigid formatting. He became a producer for Atlantic, doing sessions with Dave Brubeck and the Art Ensemble before going on to work with Motown for a short while, and then began a reissue line for ABC, which had the Impulse catalog in the '70s. Cuscuna also produced sessions for Arista and Muse. He coproduced with Alan Douglas the extensive late '70s loft jazz "Wildflowers," a magnificent, now-deleted five-volume set of performances recorded at Sam Rivers's Studio Rivbea. Cuscuna produced Anthony Braxton in the '70s and '80s, helped establish the Freedom and Novus labels, and provided a U.S. recording outlet for Cecil Taylor, Oliver Lake, Julius Hemphill, and Henry Threadgill, among others.

Cuscuna gained access to Blue Note's vaults after a five-year campaign and released nearly 100 albums of unissued classic material between 1975 and 1981. He teamed with Charlie Lourie, another jazz producer with extensive credentials, to begin Mosaic in 1983. Mosaic's operation differed markedly from that of standard jazz companies, even great ones. It did all business by mail-order and specialized in deluxe, multialbum (now multidisc) boxed sets focusing on the complete sessions of a designated artist on a particular label. Each set contained lavishly illustrated and annotated booklets, and the series has spotlighted many neglected or underrated artists such as Herbie Nichols, Tina Brooks, and Ike Quebec along with familiar giants like Charles Mingus and Thelonious Monk. Mosaic has expanded into blues with exquisite sets by T-Bone Walker and Lightnin' Hopkins, issued three massive sets dedicated to the complete output of Commodore Records, and released Nat "King" Cole's complete trio sessions. Cuscuna was voted *Down Beat*'s "Producer of the Year" in 1979 and remained high in its rankings for several years afterward. He participated in the reactivation of Blue Note in 1984 and has produced new sessions by McCoy Tyner, Tony Williams, and Don Pullen. Mosaic continued its exploits in 1993 with two huge sets devoted to live and studio recordings by Count Basie and other packages on

Louis Armstrong, Serge Chaloff, Mingus, Buck Clayton, Don Cherry, Jackie McLean, and Benny Goodman.

Tom Dowd

A staff engineer at Atlantic Records for more than 25 years, Tom Dowd is best known for his exploits on behalf of R&B, soul, and rock groups, but he also engineered numerous jazz dates by Ornette Coleman, Charles Mingus, John Coltrane, the Modern Jazz Quartet, and Ray Charles, among others. Dowd did landmark work with multitracking, helping Atlantic become one of the nation's best facilities in the early days of eight-track and stereo recording. Both a knowledgeable musician and a physics and electronics master, Dowd understood sound from the technical and performance aspects. He later went on to craft hit albums as a producer for Eric Clapton, Rod Stewart, Lynyrd Skynyrd, Chicago, Meat Loaf, and the James Gang.

Manfred Eicher

German bassist Manfred Eicher formed ECM in 1969 in Cologne, Germany. Initially the label was known for free music, issuing dates by Marion Brown, Paul Bley, and Dave Holland. But it has evolved to the point of being regarded as almost a midwife to new age, with many sessions of atmospheric, minimally improvised dates by Jan Garbarek, Ralph Towner, Terje Rypdal, Eberhard Weber, and other Europeans. Eicher's dense, expertly engineered productions have always ensured great sound. The knock on ECM is not completely fair; Jack DeJohnette, Chick Corea, Gary Burton, Keith Jarrett, Pat Metheny, Ralph Towner, Egberto Gismonti, Old and New Dreams, and Codona are among the acts who have either previously recorded or are still recording ECM dates—certainly a mixed bag. The label is still among the most prolific in recent jazz history and a place where unusual and ambitious projects often happen.

Nesuhi Ertegun

(1917-1989) The brother of Ahmet Ertegun, Nesuhi Ertegun began his involvement with jazz as a concert promoter in Washington, D.C. during the early '40s. After moving to the West Coast, Ertegun and his wife organized a band led by Kid Ory and cofounded the Crescent label in Hollywood to record it. The pair owned and operated the Jazzman label in the mid '40s and early '50s, while Ertegun was also a writer for *Clef* and record editor of *Record Changer*. He was an instructor in American music history at UCLA during the early '50s and has been cited as giving the first lectures on jazz history for college credit anywhere in the United States. Ertegun was also working part-time for both Good Time Jazz and Contemporary. He moved to New York in 1955, becoming head of Artists and Repertory (A&R) for his brother's label and started steering Atlantic toward jazz. Under Ertegun, the company at one point had John Coltrane, Charles Mingus, Milt Jackson, the Modern Jazz Quartet, Hank Crawford, David Newman, Ornette Coleman, and numerous other legendary figures under contract. He produced many Modern Jazz Quartet sessions and also helped Atlantic develop a reputation as a cutting-edge company in the '50s and '60s, while still making lucrative pop-jazz dates like Herbie Mann's *Memphis Underground* and Les McCann and Eddie Harris's *Swiss Movement*. Atlantic albums were famous for their inner sleeves, which were filled with pictures of other albums that were either available or forthcoming. Ertegun was a vice president of Atlantic until 1971 when he became president and chief executive officer under the newly merged Warner/Elektra/Atlantic situation. He helped launch Atlantic's 1976 "That's Jazz" reissue program and in 1985 became chair and co-chief executive of the joint company. He died in 1989.

Leonard Feather

(b. 1914) Best known as a syndicated critic and columnist, Leonard Feather has also been a composer, arranger, writer for radio and television, college professor, and producer. Feather attended St. Paul's School and later University College in London in the '20s and '30s, formally studying piano and clarinet and teaching himself arranging. He produced sessions in London for Benny Carter and George Chisholm and also wrote compositions. Feather came to America in the mid '30s and soon produced dates for Duke Ellington and Louis Armstrong as well as organizing jazz concerts at Carnegie Hall in the '40s. He was producer for the earliest recording dates by Dinah Washington, George Shearing, and Sarah Vaughan. Washington recorded such Feather songs as "Evil Gal Blues," "Salty Papa Blues," and "Blowtop Blues." Cleo Laine, Vaughan, Phil Woods, Sonny Stitt, Andre Previn, Cannonball Adderley, and Yusef Lateef are other noted jazz musicians who have recorded Feather numbers. Feather taught in the '70s and '80s at Loyola Marymount, the University of California at Riverside, California State University at Northridge, and UCLA. He is also a longtime columnist for the *Los Angeles Times*, the inventor of *Down Beat* magazine's blindfold test, and the compiler of several editions of *The Encyclopedia of Jazz* in various decades (a '90s edition is reportedly slated to be issued in either '94 or '95). Feather has also written several books and had numerous articles published in magazines ranging from *Metronome* to *Jazz Times*. He was an early advocate for women in jazz, helping such artists as Jutta Hipp, Yma Sumac, and others, at one point trying to establish a label devoted to recording women artists.

Joe Fields

Joe Fields established his first label, Cobblestone, in 1972 in New York as a Buddah subsidiary . He hired Don Schlitten as executive producer and the duo moved on after a few months to establish Muse and then Onyx in 1973. After dissolving the partnership when he and Schlitten had a dispute in the late '70s, Fields not only managed the company but began producing sessions himself as well as hiring Michael Cuscuna, Herb Wong, Bob Porter, and other name producers to do some sessions and having some musicians produce themselves. Muse acquired the Savoy catalog from Arista in 1985 and launched a reissue series before selling the catalog to Denon in 1993. It acquired the Landmark catalog from Fantasy and the Trix blues masters from former owner and producer Pete Lowry that same year. Muse has also distributed Enja and Sunnyside at various times.

Milt Gabler

(b. 1911) Milt Gabler's father got him involved in the music business at an early age. The senior Gabler owned a record store, the Commodore Music Shop, at 144 East 42nd Street in New York City. Milt took over the operation in the '30s and initially sold sporting goods and novelty items in addition to records. His habit of playing records all day attracted many top journalists and researchers to the store. After convincing major record labels to reissue rare out-of-print items by guaranteeing orders prior to sales, Gabler founded Commodore Records in 1938 with the assistance of Eddie Condon. Coleman Hawkins, Hot Lips Page, the Kansas City Five, and Edmond Hall were among early signees. Billie Holiday issued "Strange Fruit" on Commodore, one of four songs she cut in 1939. With Condon Gabler also started a series of jam sessions at Jimmy Ryan's on 52nd Street, and he eventually opened a second store across the street from Ryan's. Commodore was among the first companies to issue material on 12-inch 78 rpm discs, and Gabler operated Commodore until the mid '40s. He then joined Decca, where

he remained until the late '70s. Louis Jordan, Holiday, and Lionel Hampton were among the artists Gabler helped bring to Decca before it was acquired by the Music Corporation of America (MCA) in 1959. Mosaic issued three massive multi-album volumes in 1992 comprising the entire Commodore output. Previously, Commodore reissues appeared on Mainstream in the '60s and overseas on London in the '70s. Columbia reissued Commodore sessions Gabler prepared when he revived the label in the '70s after retiring from Decca. There was also a German Commodore series in the late '80s.

Ira Gitler

(b. 1928) An acclaimed and extremely knowledgeable critic whose writings on jazz have been published in numerous magazines, Ira Gitler was also a staff producer for Prestige from 1950 to 1955. He produced dates by Thelonious Monk, the Modern Jazz Quartet, Miles Davis, Billy Taylor, Art Farmer, and Teddy Charles, among others. He collaborated with Leonard Feather and served as assistant writer and editor on the 1955 edition of *The Encyclopedia of Jazz* as well as *The Encyclopedia of Jazz in the Sixties* and coauthored with Feather *The Encyclopedia of Jazz in the Seventies.* Gitler was an associate editor of *Down Beat,* has written for such publications as *Metronome, Jazz Magazine,* and *Jazz Times,* produced film scripts on Louis Armstrong and Lionel Hampton for the United States Information Service, and been a host and commentator at radio station WBAI in New York. He has also been an instructor at CUNY in New York and wrote *Swing to Bop: an Oral History of the Transition in Jazz in the 1940s* in 1985.

Norman Granz

(b. 1918) A record producer, longtime concert promoter, and manager, Norman Granz has been associated with jazz since the '40s. He attended UCLA and, following army service in World War II, worked as a film editor. Granz began a series of concerts at the Los Angeles Philharmonic Auditorium in 1944; the response was so great, he took the shows on the road, completing the tour in Canada. From this emerged the "Jazz at the Philharmonic" series, a legacy of fervent, flamboyant, and intense jam sessions that became world famous. Numerous classic live albums were recorded at JATP shows. That same year Granz supervised production of the classic film *Jammin' the Blues.* It received an Oscar nomination. He established Clef and Norgran in the late '40s and early '50s and also temporarily leased records to Mercury during that time. Hank Jones, Charlie Parker, Lester Young, Flip Phillips, Johnny Hodges, Artie Shaw, Stan Getz, Charlie Barnet, and Illinois Jacquet were some of the artists Granz recorded and produced on Clef, while Don Byas, Charlie Ventura, Bud Powell, George Wallington, and Buddy Rich cut Norgran sessions. Granz eventually bought all rights to his recordings and formed the Verve label in 1956, then moved to Switzerland in 1960 and has resided in Europe ever since. He has managed Ella Fitzgerald, Oscar Peterson, and Duke Ellington, while Roy Eldridge, Dizzy Gillespie, Art Tatum, Joe Pass, Young, Parker, and Fitzgerald have ranked among his favorite artists. Granz finally sold Verve to Polygram, but began a new label, Pablo, in 1973. He maintained it into the late '80s before selling it to Fantasy.

Dave Grusin

While best known as a pianist, composer, arranger, and bandleader (see bio), Dave Grusin has also been a producer and record executive. He started GRP records with partner Larry Rosen (Grusin-Rosen Productions) in 1974 and procured a deal with Arista a few years later. MCA has owned GRP since the mid '80s and the roster has included both fusion and instrumental pop acts like Chick Corea's Elektric

Band, Spyro Gyra, Lee Ritenour, the Yellowjackets, Dave Weckl, and David Benoit and also more conventional jazz performers like Gary Burton, Michael Brecker, Kenny Kirkland, and Afro-Latin trumpeter Arturo Sandoval. GRP is now also responsible for Impulse and Decca reissues through MCA.

John Hammond

(1910-1987) A legendary producer as well as talent scout, promoter, and advocate for social causes, John Hammond was drawn to the music of African Americans as a teenager listening to Bessie Smith in Harlem. The fact that he came from a wealthy family enabled Hammond to purchase jazz and blues records early and often and to become intimately familiar with the styles, nuances, and tendencies of jazz. His very first production was pianist Garland Wilson on a 12-inch 78 rpm. Some of his earliest sessions included producing and recording a series for Columbia in England featuring Fletcher Henderson, Benny Carter, and Benny Goodman. Hammond produced Bessie Smith's final session and Billie Holiday's first, and he later supervised several Teddy Wilson dates with Holiday as soloist in the late '30s and organized the classic "Spirituals to Swing" concerts in 1938 and 1939. Hammond's many other exploits include introducing guitarist Charlie Christian to Goodman, overcoming Goodman's initial skepticism, and getting some fabulous music recorded as a result.

Hammond served as executive producer or president at various times for Brunswick/Vocalion, Keynote, Majestic, Mercury, and Vanguard in addition to his longtime affiliation with Columbia. He was also an officer in the NAACP and wrote several nonmusical articles on political injustices dating back to the Scottsboro Boys atrocity in 1931. Hammond was responsible for the casting in the all-Black opera *Carmen Jones*. He was also a prolific critic of both jazz and popular music. Count Basie, Mildred Bailey, George Benson, Pete Seeger, Carolyn Hester, Leonard Cohen, Aretha Franklin (one of the few great artists with whom he had relatively little popular success), Bob Dylan, and Bruce Springsteen are only a few of the many great artists Hammond worked with throughout his exemplary career. He was given a special Grammy in 1971, and Dylan broke an embargo on television appearances to be on one of the Public Broadcasting System's "The World of John Hammond" specials in 1975. His son John Hammond (also known as John Hammond, Jr.) is a longtime blues guitarist. His autobiography *John Hammond on Record,* cowritten with Irving Townsend in 1977, outlined the triumphs of a remarkable lifetime.

Nat Hentoff

(b. 1925) Today an award-winning columnist on political and educational issues for the *Village Voice* specializing in First Amendment cases, Nat Hentoff was a distinguished writer and producer of jazz in the '50s. Hentoff attended Northeastern University and Harvard in the '40s and was a disc jockey at WMEX radio station in the '40s and '50s. He was the author of several profiles that were later issued in the book *The Jazz Life* and coeditor with Nat Shapiro of *Hear Me Talkin' To Ya: The Story of Jazz by the Men Who Made It* in 1955. This book was one of the earliest jazz oral histories told by the musicians. He coedited *Jazz: New Perspectives on the History of Jazz by Twelve of the World's Foremost Jazz Critics and Scholars* with A.J. McCarthy in 1959. Hentoff also cowrote *Jazz Street* with D. Stock in 1960 and wrote *Jazz Maker* in 1957. He was coeditor of the *Jazz Review* in the late '50s and early '60s and associate editor of *Down Beat* in the mid and late '50s. Hentoff was also executive and principal producer for the Candid record label in the early '60s, producing sessions by Cecil Taylor, Charles Mingus, Lightnin'

Hopkins, and Otis Spann, among others. His notes have appeared on numerous albums as well.

Carl Jefferson

Carl Jefferson established the Concord record label in 1973. The company became a prime outlet for swing-influenced, mainstream, and bebop dates by jazz veterans, although it had its own version of the "Young Lions" movement as well with several contemporary musicians like Scott Hamilton and Warren Vaché playing in an older style. Jefferson has developed the company into an independent power that now has separate divisions for Latin (Concord Picante), classical (Concord Concerto), fusion/contemporary jazz and pop (Concord Crossover), and reissues (Collector's series) and has issued 30 volumes of solo piano dates recorded at the Maybeck Recital Hall in Berkeley, California. The roster ranges from George Shearing, Mel Torme, and Dave McKenna to relative newcomers like Jesse Davis, Eden Atwood, and even some individuals with thin jazz connections like Lucie Arnaz or minimal jazz importance like Steve Allen. While it has never issued any free sessions, Jefferson's label has released dates by Marvin "Smitty" Smith, Art Blakey and the Jazz Messengers, and the duo of Donald Harrison and Terence Blanchard.

Quincy Jones

(b. 1933) A multitalented individual who has been a successful instrumentalist, composer, arranger, and record label executive, Quincy Jones possesses production credentials that are equally impressive. He was a producer for Barclay Records in Paris during the late '50s and produced sessions for Lesley Gore and Frank Sinatra in the '60s. He also produced his own successful albums for A&M like *Walking In Space* and *Gula Matari.* Jones did the scores and production for soundtracks of more than 40 films and numerous television programs during the '60s and '70s. During the '70s and early '80s, Jones produced the biggest-selling album of all time, Michael Jackson's *Thriller,* and the top-selling single, "We Are The World," as well as sessions for Al Jarreau, Chaka Khan, and other soul, R&B, and pop acts. Jones produced dates for his own Qwest label in the '80s including *Patti Austin,* the Sinatra comeback album *L.A. Is My Lady,* and tracks on a George Benson date, plus his own hit releases. He produced a Ray Charles date in the '90s and the session *Miles and Quincy at Montreux* in 1993. Jones's list of performances, arrangements, compositions, and productions is among the most extensive in popular music history.

Orrin Keepnews

(b. 1923) A critic before he became a producer, Orrin Keepnews produced numerous seminal albums by Thelonious Monk and Bill Evans, among many others. A native New Yorker, Keepnews graduated from Columbia University in the early '40s. By the late '40s he was writing for the *Record Changer,* a magazine published by former Columbia classmate Bill Grauer. They started a reissue series of 10-inch albums for RCA Victor's X label featuring classic dates by Jelly Roll Morton, King Oliver, and others. The pair cofounded Riverside Records in 1953 and initially specialized in similiar reissues. But they quickly ventured into new material, and Riverside became one of the places to hear bebop and other adventurous styles of the day. Keepnews personally produced all of Monk's dates for the label and most of Evans's. By the mid '60s, Keepnews was in charge of both the Riverside and Milestone labels, a position he held until 1972. He then became director of jazz productions for Fantasy, and when Fantasy acquired the Riverside, Milestone, and Prestige catalogs, he was in charge of reissuing a series of acclaimed two-record sets that laid the groundwork for the reissue boom of the '80s and '90s. Keepnews resigned as vice president of Fantasy in 1980 and returned to producing. He established a new company, Landmark, in 1985 and doubled as owner and producer of many dates by such musicians as Mulgrew Miller and Buddy Montgomery. Keepnews sold the Landmark masters to Muse in 1993. His book *The View from Within*, a critically praised collection of various writings, was issued in the late '80s.

Lester Koenig

(1918-1977) Lester Koenig established the Contemporary record label in 1951 and maintained it until 1977. While it earned the reputation in some circles as a "cool" label because of the predominance of such artists as Art Pepper and Chet Baker, Koenig was a fair-minded, open individual who did not close his doors to anyone. Hampton Hawes made many tremendous albums for the label and Ornette Coleman made his debut there. Koenig was the principal producer for such artists as Coleman, Pepper, Phineas Newborn, Sonny Rollins, Art Farmer, Baker, Shelly Manne, and Hawes while also establishing a subsidiary label, Good Time Jazz, for traditional material. Koenig's son took over the operation after his death, until it was acquired by Fantasy.

Bob Koester

Bob Koester established Delmark Records in 1953 in St. Louis. It was known then as Delmar and was one of the first companies that issued entire 10-inch albums of traditional New Orleans jazz rather than 7-inch or 12-inch singles. Koester moved to Chicago in 1959 and changed the label's name to Delmark. The company had a threefold strategy: Koester released traditional New Orleans jazz by people like George Lewis, Art Hodes, Albert Nicholas, and Earl Hines; expanded into modern material with releases from Ira Sullivan, Sonny Stitt, and Jimmy Forrest; and then put a foot into the free arena with albums by Sun Ra and many members of the Association for the Advancement of Creative Musicians (AACM) in the late '60s and early '70s. Delmark issued albums by The Art Ensemble and individual members including Roscoe Mitchell and Joseph Jarman, plus Muhal Richard Abrams, Anthony Braxton, Kalaparusha Maurice McIntyre, and others. Its series of brilliant blues dates in the '60s by Junior Wells, Magic Sam, Otis Rush, J.B. Hutto, and early stars like Big Joe Williams and Sleepy John Estes are justly celebrated, as were its free releases. During the '70s, Koester acquired the rights to the United label as well as two pioneering Black-owned companies, Pearl and States, and reissued sessions by J.T. Brown, Robert Nighthawk, Paul Bascomb, and Johnny Wicks. During the '90s, Delmark began an Apollo reissue line with titles from Coleman Hawkins, Willis Jackson, and Sir Charles Thompson. It has also issued new jazz by Malachi Thompson, Brad Goode, Frank Walton, and others. Koester operates the Jazz Record Mart as well, one of the nation's premier mail-order and retail record stores. Delmark has actively entered the CD reissue market.

Bill Laswell

(b. 1950) Still an active musician, Bill Laswell has also been a prominent producer in pop/rock and improvisational circles, though he's never done bebop, hard bop, or soul-jazz dates. A one-time guitarist who later switched to bass, Laswell hit the big time with his '84 production of Herbie Hancock's album *Future Shock*, notably the smash single "Rockit." He also produced a less successful followup *Sound System*, but at that point his reputation had already been established. Laswell produced releases by Mick Jagger, Laurie Anderson, Fela Kuti, Gil Scott-Heron, Manu Dibango, Yoko Ono, Nona Hendryx, James "Blood" Ulmer (arguably his best major label effort with 1987's *America — Do You Remember*

The Love), and Public Image, Ltd. Some artists have been less than thrilled by Laswell productions, despite his reputation for being a musicians' rather than a company advocate. He erased Kuti's sax solos on "Army Arrangement" and substituted organ parts, a decision that outraged world music purists. Laswell defended it, saying Fela couldn't play it and it was obvious. Scott-Heron was also unhappy about Laswell's productions and said so publicly. But Laswell remains a prime producer and doubles as a periodic member of the group Last Exit with Peter Brotzmann, Sonny Sharrock, and Ronald Shannon Jackson. He also established the record labels OAO and Celluloid and had previously organized the bands Material and Curlew.

Harry Lim

(b. 1919) Harry Lim learned about many things, including jazz, in the Netherlands. He was hooked by the music and pursued this love when he returned to his native Batavia in what was then the Dutch East Indies (now Jakarta, Indonesia). Lim followed the muse to the United States in 1939. After working as a producer in New York and Chicago, he produced dates for Keynote in the mid '40s, doing sessions by Lester Young, Coleman Hawkins, and Red Norvo as well as Milt Hinton's earliest recordings, Lennie Tristano's first commercial sessions, a date by a Charlie Shavers-led band with Earl Hines, and another composed of musicians from Woody Herman's first band with bandleader Chubby Jackson. Dave Lambert and Buddy Stewart recorded some of the first scat singing on record during a Lim production. He supervised sessions in New York, Chicago, New Orleans, and Los Angeles. Keynote later replaced Lim with another legendary figure, John Hammond, in 1947. Lim formed his own short-lived label, HL, in 1949 and produced and recorded Al Haig. He did a few sessions for Seeco, including a date by Wardell Gray, before reviving Keynote in 1955 to record material for Nat Pierce. Lim later founded Famous Door, named for the New York nightclub, in 1972. It issued sessions by George Barnes, Bill Watrous, Mundell Lowe, Zoot Sims, Red Norvo, Eddie Barefield, Scott Hamilton, George Masso, and others in the '70s and early '80s. Lim was the jazz advisor and expert for Sam Goody's record store in New York from 1956 until 1973. *The Complete Keynote Collection*, an elaborate boxed set, was issued in 1986, as well as some subsequent special collections culled from the main package.

Alfred Lion

(1908-1987) The founder of one of jazz's greatest all-time labels fell in love with the music after hearing Sam Woodling's band in Berlin in the '20s. Alfred Lion came to the United States in 1938 and attended John Hammond's "Spirituals to Swing" concert that December. The next month Lion cofounded Blue Note with Francis Wolff. The label was initially famous for great swing and traditional jazz sessions. James P. Johnson, Art Hodes, Edmond Hall, and Sidney Bechet were among their earliest artists. One of Lion's innovations was the use of 12-inch 78 rpm discs to accommodate longer sessions. Lion owned Blue Note until he sold it to Liberty in 1966. He worked another year for the new label, then retired for health reasons. Lion was honored at EMI's ceremonies reviving Blue Note in 1985 and attended a Blue Note festival in Japan the next year. (See also Blue Note in the Labels section.)

Herman Lubinsky

(1896-1974) A record dealer, electronics parts salesman, and operator of the first radio station in New Jersey, Herman Lubinsky nevertheless is a major name in jazz history as the founder of Savoy Records. Lubinsky devoted himself to the business side, leaving the production and musical decisions to his staff of A&R professionals. He was responsible for Savoy being one of the earliest labels to embrace and actively issue 12-inch albums and began the MG 1200 series, an extremely influential move. Lubinsky was sole owner until his death in 1974, and Savoy was sold the next year to Arista, which began a reissue campaign. Muse operated a similar line in the '80s, and Denon currently owns the masters and has been reissuing classic titles on a single-item basis.

Teo Macero

(b. 1925) He had an extensive performing career long before turning to production (see bio), but Teo Macero's fortunes took a major turn when he joined the CBS staff as a music editor in 1957. Among his earliest exploits was working with Charles Mingus on the great *Mingus Ah Um* and *Mingus Dynasty* releases (the eventual debacle with Mingus's material cannot be blamed on Macero). He produced Thelonious Monk during his stay on the label, though Monk's tenure was marred by the company's failure to understand his talents and refusal to issue quality material when it was fresh. Macero became Miles Davis's producer in 1959, replacing George Avakian. He and Davis worked together through the '60s and '70s, making many landmark sessions despite frequent personality clashes. His production imprint and hand in editing on numerous albums from *Sketches of Spain* to *Bitches Brew* was immense. Macero finally left Columbia in 1980 and has since issued albums on American Clave and Palo Alto and produced a date for Loose Tubes in 1987.

Sid McCoy

Although he is much better known for his radio stints as a soul music disc jockey and also an announcer on the "Soul Train" program, Sid McCoy was the principal jazz producer for Vee Jay. He produced dates by Wayne Shorter, Wynton Kelly, Lee Morgan, Eddie Harris, and others on Vee Jay from the late '50s to the early '60s.

Chuck Nessa

Michigan native Charles T. Nessa started his Chicago-based company in 1967. He produced and recorded formative sessions by Roscoe Mitchell and Lester Bowie before they became members of the Art Ensemble of Chicago, which he produced and recorded in turn. Nessa's releases were among the finest produced, packaged, and mastered of their day, and he was among the earliest sources for recordings by Bobby Bradford, John Stevens, Leo Smith, Hal Russell, Charles Tyler, and Fred Anderson. But Nessa did not restrict himself to free material; he also issued fine dates by Von Freeman, Warne Marsh, Lucky Thompson, and Ben Webster. His label was dormant for a time in the early '70s, though it kept everything in print. It became active again in the late '70s, with new dates by Marsh and Freeman. Nessa issued a limited-edition boxed set of Art Ensemble recordings, including several previously unissued tracks, in 1993.

Hughes Panassie

(1912-1974) Without question the first great non-American jazz critic, Hughes Panassie studied saxophone and began writing about the music at 18. He was a founder and later president of "The Hot Club De France" and edited *Jazz Hot* from 1936 to 1947. He also wrote the book *Le jazz Hot*, a mid-'30s treatise that was a leader in addressing the music as a serious art form. Panassie organized a series of small-group recording sessions in 1938 with Mezz Mezzrow, Tommy Ladnier, and Sidney Bechet that reportedly led to Eddie Condon's famous comment that "he didn't go over there (to France) and tell him how to stomp a grape." Count Basie recorded *Panassie Stomp* that same year. Panassie recorded and produced a swing date led by Frankie Newton in 1939.

But he was an avowed, unrepentant anti-bebop scribe, repeatedly denouncing the form as the antithesis of jazz. He continued the charges until his death in the mid '70s. Panassie's extensive private collection now resides in the Discothèque Municipale at Villefranche-de-Rougergue.

Duke Pearson

Though also well known as a musician and a bandleader, Duke Pearson had an equally important role as an A&R head and codirector of Blue Note in the '60s and early '70s. During Pearson's run from 1963 to 1971, Blue Note issued pivotal sessions by Herbie Hancock, Wayne Shorter, McCoy Tyner, Andrew Hill, Joe Henderson, and Bobby Hutcherson, among others. After Francis Wolff died in 1971 and the label began issuing jazz-rock, fusion, and instrumental pop, Pearson departed.

Ike Quebec

(1918-1963) Besides having an extensive recording career (see bio), Ike Quebec played a pivotal role in the evolution of Blue Note Records from being mainly a swing and traditional jazz company into its involvement in soul-jazz, hard bop, and even some free music. Quebec began recording for Blue Note in the mid '40s and was one of only four artists to issue an album in the 78 rpm format complete with artwork and photos. He became a close friend of label owner Alfred Lion and encouraged him to pay attention to intriguing, fresh developments coming from such then-unheralded artists as Bud Powell and Thelonious Monk. Quebec soon became a combination Artists and Repertory (A&R) head, talent scout, writer (he provided the song "Suburban Eyes," which appeared on the first Monk Blue Note date), and de facto producer. Quebec remained in this role for the rest of his life, helping the label become the premier hard bop and soul-jazz company with landmark dates by Horace Silver, Art Blakey and the Jazz Messengers, Lee Morgan, Johnny Griffin, and many more. Quebec battled heroin addiction and recovered enough to resume his recording career until his death in 1963.

Teddy Reig

Teddy Reig ranks among the greatest Artists and Repertory (A&R) people in modern music history. He was a staff producer and A&R man at Savoy and Roulette. Reig produced sessions for Charlie Parker, Miles Davis, Sonny Stitt, Kenny Dorham, Kai Winding, and Leo Parker among others at Savoy. He also played a major role in the explosion of instrumental R&B by producing and in some cases actually discovering such artists as Hal Singer, Paul Williams, and Wild Bill Moore. Reig founded the (Royal) Roost label before returning to Savoy, then moved on to Roulette in the '50s and '60s. He produced early sessions by Stan Getz and Roost reissued Charlie Parker tracks made for Dial and Bud Powell material originally recorded for Deluxe in the late '40s. Coleman Hawkins, Billy Taylor, Seldon Powell, and Gene Quill were other acts that recorded for Roost. Reig also reissued some Roost sessions through Roulette while overseeing major issue dates by Count Basie, Joe Williams, Maynard Ferguson, Harry Edison, Jack Teagarden, Randy Weston, and Sarah Vaughan.

Larry Rosen

The partner of pianist Dave Grusin and cofounder of GRP Records in 1974.

Bob Rusch

(b. 1945) A former drummer who played in '70s workshops with Jaki Byard and Cedar Walton, Bob Rusch was a writer for such publications as *Down Beat*, *Jazz Journal*, and *Jazz*

Forum before he established *Cadence* magazine in 1975. It has become perhaps the nation's premier jazz journal, with loads of reviews covering independent and small jazz labels and also extensive oral interviews, histories, and commentary. In 1980 Rusch formed Cadence Jazz Records, which distributes jazz and blues recordings for hundreds of small labels. Rusch also operates North County Audio, one of the nation's finest audio/video outlets. The book *Jazz Talk: The Cadence Interviews* (1984) is a collection of several of his interviews in book form. Rusch has also donated his exhaustive indexed collection of periodicals on jazz and blues literature to the Schomburg Center for Research in Black Culture of the New York Public Library.

Bill Russell

(b. 1905) A musician, composer, and historian in addition to being a producer, Bill Russell began collecting jazz records in the '30s. He resold them through the Hot Record Exchange, a business he co-operated with painter Steve Smith. Russell helped rediscover Bunk Johnson in the early '40s and recorded him in 1942. He later recorded Baby Dodds, Dink Johnson, George Lewis, Wooden Joe Nicholas, and others in Los Angeles, New Orleans, and New York for his American Music label. Russell was later curator of Tulane University's jazz archive from 1958 to 1965 and co-interviewed dozens of musicians for its oral history project with Richard B. Allen. He also played in the New Orleans ragtime festival through the '60s, '70s, and '80s. The William Ransom Hogan Jazz Archive at Tulane has a collection of Russell's published and unpublished writings as well as other materials.

Ross Russell

(b. 1920) Ross Russell's exploits in jazz include involvement in the entrepreneurial, production, journalistic, and management ends. Russell founded Dial Records in 1946 and was Charlie Parker's manager for a couple of years in the late '40s. He was also a journalist who wrote for *Down Beat* and the *Jazz Review*, among others. His book *The High Life and Hard Times of Charlie "Yardbird" Parker,* which was issued in 1973, was quite controversial, with some critics disputing the accuracy of accounts and validity of his contentions. Russell also penned the less-disputed *Jazz Style in Kansas City and the South* and was an instructor in African-American music history at the University of California and Palomar College in the '60s and '70s. The University of Texas purchased the Russell collection in 1981.

Don Schlitten

(b. 1932) Don Schlitten's experiences and credentials in jazz are extensive and varied. He cofounded Signal Records in New York with Jules Colomby and Harold Goldberg in 1955. Signal had a reputation for superbly engineered sessions with comprehensive liner notes and attractive packaging. The roster featured such artists as Duke Jordan, Cecil Payne, Red Rodney, and Gigi Gryce. After the label folded and its catalog was sold to Savoy, Schlitten became executive producer for Joe Fields's Cobblestone label, a subsidiary of Buddah, in New York in the early '70s. Schlitten produced dates by Jimmy Heath, Sonny Stitt, and Pat Martino and was responsible for a six-album series featuring highlights from the 1972 Newport in New York Jazz Festival, covering the first season the storied event moved to New York from Newport. Cobblestone also issued a previously unreleased date by Grant Green with Big John Patton. Schlitten departed Cobblestone for Muse in 1972, joining Fields in the same capacity as executive producer. The duo also formed Onyx in 1973, and during the mid '70s, Schlitten produced dates by Stitt, Kenny Barron, Willis Jackson, Woody Shaw, Kenny Burrell, and Red Rodney before a dispute between Fields and him escalated into an unsolvable feud. Their partnership was

dissolved and Schlitten established Xanadu, turning it into one of the late '70s and '80s finest hard bop, bebop, and historical labels. Xanadu issued over 200 albums, with Schlitten producing new dates by Al Cohn, Barry Harris, Bob Mover, Frank Butler, and others on the Xanadu Silver series and reissuing vintage sessions on the Gold line, including seminal material by Billy Eckstine, Sonny Criss, and others. Schlitten designed all album liners, took every photograph, and wrote most of the notes for the newer Xanadu sessions. While the company has not issued any new material since the late '80s, it has kept most of its catalog in print, though it had not entered the CD reissue market as of 1993.

Bob Shad

(1920-1985) Bob Shad was not only an outstanding jazz producer, but he supervised several major blues, pop, rock, and R&B dates as well. Shad started his production career with Savoy in the '40s, producing jazz sessions for Charlie Parker and blues and R&B albums for National. He founded the Sittin' In With label in 1948 and produced albums by Lightnin' Hopkins, Sonny Terry and Brownie McGhee, Smokey Hogg, Peppermint Harris, and Curley Weaver as well as jazz and R&B albums. Shad became director of Artists and Repertory (A&R) for Mercury in 1951 and launched its EmArcy division, producing dates by Sarah Vaughan, Maynard Ferguson, the Clifford Brown/Max Roach Quintet, and Dinah Washington, among many others. Shad produced Washington's first album with strings, which proved a huge hit. He also supervised pop dates by Patti Page and Vic Damone, R&B by the Platters, and blues sessions by Hopkins, Big Bill Broonzy, and several others. Shad founded Mainstream in the '60s after leaving Mercury and reissued several Sittin' In With albums as well as new dates by Shelly Manne, Dizzy Gillespie, Roy Haynes, Buddy Terry, Pete Yellin, and others. He continued at Mainstream through the '70s and also served as a producer for the debuts of Ted Nugent and Janis Joplin.

Nat Shapiro

(1922-1983) Nat Shapiro was not only a talented and influential writer but a longtime producer and record executive. He was Mercury Records' national director of promotion from 1948 to 1950 and the public relations representative for Broadcast Music Incorporated (BMI) in 1954 and 1955 as well as head of Columbia Records Artists and Repertory (A&R) from 1956 to 1966. Shapiro produced albums for Columbia, Philips, Vanguard, Epic, and RCA, among other companies, doing over 100 sessions by everyone from Miles Davis to Michel Legrand. Shapiro coedited *Hear Me Talkin' to Ya: The Story of Jazz by the Men Who Made It* and *The Jazz Masters* with Nat Hentoff in 1953 and 1957, respectively, and also compiled and revised *An Annotated Index of American Popular Songs* from 1964 until 1979.

John Snyder

John Snyder got his start working for CTI in the early '70s. A music education major and law school graduate, Snyder worked with such artists as Jim Hall and Paul Desmond. He then moved to A&M, where he created Horizon, a label famed for its great sound, exhaustively annotated albums, and eclectic roster. Snyder produced and issued sessions by Ornette Coleman, Charlie Haden, Dave Brubeck and Paul Desmond, Jim Hall, the Revolutionary Ensemble, and the Thad Jones-Mel Lewis orchestra. He was reportedly dismissed from A&M for presenting a company executive a present of a clock made from a Revolutionary Ensemble record. Snyder then began the Artists House series, another acclaimed but low-selling label. This time, in addition to retaining all the things that made Horizon such a great label, Snyder also gave the musicians partial ownership and creative control of the sessions, as well as paying them 67½ cents per record pressed. He used virgin vinyl and generally operated on behalf of the music and musicians, rather than strictly for profit. Unfortunately, Artists House did not succeed either. Snyder is currently a freelance producer.

Creed Taylor

(b. 1929) One of jazz's most commercially successful and controversial producers, Creed Taylor was a trumpeter in the Duke Ambassadors Dance Orchestra in the early '50s before moving into the production end of the business. A psychology major and Duke graduate, Taylor became head of A&R at Bethlehem Records in 1954. Charlie Mariano, Chris Connor, Oscar Pettiford, Bobby Scott, Ruby Braff, Carmen McRae, Charlie Shavers, Jack Teagarden, Charles Mingus, Herbie Mann, and the duo of J.J. Johnson and Kai Winding were some artists who recorded Bethlehem sessions during Taylor's two-year stay. He joined ABC-Paramount in 1956 and started the Impulse division in 1960. Taylor signed John Coltrane and produced the *Africa/Brass* sessions. He launched the label with an album by the Johnson/Winding duo but left to go to Verve in 1962. Taylor produced the Charlie Byrd/Stan Getz hit LP *Jazz Samba* that topped the charts in 1962 and launched the bossa nova trend. He also produced the Grammy-winning smash hit album *Getz/Gilberto* that was number two on the pop charts in 1964 and included the top-five single *The Girl from Ipanema.* After so much success at Verve, Taylor moved to A&M in 1967 where he enjoyed more commercial winners with Wes Montgomery, although the results were extremely controversial. Taylor's productions for Montgomery on such albums as *A Day in the Life, Down Here on the Ground,* and *Road Song* immersed the guitarist in arrangements with large orchestras and featured an exclusive diet of light pop and rock covers with minimal solo space and short playing times. Montgomery was supposedly so disillusioned by these albums that he refused to play them for friends at home. They certainly did well on the charts.

But Taylor wanted his own operation and got that in 1970, starting CTI, Kudu, and Salvation Records. CTI became the '70s' dominant pop jazz label, with a lineup that at one point included Freddie Hubbard, Hubert Laws, George Benson, Stanley Turrentine, Chet Baker, Deodato, and Joe Farrell. Kudu issued more funk/soul and pop material by such artists as Esther Phillips, Johnny "Hammond" Smith, and Lonnie Smith. CTI was famous for its cover art, and at one time their albums included ads for separate purchases of cover illustrations. Some releases like Turrentine's *Sugar, Cherry,* and *Don't Mess with Mister T,* Hubbard's *Red Clay, Straight Life,* and *Sky Dive,* Benson's *White Rabbit,* Laws's *Afro-Classic* and *The Rite of Spring,* and Milt Jackson's *Sunflower* were fine releases in their genre. Grover Washington became an instrumental pop superstar through Kudu albums *Inner City Blues* and *Mister Magic,* while Esther Phillips scored her last hit with a disco version of *What a Difference a Day Makes* from her '75 Kudu album. But the productions became increasingly predictable and boring even to the legions who had earlier embraced them. That, coupled with financial problems, finally caused the labels to go into bankruptcy. At one point they were owned by Motown. But CTI has resurfaced in the '90s as both a new and reissue label through a tie-in with Sony/Columbia. Columbia has reissued '70s CTI dates as part of their Contemporary Masters and Associated labels line. Bassist Charles Fambrough, a former member of Art Blakey's Jazz Messengers, has three releases on CTI including *Blues At Bradley's* in 1993.

Bob Thiele

(b. 1922) Bob Thiele's involvement in the music industry dates back to his days as a radio announcer in the '30s. Thiele was the leader of a 14-piece dance band and editor/publisher of *Jazz* magazine from 1939 to 1941. He was the first person to record pianist Erroll Garner on his Signature label, which began in 1939 and continued until 1948. Thiele also produced sessions by Coleman Hawkins, Lester Young, Eddie "Lockjaw" Davis, Julian Dash, Flip Phillips, and Anita O'Day. He joined Decca in 1952 and was responsible for productions on the Coral and Brunswick labels. Some of the artists Thiele produced were Teresa Brewer, Pearl Bailey, the McGuire Sisters, Johnny and Dorsey Burnette, and even Lawrence Welk. Thiele signed Buddy Holly after Decca rejected him, and he helped launch the careers of Jackie Wilson, Henry Mancini, Eydie Gorme, and Steve Lawrence. Thiele moved to Dot in 1959 where he produced the Mills Brothers, recorded the Clara Ward Singers live at the Apollo Theater, and did sessions with Pat Boone. He edited the soundtrack for a Red Nichols film. When Dot head Randy Wood nixed the release of a Jack Kerouac album with comedian/writer Steve Allen on piano, Thiele quit and took the session with him. He and Allen coformed the short-lived Hanover-Signature label. Thiele produced another Kerouac session with special guests Zoot Sims and Al Cohn. Others on the label included Ray Bryant, who scored a 1960 R&B hit with "Little Susie," and the team of Don Elliot and Sascha Burland, who had a novelty smash under the guise of the Nutty Squirrels. Thiele produced a classic album for Roulette of Louis Armstrong performing Duke Ellington selections with the Duke on piano.

Thiele moved to ABC-Impulse in 1961 and remained there until 1969, producing and recording more than 100 albums that were some of the turbulent '60s' greatest jazz statements. These included landmark sessions by Charles Mingus, Archie Shepp, Pharoah Sanders, Oliver Nelson, Albert Ayler, Charlie Haden's Liberation Music Orchestra, and, of course, John Coltrane. Thiele took little credit for his Coltrane productions, often saying he gave Coltrane his head in the studio and recorded the results. He also produced fine dates by Earl Hines, Johnny Hodges, Quincy Jones, Count Basie, Coleman Hawkins, and Duke Ellington, devising inspired pairings of Ellington and Coltrane, Ellington and Hawkins, and Coltrane and Johnny Hartman. Thiele also launched the Bluesway label, with remarkable albums by B.B. King, T-Bone Walker, and John Lee Hooker, and produced Frankie Laine, Della Reese, and other pop acts for ABC. In addition to all this, he composed lyrics for the song "Duke's Place" (with the melody for *C-Jam Blues*) and wrote "Bean's Place" and "Dear John C." Thiele started the Flying Dutchman, BluesTime, and Amsterdam labels after leaving ABC-Impulse. Among his activities there were Armstrong's final sessions, co-writing "What A Wonderful World," producing albums by Gato Barbieri, Eddie "Cleanhead" Vinson, Nelson, Otis Spann, Big Joe Turner, and Count Basie. Thiele helped turn poet/musician Gil Scott-Heron into a '70s campus hero by issuing his early albums of poetry and music on Flying Dutchman. He formed the Mysterious Flying Orchestra that included Larry Coryell and Lonnie Liston Smith, which wasn't one of his stellar accomplishments, though it recorded for RCA. Thiele did productions for CBS in the '70s, among them Smith and Arthur Blythe. He married Teresa Brewer in 1972 and has frequently recorded her with everyone from Count Basie to Stephane Grappelli, Hines, and Oily Rags. He started more new labels in the '80s, including Dr. Jazz and the revived Signature. He produced dates by Arnie Lawrence and Smith and issued vintage unreleased material by Ellington and Basie, plus other items from the early Signature days on Dr. Jazz. Thiele has continued his production/label exploits in the '90s with the Red Baron company. At the end of '93 the label issued new releases by David Murray, Jackie Cain and Roy Kral, Clark Terry, Thiele's own collective all-star band, and reissues featuring Paul Desmond with the Modern Jazz

Quartet and Al Cohn backed by a big band led by Al Porcino. He is still active as a producer, performer, and composer.

Rudy Van Gelder

Rudy Van Gelder is perhaps modern jazz's greatest engineer. He began engineering Blue Note sessions in 1953 and was famous for clean, sonically impeccable, and sharp recordings that were expertly balanced and ideal for jazz fans, critics, and anyone eager to hear accurate sound reproduction. Van Gelder initially juggled an optometry business and engineering before becoming a full-time sound man in 1959. He initially operated in his home studio in Hackensack, New Jersey, before moving to Englewood Cliffs in 1959. There he designed a home and studio intended for optimum recording production. Van Gelder was Blue Note's surrogate producer as well as engineering mainstay throughout its greatest days in jazz. He has remained active in jazz as a free-lance engineer and continues recording at his Englewood Cliffs home; among his most recent dates are a '93 session by trumpeter Wallace Roney. Many of Van Gelder's vintage Blue Note sessions have been reissued on CD with little or no remastering other than conversion from analog to digital. Amazingly, many ostensibly comprehensive jazz reference guides carry little or no mention of his role in jazz history, an astonishing oversight.

George Wein

(b. 1925) He studied classical piano at seven with Serge Chaloff's mother and took lessons from Sam Saxe and Teddy Wilson, but George Wein's ultimate greatness came in the promotional, not the performance end of jazz. He was the first director and ultimate impresario of the Newport Jazz Festival and numerous other related festivals across the nation and around the world. The Newport Jazz Festival has been in operation since 1954 and survived fiascoes in the '60s and '70s that could have brought it to a permanent end. Wein formed a 13-piece jazz band and led it until 1941. As a teen, he played several Boston nightclubs, working with Max Kaminsky, Edmond Hall, and Wild Bill Davison before graduating from Boston University in 1950. Wein initially organized and presented groups at the Savoy in New York, then opened his own club, Storyville, featuring famous traditional jazz musicians. During the early '50s, Wein played with Bobby Hackett and recorded with Ruby Braff, Pee Wee Russell, Vic Dickenson, Jimmy McPartland, and Papa Jo Jones. He opened a second traditional jazz club, Mahogany Hall, and later recorded with the Mahogany Hall All-Stars including Doc Cheatham and Vic Dickenson.

But all those achievements take second place to his role in helping to establish the Newport Jazz Festival in 1954, serving as its director. With the financial impetus of Louis and Elaine Lorillard, Wein initiated the festival at Newport. It became so successful that it led to the inception of many other related events ranging from the Boston Globe Jazz & Heritage Festival to the Grande Parade Du Jazz. The Newport Jazz Festival was featured in the film *Jazz on a Summer's Day* in 1958. The Newport City Council canceled it in 1961 due to unruly crowds, but it returned the next season. Wein also began a Newport Jazz Festival in Europe in 1962. A 1971 riot caused its premature end and subsequent move to New York, where it has remained ever since. The festival has grown in scope to the point that it now utilizes multiple venues, presents many special events and concerts, and remains a premier event despite continual grousing each year over conservative policies regarding invited performers and overall musical direction. Its sponsorship affiliation has changed from Kool cigarettes in the early '80s to its current JVC. Wein has also produced adjacent festivals held under the Newport banner in many cities and returned to Newport with a scaled-down version of the original. The festival's 25th anniversary was celebrated at the White House in 1978. But while he has remained busy as the head and director of Festival Productions, Inc., Wein's performing career has not ended. As early as the late '50s he was touring with a hand-picked group of top musicians called the Newport Festival All-Stars. He formed the New York Jazz Repertory Company in 1974 and created another edition of the Newport Jazz Festival All-Stars in the '80s with such musicians as Scott Hamilton, Oliver Jackson, Harold Ashby, Slam Stewart, Norris Turney, and Warren Vaché. They have recorded for Concord in the '80s and '90s. Wein has also been a jazz history instructor at Boston University since the mid '50s.

Bob Weinstock

Bob Weinstock founded Prestige Records in 1949 at 446 West 50th Street in New York. Under his leadership the label evolved into a premier outlet for cool, hard bop, and soul-jazz dates. Prestige sessions were produced by Chris Albertson, Ozzie Cadena, Esmond Edwards, Ira Gitler, Cal Lampley, Bob Porter, and Don Schlitten, and mainly engineered by Rudy Van Gelder. Weinstock also produced many sessions by such musicians as Sonny Rollins, Miles Davis, the Modern Jazz Quartet, Art Farmer, James Moody, and several other individuals and groups. Prestige was sold to Fantasy, along with subsidiary companies Bluesville, Swingville, and Moodsville, in 1971.

Martin Williams

(1924-1992) While he was first and foremost one of the greatest and most knowledgeable critics in jazz history, Martin Williams was also director of the Smithsonian's jazz program and an acquisitions editor at the Smithsonian Institution Press. He was the person who selected and helped to sequence and/or annotate the sessions included in several notable releases through the '70s, '80s, and '90s. These include *The Smithsonian Collection of Classic Jazz* and other valuable releases by Duke Ellington, Fletcher Henderson, Dizzy Gillespie, and Jelly Roll Morton and anthologies of jazz piano and American popular song. He coprogrammed and annotated *Big Band Jazz: From the Beginnings to the Fifties* with Gunther Schuller; it was issued in 1993. Williams also wrote many valuable books and wrote commentaries on jazz for the Encyclopedia Britannica. He died in 1992.

—Ron Wynn

VENUES

52nd Street

Like Storyville in New Orleans, 52nd Street in New York wasn't a club but an entity and spawning ground for superb talent. When the center of jazz headed downtown from Harlem, 52nd Street was for many years the city's jazz mecca and main headquarters. It offered diverse clubs and incredible talent at numerous locations. The Onyx opened first, followed by the Famous Door, then the Hickory House, Downbeat, Three Deuces and Jimmy Ryan's. The styles ranged from traditional New Orleans to bebop, and the roster of stars included Art Tatum, Coleman Hawkins, Erroll Garner, Charlie Parker, Billie Holiday, Hot Lips Page, Count Basie, Woody Herman, Buddy Rich, Charlie Barnet, and Fats Waller. The street reigned supreme in the '30s and early '40s, but began coming undone after World War II ended. Gradually, strip bars and clip joints replaced the jazz clubs. Today there are some commemorative signs and sidewalk plaques that recognize past achievements and heroes.

Alhambra

Though not as well known as some other New York clubs, the Alhambra has a special place in the hearts of jazz fans. It was here that the 16-year-old John Hammond, supposedly out to practice music with his friends, slipped instead into the Alhambra and heard Bessie Smith. The club opened in the '20s under the direction of Milton Gosdorfer. He presented variety shows with major blues and jazz stars. In addition to Smith, Cab Calloway performed there in the '30s, as did Billie Holiday. Edgar Hayes was the resident bandleader from 1927 to 1930 and then the Emmett Mathews band was employed. It is currently an office building of the New York Department of Motor Vehicles.

Ali's Alley

Drummer Rashied Ali opened Ali's Alley in New York at North Green Street between Spring Street and Broome Street in 1973. It was located in a loft in Greenwich Village that was formerly named Studio 77. Ali was initially the principal performer, and later such musicians as Archie Shepp and Gunter Hampel were featured with their bands. It closed in 1979.

Apollo Theater

The greatest entertainment venue in African-American cultural history and one of the most significant in popular music annals, the Apollo Theater opened in New York in 1913. Frank Schiffman and Leo Brecher had earlier operated the Lafayette Theatre. The Apollo had some jazz presentations in the '20s but came of age in the '30s. Sidney Cohen bought and renovated the building in 1933 and reopened in January of 1934. The club then evolved into the premier facility for jazz and African-American popular music. Big bands from Count Basie and Duke Ellington to Chick Webb, as well as classic blues vocalists; jazz, R&B, and soul singers; tap and jazz dancers; comedians; and gospel acts appeared

there. Only down-home and urban blues vocalists found the going a bit rough at the Apollo, where the audiences were known as the nation's toughest—and most loyal once they were on an act's side. The weekly amateur competitions were a launching pad for many great careers. The Apollo's importance as a jazz center dimmed after the '40s, was limited in the '50s and '60s, and almost nil after that, though some jazz performers still appeared there out of loyalty and a desire to remain close to the black community. R&B, soul, and gospel flourished there. Contrary to the film *The Buddy Holly Story*, White bandleader Johnny Otis appeared there long before Holly. Jerry Lee Lewis and Wayne Cochran were other White acts who headlined there and were a big success. Though threatened with extinction many times, the club has been saved through ventures with Inner City Broadcasting and with the help of national appeals to famous African-American entertainers. Television specials have been held at the refurbished and restored center in the '80s and '90s, and a syndicated program reprising the old Amateur Night contests also aired for a number of seasons.

Baby Grand

Once a great cabaret club, the Baby Grand at 319 W. 125th Street, on what is now Frederick Douglass Boulevard in New York City, operated for over 40 years as a hot spot where musicians like Joe Turner and Jimmy Butts were featured, as well as comedians like Nipsey Russell and Manhattan Paul. It opened its doors in the mid '40s, and kept going until 1989. Ruth Brown taped a nationally televised birthday special there in 1988. It is now a clothing store.

Beale Street

While it can be debated whether Beale Street in Memphis was ever as much the national center of African-American cultural activities as its admirers claim, its importance as a business and musical mecca for Blacks in the South is indisputable. Much as Storyville in New Orleans and Central Avenue in Los Angeles were much more than places to simply hear music, Beale Street was a thriving, constantly busy hub for Black financial, social, and political affairs throughout the mid-South. W.C. Handy arrived there in the '20s, and through the '30s, '40s, and into the '50s, jazz, followed closely by blues and later rhythm and blues and soul, seemed to constantly be in the air. Legendary names from Furry Lewis to B.B. King to Rufus Thomas and even Elvis Presley put in their time on Beale. Memphis' longtime political ruler and mayor, E. H. "Boss" Crump, the subject of many a great blues tune, essentially left the street alone. As a result it had the good (banks, numerous businesses, clubs), the bad (prostitution, gambling), and the ugly (a sky-high murder rate long before discussions about so-called Black-on-Black crime were in vogue). When Crump began closing down certain establishments in the '50s, legitimate businesses gradually faded away. A combination of urban renewal, neglect from city administrations, and the pall cast over Memphis by Dr.

Martin Luther King Jr.'s assassination in 1968 left the old Beale Street dead and almost completely abandoned at one point. But today the area is a historic district, with small reminders of what life was like in the glory years.

Bee Hive

The Bee Hive opened in 1948, right when jazz activity in Chicago was at its peak. It was located at East 55th Street and South Harper Avenue. Many of the city's greatest musicians such as Sonny Stitt, Johnny Griffin, and Eddie "Lockjaw" Davis played there, while Charlie Parker and the Clifford Brown-Max Roach quartet, among other national headliners, also appeared there. (A two-album set of performances by the Brown/Roach quartet at the Bee Hive was issued by Columbia but hasn't been reissued on CD.) It was also known for featuring jazz veterans like Chippie Hill, Miff Mole, Baby Dodds, and Lester Young. Norman Simmons was the house pianist in the mid '50s. The Bee Hive closed in 1956.

Birdland

One of several clubs near 52nd Street in New York, Birdland opened on Broadway in 1949 as a shrine to Charlie Parker, complete with his nickname as its signature. Morris Levy, not exactly an altar boy, operated it; and many top bebop and swing stars regularly appeared there. The club initially had parakeets in cages, but they soon died from the smoke and air conditioning. It also had tables on the dance floor, bleachers for anyone who only wanted, or could only afford, to pay the cover charge, and a milk bar for nondrinkers. Count Basie used the club as his New York headquarters in the '50s, and it had its own radio wire, broadcast booth, and eventually an NBC affiliation. Symphony Sid Torin held court there, and many Birdland shows were recorded and issued on labels owned by Boris Rose. Impulse released a 1963 John Coltrane concert, and Count Basie's 1955 recording of George Shearing's "Lullaby of Birdland" was also issued. Art Blakey recorded some superb Blue Note dates at Birdland. The pint-sized emcee Pee Wee Marquette can be heard shouting out calls for applause and announcing acts on various albums. Unfortunately, the club was just as famous for some unsavory events as for musical ones. Miles Davis was savagely beaten by two policemen outside the club one night for "loitering," an incident that led to his being jailed and needing five stitches. The club got massive unfavorable publicity before the charges were dropped. Charlie Parker had a number of horrible encounters, including one that turned into a suicide attempt. He was ultimately banned from the place bearing his nickname. The club declined in the '60s and was eventually taken over by R&B vocalist Lloyd Price. The great place that was immortalized in song by Joe Zawinul in 1976 with the composition "Birdland" was finally replaced by a strip joint.

Blackhawk

A principal San Francisco spot for hard bop and bebop in the '50s and early '60s, the Blackhawk was the site where Art Tatum had one of his last extended engagements in 1955 and the location for a pair of famous Miles Davis albums in the early '60s, *Friday and Saturday Nights at the Blackhawk.* It didn't have a long run, opening in the '50s and closing in the '60s.

Boomer's

A hard bop, bebop, and soul-jazz center in New York in the '70s, Boomer's began in 1971 at 340 Bleecker Street at Christopher Street. Cedar Walton recorded there for Muse in 1973; others who appeared included Barry Harris, Junior Mance, Joe Newman, Junior Cook and Woody Shaw. It closed six years later in 1977.

Bottom Line

This has never been exclusively or even mainly a jazz club, but it has certainly presented its share of great jazz performers since it opened in 1974. More so than the Fillmore East or West or any other major rock and pop club, the Bottom Line has featured top jazz stars like Charles Mingus, Sun Ra, Dexter Gordon, Sonny Rollins, Ralph Towner, John Abercrombie, Andrew Cyrille, and Lester Bowie. It is still in operation at 15 West Fourth Street at Mercer Street in Greenwich Village in New York.

Cafe Bohemia

Jimmy Garofolo owned and operated the Cafe Bohemia at 15 Barrow Street. This New York spot opened in 1955 and had the great bassist/cellist Oscar Pettiford as its music director, doubling as a bandleader. Cannonball Adderley made his New York debut here in 1955. Kenny Clarke immortalized it on his album *Bohemia After Dark* for Savoy. It is now a residential building.

Cafe Carlyle

This isn't a jazz club, but it possesses a special significance as the New York home for noted cabaret artist Bobby Short for well over two decades. Located in the Hotel Carlyle, Madison Avenue at East 76th Street, it enjoys an elegant, old-fashioned, intimate setting. Other top pianists such as George Shearing, Marian McPartland, and Joe Bushkin have had extended residencies there.

Cafe Society

Before he began operating the Cookery, Barney Josephson blazed some social trails with his Cafe Society clubs. The downtown New York location opened in 1939 at 2 Sheridan Square with another venue in midtown New York at 128 East 58th Street starting in October of 1940. Josephson ran a truly integrated operation in every sense of the word, right down to being unfazed by interracial couples dancing and openly associating in public during the '40s. Billie Holiday helped get the downtown club going, as did the boogie-woogie trio of Albert Ammons, Pete Johnson, and Meade "Lux" Lewis, who made their New York debut there. Lena Horne followed Holiday and remained until 1941. James P. Johnson, Teddy Wilson, Art Tatum, and Sarah Vaughan were others who played there, while Fletcher Henderson held his final gig there in 1950. George Simon and Leonard Feather directed jam sessions there in 1941. Edmond Hall, Mary Lou Williams, and several others played at both Cafe Society clubs, but others like John Kirby, Mildred Bailey, and Count Basie only appeared at the midtown spot. Both clubs closed in 1950, but Josephson would go on to run the Cookery in the '70s.

Carnegie Hall

Carnegie Hall has been in business on West 57th Street and Seventh Avenue in New York since 1891 and has featured many magnificent jazz concerts in its array of showcase entertainment. James Reese Europe organized a series of events from 1912 to 1914 to assist the Clef Club, an organization that promoted African-American artists. A 1928 tribute to W.C. Handy featured performances by James P. Johnson and Fats Waller, while the immortal 1938 "Spirituals to Swing" concert organized by John Hammond in memory of Bessie Smith featured Sidney Bechet, Jo Jones, Meade "Lux" Lewis, Albert Ammons, Pete Johnson, and Tommy Ladnier. Benny Goodman also had a famous 1938 concert there, and he returned in 1978 to celebrate that concert's 40th anniversary. Duke Ellington's *Black, Brown and Beige* suite debuted in 1943, and he presented six more concerts between 1943 and 1948. There was also Woody Herman's *Ebony Concerto* debut in 1946, Charlie Parker's late '40s and mid-'50s concerts and '60s appearances by Miles Davis, Charles Mingus, and John Coltrane. The Newport Jazz Festival has been presenting shows there since the '70s, and many other major stars have appeared in the last three decades.

Central Avenue

In its heyday, Central Avenue was the Los Angeles counterpart to New York's 52nd Street or New Orleans' Storyville, though not quite that wide open. It was not a site or a club but a lifestyle and environment. It had dozens of clubs and, with its 100-block radius, featured numerous musicians going from place to place seeking a chance to play. There were also dance halls, theaters, and other diverse forms of entertainment, some legitimate, some not so legitimate. When Los Angeles disbanded the Red Car trolley system, it spelled the doom of Central Avenue. Currently, one blues club plus the Hotel Dunbar and Lincoln Theater remain of what was once a creative oasis.

Condon's

A traditional New Orleans jazz impresario and jack-of-all-trades, Eddie Condon opened the original Condon's in New York in 1945 at 47 West Third Street. Condon co-operated the club with Pete Pesci. Its specialty was Chicago jazz of the vintage (and predominantly White) variety, though Condon certainly did not adopt any color-conscious booking policies. Sammy Price, James P. Johnson, and Walter Page also often played there along with George Wettling, Pee Wee Russell, Herb Hall, Tony Parenti, Yank Lawson, and Wild Bill Davison, though not all appeared at the same location. Condon moved the club in 1957 to 330 East 56th Street. The second club closed in 1967. A third club bearing Condon's name was opened after his death in 1975 on West 54th Street next to Jimmy Ryan's. Red Balaban led the house band and they recorded a combination tribute/live album at the newly opened club that Concord Records later issued. This club closed in 1985. A fourth Condon's opened in 1990 at 117 East 15th Street. This club has featured a more diverse lineup with Jimmy Witherspoon, Ernestine Anderson, and Harry "Sweets" Edison among its earliest performers.

Cookery

Barney Josephson, who at one time ran the Cafe Society clubs, owned and operated the Cookery in New York at 21 University Place at East Eighth Street. It began as a restaurant and then started offering music in the early '70s. It featured either solo or small combo acts. Mary Lou Williams's early '70s appearances there rekindled memories of her past achievements among some critics, while Alberta Hunter was "rediscovered" performing there in the late '70s. Teddy Wilson, Blossom Dearie, Helen Humes, and Jimmy Rowles are some of the artists who appeared there in the '70s and '80s.

Cotton Club

Jack Johnson, the first undisputed African-American heavyweight boxing champion, was the owner of the Club Deluxe in New York. This club was overrun and taken over by Owney Madden's gang in 1922. Madden hired Andy Preer's Cotton Club syncopators, complete with a chorus line composed exclusively of light-skinned Black women, all of whom had to be under 21 and at least five feet, six inches tall. It was Madden who recruited Duke Ellington to replace Preer after Preer's death in 1927. The small matter of a contract Ellington had in Philadelphia was considered of no consequence. Ellington became a hit at the Cotton Club, and his "jungle band" sound with its inspired arrangements and creative use of mutes and plungers was on its way to glory. Ellington made it his home base as did Cab Calloway. Ethel

Waters, Louis Armstrong, and many other seminal figures also appeared there. The Cotton Club relocated to West 48th Street from Lenox Avenue in 1936 following the bloody Harlem riots but failed to generate the same excitement and buzz in its new headquarters. It closed a few years later and was torn down in the '50s to make room for a housing project. A fictional film about the Cotton Club starring Richard Gere was made in 1986. It won Bob Wilber a Grammy award for his music.

Earle

Another now defunct Philadelphia nightclub, the Earle was famous for both traditional jazz and bebop performers, among them Louis Armstrong, Jack Teagarden, and Lucky Millinder with Dizzy Gillespie. It stood at the Southeast corner of 11th and Market streets; now in its place stands a Woolworth's.

Five Spot

Joe and Iggy Termini opened the original Five Spot on the edge of the Bowery in the early '50s and made it a showcase for every style. But the Five Spot was most famous for on-the-edge performances. Cecil Taylor had a residency there in 1956, and that same year an all-star tribute to Charlie Parker featuring Phil Woods, Duke Jordan, Art Taylor, and Cecil Payne was recorded at the club. Thelonious Monk played and recorded there in the late '50s with John Coltrane, and Ornette Coleman made his controversial New York debut at the Five Spot. Eric Dolphy's incendiary club performances with a quintet that included Booker Little, Mal Waldron, Richard Davis, and Ed Blackwell were recorded in 1961. Charles Mingus also played there in both the '50s and mid '60s and was famous for reportedly destroying a $20,000 bass in response to heckling from some partisans. Monk returned in 1963 after the club had moved to Third Avenue and East Seventh Street. The Five Spot changed both its name and its booking policies when it opened at St. Marks Place east of Seventh Avenue in 1972. Now called the Two Saints, the club booked jazz-rock and fusion acts. But the old Five Spot name and entertainment style returned in 1975. Art Blakey's Jazz Messengers were the opening act, and later came Jackie McLean and Coleman again. The Termini brothers lost their cabaret license and had to close the Five Spot. A horribly anti-Semitic characterization of two Jewish club owners featured in Spike Lee's film *Mo' Better Blues* may have been based on them though, wisely, no one admitted that for the record.

Hi-Hat

The Hi-Hat was located at Columbus and Mass. Ave., right at the two streets' intersection. It was the first club to present bebop to Boston audiences. Charlie Parker did several concerts there, which were broadcast, and selections were later issued in an album on the Phoenix Jazz label. They were reissued on CD in 1993 by Blue Note. The club closed in the late '50s.

Jazz Workshop/Paul's Mall

The Jazz Workshop opened in 1964 at 733 Boylston Street in Boston and was originally managed by Fred Taylor and Tony Mauriello. There was a separate club in an adjacent room in the same basement called Paul's Mall. While they both featured jazz, the Workshop was more of a mainstream and exclusive jazz venue, while Paul's Mall also presented fusion, jazz-rock, and various types of popular music. Charles Mingus, Rahsaan Roland Kirk, Miles Davis, and many others appeared at the Workshop until both clubs closed in 1978.

Keystone Korner

During the '70s, the Keystone Korner on Vallejo Street at Stockton in San Francisco was a top West Coast attraction.

Todd Barkan directed its booking and also doubled as a liner note writer and producer. It was famous for great acoustics, knowledgeable audiences, and a good environment. Many jazz acts recorded there, among them Art Blakey, Tete Montoliu, and Bobby Hutcherson. It was from this locale that National Public Radio broadcast during New Year's Eve celebrations for several years. It closed in 1982.

Lafayette Theater

The Lafayette opened in New York in 1915 and became most famous for its great variety shows and revues in the '20s. The Coleman brothers were its original owners, followed by Frank Schiffman and Leo Brecher, who also took over the Apollo Theater and Harlem Opera House in the '30s. The Lafayette was one of Harlem's two biggest theaters, and Duke Ellington made his New York debut there in 1923 playing with Wilbur Sweatman's band. Fats Waller also played there, while *Shuffle Along,* the first major African-American theatrical presentation to make it to Broadway, was initially produced at the Lafayette. Sissle and Blake presented *The Chocolate Dandies* there, and Lew Leslie's *Blackbyrds* and *The Plantation Revue* with Florence Mills were also staged at the Lafayette. Fletcher Henderson, Bennie Moten, Chick Webb, Zutty Singleton, and Ellington, this time leading a band, were among other major performers who played the Lafayette. It was turned into a full-time film theater in 1935.

Lighthouse

It is now a rock and pop outlet, but for over 20 years the Lighthouse was the center for recurring jam and recording sessions in Hermosa Beach, CA. Bandleader Howard Rumsey began the Lighthouse in 1949, and its Sunday jam sessions ran from two in the afternoon until two the next morning and sometimes longer. Shorty Rogers, Art Pepper, Hampton Hawes, Sonny Criss, Teddy Edwards, and Shelly Manne were among the musicians who regarded it as home, and a group of regulars known as the Lighthouse All-Stars cut several records in the '50s. Many are currently available on reissued CDs.

Lincoln

The Lincoln had a short but influential run. Marie Downs built a small theater at 58 West 135th Street in New York in 1909. Her theater was demolished and replaced by the Lincoln in 1915. Frank Schiffman and Leo Brecher operated it for a short time before moving on to the Lafayette and eventually the Apollo. This theater catered to an African-American audience from its inception and included many jazz performers on its variety bills. Fats Waller served as house organist in the '20s, and a young Count Basie was a regular visitor, occasionally getting some free organ lessons. Victoria Spivey was also a resident vocalist there in 1927. It is now a church.

Lincoln Theater

Though not in operation today, Philadelphia's Lincoln Theater was a busy nightspot in the '30s. It wasn't so much a jazz club as a site for variety acts that included jazz musicians. Fletcher Henderson, Noble Sissle, Duke Ellington, Jimmie Lunceford, and Don Redman were among the bands that appeared on various Lincoln Theater bills. It was located across the street from the Showboat at South Broad Street and Lombard Street.

Lulu White's

A much-beloved though short-lived institution, Lulu White's began in the late '70s on 3 Appleton Street in Boston.. It mixed both bebop and adventurous free music during its brief tenure and was one of the few places in the city that had no problems booking Dizzy Gillespie, Harry Edison, the Art Ensemble of Chicago, and Air. It closed in 1980.

Lulu White's Mahogany Hall

Both an expensive brothel and home of superb pianists, Lulu White's Mahogany Hall was operated by Lulu White, Storyville's reigning madam. White was the aunt of composer Spencer Williams and was known either as "The Queen of Demimonde" or "The Queen of Diamonds." Among the great players White employed to provide suitable "background" music were Kid Ross, Tony Jackson, and Jelly Roll Morton. The building was demolished in the '50s, though the saloon still stands.

Maybeck Recital Hall

Concord Records has made the Maybeck Recital Hall a status symbol with its series of solo piano concerts recorded there at 1537 Euclid Avenue in Berkeley, California. The hall's acoustics, coupled with the company's choice of artists and exquisite recorded results, have generated massive favorable publicity. In some cases, players who lack big reputations, like Buddy Montgomery and Gerry Wiggins, have turned in stunning performances. The 30th volume in the series was issued in 1993. Architect Bernard Maybeck built the hall in 1914 for a classical piano teacher who used it for student recitals. Nonpianists like Dizzy Gillespie and Joe Henderson have also played the intimate building. Weekly jazz concerts are now held there on Sundays, with room for only 50 guests.

Metropole

It did not begin offering jazz until the '50s, but the Metropole made up for its absence with a full slate of performers. Tony Scott, Max Kaminsky, and Sol Yaged were among the early attractions at the Metropole, located at Seventh Avenue and 48th Street in New York. Red Allen served as emcee and resident musician from 1954 until 1967. The club presented trios in the afternoon and bands at night as well as occasional featured performances by single acts like Louis Armstrong or Gene Krupa or periodic big band concerts with such bands as Lionel Hampton or Woody Herman. Zutty Singleton and Tony Parenti led groups there for long periods, and Allen headed one evening band, Coleman Hawkins and Roy Eldridge the other. Cozy Cole, Claude Hopkins, and Buster Bailey were among the resident players. The club continued presenting jazz through the '60s and for a short time also featured more modern fare. It is currently called the Metropole à Go-Go.

Minton's

Tenor saxophonist Henry Minton opened this club at 210 West 118th Street in New York in 1938. It was located in a hotel named the Cecil. Teddy Hill took over its operation two years later, and the Monday night jam sessions were widely regarded as bebop incubators in the '40s. Dizzy Gillespie, Charlie Parker, Hot Lips Page, Roy Eldridge, Charlie Christian, and Don Byas were among the guest performers, while Thelonious Monk, Kenny Clarke, Rudy Williams, and Joe Guy played in the house band. The jam sessions and late-night after-hours dates provided opportunities for major woodshedding and exchanges of ideas. Tony Scott and Jerome Richardson were some of the musicians featured at Minton's in the '50s. The old club is now a tourist attraction in the restored Cecil, and rumors abound that it will be reopened as a music facility.

Monroe's

Clark Monroe opened Monroe's Uptown House at 198 West 134th Street in New York in the '30s. The Theatrical Grill had previously occupied the location. It was a premier swing and bebop venue in the '30s and '40s with Billie Holiday performing there in 1937. The jam sessions in the '40s rivaled those at Minton's, and Charlie Parker was a featured soloist in 1943. Monroe opened a second club, Spotlite, for a couple of years in the mid '40s but eventually ran into financial difficulties with both operations. Monroe's is currently a deli.

Nick's

Nick Rongetti turned Nick's Tavern at 140 Seventh Avenue South into New York's mainline traditional jazz center beginning in the mid '30s. Bobby Hackett led the house band and regulars included Eddie Condon, Pee Wee Russell, and Zutty Singleton, while Russell and Singleton also brought in their own bands. Sidney Bechet was a bandleader there in the late '30s and early '40s. George Brunies, Meade "Lux" Lewis, Muggsy Spanier, Wild Bill Davison, Miff Mole, Billy Butterfield, Phil Napoleon, and Kenny Davern were among those who had extended club residences in the '30s, '40s, '50s, and early '60s. Nick's closed in 1963.

Palace

Once Memphis' predominant nightspot, the Palace had an importance to the local Black community that transcended its musical role, though it did occasionally feature jazz musicians. It was located at 318 Beale Street near Hernando and had a Wednesday night amateur contest, which was initially hosted by influential newspaper columnist and radio disc jockey Nat D. Williams and later by the great musician and fellow disc jockey Rufus Thomas. B.B. King, Johnny Ace, and Bobby "Blue" Bland were among the stars who got their start at the Palace. It was also the site of many spectacular concerts. It is now demolished.

Paradise Theater

The Paradise Theater is still operational in Detroit, though it encountered rough going in the '70s. Originally called Orchestra Hall, it opened in 1919 at 3711 Woodward Avenue. The place was built for the Detroit Symphony Orchestra but was renamed the Paradise Theater in recognition of the fact that it had become the prime venue for touring African-American acts that came to the city in the '40s and '50s. Count Basie and the Earl Hines band with Charlie Parker as well as many Detroit greats like Kenny Burrell, Hank Jones, and Yusef Lateef played at the Paradise. It closed temporarily in the '70s, then reopened in the late '80s with its old name again. The Detroit Symphony Orchestra, which vacated the premises in 1939, returned with the renovations in the '80s.

Plugged Nickel

Another club that did not have a long existence but burned brightly while it was active was the Plugged Nickel on North Wells Street in Chicago, a major hard bop and bebop venue in the '60s. Miles Davis recorded there during a two-week residency from December 21, 1965, to January 2, 1966, but for reasons known only to the company, Columbia did not issue the recordings until the mid '70s and then only in limited form. They have finally been made available in the CD era. Gene Ammons also appeared there when he returned to public dates in 1969. The club closed in the '70s.

Preservation Hall

Larry Borenstein had been presenting informal performances by veteran New Orleans musicians in a location directly adjacent to his art gallery. He opened Preservation Hall at 726 Peter Street in June of 1961 along with Grayson Mills and Allan and Sandra Jaffe. Preservation Hall is now a shrine to traditional New Orleans music where such venerable players as Kid Thomas, Punch Miller, and George Lewis have led

the band. There have also been many albums recorded there by both small jazz independents and major operations like Columbia. A Preservation Hall Jazz Band has also periodically toured nationally and internationally.

Regal Theatre

The Midwestern version of the Apollo, the Regal opened in 1928. Situated at 4719 South Parkway Boulevard in Chicago, it was a theater with a grand architecture and huge capacity. It could seat 3,500 with room in the foyer for 1,500. During the '30s and '40s, Louis Armstrong, Duke Ellington, Count Basie, Jimmie Lunceford, Lucky Millinder, and many others appeared at the Regal, which was also the site of several major concerts in the '50s and '60s by Miles Davis, Dizzy Gillespie, and Sonny Stitt. It also had its own tradition of amateur contests, which helped launch almost as many careers as those at the Apollo. Ken Blewett was manager from 1939 to 1959. While it is equally famous for its blues shows, particularly a '60s B.B. King concert that was recorded and released by ABC/Bluesway, the Regal had its share of remarkable jazz concerts. A new Regal Theatre was opened in 1987, built along the same architectural lines as the original, but it is otherwise unconnected. The original building was demolished in the '70s.

Roseland

While two places used this name, the one that is most synonymous with jazz was opened in 1919 on New Year's Day by Louis J. Brecker. It was one of New York's largest ballrooms and was lavishly designed and maintained, then refurbished in 1930. Like the Cotton Club, Roseland attracted White customers but began hiring Black bands in the early '20s. A.J. Piron appeared in 1924, and Fletcher Henderson began a residency that same year and stayed until 1941. The best White musicians also played at the ballroom, notably Bix Beiderbecke, who appeared with Jean Goldkette's band from 1926 to 1931. The Goldkette and Henderson bands battled in 1926. Other famous orchestras such as McKinney's Cotton Pickers, the Casa Loma orchestra, Marion Hardy's Alabamians, and the bands of Luis Russell, Cab Calloway, Chick Webb, Andy Kirk, and Benny Carter also appeared there. Roseland had regular live broadcasts transmitted throughout the country by landline. The ballroom remained open until 1955 and was demolished shortly after closing. A new, larger Roseland opened at 239 West 52nd Street a few months later. Count Basie's was one of many bands that played there in the '60s and '70s. A second Roseland ballroom opened in Brooklyn during the '30s; Woody Herman's band played there in 1936.

Ryles

Cambridge's oldest jazz club and the second oldest in the Greater Boston area, Ryles has been a boon for local talent, particularly Berklee students. But it has also welcomed national headliners like Pat Metheny, Robben Ford, and Grover Washington, Jr. It is located at 212 Hampshire Street in the Inman Square area. Ryles has not completely filled the void left by the disappearance of such places as Paul's Mall and the Jazz Workshop, but at least it is still active.

Savoy

Moses Galewski, better known as Moe Gale, along with Charles Galewski and Charles Buchanan, opened the Savoy Ballroom in New York on West 140th Street in March of 1926. It occupied the entire second floor of a building extending along the entire block between 140th and 141st streets in New York. There was a huge dance floor, two bandstands, and a retractable stage. The Savoy became Harlem's hottest club and the site where many dance crazes were launched in the '20s and '30s. It was also famous for its band battles, with the ballroom engaging two bands playing alternate sets. On special occasions they would book three or more bands for all-out warfare. A 1927 duel pitted King Oliver's Dixie Syncopators against resident performers Fess Williams and His Royal Flush Orchestra and Chick Webb's Harlem Stompers. During the '30s, Webb's band was linked with the Savoy on a long-running basis. Others with similiar arrangements were Al Cooper's Savoy Sultans and Erskine Hawkins's Orchestra. Many other landmark bands and performers made regular appearances, among them Coleman Hawkins, Count Basie, the Mills Brothers, Andy Kirk, Sidney Bechet, and Benny Carter, whose big band debuted there in 1939. The Savoy had its own radio line and several concerts were broadcast as well as recorded during its heyday. A Woolworth's now occupies the spot where the Savoy once stood.

Showboat

The Showboat was Philadelphia's reigning jazz club in the '50s. The club at 1409 Lombard Street near South Broad Street featured entertainment by John Coltrane, Thelonious Monk, Sonny Rollins, and Dizzy Gillespie, among others. It is now a mental health facility.

Slugs

Despite having a short tenure, Slugs was a hard bop haven from the mid '60s until 1972. It was located at 242 East Third Street in New York and featured performances from Jackie McLean, Joe Henderson, Philly Joe Jones, Yusef Lateef, Stanley Turrentine, Charles Lloyd, Ornette Coleman, Freddie Hubbard, Sun Ra, Art Blakey, and many others. Charles Tolliver's 1972 date there was recorded and issued on the Strata-East label. Slugs also has a tragic place in jazz annals: trumpeter Lee Morgan was shot and killed there by a distraught woman in a bizarre incident that may or may not have been a case of mistaken identity. The club closed shortly after that, ending a bright but quick chapter in hard bop and jazz club history.

Smalls' Paradise

Ed Smalls opened Smalls' Paradise at 2294½ Seventh Avenue, at West 135th Street, in 1925. The New York basement club featured music and dancing and was one of Harlem's most successful clubs even during the Depression. It was one of New York's piano centers in the '20s and '30s, with such legendary figures as Willie "The Lion" Smith, Jimmy Archey, Fletcher Henderson, and Charlie Johnson playing there, and Smith and Johnson having lengthy extended tours. Elmer Snowden served as bandleader of the Smalls' Paradise Orchestra in the early '30s and made the film Smash Your Baggage in 1932. James P. Johnson led a revised, scaled-down band in the mid 30s, but Hot Lips Page was back at the helm of a big band by 1937. Gene Sedric, Harry Dial, Happy Caldwell, and Gus Aitken were resident bandleaders in the '40s and '50s. Smalls' finally ceased operation in 1986.

Sportsmen Lounge

The Sportsmen Lounge in Baltimore still remains a perennial nightspot for both local and visiting music fans, though not as prominent now in the '90s as it was in the '50s and '60s. As one of the relatively few jazz clubs still in the heart of an African-American neighborhood, it has a cultural status as important as its legacy of great performances by such names as Gene Ammons, Gary Bartz, Count Basie, and Sonny Stitt. National Football League great and ex-Baltimore Colt Lenny Moore owned the club in the '60s, when its en-

tertainment roster would be headline material in national Black newspapers.

Storyville

Not to be confused with the relatively new Storyville Jazz Hall, which opened in the mid '80s at 1104 Decatur Street, Storyville was once a 16-block district of New Orleans located adjacent to the French Quarter. It was created January 1, 1898, out of the notion that if prostitution could not be eliminated it could be confined. But by forging this monument to hedonism, the New Orleans power brokers created both a mini-empire of vice and an area where musical creativity flourished. While full-time pimp and part-time state legislator Tom Anderson operated as mayor and principal flesh broker, the multitude of dance halls and night clubs all needed entertainment. An array of great musicians from Jelly Roll Morton to King Oliver and Clarence Williams regularly played Storyville. The district was finally shut down by the Secretary of the Navy in 1917. There are some who claim jazz got its name from the Storyville/whorehouse connection. Other insist there is little, if any, direct link.

Storyville

Longtime concert promoter and part-time musician George Wein opened Storyville in Boston in 1950. It was located initially in Kenmore Square and featured traditional jazz and swing. The club was later situated in the Copley Square Hotel. Sidney Bechet worked there extensively in 1951 and 1953. Wein also did several recording sessions there, using such musicians as Wild Bill Davison, Bechet, Ruby Braff, and Pee Wee Russell. Duke Ellington, Count Basie, Billie Holiday, and Charlie Parker were among others who appeared there.

Studio Rivbea

Multi-instrumentalist and composer Sam Rivers opened the doors of the loft Studio Rivbea, named after his wife Bea Rivers, in 1970 in New York City. It soon became one of the principal homes of what was deemed "loft jazz," free jazz played in loft apartments and clubs. The high point was a series of concerts recorded there by Douglas Records in the late '70s featuring the movement's biggest names. Unfortunately, the "Wildflowers" concert series has yet to be issued on CD and was poorly promoted and distributed during its vinyl lifetime. Sam Rivers kept the club going untl 1980.

Subway

It has been demolished for many years, but Kansas City swing veterans have fond memories of the Subway Club at 18th and Vine streets. Felix Payne and Piney Brown managed it in the '30s, and it was the haven for all the top touring big bands. It was also the spot of some savage band battles; drummer Jessie Price is reported to have once played a hour-long-plus solo (over 100 choruses) of Nagasaki in response to a challenge from two out-of-town drummers.

Theresa

Not a club but a hotel, the Theresa was formerly Harlem's largest and most famous hotel. Lena Horne, Lester Young, Joe Louis, and Fidel Castro were among its residents at various times. Cab Calloway's band once resided there, and Andy Kirk was its manager in the '50s. The grand edifice at 2090 Adam Clayton Powell Boulevard at 125th Street is now an office building.

Tipitina's

Though not exclusively or even predominantly a jazz club, Tipitina's is a special place for anyone who loves great piano and/or great music. It was founded in 1977 by some local

New Orleans citizens who wanted a place in the area for venerable Crescent City musicians, regardless of idiom, to play. Professor Longhair, whose rumbling, yodeling vocals immortalized the song "Tipitina," was among the acts who appeared at the club on 500 Napoleon Avenue. It is the home base for the Neville Brothers as well as Dr. John and the Radiators. Longhair was a part owner and frequent guest during his lifetime. Tipitina's also has a colorful past: it was once a bordello and also a meeting place for the New Orleans chapter of the Ku Klux Klan.

Village Gate

One of the New York jazz club mainstays that has survived, the Village Gate opened in 1958 at 160 Bleecker Street at Thompson Street. Numerous bebop and hard bop greats have appeared there as well as many great blues artists. Miles Davis, Erroll Garner, Cecil Taylor, Horace Silver, Lee Konitz, Rahsaan Roland Kirk, McCoy Tyner, and Art Blakey are among musicians who have worked the club. Over 60 albums have been recorded at the Village Gate over the years; Herbie Mann cut one of his finest straight jazz dates there, while B.B. King was welcomed in one of his first engagements before a predominantly White audience. Otis Rush, John Lee Hooker, Memphis Slim, and Thelonious Monk are others who have given historic Village Gate performances. The club instituted a Monday night Latin music policy in the '70s, and it is currently still in effect. The series was initially straight salsa but is now called "Salsa Meets Jazz." Willie Colón and Tito Puente have been among featured performers. While the original Village Gate was part of a decrepit, dilapidated flophouse, it is now in a luxury apartment building.

Village Vanguard

The Village Vanguard became a jazz mecca despite its tiny size and dingy look. It has operated since the early '30s and was run for many years by Max Gordon, who started it as a place for writers and artists. Gordon gradually altered the club's live entertainment policy from folk, comedy, and poetry to exclusively jazz. Many spectacular albums were recorded there, including a pair of remarkable dates by John Coltrane and Sonny Rollins. The Thad Jones-Mel Lewis orchestra, later the Mel Lewis orchestra, performed there Monday nights for over 20 years. The first Village Vanguard was located in a basement on Charles Street in Greenwich Village. Gordon was denied a cabaret license when he wanted to introduce music there because the place was deemed unsuitable. He had previously opened the Village Fair on Sullivan Street and moved the Vanguard to Seventh Avenue in a location formerly owned by a speakeasy called the Golden Triangle. From Sidney Bechet and Mary Lou Williams to Dizzy Gillespie, Art Blakey, Thelonious Monk, and Charles Mingus, headlining at the Vanguard signaled "making it" as a top jazz artist. Major folk acts such as the Weavers, Woody Guthrie, and Leadbelly; comedians like Lenny Bruce; and other miscellaneous performers such as Eartha Kitt and Burl Ives also appeared at the Vanguard at various times. It continues today as a jazz club mainstay and is now operated by Max's widow Lorraine Gordon, who is credited with the club's initial booking of Monk. It will mark its 60th anniversary in 1995. Gordon wrote a combination club history and memoir *Live at the Village Vanguard* in 1980.

—Ron Wynn

MAGAZINES

Cadence

The premier magazine about improvised music in the world, *Cadence* recently celebrated its 18th birthday. It is a monthly, edited and published by Bob Rusch, and its range of coverage for improvised music worldwide ranks second to none. *Cadence* also has a subsidiary audio department that sells numerous brands of equipment, including many fine ones that aren't commonly advertised in national audio publications. They sell a host of albums each month in their center sale, and their reviews encompass books, other periodicals, and various current and reissued discs, albums, and videos. You'll also find analysis, reviews, and commentary on blues, zydeco, and gospel. Cadence's oral history/interview/ profiles each month are thorough and no-holds-barred, usually conducted by Rusch but also at times featuring other interviewers. They are among the few places musicians openly discuss political and extramusical considerations freely and without fear. The magazine is not to be missed. It's not sold on newsstands, or at least most of them. Subscriptions are currently $30 a year, $35 outside the United States. All types of additional inducements are available as well, including lists of audio specials and available records. The address is Cadence, Cadence Building, Redwood, New York 13679.

Down Beat

Perhaps jazz's most prestigious general audience publication, as witnessed by the celebration in 1994 of its 60th birthday. *Down Beat* has made many features mandatory reading, among them the "Blindfold Test," "Caught in the Act," "Final Bar," and "Pro Session." It has had numerous esteemed critics in its regular lineup through the years, among them Dan Morgenstern, Leonard Feather, and Amiri Baraka (LeRoi Jones). It expanded its coverage range several years ago and now advertises as "Jazz, Blues & Beyond," a move that angered more conservative readers but has undeniably enhanced its profile among the general audience. It's also a monthly, with subscriptions being currently $26 for one year, $44 for two, and an additional $9 for foreign subscriptions. The address for subscription information is *Down Beat*, P.O. Box 906, Elmhurst, Illinois 60126-0906.

Jazz Times

The growth and evolution of *Jazz Times* from a small, newspaper-styled publication into a glossy magazine has been most impressive. While there are similarities in some departments to *Down Beat*, *Jazz Times* has its own look, identity, and slant. It covers plenty of blues in addition to every area of jazz and also includes discussion of videos, concerts, books, and at times sound equipment and jazz-related issues. *Jazz Times* has been willing to embrace fusion, or at least attempt to discuss it fairly, and the esteemed swing critic Stanley Dance serves as the book editor. It is also a monthly, with subscriptions currently $21.95 per year, $39.95 for two, and $59.95 for overseas subscription for one year.

The address is *Jazz Times*, 7961 Eastern Avenue, Suite #303, Silver Spring, Maryland 20910-4898.

Coda

The international perspective in jazz is well documented by *Coda*, Canada's premier publication for improvising music. It has been published since 1958, with January 1994 marking its 253rd issue and counting. It is now a bimonthly, which requires a bit more generic, nonnews approach to jazz issues, but *Coda* also manages to include plenty of still-topical information about European and/or Canadian events, concerts, news, etc. It also carries a regular column by the ubiquitous Kevin Whitehead (currently also available via *Down Beat, Pulse, CD Review,* and National Public Radio), but his "New York Notes" is quite informative when not used to slay the dragon, Wynton Marsalis. It is also second only to *Cadence* in its inclusion of independent label and underground new and free music acts. Subscriptions are currently $24 per year in the United States and $27 everywhere else. The address is *Coda*, P.O. Box 1002, Station O, Toronto, Ontario M4A 2N4, Canada.

Living Blues

The nation's foremost publication devoted to the blues, *Living Blues* stays true to the values established by its founding editors, Jim O'Neal and Amy van Singel. It covers the blues, mainly the genuine article, with occasional forays into its R&B and soul branches. *Living Blues* published issue number 113 in February of 1994, and it comes out six times each year. It includes extensive interviews with both well-known musicians and artists who are famous only within the blues sphere, as well as plenty of reviews and features. During 1993, its Letters to the Editor page demonstrated how truly little has changed in the world of blues (and music), as its policy of reserving coverage primarily for Black blues artists was debated, attacked, praised, and excoriated both nationally and internationally. It wasn't hard to figure out from the content of the letters who took what positions. It is hard to imagine any hard-core jazz fan not wanting to know the lowdown on the blues. Subscriptions for *Living Blues* are currently $18 for one year, $35 for two, with an additional $10 added for international subscribers. The address: *Living Blues*, The University of Mississippi, University, Mississippi 38677.

Jazziz

An aggressive, if sometimes puzzling, challenger to *Cadence, Down Beat,* and *Jazz Times* on the domestic front is *Jazziz*. It has also done extensive modification over the years in everything from graphic design and layout to the range of its coverage. *Jazziz* pays considerable attention to international music and also gives more space to fusion and pop-oriented sounds than its competitors. Other coverage areas include video, equipment, and jazz-influenced or related styles such as blues and Cajun. *Jazziz* also carries a radio survey, with a Top 40 chart and station listings. Subscriptions are currently $12.95 for one year or $25 for two. The address: *Jazziz*, 3620 N.W. 43rd Street, Gainesville, Florida 32606.

Latin Beat

No publication covers Afro-Latin music in such a comprehensive manner. From salsa to Latin jazz and all things in between, *Latin Beat* is the best bet. It is even a great inducement to polish up on your high school Spanish, as it is a true bilingual magazine. It comes out 10 times a year. Subscriptions are currently $25 for 10 issues. International orders need an additional $10 for postage. The address: *Latin Beat*, 15900 Crenshaw Blvd., Suite 1-223, Gardena, California 90249.

Additional magazines

The following publications are not exclusively or even predominantly jazz magazines, but do include columns and/or features, reviews, and commentary of interest. *Entertainment Weekly* offers jazz reviews by Chip Deffaa, David Hajdu, Josef Woodard, and (sadly, not too often recently) Gary Giddins. The *Village Voice* carries the aforementioned Giddins's comprehensive, essential "Weather Bird" column and periodic jazz consumer guides by Francis Davis, a great critic (who has also done several superb profiles and columns in *The Atlantic*). *Musician* often runs a monthly jazz column and some jazz reviews. Chip Stern and Peter Watrous of *The New York Times* have alternated doing the column and contributed reviews. *Stereo Review* carries jazz reviews by noted jazz critic, author, and one-time producer Chris Albertson, with some backup from, among others, Phyl Garland, who many years ago was *Ebony*'s regular music critic (she is sorely missed). *CD Review* includes extensive jazz columns, commentary, and criticism by a corps of writers, among them the prolific Kevin Whitehead, outstanding Bob Blumenthal, and others including David Okamoto, Tom Krebbiel, Michael Ullman, Myles Boisen, Brian Rabey, and Thomas Conrad. Onetime *Village Voice* (and in another time and place, before his days as a right-wing Renaissance man, *Players* magazine) jazz critic Stanley Crouch can now be found in the pages of *The New Republic*. *Rolling Stone*'s occasional jazz columns are written by Steve Futterman. Neil Tesser pens *Playboy*'s jazz column and provides one of those articles you can claim you're reading when someone accuses you of sexist insensitivity and pornographic pandering. When he gets around to jazz, Whitney Balliett can still turn some fine phrases at *The New Yorker*. *Ice*, Pete Howard's outstanding and thorough monthly CD newsletter that provides vital information about upcoming discs months ahead of everyone else, recently added a jazz column by David Okamoto, also of *CD Review* and the *Dallas Morning News*. Though it's almost totally a classical magazine, *Schwann's Opus* includes a regular jazz column from Michael Ullman. We don't have anywhere near the room to mention all the valuable daily and weekly newspaper writers who struggle to provide jazz exposure in an arena that doesn't ascribe much importance to the arts, period, let alone jazz. We salute any and all those toiling in that vineyard; certainly the quality varies, but anyone who has ever had to deal with the attitudes toward jazz emanating from a newspaper's arts desk has my empathy.

Rock & Rap Confidential

While an endorsement of a magazine like this in a jazz publication may seem like sacrilege to the "purists," it is here for two reasons: It has been among the few publications that understands the link between cultural and political struggles and has sought to inform and unite diverse musical audiences behind battles against racism, sexism, censorship, and political hypocrisy. It has also been the rare pop periodical that doesn't view jazz as museum-piece fodder, but also doesn't mistake fraudulent pap for the genuine article. In recent months, it's spotlighted more jazz albums and examined several jazz-related issues. The audience is one that the jazz world should court—music lovers with a social conscience anxious to hear something other than the same 30 songs recycled hourly. Subscriptions are currently $27 a year, $44 for two, with the rates being $36 and $60 for foreign subscriptions. The address is *Rock & Rap Confidential*, P.O. Box 341305, Los Angeles, California 90034.

—Ron Wynn

MAIL ORDER SOURCES

For those millions of us unlucky enough to reside in places outside the realm of superstores (in other words, most folks), trying to find even the latest hyped major-label jazz item in a mall store, standard retail outlet, or neighborhood mom-and-pop one-stop can be disastrous. Assuming the clerk even knows what you're talking about ("Duke who?"), you've got a better chance of striking oil in the back yard than you do of finding much jazz. Thus, you're forced to the option of mail order. Granted, there are many disadvantages to this. For one, unless you're a preferred customer, by the time you find out about sales, most of the prime items are gone. Frequently, you send the money in for six titles and two weeks later get four, with either a refund check or an inquiry asking if you want to backorder. Plus, nothing's preferable to walking in to a store, browsing, winnowing down a pile of potential buys, and finally walking out with records (discs/tapes) in hand. Anyway, here are a few places that we've personally dealt with over the years with no problems. This means they have reasonable shipping rates and will actually send you what you order, the product arrives in playable shape, and they issue catalogs in a timely manner. By no means are these the only options available: such magazines as *Goldmine, Record Collector,* and *Discoveries* are full of ads for stores that deal in jazz mail order; there are also many collectors nationwide who regularly hold auctions and set sales. But if you have never ventured into the wild world of mail order, here are some good places to start.

Cadence Mail Order

Among its many other functions, each month *Cadence* magazine also conducts monthly sales of CDs, books, and records. It carries numerous labels, including many European imports and American independents. The address is *Cadence,* Cadence Building, Redwood, New York 13679.

Coda Sales

Canada's premier jazz publication also sells records, videos, and books. Specific price information may be obtained by contacting Coda Publications, P.O. Box 1002, Station O, Toronto, Ontario M4A 2N4, Canada.

Record Roundup

Though not a jazz specialty operation, Rounder's mail-order service, Roundup, can help you find several independent-label current and classic sessions. It publishes a newsletter periodically that lists current specials, and also prints a catalog each year with more detailed listings. The address is Roundup Records, One Camp Street, Cambridge, Massachusetts 02140.

Roots and Rhythm

For many years known as Down Home Music, Inc., this operation is now Roots and Rhythm. Otherwise, nothing has changed. It remains among the finest and most diverse mail-order services in the world. It has plenty of domestic and for-

eign label/import jazz, though some of the import prices are a bit to the high side. It also publishes periodic newsletters and has catalogs for many categories, though surprisingly it hasn't as yet (March 1994) issued a strictly jazz catalog. The address: Roots and Rhythm, 10341 San Pablo Avenue, El Cerrito, California 94530.

Stash-Daybreak Express

For pure jazz, the number of labels carried by Stash-Daybreak Express rivals any mail operation. It also carries blues, R&B, soul, and doo-wop, but jazz is its specialty and it is very impressive in the caliber and volume that is available. Stash-Daybreak Express, 140 W. 22nd Street, 12th Floor, New York, New York 10011.

I.M.D.

If you haven't yet disposed of your records, or are looking for recent and/or reissued items that have been deleted and/or cut out, here is a great source. I.M.D. carries both cutout vinyl LPs and records and is particularly good for such treasured items as Smithsonian and Arista/Freedom albums. It also has a free catalog available. I.M.D., 160 Hanford Street, Columbus, Ohio 43206.

Audiophile Imports

Yes, even fusion has its champions, and Audiophile Imports offers an extensive variety of fusion and jazz-rock titles. It is a great source for Miles Davis Japanese imports for one, and Jaco Pastorius titles for another. Audiophile, Dept. JT, P.O. Box 4801, Lutherville, Maryland 21094-4801.

Double-Time Jazz

Double-Time can compete with any mail-order service for volume in old and new titles. It handles domestic independent and major-label products, as well as reissues, cutouts, and imports, while also carrying albums and videos in addition to CDs. Double-Time, P.O. Box 1244, New Albany, Indiana 47151-1244.

Worlds Records

If you're a fan of big band or blues, Worlds may prove your best bet for mail-order service. It also carries a full line of major-label, domestic independent, and foreign import titles. Worlds Records, P.O. Box 1922, Novato, California 94948.

Jaybee Jazz

Another excellent source for cutouts and deleted titles, Jaybee is quite strong with big-band items, records, CDs, and cassettes, as well as other styles. Jaybee Jazz, P.O. Box 411004, Creve Coeur, Missouri 63141.

Rick Ballard Imports

If your tastes run predominantly to styles that are mostly available on imports, here is a good source. Rick Ballard

Imports carries an extensive number of titles for such labels as Black Saint/Soul Note, DIW, Philology, Timeless, and many others. Rick Ballard Imports, P.O. Box 5063, Dept DB, Berkeley, California 94705.

Sonic Tiger

Yet another excellent source for cutouts in both domestic and import areas, and at extremely competitive prices. Sonic Tiger, P.O. Box 715, Cambridge, Massachusetts 02140.

Descarga

A great Afro-Latin mail-order service. Here is a major option for Latin jazz and salsa that is on the myriad labels out of the American major-label/independent loop. Descarga carries contemporary and classic titles, publishes a newsletter, and qualifies as a first-class operation. Descarga Records, 328 Flatbush Avenue, Suite 180-L, Brooklyn, New York 11238.

Africassette

While world music is its bailiwick, Africassette does also carry quite a bit of Afro-Latin material, including Latin jazz and salsa. It also periodically gets in jazz titles from Africa and the Caribbean, which adds other ingredients to the mix. Africassette, P.O. Box 24941, Detroit, Michigan 48224.

Original Music

While not jazz specialists, Original Music boasts a roster that includes many Afro-Latin titles. It is the company founded and still operated by John Storm Roberts. If there is anyone who knows more about "world" music and its permutations, combinations, hybrids, and multiple genres, I'd sure like to know who it is. Original Music, R.D. 1, P.O. Box 190, Lasher Road, Tivoli, New York 12583

—Ron Wynn

BIBLIOGRAPHY

This is not a list of recommended reading, although I'd certainly endorse and recommend the majority of items cited here. Nor are these all the books that would appear on a suggested list for someone anxious to learn as much as possible about jazz and, to a lesser extent, blues. These are all books that were specifically used to some extent for this project. Many are seminal; some contain viewpoints that I disagree with *(violently in one or two cases)*, but all were stimulating and deserving of scrutiny and consideration.

Reference Works

Gunther Schuller. *The Swing Era* (Oxford)

Joachim Berendt/Gunther Huesman. *The Jazz Book* (Lawrence Hill)

Linda Dahl. *Stormy Weather: The Music & Lives of a Century of Jazz Women* (Limelight)

Samuel Charters and Leonard Kunstadt. *A History of the New York Scene* (Da Capo)

Stanley Dance. *The Jazz Era–The Forties* (Da Capo)

Barry Ulanov. *A Handbook of Jazz* (GP)

Frank Driggs and Harris Levine. *Black Beauty, White Heat–A Pictorial History of Classic Jazz* (Morrow)

James Lincoln Collier. *The Making of Jazz* (Dell)

Frank Tirro. *Jazz, A History,* second edition *(Norton)*

Leo Walker. *The Big Band Almanac* (Da Capo)

Ira Gitler. *Swing To Bop* (Oxford)

Andre Hodeir. *Jazz, Its Evolution & Essence* (Grove)

Larry Coryell and Julie Friedman. *Jazz-Rock Fusion* (Delta)

David Rosenthal. *Hard Bop–Jazz & Black Music 1955-1965* (Oxford)

Len Lyons. *The Great Jazz Pianists* (Da Capo)

Gunther Schuller. *Early Jazz (Oxford)*

Martin Williams. *Jazz Masters of New Orleans* (Macmillan)

Martin Williams. *Jazz Masters in Transition* (Macmillan)

Mark Gridley. *Jazz Styles History & Analysis,* fifth edition (Prentice-Hall)

Al Rose and Edmund Souchon. *New Orleans Jazz* (LSU)

Ian Carr, Digby Fairweather, and Brian Priestly. *Jazz: The Essential Companion* (Prentice-Hall)

William Howland Kenney. *Chicago Jazz: A Cultural History 1930-1940* (Oxford)

Jon Schaefer. *New Sounds* (Perennial)

Barry McRae. *The Jazz Handbook* (GKD)

Discographies/Guides

Albert McCarthy, Alun Morgan, Paul Oliver, and Max Harrison. *Jazz On Record–A Critical Guide to the First 50 Years: 1917-1967* (Oak)

Christiane Bird. *The Jazz & Blues Lover's Guide to the U.S.* (Addison-Wesley)

Max Harrison, Charles Fox, and Eric Thacker. *The Essential Jazz Records* (Da Capo)

Donald Clarke, editor. *The Penguin Encyclopedia of Popular Music* (Penguin)

Richard Look and Brian Morton. *The Penguin Guide to Jazz* (Penguin)

Frank Scott, editor. *The Down Home Guide to the Blues* (A Cappella)

Barry Kernfield, editor. *The Blackwell Guide to Recorded Jazz* (Blackwell)

Tom Lord. *The Jazz Discography, Volumes 1-7* (Cadence Jazz Books)

Michel Ruppli, compiler. *The Clef/Verve Labels, Volumes 1 & 2* (Greenwood)

Michel Ruppli, compiler. *The King Labels, Volumes 1 & 2* (Greenwood)

Dennis Brown, compiler. *Sarah Vaughan–A Discography* (Greenwood)

Michel Ruppli, compiler. *The Prestige Label* (Greenwood)

Michel Ruppli, compiler. *The Aladdin/Imperial Label* (Greenwood)

Patti Jean Birosik. *The New Age Guide* (Collier)

John Fordham. *Jazz On CD–The Essential Guide* (KC)

Frank-John Hadley. *The Grove Press Guide to the Blues on CD* (Grove)

Michel Ruppli, compiler. *Atlantic Records Volumes 1 & 2* (Greenwood)

Michel Ruppli, compiler, with assistance from Bob Porter. *The Savoy Label* (Greenwood)

Michel Ruppli and Michael Cuscuna, compilers. *The Blue Note Label* (Greenwood)

John Lohmann. *The Sound of Miles Davis–The Discography 1945-1991* (Jazz Media)

Shinichi Iwamoto, compiler/editor. *Have You Met Mister Jones–A Hank Jones Discography* (Japan)

Luciano Massagli, compiler. *Duke Ellington's Story on Records, 1968-1970* (Italy)

Jack Millar, compiler. *Born to Sing–A Discography of Billie Holiday* (Jazz Media/Denmark)

Hans Westerberg, compiler. *Boy from New Orleans–Louis Satchmo Armstrong on Records, Films, Radio and Television* (Jazz Media/Denmark)

François-Xavier Moule, compiler. *A Guide to the Duke Ellington Recorded Legacy on LPs & CDs, Volume 1* (Madly/France)

Encyclopedias/Dictionaries

Leonard Feather. *The Encyclopedia of Jazz* (Da Capo)

Leonard Feather. *The Encyclopedia of Jazz in the Seventies* (Horizon)

Michael Kennedy. *The Oxford Dictionary of Music* (Oxford)

Oscar Thompson, editor. *The International Cyclopedia of Music* (Dodd, Mead)

J. Gordon Melton. *The New Age Encyclopedia* (Gale)

Philip Morehead. *The American Dictionary of Music* (Dutton)

Stanley Sadie, editor. *The Norton/Grove Concise Encyclopedia of Music* (Norton)

Barry Kernfield, editor. *The Grove Dictionary of Jazz, Volumes 1 & 2* (Grove)

The Guinness Encyclopedia of Popular Music, Volumes 1-4 (Guinness)

Gerard Herzhat. *Encyclopedia of the Blues* (University of Arkansas)

Sheldon Harris, editor. *Blues Who's Who* (Da Capo)

John Chilton. *Who's Who of Jazz* (Da Capo)

Biographies/Portraits

Dizzy Gillespie and Al Fraser. *To Be or Not to Bop* (Doubleday)

Michael Ullman. *Jazz Lives* (New Republic)

Barry Lee Pearson. *Sounds So Good to Me* (University of Pennsylvania)

Len Lyons/Don Perlo. *Jazz Portraits* (Quill)

Jack Chambers. *The Life of Miles Davis: Milestones 1 & Milestones 2* (Beach Tree/Morrow)

Edward Berger. *Benny Carter–A Life in American Music* (Scarecrow)

Stan Britt. *Dexter Gordon* (Da Capo)

Robert Hilbert. *Pee Wee Russell–The Life of a Jazz Man* (Oxford)

John Litweiler. *Ornette Coleman* (Morrow)

Brice Turner. *Hot Air, Cool Music* (Quartet)

Criticism/Essays

Martin Williams. *Jazz Changes* (Oxford)

Philip Larkin. *All What Jazz* (FSG)

Mark Tucker, editor. *The Duke Ellington Reader* (Oxford)

Albert Murray. *Stomping the Blues* (Vintage)

Arthur Taylor. *Notes & Tones* (Perigee)

Gary Giddins. *Rhythm-A-Ning* (Oxford)

Francis Davis. *In the Moment* (Oxford)

James Lincoln Collier. *Jazz: The American Theme Song* (Oxford)

INDEX

Also available from Miller Freeman Books

All Music Guide
The Best CDs, Albums & Tapes
Edited by Michael Erlewine

This is the most comprehensive, easy-to-use guide to virtually all kinds of recorded music, compiled by some of the best music critics in the nation. These critics have selected 23,000 of the the best recordings in 26 categories, produced by more than 6,000 artists and groups. Categories include classical, jazz, country, blues, pop, rock, world beat, children's, and more. 1180 pages, $24.95.

Available at bookstores and music stores everywhere, or directly from the publisher (add $5.00 for shipping and handling in the U.S., plus sales tax in CA, FL, GA, IL, NY, TX, and GST in Canada):

> Miller Freeman Books
> 600 Harrison Street
> San Francisco, CA 94107
> Phone 408-848-5296
> Fax 408-848-5784
> E-mail: mfbooks@mfi.com

Related Products

Miller Freeman publishes many other books for musicians, popular music enthusiasts, fans, and instrument collectors. For a complete list of books, please contact the address above.

Miller Freeman also publishes *Guitar Player, Bass Player, Keyboard,* and *Vintage Gallery* magazines, available at newstands everywhere. For subscription information, please call 415-905-2200.

The *All Music Guide* is also available on CD-ROM (from Selectware Technology, 29200 Vassar, Ste. 200, Livonia, MI 48152; phone 313-477-7340), for hard disk (from Great Bear Technologies, 100 Moraga Way, Moraga, CA 94556; phone 800-795-4325), on CompuServe (GO ALLMUSIC), and on Internet (ALLMUSIC.MSEN.COM and ALLMUSIC.FERRIS.EDU).